Y0-ARV-576

THE BIBLE COMMENTARY

F. C. Cook, Editor

VOLUME I

Genesis to Deuteronomy

BAKER BOOK HOUSE
Grand Rapids, Michigan 49506

Reprinted 1981
from the edition published by
Charles Scribner's Sons, New York, 1871-1881
under the title,
*The Holy Bible...with an Explanatory
and Critical Commentary...*

Ten Volumes

ISBN: 0-8010-2431-5

Printed in the United States of America

PREFACE

IT is about seven years since the Speaker of the House of Commons, the Right Hon. J. Evelyn Denison, conceived the idea of the present Commentary, and suggested its execution.

It appeared to him that in the midst of much controversy about the Bible, in which the laity could not help feeling a lively interest, even where they took no more active part, there was a want of some Commentary upon the Sacred Books, in which the latest information might be made accessible to men of ordinary culture. It seemed desirable that every educated man should have access to some work which might enable him to understand what the original Scriptures really say and mean, and in which he might find an explanation of any difficulties which his own mind might suggest, as well as of any new objections raised against a particular book or passage. Whilst the Word of God is one, and does not change, it must touch, at new points, the changing phases of physical, philological, and historical knowledge, and so the Comments that suit one generation are felt by another to be obsolete.

The Speaker, after mentioning this project to several prelates and theologians, consulted the Archbishop of York upon it. Although the difficulties of such an undertaking were very great, it seemed right to the Archbishop to make the attempt to meet a want which all confessed to exist; and accordingly he undertook to form a company of divines, who, by a judicious distribution of the labour amongst them, might expound, each the portion of Scripture for which his studies might best have fitted him.

The difficulties were indeed many. First came that of

treating a great and almost boundless subject upon a limited scale. Let any one examine the most complete Commentaries now in existence, and he will find that twenty or thirty ordinary volumes are not thought too many for the exhaustive treatment of the Scripture text. But every volume added makes a work less accessible to those for whom it is intended; and it was thought that eight or ten volumes ought to suffice for text and notes, if this Commentary was to be used by laymen as well as by professed divines. Omission and compression are at all times difficult; notes should be in proportion to the reader's needs, whereas they are more likely to represent the writer's predilections. The most important points should be most prominent; but the writer is tempted to lay most stress on what has cost him most labour.

Another difficulty lay in the necessity of treating subjects that require a good deal of research, historical and philological, but which could not be expected to interest those who have had no special preparation for such studies. In order to meet this, it was resolved that subjects involving deep learning and fuller illustration should be remitted to separate essays at the end of each Chapter, Book or division; where they can be found by those who desired them.

The general plan has been this. A Committee was formed to select the Editor and the Writers of the various sections. The Rev. F. C. Cook, Canon of Exeter, and Preacher of Lincoln's Inn, was chosen Editor. The work has been divided into Eight Sections, of which the present volume contains the Pentateuch. Each book has been assigned to some writer who has paid attention to the subject of it. The Editor thought it desirable to have a small Committee of reference, in cases of dispute; and the Archbishop of York with the Regius Professors of Divinity of Oxford and Cambridge agreed to act in this capacity. But in practice it has rarely been found necessary to resort to them.

The Committee were called upon, in the first place, to consider the important question, which has since received a much fuller discussion, whether any alterations should be made in the authorized English Version. It was decided to reprint that Version, without alteration, from the edition of 1611, with the marginal references and renderings; but to supply in the notes amended translations[1] of all passages proved to be incorrect. It was thought that in this way might be reconciled the claims of accuracy and truth with that devout reverence, which has made the present text of the English Bible so dear to all Christians that speak the English tongue. When the Prayer Book was revised, the earlier Psalter of Coverdale and Cranmer was left standing there, because those who had become accustomed to its use would not willingly attune their devotions to another, even though a more careful, Version: the older Psalter still holds its place, and none seem to desire its removal. Since then, knowledge of the Bible has been much diffused, and there seems little doubt that the same affection, which in the middle of the seventeenth century clung to the Psalter and preserved it, has extended itself by this time to the Authorized Version of 1611. Be that as it may, those who undertook the present work desired that the layman should be able to understand better the Bible which he uses in Church and at home; and for this purpose that Bible itself gives the best foundation, altered only where alteration is required to cure an error, or to make the text better understood.

This volume is sent forth in no spirit of confidence, but with a deep sense of its imperfections. Those who wish to condemn will readily extract matter on which to work. But those who receive it willing to find aid in it, and ready to admit that it is no easy matter to expound, completely, fully and popularly, that Book which has been the battle-field of all sects and parties, which has been interpreted by all the ages, each according to its measure of light, will do justice to the spirit that has guided the writers. Such will find in it something that may help them better to appreciate the Sacred Text.

[1] These emendations are printed throughout in a distinctive type, darker than the rest of the note.

"As for the commendation," says Coverdale, "of God's holy Scripture, I would fain magnify it as it is worthy, but I am far insufficient thereto, and therefore I thought it better for me to hold my tongue than with few words to praise or commend it." Our English Bible has come down to us, won for us by much devoted labour, by persecution, by exile, even by blood of martyrdom. It has still much work to do, and when we consider the peoples to whom we have given our language, and the vast tracts over which English-speaking peoples rule, we feel how impossible it is for us to measure the extent of that work. We humbly desire to further it in some small measure, by removing a stumblingblock here, and by shedding light upon some dark places there. Such human efforts are needed, but the use of them passes, whilst the Word of God of which they treat will endure to the end. Yet it is permitted to offer them with an aspiration after the same result that attends the Word of God itself; and that result is, in the words of inspiration, "that ye might believe that Jesus is the Christ, the Son of God; and that believing ye might have life through His name." (John xx. 31.)

More than seven years have elapsed since this Commentary was first projected. It will, doubtless, be admitted that this period is not longer than might be reasonably demanded for the preparation of any considerable portion of such a work: but it is due to all concerned with this volume to state that but for unforeseen circumstances it would have been published much earlier. We have to deplore the premature death of no less than three contributors, two of whom had undertaken the commentary on Exodus and Numbers. All the writers in this volume had, in consequence of this and of other circumstances, a much larger amount of work imposed upon them than they were prepared for, long after the commencement of the undertaking. For one book they had to write the entire commentary; for another to re-write, with a special view to condensation, notes which had been prepared with great ability and learning by Mr Thrupp. This statement is made simply to account for the delay in the publication. The other parts of the work are now far advanced, and two volumes, including the historical and poetical books, will probably be printed within twelve months.

CONTENTS

THE PENTATEUCH

GENERAL INTRODUCTION. BY E. HAROLD BROWNE, D.D., BISHOP OF ELY.

GENESIS

INTRODUCTION. BY THE BISHOP OF ELY.

GENESIS—*continued*

COMMENTARY AND CRITICAL NOTES. BY THE BISHOP OF ELY.

pp. 31—236.

EXODUS

INTRODUCTION. BY F. C. COOK, M.A., CANON OF EXETER.

COMMENTARY AND CRITICAL NOTES, CHAP. i.—xix. BY CANON COOK. pp. 253—329.

COMMENTARY AND CRITICAL NOTES, CHAP. xx.—xl. BY SAMUEL CLARK, M.A., VICAR OF BREDWARDINE. pp. 330—434.

TWO ESSAYS. BY CANON COOK.

LEVITICUS

INTRODUCTION. BY SAMUEL CLARK, M.A., VICAR OF BREDWARDINE.

COMMENTARY AND CRITICAL NOTES. BY SAMUEL CLARK, M.A.

NUMBERS

INTRODUCTION. BY T. E. ESPIN, B.D., RECTOR OF WALLASEY.

COMMENTARY AND CRITICAL NOTES. BY T. E. ESPIN, B.D., AND J. F. THRUPP, M.A., LATE VICAR OF BARRINGTON.

DEUTERONOMY

INTRODUCTION. BY T. E. ESPIN, B.D.

COMMENTARY AND CRITICAL NOTES. BY T. E. ESPIN, B.D.

THE PENTATEUCH

INTRODUCTION

THE title, Pentateuch, is the Greek name given by the LXX. translators to the five books of Moses, the name by which they were known among the Jews being "the Law," *Torah.* In the Scriptures it is called "the Book of the Law" (2 K. xxii. 8), "the Book of the Covenant" (2 K. xxiii. 2, 21; 2 Chr. xxxiv. 30), "the Book of the Law of the Lord" (2 Chr. xvii. 9, xxxiv. 14), "The Law of Moses," "The Book of Moses," or "The Book of the Law of Moses." (See 2 Chr. xxv. 4, xxxv. 12; Ezra vi. 18, vii. 6; Neh. viii. 1, xiii. 1).

The division into five books is by many thought to be also due to the LXX. interpp. The Jews, however, retain the division, calling the whole *chamishah chomeshe torah,* "The five quinquernions of the Law," though they only distinguish the several books by names derived from a leading word in the first verse in each. Thus Genesis they call *Bereshith, i.e.* "in the Beginning," Exodus *Shemoth,* "the Names," &c.

The Mosaic Origin of the Pentateuch.

That Moses was the author and writer of the Pentateuch was the belief of all Jewish and Christian antiquity, if at least we except some heretical sects in the early Christian centuries, who desired in all ways to disparage the Old Testament. The sacred narrative itself contains assertions of this authorship. Thus, Ex. xvii. 14, after a memorable battle, "The Lord said unto Moses, Write this for a memorial in the book (בַּסֵּפֶר);" as though there were a regular account kept in a well-known book. Again, Ex. xxiv. 4, "Moses wrote all the words of the Lord." So Ex. xxxiv. 27, "The Lord said unto Moses, Write thou these words." In Num. xxxiii. 2, we read that "Moses wrote their goings out according to their journeys by the commandment of the Lord." In Deut. xvii. 18, 19, it is commanded that the king, who should hereafter reign, should "write him a copy of this law in a book out of that which is before the priests the Levites;" and in Deut. xxxi. 9, 10, 11, at the very end of the Pentateuch, we read, "Moses wrote this law, and delivered it unto the priests the sons of Levi," commanding, that "at the end of every seven years" they should "read this law before all Israel in their hearing." Several times Moses himself in Deuteronomy names "this law," and "the Book of this law" (Deut. xxviii. 61, xxix. 19, 20, 29), as though he had written a book for his people to keep. With this uniformity of tradition and these claims, there is at least a presumption in favour of the Mosaic authorship. It will however be well to shew,

1. That Moses could have written the Pentateuch.

2. That the concurrent testimony of all subsequent times proves that he did write the Pentateuch.

3. That the internal evidence points to him, and to him only, as the writer of the Pentateuch.

Let it only be understood, *in limine*, that this authorship thus claimed for Moses is not inconsistent with certain admissions.

(*a*) For instance, it is not necessary to insist, that every word of the Pentateuch was written down by the hand of Moses in his own autograph. He may have dictated much, or all of it, to Joshua, or to some secretary or scribe. He may have merely superintended its writing, and stamped it with his own authority, as perhaps St Peter did the Gospel according to St Mark. This may explain (though it is not necessary to assume this in order to explain) the fact, that Moses is always spoken of in the third person[1]. This may explain also some things said concerning Moses, which he might have allowed others to write, but would not have been likely to write himself. This may explain the difficulty, if difficulty indeed it be, that the last chapter of Deuteronomy relates the death of Moses; for what more likely, than that he, who wrote at Moses' dictation the acts and the words of Moses, should have finished the work by recording Moses' death?

[1] When Caesar always writes of himself in the third person, and when the like practice has been known to most nations, it seems hard to deny that Moses could have so written.

(*b*) It is not necessary to deny, that the Pentateuch, though the work of the great Prophet and Lawgiver whose name it bears, may have undergone some recension in after times, as by Ezra or others. The Jews hold that all the books of the Old Testament were submitted to a careful review by Ezra and the Great Synagogue (Buxtorf, 'Tiberias,' Lib. I. c. 10); and the fathers of the Church generally believed in some such supervision. "Omne instrumentum Judaicæ literaturæ per Esdram constat restauratum" (Tertull. 'De Cultu Femin.' c. 3). "Sive Mosen dicere volueris auctorem Pentateuchi, sive Esram ejusdem instauratorem operis, non recuso" (Hieron. 'ad Helvidium,' edit. Vall. Tom. II. p. 212). If Ezra collated MSS. and carefully edited the books of Moses, it is not impossible, and is not inconsistent with the original authorship, that he should have admitted explanatory notes, which some think (rightly or wrongly) to betray a post-Mosaic hand.

(*c*) It is not necessary to deny that Moses had certain documents or traditions referring to the patriarchal ages, which he incorporated into his history. Indeed it is most likely that such traditions should have come down through Shem and Abraham to Joseph and the Israelites in Egypt: and there can be no reason why an inspired historian should not have worked up such trustworthy materials into the history of the ancestors of his people.

1. *Moses could have written the Pentateuch.*

The most sceptical of modern objectors do not deny the existence of Moses, nor that he was the leader of his own people out of Egypt into Canaan. We have then the fact, that there was a man, evidently of some genius and energy, who led a nation out of captivity, and settled them in a state of civil government in another land. He came out of the most civilized country in the world, and he most probably had acquired much of its civilization.

The first question then, which naturally occurs is, Was the art of writing known so early as Moses? and especially was it known to the Egyptians and the Jews?

Recent researches prove the early existence of writing power in Egypt. Hieroglyphics are as ancient as the earliest Egyptian monuments, and the cursive hieratic character is to be found in monuments, parchments, and papyri centuries before the time of Moses. A few examples will clearly prove this. The famous group of figures in the tomb of Chnoumhotep at Beni Hassan, which belongs to the twelfth dynasty, represents a scribe as presenting to the governor a roll of papyrus covered with an inscription, bearing the date of the sixth year of Osirtasen II. This was certainly many centuries before the Exodus, according to most scholars even before the time of Abraham (see Brugsch, 'Hist. d'Egypte,' p. 63). At a later period, in the reign of Menephthah I., of the nineteenth dynasty, whom many have identified with the Pharaoh of the Exodus, we have a papyrus in the cursive hieratic character, (the Papyrus Anastasi, No. 1), which gives a list of nine authors distinguished for their writings in theology, philosophy, history, and poetry (Brugsch, p. 177, note). But the most remarkable of all is the papyrus found by M. Prisse, written in the hieratic character, and translated by M. Chabas, which contains two treatises; the first, consisting of twelve pages, is the conclusion of a work, of which the earlier part is destroyed. It treats of moral subjects, and is written in an elaborate and elevated style. The second treatise is by a royal author, son of the king next preceding Assa, in whose reign the work was composed. This is considered to be the most ancient of existing MSS. It is attributed to a prince of the fifth dynasty, who represents himself as weighed down with age, and invokes the aid of Osiris to enable him to give to mankind the fruits of his long experience. (See De Rougé, 'Recueil de Rapports, Progrès des Études Relatives à l'Égypte et à l'Orient,' p. 55, Paris, 1867. Also Brugsch, pp. 29—32.) The antiquity of this document is incalculable. There can therefore be no reason to doubt, that Moses, brought up in the house of Pharaoh, and learned in all the learning of the Egyptians, had acquired the art of writing.

But the Semitic nations had also a knowledge of the same art from the most ancient times. The traditions of Greece point to Cadmus (*i.e.* "the eastern"), the brother of Europa, as having introduced letters from Phœnicia into Europe. These traditions belong to the mythic ages of Greece, and, having been varied by later authors, can only be taken for what they are worth; but in their earliest form they point to Phœnicia as the teacher of Greece, and go on to say that parchments of goat and sheep skin were used by the Phœnicians for the purposes of writing (Herod. v. 58). Moreover, these traditions are confirmed by the fact that the letters of the Greek alphabet have the same names and order with those of the alphabets of the Semitic races; and the names have a meaning in Semitic but none in Greek, which proves that the Greeks took them from the Phœnicians, not the Phœnicians from the Greeks. In an Egyptian monument a Hittite is specially named as a writer. Pentaour, a royal scribe of the reign of Rameses the Great (as some think before, but more probably soon after, the Exodus), composed a poem, which is described as a kind of Egyptian Iliad, and which was engraved on the walls of the temple of Karnac. This mentions by name Chirapsar, among the Kheta (*i.e.* the Hittites), as a writer of books (Brugsch, p. 139); with which has been compared the fact, that Joshua took a city of the Hittites, the ancient name of which was Kirjath-sepher, *i.e.* "the city of the book" (Josh. xv. 15), and that he changed that name to Debir, a word of similar significance.

It is observed by Ewald ('Geschichte des Volkes Israel,' Vol. I. p. 77. Eng. Tr. by Martineau, pp. 50, 51), that the words for "write," "book," and "ink" (כתב, ספר, דיו), belong to all the branches and dialects of Semitic (except that the Ethiopic and south Arabic have צחק for "to write"). From this he infers that writing in a book with ink must have been known to the earliest Semites before they separated off into their various tribes, nations, and families. He concludes, and he cannot be accused of over credulity, that "Whatever the Semitic people may be, to which half the civilized world owes this invaluable invention, so much is incontrovertible, that it appears in history as a possession of the Semitic nations long before Moses; and we need not scruple to assume that Israel knew and used it in Egypt before Moses."

If then writing existed in Egypt and Israel, it is certain that Moses could have written a history, first, of the ancestors of his race, if it were only from the traditions which were sure to have been preserved among them, and secondly, of their wars and their wanderings, in which he himself had been their leader. These wars and wanderings extended over a period of forty years, during which there must have been frequent and long intervals of comparative leisure, which would have afforded ample time, to a man of energy and diligence, to compose a long and elaborate work. We may add that, if Moses could have written such a book, then it is almost certain, that he would have wished to do so. If we admit but the barest outline of the history of the Exodus, derivable not from the Jews only, but confirmed by the adverse traditions of their enemies, there can be no doubt of the following facts, viz. that the Hebrews were an oppressed race who, escaping from their captivity in Egypt, made a settlement in the land of Canaan, and by degrees grew into a powerful people, having a code of laws and a system of worship, markedly distinguishing and keeping them apart from the nations round about them. Now it is plain, that to fit such a people to be their own masters, and to maintain themselves in a condition of civil polity and social independence, there were needed wise laws and good training. If there be any truth at all in history and tradition, Moses, their wise leader, gave them laws and subjected them, before their settlement in Canaan, to a system of training. Moreover, he gave them a nationality. Was it not almost certain that he would commit his laws to writing? Is it not highly probable, that he should have tried to call out their national spirit by giving them a history of their ancestry and of their own assertion of their national independence? Such a body of men would not very easily settle by conquest among people more civilized than themselves, and retain independent laws, customs and rites, notwithstanding all surrounding influences. Yet that this was done by the Israelites no scepticism has yet denied. Nothing short of all that we read in the Pentateuch can fully explain this. But, at all events, it is clear, that in order to effect it, a wise leader and legislator would have committed his laws, and very probably his history, to writing.

We conclude then, that Moses could have written a work such as the Pentateuch, and that, if he could, most probably he would have written such a work.

2. Our next position is, that *The concurrent testimony of subsequent times proves, that Moses did write the books now known by his name.*

Beginning with the earliest books of the Old Testament we can trace a constant stream of reference and quotation to the laws, the history, and the words of Moses, which shew them all to have been well-known and universally accepted.

In *Joshua*, the Law of Moses, the Book of the Law, which had been written and was to be read, is continually spoken of (Josh. i. 7, 8, viii. 31, 34, xxiii. 6). In the first chapter the very words of Deuteronomy are twice quoted at length by Joshua. (See Josh. i. 3—8, where Deut. xi. 24, 25, xxxi. 6—12 are recited, and Josh. i. 13—18, where Deut. iii. 18—20 is recited). The constitution, both ecclesiastical and temporal, of the Israelitish people exactly corresponds with that ordained by Moses. Thus the priesthood is in the family of Aaron. Eleazar, the son of Aaron, is High priest (Josh. xiv. 1). He holds the same high place in the nation that his father did, being associated with Joshua, as Aaron was with Moses (see xiv. 1, xxi. 1). He and Joshua divide the land (xxi. 1), according to the ordinance in Num. xxxiv. 17. The tribe of Levi perform the sacred functions, being scattered among the tribes, with forty-eight cities assigned to them (Josh. xiii. 14, 33; xiv. 3, 4; xviii. 7; xxi.), as had been commanded by the Lord by the hand of Moses (Num. xxxv. 7).

The Tabernacle, which had been made by Moses and pitched in the wilderness, is now set up at Shiloh (Josh. xviii. 1). The sacrifices (Josh. viii. 31, xxii. 23, 27, 29) are exactly those enjoined in Lev. i., ii., iii. The altar which Joshua builds is constructed "as Moses the servant of the LORD commanded the children of Israel, as it is written in the book of the Law of Moses" (Josh. viii. 30, 31. Cp. Ex. xx. 25). The ark of the covenant occupies the same position as it did in the wilderness. It is carried on the shoulders of the Levites, and considered as the symbol and the special place of the presence of God (Josh. iii. 3, 6, 8, vii. 6). Circumcision (v. 2) and the passover (v. 10) are observed as in the Pentateuch.

There is the same general assembly of the people in council with the same princes of the assembly (Josh. ix. 18—21, xx. 6, 9, xxii. 30. Cp. Ex. xvi. 22, &c.), the same elders of Israel (Josh. vii. 6; Deut. xxxi. 9), the same elders of the city (Josh. xx. 4; Deut. xxv. 8), the same officers called *shoterim* and *shophetim* (Josh. viii. 33; Deut. xvi. 18), the same heads of thousands (Josh. xxii. 21; Num. i. 16), and other functionaries of state or of law. The ordinances of the Mosaic law are adhered to. Thus the bodies of those who have been hung are taken down before sunset (Josh. viii. 29, x. 27), as it was commanded in Deut. xxi. 23. No league is made with the people of Canaan (Josh. ix.), according to Exod. xxiii. 32. Cities of refuge are appointed (Josh. xx.) in strict accordance with the rules laid down in Num. xxxv. 11—15; Deut. iv. 41—43; xix. 2—7. The land is divided by lot (Josh. xiv. 2), as enjoined in Num. xxxiv. 13. The daughters of Zelophehad have their inheritance given them in the way prescribed Num. xxvii. 1—12, xxxvi. 6—9.

This is no place to discuss the genuineness and antiquity of the Book of Joshua; we may simply observe that its testimony to the Pentateuch is such that adverse criticism has found no escape but in saying that the author of Joshua must also have been the author of the Pentateuch, or (perhaps *and*) that the Book of Joshua was a recent production of the time of the kings or of the captivity.

The Book of Judges is of a somewhat fragmentary character describing a disordered condition of society, and the nature of its history is such as to call forth but few references to the history or the laws of Moses. The Book, however, appears in the first place to be a continuation of the history of Israel from the death of Joshua, and so thoroughly joins on to the Book of Joshua, that it can hardly be explained except on the belief that the Book of Joshua was written before it (see ch. i. 1. sqq. ii. 6—8). The laws of Moses, and God's commandments by him, seem to be frequently referred to (see ii. 1, 2, 3, 11, 12, 20; vi. 8—10; xx. 6, 2, 13. Cp. Deut. xiii. 5; xxii. 21). We find the same ordinances of law and worship as are prescribed in the Pentateuch and observed in Joshua. Thus Judah has the pre-eminence among the tribes and the chief command (Judg. i. 2; xx. 18. Cp. Gen. xlix. 8; Num. ii. 3, x. 14). The office of Judge, which here appears so conspicuously, corresponds with what Moses had said in Deut. xvii. 9. The Theocratic character of the nation is fully recognized by Gideon, who refuses to be king (Judg. viii. 22), in accordance with the sayings of Moses (Ex. xix. 5, 6; Deut. xvii. 14, 20; xxxiii. 5). The Tabernacle is still, as set up by Joshua, at Shiloh (Judg. xviii. 31). In case of danger we find the Israelites going to ask counsel of the Lord, probably by the High priest with Urim and Thummim (Judg. xx. 23. Cp. Ex. xxviii. 30; Num. xxvii. 21): and again after defeat we find them going up to the house of the Lord, weeping and fasting and offering there burnt offerings and sacrifices in conformity with Deut. xii. 5; there enquiring of the Lord by means of Phinehas, the son of Eleazar, the son of Aaron, the High priest, in the presence of the ark of the Covenant of God (Judg. xx. 26—28). The Ephod is still the priestly garment, and so honoured as to become an object of idolatry (Judg. viii. 27; xvii. 5; xviii. 14—17). The Levites, dispersed about the tribes and cities, appear as the only legitimate ministers of religion, so that their services are sought even for idolatrous worship (Judg. xvii. 7—13; xix. 1, 2). Circumcision distinguishes the Israelite from the neighbouring tribes (Judg. xiv. 3; xv. 18).

There are numerous historical references in Judges to the facts recorded in the Pentateuch (*e.g.* i. 16, 20, 23; ii. 1, 10; vi. 13). Especially Judg. xi. 15—27 is a complete epitome of Num. xx, xxi. The language is frequently borrowed in great degree from the language of the Pentateuch (compare Judg. ii. 1—23 with Ex. xx. 5; xxxiv. 13; Lev. xxvi. 13—17, 36; Num. xxxii. 13; Deut. vii. 2, 5, 16; ix. 18; xii. 3; xvii. 2; xxxi. 16; and in the Song of Deborah, Judg. v. compare vv. 4, 5 with Deut. xxxiii. 2; v. 8 with Deut. xxxii. 17.

In the unsettled state of the country during the reigns of most of the judges it is only natural to expect that there would be some departure from the strict observance of the law: but the facts above referred to are consistent only with the belief that the events and ordinances of the Pentateuch had preceded the history and were known to the actors and writers of the Book of Judges.

The History of Samuel. Here again we meet from the first with the ordinances of the Law and the history of the Pentateuch, referred to, recognized and acted on.

We meet at once with Eli, the High priest of the race of Aaron, though of the house of Ithamar (1 Chr. xxiv. 3. Cp. 2 S. viii. 17; 1 K. ii. 27); and his sons' wickedness is related with the threat of punishment, fulfilled in the reign of Solomon (1 K. ii. 27), which sustains the truth of God's promise (Num. xxv. 10 sqq.) that the High priesthood should remain in the family of Eleazar. The tabernacle is still at Shiloh, where it was pitched by Joshua (1 S. ii. 14, iv. 3), probably somewhat more solidly fixed than it had been in the wilderness, perhaps according to the rabbinical traditions having now become "a structure of low stone walls with the tent drawn over the top" (Stanley 'S. and P.' p. 233); so that it had apparently a warder's house attached to it, where Samuel slept[1]. The lamp burns in it according to the ordinance in Exod. xxvii. 20, 21; Lev. xxiv. 2, 3; though either that ordinance was not interpreted to mean that the light might never go out, or the carelessness, which had come on in Eli's old age and in the disordered state of Israel, had let that ordinance fall into disuse. The ark of the covenant is in the sanctuary and is esteemed the sacred symbol of the presence of God (1 S. iv. 3, 4, 18, 21, 22; v. 3, 4, 6, 7; vi. 19). The Cherubim are there, and the LORD of hosts is spoken of as dwelling between the Cherubim (1 S. iv. 4). There is the altar, and the incense, and the Ephod worn by the High priest (1 S. ii. 28). The various kinds of Mosaic sacrifices are referred to: the burnt-offering (*Olah*, 1 S. x. 8; xiii. 9; xv. 22), the whole burnt-offering (*Calil*, 1 S. vii. 9. Comp. Deut. xxxiii. 10), the peace-offerings (*Shelamim*, 1 S. x. 8; xi. 15; xiii. 9. Cp. Ex. xxiv 5), the bloody sacrifice (*Zebach*, 1 S. ii. 19), and the unbloody offering (*Minchah*, 1 S. ii. 19; iii. 14; xxvi. 19). The animals offered in sacrifice, the bullock (1 S. i. 24, 25), the lamb (1 S. vii. 9), the heifer (1 S. xvi. 2), and the ram (1 S. xv. 22), are those prescribed in the Levitical code. The especial customs of the sacrifice alluded to in 1 S. ii. 13, were those prescribed in Lev. vi. 6, 7; Num. xviii. 8—19, 25, 32; Deut. xviii. 1 sqq.: but the sons of Eli knew not the Lord, and so would not acknowledge the ordinance: ("The sons of Eli...knew not the Lord, nor the ordinance of the priests in reference to the people," 1 S. ii. 12, 13). The Levites alone were permitted to handle the sacred vessels and to convey the ark of the Lord (1 S. vi. 15). Historical events are referred to as related in the Pentateuch; Jacob's going down to Egypt, the oppression of the people there and their deliverance by the hand of Moses and Aaron (1 S. xii. 8), the plagues of Egypt (1 S. iv. 8), and the wonders of the Exodus (1 S. viii. 8), the kindness

[1] The objection (Colenso, Pt. v. p. 97) that the Tabernacle could not be the tabernacle of the wilderness, because it had "a door," 1 Sam. ii. 22, is rather singular, if we observe that the words in Samuel on which the objection is founded, "the women that assembled at the door of the tabernacle of the congregation," are literally a quotation from Ex. xxxviii. 8, "the women assembling, which assembled at the door of the tabernacle of the congregation." Of course the word for "door" (פֶּתַח) is as applicable to a tent door as to a house door; and is constantly used of the door of the tabernacle in the Pentateuch.

shewn by the Kenites to Israel in the wilderness (1 S. xv. 6).

Even verbal quotations from the Pentateuch are pointed out. The reference in 1 S. ii. 22 to Ex. xxxviii. 8, has been already mentioned. The people ask them a king (1 S. viii. 5, 6), in language which shews that they had the very words of Moses (Deut. xvii. 14) in their minds. The words of 1 S. viii. 3 are evidently written with allusion to Deut. xvi. 19. The only inconsistencies which appear are readily explicable by the peculiar, unsettled condition of the nation in the days of Samuel and the early days of David. Especially when the ark was in captivity and there was no longer the sacred presence of God at Shiloh, Samuel sanctioned the offering of sacrifice in other places beside the Tabernacle (1 S. vii. 17; x. 8; xvi. 2—5). But indeed the command to sacrifice only in the place to be chosen by God was not binding until that place had been chosen, viz. Mount Zion, and the tabernacle, to be succeeded by the Temple, had been set up there. The difficulty that Samuel a Levite (1 Chron. vi. 22—28), but not a priest, should be said to have sacrificed (1 S. ix. 13), is removed, if we consider how frequently it is said of others, of Joshua (viii. 30, 31), of Saul (1 S. xiii. 9, 10), of David (2 S. xxiv. 25), of Solomon (1 K. iii. 4), of the people (1 K. iii. 2), that they sacrificed, it being in all these cases apparently understood that a priest was present to offer the sacrifice (see Deut. xviii. 3; 1 S. ii. 13; 1 K. iii. 1—4. Comp. 1 Chron. xvi. 39, 40). Samuel, as prophet and prince, blesses the sacrifice (1 S. ix. 13): but there is no evidence that he slew it. If he slew it, still the man who brought the offering might slay it, but he could not sprinkle the blood on the altar.

This is an important point in the history of Israel. Supposing Moses to have been the author of the Pentateuch and the facts recorded in it to be historical, we have now found just what we might expect to find. The land of Canaan is conquered by Joshua, the lieutenant and successor of Moses, who endeavours to establish his people in their new settlements by enforcing upon them a strict observance of all the ordinances of the Mosaic Law. After his death, and even during his failing years, we find the Israelites demoralized by long wars, settling imperfectly down to their civil duties and institutions, acknowledging, and in the main, both ecclesiastically and politically, guided by the laws of the Pentateuch, yet without a strong and settled government to enforce their strict and constant observance. Samuel, prophet, judge, and almost priest, becomes at length the chief ruler. He consistently aims at consolidating and reforming the state of society. To this end, though he apparently makes no change in the established worship of the country, which had not widely departed from that ordained by Moses, yet he strives to bring all the ordinances both of Church and State back to conformity with the institutions of the Pentateuch. This is pretty certain, either that he followed these institutions or that he invented them. The only record we have of him and of his acts is to be found in the first book called by his name. There certainly he appears as a follower not as an inventor; and the Book of Judges, which most of the modern critics admit to be ancient, testifies to the existence and authority (though at times to the popular neglect) of these ordinances, as much as do the books of Samuel. The reason, why he is charged with the invention, is that after him the main facts of the history and the principal laws of the Pentateuch were undoubtedly known, and there is the utmost anxiety on the part of the objectors to prove that they had not been known before. But, besides what we shall endeavour to shew presently, viz. that Samuel could not except by a miracle have invented the institutions of the Law, the history of Samuel is wholly inconsistent with the theory that he was a forger. "In his history there is too much of the Mosaic element to do without Moses and the Pentateuch, there is too little to betray his intention to bring the system into prominence." (Smith, 'Pentateuch,' I. p. 172.) The Pentateuch and the Mosaic system silently underlie the whole history of Samuel; but, in the midst of a general subjection to it, there are at least some apparent departures from it, which are utterly inconsistent with the belief that Samuel was its forger. It is there: but it is there without parade or observation.

The times of David and Solomon.

It is perhaps scarcely necessary to trace minutely the references to the Pentateuch, and the observance of the Law of Moses through these reigns. The facts are the same as before; the Levitical priesthood, the tabernacle, the ark, the sacrifices, all are the same; but there are two things to be observed now, which bring us fresh evidence of the existence of, and the respect paid to, the Pentateuch, and of the acceptance by the nation of the ordinances of the Tabernacle.

1. In David we have not only a king but an author. A large number of the Psalms are assignable to him, either as their author or as their compiler. Now it is true, that the later Psalms (such as the 78th, 105th, 106th, 136th) are much fuller of historical references to the Exodus than the earlier Psalms, the Psalms of David: but it will be found that the passing allusions, and the similarity of expressions and sentences, amounting sometimes to evident quotations, are far more abundant in the Psalms of David. It is impossible to compare the following, even in the English Version (but in the Hebrew it is much more apparent), without being convinced that David had in his mind the words or the thoughts of the author of the Pentateuch.

Ps. i. 3.	Gen. xxxix. 3, 23.
„ iv. 5 (Heb. 6).	Deut. xxxiii. 19.
„ „ 6 (Heb. 7).	Num. vi. 26.
„ viii. 6, 7, 8.	Gen. i. 26, 28.
„ ix. 12.	Gen. ix. 5.
„ xv. 5.	Ex. xxii. 25, Lev. xxv. 36. Ex. xxiii. 8. Deut. xvi. 19.
„ xvi. 4.	Ex. xxiii. 13.
„ „ 5, 6.	Deut. xxxii. 9.
„ xvii. 7.	Deut. xxxii. 10.
„ xxiv. 1.	Ex. xix. 5. Deut. x. 14.
„ xxvi. 6.	Ex. xxx. 19, 20.
„ xxx. Heading.	Deut. xx. 5.
„ xxxix. 12.	Lev. xxv. 23.
Ps. lxviii. 1.	Num. x. 35.
„ „ 4.	Deut. xxxiii. 26.
„ „ 7.	Ex. xiii. 21.
„ „ 8.	Ex. xix. 16.
„ „ 17.	Deut. xxxiii. 2.
„ lxxxvi. 8.	Ex. xv. 11.
„ „ 15.	Ex. xxxiv. 6.
„ ciii. 17, 18.	Ex. xx. 6. Deut. vii. 9.
„ cx. 4.	Gen. xiv. 18.
„ cxxxiii. 2.	Ex. xxx. 25, 30.

2. In Solomon we have also a royal author. His language, however, is not so much penetrated with the language of the Pentateuch as is that of David. Indeed the nature of his writings, which are mostly proverbs or apophthegms, does not admit of much reference to earlier works. Yet, even so, where the subject leads to it, we may trace an evident acquaintance with the language of Moses. See for instance the third chapter of Proverbs, where v. 3 appears to allude to Ex. xxii. 9, Deut. vi. 1; v. 9 to Ex. xxii. 29, Deut. xxvi. 2; v. 12 to Deut. viii. 5; v. 18 to Gen. ii. 9. Many other phrases in the Proverbs are borrowed directly from the Pentateuch. Thus in Prov. x. 18, "He that uttereth slander," is a Hebrew phrase of peculiar significance occurring only here and Num. xiii. 32; xiv. 36, 37; the expressions in Prov. x. 1; xx. 10, 23, are taken from the very words of Lev. xix. 36; Deut. xxv. 13. The words of xi. 13; xx. 19, "the talebearer" (literally "he that walketh being a talebearer"), are taken from Lev. xix. 16, "Thou shalt not go up and down as a talebearer," lit. "Thou shalt not walk being a talebearer."

But that which specially connects Solomon with the history of the Exodus, is that he was the builder of the Temple. Now the Temple is a fixed and enlarged Tabernacle. All the proportions of the Tabernacle are carefully retained, but the size is exactly doubled. All the instruments and the sacred vessels are the same, except that they are magnified. Nothing material is altered, except that the Temple is a structure of stone, whilst the Tabernacle was a tent covered with skin; and in the Temple there is magnificence, whereas in the Tabernacle, notwithstanding the gold and embroidery, there was comparative simplicity.

Mr Fergusson, the able writer of the article *Temple* in Smith's 'Dict. of the Bible,' has shewn with great clearness, that the proportions and construction of the Tabernacle were those of a tent, most admirably suited for its purpose in the wilderness, having every requisite which a Tent-temple ought to have. It is a strong proof of the reverence in which Solomon held the original pattern, that he and his architects should have so closely imitated the Tent in their erection of a stone Temple. Unless the Tent and all its accompaniments had existed and been described, the Temple of Solomon would have been almost impossible. No one would have thought of building a house with all the proportions of a tent, except to perpetuate the relation of the house to the tent, the Temple's ancestral rights in the Tabernacle. In the words of Ewald, "The Temple of Solomon itself, notwithstanding all its splendour and its expanded proportions, shews itself to be only a tent on a large scale, though no longer portable."

The divided kingdom.

After the separation of the ten tribes from Judah, though the worship of the true God was preserved only in Judah, and idolatry prevailed in Israel, there is still evidence that in both kingdoms the Pentateuch was acknowledged, both as a history and a law. In Judah, we find "the Book of the Law of the Lord" used as the great text-book for teaching the people in the reign of Jehoshaphat (2 Chron. xvii. 9). In another reign the king, Uzziah, ventures to offer incense contrary to the Law (Num. xvi. 1 sqq.), and he is stricken with leprosy as a punishment (2 Chron. xxvi. 16—21). Hezekiah, a great reformer in Judah, institutes all his reforms on principles strictly according with the law of the Pentateuch, and is specially noted as having "kept all the commandments, which the Lord commanded Moses." 2 K. xviii. 6. To his day had descended that venerable relic of the wilderness "the brazen serpent which Moses had made." The honour paid to it clearly proves the acceptance of its history by the Jewish people: but, because that honour had then become excessive, Hezekiah in his ardent zeal for purity of worship brake it in pieces, 2 K. xviii. 4. We turn to the kingdom of Israel. Jeroboam is warned by Ahijah the Prophet that he should keep the statutes and commandments of God (1 K. xi. 38), evidently the well-known statutes and commandments of the law. When, instead of doing so, he seduces the people to idolatry, it is still with reference to the history of the Exodus, "Behold thy gods, O Israel, which brought thee up out of the land of Egypt," 1 K. xii. 28. The very place of his worship, Bethel, was probably consecrated by the history of Jacob and the appearance of God to him there. The feast appointed 1 K. xii. 32, was an imitation of the feast of Tabernacles. Though it was "in a month devised in his own heart" (v. 33), and not at the time decreed in the Law, yet it was "like unto the feast that is in Judah," and ordained on purpose to prevent the people from going up "to the sacrifice in the house of the Lord at Jerusalem" (v. 27). The Levites appear to have remained faithful, and hence Jeroboam is obliged to make the lowest of the people priests (v. 31). We have here the clearest testimony to the existence and authority of the Law even in the description of the most flagrant breach of it.

For the history of the succeeding reigns it may suffice to point attention to the following references in the books of Kings to the laws of the Pentateuch.

1 K. xxi. 3 to Lev. xxv. 23; Num. xxxvi. 8.
" xxi. 10 to Num. xxxv. 30; Deut. xvii. 6, 7; xix. 15.
" xxii. 17 to Num. xxvii. 16, 17.
2 K. iii. 20 to Ex. xxix. 38 sqq.
" iv. 1 to Lev. xxv. 39 &c.
" vi. 18 to Gen. xix. 11.
" vii. 3 to Lev. xiii. 46; Num. v. 3.

But at one period in this history we find a body of illustrious prophets warning the people both of Judah and of Israel or Samaria. Isaiah, Hosea, Amos and Micah, all prophesied during the reigns or part of the reigns of Uzziah, Jotham, Ahaz and Hezekiah, kings of Judah. Isaiah's prophecy was confined to Judah, but Amos and Micah prophesied in both kingdoms, and Hosea wholly or chiefly in the kingdom of Israel.

In all these prophets there are frequent references to the Law, which three of them distinctly name (Is. v. 24; xxx. 9; Hos. iv. 6; viii. 1; Amos ii. 4). Isaiah seems to speak of it as "the Book" (ch. xxix. 12), just as Moses himself speaks of his own record as "the Book" (Ex. xvii. 14, see above). The familiarity of this great prophet and probably of his hearers with the Pentateuch may be seen by comparing Is. i. 10—14 with Ex. xxxiv. 24; Lev. ii. 1, 16; vi. 14, 15; xxiii. passim. Is. ii. 7, xxxi. with Deut. xvii. 16; Is. iii. 14 with Exod. xxii. 5, 26; Is. v. 26 with Deut. xxviii. 49; Is. xxx. 16, 17 with Lev. xxvi. 8; Deut. xxxii. 30, &c.

It is, however, more important for our present purpose to pass on to the other three prophets, as they prophesied in Israel, and so their references will shew, that the Pentateuch, whether as Law or as history, was assumed as the basis of truth even in appeals to the apostate and idolatrous kingdom of Ephraim.

In Hosea we have such references as these, "They have transgressed the covenant like Adam" (not "like men" as Authorized Version), Hos. vi. 7. Jacob "took his brother by the heel in the womb, and by his strength he had power with God: yea, he had power over the angel and prevailed, he wept and made supplication unto him: he found him in Bethel" &c. (Hos. xii. 3, 4, the allusions being to Gen. xxv. 26; xxviii. 11; xxxii. 24). "She shall sing there, as in the days of her youth, and as in the day when she came out of the land of Egypt" (ii. 15). "When Israel was a child, then I loved him, and called my son out of Egypt" (xi. 1, cp. Ex. iv. 22, 23). "I have written to him the great things of my law" (viii. 12).

Amos says, "I brought you up from the land of Egypt, and led you forty years through the wilderness, to possess the land of the Amorite," (ii. 10, the last words being in allusion to Gen. xv. 16), "the whole family which I brought up from the land of Egypt" (iii. 1). He speaks of "the horns of the altar" (iii. 14), in allusion to Ex. xxvii. 2, xxx. 10, and Lev. iv. 7. He speaks of the Nazarites (ii. 11, 12), which doubtless sprang out of the ordinance in Num. vi. 1—21. In chap. iv. 4, 5 he writes, "Come to Bethel, and transgress; at Gilgal multiply transgression; and bring your sacrifices every morning, and your tithes after three years: and offer a sacrifice of thanksgiving with leaven, and proclaim and publish the freewill offerings." These allusions shew an intimate acquaintance with many of the Levitical Laws. One is to the continual burnt-offering, Num. xxviii. Another to the tithe to be laid up at the end of three years, Deut. xiv. 28; xxvi. 13. A third to the prohibition to burn leaven with a meat-offering (Lev. ii. 11), and the exception made in the case of a thank-offering, where direction is given to offer besides the unleavened cakes also an offering of *leavened* bread (Lev. vii. 12, 13). A fourth allusion is to the freewill offering mentioned Lev. xxii. 18—21; Deut. xii. 6. Indeed the accuracy of agreement in this one passage goes far to prove that the law of which Amos speaks was identical with that which we now possess[1].

Micah refers to Genesis. "They shall lick the dust like *the* serpent" (כַּנָּחָשׁ) (vii. 17), in allusion to Gen. iii. 14. He mentions the promises to Abraham and to Jacob (vii. 20). He alludes to the history of the Exodus and of the book of Numbers. "I brought thee up out of the land of Egypt, and redeemed thee out of the house of servants; and I sent before thee Moses, Aaron, and Miriam. O my people, remember now what Balak king of Moab consulted, and what Balaam the son of Beor answered him," &c. (vi. 4, 5).

Is it possible that these prophets, thus speaking, or the people among whom they spoke, should not have had the Books of Moses before them?

The reign of Josiah.

We come now to the time of Josiah. In his reign we have abundant evidence that the ordinances observed, when the temple had been purified, were those of the Mosaic Law. The Passover was then held unto the Lord God, as it was written

1 McCaul, 'Examination of Bp. Colenso's Difficulties,' p. 183, third Edition, 1863.

in the book of the Covenant (2 K. xxiii.), "according to the word of the Lord by the hand of Moses" (2 Chron. xxxv. 6). The 14th day of the first month is the day appointed (2 Chr. xxxv. 1). The sacrifices are Mosaic (2 Chr. xxxv. 7—10). The priests assisted by the Levites kill the Passover and sprinkle the blood (Ib. v. 11). The priests are the sons of Aaron (v. 14). The custom of the Passover is traced from the time of Samuel to that of Josiah (v. 18), &c., &c.

But in this reign we meet with that remarkable event, the finding of the Book of the Law in the Temple by Hilkiah the High priest. It is unnecessary to determine here what may be meant by "the book of the Law" (2 K. xxii. 8), or "a book of the Law of the Lord by Moses" (2 Chr. xxxiv. 14). Whether it were the whole Pentateuch, or Deuteronomy only, or portions of the whole, has been often questioned. It seems however pretty clear, that Deuteronomy was at least a portion of the book thus found. The curses referred to in 2 Chr. xxxiv. 24, are either those in Lev. xxvi. or those in Deut. xxvii. xxviii. The effect which they produce upon the king, and his evident conviction that they concern himself especially, "for *me*, and for the people, and for all Judah," (2 K. xxii. 13), seem to point to the curses in Deuteronomy; as there only the king is threatened (Deut. xxviii. 36), there too the judgments denounced seem more specially national, and such as would most signally apply to the condition of Judah in the days of Josiah.

But it is a natural question, Whence came it that the book thus found should so have awakened the conscience and aroused the anxieties of the king, if the Pentateuch had all along been the acknowledged statute book of his people, and the text book of their faith?

Let us then notice first, that the Law was to be kept carefully in the Tabernacle or Temple. Moses commanded that the book of the law, which he had written, should be put in the side of the ark of the covenant and there preserved (Deut. xxxi. 26). It is extremely probable (the language seems to imply it) that the very autograph of Moses was thus stored up, first in the Tabernacle and afterwards in the Temple. We, who have manuscripts of the New Testament in the fullest preservation 14 or 15 centuries old, and Egyptian papyri, some unquestionably much older than Moses still legible, others written in the 14th century B. C. in perfect preservation, need not wonder if this treasured MS. of the Pentateuch had lasted from Moses to Josiah, a period of only 700 years, and that in the dry climate of Palestine. Let us next observe the long prevalence of idolatry and ungodliness in the reigns preceding that of Josiah. There is a ray of light in the reign of Hezekiah, but the darkness settles down again more thickly than ever in the reign of his son Manasseh. That reign, extending over more than half a century (2 K. xxi. 1), witnessed the greatest spread of idolatry, and of all the vices which accompanied idolatry in Palestine, the most cruel persecution of the faithful, and the most outrageous profanation of the sanctuary ever known in Israel. Manasseh built the high places and reared up altars for Baal; he built idolatrous altars in the courts of the temple, made his sons to pass through fire, dealt with wizards, and even set up a graven image, probably of the foulest possible character, "in the house of which the Lord said to David and to Solomon his son, In this house and in Jerusalem......... will I put my name for ever" (vv. 3—7, 2 Chr. xxxiii. 7). Thus he seduced the people "to do more evil than did the nations whom the Lord destroyed before the children of Israel" (v. 9). "Moreover Manasseh shed innocent blood very much, till he had filled Jerusalem from one end to another" (v. 16, also Joseph. 'Ant.' x. 3. 1). There was no doubt a short season of repentance at the end of his reign (2 Chron. xxxiii. 12 sqq.) in which the idol was taken from the Temple and the altar of the Lord repaired; but his son Amon succeeded, and again did evil in the sight of the Lord, and served the idols which his father served, and worshipped them (2 K. xxi. 19, sq). To these two evil reigns and to a long inheritance of corruption, Josiah succeeded at eight years of age. He early shewed his piety, even from the age of sixteen turning to the Lord, and at the age of twenty commencing the purification of worship (2 Chr. xxxiv. 3). At the age of 26 (the 18th of his reign) the book of the Law was found by Hilkiah in the Temple (2 K. xxii. 3). The ark which had been removed from the Temple (2 Chr. xxxv. 3) during the sacrilegious reign of Manasseh, had been brought back again: and wherever the book of the Law may have been concealed, very likely built into a wall by the priests to keep it from the hand of the spoiler, it was now brought to light again by the High priest Hilkiah.

Let us remember then, 1st, that very probably this was the autograph of Moses; 2ndly, that since the reign of Hezekiah, a period of seventy-five years, it is very unlikely that any king should have made a copy of the law, as commanded in Deuteronomy (xvii. 18); moreover it is very likely that Hezekiah's copy should have been destroyed or laid aside and forgotten; 3rdly, that by a cruel persecution idolatrous worship had long been upheld, and the worshippers of the Lord prohibited from exercising or teaching their faith; the prophets having been silenced, Isaiah according to Jewish tradition having been sawn asunder early in Manasseh's reign; 4thly, that Josiah was still young and only feeling his way to truth and to the restoration of religion. We shall then not think it strange that he should have been ignorant of much of the purport of the Pentateuch, nor that when the book, perhaps written by the very hand of Moses under the direction of God, was brought out and read to him, he should have been deeply impressed by its burning words, seeming to come straight into his soul as if they had been sent down to him from the cloud and the tempest and the mountain which burned with fire. Writing in those early days was very scarce; reading was probably confined to very few. In the middle ages of Europe, if it were possible to conceive such a state of corruption as that in the reign of Manasseh overspreading any Christian nation, it would not have been impossible for a young king to be ignorant of the contents of the Scriptures of the New Testament. Yet there can be no period of Christian history in which copies of the Scriptures were not far more abundant in every Christian country in Europe, and the power of reading them far more general, than can have been the case in Palestine at any time before the captivity.

There is nothing then to astonish us in the effect produced on Josiah by the reading of the threats of judgment from the Temple copy of the Law. That it was the Temple copy of the Law, all the most competent witnesses were satisfied. The High priest, the Scribes, Huldah the Prophetess (see 2 K. xxii. 8, 12, 14), the elders of the people (ch. xxiii. 1), the priests and Levites (xxiii. 4), those to whom some knowledge at least of the past had come down, some acquaintance with the Scriptures must have remained, all apparently acknowledged that the book found was the book of the Law by the hand of Moses. Had it been possible that a forger should then for the first time have produced it, it cannot be that so many independent witnesses should have been imposed upon to receive it. The story of its finding is told simply and without parade. It is what might very easily have happened, for it is like enough that the book would have been hidden, and Josiah's repairing of the Temple would bring it to light. The effect produced on Josiah's pious mind is exactly what might have been looked for. But, that, under all the circumstances of long continued corruption and apostasy, any one should have been able to impose such a work and such a law, as the Pentateuch, on king, priests, elders and people, even if any one at that time could possibly have written it, exceeds all power of credence.

The Captivity and the Return.

The Prophets of the Captivity acknowledge the Law, and refer to the Pentateuch as much as any of those that preceded them. Jeremiah began to prophesy in the 13th year of the reign of Josiah. The portion of his book from ch. ii. 1 to ch. viii. 17, is generally acknowledged to have been written before the finding of the Book of the Law by Hilkiah; but in those chapters there are statements concerning the Law and quotations from the books of Moses, which shew that Jeremiah was then well acquainted with the Pentateuch. "They that handle the Law know me not" (Jer. ii. 8). "How say ye, We are wise, and the Law of the Lord is with us?" (viii. 8). Here we have the common mode of referring to the Law, as a well-known authority. Chap. ii. 6 has allusions to Deut. viii. 15; Numb. xiv. 7, 8; Lev. xviii. 25—28; Numb. xxxv. 33, 34. Again, ch. ii. 28 is a quotation from Deut. xxxii. 37, 38. Chap. iv. 4 is a virtual quotation from Deut. x. 16, xxx. 6; and the figure used occurs nowhere else in the Scriptures. Ch. v. 15, 17 contains unmistakeable quotations from Deut. xxviii. 31, 49. It is of less importance to multiply examples of this kind, because it is now admitted that the writings of Jeremiah are throughout impregnated with the language of Deuteronomy, insomuch that the modern critics have argued from this that Jeremiah must himself have been the Deuteronomist.

Ezekiel prophesied during the captivity. Dr M'Caul has observed that in the one short passage (Ezek. xxii. 7—12), there are at least twenty-nine references to, or rather quotations from, Exodus, Leviticus, and Deuteronomy, perceptible in the English version, and which the marginal references in an ordinary Bible sufficiently point out, but which by consulting the original will be found to contain the very words of the Hebrew. In v. 26 again, where the Law is distinctly named, there are at least four more references to Lev. x. 10, xi. 45, xx. 25, Ex. xxxi. 13. Chapters xviii. and xx. contain references and quotations innumerable; ch. xx. being a recapitulation of all that happened in the wilderness[1].

On the return from captivity we learn, that at the Feast of Tabernacles (according to the ordinance in Deut. xxxi. 10—13), Ezra brought the book of the Law of Moses, which the Lord had commanded Israel, that he read it from morning till midday "before the men and the women, and those that could understand; and the ears of all the people were attentive unto the book of the Law" (Neh. viii. 3). That they accepted it against their own interests and affections is evident from their being induced to put away their heathen wives (see Ezra, ch. x). Some of them it is plain, understood the book as it was read to them; but to some of them, we are told, Jeshua, with the Levites and others, "read in the book of the Law distinctly (or rather 'giving an explanation'), and caused them to understand the reading" (Neh. viii. 7, 8). The older men and women, no doubt, retained their knowledge of the ancient Hebrew, but the younger men, who were grandchildren or great-grandchildren of those who were first carried captive, had almost lost the language of their forefathers, and had brought from the land of the Chaldees that Aramaic tongue, Chaldee or Syriac, which soon became the vernacular language of Judea. Hebrew was not quite lost, or Haggai and Malachi would not have written their prophecies in Hebrew; but the change was rapidly taking place. It is the constant Jewish tradition that Ezra (besides writing Ezra, Nehemiah, Esther, and 1 and 2 Chronicles) collected and reduced to order all the earlier books of the Old Testament. It is said, moreover, that "the reading distinctly the Law and causing the people to understand," referred to above, was the introduction by Ezra of the custom, which prevailed afterwards, of having Chaldee translations or paraphrases read with the Hebrew Scriptures, for the use of the Chaldee speaking Jews. It is also said, that it was Ezra who transcribed the Scriptures from the ancient Hebrew character (now known as Samaritan) into the modern Hebrew or Chaldee character. Whether or not Ezra did all this, it certainly was done no very long time after the captivity; and Ezra, who was "a ready scribe in the Law of Moses," who bore a high commission to restore the Temple and the worship of God, was the most likely person to have been intrusted with this great work.

However this may be, we are brought now to a new kind of testimony. The Pentateuch, as preserved by the Jews, has come down to us in the modern Hebrew or Chaldee character. It was known to the ancient Jews and to the Christian fathers, that there was also a copy of the Pentateuch preserved by the Samaritans in a different character. For a thousand years that Samaritan Pentateuch was lost to the Christian Church,

[1] M'Caul's 'Examination of Bp. Colenso's Difficulties,' pp. 163 sqq.

and it was almost doubted whether it had ever existed; but in the year 1616, Pietro della Valle obtained a complete MS. of it from the Samaritans in Damascus. Several other copies have since been discovered, one of which is believed to be of the most remote antiquity. In almost all particulars (dates being the principal exception) this Samaritan Pentateuch agrees with the Jewish Pentateuch. There can have been no collusion between Jews and Samaritans, for they were at mortal feud: and there are but two periods in which we can suppose the Samaritans to have become possessed of this copy of the Pentateuch. Manasseh, brother of the High priest Jaddua, being expelled from his priesthood for marrying the daughter of Sanballat the Horonite (Neh. xiii. 28), became the first High priest of the Samaritans and of the temple erected on Mount Gerizim. He was joined by many priests and Levites, who, like himself, refused to put away their heathen wives[1]. It is the belief of many, that the so-called Samaritan Pentateuch was carried by these priests from Jerusalem to Samaria. Now they would certainly not have taken it with them, testifying as it did against their heathen marriages and their schismatical worship, had they not fully believed in its genuineness and Divine authority: nor would the Samaritans have accepted it but for a like conviction on their parts. At all events, at no later period could the Hebrew Scriptures have been imposed on the dissentient Samaritans. This document therefore preserved in Samaria by the Samaritans is an independent witness, from at least the time of Ezra, to the integrity of the five books of Moses. Its witness may go back to a much earlier date; for many think, and that with much ground of reason, that the Pentateuch was carried to the Cuthites who had peopled Samaria by that Israelitish priest, who was sent by Esarhaddon, that he might teach them the worship of the Lord. (See 2 K. xvii. 28; Ezra iv. 2.). This if it be correct would carry back the independent testimony of the Samaritan Pentateuch not only to the time of Ezra but to the reign of Manasseh, the grandfather of Josiah, about B. C. 680.

[1] Joseph. 'Ant.' XI. 8, §§ 2, 4.

We pass on to the translation into Greek of B.C. 280, the famous translation of the LXX, which has a remarkable resemblance to the text of the Samaritan Pentateuch, and which proves the acceptance of the Pentateuch by the Jews in Egypt. Another link in the chain is the First Book of Maccabees, where we read of the fury of Antiochus Epiphanes, who strove to destroy the books of the Law, and of the zeal of the priests and people, who chose rather to die than to submit to his cruel edicts (1 Macc. i. 56 sqq.) The books of the Apocrypha perpetually refer to and quote the Pentateuch. Ecclesiasticus especially (perhaps the most ancient and most important) is full of such references. (See for instance ch. xvi. 8, 10; xvii. 1—4.)

That Chaldee paraphrases were made very soon after the return from captivity we are well assured. The earliest which is extant is that of Onkelos; the date of which is uncertain, by some placed in the century before our Saviour, but most probably to be referred to a date nearly coincident with the earthly life of Christ. The Targum of Onkelos is a paraphrase of the Pentateuch as we have it now. These Targums had been in use long before they were written down. When writing was comparatively scarce, the memory was so exercised, that a Targum on the Pentateuch would easily be handed down memoriter, so that probably the Targum of Onkelos really represents that which is much more ancient than itself.

Lastly, we come to the *New Testament itself.* As our purpose is to trace evidence, rather than to adduce authority, it may be sufficient here to say that, wherever the Pentateuch is referred to by the Apostles or by the Lord Himself, its Mosaic origin, as well as its Divine authority, is clearly expressed or implied. (See for instance, Matt. xix. 8; Mark x. 5; xii. 26; Luke xx. 37; Joh. i. 17; v. 46, 47; viii. 5; Acts iii. 22; vii. 37 sqq. &c. &c.).

The chain then is unbroken from the books of Joshua and Judges to the New Testament, and the words of Jesus Christ. We may fairly ask, whether any book, ancient or modern, has such a stream of concurrent and credible testimony in support of its claims to genuineness and authenticity.

3. The third point to be proved is, *That the internal evidence points to Moses and to him only as the writer of the Pentateuch.*

(1) The author of the Pentateuch and the giver of the Levitical Law had an intimate acquaintance with Egypt, its literature, its laws and its religion. This is a wide subject, and one which branches out into numerous details. It can only be briefly touched on here. Spencer ('de Legibus Hebræorum') shewed at great length that no one could have invented the Laws of Moses who was not well skilled in Egyptian learning. Bryant ('On the Plagues of Egypt') has shewn how the plagues were but an extension and accumulation of the natural evils of the country intensified by the Divine Judgment. Hengstenberg ('Egypt and the Books of Moses') has shewn how thoroughly an acquaintance with Egypt permeates the whole Pentateuch. This will appear in the following pages, when we come to the history of Joseph, to the Exodus, and to the laws of Moses. It would be impossible to enter into all the details here. Let us take a very few.

The making of bricks among the Egyptians by captives is pourtrayed on the monuments, especially of the 18th dynasty (most probably the dynasty of the Exodus) in such close conformity with the language of the Book of Exodus i. 14; v. 7, 8, 18, that the one might seem to be a description of the other (see Brugsch, 'Hist. d'Egypte,' p. 106). "Ruins of great brick buildings are found throughout Egypt" (Rosellini). "The use of crude bricks baked in the sun was universal in Egypt" (Wilkinson, II. p. 96, Hengst. p. 2). Bricks were made in Egypt under the direction of the king, as may appear by the impressions found on some of them. And in the composition of the Egyptian bricks there is generally found a certain quantity of chopped straw (Hengst. p. 79).

The ark of papyrus smeared with bitumen in which Moses was exposed, Ex. ii. 3, is suited to Egypt and Egypt only. There only was papyrus employed in the manufacture of many articles, such as mats, baskets, sandals (Herod. II. 37), sails for ships (Herod. II. 96), and even boats; for according to Plutarch ('De Is. et Osiri') Isis was borne upon a boat of papyrus. Bitumen too was of great use in Egypt. It was one of the chief ingredients in embalming; and mummy-shaped figures are found covered with a coating of bitumen (Hengstenb. p. 85).

The plagues of Egypt may be seen either in Bryant (*passim*) or Hengstenberg (p. 103—125), to be the natural troubles of the country magnified, their miraculous character resulting from their appearance and accumulation at the word of Moses and their removal at his prayer.

The Mosaic laws and institutions of worship are penetrated throughout by a knowledge of Egyptian customs.

The connection between the cherubic figures overshadowing the mercy seat and the Egyptian sculptures is traced in the note at end of Gen. iii. infra.

The distinction of clean and unclean meats is eminently Levitical, but it is eminently Egyptian also (Hengstenb. p. 180 sqq.). The Egyptian priesthood was by inheritance (Herod. II. 37); so was the Levitical. The Egyptian priests shaved their whole bodies (Herod. ib.); so the Levites were to "shave all their flesh" (Num. viii. 7). The Egyptian priests had to bathe continually (Herod. ib.); so the priests and Levites had to purify themselves by bathing (Ex. xl. 12—15, Num. viii. 7). The priests of Egypt wore none but linen garments (Herod. ib.), so was it with the Israelitish priests (Ex. xxviii. 39—42; xxxix. 27, 28; Lev. vi. 10): and there is no known example of any other priesthood of antiquity clothed only in linen (Hengst. p. 145—149). The anointing of Aaron (Lev. viii. 7—12, 30) when clothed in his priestly robes has an exact parallel in the Egyptian sculptures, where the king is anointed, clothed in royal robes and with cap and crown on his head (Wilkinson, i. p. 275; Smith on the 'Pentateuch,' p. 295).

The ceremony of the scapegoat, where the priest confesses the sins of the people on the head of the goat, which is then sent away into the wilderness, finds a parallel in what Herodotus tells us, viz. that the Egyptians heaped curses on the head of the victim and then carried it and sold it to Greek traders, or, if there were no Greeks among them, threw it into the river (Herod. II. 39).

The Urim and Thummim (Ex. xxviii. 30) on the breastplate of the High priest correspond with what we learn from Ælian ('Var. Hist.' lib. XIV. c. 34) and Diodorus (lib. XXXI. c. 75), as also from the monuments, that the chief priest among the Egyptians, when acting the part of judge, wore round his neck an image of sapphire, which was called *Truth* (Hengstenb. p. 149—153).

The writing of the commandments of God on the door-posts and gates (Deut. xi. 20) is in strict accordance with the drawings of Egyptian architecture, where the door-posts of temples and tombs are covered with hieroglyphics (Smith, 'Pentateuch,' I. p. 257).

The erecting pillars and coating them with plaster to prepare for inscriptions (Deut. xxvii. 2, 3) is in strict conformity with Egyptian custom (Hengst. p. 90).

The infliction of the bastinado as prescribed in Deut. xxv. 2, is graphically illustrated in the sculptures at Beni Hassan (Smith, p. 258). The ox treading out the corn unmuzzled (Deut. xxv. 4) was the custom in Egypt, as the monuments also prove (Smith, ib., Hengst. p. 223). The offerings for the dead forbidden in Deut. xxvi. 14, are evidently such as were prevalent in Egypt, where small tables were placed in the tombs, bearing offerings of ducks, cakes and the like (Smith, ib.).

These are a few of the parallels, which prove an intimate acquaintance with the customs of Egypt in him who wrote the Pentateuch and delivered the Mosaic Law.

(2) The history and the Law of the Israelites both bear marks and tokens of their passage through the wilderness, and long residence in it.

This is specially to be observed concerning the Tabernacle. "It is proved," says Ewald, "to have been derived from the early times of the wanderings. It was only the most sacred of the many tents of a migratory people, resembling the general's tent in the midst of a camp; and according to the minute descriptions of it, all the objects belonging to it were adapted for carrying, like those of an ordinary tent[1]."

The memory of their long dwelling in tents was preserved among the Israelites throughout their generations. Not only was the feast of Tabernacles observed from the time of Moses to that of Christ, but their language and monuments continually bore witness to the same. "The very words 'camps' and 'tents' remained long after they had ceased to be literally applicable. The 'tents of the Lord' were in the precincts of the temple. The cry of sedition, evidently handed down from ancient times was, 'To your tents, O Israel!' 'Without the camp' (Heb. xiii. 13) was the expression applied to the very latest events of Jerusalem. 'Thou that dwellest between the Cherubim, shine forth! Before Ephraim, Benjamin and Manasseh, stir up Thy strength, and come, and help us' (Ps. lxxx. 1) ... We see in this the reflected image of the ancient march, when the ark of God went forth, the pillar of fire shining high above it, surrounded by the warrior tribes of Ephraim, Benjamin, and Manasseh[2]." The elders or chiefs of the tribes correspond with the Sheykhs of the desert, the office never disappears in the history of the people, till out of the Sheykhs of the desert grew the elders of the synagogues[3]. The materials which are recorded as used in the construction of the Tabernacle and its vessels were such as could be best obtained in the desert. The ark was not made "of oak, the usual wood of Palestine, nor of cedar, the usual wood employed in Palestine for sacred purposes, but of *shittim* or acacia, a tree of rare growth in Syria, but the most frequent, not even excepting the palm, in the peninsula of Sinai[4]." The coverings of the Tabernacle were goat's hair and ram-skin dyed red after the Arabian fashion, seal-skin (*Tachash*, see Gesen. s. v.) from the adjoining gulfs of the Red Sea, and fine linen from the Egyptian spoils[5]. Even the distinc-

[1] Ewald, Translated by Martineau, p. 441.
[2] Stanley, 'Jewish Church,' I. p. 163.
[3] Ibid. p. 161.
[4] Ibid. p. 163.
[5] Ibid. p. 165.

tion of the different kinds of food permitted or forbidden in the Law "may be traced with the greatest probability to the peculiarities of the condition of Israel at the time of the giving of that Law. The animals of which they might freely eat were those that belonged especially to their pastoral state—the ox, the sheep, the goat, to which were added the various classes of the chamois and gazelle. As we read the detailed permission to eat every class of what may be called the game of the wilderness, 'the wild goat and the roe and the red deer and the ibex and the antelope and the chamois,' a new aspect is suddenly presented to us of a large part of the life of the Israelites in the desert. It reveals them to us as a nation of hunters, it shews them to us clambering over the smooth rocks, scaling the rugged pinnacles of Sinai, as the Arab chamois hunters of the present day, with bows and arrows instead of guns. Such pursuits they could only in a limited degree have followed in their own country. The permission, the perplexity implied in the permission, could only have arisen in a place where the animals in question abounded[1]." The inevitable conclusion is, that the Law had its origin in, and the Legislator was intimately acquainted with, the wilderness of Sinai.

(3) Thirdly, the language and the legislation of the Pentateuch has Canaan only in prospect. It is patent throughout that the wording, both of the laws and of the language of the lawgiver, looks forward to a future in Canaan. See Ex. xii. 25—27; xiii. 1. 5; xxiii. 20—33; xxxiv. 11; Lev. xiv. 34; xviii. 3, 24; xix. 23; xx. 22; xxiii. 10; xxv. 2; Num. xv. 2, 18; xxxiv. 2; xxxv. 2—34; Deut. iv. 1; vi. 10; vii. 1; ix. 1; xii. 10, &c.

It has been objected, that the writer of the Pentateuch knew too much of the geography of Palestine for one who had never been there, and that this is an argument against its Mosaic origin. This surely cannot be a valid objection, when we remember, first, that Moses with his knowledge of the history of Genesis and of the wanderings of the old Patriarchs, must have become familiarized with the geography of the land of these wanderings; secondly, that Palestine was well known to the Egyptians, who repeatedly traversed it from the reign of Thothmes I.; thirdly, that Moses had lived for forty years in the wilderness of Sinai feeding the flocks of Jethro, and with his active mind and his deep interest in the country of his forefathers, he was sure to have enquired about, most probably even to have visited, the neighbouring plains of Palestine; fourthly, that he had taken pains to ascertain all the character of the country, of its people, its cities and its fortresses by means of spies, and that probably for many years, as every wise general would do, when preparing to invade a hostile and powerful people. But the very prophecies, which speak so clearly of the future possession of Canaan, and which sceptical criticism will therefore have to be predictions after the event, are just such as would not have been written when the event had become known. Take for instance Deut. xii. 10, "When ye go over Jordan, and dwell in the land which the Lord your God giveth you to inherit, and when He giveth you rest from all your enemies round about, so that ye dwell in safety," &c. This prophecy is indeed referred to in Josh. xxiii. 1, and is spoken of there as though it had been fulfilled in the conquests of Joshua. Yet, when we consider how partially those conquests really gave rest to Israel, how the sins of the people conditioned and, as it were, impaired their fulfilment, how long it was before the words were proved to be true indeed, it will be hardly possible to find any time when a forger could have written them. For instance, could Samuel have written them, with the history of the Book of Judges, a record eminently of unrest and insecurity, before his eyes, himself judging Israel, with the ark of the covenant in the hands of the Philistines, and to be succeeded in his Judgeship by the warlike and turbulent reign of Saul? Indeed the reign of Solomon is the one only reign in the whole history of Israel, in which we witness anything like an united people with a wide dominion and with peace from the neighbouring tribes. That reign was 500 years after the Exodus.

[1] Ibid. pp. 168, 169. See the same subject further discussed, Smith's 'Pentateuch,' pp. 285 sqq.

Would any skilful forger have put words into the mouth of Moses apparently promising, immediately on the conquest of Canaan, rest and peace and security, when it took 500 years of restless and often unsuccessful war to attain security, and even so, when the very next reign saw the nation rent by an incurable schism?

We conclude, that, as the Pentateuch bears all the traces on its brow of Egypt and of the Desert, so also it must have had its origin before the occupation of Canaan.

(4) The language of the Pentateuch is such as to suit the age and character of Moses. The language is undoubtedly archaic. There are several words and forms to be found in the Pentateuch, and to be found nowhere else[1].

It is argued indeed, that these are not so much archaisms as peculiarities; but it is very singular that they should pervade the Pentateuch, which has, till of late, been universally esteemed the most ancient portion of the Bible, and that they should be unknown in the other books, even in those connected with the writers who have been fixed on as probable forgers of the Pentateuch, such as Samuel or Jeremiah.

It is argued again, that the language of the Pentateuch, although in some few fragments (such as Gen. iv. 23, 24, xiv. Gen. xlix. &c.) apparently archaic, is for the most part too like to later Hebrew for us to believe that it came from Moses. To this it may be replied that this is really what we might expect. A language is fixed by its great, and especially by its popular, authors. It is commonly said, that English has been fixed by Shakspeare and the translators of the Bible. Moses, putting aside all question of inspiration, was a man of extraordinary powers and opportunity. If he was not divinely guided and inspired, as all Christians believe, he must have been even a greater genius than he has been generally reckoned. He had had the highest cultivation possible in one of Egypt's most enlightened times; and, after his early training in science and literature, he had lived the contemplative life of a shepherd in Midian. We find him then, with a full consciousness of his heavenly mission, coming forth as legislator, historian, poet, as well as prince and prophet. Such a man could not but mould the tongue of his people. To them he was Homer, Solon, and Thucydides, all in one. Every one that knew anything of letters must have known the books of the Pentateuch. All Hebrew literature, as far as we know, was in ancient times of a sacred character, at all events no other has come down to us; and it is certain that writers on sacred subjects would have been deeply imbued with the language and the thoughts of the books of Moses. Eastern languages, like eastern manners, are slow of change; and there is certainly nothing strange in our finding that in the thousand years from Moses to Malachi, the same tongue was spoken and the same words intelligible; especially in books treating on the same subjects, and where the earlier books must have been the constant study of all the writers down to the very last. It is said, on the authority of Freytag, that the inhabitants of Mecca still speak the pure language of the Koran, written 1200 years ago. Egyptian papyri, with an interval of 1000 years between them,

[1] The most familiar and undoubted are the following:

(α) The Pronoun of the third person singular, except as pointed by the Masoretic Jews, has no variety of gender. Everywhere else we have הוּא (*hoo*) for "he," and הִיא (*hee*) for "she." In the Pentateuch we have הוא doing equal duty for both.

(β) In like manner נַעַר (*nangar*), "a youth," is common to both genders in the Pentateuch, meaning indifferently "boy" or "girl." In all other books נַעַר (*nangar*) is "a boy," but נַעֲרָה (*nangarah*) is "a girl."

(γ) Then we have הָאֵל, "these," constantly for אֵלֶּה, the later form. We have the infinitive of verbs in ה ending in וֹ instead of וֹת, as עֲשׂוֹ, Gen. xxxi. 28; עֲשׂוֹהוּ, Ex. xviii. 18; רְאֹה, Gen. xlviii. 11. So the third person plural præt. constantly ends in וּן instead of the later form in וּ.

(δ) We have words peculiar to the Pentateuch, as אָבִיב, "an ear of corn;" אַמְתַּחַת, "a sack;" בֶּתֶר, "a piece," and בָּתַר to "divide into pieces;" גּוֹזָל, "a young bird;" זֶבֶד, "a present," and זָבַד, "to present;" חֶרְמֵשׁ, "a sickle;" טֶנֶא, "a basket;" הַיְקוּם, "a substance, an existing thing;" כֶּשֶׂב (for כֶּבֶשׂ), "a lamb;" מַסְוֶה, "a veil;" עַר (for עִיר), "a city;" שְׁאֵר, "a blood relation."

are said by Egyptologists to exhibit no change of language or of grammar[1]. We must not reason about such nations as the Israelites, with their comparative isolation and fixedness, from the Exodus to the captivity, on the same principles as we should think of the peoples of modern Europe, where so many elements of change have conspired to alter and to mould their language and their literature. The language of the Pentateuch then is just what the language of Moses would probably have been, simple, forcible, with archaic forms and expressions, but, having formed and stamped all future language, still readily intelligible to the last.

Question of Post-Mosaic Authorship.

Having now seen that so many notes, both external and internal, combine to point out Moses as the author of the Pentateuch, let us enquire whether all or any of them belong to any later prince or prophet.

Joshua may perhaps have been employed by Moses to assist him in his writings, as he was employed to assist him in his wars; and, of course, Joshua had some of the experience of Moses and all the teaching which Moses could give him. Yet nothing points to Joshua as the writer of the Pentateuch. He was eminently a man of war in his early and middle life, and in his old age he had enough and more than enough to do in holding his people in their obedience to the laws.

Samuel was a prophet and a reformer, but he is nowhere presented to us as a legislator; especially it is impossible that Samuel, except by a miracle, could have written books which are so thick set with indications of a knowledge of Egypt, and a knowledge of Sinai. The laws of Moses bear the mark of Egypt from end to end; but Samuel could never have come into contact with Egypt at all: and indeed, as far as history shews us, the Israelites from Joshua to Samuel were utterly isolated from contact with any, except the Canaanites and Philistines, who were mixed up with them, spread all around them, and with whom they were at constant war.

David is as little likely as Samuel to have had time for composing the Pentateuch or drawing up its sanctions. He was a man of war, and though the darling and the hero of his people, yet by no means exercising that kind of control and influence, which is needful for one who would impose a new code of civil and religious laws.

Solomon is the first who appears to have had much intercourse with Egypt after the time of the Exodus, and his extensive and comparatively peaceful reign may appear more suited to the introduction of a new code of legislation than the reigns of any of his predecessors or successors. We have seen, however, how Solomon in his building of the Temple followed the pattern of the Tabernacle. The reverse process, though it has been suggested, is simply impossible[1]. His whole organization indeed proceeds on the basis of the Pentateuch. But his own history is the clearest proof, that he was not the author of the laws contained in it, or the history related in it. In his earlier days we find him a pious and a wise king. He follows out the intentions of his father, and builds a temple to succeed the old tabernacle of the wilderness. But, as he advances in years, he is spoiled by the wealth and luxury, which his power has brought around him. He multiplies wives and lapses into idolatry, a sad instance of one hardened by the deceitfulness of sin,

[1] See Brugsch, 'Revue Archéologique,' 1867, September, p. 179: "In comparing the demotic papyrus (which Brugsch translates) with the romance of the two brothers, even a superficial examination shows not only that the language and the formulæ in the two papyri, separated from each other by an interval of some thousand years, are of the same kind; but also, a point of most special interest, even the grammar has not undergone the least change." It may be added that between the papyrus of the two brothers, written under the 3rd king of the 19th dynasty, and the earliest inscriptions and papyri at least 1000 years earlier, there is nearly the same identity of language.

[1] Is it conceivable that Solomon, about to build a Temple to be the glory of his nation and for the special honour of his God, would have constructed it in fashion like a tent of the desert, in order that it might fit into the story of the desert wanderings and the sacred tabernacle carried through the desert?

and so falling from the living God. Can we conceive the author, or even the chief compiler and enlarger, of the laws and ordinances of the Mosaic code and worship, so carefully and so wisely framed to guard against the seductions of idol worship, being himself the first to fall away under those seductions?

But after the time of Solomon, the possibility of the Pentateuch having been written, and thus the laws of Moses enforced, becomes less and less. The schism of the ten tribes constituted a second kingdom, and the testimony, not of one only, but of two nations, would have been raised against such an attempt. It is impossible to believe, that in any subsequent reign such a book as the Pentateuch, and such a code as that of the Levitical law, with all its strictness and the heavy burden of its observances, should have been imposed upon the kingdom of Judah, either whilst the ten tribes were still living in their own land, or after they had been carried captive to Assyria, and a remnant only remained in Samaria. That the like should have been attempted after the return from captivity is even more impossible, and perhaps is not asserted by any one. The Hebrew language was then dying out, Chaldee rapidly taking its place; and the classic simplicity of the Pentateuch could not have had its origin in the last days of the degeneracy of language and literature.

It must be borne in mind, that any man or succession of men, attempting to write or even extensively to rearrange and enlarge such a book as the Pentateuch, must have set to work in the most diligent and systematic manner to do so. It has been shewn, that from end to end the Pentateuch and the laws of the Pentateuch have deeply imbedded in their words and thoughts ancient Egypt and ancient Sinai. A forger or redactor could only have exhibited such a phenomenon by devoting himself with the utmost care and attention to the study of Egyptian customs and antiquities, and to an acquaintance with the Sinaitic peninsula; and that too on the spot, in the midst of those very countries. Nothing less could have enabled him to produce such a work. He must have studied this with the most deliberate purpose, and must have brought his study to bear with the most consummate skill. Where in the times of Samuel, Solomon, Hezekiah, Josiah, or Ezra, can we look for such a man? And beyond this, if modern critical theories be true, we must look not for one wise head and skilful hand, that should have produced such a result: but the fabric must have grown up bit by bit; an Elohist first, then a first, second, third, fourth, or even more Jehovists, who dovetailed their respective stories and their laws of many colours one into another, making a thing of shreds and patches, which nevertheless, when compacted together, has commanded the wonder of all ages, and every portion of which has the same archaic character, the same familiarity with the Egypt of early dynasties, the same air of the desert, the same apparent impress of the great master's hand. Such a result, under the conditions of Jewish history, is inconceivable as the work of any man; but it is such as the wildest fancy cannot attribute to an indefinite and widely separated succession of many men.

GENESIS.

INTRODUCTION.

IF it be once admitted that the Pentateuch, as a whole, is due to Moses, there can be no difficulty in admitting that Genesis, the most ancient part of the Pentateuch, is due to him. If he wrote the history of the Exodus, he, either as author or compiler, must have written the introductory history of the times of the patriarchs. The unity of design is very manifest throughout. Moses was employed to mould and form a simple and previously enslaved people into an organized nation. He had to give them a code of laws, civil and ecclesiastical, for the guidance of their national life. The infant people was to be a theocracy, the germ and embryo of a theocracy greater than itself, guarded and isolated for fifteen centuries, till by a new revolution it should expand into the Church of Christ. It was obvious therefore, that he, who had to write the earliest chapters of its history, should begin by tracing down its descent from those who had from the first been the depositaries and witnesses of the truth.

If, however, adverse criticism has been busy in trying to dislocate all portions of the Pentateuch, to disprove its unity, and so to shake the evidence for its Mosaic origin; it has been signally busy in so dealing with Genesis. If Moses wrote the later books, he certainly wrote Genesis; and on the other hand, if he did not write Genesis, he wrote nothing. Hence to shake the foundation of Genesis is to destroy the fabric of the Pentateuch. The progress of the criticism has been sufficiently gradual. It was suggested long since by Vitringa, that Moses may have had before him "documents of various kinds coming down from the times of the patriarchs and preserved among the Israelites, which he collected, reduced to order, worked up, and where needful, filled in," *schedas et scrinia patrum, apud Israelitas conservata, Mosem collegisse, digessisse, ornasse, et ubi deficiebant, complesse* ('Obs. Sac.' I. c. 4). A conjecture of this kind was neither unnatural nor irreverent. It is very probable that, either in writing or by oral delivery, the Israelites possessed traditions handed down from their forefathers. It is consistent with the wisdom of Moses, and not inconsistent with his Divine inspiration, that he should have preserved and incorporated with his own work all such traditions, written or oral, as had upon them the stamp of truth.

The next step in the theory was, that taken by Astruc in 1753, who taught, that the names of God (Elohim and JEHOVAH), occurring in the book of Genesis may distinguish respectively the documents or memoirs from which Moses compiled his history. He believed that there were no fewer than twelve documents, the two chief being the Elohistic and the Jehovistic.

Later writers again have varied this theory with every possible variation; some believing that there was one Elohist, and one Jehovist document; others that there were more than one Elohist, and many Jehovists; and exercising a subtle ingenuity, most convincing at least to themselves, they have traced minutely the transitions from one document to another, sometimes even in the midst of a sentence, guided by some catchword or form of expression, which they have, as others think most arbitrarily, assigned to the first or second Elohist, to the first, second, third, or fourth Jehovist, according to the number of authors in which they respectively believe[1]. Another step has been to suggest, that the different documents, often, as it is alleged, giving different versions of the same story, have been carelessly and clumsily put together. And a further still has been to deny, that Moses could be either the Elohist, the Jehovist, or the compiler and redactor, it being evident that the whole was a later work, due perhaps to Samuel, perhaps to Hilkiah or Jeremiah, perhaps still later to Ezra or some survivor from the captivity, or possibly to a collection of the labours, the piously fraudulent labours, of them all.

The salient points in their arguments are these. There appear to be two versions of the history of the creation, the first from Gen i. 1 to Gen. ii. 3, in which only the name Elohim occurs, the other from Gen. ii. onwards, in which the name of JEHOVAH occurs in combination with Elohim. Again, there appear two accounts of the Flood, which though interlaced in the book of Genesis, may be disentangled. These also are characterized respectively by the same variety in the names of God. Similar phenomena are said to prevail throughout the book, and even throughout the Pentateuch, but these are the two most observable. Then comes the well-known passage in Ex. vi. 3, where the Most High says to Moses that He was known to the fathers by the name of El-Shaddai, but by the name JEHOVAH He was not known to them; whence the introduction of the name Jehovah in the history of Adam, Noah, Abraham, &c., is argued to be a proof of later authorship.

It may be well then to shew:

First, that the Book of Genesis is not an ill-digested collection of fragmentary documents, but a carefully arranged narrative with entire unity of purpose and plan.

Secondly, that the use of the names of God is neither arbitrary nor accidental, but consistent throughout with the Mosaic authorship, and the general scope of the history.

1. *Unity of plan and purpose throughout.*

First then, as to the organic structure of the book, though it may be somewhat obscured by the modern division into chapters and verses, as it was of old by the Jewish division of the Pentateuch into *perashim* or sections; careful examination will shew, that the arrangement is methodical and orderly from first to last.

The book begins with a general introduction, from ch. i. 1 to ch. ii. 3, wherein the creation of the universe is related in language of simple grandeur, very possibly in words handed down from the remotest antiquity, than which none could be more fitted here for the use of the sacred historian.

After this the book consists of a series of *Toledoth*, or genealogical histories, the first of which is called "the Toledoth of the heavens and the earth," ch. ii. 4; the others being the respective histories of the different families of man, especially of the ancestors of the people of Israel, from Adam to the death of Joseph[1]. The

[1] An abstract of the different theories from Astruc to the present day may be seen in Havernick ('Int. to Pent.' p. 45, Translation, Clark, Edinburgh), and 'Aids to Faith,' M'Caul's Essay on 'Mosaic Record of Creation,' p. 191.

[1] The word *Toledoth* has by some been rendered "origins," as "generations" cannot properly be used of the creation of heaven and earth; but it is not necessary to drop the figurative language in a translation. By an easy metaphor, the word, which described well the family history of a race of men, was applied to the history of the material creation. The word, moreover, as used in Genesis, does not mean a

great divisions of the book will be found to be:

1. The Introduction, from ch. i. 1 to ch. ii. 3.

2. "The generations of the heavens and the earth," beginning with ch. ii. 4, and extending on through the history of the fall to the birth of Seth, ch. iv.

3. "The book of the generations of Adam," from ch. v. to vi. 8.

4. "The generations of Noah," giving the history of Noah's family till his death, from vi. 9 to end of ix.

5. "The generations of the sons of Noah," giving an account of the overspreading of the earth, from x. 1 to xi. 9.

6. "The generations of Shem," the line of the promised seed, down to Abram, Nahor, and Haran, the sons of Terah, xi. 10 to 26.

7. "The generations of Terah," the father of Abraham, from whom also in the female line the family was traced through Sarah and Rebekah, from xi. 27 to xxv. 11[1].

8. "The generations of Ishmael," from xxv. 12 to xxv. 18.

9. "The generations of Isaac," containing the history of him and his family from the death of his father to his own death, xxv. 19 to end of xxxv.

10. "The generations of Esau," xxxvi. 1—8.

11. "The generations of Esau in Mount Seir," xxxvi. 9 to xxxvii. 1.

12. "The generations of Jacob," giving the history of Jacob and his sons to his own death and the death of Joseph, xxxvii. 2 to the end of ch. l.

history of the mode in which persons or things came into existence, but rather the history of those who descended from them. Thus "the Toledoth of Adam" gives the history of Adam and his posterity. In like manner "the Toledoth of the heavens and the earth" is the history of the material universe and its productions. See Keil on the 'Pentateuch,' Vol. I. pp. 70 sqq. (Clark, Edinburgh).

[1] It seems strange that the "generations of Abraham" should not be given distinctly from those of his father, and Quarry thinks that the title may have existed, and have fallen out of the MS. just before the last clause of xii. 4. The reason, however, which he himself assigns, seems sufficient to account for the omission, viz. that the history contained in this section is that of Abraham, Lot, Sarah, and of Isaac and Rebekah (all descendants of Terah), down to the death of Abraham.

Some of these sections relate only to collateral branches and are brief. The larger sections will be found to have subdivisions within them, which are carefully marked and arranged. As a rule, in each of these successive *Toledoth*, the narrative is carried down to the close of the period embraced, and at the beginning of each succeeding portion a brief repetition of so much as is needed of the previous account is given, and with it, very often, a note of time. Thus the Introduction is ushered in with the words "In the Beginning." Then the second section, referring to what has just been recorded, announces "The generations of the heavens and of the earth when they were created, in the day that the Lord God made the earth and the heavens," ch. ii. 4. Then again ch. v. 1, having the same note of time ("In the day," &c.) refers back to the account of creation, "In the likeness of God made He him, male and female created He them," &c. The next section, vi. 9, "The Toledoth of Noah," recapitulates the character of Noah, the degeneracy of man, and God's purpose to destroy all flesh. In xi. 10, the age of Shem and the birth of his son two years after the flood, are named. The like plan is observable in the "Toledoth of Terah," xi. 27; "the Toledoth of Ishmael," xxv. 12; "of Isaac," xxv. 19, "who was forty years old when he took Rebekah to wife;" "of Esau," xxxvi. 1, where his marriages are recorded again: and lastly, in the case of Jacob (xxxvii. 2), we find, in the verse immediately preceding (viz. xxxvii. 1), a note telling us the position of Jacob at the time, and again in vv. 2 and 3 the age of Joseph ("Joseph was seventeen years old"), taking us back to a point of time twelve years before the death of Isaac, which had been before recorded, that so we might see the new starting-point of the history.

Space will not allow the tracing of similar recapitulations and notes of time in the smaller sub-sections of the history. It must suffice to observe that they are very characteristic of the whole book, and are had recourse to wherever perspicuity of narrative seems to require[1].

[1] They are traced at length by Quarry ('Genesis,' pp. 326 to 340).

This brief review of the divisions of Genesis shews that it was not a loosely compacted structure, carelessly or clumsily thrown together by some one, who found a variety of heterogeneous materials and determined to mass them all in one: but that it was drawn up carefully, elaborately, and with distinct unity of purpose; whether from pre-existing documents or not it matters comparatively little to enquire.

2. *Of the names of God as used in the Book of Genesis.*

The names by which the Supreme Being is called in the Old Testament, and especially in Genesis, are chiefly two, *Elohim* and JEHOVAH, the one generally rendered in the versions God, the other LORD. We meet also with *El* (which is but a shorter form of Elohim), with *Elion*, Most High, (in the Pentateuch occurring only in Gen. xiv. 18 in connection with *El; El-Elion*, God most High, though in the Psalms it is found with Elohim and Jehovah, and also stands alone), and *Shaddai*, Almighty (in the Pentateuch generally with *El*, *El-Shaddai;* elsewhere standing alone).

The name *Elohim* is derived either from the Arabic root *Alaha*, "to fear, reverence, worship," or, much more probably, from אָלָה (*alah*) = אול "to be strong, to be mighty[1]." It is the simple, generic name of God, "The Mighty." It does not occur in the singular in the earlier books of Scripture, except in the abbreviated form of El. The plural is probably a plural of excellence and majesty. As in Prov. ix. 1, "wisdom," occurs in the plural *Chochmoth*, to signify wisdom in the abstract, including in itself all the treasures of wisdom and knowledge; so *Elohim* in the plural is applied to God, as comprehending in Himself the fulness of all power and all the attributes which the heathen ascribe to their several divinities (see Smith's 'Dict. of Bible,' Art. JEHOVAH). Still the word is a title rather than a name. It is applied to false gods, as well as to the true. The heathen nations round about the Israelites would have recognized the existence and the divinity of El and of the Elohim.

[1] It is more probable that the verb to signify "fear and worship" is derived from the name of the Deity, than that the name of the Deity was derived from the verb signifying "to fear."

JEHOVAH, on the contrary, is as clearly a proper name as Jupiter or Vishnu. *Elohim* and *Jehovah* are therefore as distinguishable as *Deus* and *Jupiter;* the difference being only in this, that, whereas the worshippers of Jupiter admitted "gods many and lords many," a multitude of *Dii*, the worshippers of Jehovah, on the other hand, believe in no Elohim except JEHOVAH. We may see at once, then, that there may be good reasons for expecting the title Elohim to be chiefly employed in some passages, whilst the proper name JEHOVAH would be chiefly employed in others. For instance, in the general account of creation it is very natural that Elohim, the Mighty One, the God of creation and providence, should be the word in use. So, where foreigners, people of heathen nations, as Hagar, Eliezer of Damascus, the Egyptians, &c. are introduced, it is most natural that the word Elohim should be more frequent than JEHOVAH, unless where some distinct acknowledgment of JEHOVAH is intended. On the contrary, when the history of the chosen people or their ancestors is specially concerned, and the stream of the Theocracy traced down from its fountain head, then the special name of Him, who was not ashamed to be called their God, would probably be of more frequent use. This, if kept clearly in view, will explain many of the so-called Elohistic and Jehovistic phenomena in Genesis. Another thing to be noted is this. The Semitic tongues, especially the more ancient and simpler forms of them, deal much in repetition, and where our modern Aryan languages would put a pronoun, they very frequently repeat the noun. From this general habit of repetition, and especially the habit of repeating the noun rather than using the pronoun, when in any one chapter or section we find either the word Elohim or the name JEHOVAH, we are very likely to find the same frequently recurring. In consequence of this, the several passages will to an European eye look as if they were strongly marked either by the title Elohim, or by the name JEHOVAH. For instance, it is alleged that in the first account of creation, ch. I, ii. 1—3, Elohim occurs thirty-five times, and that there is here no other name of God: but it has been replied, that, if it occurred once, it was only natural, owing to the uniformity of the whole passage, that it should have occurred again at each account of a separate creation, and also that in modern language a pronoun would have been substituted in many cases for the repeated title or name. Hence the thirty-five are in effect reducible to one. The passage is scarcely more really marked as Elohistic by the name Elohim occurring thirty-five times, than if it had occurred but once; for its having occurred once would inevitably lead to its continued and frequent recurrence[1].

The most important passage in relation to this question is, of course, Exod. vi. 2, 3, where according to the Authorized Version, "God spake unto Moses, and said unto him, I am JEHOVAH; and I appeared unto Abraham, unto Isaac, and unto Jacob, by the name of God Almighty, but by my name JEHOVAH was I not known to them." The inference derived from this passage has been this. The person, who recorded these words of God to Moses, would never have written a history of still earlier times, in which the name JEHOVAH should be introduced not only in the narrative, but in the mouths of the various speakers, from Eve downwards. Hence, no doubt, in his earlier history the writer of this passage would surely have been an Elohist. The parts of Genesis then, which are characterized by the use of the title Elohim, may probably be attributed to him: but all the parts in which JEHOVAH predominates were evidently added afterwards, and must be due to some one who was not alive to the incongruity of introducing Jehovistic language into a history of events and speeches prior to the revelation of the name JEHOVAH. It follows, of course, that the very first who could possibly have written the original Elohistic narrative was Moses, the Jehovistic portions being necessarily much later than Moses. It is further argued, however, that names compounded with the sacred name of JAH or JEHOVAH do not occur till the time of Samuel, hence it is added that the name could not have been known, nor the sixth chapter of Exodus written, till the time of Samuel: and further, it is now alleged that the name JEHOVAH is unknown even to the writer of the earlier Psalms, and that therefore probably David learned it late in life from its inventor Samuel.

The romance of modern criticism is as remarkable as its perverse ingenuity: for when once a theory has been suggested, its author and his followers proceed forthwith to construct an elaborate history upon it, as much as if, instead of excogitating a theory, they had discovered a library of authentic records. The wider the theory is from all that has hitherto been believed from concurrent testimony and careful enquiry, the more it finds acceptance and is hailed as a discovery. If we look a little closely

[1] Quarry, 'on Genesis,' pp. 341, 400, 401. The following table of the alternation of the names in the first 11 chapters is given by the learned author, and will shew how different the *virtual* occurrence of the respective names is from the apparent, superficial occurrence on which so much has been built:

					E.	J.
Ch. i. ii.	1—3.	Elohim	35 times		=1	
iii.	1—5.	Elohim	3	...	=1	
iv.	1.	Jehovah	1	...		=1
	2—16.	Jehovah	8	...		=1
	25.	Elohim	1	...	=1	
	26.	Jehovah	1	...		=1
v.	1.	Elohim	2	...	=1	
	22—24.	Elohim	3	...	=1	
	29.	Jehovah	1	...		=1
vi.	2—4.	Elohim	2	...	=1	
	3.	Jehovah	1	...		=1
	5—8.	Jehovah	4	...		=1
	9—22.	Elohim	5	...	=1	
vii.	1—5.	Jehovah	2	...		=1
	9.	Elohim	1	...	=1	
	16.	Elohim	1	...	=1	
		Jehovah	1	...		=1
viii.	1.	Elohim	2	...	=1	
	15.	Elohim	1	...	=1	
	20—21.	Jehovah	3	...		=1
ix.	1—6.	Elohim	2	...	=1	
	8—17.	Elohim	4	...	=1	
	26.	Jehovah	1	...		=1
		Elohim	1	...	=1	
	27.	Elohim	1	...	=1	
x.	9.	Jehovah	2	...		=1
xi.	5—9.	Jehovah	5	...		=1
					15	12

"Hence for the purposes of the present enquiry, and as evidence of any predilection of either name, the case is just as if in these eleven chapters, in the order of succession and at the distances here indicated, the name Elohim had recurred singly 15 times, and the name Jehovah 12 times."

into the foundations of the theory, it will appear as baseless as other dreams.

First, as regards the names compounded with JAH, we have at all events Jochebed, Joshua, Jonah, Jotham, Micah and Jonathan and mount Moriah, besides three named in Chronicles, Azariah (1 Chr. ii. 8), Abiah (1 Chr. ii. 24), Ahijah (1 Chr. ii. 25), all of which at least appear to have been so compounded, and which it is a gratuitous slander to say were the inventions of later days. Moreover, it by no means follows, that one age should have had the fashion of a special form for the composition of names, because we find that fashion prevailing some centuries later. Names compounded with *any* name of God are rare in the early ages, but became common in the later. Secondly, as regards the Psalms, there is no foundation whatever for saying that the earlier Psalms are Elohistic and the later only Jehovistic. Many of the manifestly and confessedly later Psalms (as the 78th, 82nd, 114th, &c.) are eminently Elohistic, whilst many of the earliest (as the 24th, 27th, 34th, &c.) are as eminently Jehovistic[1].

But again, the form and derivation of the name JEHOVAH points to a pre-Mosaic origin. Some of the German writers indeed have tried to trace the name to an attempt at expressing in Hebrew letters the name of the Phœnician god, *Iao*. Time will not allow of a lengthened consideration of this theory here. Suffice it to say that its chief support is an oracular response of the Clarian Apollo quoted by Macrobius ('Sat.' I. c. 18) about 400 A.D.; which has been clearly proved by Jablonsky to have originated in a Judaizing gnostic[2].

It is now generally admitted by competent Semitic scholars, that the word signifies "the existent" or something nearly akin to this. The true pronunciation, of course, is lost; but there can be no reasonable doubt, that, as the name of God declared to Moses in Ex. iii. 14, viz. אהיה, I AM, is the first person present of the substantive verb, so the name

[1] The Editor has shewn this more at length in his tract, called 'The Pentateuch and the Elohistic Psalms' (Longman).

[2] See the whole question discussed in Smith's 'Dict. of Bible,' I. p. 953, and Quarry, 'Genesis,' p. 300 sqq.

JEHOVAH is part of the same, but probably the third person present, or, as others think, the same tense of a causative (Hiphil) form[1]. But if so, there can be no question, as even Ewald fully admits, that the name must have been pre-Mosaic. In Hebrew the verb is always *hayah*, though in Syriac and Chaldee it is always *havah*. A name therefore derived from *havah* and existing in ancient Hebrew, must have come down from a time prior to the separation of the Hebrews from their kindred Aramæans, *i.e.* not later than the time of Abraham. In fact the name יהוה (IHVH) could not have been found among the Hebrews, at any period of history from the descent into Egypt to the captivity of Babylon: and as it undoubtedly exists in Hebrew writings prior to the captivity, so it must have originated before the time of Joseph.

We must conclude, then, that the name JEHOVAH was not unknown to the patriarchs, nor do the words of Exodus necessarily mean that it was. These words literally are, "I am JEHOVAH: and I appeared (or was manifested) to Abraham and to Isaac and to Jacob by El-Shaddai, but My name JEHOVAH was I not known to them:" that is to say, "I manifested myself to the patriarchs in the character of El-Shaddai, the Omnipotent God, able to fulfil that which I had promised; but as to my name (*i.e.* my character and attributes of) JEHOVAH I was not made manifest to them[2]." (So LXX. Vulg. οὐκ ἐδήλωσα, *non indicavi*). The words strictly and naturally imply this. The ancient versions seem to confirm this interpretation. It is no new one framed to meet modern objections, but was propounded by Aben Ezra and Rashi among the Jews, and by many of the most illustrious Christian commentators of past times.

The theory then of the late invention of this sacred name has really no foundation. That its use was very much more

[1] Thus it corresponds in form with such names as Isaac, Jacob, Joseph, which are all the third persons singular present of verbs.

[2] "In El-Shaddai" is interpreted to mean "as El-Shaddai," "in the character of El-Shaddai," (Gesen. Lex. s.v. בְּ div. C.). "The name of Jehovah," as meaning the character of Jehovah, is very common. Cf. Ps. v. 11, viii. 1, ix. 10, Is. xxvi. 8, xxx. 27.

prevalent after the revelation to Moses in Exodus than it had been before, there can be no reasonable doubt. God made His special covenant with Abram, beginning with the emphatic words, "I am El-Shaddai," Gen. xvii. 1. So again on a like occasion He spake to Jacob, Gen. xxxv. 11. Hence both Isaac and Jacob seemed to lay especial stress upon that name in times of trouble and anxiety (see Gen. xxviii. 3, xliii. 14), as recalling to them the faithfulness and the power of their covenant God. But to Moses the words are frequently spoken, "I am JEHOVAH," and the covenant, which had been assured to the patriarchs by God as El-Shaddai, the Mighty God, is now assured to the people of Israel, by the same God, as JEHOVAH, the self-existent, the cause of all being, governing the past, the present, and the future. Let us then suppose, that Moses had access to, or knowledge of, oral or written traditions concerning the Creation, which must from the nature of the case have been originally matter of revelation, the Flood, the history of Abraham, Isaac and Jacob; it is most likely that he would have made these the ground-work of his history. If the name, JEHOVAH, was known to the patriarchs, but had, as seems most likely from the first chapters of Exodus, been latterly but little used, perhaps wholly disused, among the Israelites in Egypt; then it is pretty certain that these traditions or documents would have had El, Elohim, or Elion, for the name of God, perhaps even to the exclusion of the name JEHOVAH. In working up these materials into a continuous history, some of the documents would be preserved entire, others might be so arranged and so worded as to fit them to be connecting links one with the other, while we should probably find many portions of the history in the hand of the author or compiler himself. If Moses was that author, though he would often use the name Elohim, we might naturally expect to find that he had a fondness for that sacred name by which the Most High had declared Himself as the special Protector of His people; and hence we might look for that name in passages where another writer perhaps would not have introduced it. If, as we infer from Josh. xxiv. 14, the Israelites in Egypt had learned to serve strange gods, there would be the more reason why Moses should set before them the one true God, as their own God, and exhibit Him under His name, JEHOVAH, thereby the more clearly to mark Him off from the false Elohim of Egypt, and the false Elohim of Canaan.

Now the facts of Genesis remarkably coincide with all this probability. Some portions of the narrative do indeed present what is called an Elohistic aspect; and especially those portions, which, of their very nature, are most likely to have existed in the traditions current from old time among the Israelites, viz. the general account of the Creation, the Flood, the covenant of circumcision made with Abraham, and the genealogical tables. These then Moses appears to have adopted, much as he found them, perhaps perpetuating, word for word, in his writings what before had been floating in unwritten record. Yet these portions of the narrative are not loosely thrown in, but rather carefully and organically incorporated and imbedded in the whole.

For instance, in the history of creation, we have first, in Gen. i. ii. 1—3, that which was very probably the ancient primeval record of the formation of the world. It may even have been communicated to the first man in his innocence. At all events, it very probably was the great Semitic tradition, handed down from Noah to Shem, from Shem to Abraham, and from Abraham through Isaac, Jacob and Joseph, to the Israelites who dwelt in Egypt. Without interfering with the integrity of this, the sacred author proceeds in the same chapter to add a supplementary history, briefly recapitulating the history of creation, with some little addition (in vv. 4—7), and then proceeding to the history of Paradise, the Fall, the expulsion, and the first bitter fruits of disobedience. In the first part of this second or supplementary history we meet with a signal phenomenon, viz. that, from ch. ii. 4 to the end of chapter iii. the two names (or rather the generic and the personal names) of God, JEHOVAH and Elohim, are used continually together. There is no other instance in Scripture of this continued and repeated use of the united names. It is evident, that the author, who adopted the first ancient record and stamped it with authority, and who desired to bring his people to a worship of the great self-existent JEHOVAH, used this method of transition from the ancient Elohistic document to his own more immediate narrative, in order that he might more forcibly impress upon his readers, that the Elohim who created all things was also the JEHOVAH, who had revealed Himself to Moses, and who was now to be spoken of as the Protector and King of the great Theocratic race, whose history was to be traced down even from the very creation of Adam. The consistency and close connection of the two parts is admitted by some, who are far from admitting the Divine original or high inspiration of the Pentateuch. "The second account," says Kalisch (*in loc.*) "is no abrupt fragment; it is not unconnected with the first; it is not superfluous repetition; it has been composed with clear consciousness after, and with reference to, the first. The author of the Pentateuch added to an ancient document on creation the history of man's disobedience and its consequence. ...The first account was composed independently of the second; but the second is a distinct and deliberate continuation of the first....It does not merely recapitulate, but it introduces new facts and a new train of thought." The consistency of the two narratives, and a consideration of the alleged inconsistencies, will be seen in the commentary (on ch. ii. especially). One singular point of resemblance it may be well to point out here. In ch. i. 26, in the so called Elohistic document, we have the remarkable words, "Let us make man," the plural pronoun used by the Almighty Himself, and the appearance of deliberation. In ch. iii. 22 (in the so called Jehovistic portion) we have again, "Behold the man is become as one of us:" again the very observable plural, and again perhaps even more markedly anthropomorphic language, as though the Most High were taking counsel, before executing His judgments. This identity of thought and speech is very observable, The like occurs again in ch. xi. 6; where neither Elohim, nor JEHOVAH-Elohim, but JEHOVAH alone is the name of God made use of[1]. There is not space to go through the book of Genesis and shew how similar principles prevail throughout. If the basis of the history of the Flood were an ancient Elohistic document, Moses appears to have interwoven it with a further narrative of his own. The one portion may be marked by the prevalence of one name, the other by that of another name of God; but the consistency of the one with the other is complete throughout (see notes on the history, infra). The same will appear in other portions of Genesis, though the creation and the flood most clearly exhibit both the phenomena relied on by the theorists and the facts leading to a refutation of their theory.

It must not, however, be thought that the variety in the employment of the sacred names could have resulted only from the variety of the materials used by Moses and the additional matter introduced by himself. Careful observation will shew, that, whilst often it was a matter of indifference whether the one or the other name was introduced, yet there was no mere carelessness in the introduction. On the contrary, in most passages it is impossible to doubt that the choice of the name adopted is the happiest possible.

Thus in the first history of creation we have Elohim, the mighty one, God of Creation and Providence, then in order to mark the transition of subject and yet the unity of the Being spoken of, we have for two chapters JEHOVAH Elohim; but when we come to the ivth chapter and to Eve's exclamation, when she hoped that her firstborn should be the ancestor of the promised seed, the words ascribed to her connect her hope with JEHOVAH, Him whom the Israelites learned to look on as their covenant God, who was to make good all the promises to the fathers. Again, in ch. v. the genealogy from Adam to Noah has no Divine name except Elohim, till we come, in v. 29, to the birth of Noah, and his father's pious anticipation that he should be a comfort to his race, in

[1] See Quarry, p. 348.

reference to the earth, which had been cursed. The use of the name JEHOVAH in this verse points us at once to the fact that Noah became the second head of the Theocratic race, the new depositary of the promises of God. If we pass on to ch. xiv. we are introduced to Melchizedek, priest and king of a Canaanitish people. He is a worshipper of *El-Elion*, God most High, this being evidently the name by which the Almighty was known to him and to his countrymen. Once, however, the name JEHOVAH occurs in the chapter, but it is in the mouth of Abraham, and Abraham evidently uses it that he may shew that he acknowledges the El-Elion worshipped by Melchizedek to be one and the same with the JEHOVAH, who was the God of Hebrews. "I have lift up my hand to JEHOVAH, El-Elion, possessor of heaven and earth," xiv. 22. A similar propriety of usage prevails throughout Genesis, and will frequently be referred to in the notes.

Again, verbal peculiarities are said to distinguish the so called Jehovistic from the so called Elohistic portions of the Pentateuch, so that, besides the variety in the use of the names of God, it is possible for a keen eye to disentangle the different documents the one from the other by noting the phraseology peculiar to each. It will be plain that, if even this were proved and patent, it would still not interfere with the Mosaic origin of Genesis, so long as we admit that Moses may have used the so called Elohistic MSS. or traditions. The Elohistic phraseology would then be characteristic of the more ancient documents, the Jehovistic would belong to Moses himself. It is, however, very clear, that the peculiarities are greatly magnified, if they exist at all. Sometimes indeed the theorists discover that a passage must belong to the Elohist for instance, because it contains Elohistic expressions; but then, though the name JEHOVAH occurs in it, that name must be a later insertion because it does not correspond with the general wording of the chapter. Thus the name JEHOVAH in ch. xvii. 1 is argued to be evidently out of place, because Elohim occurs everywhere else (ten times) in the chapter. Surely this is constructing a theory in despite, not in consequence, of the facts on which it ought to stand[1].

Again anthropomorphisms are said to characterise the Jehovist passages. This is by no means unlikely, considering that JEHOVAH is the personal name of God, and that by which He was pleased to reveal Himself familiarly to His people; yet they are far from exclusively belonging to the Jehovistic portions. Lastly, all the indications of a more advanced civilization, such as the use of gold, jewels, earrings, musical instruments, camels, servants, &c. are assigned to the Jehovist, and are thought to mark a period later than that of Moses. But surely the Israelites, who had dwelt for centuries in the fairest province in Egypt, and Moses who had been bred up in the court of a powerful and luxurious Pharaoh, must have been familiar with a civilization considerably in advance of anything that we read of in Genesis. Indeed the graphic account which Genesis gives of the simple habits of Abraham and the other patriarchs is one proof of its antiquity and its truth. It is very doubtful whether an author even in the time of Samuel, more than doubtful whether one in the reign of Solomon, of Josiah, or one of those who returned with Ezra from captivity, could have written the history of the forefathers of his race with all the truthfulness, all the simplicity, and all the accuracy of detail to be found in the Book which is called the First Book of Moses. Moses could have written it, for he had every conceivable qualification for writing it. The writer of after times, who could have produced that book, must have been himself a wonder, unsurpassed by any of those wonders which he is supposed to have devised and recorded.

The supposed inconsistency of the statements in Genesis with the recent

[1] The distinction between the Elohistic and Jehovistic words and phrases is carefully and elaborately investigated by Mr Quarry ('Genesis,' pp. 578 sqq.). The conclusion at which he arrives is the very reverse of the conclusion arrived at by the believers in the fragment theory.

discoveries of science will be found treated of in the notes to the earlier chapters. It may be well here only to say, that in the present state of our knowledge, both critical and scientific, a patient suspension of judgment on many points seems our wisest attitude. It is plain that a miraculous revelation of scientific truths was never designed by God for man. The account of creation is given in popular language; yet it is believed that it will be found not inconsistent with, though not anticipatory of, modern discovery. And after all, modern discovery is yet in a most imperfect condition, the testimony of the rocks and of the stars but imperfectly read, whilst there is room for no small diversity of sentiment on the meaning of many of the expressions in Genesis. At present the greatest inconsistency alleged as between Genesis and science is to be found in the question of the antiquity of man. Whilst there is at least good reason for withholding confident assent from the conclusions of some eminent geologists as to the evidence of the drift; it is quite possible to believe that Genesis gives us no certain data for pronouncing on the time of man's existence on the earth. The only arguments are to be drawn from the genealogies. As those given by the Evangelists are confessedly incomplete, there cannot be sufficient reason for maintaining that those in Genesis must have been complete. It is true that we have only conjecture to lead us here: but if the genealogies, before and after the Flood, present us only with the names of leading and "representative" men; we can then allow no small latitude to those who would extend the duration of man upon the earth to more than the commonly received six thousand years. The appearance of completeness in the genealogies is an undoubted difficulty; yet perhaps not insuperable, when we consider all that may have happened (no where more probably than here) in the transmission of the text from Moses to Ezra and from Ezra to the destruction of Jerusalem.

Let us suppose that it had pleased God to reveal to Moses the fact that the earth revolves round the sun, a fact familiar now to children, but unknown to astronomers for more than three thousand years after the Exodus. The effect of such a revelation would probably have been to place the believer and the astronomer in a state of antagonism. The ancient believer would have believed the truth; yet the observer of the heavens would have triumphantly convicted him of ignorance and error. We can see plainly that the wise course for both would have been to suspend their judgments, believing the Bible and yet following out the teaching of nature. A Galileo would then have been, not feared as a heretic, but hailed as a harmonist. There appears now to some an inconsistency between the words of Moses and the records of creation. Both may be misinterpreted. Further research into science, language, literature and exegesis, may shew that there is substantial agreement, where there now appears partial inconsistency. It would evidently have served no good purpose, had a revelation been vouchsafed of the Copernican system, or of modern geological science. Yet there may be in Scripture truth popularly expressed concerning the origin of all things, truth not apparent to us, because we have not yet acquired the knowledge to see and appreciate it. Certainly as yet nothing has been proved which can disprove the records of Genesis, if both the proof and the records be interpreted largely and fairly.

THE FIRST BOOK OF MOSES,

CALLED

GENESIS

CHAPTER I.

The creation of heaven and earth, 3 *of the light,* 6 *of the firmament,* 9 *of the earth separated from the waters,* 11 *and made fruitful,* 14 *of the sun, moon, and stars,* 20 *of fish and fowl,* 24 *of beasts and cattle,* 26 *of man in the image of God.* 29 *Also the appointment of food.*

[a] Psal. 33. 6. & 136. 5. Acts 14. 15. & 17. 24. Hebr. 11. 3.

IN [a] the beginning God created
the heaven and the earth.

2 And the earth was without form,
and void; and darkness *was* upon the
face of the deep. And the Spirit of God
moved upon the face of the waters.
3 And God said, [b] Let there be [b] 2 Cor. 4. 6
light: and there was light.
4 And God saw the light, that *it*
was good: and God divided † the
light from the darkness.

† Heb. *between the light and between the darkness.*

CHAP. I. 1. *In the beginning*] Not "first in order," but "in the beginning of all things." The same expression is used in Joh. i. 1, of the existence of the "Word of God," "In the beginning was the Word." The one passage illustrates the other, though it is partly by the contrast of thoughts. The Word *was*, when the world was *created*.

God created] In the first two chapters of Genesis we meet with four different verbs to express the creative work of God, viz. 1, to create; 2, to make; 3, to form; 4, to build. The first is used of the creation of the universe (v. 1); of the creation of the great sea-monsters, whose vastness appears to have excited special wonder (v. 21); and of the creation of man, the head of animated nature, in the image of God (v. 27). Everywhere else we read of God's *making*, as from an already created substance, the firmament, the sun, the stars, the brute creation (vv. 7, 16, 25, &c.); or of His *forming* the beasts of the field out of the ground (ch. ii. 19); or lastly, of His *building up* (ii. 22, margin) into a woman the rib which He had taken from man. In Isai. xliii. 7, three of these verbs occur together. "I have *created* him for my glory, I have *formed* him, yea, I have *made* him." Perhaps no other ancient language, however refined or philosophical, could have so clearly distinguished the different acts of the Maker of all things, and that because all heathen philosophy esteemed matter to have been eternal and uncreated. It cannot justly be objected that the verb *create*, in its first signification, may have been sensuous, meaning probably to *hew* stone or to *fell* timber. Almost all abstract or spiritual thoughts are expressed by words which were originally concrete or sensuous; and in nearly all the passages of Scripture in which the verb in question occurs, the idea of a true creation is that which is most naturally implied. Even where the translators have rendered it otherwise, the sense is still clearly the same, *e.g.* in Numb. xvi. 30, "If the LORD *make a new thing* (lit. *create a creation*), and the earth open her mouth;" or again, Ps. lxxxix. 47, "Wherefore hast Thou *made* (Heb. *created*) all things for nought?" The word is evidently the common word for a true and original creation, and there is no other word in Hebrew which can express that thought.

the heaven and the earth] The universe popularly described according to its appearance as earth and sky. In similar language, as Grotius notes, the new creation, to be hereafter looked for, is described 2 Pet. iii. 13, as "new heavens and a new earth." The Hebrew word for *heaven* is always plural, whether as expressive of greatness, or perhaps of multitude, like the old English plural, *welkin*.

2. *And the earth was without form, and void*] **Desolate and void.** These two words express devastation and desolation. They are used of the desert, Job xii. 24; xxvi. 7; of the devastated city, Isa. xxiv. 10; of "the line of wasting, and the plummet of destruction," Isa. xxxiv. 11. In Jer. iv. 23 they describe the utter wasting of a condemned and desolated land. Whether in the present verse they indicate entire absence of life and order, or merely that the world was not then, as now, teeming with life; whether they express primeval emptiness, or rather desolation and disorder succeeding to a former state of life and harmony, cannot immediately be determined. The purpose of the sacred writer is to give a history of man, his fall,

5 And God called the light Day, and the darkness he called Night. †And the evening and the morning were the first day.

† Heb. *And the evening was, and the morning was, &c*

his promised recovery, then specially of the chosen seed, and of the rise of the Theocracy. He therefore contents himself with declaring in one verse generally the creation of all things, and then in the next verse passes to the earth, man's place of abode, and to its preparation for the habitation of man. Countless ages may have elapsed between what is recorded in v. 1, and what is stated in v. 2. Some indeed have insisted on the close connection of v. 2 with v. 1, because they are united by the word *And:* but this particle, though necessarily implying transition, does by no means necessarily imply close connection. The Book of Leviticus begins with "And the Lord called unto Moses." The Book of Exodus begins with the same word *And*, though centuries intervene between its history and that of the Book of Genesis; and so our translators have very reasonably rendered the Hebrew particle in that passage not *And*, but *Now*. The meaning of the verse before us evidently is, "In the beginning God created the universe;" but, at the time now to be spoken of, the earth, which is our chief concern, was shapeless and waste. The verb "was" as used in this verse implies, not succession, but condition at the time in question.

darkness was upon the face of the deep] No light penetrated to the desolate and disordered ruin. The *deep* may mean either the confused mass itself, or, as more frequently, the abyss of waters and the clouds and mists with which the earth was surrounded.

the Spirit of God moved upon the face of the waters] The Targum of Onkelos and many Jewish commentators render "a mighty wind was moving," &c., which is favoured, though not proved, by the absence of the article. The common rendering is the more natural, especially if the word "moved" signifies, as some think, not merely *fluttering* or *hovering*, as of a bird over its nest, but also *brooding*, as of a bird sitting on its eggs. (See Deut. xxxii. 11, where it is used of the eagle fluttering over her young.) The Spirit of God appears to be represented as the great quickening principle, hovering or brooding over the earth and the ocean, and breathing forth upon them light and life.

3. *God said*] In the cognate languages the word here rendered *said* has the force of *commanded*.

Let there be light: and there was light] Was light created before the creation of the sun and other luminous bodies? That this is possible has been shewn by Dr M[c]Caul, 'Aids to Faith,' p. 210, &c.; but very probably the creation of the sun is related in v. 1, where under the word heaven (or heavens) may be comprehended the whole visible universe of sun, moon, and stars. Now, the history is going on to the adaptation of the earth for man's abode. In v. 2 a thick darkness had enveloped it. In this 3rd verse the darkness is dispelled by the word of God, the light is separated from the darkness, and the regular succession of day and night is established. Still probably there remains a clouded atmosphere, or other obstacle to the full vision of sun and sky. It is not till the fourth day that these impediments are removed and the sun appears to the earth as the great luminary of the day, the moon and the stars as reigning in the night. Light may, perhaps, have been created before the sun. Yet the statement, that on the first day, not only was there light, but the succession of day and night, seems to prove that the creation of the sun was "in the beginning," though its visible manifestation in the firmament was not till the fourth day.

4. *God saw the light, that it was good*] The earlier the records, the more we find in them of anthropopathic language, as the better fitted to simple understandings. The design of words like these is to express emphatically, that all the works, as they came direct from the hand of God, were good, and that the evil did not result from any defect in the workmanship, but from the will of the creature not according with the will of the Creator.

divided the light from the darkness] In the chaotic condition described in v. 2, all things were confused and commixed; but, when God called the light out of darkness, He set bounds to both of them, and caused a succession of day and night, calling the light day and the darkness night.

5. *And the evening and the morning were the first day*] Literally, "And it was (or became) evening, and it was (or became) morning, day one."

Some think the evening is put before the morning, because the Jews reckoned their days from evening to evening. Others think, that, as the darkness was first and the light called out of darkness, so the evening (in Heb. *ereb*, the time when all things are mixed and confounded) is placed before the morning; and thus the whole period of chaotic darkness may have been the first night, and the first day that period of light which immediately succeeded the darkness.

See Note A at end of the Chapter.

[c] Psal. 136. 5. Jer. 10. 12. & 51. 15. † Heb. *expansion.*

6 ¶ And God said, [c]Let there be
a †firmament in the midst of the
waters, and let it divide the waters
from the waters.
7 And God made the firmament,
and divided the waters which *were*
under the firmament from the waters
which *were* above the firmament:
and it was so.

[d] Jer. 51. 15.

8 And God called the [d]firmament Heaven. And the evening and
the morning were the second day.

[e] Psal. 33. 7. & 136. 5. Job 38. 8.

9 ¶ And God said, [e]Let the
waters under the heaven be gathered
together unto one place, and let the
dry *land* appear: and it was so.
10 And God called the dry *land*
Earth; and the gathering together of
the waters called he Seas: and God
saw that *it was* good.
11 And God said, Let the earth
bring forth †grass, the herb yielding
seed, *and* the fruit tree yielding fruit
after his kind, whose seed *is* in itself,
upon the earth: and it was so.

† Heb. *tender grass.*

12 And the earth brought forth
grass, *and* herb yielding seed after his
kind, and the tree yielding fruit,
whose seed *was* in itself, after his
kind: and God saw that *it was* good.
13 And the evening and the morning were the third day.
14 ¶ And God said, Let there
be [f]lights in the firmament of the

[f] Deut. 4. 19. Psal. 136. 7.

---

6. *Let there be a firmament*] The earth is spoken of as covered with waters, partly, that is, the waters of the sea, partly the heavy clouds and vapours, which hung round it in its state of desolation and darkness. The dispersion of some of these vapours lets in the light. Then, in the present verse, the clouds and mists are described as raised up above the firmament, the firmament itself dividing between the waters of the ocean and the clouds of heaven. It is plain from this that the word rendered *firmament* embraces the atmosphere immediately surrounding the surface of the earth, which bears up the clouds floating in it, in or on the face of which also the birds are described as flying (see v. 20). In v. 14 the word is extended further to embrace the whole region of the sky in which sun and moon and stars appear. In this respect, as Le Clerc notices, it corresponds with the classical word *cœlum*, which meant at times the air just round us, at other times the place of the stars and planets; and so likewise of our own English word *heaven*, we may say the birds of heaven, the clouds of heaven, or the stars of heaven. The original sense of the word has been much debated, but is of little consequence; for the sacred writer would use the common language of his people, and not go out of his way to devise one which would be philosophically accurate. The verb, from which the substantive is derived, signifies (1) to beat or stamp upon, Ezek. vi. 11, xxv. 6; (2) to spread abroad by stamping, 2 S. xxii. 43; (3) to beat out metal into thin plates, or gold into gold leaf, Ex. xxxix. 3, Num. xvi. 38, Isai. xl. 19; (4) to spread forth, extend, stretch out, Job xxxvii. 18, Ps. cxxxvi. 6, Is. xlii. 5, xliv. 24. The most probable meaning of the substantive therefore is *the expanse* or *the expansion*. The LXX. rendered it *firmament* (see here Quarry 'on Genesis,' p. 79); and hence it has been argued that Moses taught the sky to be a hard, metallic vault, in which the sun and stars were fixed; but the most learned modern commentators, including Gesenius, Kalisch, &c., believe the true etymology of the word to shew that *expanse*, not *firmament*, is the right translation. The teaching however of the present passage does not depend on the etymology of the word. If a writer in the present day uses the English word *heaven*, it does not follow, that he supposes the sky to be a vault *heaved* up from the earth. Neither would it follow that the inspired writer had taught, that the portion of atmosphere, intervening between the sea and the clouds, was a solid mass, even if the word used for it had etymologically signified *solidity*.

11. *Let the earth bring forth grass*] We have here the first calling forth of life upon the earth, vegetable life first, soon to be succeeded by animal life. The earth was made fruitful, and three kinds of vegetation were assigned to it; the tender grass, the common covering of the soil, fit chiefly for the use of the lower animals; herb bearing seed, which should be adapted to the service of man; and trees, with their conspicuous fruits; all three so ordained, that their seed should be in themselves, that they should contain, not a principle of life only, but a power also of fecundity, whereby the race should be perpetuated from generation to generation.

14. *Let there be lights*] Lit. **luminaries**, *light-bearers*, spoken of lamps and candlesticks, Ex. xxv. 6, Num. iv. 9, 16. The narrative only tells what sun, moon, and stars are in relation to the earth. When the clouds and mists are dispelled from its surface, the

† Heb. *between the day and between the night.*

heaven to divide †the day from the
night; and let them be for signs,
and for seasons, and for days, and
years:
15 And let them be for lights in
the firmament of the heaven to give
light upon the earth: and it was so.
16 And God made two great
lights; the greater light †to rule the
day, and the lesser light to rule the
night: *he made* the stars also.
17 And God set them in the
firmament of the heaven to give light
upon the earth,
18 And to [g]rule over the day
and over the night, and to divide the
light from the darkness: and God
saw that *it was* good.
19 And the evening and the morning were the fourth day.
20 And God said, [h]Let the waters
bring forth abundantly the ‖moving
creature that hath †life, and fowl
that may fly above the earth in the
†open firmament of heaven.
21 And God created great whales,
and every living creature that moveth,
which the waters brought forth abundantly, after their kind, and every
winged fowl after his kind: and God
saw that *it was* good.
22 And God blessed them, saying,
[i]Be fruitful, and multiply, and fill
the waters in the seas, and let fowl
multiply in the earth.
23 And the evening and the morning were the fifth day.
24 ¶ And God said, Let the earth
bring forth the living creature after
his kind, cattle, and creeping thing,
and beast of the earth after his kind:
and it was so.

† Heb. *for the rule of the day, &c.*

[g] Jer. 31. 35.

[h] 4 Esdr. 6. 47.

‖ Or, *creeping.*

† Heb. *soul.*

† Heb. *face of the firmament of heaven.*

[i] chap. 8. 17. & 9. 1.

---

seas confined within their boundaries, and the first vegetation springs up; then the sky is cleared up, the sun, moon, and stars appear and assume their natural functions, marking days and nights, seasons and years; and God makes or appoints them, the sun to rule the day, and the moon to rule the night.

16. *he made the stars also*] The purpose of the sacred narrative being to describe the adaptation of the earth to the use of man, no account is taken of the nature of the stars, as suns or planets, but merely as signs in the heavens. The words in the text may be a kind of parenthesis, not assigning the special time of the creation of the stars. Moreover, the word used is "made," not "created," see on v. 1. When the Sun and Moon became great lights to rule the day and to rule the night, then also the stars shone forth; the heavens were lit up by the sun in the day-time, by the moon and stars in the night-season, all of them declaring the glory of God and shewing His handy-work.

20. *the moving creature*] The versions render *reptiles*. The word is of wide significance, most frequently used of reptiles and fishes; the verb from which it comes, and which is here translated "bring forth abundantly," means *to swarm, to creep, to propagate itself rapidly*. We may probably therefore understand here the insect creation, the fishes of the sea, and the reptiles and saurians of sea and land.

that hath life] Literally perhaps, "Let the waters swarm with swarms of the breath of life." Let the waters teem with innumerable creatures, in which is the breath of life. The word *nephesh*, which we have rendered *breath*, corresponds nearly with the classical *psyche*, the vital principle. It is used of the breath, of the living principle, of the soul or seat of feelings and affections, and of living beings themselves.

and fowl, &c.] **and let fowl fly.**

21. *great whales*] **Great sea monsters.** The word is used of serpents, Ex. vii. 9, Deut. xxxii. 33, Ps. xci. 13, Jer. li. 34, and of the crocodile, Ezek. xxix. 3, xxxii. 2. It is not likely that the Israelites should have had much knowledge of the larger species of whales which do not frequent the shores of the Mediterranean. Their early acquaintance with Egypt had impressed them with a horror of the crocodile, and in the desert they had become familiar with large serpents. In Is. xxvii. 1, and perhaps in Job vii. 12, this name apparently belongs to sea monsters; but we may remember that the Hebrews applied the term *sea* to great rivers also, like the Nile and the Euphrates. (See Is. xix. 5, Jer. li. 36, Ezek. xxxii. 2, Nahum iii. 8.) It seems, on the whole, most probable, that the creatures here said to have been created were serpents, crocodiles, and other huge saurians, though possibly any large monsters of sea or river may be included. The use of the word *created* in this place has already been remarked on v. 1. Another reason for its use may be, that, as the Egyptians paid idolatrous worship to crocodiles, the sacred historian would teach that they also were creatures of God.

24. The fifth day was chiefly occupied in peopling the waters with fishes and reptiles,

25 And God made the beast of the
earth after his kind, and cattle after
their kind, and every thing that creepeth upon the earth after his kind: and
God saw that *it was* good.

26 ¶ And God said, [k] Let us make
man in our image, after our likeness:
and let them have dominion over the
fish of the sea, and over the fowl of
the air, and over the cattle, and over

[k] chap. 5. 1. & 9. 6. 1 Cor. 11. 7. Ephes. 4. 24. Col. 3. 10.

---

and the air with birds. The work of the sixth day gives inhabitants to the land, "cattle" (*i.e.* the well-known animals, which afterwards became domesticated, though the name was not exclusively attached to them), "and creeping things," such as serpents, lizards, crawling insects and the like, "and beast of the earth," *i. e.* either the wilder and fiercer beasts, as distinguished from cattle, or perhaps more generally animals of all kinds.

26. *And God said, Let us make man*] It has been observed by commentators, both Jewish and Christian (*e. g.* Abarbanel, *in loc.* Chrysost. *in loc.*), that the deliberation of the Creator is introduced, not to express doubt, but to enhance the dignity of the last work, the creation of man. So even Von Bohlen, "A gradual ascent is observed up to man, the chief work of creation, and in order to exalt his dignity, the act of his creation is accompanied by the deliberations of the Creator." The creative fiat concerning all other creatures runs, "Let the waters bring forth abundantly," "Let the earth bring forth," &c. Man is that great "piece of work," concerning which God is described as taking forethought and counsel, as making him in His own image, and (ch. ii. 7) as breathing into him the breath of life. Three times in v. 27 the verb *created* is used concerning the production of man; for, though his bodily organization may, like that of the beasts, have been produced from already created elements ("the dust of the ground," ch. ii. 7); yet the complex being, man, "of a reasonable soul and human flesh subsisting," was now for the first time called into being, and so was, unlike the beasts, wholly a new creation.

Let us make] The Jews vary much in their explanation of these words. Philo speaks of "the Father of all things addressing his own powers" ('De Profugis,' p. 359). The Talmud says, "The Holy One, Blessed be He, does nothing without consulting the family which is above" (*Sanhed.* c. iv.). Moses Gerundinus says, that God addressed the earth, for, as the earth was to give man the body, whilst God was to infuse the spirit, so "in our likeness" was to be referred both to God and to the earth. Abenezra writes, "When, according to God's commandment, the earth and the sea had brought forth plants and living beings, then God said to the angels, 'Let us make man, we will be occupied in his creation, not the seas and the earth.'" So he considers man to have been made after the likeness of the angels. To a similar effect Maimonides, 'More Nevochim,' p. ii. ch. 6. See Munster *in loc.*, Cleric. *in loc.*, Heidegger, p. 32.

Some interpreters, both Jewish and Christian, have understood a plural of dignity, after the manner of kings. This is the opinion of Gesenius and most of the Germans. But the royal style of speech was probably a custom of much later date than the time of Moses. Thus we read Gen. xli. 41–44, "I have set thee over the land of Egypt . . . . I am Pharaoh." Indeed this royal style is unknown in Scripture. Some of the modern rationalists believe (or affect to believe) that the plural name of God, *Elohim*, was a mere relic of ancient polytheism, and that though Moses habitually attaches a singular verb to the plural nominative, yet here "the plural unconsciously escaped from the narrator's pen" (Von Bohl.). The ancient Christians with one mind see in these words of God that plurality in the Divine unity, which was more fully revealed, when God sent His only begotten Son into the world, and when the only begotten Son, who was in the bosom of the Father, declared Him to mankind. So *e. g.* Barnabas (ch. iv.), Justin M., Irenæus, Theophil., Epiphan. ('Hæres.' xxxiii. 4–2), Theodoret ('Quæst. in Gen.').

in our image, after our likeness] Many Christian writers think that nothing is meant except that man was created holy and innocent, and that this image of God was lost when Adam fell. That holiness, indeed, formed part of the likeness may be inferred from Col. iii. 10, "the new man, which is renewed after the image of Him that created him;" but that the image of God was not wholly obliterated by the fall seems clear from Gen. ix. 6, Jas. iii. 9. And, if so, then that image did not simply consist in perfect holiness. Some, both Jewish and Christian, have supposed that it referred to that dominion, which is here assigned to man. As God rules over all, so man was constituted the governor of the animal world. St Basil M. in 'Hexaemeron' (qu. by Clericus) considers that the likeness consisted in freedom of will. This probably is a most important point in the resemblance. The brute creatures are gifted with life and will and self-consciousness, and even with some powers of reason; but they have no self-determining will, no choice between good and evil, no power of self-education, no proper moral character,

all the earth, and over every creeping
thing that creepeth upon the earth.
27 So God created man in his *own*
image, in the image of God created he
[l] Matt. 19. 4. Wisd. 2. 23. him; [l] male and female created he them.
28 And God blessed them, and God
[m] chap. 9. 1. said unto them, [m] Be fruitful, and multiply, and replenish the earth, and sub-
due it: and have dominion over the
fish of the sea, and over the fowl of
the air, and over every living thing
† Heb. *creepeth.* that † moveth upon the earth.
29 ¶ And God said, Behold, I have
† Heb. *seeding seed.* given you every herb † bearing seed,
which *is* upon the face of all the earth,
and every tree, in the which *is* the fruit
of a tree yielding seed; [n] to you it [n] chap. 9. 3.
shall be for meat.
30 And to every beast of the earth,
and to every fowl of the air, and to
everything that creepeth upon the
earth, wherein *there is* † life, *I have given* † Heb. *a living soul.*
every green herb for meat: and it
was so.
31 And [o] God saw every thing that [o] Ecclus. 39. 16.
he had made, and, behold, *it was* very
good. And the evening and the morning were the sixth day.

---

and so no true personality. God is the essentially personal Being, and in giving to man an immortal soul, He gave him also a true personality, self-consciousness, power of free choice, and so distinct moral responsibility. All this was accompanied at first with perfect purity and innocence; and thus man was like his Maker, intelligent, immortal, personal, with powers of forethought and free choice, and at the same time pure, holy and undefiled.

NOTE A on CHAP. I. V. 5. ON THE DAYS OF CREATION.

THE vexed question of the duration of the days of creation cannot readily be solved from consideration of the wording of this verse. The English Version would seem to confine it to natural days; but the original will allow much greater latitude. Time passed in regular succession of day and night. It was an ingenious conjecture of Kurtz, adopted by Hugh Miller, that the knowledge of pre-Adamite history, like the knowledge of future ages, may have been communicated to Moses, or perhaps to the first man, in prophetic vision, that so perhaps vast geological periods were exhibited to the eye of the inspired writer, each appearing to pass before him as so many successive days. It has been said moreover that the phenomena under the earth's surface correspond with the succession as described in this chapter, a period of comparative gloom, with more vapour and more carbonic acid in the atmosphere, then of greater light, of vegetation, of marine animals and huge reptiles, of birds, of beasts, and lastly of man. (See Kurtz, Vol. I. p. xxvii. sq., Hugh Miller, 'Test. of Rocks,' passim, &c.) In the present condition of geological science, and with the great obscurity of the record of creation in this chapter, it may be wise not to attempt an accurate comparison of the one with the other. Some few points, however, seem clearly to come out. In Genesis, first of all, creation is spoken of as "in the beginning," a period of indefinite, possibly of most remote distance in the past; secondly, the progress of the preparation of the earth's surface is described as gradually advancing from the rocks to the vegetable world, and the less perfectly organised animal creation, then gradually mounting up through birds and mammals, till it culminates in man. This is the course of creation as popularly described in Genesis, and the rocks give their testimony, at least in the general, to the same order and progress. The chief difference, if any, of the two witnesses would seem to be, that the Rocks speak of (1) marine plants, (2) marine animals, (3) land plants, (4) land animals in their successive developements; whereas Moses speaks of (1) plants, (2) marine animals, (3) land animals; a difference not amounting to divergence. As physiology must have been nearly and geology wholly unknown to the Semitic nations of antiquity, such a general correspondence of sacred history with modern science is surely more striking and important than any apparent difference in details. Efforts have been made to compare the Indian cosmogony with the Biblical, which utterly fail. The cosmogony of the Hindoos is thoroughly adapted to their Pantheistic Theology, the Hebrew corresponding with the pure personal Monotheism of the Old Testament. The only important resemblance of any ancient cosmogony with the Scriptural account is to be found in the Persian or Zoroastrian; which is most naturally accounted for, first by the fact, which will be noticed hereafter, that the Persians, of all people, except the Hebrews, were the most likely to have retained the memory of primitive traditions, and secondly, that Zoroaster was probably brought into contact with the Hebrews, and perhaps with the prophet Daniel in the court of Darius, and may have learned much from such association.

CHAPTER II.

1 *The first sabbath.* 4 *The manner of the creation.* 8 *The planting of the garden of Eden,* 10 *and the river thereof.* 17 *The tree of knowledge only forbidden.* 19, 20 *The naming of the creatures.* 21 *The making of woman, and institution of marriage.*

THUS the heavens and the earth were finished, and all the host of them.

2 [a] And on the seventh day God
ended his work which he had made;
and he rested on the seventh day from
all his work which he had made.

3 And God blessed the seventh day,
and sanctified it: because that in it
he had rested from all his work which
God [†] created and made.

4 ¶ These *are* the generations of

[a] Exod. 20. 11. & 31. 17. Deut. 5. 14. Heb. 4. 4.

[†] Heb. *created to make.*

CHAP. II. 3. *And God blessed the seventh day*] The natural interpretation of these words is that the blessing of the Sabbath was immediately consequent on the first creation of man, for whom the Sabbath was made (Mar. ii. 27). It has been argued from the silence concerning its observance by the patriarchs, that no Sabbatic ordinance was really given until the promulgation of the Law, and that this passage in Genesis is not *historical* but *anticipatory*. There are several objections, which seem fatal to this theory. It is first to be observed, that this verse forms an integral part of that history of the creation, which, if there be any truth in the distinction, is the oldest portion of the Pentateuch, the work of the Elohist, very possibly handed down from the earliest ages of the world, and taken by Moses as the very groundwork of his inspired narrative. Secondly, the history of the patriarchs extending over at least 2500 years is all contained in the book of Genesis, and many things must have been omitted, much more memorable than the fact of their resting on the Sabbath, which in their simple pastoral life would seldom have called for special notice. Thirdly, there are indications even in Genesis of a division of days into weeks or hebdomades. Thus Noah is said twice to have waited seven days, when sending the dove out of the ark, Gen. viii. 10, 12. And the division of time into weeks is clearly recognized in the history of Jacob, Gen. xxix. 27, 28. The same hebdomadal division was known to other nations, who are not likely to have borrowed it from the Israelites after the time of the Exodus. Moreover, it appears that, before the giving of the commandments from Mount Sinai, the Israelites were acquainted with the law of the Sabbath. In Ex. xvi. 5 a double portion of manna is promised on the sixth day, that none need be gathered on the Sabbath. This has all the appearance of belonging to an acknowledged, though perhaps neglected, ordinance of Divine Service, not as if then for the first time the Sabbath were ordained and consecrated. The simple meaning of the text is therefore by far the most probable, viz. that God, having divided His own great work into six portions, assigned a special sacredness to the seventh on which that work became complete; and that, having called man into being, He ordained him for labour, but yet in love and mercy appointed that one-seventh of his time should be given to rest and to the religious service of his Maker. This truth is repeated in the IVth Commandment, Ex. xx. 11; though there was a second and special reason why the Jews should observe the Sabbath day, Deut. v. 15: and very probably the special day of the seven, which became the Jewish Sabbath, was the very day on which the Lord brought them from the land of bondage, and gave them rest from the slavery of Egypt. If this reasoning be true, all mankind are interested in the sanctification of the Sabbath, though Jews only are required to keep that Sabbath on the Saturday; and not only has it been felt by Divines that the religious rest of the seventh day is needful for the preservation of the worship of God, but it has been acknowleged even by statesmen and physiologists that the ordinance is invaluable for the physical and moral benefit of mankind. The truly merciful character of the ordinance is fully developed in the Law, where it is extended not only to the manservant and maidservant, but to the ox and the ass and the cattle, that they also should rest with their masters, Ex. xx. 10, Deut. v. 14.

which God created and made] Lit. "**which God created to make.**" So the Targum of Onkelos and the Syriac version render it. The Vulgate has "which God created that He might make it." On the difference between the verbs *create* and *make* see on ch. i. 1. The natural meaning of the words here is, that God first created the material universe, "the heavens and the earth," and then made, moulded and fashioned the new created matter into its various forms and organisms. This is the explanation of the R. Nachmanides, "all His work which He had created out of nothing, in order that He might make out of it all the works which are recorded in the six days." (Quoted by Fagius, 'Crit. Sacri.')

4. *These are the generations*, &c.] The Jews tell us, that, when these words occur without the copulative *and*, they separate the words following from those preceding, but

the heavens and of the earth when they were created, in the day that the LORD God made the earth and the heavens,

5 And every plant of the field before it was in the earth, and every herb of the field before it grew: for the LORD God had not caused it to

---

that when they have the *and*, then they unite with the preceding. It is apparent, that the narrative proceeds in direct order from Gen. i. 1 to this verse, ii. 4, and that from this verse there is a return to the first formation of plants and vegetables and to the creation of man, a kind of recapitulation, yet with some appearance of diversity. This has been noticed long ago. In the 17th century (1655) Is. Peyreyrius wrote a book to prove, that the account of the creation of man in ch. i. related to a pre-Adamite race, from which sprang a great majority of the Gentiles, whereas the account in ch. ii. was of the creation of Adam, the direct ancestor of the Israelites and of the nations in some degree related to them. The book was condemned and suppressed. Some modern writers have more or less embraced its views, but it seems that the whole Bible, both Old and New Testament, refers to Adam as the head of the whole human race, so that, if pre-Adamite man existed at all, the race must probably have been extinguished before Adam was created. Moreover, ch. ii. 4 sqq. is evidently a continuation of ch. i., although there is a return or recapitulation in vv. 4, 5, 6, 7, in order to prepare the way for an account of Paradise and the fall. See note at end of the chapter.

The word "generations," *toledoth*, which occurs for the first time in this verse, meets us again continually at the head of every principal section of the Book of Genesis. Thus ch. v. 1, we have "the book (or account) of the generations of Adam," in which the descendants of Adam are traced to Noah. From ch. vi. 9 we have the generations of Noah, where the history of Noah and his sons is given. In ch. x. 1 we come upon the generations of the sons of Noah, where the genealogical table and the history of the descendants of Shem, Ham, and Japhet are recorded. Ch. xi. (10—26) gives us the generations (or genealogical table) of Shem. Ch. xi. 27 begins the generations of Terah, the father of Abram. Ch. xxv. 12 gives us the generations of Ishmael. Ch. xxv. 19 the generations of Isaac. Ch. xxxvi. 1, the generations of Esau; xxxvii. 2, the generations of Jacob, which are continued to the end of the book.

The word itself naturally signifies the generation or posterity of any one. It is used in general to usher in a history of the race or descendant of the heads of the great patriarchal families. The application of the word here is very appropriate. The primary creation of all things had just been recorded; the sacred writer is about to describe more in detail the results of creation. The world had been made; next comes a history of its natural productions, its plants and trees, and chief inhabitants. And as the history of a man's family is called the "book of his generations," so the history of the world's productions is called "the generations of the heavens and the earth."

when they were created] By these words the inspired writer reveals the truth set forth in the former chapter, that heaven and earth were creatures of God, "the generations" referring to what is to come after, not to what preceded, as though the universe had sprung from generation or natural production.

the LORD *God*] It has long ago been observed that the sacred name JEHOVAH occurs for the first time here in verse 4. The Jews give as a reason, that the works being now perfected, the perfect name of God, "the LORD God," is for the first time adopted. It seems most probable, that the sacred writer, having in the first chapter recorded the creation as the act of God, giving to Him then His generic name as the Supreme Being, now passes to the more personal history of man and his immediate relation to his Maker, and therefore introduces the more personal name of God, the name by which He became afterwards known to the patriarchs, as *their* God. The union of the two names JEHOVAH Elohim throughout chapters ii. iii. is singularly appropriate, as indicating that the Elohim of the first chapter is the same as the JEHOVAH who appears afterwards in the fourth chapter, and from time to time throughout the history. On the names of God and the documents in Genesis, see Introduction to Genesis.

5. *And every plant of the field*] So the LXX. and the Vulg. But the Targums, the Syr., Rashi, and the most distinguished modern Hebraists, such as Rosenmüller, Gesenius, &c., translate, **"Now no plant of the field was yet in the earth, and no herb of the field had yet sprouted forth; for the LORD God had not caused it to rain upon the earth, and there was not a man to till the ground."**

It was objected long ago, and the objection is repeated with all its force by the German critics of the day, that this is opposed to ch. i. 11; where we read, "God said, Let the earth bring forth grass," &c. Hence it is

rain upon the earth, and *there was* not
a man to till the ground.
6 But ‖there went up a mist from
the earth, and watered the whole face
of the ground.
7 And the LORD God formed man
†*of* the [b]dust of the ground, and breathed into his nostrils the breath of life;
and [c]man became a living soul.
8 ¶ And the LORD God planted a
garden eastward in Eden; and there
he put the man whom he had formed.

‖ Or, *mist which went up from, &c.*

† Heb. *dust of the ground.*

b 1 Cor. 15. 47.

c 1 Cor. 15. 45.

---

inferred that the first and second chapters constituted two independent and contradictory traditions, clumsily put together by the compiler of Genesis. The difficulty had been anticipated by R Nachman, who observes, that this passage does not refer to the produce of the earth created on the third day, but to those herbs and plants, which are raised by the cultivation of man. L. de Dieu also ('Critica Sacr.' in loc.) notices, that the words rendered *plant*, *field* and *grew*, never occur in the first chapter, they are terms expressive of the produce of labour and cultivation; so that the historian evidently means, that no cultivated land and no vegetables fit for the use of man were yet in existence on the earth.

the LORD *God had not caused it to rain upon the earth, and there was not a man to till the ground.* (6). *But there went up a mist,* &c.] It is objected here also, that the first chapter speaks of the earth as enveloped in waters and vapours, and that there could therefore have been no lack of rain and moisture. The inconsistency is again more apparent than real. In the first place, the mist, or vapour, or cloud, here mentioned as watering the ground, may perhaps tally well with that watery condition of the atmosphere, of which we read in ch. i. But next, the purpose of ch. ii. is to give an account, not of the creation or adaptation of the whole earth, but of the preparation of a special chosen spot for the early abode of man. That spot may have been in a region where little or no rain fell, and which derived all its moisture from vapours or dews. It may not have been wholly without vegetation, but it was not a cultivated field; no herbs, or shrubs, or fruit-trees fitted for man's use grew there; no rain was wont to fall there (as some render it, "not even a mist went up to water the ground," or more probably), "yet there went up a mist and watered the whole face of the ground." When the Creator made Adam, that he might not wander about a helpless savage, but that he might have a habitation suited to civilized life, a garden or cultivated field was planted for him, provided with such vegetable produce as was best adapted to his comforts and wants.

7. *And the* LORD *God formed man of the dust of the ground,* &c.] Here again, as in i. 26, 27, the formation of man is ascribed to the direct workmanship of God. In ch. i. God is said to have *created* man in His own image, because the production of a rational, personal, responsible being clothed with a material body was a new creation. Spiritual beings existed before; animal natures had been called forth from earth and sea; man had an animal nature like the beasts, but his spiritual nature was in the likeness of his Maker. So in this chapter again the Creator is described as forming man from the earth, and then breathing into him a living principle. It is probably not intended that the language should be philosophically accurate, but it clearly expresses that man's bodily substance was composed of earthly elements, whilst the life breathed by God into his nostrils plainly distinguishes that life from the life of all inferior animals. All animals have the body, all the living soul, ch. i. 20, 21, but the breath of life, breathed into the nostrils by God Himself, is said of man alone. Cp. "the body, soul and spirit" of ancient philosophy and of the Apostle Paul.

See note A at the end of this chapter.

8. *a garden*] The versions render *a Paradise*, which is a Persian word, signifying rather a park than a garden, pleasure grounds laid out with shrubs and trees.

in Eden] The word *Eden* signifies delight, and the Vulgate renders *a garden of delight, a pleasure garden;* but the word is a proper name, and points to a region, the extent of which is unknown. Two countries are mentioned in Scripture with the same name, viz., one in Mesopotamia near the Tigris, 2 K. xix. 12, Is. xxxvii. 12, Ez. xxvii. 23; the other in the neighbourhood of Damascus, Amos i. 5; but neither of these can be identified with the region in which Paradise was placed. Much has been written on the site of Paradise, but with no very definite result. The difficulty consists in discovering the four rivers mentioned in vv. 11, 12, 13, 14. It is generally agreed that one, Phrath (v. 14) is the Euphrates, and that another, Hiddekel, is the Tigris, and so it is rendered by all the ancient VSS. The name of the Tigris in Chaldee is Diglath, in Syriac Diklath, in Arabic Dijlat, all closely corresponding with Hiddekel, and from one of them the word Tigris itself is probably a corruption. The following are the principal opinions as to the names of the other rivers, and consequently as to the site of Paradise.

9 And out of the ground made the LORD God to grow every tree that is pleasant to the sight, and good for food; the tree of life also in the midst of the garden, and the tree of knowledge of good and evil.

---

1. Josephus identified the Gihon with the Nile.

2. Calvin, Huet, Bochart, and others believed the river of Paradise to have been the united streams of the Tigris and Euphrates called the Shat-el-Arab, which flows by Bassora. Its four heads, on their shewing, would have been, on the north, the two separate streams of the Tigris and Euphrates, on the south, Gihon, the eastern, and Pison, the western channels, into which the united stream again branches out below Bassora, before it falls into the sea. Havilah would then be the north-eastern part of Arabia, and Cush the region of Kissia, Susiana or Chuzestan. A general exposition of this view may be found in Wells, 'Geog. of the O. T.,' ch. i.

3. J. D. Michaelis, Rosenmüller, and Karl Von Raumer, who appear to be followed by Kurtz, identify Eden with the Armenian highlands, making Pison to be the Phasis or Araxes, and Gihon to be the Oxus. Havilah is with them the country of the Chwalissi, which is said even now to be called by the Russians Chwaliskoje More.

4. Heidegger believed that Eden was a portion of the Holy Land.

5. Others again find the site in India or Circassia.

Of these opinions No. 1 is utterly untenable. The identification of Gihon with the Nile probably originated with the Alexandrian Jews, who for the honour of their country would have had the Nile to be one of the rivers of Paradise. This was confirmed by the mistranslation of *Cush* into *Ethiopia*. It is impossible, however, setting aside all questions of inspiration, that one so familiar with Egypt as the writer of Genesis should have conceived of the Nile as connected with the Tigris and Euphrates. See Kurtz, 'Hist. of Old Covenant' (Clark's Library), Vol. I. p. 73.

No. 2 has the advantage of pointing to a single river, which might in primitive times have been described as branching out into four divisions or heads. Moreover, Arabia, in which certainly was a region called Havilah, is near to the western channel, whilst Chuzestan, which may have corresponded with the land of Cush, borders on the eastern channel.

The chief difficulty in No. 3 is that at present there is no junction between the heads of the four rivers, Tigris, Euphrates, Oxus, and Araxes, though all may take their rise in the same mountain system, and may possibly in more ancient times have been more nearly related. The question is one which has been much discussed, and is not likely soon to be set at rest: but the weight of argument and of authority seems in favour of No. 2, or something nearly corresponding with it; and it is the solution (more or less) adopted by the best modern interpreters.

9. *made the* LORD *God to grow*] We must understand this of the trees of Paradise only.

the tree of life also in the midst of the garden] Jewish and many Christian commentators consider that there was a virtue in this tree, which was calculated to preserve from diseases and to perpetuate animal life. Kennicott ('Two Dissertat.' Diss. i.) argued that the word "tree" is a noun of number, whether in the Hebrew or the Greek (comp. Rev. xxii. 2), and that all the trees of Paradise, except the tree of knowledge, "the true test of good and evil," were trees of life, in the eating of which, if man had not sinned, his life would have been perpetuated continually. The fathers inclined to the belief that the life to be supported by this tree was a spiritual life. So St Augustine ('De Gen. ad lit.' VIII. 4) says, "In other trees there was nourishment for Adam; but in this a sacrament," *i.e.* The tree was a sacrament or mystic image of, and perhaps also supporting, life eternal. Its reference, not to temporal, but to eternal life, seems to be implied in Gen. iii. 22. In Prov. iii. 18, Wisdom is compared to the tree of life: and in Prov. xiii. 12, we read, "When the desire cometh, it is a tree of life," which connects it with the hope of the future. And so perhaps we may say pretty confidently, that whatever was the physical effect of the fruit of this tree, there was a lesson contained in it, that life is to be sought by man, not from within, from himself, in his own powers or faculties, but from that which is without him, even from Him who only hath life in Himself. God only hath life in Himself; and the Son of God, who by eternal generation from the Father hath it given to Him to have life in Himself, was typified to Adam under this figure as "the Author of eternal salvation." Joh. i. 4, xiv. 6, Rev. ii. 7, xxii. 2 (see Fagius in loc. and Heidegger, 'Hist. Patriarch.' Exerc. IV.).

the tree of knowledge of good and evil] Onkelos paraphrases, "of the fruit of which they who eat learn to distinguish between good and evil." The tree appears to have been the test, whether man would be good or bad; by it the trial was made whether in keeping God's commandments he would attain to good, *i.e.* to eternal life, or by breaking them he should have evil, *i.e.* eter-

10 And a river went out of Eden to
water the garden; and from thence
it was parted, and became into four
heads.
11 The name of the first *is* [d]Pison:
that *is* it which compasseth the whole
land of Havilah, where *there is* gold;
12 And the gold of that land *is*
good: there *is* bdellium and the onyx
stone.
13 And the name of the second
river *is* Gihon: the same *is* it that
compasseth the whole land of †Ethiopia.

d Ecclus. 24. 29.

† Heb. *Cush.*

14 And the name of the third river
is Hiddekel: that *is* it which goeth
‖toward the east of Assyria. And the
fourth river *is* Euphrates.
15 And the LORD God took ‖the
man, and put him into the garden of
Eden to dress it and to keep it.
16 And the LORD God commanded the man, saying, Of every tree
of the garden †thou mayest freely
eat:
17 But of the tree of the knowledge
of good and evil, thou shalt not eat of

‖ Or, *eastward to Assyria.*

‖ Or, *Adam.*

† Heb. *eating thou shalt eat.*

---

nal death. The lesson seems to be, that man should not seek to learn what is good and evil from himself but from God only; that he should not set up an independent search for more knowledge than is fitting, throwing off the yoke of obedience and constituting himself the judge of good and ill. Some have thought that the tree had not this name from the first, but that it was given it after the temptation and the fall, either because the tempter had pretended that it would give wisdom, or because Adam and Eve, after they had eaten of it, knew by bitter experience the difference between good and evil.

12. *bdellium*] a transparent gum obtained from a tree (*Borassus flabelliformis*) which grows in Arabia, India, and Media (Plin. 'H. N.' XII. 9. § 19). This is the translation of Aqu., Symm., Theod., Vulg.: Josephus and many moderns, as Celsius ('Hierob.' I. 324), Cleric. in loc. adopt it. The LXX. renders "the carbuncle;" the Arabic, "sardius;" Kimchi, Grotius, Bochart, Gesenius, and others, with great probability take it to mean "pearls," of which great abundance was found in India and the Persian Gulf, and this falls in well with Bochart's belief, that Havilah bordered on the Persian Gulf. It appears far more probable that it should mean either pearls or some precious stone than a gum like bdellium, which is of no great value.

the onyx] Most of the versions give "onyx" or "sardonyx;" Onkelos has "beryl."

13. *Ethiopia*] **Cush.** This is a word of wide extent. It generally belongs either to Arabia or to Ethiopia. From Gen. x. 7 sqq. it will appear how widely the sons of Cush spread forth: their first settlement appears to have been in Arabia. Nimrod founded the kingdom of Babylon. Afterwards they settled largely in Ethiopia. In the more ancient books of Scripture, the Asiatic Cush is more frequently, perhaps exclusively, intended. Later the name applies more commonly to African Cush, *i.e.* Ethiopia.

14. *toward the east of Assyria*] The name Asshur included Babylonia, and even Persia: see Ezra vi. 22, where Darius is called King of Assyria: but in the time of Moses probably Assyria proper would be understood, a region of low land on the left bank of the Tigris, perhaps only including the country afterwards called Adiabene. It is hardly correct to say, that the Tigris runs "to the East of Assyria." Perhaps the renderings in some of the versions "towards" or "before Assyria" may be correct.

17. *thou shalt not eat of it*] It has been questioned why such a test as this should have been given; whether it be consistent with God's goodness to create a sin by making an arbitrary enactment; and how "the act of eating a little fruit from a tree could be visited with so severe a penalty." But we may notice that if there was to be any trial of man's obedience in Paradise, some special test was almost necessary. His condition of simple innocence and happiness, with no disorder in the constitution of his body or in the affections of his soul, offered no natural temptations to sin. Adam and Eve had none but each other and their Creator near them; and they could have had no natural inclination to sin against God or against their neighbour. If we take the ten Commandments as the type of the moral law, we shall find none that in their state of healthy innocence they could naturally desire to break (see Joseph Mede, Bk. I. Disc. 40). Their position was one of freedom indeed, but of dependence. Their only danger was that they should prefer independence upon God, and so seek for themselves freedom in the direction of evil as well as in the direction of good; and the renouncing dependence upon God is the very essence of evil in the creature. Now the command concerning the fruit of the tree, simple and childish as it may appear, was one exactly suited to their sim-

it: for in the day that thou eatest
thereof †thou shalt surely die.
† Heb. *dying thou shalt die.*
18 ¶ And the LORD God said, *It*
is not good that the man should be
alone; I will make *e*him an help †meet
for him.
e Ecclus. 17. 5.
† Heb. *as before him.*
19 And out of the ground the LORD
God formed every beast of the field,
and every fowl of the air; and brought
them unto ‖Adam to see what he would
call them: and whatsoever Adam called every living creature, that *was* the
name thereof.
‖ Or, *the man.*
20 And Adam †gave names to all
cattle, and to the fowl of the air, and
† Heb. *called.*
to every beast of the field; but for
Adam there was not found an help
meet for him.
21 And the LORD God caused a
deep sleep to fall upon Adam, and he
slept: and he took one of his ribs,
and closed up the flesh instead thereof;
22 And the rib, which the LORD
God had taken from man, †made he
a woman, and brought her unto the
man.
† Heb. *builded.*
23 And Adam said, This *is* now
bone of my bones, and flesh of my
flesh: she shall be called Woman,
because she was *f*taken out of man.
f 1 Cor. 11. 8.

---

ple and childlike state. Moreover it is not inconsistent with God's general dealings with mankind, that he should at times see fit to test faith and obedience by special and unusual trials. Compare Gen. xxii. 1, Matt. xix. 21.

thou shalt surely die] St Jerome ('Qu. in Gen.') proposes to adopt the translation of Symmachus, "Thou shalt become mortal or liable to death." It is needless so to translate, but the meaning of the threat probably was that the effect of eating of the fruit of that tree should be to poison the whole man, soul and body, with a deadly poison, making the body mortal, and the soul "dead in trespasses and sins." With the day of transgression a life commences, which is a living death. St Paul uses the expression, "Death worketh in us." There was, however, doubtless some remission of the sentence, so that they did not die instantly, as was the case with the Ninevites (Jonah iii. 10); and then a remedy was provided which might ultimately turn the curse into a blessing. Still the sentence was never wholly reversed, but the penalty took effect at once.

19. *the* LORD *God formed*] The account of the formation of the brute animals here does not, as some have supposed, necessarily imply that they were created after Adam; but it is introductory to the bringing them one by one to Adam that he may name them, and it is intended to lead up to the statement that they were none of them suited to be Adam's chief companions. They were formed by God of earthly materials; but the breath of Divine life had not been breathed into them.

brought them unto Adam to see what he would call them] The power of speech was one of those gifts which from the first distinguished man from all other animals; but, as tending to that civilized condition in which it was God's will to place Adam, in order to mature his mental powers, and to teach him the use of language, the animals are brought to him that he might name them. Nouns are the first and simplest elements of language; and animals, by their appearance, movements and cries, more than any other objects suggest names for themselves.

20. *there was not found an help meet for him*] There is some obscurity in the original of the words "an help meet for him;" they probably mean "a helper suited to," or rather "matching him."

22. *the rib...made He a woman*] lit. **The side He built up into a woman.** The word which primarily means "rib" more frequently signifies "side:" whence many of the rabbins adopted the Platonic myth (see Euseb. 'Præp. Evang.' XII. 12), that man and woman were originally united in one body, till the Creator separated them. The formation of woman from the side of man is without question most mysterious: but it teaches very forcibly and beautifully the duty of one sex towards the other, and the close relationship between them, so that neither should despise or treat with unkindness the other. That respect for the weaker sex, which we esteem a mark of the highest refinement, is taught by the very act of creation as recorded in the earliest existing record. The New Testament tells us that marriage is a type of the union of Christ and His Church; and the fathers held that the formation of Eve from the side of Adam typified the formation of the Church from the side of the Saviour. The water and blood which flowed from that side were held the one to signify baptism, the other to belong to the other great Sacrament, both water and blood cleansing from sin and making the Church acceptable to God.

23. *Woman, because she was taken out of*

Matt. 19. 24 [g]Therefore shall a man leave
Mark 10. 7. his father and his mother, and shall
Cor. 6. 5. cleave unto his wife: and they shall be
Eph. 5. 31. one flesh.

25 And they were both naked, the
man and his wife, and were not a-
shamed.

---

man] Hebrew "Ishsha because she was taken out of Ish." Hence many have argued that Hebrew must have been the primitive language. The same, of course, is inferred from other names, as Eve, Cain, Abel, &c., all having appropriate significance in Hebrew. The argument is inconclusive, because it is quite possible to translate names from one language into another, and to retain the meaning which those names had in their original tongue.

24. *Therefore*, &c.] These may have been the words of Adam, or of the inspired historian. Matt. xix. 5 seems to refer them to the latter, which also is the more natural interpretation. Then too they have more obviously that Divine authority which our Lord so emphatically ascribes to them. Such incidental remarks are not uncommon in Scripture; see for instance ch. xxxii. 32.

NOTE A on CHAP. II. v. 7. ON THE IMMEDIATE CREATION AND PRIMITIVE STATE OF MAN.

ON the question of man's direct creation in distinction to the hypothesis of development, and on his original position as a civilized being, not as a wild barbarian, we may remark, 1st, It is admitted even by the theorists themselves, that in the present state of the evidence the records beneath the earth's surface give no support to the hypothesis that every species grew out of some species less perfect before it. There is not an unbroken chain of continuity. At times, new and strange forms suddenly appear upon the stage of life, with no previous intimation of their coming. 2ndly, In those creatures, in which instinct seems most fully developed, it is impossible that it should have grown by cultivation and successive inheritance. In no animal is it more observable than in the bee: but the working bee only has the remarkable instinct of building and honey-making so peculiar to its race; it does not inherit that instinct from its parents, for neither the drone nor the queen-bee builds or works; it does not hand it down to its posterity, for itself is sterile and childless. Mr Darwin has not succeeded in replying to this argument. 3rdly, Civilization, as far as all experience goes, has always been learned from without. No extremely barbarous nation has ever yet been found capable of initiating civilization. Retrogression is rapid, but progress unknown, till the first steps have been taught. (See Abp. Whately, 'Origin of Civilization,' the argument of which has not been refuted by Sir John Lubbock, 'Prehistoric Man.' Both have been ably reviewed by the Duke of Argyll, 'Primeval Man'). Moreover, almost all barbarous races, if not wholly without tradition, believe themselves to have been once in a more civilized state, to have come from a more favoured land, to have descended from ancestors more enlightened and powerful than themselves. 4thly, Though it has been asserted without any proof that man, when greatly degenerate, reverts to the type of the monkey, just as domesticated animals revert to the wild type; yet the analogy is imperfect and untrue. Man undoubtedly, apart from ennobling influences, degenerates, and, losing more and more of the image of his Maker, becomes more closely assimilated to the brute creation, the earthly nature overpowering the spiritual. But that this is not natural to him is shewn by the fact, that, under such conditions of degeneracy, the race gradually becomes enfeebled, and at length dies out; whereas the domesticated animal, which reverts to the type of the wild animal, instead of fading away, becomes only the more powerful and the more prolific. The wild state is natural to the brutes, but the civilized is natural to man.

Even if the other parts of the Darwinian hypothesis were demonstrable, there is not a vestige of evidence that there ever existed any beast intermediate between apes and men. Apes too are by no means the nearest to us in intelligence or moral sense or in their food and other habits. It also deserves to be borne in mind, that even if it could be made probable that man is only an improved ape, no physiological reason can touch the question, whether God did not when the improvement reached its right point, breathe into him "a living soul," a spirit "which goeth upward," when bodily life ceases. This at least would have constituted Adam a new creature, and the fountain head of a new race.

On the derivation of mankind from a single pair, see Prichard's 'Physical Hist. of Mankind,' Bunsen, 'Philosophy of Universal History,' Smyth, 'Unity of the Human Race,' Quatrefages, 'L'unité de l'espèce Humaine,' &c.

CHAPTER III.

1 The serpent deceiveth Eve. 6 Man's shameful fall. 9 God arraigneth them. 14 The serpent is cursed. 15 The promised seed. 16 The punishment of mankind. 21 Their first clothing. 22 Their casting out of paradise.

NOW the serpent was more sub-
til than any beast of the field
which the LORD God had made. And
he said unto the woman, †Yea, hath † Heb. *Yea, because, &c.*
God said, Ye shall not eat of every
tree of the garden?
2 And the woman said unto the
serpent, We may eat of the fruit of
the trees of the garden:
3 But of the fruit of the tree which
is in the midst of the garden, God hath
said, Ye shall not eat of it, neither
shall ye touch it, lest ye die.
4 [a]And the serpent said unto the [a] 2 Cor. 11. 3. 1 Tim. 2. 14.
woman, Ye shall not surely die:
5 For God doth know that in the
day ye eat thereof, then your eyes
shall be opened, and ye shall be as
gods, knowing good and evil.
6 And when the woman saw that
the tree *was* good for food, and that
it *was* †pleasant to the eyes, and a † Heb. *a desire.*
tree to be desired to make *one* wise,
she took of the fruit thereof, [b]and [b] Ecclus. 25. 26. 1 Tim. 2. 14.
did eat, and gave also unto her hus-
band with her; and he did eat.
7 And the eyes of them both
were opened, and they knew that
they *were* naked; and they sewed fig
leaves together, and made themselves ‖ Or, *things to gird about*
‖aprons.

CHAP. III. 1. *Now the serpent*] "Almost throughout the East the serpent was used as an emblem of the evil principle," Kalisch, ad h. l.: but Kalisch himself, Tuch and others deny that the evil spirit is to be understood in this narrative of Genesis. Yet not only did the East in general look on the serpent as an emblem of the spirit of evil, but the earliest traces of Jewish or Christian interpretations all point to this. The evil one is constantly called by the Jews "the old serpent," *Hannachash hakkadmoni* (so also in Rev. xii. 9, "that old serpent the devil"). In Wisd. ii. 24, we read, "By the envy of the devil death entered into the world." Our Lord Himself says, "the Devil was the murderer of man from the beginning" (Joh. viii. 44). Von Bohlen observes that "the pervading Jewish view is the most obvious, according to which the serpent is considered as Satan; and the greatest confirmation of such an interpretation is the very general agreement of the Asiatic myths" (ad h. l.). Some have thought that no serpent appeared, but only that evil one, who is called the serpent; but then he could not have been said to be "more subtle than all the beasts of the field." The reason why Satan took the form of a beast remarkable for its subtlety may have been, that so Eve might be the less upon her guard. New as she was to all creation, she may not have been surprised at speech in an animal which apparently possessed almost human sagacity.

Fit vessel, fittest imp of fraud...
...For in the wily snake
Whatever sleights none would suspicious mark,
As from his wit and nature subtlety
Proceeding, which in other beasts observed
Doubt might beget of diabolic power,
Active within beyond the sense of brute.
'Paradise Lost,' IX. 91.

5. *God doth know*] The tempter represents God as envious of His creatures' happiness, the ordinary suggestion of false religion and unbelief. Then he suggests to Eve the desire of self-dependence, that which is in fact the origin of all sin, the giving up of dependence on God, and the seeking for power, wisdom, happiness in self.

as gods] Or more probably, "as God." The plural word *Elohim* stands at times for false gods, at times for angels, but most commonly for the one true God.

knowing good and evil] Having a clear understanding of all great moral questions; not like children, but like those of full age, who "by reason of use have their senses exercised to discern both good and evil" (Heb. v. 14). This was the serpent's promise, though he knew that the result would be really a knowledge of evil through the perversion of their own will and their own ill choice.

6. *to make one wise*] Gesenius and others, after the LXX. and Vulgate, render *to look upon*.

7. *the eyes of them both were opened*, &c.] "Their eyes were truly opened as the serpent had promised them, but only to see that in the moment when they departed from God they became slaves of the flesh, that the free-will and independence of God, and knowing the good and the evil, delivers them up to the power of evil. Man, who had his glorious destiny before him of becoming by means of the knowledge and love of God, and by obedience, the free lord of the world, ceases, by disobedience, to be master of himself." (O. Von Gerlach, 'Comment.' ad h. l.).

fig leaves] Celsius, Tuch, and Gesenius, have doubted whether this was the Ficus

8 And they heard the voice of the LORD God walking in the garden in the †cool of the day: and Adam and his wife hid themselves from the presence of the LORD God amongst the trees of the garden.

† Heb. *ind.*

9 And the LORD God called unto Adam, and said unto him, Where *art* thou?

10 And he said, I heard thy voice in the garden, and I was afraid, because I *was* naked; and I hid myself.

11 And he said, Who told thee that thou *wast* naked? Hast thou eaten of the tree, whereof I commanded thee that thou shouldest not eat?

12 And the man said, The woman whom thou gavest *to be* with me, she gave me of the tree, and I did eat.

13 And the LORD God said unto the woman, What *is* this *that* thou hast done? And the woman said, The serpent beguiled me, and I did eat.

14 And the LORD God said unto the serpent, Because thou hast done this, thou *art* cursed above all cattle, and above every beast of the field; upon thy belly shalt thou go, and dust shalt thou eat all the days of thy life:

15 And I will put enmity between thee and the woman, and between thy seed and her seed; and it shall

---

Carica of Linnæus, supposing it to have been the *Musa Paradisiaca;* but the word is that used throughout Scripture for the well known fig tree (see Rœdiger in Ges. 'Lex.' p. 1490).

8. *the voice of the* LORD *God*] The whole of this history of the creation and the fall is full of these anthropomorphic representations. The Creator is spoken of as if consulting about the formation of man (i. 26), as reflecting on the result of His creation, and declaring it all very good (i. 31), as resting from His work (ii. 2), as planting a garden for Adam (ii. 8), bringing the animals to him to name them (ii. 19), then building up the rib of Adam into a woman, and bringing her to Adam to be his bride (ii. 22). Here again Adam hears His voice as of one walking in the garden in the cool of the day. All this corresponds well with the simple and childlike character of the early portions of Genesis. The Great Father, through His inspired word, is as it were teaching His children, in the infancy of their race, by means of simple language, and in simple lessons. Onkelos has here "The Voice of the Word of the LORD." It is by this name, "the Word of the LORD," that the Targums generally paraphrase the name of the Most High, more especially in those passages where is recorded anything like a visible or sensible representation of His Majesty. The Christian fathers almost universally believed that every appearance of God to the patriarchs and prophets was a manifestation of the eternal Son, judging especially from Joh. i. 18.

cool of the day] Lit. "wind of the day," which is generally understood of the cool breezes of evening. Paradise had been to man the place of God's presence, which brought heretofore happiness, and security. Now that sin had come upon him, the sense of that presence was accompanied with shame and fear.

14. *cursed above all cattle*] We can hardly doubt that these words were in part directed against the animal, which was made the instrument of man's ruin, as in the law the ox which gored a man was to be put to death like a malefactor. Thus the serpent was ever to bear about the remembrance of that evil, which he had been made the means of producing, was to be the enemy of man, causing him suffering, but in the end suffering from him utter destruction; yet, as the serpent was but the outward form of the spirit of evil, so the language of the Almighty, which outwardly refers to the serpent, in its spiritual significance is a curse upon the evil one. And as the curse is for the sake of man; so in it is contained a promise that the human race shall finally triumph over that which first caused its fall. The most natural interpretation of the curse might indicate, that the serpent underwent some change of form. It would, however, be quite consistent with the narrative, even in its most literal acceptance, to understand that it merely implied continued and perpetual degradation coupled with a truceless war against mankind.

15. *seed*] Allix, as quoted by Bishop Patrick, observes that in this promise God did a kindness to Adam, who otherwise by the temptation might have been estranged from his wife; but here the promise of redemption is through the seed of the *woman.* "Marriage, which had been the vehicle of the fall, is now also to become that of salvation; the seed of the woman is to bruise the head of the Serpent." (Kurtz, I. 78.) The promise is, no doubt, general, that, though the seed of the serpent (mystically Satan and all his servants) shall continually wage war against the descendants of Eve, yet ultimately by God's appointment mankind (the whole seed of the woman) shall triumph over their spi-

bruise thy head, and thou shalt bruise
his heel.
16 Unto the woman he said, I will
greatly multiply thy sorrow and thy
conception; in sorrow thou shalt bring
forth children; and thy desire *shall be*
‖to thy husband, and he shall [c]rule
over thee.
17 And unto Adam he said, Because thou hast hearkened unto the
voice of thy wife, and hast eaten of the
tree, of which I commanded thee, saying, Thou shalt not eat of it: cursed
is the ground for thy sake; in sorrow
shalt thou eat *of* it all the days of thy life;
18 Thorns also and thistles shall
it †bring forth to thee; and thou shalt
eat the herb of the field;
19 In the sweat of thy face shalt
thou eat bread, till thou return unto

‖ Or, *subject to thy husband.*
c 1 Cor. 14. 34.
† Heb *cause to bud.*

---

ritual enemy. If there were no more than this in the language used, even so there would be, an obscure indeed, but still a significant promise of some future deliverance. But the last words of the verse seem not merely general but personal. In the first clause it is said, that there should be "enmity between thy *seed* and her *seed*;" but in the second clause it is said, "It (or he) shall bruise *thy* head." It was the head of the particular serpent (not of the seed of the serpent only), which the seed of the woman was to bruise. And though we must not lay stress on the masculine pronoun "*he*," because the word for *seed* is masculine in Hebrew, yet there is the appearance here of a personal contest, and a personal victory. This inference is strengthened by the promise being made to the seed of the *woman*. There has been but one descendant of Eve, who had no earthly father; and He was "manifested that He might destroy the works of the devil." Though the Jewish writers do not directly interpret the promise of the Messiah; yet the Targums of Jerusalem and of the Pseudo-Jonathan both say that this victory over the serpent shall be "in the days of the Messiah."

It is well known that Roman Catholic divines have attributed the victory to the Virgin Mary, misled by the rendering of some MSS. of the Latin, *Ipsa*, she. The original Hebrew is perfectly unequivocal; for, though the pronoun might be so pointed as to signify either *he* or *she*, yet the verb is (according to the Hebrew idiom) masculine. Moreover the LXX. has *seed* in the neuter, but the pronoun referring to it, "*he*," in the masculine, which would naturally refer it to some individual son of the woman. The Syriac Version also has a masculine pronoun.

shall bruise] The LXX. followed by the Vulgate and Onkelos has "shall watch," probably meaning to watch and track as a hunter does his prey; but the word in Chaldee signifies "to bruise or crush." In this, or nearly this sense it is used in the only other passages in which it occurs in Scripture, viz. Job ix. 17, Ps. cxxxix. 11, and so it is rendered by most ancient Versions and Comm. as Syr. Sam. Saad. St Paul refers to it in the words "The God of peace shall bruise Satan under your feet shortly." Rom. xvi. 20.

16. *Unto the woman He said*] It is noticed by Tertullian, that though God punished Adam and Eve, He did not curse them, as He did the Serpent, they being candidates for restoration ('adv. Marcion.' ii. 25).

I will greatly multiply thy sorrow and thy conception] Some suppose this to be a *hendiaduoin* for "the sorrow of thy conception." The words rather mean that woman's sorrow and her conception should both be multiplied. The mother has not only the pains of childbirth, but from all the cares of maternity greater sorrow connected with her common offspring than the father has. The threat of multiplying conception indicates, not that Eve had already borne children, but that childbirth would not have been unknown had the first pair remained in Paradise.

Thy desire shall be] Desire here expresses that reverential longing with which the weaker looks up to the stronger. The Vulgate therefore renders, "Thou shalt be under the power of thy husband." This is also the interpretation of Abenezra and of many moderns. The comparison with ch. iv. 7 shews that there is somewhat of dependence and subjection implied in the phrases.

17. *And unto Adam He said*] Here for the first time *Adam* occurs without an article, as a proper name.

cursed is the ground for thy sake] The whole earth partakes of the punishment, which the sin of man, its head and destined ruler, has called down. The creature itself is subjected to vanity, Rom. viii. 20. Death reigns. Instead of the blessed soil of Paradise, Adam and his offspring have to till the ground now condemned to bear thorns and thistles, and this is not to end, until the man returns to the earth from which he was taken. Yet even here there is some mark of mercy: for, whereas the serpent is cursed directly, and that with a reference to the earth he was

the ground; for out of it wast thou
taken: for dust thou *art*, and unto
dust shalt thou return.
20 And Adam called his wife's
Heb. Chavah. name †Eve; because she was the
mother of all living.
21 Unto Adam also and to his wife
did the LORD God make coats of
skins, and clothed them.
22 ¶ And the LORD God said, Behold,
the man is become as one of
us, to know good and evil: and now,
lest he put forth his hand, and take
also of the tree of life, and eat, and
live for ever:
23 Therefore the LORD God sent
him forth from the garden of Eden,
to till the ground from whence he was
taken.
24 So he drove out the man; and
he placed at the east of the garden
of Eden Cherubims, and a flaming
sword which turned every way, to
keep the way of the tree of life.

---

to travel over; here on the contrary the earth, rather than the man, is cursed, though for the man's sake and with reference to him. (Tuch.)

19. See note A at end of Chapter.

20. *Eve*] *Chavvah*, *Life*. Not only because she gave birth to all living, but perhaps with a further prophetic meaning, in reference to the promise just given, because the race of man, now subject to death, should be made alive by the Offspring of the woman.

22. *the man is become as one of us*] Man was not a mere animal, following the impulse of sense, without distinction of right and wrong. He had also a spiritual personality, with moral will and freedom of forechoice. His lower nature, though in subjection to the higher, as that was in subjection to God, yet acted as a veil, screening from him what might have been visible to pure spiritual intelligence: hence, though he knew good from knowing God and living in dependence on Him, yet he knew not evil, having had no experience of it hitherto. His fall therefore, although sinful, was not like the sin of angels, who had no animal nature to obscure vision or to tempt by sense. *Their* fall must have been more deliberate, more wilful, less pardonable. But, when man by fatal mischoice learned that there was evil in the universe as well as good, then he had acquired a condition like to that of spiritual beings, who had no veil to their understanding, and could see both on the right hand and on the left. The meaning then of this mysterious saying of the Most High may be, that now by sin man had attained a knowledge like the knowledge of pure spiritual existences, a knowledge which God has of necessity, a knowledge which the angels have, who might have fallen but who stood upright, a knowledge, which evil angels have from their own deliberate choosing of evil instead of good. The difficulty of this interpretation is, that it supposes God to speak of Himself as One among other spiritual beings, whereas He cannot be likened to any one, but is infinitely above and beyond all created natures. Some therefore would understand here and elsewhere, the plural as a mere plural of majesty. Still there is a manifest plurality of person. It is not merely "like Us," but "like one of Us." Hence it was the universal belief of the early Christians, that here as in Gen. i. 20, God was speaking to, and of, His coeternal Son and Spirit.

See note B at end of Chapter.

lest he put forth his hand] Vatablus, who looks on the tree of life as no more than a mystical emblem, understands that it was as though God had said, "Lest he should have a vain expectation excited in him by laying hold of this symbol of My promise; that shall be taken from him which might give him such a hope of immortality," ad h. l. But Augustine, who spoke of the tree of life as a sacrament, probably meant by a sacrament something more than a mere emblem; and many of the fathers looked on this judgment of God, whereby man was excluded from the reach of that, which might have made him immortal, as rather a mercy than a judgment. If his life had now been perpetuated, it would have been an immortality of sin. So Gregory Nazianzen says the exclusion from the tree of life was "that evil might not be immortal, and that the punishment might be an act of benevolence." (Greg. Naz. 'Orat.' XXXVII. n. 1. See Patrick).

24. *Cherubims*] See note C at end of Chapter.

NOTE A on CHAP. III. v. 19. ON THE EFFECT OF THE FALL.

NOTHING can really be plainer than that the narrative describes a most deplorable change in the condition of the first parents of mankind, a change from a state of holiness resulting from the presence of God and a life in dependence on His support, to a state of sin and shame following on disobedience to His will and a desire to become independent of Him. It is the distinctest possible account of a sin and of its punishment. Moreover in all subsequent teaching of Scripture the whole human race is represented as sharing in the exile of Adam from his Maker, and hence in his sinfulness; for holiness and happiness are inseparable from the presence and the Spirit of God. It may be impossible fully to explain all the justice or the mercy of this dispensation. Yet we may reflect that man was created a reasonable, free-willing, responsible being. All this implies power to will as God wills, and power to will as God does not will. It implies too something like a condition of trial, a state of probation. If each man had been put on his trial separately, as Adam was; judging from experience as well as from the history of Adam, we may see the probability that a large number of Adam's descendants would have sinned as he sinned. The confusion so introduced into the world would have been at least as great as that which the single fall and the expulsion once for all of our first parents from Paradise have actually brought in. And the remedy would have been apparently less simple and more complicated. As the Scripture history represents it to us, and as the New Testament interprets that history, the Judge of all the earth punished the sin of Adam by depriving him of His presence and His Spirit (that "original righteousness" of the fathers and the schoolmen, see Bp. Bull, Vól. II. Dis. V. and Aquinas, 'Summa,' ii. I. qu. 82. art. 4), and thus subjecting him to death. But though He thus "concluded all under sin," it was indeed "that He might have mercy on all," Rom. xi. 32. The whole race of man condemned in Adam, receives in Adam also the promise of recovery for all. And in the Second Adam, that special *Seed of the woman*, the recovery of the whole race is effected, insomuch that as in Adam all died, even so in Christ all shall be made alive. And thus in truth the mystery of sin can only be cleared up by the mystery of redemption; whilst both exhibit the justice of God brought out into its fullest relief only under the light of His love.

NOTE B on CHAP. III. V. 22. ON THE HISTORICAL CHARACTER OF THE TEMPTATION AND THE FALL.

THE traditions of all, especially Eastern nations, have more or less of resemblance to the record of the first three chapters of Genesis. This is, according to some, to be explained by mere similarity in all early mythology. According to others it results from the Hebrew histories borrowing the myths of neighbouring countries and propounding them as historical truths. There can be no reasonable doubt, that the writer of Genesis puts forth his history as history. Hence some of the early rationalists admitted an historical foundation, though they thought it coloured by subsequent fancy. Eichhorn for instance ('Urgeschichte,' Th. 2. B. 2) supposed that Adam dreamed of the formation of Eve out of his side. Eve (as Abarbanel had also imagined) saw the serpent eating poisonous fruit, then ate of it herself and gave it to her husband; and thus awakened in them both sensual thoughts and the first feelings of shame. A thunderstorm seemed to them the voice of God; they fled in terror from Paradise, and in the unkindliness of a sterile land, the toils of agriculture and the pangs of childbirth found a punishment for their fault. But such forced explanations soon gave way to mythical interpretation. Paradise is but the golden age of the Hebrews; the tree of life is the Ambrosia or Amrita of Greece or India; the tempter finds a parallel in the contests of Krishna with the serpent, or in the Persian myth of Ahriman deceiving the first human beings under a serpent's form. The Indian cosmogony and the history of Krishna certainly bear some resemblance to the Jewish history, though widely distinguished from it by the gross Pantheism of the Hindoo Theology: but that the Hebrews can owe nothing to these is evident from the fact that they are not contained in the Vedas and the most ancient Sanscrit literature, from which alone it is possible that even the later Jewish writers could have borrowed. Indeed the history of Krishna first appears in the 'Bhagavat Gita,' a work assigned to the 3rd century after Christ, and which is supposed to have drawn largely from Christian or Pseudo-Christian sources. The nearest resemblance, however, is traceable between the Biblical record and the teaching of the Zendavesta. As there is a likeness in the history of Creation and in the description of Paradise, so there is a special similarity in the account of the fall. According to the doctrine of Zoroaster, the first human beings, created by Ormuzd, the good principle, lived in a state of innocence in a happy garden with a tree which gave them life and immortality; but Ahriman, the evil principle, assuming the form of a serpent, offered them the fruit of a tree, which he had himself created; they ate and became subject to evil and to a continual contest between light and darkness, between the good motions of Ormuzd, and the evil suggestions of Ahriman. As the Hindoo traditions are disfigured by Pantheism, so are the Persian by dualism; and both are markedly contrasted with the pure monotheism of the Bible History. But Hartmann, Von Bohlen, and other mythical interpreters, have imagined that the Mosaic account was really borrowed from the Zoroastrian; a theory which could only be established by proving that the early chapters of Genesis were not written till after the Babylonish captivity; for it was then that the Jews first came into close contact with the Persians, and might have borrowed some of their superstitions.

Against so late a date the language of the first chapter of Genesis is conclusive. There are indeed a few Aramaisms in Genesis; but it has been ruled most justly, that "Aramaisms in a book of the Bible are proof either of a very early or of a very late origin." The Patriarchs, who came from Ur of the Chaldees, may have naturally spoken a Hebrew not unmixed with Chaldaisms, and some names, as that of Eve (Chava) and that of the *LORD* (JEHOVAH), both of which have a Chaldee or Aramaic form, could not possibly have been invented later than the age of Moses, unless they were invented after the Babylonian Captivity, when the Jews again came into contact with the Chaldeans in Babylonia. That the Aramaisms of Genesis really mark antiquity, not novelty, should almost be self apparent to one familiar with the original. The Hebrew of the first three chapters of the Bible is most emphatically archaic. It cannot therefore be a modern Chaldaized Hebrew, but is a Hebrew so ancient as still to retain strong traces of its original union with its sister dialect Chaldee. Its peculiar conciseness is the exact opposite of the diffuse and verbose style of the Chaldee in Daniel or Ezra. The 3rd verse of Genesis owes much of its proverbial grandeur to this very conciseness. So many thoughts are perhaps nowhere else in the world uttered in so few syllables. The very reverse of this is true of the language when it had become infected by the Chaldee of the Captivity. But, if the legends of the Zendavesta were not borrowed by the Jews in their captivity, then the real contact point between them and the Jewish history must be found in pre-Mosaic times, in the days of the early patriarchs; and then the fact, that the traditions of Persia were of all others the nearest to the Jewish traditions may easily be explained. Let us suppose the account in Genesis to be the great Semitic tradition, perhaps delivered direct from Shem to Abraham, from Abraham to Jacob, from Jacob to Joseph, and incorporated under Divine guidance by Moses in his history. Is it unlikely that Japhet may have given the very same account of his own posterity? and where would it have been so well preserved, as in Iran, that spot, or at least near to that spot, where the Aryan races seem longest to have dwelt together, and where the tradition was most likely to have been undisturbed by constant migrations? The Persians prided themselves on their pure and ancient descent; and modern ethnologists have given to those tribes which peopled India and Europe the name of Aryan, after the inhabitants of Iran and the noblest race among them, the Arii. If the Hebrews retained the Semitic tradition pure and uncorrupted, through their adherence to the worship of the true God, whilst the Persians had the Japhetic tradition, though corrupted by dualism, the resemblance between their respective accounts would be in every way natural, and the real historical basis of them both would be the simplest solution of the difficulty.

It may only be necessary to add that this reasoning will not be affected, even if we should concur with those who argue, that the history of the fall is a true history though veiled under allegorical imagery, *i. e.* that Adam and Eve were created innocent and holy, that they were subjected to a trial and fell under it, thereby bringing in sin and death upon mankind, but that the description given of this in Genesis is not literal but emblematical and mystical (see for instance Quarry 'on Gen.' p. 112, and Warburton quoted by him).

NOTE C on CHAP. III. V. 24. CHERUBIM.

(1) Traditional accounts of the Cherubim. (2) Cherubim figured in Tabernacle and Temple. (3) Cherubim seen in visions of Isaiah, Ezekiel, St John. (4) Cherubim of Paradise. (5) Etymology of name.

IN this passage the Cherubim appear to be living beings, angels of God, fulfilling the will of God. Elsewhere (except in brief allusions as Ps. xviii. 10; 2 Sam. xxii. 11) we find them as sculptured or wrought figures in the Tabernacle and the Temple; or as images in the visions of prophets, which visions have always more or less of the other imagery of the Temple presented in them (Ez. i. x; Rev. iv. and perhaps Is. vi.).

Tradition gives no satisfactory account of the appearance of these cherubic figures. Josephus, ('Ant.' III. 6. § 5) says that they were "winged animals in form like nothing seen by man." It is possible that Josephus' Pharisaic prejudice in interpreting the second commandment may have led him to this profession of utter ignorance concerning the forms of the Cherubim, for he charges Solomon with a breach of the law on account of the oxen under the brazen sea ('Ant.' VIII. 7. § 3), and in the face of Exod. xxvi. 31 (compared with Ezek. x. 20), he denies that the veil of the tabernacle had any living creatures on it ('Ant.' III. 5. § 6). Still the Apostle (Heb. ix. 5), who speaks of "the Cherubim of glory shadowing the mercy seat," adds, "of which we cannot now speak particularly," as though, after the captivity and the destruction of the first Temple, not only had the sacred figures never been restored, but even the memory of their shapes had been lost.

1. *The Tabernacle and the Temple*] When Moses is commanded to make the ark, we learn that he was to make the *Capporeth*, the mercy seat or covering of the ark, of pure gold, and Cherubim looking towards the mercy seat, stretching forth their wings on high to cover the mercy seat. The Cherubim were to be of a piece with the mercy seat, or at least of the same material (Ex. xxv. 17—20). There is no appearance of more than one face to each Cherub, nor of more than two wings. The Cherubim on the mercy seat in the Tabernacle appear to have been exactly imitated by Solomon in the Temple, unless they were the very Cherubim of the Tabernacle removed to the Temple. Their height is said to have been ten cubits, and their wings touched the walls on either side (1 K. vi. 27). Besides the two Cherubim on the mercy seat, figures of Cherubim were wrought on the curtains of the Tabernacle (Ex. xxvi. 1, 31, xxxvi. 8, 35), and were afterwards engraven on the walls and doors of the Temple, along with palms and flowers, (1 K. vi. 29, 32, 35): also on the bases of the ten lavers, on the borders that were between the ledges were "lions, oxen and Cherubims." (1 K. vii. 29). Then again were four wheels a cubit and a half high, and again we find "Cherubims, lions and palm trees." (v. 36.)

The special offices of the Cherubic figures in the Tabernacle appear to have been, first, the watching and guarding of the ark and the sacred law deposited within the ark, towards which they are represented as looking and over which they spread their outstretched wings, and secondly, to attend and bear up that mystic presence of God, which appeared in the Cloud of glory over the mercy seat. That Cloud of glory had led Israel through the Red Sea and the wilderness, the guide and guardian of God's people, the symbol of His presence, especially in the giving of the law, having a twofold aspect, at times as darkness, at times as a pillar of light; now a glory settling on the Tabernacle or resting above the ark, at another time accompanied with fire and lightnings, so that the people durst not look on it. (Ex. xiii. 21, 22, xiv. 19, 24, xvi. 10, xix. 16, 18, 20, xx. 18, xxiv. 16, 17, xxxiii. 9, xxxiv. 5, xxxvii. 6—9, xl. 34—38; Num. ix. 15—23, xii. 5—10, xvi. 19—42). When the Tabernacle is set up, the Law is deposited in the Ark, the cloud is promised to rest upon the covering of the Ark, and, as the Cherubim guard the Law and the Testimony of God, so they may be supposed reverently to surround the throne of His glory.

If we went no farther, we should naturally conclude, that the Cherubim were winged human figures, sculptured in the Tabernacle and the Temple, representing either the personal angels of God, or at least those ministers and agents of His in creation which do His pleasure and wait upon His will. We should infer, that their offices were (1) to guard what is sacred and unapproachable, the gate of Paradise (Gen. iii. 24), the ark of the covenant of the LORD, in which were deposited the two tables of the Law (compare Ezek. xxviii. 14—16, where the Prince of Tyre is compared to a Cherub, who in Eden covers with his wings the precious stones): (2) to surround the mystic throne of God and to attend His presence (hence the Most High is constantly spoken of as dwelling between the Cherubim, *i.e.* by His Shechinah on the mercy seat, 1 S. iv. 4; 2 S. vi. 2; 2 K. xix. 15; Ps. lxxx. 2, xcix. 1; Is. xxxvii. 16): (3) perhaps to bear up the throne of God upon their wings, and to carry Him when He appeared in His glory. (Comp. 2 S. xxii. 11; Ps. xviii. 10, "He rode upon a Cherub, and did fly: yea, He did fly upon the wings of the wind.")

2. *The visions of Isaiah, Ezekiel and St John*] It is doubtful whether the Seraphim in the vision of Isaiah ch. vi. (the only place in which they are named in Scripture) be the same as the Cherubim or not. The scene is the same as in the Cherubic visions of Ezekiel and St John, viz. in the Temple (vv. 1. 6). The Seraphim occupy a place like that of the Cherubim, viz. just by the Throne of God; and their taking the live coal from the altar seems to connect them with the burning coals of Ezekiel's Cherubim (Ez. i. 13). As far as we can judge these Seraphim resemble the Cherubim of the Tabernacle and the Temple in having human forms and single faces, but they have six wings each: "With twain he covered his face, and with twain he covered his feet, and with twain he did fly."

We come now to the visions of Ezekiel and St John. These visions also have their seat in the Temple as the image of Heaven. (See Ezek. x. 2, 3, 5, 18, where we meet with the altar fire and the courts of the Temple: and Rev. *passim*, where all the imagery is drawn from the Temple, *e.g.* the candlestick ch. i. 12, the High Priest ch. i. 13, the altar ch. vi. 9, &c.) In both visions the throne corresponds with the place on which the Cloud of glory rested between the Cherubim. The Cherubim then are described as living creatures (Ezek. i. 5; Rev. iv. 6), in the form of a man (Ezek. i. 5) with four (Ezek. i. 8, ii. 23, x. 7, 8—21), or with six wings (Rev. iv. 8), having eyes all over (Ezek. i. 18, x. 12; Rev. iv. 8). In Ezekiel they have each four faces, viz. of a man, of a lion, of an ox, of an eagle (Ezek. i. 10, x. 16). In St John they have but one face each, these faces being respectively of a man, of a lion, of a calf and of an eagle (Rev. iv. 7). Their feet appear to Ezekiel as straight feet, like the feet of oxen (Ezek. i. 7). In Ezek. x. 14, we have the very singular phenomenon that the face of a Cherub seems identified or synonymous with the face of a calf or an ox. (Comp. Ezek. i. 10; Rev. iv. 7.) It is thought by many, that in these latter visions we have a fuller description of the Cherubim of the Tabernacle and the Temple than we could gather from the earlier accounts in Holy Scripture. It is supposed that they too, like the Cherubim in the visions, must have been composite creatures, if of human form, yet with heads of other animals, either as described by Ezekiel or by St John. Moreover, as such composite figures must plainly have been emblematical, it has been thought that the Cherubim by their faces of a man, a lion, a bull and an eagle, perhaps expressed the strength and wisdom of the Divine Majesty, or perhaps the strength and the swiftness, with which His ministers do His will. Again, as they surround the throne and guard the Law of the Most High, so perhaps we may understand, that the natural and the spiritual creation being knit up together in one great scheme, these symbolic creatures indicate that all things, all creation, wait upon God, all do His will, all work together for good to the godly and for judgment on the ungodly. They guard His law, and execute its judgments, and keep off the sinner from the blessing of its rewards.

The existence of composite winged emblematical figures amongst nations more or less connected with the Hebrews is now well known. The Sphinx and the Griffin have long been familiar to us: but it has been remarked as singular that Mr Layard should have discovered in Nineveh gigantic winged bulls with human heads, winged lions, and human figures with hawk or eagle heads, corresponding so nearly with the winged Cherubim of the visions of Ezekiel and St John. These gigantic figures too are generally placed as guards or sentinels at the entrances of temples and palaces, like the guarding Cherubim of Holy Writ. Moreover, they are evidently not objects of idolatrous worship, but appear rather as worshippers than as divinities. It is argued, that it is not improbable that Moses should have adopted similar emblems, opposing the true worship to the false, and placing in the temple of the true God emblems of protection, watchfulness, power, and glory, similar to those used in the temples of the gods of the nations. (See Lämmert, 'Die Cherubim' in 'Jahrbücher für Deutsche Theol.' Zwölfter Band, Viertes Heft, Gotha, 1867). It is, however, to be observed, that nothing connects Moses with Assyria or the Assyrian sculptures: and indeed those found by Mr Layard in the Temple of Kojundjik, which are most to the point, are not considered by him to be of great antiquity. Far more likely is it that some Egyptian type should have been followed: and we find in the Egyptian Sculptures, and in the 18th dynasty, which was probably the dynasty of the Exodus, examples of a shrine or ark wonderfully calculated to remind us of the ark of the Covenant made by Moses. It is carried by persons of the sacerdotal race, by staves, as the Levites carried the ark. In the centre is the symbol of the Deity, and two winged human figures spread out their wings around and over it. (Lepsius, 'Denkm.' III. Bl. 14.) These two figures, however, represent the goddess Ma, under the two-fold notion of "justice" and "truth." This is clear from the ostrich feathers on the heads of the figures. This goddess is often called "the double Ma," and it is very doubtful, whether, notwithstanding this apparent similarity, there is any relation between these figures and the Cherubim of the Tabernacle.

What then is to be said of the vision of Ezekiel and of St John who nearly repeats the imagery in Ezekiel? We may observe, that Ezekiel was a priest (Ezek. i. 3). He was therefore probably familiar with the sculptures in the Temple, especially the Cherubim carved on the bases of the ten lavers, along with bulls and lions, and with four wheels curiously connected with them. His vision, the scene of which was the Temple, naturally was mixed up with objects in the Temple. The connection of his Cherubic figures with wheels is explained by 1 Kings vii. 29, 30, 33. Even the lion and bull-heads of these figures may have come from the mingling of the Cherubim with the bulls and lions in the Temple. But, besides this, he saw these visions by the river Chebar in the land of the Chaldeans; and there he and his people would, no doubt, have become familiarized with the gigantic winged guardians of the temples and the palaces in Babylonia and Assyria, the bulls and lions and eagle-headed men, and human-headed bulls. It is highly probable that the difference between the Cherubim in Ezekiel's vision (repeated with certain variations in St John's), and the Cherubim in the Tabernacle and the Temple resulted in part from this. In God's dealings with man, He constantly uses for lessons things just before men's eyes. And so He may have done in this case with Ezekiel. It is almost certain that Ezekiel's visions did not represent accurately that to which he had been used in the Temple. Hence he appears not at first to have recognized them as being Cherubim; but at the end of his second vision he tells us, that now he knew they were Cherubim (Ezek. x. 20). To Moses, on the other hand, but still on the same principle, God had dictated the carving of figures like those which he had seen in Egypt, figures emblematical of guardianship, and of the reverence of those who wait constantly upon God, but which had never been objects of idolatrous worship. Thus He sanctioned, or at least tolerated, that which seems so dear to religious humanity, the use of symbolism, where dangers from its abuse were not great. We conclude, therefore, notwithstanding much authority to the contrary, that in all probability the Cherubim of glory shadowing the mercy seat were winged human figures, with human faces too.

The Cherubim of Paradise] It is noticed that Moses describes the placing of the Cherubim at the gates of Eden in words suggested by that which he had to carve in the Tabernacle. "He placed...Cherubim" is in the Hebrew יַשְׁכֵּן "He made to dwell," a term specially belonging to the dwelling of the glory of God in the Shechinah, the cloud of glory. And the Paradise Cherubim were to keep, lit. "to guard," (לִשְׁמֹר) the way to the tree of life, as the Cherubim in the Tabernacle guarded the Ark of the Covenant. Those, who believe the Cherubim in the Tabernacle to have been like those seen by Ezekiel, naturally believe also that they were but emblems of those powers of nature and creation by which the Creator so constantly works His will. The Cherubim and the flaming sword at the East Gate of Paradise to them mean only that the way back to Eden and to the tree of life was closed by such natural hindrances as the Author of nature saw fit to interpose. It is not impossible that even if the Cherubim of the Tabernacle were not composite creatures, but simply winged human figures, much the same may have been meant. There are doubtless hosts of spiritual beings that surround the throne of God and do His will; but all things serve Him. He maketh the winds His angels, and a flame of fire His ministers. The stern, mechanical, turning every way of the sword of flame perhaps points to this; and the sacred writer may possibly have signified under the symbols of angelic beings the great ministering powers of nature.

This at least is taught us by the Cherubim guarding the way to the Tree of life. Paradise had been lost by sin; but it was not gone for ever. The tree of life, and the garden where it grew, were still in full glory under the keeping of God and of His holy angels. The forfeited life is not irrecoverable: but it can only be recovered through fighting and conquest, suffering and death. There were between it and man the ministers of righteous vengeance and the flaming sword.

The Etymology of the word *Cherub* is very obscure. Some derive it from כְּרַב (Cherab) "to plough," it being inferred from Ezek. i. 10 compared with x. 14, that the true Cherub form was that of an ox. Others compare קָרוֹב (Kerob) "near," *i.e.* admitted to the special presence of God. The Talmudists assert that the name signifies "a child," and that the faces of the Cherubim were the faces of children. Eichhorn and others compare the Greek γρύψ, γρύπος, from the Persian *greifen* "to hold," and consider the name to be nearly equal in significance, as well as in derivation, with the fabulous Griffin or Gryphon of the East. Gesenius suggests the root כרב (Charab) = חרם (Charam) "to shut out," "to consecrate" (hence *haram*, a sacred shrine). According to this derivation, the Cherubim would be the guardians and defenders of that which is consecrated, of the Shrine or the Paradise. Canon Cook (see Appendix to this volume) has traced the word to an Egyptian root, which probably means "carve," or at any rate "shape." In Matt. xviii. 2, χερεβ is the Coptic for μορφή.

CHAPTER IV.

1 *The birth, trade, and religion of Cain and Abel.* 8 *The murder of Abel.* 11 *The curse of Cain.* 17 *Enoch the first city.* 19 *Lamech and his two wives.* 25 *The birth of Seth,* 26 *and Enos.*

AND Adam knew Eve his wife;
and she conceived, and bare
Cain, and said, I have gotten a man
from the LORD.
2 And she again bare his brother
†Abel. And Abel was †a keeper of † Heb. *Hebel.*
sheep, but Cain was a tiller of the † Heb. *a feeder.*
ground. † Heb.
3 And †in process of time it came *at the end of days.*

CHAP. IV. 1. The last Chapter was a history of the first birth of sin; this gives us an account of its developement, as also of the first out-spreading of the human race. Cain and Abel are respectively types of the two opposing principles discernible throughout the sacred history; Cain of the unchecked dominion of evil, Abel of the victory of faith.

I have gotten a man from the LORD] LXX. "by means of the Lord;" Onk. "from the Lord;" Syriac "for the Lord;" Pseudo-Jonathan "a man, the angel of the LORD." Following the latter paraphrast, Luther, Munster, Fagius, Schmidt, Pfeiffer, Baumgart. and others, have rendered "I have gotten a man, even JEHOVAH," as though Eve understood that the *seed*, who was to bruise the serpent, should be incarnate Deity, and supposed that Cain was that seed. We can, however, scarcely see ground enough to believe that Eve's knowledge was so advanced, or her faith in the Messiah so lively as to

to pass, that Cain brought of the fruit
of the ground an offering unto the
LORD.
4 And Abel, he also brought of the
firstlings of his †flock and of the fat
thereof. And the LORD had [a]re-
spect unto Abel and to his offering:

† Heb. *sheep, or goats.*
[a] Heb. 4.

---

have called forth such an exclamation. It is more probable that the particle rendered in our Version *from* is a preposition (it is in the next chapter (v. 24) rendered *with*), and that it signifies, as the LXX. has it, *by means of*, or, as Gesenius, *by the help of*. There is, however, little doubt that her words had some pregnant meaning, and that she looked on Cain as at all events one of that race which was destined to triumph over the seed of the Serpent.

"The use of the name (JEHOVAH) is significant, though we cannot think that Eve already knew this name of God, which was first revealed to man at a later period of his history, and which is of Hebrew origin, whereas that language probably did not exist until the time of the dispersion at Babel. Yet, doubtless, the historian expresses the true meaning of Eve's speech which she spoke, inspired by that help which had been graciously given her of God" (Keil, 'Bibl. Comment.').

2. *Abel.*] She called her first-born Cain (*possession*), but this second Hebel (*breath, vapour, vanity, nothingness*), because all human possession is but vanity. Yet it is not said, that Abel was so named by Eve herself, as Cain had been. Hence it is possible, that the name Abel was that by which he became known, after his life had passed away like a breath or a vapour.

Abel was a keeper of sheep, but Cain was a tiller of the ground] The word rendered *sheep* includes sheep and goats. It is observed that the wildest nations live by hunting, those, who have thrown off the first barbarism, are nomadic, feeding sheep and cattle, those more civilized are agriculturists (see Rosen.). Hence the rationalist view coincides with the heathen, that a state of nature was pure barbarism, and that man gradually emerged from it into nomadic, then into agricultural, and finally into civilized life. In contradistinction to this, the account of Genesis represents man as placed by his Maker in a state of very simple civilization. Adam in Paradise was "to dress and to keep" the garden (Gen. ii. 15). His sons must have learned from him the knowledge which he had thus acquired. It is not likely to have been extensive knowledge, probably the very simplest possible, but still sufficient to rescue them from a state of pure barbarism, and from the necessity of living by the chase.

See note A at the end of this Chapter.

3. *in process of time*] Lit. "at the end of days." Abenezra understands "at the end of the year." So Fagius, Bochart, Clericus, Dathe, Rosenmüller, and many others. Clericus quotes from Aristot. 'Ethics,' VIII. 2. "It appears that ancient sacrifices were offered after the gathering of the fruits of the earth, they being a kind of first fruits. Moreover, at that time, men were most at leisure."

an offering] The word here used always signifies an unbloody oblation. It is frequently translated "a meat offering." Its nature is defined, Lev. xi. 1 seq.

4. *of the firstlings of his flock and of the fat thereof*] There has been in all times a difference of opinion as to the Divine or human origin of sacrifice. Sacrifices were so thoroughly sanctioned by the Divine law in after times, so generally accepted by God, and made so conspicuously types of the Lamb of God, that it is difficult to conceive how they should have arisen but from a Divine command. Yet, there is a deep silence as to any such command, whilst the institution of the Sabbath and of other positive ordinances is distinctly recorded. Hence, many have thought that sacrifice was dictated by an instinct of natural religion, and then, by a condescension to man's infirmity, sanctioned for a temporary purpose, and constituted an image of redemption. It is impossible to say what the view of the Apostolic fathers was; but from the time of Justin Martyr ('Apol.' II. 5; 'Dial.' pp. 237, 292), the fathers generally adopted the belief that sacrifice was a human, not a Divine ordinance. A remarkable exception to this appears in a passage of the most learned of the 4th century divines (Euseb. 'Dem. Evang.' I. 10), in which he distinctly ascribes the origin of sacrifice to a Divine inspiration, though even this does not necessarily imply a Divine command. It may be fairly said, that no certain conclusion on this question can possibly be arrived at, in the silence of Scripture. The principal arguments on the side of the Divine origin may be seen in Bp. Jer. Taylor, 'Duct. Dub.' Bk. II. R. XIII. §§ 27, 30; Witsii 'Ægypt.' III. 14; Kennicott, 'Two Dissertations,' II. p. 184 sq.; Magee 'On Atonement,' Disc. II. and notes; Faber, 'Three Dispensations,' Vol. I. The arguments on the opposite side may be found in Spencer, 'De Legibus Heb.' Lib. III. Diss. ii.; Warburton, 'Div. Legat.' Bks. VI. IX.; Davison's 'Remains,' art. *on origin of Sacrifice*. The work of Outram, 'De Sacrificiis,' should by all means be consulted, which takes an impartial survey of the whole question.

had respect unto] Comp. Num. xvi. 15;

5 But unto Cain and to his offering
he had not respect. And Cain was
very wroth, and his countenance
fell.

6 And the LORD said unto Cain,
Why art thou wroth? and why is thy
countenance fallen?

7 If thou doest well, shalt thou not
‖be accepted? and if thou doest not
well, sin lieth at the door. And ‖unto
thee *shall be* his desire, and thou shalt
rule over him.

8 And Cain talked with Abel his
brother: and it came to pass, [b]when

‖ Or, *have the excellency?*
‖ Or, *subject unto thee.*
[b] Wisd. 1[0]. 3. Matt. 23. 35. 1 John 3. 12. Jude 1[1].

Amos v. 22. How did the Almighty express His approval of Abel's offering? According to the ancient Greek translation of Theod., it was by sending down fire to consume the sacrifice, as in Lev. ix. 24; Jud. vi. 21; 1 K. xviii. 38; 1 Chr. xxi. 26; 2 Chr. vii. 1. This explanation has been adopted by St Jerome, Rashi, Abenezra, Kimchi, Luther, Grotius, Delitzsch, and many others. Nothing but conjecture can guide us in this matter. We must be content to suppose, that some sign, intelligible to both the brothers, was given from above. The reason, as well as the mode, of the acceptance of Abel's gift has been greatly debated. Ver. 7, and Heb. xi. 4, seem to prove that the difference of spirit in which the two offerings were made caused the diversity of acceptance. The Apostle says, "By faith Abel offered a more excellent sacrifice." Faith, therefore, was the motive power; yet the result may have been that the sacrifice so offered was a better, fuller, and more acceptable sacrifice. Some have maintained that Cain brought fruits only, that Abel brought both fruits and the firstlings of his flock (see Kennicott, as above, p. 194). The wording of the original does not seem to warrant this. But, whilst we may see in the different spirit and disposition of the offerers a reason why one should be accepted and the other rejected, still "the view so often expressed, that Abel's bloody sacrifice resulted from a more profound religious apprehension than that of Cain, which was 'without shedding of blood,' seems to agree with the general bearing of the text" (Kurtz, 'Hist. of O. C.' Vol. I. p. 89); even if it be not admitted that a Divine ordinance had already sanctioned animal sacrifices.

5. *countenance fell*] Cp. the original of Nehem. vi. 16.

7. *shalt thou not be accepted*] **Is there not acceptance?** Lit. "lifting up" either of guilt (*i.e.* pardon), or of the countenance, as when a suppliant bending down his face is accepted, and so his face raised up and cheered. Or more probably as the A. V., Is there not acceptance? Shalt thou not be accepted by God?

if thou doest not well, sin lieth at the door] This is generally explained as meaning that sin crouches at the door of the soul, like a wild beast, ready to devour it. Others understand *sin* to mean *the punishment of sin*, in which sense the word is sometimes used, see Zech. xiv. 19 (so Onk., Vatablus, Cornel. a Lapide). Some again interpret "a sin offering" (another frequent sense of the Hebrew word) which in the form of an animal victim lies or crouches at your door (see Kennicott, as above, p. 216, and Lee, 'Lex.' s. v. חַטָּאת). The chief objection to this latter interpretation is that there is no instance of this use of the word before the giving of the Law; which Law appears to have brought out into clearer relief the knowledge of sin and the need of sin-offering. See Rom. iii. 20.

And unto thee shall be his desire, &c.] There are two principal interpretations of these words, which have divided commentators in all times, the one set referring *his desire* to *Abel*, the other to *sin*. The LXX. Version clearly refers it to Abel, which interpretation is adopted by Chrysost., Ambrose, Augustine, and most of the fathers, by Grotius, Vossius, Heidegger, by our own translators, and by a majority of English commentators. The sense will then be, that Cain, whose jealousy had been excited by God's acceptance of Abel, need not, if he behaved well, fear that Abel should be preferred before him; his pre-eminence of birth should still be preserved to him: the desire of the younger brother should be towards him (an idiomatic expression specially noting the longing of one who looks up to another as an object of reverence, and so noting dependence, as of a younger brother on an elder, cp. Gen. iii. 16). The other interpretation, which is apparently, though not certainly, favoured by the Vulgate, is given in the Targums of Jerusalem and Pseudo-Jonathan, and adopted by Rashi, and most Jewish writers, by Luther's translation, Munster, Pererius, Rosenmüller, Von Bohlen, Delitzsch, Knobel, Keil, and most of the Germans. The sense of the passage on this supposition would be, "Sin lieth crouching like a wild beast at the door of the soul; its desire is towards thee, yet thou art not given over into its power; but if thou wilt, thou shalt be able to keep it in subjection." The former of these interpretations, which is also the more ancient, seems both more natural and more according with the simple meaning of the original.

8. *Cain talked with Abel*] The original

they were in the field, that Cain rose
up against Abel his brother, and slew
him.

9 ¶ And the LORD said unto Cain,
Where *is* Abel thy brother? And he
said, I know not: *Am* I my brother's
keeper?

10 And he said, What hast thou
done? the voice of thy brother's †blood
crieth unto me from the ground.

† Heb. *bloods.*

11 And now *art* thou cursed from
the earth, which hath opened her
mouth to receive thy brother's blood
from thy hand;

12 When thou tillest the ground, it
shall not henceforth yield unto thee
her strength; a fugitive and a vagabond
shalt thou be in the earth.

13 And Cain said unto the LORD,
‖My punishment *is* greater than I can
bear.

‖ Or, *My iniquity* is *greater than that it may be forgiven.*

14 Behold, thou hast driven me
out this day from the face of the
earth; and from thy face shall I be
hid; and I shall be a fugitive and a
vagabond in the earth; and it shall
come to pass, *that* every one that
findeth me shall slay me.

---

means more naturally "Cain *said* to Abel." Accordingly in some few of the Masoretic MSS. there is the mark of an omission here. The Samaritan Pentateuch, the LXX., Syr., Vulg., read "Cain said to Abel his brother, Let us go into the field." These latter words, however, do not occur in the Greek Versions of Aquila, Symmachus, Theodotion, or the most ancient Targum, that of Onkelos. It is probable that the words were inserted in the Sam., LXX., &c. as a gloss, from the difficulty of explaining the passage without them; and that this is really an example of an ancient and obsolete usage of the verb *to say*, which here means either *to talk with*, as the A. V., or to *tell*, as Jerome, or to *command*, to *lay a command upon*, according to Arabic usage, as Prof. Lee.

10. *the voice of thy brother's blood crieth unto me*] The verb "crieth" here agrees with "blood," which is in the plural, in which form it is used specially of blood shed, drops of blood, above all of blood shed by violence and murder. Murder is a crime which cries to heaven for vengeance, and though the blood may be hidden, its voice cannot be silenced.

11. *now art thou cursed from the earth*] The words are variously rendered (1) "Cursed art thou from the ground," *i.e.* the curse shall come upon thee from the earth, which shall not yield thee her fruit (Abenezra, Kimchi, Knobel). (2) "Cursed art thou away from the land," *i.e.* Thou art cursed and banished from the land, in which thou hast dwelt, and in which thy father and brethren are dwelling (Rosenm., Vater, Tuch, Knobel). (3) "Cursed art thou even more than the earth" which had been cursed (ch. iii. 17). Of these (3) seems quite inadmissible; either of the others yields a pertinent sense. The second is the most probable.

12. *When thou tillest*, &c.] The curse was in effect, that Cain should be banished from the land inhabited and cultivated by Adam and his family, should wander about without a settled habitation or a fertile dwelling place, living hardly in a barren and inhospitable wilderness.

13. *My punishment*] There is great variety of interpretation here. The Hebrews constantly expressed *sin* and *punishment for sin* by the same words; moreover to *bear*, and *to take away* or *forgive*, were thoughts closely connected. Hence (1) "My sin is too great to be forgiven" (as in the Marg.) is the rendering of LXX., Onk., Syr., Vulg., Saad. Whilst (2) Abenezra, Kimchi, and the majority of modern commentators, render as the A. V., "My punishment is greater than I can bear." Both these renderings can be defended on good grounds by Hebrew usage. The latter seems more accordant with the temper of Cain's mind, and is probably correct.

14. *from thy face shall I be hid*] Though God no longer constantly manifested His presence as in Eden, yet there were at times some indications of that presence, (*e.g.* see v. 4). It may perhaps be inferred that some special place had already been set apart for Divine worship and sacred service. (On this subject see Blunt, 'Undesigned Coincidences,' I. p. 9, eighth Edition, 1863).

every one that findeth me shall slay me] Josephus, Kimchi, Michaelis, and others, have supposed that Cain feared death from the beasts of the field; but most commentators rightly understand that his fear was from the vengeance of his own kindred. It is observed by Kurtz that, according to hints gathered from Gen. iv. 25, the murder of Abel probably took place just before the birth of Seth, *i.e.* 130 years after the creation of man, Gen. v. 3. We need not suppose that Cain, Abel, and Seth, were the only sons of Adam. Indeed, from Gen. v. 4, we infer that there were others. Cain, Abel, and Seth, are mentioned for obvious reasons; Abel for his piety and his early death, Cain for his wickedness

15 And the LORD said unto him, Therefore whosoever slayeth Cain, vengeance shall be taken on him sevenfold. And the LORD set a mark upon Cain, lest any finding him should kill him.

16 ¶ And Cain went out from the presence of the LORD, and dwelt in the land of Nod, on the east of Eden.

17 And Cain knew his wife; and she conceived, and bare †Enoch: and he builded a city, and called the name of the city, after the name of his son, Enoch.

† Heb. *Chanoch.*

18 And unto Enoch was born Irad: and Irad begat Mehujael: and Mehujael begat Methusael: and Methusael begat †Lamech.

† Heb. *Lemech*

19 ¶ And Lamech took unto him two wives: the name of the one *was* Adah, and the name of the other Zillah.

---

and the worldly wisdom of his posterity, Seth because he was the ancestor of the promised seed. There may then, in 130 years, have grown up a very considerable number of children and grandchildren to Adam and Eve. An Eastern tradition assigns to them no less than 33 sons and 27 daughters.

15. *Therefore*] The LXX., Symm., Theodot., Vulg., Syr., read *Not so.* So Dathe and others.

whosoever slayeth] Cain, though guilty of a terrible sin, may not have had the full and fixed purpose to commit murder, but in a moment of furious anger have seized a weapon and dealt a murderous blow, perhaps hardly aware of its deadly consequences. Hence, it may be, the Most High forbids him to be put to death, but sentences him to a perpetual banishment from his early home, and to a life of misery and sorrow. Kalisch well observes, "The early death of Abel can be no punishment; he seemed in fact to enjoy the peculiar favour of God; his offering was graciously accepted. We find, therefore, in this narrative the great and beautiful thought, that life is not the highest boon; that the pious find a better existence and a more blessed reward in another and a purer sphere; but that crime and guilt are the greatest evils; that they are punished by a long and wearisome life, full of fear and care and compunction of conscience."

set a mark upon Cain] **Gave a sign to Cain.** LXX. The interpretation that God provided Cain with some mark which would make him known is adopted by Pseudo-Jonathan, most of the Jewish Commentators, Luther, Calvin, Piscator, Wogal, &c. Most modern commentators agree that God gave some sign to Cain to assure him that he should not be slain, (Abenezra, Gabe, Dathe, Rosenm., Gesen., Maurer, Hitzig, V. Bohl., Tuch, Baumg., Kalisch, Delitzsch). Of what nature the sign may have been, we have now no means of learning.

16. *the presence of the Lord*] It is questioned whether this means merely from conversing with the Lord, or whether Eden, though not the *garden* of Eden, in which Adam had dwelt since the fall, was esteemed a sacred spot, a spot in which still a peculiar presence of God was looked for by man. See on v. 14.

Nod] *i.e.* "wandering." It is impossible to say where Nod was situated, except that it lay east of Eden.

17. *Enoch*] It has been contended that in these genealogies Adam = Enosh, Enoch or Chanoch = Enoch, Cain = Kenan, Irad = Jered, Mehujael = Mahalaleel, Methusael = Methuselah. In the first place, however, there is a manifest difference in the roots of the names so identified; next, the paucity of names at this early period may have naturally led to similar names being adopted in different families; 3rdly, the relationship of the families of Seth and Cain, and the probably occasional intercourse between them, would not unnaturally tend to the same result. Dettinger is quoted by Kurtz (Vol. I. p. 91), as having called attention to the fact, that the text furnishes more detailed particulars about Enoch and Lamech, whose names were so similar to Sethite names, in order to prevent the possibility of their being confounded, and to shew more clearly that the direction in which these two lines tended was markedly opposite. See Kurtz as above, Hävernick, 'Introd. to Pentateuch,' p. 109.

builded a city] Rather "began to build a city," lit. "was building a city." It is not necessary to suppose that the city was built immediately on the birth of Enoch. It may have been built when Cain had lived many years and was surrounded by children and grandchildren. The word *city* is, of course, not to be interpreted by modern ideas: a village of rude huts, which was distinguished from the booths or tents of the nomads, would satisfy all the conditions of the text.

19. *Lamech took unto him two wives*] Here we have the first example of polygamy; which, though afterwards tolerated, had its rise among the sons of Cain, and is evidently mentioned for reprobation.

20 And Adah bare Jabal: he was
the father of such as dwell in tents,
and *of such as have* cattle.
21 And his brother's name *was*
Jubal: he was the father of all such
as handle the harp and organ.
22 And Zillah, she also bare Tubal-cain, an †instructer of every artificer in brass and iron: and the sister
of Tubal-cain *was* Naamah.
23 And Lamech said unto his wives,
Adah and Zillah, Hear my voice; ye
wives of Lamech, hearken unto my
speech: for ‖I have slain a man to
my wounding, and a young man ‖to
my hurt.

† Heb. *whetter.*

‖ Or, *I would slay a man in my wound, &c.*

‖ Or, *in my hurt.*

---

20. *the father of such as dwell in tents, and...have cattle*] Jabal invented tents and introduced the custom of pasturing cattle round the tents, and perhaps even of stalling them in tents. Moreover, the word here used for cattle implies larger cattle, whereas that used of Abel v. 2 applied only to smaller cattle: Jabal therefore was the first who introduced the thorough nomadic life. (See Bochart, 'Hieroz.' P. I. Lib. II. c. 44.)

21. *the harp and the organ*] The *kinnur*, which descended to the Greeks and was by them called Kinura, is described by Josephus as having ten strings and as played on by a plectrum; but in 1 Sam. xvi. 23, xviii. 10, xix. 9, David is said to have played on it with his hand. It was probably, when invented by Jubal, the simplest form of stringed instrument. The word rendered *organ* was apparently a pipe, bagpipe, panpipe, or some very simple wind instrument: Onkelos renders it by pipe or flute. "It is not an accidental fact, that the lyre and the flute were introduced by the brothers of a nomadic herdsman. It is in the happy leisure of this occupation that music is generally first exercised and appreciated." Kalisch.

22. *an instructer of every artificer in brass and iron*] So Onkelos. Perhaps (with LXX. and Vulg.) *a sharpener of every instrument in bronze and iron.* The word rendered *brass* is certainly either *bronze*, or, more probably, a native metal, *copper* (see Smith's 'Dict. of the Bible,' art. *Brass*). Bronze is an alloy of copper and tin, very much harder than either of them and also than brass, with a little more tin it becomes bell-metal. Previously to this time all weapons for defence or instruments of husbandry may have been of flint, or wood, or bone. Uncivilized nations at the present time have weapons made of flint, wood, bone, shark's teeth, &c. Where nations have lost the usages of more civilized life, they seem to have fallen back on a flint age, then to have invented bronze weapons (in the case of South America weapons of gold), and lastly to have discovered the use of iron. Tubal Cain is here described as the first who made metal instruments and sharpened them. It is not to be objected, that this was too early for the invention of metals. If Tubal Cain was contemporary with Enoch (the descendant of Seth in the same degree) he must have been born at least 500 years after the creation of Adam, according to the Hebrew Chronology, or 1000 years according to the LXX. Chronology. Whether we must understand that he invented the use of both copper and iron, or only of copper or bronze, which led in course of time to the farther invention of iron, it may be difficult to decide from the concise and obscure wording of the text. That the most ancient inhabitants of Europe were ignorant of the use of metal, as indicated by the discovery of flint weapons in the gravel, can be no proof that they were unknown to the early descendants of Adam. If the colonists of Australia were for the next thousand years to be separated from all connection with the rest of the world, it is quite possible, notwithstanding their present high state of civilization, that they might utterly lose many of the arts of civilized life, and perhaps, if there were a deficiency of coal, or lime, or native metals, even the use of metallic instruments.

Nothing can be more natural or probable than the difference of character and development in the descendants of Cain and Seth respectively. In the former we see the children of this world wise in their generation, rapidly advancing in art and the acquirement of riches, but sensual, violent and godless. In the latter we find less of social and political advancement, but a life more regulated by the dictates of conscience and by faith in the Providence and Grace of God.

Resemblances to the names of Lamech's family have been traced in the names of those to whom the Latins attributed similar inventions. Thus Tubal Cain has been thought = Vulcan, Naamah, "the lovely, or beautiful," may then = Venus, Jubal, the inventor of the lyre = Apollo. It is observed also that the refinement and perhaps the luxury of the descendants of Cain appear in the names of their wives and daughters, Naamah, lovely, Adah, beauty or ornament, Zillah, shadow.

23, 24. *And Lamech said*, &c.]

And Lamech said unto his wives,
Adah and Zillah, hear my voice,
Ye wives of Lamech, give ear unto my speech;
For I slay a man if he woundeth me,
Even a young man, if he hurteth me,
Lo! Cain would be avenged seven-fold,
But Lamech seventy-and-seven fold.

24 If Cain shall be avenged sevenfold, truly Lamech seventy and sevenfold.
25 ¶ And Adam knew his wife
again; and she bare a son, and called
his name †Seth: For God, *said she*,
hath appointed me another seed instead of Abel, whom Cain slew.
26 And to Seth, to him also there
was born a son; and he called his
name †Enos: then began men ‖to
call upon the name of the LORD.

† Heb. *Sheth.*

† Heb. *Enosh.* ‖ Or, *to call themselves by the name of the LORD.*

The speech of Lamech has exercised the skill of translators and interpreters of all times. Its obscure and enigmatical character is admitted as a mark of its remote antiquity even by the most unfavourable critics. The apparent meaning of the words is this. Amid the violence of the times, especially among the descendants of Cain, Lamech comforts his wives with the assurance that with the aid of the bronze and iron instruments now in his hands, he could kill any one who injured him ("I slay or would slay a man for wounding me"); and that, if it had been promised to Cain, that he should be avenged seven fold, there was power in the hands of Lamech's family to avenge seventy-seven fold. The speech is one of confident boasting. Lamech trusts in his weapons of brass and steel to maintain his cause, even when referring to words used by God to his forefather Cain.

The chief difficulty lies in the use of the perfect tense in the verb *slay:* lit. "I have slain," (which is the rendering of the LXX. Vulg., Syr., &c.). That difficulty seems to have suggested the supposition that a *not* may have fallen out (which is the rendering of Onkelos, "I have not slain,") or that it should be rendered interrogatively ("Have I slain?"): but the more probable explanation is, that in this ancient distich the perfect tense is used to express the arrogant confidence of the boaster; even as at times the perfect is adopted in the most sure word of prophecy, the future being represented as having all the certainty of the past. The words rendered in the A. V. "to my wounding"—"to my hurt"—probably mean "for my wounding," &c. *i. e.* "for wounding me," or "in revenge for his wounding me."

25. *Seth*] *i.e.* "Foundation," from the word signifying *to place*, rendered here "appointed." Seth came into the place of Abel, as the ancestor of the Theocratic race and of the promised seed.

26. *then began men to call upon the name of the Lord*] **Then began he to call on the name of the LORD.** There is great diversity in the interpretation of these words. The Samaritan Pentateuch and the Vulgate refer them to Enos, "Then he, *i.e.* Enos, began to call on the name of the LORD." The LXX. has "Then he hoped," &c. it being possible to refer the verb to a root signifying "to hope," whence some have understood, that the birth of Enos inspired a new hope that the promise to Eve should be fulfilled. The Targum of the Pseudo-Jonathan has "In those days men began to make themselves idols, which they called after the name of the Word of the LORD." This interpretation is adopted by some celebrated Jewish commentators (Kimchi, Rashi, &c.), who derive the verb from a root signifying "to profane," and render "Then was there profanation in calling on the name of the LORD." Jerome ('Quæst.') mentions this as the opinion of many Jews in his days. The most natural sense of the Hebrew is, that when Enos was born, Seth his father in gratitude and hope then began to praise the LORD and to call on Him with reassured hope in His mercy and His promises. There is nothing to connect the verb with Enos as its nominative case rather than with Seth; nor again is there any good ground for the notion that emphasis is to be placed on the special name of God, JEHOVAH; as though then for the first time He was invoked under that name. The sacred narrative has all along used the name JEHOVAH; and whether we believe it to have been known from earlier times or to have been revealed first to Moses, there is nothing whatever to connect its revelation and acknowledgment with the birth of Enos.

NOTE A. ADDITIONAL NOTE ON CHAP. IV. V. 2. ON THE EARLY CIVILIZATION OF MANKIND.

HAVERNICK ('Introd. to the Pentateuch,' Translation, p. 104) has shewn that the traditions of ancient nations, the Phœnicians, Egyptians, Greeks, &c. refer the invention of agriculture to the earliest mythic ages; and that the investigators of history, Herder, Link, Schlosser, &c. have been led to the conclusion that "the discovery of the breeding of cattle, of agriculture, and of the preparation of metals, belong to prehistoric times, and that in the historic period these arts have made comparatively no great advances." The recent discoveries of human remains, and of the implements of human industry in the gravel and drift formations on the Earth's surface, may seem to contradict all this. Ethnologists distinguish a flint age, a bronze age, and an iron age, as having existed in ancient Europe; during the first of which only flint instruments, during the second bronze, during the third, iron instruments appear to have been in use. And, as for the most part in the earlier periods, the skulls seem to have been smaller and of a lower type than those of later date, the theory of early barbarism and of progressive civilization has been thought to derive confirmation from Geology. Sir Charles Lyell says also, that "had the original stock of mankind been really endowed with superior intellectual power and with inspired knowledge, and had possessed the same improvable nature as their posterity, the point of advancement, which they would have realized ere this, would have been immeasurably higher" ('Antiquity of Man,' p. 378). He goes on to say that, instead of rude pottery and flint weapons, we should in that case have found works like those of Phidias and Praxiteles. It may be answered, that Scripture does not represent the first man as "endowed with superior intellectual power and with inspired knowledge." All that we learn is, that Adam was placed in Eden to till it, that his power of speech was exercised by having to name the brute creation, that he had a simple command given him, and afterwards a special promise. Morally he may have been, in the first instance, in a state of innocence, without being intellectually in a condition of eminence. As for the advance of knowledge, many nations have been in a state of mental cultivation and of art knowledge incomparably beyond that of Adam and his children, and yet have remained for centuries upon centuries without any apparent progress; for instance, the people of China. All that we say is, that his primary state was not a state of savageness, but rather of rudimentary civilization. And this is really not opposed, but confirmed, by the records of Geology. "We must remember, that as yet we have no distinct geological evidence, that the appearance of what are called the inferior races of mankind has always preceded in chronological order that of the higher races" (Lyell, as above, p. 90). On the contrary, some of the most ancient remains of man and man's art give indications of considerable civilization. In the valley of the Ohio there are hundreds of mounds, which have served for temples, for places of defence and of sepulture, containing pottery, ornamental sculpture, articles in silver and copper, and stone weapons, with skulls of the Mexican type. Above these have grown a succession of forests, in which the Red Indians for centuries may have housed and hunted (Lyell, pp. 39, 40). They prove that in those very ancient days there must have been a civilization, of which all traces have vanished above the surface of the earth. As regards the fossil skulls found in Europe, that known as "the Neanderthal Skull" is of the lowest type, and is said to be the most apelike skull ever seen, though its capacity, 75 cubic inches, is greater than that of some individuals of existing races. It was discovered in a cavern with the thigh of a bear: but there is nothing to prove its great antiquity. It may be very ancient, but may be comparatively modern. But the skull found at Engis near Liege, which appears to have been contemporary with the Mammoth, and is assigned by Lyell to the post-pliocene age, although the forehead is somewhat narrow, may be matched by the skulls of individuals of European race (Lyell, p. 80): and the skull of the fossil man of Denise, though said to be contemporary with the Mammoth and coeval with the last eruption of the Puy Volcanoes, and therefore as old as, or older than, any other human skull yet discovered, is of the ordinary Caucasian or European type (Lyell, p. 200). No prudent Geologist will admit, concerning any of these crania, more than that they bear marks of rude as compared with civilized races, rather more mastication, more prominent marks of muscular attachment and the like, all things of every day occurrence. So, in fact, the argument from Geology is really coincident with the testimony of Scripture and of universal primitive tradition, viz. that man, in his original condition, was not a helpless savage, but had at least the rudiments of civilization and intelligence.

When we read that Cain was a tiller of the ground, we do not necessarily conclude, that he cultivated wheat and barley; he may have known only of fruits, vegetables, roots, &c. Yet it is observable, that cereals have been discovered with some of the very early remains of human industry.

CHAPTER V.

1 The genealogy, age, and death of the patriarchs from Adam unto Noah. 24 The godliness and translation of Enoch.

[a] 1 Chron. 1. 1.

THIS *is* the [a]book of the generations of Adam. In the day that
God created man, in the likeness of
God made he him;
2 [b]Male and female created he [b] Wisd. 2. 23.
them; and blessed them, and called
their name Adam, in the day when
they were created.

CHAP. V. 1. *the book of the generations*] The record or recounting of the genealogical history of Adam and his descendants. See ch. ii. 4.

3 ¶ And Adam lived an hundred
and thirty years, and begat *a son* in
his own likeness, after his image; and
called his name Seth:
4 *c* And the days of Adam after he
had begotten Seth were eight hundred
years: and he begat sons and daughters:
5 And all the days that Adam lived
were nine hundred and thirty years:
and he died.
6 And Seth lived an hundred and
five years, and begat †Enos:
7 And Seth lived after he begat
Enos eight hundred and seven years,
and begat sons and daughters:
8 And all the days of Seth were
nine hundred and twelve years: and
he died.
9 ¶ And Enos lived ninety years,
and begat †Cainan:
10 And Enos lived after he begat
Cainan eight hundred and fifteen
years, and begat sons and daughters:
11 And all the days of Enos were
nine hundred and five years: and he
died.

c 1 Chron. 1, 1. &c.

† Heb. *Enosh.*

† Heb. *Kenan.*

12 ¶ And Cainan lived seventy
years, and begat †Mahalaleel:
13 And Cainan lived after he begat Mahalaleel eight hundred and
forty years, and begat sons and
daughters:
14 And all the days of Cainan were
nine hundred and ten years: and he
died.
15 ¶ And Mahalaleel lived sixty
and five years, and begat †Jared:
16 And Mahalaleel lived after he
begat Jared eight hundred and thirty
years, and begat sons and daughters:
17 And all the days of Mahalaleel
were eight hundred ninety and five
years: and he died.
18 ¶ And Jared lived an hundred
sixty and two years, and he begat
Enoch.
19 And Jared lived after he begat
Enoch eight hundred years, and begat
sons and daughters:
20 And all the days of Jared were
nine hundred sixty and two years:
and he died.

† Gr. *Maleleel.*

† Heb. *Jered.*

---

3. *Adam lived*, &c.] The genealogy given is that of the Sethites, probably as the line of the promised seed. The genealogy of the Cainites was given much more imperfectly in the last chapter, and with no dates or chronological marks, because, says Keil, being under the curse of God, they had no future. He quotes Baumgarten as saying, that this genealogy was "a memorial witnessing both the truth of God's promises and also the faith and patience of the fathers." The chronology of this chapter is very different in the Hebrew, the Samaritan and the Septuagint, as will be seen in the following table of the generations from Adam to the flood (see also note infra).

	Hebrew Text.			Samaritan Text.			Septuagint.		
	Years before birth of Son.	Rest of Life.	Whole Life.	Years before birth of Son.	Rest of Life.	Whole Life.	Years before birth of Son.	Rest of Life.	Whole Life.
Adam	130	800	930	130	800	930	230	700	930
Seth	105	807	912	105	807	912	205	707	912
Enosh	90	815	905	90	815	905	190	715	905
Cainan	70	840	910	70	840	910	170	740	910
Mahalaleel	65	830	895	65	830	895	165	730	895
Jared	162	800	962	62	785	847	162	800	962
Enoch	65	300	365	65	300	365	165	200	365
Methuselah	187	782	969	67	653	720	187	782	969
Lamech	182	595	777	53	600	653	188	565	753
Noah	500			500			500		
Shem at the Flood	100			100			100		
Date of Flood	1656			1307			2262		

6. *Enos*] *i.e.* man. Adam signifies *man*, *mankind*, generally. Enos, or Enosh, is rather *mortal*, *miserable man*. The now growing experience of human sorrow and fragility may have suggested this name.

9. *Cainan*] *i.e.* possession.

12. *Mahalaleel*] The Praise of God.

15. *Jared*] The root of this name signifies *to descend*, Descent.

18. *Enoch*] *i. e.* consecrated.

21 ¶ And Enoch lived sixty and
five years, and begat †Methuselah:
22 And Enoch walked with God
after he begat Methuselah three hundred years, and begat sons and daughters:
23 And all the days of Enoch were
three hundred sixty and five years:
24 And [d]Enoch walked with
God: and he *was* not; for God took
him.
25 And Methuselah lived an hundred eighty and seven years, and begat
†Lamech:
26 And Methuselah lived after he
begat Lamech seven hundred eighty
and two years, and begat sons and
daughters:
27 And all the days of Methuselah
were nine hundred sixty and nine
years: and he died.
28 ¶ And Lamech lived an hundred eighty and two years, and begat
a son:
29 And he called his name †Noah,
saying, This *same* shall comfort us
concerning our work and toil of our
hands, because of the ground which
the LORD hath cursed.
30 And Lamech lived after he begat Noah five hundred ninety and five
years, and begat sons and daughters:
31 And all the days of Lamech
were seven hundred seventy and seven
years: and he died.
32 And Noah was five hundred
years old: and Noah begat Shem,
Ham, and Japheth.

† Gr. *Mathusala.*
[d] Ecclus. 44. 16. Heb. 11. 5.
† Heb. *Lemech.*
† Gr. *Noe.*

---

21. *Methuselah*] Perhaps "the missive of death." Bochart interprets "His death the sending forth," as indicating that his death was contemporary with the pouring forth of the waters, for Methuselah must have died in the very year of the flood. Gesenius gives the sense of the word as *vir teli*, "the man of the sword" or "of the dart." From its frequent occurrence in Phœnician inscriptions, &c., there can be little doubt that Methu = Betha = man.

24. *he was not; for God took him*] The LXX. rendering seems to interpret this of translation. So do all the Targums. In Ecclus. xliv. 16, we read "He pleased the Lord and was translated (into Paradise, according to the Vulgate), being a pattern of repentance." The words are, no doubt, obscure. Yet, when we remember how universally the promise of the Old Testament is of life and blessing in this world, not of an early and happy death, we could scarcely doubt that the ancient interpretation was the true one, even if it had not been that given in Heb. xi. 5. The history of Enoch is reasonably supposed to be the origin of the Phrygian tradition concerning a certain Annacus or Nannacus, who lived upwards of 300 years, concerning whom it was prophesied that after him all would be destroyed. This caused great grief among the Phrygians, whence "to weep as in the days of Annacus" became a proverb. At his death came the deluge of Deucalion, and all men were destroyed (Suidas, v. Νάννακος, Steph. Byz. v. Ἰκόνιον).

29. *he called his name Noah, saying, This same shall comfort us*, &c.] The name "Noah" signifies "Rest," and the connection between the thought of rest and that of comfort is obvious. Lamech appears as one oppressed with the toil and labour needful to subdue the earth, and with the feeling that God had cursed it and made it sterile. He expresses a hope, that Noah would be a comfort to his parents and the bringer of rest; whether the mere natural hope of a father that his son should be a support and comfort to him, or a hope looking to the promise made of old to Eve, or a hope inspired by prophetic vision that Noah should become the second founder of a race, the head of a regenerated world, it may be hard to say. There may have been an unconscious prophecy in the expression of a merely pious hope.

Which the LORD *hath cursed*] This occurs in a chapter which modern critics call Elohistic. Therefore they consider this an interpolation. The truer inference would be that the Elohistic theory is unfounded.

NOTE A. ON THE CHRONOLOGY IN CH. V.

Difficulties in the Chronology. 1 Difference of texts. 2 Longevity of Patriarchs. 3 Antiquity of human race, as deduced (1) from Geology, (2) from History, (3) from Language, (4) from Ethnology.

THE genealogies in this chapter and in chapter xi. are the only sources extant for the construction of a chronology of the patriarchal ages. The questions which arise are of the same kind in both genealogies, and may be considered together. The difficulties which suggest themselves may be arranged as follows:

1. The disagreement between the Hebrew, Samaritan and Septuagint texts.

2. The extreme longevity assigned to the patriarchs.

3. The insufficient time allowed for the existence of man upon the earth.

1. The first of these difficulties is such as to render it impossible to arrive at a certain conclusion as to the exact dates of the creation of man, the Deluge and the call of Abraham; but it in no degree affects the veracity of the Sacred Record. It is true, that there appears something like design in the alterations which must have taken place; thus the Hebrew gives the age of Adam as $130 + 800 = 930$, whilst the LXX. give $230 + 700 = 930$, and so on in the case of most of the Patriarchs, the results being frequently made to tally, whilst the constituents of these results disagree. Hence, whilst some have charged the Alexandrian translators with lengthening the periods, in order more nearly to satisfy the demands of Egyptian chronology, others have supposed that the rabbins shortened the time, to escape the force of the Christian's argument, that the world was six thousand years old, and that therefore the Messiah must have come. If either of these charges be true, it only brings us in face of what is already familiar to all critics, viz. that the errors of copyists were sometimes intentional, but that even these do not affect the general integrity of the text. It is well known that there have been some few designed corruptions in the text of the New Testament. It need not surprise us therefore, if we find reason to think that there were some attempts of a like kind in the text of the Old Testament. If anywhere the temptation to correct existed, it could never be stronger than in the genealogical tables of the ancestors of the Jewish race. Indeed, as numbers are of all things the most liable to become confused in ancient documents, very great errors in restoring them may be consistent with the most honest intention on the part of the restorers. And, though we believe in the Divine guidance and inspiration of the original writer, we have no right to expect that a miraculous power should have so watched over the transmission of the records, as to have preserved them from all possible errors of transcription, though a special Providence may have guarded them from such loss or mutilation, as would have weakened their testimony to Divine and spiritual truth.

2. As to the extreme longevity of the Patriarchs, it is observable that some eminent physiologists have thought this not impossible; and even Buffon, by no means inclined to credulity on the side of Scripture, admitted the truth of the record, and could see physical causes for such long life in early times. (See 'Aids to Faith,' p. 278.) It is undoubted, that the traditions of ancient nations, as Greeks, Babylonians, Egyptians, Hindoos, and others, point to the great longevity of the early inhabitants of the globe; and though sceptics argue that this only places the Scriptural account on a level with other mythic histories (see Von Bohlen, Vol. II. p. 100), yet we may reply that, if the Scripture account were true, the traditions of other nations would be almost sure to preserve some traces of the truth, and that this is a more probable explanation of the fact, than the supposition that all these nations, however unconnected with each other, should have stumbled upon the same fabulous histories.

It is well observed by Delitzsch; "We must consider that all the old-world population was descended from a nature originally immortal (in Adam and Eve), that the climate, weather, and other natural conditions were very different from those which succeeded, that the life was very simple and even in its course, and that the after-working of the Paradisiacal state was not at once lost in the track of antiquity." To this Keil adds, that this long life must have been very favourable to the multiplication of mankind, for the formation of marked characters, and the developement of the good and evil qualities of different races. Family affection, piety, good discipline and morality would strike their roots deeper in pious families; whilst evil propensities would be more and more developed in godless races. Supposing, however, that physiology should ultimately decide that the extreme longevity of the patriarchs was not possible, without a continued miracle, we should only be driven to the principle already conceded, that numbers and dates, especially in genealogical tables, are liable in the course of transcription to become obscured and exaggerated.

3. The third objection is derived from the opinion now very generally gaining strength, that man must have been in existence on the earth more than four or even six thousand years before the Christian era.

The arguments for the antiquity of man are:

(1) Geological.
(2) Historical.
(3) Linguistic.
(4) Ethnological.

(1) The very eminent British geologist, Sir C. Lyell, has attempted to prove, that man, having been contemporary with the mammoth and other extinct mammalia, must have been living at least 100,000 years on the earth. Although unfortunately in physical science a great name always carries with it a crowd of followers, far more than in politics, literature or religion, yet in the present instance Sir C. Lyell has failed to carry conviction to some of the most eminent of his contemporaries. Elie de Beaumont on the continent and several of the most distinguished geologists in England demur to his conclusions. The conclusions are based on two principal assumptions; first, that relics of

man, flint instruments or the like, are found in recent and post-pliocene formations, which have been deposited in juxtaposition with bones of the mammoth and other extinct mammalia; secondly, that the present rate of deposition must be reckoned as the normal rate, and that at that rate the beds, which overlie the extinct mammal and human remains, must have taken a vast time to form. Of course much depends on the argument from uniformity. There are many men of science, who, accepting Lyell's general principles, yet believe that in former ages there were causes at work, which would have produced much speedier deposition and greater rapidity in the formation of beds of all kinds, than we see going on at present. It may perhaps be true, that man was coeval with the mammoth; but a mammoth was found early in this century in Siberia preserved in the ice, with skin and hair fitting it to live in a cold climate, and with flesh upon it, of which it was possible to make soup. Now, even allowing for the great preserving power of ice, there is neither proof nor probability that this animal had been dead 100,000 years or even more than 6,000 years. But again, it seems probable that man was in existence at a time when animals now inhabiting tropical climates roamed at large in the forests of Gaul and Britain. How long it may have taken to reduce the climate of Great Britain from a tropical to its present temperate condition, is a question very difficult to solve. A change in the Gulf Stream, an alteration in the respective elevation of land and water, let alone all question of the gradual cooling down of the earth itself, would do much towards this. Besides, not *human bones*, but only flint instruments are found in the gravel and caverns with bones of extinct mammals. Moreover, the present opinions of geologists rather go to negative entirely the tropical character of the British climate in the mammoth and tiger periods. Sir Chas. Lyell admits that even now "the Bengal tiger ranges occasionally to latitude 52° North" (*i.e.* the latitude of England, and probably in a climate much colder than England), "and *abounds* in latitude 48°, to which the small tailless hare or pika, a polar resident, sometimes wanders southwards" ('Antiq. of Man,' p. 158). We may see therefore many contingencies which might have brought human remains into contact with the remains of tropical animals, at a period much more recent than that assigned to such proximity by this eminent writer.

Difficulties of various kinds attach to Sir Charles Lyell's very large numbers; for instance, at anything approaching to the present rate of increase the descendants of a single couple would have multiplied to nearly the number of the present population in about 6000 years. Again, according to Sir C. Lyell's own admission, "we must remember, that as yet we have no distinct geological evidence that the appearance of what are called the inferior races of mankind has always preceded in chronological order that of the higher races." p. 90. On the contrary, it was shewn above that the evidence which we have points to some degree of civilization in the earliest periods. Indeed had it not been so, it is hardly possible that man should not soon have become extinct in the presence of so many animals whose mere physical powers were so much greater than man's. But then is it credible, that for some 90,000 years the human race should have been stationary, having acquired almost from the first the art of making flint instruments, but all farther progress in the arts of civilization having apparently been reserved to the last 6,000 years? On the whole, it seems impossible not to conclude that the geological evidence as to the antiquity of man is as yet imperfect and imperfectly read.

(2) The historical arguments are chiefly derived from Egyptian sources; for, though the Indians, the Chinese, and the Babylonians profess to go back to hundreds of thousands of years of past history, it is generally admitted that their historic times do not at the very utmost extend farther back than to the 27th century B.C. The eminent Egyptologers, Bunsen and Lepsius, relying on the monuments of Egypt and the statements of Manetho, claim for Egypt a national history from nearly 10,000 years B.C. It is, however, quite certain that much of the evidence for this is of the vaguest possible character, and that very large deductions must be made for myth and for contemporary dynasties. In all probability the earliest Egyptian dynasty cannot be dated farther back than B.C. 2700. (See 'Aids to Faith,' Essay VI. 17, pp. 252 sq., also 'Biblical Dict.' Arts. *Chronology*, *Egypt*, and the Excursus at the end of this volume).

(3) The linguistic argument is of this nature. Languages are of slow growth. The divergence of several modern European languages from Latin has been comparatively inconsiderable in 1500 years. Can we then believe all languages to have been formed, and to have diverged so widely from each other, since the dispersion at Babel? One answer to this is, that only those languages which have a literature change slowly. As long as the Authorised Version of the Scriptures and the works of Shakspeare are read in English, the English language will never be much unlike what it is now, or what it was three centuries ago. But where there is no literature, a few years create a complete revolution; wild tribes in a single generation cease to understand each other. And, even keeping out of sight the miracle of the dispersion at Babel, emigration, which carried no literature with it, would soon have created an endless diversity of tongues. The chief difficulty, however, is in the slow growth of

languages to a high degree of grammatical perfection, such as of Greek to the language of Homer some 900 years B.C., and of Sanskrit to the language of the Vedas, nearly 1200 years B.C. But we must remember, that the Samaritan and LXX. chronology allow an interval of more than 3000 years from the Flood to the Christian era, and 1800 years (the difference between 3000 and 1200) will give considerable scope for grammatical developement.

(4) The ethnological argument is grounded principally on the apparently unchanging character of some of the races of mankind. Especially it is observed, that in very ancient Egyptian monuments the negro race is depicted with all its present features and peculiarities. It would therefore be impossible, it is argued, that all the varieties of man should have sprung up, if their ancestors were a single pair, brought into being not more than 6000 or 8000 years since. It is replied, that supposing, which is disputed, the alleged antiquity of the monuments in question, still a race, continuing under nearly the same circumstances, is not likely to change since first its peculiarities were produced by those very circumstances. Such has been the case with the negroes since the time of the Egyptian monuments. If we take the LXX. chronology as correct, the negroes may have been in Africa for nearly 1500 years before the reign of Sethos I., when we find them so clearly depicted on the monuments. Their change to that climate, their fixed habits of life, and isolation from other races, may have soon impressed a character upon them, which whilst continuing to live under the same condition ever since, they have never lost for a period extending now to more than 3000 years. But we witness rapid changes in race when circumstances rapidly change. The European inhabitants of the North American States are said even in two or three generations to be rapidly acquiring a similarity of feature and conformation to the original inhabitants of the soil, though not losing their European intelligence and civilization. Many similar facts are noticed; which prove that changes of race, though sometimes so slow as to be imperceptible, are at other times extremely rapid. The early condition of mankind, with its frequent migrations, wide separations and little intercommunion, must have been favourable to rapid change, whilst its later more stationary condition is favourable to continuance and perpetuity of type.

There is one other important objection made to the genealogies in this chapter and in Chapter xi. viz. that each gives a catalogue of but ten generations; which looks as if neither were historical. A probable solution of this difficulty would seem to be, that the genealogies neither were, nor were intended to be, complete. Like other genealogies or pedigrees, sacred and profane, they omitted certain links, and perhaps only recorded and handed down to posterity those ancestors of the race who, for some reason or other, were more than the rest deserving of remembrance. This solution would be entirely satisfactory, if it were not for the appearance of chronological completeness which both the genealogies exhibit in their present form; the age of the patriarch at the birth of his son and successor, and the number of years which he lived after that birth, being given in every case. If therefore the above explanation be adopted, it would almost be necessary to add that, in the course of transmission and transcription, a greater appearance of completeness had been given to the catalogues than had existed in the original record. Such hypotheses are never to be too lightly adopted; but they are far more probable than those of the modern critical school, which reject the historical truth of the earlier books of the Bible. The genealogies of our Lord given in the Gospels have undoubtedly some links omitted, and yet are reduced to a form of great completeness. This is a strong argument for believing that the genealogies in Genesis may have been treated in the same manner. We may observe that this supposition, viz. that some links are omitted, will allow a much greater antiquity to the race of man, than may at first appear on the face of the text of Scripture. In fact, if it be correct, the time which it would allow, is almost unlimited.

CHAPTER VI.

1 *The wickedness of the world, which provoked God's wrath, and caused the flood.* 8 *Noah findeth grace.* 14 *The order, form, and end of the ark.*

AND it came to pass, when men
began to multiply on the face of
the earth, and daughters were born
unto them,
2 That the sons of God saw the
daughters of men that they *were* fair;
and they took them wives of all which
they chose.
3 And the LORD said, My spirit

CHAP. VI. 1. *And it came to pass*] The inspired writer has now given us an account of the first rise of sin, of its terrible manifestation in the murder of Abel, of its further

shall not always strive with man, for that he also *is* flesh: yet his days shall be an hundred and twenty years.

---

developement in the race of the first murderer, and of the separation from the profane of the descendants of the pious Seth. He proceeds in this chapter to assign a reason for the still more universal spread of ungodliness throughout the world, such as to call down from heaven a great general judgment on mankind.

2. *the sons of God saw the daughters of men*] Who were the sons of God? and who the daughters of men?

1. Perhaps the most ancient opinion was that the sons of God were the young men of high rank (as in Ps. lxxxii. 6, "I have said, Ye are gods, and ye are all the sons of the most Highest"), whilst the daughters of men were the maidens of low birth and humble condition; the word for *men* in this passage being a word used at times to signify men of low estate (cp. Isai. ii. 9, v. 15). According to this interpretation the sin lay in the unbridled passions of the higher ranks of society, their corrupting the wives and daughters of their servants and dependants, and the consequent spread of universal licentiousness. This seems to have been the earliest interpretation among the Jews. It is adopted by the Targums of Onkelos and Jonathan, by Symmachus, Abenezra, Rashi, Kimchi, and by some moderns, Selden, Vorstius, and others. The chief objection to this is that there is scarcely proof enough that the name "sons of God" was ever given to men of high rank, or that the word for man (*Adam*) ever meant people of low rank, except when contrasted with another word for man (namely, *Ish*). Compare *vir* and *homo* in Latin.

2. A second interpretation, also of great antiquity, is that the sons of God were the angels, who, moved to envy by the connubial happiness of the human race, took to themselves human bodies, and married the fair daughters of men. This interpretation is supposed to have the support of some ancient MSS. of the LXX. (as mentioned by August. 'De Civ. Dei,' XV. 23). It is argued that St Jude (6, 7) evidently so understood it, as he likens the sin of the angels to the sin of the cities of the plain, "the going after strange flesh." The same is thought to be alluded to in 2 Pet. ii. 4. Philo ('De Gigant.' Vol. I. p. 262); Josephus ('Antiq.' Lib. I. c. 4, § 1): and the most ancient of the Christian fathers, as Justin Martyr, Tatian, Athenagoras, Clement of Alexandria, Tertullian, Cyprian, Lactantius, moved probably by their reading of the LXX. and being ignorant of Hebrew, adopted this interpretation. The Apocryphal Book of Enoch and some of the Jewish writers also expounded it so. The later fathers, Chrysostom, Cyril of Alexandria, and Theodoret, condemn this view as monstrous and profane. The rationalistic interpreters (Gesenius, Rosenmüller, Von Bohlen, Tuch, Knobel, Ewald, Hupfeld, Kalisch, Davidson, &c.) naturally prefer it, as favouring their belief, that the first chapters of Genesis exhibit merely the Hebrew mythology. But it is also adopted by several of the more orthodox German commentators, as Hofmann, Baumgarten, Delitzsch, Kurtz, who contend that some very portentous wickedness and excess of sin must have been the cause of the Deluge; a complete subverting of the whole order of God's creation, so that the essential condition of man's social life was imperilled and overthrown. The chief arguments in favour of this view are (1) that "sons of God" mostly mean angels, see Ps. xxix. 1, lxxxix. 7; Job i. 6, ii. 1, xxxviii. 7; Dan. iii. 25; (2) that the "daughters of men" can only be antithetic to something not human; (3) that the context assigns a monstrous progeny to this unnatural union; (4) that St Jude and St Peter appear to sanction it; (5) that any ordinary promiscuous marriages are not sufficient to account for the judgment of the flood.

3. The third interpretation is that "the sons of God" were the descendants of Seth, who adhered to the worship and service of the true God, and who, according to some interpretations of ch. iv. 26, were from the time of Enos called by the name of the Lord, and that "the daughters of men" were of the race of the ungodly Cain. This was the belief of the eminent Church fathers, Chrysostom, Cyril of Alexandria, Theodoret, Augustine, and Jerome. It was adopted by Luther, Calvin, and most of the reformers, and has been the opinion of a great majority of modern commentators.

4. It was suggested, by Ilgen, that the Cainites were called "sons of the gods" because of their ingenuity and inventions, and that their intermingling themselves with the other races of men caused the general corruption of mankind.

5. The author of 'the Genesis of the earth and of man' suggests that "the sons of the gods" (so he would render it) may mean the worshippers of false gods. These he looks on as a pre-Adamite race, and would render, not "daughters of men," but "daughters of Adam." The pre-Adamite worshippers of the false gods intermarried with the daughters of Adam.

Of these interpretations it appears most probable that the right is a modification of 3. We are not probably justified in saying that there were but two races descended from

4 There were giants in the earth in those days; and also after that, when the sons of God came in unto the daughters of men, and they bare *children* to them, the same *became* mighty men which *were* of old, men of renown.

5 ¶ And GOD saw that the wicked-

Adam, the race of Cain and the race of Seth. Adam may have had many sons; but the history of the Cainites is preserved because both of their impiety, and of their ingenuity; that of the Sethites, because at least in one line of that race piety and true religion flourished, and of them came the family of Noah which was preserved in the ark. There appears to have been a growing corruption of mankind, more rapid, no doubt, in the family of Cain than in any other race, but still spreading far and wide. The line of the Sethites, traced in ch. v., alone appears to have kept itself pure, the little Church of God, in the midst of gathering darkness of the world around. This little Church may well have been called "the children of God," a term by no means limited in Scripture to the holy angels. They alone were the salt of the earth; and if that salt should lose its savour, all would become worthless and vile. When therefore some of these "sons of God" went out from their own little home circle, to make mixed marriages with the general heathenized races round them, the elements of corruption were brought from the world into the Church, the Church itself became corrupted, and the single family of Noah appears to have been kept pure from that corruption, just as afterwards the family of Lot was the only family in Sodom free from the pollution and depravity of the cities of the plain. The salt had lost its savour. At all events too little was left to purify and to save the world. It could but save the souls of the few righteous that were therein.

Concerning the *giants*, see note on v. 4.

3. *My spirit shall not always strive*] Is rendered, (1) "shall not dwell" by LXX., Vulg., Syr., Onk., Saad., and others. (2) "Shall not judge," or which probably is the same thing, "shall not strive," by Symm., Targg. Joh. and Jerus., Rashi, Kimchi, Luther, Rosenmüller, &c. This is the rendering of the A. V. and is probably correct. (3) "Shall not rule," by De Wette, Rosenmüller, Maurer, Knobel, Delitzsch, &c. (4) "Shall not be humbled," Gesenius, Tuch, &c. No great difference in the general significance of the passage will be produced by adopting a different translation. Kimchi, and some of the German commentators, understand, not that the Holy Ghost shall no longer dwell or strive with man, but that the spiritual principle implanted by God in man shall no longer rule in him, or no longer contend against his animal nature.

for that he also is flesh] The modern interpreters, Gesenius, Vater, Schum, Tuch, render "Because of his error he is become wholly flesh," or, as Rosenmüller, "whilst their flesh causeth them to err." The objection to the reading of the Authorized Version, which is that of all ancient Versions and commentators, is that the particle rendered *that* never occurs in the Pentateuch, but only in the later Psalms and other clearly more modern books of the Old Testament. It is in fact an Aramæan particle. But it must never be forgotten, that Aramaisms are to be expected, either in the most modern, or *in the most ancient portions of Scripture.* There is therefore good reason to adhere to the Authorized Version.

yet his days shall be an hundred and twenty years] Josephus ('Ant.' I. 3, 2) and after him, Tuch, Ewald, Hävernick, Baumgarten, Knobel, Hupfeld, Davidson, &c., suppose that this alludes to the shortening of the term of human life. But all the Targums, Saad., Luther's Version, Rosenm., Hengst., Ranke, Hofmann, Kurtz, Delitzsch, understand "There shall yet be a respite or time for repentance of 120 years, before the threatened vengeance shall overtake them." The normal duration of human life did not, as Delitzsch truly observes, become from this time 120 years, and the whole context shews, that the judgment impending was that of the Flood, and that it was a respite from that, which is here promised, that time might be given for Noah's preaching, and man's repentance. The only argument, that can even appear to have weight against this interpretation is that of Tuch, repeated by Bp. Colenso, viz. that Noah was 500 years old (cp. ch. v. 32) when this saying, "His days shall be 120," is ascribed to the Almighty, and that he was 600 years old (c. vii. 6) when the Flood came. Hence there were but 100 years, not 120 given as a respite. But there is really no ground whatever for asserting that all which is related in ch. vi. took place after Noah was 500 years old. What is said in v. 32 is that Noah was 500 years old, when his three sons were born. The Deluge may have been threatened long before this.

4. *There were giants in the earth in those days, and also after that,* &c.] It is hence argued that by "Sons of God" must be meant angels or fallen angels; from the union of whom with the daughters of man sprang the race of giants. But there is no-

ness of man *was* great in the earth, and
that ‖every imagination of the thoughts
of his [a]heart *was* only evil †continu-
ally.
6 And it repented the LORD that
he had made man on the earth, and
it grieved him at his heart.
7 And the LORD said, I will destroy man whom I have created from
the face of the earth; †both man, and
beast, and the creeping thing, and the
fowls of the air; for it repenteth me
that I have made them.
8 But Noah found grace in the
eyes of the LORD.
9 ¶ These *are* the generations of
Noah: [b]Noah was a just man *and*
‖perfect in his generations, *and* Noah
walked with God.

‖ Or, *the whole imagination.* The Hebrew word signifieth not only *the imagination,* but also *the purposes and desires.*
[a] chap. 8. 21. Matt. 15. 19.
† Heb. *every day.*
† Heb. *from man unto beast.*
[b] Ecclus. 44. 17. 2 Pet. 2. 5.
‖ Or, *upright.*

10 And Noah begat three sons,
Shem, Ham, and Japheth.
11 The earth also was corrupt before God, and the earth was filled
with violence.
12 And God looked upon the earth,
and, behold, it was corrupt; for all
flesh had corrupted his way upon the
earth.
13 And God said unto Noah, The
end of all flesh is come before me;
for the earth is filled with violence
through them; and, behold, I will
destroy ‖them with the earth.
14 ¶ Make thee an ark of gopher
wood; †rooms shalt thou make in the
ark, and shalt pitch it within and
without with pitch.
15 And this *is the fashion* which

‖ Or, *from the earth.*
† Heb. *nests.*

---

thing said of a race of giants springing from this union. "In those days were the (well-known) *Nephilim* in the earth" cannot have such a sense, especially when what follows is taken into account, "and also after that, when the sons of God went in unto the daughters of men, and they bore children to them, these became mighty men, men of renown." Evidently the passage shews, that *Nephilim* were on earth before this union, and afterwards also from these marriages sprang men of warlike spirit, who made themselves a name. The result was, as when the Israelites afterwards made marriages with the Midianites, a great and general corruption of manners. The warlike character and perhaps bodily strength of these *Nephilim* is specially noted, as explaining what is said in v. 13, that the earth was filled with *violence.*

Nephilim. The LXX., Vulg., Syr., and Targum render "Giants;" Aq. and Symm. "violent men." Most derive the word from a root signifying to *fall;* and understand "the fallen" (whether men or angels), or, more probably, "those who fall on others," *robbers* or *tyrants.* (Aquila, Rosenm., Gesenius, Kurtz.) Others (among whom Tuch and Knobel) derive from a root signifying *wonder*, and understand *monsters*, *prodigies.* We meet with the name again Num. xiii. 33, as that of one of the Canaanitish tribes, who appear to have been men of large stature, as were the Rephaim, the Anakim and others. This very likely was the reason, why the word came to be rendered "giants," which does not seem to have been its original meaning.

6. *it repented the* LORD] All the language of this portion of Scripture is suited to the infant condition of the world. Hence human sentiments are even more than in the later books of Scripture attributed to the Almighty. No sound criticism would see any appearance of myth in this.

9. *These are the generations of*] See note on ch. ii. 4.

14. *an ark of gopher wood*] The word for *ark* occurs only here and in Exod. ii. 3, 5 of the ark or boat of papyrus or bulrushes. This word might perhaps lead us to suppose that the ark was of the form of a vast chest or coffer, rather than of the form of a ship; fitted to carry a heavy burden, not to sail over the waters; yet the proportions given are those of a ship, though of rather greater width than usual, *see on* v. 15.

gopher wood] It is uncertain what this wood was. The Targumists followed by many Jewish and Christian commentators rendered *Cedar*, others *Juniper* or *Box.* Fuller, Bochart and Celsius suggested *Cypress*, in which they have been followed by most modern commentators. The affinity between the roots *gophar* and *cupar* is great, and cypress is a wood well fitted for ship-building and abounding in the parts of Syria next to Babylon, which many have supposed to be the country inhabited by Noah.

rooms] literally *nests*, different compartments fitted for the habitation of men and animals.

pitch] more probably asphaltos, **bitumen**, which is said to be particularly suited for closing up the interstices of the timbers and making a vessel watertight.

15. *this is the fashion*] The actual form of the ark is not described. The proportions only are given, which are not very

thou shalt make it *of:* The length of
the ark *shall be* three hundred cubits,
the breadth of it fifty cubits, and the
height of it thirty cubits.
16 A window shalt thou make to
the ark, and in a cubit shalt thou
finish it above; and the door of the
ark shalt thou set in the side thereof;
with lower, second, and third *stories*
shalt thou make it.
17 And, behold, I, even I, do bring
a flood of waters upon the earth, to
destroy all flesh, wherein *is* the breath
of life, from under heaven; *and* every
thing that *is* in the earth shall die.
18 But with thee will I establish
my covenant; and thou shalt come
into the ark, thou, and thy sons, and
thy wife, and thy sons' wives with
thee.
19 And of every living thing of all
flesh, two of every *sort* shalt thou

---

different from those of "The Great Eastern." Reckoning the cubit at 21 inches; the proportions would be length 525 ft., breadth 87 ft. 6 in., height 52 ft. 6 in.; those of "The Great Eastern" being length 680, breadth 83, depth 58. (See Smith's 'Dict. of Bible,' Art. *Noah.*) The length of the cubit is doubtful, as there appear to have been 2 or 3 different measures so called. In all probability it means the length from the elbow to the end of the hand, a variable measure, of course, but sufficiently accurate for the purposes of those simple times. It is mentioned by the German commentators that Peter Jansen in 1609 built a vessel of the same proportions as the ark, though smaller, viz. Length 120, width 20, depth 12 ft. It was found most convenient for stowage, containing one-third more freight than ordinary vessels of the same tonnage, though it was unsuited for making way quickly through the water.

John Temporarius quoted by Heidegger ('Historia Sacra,' I. p. 338) made a curious calculation, according to which the ark would have afforded abundant room for all the animals then known, and food for their voyage. Tiele also in his commentary calculates that there was room for 7000 distinct species. (See Kurtz, I. p. 101.)

16. *A window shalt thou make to the ark, and in a cubit shalt thou finish it above*] There is a great variety of interpretation here, some rendering *a window*, others *light*, or *daylight* or a *transparent substance*, others, after the LXX., *an inclined roof*, or *sloping deck*. Much too has been said against the historical truth of a narrative, which could assign but one window of a cubit long to so vast a ship. The interpretation of Gesenius seems evidently the true, viz. that the unusual word translated "window" (the word in ch. viii. 6, is quite another word) means really a set of windows, a window course, a system of lighting: and the use of the feminine gender in the pronoun suggests to the same high authority, that the right rendering would be, "A window system shalt thou make to the ark, and in a cubit shalt thou finish them from above." It is quite possible that it may have been a window course running for a cubit long under the top or deck of the ark, lighting the whole upper story very similar to the clerestory of churches (see Knobel here). The word is translated by Symmachus "*a transparency*." It seems not impossible that some transparent substance was used. This may easily have been known to the Antediluvians, who had made the progress in arts described ch. iv. 21, 22. Perhaps the invention was lost after the Deluge, an event which must have reduced mankind to almost original simplicity and rudeness. It is by no means clear, that these windows were all in the roof or deck. They may have been in the gunwales, *i.e.* on the higher part of the sides of the vessel, like the port-holes of a modern ship of war. And, if they were covered with a transparent substance, it is quite possible that they may not have been confined to the upper story of the ship, as the word "*above*" does not necessarily mean on the upper part of the vessel, but may mean the top of the window course.

the door of the ark] There was naturally but one opening beside the window course, through which all the inhabitants of the ark were to be let into it.

19. *two of every sort shalt thou bring into the ark*] Of course if we will admit nothing out of the ordinary course of nature, we shall be unable to receive the Mosaic history of the Deluge. Yet, even on natural principles, we may in some measure explain Noah's power over the beasts. When a terrible catastrophe is closely impending, there is often a presentiment of it in the brute creation. Under the pressure of great danger or great suffering, the wildest animals will at times become perfectly tame and tractable. Most likely too, Noah and his family would choose pairs of very young animals, just old enough to feed themselves, as being the most tractable and as requiring less room than those full grown.

bring into the ark, to keep *them* alive
with thee; they shall be male and
female.
20 Of fowls after their kind, and
of cattle after their kind, of every
creeping thing of the earth after his
kind, two of every *sort* shall come
unto thee, to keep *them* alive.
21 And take thou unto thee of all
food that is eaten, and thou shalt
gather *it* to thee; and it shall be for
food for thee, and for them.
[c] Heb. 11. 22 [c]Thus did Noah; according to
all that God commanded him, so did he.

CHAPTER VII.

1 Noah, with his family, and the living creatures, enter into the ark. 17 The beginning, increase, and continuance of the flood.

AND the [a]LORD said unto Noah, [a] 2 Pet. 2. 5.
Come thou and all thy house
into the ark; for thee have I seen
righteous before me in this generation.
2 Of every clean beast thou shalt
take to thee by †sevens, the male and † Heb. seven seven.
his female: and of beasts that *are* not
clean by two, the male and his female.
3 Of fowls also of the air by sevens,
the male and the female; to keep
seed alive upon the face of all the
earth.
4 For yet seven days, and I will
cause it to rain upon the earth forty
days and forty nights; and every living
substance that I have made will I
†destroy from off the face of the earth. † Heb. blot out.

If the ark was to hold, not only birds and quadrupeds, but insects and reptiles, possibly eggs or larvæ may have been preserved.

CHAP. VII. 1. *And the* LORD *said unto Noah*] The preceding chapter accounts for a period of 120 years. At the beginning of that period, God had declared His will to destroy mankind by a flood, unless they profited by the time still given them for repentance. Noah is ordered to prepare an ark, the building of which may have occupied the greater part of this season of respite He is told at the very first that he and his sons are to go into the ark, and that a pair of every kind of cattle and fowls and moving things should go in with him and be preserved alive. In the present chapter we reach the end of the 120 years. The ark has been built in the prescribed form with due preparation and capacity. Noah has done according to all that God had commanded him (ch. vi. 22), and now the Lord gives to Noah fuller directions concerning the animals which he was to take with him.

2. *Of every clean beast thou shalt take to thee by sevens, the male and his female*] It is questioned whether there were to be seven or seven pairs of every clean beast. Some think there were to be only seven, the odd number being accounted for by the fact that the clean beasts were preserved for sacrifice, that therefore more of them were needed than of unclean beasts, and the number seven was adopted as a sacred number. The addition of the words "the male and his female" (comp. v. 9), seems to favour the belief that seven pairs are intended. In any case there is no inconsistency between this verse and ch. vi. 20, "two of every sort." The command here is but an amplification of the former injunction, which had probably been given 120 years before. In the first instance it was said that Noah's family should be preserved together with a pair of every kind of beast. In the second, that, whilst the general rule should be the saving of a single pair, yet, in the case of the few clean beasts, there should be preserved, not one pair only but seven. The objection that this was an anticipation of the Levitical distinction of beasts into clean and unclean, is wholly groundless. The boundary line between clean and unclean animals is marked by nature. Every tribe of mankind would distinguish between the sheep and the hyæna, between the dove and the vulture. Whether animal food was eaten before the Deluge or not, it is certain that flocks and herds were fed for the sake of their milk and wool, and that of them victims were offered in sacrifice. This alone would separate between the clean and the unclean. It is not improbable, that the distinction even of the names "clean and unclean" had been fully established by custom, long before it was recognized and ratified by the Law.

3. *Of fowls also of the air by sevens*] In the Samaritan, the LXX. and Syr. this verse runs, "And of all the fowls of the air which are clean by sevens, the male and the female, and of all fowls which are not clean by two, the male and the female, to keep seed alive upon the face of all the earth." This must have been a very ancient reading; but it appears to have arisen from a gloss or commentary having crept into the text. It probably gives the true sense of the passage.

4. *yet seven days*] The 120 years ended and the ark prepared for the saving of his house, Noah is allowed yet seven days more

5 And Noah did according unto all
that the LORD commanded him.
6 And Noah *was* six hundred years
old when the flood of waters was upon the earth.
7 ¶ And Noah went in, and his
sons, and his wife, and his sons' wives
with him, into the ark, because of the
waters of the flood.
8 Of clean beasts, and of beasts
that *are* not clean, and of fowls, and
of every thing that creepeth upon the
earth,
9 There went in two and two unto
Noah into the ark, the male and the
female, as God had commanded
Noah.
‖ Or, *on the seventh day.* 10 And it came to pass ‖ after seven
days, that the waters of the flood were
upon the earth.
11 ¶ In the six hundredth year of
Noah's life, in the second month, the
seventeenth day of the month, the
same day were all the fountains of
the great deep broken up, and the
‖ windows of heaven were opened. ‖ Or, *floodgates.*
12 And the rain was upon the
earth forty days and forty nights.
13 In the selfsame day entered
Noah, and Shem, and Ham, and Japheth, the sons of Noah, and Noah's
wife, and the three wives of his sons
with them, into the ark;
14 They, and every beast after his
kind, and all the cattle after their kind,
and every creeping thing that creepeth
upon the earth after his kind, and
every fowl after his kind, every bird
of every † sort. † Heb. *wing.*
15 And they went in unto Noah
into the ark, two and two of all flesh,
wherein *is* the breath of life.

---

for gathering all safely into the place of refuge before the flood sets in.

9. *two and two*] This again is no contradiction to v. 2. The rule was that all animals, clean or unclean, should go in two and two, that rule was not broken, but amplified, by the direction in verse 2, that of clean animals there should be more than a single pair, viz. seven or seven pairs.

11. *In the six hundredth year of Noah's life, in the second month, the seventeenth day of the month*] The questions concerning the Deluge year are complicated by the uncertainty, 1. whether the year was the old civil year beginning with the month Tisri in the autumn, or the sacred year which from the time of the Exodus was appointed to begin with the month Abib, the Passover month, in the spring: 2. whether the calculation be Lunar or Solar.

As regards the first question, we may notice that the year did not begin from Abib, until the time of the Exodus, and that even then the civil year was reckoned from Tisri. Hence we may naturally conclude, that the year of the Flood began with Tisri, or about the autumnal Equinox. If so, the 17th day of the second month would bring us to the middle of November, the beginning of the wintry and rainy season.

The second question seems at first sight resolved by comparing this verse (vii. 11) with vii. 24 and viii. 4, from which comparison it appears that the flood began on the 17th of the second month, lasted 150 days, i.e. five months of 30 days, and had subsided, so that the ark could rest on Ararat on the 17th of the seventh month. Thus the 17th of the seventh month appears to have been exactly five months of thirty days after the 17th of the second month. This would make the Noachic year a year of 360 days, corresponding with the old Egyptian year, unless any intercalation of five days was made use of. On the presumption that this reckoning is conclusive, it has been argued that the account of the Flood must have been of much later date than Moses, as the Israelites never learned to reckon by solar time till after the Babylonish captivity. It is certain however that the Egyptians used solar time long before the date of the Exodus, which is answer enough to this difficulty.

With regard to the forty days' rain, it seems pretty certain that those were not additional to, but part of, the 150 days of the prevalence of the flood. Supposing the above calculation to be correct, we have the very remarkable coincidences that on the 17th day of Abib the ark rested on Mount Ararat—on the 17th day of Abib the Israelites passed over the Red Sea—on the 17th day of Abib Christ our Lord rose again from the dead.

were all the fountains of the great deep broken up, and the windows of heaven were opened] It cannot be imagined, that this is a philosophical explanation of the flood. The use of Scripture is always to describe the phenomena of nature, not to trace their hidden causes. The words here written express only the effect produced upon man's senses. There was a flood of waters from above and

16 And they that went in, went
in male and female of all flesh, as God
had commanded him: and the LORD
shut him in.
17 And the flood was forty days
upon the earth; and the waters increased, and bare up the ark, and it
was lift up above the earth.
18 And the waters prevailed, and
were increased greatly upon the earth;
and the ark went upon the face of
the waters.
19 And the waters prevailed exceedingly upon the earth; and all the
high hills, that *were* under the whole
heaven, were covered.
20 Fifteen cubits upward did the
waters prevail; and the mountains
were covered.
21 [b]And all flesh died that moved
upon the earth, both of fowl, and of
cattle, and of beast, and of every creeping thing that creepeth upon the earth,
and every man:
22 All in whose nostrils *was* †the
breath of life, of all that *was* in the
dry *land*, died.
23 And every living substance was
destroyed which was upon the face of
the ground, both man, and cattle, and
the creeping things, and the fowl of
the heaven; and they were destroyed
from the earth: and [c]Noah only remained *alive*, and they that *were* with
him in the ark.
24 And the waters prevailed upon
the earth an hundred and fifty days.

[b] Wisd. 10.
† Heb. the breath of the spirit of &c.
[c] Wisd 10. 4. 2 Pet. 2. 5.

CHAPTER VIII.

1 *The waters asswage.* 4 *The ark resteth on Ararat.* 7 *The raven and the dove.* 15 *Noah, being commanded,* 18 *goeth forth of the ark.* 20 *He buildeth an altar, and offereth sacrifice,* 21 *which God accepteth, and promiseth to curse the earth no more.*

AND God remembered Noah, and
every living thing, and all the
cattle that *was* with him in the ark:
and God made a wind to pass over
the earth, and the waters asswaged;
2 The fountains also of the deep
and the windows of heaven were
stopped, and the rain from heaven
was restrained;
3 And the waters returned from off
the earth †continually: and after the
end of the hundred and fifty days
the waters were abated.
4 And the ark rested in the seventh
month, on the seventeenth day of the
month, upon the mountains of Ararat.

† Heb. in *going and returning.*

---

from beneath. The clouds poured down rain, and the seas and rivers swelled and burst their boundaries; so that to one who witnessed it it seemed as though "the fountains of the great deep were broken up, and the windows of heaven were opened."

16. *and the* LORD *shut him in*] By some providential or supernatural agency the door of the ark, which could not have been secured with pitch or bitumen by Noah, was secured and made water-tight.

17, 18, 19. In these verses the frequent repetition of the same thought in almost the same words has been supposed by Astruc and others to evidence the work of different hands. Repetition, however, is universal in a simple state of society, wherever great strength of expression is aimed at. Even in late Hebrew such repetition is familiar, but in early Hebrew it meets us at every turn.

20. *Fifteen cubits upward*] *i. e.* from 25 to 28 feet: a depth apparently above the neighbouring mountains, perhaps depressed by convulsion, or otherwise. See note on the Deluge at the end of the eighth chapter.

CHAP. VIII. 1. *God remembered Noah*] As it is said, 1 Sam. xv. 11, "It repenteth Me that I have anointed Saul to be king," *i.e.* I have decreed to put another in his place, and above (Gen. vi. 7), "It repenteth Me that I have made man," *i.e.* I have determined to destroy man; so here "The Lord remembered Noah" does not point to a previous forgetfulness, but to God's great mercy towards him (Theodoret).

2. *The fountains*, &c.] The clouds were dispersed by a wind, the waters no longer increased, and the effect was, as though, after the forty days of rain and flood, the fountains of the deep and the windows of heaven were closed.

4. *Ararat*] The belief that this is the mountain-range now commonly called Mount Ararat, the highest peak of which rises nearly 17,000 feet above the level of the sea, rests on a very uncertain foundation. Far more probable is the opinion that Ararat was the ancient name of Armenia itself, or, rather, of the Southern portion of Armenia. The name occurs only here, and in 2 Kings xix. 37; Is. xxxvii. 38, where it is mentioned as the place

† Heb. were *in going and decreasing.*

5 And the waters †decreased continually until the tenth month: in the
tenth *month*, on the first *day* of the
month, were the tops of the mountains
seen.
6 ¶ And it came to pass at the end
of forty days, that Noah opened the
window of the ark which he had
made:
7 And he sent forth a raven, which
went forth †to and fro, until the waters
were dried up from off the earth.

† Heb. *in going forth and returning.*

8 Also he sent forth a dove
from him, to see if the waters were
abated from off the face of the
ground;
9 But the dove found no rest for
the sole of her foot, and she returned
unto him into the ark, for the waters
were on the face of the whole earth:
then he put forth his hand, and took
her, and †pulled her in unto him into
the ark.
10 And he stayed yet other seven

† Heb. *caused her to come.*

---

to which the sons of Sennacherib fled, after the murder of their father. Most of the ancient VSS. render the word by *Armenia* (Aq., Symm., Theod., Vulg., and in Kings and Isaiah the LXX., though in Gen. the LXX. leave it untranslated). The Targums render Kardu or Kardon, probably meaning Kurdistan, or the Gordyæan mountains, which run to the South of Armenia, dividing the valley of the Tigris from Iran, on, or near to which mountains, in the Chaldæan tradition of the Deluge preserved by Berosus, Xisuthrus is said to have landed. Jerome ('on Isai.' xxxvii.) tells us, that "Ararat is a champaign country of incredible fertility, situated in Armenia, at the base of Mount Taurus, through which flows the river Araxes." Moses, Archbishop of Chorene, A.D. 460, the famous historian of Armenia, also tells us that Ararat was a region, not a mountain. A Mohammedan tradition has no doubt placed the site of the ark's resting on the top of the highest ridge of the mountain, called anciently Macis, by the Persians Coh Noah; and this has been thought to correspond with what is related by Nicolaus of Damascus, that there was a mountain in Armenia called Baris, to which people escaped in the general Deluge, and on which a vessel struck, parts of which long remained (Joseph. 'Ant.' I. 4). All this, however, is somewhat vague. We can only say with certainty that, so long as the time when the LXX. VS. was made, Ararat was believed to correspond with, or to constitute a part of Armenia. Moreover, general belief has pointed to the neighbourhood of Armenia as the original dwelling-place of the first fathers of mankind.

Yet the claims, not only of the central mountain peak, but even of any portion of Armenia, to be the site of Noah's landing-place, have been disputed by many. In Gen. xi. 2 the migration of the sons of Noah towards Shinar is said to be "from the East." If so, it could not have been from Armenia. It is, however, most probable that the right rendering should be, as in Gen. ii. 8, xiii. 11, not "from the East" but "eastward," and such is the marginal rendering of the A.V. which though not supported by the VSS. is accordant with other Hebrew idioms (see Quarry, 'Gen.' p. 397). Another objection to Armenia is found in the statement of Strabo (lib. XI. p. 527), that the vine does not grow there (cp. Gen. ix. 20). Accordingly Hardouin contends that Ararat could not have been in Armenia, but is to be sought for in the North of Palestine, where it borders on Antilibanus and Syria ('De Situ Parad. terres.' in Franzii, Edit. Plin. 'Nat. Hist.' Tom. X. pp. 259, 260). Yet the 10,000 are said to have found old wine in Armenia (Xen. 'Anab.' 4. 4, 9); and vines are said at this day to grow in the highlands of Armenia, at a level of 4000 feet above the sea. (See Ritter, quoted by Knobel, on ch. IX. 20.) Von Bohlen, arguing from Gen. xi. 2 that Ararat lay eastward of Shinar, identifies it with Aryavarta, the sacred land to the North of India, to which the Hindoo tradition points. The Samaritan VS. places it in the Island of Ceylon. Though on such a question certainty is impossible, the arguments in favour of Armenia are very strong.

6. *the window*] or *opening*, from a verb meaning *to perforate* or *open*. This is quite a different word from that used vi. 16. The A.V. would suggest the idea, that Noah was commanded (vi. 16) to make a window, and that now he opened that window; whereas the original expresses the fact, that Noah was commanded to make a window-course, or light system, and that now he opens the window, or casement, in the ark, which he had made on purpose to open.

7. *went forth to and fro*] It has been supposed that there were carcases of men and beasts floating on the waters, that from them the raven found a place to light upon, and also food; and hence, though it returned from time to time and rested on the ark, it never again sought an entrance into it.

8. *a dove*] Noah, finding no sufficient indication from the raven, now sends forth the dove, a bird which rests only on dry places and feeds only on grain.

days; and again he sent forth the
dove out of the ark;
11 And the dove came in to him
in the evening; and, lo, in her mouth
was an olive leaf pluckt off: so Noah
knew that the waters were abated
from off the earth.
12 And he stayed yet other seven
days; and sent forth the dove; which
returned not again unto him any more.
13 ¶ And it came to pass in the
six hundredth and first year, in the
first *month*, the first *day* of the month,
the waters were dried up from off the
earth: and Noah removed the covering of the ark, and looked, and, behold, the face of the ground was dry.
14 And in the second month, on
the seven and twentieth day of the
month, was the earth dried.
15 ¶ And God spake unto Noah,
saying,
16 Go forth of the ark, thou, and
thy wife, and thy sons, and thy sons'
wives with thee.
17 Bring forth with thee every
living thing that *is* with thee, of all
flesh, *both* of fowl, and of cattle, and
of every creeping thing that creepeth
upon the earth; that they may breed
abundantly in the earth, and be
fruitful, and multiply upon the
earth.
18 And Noah went forth, and his
sons, and his wife, and his sons' wives
with him:
19 Every beast, every creeping
thing, and every fowl, *and* whatsoever creepeth upon the earth, after
their †kinds, went forth out of the † Heb. *families.*
ark.
20 ¶ And Noah builded an altar
unto the LORD; and took of every
clean beast, and of every clean fowl,

---

11. *an olive leaf*] Theophr. 'Hist. Plant.' L. IV. c. 8, and Pliny, 'Hist. Nat.' L. XIII. c. 25, are cited as saying that the olive grew under water in the Red Sea, and bore berries there. Whether this be so or not, it is probable that the olive may live more healthily under a flood than most other trees. It is eminently hardy, and will grow in a favourable soil without care or culture. The following passage illustrates the extraordinary powers of adaptation to circumstances possessed by some plants. "The formation of sprouts gives the plant the means of attaching itself to the most varied conditions, of persisting through periods of continued cold and heat, damp or drought, according as the climate may produce, and guarding against death in all cases of frustrated seed-development...... Thus *Littorella lacustris*, which never flowers under water, maintains and increases itself by lateral runners, year after year, at the bottom of the lakes of the Black Forest, and only comes into flower when the water retreats in the driest years, which scarcely occur oftener than once in ten" (A. Braun, 'Rejuvenescence in Nature,' p. 41, 42, Ray Society). The olive (Olea Europea) is generally a plant of the Mediterranean: other species occur at the Cape of Good Hope, the Himalaya mountains, and elsewhere.

pluckt off] rather, as Vulg., **fresh**.

20. *every clean beast*] Probably not every beast which was afterwards permitted to the Israelites for food, but those which were esteemed clean for sacrifice; viz. oxen, sheep and goats, doves and pigeons. Some of the German commentators see in the account of this sacrifice a late interpolation, derived from the Mosaic or Levitical customs of sacrifice. Delitzsch justly observes that in most of the traditions of the Deluge, external to the Israelites, as the Phœnician, Indian, Greek, &c., a sacrifice forms part of the legend. The pretence, therefore, that in the Biblical narrative this was an afterthought of a Jehovist interpolater must be gratuitous.

21. *a sweet savour*] Lit. "the savour of satisfaction or delectation," the word *Nichoach*, "satisfaction," having a reference to *Noach*, "rest." Cp. like expressions in Lev. ii. 12, xxvi. 31; Ezek. vi. 13, xx. 41. The gratitude of Noah, and his faith as manifested by the sacrifice, were acceptable to God.

for the imagination of man's heart is evil from his youth] In ch. vi. 5, it is written that God's anger was moved, "because every imagination of the thoughts of his heart was only evil continually." Here, on the contrary it is said, that "the Lord said in His heart, I will not curse the ground any more for man's sake, for the imagination of his heart is evil from his youth." The Germans discover an inconsistency between the words of the Elohist in vi. 5, and those of the Jehovist here. Some have endeavoured to reconcile these passages by translating "although" instead of "for." The true solution is, that in the first instance (ch. vi. 5) the actual sinfulness of man, the constant tendency of every imagination of his thoughts to evil, is represented as moving the anger of God, and tend-

and offered burnt offerings on the
altar.
21 And the LORD smelled †a sweet
savour; and the LORD said in his
heart, I will not again curse the
ground any more for man's sake;
for the [a]imagination of man's heart
is evil from his youth; neither will I
again smite any more every thing living,
as I have done.
22 †While the earth remaineth,
seedtime and harvest, and cold and
heat, and summer and winter, and
day and night shall not cease.

† Heb. *a savour of rest.*

[a] chap. 6. 5. Matt. 15. 19.

† Heb. *as yet all the days of the earth.*

---

ing to man's destruction; but in the present instance (ch. viii. 21) the Lord is described as considering the feebleness of his nature, and pitying that natural propensity to evil, which every man inherits at his birth.

The word in the original for *imagination*, is the word which the Rabbins used to express that desire of evil, which results from original sin (Buxt. 'Lex. Chald.' p. 973; Ges. 'Thes.' p. 619). Accordingly in ch. vi. we see God's righteous indignation against the hardened, impenitent, unbelieving sinner. Here, on the contrary, we read of the Lord's compassionate kindness to His feeble and erring creatures, and how He is moved not to curse, but to pity and to bless those who turn to Him with penitent hearts, and faith in that great Sacrifice, of which Noah's offering was a type and a prophecy.

22. *seedtime and harvest*] The Deluge had confounded earth and sea. There reigned as it were one long winter, almost one unbroken night, over the whole world. But thenceforth the Lord decreed, that seasons should follow in their course, the season of sowing and the season of reaping, the cold and the heat, the summer and the winter, the day and the night.

NOTE A on CHAP. VIII. THE DELUGE.

1. Was it historical? (α) Traditions among all races of men. (β) Explicable only on the supposition of historical foundation. 2. Was it universal? (α) How to judge of the narrative. (β) Universal probably to mankind. (γ) Geological difficulties. (δ) Rationale of Deluge.

Two great questions concerning the Flood of Noah naturally present themselves: 1. Is the account of it historical or mythical? 2. Was the Deluge partial or universal?

1. Many of the Germans, and according to Davidson "all good critics" have abandoned the historical character of the narrative. The physical difficulties are supposed to be insuperable. The whole therefore is said to be "mythical, embodying the old Hebrew belief in the retributive character of sin" (Davidson, 'Introd. to O. T.' Vol. I. p. 187). How then, it may be asked, does it happen, that so many nations retained a recollection of the same great event? The races of mankind have been divided by modern Ethnologists into Semitic, Aryan (Iranian or Indo-European) and Turanian. It will be found, that in all these races there are traditions of a flood, which destroyed all mankind except one family. The Semitic account is to be found in the Bible and in the Chaldæan tradition, which is the nearest to that of the Bible, and which comes down to us in the fragments of Berosus preserved by Josephus and Eusebius. According to that tradition, Sisuthrus or Xisuthrus being warned of a flood by the god Cronus, built a vessel and took into it his relatives and near friends, and all kinds of birds and quadrupeds. The vessel was five stadia in length and two in breadth. When the flood had abated, he sent out birds, which first of all returned to him, but, after the second trial, returned no more. Judging then that the flood was abated, he took out some of the planks of the vessel, and found that it had stranded on the side of a mountain. Whereupon he and all his left the ship, and offered sacrifice to the gods. The place of landing was in Armenia; where part of the vessel still remained, from which the people of the country scraped off the bitumen and made amulets (see Cory's 'Ancient Fragm.' pp. 22, 29, 1st Edition). Of the Aryan traditions, first, the Greek is to be found in the well known classical legend of the floods of Ogyges and Deucalion. Pindar ('Ol.' IX. 37), first mentions the flood of Deucalion. The account is given at length by Ovid; by whom the reason assigned is the general prevalence of violence and wickedness ('Metam.' I. 240, &c.). Apollodorus (Lib. I.) ascribes the deluge of Deucalion to the determination of Jupiter to destroy the men of the brazen age. And Lucian ('De Syra Dea') speaks of it as having destroyed the whole human race. The Persian tradition may be that embodied in the Koran, though there probably incorporated with the Scriptural narrative. The Hindoo tradition represents Manu as warned by a great fish to build a ship, that he might be preserved during an impending deluge. The ship was saved by being lashed on to the horn of the fish, and was ultimately landed on a northern mountain. (See the tradition at length, Hardwick, 'Christ and other Masters,'

p. ii. ch. III. § 3.) The Phrygian story of Annakos (supposed to be Enoch) who foretold the Deluge, is singularly confirmed by a medal struck at Apamea (called Apamea Kibotus, i.e. Apamea, the Ark) in the reign of Septimius Severus, on which is depicted an ark or chest floating on the waters. Two people are seen within it and two going out of it. On the top of the ark a bird perches, and another flies towards it with a branch between its feet, on the vessel; in some specimens of this coin, are the letters ΝΩ. It can hardly be doubted, however, that this coin, and the tradition connected with it, come somewhat directly from Hebrew sources. The third division of the Human Race, the Turanian, has also everywhere traditions of the Deluge. In China, Fa-he, the reputed founder of Chinese civilization, is represented as escaping from the waters of a deluge, and he reappears as the first man at the production of a renovated world, attended by his wife, three sons and three daughters (Hardwick; Part III. p. 16). The inhabitants of the Polynesian Islands, who are probably of Malay origin, especially the Figi islanders, have distinct accounts of a deluge, in which a family, eight in number, was saved in a canoe (Hardwick, III. 185). Similar traditions prevailed throughout the continent of America, the aboriginal inhabitants of which are now generally believed to be all of one stock, and by their physical and linguistic peculiarities are by the greatest ethnologists identified with the Turanian races of Asia. (See Bunsen, 'Philos. of Univ. Hist.' Vol. II. p. 112.) In South America, the inhabitants of Mexico had paintings representing the Deluge, a man and his wife in a bark or on a raft, a mountain rising above the waters, and birds, the dove, the vulture, &c. taking part in the scene. In North America, the Cherokee Indians had a legend of all men destroyed by a deluge, except one family saved in a boat, to the building of which they had been incited by a mysterious dog, which recalls the Indian fable of the friendly fish (see Hardwick, Part III. pp. 161—164).

Thus among the more civilized countries of Europe, and in well nigh every portion of Asia and America, in every different race of mankind, we find traditionary accounts of this great catastrophe, and of the miraculous deliverance of a single family. The mythical interpreters insist, that every nation had its mythic age, its mythic traditions, and that as we discover the same myth of a deluge in all other nations, we naturally conclude that the Hebrew narrative is in like manner mythical. But how can it be explained, that in all parts of the world, people have stumbled on the same myth? What is there, apart from tradition, that so commends the fable of a Deluge and of the saving of one household to the imagination and invention of mankind? The existence of cosmogonies, more or less alike, may be easily conceived of. But, that in all parts of the world, among races the most remote and dissimilar, there should prevail a belief, that, after man was created on the earth, all men but one family, were destroyed by a Deluge, is intelligible only on the supposition, that some such event actually did occur; an event simply, graphically and accurately related in the Book of Genesis, but variously distorted and disguised in the legends of the heathen world. An universal belief, not springing directly from some instinctive principle in our nature, can with reason only be ascribed to tradition of an historical fact. The only other explanation suggested is utterly impossible, viz. that in many parts of the world among the more civilized and the most barbarous alike, remains of marine animals found beneath the Earth's surface had suggested the same belief, viz. that there must have been an universal Flood. Even supposing this possible, how does this account for the similarity of the tradition not generally only, but in minute particulars in the remotest parts of the inhabited world?

2. The second question, Was the Deluge Universal? has long divided those who believe that it was historically true, and that it is correctly related by Moses. The most literal interpretation of the language, especially of the words, Gen. vii. 19, "all the high hills that were under the whole heaven, were covered," would lead to the conviction that it must have been universal. Yet it is certain, that many, who accept implicitly the historical truth of the narrative, believe the inundation to have been partial. Of such we may distinguish two classes of writers, 1st those who think that all the then living race of man was destroyed; but that those regions of the earth not then inhabited by man were unaffected by the Flood: 2nd, those who believe that the Flood swept away only that portion of mankind with which the Sacred narrative is chiefly concerned; and which had become corrupted and vitiated by the promiscuous marriages mentioned in ch. vi. 1, 2.

In order to place ourselves in a fair position for judging of these questions, it may be well to consider the nature of the narrative, and the common use of language among the Hebrews. And if we do so carefully, we shall surely be led to conclude, that the Deluge is described as from the point of view of an eye-witness. It has been so much our wont to look on all the early portions of Genesis as a direct revelation from God to Moses, that we rather consider the picture to be drawn, if we may speak so, as from the point of view of the Omnipotent. Yet, even if we are right in esteeming all as a simply direct revelation, it may be, that the revelation was given in prophetic vision, and that Moses wrote, not merely what he had heard, but also, and rather, what he had seen. But we may remember too, that the custom of Scripture is to refer historical records to the evidence of eye-witnesses. This is very much the case in the New Testament. The Apostles and Evangelists constantly claim to have been present at the scenes which they relate (see especially Luke i. 1, 2; Joh. xix. 35, xxi. 24; Acts i. 3; 1 Cor. xv. 3—8; 2 Pet. i. 16; 1 Joh. i. 1); and they relate them as those scenes appeared to them. The baptism of Jesus, the transfiguration, the walking on the waters, the multiplying the loaves and fishes, the Crucifixion, the Resurrection, the Ascension, the tongues of fire at Pentecost, are all simply painted as they who were present saw and conceived of them. And this is equally true in the Old Testament. Take for instance the much debated miracle of the sun and the moon standing still at the command of Joshua. The phenomenon is related just as the contending armies witnessed it. It is not referred to its natural causes, whatever they may have been. That merely is related which actually appeared. At Joshua's command, and of course by Divine intervention, the Sun and the Moon, which would naturally have seemed to describe an arc in the heavens and to descend into the west, then, on the contrary, seemed to stand still in the midst of heaven. Now just so is the Deluge described in Genesis. It is pictured, as it would have presented itself to the eyes of Noah and his family. Moreover, on the principle just mentioned, it is in the highest degree probable, that the description is really that which was given by one of such eye-witnesses. It would have been very strange if no such description had been given and preserved. Shem would almost certainly have related it, over and over again, to his children and grand-children. They would have treasured it up in their memories and have handed it on. As has been so notoriously the case among later nations (see Max Müller's 'Sans. Lit.' p. 500) the very words of the original narrative would be carefully recorded from father to son, whether in writing or by oral tradition; and so, in all probability, we have in Genesis the very syllables in which the Patriarch Shem described to the ancestors of Abraham that which he himself had seen, and in which he had borne so great part. The Divine authority of the narrative would be no more affected by this, than the authority of the Gospel of St Mark is affected by the probable fact that St Mark relates that which St Peter communicated to him as the result of his own ocular and aural experience. Let us then view it thus. One of the eight human beings saved in the ark relates all that he saw. He mentions first God's warning to Noah and denunciation of judgment on mankind. He describes the building and the proportions of the ark. He narrates the 40 days of rain and the swelling of the rivers and of the ocean, in the words which most forcibly describe that great catastrophe (Gen. vii. 11). He then describes how the waters prevailed, till the ark was raised up and floated over them (v. 18). At length, not only did the ark float, but the highest hills disappeared (v. 19); nothing was visible under the whole vault of heaven, but sea and air. The very words are "All the high hills under the whole heaven were covered." Where the ark was at this time, or where Noah and his family had been dwelling before, we cannot tell. The country may have been mountainous, and so, in order to hide the hills from view, the waters must have been very deep, or it may have been a plain country, as many think the region round about Babylon, with few hills in sight and those not of great altitude; in which case but a moderate depth of water would have sufficed to cover all the highest hills under the whole canopy of heaven. The inhabitants of the ark probably tried the depth of the Deluge by a plumb line, an invention surely not unknown to those who had acquired the arts of working in brass and iron (ch. iv. 22), and they found a depth of 15 cubits. Then all flesh, all that was on the dry land, died. And, as the gathering of the waters is thus described, so in ch. viii. the subsidence is given in the same simple graphic style. At length, on a specified day, the ark rests. It is found that it had stranded near to some of the hills in a generally plain country, perhaps to the south of Armenia, perhaps in the north of Palestine, perhaps somewhere in Persia, or in India or elsewhere. The waters continually decrease, it may be the vapours also clear off; and at length the summits of the surrounding hills become visible, though the plain country still is flooded. Noah then sends out the Raven. It goes to and fro, but returns no more to the ark. No account is given of its wanderings; what appears to Noah and his family is all that we learn. So too of the Dove. It goes forth and, finding no rest, comes back again. Once more it is sent out. Whither it goes no one can tell, all that appears is, that it has found dry land. It brings back an olive leaf in its beak; and Noah judges that the waters were abated. From first to last the description is just that which Shem or Noah would have given of all that he had himself seen.

If this be the true explanation of the narrative, we may then more readily see how the question of the universality of the Deluge stands. The words used may certainly mean that the Deluge was universal, that it overwhelmed, not only all the inhabited parts of Asia, but also Europe, Africa, and America, Australia, New Zealand, and Oceanica; most, if not all, of which Islands and Continents were probably then without human inhabitants. Yet, if only the inhabited world was inundated, and all its inhabitants destroyed; the effect would have been the same to Noah, and would, most likely, have been described in the same words. The purpose of God was to sweep away the sinful race of Adam. That purpose would have been effected by a Deluge, which covered the whole of that portion of the globe, which may be called the cradle of the human race. The words of the narrative are perhaps no stronger than would have been naturally used to describe such a catastrophe. The most striking is the passage, "All the high hills under the whole heaven," ch. vii. 19. But this is no more than such expressions as, "I begin to put the dread of thee upon the nations that are under the whole heaven," Deut. ii. 25: "all countries came into Egypt to Joseph to buy corn," Gen. xli. 57: "as the Lord thy God liveth, there is no nation or kingdom whither my lord hath not sent to seek thee, &c.," 1 Kings xviii. 10. When the ancients speak of the whole world, they mean at most the whole world as known to the ancients. When they speak of the whole heaven, they mean the whole visible canopy or expanse of the sky; and so, when they speak of the earth, the land, the dry ground, they mean at times very limited portions indeed of the earth's surface. The strictest interpretation of the record, according to the habit of speech among Semitic nations, will allow us to understand that a Deluge prevailed, extensive enough to destroy all the living race of man, and to cover with water the whole visible face of nature. It is another question, whether we may admit, that any portion of the human race, except the eight persons miraculously preserved, can have escaped. Some suppose the descendants of Cain to have peopled China, and not to have been involved in the Deluge, which, in their belief, was sent on purpose to destroy those apostate and degenerate Sethites, who had defiled the chosen race by intermarrying with unbelievers. Others think that the Nephilim of Numb. xiii. 33 were descendants of the Nephilim of Gen. vi. 4, who must therefore have survived the Deluge. Others, again, as the authors of 'The Genesis of the Earth and Man,' and of 'Adam and the Adamites,' suppose that there was a pre-Adamite race of men, and that the history in Genesis relates only the fortunes of the Adamites, having no reference to the rest. Without pronouncing too hastily on any fair inference from the words of Scripture, we may reasonably say, that their most natural interpretation is, that the whole race of man had become grievously corrupted, since the faithful had intermingled with the ungodly; that the inhabited world was consequently filled with violence, and that God had decreed to destroy all mankind, except one single family; that therefore all that portion of the earth, perhaps as yet a very small portion, into which mankind had spread, was overwhelmed by water. The ark was ordained to save the one faithful family; and lest that family, on the subsidence of the waters, should find the whole country round them a desert, a pair of all the beasts of the land and of the fowls of the air were preserved along with them, and along with them went forth to replenish the now desolated continent. The words of Scripture (confirmed as they are by an universal tradition), appear, at least, to mean as much as this. They do not necessarily mean more.

The geological objections to the history of the Deluge are chiefly such as the discovery of loose scoriæ on the tops of the extinct volcanoes of Auvergne and Languedoc, the impossibility of the waters extending to the height of 15 cubits above the mountains, and the permanent distribution of the animal kingdom over the different parts of the world.

It is said the loose scoriæ on the mountains of Auvergne and Languedoc must have been swept away by an universal flood. It is, however, quite conceivable, even if the Deluge extended to those regions and to the tops of those hills, that the gradual rise and subsidence of the waters may have left there remains of volcanic action, which are not so light as has been asserted, almost untouched. The difficulty in conceiving of the waters rising 15 cubits above the highest mountains is a difficulty in the mind of the objector, not in the text of Scripture, which nowhere speaks of such a rise. (See the earlier part of this note.) The possibility of vegetation surviving has been considered in the note on ch. viii. 11. The most serious difficulty in conceiving of a Flood universal (not only to the world inhabited by man, but to the whole surface of the globe) is in the history of the distribution of the animal kingdom. For example, the animals now living in South America and in New Zealand are of the same type as the fossil animals which lived and died there before the creation of man. Is it conceivable that all should have been gathered together from their original habitats into the ark of Noah and have been afterwards redistributed to their respective homes? The difficulty, however, vanishes entirely, if the sacred narrative relates only a submersion of the human race and of its then dwelling-place, a sense of that narrative, which exact criticism shews to be possible, perhaps even the most probable, irrespective of all questions of natural science. The cavils against the single window, the proportions of the ark, &c. have been considered in their respective places. The peculiar unfairness of the objections urged is to be found, not so much in the objections themselves, as in the insisting at the same time on an interpretation of the Scripture narrative, on principles which would not be applied to any other history whatever. Not only are we required to expound ancient and Eastern phraseology with the cold exactness applicable only to the tongues of Northern Europe, but moreover to adhere to all the interpretations of past uncritical ages, to believe that there was but a single window in the ark, that the ark stranded on the top of a mountain, within sight of which it very probably never sailed, that the waters of the Flood rose three, or even five miles above the sea level, and other prodigies, which the sacred text, even in its most natural significance, nowhere either asserts or implies.

If it be inquired, why it pleased God to save man and beast in a huge vessel, instead of leaving them a refuge on high hills or in some other sanctuary, we perhaps inquire in vain. Yet surely we can see, that the great moral lesson and the great spiritual truths exhibited in the Deluge and the ark were well worth a signal departure from the common course of nature and Providence. The judgment was far more marked, the deliverance far more manifestly Divine, than they would have been, if hills or trees or caves had been the shelter provided for those to be saved. The great prophetic forepicturing of salvation from a flood of sin by Christ and in the Church of Christ would have lost all its beauty and symmetry, if mere earthly refuges had been sufficient for deliverance. As it is, the history of Noah, next after the history of Christ, is that which perhaps most forcibly arrests our thoughts, impresses our consciences and yet revives our hopes. It was a judgment signally executed at the time. It is a lesson deeply instructive for all time.

CHAPTER IX.

1 *God blesseth Noah.* 4 *Blood and murder are forbidden.* 8 *God's covenant,* 13 *signified by the rainbow.* 18 *Noah replenisheth the world,* 20 *planteth a vineyard,* 21 *is drunken, and mocked of his son,* 25 *curseth Canaan,* 26 *blesseth Shem,* 27 *prayeth for Japheth,* 29 *and dieth.*

AND God blessed Noah and his
[a] chap. 1. 28. & 8. 17. sons, and said unto them, [a]Be
fruitful, and multiply, and replenish
the earth.

2 And the fear of you and the
dread of you shall be upon every beast
of the earth, and upon every fowl of
the air, upon all that moveth *upon* the
earth, and upon all the fishes of the
sea; into your hand are they delivered.
3 Every moving thing that liveth
shall be meat for you; even as the
[b]green herb have I given you all [b] chap 1. 29.
things.

CHAP. IX. 1. *And God blessed Noah*, &c.] Noah, now become the second head of the human family, receives a blessing, the former part of which is but a repetition of the blessing first pronounced on Adam, ch. i. 28. The sin of man had frustrated the intent of the first blessing. The earth had been filled with licentiousness and violence, fatal to the increase of mankind, and at length bringing down a judgment, which swept all but one family away. Now all begins anew; and God repeats the promise of fecundity, which sin had made of none effect.

2. *the fear of you and the dread of you*] The small remnant of mankind just rescued from the Deluge might have perished from the attacks of wild beasts, which had probably been young and tame in the ark, but were now adult or adolescent and returning to their own wild natures. The assurance given in this verse was therefore a very needful comfort to Noah and his family.

3. *Every moving thing that liveth shall be meat for you*] In the primal blessing (ch. i. 28, 29, 30) there had been mention of man's supremacy and power over the inferior animals. It has been a question whether there had been a permission of animal food or not. The almost universal opinion of the ancients was that only vegetable food was then permitted; and if we remember that most probably the early race of men lived in a warm and genial climate, and that even now some of the Eastern nations are contented and healthy upon a vegetable diet, we shall be the more disposed to acquiesce in an interpretation which seems to do less violence to the text. It cannot, however, be said that there was from the first a *prohibition* of animal food. From very early times we find sheep and cattle kept at least for milk and wool, and slain for sacrifice, ch. iv. 2, 20. Whether then it had been conceded or not from the first; it is likely that those who fed and sacrificed sheep, like Abel, who kept cattle, like Jabal, or who handled instruments of bronze and iron, like Tubal Cain, would in the course of time have learned the use of animal food. If so, we may consider the words of this verse as a concession to the infirmities or the necessities of mankind, coupled with restrictions,

ev. 17. 4 [c]But flesh with the life thereof,
which is the blood thereof, shall ye
not eat.
5 And surely your blood of your
lives will I require; at the hand of
every beast will I require it, and at
the hand of man; at the hand of
every man's brother will I require the
att. 26. life of man.
6 [d]Whoso sheddeth man's blood,
v. 13. by man shall his blood be shed: [e]for
ap. 1. in the image of God made he man.
7 And you, be ye fruitful, and
multiply; bring forth abundantly in
the earth, and multiply therein.
8 ¶ And God spake unto Noah,
and to his sons with him, saying,
9 And I, behold, I establish my
covenant with you, and with your
seed after you;
10 And with every living creature
that *is* with you, of the fowl, of
the cattle, and of every beast of the
earth with you; from all that go

---

which may have been called for by the savage practices of the Antediluvians.

4. *flesh with the life thereof*] Rashi and some other Jewish commentators understand a prohibition of the practice of eating flesh cut from the living animal, and so Luther translated, "the flesh which yet lives in its blood." The monstrous wickedness of the Antediluvians, by which the earth was filled with violence, may have taken this form among others; and these words without doubt condemn by implication all such fiendish cruelty. They prohibit also the revolting custom of eating raw flesh; for civilization is ever to be a handmaid to religion. But over and above all this, there is reference to that shedding of blood, or pouring out of life, which formed so great a part of typical sacrifice, and which had its full significance in that pouring out of the soul unto death, which won for man the resurrection to eternal life. We need not look for any scientific explanation of the connection between life and blood here, or in the subsequent legal enactments (*e.g.* Lev. iii. 17, vii. 26, xvii. 10; 1 Sam. xiv. 32; Ez. xxxiii. 25). The ancients no doubt generally believed the blood to be the seat of the life; but it is also literally true, that the shedding of blood is equivalent to the destruction of life; and so in these early injunctions the God of mercy taught the value not only of human, but of all animal being, and along with the forbidding of manslaughter forbade wanton cruelty and indifference to the sufferings of His brute creatures.

5. *And surely your blood of your lives will I require*, &c.] There have been many proposed translations of this verse. The A.V., which accords with the most important ancient versions, no doubt gives the true meaning. "The blood of your lives" probably signifies "your life blood." Under the law the ox that gored was to be killed (Ex. xxi. 28), which seems a comment on this passage. In Ps. ix. 12 God is said to be the requirer of blood, a phrase identical with that made use of here.

6. *Whoso sheddeth man's blood*] Here the manner in which God will require the blood of the murdered man is specified. There shall be a legal retribution, life for life.

for in the image of God made he man] The slaughter of brute animals was permitted, though wanton cruelty towards them was forbidden; but man was made in the image of God, and to destroy man's life has in it the sin of sacrilege. Moreover, the image of God implies the existence of a personal, moral, and therefore, in the creature, a responsible will. Though the holiness, which was part of the likeness, was lost in the fall, still the personality and the moral being remained. To destroy the life of such an one is therefore to cut short his time of probation, to abridge his day of grace, to step in between him and his moral Governor, to frustrate, as far as may be, God's purposes of love and mercy to his soul. Hence the sin of murder is the greatest wrong which man can do to his brother man; perhaps also the greatest insult which man can offer to Him who is the loving Father of all men. The Jews held that there were seven precepts given to Noah, which were binding on all mankind, to be observed by proselytes of the gate and by pious Gentiles, viz. abstinence from murder, from eating the flesh of living animals, from blasphemy, idolatry, incest, theft, and the submission to constituted authority; the first two and the last are expressly enjoined in the words recorded in this chapter, the other four result from the dictates of natural religion.

9. *I establish my covenant with you, and with your seed after you*] A new covenant is now made with all the human beings rescued from the flood, and through them even with the beasts of the field, that there should not again be a flood to destroy all flesh. This, perhaps, more than any other part of the history, seems to prove that the Deluge extended at least to the destruction of all the then living race of man.

10. *from all that go out of the ark, to every beast of the earth*] An idiomatic ex-

out of the ark, to every beast of the earth.

[f] Isai. 54. 9.

11 And [f]I will establish my covenant with you; neither shall all flesh be cut off any more by the waters of a flood; neither shall there any more be a flood to destroy the earth.

12 And God said, This *is* the token of the covenant which I make between me and you and every living creature that *is* with you, for perpetual generations:

13 I do set my bow in the cloud, and it shall be for a token of a covenant between me and the earth.

[g] Ecclus. 43. 11, 12.

14 [g]And it shall come to pass, when I bring a cloud over the earth, that the bow shall be seen in the cloud:

15 And I will remember my covenant, which *is* between me and you and every living creature of all flesh; and the waters shall no more become a flood to destroy all flesh.

16 And the bow shall be in the cloud; and I will look upon it, that I may remember the everlasting covenant between God and every living creature of all flesh that *is* upon the earth.

17 And God said unto Noah, This *is* the token of the covenant, which I have established between me and all flesh that *is* upon the earth.

18 ¶ And the sons of Noah, that went forth of the ark, were Shem, and Ham, and Japheth: and Ham *is* the father of †Canaan.

† Heb. *Chenaan.*

19 These *are* the three sons of Noah: and of them was the whole earth overspread.

20 And Noah began *to be* an husbandman, and he planted a vineyard:

21 And he drank of the wine, and was drunken; and he was uncovered within his tent.

---

pression, signifying that the covenant shall extend not only to those that go out of the ark, but also to every beast of the earth. Not only those preserved in the ark, but all other animals are to be interested in this promise. From which we can hardly fail to infer that the destruction of the lower animals was confined to a certain district, and not general throughout the earth.

13. *I do set my bow in the cloud*] Lit. **I have set My bow.** The covenant was an universal covenant; the sign of the covenant was therefore to be one visible to all nations, and intelligible to all minds. It appears at first sight as if the words of the sacred record implied that this was the first rainbow ever seen on earth. But it would be doing no violence to the text to believe, that the rainbow had been already a familiar sight, but that it was newly constituted the sign or token of a Covenant, just as afterwards the familiar rite of baptism and the customary use of bread and wine were by our Blessed Lord ordained to be the tokens and pledges of the New Covenant in Christ between His Heavenly Father and every Christian soul.

20. *Noah began to be an husbandman*] Husbandry had been much used before the flood; but now there was a new condition of the earth, and all was, as it were, begun again. As an incursion of barbarians has often swept away the civilization of a whole region or continent, so the flood had reduced mankind almost to the simplicity of the days of Adam. Still, without doubt, many of the inventions of the antediluvian race would have been preserved by the family of Noah; and probably among the rest the cultivation of the vine.

21. *he drank of the wine*] Many have supposed that Noah was the discoverer of the art of making wine, and even that he was the great planter of the vine. So they have palliated his fault by ascribing it to ignorance of the effects of wine. It is hardly probable that, with all the difficulties of his new position, Noah should have invented fermentation. More likely is it, that the ingenious and intemperate descendants of Cain had long before discovered it. Noah may have been but little used to strong drink, and hence may not have known that it would so soon overcome him; yet we may well follow the wisdom of Calvin, and say, "Leaving all this in uncertainty, let us learn from Noah's intemperance how foul and detestable a vice drunkenness is." The Holy Scriptures never conceal the sins even of God's greatest saints, and the sins of saints are sure to meet with chastisement. Noah's piety is plainly recorded. It is also plainly recorded that he fell into sin, whether partly of ignorance or wholly of infirmity; that sin brought with it shame, and, as is so often found, was the occasion of sin to others, and led on to consequences disastrous to the descendants of all those who

22 And Ham, the father of Canaan, saw the nakedness of his father, and told his two brethren without.

23 And Shem and Japheth took a garment, and laid *it* upon both their shoulders, and went backward, and covered the nakedness of their father; and their faces *were* backward, and they saw not their father's nakedness.

24 And Noah awoke from his wine, and knew what his younger son had done unto him.

25 And he said, Cursed *be* Canaan; a servant of servants shall he be unto his brethren.

26 And he said, Blessed *be* the LORD God of Shem; and Canaan shall be ‖his servant.

27 God shall ‖enlarge Japheth, and

‖ Or, *servant to them.*
‖ Or, *persuade.*

---

in any degree shared in the guilt of it. Noah sinned, Ham sinned, perhaps, too, Canaan sinned. So there was a heritage of sorrow to the descendants of Noah in the line of Ham, to the descendants of Ham in the line of Canaan.

22. *Ham, the father of Canaan*] The great difficulty in this history is that Ham appears to have sinned, and Canaan is cursed. Some see in this simply the visiting of the sins of the fathers on their children. But then why only on one of those children? A propriety has been discovered in the curse on Canaan, as he was Ham's youngest son, just as Ham was the youngest son of Noah. Yet this is all gratuitous and without authority from the text of Scripture. It has been thought, once more, that Noah's prophecy extended to all the posterity of Ham, but that only that portion which affected Canaan was preserved by Moses, in order to animate the Israelites in their wars against the Canaanites; others again have conjectured, that in the prophecy of Noah, instead of "cursed be Canaan," we ought to read, "cursed be Ham the father of Canaan," but such conjectures, without authority of MSS. are quite inadmissible. The extreme brevity of the narrative renders it impossible to explain it fully. Nothing is said, save only that Ham saw his father naked, and then told his brethren. We are even left to infer that he told this scoffingly; but for the curse that follows, we might suppose that he had only consulted them as to how best to conceal their father's shame. Something therefore there plainly is, which requires to be supplied in order fully to clear up the obscurity. Yet this cannot now be discovered. Conjecture only is possible.

Origen mentions as a tradition among the Jews, that Canaan first saw the shame of his grandfather and told it to his father. In that case, it may have been that the chief sin lay with Canaan, and hence that he especially inherited the curse. Many commentators have adopted this opinion, and it would certainly solve most of the difficulty.

24. *His younger son*] Ham is always named second among the sons of Noah; but it has sometimes been thought, that Japheth was the eldest and Ham the youngest, the order being changed for the sake of putting first Shem, who was the progenitor of the chosen seed. Yet many writers of great authority, both Jewish and Christian, understand by the term here used, "his younger (lit. little) son," not his son Ham, but his grandson Canaan. (So Levi Ben Gerson, Abenezra, Theodoret, Procopius, Joseph Scaliger, &c.). This would correspond with the tradition mentioned by Origen (see last note), that the sin of Ham was shared by Canaan, or perhaps that Canaan was the guilty person, his father only not having condemned, but rather joined in his wickedness.

25. *Cursed be Canaan*, &c.] In the patriarchal ages, when there was no regular order of priests or prophets, the head of the family was the priest, and these blessings and curses spake they not of themselves, but being high priests they prophesied. Yet we can hardly fail to see also in these histories a lesson, that a parent's blessing is to be valued, a parent's curse to be dreaded.

26. *Blessed be the* LORD *God of Shem*] The prophecy here assumes the form of a thanksgiving to God, from whom all holy desires and good counsels come, and who had put into the heart of Shem to act piously. At the same time, it is clearly implied, that the Lord, JEHOVAH, should be very specially the God of Shem, which was fulfilled in the selection of the descendants of Abraham to be the peculiar people of God.

Canaan shall be his servant] Noah foretells the subjugation of the land of Canaan by the people of Israel, when the Canaanites should become servants of the descendants of Shem.

27. *God shall enlarge Japheth*] There is a paronomasia on the name Japheth, which probably signifies "enlarged." The Hebrew word "shall enlarge" is, neglecting the vowel points, letter for letter the same as the word Japheth. The prophecy looked forward to the wide territory which was assigned to the descendants of Japheth, reaching from India and Persia in the East to the remotest boun-

he shall dwell in the tents of Shem;
and Canaan shall be his servant.
28 ¶ And Noah lived after the
flood three hundred and fifty years.
29 And all the days of Noah were
nine hundred and fifty years: and he
died.

CHAPTER X.

1 The generations of Noah. 2 The sons of Japheth. 6 The sons of Ham. 8 Nimrod the first monarch. 21 The sons of Shem.

NOW these *are* the generations
of the sons of Noah, Shem,

---

daries of Europe in the West, and now spreading over America and Australia.

and he shall dwell in the tents of Shem] (1) The Targum of Onkelos, Philo, Theodoret and some other interpreters, Jewish and Christian, understood He *i.e.* God, shall dwell among the descendants of Shem." (2) Many more, (*e.g.* Calvin, Bochart, Rosenm., Tuch, Del., Reinke, Keil), following the Targum of the Pseudo-Jonathan, consider Japheth to be the subject of the proposition. Jonathan's paraphrase is "The sons of Japheth shall be proselyted and dwell in the schools of Shem," and the majority of Christian interpreters understood the prophecy to be similar to that in Isai. lx. 3, 5, "Gentiles shall come to thy light, and kings to the brightness of thy rising ...the abundance of the sea shall be converted unto thee, the forces of the Gentiles shall come unto thee." Nearly all those nations whose history and language shew them to be Japhetic have been converted to a belief in the religion of the God of Shem, which has long been the religion of all Europe, and which is now making way even among the Aryan races of Asia. (3) It has been suggested by some, though with little ground of probability, that instead of "tents of Shem," we should render "tents of renown," the tabernacles of Japheth being spoken of as famous and illustrious. Of the three interpretations, (2) may be pronounced somewhat confidently to be the true. By that the continuity of the whole prophecy is preserved. The first part, v. 25, refers only to the descendants of Ham and Canaan. The second is the blessing on Shem, with a repetition of the condemnation of Canaan. The third is the blessing on Japheth, concluding also with the condemnation of Canaan.

The prophecy then embraces the following particulars: 1. That the world should be divided among the descendants of Noah, but that Japheth should have the largest portion for his inheritance. 2. That the descendants of Shem should preserve the knowledge of the true God, and be specially chosen to be His inheritance and His peculiar people. 3. That the descendants of Japheth should ultimately dwell in the tents of Shem, that is, according to Jewish interpretation, should learn from the descendants of Shem the knowledge of the true God. 4. That Canaan, and perhaps other Hamitic nations, should be depressed and reduced to a condition of servitude.

How fully all these predictions have been carried out in the history of Asia, Europe and Africa, hardly need be said.

28. *And Noah lived*, &c.] These two verses seem the natural conclusion of ch. v. but are disjoined from it in order to insert the history of the life of Noah.

CHAP. X. **1.** *Now these are the generations*] From the history of Noah the sacred narrative proceeds to the genealogy of the sons of Noah. It is admitted on all hands that there exists no more interesting record, ethnological and geographical, independently of its Scriptural authority.

The genealogy traces the origin of all nations from a single pair. The human race descended from Adam had been destroyed by the flood, with the exception of Noah and his family. Though it is quite possible to interpret the language of the sacred narrative consistently with the belief that the Deluge was not universal, it at least appears most probable that the man-inhabited world was submerged. And again, although some have contended that the different races of man are so dissimilar, that they must have descended from different primitive stocks; yet the inquiries of naturalists and physiologists at present tend rather to diminish than to increase the number of distinct species, both in the animal and the vegetable world, and so to make it even the more certain that human beings constitute but one species deducible from a single pair. The same anatomical structure, especially of the skull and brain, the same intellectual capacities, though differently developed in different nations, the same general duration of life, the same liability to disease, the same average temperature of the body, the same normal frequency of the pulse, the fruitful intermarriage of all races, and that with no instinctive natural repugnances, are manifest indications of an unity of species (Del.). From the time of Blumenbach (whose book 'De naturæ generis humani unitate' is still a standard work on this subject) down to the present day, the most eminent physiologists agree in considering these and similar arguments well nigh conclusive in favour of the unity of the human race. (Consult especially Prichard, 'Phys. Hist. of Mankind;' Smyth, 'Unity of Human Race;' Quatrefages, 'L'unité de l'espèce humaine,' and his report on 'Anthropologie'). To these physiological considera-

Ham, and Japheth: and unto them
were sons born after the flood.
2 [a]The sons of Japheth; Gomer,
and Magog, and Madai, and Javan,
and Tubal, and Meshech, and Tiras.

[a] 1 Chron. 1. 5.

---

tions we may now add the evidence to be derived from human language. "It was a profound saying of William Humboldt, that man is man only by means of speech, but that in order to invent speech, he must be man already" (Lyell, 'Antiquity of Man,' 468). This alone is an argument for the unity of that race which is distinguished from all other animals by the possession of articulate language. But, moreover, the greatest philologists of the present day seem to be approaching the conclusion that the evidence of comparative grammar, so far as it goes, is in favour of the original unity of human language. "One of the grandest results of modern comparative philology has been to shew that all languages belonging to one common stock—and we may say, enlarging this view, all languages of the earth—are but scattered indications of that primitive state of human intellect, and more particularly of the imitative faculty, under the higher excitement of poetical inspiration, in which the language originated, and with which every language remains connected, as well through the physiological unity of the human race, as through the historical unity of the family to which it more especially belongs" (Meyer ap. Bunsen, 'Christianity and Mankind,' Vol. III. p. 163). So writes Dr Meyer: and Prof. Max Müller says, "These two points Comparative Philology has gained. (1) Nothing necessitates the admission of different independent beginnings for the material elements of the Turanian, Semitic, and Aryan branches of speech: nay, it is possible even now to point out radicals, which, under various changes and disguises, have been current in these three branches ever since their first separation. (2) Nothing necessitates the admission of different beginnings for the formal elements of the Turanian, Semitic, and Aryan branches of speech; and though it is impossible to derive the Aryan system of grammar from the Semitic, or the Semitic from the Turanian, we can perfectly understand how, either through individual influences, or by the wear and tear of grammar in its own continuous working, the different systems of grammar of Asia and Europe may have been produced" (Max Müller, *Ibid.* pp. 479, 480). Once more, although it may not be possible simply to assign all Semitic tongues to the descendants of Shem, Aryan to the descendants of Japhet, and Turanian to the descendants of Ham; it is still observable that comparative philology seems to have reduced all languages to three distinct stocks, even the rapid degeneracy of barbarian dialects not wholly obscuring their relationship to one of these three families. This is the more to be noticed, when we learn that in savage tribes those who speak the same dialect will sometimes, by separation and estrangement, become in the course of a single generation unintelligible to each other.

Certain rules are to be observed for the clearing up of some difficulties in the genealogy of this chapter. 1. Though some notice may be taken of the progenitors of all nations, yet naturally those families, more or less connected with the Hebrews, are the longest dwelt upon. 2. Whereas all are said to have settled and dispersed themselves "after their families in their nations," it will appear that only the larger division by *nations* is traced in the case of more remote peoples, whereas those related to or bordering on the Hebrews are traced both according to the wider division of *nations*, and the narrower of *families*. 3. Although the first division of the earth is spoken of as made in the time of Peleg, and some families may be traced no farther than up to the time of such division, yet the developement of those more specially treated of is brought down to the time of Moses. 4. For none, however, must we seek a very remote settlement, as the original dispersion could not have extended so far. 5. In some cases the names of nations or tribes appear to be substituted for the names of individuals, such as the Jebusite, the Hivite, the Arkite &c., very probably also such as Kittim, Dodanim, Mizraim &c.; and even perhaps Aram, Canaan and the like. This may be accounted for in more than one way. The purpose of the sacred writer was to trace nations and families, rather than to give a history of individuals, and he therefore speaks of nations known by name to the Israelites as begotten by (*i.e.* descended from) certain patriarchs, in preference to tracing their descent through unknown individuals. Perhaps too individual patriarchs and progenitors had become known by tradition to posterity, not by their own original names, but by the name of the place they had settled in, or by the name of the tribe which they had founded and ruled. The origin of names is often very obscure, and it has been common in most rude societies for persons to be called after places or properties. It is quite possible that even the very earliest patriarchs, as, Shem, Ham and Japheth, Canaan and the like, may have been known in after ages by names which adhered to them through events in their history or places where they had fixed themselves. Thus Shem may have been the man of *name*, the most renowned of Noah's sons, Ham, the

3 And the sons of Gomer; Ash- kenaz, and Riphath, and Togarmah.

man who settled in the *warm regions* of Africa, Japheth the father of the *fair* people of Europe, or perhaps the man whose descendants *spread abroad* more widely than the rest. Canaan again may have been the dweller in *low* lands, while *Aram* may have derived a title from having chosen the *high* lands for his home. This theory, if true, would not interfere with the historical character of this Chapter; especially if we consider that Hebrew may not have been the primitive tongue, in which case all these names must either have been translations of the original names, or names by which the bearers had become known to posterity. We have many examples in Scripture of persons changing their names or adopting new names from events in their history, *e.g.* Abram changing into Abraham; Esau to Edom; Jacob to Israel; Saul to Paul, &c., &c. The whole number of families noticed in this chapter amounts to 70; but it is to be observed that in some cases the descent is traced only to the grandsons, in other cases to the great grandsons of Noah: in the family of Shem only, the ancestor of the Hebrews, the descent is traced through six generations.

2. *Japheth*] It is doubtful whether Japheth was the eldest or the second son of Noah, see in v. 21. He is generally mentioned last in order, Shem, Ham and Japheth, but from ix. 24, it is generally inferred that Ham was the youngest. In this genealogy he occurs first, the reason being probably this; Shem is reserved to the last that his descent may be traced to a greater length, and Ham last but one, because his descendants were those most closely connected with the descendants of Shem. The etymology of the name Japheth should seem from ix. 27 to be from the root *Pathah*, *to extend*. But the language in ix. 27, may be only an example of the paronomasia so common in Hebrew poetry; and Gesenius, Knobel and others prefer to derive from *Yaphah*, *to be fair*, from the fair complexion of Japheth and his descendants.

Gomer] Josephus ('Ant.' I. 7) says that Gomer was the ancestor of those whom the Greeks called Galatians, who were formerly called Gomarites. The descendants of Gomer have accordingly been generally identified with the Celtic race called in the time of Homer Cimmerii, who are first known as inhabiting the Chersonesus Taurica, which still retains the name *Crimea*. (See Herod. IV. 12, 45. Æsch. 'Prom.' v. 729.) The relation of Gomer to Magog and Madai corresponds with the original juxtaposition of the Cimmerians to the Scythians and Medes, the Cimmerians dwelling first on the confines of Asia and Europe. Being driven thence by the Scythians in the reign of Cyaxares, they made an irruption into Asia Minor, from which they were driven back again by Alyattes. Their name, which then nearly disappears in Asia, is recognized again in the Cimbri, who occupied the Cimbrian Chersonesus and other parts of the North of Europe, and in the great Celtic tribe of Cymry, the ancient inhabitants of Britain and the present inhabitants of Wales.

Magog] The statement of Josephus ('Ant.' I. 6), that the descendants of Magog were the Scythians is generally accepted as true. In Ezek. xxxviii. 2, 14; xxxix. 2. 6, we find Magog as the name of a people inhabiting "the sides of the North" closely connected with Meshech, the Moschi, and Tubal, the Tibarenes, with a prince named Gog, having horses and armed with bows, which corresponds with the local position and military habits of the Scythians. The Scythians, according to their own traditions, lived first in Asia near the river Araxes, afterwards they possessed the whole country to the ocean and the lake Mæotis, and the rest of the plain to the river Tanais (Diod. Sic. II. 3). Herodotus (I. 103—106) relates their descent upon Media, and Egypt, till they were surprised and cut off at a feast by Cyaxares. From their intermixture with the Medes, the Sarmatians appear to have arisen, and from them the Russians. See Knobel.

Madai] The Medes were called *Mada* by themselves, as appears from the arrowheaded inscriptions, changed in the Semitic to Madai, and by the Greeks to Medoi. They dwelt to the S. and S. W. of the Caspian, and coming over to Europe in small parties mingled with the Scythians, whence sprang the Sarmatians.

Javan] From Javan was "Ionia and the whole Hellenic people" (Jos. 'Ant.' i. 6). Cp. Is. lxvi. 19, Ezek. xxvii. 13, Daniel viii. 21, where Alexander is called king of Javan; Joel iii. 6, where "the sons of the Javanites" are put for the Grecians (υἷες Ἀχαίων), Zech. ix. 13. Greece is called *Ionia* in Egyptian hieroglyphics and Yuna in a Cuneiform inscription at Persepolis (Gesen. s. v.). The Ionians were the most Eastern of the Hellenic races, and so were the best known to the Asiatics. The course of migration had evidently been from Ionia to Attica and other parts of Greece.

Tubal, and Meshech] These names constantly occur together; see Ezek. xxvii. 13, xxxii. 26, xxxviii. 2, 3, xxxix. 1; where we find them joined with the invading army of Gog and Magog, and going with Javan to Tyre to purchase slaves and vessels of brass. Meshech is by Josephus said to be the father

4 And the sons of Javan; Elishah, and Tarshish, Kittim, and Dodanim.

of the Cappadocians, who had, he tells us, a city called Mazacha, and to Tubal he traces the Iberians who dwelt between the Euxine and the Caspian. Later writers have long identified Meshech with the Moschi, inhabitants of the Moschian mountains between Armenia, Iberia and Colchis. Bochart was the first to identify Tubal with the Tibareni, who dwelt on the Southern shore of the Euxine towards the East and near to the Moschi. Knobel considers the Tibareni to be connected with the Iberians: Tubal = Tibar = Iber.

Tiras] Josephus identifies the descendants of Tiras with the Thracians. So Jerome, the Targums, and most modern commentators. The Getæ and Daci, north of the Danube, belonged to the Thracian stock. According to Grimm and some other authorities, the Getæ were the ancestors of the Goths, which would immediately connect the Thracian and Teutonic races together. The chief reason, however, for considering Tiras the ancestor of the Thracians seems to be the similarity of the names. Accordingly other resemblances have been found. Tuch for instance is in favour of the Tyrseni or Tyrrheni.

3. *the sons of Gomer; Ashkenaz*] There is little to guide us to the identification of Ashkenaz, except the name and the mention of Ashkenaz Jer. li. 27 in company with Ararat and Minni, which makes it probable that the descendants of Ashkenaz dwelt near the Euxine and the Caspian. Bochart suggests Phrygia, where were the lake and river Ascanius. The Rabbi Saadias says the Slavi. Targ. of Jonathan gives Adiabene. Some have discovered a resemblance of sound in *Scandinavia*, and also to *Saxon*. The modern Jews called Germany Ashkenaz; and Knobel considers this to be the true interpretation of the name; though etymologically he finds in it the race of Asa or the Asiatics, Ash-genos. These Asa or Asiatics he thinks, dwelt in Asia Minor (comp. *Ascania*), and after the Trojan war migrated towards Pannonia and thence towards the Rhine. The Scandinavians traced their origin to Asia, and called the home of their gods Asgard. It has been conjectured by Bochart and others, that the Black sea was called the sea of Ashkenaz, which sounded to the Greeks like Axenos, their original name for it, and which by an euphemism they changed to Euxeinos.

Riphath] Josephus says Paphlagonia, in which he is followed by Bochart, Le Clerc, &c. Most modern commentators compare the Riphæan mountains, which the ancient geographers (Strab. VII. 3, § 1. Plin. 'H, N.' IV. 12. Mela, I. 19, &c.) place in the remote North. Mela (II. 2) places them East of the Tanais. Knobel conjectures that the Celts or Gauls were the descendants of Riphath, and that they first lived near the Carpathians, which he identifies with the Montes Riphæi.

Togarmah] Mentioned again Ez. xxvii. 14, xxxviii. 6. Josephus identifies with the Phrygians, Bochart with the Cappadocians. Michaelis, and after him most moderns, prefer the Armenians; so Rosenm., Gesen., Winer, Knobel, &c. The Armenians themselves traced their origin to Haic the son of Thogoreu or Thorgau (Mos. Choren. I. 4, § 9). Ezekiel (xxvii. 14) attributes to Togarmah great traffic in horses; and Strabo (XI. 13, § 9) speaks of the Armenians as famous for breeding horses. Modern philologists consider the Armenian as an Aryan or Indo-European language, which corresponds with the descent from Japheth.

4. *And the sons of Javan; Elishah*] Ezekiel (xxvii. 7) mentions the isles of Elishah as those whence the Tyrians obtained their purple and scarlet. Some of the Targums identify with Hellas, in which they are followed by Michaelis, Rosenm., and others. Josephus ('Ant.' I. 6) identifies with the Æolians, which is the view adopted by Knobel. Bochart preferred the Peloponnesus, which was famous for its purple dye, and of which the most important district was called *Elis*. Whichever view he adopted, there is little doubt that the descendants of Elishah in the time of Ezekiel were a maritime people of the Grecian stock.

Tarshish] By Josephus identified with Tarsus in Cilicia; by the LXX. (Is. xxiii. 1, &c.), Theodoret, and others, with Carthage; by Eusebius, who is followed by Bochart and most moderns, with Tartessus in Spain. Tarshish, from the various notices of it, appears to have been a seaport town towards the West (cp. Ps. lxxii.; Is. lx. 9); whither the Phœnicians were wont to traffic in large ships, "ships of Tarshish" (see 1 K. x. 22, xxii. 48; Ps. xlviii. 7; Is. ii. 16, xxiii. 1, 14, lx. 9) sailing from the port of Joppa (Jon. i. 3, iv. 2). It was a most wealthy and flourishing mart, whence came silver, iron, tin, and lead (Ps. lxxii. 10; Is. lxvi. 19; Jer. x. 9; Ezek. xxvii. 12, 25). The name Tartessus is identical with Tarshish, the *t* being constantly substituted by the Syriac for the Hebrew sibilant (cp. Bashan = Batanæa, Zor = Tyre, &c.). The Spanish were among the most famous of the Phœnician colonies, and were specially rich in metal (Diod. Sic. V. 35—38; Arrian. II. 16; Plin. 'H. N.' III. 3; Mela, II. 6, &c.); of which colonies Tartessus was the most illustrious. It appears to have been situated at the mouth of the Guadalquiver (Strabo, III. p. 148). Two passages in Chronicles (2 Chron. ix. 21, xx. 36) seem irre-

5 By these were the isles of the Gentiles divided in their lands; every one after his tongue, after their families, in their nations.

6 ¶ [b] And the sons of Ham; Cush, and Mizraim, and Phut, and Canaan.

7 And the sons of Cush; Seba, and Havilah, and Sabtah, and Raamah,

b 1 Chron. 1. 8.

---

concilable with this, and induced St Jerome ('in Jerem.' x. 9), and after him Bochart and others, to suppose that there must have been another Tarshish in the Indian Ocean, which could be approached by the Red Sea, an opinion now generally rejected. Knobel supposes that the original inhabitants of Tarshish were the Tusci, Tyrsenians, or Tyrrhenians, a Pelasgic, though not Hellenic race, inhabiting great part of Italy, Corsica, and Sardinia, and that very probably Tartessus in Spain was a colony or offshoot from these people.

Kittim (or *Chittim*)] Identified by Josephus with Cyprus, in which we meet with the town of Cittium; by Eusebius, and after him by Bochart, with the inhabitants of the part of Italy contiguous to Rome. In 1 Maccab. i. 1 Alexander is said to come from Chittim, and (1 Macc. viii. 5) Perseus is called King of the Kitiæans, which induced Michaelis and others to suppose the Chittim to be the Macedonians. Most modern interpreters seem to acquiesce in the opinion of Josephus, that Cyprus (see Is. xxiii 1, 12) may have been a chief seat of the Chittim, but add that probably their colonies extended to the isles of the Eastern Mediterranean (see Jer. ii. 10; Ezek. xxvii. 6). So Gesen., Knobel, Delitz., Kalisch.

Dodanim] has been compared with Dodona in Epirus. By Kalisch it is identified with the Daunians. Gesenius suspects Dodanim to be equivalent (perhaps by contraction) with Dardanim = Dardani or Trojans, an opinion which he confirms by the authority of the Bereschit Rabba on this verse. Knobel conjectures that we have traces of Dodanim both in Dodona (a name which he says prevailed through Illyricum and Northern Greece) and also in Dardania and the Dardans. There is another reading in 1 Chr. i. 7, and here also (Gen. x. 4) in the Gr. and Samaritan, viz. Rodanim, Rhodii, the people of Rhodes.

5. *isles of the Gentiles*] The word here rendered *Isle* very probably meaning originally "habitable region" (Is. xlii. 15), is generally used either of islands or of places on the sea coast. On the whole of this verse see Jos. Mede, Bk. I. 'Disc.' XLIX. L. By the phrase "Isles of the Gentiles" were understood those countries of Europe and Asia Minor to which the inhabitants of Egypt and Palestine had access only by sea.

6. *Ham*] It is generally thought that the name means warm, which is to be compared with the Greek Aithiops (Ethiopian), which has a similar significance. The word *Kem*, the Egyptian name for Egypt, probably the same word as Ham, signifies *blackness*, with perhaps some notion of heat (see Plutarch, 'De Iside et Osiride,' § 33). The blackness is now generally admitted to refer to the soil, denoting its colour and fertility. (See Excursus.) In Ps. lxxviii. 51, cv. 23, cvi. 22, Egypt is called the land of Ham, which seems to confirm the belief that Kem (in Greek Chemia) is the same as Ham. The descendants of Ham appear to have colonized Babylonia, Southern Arabia, Egypt, Ethiopia, and other portions of Africa.

Much has been written of late about the Hamitic languages. The frequent mixture of the Hamites with the descendants of Shem makes it very difficult to discern clearly between their tongues. Bunsen considers Chamitism to be the most ancient form of Semitism, in fact Semitism, before the Hamites and Shemites thoroughly parted off from each other and from their primeval dwelling-place. The ancient Egyptian has a Semitic base with Turanian (negro) infusion, but the Hamitic races have so frequently been conquered, morally and physically, by the descendants of Shem and Japheth, that their original languages have been lost or corrupted by the prevalence of Semitism or Aryanism.

Cush] The name Cush is generally translated Ethiopia. The Ethiopians at the time of Josephus were called Chusæi, Cushites, and that is still the Syriac name for the Abyssinians. There is, however, good reason to believe, with Bochart, and others, that the first home of the Cushites was Chuzistan and the adjoining parts of Southern Asia, from whence they spread in different directions, a main body having crossed the sea and settled in Ethiopia.

Certainly some of those, who are here mentioned (*e.g.* Raamah, Sheba, Dedan, vv. 7, 8) as the descendants of Cush, established colonies in Asia. Some passages in the Old Testament seem to require that we should place Cush in Asia, as Gen. ii. 13; so also Exod. ii. 16, 21, compared with Num. xii. 1; in the latter of which Zipporah is called a Cushite, whilst in the former she is said to be a daughter of the priest of Midian. This connects Cush with Midian, which was in Arabia Felix, near the Red Sea. Again, in Hab. iii. 7 Cush and Midian appear to be connected. In Job xxviii. 19 we read of "the topaz of Cush." Now, there is no reason to suppose that Ethiopia produced topazes, but Pliny (XXXVII. 8) speaks of an island of Arabia in the Red Sea as famous for this

and Sabtechah: and the sons of Raamah; Sheba, and Dedan.
8 And Cush begat Nimrod: he began to be a mighty one in the earth.

---

gem, which is also noted by Diodorus (III. 39). All this connects Cush with Asia, and seems to prove that the first settlement of the Cushites was in Asia. Their subsequent emigration into Africa, so that one division was on the East and the other on the West of the Gulf of Arabia, may account for the language of Homer, who speaks of the Æthiopians as divided into two distinct tribes ('Od.' I. 23), a distinction observed by Strabo ('Geogr.' I. p. 21), by Pliny (lib. V. c. 8), and by Pomponius Mela (lib. I. cap. 2).

Mizraim] is undoubtedly Egypt. The origin and meaning of the word has been much debated, but with no certain conclusion. If the singular be the Hebrew Mazor, it should signify a *mound* or *fortified place*. Gesenius and others prefer the Arabic Meser, *a limit* or *boundary*. The dual form has been supposed to indicate Upper and Lower Egypt. It perhaps may be the rendering or transcription of Mes-ra-n "children of Ra," i.e. of the Sun. The Egyptians claimed to be sons of Ra. (See Excursus.) It certainly seems as if the name belonged rather to a race or nation than to a man; and, therefore, the son of Ham here named is probably designated as the founder or ancestor of the Egyptians or people of Mizraim.

Phut] The name *Phut* occurs several times in the Old Testament, and generally in connection with the Egyptians and Ethiopians, sometimes with Persia and Lud. See Jer. xlvi. 9; Ezek. xxvii. 10, xxx. 5, xxxviii. 5; Nah. iii. 9. The LXX. in Jeremiah and Ezekiel always render *Libyans*. So Josephus says ('Ant.' I. 6), that Phut colonized Libya, and that the people were from him called Phutites. The Coptic name of Libya is Phaiat ⲫⲁⲓⲁⲧ. St Jerome speaks of a river of Mauritania, and the region round it, as called Phut to his time. ('Tradit. Hebr.')

Canaan] The name is thought by some to be derived from the nature of the country in which the descendants of Canaan lived, viz. a flat, depressed region, from the Hebrew root *Cana* (hiph.) to depress. The fact, that the Canaanites appear to have spoken a Semitic tongue has been alleged as a reason why they should not have been of Hamitic descent. Knobel has well observed, however, that they are said by the ancients to have removed from the Red Sea to the Mediterranean, with which agrees the mythology which brought into relation the Phœnicians' ancestors Agenor and Phœnix sometimes with Belus and Babylonia, sometimes with Ægyptus and Danaus (the Æthiop), Cepheus and Libya. In the earliest days the Hamites and Shemites were near neighbours; there may have sprung from them a mixed race, which spread toward Tyre and Sidon and dispossessed, partly also intermingled with, a Semitic race originally inhabiting the region of Palestine and Phœnicia. As Abraham and his descendants appear to have changed their native Aramean for the Hebrew of Palestine, so very probably the Hamitic Canaanites, long mingled with Shemitic races, acquired the language of the children of Shem. The whole character of the Canaanitish civilization and worship was Hamite, not Semitic. Like the sons of Seth, the sons of Shem lived a nomadic, pastoral life; whilst, with a like resemblance to the descendants of Cain, the Hamites were builders of cities and fortresses, and rapidly grew into prosperous, mercantile races, with an advanced, but corrupt civilization. Compare Egypt, Babylon, Nineveh, Tyre, Sidon, and contrast with them the Israelites, Ishmaelites, Arabs, &c.

7. *the sons of Cush; Seba*] Seba appears to be the name of a commercial and wealthy region of Ethiopia; see Ps. lxxii. 10; Is. xliii. 3, xlv. 14. In the last passage the Sabeans (Sebaim) are called "men of stature;" and Herodotus says that the Macrobian Ethiopians "were reported to be the tallest and comeliest of men" (III. 20). According to Josephus ('Ant.' II. 10), Meroë was anciently called Seba, until Cambyses gave it the name of his sister Meroë. Meroë is described as a strong fortress situated in a most fertile country at the confluence of the rivers Astophus and Astaborus. The ruins of Meroë still remain to the north-east of the Nubian town of Shendy.

Havilah] Havilah, the son of Joktan, occurs, v. 29, among the descendants of Shem. Some identify the descendants of Havilah the son of Cush with the Avalitæ on the coast of Africa; whilst others place them in Chawlan of Arabia Felix. There is an inevitable confusion from the name of a grandson of Ham being the same as that of a descendant of Shem. Niebuhr and others have asserted that there were two Chawlans, and have ascribed one to the Shemite, the other to the Hamite. It seems very possible that the descendants of Havilah the son of Cush intermingled with the descendants of Havilah the Joktanide, and so ultimately formed but one people, whose dwelling-place was Chawlan, the well-known fertile region of Yemen.

Sabtah] By Gesenius and others, who confine the Cushites to Africa, the descendants of Sabtah are placed on the African shore of the Gulf of Arabia. More commonly, and more probably, their home is sought for in

9 He was a mighty hunter before the LORD: wherefore it is said, Even as Nimrod the mighty hunter before the LORD.

10 And the beginning of his kingdom was † Babel, and Erech, and Accad, and Calneh, in the land of Shinar.

† Gr. *Babylon.*

Hadramaut, a province of Southern Arabia, where Pliny (VI. 32) places the city of Sabbatha or Sabotha. It is said, that to this day in Yemen and Hadramaut there is a dark race of men distinguished from the fairer Arabs, and belonging evidently to a different original stock. (Knobel.)

Raamah] LXX. Rhegma. The connection of Raamah with Sheba and Dedan, of whom he is here said to be the father (cp. Ezek. xxvii. 22), leaves no doubt, even with those who confine the other Cushites to Ethiopia, that the settlement of Raamah must be sought for in Southern Arabia, in the neighbourhood of Sheba and Dedan. Ptolemy (VI. 7) places Rhēgma, and Steph. Byzant. Rhēgma on the shore of the Persian Gulf.

Sabtechah] is by some placed in Ethiopia. Bochart, who is followed by Knobel, places it in Caramania, on the Eastern shore of the Persian Gulf, where the ancients (Ptolem. VI. 8; Steph. Byz. 2) mention Samidace or Samydace.

Sheba, and Dedan] Sheba occurs again in v. 28 as a son of Joktan, and Sheba and Dedan together, Gen. xxv. 3, as children of Joktan, the son of Abraham and Keturah. This is evidently another example of the intermingling of the Cushites with the Joktanides, and generally of the early descendants of Shem and Ham. In Ezek. xxvii. 15—20 we find the Cushite Dedan supplying Tyre with merchandise brought from beyond the sea, while the Shemite Dedan supplies the produce of flocks. Sheba is known to us as an important and opulent region of Arabia Felix. (1 K. x. 1; Ps. lxxii. 10. 15; Job i. 15, vi. 19; Is. lx. 6; Jer. vi. 20; Ezek. xxvii. 22; Joel iii. 8.) The Sabeans are spoken of by Strabo (XVI. p. 777) as a most opulent and powerful people, famous for myrrh, frankincense, and cinnamon, their chief city being Mariaba, (in Arab. Marib). This was afterwards the famous kingdom of the Himyaritic Arabs, so called probably from the ruling family of Himyar. It is probable, that the Cushite Sheba, and his brother Dedan, were settled on the shore of the Persian Gulf (see Raamah above); but afterwards were combined with the great Joktanide kingdom of the Sabeans.

8. *Cush begat Nimrod*] Nimrod is here separated from the other sons of Cush, perhaps because of his great fame and mighty prowess; but it is quite possible, that the words "Cush begat Nimrod" may only mean that Nimrod was a descendant of Cush, not immediately his son, the custom of the Hebrews being to call any ancestor a father, and any descendant a son. The name Nimrod is commonly derived from the Hebrew *marad*, to *rebel*. The Eastern traditions make him a man of violent, lawless habits, a rebel against God, and an usurper of boundless authority over his fellow-men, at whose instigation men began the building of the tower of Babel. (Jos. 'Ant.' I. 4.) He has accordingly been identified with the Orion of the Greeks, and it has been thought that the constellation Orion, called by the Hebrew *Kesil* "the fool, the impious," and by the Arabs "the giant," was connected with Nimrod, who is said in the LXX. to have been a "giant on the earth." The Scripture narrative, however, says nothing of this violence and lawlessness, and the later tradition is very doubtful and vague. The LXX. spell the name Nebrod, so also Josephus, which some have referred to a Persian root signifying *war*, a warrior; but this etymology is altogether uncertain, and not to be relied on.

he began to be a mighty one in the earth] He was the first of the sons of Noah distinguished by his warlike prowess. The word "mighty one" (in the LXX. "giant") is constantly used for a great warrior, a hero, or man of renown. Cp. Gen. vi. 4; Judg. vi. 12; xi. 1; 1 S. ix. 1; 2 K. v. 1; Ps. xxxiii. 16, lxxviii. 65; Is. xiii. 3, &c.

9. *He was a mighty hunter*] LXX. "a giant hunter." Bochart says that by being a famous hunter, he gathered to himself all the enterprising young men of his generation, attached them to his person, and so became a kind of king among them, training his followers first in the chase, and then leading them to war. Compare Hercules, Theseus, Meleager, &c. among the Greeks. The Jerusalem Targum renders "He was mighty in hunting and in sin before the Lord, for he was a hunter of the sons of men in their languages." The Syriac also renders "a warrior." Following these, many have understood, that he was a hunter of men, rather than a hunter of beasts.

before the LORD] Is most likely added only to give emphasis, or the force of a superlative (cp. Gen. xiii. 10, xxx. 8, xxxv. 5; 1 S. xi. 7, xiv. 15, xxvi. 12; Ps. civ. 16; Jonah iii. 3; Acts vii. 20): though some understand "against the Lord," as 1 Chron. xiv. 8, where it is said "David went out against them," literally "before them."

10. *And the beginning of his kingdom was Babel*] The later Chaldæans and Babylonians

‖ Or, *he went out into Assyria.*
‖ Or, *the*

11 Out of that land ‖went forth
Asshur, and builded Nineveh, and
‖the city Rehoboth, and Calah,

12 And Resen between Nineveh
and Calah: the same *is* a great
city.

streets of the city.

---

spoke a Semitic language, but the most ancient Babylonian inscriptions shew that the earliest inhabitants spoke a Turanian or Cushite tongue, and were therefore of the same race as the Ethiopians and Southern Arabians. Moreover, the most ancient traditions bring the first colonists of Babylon from the South. Thus Belus, son of Poseidon and Libya, is said to have led a colony from Egypt into Babylonia, and there fixing his seat on the Euphrates, to have consecrated the priests called in Babylon Chaldæans (Diod. Sic. lib. I. c. ii.): and the fish-god Oannes, the great civilizer of Babylon, is said to have risen out of the Red Sea (Syncell. 'Chron.' p. 28). Nimrod is probably to be identified with Belus; but the word Belus itself (= Bel = Baal) is not so much a name as a title, meaning *lord* or *master*, and may have been given traditionally to the first founder of empire in the earth. The words "beginning of his kingdom" may signify that Babel was the *first*, or possibly that it was the chief city founded by Nimrod.

Erech] The Targums, Ephraim Syr. and Jerome, render *Edessa.* Bochart says Areca on the confines of Babylonia and Susiana: but it is now generally agreed to be Archoë, the ruins of which, called Warka, lie about thirty hours to the south east of Babylon. The numerous mounds and remains of bricks and coffins indicate that this was probably the burying place of the kings of Assyria. (See Rawlinson, 'Five Monarchies,' Vol. I. p. 23.)

Accad] Spelt Archad by the LXX. and Achar by the Syr., has been compared by Bochart with the river Argades in Sithacene, the whole region having perhaps been called Archada. Le Clerc, who is followed by Gesenius, suggests Sacada, a town lying not far below Nineveh, where the Lycus falls into the Tigris. Knobel proposes a tract north of Babylon called Accete. The only ancient authorities (the Targums of Jerusalem and Pseudo-Jonathan, Ephraim Syrus, Jerome, Barhebræus) render the word by *Nisibis*, a city on the river Khabour. Michaelis and many moderns adopt this as the probable site of Accad.

Calneh] (Calneh, Amos vi. 2. Calno, Is. x. 9, perhaps Canneh, Ezek. xxvii. 23, where one of De Rossi's MSS. reads Kalneh). Targg. Jer. and Pseudo-Jon., Euseb., Jerome, Ephr. Syr. give Ctesiphon on the east bank of the Tigris, opposite Seleucia, N.E. of Babylon. The name Calneh survived in Chalonitis, a region of Assyria, where Pliny places Ctesiphon. In this identification of Calneh with Ctesiphon most modern interpreters agree.

Shinar] Unquestionably the country round about Babylon, the great plain or alluvial country watered by the Tigris and Euphrates. The name seems to have been Jewish; though there was a town in Mesopotamia known to the ancients, called Singara (Arab. Sinjar); and Rawlinson found in the Assyrian and Babylonian inscriptions the name *Sinkareh* in cuneiform characters. The name too is found in Egyptian monuments of the 18th dynasty, from Thothmes I.

11. *Out of that land went forth Asshur*] So LXX., Syr., Vulg., Saad., Luth., Calv., J. D. Michael., Dathe, Ros., V. Bohlen. But the reading of the margin, "**From this land he went out into Assyria,**" is the rendering of all the Targums, of Nachmanides, and after them, of Drusius, Bochart, Le Clerc, De Wette, Baumg., Tuch, Gesenius, Knobel, Delitzsch, Kalisch, and most modern interpreters. The syntax fully admits of this interpretation; and the general sense of the passage requires it. Nimrod is the subject here treated of. Asshur, the son of Shem, v. 22, was at least a generation older than Nimrod, who may probably have first colonized the country called after him, Asshur (or Assyria); Nimrod, or one of his descendants, afterwards invading and governing that country. Asshur was a region through which the Tigris flowed, to the N.E. of Babylonia, including a portion of Mesopotomia.

and builded Nineveh] According to Herodotus, Ninus (the mythic founder of Nineveh) was the grandson of Belus, the mythic founder of Babylon (Herod. I. 7). This, the most ancient Greek tradition, well corresponds with the account of Scripture, for the words "he went out into Asshur," might be rendered "one went out into Asshur," not distinctly defining Nimrod as the individual who built Nineveh.

Nineveh, the ancient metropolis of Assyria, on the East branch of the Tigris, became in after ages the largest and most flourishing city of the old world. It is described in the book of Jonah as "an exceeding great city of three days' journey" (Jon. iii. 3), with 120,000 children "who knew not their right hand from their left" (Jon. iv. 11), which would make a population of about 2,000,000. According to Diodorus Siculus, it was no less than 55 miles in circumference (Diod. II. 3), built, no doubt, like the ancient cities of the East, with pastures and pleasure grounds interspersed among streets and houses. Even in Babylon, which was of less extent than Nineveh, Diodorus (II. 9) says, that there were gardens and orchards, and land sufficient

13 And Mizraim begat Ludim, and Anamim, and Lehabim, and Naphtuhim,

14 And Pathrusim, and Casluhim, (out of whom came Philistim,) and Caphtorim.

---

to provide corn for all the people in case of a siege. Nineveh is mentioned among the cities or fortresses captured by Thothmes III. (see Excursus, p. 1). It was attacked by Phraortes the Mede, who perished in the attempt to take it (Herod. I. 102). His successor, Cyaxares, having laid siege to it, B.C. 625, was obliged to raise the siege by an incursion of Scythians (Herod. I. 103); but finally succeeded in reducing it, B.C. 597 (Herod. I. 106). From that time it lay desolate, though Tacitus ('Ann.' XII. 13) and Ammianus (XVIII. 7) mention a fortress of the name. Its site has been identified by modern travellers with the ruins of Nebbi Yunus and Koyunjik, nearly opposite to Mosul on the East banks of the Tigris. (See esp. Layard, 'Ninev.' Vol. II. pp. 136 ff.) The language of the inscriptions discovered in these ruins appears to be an ancient Semitic dialect. This is not inconsistent with the foundation of the city by a descendant of Nimrod; for the indigenous race was no doubt derived from the colonization by Asshur, the son of Shem, and the adoption of the Semitic language has parallels in the cases of Babylon and Canaan (see above on v. 6). Moreover, it is thought that in Assyria, as well as in Babylonia, two distinct languages existed, the older being Turanian, the other Semitic; accordingly, at Koyunjik, vocabularies have been discovered with two languages arranged in parallel columns, and tablets apparently in a Turanian dialect have been found in the ruins.

11. *and the city Rehoboth*] Lit. "the streets of the city."

12. *the same is a great city*] It is extremely difficult to identify Rehoboth, Resen and Calah with any known sites. Perhaps the most probable conjecture is, that the four cities here named, viz. Nineveh, Rehoboth-Ir, Resen, and Calah, were all afterwards combined under the one name of Nineveh, and that the words, v. 12, "the same is a great city," applied to this united whole, not to the single state of Resen. This is adopted by Niebuhr, Grote, Knobel, Rawlinson, Delitzsch.

13. *Ludim*] There was also a son of Shem named Lud, v. 22; but these Ludim were an African tribe. They are probably the same as Retu, the Egyptian name for "man," especially the Egyptians. The name appears to have belonged to the old population of Central Egypt. In Jerem. xlvi. 9, Cush, Phut, and Ludim are mentioned together, the Ludim are said to "handle and bend the bow," and all are placed in the army of Pharaoh-Necho, king of Egypt. Again, in Ezek. xxx. 4, 5, Cush, Phut, and Lud are connected with Mizraim. In Isaiah, on the contrary, we find (lxvi. 19) Lud "that draw the bow" connected with Asiatic and European tribes, Tarshish, Pul, Tubal, and Javan. The existence of the two tribes both called Lud, the one Semite and the other Hamite, is inevitably a cause of confusion.

Anamim] Another Mizraite race, concerning whom no certain or very probable conjecture can be made. Knobel identifies them with an Egyptian name of the Delta.

Lehabim] Generally agreed to be the same as the Lubim, 2 Chr. xii. 3, xvi. 8, reckoned among the Ethiopian forces, and in Nah. iii. 9, Dan. xi. 43, named with the Egyptians; according to Josephus, the Libyans. The original home of this people appears to have been to the west of the Delta.

Naphtuhim] Mentioned only here and 1 Chr. i. 11. Bochart, followed by Michaelis, Jablonski, Gesenius and others, compares the name of the Egyptian goddess Nephthys, the wife of Typhon, to whom the parts of Egypt bordering on the Red Sea were consecrated. Plutarch ('De Is.' p. 355) says, "The Egyptians call the extremities of the land bordering on the sea by the name of Nephthys." If this be so, the Naphtuchim were probably a people dwelling on the Red Sea on the confines of Egypt. Knobel supposes them to have been the midland Egyptians, who in their great city Memphis worshipped Phthah, and were called in Coptic Phaphthah, "the (people) of Phthah."

14. *Pathrusim*] The people of Pathros, mentioned often in the prophets (as Is. xi. 11; Jer. xliv. 1; Ezek. xxix. 14, xxx. 14). The name Pathros occurs, sometimes as if it were separate from Egypt, sometimes as if it were part of Egypt; whence Bochart concluded that the Thebaid was intended, which at times is reckoned as in Upper Egypt, at times as distinct from it. Pliny mentions Phaturites as a præfecture of the Thebaid, ('Hist. Nat.' l. v. c. 9, § 47). The words of Ezekiel (xxix. 14), where Pathros is called the land of the Egyptians' birth, is compared with Herod. (II. 15), who says Thebes was anciently called Egypt. Pa-t-res in Egyptian means "the land of the south."

Casluhim] Bochart conjectured the Colchians, who were an Egyptian colony (Herod. II. 104; Diod. Sic. I. 28; Strabo. I. 3). In this he is followed by Gesenius and others, though the similarity of name seems the chief reason for the identification. Forster ('Ep. ad Michael.' p. 16 sqq.) conjectured Casiotis,

† Heb. *Tzidon.*

15 ¶ And Canaan begat †Sidon his firstborn, and Heth,

16 And the Jebusite, and the Amorite, and the Girgasite,

---

a region between Gaza and Pelusium, so called from Mount Casius. He is followed in this by Knobel, who says the name in Coptic signifies *burning*, hence applicable to a dry, arid, desert region. He combines Bochart's view with Forster's, supposing that the Colchians were a colony from Casiotis. This view is adopted and ably defended by Ebers ('Ægypten,' &c. p. 120).

Out of whom came Philistim] In Jer. xlvii. 4, Amos ix. 7, the Philistines are traced to the Caphtorim. Hence Michaelis and others think that there has been a transposition in this verse, and that it ought to run "and Caphtorim, out of whom came Philistim." The Samaritan text, however, and all Versions read as the Hebrew. Bochart therefore has conjectured, that the Casluchim and Caphtorim were tribes which intermingled, the Caphtorim having strengthened the Casluchian colony by immigration, and that hence the Philistines may have been said to have come from either. The name Philistine, which probably comes from an Æthiopic verb fălăsă, *to emigrate*, is often rendered by the LXX. (as Judg. xiv. 3, xiv. 1) by *allophyloi*, aliens, foreigners.

The following difficulties are urged against the Egyptian origin of the Philistines; first, that their language was probably, like that of the other inhabitants of Canaan, Semitic; secondly, that they were uncircumcised (1 S. xvii. 26), whilst Herodotus tells us that the Egyptians were circumcised. The linguistic difficulty may be explained by the very probable supposition, that the invading Philistines or Caphtorim adopted the language of the conquered Avim (Deut. ii. 23), or other tribe amongst whom they settled. The other disappears, if we consider, that everything in dress, customs, and religion of the Philistines indicates that they separated off from the other Mizraic tribes at a very early period, and that circumcision was probably adopted by the Egyptians at a much later date.

Caphtorim] It is plain from Jer. xlvii. 4, where the Philistines are called "the remnant of the isle (or maritime country) of Caphtor," that we must look for the site of the Caphtorim near the sea. The Targums and ancient Versions render Cappadocia, followed by most of the ancients, and by Bochart. Others (Swinton, Michaelis, Rosenmüller, &c.) have conjectured Cyprus, the original name of which has been thought to have been Cubdr or Cyptrus. Calmet and others prefer Crete, comparing the statement of Tacitus ('Hist.' v. 2) concerning the Cretan origin of the Jews, and supposing that he may have confounded the Jews with the Philistines. Gesenius mentions this with approval, and it is advocated by Knobel. Recent investigations in Egyptian identify Caphtor with Capht-ur, i.e. the Great Capht. This is compared with the Egyptian name Coptos. Again, the name Ægyptus is probably identical with Ai-Capht, i.e. the coast of Capht, (compare אִי כַּפְתּוֹר, *I-Caphtor*, "the isle or coast of Caphtor," Jer. xlvii. 4). This Capht, or Capht-ur, was probably the Northern Delta, from which the Phœnicians emigrated into Asia. Thus Capht became the Egyptian name for the oldest Phœnicians, whether in Asia or in Africa. (See Ebers, 'Ægypt.' &c. voc. *Caphtorim;* see also Excursus.)

15. *Sidon his first-born*] Sidon was, according to Justin (XVIII. 3), the oldest Phœnician state. Of all the Phœnicians Homer knew only Sidon. The city stood on the Eastern coast of the Mediterranean, about 20 miles North of Tyre, which latter is said by Justin to have been a colony of Sidon. So important was Sidon in most ancient times, that all the Phœnicians are comprised under the name of Sidonians (Josh. xiii. 6; Judg. xviii. 7): and this extension of the name was known to the Greeks and Romans (compare *Urbs Sidonia, i.e.* Carthage, which was a colony of Tyre, Virg. 'Æn.' I. 677; and *Sidonia Dido*, 'Æn.' I. 446, 613, &c.). The name Sidon is supposed to be derived from *fishing;* for the Phœnicians called fish Sidon (Gesen. 'Thesaur.' p. 1153).

Heth] The ancestors of the Hittites, who inhabited the hill country of Judea, especially in the neighbourhood of Hebron. These, however, were but one portion of the race, which according to Josh. i. 4 (cp. Ezek. xvi. 3) became more important. In the time of Solomon and Joram there were independent kings of the Hittites, 1 K. x. 29; 2 K. vii. 6. They are by most Egyptologers identified with the Kheta, a very powerful tribe, and masters of Syria.

16. *the Jebusite*] Inhabitants of Jebus, the ancient name of Jerusalem, mentioned Judg. xix. 10, 11; 1 Chr. xi. 4, 5. The Jebusites, a mountain tribe (Num. xiii. 29; Josh. xi. 3), seem never to have been conquered, or to have recovered possession of Jerusalem and to have retained it, till David took Jebus, 1 Chr. xi. 4, 5: and even after the conquest we find Araunah the Jebusite, who is called "Araunah the king" (2 S. xxiv. 23) living in peace and prosperity in the land.

the Amorite] Apparently the most powerful and widespread of all the Canaanitish tribes, dwelling chiefly in the hill-country of Judæa, subject to five kings (Josh. x. 5), but

17 And the Hivite, and the Arkite,
and the Sinite,
18 And the Arvadite, and the Zemarite, and the Hamathite: and afterward were the families of the Canaanites spread abroad.
19 And the border of the Canaanites was from Sidon, as thou comest
to Gerar, unto †Gaza; as thou goest,
unto Sodom, and Gomorrah, and Admah, and Zeboim, even unto Lasha.
20 These *are* the sons of Ham,
after their families, after their tongues,
in their countries, *and* in their nations.
21 ¶ Unto Shem also, the father
of all the children of Eber, the brother of Japheth the elder, even to
him were *children* born.

† Heb. *Azzah.*

---

also spreading to the other side of Jordan, to the North of the Arnon (Numb. xxi. 13), even to the river Jabbok (Num. xxi. 24). Simonis, followed by Gesenius, traces the name to an old word Amor or Emor, *elevation*, *mountain*, the Amorites being mountaineers or highlanders.

the Girgasite] Josephus ('Ant.' I. 6) says we have the name and nothing else of this people. Eusebius and others have identified them with the Gergesenes (Matt. viii. 28), who lived to the East of the Lake of Gennesaret. There is a difference of reading in St Matt.; some MSS. having Gerasenes, others Gadarenes; but Gesenius thinks, that Gerasa is but a corruption by the omission of *g* from Girgasa.

17. *the Hivite*] A people living in the neighbourhood of Hermon and Lebanon (Josh. xi. 3, Judg. vi. 3), near Sichem also (Gen. xxxiv. 2), and Gibeon (Josh. ix. 1, 7): Gesenius interprets the name to signify *pagani*, the inhabitants of villages.

the Arkite] Inhabitants, according to Josephus, of Arca a city of Phœnicia, near Libanus, 12 miles to the north of Tripoli. It was afterwards called Cesarea Libani, a name found on coins of the reign of Vespasian. Alexander Severus was born here. Shaw and Burckhardt describe the ruins of a fine city as still to be found there, called *Tell Arka*.

the Sinite] St Jerome ('Quæst. in Genes.' ad h. l.) says, that "near Arca was another city called Sini, which, though ruined, still retained its ancient name." Michaelis ('Spicil.' Pt. II. p. 29) quotes Breidenbach ('Itiner.' p. 47) as mentioning a city of the name of *Syn* in the same neighbourhood in the fifteenth century.

18. *the Arvadite*] Inhabitants probably of the city of Aradus, on an island of the same name, about three miles from the Phœnician coast. The LXX. render here and elsewhere the Aradite, and Josephus ('Ant.' I. 6) says "the Aradite inhabited the island of Aradus." Gesenius derives the name from a root, signifying "to wander," and quotes Strabo (XVI. 2, § 13) as saying that the city was built by fugitives from Sidon.

the Zemarite] There is little certainty as to the habitation of this race. The ancient interpreters, Targg., Rashi, Saad., and probably Jerome, give Emesa; Michaelis, led by Bochart's conjecture and followed by Rosenm., Gesen., Knobel, suggests Samyra, a city of Phœnicia on the sea coast, near the river Eleutherus, the ruins of which are still called Samra.

the Hamathite] Hamath was an important city, called by Amos (vi. 2) "Great Hamath," the chief city of Upper Syria on the Orontes at the foot of Libanus (Judg. iii. 3; Jer. xlix. 23; Zech. ix. 2), the metropolis of a region called the "land of Hamath" (2 K. xxiii. 33). It was called Epiphaneia by the Macedonians (Jos. 'Ant.' I. 6). It still however in the East retains the name of Hamah, and has been visited and described by Burckhardt and other modern travellers.

and afterward were the families of the Canaanites spread abroad] The first place of habitation of the Canaanites was probably on the Mediterranean, in Phœnicia, in the neighbourhood of Tyre and Sidon; but by degrees they spread abroad through the whole of Palestine, from Tyre and Sidon on the North to Gerar and Gaza and even to Lasha.

19. *Lasha*] The Targum of Jerusalem and Jerome ('Quæst. ad Genes.') identify Lasha with Callirrhoë, which Pliny ('N. H.' v. c. 6) and Josephus ('B. J.' I. 33) speak of as famous for its warm springs. It was situated on the East of the Red Sea.

21. *Shem also, the father of all the children of Eber*] As Ham is specially called the father of Canaan, so probably Shem is designated as the father of Eber. The Hebrews and the Canaanites were brought into constant conflict and exemplified respectively the characters of the Hamites and the Shemites, their characters and their destinies.

the brother of Japheth the elder] There is a great ambiguity in the original of these words. The LXX., Symm., Targ. of Onkelos render as in the English text; so Rashi, Abenezra, Luther, Cleric., J. D. Michael., Dathe, &c. But the Syriac, Arab., Vulg. render "the elder brother of Japheth," in which they are followed by Rosenm., Gesenius, Knobel, Delitzsch and most modern com-

[c] 1 Chron. 1. 17. † Heb. *Arpachshad.*

22 The [c]children of Shem; Elam,
and Asshur, and †Arphaxad, and Lud,
and Aram.
23 And the children of Aram; Uz,
and Hul, and Gether, and Mash.
24 And Arphaxad begat †Salah;
and Salah begat Eber.
25 [d]And unto Eber were born two
sons: the name of one *was* Peleg;
for in his days was the earth divid-

† Heb. *Shelah.* [d] 1 Chron. 1. 19.

---

mentators, who say, that if "the brother of Japheth the Elder" had been meant, the Hebrew idiom would have required the addition of "*son*"—"the elder son of Noah." This appears to be true: moreover, Shem is generally mentioned first, and is perhaps put last here, because the writer proceeds almost without interruption from this point with the history of the descendants of Shem. In Gen. ix. 24, Ham appears to be called the youngest son of Noah; but see note on that verse. On the whole, the common order of enumeration is probably the order of age.

22. *The children of Shem*] The Shemites dwelt chiefly in Western Asia, South of the Asiatic Japhethites.

Elam] Elymais, a region adjoining Susiana and Media, called by the Arabs Chuzistan. Daniel (viii. 2) places Shushan (*i. e.* Susa) in Elam, which immediately connects Elam with Susiana.

Asshur] Without doubt the ancestor of the Assyrians. At first, perhaps, the name Asshur or Assyria was restricted to the region round about Nineveh, known to the Greeks as Adiabene. Afterwards it spread, especially to the North-west, and embraced the Syrians. The foundation of its principal greatness is ascribed to the Babylonians in v. 11. This corresponds with the tradition in Herodotus (I. 7), which attributes the foundation of Nineveh to Ninus, the son of Belus, the founder of Babylon.

Arphaxad] Bochart conjectured that the name Arrapachites, a province in Northern Assyria, bordering on Armenia, was derived from Arphaxad; and as this was the country of the Chaldees, it has been thought that in the three last consonants of the name Arphaxad, viz. ch-s-d, are contained the elements of the name Chasdim (i. e. Chaldæans). Josephus certainly tells us that "Arphaxad gave the name Arphaxadæans to those afterwards called Chaldæans" ('Ant.' I. 6).

Lud] Josephus says the Lydians ('Ant.' I. 6). He is followed by Euseb., Jerome, and by Bochart, and most moderns. The resemblance of their manners and of their more ancient names to the Semitic confirms this tradition. It is probable, that their first home was not far from Armenia, whence they migrated into Asia Minor.

Aram] The country called Aram in Scripture was the highland region lying to the north-east of the Holy Land, extending from the Jordan and the Sea of Galilee to the Euphrates. The name Aram has been supposed to mean *high* (from *Aram* = *rūm*, to be high). In Genesis we read of Aram-Naharaim, *i.e.* Aram between the two rivers = Mesopotamia, which, or part of which, is also called Padan-Aram; and Laban who dwelt there is called the Aramean (Gen. xxv. 20, &c.). Homer ('Il.' II. 783); Hesiod ('Th.' 304); Pindar ('Fr.' v. 3), &c. speak of the Syrians as Arimi.

23. *Uz*] From him no doubt was named "the land of Uz," in which Job lived. (Job i. 1.) It is there rendered by the LXX. Ausitis. Ptolemy (V. 19) mentions the Æsitæ as inhabiting the northern part of Arabia Deserta, near to Babylon and the Euphrates, which Bochart, Gesenius, and others, identify with the inhabitants of Uz or Ausitis. The name Uz occurs also among the descendants of Abraham (Gen. xxii. 21), and again (Gen. xxxvi. 28) among the descendants of Seir the Hivite; and it has been conjectured, with more or less probability, that these different Semitic families may have coalesced.

Hul] Josephus places in Armenia, according to Bochart, that part called Cholobotene by the Greeks, as though it were Beth-Chul, the home of Hul. Michaelis, followed by Knobel, suggests that the name Cœlesyria may have come from Hul or Chul. Rosenmüller has suggested the Ard el Hhuleh, a district near the sources of the Jordan.

Gether] No probable site has been fixed on for the descendants of Gether.

Mash] Josephus ('Ant.' I. 6) says, "Mash founded the Mesanæans," *i.e.* the inhabitants of Mesene, near Bassora, where the Tigris and Euphrates fall into the Persian Gulf. The opinion of Bochart is adopted by Gesenius, Winer, Knobel, and others, that the descendants of Mash were the inhabitants of Mons Masius, a range of hills to the North of Mesopotamia.

24. *Arphaxad begat Salah; and Salah begat Eber*] The name *Salah* appears to signify *sending forth*, *extension*, as *Eber*, the name of his son, signifies *passing over*. Many of the names in these genealogies are significant, and were probably given to their bearers late in life, or even historically, after their deaths. Salah and Eber seem to point to this fact, that the descendants of Arphaxad were now beginning to spread forth from the first cradle of the Semitic race, and to cross over the

ed; and his brother's name *was* Joktan.
26 And Joktan begat Almodad, and Sheleph, and Hazarmaveth, and Jerah,
27 And Hadoram, and Uzal, and Diklah,
28 And Obal, and Abimael, and Sheba,
29 And Ophir, and Havilah, and

---

great rivers on their way to Mesopotamia, and thence to Canaan.

25. *Peleg; for in his days was the earth divided*] It is generally supposed from this, that Peleg lived contemporaneously with the dispersion of Babel. It is, however, quite possible, that the reference is to a more partial division of regions and separation of races. The genealogy is now specially concerned with the descendants of Shem and the ancestry of the promised race, which is here traced down to Peleg to be continued farther in ch. xi. 18 sqq. The two races, which sprang from Eber, soon separated very widely from each other, the one, Eber and his family, spreading north-westward towards Mesopotamia and Syria, the other, the Joktanides, southward into Arabia. As the sacred narrative in vv. 31, 32, speaks expressly of the general spreading forth of the sons of Noah, and in ch. xi. 1—9 relates the confusion of their languages, it is very probable that in this verse the division of the land concerns only the separation of the Shemites.

Joktan] There is a general consent in favour of the colonization of Southern Arabia by the descendants of Joktan, with the names of whom correspond several of the districts and cities of that country. The Arabs identify Joktan with Kahtan, who was the traditional ancestor of the Beni Kahtan, inhabitants of Yemen or Arabia Felix. In Arabia the Joktanides, no doubt, found some peoples settled there already, viz. the Cushite descendants of Ham (ver. 7), and the Ludite descendants of Shem (ver. 22). The Arabic authors are silent concerning any Cushites, but derive the ancient Arabic races from the Kahtanides (*i.e.* the Joktanides).

26. *Almodad*] The names Modad and Morad (*r* being often a corruption of *d* by a clerical error) occur frequently in Arabic genealogies. The syllable *Al* is probably the definite article.

Sheleph] has been compared by Bochart with the Salopeni of Ptolemy (VI. 7), inhabiting the interior of Arabia, and is identified with a tribe of Sulaph or Seliph in Yemen. The Arabic writers speak of a large region called Salfie, south-west of Sanaa.

Hazarmaveth] The name agrees in every letter with Hadramaut, the name of a province on the southern coast of Arabia, famous for its fertility in myrrh and frankincense, and for the unhealthiness of its climate.

Jerah] The name in Hebrew signifies the *moon*. Bochart has suggested the identification of his descendants with the Alilæi (Agatharch. c. 49; Strabo, XVI. p. 277) = the Beni Hilal ("the sons of the new moon"), who dwelt south of Chawlan.

27. *Hadoram*] There has been no satisfactory identification of the descendants of Hadoram with any known race, though Bochart compared the Adramitæ of Ptolemy (VI. 7) and the Atramitæ of Pliny (VI. 28) in the south of Arabia.

Uzal] This name is identified with Awzal, the ancient name of Sanaa, the capital city of Yemen.

Diklah] in Syriac signifies *Palm;* whence Bochart and Gesenius identified the descendants of Diklah with the Minæi, a people of Yemen, who inhabited a palm-growing country. Michaelis conjectured a people contiguous to the Tigris, the name of which river in Syriac and Arabic was Diklat.

28. *Obal, and Abimael*] Only very uncertain conjectures have been made as to these names.

Sheba] We read much of Sheba, a country in Arabia Felix, abounding in gold, precious stones, frankincense, and famous for its merchandise (1 K. x. 10; Job vi. 19; Ps. lxxii. 10, 15; Is. lx. 6; Jer. vi. 20; Ezek. xxvii. 22; Joel iii. 8). The Arabic and Greek accounts of the Sabæans, a people, whose capital was Saba or Mariaba, three or four days' journey from Senaa, correspond thoroughly with all this. See on ver. 7 above.

29. *Ophir*] On no geographical question has a greater diversity of opinion existed than on the site of Ophir. The position of Ophir, as a son of Joktan, and the settlement of the other Joktanides in Arabia, form a strong argument in favour of placing Ophir in Arabia also. The historical notices, however, in the books of Kings and Chronicles (1 K. ix. 26—28, x. 11, xxii. 48; 2 Chr. viii. 18, ix. 10) have inclined many to place Ophir either in India or in Africa: whilst others have thought, that two Ophirs are mentioned in Scripture, one in Arabia, the other in India or Ceylon. The question is discussed at length by Gesenius, 'Thes.' p. 142. See also 'Dict. of Bible,' s. v. Ophir.

Havilah] It is generally thought that Chawlan, in Arabia Felix, was the home of the descendants of Havilah. (On the Cushite Havilah, see note on v. 7.) Whilst some have thought that there were two Chaw-

Jobab: all these *were* the sons of Joktan.

30 And their dwelling was from Mesha, as thou goest unto Sephar a mount of the east.

31 These *are* the sons of Shem, after their families, after their tongues, in their lands, after their nations.

32 These *are* the families of the sons of Noah, after their generations, in their nations: and by these were the nations divided in the earth after the flood.

CHAPTER XI.

1 *One language in the world.* 3 *The building of Babel.* 5 *The confusion of tongues.* 10 *The generations of Shem.* 27 *The generations of Terah the father of Abram.* 31 *Terah goeth from Ur to Haran.*

AND [a] the whole earth was of one [a] Wisd. 10. 5.
†language, and of one †speech. † Heb. *lip.*
2 And it came to pass, as they † Heb. *words.*
journeyed from the east, that they
found a plain in the land of Shinar;
and they dwelt there.
3 And †they said one to another, † Heb. *a man said to his neighbour.*
Go to, let us make brick, and †burn
them throughly. And they had brick † Heb. *burn them to a burning.*
for stone, and slime had they for
morter.
4 And they said, Go to, let us

lans, one belonging to the descendants of the Joktanide and the other to the sons of the Cushite Havilah; others have thought that the two races were intermingled and confounded.

Jobab] Ptolemy (VI. 7) mentions the Jobaritæ near the Indian Sea, which Bochart conjectured to have been Jobabitæ, in which he is followed by Gesenius. Bochart and Gesenius think the name to be = the Arabic Jebab, *a desert.*

30. *And their dwelling was from Mesha, as thou goest unto Sephar a mount of the East*] Mesha has been identified by Bochart with the seaport of Musa or Muza, mentioned by Ptolemy VI. 8; Pliny VI. 23, &c. Michaelis, followed by Rosenmüller, Gesenius, &c. preferred Mesene, a place at the mouth of the Tigris and Euphrates, not far from Bassora.

Sephar] is pretty certainly Zafâr or Dhafari, a seaport on the coast of Hadramaut. It is pronounced in modern Arabic Isfor, and is not so much one town as a series of villages near the shore of the Indian Ocean. (Fresnel, quoted by Gesenius, p. 968.)

CHAP. XI. **1.** *one language*] The general opinion of the Jews and ancient Christians was that this language was Hebrew. The names of the most ancient places and persons mentioned in Scripture being Hebrew seems to countenance this belief. But it is impossible to arrive at any certainty on the question, it being notorious that names have been translated from one language into another in many instances.

2. *it came to pass, as they journeyed from the east*] On the difficulty in these words, and on the first home of the descendants of Noah, see note on viii. 4. If Armenia was that first home, we must suppose either that they had journeyed in a south-easterly direction before they turned towards Shinar, and then they would journey from the east, or we must render "eastward," lit. "on the sides of the east."

a plain] The word more naturally means a deep valley, but it is often used of a wide vale or plain.

Shinar] Without doubt the region round about Babylon, to which, besides Babylon, pertained the cities of Erech, Kalneh and Accad (Gen. x. 10, where see note). The fertility of this country for the production of wheat is greatly praised by Herodotus (I. 193).

3. *let us make brick, and burn them throughly*] The regions of Assyria and Babylonia consisting of rich alluvial plains would provide no stone and were specially abundant in brick earth. Hence, when Nimrod built Babel and other towns in Shinar (ch. x. 10), he and those with him must have learned the art of brick-making. The building of villages in the earlier settlements of the Noachidæ had been probably of wood or stone.

they had brick for stone, and slime had they for morter] All the versions give *asphalte* or **bitumen** for the word *chemer*, "slime". Herod. (I. 179) describes the building of the walls of Babylon much as the sacred history describes this building of the tower of Babel. He says a deep foss was dug all round the city, from which the mud was taken in large bricks and burnt in furnaces. Then for mud or mortar, they used hot bitumen, and so built the walls of the city. He mentions a town called Is, with a river of the same name near it, about eight days' journey from Babylon, where much bitumen was obtained and carried to Babylon for the building of the city. See also Strabo (Lib. XVI. p. 74), who speaks of the excellence of the Babylonian bitumen for building. Justin also (Lib. I. 2) speaks of Semiramis as having built Babylon with brick and liquid bitumen, which flowed in great abundance in the neighbourhood. Diodor. Sicul. (II. 12),

build us a city and a tower, whose
top *may reach* unto heaven; and let
us make us a name, lest we be scattered abroad upon the face of the
whole earth.

5 And the LORD came down to
see the city and the tower, which the
children of men builded.

6 And the LORD said, Behold, the
people *is* one, and they have all one

Pliny ('H. N.' XXXI. 5), Athenæus (Lib. II. 5), and other ancient writers, mention a lake close to Babylon abounding in bitumen, which floated on the waters. (See Reland, 'Palestin.' II. pp. 244, 245). The town of Is, mentioned by Herodotus (as above), is identified by modern travellers with Heets, where bitumen pits are still found on the western bank of the Euphrates. Some of the heaps of ruins, which have been identified with the ruins of Babylon, exhibit specimens of sun-dried bricks laid in bitumen, producing walls of great strength and solidity. Mr Layard tells us that at Birs Nimrod, "The cement, by which the bricks were united, is of so tenacious a quality, that it is almost impossible to detach one from the other," ('Nineveh and Babylon,' p. 499).

4. *a tower, whose top may reach unto heaven*] That is to say "a very high tower," just as the cities of the Canaanites were said to be "great and walled up to heaven" (Deut. i. 28, ix. 1), or as Homer ('Od.' V. 239), speaks of a pine tree "high as heaven." Many have identified this tower with the temple of Belus (Herod. I. 181), which is described as consisting of eight squares one upon the other, the dimensions of the lowest or base being a stadium in length and in breadth. The mound called Birs Nimroud is generally supposed to be the ruin of the temple of Belus.

let us make us a name, lest we be scattered abroad upon the face of the whole earth] Josephus gives as the motive for building the tower of Babel, that the builders feared another deluge, and hoped that the tower would be high enough to save them from its waters; Nimrod, the leader in the scheme, boasting that he could so defy the vengeance of God. Again some have thought, that Noah had deliberately marked out the settlements of his posterity (Usher, ad A. M. 1757), and that Nimrod and his followers were unwilling to submit to this. Then some Jewish writers have interpreted the word *name* (Shem) to mean God, "the name of God" being often put for God Himself; and so have imagined that the builders of the tower proposed to make an idol temple. Others have supposed that the descendants of Ham under Nimrod made here some reference to Shem, the favoured son of Noah, as though they would have said, "A blessing has been promised to Shem, but we will make a Shem for ourselves." Clericus suggested that the word Shem meant here a monument (cp. 2 S. viii. 13). The simplest sense of the passage seems the true. In ch. x. 10, we find that Nimrod founded a kingdom in Shinar. He and his followers were apparently actuated by an ambitious spirit, not satisfied with the simplicity of a patriarchal life, nor willing to be scattered abroad, as so many were, by the migratory instinct that seems to have led the descendants of Noah thus early to form extensive settlements, but desiring to found an empire, to build a city, with a strong citadel, and so to hold together in a powerful commonwealth, and to establish for themselves a name, fame, importance, renown, thereby, it may be, attracting others to join their community. Perhaps there was an allusion to this in the prophecy (Is. xiv. 22), "I will . . . cut off from Babylon *the name* and remnant and son and nephew" (*i. e.* grandson or posterity) "saith the LORD." The tradition which assigns the lead in the building of the tower of Babel to Nimrod was ancient and general. (See Joseph. 'Ant.' I. 4, Aug. 'De Civit. Dei,' XVI. 4, &c.) It may have arisen chiefly from what is said of him in ch. x. 9, 10, 11. It is worthy of remark, that, though the descendants of Shem and Japheth shared in the judgment which confounded the tongues, yet their dialects have to this day a nearer resemblance between themselves than those which may perhaps be attributed to the children of Ham. As the Shemites and Japhethites have had a higher civilization, so they have retained a purer language. The Semitic dialects all have a strong family likeness. The Aryan or Indo-European (*i.e.* probably the Japhetic) dialects, though more diverse than the Semitic, are yet all easily assignable to a common origin; whilst the Turanian and other languages branch off into endless varieties.

5. *the LORD came down to see*] An instance of the natural anthropomorphic language suited to the teaching of man in a state of simple and partial civilization.

the children of men builded] It has been thought, though perhaps on insufficient ground, that "children of men" as in ch. vi. 2, designates the impious portion of the human race, bad men, as opposed to "children of God;" and possibly the rebellious offspring of Ham.

6. *this they begin to do*] Perhaps rather "this is the beginning of their deeds." This is their first act of daring and impiety, and unless they be effectually checked, nothing will restrain them from going farther and farther.

language; and this they begin to do:
and now nothing will be restrained
from them, which they have imagined
to do.
7 Go to, let us go down, and there
confound their language, that they
may not understand one another's
speech.
8 So the LORD scattered them
abroad from thence upon the face of
all the earth: and they left off to
build the city.
9 Therefore is the name of it called
[That is, confusion.] ‖Babel; because the LORD did there
confound the language of all the
earth: and from thence did the LORD
scatter them abroad upon the face of
all the earth.
10 ¶ [b]These *are* the generations [b 1 Chron. 1. 17.]
of Shem: Shem *was* an hundred years
old, and begat Arphaxad two years
after the flood:
11 And Shem lived after he begat
Arphaxad five hundred years, and begat sons and daughters.
12 And Arphaxad lived five and
thirty years, and begat Salah:
13 And Arphaxad lived after he

---

8. *they left off to build the city*] It seems, therefore, very doubtful how far the builders could have proceeded in building their tower, and hardly likely that the famous temple of Belus should have been to any considerable extent erected by them, though not improbably that great structure may have been raised on the foundation laid at this time. The tradition that God overturned it with a tempest (Jos. 'Ant.' I. 6; Euseb. 'Præp. Evang.' IX. 4), though probably unfounded, witnesses to its not having been completed.

9. *Babel*] From *Balal*, to *confound*, contracted from *Balbal*, *confusion*. The Greek tradition was, that the city was named after Belus, its mythic founder. So the Etymologicum Magnum says that "Babylon was named after Belus, who founded it." Hence Eichhorn suggested, that the name originally was Bāb Bel, "the gate or court of Bel," *i.e.* Baal or Belus. So Rosenmüller, Gesenius and others have thought it might be Bāb Il, the "Gate of God." These derivations are really much less likely than that given by Moses. There was no such person as Belus, except that Nimrod, whose scriptural name probably signifies *rebel*, may by his own people have been called Baal, Belus, Lord.

10. *These are the generations of Shem*] We have here the third genealogical table. The 1st was given in ch. v. from Adam to Noah; the 2nd in ch. x, the genealogy of the three sons of Noah, the descendants of Shem being traced down as far as Peleg. Now we have the line of Shem farther carried down to Abraham, the father of the faithful, the ancestor of the promised seed. In ch. x. no account is given of the length of the generations or of the duration of life; but here in ch. xi. as before in ch. v., both these are supplied. Concerning the chronological question and the ages of the patriarchs, see Introduction and on ch. v. note A. It may be observed here, that we mark at once the transition from the antediluvian to the postdiluvian duration of life. Noah lived 950 years, Shem only 600, Arphaxad, the first born of Shem after the deluge, only 438; when we come to Peleg, who seems to have been contemporary with the dispersion, life is still shorter, Peleg lived 239 years, Reu 239, Serug 230, Nahor 148.

The following table exhibits the different calculations according to the Hebrew, the Samaritan, and the Septuagint texts respectively.

	Hebrew Text.			Samaritan.			Septuagint.			Hebrew Text.	
	Years before birth of Son.	Rest of Life.	Whole Life.	Years before birth of Son.	Rest of Life.	Whole of Life.	Years before birth of Son.	Rest of Life.	Whole Life.	Year of birth A.M.	Year of death A.M.
Shem	100	500	600	100	500	600	100	500	600	1558	2158
Arphaxad	35	403	438	135	303	438	135	400	535	1658	2097
Kainan							130	330	460		
Salah	30	403	433	130	303	433	130	330	460	1693	2126
Eber	34	430	464	134	270	404	134	270	404	1723	2187
Peleg	30	209	239	130	109	239	130	209	339	1757	1996
Reu	32	207	239	132	107	239	132	207	339	1787	2026
Serug	30	200	230	130	100	230	130	200	330	1819	1997
Nahor	29	119	148	79	69	148	179	125	304	1849	1997
Terah	70	135	205	70	75	145	70	135	209	1878	2083
Abraham										1948	2123

begat Salah four hundred and three
years, and begat sons and daughters.
14 And Salah lived thirty years,
and begat Eber:
15 And Salah lived after he begat
Eber four hundred and three years,
and begat sons and daughters.
16 [c]And Eber lived four and thirty years, and begat [d]Peleg:
17 And Eber lived after he begat
Peleg four hundred and thirty years,
and begat sons and daughters.
18 And Peleg lived thirty years,
and begat Reu:
19 And Peleg lived after he begat
Reu two hundred and nine years, and
begat sons and daughters.
20 And Reu lived two and thirty
years, and begat [e]Serug:
21 And Reu lived after he begat
Serug two hundred and seven years,
and begat sons and daughters.

[c] 1 Chron. 1. 19.
[d] Called, Luke 3. 35 *Phalec.*
[e] Luke 3. 35, *Saruch.*

22 And Serug lived thirty years,
and begat Nahor:
23 And Serug lived after he begat
Nahor two hundred years, and begat
sons and daughters.
24 And Nahor lived nine and
twenty years, and begat [f]Terah:
25 And Nahor lived after he begat
Terah an hundred and nineteen years,
and begat sons and daughters.
26 And Terah lived seventy years,
and [g]begat Abram, Nahor, and Haran.
27 ¶ Now these *are* the generations of Terah: Terah begat Abram,
Nahor, and Haran; and Haran begat
Lot.
28 And Haran died before his father Terah in the land of his nativity,
in Ur of the Chaldees.
29 And Abram and Nahor took
them wives: the name of Abram's
wife *was* Sarai; and the name of
Nahor's wife, Milcah, the daughter

[f] Luke 3. 34, *Thara.*
[g] Joshua 24. 2. 1 Chron. 1. 26.

---

27. *Now these are the generations of Terah*] Not perhaps a distinct genealogy, but the winding up of the genealogy which had already been traced to the sons of Terah, and the expanding it into a fuller account of the families of these sons and especially of Abraham.

28. *Ur of the Chaldees*] Mentioned only here. There is great diversity of opinion as to the site of this city, except that it was in Chaldæa, i.e. the southern part of Babylonia. Bochart, followed by Michaelis, Rosenmüller and many others, identified it with *Ur*, which is mentioned by Ammianus Marcellinus (XXV. 8. col. 26), when describing the return of the Roman army under Jovian after the death of Julian, as lying between Nisibis and the Tigris. Ancient tradition and the opinion of many moderns connect it with the modern Orfa, the Edessa of the Greeks, well known in Christian times as the capital of Abgarus, its first Christian King, who is said to have written a letter to, and to have received a letter from our Saviour. "The traditions of Abraham still live in the mouths of the Arab inhabitants of Orfa. The city lies on the edge of one of the bare rugged spurs which descend from the mountains of Armenia, into the Assyrian plains in the cultivated land, which, as lying under the mountains, was called Padan-Aram. Two physical features must have secured it from the earliest times as a nucleus for the civilization of those regions. One is a high crested crag, the natural fortification of the present citadel, doubly defended by a trench of immense depth, cut out of the living rock behind it. The other is an abundant spring (the Callirrhoe of the Greek writers) issuing in a pool of transparent clearness and embosomed in a mass of luxuriant verdure, which, amidst the dull brown desert all around, makes, and must always have made, this spot an oasis, a Paradise in the Chaldæan wilderness." (Dean Stanley 'On the Jewish Church,' I. p. 7.) Eupolemus as quoted by Euseb. 'Præp. Evang.' IX. 17, says that Abraham was born in the city of Babylonia called Camarine, which some say is the city Uria, and by interpretation city of the Chaldees, which Gesenius explains by saying that *Ur* in Sanscrit signifies *city*, *country*, (cognate perhaps with the Hebrew *Ir*, עִיר), the original language of the Chaldees having been cognate with the Indian and Persian. This city is supposed to be now represented by the ruins Umgheir on the right bank of the Euphrates, which appears by its bricks to have been called Hur by the natives. (Professor Rawlinson in 'Dict. of Bible.')

29. *Iscah*] According to Josephus ('Ant.' I. 6), Targum Pseudo-Jonathan and Jerome ('Qu. in Genes.') the same as Sarai. This, however, hardly seems consistent with Gen. XX. 12, where Abram speaks of Sarai as daughter of his father but not of his mother; though it is very difficult to say with what exactness the terms father, daughter, brother, &c. are used. Ewald has conjectured that Iscah was Lot's wife and therefore mentioned here; but there is no evidence for this.

of Haran, the father of Milcah, and
the father of Iscah.
30 But Sarai was barren; she *had*
no child.
31 And Terah took Abram his
son, and Lot the son of Haran his
son's son, and Sarai his daughter in
law, his son Abram's wife; and they
h Neh. 9. 7. went forth with them from [h] Ur of
Judith 5. 7. the Chaldees, to go into the land of
Acts 7. 4. Canaan; and they came unto Haran,
and dwelt there.
32 And the days of Terah were
two hundred and five years: and Terah died in Haran.

CHAPTER XII.

1 *God calleth Abram, and blesseth him with a promise of Christ.* 4 *He departeth with Lot from Haran.* 6 *He journeyeth through Canaan,* 7 *which is promised him in a vision.* 10 *He is driven by a famine into Egypt.* 11 *Fear maketh him feign his wife to be his sister.* 14 *Pharaoh, having taken her from him, by plagues is compelled to restore her.*

NOW the [a] LORD had said unto a Acts 7. 3.
Abram, Get thee out of thy
country, and from thy kindred, and
from thy father's house, unto a land
that I will shew thee:
2 And I will make of thee a great
nation, and I will bless thee, and

---

31. *and they went forth with them*] i.e. Terah and Abram went forth with Lot and Sarai. The Samaritan (followed by LXX. and Vulg.) by a slight transposition of the letters and different pointing reads "He brought them forth."

Haran] The Carrhæ of the Greeks and Romans, where Crassus fell, defeated by the Parthians (Plutarch, 'Vit. Cras.' 25. 27. 28. Plin. v. 24). It is called Charran in Acts vii. 4.

32. *two hundred and five years*] The Samaritan Pentateuch has here *one hundred and forty five*, which Bochart and others consider the right number. St Stephen (Acts vii. 4) says the migration of Abram into Canaan was after his father's death: but from v. 26 *supra* it seems as if Terah was only 70 when Abram was born, and by xii. 4 we find that Abram was 75 when he left Haran. This, according to the Samaritan, would appear to be the very year of his father's death. It is certain that the Samaritan text cannot have been tampered with by any Christian hand to bring it into conformity with St Stephen's statement, and it may very likely have preserved the true reading. It is possible, however, that Terah may have been really 130 years old when Abram was born: for though it is said in ver. 26 that Terah lived seventy years and begat Abram, Nahor and Haran, yet it does not follow that Abram was the eldest son, having been named first as being the heir of the promises and the subject of the future history. Indeed some of the rabbins consider Abram to have been the youngest son, in which case he may have been born when his father was 130 years old (see Wordsworth on Acts vii. 4).

CHAP. XII. 1. *Now the LORD had said*] **Now the LORD said.** The former chapter had carried the history down to the death of Terah. The present chapter returns to the date of the call of Abram. In Acts vii. 2 St Stephen tells us, what also appears most likely from the history in Gen., that God appeared to Abram "when he was in Mesopotamia, before he dwelt in Charran." This led our translators to render "*had said.*" The Hebrew lacks the pluperfect tense; but the continuous character of the narrative from this point marks the propriety of adopting a simple perfect, which is also the rendering of the ancient versions. The recounting briefly of events up to the death of Terah in the last chapter was by a prolepsis. We have here the beginning of a new Chapter in the history, of a new dispensation and a new covenant. Henceforth the narrative concerns only the chosen people of God and those who affect them and their fortunes.

Get thee out of thy country] Lit. *Go thee*, a pleonasm of the pronoun, common in many languages. The call was evidently from the birthplace of Abram, Ur of the Chaldees; and not only Abram, but his father and other of his family seem at first to have obeyed the call: for Terah took Abram and Lot and Sarai, and "they went forth from Ur of the Chaldees to go into the land of Canaan" (ch. xi. 31). The land is here called by the Almighty "the land that I will shew thee," but Moses, in ch. xi. 31, calls it the land of Canaan, the destination of Abram being known to Moses, though it was not at the time of his call known to Abram himself.

2. *I will make of thee a great nation*] Literally fulfilled in the glories of Israel, spiritually and more largely in the spiritual sons of Abraham, "Abraham's seed and heirs according to the promise," Gal. iii. 29.

and thou shalt be a blessing] Kimchi on Zech. viii. 12, followed by Clericus and Knobel, interprets "shalt be an example or type of blessing," so that men shall say "Blessed be thou, as Abraham was blessed." Others, as Rosenmüller, Gesenius, &c. consider the substantive to be put for the parti-

make thy name great; and thou shalt
be a blessing:
3 And I will bless them that bless
thee, and curse him that curseth thee:
[b]and in thee shall all families of the
earth be blessed.
4 So Abram departed, as the LORD
had spoken unto him; and Lot went
with him: and Abram *was* seventy
and five years old when he departed
out of Haran.
5 And Abram took Sarai his wife,
and Lot his brother's son, and all
their substance that they had gathered, and the souls that they had gotten
in Haran; and they went forth to go
into the land of Canaan; and into the
land of Canaan they came.
6 ¶ And Abram passed through
the land unto the place of Sichem,
unto the plain of Moreh. And the
Canaanite *was* then in the land.

[b] chap. 18. 18. & 22. 18. Acts 3. 25. Gal. 3. 8.

---

ciple, *a blessing* for *blessed*, comp. Zech. viii. 12. More probable, as well as more natural, is the interpretation adopted by Tuch, Delitzsch, Keil, and others, and commended by the last words of v. 3, "Thou shalt be a blessing or cause of blessing to others besides thyself."

3. *I will bless them that bless thee, and curse him that curseth thee*] God's blessing was to extend to Abram's friends and followers, and the enemies of Abram were to be subject to God's curse. Two different Hebrew words are here translated by the one English word *curse*. Some think that the one expresses more properly the reviling and malediction of man, the other the withering curse of God. Both, however, are used of God and of man, cp. Job iii. 8; Deut. xxi. 23. The first in the English Version, that used of God, is undoubtedly the stronger of the two.

in thee shall all families of the earth be blessed] Here again Rashi, Cleric., Knobel, and some others interpret the words to mean that Abram should be so blessed in his family that all families of the earth should wish for like blessings (comp. Gen. xlviiii. 20, "In thee shall Israel bless, saying, God make thee as Ephraim and Manasseh"). The words, however, can with no shew of reason be rendered otherwise than as rendered in the Authorized Version, following the LXX. and Vulg. Nor can it be understood otherwise than that all families of men should in some manner derive blessing through Abram. The Targum of Onkelos has *for thy sake*, and so the Jerusalem Targum; but this is an unauthorized exposition.

It is not necessary to assert that the prediction here given was such as to enlighten Abram with any full clearness as to the way in which his seed should bless all nations. Indeed the promise is twofold, general and particular. Generally it is true, that Abram's seed was for centuries the sole depositary of God's objective revelations, and that that knowledge of God which was confided to them has by them been spread to all nations. "Out of Zion went forth the law, and the word of the LORD from Jerusalem" (Is. ii. 3). It has indeed been said with truth, that the Semitic nations, and especially the descendants of Abram, were from the time of Abram to Christ the only believers in the unity of the Godhead, and that ever since the Christian era they only have taught monotheism to mankind. But that which was the special blessing to Abram's race, has also, springing from that race, become the universal blessing to mankind. Of him "as concerning the flesh Christ came."

4. *seventy and five years old*] See on ch. xi. 32.

5. *the souls that they had gotten*] that is, the slaves or dependants whom they had attached to them. So in Ezek. xxvii. 13, slaves are spoken of as "souls of men." Onkelos renders, "The souls which they had converted to the law in Charran." So the Pseudo-Jonathan and Jerusalem Targums render, "the souls whom they had proselyted." And following this tradition, Rashi says that Abram made proselytes of the men and Sarai of the women.

into the land of Canaan they came] Leaving Haran they must have crossed the river Euphrates, from which crossing it is very commonly supposed the name Hebrew was derived (rendered by the LXX. in Gen. xiv. 13, ὁ περάτης, *the crosser over*). Thence their course must have been southward over the desert, probably near to Mount Lebanon, and thence to the neighbourhood of Damascus. Josephus ('Ant.' I. 7) quotes from Nicolaus of Damascus ('Hist.' bk. IV.), "Abraham reigned in Damascus, being come with an army from the country beyond Babylon called the land of the Chaldæans. But not long after, leaving this country with his people he migrated into the land of Canaan, which is now called Judæa." Josephus adds, that the name of Abraham was even in his days famous in the country of the Damascenes, and a village was pointed out there, which was called Abraham's habitation.

6. *the place of Sichem*] So named by anticipation. The word *place* may perhaps indicate that the town did not yet exist.

7 And the LORD appeared unto
chap. 13. 5. Abram, and said, [c] Unto thy seed will
I give this land: and there builded he
an [d] altar unto the LORD, who ap- d chap. 13. 4.
peared unto him.
8 And he removed from thence

It is generally supposed that Sychar (Joh. iv. 5) is the name by which it was known among the later Samaritans, though the identity of Sychar with Shechem is not quite certain (see Smith's 'Dict. of the Bible,' Art. 'Sychar'). The word Shechem signifies *a shoulder*, and, unless the town derived its name from Shechem the son of Hamor, it probably was situated on a *shoulder* or *ridge* of land connected with the hills of Ebal and Gerizim. Josephus ('Ant.' IV. 8) describes the city of Shechem or Sicima as lying between Gerizim on the right and Ebal on the left. The name Neapolis was given to it by Vespasian; and the ancients clearly identify the later Neapolis with the ancient Shechem; *e.g.* Epiphanius ('Hær.' III. 1055), "In Sichem, that is in the present Neapolis." The modern name is Nabulus. The situation of the town is described by modern travellers as one of exceeding beauty. Dr Robinson writes, "All at once the ground sinks down to a valley running toward the West, with a soil of rich black vegetable mould. Here a scene of luxuriant and almost unparalleled verdure burst upon our view. The whole valley was filled with gardens of vegetables and orchards of all kinds of fruits, watered by several fountains which burst forth in various parts and flow westward in refreshing streams. It came suddenly upon us like a scene of fairy enchantment, we saw nothing to compare to it in all Palestine" (Vol. II. p. 275. See also Stanley's 'Sinai and Palestine,' p. 234.) This spot, probably not yet so cultivated, but even then verdant and beautiful, was the first dwellingplace of the Patriarch in the land of promise.

the plain of Moreh] **The oak** (or terebinth) **of Moreh.** There is considerable variety of opinion as to the nature of the tree here mentioned, called *Elon* in Hebrew. Celsius ('Hierob.' I. p. 34) has argued that all the cognate words, *El*, *Elon*, *Elah*, &c. signify the terebinth tree, the word *allon* only being the oak. So Michaelis ('Supplem.' p. 72), Rosenm., Delitzsch, Keil, &c. The question is discussed at great length by Gesen. ('Thes.' p. 50), who doubts the distinction between *Allon* and *Elon* (a distinction merely of vowel points), and interprets both by *oak*, or perhaps generally a *large forest tree*. The LXX. and Vulg. render *oak*. The Targums (followed by the English Version) render *plain* (see also Stanley, 'Sinai and Palestine,' p. 141). It may be a question also whether the *oak of Moreh* was a single tree, or whether the word used may be a noun of multitude, signifying *the oak grove*. A single tree of large size and spreading foliage would, no doubt, be a natural resting place for a caravan or Arab encampment in the desert; but the great fertility of the valley of Shechem favours the belief that there may have been a grove rather than a single tree. Nothing is known as to the meaning of the word *Moreh:* it may have probably been the name of a man, a prince of the land, or owner of the property.

the Canaanite was then in the land] The original settlement of the sons of Canaan seems to have been in the South near the Red Sea; a Semitic race probably occupied the regions of Palestine and Phœnicia; a colony of the Canaanites afterwards spreading northwards, partly dispossessed and partly mingled with the ancient Shemite inhabitants, and adopted their language (see note on ch. x. 6, see also Epiphan. 'Hæres.' LXVI. n. 84). The historian therefore most appropriately relates that, at the time of the emigration of Abram and his followers, the Canaanite was already in possession of the land. The conjecture, therefore, that these words were written by a later hand than that of Moses, after the ancient Canaanite inhabitants had been expelled, is altogether beside the mark.

7. *And the LORD appeared unto Abram*] This is the first mention of a distinct appearance of the LORD to man. His voice is heard by Adam, and He is said to have spoken to Noah and to Abram: but here is a visible manifestation. The following questions naturally arise, 1. Was this a direct vision of JEHOVAH in Bodily shape? 2. Was it an impression produced on the mind of the seer, but not a true vision of God? 3. Was it an angel personating God? 4. Was it a manifestation of the Son of God, a Theophania, in some measure anticipating the Incarnation? (1) The first question seems answered by St John (Joh. i. 18), "No man hath seen God (the Father) at any time." (2) The second to a certain extent follows the first. Whether there was a manifestation of an objective reality, or merely an impression on the senses, we cannot possibly judge; but the vision, whether seen in sleep or waking, cannot have been a vision of God the Father. (3) The third question has been answered by many in the affirmative, it being concluded that "the Angel of the LORD," a created Angel, was always the means of communication between God and man in the Old Testament. The great supporter of this opinion in early times was St Augustine ('De Trin.' III. c. xi. Tom. VIII. pp. 805—810), the chief arguments in its favour being the statements of the New Testament that the

unto a mountain on the east of Beth-
el, and pitched his tent, *having* Bethel
on the west, and Hai on the east:
and there he builded an altar unto the
LORD, and called upon the name of
the LORD.
9 And Abram journeyed, †going on
still toward the south.
10 ¶ And there was a famine in
the land: and Abram went down
into Egypt to sojourn there; for the
famine *was* grievous in the land.
11 And it came to pass, when he
was come near to enter into Egypt,
that he said unto Sarai his wife, Behold now, I know that thou *art* a fair
woman to look upon:
12 Therefore it shall come to pass,

† Heb. *in going and journeying.*

---

law was given "by disposition of angels," "spoken by angels," &c. (Acts vii. 53; Gal. iii. 19; Heb. ii. 22). It is further argued by the supporters of this view, that "the angel of the LORD" is in some passages in the Old Testament, and always in the New Testament, clearly a created angel (*e.g.* Zech. i. 11, 12, &c.; Luke i. 11; Acts xii. 23); and that therefore it is not to be supposed that any of these manifestations of the Angel of God or Angel of the Lord, which seem so markedly Divine, should have been anything more than the appearance of a created Angel personating the Most High. (4) The affirmative of the fourth opinion was held by the great majority of the fathers from the very first (see, for instance, Justin. 'Dial.' pp. 280—284; Tertull. 'adv. Prax.' c. 16; Athanas. 'Cont. Arian.' IV. pp. 464, 465 (Ed. Col.); Basil, 'adv. Eunom.' II. 18; Theodoret, 'Qu. V. in Exod.' The teaching of the fathers on this head is investigated by Bp. Bull, 'F. N. D.' IV. iii. In like manner the ancient Jews had referred the manifestation of God in visible form to the *Shechinah*, the *Metatron*, or the *Memra de Jah*, apparently an emanation from God, having a semblance of diversity, yet really one with Him, coming forth to reveal Him, but not truly distinct from Him. The fact, that the name *Angel of the Lord* is sometimes used of a created Angel, is not proof enough that it may not be also used of Him who is called "the Angel of mighty counsel" (μεγάλης βουλῆς Ἄγγελος, Is. ix. 6, Sept. Trans.), and "the Angel of the covenant" (Mal. iii. 1). and the apparent identification of the Angel of God with God Himself in very many passages (*e.g.* Gen. xxxii. 24, comp. vv. 28, 30, Hos. xii. 3, 4; Gen. xvi. 10, 13, xlviii. 15, 16; Josh. v. 14, vi. 2; Judg. ii. 1, xiii. 22; Isa. vi. 1; cp. Joh. xii. 41; Is. lxiii. 9) leads markedly to the conclusion, that God spake to man by an Angel or Messenger, and yet that that Angel or Messenger was Himself God. No man saw God at any time, but the only begotten Son, who was in the Bosom of the Father, declared Him. He, who was the Word of God, the Voice of God to His creatures, was yet in the beginning with God, and He was God.

Unto thy seed will I give this land: and there builded he an altar] This is the first definite promise to Abram, that the land of Canaan should be the inheritance of his children. Accordingly, he built an altar there, as consecrating the soil and dedicating it to God. It is not mentioned that he offered sacrifice, but as the Hebrew word for *altar* means the *place of slaughter* or *of sacrifice*, there can be no doubt, that it was an altar of burnt offering, which he built, as was Noah's altar (ch. viii. 20), the only altar spoken of prior to this time.

8. *he removed*] lit. *he plucked up* his tent pegs. The journeying was by repeated encampments, after the manner of the Bedouins.

Beth-el,] *i.e.* the House of God. This is by anticipation. It was called *Luz* at this time (see ch. xxviii. 19; Judg. i. 23). The present name is Beitan.

Hai] was about five miles to the East of Beth-el, the ruins of which bear the name of Medinet Gai.

called upon the name of the LORD.] See ch. iv. 26.

9. *going on still toward the south*] The words express a gradual change of place, after the nomadic fashion. As food offered itself he pitched his tent and fed his cattle, and when food failed he went onwards to fresh pastures.

10. *a famine*] A country like Canaan, imperfectly cultivated, would be very subject to droughts and famine. The part of Egypt, which lay immediately South of Canaan, appears to have been especially fertile. It was at that time inhabited by a people skilled in agriculture, and flooded periodically by the Nile. Egypt is still the refuge for neighbouring nations when afflicted with drought. It is said that Abram went down to Egypt "to sojourn," not to live there; for he had received the promise of inheritance in Canaan, and, though this famine may have tried, it did not shake his faith.

11. *Behold...thou art a fair woman*] Sarai was now more than sixty years old: but her life extended to 127 years, so that she was only then in middle life; she had borne no children, and at the age of ninety, though not naturally young enough to have a son, was yet preserved in a condition of unusual and

when the Egyptians shall see thee,
that they shall say, This *is* his wife:
and they will kill me, but they will
save thee alive.
13 Say, I pray thee, thou *art* my
sister: that it may be well with me
for thy sake; and my soul shall live
because of thee.
14 ¶ And it came to pass, that,
when Abram was come into Egypt,
the Egyptians beheld the woman that
she *was* very fair.
15 The princes also of Pharaoh
saw her, and commended her before
Pharaoh: and the woman was taken
into Pharaoh's house.
16 And he entreated Abram well
for her sake: and he had sheep, and
oxen, and he asses, and menservants,
and maidservants, and she asses, and
camels.
17 And the LORD plagued Pharaoh
and his house with great plagues because of Sarai Abram's wife.
18 And Pharaoh called Abram,
and said, What *is* this *that* thou hast
done unto me? why didst thou not
tell me that she *was* thy wife?
19 Why saidst thou, She *is* my
sister? so I might have taken her to
me to wife: now therefore behold
thy wife, take *her*, and go thy way.

---

preternatural youth, so that she bore Isaac; her fair complexion would contrast favourably with the swarthy complexion of the Egyptians. The Arab life of Abram naturally made him wary of danger. He was about to sojourn in a country with a despotic government, and among a licentious people. We see in the conduct of Abram an instance of one under the influence of deep religious feeling and true faith in God, but yet with a conscience imperfectly enlightened as to many moral duties, and when leaning to his own understanding suffered to fall into great error and sin. The candour of the historian is shewn by his exhibiting in such strong relief the dissimulation of Abram as contrasted with the straightforward integrity of Pharaoh.

15. *Pharaoh*] The name or title, by which the kings of Egypt are called in the Old Testament. Josephus tells us that "Pharaoh among the Egyptians signifies *king*." It used to be thought that it was the Coptic word *Ouro* with the article *Pi* or *Ph*. (Jablonski, Diss. iv. section 3, 'De Terra Gosen.') Later the opinion of Rosellini, Lepsius, Rawlinson, Poole and others has been that it corresponded with the title of the Sun-God RA, with the article, PH—RA, a name which was given to some of the kings of Egypt. Gesenius objects to this from its lacking the final *oh* ('Thes.' p. 1129); and there is insufficient evidence that the title was really a common title of the kings. Very recently M. De Rougé has shewn that the hieroglyphic, which is the regular title of the Egyptian kings, and which signifies "the great house" or "the double house," must be read Peraa or Perao. This singularly corresponds with the statement of Horapollo (I. 61), that the king was called οἶκος μέγας, "the great house." The identity of this with the name Pharaoh is admitted by Brugsch, Ebers ('Ægypten, &c.' p. 26), and is argued at length in the "Excursus on Egyptian Words" (by the Rev. F. C. Cook) at the end of this volume. It may be compared with the title "Sublime Porte."

It is difficult to fix the particular Pharaoh or dynasty under which Abram came into Egypt. Generally the characteristics of the Court, as briefly described in Genesis, point to a native dynasty of very remote date. Some circumstances, the friendly reception of a Semitic nomade and the use of camels (v. 16) among the Egyptians, have suggested the belief that Abram's Pharaoh must have been a shepherd king (see Smith's Dict. of the Bible, Artt. *Pharaoh* and *Zoan*); and Sir Gardiner Wilkinson ('Ancient Egyptians,' Vol. I. chap. ii. p. 42) has identified him with Apophis or Apepi, the sixth monarch of Manetho's 15th dynasty. It is, however, impossible to admit so late a date. The Pharaoh of Joseph was almost certainly a king of the 12th dynasty. Abram's Pharaoh must therefore at latest have been one of the first kings of that same dynasty, if not belonging to a dynasty earlier still. The objections, derived from the camels, and other apparent indications of a shepherd reign, are fully considered in Excursus I. "On the Bearings of Egyptian History on the Pentateuch," at the end of this volume, by Rev. F. C. Cook: and the period of Abram's sojourn in Egypt is shewn to be most probably under one of the earlier sovereigns of the 12th dynasty.

the woman was taken into Pharaoh's house] Probably even at that early period Egypt had reached such a pitch of corrupt civilization that the sovereign had a hareem, and Sarai was chosen to be one of his wives.

18. *Pharaoh called Abram*] Josephus says, that the priests told Pharaoh for what cause that plague had fallen on him ('Ant.' I. 8). It is more likely that Sarai herself, being

20 And Pharaoh commanded *his*
men concerning him: and they sent
him away, and his wife, and all that
he had.

CHAPTER XIII.

1 *Abram and Lot return out of Egypt.* 7 *By disagreement they part asunder.* 10 *Lot goeth to wicked Sodom.* 14 *God reneweth the promise to Abram.* 18 *He removeth to Hebron, and there buildeth an altar.*

AND Abram went up out of E-
gypt, he, and his wife, and all
that he had, and Lot with him, into
the south.
2 And Abram *was* very rich in
cattle, in silver, and in gold.
3 And he went on his journeys
from the south even to Beth-el, unto
the place where his tent had been at
the beginning, between Beth-el and
Hai;
4 Unto the [a]place of the altar, [a] chap. 12. 7.
which he had made there at the first:
and there Abram called on the name
of the LORD.
5 ¶ And Lot also, which went
with Abram, had flocks, and herds,
and tents.
6 And the land was not able to
bear them, that they might dwell together: for their substance was great,
so that they could not dwell together.
7 And there was a strife between
the herdmen of Abram's cattle and
the herdmen of Lot's cattle: and the

---

interrogated about it, confessed the truth (Patrick).

19. *so I might have taken her*] Heb. **So I took her.** LXX. Syr. Onk. Though the Vulgate followed by the Arabic has, "so that I might have taken her." The meaning is, Deceived by Abram's words, Pharaoh took her with the intention of making her his wife, but was hindered from doing so by the afflictions with which God visited him (see Theodoret, 'Qu. LXXII. in Gen.' Op. XII. Augustin, 'De Civit. Dei,' XVI. 18). St Jerome ('Trad. Heb. in Genes.') refers to Esth. ii. 12, where we learn that the custom of Eastern monarchs was, that a maiden should undergo twelvemonths of purification before she was actually taken to wife. It was, he thinks, during some such period that Pharaoh was plagued and prohibited from marrying Sarai. It deserves to be noticed, that throughout the history of the chosen race, Egypt was to them the scene of spiritual danger, of covetousness and love of riches, of worldly security, of temptation to rest on an arm of flesh, on man's own understanding, and not on God only. All this appears from the very first, in Abraham's sojourn there, Sarai's danger, their departure full of wealth and prosperity.

CHAP. XIII. **1.** *and Lot with him*] Lot is not mentioned in the descent into Egypt, because no part of the narrative there concerns him. On the return to Canaan he becomes a principal actor.

into the south] That southern part of Canaan, whence he had gone down into Egypt, The south, or *Negeb*, is almost a proper name.

2. *very rich*] He had grown rich in Egypt. He has now to experience some of the dangers and evils of prosperity.

3. *on his journeys*] By his stations, or according to his encampments, *i.e.* either station by station, as before, pitching his tent for a time at one station and then removing it to another; or perhaps, returning by his former stations, according to his original encampments when he was journeying southwards.

unto the place where his tent had been at the beginning] Shechem was the first place at which he rested and built an altar; but he probably remained there a comparatively short time. The Canaanites then in the land (ch. xii. 6) would doubtless have occupied all the most fertile country about Shechem. His second place of sojourn was the mountain near Bethel, where he is said to have built an altar and called on the name of the Lord, and where very probably he had continued until the famine began to prevail. (See ch. xii. vv. 7, 8, 9, 10.)

6. *the land was not able to bear them*] Lot was the sharer of Abram's prosperity. They came up out of Egypt with much larger possessions than before, more "flocks and herds and tents" for their now more numerous retainers. The land too had but just recovered from a state of drought and dearth: "and the Canaanite and the Perizzite dwelt then in the land" (v. 7), and probably by their occupation contributed to the scarcity of pasture.

7. *Perizzite*] But little is known of this people. They are not mentioned in the catalogue of nations in Gen. x. They are mostly coupled, as here, with the Canaanites. They appear from Josh. xi. 3, xvii. 15, to have dwelt in the woods and mountains. Bochart describes them ('Phaleg.' IV. 36) as a rustic, agrarian race, living without cities and in villages only, the name itself signifying ***pagani***, *villagers*, *rustics*.

Canaanite and the Perizzite dwelled
then in the land.
8 And Abram said unto Lot,
Let there be no strife, I pray thee,
between me and thee, and between
my herdmen and thy herdmen; for
we *be* †brethren. (Heb. *men brethren.*)
9 *Is* not the whole land before
thee? separate thyself, I pray thee,
from me: if *thou wilt take* the left
hand, then I will go to the right; or
if *thou depart* to the right hand, then
I will go to the left.
10 And Lot lifted up his eyes, and
beheld all the plain of Jordan, that it
was well watered every where, before
the LORD destroyed Sodom and Gomorrah, *even* as the garden of the
LORD, like the land of Egypt, as thou
comest unto Zoar.
11 Then Lot chose him all the
plain of Jordan; and Lot journeyed
east: and they separated themselves
the one from the other.
12 Abram dwelled in the land of
Canaan, and Lot dwelled in the cities
of the plain, and pitched *his* tent toward Sodom.
13 But the men of Sodom *were*
wicked and sinners before the LORD
exceedingly.
14 ¶ And the LORD said unto A-
bram, after that Lot was separated
from him, Lift up now thine eyes,
and look from the place where thou
art northward, and southward, and
eastward, and westward:
15 For all the land which thou
seest, [b]to thee will I give it, and to
thy seed for ever.

[b] chap. 12. 7. & 26. 4. Deut. 34. 4.

---

dwelled then in the land] See on xii. 6.

8. *Let there be no strife*] A noble example of disinterestedness and love of peace exhibited by the father of the faithful.

10. *Lot lifted up his eyes*] They were probably encamped on that mountain on the east of Bethel, having Bethel on the west and Hai on the east, where Abram had built the altar and called on the name of the Lord (ch. xii. 8). The very spot can be traced from the indications of the sacred text (Stanley's 'Jewish Church,' Vol. I. p. 32). From this spot Lot and Abram chose their respective possessions. Lot saw the plains of Jordan, watered by fertilizing rivers, not yet broken up by the overflowing or outbursting of the great salt lake, very probably irrigated like the land of Egypt which he had lately left, where the Nile refreshed the soil, and the plague of famine never came. Taking no warning by the dangers, bodily and spiritual, which had beset them in Egypt, he feared not the proximity of the wealthy and luxurious inhabitants of Sodom and Gomorrah, but thought their land pleasant even as the garden of the Lord. He chose the rich pastures of the plain, and left Abram the less promising, but, as it proved, the safer inheritance of the hill country of Judæa. It was a selfish choice, and it proved a sad one.

as thou comest unto Zoar] See on ch. xiv. 3.

12. *land of Canaan*] That is, Canaan strictly so called.

the plain] Lit. "the circuit or neighbourhood," the country round about Jordan. So the LXX. (Ges. 'Thes.' p. 717. Stanley, 'Sinai and Palestine,' p. 287.) The low tract or plain along the river—through which it flows, perhaps as comprehensive as the Ghor itself. (Robinson, 'Phys. Geog.' p. 73.)

13. *sinners before the LORD*] Sodom, Gomorrah, Admah and Zeboim are mentioned, Gen. x. 19, as among the first settlements of the Canaanites. The fertility of the soil in this Valley of the Jordan, with the luxurious and enervating character of the climate, rapidly developed the sensual vices of this early civilized but depraved race. Their wickedness is mentioned here perhaps in anticipation of the history in ch. xix., but partly also in order to exhibit more clearly the thoughtlessness and worldliness of Lot in choosing their neighbourhood for his residence, as distinguished from the humility and unselfish spirit of Abram.

14. *Lift up now thine eyes*, &c.] He was probably still on the hill east of Bethel. Here once again, on his return from Egypt to the land of his inheritance, God renews his promise to Abram. The world, with its dangers and its honours, may have tempted Abram, but it had not corrupted him. He came back from Egypt with larger knowledge, probably all the more armed against sin by having had some experience of its seductions. He is still the chosen of God; and he is comforted under separation from his kinsman, and the discovery of that kinsman's lower motives and less disinterestedness, by the assurance that God was still ever with him and pledged to preserve and provide for him.

15. *to thee*] The land even in present possession was his, so far as was needed by him as a nomade chief, though its permanent occupation was to him and his seed after him.

16 And I will make thy seed as the dust of the earth: so that if a man can number the dust of the earth, *then* shall thy seed also be numbered.

17 Arise, walk through the land in the length of it and in the breadth of it; for I will give it unto thee.

18 Then Abram removed *his* tent, and came and dwelt in the †plain of Mamre, which *is* in Hebron, and built there an altar unto the LORD.

† Heb. *plains.*

CHAPTER XIV.

1 The battle of four kings against five. 12 Lot is taken prisoner. 14 Abram rescueth him. 18 Melchizedek blesseth Abram. 20 Abram giveth him tithe. 22 The rest of the spoil, his partners having had their portions, he restoreth to the king of Sodom.

AND it came to pass in the days of Amraphel king of Shinar, Arioch king of Ellasar, Chedorlaomer king of Elam, and Tidal king of nations;

2 *That these* made war with Bera king of Sodom, and with Birsha king of Gomorrah, Shinab king of Admah, and Shemeber king of Zeboiim, and the king of Bela, which is Zoar.

---

for ever] *i.e.* in perpetuity. But, when we consider that the promises to Abram have their full completion in Christ, to whom are given "the uttermost parts of the earth for a possession," there need be no limit to the sense of the words "for ever."

18. *the plain of Mamre*] **The Oaks** (or terebinths) **of Mamre**, see on ch. xii. 6. Probably it means "the oak grove" or "wood of Mamre," called after Mamre the Amorite, the friend and ally of Abram (ch. xiv. 13, 24).

Hebron] Called *Arba* or *Kirjath-arba* (see ch. xxiii. 2, xxxv. 4. Judg. i. 10) till after the death of Moses, when Caleb took the city and changed its name to Hebron. It has been thought therefore that the words here "which is Hebron," must have been inserted by a later hand than that of Moses. It is more probable that Hebron was the original name, changed to Kirjath-arba during the sojourn of the descendants of Jacob in the land of Egypt, and restored by Caleb at the conquest of Palestine. So Karme (cited by Rosenmüller), Hengstenberg, Keil, &c.; see also on ch. xxiii. 2. This was the third resting place of Abram: 1. Shechem, 2. Bethel, 3. Hebron. Near it was the cave of Machpelah, where he and Sarah were buried. It is now called *El Khalil*, "the friend," *i. e.* the house of the friend of God. Near to it stands an ancient Terebinth, once a place of heathen worship (Delitzsch). The cave of Machpelah still is there, surrounded by a mosque, in which lie probably the dust of Abraham and Isaac, and perhaps the embalmed body, the mummy, of Jacob, brought up in solemn state from Egypt, ch. l. 13 (Stanley, 'Sinai and Palestine,' p. 102).

CHAP. XIV. 1. *And it came to pass*] We come now upon a new scene in the life of Abram. The choice of Lot was soon seen not to be a wise choice, even for earthly happiness. The rich plains of Sodom and Gomorrah were likely to be scenes of strife, as in early times was the case with all fertile countries (Thucyd. I. 2). The history of this war is a remarkable episode, and is thought by many to be a very ancient document incorporated by Moses in his great work. So Tuch, Ewald, Kurtz, &c. who all bear testimony to its internal proofs of historical accuracy. The occurrence of the name JEHOVAH in it is inconsistent with the theory, which assigns the use of that name only to the later portions of the book of Genesis.

in the days of Amraphel king of Shinar] The king of Shinar, (*Babel*, Onkel., *Bagdad*, Arab. Erpen., *Pontus*, Jonathan,) as being the representative of Nimrod, founder of the great Babylonian Empire, is mentioned first. The name Amraphel is probably Assyrian, its derivation unknown.

Arioch] If, as it is supposed, the root of this word be *ari*, a *lion*, the bearer of it would appear to have been Semitic.

Ellasar] Jonathan *Telassar* (see 2 K. xix. 12; Isa. xxxvii. 12), a place not far off. It is more probably identified with Larsa or Larancha, the Larissa of the Greeks, a town in Lower Babylonia, or Chaldæa, between Ur and Erech, on the left bank of the Euphrates (Rawlinson, Kalisch, &c.).

Chedorlaomer king of Elam] It seems from the narrative that at this time the king of Elam was the most powerful of the Asiatic princes (Le Clerc). The Elamites appear to have been originally a Semitic people (ch. x. 22). If then they had now gained a superiority over the Hamitic races, it is not improbable that the Canaanites of the plain of Jordan, having been originally subject to the kings of Shinar, or Babylon, bore unwillingly the transference of their fealty to the Shemite king of Elam, and took the first opportunity of throwing off their allegiance, whereupon the king of Elam, now the head of the four kingdoms named in this verse, gathered his subjects or tributary allies, and strove to reduce the Canaanites again to subjection. Re-

3 All these were joined together
in the vale of Siddim, which is the
salt sea.

4 Twelve years they served Chedorlaomer, and in the thirteenth year
they rebelled.

5 And in the fourteenth year came
Chedorlaomer, and the kings that
were with him, and smote the Rephaims in Ashteroth Karnaim, and
the Zuzims in Ham, and the Emims
in ‖Shaveh Kiriathaim,

‖ Or, *the plain of Kiriathaim.*

---

cent discoveries shew that Susa (the capital of Elymais) must have been one of the most ancient cities of the East. Sir Henry Rawlinson thought he discovered a name coresponding with Chedorlaomer on Chaldæan bricks, viz. Kadur-Mapula, the second portion of the word being of course distinct. Another title by which Kadur-Mapula was known was "Ravager of the West," which corresponds with the account here given of Chedorlaomer. Rawlinson and others consider the dynasty of Chedorlaomer not to have been Semitic, but belonging to a race of Hamites, who had subdued the original Elymæans.

Tidal king of nations] Symmachus renders "King of the Scythians," which is approved by some commentators, because Scythia was inhabited by many different tribes (Fuller, 'Miscell. SS.' Lib. II. c. 4, quoted by Rosenm.). Le Clerc, followed by Rosenmüller, prefers Galilee, called "Galilee of the Gentiles" or "nations" (Is. ix. 1; Matt. iv. 15. See also Strabo, Lib. XVI. § 34, who says that these northern parts of Judæa were inhabited by various mixed tribes, Egyptians, Arabs, Phœnicians). But all this was probably later in history, and the name Galilee of the nations was given to Galilee, because it was still inhabited by other tribes, whilst Judæa was inhabited by none but Israelites (Gesenius, 'Thes.' p. 272). We may most probably conjecture that Tidal was owned as the chief of several nomade tribes, who, like Abram, had no stationary home. For Tidal, the LXX. has *Thargal*, which is preferred by some, as having the meaning of "Great chief" in the early Hamitic dialect of the lower Tigris and Euphrates country (Rawlinson, in Smith's 'Dict. of Bible').

3. *vale of Siddim*] The meaning of this name has been a great puzzle to interpreters. The LXX. render it "the salt valley." Onkelos evidently refers the derivation to *Sadeh*, a plain (as though שִׂדִּים was plural of שָׂדֶה). So Aquila and Rashi. They are followed by Stanley ('Sinai and Palestine,' p. 491). Aben Ezra derives it from *Sid* (שִׂיד), *lime*, because of the abundance of bitumen, which was used as lime (see ch. xi. 3). Gesenius suggests an Arabic root signifying an obstacle, and so concludes that the valley of Siddim was a plain full of rocky valleys and irregularities. In v. 10 it is said to be full of bitumen pits, which was perhaps the reason why the five kings chose it for the field of battle, as being more favourable to the weaker party.

which is the salt sea] The extreme depression of the Dead Sea, 1316 feet (Robinson, 'Phys. Geog.' p. 190), and other geological phenomena, are thought to favour the belief, that there must have been originally some lake at the extremity of the valley of the Jordan; but perhaps after the destruction of Sodom and Gomorrah the lake greatly extended itself, so as to cover much which before may have been low valley land. The vale of Siddim is generally thought to have been at the southern extremity of the Dead Sea, where are now to be seen the principal deposits of salt and bitumen, the site being occupied by the shallow southern portion of that sea (see Robinson, 'Physical Geography of the Holy Land,' pp. 73, 213).

4. *Twelve years*, &c.] See on v. 1.

5. *Rephaims*] The LXX. renders "Giants," so virtually do Onk. and Syr. It is, no doubt, the name of an ancient people; very probably a tribe resident in the Holy Land before the immigration of the Canaanites. They appear to have been a people of large stature. Og, the king of Bashan, at the time of the Exodus, is mentioned as the last remaining of their race (Deut. iii. 11). Their habitation was to the north-east of the valley of the Jordan, the country afterwards called Peræa. They must also have extended to the south-west; for the valley of Rephaim, named after them, appears to have been in the neighbourhood of the valley of Hinnom and Bethlehem, to the south of Jerusalem (see Josh. xv. 8, xviii. 16; 2 S. v. 18, 22, xxiii. 13). The name "Rephaim," in later times, is constantly used for "the dead," or rather for the "ghosts or manes of the dead" (Job xxvi. 5; Ps. lxxxviii. 11; Prov. ii. 18; Is. xiv. 9, xxvi. 14). Whether there is a connection between the name of this ancient and afterwards extinct people, and this word thus used for "the dead," is very doubtful (Gesen. 'Thes.' p. 1302).

Ashteroth Karnaim] "Ashteroth of the two horns." It is most probable that this was the same as the Ashtaroth, where Og the king of Bashan dwelt (Deut. i. 4; Josh. ix. 10), in the east of the inheritance of the tribe of Manasseh; and that it was named from the worship of Astarte (Ashtoreth), whose image

6 And the Horites in their mount Seir, unto ‖El-paran, which *is* by the wilderness.

‖ Or, *the plain of Paran.*

7 And they returned, and came to En-mishpat, which *is* Kadesh, and smote all the country of the Amalekites, and also the Amorites, that dwelt in Hazezon-tamar.

---

was such as to suggest the idea of a horned figure (see Gesen. 'Thes.' p. 1082). In like manner Athor (the Egyptian Venus, as Astarte was the Phœnician) was depicted with horns like a cow (see Rawlinson's 'Herod.' Vol. II. pp. 61, 62). Some, however, think the two horns to refer to two hills, between which the city lay, and the name "horned" was intended to distinguish this town from the city commonly called Ashtaroth only (see Rosenm. in loc. and Smith's 'Dict. of Bible,' s. v. *Ashtaroth*).

Zuzims] Little is known concerning the name or place of this people. The LXX. and Onk. render "the strong or mighty ones." Le Clerc thinks the name means "wanderer," from the root Zuz זוּז, "to move oneself." Michaelis understands "dwarfs." Both derivations are rejected by Gesen. ('Thes.' p. 410). They are very generally thought to be the same with the Zamzummims (Deut. ii. 20), who are spoken of as a race of great stature, and connected with the Horim, as are the Zuzims here.

in Ham] If the Zuzim be the same as the Zamzummim, they must have dwelt in the territory of the Ammonites, and Tuch, followed by Knobel, considers that Ham here is the same as Rabbath-Ammon. There is another reading in seven Samaritan MSS. followed by the LXX. and Vulg. viz. (בָּהֶם *ἅμα αὐτοῖς, cum illis*) "with them;" but the pointing of the Masorites seems more likely to be the true.

the Emims] The name is supposed to be the Hebrew for "terrible ones." The Rev. F. C. Cook identifies the name with Amu, the Egyptian word for nomad Semites. In Deut. ii. 10, 11, where they are mentioned in the same connection as here, they are spoken of as "a people great and many and tall." They dwelt in the country afterwards occupied by the Moabites.

Shaveh Kiriathaim] or "the plain of Kiriathaim," or "the plain of the two cities." Kiriathaim is mentioned, Num. xxxii. 37, Josh. xiii. 19, as in the possession of the sons of Reuben. Eusebius says it was well known in his day, a village inhabited by Christians, close to the Baris, about 10 miles west of Medeba ('Onom.' Κιριαθιείμ).

6. *the Horites in their mount Seir*] The name "Horites" means "inhabitants of caves." These people dwelt in the mountain region called Seir (lit. "the hirsute," probably from its thick forests and brushwood), extending from the Dead Sea southward to the Elamitic Gulf. Mount Seir is called in the Samaritan Pentateuch and the Jerusalem Targum "Gabla," and the northern part of the range is still called "Jebal," or "the mountain," by the Arabs. The wonderful excavations in the rocks near Petra may very possibly be due to these "Horim," or cave-dwellers. They were driven out by the Edomites (Deut. ii. 12), who also after the manner of their predecessors "made their nest high like the eagle."

El-paran] *i.e.* "the oak or terebinth wood of Paran." The great wilderness, extending to the south of Palestine, the south-west of Idumæa, and thence to the Sinaitic range, appears to have been called the wilderness of Paran. It probably lay to the west of the wilderness of Sin, but at times is to be taken in a wider sense, as comprehending the desert of Sin (see Gesen. 'Thes.' pp. 47, 1090). El-paran is here said to be by the wilderness, *i.e.* on the eastern side of the great desert, marking the farthest point to which the expedition of Chedorlaomer reached. The wilderness of Paran is identified with the modern desert of El-Tih, the wilderness of Zin or Sin being the Wady-el-Arabah (Stanley, 'Sinai and Palestine,' p. 92).

7. *to En-mishpat, which is Kadesh*] The LXX. renders "to the well of judgment," the Vulg. "to the well of Mishpat." Some suppose it to have derived its name from the *judgment* pronounced on Moses and Aaron (Num. xx. 12), and that the name is here given proleptically; but it is evidently here given as the ancient name to which the more modern *Kadesh* corresponded. Syr., Onk., Jerus. render Kadesh by Rekam. Josephus calls it Arekem, which he says now bears the name of Petra ('A. J.' IV. 4). This identity of Kadesh with Petra is ably defended by Dean Stanley ('S. and P.' pp. 94, 95). Another site for the ancient Kades, or Ain-Mishpat, is vindicated for Kudes or Kades, lying to the east of the highest part of Djebel-Halal, about 12 miles to the E.S.E. of Morlakhi (see Williams, 'Holy City,' Vol. I. p. 467; Kalisch, Delitzsch, Keil, in loc.) Strong objections to both these sites are urged in the art. *Kades* in Smith's 'Dict. of the Bible.'

Amalekites] See note on ch. xxxvi. 12.

Hazezon-tamar] *i.e.* "The pruning of the palm," the same place which was afterwards called Engedi, "the fountain of the wild-goat" (2 Chr. xx. 2). The palm-groves, which gave the original name, and for which Pliny says Engedi was famous ('Nat. Hist.' v. 17), have

8 And there went out the king of
Sodom, and the king of Gomorrah,
and the king of Admah, and the king
of Zeboiim, and the king of Bela
(the same *is* Zoar;) and they joined
battle with them in the vale of Siddim;
9 With Chedorlaomer the king of
Elam, and with Tidal king of nations,
and Amraphel king of Shinar, and
Arioch king of Ellasar; four kings
with five.
10 And the vale of Siddim *was full
of* slimepits; and the kings of Sodom
and Gomorrah fled, and fell there;
and they that remained fled to the
mountain.
11 And they took all the goods of
Sodom and Gomorrah, and all their
victuals, and went their way.
12 And they took Lot, Abram's
brother's son, who dwelt in Sodom,
and his goods, and departed.
13 ¶ And there came one that had
escaped, and told Abram the Hebrew;
for he dwelt in the plain of Mamre
the Amorite, brother of Eshcol, and
brother of Aner: and these *were* confederate with Abram.
14 And when Abram heard that
his brother was taken captive, he
‖ armed his ‖ trained *servants*, born in his ‖ Or, *led forth.*
own house, three hundred and eigh- ‖ Or, *instructed.*
teen, and pursued *them* unto Dan.
15 And he divided himself against
them, he and his servants, by night,

---

disappeared, but the ibex, or Syrian chamois, still inhabits the cliffs in the neighbourhood (Stanley, 'S. and P.' p. 295). The place was situated in the wilderness of Judæa, to the west of the Dead Sea, according to Josephus 300 stadia from Jerusalem ('Ant.' IX. c. 1). The ruins found at a place called Ain Jiddi, with a fountain in the midst of a mountain country, to the west of the Dead Sea and of about the latitude of Hebron, are supposed to mark the original site of Engedi or Hazezon-tamar.

10. *slimepits*] **Bitumen-pits**: of asphalt or bitumen, from which the Dead Sea was afterwards called Lacus Asphaltites, or Sea of Asphalt.

fell there] *i.e.* were overthrown there; for the king of Sodom seems to have been one of those who fled to the mountains and escaped, see v. 17.

13. *one that had escaped*] Rather **those that escaped** (Ew. 277; Ges. 'Thes.' p. 1105).

the Hebrew] *i.e.* either "the descendant of Eber," which seems most accordant with the words in ch. x. 21, where Eber seems to have given a general name to his descendants, or (as the LXX., Aq., Vulg., and most ancient interpreters), "the stranger from beyond the Euphrates," an appellative from the Hebrew noun or preposition *Eber*, עֵבֶר, signifying the "opposite side, beyond." The mention of Abram as the Hebrew is due to the fact, that the messenger, who came and told him what had happened, was an inhabitant of the land, and Abram was to him one of a strange country and strange race.

the plain] **The oaks or oak groves.**

14. *He armed his trained servants*] **He led out his trained servants.** The verb here used means "to draw out," as a sword from its sheath: and the word *trained* is applied to the teaching of children (Prov. xxii. 6), and to initiation or consecration, as of a house (Deut. xx. 5), or a temple (1 K. viii. 63).

born in his own house] Of his own patriarchal family, not bought, hired, or taken in war.

unto Dan] Some taking this Dan to be the same as Laish, which was not called Dan till after the country was conquered by the Danites (Josh. xix. 47; Judg. xviii. 29), have thought that this passage was not from the hand of Moses. So Ewald ('Gesch.' I. 53), who supposes *Dan* to have been substituted by a later hand for Laish in the original MS. Others have thought that another place was meant here (so Deyling, Hävernick, Kalisch, Keil). Keil contends that the Dan, formerly called Laish, which was on the central source of the Jordan (see Joseph. 'Ant.' I. 10; Stanley, 'S. and P.' p. 395), could not have been the Dan here mentioned, as it did not lie in either of the two roads leading from the vale of Siddim to Damascus. Both he and Kalisch think this Dan to be the same as Dan-jaan (2 S. xxiv. 6), apparently belonging to Gilead, and to be sought for in northern Peræa, to the south-west of Damascus. The chief objection to this is, that Josephus (as above, 'Ant.' I. 10) and Jerome ('Qu. Hebr. in Gen.' ad h.l.) distinctly speak of the Dan here mentioned, as situated at the source of the Jordan. The conjecture of Le Clerc (Cleric. *in loc.*) is not contemptible, viz. that the original name of the fountain was "Dan," *i.e.* "judge," (cp. Ain-mishpat, the fountain of justice), the neighbouring town being called Laish; but that the Danites gave the name of the well, which corresponded with that of their own tribe, to the city as well as the fountain.

15. *he divided himself against them, he*

and smote them, and pursued them unto Hobah, which *is* on the left hand of Damascus.

16 And he brought back all the goods, and also brought again his brother Lot, and his goods, and the women also, and the people.

17 ¶ And the king of Sodom went
out to meet him after his return from
the slaughter of Chedorlaomer, and
of the kings that *were* with him, at
the valley of Shaveh, which *is* the
[a]king's dale.
18 And [b]Melchizedek king of Sa-

[a] 2 Sam. 18. 18.
[b] Heb. 7. 1.

---

and his servants, by night] From v. 24 it appears that besides Abram's own servants there went out with him Aner, Eshcol and Mamre, with their followers. These divided their forces, surprised the invaders at different points of attack during the darkness, and so routed them.

Hobah, which is on the left hand of Damascus] *i.e.* to the north of Damascus, the north being to the left of a man, who looks toward the sunrising. A place called Choba is mentioned, Judith xv. 6; Eusebius ('Onom.' v. Χωβά) says that in his day a village existed in the neighbourhood of Damascus called by this name, which was inhabited by Ebionites. About two miles from Damascus is now a village called Hobah, said to be the place to which Abram pursued the kings (Stanley, 'S. and P.' p. 414 k).

17. *the valley of Shaveh, which is the king's dale*] In 2 S. xviii. 18, we read that Absalom in his lifetime "took and reared up for himself a pillar, which is in the king's dale: for he said, I have no son to keep my name in remembrance: and he called the pillar after his own name, and it is called unto this day, Absalom's place." Josephus ('Ant.' VII. 10) says, that the monument was two stadia from Jerusalem. This would correspond well with the valley of the Upper Kidron, where are the tombs of the judges and other ancient sepulchres, a very likely place for Absalom to have erected what was evidently intended as a sepulchral monument. The tomb now known as Absalom's is probably not his, as it appears to be of later date, corresponding with the rock-tombs of Petra belonging to a period later than the Christian era (Robinson, 'Phys. Geog.' p. 92). It is not, however, possible to determine the situation of the valley of Shaveh, and its identity with the later King's Dale of 2 S. xviii. 18, without first fixing the site of Salem, of which Melchizedek was king. If Salem be Jerusalem, then Shaveh may well have been the valley of the Kidron, close to Jerusalem: but if Salem were some more northern city, we must leave the position of Shaveh undetermined. See on v. 18.

18. *Melchizedek*] Various have been the conjectures in all ages as to the person of Melchizedek. Some have supposed the name to be a title, like Augustus or Pharaoh, rather than a proper name, comparing Malek-ol-Adel and Adel-Chan, *i. e.* "the just king," a title common to some Mahommedan kings, as the princes of the Deccan and Golconda: but the Hebrew form of the word seems to point to a proper name rather than to a title. Cp. Abi-melech, Gen. xx. 2, Adoni-zedek, Josh. x. 3. The Targums of Jerusalem and Pseudo-Jonathan say, that Melchizedek was Shem, and St Jerome ('Qu. ad Genes.' in loc.) tells us that the Jews of his day said he was Shem the son of Noah, and calculating the days of his life, shewed that he must have lived to the time of Isaac. (See also Epist. LXXIII. 'ad Evang.' Opp. I. p. 438). This opinion has been adopted by many moderns, and is defended at length by Jackson 'On the Creed,' Bk. IX. It probably arose from considerations of the great dignity of the king and priest, who blessed Abraham and took tithes of him, and from the readiness of the Jews to ascribe such dignity only to an ancestor of their own. The Jews very anciently considered him at least to be a type of Messiah (Schœttgen. 'Hor. Hebr.' T. II. p. 645); but they generally seem to have believed that he was a prince of the country, as the Targum of Onkelos and Josephus, which both describe him simply as king of Jerusalem, in which they are followed by most commentators of modern times. It is a question of interest, but impossible to solve, Was he of the Canaanitish race or Semitic? On ch. x. 6, some explanation is given of the fact that the Canaanites spoke a Semitic tongue. The name and titles of Melchizedek are Semitic, but this proves nothing. He dwelt among Canaanites; but there had probably been Semitic inhabitants of the land before the immigration of the Canaanites (see on ch. xii. 6); and so Melchizedek, who was a worshipper of the true God, may have been one of the original Shemite stock. There were, however, worshippers of the true God, besides the Israelites, retaining patriarchal truth, as Job, and Balaam, and so it is not certain that Melchizedek was a descendant of Shem. He is, in fact, as the Apostle tells us, introduced "without father, without mother, without descent," with no mention of the beginning of his priesthood or the ending of it, and so specially suited to be a type of the Son of God. He is mentioned once besides in the Old Testament, viz. in Ps. cx. 4, where the priesthood of Messiah is said to be after the

lem brought forth bread and wine: and he *was* the priest of the most high God.

19 And he blessed him, and said, Blessed *be* Abram of the most high God, possessor of heaven and earth:

order of Melchizedek; and again in the New Testament, Heb. v. vi. vii., where the comparison between the royal priesthood of Melchizedek and that of Jesus is drawn out at length. The special points of resemblance of Melchizedek to Christ are: 1. that he was not of the Levitical order, local, national, but previous to the giving of the Law, catholic, universal; 2. that he was superior to Abraham, blessed and took tithes of him; 3. that (as often in old times, Virg. 'Æn.' III. 80; Arist. 'Pol.' III. 14, &c.), he was both king and priest; 4. that no beginning and no end are assigned either to his priesthood or his life; 5. his name too "king of righteousness and king of peace," are eminently suited to a type of the Son of God (Heb. vii. 2, 3). The bringing forth bread and wine is not referred to by the Apostle; but the ancient Church loved to dwell on this as typical of the institution by the Saviour of the θυσία ἀναίμακτος, the *incruentum sacrificium*, as they were wont to call the Holy Eucharist; and later ages may have made more of it than Scripture will warrant. (See Jackson, as above, Bk. IX. sect. ii. ch. x.)

king of Salem] Josephus ('Ant.' I. 10), Onkelos and all the Targg. understand Jerusalem, which is called Salem in Ps. lxxvi. 2, and this is pretty certainly the true interpretation. Jerome however ('Epist. LXXIII. ad Evang.' Tom. I. p. 446, edit. Vallars.), says it was not Jerusalem, but a city near Scythopolis, called Salem up to his time, where the ruins of Melchizedek's palace were shewn, and of which it is written (Gen. xxxiii. 18), "Jacob came to Shalem." Yet *Shalem*, in Gen. xxxiii. is rendered by Onkelos and a majority of modern commentators, not as a proper name, but rather "in peace" (see note on ch. xxxiii. 19). Moreover, Jerome elsewhere ('Qu. in Gen.') speaks of Melchizedek as "king of Salem, which was the former name of Jerusalem." Probably Salem was the oldest, Jebus the next, and Jerusalem the more modern name of the same city, though some think that the Salem here was the same as Salim near Ænon, where John baptized (Joh. iii. 23). If, as is most probable, Siddim, Sodom and Gomorrah, lay to the south of the Dead Sea, there is no reason why Salem should not have been Jerusalem, or that the valley of Shaveh, which is the "king's dale," should not have been the valley of the Kidron. If the view advocated by Mr Grove ('Dict. of Bible,' art. *Shaveh*, *Siddim*, *Sodom*, *Zoar*), and defended by Dean Stanley ('S. and P.' pp. 249, &c.), viz. that the valley of Siddim was north of the Dead Sea, be correct, then no doubt, Salem must have been a place far north of Jerusalem; but the more ancient opinion, viz. that the cities of the plain lay south of the Dead Sea is ably defended by Kuinoel ('Ep. ad Hebr.' VII. 1), Robinson ('B. R.' II. 188, 'Phys. Geog.' 213), Kurtz, Knobel, Delitzsch, Kalisch, Keil, &c., and is most probably the true. See also note on the Dead Sea at the end of ch. xix.

the priest] This is the first time that the word *priest*, *Cohen*, ἱερεὺς, *sacerdos*, occurs in the Bible, and it is in connection with the worship of an ancient people, perhaps not related by blood to the chosen race. The etymological meaning of the word is unknown. The word itself is applied afterwards both to the Levitical priesthood and to the priesthood of false religions. The patriarchs seem to have had no other priesthood than that of the head of the family (Gen. viii. 20, xii. 8, xxii., xxvi. 25, xxxiii. 20; Job i. 5); but here we find Melchizedek designated as a priest and as performing many priestly acts, solemnly blessing, taking tithes, &c. There is no distinct mention of sacrifice, which was afterwards the most special function of the priesthood. As, however, sacrifice was a rite of common use among the patriarchs, and, later at least, among all surrounding nations, there is no reasonable doubt but that Melchizedek was a sacrificing priest, and so more fitly a type of Christ, who offered Himself a sacrifice without spot to God (see Kuinoel on Heb. vii. 1). Philo indeed asserts that Melchizedek offered the first fruits of the spoil in sacrifice, ἐπινίκια ἔθυε ('De Abrah.' p. 381), a thing by no means improbable; and connected with such a sacrifice may have been the bread and wine, corresponding with the *mola* and libations of later days.

the most high God] This is the first time we meet with this title, *Elion*. It occurs frequently afterwards, as Num. xxiv. 16 (where it is used by Balaam, also an alien from the family of Abraham), Deut. xxxii. 18, Ps. vii. 18, ix. 2, xviii. 13, xlvii. 2, lxxviii. 35, &c., where sometimes we have *Elion* alone, sometimes joined with *El*, sometimes with JEHOVAH. It is observed that Sanchoniathon (ap. Euseb. 'Præp. Evang.' I. 10) mentions *Elion* as the name of the Phœnician Deity. So the words *alonim walonuth*, which occur in the well-known Punic passage in the Pœnulus of Plautus, are supposed to correspond with the Hebrew *Elionim velionoth*, "gods and goddesses." This may be true; the worship of the Phœnicians, as of other heathen nations, was, no doubt, a corruption of the ancient patriarchal faith: but it is plain, that Abram here acknowledges Melchizedek as a worshipper of the true God: and in v. 22,

20 And blessed be the most high
God, which hath delivered thine enemies into thy hand. And he gave
c Heb. 7. 4. him [c]tithes of all.
21 And the king of Sodom said
† Heb. souls. unto Abram, Give me the †persons,
and take the goods to thyself.
22 And Abram said to the king of
Sodom, I have lift up mine hand unto
the LORD, the most high God, the
possessor of heaven and earth,
23 That I will not *take* from a
thread even to a shoelatchet, and
that I will not take anything that *is*
thine, lest thou shouldest say, I have
made Abram rich:
24 Save only that which the young
men have eaten, and the portion of
the men which went with me, Aner,
Eshcol, and Mamre; let them take
their portion.

CHAPTER XV.

1 *God encourageth Abram.* 2 *Abram complaineth for want of an heir.* 4 *God promiseth him a son, and a multiplying of his seed.* 6 *Abram is justified by faith.* 7 *Canaan is promised again, and confirmed by a sign,* 12 *and a vision.*

AFTER these things the word of
the LORD came unto Abram in
a vision, saying, Fear not, Abram: I
am thy shield, *and* thy exceeding
[a]great reward. a Ps. 16. 5.

Abram uses the very titles of God, which had been used by Melchizedek before, coupling with them the most sacred name JEHOVAH, the name of the Covenant God, under which He was ever adored by the chosen seed as specially their God.

19. *possessor of heaven and earth*] The LXX. and Vulg. have "Maker of heaven and earth." This is probably the true meaning, but the word may have either significance (Ges. 'Th.' p. 1221. So Delitzsch and Keil).

20. *he gave him tithes of all*] The sentence, as it stands, is ambiguous, but the sense is obviously (as LXX., Joseph., Jonathan, and Heb. vii. 6) "Abram gave Melchizedek tithes of all," *i. e.* the *spolia opima*, the tenth part of the spoil which he had taken from the enemy (Joseph. 'Ant.' I. 10).

21. *Give me the persons, and take the goods to thyself.*] *i. e.* restore those of my people, whom you have rescued, but keep whatever other property of mine you may have lighted on.

22. *I have lift up mine hand unto the LORD*] A common form of solemn attestation in all nations. (See Dan. xii. 7, Virg. 'Æn.' XII. 195.) On the identification of the name El-elion with JEHOVAH, and on the use of the latter name, see notes on vv. 1, 18.

23. *That I will not take*] Lit. "If I will take." The particle *if* was constantly used in swearing, there being an ellipsis of some such expression as "God do so to me and more also if," (1 S. iii. 17). The particle is literally rendered in Heb. iii. 11. There is a marked difference between Abram's conduct to Melchizedek, and his conduct to the king of Sodom. From Melchizedek he receives refreshment and treats him with honour and respect. Towards the king of Sodom he is distant and reserved. Probably the vicious lives of the inhabitants of Sodom made him careful not to lay himself under any obligation to their king, lest he should become too much associated with him and them.

24. *the young men*] Abram's trained servants, whom he had led to the fight (Cp. 2 S. ii. 14, 1 K. xx. 14).

CHAP. XV. **1.** *After these things the word of the LORD came unto Abram in a vision*] We have in this chapter a repetition of the promises to Abram, given when he was first called (ch. xii. 1), and when he first entered into the land of Canaan (ch. xii. 7), with the farther assurance that his own son should be his heir. This is the first time that the expression so frequent afterwards "the word of the LORD" occurs in the Bible. It has been questioned whether the "vision" was a dream or waking vision. The same word is used of Balaam, "which saw the *vision* of the Almighty, falling, but having his eyes open" (Num. xxiv. 4, 16). The way in which Abram was led out and saw the stars, and the subsequent reality of the sacrifice, look like a waking vision, and it is not till v. 12, that he falls into a deep sleep.

Fear not] Abram had now become a great man, with wealth and a comparatively settled home: but he was in a land of strangers, and many of them of godless life. He had been engaged in a war, and his very victory might bring reprisals. In his old age he had no children to support and defend him. Accordingly he now is assured of God's farther protection, and secured against those feelings of despondency natural to one who was lonely, childless, and in danger. It is observed that the words "fear not" have introduced many announcements of Messiah, as Joh. xii. 15; Luke i. 13, 30, ii. 10 (Wordsworth).

thy exceeding great reward] The word *great* is here an infinitive absolute used ad-

2 And Abram said, Lord God,
what wilt thou give me, seeing I go
childless, and the steward of my house
is this Eliezer of Damascus?
3 And Abram said, Behold, to me
thou hast given no seed: and, lo, one
born in my house is mine heir.
4 And, behold, the word of the
Lord *came* unto him, saying, This
shall not be thine heir; but he that
shall come forth out of thine own
bowels shall be thine heir.
5 And he brought him forth a-
broad, and said, Look now toward
heaven, and tell the stars, if thou be
able to number them: and he said
unto him, [b]So shall thy seed be. [b] Rom. 4. 18.
6 And he [c]believed in the Lord; [c] Rom. 4. 3. Gal. 3. 6. Jam. 2. 23.
and he counted it to him for right-
eousness.

---

verbially, so that the more exact rendering may be, "Thy reward exceeding abundantly." The LXX. render "Thy reward shall be exceeding great," which is approved by Rœdiger (in Ges. 'Thes.' p. 1257), Rosenm., Delitzsch.

2. *Lord God*] *Adonai* Jehovah. This is the first use of these two words together. When separate, both are rendered by versions, ancient and modern, by the same word Lord. Except in v. 8, the same combination occurs again in the Pentateuch, only in Deut. iii. 24, ix. 26. In all these passages it is in the vocative case, and Jehovah alone does not occur in Genesis as a vocative (Quarry, 'Genesis,' p. 234).

seeing I go childless] Abram, though blessed personally, feels that the promises of God seem to extend into the future, and does not understand that they can be fulfilled in him alone.

the steward of my house is this Eliezer of Damascus] The literal rendering is "The son of the business" (or perhaps "of the possession") "of my house, he is Damascus Eliezer." It is most probable that "Damascus" is put for "a man of Damascus," as the Authorized Version. The words rendered "steward of my house" are very obscure, so that some ancient versions leave them untranslated. The older critics generally render "son of the business," *i.e.* "steward;" the majority of modern commentators, after the Syriac, preferring "son of possession," *i.e.* "heir." The passage, therefore, must be read either "the steward," or "the heir of my house is Eliezer of Damascus." The tradition of Abram's connection with Damascus has already been referred to (see Nicol. Damasc. Ap. Joseph. 'Ant.' I. 7; Justin. XXXVI. 2). If Abram came into Palestine by the way of Damascus, it is not unlikely that he should have taken his principal retainer from that place.

3. *one born in my house*] Lit. "son of my house." The expression is like, but not necessarily equivalent to that in ch. xvii. 12, 27 (יְלִיד־בָּיִת), *he that is born in the house*, as opposed to those *bought with money of any stranger*. It is quite possible that the title "son of my house," was applied to inmates of the house, especially those in honourable office in the household, whether born in the family, or afterwards adopted into it. The relation of the head of a family to his retainers was, in the case of Abram at least, truly paternal. It evidently more resembled the connection between a feudal chief and his vassals than that between a master and his slaves. That some of them were "bought with money," appears indeed from the passages above referred to; but they were evidently not in the abject condition which attached to slavery in later days, and the principal among them was marked out in default of his own offspring as heir to his master, though Abram had near relations, and some of them at no greater distance from him than Lot and his family, then living in the plains of Jordan.

5. *tell the stars*] In the promise to Noah the rainbow had been the sign given from on high, a sacramental promise of mercy to mankind. Now to Abram the still brighter and more enduring token is the starry firmament. His seed should abide as "the faithful witness in heaven." There is the pledge of a brilliant future for his house, even as regards material prosperity; the pledge of still greater blessings to that spiritual family, which by baptism into Christ became "Abraham's seed, and heirs according to the promise" (Gal. iii. 27, 29).

6. *And he believed in the Lord; and he counted it to him for righteousness*] The root of the word rendered *believed* has the sense of supporting, sustaining, strengthening. Hence in the Hiphil conjugation (as here), it signifies to hold as firm, to rest upon as firm, hence to believe and rely upon as true and stable (Ges. 'Thes.' p. 114). The promise here made by the Lord to Abram was given to him before circumcision, whilst there was yet not even the germ of Levitical Law. It contained in it the promise of Christ. It elicited from Abram the great evangelical principle of faith. God promised that which was opposed to all appearance and likelihood. Abram relied on that promise. He surrendered his own wisdom

7 And he said unto him, I *am* the
LORD that brought thee out of Ur of
the Chaldees, to give thee this land
to inherit it.
8 And he said, Lord GOD, whereby shall I know that I shall inherit it?
9 And he said unto him, Take me
an heifer of three years old, and a she
goat of three years old, and a ram of
three years old, and a turtledove, and
a young pigeon.
10 And he took unto him all these,
and divided them in the midst, and
laid each piece one against another:
but the birds divided he not.
11 And when the fowls came down
upon the carcases, Abram drove them
away.

---

to the wisdom of God, and so gave up his own will to the will of God. So he became the heir of the promises; and the internal principle of faith became to him the true principle of righteousness. It was the only righteousness possible for the feeble and the sinful; for it was a reposing on the power and the love of the Almighty and the Holy One. It was therefore reckoned to him as what may be called a passive righteousness, and at the same time it was productive in him of an active righteousness: for the soul which relies on the truth, power, and goodness of another, in the strength of that truth, power, and goodness, can itself be active in them all: taking advantage of the power and goodness relied upon, it becomes itself powerful and good and true. The Apostles naturally dwell upon this first recorded instance of faith, faith in God, implied faith in Christ, and consequent accounting of righteousness, recorded before all legal enactments, as illustrative of the great evangelical grace of faith, its power as resting on One who is all powerful, and its sanctifying energy, as containing in itself the principle of holiness and the germ of every righteous act. (Rom. iv. v.; Gal. iii.; Heb. xi.; Jas. ii., &c. &c.)

7. *I am the LORD that brought thee out of Ur of the Chaldees*] In ch. xi. 31, Terah is represented as having left Ur of the Chaldees and settled in Haran with Abram, Sarai and Lot; whilst in ch. xii. 1, Abram is represented as having been called by the Lord to go *out* of Haran, cp. v. 4. These different statements are thought to be inconsistent with each other and referable to three different hands. Whether there was a distinct command to Abram to leave Ur does not appear. The LORD by His Providence may have led him and his father out of Ur to Haran, with the design of leading him further onward, and afterwards by special revelation have called him to leave Haran and to go to Canaan (see Quarry, p. 430).

8. *whereby shall I know*] Abram believed God; but there may have been some misgiving as to the reality of what he saw and heard; like St Peter, who "wist not that it was true which was done by the angel, but thought he saw a vision" (Acts xii. 9): and even where there is much faith, a man may distrust himself, may feel that though now the belief is strong, yet ere long the first impression and so the firm conviction may fade away. Thus Gideon (Jud. vi. 17), Hezekiah (2 K. xx. 8), the Blessed Virgin (Luk. i. 34) asked a sign in confirmation of their faith, and, as here to Abram, it was graciously given them.

9. *Take me an heifer of three years old*] The age chosen was probably because then the animals were in full age and vigour (Chrysost. 'in Gen. Hom. XXVI.'). The animals were those which specially formed the staple of Abram's wealth: they were also those, which in after times were specially ordained for sacrificial offerings. It has been said, that the transaction was not a real sacrifice, as there was no sprinkling of blood, nor offering on an altar: but the essence of the true Hebrew sacrifice was in the slaying of the victim, for the very word זָבַח (*Zebach*, sacrifice) signifies *slaying:* and it was rather with the shedding of blood than with its sprinkling that atonement was made (Heb. ix. 22). The covenant was made according to the custom of ancient nations. The sacrificed victims were cut into two pieces, and the covenanting parties passed between them (see Jerem. xxxiv. 18, 19). The very word covenant in Hebrew, *Berith*, is supposed by Gesenius to be from a root signifying *to cut* ('Thes.' p. 238); and the common formula for "to make a covenant" is *carath berith*, "to cut a covenant" (so v. 18), comp. the Greek ὅρκια τέμνειν (Hom. 'Il.' v. 124) and the Lat. *fœdus ferire* (see Bochart, 'Hieroz.' I. 332). The division into two is supposed to represent the two parties to the covenant; and their passing between the divided pieces to signify their union into one. In this case Abram was there in person to pass between the pieces, and the manifested presence of God passed between them under the semblance of fire (v. 17).

10. *the birds divided he not*] So under the Law the doves offered as burnt offerings were not cleft in two (Lev. i. 17).

11. *the fowls*] The birds of prey. The

12 And when the sun was going
down, a deep sleep fell upon Abram;
and, lo, an horror of great darkness
fell upon him.
13 And he said unto Abram, Know
Acts 7. 6. of a surety [d]that thy seed shall be a
stranger in a land *that is* not theirs,
and shall serve them; and they shall
afflict them four hundred years;
14 And also that nation, whom
they shall serve, will I judge: and
afterward shall they come out with
great substance.
15 And thou shalt go to thy fathers
in peace; thou shalt be buried in a
good old age.
16 But in the fourth generation
they shall come hither again: for the
iniquity of the Amorites *is* not yet
full.
17 And it came to pass, that, when
the sun went down, and it was dark,
behold a smoking furnace, and †a burn- † Heb.
ing lamp that passed between those *a lamp of fire.*
pieces. [e] chap. 12.
18 In the same day the LORD 7. & 13. 15.
made a covenant with Abram, say- & 26. 4.
ing, [e]Unto thy seed have I given this Deut. 34. 4.

---

word used (*ait*) means any rapacious animal, especially vultures or other birds of prey. It is probably of the same root as the Greek ἀετός, eagle.

Abram drove them away] It is generally thought, that the vultures seeking to devour the sacrifice before the covenant was ratified typified the enemies of Israel, especially the Egyptians; and in a spiritual sense they represent the spiritual enemies, which seek to destroy the soul, keeping it from union with God through the accepted sacrifice of His Son (see Knobel in loc.).

12. *when the sun was going down*] The evening came on before all the preparations were made, a solemn time for concluding the covenant between God and the seed of Abram; but it may have been said that it was evening, not night, in order to shew that the great darkness was preternatural (V. Gerlach).

a deep sleep] The same word as that used Gen. ii. 21, when Eve was taken from Adam's side. The constant translation, ἔκστασις (ecstasy), by the LXX. shews the belief that the sleep was sent by God for purposes of Divine revelation.

an horror of great darkness] Lit. **a horror, a great darkness.** The prophets were frequently appalled when admitted to the special presence of God: but here perhaps the horror was connected also with the announcement about to be made to Abram of the sufferings of his posterity.

13. *four hundred years*] In Ex. xii. 40 it is called 430. Possibly here the reckoning is in round numbers; also the Hebrews were not ill-treated during the whole 430 years.

15. *And thou shalt go to thy fathers in peace*] A similar expression occurs ch. xxv. 8, xxxv. 29, xlix. 33. It is interpreted to mean either going to the grave, in which his father or his people had been buried, or, (as by Knobel and others) going to that place, where the souls of his ancestors are in the state of separate spirits. That it cannot mean the former here seems to follow from the fact, that Abram was not to be buried in his father's burying-place, but in a grave which he himself purchased in the land of his adoption.

16. *in the fourth generation*] On the chronology from the Descent into Egypt to the Exodus, see note on Exod.

the iniquity of the Amorites is not yet full] The Amorites, the most powerful people in Canaan, are here put for the Canaanites in general. Their state of moral corruption is abundantly manifest in the early chapters of Genesis; and in the Divine foreknowledge it was seen that they would add sin to sin, and so at length be destroyed by the Divine vengeance. Still the long-suffering of God waited for them, giving time for repentance, if they would be converted and live.

17. *when the sun went down, and it was dark*] Or, "when the sun had gone down, that there was a thick darkness." So the Vulgate.

a smoking furnace, and a lamp of fire] This was the token of the presence of God, as when He appeared to Moses in the burning bush, and to the Israelites in a pillar of fire. The word *lamp* may very probably here signify a flame or tongue of fire. The Hebrew word which is cognate with *lamp*, and the other Aryan words of like sound (λάμπω, λαμπὰς, &c.) has probably its radical significance *a lambendo*, a lambent flame. Compare *labium*, *lip*, &c. (see Ges. 'Th.' p. 759)

18. *made a covenant*] Lit. "cut a covenant." See above on v 9.

land, from the river of Egypt unto the
great river, the river Euphrates:
19 The Kenites, and the Kenizzites, and the Kadmonites,
20 And the Hittites, and the Perizzites, and the Rephaims,
21 And the Amorites, and the Canaanites, and the Girgashites, and the
Jebusites.

CHAPTER XVI.

1 Sarai, being barren, giveth Hagar to Abram. 4 Hagar, being afflicted for despising her mistress, runneth away. 7 An angel sendeth her back to submit herself, 11 and telleth her of her child. 15 Ishmael is born.

NOW Sarai Abram's wife bare
him no children: and she had
an handmaid, an Egyptian, whose
name *was* Hagar.
2 And Sarai said unto Abram, Behold now, the LORD hath restrained
me from bearing: I pray thee, go in
unto my maid; it may be that I
may †obtain children by her. And † Heb.
Abram hearkened to the voice of *be builded by her.*
Sarai.

---

the river of Egypt] Many understand not the Nile but the *Wady-El-Arisch* which, however, is called "the brook or stream of Egypt" as in Is. xxvii. 12, not "the river of Egypt." The boundaries of the future possession are not described with minute accuracy, but they are marked as reaching from the valley of the Euphrates to the valley of the Nile. And in 2 Chron. ix. 26, it is distinctly stated that "all the Kings from the river (i.e. Euphrates) even unto the land of the Philistines and to the border of Egypt" were tributary to Solomon. Cp. 2 S. viii. 3.

19. *The Kenites*] An ancient people inhabiting rocky and mountainous regions to the south of Canaan, near the Amalekites (Num. xxiv. 21 seq.; 1 S. xv. 6, xxvii. 10, xxx. 29), a portion of which afterwards migrated to Canaan (Judg. i. 16, iv. 11, 17).

the Kenizzites] Mentioned only here. Bochart ('Phaleg,' IV. 36) conjectures that they had become extinct in the period between Abraham and Moses.

the Kadmonites] i. e. "the Eastern people." They are not elsewhere named. Bochart thought they might be the Hivites, elsewhere enumerated among the Canaanites, and spoken of as inhabiting the neighbourhood of Mount Hermon (Josh. xiii. 3; Judg. iii. 3), which was to the east of Canaan.

20. *the Hittites, and the Perizzites, and the Rephaims*] See on ch. x. 15, xiii. 7, xiv. 5.

21. *the Amorites, the Girgashites, and the Jebusites.*] See on ch. x. 15, 16.

the Canaanites] here distinguished from the kindred tribes, are described as inhabiting the low country "from Sodom to Gerar, unto Gaza; as thou goest, unto Sodom, and Gomorrha, and Admah, and Zeboim, even unto Lasha" (Gen. x. 19).

CHAP. XVI. **1.** *Now Sarai*, &c.] The recapitulatory character of this verse is consistent with the general style of the book of Genesis, and the connection of the first four verses perfectly natural. The promise of offspring had been made to Abram, and he believed the promise. It had not, however, been distinctly assured to him that Sarai should be the mother of the promised seed. The expedient devised by Sarai was according to a custom still prevalent in the east. Laws concerning marriage had not been so expressly given to the patriarchs as they afterwards were. Yet the compliance of Abram with Sarai's suggestion may be considered as a proof of the imperfection of his faith; and it is justly observed, that this departure from the primeval principle of monogamy by Abraham has been an example followed by his descendents in the line of Ishmael, and has proved, morally and physically, a curse to their race.

an handmaid, an Egyptian, whose name was Hagar] Hagar, no doubt, followed Sarai from Egypt after the sojourn there recorded in ch. xii., when it is said that Abraham obtained great possessions, among other things, in "menservants and maidservants," v. 16. It is generally thought that the name Hagar signifies *flight*, a name which may have been given her after her flight from her mistress, recorded in this chapter, in which case the name is here given her proleptically, a thing not uncommon in Scripture history. Others suppose that she derived her name from having fled with her mistress out of Egypt. As she was an Egyptian, it is not likely that the Hebrew or Arabic name of Hagar should have been given her by her own parents.

2. *it may be that I may obtain children by her*] Lit. "I may be built up by her." The words "house" and "family" are in most languages used figuratively the one of the other. The house, considered as representing the family, is built up by the addition of children to it, and so the very word for son, in Hebrew, *Ben*, is most probably connected with the root *banah*, "to build" (see Ges. 'Th.' p. 215). Comp. ch. xxx. 3, where also it appears that the wife, when she gave her handmaid to her

3 And Sarai Abram's wife took
Hagar her maid the Egyptian, after
Abram had dwelt ten years in the
land of Canaan, and gave her to her
husband Abram to be his wife.
4 ¶ And he went in unto Hagar,
and she conceived: and when she saw
that she had conceived, her mistress
was despised in her eyes.
5 And Sarai said unto Abram, My
wrong *be* upon thee: I have given
my maid into thy bosom; and when
she saw that she had conceived, I was
despised in her eyes: the LORD judge
between me and thee.
6 But Abram said unto Sarai, Behold, thy maid *is* in thy hand; do to
her †as it pleaseth thee. And when
Sarai †dealt hardly with her, she fled
from her face.
7 ¶ And the angel of the LORD
found her by a fountain of water in
the wilderness, by the fountain in the
way to Shur.
8 And he said, Hagar, Sarai's maid,
whence camest thou? and whither
wilt thou go? And she said, I flee
from the face of my mistress Sarai.
9 And the angel of the LORD said
unto her, Return to thy mistress, and
submit thyself under her hands.
10 And the angel of the LORD said
unto her, I will multiply thy seed
exceedingly, that it shall not be numbered for multitude.
11 And the angel of the LORD said
unto her, Behold, thou *art* with child,
and shalt bear a son, and shalt call
his name ‖Ishmael; because the LORD
hath heard thy affliction.
12 And he will be a wild man; his
hand *will be* against every man, and

† Heb. *that which is good in thine eyes.*
† Heb. *afflicted her.*
‖ That is, *God shall hear.*

---

husband, esteemed the handmaid's children as her own.

3. *after Abram had dwelt ten years in the land of Canaan*] Abram was now 85 and Sarai 75 years old (cp. xii. 4, xvi. 16, xvii. 17). These words are doubtless intended to account for the impatience produced in them by the delay of the Divine promise.

4. *her mistress was despised in her eyes*] Among the Hebrews barrenness was esteemed a reproach (see ch. xix. 31, xxx. 1, 23; Lev. xx. 20, &c.): and fecundity a special honour and blessing of God (ch. xxi. 6, xxiv. 60; Ex. xxiii. 26; Deut. vii. 14): and such is still the feeling in the east. But, moreover, very probably Hagar may have thought that now Abram would love and honour her more than her mistress (cp. ch. xxix. 33).

5. *My wrong be upon thee*] *i.e.* "my wrong, the injury done to me is due to thee, must be imputed to thee, thou art to be blamed for it, inasmuch as thou sufferest it and dost not punish the aggressor." So in effect all the versions, LXX., Vulg., Targg., &c.

7. *the angel of the LORD*] In v. 13 distinctly called *the* LORD. See on ch. xii. 7.

Shur] according to Joseph. ('Ant.' VI. 7) is Pelusium, near the mouth of the Nile, which, however, seems more probably to be the equivalent for Sin (see Ges. 'Thes.' p. 947). Onkelos renders here "Hagra." The desert of Shur is generally thought to be the north eastern part of the wilderness of Paran, called at present *Al-jifar*. Hagar, no doubt, in her flight from Sarai, took the route most likely to lead her back to her native land of Egypt; and Gesenius supposes that Shur very probably corresponded with the modern Suez.

8. *Hagar, Sarai's maid*] The words of the angel recal to Hagar's mind that she was the servant of Sarai, and therefore owed her obedience.

11. *Ishmael; because the LORD hath heard*] *i.e.* "God heareth, because JEHOVAH hath heard." The name of God, by which all nations might acknowledge Him, is expressed in the name Ishmael, but the name JEHOVAH, the covenant God of Abraham, is specially mentioned, that she may understand the promise to come to her from Him, who had already assured Abraham of the blessing to be poured upon his race.

12. *a wild man*] Lit. "a wild ass of, or among men;" *i.e.* wild and fierce as a wild ass of the desert. A rendering has been suggested, "a wild ass, a man, whose hand is against every man." The suggestion is very ingenious; but for such a rendering we should have expected to find the word *Ish* (*vir*) not, as it is in the original, *Adam* (*homo*). The word *pere*, wild ass, is probably from the root *para*, signifying "to run swiftly." This animal is frequently mentioned in Scripture, and often as a type of lawless, restless, unbridled dispositions in human beings (see Job xi. 12, xxiv. 5; Ps. civ. 11; Is. xxxii. 14; Jer. ii. 24; Dan. v. 21; Hos. viii. 9). In Job xxxix. 5, another Hebrew word is used, but most commentators consider that the same animal is meant. The description of their

[a chap. 25. 18.] every man's hand against him; [a]and
he shall dwell in the presence of all
his brethren.

13 And she called the name of the
LORD that spake unto her, Thou
God seest me: for she said, Have
I also here looked after him that
seeth me?

14 Wherefore the well was called
[b chap. 24. 62.] [b]‖ Beer-lahai-roi; behold, *it is* between
[‖ That is, *the well of him that liveth* and *seeth me*.] Kadesh and Bered.

15 ¶ And Hagar bare Abram a son:
and Abram called his son's name,
which Hagar bare, Ishmael.

16 And Abram *was* fourscore and
six years old, when Hagar bare Ishmael to Abram.

CHAPTER XVII.

1 *God reneweth the covenant.* 5 *Abram his name is changed in token of a greater blessing.* 10 *Circumcision is instituted.* 15 *Sarai her name is changed, and she blessed.* 17 *Isaac is promised.* 23 *Abraham and Ishmael are circumcised.*

AND when Abram was ninety
years old and nine, the LORD
appeared to Abram, and said unto [a chap. 5. 22.]
him, I *am* the Almighty God; [a]walk [‖ Or, *upright*, or, *sincere*.]
before me, and be thou ‖ perfect.

---

great speed in Xen. 'Anab.' Lib. I. is well known. Gesenius refers to a picture of the wild ass of Persia in Ker Porter's 'Travels in Georgia and Persia,' Vol. I. p. 459, and says, that a living specimen which he saw in the London Zoological Gardens in 1835 exactly corresponded with this picture ('Thes.' p. 1123).

his hand will be against every man, &c.] or "upon every man," a common phrase for violence and injury (cp. Gen. xxxvii. 27; Exod. ix. 3; Deut. ii. 16; Josh. ii. 19; 1 S. xviii. 17, 21, xxiv. 13, 14). The violent character and lawless life of the Bedouin descendants of Ishmael from the first till this day is exactly described in these words.

in the presence of all his brethren]. Lit. "in front" or "before the face of all his brethren." This may point to that constant attitude of the Bedouin Arabs, living every where in close proximity to their kindred races, hovering round them, but never mingling with them: or, we may render "to the east of all his brethren," a translation adopted by Rosenm., Gesen., Tuch, Knobel, Delitzsch, &c. The Arabs are called in Job i. 3, "the children of the east," and in some passages of Scripture the phrase "in the presence of," is explained to mean "eastward of" (see Numb. xxi. 11; Josh. xv. 8; Zech. xiv. 4); the rationale of this being, that when a man looked toward the sunrise, the east was *before* him.

13. *Thou God seest me: for she said, Have I also here looked after him that seeth me?*] **Thou art a God of seeing, for have I also seen here after seeing?** The Authorized Version has nearly followed the rendering of the LXX. and Vulg., which is inadmissible. The meaning of the words is probably, "Thou art a God that seest all things," (or perhaps "that revealest Thyself in visions"); "and am I yet living and seeing, after seeing God?" (cp. Judg. xiii. 21). So apparently Onkelos; and this rendering is adopted by Rosenm., Gesen., Tuch, Kalisch, Delitzsch, and most moderns. The name of God throughout this chapter is JEHOVAH, except when Hagar the Egyptian speaks; yet the God of vision who reveals Himself to her is carefully identified with the JEHOVAH of Abraham.

14. *Beer-lahai-roi*] "The well of life of vision," *i.e.* where life remained after vision of God. (See Ges. 'Thes.' p. 175.) This seems to be the meaning of the name according to the etymology derived from the last verse, though others render it "the well of the living One (*i.e.* the living God) of vision."

between Kadesh and Bered] On the site of Kadesh and its uncertainty see on ch. xiv. 7. The uncertainty of the site of Bered is still greater, and therefore the difficulty of arriving at the exact position of Beer-lahai-roi is almost insuperable. Mr Rowlands (in Williams' 'Holy City,' I. 465) thinks that he has discovered its site at a place called Moilahhi, about 10 hours south of Ruheibeh, in the road from Beersheba to Shur, or Jebel-es-sur, a mountain range running north and south in the longitude of Suez.

CHAP. XVII. **1.** *And when Abram was ninety years old and nine*] *i.e.* just thirteen years after the events related in the last chapter, compare v. 25, where Ishmael is said to be now thirteen years old.

the Almighty God] El-Shaddai. The word Shaddai, translated by most versions "mighty," or "Almighty," is generally thought (by Gesen., Rosenm., Lee, &c. &c.) to be a plural of excellence (in this respect like Elohim), derived from the root *Shadad*, the primary meaning of which appears to have been "to be strong," "to act strongly," though more commonly used in the sense of "to destroy, to devastate." The later Greek versions Aq., Sym., Theod., render ἱκανός, "sufficient," "all-sufficient." So Theodoret, Hesych., Saad. Accordingly, Rashi and some of the Jewish writers consider it to be compounded of two words, signifying "who is sufficient?" the improbability

2 And I will make my covenant
between me and thee, and will multiply thee exceedingly.
3 And Abram fell on his face: and
God talked with him, saying,
4 As for me, behold, my covenant
is with thee, and thou shalt be a
† Heb. father of † many nations.
multitude of nations. 5 Neither shall thy name any more
be called Abram, but thy name shall
Rom. 4. be Abraham; [b]for a father of many
nations have I made thee.
6 And I will make thee exceeding
fruitful, and I will make nations of
thee, and kings shall come out of thee.
7 And I will establish my covenant between me and thee and thy
seed after thee in their generations
for an everlasting covenant, to be a
God unto thee, and to thy seed after
thee.
8 And I will give unto thee, and to
thy seed after thee, the land † wherein † Heb.
thou art a stranger, all the land of *of thy sojournings.*
Canaan, for an everlasting possession;
and I will be their God.
9 ¶ And God said unto Abraham,
Thou shalt keep my covenant therefore, thou, and thy seed after thee in
their generations.
10 This *is* my covenant, which ye
shall keep, between me and you and
thy seed after thee; [c]Every man child [c] Acts 7. 8.
among you shall be circumcised.
11 And ye shall circumcise the flesh
of your foreskin; and it shall be a
[d]token of the covenant betwixt me [d] Acts 7. 8. Rom. 4. 11.
and you.
12 And he that is † eight days old † Heb. *a son of eight days.*
[e]shall be circumcised among you, every [e] Lev. 12. 3.
man child in your generations, he that
is born in the house, or bought with Luke 2. 21. John 7. 22.
money of any stranger, which *is* not
of thy seed.

---

of which derivation is very great. The title, or character, El-Shaddai, is said, Exod. vi. 2, 3, to have been that by which God was revealed to the patriarchs, not then, at least in its full meaning, by the name JEHOVAH; and it is noted as occurring in those passages which the German critics call Elohistic. In this very verse, however, we read it in immediate juxtaposition with the name JEHOVAH, and in Ruth i. 20, 21, we find the identification of JEHOVAH with Shaddai. Probably, like Elohim, and Adonai, we may consider El-Shaddai (a title known to Balaam, Num. xxiv. 4, 16, and constantly used in Job), to have been one of the more general world-wide titles of the Most High, whilst JEHOVAH was rather the name by which His own chosen people knew and acknowledged Him. The title, which especially points to power, seems most appropriate when a promise is made, which seems even to Abram and Sarai to be well-nigh impossible of fulfilment.

2. *I will make my covenant*] The word for "make" is different from that used in xv. 18. There God is said to have "cut" a covenant with Abram by sacrifice, which phrase has probably special reference to the sacrifice and also to the two parties who made the covenant by sacrifice (see on xv. 9). Here He says, "I will *give* my covenant between Me and thee." The freedom of the covenant of promise is expressed in this latter phrase. It was a gift from a superior, rather than a bargain between equals; and as it was accompanied by the rite of circumcision, it was typical of the freedom of that covenant made afterwards to Christians in Christ, and sealed to them in the sacred rite of baptism.

4. *of many nations*] **Of a multitude of nations**; as in margin.

5. *Abraham*] *i.e.* "father of a multitude." He was originally *Ab-ram*, "exalted father." Now he becomes *Ab-raham*, "father of a multitude;" *raham*, in Arabic, being a vast number, a great multitude. Abraham was literally the ancestor of the twelve tribes of Israel, of the Ishmaelites, of the descendants of Keturah and of the Edomites; but spiritually he is the father of all the faithful, who by faith in Christ are "Abraham's seed, and heirs according to the promise" (Gal. iii. 29). It has been very generally believed that the letter *H* here introduced into the names both of Abraham and Sarah is one of the two radical letters of the name JEHOVAH (as the other radical *J* was introduced into the name Joshua), whereby the owner of the name is doubly consecrated and bound in covenant to the LORD (see Delitzsch, in loc.). The custom of giving the name at the time of circumcision (Luke i. 59) probably originated from the change of Abraham's name having been made when that rite was first instituted.

10. *This is my covenant*] *i.e.* the sign, token and bond of the covenant.

12. *eight days old*] Seven days, a sacred number, were to pass over the child before he was so consecrated to God's service. There was a significance in the number 7, and there was a reason for the delay that the child might grow strong enough to bear the operation.

13 He that is born in thy house,
and he that is bought with thy money,
must needs be circumcised: and my
covenant shall be in your flesh for an
everlasting covenant.
14 And the uncircumcised man
child whose flesh of his foreskin is not
circumcised, that soul shall be cut off
from his people; he hath broken my
covenant.
15 ¶ And God said unto Abraham,
As for Sarai thy wife, thou shalt not
call her name Sarai, but Sarah *shall*
her name *be*.
16 And I will bless her, and give
thee a son also of her: yea, I will bless
her, and †she shall be *a mother* of na- † Heb.
tions; kings of people shall be of *she shall*
her. *become nations.*
17 Then Abraham fell upon his
face, and laughed, and said in his
heart, Shall *a child* be born unto him
that is an hundred years old? and
shall Sarah, that is ninety years old,
bear?
18 And Abraham said unto God,
O that Ishmael might live before
thee!

---

13. *He that is born in thy house*, &c.] "Moses has nowhere given any command, nor even so much as an exhortation, inculcating the duty of circumcision upon any person not a descendant, or a slave of Abraham, or of his descendants, unless he wished to partake of the passover .... In none of the historical books of the Old Testament do we find the smallest trace of circumcision as necessary to the salvation of foreigners, who acknowledge the true God, or requisite even to the confession of their faith: no not so much as in the detailed story of Naaman (2 K. v.); in which indeed every circumstance indicates that the circumcision of that illustrious personage can never be supposed" (Michaelis, 'Laws of Moses,' Bk. IV. Art. 184). There is a marked distinction in this between circumcision and baptism. Judaism was intended to be the religion of a peculiar isolated people. Its rites therefore were for them alone. Christianity is for the whole human race; the Church is to be catholic; baptism to be administered to all that will believe.

14. *that soul shall be cut off from his people*] The rabbinical writers very generally understand that the excision should be by Divine judgment. Christian interpreters have mostly understood the infliction of death by the hand of the magistrate: some (Cleric. and Michael. in loc.) either exile or excommunication. The latter opinion was afterwards retracted by Michaelis, and it is pretty certain that death in some form is intended (see Gesen. 'Thes.' p. 718).

15. *thou shalt not call her name Sarai, but Sarah shall her name be*] There is but little doubt that Sarah signifies "Princess," in allusion probably to the princely race which was to spring from her, though Ikenius, followed by Rosenmüller, argues in favour of a meaning to be derived from the Arabic root *Saraa*, signifying, "to have a numerous progeny." As to the original name *Sarai*, the older interpreters generally understood it to signify "my princess:" the change to Sarah indicating that she was no longer the princess of a single race, but rather that all the families of the earth should have an interest in her (Jerome, 'Qu. Hebr.' p. 522); many think that Sarai means simply "noble, royal," whilst Sarah more definitely means "princess;" which, however, seems neither etymologically nor exegetically probable. Ewald explains Sarai as meaning "contentious," from the verb Sarah, שָׂרָה, which (Gen. xxxii. 29; Hos. xii. 4) occurs in the sense of "to fight, to contend." This meaning is approved by Gesenius ('Thes.' p. 1338), but the more usual derivation is probably the true.

16. *she shall be a mother of nations*] Heb. "she shall become nations."

17. *laughed*] Onkel. renders "rejoiced." Pseudo-Jon. "marvelled." The Jewish commentators, and many of the Christian fathers, understood this laughter to be the laughter of joy not of unbelief (Aug. 'De Civ.' XVI. 26). So also many moderns, *e.g.* Calvin, "partly exulting with gladness, partly carried beyond himself with wonder, he burst into laughter." It is thought also that our Blessed Lord may have alluded to this joy of Abraham (Joh. viii. 56), "Your father Abraham rejoiced to see My day, *and* he saw it and was glad;" for it was at the most distinct promise of a son, who was to be the direct ancestor of the Messiah, that the laughter is recorded (cp. also the words of the Blessed Virgin, Luke i. 47). On the other hand it must be admitted, that Abraham's words immediately following the laughter, seem at first sight as implying some unbelief, or at least weakness of faith, though they may be interpreted as the language of wonder rather than of incredulity.

18. *O that Ishmael might live before thee!*] These words may be interpreted in two ways, according as we understand the laughter of Abraham. They may mean, "I dare not hope for so great a boon as a son to be born hereafter to myself and Sarah in our old

f chap. 18. 10. & 21. 2.

19 And God said, f Sarah thy wife
shall bear thee a son indeed; and thou
shalt call his name Isaac: and I will
establish my covenant with him for
an everlasting covenant, *and* with his
seed after him.
20 And as for Ishmael, I have heard
thee: Behold, I have blessed him,
and will make him fruitful, and will
multiply him exceedingly; g twelve
princes shall he beget, and I will
make him a great nation.
21 But my covenant will I establish
with Isaac, which Sarah shall bear unto
thee at this set time in the next year.
22 And he left off talking with him,
and God went up from Abraham.
23 ¶ And Abraham took Ishmael
his son, and all that were born in his
house, and all that were bought with
his money, every male among the men
of Abraham's house; and circumcised
the flesh of their foreskin in the selfsame day, as God had said unto him.
24 And Abraham *was* ninety years
old and nine, when he was circumcised in the flesh of his foreskin.
25 And Ishmael his son *was* thirteen years old, when he was circumcised in the flesh of his foreskin.
26 In the selfsame day was Abraham circumcised, and Ishmael his son.
27 And all the men of his house,
born in the house, and bought with
money of the stranger, were circumcised with him.

g chap. 25. 12.

---

age, but O that Ishmael may be the heir of Thy promises!" or they may imply only a fear, that now, when another heir is assured to Abraham, Ishmael should be excluded from all future inheritance.

19. *Isaac*] *i.e.* "he laughs," the third person singular of the present tense: similar forms are Jacob, Jair, Jabin, &c.

20. *as for Ishmael, I have heard thee*] There is an allusion to the significance of the name Ishmael, viz. "God heareth."

25. *Ishmael his son was thirteen years old*] The Arabs have in consequence always circumcised their sons at the age of 13. Josephus mentions this ('Ant.' I. 13), and it is well known that the custom still prevails among the Mahometan nations.

NOTE A on CHAP. XVII. v. 10. CIRCUMCISION.

(1) Reasons for the rite. (2) Origin of circumcision, whether pre-Abrahamic or not. (*a*) Egyptians said to have first used it. (*β*) Answer from lateness and uncertainty of the testimony. (*γ*) Balance of arguments.

THE reasons for this rite may have been various, 1st, to keep the descendants of Abraham distinct from the idolatrous nations round about them, the other inhabitants of Palestine not being circumcised, 2ndly, to indicate the rigour and severity of the Law of God, simply considered as Law, in contrast to which the ordinance that succeeded to it in the Christian dispensation indicated the mildness and mercy of the new covenant, 3rdly, to signify that the body should be devoted as a living sacrifice to God, "our hearts and all our members being mortified from all carnal and worldly lusts," and so to typify moral purity. (See Deut. x. 16; Jer. iv. 4; Acts vii. 51).

An important question arises as to the origin of circumcision. Was it first made known and commanded to Abraham, having nowhere been practised before? Or, was it a custom already in use, and now sanctified by God to a higher end and purport? A similar question arose concerning sacrifice. Was it prescribed by revelation or dictated by natural piety and then sanctioned from above? As the rainbow probably did not first appear after the flood, but was then made the token of the Noachic covenant; as the stars of heaven were made the sign of the earlier covenant with Abraham (ch. xv. 5); may it have been also, that circumcision already prevailed among some nations, and was now divinely authorized and made sacred and authoritative? There would be nothing necessarily startling in the latter alternative, when we remember that the corresponding rite of baptism in the Christian dispensation is but one adaptation by supreme authority of natural or legal washings to a Christian purpose and a most spiritual significance.

It is certain that the Egyptians used circumcision (Herod. II. 36, 37, 104; Diod. Sicul. I. 26, 55; Strabo, XVII. p. 524; Phil. Jud. 'De Circumcis.' II. p. 210; Joseph. 'Ant.' VIII. 10; 'Cont. Apion.' I. 22; II. 13). The earliest writer who mentions this is Herodotus. He says, indeed, that the Egyptians and Ethiopians had it from the most remote antiquity, so that he cannot tell which had it first; he mentions the Colchians as also using it (whence Diodorus inferred that they were an Egyptian colony), and says that the Phœnicians and Syrians in Palestine admit that they "learned this practice from the Egyptians" (Herod. II. 104). This is evidently a very loose statement. The Phœnicians probably did not use it, and the Jews, whom Herodotus here calls "the Syrians in Palestine," admitted that they had once dwelt in Egypt, but never admitted that they derived circumcision from thence. The statements of Diodorus and Strabo, which are more or less similar to those of Herodotus, were no doubt partly derived from him, and partly followed the general belief among the Greeks, that the "Jews were originally Egyptians" (Strabo, as above). It is stated by Origen ('in Epist. ad Rom.' ch. II. 13) that the Egyptian priests, soothsayers, prophets, and those learned in hieroglyphics were circumcised; and the same is said by Horapollo (I. 13, 14). If these ancient writers were unsupported by other authorities, there would be no great difficulty in concluding that Herodotus had found circumcision among the Egyptian *priests*, had believed the Jews to be a mere colony from Egypt, and had concluded that the custom originated in Egypt, and from them was learned by the Ishmaelites and other races. It is, however, asserted by some modern Egyptologists, that circumcision must have prevailed from the time of the fourth dynasty, *i.e.* from at least 2400 B.C., therefore much before the date generally assigned to Abraham, B.C. 1996, and that it was not confined to the priests, as is, they say, learned from the mummies and the sculptures, where circumcision is made a distinctive mark between the Egyptians and their enemies (see Sir Gardiner Wilkinson, in Rawlinson's 'Herodotus,' pp. 52, 146, 147, notes). If this be correct, we must conclude, that the Egyptians practised circumcision when Abraham first became acquainted with them, that probably some of Abraham's own Egyptian followers were circumcised, and that the Divine command was not intended to teach a new rite, but to consecrate an old one into a sacramental ordinance. Some even think that they see in the very style of this and the following verses indications that the rite was not altogether new and before unknown; for had it been new and unknown, more accurate directions would have been given of the way in which a painful and dangerous operation should be performed (Michaelis, 'Laws of Moses,' Bk. IV. Ch. iii. Art. 185). The Egyptians, Ethiopians, and perhaps some other African races, are supposed to have adopted it, partly from regard to cleanliness (Herod. II. 36), which the Egyptians, and above all the Egyptian priests, especially affected, partly to guard against disease incident in those hot climates (see Philo, as above, p. 211; Joseph. 'C. Apion.' II. 13), partly for other reasons, which may have been real or imaginary (see Michaelis, as above, Art. 186). This side of the question is ably defended by Michaelis, 'Laws of Moses,' as above, and Kalisch, in loc.

In answer it is truly said, that the Greek historians are too late and too loose in their statements to command our confidence; that the tribes cognate with the Egyptians, such as the Hamite inhabitants of Palestine, were notoriously uncircumcised, that the Egyptians, especially the Egyptian priests, are not unlikely to have adopted the rite at the time when Joseph was their governor and in such high estimation among them, and that the question concerning the relative dates of Abraham and the different Egyptian dynasties is involved in too much obscurity to be made a ground for such an argument as the above to be built upon it. (See Bp. Patrick, in loc.; Heidegger, 'Hist. Patr.' II. 240; Wesseling and Larcher, 'ad Herod.' II. 37, 104; Graves 'on the Pentateuch,' Pt. II. Lect. v.; Wordsworth, in loc.) Again, the argument derived from the ancient Egyptian language proves nothing, the words are lost or doubtful. The argument from the mummies proves nothing, as we have no mummies of the ancient empire. The figures in the hieroglyphics are later still. The only argument of weight is that derived from the old hieroglyphic, common in the pyramids, which is *thought* to represent circumcision. It may on the whole be said, that we cannot conclude from the loose statements of Greek writers 15 centuries later than Abraham, nor even from the evidence of monuments and sculptures as yet perhaps but imperfectly read and uncertain as to their *comparative* antiquity, that circumcision had been known before it was given to Abraham; yet that on the other hand, there would be nothing inconsistent with the testimony of the Mosaic history in the belief, that it had been in use among the Egyptians and other African tribes, before it was elevated by a Divine ordinance into a sacred rite for temporary purposes, to be served in the Mosaic dispensation. A very able summary of the arguments on both sides, not, of course, embracing those drawn from the more recent discoveries in Egypt, is given by Spencer, 'De Legg. Heb.' lib. I. c. 5. § 4. See Deut. x. 16 and Note.

CHAPTER XVIII.

1 *Abraham entertaineth three angels.* 9 *Sarah is reproved for laughing at the strange promise.* 17 *The destruction of Sodom is revealed to Abraham.* 23 *Abraham maketh intercession for the men thereof.*

AND the [a] LORD appeared unto him in the plains of Mamre:
and he sat in the tent door in the
heat of the day;
2 And he lift up his eyes and

[a] Heb. 13. 2.

looked, and, lo, three men stood by
him: and when he saw *them*, he ran
to meet them from the tent door, and
bowed himself toward the ground,
3 And said, My Lord, if now I have
found favour in thy sight, pass not
away, I pray thee, from thy servant:
4 Let a little water, I pray you, be
fetched, and wash your feet, and rest
yourselves under the tree:
5 And I will fetch a morsel of bread,
and †comfort ye your hearts; after † Heb. *stay.*
that ye shall pass on: for therefore
†are ye come to your servant. And † Heb. *you have passed.*
they said, So do, as thou hast said.
6 And Abraham hastened into the
tent unto Sarah, and said, †Make ready † Heb. *Hasten.*
quickly three measures of fine meal,
knead *it*, and make cakes upon the
hearth.
7 And Abraham ran unto the herd,
and fetcht a calf tender and good, and

CHAP. XVIII. 1. *plains of Mamre*] **Oaks or oak grove of Mamre**, see xiii. 18; xiv. 13.

in the heat of the day] Abraham was sitting in his tent under the shade of the trees, at the noon day when the sun was oppressive, and when the duty of hospitality specially suggested to him the receiving of travellers, who might be wearied with their hot journey. The time of the day may be also mentioned, that it might be the more certain that this was an open vision, not a dream of the night.

2. *three men*] In v. 1 it is said, "The LORD appeared unto him;" in v. 22 it is said, "The *men* turned their faces from thence, and went towards Sodom; but Abraham stood yet before the LORD;" in ch. xix. 1 it is said, "There came *two Angels* to Sodom at even." It appears from the comparison of these passages, and indeed from the whole narrative, that of the three men who appeared to Abraham, two were angels, and one was JEHOVAH Himself. On the belief of the ancient Church that these manifestations of God were manifestations of God the Son, anticipations of the Incarnation, see note on ch. xii. 7. See also on this passage, Euseb. 'Demonst. Evan.' Lib. v. c. 9. There was, however, a belief among many of the ancients that the three men here appearing to Abraham symbolized the three Persons of the Trinity; and the Church by appointing this chapter to be read on Trinity Sunday seems to indorse this belief. This need not conflict with the opinion, that the only Person in the Trinity really manifested to the eyes of Abraham was the Son of God, and that the other two were created angels. Indeed such a manifestation may have been reason enough for the choice of this lesson on Trinity Sunday. It has been observed that One of the three mentioned in this chapter is called repeatedly JEHOVAH, but neither of the two in ch. xix. is ever so called.

bowed himself toward the ground] This was merely the profound eastern salutation (cp. ch. xxiii. 7, 12, xxxiii. 6, 7). Abraham as yet was "entertaining angels *unawares*" (Heb. xiii. 2). He may have observed a special dignity in the strangers, but could not have known their heavenly mission.

3. *My Lord*] It is to be noticed that Abraham here addresses One of the three, who appears more noble than the rest. The title which he gives Him is *Adonai*, a plural of excellence, but the Targum of Onkelos has rendered JEHOVAH (יְיָ), as supposing that Abraham had recognized the divinity of the visitor.

4. *wash your feet*] In the hot plains of the east travellers shod only with sandals found the greatest comfort in bathing their feet, when resting from a journey. (See ch. xix. 2, xxiv. 32; Judg. xix. 21; 1 Tim. v. 10.)

5. *comfort ye your hearts*] Lit. "support your hearts." The heart, considered as the centre of vital functions, is put by the Hebrews for the life itself. To support the heart therefore is to refresh the whole vital powers and spirits. (See Ges. 'Thes.' p. 738, 6, לבב, 1. *a.*)

for therefore are ye come to your servant] The patriarch recognizes a providential call upon him to refresh strangers of noble bearing, come to him on a fatiguing journey.

6. *three measures of fine meal*] **Three seahs of the finest flour.** A *seah* was the third part of an ephah according to the Rabbins. Josephus ('Ant.' IX. 4) and Jerome ('Comm. on Matt.' xiii. 33), say that the seah was a modius and a half. The accuracy of this comparison between the Hebrew and Roman measures is doubted, as it does not correspond with the calculations of Rabbinical writers. (See Ges. 'Thes.' pp. 83, 932; Smith, 'Dict. of Bible,' Vol. III. pp. 1741, 1742.) The two words, *Kemach soleth*, rendered "fine meal," are nearly synonymous, both appearing to mean fine flour, the latter being the finer of the two. They might be rendered "flour of fine flour." According to the Rabbinical Commentary, 'Vajikra Rabba,' *soleth* is the *kemach* of *kemachs*, the fine flour of fine flour. (See Ges. 'Thes.' p. 959.)

cakes upon the hearth] Probably the simpler form of cake baked in the midst of hot cinders.

gave *it* unto a young man; and he
hasted to dress it.
8 And he took butter, and milk, and
the calf which he had dressed, and set
it before them; and he stood by them
under the tree, and they did eat.
9 ¶ And they said unto him, Where
is Sarah thy wife? And he said, Behold,
in the tent.
10 And he said, I will certainly
return unto thee according to the time
of life; and, lo, [b]Sarah thy wife shall
have a son. And Sarah heard *it* in
the tent door, which *was* behind
him.
11 Now Abraham and Sarah *were*
old *and* well stricken in age; *and* it
ceased to be with Sarah after the
manner of women.
12 Therefore Sarah laughed within
herself, saying, After I am waxed old
shall I have pleasure, my [c]lord being
old also?
13 And the LORD said unto Abraham,
Wherefore did Sarah laugh,
saying, Shall I of a surety bear a
child, which am old?
14 Is any thing too hard for the
LORD? At the time appointed I will
return unto thee, according to the
time of life, and Sarah shall have a son.
15 Then Sarah denied, saying, I
laughed not; for she was afraid. And
he said, Nay; but thou didst laugh.

[b] chap. 17. 19. & 21. 2.

[c] 1 Pet. 3. 6.

---

8. *butter*] *i.e.* thick milk or clotted cream. The modern Arabs have a simple mode of churning, and make very good butter. Robinson ('Res.' II. p. 180) describes the baking of cakes and making of butter among them in the present day. It is, however, most probable, that the word, rendered *butter* in the Old Testament, was rather thick milk, or more probably, thick cream, though in one place (Prov. xxx. 33), it may perhaps be rendered *cheese*. The ancient inhabitants of Palestine used olive oil where we use butter. (See Rosenm. and Ges. 'Thes.' p. 486.)

they did eat] That spiritual visitants, though in human form, should eat, has been a puzzle to many commentators. Josephus ('Ant.' I. 11) and Philo ('Opp.' II. 18), say it was in appearance only, which is implied by Pseudo-Jonathan, Rashi and Kimchi. If the angels had assumed human bodies, though but for a time, there would have been nothing strange in their eating. In any case, the food may have been consumed, miraculously or not; and the eating of it was a proof that the visit of the angels to Abraham was no mere vision, but a true manifestation of heavenly beings.

10. *he said*] In v. 9 we read "they said," *i.e.* one of the three heavenly guests spoke for the others. Now we have the singular number, and the speaker uses language suited only to the Ruler of nature and of all things.

according to the time of life] There is some difficulty in the rendering of these words. The phrase occurs again, 2 K. iv. 16. It is now generally thought that the sense is the same as in ch. xvii. 21, "at this set time in the next year" (cp. xviii. 14); and that the words should be translated, "when the season revives," *i.e.* when spring or summer comes round again. Compare

χαῖρε, γύναι, φιλότητι· περιπλομένου δ' ἐνιαυτοῦ
τέξεις ἀγλαὰ τέκνα.

Hom. 'Od.' Λ. 247.

(See Rosenm. in loc.; Ges. 'Thes.' p. 470.) Prof. Lee ('Lex.' p. 193) denies the soundness of this criticism, and virtually indorses the Authorized Version, "as (at) the season, period, of a vigorous woman." There is, however, very little doubt that the criticism is correct.

12. *laughed*] Whatever may have been the nature of Abraham's laughter (see xvii. 17), this of Sarah's seems to have resulted from incredulity. She may scarcely have recognized the Divinity of the speaker, and had not perhaps realized the truth of the promise before made to Abraham. St Augustine distinguishes between the laughter of Abraham and that of Sarah thus, "The father laughed, when a son was promised to him, from wonder and joy; the mother laughed, when the three men renewed the promise, from doubtfulness and joy. The angel reproved her, because though that laughter was from joy, yet it was not of full faith. Afterwards by the same angel she was confirmed in faith also." 'De C. D.' XVI. 31.

my lord] See 1 Pet. iii. 6.

13. *the LORD said*] Here the speaker is distinctly called JEHOVAH, and it seems much more reasonable to believe that there was a Theophania of the Son of God, than that a created angel was personating God and speaking in His name.

14. *Is any thing too hard for the LORD?*] Lit. "Is anything too wonderful for the Lord?" Cp. Luke i. 37.

At the time appointed I will return unto thee, according to the time of life] See on v. 10.

16 ¶ And the men rose up from
thence, and looked toward Sodom:
and Abraham went with them to
bring them on the way.
17 And the LORD said, Shall I
hide from Abraham that thing which
I do;
18 Seeing that Abraham shall surely
become a great and mighty nation,
and all the nations of the earth shall
chap. 12. be [d]blessed in him?
& 22. 18. 19 For I know him, that he will
cts 3. 25. command his children and his house-
al. 3. 8. hold after him, and they shall keep
the way of the LORD, to do justice
and judgment; that the LORD may
bring upon Abraham that which he
hath spoken of him.
20 And the LORD said, Because the
cry of Sodom and Gomorrah is great,
and because their sin is very grievous;
21 I will go down now, and see
whether they have done altogether
according to the cry of it, which is
come unto me; and if not, I will
know.
22 And the men turned their faces
from thence, and went toward Sodom:
but Abraham stood yet before the
LORD.
23 ¶ And Abraham drew near,
and said, Wilt thou also destroy the
righteous with the wicked?
24 Peradventure there be fifty righteous within the city: wilt thou also
destroy and not spare the place for
the fifty righteous that *are* therein?
25 That be far from thee to do after
this manner, to slay the righteous with
the wicked: and that the righteous
should be as the wicked, that be far
from thee: Shall not the Judge of all
the earth do right?
26 And the LORD said, If I find in
Sodom fifty righteous within the city,
then I will spare all the place for their
sakes.
27 And Abraham answered and
said, Behold now, I have taken upon
me to speak unto the Lord, which *am
but* dust and ashes:
28 Peradventure there shall lack
five of the fifty righteous: wilt thou
destroy all the city for *lack of* five?

---

16. *Abraham went with them*] The three heavenly visitors all go towards Sodom. Abraham goes some way with them, how far is not said. There is a tradition that he went as far as Caphar-berucha, from which the Dead Sea is visible, through a ravine.

17. *Shall I hide from Abraham*] The LXX. adds here "my son," which is quoted by Philo (I. p. 401, Mangey) as "Abraham, my friend:" so that in all probability, copies of the LXX. in the time of Philo had this afterwards familiar name of Abraham expressed in this verse. Cp. 2 Chr. xx. 7; Isa. xli. 8; James ii. 23.

19. *For I know him, that*] This is the general reading of the ancient Versions, LXX., Vulg., Targg., &c. &c. It does not, however, seem to correspond with the Hebrew idiom. The literal rendering would be, "I have known him, to the end that, in order that, he should command his children, &c." The word (ידע, *to know*) is sometimes used of the eternal foreknowledge and election of God, as in Amos iii. 2, "You only have I known of all the families of the earth." Cp. Exod. xxxiii. 12; Job xxii. 13; Ps. lxxiii. 11, cxliv. 3; Is. lviii. 3; Nah. i. 7. And compare a similar use in the Greek Testament, Rom. viii. 29, xi. 2. The meaning would then be, "I have foreknown and chosen Abraham, that he should be the depositary of my truth, and should teach his children in the way of religion and godliness, that so the promises made to him should be fulfilled in his seed and lineage. So Ges. ('Thes.' p. 571), Rosenm., Tuch, Knobel, Delitzsch, Keil, &c.

20. *the cry*] Cp. ch. iv. 10; Ps. ix. 13.

21. *I will go down*] Ch. xi. 5, 7; Ex. iii. 8. The reason for God's thus revealing His purpose to Abraham seems to have been, that, as Abraham was to be the heir of the promises, he might be taught and might teach his children, who were afterwards to dwell in that very country, that God is not a God of mercy only, as shewn to Abraham and his descendants, but a God of judgment also, as witnessed by His destruction of the guilty cities of the plain.

22. *the men turned their faces from thence, &c.*] The two created angels went on to Sodom (see ch. xix. 1), "but Abraham stood yet before the LORD," stood yet in the presence of that third Being who was not a created angel, but the eternal Word of God, "the Angel of Mighty counsel" (Isai. ix. 6, LXX.); "the Messenger of the covenant" (Mal. iii. 1).

And he said, If I find there forty and five, I will not destroy *it*.

29 And he spake unto him yet again, and said, Peradventure there shall be forty found there. And he said, I will not do *it* for forty's sake.

30 And he said *unto him*, Oh let not the Lord be angry, and I will speak: Peradventure there shall thirty be found there. And he said, I will not do *it*, if I find thirty there.

31 And he said, Behold now, I have taken upon me to speak unto the Lord: Peradventure there shall be twenty found there. And he said, I will not destroy *it* for twenty's sake.

32 And he said, Oh let not the Lord be angry, and I will speak yet but this once: Peradventure ten shall be found there. And he said, I will not destroy *it* for ten's sake.

33 And the LORD went his way, as soon as he had left communing with Abraham: and Abraham returned unto his place.

CHAPTER XIX.

1 Lot entertaineth two angels. 4 The vicious Sodomites are stricken with blindness. 12 Lot is sent for safety into the mountains. 18 He obtaineth leave to go into Zoar. 24 Sodom and Gomorrah are destroyed. 26 Lot's wife is a pillar of salt. 30 Lot dwelleth in a cave. 31 The incestuous original of Moab and Ammon.

AND there came two angels to Sodom at even; and Lot sat in the gate of Sodom: and Lot seeing *them* rose up to meet them; and he bowed himself with his face toward the ground;

2 And he said, Behold now, my lords, turn in, I pray you, into your servant's house, and tarry all night, and [a] wash your feet, and ye shall rise up early, and go on your ways. And they said, Nay; but we will abide in the street all night.

[a] chap. 18. 4.

3 And he pressed upon them greatly; and they turned in unto him, and entered into his house; and he made them a feast, and did bake unleavened bread, and they did eat.

---

32. *I will not destroy it for ten's sake*] A noted example of the efficacy of prayer, of the blessedness of a good leaven in a city or nation, and of the longsuffering mercy of God.

CHAP. XIX. **1.** *two angels*] Lit. **the two angels**. So LXX. The two men, who left Abraham still standing in the presence of the LORD (ch. xviii. 22) now came to Sodom at even.

Lot sat in the gate of Sodom] The gate of the city was, in the ancient towns of the east, the common place of public resort, both for social intercourse and public business. This gate of the city nearly corresponded with the forum or market-place of Greece and Rome. Not only was it the place of public sale, but judges and even kings held courts of justice there. The gate itself was probably an arch with deep recesses, in which were placed the seats of the judges, and benches on either side were arranged for public convenience. (Cp. ch. xxxiv. 20; Deut. xxi. 19, xxii. 15; Ruth iv. 1. See also Hom. 'Il.' Lib. III. 148.)

bowed himself] See on ch. xviii. 2.

2. *my lords*] The Masorites mark this word as "profane," *i. e.* as not taken in the divine, but in the human sense. Lot, like Abraham, only saw in the angels two men, travellers apparently wearied with the way, and he offers them all the rites of hospitality. In those days there were neither inns nor perhaps even caravanserais, so that private houses only could give lodging to strangers.

we will abide in the street all night] The "street," lit. "the broad, open space," probably included all the streets, squares, and inclosures, frequently extensive in an eastern city, and in these early days perhaps less built over than in modern towns. The warmth of the climate would make it easy to pass the night in such a place. The words of the angels may be compared with our Lord's manner as recorded Luke xxiv. 28, "He made as though He would have gone further." The visit of the angels was one of trial previous to judgment (see ch. xviii. 21), trial of Lot as well as of the people of Sodom. Lot's character, though he is called "a righteous" or upright "man" (2 Pet. ii. 7), was full of faults and infirmities, but here he comes out well under the trial. His conduct is altogether favourably contrasted with that of the inhabitants of the city, and so he is delivered, whilst they are destroyed.

3. *a feast*] Lit. "a drink, or banquet, symposium." It is the word used commonly for a sumptuous repast.

unleavened bread] As having no time to leaven it. Literally the words mean "bread of sweetness," *i. e.* bread which had not been made bitter by leaven.

4 ¶ But before they lay down, the
men of the city, *even* the men of
Sodom, compassed the house round,
both old and young, all the people
from every quarter:
5 And they called unto Lot, and
said unto him, Where *are* the men
which came in to thee this night?
bring them out unto us, that we may
know them.
6 And Lot went out at the door
unto them, and shut the door after
him,
7 And said, I pray you, brethren,
do not so wickedly.
8 Behold now, I have two daughters
which have not known man; let me,
I pray you, bring them out unto you,
and do ye to them as *is* good in your
eyes: only unto these men do nothing;
for therefore came they under the
shadow of my roof.
9 And they said, Stand back. And
they said *again*, This one *fellow* came
in to sojourn, and he will needs be a
judge: now will we deal worse with
thee, than with them. And they
pressed sore upon the man, *even* Lot,
and came near to break the door.
10 But the men put forth their
hand, and pulled Lot into the house
to them, and shut to the door.
11 And they smote the men [b]that [b] Wisd. 19. 16.
were at the door of the house with
blindness, both small and great: so
that they wearied themselves to find
the door.
12 ¶ And the men said unto Lot,
Hast thou here any besides? son in
law, and thy sons, and thy daughters,
and whatsoever thou hast in the city,
bring *them* out of this place:
13 For we will destroy this place,
because the [c]cry of them is waxen [c] chap. 18. 20.

---

4. *all the people from every quarter*] The utter shamelessness of the inhabitants of Sodom, as well as their unbridled licentiousness, is briefly but most emphatically expressed in this verse. The Canaanitish nations in general, and the cities of the plain especially, were addicted to those deadly sins so strictly forbidden to the Israelites. See Lev. xx. 22, 23.

6. *Lot went out at the door unto them, and shut the door after him*] Lit. "went out at the doorway, and shut the door after him."

8. *I have two daughters*] These words of Lot have been much canvassed in all times. St Chrysostom thought it virtuous in him not to spare his own daughters, rather than sacrifice the duties of hospitality, and expose his guests to the wickedness of the men of Sodom ('Hom. XXIII. in Gen.'). So St Ambrose ('De Abrah.' Lib. I. c. 6), speaking as if a smaller sin were to be preferred to a greater. But St Augustine justly observes, that we should open the way for sin to reign far and wide, if we allowed ourselves to commit smaller sins, lest others should commit greater ('Lib. contr. Mend.' c. 9. See also 'Qu. in Gen.' 42). We see in all this conduct of Lot the same mixed character. He intended to do rightly, but did it timidly and imperfectly. He felt strongly the duty of hospitality, perhaps by this time he had even some suspicion of the sacred character of his guests, but his standard of right, though high when compared with that of his neighbours, was not the highest. The sacred writer relates the history simply and without comment, not holding up Lot as an example for imitation, but telling his faults as well as his virtues, and leaving us to draw the inferences. He brought all his troubles on himself by the home he had chosen. He was bound to defend his guests at the risk of his own life, but not by the sacrifice of his daughters.

9. *Stand back*] Lit. "Come near, farther off."

will needs be a judge] or, "judging, he will judge," referring, probably, as Tuch observes, to Lot's frequent remonstrances with them for their licentiousness and violence, which is referred to in 2 Pet. ii. 7, 8.

11. *they smote the men that were at the door of the house with blindness*] Perhaps the word for blindness rather indicates confused vision, LXX. ἀορασία. In Wisd. xix. 17, the darkness in which these men were involved is compared with the plague of 'darkness which may be felt," which fell on the Egyptians (Ex. x. 22). If it had been actual blindness, they would hardly have wearied themselves to find the door, but would have sought some one to lead them by the hand (August. 'De Civit. Dei.' XXII. 19). The same word, the root of which is very doubtful (see Gesen. 'Thes.' p. 961), occurs only once again, in 2 K. vi. 18, where, apparently (see vv. 19, 20), not real blindness, but indistinctness of vision and misleading error are described. Aben Ezra interprets it as meaning "blindness of eye and mind."

great before the face of the LORD;
and the LORD hath sent us to destroy it.
14 And Lot went out, and spake
unto his sons in law, which married
his daughters, and said, Up, get you
out of this place; for the LORD will
destroy this city. But he seemed as
one that mocked unto his sons in
law.
15 ¶ And when the morning arose,
then the angels hastened Lot, saying,
Arise, take thy wife, and thy two
† Heb. *are found.* daughters, which †are here; lest thou
‖ Or, *punishment.* be consumed in the ‖iniquity of the
city.
d Wisd. 10. 6. 16 And [d]while he lingered, the
men laid hold upon his hand, and
upon the hand of his wife, and upon
the hand of his two daughters; the
LORD being merciful unto him: and
they brought him forth, and set him
without the city.
17 ¶ And it came to pass, when
they had brought them forth abroad,
that he said, Escape for thy life; look
not behind thee, neither stay thou in
all the plain; escape to the mountain,
lest thou be consumed.
18 And Lot said unto them, Oh,
not so, my Lord:
19 Behold now, thy servant hath
found grace in thy sight, and thou
hast magnified thy mercy, which thou
hast shewed unto me in saving my
life; and I cannot escape to the mountain, lest some evil take me, and I
die:
20 Behold now, this city *is* near to
flee unto, and it *is* a little one: Oh,
let me escape thither, (*is* it not a little
one?) and my soul shall live.
21 And he said unto him, See, I
have accepted †thee concerning this † Heb. *thy face.*
thing also, that I will not overthrow
this city, for the which thou hast
spoken.
22 Haste thee, escape thither; for

13. *the LORD hath sent us to destroy it*] The angels speak here as messengers of judgment, not as He, who conversed with Abraham, ch. xviii. 17—33.

14. *which married his daughters*] Lit. "the takers of his daughters." LXX. "who had taken his daughters." Vulg. "who were about to marry his daughters." Some, Knobel, Delitzsch, &c., have held that besides those mentioned, vv. 8, 30, Lot had other daughters, who had married men of the city, and who perished in the conflagration with their husbands. It is more commonly thought that he had only two daughters, who were betrothed, but not yet married; betrothal being sufficient to give the title "son in law" or "bridegroom" to their affianced husbands.

15. *which are here*] Lit. "which are found." This seems to Knobel and others to indicate that there were other daughters, but that these two only were at home, the others being with their husbands in the city (see on v. 14); but it very probably points only to the fact, that Lot's wife and daughters were at home and ready to accompany him, whilst his sons in law scoffed and refused to go.

16. *the LORD being merciful unto him*] Lit. "in the mercy" (the sparing pity) "of the LORD to him."

17. *that he said*] *i.e.* one of the angels.

the plain] The *kikkar*, the circuit of the Jordan. Lot was to escape from the whole of the devoted region, which he had formerly coveted for his own, and where, when he parted from Abraham, he had made his habitation, and sought to enrich himself.

18. *my Lord*] The Masorites have the note *kadesh*, *i.e.* "holy," but it is probably no more than the salutation of reverence, see v. 2. For, though Lot had now found out the dignity of his guests, there is no evidence that he thought either of them to be the Most High. Indeed the word might be rendered in the plural "my lords," as the Syr. and Saad.

19. *I cannot escape to the mountain*] Lot and his family were, no doubt, exhausted by fear and anxiety, and he felt that, if he had to go to the mountains of Moab, he would be exposed to many dangers, which might prove his destruction; another instance of defective courage and faith, which yet is pardoned by a merciful God.

some evil] The evil, *i.e.* the destruction about to fall on Sodom; all Lot's conduct here denotes excessive weakness.

20. *is it not a little one?*] Though Zoar may have been involved in the guilt of the other cities of the plain, Lot pleads that it has but few inhabitants, and that the sins of such a small city can be but comparatively small. So Rashi.

21. *I have accepted thee*] Lit. "I have lifted up thy face." It was the custom in the

I cannot do anything till thou be
come thither. Therefore the name
of the city was called Zoar.
23 ¶ The sun was † risen upon the
earth when Lot entered into Zoar.
24 Then [e] the LORD rained upon
Sodom and upon Gomorrah brimstone and fire from the LORD out of
heaven;
25 And he overthrew those cities,
and all the plain, and all the inhabitants
of the cities, and that which grew upon
the ground.
26 ¶ But his wife looked back from
behind him, and she became a pillar of
salt.
27 ¶ And Abraham gat up early in
the morning to the place where he
stood before the LORD:
28 And he looked toward Sodom

† Heb. *gone forth.*

[e] Deut. 29. 23. Luke 17. 29. Isai. 13. 19. Jer. 50. 40. Amos 4. 11. Jude 7.

East to make supplication with the face to the ground; when the prayer was granted, the face was said to be raised.

22. *Zoar*] *i.e.* "little." It appears by several ancient testimonies to have been believed that Zoar or Bela, though spared from the first destruction of the cities of the plain, was afterwards swallowed up by an earthquake, probably when Lot had left it, v. 30. (See Jerom 'ad Jos.' XV. and 'Qu. in Gen.' c. XIV.; Theodoret 'in Gen.' XIX.). This tradition may account for the statement in Wisdom x. 6, that five cities were destroyed, and of Josephus ('B. J.' IV. 8. 4), that the "shadowy forms of five cities" could be seen; whereas Deut. xxix. 23 only mentions four, viz. Sodom, Gomorrah, Admah and Zeboim: yet, on the other hand, Eusebius (v. βαλὰ) witnesses that Bela, or Zoar, was inhabited in his day, and garrisoned by Roman soldiers.

24. *the LORD rained upon Sodom and upon Gomorrah brimstone and fire from the LORD out of heaven*] The LORD is said to have rained from the LORD, an expression much noted by commentators, Jewish and Christian. Several of the Rabbins, Manasseh Ben Israel, R. Simeon, and others, by the first JEHOVAH understand the angel Gabriel, the angel of the LORD: but there is certainly no other passage in Scripture, where this most sacred name is given to a created angel. Many of the fathers, Ignatius, Justin M., Tertullian, Cyprian, Athanasius, Hilary, The Council of Sirmium, &c. see in these words the mystery of the Holy Trinity, as though it were said, "GOD the Word rained down fire from GOD the Father;" an interpretation which may seem to be supported by the Jerusalem Targum, where "the Word of the LORD" is said to have "rained down fire and bitumen from the presence of the LORD." Other patristic commentators of the highest authority (as Chrysostom, Jerome and Augustine) do not press this argument. Aben Ezra, whom perhaps a majority of Christian commentators have followed in this, sees in these words a peculiar "elegance or grace of language;" "The LORD rained...from the LORD" being a grander and more impressive mode of saying, "The LORD rained from Himself." It is a common idiom in Hebrew to repeat the noun instead of using a pronoun.

brimstone and fire...out of heaven] Many explanations have been offered of this. Whether the fire from heaven was lightning, which kindled the bitumen and set the whole country in a blaze, whether it was a great volcanic eruption overwhelming all the cities of the plain, or whether there was simply a miraculous raining down of ignited sulphur, has been variously disputed and discussed. From comparing these words with Deut. xxix. 23, where it is said, "The whole land thereof is brimstone and salt and burning," it may be reasonably questioned, whether the "brimstone" in both passages may not mean *bitumen*, with which unquestionably, both before (see ch. xiv. 10), and after the overthrow, the whole country abounded (see also Jerusalem Targum quoted in the last note). The Almighty, in His most signal judgments and even in His most miraculous interventions, has been pleased often to use natural agencies; as, for instance, He brought the locusts on Egypt with an East wind and drove them back with a West wind (Ex. x. 13, 19). Possibly therefore the bitumen, which was the natural produce of the country, volcanic or otherwise, was made the instrument by which the offending cities were destroyed. The revelation to Abraham, the visit of the angels, the deliverance of Lot, mark the whole as miraculous and the result of direct intervention from above, whatever may have been the instrument which the Most High made use of to work His pleasure.

26. *a pillar of salt*] All testimony speaks of the exceeding saltness of the Dead Sea, and the great abundance of salt in its neighbourhood (*e.g.* Galen. 'De Simp. Medic. Facult.' IV. 19). In what manner Lot's wife actually perished has been questioned. Aben-Ezra supposed that she was first killed by the brimstone and fire and then incrusted over with salt, so as to become a statue or pillar of salt. There was a pillar of salt near the Dead Sea, which later tradition identified with Lot's wife (Joseph. 'Ant.' I. 11; Iren. IV. 51; Tertullian, 'Carmen de Sodoma;' Benjamin of

and Gomorrah, and toward all the
land of the plain, and beheld, and, lo,
the smoke of the country went up as
the smoke of a furnace.

29 ¶ And it came to pass, when
God destroyed the cities of the plain,
that God remembered Abraham, and
sent Lot out of the midst of the overthrow, when he overthrew the cities
in the which Lot dwelt.

30 ¶ And Lot went up out of
Zoar, and dwelt in the mountain, and
his two daughters with him; for he
feared to dwell in Zoar: and he dwelt
in a cave, he and his two daughters.

31 And the firstborn said unto the
younger, Our father *is* old, and *there*
is not a man in the earth to come in
unto us after the manner of all the
earth:

32 Come, let us make our father
drink wine, and we will lie with him,
that we may preserve seed of our
father.

33 And they made their father
drink wine that night: and the firstborn went in, and lay with her father;
and he perceived not when she lay
down, nor when she arose.

34 And it came to pass on the
morrow, that the firstborn said unto
the younger, Behold, I lay yesternight
with my father: let us make him drink
wine this night also; and go thou in,
and lie with him, that we may preserve seed of our father.

35 And they made their father
drink wine that night also: and the
younger arose, and lay with him; and
he perceived not when she lay down,
nor when she arose.

36 Thus were both the daughters
of Lot with child by their father.

37 And the firstborn bare a son,

Tudela, 'Itin.' p. 44. See Heidegger, II. p. 269). The American expedition, under Lynch, found to the East of Usdum a pillar of salt about forty feet high, which was perhaps that referred to by Josephus, &c.

29. *God remembered Abraham*] He remembered Abraham's intercession recorded in ch. xviii. and also the covenant which He had made with Abraham, and which was graciously extended so as to benefit his kinsman Lot.

30. *he feared to dwell in Zoar*] Jerome ('Qu.' ad h.l.) supposes that Lot had seen Zoar so often affected by earthquakes that he durst no longer abide there, see on v. 22. Rashi thought that the proximity to Sodom was the reason for his fear. The weakness of Lot's character is seen here again, in his not trusting God's promises.

dwelt in a cave] These mountainous regions abound in caves, and the early inhabitants formed them into dwellingplaces; see on ch. xiv. 6.

31. *there is not a man in the earth*] Iren. (IV. 51;) Chrysostom ('Hom. 34 in Genes.'), Ambros. ('De Abrahamo,' I. 6), Theodoret, ('Qu. in. Gen.' 69), excuse this incestuous conduct of the daughters of Lot on the ground, that they supposed the whole human race to have been destroyed, excepting their father and themselves. Even if it were so, the words of St Augustine would be true, that "they should have preferred to be childless rather than to treat their father so." (*Potius nunquam esse matres quam sic uti patre debuerunt*, 'C. Faustum,' XXII. 43.) It is too apparent that the licentiousness of Sodom had had a degrading influence upon their hearts and lives.

32. *let us make our father drink wine*] It has been suggested in excuse for Lot, that his daughters drugged the wine. Of this, however, there is no intimation in the text. But the whole history is of the simplest character. It tells plainly all the faults, not of Lot only, but of Abraham and Sarah also. Still though it simply relates and neither praises nor blames, yet in Lot's history we may trace the judgment as well as the mercy of God. His selfish choice of the plain of Jordan led him perhaps to present wealth and prosperity, but withal to temptation and danger. In the midst of the abandoned profligacy of Sodom he indeed was preserved in comparative purity, and so, when God overthrew the cities of the plain, he yet saved Lot from destruction. Still Lot's feebleness of faith first caused him to linger, v. 16, then to fear escape to the mountains, v. 19, and lastly to doubt the safety of the place which God had spared for him, v. 30. Now again he is led by his children into intoxication, which betrays him, unconsciously, into far more dreadful wickedness. And then we hear of him no more. He is left by the sacred narrative, saved indeed from the conflagration of Sodom, but an outcast, widowed, homeless, hopeless, without children or grandchildren, save the authors and the heirs of his shame.

and called his name Moab: the same
is the father of the Moabites unto
this day.
38 And the younger, she also bare
a son, and called his name Ben-
ammi: the same *is* the father of
the children of Ammon unto this
day.

---

37. *Moab*] According to the LXX.=*me-ab*, *i.e.* "from the father." So also the Targ. of Pseudo-Jonathan, Augustine, Jerome, &c. alluding to the incestuous origin of Moab. The Moabites dwelt originally to the East of the Dead Sea, from whence they expelled the Emims (Deut. ii. 11). Afterwards they were driven by the Amorites to the South of the river Arnon, which formed their Northern boundary.

38. *Ben-ammi*] *i.e.* "son of my people," in allusion to his being of unmixed race. The Ammonites are said to have destroyed the Zam-zummim, a tribe of the Rephaim, and to have succeeded them and dwelt in their stead. (Deut. ii. 22.) They appear for the most part to have been an unsettled marauding violent race, of Bedouin habits, worshippers of Molech, "the abomination of the Ammonites." 1 K. xi. 7.

De Wette and his followers, Rosenmüller, Tuch, Knobel, &c. speak of this narrative, as if it had arisen from the national hatred of the Israelites to the Moabites and Ammonites, but the Pentateuch by no means shews such national hatred (see Deut. ii. 9, 19): and the book of Ruth gives the history of a Moabitess who was ancestress of David himself. It was not till the Moabites had seduced the Israelites to idolatry and impurity, Num. xxv. 1, and had acted in an unfriendly manner towards them, hiring Balaam to curse them, that they were excluded from the congregation of the Lord for ever. Deut. xxiii. 3, 4.

NOTE A on CHAP. XIX. 25. THE DEAD SEA, SITE OF SODOM AND ZOAR.

(1) Characteristics of Dead Sea. Testimonies ancient and modern. (2) Geological formation. (3) Were Sodom, Zoar, &c. on the North or South of the Dead Sea?

THE Dead Sea, if no historical importance attached to it, would still be the most remarkable body of water in the known world. Many fabulous characteristics were assigned to it by ancient writers, as that birds could not fly over it, that oxen and camels floated in it, nothing being heavy enough to sink (Tacit. 'Hist.' v. 6; Plin. 'H. N.' v. 16; Seneca, 'Qu. Nat.' lib. III.). It has been conjectured by Reland, with some probability, that legends belonging to the lake of Asphalt said to have existed near Babylon (see on ch. xi. 3) were mixed up with the accounts of the Dead Sea, and both exaggerated (Reland, 'Palest.' II. pp. 244 seq.).

The Dead Sea called in Scripture the Salt Sea (Gen. xiv. 3; Numb. xxxiv. 3, 12), the Sea of the Plain (Deut. iii. 17, iv. 49; Josh. iii. 16), and in the later books, "the East Sea" (Ezek. xlvii. 18; Joel ii. 20; in Zech. xiv. 8, "the former sea" should be rendered "the East Sea"), is according to Lynch 40 geographical miles long by 9 to $9\frac{3}{4}$ broad. Its depression is 1316 feet below the level of the Mediterranean. Its depth in the northern portion is 1308 feet. Its extreme saltness was known to the ancients. Galen. ('De Simplic. Medicam. Facultat.' c. 19) says that "its taste was not only salt but bitter." Modern travellers describe the taste as most intensely and intolerably salt, its specific gravity and its buoyancy being consequently so great that people can swim or float in it, who could not swim in any other water. This excessive saltness is probably caused by the immense masses of fossil salt which lie in a mountain at its South-west border, and by the rapid evaporation of the fresh water, which flows into it (Stanley, 'S. and P.' p. 292; Robinson's 'Phys. Geog.' p. 195). Both ancient and modern writers assert that nothing animal or vegetable lives in this sea (Tacit. 'Hist.' v. 6; Galen. 'De Simpl. Med.' IV. 19; Hieron. ad Ezech. XLVII. 18; Robinson, 'Bib. Res.' II. p. 226). The few living creatures which the Jordan washes down into it are destroyed (Stanley, 'S. and P.' p. 293). No wonder, then, that the Salt Sea should have been called the Dead Sea, a name unknown to the sacred writers, but common in after times. Even its shores, incrusted with salt, present the appearance of utter desolation. The ancients speak much of the masses of asphalt, or bitumen, which the lake threw up. Diodorus Sic. affirms that the masses of bitumen were like islands, covering two or three plethra (Diod. Sic. II. 48); and Josephus says that they were of the form and magnitude of oxen ('B. J.' IV. 8. 4). Modern travellers testify to the existence of bitumen still on the shores and waters of the Dead Sea, but it is supposed by the Arabs, that it is only thrown up by earthquakes. Especially after the earthquakes of 1834 and 1837, large quantities are said to have been cast upon the Southern shore, probably detached by shocks from the bottom of the Southern bay (Robinson, 'B. R.' II. p. 229; 'Physical Geog.' p. 201. See also Thomson, 'Land and Book,' p. 223).

There is great difference between the Northern and Southern portions of the sea. The great depth of the Northern division does not extend to the South. The Southern bay is shallow, its shores low and marshy, almost like a quicksand, (Stanley, 'S. and P.' p. 293). It has been very generally supposed from Gen. xiv. 3, that the Dead Sea now occupies the site of what was originally the Plain of Jordan, the vale of Siddim, and to this has been added the belief that the cities of Sodom, Gomorrah, &c. were situated in the vale of Siddim, and that they too were covered by the Dead Sea. Recent observations have led many to believe that probably a lake must have existed here before historic times. Yet it is quite conceivable that the terrible catastrophe recorded in Genesis, traces of which are visible throughout the whole region, may have produced even the deep depression of the bed of the Dead Sea, and so have arrested the streams of the Jordan, which may before that time have flowed onwards through the Arabah, and emptied itself into the Gulph of Akabah. At all events, it is very probable that the Southern division of the lake may have been formed at a comparatively recent date. The character of this Southern part, abounding with salt, frequently throwing up bitumen, its shores producing sulphur and nitre (Robinson, 'Phys. Geog.' p. 204), corresponds accurately with all that is told us of the valley of Siddim, which was "full of slime pits" (Gen. xiv. 10), and with the history of the destruction of the cities by fire and brimstone and the turning of Lot's wife into a pillar of salt. Very probably therefore the vale of Siddim may correspond with what is now the Southern Bay of the Dead Sea. There is, however, no Scriptural authority for saying that Sodom and the other guilty cities were immersed in the sea. They are always spoken of as overthrown by fire from heaven (cf. Deut. xxix. 23; Jer. xlix. 18, l. 40; Zeph. ii. 9; 2 Pet. ii. 6). And Josephus ('B. J.' IV. 8. 4) speaks of "Sodomitis, once a prosperous country from its fertility and abundance of cities, but now entirely burnt up," as adjoining the lake Asphaltites. This was observed long ago by Reland (II. p. 256), and is now generally admitted by travellers and commentators. All ancient testimony is in favour of considering the cities of the plain as having lain at this Southern extremity of the sea. The general belief at present that that portion only of the sea can have been of recent formation, and hence that that only can have occupied the site of the vale of Siddim, the belief that Sodom was near the vale of Siddim, the bituminous, saline, volcanic aspect of the Southern coast, the traditional names of Usdum, &c., the traditional site of Zoar, called by Josephus (as above) Zoar of Arabia, the hill of salt, said to have been Lot's wife, and every other supposed vestige of the destroyed cities being to the South, all tend to the general conviction that the cities of the plain (of the Kikkar) lay either within or around the present South bay of the Dead Sea. On the other hand, Mr Grove (in Smith's 'Dict. of the Bible') has argued with great ability in favour of a Northern site for these cities, and he is supported by Tristram ('Land of Israel,' pp. 360—363). The chief grounds for his argument are 1st, that Abraham and Lot, at or near Bethel, could have seen the plain of Jordan to the North of the Dead Sea, but could not have seen the Southern valleys (see Gen. xiii. 10): 2ndly, that what they saw was "the Kikkar of the Jordan," whereas the Jordan flowed into the Dead Sea at its Northern extremity, but probably never flowed to the South of that sea: 3rdly, that later writers have been misled by apparent similarity of names, by the general belief that the sea had overflowed the sites of the cities and by uncertain traditions. It is, however, to be observed, that Mr Grove's arguments rest on two somewhat uncertain positions: first, that, in Gen. xiii. 10—13, Lot must have been able to see, from between Bethel and Ai, the cities of the plain; whereas it is possible that the language is not to be pressed too strictly, Lot seeing at the time the river Jordan North of the present Dead Sea, and knowing that the whole valley both North and South was fertile and well watered; secondly, that no part of the Dead Sea can be of recent formation, notwithstanding the terrible catastrophes all around it, to which not only Scripture but tradition and the present appearance of the whole country bear testimony. On the other hand, both tradition, local names and local evidences are strongly in favour of the Southern site of the cities destroyed.

CHAPTER XX.

1 *Abraham sojourneth at Gerar,* 2 *denieth his wife, and loseth her.* 3 *Abimelech is reproved for her in a dream.* 9 *He rebuketh Abraham,* 14 *restoreth Sarah,* 16 *and reproveth her.* 17 *He is healed by Abraham's prayer.*

AND Abraham journeyed from
thence toward the south country, and dwelled between Kadesh
and Shur, and sojourned in Gerar.
2 And Abraham said of Sarah his
wife, She *is* my sister: and Abime-

CHAP. XX. 1. *From thence*] *i.e.* from Mamre, where he had received the heavenly visitors, and whence he had beheld the smoke from the conflagration of the cities of the plain.

lech king of Gerar sent, and took
Sarah.
3 But God came to Abimelech in
a dream by night, and said to him,
Behold, thou *art but* a dead man, for
the woman which thou hast taken;
for she *is* †a man's wife.
4 But Abimelech had not come
near her: and he said, Lord, wilt
thou slay also a righteous nation?
5 Said he not unto me, She *is* my
sister? and she, even she herself said,
He *is* my brother: in the [1]integrity
of my heart and innocency of my
hands have I done this.
6 And God said unto him in a
dream, Yea, I know that thou didst
this in the integrity of thy heart; for
I also withheld thee from sinning
against me: therefore suffered I thee
not to touch her.
7 Now therefore restore the man
his wife; for he *is* a prophet, and he
shall pray for thee, and thou shalt

† Heb. *married to an husband.*

1 Or, *simplicity,* or, *sincerity.*

It may have been painful to him to abide in a place where he would be hourly reminded of this terrible catastrophe, or he may merely have travelled onward in search of fresh pasturage.

dwelled between Kadesh and Shur, and sojourned in Gerar] He settled apparently in a fertile country lying between the two deserts of Kadesh and Shur, and finally took up his residence as a stranger or sojourner (so the word "sojourned" signifies) at Gerar, a place which, St Jerome says, was on the southern border of the Canaanites. Gerar was not far from Gaza (Gen. x. 19), and Beersheba (xxvi. 26). Its site has probably been identified by Rowlands (Williams' 'Holy City,' I. 465) with the traces of an ancient city now called *Khirbet-el-Gerar*, near a deep Wady called *Jurf-el-Gerar*, about three hours to the south-south-east of Gaza.

2. *She is my sister*] This was Abraham's plan of action, when sojourning among strangers, of whose character he was ignorant, see v. 13. He has been defended as having "said she was his sister, without denying that she was his wife, concealing the truth but not speaking what was false" (August. 'c. Faust.' XXII. 3). But, though concealment may not necessarily be deception, we can scarcely acquit Abraham either of some disingenuousness or of endangering his wife's honour and chastity, in order to save his own life.

Abimelech] *Father of the king*, or perhaps *father king*, the common title of the Philistine kings, as Pharaoh was of the Egyptians. The age at which Sarah must have been at this time, some twenty-three or twenty-four years older than when Pharaoh took her into his house (ch. xii. 15), creates a considerable difficulty here. We may remember that Sarah after this became a mother, that though too old for childbearing under normal conditions, she had had her youth renewed since the visit of the angels (Kurtz), when it was promised that she should have a son. The assertion of modern critics that this is merely another version of ch. xii. 10—20, the work of the Elohist, whilst that was by the Jehovist, is ably combated by Keil (p. 170, Eng. Trans. p. 242). He observes, that the name *Elohim* indicates the true relation of God to Abimelech; but that in v. 18, JEHOVAH, the covenant God of Abraham, interposes to save him. All the more minute details of this history are different from that in ch. xii. In Abimelech we see a totally different character from that of Pharaoh; the character, namely, of a heathen imbued with a moral consciousness of right and open to receive a divine revelation, of which there is no trace in the account of the king of Egypt. It is not to be wondered at that the same danger should twice have occurred to Sarah, if we remember that the customs of the heathen nations, among which he was sojourning, were such as to induce Abraham to use the artifice of calling his wife his sister.

4. *had not come near her*] Apparently a divinely sent illness had been upon him, vv. 6, 18.

a righteous nation] *i.e.* a nation guiltless as regards this act of their king; but it may be, that the people of Gerar were really exempt from the worst vices of Canaan, and living in a state of comparative piety and simplicity.

6. *suffered I thee not to touch her*] See on v. 4.

7. *he is a prophet*] *i.e.* one inspired by God, or the medium of God's communications and revelations to mankind. Thus Exod. vii. 1, Aaron is said to be Moses' prophet, because he was to convey the messages and commands of Moses to Pharaoh. An objection has been made to the antiquity of the Pentateuch from the statement in 1 S. ix. 9, that "he that is now called a Prophet was beforetime called a Seer." Hence it is argued that the Pentateuch, which always uses the word prophet, cannot be of the great antiquity assigned to it. The difficulty is only on the surface. "Prophet" was the genuine name applied to all who declared God's will, who foretold the future, or even to great religious teachers. "Seer" had a more restricted sense, and was appropriated to those only who were favoured with visions from heaven. The word *prophet* occurs constantly in the Pentateuch in the

live: and if thou restore *her* not, know thou that thou shalt surely die, thou, and all that *are* thine.

8 Therefore Abimelech rose early in the morning, and called all his servants, and told all these things in their ears: and the men were sore afraid.

9 Then Abimelech called Abraham, and said unto him, What hast thou done unto us? and what have I offended thee, that thou hast brought on me and on my kingdom a great sin? thou hast done deeds unto me that ought not to be done.

10 And Abimelech said unto Abraham, What sawest thou, that thou hast done this thing?

11 And Abraham said, Because I thought, Surely the fear of God *is* not in this place; and they will slay me for my wife's sake.

12 And yet indeed *she is* my sister; she *is* the daughter of my father, but not the daughter of my mother; and she became my wife.

13 And it came to pass, when God caused me to wander from my father's house, that I said unto her, This *is* thy kindness which thou shalt shew unto me; at every place whither we shall come, [a]say of me, He *is* my brother.

[a] chap. 12. 13.

14 And Abimelech took sheep, and oxen, and menservants, and womenservants, and gave *them* unto Abraham, and restored him Sarah his wife.

15 And Abimelech said, Behold, my land *is* before thee: dwell †where it pleaseth thee.

† Heb. *as is good in thine eyes.*

16 And unto Sarah he said, Behold, I have given thy brother a thousand *pieces* of silver: behold, he *is* to thee

---

general sense of one in communion with God, and made the medium of God's communications to man. The word "seer" would generally be out of place in such a passage as this, or such as Ex. vii. 1, xv. 20; Num. xi. 29, xii. 6, &c.; but in the time of Samuel, when "the word of the LORD was precious there was no open vision," (1 S. iii. 1;) the application of the title "seer" to Samuel, who had visions specially vouchsafed to him, was very appropriate; yet after his time, though the name was sometimes employed to designate the inspired teachers of mankind, the older and more comprehensive title of "prophet" again came into common use, not only for teachers of religion generally, but also for the most favoured of God's servants. (See 'Mosaic Origin of the Pentateuch,' by a Layman, p. 97.)

he shall pray for thee] As the prophets were the instruments of God's revelations, His messengers, to man; so men made the prophets instruments for sending their prayers up to God (Cleric.). Cp. Jer. vii. 16, xi. 14, xiv. 11.

10. *What sawest thou*] Many recent commentators, Knobel, Delitzsch, Keil, &c., render, "What hadst thou in view?" The more simple sense is, what didst thou see in the conduct and manners of me or my people, that thou shouldest have done so to us? Didst thou see us taking away the wives of strangers and murdering the husbands?

11. *Surely the fear of God is not in this place*] Abraham had seen the impiety and heathenism of the Canaanitish races, and had lately witnessed the overthrow of Sodom for the licentiousness of its people, and he naturally thought that the inhabitants of Gerar might be equally forgetful of God, and therefore prone to all wickedness.

12. *she is my sister; she is the daughter of my father, but not the daughter of my mother*] Sarah's name does not occur in the genealogies, and we do not know any thing of her birth but that which is here stated. Such marriages, though afterwards forbidden (Lev. xviii. 9, 11, xx. 17; Deut. xxvii. 22), may not have been esteemed unlawful in patriarchal times, and they were common among the heathen nations of antiquity (Ach. Tatius, Lib. I.; Diod. I. 27; Herod. III. 31; Nepos, 'Cimon,' c. 1.) Many Jewish and Christian interpreters, however, think that *daughter* here means *granddaughter*, and that Sarah was the same as Iscah, the sister of Lot (ch. xi. 29), who is called "the brother of Abraham" (ch. xiv. 16).

13. *God caused me to wander*] In general the name of GOD (Elohim), though of plural form, is joined with a singular verb. In this case, however, the verb is in the plural. Similar constructions occur ch. xxxv. 7; Exod. xxii. 8; 2 S. vii. 23; (cp. 1 Chr. xvii. 21); Ps. lviii. 12. In Josh. xxiv. 19, the adjective is in the plural. The Samaritan Pentateuch here and in ch. xxxv. 7 has the verb in the singular.

16. *a thousand pieces of silver*] Lit. "a thousand of silver." The versions insert "shekels" or "didrachmas;" nothing can be known of the weights and measures of this early time.

a covering of the eyes, unto all that
are with thee, and with all *other:* thus
she was reproved.
17 ¶ So Abraham prayed unto
God: and God healed Abimelech,
and his wife, and his maidservants;
and they bare *children*.
18 For the LORD had fast closed
up all the wombs of the house of
Abimelech, because of Sarah Abraham's wife.

CHAPTER XXI.

1 *Isaac is born.* 4 *He is circumcised.* 6 *Sarah's joy.* 9 *Hagar and Ishmael are cast forth.* 15 *Hagar in distress.* 17 *The angel comforteth her.* 22 *Abimelech's covenant with Abraham at Beer-sheba.*

AND the LORD visited Sarah as he
had said, and the LORD did
unto Sarah [a]as he had spoken. [a] chap. 17. 19. & 18. 10.
2 For Sarah [b]conceived, and bare
Abraham a son in his old age, at the [b] Acts 7. 8. Gal. 4. 22. Heb. 11. 11.
set time of which God had spoken to
him.
3 And Abraham called the name
of his son that was born unto him,
whom Sarah bare to him, Isaac.
4 And Abraham circumcised his
son Isaac being eight days old, [c]as God [c] chap. 17. 12.
had commanded him.
5 And Abraham was an hundred
years old, when his son Isaac was
born unto him.
6 ¶ And Sarah said, God hath

Probably the thousand pieces of silver indicate the value of the sheep and oxen, which Abimelech gave to Abraham, though some think it was an additional present.

16. *he is to thee a covering of the eyes*] There is great variety of opinion as to the sense of these words. If we follow the rendering of the Authorized Version, the most probable interpretation is that of Heidegger, Schrœder, Rosenmüller, &c., viz. this, that in early times in the East unmarried women often went unveiled, but married women always veiled themselves. Cp. Gen. xxiv. 65. Hence Abimelech meant to say, that Abraham should be like a veil to Sarah, screening her from the eyes of all other men. See Rosenm. in loc. Heidegger, II. p. 163. The words might have been rendered, as by the LXX., Vulg., Targg., Syr., "it" or "they," *i.e.* the one thousand pieces of silver "are to thee a covering of the eyes," in which case the meaning would probably be "this gift is to thee for a covering to the eyes, so that thou shouldest overlook or condone the injury done to thee." So St Chrysostom, and among moderns, Gesenius, Tuch, Knobel, &c.

thus she was reproved] Here also there is great diversity of interpretation; but the Authorized Version is probably correct, and we must understand the words to be those of the historian, not of Abimelech. So apparently Onk., Arab., Saad., Kimchi, Gesen., Rosenm., &c.

18. *the LORD*] Keil has observed, that the various names of the Most High are used very significantly in these two last verses. The care of Abimelech and his wives belonged to the Deity (*Elohim*). Abraham directed his intercession not to *Elohim*, an indefinite and unknown god, but to *Ha-Elohim*, "the" true "God;" and it was JEHOVAH, the covenant God, who interposed for Abraham and preserved the mother of the promised seed.

CHAP. XXI. **1.** *the LORD did unto Sarah as he had spoken*] In ch. xvii. 16, GOD promised that He would give Abraham a son by Sarah his wife, on which promise Abraham fell on his face and laughed, whether from incredulity or for joy. What God (Elohim) then promised here the LORD (JEHOVAH) fulfils.

2. *at the set time of which God had spoken to him*] The "set time" was fixed, ch. xvii. 21, and xviii. 10, 14. (See note on ch. xviii. 10.) Modern critics see in ch. xvii. and in this ch. xxi. an Elohistic portion of the history of Abraham, and in ch. xviii. a Jehovistic portion. Yet this present chapter seems clearly to point back to both ch. xvii. and ch. xviii., and in its first verse it uses twice the name JEHOVAH, whilst in the second and subsequent verses it has constantly the name Elohim until we come to v. 33, when both names are conjoined, for Abraham is said to have called on the name of "The LORD, the everlasting God."

3. *Isaac*] The name which God had appointed for him, ch. xvii. 19. See also note on ch. xviii. 12.

6. *God hath made me to laugh*] Whatever was the nature of Sarah's laughter when the promise was made to her (see ch. xviii. 12), she now acknowledges that God had made her to laugh for joy; and she recognizes that He, whom she then took for a traveller and who made the promise, at which she laughed, was truly GOD.

will laugh with me] The Hebrew might mean "laugh at me" or "laugh with me." The Authorised Version rightly follows the LXX., Vulg., Targg., &c.

made me to laugh, *so that* all that
hear will laugh with me.
7 And she said, Who would have
said unto Abraham, that Sarah should
have given children suck? for I have
born *him* a son in his old age.
8 And the child grew, and was
weaned: and Abraham made a great
feast the *same* day that Isaac was
weaned.
9 ¶ And Sarah saw the son of
Hagar the Egyptian, which she had
born unto Abraham, mocking.
10 Wherefore she said unto Abraham, [d]Cast out this bondwoman and
her son: for the son of this bondwoman shall not be heir with my son,
even with Isaac.
11 And the thing was very grievous in Abraham's sight because of his
son.
12 ¶ And God said unto Abraham,
Let it not be grievous in thy sight
because of the lad, and because of thy
bondwoman; in all that Sarah hath
said unto thee, hearken unto her
voice; for in Isaac shall thy seed be
called.
13 And also of the son of the bondwoman will I make a nation, because
he *is* thy seed.
14 And Abraham rose up early in

[d] Gal. 4. 30.

---

7. *Who would have said*] The rendering of the Authorised Version is most likely correct. The obscurity of the passage probably arises from its poetical form. It has been long ago observed, that the words are apparently those of a short poem or hymn, like the hymn of Hannah, 1 S. ii. 1—7, or the Magnificat of the Blessed Virgin, Luke i. 46—55, the resemblance to which is the more noticeable, as Isaac was an eminent type of the Lord Jesus (see Wordsworth ad loc.). That these words were of the nature of a hymn or poem is seen in the use of a poetical word (*millel*) for "said," instead of the more common words (*dibber* or *amar*); and also in the appearance of regular parallelism of the members of the sentence.

8. *the child grew, and was weaned*] From 1 S. i. 23, 24; 2 Macc. vii. 27; Joseph. 'Ant.' II. 9. 6, it has been inferred that children were not weaned among the Hebrews till they were three years old. Ishmael was thirteen years old when he was circumcised, ch. xvii. 25, and one year after Isaac was born, ch. xvii. 21. If therefore Isaac was three years old at his weaning, Ishmael must have been then seventeen. If Isaac was but one year old, Ishmael would have been fifteen.

made a great feast] By comparing 1 S. i. 24, 25, it would seem that this was very probably a religious feast.

9. *mocking*] The word, which naturally means *to laugh*, is rendered by the LXX. and Vulg., "playing with Isaac." Tuch, Knobel, &c. say the word means merely, "playing like a child." Gesenius thinks it was "playing and dancing gracefully," and so attracting the favour of his father, which moved the envy of Sarah. The Targum of Onkelos appears to give the sense of "deriding" (see Buxtorf, 'Lex. Chald. and Talmud.' p. 719), as does the Syriac. The later Targums (Pseudo-Jon. and Jerusalem) understand some acts of idolatrous worship or perhaps impurity, (comp. Ex. xxxii. 6, where the same word is used for "play," and 1 Cor. x. 7). It is quite untrue that the word "laugh," here rendered "mocking," is never used but in a good sense. In ch. xix. 14, it is rightly rendered "mocked." See also Gen. xxvi. 8, xxxix. 14, 17; Ex. xxxii. 6. It probably means in this passage, as it has generally been understood, "mocking laughter." As Abraham had laughed for joy concerning Isaac, and Sarah had laughed incredulously, so now Ishmael laughed in derision, and probably in a persecuting and tyrannical spirit (see Gal. iv. 29).

10. *Cast out*] These words are quoted by St Paul (Gal. iv. 30), introduced by "But what saith the Scripture?" The words were those of Sarah, but they are confirmed by the Almighty, v. 12.

12. *in Isaac shall thy seed be called*] Here is the distinct limitation of the great promises of God to the descendants of Abraham in the line of Isaac (see Rom. ix. 7). God's promises gradually developed themselves in fulness, and yet were gradually restricted in extent: to Adam first; then to Noah; to Abraham; then to one race or seed of Abraham, viz. Isaac; to one of Isaac's children, viz. Jacob; to one of the twelve patriarchs, viz. Judah; then to his descendant David; and lastly to the great Son of David, the true promised Seed; but as all centred in Him, so too from Him they have spread out to all redeemed by Him, though more especially taking effect in those, who are "the children of God by faith in Christ Jesus" (Gal. iii. 26).

the morning, and took bread, and a bottle of water, and gave *it* unto Hagar, putting *it* on her shoulder, and the child, and sent her away: and she departed, and wandered in the wilderness of Beer-sheba.

15 And the water was spent in the bottle, and she cast the child under one of the shrubs.

16 And she went, and sat her down over against *him* a good way off, as it were a bowshot: for she said, Let me not see the death of the child. And she sat over against *him*, and lift up her voice, and wept.

17 And God heard the voice of the lad; and the angel of God called to Hagar out of heaven, and said unto

---

14. *a bottle*] A skin or leathern bottle, probably made of the skin of a goat or a kid. (See the word *bottle* in Smith's 'Dict. of the Bible.')

putting it on her shoulder] Hagar was an Egyptian, and Herod. (II. 35) says that the women in Egypt carried burdens on their *shoulders*, but the men carried them on their heads. According to the testimony of the sculptures both men and women carried burdens on their shoulders. It is common now in the East to see women carrying skins of water in this way. (See Robinson, 'B. R.' I. p. 340, II. pp. 163, 276.)

and the child] The sacred writer has been charged with an anachronism here, both from his use of the word "child," when Ishmael must have been from fifteen to seventeen years old (see note on v. 8), and because it is said that the original indicates that he, as well as the bread and water, was placed on Hagar's shoulder. The word for "child" (*yeled*), however, is used for boys of adolescent age, as in Gen. xlii. 22, of Joseph, when he was seventeen. It is true, the Vatican MS. of the LXX. renders "he placed the boy on her shoulders," which Tuch adopts as the right rendering; but the Alexandrian MS. of the LXX. has simply "and the boy," whilst the Vulg., Targg., Syr., connect the words "putting it on her shoulder" only with the bread and the bottle of water, which is perfectly consistent with the Hebrew, whether the verb be rendered by the past tense, or, as probably with accuracy in the Authorised Version, by the participle. The promise, which Abraham had just received, that God would make a nation of Ishmael also, v. 13, may probably have led him to trust that the boy and his mother would be provided for, and so to leave them with only provision for their immediate wants.

in the wilderness of Beer-sheba] Abraham, who had been now for at least a year dwelling in the neighbourhood of Gerar (ch. xx. 1), may very probably have by this time taken up his residence at Beersheba (see vv. 33, 34). The name Beersheba is here given proleptically (see v. 31), unless the events in the latter part of this chapter took place before those in the former part, not having been related at first, lest there should be a break in the continuity of the history of Isaac and Ishmael.

15. *she cast the child under one of the shrubs*] From this expression again it is inferred that Ishmael must have been a child in arms. Such a conclusion, however, is not borne out by these words, nor by the whole narrative. The boy was young, but he was evidently old enough to give offence to Sarah by mocking (v. 9). At a time when human life was much longer than it is now (Ishmael himself died at 137), fifteen or sixteen would be little removed from childhood. The growing lad would easily be exhausted with the heat and wandering; whilst the hardy habits of the Egyptian handmaid would enable her to endure much greater fatigue. She had hitherto led the boy by the hand, now she left him fainting and prostrate under the shelter of a tree. (So Le Clerc followed by Rosenmüller.)

16. *a good way off, as it were a bowshot*] Lit. "as far off as the drawers of a bow," or "as they who draw a bow," *i.e.* as far as archers can shoot an arrow.

17. *the angel of God*] No where else in Genesis does this name occur. Elsewhere it is always "the Angel of the LORD." We meet with it again in Exod. xiv. 19, "And the Angel of God, which went before the camp of Israel, removed, and went behind them." The identification of the *Malach Elohim* with *Elohim* (cp. vv. 17, 19, 20,) here is exactly like the identification of the *Malach* JEHOVAH with JEHOVAH in other passages; a clear proof that there is not that difference between the Elohistic and Jehovistic passages in the Pentateuch, of which so much has been written. In ch. xvi. 7, whilst Hagar was still Abraham's secondary wife, we read that the Angel of the LORD, the covenant God of Abraham, appeared to her. She and her son, by Isaac's birth and their expulsion from Abraham's household, are now separated from the family and covenant of promise, yet still objects of care to Him who is "the God of the spirits of all flesh," and "of all the ends of the earth."

her, What aileth thee, Hagar? fear
not; for God hath heard the voice of
the lad where he *is*.
18 Arise, lift up the lad, and hold
him in thine hand; for I will make
him a great nation.
19 And God opened her eyes, and
she saw a well of water; and she
went, and filled the bottle with water,
and gave the lad drink.
20 And God was with the lad; and
he grew, and dwelt in the wilderness,
and became an archer.
21 And he dwelt in the wilderness
of Paran: and his mother took him a
wife out of the land of Egypt.
22 ¶ And it came to pass at that
time, that Abimelech and Phichol
the chief captain of his host spake
unto Abraham, saying, God *is* with
thee in all that thou doest:
23 Now therefore swear unto me
here by God †that thou wilt not deal
falsely with me, nor with my son, nor
with my son's son: *but* according to
the kindness that I have done unto
thee, thou shalt do unto me, and to
the land wherein thou hast sojourned.

† Heb. *if thou shalt lie unto me.*

24 And Abraham said, I will swear.
25 And Abraham reproved Abimelech because of a well of water,
which Abimelech's servants had violently taken away.
26 And Abimelech said, I wot not
who hath done this thing: neither
didst thou tell me, neither yet heard
I *of it*, but to day.
27 And Abraham took sheep and
oxen, and gave them unto Abimelech;
and both of them made a covenant.
28 And Abraham set seven ewe
lambs of the flock by themselves.
29 And Abimelech said unto Abraham, What *mean* these seven ewe
lambs which thou hast set by themselves?
30 And he said, For *these* seven
ewe lambs shalt thou take of my hand,
that they may be a witness unto me,
that I have digged this well.
31 Wherefore he called that place
‖Beer-sheba; because there they sware
both of them.
32 Thus they made a covenant at
Beer-sheba; then Abimelech rose up,
and Phichol the chief captain of his

‖ That is, *The well of the oath.*

---

18. *Arise, lift up the lad, and hold him in thine hand*] So the Versions, according to the common use of the same verb with the same preposition. Cp. Deut. xxii. 25; Judg. xix. 25, 29; 2 S. xiii. 11, &c.; and see Gesen. 'Thes.' p. 463. "From this," says St Jerome, "it is plain that the boy whom she held in her hand had been her companion on the journey, not a burden on her shoulders," 'Qu. in Gen'.

19. *God opened her eyes, and she saw a well of water*] Very probably the mouth of the well had been purposely covered by the inhabitants of the desert, and was now by God's gracious intervention discovered to Hagar.

21. *in the wilderness of Paran*] (See on ch. xiv. 6). Probably the great desert, now called the desert El-Tih, *i.e.* "the wanderings," extending from the Wady-el-Arabah on the east, to the gulf of Suez on the west, and from the Sinaitic range on the south to the borders of Palestine on the north.

took him a wife out of the land of Egypt] According to the custom then prevalent in the East for parents to choose wives for their sons. (See ch. xxiv. 4, 55; Exod. xxi. 10.)

22. *Phichol*] The name occurs again in ch. xxvi. 26, and, as it signifies "the mouth of all," it has been supposed to have been the name of an officer, the grand vizier or prime minister of the king, through whom all complaints and petitions were to be made to him. Abimelech was also an official name. See on ch. xx. 2.

23. *that thou wilt not deal falsely with me*] Lit. "if thou shalt lie unto me;" the common form of an oath in Hebrew. See above, on xiv. 23.

31. *Beer-sheba*] *i.e.* "the well of the oath," or, it might be, "the well of the seven." There was a connection between the sacred number seven and an oath; oaths being ratified with the sacrifice of seven victims or by the gift of seven gifts (as seems to have been the case here), or confirmed by seven witnesses and pledges. (See Herod. III. 8; Hom. 'Il.' XIX. 243). Beer-sheba was in the Wady-es-Seba, a wide water-course or bed of a torrent, twelve hours south of Hebron, in which there are still relics of an ancient town or village, called Bir-es-Seba, with two deep wells of good water. See Robinson, 'B. R.' I. p. 204, seq. St Jerome speaks of the city as remaining in his day ('Qu. ad Gen.' XXI. 31).

host, and they returned into the land of the Philistines.

‖ Or, *tree*. 33 ¶ And *Abraham* planted a ‖ grove in Beer-sheba, and called there on the name of the LORD, the everlasting God.

34 And Abraham sojourned in the Philistines' land many days.

CHAPTER XXII.

1 *Abraham is tempted to offer Isaac.* 3 *He giveth proof of his faith and obedience.* 11 *The angel stayeth him.* 13 *Isaac is exchanged with a ram.* 14 *The place is called Jehovah-jireh.* 15 *Abraham is blessed again.* 20 *The generation of Nahor unto Rebekah.*

AND it came to pass after these
things, that [a]God did tempt [a] Heb. 11. 17.

---

33. *Abraham planted a grove*] Rather **a tamarisk tree.** This is the rendering of Kimchi, which is adopted by Gesenius ('Th.' p. 159), Rosenm., and most of the German critics. (The ancient versions vary very much in their interpretation.) The hardiness of this evergreen shrub would fit it to be a perpetual memorial to Abraham and his followers that this well was theirs.

the LORD, the everlasting God] "JEHOVAH, the God of eternity." The word, rendered everlasting, means probably "the hidden time," that, whose beginning and ending are hidden in darkness, hence "eternity" (Ges. 'Th.' p. 1035). It signifies also "the world," "the universe," and hence, according to Maimonides, it means here the God of the universe, the Creator of the world. So the Samaritan, Syr., and Arab. versions. The more probable sense, however, is that given in the Authorised Version, which corresponds with the LXX., Vulg., Onk., and other Targg. The JEHOVAH whom Abraham worshipped is here identified with "El-Olam," the God of eternity, which was very probably a local name for the supreme Being. Compare "Elion" in ch. xiv. 22.

CHAP. XXII. 1. *And it came to pass after these things*] This is the only note of time that we have in this chapter, excepting the fact that Isaac was now grown old enough to bear the wood of the burnt offering, and to carry it up the mountain. The words "after these things," rather refer us to all that had been passing before. Abraham, after long wanderings and many trials, is presented to us in the last chapter, as eminently comforted and in a condition of peaceful prosperity. The promised, longed-for son has been given to him; his other son Ishmael, though no longer in his household, is growing up and prospering, Abraham is in treaty and at peace with his neighbours the Philistines, he sojourns for many days at Beer-sheba and its neighbourhood, with abundance of cattle, in a place well watered and fertile. Thus it appears to have been with him till now, when his son, his only son Isaac, whom he loved, is growing up to early manhood, his chief comfort and stay and hope in this world. But times of prosperity are often times when trial is needed for us, and so we find it here. There is great variety of tradition, but no evidence, as to the age of Isaac in this chapter. According to Josephus ('Ant.' I. 14), he was twenty-five. Aben-Ezra supposes that he was only thirteen, whilst some of the rabbins put him even at thirty-seven (see Heidegger, II. 282).

God did tempt Abraham] Lit. "The God did tempt," &c. possibly referring to the last two verses of the last chapter (where JEHOVAH is called El-olam), meaning "this same God." Much difficulty has been most needlessly found in these words. St James tells us (i. 13) that "God cannot be tempted with evil, neither tempteth He any man," language which it has been thought difficult to reconcile with this history in Genesis. So, some have endeavoured to explain away the words of this passage, as though Abraham had felt a strong temptation rising in his own heart, a temptation from Satan, or from self, a horrible thought raised perhaps by witnessing the human sacrifices of the Phœnicians, and had then referred the instigation to God, thinking he was tempted from above, whereas the real temptation was from beneath. The difficulty, however, has arisen from not observing the natural force of the word here rendered "did tempt," and the ordinary use of that word in the language of the Old Testament, especially of the Pentateuch. According to the highest authorities, the primary sense of the verb corresponds with that of a similar word in Arabic, viz. "to smell," and thence "to test by smelling" (see Ges. 'Thes.' p. 889, and the testimonies there cited). Hence it came to signify close, accurate, delicate testing or trying. It is translated by "prove," "assay," "adventure," "try," and that very much more frequently than it is translated by "tempt." For instance, David would not take the sword and armour of Saul, because he had not "proved them," 1 S. xvii. 39. Again, he prayed in the words "examine me, O LORD, and *prove* me" (Ps. xxvi. 2); and in very numerous and familiar passages in the Pentateuch, we read of God "proving" men, whether they would be obedient or disobedient, the same Hebrew verb being constantly made use of. (See Ex. xv. 25, xvi. 4, xx. 20; Deut. iv. 34, viii. 2, 16, xiii. 3, xxxiii. 8). Accordingly, whilst most of the versions adhere closely to the sense of

Abraham, and said unto him, Abraham: and he said, [†]Behold, *here* I
am.

† Heb. *Behold me.*

2 And he said, Take now thy son,
thine only *son* Isaac, whom thou lovest,
and get thee into the land of Moriah;

"try," *tentare*, in this passage, the Arabic renders it very correctly, "God did prove Abraham." Words having the sense of "try" may generally be used either in a good or a bad sense. This particular word has generally a good sense, except where men are said to try or tempt God, *e.g.* Ex. xvii. 2; Num. xiv. 22; Deut. vi. 16; Ps. lxxviii. 18; cvi. 14, &c. The whole history of Abraham is a history of his moral and spiritual education by the teaching of God himself. He was to be the head of the chosen seed, the father of the faithful; himself the type of justifying faith. Here then, after long schooling and training, in which already there had been many trials (such as his first call, his danger in Egypt, his circumcision, his parting with Lot, &c. &c.), one great test of his now matured and strengthened faith is ordained by God. We have many instances of the trial of men's faith by the Most High. One remarkable example is that recorded in Matt. xix. 21. It cannot be that He who sees the heart needs such trials for His own information: but it is important for our instruction and correction, for example to future ages, and for the vindication of God's justice, that such trials should be permitted, and that so men's characters should be drawn out and exhibited to themselves and others. So St Augustine, "all temptation is not to be blamed, but that whereby probation is made is rather to be welcomed. For the most part a man's spirit cannot be known to himself, unless his strength be proved not by word but by actual trial." ('De Civit. Dei,' XVI. 32. See also Ambros. 'De Abr.' I. 8.)

2. *Take now thy son, thine only son*] In more ways than one Isaac might be called his "only son." He was the only son by his wife Sarah: he was the only son of promise, and to whom the promises were given and assured: by the expulsion of Hagar and Ishmael he was the only son left to his father's house. The rendering therefore of the LXX. "beloved" is not necessary. The words, emphatic as they are, "Thy son, thine only son, whom thou lovest," are all calculated to impress and enhance the sacrifice which Abraham is called on to make.

Moriah] The meaning of the name seems clearly to be *Mori-jah*, "the vision" or "the manifested of JEHOVAH." To this root it is evidently referred by Sym., Vulg. ("the land of vision"), Aq. ("the conspicuous land"), LXX. ("the lofty land"). In 2 Chr. iii. 1, Solomon is said to have built his temple on Mount Moriah; and the Jewish tradition (Joseph. 'Ant.' I. 13. 2; VII. 13. 4) has identified this Mount Moriah of the temple with the mountain in the land of Moriah, on which Abraham was to offer his son, whence probably here Onkelos and the Arab. render "the land of worship." No sufficient reason has been alleged against this identification except that in v. 4, it is said that "Abraham lifted up his eyes, and saw the place afar off," whereas Mount Zion is said not to be conspicuous from a great distance. Thence Bleek, De Wette, Tuch, Stanley ('S. and P.' p. 251, 'Jewish Church,' I. 49), and Grove ('Dict. of Bible,' s. v. *Moriah*), have referred to Moreh (Gen. xii. 6), and attempted to identify the site of the sacrifice with "the natural altar on the summit of Mount Gerizim," which the Samaritans assert to be the scene of the sacrifice. Really, however, the words in v. 4, mean nothing more than this, that Abraham saw the spot to which he had been directed at some little distance off, not farther than the character of the place readily admits. The evident meaning of the words "the mount of the vision of the LORD" (see v. 14); the fact that the mount of the temple bore the same name (2 Chr. iii. 1), the distance, two days' journey from Beer-sheba, which would just suffice to bring the company to Jerusalem, whereas Gerizim could not have been reached from Beer-sheba on the third day, are arguments too strong to be set aside by the single difficulty mentioned above, which is in fact no difficulty at all. This identity is ably defended by Hengstenberg ('Genuineness of the Pentateuch,' II. 162, translated by Ryland), Knobel (*in loc*), Kalisch (*in loc.*), Kurtz ('Hist. of Old Covenant,' Vol. I. 271), Thomson ('The Land and the Book', p. 475), Tristram ('Land of Israel,' p. 152).

offer him there for a burnt offering] It cannot justly be urged that the command was (1) in itself immoral, or (2) that it was a virtual sanction of human sacrifice. (1) As to the objection that it was immoral, it may be said, that the true basis of all morality is obedience to the will of God; but further than this, it is plain from the whole story, that the command was wholly of the nature of a trial. Abraham was the special type of trustful, obedient, loving faith. He believed that all which God commanded must be right, all that He promised must be true. Hence he knew that when the injunction was clear, the obedience must be undoubting. The wisdom, the justice, and the goodness of God, were such that, though he might not understand the reason of the dispensation, he must reverently and patiently submit to it. This too was not a mere blind credulity. He had lived a long life under the special guiding,

and offer him there for a burnt offering upon one of the mountains which
I will tell thee of.
3 ¶ And Abraham rose up early in
the morning, and saddled his ass, and
took two of his young men with him,
and Isaac his son, and clave the wood
for the burnt offering, and rose up,
and went unto the place of which God
had told him.
4 Then on the third day Abraham
lifted up his eyes, and saw the place
afar off.
5 And Abraham said unto his young
men, Abide ye here with the ass; and
I and the lad will go yonder and worship, and come again to you.
6 And Abraham took the wood of
the burnt offering, and laid *it* upon
Isaac his son; and he took the fire in
his hand, and a knife; and they went
both of them together.
7 And Isaac spake unto Abraham
his father, and said, My father: and
he said, †Here *am* I, my son. And † Heb. *Behold me.*
he said, Behold the fire and the wood:
but where *is* the ‖lamb for a burnt ‖ Or, *kid.*
offering?
8 And Abraham said, My son, God
will provide himself a lamb for a burnt
offering: so they went both of them
together.
9 And they came to the place which
God had told him of; and Abraham

---

training, and teaching of the Lord, and so he knew in whom he had believed. The command therefore, strange as it was, was but a final test of the firmness of his faith; and his obedience to that command testified that the faith was intelligent as well as unconditional and unwavering. (2) The objection that this was a virtual sanction to the heathen custom of offering human sacrifices is still less tenable. That such sacrifices were common in later times is unquestionable, and probably they may have been already adopted by the Canaanites, who certainly were afterwards much addicted to them. Although we must ascribe them not to Divine but to Satanic influence, their observance plainly shewed the devotion of the offerers to the religion of their demon gods. The God of Abraham would have His special servant, the father of the chosen race and of the promised Seed, manifest his faith and obedience to the true God to be not less than the faith and obedience of idolaters to their false gods. This could not be more signally done than by his readiness to overcome all scruples and all natural feelings at the command of Him whose voice he knew, and whose leading he had so long followed. But the conclusion of the history is as clear a condemnation of human sacrifice as the earlier part might have seemed, had it been left incomplete, to sanction it. The intervention of the angel, the substitution of the lamb, the prohibition of the human sacrifice, proved that in no case could such an offering be acceptable to God, even as the crowning evidence of faith, devotion, and self-sacrifice. The following is the well-known perverted account of the sacrifice of Isaac in the Phœnician traditions, as preserved from Sanchoniatho by Philo Byblius, "Cronus, whom the Phœnicians call Israel, being king over that country, who after his death was deified and consecrated into the planet bearing his name, having an only son by a nymph named Anobret, called therefore *Jehoud*" (= Heb. Jahid), "which is even now the name for *only-begotten* among the Phœnicians, when great perils from wars were impending over the land, having clothed his son in royal apparel offered him up upon an altar which he had built," (Euseb. 'Præp. Evang.' Lib. I. c. 10).

3. *rose up early in the morning*] The promptness and steadiness of Abraham's obedience are plainly marked in all the simple details of this verse.

5. *come again to you*] It may be questioned whether this had in it a prophetic significance, Abraham "accounting that God was able to raise his son up even from the dead" (Heb. xi. 17). In fact it was proved by the event to be a prophecy, though Abraham may have uttered it unconsciously (so Rashi): and that faith in God, which never forsook the patriarch, probably in the lowest depth of his anxiety brought a gleam of hope, that in some unforeseen way his son, even though slain, should yet be restored to him at last (see Origen, 'Homil. VIII. in Gen.' § 5).

6. *laid it upon Isaac his son*] Compare Joh. xix. 17, the great Antitype bearing the wood for the sacrifice of Himself (Origen, 'Hom. VIII. in Gen.' § 6; Aug. 'De C. D.' XVI. 32; 'De Trin.' III. 6).

8. *God will provide himself a lamb for a burnt offering*] **The lamb.** The fathers see in this again an unconscious prophecy by Abraham (see Origen as above, and Ambrose 'De Abr.' lib. I. 8). He probably meant to say that God had provided that Isaac should be the lamb or victim for the burnt-offering: but his words were more literally fulfilled in the

built an altar there, and laid the wood
in order, and bound Isaac his son, and
[b] James 2. 21. [b]laid him on the altar upon the wood.
10 And Abraham stretched forth
his hand, and took the knife to slay
his son.
11 And the angel of the LORD
called unto him out of heaven, and
said, Abraham, Abraham: and he said,
Here *am* I.
12 And he said, Lay not thine hand
upon the lad, neither do thou any thing
unto him: for now I know that thou
fearest God, seeing thou hast not withheld
thy son, thine only *son* from
me.
13 And Abraham lifted up his eyes,
and looked, and behold behind *him* a
ram caught in a thicket by his horns:
and Abraham went and took the ram,

---

unexpected event, the ram caught in a thicket, and in a deeper spiritual significance when God sent His Son to be "the Lamb of God that taketh away the sin of the world."

9. *Abraham built an altar there*] R. Eliezer in 'Pirke Avoth,' c. 31, has a tradition that this was the same place at which Adam sacrificed, at which Abel offered his burnt-offering, and where Noah built an altar and offered a sacrifice: so that it was apparently supposed that Abraham merely repaired the ruins of the ancient altar. Whatever the tradition is worth, it may illustrate the history. An altar of earth or of loose stones would be very quickly raised.

bound Isaac his son] It was common to bind victims, especially human victims (Ovid, 'Eleg. ex. Ponto.' III. 2; Virg. 'Æn. II. 134). The Jews agree that Isaac yielded submissively to his father's will and consented to be bound and sacrificed (Joseph. 'A. J.' I. 13; Eliezer, 'in Pirke,' c. 31; so also Chrysost. 'Homil. in Gen.' 46). Herein he was the truer type of Him, "who, when He was reviled, reviled not again; when He suffered, He threatened not; but committed Himself to Him that judgeth righteously" (1 Pet. ii. 23).

10. *stretched forth his hand*] The steady deliberate purpose of Abraham, and yet all the natural shrinking of his spirit, are admirably expressed in the details of the history.

11. *the Angel of the LORD*] Up to this verse we have only the name Elohim, God. Now that the Divine intervention to save Isaac and to accept a ransom for his life is related, we find the name, JEHOVAH, the great covenant name frequently made use of, though the name Elohim occurs again in the next verse. The Being here called "the Angel of JEHOVAH," who speaks as with Divine, supreme authority, is doubtless the Angel of the Covenant (Mal. iii. 1), the everlasting Son of the Father, who alone "hath declared Him" (John i. 18).

12. *now I know that thou fearest God*] "God tried Abraham," says Theodoret, "not that He might learn what He knew already, but that He might shew to others, with how great justice He loved the patriarch" ('Qu. in Gen.' LXXIII). Compare Origen ('Homil. VIII. 8), who refers to those words of the Apostle: "God spared not His own Son, but freely gave Him up for us all."

thou hast not withheld thy son] These words in the LXX. (*οὐκ ἐφείσω τοῦ υἱοῦ σου*) appear to be referred to in Rom. viii. 32 (*τοῦ ἰδίου υἱοῦ οὐκ ἐφείσατο*). Whence we may learn that St Paul held the sacrifice of Isaac to be prophetic of Christ.

13. *behold behind him a ram caught in a thicket by his horns*] There is a various reading (supported by many MSS., by the Samaritan Pentateuch, LXX., Vulg., Syr., Sam., and perhaps Onkelos), which might be rendered thus: "Behold a single ram caught," &c. a ram, that is, separated from the flock. There is a similar expression in Dan. viii. 3: "Behold, there stood before the river a ram," lit. "one ram," or a "single ram." The separation of the ram thus caught is significant, both historically, as shewing the Providential agency of God, and also as pointing to that Lamb of God, who was "separate from sinners" (Heb. vii. 26), bearing alone the burden of our iniquities. St Augustine thinks the horns caught in the thicket typical of the Lord Jesus crowned with thorns before His sacrifice ('De C. D.' XVI. 32).

offered him up for a burnt offering in the stead of his son] It has been argued that the lamb substituted for Isaac, not Isaac himself, was the true type of the Lord Jesus, who died that we might live. This, however, would be a very imperfect explication of the mystery. The antitype is always greater than the type, and hence in the prophetic system of the Old Testament, types are multiplied that they may express collectively that which can but partially be expressed by one of them. The fathers recognize the double type in this whole history. The father with full deliberate purpose offering up his dearly beloved, only-begotten son, the son willingly obedient unto death, the wood for the sacrifice carried by the victim up the hill, the sacrifice fulfilled in purpose though not in act, and then the father receiving his son in a figure from the dead (Heb. xi. 19) after three days of death in the father's purpose and belief; all

and offered him up for a burnt offering in the stead of his son.
14 And Abraham called the name of that place ‖ Jehovah-jireh: as it is said *to* this day, In the mount of the LORD it shall be seen.

‖ That is, *The LORD will see, or, provide.*

15 ¶ And the angel of the LORD called unto Abraham out of heaven the second time,
16 And said, [c] By myself have I sworn, saith the LORD, for because thou hast done this thing, and hast

[c] Ps. 105. 9. Ecclus. 44. 21. Luke 1. 73. Heb. 6. 13.

---

this is as much an actual prophecy of the sacrifice and resurrection of the Son of God as was possible without a true slaying of Isaac, for which was substituted the slaying of the ram. That which Isaac's sacrifice wanted to make it perfect as a type was actual death and the notion of substitution. These therefore were supplied by the death of the ram, and his substitution for a human life. Theodoret says ('Qu. in Gen.' LXXIII.) that "Isaac was the type of the Godhead, the ram of the manhood." This perhaps sounds fanciful at first; but the correspondence is in truth very exact. Isaac was of too noble a nature to be slain upon the altar; God would have abhorred such an offering. Hence the Most High prepares a victim to be as it were joined with Isaac and then to suffer, that thus the sacrifice should not be imperfect. So the ever blessed Son of God was by nature above the possibility of suffering; hence the Eternal Father prepares for Him a perfect humanity ("a Body hast Thou prepared me"), that He might die in that nature which was mortal, the immortal, impassible nature being yet inseparably united with it. Thus, Isaac and the ram together symbolized and typified in almost all particulars the sacrifice, the death and the resurrection of the Son of God, who also was the Son of man.

We may observe too, that not only was Isaac thus made the most memorable type of the Redeemer of the world (Isaac, who otherwise seems less noticeable than either Abraham or Jacob), but also that Abraham had the singular honour of representing the highest, holiest God and Father, who "spared not His own Son, but freely gave Him up for us all" (Rom. viii. 32. See Aug. 'De Civ. D.' XVI. 32).

14. *JEHOVAH-jireh*] *i.e.* "the Lord will see," or "the Lord will provide." The same words which Abraham had used in v. 8, but with a change in the sacred names. In v. 8, when Isaac had asked, "where is the Lamb?" Abraham answered, *Elohim jireh*, "God will see," or "provide a lamb for Himself." Now he perceives that he had uttered an unconscious prophecy, and that the God (Elohim) in whom he trusted had shewn Himself indeed JEHOVAH, the Eternal Truth and the covenated Saviour of his servants, and so he names the place JEHOVAH-jireh. The connection which there is between these words and the word Moriah (see on v. 2) has suggested the belief, that the name Moriah in v. 2 is used proleptically, and that it really originated in this saying of Abraham.

as it is said to this day, In the mount of the LORD it shall be seen] Or, "it shall be provided."

There is great variety of renderings in the ancient Versions. Indeed, if we disregard the vowel points, it would be equally possible to translate "In the mount of the Lord it shall be seen or provided," or "In the mount the Lord will see or provide," or "In the mount the Lord will be seen." The LXX. takes the last, the Vulgate, Syriac and Samaritan take the second. Onkelos departs from his habit of translating, and paraphrases, like the late Targums; "And Abraham worshipped and prayed there and said before the Lord, Here shall generations worship; whereupon it shall be said in that day, In this mountain Abraham worshipped before the Lord." St Jerome, taking the Latin, explained it thus: "This became a proverb among the Hebrews, that if any should be in trouble and should desire the help of the Lord, they should say, *In the mount the Lord will see*, that is, as He had mercy on Abraham, so will He have mercy on us" ('Qu. Hebraic. in Gen.' XXII).

On the whole, the pointing of the Masorites, a tradition never lightly to be rejected, which is followed by the Authorised Version, seems to give the most probable sense of the passage (So Ges. 'Thes.' p. 1246; Rosemn., Knobel). But, in any case, there seems not only a general assurance of God's providential care of His people, who in trouble may remember that "the Lord will provide," but also a special prophecy, 1st of the manifestation of the Lord in His temple at Jerusalem, where He was to be seen in the Shechinah or cloud of glory between the Cherubim, where He provided access to Himself and sacrifices for His service; 2ndly, of the coming of the Lord to His temple (Mal. iii. 1), thereby making "the glory of the latter house greater than of the former" (Hagg. ii. 9); and of His providing there a Lamb for a sacrifice, which should save not only from temporal but from eternal death, taking away the sin of the world.

16. *by myself have I sworn*] This is the final promise of the Lord to Abraham, confirming all the former promises by the solemnity of an oath, and "because He could swear by no greater, He sware by Himself"

not withheld thy son, thine only
son:
17 That in blessing I will bless
thee, and in multiplying I will multiply thy seed as the stars of the heaven,
and as the sand which *is* upon the sea
† Heb. *lip.* †shore; and thy seed shall possess the
gate of his enemies;
[d] chap. 12. 3. & 18. 18. Ecclus. 44. 22. Acts 3. 25. Gal. 3. 8.
18 [d]And in thy seed shall all the
nations of the earth be blessed; because thou hast obeyed my voice.
19 So Abraham returned unto his
young men, and they rose up and went
together to Beer-sheba; and Abraham
dwelt at Beer-sheba.

20 ¶ And it came to pass after
these things, that it was told Abraham, saying, Behold, Milcah, she hath
also born children unto thy brother
Nahor;
21 Huz his first-born, and Buz his
brother, and Kemuel the father of
Aram,
22 And Chesed, and Hazo, and
Pildash, and Jidlaph, and Bethuel.
23 And Bethuel begat [e]Rebekah: [e] Called, Rom. 9. 10, *Rebecca.*
these eight Milcah did bear to Nahor,
Abraham's brother.
24 And his concubine, whose name
was Reumah, she bare also Tebah,

(Heb. vi. 13). The vast importance of the revelation and of the promise here recorded is proved by this remarkable act of the Most High. "God, willing more abundantly to shew unto the heirs of promise the immutability of His counsel, interposed Himself by an oath" (or "made Himself the Mediator to be sworn by," ἐμεσίτευσεν ὅρκῳ); "that by two immutable things" (*i.e.* His word and His oath, Chrysost., Theod., Theophyl.), "in which it was impossible for God to lie, we might have a strong consolation, who have fled for refuge to lay hold upon the hope set before us" (Heb. vi. 17, 18). Abraham had by Divine grace achieved a victory of faith unheard of before in the world's history; and so to him personally a most blessed and most solemn promise is given of prosperity, honour and enlargement to him and to his seed after him. But this great victory of Abraham's was the type of a still greater victory to be won hereafter by God and God's only begotten Son; and so the promise to Abraham includes a promise still greater to all mankind, for in the seed of Abraham all the nations of the earth were to be blessed for ever. N. B. Onkelos renders here, "I have sworn by My Word," *Memra;* and the Arabic, "I have sworn by My own Name."

20. *it was told Abraham*] This is introduced for the sake of tracing the genealogy of Abraham's brother Nahor down to Rebekah the wife of Isaac, v. 23.

21. *Huz*] See on ch. x. 23, where we have seen Uz and Aram together before. It is only natural that names should have been repeated in the same race, the race of Shem. Uz and Aram also occur among the posterity of Esau (Gen. xxxvi. 28), whence Idumea is called "the land of Uz" (Lam. iv. 21). This recurrence of names in juxtaposition creates some obscurity as to the sites to be assigned to their descendants in the division of the nations. St Jerome ('Qu. in Gen.') thinks that Job was a descendant of Huz or Uz the son of Nahor. It is said that Job was of the land of Uz (Job i. 1), and his friend Elihu was "a Buzite of the kindred of Ram" (xxxii. 2). If Ram be the same as Aram, we have then the three names in this verse—Huz, Buz and Aram occurring in the history of Job. In Jerem. xxv. 23 Buz is placed with Dedan and Tema, apparently in Arabia Petræa.

22. *Chesed*] Jerome supposes the Chasdim (or Chaldæans) to have derived their name from him, to which conjecture the occurrence of the Chasdim also in the Book of Job, gives some colour (see on v. 21). If, indeed, "Ur of the Chaldees" was so called when Abraham dwelt there (Gen. xi. 31), this would be an anachronism, but very probably it may have been known as Ur of the Chaldees when Moses wrote, and so designated by him, though the Chaldees or Chasdim may not have been in existence in the days of Abraham.

23. *Bethuel begat Rebekah*] The relationship therefore of Rebekah to Isaac was that Rebekah was daughter of Isaac's first cousin. They were, as we should say, first cousins once removed. Nahor was the elder brother of Abraham, and his granddaughter may have been of a suitable age to be the wife of Abraham's son.

these eight] The sons of Nahor, like the sons of Ishmael and of Jacob, were twelve in number. But though it happens that among the descendants of Terah three persons had twelve sons, there is such a diversity in the other circumstances of the family, such a difference with regard to their mothers, and there are so many other patriarchs, Abraham, Isaac, &c., the numbering of whose children were quite unlike these, that the notion of a mystic number is utterly untenable (see Keil in loc.).

and Gaham, and Thahash, and Maachah.

CHAPTER XXIII.

1 *The age and death of Sarah.* 3 *The purchase of Machpelah,* 19 *where Sarah was buried.*

AND Sarah was an hundred and
seven and twenty years old:
these were the years of the life of Sarah.
2 And Sarah died in Kirjath-arba;
the same *is* Hebron in the land
of Canaan: and Abraham came to
mourn for Sarah, and to weep for
her.
3 ¶ And Abraham stood up from
before his dead, and spake unto the
sons of Heth, saying,
4 I *am* a stranger and a sojourner
with you: give me a possession of a
buryingplace with you, that I may
bury my dead out of my sight.
5 And the children of Heth answered Abraham, saying unto him,
6 Hear us, my lord: thou art a
†mighty prince among us: in the choice
of our sepulchres bury thy dead; none
of us shall withhold from thee his
sepulchre, but that thou mayest bury
thy dead.
7 And Abraham stood up, and

† Heb. *a prince of God.*

CHAP. XXIII. 1. *And Sarah was an hundred and seven and twenty years old*] Sarah is the only woman whose age is mentioned in the Scriptures (Lightfoot, 'Har. of Old Testament,' Gen. xxiii.), because as the mother of the promised seed, she became the mother of all believers. (1 Pet. iii. 6) (Del., Keil.) She died 37 years after the birth of Isaac, as she was 90 when he was born.

2. *Kirjath-arba; the same is Hebron in the land of Canaan*] See on ch. xiii. 18. The supposition that the name Hebron was not given till the time of Joshua, and that the use of it in Genesis indicates a later hand, is contradicted by the natural force of these words. They appear plainly to have been written by some one not then living in the land of Canaan. Hebron was apparently the original name, which was changed to Kirjath-arba, and restored again by Caleb, Josh. xiv. 15.

Abraham came to mourn for Sarah] Aben-ezra and others infer from this that Abraham was not with Sarah when she died. It may mean no more than that Abraham went into Sarah's tent to mourn for her.

4. *I am a stranger and a sojourner*] (Cp. Heb. xi. 13). Abraham had only pastured his flocks, moving from place to place, as a nomad chief; but the various Canaanitish tribes had settled in the land, building cities and cultivating fields; and so as Lightfoot observes ('Harm.:' on Gen. xxiii.), "a burial place is the first land that Abraham has in Canaan." The heir of the promises was but a stranger and a pilgrim, never to rest but in the grave, but with a glorious future before him for his race and for himself; assured that his seed should possess the land, and himself "desiring a better country, that is a heavenly."

Give me a possession of a buryingplace with you] This is the first mention of burial. It was noted by the heathen historian as a characteristic of the Jews, that they preferred to bury their dead rather than to burn them; *corpora condere quam cremare* (Tac. 'Hist.' v. 5). It is observable that this is thus mentioned first, when the first death takes place in the family of him, who had received the promises. The care of the bodies of the departed is a custom apparently connected with the belief in their sanctity as vessels of the Grace of God, and with the hope that they may be raised again in the day of the restitution of all things. The elaborate embalming of the Egyptians had perhaps a very different significance, looking rather to retain the beloved body in its former shape, and perhaps to preserve the living principle in permanent existence with it, rather than hoping that the body, being "sown a natural should be raised a spiritual body."

5. *saying unto him*] The Sam. Pent. and LXX. read (by the variation of a single letter), "saying, Not so."

6. *thou art a mighty prince among us*] lit. "a prince of God." See on ch. x. 9, the name of God being apparently added to give a superlative force: cp. 1 Sam. xxvi. 12, where R. D. Kimchi writes, "When the Scripture would magnify anything, it joins it to the name of God."

in the choice of our sepulchres bury thy dead] The Hittites in the complimentary manner common in oriental bargains (see Thomson, 'Land and Book,' p. 578) offer Abraham to bury his dead in their sepulchres; but there was a separation between them of faith and life, which forbade Abraham to deposit the body of Sarah in the same grave with the people of the land. We know nothing of the funeral rites of the Canaanites at this early period, nor whether they buried the bodies of the departed or only their ashes. It is, however, very probable, that there were idolatrous rites connected with their sepulture, which it would have been unlawful for Abraham to countenance.

bowed himself to the people of the
land, *even* to the children of Heth.
8 And he communed with them,
saying, If it be your mind that I
should bury my dead out of my sight;
hear me, and intreat for me to Ephron
the son of Zohar,
9 That he may give me the cave
of Machpelah, which he hath, which
is in the end of his field; for †as
much money as it is worth he shall
give it me for a possession of a buryingplace amongst you.
10 And Ephron dwelt among the
children of Heth: and Ephron the
Hittite answered Abraham in the †au-
dience of the children of Heth, *even*
of all that went in at the gate of his
city, saying,
11 Nay, my lord, hear me: the
field give I thee, and the cave that
is therein, I give it thee; in the presence of the sons of my people give I
it thee: bury thy dead.
12 And Abraham bowed down himself before the people of the land.
13 And he spake unto Ephron in
the audience of the people of the land,
saying, But if thou *wilt give it*, I pray
thee, hear me: I will give thee money
for the field; take *it* of me, and I
will bury my dead there.
14 And Ephron answered Abraham, saying unto him,
15 My lord, hearken unto me: the
land *is worth* four hundred shekels
of silver; what *is* that betwixt me
and thee? bury therefore thy dead.

† Heb. *full money.*

† Heb. *ears.*

---

7. *bowed himself*] The Vulgate has "adoravit coram populo." It was simply the deep reverence common in the East (cp. 1 Sam. xxv. 24; xxviii. 14; 1 Kings xviii. 7; 2 Kings ii. 15; Esth. viii. 3). It was a matter of courtesy and respect, also of entreaty or of gratitude.

9. *the cave of Machpelah*] The soil of Palestine being rocky naturally suggested sepulture in caves (see Winer, 'Realw.' s.v. *Grabes*, Smith, 'Dict. of Bible,' s.v. *Burial*). All the ancient Versions render the words "cave of Machpelah" by "the double cave," deriving Machpelah from the verb *Caphal* to divide, to double. Interpreters have explained this in various ways, as either that there were two entrances to the cave, or that it had a double structure such that two bodies (as e.g. that of Abraham and Sarah) might be laid there (see Heidegger, II. 131). Others, however, treat the word as a proper name, and Gesenius considers it more probably to signify "portion" than "duplication." The site of this ancient burialplace is well ascertained. Josephus tells us that "Abraham and his descendants built monuments over the sepulchres" here (A. J. I. 14), which were said to be still visible in the days of Jerome ('Onomast.'). Now a mosque is erected over the ground believed to cover the sepulchres. The Haram or sacred precinct of the mosque is surrounded by a wall, believed to be as ancient as anything now remaining in Palestine. The present condition and appearance of it are described by Robinson ('B. R.' II. p. 431 sq.), see also Thomson, 'Land and Book,' p. 580, and a full account of the sepulchre in the appendix to Stanley's 'Sermons in the East.'

for as much money as it is worth] lit. "for full money." The same words are rendered 1 Chron. xxi. 22, "for the full price."

10. *all that went in at the gate of his city*] The transaction took place publicly at the gate of the city, the forum or public place of the ancient cities of the East, see on ch. xix. 1.

11. *the field give I thee*] Compare 2 Sam. xxiv. 20, 24. Both conversations, that between Abraham and Ephron, and that between David and Araunah, are specimens of the extreme courtesy of the Eastern people in the transaction of business.

13. *But if thou wilt give it, I pray thee, hear me*] Rather perhaps, "But do thou, I pray thee, hear me." Two particles of wishing or intreating are used.

money for the field] Lit. "the money of the field," i.e. the value of the field.

15. *four hundred shekels of silver*] The word *shekel* means merely *weight*, cp. *pondus*, *pound*. See on ch. xx. 16, where no name fo a coin or weight occurs, but only the words "a thousand of silver." Here we first have the name of a weight, though probably not of a coin. There is no mention of coinage in Scripture before the Babylonish Captivity; but the Egyptians had rings of gold and silver of fixed weight long before Moses, which are represented on the monuments. The first actual Jewish money appears to have been coined by Simon Maccabæus (1 Macc. xv.). It is not easy to conjecture accurately what the value of a shekel may have been in the time of Abraham. In later times the LXX. and the New Testament (Matt. xvii. 24)

16 And Abraham hearkened unto Ephron; and Abraham weighed to Ephron the silver, which he had named in the audience of the sons of Heth, four hundred shekels of silver, current *money* with the merchant.

17 ¶ And the field of Ephron, which *was* in Machpelah, which *was* before Mamre, the field, and the cave which *was* therein, and all the trees that *were* in the field, that *were* in all the borders round about, were made sure

18 Unto Abraham for a possession in the presence of the children of Heth, before all that went in at the gate of his city.

19 And after this, Abraham buried Sarah his wife in the cave of the field of Machpelah before Mamre: the same *is* Hebron in the land of Canaan.

20 And the field, and the cave that *is* therein, were made sure unto Abraham for a possession of a buryingplace by the sons of Heth.

CHAPTER XXIV.

1 *Abraham sweareth his servant.* 10 *The*
servant's journey: 12 *his prayer:* 14 *his sign.*
15 *Rebekah meeteth him,* 18 *fulfilleth his sign,*
22 *receiveth jewels,* 23 *sheweth her kindred,*
25 *and inviteth him home.* 26 *The servant*
blesseth God. 29 *Laban entertaineth him.*
34 *The servant sheweth his message.* 50
Laban and Bethuel approve it. 58 *Rebekah*
consenteth to go. 62 *Isaac meeteth her.*

AND Abraham was old, *and* † well stricken in age: and the LORD had blessed Abraham in all things. † Heb. *gone into days.*

2 And Abraham said unto his eldest servant of his house, that ruled over all that he had, [a] Put, I pray thee, thy hand under my thigh: [a] chap. 47. 29.

3 And I will make thee swear by the LORD, the God of heaven, and the God of the earth, that thou shalt not take a wife unto my son of the daughters of the Canaanites, among whom I dwell:

---

identify the half shekel with the didrachma, which would make the shekel nearly half an ounce, 220 grains of our weight, or a little less in value than half-a-crown of our present money. The field therefore would have been purchased for about fifty guineas, 52*l.* 10*s.* (See Gesenius, 'Thes.' p. 1474; Winer, 'R. W. B.' s.v. *sekel;* Smith's 'Dict. of Bib.' s.vv. *money*, *shekel*, *weights and measures.*)

16. *current money with the merchant*] Lit. "silver passing with the merchant." The Canaanites were great merchants, so much so that the very word Canaanite became a synonym for merchant, see Job xl. 30 (in Authorised Version xli. 6); Prov. xxxi. 24. It is therefore very probable that they early learned the use of silver as a means of barter: and though it may not have been coined, yet the masses or bars of silver may have been early formed into conventional shapes, or marked with some rude sign to indicate their weight (see Ges. 'Thes.' p. 982).

17. *the field*, &c.] Not only the cave, as first proposed by Abraham, but the whole field with trees in it, which may have formed part of that grove of Mamre, where Abraham dwelt before the overthrow of Sodom and where he built an altar to the Lord.

were made sure unto Abraham] Lit. "stood firm to Abraham."

CHAP. XXIV. 1. *Abraham was old*] He was 137 at the death of Sarah. Isaac was then 37; and when he married Rebekah, he was 40 (see ch. xxv. 20). Abraham therefore must have been in his 140th year at this time, and he lived 35 years after it (ch. xxv. 7).

2. *unto his eldest servant of his house*] Lit. "to his servant, the elder of his house." The word *elder* in Hebrew as in most languages is used as a title of honour, cp. *Sheykh*, *Senatus*, *γέροντες*, *presbyter*, *Signor*, *Mayor*, &c. (Ges. 'Thes.' p. 427; Hammond, on Acts xi. 30). It is generally supposed that this was Eliezer of Damascus, see ch. xv. 2.

Put, I pray thee, thy hand under my thigh] A form of adjuration mentioned only here and of Jacob, ch. xlvii. 29. Various conjectures have been made by Jews (Joseph. 'Ant.' I. 16; Hieron. 'Qu. in Gen.;' Ambrose, 'De Abraham.' I. 6; Eliezer, in 'Pirke,' c. 39), and by the fathers (Ambros. 'De Abrahamo, I. 9; Hieron. ubi supra; August. 'De C. D.' XVI. 33); but nothing is known with certainty of the signification of the action. Aben-Ezra supposes that it was a form of oath prevalent in patriarchal times but only taken by inferiors, as here by Abraham's steward, and in Gen. xlvii. 29 by a son to his father; that accordingly it was a kind of homage, the servant or son thereby indicating subjection and the purpose of obedience. (See Heidegger, II. pp. 134, 135; Rosenm. in loc.)

3. *of the daughters of the Canaanites*]

4 But thou shalt go unto my country, and to my kindred, and take a wife unto my son Isaac.

5 And the servant said unto him, Peradventure the woman will not be willing to follow me unto this land: must I needs bring thy son again unto the land from whence thou camest?

6 And Abraham said unto him, Beware thou that thou bring not my son thither again.

7 ¶ The LORD God of heaven, which took me from my father's house, and from the land of my kindred, and which spake unto me, and that sware unto me, saying, [b]Unto thy seed will I give this land; he shall send his angel before thee, and thou shalt take a wife unto my son from thence.

[b] chap. 12. 7. & 13. 15. & 15. 18. & 26. 4.

8 And if the woman will not be willing to follow thee, then thou shalt be clear from this my oath: only bring not my son thither again.

9 And the servant put his hand under the thigh of Abraham his master, and sware to him concerning that matter.

10 ¶ And the servant took ten camels of the camels of his master, and departed; ‖for all the goods of his master *were* in his hand: and he arose, and went to Mesopotamia, unto the city of Nahor.

‖ Or, *and*.

11 And he made his camels to kneel down without the city by a well of

---

The licentiousness of the Canaanites had probably determined Abraham against marrying his son to one of their daughters. He had also, no doubt, reference to the Promised Seed, and desired that the race from which He was to come should be kept pure from admixture with the race of Ham.

6. *Beware thou that thou bring not my son thither again*] Abraham had been distinctly called of God to leave his own country, and to be a stranger and sojourner in the land which was to be his hereafter. It would therefore have been an act both of unbelief and of disobedience, to send his son back again. He trusted that He, who had so called him, would provide his son with a wife from his own kindred, not defiled, at least as the Canaanites were, with heathen worship and heathen morality; but in any case he would rather his son should wed among the aliens than return to the place whence he himself had been bidden to depart.

10. *ten camels*, &c.] The journey was long and could only be performed in safety by a considerable company or caravan. The words which follow, "for all the goods of his master were in his hand," very probably are no more than an explanation of his taking so many camels with him, his master sparing nothing to make the journey successful. The LXX. and Vulgate render "and he took part of all his master's goods in his hand," as though Abraham had sent a present with the servant to conciliate the favour of the bride's family.

to Mesopotamia] Lit. "Aram of the two rivers," or "Aram-Naharaim." The name *Naharina* constantly occurs in Egyptian inscriptions of the 18th and 19th dynasties. In other passages in Genesis (xxv. 20; xxviii. 2, 6, 7; xxxi. 18; xxxiii. 18; xxxv. 9, 26; xlvi. 15) we read of Padan Aram or simply Padan (Gen. xlviii. 7), "the Plain of Syria," "the flat land of Syria." *Aram-Naharaim* occurs again Deut. xxiii. 5; Judg. iii. 8; Ps. lx. 2 (Heb.). Both names describe the low flat country lying between the two rivers Tigris and Euphrates, though Padan Aram was more limited in extent than Aram-Naharaim. The whole highland country of Syria appears to have been called Aram, as many think to distinguish it from Canaan, the low country, Aram meaning "high" and Canaan "low" land. The country, however, which lies between the two rivers, is chiefly a vast plain, though intersected by the Sinjar range, and becoming more mountainous towards the North (see Stanley, 'S. and P.' p. 129; Smith's 'Dict. of Bible,' II. p. 338). Aram-Naharaim was the whole region afterwards called Mesopotamia, lying between the two rivers: Padan Aram being a limited portion of this country of flat character in the neighbourhood of Haran (see on xxv. 20, xxvii. 43).

the city of Nahor] i. e. Haran or Charran (compare ch. xxvii. 43, and see ch. xi. 31; Acts vii. 2).

11. *made his camels to kneel down*] That they might be unloaded, and rest there. (See on the whole of this scene, Thomson, 'Land and Book,' p. 592.)

the time that women go out to draw water] Le Clerc compares Hom. Od. VII. 20, where Minerva, in the form of a girl carrying a pitcher, meets Ulysses as he is about to enter the city of the Phœnicians in the evening. See also Robinson, 'B. R.' vol. II. p. 368, where a somewhat similar scene to this is described.

water at the time of the evening, *even*
the time †that women go out to draw
water.

† Heb. *that women which draw* water *go forth.*

12 And he said, O LORD God of
my master Abraham, I pray thee,
send me good speed this day, and shew
kindness unto my master Abraham.
13 Behold, [c]I stand *here* by the
well of water; and the daughters of
the men of the city come out to draw
water:

c Ver. 43.

14 And let it come to pass, that
the damsel to whom I shall say, Let
down thy pitcher, I pray thee, that I
may drink; and she shall say, Drink,
and I will give thy camels drink also:
let the same be she *that* thou hast
appointed for thy servant Isaac; and
thereby shall I know that thou hast
shewed kindness unto my master.
15 ¶ And it came to pass, before
he had done speaking, that, behold,
Rebekah came out, who was born to
Bethuel, son of Milcah, the wife of
Nahor, Abraham's brother, with her
pitcher upon her shoulder.
16 And the damsel *was* †very fair
to look upon, a virgin, neither had
any man known her: and she went
down to the well, and filled her pitcher,
and came up.

† Heb. *good of countenance.*

17 And the servant ran to meet
her, and said, Let me, I pray thee,
drink a little water of thy pitcher.
18 And she said, Drink, my lord:
and she hasted, and let down her
pitcher upon her hand, and gave him
drink.
19 And when she had done giving
him drink, she said, I will draw *water*
for thy camels also, until they have
done drinking.
20 And she hasted, and emptied
her pitcher into the trough, and ran
again unto the well to draw *water*,
and drew for all his camels.
21 And the man wondering at her
held his peace, to wit whether the
LORD had made his journey prosperous
or not.
22 And it came to pass, as the
camels had done drinking, that the
man took a golden ‖earring of half a
shekel weight, and two bracelets for

‖ Or, *jewel for the forehead.*

---

12. *O LORD God of my master Abraham*] The Damascene recognizes JEHOVAH, the God of his master Abraham, the Supreme Disposer of all things. He had probably been born a heathen idolater; but Abraham, to whom God had been revealed as JEHOVAH, the eternal self-existing, had no doubt taught his household to acknowledge Him as the Covenant God of Abraham and his family. It is very observable, however, that when Abraham administers an oath to his servant, he makes him swear not only by JEHOVAH, but adds the God of heaven and the God of the earth, which might be a stronger sanction to one brought up in ignorance of the faith of his master.

give me good speed] Lit. "cause to meet me," i. e. the person of whom I am in quest.

14. *the damsel*] The word here used for *damsel* is of common gender, signifying a child or young person of either sex. This is a peculiarity of the Pentateuch. In all the later books the distinction of gender is observed, the feminine affix (ה) being used when a girl is intended. It is important to notice this here; first as shewing the antiquity of the Pentateuch generally; secondly, as shewing that this chapter, which is markedly Jehovistic, is also of marked antiquity. Those, who accuse the so-called Jehovistic chapters of being modern (of the date of Samuel for instance), ground their arguments on a minute criticism of the difference of the words used by the Elohist and the Jehovist writers respectively. It is, however, here very apparent that the word child, "nangar," had not, in the time of the writer of this most Jehovistic history, been distinguished in the singular number into masculine and feminine, *nangar* and *nangarah*, boy and girl.

thereby shall I know] Perhaps more correctly "by her shall I know;" though the Versions generally render the feminine pronoun here by a neuter, the Hebrew having no neuter gender.

15. *who was born to Bethuel*] See ch. xxii. 20 and note.

21. *wondering at her*] "Amazed and astonished" at finding his prayer so suddenly answered.

22. *earring*] So LXX., Vulg., but perhaps more probably "nose-ring." St Jerome in Ezek. xvi. 11, 12, mentions that to his day the women in the East wore golden rings hanging down from their foreheads, on their noses. Hence here the marginal reading gives "jewel for the forehead." To the present

her hands of ten *shekels* weight of gold;

23 And said, Whose daughter *art* thou? tell me, I pray thee: is there room *in* thy father's house for us to lodge in?

24 And she said unto him, I *am* the daughter of Bethuel the son of Milcah, which she bare unto Nahor.

25 She said moreover unto him, We have both straw and provender enough, and room to lodge in.

26 And the man bowed down his head, and worshipped the LORD.

27 And he said, Blessed *be* the LORD God of my master Abraham, who hath not left destitute my master of his mercy and his truth: I *being* in the way, the LORD led me to the house of my master's brethren.

28 And the damsel ran, and told *them of* her mother's house these things.

29 ¶ And Rebekah had a brother, and his name *was* Laban: and Laban ran out unto the man, unto the well.

30 And it came to pass, when he saw the earring and bracelets upon his sister's hands, and when he heard the words of Rebekah his sister, saying, Thus spake the man unto me; that he came unto the man; and, behold, he stood by the camels at the well.

31 And he said, Come in, thou blessed of the LORD; wherefore standest thou without? for I have prepared the house, and room for the camels.

32 ¶ And the man came into the house: and he ungirded his camels, and gave straw and provender for the camels, and water to wash his feet, and the men's feet that *were* with him.

33 And there was set *meat* before him to eat: but he said, I will not eat, until I have told mine errand. And he said, Speak on.

34 And he said, I *am* Abraham's servant.

35 And the LORD hath blessed my master greatly; and he is become great: and he hath given him flocks, and herds, and silver, and gold, and menservants, and maidservants, and camels, and asses.

36 And Sarah my master's wife bare a son to my master when she was old: and unto him hath he given all that he hath.

37 And my master made me swear, saying, Thou shalt not take a wife to my son of the daughters of the Canaanites, in whose land I dwell:

38 But thou shalt go unto my father's house, and to my kindred, and take a wife unto my son.

39 And I said unto my master, Peradventure the woman will not follow me.

40 And he said unto me, The LORD, before whom I walk, will send his angel with thee, and prosper thy way; and thou shalt take a wife for my son of my kindred, and of my father's house:

41 Then shalt thou be clear from *this* my oath, when thou comest to

---

day some Eastern nations wear nose-rings. Schrœder ('De Vest. Mul. Hebr.' c. xxii. § 2). Hartmann ('Hebr.' II. 166); Winer ('R. W.B.' II. 162); Gesen. ('Th.' p. 870); Rosenmüller (in loc.), argue for the rendering "nose-ring" in this passage. The word, however, simply signifies a ring.

half a shekel] Probably about 2 drachms or a quarter of an ounce. See on ch. xxxiii. 14.

28. *her mother's house*] Her father Bethuel was still living (see v. 50); but the mother is mentioned, perhaps because even thus early women may have lived in separate tents from the men (Rashi): which appears also from v. 67, where Sarah's tent is named, and Rebekah is installed in it at her marriage. The daughter naturally went to tell her mother rather than her father of what the servant of Abraham had done; the jewel, which he gave her, being perhaps intended to denote the nature of his embassage.

33. *I will not eat, until I have told mine errand*] Ancient hospitality taught men to set meat before their guests before asking them their names and their business; but here the servant of Abraham felt his message to be so momentous, that he would not eat till he had unburdened himself of it.

my kindred; and if they give not
thee *one*, thou shalt be clear from my
oath.
42 And I came this day unto the
well, and said, O LORD God of my
master Abraham, if now thou do prosper my way which I go:
Ver. 13. 43 [d]Behold, I stand by the well of
water; and it shall come to pass, that
when the virgin cometh forth to draw
water, and I say to her, Give me, I
pray thee, a little water of thy pitcher
to drink;
44 And she say to me, Both drink
thou, and I will also draw for thy
camels: *let* the same *be* the woman
whom the LORD hath appointed out
for my master's son.
45 And before I had done speaking
in mine heart, behold, Rebekah came
forth with her pitcher on her shoulder;
and she went down unto the well, and
drew *water:* and I said unto her, Let
me drink, I pray thee.
46 And she made haste, and let
down her pitcher from her *shoulder*,
and said, Drink, and I will give thy
camels drink also: so I drank, and
she made the camels drink also.
47 And I asked her, and said,
Whose daughter *art* thou? And she
said, The daughter of Bethuel, Nahor's
son, whom Milcah bare unto him: and
I put the earring upon her face, and
the bracelets upon her hands.
48 And I bowed down my head,
and worshipped the LORD, and blessed
the LORD God of my master Abraham, which had led me in the right
way to take my master's brother's
daughter unto his son.
49 And now if ye will deal kindly
and truly with my master, tell me:
and if not, tell me; that I may turn
to the right hand, or to the left.
50 Then Laban and Bethuel answered and said, The thing proceedeth
from the LORD: we cannot speak unto thee bad or good.
51 Behold, Rebekah *is* before thee,
take *her*, and go, and let her be thy
master's son's wife, as the LORD hath
spoken.
52 And it came to pass, that, when
Abraham's servant heard their words,
he worshipped the LORD, *bowing himself* to the earth.
53 And the servant brought forth
†jewels of silver, and jewels of gold, † Heb.
and raiment, and gave *them* to Re- *vessels*.
bekah: he gave also to her brother
and to her mother precious things.
54 And they did eat and drink, he
and the men that *were* with him, and
tarried all night; and they rose up in
the morning, and he said, [e]Send me [e] Ver. 56.
away unto my master. & 59.
55 And her brother and her mother
said, Let the damsel abide with us ‖*a* ‖ Or, *a*
few days, at the least ten; after that *full year*,
she shall go. or, *ten* months.
56 And he said unto them, Hinder
me not, seeing the LORD hath prospered my way; send me away that
I may go to my master.
57 And they said, We will call the
damsel, and inquire at her mouth.
58 And they called Rebekah,

---

50. *Laban and Bethuel*] The brother is here put before the father, and in v. 39 the brother only is mentioned. It appears that in those days the brother was much consulted concerning the marriage of his sisters (Cp. ch. xxxiv. 13; Judg. xxi. 22): but it has also been observed that Bethuel is altogether kept in the background in this history, as though he were a person of insignificant character, see ch. xxix. 6, where he is altogether passed over, Laban being called the son of Nahor, who was his grandfather. (See Blunt's 'Coincidences,' p. 35, and Wordsworth in loc.) Laban was evidently an active stirring man, as is manifested throughout the subsequent history of Jacob. The Hebrew tradition was that Bethuel died on the day that Eliezer, Abraham's servant, arrived (Targum of Pseudo-Jonathan, on v. 55). Josephus ('Ant.' I. 16) speaks of him as dead, which, however, is unlikely, see on ch. xxvii. 2.

53. *jewels of silver*, &c.] Lit. "vessels of silver," &c.

55. *days, at the least ten*] Lit. "days or ten." Certain days or at least ten; unless "days" be a phrase for the regular period of seven days, i.e. a week, when it would be "a week of days or ten days."

and said unto her, Wilt thou go with
this man? And she said, I will go.
59 And they sent away Rebekah
their sister, and her nurse, and Abraham's servant, and his men.
60 And they blessed Rebekah, and
said unto her, Thou *art* our sister, be
thou *the mother* of thousands of millions, and let thy seed possess the gate
of those which hate them.
61 ¶ And Rebekah arose, and her
damsels, and they rode upon the
camels, and followed the man: and
the servant took Rebekah, and went
his way.
62 And Isaac came from the way
f chap. 16. of the f well Lahai-roi; for he dwelt
14. & 25. 11. in the south country.
‖ Or, *to pray.* 63 And Isaac went out ‖ to meditate in the field at the eventide: and
he lifted up his eyes, and saw, and,
behold, the camels *were* coming.
64 And Rebekah lifted up her eyes,
and when she saw Isaac, she lighted
off the camel.
65 For she *had* said unto the servant, What man *is* this that walketh
in the field to meet us? And the servant *had* said, It *is* my master: therefore she took a vail, and covered herself.
66 And the servant told Isaac all
things that he had done.
67 And Isaac brought her into his
mother Sarah's tent, and took Rebekah, and she became his wife; and he
loved her: and Isaac was comforted
after his mother's *death*.

CHAPTER XXV.

1 *The sons of Abraham by Keturah.* 5 *The division of his goods.* 7 *His age, and death.* 9 *His burial.* 12 *The generations of Ishmael.* 17 *His age, and death.* 19 *Isaac prayeth for Rebekah, being barren.* 22 *The children*

---

59. *their sister*] Only one brother is mentioned, viz. Laban: but her relatives generally are spoken of here, as saying of her, "Thou art our sister," sister being used in that wide sense for relation, in which brother is so often found in Scripture.

her nurse] Her name, Deborah, and her death are mentioned ch. xxxv. 8.

62. *And Isaac came from the way of the well of Lahai-roi*] Perhaps "Isaac had come from a journey to Lahai-roi," or "had returned from going to Lahai-roi."

for he dwelt in the south country] Probably at Beer-sheba. Abraham's later dwelling places had been Hebron and Beer-sheba. After the sacrifice of Isaac, we find him dwelling at Beer-sheba (xxii. 19), until we hear of the death of Sarah at Hebron. Very probably Abraham returned after this to Beer-sheba. And so Isaac, whether living with his father, or pitching his tent and feeding his flocks near him, is here represented as dwelling in the south country. In ch. xxv. 11 we find that, after Abraham's death, Isaac took up his residence at Lahai-roi, to which we find that he had been on a visit, when Rebekah arrived, where perhaps he had already been pasturing his flocks and herds (Knobel). All this is in the strictest harmony; though the German critics discover the hand of the Elohist in chapter xxiii., and in the earlier verses of xxv., and that of the Jehovist throughout xxiv.

63. *to meditate*] So LXX., Vulg., but the Targg., Sam., Arab., Saad., Rashi, render "to pray;" some (Syr., Aben-Ezra) "to walk." The word, however, appears most probably to signify religious meditation (see Ges. 'Thes.' p. 1322). Such occupation seems very characteristic of Isaac, whose whole life was so tranquil, and his temper and spirit so calm and submissive, as suiting one who was made an eminent type of Him, who "was oppressed and afflicted, yet He opened not His mouth: He was brought as a lamb to the slaughter; and as a sheep before her shearers is dumb, so He opened not His mouth" (Is. liii. 7). St Jerome ('Qu. in Gen.') sees in this quiet meditation and prayer a type of Him "who went out into a mountain apart to pray" (Matt. xiv. 23).

64. *lighted off the camel*] "It is customary for both men and women, when an Emir or great personage is approaching, to alight some time before he comes up with them. Women frequently refuse to ride in the presence of men; and when a company of them are to pass through a town, they often dismount and walk." (Thomson, 'Land and Book,' p. 593.)

65. *a vail*] The long cloak-like vail, with which the Eastern women covered their faces (see Jerome in loc. and in 'Comment. ad Jes.' III.; Tertullian, 'De velandis Virginibus' (Cap. XVI.). Even at this early period it seems to have been the custom for brides not to suffer the bridegroom to see their faces before marriage (cp. ch. xxix. 23, 25).

67. *Sarah's tent*] See on v. 28.

strive in her womb. 24 *The birth of Esau and*
Jacob. 27 *Their difference.* 29 *Esau selleth*
his birthright.

THEN again Abraham took a wife,
and her name *was* Keturah.
a 1 Chron. i. 32. 2 And [a] she bare him Zimran, and
Jokshan, and Medan, and Midian, and
Ishbak, and Shuah.
3 And Jokshan begat Sheba, and
Dedan. And the sons of Dedan
were Asshurim, and Letushim, and
Leummim.
4 And the sons of Midian; Ephah,
and Epher, and Hanoch, and Abidah,
and Eldaah: All these *were* the children of Keturah.
5 ¶ And Abraham gave all that he
had unto Isaac.
6 But unto the sons of the concubines, which Abraham had, Abraham
gave gifts, and sent them away from
Isaac his son, while he yet lived, eastward, unto the east country.
7 And these *are* the days of the years

CHAP. XXV. 1. *Then again Abraham took a wife, and her name was Keturah*] The later Targg. and some other Jewish commentators (Rashi and R. Eliezer, in 'Pirke,' c. 30; see also Jerome, 'Qu. in Gen.'), say that Keturah was the same as Hagar, whom Abraham took again, after Sarah's death. This seems inconsistent with v. 6, which speaks of "the concubines" in the plural, meaning, doubtless, Hagar and Keturah. The latter, though called wife here, is called concubine in 1 Chron. i. 32. Moreover, in 1 Chron. i. 28, 32, the sons of Keturah are named separately from Isaac and Ishmael. The concubine (Pilegesh) was a kind of secondary wife, sometimes called "the concubine wife," Judg. xix. 1; 2 S. xv. 16; xx. 3. It is generally supposed, that Abraham did not take Keturah to wife, till after Sarah's death. So the fathers generally. Abraham lived to the age of 175. If we consider this extreme old age as equivalent to eighty-five or ninety in the present day, his age at the time of Sarah's death would correspond to that of a man of from sixty-five to seventy now.

Some, however, think, that Abraham took Keturah to be a secondary wife, during Sarah's life, though no mention is made of this marriage till this time, as the chief purpose of mentioning it was that some account should be given of Keturah's children. So Keil, Poole (in 'Dict. of Bible'), &c. It is impossible to decide this question, as the text gives no note of time. The Authorised Version indeed renders, "Then again Abraham took a wife," but the Hebrew only conveys the notion that Abraham took another wife.

2. *she bare him Zimran*] Josephus ('A. J.' I. 15) tells us that the descendants of Keturah occupied the Troglodyte country and Arabia Felix, which statement is repeated by Jerome ('Qu. Heb. in Gen.'). Some of their names occur among the Arab tribes, but it is not easy to identify them all clearly

Zimran has been thought to be identified with the Zabram of Ptolemy (VI. 7, 5), the royal city of the Cinædocolpitæ to the West of Mecca, on the Red Sea; Jokshan with the Cassanitæ on the Red Sea (Ptol. VI. 7, 6); Ishbak with Shobek, in Idumæa (Knobel, Del., Keil).

Medan, and Midian] In ch. xxxvii. 28, 36, the Midianites and Medanites are identified. The Midianites dwelt partly in the peninsula of Sinai, partly beyond Jordan, in the neighbourhood of the Moabites. We meet with them first as the merchants to whom Joseph was sold by his brethren (as ch. xxxvii. 28 sqq.), trafficking between Egypt and Canaan. Next we find Moses flying to the land of Midian, and marrying the daughter of a priest of Midian, Exod. ii. 15, 16, 21, whose flocks pastured in the desert, in the neighbourhood of Mount Horeb (Ex. iii. 1). Later we find the people of Midian in immediate juxta-position with the Moabites (Num. xxii. 4, xxv. 6, 17, 18). We find them afterwards as formidable neighbours to the Israelites, invading and oppressing them, though afterwards expelled and conquered (Judg. vi. vii. viii.). It has been thought that traces of the name of Midian may be found in Modiana on the Eastern coast of the Elanitic Gulf mentioned by Ptolemy (VI. 7), (Knobel).

3. *Sheba, and Dedan*] Are named, ch. x. 7, among the descendants of Cush. It has been thought that in these, as in other instances, the Shemite and Hamite races intermarried, and that there consequently arose a certain confusion in their names, or that very probably they adopted names from those with whom they were thus connected (see on ch. x. 6, 7; also Ges. 'Thes.' p. 322).

4. *Ephah*] We meet with this Midianitish tribe in Is. lx. 6, as a people rich in camels and gold and incense. The attempts to identify the various descendants of Keturah, mentioned in this chapter, with the names of tribes or cities known to later geographers and historians, may be seen in Knobel, Del., Keil, &c. The uncertainty of such identification is very great.

6. *eastward, unto the east country*] That

of Abraham's life which he lived, an
hundred threescore and fifteen years.
8 Then Abraham gave up the
ghost, and died in a good old age, an
old man, and full *of years;* and was
gathered to his people.
9 And his sons Isaac and Ishmael
buried him in the cave of Machpelah,
in the field of Ephron the son of
Zohar the Hittite, which *is* before
Mamre;
10 [b]The field which Abraham pur- [b chap. 23. 16.]
chased of the sons of Heth: there was
Abraham buried, and Sarah his wife.
11 ¶ And it came to pass after the
death of Abraham, that God blessed
his son Isaac; and Isaac dwelt by the
[c]well Lahai-roi. [c chap. 16. 14. & 24. 62.]
12 ¶ Now these *are* the generations
of Ishmael, Abraham's son, whom
Hagar the Egyptian, Sarah's handmaid, bare unto Abraham:
13 And [d]these *are* the names of [d 1 Chron. 1. 29.]
the sons of Ishmael, by their names,
according to their generations: the
firstborn of Ishmael, Nebajoth; and
Kedar, and Adbeel, and Mibsam,
14 And Mishma, and Dumah, and
Massa,
15 ‖Hadar, and Tema, Jetur, Na-
phish, and Kedemah:
16 These *are* the sons of Ishmael,
and these *are* their names, by their
towns, and by their castles; twelve
princes according to their nations.
17 And these *are* the years of the
life of Ishmael, an hundred and thirty
and seven years: and he gave up the
ghost and died; and was gathered
unto his people.
18 And they dwelt from Havilah
unto Shur, that *is* before Egypt, as
thou goest toward Assyria: *and* he
†died in the presence of all his bre- [† Heb. *fell.*]
thren.
19 ¶ And these *are* the generations of Isaac, Abraham's son: Abraham begat Isaac:
20 And Isaac was forty years old
when he took Rebekah to wife, the
daughter of Bethuel the Syrian of
Padan-aram, the sister to Laban the
Syrian.
21 And Isaac intreated the LORD

---

is into Arabia, the inhabitants of which were called Bene-Kedem, "children of the East" (Judg. vi. 3; 1 K. iv. 30; Job i. 3, Is. xi. 14), and afterwards "Saracens," i.e. "Easterns."

8. *Abraham gave up the ghost*] The history of Abraham is thus wound up before the history of Isaac's family is told. Abraham did not die till Jacob and Esau were born. Indeed they were fifteen years old at Abraham's death: for he died at 175, Isaac was then seventy-five years old, but Esau and Jacob were born when Isaac was sixty (see v. 26).

was gathered to his people] This cannot mean that he was buried where his fathers had been buried, for he had been a hundred years a pilgrim in the land of Israel, far from the home of his ancestors, and he was buried in the cave of Machpelah. The place therefore seems to indicate the belief of the patriarchal ages in a place of departed spirits, to which the souls of the dead were gathered. Thus Jacob expected to "go down into the grave (to Sheol) unto his son," though he did not believe his son to have been buried, but to have been devoured by wild beasts (ch. xxxvii. 35; compare also Deut. xxxii. 50). St Augustine ('Qu. in Gen.' 268) interprets the words "his people," of "the people of that city, the heavenly Jerusalem," spoken of in Heb. xii. 22, and which God is said to have prepared for the faithful patriarchs, Heb. xi. 16.

9. *his sons Isaac and Ishmael*] From this we see that Ishmael, though sent to dwell Eastward, had not lost sight of his father and Isaac; and very probably their father's death reconciled the two brothers to each other. Isaac is put first as the heir, and the heir of the promises.

16. *castles*] See on Num. xxxi. 10.

19. *And these are the generations of Isaac, Abraham's son*] This is the beginning of a new Section in the history of Genesis, which continues to the end of ch. xxxv. According to the uniform plan of the author, there is a brief recapitulation, in order to make the Section complete. In this case it is very brief, consisting of the latter part of v. 19, and v. 20.

20. *the Syrian of Padan-aram*] **The Aramean of Padan-aram.** Padan-aram is the "plain or flat land of Aram," translated or paraphrased in Hosea xii. 12 by Sĕdeh-Aram, "the field or plain of Aram." In the last chapter the country of Rebekah is called Aram-Naharaim, or Aram of the two rivers. See on ch. xxiv. 10. There is no reasonable foundation for the belief that Padan-aram

for his wife, because she *was* barren:
and the LORD was intreated of him,
and Rebekah his wife conceived.
22 And the children struggled together within her; and she said, If *it*
be so, why *am* I thus? And she went
to inquire of the LORD.
23 And the LORD said unto her,
Two nations *are* in thy womb, and
two manner of people shall be separated from thy bowels; and *the one*
people shall be stronger than *the other*
people; and [e] the elder shall serve the
younger.
24 ¶ And when her days to be delivered were fulfilled, behold, *there*
were twins in her womb.
25 And the first came out red, all

[e] Rom. 9. 12.

---

was the old name used by the so-called Elohist, Aram-Naharaim being the name which had been adopted by the later Jehovist. It was natural that the historian, when relating the embassy of Eliezer of Damascus to Mesopotamia to seek a wife for Isaac, should have used the general name of the country into which Eliezer was sent, whereas in the present Section more particularity is to be expected, where Jacob is described as sojourning for years in Padan-aram, the land of Laban; just as in one case it might be natural to speak of going into Scotland, whilst in a more detailed account, we might prefer to speak of the Highlands of Scotland, or the Lowlands, or of some particular county or district.

21. *Isaac intreated the* LORD *for his wife, because she was barren*] This barrenness had lasted twenty years (v. 26). Another instance of the delay in the fulfilment of God's promises, and of the trial of the faith of those for whom the greatest blessings are reserved. The word here used for prayer is by many thought to mean frequent and repeated prayer; implying the anxious desire of Isaac to be blessed with offspring. Gesenius (p. 1085) thinks the word is connected with a root signifying "to offer incense," which certainly appears to belong to it in Ezek. viii. 11. If it be so, we must believe that the patriarchal worship, which from the earliest times was accompanied with sacrifice, had also, whether from Divine revelation or from an instinctive feeling, adopted the use of incense.

22. *If it be so, why am I thus?*] An obscure saying. The Vulg. and Targums render, "If it was to be thus with me, why did I conceive?" The Arabic has, "If I had known it would be thus, I would not have sought for offspring." Much to the same effect Rashi, "If such be the sufferings of pregnancy, why did I desire it?" The Syriac and most of the German Comm. understand it, "If it be so, wherefore do I live?"

And she went to inquire of the LORD] By prayer, or by sacrifice, perhaps at some special place of prayer; as to the domestic altar of Isaac (Theodor. 'Qu. in Gen.'), or more likely, by going to a prophet. The Jerusalem Targum, followed by several Jewish commentators says, she went to Shem; others say to Melchizedec. Abraham, who was still living, was the head of the family then dwelling in Palestine; he had been specially honoured by revelations from heaven; and was probably esteemed the patriarch-priest of the whole race. It is most likely, therefore, that if the inquiry was made through a man, it would have been made through him. Still we may conclude with St Augustine ('Qu.' 72), that nothing is certain except that Rebekah went to ask of the Lord, and that the Lord answered her.

23. *Two nations*, &c.] The response is in antistrophic parallelisms, a poetic form, in which no doubt it was more readily handed down from father to son:

Two nations are in thy womb:
and two peoples shall be separated from thy bowels;
and nation shall be stronger than nation,
and the elder shall serve the younger.

To this see the reference Mal. i. 2, 3, "Jacob have I loved, and Esau have I hated," and in Rom. ix. 10—13, where St Paul shews that election to the privilege of being the depositories of God's truth and the Church of God on earth is inscrutable, but not therefore necessarily unjust or unmerciful. Such election indeed plainly marks that God does not choose men as His instruments because of their merits, but it does not shew that He is therefore simply arbitrary. In all there is a hidden stream of mercy flowing. The chosen race shall be made the means of salvation to others as well as to themselves. Their privileges will be blessed to them, if they use those privileges faithfully. Otherwise whilst they are the channels of God's grace to their brethren, they themselves will be cast out, and others shall come into their inheritance.

25. *red, all over like an hairy garment*] He seemed as if covered with a kind of fur, a thick down, which is said to be found on some new born infants. It gave an animal appear-

over like an hairy garment; and they
called his name Esau.
26 And after that came his brother
f Hos. 12. 3. out, and *f* his hand took hold on Esau's
heel; and his name was called Jacob:
and Isaac *was* threescore years old
when she bare them.
27 And the boys grew: and Esau
was a cunning hunter, a man of the
field; and Jacob *was* a plain man,
dwelling in tents.
28 And Isaac loved Esau, because
† he did eat of *his* venison: but Rebe- † Heb. *venison was in his mouth.*
kah loved Jacob.
29 ¶ And Jacob sod pottage: and
Esau came from the field, and he *was*
faint:
30 And Esau said to Jacob, Feed
me, I pray thee, † with that same red † Heb. *with that red, with that red pottage.*
pottage; for I *am* faint: therefore was
his name called ‖ Edom. ‖ That is, *Red.*
31 And Jacob said, Sell me this
day thy birthright.
32 And Esau said, Behold, I *am*

---

ance to Esau, and probably indicated his more sensual nature. Owing to this he was called Esau, "hairy."

Jacob] Meaning, literally, "he holds the heel;" but, from the act of a person tripping up an adversary in wrestling or running by taking hold of the heel, it signifies also to "trip up," "to outwit," "to supplant." (See xxvii. 36).

27. *a cunning hunter*] **Skilled in hunting.** Instead of following the quiet pastoral life of his forefathers, Esau preferred the wilder life of a hunter, betokening his wild, restless, self-indulgent character, and leading him probably to society with the heathen Canaanites round about.

a man of the field] This is antithetic to what follows, "a dweller in tents." It probably indicates still more fully the wild life of Esau. Instead of spending his life in the society of his family, returning to his tent after the day's labour at night, he roved over the country, like the uncivilized hunters in half savage lands.

Jacob was a plain man] **An upright man,** a man of steady, domestic, moral habits.

dwelling in tents] *i.e.* staying at home, attending to the pasturing of the flocks and the business of the family, instead of wandering abroad in search of pleasure and amusement. (See Ges. 'Thes.' p. 634.)

28. *Isaac loved Esau, because he did eat of his venison*] Lit. "because venison was in his mouth." The bold daring of Esau was, perhaps by force of contrast, pleasant to the quiet spirit of Isaac. That quiet temper was not strong enough to rule such a restless youth; there was also a marked selfishness in Isaac's affection, which brought with it its own punishment. The mother, on the contrary, loved the well-conducted and helpful Jacob. Yet her love too was not guided by the highest principle, and so led her and her favourite son to sin against truth and justice, and brought heavy trials and sorrows on them both.

30. *Feed me, I pray thee, with that same red pottage*] **Let me, I pray thee, devour some of that red, that red.** The words express the vehemence of the appetite, and probably the very words uttered by Esau in his impatient hunger and weariness. The red lentil is still esteemed in the East, and has been found very palatable by modern travellers (Robinson, 'Bib. Res.' I. 246). Dr Kitto says he often partook of a red pottage made of lentils. "The mess had the redness, which gained for it the name of red" ('Pict. Bib.' Gen. xxv. 30, quoted in Smith's 'Dict. of Bib.' II. 92). It is also described by Thomson, 'Land and Book,' p. 587, as exhaling an odour very tempting to a hungry man.

therefore was his name called Edom] Names appear to have been frequently given from accidental causes, especially in the East; and sometimes the occurrence of more than one circumstance to the same person seems to have riveted a name. Thus we read above that Esau was born with red hair and colour. His frantic demand for *red* pottage and selling his birthright to gain it, may have conspired with his hair and complexion to stamp the name Edom (or Red) upon him. The conjecture of Tuch and others, that the name was connected with the Red Sea, near which the Edomites dwelt, is wholly groundless. The Red Sea was never so called in early times, or in Semitic tongues. The name Red was given in later days to this sea by the Greeks.

31. *Sell me this day thy birthright*] It is doubtful what privileges the birthright carried with it in patriarchal times. In after times a double portion of the patrimony was assigned to the firstborn by law (Deut. xxi. 15—17); but in the earliest days the respect paid to the eldest son is very apparent; and as the family spread out into a tribe, the patriarchal head became a chieftain or prince.

† Heb. *going to die.* †at the point to die: and what profit
shall this birthright do to me?
33 And Jacob said, Swear to me
this day; and he sware unto him:
g Heb. 12. 16. and [g]he sold his birthright unto
Jacob.
34 Then Jacob gave Esau bread
and pottage of lentiles; and he did
eat and drink, and rose up, and went
his way: thus Esau despised *his* birthright.

CHAPTER XXVI.

1 *Isaac because of famine went to Gerar.* 2 *God instructeth, and blesseth him.* 7 *He is reproved by Abimelech for denying his wife.* 12 *He groweth rich.* 18 *He diggeth Esek, Sitnah, and Rehoboth.* 26 *Abimelech maketh a covenant with him at Beer-sheba.* 34 *Esau's wives.*

AND there was a famine in the
land, beside the first famine that
was in the days of Abraham. And

It also looks as if the head of the family exercised a kind of priesthood. Then the father's chief blessing was given to his firstborn son. Above all, in the family of Abraham, there was a promise of peculiar spiritual privileges, which, if not fully understood, would have been much dwelt upon by believing minds. All this was to Esau of little account compared with the desire of present gratification of appetite. It has been thought, not improbably, that the famine impending (see xxvi. 1) was already, more or less, pressing on the family of Isaac (Lightfoot, 'Harm. of O. T.' in loc.). Esau had perhaps been seeking in vain for food in the chase, whilst Jacob had prepared a mess of pottage, sufficient to relieve the pains of hunger. If it were so, Esau, wearied and famished, may have been strongly tempted to give up much for food. But his worldly and "profane" character is exhibited in his contempt for that, which was, whether in a worldly or in a spiritual point of view, rather an object of faith or sentiment, than of sight and sense. Jacob, a man of widely different character, had probably looked with reverence on the spiritual promises, though with culpable ambition for the personal preeminence of the firstborn. He and Esau were twins, and it may have seemed hard to him to be shut out from the chief hope of his house by one not older than himself, and whose character was little worthy of his position. This may be some excuse for his conduct, but the sacred history, whilst exposing the carnal indifference of Esau, does not extenuate the selfishness of Jacob. Throughout their history, Esau is the bold, reckless, but generous and openhearted man of this world; Jacob, on the contrary, is a thoughtful, religious man, but with many infirmities, and especially with that absence of simplicity and uprightness, which often characterizes those who have made their choice of heaven and yet let their hearts linger too much on earth.

The events correspond with the characters of the men. Esau lives on his rough and reckless life; though towards the end of it we see his better feelings overcoming his vindictiveness. Whatever his own final state with God may have been, he has disinherited his children, left them wild men of the desert and the rocks, instead of leaving them heirs of the promises and ancestors of the Messiah. Jacob, with a less prosperous life, has yet gone through a long training and chastening from the God of his fathers, to whose care and guidance he had given himself; he suffers heavily, but he learns from that he suffered; at last he goes down to Egypt to die, comforted in having his children yet alive, confessing that few and evil had been the days of the years of his pilgrimage, but yet able to say in peaceful confidence upon his deathbed, "I have waited for thy salvation, O LORD." He has inherited the promises; but for trying by unworthy means to anticipate the promise of inheritance, he has to go through a life of trial, sorrow, and discipline, and to die at last, not in the land of promise, but in the house of bondage.

CHAP. XXVI. 1. *Abimelech*] It has been doubted whether this be the Abimelech with whom Abraham was concerned or not. The events related in this chapter took place about eighty years after those related in ch. xx. It is not therefore impossible, when men lived to 180, that the same king may still have been reigning over the Philistines; and it has been thought that the character described here is very similar to that in ch. xx. It seems more probable that the present Abimelech should have been the son or successor of the earlier king. Names were very frequently handed down to the grandson, recurring alternately, and this may very possibly have been the case here: but moreover, *Abimelech* (*father king*, or *father of the king*), may very likely have been, like Pharaoh, a title rather than a name, so also Phichol (*the mouth of all*, i.e. commanding all), sounds like the title of the commander in chief or the grand vizier. Cp. xxi. 22, xxvi. 26.

Gerar] The chief city of the Philistines, now Kirbet el Gerar.

Isaac went unto Abimelech king of
the Philistines unto Gerar.
2 And the LORD appeared unto
him, and said, Go not down into
Egypt; dwell in the land which I
shall tell thee of:
3 Sojourn in this land, and I will
be with thee, and will bless thee; for
[a] chap. 13. 15. & 15. 18. unto thee, and unto thy seed, [a]I will
give all these countries, and I will
perform the oath which I sware unto
Abraham thy father;
4 And I will make thy seed to
multiply as the stars of heaven, and
will give unto thy seed all these countries; and in thy seed shall all the
[b] chap. 12. 3. & 15. 18. & 22. 18. nations of the earth be [b]blessed;
5 Because that Abraham obeyed
my voice, and kept my charge, my
commandments, my statutes, and my
laws.
6 ¶ And Isaac dwelt in Gerar:
7 And the men of the place asked
him of his wife; and he said, She *is*
my sister: for he feared to say, *She is*
my wife; lest, *said he*, the men of
the place should kill me for Rebekah;
because she *was* fair to look upon.
8 And it came to pass, when he
had been there a long time, that
Abimelech king of the Philistines looked out at a window, and saw, and,
behold, Isaac *was* sporting with Rebekah his wife.
9 And Abimelech called Isaac, and
said, Behold, of a surety she *is* thy
wife: and how saidst thou, She *is* my
sister? And Isaac said unto him, Because I said, Lest I die for her.
10 And Abimelech said, What *is*
this thou hast done unto us? one of
the people might lightly have lien with
thy wife, and thou shouldest have
brought guiltiness upon us.
11 And Abimelech charged all *his*
people, saying, He that toucheth this
man or his wife shall surely be put to
death.
12 Then Isaac sowed in that land,
and †received in the same year an † Heb. found

2. *the LORD appeared unto him*] The last recorded vision was at the sacrifice of Isaac more than sixty years before, ch. xxii. These revelations were not so frequent as they seem to us, as we read one event rapidly after the other, but just sufficient to keep up the knowledge of God and the faith of the patriarchs in the line of the chosen people and of the promised seed.

Go not down into Egypt] "In the first famine, which was in the days of Abraham," Abraham had gone down to Egypt. Probably, after this example, and from the plenty with which Egypt was blessed, Isaac had purposed to go down there now.

3. *Sojourn in this land*] He was the heir, to whom the land had been promised. He is to dwell in it, as a stranger and sojourner, and not to be tempted by suffering to go down to that land of spiritual danger, from which his father so narrowly escaped.

4. *all these countries*] The lands of the different Canaanitish tribes named in ch. xv. 19—21. The pronoun here rendered "these" is one of those ancient forms peculiar to the Pentateuch (*ha-el;* in the later books it would be *ha-eleh*).

7. *She is my sister*] Isaac acted on this occasion just as Abraham had done in Egypt and in Philistia. Probably too, he called Rebekah his sister because she was his cousin, and the deep importance of strict truthfulness had not been fully unfolded to the patriarchs in their twilight state of faith. The difference in the details of this story and the events in the life of Abraham is too marked to allow it to be thought that this is only a repetition of the histories in ch. xii. and xx. In the history of Abraham Sarah was taken into the house of Pharaoh, and afterwards into that of Abimelech, and in both cases preserved by Divine intervention. In the history of Isaac, there is no apparent intention on the part of Abimelech to take Rebekah into his house, but he accidentally discovers that Isaac and Rebekah were not brother and sister but husband and wife, and then reproves Isaac for his concealment of the truth, on the ground that so some of his people might have ignorantly taken Rebekah to wife.

12. *sowed in that land*] The patriarchs were not so wholly nomadic and pastoral in their habits of life as to neglect agriculture entirely. Even the Bedouins practise agriculture at the present day as well as grazing (Robinson, 'B. R.' Vol. I. p. 77).

an hundredfold] **An hundred measures;** *i.e.* probably a hundred measures for each measure sown, a very unusual increase, though not quite unknown in a virgin soil, especially if the corn were barley. (The LXX. and Syr. render here "a hundred of barley,"

hundredfold: and the LORD blessed
him.
13 And the man waxed great, and
† Heb. *went going.* †went forward, and grew until he became very great:
14 For he had possession of flocks,
and possession of herds, and great
‖ Or, *husbandry.* store of ‖servants: and the Philistines
envied him.
15 For all the wells which his father's servants had digged in the days
of Abraham his father, the Philistines
had stopped them, and filled them
with earth.
16 And Abimelech said unto Isaac,
Go from us; for thou art much
mightier than we.
17 ¶ And Isaac departed thence,
and pitched his tent in the valley of
Gerar, and dwelt there.
18 And Isaac digged again the
wells of water, which they had digged
in the days of Abraham his father;
for the Philistines had stopped them
after the death of Abraham: and he
called their names after the names by
which his father had called them.
19 And Isaac's servants digged in
the valley, and found there a well of
† Heb. *living.* †springing water.
20 And the herdmen of Gerar did
strive with Isaac's herdmen, saying,
The water *is* ours: and he called the
‖ That is, *Contention.* name of the well ‖Esek; because they
strove with him.
21 And they digged another well,
and strove for that also: and he called
‖ That is, *Hatred.* the name of it ‖Sitnah.
22 And he removed from thence,
and digged another well; and for that
they strove not: and he called the
name of it ‖Rehoboth; and he said, ‖ That is, *Room.*
For now the LORD hath made room
for us, and we shall be fruitful in the
land.
23 And he went up from thence
to Beer-sheba.
24 And the LORD appeared unto
him the same night, and said, I *am*
the God of Abraham thy father: fear
not, for I *am* with thee, and will bless
thee, and multiply thy seed for my
servant Abraham's sake.
25 And he builded an altar there,
and called upon the name of the LORD,
and pitched his tent there: and there
Isaac's servants digged a well.
26 ¶ Then Abimelech went to him
from Gerar, and Ahuzzath one of his
friends, and Phichol the chief captain
of his army.
27 And Isaac said unto them,
Wherefore come ye to me, seeing ye
hate me, and have sent me away from
you?
28 And they said, †We saw cer- † Heb. *Seeing we saw.*
tainly that the LORD was with thee:
and we said, Let there be now an oath
betwixt us, *even* betwixt us and thee,
and let us make a covenant with thee;
29 †That thou wilt do us no hurt, † Heb. *If thou shalt, &c.*
as we have not touched thee, and as
we have done unto thee nothing but
good, and have sent thee away in
peace: thou *art* now the blessed of
the LORD.

---

which Michaelis and others have adopted. The reading and rendering of the Authorised Version are more generally supported, and are probably correct.) The fertility of the soil in this neighbourhood is still very great.

17. *the valley of Gerar*] The word for *valley* signifies properly the bed or course of a stream or mountain torrent, a *wady*. It is not easy to say which of the valleys running to the sea, South of Beer-sheba, may be identified with this valley of Gerar (see Robinson, 'Physical Geography,' p. 112).

22. *Rehoboth*] Probably identified as to site with the Wady er-Ruhaibeh, where are the ruins of an extensive city, eight hours South of Beer-sheba. Here is an ancient well, now filled up, twelve feet in diameter, and regularly built with hewn stone (Robinson, 'Phys. Geog.' p. 243; see also 'B. R.' p. 289).

26. *Phichol*] See on v. 1. The name signifies "the mouth of all," which would be applicable to a grand vizier, through whom all might have access to the sovereign, or to a general whose voice gave command to all. The former sense would seem the more probable, if it had not been said that Phichol was "the chief captain of the army."

29. *thou art now the blessed of the LORD*] We have here twice (see v. 28) the sacred name JEHOVAH, used by the heathen king of Gerar. This does not, however, indicate that the writer of this portion of the

30 And he made them a feast, and
they did eat and drink.
31 And they rose up betimes in
the morning, and sware one to another: and Isaac sent them away, and
they departed from him in peace.
32 And it came to pass the same
day, that Isaac's servants came, and
told him concerning the well which
they had digged, and said unto him,
We have found water.
33 And he called it ‖ Shebah: therefore the name of the city *is* ‖ Beer-
sheba unto this day.
34 ¶ And Esau was forty years
old when he took to wife Judith the
daughter of Beeri the Hittite, and
Bashemath the daughter of Elon the
Hittite:
35 Which [c] were † a grief of mind
unto Isaac and to Rebekah.

‖ That is, *an oath.* ‖ That is, *the well of the oath.*

c chap. 27. 46. † Heb. *bitterness of spirit.*

CHAPTER XXVII.

1 *Isaac sendeth Esau for venison.* 6 *Rebekah instructeth Jacob to obtain the blessing.* 15 *Jacob under the person of Esau obtaineth it.* 30 *Esau bringeth venison.* 33 *Isaac trembleth.* 34 *Esau complaineth, and by importunity obtaineth a blessing.* 41 *He threateneth Jacob.* 42 *Rebekah disappointeth it.*

AND it came to pass, that when
Isaac was old, and his eyes were
dim, so that he could not see, he
called Esau his eldest son, and said

---

history had so-called Jehovistic tendencies, or that he simply identified the name JEHOVAH with the name Elohim. Abraham had dwelt for some time in Gerar, either under this very Abimelech, or under his immediate predecessor. Abraham was known as a worshipper of JEHOVAH, and was seen to be blessed and prospered by his God. Now again Abraham's son Isaac comes and sojourns for a long time in the same country. He too worships his father's God, and is seen, like his father, to prosper abundantly. The Philistines therefore recognize him, as his father, to be a worshipper of JEHOVAH, and perceive that he has succeeded to his father in the favour of their great Protector. Abimelech does not profess himself a worshipper of the LORD, but looks on the LORD as the God of Abraham, and sees that Abraham's son Isaac is "*now* the blessed of the LORD."

33. *he called it Shebah: therefore the name of the city is Beer-sheba unto this day*] "Shebah" means both *seven* and *oath;* the number seven being a sacred number among the Hebrews, and oaths being apparently ratified with presents or sacrifices seven in number (see ch. xxi. 28). There is no inconsistency in the history which tells us that Abraham gave the name of Beer-sheba to this well long before, and under similar circumstances. The well, dug by Abraham, and secured to him by oath, had been covered and lost. It is found by Isaac's servants just after the covenant made between him and Abimelech. The whole series of events recalls to Isaac's mind the original name, and that which gave rise to the name, and so he restores, not the well only, but the name also. "Upon the Northern side of the Wady es-Seba are the two deep and ancient wells, which gave occasion to this name" (Robinson, 'Phys. Geog.' p. 242; 'B. R.' I. p. 300). It is supposed by Robinson, that the one is that dug by Abraham, the other that dug by Isaac; the name having been afterwards given to both.

34. *Esau was forty years old,* &c.] Isaac was now a hundred years old. Esau marries two wives and both of them Canaanites. On account of his polygamy and his marrying without consent of his parents from among the idolatrous Hittites and Hivites (see ch. xxxvi. 2), he is called "a fornicator" by the Apostle (Heb. xii. 16). These two verses do not belong so much to this chapter as to the next. The account of Esau's marriage, and the consequent grief of Isaac and Rebekah, is intended to prepare the way for the succeeding history.

35. *a grief of mind*] **A bitterness of spirit.**

CHAP. XXVII. 1. *Isaac was old*] The Jewish intepreters say he was now one hundred and thirty-seven years old, the age at which Ishmael died fourteen years before, and it is not improbable that the thought of his brother's death at this age put Isaac in mind of his own end. The calculation on which it is inferred that Isaac was one hundred and thirty-seven, Esau and Jacob being seventy-seven at this time, is as follows; Joseph was thirty years old when he stood before Pharaoh (Gen. xli. 46), then came seven years of plenty (v. 47—53), which made Joseph thirty-seven; then two years of famine ere Jacob came into Egypt (ch. xlv. 6), which brings Joseph's age to thirty-nine; but at this time Jacob was one hundred and thirty; therefore Jacob must have been ninety-one when Joseph was born. Now Joseph was born in the last year of the second seven, or in the fourteenth year of Jacob's service with Laban, at the very end of that year

unto him, My son: and he said unto him, Behold, *here am* I.

2 And he said, Behold now, I am old, I know not the day of my death:

3 Now therefore take, I pray thee, thy weapons, thy quiver and thy bow, and go out to the field, and †take me *some* venison;

† Heb. *hunt.*

4 And make me savoury meat, such as I love, and bring *it* to me, that I may eat; that my soul may bless thee before I die.

5 And Rebekah heard when Isaac spake to Esau his son. And Esau went to the field to hunt *for* venison, *and* to bring *it*.

6 ¶ And Rebekah spake unto Jacob her son, saying, Behold, I heard thy father speak unto Esau thy brother, saying,

7 Bring me venison, and make me savoury meat, that I may eat, and bless thee before the LORD before my death.

8 Now therefore, my son, obey my

(ch. xxx. 25, 26). Take fourteen years out of ninety-one, Jacob's age when Joseph was born, and we have seventy-seven for the age of Jacob, when he was sent away from the wrath of Esau to the house of Laban. (See Lightfoot's 'Harmony of Old Testament' in loc., works by Pitman, 1822, Vol. II. pp. 96, 97). If this calculation be true, Isaac had still forty-three years to live, his quiet life having been extended to an unusual length. There is however great risk of numerical calculations from various causes being inexact. The last chapter had brought us down only to the hundredth year of Isaac's life, Esau being then but forty; and in some respects an earlier date seems more accordant with the tenor of the subsequent history, it being hardly probable that Jacob should have been seventy-seven when he fled to Laban and served seven years for his wife, and then another seven years for his second wife; even at a period when human life was still extended so far beyond that of future generations. On the chronology of Jacob's life see note at the end of ch. xxxi.

3. *quiver*] So LXX., Vulg., Pseudo-Jon.: but Onkelos, Syr. have "sword." The Jewish commentators are divided between the two senses. The word occurs nowhere else, but is derived from a verb meaning to "hang," to "suspend," which would suit either the quiver which hung over the shoulder, or the sword. the "hanger," which was suspended by the side.

4. *that my soul may bless thee*] There appears a singular mixture of the carnal and the spiritual in this. Isaac recognizes his own character as that of the priestly and prophetic head of his house, privileged to bless as father and priest, and to foretell the fortunes of his family in succession to Abraham in his office of the prophet of God. Yet his carnal affection causes him to forget the response to the enquiry of Rebekah, "the elder shall serve the younger," and the fact that Esau had sold his birthright and alienated it from him for ever by a solemn oath. Moreover, in order that his heart may be the more warmed to him whom he desires to bless, he seeks to have some of that savoury meat brought to him which he loved.

6. *Rebekah spake unto Jacob*] She had no doubt treasured up the oracle which had assured her, even before their birth, that her younger son Jacob, whom she loved, should bear rule over Esau, whose wild and reckless life, and whose Canaanitish wives had been a "bitterness of soul" to her. She probably knew that Jacob had bought Esau's birthright. Now, believing rightly that the father's benediction would surely bring blessing with it, she fears, that these promises and hopes would fail. She believed, but not with that faith, which can patiently abide till God works out His plans by His Providence. So she strove, as it were, to force forward the event by unlawful means; even, as some have thought that Judas betrayed Christ that he might force Him to declare Himself a king and to take the kingdom. Every character in this remarkable history comes in for some share of blame, and yet some share of praise. Isaac, with the dignity of the ancient patriarch and faith in the inspiring Spirit of God, prepares to bless his son, but he lets carnal and worldly motives weigh with him. Rebekah and Jacob, seeing the promises afar off and desiring the spiritual blessings, yet practise deceit and fraud to obtain them, instead of waiting till He who promised should shew Himself faithful. Esau, defrauded of what seems his right, exhibits a natural feeling of sorrow and indignation, which excites our pity and sympathy; but we have to remember how "for a morsel of meat he sold his birthright," and that so, when he would have inherited the promises he was rejected, being set forth as an example of the unavailing regret of such as wantonly despise spiritual privileges, and when they have lost them, seek too late for the blessings to which they lead.

voice according to that which I command thee.
9 Go now to the flock, and fetch
me from thence two good kids of the
goats; and I will make them savoury
meat for thy father, such as he loveth:
10 And thou shalt bring *it* to thy
father, that he may eat, and that he
may bless thee before his death.
11 And Jacob said to Rebekah his
mother, Behold, Esau my brother *is*
a hairy man, and I *am* a smooth man:
12 My father peradventure will feel
me, and I shall seem to him as a de-
ceiver; and I shall bring a curse upon
me, and not a blessing.
13 And his mother said unto him,
Upon me *be* thy curse, my son: only
obey my voice, and go fetch me *them*.
14 And he went, and fetched, and
brought *them* to his mother: and his
mother made savoury meat, such as
his father loved.
15 And Rebekah took † goodly rai- († Heb. *desirable.*)
ment of her eldest son Esau, which
were with her in the house, and put
them upon Jacob her younger son:
16 And she put the skins of the
kids of the goats upon his hands, and
upon the smooth of his neck:
17 And she gave the savoury meat
and the bread, which she had prepared,
into the hand of her son Jacob.
18 ¶ And he came unto his father,
and said, My father: and he said,
Here *am* I; who *art* thou, my son?
19 And Jacob said unto his father,
I *am* Esau thy firstborn; I have done
according as thou badest me: arise, I
pray thee, sit and eat of my venison,
that thy soul may bless me.
20 And Isaac said unto his son,
How *is it* that thou hast found *it* so
quickly, my son? And he said, Because the LORD thy God brought *it*
† to me. († Heb. *before me.*)
21 And Isaac said unto Jacob,
Come near, I pray thee, that I may
feel thee, my son, whether thou *be*
my very son Esau or not.
22 And Jacob went near unto Isaac
his father; and he felt him, and said,
The voice *is* Jacob's voice, but the
hands *are* the hands of Esau.
23 And he discerned him not, because his hands were hairy, as his
brother Esau's hands: so he blessed
him.
24 And he said, *Art* thou my very
son Esau? And he said, I *am*.

---

15. *goodly raiment of her elder son Esau*] St Jerome ('Qu. Hebr.' in loc.) mentions it as a tradition of the rabbins, that the firstborn in the patriarchal times, holding the office of priesthood, had a sacerdotal vestment in which they offered sacrifice; and it was this sacerdotal vestment which was kept by Rebekah for Esau, and which was now put upon Jacob. See on ch. xxxvii. 3.

16. *the skins of the kids of the goats*] Martial (Lib. XII. Epig. 46) alludes to kid skins as used by the Romans for false hair to conceal baldness. The wool of the oriental goats is much longer and finer than of those of this country. (Cp. Cant. iv. 1. See Bochart, 'Hieroz.' p. 1, Lib. II. c. 51. See also Rosenm., Tuch, &c.)

18. *who art thou, my son?*] The anxiety and trepidation of Isaac appear in these words. He had perhaps some misgiving as to the blessing of Esau, and doubted whether God would prosper him in the chase and bring him home with venison to his father.

20. *Because the LORD thy God brought it to me*] The covering of his falsehood with this appeal to the Most High is the worst part of Jacob's conduct. In the use of the names of God, Jacob speaks of JEHOVAH as the God of his father. A little further on in the history, Jacob vows that, if he is prospered in his journey, then JEHOVAH shall be his God (ch. xxviii. 21). This is exactly accordant with the general use of these sacred names. Elohism would, so to speak, correspond with our word Theism. Though Jacob was a believer in JEHOVAH, yet revelation in those early days was but slight, and the knowledge of the patriarchs imperfect. There were gods of nations round about. JEHOVAH had revealed Himself to Abraham and was Abraham's God, and again to Isaac, and Isaac had served Him as his God. It is quite possible that Esau, with his heathen wives, may have been but a half worshipper of JEHOVAH; but Jacob recognizes Him as the God of his father Isaac (cp. ch. xxxi. 53), and afterwards solemnly chooses Him as the object of his own worship and service. See however note on ch. xxviii. 2.

25 And he said, Bring *it* near to
me, and I will eat of my son's venison, that my soul may bless thee.
And he brought *it* near to him, and
he did eat: and he brought him wine,
and he drank.
26 And his father Isaac said unto
him, Come near now, and kiss me,
my son.
27 And he came near, and kissed
him: and he smelled the smell of his
raiment, and blessed him, and said,
See, the smell of my son *is* as the
smell of a field which the LORD
hath blessed:
28 Therefore [a]God give thee of
the dew of heaven, and the fatness of
the earth, and plenty of corn and
wine:
29 Let people serve thee, and nations bow down to thee: be lord over
thy brethren, and let thy mother's
sons bow down to thee: cursed *be*
every one that curseth thee, and
blessed *be* he that blesseth thee.
30 ¶ And it came to pass, as soon
as Isaac had made an end of blessing
Jacob, and Jacob was yet scarce gone
out from the presence of Isaac his
father, that Esau his brother came in
from his hunting.
31 And he also had made savoury
meat, and brought it unto his father,
and said unto his father, Let my father arise, and eat of his son's venison,
that thy soul may bless me.
32 And Isaac his father said unto
him, Who *art* thou? And he said, I
am thy son, thy firstborn Esau.
33 And Isaac †trembled very exceedingly, and said, Who? where *is*
he that hath †taken venison, and
brought *it* me, and I have eaten of
all before thou camest, and have blessed him? yea, *and* he shall be blessed.
34 And when Esau heard the words
of his father, he cried with a great and
exceeding bitter cry, and said unto his
father, Bless me, *even* me also, O my
father.
35 And he said, Thy brother came
with subtilty, and hath taken away
thy blessing.
36 And he said, Is not he rightly
named ‖Jacob? for he hath supplanted me these two times: he took away
my birthright; and, behold, now he
hath taken away my blessing. And
he said, Hast thou not reserved a
blessing for me?
37 And Isaac answered and said
unto Esau, Behold, I have made him

[a] Heb. 11. 20.

† Heb. *trembled with a great trembling greatly.*

† Heb. *hunted.*

‖ That is, *a supplanter.*

---

26. *kiss me*] Tuch has suggested that Isaac asked his son to kiss him, that he might distinguish the shepherd who would smell of the flock from the huntsman who would smell of the field. It may have been so (see next verse), or it may have only been paternal love.

28. *God*] Lit. *The God*, i.e. that God just named, the God of thy Father, viz. JEHOVAH. It does not indicate (as Keil) "the personal God," nor is it (as some would have it) a Jehovistic formula. The article is perfectly natural as referring to Jacob's words v. 20. The blessing is, as usual, thrown into the poetic form of an anti-strophic parallelism.

29. *Let people serve thee, and nations bow down to thee*] This was fulfilled in the extensive dominions of the descendants of Jacob under David and Solomon, but, no doubt, has a fuller reference to the time when "the LORD should arise upon Israel, and His glory should be seen on her, when Gentiles should come to her light, and kings to the brightness of her rising"...when "the abundance of the sea should be converted unto her, the forces of the Gentiles should come unto her" (Isa. lx. 5, 6. Cp. Rom. xi. 25).

29. *cursed be every one*, &c.] This is the continued promise to the chosen race, first given (Gen. xii. 3) to Abraham. It is observed, however, that Isaac does not pronounce on Jacob that emphatic spiritual blessing, which God Himself had assured to Abraham twice (xii. 3; xxii. 18), and to Isaac once (xxvi. 4), "In thy seed shall all the nations of the earth be blessed." There was something carnal and sinful in the whole conduct of the persons concerned in the history of this chapter, Isaac, Rebekah, Jacob, Esau: and it may have been this which withheld for the time the brightest promise to the family of Abraham; or perhaps it may have been that that promise should come only from the mouth of God Himself, as it is given afterwards in ch. xxviii. 14.

36. *Is not he rightly named Jacob?*] Lit. "Is it that he is called Jacob, and he supplanteth or outwitteth me these two times?"

thy lord, and all his brethren have I
given to him for servants; and with
‖ Or, *supported.* corn and wine have I ‖sustained him:
and what shall I do now unto thee,
my son?
38 And Esau said unto his father,
Hast thou but one blessing, my father?
bless me, *even* me also, O my
father. And Esau lifted up his voice,
b Heb. 12. 17. *b*and wept.
39 And Isaac his father answered
c ver. 28. and said unto him, Behold, *c*thy dwelling
‖ Or, *of the fatness.* shall be ‖the fatness of the earth,
and of the dew of heaven from above;
40 And by thy sword shalt thou
live, and shalt serve thy brother; and
it shall come to pass when thou shalt
have the dominion, that thou shalt
break his yoke from off thy neck.
41 ¶ And Esau hated Jacob because
of the blessing wherewith his
father blessed him: and Esau said in
his heart, The days of mourning for
my father are at hand; *d*then will I *d* Obad. 10
slay my brother Jacob.
42 And these words of Esau her
elder son were told to Rebekah: and
she sent and called Jacob her younger
son, and said unto him, Behold, thy
brother Esau, as touching thee, doth
comfort himself, *purposing* to kill thee.
43 Now therefore, my son, obey
my voice; and arise, flee thou to
Laban my brother to Haran;
44 And tarry with him a few days,
until thy brother's fury turn away;
45 Until thy brother's anger turn
away from thee, and he forget *that*
which thou hast done to him: then I
will send, and fetch thee from thence:
why should I be deprived also of you
both in one day?

A paronomasia on the name Jacob. See on ch. xxv. 26. The words seem to mean, Is there not a connection between the meaning of his name Jacob, and the fact that he thus supplants or outwits me?

39. *thy dwelling shall be the fatness of the earth, and of the dew of heaven from above*] Lit. "from the fatness of the earth and from the dew of heaven." Castalio, Le Clerc, Knobel, Del., Keil, render the preposition "from" by "far from." So apparently Gesenius ('Thes.' p. 805, *absque, sine*). But the Authorized Version corresponds with the ancient versions. The very same words with the very same preposition occur in v. 28, and it is difficult to make that preposition partitive in v. 28, and privative in v. 39.

40. *by thy sword thou shalt live, and shalt serve thy brother*, &c.] Josephus ('B. J.' IV. 4. 1) describes the Edomites as a tumultuous, disorderly race, and all their history seems to confirm the truth of this description. The prophecy thus delivered by Isaac was fulfilled in every particular. At first Esau, the elder, seemed to prosper more than his brother Jacob. There were dukes in Edom before there reigned any king over the children of Israel (Gen. xxxvi. 31); and whilst Israel was in bondage in Egypt, Edom was an independent people. But Saul defeated and David conquered the Edomites (1 S. xiv. 47; 2 S. viii. 14), and they were, notwithstanding some revolts, constantly subject to Judah (see 1 K. xi. 14; 2 K. xiv. 7, 22; 2 Chr. xxv. 11; xxvi. 2) till the reign of Ahaz, when they threw off the yoke (2 K. xvi. 6; 2 Chr. xxviii. 7). Judas Maccabæus defeated them frequently (1 Macc. v.; 2 Macc. x.). At last his nephew Hyrcanus completely conquered them, and compelled them to be circumcised, and incorporated them into the Jewish nation (Joseph. 'Ant.' XIII. 9. 1); though finally under Antipater and Herod they established an Idumæan dynasty, which continued till the destruction of the Jewish polity.

when thou shalt have dominion] More probably **when thou shalt toss** (the yoke). So the LXX., Vulg. (*excutias*); Gesen. 'Thes.' p. 1269; Hengst., Keil, &c. The allusion is to the restlessness of the fierce Edomite under the yoke of the Jewish dominion. The prophecy was fulfilled when they revolted under Joram and again under Ahaz; and finally when they gave a race of rulers to Judæa in the persons of Herod and his sons (see last note).

43. *Haran*] It appears that not only Abraham and the family of his brother Haran must have left Ur of the Chaldees (see ch. xi. 31); but that the family of Nahor must have followed them to Haran, which is therefore called "the city of Nahor" (ch. xxiv. 10). The name Harran still remains in the centre of the cultivated district at the foot of the hills lying between the Khabour and the Euphrates.

45. *why should I be deprived also of you both in one day?*] *i.e.* of Jacob by the hand of Esau, and of Esau by the hand of justice (ch. ix. 6). The sacred history has shewn us the sins and errors of the family of Isaac; it here briefly but emphatically exhibits the distress

[e] chap. 26. 35. 46 And Rebekah said to Isaac, [e] I
am weary of my life because of the
daughters of Heth: if Jacob take a
wife of the daughters of Heth, such
as these *which are* of the daughters of
the land, what good shall my life
do me?

CHAPTER XXVIII.

1 *Isaac blesseth Jacob, and sendeth him to Padan-aram.* 6 *Esau marrieth Mahalath the daughter of Ishmael.* 10 *The vision of Jacob's ladder.* 18 *The stone of Beth-el.* 20 *Jacob's vow.*

AND Isaac called Jacob, and blessed him, and charged him, and
said unto him, Thou shalt not take a
wife of the daughters of Canaan.
[a] Hos. 12. 12. 2 [a] Arise, go to Padan-aram, to
the house of Bethuel thy mother's
father; and take thee a wife from
thence of the daughters of Laban thy
mother's brother.
3 And God Almighty bless thee,
and make thee fruitful, and multiply
† Heb. *an assembly of people.* thee, that thou mayest be † a multitude of people;
4 And give thee the blessing of
Abraham, to thee, and to thy seed
with thee; that thou mayest inherit
the land † wherein thou art a stranger, † Heb. *of thy sojournings.*
which God gave unto Abraham.
5 And Isaac sent away Jacob:
and he went to Padan-aram unto
Laban, son of Bethuel the Syrian,
the brother of Rebekah, Jacob's and
Esau's mother.
6 ¶ When Esau saw that Isaac
had blessed Jacob, and sent him away
to Padan-aram, to take him a wife
from thence; and that as he blessed
him he gave him a charge, saying,
Thou shalt not take a wife of the
daughters of Canaan;
7 And that Jacob obeyed his father
and his mother, and was gone to
Padan-aram;
8 And Esau seeing that the daugh-
ters of Canaan † pleased not Isaac his † Heb. *were evil in the eyes, &c.*
father;
9 Then went Esau unto Ishmael,
and took unto the wives which he
had Mahalath the daughter of Ishmael Abraham's son, the sister of
Nebajoth, to be his wife.
10 ¶ And Jacob went out from
Beer-sheba, and went toward [b] Haran. [b] Called, Acts 7. 2, *Charran*
11 And he lighted upon a certain
place, and tarried there all night,

---

and misery which at once followed; Isaac and Rebekah left in their old age by both their children; idols become scourges; Esau disappointed and disinherited; Jacob banished from his home, destined to a long servitude and a life of disquietude and suffering. Even those, whom God chooses and honours, cannot sin against Him without reaping, at least in this world, the fruit of evil doings (1 Cor. xi. 32).

CHAP. XXVIII. **1.** *Isaac called Jacob, and blessed him*] Isaac has learned that God had decreed that Jacob should be the heir of the promises, the recipient of the blessings. Accordingly, in v. 4, he invokes on Jacob "the blessing of Abraham," that "he and his seed should inherit the land of his sojourning," and no doubt also the spiritual blessings pronounced on the descendants of Abraham.

2. *Padan-aram*] See on xxiv. 10, xxv. 20, xxvii. 43.

Bethuel] This looks as if Bethuel were still living, not as the Jewish tradition says, that he died before Isaac's marriage. It is more likely that he was either naturally of weak character, or enfeebled by age. (See on ch. xxiv. 50.)

3. *God Almighty*] "El-Shaddai." It was under this name that God appeared to Abraham, ch. xvii. 1, and gave him the blessing to which Isaac now refers.

4. *the land wherein thou art a stranger*] Lit. **the land of thy sojournings.**

8. *pleased not*] Lit. **were evil in the eyes of.**

11. *he lighted upon a certain place*] Lit. **he lighted on the place.** The definite article probably indicates either that it was the place appointed by God, or that it was the place afterwards so famous from God's revelation to Jacob. We may well picture to ourselves the feelings of Jacob on this night, a solitary wanderer from his father's house, going back from the land of promise, conscious of sin and in the midst of danger, with a dark and doubtful future before him, yet hitherto having always cherished the hope of being the chosen of God to bear the honours and privileges of his house, to have the inheritance promised to Abraham, and now too with

because the sun was set; and he
took of the stones of that place, and
put *them for* his pillows, and lay down
in that place to sleep.
12 And he dreamed, and behold a
ladder set up on the earth, and the
top of it reached to heaven: and behold the angels of God ascending and
descending on it.
c chap. 35. 1. 13 [c] And, behold, the LORD stood
& 48. 3. above it, and said, I *am* the LORD
God of Abraham thy father, and the
God of Isaac: the land whereon thou
liest, to thee will I give it, and to thy
seed;
14 And thy seed shall be as the
† Heb. *break forth.* dust of the earth, and thou shalt
† spread abroad [d] to the west, and to
d Deut. 12. 20. the east, and to the north, and to the
e chap. 12. 3. south: and in thee and [e] in thy seed
& 18. 18. shall all the families of the earth be
& 22. 18. & 26. 4. blessed.
15 And, behold, I *am* with thee,
and will keep thee in all *places* whither thou goest, and will bring thee
again into this land; for I will not
leave thee, until I have done *that*
which I have spoken to thee of.
16 ¶ And Jacob awaked out of his
sleep, and he said, Surely the LORD is
in this place; and I knew *it* not.
17 And he was afraid, and said,
How dreadful *is* this place! this *is*
none other but the house of God,
and this *is* the gate of heaven.
18 And Jacob rose up early in the
morning, and took the stone that he
had put *for* his pillows, and set it up
for a pillar, and poured oil upon the
top of it.
19 And he called the name of that
place ‖ Beth-el: but the name of that ‖ That is, *the house of God.*
city *was called* Luz at the first.
20 And Jacob vowed a vow, say-

---

the words of Isaac's blessing just ringing in his ears. Whether would fear or faith prevail?

12. *a ladder*] God takes this opportunity to impress Jacob more deeply with the sense of His presence, to encourage him with promises of protection and to reveal to him His purpose of mercy and love.

The ladder might only indicate that there was a way from God to man, and that man might by God's help mount up by it to heaven, that angels went up from man to God, and came down from God to man, and that there was a continual providence watching over the servants of God. So the dream would teach and comfort the heart of the dreamer. But we cannot doubt, that there was a deeper meaning in the vision thus vouchsafed to the heir of the promises, in the hour of his greatest desolation, and when the sense of sin must have been most heavy on his soul. Our Lord Himself teaches (John i. 51), that the ladder signified the Son of Man, Him, who was now afresh promised as to be of the Seed of Jacob (v. 14); Him, by whom alone we go to God (John xiv. 6); who is the way to heaven, and who has now gone there to prepare a place for us.

13. *the LORD stood above it*] Onkelos renders "the glory of the LORD."

16. *Surely the LORD is in this place*] It is possible that Jacob may not have had quite so intelligent a conviction of God's omnipresence as Christians have; but it is apparent throughout the patriarchal history that special sanctity was attached to special places. This feeling is encouraged by the highest sanction in Ex. iii. 5.

18. *set it up for a pillar, and poured oil upon the top of it*] This was probably the most ancient and simplest form of temple or place for religious worship; excepting the altar of stones or earth for a burnt sacrifice. Whether this is the first example of such an erection we cannot judge. It was a very natural and obvious way of marking the sanctity of a spot; as in Christian times wayside crosses and the like have been set up so frequently. The pouring oil on it was a significant rite, though what may have been the full significance to Jacob's mind it is not easy to say. St Augustine ('De C. D.' XVI. 38) says that it was not that he might sacrifice to the stone or worship it, but that as *Christ* is named from *chrism*, or unction, so there was a great mystery (*sacramentum*) in this anointing of the stone with oil. The constant connection in religious thought between unction and sanctification seems a more probable solution of the question.

19. *Beth-el*] Abraham had built an altar in this neighbourhood (xii. 8, xiii. 4); and it is possible that the spot thus sanctified may have been the very place which Jacob lighted on (v. 11), and which he found to be the house of God and the gate of heaven.

The place consecrated perhaps first by Abraham's altar, and afterwards by Jacob's vision and pillar, was plainly distinct from the *city* which was "called Luz at the first," and which afterwards received the name of Bethel

ing, If God will be with me, and
will keep me in this way that I go,
and will give me bread to eat, and
raiment to put on,
21 So that I come again to my
father's house in peace; then shall the
LORD be my God:
22 And this stone, which I have
set *for* a pillar, shall be God's house:
and of all that thou shalt give me I
will surely give the tenth unto thee.

CHAPTER XXIX.

1 Jacob cometh to the well of Haran. 9 He taketh acquaintance of Rachel. 13 Laban entertaineth him. 18 Jacob covenanteth for Rachel. 23 He is deceived with Leah. 28 He marrieth also Rachel, and serveth for her seven years more. 32 Leah beareth Reuben, 33 Simeon, 34 Levi, 35 and Judah.

THEN Jacob † went on his jour- † Heb. *lift up his*
ney, and came into the land of *feet.*
the † people of the east. † Heb. *children.*
2 And he looked, and behold a
well in the field, and, lo, there *were*
three flocks of sheep lying by it; for
out of that well they watered the
flocks: and a great stone *was* upon
the well's mouth.
3 And thither were all the flocks

---

from its proximity to the sanctuary. So late as the time of Joshua (see Josh. xvi. 1, 2) the two places were distinct. When the tribe of Joseph took the city (Judg. i. 21—26), they appear to have given to the *city* the name of Bethel, formerly attaching only to the sanctuary, and thenceforward, the name Luz having been transferred to another town, the old town of Luz is always called Bethel. According to Eusebius and Jerome ('Onomast.' art. βαιθήλ) it lay about twelve miles from Jerusalem on the road to Sichem. Its ruins are still called by the name of *Beitin*. The rocky character of the hills around, and the stony nature of the soil, have been much noted by travellers (see Robinson, 'B. R.' II. pp. 127—130, and Stanley, 'Sinai and Palestine,' pp. 217—223). It has been thought by many that this act of Jacob, in setting up a stone to mark a sacred spot, was the origin of Cromlechs and all sacred stones. Certainly we find in later ages the custom of having stones, and those too anointed with oil, as objects of idolatrous worship. Clem. Alex. ('Stromat.' Lib. VII. p. 713) speaks of "worshipping every oily stone," and Arnobius, ('Adv. Gentes,' Lib. I. 39), in like manner, refers to the worshipping of "a stone smeared with oil, as though there were in it a present power." It has been conjectured farther that the name *Bætulia*, given to stones, called animated stones (λίθοι ἔμψυχοι), by the Phœnicians (Euseb. 'Præp. Evang.' I. 10) was derived from this name of Bethel. (See Spencer, 'De Legg.' I. 2; Bochart, 'Canaan,' II. 2.) These Bætulia, however, were meteoric stones, and derived their sanctity from the belief that they had fallen from heaven: and the name has probably but a fancied likeness to the name Bethel. Still the connection of the subsequent worship of stones with the primitive and pious use of them to mark places of worship is most probably a real connection. The erection of all such stones for worship was strictly forbidden in later times (see Lev. xxvi. 1; Deut. xvi. 22, &c.). What was good in its origin had become evil in its abuse.

21. *then shall the* LORD *be my God*] So the LXX., Vulg., Syr.; but the Arab. and several of the Hebrew commentators put these words in the protasis; "And if the LORD will be my God, then shall this stone be God's house," &c. The Hebrew is ambiguous, and so is the Targum of Onkelos: but the change of construction and of tense certainly appears to be at the beginning of v. 22, for all the verbs, beginning with "will keep me" in v. 20 to the end of v. 21, are in the same form (the perfect with vau conversive); and in verse 22 there is a change to the future. If this be so, the whole passage will then run, "If God will be with me and will keep me in the way that I go, and will give me bread to eat, and raiment to put on, and if I come again to my father's house in peace, and if the LORD will be my God, then shall this stone, which I have set for a pillar, be the house of God, and of all that Thou shalt give me, I will surely give a tenth unto Thee." The fulfilment of this vow is related in ch. xxxv. 15, where God again appears to Jacob on his return from Padan-aram, and Jacob restores the pillar which he had before set up, and again solemnly gives it the name of Beth-el, "the house of God" (see Quarry, 'on Genesis,' p. 486).

22. *give the tenth unto thee*] In ch. xiv. 20, we have an instance of Abraham giving tithes to Melchizedek. Here we have another proof that the duty of giving a tenth to God was recognized before the giving of the Law.

CHAP. XXIX. **1.** *Then Jacob*, &c.] Lit. "Then Jacob lifted up his feet and came into the land of the children of the East," *i.e.* into Mesopotamia, which lies East of Judæa.

2. *he looked, and behold a well*] Cp. ch. xxiv. 11—15. The similarity of the two stories results from the unvarying customs of

gathered: and they rolled the stone
from the well's mouth, and watered
the sheep, and put the stone again
upon the well's mouth in his place.
4 And Jacob said unto them, My
brethren, whence *be* ye? And they
said, Of Haran *are* we.
5 And he said unto them, Know
ye Laban the son of Nahor? And
they said, We know *him*.
† Heb. Is there *peace to him?* 6 And he said unto them, †*Is* he
well? And they said, *He is* well:
and, behold, Rachel his daughter cometh with the sheep.
† Heb. *yet the day is great.* 7 And he said, Lo, †*it is* yet high
day, neither *is it* time that the cattle
should be gathered together: water ye
the sheep, and go *and* feed *them*.
8 And they said, We cannot, until
all the flocks be gathered together,
and *till* they roll the stone from the
well's mouth; then we water the
sheep.
9 ¶ And while he yet spake with
them, Rachel came with her father's
sheep: for she kept them.
10 And it came to pass, when Jacob saw Rachel the daughter of Laban his mother's brother, and the
sheep of Laban his mother's brother,
that Jacob went near, and rolled the
stone from the well's mouth, and watered the flock of Laban his mother's
brother.
11 And Jacob kissed Rachel, and
lifted up his voice, and wept.
12 And Jacob told Rachel that he
was her father's brother, and that he
was Rebekah's son: and she ran and
told her father.
13 And it came to pass, when La-
ban heard the †tidings of Jacob his † Heb. *hearing.*
sister's son, that he ran to meet him,
and embraced him, and kissed him,
and brought him to his house. And
he told Laban all these things.
14 And Laban said to him, Surely
thou *art* my bone and my flesh. And
he abode with him †the space of a † Heb. *a month of days.*
month.
15 ¶ And Laban said unto Jacob,
Because thou *art* my brother, shouldest
thou therefore serve me for nought?
tell me, what *shall* thy wages *be?*
16 And Laban had two daughters:
the name of the elder *was* Leah, and
the name of the younger *was* Rachel.
17 Leah *was* tender eyed; but
Rachel was beautiful and well favoured.
18 And Jacob loved Rachel; and
said, I will serve thee seven years for
Rachel thy younger daughter.
19 And Laban said, *It is* better

---

the East, and from the natural halting place being a well outside a city.

5. *Laban the son of Nahor*] *i.e.* the descendant, the grandson of Nahor. Just as in v. 12, Jacob calls himself the brother of Laban, being in truth his nephew. The omission of Bethuel is here again observable.

6. *Is he well?*] Lit. "Is it peace to him?"

8. *We cannot*] Probably because there was an agreement not to roll away the stone till all were assembled, not because the stone was too heavy for three shepherds to move.

9. *Rachel came with her father's sheep*] So Ex. ii. 16, the daughters of Reuel, the priest of Midian, led their father's sheep to water. And even now among the Arabs it is not beneath the daughter of an Emir to water the sheep.

13. *he told Laban all these things*] *i.e.* probably the cause of his exile from home, his father's blessing and command to him to marry a wife of his mother's kindred, and the various events of his journey.

14. *the space of a month*] Lit. "a month of days;" the word "days" being frequently added to a note of time, as we might say "a month long," or as here in the Authorized Version, "the space of a month."

17. *tender eyed*] *i.e.* weak eyed, so LXX., Vulg., &c.

18. *I will serve thee seven years for Rachel*] In the case of Isaac and Rebekah, Abraham's servant gives handsome presents to Rebekah, ch. xxiv. 53, the Eastern custom at marriages. Jacob could give neither presents nor dowry, for he was a fugitive from his father's house, and describes himself as having passed over Jordan with only his staff (ch. xxxii. 10). He proposes therefore to serve Laban seven years, if he will give him his daughter to wife, a proposal, which Laban's grasping disposition prompts him to accept, even from one whom he calls brother and of his own bone and flesh (vv. 14, 15).

19. *It is better that I should give her to thee*, &c.] It has always been the custom

that I give her to thee, than that I
should give her to another man: abide
with me.
20 And Jacob served seven years
for Rachel; and they seemed unto
him *but* a few days, for the love he
had to her.
21 ¶ And Jacob said unto Laban,
Give *me* my wife, for my days are
fulfilled, that I may go in unto her.
22 And Laban gathered together all
the men of the place, and made a feast.
23 And it came to pass in the evening, that he took Leah his daughter,
and brought her to him; and he went
in unto her.
24 And Laban gave unto his daughter Leah Zilpah his maid *for* an handmaid.
25 And it came to pass, that in the
morning, behold, it *was* Leah: and
he said to Laban, What *is* this thou
hast done unto me? did not I serve
with thee for Rachel? wherefore then
hast thou beguiled me?
26 And Laban said, It must not
be so done in our †country, to give
the younger before the firstborn.

† Heb. *place.*

27 Fulfil her week, and we will
give thee this also for the service which
thou shalt serve with me yet seven
other years.
28 And Jacob did so, and fulfilled
her week: and he gave him Rachel
his daughter to wife also.
29 And Laban gave to Rachel his
daughter Bilhah his handmaid to be
her maid.
30 And he went in also unto Rachel, and he loved also Rachel more
than Leah, and served with him yet
seven other years.
31 ¶ And when the LORD saw
that Leah *was* hated, he opened her
womb: but Rachel *was* barren.
32 And Leah conceived, and bare
a son, and she called his name ‖Reu-
ben: for she said, Surely the LORD
hath looked upon my affliction; now
therefore my husband will love me.
33 And she conceived again, and
bare a son; and said, Because the
LORD hath heard that I *was* hated,
he hath therefore given me this *son*
also: and she called his name ‖Si-
meon.

‖ That is, *see a son.*

‖ That is, *hearing.*

---

with Eastern tribes to prefer marrying among their own kindred.

20. *but a few days, for the love he had to her*] He loved Rachel so much, that he valued the labour of seven years as though it were the labour of but few days in comparison with the great prize, which that labour was to bring him.

24. *Zilpah his maid for an handmaid*] So ch. xxiv. 61.

25. *it was Leah*] This deception was possible, because there appears to have been no religious or other solemn ceremony, in which the bride was presented to the bridegroom, and the veil in which brides were veiled was so long and close that it concealed, not only the face, but much of the figure also.

27. *Fulfil her week*] *i.e.* celebrate the marriage feast for a week with Leah (cp. Judg. xiv. 12); and after that we will give thee Rachel also. "It was not after another week of years that he should receive Rachel to wife; but after the seven days of the first wife's nuptials." (St Jerome, 'Qu. Hebr.' in loc.) It has been observed that the fraud practised by Laban on Jacob was a fit penalty for the fraud practised by Jacob on Isaac and Esau. The polygamy of Jacob must be explained on the same principle as that of Abraham. It had not yet been expressly forbidden by the revealed law of God. The marriage of two sisters also was afterwards condemned (Lev. xviii. 18), but as yet there had been no such prohibition.

31. *was hated*] *i.e.* less loved (cp. Mal. i. 3).

32. *Reuben*] *i.e.* "Behold a son." The words which follow are but one of those plays on a name so general in these early days; they do not give the etymology of the name; they have however led some to think that the meaning of "Reuben" is rather "the son of vision," or as Jerome interprets it, "the son of God's gracious regard," *filium respectus gratuiti.* The Syr. and Josephus give the name as Reubel, the latter explaining it as "the pity of God" ('Ant.' I. 19. 8), which is supported by Michaelis, though it is obviously a corrupt reading (see Rosenm. in loc. and Gesen. p. 1247).

33. *Simeon*] *i.e.* "hearing." The birth of her first son convinces her that God hath *seen* her, the second that God hath *heard* her.

34 And she conceived again, and
bare a son; and said, Now this time
will my husband be joined unto me,
because I have born him three sons:
therefore was his name called ‖Levi.
35 And she conceived again, and
bare a son: and she said, Now will I
praise the LORD: therefore she called
his name *a*‖Judah; and †left bearing.

‖ That is, *joined.*
a Matt. 1. 2.
‖ That is, *praise.*
† Heb. *stood from bearing.*

CHAPTER XXX.

1 *Rachel, in grief for her barrenness, giveth Bilhah her maid unto Jacob.* 5 *She beareth Dan and Naphtali.* 9 *Leah giveth Zilpah her maid, who beareth Gad and Asher.* 14 *Reuben findeth mandrakes, with which Leah buyeth her husband of Rachel.* 17 *Leah beareth Issachar, Zebulun, and Dinah.* 22 *Rachel beareth Joseph.* 25 *Jacob desireth to depart.* 27 *Laban stayeth him on a new covenant.* 37 *Jacob's policy, whereby he became rich.*

AND when Rachel saw that she
bare Jacob no children, Rachel
envied her sister; and said unto Jacob,
Give me children, or else I die.
2 And Jacob's anger was kindled
against Rachel: and he said, *Am* I in
God's stead, who hath withheld from
thee the fruit of the womb?
3 And she said, Behold my maid
Bilhah, go in unto her; and she shall
bear upon my knees, that I may also
†have children by her.

† Heb. *be built by her.*

4 And she gave him Bilhah her
handmaid to wife: and Jacob went
in unto her.
5 And Bilhah conceived, and bare
Jacob a son.
6 And Rachel said, God hath
judged me, and hath also heard my
voice, and hath given me a son: therefore
called she his name ‖Dan.
7 And Bilhah Rachel's maid conceived
again, and bare Jacob a second
son.
8 And Rachel said, With †great
wrestlings have I wrestled with my
sister, and I have prevailed: and she
called his name ‖*a*Naphtali.
9 When Leah saw that she had left
bearing, she took Zilpah her maid, and
gave her Jacob to wife.
10 And Zilpah Leah's maid bare
Jacob a son.
11 And Leah said, A troop cometh:
and she called his name ‖Gad.
12 And Zilpah Leah's maid bare
Jacob a second son.
13 And Leah said, †Happy am I, for
the daughters will call me blessed: and
she called his name ‖Asher.
14 ¶ And Reuben went in the days
of wheat harvest, and found mandrakes
in the field, and brought them

‖ That is, *judging.*
† Heb. *wrestlings of God.*
‖ That is, *my wrestling.*
a Called, Matt. 4. 13, *Nephthalim.*
‖ That is, *a troop, or company.*
† Heb. *In my happiness.*
‖ That is, *happy.*

---

34. *Levi*] "Association" or "associated."

35. *Judah*] *i. e.* "praised" (from the Hophal future of *Jadah*).

CHAP. XXX. 3. *that I may also have children by her*] Lit. "that I may be built up by her." (See on ch. xvi. 2.)

6. *Dan*] *i. e.* "judge."

8. *With great wrestlings*] Lit. "with wrestlings of God." The LXX. renders "God has helped me," and Onkelos, "God has received my prayer." So virtually the Syriac. Though the addition of the name of God often expresses a superlative, yet "wrestling" being a type of prayer, it is most probable that in this passage the allusion is to Rachel's earnest striving in prayer with God for the blessing of offspring. (So Hengst., Del., Keil.) Above, v. 1, Rachel had manifested impatience and neglect of prayer, seeking from Jacob what only could be given of God. Jacob's remonstrance with her, v. 2, may have directed her to wiser and better thoughts.

11. *A troop cometh*] Rather, **Good fortune cometh**, or, "in good fortune," *i. e.* happily, prosperously. The rendering of the Authorized Version is favoured by the Samaritan version, and has been supposed to be in accordance with ch. xlix. 19. The latter, however, may have no reference to the derivation, but be only the common Oriental play upon a word. The LXX., Vulg., Syr., Onk., Jerus., Pseudo-Jon., all interpret *Gad* to mean "success," "good fortune," "prosperity." So Gesen., Rosenm., Knobel, Del., Keil, &c.

13. *Happy am I*, &c.] Lit. **in my happiness** (*am I*), **for the daughters call me happy; and she called his name Asher,** *i. e.* happy.

14. *mandrakes*] So with great unanimity the ancient versions and most of the Jewish commentators. There is little doubt that the plant was really the *atropa mandragora*, a species closely allied to the deadly nightshade (*atropa belladonna*). It is not uncommon in Palestine (Tristram, pp. 103, 104). It is said to be a narcotic, and to have stupefying and even intoxicating properties. It has

unto his mother Leah. Then Rachel
said to Leah, Give me, I pray thee,
of thy son's mandrakes.
15 And she said unto her, *Is it* a
small matter that thou hast taken my
husband? and wouldest thou take
away my son's mandrakes also? And
Rachel said, Therefore he shall lie
with thee to night for thy son's mandrakes.
16 And Jacob came out of the
field in the evening, and Leah went
out to meet him, and said, Thou
must come in unto me; for surely
I have hired thee with my son's mandrakes. And he lay with her that
night.
17 And God hearkened unto Leah,
and she conceived, and bare Jacob the
fifth son.
18 And Leah said, God hath given
me my hire, because I have given my
maiden to my husband: and she called
his name ‖ Issachar. ‖ That is, *an hire.*
19 And Leah conceived again, and
bare Jacob the sixth son.
20 And Leah said, God hath endued me *with* a good dowry; now
will my husband dwell with me, because I have born him six sons: and
she called his name ‖ [b] Zebulun. ‖ That is, *dwelling.*
21 And afterwards she bare a daugh- [b] Called, Matt. 4. 13, *Zabulon.*
ter, and called her name ‖ Dinah. ‖ That is, *judgment.*
22 ¶ And God remembered Rachel,
and God hearkened to her, and opened
her womb.
23 And she conceived, and bare a
son; and said, God hath taken away
my reproach:
24 And she called his name ‖ Jo- ‖ That is, *adding.*
seph; and said, The LORD shall add
to me another son.
25 ¶ And it came to pass, when
Rachel had born Joseph, that Jacob

---

broad leaves and green apples, which become pale yellow when ripe, with a strong tuberous bifid root, in which Pythagoras discerned a likeness to the human form, whence many ancient fables concerning it. They are still found ripe about the time of wheat harvest on the lower ranges of Lebanon and Hermon. The apples are said to produce dizziness; the Arabs believe them to be exhilarating and stimulating even to insanity; hence the name *tuffah el jan*, "apples of the jan" (Thomson, 'Land and Book,' p. 577). The ancients believed them calculated to produce fruitfulness, and they were used as philtres to conciliate love, hence their name in Hebrew, *dudaim*, *i. e.* love-apples. Rachel evidently shared in this superstitious belief. (See Heid. Tom. II. Ex. xix.; Winer, 'R. W. B.' voc. *Abram;* Ges. 'Thes.' p. 324; Rosenm. in loc.; Smith's 'Dict.' voc. *mandrake*), &c.

18. *Issachar*] *i. e.* "there is a reward."

20. *Zebulun*] *i. e.* "dwelling," derived from *zabal*, to dwell, with a play on the word *Zabad*, "to give, to endow."

21. *Dinah*] *i. e.* "judgment." It is thought that Jacob had other daughters (see ch. xxxvii. 35; xlvi. 7). Daughters, as they did not constitute links in a genealogy, are not mentioned except when some important history attaches to them, as in this case the history in ch. xxxiv.

24. *Joseph*] *i. e.* "adding," from *jasaph*, "to add," with a play on *asaph*, "to take away."

25. *when Rachel had born Joseph*] It has been inferred from this, that Joseph was born at the end of the second seven years of Jacob's servitude; though it is by no means certain that Jacob demanded his dismissal at the first possible moment. The words of this verse seem to indicate that Jacob did not desire to leave Laban, at all events till after Joseph's birth. Many reasons may have induced him to remain in Padan-aram longer than the stipulated fourteen years; the youth of his children unfitting them for a long journey, the pregnancy of some of his wives, the unhappy temper of his beloved Rachel, whom he may have been unwilling to take from her parents, till she had a son of her own to comfort her; above all, the fear of Esau's anger, who had resolved to slay him. There is nothing necessarily inconsistent in the narrative. It is possible that Leah should have borne 6, Rachel 1, Bilhah 2, and Zilpah 2 sons in seven years. It is not certain that Dinah was born at this time at all. Her birth is only incidentally noticed. It would be possible even that Zebulun should have been borne by Leah later than Joseph by Rachel; it being by no means necessary that we should believe all the births to have followed in the order in which they are enumerated, which is in the order of mothers, not of births. The common explanation is, that the first four sons of Leah were born as rapidly as possible, one after the other, in the first four years of marriage. In the meantime, not necessarily after the birth of Leah's fourth son, Rachel gives her maid to Jacob, and so very probably Bilhah gave birth to Dan and Naphtali before the birth of Ju-

said unto Laban, Send me away, that
I may go unto mine own place, and
to my country.
26 Give *me* my wives and my
children, for whom I have served
thee, and let me go: for thou knowest my service which I have done
thee.
27 And Laban said unto him, I
pray thee, if I have found favour in
thine eyes, *tarry: for* I have learned
by experience that the LORD hath
blessed me for thy sake.
28 And he said, Appoint me thy
wages, and I will give *it*.
29 And he said unto him, Thou
knowest how I have served thee, and
how thy cattle was with me.
30 For *it was* little which thou
hadst before I *came*, and it is *now* †in-
creased unto a multitude; and the
LORD hath blessed thee †since my
coming: and now when shall I provide for mine own house also?
31 And he said, What shall I give
thee? And Jacob said, Thou shalt
not give me any thing: if thou wilt
do this thing for me, I will again feed
and keep thy flock:
32 I will pass through all thy flock
to day, removing from thence all the
speckled and spotted cattle, and all
the brown cattle among the sheep,
and the spotted and speckled among
the goats: and *of such* shall be my
hire.
33 So shall my righteousness answer for me †in time to come, when
it shall come for my hire before thy
face: every one that *is* not speckled
and spotted among the goats, and
brown among the sheep, that shall be
counted stolen with me.
34 And Laban said, Behold, I
would it might be according to thy
word.
35 And he removed that day the
he goats that were ringstraked and
spotted, and all the she goats that were
speckled and spotted, *and* every one
that had *some* white in it, and all the
brown among the sheep, and gave
them into the hand of his sons.
36 And he set three days' journey

† Heb. *broken forth.*
† Heb. *at my foot.*
† Heb. *to morrow.*

---

dah. Leah, then finding that she was not likely to bear another son soon, may, in the state of jealousy between the two sisters, have given Zilpah to Jacob, of whom were born Asher and Naphtali, and then again in the very last year of the seven, at the beginning of it, Leah may have borne Issachar, and at the end of it Zebulun. Another difficulty has been found in Reuben's finding the mandrakes: but there is no reason why he should have been more than four years old, when he discovered them, and attracted by their flowers and fruits, brought them to his mother. (See Petav. 'De Doct. Temp.' X. 19; Heid. II. Exer. xv. xviii.; Kurtz 'on the Old Covenant,' in loc.; Keil in loc. &c., and note at end of ch. xxxi.)

27. *I have learned by experience*] **I have learned by divination**, literally either "I have hissed, muttered" (so Knobel on ch. xliv. 5), or more probably, "I have divined by omens deduced from serpents" (Boch. 'Hier.' I. 20; Gesen. 'Th.' p. 875). The heathenism of Laban's household appears by ch. xxxi. 19, 32; and though Laban acknowledged the LORD as Jacob's God, this did not prevent him from using idolatrous and heathenish practices. It is however quite possible that the word here used may have acquired a wider signification, originally meaning to "divine," but then having the general sense of "investigate," "discover," "learn by enquiry," &c.

30. *increased*] Lit. **broken forth.**

since my coming] Lit. "at my foot," *i.e.* God sent blessing to thee following on my footsteps, wherever I went. (See Ges. 'Th.' p. 1262.)

32. *removing from thence all the spotted and speckled cattle*]. It is said, that in the East the sheep are generally white, very rarely black or spotted, and that the goats are black or brown, rarely speckled with white. Jacob therefore proposes to separate from the flock all the spotted and speckled sheep and goats, which would be comparatively few, and to tend only that part of the flock which was pure white or black. He is then to have for his hire only those lambs and kids, born of the unspeckled flock, which themselves should be marked with spots and speckles and ringstrakes. Laban naturally thinks that these will be very few; so he accepts the offer, and, to make matters the surer, he removes all the spotted and ringstraked goats, and all the sheep with any brown in them, three days' journey from the flock of white sheep and brown goats to be left under Jacob's care (see

betwixt himself and Jacob: and Jacob
fed the rest of Laban's flocks.

37 ¶ And Jacob took him rods of
green poplar, and of the hazel and
chesnut tree; and pilled white strakes
in them, and made the white appear
which *was* in the rods.

38 And he set the rods which he
had pilled before the flocks in the
gutters in the watering troughs when
the flocks came to drink, that they
should conceive when they came to
drink.

39 And the flocks conceived before
the rods, and brought forth cattle
ringstraked, speckled, and spotted.

40 And Jacob did separate the
lambs, and set the faces of the flocks
toward the ringstraked, and all the
brown in the flock of Laban; and he
put his own flocks by themselves, and
put them not unto Laban's cattle.

41 And it came to pass, whensoever the stronger cattle did conceive,
that Jacob laid the rods before the
eyes of the cattle in the gutters, that
they might conceive among the rods.

42 But when the cattle were feeble,
he put *them* not in: so the feebler were
Laban's, and the stronger Jacob's.

43 And the man increased exceedingly, and had much cattle, and maidservants, and menservants, and camels,
and asses.

CHAPTER XXXI.

1 Jacob upon displeasure departeth secretly. 19 Rachel stealeth her father's images. 22 Laban pursueth after him, 26 and complaineth of the wrong. 34 Rachel's policy to hide the images. 36 Jacob's complaint of Laban. 43 The covenant of Laban and Jacob at Galeed.

AND he heard the words of Laban's sons, saying, Jacob hath
taken away all that *was* our father's;
and of *that* which *was* our father's
hath he gotten all this glory.

2 And Jacob beheld the countenance of Laban, and, behold, it *was*
not toward him † as before.

3 And the LORD said unto Jacob,
Return unto the land of thy fathers,
and to thy kindred; and I will be
with thee.

4 And Jacob sent and called Rachel and Leah to the field unto his
flock,

5 And said unto them, I see your
father's countenance, that it *is* not
toward me as before; but the God
of my father hath been with me.

6 And ye know that with all my
power I have served your father.

7 And your father hath deceived
me, and changed my wages ten times;
but God suffered him not to hurt
me.

8 If he said thus, The speckled
shall be thy wages; then all the cattle bare speckled: and if he said thus,

† Heb. *as yesterday and the day before.*

---

vv. 35, 36), lest any of them might stray unto Jacob's flock and so be claimed by him, or any lambs or kids should be born like them in Jacob's flock.

37. *poplar*] So Celsius ('Hierobot.' I. 292), and many other authorities after the Vulg., but the LXX. and Arab. have the storax tree, which is adopted by Gesenius (p. 740) and many others.

hazel] **Almond**, Ges. (p. 747).

chesnut tree] **Plane-tree**, Ges. (p. 1071).

40. *And Jacob did separate the lambs*] The apparent inconsistency of this with the rest of the narrative, especially with v. 36, has induced some commentators to suspect a corruption in the text. The meaning, however, appears to be, that Jacob separated those lambs, which were born after the artifice mentioned above, keeping the spotted lambs and kids apart; but though he thus separated them, he contrived that the ewes and she goats should have the speckled lambs and kids in sight. "His own flocks" mentioned in the latter part of the verse were the young cattle that were born ringstraked and speckled; "Laban's cattle," on the contrary, were those of uniform colour in the flock tended by Jacob; not that flock which Laban had separated by three days' journey from Jacob.

CHAP. XXXI. **2.** *as before*] Lit. "as yesterday and the day before."

5. *the God of my father hath been with me*] *i.e.* God has been present with me and has protected me. Jacob calls him the God of his father, so distinguishing the Most High from the gods of the nations and from the idols, which perhaps the family of Laban had worshipped. vv. 19, 30.

7. *ten times*] *i.e.* probably "very frequently." Cp. Num. xiv. 22; Job xix. 3.

The ringstraked shall be thy hire;
then bare all the cattle ringstraked.

9 Thus God hath taken away the
cattle of your father, and given *them*
to me.

10 And it came to pass at the time
that the cattle conceived, that I lifted
up mine eyes, and saw in a dream,
|| Or, *he goats.* and, behold, the ||rams which leaped
upon the cattle *were* ringstraked, speckled, and grisled.

11 And the angel of God spake
unto me in a dream, *saying*, Jacob:
And I said, Here *am* I.

12 And he said, Lift up now thine
eyes, and see, all the rams which leap
upon the cattle *are* ringstraked, speckled, and grisled: for I have seen all
that Laban doeth unto thee.

a chap. 28. 18. 13 I *am* the God of Beth-el, [a] where
thou anointedst the pillar, *and* where
thou vowedst a vow unto me: now
arise, get thee out from this land, and
return unto the land of thy kindred.

14 And Rachel and Leah answer-
ed and said unto him, *Is there* yet any
portion or inheritance for us in our
father's house?

15 Are we not counted of him
strangers? for he hath sold us, and
hath quite devoured also our money.

16 For all the riches which God
hath taken from our father, that *is*
ours, and our children's: now then,
whatsoever God hath said unto thee,
do.

17 ¶ Then Jacob rose up, and set
his sons and his wives upon camels;

18 And he carried away all his
cattle, and all his goods which he had
gotten, the cattle of his getting, which
he had gotten in Padan-aram, for to
go to Isaac his father in the land of
Canaan.

19 And Laban went to shear his
sheep: and Rachel had stolen the † Heb. *teraphim.*
†images that *were* her father's.

20 And Jacob stole away †una- † Heb. *the heart of Laban.*

10. *the rams*] **The he goats.**

grisled] *i.e.* "sprinkled as with hail," the literal meaning of the word "grisled."

13. *I am the God of Beth-el*] (Heb. "El-Beth-el.") In v. 11 it is said, "the angel of God spake unto me." The Jewish commentators explain this by saying that God spoke through the mouth of the angel, and therefore though the angel actually spoke to Jacob, yet the words are the words of God. The Christian fathers generally believe all such visions to have been visions of the Son of God, who is both God and the angel of God: see on ch. xvi. 7.

There is no necessary contradiction between this dream and the account of Jacob's artifice given in the last chapter. If the dream occurred just before the flight of Jacob from Laban, it would be an indication to Jacob that all his artifices would have had no effect, had it not been God's pleasure that he should grow rich. The labours of the husbandman do not prosper but through the blessing of God. It seems, however, not improbable that Jacob is here relating to his wives two dreams, that concerning the sheep and goats having occurred at the beginning of his agreement with Laban, and that in which he was commanded to depart from Padan-aram just before his actual departure. This was suggested by Nachmanides and is approved by Rosenmüller. If so, we may infer, that Jacob believed the promise that the sheep which were to be his hire should multiply rapidly: but yet consistently with his mixed character, partly believing and partly impatient of the fulfilment, he adopted natural means for bringing about this event which he desired (so Kurtz and apparently Keil).

15. *he hath sold us*] Probably referring to Laban's giving his daughter to Jacob as wages for his service.

19. *And Laban went to shear his sheep*] The force of the tenses in the Hebrew will perhaps be better explained as follows: "Now Laban had gone to shear his sheep, and (or, whereupon) Rachel stole the Teraphim which were her father's, and Jacob stole away unawares to (lit. stole the heart of) Laban the Syrian." There may be a series of paronomasias in the Hebrew, "Rachel *stole* the Teraphim," "Jacob *stole* the heart of Laban;" and again, "the heart of Laban" is *Leb-Laban*, the first syllable of Laban corresponding with the word for "heart."

images] **Teraphim.** These were undoubtedly images in the human form, but whether whole length figures or only busts has been much doubted. In 1 S. xix. 13, Michal puts teraphim (the plural perhaps for a single image) in David's bed to deceive the messengers of Saul; which looks as if the image was of the size of life. In the present history as Rachel hides them under the camel's saddle, they were probably not so large. Laban calls them his gods v. 30, which corresponds with

wares to Laban the Syrian, in that he
told him not that he fled.
21 So he fled with all that he had;
and he rose up, and passed over the
river, and set his face *toward* the
mount Gilead.
22 And it was told Laban on the
third day that Jacob was fled.
23 And he took his brethren with
him, and pursued after him seven
days' journey; and they overtook him
in the mount Gilead.
24 And God came to Laban the
Syrian in a dream by night, and said
unto him, Take heed that thou speak
not to Jacob †either good or bad.
25 ¶ Then Laban overtook Jacob.
Now Jacob had pitched his tent in
the mount: and Laban with his brethren pitched in the mount of Gilead.
26 And Laban said to Jacob,
What hast thou done, that thou hast
stolen away unawares to me, and
carried away my daughters, as captives *taken* with the sword?
27 Wherefore didst thou flee away
secretly, and †steal away from me;
and didst not tell me, that I might
have sent thee away with mirth, and
with songs, with tabret, and with harp?

† Heb. *from good to bad.*

† Heb. *hast stolen me.*

28 And hast not suffered me to
kiss my sons and my daughters? thou
hast now done foolishly in *so* doing.
29 It is in the power of my hand
to do you hurt: but the God of your
father spake unto me yesternight, saying, Take thou heed that thou speak
not to Jacob either good or bad.
30 And now, *though* thou wouldest needs be gone, because thou sore
longedst after thy father's house, *yet*
wherefore hast thou stolen my gods?
31 And Jacob answered and said
to Laban, Because I was afraid: for
I said, Peradventure thou wouldest
take by force thy daughters from
me.
32 With whomsoever thou findest
thy gods, let him not live: before
our brethren discern thou what *is*
thine with me, and take *it* to thee.
For Jacob knew not that Rachel had
stolen them.
33 And Laban went into Jacob's
tent, and into Leah's tent, and into
the two maidservants' tents; but he
found *them* not. Then went he out
of Leah's tent, and entered into Rachel's tent.
34 Now Rachel had taken the im-

---

what we find afterwards concerning their worship (see Judg. xvii. 5; xviii. 14, 17, 18, 20). They are condemned with other idolatrous practices (1 S. xv. 23; 2 K. xxiii. 24), and in later times we find that they were consulted for purposes of divination (Ezek. xxi. 21; Zech. x. 2). They have been generally considered as similar to the Penates of the classical nations. Most probably they were of the nature of a fetish, used for purposes of magic and divination, rather than strictly objects of divine worship. In them we perhaps see the earliest form of patriarchal idolatry; a knowledge of the true God not wholly gone, but images, perhaps of ancestors, preserved, revered and consulted. There have been numerous conjectures as to the derivation of the name. The majority of recent Hebraists refer to the Arab. root *tarafa*, "to enjoy the good things of life," and think that teraphim were preserved and honoured, like the penates, or the household fairy, to secure domestic prosperity (see Ges. 'Thes.' p. 1520). Other but improbable derivations are that suggested by Castell from the Syriac *Teraph*, "to enquire," alluding to their use as oracles; and that by Prof. Lee, from the Æthiopic root, signifying "to remain, survive," so that the name may originally have meant "relics." The motive of Rachel's theft has been as much debated as the root of the word and the use of the images. It is at all events probable, that Rachel, though a worshipper of Jacob's God, may not have thrown off all the superstitious credulity of her own house, and that she stole the teraphim for some superstitious purpose.

20. *stole away unawares to Laban*] Lit. "stole the heart of Laban," i.e. deceived his mind and intelligence.

21. *the river*] The Euphrates.

mount Gilead] So called by anticipation. It received the name from what occurred below, vv. 46, 47.

26. *as captives taken with the sword*] **As captives of the sword.**

29. *It is in the power of my hand*] So probably, not as Hitzig, Knobel, Keil, &c., "my hand is for God," i.e. my hand serves me for God, is powerful.

ages, and put them in the camel's
furniture, and sat upon them. And
† Heb. felt. Laban †searched all the tent, but
found *them* not.
35 And she said to her father, Let
it not displease my lord that I cannot
rise up before thee; for the custom of
women *is* upon me. And he searched, but found not the images.
36 ¶ And Jacob was wroth, and
chode with Laban: and Jacob answered and said to Laban, What *is*
my trespass? what *is* my sin, that
thou hast so hotly pursued after me?
† Heb. felt. 37 Whereas thou hast †searched
all my stuff, what hast thou found of
all thy household stuff? set *it* here
before my brethren and thy brethren,
that they may judge betwixt us both.
38 This twenty years *have* I *been*
with thee; thy ewes and thy she
goats have not cast their young, and
the rams of thy flock have I not eaten.
39 That which was torn *of beasts*
I brought not unto thee; I bare the
b Ex. 22. 12. loss of it; of [b]my hand didst thou
require it, *whether* stolen by day, or
stolen by night.
40 *Thus* I was; in the day the
drought consumed me, and the frost
by night; and my sleep departed from
mine eyes.
41 Thus have I been twenty years
in thy house; I served thee fourteen
years for thy two daughters, and six
years for thy cattle: and thou hast
changed my wages ten times.
42 Except the God of my father,
the God of Abraham, and the fear of
Isaac, had been with me, surely thou
hadst sent me away now empty. God
hath seen mine affliction and the labour of my hands, and rebuked *thee*
yesternight.
43 ¶ And Laban answered and
said unto Jacob, *These* daughters *are*
my daughters, and *these* children *are*
my children, and *these* cattle *are* my
cattle, and all that thou seest *is* mine:
and what can I do this day unto
these my daughters, or unto their
children which they have born?
44 Now therefore come thou, let
us make a covenant, I and thou; and
let it be for a witness between me
and thee.
45 And Jacob took a stone, and
set it up *for* a pillar.
46 And Jacob said unto his brethren, Gather stones; and they took
stones, and made an heap: and they
did eat there upon the heap.
47 And Laban called it ‖ Jegar-sa- ‖ That is, *the heap of witness.*
hadutha: but Jacob called it Galeed.

34] *the camel's furniture*] The word for furniture (*Car*, perhaps cognate with *currus*, *car*, *carry*, *carriage*, &c.), seems to have signified a covered seat, litter, or palanquin, which was placed on the back of the camel for carrying women and children and supplied with curtains for concealing them, not only from sun and wind, but also from public view (see Ges. 'Thes.' p. 715 and the authorities there referred to). The Teraphim, being probably not of large size, would easily be concealed under such apparatus.

38. *This twenty years*] See above, v. 41. On the chronology, see Note A at the end of this chapter.

40. *in the day the drought consumed me, and the frost by night*] In the East it is common for extremely hot days to be succeeded by very cold nights.

42. *the fear of Isaac*] That is to say, the object of Isaac's reverential awe. The whole history of Isaac points him out to us as a man of subdued spirit, whilst his father Abraham appears as of livelier faith and as admitted to a more intimate communion with God. Hence Jacob not unnaturally calls his father's God "the fear of Isaac."

47. *Laban called it Jegar-sahadutha: but Jacob called it Galeed*] Jegar-sahadutha is the Aramaic (Chaldee or Syriac) equivalent for the Hebrew Galeed; both meaning the "heap of witness." It appears therefore that at this time Jacob spoke Hebrew whilst his uncle Laban spoke Syriac. We can only account for this by supposing either that the family of Nahor originally spoke Syriac and that Abraham and his descendants learned Hebrew in Canaan, where evidently the Hebrew language was indigenous when he first went there, having probably been acquired by the Hamitic Canaanites from an earlier Shemite race—or else, which is not otherwise supported, that the ancestors of Laban having left the early seat of the family had unlearned their original Hebrew and acquired the Syriac dialect of Padan-aram.

48 And Laban said, This heap *is*
a witness between me and thee this
day. Therefore was the name of it
called Galeed;
49 And ‖Mizpah; for he said, The
LORD watch between me and thee,
when we are absent one from another.
50 If thou shalt afflict my daughters, or if thou shalt take *other* wives
beside my daughters, no man *is* with
us; see, God *is* witness betwixt me
and thee.
51 And Laban said to Jacob, Behold this heap, and behold *this* pillar,
which I have cast betwixt me and
thee;
52 This heap *be* witness, and *this*
pillar *be* witness, that I will not pass
over this heap to thee, and that thou
shalt not pass over this heap and this
pillar unto me, for harm.
53 The God of Abraham, and the
God of Nahor, the God of their father, judge betwixt us. And Jacob
sware by the fear of his father Isaac.
54 Then Jacob ‖offered sacrifice
upon the mount, and called his brethren to eat bread: and they did eat
bread, and tarried all night in the
mount.
55 And early in the morning Laban rose up, and kissed his sons and
his daughters, and blessed them: and
Laban departed, and returned unto
his place.

‖ [That is,] [Be]acon, [or] watch-[tow]er.

‖ Or, *killed beasts.*

---

49. *Mizpah*] *i.e.* "watch-tower."

The LORD watch] Here Laban adopts both the language and the theology of Jacob. He calls the place Mizpah, which is a Hebrew name, and he acknowledges the watchfulness of JEHOVAH the God of Abraham.

53. *The God of Abraham, and the God of Nahor, the God of their father, judge between us*] The verb *judge* is in the plural. This looks as if Laban acknowledged JEHOVAH as Jacob's God and Abraham's God, but being himself descended from Nahor and Terah and doubting whether the God who called Abraham from his father's house was the same as the God whom Terah and Nahor had served before, he couples the God of Abraham with the God of Nahor and Terah, and calls on both to witness and judge. Polytheism had still hold on Laban, though he felt the power of the God of Jacob. We learn from Josh. xxiv. 2, that the ancestors of Abraham worshipped strange gods. There is a very marked unity of purpose throughout this chapter in the use of the names of the Most High, utterly inconsistent with the modern notion of a diversity of authors, according to some not fewer than four, in the different portions of the same chapter. To Jacob He is JEHOVAH, v. 3, and the God of his father, v. 5, &c., whilst Laban acknowledges Him as the God of Jacob's father, v. 29. Once more Jacob refers to Him as the God of Abraham and the fear of Isaac (v. 42), by appeal to whom it was but likely that Laban would be moved; and lastly Laban, being so moved, himself appeals to the watchfulness of JEHOVAH, v. 49, but yet joins with Him, as possibly a distinct Being, the God of their common ancestor Nahor.

NOTE A on CHAP. XXXI. V. 41. ON THE CHRONOLOGY OF JACOB'S LIFE.

(1) Difficulty of the question. Common reckoning. (2) Suggestion of Dr Kennicott. (3) Dates on this hypothesis. (4) Greater facility for explaining the events thus obtained.

THE difficulties in the Chronology of the life of Jacob and his sons are very great, so great that Le Clerc has said, "There occur entanglements (*nodi*) in these things which no one has yet unravelled, nor do I believe will any one ever unravel them." It has been generally held by commentators, Jewish and Christian, that Isaac was 137 and Jacob 77 when Jacob received his father's blessing, and left his father's house to go to Padan-aram. (See note, ch. xxxvii. 1.) This calculation rests mainly on the following two points: the 1st is that Joseph was born just fourteen years after Jacob went to Haran, *i.e.* at the end of the second hebdomade which Jacob served for his wives; an inference, which would oblige us to conclude that all the sons of Jacob except Benjamin, eleven in number, were born in six years, a thing not quite impossible, but highly improbable (see on ch. xxx. 25). The second is, that Jacob, in vv. 38, 41, of this ch. xxxi. seems to say that his whole sojourn in Padan-aram was only twenty years. If these points be made out, we cannot deny the conclusion, that as Joseph was 39 when Jacob was 130, and so born when Jacob was 91, therefore Jacob must have been $91-14=77$, when he fled from Beer-sheba to Padan-aram.

As regards the first point, however, it has

already been seen (note on ch. xxx. 23), that it is not necessary to conclude that Jacob should have wished to leave Laban immediately on the conclusion of his 14 years' servitude. On the contrary, with his children too young to carry on so long a journey, with but little independent substance, and with the fear of Esau before his eyes, it is far more likely that he should have been willing to remain longer in the service of Laban. But, if this be so, we have then an indefinite time left us for this additional sojourn, limited only by the words "when Rachel had born Joseph" (ch. xxx. 25). Jacob may have lived and worked for twenty years longer with Laban, and not have asked for his dismissal, till Joseph was old enough to travel, or at all events till he was born.

As to the second point, almost all commentators take the statements in vv. 38 and 41 as identical, v. 41 being but a repetition, with greater detail, of the statement in v. 38, as appears in the translation of the Authorized Version. It has, however, been suggested by Dr Kennicott, that very probably the twenty years in v. 38 are not the same twenty years as those mentioned in v. 41, and that the sense of the Hebrew would be better expressed as follows, v. 38, "one twenty years I was with thee" (*i.e.* taking care of thy flocks for thee but not in thy house); and (v. 41), "another twenty years I was for myself in thy house, serving thee fourteen years for thy two daughters and six years for thy cattle." This, he contends, is a legitimate mode of rendering the repeated particle (*zeh*, *zeh*). Each mention of the twenty years is introduced with the word *zeh*, "this," which word, when repeated, is used in opposition or by way of distinction (see Ex. xiv. 20; Job xxi. 23, 25; Eccl. vi. 5). He understands Jacob therefore as saying, that he had served Laban fourteen years for his wives, after that he had for twenty years taken care of his cattle, not as a servant but as a neighbour and friend; and then, not satisfied to go on thus without profit, at last for six years more he served for wages, during which short period Laban had changed his hire 10 times.

If this reasoning be correct, and Bp Horsley has said that Dr Kennicott assigns unanswerable reasons for his opinion, then the following table will give the dates of the chief events in Jacob's life.

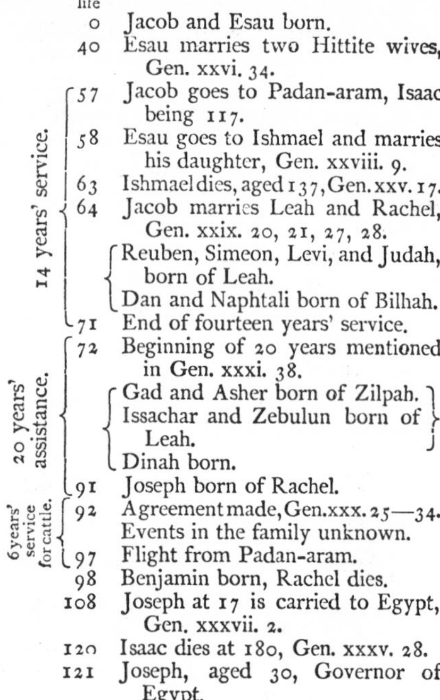

	Years of Jacob's life	
	0	Jacob and Esau born.
	40	Esau marries two Hittite wives, Gen. xxvi. 34.
14 years' service.	57	Jacob goes to Padan-aram, Isaac being 117.
	58	Esau goes to Ishmael and marries his daughter, Gen. xxviii. 9.
	63	Ishmael dies, aged 137, Gen. xxv. 17.
	64	Jacob marries Leah and Rachel, Gen. xxix. 20, 21, 27, 28.
		Reuben, Simeon, Levi, and Judah, born of Leah. Dan and Naphtali born of Bilhah.
	71	End of fourteen years' service.
20 years' assistance.	72	Beginning of 20 years mentioned in Gen. xxxi. 38.
		Gad and Asher born of Zilpah. Issachar and Zebulun born of Leah. Dinah born.
	91	Joseph born of Rachel.
6 years' service for cattle.	92	Agreement made, Gen. xxx. 25—34. Events in the family unknown.
	97	Flight from Padan-aram.
	98	Benjamin born, Rachel dies.
	108	Joseph at 17 is carried to Egypt, Gen. xxxvii. 2.
	120	Isaac dies at 180, Gen. xxxv. 28.
	121	Joseph, aged 30, Governor of Egypt.
	130	Jacob goes down to Egypt, Gen. xlvi. 1.
	147	Jacob dies, Gen. xlvii. 28.

It is not possible to date accurately the events in ch. xxxiv., xxxviii., but the above seems a far more probable chronology than that commonly acquiesced in. According to the common calculation, Judah and his sons Er and Onan must have been quite children when they married, whereas the assigning 40 instead of 20 years to the sojourn of Jacob in Padan-aram, will allow time for them to have grown up, though even so their marriages must have been for that time unusually early. The common calculation, which makes Jacob 84 at his marriage, whilst his son Judah could not have been more than 20, and his grandchildren Er and Onan not above 15 when they married (see Keil on ch. xxxviii.), must surely require some correction, even allowing for the length of patriarchal lives on the one side and for the early age of eastern marriages on the other.

CHAPTER XXXII.

1 *Jacob's vision at Mahanaim.* 3 *His message to Esau.* 6 *He is afraid of Esau's coming.* 9 *He prayeth for deliverance.* 13 *He sendeth a present to Esau.* 24 *He wrestleth with an angel at Peniel, where he is called Israel.* 31 *He halteth.*

AND Jacob went on his way, and the angels of God met him.

2 And when Jacob saw them, he
said, This *is* God's host: and he
called the name of that place ‖ Mahanaim.

3 And Jacob sent messengers before him to Esau his brother unto the
land of Seir, the † country of Edom.
4 And he commanded them, say-

‖ That two h[illegible] or, c[illegible]

† Heb. *field.*

ing, Thus shall ye speak unto my
lord Esau; Thy servant Jacob saith
thus, I have sojourned with Laban,
and stayed there until now:
5 And I have oxen, and asses,
flocks, and menservants, and womenservants: and I have sent to tell my
lord, that I may find grace in thy
sight.
6 ¶ And the messengers returned
to Jacob, saying, We came to thy
brother Esau, and also he cometh to
meet thee, and four hundred men
with him.
7 Then Jacob was greatly afraid
and distressed: and he divided the
people that *was* with him, and the
flocks, and herds, and the camels, into two bands;
8 And said, If Esau come to the
one company, and smite it, then the
other company which is left shall
escape.
9 ¶ And Jacob said, O God of
my father Abraham, and God of my
father Isaac, the LORD which saidst
unto me, [a] Return unto thy country, [a] chap. 31
and to thy kindred, and I will deal 13.
well with thee:
10 † I am not worthy of the least

† Heb. *I am less than all, &c.*

CHAP. XXXII. 1. *the angels of God met him*] The conjectures of various Jewish interpreters concerning this vision of angels may be seen in Heidegger, Tom. II. Ex. XV. § 37. The real purpose of it seems to have been this. When Jacob was flying from Esau's anger into Mesopotamia, he had a vision of angels ascending and descending on the ladder of God. He was thus assured of God's providential care over him, and mysteriously taught that there was a way from heaven to earth and from earth to heaven. Now he is again about to fall into the power of Esau; and so the angels encamped, perhaps on each side of him (*Mahanaim*, v. 2, signifying "two camps"), may have been sent to teach him, as a similar vision taught afterwards the servant of Elisha (2 K. vi. 16, 17), that, though he was encompassed with danger, there were more with him than could be against him, or, as the Psalmist wrote afterwards, that "the angel of the LORD encampeth round about them that fear him, and delivereth them" (Ps. xxxiv. 7). Thus Josephus ('A. J.' I. 20) says, "these visions were vouchsafed to Jacob returning into Canaan, to encourage him with happy hopes of what should befal him afterwards," and St Chrysost. ('Hom. 58 in Gen.'), "the fear of Laban having passed away, there succeeded to it the fear of Esau; therefore the merciful Lord, willing that the pious man should be encouraged and his fear dispelled, ordained that he should see this vision of angels."

2. *Mahanaim*] *i.e.* "two camps." Some have thought the dual here used for the plural; others that Jacob thought of his own camp and the camp of angels. (So Abenezra, and after him Clericus.) More likely the angels were encamped on the right-hand and on the left, so seeming to surround and protect Jacob (see on v. 1). The place called Mahanaim was in the tribe of Gad, and was assigned to the Levites, Josh. xxi. 38. The name *Mahneh* is still retained in the supposed site of the ancient town (Robinson).

3. *unto the land of Seir, the country of Edom*] It does not follow necessarily from this verse, that Seir had by this time become Esau's permanent place of residence. The historian calls Seir the country of Edom, because it had become so long before Moses wrote. Esau was a great hunter, and very probably a conqueror, who took possession of Seir, driving out or subjugating the Horites. It may have been for this very conquest, that he was now at the head of 400 armed men (v. 6). He had not yet removed his household from Canaan (ch. xxxvi. 6); and did not settle permanently in his newly conquered possession till after his father's death, when, yielding to the assignment made to Jacob by Isaac's blessing, he retires to Idumæa, and leaves Canaan to Jacob (ch. xxxvi. 1—8). (See Kurtz in loc.)

7. *Jacob was greatly afraid and distressed*] Though he had just seen a vision of angels, he was not unnaturally alarmed at the apparently hostile approach of Esau. He makes therefore all preparation for that approach, and then takes refuge in prayer. His faith was imperfect, but he was a religious man, and so he seeks in his terror help from God.

9. *O God of my father Abraham, and God of my father Isaac, the LORD*] This combination of names is natural and exact. He appeals to the Most High as the Covenant God, who had given promises to his fathers, of which promises he himself was the heir, and who had revealed Himself to the chosen family as the self-existent JEHOVAH, who would be their God. The whole prayer is one of singular beauty and piety.

10. *I am not worthy of the least of all the mercies*] Lit. "I am less than all the mercies."

of all the mercies, and of all the
truth, which thou hast shewed unto
thy servant; for with my staff I
passed over this Jordan; and now I
am become two bands.
11 Deliver me, I pray thee, from
the hand of my brother, from the
hand of Esau: for I fear him, lest
he will come and smite me, *and* the
mother † with the children.
12 And thou saidst, I will surely
do thee good, and make thy seed as
the sand of the sea, which cannot be
numbered for multitude.
13 ¶ And he lodged there that
same night; and took of that which
came to his hand a present for Esau
his brother;
14 Two hundred she goats, and
twenty he goats, two hundred ewes,
and twenty rams,
15 Thirty milch camels with their
colts, forty kine, and ten bulls, twenty
she asses, and ten foals.
16 And he delivered *them* into the
hand of his servants, every drove by
themselves; and said unto his servants, Pass over before me, and put
a space betwixt drove and drove.
17 And he commanded the foremost, saying, When Esau my brother meeteth thee, and asketh thee,
saying, Whose *art* thou? and whither goest thou? and whose *are* these
before thee?
18 Then thou shalt say, *They be*
thy servant Jacob's; it *is* a present
sent unto my lord Esau: and, behold,
also he *is* behind us.
19 And so commanded he the second, and the third, and all that followed the droves, saying, On this
manner shall ye speak unto Esau,
when ye find him.
20 And say ye moreover, Behold,
thy servant Jacob *is* behind us. For
he said, I will appease him with the
present that goeth before me, and
afterward I will see his face; peradventure he will accept † of me.
21 So went the present over before
him: and himself lodged that night in
the company.
22 And he rose up that night,
and took his two wives, and his
two womenservants, and his eleven
sons, and passed over the ford Jabbok.
23 And he took them, and † sent
them over the brook, and sent over
that he had.
24 ¶ And Jacob was left alone;

† Heb. *upon.*

† H[eb.] *my* [face.]

† H[eb.] *cau[sed to] pass.*

---

11. *the mother with the children*] Lit. "upon the children." Whence some have thought that there was allusion to the mother protecting the child, as a bird covers its young (Tuch, Knobel, Keil), or to the slaying of the child before the parent's eyes, and then the parent upon him (Ros.); but the sense seems correctly expressed by "with," as in Ex. xxv. 22; Num. xx. 11; Deut. xvi. 3; Job xxxviii. 32, &c. (See Ges. 'Thes.' p. 1027.)

13. *of that which came to his hand*] or perhaps "that which had come to his hand," *i.e.* into his possession, what he possessed.

20. *I will appease him*, &c.] The sentence literally rendered would be, "I will cover his face with the present that goeth before me, and afterward I will see his face, peradventure he will accept my face." "To cover the eyes or the face" was an expression apparently signifying to induce the person to turn away from or connive at a fault. (Ges. pp. 700, 706.) "To accept or lift up the face" was equivalent to accepting a person favourably (*Ib.* p. 915).

22. *the ford Jabbok*] or "the ford of Jabbok." The name Jabbok is either derived from *bakak*, "to pour forth, to gush forth," or from *abak*, "to wrestle," from the wrestling of Jacob there. It flowed into the Jordan about half way between the Dead Sea and the sea of Galilee, at a point nearly opposite to Shechem. It is now called *Zerka*, *i.e.* "blue" (Ges. 'Thes.' p. 232).

23. *the brook*] The word signifies either a brook, a torrent, or the bed of a torrent, sometimes dry and sometimes flowing, like the Arabic *Wady*.

24. *Jacob was left alone*] He remained to the last that he might see all his family pass safely through the ford, that he might prevent anything being left behind through carelessness; and most probably that he might once more give himself to earnest prayer for God's protection in his expected meeting with his brother Esau.

and there wrestled a man with him
until the † breaking of the day.
25 And when he saw that he prevailed not against him, he touched
the hollow of his thigh; and the
hollow of Jacob's thigh was out of
joint, as he wrestled with him.
26 And he said, Let me go, for the
day breaketh. And he said, [b] I will
not let thee go, except thou bless me.

† Heb. *ascending of the morning.*

[b] Hos. 12. 4.

---

there wrestled a man with him] He is called "the angel," Hos. xii. 4, and Jacob says of him (v. 30), "I have seen God face to face." The Jews of course believed that he was a created angel, and said that he was the angel of Esau, *i.e.* either Esau's special guardian angel (cp. Acts xii. 15), or the angel that presided over Esau's country (cp. Dan. x. 13). So Abenezra and Abarbanel. Many Christian commentators also prefer to consider this a vision of a created angel, as thinking it inconsistent with the greatness of the Creator to have manifested Himself in this manner to Jacob. Most of the fathers, however, thought this to have been one of the manifestations of the Logos, of the eternal Son, anticipatory of His incarnation. Theodoret (Qu. 92 in Gen.) argues thus at length. (See also Justin M. 'Dial.' § 126; Tertull. 'Contra Marcion.' c. 3; Euseb. 'H. E.' I. 22; August. 'De C. D.' XVI. 39, &c. &c.). From vv. 29, 30, this seems the true opinion. The word for 'wrestle" (*abak*) is derived from *abak*, "dust," from the rolling of athletes in the dust when wrestling with each other.

until the breaking of the day] lit. "till the rising of the dawn."

25. *when he saw that he prevailed not against him*] There must have been some deep significance in this wrestling, in which an Angel, or more probably the God of angels, Himself "the Angel of the LORD," prevailed not against a man. The difficulty of believing that man could prevail against God led to some forced interpretations, such as that of Origen ('De Principiis,' Lib. III.), and Jerome ('in Epist. ad Ephes.' c. VI.), that Jacob wrestled against evil spirits, and that the "Man" is said to have wrestled *with* him in the sense of assisting him, wrestling on his side; an interpretation refuted by the words of the "Man" Himself in v. 28. The mystical meaning of the whole transaction seems probably to be of this kind. The time was an important epoch in Jacob's history. It was a turning-point in his life. There had been much most faulty in his character; which had led him to much trouble, and subjected him to a long penitential and reformatory discipline. He was now returning after an exile, of 20 or more probably 40 years, to the land of his birth, which had been promised to him for his inheritance. It was a great crisis. Should he fall under the power of Esau and so suffer to the utmost for his former sins? or should he obtain mercy and be received back to his father's house as the heir of the promises? This eventful night, this passage of the Jabbok, was to decide; and the mysterious conflict, in which by Divine mercy and strength he is permitted to prevail, is vouchsafed to him as an indication that his repentance, matured by long schooling and discipline and manifested in fervent and humble prayer, is accepted with God and blessed by the Son of God, whose ancestor in the flesh he is now once more formally constituted.

the hollow of the thigh] The socket of the hip-joint, the hollow place like the palm of a hand (Heb. *Caph*) into which the neck-bone of the thigh is inserted. The reason of this act of the Angel was very probably lest Jacob should be puffed up by the "abundance of the revelations;" he might think that by his own strength and not by grace he had prevailed with God; as St Paul had the thorn in the flesh sent to him lest he "should be exalted above measure," 2 Cor. xii. 7. (So Theodoret in loc.).

26. *Let me go, for the day breaketh*]. Lit. "for the dawn ariseth." The contest had taken place during the later hours of the night. It was now right that it should be ended: for the time had arrived, the breaking of the day, when Jacob must prepare to meet Esau and to appease his anger. It was for Jacob's sake, not for His own convenience, that the Divine wrestler desired to go. (So Abarbanel, Heidegger, &c. &c.).

except thou bless me] Jacob had plainly discovered that his antagonist was a heavenly Visitor. Though he had been permitted to prevail in the contest, he still desired blessing for the future.

28. *Israel: for as a prince hast thou power*], The verb *Sarah* and its cognate *Sūr* signify "to contend with," and also "to be a prince or leader." See Judg. ix. 22; Hos. xii. 4 (Ges. pp. 1326, 1338, Ros. in loc.). It is quite possible that both senses are conveyed by the word, and it might be rendered either, "thou hast contended with God," or "thou hast been a prince with God." The Authorised Version combines both. The best Vss., LXX., Vulg., render, "Thou hast had power with God, and how much more wilt thou prevail with men," which has been followed by many moderns, as Heidegger, Rosenm., &c. The sense is thus rendered more perspicuous, as implying a promise of safety from

27 And he said unto him, What *is*
thy name? And he said, Jacob.
[c chap. 35. 10.] 28 And he said, [c] Thy name shall
be called no more Jacob, but Israel:
for as a prince hast thou power with
God and with men, and hast prevailed.
29 And Jacob asked *him*, and said,
Tell *me*, I pray thee, thy name. And
he said, Wherefore *is* it *that* thou
dost ask after my name? And he
blessed him there.
30 And Jacob called the name of
[‖ That is, *the face of God.*] the place ‖ Peniel: for I have seen
God face to face, and my life is pre-
served.
31 And as he passed over Penuel
the sun rose upon him, and he halted
upon his thigh.
32 Therefore the children of Israel
eat not *of* the sinew which shrank,
which *is* upon the hollow of the
thigh, unto this day: because he
touched the hollow of Jacob's thigh
in the sinew that shrank.

CHAPTER XXXIII.

1 *The kindness of Jacob and Esau at their meeting.* 17 *Jacob cometh to Succoth.* 18 *At Shalem he buyeth a field, and buildeth an altar called El-elohe-Israel.*

AND Jacob lifted up his eyes, and
looked, and, behold, Esau came,
and with him four hundred men. And
he divided the children unto Leah,
and unto Rachel, and unto the two
handmaids.
2 And he put the handmaids and
their children foremost, and Leah and
her children after, and Rachel and
Joseph hindermost.
3 And he passed over before them,
and bowed himself to the ground
seven times, until he came near to
his brother.
4 And Esau ran to meet him, and
embraced him, and fell on his neck,
and kissed him: and they wept.
5 And he lifted up his eyes, and
saw the women and the children;
and said, Who *are* those † with thee? [† Heb. *to thee*]
And he said, The children which God
hath graciously given thy servant.
6 Then the handmaidens came
near, they and their children, and
they bowed themselves.
7 And Leah also with her children
came near, and bowed themselves:
and after came Joseph near and Ra- [† Heb. *What all this band to thee?*]
chel, and they bowed themselves.
8 And he said, † What *meanest* thou

Esau. The difficulty, however, of thus explaining the particle *Vau* before "hast prevailed" is great.

29. *Wherefore is it that thou dost ask after my name?*] Comp. Judg. xiii. 18, "And the Angel of the Lord said unto him (*i. e.* Manoah), Why askest thou after my name seeing it is secret?" lit. "wonderful." In the present instance perhaps the words mean, "Why dost thou ask my name? as it may be plain to you who I am."

30. *Peniel*] *i. e.* "the face of God." Elsewhere it is always *Penuel*, and the Samaritan Pentateuch and the Vulg. have Penuel here. The LXX. does not give this name itself, but translates it both here and in v. 31. Josephus has Phanuel only. The words only differ by a single line in one letter, and have no difference of meaning. Strabo ('Geogr.' L. XVI. c. 2, §§ 15, 18) mentions a town among the Phœnician cities with a Greek name of the same meaning, viz. *Theou prosopon.*

32. *the sinew which shrank*] This is the rendering of LXX., Vulg., Onk. Many Jewish and Christian commentators have rendered it "the nerve of contraction" or "the nerve of oblivion." Whatever be the literal sense of the words, they doubtless mean the "sciatic nerve," the *nervus ischiadicus*, which is one of the largest in the body, and extends down the thigh and leg to the ankle. The Arabs still use this same word (*Nasheh* or *Naseh*) to designate the sciatic nerve (see Ros. in loc., Ges. 'Thes.' p. 924). The custom prevailing among the Jews to this day of abstaining religiously from eating this sinew seems a lasting monument of the historical truth of this wonderful event in the life of Jacob.

CHAP. XXXIII. **3.** *bowed himself to the ground*] A deep oriental bow, not probably such profound prostration as is expressed in ch. xix. 1: "he bowed himself with his face to the ground."

5. *Who are those with thee?*] Lit. "to thee;" *i. e.* that thou hast.

8. *What meanest thou by all this drove*] Lit. "What to thee is all this camp?" The sheep with their shepherds, assumed the appearance of a band or troop, hence called "camp."

by all this drove which I met? And
he said, *These are* to find grace in the
sight of my lord.
9 And Esau said, I have enough,
my brother; †keep that thou hast
unto thyself.
10 And Jacob said, Nay, I pray
thee, if now I have found grace in
thy sight, then receive my present at
my hand: for therefore I have seen
thy face, as though I had seen the
face of God, and thou wast pleased
with me.
11 Take, I pray thee, my blessing
that is brought to thee; because God
hath dealt graciously with me, and
because I have enough. And he
urged him, and he took *it*.
12 And he said, Let us take our
journey, and let us go, and I will go
before thee.
13 And he said unto him, My
lord knoweth that the children *are*
tender, and the flocks and herds with
young *are* with me: and if men should
overdrive them one day, all the flock
will die.
14 Let my lord, I pray thee, pass
over before his servant: and I will
lead on softly, †according as the cattle
that goeth before me and the children
be able to endure, until I come unto
my lord unto Seir.
15 And Esau said, Let me now
†leave with thee *some* of the folk that
are with me. And he said, †What
needeth it? let me find grace in the
sight of my lord.
16 ¶ So Esau returned that day on
his way unto Seir.
17 And Jacob journeyed to Succoth, and built him an house, and
made booths for his cattle: therefore
the name of the place is called ‖Suc-
coth.
18 ¶ And Jacob came to Shalem,

† Heb. *that to thee that is thine.*

† Heb. *according to the foot of the work, &c. and according to the foot of the children.*

† Heb. *set, or, place.*

† Heb. *Wherefore is this?*

‖ That is, *booths.*

---

10. *for therefore I have seen thy face, &c.*] Rather "for I have seen thy face, as though I had seen the face of God." The same particles are rendered "because," Gen. xxxviii. 26; "forasmuch as," Num. x. 31; "because," Num. xiv. 43 (see Ges. 'Thes.' p. 682). Jacob pleads as a reason why Esau should accept his present, that Esau's face had seemed as gracious and favourable to him as though it had been God's face. It is highly probable that Jacob here refers to his vision of God in the night past at Peniel. The words he uses are "for I have seen thy face, like a vision of *Peney El-ohim*," *i.e.* "the face of God." It might have seemed likely that Jacob on his meeting with Esau would use the special name of their father's God, JEHOVAH; but this, in addition to the reason given above, would have been like claiming to be the heir of the promises and under the peculiar care of JEHOVAH, which would have been very offensive to Esau.

11. *my blessing*] That is, "this gift which is meant to express good will and affection, offered with prayers for blessing on the recipient" (cp. Judg. i. 15; 1 S. xxv. 32, xxx. 26; 2 K. v. 15).

I have enough] Lit. "I have all."

13. *with young*] **In milk.**

if men should overdrive them one day] Esau's 400 horsemen would be likely to move too rapidly for the milch cattle.

14. *according as the cattle that goeth before me and the children be able to endure*] **According to the pace** (lit. "the foot") **of the cattle that is before me, and according to the pace of the children.** The word for cattle is literally "work;" thence anything acquired by labour, property, and hence cattle, the chief possession of a pastoral people.

until I come unto my lord unto Seir] It is probable that Jacob here intimated a hope that he might one day visit Esau at Seir. It does not necessarily mean that he was directly on his way thither; his course being evidently towards Shechem.

17. *booths*] Perhaps only wattled enclosures, or very possibly some simple contrivance of branches and leaves made for sheltering the milch cattle from the heat of the sun.

Succoth] "Booths," from *saccac*, to entwine, to shelter. Jacob could easily visit his father from this place. Jerome ('Qu. Heb.' ad h.l.) says that "Sochoth is to this day a city beyond Jordan in Scythopolis." According to Josh. xiii. 27, Judg. viii. 4, 5, Succoth was in the valley of the Jordan, "on the other side of the Jordan eastward," and was allotted to the tribe of Gad.

18. *to Shalem*] Or "in peace." The LXX., Vulg., Syr. render "Shalem." Robinson ('B. R.' III. 322) and Wilson ('Lands of the Bible,' II. 72) mention a place still called Salim to the east of Nablus. On the other hand the Sam. Pent. has *Shalom*, *i.e.* "safe."

‖ Called, Acts 7. 16, *Sychem*.

a city of ‖ Shechem, which *is* in the
land of Canaan, when he came from
Padan-aram; and pitched his tent
before the city.
19 And he bought a parcel of a
field, where he had spread his tent,
at the hand of the children of ‖ Hamor, Shechem's father, for an hundred
‖ pieces of money.
20 And he erected there an altar,
and called it ‖ El-elohe-Israel.

‖ Called, Acts 7. 16, *Emmor*.

‖ Or, *lambs*.

‖ That is, *God the God of Israel*.

CHAPTER XXXIV.

1 *Dinah is ravished by Shechem.* 4 *He sueth to marry her.* 13 *The sons of Jacob offer the condition of circumcision to the Shechemites.* 20 *Hamor and Shechem persuade them to accept it.* 25 *The sons of Jacob upon that advantage slay them,* 27 *and spoil their city.* 30 *Jacob reproveth Simeon and Levi.*

AND Dinah the daughter of Leah,
which she bare unto Jacob, went
out to see the daughters of the land.
2 And when Shechem the son of
Hamor the Hivite, prince of the
country, saw her, he took her, and
lay with her, and † defiled her.
3 And his soul clave unto Dinah
the daughter of Jacob, and he loved
the damsel, and spake † kindly unto
the damsel.
4 And Shechem spake unto his father Hamor, saying, Get me this damsel to wife.
5 And Jacob heard that he had defiled Dinah his daughter: now his
sons were with his cattle in the field:
and Jacob held his peace until they
were come.
6 ¶ And Hamor the father of Shechem went out unto Jacob to commune with him.
7 And the sons of Jacob came out
of the field when they heard *it*: and
the men were grieved, and they were
very wroth, because he had wrought

† Heb. *humbled her*.

† Heb. *to her heart*.

Onkelos renders "in peace," and he is followed by Saadias, Rashi and most Jewish commentators, by Rosenm., Schum, Gesen., Tuch, Del., Knobel, Keil.

a city of Shechem] If instead of "to Shalem" we adopt the rendering "in peace," or "in safety;" then we must render here "to the city of Shechem." It was perhaps called after Shechem the son of Hamor (v. 19). In ch. xii. 6 (where see note), we read of "the place of Sichem," *i.e.* perhaps the site on which Sichem or Shechem was afterwards built. It was the first place in which God appeared to Abraham, and it is the place at which Jacob re-enters the promised land; for Succoth, whence he came to it, was on the other side of Jordan. Abraham only purchased a burial-place, Jacob purchases a dwelling-place. Perhaps the country had now become more fully inhabited, and therefore land must be secured before it could be safely lived upon.

19. *an hundred pieces of money*] "A hundred Kesita." All the ancient Versions (except Targg. Jerus. and Jonath.) render "a hundred lambs," whence it has been inferred that the *Kesita* was a piece of money bearing the impression of a lamb. It appears however to have been either an ingot or bar of silver of certain weight, or perhaps merely a certain weight of silver; a word of the same root in Arabic signifying "a balance," "a pair of scales." (See Ges. 'Thes.' p. 1241. Lee, 'Lex.' in voc.).

20. *El-elohe-Israel*] The name *Israel* contains in it the syllable *El*, one of the names of God. Jacob therefore calls *El* the God of Israel, and gives this title to the altar, which he built on the spot which had already been consecrated by Abraham (ch. xii. 7). Jacob had hitherto always spoken of JEHOVAH as the God of Abraham, and the God, or the Fear, of his father Isaac. Now on his gracious acceptance by Him, his change of name by His appointment, his return to Canaan as the heir of the land, he calls Him his own God, El, the God of Israel.

CHAP. XXXIV. **1.** *Dinah the daughter of Leah*] Her birth is mentioned (ch. xxx. 21) before the birth of Joseph (vv. 22, 23). If Jacob's sojourn in Padan-aram was 40 years long and not 20 only (see note at the end of ch. xxxi.), it is quite possible that Dinah may have been some years older than Joseph, who was 17 at the beginning of the history related in ch. xxxvii. (see v. 2), *i.e.* probably about a year or two after the events related in this present chapter. In any case therefore she was not less than 15 years old at this time, supposing her to have been no older than Joseph; so that the objection urged by Tuch and others that at this time she was but 6 or 7 years old cannot be maintained.

went out to see the daughters of the land] Josephus ('Ant.' I. 21) states that a feast among the Shechemites was the occasion of this visit.

3. *spake kindly unto the damsel*] Lit. "Spake to the heart of the damsel." So ch. l. 21; Judg. xix. 3; Isa. xl. 2; Hos. ii. 14, &c.

7. *he had wrought folly in Israel...which*

folly in Israel in lying with Jacob's
daughter; which thing ought not to
be done.
8 And Hamor communed with
them, saying, The soul of my son
Shechem longeth for your daughter:
I pray you give her him to wife.
9 And make ye marriages with us,
and give your daughters unto us, and
take our daughters unto you.
10 And ye shall dwell with us:
and the land shall be before you; dwell
and trade ye therein, and get you possessions therein.
11 And Shechem said unto her father and unto her brethren, Let me
find grace in your eyes, and what ye
shall say unto me I will give.
12 Ask me never so much dowry
and gift, and I will give according as
ye shall say unto me: but give me
the damsel to wife.
13 And the sons of Jacob answered
Shechem and Hamor his father deceitfully, and said, because he had
defiled Dinah their sister:
14 And they said unto them, We
cannot do this thing, to give our sister
to one that is uncircumcised; for that
were a reproach unto us:
15 But in this will we consent unto you: If ye will be as we *be*, that
every male of you be circumcised;
16 Then will we give our daughters unto you, and we will take your
daughters to us, and we will dwell
with you, and we will become one
people.
17 But if ye will not hearken unto us, to be circumcised; then will
we take our daughter, and we will be
gone.
18 And their words pleased Hamor,
and Shechem Hamor's son.
19 And the young man deferred
not to do the thing, because he had
delight in Jacob's daughter: and he
was more honourable than all the
house of his father.
20 ¶ And Hamor and Shechem his
son came unto the gate of their city,
and communed with the men of their
city, saying,
21 These men *are* peaceable with
us; therefore let them dwell in the
land, and trade therein; for the land,
behold, *it is* large enough for them;
let us take their daughters to us for
wives, and let us give them our
daughters.
22 Only herein will the men consent unto us for to dwell with us, to
be one people, if every male among
us be circumcised, as they *are* circumcised.
23 *Shall* not their cattle and their
substance and every beast of theirs *be*
ours? only let us consent unto them,
and they will dwell with us.
24 And unto Hamor and unto Shechem his son hearkened all that went
out of the gate of his city; and every
male was circumcised, all that went
out of the gate of his city.
25 ¶ And it came to pass on the
third day, when they were sore, that

---

thing ought not to be done] Lit. "and so it is not done." These are not the words of the sons of Jacob, but of the sacred historian. It is not likely that the family of Jacob should by this time have acquired the generic name of Israel; but Moses uses the designation which had become familiar in his own day. The words of this verse seem to have become proverbial, they are almost repeated in 2 S. xiii. 12. But this is no reason for supposing that the words of this present verse should be ascribed to a later hand than that of Moses.

13. *and said*] Schultens, Gesen. (p. 315), Knobel, Del., &c. translate here "and plotted" or "laid snares:" others repeat the word "deceitfully" from the former clause, rendering and "spoke deceitfully:" but the rendering of the Authorised Version seems preferable.

18. *their words pleased Hamor*, &c.] The readiness of the Shechemites to submit to circumcision may be accounted for, if circumcision had by this time become a rite known to others besides the descendants of Abraham (Herod. II. 104). At all events, it was now practised not only by the sons of Jacob and his household, but by the Ishmaelites, and the family and household of Esau, all growing into important tribes in the neighbourhood of the Shechemites.

25. *Simeon and Levi, Dinah's brethren, took each man his sword*] *i.e.* sons of the same

two of the sons of Jacob, Simeon and
Levi, Dinah's brethren, took each man
his sword, and came upon the city
a chap. 49. 6. boldly, and [a]slew all the males.
26 And they slew Hamor and She-
† Heb. *mouth.* chem his son with the †edge of the
sword, and took Dinah out of She-
chem's house, and went out.
27 The sons of Jacob came upon
the slain, and spoiled the city, because
they had defiled their sister.
28 They took their sheep, and their
oxen, and their asses, and that which
was in the city, and that which *was*
in the field,
29 And all their wealth, and all
their little ones, and their wives took
they captive, and spoiled even all that
was in the house.
30 And Jacob said to Simeon and
Levi, Ye have troubled me to make
me to stink among the inhabitants of
the land, among the Canaanites and
the Perizzites: and I *being* few in
number, they shall gather themselves
together against me, and slay me; and
I shall be destroyed, I and my house.
31 And they said, Should he deal
with our sister as with an harlot?

CHAPTER XXXV.

1 *God sendeth Jacob to Beth-el.* 2 *He purgeth his house of idols.* 6 *He buildeth an altar at Beth-el.* 8 *Deborah dieth at Allon-bachuth.* 9 *God blesseth Jacob at Beth-el.* 16 *Rachel travaileth of Benjamin, and dieth in the way to Edar.* 22 *Reuben lieth with Bilhah.* 23 *The sons of Jacob.* 27 *Jacob cometh to Isaac at Hebron.* 28 *The age, death, and burial of Isaac.*

AND God said unto Jacob, Arise,
go up to Beth-el, and dwell there:
and make there an altar unto God,
that appeared unto thee [a]when thou a chap. 27. 43.
fleddest from the face of Esau thy
brother.
2 Then Jacob said unto his household, and to all that *were* with him,
Put away the strange gods that *are*
among you, and be clean, and change
your garments:
3 And let us arise, and go up to

---

mother, Leah, as well as of the same father, Jacob. In ch. xxiv. 50, 55, &c. we saw Laban taking a principal part in giving his sister in marriage Michaelis (in loc.) mentions it as a prevalent opinion in the East that a man is more affected by the dishonour of his sister than even by the dishonour of his wife, as he may divorce his wife but can never cease to be his sister's brother. We are not to suppose that Simeon and Levi without help from others attacked and slew all the males: they had no doubt a retinue from their father's household with them, and perhaps were accompanied by some of their brothers, though they only are specially mentioned, as having taken the lead in the assault, and as most strongly actuated by the spirit of revenge.

27. *the sons of Jacob*] *i.e.* others beside Simeon and Levi, for all appear to have joined in the original stratagem (see v. 13), and probably all assisted in spoiling the city.

30. *I being few in number*] Lit. "I being men of number." That is, I and my family and followers (compare "I am become two bands," ch. xxxii. 10) are men so few that we can easily be numbered. A common idiom: see Deut. iv. 27; 1 Chr. xvi. 19; Ps. cv. 12; Isa. x. 19; Jer. xliv. 28.

It seems strange that Jacob should have reproached his sons as having brought him into danger, not as having been guilty of treachery and murder. This is only another instance of Jacob's weak character, and of the fidelity of the historian. Jacob's own fault was want of straightforward honesty. It is reproduced with grievous aggravations in his sons. The timidity of his disposition, a kindred defect with untruthfulness, shews itself now in his exclamation of fear rather than of moral horror. His more righteous indignation, the result of calmer thought, is expressed in his final judgment on the fierceness of their anger and the cruelty of their wrath (ch. xlix. 5, 6, 7).

CHAP. XXXV. 1. *Beth-el*] See on ch. xxviii. 19.

2. *strange gods*] Not only had Rachel stolen her father's teraphim, but probably others of Jacob's company had secreted instruments of idolatrous worship in the camp. As they had just spoiled a heathen city (ch. xxxiv. 27), it is not unlikely that they brought such instruments from that also.

be clean] "Purify yourselves." The same word is frequently used under the Law for purification from legal uncleanness before access to sacred ordinances (Lev. xiv. 4; Num. viii. 7; 2 Chr. xxx. 18; Ezra vi. 20; Neh. xii. 30; xiii. 22). Such purification was probably in the patriarchal times, as often even under the law, by washing merely, all such

Beth-el; and I will make there an
altar unto God, who answered me in
the day of my distress, and was with
me in the way which I went.
4 And they gave unto Jacob all the
strange gods which *were* in their hand,
and *all their* earrings which *were* in
their ears; and Jacob hid them under
the oak which *was* by Shechem.
5 And they journeyed: and the
terror of God was upon the cities that
were round about them, and they did
not pursue after the sons of Jacob.
6 ¶ So Jacob came to Luz, which
is in the land of Canaan, that *is*,
Beth-el, he and all the people that
were with him.
7 And he built there an altar, and
[b]called the place ‖El-beth-el: because [b] chap. 28. 19.
there God appeared unto him, when ‖ That is, *the God of Beth-el.*
he fled from the face of his brother.
8 But Deborah Rebekah's nurse
died, and she was buried beneath
Beth-el under an oak: and the name
of it was called ‖Allon-bachuth. ‖ That is, *the oak of weeping.*
9 ¶ And God appeared unto Jacob
again, when he came out of Padan-aram,
and blessed him.
10 And God said unto him, Thy
name *is* Jacob: thy name shall not be
called any more Jacob, [c]but Israel [c] chap. 32. 28.
shall be thy name: and he called his
name Israel.
11 And God said unto him, I *am*
God Almighty: be fruitful and multiply; a nation and a company of na-

---

ceremonial washings being the prototypes of baptism, by which, false religions being rejected, men are brought into the Church of the living God.

4. *ear-rings*] perhaps talismans or idolatrous symbols worn in the ear. Augustine ('Qu.' ad h. l.) calls them "idolatrous phylacteries," *idolorum phylacteria*, and ('Epist.' CCXLV.) he mentions a superstitious use of earrings even in his own day among the African Christians "not to please men but to serve demons."

the oak which was by Shechem] See note on ch. xii. 6. It may have been under the very oak, or oak-grove, where Abraham pitched his tent, and which seems to have been sacred even in Joshua's time (Josh. xxiv. 26).

5. *the terror of God*] God inspired into the minds of the neighbouring tribes a sense of fear, so that they did not pursue Jacob in order to avenge the slaughter of the Shechemites.

6. *Luz*] See ch. xxviii. 19.

7. *El-beth-el*] *i.e.* "the God of Beth-el," or "the God of the House of God." At Bethel God first appeared to him. Then he devoted himself to God's service and received the promises of God's protection. He accordingly called the place Bethel, which name he now renews with addition of *El.*

God appeared unto him] The word for God, "Elohim," being here as generally in the plural, the verb is by a kind of attraction put in the plural also. Some have discovered in this a relic of polytheism, and Onkelos has rendered angels, a most unwarrantable translation. The Samaritan Pentateuch and the LXX. and Vulg. Versions have the verb in the singular, which may be the true reading; but see on ch. xx. 13.

8. *Allon-bachuth*] "The oak of weeping."

9. *God appeared unto Jacob again, when he came out of Padan-aram*] He was now at Bethel, the place from which he may be considered to have set out for Padan-aram, and where he made his vow that if God would be with him and be his God, he would make that place the house of God. He had now come back again to the same spot; he had fulfilled his vow by consecrating Bethel as the temple of God; this might then well be considered as the accomplishment of his return from Padan-aram. Accordingly God appears to him here once more, promises him again, and more emphatically, protection, blessing, inheritance, confirms the name of Israel to him, a name given by the angel at the ford of the brook Jabbok, but now fixed and ratified, and assures him that his posterity shall be numerous, powerful and blessed Accordingly Jacob, recognizing the fulfilment of all that had been promised him when he fled from Esau, and of all that his vows had pointed to, rears again a stone pillar as he had done forty years before, and again solemnly names the place Bethel. The whole of this history thoroughly fits in to all that has gone before, there being nothing whatever to support the notion that it is a mere legendary repetition of the previous vision.

11. *I am God Almighty*] *El-Shaddai.* It was by this name that God revealed Himself to Abram, when he changed his name to Abraham, and promised him the land of Canaan for an everlasting possession (see ch. xvii. 8). The use of the same name here is

tions shall be of thee, and kings shall
come out of thy loins;
12 And the land which I gave
Abraham and Isaac, to thee I will
give it, and to thy seed after thee will
I give the land.
13 And God went up from him in
the place where he talked with him.
14 And Jacob set up a pillar in the
place where he talked with him, *even*
a pillar of stone: and he poured a
drink offering thereon, and he poured
oil thereon.
15 And Jacob called the name of
the place where God spake with him,
Beth-el.
16 ¶ And they journeyed from
Beth-el; and there was but †a little
way to come to Ephrath: and Rachel
travailed, and she had hard labour.
17 And it came to pass, when she
was in hard labour, that the midwife
said unto her, Fear not; thou shalt
have this son also.
18 And it came to pass, as her soul
was in departing, (for she died) that
she called his name ‖Ben-oni: but
his father called him ‖Benjamin.
19 And Rachel died, and was buried in the way to Ephrath, which *is*
Beth-lehem.
20 And Jacob set a pillar upon her
grave: that *is* the pillar of Rachel's
grave unto this day.
21 ¶ And Israel journeyed, and
spread his tent beyond the tower of
Edar.
22 And it came to pass, when Israel dwelt in that land, that Reuben
went and [d]lay with Bilhah his father's concubine: and Israel heard *it*.
Now the sons of Jacob were twelve:
23 The sons of Leah; Reuben,
Jacob's firstborn, and Simeon, and
Levi, and Judah, and Issachar, and
Zebulun:
24 The sons of Rachel; Joseph,
and Benjamin:
25 And the sons of Bilhah, Rachel's
handmaid; Dan, and Naphtali:
26 And the sons of Zilpah, Leah's
handmaid; Gad, and Asher: these
are the sons of Jacob, which were
born to him in Padan-aram.
27 ¶ And Jacob came unto Isaac
his father unto Mamre, unto the city
of Arbah, which *is* Hebron, where
Abraham and Isaac sojourned.

† Heb. *a little piece of ground.*

‖ That is, *the son of my sorrow.*

‖ That is, *the son of the right hand.*

d chap. 49. 4.

---

therefore singularly appropriate, and Jacob refers to it with evident comfort and satisfaction at the close of his life (see ch. xlviii. 3).

16. *a little way*] These words probably in the original denote a definite space. The LXX. does not translate the principal word. The Vulg. improperly renders "in the Spring time." Onk. has "an acre of land;" the Syr. "a parasang;" Saad. and Arab. Erpen. "a mile." The Jews generally incline to understand "a mile," because of the traditions that Rachel's tomb was a mile from Bethlehem or Ephrath (v. 19).

18. *Ben-oni*] *i.e.* "son of my sorrow."

Benjamin] *i.e.* "son of the right hand," a name of good significance, the right hand being connected with prosperity, as the left hand was with calamity. Some ancient versions (favoured by the Samaritan Pentateuch) interpret Benjamin as "son of days," *i.e.* "son of old age." There is evidently, however, an antithesis between Benoni, "son of sorrow," and Benjamin, "son of prosperity." It might possibly be interpreted "son of strength," from the "strong right hand."

20. *unto this day*] *i.e.* till Moses wrote. It was worthy of notice that the pillar still stood after the land had been so long inhabited by unfriendly tribes. On the knowledge of the geography of Palestine by Moses, see Introduction to the Pentateuch, p. 17.

21. *tower of Edar*] *i.e.* "tower of the flock." It was apparently a watch-tower for the protection of flocks against robbers and wild beasts. (Cp. 2 K. xviii. 8; 2 Chr. xxvi. 10, xxvii. 4.)

22. *Reuben*] The incest of Reuben is punished by his being deprived of his right of primogeniture, ch. xlix. 3, 4; 1 Chr. v. 1.

and Israel heard it] The LXX. adds "and it was evil in his sight." The silence of the Hebrew expresses more eloquently the indignation of the offended patriarch.

26. *in Padan-aram*] *i.e.* except Benjamin, whose birth has just been recorded in Canaan (v. 18).

27. *Jacob came unto Isaac his father*] Whether this was just before Isaac's death, or whether Jacob spent some time at Mamre with his father, we do not read. If this were only just before his death it is very probable that Jacob had visited him from time to time before.

28 And the days of Isaac were an
hundred and fourscore years.
29 And Isaac gave up the ghost,
e chap. 25. 8. and died, and [e] was gathered unto his
people, *being* old and full of days: and
his sons Esau and Jacob buried him.

CHAPTER XXXVI.

1 *Esau's three wives.* 6 *His removing to mount Seir.* 9 *His sons.* 15 *The dukes which descended of his sons.* 20 *The sons and dukes of Seir.* 24 *Anah findeth mules.* 31 *The kings of Edom.* 40 *The dukes that descended of Esau.*

NOW these *are* the generations
of Esau, who *is* Edom.
2 Esau took his wives of the daughters
of Canaan; Adah the daughter
of Elon the Hittite, and Aholibamah
the daughter of Anah the daughter
of Zibeon the Hivite;
3 And Bashemath Ishmael's daughter,
sister of Nebajoth.
a 1 Chron. 1. 35. 4 And [a] Adah bare to Esau Eliphaz;
and Bashemath bare Reuel;
5 And Aholibamah bare Jeush, and
Jaalam, and Korah: these *are* the
sons of Esau, which were born unto
him in the land of Canaan.
6 And Esau took his wives, and
his sons, and his daughters, and all
the † persons of his house, and his cat- † Heb. souls.
tle, and all his beasts, and all his
substance, which he had got in the
land of Canaan; and went into the
country from the face of his brother
Jacob.
7 For their riches were more than
that they might dwell together; and
the land wherein they were strangers
could not bear them because of their
cattle.
8 Thus dwelt Esau in [b] mount Seir: b Josh. 24. 4.
Esau *is* Edom.
9 ¶ And these *are* the generations
of Esau the father of † the Edomites † Heb. Edom.
in mount Seir:
10 These *are* the names of Esau's
sons; [c] Eliphaz the son of Adah the c 1 Chron. 1. 35, &c.
wife of Esau, Reuel the son of Bashemath
the wife of Esau.
11 And the sons of Eliphaz were
Teman, Omar, Zepho, and Gatam,
and Kenaz.
12 And Timna was concubine to
Eliphaz Esau's son; and she bare to
Eliphaz Amalek: these *were* the sons
of Adah Esau's wife.
13 And these *are* the sons of Reu-

CHAP. XXXVI. 2, 3. *Adah*, &c.] See note A at the end of the Chapter.

6. *went into the country*] Lit. "into a land." Onk. and Vulg. has "into another land." The Sam. Pentat. has "from the land of Canaan." The LXX. "from the land." The Syr. reads "into the land of Seir," which is adopted by Ewald, Knobel, Delitzsch, Keil, &c. In ch. xxxii. 3, Esau is mentioned as in the land of Seir, but then probably he was only there for a time, perhaps engaged in its conquest, now he finally takes up his abode there. See note on xxxii. 3.

7. *the land wherein they were strangers could not bear them because of their cattle*] They were not settled inhabitants, but only sojourners in the land: and though they were allowed to pasture their flocks in the land, yet it was not to be expected that the settled inhabitants would tolerate more than a reasonable number of cattle from one family to eat up the produce of their fields.

8. *mount Seir*] Mount Seir was the mountainous country between the Dead Sea and the Elamitic Gulf, the northern part of which is called *Jebal*, *i.e.* "the hill country," by the Arabs. So the Targums of Jerusalem and Pseudo-Jonathan put here *Gabala* for *Seir*. The southern part is called Sherah.

9. *the father of the Edomites*] Lit. "the father of Edom," *i.e.* either "the father of the Edomites," or "the founder of Idumæa."

11. *Teman*] We read elsewhere of a district in Idumæa called Teman, famous for its wisdom (Jer. xlix. 7, 20; Amos i. 12; Hab. iii. 3); and in Job we meet with Eliphaz the Temanite, probably descended from this Teman, the son of Eliphaz, the son of Esau. Pliny ('H. N.' VI. 32) speaks of the Thimanæi in connection with Petra.

Omar] is compared by Knobel with the Beni Ammer in Southern Palestine and Northern Idumæa, and with the Amarin Arabs and the Amir Arabs, all mentioned by Seetzen, Burckhardt, and Robinson.

Zepho] Compare Zaphia, a place to the south of the Dead Sea (Knobel).

Kenaz] Compare Aneizeh, the name of an Arab tribe, and of a fortress to the north-east of Petra (Knobel).

12. *Amalek*] The ancestor of the Amalekites, who probably at an early period separated themselves from the rest of the Edom-

el; Nahath, and Zerah, Shammah, and Mizzah: these were the sons of Bashemath Esau's wife.

14 ¶ And these were the sons of Aholibamah, the daughter of Anah the daughter of Zibeon, Esau's wife: and she bare to Esau Jeush, and Jaalam, and Korah.

15 ¶ These *were* dukes of the sons of Esau: the sons of Eliphaz the firstborn *son* of Esau; duke Teman, duke Omar, duke Zepho, duke Kenaz,

16 Duke Korah, duke Gatam, *and* duke Amalek: these *are* the dukes *that came* of Eliphaz in the land of Edom; these *were* the sons of Adah.

17 ¶ And these *are* the sons of Reuel Esau's son; duke Nahath, duke Zerah, duke Shammah, duke Mizzah: these *are* the dukes *that came* of Reuel in the land of Edom; these *are* the sons of Bashemath Esau's wife.

18 ¶ And these *are* the sons of Aholibamah Esau's wife; duke Jeush, duke Jaalam, duke Korah: these *were* the dukes *that came* of Aholibamah the daughter of Anah, Esau's wife.

19 These *are* the sons of Esau, who *is* Edom, and these *are* their dukes.

20 ¶ [d] These *are* the sons of Seir the Horite, who inhabited the land; Lotan, and Shobal, and Zibeon, and Anah, [d] 1 Chron. 1. 38.

21 And Dishon, and Ezer, and Dishan: these *are* the dukes of the Horites, the children of Seir in the land of Edom.

22 And the children of Lotan were Hori and Hemam; and Lotan's sister *was* Timna.

23 And the children of Shobal *were* these; Alvan, and Manahath, and Ebal, Shepho, and Onam.

24 And these *are* the children of

---

ites, and formed a distinct and powerful tribe. The Arabs have a legend concerning an aboriginal tribe of Amalek, with whom it has been thought that the Edomitish Amalekites were fused. Nöldeke has a monograph on the Amalekites, in which he shews that the Arabian legends concerning them are drawn directly or indirectly from the Old Testament, and are utterly valueless when they depart from that only historical source. There is no authority in the Old Testament for the existence of this aboriginal tribe, except the mention in ch. xiv. 7 of "the country of the Amalekites." This name, however, is probably given by anticipation, not because the country was so called in Abraham's time, but because it had become known by that title before the time of Moses and the Exodus. The Amalekites, having their chief seat to the south of the mountains of Judah, as far as Kadesh (Num. xiii. 29, xiv. 43, 45), spread over the whole of the northern part of Arabia Petræa, from Havilah to Shur on the border of Egypt (1 S. xv. 3, 7, xxvii. 8); whilst one branch penetrated into the heart of Canaan (Judg. xii. 15).

13. *Nahath*] "A descent." Cp. with the valley of Akaba of like significance (Knob.).

Shammah] Cp. the Sameni, a tribe of Nomad Arabs mentioned by Steph. Byzant. (Knob.)

14. *Aholibamah*] See note A on vv. 2, 3 below.

Korah] Perhaps perpetuated in the modern tribe of Kurayeh (Knobel).

15. *dukes*] *i.e. duces*, leaders of tribes, phylarchs. The Hebrew *alluph* is connected with *eleph*, which signifies either "a thousand" or "a family." Hence Bochart and others understand here *chiliarchs*, leaders of thousands; whilst others, with more probability, understand *phylarchs*, heads of tribes or families, (see Ges. 'Thes.' pp. 105, 106). Rosenmüller thinks that the word is used metonymically for a family, and would render "These are the families (or tribes) of the sons of Esau." This interpretation would apply well throughout the catalogue, but does not so well correspond with the etymology and formation of the word.

16. *Duke Korah*] These words are omitted in one MS. in the Sam. Pent. and Version. They are considered as having crept in through a clerical error from v. 18, by Kennicott, Tuch, Knobel, Delitzsch, Keil, &c.

20. *sons of Seir the Horite*] The inhabitants of the country previously to the Edomitish invasion. The Horites (*i.e.* Troglodytes or dwellers in caves), mentioned ch. xiv. 6 as an independent people, were partly exterminated and partly subdued by Esau and his descendants (Deut. ii. 12, 22).

Lotan] is compared with *Leyathan*, the name of a fierce tribe in the neighbourhood of Petra (Knobel).

22. *Hemam*] Cp. *Homaima*, a place to the south of Petra (Knobel).

23. *Alvan*] Cp. the *Alawin*, a tribe of Arabs of evil notoriety to the north of Akaba (Knobel).

Zibeon; both Ajah, and Anah: this
was that Anah that found the mules
in the wilderness, as he fed the asses
of Zibeon his father.
25 And the children of Anah *were*
these; Dishon, and Aholibamah the
daughter of Anah.
26 And these *are* the children of
Dishon; Hemdan, and Eshban, and
Ithran, and Cheran.
27 The children of Ezer *are*
these; Bilhan, and Zaavan, and A-
kan.
28 The children of Dishan *are*
these; Uz, and Aran.
29 These *are* the dukes *that came*
of the Horites; duke Lotan, duke
Shobal, duke Zibeon, duke Anah,
30 Duke Dishon, duke Ezer, duke
Dishan: these *are* the dukes *that came*
of Hori, among their dukes in the
land of Seir.
31 ¶ And these *are* the kings that
reigned in the land of Edom, before
there reigned any king over the children of Israel.
32 And Bela the son of Beor
reigned in Edom: and the name of
his city *was* Dinhabah.
33 And Bela died, and Jobab the

Manahath] Ptolemy, v. 17, 3, mentions *Manychiates* west of Petra (Knobel).

Shepho] Cp. the hill *Shafeh* north of Akaba (Robinson, 'B. R.' I. 256; Knobel).

24. *Anah that found the mules*] **Anah that found the hot springs.** (See note on vv. 2, 3 below.) The Greek Versions do not translate the word *yemim* (the LXX. has τὸν Ἰαμείν). The Samaritan text has "the Emim," a gigantic people, with which agrees the Targum of Onkelos, "the giants." This is followed by Bochart, Patrick, and others. The Targum of Pseudo-Jonathan renders "mules," being followed herein by Saad., Kimchi, and many Rabbins, by Luther, and the Authorised Version. The Vulgate renders "warm waters," *aquas calidas*, and the Syriac has "waters," a rendering adopted by Gesen. (see 'Thes.' p. 586), Rosenm., Schumann, and most modern interpreters. There were many warm springs in this region, the most famous being Callirrhoe, in the Wady Zerka Maein, which some suppose to have been the very springs discovered by Anah.

31. *And these are the kings that reigned in the land of Edom, before there reigned any king over the children of Israel*] These words have led many to suppose that this and the following verses were a late interpolation, as, it is thought, they must have been written after kings had reigned in Israel. Spinoza argued from them that it was clearer than midday that the whole Pentateuch was written centuries after the time of Moses; a most illogical conclusion, for the utmost that could be inferred would be that (as Kennicott supposed) these verses were taken from 1 Chron. i. 43—54, and having been inserted in the margin of a very ancient MS. of Genesis, had crept into the text.

There is however nothing inconsistent with the Mosaic origin of the whole passage. In the last chapter (ch. xxxv. 11) there had been an emphatic promise from God Almighty (El-Shaddai) to Jacob that "kings should come out of his loins." The Israelites, no doubt, cherished a constant hope of such a kingdom and such a kingly race. Moses himself (Deut. xxviii. 36) prophesied concerning the king that the Israelites should set over them; and hence it was not unnatural that, when recording the eight kings, who had reigned in the family of Esau up to his own time, he should have noted that as yet no king had risen from the family of his brother Jacob, to whom a kingly progeny had been promised. The words in the original are "before the reigning of a king to the sons of Israel;" and might be rendered, "whilst as yet the children of Israel have no king;" there being nothing in the words expressive of a past tense, or indicating that before the writing of the sentence a king had reigned in Israel.

The other difficulty in the passage is chronological, it being thought that so many dukes and kings could not have succeeded one another in the period which elapsed from Esau to Moses. But there is no reason to suppose that the dukes, mentioned from v. 15 to 19, reigned in succession, then the kings from v. 31 to 39, and then again the dukes mentioned from v. 40 to 43. On the contrary, a comparison of Num. xx. 14 with Exod. xv. 15 shews, that a single king was reigning in Edom contemporaneously with several dukes or phylarchs. The dukes (as their title indicates) were not sovereigns of the whole of Idumæa, but princes or rulers of tribes or provinces: moreover the kings do not appear to have succeeded by inheritance, the son never succeeding to his father. Hence they were probably elected by the dukes.

33. *Jobab*] The LXX. and some of the fathers consider this to have been the same person as Job; and the mention of Eliphaz in v. 11 in connection with Teman, and of Elison of Zerah of Bozrah reigned in his stead.

34 And Jobab died, and Husham of the land of Temani reigned in his stead.

35 And Husham died, and Hadad the son of Bedad, who smote Midian in the field of Moab, reigned in his stead: and the name of his city *was* Avith.

36 And Hadad died, and Samlah of Masrekah reigned in his stead.

37 And Samlah died, and Saul of Rehoboth *by* the river reigned in his stead.

38 And Saul died, and Baal-hanan the son of Achbor reigned in his stead.

39 And Baal-hanan the son of Achbor died, and Hadar reigned in his stead: and the name of his city *was* Pau; and his wife's name *was* Mehetabel, the daughter of Matred, the daughter of Mezahab.

40 And these *are* the names of the dukes *that came* of Esau, according to their families, after their places, by their names; duke Timnah, duke Alvah, duke Jetheth,

41 Duke Aholibamah, duke Elah, duke Pinon,

42 Duke Kenaz, duke Teman, duke Mibzar,

43 Duke Magdiel, duke Iram: these *be* the dukes of Edom, according to their habitations in the land of their possession: he *is* Esau the father of † the Edomites.

† Heb. *Edom*.

---

phaz the Temanite in the book of Job favours this belief.

Bozrah] A famous city of Idumæa (see Isa. xxxiv. 6, lxiii. 1, &c.), remains of which are still traced in *El Buseireh*, a ruined village in *Jebal*. (Burckhardt, 'Syr.' 407; Robinson, II. 167.)

37. *Rehoboth by the river*] or *Rehoboth Hannahar*, so distinguished from *Rehoboth Ir*, ch. x. 11. The river here is probably the Euphrates.

39. *Hadar*] Called Hadad in 1 Chr. i. 50, and here also in the Samaritan text. He probably was living when Moses wrote, as no mention is made of his death, an argument for the Mosaic origin of this chapter; for Hadad could hardly have been living after the time of the kings of Israel, to which period those who from v. 31 consider it to be an interpolation would assign this genealogy, or perhaps the whole chapter.

40. *And these are the names of the dukes*, &c.] From comparing the words in this verse "after their places, by their names" with those in v. 43, "according to their habitations in the land of their possession," it is inferred with great probability, that this second catalogue of dukes is, not a catalogue of dukes who reigned subsequently to the kings of the preceding verses, nor a different version of the catalogue given in vv. 15 to 19, but rather a territorial catalogue, recounting, not the names, but the cities in which the various dukes or phylarchs before named had their seat of government. If so, we must render "the duke of Timnah, the duke of Alvah, the duke of Jetheth, &c." Two of the names in this list correspond with two in the former list, viz. Timnah and Kenaz, because, as it is supposed, the dukes Timnah and Kenaz called their cities after their own names. Aholibamah may have been a city called after the Horite princess (v. 25). (So Schumann, Knobel, Del., Keil, Kalisch, &c.).

43. *the father of the Edomites*] See on v. 9.

NOTE A on CHAP. XXXVI. VV. 2, 3.

Adah the daughter of Elon the Hittite, and Aholibamah the daughter of Anah, the daughter of Zibeon the Hivite; and Bashemath, Ishmael's daughter, sister of Nebajoth] The difficulty of reconciling this with the names of the three wives of Esau, as given in ch. xxvi. 34, xxviii. 3, will be seen by comparing the two accounts as follows:

Ch. xxvi. 34, xxviii. 9.

1. Judith, daughter of Beeri the Hittite.
2. Bashemath, daughter of Elon the Hittite.
3. Mahalath, daughter of Ishmael, sister to Nebaioth.

Ch. xxxvi. 2.

1. Aholibamah, daughter of Anah daughter of Zibeon the Hivite.
2. Adah, daughter of Elon the Hittite.
3. Bashemath, daughter of Ishmael, sister to Nebaioth.

From this table it appears that every one of the three wives is designated by a different name in the earlier history from that in the later genealogy. Yet there can be little doubt that 2 Bashemath the daughter of Elon = Adah the daughter of Elon, nor that 3 Mahalath = Bashemath, both being described as daughter of Ishmael, and sister of Nebaioth. We may therefore conclude also that 1 Judith = Aholibamah. This excludes the explanation suggested by several commentators, that the wives of Esau, named in ch. xxvi. 34 had died without offspring, and that Esau had married others. It seems far more probable that the one set of names were those which they bore in their father's house, the other set having been given to them by Esau, or by the Edomites, after they had become mothers of tribes.

1. The identity of Judith and Aholibamah may appear thus. Judith is called the daughter of Beeri the Hittite, whilst Aholibamah is called "the daughter of Anah, the daughter of Zibeon the Hivite." Anah was probably not the mother, but the father of Aholibamah, the second "daughter" being referrible back to Aholibamah, and not attributable to Anah (unless the reading of the Samaritan, LXX., and Syriac, "the son of Zibeon," be the right reading); for in v. 24 we find that Anah was the son of Zibeon, and the grandson of Seir the Horite. The reason why the same person has been called Anah and Beeri has been derived by Hengstenberg and others from the fact that Anah is said, in v. 24, to have discovered the hot springs, from which very probably he acquired the name of Beeri, *i.e. fontanus*, "the well-finder." A greater difficulty is apparent in his being called a "Hittite" (xxvi. 34), a "Hivite" (xxxvi. 2), and a "Horite" (xxxvi. 20). It is observed that these three words "Hittite," "Hivite," and "Horite," differ in Hebrew by one letter only, and that they were easily interchanged in transcription. It is, however, clear (from xxvii. 46) that Rebekah calls Judith a daughter of Heth. And from xxxvi. 20, 24, 25, that Aholibamah, the daughter of Anah, was a Horite. The difficulty seems therefore rather to admit of solution by saying that Hittite (like Amorite) was a generic name for a large portion of the Canaanitish people, comprehending both Hivites and Horites. It is not improbable that Hivite in v. 2 may be an error of transcription for Horite (חוי for חרי), in which case we have only to conclude that the Horites of Mount Seir were reckoned by Isaac and Rebecca as among the Hittite inhabitants of Canaan. If, however, the reading Hivite be correct, it is not impossible that the Hivites, a southern people, may originally have come from Mount Seir, and have been dwellers in its rocky fastnesses, which is the meaning of the word Horite (troglodyte, dweller in caves). If this be correct, then we must conclude that Judith the daughter of Anah, called Beeri, from his finding the hot springs, and the granddaughter of Zibeon the Horite, one of the tribes reckoned in the great Hittite family, when she married Esau, assumed the name of Aholibamah ("the tent of the height").

2. Bashemath is described exactly as Adah is, *i.e.* as the daughter of Elon the Hittite. There is no difficulty here except in the change of name into Adah, "ornament," a change not improbable for Esau to have made.

3. In the same manner Mahalath is the daughter of Ishmael the sister of Nebaioth, and Bashemath is the daughter of Ishmael the sister of Nebaioth. There would be no difficulty in this, except that Bashemath, the second name of the daughter of Ishmael, is the same with the first name of the daughter of Elon the Hittite. If this seems to some irreconcileable with probability, it may be ascribed to an error of transcription, likely enough to occur in the writing out of genealogies, and the Samaritan text reads Mahalath in the genealogy as well as in the history.

CHAPTER XXXVII.

2 Joseph is hated of his brethren. 5 His two dreams. 13 Jacob sendeth him to visit his brethren. 18 His brethren conspire his death. 21 Reuben saveth him. 26 They sell him to the Ishmeelites. 31 His father, deceived by the bloody coat, mourneth for him. 36 He is sold to Potiphar in Egypt.

AND Jacob dwelt in the land
†wherein his father was a stranger, † Heb. *of his father's sojournings.*
in the land of Canaan.
2 These *are* the generations of Jacob. Joseph, *being* seventeen years
old, was feeding the flock with his
brethren; and the lad *was* with the

CHAP. XXXVII. 1. *And Jacob dwelt in the land*, &c.] Ch. xxxv. concluded the history of Isaac. Ch. xxxvi. disposed of the history of Esau and his descendants down to the very time of the Exodus. (See on ch. xxxvi. 39.) This first verse of ch. xxxvii. now lands us in the time and place, from whence the succeeding history is to begin. **Jacob dwelt in the land of his father's sojournings, in the land of Canaan.** Esau had left Canaan to Jacob, who after their father's death became the sojourner in the land, which his posterity were to possess.

2. *These are the generations of Jacob.*] The *Toledoth*, or genealogical history of Isaac began (ch. xxv. 19) after the death of his father Abraham, a few verses having been allotted (vv. 12—18) to dispose of the history of his brother Ishmael. In the same manner, the *Toledoth* of Jacob are given in this chapter after the death of his father Isaac, ch. xxxvi. having intervened to account for Esau and his family. Many of the preceding chapters had been occupied with the history of Jacob and his sons, but Jacob's *Toledoth* begin at this point, because now he has become

sons of Bilhah, and with the sons of Zilpah, his father's wives: and Joseph
brought unto his father their evil report.
3 Now Israel loved Joseph more
than all his children, because he *was*
the son of his old age: and he made
him a coat of *many* ‖colours. (‖ Or, *pieces.*)
4 And when his brethren saw that
their father loved him more than all
his brethren, they hated him, and
could not speak peaceably unto him.
5 ¶ And Joseph dreamed a dream,
and he told *it* his brethren: and they
hated him yet the more.
6 And he said unto them, Hear, I
pray you, this dream which I have
dreamed:
7 For, behold, we *were* binding
sheaves in the field, and, lo, my sheaf
arose, and also stood upright; and, behold, your sheaves stood round about,
and made obeisance to my sheaf.
8 And his brethren said to him,
Shalt thou indeed reign over us? or
shalt thou indeed have dominion over
us? And they hated him yet the
more for his dreams, and for his
words.
9 ¶ And he dreamed yet another
dream, and told it his brethren, and
said, Behold, I have dreamed a dream
more; and, behold, the sun and the
moon and the eleven stars made obeisance to me.
10 And he told *it* to his father,
and to his brethren: and his father

---

the sole head and father of the chosen seed. The *Toledoth*, or family history, of Jacob continues now till his death ch. l.

2. *Joseph, being seventeen years old.*] This history goes back a few years; for Isaac must have been living when Joseph was seventeen. (See note at the end of ch. xxxi.) But the historian had fully wound up the history of Isaac, before commencing the *Toledoth* of Jacob; and he now gives unity to the history of the descent into Egypt by beginning with the adolescence of Joseph, his father's fondness for him, and his brothers' jealousy of him.

3. *the son of his old age*] It is not impossible that the greater part of this narrative may have been chronologically before the birth of Benjamin and the death of Rachel, related in ch. xxxv. 18.

coat of many colours] (1). The LXX. Vulg. and most modern versions render a garment made of different pieces, of patchwork, and so of many colours. In the well-known scene from the tomb of Chnoumhotep at Beni Hassan, a tomb of the XIIth dynasty, the Semitic visitors who are offering presents to the Governor are dressed in robes of rich colouring, apparently formed of separate small pieces or patches sewn together. There is an excellent engraving and explanation in Brugsch, 'Histoire d'Egypte,' p. 63.

(2). The versions of Aquila, Symm., Syr. render a tunic with sleeves or fringes extending to both hands and feet, *tunica manicata et talaris* (see Hieron. 'Qu.' ad h. l.), which is the interpretation adopted by most modern Hebraists (see Ges. 'Thes.' p. 1117). We find Thamar, the daughter of David, wearing this same dress (2 S. xiii. 18): and Josephus ('Ant.' vii. 8. 1) speaks of long garments reaching to the hands and ankles as worn by Jewish maidens. But the engraving at Beni Hassan just mentioned makes the former interpretation (1) the more probable.

It has been thought by some that Jacob, in his anger at the sins of his elder sons, especially of Reuben his firstborn, and in his partiality for Joseph, the firstborn of Rachel, designed to give him the right of primogeniture, that this robe was the token of birthright, and perhaps even designating the priestly office of the head of the family. (See Heidegger, Tom. II. p. 581. Braunius 'de Vestitu sacerdotali,' pp. 473 sqq., Kurtz, Vol. I. p. 378, Clark's translation, Blunt, 'Undesigned Coincidences,' p. 15.)

7. *we were binding sheaves in the field*] It appears from this, that Jacob was not a mere nomad, but, like his father Isaac (ch. xxvi. 12), had adopted agricultural as well as pastoral employments.

10. *his father rebuked him*] Joseph may have told the dream in the simplicity of his heart, or perhaps he may have been elated by his father's partiality and by "the abundance of the revelations" (2 Cor. xii. 7).

thy mother] It is possible that Rachel may have been living now, for neither the date of the dream nor of Rachel's death are clearly given. The dream may have been some time before the selling of Joseph, and is only related here as one of the reasons which caused his brethren to hate him. If, however, Rachel was dead, we must then understand Jacob to mean by "thy mother" either Leah, who would be his step-mother, or perhaps more likely Bilhah, who was Rachel's handmaid, and at once nurse and step-mother to Joseph; and it is not impossible that in either Leah or Bilhah the dream may have been fulfilled; for we do not know whether they were

rebuked him, and said unto him,
What *is* this dream that thou hast
dreamed? Shall I and thy mother
and thy brethren indeed come to bow
down ourselves to thee to the earth?
11 And his brethren envied him;
but his father observed the saying.
12 ¶ And his brethren went to feed
their father's flock in Shechem.
13 And Israel said unto Joseph,
Do not thy brethren feed *the flock*
in Shechem? come, and I will send
thee unto them. And he said to
him, Here *am I*.
14 And he said to him, Go, I pray
thee, † see whether it be well with thy
brethren, and well with the flocks;
and bring me word again. So he
sent him out of the vale of Hebron,
and he came to Shechem.
15 ¶ And a certain man found
him, and, behold, *he was* wandering
in the field: and the man asked him,
saying, What seekest thou?
16 And he said, I seek my brethren: tell me, I pray thee, where
they feed *their flocks*.
17 And the man said, They are
departed hence; for I heard them say,
Let us go to Dothan. And Joseph
went after his brethren, and found
them in Dothan.
18 And when they saw him afar
off, even before he came near unto
them, they conspired against him to
slay him.
19 And they said one to another,
Behold, this † dreamer cometh.
20 Come now therefore, and let
us slay him, and cast him into some
pit, and we will say, Some evil beast
hath devoured him: and we shall see
what will become of his dreams.
21 And [a] Reuben heard *it*, and he
delivered him out of their hands; and
said, Let us not kill him.
22 And Reuben said unto them,
Shed no blood, *but* cast him into this
pit that *is* in the wilderness, and lay
no hand upon him; that he might rid
him out of their hands, to deliver him
to his father again.
23 ¶ And it came to pass, when
Joseph was come unto his brethren,
that they stript Joseph out of his
coat, *his* coat of *many* ‖ colours that
was on him;
24 And they took him, and cast
him into a pit: and the pit *was* empty,
there was no water in it.

† Heb. *see the peace of thy brethren, &c.*

† Heb. *master of dreams.*

[a] chap. 42. 22.

‖ Or, *pieces.*

---

alive or not when Jacob went down into Egypt.

14. *out of the vale of Hebron, and he came to Shechem*] It appears from this that Jacob was now dwelling in the neighbourhood of Hebron where his father Isaac was still living (see on v. 3). After the slaughter of the Shechemites (see ch. xxxiv.) Jacob journeyed southward; but from the fact that his sons were sent to feed sheep in Shechem, it is not impossible that he may have left some of his cattle still in their old pastures, and his anxiety here about his sons, who were thus feeding in Shechem, may have arisen in part from the enmity excited against them in that neighbourhood by their violence. In ch. xxxv. we trace Jacob's southward journeyings from Shechem first to Bethel, v. 6; then to Bethlehem, vv. 16, 19; then to the tower of Edar, v. 21; and finally to Hebron, v. 27, where Isaac died, v. 29. But from this verse, ch. xxxvii. 14, we infer that Jacob must have arrived at Hebron several years before his father's death.

17. *Dothan*] or *Dothain*, the two wells or cisterns. They may have gone there because of the water in these wells. Dothan is said (Euseb. 'Onomasticon') to have been twelve Roman miles north of Sebaste (*i.e.* Shechem or Samaria) towards the plain of Jezreel. It still retains its ancient name (Robinson, 'B. R.' III. 122).

20. *some pit*] A cistern, or well, dug by the shepherds of the country, to catch and preserve the rain-water. Some of these cisterns were very deep, and a lad thrown into one of them would have been unable to escape.

24. *the pit was empty, there was no water in it*] Apparently referred to by Zech. ix. 11, in a prophecy of the Messiah. Joseph has been recognised by most Christian interpreters as a type of Christ; in his father's love for him, in his being sent to his brethren, rejected by them, sold to the Gentiles, delivered to death, in the sanctity of his life, in his humiliation, in his exaltation to be a Prince and a Saviour, in that his father and mother and brethren all came and bowed down to him. We may notice here, that the counsels of his brethren to prevent the fulfilment of his dreams, like the counsels of Herod and the Jews to prevent the fulfilment of the prophecies con-

25 And they sat down to eat bread: and they lifted up their eyes and looked, and, behold, a company of Ishmeelites came from Gilead with their camels bearing spicery and balm and myrrh, going to carry *it* down to Egypt.

26 And Judah said unto his brethren, What profit *is it* if we slay our brother, and conceal his blood?

27 Come, and let us sell him to the Ishmeelites, and let not our hand be upon him; for he *is* our brother *and* our flesh. And his brethren †were content.

† Heb. *hearkened.*

28 Then there passed by Midianites merchantmen; and they drew and lifted up Joseph out of the pit, [b]and sold Joseph to the Ishmeelites for twenty *pieces* of silver: and they brought Joseph into Egypt.

[b] Psal. 105. 17. Wisd. 10. 13. Acts 7. 9.

29 ¶ And Reuben returned unto the pit; and, behold, Joseph *was* not in the pit; and he rent his clothes.

30 And he returned unto his brethren, and said, The child *is* not; and I, whither shall I go?

31 And they took Joseph's coat, and killed a kid of the goats, and dipped the coat in the blood;

32 And they sent the coat of *many* colours, and they brought *it* to their father; and said, This have we found: know now whether it *be* thy son's coat or no.

33 And he knew it, and said, *It is* my son's coat; an [c]evil beast hath devoured him; Joseph is without doubt rent in pieces.

[c] chap. 44. 28.

34 And Jacob rent his clothes, and put sackcloth upon his loins, and mourned for his son many days.

35 And all his sons and all his daughters rose up to comfort him; but he refused to be comforted; and he said, For I will go down into the grave unto my son mourning. Thus his father wept for him.

---

cerning Jesus, only served to bring about God's counsels, which were wrought out by the very means taken to defeat them. If Joseph had not been sold to the Midianites, he would never have been exalted to be governor in Egypt. If Christ had not been persecuted and at last crucified, He would not have worked out redemption for us, have risen from the dead, and ascended up into His glory.

25. *they sat down to eat bread*] In this heartless meal Reuben can have taken no part. It appears from verse 29, that he must have left his brethren, perhaps with the very purpose of seeking means to rescue Joseph. The simplicity and truthfulness of the narrative are all the more apparent by the indifference of the writer to the question how and why it was that Reuben was absent at this point of the history. A forger would have been likely to tell all about it, and make it all plain. Yet strangely enough, this very artlessness has been made an argument against the historical truth of the narrative, as being clumsily arranged, and inconsistent in these details.

25. *a company of Ishmeelites*] "A travelling company" or "caravan." Ishmaelites afterwards called Midianites in v. 28, and Medanim in v. 36. See note on ch. xxv. 2. Medan and Midian were sons of Abraham by Keturah; Ishmael his son by Hagar. The Ishmaelites and Midianites were near neighbours, and very probably joined together in caravans and commercial enterprizes. Very probably too the Ishmaelites, being the more powerful tribe, may have by this time become a general name for several smaller and associated tribes.

spicery] probably "storax," the gum of the styrax-tree. So Aqu. followed by Bochart, 'Hieroz.' II. p. 532, Gesen. 'Thes.' p. 883, &c. The LXX. and Vulg. give only "perfumes."

balm] Probably the gum of the opobalsam or balsam-tree, which grew abundantly in Gilead, and was especially used for healing wounds. This is the interpretation commonly given by the Jews, and adopted by Bochart ('Hieroz.' I. 628); Celsius ('Hierob.' II. 180); Ges. 'Thes.' 1185, &c.). Lee (Lex. in loc.) contends for "mastich" as the right rendering.

myrrh] According to almost all modern interpreters Ladanum, an odoriferous gum found on the leaves of the *cistus creticus* or *cistus ladanifera*. (See Celsius, 'Hierob.' I. 280—288, Gesen. 'Thes.' p. 748, Smith, 'Dict. of Bible,' s.v. *Myrrh*.)

27. *were content*] **hearkened.**

35. *his daughters*] See on ch. xxx. 21.

into the grave] **To sheol.** He thought his son devoured by wild beasts, therefore the word *Sheol* translated "grave" must here mean the place of the departed. The word appears to signify a hollow subterraneous place (comp. *hell*, *hole*, &c.). (See Ges. 'Thes.' p. 1348.)

36 And the Midianites sold him
into Egypt unto Potiphar, an †officer
of Pharaoh's, *and* †‖captain of the
guard.

† Heb. *eunuch.* But the word doth signify not only *eunuchs*, but also *chamberlains, courtiers*, and *officers*.
† Heb. *chief of the slaughter-men*, or, *executioners.*
‖ Or, *chief marshal.*

CHAPTER XXXVIII.

1 *Judah begetteth Er, Onan, and Shelah.* 6 *Er marrieth Tamar.* 8 *The trespass of Onan.* 11 *Tamar stayeth for Shelah.* 13 *She deceiveth Judah.* 27 *She beareth twins, Pharez and Zarah.*

AND it came to pass at that time,
that Judah went down from his
brethren, and turned in to a certain
Adullamite, whose name *was* Hirah.
2 And Judah saw there a daughter
of a certain Canaanite, whose name
was [a] Shuah; and he took her, and [a] 1 Chron. 2. 3.
went in unto her.
3 And she conceived, and bare a
son; and he called his name Er.
4 [b] And she conceived again, and [b] Numb. 26. 19.
bare a son; and she called his name
Onan.
5 And she yet again conceived,
and bare a son; and called his name
Shelah: and he was at Chezib, when
she bare him.
6 And Judah took a wife for Er

---

36. *Potiphar*] Generally supposed to be the same as Potiphera, *i.e.* "devoted to Ra," the Sun-God. (See Ges. 'Thes.,' p. 1094.) It is far more probably "devoted to Par or Phar," *i.e.* to the Royal House or Palace. (See 'Excursus on Egyptian Words' at the end of this volume.)

an officer of Pharaoh's] Heb. "an eunuch;" but used also of chamberlains and other officers about the court. The immediate predecessor in Manetho of Sesostris, who was of the same dynasty with Joseph's Pharaoh, was slain by his eunuchs.

captain of the guard] **Chief of the executioners**, or "commander of the body guard," who executed the sentences of the king. (Cp. 2 K. xxv. 8; Jer. xxxix. 9, lii. 12.) Herod. (II. 168) tells us that "a thousand Calasirians and the same number of Hermotybians formed in alternate years the body-guard of the king" of Egypt.

CHAP. XXXVIII. **1.** *it came to pass at that time*] This chapter may appear to be an useless digression inserted at an inconvenient time; but in reality it supplies a very important link, and this was probably the best place for its introduction. In the *Toledoth*, or family history, of Jacob, the two chief persons were Joseph and Judah; Joseph from his high character, his personal importance, his influence in the future destinies of the race, and his typical foreshadowing of the Messiah; Judah, from his obtaining the virtual right of primogeniture, and from his being the ancestor of David and of the Son of David. Hence, at a natural pause in the history of Joseph, viz. when he had been now sold into Egypt and settled in Potiphar's house, the historian recurs to the events in the family of Judah, which he carries down to the birth of Pharez, the next link in the ancestry of the Saviour. Thus he clears away all that was necessary to be told of the history of the twelve patriarchs, with the exception of that which was involved in the history of Joseph. There is also a remarkable contrast brought vividly out by this juxtaposition of the impure line of Judah and his children with the chastity and moral integrity of Joseph as seen in the succeeding chapter.

at that time] It is by no means certain that this note of time is to be immediately connected with the events in the last chapter. The strict chronological sequence in these *Toledoth* is not always followed. Episodes, like the genealogies of Ishmael and Esau above referred to, are introduced here and there, in order to avoid interrupting the general order of another narrative, and so this episode of the history of Judah is brought in to prevent an interruption in the history of Joseph. If the chronology in note at the end of ch. xxxi. be adopted, Judah would have been at least 26 at the time of Jacob's flight from Padan-aram, and from that time to the going down to Egypt there would be an interval of 33 years.

went down from his brethren] *i.e.* went southward (Abenezra, Rosenm. &c.).

Adullamite] Adullam, a place afterwards famous in the history of David, 1 S. xxii. 1 (see also Josh. xii. 15; 2 S. xxiii. 13; 1 Chr. xi. 15; 2 Chr. xi. 7; Micah i. 15), is mentioned by Jerome as existing in his day, then a small village to the east of Eleutheropolis. It must have lain in the southern part of the plain of Judah, but its site has not been discovered by modern travellers.

2. *a certain Canaanite, whose name was Shuah*] Shuah was the name of the father of Judah's wife, not of the wife herself, as appears from the Hebrew and from v. 12. This marriage of Judah with one of the daughters of the land was the fruitful source of sin and misery in his family.

5. *at Chezib*] Probably the same as Achzib mentioned with Adullam, Mic. i. 14, 15.

his firstborn, whose name *was* Tamar.
7 And [c] Er, Judah's firstborn, was
wicked in the sight of the LORD; and
the LORD slew him.
8 And Judah said unto Onan, Go
in unto thy brother's wife, and marry
her, and raise up seed to thy brother.
9 And Onan knew that the seed
should not be his; and it came to
pass, when he went in unto his brother's wife, that he spilled *it* on the
ground, lest that he should give seed
to his brother.
10 And the thing which he did
† displeased the LORD: wherefore he
slew him also.
11 Then said Judah to Tamar his
daughter in law, Remain a widow at
thy father's house, till Shelah my son
be grown: for he said, Lest peradventure he die also, as his brethren
did. And Tamar went and dwelt in
her father's house.
12 ¶ And † in process of time the
daughter of Shuah Judah's wife died;
and Judah was comforted, and went
up unto his sheepshearers to Timnath, he and his friend Hirah the
Adullamite.
13 And it was told Tamar, saying,
Behold thy father in law goeth up to
Timnath to shear his sheep.
14 And she put her widow's garments off from her, and covered her
with a vail, and wrapped herself, and
sat in † an open place, which *is* by the
way to Timnath; for she saw that
Shelah was grown, and she was not
given unto him to wife.
15 When Judah saw her, he thought
her *to be* an harlot; because she had
covered her face.
16 And he turned unto her by the
way, and said, Go to, I pray thee,
let me come in unto thee; (for he
knew not that she *was* his daughter
in law.) And she said, What wilt
thou give me, that thou mayest come
in unto me?
17 And he said, I will send *thee*
† a kid from the flock. And she said,
Wilt thou give *me* a pledge, till thou
send *it?*

[c] Numb. 26. 19.

† Heb. *was evil in the eyes of the LORD.*

† Heb. *the days were multiplied.*

† Heb. *the door of eyes, or, of Enajim.*

† Heb. *a kid of the goats.*

---

6. *Tamar*] *i.e.* "a palm-tree."

8. *raise up seed to thy brother*] As this was before the law of Moses, it would appear probable that this *lex leviratus*, law of marriage with a brother's widow, rested on some traditional custom, very probably among the Chaldees. The law of Moses did not abolish it, but gave rules concerning it (Deut. xxv. 5), as was the case as regards many other ancient practices. This law of levirate marriage prevailed among Indian, Persian, African, and some Italian races (Diod. Sic. XII. 18).

11. *Then said Judah to Tamar*] Judah perhaps superstitiously seems to have thought Tamar in some way the cause of his son's death (cp. Tobit iii. 7); or he may have thought Shelah too young to marry.

12. *Timnath*] Probably not the border town of Dan and Judah, between Ekron and Beth Shemesh (Josh. xv. 10), but Timnah in the mountains of Judah (Josh. xv. 57).

his friend] The LXX., and Vulg. have "his shepherd," but Onkelos, Syr., Arab. and most modern interpreters, render as the Authorised Version, which is probably right.

14. *in an open place*] **In the gate of Enaim.** So the LXX., Jerome (in 'Loc. Heb.'), Gesen., Winer and most modern interpreters. Enaim is probably the same as Enam, Josh. xv. 34. Enam is a place in the plain which lay on the road from Judah's dwelling-place to Timnath (Knobel). Other possible renderings are "at the opening of the eyes," *i.e.* in a public place, such as "the crossing of two roads," (so Vulg., Syr., and many Jewish interpreters); and "at the breaking forth of two fountains" (so Abenezra, Rosenm. and others): but the first is pretty certainly the true.

15. *an harlot; because she had covered her face*] Probably Judah thought her to be a woman having a vow. In v. 21, he calls her by a title translated "harlot," meaning literally "consecrated," *i.e.* to the impure worship of Astarte, as was the custom of Babylon in the worship of Mylitta (Herod. I. 199). This abominable worship was very early introduced into Canaan and Egypt. So *Kedeshah*, "a consecrated woman," appears to have come into use as a kind of euphemism. The veil probably led Judah to think her thus under a vow: for there is no reason to suppose that mere profligates so covered their faces (see Ges. 'Thes.' p. 1197). The worship of the *Dea Syra* at Byblos is recorded at a very early age. In the time of Rameses II. it was already very ancient.

18 And he said, What pledge shall I give thee? And she said, Thy signet, and thy bracelets, and thy staff that *is* in thine hand. And he gave *it* her, and came in unto her, and she conceived by him.

19 And she arose, and went away, and laid by her vail from her, and put on the garments of her widowhood.

20 And Judah sent the kid by the hand of his friend the Adullamite, to receive *his* pledge from the woman's hand: but he found her not.

21 Then he asked the men of that place, saying, Where *is* the harlot, that *was* ‖ openly by the way side? And they said, There was no harlot in this *place*.

‖ Or, *in Enajim.*

22 And he returned to Judah, and said, I cannot find her; and also the men of the place said, *that* there was no harlot in this *place*.

23 And Judah said, Let her take *it* to her, lest we † be shamed: behold, I sent this kid, and thou hast not found her.

† Heb. *become a contempt.*

24 ¶ And it came to pass about three months after, that it was told Judah, saying, Tamar thy daughter in law hath played the harlot; and also, behold, she *is* with child by whoredom. And Judah said, Bring her forth, and let her be burnt.

25 When she *was* brought forth, she sent to her father in law, saying, By the man, whose these *are*, *am* I with child: and she said, Discern, I pray thee, whose *are* these, the signet, and bracelets, and staff.

26 And Judah acknowledged *them*, and said, She hath been more righteous than I; because that I gave her not to Shelah my son. And he knew her again no more.

27 ¶ And it came to pass in the time of her travail, that, behold, twins *were* in her womb.

28 And it came to pass, when she travailed, that *the one* put out *his* hand: and the midwife took and bound upon his hand a scarlet thread, saying, This came out first.

29 And it came to pass, as he drew back his hand, that, behold, his brother came out: and she said, ‖ How hast thou broken forth? *this* breach *be* upon thee: therefore his name was called ‖ [d] Pharez.

‖ Or, *Wherefore hast thou made* this *breach against thee?*
‖ That is, *a breach.*
d 1 Chron. 2. 4. Matt. 1. 3.

30 And afterward came out his brother, that had the scarlet thread upon his hand: and his name was called Zarah.

CHAPTER XXXIX.

1 *Joseph advanced in Potiphar's house.* 7 *He resisteth his mistress's temptation.* 13 *He is falsely accused.* 20 *He is cast in prison.* 21 *God is with him there.*

AND Joseph was brought down to Egypt; and Potiphar, an officer of Pharaoh, captain of the guard, an Egyptian, bought him of the hands

---

18. *Thy signet*] A seal or signet-ring. The ancients wore it sometimes, not as a ring on the finger, but hanging round the neck by a cord or chain (Ges. 'Thes.' p. 534).

thy bracelets] **Thy cord**: the cord or string by which the seal was suspended (so Ges., Rosenm., Schum., Lee).

staff] It was probably of considerable value, as among the Babylonians, and on Egyptian monuments.

21. *openly*] **At Enaim.** See on v. 14.

26. *She has been more righteous than I*] Judah acknowledges that he had done wrong to Tamar in not giving her his son Shelah, according to the *lex leviratus*, that the brother should raise up seed to his brother. It appears further from Ruth ch. iii. iv. that, according to the patriarchal custom, the nearest of kin was to take the widow to wife, hence when Shelah does not take her, she considers Judah the right person with whom to form such an alliance.

29. *How hast thou broken forth? this breach be upon thee*] Or, "why hast thou made a rent for thyself?" or "hast rent a rent for thyself?"

Pharez] *i.e.* "breach" or "breaking forth."

30. *Zarah*] *i.e.* "rising."

Chap. XXXIX. 1. *And Joseph was brought down to Egypt*, &c.] A recapitulation of the narrative in ch. xxxvii. 36, which had been interrupted by the history of Judah's family in ch. xxxviii.

Ishmeelites] See on ch. xxxvii. 25.

of the Ishmeelites, which had brought him down thither.

2 And the LORD was with Joseph, and he was a prosperous man; and he was in the house of his master the Egyptian.

3 And his master saw that the LORD *was* with him, and that the LORD made all that he did to prosper in his hand.

4 And Joseph found grace in his sight, and he served him: and he made him overseer over his house, and all *that* he had he put into his hand.

5 And it came to pass from the time *that* he had made him overseer in his house, and over all that he had, that the LORD blessed the Egyptian's house for Joseph's sake; and the blessing of the LORD was upon all that he had in the house, and in the field.

6 And he left all that he had in Joseph's hand; and he knew not ought he had, save the bread which he did eat. And Joseph was *a* goodly *person*, and well favoured.

7 ¶ And it came to pass after these things, that his master's wife cast her eyes upon Joseph; and she said, Lie with me.

8 But he refused, and said unto his master's wife, Behold, my master wotteth not what *is* with me in the house, and he hath committed all that he hath to my hand;

9 *There is* none greater in this house than I; neither hath he kept back any thing from me but thee, because thou *art* his wife: how then can I do this great wickedness, and sin against God?

10 And it came to pass, as she spake to Joseph day by day, that he hearkened not unto her, to lie by her, *or* to be with her.

11 And it came to pass about this time, that *Joseph* went into the house to do his business; and *there was* none of the men of the house there within.

12 And she caught him by his garment, saying, Lie with me: and he left his garment in her hand, and fled, and got him out.

13 And it came to pass, when she

---

2. *the* LORD *was with Joseph*] The variety in the use of the Divine names in the history of Joseph is very observable. The name JEHOVAH occurs only where the narrator is speaking in his own person; until we come to ch. xlix. where Jacob uses it in the midst of his blessing on Dan, ch. xlix. 18. In all other speeches in the history we have Elohim, sometimes Ha-Elohim with the article, and sometimes El, or Ha-El. The reason of this is generally apparent. The whole history, though given by an inspired writer to whom the name JEHOVAH was familiar, concerns the history of Joseph and his kindred in contact with a heathen people. It is therefore on all accounts natural that the general name Elohim, and not the specially revealed name JEHOVAH, should be used in dialogue. Even the narrative, as in ch. xlvi., is most naturally carried on in a so-called Elohistic form, the name Elohim being of common use to both Hebrews and Egyptians. The adoption of the name *El* (or Ha-El) in xlvi. 3, is probably with marked reference to the blessing on Abraham pronounced in the name of *El-Shaddai* in ch. xvii. 1.

4. *overseer*] The Egyptian sculptures represent the property of rich men as superintended by scribes or stewards, who are exhibited as carefully registering all the operations of the household, the garden, the field, &c.

6. *Joseph was a goodly person, and well favoured*] Lit. "was fair of form and fair of aspect," or "appearance."

7. *his master's wife*] The licentiousness of the Egyptian women has always been complained of (see Herod. II. 111; Diod. I. 59). The same appears from the monuments, which prove also that women did not live so retired a life in Egypt as in other ancient and especially Eastern countries (Wilkinson, Vol. II. p. 389, Hengstenb. 'Egypt.' p. 26). There is a very remarkable resemblance between this passage in the history of Joseph and a very ancient Egyptian Romance in the Papyrus d'Orbiney in the British Museum, called "The Two Brothers," in which the wife of the elder brother acts in the same manner and uses almost the same words towards the younger brother as Potiphar's wife uses towards Joseph (see Ebers, 'Ægypten,' p. 311).

9. *sin against God*] The direct sin would have been against his master; but Joseph clearly recognized that the true guilt of all sin consists in its breach of the law, and disobedience to the will of God.

saw that he had left his garment in
her hand, and was fled forth,
14 That she called unto the men
of her house, and spake unto them,
saying, See, he hath brought in an
Hebrew unto us to mock us; he came
in unto me to lie with me, and I cried
with a †loud voice:
15 And it came to pass, when he
heard that I lifted up my voice and
cried, that he left his garment with
me, and fled, and got him out.
16 And she laid up his garment
by her, until his lord came home.
17 And she spake unto him according to these words, saying, The Hebrew servant, which thou hast brought
unto us, came in unto me to mock me:
18 And it came to pass, as I lifted
up my voice and cried, that he left his
garment with me, and fled out.
19 And it came to pass, when his
master heard the words of his wife,
which she spake unto him, saying,
After this manner did thy servant to
me; that his wrath was kindled.
20 And Joseph's master took him,
and put him into the prison, a place
where the king's prisoners *were* bound:
and he was there in the prison.
21 ¶ But the LORD was with Joseph, and †shewed him mercy, and
gave him favour in the sight of the
keeper of the prison.
22 And the keeper of the prison
committed to Joseph's hand all the
prisoners that *were* in the prison; and
whatsoever they did there, he was the
doer *of it*.
23 The keeper of the prison looked
not to anything *that was* under his
hand; because the LORD was with
him, and *that* which he did, the LORD
made *it* to prosper.

† Heb. *great.*

† Heb. *extended kindness unto him.*

CHAPTER XL.

1 The butler and baker of Pharaoh in prison. 4 Joseph hath charge of them. 5 He interpreteth their dreams. 20 They come to pass according to his interpretation. 23 The ingratitude of the butler.

AND it came to pass after these
things, *that* the butler of the
king of Egypt and *his* baker had offended their lord the king of Egypt.
2 And Pharaoh was wroth against
two *of* his officers, against the chief
of the butlers, and against the chief
of the bakers.
3 And he put them in ward in the
house of the captain of the guard,
into the prison, the place where Joseph *was* bound.

---

20. *prison*] The word here used occurs only here and in ch. xl. It probably means a turret or rounded (perhaps arched) building or apartment, arched or rounded for strength, used as a prison or dungeon. It appears from ch. xl. 3, to have been a part of the house of the captain of the guard or chief of the executioners, in which the state prisoners were kept, and to have had a special jailer or keeper of the prison, an officer of the chief of the executioners, placed over it. In ch. xl. 15, Joseph speaks of it as "a dungeon" or pit, which would quite correspond with the character of an arched or vaulted room. In Ps. cv. 17, 18, the imprisonment of Joseph is represented as having been very severe, "whose feet they afflicted with the fetters, the iron entered into his soul." It is most probable that at first Joseph's treatment may have been of this character, the crime with which he was charged having been such that a slave would most likely have been instantly put to death for it. By degrees, however, he gained, under God's Providence, the confidence of the jailer (v. 22), when the rigour of his confinement was mitigated, and at length the chief of the executioners himself (either Potiphar, or, as some think, his successor) intrusts him with the care of important state prisoners. The fact that Joseph was not put to death, and by degrees treated kindly in prison, has given rise to the conjecture, that Potiphar did not wholly believe his wife's story, though he to a certain extent acted on it (Cleric in loc., Keil, &c.).

CHAP. XL. 2. *the chief of the butlers*] **The chief of the cupbearers.** The office of cupbearer to the sovereign was one of importance and high honour in the East. See Herod. III. 34.

chief of the bakers] or "confectioners." The Targum of Pseudo-Jonathan adds that "they had taken counsel to throw the poison of death into his food and into his drink, to kill their master, the king of Mizraim." This is probably only a conjecture from the fact that the two offending persons were immediately concerned with the food and the drink of the king.

4 And the captain of the guard
charged Joseph with them, and he
served them: and they continued a
season in ward.
5 ¶ And they dreamed a dream
both of them, each man his dream in
one night, each man according to the
interpretation of his dream, the butler
and the baker of the king of Egypt,
which *were* bound in the prison.
6 And Joseph came in unto them
in the morning, and looked upon them,
and, behold, they *were* sad.
7 And he asked Pharaoh's officers
that *were* with him in the ward of his
lord's house, saying, Wherefore †look
ye *so* sadly to day?

† Heb. are *your faces evil?*

8 And they said unto him, We
have dreamed a dream, and *there is*
no interpreter of it. And Joseph said
unto them, *Do* not interpretations *be-*
long to God? tell me *them*, I pray you.
9 And the chief butler told his
dream to Joseph, and said to him, In
my dream, behold, a vine *was* before
me;
10 And in the vine *were* three
branches: and it *was* as though it
budded, *and* her blossoms shot forth;
and the clusters thereof brought forth
ripe grapes:
11 And Pharaoh's cup *was* in my
hand: and I took the grapes, and
pressed them into Pharaoh's cup, and
I gave the cup into Pharaoh's hand.
12 And Joseph said unto him, This
is the interpretation of it: The three
branches *are* three days:
13 Yet within three days shall
Pharaoh ‖lift up thine head, and restore thee unto thy place: and thou
shalt deliver Pharaoh's cup into his
hand, after the former manner when
thou wast his butler.

‖ Or, *reckon.*

14 But †think on me when it shall
be well with thee, and shew kindness,
I pray thee, unto me, and make mention of me unto Pharaoh, and bring
me out of this house:

† Heb. *remember me with thee.*

15 For indeed I was stolen away
out of the land of the Hebrews: and
here also have I done nothing that
they should put me into the dungeon.
16 When the chief baker saw that

---

4. *they continued a season*] Lit. "days," by which the Jews very generally understand a year.

9. *a vine*] Herodotus denies the existence of vines in ancient Egypt, and says that the Egyptian wine was made of barley (II. 77). Yet Herodotus himself (II. 42, 48, 144) and Diodorus (I. 11) identify Osiris with the Greek Bacchus, the discoverer of the vine, and Diodorus (I. 15) expressly ascribes to Osiris the first cultivation of the vine. But, moreover, it now appears from the monuments that both the cultivation of grapes and the art of making wine were well known in Egypt from the time of the Pyramids. Wine was universally used by the rich throughout Egypt, and beer supplied its place at the tables of the poor, not because "they had no vines in the country, but because it was cheaper." (Sir G. Wilkinson's note in Rawlinson's Herod. II. 77. See also Rosellini, Vol. II. pp. 365, 373, 377; Wilkinson, Vol. II. 143; Hengstenberg, 'Egypt,' &c. p. 16; Hävernick, 'Introd. to Pentateuch,' in h.l.; Ebers, 'Ægypten,' p. 323.)

11. *I took the grapes, and pressed them*] Some have thought that this indicates that the Egyptians did not at this time practise the fermentation of the grape, but merely drank the fresh juice, which would accord with the statement of Plutarch ('Is. et Osir.' § 6) that the Egyptians before the time of Psammetichus neither drank wine nor made libations thereof, as esteeming it to have sprung from the blood of those who made war with the gods; but the monuments represent the process of fermenting wine in very early times. See last note.

13. *shall Pharaoh lift up thine head*] Some think this expression merely means "will take count of thee," "will remember thee." Cp. Ex. xxx. 12; Num. i. 49; where the marginal reading is "reckon." More probably the meaning is, "will take thee out of prison" (see Ges. p. 914).

15. *the land of the Hebrews*] Though the patriarchs had been strangers and pilgrims, yet Abraham, Isaac and Jacob had effected something like permanent settlements in the neighbourhood of Mamre, Hebron, Shechem, &c. Probably too the visit of Abraham to Egypt and the intercourse of the Egyptians with the Hittites and other Canaanitish tribes, had made the name of Hebrew known to the Egyptians. Joseph does not say "the land of Canaan," lest he should be confounded with the Canaanites, who were odious to himself as being idolaters.

the interpretation was good, he said
unto Joseph, I also *was* in my dream,
and, behold, *I had* three ‖white baskets on my head:

‖ Or, *full of holes.*

17 And in the uppermost basket
there was of all manner of †bakemeats
for Pharaoh; and the birds did eat
them out of the basket upon my head.

† Heb. *meat of Pharaoh, the work of a baker,* or, *cook.*

18 And Joseph answered and said,
This *is* the interpretation thereof:
The three baskets *are* three days:
19 Yet within three days shall
Pharaoh ‖lift up thy head from off
thee, and shall hang thee on a tree;
and the birds shall eat thy flesh from
off thee.

‖ Or, *reckon thee,* and take thy office *from thee.*

20 ¶ And it came to pass the third
day, *which was* Pharaoh's birthday,
that he made a feast unto all his servants: and he ‖lifted up the head of
the chief butler and of the chief baker
among his servants.

‖ Or, *reckoned.*

21 And he restored the chief butler unto his butlership again; and he
gave the cup into Pharaoh's hand:
22 But he hanged the chief baker:
as Joseph had interpreted to them.
23 Yet did not the chief butler remember Joseph, but forgat him.

CHAPTER XLI.

1 *Pharaoh's two dreams.* 25 *Joseph interpreteth them.* 33 *He giveth Pharaoh counsel.* 38 *Joseph is advanced.* 50 *He begetteth Manasseh and Ephraim.* 54 *The famine beginneth.*

AND it came to pass at the end
of two full years, that Pharaoh
dreamed: and, behold, he stood by
the river.
2 And, behold, there came up out
of the river seven well favoured kine
and fatfleshed; and they fed in a
meadow.
3 And, behold, seven other kine
came up after them out of the river,
ill favoured and leanfleshed; and stood
by the *other* kine upon the brink of
the river.
4 And the ill favoured and leanfleshed kine did eat up the seven well
favoured and fat kine. So Pharaoh
awoke.
5 And he slept and dreamed the
second time: and, behold, seven ears
of corn came up upon one stalk,
†rank and good.
6 And, behold, seven thin ears and
blasted with the east wind sprung up
after them.

† Heb. *fat.*

---

16. *three white baskets*] Probably "baskets of white bread;" so LXX., Aq., Vulg., Syr., Onk. Some prefer "baskets full of holes," "perforated," or "wicker baskets."

on my head] See Herod. II. 35, of the men bearing burdens on their heads.

17. *bakemeats for Pharaoh*] Lit. "food for Pharaoh, the work of a baker." The Egyptians appear to have been very luxurious in the preparation of different kinds of bread and pastry. (See Rosellini, Vol. II. 264; Wilkinson, II. 384; Hengstenberg, p. 27.)

19. *shall Pharaoh lift up thy head from off thee*] The same words as those used in v. 13, with the addition of "from off thee," making the most vital difference. The mode of punishment was probably decapitation, the most common form of execution in Egypt (Ges. p. 915); though some have thought hanging or crucifixion, as Onkelos in loc. Possibly the words may only indicate *capital* punishment, like the *capite plecti* of the Latins.

CHAP. XLI. 1. *the river*] The "yeor," an Egyptian word signifying "great river," or "canal," used in Scripture for the Nile. The Nile had a sacred and a profane name. The sacred name was *Hapi*, i. e. Apis. The profane name was *Aur*, with the epithet *aa* great. The Coptic forms ⲓⲁⲣⲟ, ⲓⲁⲣⲱ, correspond exactly to the Hebrew *yeor*.

2. *kine*] The Egyptians esteemed the cow above all other animals. It was sacred to Isis (Herod. II. 41), or rather to Athor, the Venus Genetrix of Egypt, and was looked on as "a symbol of the Earth and its cultivation and food" (Clem. Alex. 'Strom.' v. p. 671). Hence it was very natural that in Pharaoh's dream the fruitful and unfruitful years should be typified by well-favoured and ill-favoured kine (see Hengstenb. 'Egypt,' p. 28).

in a meadow] **In the reed grass.** The word (Achu) is of Egyptian origin. It is not common, but occurs in a papyrus of early date (*akh-akh*, green, verdant). Jerome (on Isai. xix. 7) says that "when he enquired of the learned what the word meant, he was told by the Egyptians that in their tongue every thing green that grows in marshes is called by this name." It probably therefore means the sedge, reed, or rank grass by the river's side.

7 And the seven thin ears devoured the seven rank and full ears. And
Pharaoh awoke, and, behold, *it was* a
dream.
8 And it came to pass in the
morning that his spirit was troubled; and he sent and called for
all the magicians of Egypt, and all
the wise men thereof: and Pharaoh
told them his dream; but *there was*
none that could interpret them unto
Pharaoh.
9 ¶ Then spake the chief butler
unto Pharaoh, saying, I do remember my faults this day:
10 Pharaoh was wroth with his
servants, and put me in ward in the
captain of the guard's house, *both* me
and the chief baker:
11 And we dreamed a dream in
one night, I and he; we dreamed
each man according to the interpretation of his dream.
12 And *there was* there with us a
young man, an Hebrew, servant to
the captain of the guard; and we told
him, and he [a] interpreted to us our [a] chap. 40. 12, &c.
dreams; to each man according to
his dream he did interpret.
13 And it came to pass, as he interpreted to us, so it was; me he
restored unto mine office, and him
he hanged.
14 ¶ [b] Then Pharaoh sent and [b] Psal. 105. 20.
called Joseph, and they † brought him † Heb. *made him run.*
hastily out of the dungeon: and he
shaved *himself*, and changed his raiment, and came in unto Pharaoh.
15 And Pharaoh said unto Joseph,
I have dreamed a dream, and *there*
is none that can interpret it: and
I have heard say of thee, *that* ‖ thou ‖ Or, when *thou hearest a dream, thou canst interpret it.*
canst understand a dream to inter-
pret it.
16 And Joseph answered Pharaoh,
saying, *It is* not in me: God shall
give Pharaoh an answer of peace.
17 And Pharaoh said unto Joseph,
In my dream, behold, I stood upon
the bank of the river:
18 And, behold, there came up
out of the river seven kine, fatfleshed
and well favoured; and they fed in a
meadow:

---

6. *east wind*] Probably put for the S. E. wind (Chamsin), which blows from the desert of Arabia. The East wind of Egypt is not the scorching wind, and indeed seldom blows; but the South-east wind is so parching as to destroy the grass entirely, if it blows very long (see Hengstenberg, p. 10).

7. *behold, it was a dream*] The impression on Pharaoh's mind was so strong and vivid, that he could hardly believe it was not real. The particulars of the dream are all singularly appropriate. The scene is by the Nile, on which depends all the plenty of Egypt. The kine and the corn respectively denote the animal and the vegetable products of the country. The cattle feeding in the reed grass shewed that the Nile was fertilizing the land and supporting the life of the beasts. The lean cattle and the scorched-up corn foreshadowed a time when the Nile, for some reason, ceased to irrigate the land. The swallowing up of the fat by the lean signified that the produce of the seven years of plenty would be all consumed in the seven years of scarcity.

8. *magicians*] Apparently "sacred scribes;" the name, if Hebrew, being composed of two words signifying respectively *a style* and *sacred*. Some have thought the word to be of Egyptian origin, or perhaps a Hebrew compound imitating an Egyptian name (see Ges. 'Thes.' p. 521). There has, however, no Egyptian name been found like it. The magicians appear to have been a regular order of persons among the Egyptians, learned priests, who devoted themselves to magic and astrology (see Hengstenberg, p. 28, and Poole in Smith's 'Dict. of the Bible,' art. *Magic*).

13. *me he restored*] Joseph prophesied that I should be restored, and, as he prophesied, so it came to pass.

14. *shaved himself*] The Hebrews cherished long beards, but the Egyptians cut both hair and beard close, except in mourning for relations, when they let both grow long (Herod. II. 36). On the monuments when it was "intended to convey the idea of a man of low condition or a slovenly person, the artists represented him with a beard" (Wilkinson, Vol. III. p. 357; Hengstenberg, p. 30). Joseph, therefore, when about to appear before Pharaoh, was careful to adapt himself to the manners of the Egyptians.

15. *that thou canst understand a dream to interpret it*] Lit. **that thou hearest a dream to interpret it.**

18. *in a meadow*] **In the reed grass.** See on v. 2.

19 And, behold, seven other kine
came up after them, poor and very
ill favoured and leanfleshed, such as
I never saw in all the land of Egypt
for badness:
20 And the lean and the ill favoured kine did eat up the first seven
fat kine:
21 And when they had † eaten
them up, it could not be known that
they had eaten them; but they *were*
still ill favoured, as at the beginning.
So I awoke.

† Heb. *come to the inward parts of them.*

22 And I saw in my dream, and,
behold, seven ears came up in one
stalk, full and good:
23 And, behold, seven ears, ‖ withered, thin, *and* blasted with the
east wind, sprung up after them:

‖ Or, *small.*

24 And the thin ears devoured the
seven good ears: and I told *this* unto
the magicians; but *there was* none
that could declare *it* to me.
25 ¶ And Joseph said unto Pharaoh, The dream of Pharaoh *is* one:
God hath shewed Pharaoh what he *is*
about to do.
26 The seven good kine *are* seven
years; and the seven good ears *are*
seven years: the dream *is* one.
27 And the seven thin and ill
favoured kine that came up after
them *are* seven years; and the seven
empty ears blasted with the east wind
shall be seven years of famine.
28 This *is* the thing which I have
spoken unto Pharaoh: What God *is*
about to do he sheweth unto Pharaoh.
29 Behold, there come seven years
of great plenty throughout all the
land of Egypt:
30 And there shall arise after them
seven years of famine; and all the
plenty shall be forgotten in the land
of Egypt; and the famine shall consume the land;
31 And the plenty shall not be
known in the land by reason of that
famine following; for it *shall be* very
† grievous.

† Heb. *heavy.*

32 And for that the dream was
doubled unto Pharaoh twice; *it is*
because the thing *is* ‖ established by
God, and God will shortly bring it
to pass.

‖ Or, *prepared of God.*

33 Now therefore let Pharaoh look
out a man discreet and wise, and set
him over the land of Egypt.
34 Let Pharaoh do *this*, and let
him appoint ‖ officers over the land,
and take up the fifth part of the
land of Egypt in the seven plenteous
years.

‖ Or, *overseers.*

35 And let them gather all the
food of those good years that come,
and lay up corn under the hand of
Pharaoh, and let them keep food in
the cities.
36 And that food shall be for store
to the land against the seven years of
famine, which shall be in the land of
Egypt; that the land † perish not
through the famine.

† Heb. *be not cut off.*

37 ¶ And the thing was good in
the eyes of Pharaoh, and in the eyes
of all his servants.
38 And Pharaoh said unto his servants, Can we find *such a one* as
this *is*, a man in whom the Spirit of
God *is?*
39 And Pharaoh said unto Joseph,
Forasmuch as God hath shewed thee
all this, *there is* none so discreet and
wise as thou *art:*
40 [c] Thou shalt be over my house,
and according unto thy word shall all
my people be † ruled: only in the
throne will I be greater than thou.

[c] Psal. 105. 21. 1 Mac. 2. 53. Acts 7. 10.

† Heb. *armed,* or, *kiss.*

---

34. *take up the fifth part of the land*] *i. e.* Let him exact a fifth of the produce of the land. The Hebrew is literally "let him fifth the land." (Compare our phrase "to tithe the land.") It has been questioned whether the advice was to purchase a fifth of all the produce, or rather to impose a tax amounting to one fifth of the produce of the land. It has been not improbably conjectured that the Egyptian kings usually imposed a tribute of one tenth, and that in this season of unusual abundance Joseph advises Pharaoh to double the impost, with the benevolent intention of afterwards selling the corn so collected in the time of famine (Cleric. in loc.). On the large storehouses and granaries of Egypt, see Hengstenb., p. 36, Wilkinson, II. 135.

40. *according unto thy word shall all my*

41 And Pharaoh said unto Joseph,
See, I have set thee over all the land
of Egypt.
42 And Pharaoh took off his ring
from his hand, and put it upon Joseph's hand, and arrayed him in ves-
tures of ‖ fine linen, and put a gold ‖ Or, *silk.*
chain about his neck;
43 And he made him to ride in
the second chariot which he had; and
they cried before him, ‖† Bow the ‖ Or, *Tender father.*
knee: and he made him *ruler* over † Heb. *Abrech.*
all the land of Egypt.
44 And Pharaoh said unto Joseph,
I *am* Pharaoh, and without thee shall
no man lift up his hand or foot in all
the land of Egypt.
45 And Pharaoh called Joseph's
name Zaphnath-paaneah; and he gave
him to wife Asenath the daughter

---

people be ruled] So, or nearly so, ("at thy word shall all my people arm themselves, or dispose themselves,") the Versions, Targg. and most commentators. But Kimchi, Gesenius, Knobel, &c., render "and all my people shall kiss thy mouth," as a token of reverence and obedience. The objections to the latter interpretation are that the kiss of reverence was on the hand or the foot, not on the mouth, which was the kiss of love, and that the construction here is with a preposition never used with the verb signifying "to kiss."

42. *ring*] The signet-ring was the special symbol of office and authority. The seal to this day in the East is the common mode of attestation, and therefore when Pharaoh gave Joseph his ring he delegated to him his whole authority.

fine linen] The byssus or fine linen of the Egyptians. The word used for it is *Shes*, a well-ascertained Egyptian word. It is mentioned in Ezek. xxvii. as imported into Tyre from Egypt. It was the peculiar dress of the Egyptian priests.

a gold chain] Probably "a simple gold chain in imitation of string, to which a stone scarabæus set in the same precious metal was appended." (Wilkinson, III. 376. See also Hengstenberg, p. 31.)

43. *Bow the knee*] **Abrech.** If the word be Hebrew, the rendering of the Authorised Version is probably correct. The Targums all give "father of the king" (cp. ch. xlv. 8), deriving from the Hebrew *Ab*, a father, and the Chaldee *Rech*, a king, which, however, is thought to be a corruption of the Latin *Rex*. It is generally thought to be an Egyptian word signifying "Bow the head," having some resemblance in form to the Hebrew (De Rossi, 'Etymol. Egypt.' p. 1. So Gesen. 'Thes.,' p. 19, and most of the Germans). A more probable interpretation is that which is given in the Excursus on Egyptian Words at the end of this volume, viz. "Rejoice" or "Rejoice thou!"

45. *Zaphnath-paaneah*] In the LXX. *Psonthomphanek*. The Vulg. renders *Salvator Mundi*, "Saviour of the World." Several learned in the language and antiquities of Egypt, Bernard (in Joseph, 'Ant.' II. 6); Jablonski ('Opusc.' I. 207); Rosellini ('Monuments,' I. p. 185), have so interpreted it. They are followed in the main by Gesenius (p. 1181, "the supporter or preserver of the age") and a majority of modern commentators. The true meaning appears to be "the food of life," or "of the living." (See Excursus on Egyptian Words at the end of this volume.) The Targg., Syr., Arab. and Hebrew interpp. render "a revealer of secrets," referring to a Hebrew original, which is on every account improbable. There can be no doubt that Pharaoh would have given his Grand Vizier an Egyptian name, not a Hebrew name, just as the name of Daniel was changed to Belteshazzar, and as Hananiah, Azariah and Mishael, were called by Nebuchadnezzar, Shadrach, Meshach, and Abednego.

Asenath] either "devoted to Neith," the Egyptian Minerva (Ges. 'Thes.' p. 130), or perhaps compounded of the two names Isis and Neith, such a form of combination of two names in one being not unknown in Egypt. (See Excursus on Egyptian Words at the end of this volume.)

Poti-pherah] *i.e.* "belonging" or "devoted to Ra," *i.e.* the Sun, a most appropriate designation for a priest of On or Heliopolis, the great seat of the Sun-worship. (See Excursus on Egyptian Words at the end of this volume.)

On] Heliopolis (LXX), called, Jer. xliii. 13, Beth-shemesh, the city of the Sun. Cyril (ad. Hos. v. 8), says, "On is with them the Sun." The city stood on the Eastern bank of the Nile a few miles north of Memphis, and was famous for the worship of Ra, the Sun, as also for the learning and wisdom of its priests (Herod. II. 3). There still remains an obelisk of red granite, part of the Temple of the Sun, with a dedication sculptured by Osirtasen or Sesortasen I. It is the oldest and one of the finest in Egypt; of the 12th dynasty. (Ges. p. 52, Wilkinson, Vol. I. p. 44; also Rawlinson's Herod. II. 8, Brugsch, 'H. E.' p. 254.)

The difficulty of supposing that the daughter of a priest of On should have been married to Joseph, a worshipper of JEHOVAH, has been unduly magnified. Neither the Egyptians nor the Hebrews were at this time as exclusive as

‖ Or, *prince.* of Poti-pherah ‖ priest of On. And
Joseph went out over *all* the land of
Egypt.
46 ¶ And Joseph *was* thirty years
old when he stood before Pharaoh
king of Egypt. And Joseph went
out from the presence of Pharaoh,
and went throughout all the land of
Egypt.
47 And in the seven plenteous
years the earth brought forth by
handfuls.
48 And he gathered up all the
food of the seven years, which were
in the land of Egypt, and laid up
the food in the cities: the food of
the field, which *was* round about
every city, laid he up in the same.
49 And Joseph gathered corn as
the sand of the sea, very much, until
he left numbering; for *it was* without number.
d chap. 46. 20. & 48. 5. 50 *d* And unto Joseph were born
two sons before the years of famine
came, which Asenath the daughter
‖ Or, *prince.* of Poti-pherah ‖ priest of On bare
unto him.
51 And Joseph called the name of
‖ That is, *Forgetting.* the firstborn ‖ Manasseh: For God,
said he, hath made me forget all my
toil, and all my father's house.
52 And the name of the second
‖ That is, *Fruitful.* called he ‖ Ephraim: For God hath
caused me to be fruitful in the land
of my affliction.
53 ¶ And the seven years of plen-
teousness, that was in the land of
Egypt, were ended.
54 *e* And the seven years of dearth *e* Psal. 105. 16.
began to come, according as Joseph
had said: and the dearth was in all
lands; but in all the land of Egypt
there was bread.
55 And when all the land of Egypt
was famished, the people cried to Pharaoh for bread: and Pharaoh said unto all the Egyptians, Go unto Joseph;
what he saith to you, do.
56 And the famine was over all
the face of the earth: And Joseph
opened † all the storehouses, and sold † Heb. *all wherein* was.
unto the Egyptians; and the famine
waxed sore in the land of Egypt.
57 And all countries came into
Egypt to Joseph for to buy *corn*;
because that the famine was *so* sore
in all lands.

CHAPTER XLII.

1 *Jacob sendeth his ten sons to buy corn in Egypt.* 16 *They are imprisoned by Joseph for spies.* 18 *They are set at liberty, on condition to bring Benjamin.* 21 *They have remorse for Joseph.* 24 *Simeon is kept for a pledge.* 25 *They return with corn, and their money.* 29 *Their relation to Jacob.* 36 *Jacob refuseth to send Benjamin.*

NOW when *a* Jacob saw that *a* Acts 7. 12.
there was corn in Egypt, Ja-
cob said unto his sons, Why do ye
look one upon another?
2 And he said, Behold, I have

---

they became afterwards. The Semitic races were treated with respect in Egypt. Joseph had become thoroughly naturalized (see v. 51 and ch. xliii. 32), with an Egyptian name and the rank of Viceroy or Grand Vizier. Abraham had before this taken Hagar, an Egyptian, to wife, which would make such an alliance less strange to Joseph. Whether Asenath adopted Joseph's faith we are not told, but, in the end at least, she probably did. (See also Excursus on Egyptian Words, on "Asenath wife of Joseph," at the end of this volume.)

46. *thirty years old*] He must therefore have been thirteen years in Egypt, either in Potiphar's house or in prison. (See ch. xxxvii. 2.)

51. *Manasseh*] *i.e.* "causing to forget." He was comforted by all his prosperity, so that he no longer mourned over his exile. It does not follow that he was ungratefully forgetful of his home.

52. *Ephraim*] *i.e.* "doubly fruitful," a dual form.

54. *the dearth*] Notwithstanding the fertility generally produced in Egypt by the overflowing of the Nile, yet the swelling of the Nile a few feet above or below what is necessary, has in many instances produced destructive and protracted famines, such that the people have been reduced to the horrible necessity of eating human flesh, and have been almost swept away by death. (See Hengstenberg, 'Egypt,' &c., pp. 37, 38; Hävernick, Int. to Pentateuch, p. 218; also Smith's 'Dict. of Bible,' art. *Famine.*)

in all lands] The drought which affected Egypt reached the neighbouring countries also. Ethiopia, Arabia, Palestine, and Syria, would be especially affected by it; and the Egyptians, and Hebrews also, would look on these lands as comprehending the whole known world.

heard that there is corn in Egypt:
get you down thither, and buy for
us from thence; that we may live,
and not die.
3 ¶ And Joseph's ten brethren
went down to buy corn in Egypt.
4 But Benjamin, Joseph's brother,
Jacob sent not with his brethren; for
he said, Lest peradventure mischief
befall him.
5 And the sons of Israel came to
buy *corn* among those that came: for
the famine was in the land of Canaan.
6 And Joseph *was* the governor
over the land, *and* he *it was* that
sold to all the people of the land: and
Joseph's brethren came, and bowed
down themselves before him *with*
their faces to the earth.
7 And Joseph saw his brethren,
and he knew them, but made himself strange unto them, and spake
† Heb. *hard things with them.* † roughly unto them; and he said unto them, Whence come ye? And
they said, From the land of Canaan
to buy food.
8 And Joseph knew his brethren,
but they knew not him.
b chap. 37. 5. 9 And Joseph [b] remembered the
dreams which he dreamed of them,
and said unto them, Ye *are* spies; to
see the nakedness of the land ye are
come.
10 And they said unto him, Nay,
my lord, but to buy food are thy
servants come.
11 We *are* all one man's sons; we
are true *men*, thy servants are no spies.
12 And he said unto them, Nay,
but to see the nakedness of the land
ye are come.
13 And they said, Thy servants
are twelve brethren, the sons of one
man in the land of Canaan; and,
behold, the youngest *is* this day with
our father, and one *is* not.
14 And Joseph said unto them,
That *is it* that I spake unto you,
saying, Ye *are* spies:
15 Hereby ye shall be proved: By
the life of Pharaoh ye shall not go
forth hence, except your youngest
brother come hither.
16 Send one of you, and let him
fetch your brother, and ye shall be
† kept in prison, that your words may † Heb. *bound.*
be proved, whether *there be any* truth
in you: or else by the life of Pharaoh
surely ye *are* spies.
17 And he † put them all together † Heb. *gathered.*
into ward three days.
18 And Joseph said unto them the
third day, This do, and live; *for* I
fear God:
19 If ye *be* true *men*, let one of
your brethren be bound in the house
of your prison: go ye, carry corn for
the famine of your houses:

CHAP. XLII. 6. *he it was that sold to all the people of the land*] We are not to suppose that Joseph personally sold the corn to all buyers, but that he ordered the selling of it, and set the price upon it; and very probably, when a company of foreigners came to purchase in large quantities, they were introduced personally to Joseph, that he might enquire concerning them and give directions as to the sale of corn to them.

7. *spake roughly unto them*] Lit. "spake hard things with them," as the margin. This did not arise from a vindictive spirit. It was partly that he might not be recognized by them, and partly that he might prove them and see whether they were penitent for what they had done to him.

8. *they knew not him*] He was only 17 when they sold him; he was now at least 37, and had adopted all the habits and manners of the Egyptians; probably even his complexion had been much darkened by living so long in a southern climate.

9. *the nakedness of the land*] *i.e.* the defenceless and assailable points of the country; like the Latin phrases, *nuda urbs præsidio, nudata castra, nudi defensoribus muri* (Ros.; Cp. Hom. 'Il.' XII. 399, τεῖχος ἐγυμνώθη). The Egyptians were always most liable to be assailed from the East and North-east. (See Herod. III. 5.) The various Arab and Canaanitish tribes seem to have constantly made incursions into the more settled and civilized land of Egypt. Particularly the Hittites were at constant feud with the Egyptians. Moreover the famous Hycsos invasion and domination may have been very nearly impending at this period.

15. *By the life of Pharaoh*] Cp. similar phrases (1 S. i. 26; xvii. 55; 2 S. xiv. 19; 2 K. ii. 2, 4, 6). Not distinctly an oath, but a strong asseveration.

[c] chap. 43. 5. 20 But [c] bring your youngest brother unto me; so shall your words be
verified, and ye shall not die. And
they did so.
21 ¶ And they said one to another, We *are* verily guilty concerning our brother, in that we saw the
anguish of his soul, when he besought us, and we would not hear;
therefore is this distress come upon us.
22 And Reuben answered them,
[d] chap. 37. 21. saying, [d] Spake I not unto you, saying, Do not sin against the child;
and ye would not hear? therefore,
behold, also his blood is required.
23 And they knew not that Joseph
† Heb. *an interpreter* was *between them.* understood *them;* for † he spake unto
them by an interpreter.
24 And he turned himself about
from them, and wept; and returned
to them again, and communed with
them, and took from them Simeon,
and bound him before their eyes.
25 ¶ Then Joseph commanded to
fill their sacks with corn, and to
restore every man's money into his
sack, and to give them provision for
the way: and thus did he unto them.
26 And they laded their asses with
the corn, and departed thence.
27 And as one of them opened his
sack to give his ass provender in the
inn, he espied his money; for, behold,
it *was* in his sack's mouth.
28 And he said unto his brethren,
My money is restored; and, lo, *it*
is even in my sack: and their heart
† failed *them*, and they were afraid, † Heb. *went forth.*
saying one to another, What *is* this
that God hath done unto us?
29 ¶ And they came unto Jacob
their father unto the land of Canaan,
and told him all that befell unto
them; saying,
30 The man, *who is* the lord of
the land, spake † roughly to us, and † Heb. *with us hard things.*
took us for spies of the country.
31 And we said unto him, We *are*
true *men;* we are no spies:
32 We *be* twelve brethren, sons of
our father; one *is* not, and the youngest *is* this day with our father in the
land of Canaan.
33 And the man, the lord of the
country, said unto us, Hereby shall
I know that ye *are* true *men;* leave
one of your brethren *here* with me,
and take *food for* the famine of your
households, and be gone:
34 And bring your youngest brother unto me: then shall I know
that ye *are* no spies, but *that* ye
are true *men: so* will I deliver you
your brother, and ye shall traffick in
the land.
35 ¶ And it came to pass as they
emptied their sacks, that, behold,
every man's bundle of money *was* in

---

20. *bring your youngest brother unto me*] There seems some needless severity here on the part of Joseph in causing so much anxiety to his father. We may account for it perhaps in the following ways. 1st, Joseph felt that it was necessary to test the repentance of his brethren and to subject them to that kind of discipline which makes repentance sound and lasting. 2ndly, He may have thought that the best mode of persuading his father to go down to him in Egypt was first of all to bring Benjamin thither. 3rdly, He was manifestly following a Divine impulse and guiding, that so his dreams should be fulfilled, and his race brought into their house of bondage and education.

24. *Simeon*] It has been thought that he took Simeon, either because he was the next in age to Reuben, whom he would not bind as having been the brother that sought to save him, or perhaps because Simeon had been one of the most unfeeling and cruel towards himself, according to the savage temper which he shewed in the case of the Shechemites. See ch. xxxiv, xlix. 5.

25. *their sacks*] Rather, **their vessels**; the word is different from that elsewhere used for sacks, and apparently indicates that they had some kind of vessel for corn which they carried within their sacks.

27. *in the inn*] The khan, or caravanserai, in the East was, and is still, a place, where men and cattle can find room to rest, but which provides neither food for man nor fodder for cattle. It is doubtful, however, whether anything of this kind existed so early as the time of Joseph. The word means only "a resting place for the night," and very probably was only a station, at which caravans were wont to rest, near to a well, to trees, and to pasture, where the tents were pitched and the cattle were tethered.

his sack: and when *both* they and their father saw the bundles of money, they were afraid.

36 And Jacob their father said unto them, Me have ye bereaved *of my children:* Joseph *is* not, and Simeon *is* not, and ye will take Benjamin *away:* all these things are against me.

37 And Reuben spake unto his father, saying, Slay my two sons, if I bring him not to thee: deliver him into my hand, and I will bring him to thee again.

38 And he said, My son shall not go down with you; for his brother is dead, and he is left alone: if mischief befall him by the way in the which ye go, then shall ye bring down my gray hairs with sorrow to the grave.

CHAPTER XLIII.

1 *Jacob is hardly persuaded to send Benjamin.* 15 *Joseph entertaineth his brethren.* 31 *He maketh them a feast.*

AND the famine *was* sore in the land.

2 And it came to pass, when they had eaten up the corn which they had brought out of Egypt, their father said unto them, Go again, buy us a little food.

3 And Judah spake unto him, saying, The man †did solemnly protest unto us, saying, Ye shall not see my face, except your [a]brother *be* with you.

† Heb. *protesting he protested.* [a] chap. 42. 20.

4 If thou wilt send our brother with us, we will go down and buy thee food:

5 But if thou wilt not send *him*, we will not go down: for the man said unto us, Ye shall not see my face, except your brother *be* with you.

6 And Israel said, Wherefore dealt ye *so* ill with me, *as* to tell the man whether ye had yet a brother?

7 And they said, The man †asked us straitly of our state, and of our kindred, saying, *Is* your father yet alive? have ye *another* brother? and we told him according to the †tenor of these words: †could we certainly know that he would say, Bring your brother down?

† Heb. *asking he asked us.* † Heb. *mouth.* † Heb. *knowing could we know.*

8 And Judah said unto Israel his father, Send the lad with me, and we will arise and go; that we may live, and not die, both we, and thou, *and* also our little ones.

9 I will be surety for him; of my hand shalt thou require him: [b]if I bring him not unto thee, and set him before thee, then let me bear the blame for ever:

[b] chap. 44. 32.

10 For except we had lingered, surely now we had returned ǀthis second time.

ǀ Or, *twice by this.*

11 And their father Israel said unto them, If *it must be* so now, do this; take of the best fruits in the land in your vessels, and carry down the man a present, a little balm, and a little honey, spices, and myrrh, nuts, and almonds:

---

36. *Me have ye bereaved*] Jacob suspects that they had been in some way the cause of Joseph's supposed death and of Simeon's captivity.

against me] Lit. "upon me," *i.e.* upon me as a burden too heavy for me to bear.

CHAP. XLIII. 11. *of the best fruits in the land*] Lit. "of the song of the land," *i.e.* the most praised produce, the fruits celebrated in song.

balm] See xxxvii. 25.

honey] So rendered in all the Versions, though some think that it was composed of the juice of grapes boiled down to a syrup of the consistency of honey, called in Arabic *Dibs;* which even in modern times has been imported into Egypt annually from the neighbourhood of Hebron (see Ros. and Ges. p. 319).

spices] Probably *Storax*. See on xxxvii. 25.

myrrh] **Ladanum.** See on xxxvii. 25.

nuts] **Pistachio nuts.** So Bochart ('Hieroz.' II. iv. 12); Ceis. ('Hierobot.' Tom. I. p. 24); Ges. (p. 202). The LXX., followed by Onk., Syr., Arab., renders *terebinth*, probably because the pistachio nut tree was considered as a species of terebinth. All these fruits may have grown in the land of Canaan, though the corn-harvest may have utterly failed. Thus also may we account for the fact, that the small supply, which could be carried from Egypt by ten asses, sufficed for a time to sup-

12 And take double money in your
hand; and the money that was brought
again in the mouth of your sacks,
carry *it* again in your hand; peradventure it *was* an oversight:
13 Take also your brother, and
arise, go again unto the man:
14 And God Almighty give you
mercy before the man, that he may
send away your other brother, and
Benjamin. ‖If I be bereaved *of my*
children, I am bereaved.
15 ¶ And the men took that present, and they took double money in
their hand, and Benjamin; and rose
up, and went down to Egypt, and
stood before Joseph.
16 And when Joseph saw Benjamin with them, he said to the ruler of
his house, Bring *these* men home, and
†slay, and make ready; for *these* men
shall †dine with me at noon.
17 And the man did as Joseph
bade; and the man brought the men
into Joseph's house.
18 And the men were afraid, because they were brought into Joseph's
house; and they said, Because of the
money that was returned in our sacks
at the first time are we brought in;
that he may †seek occasion against us,
and fall upon us, and take us for bondmen, and our asses.
19 And they came near to the
steward of Joseph's house, and they
communed with him at the door of
the house,
20 And said, O sir, [c]†we came in-

‖ Or, *And I, as I have been, &c.*
† Heb. *kill a killing.*
† Heb. *eat.*
† Heb. *roll himself upon us.*
[c] chap. 42. 3.
† Heb. *coming down we came down.*

deed down at the first time to buy
food:
21 And it came to pass, when we
came to the inn, that we opened our
sacks, and, behold, *every* man's money
was in the mouth of his sack, our
money in full weight: and we have
brought it again in our hand.
22 And other money have we
brought down in our hands to buy
food: we cannot tell who put our
money in our sacks.
23 And he said, Peace *be* to you,
fear not: your God, and the God of
your father, hath given you treasure
in your sacks: †I had your money.
And he brought Simeon out unto them.
24 And the man brought the men
into Joseph's house, and [d]gave *them*
water, and they washed their feet;
and he gave their asses provender.
25 And they made ready the present against Joseph came at noon:
for they heard that they should eat
bread there.
26 ¶ And when Joseph came home,
they brought him the present which
was in their hand into the house, and
bowed themselves to him to the earth.
27 And he asked them of *their*
†welfare, and said, †*Is* your father well,
the old man of whom ye spake? *Is*
he yet alive?
28 And they answered, Thy servant our father *is* in good health, he
is yet alive. And they bowed down
their heads, and made obeisance.
29 And he lifted up his eyes, and

† Heb. *your money came to me.*
[d] chap. 18. 4 & 24. 32.
† Heb. *peace.*
† Heb. Is there *peace to your father.*

---

ply Jacob's household. There was a grievous famine, but still all the fruits of the earth had not failed. Corn was needed; but life can be supported, especially in a warm climate, with but a moderate amount of the more solid kinds of food.

14. *God Almighty*] *El Shaddai.* Jacob here uses that name of the Most High, by which He made Himself known to Abraham, and afterwards renewed His covenant with Jacob himself (ch. xvii. 1, xxxv. 11; where see note). Hereby he calls to mind the promise of protection to himself and his house, as well as the power of Him who had promised.

If I be bereaved of my children, I am bereaved.] Cp. Esth. iv. 16; 2 K. vii. 4. The expression seems partly of sorrow and partly of submission and resignation.

18. *that he may seek occasion against us*] Lit. "that he may roll himself upon us," that is, probably, "that he may rush out upon us."

20. *O Sir*] "Pray, my lord," or "Hear, my lord," the word translated *O* is a particle of earnest entreaty.

26. *and bowed themselves*] Joseph's first dream is now fulfilled. The eleven sheaves make obeisance to Joseph's sheaf. It is observable, that Joseph's dream, like Pharaoh's, had reference to sheaves of corn, evidently pointing to the supply of food sought by the brethren.

saw his brother Benjamin, his mother's
son, and said, *Is* this your younger
brother, of whom ye spake unto me?
And he said, God be gracious unto
thee, my son.
30 And Joseph made haste, for
his bowels did yearn upon his brother:
and he sought *where* to weep; and he
entered into *his* chamber, and wept
there.
31 And he washed his face, and
went out, and refrained himself, and
said, Set on bread.
32 And they set on for him by
himself, and for them by themselves,
and for the Egyptians, which did eat
with him, by themselves: because the
Egyptians might not eat bread with
the Hebrews; for that *is* an abomination unto the Egyptians.
33 And they sat before him, the
firstborn according to his birthright,
and the youngest according to his
youth: and the men marvelled one
at another.
34 And he took *and sent* messes
unto them from before him: but
Benjamin's mess was five times so
much as any of theirs. And they
drank, and †were merry with him.

† Heb. *they drank largely.*

CHAPTER XLIV.

1 *Joseph's policy to stay his brethren.* 14 *Judah's humble supplication to Joseph.*

AND he commanded †the steward
of his house, saying, Fill the
men's sacks *with* food, as much as
they can carry, and put every man's
money in his sack's mouth.
2 And put my cup, the silver cup,
in the sack's mouth of the youngest,
and his corn money. And he did
according to the word that Joseph had
spoken.
3 As soon as the morning was light,
the men were sent away, they and
their asses.
4 *And* when they were gone out
of the city, *and* not *yet* far off, Joseph
said unto his steward, Up, follow after
the men; and when thou dost overtake them, say unto them, Wherefore
have ye rewarded evil for good?
5 *Is* not this *it* in which my lord
drinketh, and whereby indeed he ‖di-
vineth? ye have done evil in so doing.

† Heb. him *that* was *over his house.*

‖ Or *maketh trial?*

---

29. *my son*] Joseph addresses Benjamin his younger brother with this paternal salutation, not only from the difference in their ages, but as being a governor he speaks with the authority and dignity of his position.

32. *the Egyptians might not eat bread with the Hebrews*] The Egyptians feared to eat with foreigners, chiefly because they dreaded pollution from such as killed and ate cows, which animals were held in the highest veneration in Egypt. Hence Herodotus says, that an Egyptian would not kiss a Greek, nor use a knife or a spit belonging to a Greek, nor eat any meat that had been cut with a Greek knife (Her. II. 45). Joseph probably dined alone from his high rank, the distinctions of rank and caste being carefully observed; but, as he was naturalized in Egypt, and had, no doubt, conformed to their domestic customs, he would probably not have needed to separate himself at meals from the native Egyptians, as would his brethren from the land of the Hebrews.

33. *they sat before him*] The Egyptians sat at their meals, though most of the ancients, and, in later times at least, the Hebrews, reclined.

the men marvelled one at another] They marvelled that strangers should have seated them exactly according to their ages.

34. *sent messes unto them*] The custom is met with elsewhere, as a mark of respect to distinguished guests (see 1 S. ix. 23, 24).

five times so much] Herodotus mentions the custom of giving double portions as a mark of honour. The Spartan kings "are given the first seat at the banquet, they are served before the other guests, and have a double portion of everything" (VI. 57; cp. also Hom. 'Il.' VII. 321, VIII. 162).

were merry] **Drank freely.** The word is chiefly used of drinking to excess, but not always; see for instance Hagg. i. 6.

CHAP. XLIV. 2. *my cup*] or rather **bowl.** In Jer. xxxv. 5 the word is rendered "pots." In Ex. xxv. 31, xxxvii. 17, it is used of the "bowl" or calix of the sculptured flowers. It was evidently a larger vessel, flagon or bowl, from which the wine was poured into the smaller cups.

5. *divineth*] Divination by cups was frequent in ancient times. Jamblichus ('De Myst.' III. 14) mentions it, so Varro (ap. August. 'Civ. Dei,' VII. 35), Pliny ('H. N.' XXXVII. 73, &c.). The latter says that "in

6 ¶ And he overtook them, and he
spake unto them these same words.
7 And they said unto him, Wherefore saith my lord these words? God
forbid that thy servants should do
according to this thing:
8 Behold, the money, which we
found in our sacks' mouths, we brought
again unto thee out of the land of
Canaan: how then should we steal
out of thy lord's house silver or gold?
9 With whomsoever of thy servants
it be found, both let him die, and we
also will be my lord's bondmen.
10 And he said, Now also *let* it *be*
according unto your words: he with
whom it is found shall be my servant;
and ye shall be blameless.
11 Then they speedily took down
every man his sack to the ground, and
opened every man his sack.
12 And he searched, *and* began at
the eldest, and left at the youngest:
and the cup was found in Benjamin's
sack.
13 Then they rent their clothes,
and laded every man his ass, and returned to the city.
14 ¶ And Judah and his brethren
came to Joseph's house; for he *was*
yet there: and they fell before him
on the ground.
15 And Joseph said unto them,
What deed *is* this that ye have done?
wot ye not that such a man as I can
certainly ‖divine? ‖ Or, *make trial?*
16 And Judah said, What shall we
say unto my lord? what shall we
speak? or how shall we clear ourselves? God hath found out the iniquity of thy servants: behold, we *are*
my lord's servants, both we, and *he*
also with whom the cup is found.
17 And he said, God forbid that
I should do so: *but* the man in whose
hand the cup is found, he shall be my
servant; and as for you, get you up
in peace unto your father.
18 ¶ Then Judah came near unto
him, and said, Oh my lord, let thy

---

this hydromantia images of the gods were called up." It was practised either by dropping gold, silver, or jewels, into the water, and then examining their appearance; or simply by looking into the water as into a mirror, somewhat probably as the famous Egyptian magician did into the mirror of ink, as mentioned by the duke of Northumberland and others in the present day. (See Lane, 'Mod. Egypt.' II. 362.)

The sacred cup is a symbol of the Nile, into whose waters a golden and silver patera were annually thrown. The Nile itself, both the source and the river, was called "the cup of Egypt" (Plin. 'H. N.' VIII. 71). This cup of Joseph was of silver, while in ordinary cases the Egyptians drank from vessels of brass (Hecatæus in 'Athen.' XI. 6; Herod. II. 37; see Hävernick, 'Introd. to Pentateuch,' ad h. l.).

15. *wot ye not that such a man as I can certainly divine?*] Joseph here adapts himself and his language to his character as it would naturally appear in the eyes of his brethren. We are not to assume that he actually used magical arts. This would be quite inconsistent with what he said to Pharaoh, ch. xli. 16, disclaiming all knowledge of the future, save as revealed by God. It has been questioned how far Joseph was justified in the kind of dissimulation which he thus used to his brethren. That he was perfectly justified in not declaring himself to them until he had tested their repentance and had brought his schemes concerning his father to a point, there can be little doubt. He was never tempted to deny that he was Joseph, for no one suspected that he was. In fact he simply preserved his disguise. But in the present passage he seems to have used words which, though not affirming that he could divine, yet nearly implied as much. It is to be observed, however, that whatever may be thought on this head, Joseph is not held up to us as absolutely perfect. As it was in the case of Abraham, Isaac, and Jacob, the history is simply told of the events as they occurred. Joseph was a man of singular piety, purity, and integrity, in high favour with Heaven, and even at times inspired to declare the will of God. It does not follow that he was perfect. If inspired apostles were sometimes to be blamed (Gal. ii. 11, 13), the holiest patriarchs are not likely to have been incapable of error. If the act was wrong, we must not consider it as the result of Divine guidance, but as the error of a good but fallible man, whilst in the main carrying out the designs of Providence. Making the worst that can be made of it, it is difficult to say that any character in Scripture, save One, (of which at least we have any detailed account) comes out more purely and brightly in the whole course of its history than the character of Joseph.

servant, I pray thee, speak a word in my lord's ears, and let not thine anger burn against thy servant: for thou *art* even as Pharaoh.

19 My lord asked his servants, saying, Have ye a father, or a brother?

20 And we said unto my lord, We have a father, an old man, and a child of his old age, a little one; and his brother is dead, and he alone is left of his mother, and his father loveth him.

21 And thou saidst unto thy servants, Bring him down unto me, that I may set mine eyes upon him.

22 And we said unto my lord, The lad cannot leave his father: for *if* he should leave his father, *his father* would die.

23 And thou saidst unto thy servants, [a]Except your youngest brother come down with you, ye shall see my face no more.

[a] chap. 43. 3.

24 And it came to pass when we came up unto thy servant my father, we told him the words of my lord.

25 And our father said, Go again, *and* buy us a little food.

26 And we said, We cannot go down: if our youngest brother be with us, then will we go down: for we may not see the man's face, except our youngest brother *be* with us.

27 And thy servant my father said unto us, Ye know that my wife bare me two *sons:*

28 And the one went out from me, and I said, [b]Surely he is torn in pieces; and I saw him not since:

[b] chap. 37. 33.

29 And if ye take this also from me, and mischief befall him, ye shall bring down my gray hairs with sorrow to the grave.

30 Now therefore when I come to thy servant my father, and the lad *be* not with us; seeing that his life is bound up in the lad's life;

31 It shall come to pass, when he seeth that the lad *is* not *with us*, that he will die: and thy servants shall bring down the gray hairs of thy servant our father with sorrow to the grave.

32 For thy servant became surety for the lad unto my father, saying, [c]If I bring him not unto thee, then I shall bear the blame to my father for ever.

[c] chap. 43. 9.

33 Now therefore, I pray thee, let thy servant abide instead of the lad a bondman to my lord; and let the lad go up with his brethren.

34 For how shall I go up to my father, and the lad *be* not with me? lest peradventure I see the evil that shall † come on my father.

† Heb. *find my father.*

CHAPTER XLV.

1 Joseph maketh himself known to his brethren. 5 He comforteth them in God's providence. 9 He sendeth for his father. 16 Pharaoh confirmeth it. 21 Joseph furnisheth them for their journey, and exhorteth them to concord. 25 Jacob is revived with the news.

THEN Joseph could not refrain himself before all them that stood by him; and he cried, Cause every man to go out from me. And there stood no man with him, while Joseph made himself known unto his brethren.

2 And he † wept aloud: and the Egyptians and the house of Pharaoh heard.

† Heb. *gave forth his voice in weeping.*

3 And Joseph said unto his brethren, [a]I *am* Joseph; doth my father yet live? And his brethren could not answer him; for they were ‖ troubled at his presence.

[a] Acts 7. 13.

‖ Or, *terrified.*

4 And Joseph said unto his bre-

---

28. *Surely he is torn in pieces*] From these words probably for the first time Joseph learns what had been Jacob's belief as to his son's fate.

34. *how should I go up to my father*] The character of Judah comes out most favourably in this speech. He had, in the first instance, saved Joseph from death, but yet he had proposed the alternative of selling him as a slave. He is evidently now much softened; has witnessed Jacob's affliction with deep sympathy and sorrow, and so has been brought to contrition and repentance. The sight of his repentance finally moves Joseph at once to make himself known to his brethren.

CHAP. XLV. **2.** *wept aloud*] Lit., as the margin, "gave forth his voice in weeping."

thren, Come near to me, I pray you.
And they came near. And he said,
I *am* Joseph your brother, whom ye
sold into Egypt.
5 Now therefore be not grieved,
† nor angry with yourselves, that ye
sold me hither: [b] for God did send
me before you to preserve life.
6 For these two years *hath* the
famine *been* in the land: and yet *there*
are five years, in the which *there shall*
neither *be* earing nor harvest.
7 And God sent me before you † to
preserve you a posterity in the earth,
and to save your lives by a great deliverance.
8 So now *it was* not you *that* sent
me hither, but God: and he hath
made me a father to Pharaoh, and lord
of all his house, and a ruler throughout all the land of Egypt.
9 Haste ye, and go up to my father,
and say unto him, Thus saith thy son
Joseph, God hath made me lord of
all Egypt: come down unto me, tarry
not:
10 And thou shalt dwell in the
land of Goshen, and thou shalt be
near unto me, thou, and thy children,
and thy children's children, and thy
flocks, and thy herds, and all that thou
hast:
11 And there will I nourish thee;
for yet *there are* five years of famine;
lest thou, and thy household, and all
that thou hast, come to poverty.
12 And, behold, your eyes see, and
the eyes of my brother Benjamin, that
it is my mouth that speaketh unto
you.
13 And ye shall tell my father of
all my glory in Egypt, and of all that
ye have seen; and ye shall haste and
bring down my father hither.
14 And he fell upon his brother
Benjamin's neck, and wept; and
Benjamin wept upon his neck.
15 Moreover he kissed all his bre-

† Heb. *neither let there be anger in your eyes.*
[b] chap. 50. 20.
† Heb. *to put for you a remnant.*

---

6. *earing*] *i.e.* "ploughing." To "ear" is an old English word from the Anglo-Saxon root *erian*, "to plough," cognate with the Latin *arare*. (See Bosworth, 'Anglo-Saxon Dict.' 25 k.) It occurs in the Authorised Version; Ex. xxxiv. 21; Deut. xxi. 4; 1 S. viii. 12; Isa. xxx. 24.

7. *to preserve you a posterity in the earth, and to save your lives by a great deliverance*] **To make you a remnant in the earth** (that is, to secure you from utter destruction), **and to preserve your lives to a great deliverance** (*i.e.* to preserve life to you, so that your deliverance should be great and signal).

8. *but God*] Lit. "The God." That great Personal God, who had led and guarded Abraham, Isaac, and Jacob, and who still watched over the house of Israel.

a father to Pharaoh] *i.e.* a wise and confidential friend and counsellor. The Caliphs and the Sultan of Turkey appear to have given the same title to their Grand Viziers. (See Burder, 'Oriental Customs,' ad h. l.; Gesen. p. 7; Ros. in loc.).

10. *the land of Goshen*] The land of Goshen was evidently a region lying to the north-east of lower Egypt, bounded apparently by the Mediterranean on the north, by the desert on the east, by the Tanitic branch of the Nile on the west (hence called "the field of Zoan" or Tanis, Ps. lxxviii. 12, 43), and probably extending south as far as to the head of the Red Sea, and nearly to Memphis. It appears, in Gen. xlvii. 11, to be called the land of Rameses, and the Israelites, before the Exodus, are said to have built in it the cities of Raamses and Pithom (Exod. i. 11). It was probably, though under the dominion of the Pharaohs, only on the confines of Egypt. Hence the LXX. here renders "Gesen of Arabia." In ch. xlvi. 28, where Goshen occurs twice, the LXX. call it "the city of Heroopolis in the land of Ramasses." Joseph placed his brethren naturally on the confines of Egypt, nearest to Palestine, and yet near himself. It is probable, that either Memphis or Tanis was then the metropolis of Egypt, both of which are in the immediate neighbourhood of the region thus marked out. (See Ges. p. 307; Poole, in Smith, 'Dict. of Bible' Art. *Goshen;* Hengstenb. 'Egypt,' &c. p. 42 sq.).

11. *and thy household*] The household of Abraham and of Isaac consisted of many servants and dependents, besides their own families. So Jacob, when he came from Padan-aram, had become "two bands." It is probable that some hundreds of dependents accompanied Jacob in his descent into Egypt, and settled with him in Goshen. So again in v. 18, Joseph's brethren are bidden to take their "father and their *households*."

thren, and wept upon them: and after
that his brethren talked with him.
16 ¶ And the fame thereof was
heard in Pharaoh's house, saying,
Joseph's brethren are come: and it
† pleased Pharaoh well, and his servants.
17 And Pharaoh said unto Joseph,
Say unto thy brethren, This do ye;
lade your beasts, and go, get you unto
the land of Canaan;
18 And take your father and your
households, and come unto me: and
I will give you the good of the land
of Egypt, and ye shall eat the fat of
the land.
19 Now thou art commanded, this
do ye; take you wagons out of the
land of Egypt for your little ones,
and for your wives, and bring your
father, and come.
20 Also † regard not your stuff; for
the good of all the land of Egypt *is*
yours.
21 And the children of Israel did
so: and Joseph gave them wagons,
according to the † commandment of
Pharaoh, and gave them provision for
the way.
22 To all of them he gave each
man changes of raiment; but to Benjamin he gave three hundred *pieces* of
silver, and five changes of raiment.
23 And to his father he sent after
this *manner;* ten asses † laden with the
good things of Egypt, and ten she asses
laden with corn and bread and meat
for his father by the way.
24 So he sent his brethren away,
and they departed: and he said unto
them, See that ye fall not out by the
way.
25 ¶ And they went up out of
Egypt, and came into the land of
Canaan unto Jacob their father,
26 And told him, saying, Joseph
is yet alive, and he *is* governor over
all the land of Egypt. And † Jacob's
heart fainted, for he believed them not.
27 And they told him all the words
of Joseph, which he had said unto
them: and when he saw the wagons
which Joseph had sent to carry him,
the spirit of Jacob their father revived:
28 And Israel said, *It is* enough;
Joseph my son *is* yet alive: I will go
and see him before I die.

† Heb. *was good in the eyes of Pharaoh.*
† Heb. *let not your eye spare, &c.*
† Heb. *mouth.*
† Heb. *carrying.*
† Heb. *his.*

CHAPTER XLVI.

1 *Jacob is comforted by God at Beer-sheba:* 5 *Thence he with his company goeth into Egypt.* 8 *The number of his family that went into Egypt.* 29 *Joseph meeteth Jacob.* 31 *He instructeth his brethren how to answer to Pharaoh.*

AND Israel took his journey with
all that he had, and came to
Beer-sheba, and offered sacrifices unto
the God of his father Isaac.
2 And God spake unto Israel in
the visions of the night, and said,

---

24. *See that ye fall not out by the way*] So all the Versions; but as the word rendered "fall out" expresses any violent emotion as of fear or anger, some prefer to render, "Be not afraid in the journey;" so Tuch, Baumg., Gesen., and many moderns. The ancient interpretation is more probable. They had already travelled on that journey several times without meeting with any evil accident; but there was some danger that they might quarrel among themselves, now that they were reconciled to Joseph, perhaps each one being ready to throw the blame of former misconduct on the others (Calvin).

27. *wagons*] Carts and wagons were known early in Egypt, which was a flat country and highly cultivated; but they were probably unknown at this time in Palestine and Syria. The Egyptian carts, as depicted on the monuments, are of two wheels only, when used for carrying agricultural produce. The four-wheeled car, mentioned by Herodotus, was used for carrying the shrine and image of a deity. (See Sir G. Wilkinson's note to Rawlinson's Herodotus, II. 63, and the engraving there.) When Jacob saw the wagons, he knew that they had come from Egypt, and so he believed his sons' report, and was comforted.

CHAP. XLVI. 1. *to Beer-sheba, and offered sacrifices*, &c.] Here Abraham and Isaac, built altars (ch. xxi. 33, xxvi. 25), and worshipped. Jacob naturally felt it to be a place hallowed by sacred memories, and being anxious as to the propriety of leaving the land of promise and going down into Egypt, he here sacrificed to the God of his fathers, and no doubt sought guidance from Him. Beer-sheba was South of Hebron on the road by which Jacob would naturally travel into Egypt.

Jacob, Jacob. And he said, Here
am I.
3 And he said, I *am* God, the God
of thy father: fear not to go down
into Egypt; for I will there make of
thee a great nation:
4 I will go down with thee into
Egypt; and I will also surely bring
thee up *again:* and Joseph shall put
his hand upon thine eyes.
5 And Jacob rose up from Beer-
sheba: and the sons of Israel carried
Jacob their father, and their little ones,
and their wives, in the wagons which
Pharaoh had sent to carry him.
6 And they took their cattle, and
their goods, which they had gotten in
[a] Josh. 24. 4. the land of Canaan, and came into
Psal. 105. 23. Egypt, [a] Jacob, and all his seed with
Is. 52. 4. him:
7 His sons, and his sons' sons with
him, his daughters, and his sons'
daughters, and all his seed brought
he with him into Egypt.
8 ¶ And [b] these *are* the names of [b] Exod. 1.
the children of Israel, which came into 1. & 6. 14.
Egypt, Jacob and his sons: [c] Reuben, [c] Numb. 26. 5.
Jacob's firstborn. 1 Chron. 5. 1.
9 And the sons of Reuben; Hanoch, and Phallu, and Hezron, and
Carmi.
10 ¶ [d] And the sons of Simeon; [d] Exod. 6. 15.
Jemuel, and Jamin, and Ohad, and 1 Chron. 4. 24.
Jachin, and Zohar, and Shaul the
son of a Canaanitish woman.
11 ¶ And the sons of [e] Levi; Ger- [e] 1 Chron. 6. 1.
shon, Kohath, and Merari.
12 ¶ And the sons of [f] Judah; Er, [f] 1 Chron.
and Onan, and Shelah, and Pharez, 2. 3. & 4. 21.
and Zarah: but Er and Onan died in chap. 38. 3.

---

3. *I am God, the God of thy father*] "I am *El*"—a reference again to the name "El-Shaddai," by which the Most High so specially made covenant with the patriarchs. See on ch. xliii. 14.

fear not to go down into Egypt] Abraham had gone down there and been in great danger. Isaac had been forbidden to go thither (ch. xxvi. 2). Abraham, Isaac, Jacob had all been placed and settled in Canaan with a promise that they should in future possess the land. Moreover, Egypt was, not only a heathen land, but one in which heathenism was specially developed and systematized. Jacob might therefore naturally fear to find in it dangers both worldly and spiritual. Hence the promise of God's presence and protection was signally needed.

4. *Joseph shall put his hand upon thine eyes*] The ancients, Gentiles as well as Jews, desired that their dearest relatives should close their eyes in death (Hom. 'Il.' XI. 453; 'Od.' XXIV. 296; Eurip. 'Hec.' 430; 'Phœn.' 1465; Virg. 'Æn.' IX. 487; Ov. 'Heroid.' I. 162).

5. *the sons of Israel carried Jacob their father*] The scene depicted on the tomb of Chnoumhotep at Beni Hassan cannot be the Egyptian version of the arrival of the Israelites in Egypt; but it is strikingly illustrative of the history of that event. The date of the inscription is that of the 12th dynasty, which was probably the dynasty under which Joseph lived; a number of strangers, with beards (which the Egyptians never wore, but which in the sculptures indicate uncivilized foreigners), and with dress and physical characteristics belonging to the Semitic nomads, appear before the governor offering him gifts. They carry their goods with them on asses, have women and children with them, and are armed with bows and clubs. They are described as Absha and his family, and the number 37 is written over in hieroglyphics. The signs, which accompany the picture, indicate that they were either captives or tributaries. Sir G. Wilkinson, however, has suggested that possibly this indication may result from the contemptuous way in which the Egyptians spoke of all foreigners, and the superiority which they claimed over them. Moreover, they are armed, one of them is playing on a lyre, and others bring presents; which things point rather to an immigration than to a captivity. (See Wilkinson, Vol. II. p. 296, and plate. Brugsch, 'H. E.' p. 63, where the scene is well engraved, and a good description annexed.)

7. *his daughters*] Only one daughter is named and one granddaughter. This verse implies that there were more. Married women would not be mentioned in a Hebrew genealogy; hence Jacob's sons' wives are not recounted among the seventy souls that came into Egypt. See v. 26. Dinah remained unmarried. Hence she only of Jacob's daughters is named.

10. *Jemuel*] Called Nemuel, Num. xxvi. 12; 1 Chron. iv. 24.

Ohad] Not named in Num. xxvi. 12; 1 Chr. iv. 24.

Jachin] "Jarib," 1 Chr. iv. 24.

Zohar] "Zerah," Num. xxvi. 13; 1 Chr. iv. 24.

11. *Gershon*] 'Gershom,' 1 Chr. vi. 16.

12. *And the sons of Pharez were Hezron and Hamul*] The difficulties in the chro-

the land of Canaan. And the sons of
Pharez were Hezron and Hamul.
g 1 Chron. 7. 1. 13 ¶ [g]And the sons of Issachar;
Tola, and Phuvah, and Job, and
Shimron.
14 ¶ And the sons of Zebulun;
Sered, and Elon, and Jahleel.
15 These *be* the sons of Leah,
which she bare unto Jacob in Padan-
aram, with his daughter Dinah: all
the souls of his sons and his daughters
were thirty and three.
16 ¶ And the sons of Gad; Ziphion, and Haggi, Shuni, and Ezbon,
Eri, and Arodi, and Areli.
h 1 Chron. 7. 30. 17 ¶ [h]And the sons of Asher; Jimnah, and Ishuah, and Isui, and Beriah,
and Serah their sister: and the sons of
Beriah; Heber, and Malchiel.
18 These *are* the sons of Zilpah,
whom Laban gave to Leah his daughter, and these she bare unto Jacob,
even sixteen souls.
19 The sons of Rachel Jacob's
wife; Joseph, and Benjamin.
20 ¶ [i]And unto Joseph in the land i chap. 41. 50.
of Egypt were born Manasseh and
Ephraim, which Asenath the daughter
of Poti-pherah ‖priest of On bare unto ‖ Or, *prince.*
him.
21 ¶ [k]And the sons of Benjamin k 1 Chron. 7. 6. & 8. 1.
were Belah, and Becher, and Ashbel,

---

nology of this catalogue have suggested the thought that it did not form a part of the original history of Genesis. The difficulties are really no greater than we might expect to find in a document so ancient, and where names and numbers are concerned, which of all things are most likely to puzzle us. In this verse it appears that Er and Onan having died in Canaan, two of Judah's grandchildren are substituted for them. It has been said that Hezron and Hamul could not have been born before the descent into Egypt, as the events related in ch. xxxviii. took place after the selling of Joseph, and that, therefore, Pharez could not have been old enough to have two sons at the time of that descent. Moreover, it is argued, that Judah himself could not have been more than 42 at this time, which is inconsistent with the apparent statement that his third son, Pharez, not born till after the marriage and death of his two elder brothers, Er and Onan, should himself have had two sons. To this it may be replied, (1), that we must not assume that the events in chap. xxxviii. necessarily took place after those in ch. xxxvii. It is most likely that ch. xxxviii. was introduced episodically at a convenient point in the history, to avoid breaking the continuity of the story. (See note on xxxviii. 1.) (2) Again, if the chronology of the life of Jacob proposed in the note at the end of ch. xxxi. be correct, Judah was, not 42, but 62, at the descent into Egypt, in which case the two sons of Pharez may easily have been born then. (3) Moreover, it is quite possible that the names in this catalogue may have comprised, not only those that were actually of the company, which went down into Egypt, but also all the grandchildren or great grandchildren of Jacob born before Jacob's death. This would not be inconsistent with the common usage of Scripture language, and it would allow 17 years more for the birth of those two grandsons of Judah and for the ten sons of Benjamin. Now Judah was probably 79 at Jacob's death, at which age his son Pharez may easily have had two sons. Indeed, the statement immediately coupled with the names of Hezron and Hamul, viz. that Er and Onan had died in Canaan, seems introduced on purpose to account for the reckoning of these grandchildren of Judah, born in Egypt, with others who had been born in Canaan.

13. *Job*] Called 'Jashub' Num. xxvi. 24; 1 Chr. vii. 1.

15. *thirty and three*] that is, including Jacob himself, but not Er, or Onan, who were dead, nor perhaps Leah.

16. *Ziphion*] 'Zephon' in Num. xxvi. 15.

Ezbon] 'Ozni,' Num. xxvi. 16.

Arodi] 'Arod,' Num. xxvi. 17.

17. *Ishuah*] Not mentioned in Numbers. Probably he had not left descendants and founded families.

20. *And unto Joseph*, &c.] At the end of this verse the LXX. insert the names of Machir the son of Manasseh, and Galaad the son of Machir, and Sutalaam and Taam the sons of Ephraim, and Edem the son of Sutalaam. (See Numb. xxvi. 28—37; 1 Chr. vii. 14.) Thus the whole number of persons becomes 75. The passage however is not in the Samaritan, with which the LXX. mostly agrees.

21. *the sons of Benjamin*] These are ten in number. According to Numb. xxvi. 40 two of them, Naaman and Ard, were grandsons of Benjamin. According to the common chronology Benjamin was only 23 at the coming into Egypt; an age at which he could hardly have had ten sons, or eight sons and two grandsons, even if he had two wives and some of the children had been twins. The considerations alluded to at v. 12, however, will allow us to calculate that Benjamin was 32 at

Gera, and Naaman, Ehi, and Rosh,
Muppim, and Huppim, and Ard.
22 These *are* the sons of Rachel,
which were born to Jacob: all the
souls *were* fourteen.
23 ¶ And the sons of Dan; Hushim.
24 ¶ And the sons of Naphtali;
Jahzeel, and Guni, and Jezer, and
Shillem.
25 These *are* the sons of Bilhah,
which Laban gave unto Rachel his
daughter, and she bare these unto
Jacob: all the souls *were* seven.
26 [l] All the souls that came with [l] Deut. 10. 22.
Jacob into Egypt, which came out
of his † loins, besides Jacob's sons' † Heb. *thigh.*
wives, all the souls *were* threescore
and six;
27 And the sons of Joseph, which
were born him in Egypt, *were* two
souls: all the souls of the house of
Jacob, which came into Egypt, *were*
threescore and ten.
28 ¶ And he sent Judah before
him unto Joseph, to direct his face
unto Goshen; and they came into
the land of Goshen.
29 And Joseph made ready his
chariot, and went up to meet Israel
his father, to Goshen, and presented
himself unto him; and he fell on his
neck, and wept on his neck a good
while.
30 And Israel said unto Joseph,
Now let me die, since I have seen
thy face, because thou *art* yet alive.
31 And Joseph said unto his brethren, and unto his father's house,
I will go up, and shew Pharaoh, and
say unto him, My brethren, and my
father's house, which *were* in the
land of Canaan, are come unto me;
32 And the men *are* shepherds,
for † their trade hath been to feed † Heb. *they are men of cattle.*
cattle; and they have brought their
flocks, and their herds, and all that
they have.
33 And it shall come to pass, when
Pharaoh shall call you, and shall say,
What *is* your occupation?
34 That ye shall say, Thy servants'
trade hath been about cattle from our
youth even until now, both we, *and*
also our fathers: that ye may dwell
in the land of Goshen; for every
shepherd *is* an abomination unto the
Egyptians.

---

the going down to Egypt (see note at the end of ch. xxxi.), and therefore forty-nine at the death of Jacob, by which age he might easily have been the father of ten sons.

Three of Benjamin's sons, Becher, Gera and Rosh, are wanting in the table given in Num. xxvi., probably because they had not left children enough to form independent families.

Ehi, Muppim, and Huppim] Called 'Shupham, Hupham, and Ahiram,' in Num. xxvi. 38, 39.

27. *all the souls of the house of Jacob, which came into Egypt, were threescore and ten*] The number is made up of the 66 mentioned in the last verse, Jacob himself, Joseph, and the two sons of Joseph. The LXX. reads here "The sons of Joseph, which were born to him in Egypt, were nine souls. All the souls of the house of Jacob, who came with Jacob into Egypt, were seventy-five." See above note on verse 20. St Stephen (Acts vii. 14) adopts the number 75, probably because he, or St Luke, quotes the LXX. version, as all Greek-speaking Jews would naturally have done; and it may be fairly said, that both numbers were equally correct, and that the variation depends on the different mode of reckoning. The genealogical tables of the Jews were drawn up on principles unlike those of modern calculation. And there would be no impropriety, on these principles, in reckoning the children of Joseph only, or in adding to them his grandchildren also, especially if the latter became founders of important families in Israel.

28. *he sent Judah before him unto Joseph, to direct his face unto Goshen*] *i.e.* He sent Judah before himself (Jacob) to Joseph, that Joseph might direct him to Goshen.

34. *every shepherd is an abomination unto the Egyptians*] Herodotus speaks of the aversion of the Egyptians for swineherds (II. 47). The monuments indicate their contempt for shepherds and goatherds by the mean appearance always given to them. Neither mutton nor the flesh of goats was ever eaten or offered. Even woollen garments, though sometimes worn over linen, were esteemed unclean. No priest would wear them. They were never worn in temples, nor were the dead buried in them. To this day, sheep-feeding is esteemed the office of women and slaves. The fact that the Egyptians themselves were great agriculturists, tillers of land, and

CHAPTER XLVII.

1 *Joseph presenteth five of his brethren,* 7 *and his father, before Pharaoh.* 11 *He giveth them habitation and maintenance.* 13 *He getteth all the Egyptians' money,* 16 *their cattle,* 18 *their lands to Pharaoh.* 22 *The priests' land was not bought.* 23 *He letteth the land to them for a fifth part.* 28 *Jacob's age.* 29 *He sweareth Joseph to bury him with his fathers.*

THEN Joseph came and told
Pharaoh, and said, My father
and my brethren, and their flocks,
and their herds, and all that they
have, are come out of the land of
Canaan; and, behold, they *are* in the
land of Goshen.
2 And he took some of his brethren, *even* five men, and presented
them unto Pharaoh.
3 And Pharaoh said unto his brethren, What *is* your occupation?
And they said unto Pharaoh, Thy
servants *are* shepherds, both we, *and*
also our fathers.
4 They said moreover unto Pharaoh, For to sojourn in the land are
we come; for thy servants have no
pasture for their flocks; for the famine *is* sore in the land of Canaan:
now therefore, we pray thee, let thy
servants dwell in the land of Goshen.
5 And Pharaoh spake unto Joseph,
saying, Thy father and thy brethren
are come unto thee:
6 The land of Egypt *is* before
thee; in the best of the land make
thy father and brethren to dwell; in
the land of Goshen let them dwell:
and if thou knowest *any* men of acti-
vity among them, then make them
rulers over my cattle.
7 And Joseph brought in Jacob
his father, and set him before Pharaoh: and Jacob blessed Pharaoh.
8 And Pharaoh said unto Jacob,
† How old *art* thou? † Heb. *How many* are *the days of the years of thy life?*
9 And Jacob said unto Pharaoh,
[a] The days of the years of my pilgrimage *are* an hundred and thirty
years: few and evil have the days of
the years of my life been, and have a Heb. 11. 9, 13.

---

that their neighbours the Arab tribes of the desert, with whom they were continually at feud, were nomads only, may have been sufficient to cause this feeling. The Egyptians looked on all the people of Egypt as of noble race (Diod. v. 58), and on all foreigners as low-born. Hence they would naturally esteem a nomadic people in close proximity to themselves, and with a much lower civilization than their own, as barbarous and despicable. Whatever be the historical foundation for the existence of three dynasties of Hycsos or Shepherd-kings extending over a period of from 500 to 1000 years, there can be little doubt that the Egyptians were frequently harassed by incursions from the nomadic tribes in their neighbourhood. Some of these tribes appear to have subdued portions of Lower Egypt and to have fixed their seat of government at Tanis (Zoan), or even at Memphis. The great Hycsos invasion was after the time of Joseph, who probably lived under a Pharaoh of the twelfth dynasty (see Excursus); but the hostility between the Egyptians and the nomad tribes of Asia had no doubt been of long duration.

CHAP. XLVII. 6. *in the best of the land*] The modern province of Es-Shurkiyeh, which appears nearly to correspond with the land of Goshen, is said to "bear the highest valuation and to yield the largest revenue" of any in Egypt. (Robinson, 'B. R.' I. p. 78, 79; Kurtz, Vol. II. p. 15.) M. Chabas has collected notices of great interest showing the riches and beauty of the district under the 19th dynasty ('Mél. Egypt.' II.)

7. *and Jacob blessed Pharaoh*]. Some here render "Jacob saluted Pharaoh," a possible translation, as the Eastern salutation is often with words of blessing: but the natural sense of the word is "to bless;" and if Jacob had bowed himself to the ground before Pharaoh according to a familiar Eastern custom, it would probably have been so related in the history. More probably the aged patriarch, with the conscious dignity of a prophet and the heir of the promises, prayed for blessings upon Pharaoh.

8. *How old art thou?*] **How many are the days of the years of thy life?**

9. *my pilgrimage*] Lit. "my sojournings." Pharaoh asked of the days of the years of his life, he replies by speaking of the days of the years of his pilgrimage. Some have thought that he called his life a pilgrimage, because he was a nomad, a wanderer in lands not his own: but in reality the patriarchs spoke of life as a pilgrimage or sojourning, because they sought another country, that is a heavenly (Heb. xi. 9, 13). Earth was not their home, but their journey homewards.

few and evil] The Jews speak of Jacob's

not attained unto the days of the
years of the life of my fathers in the
days of their pilgrimage.
10 And Jacob blessed Pharaoh, and
went out from before Pharaoh.
11 ¶ And Joseph placed his father
and his brethren, and gave them a
possession in the land of Egypt, in
the best of the land, in the land of
Rameses, as Pharaoh had commanded.
12 And Joseph nourished his father,
and his brethren, and all his
father's household, with bread, ‖ † according
to *their* families.
13 ¶ And *there was* no bread in
all the land; for the famine *was* very
sore, so that the land of Egypt and
all the land of Canaan fainted by reason
of the famine.
14 And Joseph gathered up all the
money that was found in the land of
Egypt, and in the land of Canaan,
for the corn which they bought: and
Joseph brought the money into Pharaoh's
house.
15 And when money failed in the
land of Egypt, and in the land of
Canaan, all the Egyptians came unto
Joseph, and said, Give us bread: for
why should we die in thy presence?
for the money faileth.

‖ Or, *as a little child is nourished.* † Heb. *according to the little ones.*

16 And Joseph said, Give your
cattle; and I will give you for your
cattle, if money fail.
17 And they brought their cattle
unto Joseph: and Joseph gave them
bread *in exchange* for horses, and for
the flocks, and for the cattle of the
herds, and for the asses: and he † fed
them with bread for all their cattle
for that year.
18 When that year was ended,
they came unto him the second year,
and said unto him, We will not hide
it from my lord, how that our money
is spent; my lord also hath our herds
of cattle; there is not ought left in
the sight of my lord, but our bodies,
and our lands:
19 Wherefore shall we die before
thine eyes, both we and our land?
buy us and our land for bread, and
we and our land will be servants unto
Pharaoh: and give *us* seed, that we
may live, and not die, that the land
be not desolate.
20 And Joseph bought all the land
of Egypt for Pharaoh; for the Egyptians
sold every man his field, because
the famine prevailed over them: so
the land became Pharaoh's.
21 And as for the people, he re-

† Heb. *led them.*

---

seven afflictions: (1) the persecution of Esau; (2) the injustice of Laban; (3) the result of his wrestling with the Angel; (4) the violation of Dinah; (5) the loss of Joseph; (6) the imprisonment of Simeon; (7) the departure of Benjamin for Egypt. They might well have added the death of Rachel and the incest of Reuben (Schumann).

11. *the land of Rameses*] In Ex. i. 11, the Israelites are said to have built treasure cities for Pharaoh, Pithom and Raamses. It is possible that Goshen is here called the land of Rameses by anticipation, as it may have become familiarly known to the Israelites by the name "land of Rameses" after they had built the city Rameses in it. Very probably, however, the Israelites in the captivity only fortified and strengthened the city of Rameses then already existing, and so fitted it to be a strong treasure-city. The name Rameses became famous in after times from the exploits of Rameses II., a king of the 19th dynasty: but he was of too late a date to have given name to a city, either in the time of Joseph, or even at the time of the Exodus. Rameses, according to the LXX. corresponded with the Heroopolis of after times. (See on this city Hengstenberg, 'Egypt,' p. 51, and Excursus at the end of the volume.)

12. *according to their families*] Lit. "to the mouth of their children;" meaning very probably, "even to the food for their children."

20. *Joseph bought all the land of Egypt for Pharaoh*] All the main points in the statements of this chapter are confirmed by Herodotus, Diodorus, Strabo, and the monuments. Herodotus (II. 109) says that Sesostris divided the soil among the inhabitants, assigning square plots of land of equal size to all, and obtained his revenue from a rent paid annually by the holders. Diodorus (I. 54) says that Sesoösis divided the whole country into 36 nomes and set nomarchs over each to take care of the royal revenue and administer their respective provinces. Strabo (XVII. p. 787) tells us that the occupiers of land held it subject to a rent. Again, Diodorus (I. 73, 74) represents the land as possessed only by the priests, the king, and the warriors, which

moved them to cities from *one* end
of the borders of Egypt even to the
other end thereof.
‖ Or, *princes.*
22 Only the land of the ‖ priests
bought he not; for the priests had
a portion *assigned them* of Pharaoh,
and did eat their portion which Pharaoh gave them: wherefore they sold
not their lands.
23 Then Joseph said unto the people, Behold, I have bought you this
day and your land for Pharaoh: lo,
here is seed for you, and ye shall sow
the land.
24 And it shall come to pass in
the increase, that ye shall give the
fifth *part* unto Pharaoh, and four
parts shall be your own, for seed of
the field, and for your food, and for
them of your households, and for food
for your little ones.
25 And they said, Thou hast saved
our lives: let us find grace in the
sight of my lord, and we will be
Pharaoh's servants.
26 And Joseph made it a law over
the land of Egypt unto this day, *that*
Pharaoh should have the fifth *part;*

---

testimony is confirmed by the sculptures (Wilkinson, I. p. 263). The discrepancy of this from the account in Genesis is apparent in the silence of the latter concerning the lands assigned to the warrior caste. The reservation of their lands to the priests is expressly mentioned in v. 22; but nothing is said of the warriors. There was, however, a marked difference in the tenure of land by the warriors from that by the priests. Herodotus (II. 168) says that each warrior had assigned to him twelve *aruræ* of land (each *arura* being a square of 100 Egyptian cubits); that is to say, there were no landed possessions vested in the caste, but certain fixed portions assigned to each person: and these, as given by the sovereign's will, so apparently were liable to be withheld or taken away by the same will; for we find that Sethos, the contemporary of Sennacherib and therefore of Hezekiah and Isaiah, actually deprived the warriors of these lands, which former kings had conceded to them (Herod. II. 141). It is therefore, as Knobel remarks, highly probable that the original reservation of their lands was only to the priests, and that the warrior caste did not come into possession of their twelve *aruræ* each, till after the time of Joseph. In the other important particulars the sacred and profane accounts entirely tally, viz. that, by royal appointment, the original proprietors of the land became crown tenants, holding their land by payment of a rent or tribute; whilst the priests only were left in full possession of their former lands and revenues. As to the particular king to whom this is attributed by Herodotus and Diodorus, Lepsius ('Chronol. Egypt.' I. p. 304) supposes that this was not the Sesostris of Manetho's 12th dynasty (Osirtasen of the Monuments), but a Sethos or Sethosis of the 19th dynasty, whom he considers to be the Pharaoh of Joseph. The 19th dynasty is, however, certainly much too late a date for Joseph. It may be a question whether the division of the land into 36 nomes and into square plots of equal size by Sesostris be the same transaction as the purchasing and restoring of the land by Joseph. The people were already in possession of their property when Joseph bought it, and they received it again on condition of paying a fifth of the produce as a rent. But whether or not this act of Sesostris be identified with that of Joseph (or the Pharaoh of Joseph), the profane historians and the monuments completely bear out the testimony of the author of Genesis as to the condition of land tenure and its origin in an exercise of the sovereign's authority.

21. *he removed them to cities*] He had collected all the corn, which he had stored up for the famine, into the various cities of Egypt, and so he removed the people into the cities and their neighbourhood, that he might the better provide them with food (Schum.).

22. *Only the land of the priests bought he not*] See on v. 20.

the priests had a portion assigned them of Pharaoh, and did eat their portion which Pharaoh gave them] This does not mean that the priests were Pharaoh's stipendiaries, which would be inconsistent with the immediately preceding words, as well as with the statement of profane authors as to the landed possessions of the priests. On the contrary, it means, that Pharaoh had such respect for the ministers of religion, that, instead of suffering Joseph to sell corn to them and so to buy up their land, he ordered a portion of corn to be regularly distributed to them during the famine, and so they were not reduced to the necessity of selling their lands. This regard for the priests is expressly assigned to Pharaoh, not to Joseph, and so there can be no need to apologize for Joseph's respect to an idolatrous priesthood.

26. *Joseph made it a law*] The final result of Joseph's policy was that the land was restored to the Egyptians, with an obligation to pay one fifth of it to Pharaoh for the

except the land of the [‖] priests only, (‖Or, princes.)
which became not Pharaoh's.
27 ¶ And Israel dwelt in the land
of Egypt, in the country of Goshen;
and they had possessions therein, and
grew, and multiplied exceedingly.
28 And Jacob lived in the land of
Egypt seventeen years: so [†] the whole (†Heb. the days of the years of his life.)
age of Jacob was an hundred forty
and seven years.
29 And the time drew nigh that
Israel must die: and he called his son
Joseph, and said unto him, If now
I have found grace in thy sight,
[b] put, I pray thee, thy hand under (b chap. 24. 2.)
my thigh, and deal kindly and truly
with me; bury me not, I pray thee,
in Egypt:
30 But I will lie with my fathers,
and thou shalt carry me out of Egypt,
and bury me in their buryingplace.
And he said, I will do as thou hast
said.
31 And he said, Swear unto me.
And he sware unto him. And [c] Is- (c Heb. 11. 21.)
rael bowed himself upon the bed's
head.

CHAPTER XLVIII.

1 Joseph with his sons visiteth his sick father. 2 Jacob strengtheneth himself to bless them. 3 He repeateth the promise. 5 He taketh Ephraim and Manasseh as his own. 7 He telleth Joseph of his mother's grave. 9 He blesseth Ephraim and Manasseh. 17 He preferreth the younger before the elder. 21 He prophesieth their return to Canaan.

AND it came to pass after these
things, that *one* told Joseph,
Behold, thy father *is* sick: and he

---

purpose of maintaining the revenues of the state. Much has been written in condemnation, and again in vindication of these proceedings. Was Joseph a mere creature of Pharaoh's, desirous only of his master's aggrandizement? or was he bent on establishing a tyrannical absolutism in violation of the rights and liberties of the subject? The brevity of the narrative and our imperfect acquaintance with the condition of the people and the state of agriculture in ancient Egypt make it impossible fully to judge of the wisdom and equity of Joseph's laws. This much, however, is quite evident. The land in favourable years was very productive. In the plenteous years it brought forth by handfuls (ch. xli. 47). Even the fifth part of the revenue of corn (v. 34) was so abundant that it is described as like "the sand of the sea," and "without number" (v. 49). Yet there was a liability to great depression, as shewn by the seven years of famine: the monuments too indicate the frequent occurrence of scarcity, and there was evidently no provision against this in the habits of the people or the management of the tillage. If Pharaoh had not been moved to store up corn against the famine years, the population would most probably have perished. The peculiar nature of the land, its dependence on the overflow of the Nile, and the unthrifty habits of the cultivators, made it desirable to establish a system of centralization, perhaps to introduce some general principle of irrigation, in modern phraseology, to promote the prosperity of the country by great government works, in preference to leaving all to the uncertainty of individual enterprize. If this was so, then the saying, "Thou hast saved our lives," was no language of Eastern adulation, but the verdict of a grateful people.

The "fifth part" which was paid to Pharaoh for the revenues of the state, and perhaps for public works of all kinds, agricultural and others, was not an exorbitant impost. The Egyptians appear to have made no difficulty in paying one-fifth of the produce of their land to Pharaoh during the years of plenty; and hence we may infer that it would not have been a burdensome rent when the system of agriculture was put on a better footing.

28. *the whole age of Jacob*] Lit. **the days of Jacob, even the years of his life.**

29. *bury me not...in Egypt*] Jacob had a firm faith that his descendants should inherit the land of Canaan, and therefore desired to be buried there. Moreover, he very probably wished to direct the minds of his children to that as their future home, that they might be kept from setting up their rest in Egypt.

31. *bowed himself upon the bed's head*] So the Masorites point it. So the Targg., Symm., Aquila, Vulg., but the LXX., Syr., and Epistle to the Hebrews (xi. 21), read "on the top of his staff." The Hebrew word without the vowel points means either "bed" or "staff." The only distinction is in the vowel points, which do not exist in the more ancient MSS. It is therefore impossible to decide with certainty which was the original sense of the word. It is quite possible that the meaning is, as the Apostle quotes the passage, that after Joseph had sworn to bury him in Canaan, Jacob bowed himself upon the staff which had gone with him through all his wanderings (Gen. xxxii. 10), and so worshipped God. And this seems the more likely from the fact that it is not till after these things that one told Joseph, "Behold, thy father is

took with him his two sons, Manasseh and Ephraim.

2 And *one* told Jacob, and said, Behold, thy son Joseph cometh unto thee: and Israel strengthened himself, and sat upon the bed.

3 And Jacob said unto Joseph, God Almighty appeared unto me at
a chap. 28. 13. & 35. 6. [a]Luz in the land of Canaan, and blessed me,

4 And said unto me, Behold, I will make thee fruitful, and multiply thee, and I will make of thee a multitude of people; and will give this land to thy seed after thee *for* an everlasting possession.

b chap. 41. 50. Josh. 13. 7. 5 ¶ And now thy [b]two sons, Ephraim and Manasseh, which were born unto thee in the land of Egypt before I came unto thee into Egypt, *are* mine; as Reuben and Simeon, they shall be mine.

6 And thy issue, which thou begettest after them, shall be thine, *and* shall be called after the name of their brethren in their inheritance.

7 And as for me, when I came
from Padan, [c]Rachel died by me in c chap. 35. 19.
the land of Canaan in the way, when yet *there was* but a little way to come unto Ephrath: and I buried her there in the way of Ephrath; the same *is* Beth-lehem.

8 And Israel beheld Joseph's sons, and said, Who *are* these?

9 And Joseph said unto his father, They *are* my sons, whom God hath given me in this *place*. And he said, Bring them, I pray thee, unto me, and I will bless them.

10 Now the eyes of Israel were
†dim for age, *so that* he could not see. † Heb. *heavy*.
And he brought them near unto him; and he kissed them, and embraced them.

11 And Israel said unto Joseph, I had not thought to see thy face: and, lo, God hath shewed me also thy seed.

12 And Joseph brought them out from between his knees, and he bowed himself with his face to the earth.

---

sick" (ch. xlviii. 1), so that Jacob probably had not as yet taken to his bed. At the same time we must not always press the quotations in the New Testament as proof of the true sense of the Hebrew original, for it is natural for the Apostles to quote the LXX. as being the Authorised Version, just as modern divines quote modern versions in the vernacular languages without suggesting a correction of their language, when such correction is unnecessary for their argument.

CHAP. XLVIII. 3. *God Almighty*] "El-Shaddai." See on ch. xliii. 14.

at Luz] *i.e.* Bethel. See ch. xxviii. 17, 19, xxxv. 6, 7.

5. *as Reuben and Simeon, they shall be mine*] Thy two sons shall be as much counted to be my sons, as Reuben and Simeon, my own two eldest sons, are counted to be mine; accordingly Ephraim and Manasseh became patriarchs, *eponymi*, heads of tribes. Some think that, as Reuben was deprived of his birthright, so here the birthright is given to Ephraim, the elder son of the firstborn of Rachel. But the birthright seems rather to have been transferred to Judah, his three elder brothers being disinherited, the first for incest, the other two for cruelty (see ch. xlix. 8-10) Accordingly, Judah became the royal tribe, from whom as concerning the flesh Christ came, who is over all God blessed for ever. There was, however, a kind of secondary birthright given to Ephraim (see xlix. 22 sq.), who became ancestor of the royal tribe among the ten tribes of Israel.

6. *shall be called after the name of their brethren*] Shall not give names to separate tribes, but shall be numbered with the tribes of Ephraim and Manasseh. We hear nothing of any younger sons of Joseph, and do not know for certain that any were born to him; but it has been thought that they may be mentioned in Num. xxvi. 28—37, 1 Chr. vii. 14—29.

7. *Rachel died by me*] When adopting the sons of Joseph, Jacob turns his thoughts back to his beloved Rachel, for whose sake especially he had so dearly loved Joseph. Rosenm., Gesenius and some others propose to translate here "Rachel died to my sorrow," lit. "upon me," and therefore as a heavy burden to me; but the received translation is supported by the Versions, and by the frequent use of the preposition in the sense of "near me," "by my side."

12. *Joseph brought them out from between his knees*] Joseph brought them out from between Jacob's knees, where they had gone that he might embrace them, and probably placed them in a reverent attitude to receive the patriarch's blessing

13 And Joseph took them both,
Ephraim in his right hand toward
Israel's left hand, and Manasseh in
his left hand toward Israel's right
hand, and brought *them* near unto him.
14 And Israel stretched out his
right hand, and laid *it* upon Ephraim's head, who *was* the younger,
and his left hand upon Manasseh's
head, guiding his hands wittingly; for
Manasseh *was* the firstborn.
15 ¶ And [d]he blessed Joseph, and (d Heb. 11. 21.)
said, God, before whom my fathers
Abraham and Isaac did walk, the God
which fed me all my life long unto
this day,
16 The Angel which redeemed me
from all evil, bless the lads; and let
my name be named on them, and the
name of my fathers Abraham and
Isaac; and let them †grow into a († Heb. *as fishes do increase.*)
multitude in the midst of the earth.
17 And when Joseph saw that his
father laid his right hand upon the
head of Ephraim, it displeased him:
and he held up his father's hand, to
remove it from Ephraim's head unto
Manasseh's head.
18 And Joseph said unto his father, Not so, my father: for this *is*
the firstborn; put thy right hand upon
his head.
19 And his father refused, and said,
I know *it*, my son, I know *it*: he
also shall become a people, and he
also shall be great: but truly his
younger brother shall be greater than
he, and his seed shall become a †mul- († Heb. *fulness.*)
titude of nations.
20 And he blessed them that day,
saying, In thee shall Israel bless, saying, God make thee as Ephraim and
as Manasseh: and he set Ephraim
before Manasseh.
21 And Israel said unto Joseph,
Behold, I die: but God shall be with
you, and bring you again unto the
land of your fathers.
22 Moreover I have given to thee
one portion above thy brethren, which
I took out of the hand of the Amorite
with my sword and with my bow.

---

and he bowed himself with his face to the earth] i.e. Joseph bowed down respectfully and solemnly before his father. The LXX. has "They bowed themselves," which differs but by the repetition of one letter from the received reading.

14. *guiding his hands wittingly*] So Gesen., Rosenm., and most modern interpreters; but the LXX. Vulg. &c. "putting his hands crosswise." This has been defended by some, comparing an Arabic root, which has the sense "to bind, to twist," but it cannot be shewn ever to have had the sense "to cross."

16. *The Angel which redeemed me from all evil*] There is here a triple blessing:

"The God, before whom my fathers walked,
"The God, which fed me like a shepherd, all my life long,
"The Angel, which redeemed (or redeemeth me) from all evil."

It is impossible that the Angel thus identified with God can be a created Angel. Jacob, no doubt, alludes to the Angel who wrestled with him and whom he called God (ch. xxxii. 24—30), the same as the Angel of the Covenant, Mal. iii. 1. Luther observes that the verb "bless," which thus refers to the God of his fathers, to the God who had been his Shepherd, and to the Angel who redeemed him, is in the singular, not in the plural, showing that these three are but one God, and that the Angel is one with the fathers' God and with the God who fed Jacob like a sheep.

22. *Moreover I have given to thee one portion*] There is little doubt but that this rendering is correct. The past tense is used by prophetic anticipation, and the meaning is, "I have assigned to thee one portion of that land, which my descendants are destined to take out of the hands of the Amorites." The word rendered portion is *Shechem*, meaning literally "a shoulder," thence probably a ridge or neck of land, hence here rendered by most versions and commentators "portion." Shechem, the city of Samaria, was probably named from the fact of its standing thus on a ridge or shoulder of ground. (See on Gen. xii. 6.) Accordingly here the LXX., Targ. of Pseudo-Jonath., as also Calvin, Rosenm., and some moderns, have rendered not "portion," but "Shechem," a proper name. The history of Shechem is doubtless much mixed up with the history of the Patriarchs, and was intimately connected with all their blessings. It was Abraham's first settlement in Palestine, and there he first built an altar (ch. xii. 6). There too Jacob purchased a piece of ground from Hamor the father of Shechem, and built an altar (xxxiii. 18—20). This was, however, not "taken out of the hand of the Amorite with sword and bow," but obtained peaceably

CHAPTER XLIX.

1 *Jacob calleth his sons to bless them.* 3 *Their blessing in particular.* 29 *He chargeth them about his burial.* 33 *He dieth.*

AND Jacob called unto his sons,
and said, Gather yourselves together, that I may tell you *that* which
shall befall you in the last days.
2 Gather yourselves together, and
hear, ye sons of Jacob; and hearken
unto Israel your father.
3 ¶ Reuben, thou *art* my firstborn,
my might, and the beginning of my
strength, the excellency of dignity,
and the excellency of power:
4 Unstable as water, †thou shalt
not excel; because thou [a]wentest up
to thy father's bed; then defiledst
thou *it:* ‖he went up to my couch.
5 ¶ Simeon and Levi *are* brethren;
‖instruments of cruelty *are in* their
habitations.

† Heb. *do not thou excel.*
[a] chap. 35. 22. 1 Chron. 5. 1.
‖ Or, *my couch is gone.*
‖ Or, *their swords* are *weapons of violence.*

---

by purchase. Some have thought therefore that the allusion is to the victory over the Shechemites by Simeon and Levi related in ch. xxxiv., the Shechemites being here called Amorites, though there Hivites, because Amorite was a generic name, like Canaanite: but it is hardly likely that Jacob should boast of a conquest by his sons, as though it were his own, when he strongly reprobated their action in it, and even "cursed their anger, for it was fierce, and their wrath, for it was cruel" (ch. xlix. 7). Though, therefore, it is undoubtedly told us, that Jacob gave Shechem to Joseph, and that Joseph was therefore buried there (Josh. xxiv. 32; John iv. 5. See also Jerome, 'Qu. in Gen.' xlix.); and though there may be some allusion to this gift in the words here made use of, by a paronomasia so common in Hebrew, it is most likely that the rendering of the Authorised Version is correct. The addition of "one" to "portion" seems to decide for this interpretation. "I have given thee one Shechem," would be very hard to interpret.

CHAP. XLIX. 1. *in the last days*] The future generally, but with special reference to the times of Messiah. The Rabbi Nachmanides says, "According to the words of all, the last days denote the days of Messiah." The passages in which it occurs are mostly Messianic predictions (see Num. xxiv. 14; Isa. ii. 2; Jer. xxx. 24; Ezek. xxxviii. 16; Dan. x. 14; Hos. iii. 5; Mic. iv. 1). The exact words of the LXX. are used in Heb. i. 1, and virtually the same in Acts ii. 17; 2 Tim. iii. 1; 1 Pet. i. 20; 2 Pet. iii. 3, where the reference is to the times of Christ. (See Heidegger, Vol. II. XXIII. 6; Gesen. 'Thes.' p. 73.) The prophecy of Jacob does not refer exclusively to the days of Messiah, but rather sketches generally the fortunes of his family; but all is leading up to that which was to be the great consummation, when the promised Seed should come and extend the blessings of the Spiritual Israel throughout all the world. It is to be carefully noted, that the occupation of Canaan by the twelve tribes under Joshua was not the point to which his expectations pointed as an end, but rather that from which his predictions took their beginning. It was not the *terminus ad quem*, but the *terminus a quo.* The return to Canaan was a fact established in the decrees of Providence, the certainty of which rested on promises given and repeated to the Patriarchs. Jacob therefore does not repeat this, farther than by the injunction, in the last chapter, and again at the end of this, that he should be buried, not in Egypt, but at Machpelah, the buryingplace of his fathers.

3. *the beginning of my strength*] Some important Versions (Aquila, Symm., Vulg.) render "the beginning of my sorrow," a possible translation, but not suited to the parallelisms. For the expression, as applied to firstborn sons, comp. Deut. xxi. 17; Ps. lxxviii. 51, cv. 36.

4. *Unstable as water*] or "boiling over like water." The meaning of the word is uncertain. The same root in Syriac expresses "wantonness;" in Arabic, "pride," "swelling arrogance." In this passage it is clearly connected with water. The Vulgate translates, "Thou art poured out like water." Symmachus renders "Thou hast boiled over like water." The translation of the LXX. is peculiar, but it also seems to point to boiling as well as to the insolence of pride (ἐξύβρισας ὡς ὕδωρ, μὴ ἐκζέσῃς). Modern lexicographers (as Gesen., Lee, &c.) generally give "boiling over."

thou shalt not excel] Perhaps, though, through thy swelling wantonness, thou risest up like water when it boils, yet it shall not be so as to excel and surpass thy brethren. Not one great action, not one judge, prophet, or leader from the tribe of Reuben is ever mentioned in history.

then defiledst thou it] "Thou hast polluted" or "desecrated it."

5. *instruments of cruelty are in their habitations*] Probably, "Their swords are instruments of violence;" so the Vulg., several Rabbins, and the most eminent moderns. The word occurs only here, is very variously rendered by the Versions, and is of doubtful derivation.

6 O my soul, come not thou into
their secret; unto their assembly,
mine honour, be not thou united:
for in their anger they slew a man,
and in their selfwill they ‖digged down
a wall.

‖ Or, *houghed oxen.*

7 Cursed *be* their anger, for *it was*
fierce; and their wrath, for it was
cruel: I will divide them in Jacob,
and scatter them in Israel.

8 ¶ Judah, thou *art* *he* whom thy
brethren shall praise: thy hand *shall*
be in the neck of thine enemies; thy
father's children shall bow down before thee.

9 Judah *is* a lion's whelp: from
the prey, my son, thou art gone up:
he stooped down, he couched as a
lion, and as an old lion; who shall
rouse him up?

10 The sceptre shall not depart
from Judah, nor a lawgiver from be-

---

6. *mine honour*] Probably a synonym for "my soul" in the first clause of the parallelism: The soul as being the noblest part of man is called his glory. See Ps. viii. 5 (6 Heb.), xvi. 9, xxx. 12 (13 Heb.), lvii. 8 (9 Heb.), cviii. 1 (2 Heb.); (Ges. 'Thes.' p. 655).

digged down a wall] **Hamstrung an ox.** So the margin "houghed oxen." The singular "an ox" must be used to retain the parallelism with "a man" in the former clause, both have a collective intention. This is the rendering of the LXX. and gives the commoner sense of the verb. It is therefore adopted by most recent commentators. The same Hebrew word, with a distinction only in the vowel point, means "ox" and "wall."

7. *I will divide them in Jacob, and scatter them in Israel*] This was most literally fulfilled, for when Canaan was conquered, on the second numbering under Moses, the tribe of Simeon had become the weakest of all the tribes (Numb. xxvi. 14); in Moses' blessing (Deut. xxxiii.) it is entirely passed over; and in the assignment of territory it was merely mingled or scattered among the tribe of Judah, having certain cities assigned it within the limits of Judah's possession (Josh. xix. 1—9); whilst the Levites had no separate inheritance, but merely a number of cities to dwell in, scattered throughout the possessions of their brethren (Josh. xxi. 1—40). With regard to the latter, though by being made dependent on the tithes and also on the liberality of their fellow countrymen, they were punished, yet in process of time the curse was turned into a blessing. (See Mede, 'Works,' Bk. I. Disc. xxxv.) Of this transformation of the curse into a blessing there is not the slightest intimation in Jacob's address: and in this we have a strong proof of its genuineness. After this honourable change in the time of Moses (due in great part to the faithfulness of Moses himself and of the Levites with him), it would never have occurred to the forger of a prophecy to cast such a reproach, and to foretell such a judgment on the forefather of the Levites. In fact, how different is the blessing pronounced by Moses himself upon the tribe of Levi in Deut. xxxiii. 8 sqq. (See Keil.)

8. *Judah, thou art he whom thy brethren shall praise*] **Judah, thou, thy brethren shall praise thee.** The word "thou" is emphatic, probably, like "Judah," in the vocative, not, as some would render it, "Thou art Judah," which is far tamer. The reference is to the meaning of the name. Leah said, "Now will I *praise* the Lord, therefore she called his name *Judah*" (ch. xxix. 35). Judah, notwithstanding the sad history of him and his house in ch. xxxviii., shewed on the whole more nobleness than any of the elder sons of Jacob. He and Reuben were the only two who desired to save the life of Joseph (ch. xxxvii. 22, 26); and his conduct before Joseph in Egypt is truly noble and touching (see ch. xliv. 18—34). Hence, when Reuben is deprived of his birthright for incest, Simeon and Levi for manslaughter, Judah, who is next in age, naturally and rightly succeeds to it.

thy hand shall be in the neck of thine enemies; thy father's children shall bow down before thee] He was to be victorious in war, and the leading tribe in Israel; the former promise being signally fulfilled in the victories of David and Solomon, the latter in the elevation of Judah to be the royal tribe; but both most fully in the victory and royalty of David's Son and David's Lord.

9. *Judah is a lion's whelp: from the prey, my son, thou art gone up*] Judah is compared to the most royal and the most powerful of beasts. The image is from the lion retiring to the mountains after having devoured his prey: not probably, as Gesenius and others, "thou hast grown up from feeding upon the prey."

as an old lion] **As a lioness** (Bochart, 'Hieroz.' I. p. 719; Ges. 'Thes.' p. 738). The standard of Judah was a lion, very probably derived from these words of Jacob.

10. *The sceptre shall not depart from Judah, &c.*] Render

A sceptre shall not depart from Judah
Nor a lawgiver from between his feet,
Until that Shiloh come,
And to him shall be the obedience of the peoples.

tween his feet, until Shiloh come;
and unto him *shall* the gathering of
the people *be*.
11 Binding his foal unto the vine,
and his ass's colt unto the choice vine;
he washed his garments in wine,
and his clothes in the blood of grapes:
12 His eyes *shall be* red with wine,
and his teeth white with milk.
13 ¶ Zebulun shall dwell at the

A remarkable prophecy of the Messiah, and so acknowledged by all Jewish, as well as Christian, antiquity. The meaning of the verse appears to be "The Sceptre (either of royal, or perhaps only of tribal, authority) shall not depart from Judah, nor a lawgiver (senator or scribe) from before him, until Shiloh (*i.e.* either 'the Prince of peace,' or 'he whose right it is') shall come, and to him shall the nations be obedient." There are some obscure expressions, but we may confidently hold that the above paraphrase conveys the true sense of the passage.

1. The word *sceptre*, originally denoting a staff of wood, a strong rod taken from a tree and peeled as a wand, is used (1) for "the rod of correction, (2) for "the staff of a shepherd," (3) for "the sceptre of royalty" (as Ps. xlv. 7; cp. Hom. 'Il.' II. 46, 101), (4) for "a tribe," which may be because the sceptre denoted tribal as well as regal authority, or because tribes were considered as twigs or branches from a central stem. (See Ges. p. 1353.) It is probable that the sceptre in Balaam's prophecy (Num. xxiv. 17) has a reference to these words of Jacob.

2. "A lawgiver," so, more or less, all the Ancient Versions. The LXX. and Vulg. render "a leader," the Targums paraphrasing by "scribe or interpreter of the law." The word certainly means "a lawgiver" in Deut. xxxiii. 21; Isa. xxxiii. 22; and all ancient interpretation was in favour of understanding it of a person. The R. Lipmann, however, proposed the sense of "a rod or staff" answering to "the sceptre" in the former clause, in which he has been followed by eminent critics, such as Gesenius, Tuch, Knobel, who think that this sense is more pertinent here, and in Num. xxi. 18; Ps. lx. 7 (see Heidegger, Vol. II. p. 738; Ges. p. 514); but it requires proof that the word, naturally signifying "lawgiver," sometimes undoubtedly meaning "lawgiver," and always so rendered in the Versions, can mean lawgiver's staff or sceptre.

3. "From between his feet" is rendered by the Versions, and generally by commentators "from among his posterity. (See Ges. p. 204.)

4. "Until Shiloh come." For fuller consideration of the name "Shiloh," see Note A at the end of the Chapter. The only two admissible interpretations are that the word is (1) a proper name, meaning "the Peace-maker," "the Prince of peace," or, (2) according to the almost unanimous consent of the Versions and Targums, "He, whose right it is." All the Targums add the name of Messiah, and all the more ancient Jews held it to be an undoubted prophecy of Messiah.

5. "Unto him shall the gathering of the people be." Rather, "Unto him shall be the obedience of the nations." The word for obedience occurs only once besides, in Prov. xxx. 17; but, if the reading be correct, there is little doubt of its significance. (See Ges. pp. 620, 1200; Heidegger, Tom. II. p. 748.)

As regards the fulfilment of this prophecy, it is undoubted that the tribal authority and the highest place in the nation continued with Judah until the destruction of Jerusalem. It is true that after the Babylonish Captivity the royalty was not in the house of Judah; but the prophecy is not express as to the possession of absolute royalty. Israel never ceased to be a nation, Judah never ceased to be a tribe with at least a tribal sceptre and lawgivers, or expositors of the law, Sanhedrim or Senators, and with a general pre-eminence in the land, nor was there a foreign ruler of the people, till at least the time of Herod the Great, just before the birth of the Saviour; and even the Herods, though of Idumæan extraction, were considered as exercising a native sovereignty in Judah, which did not quite pass away till a Roman procurator was sent thither after the reign of Archelaus, the son of Herod the Great: and at that very time the Shiloh came, the Prince of peace, to whom of right the kingdom belonged. (On the meaning of the name *Shiloh*, see Note A at the end of the Chapter.)

11. *Binding his foal unto the vine*, &c.] Many think that the patriarch, having spoken of the endurance of the reign of Judah till the coming of Christ, returns to speak of Judah's temporal prosperity during all that period; but the Targums of Jerusalem and Pseudo-Jonathan refer this verse to the Messiah. So also several Christian fathers (*e.g.* Chrysostom, in loc., Theodoret, 'Qu. in Gen.'); interpreting the vine of the Jewish people, and the wild ass of the gentile converts brought into the vineyard of the Church. The washing of the garments in wine they consider an allusion to Christ as the true vine (John xv. 1), to His treading "the winepress alone" (Isa. lxiii. 1—3), and empurpling His garments with His own Blood. (See Heidegger, II. pp. 752, sqq.)

12. *His eyes shall be red with wine,*] &c. Or perhaps (as the LXX., Vulg., Targg. Jerus., and Pseudo-Jon.), "His eyes shall be

haven of the sea; and he *shall be* for an haven of ships; and his border *shall be* unto Zidon.

14 ¶ Issachar *is* a strong ass couching down between two burdens:

15 And he saw that rest *was* good, and the land that *it was* pleasant; and bowed his shoulder to bear, and became a servant unto tribute.

16 ¶ Dan shall judge his people, as one of the tribes of Israel.

17 Dan shall be a serpent by the way, †an adder in the path, that biteth the horse heels, so that his rider shall fall backward.

† Heb. *an arrow-snake.*

18 I have waited for thy salvation, O LORD.

19 ¶ Gad, a troop shall overcome

---

redder than wine, and His teeth whiter than milk." This is generally supposed to refer to the land flowing with milk and honey, and abounding in vineyards; but the fathers applied it to the Messiah's kingdom in the same manner with the last verse, *e.g.* "That His eyes shine as with wine know all those members of His Body mystical, to whom it is given with a sort of sacred inebriation of mind, alienated from the fleeting things of time, to behold the eternal brightness of wisdom." (Augustin. 'C. Faust.' XII. 42, Tom. VIII. p. 24).

13. *Zebulun shall dwell at the haven of the sea*] "Zebulun shall dwell on the shore of the sea, and he shall be for a shore of ships," (*i.e.* suited for ships to land on), "and his border" (or farthest extremity) "shall be by Zidon." As far as we know of the limits of Zebulun, after the occupation of Canaan, it reached from the sea of Gennesareth to Mount Carmel, and so nearly to the Mediterranean. It did not reach to the city of Zidon, but its most western point reaching to Mount Carmel brought it into close proximity to Zidonia, or the territory of Tyre and Sidon. The language here used, though in all material points fulfilled in the subsequent history, is just what would not have been written by a forger in after times. Zebulun had not properly a maritime territory; yet its possessions reached very nearly to both seas. It was far from the city of Zidon; and yet, as approximating very closely to the land of the Syrians, might well be said to have its border by or towards Zidon. Tyre probably was not built at this time, and therefore is not named in the prophecy.

14. *Issachar is a strong ass couching down between two burdens*] Probably "Issachar is a strong-boned ass, couching down between the cattle pens," or "sheepfolds." The last word occurs only here and in Judg. v. 16, where it is rendered sheepfolds (see Rœdiger in Ges. 'Thes.' p. 1470). The prediction all points to the habits of an indolent agricultural people, and to what is likely to accompany such habits, an endurance of oppression in preference to a war of independence.

16. *Dan shall judge his people*, &c.] A paronomasia on *Dan* (*i.e.* a judge). The words may mean that, though he was only a son of Bilhah, he shall yet have tribal authority in his own people. The word translated "tribe" is the same as that translated "sceptre" in v. 10. Onkelos and others after him suppose the allusion to be to the judgeship of Samson, who was of the tribe of Dan (Judg. xv. 20).

17. *Dan shall be a serpent by the way, an adder in the path*] The word for adder, *Shephiphon*, is translated by the Vulg. *cerastes* the horned snake, the *coluber cerastes* of Linnæus, a small snake about 14 inches long and one inch thick, lurking in the sand and by the way side, very poisonous and dangerous. (Bochart, 'Hieroz.' Pt. ii. Lib. III. c. 12.) The people of Dan in Judges xviii. 27, shewed the kind of subtlety here ascribed to them. Perhaps the local position of the tribe is alluded to. It was placed originally on the outskirts of the royal tribe of Judah, and might in times of war have to watch stealthily for the enemy and fall on him by subtlety as he was approaching. The comparison of Dan to a serpent lying in wait and biting the heel seems to imply some condemnation. It is certainly observable that the first introduction of Idolatry in Israel is ascribed to the tribe of Dan (Judg. xviii.), and that in the numbering of the tribes in Rev. vii., the name of Dan is omitted. From these or other causes many of the fathers were led to believe that antichrist should spring from the tribe of Dan (Iren. V. 30, 32; Ambros. 'De Benedict. Patriarch.' c. 7; Augustin. 'In Josuam,' Quæst. 22; Theodoret, 'In Genes.' Quæst. 109; Prosper, 'De Promiss. et Prædict.' p. 4; Gregorius, 'Moral.' c. 18, &c.).

18. *I have waited for thy salvation, O LORD*] This ejaculation immediately following the blessing on Dan is very remarkable, but not easy to interpret. The Targg. Jerus. and Pseudo-Jonath. (and according to the Complutensian Polyglot Onkelos also, though the passage is probably spurious) paraphrase the words by saying that Jacob looked not for temporal redemption, such as that wrought by Gideon or Samson, but for the eternal redemption promised by Messiah. Is it not possible, that Jacob, having been moved

him: but he shall overcome at the last.
20 ¶ Out of Asher his bread *shall be* fat, and he shall yield royal dainties.
21 ¶ Naphtali *is* a hind let loose: he giveth goodly words.
22 ¶ Joseph *is* a fruitful bough, *even* a fruitful bough by a well; *whose* †branches run over the wall:

† Heb. *daughters.*

23 The archers have sorely grieved him, and shot *at him*, and hated him:
24 But his bow abode in strength, and the arms of his hands were made strong by the hands of the mighty *God* of Jacob; (from thence *is* the shepherd, the stone of Israel:)
25 *Even* by the God of thy father,

---

by the Spirit of God to speak of the serpent biting the heel, may have had his thoughts called back to the primal promise made to Eve, the Protevangelium, where the sentence that the serpent should bruise the heel was succeeded by the promise that the serpent's head should be crushed by the coming Seed? This combination of thoughts may easily have elicited the exclamation of this verse.

19. *Gad, a troop shall overcome him: but he shall overcome at the last*] Perhaps "Gad, troops shall press on him, but he shall press upon their rear" (so Gesen. p. 271; Ros., Schum.); the allusion being to the Arab tribes in the neighbourhood of Gad, who would invade him, and then retire, Gad following them and harassing their retreat. Every word but two in the verse is some form of the same root, there being a play of words on the name *Gad* and *Gedud*, *i.e.* a troop; we might express it, "Gad, troops shall troop against him, but he shall troop on their retreat." (See on ch. xxx. 11.)

20. *Out of Asher his bread shall be fat, and he shall yield royal dainties*] The translation may be a little doubtful; but the sense is probably that expressed by the Authorised Version. The allusion is to the fertility of the territory of Asher extending from Mount Carmel along the coast of Sidonia nearly to Mount Lebanon. It was specially rich in corn, wine and oil (Heidegger), containing some of the most fertile land in Palestine (Stanley, 'S. and P.' p. 265).

21. *Naphtali is a hind let loose: he giveth goodly words*] The Targg. Pseudo-Jon. and Jerus. explain this that "Naphtali is a swift messenger, like a hind that runneth on the mountains, bringing good tidings." So virtually the Syr. and Sam. Versions. The allusion is obscure, as we know so little of the history of Naphtali. The Targums above cited say that Naphtali first declared to Jacob that Joseph was yet alive. As the tribe of Naphtali occupied part of that region which afterwards became Galilee, some have supposed that there was contained in these words a prophecy of the Apostles (in Hebrew *Sheluchim*, the same word with *Shelucha* here rendered "let loose"), who were Galileans and of whom it was said, "How beautiful upon the mountains are the feet of him that bringeth good tidings."

Bochart, after whom Michaelis, Schulz, Dathe, Ewald and others, follow the LXX. altering the vowel points, and render, "Naphtali is a spreading tree, which puts forth goodly branches."

22. *Joseph is a fruitful bough*] Perhaps "Joseph is the son," or branch, "of a fruitful tree, the son of a fruitful tree by a well, as for the branches" (lit. the daughters) "each one of them runneth over the wall" (see Ges. 218, 220). The construction is difficult and the difference of translations very considerable; but so, or nearly so, Gesen., Tuch, Knobel, Delitzsch, &c. The prophecy probably refers to the general prosperity of the house of Joseph. The fruitful tree is by some supposed to be Rachel. The luxuriance of the tendrils running over the wall may point to Joseph's growing into two tribes, whilst none of his brethren formed more than one: so Onkelos.

23. *The archers have sorely grieved him*] Though the Targums and others have referred this to Joseph's trials in Egypt, the prophetic character of the whole chapter shows that they point rather to the future wars of his tribes and the strength which he received from the hands of the mighty God of Jacob.

24. *from thence is the shepherd, the stone of Israel*] "From thence," referring to "the mighty one of Jacob" in the last clause. Some understand here that Joseph, having been defended from the malice of his enemies, was raised up by God to be a Shepherd or Guardian both to the Egyptians and to his own family, and a stone or rock of support to the house of Israel. Others see in this a prophecy of Joshua, the great captain of his people, who came of the tribe of Ephraim, and led the Israelites to the promised land. Others again have thought that, when Jacob was speaking of the sufferings and subsequent exaltation of his son Joseph, his visions were directed forward to that greater Son, of whom Joseph was a type, whom the archers vexed, but who was victorious over all enemies, and that of Him he says "From GOD cometh the Shepherd, the

who shall help thee; and by the Almighty, who shall bless thee with blessings of heaven above, blessings of the deep that lieth under, blessings of the breasts, and of the womb:

26 The blessings of thy father have prevailed above the blessings of my progenitors unto the utmost bound of the everlasting hills: they shall be on the head of Joseph, and on the crown of the head of him that was separate from his brethren.

27 ¶ Benjamin shall ravin *as* a wolf: in the morning he shall devour the prey, and at night he shall divide the spoil.

28 ¶ All these *are* the twelve tribes of Israel: and this *is it* that their father spake unto them, and blessed them; every one according to his blessing he blessed them.

29 And he charged them, and said unto them, I am to be gathered unto my people: [b] bury me with my fathers in the cave that *is* in the field of Ephron the Hittite,

[b] chap. 47. 30.

30 In the cave that *is* in the field of Machpelah, which *is* before Mamre, in the land of Canaan, [c] which Abraham bought with the field of Ephron the Hittite for a possession of a buryingplace.

[c] chap. 23. 16.

31 There they buried Abraham and Sarah his wife; there they buried Isaac and Rebekah his wife; and there I buried Leah.

32 The purchase of the field and of the cave that *is* therein *was* from the children of Heth.

33 And when Jacob had made an end of commanding his sons, he gathered up his feet into the bed, and yielded up the ghost, and was gathered unto his people.

Rock of Israel." As both Joseph and Joshua were eminent shadows and forerunners of the Saviour, it is quite possible that all these senses, more or less, belong to the words, though perhaps with special reference to the last. The translation advocated by many recent commentators, "From thence—from the Shepherd—the Rock of Israel" is against the original and the Versions.

25. *Even by the God of thy father, who shall help thee*, &c.] Rather "From the God of thy father and He shall help thee, and with (the aid of) the Almighty, even He shall bless thee."

26. *The blessings of thy father have prevailed above the blessings of my progenitors unto the utmost bound of the everlasting hills*] If this be the right rendering of a very obscure passage in the original, the meaning obviously is, that the blessings of Jacob on the head of Joseph and his offspring are greater than those which Abraham had pronounced on Isaac and Isaac on Jacob, and that they should last as long as the everlasting hills. This is more or less the interpretation of all the Jewish commentators following the Targums and the Vulg. The LXX (with which agrees the reading of the Samaritan Pentateuch) has a rendering which is adopted by Michaelis, Dathe, Vater, Tuch, Winer, Maurer, Schumann, Knobel, and Gesen. (see Ges. pp. 38, 391), "The blessings of thy father prevail over the blessings of the eternal mountains, even the glory of the everlasting hills." By this the parallelism of the two clauses is preserved, and the violence done to the two words translated in Authorised Version "progenitors" and "utmost bounds" is avoided.

separate from his brethren] So Onkelos. The Vulg. and Saad. have "the Nazarite among his brethren." Either of these translations would allude to the separation of Joseph from his family, first by his captivity and afterwards by his elevation. The word for "separate" means "one set apart," "consecrated," especially used of a Nazarite like Samson (Judg. xiii., xvi. 17), and of the Nazarite under the law (Num. vi. 2). It is possible that this consecration may apply also to princes who are separated to higher rank in dignity, just as the word *nezer*, "consecration," signifies a royal or high-priestly diadem. Accordingly, the LXX., Syr., Targg. Jerus., Pseudo-Jon. and many recent interpreters, render "a prince or leader of his brethren" (see Ges. p. 871).

27. *Benjamin shall ravin as a wolf*, &c.] The reference is, no doubt, to the warlike character of the tribe of Benjamin. Examples of this may be seen Judg. v. 14, xx. 16; 1 Chron. vii. 7, xii. 17; 2 Chron. xiv. 8, xvii. 17. Also Ehud the Judge (Judg. iii. 15) and Saul the king, with his son Jonathan, were Benjamites. The fathers (Tertul., Ambrose, August., Jerom.) think that there is a reference also to St Paul, who before his conversion devastated the Church and in later life brought home the spoils of the Gentiles.

NOTE A on Chap. xlix. v. 10. Shiloh.

i. Different renderings of word. 1. "He who shall be sent." 2. "His son." 3. "Until he come to Shiloh." 4. "The Peace-Maker." 5. "He, whose right it is." ii. Choice of renderings, either 4 or 5. iii. Messianic, by consent of Jewish and Christian antiquity. iv. Answer to objections.

Shiloh. A word of acknowledged difficulty.

1. The Vulgate renders "He, who shall be sent" (comp. *Shiloah*, Isai. viii. 6; John ix. 7—11). This would correspond with a title of the Messiah, "He that should come" (Matt. xi. 3). Such a translation is unsupported from other sources and rests on a different reading of the original, the letter ח (cheth) being substituted for ה (he) of the received text.

2. The Targum of Pseudo-Jonathan and some rabbins render "his son." So Kimchi, Pagninus, Calvin and others: but it requires proof that the word *shil*, "a son," has any existence in Hebrew.

3. The Rabbi Lipmann, in his book called "Nizzachon," suggests that it was the name of the city Shiloh, and that we should render "until he (Judah) shall come to Shiloh." A similar construction occurs 1 S. iv. 12 (he "came to Shiloh"), and it is said that Judah, in the march to the encampments in the wilderness, always took the first place (Num. ii. 3—9, x. 14), but that, when the Israelites came to Shiloh, they pitched the tabernacle there (Josh. xviii. 1—10), and, the other tribes departing from Judah, his principality closed.

It seems fatal to this theory, that every ancient Version, paraphrase and commentator make Shiloh, not the objective case after the verb, but the subject or nominative case before the verb. Moreover, whether it were a prophecy by Jacob, or, as many who adopt this theory will have it, a forgery of after date, nothing could be less pertinent than the sense to be elicited from the words, "till he come to Shiloh." Probably the town of Shiloh did not exist in Jacob's time, and Judah neither lost nor acquired the pre-eminence at Shiloh. He was not markedly the leader in the wilderness, for the people were led by Moses and Aaron; nor did he cease to have whatever pre-eminence he may have had when they came to Shiloh. This has induced some to vary the words, by translating, "*when* he comes to Shiloh," a translation utterly inadmissible; but it will give no help to the solution of the passage, for Judah did not acquire any fresh authority at Shiloh. It was the place of the rest of the tabernacle and therefore perhaps was named Shiloh, "Rest:" but it was no turning point in the history of Judah. Notwithstanding therefore the authority of Teller, Eichhorn, Bleek, Hitzig, Tuch, Ewald, Delitzsch, Kalisch, &c., we may pronounce with Hofmann, that the rendering is utterly impossible.

4. Far more probable is the rendering which makes Shiloh a proper name, and the subject of the verb, signifying "Peace," or rather, "the Peace-maker," the "Prince of peace." So, with slight variations, Luther, Vater, Gesenius, Rosenmüller, Hengstenberg, Knobel, Keil and others of the highest authority. The title is one most appropriate to Messiah (see Isai. ix. 6). The word is legitimately formed from the verb *Shalah*, to rest, to be at peace; and if the received reading be the true reading, there need be little doubt that this is its meaning. It has been thought by some that Solomon received his name *Shelomo*, the "peaceful," with an express reference to this prophecy of Shiloh, and it may be said that in Solomon was a partial fulfilment of the promise. Solomon was very markedly a type of the Messiah, himself the son of David, whose dominion was from sea to sea, who established a reign of peace in the land and who built the temple of the Lord; but Solomon was not the true Shiloh, any more than he was the true "Son of David."

5. The authority of the Ancient Versions is all but overwhelming in favour of the sense, "He, to whom it belongs," or "He, whose right it is." So, more or less, LXX., Aq., Symm., Syr., Saad., Onk., Targ. Jer., all, in fact, except Vulg. and Pseudo-Jonathan.

The objections to this are:

(1) That if the letter *yod* (expressed by the *i* in Sh*i*loh) be genuine, the translation is inadmissible: but it is replied that very many Hebrew MSS. and all Samaritan MSS. are without the *yod*, and that the evidence is much in favour of the belief that the *yod* did not appear till the 10th century (see Prof. Lee, 'Lex.' in voc.). It may be added that, as the reading without the *yod* is the harder and apparently the less probable, the copyists were more likely to have inserted it by mistake than to have omitted it by mistake.

(2) It is said, that by this reading so interpreted, a form is introduced unknown to the Pentateuch, Aramæan and of later date. To this it is replied, that the form occurs in the Song of Deborah (Judg. v. 7), which is very ancient; that Aramæan forms were either very ancient or decidedly modern, to be met with in Hebrew when the patriarchs were in contact with the Chaldæans (and Jacob had been forty years in Mesopotamia), or not again till the Jews were in captivity at Babylon. An Aramaism or Chaldaism therefore was na-

tural in the mouth of Jacob, though not in the mouth of David or Solomon.

This rendering of the Vss. is supported by the early Christian writers, as Justin M. ('Dial.' § 120) and many others. It is thought that Ezekiel (xxi. 27) actually quotes the words, "Until he come whose right it is," expanding them a little, and St Paul (in Gal. iii. 19) is supposed to refer to them.

On the whole, rejecting confidently the senses 1, 2, 3, we may safely adopt either 4 or 5; 4, if the reading be correct; 5, if the reading without the *yod* be accepted.

All Jewish antiquity referred the prophecy to Messiah. Thus the Targum of Onkelos has "until the Messiah come, whose is the kingdom;" the Jerusalem Targum, "until the time that the king Messiah shall come, whose is the kingdom." The Targum of Pseudo-Jonathan, "till the king the Messiah shall come, the youngest of his sons." So the Babylonian Talmud ('Sanhedrim,' cap. II. fol. 98*x*), "What is Messiah's name? His name is Shiloh, for it is written, Until Shiloh come." So likewise the Bereshith Rabba, Kimchi, Aben-ezra, Rashi, and other ancient Rabbins. The more modern Jews, pressed by the argument, that the time appointed must have passed, refer to David, Saul, Nebuchadnezzar and others (see Schœttgen, 'Hor. Heb.' p. 1264). There can be no doubt that this prophecy was one important link in the long chain of predictions which produced that general expectation of a Messiah universally prevalent in Judæa at the period of the Christian era, and which Suetonius, in the well-known passage in his life of Vespasian, tells us had long and constantly pervaded the whole of the East. With the Jewish interpreters agreed the whole body of Christian fathers, *e.g.* Justin M. 'Apol.' I. §§ 32, 54; 'Dial.' §§ 52, 20; Iren. IV. 23; Origen, 'C. Cels.' I. p. 41, 'Hom.' in Gen. 17; Cyprian, 'C. Jud.' I. 20; Cyril. Hieros. 'Cat.' XII.; Euseb. 'H. E.' I. 6; Chrys. 'Hom. 67, in Gen.'; Augustine, 'De Civ. D.' XVI. 41; Theodoret, 'Quæst. in Gen.' 110; Hieron. 'Quæst. in Gen.', &c.

The only arguments of any weight against the Messianic character of the prophecy, except of course a denial that prophecy is possible at all, seem to be the following.

1. The patriarchal age had no anticipation of a personal Messiah, though there may have been some dim hope of a future deliverance. This is simply a gratuitous assertion. Admitting even that the promise to Adam may have been vaguely understood, we cannot tell how much the rite of sacrifice, the prophecies of men like Enoch and Noah, and the promises to Abraham and Isaac, had taught the faith of the fathers. There is the highest of all authority for saying that "Abraham rejoiced to see the day of Christ; he saw it, and was glad" (Joh. viii. 56). It was not indeed to be expected, that much beyond general intimations should be given in very early times, the light gradually increasing as the Sun-rise was drawing near: but there seems no more likely time for a special teaching on this vital point than the time of Jacob's death. He was the last of the three patriarchs to whom the promises were given. He was leaving his family in a foreign land, where they were to pass some generations surrounded by idolatry and error. He was foretelling their future fortunes on their promised return to Canaan. What more natural than that he should be moved to point their hopes yet farther forward to that, of which the deliverance from Egypt was to be an emblem and type?

2. The New Testament does not cite this as a prediction of Christ.

Bishop Patrick has well observed, that the fulfilment of the prophecy was not till the destruction of Jerusalem, when not only the Sceptre of Royalty, but even the tribal authority, and the Sanhedrim or council of elders ("the lawgiver") wholly passed from Judah. Then, and not till then, had the foretold fortunes of Judah's house been worked out. The sceptre and the lawgiver had departed, and "He, whose right it was," had taken the kingdom. The "Prince of peace" had come, and nations were coming into His obedience. But it would have been no argument to the Jew to cite this prophecy, whilst the Jewish nation was still standing and still struggling for its freedom, still possessing at least a shadow of royal authority and judicial power. There is therefore abundant reason why the New Testament should not refer to it.

CHAPTER L.

1 *The mourning for Jacob.* 4 *Joseph getteth leave of Pharaoh to go to bury him.* 7 *The funeral.* 15 *Joseph comforteth his brethren, who craved his pardon.* 22 *His age.* 23 *He seeth the third generation of his sons.* 24 *He prophesieth unto his brethren of their return.* 25 *He taketh an oath of them for his bones.* 26 *He dieth, and is chested.*

AND Joseph fell upon his father's face, and wept upon him, and kissed him.

2 And Joseph commanded his servants the physicians to embalm his

CHAP. L. 2. *his servants the physicians*] Herod. (II. 84) tells us, that in Egypt all places were crowded with physicians for every different kind of disease. The physi-

father: and the physicians embalmed
Israel.
3 And forty days were fulfilled for
him; for so are fulfilled the days of
those which are embalmed: and the
Egyptians †mourned for him threescore and ten days.
4 And when the days of his mourning were past, Joseph spake unto the
house of Pharaoh, saying, If now I
have found grace in your eyes, speak,
I pray you, in the ears of Pharaoh,
saying,
5 [a]My father made me swear, saying, Lo, I die: in my grave which
I have digged for me in the land
of Canaan, there shalt thou bury me.
Now therefore let me go up, I pray
thee, and bury my father, and I will
come again.
6 And Pharaoh said, Go up, and
bury thy father, according as he made
thee swear.

† Heb. *wept.*

[a] chap. 47. 29.

7 ¶ And Joseph went up to bury
his father: and with him went up all
the servants of Pharaoh, the elders of
his house, and all the elders of the
land of Egypt,
8 And all the house of Joseph,
and his brethren, and his father's
house: only their little ones, and
their flocks, and their herds, they left
in the land of Goshen.
9 And there went up with him
both chariots and horsemen: and it
was a very great company.
10 And they came to the threshing-
floor of Atad, which *is* beyond Jordan,
and there they mourned with a great
and very sore lamentation: and he made
a mourning for his father seven days.
11 And when the inhabitants of
the land, the Canaanites, saw the
mourning in the floor of Atad, they
said, This *is* a grievous mourning to
the Egyptians: wherefore the name

---

cians of Egypt were famous in other lands also (Herod. III. 1, 129). It is not wonderful therefore that Joseph, with all his state, should have had several physicians attached to his establishment. Physicians, however, were not ordinarily employed to embalm, which was the work of a special class of persons (Herod. II. 85; Diodor. I. 91); and the custom of embalming and the occupation of the embalmer were probably anterior to Moses and to Joseph. Very probably the physicians embalmed Jacob because he was not an Egyptian, and so could not be subjected to the ordinary treatment of the Egyptians, or embalmed by their embalmers.

3. *And forty days were fulfilled for him*] The account given by Diodorus (I. 91) is that the embalming lasted more than 30 days, and that when a king died they mourned for him 72 days. This very nearly corresponds with the number in this verse. The mourning of 70 days probably included the 40 days of embalming. Herodotus (II. 86), who describes at length three processes of embalming, seems to speak of a subsequent steeping in natron (*i.e.* subcarbonate of soda) for 70 days. He probably expresses himself with some inaccuracy, as both the account in Genesis, which is very much earlier, and the account in Diodorus which is later, give a much shorter time for the whole embalming, *i.e.* either 30 or 40 days, and seem to make the whole mourning last but 70 days. It is possible, however, to understand Herodotus as meaning the same as the Scriptural account and that of Diodorus. His words are, "Having done this they embalm in natron, covering it up for 70 days. Longer than this it is not lawful to embalm." (See Sir G. Wilkinson in Rawlinson, 'Herod.' II. 86; Hengstenb. 'Egypt,' &c. p. 68.)

4. *Joseph spake unto the house of Pharaoh*] He probably did not go himself to Pharaoh, because in mourning for his father he had let his hair and beard grow long, which was the custom in Egypt at the death of relations (Herod. II. 36): and it would have been disrespectful to go into the presence of Pharaoh without cutting the hair and shaving the beard. (See on ch. xli. 14. and Hengstenb. 'Egypt,' p. 71.)

7. *with him went up all the servants of Pharaoh*] Such large funeral processions are often seen on the Egyptian monuments (Rosellini, II. p. 395; Hengstenb. p. 71; Wilkinson, 'A. E.' Vol. V. ch. XVI. and plates there).

10. *threshingfloor of Atad*] Or "Goren-Atad," or "the threshingfloor of thorns."

beyond Jordan] *i.e.* to the West of Jordan. Moses wrote before the Israelites had taken possession of the land of Israel, and therefore whilst they were on the East of Jordan. This accords with what we hear of the site of Goren-Atad and Abel-Mizraim; for Jerome ('Onom.' s. v. *Area-Atad*) identi-

‖ That is, *the mourning of the Egyptians.*
of it was called ‖ Abel-mizraim, which
is beyond Jordan.
12 And his sons did unto him according as he commanded them:
b Acts 7. 16.
13 For *b* his sons carried him into
the land of Canaan, and buried him
in the cave of the field of Machpe-
c chap. 23. 16.
lah, which Abraham *c* bought with
the field for a possession of a buryingplace of Ephron the Hittite, before Mamre.
14 ¶ And Joseph returned into
Egypt, he, and his brethren, and all
that went up with him to bury
his father, after he had buried his
father.
15 ¶ And when Joseph's brethren
saw that their father was dead, they
said, Joseph will peradventure hate
us, and will certainly requite us all
the evil which we did unto him.
† Heb. *charged.*
16 And they † sent a messenger
unto Joseph, saying, Thy father did
command before he died, saying,
17 So shall ye say unto Joseph,
Forgive, I pray thee now, the trespass of thy brethren, and their sin;
for they did unto thee evil: and now,
we pray thee, forgive the trespass of
the servants of the God of thy father.
And Joseph wept when they spake
unto him.
18 And his brethren also went
and fell down before his face; and
they said, Behold, we *be* thy servants.
19 And Joseph said unto them,
d Fear not: for *am* I in the place of
God? *d* chap. 45. 5.
20 But as for you, ye thought evil
against me; *but* God meant it unto
good, to bring to pass, as *it is* this
day, to save much people alive.
21 Now therefore fear ye not: I
will nourish you, and your little ones.
And he comforted them, and spake
† kindly unto them. † Heb. *to their hearts.*
22 ¶ And Joseph dwelt in Egypt,
he, and his father's house: and Joseph
lived an hundred and ten years.
23 And Joseph saw Ephraim's
children of the third *generation*: *e* the
children also of Machir the son of *e* Numb. 32. 39.
Manasseh were † brought up upon Jo-
seph's knees. † Heb. *borne.*
24 And Joseph said unto his brethren, I die: and *f* God will surely
visit you, and bring you out of this *f* Heb. 11. 22.
land unto the land which he sware
to Abraham, to Isaac, and to Jacob.
25 And *g* Joseph took an oath of
the children of Israel, saying, God *g* Exod. 13. 19.
will surely visit you, and ye shall
carry up my bones from hence.

---

fies it with Beth-Hoglah, which lay between the Jordan and Jericho, the ruins of which are probably still to be seen (Rob. I. 544; see Smith's 'Dict. of Bible,' I. p. 200.)

11. *Abel-mizraim*] Means either "the field of Egypt," or "the mourning of Egypt," according to the vowel-points. The violence of the Egyptian lamentations is described by Herodotus (II. 85). See also Wilkinson, 'A. E.' ch. XVI.

19. *Am I in the place of God?*] *i.e.* it is God's place to avenge, not mine. See Rom. xii. 19.

23. *Were brought up upon Joseph's knees*] Lit. "were born on Joseph's knees." Comp. the phrase ch. xxx. 3. It seems as if they were adopted by Joseph as his own children from the time of their birth.

26. *They embalmed him, and he was put in a coffin*] The word for coffin is literally "ark" or "chest;" a word used always of a wooden chest, elsewhere almost exclusively of "the ark of the covenant." Herodotus, after describing the embalming, says, "The relatives inclose the body in a wooden image which they have made in the shape of a man. Then fastening the case, they place it in a sepulchral chamber, upright against the wall. This is the most costly way of embalming the dead" (II. 86). The description is of that which we commonly call a mummy-case. Such coffins, made of wood, chiefly of sycamore wood, were the commonest in Egypt; and though some very rich people were buried in basaltic coffins, yet, both from Herodotus' description above and from other sources, we know that wooden coffins were frequent, for great men, even for kings. The coffin of king Mycerinus, discovered A.D. 1837 in the third Pyramid of Memphis, is of sycamore wood. The command of Joseph and the promise of the Israelites, that his bones should be carried back into Canaan, were reason enough for preferring a wooden to a stone coffin. (See Hengstenb. 'Egypt,' pp. 71, 72. Various coffins of wood, stone, and

26 So Joseph died, *being* an hundred and ten years old: and they embalmed him, and he was put in a coffin in Egypt.

---

earthenware are described and engraved in Wilkinson's 'A. E.' Vol. v. p. 479.) The coffin was, no doubt, deposited in some sepulchral building (see Herod. above) and guarded by his own immediate descendants till the time of the Exodus, when it was carried up out of Egypt and finally deposited in Shechem (Josh. xxiv. 32). The faith of Joseph (Heb. xi. 22) must have been a constant remembrance to his children and his people, that Egypt was not to be their home. His coffin laid up by them, ready to be carried away according to his dying request whenever God should restore them to the promised land, would have taught them to keep apart from Egypt and its idolatries, looking for a better country, which God had promised to their fathers.

EXODUS

INTRODUCTION.

§ 1. THE Book of Exodus consists of two distinct portions. The former (cc. i—xix) gives a detailed account of the circumstances under which the deliverance of the Israelites was accomplished. The second (cc. xx—xl) describes the giving of the law, and the institutions which completed the organization of the people as "a kingdom of priests, and an holy nation," c. xix. 6.

These two portions are unlike in style and structure, as might be expected from the difference of their subject-matter: but their mutual bearings and interdependence are evident, and leave no doubt as to the substantial unity of the book. The historical portion owes all its significance and interest to the promulgation of God's will in the law. The institutions of the law could not, humanly speaking, have been established or permanently maintained but for the deliverance which the historical portion records.

The name Exodus, *i. e.* "the going forth," applies rather to the former portion than to the whole book. It was very naturally assigned to it by the Alexandrian Jews, by whom the most ancient translation was written. Like their forefathers they were exiles in Egypt, and looked forward to their departure from that land as the first condition of the accomplishment of their hopes. The Hebrews of Palestine simply designated the book by its first words Elleh Shemoth, *i. e.* "these are the names," regarding it not as a separate work, but as a section of the Pentateuch.

The narrative, indeed, is so closely connected with that of Genesis as to shew not only that it was written by the same author, but that it formed part of one general plan. Still it is a distinct section; the first events which it relates are separated from the last chapter in Genesis by a considerable interval, and it presents the people of Israel under totally different circumstances. Its termination is marked with equal distinctness, winding up with the completion of the tabernacle.

The book is divided into many smaller sections; each of which has the marks which throughout the Pentateuch indicate a subdivision. They are of different lengths, and were probably written on separate parchments or papyri, the longest not exceeding the dimensions of contemporary documents in Egypt[1]. They

[1] A single page of Egyptian papyrus contains very frequently as much subject-matter as is found in any section of the Pentateuch. Thus, for instance, the 17th chapter of the Ritual in a papyrus, of which a facsimile has been published by M. de Rougé, occupies one page of 49 lines: each line is equivalent to three lines of Hebrew, as may be proved by transcription of the two languages in Egyptian and Phœnician

were apparently so arranged for the convenience of public reading. This is a point of importance, accounting to a great extent for apparent breaks in the narrative, and for repetitions, which have been attributed to the carelessness of the compiler, who is supposed to have brought separate and unconnected fragments into a semblance of order.

The first seven verses are introductory to the whole book. In accordance with the almost invariable custom of the writer, we find a brief recapitulation of preceding events, and a statement of the actual condition of affairs. The names of the Patriarchs and the number of distinct families at the time of the immigration into Egypt are stated in six verses: a single paragraph then records the rapid and continuous increase of the Israelites after the death of Joseph and his contemporaries.

The narrative begins with the 8th verse, c. i. The subdivision which includes the first two chapters relates very briefly the events which prepared the way for the Exodus: the accession of a new king, followed by a change of policy and measures of extreme cruelty towards the Israelites; and the birth and early history of Moses, destined to be their deliverer. The second division, from c. iii. 1 to vi. 1, opens after an interval of some forty years. From this point the narrative is full and circumstantial.

letters. The longest section in the Pentateuch scarcely exceeds 150 lines in Van der Hooght's edition. Several papyri of the 18th dynasty are of considerable length. Thus, the papyrus called Anastasi I., in the British Museum, contains 28 pages, each page of 9 lines, equal to three lines of ancient Hebrew characters. This exceeds the length of any one division of the Pentateuch. The papyrus in question is undoubtedly of the age in which the generality of modern critics hold the Exodus to have occurred. The assertion that Moses probably used parchment rests on the fact that it was commonly employed at an early time, and more especially, as it would seem, for sacred compositions. Thus, in an inscription of Thotmes III., either contemporary with Moses, or much older, we read that an account of his campaigns was written on parchment, and hung up in the temple of Ammon. See Brugsch, 'Dictionnaire Hieroglyphique,' p. 208. A far more ancient instance of the use of parchment in sacred writings is given by M. Chabas and Mr Goodwin in the 'Egyptische Zeitschrift' for Nov. 1865 and June 1867.

It describes the call of Moses; the revelation of God's will and purpose; the return of Moses to Egypt, and his first application to Pharaoh, of which the immediate result was a treatment of the Israelites, which materially advanced the work, on the one hand preparing them for departure from their homes, and on the other attaching them more closely to their native officers by the bonds of common suffering.

c. vi. 2—27 forms a distinct portion. Moses is instructed to explain the bearings of the Divine name (of which the meaning had been previously intimated, see iii. 14) upon the relations of God to the people. He then receives a renewal of his mission to the Israelites and to Pharaoh, Aaron being formally appointed as his coadjutor: the genealogy of both is then introduced, marking their position as leaders of the people.

This portion stands in its right place. It is necessary to the full understanding of the following, and is closely connected with the preceding section; but it stands apart from both, it begins with a solemn declaration and ends with a distinct announcement.

c. vi. 28 to the end of c. xi. In this division the narrative makes a fresh start. It begins, as usual in a new section, with a brief statement to remind the reader of the relative position of Moses and Aaron and of the work appointed to them. Then follows in unbroken order the history of nine plagues, in three groups, each increasing in severity. At the close of this division the tenth and most terrible plague is denounced, and the failure of the other nine, in turning Pharaoh, is declared in the often recurring form, "the Lord hardened Pharaoh's heart, so that he would not let the children of Israel go out of his land" (xi. 10).

The next section, xii. 1—42, gives an account of the institution of the Passover, and the departure of the Israelites from Rameses: the close of the section is distinctly marked by the chronological statement. This important section is closely connected with the preceding narrative, but it was evidently intended to be read as a separate lesson, and may possibly have been rewritten or revised for that purpose towards the close of the life of Moses. From xii. 43 to xiii. 16 special injunctions touching the Passover are recorded; they may have been inserted here as the most appropriate place when the separate documents were put together.

The narrative begins again c. xiii. 17. After a brief introduction, stating the general direction of the journey, comes the history of the march towards the Red Sea, the passage across it, and the destruction of Pharaoh's host. This subdivision extends to the end of the xivth chapter.

The Song of Moses[1] is inserted here: it does not interrupt the narrative, which proceeds without a break until, in the third month after the Exodus, Israel came to the Wilderness of Sinai and camped before the Mount: c. xix. In this chapter and the next the promulgation of the law is described. The remainder of the book gives the directions received by Moses touching the Tabernacle and its appurtenances, and the institution of the Aaronic priesthood. It then relates the sin of the Israelites, and their forgiveness at the intercession of Moses: and concludes with an account of the making of the tabernacle, and a description of the symbolical manifestation of God's Presence with His people.

This general view of the structure of the book meets several questions which have been raised as to its integrity. That the several portions are distinct, forming complete subdivisions, may not only be admitted without misgiving, but this fact is best accounted for by the circumstances under which the work must have been composed, if Moses was its author. It was the form in which a man engaged in such an undertaking would naturally present at intervals an account of each series of transactions, and in which such an account would be best adapted for the instruction of the people. The combination of all the documents into a complete treatise might naturally occupy the period of comparative leisure towards the end of his life, and, while it involved some few additions and explanations, would be effected without any substantial change.

§ 2. The principal arguments for the Mosaic authorship have been stated in the Introduction to the Pentateuch: but many objections apply especially to this book; and some of the most convincing evidences are supplied by its contents. This might be expected. On the one hand the question of authorship is inseparably bound up with that of the miraculous character of many transactions which are recorded. Critics who reject miracles as simply incredible under any circumstances, have ever felt that the narrative before us could scarcely have been written by a man in the position and with the character of Moses, and could not certainly have been addressed to eye-witnesses or contemporaries of the events which it relates. It is a foregone conclusion with writers of this school. On the other hand a narrative of the personal history of Moses, of the circumstances under which the greatest work in the world's annals was accomplished, if it be authentic and veracious, must abound in internal coincidences and evidences sufficient to convince any inquirer not shut up to the opposite theory. In fact no critic of any weight, either in France or Germany, who admits the supernatural character of the transactions, rejects the authorship of Moses.

[1] The length and structure of this great hymn have been represented as proofs of a later origin. A comparison with Egyptian poems of the age of Moses, or much earlier, gives these results. The hymn to the Nile, in the 'Pap. Sallier,' II., was written at the time when the Exodus is fixed by most Egyptologers. It is more than twice the length of the Song of Moses. The structure is elaborate and the cadences resemble the Hebrew. It begins thus, "Hail, O Nile, thou comest forth over this land, thou comest in peace, giving life to Egypt, O hidden God." Again, a poem inscribed on the walls of a temple built by Thotmes III. is about twice as long as the Song. Its style is artificial and the cadences even more strongly marked. It is some two centuries older than the hymn to the Nile. We have also exact information as to the time which it would take to write out such a hymn. An Egyptian scribe writing, with the greatest care, with rubrical headings, &c. would have done it in half a day: a few hours would suffice in the simpler characters used by the Semitic races. This comparison leaves no doubt as to the possibility of such a hymn being written by Moses, who was trained in the schools of Egypt; and no one denies his genius.

One argument is drawn from the representation of the personal character and qualifications of Moses. In its most important features it is such as could never have been produced by a writer collecting the traditional reminiscences or legends of a later age: not such even as might have been drawn by a younger contemporary. To posterity, to Israelites of his own time, Moses was simply the greatest of men: but it is evident that the writer of this book was unconscious of the personal greatness of the chief actor. He was indeed thoroughly aware of the greatness of his mission, and consequently of the greatness of the position, which was recognized at last by the Egyptians, see ch. xi. 3; but as to his personal qualifications, the points which strike him most forcibly are the deficiencies of natural gifts and powers, and the defects of character, which he is scrupulously careful to record, together with the rebukes and penalties which they brought upon him, and the obstacles which they opposed to his work. His first attempt to deliver the people is described as a complete failure; an act which, however it might be palliated by the provocation, is evidently felt by the writer to have been wrongful, punished by a long exile extending over the best years of his life. When he receives the Divine call he is full of hesitation, and even when his unbelief is overcome by miracles he still recoils from the work, dwelling with almost irreverent pertinacity upon his personal disqualifications, ch. iii. 10—13. On his homeward journey he is severely chastised for neglect of a religious duty, ch. iv. 24—26. When his first application to Pharaoh brings increased suffering to his people, he bursts out into passionate remonstrance. The courage and magnanimity of his conduct to Pharaoh are never the subject of direct commendation. No act is attributed to his personal character. Even in the passage over the Red Sea and in the journeying through the wilderness, nothing recalls his individuality. Each step is under Divine guidance: no intimation is given of wisdom, skill, or foresight in the direction of the march. The first conflict with assailants is conducted by Joshua. The only important act in the organization of the nation, which is not distinctly assigned to a Divine revelation, is attributed to the wisdom, not of Moses, but of his kinsman Jethro. The few notices of personal character in the other books accord with this portraiture: the repugnance to all self-assertion in the controversy with Aaron and Miriam; the hasty and impetuous temper which, manifested on one important occasion, brought upon him the lasting displeasure of God, and ultimately transferred the execution of his great work to the hands of his successor Joshua.

Such a representation is perfectly intelligible, as proceeding from Moses himself: but what in him was humility would have been obtuseness in an annalist: such as never is found in the accounts of other great men, nor in the notices of Moses in later books[1]. What other men have seen in Moses is the chief agent in the greatest work ever intrusted to man, an agent whose peculiar and unparalleled qualifications are admitted alike by those who accept and by those who deny the Divine interposition[2]: what the writer himself sees in Moses is a man whose only qualification is an involuntary and reluctant surrender to the will of God. The only rational account of the matter is, that we have Moses' own history of himself and of his work.

The next argument is even less open to objection, since it rests not on subjective impressions, but on external facts. The book of Exodus could not have been written by any man who had not passed many years in Egypt, and who had not also a thorough knowledge, such as could only be acquired by personal observation, of the Sinaitic Peninsula. But it is improbable that any Israelite between the time of Moses and Jeremiah could have possessed either of these qualifications; it is not credible, or even possible, that any should have

[1] See especially the three last verses of Deuteronomy, added either by a younger contemporary of Moses, or at a later time by a reviser.

[2] The two writers by whom the greatness of the character and work of Moses are perhaps most thoroughly appreciated and developed with greatest power are Ewald, 'G. I.' vol. II., and Salvador, 'Histoire des Institutions de Moïse et du peuple Hebréu.'

combined both. Israelites may have been, and probably were, brought into Egypt as captives by the Pharaohs in their not unfrequent invasions of Syria, but in that position they were not likely to become acquainted with the institutions of Egypt: still less likely is it that any should have returned to their native land. Again, no Israelite, for centuries after the occupation of Palestine, is likely to have penetrated into the Sinaitic Peninsula, occupied as it was by hostile tribes, while it is certain that none could have had any motive, or opportunity, for traversing the route from Egypt to Horeb, with which no one doubts the writer of the Pentateuch was personally familiar. The notices are too numerous, and interwoven with the narrative too intimately, to be accounted for as mere traditional reminiscences, or even as derived from scanty records in the possession of the Israelites at a later period. We have no probable alternative but to admit that the narrative in its substance came from Moses, or from a contemporary. Either alternative might suffice so far as regards the accuracy and trustworthiness of the narrative, and consequently the miraculous character of the transactions which it records; but we can have little hesitation as to our choice between these alternatives, when we consider that none of the contemporaries of Moses had equal opportunities of observation, and that none were likely to have received the education and training[1] which would have enabled them to record the events.

§ 3. A weighty argument is drawn from the accounts of the miracles, by which Moses was expressly bidden to attest his mission, and by which he was enabled to accomplish the deliverance of his people. One characteristic, common to all scriptural miracles, but in none more conspicuous than in those recorded in the book of Exodus, is their strongly marked, and indeed unmistakeable, local colouring. They are such as no later writer living in Palestine could have invented for Egypt. From beginning to end no miracle is recorded which does not strike the mind by its peculiar suitableness to the place, time, and circumstances under which it was wrought. The plagues are each and all Egyptian; and the modes by which the people's wants are supplied in the Sinaitic Peninsula recall to our minds the natural conditions of such a journey in such a country. We find nature everywhere, but nature in its master's hand.

Detailed accounts of the plagues and of the natural phenomena in Egypt with which they were severally connected will be found in the notes; but it may be well to bring together a few points which shew the effects produced both by the miracles, and by the apparent failure of all but the last in determining the immediate deliverance of the people. The direct and indirect effects were in fact equally necessary, humanly speaking, for the accomplishment of that event.

In the first place it must be remarked, that the delay occasioned by Pharaoh's repeated refusals to listen to the commands afforded ample time for preparation. Two full months elapsed between the first and second interview of Moses with the king; see notes on v. 7 and vii. 17. During that time the people, uprooted for the first time from the district in which they had been settled for centuries, were dispersed throughout Egypt, subjected to severe suffering, and impelled to exertions of a kind differing altogether from their ordinary habits, whether as herdsmen or bondsmen. This was the first and a most important step in their training for a migratory life in the desert.

Towards the end of June, at the beginning of the rise of the annual inundation, the first series of plagues began. The Nile was stricken. Egypt was visited in the centre both of its physical existence, and of its national superstitions. Pharaoh did not give way, and no intimation as yet was made to the people that permission for their departure would be extorted; but the intervention of their Lord was now certain, the people, on their return wearied and exhausted from the search for stubble, had an interval of suspense. Three

[1] On the education of Moses see note at the end of ch. ii.

months appear to have intervened between this and the next plague. There must have been a movement among all the families of Israel; as they recapitulated their wrongs and hardships, the sufferings of their officers, and their own position of hopeless antagonism to their oppressors, it is impossible that they should not have looked about them, calculated their numbers and resources, and meditated upon the measures which, under the guidance of a leader of ability and experience, might enable them to effect their escape from Egypt. Five months might not be too much, but were certainly sufficient, to bring the people so far into a state of preparation for departure.

The plague of frogs followed. It will be shewn in the notes that it coincided in time with the greatest extension of the inundation in September. Pharaoh then gave the first indication of yielding; the permission extorted from him, though soon recalled, was not therefore ineffectual. On the one hand native worship in one of its oldest and strangest forms was attacked[1]; on the other hand Moses was not likely to lose any time in transmitting instructions to the people. The first steps may have been then taken towards an orderly marshalling of the people.

The third plague differed from the preceding in one important point. There was no previous warning[2]. It must have followed soon after that of frogs, early in October. It marks the close of the first series of inflictions, none of them causing great suffering, but quite sufficient on the one hand to make the Egyptians conscious of danger, and to confirm in the Israelites a hope of no remote deliverance.

The second series of plagues was far more severe; it began with swarms of poisonous insects, probably immediately after the subsidence of the inundation. It is a season of great importance to Egypt; from that season to the following June the land is uncovered; cultivation begins; a great festival (called Chabsta) marks the period for ploughing. At that time there was the first separation between Goshen and the rest of Egypt. The impression upon Pharaoh was far deeper than before, and then, in November, the people once more received instructions for departure; there was occasion for a rehearsal, so to speak, of the measures requisite for the proper organization of the tribes and families of Israel.

The cattle plague broke out in December, or at the latest in January. It was thoroughly Egyptian both in season[3] and in character. The exemption of the Israelites was probably attributed by Pharaoh to natural causes; but the care then bestowed by the Israelites upon their cattle, the separation from all sources of contagion, must have materially advanced their preparation for departure.

Then came the plagues of boils, severe but ineffectual, serving however to make the Egyptians understand that continuance in opposition would be visited on their persons. With this plague the second series ended. It appears to have lasted about three months.

The hailstorms followed, just when they now occur in Egypt, from the middle of February to the early weeks of March. The time was now drawing near. The Egyptians for the first time shew that they are seriously impressed. There was a division among them, many feared the word of the Lord, and took the precautions, which, also for the first time, Moses then indicated. This plague

[1] This has been shewn by Lepsius; see note in loc. There is a curious vignette in Mariette's work, 'Fouilles d'Abydos,' Part II. Vol. I. p. 30, No. CVIII. It represents Seti, the father of Rameses II., offering two vases of wine to a frog inshrined in a small chapel with the legend, 'The Sovereign Lady of both worlds.' Mariette's work has been withdrawn from circulation.

[2] This peculiarity, which applies to the third plague in each group, was pointed out by Maimonides.

[3] In an Egyptian calendar, written in the reign of Rameses II., and lately translated by M. Chabas, the 22nd of Tobi, corresponding to January, has this notice, "Il y a des ouragans dans le ciel ce jour-là, la contagion annuelle s'y mêle abondamment." 'Pap. Sallier,' IV. pp. 14, 15. This applies even more specially to the following plague.

drew from Pharaoh the first confession of guilt; and now for the third time, between one and two months before the Exodus, the Israelites receive permission to depart, when formal instructions for preparation were of course given by Moses. The people now felt also for the first time that they might look for support or sympathy among the very servants of Pharaoh.

The plague of locusts, when the leaves were green, towards the middle of March, was preceded by another warning, the last but one. The conquest over the spirit of Egypt was now complete. All but the king gave way; see x. 7. Though not so common in Egypt as in adjoining countries, the plague occurs there at intervals, and is peculiarly dreaded. Pharaoh once more gives permission to depart; once more the people are put in an attitude of expectation.

The ninth plague concludes the third series. Like the third and the sixth, each closing a series, it was preceded by no warning. It was peculiarly Egyptian. Though causing comparatively but little suffering, it was felt most deeply as a menace and precursor of destruction. It took place most probably a very few days before the last and crowning plague, a plague distinct in character from all others, the first and the only one which brought death home to the Egyptians, and accomplished the deliverance of Israel.

We have thus throughout the characteristics of local colouring, of adaptation to the circumstances of the Israelites, and of repeated announcements followed by repeated postponements, which enabled and indeed compelled the Israelites to complete that organization of their nation, without which their departure might have been, as it has been often represented, a mere disorderly flight.

There are some who fear to compromise the miraculous character of events by admitting any operation of natural causes to a share of them. Yet the inspired writer does not fail to record that it was by the east wind that the Lord brought the locusts (Exod. x. 12) and sent back the sea (xiv. 21), and by the mighty strong west wind (x. 19) took back the plague that he had sent. Nor is the miracle at all lessened, because the winds of heaven were made God's messengers and instruments in the doing it. In order to guard against misapprehensions from such readers, let us state with some precision the view we take of the miracles in Egypt. They were supernatural in their greatness, in their concentration upon one period, in their coming and going according to the phases of the conflict between the tyrant and the captive race, in their measured gradation from weak to strong, as each weaker wonder failed to break the stubborn heart. And king and people so regarded them; they were accustomed perhaps to frogs and lice and locusts; but to such plagues, so intense, so threatened, and accomplished, and withdrawn, as it were so disciplined to a will, they were not accustomed; and they rightly saw them as miraculous and divinely sent. This being clearly laid down it is most desirable to notice that the phenomena that are put to this use are such as mark the country where this great history is laid. No Jewish writer, who had lived in Palestine alone, could have imagined a narrative so Egyptian in its marks. Much evidence will appear in the course of the Commentary tending this way; that the history was written by some one well conversant with Egypt; and we shall look in vain for any one, other than Moses himself, who possessed this qualification for writing under divine guidance the history of the emancipation of the Israelites.

A point of subordinate, but in the present state of biblical criticism of practical importance, is suggested by the view here presented. The two facts that between all the miracles there is an intimate connection, and that each and all are shewn to be nearly allied to analogous phenomena recorded in ancient and modern accounts of Egypt, leave no place for interpolations of any considerable extent, none certainly for the introduction of any single visitation. In the commentaries of some scholars, to whose learning and ability the student of Holy Scripture is deeply indebted, some of the accounts are attributed to the Elohistic, others to the Jehovistic writer. The arguments based upon language are considered in their proper places[1]; those resting on merely subjective impressions, varying to a most remarkable extent in writers of the same school, are too vague and indefinite to be capable of disproof, as they are incapable of demonstration, and will probably leave no trace in biblical literature; but the characteristics here pointed out are common to all the plagues, and they are conclusive. In fact no one plague could be omitted without dislocating the whole narrative, and breaking the order distinctly intimated, though nowhere formally stated, by the writer. The results were brought about by the combined operation of all the plagues; they could never have been produced by a merely fortuitous concurrence of natural events, and the narrative which records them, remarkable as it is for artlessness and simplicity, is certainly not one which could have been concocted from documents of different ages, constructed on different principles, and full of internal discrepancies and contradictions. It is the production of one mind, written by one man, and by one who had alone witnessed all the events which it records, who alone was at that time likely to possess the knowledge or ability required to write the account.

§ 4. The portion of the book, which follows the account of the departure from Egypt, has characteristics marked with equal distinctness, and bearing with no less force upon the question of authorship. It has never occurred to any traveller who has traversed the route from Suez to Sinai, or from Sinai to Palestine, to doubt that the chapters of Exodus which touch that ground were written by one to whom the localities were known from personal observation. It is not merely that the length of each division of the journey, the numerous halting places are distinctly marked; for although such notices could not possibly have been invented, or procured at any later period by a dweller in Palestine, the fact might be accounted for by the supposition, gratuitously made, but hard to be rebutted, that some ancient records of the journey had been preserved by written or oral tradition; but the chapters which belong either to the early sojourn of Moses, or to the wanderings of the Israelites, are pervaded by a peculiar tone, a local colouring, an atmosphere so to speak of the desert, which has made itself felt by all those who have explored the country, to whatever school of religious thought they may have belonged. And this fact is the more striking when we bear in mind that, although the great general features of the Peninsula, the grouping of its arid heights and the direction of its innumerable wadys are permanent, still changes of vast, and scarcely calculable importance in matters which personally affect the traveller and modify his impressions, have taken place since the time of Moses; changes to which, for obvious reasons, it is necessary to call special attention.

At present one great difficulty felt by all travellers is the insufficiency of the resources of the Peninsula to support such a host as that which is described in

[1] The attention of scholars is specially called to the following list of words. They are either found only in this book and marked ἁ. λ., or in the Pentateuch and later Psalms taken directly from it, marked P. All marked E. have Egyptian equivalents, and are derived from roots either common to Egyptian and Hebrew, or found only in Egyptian.

Ch. i. 7, were fruitful, E., increased exceedingly, P. E. *v.* 11, taskmasters, ἁ. λ., E. Pithon and Rameses, E. *v.* 16, the stools, ἁ. λ. ii. 3, ark, P. E. bulrushes, E. pitch, E. flags, E. river's brink, E. *v.* 5, wash, E. *v.* 10, drew out, P. E. *v.* 16, troughs, P., once in Cant. iii. a bush, P. E. v. 12, stubble and straw, E. vii. 3, magicians, sorcerers, E. *v.* 22, enchantments, ἁ. λ., E. *v.* 27, frogs, P. E. viii. 13, lice, ἁ. λ., *i.e.* here and Ps. cv. 31, E. *v.* 17, swarms of flies, ἁ. λ., E. ix. 8, ashes, ἁ. λ., E. furnace, P. E. *v.* 9, a boil, E. breaking forth, E., blains, ἁ. λ., E. x. 31, flax, E. bolled, ἁ. λ., E. *v.* 32, spelt, E. not grown up, ἁ. λ., E. xii. 4, number, ἁ. λ. *v.* 6, two evenings, ἁ. λ. *v.* 7, lintel, ἁ. λ. *vv.* 8, 11, passover, E. *v.* 15, leaven, ἁ. λ., E. xiii. 16, frontlets, P. xiv. horse, E. xv. 1, hath triumphed gloriously, E. *v.* 2, I will prepare him an habitation? ἁ. λ. *v.* 7, heaped up, ἁ. λ. *v.* 8, congealed: in this sense, ἁ. λ., E. *v.* 20, timbrel, E. xvi. 3, flesh-pots, E. *v.* 15, manna, E. *v.* 16, omer, P. E. *v.* 33, pot, P. E.

It is to be observed that these words occur indiscriminately in the so-called Jehovistic and Elohistic passages. The list may be extended.

the narrative; a difficulty not wholly removed by the acceptance of the accounts of providential interventions, which appear to have been not permanent, but limited to special occasions. But facts can be adduced which confirm, and indeed go far beyond, the conjectures of travellers, who have pointed out that the supply of water, and the general fertility of the district, must have been very different before the process of denudation, which has been going on for ages, and is now in active progress, had commenced. We have now proofs from inscriptions coeval with the pyramids, both in Egypt and in the Peninsula, that under the Pharaohs of the third to the eighteenth dynasty, ages before Moses, and up to his time, the whole district was occupied by a population, whose resources and numbers must have been considerable, since they were able to resist the forces of the Egyptians, who sent large armies in repeated, but unsuccessful, attempts to subjugate the Peninsula. Their principal object however was effected, since they established permanent settlements at Sarbet el Khadim, and at Mughara, to work the copper-mines[1]. These settlements were under the command of officers of high rank, and are proved by monuments and inscriptions to have been of an extent, which implies the existence of considerable resources in the immediate neighbourhood. It is well known that the early Egyptian kings were careful to provide for the security and sustentation of the caravans and bodies of troops, by which the communications with settlements under such circumstances were carried on: and every spot where the modern traveller still finds water on the route was doubtless then the object of special attention[2]. The vegetation which even now protects the wells of Moses, from which the dwellers at Suez obtain a supply of brackish water, must have been then far more luxuriant; and the seventy palm-trees, which Moses found at Elim, doubtless sheltered fountains, from which streams far more copious than those which now water the wady, flowed over the adjoining district. See note, ch. xv. 27. Where the superficial water was insufficient, it was customary in that early age to dig wells of whatever depth might be needed[3]; and every tree, now recklessly destroyed, was the object of special care, and even superstitious reverence. During the long ages which have elapsed since the Egyptian power passed away, the Peninsula has never been subjected to an Empire which has had a sufficient motive, or sufficient wisdom and resources, to arrest the process of deterioration: and every horde of Arabs, who have since been virtually its masters, bent only on supplying their own limited wants, cut down without remorse the shrubs and trees, on which the water supply, and consequently the general fertility of the district, mainly depend. The aspect of the whole country when

[1] Brugsch differs from all Egyptian scholars in a point of secondary importance, holding that the mines here were worked chiefly for the sake of turquoises (see Leps. 'Zeits.' 1866, p. 74, n. 3); but his treatise, entitled 'Wanderung nach den Türkis Minen,' gives a good account of the inscriptions. They are very numerous in the Wady Mughara; the earliest dates from Snefru, of the third dynasty; 8 Pharaohs of the three following dynasties have left many inscriptions, a considerable number belong to Amenemha III., dating from his 2nd to his 42nd year; and one of great importance describes an expedition under Ramaaka, *i.e.* Hatasu, the widow of Thotmes II. These inscriptions repeatedly speak of victories over native tribes: the very earliest inscription in existence, earlier than any in Egypt, records a victory achieved by Snefru over the Mentu, the general designation of the mountaineers of the Peninsula. The mines were lately worked by an Englishman, Major Macdonald, of whom Brugsch gives a full and very interesting account.

[2] In one of the most ancient papyri we find a notice of a place called She-Snefru, that is, the reservoir of Snefru, named after Snefru, the earliest Pharaoh who is known to have established an Egyptian settlement in the Peninsula of Sinai. M. Chabas remarks "She-Snefru était sans doute l'une des stations qu'il avait disposées au desert d'Arabie, sur la route de la Mer-Rouge." 'Les Papyrus Hiératiques de Berlin,' p. 39.

[3] See, for instance, the inscription relating to the gold mines near Dakkeh, explained by Mr Birch. It mentions a well 180 feet deep, and another still deeper, on a route where water could not be procured, dug by the order of Seti I. and Rameses II. The works of preceding Pharaohs, especially under the 12th dynasty, were equally remarkable for forethought.

it was first visited by Christian pilgrims who have left us accounts of their journeyings, must have differed greatly from that which it presented to the Israelites, when, under the guidance of Moses, they found pasturage for their flocks and herds. But far greater is the difference at present. Under Turkish misrule the Arabs carry on the work of desolation with no effective interference; no plantations are made, no wells are dug, the fountains are unprotected; and as though natural causes were insufficient, the annual tribute demanded by the Pasha consists in charcoal, each contribution laying waste a whole district. The devastation which began ages ago has in fact continued without cessation, and if it goes on at the present rate of increase, will ere long reduce the whole district to a state of utter aridity and barrenness. When Niebuhr visited the country, at the beginning of the last century, large supplies of vegetable produce were exported regularly to Egypt, shewing that the original fertility was not even then exhausted. Those supplies have ceased; and the only wonder is that so much remains to satisfy a careful inquirer of the possibility of the events recorded in Exodus.

Taking summarily the points in this part of the argument, we find the following coincidences between the narrative and accounts of travellers. Absence of water where no sources now exist, abundance of water where fountains are still found, and indications of a far more copious supply in former ages; tracts, occupying the same time in the journey, in which food would not be found; and in some districts a natural production similar to manna, most abundant in rainy seasons (such as several notices shew the season of the Exodus to have been), but not sufficient for nourishment, nor fit for large consumption, without such modifications in character and quantity as are attributed in the narrative to a divine intervention. We have the presence of Nomad hordes, and an attack made by them precisely in the district, and under the circumstances when their presence and attack might be expected. We have a route which the late exploration of the Peninsula, of which an account will be found at the end of the notes on this book, will shew to have been probably determined by conditions agreeing with incidental notices in the history; and when we come to the chapters in which the central event in the history of Israel, the delivery of God's law, is recorded, we find localities and scenery which travellers concur in declaring to be such as fully correspond to the exigencies of the narrative, and which in some accounts (remarkable at once for scientific accuracy and graphic power) are described in terms which shew they correspond, so far as mere outward accessories can correspond, to the grandeur of the manifestation.

Throughout this portion it will be observed that the notices on which the argument mainly rests are interwoven with the narrative and inseparable from it. It is easy to assert that any single notice may have been retained by oral tradition, or preserved for ages in scanty documents, such as were formerly supposed to be alone likely or possible to have been produced in the time of Moses; and such is the course generally adopted when any coincidence is pointed out too clear to be explained away; a course which, were it applied to any secular history, would be condemned as disingenuous or uncritical, making it in fact impossible to establish the authenticity of any ancient writing. But in addition to the positive arguments thus adduced, a negative argument at least equally conclusive demands attention. No history or composition in existence, which is known to have been written long after the events which it describes, is without internal indications which conclusively prove its later origin; contemporary documents may be interwoven with it, and great pains taken in ages of literary refinement and artifice to disguise its character, but even when anachronisms and errors of detail are avoided, which is seldom, if ever, effectually done, the genuine touch of antiquity, the χνοῦς ἀρχαιοπρεπής, is invariably and inevitably absent. Whether we look at the general tone of this narrative, the style equally remarkable for artlessness and power, or at the innumerable points of contact with external facts capable of exact determination, we are impressed by the weight of this internal evidence, supported as it has been shewn to be by the unbroken and unvarying tradition of the nation to whom the narrative was addressed, and by whom it was held too sacred not to be preserved from wilful mutilation or interpolation.

§ 5. An argument which many readers may feel to be even less open to objection is drawn from the account of the Tabernacle. In the notes on this part of the work the following facts are demonstrated.

In form, structure, and materials, the tabernacle belongs altogether to the wilderness. The wood used in the structure is found there in abundance. It appears not to have been used by the Israelites in Palestine; when the temple was rebuilt it was replaced by cedar. (See note on xxv. 10.) The whole was a tent, not a fixed structure, such as would naturally have been set up, and in point of fact was very soon set up, in Palestine; where wooden doors and probably a surrounding wall existed under the Judges of Israel. The skins and other native materials belong equally to the locality. One material which entered largely into the construction, the skin of the Tachash, was in all probability derived from the Red Sea; with the exception of one reference in Ezekiel xvi. 10, no traces of its use are found at a later period, or in any other district. The metals, bronze, silver and gold, were those which the Israelites knew, and doubtless brought with them from Egypt; nor is it probable that they possessed equal resources for a long time after their settlement in Palestine. The names of many of the materials and implements which they used, and the furniture and accessories of the tabernacle, the dress and ornaments of the priests, are shewn to have been Egyptian. It is also certain that the arts required for the construction of the tabernacle, and for all its accessories, were precisely those for which the Egyptians had been remarkable for ages; such as artizans who had lived under the influence of Egyptian civilization would naturally have learned. The rich embroidery of the hangings, the carving of the cherubic forms, the ornamentation of the capitals, the naturalistic character of the embellishments, were all things with which the Israelites had been familiar in Egypt; but which for ages after their settlement in Palestine, in which the traces of Canaanitish culture had been destroyed as savouring of idolatry, and where the people were carefully separated from the contagious influences of other nations on a par with Egypt, must have died out, if not from their remembrance, yet from all practical application. There are exceedingly few indications of any such arts among the Israelites during the period from the occupation of Palestine to the accession of Solomon; the ephod of Micah, and the teraphim in David's bed, being scarcely noticeable exceptions. It is improbable that any portion of the decorations of the tabernacle could have been produced, even had the rich materials been forthcoming; and it is to be noted as a fact of very special importance in this inquiry, that when Solomon, in the height of his prosperity, with the resources of a vast empire at his disposal, erected the temple which was to replace the tabernacle, he was compelled to seek the aid of foreigners, and to bring Tyrian artists to accomplish the work which Bezaleel had produced, when his native genius, trained in the school of Egypt, was developed by the Spirit of God.

The peculiar way in which the history of the erection of the Tabernacle is recorded suggests another argument, which has not hitherto received due attention. Two separate accounts are given. In the first Moses relates the instructions which he received, in the second he describes the accomplishment of the work. Nothing would be less in accordance with the natural order of a history written at a later period than this double account. It has been represented as an argument for a double authorship, as though two sets of documents had been carelessly or superstitiously adopted by a compiler. It is however fully accounted for by the obvious hypothesis, adopted throughout this part of the commentary, that each part of the narrative was written at the time, and on the occasion, to which it immediately refers. When Moses received these instructions he wrote a full account of them for the information of the people. This was on all accounts probable and necessary: among other obvious reasons it was necessary in order that the people might learn exactly what amount of materials and what amount of work would be required of them. When again he had executed his task, it was equally proper, and doubtless also in accordance with the habits of a people keen and jealous in the management of their affairs, and at no time free from tendencies to suspicion, that he should give a formal account of every detail in its execution[1]: a proof, to such as might call for proof, that all their precious offerings had been devoted to the purpose; and what was of far more importance, that the divine instructions had been completely and literally obeyed. It is a curious fact, that in the two accounts the order of the narrative is systematically reversed. In the instructions given to Moses and recorded for the information of the people, the most important objects stand first. The ark, the mercy-seat, the cherubs, the table of shew-bread, the golden candlestick, the whole series of symbolic forms by which the national mind was framed to comprehend the character of the divine revelation, are presented at once to the worshippers. Then come instructions for the tabernacle, its equipments and accessories; and when all else is completed, the dress and ornaments of the officiating priests. But when the work of Bezaleel and his assistants is described, the structure of the tabernacle comes first, as it naturally would do when the work was commenced; the place was first prepared, and then the ark and all the sacred vessels, according to all that the Lord commanded Moses.

[1] It is also to be observed that a very large portion of the papyri, written at nearly the same period in Egypt, consist of minute accounts of the work done, and the sums expended under the superintendence of the writers. In an inscription on the statue of an Egyptian architect, Bokenchons, who lived under Sethos I. and Rameses II., special note is made of his accuracy in accounting for expensive buildings.

§ 6. The Chronology of Exodus involves two questions, the duration of the sojourn of the Israelites in Egypt, and the date of their departure. So far as regards the direct statements in the Hebrew text, the answers to both questions are positive and unambiguous. Exodus xii. 40 gives 430 years for the sojourn, Genesis xv. 13 gives 400 years for the whole, or the greater portion of the same period. Again, the 1st book of Kings, c. vi. 1, fixes the Exodus at 480 years before the building of the Temple in the fourth year of Solomon's reign. This would settle the date within a few years, about 1490 B.C. See note on c. xii. 40.

Both statements are taken in their obvious and literal meaning by critics of different schools in Germany and England. The latter statement presents some difficulties. On the one hand it involves a longer period than appears to be consistent with the genealogies, especially with the genealogy of David. This objection loses its weight if the omission of several links in the genealogies be admitted as probable: in some cases of the highest importance it is certain, *e.g.* in that of Ezra and of our Lord. On the other hand it involves a shorter period than is deduced from notices in the book of Judges; an objection met by the probable hypothesis that many transactions in that book may have taken place at the same period in different parts of Palestine. Egyptian chronology is too uncertain to determine the question, as is shewn in the Appendix. The date appears on the whole to be reconcileable with the facts of history, and to rest on higher authority than any other which has been proposed.

The grounds on which the duration of the sojourn is determined are considered in the note at the end of c. xii. It is especially important with reference to the number of the Israelites, which amounted to 600,000 males at the time of the Exodus. Such an increase of a patriarchal family within 215 years, the period deduced by the Rabbins from genealogical computations, and adopted by many theologians, presents great, if not insuperable difficulties, which are removed if we accept the statement of Moses in the sense attached to it by most commentators. It needs no elaborate calculation to shew that in a period extending over more than four centuries, a family which counted 70 males with their households, probably amounting to many hundreds, occupying the most fertile district in Egypt, under circumstances most favourable to rapid and continuous increase specially recorded in this book, should become a mighty nation, such as they are represented in the narrative, and as critics admit they must have been to effect the conquest of Canaan and to retain their national integrity in the midst of a hostile population.

The commentary on this book was originally assigned to the Rev. R. C. Pascoe, Principal of the Theological college at Exeter. His death in June 1868 was preceded by a long illness, which prevented him from preparing notes which could be used for this work. In consequence of this very serious loss the first 19 chapters, together with the Introduction and appendices on Egyptian subjects, were undertaken by the Editor, and the remainder by the Rev. S. Clarke.

THE SECOND BOOK OF MOSES,

CALLED

EXODUS.

CHAPTER I.

1 The children of Israel, after Joseph's death, do multiply. 8 The more they are oppressed by a new king, the more they multiply. 15 The godliness of the midwives, in saving the men children alive. 22 Pharaoh commandeth the male children to be cast into the river.

NOW these *are* the names of the
[a] Gen. 46. 8. [a]children of Israel, which came
chap. 6. 14. into Egypt; every man and his household came with Jacob.
2 Reuben, Simeon, Levi, and Judah,
3 Issachar, Zebulun, and Benjamin,
4 Dan, and Naphtali, Gad, and Asher.
5 And all the souls that came out
of the † loins of Jacob were [b] seventy † Heb. *thigh.*
souls: for Joseph was in Egypt *al-* [b] Gen. 46.
ready. 27. Deut. 10.
6 And Joseph died, and all his 22.
brethren, and all that generation.
7 ¶ [c] And the children of Israel [c] Acts 7.
were fruitful, and increased abundant- 17.
ly, and multiplied, and waxed exceeding mighty; and the land was filled
with them.
8 Now there arose up a new king
over Egypt, which knew not Joseph.

CHAP. I. 1. *Now*] Literally "and." This conjunction is omitted by the LXX. but it is commonly used at the beginning of the historical books after Genesis, and here indicates a close connection with the preceding narrative. This chapter in fact contains a fulfilment of the predictions recorded in Gen. xlvi. 3, that God would make of Jacob "a great nation" in Egypt: and in Gen. xv. 13, that the people of that land would "afflict them four hundred years."

every man and his household] It may be inferred from various notices that the total number of dependents was considerable, a point of importance in its bearings upon the history of the Exodus. See Gen. xiii. 6, xiv. 14, from which we learn that Abram had 318 trained servants born in his house. The daughters are not mentioned, nor are the names of their husbands given; it is more likely that they were married to their near relations, or to dependents than to heathens; and in that case they with their families would form part of the patriarchal households.

5. *seventy*] This number includes Joseph, his two sons, and by a mode of reckoning not uncommon, Jacob himself; see Gen. xlv. 11, xlvi. 27; Deut. x. 22. The object of the writer in this introductory statement is to give a complete list of the heads of separate families at the time of their settlement in Egypt. See note on Num. xxvi. 5. The LXX. place the last clause, "Joseph was in Egypt," at the beginning of the verse, an arrangement which seems preferable, and is defended by Egli; see 'Zeitschrift für wissenschaftliche Theologie,' 1870, p. 326.

7. The narrative begins, properly speaking, with this paragraph. This is clearly shewn by the construction of the Hebrew, which does not connect the word "was fruitful" with the preceding verse. Egypt was always celebrated for its fruitfulness, and in no province does the population increase so rapidly as in that occupied by the Israelites. See notes on Gen. xlvii 6. At present it has more flocks and herds than any province in Egypt, and more fishermen, though many villages are deserted; it is calculated that another million might be sustained in it. (See Robinson, Vol. I. p. 55.) Until the accession of the new king, the relations between the Egyptians and the Israelites were undoubtedly friendly. The expressions used in this verse imply the lapse of a considerable period after the death of Joseph.

the land was filled with them] *i.e.* the district allotted to them, extending probably from the Eastern branch of the Nile to the borders of the desert. It appears from other passages (see iii. 22) that they did not occupy this land exclusively, but were intermingled with the native Egyptians.

8. The expressions in this verse are peculiar, and emphatic. "A new king" is a phrase not found elsewhere. It is understood by most commentators to imply that he did not succeed his predecessor in natural order of descent and inheritance. He "arose up over Egypt," occupying the land, as it would seem, on different terms from the king whose place he took, either by usurpation or conquest. The fact that he knew not Joseph implies a complete separation from the tradi-

9 And he said unto his people,
Behold, the people of the children of
Israel *are* more and mightier than we:
10 Come on, let us deal wisely
with them; lest they multiply, and
it come to pass, that, when there
falleth out any war, they join also
unto our enemies, and fight against
us, and *so* get them up out of the land.
11 Therefore they did set over
them taskmasters to afflict them with
their burdens. And they built for
Pharaoh treasure cities, Pithom and
Raamses.
12 † But the more they afflicted
them, the more they multiplied and
grew. And they were grieved because of the children of Israel.

† Heb. *And as they afflicted them, so they multiplied, &c*

---

tions of Lower Egypt. At present the generality of Egyptian scholars identify this Pharaoh with Rameses II. The question is discussed in the Appendix, where it is shewn that all the conditions of the narrative are fulfilled in the person of Amosis I., the head of the 18th Dynasty. He was the descendant of the old Theban sovereigns, but his family resided for many years at Eileithyia, (El Kab, south of Thebes,) and was tributary to the Dynasty of the Shepherds, the Hyksos of Manetho, then ruling in the North of Egypt. Amosis married an Ethiopian princess, Nephertari, and in the third year of his reign captured Avaris, or Zoan, the capital of the Hyksos, and completed the expulsion of that race.

9. *unto his people*] This expression has a peculiar fitness as addressed by the representative of the old Egyptian kings to his countrymen immediately after their emancipation from the dominion of aliens.

more and mightier] This may have been literally true, if, as was natural, the king compared the Israelites of Goshen with the population of the North Eastern district after the expulsion of the shepherds. The first impression made upon his mind would be the insecurity of a frontier occupied by a foreign race.

10. *any war*] The king had good cause to anticipate war. The North Eastern frontier was infested by the neighbouring tribes, the Shasous of Egyptian monuments, and war was waged with Egypt by the confederated nations of Western Asia under the reigns of his successors. These incursions were repulsed with extreme difficulty. In language, features, costume, and partly also in habits, the Israelites probably resembled those enemies of Egypt, and were regarded by the Egyptians as their natural allies.

out of the land] This is important as the first indication of a motive which determined the policy of the Pharaohs in dealing with the Israelites: they apprehended the loss of revenue and power, which would result from the withdrawal of a peaceful and industrious race.

11. *taskmasters*] The writer uses the proper Egyptian designation for these officers, viz. Chiefs of tributes (see Note at the end of the Chapter). They were men of rank, superintendents of the public works (LXX. ἐπιστάται τῶν ἔργων), such as are often represented on Egyptian monuments, and carefully distinguished from the subordinate overseers. The Israelites were employed in forced labours, probably in detachments, each under an Egyptian "taskmaster:" but they were not reduced to slavery, properly speaking, nor treated as captives of war. They continued to occupy and cultivate their own district, and they retained possession of their houses, flocks, herds, and other property until they emigrated from Egypt. Amosis had special need of such labourers. He restored the temples and other buildings destroyed by the shepherds, employing foreigners, either as subjects or mercenaries, for the transport of materials. This is proved by an inscription, dated in his 22nd year, see 'Æg. Zeitschrift,' November 1867.

treasure cities] The Hebrew word corresponds very closely both in form and meaning with "magazines," depots of ammunition and provisions: the same word is used 1 Kings ix. 19; 2 Chron. viii. 4 and xxxii. 28. Captives were employed in great numbers for building and enlarging such depots under the Egyptian kings of the 18th and 19th dynasties.

Pithom and Raamses] Both cities were situate on the canal, which had been dug or enlarged long before, under Osertasen, of the 12th dynasty. The names of both cities are found on Egyptian monuments: the former is known to have existed under the 18th dynasty: both were in existence in the beginning of the reign of Rameses II., by whom they were fortified and enlarged. The name "Pithom" means "House or temple of Tum," the Sun God of Heliopolis. The name of Raamses, or Rameses is generally assumed to have been derived from Rameses II., the Sesostris of the Greeks, but it was previously known as the name of the district. See Genesis xlvii. 11, and Appendix. The LXX. add "On, which is Heliopolis:" a reading commended by Egli, l.c. but On existed long before that age.

12. *they were grieved*] The Hebrew expresses a mixture of loathing and alarm. For "they" the LXX. read "the Egyptians."

13 And the Egyptians made the
children of Israel to serve with rigour:
14 And they made their lives bitter with hard bondage, in morter,
and in brick, and in all manner of
service in the field: all their service,
wherein they made them serve, *was*
with rigour.
15 ¶ And the king of Egypt spake
to the Hebrew midwives, of which
the name of the one *was* Shiphrah,
and the name of the other Puah:
16 And he said, When ye do the
office of a midwife to the Hebrew
women, and see *them* upon the stools;
if it *be* a son, then ye shall kill him:
but if it *be* a daughter, then she shall
live.
17 But the midwives feared God,
and did not as the king of Egypt
commanded them, but saved the men
children alive.
18 And the king of Egypt called
for the midwives, and said unto them,
Why have ye done this thing, and
have saved the men children alive?
19 And the midwives said unto
Pharaoh, Because the Hebrew women *are* not as the Egyptian women;
for they *are* lively, and are delivered ere the midwives come in unto
them.
20 Therefore God dealt well with
the midwives: and the people multiplied, and waxed very mighty.
21 And it came to pass, because

---

13. *with rigour*] The word is repeated v. 14; but does not occur elsewhere.

14. *morter and brick*] The use of brick, at all times common in Egypt, was especially so under the 18th dynasty. An exact representation of the whole process of brickmaking is given in a small temple at Thebes, erected by Thotmes III., the fourth in descent from Amosis. The persons there employed are captives, taken by that Pharaoh in his Asiatic campaigns. They are under a general superintendent, or "taskmaster," and are driven to work by overseers, armed with heavy lashes, who cry out "work without fainting." A report from a scribe at a later date, under the 19th dynasty, shews the rigour with which the labour, generally assigned to captives or to slaves, was enforced. See Brugsch, 'Histoire d'Egypte,' p. 174, and Chabas, 'Mélanges égyptologiques,' II. p. 121. Immense masses of brick are found at Belbeis, the modern capital of Sharkiya, *i.e.* Goshen, and in the adjoining district. There is no intimation that the Israelites were employed in building pyramids, which were erected by kings of Lower Egypt, with few exceptions, long before this period.

all manner of service in the field] Not merely agricultural labours to which the Israelites were accustomed, but probably the digging of canals and processes of irrigation which are peculiarly onerous and unhealthy, and on both accounts likely to have been imposed upon the Israelites. The word used throughout by the Targumist (see Note at the end of the Chapter) is interesting; the designation Fellahs, forced workers, is derived from it.

15. *Hebrew midwives*] Or "midwives of the Hebrew women." This measure at once attested the inefficacy of the former measures, and was the direct cause of the event which issued in the deliverance of Israel, viz. the exposure of Moses. Two midwives only are named. They may have been the two chief midwives, but it is not improbable that they were the only ones in Goshen. At present all travellers state that midwives are very seldom employed by Egyptian women, never by the common people, and by women of station only in cases of peculiar difficulty. Two might therefore have sufficed for the Israelites. It may perhaps be inferred from this statement that the object of the king was not to destroy all the male infants, a course obviously contrary to his interests, but those of the chiefs, whose wives were alone likely to call in the midwives. Both midwives bear names which are supposed by some to be of Hebrew origin, signifying personal beauty. They were however probably Egyptians, as would seem to be implied in the expressions in *vv.* 17 and 19: an Egyptian etymology of each name may be suggested: Puah from a word which means "child bearing," and Shiphrah, "prolific." See Note below.

16. *upon the stools*] The Hebrew means literally "two stones." The meaning is doubtful, as the expression does not occur elsewhere, but it probably denotes a peculiar seat, such as is represented on monuments of the 18th dynasty, and according to Lane is still used by Egyptian midwives. So it is understood by our translators, by the Targumist, and the Arabian translator, Saadia, a resident in Egypt and a man of great learning, whose authority on such a point has considerable weight. Gesenius, however, takes it to mean the stone

the midwives feared God, that he made them houses.

22 And Pharaoh charged all his people, saying, Every son that is born ye shall cast into the river, and every daughter ye shall save alive.

---

laver in which the newborn infant was washed, and he quotes a striking passage from Thevenot, stating that the Persian kings order the newborn male infants of their relatives to be killed in the stone basin in which they are washed. See Note below.

21. *made them houses*] *i.e.* they married Hebrews and became mothers in Israel. The expression is proverbial. See 2 Sam. vii. 11, 27.

22. Pharaoh thus made the people agents in the crime. The command, though general, may have been understood to apply to the leading families by whom the midwives had been employed, or to be in force until the population was reduced, so as to remove all apprehensions for the security of the frontier. The extreme cruelty of the measure does not involve improbability. Hatred of strangers was always a characteristic of the Egyptians, see Gen. xliii. 32, and was likely to be stronger than ever after the expulsion of an alien race. Before Psammetichus chance visitors were taken as slaves or put to death, see Diod. Sic. I. 67. Under the 12th dynasty, in the time of Abraham, the wives and children of foreigners were the property of the king (Chabas, 'Pap. Hier.' p. 14). The Spartans were even more guilty; they systematically murdered their Helots when their increased numbers excited alarm; on one occasion they slew 2,000, who had offered themselves as volunteers at the invitation of the state. Plut. 'Lyc.' § 28, and Thuc. IV. 80.

NOTES on vv. 11, 14, 15, 16.

11. The Hebrew is שרי־מסים, Sare massim. Sar means chief, or prince in Semitic languages, in Assyrian it has lately been shewn to be the proper phonetic for king; and it is common in Hebrew: but it is an Egyptian title, found on very ancient monuments, and it is the title specially given to the head of the works in the representation of brick making under Thotmosis III., to which allusion is more than once made in these notes. The word *massim* has no satisfactory etymology in Hebrew. Gesenius supposes it to be a contracted form, Michaelis suggests an improbable derivation from Arabic. The Egyptian *mas*, gives a good and natural sense, it means to bring tribute, *mas-mas* to divide or number in portions. See the Egyptian forms in the Appendix.

14. The Chaldee paraphrase of Onkelos is always meant when reference is made to the Targum in these notes; it is of great antiquity and authority. The Targum attributed to Jonathan is of late date and comparatively of little value. Saadia, who is often mentioned, was a Jew of great learning, a native of Fayoum in Egypt, towards the end of the 9th century. His Arabic translation is printed in Walton's Polyglott.

15. The Hebrew derivations of the two names are not satisfactory. Simonis makes פועה equivalent to יפועה, splendid, from יפע, a form for which there is no authority. Gesenius suggests the Arabic فوهة, countenance; this would require a change of letters, and is quite improbable. The Egyptian gives a simple and very satisfactory etymology; pā = פע with one determinative or explanatory sign means "splenduit" (coinciding in sense with Simonis' conjecture); with another and equally common sign it means "parturio, accoucher d'un enfant." Brugsch, 'D. H.' p. 463. Shiphra is rendered "child of Ra," by Bunsen, 'Bibelwerk.' This is inadmissible; "sefi" means "child," but the transcription of both syllables is inexact. The sense "prolific" given above is derived from one of the commonest words in Egyptian, Cheper; the transcription is very close, the ch and sh being regularly interchanged; the meaning "esse, fieri, nasci, procreare," with the additional notion of rapid increase and reproduction.

16. Professor Selwyn proposes an emendation which would entirely remove the difficulty; instead of אבנים he would read בנים, when ye look upon the children. The insertion of *them* in the Authorised Version is unauthorised. The only objection to the conjecture is that the change from so plain and intelligible a reading can scarcely be accounted for. Hirsch, chief Rabbi at Frankfort, whose commentary has appeared since these notes were printed, observes very truly that there is no authority for the interpretation most commonly received of אבנים, but the explanation which he suggests is forced and improbable. Like many other words it belongs to the age of Moses.

CHAPTER II.

1 Moses is born, 3 and in an ark cast into the flags. 5 He is found, and brought up by Pharaoh's daughter. 11 He slayeth an Egyptian. 13 He reproveth an Hebrew. 15 He fleeth into Midian. 21 He marrieth Zipporah. 22 Gershom is born. 23 God respecteth the Israelites' cry.

[a] chap. 6. 20. Numb. 26. 59.

AND there went [a] a man of the
house of Levi, and took *to wife*
a daughter of Levi.

2 And the woman conceived, and
bare a son: and when she saw him
that he *was a* goodly *child*, she [b] hid
him three months.

[b] Acts 7. 20. Heb. 11. 23.

3 And when she could not longer
hide him, she took for him an ark of
bulrushes, and daubed it with slime
and with pitch, and put the child
therein; and she laid *it* in the flags by
the river's brink.

4 And his sister stood afar off, to
wit what would be done to him.

5 ¶ And the daughter of Pharaoh
came down to wash *herself* at the river;
and her maidens walked along by the
river side; and when she saw the ark
among the flags, she sent her maid to
fetch it.

CHAP. II. 1. *a man of the house of Levi*] The marriage of Amram and Jochebed took place so long after the immigration of the Israelites, that it seems scarcely possible that Amram should have been the grandson, and Jochebed the daughter of Levi. The idiom which calls even a remote descendant the son or daughter is common to the Old and New Testament, and this passage may be understood to mean that both parents of Moses were of the house and lineage of Levi. Thus the Vulgate renders the verse, "and he took a wife of his own family;" the LXX. has "a wife of the daughters of Levi." See the Introduction, and note on ch. vi. 20, and on Num. xxvi. 59.

2. *bare a son*] Not her firstborn, Aaron and Miriam were older than Moses. In this part of the book the object of the writer is simply to narrate the events which led to the Exodus, and, as usual, he omits to notice what had no direct bearing upon that object. It is remarkable that any critic conversant with the style of the sacred writers should have drawn from this omission an argument against the accuracy or veracity of the writer.

a goodly child] This is the only allusion in the Pentateuch to the personal appearance of Moses, upon which much stress is laid by later tradition. Jochebed probably did not call in a midwife, see note on ch. i. 15, and she was of course cautious not to shew herself to Egyptians. The hiding of the child is spoken of as an act of faith, see Heb. xi. 23. It was done in the belief that God would watch over the child.

3. *an ark of bulrushes*] Both of these words, like the other words used in this description, are either common to Hebrew and Egyptian, or simply Egyptian. See Appendix. The ark was made of the papyrus which was commonly used by the Egyptians for light and swift boats. The species is no longer found in the Nile below Nubia. It is a strong rush, like the bamboo, about the thickness of a finger, not quite cylindrical but three cornered, and attains the height of 10 to 15 feet. It is represented with great accuracy on the most ancient monuments of Egypt; as for instance in the tomb of Tei under the 6th dynasty. An article on the Papyrus is given in the 'Mémoires de l'Académie des Inscriptions et de belles lettres,' Tom. XIX. p. 156.

slime and pitch] The "slime" is understood by most critics to be asphalt, but it more probably means the mud, of which bricks were usually made in Egypt, and which in this case was used to bind the stalks of the papyrus into a compact mass, and perhaps also to make the surface smooth for the infant. The pitch or bitumen (commonly used in Egypt, bearing the name here used by Moses,) made the small vessel water-tight.

in the flags] This is another species of the papyrus, called tufi, or sufi, (an exact equivalent of the Hebrew *suph*,) which was less in size and height than the rush of which the ark was made. The brink, or "lip of the river" is an expression common to Egyptian and Hebrew; both words correspond in meaning and form. That which is rendered "river," viz. *Jor* is not used in the Bible of any river out of Egypt, except once by Daniel xii. 5, on which see Ges. 'Thes.' s.v.

5. *the daughter of Pharaoh*] The traditions which give a name to this princess are probably of late origin, and merely conjectural. Josephus calls her Thermuthis; which means "the great Mother," a designation of Neith, the special deity of Lower Egypt: but it does not occur as the name of a princess. The names Pharia, Merris, and Bithia are also found in Syncellus, Eusebius, and the Rabbins. It is of more importance to observe that the Egyptian princesses held a very high and almost independent position under the ancient and middle empire, with a separate household and numerous officials. This was espe-

6 And when she had opened *it*, she
saw the child: and, behold, the babe
wept. And she had compassion on
him, and said, This *is one* of the Hebrews' children.
7 Then said his sister to Pharaoh's
daughter, Shall I go and call to thee a
nurse of the Hebrew women, that she
may nurse the child for thee?
8 And Pharaoh's daughter said to
her, Go. And the maid went and
called the child's mother.
9 And Pharaoh's daughter said unto
her, Take this child away, and nurse
it for me, and I will give *thee* thy
wages. And the woman took the
child, and nursed it.
10 And the child grew, and she
brought him unto Pharaoh's daughter,
and he became her son. And she
called his name ‖Moses: and she said,
Because I drew him out of the water.
11 ¶ And it came to pass in those
days, when Moses was grown, that he
went out unto his brethren, and looked
on their burdens: and he spied an
Egyptian smiting an Hebrew, one of
his brethren.

‖ That is, *Drawn out.*

---

cially the case with the daughters of the first sovereigns of the 18th dynasty: in two instances at least they were regents or co-regents with their brothers. See Appendix.

The facts recorded in these verses, according to M. Quatremère, suggest a satisfactory answer as to the residence of the daughter of Pharaoh and of the family of Moses. It must have been in the immediate neighbourhood of the Nile, and therefore not at On or Heliopolis, at which place Amosis put down human sacrifices offered by the Hyksos: it must have been near a branch of the Nile not infested by crocodiles, or the child would not have been exposed, nor would the princess have bathed there: therefore not near Memphis, where Amosis rebuilt the great temple of Ptah, from which the city took its name. At present crocodiles are not often found below the cataracts, but under the ancient empire they were common as far north as Memphis. These and other indications agreeing with the traditions recorded by Eutychius (see Milman, 'H. J.' I. p. 68), point to Zoan, Tanis, now San, the ancient Avaris, on the Tanitic branch of the river, near the sea, where crocodiles are never found, which was probably the western boundary of the district occupied by the Israelites. Avaris was captured by Amosis, and was the most suitable place for the head quarters of the Pharaohs, both as commanding the districts liable to incursions from Asiatic nomads, and as well adapted for carrying out the measures for crushing the Israelites. The field of Zoan was always associated by the Hebrews with the marvels which preceded the Exodus. See Ps. lxxviii. 43.

to wash] It is not customary at present for women of rank to bathe in the river, but it was a common practice in ancient Egypt. See Wilkinson, III. p. 389. The Nile was worshipped as an emanation (ἀπορροή) of Osiris, and a peculiar power of imparting life and fertility was attributed to its waters, a superstition still prevalent in the country. (Thus Strabo, Ælian, and Pliny and Seetzen, Vol. III. p. 204. See also Brugsch, 'Zeitschrift,' 1868, p. 123, and 'D. H.' p. 413.) The habits of the princess, as well as her character, must have been well known to the mother of Moses, and probably decided her choice of the place.

6. *she had compassion on him*] A touch of natural feeling, to which throughout the narrative Moses is careful to direct attention. The Egyptians indeed regarded such tenderness as a condition of acceptance on the day of reckoning. In the presence of the Lord of truth each spirit had to answer, "I have not afflicted any man, I have not made any man weep, I have not withheld milk from the mouths of sucklings." See the 'Funeral Ritual,' c. 125. There was special ground for mentioning the feeling, since it led the princess to save and adopt the child in spite of her father's commands.

10. *he became her son*] This expression leaves no doubt as to the formal adoption of Moses. He became a member of the royal household, where the training and education which he received would be such as St Stephen describes, he became learned in all the wisdom of the Egyptians. (See Note at the end of the Chapter.) Such a preparation was indeed humanly speaking all but indispensable to the efficient accomplishment of his work as the predestined leader and instructor of his countrymen. Moses probably passed the early years of his life in Lower Egypt, where the princess resided; all the notices in this book indicate a thorough familiarity with that portion of the country, and scarcely refer to the Thebaid. There may however be substantial grounds for the tradition in Josephus that he was engaged in a campaign against the Ethiopians, thus shewing himself, as St Stephen says, "mighty in word and deed." See 'Excursus' I. at the end of the volume.

Moses] The Egyptian origin of this word is generally admitted. The name itself is not uncommon in ancient documents. The exact

12 And he looked this way and that
way, and when he saw that *there was*
no man, he slew the Egyptian, and
hid him in the sand.
13 And when he went out the
second day, behold, two men of the
Hebrews strove together: and he said
to him that did the wrong, Wherefore
smitest thou thy fellow?
14 And he said, Who made thee
†a prince and a judge over us? in-
tendest thou to kill me, as thou killedst
the Egyptian? And Moses feared,
and said, Surely this thing is known.
15 Now when Pharaoh heard this
thing, he sought to slay Moses. But
Moses fled from the face of Pharaoh,
and dwelt in the land of Midian: and
he sat down by a well.
16 Now the ‖priest of Midian had

† Heb. *a man, a prince.*

‖ Or, *prince.*

---

meaning is "son," but the verbal root of the word signifies "produce," "draw forth." The whole sentence in Egyptian would exactly correspond to our version. She called his name Moses, *i.e.* "son," or "brought forth," because she brought him forth out of the water. See Appendix.

11. Moses records no incident of his life during the following years. His object, as Ranke observes, was not to write his own biography, but to describe God's dealings with his people. Later tradition would have been full of details. At the end of 40 years, when according to St Stephen, Moses visited his brethren, the princess was probably dead, as Syncellus relates, and the events which follow took place under another Pharăoh.

went out unto his brethren] This shews that the Egyptian princess had not concealed from him the fact of his belonging to the oppressed race, nor is it likely that she had debarred him from intercourse with his foster-mother and her family, whether or not she became aware of the true relationship.

an Egyptian] This man was probably one of the overseers of the workmen, natives under the chief superintendent, who are represented in the well-known picture of brickmakers under Thotmes III. See note on c. i. 13. They were armed with long heavy scourges, made of a tough pliant wood imported from Syria. See Chabas, 'Voyage d'un Égyptien,' pp. 119 and 136. The discipline of the Egyptian services, both military and civil, was maintained by punishments of excessive severity, even in the case of native officers. Hence the proverbial saying, "the child grows up and his bones are broken like the bones of an ass," and again, "the back of a lad is made that he may hearken to him that beats it." (Chabas, l. c. p. 136, and 'Pap. Anast.' v. 8, 6.) The "smiting" must have been unusually cruel to excite the wrath of Moses. The slaying of the Egyptian is not to be justified, or attributed to a divine inspiration, which Moses would not have omitted to mention; but it is to be judged with reference to the provocation, the impetuosity of Moses' natural character, perhaps also to the habits developed by his training at the court of Pharaoh. See the excellent remarks of St Augustine, 'c. Faust.' XXII. 70. The act involved a complete severance from the Egyptians; but far from expediting, it delayed for many years the deliverance of the Israelites. Forty years of a very different training prepared Moses for the execution of that appointed work.

13. *did the wrong*] Lit. "the wicked one," *i.e.* the aggressor.

thy fellow] **Thy neighbour:** so the word should be rendered: the reproof was that of a legislator who established moral obligations on a recognized principle. Hence in the following verse the offender is represented as feeling that the position claimed by Moses was that of a Judge. The act could only have been made known by the Hebrew on whose behalf Moses had committed it.

14. *a prince*] lit. as in the margin, a man, a prince. The Hebrew for Prince is *Sar*, used in i. 11. The word "Sar" implies the power, "judge" the right, of interfering.

15. *Pharaoh heard it*] No Egyptian king would have left such an offence unpunished, even had it been committed by a native of high rank: it is not even necessary to assume the death of the princess (see note on *v.* 2) to rebut the objection that her adopted son found no defender. It is observed however (by Hirsch) that the expression "sought to kill him" implies that the position of Moses, as adopted son of a princess, made it necessary even for a despotic sovereign to take unusual precautions.

the land of Midian] The Midianites occupied an extensive district from the eastern coast of the Red Sea to the borders of Moab. It is not improbable that in the time of Moses they may have had a settlement in the peninsula, at Sherm, where the two harbours, the only safe ones on that coast, offered peculiar advantages to them, engaged as they were from the earliest times in the transport of merchandize. (See Note at the end of the Chapter.)

by a well] **The well.** The well is spoken of as well known, the chief feature of the locality; such was the case whichever site be accepted as the residence of Reuel.

16. *the Priest of Midian*] Not "the prince" as in the margin. The word *Cohen*

seven daughters: and they came and
drew *water*, and filled the troughs to
water their father's flock.
17 And the shepherds came and
drove them away: but Moses stood
up and helped them, and watered their
flock.
18 And when they came to Reuel
their father, he said, How *is it that* ye
are come so soon to day?
19 And they said, An Egyptian
delivered us out of the hand of the
shepherds, and also drew *water* enough
for us, and watered the flock.
20 And he said unto his daughters,
And where *is* he? why *is* it *that* ye
have left the man? call him, that he
may eat bread.
21 And Moses was content to dwell
with the man: and he gave Moses
Zipporah his daughter.
22 And she bare *him* a son, and he
called his name [c] Gershom: for he said, [c] chap. 18. 3.
I have been a stranger in a strange land.

---

may have that meaning in some passages, but there is no reason for assuming it in this. Josephus and most of the ancient versions render it "priest." A Jewish tradition, derived probably from the Targum (which styles him Rabba, or Lord), represents Reuel as the prince, or probably as combining, like Melchizedek, the hereditary offices of chieftain and priest of the tribe, the Imam, the word used in the Arabic Version. The name of Reuel, and the detailed notices in c. xviii. (where see notes), prove that he was a priest of the one true God, known to the patriarchs especially under the name El; although the great bulk of the tribe, certainly those who lived farther north and more closely in contact with the Hamites of Canaan, were already plunged in idolatry. The conduct of the shepherds may indicate that his person and office were lightly regarded by the idolatrous tribes in his immediate neighbourhood.

drew water] This act would not be unbecoming or uncommon for the daughters of a priest whether chief of his tribe or not. At present the watering of cattle in that district is a work of maidens, from which even the daughters of sheickhs are not exempt. See Burckhardt, 'Syria,' p. 531. Thus Dr Stanley speaks of flocks climbing the rocks or gathered round the brooks and springs of the valleys under the charge of the black-vested Bedouin women of the present day.

18. *Reuel*] Or as in Num. x. 29, Raguel. The name means "friend of God." It appears to have been not uncommon among Hebrews and Edomites; see Gen. xxxvi. 4, 10; 1 Chron. ix. 8; Tobit vi. 10. Commentators, who identify Reuel with Jethro, a point open to grave objections (see Note at the end of the Chapter), generally accept the conjecture of Josephus, viz. that Reuel was his proper name, and Jether or Jethro, which means "excellency" (corresponding, as Knobel observes, to Imam), was his official designation. Moses naturally used the former name when he first mentioned his father-in-law, on other occasions he might take that by which the Priest was probably best known to the Israelites.

19. *An Egyptian*] Of course they spoke judging from his costume, or language, which must have been Egyptian at that time; a slight coincidence, but such as may be looked for only in a narrative of facts. Had Moses lived long among the Israelites, the Midianitish maidens would not have mistaken him for an Egyptian: a later writer would scarcely have noted the occurrence.

21. *was content to dwell with the man*] This conveys the true sense of the Hebrew. It implies that Moses recognized in Reuel a man in whom he could confide; and in his family a fitting home. So quietly, and yet so impressively, Moses records the entrance upon a long period, extending over forty years of mature life. Moses tells us nothing of what he may have learned from his father-in-law, but he must have found in him a man conversant with the traditions of the family of Abraham; nor is there any improbability in the supposition that, as hereditary priest, Reuel may have had written documents concerning their common ancestors. The use of letters was well known to the Phœnicians, whose trade with the dwellers in that very district is recorded on Egyptian monuments of the 13th dynasty, long anterior to the age of Moses: (see Brugsch, 'Histoire d'Egypte,' p. 74,) and inscriptions which record the campaigns of Pharaohs of the 18th and 19th dynasties, make express mention of scribes and historians of nations, *e.g.* of the Kheta or Hittites, who were probably not in advance of the Midianites.

22. *Gershom*] According to most Hebrew scholars the name is derived from a word meaning "expulsion." This, however, is scarcely reconcileable with Moses' own account, of which the Egyptian supplies an exact and satisfactory explanation. The first syllable "Ger" is common to Hebrew and Egyptian, and means "sojourner." The second syllable "Shom" answers exactly to the Coptic "Shemmo," which means "a foreign or strange land." For the old Egyptian forms, see Appendix.

23 ¶ And it came to pass in process
of time, that the king of Egypt died:
and the children of Israel sighed by
reason of the bondage, and they cried,
and their cry came up unto God by
reason of the bondage.

24 And God heard their groaning, and
God remembered his [d]covenant with [d] Gen. 15. 14. & 46. 4.
Abraham, with Isaac, and with Jacob.
25 And God looked upon the
children of Israel, and God †had re- † Heb. *knew.*
spect unto *them*.

---

23. *in process of time*] Nearly forty years: some delay intervened between the call of Moses and his departure for Egypt. This verse marks the beginning of another section. We now enter at once upon the history of the Exodus.

their cry came up unto God] This statement, taken in connection with the two following verses, proves that the Israelites retained their faith in the God of their Fathers. The divine name God, Elohim, is chosen because it was that which the Israelites must have used in their cry for help, that under which the covenant had been ratified with the Patriarchs. Dr Stanley would illustrate this by an account of the cries of the Fellahs in Egypt: but the distinction ought to be marked between their execrations, and the prayers which reached God from the Israelites.

24. *remembered*] This means that God was moved by their prayers to give effect to the covenant, of which an essential condition was the faith and contrition involved in the act of supplication. The whole history of Israel is foreshadowed in these words. The accumulation of so called anthropomorphic terms in this passage is remarkable. God heard, remembered, looked upon, and knew them. It evidently indicates the beginning of a crisis marked by a personal intervention of God.

25. *had respect unto them*] lit. and God knew. The LXX. "and was known unto them." This involves only a change of punctuation and may be preferable.

NOTES on vv. 10, 13, 18.

10. The education which would be given to a youth belonging to the royal household, and destined for military or civil service under the Middle Empire, has lately been illustrated by the labours of Goodwin, Chabas, and other Egyptologers, from the select papyri published in 1844 by the Trustees of the British Museum. These documents belong for the most part to the reigns of Rameses II. and his immediate successors, but the literary habits and attainments which they describe are known to have been far more ancient; collections of manuscripts, and scribes holding high offices of state, are frequently mentioned in the monuments of the early dynasties (see M. de Rougé, 'Recherches,' p. 73), and some of the most valuable papyri are productions of the ancient empire. M. Maspero has lately collected the most important facts in the introduction to his work on a portion of a papyrus of the 19th dynasty, entitled 'Hymne au Nil.'

He observes that we know for certain that a literary education was the first condition for admission to the public service; the title of scribe was necessary in order to obtain the lowest appointment in the civil administration or in the army. Hence a real enthusiasm for study is manifested by men of letters, such as Enna and Pentaour, whose compositions, indeed whose autographs are preserved. We have addresses to Thoth, the Hermes of the Greeks, the god of learning, in which the superiority of his work to all works is passionately maintained. "Thy works are better than all works; he who devotes himself to them becomes a noble; all successes achieved in life are due to thee; under thy inspiration a man becomes great, powerful, rich; of him all the world, all generations of men cry out, 'Great is he, great is the work of Thoth.'"

The education so highly valued began at a tender age; the infant, when it was weaned, was sent to school, and there instructed by scribes officially appointed. The discipline was severe, but due care was taken for the child's maintenance: the mother brought his food daily from his home, and in the upper schools rations of bread and salt fish seem to have been supplied regularly by the government: the register of distribution being, as in our colleges, accepted as proofs of the scholars' attendance (see Chabas, 'Voyage d'un Egyptien,' p. 23).

The scholar learned the elements of letters, the rules of orthography and grammar; and as he advanced, the art of expressing his thoughts in simple and perspicuous prose, of which the story of the two brothers in the D'Orbiney papyrus is a fair specimen; or in the epistolary style adapted for official communications, which occupy a large portion of the papyri; or in poetical composition, in which extant examples shew a genuine feeling for art; resembling Hebrew poetry in the carefully balanced parallelisms, and skilful combination of antitheses, though differing from it as markedly in the absence of the essential characteristics of simplicity and grace. It was indeed no slight thing to master the qualifications of a man of letters. The mere art of writing presented difficulties so serious that we find scribes boasting of a thorough knowledge of the mysteries of sacred letters as a rare and wonderful attainment. According to Diodorus special pains were bestowed upon arithmetic and geometry, an assertion borne out by late inquiries, which shew that the system of notation was remarkably clear, and that exact accounts were kept in every large household; a treatise on geometry in the British Museum now engages the attention of scholars, and will probably be published by Mr Birch. The mystic writings, in which ancient truths were imbedded in dark and dreary superstitions, occupied much of the time, not only of the priests, but of all men of learning. Schools of interpretation existed at an age long before Moses, which have left abundant traces in various readings, glosses, and mystic explanations of the so-called Funeral Ritual or Book of the Dead, a work which the literal translation of Mr Birch, remarkable for learning and ingenuity, has made to some extent accessible to English readers. The earliest extant copy of the chapter (the 17th) which gives the deepest insight into the ancient theosophy of Egypt dates from the 11th dynasty, and has even in that form numerous glosses bearing witness to a remote antiquity. In an address to an officer of rank, whose adventures in Syria have been illustrated by Goodwin and Chabas, the scribe whose autograph is before us, says, "Thou art a scribe skilful above thy equals, learned in the sacred writings, chastened in heart, disciplined in tongue; thy words pierce me, one phrase has thrice gone forth, thou hast broken me with terror." In a work just published ('Moses der Hebräer') M. Lauth attempts to identify this personage so remarkable for talents, learning, and bold speculations on religion, with Moses the Hebrew: an identification not likely to approve itself to scholars, but which serves to show the course of thought, and to some extent the state of mental development, in Egypt at a time not far remote from that in which Moses became learned in all the wisdom of the Egyptians, and mighty in word and deed.

13. The question whether the residence of Reuel was on the eastern or western coast of the Ælanitic gulf is not easily settled. The older and more general tradition is in favour of the former. The ruins of the city of Madian, described by Édrisi and Abul-feda and visited by Seetzen, lay on the east of the gulph, five days' journey from Aila, *i. e.* Akaba, and a well was shewn there as that from which Moses watered the flocks of his father-in-law. It would seem scarcely probable that Moses would be secure from pursuit within the peninsula, which was frequented by the Egyptians, who long before that time worked the copper mines and carried on a considerable traffic. Under the 18th and 19th dynasties the power of the Pharaohs appears to have extended over the whole country. It is also to be observed that the Israelites did not come into contact with the Midianites while they were in the peninsula, and that Jethro appears from the notices in ch. xviii. vv. 1, 5, 27 to have come from some considerable distance to meet Moses. It is objected that the distance of this city would have been too great for Moses to have pastured the flocks of Jethro in the peninsula, but we find instances of much longer distances in the history of Jacob and Laban, and at present in the accounts of the Bedouins. Thus Bochart, D'Anville, Mannert, and Quatremère, 'Mémoires de l'Académie des Inscriptions et Belles Lettres.'

On the other hand it is argued by Laborde, Knobel and others, that Reuel must have lived on the west of the gulf. The communications between the two coasts have always been frequent; at present sheep and goats are brought in great numbers from Mukna, near Madian, for sale in the peninsula, and at different times settlements have been made by Bedouins from the Hedjaz. The Towara, who are now the most powerful and most civilized tribe in the Peninsula, and have been recognized as the true descendants of the Midianites by most geographers (see Ritter, 'Sinai,' p. 936), occupied Madian in the time of Mahomet, who received one of their chieftains with the exclamation, "welcome to the brothers-in-law of Moses, welcome to the race of Shoeib, *i.e.* Jethro." If Reuel lived in this district, it must have been at Sherm, about 10 miles from Ras Mohammed, the southern headland. There are proofs that peculiar sanctity attached to that place at a very early period. The notices of ancient geographers (Strabo, Artemidorus, and Agatharchides, ap. Diodor. Sic., collected and examined by Knobel) speak of extensive palm-groves, abundant sources of fresh water, and a sanctuary under the charge of an hereditary priest and priestess, who held their office for life. The same writers testify to the existence of an ancient tribe in that neighbourhood bearing a name (Μαριανεῖς) nearly resembling and probably identical with Midianites; the d and r are frequently interchanged, or confounded owing to the similarity of ד and ר, a similarity even more striking in the most archaic forms of the two letters. The place, though sharing the general desolation of Turkish provinces, is at present of some importance. "There are two large bays affording the only safe anchorage for large ships, on the southern bay is the tomb of an unknown sheickh, near the northern bay are several copious wells of brackish water, deep, and lined with ancient stones, apparently an ancient work of considerable labour." Burckhardt, 'Syria,' p. 52.

18. The identity of Reuel with Jethro rests chiefly on the assumption that חתן, which is applied to Jethro repeatedly in the 3rd and 18th chapters, means "father-in-law." If Jethro were the father-in-law of Moses he would of course be the same person as Reuel. But in all other passages when the word חתן occurs, it means simply a "relation by marriage." In the Pentateuch it is applied to the sons-in-law of Lot, Gen. xix. 12, 14: to the brother-in-law of Moses, Hobab, Num. x. 29: to Moses himself, as husband of Zipporah, Exod. iv. 25, 26. In the book of Judges it is used once (xix. 4) of "a father-in-law," twice of "a son-in-law," twice of "a brother-in-law." The meaning in other passages is far more commonly son-in-law. The LXX. uses πενθερὸς and γαμβρός. The usage in Hebrew, Syriac, and Arabic is the same. Thus Freytag, ختن socer, vel omnis propinquus ab uxoris parte, scil. pater ejus, aut frater, &c.: ita apud genuinos Arates: vulgo autem est gener. Our rendering follows the Targums and Saadia. The Coptic word "Shom" has the same range of meaning. The meaning "circumcidit" has no authority in Hebrew, unless the very improbable explanation of ch. iv. 21, proposed by Gesenius, were admitted. The relationship therefore between Jethro and Moses cannot be decided by this word: it depends upon the internal evidence of the narrative. But Reuel must have been advanced in years, having seven grown up daughters when Moses arrived in Midian. When Moses was eighty years old, it is more probable that Reuel's son had succeeded him in his hereditary priesthood than that he was still living: and no difficulty is presented by the supposition that Jethro was the brother-in-law, not the father-in-law of Moses. The identity in that case of Jethro and Hobab, see Numb. x. 29, may be regarded as possible, but by no means as certain. Jethro returned to his own land before the promulgation of the law on Sinai, nor does his name occur afterwards. Hobab appears to have accompanied Moses on his journey, casting in his lot with the Israelites (see Judges iv. 11). He may have been, and very probably was, a younger brother of Jethro, not bound, like him, to his own tribe by the duties of an hereditary priesthood. This combination seems to meet all the conditions of the narrative, which would otherwise present serious, if not insuperable, difficulties.

CHAPTER III.

1 Moses keepeth Jethro's flock. 2 God appeareth to him in a burning bush. 9 He sendeth him to deliver Israel. 14 The name of God. 15 His message to Israel.

NOW Moses kept the flock of Jethro his father in law, the priest of Midian: and he led the flock to the backside of the desert, and

---

CHAP. III. The connection between this chapter and the preceding is very close, although many years intervened between the arrival of Moses in Midian and the transactions described in it. It marks however a distinct epoch, the commencement of the series of events which immediately preceded the Exodus. Hitherto the narrative has been studiously brief, stating only what was necessary to be known as preparatory to those events; but from this point Moses dwells minutely on the details, and enables us to realize the circumstances of the catastrophe which in its immediate and remote consequences stands alone in the world's history. This chapter is attributed by some writers to the so-called Jehovist; by others it is broken up into fragments, in order to meet the obvious objection that the name Elohim is found in it seventeen times, that of Jehovah six times only. But the internal evidence of unity is irresistible, and the fact that both the divine names occur far more frequently than in the preceding chapters is sufficiently accounted for by our having here a record of the personal intervention of the Lord God.

1. *the flock*] The expression is precise in Hebrew as in English, meaning not the cattle, but the sheep and goats. At present neither oxen nor horses are kept in the Peninsula, which does not supply fodder for them, under ordinary circumstances. It was however far more fertile in the time of Moses.

Jethro his father-in-law] Or "brother-in-law," see note above. An indefinite word such as affinis, signifying relation by marriage, would be preferable, but Jethro was probably the brother-in-law of Moses.

the backside] Gesenius explains this to mean "to the west of the district." This follows from the Hebrew system of orientation. The East is the region which is looked upon as before a man, the west behind him, the south and north as the right and left hand.

desert] Or **wilderness**. The word here used does not mean a barren waste, but a district supplying pasturage. The district near

came to the mountain of God, *even*
to Horeb.
2 And the angel of the LORD ap-
[a] Acts 7. 30. peared unto him in a [a]flame of fire
out of the midst of a bush: and he
looked, and, behold, the bush burned
with fire, and the bush *was* not consumed.
3 And Moses said, I will now turn
aside, and see this great sight, why the
bush is not burnt.
4 And when the LORD saw that he
turned aside to see, God called unto
him out of the midst of the bush, and
said, Moses, Moses. And he said,
Here *am* I.
5 And he said, Draw not nigh
hither: [b]put off thy shoes from off [b] Josh. 5.
thy feet, for the place whereon thou 15. Acts 7. 33.
standest *is* holy ground.
6 Moreover he said, [c]I *am* the God [c] Matt. 22.
of thy father, the God of Abraham, 32. Acts 7. 32.

Sherm, where Jethro may have resided, is described by ancient and modern travellers as barren and parched; on the west and east are rocky tracts, but to the north-west, at a distance of three or four days' journey, lies the district of Sinai, where the pasturage is good and water abundant. The Bedouins drive their flocks thither from the lowlands at the approach of summer. From this it may be inferred that the events here recorded took place at that season.

the mountain of God, even to Horeb] More exactly, **To the mountain of God, towards Horeb.** The meaning is that Moses came to the mountain of God, *i.e.* Sinai, on his way towards Horeb. The name Horeb appears to belong to the northern part of the Sinaitic range, and to reach it Moses probably followed the road from Sherm, which passes through the deep valley between the Gebel ed Deir and the range terminated on the south by the commanding height called Gebel Musa. The tract which leads to the height is half way between the two extremities, about three miles distant from each other: this would bring Moses to the lower part of the range towards the north, which is best adapted for pasturage. An argument is drawn from the expression "mountain of God" against the Mosaic authorship: but Moses, who appears to have written, or to have revised, this book towards the end of his life, may naturally have given this name by anticipation, with reference to the manifestation of God. The paraphrase in the Targum gives the true meaning, "the mountain in which the glory of Jah was revealed to him." On the other hand, it is assumed that the spot was previously held sacred. For this there is no ancient authority; though it has been lately shewn that the whole Peninsula was regarded by the Egyptians as specially consecrated to the gods from a very early time. An inscription at Sarbut el Chadem, dated the 25th year of Thotmes III., speaks of an officer charged to bring copper from the land of the gods.

2. *the angel of the LORD*] Or **an angel of Jehovah**; the article is not in the Hebrew. On the meaning and usage of the expression see note on Gen. xii. 7. In this passage it appears to designate a manifestation of God by the agency, or instrumentality of a created being. What Moses saw was the flame of fire in the bush; what he recognised therein was an intimation of the presence of God, who maketh "a flame of fire His angel." Ps. civ. 4. The words which Moses heard were those of God Himself, as all ancient and most modern divines have held, manifested in the Person of the Son.

out of the midst of a bush] Literally "**of the bush**, or seneh," a word which ought perhaps to be retained as the proper name of a thorny shrub common in that district, a species of acacia according to Dr Stanley. The name is very ancient, in Coptic *Sheno;* it is found in papyri of the 19th dynasty and in inscriptions quoted by Brugsch, 'D. H.' p. 1397, who translates it Dorn-Acacia, thorny acacia. The use of the article is peculiar: it seems to mean that bush of which Moses must have spoken frequently to the Israelites.

4. *the LORD saw*] The interchange of the two divine names is to be observed; *Jehovah* saw, *God* called.

5. *put off thy shoes*] The reverence due to holy places thus rests on God's own command. The custom itself is well known from the observances of the Temple, it was almost universally adopted by the ancients, and is retained in the East.

holy ground] This passage is almost conclusive against the assumption that the place was previously a sanctuary. Moses knew nothing of its holiness after some 40 years spent on the Peninsula. It became holy by the presence of God.

6. *Moreover*] Literally **And.**

thy father] The word seems to be used collectively for the forefathers of Moses; it may, however, refer specially to Abraham, the father of the faithful; with whom the covenant was first made.

Our Saviour adduces the passage as a proof that the doctrine of the resurrection was taught in the Old Testament, and he calls this

the God of Isaac, and the God of Jacob. And Moses hid his face; for he was afraid to look upon God.

7 ¶ And the LORD said, I have surely seen the affliction of my people which *are* in Egypt, and have heard their cry by reason of their taskmasters; for I know their sorrows;

8 And I am come down to deliver them out of the hand of the Egyptians, and to bring them up out of that land unto a good land and a large, unto a land flowing with milk and honey; unto the place of the Canaanites, and the Hittites, and the Amorites, and the Perizzites, and the Hivites, and the Jebusites.

9 Now therefore, behold, the cry of the children of Israel is come unto me: and I have also seen the oppression wherewith the Egyptians oppress them.

10 Come now therefore, and I will send thee unto Pharaoh, that thou mayest bring forth my people the children of Israel out of Egypt.

11 ¶ And Moses said unto God, Who *am* I, that I should go unto Pharaoh, and that I should bring forth the children of Israel out of Egypt?

12 And he said, Certainly I will be with thee; and this *shall be* a token unto thee, that I have sent thee:

---

book the book of Moses (see marg.), two points to be borne in mind by readers of the Pentateuch.

7. *taskmasters*] A different word from that used in ch. i. 11. It means oppressors.

I know] The expression implies a personal feeling, tenderness, and compassion.

8. *a good land*, &c.] The natural richness of Palestine, the variety and excellence of its productions, are attested by all ancient writers, whose descriptions are strongly in contrast with those of later travellers. The expression "flowing with milk and honey" is used proverbially by Greek poets. Knobel assumes very unnecessarily, that the honey of wine, not of bees, is meant; Euripides, describing a paradisiacal state, says: "It flows with milk, it flows with the honey of bees," 'Bacchæ,' l. 142. On the abundance of honey in Palestine see Tristram, 'Land of Israel,' p. 88.

the place of the Canaanites] This is the first passage in this book where the enumeration, so often repeated, of the nations then in possession of Palestine, is given. Moses was to learn at once the extent of the promise, and the greatness of the enterprise. In Egypt, the forces, situation, and character of these nations were then well known. Aahmes I. had invaded the south of Palestine in his pursuit of the Shasous; Thotmes I. had traversed the whole land on his campaign in Syria and Mesopotamia; representations of Canaanites, of the Cheta, identified by most Egyptologers with the Hittites, are common on monuments of the 18th and 19th dynasties, and give a strong impression of their civilization, riches, and especially of their knowledge of the arts of war. In this passage, the more general designations come first—"Canaanites" probably includes all the races; the Hittites, who had great numbers of chariots (892 were taken from them by Thotmes III. in one battle), occupied the plains; the Amorites were chiefly mountaineers, but gave their name to the whole country in Egyptian inscriptions; the name Perizzites probably denotes the dwellers in scattered villages, the half-nomad population; the Hivites, a comparatively unwarlike, but influential people, held 4 cities in Palestine proper, but their main body dwelt in the north-western district, from Hermon to Hamath (see Josh. xi. 3, and Judg. iii. 3); the Jebusites at that time appear to have occupied Jerusalem and the adjoining district. Soon after their expulsion by Joshua, they seem to have recovered possession of part of Jerusalem, probably Mount Zion, and to have retained it until the time of David.

11. *Who am I*] The change in the character of Moses since his first attempt, is strongly marked by these words, which, however, indicate humility, not fear. Among the grounds which he alleges for his hesitation, in no instance is there any allusion to personal danger; what he feared was failure owing to incompetency, especially in the power of expression. This shrinking from self-assertion is the quality which seems to be specially intimated by the word rendered "meek" in Numbers ch. xii. 3.

12. *a token unto thee*] Or **the sign.** This passage illustrates a peculiar use of the word. It generally means any act, whether supernatural or not, which is made the pledge of some future event; but sometimes, as undoubtedly in this place, it means a declaration or promise of God, which rests absolutely on His word, and demands faith. The promise that God would have the people serve Him in that place was an assurance, if fully believed, that all intervening obstacles would be removed by His power.

When thou hast brought forth the
people out of Egypt, ye shall serve
God upon this mountain.
13 And Moses said unto God, Behold, *when* I come unto the children
of Israel, and shall say unto them,
The God of your fathers hath sent
me unto you; and they shall say to
me, What *is* his name? what shall I
say unto them?
14 And God said unto Moses, I
AM THAT I AM: and he said,
Thus shalt thou say unto the children
of Israel, I AM hath sent me unto
you.
15 And God said moreover unto
Moses, Thus shalt thou say unto the
children of Israel, The LORD God of
your fathers, the God of Abraham,
the God of Isaac, and the God of Jacob, hath sent me unto you: this *is*
my name for ever, and this *is* my
memorial unto all generations.
16 Go, and gather the elders of
Israel together, and say unto them,
The LORD God of your fathers, the
God of Abraham, of Isaac, and of
Jacob, appeared unto me, saying, I
have surely visited you, and *seen* that
which is done to you in Egypt:
17 And I have said, I will bring
you up out of the affliction of Egypt
unto the land of the Canaanites, and
the Hittites, and the Amorites, and
the Perizzites, and the Hivites, and
the Jebusites, unto a land flowing with
milk and honey.
18 And they shall hearken to thy
voice: and thou shalt come, thou and
the elders of Israel, unto the king of
Egypt, and ye shall say unto him,
The LORD God of the Hebrews hath

---

13. *What is his name*] The meaning of this question is evidently: By which name shall I tell them the promise is confirmed? Each name of the Deity represented some aspect or manifestation of His attributes. El, Elohim, or Shaddai would speak of majesty, or might; either would probably have sufficed for Moses, but he would not use any one of them without God's special permission. What he needed was not a new name, but direction to use that Name which would bear in itself a pledge of accomplishment. It is not probable that Moses alluded to the multitudinous gods of Egypt; but he was familiar with the Egyptian habit of choosing from their many names that which bore specially upon the wants and circumstances of their worshippers (see especially the formulæ in the 'Papyrus magique d'Harris,' Chabas), and this may possibly have suggested the question which he was of course aware would be the first his own people would expect him to answer.

14. *I am that I am*] That is "I am what I am." The words express absolute, and therefore unchanging and eternal Being. So they are understood by ancient and modern interpreters (On the meaning and use of the name see the General Introduction). To Moses and the Israelites this was an explanation of the name Jehovah, which had been known from the beginning, but of which probably the meaning, certainly the full import, was not comprehended. The word "I am" in Hebrew is equivalent in meaning to Jehovah, and differs from it very slightly in form. This is much obscured by our substitution of **Lord** for Jehovah. The name, which Moses was thus commissioned to use, was at once new and old; old in its connection with previous revelations; new in its full interpretation, and in its bearing upon the covenant of which Moses was the destined mediator.

15. *The LORD God*] In this passage it is of great importance to keep the divine name **Jehovah God of your fathers, God of Abraham, God of Isaac, and God of Jacob.** It corresponds exactly to the preceding verse, the words **I am** and **Jehovah** being equivalent. This enables us to omit the article before "God," which is not in the Hebrew, and may be misunderstood, as though distinguishing Jehovah from other gods. The name met all the requirements of Moses, involving a twofold pledge of accomplishment; the pledges of ancient benefits and of a new manifestation.

name...memorial] The name signifies that by which God makes himself known, the *memorial* that by which His people worship Him; or as Bishop Wordsworth, following Keil, expresses it "the name declares the objective manifestation of the Divine Nature; the memorial, the subjective recognition by man."

18. *hath met with us*] This translation has been questioned, but it is now generally adopted. The Ancient Versions generally have "hath commanded or called us."

met with us: and now let us go, we
beseech thee, three days' journey into
the wilderness, that we may sacrifice
to the LORD our God.
19 ¶ And I am sure that the king
of Egypt will not let you go, ‖no, not
by a mighty hand.
20 And I will stretch out my hand,
and smite Egypt with all my wonders
which I will do in the midst thereof:
and after that he will let you go.

‖ Or, but by strong hand.

21 And I will give this people favour in the sight of the Egyptians:
and it shall come to pass, that, when
ye go, ye shall not go empty:
22 [d] But every woman shall borrow
of her neighbour, and of her that
sojourneth in her house, jewels of
silver, and jewels of gold, and raiment:
and ye shall put *them* upon your sons,
and upon your daughters; and ye shall
spoil ‖the Egyptians.

d chap. 11. 2. & 12. 35.

‖ Or, Egypt.

---

three days' journey] *i.e.* A journey which would occupy three days in going and returning. The request which the Israelites were instructed to make was therefore most probably not a permission to go beyond the frontier, but into the part of the desert adjoining Goshen. In this there was no deception. The Israelites were to ask what could not reasonably be refused, being a demand quite in accordance with Egyptian customs. The refusal of Pharaoh and his subsequent proceedings led to the accomplishment of the ultimate purpose of God, which was revealed to Moses at once, since without it his mission would have had no adequate object. It is important to observe that the first request which Pharaoh rejected could have been granted without any damage to Egypt, or any risk of the Israelites passing the strongly fortified frontier. The point is well drawn out by M. de Quatremère. See 'Mémoires de l'Académie des Inscriptions et Belles Lettres,' Vol. XIX.

19. *And I am sure*] Or, **I know.**

no, not] The marginal rendering "but by a mighty hand" probably gives the true meaning, but the construction presents some difficulty. The LXX. have ἐὰν μή, unless. Keil renders the phrase "not even by a mighty hand," and explains it to mean Pharaoh will not let the people go even when severely smitten. This is a satisfactory explanation, and is borne out by the history; even after the 8th plague, we read "Pharaoh would not let them go."

22. *shall borrow*] or **shall ask.** (See Note at the end of the Chapter.) Our translation is unfortunate. The word is exceedingly common, and always means **ask** or demand. Setting aside this passage no proof or justification of the rendering "borrow" is adduced, except 1 Sam. i. 28, and 2 Kings vi. 5. In the former passage the meaning is "asked," and granted, not "borrowed." In the latter the meaning "borrowed" is true, but secondary. Of course "asked" may apply either to a gift or a loan, a sense to be determined by the context, as in Exod. xxii. 14, where the construction is different. In this case there is no indication that the jewels which were demanded when the final departure of the Israelites was settled, and strongly urged upon their acceptance by the Egyptians, were expected to be returned. The Egyptians had made the people serve "with rigour, in all manner of service in the fields," and the Israelites when about to leave the country for ever were to ask, or claim the jewels as a just, though very inadequate remuneration for services which had made "their lives bitter." The Egyptians doubtless would have refused had not their feelings towards Moses (see ch. xi. 3) and the people been changed under God's influence, by calamities in which they recognized a divine interposition, which also they rightly attributed to the obstinacy of their own king, (see ch. x. 7). The Hebrew women were to make the demand, and were to make it to women, who would of course be specially moved to compliance by the loss of their children, the fear of a recurrence of calamity, perhaps also by a sense of the fitness of the request in connection with a religious festival.

jewels] The Hebrew may be rendered more generally "vessels" or simply "articles." (The Vulgate has vasa, the LXX. σκεύη.) But the word probably refers chiefly to trinkets. The ornaments of gold and silver worn at that time by Egyptian women were beautiful and of great value. It is probable that, as at present, husbands invested their earnings in jewels. The wife of a tradesman or of a dragoman is thus often in possession of bracelets and collars of gold which in Europe would indicate wealth or high station. It is to be observed that these ornaments were actually applied to the purpose for which they were probably demanded, being employed in making the vessels of the sanctuary.

sojourneth in her house] This indicates a degree of friendly and neighbourly intercourse, which could scarcely be inferred from the preceding narrative, but it is in accordance with several indirect notices, and was a natural result of long and peaceable sojourn in the district. The Egyptians did not all necessarily share the feelings of their new king.

NOTE on CHAP. III. V. 22.

The true translation is important. The word has in fact but one true meaning, 'ask.' The ancient Versions take it in this sense. The LXX. has αἰτήσει, the Vulgate, postulabit. The Syriac and the Targum use the same word, in the same sense as the Hebrew. Thus too the Samaritan paraphrase. Saadia has تستوهب, which is incorrectly rendered in Walton's Polyglott, mutuabitur. Freytag, 'Lex. Arab.' s. v., gives the true sense, rogavit donum, aut petiit dono sibi dari quid. See also the note on c. xii. 36.

CHAPTER IV.

1 Moses's rod is turned into a serpent. 6 His hand is leprous. 10 He is loth to be sent. 14 Aaron is appointed to assist him. 18 Moses departeth from Jethro. 21 God's message to Pharaoh. 24 Zipporah circumciseth her son. 27 Aaron is sent to meet Moses. 31 The people believeth them.

AND Moses answered and said,
But, behold, they will not believe me, nor hearken unto my voice:
for they will say, The LORD hath not
appeared unto thee.
2 And the LORD said unto him,
What *is* that in thine hand? And
he said, A rod.
3 And he said, Cast it on the
ground. And he cast it on the
ground, and it became a serpent;
and Moses fled from before it.
4 And the LORD said unto Moses,
Put forth thine hand, and take it by
the tail. And he put forth his hand,
and caught it, and it became a rod in
his hand:
5 That they may believe that the
LORD God of their fathers, the God
of Abraham, the God of Isaac, and
the God of Jacob, hath appeared unto
thee.
6 ¶ And the LORD said furthermore unto him, Put now thine hand
into thy bosom. And he put his
hand into his bosom: and when he
took it out, behold, his hand *was*
leprous as snow.
7 And he said, Put thine hand into
thy bosom again. And he put his
hand into his bosom again; and plucked it out of his bosom, and, behold, it
was turned again as his *other* flesh.
8 And it shall come to pass, if they
will not believe thee, neither hearken
to the voice of the first sign, that they
will believe the voice of the latter sign.

CHAP. IV. With this chapter begins the series of miracles which resulted in the deliverance of Israel. Long intervals of sacred history pass without any notice of miracle; not one, properly speaking, is recorded in connection with the previous history of the children of Jacob; but they cluster around great and critical events, occurring where they are demonstrably necessary. It is clear that unless a spiritual miracle transcending outward marvels had been wrought in the hearts both of the Israelites and of their oppressors, some special manifestations of divine power were indispensable. The first miracle was wrought to remove the first obstacle, viz. the reluctance of Moses, conscious of his own weakness, and of the enormous power with which he would have to contend. The LXX. add, "what shall I say unto them?" a probable, but not a necessary reading.

2. *A rod*] The word seems to denote the long staff which on Egyptian monuments is borne by men in positions of authority. See Wilkinson, III. pp. 367 and 386. It was usually made of acacia wood, such as is still sold for that purpose by the monks of the convent of Mount Sinai.

3. *a serpent*] This miracle had a meaning which Moses could not mistake. The serpent was probably the basilisk or Uræus, the Cobra. See Tristram, 'Nat. Hist.' p. 271. This was the symbol of royal and divine power on the diadem of every Pharaoh. It was a poisonous snake, as is shown by the flight of Moses and by most passages in which the same word occurs, *nahash*, derived from hissing. This snake never attacks without first inflating its neck, and then hissing; on the monuments it is always represented with its neck enormously swollen. The conversion of the rod was not merely a portent (τέρας), it was a sign (σημεῖον), at once a pledge and representation of victory over the king and gods of Egypt.

6. *leprous*] The instantaneous production and cure of the most malignant and subtle disease known to the Israelites was a sign of their danger if they resisted the command, and of their deliverance if they obeyed it. The infliction and cure were always regarded as special proofs of a divine intervention.

9 And it shall come to pass, if they
will not believe also these two signs,
neither hearken unto thy voice, that
thou shalt take of the water of the
river, and pour *it* upon the dry *land*:
and the water which thou takest out
of the river †shall become blood upon
the dry *land*.
10 ¶ And Moses said unto the
LORD, O my Lord, I *am* not †eloquent,
neither †heretofore, nor since
thou hast spoken unto thy servant:
but I *am* slow of speech, and of a
slow tongue.
11 And the LORD said unto him,
Who hath made man's mouth? or
who maketh the dumb, or deaf, or
the seeing, or the blind? have not I
the LORD?
12 Now therefore go, and I will
be [a]with thy mouth, and teach thee
what thou shalt say.
13 And he said, O my Lord, send,
I pray thee, by the hand *of him whom*
thou [1]wilt send.
14 And the anger of the LORD was
kindled against Moses, and he said, *Is*
not Aaron the Levite thy brother? I
know that he can speak well. And
also, behold, he cometh forth to meet
thee: and when he seeth thee, he
will be glad in his heart.
15 And thou shalt speak unto him,
and put words in his mouth: and I
will be with thy mouth, and with his
mouth, and will teach you what ye
shall do.
16 And he shall be thy spokesman

† Heb. *shall be and shall be.*

† Heb. *a man of words.*

† Heb. *since yesterday, nor since the third day.*

[a] Matt. 10. 19. Mark 13. 11. Luke 12. 11.

[1] Or, *shouldest.*

---

9. *shall become*] This rendering is preferable to that in the margin.

10. *eloquent*] Lit. a **man of words**, as in margin. The expressions which Moses uses do not imply a natural defect or impediment, but an inability to speak fluently. "Slow of speech," literally **heavy**, is specially used of persons speaking a foreign language imperfectly (see Ezek. iii. 5). The double expression slow of speech and of a slow tongue seems to imply a difficulty both in finding words and in giving them utterance, a very natural result of so long a period of a shepherd's life, passed in a foreign land, and as such to be counted among the numerous latent coincidences of the narrative.

since thou hast spoken] This expression seems to imply that some short time had intervened between this address and the first communication of the divine purpose to Moses.

12. Compare with this our Lord's promise to His Apostles; Matt. x. 19, Mark xiii. 11. It applies to both difficulties; "be with thy mouth" giving prompt utterance, and "teach thee" supplying or eliciting the best expression of the right thought.

13. *And he said*] The reluctance of Moses is a point of great moment. It had a permanent effect, for it caused the transfer of a most important part of his work to his brother, and its record supplies a strong evidence of the Mosaic authorship of this portion, attributed by Knobel to the so-called Jehovist. Like every other circumstance in the narrative it is in accordance with the inner law of man's spiritual development, and specially with the character of Moses; but under the circumstances it indicates a weakness of faith, such as no late writer would have attributed to the greatest of the descendants of Abraham.

send...by the hand] The Hebrew phrase is curt, so to speak, and ungracious; literally "send I pray by hand, thou wilt send," *i.e.* by whomsoever thou wilt; an expression which has scarcely a precedent and which may serve to illustrate Moses' own account of his heavy and awkward utterance: cf. Note on Numb. xiv. 13—17.

14. *anger*] This proves that the words of Moses indicated more than a consciousness of infirmity; somewhat of the vehemence and stubbornness, characteristic failings of strong, concentrated natures, which had previously been displayed in the slaying of the Egyptian.

Aaron] This is the first mention of Aaron. The exact meaning of the words "he can speak well," lit. "speaking he can speak," has been questioned, but they probably imply that Aaron had both the power and will to speak. Aaron is here called "the Levite," with reference, it may be, to the future consecration of this tribe; but not, as Knobel assumes, as though at that time the office and duties of the priesthood were assigned to him.

he cometh forth] *i.e.* is on the eve of setting forth. The Hebrew does not imply that Aaron was already on the way, but that he had the intention of going to his brother, probably because the enemies of Moses were now dead, see v. 19. The divine intimation was given afterwards, v. 27; it told Aaron where his brother was to be found. The expression "glad in his heart" should be noted as one of many indications of the divine sympathy with strong and pure natural affections.

15. *thou shalt speak*] Moses thus retains his position as "mediator;" the word comes to him first, he transmits it to his brother.

unto the people: and he shall be,
even he shall be to thee instead of a
[b] chap. 7. 1. mouth, and [b]thou shalt be to him instead of God.
17 And thou shalt take this rod in
thine hand, wherewith thou shalt do
signs.
18 ¶ And Moses went and returned to †Jethro his father in law, and
said unto him, Let me go, I pray
thee, and return unto my brethren
which *are* in Egypt, and see whether
they be yet alive. And Jethro said
to Moses, Go in peace.
19 And the LORD said unto Moses
in Midian, Go, return into Egypt:
for all the men are dead which sought
thy life.
20 And Moses took his wife and
his sons, and set them upon an ass,
and he returned to the land of Egypt:
and Moses took the rod of God in his
hand.
21 And the LORD said unto Moses,
When thou goest to return into Egypt,
see that thou do all those wonders before Pharaoh, which I have put in
thine hand: but I will harden his heart,
that he shall not let the people go.
22 And thou shalt say unto Pharaoh, Thus saith the LORD, Israel *is*
my son, *even* my firstborn:

---

16. *instead of a mouth*] We may bear in mind Aaron's unbroken habitude of speaking Hebrew and his probable familiarity with Egyptian. The Arabic translator (Saadia) uses the word tarjaman, *i.e.* dragoman, interpreter. Thus also the Syriac and the Targum.

instead of God] The word God is used of persons who represent the Deity, as kings, or judges, and it is understood in this sense by the Targumist and Saadia: "Thou shalt be to him a master."

18. *Jethro*] In the Hebrew Jether, see note on ch. II. Moses says nothing of his divine mission to Jethro; it was a secret thing between him and God.

19. *in Midian*] The LXX. insert before this verse "but after those many days the king of Egypt died." Egli, l. c., holds this to be the ancient reading, but it was probably introduced to explain the following statement, which is clear without it. There was apparently some delay on the part of Moses, who did not set out until he received a distinct assurance that all his enemies were removed. Such notices would never have occurred to a later writer, nor could they have originated in popular impressions. They show moreover how entirely Moses acted under an influence overruling the feelings, in which some would find the key to his acts.

20. *an ass*] Lit. "the ass," which according to Hebrew idiom means that he set them upon asses, not upon one ass, which would imply that they were both infants. This is the first notice of other sons besides Gershom.

the rod of God] The reference to the miracle recorded in v. 2, and to the express command in v. 17, is so obvious that it would be unnecessary to point it out but for the strange statement (Knobel) that the rod is here first mentioned. The staff of Moses was consecrated by the miracle and became the rod of God.

21. *see that thou do*, &c.] The Hebrew has, See all the wonders which I have put into thy hand, and do them before Pharaoh. Moses is called upon to consider the signs and to be prepared to produce them. The construction however is not certain; and the old Versions for the most part agree with our Authorised Version, which gives the general sense.

I will harden] Calamities which do not subdue the heart harden it; and the effects of God's judgments being foreknown are willed by Him. We should not therefore adopt a forced interpretation of this expression in order to explain away its apparent harshness. The hardening itself is judicial, and just, when it is a consequence of previously formed habits; in the case of Pharaoh it was at once a righteous judgment, and a natural result of a long series of oppressions and cruelties. Theodoret thus deals with the question: "The sun by the action of heat makes wax moist, and mud dry, hardening the one while it softens the other, by the same operation producing exactly opposite results; thus from the long-suffering of God some derive benefit and others harm, some are softened while others are hardened." 'Quæst. XII. in Exod.' The reason why the action of God rather than the character of Pharaoh is dwelt on in this passage would seem to be that it was necessary to sustain the spirit of Moses and the people during the process of events, which they were thus taught were altogether foreseen and predetermined by God.

22. *my firstborn*] The expression would be perfectly intelligible to Pharaoh, whose official designation was Si Ra, son of Ra. In numberless inscriptions the Pharaohs are styled "own sons" or "beloved sons" of the deity. It is here applied for the first time to Israel; and as we learn from *v.* 23, emphatically in antithesis to Pharaoh's own firstborn. The menace however was not uttered until it was called forth by Pharaoh's sin. See ch. xi. 5.

23 And I say unto thee, Let my son go, that he may serve me: and if thou refuse to let him go, behold, I will slay thy son, *even* thy firstborn.

24 ¶ And it came to pass by the way in the inn, that the LORD met him, and sought to kill him.

25 Then Zipporah took a sharp [1]stone, and cut off the foreskin of her son, and [†]cast *it* at his feet, and said, Surely a bloody husband *art* thou to me.

[1] Or, *knife.*
[†] Heb. *made it touch.*

26 So he let him go: then she said, A bloody husband *thou art*, because of the circumcision.

27 ¶ And the LORD said to Aaron, Go into the wilderness to meet Moses. And he went, and met him in the mount of God, and kissed him.

28 And Moses told Aaron all the words of the LORD who had sent him, and all the signs which he had commanded him.

29 ¶ And Moses and Aaron went

---

24. *in the inn*] Or "resting place," it probably does not mean a building, but the place where they rested for the night, whether under a tent, or in the open air. The khans or caravanserais, now common in the East, appear to have been unknown to the ancient Israelites and Egyptians.

met him, and sought to kill him] The expression is obscure, but is understood to mean that Moses was attacked by a sudden and dangerous illness, which he knew was inflicted by God. The word 'sought to kill' implies that the sickness, whatever might be its nature, was one which threatened death had it not been averted by a timely act. We are not told for what cause the visitation came; but from the context it may be inferred that it was because Moses had neglected the duty of an Israelite and had not circumcised his son. From the words of Zipporah it is evident that she believed the illness of Moses was to be thus accounted for; the delay was probably owing to her own not unnatural repugnance to a rite, which though practised by the Egyptians under the 19th dynasty, and perhaps earlier, was not adopted generally in the East, even by the descendants of Abraham and Keturah. Moses appears to have been utterly prostrate and unable to perform the rite himself.

25. *sharp stone*] Not "knife," as in the margin. Zipporah used a piece of flint, in accordance with the usage of the patriarchs. The Egyptians never used bronze or steel in the preparation of mummies because stone was regarded as a purer and more sacred material than metal. See Wilkinson, Vol. II. p. 164; and M. de Rougemont, 'Age du Bronze,' p. 152.

cast it at his feet] The Hebrew is obscure, but the Authorised Version probably gives the true meaning. Zipporah threw it at the feet of Moses, not of her son, as some commentators suppose; showing at once her abhorrence of the rite, and her feeling that by it she had saved her husband's life.

a bloody husband] Lit. "A husband of blood;" or "bloods:" the plural form signifies effusion of blood; the word (חתן) rendered husband (as in Psalm xix. 5, bridegroom) includes all relations by marriage; see note at the end of c. ii. The meaning is, the marriage bond between us is now sealed by blood. In the next verse Zipporah repeats the expression, as though she would say, thou art bound to me by a second covenant of which this bloody rite is the sign and pledge. By performing it Zipporah had recovered her husband; his life was purchased for her by the blood of her child. See the remarks of Hooker, 'E. P.' v. 62. The Targum Onk. gives a paraphrase, "had it not been for the blood of this circumcision my husband had been condemned to death." This appears to be the true explanation of a very obscure passage; other interpretations, which make the words refer to the child, or to the Angel of the Covenant, are generally admitted to be untenable.

26. *So he let him go*] *i.e.* God withdrew His visitation from Moses. The Hebrew allows no other interpretation.

We learn from ch. xviii. 2, that Moses sent Zipporah and her children back to Jethro before he went to Egypt. It was probably on this occasion. The journey would have been delayed had he waited for the healing of the child.

27. *And the LORD said*] See *v.* 14. Aaron now receives direct intimation where he is to meet his brother. He might otherwise have undertaken a long and fruitless journey to the residence of Jethro.

in the mount of God] Horeb lies on the direct route from Sherm to Egypt; this passage is therefore in favour of the supposition that Jethro's residence was on the west of the gulf. See note on c. ii.

28. *who had sent him*] The meaning is, probably, "which God had charged him to do." Thus the Vulgate, LXX., Knobel, and other commentators; but it is not necessary to alter the translation, which is literal and supported by Rosenmüller, who renders it, "qui eum miserat."

and gathered together all the elders of
the children of Israel:
30 And Aaron spake all the words
which the LORD had spoken unto
Moses, and did the signs in the sight
of the people.
31 And the people believed: and
when they heard that the LORD had
visited the children of Israel, and that
he had looked upon their affliction,
then they bowed their heads and worshipped.

CHAPTER V.

1 *Pharaoh chideth Moses and Aaron for their message.* 5 *He increaseth the Israelites' task.* 15 *He checketh their complaints.* 20 *They cry out upon Moses and Aaron.* 22 *Moses complaineth to God.*

AND afterward Moses and Aaron
went in, and told Pharaoh,
Thus saith the LORD God of Israel,
Let my people go, that they may hold
a feast unto me in the wilderness.
2 And Pharaoh said, Who *is* the
LORD, that I should obey his voice to
let Israel go? I know not the LORD,
neither will I let Israel go.
3 And they said, [a]The God of the
Hebrews hath met with us: let us go, [a] chap. 3. 18.
we pray thee, three days' journey
into the desert, and sacrifice unto
the LORD our God; lest he fall upon
us with pestilence, or with the
sword.
4 And the king of Egypt said unto

---

29. *all the elders*] The Israelites retained their own national organization; their affairs were administered by their own elders.

31. *the people*] This implies that the elders called a public assembly to hear the message brought by Moses and Aaron.

and worshipped] There is no reason to doubt that this act of worship was addressed to God, not to Moses and Aaron. It is important to remark that in this narrative there is no indication of ignorance of the history of the patriarchs, or of abandonment of the worship of God, sometimes attributed to the Israelites.

CHAP. V. 1. *Pharaoh*] This king, probably (see Appendix) Thotmes II. the great grandson of Aahmes, the original persecutor of the Israelites, must have been resident at this time in a city of lower Egypt, situate on the Nile. It could not therefore have been Heliopolis, and we have to choose between Memphis and Tanis; and there can be little doubt that most of the events which follow occurred at the latter city, the Zoan of Scripture. The notice in Psalm lxxviii. 12, 43, is admitted by all critics to be of great weight, and all the circumstances confirm it. See on ix. 31 and on ii. 5. Tanis was a very large city, and strongly fortified. The remains of buildings and the obelisks are numerous; they bear for the most part the name of Rameses II.; but it was the place of rendezvous for the armies of the Delta, and an imperial city in the 12th dynasty; it is identified by M. de Rougé with Avaris the capital of the Hyksos, who probably gave it its Hebrew name; both Avaris and Zoan mean "going out." This Pharaoh had waged a successful war in the beginning of his reign against the Shasous, the nomad tribes of the adjoining district, and his residence in the north-west of Egypt would be of importance at that time.

the LORD God] This version rather obscures the meaning; **Jehovah God of Israel** demanded the services of his people. The demand according to the general views of the heathens was just and natural; the Israelites could not offer the necessary sacrifices in the presence of Egyptians.

2. *I know not the LORD*] This may mean either that Pharaoh had not heard of Jehovah, or that he did not recognize Him as a God. The former is possible, for though the name was ancient, it was apparently less used by the Israelites than other designations of God. The Targum thus paraphrases: "the name of Jah has not been revealed to me."

3. *three days' journey*] This would not suffice for the journey to the "Mountain of God." See note on iii. 18. All that Moses was instructed to ask for was permission to go into a part of the desert where the people might offer sacrifices without interruption from the Egyptians; and that might be found on the frontiers of Egypt, or, at least, in a district commanded by the king's army. It is evident from Pharaoh's answer that he did not see in the request any indication of an intention to escape from Egypt. Ewald (Vol. II. pp. 84, 85) recognizes the reasonableness and modesty of this demand, which he represents as a manifest proof that the sober and noble spirit of prophecy in its best age has interpenetrated the narrative; words which do but express the old truth that the transaction and record bear equally the marks of divine governance and inspiration.

with pestilence, or with the sword] This notice is important as shewing that the plague was well known to the ancient Egyptians. It

them, Wherefore do ye, Moses and Aaron, let the people from their works? get you unto your burdens.

5 And Pharaoh said, Behold, the people of the land now *are* many, and ye make them rest from their burdens.

6 And Pharaoh commanded the same day the taskmasters of the people, and their officers, saying,

7 Ye shall no more give the people straw to make brick, as heretofore: let them go and gather straw for themselves.

8 And the tale of the bricks, which they did make heretofore, ye shall lay upon them; ye shall not diminish *ought* thereof: for they *be* idle; therefore they cry, saying, Let us go *and* sacrifice to our God.

9 †Let there more work be laid upon the men, that they may labour therein; and let them not regard vain words.

† Heb. *Let the work be heavy upon the men.*

10 ¶ And the taskmasters of the people went out, and their officers, and they spake to the people, saying, Thus saith Pharaoh, I will not give you straw.

11 Go ye, get you straw where ye can find it: yet not ought of your work shall be diminished.

12 So the people were scattered abroad throughout all the land of Egypt to gather stubble instead of straw.

13 And the taskmasters hasted *them*, saying, Fulfil your works, †*your* daily tasks, as when there was straw.

† Heb. *a matter of a day in his day.*

---

was probably less common than at present under the ancient Pharaohs, who bestowed great care on the irrigation and drainage of the country, but there are other indications of its ravages. See Chabas, 'Mél. Eg.' I. p. 40. The reference to the sword is equally natural, since the Israelites occupied the eastern district, which was frequently disturbed by the neighbouring Shasous. See note on v. 1.

6. *the taskmasters*] This word, which means "exactors" or "oppressors," designates the Egyptian overseers, who were subordinate to the officers called "taskmasters" in ch. i. 11, but whose name is different in Hebrew. See note on ch. i. 11, and 14.

their officers] Or **scribes**. These were Hebrews, appointed by the Egyptian superintendents, and responsible to them for the work; see v. 14. The Hebrew name *shoter* is equivalent to "scribe;" and it is probable that persons were chosen who were able to keep accounts in writing. Subordinate officers are frequently represented on Egyptian monuments giving in written accounts to their immediate superiors. Rosellini (II. 3, p. 272) observes that Egyptians made more use of writing on ordinary occasions than modern Europeans. "Shoterim" are often mentioned in the Old Testament, generally in connection with judges or leaders, by whom they were employed to transmit orders to the people and superintend the execution. It is evident how much this measure must have advanced the organization of the Israelites, and prepared them for their departure. See Note at the end of the Chapter.

7. *straw*] Some of the most ancient buildings in Egypt were constructed of bricks not burned, but dried in the sun; they were made of clay, or more commonly of mud, mixed with straw chopped into small pieces. Baked bricks are seldom found in ruins more ancient than the Exodus, never, according to Sir G. Wilkinson, (see Quarterly Review, 1859, April, p. 421), but there is a specimen in the British Museum belonging to the reign of Thotmosis III. An immense quantity of straw must have been wanted for the works on which the Israelites were engaged, and their labours must have been more than doubled by this requisition. In a papyrus of the 19th dynasty ('Anast.' IV. 12, 16) the writer complains: "I have no one to help me in making bricks, no straw." The expression at that time was evidently proverbial, whether or not as a reminiscence of the Israelites may be questioned, but it shows the thoroughly Egyptian character of the transaction.

9. *may labour therein*] The LXX. have "that they may attend to it and not attend to vain words:" a good and probable reading.

12. *stubble instead of straw*] Rather, **for the straw**. See Note at the end of the Chapter. The Israelites had to go into the fields after the reaping was done, to gather the stubble left by the reapers, who then, as at present in Egypt, cut the stalks close to the ears. They had then to chop it into morsels of straw before it could be mixed with the clay: see the previous note. This implies that some time must have elapsed before Moses again went to Pharaoh; and it also marks the season of the year, viz. early spring, after the barley or wheat harvest, towards the end of April. Their suffering must have been severe, since at that season the pestilential sand-wind blows over Egypt some 50 days, hence its name Chamsin.

14 And the officers of the children of Israel, which Pharaoh's taskmasters had set over them, were beaten, *and* demanded, Wherefore have ye not fulfilled your task in making brick both yesterday and to day, as heretofore?

15 ¶ Then the officers of the children of Israel came and cried unto Pharaoh, saying, Wherefore dealest thou thus with thy servants?

16 There is no straw given unto thy servants, and they say to us, Make brick: and, behold, thy servants *are* beaten; but the fault *is* in thine own people.

17 But he said, Ye *are* idle, *ye are* idle: therefore ye say, Let us go *and* do sacrifice to the LORD.

18 Go therefore now, *and* work; for there shall no straw be given you, yet shall ye deliver the tale of bricks.

19 And the officers of the children of Israel did see *that* they *were* in evil *case*, after it was said, Ye shall not minish *ought* from your bricks of your daily task.

20 ¶ And they met Moses and Aaron, who stood in the way, as they came forth from Pharaoh:

21 And they said unto them, The LORD look upon you, and judge; because ye have made our savour † to be abhorred in the eyes of Pharaoh, and in the eyes of his servants, to put a sword in their hand to slay us. († Heb. *to stink.*)

22 And Moses returned unto the LORD, and said, Lord, wherefore hast thou *so* evil entreated this people? why *is* it *that* thou hast sent me?

23 For since I came to Pharaoh to speak in thy name, he hath done evil to this people; neither hast thou † delivered thy people at all. († Heb. *delivering thou hast not delivered.*)

---

13. *hasted them*] See the words of the overseer quoted above on ch. i. 14. In a passage of the papyrus 'Anast.' III. translated by M. Chabas, 'Mél. Eg.' II. p. 122, twelve labourers employed in the same district are punished for negligence in failing to make up their daily tale of bricks.

14. *Were beaten*] The beating of these officers is quite in accordance with Egyptian customs; even natives of rank in civil and military service were subject to severe corporal punishments. See note on ch. ii. 11.

16. *the fault is in thine own people*] Lit. **thy people sin**: which may possibly mean thy subjects, *i.e.* the Israelites, are made guilty and punished: but the Authorised Version probably gives the true meaning; thus the Vulg., Targ. and Saadia. The LXX. and Syr. have "thou hast sinned against thy people."

17. *Ye are idle*] The old Egyptian language abounds in epithets which shew contempt for idleness. The charge was equally offensive and ingenious; one which would be readily believed by Egyptians who knew how much public and private labours were impeded by festivals and other religious ceremonies. Among the great sins which involved condemnation in the final judgment, idleness is twice mentioned; see funeral ritual in Bunsen's 'Egypt,' ed. 2, Vol. V. pp. 254, 255.

19. *in evil case*] They saw plainly that the object of Pharaoh was to find a pretext for further cruelty; probably for cutting off the leaders of the Israelites; see v. 21. The effect, however, would be to bring them into closer union and sympathy with the people.

20. *who stood in the way*] Or "waiting to meet them," *i.e.* Moses and Aaron stood without the palace to learn the result of the interview.

21. *in the eyes*] The change of metaphor shows that the expression was proverbial. Thus an Egyptian of rank complains to the scribe, who writes his history, "Thou hast made my name offensive, stinking, to all men." 'Anast.' I. 27, 7.

23. The earnestness of this remonstrance, and even its approach to irreverence, are quite in keeping with other notices of Moses' naturally impetuous character, see especially, ch. iii. 13; but such a speech would certainly not have been put into his mouth by a later writer. See note on ch. iv. 10.

NOTES on CHAP. V. *vv.* 6 and 12.

6. The question whether the שטרים were Egyptians or Hebrews is important in its bearings on the narrative. The word is common, and always denotes the class of persons described in the foot-note. Gesenius finds its root in the Arabic سطر, he wrote. The LXX. render it τοῖς γραμματεῦσιν: the Syr. ܣܦܪܐ, writer or scribe. Thus also the Samaritan version. The Targum Onk. uses the word סרכא, which is incorrectly rendered

"exactor" in Walton's Polyglott. It corresponds exactly to *shoter*, and is applied to the native officers of Israel: see Buxtorf, 'Lex. Chal.' s. v. Saadia uses a word which Walton renders "exactor;" but its true meaning is "cognitor, qui suos cognitos habet;" a very apt expression for these Hebrew officials.

12. The Hebrew has קַשׁ, stubble, and לְתֶבֶן, which does not mean instead of, but "for," *i.e.* to be prepared as תֶּבֶן, "straw chopped small:" stramenta minutim concisa. Thus the ancient versions and Targ. Onk., which is incorrectly translated in Walton. The etymology of תֶּבֶן is doubted; no Semitic root is found. The Egyptian has *tebu*, chaff. 'Pap. Sallier,' v. 6. Kash also is Egyptian for stubble, or stalk.

CHAPTER VI.

1 *God reneweth his promise by his name JEHOVAH.* 14 *The genealogy of Reuben,* 15 *of Simeon,* 16 *of Levi, of whom came Moses and Aaron.*

THEN the LORD said unto Moses, Now shalt thou see what I will do to Pharaoh: for with a strong hand shall he let them go, and with a strong hand shall he drive them out of his land.

2 And God spake unto Moses, and said unto him, I *am* the LORD:

3 And I appeared unto Abraham, unto Isaac, and unto Jacob, by *the name of* God Almighty, but by my name JEHOVAH was I not known to them.

4 And I have also established my covenant with them, to give them the land of Canaan, the land of their pilgrimage, wherein they were strangers.

5 And I have also heard the groaning of the children of Israel, whom the Egyptians keep in bondage; and I have remembered my covenant.

6 Wherefore say unto the children of Israel, I *am* the LORD, and I will bring you out from under the burdens of the Egyptians, and I will rid you out of their bondage, and I will redeem you with a stretched out arm, and with great judgments:

7 And I will take you to me for a people, and I will be to you a God: and ye shall know that I *am* the LORD

CHAP. VI. 1. *with a strong hand*] Or, **by a strong hand**, *i.e.* compelled by the power of God, manifested in judgments. In the 2nd clause the LXX. have "by a stretched out arm:" a probable reading, adopted by Egli, l. c.

2, 3. There appears to have been an interval of some months between the preceding events and this renewal of the promise to Moses. The oppression in the mean time was not merely driving the people to desperation, but preparing them by severe labour, varied by hasty wanderings in search of stubble, for the exertions and privations of the wilderness. Hence the formal and solemn character of the announcements in the whole chapter.

2. *I am the LORD*] See General Introduction, p. 25. The meaning, as is there shewn, seems to be this. I am Jehovah, and I appeared to Abraham, Isaac, and Jacob as El Shaddai, but as to my name Jehovah, I was not made known to them. In other words, the full import of that name was not disclosed to them. On the one hand it is scarcely possible to doubt, and it is in fact admitted by most critics, that the sacred name Jehovah was known from very early times; on the other, the revelation on Mount Sinai clearly states that the derivation and full meaning of the name were then first declared. On this special occasion it was important or necessary, for the support and encouragement of Moses and the people to whom he gave the announcement, to repeat the declaration as a pledge of the fulfilment of the promises made on the "Mountain of God."

3. *God Almighty*] Rather, "**El Shaddai**," it is better to keep this as a proper name; the meaning is correctly given in the text.

4. *And I have also*] The connection between this and the following verse is marked by the repetition of these words. Two reasons are assigned for the promise, viz. the old covenant with the patriarchs, and the divine compassion for the sufferings of Israel.

6. *with a stretched out arm*] The figure is common and quite intelligible; it may have struck Moses and the people the more forcibly since they were familiar with the hieroglyphic which represents might by two outstretched arms. On the obelisk at Heliopolis, Moses had been from infancy familiar with the symbol in the official name of Osertasen Racheperka, *i.e.* Ra is might.

your God, which bringeth you out
from under the burdens of the Egyptians.
8 And I will bring you in unto
the land, concerning the which I did
† Heb. *lift up my hand.* †swear to give it to Abraham, to Isaac,
and to Jacob; and I will give it you
for an heritage: I *am* the LORD.
9 ¶ And Moses spake so unto the
children of Israel: but they hearkened
† Heb. *shortness, or, straitness.* not unto Moses for †anguish of spirit,
and for cruel bondage.
10 And the LORD spake unto Moses, saying,
11 Go in, speak unto Pharaoh king
of Egypt, that he let the children of
Israel go out of his land.
12 And Moses spake before the
LORD, saying, Behold, the children of
Israel have not hearkened unto me;
how then shall Pharaoh hear me, who
am of uncircumcised lips?
13 And the LORD spake unto Moses and unto Aaron, and gave them a
charge unto the children of Israel, and
unto Pharaoh king of Egypt, to bring
the children of Israel out of the land
of Egypt.
14 ¶ These *be* the heads of their
fathers' houses: [a]The sons of Reuben [a] Gen. 46. 9.
the firstborn of Israel; Hanoch, and 1 Chron.
Pallu, Hezron, and Carmi: these *be* 5. 3.
the families of Reuben.
15 [b]And the sons of Simeon; Je- [b] 1 Chron.
muel, and Jamin, and Ohad, and Ja- 4. 24.
chin, and Zohar, and Shaul the son of
a Canaanitish woman: these *are* the
families of Simeon.

---

8. *I am the LORD*] Rather, **I the Lord**: the word "am" obscures the construction.

9. *they hearkened not*] The contrast between the reception of this communication and that recorded in ch. iv. 31, is dwelt upon by some critics as indicating different authors, but it is distinctly accounted for by the change of circumstances. On the former occasion the people were comparatively at ease, accustomed to their lot, sufficiently afflicted to long for deliverance, and sufficiently free in spirit to hope for it.

for anguish] Literally as in the margin, **for shortness of spirit**; out of breath, as it were, after their cruel disappointment, they were quite absorbed by their misery, unable and unwilling to attend to any fresh communication; an effect which might seem recorded expressly to preclude the notion that the deliverance of Israel was the result of a religious struggle, such as is assumed in some accounts of the transaction.

11. *go out of his land*] There is now a change in the demand; the first of a series of changes. Moses is now bidden to demand not a permission for a three days' journey, which might be within the boundaries of Egypt, but for departure from the land.

12. *uncircumcised lips*] An uncircumcised ear is one that does not hear clearly; an uncircumcised heart one slow to receive and understand warnings; uncircumcised lips, such as cannot speak fluently. Thus LXX., Syr., Targ., &c. There is no ground for assuming a natural defect. See note on ch. iv. 10. The recurrence of Moses' hesitation is natural; great as was the former trial this was far more severe; yet his words as ever imply fear of failure, not of personal danger.

13. *unto Moses and unto Aaron*] The final and formal charge to the two brothers is given, as might be expected, before the plagues are denounced. With this verse begins a new section of the history, and as in the book of Genesis "there is in every such case a brief repetition of so much of the previous account as is needed to make it an intelligible narrative in itself; a peculiarity which extends to the lesser subdivisions also." Quarry 'On Genesis,' p. 322.

14. *These be the heads*] We have in the following verses, not a complete genealogy, but a summary account of the family of the two brothers. It has been objected to as out of place, interrupting the narrative, and therefore probably an interpolation; but, as Rosenmüller and other unbiassed critics have observed, the reason is clear why Moses should have recorded his own genealogy and that of his brother, when they were about to execute a duty of the highest importance which had been imposed upon them; just then it was right and natural to state, for the satisfaction of Hebrew readers, to whom genealogical questions were always interesting, the descent and position of the designated leaders of the nation.

The sons of Reuben] Moses mentions in the first place the families of the elder brothers of Levi, in order to shew the exact position of his own tribe and family. Thus Rashi and Rosenmüller.

16 ¶ And these *are* the names of
[c] Numb. 3. 17. 1 Chron. 6. 1. the [c]sons of Levi according to their
generations; Gershon, and Kohath,
and Merari: and the years of the life
of Levi *were* an hundred thirty and
seven years.

17 The sons of Gershon; Libni,
and Shimi, according to their families.

[d] Numb. 26. 57. 1 Chron. 6. 1. 18 And [d]the sons of Kohath; Amram, and Izhar, and Hebron, and
Uzziel: and the years of the life of
Kohath *were* an hundred thirty and
three years.

19 And the sons of Merari; Ma-
hali and Mushi: these *are* the families
of Levi according to their generations.

[e] chap. 2. 1, 2. Numb. 26. 59. 20 And [e]Amram took him Jochebed his father's sister to wife; and she
bare him Aaron and Moses: and the
years of the life of Amram *were* an
hundred and thirty and seven years.

21 ¶ And the sons of Izhar; Korah, and Nepheg, and Zithri.

22 And the sons of Uzziel; Mishael, and Elzaphan, and Zithri.

23 And Aaron took him Elisheba,
daughter of Amminadab, sister of
Naashon, to wife; and she bare him
Nadab, and Abihu, Eleazar, and
Ithamar.

24 And the sons of Korah; Assir,
and Elkanah, and Abiasaph: these *are*
the families of the Korhites.

25 And Eleazar Aaron's son took
him *one* of the daughters of Putiel to
wife; and [f]she bare him Phinehas: [f] Numb. 25. 11.
these *are* the heads of the fathers of
the Levites according to their families.

26 These *are* that Aaron and Moses,
to whom the LORD said, Bring out the
children of Israel from the land of
Egypt according to their armies.

---

16. *sons of Levi*] Thus Moses shews that of the three great divisions of the tribe, the one to which he and Aaron belonged, and to which the priesthood was afterwards confined, was the second, not the first. Again, he does not trace the descent of other families, but passes at once from Kohath, the son of Levi, to the heads of Kohath's family in his own time.

the years of the life of Levi] It is usual throughout Genesis in each genealogy to give the age of the chief person in each principal family, and to omit it in the case of secondary families.

20. *Amram*] This can scarcely be the same person who is mentioned in *v.* 18; but his descendant and representative in the generation immediately preceding that of Moses. The intervening links are omitted, as is the rule where they are not needed for some special purpose, and do not bear upon the history. Between the death of Amram and the birth of Moses was an interval which can scarcely be brought within the limits assigned by any system of chronology to the sojourn in Egypt. Thus Tiele, quoted by Keil: "According to Numbers iii. 27, &c. in the time of Moses the Kohathites were divided into four branches, that of Amram, Izhar, Hebron, and Uzziel: their number amounted to 8600 males; of these the Amramites were about one fourth, *i.e.* more than 2000 males. This would be impossible were Amram the son of Kohath identical with Amram the father of Moses. We must therefore admit an omission of several links between the two." Thus in the genealogy of Ezra (Ezra vii. 3, compared with 1 Chron. v. 33—35) five descents are omitted between Azariah the son of Meraioth and Azariah son of Johanan, and several between Ezra himself and Seraiah, who was put to death by Nebuchadnezzar 150 years before the time of Ezra."

Jochebed] Here named for the first time, and, as might be expected, not in the general narrative but in a genealogical statement. The name means "the glory of Jehovah," one clear instance of the usage of the sacred name before the Exodus.

father's sister] This was within the prohibited degrees after the law was given, but not previously.

23. *Elisheba*] Her brother Naashon was at that time captain of the children of Judah, Num. ii. 3. Theodoret remarks, τῆς βασιλικῆς καὶ τῆς ἱερατικῆς φυλῆς τὴν ἐπιμιξίαν διδάσκει. 'Quæst. in Exod.' *i.e.* (Moses) shews the intermixture of the royal and priestly tribes.

25. *Putiel*] This name is remarkable, being compounded of Puti, or Poti, in Egyptian "devoted to," and "El," the Hebrew name of God. See De Vogüé, 'Inscriptions sémitiques,' p. 125.

26, 27. This emphatic repetition shews the reason for inserting the genealogy. The names of Moses and Aaron are given twice and in a different order; in the 26th verse probably to mark Aaron as the elder in the genealogy, and in the 27th to denote the leadership of Moses.

27 These *are* they which spake to
Pharaoh king of Egypt, to bring out
the children of Israel from Egypt:
these *are* that Moses and Aaron.

28 ¶ And it came to pass on the
day *when* the LORD spake unto Moses
in the land of Egypt,

29 That the LORD spake unto
Moses, saying, I *am* the LORD: speak
thou unto Pharaoh king of Egypt all
that I say unto thee.

30 And Moses said before the
LORD, Behold, I *am* of uncircumcised
lips, and how shall Pharaoh hearken
unto me?

CHAPTER VII.

1 *Moses is encouraged to go to Pharaoh.* 7 *His age.* 8 *His rod is turned into a serpent.* 11 *The sorcerers do the like.* 13 *Pharaoh's heart is hardened.* 14 *God's message to Pharaoh.* 19 *The river is turned into blood.*

AND the LORD said unto Moses,
See, I have made thee a god to
Pharaoh: and Aaron thy brother shall
be thy prophet.

---

28. This and the following verses belong to the next chapter. They mark distinctly the beginning of a subdivision of the narrative, and according to the general rule in the Pentateuch (see note on ver. 14), begin with a brief recapitulation. Moses once more, like other sacred writers, dwells strongly upon his personal deficiencies and faults of character (see Ewald, II. p. 84), an all but certain indication of autobiography in the case of great and heroic personages.

CHAP. VII. With this chapter begins the series of miracles wrought in Egypt. They are progressive. The first miracle is wrought to accredit the mission of the brothers; it is simply credential, and unaccompanied by any infliction. Then come signs which shew that the powers of nature are subject to the will of Jehovah, each plague being attended with grave consequences to the Egyptians, yet not inflicting severe loss or suffering; then in rapid succession come ruinous and devastating plagues, murrain, boils, hail and lightning, locusts, darkness, and lastly, the death of the firstborn. Each of the inflictions has a demonstrable connection with Egyptian customs and phenomena; each is directly aimed at some Egyptian superstition; all are marvellous, not, for the most part, as reversing, but as developing forces inherent in nature, and directing them to a special end. The effects correspond with these characteristics; the first miracles are neglected; the following plagues first alarm, and then for a season, subdue, the king, who does not give way until his firstborn is struck. Even that blow leaves him capable of a last effort, which completes his ruin, and the deliverance of the Israelites.

It is admitted by critics that the deliverance of the Israelites must have been the result of heavy calamities inflicted upon the Egyptians, who certainly would never have submitted to so great a loss had they been in a state to prevent it. Nor could it have been effected by a successful uprising of the Israelites, who were not in a position to resist the power of Egypt, and who, had such been the case, would certainly have preserved the record of a war issuing in so glorious a result. It is also generally admitted that the calamities, whatever they might have been, did not include an overthrow of Egyptian power by foreign enemies, or national insurrections. No notice of either, as Knobel remarks, is found in Hebrew traditions; and it may be added, that in neither of the reigns to which the Exodus has been assigned, are there any indications of either calamity. Egypt was in the highest state of power and prosperity through the whole period within which all agree that the Exodus took place. The reign of Thotmes II., which has been shewn in the Appendix to be that which tallies best with all ascertained facts, intervened between two of the ablest and most successful sovereigns in Egypt, and though obscure and uneventful, it gives no indications of loss or disturbance; the only war recorded was one that extended or confirmed his power. Late investigations have also shewn that the reigns of Merneptah and his successor (under whom these events are supposed by most critics to have occurred), were on the whole prosperous; one only invasion is recorded in the beginning of that period and it was completely repelled. A succession of such plagues as are described in Exodus must therefore be assumed, and is in fact accepted by critics, as the only conceivable cause of the result. The question whether it was miraculous, depends upon the ulterior question, whether miracles under any circumstances are conceivable; if in any case possible no case can be imagined in which the necessity of a divine interposition, and its direct and permanent results upon the whole state of humanity, could be more satisfactorily shewn.

1. *I have made thee*] Or "appointed thee." The expression "a god" is not unfrequently used of an appointed representative of God; but here it implies that Moses will stand in this peculiar relation to Pharaoh, that he will address him by a prophet, *i.e.* by one appointed to speak in his name. The pas-

2 Thou shalt speak all that I command thee: and Aaron thy brother shall speak unto Pharaoh, that he send the children of Israel out of his land.

3 And I will harden Pharaoh's heart, and multiply my signs and my wonders in the land of Egypt.

4 But Pharaoh shall not hearken unto you, that I may lay my hand upon Egypt, and bring forth mine armies, *and* my people the children of Israel, out of the land of Egypt by great judgments.

5 And the Egyptians shall know that I *am* the LORD, when I stretch forth mine hand upon Egypt, and bring out the children of Israel from among them.

6 And Moses and Aaron did as the LORD commanded them, so did they.

7 And Moses *was* fourscore years old, and Aaron fourscore and three years old, when they spake unto Pharaoh.

8 ¶ And the LORD spake unto Moses and unto Aaron, saying,

9 When Pharaoh shall speak unto you, saying, Shew a miracle for you: then thou shalt say unto Aaron, Take thy rod, and cast *it* before Pharaoh, *and* it shall become a serpent.

10 ¶ And Moses and Aaron went in unto Pharaoh, and they did so as the LORD had commanded: and Aaron cast down his rod before Pharaoh, and before his servants, and it became a serpent.

11 Then Pharaoh also called the wise men and the sorcerers: now the magicians of Egypt, they also did in like manner with their enchantments.

12 For they cast down every man his rod, and they became serpents: but Aaron's rod swallowed up their rods.

---

sage is an important one as illustrating the primary and essential characteristic of a prophet, he is the declarer of God's will and purpose.

3. *and my wonders*] The distinction between signs and the word here rendered "wonders," according to Kimchi, is that the former is used more generally, the latter only of portents wrought to prove a divine interposition; they were the credentials of God's messengers.

9. *thy rod*] Apparently the rod before described, which Moses on this occasion gives to Aaron as his representative.

a serpent] A different word is used in ch. iv. 3, when the rod of Moses is changed. In that passage the snake is called "Nahash," which corresponds to the Egyptian Arā, or Uræus. Here another and more general term, "Tannin," is employed, which in other passages includes all sea or river monsters, and is more specially applied to the crocodile as a symbol of Egypt. It occurs in the Egyptian ritual, c. 163, nearly in the same form, "Tanem," as a synonym of the monster serpent which represents the principle of antagonism to light and life. The ancient versions either render the word coluber, δράκων, or simply transcribe the Hebrew; thus Syr., Targ., Sam., and Saadia.

11. *magicians*] See Note at the end of the chapter.

with their enchantments] The derivation of the original expression is ambiguous. It may come from a word meaning "flame," or from another meaning "conceal;" in either case it implies a deceptive appearance, an illusion, a juggler's trick, not an actual putting forth of magic power. It bears a very near resemblance to an Egyptian term for a magic formula, sc. Ra, or La, ap. Chabas, 'P. M.' p. 170. Moses describes the act of the sorcerers as it appeared to Pharaoh and the spectators; living serpents may have been thrown down by the jugglers, a feat not transcending the well-known skill of their modern representatives, with whom it is a common trick to handle venomous serpents, and benumb them so that they are motionless and stiff as rods. Pharaoh may or may not have believed in a real transformation; probably he did, for the jugglers have always formed a separate caste, and have kept their arts secret; but in either case he would naturally consider that if the portent wrought by Aaron differed from theirs, it was a difference of degree only, implying merely superiority in a common art. The miracle which followed was sufficient to convince him had he been open to conviction. The accounts in the Koran, Sur. VII. and XX., are curious. They represent the magicians as deceiving the spectators by acting upon their imagination.

12. *swallowed up their rods*] The miracle here is distinctly stated, and is bound up with the very substance of the narrative. Its meaning is obvious. Ewald remarks truly that this miracle was the clearest expression of the truth which underlies all these stories, as he is pleased to call the miracles, viz. the truth and power of the religion of Jehovah in contrast with others.

13 And he hardened Pharaoh's heart, that he hearkened not unto them; as the LORD had said.

14 ¶ And the LORD said unto Moses, Pharaoh's heart *is* hardened, he refuseth to let the people go.

15 Get thee unto Pharaoh in the morning; lo, he goeth out unto the water; and thou shalt stand by the river's brink against he come; and the rod which was turned to a serpent shalt thou take in thine hand.

16 And thou shalt say unto him, The LORD God of the Hebrews hath sent me unto thee, saying, Let my people go, that they may serve me in the wilderness: and, behold, hitherto thou wouldest not hear.

17 Thus saith the LORD, In this thou shalt know that I *am* the LORD: behold, I will smite with the rod that *is* in mine hand upon the waters which *are* in the river, and they shall be turned to blood.

18 And the fish that *is* in the river shall die, and the river shall stink; and the Egyptians shall lothe to drink of the water of the river.

19 ¶ And the LORD spake unto Moses, Say unto Aaron, Take thy rod, and stretch out thine hand upon the waters of Egypt, upon their streams, upon their rivers, and upon their ponds, and upon all their † pools of water, that they may become blood; and *that* there may be blood

† Heb. *gathering of their waters.*

---

13. *And he hardened*] Or **Pharaoh's heart was hardened.** The word is here used intransitively, as in many passages: thus all the Ancient Versions.

15. *he goeth out unto the water*] The Nile was worshipped under various names and symbols, at Memphis especially, as Hapi, *i.e.* Apis, the sacred bull, or living representation of Osiris, of whom the river was regarded as the embodiment or manifestation. See 'Zeitschrift Eg.' 1868, p. 123. It is therefore probable that the king went in the morning to offer his devotions. This gives a peculiar force and suitableness to the miracle. The reason which Knobel assigns is not incompatible with this. It was the season of the yearly overflowing, about the middle of June. (The Arabic almanacs give the 18th of Payni, *i.e.* the 12th of June, for the festival of the rising of the Nile.) The daily rise of the water was accurately recorded, probably in the time of Moses, as some centuries later, under the personal superintendence of the king. In early inscriptions the Nilometer is the symbol of stability and providential care. According to Diodorus a Nilometer was erected at Memphis under the ancient Pharaohs; one is described by Lepsius which bears the name of Amenemha III., of the 12th dynasty, by whom the system of irrigation was completed. See Appendix.

The First Plague.

17. *turned to blood*] In accordance with the general character of the narrative it might be expected that this miracle would bear a certain resemblance to natural phenomena, and therefore be one which Pharaoh might see with amazement and dismay, yet without complete conviction. It is well known that before the rise the water of the Nile is green and unfit to drink. About the 25th of June it becomes clear, and then yellow, and gradually reddish like ochre; this effect has been generally attributed to the red earth brought down from Sennaar, but Ehrenberg proves that it is owing to the presence of microscopic cryptogams and infusoria. The depth of the colour varies in different years; when it is very deep the water has an offensive smell. Late travellers say that at such seasons the broad turbid tide has a striking resemblance to a river of blood. The supernatural character of the visitation was attested by the suddenness of the change; by its immediate connection with the words and act of Moses, and by its effects. It killed the fishes, and made the water unfit for use, neither of which results follows the annual discoloration.

18. *shall lothe*] Lit. "be weary of," but the Authorised Version expresses the meaning. The word has a special force as applied to the water of the Nile, which has a certain sweetness when purified of the slime, and has always been regarded by Egyptians as a blessing peculiar to their land. It is the only pure and wholesome water in their country, since the water in wells and cisterns is unwholesome, while rain water seldom falls, and fountains are extremely rare. Maillet, ap. Kalisch.

19. The expressions in this verse shew an accurate knowledge of Egypt, where the water system was complete at a period long before Moses. Lepsius ('Zeitschrift,' 1865) describes it carefully. *Their streams* mean the natural branches of the Nile in Lower Egypt. The word *rivers* should rather be *canals*. Moses uses the Egyptian word explained above (ch, ii.). It includes canals. They were of great extent, running parallel to the Nile, and

throughout all the land of Egypt,
both in *vessels of* wood, and in *vessels*
of stone.
20 And Moses and Aaron did so,
as the LORD commanded; and he
a chap. 17. 5. [a]lifted up the rod, and smote the
waters that *were* in the river, in the
sight of Pharaoh, and in the sight of
b Psal. 78. 44. his servants; and all the [b]waters that
were in the river were turned to blood.
21 And the fish that *was* in the
river died; and the river stank, and
the Egyptians could not drink of the
water of the river; and there was
blood throughout all the land of Egypt.

22 [c]And the magicians of Egypt c Wisd. 17. 7.
did so with their enchantments: and
Pharaoh's heart was hardened, neither
did he hearken unto them; as the
LORD had said.
23 And Pharaoh turned and went
into his house, neither did he set his
heart to this also.
24 And all the Egyptians digged
round about the river for water to
drink; for they could not drink of
the water of the river.
25 And seven days were fulfilled,
after that the LORD had smitten the
river.

---

communicating with it by sluices, which were opened at the rise, and closed at the subsidence of the inundation. The word rendered "*ponds*" refers either to natural fountains, or more probably to cisterns or tanks found in every town and village. The "*pools*," lit. "gathering of waters," were the reservoirs, always large and some of enormous extent, containing sufficient water to irrigate the country in the dry season.

in vessels of wood] Lit. "in wood and stone;" but the word "vessels" is understood and should be retained. This also marks the familiarity of the writer with Egyptian customs. The Nile water is kept in vessels and is purified for use by filtering, and by certain ingredients such as the paste of almonds. At present the vessels are generally earthenware. The words in the text appear to include all household vessels in which the water was kept.

21. *the fish*, &c.] The expression may not necessarily mean "all the fish;" but a great mortality is of course implied, and would be a most impressive warning. The Egyptians subsisted to a great extent on the fish of the Nile, though salt-water fish was regarded as impure. A mortality among the fish was a plague much dreaded. In a hymn to the Nile written by the scribe Enna it is said that the wrath of Hapi the Nile-God is a calamity for the fishes. See Maspero, 'Hymne au Nil,' p. 27.

22. *did so*] From this it must be inferred that the plague though general was not universal. In numberless instances the Hebrew terms which imply universality must be understood in a limited sense.

24. *digged round about the river*] This statement corroborates the explanation given above on *v.* 17. The discoloured water would be purified by a natural filtration.

25. *seven days*] This marks the duration of the plague. The natural discoloration of the Nile water lasts generally much longer, about 20 days.

NOTE on CHAP. VII. 11.

11. Three names for the magicians of Egypt are given in this verse. The first and last occur in Genesis, ch. v. The word (חכמים), wise men, is used specifically of men who know occult arts. Corresponding expressions in Arabic are well known, as araph, alam, &c. Thus in the Acts the sorcerer Bar-jesus is called Elymas, "the knowing one." In ancient Egyptian the most general name is Rechiu Chetu, *i.e.* people who know things, the word "things" being applied technically to secret and curious things. The word rendered "sorcerers" (מכשפים) occurs first in this passage. It is used in the sense "muttering magic formulæ." According to Gesenius the original meaning, as retained in Syriac and Ethiopic, is simply to worship or pray. No exact parallel is found for this word among the numerous designations for sorcerers in Egyptian documents; but it seems not improbable that it may be connected with "Chesef," a very common word used specially in the sense of repelling, driving away, conjuring all noxious creatures by magic formulæ. Thus in the funeral ritual there are no less than 11 chapters (32—42) containing forms for "stopping" or driving away crocodiles, snakes, asps, &c. It was natural that Pharaoh should have sent especially for persons armed with such formulæ on this occasion. The more general word "chartummim," which corresponds in meaning to ἱερογραμματεὺς or ἐξηγητής, "sacred scribe" or "interpreter," has not been yet traced in Egyptian. If however it is resolved into its probable elements, the first syllable חר (char) answers exactly to "cher," one of the commonest Egyptian words, used in compound terms as "bearing," "having," "possessing;" the second part corresponds to "temu" or "tum," "to speak, utter," which is applied specifically to uttering a sacred name, and apparently as "a spell." Thus on certain days of the calendar it was unlawful to utter (temu) the name of Set or Sutech, the Typhon, or spirit of force and destruction. See 'Papyrus Sallier,' IV. p. 12, last line; and Brugsch, 'D. H.' s. v. In the trilingual inscription lately discovered at San, "tum" means to recite a sacred hymn, l. 34. Cher-tum would thus mean "bearer of sacred words."

The most complete and interesting account of Egyptian magic is given by M. Chabas in his work called 'Le Papyrus Magique,' Harris, 1866. Books containing magic formulæ belonged exclusively to the king; no one was permitted to consult them but the priests and wise men, who formed a council or college, and were called in by the Pharaoh on all occasions of difficulty. These "wise men" are called "scribes" (see Brugsch, 'D. H.' p. 1576), "scribes of the sacred house," or "te-ameni," *i.e.* "scribes of occult writings," &c. Under the 20th dynasty, the use of these books was interdicted under pain of death. Two curious documents (the Papyrus Lee and Rollin explained by M. Chabas, and lately edited by Pleyte) give a full account of the trial and execution of a criminal who fraudulently obtained possession of some books kept in the archives of the palace. No formulæ are more common than those which were used to fascinate, or to repel serpents.

The names of the two principal magicians, Jannes and Jambres, who "withstood Moses" are preserved by S. Paul, 2 Tim. iii. 8. Both names are Egyptian, in which language An, or Anna, identical with Jannes, means scribe. It was also a proper name borne by a writer well known in Papyri of the time of Rameses II. Jambres may mean Scribe of the South. The tradition was widely spread. It is found in the Talmud, in the later Targum, and in other Rabbinical writings quoted by Buxtorf, 'Lex. H. C.' p. 946. Pliny, who makes Moses, Jamnes, and Jotape heads of magic factions, seems to have derived his information from other sources, and he is followed by Apuleius. Numenius, a Pythagorean, quoted by Eusebius, comes nearer to the truth, though according to Greek habit he transforms Moses into Musæus.

CHAPTER VIII.

1 *Frogs are sent.* 8 *Pharaoh sueth to Moses,* 12 *and Moses by prayer removeth them away.* 16 *The dust is turned into lice, which the magicians could not do.* 20 *The swarms of flies.* 25 *Pharaoh inclineth to let the people go,* 32 *but yet is hardened.*

AND the LORD spake unto Moses, Go unto Pharaoh, and say
unto him, Thus saith the LORD, Let
my people go, that they may serve me.
2 And if thou refuse to let *them*
go, behold, I will smite all thy borders with frogs:
3 And the river shall bring forth
frogs abundantly, which shall go up
and come into thine house, and into

The Second Plague.

CHAP. VIII. 2. *with frogs*] The annoyance and suffering caused by frogs are described by ancient writers, quoted by Bochart, 'Hier.' III. In Egypt they sometimes amount at present to a severe visitation. Some months appear to have elapsed between this and the former plague, if they made their appearance at the usual time, that is (according to Seetzen, who gives the fullest and most accurate account of them, Vol. III. p. 492) in September. He describes two species, the rana Nilotica, and the rana Mosaica, called by the natives "Dofda," which exactly corresponds to the Hebrew word used in this and no other passage, except in the psalms taken from it; it is not a general designation, but restricted to the species, and probably of Egyptian origin. See Appendix and end of volume. They are small, do not leap much, are much like toads, and fill the whole country with their croakings. They are generally consumed rapidly by the Ibis (ardea Ibis), which thus preserves the land from the stench described *v.* 14. This plague was thus, like the preceding, in general accordance with natural phenomena, but marvellous both for its extent and intensity, and for its direct connection with the words and acts of God's messengers. It had also apparently, like the other plagues, a direct bearing upon Egyptian superstitions. A female deity with a frog's head, named Heka, was worshipped in the district of Sah (*i.e.* Benihassan) as the wife of Chnum, the god of the cataracts, or of the inundation; see Brugsch, 'Geog.' p. 224. Lepsius has shewn that the frog was connected with the most

thy bedchamber, and upon thy bed,
and into the house of thy servants,
and upon thy people, and into thine
‖ Or, *dough.* ovens, and into thy ‖ kneadingtroughs:
4 And the frogs shall come up
both on thee, and upon thy people,
and upon all thy servants.
5 ¶ And the LORD spake unto
Moses, Say unto Aaron, Stretch forth
thine hand with thy rod over the
streams, over the rivers, and over the
ponds, and cause frogs to come up
upon the land of Egypt.
6 And Aaron stretched out his
hand over the waters of Egypt; and
the frogs came up, and covered the
land of Egypt.
[a] Wisd. 17. 7. 7 [a] And the magicians did so with
their enchantments, and brought up
frogs upon the land of Egypt.
8 ¶ Then Pharaoh called for Moses and Aaron, and said, Intreat the
LORD, that he may take away the
‖ Or, *Have this honour over me, &c.* frogs from me, and from my people;
and I will let the people go, that they
may do sacrifice unto the LORD.
‖ Or, *against when.* 9 And Moses said unto Pharaoh,
‖ Glory over me: ‖ when shall I in-
treat for thee, and for thy servants,
and for thy people, † to destroy the † Heb. *to cut off.*
frogs from thee and thy houses, *that*
they may remain in the river only?
10 And he said, ‖ To morrow. And ‖ Or, *Against to morrow.*
he said, *Be it* according to thy word:
that thou mayest know that *there is*
none like unto the LORD our God.
11 And the frogs shall depart from
thee, and from thy houses, and from
thy servants, and from thy people;
they shall remain in the river only.
12 And Moses and Aaron went
out from Pharaoh: and Moses cried
unto the LORD because of the frogs
which he had brought against Pharaoh.
13 And the LORD did according
to the word of Moses; and the frogs
died out of the houses, out of the
villages, and out of the fields.
14 And they gathered them together upon heaps: and the land
stank.
15 But when Pharaoh saw that
there was respite, he hardened his
heart, and hearkened not unto them;
as the LORD had said.

---

ancient forms of nature-worship in Egypt. See also Duemichen, 'Æg. Zeitschrift,' 1869, p. 6. According to Chæremon (see Bunsen's 'Egypt,' Vol. v. p. 736) the frog was regarded as a symbol of regeneration. See the note, p. 242, on the adoration of the frog by the father of Rameses II.

3. *into thine house*] This appears to have been peculiar to the plague, as such. No mention is made of it by travellers. It was specially the visitation which would be felt by the scrupulously clean Egyptians.

kneadingtroughs] Not "dough," as in the margin.

7. The magicians would seem to have been able to increase the plague, but not to remove it; hence Pharaoh's application to Moses, the first symptom of yielding. An explanation, which is certainly ingenious and not improbable, is suggested by a late commentator (Hirsch, 1869). He assumes that the words "the magicians did so," mean that they imitated the action of Aaron, stretching out their rods, but using magic formulæ with the intention of driving away the frogs, the result being not only a frustration of their object, but an increase of the plague.

9. *Glory over me*] The expression is rather obscure, but it is supposed by most of the later, and by some early commentators, to mean, as the margin renders it, "have honour over me," *i.e.* have the honour, or advantage over me, directing me when I shall entreat God for thee and thy servants, &c. Moses thus accepts the first intimation of a change of mind in Pharaoh, and expresses himself, doubtless in accordance with Egyptian usage, at once courteously and deferentially. It is, however, obvious that such an expression would not have been attributed to him by a later writer. The old versions, LXX., Vulg., Saadia, who are followed by Gesenius, generally render the word, appoint for me, determine for me when, &c., the Syriac has "ask for me a time when;" this agrees well with the answer "to-morrow."

when] Or **by when**; *i.e.* for what exact time. Pharaoh's answer in *v.* 10 refers to this, **by to-morrow**. The shortness of the time would, of course, be a test of the supernatural character of the transaction.

13. *villages*] Lit. "inclosures, or court-yards."

16 ¶ And the LORD said unto Moses, Say unto Aaron, Stretch out thy rod, and smite the dust of the land, that it may become lice throughout all the land of Egypt.

17 And they did so; for Aaron stretched out his hand with his rod, and smote the dust of the earth, and it became lice in man, and in beast; all the dust of the land became lice throughout all the land of Egypt.

18 And the magicians did so with their enchantments to bring forth lice, but they could not: so there were lice upon man, and upon beast.

19 Then the magicians said unto Pharaoh, This *is* the finger of God: and Pharaoh's heart was hardened, and he hearkened not unto them; as the LORD had said.

20 ¶ And the LORD said unto Moses, Rise up early in the morning, and stand before Pharaoh; lo, he cometh forth to the water; and say unto him, Thus saith the LORD, Let my people go, that they may serve me.

21 Else, if thou wilt not let my people go, behold, I will send ‖ swarms *of flies* upon thee, and upon thy servants, and upon thy people, and into thy houses: and the houses of the Egyptians shall be full of swarms *of flies*, and also the ground whereon they *are*.

‖ Or, *a mixture of noisome beasts, &c.*

The Third Plague.

It is observed by Hebrew commentators that the nine plagues are divided into three groups: distinct warnings are given of the first two plagues in each group; the third in each is inflicted without any previous notice, the third, *lice*, the sixth, *boils*, the ninth, *darkness*.

16. *the dust of the land*] The two preceding plagues fell upon the Nile. This fell on the earth, which was worshipped under the name Seb, its personification, regarded, in the pantheistic system of Egypt, as the father of the gods. See Brugsch, 'Zeitschrift,' 1868, p. 123. An especial sacredness was attached to the black fertile soil of the basin of the Nile, called Chemi, from which the ancient name of Egypt is supposed to be derived.

lice] In Hebrew "Kinnim." The word occurs only in connection with this plague. These insects are generally identified with mosquitos, a plague nowhere greater than in Egypt. They are most troublesome towards October, *i.e.* soon after the plague of frogs, and are dreaded not only for the pain and annoyance which they cause, but also because they are said to penetrate into the body through the nostrils and ears. Thus the LXX. (σκνίφες), Philo, and Origen, whose testimony as residents in Egypt is of great weight. The mosquito net is an indispensable article to Egyptian travellers. There are however some grave objections to this interpretation. Mosquitos are produced in stagnant waters where their larvæ are deposited, whereas these kinnim spring from the dust of the earth. The word in our version may be nearer to the original, which is probably Egyptian; see Appendix. Late travellers (*e.g.* Sir S. Baker) describe the visitation of vermin in very similar terms, "it is as though the very dust were turned into lice." The lice which he describes are a sort of tick, not larger than a grain of sand, which when filled with blood expands to the size of a hazel nut. Saadia renders the word "lice."

17. *all the dust*] The sense is here necessarily limited: the meaning being, the dust swarmed with lice in every part of the land.

19. *the finger of God*] This expression is thoroughly Egyptian; it need not imply that the magicians recognised Jehovah as the God who wrought the marvel, which they attributed generally to the act of the Deity. They may possibly have referred it to a god hostile to their own protectors, such as Set, or Sutech, the Typhon of later mythology, to whom such calamities were attributed by popular superstition.

The Fourth Plague.

20. *cometh forth to the water*] See note ch. vii. 15. It is not improbable that on this occasion Pharaoh went to the Nile with a procession in order to open the solemn festival, which was held 120 days after the first rise, at the end of October or early in November, when the inundation is abating and the first traces of vegetation are seen on the deposit of fresh soil.

The plague now denounced may be regarded as connected with the atmosphere, each element in turn being converted into a scourge. The air was an object of worship, personified in the deity Shu, the son of Ra, the sun-god; or in Isis, queen of heaven.

21. *swarms of flies*] The Hebrew has the word "Arob," which most of the ancient, and some modern interpreters, understand to mean a mixture of beasts and insects, a sense

22 And I will sever in that day
the land of Goshen, in which my
people dwell, that no swarms *of flies*
shall be there; to the end thou mayest know that I *am* the LORD in the
midst of the earth.
23 And I will put † a division between my people and thy people: ‖ to
morrow shall this sign be.
24 And the LORD did so; and
[b] there came a grievous swarm *of flies*
into the house of Pharaoh, and *into*
his servants' houses, and into all the
land of Egypt: the land was ‖ corrupted by reason of the swarm *of flies*.

† Heb. *a redemption.*
‖ Or, *by to morrow.*
[b] Wisd. 16. 9.
‖ Or, *destroyed.*

25 ¶ And Pharaoh called for
Moses and for Aaron, and said, Go
ye, sacrifice to your God in the
land.
26 And Moses said, It is not meet
so to do; for we shall sacrifice the
abomination of the Egyptians to the
LORD our God: lo, shall we sacrifice
the abomination of the Egyptians before their eyes, and will they not
stone us?
27 We will go three days' journey
into the wilderness, and sacrifice to
the LORD our God, as [c] he shall command us.

[c] chap. 3. 18.

---

derived from the Arabic "Arab," "mixed." (Thus the Vulg., Targ., Saadia, Syr., and Aquila.) It is now, however, more generally supposed that a particular species of fly is described, the dog-fly (κυνόμυια, LXX.), which at certain seasons is described as a far worse plague than mosquitos. The bite is exceedingly sharp and painful, causing severe inflammation, especially in the eyelids. Coming in immense swarms they cover all objects in black and loathsome masses and attack every exposed part of a traveller's person with incredible pertinacity. Some commentators however adopt the opinion of Œdmann, who identifies the species here described with the blatta orientalis, or the kakerlaque, a species of beetle, of which Munk ('Palestine,' p. 120) says: "Ceux qui ont voyagé sur le Nil savent combien cet insecte est incommode: les bateaux en sont infestés, et on les y voit souvent par milliers." Kalisch quotes passages which prove that they inflict painful bites and consume all sorts of materials. There would be a special fitness in this plague, since the beetle was reverenced by the Egyptians as the symbol of life, of reproductive or creative power. No object is more common in hieroglyphics, where it represents the word "cheper," "to exist," or "to become." The sun-god, as creator, bore the name Chepera, and is represented in the form, or with the head, of a beetle. The word "arob," which occurs nowhere else, moreover bears a very near resemblance to an old Egyptian word, retained in Coptic, which designates a species of beetle. See Brugsch, 'D. H.' p. 178, s.v. 'Abeb.'

22. *I will sever*, &c.] This severance constituted a specific difference between this and the preceding plagues. Pharaoh could not of course attribute the exemption of Goshen from a scourge, which fell on the valley of the Nile, to an Egyptian deity, certainly not to Chepera (see the last note), a special object of worship in lower Egypt.

in the midst] Literally "heart." The idiom is common in Hebrew, but there may possibly be an allusion to the Egyptian "heart" used specially to designate lower Egypt.

25. *to your God*] Pharaoh now admits the existence and power of the God whom he had professed not to know; but, as Moses is careful to record, he recognises Him only as the national Deity of the Israelites.

in the land] *i.e.* In Egypt, not beyond the frontier.

26. *the abomination*] The expression may mean either the object of an abominable worship (as Chemosh is called the abomination of Moab, and Moloch the abomination of Ammon, see 1 Kings xi. 7), or an animal which the Egyptians held it sacrilegious to slay. The latter meaning seems more probable, considering that the words were addressed to Pharaoh. Thus Ros., Knob., but the former meaning is preferred by Bp. Wordsworth, and is given by the LXX., Targ., Vulg., and Syr. In either case the ox, bull, or cow, is meant. The cow was never sacrificed in Egypt, being sacred to Isis; but as a general rule, no animal was slaughtered in a district where it represented a local deity. From a very early age the ox was worshipped throughout Egypt, and more especially at Heliopolis and Memphis under various designations, Apis, Mnevis, Amen-Ehe, as the symbol or manifestation of their greatest deities, Osiris, Atum, Ptah, and Isis.

27. *three days' journey*] See note on ch. iii. 18. The demand does not refer to a journey to Sinai, which would have occupied much longer time. In the next verse Pharaoh grants the permission, not however without imposing a condition which would have enabled him to take effectual measures to prevent the final emigration of the Israelites. The power of the Pharaohs extended far beyond the frontier, espscially on the road to

28 And Pharaoh said, I will let
you go, that ye may sacrifice to the
LORD your God in the wilderness;
only ye shall not go very far away:
intreat for me.
29 And Moses said, Behold, I go
out from thee, and I will intreat the
LORD that the swarms *of flies* may
depart from Pharaoh, from his servants, and from his people, to morrow: but let not Pharaoh deal deceitfully any more in not letting the
people go to sacrifice to the LORD.
30 And Moses went out from Pharaoh, and intreated the LORD.
31 And the LORD did according to
the word of Moses; and he removed
the swarms *of flies* from Pharaoh,
from his servants, and from his people; there remained not one.
32 And Pharaoh hardened his heart
at this time also, neither would he let
the people go.

CHAPTER IX.

1 *The murrain of beasts.* 8 *The plague of boils and blains.* 13 *His message about the hail.* 22 *The plague of hail.* 27 *Pharaoh sueth to Moses,* 35 *but yet is hardened.*

THEN the LORD said unto Moses, Go in unto Pharaoh, and
tell him, Thus saith the LORD God
of the Hebrews, Let my people go,
that they may serve me.
2 For if thou refuse to let *them* go,
and wilt hold them still,
3 Behold, the hand of the LORD
is upon thy cattle which *is* in the
field, upon the horses, upon the asses,
upon the camels, upon the oxen, and
upon the sheep: *there shall be* a very
grievous murrain.
4 And the LORD shall sever between the cattle of Israel and the
cattle of Egypt: and there shall nothing die of all *that is* the children's of
Israel.
5 And the LORD appointed a set
time, saying, To morrow the LORD
shall do this thing in the land.
6 And the LORD did that thing on
the morrow, and all the cattle of
Egypt died: but of the cattle of the
children of Israel died not one.
7 And Pharaoh sent, and, behold,
there was not one of the cattle of
the Israelites dead. And the heart
of Pharaoh was hardened, and he did
not let the people go.
8 ¶ And the LORD said unto Moses and unto Aaron, Take to you

Palestine, which was commanded by fortresses erected by the early sovereigns of the 18th dynasty.

The Fifth Plague.

CHAP. IX. 3. *a very grievous murrain*] Or "pestilence;" but the word murrain, *i.e.* a great mortality, exactly expresses the meaning. This terrible visitation struck far more severely than the preceding, which had caused distress and suffering; it attacked the resources of the nation. The disease does not appear to have been common in ancient times, no distinct notice is found on the monuments, unless it is included, as seems not improbable, under the term "Aat," which, as M. Chabas shews, applies to the contagious or epidemic pestilence which frequently, as it would almost seem annually, broke out after the subsidence of the inundation; see 'Mélanges Egyptologiques,' I. p. 39. Within the last few years the murrain has thrice fallen upon Egypt, in 1842, 1863, and 1866 (also 60 years previously); when nearly the whole of the herds have been destroyed. The disease appears to have been of the same kind as that which lately fell so severely upon England. The exact time of the infliction is not mentioned; but in Egypt the cattle are in the fields from December to the end of April, and the disease may have broken out in the former month when the cattle were predisposed to it by the change from confinement to the open air, and from old to fresh pastures; a change more dangerous than usual in so exceptional a year. In 1863 the murrain began in November, and was at its height in December.

the camels] These animals are only twice mentioned, here and Gen. xii. 16, in connection with Egypt. In this passage the enumeration of cattle is studiously complete. It is shewn in the Appendix, that though camels are never represented on the monuments, they were known to the Egyptians and were probably used on the frontier bordering on the desert.

7. *was hardened*] Pharaoh may have attributed to natural causes both the severity of the plague and even the exemption of the Israelites, a pastoral race well acquainted with all that appertained to the care of cattle; and dwelling in a district probably far more healthy than the rest of lower Egypt.

handfuls of ashes of the furnace, and
let Moses sprinkle it toward the heaven in the sight of Pharaoh.

9 And it shall become small dust
in all the land of Egypt, and shall be
a boil breaking forth *with* blains upon
man, and upon beast, throughout all
the land of Egypt.

10 And they took ashes of the
furnace, and stood before Pharaoh;
and Moses sprinkled it up toward
heaven; and it became a boil breaking forth *with* blains upon man, and
upon beast.

11 And the magicians could not
stand before Moses because of the
boils; for the boil was upon the magicians, and upon all the Egyptians.

12 And the LORD hardened the
heart of Pharaoh, and he hearkened
not unto them; [a]as the LORD had [a] Chap. 4. 21.
spoken unto Moses.

13 ¶ And the LORD said unto Moses, Rise up early in the morning, and
stand before Pharaoh, and say unto
him, Thus saith the LORD God of the
Hebrews, Let my people go, that
they may serve me.

14 For I will at this time send all
my plagues upon thine heart, and
upon thy servants, and upon thy
people; that thou mayest know that
there is none like me in all the
earth.

15 For now I will stretch out my
hand, that I may smite thee and thy
people with pestilence; and thou shalt
be cut off from the earth.

The Sixth Plague.

This marks a distinct advance and change in the character of the visitations. Hitherto the Egyptians had not been attacked directly in their own persons. It is the second plague which was not preceded by a demand and warning, probably on account of the peculiar hardness shewn by Pharaoh in reference to the murrain.

8. *ashes of the furnace*] The Hebrew word occurs only in the Pentateuch, and is probably of Egyptian origin. The act was evidently symbolical: the ashes were to be sprinkled towards heaven, challenging, so to speak, the Egyptian Deities, and specially it may be Neit, who bore the designation "The Great Mother Queen of highest heaven," and was worshipped as the tutelary Goddess of lower Egypt. There may possibly be a reference to an Egyptian custom of scattering to the winds ashes of victims offered to Sutech, or Typhon. Human sacrifices said to have been offered at Heliopolis under the Shepherd dynasty were abolished by Amosis I., but some part of the rite may have been retained, and the memory of the old superstition would give a terrible significance to the act. Thus Burder, Hævernick and Kurtz.

9. *a boil breaking forth with blains*] The word rendered boil is derived from "burning inflammation," and is used elsewhere of plague-boils; of the leprosy, and elephantiasis. See Deut. xxviii. 27, and 35, which may specially refer to this passage. Here it means probably a burning tumour or carbuncle breaking out in pustulous ulcers. Cutaneous eruptions of extreme severity are common in the valley of the Nile, some bearing a near resemblance to the symptoms described in this passage. The date is not marked. It was probably soon after the last plague. In an old Egyptian calendar mention is made of severe contagious diseases in December, Pap. Sall. IV. The analogy of natural law is still preserved, the miracle consisting in the severity of the plague and its direct connection with the act of Moses.

11. This verse seems to imply that the magicians now formally gave way and confessed their defeat.

The Seventh Plague.

13—34. The plague of hail: with this begins the last series of plagues, which differ from the former both in their severity and their effects. Each produced a temporary, but real change in Pharaoh's feelings.

14. *all my plagues*] This applies to all the plagues which follow; the effect of each was foreseen and foretold. The words "at this time" are understood by some to limit the application to the plague of hail, but they point more probably to a rapid and continuous succession of blows. The plagues which precede appear to have been spread over a considerable time; the first message of Moses was delivered after the early harvest of the year before, when the Israelites could gather stubble, *i.e.* in April and May: the second mission, when the plagues began, was probably towards the end of June, and they went on at intervals until the winter; this plague was in February; see note on *v.* 31.

15. *For now*, &c.] This verse (as scholars are agreed, *e.g.* Rosenmüller, Ewald, Knobel, Keil) should be rendered thus: **For now in-**

[b] Rom. 9. 17.
† Heb. *made thee stand.*

16 And in very deed for [b]this
cause have I †raised thee up, for to
shew *in* thee my power; and that my
name may be declared throughout all
the earth.
17 As yet exaltest thou thyself
against my people, that thou wilt not
let them go?
18 Behold, to morrow about this
time I will cause it to rain a very
grievous hail, such as hath not been
in Egypt since the foundation thereof
even until now.
19 Send therefore now, *and* gather
thy cattle, and all that thou hast in
the field; *for upon* every man and
beast which shall be found in the field,
and shall not be brought home, the
hail shall come down upon them, and
they shall die.
20 He that feared the word of the
LORD among the servants of Pharaoh
made his servants and his cattle flee
into the houses:

† Heb. *set not his heart unto.*

21 And he that †regarded not the
word of the LORD left his servants
and his cattle in the field.
22 ¶ And the LORD said unto Moses, Stretch forth thine hand toward
heaven, that there may be hail in all
the land of Egypt, upon man, and
upon beast, and upon every herb of
the field, throughout the land of Egypt.
23 And Moses stretched forth his
rod toward heaven: and the LORD
sent thunder and hail, and the fire
ran along upon the ground; and the
LORD rained hail upon the land of
Egypt.
24 So there was hail, and fire mingled with the hail, very grievous, such
as there was none like it in all the
land of Egypt since it became a nation.
25 And the hail smote throughout
all the land of Egypt all that *was* in
the field, both man and beast; and
the hail smote every herb of the field,
and brake every tree of the field.
26 Only in the land of Goshen,
where the children of Israel *were*, was
there no hail.
27 ¶ And Pharaoh sent, and called
for Moses and Aaron, and said unto
them, I have sinned this time: the

---

deed had I stretched forth my hand and smitten thee and thy people with the pestilence then hadst thou been cut off from the earth. The next verse gives the reason why God had not thus inflicted a summary punishment once for all.

16. *have I raised thee up*] The margin **made thee stand** is correct: the meaning is, not that God raised Pharaoh to a position of rank and power, but that he kept him standing, *i.e.* permitted him to live and hold out until His own purpose was accomplished.

18. *a very grievous hail*] This verse distinctly states that the miracle consisted in the magnitude of the infliction and in its immediate connection with the act of Moses. Travellers in lower Egypt speak of storms of snow, thunder and lightning in the winter months; and Seetzen and Willman (quoted by Knobel) describe storms of thunder and hail in March. A friend (Rev. T. H. Tooke) describes a storm of extreme severity, which lasted 24 hours, in the middle of February, at Benihassan. The natives spoke of it as not uncommon at that season.

19. *thy cattle*] In Egypt the cattle are sent to pasture in the open country from January to April, when the grass is abundant; see note on *v.* 3. They are kept in stalls the rest of the year. The word "gather" does not exactly express the meaning of the original, "cause to flee," *i.e.* bring them rapidly under cover.

20. *the word of the LORD*] This gives the first indication that the warnings had a salutary effect upon the Egyptians. See ch. xi. 3.

22. *in all the land of Egypt*] The storms described above fell on lower Egypt: the expression here may imply that this extended to the upper valley of the Nile, but it is possible that the land of Mizraim is used specially to designate the Delta and the adjoining district.

23. *and the fire ran along upon the ground*] The expression is peculiar (literally "fire walked earthwards"), and appears to describe a succession of flashes mingled with the hail: our Authorised Version seems to present a true and graphic account of the phenomenon.

25. *smote*] The words imply heavy damage both to herbs and trees, but not total destruction: the loss however must have been enormous.

27. *this time*] *i.e.* I acknowledge now that I have sinned.

LORD *is* righteous, and I and my people
are wicked.
28 Intreat the LORD (for *it is*
enough) that there be no *more* † mighty
thunderings and hail; and I will let
you go, and ye shall stay no longer.
29 And Moses said unto him, As
soon as I am gone out of the city, I
will spread abroad my hands unto the
LORD; *and* the thunder shall cease,
neither shall there be any more hail;
that thou mayest know how that the
c earth *is* the LORD'S.
30 But as for thee and thy servants,
I know that ye will not yet fear the
LORD God.
31 And the flax and the barley was
smitten: for the barley *was* in the
ear, and the flax *was* bolled.
32 But the wheat and the rie were
not smitten: for they *were* † not grown
up.
33 And Moses went out of the city
from Pharaoh, and spread abroad his
hands unto the LORD: and the thunders and hail ceased, and the rain was
not poured upon the earth.
34 And when Pharaoh saw that
the rain and the hail and the thunders
were ceased, he sinned yet more, and
hardened his heart, he and his servants.
35 And the heart of Pharaoh was
hardened, neither would he let the
children of Israel go; as the LORD
had spoken † by Moses.

† Heb. *voices of God.*

c Psal. 24. 1.

† Heb. *hidden*, or, *dark.*

† Heb. *by the hand of Moses.*

CHAPTER X.

1 *God threateneth to send locusts.* 7 *Pharaoh, moved by his servants, inclineth to let the Israelites go.* 12 *The plague of the locusts.* 16 *Pharaoh sueth to Moses.* 21 *The plague of darkness.* 24 *Pharaoh sueth unto Moses,* 27 *but yet is hardened.*

AND the LORD said unto Moses,
Go in unto Pharaoh: for *a* I
have hardened his heart, and the heart
of his servants, that I might shew
these my signs before him:

a chap. 4 21.

---

the LORD] Thus for the first time Pharaoh explicitly recognizes Jehovah as God.

28. *for it is enough*] The Authorised Version is not literal, but it probably expresses the meaning of the original, which is somewhat obscure, and it is much, *i.e.* enough, that there should be voices of God (thunderings) and hail, no more are needed now.

29. *the earth is the LORD'S*] This declaration has a direct reference to Egyptian superstition. Each God was held to have special power within a given district; Pharaoh had learned that Jehovah was *a* God, he was now to admit that his power extended over the whole earth. The unity and universality of the Divine power are tenets distinctly promulgated in the Pentateuch, and though occasionally recognized in ancient Egyptian documents (*e.g.* in the early copies of the 17th chapter of the Funeral Ritual under the 11th dynasty), were overlaid at a very early period by systems alternating between Polytheism and Pantheism.

31. *the flax was bolled*] *i.e.* in blossom. This is a point of great importance. It marks the time. In the north of Egypt the barley ripens and flax blossoms about the middle of February, or at the latest early in March, and both are gathered in before April, when the wheat harvest begins (Forskal and Seetzen ap. Knobel). The cultivation of flax must have been of great importance; linen was preferred to any material and exclusively used by the priests. It is frequently mentioned on Egyptian monuments. Four kinds are noted by Pliny (XIX. 1) as used in Egypt. He makes special mention of Tanis, *i.e.* Zoan, as one of the places famous for flax. The texture was remarkably fine, in general quality equal to the best now made, and for the evenness of the threads, without knot or break, superior to any of modern manufacture. Wilkinson on Herod. II. c. 37, p. 54.

32. *rie*] Rather **spelt**, triticum spelta, the common food of the ancient Egyptians, now called doora by the natives: the only grain, according to Wilkinson (on Herod. II. c. 36), represented on the sculptures: the name however occurs on the monuments very frequently in combination with other species. See Brugsch, 'D. H.' p. 442.

34. *hardened*] Different words are used in this and the following verse: here the word means "heavy," *i.e.* obtuse, incapable of forming a right judgment; the other, which is more frequently used in this narrative, is stronger and implies a stubborn resolution. The LXX. render the former word ἐβάρυνε, the latter ἐσκληρύνθη. The other old Versions mark the distinction with equal clearness.

The Eighth Plague.

CHAP. X. **1—20.** *I have hardened*] Literally "made heavy." This state of mind, though judicial, may be accounted for psychologically by the fact that the corn, to

2 And that thou mayest tell in the
ears of thy son, and of thy son's son,
what things I have wrought in Egypt,
and my signs which I have done among
them; that ye may know how that I
am the LORD.
3 And Moses and Aaron came in
unto Pharaoh, and said unto him, Thus
saith the LORD God of the Hebrews,
How long wilt thou refuse to humble
thyself before me? let my people go,
that they may serve me.
4 Else, if thou refuse to let my
people go, behold, to morrow will I
[b] Wisd. 16. 9. bring the [b]locusts into thy coast:
† Heb. *eye*. 5 And they shall cover the †face
of the earth, that one cannot be able
to see the earth: and they shall eat
the residue of that which is escaped,
which remaineth unto you from the
hail, and shall eat every tree which
groweth for you out of the field:
6 And they shall fill thy houses,
and the houses of all thy servants, and
the houses of all the Egyptians; which
neither thy fathers, nor thy fathers'
fathers have seen, since the day that
they were upon the earth unto this
day. And he turned himself, and went
out from Pharaoh.
7 And Pharaoh's servants said unto
him, How long shall this man be a
snare unto us? let the men go, that
they may serve the LORD their God:
knowest thou not yet that Egypt is
destroyed?
8 And Moses and Aaron were
brought again unto Pharaoh: and he

---

which he and his people attached most importance had been spared in the visitation. The word "I" is emphatic, equivalent to "as for me I have," &c.

2. *thou*] Moses is addressed as the representative of Israel.

wrought] The Hebrew word is not very commonly used. It implies an action which brings shame and disgrace upon its objects, making them, so to speak, playthings of divine power (התעלל, LXX. ἐμπέπαιχα). Ges. 'Thes.' interprets it with reference to 1 Sam. xxxi. 4, "animum explevit illudendo," which appears to be the true meaning in this passage, as in most others.

4. *the locusts*] The locust is less common in Egypt than in many eastern countries, yet it is well known, and dreaded as the most terrible of scourges. In the papyrus Anast. V. p. 10, it is mentioned as a common enemy of the husbandmen. Niebuhr and Forskal witnessed two visitations; Tischendorf describes one of unusual extent in March which covered the whole country: they come generally from the western deserts, but sometimes from the east and the south-east. Denon saw an enormous cloud of locusts in May, which came from the east, settling upon every blade of grass, and after destroying the vegetation of a district passing on to another. No less than nine names are given to the locust in the Bible, the word here used is the most common; it signifies "multitudinous," and whenever it occurs reference is made to its terrible devastations. See notes on Leviticus xi. 22.

5. *the face*] Literally "the eye of the earth," alluding doubtless to the darkness when, as Olivier describes it, "the whole atmosphere is filled on all sides and to a great height by an innumerable quantity of these insects—in a moment all the fields are covered by them."

shall eat every tree] Not only the leaves, but the branches and even the wood are attacked and devoured. Pliny says, XI. 29, "omnia morsu erodentes et fores quoque tectorum." The Egyptians were passionately fond of trees; in hieroglyphics one of the most ancient names of Egypt is "the land of the sycomore:" see De Rougé, 'Recherches,' p. 80, under the 5th dynasty; Saneha, *i.e.* "son of the sycomore," is found as a name given to a court favourite under the 12th dynasty. The widow of Thotmes II. a few years after his death, imported a large number of trees from Arabia Felix; a singular coincidence if, as seems probable, that was the date of the Exodus. See Duemichen's 'Fleet of an Egyptian Queen.'

6. *fill thy houses*] The terraces, courts, and even the inner apartments are said to be filled in a moment by a locust storm. Cf. Joel ii. 9.

7. *Pharaoh's servants*] This marks a very considerable advance in the transaction. For the first time the officers of Pharaoh intervene before the scourge is inflicted, shewing at once their belief in the threat, and their special terror of the infliction. Pharaoh also for the first time takes measures to prevent the evil; he does not indeed send for Moses and Aaron, but he permits them to be brought into his presence.

let the men go] *i. e.* the men only, not all the people; the officers assumed that the women and children would remain as hostages, and Pharaoh was now ready to consent to the proposal so limited.

said unto them, Go, serve the LORD your God: *but* †who *are* they that shall go?

† Heb. *who and who, &c.*

9 And Moses said, We will go with our young and with our old, with our sons and with our daughters, with our flocks and with our herds will we go; for we *must hold* a feast unto the LORD.

10 And he said unto them, Let the LORD be so with you, as I will let you go, and your little ones: look *to it;* for evil *is* before you.

11 Not so: go now ye *that are* men, and serve the LORD; for that ye did desire. And they were driven out from Pharaoh's presence.

12 ¶ And the LORD said unto Moses, Stretch out thine hand over the land of Egypt for the locusts, that they may come up upon the land of Egypt, and eat every herb of the land, *even* all that the hail hath left.

13 And Moses stretched forth his rod over the land of Egypt, and the LORD brought an east wind upon the land all that day, and all *that* night; *and* when it was morning, the east wind brought the locusts.

14 And the locusts went up over all the land of Egypt, and rested in all the coasts of Egypt: very grievous *were they;* before them there were no such locusts as they, neither after them shall be such.

15 For they covered the face of the whole earth, so that the land was darkened; and they did eat every herb of the land, and all the fruit of the trees which the hail had left: and there remained not any green thing in the trees, or in the herbs of the field, through all the land of Egypt.

16 ¶ Then Pharaoh †called for Moses and Aaron in haste; and he said, I have sinned against the LORD your God, and against you.

† Heb. *hastened to call.*

17 Now therefore forgive, I pray thee, my sin only this once, and intreat the LORD your God, that he may take away from me this death only.

18 And he went out from Pharaoh, and intreated the LORD.

19 And the LORD turned a mighty strong west wind, which took away

---

9. *with our young*, &c.] The demand was not contrary to Egyptian usage, as great festivals were kept by the whole population: see Herod. II. 58, "the numbers who attend (*i. e.* the festival at Bubastis) counting only the men and women, and omitting the children, amounted, according to the native reports, to seven hundred thousand."

10. *evil is before you*] The meaning is ambiguous. It may be a threat, but most commentators (LXX., Vulg., Rosen., Knobel, &c.) render it, "for your intentions are evil," and this doubtless expresses the exact motive of the king: great as the possible infliction might be, he held it to be a less evil than the loss of so large a population.

13. *an east wind*] Moses is careful to record the natural and usual cause of the evil, portentous as it was in its extent, and in its connection with his denouncement. The east wind sometimes brings locusts into Egypt, see note on *v.* 4, nor is there any reason for departing from the common meaning of the word which is given in the Authorised Version.

14. *went up*] The expression is exact and graphic; at a distance the locusts appear hanging, as it were, like a heavy cloud over the land; as they approach they seem to rise, and they fill the atmosphere overhead on their arrival.

over all the land] The expression may be taken in the broadest sense. Accounts are given by Major Moore of a cloud of locusts extending over 500 miles, and so compact while on the wing that, like an eclipse, it completely hid the sun. Brown states ('Travels in Africa'), that an area of nearly two thousand square miles was literally covered by them. This passage describes a swarm unprecedented in extent.

17. *this death only*] Pliny calls locusts "Pestis iræ Deorum," a pestilence brought on by divine wrath. Pharaoh now recognizes the justice of his servants' apprehensions, *v.* 7.

19. *west wind*] Literally "a sea wind," which in Palestine of course is from the west: but in this passage it may, and probably does, denote a wind blowing from the sea on the north-west of Egypt. A direct westerly wind would come from the Lybian desert and be far less effectual than one rushing transversely over the whole surface of lower Egypt (which was doubtless the main centre of the visitation), and driving the locusts into the Red

† Heb. *fastened.* the locusts, and †cast them into the
Red sea; there remained not one
locust in all the coasts of Egypt.
20 But the LORD hardened Pharaoh's heart, so that he would not let
the children of Israel go.
21 ¶ And the LORD said unto Moses, Stretch out thine hand toward
heaven, that there may be darkness
† Heb. *that one may feel darkness.* over the land of Egypt, †even darkness *which* may be felt.
22 And Moses stretched forth his
hand toward heaven; and there was
a thick darkness in all the land of
Egypt three days:
23 They saw not one another, neither rose any from his place for three
c Wisd. 18. 1. days: cbut all the children of Israel
had light in their dwellings.
24 ¶ And Pharaoh called unto
Moses, and said, Go ye, serve the
LORD; only let your flocks and your
herds be stayed: let your little ones
also go with you.
25 And Moses said, Thou must
give †us also sacrifices and burnt † Heb. *into our hands.*
offerings, that we may sacrifice unto
the LORD our God.
26 Our cattle also shall go with
us; there shall not an hoof be left
behind; for thereof must we take to
serve the LORD our God; and we
know not with what we must serve
the LORD, until we come thither.
27 ¶ But the LORD hardened Pharaoh's heart, and he would not let
them go.
28 And Pharaoh said unto him,
Get thee from me, take heed to thyself, see my face no more; for in *that*
day thou seest my face thou shalt die.
29 And Moses said, Thou hast
spoken well, I will see thy face again
no more.

Sea. The rendering "cast" in the text is preferable to that in the margin; the Hebrew word means to drive in by a sharp stroke or blow.

Red sea] The Hebrew has the Sea of Suph: the exact meaning of Suph is disputed. Gesenius renders it "rush" or "sea-weed;" but it is probably an Egyptian word. A sea-weed resembling wool is thrown up abundantly on the shores of the Red Sea. The origin of the modern name is uncertain. The Egyptians called it the sea of Punt, *i.e.* of Arabia. The sudden and complete disappearance of the locusts, generally effected by a strong wind (gregatim sublatæ vento in maria aut stagna decidunt, Plin. 'H. N.' XI. 35), is a phenomenon scarcely less remarkable than their coming; the putrefaction of such immense masses not unfrequently causes a terrible pestilence near the coasts of the sea into which they fall.

The Ninth Plague.

21. *darkness*] This infliction was specially calculated to affect the spirits of the Egyptians, whose chief object of worship was Ra, the Sun-god, and its suddenness and severity in connection with the act of Moses mark it as a preternatural withdrawal of light. Yet it has an analogy in physical phenomena. After the vernal equinox the south-west wind from the desert blows some fifty days, see note on v. 12, not however continuously but at intervals, lasting generally some two or three days. (Thus Lane, Willman and others quoted by Knobel.) It fills the atmosphere with dense masses of fine sand, bringing on a darkness far deeper than that of our worst fogs in winter. While it lasts no man "rises from his place; men and beasts hide themselves: people shut themselves up in the innermost apartments or vaults." "So saturated is the air with the sand that it seems to lose its transparency, so that artificial light is of little use." The expression "even darkness which might be felt," has a special application to a darkness produced by such a cause. The consternation of Pharaoh proves that, familiar as he may have been with the phenomenon, no previous occurrence had prepared him for its intensity and duration, and that he recognized it as a supernatural visitation. The rendering, which has been questioned, is correct, LXX. ψηλαφητὸν σκότος, Vulg. tam densæ ut palpari queant. Thus Rosen., Maurer, Knobel, &c.

23. *had light in their dwellings*] The sandstorm, if such were the cause, may not have extended to the district of Goshen; but the expression clearly denotes a miraculous intervention, whether accomplished or not by natural agencies.

24. *your flocks and your herds*] Pharaoh still exacts what would of course be a complete security for their return: but the demand was wholly incompatible with the object assigned for the journey into the wilderness. Every gradation in the yielding of Pharaoh and in the demands of Moses is distinctly noted: but it should be observed that these do not yet

CHAPTER XI.

1 *God's message to the Israelites to borrow jewels of their neighbours.* 4 *Moses threateneth Pharaoh with the death of the firstborn.*

AND the LORD said unto Moses,
Yet will I bring one plague
more upon Pharaoh, and upon Egypt;
afterwards he will let you go hence:
when he shall let *you* go, he shall
surely thrust you out hence altogether.
2 Speak now in the ears of the
people, and let every man borrow of
his neighbour, and every woman of
her neighbour, [a]jewels of silver, and [a] chap. 3. 22.
jewels of gold. & 12. 35.
3 And the LORD gave the people
favour in the sight of the Egyptians.
Moreover the man [b]Moses *was* very [b] Ecclus.
great in the land of Egypt, in the 45. 1.
sight of Pharaoh's servants, and in the
sight of the people.
4 And Moses said, Thus saith the
LORD, [c]About midnight will I go out [c] chap. 12.
into the midst of Egypt: 29.

---

extend to a permission to emigrate from the country. Had Pharaoh even then yielded he could have taken measures to compel them to come back, a result only at last rendered impossible by the destruction of the whole army stationed on the frontier of lower Egypt.

CHAP. XI. 1. *the LORD said*] Or "the Lord had said." Commentators generally agree that the first three verses of this chapter are parenthetical. The most probable account of their insertion in this place appears to be that, before Moses relates the last warning given to Pharaoh, he feels it right to recall to his readers' minds the revelation and command which had been previously given to him by the Lord. Thus Aben-Ezra, who proposes the rendering "had said," which is adopted by Rosenmüller, Keil, Kalisch, Ranke, Smith ('Pentateuch,' pp. 557—560), who completely disposes of the objections of German and English critics. No grammatical objection is made to this construction, which is common in the Old Testament and belongs to the simple and inartificial style of the Pentateuch. The command may have been given immediately before the last interview with Pharaoh; such repetition when a work is on the eve of accomplishment is customary in Holy Writ. Here it accounts "both for the confidence with which Moses, remembering the words of Jehovah, had just told the king that he would no more see his face, and for the prediction which immediately follows, that Pharaoh's court would come humbly to entreat him to depart." Smith, *l. c.*

when he shall let you go, &c.] The original is obscure, but it may probably be rendered **when he lets you go altogether he will surely thrust you out hence**; see note below. The meaning is, when at last he lets you depart with children, flocks, herds, and all your possessions, he will compel you to depart in haste. This part of the command is important, as shewing that Moses was already aware that the last plague would be followed by an immediate departure, and, therefore, that measures had probably been taken to prepare the Israelites for the journey. In fact on each occasion when Pharaoh relented for a season, immediate orders would of course be issued by Moses to the heads of the people, who were thus repeatedly brought into a state of more or less complete organization for the final movement. See Introduction.

2. *every man*] In ch. iii. 22 women only were named; the command is more explicit when the time is come for its execution.

borrow] Or "demand." See note on ch. iii. 22.

3. *gave the people favour*] See note on iii. 22.

Moreover the man Moses was very great] No objection would have been taken to this statement had it been found in any other book. It does not assert, however, what was perfectly true, that Moses was a great man by reason of personal qualifications, but that he was great in the estimation of Pharaoh, of his servants, and of all the Egyptians. This has a very important bearing upon the narrative, shewing the effect produced upon the Egyptians by the previous visitations, and by the conduct of Moses, especially by the care he had taken to warn them, and, so far as was practicable, to save them from suffering. See ch. ix. 19, 20. It accounts for their ready compliance with the demand of the Israelites. God gave them a kindly feeling, by an inward act, not changing their nature, but eliciting their better feelings, the sense of obligation, and gratitude for benefits which Diodorus specially mentions as a characteristic of the Egyptians. The reasons above assigned appear sufficient to account for the introduction of these verses, which undoubtedly interrupt the narrative; but there would be no objection in point of principle to the supposition that they may have been inserted either by Moses at a later period, when he probably put together and revised the detached portions of the books; or by one of his younger contemporaries, who must have been equally conversant with the facts, and aware of the

5 And all the firstborn in the land of Egypt shall die, from the firstborn of Pharaoh that sitteth upon his throne, even unto the firstborn of the maid-servant that *is* behind the mill; and all the firstborn of beasts.

6 And there shall be a great cry throughout all the land of Egypt, such as there was none like it, nor shall be like it any more.

7 But against any of the children of Israel shall not a dog move his tongue, against man or beast: that ye may know how that the LORD doth put a difference between the Egyptians and Israel.

8 And all these thy servants shall come down unto me, and bow down themselves unto me, saying, Get thee out, and all the people †that follow thee: and after that I will go out. And he went out from Pharaoh in †a great anger.

† Heb. *that is at thy feet.*

† Heb. *heat of anger.*

9 And the LORD said unto Moses, Pharaoh shall not hearken unto you; that my wonders may be multiplied in the land of Egypt.

10 And Moses and Aaron did all these wonders before Pharaoh: and the LORD hardened Pharaoh's heart, so that he would not let the children of Israel go out of his land.

---

importance of the statement in its bearings upon the whole transaction.

4. *And Moses said*] The following words must be read in immediate connection with the last verse of the preceding chapter. It is not there stated that Moses left the presence of Pharaoh; this passage tells us what took place after his declaration that this would be his last interview.

About midnight] This marks the hour, but not the day, on which the visitation would take place. There may have been, and probably was, an interval of some days, during which preparations might be made both for the celebration of the Passover, and the departure of the Israelites: in the meantime Egypt remained under the shadow of the menace.

5. *the firstborn*] Two points are to be noticed: 1, The extent of the visitation: the whole land suffers in the persons of its firstborn, not merely for the guilt of the sovereign, but for the actual participation of the people in the crime of infanticide. 2, The limitation. Pharaoh's command had been to slay all the male children of the Israelites, one child only in each Egyptian family was to die. If Thotmes II. was the Pharaoh (see Appendix) the visitation fell with special severity on his family. He left no son, but was succeeded by his widow.

the mill] The mill used by the Israelites, and probably by the Egyptians, consisted of two circular stones, one fixed in the ground, the other turned by a handle. The work of grinding was extremely laborious, and performed by women of the lowest rank.

firstborn of beasts] This visitation has a peculiar force in reference to the worship of beasts, which was universal in Egypt; each nome having its own sacred animal, adored as a manifestation or representative of the local tutelary deity.

8. *in great anger*] Or **in heat of anger**, as in the margin.

9, 10. These two verses refer to the whole preceding narrative, and mark the close of one principal division of the book.

NOTE on *v.* 1.

The force of the word כלה appears to have been overlooked by our translators, who misplace it, as also by the Vulgate, which takes no notice of it. The Targum of Onkelos renders it correctly גמירא. The LXX. σὺν παντί: the Syriac less accurately, "all of you." It reads also in both clauses, "I will dismiss you." The Arabic forcibly and correctly جملة.

CHAPTER XII.

1 *The beginning of the year is changed.* 3 *The passover is instituted.* 11 *The rite of the passover.* 15 *Unleavened bread.* 29 *The firstborn are slain.* 31 *The Israelites are driven out of the land.* 37 *They come to Succoth.* 43 *The ordinance of the passover.*

AND the LORD spake unto Moses
and Aaron in the land of Egypt,
saying,
2 This month *shall be* unto you
the beginning of months: it *shall be*
the first month of the year to you.
3 ¶ Speak ye unto all the congregation of Israel, saying, In the tenth
day of this month they shall take to
them every man a ‖lamb, according ‖ Or, *kid.*
to the house of *their* fathers, a lamb
for an house:
4 And if the household be too little
for the lamb, let him and his neighbour next unto his house take *it* according to the number of the souls;
every man according to his eating
shall make your count for the lamb.
5 Your lamb shall be without † Heb. *son of a year.*
blemish, a male †of the first year: ye

CHAP. XII. 1. *in the land of Egypt*] It seems evident that this verse, and consequently the rest of the chapter, was written some time after the Exodus, probably when Moses put together the portions of the book towards the end of his life. The statements that these instructions were given in the land of Egypt, and that they were given to Moses and Aaron, are important: the one marks the peculiar dignity of this ordinance, which was established before the Sinaitic code, the other marks the distinction between Moses and Aaron and all other prophets. They alone, as Aben-Ezra observes, were prophets of the Law, *i.e.* no law was promulgated by any other prophets.

2. *This month*] The name of the month, Abib, is given xiii. 4. It was called by the later Hebrews Nisan, a name found in early Syrian inscriptions, De Vogüé, 'Syrie centrale,' p. 5, and derived from the Nisannu of the Assyrians and Babylonians, with whom it was the first month of the year. It corresponds nearly to our April, since the last full moon in March or the first in April fell in the middle of the month. It is clear that in this passage the Israelites are directed to take Abib henceforth as the beginning of the year; the year previously began with the month Tisri, when the harvest was gathered in; see xxiii. 16. They do not appear to have adopted the Egyptian division, in which the fixed year began in June, at the rise of the Nile. The injunction touching Abib or Nisan referred only to religious rites; in other affairs they retained the old arrangement, even in the beginning of the Sabbatic year; see Levit. xxv. 9; and Josephus, 'Ant.' I. 25. 9. The assumption that an ancient festival was previously held at this season to celebrate the ripening of the wheat has no grounds in history or tradition.

3. *a lamb*] The Hebrew word, used in the same way in Arabic and Chaldee, is general, meaning either a sheep or goat, male or female, and of any age; the age and sex are therefore specially defined in the following verse. The direction to select the lamb on the tenth day, the fourth day before it was offered, is generally assumed to have applied to the first institution only, but there is no indication of this in the text, and it seems more probable that the injunction was intended to secure due care in the preparation for the greatest national festival. The custom certainly fell into desuetude at a later period, but probably not before the destruction of the Temple. The later Targum, which asserts that the rule was not intended to be of permanent obligation, records the traditions of Rabbins of the sixth century.

the house of their fathers] Lit. a house of fathers, or parents; *i.e.* for each family.

4. *if the household be too little*, &c.] The meaning is clear, if there be not persons enough to consume a lamb at one meal: tradition specifies ten as the least number; thus Josephus says, not less than ten attend this sacrifice, and twenty are generally assembled, 'De B. J.' VI. 9. 3. The later Targum paraphrases the passage thus: "If the men of the household be less than ten in number." There is, however, no indication of such a rule earlier than Josephus, and it was probably left altogether to the discretion of the heads of families. The women and children were certainly not excluded, though the Rabbins held their attendance to be unnecessary, and the Karaites permitted none but adult males to be partakers.

The last clause should be rendered: "let him and his neighbour who is near to his house take according to the number of souls, each man according to his eating ye shall count for the lamb." Our Version only requires the insertion of *ye*, or *you*, before "shall make your count." See note below.

5. *without blemish*] This is in accordance with the general rule laid down in Levit. xxii. 20: so also is the choice of a male, Levit. i. 3: although in this case there is a special reason, since the lamb was in place of the firstborn male in each household. The re-

shall take *it* out from the sheep, or
from the goats:
6 And ye shall keep it up until the
fourteenth day of the same month:
and the whole assembly of the congregation of Israel shall kill it †in the
evening.
7 And they shall take of the
blood, and strike *it* on the two side
posts and on the upper door post
of the houses, wherein they shall
eat it.
8 And they shall eat the flesh in
that night, roast with fire, and unleavened bread; *and* with bitter *herbs*
they shall eat it.

† Heb. *between the two evenings.*

---

striction to the first year is peculiar, and refers apparently to the condition of perfect innocence in the antitype, the Lamb of God.

or from the goats] There is no indication of a preference, but the Hebrews have generally held that a lamb was the more acceptable offering.

6. *ye shall keep it up*] The Hebrew implies that it was to be kept with great care, which appears to be the meaning of the expression "keep it up."

until the fourteenth day] It should be observed that the offering of our Lord on the selfsame day is an important point in determining the typical character of the transaction. Masius on Josh. v. 10 quotes a remarkable passage from the Talmud: "It was a famous and old opinion among the ancient Jews that the day of the new year which was the beginning of the Israelites' deliverance out of Egypt should in future time be the beginning of the redemption by the Messiah."

in the evening] The Hebrew has **between the two evenings.** The meaning of the expression is disputed. The most probable explanation is that it includes the time from afternoon, or early eventide, until sunset. This accords with the ancient custom of the Hebrews, who slew the paschal lamb immediately after the offering of the daily sacrifice, which on the day of the passover took place a little earlier than usual, between two and three p.m. This would allow about two hours and a half for slaying and preparing all the lambs. It is clear that they would not wait until sunset, at which time the evening meal would take place. This interpretation is supported by Rashi, Kimchi, Bochart, Lightfoot, Clericus, and Patrick. Thus Josephus: "they offer this sacrifice from the ninth to the eleventh hour." The Greeks had the same idiom, distinguishing between the early and late evening. Other interpreters understand it to mean the interval between sunset and total darkness, an exceedingly short time in the East, and quite insufficient for the work. Rosenmüller shews from the Talmud that the twilight as strictly defined did not last longer than it would take to walk half a mile, *i.e.* about ten minutes. If, moreover, the lamb were slain after sunset, it would not have been on the fourteenth day of the month, since the day was reckoned from sunset to sunset. Knobel observes that the expression is peculiar to the so-called Elohist; it is in fact peculiar to the Pentateuch, and its meaning was evidently ascertained only by conjecture at a later period. It is to be observed that the slaying of the lamb on the former hypothesis coincides exactly with the death of our Saviour, at the ninth hour of the day.

7. *the upper door post*] Or **lintel,** as it is rendered v. 23. This meaning is generally accepted, but the word occurs only in this passage; it is derived from a root which means to "look out," and may signify a lattice above the door: thus Aben-Ezra and Rosenmüller. This direction was understood by the Hebrews to apply only to the first Passover: it was certainly not adopted in Palestine. The meaning of the sprinkling of blood is hardly open to question. It was a representation of the offering of the life, substituted for that of the firstborn in each house, as an expiatory and vicarious sacrifice.

8. *in that night*] The night is thus clearly distinguished from the evening when the lamb was slain. It was slain before sunset, on the 14th, and eaten after sunset, the beginning of the 15th.

with fire] Among various reasons given for this injunction the most probable and satisfactory seems to be the special sanctity attached to fire from the first institution of sacrifice. The memory of this primeval sanctity is preserved by universal tradition, *e.g.* among the Aryans, as is shewn by the hymns in the Rig Veda to Agni, the fire-god, and by the whole system of the Zend Avesta.

and unleavened bread] Or, **and they shall eat unleavened cakes with bitter herbs.** See note below. The Hebrew word is certain in meaning, but of doubtful origin; see note below. Like many others in this account it is archaic, found only in the Pentateuch, except in passages which refer to the Passover. The importance of the injunction is admitted; the unleavened cakes give one of the two general designations to the festival. This may in part be accounted for by its being a lasting memorial of the circumstances

9 Eat not of it raw, nor sodden at all with water, but roast *with* fire; his head with his legs, and with the purtenance thereof.
10 And ye shall let nothing of it remain until the morning; and that which remaineth of it until the morning ye shall burn with fire.
11 ¶ And thus shall ye eat it; *with* your loins girded, your shoes on your

---

of the hasty departure, allowing no time for the process of leavening: but the meaning discerned by St Paul, 1 Cor. v. 7, and recognized by the Church in all ages, was assuredly implied, though not expressly declared in the original institution; and though our Lord may not directly refer to the Passover, yet His words, Matt. xiii. 33, are conclusive as to the symbolism of leaven.

bitter herbs] The word occurs only here and in Numbers ix. 11, in reference to herbs. The symbolical reference to the previous sufferings of the Israelites is generally admitted. Various kinds of bitter herbs are enumerated in the Mishna; but the expression should be taken generally; the bitter herbs of Egypt would of course differ in kind from those of other countries where the Passover was to be eaten.

9. *raw*] Another obsolete word, probably Egyptian, found only in this passage: the corresponding root in Arabic means "half-cooked," and this appears to be the sense here: raw meat was not likely to be eaten, though some interpretors find here a reference to the ὠμοφαγία, "feasting on raw food," in some Gentile festivals. The prohibition of eating it sodden with water has been considered in reference to "roast with fire:" it was probably more common to seethe than to roast meat; hence the regrets expressed by the Israelites for the seething pots of Egypt; on other occasions the flesh of sin and peace-offerings, whether consumed by the people or the priests, was ordered to be sodden: see Lev. vi. 28; Num. vi. 19.

sodden...with water] or "sodden," omitting "water," which is added in Hebrew because the word in that language may be used either of roasting (as in 2 Chron. xxxv. 13) or boiling.

the purtenance thereof] or **its intestines.** This verse directs that the lamb should be roasted and placed on the table whole. No bone was to be broken (see v. 46, and Num. ix. 12, an injunction which the LXX. insert in the next verse). According to Rashi and other Rabbins the bowels were taken out, washed and then replaced. The Talmud prescribes the form of the oven of earthenware, in which the lamb was roasted, open above and below with a grating for the fire. Lambs and sheep are roasted whole in Persia, nearly in the same manner. Thevenot describes the process, Vol. II. p. 180, ed. 1674.

This entire consumption of the lamb constitutes one marked difference between the Passover and all other sacrifices, in which either a part or the whole was burned, and thus offered directly to God. The whole substance of the sacrificed lamb was to enter into the substance of the people, the blood only excepted, which was sprinkled as a propitiatory and sacrificial offering. Another point of subordinate importance is noticed. The lamb was slain and the blood sprinkled by the head of each family: no separate priesthood as yet existed in Israel; its functions belonged from the beginning to the father of the family: when the priesthood was instituted the slaying of the lamb still devolved on the heads of families, though the blood was sprinkled on the altar by the priests; an act which essentially belonged to their office. The typical character of this part of the transaction is clear. Our Lord was offered and His blood shed as an expiatory and propitiatory sacrifice, but His whole humanity is transfused spiritually and effectually into His Church, an effect which is at once symbolized and assured in Holy Communion, the Christian Passover.

10. *And ye shall let nothing*, &c.] This was afterwards a general law of sacrifices; at once preventing all possibility of profanity, and of superstitious abuse, such as was practised among some ancient heathens, who were wont to reserve a portion of their sacrifices; see Herod. I. 132; and Baruch vi. 28. The injunction is on both accounts justly applied by our Church to the Eucharist.

burn with fire] Not being consumed by man, it was thus offered, like other sacrifices, to God.

11. *with your loins girded*, &c.] These instructions are understood by the Jews to apply only to the first Passover, when they belonged to the occasion. There is no trace of their observance at any later time; a striking instance of good sense and power of distinguishing between accidents and substantial characteristics. Each of the directions marks preparation for a journey; the long flowing robes are girded round the loins; shoes or sandals, not worn in the house or at meals, were fastened on the feet; and the traveller's staff was taken in hand.

the LORD'S *passover*] A most important statement. It gives at once the great and most significant name to the whole ordinance. The word Passover renders as nearly as pos-

feet, and your staff in your hand;
and ye shall eat it in haste: it *is* the
LORD's passover.
12 For I will pass through the land
of Egypt this night, and will smite all
the firstborn in the land of Egypt,
both man and beast; and against all
the ‖gods of Egypt I will execute
judgment: I *am* the LORD.
13 And the blood shall be to you
for a token upon the houses where ye
are: and when I see the blood, I will
pass over you, and the plague shall
not be upon you †to destroy *you*,
when I smite the land of Egypt.
14 And this day shall be unto you
for a memorial; and ye shall keep it
a feast to the LORD throughout your
generations; ye shall keep it a feast
by an ordinance for ever.

‖ Or, *princes*.

† Heb. *for a destruction*.

---

sible the true meaning of the original, of which the primary sense is generally held to be "pass rapidly," like a bird with outstretched wings, but it undoubtedly includes the idea of sparing. See Ges. 'Thes.' s.v. It is a word which occurs very seldom in other books, twice in one chapter of 1 K., xviii. 21, where it is rendered "halt," and seems to mean "waver," flitting like a bird from branch to branch, and 26, where our A.V. has in the margin "leaped up and down." A passage in Isaiah xxxi. 5 is of more importance, since it combines the two great ideas involved in the word: "As birds flying, so will the LORD of hosts defend Jerusalem; defending also he will deliver it; and PASSING OVER he will preserve it." This combination of ideas is recognized by nearly all ancient and modern critics. It is remarkable that the word is not found in other Semitic languages, except in passages derived from the Hebrew Bible. In Egyptian the word Pesh, which corresponds to it very nearly in form, means to "spread out the wings over," and "to protect;" see Brugsch, 'D. H.' p. 512.

12. *I will pass through*] The word rendered "pass through" is wholly distinct from that which means "pass over." The passing through was in judgment, the "passing over" in mercy.

against all the gods of Egypt] The meaning of this and of the corresponding passage, Num. xxxiii. 4, is undoubtedly that the visitation reached the gods of Egypt, not "the princes" as in the margin. The true explanation in this case is that in smiting the firstborn of all living beings, man and beast, God smote the objects of Egyptian worship. It is not merely that the bull and cow and goat and ram and cat were worshipped in the principal cities of Egypt as representatives, or, so to speak, incarnations, of their deities, but that the worship of beasts was universal; every nome, every town had its sacred animal, including the lowest forms of animal life; the frog, the beetle, being especial objects of reverence as representing the primeval deities of nature. In fact not a single deity of Egypt was unrepresented by some beast. This explanation, which is adopted by many critics, *e.g.* Michaelis, Rosenmüller, forces itself upon our minds in proportion to our closer and more accurate knowledge of Egyptian superstitions. It would not however have occurred to an Israelite living in Palestine, and the Rabbins in course of time adopted a different view, which approved itself to some of the early Fathers of the Church. Thus Jerome, 'Ep. ad Fabiolam,' says: "The Hebrews think that in the night when the people went forth all the temples in Egypt were destroyed either by earthquake or lightning:" and the second Targum, which gives the traditions of a still later time, asserts that each and every idol was destroyed. The explanation given above meets the whole requirement of the text.

13. *a token*] A sign to you, so to speak, a sacramental pledge of mercy.

I will pass over you] The same word as in *v.* 11. The sense of sparing is clear. The Targum renders it "I will spare you," and the LXX. "I will protect you."

to destroy you] or "to destruction," but our version gives the true sense and may be retained.

14. *a memorial*] The following verses to end of *v.* 20 contain explicit instructions for the future celebration of the Passover. They appear from *v.* 17 to have been given to Moses after the departure from Egypt, but are inserted here in their proper place, in connection with the history. The passover was to be a memorial, a commemorative and sacramental ordinance of perpetual obligation. As such it has ever been observed by the Hebrews. By the Christian it is spiritually observed; its full significance is recognized, and all that it foreshadowed is realized, in the Sacrament of Holy Communion. It is not therefore necessary to limit the meaning of the words "throughout your generations" and "for ever," although both expressions are frequently used with reference to an existing dispensation, or to a limited period.

ye shall keep it a feast] The word *chag* is used twice in this passage, for "keep a feast." The radical meaning is festivity, expressed in outward demonstrations of joy.

15 Seven days shall ye eat unleavened bread; even the first day ye shall put away leaven out of your houses: for whosoever eateth leavened bread from the first day until the seventh day, that soul shall be cut off from Israel.

16 And in the first day *there shall be* an holy convocation, and in the seventh day there shall be an holy convocation to you; no manner of work shall be done in them, save *that* which every †man must eat, that only may be done of you.

† Heb. *soul.*

17 And ye shall observe *the feast of* unleavened bread; for in this selfsame day have I brought your armies out of the land of Egypt: therefore shall ye observe this day in your generations by an ordinance for ever.

18 ¶ [a]In the first *month*, on the fourteenth day of the month at even, ye shall eat unleavened bread, until the one and twentieth day of the month at even.

a Lev. 23. 5. Numb. 28. 16.

19 Seven days shall there be no leaven found in your houses: for whosoever eateth that which is leavened, even that soul shall be cut off from the congregation of Israel, whether he be a stranger, or born in the land.

20 Ye shall eat nothing leavened; in all your habitations shall ye eat unleavened bread.

21 ¶ Then Moses called for all the elders of Israel, and said unto them, Draw out and take you a ‖lamb according to your families, and kill the passover.

‖ Or, *kid.*

---

15. *Seven days*] From the evening of the fourteenth of Nisan to the end of the 21st day. The leaven was removed from the houses before the paschal lamb was slain, in accordance with the general instruction, "Thou shalt not offer the blood of my sacrifice with leavened bread;" xxiii. 18. The unleavened bread was an essential element in the celebration: see note on *v.* 8. The penalty inflicted on those who transgressed the command may be accounted for on the ground that it was an act of rebellion; but additional light is thrown upon it by the typical meaning assigned to leaven by our Lord, Matt. xvi. 6. The period of seven days does not settle the question as to the previous observance of the week, since this command may have been first given after the institution of the Sabbath, but it adds considerable weight to the argument in its favour.

16. *an holy convocation*] This rendering exactly expresses the sense of the original; an assembly called by proclamation for a religious solemnity. The proclamation was directed to be made on some occasions by the blowing of the silver trumpets. See Num. x. 2, 3. In the East the proclamation is made by the Muezzins from the minarets of the mosques.

save that, &c.] In this the observance of the festival differed from the Sabbath, when the preparation of food was prohibited. The same word for "work" is used here and in the 4th Commandment: it is very general, and includes all laborious occupation, not however all bodily exercise, as it is understood by the stricter sects of the Rabbins.

17. *the feast of unleavened bread*] lit. "the unleavened bread;" which may mean either the festival, or the instructions relating to the unleavened bread. The Samaritan Pentateuch and the LXX. read "the precept," taking a word which differs slightly in form in the unpunctuated Hebrew: but our reading and translation are accepted by most critics.

18. *In the first month*] or "in the beginning," which may mean at the beginning of the festival, on the evening of the 14th Nisan. Thus the LXX.; but the other ancient versions agree with our own, and their rendering is supported by Rosenmüller.

19. *leaven*] The Hebrew word used here occurs only in the Pentateuch. It denotes the leaven itself; the word in the next clause, which is also found only in the Pentateuch, means the leavened dough, or bread.

born in the land] or "a native of the land;" a stranger or foreigner might be born in the land, but the word here used means indigenous, belonging to the country in virtue of descent, that descent being reckoned from Abraham, to whom Canaan was promised as a perpetual inheritance. The Hebrews had no tinge of the opinion which takes human races to be autochthonous. It is indeed remarkable that that opinion was entertained most strongly of old by the Athenians, a people whose foreign origin is incontestably proved by their language, customs and religion.

21. *Then Moses called*] From this verse to end of the 28th Moses records the directions

Heb. 11. 28. 22 [b]And ye shall take a bunch of
hyssop, and dip *it* in the blood that
is in the bason, and strike the lintel
and the two side posts with the blood
that *is* in the bason; and none of you
shall go out at the door of his house
until the morning.
23 For the LORD will pass through
to smite the Egyptians; and when he
seeth the blood upon the lintel, and
on the two side posts, the LORD will
pass over the door, and will not suffer
the destroyer to come in unto your
houses to smite *you*.
24 And ye shall observe this thing
for an ordinance to thee and to thy
sons for ever.
25 And it shall come to pass, when
ye be come to the land which the LORD
will give you, according as he hath promised, that ye shall keep this service.
26 [c]And it shall come to pass, c Josh. 4. 6.
when your children shall say unto
you, What mean ye by this service?
27 That ye shall say, It *is* the
sacrifice of the LORD's passover, who
passed over the houses of the children
of Israel in Egypt, when he smote
the Egyptians, and delivered our
houses. And the people bowed the
head and worshipped.
28 And the children of Israel went
away, and did as the LORD had commanded Moses and Aaron, so did
they.
29 ¶ [d]And it came to pass, that at d chap. 11. 4.
midnight the LORD smote all the
firstborn in the land of Egypt, [e]from e Wisd. 18. 11.
the firstborn of Pharaoh that sat on
his throne unto the firstborn of the
captive that *was* in the †dungeon; † Heb. *house of the pit.*
and all the firstborn of cattle.

---

which, in obedience to the command, he gave at the time to the people. This method of composition occurs frequently in the Pentateuch: it involves of course some repetition, from which no very ancient writer would shrink, but it would scarcely have been adopted by a compiler. Moses is ever careful to record first the commands which he receives, and afterwards the way in which he executed them.

Draw out] The expression is clear, but the sense has been questioned. Moses directs the elders to draw the lamb from the fold and then to take it to their houses.

the passover] The word is here applied to the lamb; an important fact, marking the lamb as the sign and pledge of the exemption of the Israelites.

22. *a bunch of hyssop*] The word rendered hyssop occurs only in the Pentateuch, with two exceptions, Ps. li. 7, which refers to the Mosaic rite, and 1 K. iv. 33, where it is applied to a herb growing on the wall, probably a small species of fern, mentioned as the smallest of plants and therefore not likely to be used for the sprinkling. The species here designated does not appear to be the plant now bearing the name. If we follow the Hebrew tradition, which in such matters is of weight, and is supported by most critics, it would seem to be a species of origanum, common in Palestine and near Mount Sinai, an aromatic plant with a long straight stalk and leaves well adapted for the purpose. See note on Lev. xiv. 4.

bason] The rendering rests on good authority and gives a good sense: but the word means threshold in some other passages and in Egyptian, and is taken here in that sense by the LXX. and Vulgate. If that rendering were correct it would imply that the lamb was slain on the threshold.

none...shall go out, &c.] There is no safety outside of the precincts protected by the blood of the lamb; a symbolism too obvious to require pointing out.

23. *the destroyer*] The word certainly denotes a personal agent; see note on *v.* 29.

24. *this thing*] The injunction would seem to apply specially to the sprinkling of blood on the lintel and doorposts; but the authority for changing the rite is unquestioned; see note on *v.* 9; and the Hebrew tradition is uniform. It may therefore be admitted, with Aben-Ezra and Knobel, who represent very different schools, that this charge refers to the general observance of the Passover.

27. *It is the sacrifice of the LORD's passover*] or **This is the sacrifice of the Passover to Jehovah.** The most formal and exact designation of the festival is thus given: but "the Passover" may mean either the act or God's mercy in sparing the Israelites, or the lamb which is offered in sacrifice: more probably the latter, as in *v.* 21, "and kill the passover." This gives a clear sense to the expression "to Jehovah;" it was a sacrifice offered to Jehovah by His ordinance.

The Tenth and Last Plague.

29. *smote all the firstborn*] This plague is distinctly attributed here and in *v.* 23 to

30 And Pharaoh rose up in the
night, he, and all his servants, and all
the Egyptians; and there was a great
cry in Egypt; for *there was* not a
house where *there was* not one dead.

31 ¶ And he called for Moses and
Aaron by night, and said, Rise up,
and get you forth from among my
people, both ye and the children of
Israel; and go, serve the LORD, as ye
have said.

32 Also take your flocks and your
herds, as ye have said, and be gone;
and bless me also.

33 And the Egyptians were urgent
upon the people, that they might send
them out of the land in haste;
they said, We *be* all dead *men*.

34 And the people took their dough
before it was leavened, their [1] knead- [1] Or, *dough.*
ingtroughs being bound up in their
clothes upon their shoulders.

35 And the children of Israel did
according to the word of Moses;
and they borrowed of the Egyptians
[f] jewels of silver, and jewels of gold, [f] chap. 3. 22. & 11. 2.
and raiment:

36 And the LORD gave the people
favour in the sight of the Egyptians,
so that they lent unto them *such
things as they required*. And they
spoiled the Egyptians.

---

the personal intervention of THE LORD; but it is to be observed that although the Lord Himself passed through to smite the Egyptians, He employed the agency of "the destroyer," in whom, in accordance with Heb. xi. 28, all the Ancient Versions, and most critics, recognize an angel. Such indeed is the express statement of Holy Writ with reference to other visitations, as 2 Kings xix. 35, and more especially 2 Sam. xxiv. 16. The employment of angelic agency, however, does not always exclude the operation of physical causes. In the same chapter of 2 Sam. which describes the destruction of 70,000 Israelites by an angel, whose personality is distinctly attested, see *vv.* 15—17, it is no less distinctly declared to have been effected by a pestilence; see *vv.* 13 and 25. Nature accomplishes God's purposes under His control. As in every other case the hand of God was distinctly shewn by the previous announcement, the suddenness, intensity, and limitation of the calamity. No house of the Egyptians escaped; the firstborn only perished in each; the Israelites were unscathed.

the captive] In ch. xi. 5, the woman at the mill is mentioned. Such variations are common in Holy Writ, and are to be noticed as shewing the disregard of slight or apparent discrepancies. The notices of captives under the 18th dynasty are numerous on the monuments: they were generally employed in brick-making and building, and this passage implies that they were treated to some extent as settlers in the land. The word "dungeon" translated more literally in the margin "house of the pit," corresponds to the Egyptian "Rar," or "Lar," in meaning; the same word for "pit" is found in both languages. See Brugsch, 'D. H.' p. 402, who considers it to be Semitic.

31. *the LORD*] The LXX. add "your God," a very probable reading.

32. *bless me also*] No words could shew more strikingly the complete, though temporary submission of Pharaoh.

34. *kneadingtroughs*] Not "dough" as in the margin. The same word is used in ch. viii. 3, and Deut. xxviii. 5. The troughs were probably small, such as are now used by the Arabians; wooden bowls in which the cakes when baked are preserved for use. The Hebrews used their outer garment, or mantle, in the same way as the Bedouins at present, who make a bag of the voluminous folds of their haiks or burnous. See Ruth iii. 15; 2 Kings iv. 39.

35. *borrowed*] Or "asked of." See note ch. iii. 22.

36. *lent*] Or **gave**. The word here used in the Hebrew means simply "granted their request." Whether the grant is made as a loan, or as a gift, depends in every instance upon the context. In this case the question is whether the Israelites asked for the jewels and the Egyptians granted them as a loan with reference to the festival in the wilderness; or whether this was regarded on both sides as a moderate remuneration for long service, and a compensation for cruel wrongs. The word "spoiling" (iii. 22) ought to be regarded as conclusive for the latter sense. The Arabic translator, Saadia, uses the word "gave." The Syriac and the Targum Onk. have the exact equivalent of the Hebrew. Rosenmüller says truly, in Hebrew the word means simply "to give;" often with the idea of willingness or readiness. Thus too Knobel, who altogether rejects the notion of lending; and Kalisch. Even if the word were taken, as it is by some distinguished scholars, in the sense "lent," it must be remembered that the actual cause which prevented the Egyptians from recovering their property was, that the return of the

[g Numb. 33. 3.]
37 ¶ And [g] the children of Israel
journeyed from Rameses to Succoth,
about six hundred thousand on foot
that were men, beside children.
38 And † a mixed multitude went
up also with them; and flocks, and
herds, *even* very much cattle.

[† Heb. *great mixture.*]

39 And they baked unleavened
cakes of the dough which they brought
forth out of Egypt, for it was not
leavened; because they were thrust
out of Egypt, and could not tarry,
neither had they prepared for themselves any victual.
40 ¶ Now the sojourning of the
children of Israel, who dwelt in
Egypt, *was* [h] four hundred and thirty
years.
41 And it came to pass at the
end of the four hundred and thirty
years, even the selfsame day it came
to pass, that all the hosts of the
LORD went out from the land of
Egypt.
42 It *is* † a night to be much observed unto the LORD for bringing
them out from the land of Egypt:
this *is* that night of the LORD to be
observed of all the children of Israel
in their generations.

[h Gen. 15. 13. Acts 7. 6. Gal. 3. 17.]

[† Heb. *a night of observations.*]

Israelites was cut off by the treachery of Pharaoh. Thus Ewald, 'G. I.' II. p. 87. Ewald also accepts the application of the transaction found so commonly in the Fathers, who see in it a figure of the appropriation by the Israelites of Egyptian rites and ceremonies, and of the truths thereby represented.

The Departure of the Israelites.

37. *Rameses*] See note on ch. i. 11. Rameses was evidently the place of general rendezvous, well adapted for that purpose as the principal city of Goshen. The Israelites, by whom it had been built, were probably settled in considerable numbers in it and about it. Pharaoh with his army and court were at that time near the frontier, and Rameses, where a large garrison was kept, was probably the place where the last interview with Moses occurred. Under the 19th dynasty the Pharaohs received foreign embassies, transacted treaties, and held their court in this city, which was considerably enlarged and embellished by Rameses II. A discussion on the route of the Israelites from Rameses to Sinai will be found in the Appendix to this book. The first part of the journey appears to have followed the course of the ancient canal. The site of Succoth cannot be exactly determined, but it lay about half-way between Rameses and Etham. It could not therefore have been on the road to Palestine which ran north-east of the lake of crocodiles (Birket Timseh), but to the south of that lake by the road which led by the shortest way to the edge of the wilderness. The frontier to the east of the road appears to have been covered in ancient times by the so-called bitter lakes, which extended to the Gulf of Suez. The name Succoth (*i.e.* "tents" or "booths" in Hebrew), may have been given by the Israelites, but the same, or a similar word, occurs in Egyptian in connection with the district. Thus in De Rougé, 'Recherches,' p. 50, we find an officer of state in possession of a domain called Sechet, or Sochot, in the time of Chufu. That domain was certainly in lower Egypt, and probably at no great distance from Memphis.

600,000] This includes all the males who could march. The total number of the Israelites should therefore be calculated not from the men above twenty years old, but from the males above twelve or fourteen, and would therefore amount to somewhat more than two millions. This is not an excessive population for Goshen, nor does it exceed a reasonable estimate of the increase of the Israelites, including their numerous dependents. See Payne Smith's 'Bampton Lectures,' 1869, L. III. p. 88. The number 600,000 is confirmed by many distinct statements and details, and is accepted by Ewald and other critics.

38. *a mixed multitude*] They consisted probably of remains of the old Semitic population, whether or not first brought into the district by the Hyksos is uncertain. As natural objects of suspicion and dislike to the Egyptians who had lately become masters of the country, they would be anxious to escape, the more especially after the calamities which preceded the Exodus.

very much cattle] This is an important fact, both as shewing that the oppression of the Israelites had not extended to confiscation of their property, and as bearing upon the question of their maintenance in the Wilderness.

40. *who dwelt*] Read, **which they sojourned.** The obvious intention of Moses is to state the duration of the sojourn in Egypt. On the interpretation and chronology see note below.

41. At the end of this verse the LXX. add "by night."

43 ¶ And the LORD said unto
Moses and Aaron, This *is* the ordinance of the passover: There shall
no stranger eat thereof:
44 But every man's servant that
is bought for money, when thou hast
circumcised him, then shall he eat
thereof.
45 A foreigner and an hired servant shall not eat thereof.
[i] Numb. 9. 12.
46 [i] In one house shall it be eaten;
thou shalt not carry forth ought of
the flesh abroad out of the house;
[k] John 19. 36.
[k] neither shall ye break a bone thereof.
47 All the congregation of Israel
† Heb. *do it.*
shall † keep it.
48 And when a stranger shall sojourn with thee, and will keep the
passover to the LORD, let all his
males be circumcised, and then let
him come near and keep it; and he
shall be as one that is born in the
land: for no uncircumcised person
shall eat thereof.
49 One law shall be to him that
is homeborn, and unto the stranger
that sojourneth among you.
50 Thus did all the children of
Israel; as the LORD commanded Moses and Aaron, so did they.
51 And it came to pass the selfsame day, *that* the LORD did bring
the children of Israel out of the land
of Egypt by their armies.

---

43. *And the LORD said*] The following passage, from this verse to *v.* 16 of the next chapter, contains additional instructions regarding the Passover. Such instructions were needed when the Israelites were joined by the "mixed multitudes" of strangers; and they were probably given at Succoth, on the morning following the departure from Rameses. The antiquity of this section is admitted by critics of all schools. The first point which required to be determined was the condition of participation in the rite; it is simple and complete. No one was to be admitted without being circumcised: all were to be admitted who were qualified by that rite.

no stranger] lit. "son of a stranger." The term is general; it includes all who were aliens from Israel, until they were incorporated into the nation by circumcision. The Arabic translator is probably right in using a word which involves the idea of persistence in a false religion; the Targum goes farther, and takes a word which means apostate.

44. *servant*] or "slave." It seems better to retain the word "servant," for although the servant was, strictly speaking, a slave, being the property of his master, his condition differed very widely from that of a slave in heathen countries, or those Christian nations wherein slavery is legalized. The circumcision of the slave, thus enjoined formally on the first day that Israel became a nation, in accordance with the law given to Abraham Gen. xvii. 12, made him a true member of the family, equally entitled to all religious privileges. In the household of a priest the slave was even permitted to eat the consecrated food: Lev. xxii. 11.

45. *A foreigner*] or **sojourner**. The Hebrew means one who resides in a country, not having a permanent home, nor being attached to an Israelitish household. A different word is used *v.* 43.

46. *In one house*] The Targum renders this "in one company," a translation which, though not literal, expresses the true meaning of the injunction. Each lamb was to be entirely consumed by the members of one company, whether they belonged to the same household or not.

break a bone] The typical significance of this injunction is recognized by St John; see marginal reference. It is not easy to assign any other satisfactory reason for it. This victim alone was exempt from the general law by which the limbs were ordered to be separated from the body.

48. *when a stranger shall sojourn*] or "when a stranger shall settle with thee." It is not easy to express in English the exact meaning of these words. The sojourner and the hired servant did not come under the definition of a permanent settler. When circumcised any foreigner became one of the chosen race.

50. *Thus did, &c.*] This verse and the following apply apparently to the stay of the people at Succoth, where they may have remained a short time, completing their preparation for final departure from Egypt.

NOTES on VV. 4, 8, 40.

4. The variations in translating this verse do not affect the general sense, but indicate some difficulty in the construction. "Each man according to his eating" is understood by the Vulg. to mean the number which may be sufficient to consume the lamb: but the evident sense is that the head of the family must judge what quantity each person will probably consume, a quantity varying of course according to age, strength, and other circumstances. The Hebrew root כסם, with its derivatives, does not occur in any book but the Pentateuch, and with one exception, Num. xxxi., only in connection with this special transaction, nor is it found in any of the Semitic languages. It is evidently archaic, unknown to later Hebrews except from this book. Gesenius points out the analogy with other roots with the same or similar initials, and Fuerst compares the Sanscrit *ças*, *kshi*, which however differ, having, as well as the Egyptian *kesha*, the sense of cutting, wounding, &c.

8. Hebrew מצות; derived by Gesenius from מצץ, "cum voluptate hausit, gustavit." Brugsch, 'D. H.' s. v., suggests an Egyptian etymology. The cakes offered at the festival of the New Year to Osiris were called *mest*, or *mesī-t*. It is possible that the word was commonly used while the Israelites were in Egypt to denote sweet, or unleavened, cakes used exclusively for sacred purposes. Knobel and Keil agree in referring *mazzoth* to a word extant in Arabic, in the sense "pure:" but that sense is secondary and probably not ancient; the root has the meaning assigned above to מצץ. At the end of this verse the LXX. and Vulg. omit "it" after "eat." This gives a preferable construction to that of our A.V.; and the authority of the LXX., always high in the Pentateuch, is especially so in this book.

40. The rendering of the Authorised Version, "who dwelt," is peculiar. It has no support in the Ancient Versions: (the LXX. have ἦν κατῴκησαν; the Vulg. qua manserunt; thus also the Arabic, Syriac, Chaldee and Samaritan;) nor does it appear to be adopted by any modern commentator. In fact the mention of the sojourning without reference to its duration would be beside the mind of the writer. If the Hebrew text be taken as it stands, it fixes that duration to 430 years; and this is accepted by the majority of critics of all schools. It agrees substantially with Genesis xv. 13, 14, when the announcement was first made to Abraham, "know of a surety that thy seed shall be a stranger in a land that is not theirs, and shall serve them; and they shall afflict them four hundred years; and also that nation, whom they shall serve, will I judge: and afterwards shall they come out with great substance." The expressions here used apply to Egypt and not to Canaan, in which the Patriarchs were certainly not made to serve. The additional statement in *v.* 16 of the same chapter "in the fourth generation they shall come hither again" presents some difficulty; it is however probably identical in sense with the preceding one, referring to the time during which the people would serve in a strange land; the term generation is understood by Gesenius and other Hebrew scholars to be equivalent to a century.

The correctness of the Hebrew text has however been questioned. The LXX. according to the Vatican codex inserts after Egypt, "and in the land of Canaan:" or according to the Alexandrian codex and Coptic Version, ed. De Lagarde, "which they and their fathers dwelt in the land of Egypt and the land of Canaan." The Samaritan Pentateuch has "which they dwelt in the land of Canaan and the land of Egypt." This is supposed by some to represent a various reading in the original: but the authority of both witnesses is impaired by the variations which indicate an intention to meet a difficulty, and by the fact that the most ancient Greek codices omit the words altogether and agree with the Hebrew text. For this we have the evidence of Theophilus Ant. who states twice, 'ad Aut.' III. § 9 and 24, that the Israelites sojourned 430 years in Egypt: the Samaritan text and that of one late Hebrew MS. which agrees with it are suspected of interpolation. Scholars at present generally accept the Hebrew as genuine, differing only in the interpretation.

There can be no doubt that at an early time the Jews felt the difficulty of reconciling this statement with the genealogies, which they held to be complete. If Levi were the grandfather of Moses on the mother's side through Jochebed, and separated only by two descents on the father's, through Kohath and Amram, it is clear that a space of 430 years could not be accounted for. Levi was past middle age when he went into Egypt; Moses was born 80 years before the Exodus. The difficulty however appears to be insuperable even on the hypothesis that 430 years included the whole interval between Abraham and the Exodus. Isaac was born 25 years after Abraham's arrival in Canaan, Jacob was born in Isaac's 60th year, and was 130 years old when he entered Egypt. This accounts for 215 years, leaving 215 for the sojourn. But in order to make out 215 years it is necessary to assume that Levi was 95 years old when Jochebed was born, and that Jochebed was 85 years old when she became mother of Moses. This is said by a commentator of great weight not to be improbable; but it involves two miracles, for which there is no authority in Scripture.

In the later Targum on Exodus ii. 1 a rabbinical tradition is recorded that Jochebed was miraculously restored to youth at the age of 130 years. But even these assumptions would not remove the objection, that the male descendants of Kohath (the grandfather of Moses on this hypothesis) amounted to 8600 at the time of the Exodus; see Num. iii. 28. The Kohathites were then divided into four families, each of which must have numbered, including females, about 4300, when Moses was 80 years of age. Whether the longer or shorter period be adopted it is equally necessary either to assume a succession of miracles, or to admit that an indefinite number of links in the genealogies are omitted; a fact for which we have positive evidence in the most important of all genealogies, that of our Lord, and in that of Ezra, which therefore there can be no irreverence in assuming in a case when it clears up every difficulty in the narrative.

The Jewish tradition is assumed to be in favour of 215 years; this may be true in reference to the later Rabbis: but it is far from being uniform. Josephus adopts it in one passage, 'Ant.' II. 15. 2, but in others he distinctly asserts that the period of affliction in Egypt after the death of Joseph lasted 400 years; see 'Ant.' II. 9. 1 and 'B. J.' V. 9. 4. The evidence is worth little, being self-contradictory, but it shews that both opinions were held at his time. In the New Testament St Stephen's speech, Acts vii. 6, recognizes 400 years as the period when the seed of Abraham should be in bondage and evil entreated, terms which could only apply to Egypt. St Paul however seems to support the other view, Gal. iii. 17, when he says that the law was given 430 years after Abraham: but the period accepted generally by the Jews in his time sufficed for his purpose, and a discussion upon a point which did not affect his argument would have been out of place.

It may be possible to reconcile the number of the Israelites at the time of the Exodus with the shorter period; but it certainly is far more probable if we accept without any reserve the statement of Moses in this passage, made as it is in the most formal and precise terms, with the express purpose of fixing the length of the sojourn permanently upon the national mind.

The determination of the date of the Exodus rests mainly upon the statement in 1 K. vi. 1, that 480 years elapsed between the fourth year of Solomon and the time when the children of Israel came out of the land of Egypt. That date is supported by all the ancient versions (the slight deviation in the LXX., 440 for 480, being accounted for by Winer and Thenius in loc. as a lapsus calami, מ=40 for פ=80), it is accepted by able critics, and it appears to the writer of this note to accord best with the indications of time in the historical books; but the subject belongs properly to the commentatary on Kings.

CHAPTER XIII.

1 *The firstborn are sanctified to God.* 3 *The memorial of the passover is commanded.* 11 *The firstlings of beasts are set apart.* 17 *The Israelites go out of Egypt, and carry Joseph's bones with them.* 20 *They come to Etham.* 21 *God guideth them by a pillar of a cloud, and a pillar of fire.*

AND the LORD spake unto Moses, saying,

2 *a* Sanctify unto me all the first- *a* chap. 22. 29.
born, whatsoever openeth the womb & 34. 19. Lev. 27.26.
among the children of Israel, *both* of Numb. 3. 13.
man and of beast: it *is* mine. & 8. 16.
3 ¶ And Moses said unto the peo- Luke 2. 23.
ple, Remember this day, in which
ye came out from Egypt, out of the
house of † bondage; for by strength † Heb.
of hand the LORD brought you out *servants.*

CHAP. XIII. The instructions in the first part of this chapter are not necessarily connected with the rest of the narrative, and there may have been special reasons for adding some of them, together with the grounds for their observance, when the people were preparing for the invasion of Palestine. This might have been before the beginning of their long wandering in the wilderness of Tih, at the same time when Moses sent the spies to explore Canaan. Whether written later or not, this section contains much which must have been orally given at the first celebration of the Passover.

2. *Sanctify unto me*] The command is addressed to Moses. It was to declare the will of God that all firstborn were to be consecrated to him, set apart from all other creatures. The command is expressly based upon the Passover. The firstborn exempt from the destruction became in a new and special sense the exclusive property of the Lord: the firstborn of man as His ministers, the firstborn of cattle as victims. In lieu of the firstborn of men the Levites were devoted to the temple services. The consecration of all firstborn is admitted to be peculiar to the Hebrews; nor can any satisfactory reason for such a law be assigned by those who refuse to accept the Scriptural statement, which they admit to be explicit. Knobel refutes the theories of other writers.

from this *place:* there shall no leavened bread be eaten.
4 This day came ye out in the
month Abib.
5 ¶ And it shall be when the LORD
shall bring thee into the land of the
Canaanites, and the Hittites, and the
Amorites, and the Hivites, and the
Jebusites, which he sware unto thy
fathers to give thee, a land flowing
with milk and honey, that thou shalt
keep this service in this month.
6 Seven days thou shalt eat unleavened bread, and in the seventh
day *shall be* a feast to the LORD.
7 Unleavened bread shall be eaten
seven days; and there shall no leavened bread be seen with thee, neither shall there be leaven seen with
thee in all thy quarters.
8 ¶ And thou shalt shew thy son
in that day, saying, *This is done* because of that *which* the LORD did
unto me when I came forth out of
Egypt.
9 And it shall be for a sign unto
thee upon thine hand, and for a
memorial between thine eyes, that
the LORD's law may be in thy mouth:
for with a strong hand hath the LORD
brought thee out of Egypt.
10 Thou shalt therefore keep this
ordinance in his season from year to
year.
11 ¶ And it shall be when the
LORD shall bring thee into the land
of the Canaanites, as he sware unto
thee and to thy fathers, and shall
give it thee,
12 [b]That thou shalt †set apart [b] chap. 22.
unto the LORD all that openeth the 29.
matrix, and every firstling that com- & 34. 19.
eth of a beast which thou hast; the Ezek. 44. 30.
males *shall be* the LORD's. † Heb. *cause to pass over.*
13 And every firstling of an ass
thou shalt redeem with a ‖ lamb; and ‖ Or, *kid.*

---

4. *Abib*] It is uncertain whether this name was ancient or given then for the first time. It is found only in the Pentateuch, twice in the sense of young wheat, six times as the name of the first month. The two former instances leave little doubt as to the etymology, viz. the month when the wheat began to ripen. Thus the LXX., Targ. and Saadia. In Arabic *abbon* means green herbs. The name resembles the Egyptian Epiphi, April, and may possibly have been derived from it; that name is ancient. See Brugsch, 'H. E.' p. 162.

5. *the Canaanites*] Five nations only are named in this passage, whereas six are named in iii. 8, and ten in the original promise to Abraham, Gen. xv. 19—21. The LXX. add the Perizzites and Girgashites, probably on MSS. authority. The first word Canaanite is generic, and includes all the Hamite races of Palestine.

9. *And it shall be for a sign unto thee*, &c.] Hebrew writers have generally regarded this as a formal injunction to write the precepts on slips of parchment, and to fasten them on the wrists and forehead; but other commentators are generally agreed that it is to be understood metaphorically. The words appear to be put into the mouths of the parents. They were to keep all the facts of the passover constantly in mind, and, referring to a custom prevalent ages before Moses in Egypt, to have them present as though they were inscribed on papyrus or parchment fastened on the wrists, or on the face between the eyes. It is improbable that Moses should have adopted that custom, which was scarcely separable from the Egyptian superstition of amulets; but modern Israelites generally allege this precept as a justification for the use of phylacteries. Moses states distinctly the object of the precept, which was that the law of Jehovah should be in their mouth: see *v.* 16. The expression may have been proverbial in the time of Moses, as it certainly was at a later period; see Proverbs vi. 20—22, vii. 3, where the metaphorical sense is not questioned. Jerome gives a clear and rational interpretation in his commentary on Matthew xxiii. 5, "Præcepta mea sint in manu tua, ut opere compleantur, sint ante oculos tuos ut nocte et die mediteris in illis."

12. *thou shalt set apart*] lit. as in the margin "cause to pass over," but the sense is correctly expressed in the text, which follows the Old Versions, and is preferable to the marginal rendering, which suggests a reference to the word "Passover."

13. *an ass*] The reason of the injunction is evidently that the ass could not be offered in sacrifice, being an unclean animal: possibly the only unclean animal domesticated among the Israelites at the time of the Exodus. The principle of the law being obvious, it was extended to the horse and camel, and generally to every unclean beast; see Num. xviii. 15. The mention of the ass only would scarcely have occurred to an Israelite of a

if thou wilt not redeem it, then thou
shalt break his neck: and all the firstborn of man among thy children shalt
thou redeem
14 ¶ And it shall be when thy son
asketh thee † in time to come, saying,
What *is* this? that thou shalt say
unto him, By strength of hand the
LORD brought us out from Egypt, from
the house of bondage:
15 And it came to pass, when Pharaoh would hardly let us go, that
the LORD slew all the firstborn in
the land of Egypt, both the firstborn
of man, and the firstborn of beast:
therefore I sacrifice to the LORD all
that openeth the matrix, being males;
but all the firstborn of my children I
redeem.
16 And it shall be for a token
upon thine hand, and for frontlets
between thine eyes: for by strength
of hand the LORD brought us forth
out of Egypt.
17 ¶ And it came to pass, when
Pharaoh had let the people go, that
God led them not *through* the way of
the land of the Philistines, although
that *was* near; for God said, Lest
peradventure the people repent when
they see war, and they return to
Egypt:
18 But God led the people about,
through the way of the wilderness of
the Red sea: and the children of Israel went up ‖ harnessed out of the
land of Egypt.
19 And Moses took the bones of
Joseph with him: for he had straitly
sworn the children of Israel, saying,

† Heb. *to morrow.*

‖ Or, *by five in a rank.*

---

later age. It has been observed that the ass was held by the Egyptians to be typhonic, *i.e.* in a peculiar sense unclean: but that feeling appears to belong to a comparatively later period; in early monuments the ass is frequently represented, and in the 'Ritual,' c. 40, it is even a type of Osiris.

thou shalt redeem] The lamb, or sheep, was given to the priest for the service of the sanctuary.

firstborn of man] The price of redemption was fixed at five shekels of the sanctuary: Num. iii. 47, where see note.

16. *it shall be*] This passage confirms the interpretation given above on *v.* 9.

17—19. These verses do not appear to be a continuation of the narrative, which is resumed at *v.* 20. It is not improbable that some short time was passed at Succoth, and that Moses then gave final injunctions touching the celebration of the Passover, and received general instructions as to the ultimate direction of the journey. Succoth may very probably have been the head-quarters of the Hebrews in Goshen. The name in Hebrew indicates an assemblage of booths, or moveable huts (see ch. xii. 37), such as were probably used by the Israelites, ever mindful of their condition as sojourners in a strange land: the notice in *v.* 19 naturally leaves the impression that the bones of Joseph were kept there, of course in the charge of his own descendants.

17. *the way of the land of the Philistines*] The occupancy of southern Palestine by the Philistines, at a much earlier period than is assigned by any critics to the Exodus, is attested by the narrative in Genesis xxvi. 1. It has lately been questioned on the ground that the inhabitants of Ascalon, when it was captured by Rameses II. did not wear the well-known costume of the Philistines, but that of the ancient Canaanites, and that the name Pulisha, *i.e.* Philistines, occurs first in monuments of the time of Rameses III. Brugsch, 'Geog. Ins.' II. p. 86. The objection is answered in the Appendix at the end of the volume: here it may suffice to notice that the persons represented on the monuments of Rameses II. were probably Israelites; for they actually took possession of the cities of the Philistines, who did not recover the territory until a considerable time had elapsed after the death of Joshua. The warlike character of the Philistines is equally conspicuous in the Egyptian and Hebrew records.

18. *harnessed*] This interpretation of the Hebrew word rests on the authority of some ancient versions, and a possible etymology is suggested by Rabbinical writers. It seems, however, more probable that the meaning is marshalled or in orderly array. See note below. The objection (grounded on the rendering in our version) that the Israelites were not likely to have been armed is unreasonable. There is not the least indication that they were disarmed by the Egyptians, and as occupying a frontier district frequently assailed by the nomads of the desert they would of necessity be accustomed to the use of arms. The fear expressed by Pharaoh (see ch. i. 10) that they might at any time join the invaders and fight against Egypt was the avowed and doubtless the true motive for the crafty measures by which he hoped to subdue their spirit and prevent their increase.

[e] Gen. 50. 25. Josh. 24. 32. [d] Numb. 33. 6. [e] Numb. 14. 14. Deut. 1. 33. Psal. 78. 14. 1 Cor. 10. 1.

[e]God will surely visit you; and ye
shall carry up my bones away hence
with you.
20 ¶ And [d]they took their journey
from Succoth, and encamped in E-
tham, in the edge of the wilderness.
21 And [e]the LORD went before
them by day in a pillar of a cloud, to
lead them the way; and by night in
a pillar of fire, to give them light; to
go by day and night:
22 He took not away the pillar of
the cloud by day, [f]nor the pillar of
fire by night, *from* before the people.

[f] Neh. 9. 19.

---

20. *Etham*] The Egyptian notices of Etham will be found in the Appendix at the end of this volume. The most probable result of those notices is that Etham, which means the house or sanctuary of Tum (the Sun God worshipped specially by that name in lower Egypt), was in the immediate vicinity of Heroopolis, called by the Egyptians the fortress of Zar, or Zalu (*i.e.* of foreigners); the frontier city where the Pharaohs of the 18th dynasty reviewed their forces when about to enter upon a campaign on Syria. The name Pithom has precisely the same meaning with Etham, and may possibly be identified with it. It was at this point that the Bedouins of the adjoining wilderness came into contact with the Egyptians. Under the 19th dynasty we find them applying in a time of famine for admission to the fertile district commanded by the fortress called the sanctuary of Tum.

21. *pillar of cloud*] The Lord Himself did for the Israelites by preternatural means that which armies were obliged to do for themselves by natural agents. Passages are quoted from classical writers which shew that the Persians and Greeks used fire and smoke as signals in their marches. Curtius describes the practice of Alexander, who gave the signal for departure by a fire on a tall pole over his tent, and says, observabatur ignis noctu fumus interdiu. Vegetius and Frontinus mention it as a general custom, especially among the Arabians. The success of some important expeditions, as of Thrasybulus and Timoleon, was attributed by popular superstition to a divine light guiding the leaders. To these well-known instances may be added two of peculiar interest, as bearing witness to a custom known to all the contemporaries of Moses. In an inscription of the Ancient Empire an Egyptian general is compared to "a flame streaming in advance of an army." (See Chabas 'V. E.' p. 54; the inscription is in the Denkmæler, II, pl. 150, 2). Thus too in a wellknown papyrus, (Anast. I) the commander of an expedition is called "A flame in the darkness at the head of his soldiers." By this sign then of the pillar of cloud, the Lord shewed Himself as their leader and general. "The Lord is a man of war . . . thy right hand, O Lord, hath dashed in pieces the enemy" (xv.).

NOTE on *v.* 18.

The Hebrew חמשים is rendered "armati" by the Vulg., מזרזין by Onkelos, *i.e.* accincti, expediti, rather than armati. as it is rendered in Walton's Polyglott. This would suit the etymology proposed by Abulwalid, Kimchi, and Tanchum, and adopted by Kalisch, viz. חֹמֶשׁ, ilia, abdomen. The sense however would be *not* "full-armed," but simply "with their loins girded," as men prepared for a journey. Thus in Joshua i. 14 it is rendered εὔζωνοι by the LXX. The Arabic in Walton (by Saadia) has متعبيين. *i.e.* instructi, marshalled; and this meaning is adopted by many critics, though different etymologies are proposed. Knobel says that it *must* signify assembled, arranged in orderly divisions, in contradistinction from a disorganised rabble. He derives it from Arabic roots, such as خمس &c. It seems however preferable to take the obvious Hebrew etymology from חמש, *i.e.* five, probably connected with خمس, agmen instructum, pr. quinquepartitum, which is pointed at by the singular rendering of the LXX. "in the fifth generation." Ewald, 'G. I.' explains it "arranged in five divisions," *i.e.* van, centre, two wings and rear-guard. The promptitude with which so vast a multitude was marshalled and led forth justifies admiration, but is not marvellous, nor without parallels in ancient and modern history (see Introduction). The Israelites had been prepared for departure, some preliminary measures must have been taken after each of the plagues when Pharaoh had given a temporary assent to the request of Moses, see viii. 8, 28, ix. 28, x. 16, four several occasions on which notice must have been given to the people. It must also be borne in mind that the despotism of Pharaoh had supplied the Israelites with native officers whom they were accustomed to obey, and with whom they were united by the bond of a common suffering (see ch. v. 14—21). Their leader had the experience of an early life at a warlike court, and of long years passed among the fierce tribes of the desert. The nation moreover has shewn in every age a remarkable talent for prompt and systematic organization.

CHAPTER XIV.

1 *God instructeth the Israelites in their journey.* 5 *Pharaoh pursueth after them.* 10 *The Israelites murmur.* 13 *Moses comforteth them.* 15 *God instructeth Moses.* 19 *The cloud removeth behind the camp.* 21 *The Israelites pass through the Red sea,* 23 *which drowneth the Egyptians.*

AND the LORD spake unto Moses,
saying,
2 Speak unto the children of Israel,
that they turn and encamp before
[a] Pi-hahiroth, between Migdol and the [a] Numb.
sea, over against Baal-zephon: before 33. 7.
it shall ye encamp by the sea.
3 For Pharaoh will say of the
children of Israel, They *are* entangled
in the land, the wilderness hath shut
them in.

The Passage over the Red Sea.

CHAP. XIV. 2. *That they turn*] The narrative is continued from *v.* 20 of the preceding chapter. The people were then at Etham, or Pitnom, the frontier city towards the wilderness: they are now commanded to change the direction of their march, and to go southwards, to the west of the Bitter Lakes, which completely separated them from the desert: see note on c. xii. 37.

Pi-hahiroth] The derivation of this name is doubtful. If it is Semitic, like the two other names mentioned in connection with it, the meaning may be "mouth, or entrance of the holes or caverns," but it is more probably Egyptian, with the common prefix Pi, *i. e.* house. In an ancient papyrus, we read of a place called Hir, or Pe-Hir, where there was a large well, at no great distance from Rameses, which it supplied with garlands. See Chabas, 'Mél. Eg.' II. p. 123. The place is generally identified with Ajrud, a fortress with a very large well of good water (see Niebuhr, 'Voyage,' I. p. 175), situate at the foot of an elevation commanding the plain which extends to Suez, at a distance of four leagues. The journey from Etham might occupy two, or even three days; had however Etham been, as many geographers suppose, half-way between Mukfar and Ajrud (see Robinson's 'Chart'), Pharaoh could not possibly have overtaken the Israelites, whether his head-quarters were at Zoan, or even at Rameses, which was two days' journey from Etham.

Migdol] The word means a tower, or fort: it is probably to be identified with Bir Suweis, about two miles from Suez. The water is said by Niebuhr to be scarcely drinkable; according to Robinson, p. 45, it is used only for cooking and washing. This traveller observes justly, that if the wells were in existence at the time of the Exodus they would mark the site of a town. Now M. Chabas has lately shewn that Maktal, or Magdal, an Egyptian fort (which on other grounds he identifies with Migdol), visited by Sethos I. on his return from a campaign in Syria, was built over a large well: see 'Voyage d'un Egyptien,' p. 286. This leaves scarcely any room for doubt as to the locality; it is a point of importance with reference to the passage over the sea.

Baal-zephon] This appears to have been the name under which the Phœnicians, who had a settlement in lower Egypt at a very ancient period, worshipped their chief Deity. The corresponding Egyptian Deity was Sutech, who is often called Bal on monuments of the 19th dynasty. Sethos I. gave a name closely connected with this to a city in the same neighbourhood, which Chabas, l. c., holds to be Baal-Zephon. There can be no doubt it was near Kolsum, or Suez. In the time of Niebuhr there were considerable ruins close to Suez on the north. From the text it is clear that the encampment of the Israelites extended over the plain from Pi-hahiroth: their head-quarters being between Bir Suweis and the sea opposite to Baal-Zephon. At Ajrud the road branches off in two directions, one leading to the wilderness by a tract, now dry, but in the time of Moses probably impassable, see next note; the other leading to Suez, which was doubtless followed by the Israelites.

3. *They are entangled*, &c.] The meaning evidently is, in that direction they have no egress from Egypt: the latter part of the verse is generally rendered as in our Version, "the wilderness has shut them in," but the sense would rather seem to be "the wilderness is closed to them;" see note below. The original intention of Moses was to go towards Palestine by the wilderness: when that purpose was changed by God's direction and they moved southwards, Pharaoh on receiving information was of course aware that they were completely shut in, since the waters of the Red Sea then extended to the bitter lakes. It is known that the Red Sea at some remote period extended considerably further towards the north than it does at present. In the time of Moses the water north of Kolsum joined the bitter lakes, though at present the constant accumulation of sand has covered the intervening space to the extent of 8000 to 10000 yards, not however rising higher than six feet above the level of the lakes, and from 40 to 50 feet below the level of the Red Sea. Mr Malan, p. 217, observes that the lake Timseh, still further north, is full of

4 And I will harden Pharaoh's
heart, that he shall follow after them;
and I will be honoured upon Pharaoh,
and upon all his host; that the Egyptians may know that I *am* the LORD.
And they did so.
5 ¶ And it was told the king of
Egypt that the people fled: and the
heart of Pharaoh and of his servants
was turned against the people, and
they said, Why have we done this,
that we have let Israel go from serving us?
6 And he made ready his chariot,
and took his people with him:
7 And he took six hundred chosen
chariots, and all the chariots of Egypt,
and captains over every one of them.
8 And the LORD hardened the
heart of Pharaoh king of Egypt, and
he pursued after the children of Israel: and the children of Israel went
out with an high hand.
9 But the [b] Egyptians pursued after [b] Josh. 24. 6.
them, all the horses *and* chariots of 1 Mac. 4.
Pharaoh, and his horsemen, and his 9.
army, and overtook them encamping
by the sea, beside Pi-hahiroth, before
Baal-zephon.
10 ¶ And when Pharaoh drew nigh,
the children of Israel lifted up their
eyes, and, behold, the Egyptians
marched after them; and they were
sore afraid: and the children of Israel
cried out unto the LORD.
11 And they said unto Moses, Be-

---

the Saris or Shari, the arundo Egyptiaca, from which the Red Sea takes its local name.

5. *the people fled*] This was a natural inference from the change of direction, which could have no object but escape from Egypt by the pass at Suez. Up to the time when that information reached Pharaoh both he and his people understood that the Israelites would return after keeping a festival in the district adjoining Etham. From Etham the intelligence would be forwarded by the commander of the garrison to Rameses in less than a day, and the cavalry, a highly disciplined force, would of course be ready for immediate departure.

7. *six hundred chosen chariots*] The Egyptian army comprised large numbers of chariots, each drawn by two horses, with two men, one bearing the shield and driving, the other fully armed. The horses were thorough-bred, renowned for strength and spirit. Chariots are first represented on the monuments of the 18th dynasty: they were used by Amosis I. in the expedition against the shepherd kings, by Thotmes I. against Syria and Mesopotamia: under Thotmes III. we have the record of a battle at Megiddo in which 897 war-chariots were captured from the confederated forces of northern Palestine and Syria. By "all the chariots of Egypt" we are to understand all that were stationed in lower Egypt, most of them probably at Rameses and other frontier garrisons near the head-quarters of Pharaoh. According to Diodorus Siculus, I. 54, the Egyptians had 27000 chariots in the time of Rameses II.

captains over every one of them] Rather **captains over the whole of them.** Thus the LXX., Vulg., Saadia, Syr. The word rendered captains (Shalishim, lit. third or thirtieth) is supposed by Rœdiger, Ges. 'Thes.' s. v., to mean the warriors in the chariots, but the Egyptians never put more than two men in a chariot. The true meaning is captains or commanders. The word may represent an Egyptian title. The king had about him a council of thirty, each of whom bore a title corresponding to the Roman decemvir, viz. Mapu, a "thirty man." See Pleyte, 'Æg. Zeitschrift,' 1866, p. 12, and Chabas, 'Voyage d'un Égyptien.' The word occurs frequently in the books of Kings. David seems to have organized the Shalishim as a distinct corps, see 2 Sam. xxiii. 8, where it is translated, as in this passage, captains. He probably retained the old name, though it is possible that he may have adopted the Egyptian system, being on friendly terms with the contemporary dynasty, which gave a queen to Israel.

9. *and his horsemen*] Horsemen are not represented on Egyptian monuments, even on those of a later age, when they were employed in great numbers; the omission is probably connected with the strict regulations of Egyptian art; but Diodorus Siculus, whose authority is not questioned on this point, states that Rameses II. had a force of 24000 cavalry, independent of the chariotry; Isaiah makes the same distinction between the chariots and horsemen of Egypt, c. xxxi. 1. The technical expression for mounting on horseback is found in ancient papyri.

beside Pi-hahiroth] This statement is urged as an objection to the identification with Ajrud; but the encampment of the great host of Israel extended over many miles.

cause *there were* no graves in Egypt,
hast thou taken us away to die in the
wilderness? wherefore hast thou dealt
thus with us, to carry us forth out of
Egypt?
[c] chap. 6. 9. 12 [c]*Is* not this the word that we
did tell thee in Egypt, saying, Let us
alone, that we may serve the Egyptians? For *it had been* better for us
to serve the Egyptians, than that we
should die in the wilderness.
13 ¶ And Moses said unto the
people, Fear ye not, stand still, and
see the salvation of the LORD, which
‖ Or, *for whereas you have seen the Egyptians to day, &c.* he will shew to you to day: ‖for the
Egyptians whom ye have seen to day,
ye shall see them again no more for
ever.
14 The LORD shall fight for you,
and ye shall hold your peace.
15 ¶ And the LORD said unto Moses, Wherefore criest thou unto me?
speak unto the children of Israel, that
they go forward:
16 But lift thou up thy rod, and
stretch out thine hand over the sea,
and divide it: and the children of Israel shall go on dry *ground* through
the midst of the sea.
17 And I, behold, I will harden
the hearts of the Egyptians, and they
shall follow them: and I will get me
honour upon Pharaoh, and upon all
his host, upon his chariots, and upon
his horsemen.
18 And the Egyptians shall know
that I *am* the LORD, when I have
gotten me honour upon Pharaoh,
upon his chariots, and upon his horsemen.
19 ¶ And the angel of God, which
went before the camp of Israel, removed and went behind them; and
the pillar of the cloud went from before their face, and stood behind
them:
20 And it came between the camp
of the Egyptians and the camp of
Israel; and it was a cloud and darkness *to them*, but it gave light by night
to these: so that the one came not
near the other all the night.
21 And Moses stretched out his
hand over the sea; and the LORD
caused the sea to go *back* by a strong
east wind all that night, and made
the sea dry *land*, and the waters were [d] Josh. 4. 23. Psal. 114. 3.
[d]divided.

---

11. *no graves in Egypt*] This bitter taunt was probably suggested by the vast extent of cemeteries in Egypt, which might not improperly be called the land of tombs: it would scarcely have been imagined by one who had not dwelt there.

12. *Let us alone*] This is a gross exaggeration, yet not without a semblance of truth: for although the Israelites welcomed the message of Moses at first, they gave way completely at the first serious trial. See the reference in marg. The whole passage foreshadows the conduct of the people in the wilderness.

13. *for the Egyptians whom*, &c.] Rather **for as ye have seen the Egyptians** today ye shall see them again no more for ever. Our A.V. follows the Vulg., but the LXX., Targ., Saad. give the true sense, ye shall never see the Egyptians in the same way, under the same circumstances.

15. *Wherefore criest thou unto me?*] Moses does not speak of his intercession, and we only know of it from this answer to his prayer. This is a characteristic of the narrative, important to be observed with reference to other omissions less easily supplied.

19. *the angel of God*] Compare ch. xiii. 21; and see note on ch. iii. 2.

20. The words in Italics are accepted as explanatory by some commentators; but the LXX. read "and the night passed" instead of "it gave light by night." The sense is good and the reading not improbable.

21. *a strong east wind*] It is thus distinctly stated that the agency by which the object was effected was natural. It is clear that Moses takes for granted that a strong east wind blowing through the night, under given circumstances, would make the passage quite possible. It would seem to be scarcely practicable, when the wind blows from other quarters (see Tischendorf's account, 'Aus dem heiligen Lande,' p. 21). Of course this would not explain the effect, if the passage had been made, as was formerly supposed, through the deep sea near the Wady Musa, some leagues south of Suez. All the conditions of the narrative are satisfied by the hypothesis, that the passage took place near Suez.

the waters were divided] *i.e.* there was a complete separation between the water of the gulf and the water to the north of Kolsum.

e Psal. 78. 13. 1 Cor. 10. 1. Heb. 11. 29.

22 And [e] the children of Israel went
into the midst of the sea upon the dry
ground: and the waters *were* a wall
unto them on their right hand, and on
their left.
23 ¶ And the Egyptians pursued,
and went in after them to the midst
of the sea, *even* all Pharaoh's horses,
his chariots, and his horsemen.
24 And it came to pass, that in the
morning watch the LORD looked unto
the host of the Egyptians through the
pillar of fire and of the cloud, and
troubled the host of the Egyptians,
25 And took off their chariot wheels,
‖ that they drave them heavily: so
that the Egyptians said, Let us flee
from the face of Israel; for the LORD
fighteth for them against the Egyptians.
26 ¶ And the LORD said unto Moses,
Stretch out thine hand over the
sea, that the waters may come again
upon the Egyptians, upon their chariots,
and upon their horsemen.
27 And Moses stretched forth his
hand over the sea, and the sea returned
to his strength when the morning appeared;
and the Egyptians fled against
it; and the LORD † overthrew the
Egyptians in the midst of the sea.
28 And the waters returned, and
covered the chariots, and the horsemen,
and all the host of Pharaoh that
came into the sea after them; there remained
not so much as [f] one of them.

‖ Or, *made them to go heavily.*

† Heb. *shook off.*

f Psal. 106. 11.

---

22. *were a wall unto them*] The waters served the purpose of an intrenchment and wall; the people could not be attacked on either flank during the transit; to the north was the water covering the whole district; to the south was the Red Sea. For the idiom, compare Nahum iii. 8.

23. *the Egyptians pursued*] The Egyptians might be aware that under ordinary circumstances there would be abundant time for the passage of the chariots and cavalry, of which the force chiefly consisted.

24. *in the morning watch*] At sunrise, a little before 6 A.M. in April.

troubled] Threw them into confusion by a sudden panic.

25. *And took off their chariot wheels*] This translation is generally accepted. The LXX. however render the word "bound" or clogged (συνέδησε = ויאסר), a probable reading, and perhaps more suited to the context.

26. *that the waters may come*] A sudden cessation of the wind at sunrise, coinciding with a spring tide (it was full moon) would immediately convert the low flat sand-banks first into a quicksand, and then into a mass of waters, in a time far less than would suffice for the escape of a single chariot, or horseman loaded with heavy corslet.

27. *overthrew the Egyptians*] Better as in the margin, **The Lord shook them off**, hurled them from their chariots into the sea. Thus in the papyrus quoted above, when the chariot is broken the warrior is hurled out with such force that his armour is buried in the sand.

28. *not so much as one of them*] The statement is explicit, all the chariots and horsemen and that portion of the infantry which followed them into the bed of the sea. In fact, as has been shewn, escape would be impossible. A doubt has been raised whether Pharaoh himself perished: but independent of the distinct statement of the Psalmist, Ps. cxxxvi. 15, his destruction is manifestly assumed, and was in fact inevitable. The station of the king was in the vanguard: on every monument the Pharaoh is represented as the leader of the army, and allowing for Egyptian flattery on other occasions, that was his natural place in the pursuit of fugitives whom he hated so intensely. The death of the Pharaoh, and the entire loss of the chariotry and cavalry accounts for the undisturbed retreat of the Israelites through a district then subject to Egypt and easily accessible to their forces. The blow to Egypt was not fatal, for the loss of men might not amount to many thousands; but falling upon their king, their leaders and the portion of the army indispensable for the prosecution of foreign wars, it crippled them effectually. If, as appears probable, Tothmosis II. were the Pharaoh, the first recorded expedition into the Peninsula took place 17 years after his death; and twenty-two years elapsed before any measures were taken to recover the lost ascendancy of Egypt in Syria. So complete, so marvellous was the deliverance: thus the Israelites were baptized to Moses in the cloud and in the sea. When they left Baal-Zephon they were separated finally from the idolatry of Egypt: when they passed the Red Sea their independence of its power was sealed; their life as a nation then began, a life inseparable henceforth from belief in Jehovah, and His servant Moses, only to be merged in the higher life revealed by His Son.

29 But the children of Israel walked
upon dry *land* in the midst of the
sea; and the waters *were* a wall unto
them on their right hand, and on
their left.
30 Thus the LORD saved Israel
that day out of the hand of the Egyptians; and Israel saw the Egyptians
dead upon the sea shore.
31 And Israel saw that great † work
which the LORD did upon the Egyptians: and the people feared the LORD,
and believed the LORD, and his servant Moses.

† Heb. *hand.*

NOTE on *v.* 3.

The Hebrew has סגר עליהם המדבר. The LXX. and Vulg. render סגר συγκέκλεικε, conclusit: but it is not followed by an accusative in the Hebrew, and must be intransitive, as it is taken by Saadia انغلق, and the Syr. ܐܬܬܚܕ, *i.e.* conclusum est. Thus in Judges iii. 22, "The fat closed upon the blade." The correct rendering seems to be the wilderness is closed to them. In no sense could the wilderness be a barrier; the direct route led them into it, the change of route shut them out from it.

CHAPTER XV.

1 *Moses' song.* 22 *The people want water.* 23 *The waters at Marah are bitter.* 25 *A tree sweeteneth them.* 27 *At Elim are twelve wells, and seventy palm trees.*

THEN sang [a] Moses and the children of Israel this song unto
the LORD, and spake, saying, I will
sing unto the LORD, for he hath
triumphed gloriously: the horse and
his rider hath he thrown into the sea.
2 The LORD *is* my strength and
song, and he is become my salvation:
he *is* my God, and I will prepare him

[a] Wisd. 1. 20.

CHAP. XV. 1—18. With the deliverance of Israel is associated the development of the national poetry, which finds its first and perfect expression in this magnificent hymn. It is said to have been sung by Moses and the people, an expression which evidently points to him as the author. That it was written at the time is an assertion expressly made in the text, and it is supported by the strongest internal evidence. The style is admitted, even by critics who question its genuineness, to be archaic both in the language, which is equally remarkable for grandeur, and severe simplicity, and in the general structure, which, though rhythmical and systematic, differs materially from later compositions, in which the divisions are more numerous and the arrangement more elaborate. The subject matter and the leading thoughts are such as belong to the time and the occasion; unlike the imitations in the later Psalms, the song abounds in allusions to incidents passing under the eye of the composer: it has every mark of freshness and originality. The only objections are founded on the prophetic portion (15—17): but if ever there was a crisis calculated to elicit the spirit of prophecy, it was that of the Exodus, if ever a man fitted to express that spirit, it was Moses. Even objectors admit that the invasion of Palestine was contemplated by Moses: if so what more natural than that after the great catastrophe, which they accept as an historical fact, he should anticipate the terror of the nations through whose territories the Israelites would pass, and whose destruction was an inevitable condition of their success. In every age this song gave the tone to the poetry of Israel; especially at great critical epochs of deliverance. In the book of Revelation (xv. 3) it is associated with the final triumph of the Church, when the saints "having the harps of God" will sing "the Song of Moses the servant of God, and the Song of the Lamb."

The division of the Song into three parts is distinctly marked: 1—5, 6—10, 11—18: each begins with an ascription of praise to God; each increases in length and varied imagery unto the triumphant close.

FIRST DIVISION. 1—10. Ascription of praise and brief statement of the transaction.

1. *He hath triumphed gloriously*] This gives the true meaning, but not the force and grandeur of the Hebrew, literally He is gloriously glorious. Among the Ancient Versions the LXX, ἐνδόξως δεδόξασται, comes near, the Arabic of Saadia is very fine اقتدر اقتدارا.

an habitation; my father's God, and
I will exalt him.
3 The LORD *is* a man of war: the
LORD *is* his name.
4 Pharaoh's chariots and his host
hath he cast into the sea: his chosen
captains also are drowned in the Red
sea.
5 The depths have covered them:
they sank into the bottom as a stone.
6 Thy right hand, O LORD, is become glorious in power: thy right
hand, O LORD, hath dashed in pieces
the enemy.
7 And in the greatness of thine excellency thou hast overthrown them
that rose up against thee: thou sentest
forth thy wrath, *which* consumed them
as stubble.
8 And with the blast of thy nostrils
the waters were gathered together, the
floods stood upright as an heap, *and*

---

the horse and his rider] The word "rider" may include horseman, but applies properly to the charioteer: the Egyptian word for horse which corresponds exactly to the Hebrew, always designates the swift, high-bred horses used for the war-cars of nobles. Thus in the papyrus 'Anast.' I, "The horses of my chariot are swift as jackals: their eyes like fire: they are like a hurricane when it bursts."

2. *The LORD is my strength and song*] **My strength and song is Jah.** This name is specially associated with victory by the Psalmist, Ps. lxviii. 4. It was doubtless chosen here by Moses to draw attention to the promise ratified by the name "I am." The form of the word "song" in Hebrew is archaic.

I will prepare Him an habitation] **I will glorify Him.** Scholars agree that the Hebrew word means to celebrate with grateful, loving adoration. In fact this sense is given by most of the ancient Versions. Our Authorised Version is open to serious objection, as suggesting a thought (viz. of erecting a temple) which could hardly have been in the mind of Moses at that time, and unsuited to the occasion. It is one of many instances of undue deference to Rabbinical authorities on the part of our translators. The Targum of Onkelos, who is followed by Kimchi, has "I will build Him a sanctuary." Thus too the interlinear Latin in Walton's Polyglott. The LXX., Vulg. and Syr. render the word correctly. Saadia has "I will take refuge with Him."

3. *a man of war*] Compare Ps. xxiv. 8. The name has on this occasion a peculiar fitness; man had no part in the victory: the battle was the Lord's.

the LORD is his name] A pregnant expression, implying that the manifestation of might, by which the salvation of Israel was effected, accorded with the name Jehovah, the most perfect expression of the Divine Essence.

4. *hath He cast*] The Hebrew is very forcible, "hurled," as from a sling. See note on ch. xiv. 27. All the words which describe the fall of the mailed warriors of Egypt are such as one who actually witnessed their overthrow would naturally employ. See note on the next verse.

his chosen captains] The same expression is used in ch. xiv. 7, where see note. It designates officers of the highest rank, chosen specially to attend on the person of Pharaoh: probably commanders of the 2000 Calasirians who alternatively with the Hermotybians formed his body-guard. They may have been for the most part personally known to Moses.

drowned] The original is more graphic, "plunged, submerged," describing the overthrow in the rushing tide.

5. *as a stone*] The warriors on chariots are always represented on the monuments with heavy coats of mail; the corslets of "chosen captains" consisted of plates of highly tempered bronze, with sleeves reaching nearly to the elbow, covering the whole body and the thighs nearly to the knee; see the engraving of the corslet of Rameses III. in Sir G. Wilkinson, 'M. and C.' I. p. 366. They must have sunk at once like a stone, or as we read in v. 10, like lumps of lead. Touches like these come naturally from an eye-witness.

SECOND DIVISION. **6—10.** This division presents the details more fully, and completes the picture by describing the mode in which the destruction was effected, and the arrogance of the Egyptians by which it was provoked.

6. *is become glorious*] The translation is correct, but inadequately represents the force and beauty of the Hebrew word, which is archaic in form and usage.

7. *thy wrath*] lit. Thy burning, *i.e.* the fire of Thy wrath, a word chosen expressly with reference to the effect: it consumed the enemy suddenly, completely, like fire burning up stubble. The simile is not uncommon in Egyptian: thus in the poem of Pentaour addressed to Rameses II. "The people were as stubble before thy chariot:" but the superiority of the Hebrew is obvious—it represents the

the depths were congealed in the heart
of the sea.
9 The enemy said, I will pursue, I
will overtake, I will divide the spoil;
my lust shall be satisfied upon them;
I will draw my sword, my hand shall
‖destroy them.

‖ Or, *repossess.*

10 Thou didst blow with thy wind,
the sea covered them: they sank as
lead in the mighty waters.
11 Who *is* like unto thee, O LORD,
among the ‖gods? who *is* like thee,
glorious in holiness, fearful *in* praises,
doing wonders?

‖ Or, *mighty ones?*

---

flame going forth from the Presence of God. The Hebrew for stubble is also Egyptian.

8. This description has been strangely misrepresented as though it were irreconcileable with the preceding narrative. It differs from that as lyric poetry differs in its imagery from prose; and as inspired poetry it brings us into contact with the hidden and effectual causes of the natural phenomena, which it still distinctly recognizes. The blast of God's nostrils corresponds to the natural agency, the east wind (ch. xiv. 21), which drove the waters back. On each side the Psalmist describes what he must actually have seen: on the north the waters rising high, overhanging the sands, but kept back by the strong wind: on the south lying in massive rollers, kept down by the same agency in the heart, or deep bed of the Red Sea. In both descriptions we have precisely the same effects; in the former the bearings upon the passage of the Israelites are most prominent; in this the scenery is presented in the form which impressed the seer's imagination most vividly, and which fixes itself most strongly on the spirit of the reader.

as an heap] The LXX. render this "as a wall," ὡσεὶ τεῖχος. The Hebrew word probably means "a dam." It corresponds to wall, xiv. 22.

9. *The enemy said*] The abrupt, gasping utterances; the haste, cupidity and ferocity of the Egyptians, the confusion and disorder of their thoughts. are described in terms recognized by critics of all schools as belonging to the highest order of poetry; it must not be forgotten that they enable us to realize the feelings which induced Pharaoh and his host to pursue the Israelites over the treacherous sandbanks.

destroy them] Thus Vulg., Targ., Saad. and most modern critics. The margin follows the LXX. and is defensible.

10. *Thou didst blow with thy wind*] The solemn majesty of these few words, in immediate contrast with the tumult and confusion of the preceding verse, needs scarcely be noticed: it is important to observe that Moses here states distinctly the natural agency by which the destruction was effected. In the direct narrative, xiv. 28, we read only, "the waters returned," here we are told that it was because the wind blew. A sudden change in the direction of the wind would bring back at once the masses of water heaped up on the north. If the tide rose at the same time, the waters of the Red Sea would meet and overwhelm the host: but this is not said, and the Egyptians, who were close observers of natural phenomena, would probably have been aware of the danger of attempting the passage had flood-time been near at hand. One cause is assigned and it suffices for the effect.

they sank as lead] See note on *v.* 4. The sudden drowning of the charioteers as they fell headlong in their heavy panoply must have been one of the most striking features of the scene: hence the repetition, not without a variation, which gives a more exact simile: they fell like masses of lead, helpless, motionless, unable for a moment to struggle with the waters.

THIRD AND LAST DIVISION. After the ascription of praise the seer turns to the remoter, but certain consequences of this unparalleled event. It was impossible that a man in the position and with the feelings of Moses should not revert to them, and at once present them in clear strong language to His people. The deliverance was the earnest of a complete fulfilment of old promises, it was a pledge also that enemies, whom the Israelites could not but dread as their superiors in the arts and resources of war, would be disheartened, and speedily overcome, and that they themselves would be put in possession of the inheritance of Abraham.

11. *among the gods*] The marg. has "mighty ones," which is a possible rendering, adopted in the Vulg. But the translation is quite correct, and justified by other unmistakeable passages; thus in Ps. lxxxvi. 8, "Among the gods there is none like unto Thee," an expression which by no means admits the substantial power of the objects of heathen worship, in which the Israelite recognized either evil spirits or mere phantoms of superstitious imagination; see especially Deut. xxxii. 16, 17. A Hebrew just leaving the land in which Polytheism attained its highest development, with gigantic statues and temples of incomparable grandeur, might well on such an occa-

12 Thou stretchedst out thy right hand, the earth swallowed them.

13 Thou in thy mercy hast led forth the people *which* thou hast redeemed: thou hast guided *them* in thy strength unto thy holy habitation.

14 The [b]people shall hear, *and* be afraid: sorrow shall take hold on the inhabitants of Palestina.

[b] Deut. 2. 25. Josh. 2. 9.

15 Then the dukes of Edom shall be amazed; the mighty men of Moab, trembling shall take hold upon them; all the inhabitants of Canaan shall melt away.

16 [c]Fear and dread shall fall upon them; by the greatness of thine arm they shall be *as* still as a stone; till thy people pass over, O LORD, till the people pass over, *which* thou hast purchased.

[c] Deut. 2. 29. Josh. 2. 5.

---

sion dwell upon this consummation of the long series of triumphs by which the "greatness beyond compare" of Jehovah was once for all established.

12. *the earth swallowed them*] The statement is general, not dwelling on the special mode of the Egyptian overthrow, which had already been fully treated, but serving to mark the transition to a different subject, viz. the effects of the deliverance upon Israel.

13. *thou hast guided them*, &c.] Two objections are made to this, as indicating a later origin; (1) the use of the past tense; but Moses naturally and correctly speaks of the guidance as already begun, God had redeemed the Israelites, and placed them in the way towards Canaan. (2) The words "thy holy habitation" are supposed to refer to the temple at Jerusalem. It would not however be an unsuitable designation for Palestine, regarded as the land of promise, sanctified by manifestations of God to the Patriarchs, and destined to be both the home of God's people, and the place where His glory and purposes were to be perfectly revealed. It is clear that no Hebrew writing before the time of Solomon would have introduced a reference to the temple, and improbable that any one writing afterwards would have put an expression with that meaning into the mouth of Moses. But it is possible that Moses had Mount Moriah in his mind, whether in remembrance of Abraham's offering, or as the result of an immediate inspiration. If so it would be an instance of that not uncommon and most interesting form of prediction in which events separated by a wide interval from the seer's time are realized as impending. Of all predictions such are least likely to be attributed to any writer after their long deferred fulfilment.

14. *The people*] or **the peoples**, an expression now justified by usage, and necessary in this passage to give the true meaning.

the inhabitants of Palestina] In Hebrew Pelasheth, *i.e.* the country of the Philistines. They were the first who would expect an invasion, and the first whose district would have been invaded but for the faintheartedness of the Israelites. It is obvious that the order of thoughts would have been very different had the song been composed at a later period, since in fact Philistia was the last district occupied by the Israelites.

15. *the dukes of Edom*] The specific name used in Genesis xxxvi. 15, where see note It denotes the chieftains, not the kings of Edom: see also Dr W. Smith, 'The Pentateuch,' p. 385.

the mighty men of Moab] The physical strength and great stature of the Moabites are noted in other passages: see Jer. xlviii. 29, 41.

Canaan] The name in this, as in many passages of Genesis, designates the whole of Palestine: and is used of course with reference to the promise to Abraham. It was known to the Egyptians, and occurs frequently on the monuments as Pa-kanana, which according to M. Chabas designates only a large fortress in Syria, but as most Egyptologers hold, and on very solid grounds, applies, if not to the whole of Palestine, yet to the northern district under Lebanon, which the Phœnicians occupied and called Canaan.

16. *shall fall upon them*] Most of the ancient versions use the optative form. Let fear and dread fall upon them, let them be still, *i.e.* motionless, as a stone: thus LXX, Vulg. Such undoubtedly may be the meaning of the Hebrew, but the future is equally, if not more forcible; and the prediction is so general that even those, who reject specific announcements of future events, might accept it as a natural expression of the anticipations of Moses. An objection is taken by some critics to the expression "pass over" as applying specially to the passage over Jordan; the prophecy was doubtless then fulfilled, but that event could not have been in the mind of Moses, since he expected that the entrance would be by the southern frontier; and the term which he uses would be equally applicable to any passing over the physical barriers of Canaan; had indeed the song been composed after that passage it is scarcely possible that some allusion would not have been made to the resemblance between the two miracles.

17 Thou shalt bring them in, and
plant them in the mountain of thine
inheritance, *in* the place, O LORD,
which thou hast made for thee to dwell
in, *in* the Sanctuary, O Lord, *which*
thy hands have established.
18 The LORD shall reign for ever
and ever.
19 For the horse of Pharaoh went
in with his chariots and with his horsemen into the sea, and the LORD brought
again the waters of the sea upon them;
but the children of Israel went on
dry *land* in the midst of the sea.
20 ¶ And Miriam the prophetess,
the sister of Aaron, took a timbrel in
her hand; and all the women went
out after her with timbrels and with
dances.
21 And Miriam answered them,
Sing ye to the LORD, for he hath
triumphed gloriously; the horse and
his rider hath he thrown into the sea.
22 So Moses brought Israel from
the Red sea, and they went out into
the wilderness of Shur; and they went
three days in the wilderness, and found
no water.

---

17. *in the mountain of thine inheritance*] See note on v. 13. The expressions in this verse, especially the word Sanctuary, are in favour of the explanation given in the latter part of that note; but some critics (as Smith 'Pentateuch,' p. 403, and Bleek, 'Einleitung,' p. 274) consider that Palestine is meant.

The psalm closes, not with the conquest of Canaan, but with its ultimate and crowning result, the settlement of the people of Jehovah in the inheritance which he had promised, and in the place which he destined for His Sanctuary.

19. *For the horse*, &c.] This verse does not belong to the hymn, but marks the transition from it to the narrative. Writers, who attribute different portions of the book to various authors, consider that it belongs to the original composition. It is however obviously a summary statement of the cause and subject-matter of the preceding hymn, and as such, assumes its existence.

20 *And Miriam the prophetess*] The part here assigned to Miriam and the women of Israel is in accordance both with Egyptian and Hebrew customs. The men are represented as singing the hymn in chorus, under the guidance of Moses; at each interval Miriam and the women sang the refrain, marking the time with the timbrel, and with the measured rhythmical movements always associated with solemn festivities. Compare Judg. xi. 34, 1 Sam. xviii. 6, and 2 Sam. vi. 5. A representation of women dancing, some with boughs in their hand, others playing on timbrels, or tambourines of various shapes, some square and some round, is given by Wilkinson, 'M. and C.' I. p. 93. The word used in this passage for the timbrel is Egyptian, and judging from its etymology and the figures which are joined with it in the inscriptions, it was probably the round instrument. See Brugsch, 'D. H.' p. 1323, and 1534.

Miriam is called a prophetess, evidently, as appears from Numbers xii. 2, because she and Aaron had received divine communications. The word is used here in its proper sense of uttering words suggested by the Spirit of God. On the use and meaning of the word see note on Genesis xx. 7. She is called the sister of Aaron, most probably to indicate her special position as co-ordinate, not with Moses the leader of the nation, but with his chief aid and instrument. It is evident, however, that this designation, most natural in the mouth of Moses, who would be careful to record the names of his brother and sister on such an occasion, was not likely to have been applied to Miriam by a later writer.

22. *So Moses*] Lit. **And Moses.** The word *so* gives the impression of a closer connection with the preceding verse than is suggested by the Hebrew. The history of the journey from the Red Sea to Sinai begins in fact with this verse, which would more conveniently have been the commencement of another chapter.

from the Red sea] The station where Moses and his people halted to celebrate their deliverance is generally admitted to be the Ayoun Musa, *i.e.* the fountains of Moses. It is the only green spot near the passage over the Red Sea. There are several wells there (17 according to Dr Stanley, p. 67, 7 according to Robinson, p. 62). Tischendorf, whose description is fuller than that of other travellers and gives a more pleasing impression, counted 19, and observes that the vegetation indicates a still larger number. 'Aus dem heiligen Lande,' p. 22. The water, like all the water on the western coast of the Peninsula, is dark-coloured and brackish, but it is drinkable, and is said to be highly prized by the people of Suez, whose richer inhabitants formerly built country houses, and laid out gardens in the place. At present the German consul has a garden of

23 ¶ And when they came to
Marah, they could not drink of the
waters of Marah, for they *were* bitter:
therefore the name of it was called
[That is, *Bitterness*.] Marah.
24 And the people murmured
against Moses, saying, What shall we
drink?
25 And he cried unto the LORD;
[Ecclus. 38. 5.] and the LORD shewed him a [d]tree,
which when he had cast into the
waters, the waters were made sweet:
there he made for them a statute and
an ordinance, and there he proved
them,
26 And said, If thou wilt diligently
hearken to the voice of the LORD thy
God, and wilt do that which is right
in his sight, and wilt give ear to his
commandments, and keep all his statutes, I will put none of these diseases
upon thee, which I have brought upon
the Egyptians: for I *am* the LORD
that healeth thee.

---

considerable extent and beauty, described by Tischendorf. Wellsted found there about twenty clumps of palm-trees, the branches of which were so closely interwoven that they formed a dense impervious shade, affording shelter to the Arabs. According to M. Monge (quoted by Robinson, p. 62) there was formerly an aqueduct extending to the sea so as to form a watering place for ships. In the time of Moses the wells were probably inclosed and kept with great care by the Egyptians, for the use of the frequent convoys to and from their ancient settlements at Sarbut el Khadem and the Wady Mughara.

the wilderness of Shur] This name belongs to the whole district between the north-eastern frontier of Egypt and Palestine. The word is undoubtedly Egyptian, whether derived from the name of the fortress on the frontier, called the Fort of Zor, or more probably from the word Khar, which designated all the country between Egypt and Syria proper. Thus in a papyrus of the 19th dynasty ('Anast.' III. 1, l. 7) we read "The land of Khar from Zor to Aup," a city in Syria. 'Kh' and 'Sh' are constantly interchanged in transcription: see Chabas, 'V. E.' p. 97. In Numbers xxxiii. 8, the more special designation is used, viz. "the wilderness of Etham," a strong corroboration of the view that Etham was not on the west of the Bitter lakes, but at their northern extremity.

three days] The distance between Ayoun Musa and Huwara, the first spot where any water is found on the route, is 33 geographical miles. A small fountain Abu Suweira, near the sea, and another called the Cup of Sudr on the east, some hours distant from the road, were of course known to Moses, but would be of little, if any use to the host. The whole district is a tract of sand, or rough gravel; the wadys are depressions in the desert, with only a few scattered herbs and shrubs, withered and parched by drought: the road afterwards continues through hills of limestone equally destitute of vegetation, some exhibiting an abundance of crystallized sulphate of lime.

23. *Marah*] The identification of Marah with the fount of Huwara, first proposed by Burckhardt, is now generally accepted. The fountain rises from a large mound, a whitish petrifaction, deposited by the water. At present no water flows, but there are traces of a running stream, and in the time of Moses, when the road was kept by the Egyptians and vegetation was more abundant, the source was probably far more copious. The water is considered by the Arabians to be the worst in the whole district. Two stunted palm-trees now stand near it, and the ground is covered by thickets of the ghurkud (Peganum retusum, Forskal), a low bushy thorny shrub, producing a small fruit which ripens in June, not unlike the barberry, very juicy and slightly acidulous; see Robinson, p. 66. Burckhardt, 'Syria,' p. 474, suggested that the juice might possibly be used to sweeten the water, but no such process is known to the Bedouins, and the fruit would not be ripe about Easter, when the Israelites reached the place. Wellsted observes that when he tasted the water and muttered the word "Marah" his Bedouin said "You speak the word of truth: they are indeed Mara." The Arabic word Huwara means "ruin," "destruction" (Freytag); but "bitter" and "deadly" are with the Arabs, as with the Hebrews, convertible terms.

25. *a tree*] The statement evidently points to a natural agency. The miracle was not wrought without the tree. This is in accordance with the whole spirit of the narrative. There may possibly have been some resemblance to a mode of purifying stagnant waters, such as Josephus and Du Boys Aimé describe, by thrusting long sticks into the bottom of a spring and eliciting a fresh supply: but the result was manifestly supernatural.

he made, &c.] The Lord then set before them the fundamental principle of implicit trust, to be shewn by obedience. The healing of the water was a symbol of deliverance from physical and spiritual evils.

[e] Numb. 33. 9.

27 ¶ [e]And they came to Elim,
where *were* twelve wells of water, and
three score and ten palm trees: and
they encamped there by the waters.

CHAPTER XVI.

1 *The Israelites come to Sin.* 2 *They murmur for want of bread.* 4 *God promiseth them bread from heaven.* 11 *Quails are sent,* 14 *and manna.* 16 *The ordering of manna.* 25 *It was not to be found on the sabbath.* 32 *An omer of it is preserved.*

AND they took their journey from
Elim, and all the congregation
of the children of Israel came unto
the wilderness of Sin, which *is* between Elim and Sinai, on the fifteenth
day of the second month after their
departing out of the land of Egypt.

2 And the whole congregation of
the children of Israel murmured against
Moses and Aaron in the wilderness:

3 And the children of Israel said
unto them, Would to God we had
died by the hand of the LORD in the
land of Egypt, when we sat by the
flesh pots, *and* when we did eat bread
to the full; for ye have brought us
forth into this wilderness, to kill this
whole assembly with hunger.

4 ¶ Then said the LORD unto Moses, Behold, I will rain bread from
heaven for you; and the people shall
go out and gather †a certain rate every
day, that I may prove them, whether
they will walk in my law, or no.

5 And it shall come to pass, that

† Heb. *the portion of a day in his day.*

---

27. *Elim*] At a distance of two hours' journey south of Huwara is the large and beautiful valley of Gharandel (Girondel, Niebuhr, p. 183). In the rainy season a considerable torrent flows through it, discharging its waters in the Red Sea. Even in the dry season water is still found, which though somewhat brackish after long drought (Robinson), is generally good, and according to all travellers the best on the whole journey from Cairo to Sinai. The grass there grows thick and high, there is abundance of brushwood, with tamarisks and acacias; a few palm-trees still remain, relics of the fair grove which once covered this Oasis of the western side of the Peninsula. The only objection to the identification of this valley with Elim is the shortness of the distance, but the inducement for the encampment is obvious, and no other site corresponds with the main conditions of the narrative. The Israelites remained a considerable time in this neighbourhood, since they did not reach the wilderness of Sin till two months and a half after leaving Suez. They would find water and pasturage in the district between Elim and the station on the Red Sea, mentioned in Numbers xxxiii. 10: which appears to have been at the further end of the Wadi Tayibe, a journey of eight hours, near the headland of Ras Selima. The whole valley is said to be beautiful, full of tamarisks and other shrubs, the Tarfa-tree and the Palm. Water is found in it, though far inferior to that in Gharandel. The station at the Red Sea then visited by the Israelites was of considerable importance, the starting point for the roads to the copper-mines of the Wadi Mughara, Sarbut el Khadem, and the Wadi Nasb.

twelve wells] Read **springs**; the Hebrew denotes natural sources. These springs may have been perennial when a richer vegetation clothed the adjacent heights. They certainly supplied copious streams when the Israelites "encamped there by the waters."

CHAP. XVI. 1. *the wilderness of Sin*] The desert tract, called Debbet er Ramleh, extends nearly across the peninsula from the Wady Nasb in a south-easterly direction, between the limestone district of El Tih and the granite of Sinai. The journey from the station at Elim, or even from that on the Red Sea, could be performed in a day: at that time the route was kept in good condition by the Egyptians who worked the copper-mines at Sarbut el Khadim. The text seems to imply that the Israelites proceeded in detachments, and were first assembled as a complete host when they reached the wilderness of Sin.

2. *murmured*] The want of food was first felt after six weeks from the time of the departure from Egypt, see *v.* 1: we have no notice previously of any deficiency of bread.

3. *by the hand of the LORD*] This evidently refers to the plagues, especially the last, in Egypt: the death which befell the Egyptians appeared to the people preferable to the sufferings of famine.

flesh pots, and...bread] These expressions prove that the servile labours to which they had been subjected did not involve privation: they were fed abundantly, either by the officials of Pharaoh, or more probably by the produce of their own fertile district. The word used for flesh-pots is Egyptian, the name and representation are given in Brugsch, 'D. H.' p. 1264.

4. *rain bread from heaven*] This marks at the outset the strictly supernatural character of the supply. Without such supply the vast host of the Israelites could not have subsisted

on the sixth day they shall prepare
that which they bring in; and it shall
be twice as much as they gather daily.
6 And Moses and Aaron said unto
all the children of Israel, At even,
then ye shall know that the LORD
hath brought you out from the land
of Egypt:
7 And in the morning, then ye shall
see the glory of the LORD; for that
he heareth your murmurings against
the LORD: and what *are* we, that ye
murmur against us?
8 And Moses said, *This shall be*,
when the LORD shall give you in the
evening flesh to eat, and in the morning bread to the full; for that the
LORD heareth your murmurings which
ye murmur against him: and what *are*
we? your murmurings *are* not against
us, but against the LORD.
9 ¶ And Moses spake unto Aaron,
Say unto all the congregation of the
children of Israel, Come near before
the LORD: for he hath heard your
murmurings.
10 And it came to pass, as Aaron
spake unto the whole congregation of
the children of Israel, that they looked
toward the wilderness, and, behold,
the glory of the LORD [a]appeared in [a] chap. 13.
the cloud. 21.
11 ¶ And the LORD spake unto
Moses, saying,
12 I have heard the murmurings
of the children of Israel: speak unto
them, saying, At even ye shall eat
flesh, and in the morning ye shall be
filled with bread; and ye shall know
that I *am* the LORD your God.
13 And it came to pass, that at
even [b]the quails came up, and covered [b] Numb.
the camp: and in the morning the 11. 31. [c] Numb.
dew lay round about the host. 11. 7.
14 And when [c]the dew that lay Psal. 78. 24.
was gone up, behold, upon the face of Wisd. 16. 20.

---

for a considerable time in any part of the Peninsula.

a certain rate every day] Lit. as in the margin, "the portion of a day in its day:" *i. e.* the quantity sufficient for one day's consumption: this may be better expressed "a day's portion each day."

that I may prove them] The trial consisted in the restriction to the supply of their daily wants.

5. *it shall be twice as much*] The meaning evidently is that they should collect and prepare a double quantity, not (as has been assumed, in order to make out a contradiction with *v.* 22) that the quantity collected would be miraculously increased afterwards.

7. *the glory of the LORD*] Some commentators understand this to mean the manifestation of His power and goodness in supplying the people with food; but it refers to the visible appearance described in *v.* 10.

8. *not against us*] *i. e.* according to a common Hebrew idiom, not so much against us as against the Lord; the murmuring implied a distrust of the people in the divine mission of their leaders, notwithstanding the previous miracles.

9. The preceding paragraph from *v.* 3 describes the conference between the people and their leaders: the result was a summons to meet Him whom they represented, *i. e.* to assemble in the open space before the tabernacle.

10. *appeared in the cloud*] Or, "was seen in a cloud." The definite article would imply that the cloud was the same which is often mentioned in connection with the tabernacle. The people saw the cloud here spoken of beyond the camp.

12. *flesh...bread*] These expressions refer to the previous murmuring of the people, *v.* 3. God gives them in His own way that which they longed for: this is a clear proof that the narrative is continuous and that the preceding passage is not (as Knobel assumes) an interpolation: see also notes on *vv.* 16 and 27.

13. *quails*] The identification of the Hebrew, "slav," with the common quail may be assumed as certain. The name is applied in Arabic to that bird: it migrates in immense numbers in spring from the south: it is nowhere more common than in the neighbourhood of the Red Sea. When exhausted by a long flight it is easily captured even with the hand. The flesh is palatable and not unwholesome when eaten in moderation. In this passage we read of a single flight so dense that it covered the encampment. The miracle consisted in the precise time of the arrival and its coincidence with the announcement. Other explanations of the name have been given, but this alone meets all the conditions.

the dew lay round] Lit. "a lying of dew

the wilderness *there lay* a small round
thing, *as* small as the hoar frost on
the ground.
15 And when the children of Israel
saw *it*, they said one to another, ‖It
is manna: for they wist not what it
was. And Moses said unto them,
[d]This *is* the bread which the LORD
hath given you to eat.
16 ¶ This *is* the thing which the
LORD hath commanded, Gather of it
every man according to his eating, an
omer †for every man, *according to* the
number of your †persons; take ye
every man for *them* which *are* in his
tents.
17 And the children of Israel did
so, and gathered, some more, some
less.
18 And when they did mete *it* with
an omer, [e]he that gathered much had
nothing over, and he that gathered
little had no lack; they gathered every
man according to his eating.
19 And Moses said, Let no man
leave of it till the morning.
20 Notwithstanding they hearkened
not unto Moses; but some of them

‖ Or, *What is this?* or, *It is a portion.*
d John 6. 31. 1 Cor. 10. 3.
† Heb. *by the poll*, or, *head.*
† Heb. *souls.*
e 2 Cor. 8. 15.

---

round the camp." This is generally understood to mean there was a heavy fall of dew round the encampment. Knobel explains it to be a dense mist, but the usage seems to be that which is recognized by the Authorised Version and all the ancient versions. There are many indications that the season was unusually humid, natural agencies concurring with supernatural interpositions. Manna is found in abundance in wet seasons, in dry seasons it ceases altogether.

On Manna, see note at the end of the chapter.

14. *a small round thing*] The meaning of the Hebrew is questioned (see note below), but there is good authority for our version, which is true to nature: manna appears in small, compact grains. Here we have a resemblance in shape and appearance, but natural manna is not found on the open plain, "the face of the wilderness," but on dry leaves, or the ground under the tamarisk, from the trunk and branches of which it exudes.

15. *It is manna*] This rendering is disputed. The Old Versions concur in rendering the phrase "What is this?" But oriental scholars are generally agreed that this explanation is not borne out by ancient usage, and that the Israelites said "this is *man*." The word "man" they explain by reference to the Arabic, in which it means "gift." The Egyptian language seems to afford the true solution. It has been very lately shown that "man" or man-hut, *i. e.* white manna, was the name under which the substance was known to the Egyptians, and therefore to the Israelites; see note below. When they saw it on the ground they would of course at once recognize it. They wist not what it was: for in fact it was not natural manna, but a heavenly gift. Our Version should therefore be retained, and the passage may be thus explained. When the Israelites saw the small round thing, they said at once "this is manna," but with an exclamation of surprise at finding it on the open plain, in such immense quantities, under circumstances so unlike what they could have expected: in fact they did not know what it really was, only what it resembled.

16. *according to his eating*] This refers to *v.* 4; it was a trial of the faith of the people, since they were to gather just enough for a day's consumption. The reference is noticeable as an additional argument against Knobel's assumption of an interpolation; see note on *v.* 12.

an omer] *i. e.* the tenth part of an Ephah, see *v.* 36. The exact quantity cannot be determined, since the measures varied at different times. Josephus makes the omer equal to six cotylæ, or half-pints. The ephah was an Egyptian measure, supposed to be about a bushel or one-third of a hin. See Brugsch, 'D. H.' pp. 49, 50. The word omer, in this sense, occurs in no other passage. It was probably not used at a later period, belonging, like many other words, to the time of Moses. It is found in old Egyptian, but with the meaning "storehouse" (see Birch, 'D. H.' p. 363. Brugsch does not give it). See Lev. xix. 36.

man...persons] Lit. as in the margin, **head**, and **souls**, which should be retained as in many other passages.

17. *some more, some less*] It is evidently implied that the people were in part at least disobedient and failed in this first trial.

18. *had nothing over*] The result is undoubtedly represented as miraculous. The Jewish interpreters understand by this statement that whatever quantity each person had gathered, when he measured it in his tent, he found that he had just as many omers as he needed for the consumption of his family: and this is probably the true meaning. It is adopted by Knobel and Keil.

20. *it bred worms*] This result was super-

left of it until the morning, and it
bred worms, and stank: and Moses
was wroth with them.
21 And they gathered it every
morning, every man according to his
eating: and when the sun waxed hot,
it melted.
22 ¶ And it came to pass, *that* on
the sixth day they gathered twice as
much bread, two omers for one *man*:
and all the rulers of the congregation
came and told Moses.
23 And he said unto them, This
is that which the LORD hath said,
To morrow *is* the rest of the holy
sabbath unto the LORD: bake *that*
which ye will bake *to day*, and seethe
that ye will seethe; and that which
remaineth over lay up for you to be
kept until the morning.
24 And they laid it up till the morning, as Moses bade: and it did not
stink, neither was there any worm
therein.
25 And Moses said, Eat that to
day; for to day *is* a sabbath unto the
LORD: to day ye shall not find it in
the field.
26 Six days ye shall gather it; but
on the seventh day, *which is* the sabbath, in it there shall be none.
27 ¶ And it came to pass, *that*
there went out *some* of the people on
the seventh day for to gather, and
they found none.
28 And the LORD said unto Moses,
How long refuse ye to keep my commandments and my laws?
29 See, for that the LORD hath given
you the sabbath, therefore he giveth

---

natural: no such tendency to rapid decomposition is recorded of common manna.

21. *it melted*] This refers to the manna which was not gathered. It is noted in all accounts of common manna that it is melted by the heat of the sun.

22. *twice as much bread*] This was in accordance with God's command to Moses *v.* 5, which it is not probable he had omitted to communicate to the people, though the fact is unnoticed in the narrative. The rulers of the congregation appear to have applied to Moses for instructions as to what was to be done under these circumstances, fearing possibly the recurrence of the result mentioned above, *v.* 20. Knobel supposes that the people acted unconsciously, God permitting them to gather a double quantity, but the other explanation is far more natural.

From this passage and from *v.* 5 it is inferred that the seventh day was previously known to the people as a day separate from all others, and if so, it must have been observed as an ancient and primeval institution. No other account of the command (given without any special explanation), or of the conduct of the people, who collected the manna, is satisfactory: thus Rosenmüller, and others. It is at the same time evident that Moses took this opportunity of enforcing a strict and more solemn observance of the day.

23. *To morrow is the rest of the holy sabbath unto the LORD*] Or, **To-morrow is a rest, a Sabbath holy to Jehovah:** *i.e.* to-morrow must be a day of rest, observed strictly as a sabbath, or festal rest, holy to Jehovah. It is at once a statement, and an injunction. The people knew it as the Sabbath, they were to observe it as a great festival.

bake, &c.] These directions shew that the manna thus given differed essentially from the natural product. Here and in Numbers xi. 8 it is treated in a way which shews it had the properties of corn, could be ground in a mortar, baked and boiled. Ordinary manna is used as honey, it cannot be ground, it melts when exposed to a moderate heat forming a substance like barley sugar, called manna tabulata. In Persia it is boiled with water and brought to the consistency of honey. The Arabs also boil the leaves to which it adheres, and the manna thus dissolved floats on the water as a glutinous or oily substance (Rosenmüller, Niebuhr, &c.). It is obvious that these accounts are inapplicable to the manna from heaven, which had the characteristics and nutritive properties of bread.

25. *Eat that to day*] The practical observance of the Sabbath was thus formally instituted before the giving of the law. The people were to abstain from the ordinary work of every-day life: they were not to collect food, nor, as it would seem, even to prepare it as on other days.

27. *there went out some of the people*] This was an act of wilful disobedience. It is remarkable, being the first violation of the express command, that it was not visited by a signal chastisement: the rest and peace of the "Holy Sabbath" were not disturbed by a manifestation of wrath.

28. *How long*] The reference to *v.* 4 is obvious. The prohibition involved a trial of

you on the sixth day the bread of two
days; abide ye every man in his place,
let no man go out of his place on the
seventh day.
30 So the people rested on the
seventh day.
31 And the house of Israel called
the name thereof Manna: and it *was*
like coriander seed, white; and the
taste of it *was* like wafers *made* with
honey.
32 ¶ And Moses said, This *is* the
thing which the LORD commandeth,
Fill an omer of it to be kept for your
generations; that they may see the
bread wherewith I have fed you in
the wilderness, when I brought you
forth from the land of Egypt.
33 And Moses said unto Aaron,
Take a pot, and put an omer full of
manna therein, and lay it up before the
LORD, to be kept for your generations.
34 As the LORD commanded Mo-
ses, so Aaron laid it up before the
Testimony, to be kept.
35 And the children of Israel did
eat manna forty years, *f* until they *f* Josh. 5.
came to a land inhabited; they did 12. Neh. 9. 15
eat manna, until they came unto the
borders of the land of Canaan.
36 Now an omer *is* the tenth *part*
of an ephah.

---

faith, in which as usual the people were found wanting. Every miracle formed some part, so to speak, of an educational process.

29. *abide ye every man in his place*] This is an additional injunction. They were to remain within the camp. The expression in Hebrew is peculiar and seems almost to enjoin a position of complete repose, "in his place," lit. under himself, as the Oriental sits with his legs drawn up under him. The prohibition must however be understood with reference to its immediate object; they were not to go forth from their place in order to gather manna, which was on other days without the camp. The spirit of the law is sacred rest. The Lord gave them this Sabbath, as a blessing and privilege. It was "made for man." A Jewish sect called Masbothei, *i.e.* Sabbatarians, took this text as a command that no man should change his position from the morning to the evening of the Sabbath; see Routh on 'Hegesippus,' R. S. I. p. 225.

31. *Manna*] This refers of course to their first exclamation, confirmed after a week's experience. It was not indeed the common manna, as they then seem to have believed, but the properties which are noted in this passage are common to it and the natural product: in size, form and colour it resembled the seed of the white coriander, a small round grain of a whitish or yellowish grey. The wafer made with honey is called by the LXX. ἐγκρὶς ἐν μέλιτι, *i.e.* according to Athenæus a cake of meal, oil and honey.

32. *Fill an omer*] This was probably done at the end of the first week; but the order to Aaron may have been repeated when the tabernacle was fitted up with its appurtenances.

33. *a pot*] The word here used occurs in no other passage. It corresponds in form and use to the Egyptian for a casket or vase in which oblations were presented. Br. D. H. p. 1644.

35. *did eat manna forty years*] This does not necessarily imply that the Israelites were fed exclusively on manna, or that the supply was continuous during forty years: but that whenever it might be needed, owing to the total or partial failure of other food, it was given until they entered the promised land. They had numerous flocks and herds, which were not slaughtered (see Numbers xi. 22), but which gave them milk, cheese and of course a limited supply of flesh: nor is there any reason to suppose that during a considerable part of that time they may not have cultivated some spots of fertile ground in the wilderness. We may assume, as in most cases of miracle, that the supernatural supply was commensurate with their actual necessity. Dr W. Smith, p. 365, observes the peculiarity of the expression. Moses gives a complete history of manna till the end of his own life. The manna was not withheld in fact until the Israelites had passed the Jordan. Moses writes as a historian, not as a prophet. What he knew as fact was that it lasted until he penned this passage. A later writer would have been more specific.

36. *an omer*] This definition of an omer has been attributed to a later hand, a gloss inserted to explain an obsolete word, "omer" occurring only in this passage as the name of a measure; on the other hand, it has been argued that Moses, as a legislator, would be careful to define what was probably a new measure; both omer and ephah are Egyptian words.

NOTE ON MANNA.

It is well to bring together the facts which are certainly known from ancient and modern authorities. They leave no doubt, on the one hand, as to the connection between the manna of Exodus and the natural production: or on the other, as to the supernatural character of the former. Both points are admitted alike by critics who believe, or disbelieve the sacred narrative: the only question between them is the truth of the writer; his intention and meaning are unmistakeable.

The manna of the Peninsula of Sinai is the sweet juice of the Tarfa, a species of tamarisk. It exudes from the trunk and branches in hot weather, and forms small round white grains. In cool weather it preserves its consistency, in hot weather it melts rapidly. It is either gathered from the twigs of the tamarisk, or from the fallen leaves underneath the tree. The colour is a greyish yellow. It begins to exude in May, and lasts about six weeks. The Arabs cleanse it from leaves and dirt, boil it down, strain it through coarse stuff and keep it in leather bags: they use it as honey with bread. Its taste is sweet, with a slight aromatic flavour: travellers generally compare it with honey. According to Ehrenberg it is produced by the puncture of an insect. It is abundant in rainy seasons, many years it ceases altogether. The whole quantity now produced in a single year does not exceed 600 or 700 pounds. It is found in the district between the Wady Gharandel, *i.e.* Elim, and Sinai, in the Wady Sheich, and in some other parts of the Peninsula. For each of these statements we have the concurrent testimony of travellers. Seetzen in 1807 was the first who described the natural product with scientific accuracy: see Kruse's notes on Seetzen, Vol. IV. p. 416. The resemblance in colour, shape, taste, and in the time and place of the appearance is exact. The name is also that now given to the product, well known as its Arabic designation, and, as we have shewn, found also on Egyptian monuments.

The differences however are equally unmistakeable. 1. The manna of Exodus was not found under the tamarisk tree, but on the surface of the wilderness, after the disappearance of the morning dew. 2. The quantity which was gathered in a single day far exceeded the annual produce at present, and probably at the time of Moses. 3. The supply ceased on the Sabbath-day. 4. The properties differed from common manna; it could be ground, baked, and in other respects treated like meal. It was not used merely as a condiment, or medicine, but had the nutritive qualities of bread. 5. It was found after leaving the district where it is now produced, until the Israelites reached the land of Canaan.

It is to be observed that we have all the conditions and characteristics of Divine interpositions. (1) The condition of a recognized necessity: for all writers agree that under any conceivable circumstances the preservation of the Israelites would otherwise have been impossible. (2) The condition of a harmony with a Divine purpose, the preservation of a peculiar people on which the whole scheme of providential government and the salvation of mankind depended. (3) We have the usual characteristics of harmony between the natural order of events and the supernatural transaction. God fed His people not with the food which belonged to other regions, but with such as appertained to the district. The local colouring is unmistakeable. We may not attempt to give an explanation how the change was effected; to such a question we have but to answer that we know nothing. One thing certain is, that if Moses wrote this narrative, it is impossible that he could be deceived, and equally impossible that he could have deceived contemporaries and eye-witnesses. As for ourselves, we must be content to bear the reproach that we are satisfied with a reference to the Almightiness of Jehovah, in which alone faith finds any explanation of the mystery of the universe.

מְחֻסְפָּס. LXX. *ὡσεὶ κόριον λευκόν*, Vulg. quasi pilo tusum. Ch. מְקַלַּף, and Syr. ܡܩܠܦܐ, decorticatum. Saad. مدحرج, round. These renderings seem to be conjectural. Gesenius derives the word from حسف, Chal. חְסַף to peel: and explains the phrase "a small thing, as something peeled." This explanation has in its favour the Egyptian usage, in which "heseb" means "peel." Brugsch, 'D. H.' p. 994. Knobel points out that in that case a particle of comparison would be required, and compares حشف, frost, hoar-frost, understanding it to describe a small compact granular substance. In this he is followed by Keil.

מָן is the Chaldaic form for מָה, what? but there is no vestige of the use in the ancient language. Thus Gesenius and Knobel; Keil assumes it to be the popular, and old Semitic form, but gives no proof. The meaning "gift" was first suggested by Kimchi, מתנה וחלק, gift and portion. Gesenius derives it from מנה, to distribute or apportion. The Arabic من (mann) is adduced in support of the meaning "gift," but as Keil points out it is probably taken from the Hebrew Manna. Kalisch mentions the conjecture of Rashbam that the word was probably Egyptian, for which, as he observes truly, no proof could be adduced. The conjecture was a happy one, and the proof is now found. Brugsch gives the word, see 'D. H.' p. 655. "Mennu," "identical with the Hebrew מָן, Arabic من." It is found among other articles in a basket of oblations at Apollinopolis. Under another form it appears as Mannu-hut, *i.e.* white Manna, and is described as the product of a tree, probably a species of Tamarisk.

CHAPTER XVII.

1 *The people murmur for water at Rephidim.* 5 *God sendeth him for water to the rock in Horeb.* 8 *Amalek is overcome by the holding up of Moses' hands.* 15 *Moses buildeth the altar Jehovah-nissi.*

AND all the congregation of the
children of Israel journeyed
from the wilderness of Sin, after their
journeys, according to the commandment of the LORD, and pitched in
Rephidim: and *there was* no water for
the people to drink.
a Numb. 20. 4. 2 Wherefore [a] the people did chide
with Moses, and said, Give us water
that we may drink. And Moses said
unto them, Why chide ye with me?
wherefore do ye tempt the LORD?
3 And the people thirsted there for
water; and the people murmured
against Moses, and said, Wherefore
is this *that* thou hast brought us up out
of Egypt, to kill us and our children
and our cattle with thirst?
4 And Moses cried unto the LORD,
saying, What shall I do unto this
people? they be almost ready to stone
me.
5 And the LORD said unto Moses,
Go on before the people, and take
with thee of the elders of Israel; and
thy rod, wherewith [b] thou smotest the b chap. 7. 20.
river, take in thine hand, and go.
6 [c] Behold, I will stand before thee c Numb. 20. 9.
there upon the rock in Horeb; and Psal. 78. 15.
thou shalt smite the rock, and there & 105. 41.
shall come water out of it, that the Wisd. 11. 4.
people may drink. And Moses did 1 Cor. 10. 4.
so in the sight of the elders of
Israel.
7 And he called the name of the ‖ That is, *Tentation.*
place ‖ Massah, and ‖ Meribah, because ‖ That is, *Chiding,* or, *Strife.*
of the chiding of the children of Israel,

CHAP. XVII. 1. *according to their journeys*] The Israelites rested at two stations before they reached Rephidim, viz. Dophkah and Alush: see Numbers xxxiii. 12—14. According to Knobel, whose view is adopted by Keil, and appears, on the whole, to accord best with the Biblical notices and the accounts of travellers, Dophkah was in the Wady Seih, a day's journey from the Wady Nasb; traces of the ancient name were found by Seetzen at a place called El Tabbacha in a rocky pass, El Kineh, where Egyptian antiquities still remain, indicating the ancient route. The wilderness of Sin properly speaking ends here, the sandstone ceases, and is replaced by the porphyry and granite which belong to the central formation of the Sinaitic group. Alush lay on the way towards Rephidim; the identification with Ash is doubtful, the distance from Horeb exceeding a day's march. Alush may have been near the entrance to the Wady Sheich.

Rephidim] On the identification of Rephidim see note at the end of this book.

2. *tempt the LORD*] It is a general characteristic of the Israelites that the miracles, which met each need as it arose, failed to produce a habit of faith: but the severity of the trial, the faintness and anguish of thirst in the burning desert, must not be overlooked in appreciating their conduct. "I thirst" was the only expression of bodily suffering wrung from our Lord on the Cross.

4. *they be almost ready to stone me*] Lit. **yet a little and they will stone me.** The Authorised Version gives the meaning, but not the liveliness and force of the Hebrew.

6. *the rock in Horeb*] The name Horeb signifies "dry, parched," and evidently points to a distinct miracle. At what point Moses struck the rock cannot be determined; but it would seem to have been in the presence of the Elders as selected witnesses, not in the sight of the people, and therefore not near the summit.

It is questioned whether the water thus supplied ceased with the immediate occasion. St Paul calls it "a spiritual drink," and adds, "that all the Israelites drank of the spiritual rock which followed them, and that rock was Christ." 1 Cor. x. 4. The interpretation of that passage belongs to the New Testament: but the general meaning appears to be that their wants were ever supplied from Him, of whom the rock was but a symbol, and who accompanied them in all their wanderings. Two traditions of the Rabbins are noticeable: one, that the rock thus smitten actually followed the Israelites, another, that the stream of water went with them. There is no justification for these fables in the sacred narrative. The repetition of the miracle (see Numbers xx. 11) excludes the second, the first needs no refutation.

7. *Massah*] The word is derived from that which is used by Moses, *v.* 2. Meribah, as is stated in the margin, means "chiding," referring also to *v.* 2. The names were retained from that time, nor are Rephidim and Kadesh mentioned by later writers: they belong to the time of Moses. On the im-

and because they tempted the LORD,
saying, Is the LORD among us, or not?
[d] Deut. 25. 17. 8 ¶ [d]Then came Amalek, and
Wisd. 11. 3. fought with Israel in Rephidim.
[e] Called *Jesus*, Acts 7. 45. 9 And Moses said unto [e]Joshua,
Choose us out men, and go out, fight
with Amalek: to morrow I will stand
on the top of the hill with the rod of
God in mine hand.
10 So Joshua did as Moses had said
to him, and fought with Amalek: and
Moses, Aaron, and Hur went up to
the top of the hill.
11 And it came to pass, when Moses held up his hand, that Israel prevailed: and when he let down his
hand, Amalek prevailed.
12 But Moses' hands *were* heavy;
and they took a stone, and put *it* under him, and he sat thereon; and
Aaron and Hur stayed up his hands,
the one on the one side, and the other
on the other side; and his hands were
steady until the going down of the
sun.
13 And Joshua discomfited Amalek
and his people with the edge of the
sword.

---

portance of this lesson see our Lord's words, Matt. iv. 7.

8. *Then came Amalek*] The attack upon the Israelites was made under circumstances, at a time and place, fully explained by what is known of the Peninsula. It occurred about two months after the Exodus, towards the end of May or early in June, when the Bedouins leave the lower plains in order to find pasture for their flocks on the cooler heights. The approach of the Israelites to Sinai would of course attract notice, and no cause of warfare is more common than a dispute for the right of pasturage. The Amalekites were at that time the most powerful race in the Peninsula, which from the earliest ages was peopled by fierce and warlike tribes, with whom the Pharaohs, from the third dynasty downwards, were engaged in constant struggles. It may be conjectured that reports of the marvellous supply of water may have reached the natives and accelerated their movements. On this occasion Amalek took the position, recognized in the Sacred History, as the chief of the heathens, Num. xxiv. 20; the first among the heathens who attacked God's people, and as such marked out for punishment, see 1 Sam. xv. 2, especially merited by them as descendants of the elder brother of Jacob, and therefore near kinsmen of the Israelites.

9. *Joshua*] This is the first mention of the great follower and successor of Moses. He died at the age of 110, some 65 years after this transaction. His original name was Hosea, but Moses calls him by the full name, which was first given about forty years afterwards, as that by which he was to be known to succeeding generations. From this it may perhaps be inferred that this portion of Exodus was written, or revised, towards the end of the sojourn in the wilderness. A later writer, mindful of the change of name, would probably have avoided the appearance of an anachronism.

the rod of God] By using the same rod Moses gave the people an unmistakeable and much needed proof that victory over human enemies was to be attributed altogether to the divine power which had delivered them from Egypt, and saved them from perishing in the wilderness. The hill, on which Moses stood during the combat, Knobel supposed to be the height now called Feria on the north side of the plain Er Rahah; on its top is a level tract with good pasturage and plantations. The conjecture may shew the vivid impression of reality made by the narrative upon a critic who believes this very portion to be the product of a later age.

10. *Hur*] Hur is mentioned in one other passage in connection with Aaron, ch. xxiv. 14. He was grandfather of Bezaleel, the great sculptor and artificer of the tabernacle, see ch. xxxi. 2—5, and belonged to the tribe of Judah. From the book of Chronicles we learn that the name of his father was Caleb, of his mother, Ephrath. That he was a person of high station and of advanced years is evident, but the traditions that he was the husband of Miriam (Josephus), or her son by Caleb (Jarchi), would seem to be mere conjecture; such a connection would scarcely have been unnoticed in the account of Bezaleel.

11. The act represents the efficacy of intercessory prayer—offered doubtless by Moses —a point of great moment to the Israelites at that time and to the Church in all ages. This interpretation would seem too obvious to insist upon, but it has been contested by Kurtz, who regards the lifting of Moses' hands as the attitude of a general directing the battle.

12. *until the going down of the sun*] The length of this first great battle indicates the strength and obstinacy of the assailants. It was no mere raid of Bedouins, but a deliberate attack of the Amalekites, who, as we have seen, were thoroughly trained in warfare by their struggles with Egypt.

13. *with the edge of the sword*] This

14 And the LORD said unto Moses,
Write this *for* a memorial in a book,
and rehearse *it* in the ears of Joshua:
for *f* I will utterly put out the remembrance of Amalek from under
heaven.
15 And Moses built an altar, and
called the name of it ‖ Jehovah-
nissi:
16 For he said, ‖ Because † the LORD
hath sworn *that* the LORD *will have*
war with Amalek from generation to
generation.

f Numb. 24. 20. 1 Sam. 15. 3.

‖ That is, *The LORD my banner.*

‖ Or, *Because the hand* of Amalek is *against the throne of the LORD*, therefore, &c. † Heb. *the hand upon the throne of the LORD*.

---

expression always denotes a great slaughter of the enemy.

14. *in a book*] It should be rendered **in the book**. The plain and obvious meaning is that the account of this battle, and of the command to destroy the Amalekites, was to be recorded in the book which contained the history of God's dealings with His people. In this explanation nearly all critics are agreed. See Introduction to the Pentateuch, p. 1, and note below. Moses was further instructed to impress the command specially on the mind of Joshua, as the leader to whom the first step towards its accomplishment would be entrusted on the conquest of Canaan. The work was not actually completed until the reign of Hezekiah, when 500 of the tribe of Simeon "smote the rest of the Amalekites that were escaped" and retained possession of Mount Seir, when the book of Chronicles was written, 1 Chron. iv. 43. This is a point to be especially noticed. True prophecy deals often with the remote future, regardless of delays in its fulfilment; but certainly no one writing at a later time, while the Amalekites still existed as a nation, would have invented the prediction.

15. *Jehovah-nissi*] *i.e.* as in the margin, "Jehovah my banner." As a proper name the Hebrew word is rightly preserved. The meaning is evidently that the name of Jehovah is the true banner under which victory is certain; so to speak, the motto or inscription on the banners of the host. Inscriptions on the royal standard were well known. Each of the Pharaohs on his accession adopted one in addition to his official name.

16. *Because the LORD hath sworn*] This rendering is incorrect, but the Hebrew is obscure and the true meaning is very doubtful. As the Hebrew text now stands the literal interpretation is "for hand on throne of Jah," which may mean, as our margin and as Clericus and Rosenmüller explain it, "because his hand (*i.e.* the hand of Amalek) is against the throne of God, therefore the Lord hath war with Amalek from generation to generation;" and this on the whole, seems to be the most satisfactory explanation. It expresses a certain fact, and keeps most closely to the Hebrew. The word rendered "throne" occurs in the exact form in no other passage, but it may be an archaic form of the very common word from which it differs but slightly (כס for כסא), and which is found in the Samaritan. Our translators follow the general sense given by the Targum of Onkelos and Saadia, who agree in regarding the expression as a solemn asseveration by the throne of God. To this however the objections are insuperable; it has no parallel in Scriptural usage: God swears by Himself, not by His Throne.

An alteration, slight in form, but considerable in meaning, has been proposed with much confidence, viz. "Nes," standard for "Kes," throne; thus connecting the name of the altar with the sentence. But conjectural emendations are not to be adopted without necessity, and the obvious a priori probability of such a reading makes it improbable that one so far more difficult should have been substituted for it. One of the surest canons of criticism militates against its reception. The text as it stands was undoubtedly that which was alone known to the Targumists, the Samaritan, the Syriac, the Latin and the Arabic translators. The LXX. appear to have had a different reading, ἐν χειρὶ κρυφαίᾳ πολεμεῖ.

NOTE on *v.* 14.

Rosenmüller expresses himself without any doubt. In his note on the passage he says "Memoriale in libro quem scribere incepisti:" and in the Prolegg. p. 5, "Moses dicit se divino jussu (insidias) inscripsisse libro, incœpto haud dubie, et in quo jam plura exaraverat, quod cum articulo בַּסֵּפֶר (non בְּסֵפֶר) scripsit, quo innuit se de certo quodam et satis noto libro loqui." Thus Keil, "the book appointed for the record of the glorious works of God;" and Kalisch, who renders it "the book:" he quotes Aben-Ezra to prove that a particular book was referred to, and compares other passages (Exod. xxiv. 4, 7, xxxiv. 27; Num. xxxiii. 1, 2, xxxvi. 13; Deut. xxviii. 61). Knobel however proposes a different interpretation, taking "in the book" to mean simply, "in writing." He refers to Num. v. 23; 1 S. x. 25; Jer. xxxii. 10; and Job xix. 23: which prove that this expression might mean "a book" generally, provided no particular book were already in existence. It is not however by any means equivalent to our expression "in writing," which would be a strange tautology "write in writing," but in each case a book or schedule is meant: whether a book already begun, or then to be begun, is a question to be determined by the context. The argument for the positive existence of "a book" is not materially affected by the proposed change: but all probability is in favour of the natural and obvious impression that Moses was commanded to record this particular transaction in "the book" which related the history of God's dealings with His people. The evidence for the existence of books of considerable extent is stated in the Introduction to the Pentateuch. To this it may be added that under the ancient Empire, functionaries of the highest rank held the office of governor of the Palace and of the "house of manuscripts;" see De Rougé, 'Recherches,' pp. 73, 85. The tutelary Deity of writing was called Saph or Sapheh (a name apparently connected with the Hebrew "sepher"): a Pharaoh of the 5th Dynasty bears the style "beloved of Saph." l.c. p. 84.

CHAPTER XVIII.

1 *Jethro bringeth to Moses his wife and two sons.* 7 *Moses entertaineth him.* 13 *Jethro's counsel is accepted.* 27 *Jethro departeth.*

[a] chap. 2. 16. WHEN [a] Jethro, the priest of
Midian, Moses' father in law,
heard of all that God had done for
Moses, and for Israel his people, *and*
that the LORD had brought Israel out
of Egypt;
2 Then Jethro, Moses' father in
law, took Zipporah, Moses' wife, after
he had sent her back,
3 And her two sons; of which the
[b] chap. 2. 22. [b] name of the one *was* ‖ Gershom; for
‖ That is, *A stranger there.* he said, I have been an alien in a
strange land:
4 And the name of the other *was*
‖ That is, *My God is an help.* ‖ Eliezer; for the God of my father,
said he, was mine help, and delivered
me from the sword of Pharaoh:
5 And Jethro, Moses' father in law,
came with his sons and his wife unto
Moses into the wilderness, where he
encamped at the mount of God:
6 And he said unto Moses, I thy
father in law Jethro am come unto
thee, and thy wife, and her two sons
with her.
7 ¶ And Moses went out to meet
his father in law, and did obeisance,
and kissed him; and they asked each
other of *their* † welfare; and they came † Heb. *peace.*
into the tent.
8 And Moses told his father in law
all that the LORD had done unto
Pharaoh and to the Egyptians for
Israel's sake, *and* all the travail that
had † come upon them by the way, and † Heb. *found them.*
how the LORD delivered them.
9 And Jethro rejoiced for all the
goodness which the LORD had done

CHAP. XVIII. The events recorded in this chapter could not have occupied many days, fifteen only elapsed between the arrival of the Israelites in the wilderness of Sin and their final arrival at Sinai, see ch. xvi. 1, and xix. 1. This leaves however sufficient time for the interview and transactions between Moses and Jethro.

1. *Jethro*] See note on ch. ii. 18. For "father in law" the Vulgate has cognatus, an indefinite expression. Jethro was in all probability the "brother in law" of Moses. On the parting from Zipporah, see note on ch. iv. 26.

This chapter, which abounds in personal reminiscences (and gives a vivid impression of the affectionate and confiding character of Moses), stands rather apart from the general narrative. It may have been and probably was written on a separate roll. The repetition of particulars well known to the reader is a general characteristic of such distinct portions.

5. *into the wilderness*] *i.e.* according to the view which seems on the whole most probable, on the plain near the northern summit of Horeb, the mount of God. It is described by Robinson, I. p. 88, as a naked desert,—wild and desolate. The exact specification of the locality may indicate a previous engagement between Moses and Jethro to meet at this place. The valley which opens upon Er Rahah on the left of Horeb is called by the Arabs Wady Shueib, *i.e.* the vale of Hobab.

6. The LXX. read, "And it was told to Moses, saying, Lo, thy father in law Jether is come." This suits the context, and is probably the true reading.

7. *did obeisance*] As to an elder, the priest, if not the chief, of a great tribe.

asked each other of their welfare] Or, addressed each other with the customary salutation, "Peace be unto you."

to Israel, whom he had delivered out
of the hand of the Egyptians.
10 And Jethro said, Blessed *be* the
LORD, who hath delivered you out
of the hand of the Egyptians, and out
of the hand of Pharaoh, who hath delivered the people from under the hand
of the Egyptians.
11 Now I know that the LORD *is*
greater than all gods: [c]for in the thing
wherein they dealt proudly *he was*
above them.
12 And Jethro, Moses' father in
law, took a burnt offering and sacrifices
for God: and Aaron came, and all
the elders of Israel, to eat bread with
Moses' father in law before God.
13 ¶ And it came to pass on the
morrow, that Moses sat to judge the
people: and the people stood by
Moses from the morning unto the
evening.
14 And when Moses' father in law
saw all that he did to the people, he
said, What *is* this thing that thou
doest to the people? why sittest thou
thyself alone, and all the people stand
by thee from morning unto even?
15 And Moses said unto his father
in law, Because the people come unto
me to inquire of God:
16 When they have a matter, they
come unto me; and I judge between
†one and another, and I do make
them know the statutes of God, and
his laws.

[c] chap. 1. 10, 16, 22. & 5. 7. & 14. 18.

† Heb. *a man and his fellow.*

---

11. *greater than all gods*] This does not prove that Jethro recognized the existence or power of other Deities, for the expression is not uncommon in the mouth of Hebrew monotheists, and corresponds exactly to the terms in which Moses had himself celebrated the overthrow of the Egyptians; see note on ch. xv. 11. It simply indicates a conviction of the incomparable might and majesty of Jehovah.

for in...above them] Lit. **For** (*this is shewn*) **in the matter wherein they dealt proudly against them.** The construction depends upon the previous clause; the meaning is, for I know the greatness of Jehovah by the very transaction wherein the Egyptians dealt haughtily and cruelly against the Israelites. Jethro refers especially to the destruction of the Egyptian host in the Red Sea, and very probably to the words in which Moses himself had celebrated that event; see ch. xv. 11.

12. *a burnt offering and sacrifices*] This verse clearly shews that Jethro was recognized as a priest of the true God. The identity of religious faith could not be more conclusively proved than by the participation in the sacrificial feast. This passage is of great importance in its bearings upon the relation between the Israelites and their congeners, and upon the state of religion among the descendants of Abraham.

13. In the following passage the change in the organization of the people, by which the burden of judicial proceedings was transferred in great part from Moses to subordinate officers, is attributed entirely to the counsel of Jethro. This is important for several reasons. It is certain that no late writer would have invented such a story, and most improbable that tradition would have long preserved the memory of a transaction which to Israelites might naturally seem derogatory to their legislator. Nothing however can be more characteristic of Moses, who combines on all occasions distrust of himself, and singular openness to impressions, with the wisdom and sound judgment which chooses the best course when pointed out. It is remarkable that an institution so novel and important should have preceded the promulgation of the Sinaitic law.

from the morning unto the evening] It may be assumed as at least probable that numerous cases of difficulty arose out of the division of the spoil of the Amalekites: this was moreover the first station at which the Israelites appear to have rested long after their departure from Elim, and causes would of course accumulate during the journey.

15. *to inquire of God*] The decisions of Moses were doubtless accepted by the people as oracles. There is no reason to suppose that he consulted, or that the people expected him to consult, the Lord by Urim and Thummim, which are first mentioned xxviii. 30, where see note. The internal prompting of the Spirit was a sufficient guidance for him, and a sufficient authority for the people.

16. *the statutes of God, and his laws*] This would seem to imply that in deciding each particular case Moses explained the principles of right and justice on which his decision rested. It became, so to speak, a precedent; he can scarcely be supposed to refer to any existing code, the necessity for which must, however, have soon become apparent, preparing the people for the legislation given within a few days at Sinai.

17 And Moses' father in law said
unto him, The thing that thou doest
is not good.
† Heb. *Fading thou wilt fade.*
18 †Thou wilt surely wear away,
both thou, and this people that *is* with
thee: for this thing *is* too heavy for
[d] Deut. i. 9.
thee; [d]thou art not able to perform it
thyself alone.
19 Hearken now unto my voice, I
will give thee counsel, and God shall
be with thee: Be thou for the people
to God-ward, that thou mayest bring
the causes unto God:
20 And thou shalt teach them
ordinances and laws, and shalt shew
them the way wherein they must walk,
and the work that they must do.
21 Moreover thou shalt provide out
of all the people able men, such as
fear God, men of truth, hating covetousness; and place *such* over them,
to be rulers of thousands, *and* rulers of
hundreds, rulers of fifties, and rulers
of tens:
22 And let them judge the people
at all seasons: and it shall be, *that*
every great matter they shall bring
unto thee, but every small matter they
shall judge: so shall it be easier for
thyself, and they shall bear *the burden*
with thee.
23 If thou shalt do this thing, and
God command thee *so*, then thou shalt
be able to endure, and all this people
shall also go to their place in peace.
24 So Moses hearkened to the voice
of his father in law, and did all that
he had said.
25 And Moses chose able men out
of all Israel, and made them heads
over the people, rulers of thousands,
rulers of hundreds, rulers of fifties,
and rulers of tens.
26 And they judged the people at
all seasons: the hard causes they
brought unto Moses, but every small
matter they judged themselves.
27 ¶ And Moses let his father in
law depart; and he went his way into
his own land.

---

18. *Thou wilt surely wear away*] This expresses the true sense: the Hebrew word implies decay and exhaustion.

19. *counsel*] In this counsel Jethro draws a distinction, probably not previously recognized, between the functions of the legislator and the judge. Moses as legislator stands between the people and God. He brings the cause to God, and learns from Him the principle by which it is to be determined: and in the next place, sets before the people the whole system of ordinances and laws by which they are to be henceforth guided. As judge Moses decides all difficult cases in the last resort, leaving questions of detail to officers chosen by himself from the people.

to God-ward] lit. "before God," standing between them and God, both as His minister, or representative: and also as the representative of the people, their agent, so to speak, or deputy before God.

20. *teach them*] The Hebrew word is emphatic, and signifies "enlightenment." The text gives four distinct points, (*a*) the "ordinances," or specific enactments, (*b*) "the laws," or general regulations, (*c*) "the way," the general course of duty, (*d*) "the work," each specific act.

21. *able men*] This gives the true force of the Hebrew, literally "men of might;" *i.e.* strength of character and ability. The qualifications are remarkably complete, ability, piety, truthfulness and unselfishness. The recommendation leaves no doubt as to the faith of Jethro, though, with the usual care observed by Moses in relating the words of pious Gentiles, he is represented as using the general expression God, not the revealed name Jehovah. From Deut. i. 13, it appears that Moses left the selection of the persons to the people, an example followed by the Apostles; see Acts vi. 3.

rulers of thousands, &c.] This minute classification of the people is thoroughly in accordance with the Semitic character, and was retained in after ages. The numbers appear to be conventional, corresponding nearly, but not exactly, to the military, or civil divisions of the people. The number "ten" denotes in Arabic, and may have denoted in Hebrew, a family; the largest division 1000 is used as an equivalent of a gens under one head, Num. i. 16, x. 4; Josh. xxii. 14.

The word "rulers," sometimes rendered "princes," is general, including all ranks of officials placed in command. The same word is used regularly on Egyptian monuments of the time of Moses: see note on ch. i. 11.

23. *to their place*] *i.e.* to Canaan, which is thus recognized by Jethro as the appointed and true home of Israel.

27. *into his own land*] Midian. This

CHAPTER XIX.

1 The people come to Sinai. 3 God's message by Moses unto the people out of the mount. 8 The people's answer returned again. 10 The people are prepared against the third day. 12 The mountain must not be touched. 16 The fearful presence of God upon the mount.

IN the third month, when the
children of Israel were gone forth
out of the land of Egypt, the same
day came they *into* the wilderness of
Sinai.
2 For they were departed from
Rephidim, and were come *to* the desert
of Sinai, and had pitched in the wilderness; and there Israel camped before the mount.
[a] Acts 7. 38. 3 And [a] Moses went up unto God,
and the LORD called unto him out of
the mountain, saying, Thus shalt thou
say to the house of Jacob, and tell the
children of Israel;
4 [b] Ye have seen what I did unto [b] Deut. 29. 2.
the Egyptians, and *how* I bare you on
eagles' wings, and brought you unto
myself.
5 Now [c] therefore, if ye will obey [c] Deut. 5. 2.
my voice indeed, and keep my cove-
nant, then ye shall be a peculiar trea-
sure unto me above all people: for [d] all [d] Deut. 10. 14.
the earth *is* mine: Psal. 24. 1.
6 And ye shall be unto me a [e] king- [e] 1 Pet. 2. 9.
dom of priests, and an holy nation. Rev. 1. 6.
These *are* the words which thou shalt
speak unto the children of Israel.

---

expression is favourable to the view that the home of Midian was on the east of the Red Sea, and not in the Peninsula of Sinai. If the identity of Jethro with Hobab be assumed, he must have returned and met Moses once more after the departure from Sinai. See Numbers x. 29—32. It seems however far more probable that Hobab was his brother. See note on ch. ii. 18.

CHAP. XIX. 1. *In the third month*] This expression does not determine the exact day: the word "month" is not found in the Pentateuch in the sense of new moon, or the first day of the month, which has been attributed to it in this passage by many eminent critics. Still the natural impression made by this statement is that the arrival of the Israelites coincided with the beginning of the third month.

the wilderness of Sinai] See note at the end of the book.

3. *Moses went up unto God*] This seems to imply that the voice was heard by Moses as he was ascending the mount.

house of Jacob] This expression does not occur elsewhere in the Pentateuch. It has a peculiar fitness here, referring doubtless to the special promises made to the Patriarch.

4. *on eagles' wings*] Bochart, after quoting passages from Ælian, Appian and other writers, observes that Moses gives a perfect explanation of the simile in Deuteronomy xxxii. 11. He adds "It is to be observed that both in the law and in the gospel the Church is compared to fledgelings which the mother cherishes and protects under her wings: but in the law that mother is an eagle, in the gospel a hen; thus shadowing forth the diversity of administration under each Covenant: the one of power, which God manifested when He brought His people out of Egypt with a mighty hand and an outstretched arm, and led them into the promised land; the other of grace, when Christ came in humility and took the form of a servant and became obedient unto death, even the death of the Cross." Bochart however, remarks, that the simile of an eagle is applied to Christ when He vindicates His people from the Dragon, Rev. xii. 14. See Hierozoicon, lib. II. ch. 22, § 3 and 4.

5. *a peculiar treasure*] This expresses the true sense of the Hebrew word, which designates a costly possession acquired with exertion, and carefully guarded. The peculiar relation in which Israel stands, taken out of the Heathen world and consecrated to God, as his slaves, subjects, and children, determines their privileges, and is the foundation of their duties. The same principle applies even in a stronger sense to the Church. See Acts xx. 28; 1 Cor. vi. 20; 1 Pet. ii. 9.

all the earth is mine] This is added, as we may believe, to impress upon the Jews that their God was no mere national Deity, a point of great practical importance.

6. *a kingdom of priests*] The exact meaning of this expression, as it was understood by all the ancient translators, and as it is explained in the New Testament, is that Israel collectively is a royal and priestly race: a dynasty of priests, each true member uniting in himself the attributes of a king and priest. The word "kingdom" is not taken in the modern sense, as a collective name for the subjects of a king, but in the old Hebrew sense of "royalty," or "dynasty." Thus nearly all ancient and modern commentators explain the words. (The LXX. *βασίλειον ἱεράτευμα*, Targum Onk. kings and priests; Jonathan, crowned kings and ministering priests.)

7 ¶ And Moses came and called
for the elders of the people, and laid
before their faces all these words
which the LORD commanded him.

8 And [f]all the people answered
together, and said, All that the LORD
hath spoken we will do. And Moses
returned the words of the people unto
the LORD.

f chap. 24. 3, 7. Deut. 5. 27. & 26. 17.

9 And the LORD said unto Moses,
Lo, I come unto thee in a thick
cloud, that the people may hear when
I speak with thee, and believe thee
for ever. And Moses told the words
of the people unto the LORD.

10 ¶ And the LORD said unto Moses, Go unto the people, and sanctify
them to day and to morrow, and let
them wash their clothes,

11 And be ready against the third
day: for the third day the LORD will
come down in the sight of all the
people upon mount Sinai.

12 And thou shalt set bounds unto the people round about, saying,
Take heed to yourselves, *that ye* go
not up into the mount, or touch the
border of it: [g]whosoever toucheth
the mount shall be surely put to
death:

g Heb. 12. 20.

13 There shall not an hand touch
it, but he shall surely be stoned, or
shot through; whether *it be* beast or
man, it shall not live: when the
‖ trumpet soundeth long, they shall
come up to the mount.

‖ Or, *cornet.*

14 ¶ And Moses went down from
the mount unto the people, and sanctified the people; and they washed
their clothes.

15 And he said unto the people,
Be ready against the third day: come
not at *your* wives.

16 ¶ And it came to pass on the
third day in the morning, that there
were thunders and lightnings, and a
thick cloud upon the mount, and the
voice of the trumpet exceeding loud;
so that all the people that *was* in the
camp trembled.

---

an holy nation] The holiness of Israel consisted in its special consecration to God: it was a sacred nation, sacred by adoption, by covenant, and by participation in all means of grace. The radical meaning of the Hebrew "Khodesh" appears to be "pure, clean, clear from all pollution bodily or spiritual," rather than, as many critics have assumed, "separate and set apart." The distinction between official consecration, and internal holiness is secondary, and scarcely seems to have lain within the scope of the Hebrew mind: the ideas were inseparable.

8. *All that the LORD*, &c.] By this answer the people accepted the covenant. It was the preliminary condition of their complete admission into the state of a royal priesthood.

9. *in a thick cloud*] Or "in the darkness of cloud," *i.e.* in the midst of the dense cloud which indicated the Presence of Jehovah. The people were to hear the voice of God, distinctly announcing the fundamental principles of the eternal law.

10. *sanctify them*] The injunction involves bodily purification and undoubtedly also spiritual preparation. Thus Heb. x. 22, "our hearts sprinkled from an evil conscience, and our bodies washed with pure water." The washing of the clothes was an outward symbol well understood in all nations. The supply of water in the region about Sinai is repeatedly stated by Burckhardt and other travellers to be abundant. In Deut. ix. 21, we read of the brook descending from the mount.

11. *the third day*] The significance of the expression "third day" scarcely needs to be pointed out; whether this third day fell on the Jewish or Christian Sabbath is quite uncertain; but it can scarcely have corresponded to the day of Pentecost, as Bp. Wordsworth holds on the authority of an ancient and widely accredited tradition: more than 60 days had elapsed since the Passover. See the article on Pentecost in Smith's 'Dict.'

12. *set bounds unto the people*] The access to the base of the mountain is evidently shewn to have been otherwise unimpeded. Dr Stanley speaks of the low line of alluvial mounds at the foot of the cliff of Ras Safsafeh as exactly answering to the bounds which were to keep the people off from touching the mount: but the bounds here spoken of were to be set up by Moses.

13. *touch it*] Rather "touch him." The person was not to be touched, since the contact would be pollution. He was to be stoned or shot with an arrow; or probably with a javelin, as was customary in later times.

when the trumpet, &c.] When the trumpet sounded those who were specially called might ascend.

17 And Moses brought forth the people out of the camp to meet with God; and they stood at the nether part of the mount.

h Deut. 4. 11.

18 And *h* mount Sinai was altogether on a smoke, because the LORD descended upon it in fire: and the smoke thereof ascended as the smoke of a furnace, and the whole mount quaked greatly.

19 And when the voice of the trumpet sounded long, and waxed louder and louder, Moses spake, and God answered him by a voice.

20 And the LORD came down upon mount Sinai, on the top of the mount: and the LORD called Moses *up* to the top of the mount; and Moses went up.

† Heb. *contest.*

21 And the LORD said unto Moses, Go down, † charge the people, lest they break through unto the LORD to gaze, and many of them perish.

22 And let the priests also, which come near to the LORD, sanctify themselves, lest the LORD break forth upon them.

23 And Moses said unto the LORD, The people cannot come up to mount Sinai: for thou chargedst us, saying, Set bounds about the mount, and sanctify it.

24 And the LORD said unto him, Away, get thee down, and thou shalt come up, thou, and Aaron with thee: but let not the priests and the people break through to come up unto the LORD, lest he break forth upon them.

25 So Moses went down unto the people, and spake unto them.

CHAPTER XX.

1 *The ten commandments.* 18 *The people are afraid.* 20 *Moses comforteth them.* 22 *Idolatry is forbidden.* 24 *Of what sort the altar should be.*

AND God spake all these words, saying,

2 *a* I *am* the LORD thy God, which have brought thee out of the land of Egypt, out of the house of † bondage.

a Deut. 5. 6. Psal. 81. 10. † Heb. *servants.*

---

17. *out of the camp*] The encampment must have extended far and wide over the plain in front of the mountain. From one entrance of the plain to the other there is space for the whole host of the Israelites. This is a point which has been determined by accurate measurement of the valley. See note at the end of Exodus.

18. *a furnace*] The word is Egyptian, and occurs only in the Pentateuch.

22. *the priests also*] The Levitical priesthood was not yet instituted, but sacrifices had hitherto been offered by persons who were recognized as having the right or authority: according to the very probable account of Rabbinical writers these were the first-born, or the heads of families, until they were superseded by the Aaronic priesthood.

THE TEN COMMANDMENTS.
CHAP. XX. 1—17.

On the Ten Commandments, taken as a whole, see Note after *v.* 21. The account of the delivery of them in chap. xix. and in *vv.* 18—21 of this chap. is in accordance with their importance as the recognized basis of the Covenant between Jehovah and His ancient people (Exod. xxxiv. 27, 28; Deut. iv. 13; 1 K. viii. 21, &c.), and as the Divine testimony against the sinful tendencies in man for all ages. Jewish writers have speculated as to the mode in which the Divine communication was made to the people (Philo, 'de Orac.' c. 9; Palestine Targum, &c.). It may be noticed that, while it is here said that "God spake all these words," and in Deut. v. 4, that He "spake face to face," in the New Testament the giving of the Law is spoken of as having been through the ministration of angels (Acts vii. 53; Gal. iii. 19; Heb. ii. 2). We can only reconcile these contrasts of language by keeping in mind that God is a Spirit, and that He is essentially present in the agents who are performing His will. A similar difficulty was felt by some in St Augustin's time in reconciling Gen. i. 1 with John i. 3. ('Cont. Adimant. Man.' c. 1.)—Josephus appears as the only witness for the superstition, which was probably common amongst the Pharisees of his day, that it was not lawful to utter the very words in which the Ten Commandments were originally expressed ('Ant.' III. 5, § 4). It is remarkable that there seems to be no trace of this in the rabbinists.—The Two Tables of stone on which the Commandments were inscribed are mentioned ch. xxiv. 12, xxxi. 18.

2. *which have brought thee out of the land of Egypt, out of the house of bondage*] It was a rabbinical question, Why, on this occasion, was not THE LORD rather proclaimed as "the Creator of Heaven and Earth"? The true answer evidently is, That the Ten Commandments were at this time addressed by Jehovah

3 Thou shalt have no other gods before me.

b Lev. 26. 1. Psal. 97. 7. 4 b Thou shalt not make unto thee any graven image, or any likeness *of any thing* that *is* in heaven above, or that *is* in the earth beneath, or that *is* in the water under the earth:

5 Thou shalt not bow down thyself to them, nor serve them: for I the LORD thy God *am* a jealous God, visiting the iniquity of the fathers upon the children unto the third and fourth *generation* of them that hate me;

---

not merely to human creatures, but to the people whom He had redeemed, to those who had been in bondage, but were now free men. (Exod. vi. 6, 7, xix. 5.) The Commandments are expressed in absolute terms. They are not sanctioned by outward penalties, as if for slaves, but are addressed at once to the conscience, as for free men. The well-being of the nation called for the infliction of penalties, and therefore statutes were passed to punish offenders who blasphemed the name of Jehovah, who profaned the Sabbath, or who committed murder or adultery. (See on Lev. xviii. 24—30.) But these penal statutes were not to be the ground of obedience for the true Israelite according to the Covenant. He was to know Jehovah as his Redeemer, and was to obey Him as such. (Cf. Rom. xiii. 5; see Note after *v.* 21, § V.)

3. *before me*] Literally, *before my face.* The meaning is that no god should be worshipped in addition to Jehovah. Cf. *v.* 23. The rendering in our Prayer-Book, *but me*, with that of the LXX. πλὴν ἐμοῦ, does not so well represent the Hebrew. The polytheism which was the besetting sin of the Israelites in later times did not exclude Jehovah, but it associated Him with false deities. See Note on xxxiv. 13.

4. *graven image*] Any sort of image is here intended. The Hebrew word (*pesel*) strictly means a carved image, mostly denoting one of wood or stone, and in some places it is distinguished from a molten image of metal (*massēkāh*): but as molten images were finished up with a graver or carving tool, *pesel* is sometimes applied to them (Is. xl. 19, xliv. 10; Jer. x. 14, &c.), and is frequently used, as it is here, for a general name for images of all sorts.

or any likeness] This may be rendered, **even any likeness.** What follows in the verse expresses the whole material creation; it is expanded in detail in Deut. iv. 16—19.

5. *Thou shalt not bow down thyself to them, nor serve them*] The antecedent to *them* in each clause appears to be the likenesses of things in heaven and earth spoken of in the preceding verse. It has been observed that, according to the Hebrew idiom, these clauses may have a strict grammatical connection with "Thou shalt not make," &c. in *v.* 4. The meaning certainly is to prohibit the making of the likeness of any material thing, *in order to* worship it. For a similar form of expression, see Num. xxii. 12. As the First Commandment forbids the worship of any false god, seen or unseen, it is here forbidden to worship an image of any sort, whether the figure of a false deity or one in any way symbolical of Jehovah (see on xxxii. 4). The spiritual acts of worship were symbolized in the furniture and ritual of the Tabernacle and the Altar, and for this end the forms of living things might be employed as in the case of the Cherubim (see on xxv. 18): but the presence of the invisible God was to be marked by no symbol of Himself, but by His words written on stones, preserved in the Ark in the Holy of Holies and covered by the Mercy-seat. On the repudiation of images of the Deity by the ancient Persians, see Herodot. I. 131; Strabo, XV. p. 732; and by the earliest legislators of Rome, see Plut. 'Numa,' 8; Augustin. 'de Civ. Dei,' IV. 31.

The Jews, not recognizing the connection between *vv.* 4 and 5, have imagined *v.* 4 to be a prohibition of the exercise of the arts of painting and sculpture. Considering the Cherubim of the Mercy-seat and of the curtains of the Tabernacle, the pomegranates of the High-priest's robe, and the fruits and flowers of the Candlestick, to say nothing of the sculptures of the Temple in later times (1 K. vi. 23 sq., vii. 27 sq.), any such notion as this must show the prejudiced and fragmentary way in which they were tempted to study the Scriptures. Philo declares that Moses condemned to perpetual banishment the cheating arts (ἐπιβοῦλοι τέχναι) of painters and sculptors ('Quis div. rer. heres.' c. 35; 'de Orac.' c. 29). Josephus charges Solomon with a breach of the Law, on account of the oxen which supported the brazen sea, and the lions which adorned his throne ('Ant.' VIII. 7, § 5): and in direct contradiction of Exod. xxvi. 31, he denies that the vail which concealed the Most Holy Place was ornamented with living creatures. ('Ant.' III. 6, § 4.) This prejudice, from the time when the pharisaic tendency began to work on the mind of the nation, must have effectually checked the progress of the imitative arts.

for I the LORD thy God am a jealous God] Deut. vi. 15; Josh. xxiv. 19; Is. xlii. 8, xlviii. 11; Nahum i. 2. This reason applies to the First, as well as to the Second Commandment. The truth expressed in it was declared more fully

6 And shewing mercy unto thousands of them that love me, and keep
my commandments.
7 [c] Thou shalt not take the
name of the LORD thy God in
vain; for the LORD will not hold
him guiltless that taketh his name in
vain.
8 Remember the sabbath day, to
keep it holy.

[c] Lev. 19. 12. Deut. 5. 11. Matt. 5. 33.

---

to Moses when the name of Jehovah was proclaimed to him after he had interceded for Israel on account of the golden calf (xxxiv. 6, 7; see note).

visiting the iniquity of the fathers upon the children] The visitation here spoken of can hardly be any other than that which we are accustomed to witness in the common experience of life. (Cf. xxxiv. 7; Jer. xxxii. 18.) Sons and remote descendants inherit the consequences of their fathers' sins, in disease, poverty, captivity, with all the influences of bad example and evil communications. (See Lev. xxvi. 39; Lam. v. 7 sq.) The "inherited curse" seems to fall often most heavily on the least guilty persons, as is abundantly proved in all history and is pointedly illustrated in Greek tragedy. But such suffering must always be free from the sting of conscience; it is not like the visitation for sin on the individual by whom the sin has been committed. The suffering, or loss of advantages, entailed on the unoffending son, is a condition under which he has to carry on the struggle of life, and, like all other inevitable conditions imposed upon men, it cannot tend to his ultimate disadvantage, if he struggles well and perseveres to the end. He may never attain in this world to a high standard of knowledge, or of outward conduct, compared with others, but the Searcher of hearts will regard him with favour, not in proportion to his visible conduct, but to his unseen struggles. As regards the administration of justice by earthly tribunals, the Law holds good, "The fathers shall not be put to death for the children, neither shall the children be put to death for the fathers; every man shall be put to death for his own sin" (Deut. xxiv. 16). The same principle is carried out in spiritual matters by the Supreme Judge. The Israelites in a later age made a confusion in the use of their common proverb, "The fathers have eaten sour grapes, and the children's teeth are set on edge." There would have been truth in this saying had it been used only in reference to the mere natural consequences of their fathers' sins. In this sense their teeth were set on edge by the sour grapes their fathers had eaten. But the Prophets pointed out the falsehood involved in the proverb as it was understood by the people. They showed that it was utterly false when applied to the spiritual relation in which each person stands in the judgment of Him who is no respecter of persons. (Jer. xxxi. 29, 30; Ezek. xviii. 2—4 sq.)

Another explanation of the words appears in the Targums, and is favoured by some of the Fathers and other commentators, Christian and Jewish. It assumes that the words refer only to the children who go on sinning so as to fill up the measure of their fathers' iniquities in the manner spoken of Lev. xxvi. 39; Is. lxv. 7; Jer. xvi. 10—13; Matt. xxiii. 29—32. (See Hengst. 'Pent.' Vol. II. p. 446.) But this seems unworthily to reduce the Divine words to a mere truism. It makes them say in an awkward mannner no more than that the guilty sons shall be punished as well as the guilty fathers.

6. *unto thousands*] **unto the thousandth generation.** Jehovah's visitations of chastisement extend to the third and fourth generation, his visitations of mercy to the thousandth; that is, for ever. That this is the true rendering seems to follow from Deut. vii. 9. Cf. 2 S. vii. 15, 16. So Syr., Onk., Leo Juda, Geneva French, Rosen., Zunz, Schott. Knobel, Keil, Herx., and Wogue. Our version is supported by the LXX., Vulg., Saadia, Luther, and de Wette.

7. Our translators have followed the LXX., Aquila, the Vulgate, Augustin ('Serm.' VIII.), and Theodoret ('Quæst. in Exod.' 41), in making the Third Commandment bear upon any profane and idle utterance of the name of God. Saadia, the Syriac, some of the Rabbinists, and the greater number of the critics of our day, give it the sense, *Thou shalt not swear falsely by the name of Jehovah thy God.* The Hebrew word which answers to *in vain* may be rendered either way. The two abuses of the sacred name seem to be distinguished in Lev. xix. 12. Our Version is probably right in giving the rendering which is more inclusive. To swear falsely is undoubtedly a profanation of the name of God; and looking at the matter on its practical side, the man who, in a right spirit, avoids the idle use of the Name will be incapable of swearing falsely. Hence there may be a reference to this Commandment, as well as to Lev. xix. 12, in Matt. v. 33. The caution that a breach of this Commandment incurs guilt in the eyes of Jehovah is especially appropriate, in consequence of the ease with which the temptation to take God's name in vain besets men in their common intercourse with each other.

8. *Remember the sabbath day*] These words have been taken to refer to the observance of the Sabbath day as an old usage dating back

[d] chap. 23. 12. 9 [d] Six days shalt thou labour, and
Ezek. 20. 12. do all thy work:
Luke 13. 14. 10 But the seventh day *is* the sabbath of the LORD thy God: *in it*
thou shalt not do any work, thou,
nor thy son, nor thy daughter, thy
manservant, nor thy maidservant, nor
thy cattle, nor thy stranger that *is*
within thy gates:

11 For [e] *in* six days the LORD made [e] Gen. 2. 2.
heaven and earth, the sea, and all that
in them *is*, and rested the seventh
day: wherefore the LORD blessed the
sabbath day, and hallowed it.
12 ¶ [f] Honour thy father and thy [f] Deut. 5. 16.
mother: that thy days may be long Matt. 15. 4.
upon the land which the LORD thy Eph. 6. 2.
God giveth thee.

---

to the Patriarchs, or even to the creation of the world. There is however no distinct evidence that the Sabbath, as a formal ordinance, was recognized before the time of Moses. The expressions of Nehemiah (ix. 14), of Ezekiel (xx. 10, 11, 12), and, perhaps, of Moses himself (Deut. v. 15), may be taken to intimate that the observance was regarded as originating in the Law given on Mount Sinai. The most ancient testimonies favour this view. (See Note at end of this Chapter. Also note on Gen. ii. 2.) It is now generally admitted that the attempts to trace the observance in heathen antiquity have failed. It has been alleged that the word *remember* may be reasonably explained in one of two ways without adopting the inference that has been mentioned; it may either be used in the sense of *keep in mind* what is here enjoined for the first time, or it may refer back to what is related in ch. xvi. where the Sabbath day is first noticed, in giving the law for collecting the manna.

to keep it holy] See Note after *v.* 21, § I.

10. *the sabbath of the* LORD *thy God*] **a Sabbath to Jehovah thy God.** It may be observed that the word *sabbath* (more properly, *shabbath*) has no etymological connection with *sheba'*, the Hebrew for *seven*. The proper meaning of *sabbath* is, *rest after labour.*

thy stranger that is within thy gates] The Hebrew word *geer* does not mean a *stranger* (that is an unknown person), but, according to its mere derivation, a *lodger*, or *sojourner*. In this place it denotes one who had come from another people to take up his permanent abode among the Israelites, and who might have been well known to his neighbours. Our word *foreigner*, in its common use, seems best to answer to it here. The LXX. renders *geer* by προσήλυτος (*proselyte*), πάροικος, and ξένος. That the word did not primarily refer to foreign domestic servants (though all such were included under it) is to be inferred from the term used for gates (*sha'arim*), signifying not the doors of a private dwelling, but the gates of a town or camp.

11. *wherefore the* LORD *blessed the sabbath day*] Our Communion Service and Catechism follow the reading of the LXX. and the earlier English Versions, in calling this the *seventh day* instead of the *sabbath day.* On the meaning of the verse, see Note after *v.* 21.

12. *Honour thy father and thy mother*] According to our usage, the Fifth Commandment is placed as the first in the second table; and this is necessarily involved in the common division of the Commandments into our duty towards God and our duty towards men. But the more ancient, and probably the better, division allots five Commandments to each Table. The connection between the first four Commandments and the Fifth exists in the truth that all faith in God centres in the filial feeling. Our parents stand between us and God in a way in which no other beings can. It is worthy of note that the honouring of parents and the keeping of the Sabbath day, which is the same as honouring God, are combined in one precept in Lev. xix. 3.—In connection with this, it may be observed that the Fifth Commandment and the first part of the Fourth are the only portions of the Decalogue which are expressed in a positive form. See Note after *v.* 21, § IV. On the maintenance of parental authority, see xxi. 15, 17; Deut. xxi. 18—21.

that thy days may be long upon the land] Filial respect is the ground of national permanence. When the Jews were about to be cast out of their land, the rebuke of the prophet was, that they had not walked in the old paths and had not respected the voice of their fathers as the sons of Jonadab had done (Jer. vi. 16, xxxv. 18, 19). And when in later times the land had been restored to them, and they were about to be cast out of it a second time, the great sin of which they were convicted was, that they had set aside this Fifth Commandment for the sake of their own traditions. (Matt. xv. 4—6; Mark vii. 10, 11.) Every other nation that has a history bears witness to the same truth. Rome owed her strength, as well as the permanence of her influence after she had politically perished, to her steady maintenance of the *patria potestas* (Maine, 'Ancient Law,' p. 135). China has mainly owed her long duration to the simple way in which she has uniformly acknowledged the authority of fathers. The Divine words were addressed emphatically to Israel, but they

[g] Matt. 5. 21.

13 [g] Thou shalt not kill.
14 Thou shalt not commit adultery.
15 Thou shalt not steal.
16 Thou shalt not bear false witness against thy neighbour.

[h] Rom. 7. 7.

17 [h] Thou shalt not covet thy neighbour's house, thou shalt not covet thy neighbour's wife, nor his manservant, nor his maidservant, nor his ox, nor his ass, nor any thing that *is* thy neighbour's.

[i] Heb. 12. 18.

18 ¶ And [i] all the people saw the thunderings, and the lightnings, and the noise of the trumpet, and the mountain smoking: and when the people saw *it*, they removed, and stood afar off.

[k] Deut. 5. 27. & 18. 16.

19 And they said unto Moses, [k] Speak thou with us, and we will

---

set forth a universal principle of national life. St Paul calls this Commandment, "the first commandment with promise" (Eph. vi. 2); the promise is fulfilled in God's government of the whole world. The narrow view which Selden and others have taken of the Commandment, that it implied no more than a prediction that the children of Israel should possess the land of Canaan on the condition stated, is alien to the spirit of the Decalogue. (See Note after *v.* 21, § VI.)

13, 14. The Sixth and Seventh Commandments are amongst those utterances of the Law which our Saviour, in the Sermon on the Mount, took to illustrate the relation in which the Gospel stands to the Law. Whatever range of meaning we are to give to the expression in Matt. v. 17, that Christ came not to destroy but to *fulfil* (πληρῶσαι), we can hardly exclude from it, in its bearing on the discourse that follows in *vv.* 18—48, the sense, to *set forth perfectly* in the way of teaching. (Cf. Rom. xv. 19; Col. i. 25.) The Scribes and Pharisees failed perfectly to set forth the Law, in their teaching as well as in their practice; they taught the mere words in their dry external relations; "they gave the husk without the kernel." Their righteousness, both that which they taught and that which they practised, therefore fell short of the true standard (Matt. v. 20). If this view of the word *fulfil* is admitted, our Saviour's words respecting these Commandments (*vv.* 21—32) cannot be taken as an external supplement to the Law, or as a new adaptation of it to a changed order of things, but as a perfect unfolding, in the most practical form, of the meaning which the Commandments had from the beginning, and which had been, with different degrees of distinctness, shadowed forth to all who wisely and devoutly obeyed the Law under the Old Dispensation. The passage in St Matthew (v. 21—32) is therefore the best comment on these two verses of Exodus. St Augustin says that the purpose of Christ's coming was, *non ut Legi adderentur quæ deerant, sed ut fierent quæ scripta erant.* 'Cont. Faust.' XVII. 6.

15. The right of property is sanctioned in the Eighth Commandment by an external rule: its deeper meaning is involved in the Tenth Commandment.

17. As the Sixth, Seventh, and Eighth Commandments forbid us to injure our neighbour in deed, the Ninth forbids us to injure him in word, and the Tenth, in thought. No human eye can see the coveting heart; it is witnessed only by him who possesses it and by Him to whom all things are naked and open. But it is the root of all sins against our neighbour in word or in deed (Jam. i. 14, 15). The man who is acceptable before God, walking uprightly, not backbiting with his tongue, nor doing evil to his neighbour, is he who "speaketh the truth IN HIS HEART." Ps. xv. 2, 3. St Paul speaks of the operation of this Commandment on his own heart as the means of revealing to him the holiness of the Law (Rom. vii. 7). The direct connection of the Commandments of the Second Table with the principle of love between man and man, is affirmed Matt. xxii. 39, 40; Rom. xiii. 9, 10; Gal. v. 14.—On the variations between this and the parallel place in Deut. v. 21, see Note after *v.* 21, § II.

There is a curious interpolation in the Samaritan text following the Tenth Commandment. The Israelites are commanded to set up on Mount Gerizim two great plastered stones with the words of the Law inscribed on them, to build there an Altar, and to sacrifice upon it Burnt-offerings and Peace-offerings. The passage is evidently made up from Deut. xxvii. 2—7, with some expressions from Deut. xi. 30, Gerizim being substituted for Ebal. See on Deut. xxvii. 2—7.

18—21. This narrative is amplified in Deut. v. 22—31. The people had realized the terrors of the voice of Jehovah in the utterance of the Ten Words of the Testimony, and they feared for their lives. Though Moses encouraged them, they were permitted to withdraw and to stand afar off, at their tent doors (see Deut. v. 30). It would appear, according to xix. 24, that Aaron on this occasion accompanied Moses in drawing near to the thick darkness. Cf. xxiv. 18.

hear: but [d] let not God speak with us, lest we die.
20 And Moses said unto the people, Fear not: for God is come to prove you, and that his fear may be before your faces, that ye sin not.
21 And the people stood afar off, and Moses drew near unto the thick darkness where God *was*.

NOTE on CHAP. XX. *vv.* 1—17.

ON THE TEN COMMANDMENTS.

I. *The Name.* II. *What was written on the Stones?* III. *The Division into Ten.* IV. *The Two Tables.* V. *The Commandments as* A TESTIMONY. VI. *Breadth of their meaning.*

§ I.

The Hebrew name which is rendered in our Version THE TEN COMMANDMENTS (עֲשֶׂרֶת הַדְּבָרִים) occurs in Exod. xxxiv. 28; Deut. iv. 13, x. 4. It literally means *the Ten Words*, as it stands in the margin of our Bible; LXX. οἱ δέκα λόγοι, or τὰ δέκα ῥήματα; Vulg. *decem verba.* But the Hebrew substantive דָּבָר often denotes a *mandate* (Josh. i. 13; Esth. i. 19); and the common English rendering may be therefore justified. In Ex. xxiv. 12, the Ten Commandments are called **the Law, even the Commandment**: the latter word (מִצְוָה) occurs in its plural form in the Second Commandment, Ex. xx. 6; Deut. v. 10. They are elsewhere called THE WORDS OF THE COVENANT (Ex. xxxiv. 28, where the strict rendering would be, *the Words of the Covenant, even the Ten Words*), THE TABLES OF THE COVENANT (Deut. ix. 9, 11, 15), and simply THE COVENANT (Deut. iv. 13: 1 K. viii. 21; 2 Chron. vi. 11); also THE TWO TABLES (Deut. ix. 10, 17). But the most frequent name for them in the Old Testament is, THE TESTIMONY[1] (הָעֵדוּת, LXX. τὸ μαρτύριον or τὰ μαρτύρια), or THE TWO TABLES OF THE TESTIMONY[2]. In the New Testament they are called simply THE COMMANDMENTS[3] (αἱ ἐντολαί). The name DECALOGUE (ὁ δεκάλογος) is found first in Clement of Alexandria, and was commonly used by the Fathers who followed him.

We thus know that the Tables were two, and that the Commandments were ten, in number. But the Scriptures do not, by any direct statements, enable us to determine with precision how the Ten Commandments are severally to be made out, nor how they are to be allotted to the Two Tables. On each of these points various opinions have been held.

[1] Ex. xvi. 34, xxv. 16, 21, xxx. 6, xl. 20; Lev. xvi. 13, &c. &c.

[2] Ex. xxxi. 18, xxxii. 15, xxxiv. 29.

[3] Matt. xix. 17; Mark x. 19; Luke xviii. 20; Rom. xiii. 9.

§ II.

But there is a question which rightly claims precedence of these: What actually were the Words of Jehovah that were engraven on the Tables of Stone? We have two distinct statements, one in Exodus (xx. 1—17) and one in Deuteronomy (v. 6—21), apparently of equal authority, but differing from each other in several weighty particulars. Each is said, with reiterated emphasis, to contain the words that were actually spoken by the LORD, and written by Him upon the stones[4].

The variations which are of most importance are in the Commandments which we commonly call the Fourth, the Fifth, and the Tenth. The two copies of these are here placed side by side. The expressions in Deuteronomy which differ in the original Hebrew from the corresponding ones in Exodus, are in italics, and the additional clauses are in brackets.

EXODUS XX.	DEUT. V.
IV. (*vv.* 8—11.)	IV. (*vv.* 12—15.)
Remember the sabbath day, to keep it holy. Six days shalt thou labour, and do all thy work: But the seventh day is the sabbath of the LORD thy God: in it thou shalt not do any work, thou, nor thy son, nor thy daughter, thy manservant, nor thy maidservant, nor thy cattle, nor thy stranger that is within thy gates: For in six days the LORD made heaven and earth, the sea, and all that in them is, and rested the seventh day: wherefore the LORD blessed the sabbath day, and hallowed it.	*Keep* the sabbath day to sanctify it, [*as the* LORD *thy God hath commanded thee.*] Six days thou shalt labour, and do all thy work: But the seventh day is the sabbath of the LORD thy God: in it thou shalt not do any work, thou, nor thy son, nor thy daughter, nor thy manservant, nor thy maidservant, [*nor thine ox, nor thine ass,*] nor any of thy cattle, nor thy stranger that is within thy gates; [*that thy manservant and thy maidservant may rest as well as thou.*] *And remember that thou wast a servant in the land of Egypt, and that the* LORD *thy God brought thee out thence through a mighty hand and by a stretched out*

[4] Ex. xx. 1, xxiv. 12, xxxi. 18, xxxii. 15, 16; Deut. v. 4, 5, 22, iv. 13, ix. 10.

	arm: therefore the Lord *thy God commanded thee to keep the sabbath day.*
V. (*v.* 12.) Honour thy father and thy mother: that thy days may be long upon the land which the Lord thy God giveth thee.	V. (*v.* 16.) Honour thy father and thy mother, [*as the* Lord *thy God hath commanded thee*]; that thy days may be prolonged, [*and that it may go well with thee*], in the land which the Lord thy God giveth thee.
X. (*v.* 17.) Thou shalt not covet thy neighbour's house, thou shalt not covet thy neighbour's wife, nor his manservant, nor his maidservant, nor his ox, nor his ass, nor any thing that is thy neighbour's.	X. (*v.* 21.) *Neither* shalt thou desire thy neighbour's wife, *neither* shalt thou *covet* thy neighbour's house, [*his field*], or his manservant, or his maidservant, his ox, or his ass, or any thing that is thy neighbour's.

In the Fourth Commandment, it will be seen that in Deuteronomy:—

(1) "Keep (שְׁמוֹר) the Sabbath day," is read instead of "Remember (זָכוֹר) the Sabbath day."

(2) Three fresh clauses are inserted:—

"As the Lord thy God hath commanded thee."

"Nor thine ox nor thine ass."

"That thy manservant and thy maidservant may rest as well as thou."

(3) A different reason is given for the Commandment, referring to the deliverance of the Israelites from Egypt, instead of the rest of God after the six works of Creation.

In the Fifth, Deuteronomy inserts the same expression as it does in the Fourth, "as the Lord thy God hath commanded thee;" and also the words, "that it may go well with thee."

In the Tenth, it transposes "thy neighbour's house," and "thy neighbour's wife;" it inserts "his field," and it makes the two parts of the Commandment more distinct by the use of a different verb in the imperative mood in each. The verb rendered *desire* (חָמַד) is the same that is rendered *covet* in Exodus, but the one here rendered *covet* is a different one (אָוָה).

It should also be observed that, in Deut. v. verses 17, 18, 19, 20, 21 are linked together by the copulative conjunction. The few other slight variations do not affect the sense.

It has been generally assumed that the whole of one or other of these copies was written on the Tables. Most commentators have supposed that the original document is in Exodus, and that the author of Deuteronomy wrote from memory, with variations suggested at the time. Others have conceived that Deuteronomy must furnish the more correct form since the Tables must have been in actual existence when the book was written. But neither of these views can be fairly reconciled with the statements in Exodus and Deuteronomy to which reference has been made. If either copy, as a whole, represents what was written on the Tables, it is obvious that the other cannot do so.

A conjecture which seems to deserve respect has been put forth by Ewald. He supposes that the original Commandments were all in the same terse and simple form of expression as appears (both in Exodus and Deuteronomy) in the First, Sixth, Seventh, Eighth, and Ninth, such as would be most suitable for recollection, and that the passages in each copy in which the most important variations are found were comments added when the Books were written. It is not necessary to involve this theory with any question as to the authorship of the Books, or with any doubt as to the comments being the words of God[1] given by Moses as much as the Commandments, strictly so called, that were written on the Tables. In reference to the most important of the differences, that relating to the reason for the observance of the Sabbath day, the thoughts are in no degree discordant, and each sets forth what is entirely worthy of, and consistent with, the Divine Law[2]. Slighter verbal or literal variations, with no important difference of meaning (such as *keep* for *remember*), may perhaps be ascribed to copyists[3].

It may be supposed then that the Ten Words of Jehovah, with the prefatory sentence, were to this effect, assuming that each Table contained Five Commandments. See § IV.

I am Jehovah thy God who have brought thee out of the land of Egypt, out of the house of bondage.

First Table.

i. *Thou shalt have no other God*[4] *before me.*

ii. *Thou shalt not make to thee any graven image.*

iii. *Thou shalt not take the name of Jehovah thy God in vain.*

iv. *Thou shalt remember the Sabbath day, to keep it holy.*

v. *Thou shalt honour thy father and thy mother.*

[1] See Ex. xx. 1.

[2] See the following Note, § III.

[3] What is assumed, on the theory here stated, to be the comment on both the First and Second Commandments ("For I the Lord thy God am a jealous God," &c. See on Ex. xx. 5) occurs in a somewhat different and more diffuse form in Ex. xxxiv. 6, 7. Does not a comparison of the two passages tend to confirm the supposition that the words are not a part of the original Ten Commandments, but that they were quoted here in a condensed form by Moses, as bearing on the two Commandments, when the book of Exodus was put together?

[4] See on Ex. xx. 3.

SECOND TABLE.

vi. *Thou shalt not kill.*
vii. *Thou shalt not commit adultery.*
viii. *Thou shalt not steal.*
ix. *Thou shalt not bear false witness.*
x. *Thou shalt not covet.*

A practical illustration from the usage of different ages may tend to shew the probability that the Ten Commandments were familiarly known in such a compendious form as this, at a time when they were used not only as the common watchwords of duty, but as the axioms of the Law in its actual operation. In those copies of the Commandments which have been used in different branches of the Church for the instruction of its members, the form has almost always been more or less abbreviated of a part, or the whole, of those which are the most expanded in Exodus and Deuteronomy; namely, the Second, Third, Fourth, Fifth, and Tenth[1]. The earliest book of Christian instruction in which they are given at full length as they stand in Exodus, appears to be "the Prymer in English," of about A.D. 1400, printed in Maskell's 'Monumenta Ritualia" (Vol. II. p. 177). They are also given in full in the Primer of Edward VI. (A.D. 1553). When they were first introduced into our Communion Service in the Second Prayer Book of Edward VI. (A.D. 1552), the words in the introductory sentence, "which have brought thee out of the land of Egypt, out of the house of bondage," were unfortunately omitted, and have not been restored in succeeding editions. But they are not only retained in our Catechism, but are made a special topic of instruction in connection with the Commandments in Nowell's larger Catechism[2].

§ III.

The mode in which the Commandments are divided into Ten in our own Service Book agrees with the most ancient authorities, Jewish as well as Christian, and the usage of the Eastern Church. It appears to be based on the clearest view of the subject matter, as it is set forth in the sacred text[3].

But another arrangement, which is first found distinctly stated in St Augustin[4], demands attention from its having been universally adopted by the Western Church until the Reformation. The Second Commandment is added to the First (or, in some of the abridged forms, omitted altogether), and the number ten is made out by treating the Tenth as two Commandments. St Augustin, following Deuteronomy, and the LXX. in Exodus (see below), makes the Ninth "Thou shalt not covet thy neighbour's wife," and the Tenth "Thou shalt not covet thy neighbour's house," &c.: while others, following the Hebrew text of Exodus, reverse this order. In some forms used by the Western Church the whole paragraph on coveting is kept entire, but it is headed as "the Ninth and Tenth Commandments[5]." The general arrangement here spoken of was used by the Church in Britain before the Reformation[6], and is still retained by the Lutheran as well as the Romish Church.

An arrangement unlike either of these may be traced to the fourth century, is distinctly set forth in the Targum of Palestine (which probably belongs to the seventh century), and has been adopted by Maimonides, Aben-Ezra, and other Jewish authorities down to the present day. The First *Word* is identified with "I am the LORD thy God which brought thee out of the land of Egypt" (which cannot of course be properly called a *Commandment*), and the Second Word is made, as in the arrangement last mentioned, to include what we reckon as the First and Second Commandments.

The subject matter itself seems to suggest grave and obvious objections to the two latter arrangements. There is a clear distinction between polytheism and idolatry which entitles each to a distinct Commandment: and the sin of coveting our neighbour's possessions is essentially the same in its nature, whatever may be the object coveted.

It is worthy of notice in regard to the sequence of the Commandments, that the LXX. in Ex. xx. (according to the Vatican text) and Suidas (s. πλαξίν) place vii. and viii. before vi., and transpose the *house* and the *wife* in x.; and that Philo places vii. before vi. according to

[1] Sulp. Sev. 'Sac. Hist.' lib. I. 'Synopsis Sac. Script.' ascribed to St Athanasius. Suidas s. πλαξίν. King Alfred's 'Laws.' 'The Lutheran Cat.' (in which what are here called the sacred writers' comments are named *appendices*). 'The Institution,' &c. and 'The Erudition,' &c. of Henry VIII. The Catechism of Edward VI. The Douay Catechism. The Catechism of the Greek Church, &c. &c.

[2] p. 23. Edit. Jacobson.

[3] This division is recognized in Philo, 'de Orac.' c. 12, 22, 31; 'Quis rer. div. heres.' c. 35. Joseph. 'Ant.' III. 5, § 5. Origen 'Hom. in Exod.' VIII. Jerome 'in Ephes.' VI. 2. Sulp. Sev. 'Sac. Hist.' I. 'Synopsis S.S.' ascribed to Athanasius. Suidas s. πλαξίν. The Catechism of the Greek Church. 'The Institution,' &c. and 'The Erudition,' &c. of Henry VIII. The Primer of 1553, &c. &c.—The testimony of Clement of Alexandria, 'Stromat.' VI. § 137, is ambiguous, and has been quoted both for and against the arrangement; see Suicer s. δεκάλογος, and Kurtz, 'Old Covenant,' III. 124.

[4] 'Quæst. in Exod.' LXXI. Serm. VIII. IX. &c.

[5] The Trent and Lutheran Catechisms.

[6] King Alfred's 'Laws.'—The 'Speculum' of St Edmund, Archbishop of Canterbury (1234—1242), and the 'Treatises' of Richard Hampole (circ. 1340), published by the Early English Text Society.—The Primer of 1400, &c. &c.

the order recognized in Mark x. 19; Luke xviii. 20; Rom. xiii. 9; James ii. 11. The usual order is preserved by the other ancient versions in Exodus, and by the LXX. in Deut. v.; as it is also, as regards vi. and vii., in Matt. v. 21, 27, xix. 18.

§ IV.

The distribution of the Commandments between the Two Tables which is most familiar to us, allotting four to the First Table and six to the Second, is first mentioned by St Augustine, though it is not approved by him. It is based on a distinction that lies on the surface, and that easily adapts itself to modern ethical systems, between our duty towards God and our duty towards our neighbour[1]. The division approved by St Augustine was, in relation to the matter in each Table, the same; but as he united the First and Second Commandments into one, and divided the Tenth into two, he made the First Table to comprise three Commandments, and the Second Table, seven. He mystically associated the first of these numbers with the Persons of the Trinity, and the latter with the Sabbatical institution[2].

But the more symmetrical arrangement which allots five Commandments to each Table is supported by the most ancient authorities[3], and is approved by several modern critics. It is also countenanced by Rom. xiii. 9, where the complete Second Table appears to be spoken of as not including the Fifth Commandment.

Philo places the Fifth Commandment last in the First Table, and calls it a link between the Two Tables. On the reason of this designation of his, see on Ex. xx. 12. The real distinction between the Tables appears to be that the First relates to the duties which arise from our Filial relations, the Second to those which arise from our Fraternal relations[4]. But as the Commandments represent the essence of law, they assume the strict form of law. They are expressed, almost exclusively, in the prohibitory form, because it belongs to law to say what a man shall not do, rather than what he shall do. The Commandments therefore set forth neither of the relations that have been mentioned on the positive side. They contain no injunctions to love God, like that in Deut. vi. 5, x. 12, &c.; nor to love our brethren, like that in Lev. xix. 18; nor do they tell us to *love* our parents.

[1] See on Exod. xx. 12.

[2] 'Quæst. in Exod.' 71. The notion is adopted in the 'Speculum' of St Edmund. See p. 337, note 6.

[3] Philo, 'de Orac.' 25; 'Quis rer. div. heres.' 35. Josephus 'Ant.' III. 5, § 8 and § 5. Irenæus, 'Adv. hæres.' II. 24, § 4. Gregor. Naz. 'Carm. Var.' XXXV.

[4] Knobel observes that the subject of the First Table is *pietas*, that of the Second Table, *probitas*.

§ V.

The name most frequently used by Moses for the Decalogue (העדות) signifies something strongly affirmed, literally, *something spoken again and again*: it is therefore properly rendered in our version THE TESTIMONY (see § I.). Taking this in connection with the prohibitory form of the Commandments, the name must have been understood as the Testimony of Jehovah against the tendency to transgress in those to whom the document was addressed. When Moses laid up the completed Book of the Law, of which the Commandments were the central point, by the side of the Ark of the Covenant, his declared purpose was "that it may be there for a witness against thee; for I know thy rebellion and thy stiff neck" (Deut. xxxi. 26, 27)[5].

It was by the Law, as it was represented in these Commandments, that there came "the knowledge of sin[6]." The disturbance of the conscience which results from doing wrong, when there is no expressed law, is a vague discomfort to the person with no clear apprehension as to its cause. But when the voice of the Lord has given forth the Law in words intelligible to the mind, then comes *the knowledge* of sin, as the transgression of righteous obligation to a gracious God[7].

And this knowledge of sin necessarily involves a consciousness of condemnation. Hence the Tables given to Moses were "a ministration of condemnation"—"a ministration of death written and engraven on stones" (2 Cor. iii. 7, 9; cf. Eph. ii. 15). Yet was this ministration of condemnation a true revelation of Him who had redeemed His people in love, and it is, in the truest sense, a demand on them for the tribute of their love[8]. It is love in the creature which alone can obey the Law in reality and with acceptance[9].

The relation in which the condemning strictness of the Law stood to the forgiving mercy of Jehovah was distinctly shewn in the

[5] Hengstenberg takes nearly the same view as is here given of the application of the word עדות, and of the relation of the Mercy seat to the Decalogue. 'Pentateuch,' Vol. II. p. 524.

[6] Rom. iii. 20, vii. 7; cf. note on Ex. xx. 17.

[7] On the mode in which this was figured in the Sacrifices of the Law, see notes on Lev. iv.

[8] "For though the Law, being love, may seem to reveal God who is love, yet is it rather a demand for love than a revelation of love; and though it might have been, in the light of high intelligence, and where there was no darkening of sin, concluded that love alone could demand love, yet does the mere demand never so speak to sinners; but 'by the Law is the knowledge of sin:'-wherefore 'the Law worketh wrath.'" Campbell, 'The Nature of the Atonement,' p. 41. Cf. Rom. vii. 7—14.

[9] Matt. xxii. 37—40; Mark xii. 29—31; Luke x. 26, 27; Rom. xiii. 8, 10; Gal. v. 4; Jam. ii. 8. See on Ex. xx. 2.

symbolism of the Sanctuary. When the Tables of the Law were deposited in the Ark of the Covenant, they were covered by the Mercy seat, which, in accordance with its name, was the sign of the Divine lovingkindness (see Note on ch. xxv. 17). The Cherubim which were on the Mercy seat appear to have figured the highest condition of created intelligence in the act of humble adoration and service, and so to have expressed the condition on which were obtained forgiveness, deliverance from the letter that killeth (2 Cor. iii. 6), and communion with Jehovah. This view of the significance of the Ark and what pertained to it seems aptly to suit the words in which the arrangement of the symbols is prescribed; "and thou shalt put the mercy seat above upon the ark; and in the ark thou shalt put the testimony that I shall give thee. And there I will meet with thee, and I will commune with thee from above the mercy seat. from between the two cherubims which are upon the ark of the testimony," Ex. xxv. 21, 22.

The Ark, as the outward and visible sign of the Covenant between Jehovah and His people, thus expressed, in a way suited to the time and the occasion, the Divine purpose in the Atonement. The Law was the characteristic feature in the dispensation which was then present; and accordingly the essence of the Law was expressed, not in a symbol, but in plain words written by the finger of God. But the sentence of condemnation implied in the Commandments could not be exhibited in its naked severity as the basis of the Covenant. It was enclosed in the Ark, and over it the Divine mercy was symbolized in such shadowy outline as was to edify the faithful believers until the fulness of the time came, when the Son was sent "whom God hath set forth to be a propitiation (ἱλαστήριον, *a mercy seat*)[1] through faith in his blood, to declare his righteousness for the remission of sins that are past, through the forbearance of God; to declare, I say, at this time His righteousness: that He might be just, and the justifier of him that believeth in Jesus" (Rom. iii. 25, 26).

The significance of the whole Sanctuary may be said to be concentrated in the Tables of the Law, and the Mercy seat. The other holy things, with every external arrangement, were subordinated to them[2]. And hence the place in which they were deposited was the Holy of Holies, closely shut off by the vail, entered by no one but the High-priest, and by him only once in the year, Ex. xl. 20, 21; Lev. xvi. 2.

§ VI.

It is to be observed that the Decalogue, in respect to its subject-matter, does not set forth what is local, or temporary, or peculiar to a single nation[3]. Its two Tables are a standing declaration of the true relation between morality and religion for all nations and ages[4]. The Fourth Commandment is, in its principle, no exception to this[5]. The Decalogue belonged to the Israelites, not because the truths expressed in it were exclusively theirs, but because it was revealed to them in a special manner (see on Ex. xx. 2). The breadth of meaning which rightly belongs to it may be compared to that of the Lord's Prayer, which, though it was especially given by Christ to His followers for their own use, contains nothing unsuitable for any believer in One God.

NOTE on CHAP. XX. *v.* 8.

ON THE SABBATH DAY.

I. *The Sabbath according to the Law;* II. *according to Tradition.* III. *Its connection with the Creation.* IV. *Its relation to Sunday.* V. *Its connection with the deliverance from Egypt.* VI. *Its compass of meaning.*

§ I.

That the formal observance of the Sabbath day originated in the Law of Moses appears to have been the opinion of Philo and of most of the Fathers and Rabbinists[6], and is held by many modern critics[7]. But see note on Gen. ii. 3.

In what way was the Sabbath day to be kept holy in accordance with the Fourth Commandment? It is expressly said that the ordinary work of life should be intermitted by the whole community, not only the masters, servants, and foreign residents[8], but also the cattle; and the period of this intermission

[1] See Note on ch. xxv. 17.

[2] See Note at the end of ch. xl. § III.

[3] Philo seems to have been impressed with this when he lays an emphasis on the fact that the Ten Commandments were given by Him who was *the Father of the Universe* (ὁ πατὴρ τῶν ὅλων), *the God of the World* (Θεὸς κόσμου), 'de decem Orac.' 9, 10.

[4] "It was the boast of Josephus ('Cont. Ap.' II. 17), that whereas other legislators had made religion to be a part of virtue, Moses had made virtue to be a part of religion." Stanley, 'Jewish Church,' Vol. I. 175.

[5] See Note 'On the Sabbath day,' § IV.

[6] Philo, 'de Orac.' c. 20. Justin Martyr, 'Dialog. cum Tryph.' § 19. Irenæus, IV. 16. Tertullian, 'Adv. Jud.' 2, 4. Otho, 'Rabb. Lex.' p. 603.

[7] See Hengst. 'On the Lord's Day,' p. 7; Ewald, 'Alterthüm.' p. 3; 'Hist. of Israel,' I. 576. Hessey, 'Sunday,' Lect. IV., &c. On the word *Remember* in Ex. xx. 8, see note.

[8] See on Ex. xx. 10.

was from the evening of the sixth day of the week to the evening of the seventh[1]. The following occupations are expressly mentioned as unlawful in different parts of the Old Testament; sowing and reaping (Ex. xxxiv. 21), pressing grapes, and bearing burdens of all kinds (Neh. xiii. 15; Jer. xvii. 21), holding of markets and all kinds of trade (Neh. xiii. 15; Amos viii. 5), gathering wood, and kindling a fire for cooking (Ex. xxxv. 3; Num. xv. 32). The Sabbath was to be a day of enjoyment like other festivals (Isa. lviii. 13; Hos. ii. 11), and such restrictions as were imposed could have been unacceptable to none but the disobedient and the avaricious, such as are spoken of in Amos viii. 5, 6.

In the service of the Sanctuary, the Morning and Evening Sacrifices were doubled[2], the Shewbread was changed[3], and, after the courses of the Priests and Levites had been instituted by David, each course in its turn commenced its duties on the Sabbath day[4]. When the Temple was built, there is reason to believe that there was a special musical service for the day[5].

The term *Holy Convocation*, which belongs to the Sabbath day in common with certain other Festival days, would seem to imply that there was a meeting together of the people for a religious purpose[6]. From the mode in which the commands to keep the Sabbath day and to reverence the Sanctuary are associated, it may be inferred with probability that there was such a meeting in the Court of the Sanctuary[7]. At later periods, in places remote from the Temple, we know that it was a custom to resort on this day to public teachers, and to hear the reading of the Old Testament, with addresses of exposition and exhortation, in the Synagogues[8]. It is not unreasonable to suppose that some usage of this kind may have been observed at the Sanctuary itself from the first institution of the Sabbath[9].

1 See Lev. xxiii. 32.

2 Num. xxviii. 9; 2 Chro. xxxi. 3; Ezek. xlvi. 4.

3 Lev. xxiv. 8; 1 Chro. ix. 32; Matt. xii. 4, &c.

4 2 K. xi. 5; 2 Chro. xxiii. 4; cf. 1 Chro. ix. 25.

5 This is favoured by a comparison of the heading of Ps. lxxxi. with *v.* 3 of the Psalm itself, as well as by the Talmud.

6 Lev. xxiii. 2, 3.

7 Lev. xix. 30; Ezek. xxiii. 38.

8 2 K. iv. 23; Luke iv. 15, 16; Acts xiii. 14, 15, 27, xv. 21.

9 There may be references to such a custom Lev. x. 11; Deut. xxxiii. 10. The earliest and best Jewish traditions state that one great object of the Sabbath day was to furnish means and opportunity for spiritual edification. Philo, 'de Orac.' c. 20. 'Vit. Mos.' III. 27. Jos. 'Ant.' XVI. 2. § 3. 'Cont. Ap.' I. 20, II. 18. For rabbinical authorities to the same effect, see Cartwright on Ex. xx. 8, in the 'Critici Sacri.'

Such are the particulars that can be gathered out of the Scriptures as to the mode of observing the Sabbath day. In the time of the Legislator an entire rest from the work of daily life was to reign throughout the Camp: and it may be conjectured that the people assembled before the Altar at the hours of the Morning and Evening Sacrifices for prayer and contemplation, and to listen to the reading of portions of the Divine Law, perhaps from the lips of Moses himself.

The notices of the Sabbath day in the Prophets are most frequently accompanied by complaint or warning respecting its neglect and desecration[10]. But in the time of Isaiah (i. 13) a parade of observing it had become a cloak for hypocrisy, probably under a kindred influence to that which turned the public fasts into occasions for strife and debate (Isa. lviii. 4). These diverse abuses may have co-existed as belonging to two opposite parties in the community, both being in the wrong.

§ II.

In another age, after the Captivity, the Pharisees multiplied the restraints of the Sabbath day to a most burdensome extent. It was forbidden to pluck an ear of corn and rub out the grains to satisfy hunger in passing through a cornfield (Matt. xii. 2); or to relieve the sick (Matt. xii. 10; Luke xiii. 14). It was however permitted to lead an ox or an ass to water, or to lift out an animal that had fallen into a pit (Matt. xii. 11; Luke xiv. 5), to administer circumcision, if the eighth day after the birth of a child fell on a Sabbath (Joh. vii. 22), and to invite guests to a social meal (Luke xiv. 1). According to rabbinical authorities, it was forbidden to travel more than 2000 cubits on the Sabbath[11], to kill the most offensive kinds of vermin, to write two letters of the alphabet, to use a wooden leg or a crutch, to carry a purse, or, for a woman, to carry a seal-ring or a smelling bottle, to wear a high head-dress or a false tooth. Amongst other restraints laid upon animals, the fat-tailed sheep was not allowed to use the little truck on which the tail was borne to save the animal from suffering. These are a portion of 39 prohibitions of the same kind[12].

10 Is. lvi. 2—6, lviii. 13; Jer. xvii. 21, 27; Ezek. xx. 13, 16, 20; Amos viii. 5, &c.

11 On the Sabbath-day's journey, see Joseph. 'Ant.' XIII. 8. § 4 with the Note on Ex. xvi. 29: also Walther, 'de Itin. Sabb.' in 'Thes. Philolog.' II. p. 417. Winer, 'R. B.' s. 'Sabbathsweg.'

12 Mishna, 'de Sabbatho.' We are told by a eulogist of the Talmud that the rabbinical Sabbath was not "a thing of grim austerity" ('Quarterly Rev.' Dec. 1867.) Its austerity was indeed somewhat mitigated by qualifying regulations. Though the Jew could not light a fire on the Sabbath, he was formally permitted, at the latest moment of the eve of the Sabbath, to pack

Connected with this trifling of the Pharisees and the Rabbinists, is the notion that the intention of the Law was, that the Sabbath should be, as nearly as possible, a day of mere inaction. This has been held not only by Jewish writers[1], but by some Christians in the time of S. Chrysostom[2], and by critics of more modern date (Spencer, Vitringa, Le Clerc). Our Lord decides this very point by declaring that there is a kind of work which is proper for the Sabbath day[3]. See the next section.

§ III.

In examining the two distinct grounds for the observance of the Sabbath day which are assigned by Moses[4], the first step is to trace the nature of the connection between the Day and the Creation of the world. What is clearly stated is, that the Day was hallowed by the Divine Law as a memorial of the rest of God when the Creation of the world was completed[5]. Man was to rest because God had rested. But the rest of man can only partially resemble the rest of God. "The Creator of the ends of the earth fainteth not, neither is weary[6]." His work in the world did not cease at the close of the six days, nor has it ever been remitted since[7]. His hand must be ever holding the corners of the earth and the strength of the hills[8]. His rest cannot therefore be like that inaction which belongs to night and sleep, which man, in common with all animals, requires for the restoration of his wasted powers. But yet a man may have conscious experience, after well performed work, of a restful condition that bears an analogy to the occasion on which "God saw every thing that He had made, and, behold, it was very good[9]." And this Sabbath feeling is only to be enjoyed by those whose work, performed in a spirit of trustful dependence, has kept pace with the day during the week; those who obey not only the command, "Remember the Sabbath day," but also the command, "Six days shalt thou labour[10]."

The true rest of man then is so far like the rest of the Creator, that it is remote in its nature from the sleep of insensibility as it is from the ordinary struggle of the world. The weekly Sabbath, as representing that state, was "a shadow of things to come[11]," a foretaste of the life in which there is to be no more *toilsome fatigue* (πόνος[12]), that life which is the true *keeping of Sabbath* (σαββατισμός) into which our Saviour entered as our forerunner when He ceased from His works on earth, as God had ceased from His works on the seventh day (Heb. iv. 9, 10).

The works of the Creation are described as culminating in the creation of man. The Sabbath crowned the completed works, and as it was revealed to the Israelite, it reminded him of "the fact of his relation to God, of his being made in the image of God; it was to teach him to regard the universe not chiefly as under the government of sun or moon, or as regulated by their courses; but as an order which the unseen God had created, which included Sun, Moon, Stars, Earth, and all the living creatures that inhabit them. The week, then, was especially to raise the Jew above the thought of Time, to make him feel that though he was subject to *its* laws, he yet stood in direct connection with an *eternal* law; with a Being who is, and was, and is to come[13]." Philo aptly calls the day *the imaging forth* (ἐκμαγεῖον) *of the first beginning*. Some of the wisest Jewish teachers (Aben-Ezra, Abarbanel) have said that he who breaks the Sabbath denies the Creation. The Sabbath, in this connection, became to the Israelite the central point of religious observance, and represented every appropriation of time to the public recognition of Jehovah. Hence the injunction to observe it appears to be essentially connected with the warning against idolatry[14].

§ IV.

But this great idea did not exclusively belong to the Israelite, although it was revealed to him, above all men, in its true relation to God and man. Real worship for every man, always and everywhere, is of course based on the truth of a Creator distinct from the Creation. And thus the Law of the Sabbath was the expression of a universal truth. Hence, the Commandment bears its meaning for all mankind. The day which we observe, in accordance with ecclesiastical usage, holds another place in the week, and its connection with

up hot food in such a way as to keep it hot as long as possible ('de Sabb.' IV. 1. 2). Under particular conditions, the sick might be relieved (Mish. 'Joma,' VIII. 6). Fasting on the Sabbath was strictly prohibited (Otho, 'Rab. Lex.' p. 608; cf. Judith viii. 6). Whether or not a Sabbath regulated by rabbinical rules was, on the whole, grimly austere, we need not scruple to call the rules themselves grossly absurd.

1 Buxtorf. 'Synag. Jud.' CXVI.

2 'Hom. in Matt.' XXXI.

3 Matt. xii. 12; Mark iii. 4, &c.

4 See Ex. xx. 11; Deut. v. 15; Note 'On the Ten Commandments,' § II.

5 Ex. xx. 11, xxxi. 17. Cf. Gen. ii. 3.

6 Is. xl. 28.

7 See John v. 17.

8 Ps. xcv. 4, 5.

9 Gen. i. 31.

10 Moses (says Philo) ἐκέλευσεν τοὺς μέλλοντας ἐν ταύτῃ ζῆν τῇ πολιτείᾳ, καθάπερ ἐν τοῖς ἄλλοις, καὶ κατὰ τοῦθ' ἕπεσθαι θεῷ, πρὸς μὲν ἔργα τρεπομένους ἐφ' ἡμέρας ἕξ, ἀνέχοντας δὲ καὶ φιλοσοφοῦντας τῇ ἑβδόμῃ καὶ θεωρίαις μὲν τῶν τῆς φύσεως σχολάζοντας, κ.τ.λ. 'de decem Orac.' c. 20.

11 Col. ii. 16, 17.

12 Cf. Rev. xiv. 13.

13 Maurice 'On the Old Testament,' Serm. I.

14 See Lev. xix, 3. 4; Ezek. xx. 16, 20.

the Creation of the world has thus been put into the background. But the meaning of the Lord's day cannot be separated from the great meaning of the Sabbath. As the Sabbath reminded the believer under the Old Covenant that God had rested after He had created man and breathed into him the breath of life before sin had brought death into the world, so the Sunday now reminds the believer that Christ rested after He had overcome death, that he might restore all who believe in Him to a new life, that they may become the sons of God by adoption[1]. What therefore the Sunday, as a commemoration of the Resurrection, is to the dispensation of Christ, the Sabbath, in respect to its connection with the rest of God, was to the dispention of Moses. On this ground then there is reason enough why the Fourth, as well as the other Commandments, should be addressed to Christian congregations and should hold its place in our Service.

§ V.

It was at a later period that the inspired Legislator set forth a second ground on which obedience to the Commandment was required. It was said to the Israelite that he should observe the Day in order that his manservant and his maidservant might rest as well as he; and the words were added; "and remember that thou wast a servant in the land of Egypt, and that the LORD thy God brought thee out thence through a mighty hand and a stretched out arm: therefore the LORD thy God commanded thee to keep the Sabbath day[2]." By the command that the manservants and the maidservants were to rest on the Day as well as their masters, witness was borne to the equal position which every Israelite might claim in the presence of Jehovah. The Sabbath was thus made a distinguishing badge, a sacramental bond, for the whole people, according to the words, "it is a sign between me and you throughout your generations; that ye may know that I am the LORD that doth sanctify you[3]." The wealthy Israelite, in remembrance of what he himself, or his forefathers, had suffered in Egypt, was to realize the fact on this Day that the poorest of his brethren had enjoyed the same deliverances, and had the same share in the Covenant, as himself. The whole nation, as one man, was to enjoy rest. He who outraged the Sabbath, either by working himself, or by suffering his servants to work, broke the Covenant with Jehovah, and at the same time cut himself off from his people so as to incur the sentence of death[4].

This latter ground for the observance of the Sabbath day furnishes a not less strict analogy with the Sunday than that which has been noticed. What the Sabbath was to "the kingdom of priests, the holy nation[5]," on the score that they had been redeemed from the bondage of Egypt and made free men, such the Sunday is to "the chosen generation, the royal priesthood, the holy nation, the peculiar people[6]," as those whom Christ has redeemed from the bondage of corruption, and brought into the glorious liberty of the children of God[7].

§ VI.

In order rightly to apprehend the compass of the Fourth Commandment in reference to the public worship of the Israelites, it should be kept in view that the Sabbath did not stand by itself, as an insulated observance. Not only did the original ground of the Weekly Sabbath connect it with all true worship, but it formed the centre of an organized system including the Sabbatical year, and the Jubilee year[8]. Besides this, the recurrence of the Sabbatical number in the cycle of yearly festivals is so frequent and distinct, as plainly to indicate a set purpose. Without laying stress on the mystical meaning of the number *seven*, as Philo, Bähr, and others have done, it is evident that the number was the Divinely appointed symbol, repeated again and again in the public services, suggesting the connection between the entire range of the Ceremonial Law and the consecrated Seventh Day. And this may be compared with the important remark of Bähr, that the ritual of the Sabbath day, in spite of the superlative sanctity of the Day, was not, like that of other Festivals, distinguished by offerings or rites of a peculiar kind, but only by a doubling of the common daily sacrifices. It was thus not so much cut off from the Week as marked out as *the Day of Days*, and so symbolized the sanctification of the daily life of the people. In whichever way we regard it, the Fourth Commandment appears to have stood to the Israelite as an injunction in the broadest sense to maintain the national Worship of Jehovah.

[1] Rom. iv. 25, vi. 4, viii. 13, 15.
[2] Deut. v. 14, 15.
[3] Ex. xxxi. 13, 17; cf. Lev. xx. 8; Is. lvi. 2, 4; Ezek. xx. 12. 20, xxii. 8, 26.
[4] Ex. xxxi. 14, 15—xxxv. 2; Jer. xvii. 21—27.
[5] Ex. xix. 6.
[6] 1 Pet. ii. 9.
[7] Rom. viii. 21.
[8] Lev. xxv.

22 ¶ And the LORD said unto
Moses, Thus thou shalt say unto the
children of Israel, Ye have seen
that I have talked with you from
heaven.
23 Ye shall not make with me
gods of silver, neither shall ye make
unto you gods of gold.
24 ¶ An altar of earth thou shalt
make unto me, and shalt sacrifice
thereon thy burnt offerings, and thy
peace offerings, thy sheep, and thine
oxen: in all places where I record my
[l] Deut. 27. 5. name I will come unto thee, and I
Josh. 8. 31. will bless thee.
† Heb. *build them with hewing.* 25 And [l] if thou wilt make me an
altar of stone, thou shalt not † build
it of hewn stone: for if thou lift
up thy tool upon it, thou hast polluted it.
26 Neither shalt thou go up by
steps unto mine altar, that thy nakedness be not discovered thereon.

CHAPTER XXI.

1 *Laws for menservants.* 5 *For the servant whose ear is bored.* 7 *For womenservants.* 12 *For manslaughter.* 16 *For stealers of men.* 17 *For cursers of parents.* 18 *For smiters.* 22 *For a hurt by chance.* 28 *For an ox that goreth.* 33 *For him that is an occasion of harm.*

NOW these *are* the judgments
which thou shalt set before
them.

THE BOOK OF THE COVENANT.
Ch. xx. 22—xxiii. 33.
Introductory Note.

Now follows a series of laws, some of them addressed simply to the conscience, like the Ten Commandments, and others having the sanction of a penalty attached. The context seems to make it clear that we may identify this series with what was written by Moses in the book called the BOOK OF THE COVENANT, and read by him in the audience of the people (see xxiv. 4, 7). There has been a difference of opinion as to the compass of matter contained in this Book. But the weight of authority is in fávour of its comprising the last five verses of ch. xx. with chaps. xxi, xxii, xxiii (de Wette, Ewald, Hupfeld, Knobel, Keil, Herxheimer, &c.). A few would add the Ten Commandments (Hengst., Kurtz, &c.). Some Jewish Commentators imagine that the BOOK OF THE COVENANT included very considerable portions of Genesis and of the earlier part of Exodus.

Adopting the conclusion as by far the most probable one, that the Book of the Covenant included from ch. xx. 22 to xxiii. 33, it is evident that the document cannot be regarded as a strictly systematic whole. Portions of it were probably traditional rules handed down from the Patriarchs, and retained by the Israelites in Egypt. Probable traces of præ-Mosaic antiquity may be seen in xx. 24—26, xxi. 6, xxiii. 19, &c. Some of the laws relate to habits of fixed abode, not (at least if taken in their strict form) to such a mode of life as that of the Israelites in their march through the Wilderness (see xxii. 5, 6, 29, xxiii. 10, 11): some, especially those relating to slavery, would seem to have been modifications of ancient usages (see on xxi. 20, 21). These more or less ancient maxims may have been associated with notes of such decisions on cases of difference as had been up to this time pronounced by Moses and the judges whom he had appointed by the advice of Jethro. See xviii. 13—26.

In whatever way these laws may have originated, as they are here brought together, they are clearly enforced by Jehovah as conditions of conduct for the covenanted people. The adoption of Patriarchal maxims accords with the spirit of the Mosaic legislation, as expressed in the Fifth Commandment.

CHAP. XX. **22—26.** Nothing could be more appropriate as the commencement of the Book of the Covenant than these regulations for public worship.

23. Assuming this to be an old formula, its meaning is brought out more comprehensively in the Second Commandment, and is strengthened by the fact declared in *v.* 22, that Jehovah had now spoken from Heaven.

24—26. These must have been old and accepted rules for the building of altars, and they are not inconsistent with the directions for the construction of the Altar of the Court of the Tabernacle, ch. xxvii. 1—8. There is no good reason to doubt that they were observed in "the Brazen Altar," as it is called, although no reference is made to them in connection with it. That Altar, according to the directions that are given, must indeed have been rather *an altar case*, with a mass of earth or stone within, when it was put to use. See notes on xxvii. 1—8, and cf. Josh. xxii. 26—28.

CHAP. XXI. The Book of the Covenant, continued.

1. *judgments*] *i.e.* decisions of the Law. It is worthy of remark that these judgments

a Lev. 25. 41. Deut. 15. 12. Jer. 34. 14.

2 [a] If thou buy an Hebrew servant, six years he shall serve: and in
the seventh he shall go out free for
nothing.

† Heb. *with his body.*

3 If he came in † by himself, he
shall go out by himself: if he were
married, then his wife shall go out
with him.

4 If his master have given him a
wife, and she have born him sons or
daughters; the wife and her children
shall be her master's, and he shall go
out by himself.

† Heb. *saying shall say.*

5 And if the servant † shall plainly
say, I love my master, my wife, and
my children; I will not go out free:

6 Then his master shall bring him
unto the judges; he shall also bring
him to the door, or unto the door
post; and his master shall bore his
ear through with an aul; and he shall
serve him for ever.

7 ¶ And if a man sell his daughter to be a maidservant, she shall not
go out as the menservants do.

8 If she † please not her master, † Heb. *be evil in the eyes of, &c.*
who hath betrothed her to himself,
then shall he let her be redeemed: to
sell her unto a strange nation he shall
have no power, seeing he hath dealt
deceitfully with her.

9 And if he have betrothed her
unto his son, he shall deal with her
after the manner of daughters.

10 If he take him another *wife;*
her food, her raiment, and her duty
of marriage, shall he not diminish.

11 And if he do not these three
unto her, then shall she go out free
without money.

---

begin with some that relate to slavery (*vv.* 2—16); other judgments on the same subject occur in *vv.* 20, 21, 26, 27.

2. A Hebrew might be sold as a bondman in consequence either of debt (Lev. xxv. 39) or of the commission of theft (Ex. xxii. 3). But his servitude could not be enforced for more than six full years. The law is more fully expressed in Deut. xv. 12—18, where it enjoins that the bondman should not be sent away at the end of his period of service without a liberal supply of provisions; and it is further supplemented by other regulations, especially in reference to the Jubilee, in Lev. xxv. 39—43, 47—55. Foreign slaves are expressly spoken of Lev. xxv. 44, 46.

3. If a married man became a bondman, his rights in regard to his wife were respected: but if a single bondman accepted at the hand of his master a bondwoman as his wife, the master did not lose his claim to the woman, or her children, at the expiration of the husband's term of service. Such wives, it may be presumed, were always foreign slaves.

5, 6. But if the bondman loved his wife so as to be unwilling to give her up, or if he was strongly enough attached to his master's service, he might, by submitting to a certain ceremony, prolong his term "for ever;" that is, most probably, till the next Jubilee, when every Hebrew was set free. So Josephus ('Ant.' IV. 8, § 28) and the Rabbinists understood the phrase. See Lev. xxv. 40, 50. The custom of boring the ear as a mark of slavery appears to have been a common one in ancient times, observed in many nations. See Xenoph. 'Anab.' III. 1, § 31; Plaut. 'Pœnul.' V. ii. 21; Juvenal, I. 104; Plut. 'Cicero,' c. 26, &c.

6. *unto the judges*] Literally, *before the gods* (*elohim*). The word does not denote *judges* in a direct way, but it is to be understood as the name of God, in its ordinary plural form, God being the source of all justice. (So Gesen., de Wette, Knobel, Fürst, Herxh., &c.) LXX. πρὸς τὸ κριτήριον τοῦ Θεοῦ. The name in this connection always has the definite article prefixed. See xxii. 8, 9, &c.

7. A man might, in accordance with existing custom, sell his daughter to another man with a view to her becoming an inferior wife, or concubine. In this case, she was not "to go out," like the bondman; that is, she was not to be dismissed at the end of the sixth year. But women who were bound in any other way, would appear to have been under the same conditions as bondmen. See Deut. xv. 17.

8. *shall he let her be redeemed*] More strictly, **he shall cause her to be redeemed.** The meaning seems to be that he should either return her to her father as set free, or find another Hebrew master for her who would grant her the same privileges as she would have had if she had remained with himself. The latter sentence of the verse appears to signify that, although he was not forced to keep literal faith with the woman by making her his concubine, he was not permitted to sell her to a foreigner. Even in the case of a foreign captive who had been accepted as a concubine, and had displeased her master, she could not be sold as a slave,

[b] Lev. 24. 17. 12 ¶ [b] He that smiteth a man, so
that he die, shall be surely put to death.
13 And if a man lie not in wait,
but God deliver *him* into his hand;
[c] Deut. 19. 3. then [c] I will appoint thee a place whither he shall flee.
14 But if a man come presumptuously upon his neighbour, to slay
him with guile; thou shalt take him
from mine altar, that he may die.
15 ¶ And he that smiteth his father, or his mother, shall be surely
put to death.
16 ¶ And he that stealeth a man,
and selleth him, or if he be found
in his hand, he shall surely be put
to death.
17 ¶ And [d] he that ‖ curseth his [d] Lev. 20. 9. Prov. 20. 20. Matt. 15. 4. Mark 7. 10.
father, or his mother, shall surely be
put to death.
18 ¶ And if men strive together,
and one smite ‖ another with a stone, ‖ Or, *revileth.*
or with *his* fist, and he die not, but ‖ Or, *his neighbour.*
keepeth *his* bed:
19 If he rise again, and walk a-
broad upon his staff, then shall he
that smote *him* be quit: only he
shall pay *for* † the loss of his time, † Heb. *[his] ceasing.*
and shall cause *him* to be thoroughly
healed.
20 ¶ And if a man smite his servant, or his maid, with a rod, and he
die under his hand; he shall be surely
† punished. † Heb. *avenged.*

---

but was entitled to her freedom. See Deut. xxi. 14.

11. *if he do not these three unto her*] Most commentators refer these three things to the food, raiment, and duty of marriage, mentioned in *v.* 10. But Knobel and others prefer the interpretation of most of the Rabbinists, which seems on the whole best to suit the context, that the words express a choice of one of three things, in which case their sense is, *if he do neither of these three things*. The man was to give the woman, whom he had purchased from her father, her freedom, unless (i) he caused her to be redeemed by a Hebrew master (*v.* 8); or, (ii) gave her to his son, and treated her as a daughter (*v.* 9); or, (iii) in the event of his taking another wife (*v.* 10), unless he allowed her to retain her place and privileges. These rules (*vv.* 7—11) are to be regarded as mitigations of the then existing usages of concubinage. The form in which they are expressed confirms this view.

12. No distinction is expressly made here or elsewhere between the murder of a free man and that of a bondman. See on *v.* 20. The law was afterwards expressly declared to relate also to foreigners, Lev. xxiv. 17, 21, 22; cf. Gen. ix. 6.

13, 14. There was no place of safety for the guilty murderer, not even the Altar of Jehovah. Thus all superstitious notions connected with the right of sanctuary were excluded. Adonijah and Joab appear to have vainly trusted that the vulgar feeling would protect them, if they took hold of the horns of the Altar on which atonement with blood was made (1 K. i. 50, ii. 28; Lev. iv. 7). But for one who killed a man "at unawares," that is, without intending to do it, the Law afterwards appointed places of refuge, Num. xxxv. 6—34; Deut. iv. 41—43, xix. 2—10; Josh. xx. 2—9. It is very probable that there was some provision answering to the Cities of Refuge, that may have been based upon old usage, in the Camp in the Wilderness.

15, 16, 17. The following offences were to be punished with death:—

Striking a parent, cf. Deut. xxvii. 16.

Cursing a parent, cf. Lev. xx. 9.

Kidnapping, whether with a view to retain the person stolen, or to sell him, cf. Deut. xxiv. 7.

18, 19. If one man injured another in a quarrel so as to oblige him to keep his bed, he who had inflicted the injury was set free from the liability to a criminal charge (such as might be based upon *v.* 12) when the injured man had so far recovered as to be able to walk with a staff: but he was required to compensate the latter for the loss of his time until his recovery was complete, and for the cost of his healing.

20, 21. The Jewish authorities appear to be right in referring this law, like those in *vv.* 26, 27, 32, to foreign slaves (see Lev. xxv. 44—46). All Hebrew bondmen were treated, in regard to life and limb, like freemen, and the Law would take this for granted. The master was permitted to retain the power of chastising his alien slave with a rod, but the indulgence of unbridled temper was so far kept in check by his incurring punishment if the slave died under his hand. If however the slave survived the castigation a day or two, it was assumed that the offence of the master had not been so heinous, and he did not become amenable to the law, because the loss of the slave who, by old custom, was recognized as his property, was accounted, under the circumstances, as a punish-

21 Notwithstanding, if he continue
a day or two, he shall not be punished: for he *is* his money.
22 ¶ If men strive, and hurt a
woman with child, so that her fruit
depart *from her*, and yet no mischief
follow: he shall be surely punished,
according as the woman's husband
will lay upon him; and he shall pay
as the judges *determine*.
23 And if *any* mischief follow, then
thou shalt give life for life,
24 [e] Eye for eye, tooth for tooth,
hand for hand, foot for foot,
25 Burning for burning, wound for
wound, stripe for stripe.
26 ¶ And if a man smite the eye
of his servant, or the eye of his maid,
that it perish; he shall let him go free
for his eye's sake.
27 And if he smite out his manservant's tooth, or his maidservant's
tooth; he shall let him go free for his
tooth's sake.
28 ¶ If an ox gore a man or a
woman, that they die: then [f] the ox
shall be surely stoned, and his flesh
shall not be eaten; but the owner of
the ox *shall be* quit.
29 But if the ox were wont to
push with his horn in time past, and
it hath been testified to his owner,
and he hath not kept him in, but
that he hath killed a man or a woman; the ox shall be stoned, and his
owner also shall be put to death.
30 If there be laid on him a sum
of money, then he shall give for the
ransom of his life whatsoever is laid
upon him.
31 Whether he have gored a son,
or have gored a daughter, according
to this judgment shall it be done unto
him.

[e] Lev. 24. 20. Deut. 19. 21. Matt. 5. 38.

[f] Gen. 9. 5.

---

ment. It is not said how the master was to be treated in the event of the immediate death of the slave. It may have been left to the decision of the judges as to whether the case should come under the law of *v.* 12, or some secondary punishment should be inflicted.—The protection here afforded to the life of a slave may seem to us but a slight one; but it is the very earliest trace of such protection in legislation, and it stands in strong and favourable contrast with the old laws of Greece, Rome, and other nations. The same may be said of *vv.* 26, 27, 32. These regulations were most likely, as much as was feasible at the time, to mitigate the cruelty of ancient practice; they were as much as the hardness of the hearts of the people would bear, Matt. xix. 8. See Mr Goldwin Smith's admirable essay, "Does the Bible sanction American Slavery?"

22—25. The sense is rather obscure. The rule would seem to refer to a case in which the wife of a man engaged in a quarrel interfered. If the violence did no more than occasion premature birth, he who inflicted it was punished by a fine to be proposed by the husband, and approved by the magistrates. But if the injury was more serious, so as to affect life or limb, a penalty was to be inflicted in accordance with the law of suffering like for like, the *jus talionis*.—This law is repeated in substance, Lev. xxiv. 19, 20, 21; Deut. xix. 21; cp. Gen. ix. 6. It has its root in a simple conception of justice, and is found in the laws of many ancient nations. It was ascribed to Rhadamanthus (Arist. 'Ethic.' v. 5). It was recognized in the laws of Solon (Diog. Laert. I. 57), in the Laws of the Twelve Tables (Aul. Gell. X. 1; Festus, s. *talio*), by the ancient Indians (Strab. XV. p. 710), and by the Thurians (Diod. Sic. XII. 17). It appears to be regarded in this place as a maxim for the magistrate in awarding the amount of compensation to be paid for the infliction of personal injury. The sum was to be as nearly as possible the worth in money of the power lost by the injured person. This view appears to be in accordance with Jewish tradition (Mishna, 'Baba Kama,' VIII. 1). Michaelis has some good remarks on the *jus talionis* ('Laws of Moses,' Vol. III. p. 448).—Our Lord quotes *v.* 24 as representing the form of the Law, in order to illustrate the distinction between the Letter and the Spirit (Matt. v. 38). The tendency of the teaching of the Scribes and Pharisees was to confound the obligations of the conscience with the external requirements of the Law. The Law, in its place, was still to be "holy and just and good," but its direct purpose was to protect the community, not to guide the heart of the believer, who was not to exact eye for eye, tooth for tooth, but to love his enemies, and to forgive all injuries.

26, 27. When a master inflicted a permanent injury on the person of his bondservant, freedom was the proper equivalent for the disabled or lost member.

28—31. If an ox killed a person, the animal was slain as a tribute to the sanctity of human life (Gen. ix. 6; cf. Gen. iv. 11). It

32 If the ox shall push a manservant or a maidservant; he shall give unto their master thirty shekels of silver, and the ox shall be stoned.

33 ¶ And if a man shall open a pit, or if a man shall dig a pit, and not cover it, and an ox or an ass fall therein;

34 The owner of the pit shall make *it* good, *and* give money unto the owner of them; and the dead *beast* shall be his.

35 ¶ And if one man's ox hurt another's, that he die; then they shall sell the live ox, and divide the money of it; and the dead *ox* also they shall divide.

36 Or if it be known that the ox hath used to push in time past, and his owner hath not kept him in; he shall surely pay ox for ox; and the dead shall be his own.

CHAPTER XXII.

1 *Of theft.* 5 *Of damage.* 7 *Of trespasses.* 14 *Of borrowing.* 16 *Of fornication.* 18 *Of witchcraft.* 19 *Of beastiality.* 20 *Of idolatry.* 21 *Of strangers, widows, and fatherless.* 25 *Of usury.* 26 *Of pledges.* 28 *Of reverence to magistrates.* 29 *Of the first-fruits.*

IF a man shall steal an ox, or a
‖ sheep, and kill it, or sell it; he ‖ Or, *goat.*
shall restore five oxen for an ox, and
[a] four sheep for a sheep. [a] 2 Sam. 12. 6.

2 ¶ If a thief be found breaking up, and be smitten that he die, *there shall* no blood *be shed* for him.

3 If the sun be risen upon him, *there shall be* blood *shed* for him; *for* he should make full restitution; if he have nothing, then he shall be sold for his theft.

4 If the theft be certainly found in his hand alive, whether it be ox, or ass, or sheep; he shall restore double.

---

was stoned, and its flesh was treated as carrion. In ordinary cases, the owner suffered only the loss of his beast. But if the ox had been previously known to be vicious, the guilty negligence of its owner, in not keeping it under restraint, was reckoned, *prima facie*, as a capital offence. His life might however be commuted for a fine to be determined by the judges; and, as we may infer with probability, to be agreed to by the parents or near relations of the slain person.

32. If the slain person was a slave, the ox was to be stoned to death, and its owner was to pay to the master of the slain person what appears to have been the standard price of a slave, thirty shekels of silver. See on Lev. xxv. 44—46, xxvii. 3.

33, 34. If a man either left his pit (or well) exposed, or dug a new one without protecting it, and an animal fell therein, he was to pay the value of the animal to its owner, but was allowed to appropriate the carcase. The usual mode of protecting a well was probably then, as it is now in the East, by building round it a low circular wall.

35, 36. The dead ox in this case, as well as in the preceding one, must have been worth no more than the price of the hide, as the flesh could not be eaten. See Lev. xvii. 1—6. There is here the same sort of prudent restraint laid upon the owners of vicious animals as in *v.* 29.

CHAP. XXII. The Book of the Covenant, continued.

1. The theft of an ox appears to have been regarded as a greater crime than the theft of a sheep, not from the mere consideration of value, but because it shewed a stronger purpose in wickedness to take the larger and more powerful animal. It may have been on similar moral ground that the thief, when he had proved his persistency in crime by adding to his theft the slaughter, or sale, of the animal, was to restore four times its value in the case of a sheep (cf. 2 S. xii. 6), and five times its value in the case of an ox; but if the animal was still in his possession alive (see *v.* 4) he had to make only twofold restitution.

2. *breaking up*] **breaking in.**

3, 4. If a thief, in breaking into a dwelling in the night, was slain, the person who slew him did not incur the guilt of blood; but if the same occurred in daylight, the slayer was guilty in accordance with xxi. 12. The distinction may have been based on the fact that in the light of day there was a fair chance of identifying and apprehending the thief, or, at least, his design would be apparent: but in the darkness of night there could be no reckoning as to how far his purpose might extend, and there would be a great probability of his escaping unrecognized. When a thief was apprehended in the act, he could be forced to make restitution if he had the means, and if not he was to be sold as a bondslave. The latter punishment may be likened to our penal servitude; and, in the case of a Hebrew, it could not be prolonged beyond six years. See xxi. 2.

5 ¶ If a man shall cause a field or vineyard to be eaten, and shall put in his beast, and shall feed in another man's field; of the best of his own field, and of the best of his own vineyard, shall he make restitution.

6 ¶ If fire break out, and catch in thorns, so that the stacks of corn, or the standing corn, or the field, be consumed *therewith;* he that kindled the fire shall surely make restitution.

7 ¶ If a man shall deliver unto his neighbour money or stuff to keep, and it be stolen out of the man's house; if the thief be found, let him pay double.

8 If the thief be not found, then the master of the house shall be brought unto the judges, *to see* whether he have put his hand unto his neighbour's goods.

9 For all manner of trespass, *whether it be* for ox, for ass, for sheep, for raiment, *or* for any manner of lost thing, which *another* challengeth to be his, the cause of both parties shall come before the judges; *and* whom the judges shall condemn, he shall pay double unto his neighbour.

10 If a man deliver unto his neighbour an ass, or an ox, or a sheep, or any beast, to keep; and it die, or be hurt, or driven away, no man seeing *it:*

11 *Then* shall an oath of the LORD be between them both, that he hath not put his hand unto his neighbour's goods; and the owner of it shall accept *thereof*, and he shall not make *it* good.

12 And [b] if it be stolen from him, [b] Gen. 3
he shall make restitution unto the 39.
owner thereof.

13 If it be torn in pieces, *then* let him bring it *for* witness, *and* he shall not make good that which was torn.

14 ¶ And if a man borrow *ought* of his neighbour, and it be hurt, or die, the owner thereof *being* not with it, he shall surely make *it* good.

15 *But* if the owner thereof *be* with it, he shall not make *it* good: if it *be* an hired *thing*, it came for his hire.

16 ¶ And [c] if a man entice a maid [c] Deut. 2
that is not betrothed, and lie with 28.
her, he shall surely endow her to be his wife.

17 If her father utterly refuse to give her unto him, he shall † pay † Heb.
money according to the dowry of *weigh.*
virgins.

---

4. See on *v.* 1.

5. *shall put in his beast, and shall feed*] Rather, **shall let his beast go loose, and it shall feed.** (Thus the LXX., Vulg., Syr., Luther, Zunz, &c.) He who had allowed his beast to stray and consume the pasture or the grapes of his neighbour, had to restore out of the best of his possessions a like quantity of produce, without regard to the quality of that which had been consumed.

7. *pay double*] Cf. *v.* 4.

8. It would appear that if the master of the house could clear himself of imputation, the loss of the pledged article fell upon its owner.

judges] See on xxi. 6.

9. *all manner of trespass*] In every case of theft, he who was accused, and he who had lost the stolen property, were both to appear before the judges (xviii. 25, 26): the convicted thief, under ordinary circumstances, was to pay double. See *vv.* 4, 7.

10—13. This law appears to relate chiefly to herdsmen employed by the owners of cattle. It implies that, if he to whom the creatures were entrusted could prove that he had taken all reasonable care and precaution, the risk of loss or injury fell upon the owner: and if no witness could be produced, the oath of the herdsman himself that he had performed his duty was accepted. But when an animal was stolen (*v.* 12), it was presumed either that the herdsman might have prevented it, or that he could find the thief and bring him to justice (see *v.* 4). When an animal was killed by a wild beast, the keeper had to produce the mangled carcase, not only in proof of the fact, but to shew that he had, by his vigilance and courage, deprived the wild beast of its prey.

14, 15. If a man borrowed, or hired, an animal, it was at his risk, unless the owner accompanied it.

15. *it came for his hire*] These words are obscure, but they probably mean that the sum paid for hiring was regarded as covering the risk of accident.

16, 17. The man who seduced a girl that was not betrothed had to forfeit for her bene-

18 ¶ Thou shalt not suffer a witch
to live.
19 ¶ Whosoever lieth with a beast
shall surely be put to death.
[d] Deut. 13. 20 ¶ [d] He that sacrificeth unto *any*
13, 14, 15. 1 Mac. 2. god, save unto the LORD only, he
24. shall be utterly destroyed.
[e] Lev. 19. 21 ¶ [e] Thou shalt neither vex a
33. stranger, nor oppress him: for ye were
strangers in the land of Egypt.
[f] Zech. 7. 22 ¶ [f] Ye shall not afflict any
10. widow, or fatherless child.
23 If thou afflict them in any wise,
and they cry at all unto me, I will
surely hear their cry;
24 And my wrath shall wax hot,
and I will kill you with the sword;
[g] Lev. 25. and your wives shall be widows, and
37. Deut. 23. your children fatherless.
19. Psal. 15. 5. 25 ¶ [g] If thou lend money to *any*
of my people *that is* poor by thee,
thou shalt not be to him as an
usurer, neither shalt thou lay upon
him usury.
26 If thou at all take thy neighbour's raiment to pledge, thou shalt
deliver it unto him by that the sun
goeth down:
27 For that *is* his covering only, it *is*
his raiment for his skin: wherein shall
he sleep? and it shall come to pass,
when he crieth unto me, that I will
hear; for I *am* gracious.
28 ¶ [h] Thou shalt not revile the [h] Acts 23.
‖ gods, nor curse the ruler of thy 5. ‖ Or,
people. *judges.* † Heb.
29 ¶ Thou shalt not delay *to offer* *thy fulness.*
the † first of thy ripe fruits, and of † Heb.
thy † liquors: [i] the firstborn of thy *tear.* [i] chap. 13.
sons shalt thou give unto me. 2, 12. & 34. 19.

---

fit a proper sum for a dowry (see on Deut. xxii. 28, 29), and to marry her, if her father would allow him to do so. The seducer of a betrothed girl was to be stoned. See Deut. xxii. 23, 27.

18. *Thou shalt not suffer a witch to live*] The practice of witchcraft by both sexes is condemned in Lev. xx. 27; Deut. xviii. 9—12. Wizards alone are mentioned Lev. xix. 31. The witch is here named to represent the class. This is the earliest denunciation of witchcraft in the Law. In every form of witchcraft there is an appeal to a power not acting in subordination to the Divine Law. From all such notions and tendencies true worship is designed to deliver us. The practice of witchcraft was therefore an act of rebellion against Jehovah, and, as such, was a capital crime. The passages bearing on the subject in the Prophets, as well as those in the Law, carry a lesson for all ages. Isa. viii. 19, xix. 3, xliv. 25, xlvii. 12, 13, &c.

19. See Lev. xviii. 23.

20. This was probably an old formula, the sense of which, on its ethical side, is comprised in the First and Second Commandments.

shall be utterly destroyed] The Hebrew word here used is *cherem* (*i.e. devoted*). See on Lev. xxvii. 28.

21. *a stranger*] More properly, **a foreigner** (Heb. *geer*), one who dwells in a land to which he does not belong. See on xx. 10. The command is repeated xxiii. 9. See also Lev. xix. 33, 34; Deut. x. 17—19.

22—24. The meaning of the word rendered *afflict*, includes all cold and contemptuous treatment. See Deut. x. 18. The same duty is enforced with the promise of a blessing, Deut. xiv. 29.

25. See on Lev. xxv. 35—43; cf. Deut. xxiii. 19.

26, 27. The law regarding pledges is expanded Deut. xxiv. 6, 10—13.

28. *the gods*] Heb. *elohim*. See on xxi. 6. This passage has been understood in three different ways: (1) Some of the best modern authorities take it as the name of **God** (as in Gen. i. 1), and this certainly seems best to represent the Hebrew, and to suit the context. So de Wette, Knobel, Schott, Keil, Benisch, &c. (2) Our Version follows the LXX., Vulg., Luther, Cranmer, &c.; it is also countenanced by Philo ('Vit. Mos.' III. 26), and Josephus ('Ant.' IV. 8. § 10; 'Contr. Ap.' II. 34), who make a boast of the liberality of the sentiment as regards the gods of other nations. (3) The word is rendered as *judges* by the Targums, Saadia, the Syriac, Theodoret, Geneva Fr. and Eng., Zunz, Herxh., &c., and this makes good sense, but it is rightly objected that *elohim*, to have the meaning according to which alone it could be so rendered, should have the article prefixed. See on xxi. 6.

curse the ruler, &c.] Acts xxiii. 5.

29, 30. The offering of Firstfruits appears to have been a custom of primitive antiquity, and was connected with the earliest acts of sacrifice. See Gen. iv. 3, 4. The references to it here and in xxiii. 19 had probably been handed down from patriarchal times. The specific law relating to the firstborn of

30 Likewise shalt thou do with
thine oxen, *and* with thy sheep: seven
days it shall be with his dam; on the
eighth day thou shalt give it me.
31 ¶ And ye shall be holy men
k Lev. 22. 8. Ezek. 44. 31. unto me: [k] neither shall ye eat *any*
flesh *that is* torn of beasts in the
field; ye shall cast it to the dogs.

CHAPTER XXIII.

1 *Of slander and false witness.* 3, 6 *Of justice.* 4 *Of charitableness.* 10 *Of the year of rest.* 12 *Of the sabbath.* 13 *Of idolatry.* 14 *Of the three feasts.* 18 *Of the blood and the fat of the sacrifice.* 20 *An Angel is promised, with a blessing, if they obey him.*

‖ Or, *receive.* THOU shalt not ‖ raise a false
report: put not thine hand with
the wicked to be an unrighteous witness.
2 ¶ Thou shalt not follow a multitude to *do* evil; neither shalt thou
† Heb. *answer.* † speak in a cause to decline after many
to wrest *judgment:*
3 ¶ Neither shalt thou countenance a poor man in his cause.
4 ¶ If thou meet thine enemy's
ox or his ass going astray, thou shalt
surely bring it back to him again.
5 [a] If thou see the ass of him that *a* Deut. 22. 4.
hateth thee lying under his burden,
‖ and wouldest forbear to help him, ‖ Or, *wilt thou cease to help him? or, and wouldest cease to leave thy business for him: thou shalt surely leave it to join with him.*
thou shalt surely help with him.
6 Thou shalt not wrest the judgment of thy poor in his cause.
7 Keep thee far from a false matter; and the innocent and righteous
slay thou not: for I will not justify
the wicked.
8 ¶ And [b] thou shalt take no gift: *b* Deut. 16. 19. Ecclus. 20. 29.
for the gift blindeth † the wise, and † Heb. *the seeing.*
perverteth the words of the righteous.
9 ¶ Also thou shalt not oppress a
stranger: for ye know the † heart of a † Heb. *soul.*
stranger, seeing ye were strangers in
the land of Egypt.

---

living creatures was brought out in a strong light in connection with the deliverance from Egypt (xiii. 2, 12, 13). Regarding "the eighth day," see Lev. xxii. 27. The form for offering Firstfruits is described Deut. xxvi. 2—11. But besides these usages exclusively referring to Firstfruits, there were others embodying the same religious idea in the rites of the festivals of the Passover and Pentecost. See on Lev. xxiii.

the first of thy ripe fruits, and of thy liquors] The literal rendering of the Hebrew is given in the margin ("thy fulness and thy tear"), and is retained in Luther's version. Firstfruits (בכורים, xxiii. 19) are not here mentioned by name; but the connection clearly shows that they are meant. The latter of the two Hebrew substantives (דמע) does not occur elsewhere. But according to its etymology, it means that which drops like a tear. The LXX. has ἀπαρχὰς ἅλωνος καὶ ληνοῦ σου. Vulg. *decimas tuas et primitias tuas.* These renderings, as well as that in our Bible (which nearly follows Onk. and the Syr.), are of course paraphrases rather than versions.

31. The sanctification of the nation was emphatically symbolized by strictness of diet as regards both the kind of animal, and the mode of slaughtering. See Lev. chaps. xi. and xvii.

CHAP. XXIII. The Book of the Covenant, concluded.

1—3. These four commands, addressed to the conscience without sanction of punishment, are so many illustrations of the Ninth Commandment, mainly in reference to the giving of evidence in legal causes. It is forbidden:—

1. To circulate a false report (cf. Lev. xix. 16).
2. To join hand in hand with another in bearing false witness.
3. To follow a majority in favouring an unrighteous cause.
4. To shew partiality to a man's cause because he is poor (cf. Lev. xix. 15).

2. This verse might be more strictly rendered, *Thou shalt not follow the many to evil; neither shalt thou bear witness in a cause so as to incline after the many to pervert justice.*

3. *countenance*] Rather, **to show partiality to.**

4, 5. So far was the spirit of the Law from encouraging personal revenge that it would not allow a man to neglect an opportunity of saving his enemy from loss. On the apparently different spirit expressed in Deut. xxiii. 6, and on the reference to the subject in Matt. v. 43, see in loc. Cf. Deut. xxii. 1—4.

5. *wouldest forbear to help him,* &c.] The words are rather difficult, but the sense appears to be:—*If thou see the ass of thine enemy lying down under his burden, thou shalt forbear to pass by him; thou shalt help him in loosening the girths of the ass.* The passage is rendered to this effect by Saadia, Gesenius, Knobel, &c.

6—9. These verses comprise four precepts, which are evidently addressed to those in authority as judges:—

[c] Lev. 25. 3. 10 And [c] six years thou shalt sow
thy land, and shalt gather in the fruits
thereof:
11 But the seventh *year* thou shalt
let it rest and lie still; that the poor
of thy people may eat: and what
‖ Or, *olive trees.* they leave the beasts of the field shall
[d] chap. 20. 8. eat. In like manner thou shalt deal
Deut. 5. 13. with thy vineyard, *and* with thy ‖ olive-
Luke 13. 14. yard.
12 [d] Six days thou shalt do thy work,
and on the seventh day thou shalt
rest: that thine ox and thine ass may
rest, and the son of thy handmaid,
and the stranger, may be refreshed.
13 And in all *things* that I have
said unto you be circumspect: and
make no mention of the name of
other gods, neither let it be heard
out of thy mouth.
14 ¶ [e] Three times thou shalt keep [e] Deut. 16. 16.
a feast unto me in the year.

---

1. To do justice to the poor.—Comparing *v.* 6 with *v.* 3, it was the part of the judge to defend the poor against the oppression of the rich, and the part of the witness to take care lest his feelings of natural pity should tempt him to falsify his evidence.

2. To be cautious of inflicting capital punishment on one whose guilt was not clearly proved.—A doubtful case was rather to be left to God Himself, who would "not justify the wicked," nor suffer him to go unpunished though he might be acquitted by an earthly tribunal. *v.* 7.

3. To take no bribe or present which might in any way pervert judgment (*v.* 8); cf. Num. xvi. 15; 1 S. xii. 3.

4. To vindicate the rights of the stranger (*v.* 9)—rather, the **foreigner**. See on xx. 10. This verse is a repetition of xxii. 21, but the precept is there addressed to the people at large, while it is here addressed to the judges in reference to their official duties. This is Knobel's explanation; but Bleek and others, overlooking the very distinct contexts, take the repetition as merely redundant.—The word rendered *heart* is more strictly *soul* (נפשׁ), and would be better represented here by **feelings**. Cf. on xxviii. 3 and on Lev. xvii. 11.

10—12. This is the first mention of the Sabbatical year; the law for it is given at length Lev. xxv. 2. Both the Sabbatical year and the weekly Sabbath are here spoken of exclusively in their relation to the poor, as bearing testimony to the equality of the people in their Covenant with Jehovah. In the first of these institutions, the proprietor of the soil gave up his rights for the year to the whole community of living creatures, not excepting the beasts: in the latter, the master gave up his claim for the day to the services of his servants and cattle. See Note 'On the Sabbath day,' § V. after ch. xx.

11. *thou shalt let it rest and lie still*] Some understand this expression to relate to the crops, not to the land, so as to mean, *thou shalt leave them* (*i.e.* the crops) *and give them up to the poor*, &c. (Kranold, Hupfeld, Davidson.) The words, if they stood by themselves, might bear this interpretation as well as that given in our version, and neither interpretation is opposed to Lev. xxv. 2—5, where it is said that the land was to remain untilled. But it has been presumed without the least authority that the writer of Leviticus made a mistake, and that the original law, as it is here given, was not intended to prevent the land from being tilled as usual, but only to forbid that the crops should be harvested by the proprietor, in order that the poor might gather them for themselves. See on Lev. xxv. 2. It has also been objected that this original law could not have been written by Moses in the wilderness, where, of course, it could not have been observed, and that this difficulty occurred to the writer of Leviticus, and induced him to prefix the words "when ye come into the land which I give you." But surely this difficulty, if we admit it to have a real existence, would have been avoided by any one writing a clever fictitious narrative with a view to deceive his own, or later ages. It seems easier and more reasonable to regard Moses as having legislated and written with the deep conviction ever in his mind that the promise of the possession of the land made to Abraham was sure of fulfilment. See on *vv.* 20, 31.

12. *may be refreshed*] Literally, *may take breath.*

13. Cf. Deut. iv. 9, vi. 13, 14; Josh. xxii. 5.

14—17. This is the first mention of the three great Yearly Festivals. The Feast of Unleavened Bread, in its connection with the Paschal Lamb, is spoken of in ch. xii., xiii.: but the two others are here first named. The whole three are spoken of as if they were familiarly known to the people. The points that are especially enjoined are that every male Israelite should attend them at the Sanctuary (cf. xxxiv. 23), and that he should take with him an offering for Jehovah. He was, on each occasion, to present himself before his King with his tribute in his hand. That the latter condition belonged to all the Feasts,

f chap. 13. 3. & 34. 18.
15 fThou shalt keep the feast of
unleavened bread: (thou shalt eat unleavened bread seven days, as I commanded thee, in the time appointed
of the month Abib; for in it thou
g Deut. 16. 16. Ecclus. 35. 4.
camest out from Egypt: gand none
shall appear before me empty:)
16 And the feast of harvest, the
firstfruits of thy labours, which thou
hast sown in the field: and the feast
of ingathering, *which is* in the end of
the year, when thou hast gathered in
thy labours out of the field.
17 Three times in the year all thy
males shall appear before the Lord
GOD.
18 Thou shalt not offer the blood
of my sacrifice with leavened bread;
neither shall the fat of my ‖sacrifice ‖ Or, *feast.*
remain until the morning.
19 hThe first of the firstfruits of h chap. 34. 26.
thy land thou shalt bring into the

---

though it is here stated only in regard to the Passover, cannot be doubted. See Deut. xvi. 16.

15, 16. On the Feast of Unleavened Bread, or the Passover, see xii. 1—28, 43—50, xiii. 3—16, xxxiv. 18—20; Lev. xxiii. 4—14. On the Feast of the Firstfruits of Harvest, called also the Feast of Weeks, and the Feast of Pentecost, see xxxiv. 22; Lev. xxiii. 15—21. On the Feast of Ingathering, called also the Feast of Tabernacles, see Lev. xxiii. 34—36, 39—43.

16. *in the end of the year*] Cf. xxxiv. 22. The year here spoken of must have been the civil or agrarian year, which began after harvest, when the ground was prepared for sowing. Cf. Lev. xxiii. 39; Deut. xvi. 13—15. The sacred year began in spring, with the month Abib, or Nisan. See on Exod. xii. 2, and on Lev. xxv. 9.

when thou hast gathered] Rather, **when thou gatherest in.** The Hebrew does not imply that the gathering in was to be completed before the Feast was held. In some years the harvest must have fallen later than in others. It was perhaps rarely completed before the time appointed for the Feast. And hence the fitness of the expression, "which is in the end of the year," as explained in the preceding note.

18, 19. These verses comprise three maxims, each of which, according to the best interpretation, appears to relate to one of the Festivals, in due order, as named in *vv.* 14—17.

18. *the blood of my sacrifice*] It is generally considered that this must refer to the Paschal Lamb. The blood that was sprinkled on the door-posts, or (after the first occasion) on the Altar, emphatically represented "the sacrifice of the LORD's passover." See xii. 7, 11, 13, 22, 23, 27.

the fat of my sacrifice] Strictly, **the fat of my feast.** In the parallel passage xxxiv. 25, what appears to be the equivalent expression is, "the sacrifice of the feast of the passover." It has been inferred with great probability that the *fat of my feast* means not literally the *fat* of the Paschal Lamb, but the *best part* of the feast, that is, the Paschal Lamb itself (Knobel, Keil). This explanation best accords with xii. 10, where there is no mention of the fat. If we take the words in their mere literal sense, they must refer to the fat of the sacrifices in general, which, when the ritual of the sacrifices was arranged, was burnt upon the Altar by the Priests (Lev. i. 8, iii. 3—5).

19. *The first of the firstfruits of thy land*] This most probably means the *best*, or *chief* of the Firstfruits, &c. As the preceding precept appears to refer to the Passover, so it is likely that this refers to Pentecost, as especially to the offering of what are called in *v.* 16 "the firstfruits of thy labours;" that is, the two wave loaves described Lev. xxiii. 17. They are called in Leviticus, "the firstfruits unto the LORD;" and it is reasonable that they should here be designated the *chief* of the Firstfruits. If, with Keil and others, we suppose the precept to relate to the offerings of Firstfruits in general, the command is no more than a repetition of xxii. 29.

Thou shalt not seethe a kid in his mother's milk] This precept is repeated xxxiv. 26; Deut. xiv. 21. There has been much discussion as to its meaning. St Augustine and some more recent commentators have given up the explanation of it in despair. If we are to connect the first of the two preceding precepts with the Passover, and the second with Pentecost, it seems reasonable to connect this with the Feast of Tabernacles. The only explanation which accords with this connection is one which refers to some sort of superstitious custom connected with the harvest. Abarbanel speaks of such a custom, in which a kid was seethed in its mother's milk to propitiate in some way the deities. But the subject is more pointedly illustrated in an ancient commentary on the Pentateuch by a Karaite Jew, from the manuscript of which a quotation is given by Cudworth ('On the Lord's Supper,' p. 36). It is there said to have been a prevalent usage to boil a kid in its

[i] ch. 34. 26. Deut. 14. 21. house of the LORD thy God. [i] Thou
shalt not seethe a kid in his mother's
milk.

[k] chap. 33. 2. 20 ¶ [k] Behold, I send an Angel
before thee, to keep thee in the way,
and to bring thee into the place which
I have prepared.

21 Beware of him, and obey his
voice, provoke him not; for he will
not pardon your transgressions: for
my name *is* in him.

22 But if thou shalt indeed obey
his voice, and do all that I speak;
then I will be an enemy unto thine
enemies, and ‖ an adversary unto thine
adversaries.

23 [l] For mine Angel shall go before thee, and [m] bring thee in unto
the Amorites, and the Hittites, and
the Perizzites, and the Canaanites,
and the Hivites, and the Jebusites:
and I will cut them off.

‖ Or, *I will afflict them that afflict thee.*

[l] chap. 33. 2.

[m] Josh. 24. 11.

---

mother's milk, when all the crops were gathered in, and to sprinkle with the milk the fruit trees, fields and gardens, as a charm to improve the crops of the coming year. The explanation based upon this is preferred by Bochart, John Gregory, Grotius, Knobel and others. The command, so understood, is a caution against the practice of magic. See on xxii. 18. But in a matter so doubtful, it is but fair to give such other explanations as seem most worthy of notice.

1. It has been taken as a prohibition of the eating of flesh and milk together (the Targums, Erpenius). This is countenanced by the traditional custom of the Jews ('Mishna,' Cholin VIII. 1; Maimon. 'de Cit. Vel.' 9; Buxtorf, 'Syn. Jud.' p. 596).

2. It has been supposed to forbid the eating of a kid before it has been weaned from its mother—Luther, Calvin, Fagius, &c.

3. It has been referred to a custom now existing among the Arabs, which is certainly of great antiquity, of preparing a gross sort of food by stewing a kid in milk, with the addition of certain ingredients of a stimulating nature, which is commonly called in Arabic, "a kid in his mother's milk." Aben-Ezra, Keil, Thomson ('The Land and the Book,' ch. VIII.), &c.

4. It has been brought into connection with the prohibitions to slaughter a cow and a calf, or a ewe and her lamb, on the same day (Lev. xxii. 28), and to take a bird along with her young in the nest (Deut. xxii. 6). It is thus understood as a protest against cruelty and outraging the order of nature (*ne commisceatur germen cum radicibus*). Theodoret, Vatablus, Ewald, &c. See Bochart, 'Hieroz.' l. II. c. 52.

20—33. These verses appear to form the conclusion of the Book of the Covenant. They contain promises of the constant presence and guidance of Jehovah (*vv.* 20—22), of the driving out of the nations of the Canaanites by degrees (23—30), and of the subsequent enlargement of Hebrew dominion (*v.* 31). But these promises are accompanied by solemn exhortations and threatenings.—Cf. xxxiv. 10—17, where similar promises and warnings are prefixed to the shorter compendium of Law which was written down after the renewal of the Tables.

20, 21. *an Angel...for my name is in him*] The Angel appears to mean the presence and the power of Jehovah Himself, manifested in the work of leading and delivering His people, and maintaining His Covenant with them. Cf. xxxii. 34, xxxiii. 2, 15, 16, and the notes; see also on Gen. xii. 7.

20. *the place which I have prepared*] The promise of the Land may be seen to inspire the legislation and conduct of Moses throughout his career. There is no trace of uncertainty as to the ultimate aim of his mission. He had been called to lead the people to the home prepared for them, according to the promise first made to Abraham, and to discipline them in their passage through the wilderness to become a strong nation.

22. *and an adversary unto thine adversaries*] The rendering in the margin is the better one. Cf. Deut. xx. 4.

23. The nations here mentioned are those only that inhabited the land strictly called the Land of Canaan, lying between the Jordan and the Great Sea. See Num. xxxiv. 2; cf. Exod. xxxiv. 11.

I will cut them off] It has been too absolutely taken for granted that it was the Divine will that the inhabitants of Canaan should be utterly exterminated. We know that, as a matter of fact, great numbers of the Canaanite families lived on, and intermarried with the Israelites (see Judg. i., ii., with such cases as those of the Sidonians, of Araunah, of Uriah, of the family of Rahab, &c.). The national existence of the Canaanites was indeed to be *utterly* destroyed, every trace of their idolatries was to be blotted out, no social intercourse was to be held with them while they served other gods, nor were alliances of any kind to be formed with them. These commands are emphatically repeated and expanded in Deuteronomy (vii.; xii. 1—4, 29—31).

24 Thou shalt not bow down to
their gods, nor serve them, nor do
n Deut. 7. 25. after their works: n but thou shalt
utterly overthrow them, and quite
break down their images.
25 And ye shall serve the LORD
your God, and he shall bless thy bread,
and thy water; and I will take sickness away from the midst of thee.
o Deut. 7. 14. 26 ¶ o There shall nothing cast
their young, nor be barren, in thy
land: the number of thy days I will
fulfil.
27 I will send my fear before thee,
and will destroy all the people to
whom thou shalt come, and I will
make all thine enemies turn their
† Heb. *neck.* † backs unto thee.

28 And p I will send hornets before p Josh. 24. 12.
thee, which shall drive out the Hivite,
the Canaanite, and the Hittite, from
before thee.
29 I will not drive them out from
before thee in one year; lest the land
become desolate, and the beast of the
field multiply against thee.
30 By little and little I will drive
them out from before thee, until thou
be increased, and inherit the land.
31 And I will set thy bounds from
the Red sea even unto the sea of the
Philistines, and from the desert unto
the river: for I will deliver the inhabitants of the land into your hand;
and thou shalt drive them out before
thee.

They were often broken by the Israelites, who had to suffer for their transgression (Num. xxxiii. 55; Judg. ii. 3). But it is alike contrary to the spirit of the Divine Law, and to the facts bearing on the subject scattered in the history, to suppose that any obstacle was put in the way of well disposed individuals of the denounced nations who left their sins and were willing to join the service of Jehovah. The Law, as it was addressed to the Israelites, never forgets the stranger (rather, **the foreigner**, LXX. προσήλυτος) who had voluntarily come within their gates. See xx. 10. The spiritual blessings of the Covenant were always open to those who sincerely and earnestly desired to possess them. Lev. xix. 34, xxiv. 22. A narrowness and cruelty in this and other respects has been very generally ascribed to the Law of Moses, from which it has been justly vindicated by Salvador, 'Histoire des Institutions de Moïse,' Vol. I. p. 447.

24. Cf. Num. xxxiii. 52; Deut. vii. 5, 16, xii. 29, 30, xx. 18.

27. *destroy*] Rather, **overthrow**. See on *v.* 23; cf. xv. 14; Deut. ii. 25; Josh. ii. 11.

28. *hornets*] Cf. Deut. vii. 20; Josh. xxiv. 12. The Hebrew word is in the singular number, used for the species—**the hornet**. Bochart ('Hieroz.' lib. IV. c. 13) has collected instances from ancient authorities of large bodies of men being driven away by noxious insects and other small creatures; and the author of the Book of Wisdom (xii. 8, 9) with some of the commentators have supposed that hornets are literally meant (see 'Crit. Sac.'). But there seems to be no reasonable doubt that the word is used figuratively for a cause of terror and discouragement. Bees are spoken of in the like sense, Deut. i. 44; Ps. cxviii. 12. The passage has been thus understood by most critics.

29. *beast of the field*] The term is applied to any wild animal; here it means a destructive one, as it does also Deut. vii. 22: cf. Lev. xxvi. 22; 2 K. xvii. 25; Job v. 22; Ezek. xiv. 15.

31. In *v.* 23, the limits of the Land of Canaan, strictly so called, are indicated; to this, when the Israelites were about to take possession of it, were added the regions of Gilead and Bashan on the left side of the Jordan (Num. xxxii. 33—42; Josh. xiii. 29—32). These two portions made up the Holy Land, of which the limits were recognized, with inconsiderable variations, till the final overthrow of the Jewish polity. But in this verse the utmost extent of Hebrew dominion, as it existed in the time of David and Solomon, is set forth. The kingdom then reached to Eloth and Ezion-geber on the Ælanitic Gulf of the Red Sea (1 K. ix. 26), and to Tiphsah on the "River," that is, the River Euphrates (1 K. iv. 24), having for its western boundary "the Sea of the Philistines," that is, the Mediterranean, and for its southern boundary "the desert," that is, the wildernesses of Shur and Paran (cf. Gen. xv. 18; Deut. i. 7, xi. 24; Josh. i. 4). Hengstenberg thinks that these broad descriptions of the Land are to be taken as rhetorical, and not as the strict terms of the promise ('Pentateuch,' II. p. 217). He considers this to be the right way of meeting those who reject the genuineness of the narrative on the ground of the improbability that Moses should have foretold the extent of the conquests of David and Solomon. But the cavils of such objectors may be met more simply and effectively by urging that if Moses

[q chap. 34. 15. Deut. 7. 2.]

32 [q] Thou shalt make no covenant with them, nor with their gods.

33 They shall not dwell in thy land, lest they make thee sin against me: for if thou serve their gods, [r] it will surely be a snare unto thee.

[r Deut. 7. 16. Josh. 23. 13. Judg. 2. 3.]

CHAPTER XXIV.

1 *Moses is called up into the mountain.* 3 *The people promise obedience.* 4 *Moses buildeth an altar, and twelve pillars.* 6 *He sprinkleth the blood of the covenant.* 9 *The glory of God appeareth.* 14 *Aaron and Hur have the charge of the people.* 15 *Moses goeth into the mountain, where he continueth forty days and forty nights.*

AND he said unto Moses, Come up unto the LORD, thou, and Aaron, Nadab, and Abihu, and seventy of the elders of Israel; and worship ye afar off.

2 And Moses alone shall come near the LORD: but they shall not come nigh; neither shall the people go up with him.

3 ¶ And Moses came and told the people all the words of the LORD, and all the judgments: and all the people answered with one voice, and said, [a] All the words which the LORD hath said will we do.

[a chap. 19. 8. & 24. 3, 7. Deut. 5. 27.]

4 And Moses wrote all the words of the LORD, and rose up early in the morning, and builded an altar under the hill, and twelve pillars, according to the twelve tribes of Israel.

5 And he sent young men of the children of Israel, which offered burnt offerings, and sacrificed peace offerings of oxen unto the LORD.

6 And Moses took half of the blood, and put *it* in basons; and half of the blood he sprinkled on the altar.

7 And he took the book of the covenant, and read in the audience of the people: and they said, [b] All that the LORD hath said will we do, and be obedient.

[b ver. 3.]

---

was acquainted with the geography of the region (which can hardly be called in question), he might certainly have foreseen that the Hebrew power, when it became very strong in the Land of Canaan, could not fail to exercise domination over all the country from the Euphrates to the Mediterranean and the Red Sea.

CHAP. XXIV.

The Sealing of the Covenant.

1—8.

1, 2. It is not easy to trace the proper connection of these two verses as they stand here. Ewald, with great probability, thinks that their right place is between verses 8 and 9 in this chapter ('Hist. of Israel,' p. 529).—It has been suggested that they may relate to what was said to Moses immediately after the utterance of the Ten Commandments, ch. xx. 19 (Knobel).—If they are here placed in due order of time (as Rosenmüller, Keil and others suppose), the direction to Moses contained in them was delivered on the mount (see xx. 21), but its fulfilment was deferred till after he had come down from the mount and done all that is recorded in *vv.* 3—8.

3, 4. The narrative in these verses seems naturally to follow the end of the preceding chapter. Moses leaves the mount and repeats the words of the Book of the Covenant to the people, they give their assent, and the next morning he arranges the ceremony for the formal ratification of the Covenant.

4. *twelve pillars*] As the altar was a symbol of the presence of Jehovah, so these twelve pillars represented the presence of the Twelve Tribes with whom He was making the Covenant. Keil suggests that the pillars were perhaps arranged as boundary stones for the spot consecrated for the occasion.

5. *young men of the children of Israel*] The Targums and Saadia call these *the firstborn sons.* There is no fair ground for this interpretation. Moses was on this occasion performing the office of a priest (the family of Aaron not being yet consecrated), and he employed young men whose strength and skill qualified them to slaughter and prepare the sacrifices. The Law did not regard these acts as necessarily belonging to the priests, and it is probable that they were regarded in the same way in earlier times, when the sacerdotal character belonged especially to the firstborn sons. See on Lev. i. 5, and Exod. xxviii. 1.

burnt offerings...peace offerings] The Burnt offerings figured the dedication of the nation to Jehovah, and the Peace offerings their communion with Jehovah and with each other.

6. *he sprinkled*] Rather, **he cast.** See on Lev. i. 5. The same word is used *v.* 8.

7. *the book of the covenant*] See *v.* 4, and Introd. note on xx. 22. The people had to repeat their assent to the Book of the Covenant before the blood was thrown upon them. Cf. 2 K. xxiii. 2, 21; 2 Chron. xxxiv. 30.

8 And Moses took the blood, and
sprinkled *it* on the people, and said,
Behold [c] the blood of the covenant,
which the LORD hath made with you
concerning all these words.
9 ¶ Then went up Moses, and
Aaron, Nadab, and Abihu, and seventy of the elders of Israel:
10 And they saw the God of Israel: and *there was* under his feet as
it were a paved work of a sapphire
stone, and as it were the body of
heaven in *his* clearness.
11 And upon the nobles of the
children of Israel he laid not his
hand: also they saw God, and did
eat and drink.
12 ¶ And the LORD said unto Mo-

[c] 1 Pet. 1. 2. Heb. 9. 20.

---

8. *the blood of the covenant*] It should be observed that the blood which sealed the Covenant was the blood of Burnt offerings and Peace offerings. The Sin offering had not yet been instituted. That more complicated view of human nature which gave to the Sin offering its meaning, had yet to be developed by the Law, which was now only receiving its ratification. The Covenant between Jehovah and His people therefore took precedence of the operation of the Law, by which came the knowledge of sin. Rom. iii. 20; Note on the Ten Commandments, § V.

Half of the blood had been put into basins, and half of it had been cast upon the Altar. The Book of the Covenant was then read, and after that the blood in the basins was cast "upon the people." It was cast either upon the elders, or those who stood foremost; or, as Abarbanel and others have supposed, upon the twelve pillars representing the Twelve Tribes, as the first half had been cast upon the altar, which witnessed the presence of Jehovah. The blood thus divided between the two parties to the Covenant signified the sacramental union between the Lord and His people. Cf. Ps. l. 5; Zech. ix. 11.

The instances from classical antiquity adduced as parallels to this sacrifice of Moses by Bähr, Knobel and Kalisch, in which animals were slaughtered on the making of covenants, are either those in which the animal was slain to signify the punishment due to the party that might break the covenant (Hom. 'Il.' III. 298, XIX. 252; Liv. 'Hist.' I. 24, XXI. 45); those in which confederates dipped their hands, or their weapons, in the same blood (Æsch. 'Sept. c. Theb.' 43; Xenoph. 'Anab.' II. 2, § 9); or those in which the contracting parties tasted each other's blood (Herodot. I. 74, IV. 70; Tac. 'Annal.' XII. 47). All these usages are based upon ideas which are but very superficially related to the subject; they have indeed no true connection whatever with the idea of sacrifice as the seal of a covenant between God and man. See on Ex. xxix. 20.

The Feast of the Peace offerings.

9—11.

9. It would appear that Moses, Aaron with his two sons, and seventy of the elders (xix. 7) went a short distance up the mountain to eat the meal of the Covenant (cf. Gen. xxxi. 43—47), which must have consisted of the flesh of the Peace offerings (*v.* 5.). Joshua is not named here, but he accompanied Moses as his servant. See *v.* 13.

10. *And they saw the God of Israel*] As they ate the sacrificial feast, the presence of Jehovah was manifested to them with special distinctness. In the act of solemn worship, they perceived that he was present with them, as their Lord and their Deliverer. It is idle to speculate, as Keil and others have done, on the mode of this revelation. That no visible form was presented to their bodily eyes, we are expressly informed, Deut. iv. 12; see on xxxiii. 20; cf. Isa. vi. 1.

there was under his feet as it were a paved work of a sapphire stone, and as it were the body of heaven in his clearness] Rather, *under His feet, it was like a work of bright sapphire stone, and like the heaven itself in clearness.* On the sapphire, see xxviii. 18; cf. Ezek. i. 26. The pure blue of the heaven above them lent its influence to help the inner sense to realize the vision which no mortal eye could behold.

11. *he laid not his hand*] *i.e.* he did not smite them. It was believed that a mortal could not survive the sight of God (Gen. xxxii. 30; Ex. xxxiii. 20; Judg. vi. 22, xiii. 22): but these rulers of Israel were permitted to eat and drink, while they were enjoying in an extraordinary degree the sense of the Divine presence, and took no harm. "When the heads of the people venture to draw near their God, they find his presence no more a source of disturbance and dread, but radiant in all the bright loveliness of supernal glory; a beautiful sign that the higher religion and state of conformity to law, now established, shall work onwards to eternal blessedness." Ewald, 'Hist. of Israel,' Vol. I. p. 529.

Moses goes up to receive the Tables.

12—18.

12. *tables of stone, and a law, and commandments*] Maimonides and many of the Jews understand *the tables of stone* to denote the Ten Commandments; *the law*, the Law written in the Pentateuch; and *the command-*

ses, Come up to me into the mount,
and be there: and I will give thee
tables of stone, and a law, and commandments which I have written;
that thou mayest teach them.
13 And Moses rose up, and his
minister Joshua: and Moses went up
into the mount of God.
14 And he said unto the elders,
Tarry ye here for us, until we come
again unto you: and, behold, Aaron
and Hur *are* with you: if any man
have any matters to do, let him come
unto them.
15 And Moses went up into the
mount, and a cloud covered the
mount.
16 And the glory of the LORD
abode upon mount Sinai, and the
cloud covered it six days: and the
seventh day he called unto Moses out
of the midst of the cloud.
17 And the sight of the glory of
the LORD *was* like devouring fire on
the top of the mount in the eyes of
the children of Israel.
18 And Moses went into the midst
of the cloud, and gat him up into the
mount: and [d] Moses was in the mount [d] chap. 34. 28.
forty days and forty nights. Deut. 9. 9.

CHAPTER XXV.

1 *What the Israelites must offer for the making of the tabernacle.* 10 *The form of the ark.* 17 *The mercy seat, with the cherubims.* 23 *The table, with the furniture thereof.* 31 *The candlestick, with the instruments thereof.*

AND the LORD spake unto Moses, saying,

---

ments (it should be *the commandment*), the oral or traditional law which was in after ages put into writing in the Mishna and the Gemara. Ewald takes the words to mean the Ten Commandments, and "other sacred books of the Law" ('H. of I.' I. p. 606). But it is more probable that the Ten Commandments alone are spoken of, and that the meaning is, *the Tables of stone with the Law, even the Commandment.* So Knobel, Keil, Herx. See Note on the Ten Commandments, § I.

that thou mayest teach them] More strictly, **to teach them.** The promise of the Tables is fulfilled after the directions for the Tabernacle have been given, xxxi. 18.

13. *Joshua*] See on *v.* 9; cf. xxxii. 17; xxxiii. 11.

mount of God] See on iii. 1.

14. It need not be supposed that the Elders were required to remain on the very spot where Moses parted with them, but simply that they were to advance no further. Aaron and Hur were to represent the authority of Moses during his absence.

15. *Moses went up*] Moses appears to have left Joshua and gone up alone into the cloud. See *v.* 2.

16. Cf. xix. 18 sq.

18. During this period of forty days, and the second period when the Tables were renewed, Moses neither ate bread nor drank water. Deut. ix. 9; Exod. xxxiv. 28. Elijah in like manner fasted for forty days, when he visited the same spot (1 K. xix. 8). The two who met our Saviour on the Mount of Transfiguration, the one as representing the Law, the other as representing the Prophets, thus shadowed forth in their own experience the Fast of Forty days in the wilderness of Judæa.

THE ARK AND THE TABERNACLE. CHAP. XXV. XXVI.

Jehovah had redeemed the Israelites from bondage. He had made a Covenant with them and had given them a Law. He had promised, on condition of their obedience, to accept them as His own "peculiar treasure," as "a kingdom of priests and a holy nation" (xix. 5, 6). And now He was ready visibly to testify that He made his abode with them. He claimed to have a dwelling for Himself, which was to be in external form a tent of goats' hair, to take its place among their own tents, formed out of the same material (on Ex. xxvi. 7). The special mark of His presence within the Tent was to be the Ark or chest containing the Ten Commandments on two tables of stone (Ex. xxxi. 18), symbolizing the divine Law of holiness, covered by the Mercy seat, the type of reconciliation.—Moses was divinely taught regarding the construction and arrangement of every part of the Sanctuary. The directions which were given him are comprised in Ex. xxv. 1—xxxi. 11. The account of the performance of the work, expressed generally in the same terms, is given Ex. xxxv. 20—xl. 33.

The meaning of the Tabernacle, with the relation in which it stood to the Tables of the Law, is considered more at length in the Note at the end of ch. xl.

CHAP. XXV. 1—9. Moses is commanded to invite the people to bring their gifts for the construction and service of the Sanctuary and for the dresses of the Priests.

† Heb. *take for me.* ‖ Or, *heave offering.* a chap. 35. 5.

2 Speak unto the children of Israel,
that they † bring me an ‖ offering: a of
every man that giveth it willingly
with his heart ye shall take my
offering.

3 And this *is* the offering which ye
shall take of them; gold, and silver,
and brass,

4 And blue, and purple, and scarlet,
and ‖ fine linen, and goats' *hair*,

‖ Or, *silk.*

---

2. *an offering*] The Hebrew word is *tĕrumāh*, which occurs here for the first time. On the marginal rendering "heave offering," see note on Ex. xxix. 27. The word in this place appears to denote no more than *offering*, in its general sense, being equivalent to *korban*. It is used with the same compass of meaning Ex. xxx. 13, xxxv. 5, &c. In Num. xviii. 24, tithes are called a *tĕrumah*.

that giveth it willingly with his heart] Literally, **whose heart shall freely give it.** The public service of Jehovah was to be instituted by freewill offerings, not by an enforced tax. Cf. 1 Chron. xxix. 3, 9, 14; Ezra ii. 68, 69; 2 Cor. viii. 11, 12, ix. 7. On the zeal with which the people responded to the call, see Ex. xxxv. 21—29, xxxvi. 5—7.

my offering] The recipient of the offering is here denoted by the possessive case, according to the common Hebrew idiom. Ex. xxx. 13, xxxv. 5, 21, 24, &c.

3. *gold, and silver, and brass*] The supply of these metals possessed by the Israelites at this time probably included what they had inherited from their forefathers, what they had obtained from the Egyptians (Ex. xii. 35), and what may have been found amongst the spoils of the Amalekites (Ex. xvii. 8—13). But with their abundant flocks and herds, it can hardly be doubted that they had carried on important traffic with the trading caravans that traversed the wilderness, some of which, most likely, in the earliest times were furnished with silver, with the gold of Ophir (or gold of Sheba, as it seems to have been indifferently called), and with the bronze of Phœnicia and Egypt (Gen. xxxvii. 25, 28; Deut. xxxiii. 25; 1 K. ix. 28, x. 15; 1 Chron. xxix. 4; 2 Chron. ix. 14; Job xxii. 24, xxviii. 16; Ps. xlv. 9).—Cf. note on Ex. xxxviii. 24.

brass] The Hebrew word *nĕhosheth* [see on 2 K. xviii. 4] must mean pure copper in such passages as Deut. viii. 9, xxxiii. 25; Job xxviii. 2. But it commonly denotes (as it does most likely in this place) the hardened alloy of copper and tin, more strictly called **bronze** than brass, which was so largely used for weapons and implements before the art of working iron was well understood. On the bronze of the Egyptians see Wilkinson's 'Popular Account,' Vol. I. p. 148, II. p. 152, and De Rougemont, 'Age du Bronze,' p. 180. The latter writer proves that the Egyptians were well acquainted with bronze and with the art of working in all the common metals, except iron, under the fourth dynasty, ages before the time of Abraham.

4. *blue, and purple, and scarlet*] The names of the colours are used for the material which was dyed with them. The Jewish tradition has been very generally received that this material was wool. Cf. Heb. ix. 19 with Lev. xiv. 4, 49, &c. But the question is not quite without difficulty. See on xxviii. 5, and Lev. xix. 19.—The material, having been spun and dyed by the women, appears to have been delivered in the state of yarn. The Egyptians were well skilled in the art of dyeing (Wilkinson, II. p. 83). The weaving and embroidering were left to Aholiab and his assistants, Ex. xxxv., cf. *v.* 25 with *v.* 35. The Egyptians in like manner used to dye the threads of their stuffs before weaving them, and to employ women in spinning, and men in weaving and embroidering. (Wilkinson, 'Ancient Egyptians,' II. p. 79 sq.). Respecting the names of the colours, see Note at the end of the chapter.

fine linen] The word *shēsh*, which is here used, is Egyptian (Birch in Bunsen's 'Egypt,' Vol. V. p. 571). It is rendered by the LXX. βύσσος, which must be allied to *butz*, the name of the "fine linen" of Syria, in Ezek. xxvii. 16, which was that used in the time of Solomon for the hangings of the Temple and for other purposes (1 Chron. xv. 27; 2 Chron. ii. 14, iii. 14, v. 12). That the word *shēsh* denoted the fine flax, or the manufactured linen, for which Egypt was famous [see Ezek. xxvii. 7, where the original word is *shēsh:* but in Prov. vii. 16 "fine linen of Egypt" is a mistranslation, see note in loc.], and which the Egyptians were in the habit of using for dresses of state (Gen. xli. 42); and not *cotton*, as some have imagined, nor *silk* [as the word *shēsh* is rendered Prov. xxxi. 22, and in the margin here and elsewhere], is now clearly proved. Wilkinson, 'Pop. Account,' &c. II. p. 73, and his note to Herodot. II. 86. The *linen cloth* of Persia is mentioned, Esth. i. 6, by its Persian name *karpas* (the parent of κάρπασος and *carbasus*), which in our version is wrongly rendered *green*, as the name of a colour. The occurrence of these three native names, *shēsh*, *butz*, and *karpas*, for the same article produced in three different countries, in strict consistency with the narratives in which they occur, is worthy of remark. The LXX. translates each of the three by βύσσος. Cf. notes on Ex. ix. 31, xxxix. 28. The estimation in which fine linen was held in differ-

5 And rams' skins dyed red, and badgers' skins, and shittim wood,

6 Oil for the light, spices for anointing oil, and for sweet incense,

---

ent ages, before silk was generally known, may be seen 1 Chron. xv. 27; Prov. xxxi. 22; Ezek. xvi. 10, 13; Luke xvi. 19; Rev. xix. 8, 14. If silk is anywhere spoken of in the Hebrew Bible, it is only in Ezek. xvi. 10, where the word is not *shĕsh* but *meshi*, which Fuerst thinks may be of Chinese derivation.—It would seem that, for the use of the Tabernacle, the flax was spun by the women, like the coloured wools, and was delivered in the state of thread to be woven by Aholiab and his assistants (Ex. xxxv. 25, 35). The fine linen appears to have been used as the ground-work of the figured curtains of the Tabernacle as well as of the embroidered hangings of the Tent and the Court. See on xxxv. 35.

goats' hair] The hair of the goat has furnished the material for tents to the Roman armies (Virg. 'Georg.' III. 313) and to the Arabs and Eastern Nomads of all ages, as it did to the Israelites in the wilderness. The tent which was to be the chosen dwelling-place of Jehovah was to be formed of the same material as the tents of His people. See Introd. Note.

5. *rams' skins dyed red*] These skins may have been tanned and coloured like the leather now known as red morocco, which is said to have been manufactured in Libya from the remotest antiquity. On the manufacture of leather by the Egyptians, see Wilkinson, 'Pop. Account,' II. pp. 102—106.

badgers' skins] The skins here spoken of were certainly not those of the badger, as was supposed by Luther and Gesenius. That animal is often found in the Holy Land, but it is very rare in the wilderness, if it exists there at all (Tristram, 'N. H.' p. 44). The Hebrew name here used, *tachash*, occurs in the Old Testament only in connection with these skins, which were employed for the outer covering of the Tent of the Tabernacle (Ex. xxvi. 14), and in wrapping up the holy things when they were moved (Num. iv. 8, 10, &c.), and which are mentioned as the material of the shoes of the prophetic impersonation of Jerusalem by Ezekiel (xvi. 10). The word bears a near resemblance to the Arabic *tuchash*, which appears to be the general name given to the seals, dugongs and dolphins found in the Red Sea (Tristram), and, according to some authorities, to the sharks and dog-fish (Fürst). The substance spoken of would thus appear to have been leather formed from the skins of marine animals, which was well adapted as a protection against the weather. Pliny speaks of tents made of seal skins as proof against the stroke of lightning ('H. N.' II. 56), and one of these is said to have been used by Augustus whenever he travelled (Sueton. 'Octav.' 90). The skins of the dolphin and dugong are cut into sandals by the modern Arabs, and this may explain Ezek. xvi. 10. The question seems thus to be determined on pretty certain grounds. But it is remarkable that the LXX., with Josephus, the Vulgate, the Targums, and most of the ancient versions, treat the word *tachash* as the name of ordinary leather, distinguished only by a particular colour. But there is a difference as to whether the colour was black, red, violet, or blue. Most of the ancient authorities, followed by Bochart and Rosenmüller, imagine the colour to have been *hyacinthine*, the first of the three colours in the embroidered work of the Tabernacle [see Note at the end of the Chapter]. From Josephus speaking of the colour of these skins, such as he conceived it to be, as like the heavens ('Ant.' III. 6, § 4), we may infer with confidence that he conceived *hyacinthine* to be *sky-blue*. [Note, § II.]

shittim wood] The word *shittim* is the plural form of *shittah*, which occurs as the name of the growing tree Is. xli. 19. The tree is satisfactorily identified with the *Acacia seyal*, "a gnarled and thorny tree, somewhat like a solitary hawthorn in its habit and manner of growth, but much larger. [See note on Ex. xxvi. 15.] It flourishes in the driest situations, and is scattered more or less numerously over the Sinaitic Peninsula" (Tristram). It is rare in the Holy Land except in the neighbourhood of the Dead Sea, where it appears to have given its name to two places in ancient times. See Num. xxv. 1; Joel iii. 18. It grows in Egypt in some regions at a distance from the coast. The timber is hard and close-grained, of an orange colour with a darker heart, well adapted for cabinet work. The LXX. call it *wood that will not rot*, ξύλα ἄσηπτα. It appears to be the only good wood produced in the wilderness. No other kind of wood was employed in the Tabernacle or its furniture. In the construction of the Temple cedar and fir took its place (1 K. v. 8, vi. 18; 2 Chron. ii. 8). A distinct species of Acacia is mentioned by Dr Robinson, Dr Royle and others, as *A. gummifera*. But Mr Tristram states that the gum arabic of commerce is obtained from the *A. seyal*, and forms an important article of traffic on the shores of the Red Sea, as it did in ancient times. See also Bunsen, V. 414. As the plural form, *shittim*, is always applied to the wood, never being used like the singular *shittah* (Is. xli. 19) for the growing tree, the conjecture will hardly stand that the plural name is to be accounted for from "the tangled thicket into which its stem expands." (Tristram 'H. N.' p. 390; Stanley, 'S. and P.' p. 20; 'Jewish Ch.' I. p. 163; Houghton,

7 Onyx stones, and stones to be set
in the [b]ephod, and in the [c]breastplate.
8 And let them make me a sanc-
tuary; that I may dwell among them.
9 According to all that I shew thee,
after the pattern of the tabernacle,
and the pattern of all the instruments
thereof, even so shall ye make *it*.
10 ¶ [d]And they shall make an ark
of shittim wood: two cubits and a
half *shall be* the length thereof, and
a cubit and a half the breadth thereof,

[b] chap. 28. 4.
[c] chap. 28. 15.
[d] chap. 37. 1.

'Smith's Dict.' III. 1295; Royle, 'Kitto's Cycl.' III. 841.) See also on Ex. iii. 2.

6. *Oil for the light*] The oil was to be "pure olive oil beaten," see on Ex. xxvii. 20.

spices for anointing oil] What these spices were see Ex. xxx. 22—25.

sweet incense] See Ex. xxx. 34, 35.

7. On the materials and construction of the ephod and breastplate, see ch. xxviii.

8. *sanctuary*] Heb. *mikdash*, *i.e.* a hallowed place. This is the most comprehensive of the words that relate to the place dedicated to Jehovah. It included the Tabernacle with its furniture, its Tent and its Court.

that I may dwell among them] The purpose of the Sanctuary is here definitely declared by the Lord Himself. It was to be the constant witness of His presence amongst His people. xxix. 42—46, xl. 34—38, &c.

9. *According to all that I shew thee*] The Tabernacle and all that pertained to it were to be in strict accordance with the ideas revealed by the Lord to Moses: nothing in the way of form or decoration was to be left to the taste or judgment of the artificers. The command is emphatically repeated *v.* 40, xxvi. 30; cf. Acts vii. 44; Heb. viii. 5.—The word here translated *pattern* is also used in Chronicles to denote the plans for the Temple which were given by David to Solomon (1 Chron. xxviii. 11, 12, 19); it is elsewhere rendered *form*, *likeness*, *similitude*, Deut. iv. 16, 17; Ezek. viii. 3, 10. The revelation to the mind of Moses was, without doubt, such as to suggest the exact appearance of the work to be produced. But there is no need to adopt the materialistic notion of some of the rabbinists, that a Tabernacle in the heavens was set forth before the bodily eyes of the Legislator.

the tabernacle] The Hebrew word *hammishkān*, signifies the dwelling-place. It here denotes the wooden structure, containing the holy place and the most holy place, with the tent which sheltered it. See on xxvi. 1.

The Ark of the Covenant.

xxv. 10—16 (cf. xxxvii. 1—5).

The ARK is uniformly designated in Exodus the ARK OF THE TESTIMONY (xxv. 22, xxvi. 34, xxx. 6, 26, xxxi. 7, xl. 3, &c.); it is so called also Num. iv. 5, vii. 89; Josh. iv. 16; it is called simply THE TESTIMONY Ex. xvi. 34, xxvii. 21; Lev. xvi. 13, xxiv. 3; Num. xvii. 10. But in Num. x. 33 it is named THE ARK OF THE COVENANT, and this is its most frequent name in Deuteronomy and the other books of the Old Testament. In some places it is named THE ARK OF THE LORD (Josh. iii. 13, iv. 11, vii. 6; 1 S. iv. 6; 2 S. vi. 9, &c.), THE ARK OF GOD (1 S. iii. 3, iv. 11, v. 1, &c.), THE ARK OF THE STRENGTH OF THE LORD (2 Chron. vi. 41; Ps. cxxxii. 8), and THE HOLY ARK (2 Chron. xxxv. 3). Cf. note on *v.* 16.

The Ark of the Covenant was the central point of the Sanctuary. It was designed to contain the Testimony (xxv. 16, xl. 20; Deut. xxxi. 26), that is, the Tables of the Divine Law, the terms of the Covenant between Jehovah and His people: and it was to support the Mercy seat with its Cherubim, from between which He was to hold communion with them (Ex. xxv. 22). On this account, in these directions for the construction of the Sanctuary, it is named first of all the parts. But on the other hand, in the narrative of the work as it was actually carried out, we find that it was not made till after the Tabernacle (Ex. xxxvii. 1—9). It was more suitable that the receptacle should be first provided to receive and shelter the most sacred of the contents of the Sanctuary as soon as it was completed. The practical order of the works seems to be given in Ex. xxxi. 7—10, and xxxv. 11—19.—On the Golden Altar, see on xxx. 1.—The completion of the Ark is recorded xxxvii. 1—5. On its history, see concluding note on ch. xl.

10. *an ark*] The Hebrew name is *arōn*, which means a box, or coffer (Gen. l. 26; 2 K. xii. 9, 10; 2 Chro. xxiv. 8, &c.). The word *ark* exactly answers to it; but our translators have employed the same to render quite a different word (*tēbāh*), which is used nowhere in the Hebrew Bible except to denote what we familiarly call "the ark" of Noah, and the "ark of bulrushes" (Gen. vi. 14; Ex. ii. 3). In the first instance, there is the same confusion in both the LXX. and the Vulgate, but not in the latter one. The word *tēbāh* is Egyptian, having nearly the same meaning. See on Ex. ii. 3.—Taking the cubit at eighteen inches (see on Gen. vi. 15), the Ark of the Covenant was a box 3 ft. 9 in. long, 2 ft. 3 in. wide, and 2 ft. 3 in. deep.

of shittim wood] It is well observed that if the Ark, which appears to have been preserved till the destruction of Jerusalem (2 Chro. xxxv. 3; Jer. iii. 16), had originated

and a cubit and a half the height
thereof.
11 And thou shalt overlay it with
pure gold, within and without shalt
thou overlay it, and shalt make upon
it a crown of gold round about.
12 And thou shalt cast four rings
of gold for it, and put *them* in the four
corners thereof; and two rings *shall*
be in the one side of it, and two rings
in the other side of it.
13 And thou shalt make staves *of*
shittim wood, and overlay them with
gold.
14 And thou shalt put the staves
into the rings by the sides of the ark,
that the ark may be borne with them.
15 The staves shall be in the rings
of the ark: they shall not be taken
from it.
16 And thou shalt put into the ark
the testimony which I shall give thee.

---

in Palestine, it would not have been made of shittim wood, the wood of the Wilderness (see on v. 5), but either of oak, the best wood of the Holy Land, or of cedar, which took the place of shittim wood in the construction of the Temple (Stanley, 'Jewish Church,' I. p. 163).

11. *overlay it with pure gold*] According to the rabbinists, the Ark was lined and covered with plates of gold. But there is nothing in the original which might not aptly denote the common process of gilding. The Egyptians in early times were acquainted with both the art of gilding and that of covering a substance with thin plates of gold. (Wilkinson's 'Pop. Acc.' II. 145.)

a crown of gold] That is, an edging or **moulding** of gold round the top of the Ark, within which the cover or Mercy seat (*v.* 17) may have fitted (cf. Ex. xxxvii. 2). There were golden mouldings, called by the same name, to the Table of Shewbread (*v.* 24, xxxvii. 11, 12) and to the Golden Altar (xxx. 3, xxxvii. 26). The Heb. word *zeer* signifies, according to its etymology, a band, or cincture, and is naturally applied to a crown. Our Version in here rendering it *crown*, follows the Vulgate and some other ancient Versions. But the renderings of the LXX., Josephus, the Targums, Luther, de Wette, Zunz, Wogue, &c., more nearly agree with our word **moulding**, *i.e.* a small cornice, and this answers to the radical meaning of *zeer* as well as *crown* does. See Reland, 'De Spoliis Templi,' c. VII.

12. *four corners thereof*] Rather, **its four bases**, or feet. The Hebrew substantive is rendered *corners* in most of the ancient versions. But the LXX. have κλίτη (which appears to be rather vaguely used to denote *extremities*, cf. *vv.* 12, 19), and there seems no doubt that the original means *feet* (Aben-Ezra, Abarbanel, Gesen., Fürst, Knobel, &c.). The word may possibly denote the lowest part of each corner: but it is not unlikely that there were low blocks, or plinths, placed under the corners to which the rings were attached (see on *v.* 26), and that it is to them the word is here applied. The Ark, when it was carried, must thus have been raised above the shoulders of the bearers. The rings of the Golden Altar were placed immediately under the golden moulding (xxx. 4); but those of the Table of Shewbread were fastened to the feet of the four legs. It has been imagined by some Jewish and other authorities that the Ark was raised on high when it was carried in order to display the most sacred symbol of the Sanctuary. But we may infer, from there being a similar arrangement of the rings on the Table of Shewbread, as well as from the distinctive character of the Ark itself, that this could not have been the case. The Ark of the Covenant of Jehovah was never carried about like the arks of the gentile nations, for display. See Note at the end of chap. xl.

15. *they shall not be taken from it*] This direction was probably given in order that the Ark might not be touched by the hand (cf. 2 S. vi. 6). There is no similar direction regarding the staves of the Tabernacle of Shewbread (*v.* 27), those of the Golden Altar (xxx. 5), nor those of the Altar of Burnt offering (xxvii. 7). These were of less sanctity than the Ark and might be touched.—The formula in Num. iv. 6, 8, 11, 14, as it is rendered in our version, may seem to contradict the direction here given in regard to the Ark. But it might rather be translated in a more general sense, as, *put the staves in order* (see note in loc.).

16. *the testimony which I shall give thee*] The stone Tables of the Ten Commandments (Ex. xxiv. 12, xxxi. 18, xxxiv. 1, 28) are called the Testimony, or, the Tables of the Testimony (xxxi. 18, xxxii. 15, xxxiv. 29), as the Ark which contained them is called the Ark of the Testimony (see Introd.), and the Tabernacle in which the Ark was placed, the Tabernacle of the Testimony (Ex. xxxviii. 21; Num. i. 50, &c.); they are also called the Tables of the Covenant (Ex. xxxiv. 28; Deut. ix. 9, 11, 15), as the Ark is called the Ark of the Covenant. The meaning of the latter name admits of no doubt: the

17 And thou shalt make a mercy
seat *of* pure gold: two cubits and a
half *shall be* the length thereof, and
a cubit and a half the breadth thereof.
18 And thou shalt make two cherubims *of* gold, *of* beaten work shalt
thou make them, in the two ends of
the mercy seat.
19 And make one cherub on the one
end, and the other cherub on the other
end: *even*‖ of the mercy seat shall ye
make the cherubims on the two ends
thereof.
20 And the cherubims shall stretch
forth *their* wings on high, covering the
mercy seat with their wings, and their
faces *shall look* one to another; toward the mercy seat shall the faces
of the cherubims be.

‖ Or, *of the matter of the mercy seat.*

Ten Commandments contained "the word of the Covenant" between Jehovah and His people (Ex. xxxiv. 28; Deut. iv. 13). But there has been a difference regarding the interpretation of the former name, which derives additional importance from its being the name used here and in ch. xl. 20 in immediate connection with the first placing of the Tables within the Ark and under the Mercy seat. The reasons for taking the word Testimony, in its application to the Ten Commandments, as signifying the direct testimony of Jehovah against sin in man, and thus bringing it into connection with Deut. xxxi. 26, 27, is given elsewhere. See Note on the Ten Commandments, after ch. xx. 21.

The Mercy Seat.

xxv. 17—22. (Cf. xxxvii. 6—9.)

17. *a mercy seat of pure gold*] In external form, the Mercy seat was a plate of gold with the cherubim standing on it, the whole beaten out of one solid piece of metal (xxxvii. 7); it was placed upon the Ark and so took the place of a cover. Its Hebrew name is *kapporeth*, and on the true meaning of this word there is a very important difference of opinion. The greater number of recent translators and critics, Jewish and others, with the Arabic amongst the ancient versions, render it as simply *cover*. Our version, following the general voice of antiquity, with Luther, Cranmer, and others of the early translators in modern languages, gives, as we believe, the truer rendering, calling it the Mercy seat. [See Note at the end of the chapter.]

18—20. The way in which the Cherubim of the Mercy seat are here mentioned, with reference to their faces, wings and posture, is in favour of the common Jewish tradition (Otho, 'Rabb. Lex.' p. 129), that they were human figures, each having two wings. They must have been of small size, proportioned to the area of the Mercy seat. On the other notices of Cherubim in the Scriptures, see Note on Gen. iii. 24. Comparing the different references to form in this place, in 2 Sam. xxii. 11 (Ps. xviii. 10), in Ezek. ch. i., x. and in Rev. ch. iv., it would appear that the name *Cherub* was applied to various combinations of animal forms. Similar combinations were made by most ancient peoples in order to represent conceivable combinations of powers, such as are denied to man in his earthly state of existence. It is remarkable that amongst the Egyptians, the Assyrians and the Greeks, as well as the Hebrews, the creatures by very far most frequently introduced into these composite figures, were man, the ox, the lion, and the eagle. These are evidently types of the most important and familiarly known classes of living material beings. The rabbinists recognized this in the Cherubim as described by Ezekiel, which they regarded as representing the whole creation engaged in the worship and service of God (Schöttgen, 'Hor. Heb.' p. 1108). Cf. Rev. iv. 9—11, v. 13. It would be in harmony with this view to suppose that the more strictly human shape of the Cherubim of the Mercy seat represented the highest form of created intelligence engaged in the devout contemplation of the divine Law of love and justice. Cf. 1 Pet. i. 12. They were thus symbols of worship rendered by the creature in the most exalted condition (See Augustin. 'Quæst. in Exod.' cv.).—It is worthy of notice that the golden Cherubim from between which Jehovah spoke to His people bore witness, by their place on the Mercy seat, to His redeeming mercy; while the Cherubim that took their stand with the flaming sword at the gate of Eden, to keep the way to the tree of life, witnessed to His condemnation of sin in man. The most perfect finite intelligence seems thus to be yielding assent to the divine Law in its twofold manifestation.

18. *of beaten work*] *i.e.* elaborately wrought with the hammer.

19. *even of the mercy seat*] Rather, **out of the Mercy seat.** The sense appears to be that the Cherubim and the Mercy seat were to be wrought out of one mass of gold. (Cf. xxxvii. 7.) This meaning agrees with Onkelos, Saadia, and most modern interpreters. But the LXX., Vulg. and Syr. translate the words in question as if the second clause of the verse were, in sense, only a repetition of the first clause.

20. See on *v.* 18.

21 And thou shalt put the mercy
seat above upon the ark; and in the
ark thou shalt put the testimony that
I shall give thee.
22 And there I will meet with thee,
and I will commune with thee from
Numb. 7. 9. above the mercy seat, from *e* between
the two cherubims which *are* upon
the ark of the testimony, of all *things*
which I will give thee in commandment unto the children of Israel.
chap. 37. 10. 23 ¶ *f* Thou shalt also make a table
of shittim wood: two cubits *shall be*
the length thereof, and a cubit the
breadth thereof, and a cubit and a half
the height thereof.
24 And thou shalt overlay it with
pure gold, and make thereto a crown
of gold round about.
25 And thou shalt make unto it a
border of an hand breadth round
about, and thou shalt make a golden
crown to the border thereof round
about.
26 And thou shalt make for it four
rings of gold, and put the rings in the
four corners that *are* on the four feet
thereof.

---

21. *the testimony*] See on *v.* 16. Cf. xl. 20.

22. *I will commune with thee*] See Note on the Ten Commandments, § V.

The Table of Shewbread.

23—30. (Cf. xxxvii. 10—16.)

23. *a table of shittim wood*] This Table is one of the most prominent objects in the triumphal procession sculptured in relief on the Arch of Titus. The most important of the sculptures of the Arch were carefully copied under the direction of Reland in 1710. Since that time they have gone on to decay, so that the engravings of them in his work 'De Spoliis Templi,' &c., are now of great interest and value. Reland has interpreted the sculptures with his accustomed learning and sagacity.

The Shewbread Table with its incense cups and the two Silver Trumpets (Num. x. 2).

The Table which is here represented could not, of course, have been the one made for the Tabernacle. The original Ark of the Testimony was preserved until it disappeared when Jerusalem was captured by the Babylonians: it was never replaced by an Ark of more modern construction. See concluding note on ch. xl. But the Shewbread Table, the Golden Altar, and the Golden Candlestick, were renewed by Solomon for the Temple. Of the Candlestick, ten copies were then made. (1 K. vii. 48, 49; 2 Chro. iv. 19). From the omission of them amongst the spoils carried home from Babylon (Ezra i. 9—11) we may infer that the Table and the Golden Altar with a single Candlestick were re-made by Zerubbabel (see 1 Macc. i. 21, 22), and again by the Maccabees (1 Macc. iv. 49). There cannot therefore be a doubt that the Table and the Candlestick figured on the Arch are those of the Maccabæan times: and it must have been these which are described, and must have been seen, by Josephus ('Ant.' III. 6. § 6, 7; 'B. J.' VII. 5. § 5). It is however most likely that the restorations were made as nearly as possible after the ancient models. In representing the Table it will be seen that the sculptor has exhibited its two ends, in defiance of perspective. The details and size of the figure, and the description of Josephus, appear to agree very nearly with the directions here given to Moses, and to illustrate them in several particulars. Josephus says that the Table was like the so-called Delphic tables, richly ornamented pieces of furniture in use amongst the Romans, which were sometimes, if not always, covered with gold or silver (Martial, XII. 67; Cicero, 'in Verr.' IV. 59; cf. Du Cange, Art. 'Delphica').

24. *overlay it*] See on *v.* 11.

a crown of gold] Rather, **a moulding of gold.** See on *v.* 11. The moulding of the Table is still seen at the ends of the sculptured figure.

25. *a border*] Rather **a framing**, which reached from leg to leg so as to make the Table firm, as well as to adorn it with a second moulding of gold. Two fragments of such a framing are still seen in the sculpture attached to the legs half-way down.

26. *in the four corners that are on the four feet thereof*] The word here rendered *feet* is

27 Over against the border shall the rings be for places of the staves to bear the table.

28 And thou shalt make the staves *of* shittim wood, and overlay them with gold, that the table may be borne with them.

29 And thou shalt make the dishes thereof, and spoons thereof, and covers thereof, and bowls thereof, [1] to cover withal: *of* pure gold shalt thou make them.

30 And thou shalt set upon the table shewbread before me alway.

31 ¶ [g] And thou shalt make a candlestick *of* pure gold: *of* beaten work shall the candlestick be made: his shaft, and his branches, his bowls, his

[1] Or, *to pour out withal.*

[g] chap. 37. 17.

---

the common name for the feet of men or animals. Josephus says that the feet of the Table were like those that the Dorians used to put to their couches, which appear to have been famous for their splendour (Ælian, 'Var. Hist.' XII. 29; Athenæus, II. 47). Comparing this with the sculpture, it would seem that the legs terminated in something like the foot of an animal, such as in modern furniture is called *a claw*. The like device often occurs in the ancient Egyptian furniture (Wilkinson, I. pp. 59, 60, 62, &c.). The word here rendered *corner* is not the same as that so rendered in *v.* 12, and it may denote any extreme part. We might thus render the words, **upon the four extremities that are at the four feet.** Josephus speaks of the rings as having been in part attached to the claws themselves. But there is no trace of the rings in the sculpture.

27. *Over against the border*] Rather, **Over against the framing**; that is, the rings were to be placed not upon the framing itself, but at the extremities of the legs answering to each corner of it.

29. *dishes*] The Hebrew word is the same as is employed to denote the large silver vessels which were filled with fine flour and formed part of the offerings of the Princes of Israel in Num. vii. 13 sq., where it is rendered *chargers*. According to its probable etymology, it denoted a deep vessel, and therefore neither of the English words answers well to it: perhaps *bowls* would be nearer the mark. Knobel conjectures that these vessels, which belonged to the Shewbread Table, were used to bring the bread into the Sanctuary; but it is hard to imagine that vessels of sufficient size for such a purpose (Lev. xxiv. 5) were formed of gold. They may possibly have been the measures for the meal used in the loaves.

spoons] The Hebrew word is that used for the small gold **cups** that were filled with frankincense in the offerings of the Princes, Num. vii. 14 sq. The LXX. render it θυΐσκαι = *incense cups*. See on Lev. xxiv. 7. These must be the only vessels which are mentioned by Josephus in connection with the Table—δύο φιάλαι χρύσεαι λιβανωτοῦ πλήρεις ('Ant.' III. c. 6. § 6. c. 10. § 7), and which are represented on the Table in the sculpture.

covers...bowls] According to the best authority these were **flagons** and **chalices**, such as were used for Drink offerings. LXX. σπονδεῖα and κύαθοι. See the next note.

to cover withal] More correctly rendered in the margin, *to pour out withal*. It is strange that our translators in the text should have left Luther and Cranmer, backed as they are by the LXX., the Vulg., the Syriac, the Targums, and the most direct sense of the original words, to follow Saadia and the Talmud. With the exception of some recent Jewish versions, the best modern authorities apply the passage, along with the two last names of vessels, to the rite of the Drink offering, which appears to have regularly accompanied every Meat offering (Lev. xxiii. 18; Num. vi. 15, xxviii. 14, &c.). The subject is important in its bearing upon the meaning of the Shewbread: the corrected rendering of the words tends to shew that it was a true Meat offering [see on Lev. xxiv. 9].—The first part of the verse might thus be rendered;—**And thou shalt make its bowls and its incense-cups and its flagons and its chalices for pouring out** *the Drink offerings*.

30. The Shewbread Table was placed in the Holy Place on the north side (xxvi. 35). Directions for preparing the Shewbread are given in Lev. xxiv. 5—9. It consisted of twelve large cakes of unleavened bread, which were arranged on the Table in two piles, with a golden cup of frankincense on each pile (Jos. 'Ant.' III. 10. § 7). It was renewed every Sabbath day. The stale loaves were given to the priests, and the frankincense appears to have been lighted on the Altar for a memorial [see on Lev. ii. 2]. We may presume that the Drink offering was renewed at the same time. The Shewbread, with all the characteristics and significance of a great national Meat offering, in which the twelve tribes were represented by the twelve cakes, was to stand before Jehovah *perpetually*, in token that He was always graciously accepting the good works of His people, for whom Atonement had been made by the victims offered on the Altar in the Court of the Sanctuary [see notes on Lev. xxiv. 5—9].

knops, and his flowers, shall be of the same.

32 And six branches shall come out of the sides of it; three branches of the candlestick out of the one side, and three branches of the candlestick out of the other side:

33 Three bowls made like unto almonds, *with* a knop and a flower in one branch; and three bowls made like almonds in the other branch, *with* a knop and a flower: so in the six branches that come out of the candlestick.

The Golden Candlestick.

31—39. (Cf. xxxvii. 17—24).

31. *a candlestick of pure gold*] This would more properly be called a lamp-stand than a candlestick. Its purpose was to support seven oil-lamps. Like the Shewbread Table, it is a prominent object amongst the spoils of the Temple sculptured on the Arch of Titus. This figure is copied from Reland [see on *v.* 23].

The size of the Candlestick is nowhere mentioned: but we may form an estimate of it by comparing the figure with that of the Table. It is most likely that the two objects are represented on the same scale. Its height appears to have been about three feet, and its width two feet. The details of the sculpture usefully illustrate the description in the text. But the work and form of the pedestal here represented are not in accordance with Jewish taste or usage at any period. Reland conjectures that the original foot may have been broken off, and lost or stolen when the Candlestick was taken out of the Temple, and that the pedestal in the sculpture was added by some Roman artist to set off the trophy. There are other ancient representations of the Candlestick on gems, in tombs, and on the walls of synagogues. Some of these are copied in Reland's work, and one has lately been discovered by Capt. Wilson in a ruined synagogue in the valley of the Jarmuk. In most of them the stem is supported on three feet, or claws. This arrangement however is supposed to contradict Josephus, who says that the stem rose from a *pedestal:* the word he uses (βάσις) is however not quite free from ambiguity. In general form the other figures of the Candlestick copied by Reland nearly agree with that on the arch except in the limbs being more slender, in which particular they are countenanced by the description in Josephus ('B. J.' VII. 5. § 5). It is likely that the sculptor may have thickened the limbs in his work to give them better effect from the point of view from which spectators would see them.

of beaten work] See on *v.* 18.

his shaft, and his branches, his bowls, his knops, and his flowers] This might rather be rendered, **its base, its stem, its flower cups** [see next verse], **its knobs, and its lilies.**

33. *Three bowls made like unto almonds*] More strictly, **three cups of almond flowers.** These appear to be the cups in immediate contact with the knobs as shewn in the sculpture.

a flower] Most of the old versions render the word as **a lily**, and this rendering well agrees with the sculpture.

the candlestick] Here, and in the two following verses, the word appears to denote *the stem*, as the essential part of the Candlestick. It would seem from *vv.* 33—35 that the ornamentation of the Candlestick consisted of uniform members, each comprising a series of an almond flower, a knob and a lily; that the stem comprised four of these members; that each pair of branches was united to the stem at one of the knobs; and that each branch comprised three members. In comparing the description in the text with the sculptured figure, allowance may be made for some deviation in the sculptor's copy, which was pardonable enough, considering the purpose for which the representation was made.

34 And in the candlestick *shall be* four bowls made like unto almonds, *with* their knops and their flowers.

35 And *there shall be* a knop under two branches of the same, and a knop under two branches of the same, and a knop under two branches of the same, according to the six branches that proceed out of the candlestick.

36 Their knops and their branches shall be of the same: all it *shall be* one beaten work *of* pure gold.

37 And thou shalt make the seven lamps thereof: and they shall ‖light the lamps thereof, that they may give light over against † it.

‖ Or, *cause to ascend.*

† Heb. *the face of it.*

38 And the tongs thereof, and the snuffdishes thereof, *shall be of* pure gold.

39 *Of* a talent of pure gold shall he make it, with all these vessels.

40 And *h* look that thou make *them* after their pattern, † which was shewed thee in the mount.

h Acts 7. 44. Heb. 8. 5.

† Heb. *which thou wast caused to see.*

---

37. *seven lamps*] These lamps were probably like those used by the Egyptians and other nations, shallow covered vessels more or less of an oval form, with a mouth at one end from which the wick protruded. This may help us to the simplest explanation of the rather obscure words, "that they may give light over against it." The Candlestick was placed on the south side of the Holy Place (xxvi. 35), with the line of lamps parallel with the wall, or, according to Josephus, somewhat obliquely. If the wick-mouths of the lamps were turned outwards, they would give light over against the Candlestick; that is, towards the north side [see Num. viii. 2].

37. *they shall light*] See marginal rendering and note on Lev. xxiv. 2.

38. *the tongs*] The Hebrew word is the same as in Is. vi. 6. The small tongs for the lamps were used to trim and adjust the wicks.

the snuff-dishes] These were shallow vessels used to receive the burnt fragments of wick removed by the tongs. The same Hebrew word is translated, in accordance with its connection, *fire pans*, xxvii. 3, xxxviii. 3; and *censers*, Num. iv. 14, xvi. 6, &c. For the regulations respecting the Priests' tending the lamps, see xxvii. 20, 21, xxx. 8; Lev. xxiv. 2—4 (with the note); 2 Chro. xiii. 11.

39. *a talent of pure gold*] Amongst the discrepant estimates of the weight of the Hebrew talent, the one that appears to be received most generally would make it about 94 lbs. See on xxxviii. 27.

vessels] Rather, **utensils** [see on xxvii. 19].

Several writers have treated of the symbolism of the lights of the Golden Candlestick with their oil, of its ornamentation with the knobs and flowers, and of its branched form (Bähr, Hengstenberg, Keil, &c.). All these particulars might have been in later times appropriated by the prophetic inspiration as figures illustrative of spiritual truth. See Zech. iv. 1—14; Rev. i. 12, 13, 20. But in any especial connection with the place held by the Candlestick in the Sanctuary, as its plan was revealed to Moses, there appears to be only one peculiar point of symbolism on which stress can be laid—the fact that the lamps were seven in number. The general fashion of the Candlestick and its ornaments might have been a matter of taste; light was of necessity required in the Tabernacle, and whereever light is used in ceremonial observance, it may of course be taken in a general way as a figure of the Light of Truth; but in the Sanctuary of the covenanted people, it must plainly have been understood as expressly significant that the number of the lamps agreed with the number of the Covenant. The Covenant of Jehovah was essentially a Covenant of light.

40. See on *v.* 9.

NOTE ON CHAP. XXV. 4.

ON THE COLOURS OF THE TABERNACLE.

I.

Our version is most probably right in its rendering of the names of the three colours used in the curtains and vails of the Tabernacle. But the subject is a doubtful one. The names of colours in all languages appear to have been very vaguely used, until the progress of science in connection with the decorative arts has rendered greater precision both possible and desirable. Our own word *gray*, as applied not only to the mixture of black and white now so called, but also to the brown dress of the "gray friars" and to the cockchafer (the "gray fly" of Milton); and the Latin *purpureus* as applied to snow, the swan and the foam of the sea, to the rose, to a beautiful human eye, as well as to the colour now known as purple, may be taken as instances. The ἱμάτιον πορφυροῦν of John xix. 2 is called χλαμύδα κοκκίνην in Matt. xxvii. 28. Mr.

Gladstone's essay on the use of the names of colours in Homer furnishes other illustrations[1]. That the Hebrew names were used with not more stedfastness is proved by Mr Bevan in Smith's 'Dict. of the Bible' (Art. 'Colours'). The Hebrew names in the text must however have been applied at the time with distinct denotation in reference to the use of the yarn in the embroidery of the curtains. The uncertainty concerns only our discovering what the colours actually were. The earliest equivalents we have for the Hebrew words are those used by the LXX., which have been adopted by Philo and Josephus, and have been followed by the ancient versions in general. But we are unfortunately far from certain of the purport of the Greek words.

II.

The most important of the three colours mentioned in this place is the one rendered *blue*. The balance of evidence seems to be in favour of its being a pure sky blue. The Hebrew is *tĕkēleth* (תְּכֵלֶת), for which the LXX. have ὑάκινθος, and the Vulgate *Hyacinthus*. As the name of a flower, the Greek word has been taken for the iris, the gladiolus, the delphinium, or the hyacinth: as the name of a precious stone, it evidently could not, as some have supposed, belong to the amethyst, since it is mentioned with the amethyst (ἀμέθυστος) in Rev. xxi. 20; it most likely denoted the sapphire[2]: as the name of a colour, it has been supposed to denote pure blue, purple, violet, black, red or rust colour[3]. Of the different flowers to which the word has been ascribed, it may be remarked that the greater number are blue; for example, the common iris, the larkspur, the wild hyacinth, and the starch hyacinth, which is so abundant in the neighbourhood of Athens. The Hebrew word has been very generally taken to denote either blue, or bluish-purple, while "the purple" associated with it has been supposed to have had a stronger red tinge. Philo[4], Josephus[5], and Saadia, with most of the Fathers and the rabbinists, appear to have understood it as the colour of the sky. Philo, who took it to symbolize the air, in the expression which he applies to the air (φύσει γὰρ μέλας), has been reasonably supposed to allude to the dark full tinge which distinguishes the skies of southern latitudes[6].

That the Egyptians in early times used indigo as a blue dye is certain[7], and it is by no means improbable that the Israelites did the same. If, as Wilkinson and others[8] suppose, the blue border of the Israelites' garments was adopted from an Egyptian custom, the facts that the Egyptian borders were certainly dyed with indigo, and that the Hebrew and Greek words expressing the colour of the Israelites' borders (Num. xv. 38) are *tĕkēleth* and ὑάκινθος, favour the notion that these words express the colour obtained from indigo. But the etymology of the Hebrew term is supposed rather to indicate that the colour was procured, like the Tyrian purple, from a shell-fish. It is conceived that while a species of Murex produced the purple, a Buccinum produced the blue[9]. Both colours were obtained by the Tyrians from "the Isles of Elishah," that is, the Isles of the Ægean Sea, where it seems most probable that each must have been obtained from the sea[10]. The art of preparing the dye from the fish is now lost, and this, of course, increases the uncertainty of the question at issue.

It is however likely that *tĕkēleth* was the name of the well-known colour obtained from more than one kind of dye. The inquiry regarding the colour itself has peculiar interest from its having been the predominating colour in the decoration of the Sanctuary. Besides taking its place with the other two colours in the curtains and vails of the Tabernacle, it is found by itself in the loops of the curtains (Ex. xxvi. 4), in the lace of the breastplate of the High Priest (xxviii. 28), in the robe of the ephod (xxviii. 31), and the lace of the mitre (xxviii. 37). In wrapping up the sacred utensils when the host was on the march, blue cloths, purple cloths, and scarlet cloths were used for the various articles according to specific directions (Num. iv.). The national significance of blue appears to be shewn in the blue fringes that have been mentioned (Num. xv. 38; cf. Matt. xxiii. 5).

Several Jewish commentators, followed by Luther and Cranmer, have taken the word *tĕkēleth* to denote *yellow silk*. It is hardly

[1] 'Essays on Homer,' Vol. III. p. 457.

[2] Professor Maskelyne considers that the hyacinth of Pliny ('H. N.' XXXVII. 40) and other classical writers was what we call the sapphire, while the stone called sapphire by the ancients was lapis lazuli. 'Edinb. Rev.' No. 253. See note on Ex. xxviii. 18.

[3] See Liddell and Scott's 'Lex.'

[4] 'Vit. Mos.' III. 6.

[5] 'Ant.' III. 7. § 7. See also note on Ex. xxv. 5.

[6] Other grounds for rendering the Hebrew word *sky blue*, rather than *violet* or *bluish purple*, as Gesenius and others have preferred, may be found in Bochart, 'Op.' Vol. III. p. 728, and Bähr, 'Symbolik,' Vol. I. p. 303.

[7] Wilkinson, 'Pop. Acc.' Vol. II. p. 78.

[8] Henstenberg, 'Egypt and the Books of Moses,' Smith, 'The Pentateuch,' p. 302.

[9] Bochart, 'Op.' p. III. 727. Gesenius, s. v. Fürst, s.v. Wilkinson, Note on Herodot. III. 20. Tristram, 'Nat. Hist. of the Bible,' p. 297.

[10] Ezek. xxvii. 7; Jer. x. 9. Cf. Plin. 'H.N.' IX. 60, *sq*.

necessary to state that the material could not have been silk [see note on Ex. xxv. 4]. The notion that the colour was yellow seems to stand upon a mere hollow conjecture suggested by the natural colour of silk.

III.

Purple is in Heb. *argāmān* (אַרְגָּמָן), in the LXX. πορφύρα. The derivation of the Hebrew word is doubtful, but all authorities seem to be in favour of its signifying the purple obtained from more than one species of shell-fish in the Mediterranean, which became commonly known as the Tyrian purple (Ezek. xxvii. 7, 16). The colour seems to have had a strong red tinge, and to have approached what we call crimson. The fish that produced it has been supposed to be a muscle, but it is hardly to be doubted that it was in fact a Murex, two species of which (*M. brandaris* and *M. trunculus*) might have furnished it (Tristram). Hence the dye was called *murex* by the Latin writers. The colour is mentioned in connection with the Sanctuary only in combination with blue and scarlet in the curtains and vails and in some of the cloths for wrapping (Num. iv. 13). The estimation in which the dye was held may be inferred from Judg. viii. 26; Esth. i. 6; Prov. xxxi. 22.

IV.

Scarlet is in Hebrew *tola'ath shāni* (תּוֹלַעַת שָׁנִי), in LXX. κόκκινος διπλοῦς, and in Vulg. "coccus bistinctus[1]." But the literal translation of the two Hebrew words is *scarlet worm*, while in Lev. xiv. 4, 6, 49, 51, 52, the words are transposed (שְׁנִי תוֹלַעַת), so as to signify *worm scarlet*. The word *shāni*, by itself, denotes scarlet in Gen. xxxviii. 28, 30; Josh. ii. 18; Prov. xxxi. 21, &c. Ancient and modern authorities agree as to the colour, which is uniformly called scarlet in our version except in Jer. iv. 30, where it is rendered *crimson*. The dye used to produce the colour in the vail of the Temple is called *karmil* (כַּרְמִיל), 2 Chron. ii. 7, 14, iii. 14, where it is rendered *crimson*, though there is no reason to doubt that the colour was the same as the *scarlet* of the Tabernacle. It appears to have been obtained from the *coccus ilicis*, the cochineal insect of the holm oak, which was used in the East before the *coccus cacti*, the well-known cochineal of the prickly pear, was introduced from Mexico. The Arabic name for it is *kermez*, which is evidently related to the Hebrew word *karmil*. The root *karm* exists in our *crimson* and *carmine*. In the use of the Sanctuary, it is found only in the figured curtains and embroidery associated with blue and purple, and in the wrapping cloths (Num. iv. 8). It appears to have had a special connection with the rites of purification in association with hyssop and cedar (Lev. xiv. 4, 6, 49, 51, 52; Num. xix. 6; Heb. ix. 19).

V.

On the whole, there does not seem to be much ground to doubt that our version, in rendering the names of the colours of the woven and embroidered work of the Sanctuary, expresses the most probable conclusions.

The three colours, blue, scarlet and purple, have been recognized all but universally as royal colours, such as were best suited for the decoration of a palace[2]. This fact appears to furnish sufficient ground for their having been appointed as the colours for the embroidery which was to adorn the dwelling-place of Jehovah. Many have, however, imagined that there was some other symbolical significance in them. See Bähr, 'Symbolik,' Vol. I. p. 324; Dr W. L. Alexander in Kitto's 'Cyclo.' Vol. I. p. 541, &c.

NOTE ON CHAP. XXV. 17.

ON THE MERCY SEAT.

The word *kapporeth* (כַּפֹּרֶת) is never applied to anything except the golden cover of the Ark. The root from which it comes, *kāphar* (כָּפַר), without doubt signifies *to cover*, and bears an obvious resemblance to our word *cover*. In one passage of the Old Testament, but in one only, the Hebrew word, in its *Kal* or primitive form, is used in this sense in reference to covering the Ark of Noah with pitch (Gen. vi. 14). In the *Piel* form (*Kipper*, כִּפֶּר) the root is used nearly seventy times, and always in the sense of *forgiving* or *reconciling*, that is of covering up offences. Now a large number of recent authorities, Jewish and others[3], have preferred to take *kapporeth* in the simple sense of *a cover*. Josephus and Saadia give countenance to this rendering. The question thus brought before us is, was the *kapporeth* originally regarded as a mere part of the Ark, or as something having a distinct significance, and a recognized designation, of its own? The inquiry is of great importance, from its bearing on the character

[1] The Greek and Latin renderings appear to be based on a mistake in regard to the word שני, which, with other vowel points, would mean *twice*.

[2] See Esth. i. 6, viii. 15; 2 S. i. 24; Cant. iii. 10; Jer. x. 9; Ezek. xxiii. 6; Dan. v. 7; Luke xvi. 19; Rev. xviii. 12, &c.

[3] Kimchi, Mendelsohn, de Wette, Gesenius, Schott, Fürst, Zunz, Knobel, Herxheimer, Leeser, Benisch, Sharpe, &c. But amongst the Jewish commentators, Wogue and Kalisch are exceptions.

of the Mosaic ritual. The latter view appears to deserve the preference on these grounds;—

1. In the order of the sacred text, the Mercy seat is described by itself, and is directed to be placed "above upon the Ark" (Ex. xxv. 17—22, xxvi. 34): it is never called *the cover* (or *kapporeth*) *of the Ark*, but is always mentioned as a distinct thing (Ex. xxx. 6, xxxi. 7, xxxv. 12, xxxvii. 6—9, xxxix. 35; Lev. xvi. 13; Num. vii. 89, &c.).

2. The Holy of Holies is called in the first Book of Chronicles (xxviii. 11) *the house of the kapporeth* (בֵּית הַכַּפֹּרֶת); and in Leviticus (xvi. 2) it is called the place *within the vail before the kapporeth, which is upon the Ark.* Such expressions as these seem clearly to indicate that the *kapporeth* could not have been regarded as a mere subordinate part of the Ark.

3. An argument scarcely less strong may be drawn from the relationship of the word *kapporeth* to *kippurim* (כִּפֻּרִים) = *atonements*, in connection with the rites of the Day of Atonement, or (as it is literally) the Day of Atonements. No part of the Sanctuary is so intimately connected with the *kippurim* made on that day by the High Priest as the *kapporeth* (Lev. xvi. 2, 13, 14, 15). The phraseology of these passages is certainly not such as could be well accounted for by the mere position of the *kapporeth* as the cover of the Ark.

4. The general current of the most ancient Jewish tradition evidently favours the derivation of *kapporeth* from *kipper* (כִּפֵּר), the *Piel* form of the verb, which, as it has been already observed, nowhere bears any other meaning than *to atone*, or *to shew mercy*. The oldest authority is the Septuagint, in which the word is rendered ἱλαστήριον ἐπίθημα[1]. Philo speaks of the cover of the Ark being called in the Scripture ἱλαστήριον, as a symbol τῆς ἵλεω τοῦ Θεοῦ δυνάμεως[2]. Rabbinical tradition furnishes evidence to the same effect. The vowel points in the word *kapporeth* (כַּפֹּרֶת) are such as to connect it with the *Piel* form *kipper*, rather than with the *Kal* form *kāphar*. Another argument may be added from the use in the Targums of the same expression as is found 1 Chron. xxviii. 11, *the house of the kapporeth* [see § 2], to answer to "the oracle" (דְּבִיר) in 1 K. vi. 5.

5. We might at once settle the question as to the Mercy seat having a meaning of its own by referring to the passages in the New Testament in which the word ἱλαστήριον occurs (Heb. ix. 5; Rom. iii. 25). But it is satisfactory to have such clear evidence as exists that the New Testament use of the word is not a late or artificial adaptation of it, but a clear and simple application of its original meaning.

[1] Fürst, following certain Jewish authorities, conceives that ἱλαστήριον is a gloss of later date. But this is evidently a mere conjecture of prejudice.

[2] 'Vit. Mos.' III. 8.

CHAPTER XXVI.

1 *The ten curtains of the tabernacle.* 7 *The eleven curtains of goats' hair.* 14 *The covering of rams' skins.* 15 *The boards of the tabernacle, with their sockets and bars.* 31 *The vail for the ark.* 36 *The hanging for the door.*

MOREOVER thou shalt make the tabernacle *with* ten curtains *of* fine twined linen, and blue, and purple, and scarlet: *with* cherubims of † cunning work shalt thou make them.

† Heb. *the work of a cunning workman*, or, *embroiderer*.

The Tabernacle.

xxvi. 1—37. (xxxvi. 8—38.)

Chap. XXVI. The Tabernacle was to comprise three main parts, the Tabernacle, more strictly so-called, its Tent, and its Covering (Ex. xxxv. 11, xxxix. 33, 34, xl. 19, 34; Num. iii. 25, &c.). These parts are very clearly distinguished in the Hebrew, but they are confounded in many places of the English Version [see on *vv.* 7, 9, &c.], and in still more places of the LXX., the Vulgate, and other versions, ancient and modern. The Tabernacle itself was to consist of curtains of fine linen woven with coloured figures of Cherubim, and a structure of boards which was to contain the Holy Place and the Most Holy Place; the Tent was to be a true tent of goats' hair cloth to contain and shelter the Tabernacle: the Covering was to be of red rams' skins and tachash skins [see on xxv. 5], and was spread over the goats' hair tent as an additional protection against the weather. On the external form of the Tabernacle and the arrangement of its parts, see Note at the end of the chap. The account of its completion is given ch. xxxvi. 8—38.

The Tabernacle.

xxvi. 1—6. (Cf. xxxvi. 8—13.)

1. *tabernacle*] The Hebrew is *mishkān*, *i.e.* dwelling-place (Job xviii. 21, xxi. 28; Ps. xlix. 11; Is. xxii. 16, &c. &c.). When it denotes the Dwelling-place of Jehovah, it is

2 The length of one curtain *shall be* eight and twenty cubits, and the breadth of one curtain four cubits: and every one of the curtains shall have one measure.

3 The five curtains shall be coupled together one to another; and *other* five curtains *shall be* coupled one to another.

4 And thou shalt make loops of blue upon the edge of the one curtain from the selvedge in the coupling; and likewise shalt thou make in the uttermost edge of *another* curtain, in the coupling of the second.

5 Fifty loops shalt thou make in the one curtain, and fifty loops shalt thou make in the edge of the curtain that *is* in the coupling of the second; that the loops may take hold one of another.

6 And thou shalt make fifty taches

---

regularly accompanied by the definite article (*hammishkān*). The word tabernacle (which our translators took from the Vulgate) might fitly designate the structure of boards which formed the walls of the Holy Places, but its meaning does not etymologically answer to *mishkān*. The Hebrew word is however uniformly rendered tabernacle in our Bible: the confusion to which reference has been made in the preceding note occurs in rendering the names of the Tent and the Covering.

It should be noticed that in this place *hammishkān* is not used in its full sense as denoting the dwelling-place of Jehovah: it denotes only the tabernacle cloth. It was the textile work which was regarded as the essential part of the Tabernacle, and this is apparent in our version of *v.* 6. The tent-cloth in like manner and for the like reason is called simply the Tent (*v.* 11). The wooden parts of both the Tabernacle and the Tent are evidently mentioned as if they were subordinate to the textile parts.—The word *mishkān* is employed with three distinct ranges of meaning, (1) in its strict sense, comprising the cloth of the Tabernacle with its woodwork (Exod. xxv. 9, xxvi. 30, xxxvi. 13, xl. 18, &c.); (2) in a narrower sense, for the tabernacle-cloth only (Exod. xxvi. 1, 6, xxxv. 11, xxxix. 33, 34, &c.); (3) in a wider sense, for the *Mishkān* with its Tent and Covering (Exod. xxvii. 19, xxxv. 18, &c.).

with ten curtains] Rather, **of ten breadths.** The Hebrew word (*yĕrī'ah*) is everywhere in our version rendered *a curtain.* Some corresponding word is used in the Ancient Versions (LXX. αὐλαία, Vulg. *cortina*) and in some modern ones. In such places as Ps. civ. 2, Is. liv. 2, Jer. iv. 20, the Hebrew word is evidently applied to an entire tent-curtain. But in connection with the Sanctuary it always denotes what in English would more strictly be called a breadth. Five of these breadths were united so as to form what, in common usage, we should call a large curtain. (See on *v.* 3.) The word curtain will be used in this, its ordinary sense, in these notes. The two curtains thus formed were coupled together by the loops and taches to make the entire tabernacle-cloth, which is what is here called "the tabernacle." See preceding note.

fine twined linen] *i.e.* the most carefully spun thread of flax, each thread consisting of two or more smaller threads twined together (see Wilkinson, 'Pop. Account,' II. 76). On the original word for *linen*, see on xxv. 4.

blue, and purple, and scarlet] See on xxv. 4.

cherubims] See on xxv. 18.

of cunning work] More properly, **of the work of the skilled weaver.** The coloured figures of Cherubim were to be worked in the loom, as in the manufacture of tapestry and carpets: in the hangings for the Tent they were to be embroidered with the needle [see on *v.* 36]. On the different kinds of workmen employed on the textile fabrics, see on xxxv. 35.

3. Each curtain formed of five breadths (see on *v.* 1), was 42 feet in length and 30 feet in breadth, taking the cubit at 18 inches.

4. This verse is obscure as it stands in our version, nor is it easy to render the original word for word so as to make the sense clear. But the meaning appears to be, *And thou shalt make loops of blue on the selvedge of the one breadth* (*which is*) *on the side* (*of the one curtain*) *at the coupling; and the same shalt thou do in the selvedge of the outside breadth of the other* (*curtain*) *at the coupling.* The "coupling" is the uniting together of the two curtains. This explanation substantially agrees with the Ancient Versions and most of the modern ones.

5. The words "in the edge of the curtain that is in the coupling of the second," mean, *on the edge of the breadth that is at the coupling in the second* (*curtain*).—The word rendered "loops" (*lulaoth*) only occurs here and in xxxvi. 11. It is doubtful whether it has connection with any Semitic root; it is probably of Egyptian origin. Conjectures on the other side may be seen in Gesenius' 'Handwörterbuch,' and Fürst's 'Lex.'

6. *taches of gold*] Each clasp, or *tache*, was to unite two opposite loops. On the Heb. word for *tache*, see p. 375, note 7.

of gold, and couple the curtains together with the taches: and it shall
be one tabernacle.
7 ¶ And thou shalt make curtains
of goats' *hair* to be a covering upon
the tabernacle: eleven curtains shalt
thou make.
8 The length of one curtain *shall be*
thirty cubits, and the breadth of one
curtain four cubits: and the eleven
curtains *shall be all* of one measure.
9 And thou shalt couple five curtains by themselves, and six curtains
by themselves, and shalt double the
sixth curtain in the forefront of the
tabernacle.
10 And thou shalt make fifty loops
on the edge of the one curtain *that is*
outmost in the coupling, and fifty loops
in the edge of the curtain which
coupleth the second.
11 And thou shalt make fifty taches
of brass, and put the taches into the
loops, and couple the ‖tent together, ‖ Or, *covering.*
that it may be one.
12 And the remnant that remaineth
of the curtains of the tent, the half
curtain that remaineth, shall hang over
the backside of the tabernacle.
13 And a cubit on the one side,
and a cubit on the other side †of that † Heb.
which remaineth in the length of the *in the remainder.*
curtains of the tent, it shall hang over or, *surplusage.*
the sides of the tabernacle on this side
and on that side, to cover it.
14 And thou shalt make a covering for the tent *of* rams' skins dyed
red, and a covering above *of* badgers'
skins.
15 ¶ And thou shalt make boards
for the tabernacle *of* shittim wood
standing up.

---

couple the curtains] *i.e.* couple the two outside breadths mentioned in *v.* 4.

it shall be one tabernacle] The tabernacle-cloth alone is here meant. See on *v.* 1. For the mode in which the tabernacle-cloth was disposed, see Note at the end of the chap., § IV.

The Tent-cloth.

7—13 (xxxvi. 14—18).

7. *curtains*] See on *v.* 1.

of goats' hair] See on xxv. 4.

a covering upon the tabernacle] **a tent over the Tabernacle.** The same Hebrew words are rightly translated xxxvi. 14. The name *ohel*, which is here used, is the regular one for a tent of skins or cloth of any sort. See introd. note to ch. xxv., and Note at the end of this chap. § II.

9. The width of each breadth of the tent-cloth was to be four cubits, the same as that of the breadths of the figured cloth of the Tabernacle (*v.* 2). But the length was to be two cubits more, and there was to be an additional breadth (*v.* 13). One of the curtains (see on *v.* 1) was to comprise five breadths and the other six.

shalt double the sixth curtain in the forefront of the tabernacle] The last word should be **Tent**, not tabernacle. The passage might be rendered, *thou shalt equally divide the sixth breadth at the front of the Tent.* In this way, half a breadth would overhang at the front and half at the back. See *v.* 12, and Note at the end of the chapter.

10. The meaning may be thus given:—*And thou shalt make fifty loops on the selvedge of the outside breadth of the one (curtain) at the coupling, and fifty loops on the selvedge of the outside breadth of the other (curtain) at the coupling.* Cf. note *v.* 4.

11. In the Tent, clasps of bronze were used to unite the loops of the two curtains; in the Tabernacle, clasps of gold, cf. *v.* 6 and on *v.* 37.

couple the tent together] This is the right translation. The "covering," as the alternative for *tent* given in the margin, is wrong. See introd. note to this chap. By "the tent" is here meant the tent-cloth alone. See on *v.* 1.

12. *the half curtain*] See on *v.* 9, and Note at the end of the chapter, § IV.

13. The measure of the entire tabernacle-cloth was 40 cubits by 28; that of the tent-cloth was 44 cubits by 30. When the latter was placed over the former, it spread beyond it at the back and front two cubits (the "half-curtain" *vv.* 9, 12) and at the sides one cubit. See Note at the end of the chapter.

The Covering for the Tent.

v. 14. (Cf. xxxvi. 19.)

14. *rams' skins dyed red*] See on xxv. 5.

badgers' skins] The skin, not of the badger, but of a marine animal called *tachash*, perhaps the dugong or the seal. See on xxv. 5.

The Boards and Bars of the Tabernacle.

15—30 (xxxvi. 20—34).

15. *boards*] There is no reason to doubt that these were simple boards or planks (Vulg.

16 Ten cubits *shall be* the length
of a board, and a cubit and a half *shall
be* the breadth of one board.

17 Two † tenons *shall there be* in
one board, set in order one against
another: thus shalt thou make for all
the boards of the tabernacle.

† Heb. *hands.*

18 And thou shalt make the boards
for the tabernacle, twenty boards on
the south side southward.

19 And thou shalt make forty
sockets of silver under the twenty
boards; two sockets under one board
for his two tenons, and two sockets
under another board for his two tenons.

20 And for the second side of the
tabernacle on the north side *there shall
be* twenty boards:

21 And their forty sockets *of* silver;
two sockets under one board, and two
sockets under another board.

22 And for the sides of the tabernacle westward thou shalt make six
boards.

23 And two boards shalt thou make
for the corners of the tabernacle in the
two sides.

24 And they shall be † coupled together beneath, and they shall be
coupled together above the head of it

† Heb. *twinned.*

---

tabulæ), of sufficient thickness for the stability of the structure. They are called *pillars* in Greek (LXX. στῦλοι, Philo and Josephus, κίονες). Bähr adopts the rabbinical notion that they were a cubit in thickness; Josephus, with greater probability, says that they were four fingers.

of shittim wood] The shittah tree (*Acacia seyal*, see on XXV. 5) has been said to be too small to produce boards of the size here described. It has been conjectured that each board was jointed up of several pieces. But Mr Tristram regards this conjecture as needless, and states that there are acacia-trees near Engedi which would produce boards four feet in width ('Nat. Hist. of the Bible,' p. 392). If there are no trees so large in the Peninsula of Sinai at this time, liberal allowance may be made for the diminished capabilities of the region for the production of timber.

17. *tenons*] See Note at the end of the chapter.

18. The dimensions of the wooden part of the Tabernacle are not directly stated; but they are easily made out from the measurement, number and arrangement of the boards, if we estimate each of the corner boards (*v.* 23) as adding half a cubit to the width. The entire length of the structure was thirty cubits in the clear, and its width ten cubits. With this agree Philo ('Vit. Mos.' III. 7), Josephus ('Ant.' III. 6. § 3), and all tradition.

the south side southward] The Hebrew phrase, which also occurs xxvii. 9, xxxvi. 23, xxxviii. 9, is relieved from pleonasm if it is rendered, **the south side on the right.** (Geneva Fr., Zunz, Leeser; cf. Gesen. p. 600.) As the entrance of the Tabernacle was at its east end, the south side, to a person entering it, would be on the *left* hand: but we learn from Josephus ('Ant.' VIII. 3. § 6) that it was usual in speaking of the Temple to identify the south with the right hand and the north with the left hand, the entrance being regarded as the face of the structure and the west end as its back.

19. *sockets*] More literally, **bases.** The same word is rightly rendered "foundations" in Job xxxviii. 6: most versions in this place translate it by some word equivalent to *bases*. Each base weighed a talent, that is, about 94 lbs. (see xxxviii. 27), and must have been a massive block. Nothing is said of the form, but as the tenons of the boards were "set in order one against another" (*v.* 17), the bases may have fitted together so as to make a continuous foundation for the walls of boards, presenting a succession of sockets, or mortices (each base having a single socket), into which the tenons were to fit. This seems to have been the notion of Philo and Josephus [see Note at the end of chapter, § I.]. The bases served not only for ornament but also for a protection of the lower ends of the boards from the decay which would have resulted from contact with the ground. The word *socket* seems to have been adopted from Josephus. The word he uses is στρόφιγξ, which does not answer to the Hebrew etymologically, as the βάσις of the LXX. and Philo does; but there is an obvious resemblance which seems to have struck him between what is here spoken of and the socket (στρόφιγξ) in which the tenon of a door turns to serve as a hinge, according to common Eastern custom.

22. *the sides of the tabernacle westward*] Rather, **the back of the Tabernacle towards the west.** See on *v.* 18.

23. *in the two sides*] Rather, **at the back.** So LXX., Vulg., Luther, de Wette, Zunz, Herxh., &c.

24. The corner boards appear to have been of such width, and so placed, as to add

unto one ring: thus shall it be for
them both; they shall be for the two
corners.
25 And they shall be eight boards,
and their sockets *of* silver, sixteen
sockets; two sockets under one board,
and two sockets under another board.
26 ¶ And thou shalt make bars *of*
shittim wood; five for the boards of
the one side of the tabernacle,
27 And five bars for the boards of
the other side of the tabernacle, and
five bars for the boards of the side of
the tabernacle, for the two sides westward.
28 And the middle bar in the midst
of the boards shall reach from end to
end.
29 And thou shalt overlay the boards
with gold, and make their rings *of* gold
for places for the bars: and thou shalt
overlay the bars with gold.
30 And thou shalt rear up the tabernacle [a]according to the fashion
thereof which was shewed thee in the
mount.
31 ¶ And thou shalt make a vail *of*
blue, and purple, and scarlet, and fine
twined linen of cunning work: with
cherubims shall it be made:
32 And thou shalt hang it upon
four pillars of shittim *wood* overlaid
with gold: their hooks *shall be of* gold,
upon the four sockets of silver.
33 ¶ And thou shalt hang up the
vail under the taches, that thou mayest

[a] chap. 25. 9, 40. Acts 7. 44 Heb. 8. 5.

---

a cubit to the width of the structure, making up with the six boards of full width (*v.* 22) ten cubits in the clear (see on *v.* 18). There is no occasion to imagine, as some have done, that each of them consisted of two strips mitered together longitudinally so as to form a corner by itself. They may have been simple boards with the width of half a cubit added to the thickness of the boards of the sides. The boards at the corners were to be coupled together at the top "unto one ring," and at the bottom "unto one ring," and each ring was to be so formed as to receive two bars meeting at a right angle.

26, 27. See on *v.* 28, and Note at the end of the chapter, § I.

27. *for the two sides westward*] **for the back towards the west.** Cf. *v.* 22.

28. *in the midst of the boards*] The middle bar was distinguished from the other bars by its reaching from end to end. The Hebrew might mean either that the *midst* throughout which it ran was the middle between the top and the bottom of the boards, or that it was a passage for it bored through the substance of the wood out of sight. The latter would seem to have been the notion of our translators. See xxxvi. 33. But if we suppose the boards to have been of ordinary thickness [see on *v.* 16], by far the more likely supposition is that the bar was visible and passed through an entire row of rings. In either case, it served to hold the whole wall together. On the probable relation of this middle bar to the others, see Note and woodcut, p. 377.

29. *overlay ... with gold*] See on xxv. 11.
their rings] See on *v.* 28.

30. Cf. xxv. 9, 40.

The Vail and the Holy Places.

31—35. (Cf. xxxvi. 35, 36.)

31. *vail*] The Hebrew word literally means *separation* [see on xxxv. 12].
blue, and purple, and scarlet] See on xxv. 4.
twined linen] See on *v.* 1.
of cunning work, &c.] **of work of the skilled weaver** [see on *v.* 1, and on xxxv. 35] **shall it be made, with Cherubim.**
cherubims] The vail of the first Temple was in like manner adorned with Cherubim (2 Chron. iii. 14). It is remarkable that Josephus describes the vail of the Tabernacle as woven with flowers and all sorts of ornamental forms, except the figures of living creatures ('Ant.' III. 6. § 4). He himself calls the Cherubim *living creatures* ('Ant.' III. 6. § 5), and he must have known that Ezekiel does so (x. 20). He is thus plainly at variance with the statement in Exodus. But can it be that he describes the vail according to the one which existed in the Temple in his time? If so, we obtain a striking instance of the operation of the superstition with which the Jews in later times, including Josephus himself, interpreted the second commandment (see 'Ant.' VIII. 7. § 5, and note on Ex. xx. 4). It may suggest a thought, if we may conceive that the vail of the Temple which was rent at the Crucifixion had been deprived of its characteristic symbol by the dark prejudices of the chosen people.

32. *pillars of shittim wood*, &c.] Rather, pillars of shittim wood overlaid with gold, **their hooks also of gold, upon four bases of silver.** Cf. xxxvi. 36.

33. *under the taches*] These taches are not, as some suppose, the same as the *hooks* of the preceding verse. The Hebrew words

bring in thither within the vail the ark of the testimony: and the vail shall divide unto you between the holy *place* and the most holy.

34 And thou shalt put the mercy seat upon the ark of the testimony in the most holy *place*.

35 And thou shalt set the table without the vail, and the candlestick over against the table on the side of the tabernacle toward the south: and thou shalt put the table on the north side.

36 And thou shalt make an hanging for the door of the tent, *of* blue, and purple, and scarlet, and fine twined linen, wrought with needlework.

37 And thou shalt make for the hanging five pillars *of* shittim *wood*, and overlay them with gold, *and* their hooks *shall be of* gold: and thou shalt cast five sockets of brass for them.

---

are quite different. These are the taches of the tabernacle-cloth (see *v.* 6). On the difficulty of the statement, see Note at the end of the chapter, § I.

34. *mercy seat upon the ark of the testimony*] See on xxv. 10—16. The Samaritan text here inserts the passage regarding the Altar of Incense from ch. xxx. 1—10. The omission of all mention of this altar in this place is strange, but the reading of the Samaritan bears marks of an intended emendation, and cannot represent the original text.

35. *candlestick*] See on xxv. 31.

table] See on xxv. 23.

The Front of the Tent.

36, 37. (Cf. xxxvi. 37, 38.)

36. *hanging*] Rather, **curtain** [see on xxvii. 16].

the door of the tent] **the entrance to the Tent.** The word is *petkach*, that is the opening which it is the office of the door (*deleth*), or as in this place, of the curtain (*māsāk*), to close. The distinction between *door* and *entrance* is generally overlooked in our version. See on Lev. viii. 3.

wrought with needlework] **the work of the embroiderer.** The breadths of the cloth and the vail of the Tabernacle were to be of **the work of the skilled weaver;** the entrance curtain of the Tent and that of the Court (xxvii. 16) were to be of the same materials, but embroidered with the needle, not wrought in figures in the loom. [See on *v.* 1, and on xxxv. 35.]

37. *hanging*] **curtain** as in *v.* 36.

five pillars] These, it should be observed, belonged to the entrance of the Tent, not, in their architectural relation, to the entrance of the Tabernacle [see Note, § III.].

overlay them with gold] See on xxv. 11.

their hooks] See on *v.* 33. These pillars had chapiters (capitals), and fillets (**connecting rods**, see on xxvii. 10), overlaid with gold (xxxvi. 38). Their bases (see on *v.* 19) were of bronze (like the taches of the tent-cloth), not of silver, to mark the inferiority of the Tent to the Tabernacle.

NOTE ON CHAP. XXVI. 1—37.

ON THE CONSTRUCTION OF THE TABERNACLE.

I. *The Mishkān, its Tent and its Covering.* II. *Common view of the arrangement of the parts.* III. *Mr Fergusson's theory.* IV. *The place of the tabernacle cloth.* V. *Symmetry of the proposed arrangement.* VI. *The Court.*

The chief portions of the structure are described with remarkable clearness in Exodus xxvi. and a second time in ch. xxxvi. It would however seem that those parts only are distinctly mentioned which formed visible features in the completed fabric. Mere details of construction were most probably carried out according to the mechanical usage of the time.

If we take this for granted, the sacred text appears to furnish sufficient information to enable us to realize with confidence the form and the general arrangements of the Tabernacle as well as of its Court. But the subject has been encumbered ever since the time of Philo[1] with certain traditional notions which are opposed not only to the words of Exodus, but to the plainest principles of constructive art.

I.

It has been already stated[2] that three principal parts of the Sanctuary are clearly distinguished in the Hebrew, though they are confounded in most versions. These parts are—

1. THE DWELLING PLACE, OR THE TABERNACLE, strictly so called; in Hebrew, *hammishkān* (הַמִּשְׁכָּן) [note on xxvi. 1].
2. The TENT, in Heb. *ohel* (אֹהֶל).
3. The COVERING, in Heb. *mikseh* (מִכְסֶה)

[1] 'Vit. Mos.' III. 4 sq.
[2] Introd. Note to chap. xxvi.

1. The materials for THE MISHKĀN were a great cloth of woven work figured with Cherubim measuring forty cubits by twenty-eight cubits, and a quadrangular enclosure of wood, open at one end, ten cubits in height, ten cubits in width and thirty cubits in length.

The size of the Tabernacle cloth is indicated beyond the reach of doubt by the number and dimensions of the ten breadths (or "curtains") of which it consisted[1]. The size of the wooden enclosure is made out almost as certainly from the number and measurements of the boards[2].

The boards were set upright, each of them being furnished at its lower extremity with two tenons which fitted into mortices in two heavy bases of silver. The whole of these bases placed side by side probably formed a continuous wall-plinth[3]. The boards were furnished with rings or loops of gold so fixed as to form rows, when the boards were set up, and through these rings bars were thrust. There were five bars for each side of the structure and five for the back[4]. The middle bar of each wall "was to reach from end to end," and this plainly distinguished it from the other four bars. It is inferred with great probability that this middle bar was twice as long as the others, that there were three rows of rings, and that the half of each wall was fastened together by two of the shorter bars, one near the top, the other near the bottom, while the two halves were united into a whole by the middle bar reaching from end to end[5]. Thus each wall must have been furnished with four short bars and one long one. Each of the rings near the top and the bottom of the two corner boards was shaped in some way so as to receive the ends of two bars, one belonging to the back, the other to the side, meeting at a right angle. In this way the walls were "coupled together" at the corners[6].

There is nothing said from which we can decide whether the rings and bars were on the outside or the inside of the wooden structure. From the rich materials of which they were made, it seems not unlikely that they constituted an ornamental feature on the inside. It may be added, that on the inside they would tend to make the structure firm more than on the outside.

So far it is not difficult to see nearly what THE MISHKĀN must have been. But it is not so easy to determine the way in which the great figured cloth that belonged to it was arranged. The question must be considered in connection with the description of the parts of the TENT.

There is another difficulty, by far less easy of solution, which may be stated here. It affects the internal arrangement. The vail which separated the Most Holy Place from the Holy Place was suspended from golden hooks attached to four pillars overlaid with gold, standing upon silver bases. But the position of these pillars is not mentioned in Exodus. It is indeed said that the vail was hung "under the taches[7]." Now the taches of the tabernacle cloth must have been fifteen cubits from the back of the Mishkān, that is, half way between its back and front. But according to Philo, Josephus, and all tradition, supported by every consideration of probability, the vail was ten cubits, not fifteen, from the back, and the Holy of Holies was a cubical chamber of corresponding measurement. The statement that the vail was hung "under the taches" remains unexplained. But this difficulty is by no means such as to be set in opposition to any view that may meet all other conditions expressed or involved in the narrative.

2. The TENT is described as consisting of a great tent-cloth of goats' hair, which, according to the number and dimensions of its breadths, was forty-four cubits by thirty[8], and five pillars overlaid with gold standing on bases of bronze, and furnished with golden hooks from which was suspended the curtain that served to close the entrance of the Tent[9].

3. Of the COVERING of rams' skins and tachash skins, nothing whatever is said except as regards the materials of which it was composed[10].

II.

It has been usual to represent the Tabernacle as consisting of the wooden structure which has been described, with the masses of drapery and skins thrown over it "as a pall is thrown over a coffin." There was first the figured

[1] Ex. xxvi. 1—6; xxxvi. 8—13.
[2] See on Ex. xxvi. 18.
[3] See on xxvi. 19.
[4] Ex. xxvi. 26—28; xxxvi. 31—33.
[5] See on Ex. xxvi. 28, and woodcut, p. 377.
[6] Ex. xxvi. 24; xxxvi. 29.

[7] Ex. xxvi. 33. This is not mentioned in ch. xxxvi., where the manufacture of the parts, and not their arrangement, is spoken of. It has been imagined that the *taches* were the same as the *hooks* from which the vail was actually hung (Ex. xxvi. 32). But the words are quite distinct. The word rendered *tache* is *keres* (קֶרֶס), which is supposed to be derived from a root which signifies to bind; that rendered *hook*, is *vāv* (וָו), which is the name of the Hebrew letter shaped like a hook suited for hanging anything on (ו); its origin is unknown. *Keres* is used only in reference to the taches of the tabernacle-cloth and of the tent-cloth of the Sanctuary (Ex. xxvi. 6, 33, &c.), and *vāv* only in reference to the hooks of the vail and of the tent-curtain.
[8] Ex. xxvi. 7—13; xxxvi. 14—18.
[9] Ex. xxvi. 36, 37; xxxvi. 37, 38.
[10] Ex. xxvi. 14; xxxvi. 19. See on xxv. 5.

cloth recognized as part of THE MISHKĀN, then the goats' hair cloth of the TENT, and then the twofold COVERING of skins.

A modification of this arrangement was suggested by Vater and adopted by Bähr[1], which has the advantage of displaying the figured cloth and of connecting it more strictly with the Mishkān, though in no very graceful or convenient manner. It was supposed that this cloth was strained over the top of the structure like a ceiling and fastened to the top of the boards in some way, so as to hang down and cover the walls on the inside as a tapestry, leaving a cubit at the bases of the boards bare, to show as a sort of skirting.

With the exception of certain expressions in Josephus[2], the whole current of opinion seems to have been in favour of this general arrangement of the parts of the Tabernacle. But it should be kept in view that the subject is one in which tradition cannot be of much value. We may allow that it is just possible, though by no means probable, that some points of detail besides what are actually recorded, or some special knowledge of the meaning of technical terms, may have been handed down from the time of Moses. But in a case of this kind we certainly need not hesitate to set tradition aside, whenever it is in conflict either with the letter of Scripture, or with reasonable probability.

The objections to the common theory are these:—

1. The arrangement proposed makes out the fabric to have been unsightly in its form and to have had a great part of the beauty of its materials entirely concealed.

2. It would be quite impossible to strain drapery over a space of fifteen feet, so as to prevent it from heavily sagging; and no flat roof of such materials could by any means be rendered proof against the weather.

3. It is hard to assign any use to the pins and cords of the Tabernacle[4] (which would be essential in the construction of a tent[5]) if the curtains and skins were merely thrown over the woodwork and allowed to hang down on each side.

4. The shelter of the Mishkān is always called in Hebrew by a name which, in its strict use, can denote nothing but a tent, properly so called, of cloth or skins.

5. An essential part of the Tent was the row of five pillars at its entrance[3]: if we suppose these five pillars to have stood just in front of the Mishkān, they must have been strangely out of symmetry with the four pillars of the vail, and the middle pillar must have stood needlessly and inconveniently in the way of the entrance.

III.

We are indebted to Mr Fergusson[7] for what may be regarded as a satisfactory reconstruction of the Sanctuary in all its main particulars. He holds that what sheltered the Mishkān was actually a Tent of ordinary form, such as common sense and practical experience would suggest as best suited for the purpose.

According to this view the five pillars at the entrance of the tent[3] were graduated as they would naturally be at the entrance of any large tent of the best form, the tallest one being in the middle to support one end of a ridge-pole. It has been already observed that the descriptions in Exodus appear to pass over all particulars of the construction except

[1] 'Symbolik,' I. p. 63.
[2] See p. 379.
[3] Ex. xxvi. 37.

[4] See Ex. xxvii. 19; xxxv. 18. The word "tabernacle" (*mishkān*), in these places, evidently includes the Tent as well as the Mishkān itself. See note on Ex. xxvi. 1.
[5] Cf. Jer. x. 20. [6] Ex. xxvi. 37; xxxvi. 38.
[7] Smith's 'Dict. of the Bible,' Art. *Temple*.—"The Holy Sepulchre and the Temple," 1865.

those which formed visible features in the fabric. On this ground we may be allowed to suppose that there was not only a ridge-pole, but a series of pillars at the back of the Tent corresponding in height with those at the front. Such a ridge-pole, which must have been sixty feet in length[1], would have required support, and this might have been afforded by light rafters resting on the top of the boards, or, as is more in accordance with the usage of tent architecture, by a plain pole in the middle of the structure. Over this framing of wood-work the tent-cloth of goats' hair was strained with its cords and tent-pins in the usual way. There must also have been a back-cloth suspended from the pillars at the back. The heads of the pillars appear to have been united by connecting rods (in our version, "fillets") overlaid with gold. [See xxxvi. 38.]

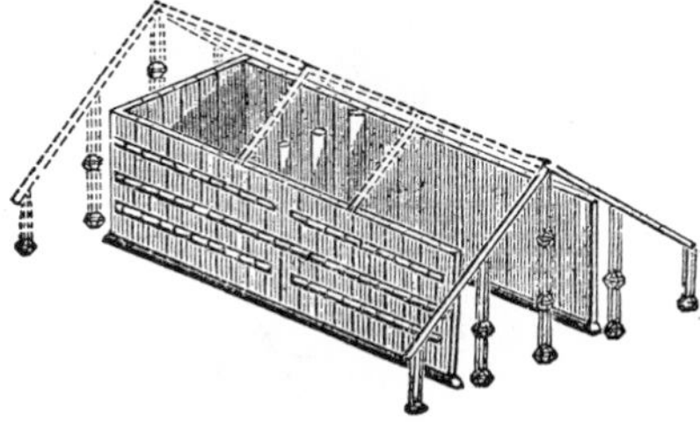

In this cut the woodwork of the Tent and Tabernacle which is described in the text is represented, the assumed positions of the portions that are not described being shown by dotted lines.

Above the tent-cloth of goats' hair was spread the covering of red rams' skins. Mr Fergusson conceives that the covering of tachash skins[2] above this did not cover the whole roof, but served only as "a coping or ridge-piece" to protect the crest of the roof.

[1] Mr Fergusson considers that "the middle bar in the midst of the boards" (Ex. xxvi. 28; xxxvi. 33) was the ridge-pole, and he would render the verse, "And the middle bar which is between the boards shall reach from end to end." But even if this rendering is allowable, we venture to think that the expression "from end to end" cannot, according to the context, refer to the Tent, but only to the wooden part of the Mishkān (see Plan, p. 378). Moreover, the methodical arrangement of the descriptions would be disturbed by the mention of the ridge-pole in Ex. xxvi. 28 and in xxxvi. 33. It could only be introduced in proper order in connection either with the cloth of the Tent (after xxvi. 13 and xxxvi. 18), or with its five pillars (after xxvi. 37 and xxxvi. 36). As however, according to the view here given, there must have been a ridge-pole of some sort, the question involves no essential particular of the construction of the fabric. See on xxvi. 28.

[2] Ex. xxvi. 14; xxxvi. 19. See note on xxv. 5.

IV.

The next inquiry relates to the position of the Tabernacle-cloth of fine linen and coloured yarns.

It is evident that the relation in which the measurement of the tabernacle-cloth stood to that of the tent-cloth had an important bearing on the place of each of them in the structure. The tent-cloth is said to have extended a cubit on each side beyond the tabernacle-cloth[3], and it appears to have extended two cubits at the back and front[4]. It would appear then that the tent-cloth was laid over the tabernacle-cloth so as to allow the excess of the dimensions of the former to be equally divided between the two sides and between the back and front. We may from these particulars infer that the tabernacle-cloth served as a lining to the other, and that they were both extended over the ridge-pole. In this way, the effect would have been produced of an ornamented open roof extending the length of the Tent.

V.

Mr Fergusson has pointed out the very remarkable consistency of the measurements of the different parts, if we accept this mode of putting them together. He assumes the angle formed by the roof to have been a right angle, as a reasonable and usual angle for such a roof, and this brings the only measurements which appear at first sight to be abnormal, into harmony. Every measurement given in the text is a multiple of five cubits, except the width of the tabernacle-cloth, which is twenty-eight cubits, and the length of the tent-cloth, which is forty-four cubits. With a right angle at the ridge, each side of the slope as shewn in this section would be within a

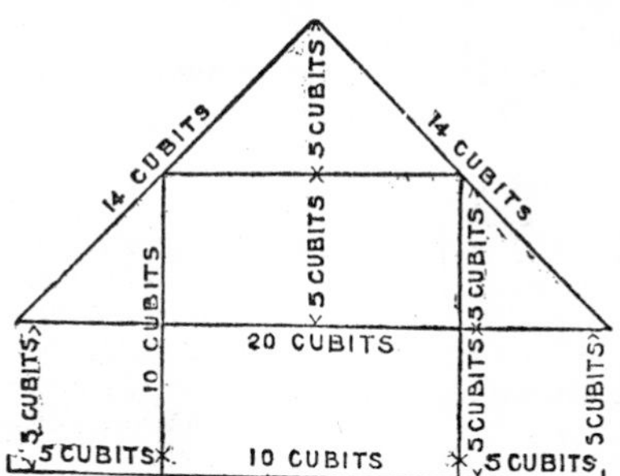

fraction of fourteen cubits (14.08), half the width of the tabernacle-cloth. The slope is here carried just five cubits beyond the wooden walls and to within just five cubits of the ground. The tent-cloth would hang down in a valance on each side, one cubit in depth[5].

[3] Ex. xxvi. 13.
[4] Ex. xxxvi. 9, 13.
[5] Ex. xxvi. 13.

If we allow the tabernacle-cloth, according to this arrangement, to determine the length of the Tent as well as its width, we obtain an area for the structure of forty cubits by twenty. The tent-cloth would of course overhang this at the back and front by two cubits, that is, half a breadth[1]. The wooden structure being placed within the Tent, there would be a space all round it of five cubits in width. This is shown in this Plan, in which one half represents the ground-plan and the other half the extended tent-cloth.

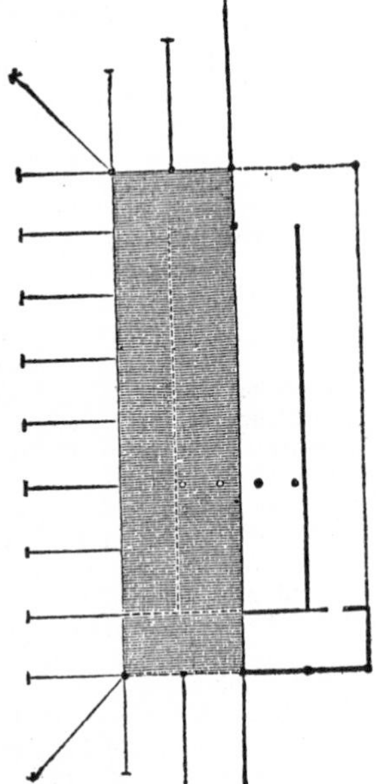

The five pillars, to reach across the front of the Tent, must have stood five cubits apart. Their heads were united by **connecting rods** ("fillets") overlaid with gold (Exod. xxxvi. 38). The space immediately within them, according to Mr Fergusson, formed a porch of five cubits in depth[2]. The spaces at the sides and back may have been wholly or in part covered in for the use of the officiating priests, like the small apartments which in after times skirted three sides of the Temple. It was probably here that those portions of the sacrifices were eaten which were not to be carried out of the sacred precinct[3].

The exact symmetrical relation which the dimensions of the Temple bore to those of the Tabernacle is not only striking in itself, but it bears a strong testimony to the correctness of Mr Fergusson's theory as regards those measurements which are not directly stated in the text, but are made out by inference from the theory. Each chief measurement of the Temple was just twice that of the Tabernacle. The Most Holy Place, a square of ten cubits in the Tabernacle[4], was one of twenty cubits in the Temple: the Holy Place, in each case, was a corresponding double square. The Porch, which was five cubits deep in the Tabernacle, was ten cubits in the Temple; the side spaces, taking account of the thickness of the walls of the Temple, were re-

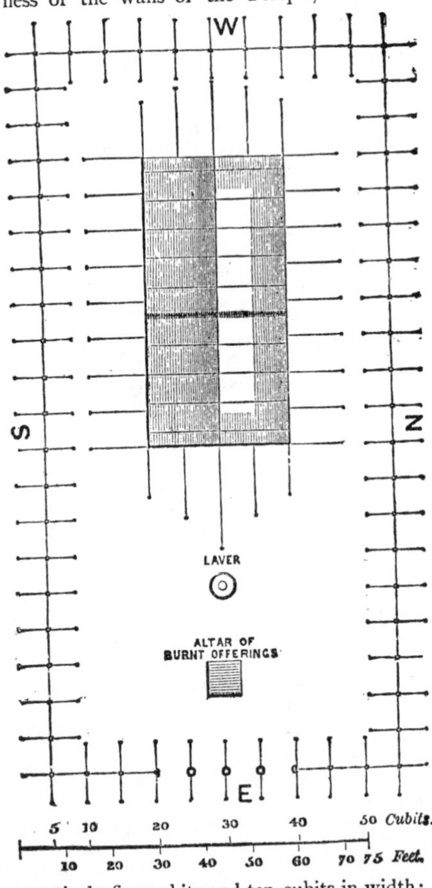

spectively five cubits and ten cubits in width; the height of the ridge-pole of the Tabernacle was fifteen cubits, that of the roof of the Holy Place in the Temple thirty cubits[5].

[1] Ex. xxvi. 9, 12.

[2] See cut, p. 376.

[3] Lev. vi. 16, 26, &c. We may infer that priests also lodged in them from Lev. viii. 33; 1 S. iii. 2, 3.

[4] It has already been observed that the length of the Most Holy Place is not given in Exodus; but ten cubits is universally accepted on the ground of inference. See § I.

[5] 1 K. vi. 2. The analogy here pointed out seems to shew the fitness of the word *tent* (Heb. *ohel*, wrongly rendered "tabernacle") as applied to the Temple in the vision of Ezekiel xli. 1).

Whether we believe the statements of Josephus to contain any elements of genuine tradition or not, it is worth noticing that in certain particulars he strikingly countenances the views of Mr Fergusson. He speaks of the Tabernacle as consisting of three parts. The third part was the Most Holy Place, the second part the Holy Place; and he seems to intimate that the remaining, or first part, was the entrance with its five pillars. He also says that the tent-curtain was so arranged in the front as to be *like a gable and a porch* (ἀετώματι παραπλήσιον καὶ παστάδι)[1].

It may perhaps be doubted whether there is, within the entire range of ancient literature (unless we should except the works of strictly technical writers), a description of any structure more clear and practical than that of the Tabernacle contained in the xxvith and xxxvith chapters of Exodus. Mr Fergusson's testimony on this head deserves to be quoted; "it seems to me clear that it must have been written by some one who had seen the Tabernacle standing. No one could have worked it out in such detail without ocular demonstration of the way in which the parts would fit together."

[1] 'Ant.' III. 6. § 4.

VI.

The second Plan in the preceding page exhibits the Tabernacle in its Court, with the cords and tent-pins in their proper places, as determined by Mr Fergusson in accordance with the practice of tent-architecture. It will be seen that the width of the Tent is the same as that of the entrance to the Court, which is a coincidence connected with the harmony of the arrangement that well deserves to be noticed.

CHAPTER XXVII.

1 *The altar of burnt offering, with the vessels thereof.* 9 *The court of the tabernacle inclosed with hangings and pillars.* 18 *The measure of the court.* 20 *The oil for the lamp.*

AND thou shalt make an altar *of*
shittim wood, five cubits long,
and five cubits broad; the altar shall
be foursquare: and the height thereof
shall be three cubits.
2 And thou shalt make the horns
of it upon the four corners thereof:
his horns shall be of the same: and
thou shalt overlay it with brass.
3 And thou shalt make his pans to
receive his ashes, and his shovels, and
his basons, and his fleshhooks, and his
firepans: all the vessels thereof thou
shalt make *of* brass.
4 And thou shalt make for it a

CHAP. XXVII.

The Altar of Burnt-offering.

1—8. (Cf. xxxviii. 1—7.)

The great Altar which stood in the Court immediately in front of the Tabernacle was commonly called the ALTAR OF BURNT-OFFERING, because on it were burnt the whole Burnt-offerings, and all those parts of the other animal sacrifices which were offered to the Lord. It was also called the BRAZEN ALTAR, because it was covered with bronze, in distinction from the Golden Altar, or Altar of Incense (Exod. xxxix. 38, 39, xl. 5, 6).

1. *an altar*] See Note at the end of ch. xl. § I.

2. *his horns shall be of the same*] These horns were projections pointing upwards in the form either of a small obelisk, or of the horn of an ox. They were to be actually parts of the Altar, not merely superadded to it. On them the blood of the Sin-offering was smeared (Exod. xxix. 12; Lev. iv. 7, viii. 15, ix. 9, xvi. 18). To take hold of them appears to have been regarded as an emphatic mode of laying claim to the right of Sanctuary (Exod. xxi. 14; 1 K. i. 50).

3. *pans to receive his ashes*] Rather **pots** as in xxxviii. 3; 1 K. vii. 45. On the use to which these pots were put in disposing of the ashes of the Altar, see Lev. i. 16.—The Heb. word here rendered *to receive his ashes*, is remarkable. In its derivation it is connected with *fat*, and it is never used in reference to any ashes except those of the Altar. It occurs Num. iv. 13, and Ps. xx. 3; where see margin. But all authorities are agreed as to what it denotes in these places.

his basons] According to the etymology of the name (from *zārak*, to scatter) it is inferred that these vessels were used for receiving the blood of the victims and casting it upon the Altar [see xxiv. 6, Lev. i. 5, &c.].

his fleshhooks] These were for adjusting the pieces of the victim upon the Altar [cf. 1 S. ii. 13].

his firepans] The same word is rendered *snuffdishes*, xxv. 38, xxxvii. 23: *censers*, Lev. x. 1, xvi. 12, Num. iv. 14, xvi. 6, &c. These utensils appear to have been shallow metal vessels which served either to catch the snuff of the lamps when they were trimmed, or to burn small quantities of incense. No-

grate of network *of* brass; and upon
the net shalt thou make four brasen
rings in the four corners thereof.
5 And thou shalt put it under the
compass of the altar beneath, that the
net may be even to the midst of the
altar.
6 And thou shalt make staves for
the altar, staves *of* shittim wood, and
overlay them with brass.
7 And the staves shall be put into
the rings, and the staves shall be upon
the two sides of the altar, to bear it.
8 Hollow with boards shalt thou
make it: as † it was shewed thee in the
mount, so shall they make *it*.
9 ¶ And thou shalt make the court
of the tabernacle: for the south side
southward *there shall be* hangings for
the court *of* fine twined linen of an
hundred cubits long for one side:
10 And the twenty pillars thereof
and their twenty sockets *shall be of*
brass; the hooks of the pillars and
their fillets *shall be of* silver.
11 And likewise for the north side

† Heb. *he shewed.*

---

thing however is said of the burning of incense in immediate connection with the Brazen Altar, and it has been supposed that the firepans were employed merely to carry burning embers from the Brazen Altar to the Altar of Incense, and that this use furnishes their only claim to the name of *censers*. See on Num. xvi. 6.

5. *the compass of the altar*] This appears to have been a shelf, or projecting ledge, of convenient width, carried round the Altar half way between the top and the base, on which the priests probably stood when they tended the fire or arranged the parts of the victims. It was supported all round its outer edge by a vertical net-like grating of bronze that rested on the ground. The name is a peculiar one, occurring only in this application and only in one other place, xxxviii. 4. But there appears to be scarcely a doubt as to its meaning.

8. *Hollow with boards*] Slabs, or **planks**, rather than *boards*. The word is that which is used for the stone tables of the Law (xxiv. 12, xxxi. 18), not that applied to the boards of the Tabernacle (xxvi. 15).

There has been considerable difference of opinion regarding some points in the description of the Brazen Altar, but the most probable account of it seems to be this. It was a hollow casing, formed of stout acacia planks covered with plates of bronze, seven feet six in length and width and four feet six in height. Jewish as well as Christian authorities have supposed that, when it was fixed for use, it was filled up with earth or rough stones. If we connect this suggestion with the old rule regarding the Altar of earth and the Altar of stone given in chap. xx. 24, 25, the woodwork might in fact be regarded merely as the case of the Altar on which the victims were actually burned. The shelf round the sides (*v.* 5) was required as a stage for the priests to enable them to carry on their work conveniently on the top of the Altar. Hence it is said of Aaron that he *came down* from the Altar (Lev. ix. 22). According to rabbinical tradition, there was a slope of earth banked up for the priest to ascend to the stage (cf. Ex. xx. 26). Such a slope could only have been at the south side, as the place of ashes was on the east (Lev. i. 16); the west side was opposite the Tabernacle, and on the north the victims appear to have been slain close to the Altar [see on Lev. i. 11]. The rings for the staves for carrying the Altar were attached to the corners of the grating (*v.* 4), which must have been proportionally strong.

The Altar of Solomon's Temple is described 2 Chro. iv. 1. It was twenty cubits in length and breadth and ten cubits in height; so that it was unlike the Altar of the Tabernacle, not only in its magnitude but in its proportions. The Altar erected by Herod is said by Josephus to have been fifty cubits square and fifteen cubits high ('Bell. Jud.' v. 5. § 6).

as it was shewed thee in the mount] See on xxv. 40.

The Court of the Tabernacle.

9—19. (Cf. xxxviii. 9—20.)

9. *the south side southward*] **the south side on the right.** See on xxvi. 18.

fine twined linen] See on xxvi. 1.

10. *sockets*] **bases.** See on xxvi. 19.

fillets] Rather, **connecting rods.** So the Targums. The Hebrew word is peculiar, and may mean any sort of bonds or fastenings. What are spoken of in this place appear to have been curtain-rods of silver connecting the heads of the pillars. The hangings were attached to the pillars by the silver hooks; but the length of the space between the pillars would render it most probable that they were also in some way fastened to these rods. The capitals of the pillars were overlaid with silver, as we learn from chap. xxxviii. 17.

11. *sockets*] **bases.**

fillets] **connecting rods.**

in length *there shall be* hangings of an hundred *cubits* long, and his twenty pillars and their twenty sockets *of* brass; the hooks of the pillars and their fillets *of* silver.

12 ¶ And *for* the breadth of the court on the west side *shall be* hangings of fifty cubits: their pillars ten, and their sockets ten.

13 And the breadth of the court on the east side eastward *shall be* fifty cubits.

14 The hangings of one side *of the gate shall be* fifteen cubits: their pillars three, and their sockets three.

15 And on the other side *shall be* hangings fifteen *cubits:* their pillars three, and their sockets three.

16 ¶ And for the gate of the court *shall be* an hanging of twenty cubits, *of* blue, and purple, and scarlet, and fine twined linen, wrought with needlework: *and* their pillars *shall be* four, and their sockets four.

17 All the pillars round about the court *shall be* filleted with silver; their hooks *shall be of* silver, and their sockets *of* brass.

18 ¶ The length of the court *shall be* an hundred cubits, and the breadth † fifty every where, and the height five cubits *of* fine twined linen, and their sockets *of* brass.

† Heb. *fifty by fifty.*

19 All the vessels of the tabernacle in all the service thereof, and all the

---

13. *the east side eastward*] **on the front side eastward.** The front [see on xxvi. 18, cf. *v.* 9].

14, 15, 16. See on *v.* 18, note (*c*).

16. *an hanging*] The Hebrew word is not the same as that rendered *hanging* in *vv.* 11, 12, 14, 15, and it would be better represented by **curtain.** It strictly denotes an entrance curtain, which, unlike the hangings at the sides and back of the Court, could be drawn up, or aside, at pleasure. The words are rightly distinguished in our Bible in Num. iii. 26.

wrought with needlework] **the work of the embroiderer.** See on xxvi. 36, xxxv. 35. On the materials, see xxv. 4.

sockets] **bases.**

17. *filleted with silver*] **connected with silver rods.** See on *v.* 10.

18. (*a*) The size and general construction of the Court of the Tabernacle are described in such a way as to leave no important doubt. Its area was one hundred and fifty feet (taking the cubit at eighteen inches) in length, and seventy-five feet in width. It was enclosed by hangings of fine linen suspended from pillars seven feet six inches in height, and standing seven feet six inches apart. These pillars were connected at their heads by silver rods [see on *v.* 10]; they had silver hooks for the attachment of the hangings, and their capitals were overlaid with silver; they stood on bases of bronze. At the east end of the enclosure the linen hangings on each side were continued for twenty-two feet six inches, and the intermediate space of thirty feet was the entrance, which was closed by an embroidered curtain (*vv.* 14, 15, 16). The pillars were kept firm by cords and tent-pins of bronze [see *v.* 19, cf. Num. iii. 26].

(*b*) The position of the Tabernacle in the Court could hardly have been in the middle, as Josephus imagined ('Ant.' III. 6. § 3). It is most probable that its place was, as Philo conceived ('Vit. Mos.' III. 7), equidistant from the west, the north and the south walls of the Court, so as to leave between it and the entrance of the Court a suitable space for the Brazen Altar and the Laver. See Note at the end of ch. xxvi. with the plan of the Court, according to Fergusson, in which the feasibility of this arrangement is strikingly apparent.

(*c*) There has been a difficulty raised regarding the number and distribution of the pillars of the Court. Knobel, taking up the notion of Philo and some other interpreters, supposes that the number was fifty-six, each corner pillar being reckoned both as one for the side and as one for the end. Keil, who contends for sixty as the number, has not made the matter much clearer by his mode of explanation. The mode of stating the numbers involved in the arrangement in *vv.* 10, 11, 12, 14, 15, 16 is perhaps a technical one. Taking it for granted that the number sixty, as given in those verses, is the true one, and that the Court measured precisely one hundred cubits by fifty, the pillars must have stood five cubits apart, which is in accordance with the general symmetry of the Sanctuary [see Note at the end of ch. xxvi. § V.]. If we may suppose the numbers, referring to each side of the enclosure, to have belonged to the spaces between the pillars rather than to the pillars themselves, the statements become clear, in reference both to the sides with their continuous hangings, and to the front where there was the entrance. See Mr Fergusson's plan, p. 378.

19. *All the vessels*, &c.] Our version here follows the Vulgate, and is obviously wrong.

pins thereof, and all the pins of the
court, *shall be of* brass.
20 ¶ And thou shalt command the
children of Israel, that they bring thee
pure oil olive beaten for the light, to
cause the lamp † to burn always.
21 In the tabernacle of the congregation without the vail, which *is* before
the testimony, Aaron and his sons
shall order it from evening to morning
before the LORD: *it shall be* a statute
for ever unto their generations on the
behalf of the children of Israel.

† Heb. *to ascend up.*

CHAPTER XXVIII.

1 *Aaron and his sons are set apart for the priest's office.* 2 *Holy garments are appointed.* 6 *The ephod.* 15 *The breastplate with twelve precious stones.* 30 *The Urim and Thummim.* 31 *The robe of the ephod, with pomegranates and bells.* 36 *The plate of the mitre.* 39 *The embroidered coat.* 40 *The garments for Aaron's sons.*

AND take thou unto thee Aaron
thy brother, and his sons with
him, from among the children of Israel,
that he may minister unto me in the
priest's office, *even* Aaron, Nadab and

We know that the vessels of the Tabernacle were of gold, xxv. 29, 39. The Hebrew word rendered *vessels* means in the broadest sense *utensils:* it is in different places rendered *furniture*, *stuff*, *sacks*, *jewels*, *weapons*, &c. In the same connection as in this place, it is not incorrectly represented by *instruments*, Num. iii. 8. The verse might be thus translated; **All the tools of the Tabernacle** *used* **in all its workmanship, and all its tent-pins, and all the tent-pins of the court, shall be of bronze.**—The working tools of the Sanctuary were most probably such things as axes, knives, hammers, &c. that were employed in making, repairing, setting up and taking down the structure. Cf. Num. iii. 36.

the tabernacle] Heb. *hammishkān*. The word is here to be taken as including both the Mishkān and the Tent, as in Num. i. 51, 53, &c. [see on xxvi. 1].

the pins thereof,...the pins of the court] The Hebrew word is the regular name for tent-pins.

The Lamps of the Sanctuary.

vv. 20, 21.

It is not quite easy to see the reason of the insertion of these verses in this place. The passage, with unimportant verbal alterations, is repeated Lev. xxiv. 2, 3, where it is connected in a natural manner with the rules for the supplying and ordering of the Shewbread. Cf. Exod. xxv. 6, 37; xxxv. 14, xl. 4, 24, 25.

20. *pure oil olive beaten*] The oil was to be of the best kind. It is called *beaten*, because it was obtained by merely bruising the olives in a mortar or mill, without the application of heat. The finest oil is now thus obtained from young fruit freshly gathered, and hence it is sometimes distinguished as "cold drawn." The inferior kind is expressed from unselected fruit, under stronger pressure, with the application of heat.

the lamp] *i.e.* the lamps of the Golden Candlestick. [See xxv. 37.]

to burn] The word is literally rendered in the margin *to ascend up*. It should be observed that it does not properly mean to burn in the sense of to consume, and that it is the word regularly used to express the action of fire upon what was offered to Jehovah [see on Lev. i. 9].

always] *i.e.* every night "from evening till morning." Cf. xxx. 8.

21. *the tabernacle of the congregation*] More literally, **the Tent of meeting** [see Note at the end of ch. xl. § II.]. This is the first occurrence of this designation of the Tabernacle.

without the vail, which is before the testimony] *i.e.* the Holy Place [see on xxv. 16].

CHAP. XXVIII.

THE INVESTITURE OF AARON AND HIS SONS.

1—43 (Cf. xxxix. 1—31).

Moses is now commanded to commit all that pertains to the Offerings made to the Lord in the Sanctuary to the exclusive charge of the members of a single family, who were to hold their office from generation to generation. In the patriarchal times, the external rites of worship had generally been conducted by the head of the tribe or family, in accordance with the principle involved in the dedication of the firstborn (Ex. xiii. 2; Num. iii. 12, 13). Moses, as the divinely appointed and acknowledged leader of the nation, had, on a special occasion, appointed those who were to offer sacrifice, and had himself sprinkled the consecrating blood of the victims on the people (xxiv. 5, 6, 8). On the completion of the Tabernacle, after Aaron and his sons had been called to the priesthood, he took chief part in the daily service of the Sanctuary (xl. 23—29, 31, 32) until the consecration of the family of Aaron, on which occasion he appears to have exercised the priest's office for the last time (Lev. viii. 14—29; cf. Ex. xxix. 10—26). The setting apart of the whole tribe of Levi for the entire cycle of religious services is mentioned Num. iii. 5—13, viii. 5—26, xviii. 1—32.

Abihu, Eleazar and Ithamar, Aaron's sons.

2 And thou shalt make holy garments for Aaron thy brother for glory and for beauty.

3 And thou shalt speak unto all *that are* wise hearted, whom I have filled with the spirit of wisdom, that they may make Aaron's garments to consecrate him, that he may minister unto me in the priest's office.

4 And these *are* the garments which they shall make; a breastplate, and an ephod, and a robe, and a broidered coat, a mitre, and a girdle: and they shall make holy garments for Aaron thy brother, and his sons, that he may minister unto me in the priest's office.

5 And they shall take gold, and blue, and purple, and scarlet, and fine linen.

---

1. Nadab and Abihu, the two elder sons of Aaron, had accompanied their father and the seventy Elders when they went a part of the way with Moses up the mountain (xxiv. 1, 9). Soon after their consecration they were destroyed for "offering strange fire before the Lord" (Lev. x. 1, 2). Eleazar and Ithamar are here mentioned for the first time, except in the genealogy, vi. 23. Eleazar succeeded his father in the High-priesthood, and was himself succeeded by his son Phinehas (Judg. xx. 28). But Eli, the next High-priest named in the history, was of the line of Ithamar. The representatives of both families held office at once in the time of David. See 1 Chro. xxiv. 1—3; 2 S. viii. 17.

3. *wise hearted*] The heart was frequently spoken of as the seat of wisdom (Ex. xxxi. 6, xxxv. 10, 25, xxxvi. 1; Job ix. 4; Prov. xi. 29, xvi. 21, 23, &c.). The same notion is traced in the Latin phrase *homo cordatus;* also in the language of Homer, 'Il.' XV. 52; 'Od.' VII. 82, XVIII. 344. The bowels, as distinguished from the heart, were commonly recognized as the seat of the affections (Gen. xliii. 30; 1 K. iii. 26; Is. lxiii. 15: and, in the Hebrew text, Deut. xiii. 6; 2 S. xxiv. 14, &c. See also Luke i. 78; 2 Cor. vi. 12, vii. 15; Phil. i. 8, ii. 1; Philemon, *v.* 7, &c.).

the spirit of wisdom] See on xxxi. 3. What may be especially noticed in this place is, that the spirit of wisdom given by the Lord is spoken of as conferring practical skill in the most general sense: those who possess it are called *because* they possess it; they are not first called and then endowed with it.

garments to consecrate him] There is here a solemn recognition of the significance of an appointed official dress. It expresses that the office is not created or defined by the man himself (Heb. v. 4), but that he is *invested* with it according to prescribed institution. The rite of anointing was essentially connected with investiture in the holy garments (xxix. 29, 30; xl. 12—15).—The history of all nations shews the importance of these forms. As time goes on, their "ancient and well-noted face" becomes more and more valuable as a witness against restless longing for change. The following points in this divinely ordained investiture of the Priests of Jehovah seem to be worthy of special notice in our own day:—(1) there was nothing left to individual taste or fancy, every point was authoritatively laid down in minute detail: (2) the High-priest, when performing his highest and holiest functions, was attired in a plain white dress (Lev. xvi. 4): (3) the only garments worn by the other priests "for glory and for beauty" (*v.* 40), when they were engaged in the service of both the Golden Altar and the Brazen Altar (see Lev. vi. 10), were also white, with the exception of the Girdle (*v.* 40): (4) there were no changes in the dresses of the priests at the three Great Festivals, nor any periodical change whatever, except when the High-priest, on the Day of Atonement, put off his robes of office for the dress of white linen.

4. There are here mentioned six articles belonging to the official dress of the High-priest, which are described in the verses that follow; but the description does not follow the order of this enumeration, and it comprises, in addition, the gold plate of the mitre (*v.* 36) and the garments which were common to all the priests.

and his sons] These, it is evident, were the representatives of the family who, in the ages that followed, inherited the High-priesthood in succession. But the sons who were consecrated at this time with Aaron as common priests, are designated in the same way in *v.* 40 and elsewhere.

5. *gold, and blue,* &c.] **the gold and the blue and the scarlet and the fine linen.** The definite article is prefixed to each substantive to denote specially the quantity and the quality of the material required for the dresses. With the exception of the gold, the materials were the same as those of the tabernacle-cloth, the vail of the Tabernacle and the entrance-curtain of the Tent (xxvi. 1, 31, 36. See on xxv. 4). The gold was wrought into thin flat wires which could either be woven with the woollen and linen threads, or worked with the needle (see

6 ¶ And they shall make the ephod *of* gold, *of* blue, and *of* purple, *of* scarlet, and fine twined linen, with cunning work.

7 It shall have the two shoulder-pieces thereof joined at the two edges thereof; and *so* it shall be joined together.

8 And the [1]curious girdle of the ephod, which *is* upon it, shall be of the same, according to the work thereof; *even of* gold, *of* blue, and purple, and scarlet, and fine twined linen.

[1] Or, *embroidered.*

9 And thou shalt take two onyx stones, and grave on them the names of the children of Israel:

10 Six of their names on one stone, and *the other* six names of the rest on the other stone, according to their birth.

11 [a]With the work of an engraver in stone, *like* the engravings of a signet, shalt thou engrave the two stones with the names of the children of Israel: thou shalt make them to be set in ouches of gold.

[a] Wisd. 18. 24.

---

xxxix. 3 and on xxxv. 35). In regard to the mixture of linen and woollen threads in the Ephod and other parts of the High-priest's dress, a difficulty seems to present itself in connection with the law which forbad garments of linen and woollen mixed to be worn by the Israelites (Lev. xix. 19; Deut. xxii. 11). It has been conjectured that the coloured threads here mentioned were not woollen but dyed linen (Knobel). But see on Lev. xix. 19.

The Ephod.

6—12 (xxxix. 2—7).

6. *the ephod*] The Hebrew word is here retained, which, according to its etymology, has the same breadth of meaning as our word *vestment.* The garment being worn over the shoulders, the word is rendered by the LXX. ἐπωμίς (which occurs also Ecclus. xlv. 8), and by the Vulgate *superhumerale.* It consisted of blue, purple and scarlet yarn and "fine twined linen" (on xxvi. 1) wrought together in **work of the skilled weaver** (on xxvi. 1 and xxxv. 35). It was the distinctive vestment of the High-priest, to which "the breastplate of judgment" was attached (*vv.* 25—28).

7. From this verse, and from xxxix. 4, it would seem that the Ephod consisted of two principal pieces of cloth, one for the back and the other for the front, joined together by shoulder straps (see on *v.* 27). Below the arms, probably just above the hips, the two pieces were kept in place by a band attached to one of the pieces, which is described in the next verse. Most Jewish authorities have thus understood the description. But Josephus describes the Ephod as a tunic (χιτών) having sleeves ('Ant.' III. 7. § 5). It is just possible that the fashion of it may have changed before the time of the historian. On the respect in which this Ephod of the High-priest was held, see 1 S. ii. 28, xiv. 3, xxi. 9, xxiii. 6, 9, xxx. 7. But an Ephod made of linen appears to have been a recognized garment not only for the common priests (1 S. xxii. 18) but also for those who were even temporarily engaged in the service of the Sanctuary (1 S. ii. 18; 2 S. vi. 14; 1 Chro. xv. 27).

8. *the curious girdle of the ephod, which is upon it, shall be of the same*] The meaning might rather be expressed:—*the band for fastening it, which is upon it, shall be of the same work, of one piece with it.* So de Wette, Knobel, Zunz, Herx., &c. This band being woven on to one of the pieces of the Ephod was passed round the body, and fastened by buttons, or strings, or some other suitable contrivance.

9. *two onyx stones*] The Hebrew name of the stone here spoken of is *shoham.* It is uniformly rendered *onyx* in our Bible and in the Vulgate; Josephus calls it the *sardonyx.* The LXX. and Philo, on the other hand, call it the *beryl.* But the Greek translators are inconsistent in translating the word in different places, so that, as regards this question, no confidence can be placed in them. The stone was most likely one well adapted for engraving; in this respect the onyx is preferable to the beryl See on *v.* 17.

11. *an engraver in stone*] **an artificer in stone.** See on xxxv. 35.

like the engravings of a signet] Cf. *vv.* 21, 36. These words probably refer to a peculiar way of shaping the letters, adapted for engraving on a hard substance.—Seal engraving on precious stones was practised in Egypt from very remote times, and in Mesopotamia, probably, from 2000 A.C.

ouches of gold] The gold settings of the engraved stones are here plainly denoted; but, according to the derivation of the Hebrew word, they seem to have been formed not of solid pieces of metal, but of woven wire, wreathed round the stones in what is called *cloisonnée* work, a sort of filigree, often found in Egyptian ornaments. Mr King conjectures that these stones, as well as those on the breastplate, were "in the form of ovals, or rather ellipses, like the cartouches, containing proper names, in hieroglyphic inscriptions."

12 And thou shalt put the two
stones upon the shoulders of the ephod
for stones of memorial unto the children of Israel: and Aaron shall bear
their names before the LORD upon his
two shoulders for a memorial.
13 ¶ And thou shalt make ouches
of gold;
14 And two chains *of* pure gold at
the ends; *of* wreathen work shalt thou
make them, and fasten the wreathen
chains to the ouches.
15 ¶ And thou shalt make the
breastplate of judgment with cunning
work; after the work of the ephod
thou shalt make it; *of* gold, *of* blue,
and *of* purple, and *of* scarlet, and
of fine twined linen, shalt thou
make it.
16 Foursquare it shall be *being*
doubled; a span *shall be* the length
thereof, and a span *shall be* the breadth
thereof.
17 And thou shalt † set in it set- † Heb.
tings of stones, *even* four rows of *fill in it fillings of stone.*
stones: *the first* row *shall be* a ‖ sar- ‖ Or, *ruby.*
dius, a topaz, and a carbuncle: *this*
shall be the first row.

'Ancient Gems,' p. 136. The same word is used in *vv.* 13, 14, 25, where it seems to express an ornamental gold button, without a stone. The word *ouches* is used by Shakspeare, Spenser, and some of their contemporaries in the general sense of jewels. See Nares' 'Glossary.'

12. *upon the shoulders of the ephod*] *i.e.* upon the **shoulder-pieces** of the ephod. See *v.* 7.

upon his two shoulders] Cf. Isa. ix. 6, xxii. 22. The High-priest had to represent the Twelve Tribes in the presence of Jehovah; and the burden of his office could not be so aptly symbolized anywhere as on his shoulders, the parts of the body fittest for carrying burdens. The figure is familiar enough in all languages. Cf. on *v.* 29.

The Breastplate.

13—30. (Cf. xxxix. 8—21.)

13. *ouches*] See on *v.* 11. These were two in number, to suit the chains mentioned in the next verse. Cf. *v.* 25 and xxxix. 18.

14. *two chains of pure gold at the ends; of wreathen work shalt thou make them*] Rather, two chains of pure gold **shalt thou make of wreathen work, twisted like cords.**—They were more like cords of twisted gold wire than chains in the ordinary sense of the word. Such chains have been found in Egyptian tombs, and some of these were exhibited in the Paris Exhibition of 1867.

15. *the breastplate of judgment*] The meaning of the Hebrew word (*choshen*) rendered *breastplate*, appears to be simply *ornament*. The names given to it in nearly all versions must therefore be regarded as glosses. The LXX., Philo, Josephus and the son of Sirach (Ecclus. xlv. 10) call it λογεῖον, or λόγιον, and the Vulgate *rationale*, in reference to its use as an oracle in making known the judgments of the Lord. It was from this use that it was designated the *Choshen of Judgment*. Symmachus renders the word as a receptacle, or bag (δόχιον), from what appears to have been its form. The names given to it by most modern translators (like our own *breastplate*) relate merely to its place in the dress. It was to be made of a piece of *cunning work* (**the work of the skilled weaver**, see xxxv. 35), the same in texture and materials as the Ephod. This piece was a cubit (two spans) in length and half a cubit (a span) in width, and it was to be folded together so as to form a square of half a cubit. Whether it was doubled with no other purpose than to give it stability (Rosenmüller, Knobel, Kalisch), or in order to form what was used as a bag (Gesenius, Bähr, Fürst), has been questioned: but the latter appears to be by far the more likely alternative. On the mode in which it was attached to the Ephod, see *v.* 22 sq., and on its probable use as a bag, see Note at the end of the Chapter.

17. *settings*] The same Hebrew word is less aptly rendered "inclosings" in *v.* 20. From xxxix. 13 it appears that they were ouches of *cloisonnée* work, like those mentioned in *v.* 11 as the settings of the gems on the shoulder-pieces of the ephod.

four rows of stones] No very near approach to certainty can be obtained in the identification of these precious stones. In several instances the Hebrew names themselves afford some light on the subject. The oldest external authority to help us is the LXX., and next to it come Josephus ('Ant.' III. 7. § 5; 'Bel. Jud.' V. 5. § 7) and the other old versions, especially the Vulgate. It must however be observed that the Greek and Latin names are not always consistently applied to the same Hebrew word in different places (see on *v.* 9). One point of interest in the inquiry appears to be the etymological identity of several of the names of stones in Hebrew, Greek, Latin and the modern languages of Europe. These names were probably transmitted to the Greeks and Romans by the Phœnician merchants, whose traffic in most of the precious stones

18 And the second row *shall be* an emerald, a sapphire, and a diamond.

19 And the third row a ligure, an agate, and an amethyst.

---

here mentioned is alluded to by Ezekiel (xxviii. 13). But, unfortunately, the identity of the stone denoted by no means follows from the identity of the name. A name was often given in ancient times to a substance on account of some single characteristic, such as its colour or its hardness. Hence *adamant* was applied to the diamond, to steel, and to other hard bodies: *sapphire* was certainly applied to the lapis-lazuli, and, though not till a much later age, to what we call the sapphire. Hence it is plain that our conclusions on the subject can rarely be quite certain. The field of conjecture in the present inquiry may however be somewhat narrowed from the results of the study of the antique gems of Assyria, Egypt and Ancient Greece. We need not hesitate to exclude those stones which appear to have been unknown to the ancients, and those which are so hard that the ancients did not know how to engrave them. On such grounds, according to Prof. Maskelyne, we must at once reject the diamond, the ruby, the sapphire, the emerald, the topaz, and the chrysoberyl.—The best information on the subject may be found in two articles in the 'Edinb. Rev.' Nos. 253, 254, by Prof. Maskelyne, to whom these notes on the breastplate are greatly indebted.

a sardius] Heb. *odem*, i.e. *the red stone;* LXX. σάρδιον; Vulg. *sardius*; Jos. σαρδόνυξ in one place ('Ant.' III. 7. § 5), but σάρδιον in another ('Bel. Jud.' V. 5. § 7). The Sardian stone, or **sard**, was much used by the ancients for seals; and it is perhaps the stone of all others the best for engraving (see Theophrastus, 'de Lapid.' 8; Pliny, 'H. N.' XXXVII. 23, 31). It is mentioned Ezek. xxviii. 13.

topaz] Heb. *pitdāh*; LXX. and Jos. τοπάζιον; Vulg. *topazius*. The word *topaz* appears to have been formed by metathesis from *pitdāh* (Gesenius, Knobel, Fürst). The *pitdāh* is mentioned by Ezekiel (xxviii. 13); and it is spoken of in Job (xxviii. 19) as a product of Ethiopia, which tends to confirm its identity with the topaz which is said by Strabo (XVI. p. 770), Diodorus (III. 39), and Pliny (XXXVII. 32), to have been obtained from Ethiopia. It was not however the stone now called the topaz: it may have been the peridot, or chrysolite, a stone of a greenish hue.

a carbuncle] Heb. *bāreketh*; LXX. and Jos. σμάραγδος, Vulg. *smaragdus*. It was certainly not the carbuncle; it is not improbable that it was the **beryl**, which is a kind of emerald (Plin. XXXVII. 16, Solinus XV. 23). The Greek name sometimes appears as μάραγδος, supposed to be identical with the Sanskrit name of the beryl, *marakata* (Fürst), which plainly appears to be allied to the Heb. *bāreketh*, and probably to our own *emerald*. Gesenius and Liddell and Scott severally ascribe the Hebrew name and the Greek to roots signifying to *glitter*, or *sparkle:* but the characteristic quality thus suggested is not one that particularly distinguishes the beryl amongst precious stones. The *bāreketh* is mentioned Ezek. xxviii. 13.

18. *an emerald*] Heb. *nophek*, i.e. *the glowing stone* (Knobel, Fürst); LXX. and Jos. ἄνθραξ; Vulg. *carbunculus*. There seems no reason to doubt that the garnet, which when cut with a convex face is termed the **carbuncle**, is meant. (See Theoph. 'de Lapid.' 18). The same stone is mentioned Ezek. xxvii. 16, xxviii. 13.

a sapphire] Heb. *sappīr;* LXX. σάπφειρος; Vulg. *sapphirus*. Josephus appears to have transposed this name and the next, and may fairly be regarded as agreeing with the LXX. as to its meaning. It is conceived to have been the sapphire of the Greeks, not only from the identity of the name, but from the evident references to the colour in Exod. xxiv. 10; Ezek. i. 26, x. 1. The name also occurs Job xxviii. 6, 16; Cant. v. 14; Isa. liv. 11; Lam. iv. 7; Ezek. xxviii. 13. Michaelis and others objected to what is now called the sapphire on account of its hardness, and supposed that the lapis-lazuli is most probably meant. The best recent authorities justify this conjecture, in reference not only to the *sappīr* of the Old Testament, but to the sapphire of the Greeks and Romans (see the first note on this verse). According to a Jewish fancy in the Talmud, the Tables of the Law were formed of *sappīr*.

a diamond] Heb. *yahalom*. The etymology of the word is supposed to be similar to that ascribed to the Greek ἀδάμας, so as to give it the meaning of *the unconquerable*. Hence some of the ancient versions, with Aben-Ezra, Abarbanel, and Luther (whom our translators followed), have taken the diamond as the stone denoted. But there is no trace of evidence that the ancients ever acquired the skill to engrave on the diamond, or even that they were acquainted with the stone. The LXX. render *yahalom* by ἴασπις, and the Vulg. by *jaspis;* but these words answer more satisfactorily to the jasper (see on *v.* 20). Some imagine it to be the onyx, which is more likely the *shoham* (*v.* 9): but it may possibly be some other variety of chalcedony, or (perhaps) rock crystal. In the uncertainty which exists, the original name **yahalom** might be retained in the version. The word is found in Ezek. xxviii. 13: but it is another word (*shamīr*) which is rendered *diamond* or *adamant* in Jer. xvii. 1; Ezek. iii. 9; Zech. vii. 12.

20 And the fourth row a beryl, and an onyx, and a jasper: they shall be set in gold in their † inclosings.

† Heb. *fillings*.

21 And the stones shall be with the names of the children of Israel, twelve, according to their names, *like* the engravings of a signet; every one with his name shall they be according to the twelve tribes.

22 ¶ And thou shalt make upon the breastplate chains at the ends *of* wreathen work *of* pure gold.

23 And thou shalt make upon the breastplate two rings of gold, and shalt put the two rings on the two ends of the breastplate.

24 And thou shalt put the two wreathen *chains* of gold in the two rings *which are* on the ends of the breastplate.

25 And *the other* two ends of the two wreathen *chains* thou shalt fasten in the two ouches, and put *them* on the shoulderpieces of the ephod before it.

26 ¶ And thou shalt make two rings of gold, and thou shalt put them upon the two ends of the breastplate in the border thereof, which *is* in the side of the ephod inward.

27 And two *other* rings of gold thou shalt make, and shalt put them on the two sides of the ephod underneath, toward the forepart thereof, over against the *other* coupling thereof, above the curious girdle of the ephod.

---

19. *a ligure*] Heb. *leshem*, LXX. and Jos. λιγύριον, Vulg. *ligurius*. According to Theophrastus ('de Lapid.' 29) and Pliny ('H. N.' XXXVII. 11), **amber** came from Liguria, and this would exactly account for the names used by the LXX. and Vulg., if, as is not in any respect improbable, amber is here meant. On the name λυγκούριον, see Liddell and Scott. The *leshem* is not mentioned elsewhere in the Old Testament except in xxxix. 12.

an agate] Heb. *shevoo*, LXX. ἀχάτης, Vulg. *achates*. Josephus appears to have transposed ἀχάτης with the next name: he makes several other changes in the order of the stones in the list given, 'Bel. Jud.' v. 5. § 7. No question has been raised that the agate is here meant. The word *shevoo* occurs only here and xxxix. 12; but another word (*kadkod*) is rendered *agate* in our version, Isa. liv. 12; Ezek. xxvii. 16.

an amethyst] Heb. *achlāmāh*, LXX. and Josephus ἀμέθυστος, Vulg. *amethystus*. Mentioned only here and xxxix. 12.

20. *a beryl*] Heb. *tarshish*, LXX. and Jos. χρυσόλιθος, Vulg. *chrysolithus*. This could hardly have been the beryl (see on *v.* 17) or the turkois, as Luther and Cranmer imagined. The Hebrew name is reasonably supposed to have been given to the stone because it came from Tarshish. A kind of carbuncle, or garnet, is spoken of by Pliny, called *carchedonius*, in connection with Carthage ('H. N.' XXXVII. 25), and this is supposed by some to be the *tarshish* (Knobel, Fürst). Others suppose that it was what Pliny calls the chrysolite, a brilliant yellow stone (see Plin. XXXVII. 42), which they identify with what is now known as the Spanish topaz (Gesenius, &c.). It would seem to be best, in such uncertainty, to retain the name **tarshish** in translating. The stone is mentioned Cant. v. 14; Ezek. i. 16, x. 9, xxviii. 13; Dan. x. 6.

an onyx] Heb. *shoham*. Josephus and the Vulgate take it for the onyx (see on *v.* 9); but the LXX., apparently by a copyist's transposition, have βηρύλλιον here, and ὀνύχιον for the next stone. The *shoham* is mentioned Gen. ii. 12; Ex. xxv. 7; 1 Chro. xxix. 2; Job xxviii. 16; Ezek. xxviii. 13.

a jasper] Heb. *yashpeh*. The similarity of the Hebrew name to our word *jasper*, to the Greek ἴασπις, the Latin *jaspis*, and the Arabic *jasb*, is obvious. Josephus and the Vulgate render it as *beryl*, and the LXX. as onyx (but see preceding note). The best authorities take it for jasper (Gesen., Bähr, Knobel, Fürst): it was probably the green jasper. It is mentioned nowhere else except Ex. xxxix. 13; Ezek. xxviii. 13.

their inclosings] **their settings** (see on *v.* 17).

22. *chains at the ends of wreathen work*] **chains of wreathen work, twisted like cords** (see on *v.* 14).

23. *on the two ends of the breastplate*] The extremities spoken of here, and in the next verse, must have been the upper corners of the square. The chains attached to them (*v.* 25) suspended the Breastplate from the ouches of the shoulder-pieces (*vv.* 9, 11, 12).

26. *two rings*] These two rings appear to have been fastened to the Breastplate, near its lower corners upon the inner side, so as to have been out of sight. See on the following two verses.

27. "And two rings of gold shalt thou make and put them on **the two shoulder-pieces of the Ephod, low down in the**

28 And they shall bind the breastplate by the rings thereof unto the
rings of the ephod with a lace of
blue, that *it* may be above the curious
girdle of the ephod, and that the
breastplate be not loosed from the
ephod.
29 And Aaron shall bear the
names of the children of Israel in the
breastplate of judgment upon his heart,
when he goeth in unto the holy *place*,
for a memorial before the LORD continually.
30 ¶ And thou shalt put in the
breastplate of judgment the Urim and
the Thummim; and they shall be
upon Aaron's heart, when he goeth
in before the LORD: and Aaron shall
bear the judgment of the children of
Israel upon his heart before the LORD
continually.
31 ¶ And thou shalt make the
robe of the ephod all *of* blue.
32 And there shall be an hole in
the top of it, in the midst thereof:
it shall have a binding of woven work
round about the hole of it, as it were
the hole of an habergeon, that it be
not rent.
33 ¶ And *beneath* upon the ‖ hem ‖ Or, *skirts*.
of it thou shalt make pomegranates
of blue, and *of* purple, and *of* scarlet,

---

front of it, near the joining, above the band for fastening it." It would seem that the shoulder-pieces were continued down the front of the Ephod as far as the band (see on *v.* 8); **the joining** appears to have been the meeting of the extremities of the shoulder-pieces with the band. These rings were attached to the shoulder-pieces just above this joining.

28. *the curious girdle of the ephod*] **the band for fastening it** (see on *v.* 8). The two lower rings of the Breastplate were to be tied to the rings near the ends of the shoulder-pieces, opposite to which they seem to have been placed, by laces of blue, so as to keep the Breastplate firmly in its place just above the band.

29. The names of the Tribes on the two onyx stones were worn on the shoulders of the High-priest to indicate the burden of the office which he bore (see on *v.* 12); the same names engraved on the stones of the Breastplate were worn over his heart, the seat of the affections, as well as of the intellect (see on *v.* 3), to symbolize the relation of love and of personal interest which the Lord requires to exist between the Priest and the People.

30. *put in the breastplate of judgment the Urim and the Thummim*] It is not questioned that this rendering (which agrees with the Vulgate, Saadia, Luther, and most modern versions) fairly represents the original words; and it most naturally follows that the Urim and the Thummim (whatever they were) were *put into* the bag that was formed by the doubling of the *Choshen* (see on *v.* 15), as the Tables of the Law were *put into* the Ark, the same verb and preposition being used in each case (xxv. 16). Most critics are in favour of this view. But it cannot be denied that the words may also mean, *upon the Breastplate.* So the LXX., the Syriac, de Wette, Knobel. See Note at the end of the Chapter.

the Urim and the Thummim] These were probably some well-known means for casting lots which, from this time forward, were kept in the bag of the *Choshen.* See Note.

The Robe of the Ephod.

31—35. (xxxix. 22—26.)

31. *the robe of the ephod*] The Robe of the Ephod was a frock or robe of the simplest form, woven without seam, wholly of blue (see Note at the end of ch. xxv. § II.). It was put on by being drawn over the head. It appears to have had no sleeves. It probably reached a little below the knees. It must have been visible above and below the Ephod, the variegated texture of which it must have set off as a plain blue groundwork.

32. *And there shall be an hole in the top of it, in the midst thereof*] **And its opening for the head shall be in the middle of it.** So de Wette, Knobel, Kalisch, Herx., &c. The meaning appears to be that the opening through which the head was to be put should be a mere round hole, not connected with any longitudinal slit before or behind.

of woven work] **of the work of the weaver** (see on xxvi. 1, xxxv. 35). This was probably a stout binding of woven thread, sewn over the edge of the hole for the head, to strengthen it and preserve it from fraying.

an habergeon] The original word, *tacharāh*, is found in Egyptian papyri of the 19th dynasty (Brugsch, 'D. H.,' p. 1579), though its root appears to be Semitic (Gesen. 'Thes.' p. 518). Corselets of linen, such as appear to be here referred to, were well known amongst the Egyptians (Herodot. II. 182, III. 47; Plin. XIX. 2. Cf. Hom. 'Il.' II. 529).

33, 34. The skirt was to be adorned with a border of pomegranates in colours, and a

round about the hem thereof; and bells
of gold between them round about:
34 A golden bell and a pomegranate,
a golden bell and a pomegranate,
upon the hem of the robe
round about.
b Ecclus. 45. 9. 35 [b] And it shall be upon Aaron to
minister: and his sound shall be heard
when he goeth in unto the holy *place*
before the LORD, and when he cometh
out, that he die not.
36 ¶ And thou shalt make a plate
of pure gold, and grave upon it, *like*
the engravings of a signet, HOLINESS
TO THE LORD.
37 And thou shalt put it on a
blue lace, that it may be upon the
mitre; upon the forefront of the mitre
it shall be.
38 And it shall be upon Aaron's
forehead, that Aaron may bear the
iniquity of the holy things, which
the children of Israel shall hallow in
all their holy gifts; and it shall be
always upon his forehead, that they
may be accepted before the LORD.
39 ¶ And thou shalt embroider
the coat of fine linen, and thou shalt
make the mitre *of* fine linen, and thou
shalt make the girdle *of* needlework.

---

small golden bell was to be attached to the hem between each two of the pomegranates.

35. *his sound*] **its** sound, i.e. the sound of the Robe. Some conceive that the bells furnished a musical offering of praise to the Lord (Knobel, &c.). But it seems more likely that their purpose was that the people, who stood without, when they heard the sound of them within the Tabernacle, might have a sensible proof that the High-priest was performing the sacred rite in their behalf, though he was out of their sight. The bells thus became an incentive to devotional feelings. This accords with very early tradition. See Ecclus. xlv. 9.

that he die not] The bells also bore witness that the High-priest was, at the time of his ministration, duly attired in the dress of his office, and so was not incurring the sentence of death which is referred to again in *v.* 43 in connection with the linen drawers that were worn by the whole body of the priests. An infraction of the laws for the service of the Sanctuary was not merely an act of disobedience; it was a direct insult to the presence of Jehovah from His ordained minister, and justly incurred a sentence of capital punishment. Cf. Ex. xxx. 21; Lev. viii. 35, x. 7.

The Mitre and the Garments of Fine Linen.

36—43. (xxxix. 27—31.)

36. In the narrative of the making of the holy things (xxxix. 28, 30) the Mitre of fine linen is mentioned before the Golden Plate, as having been first completed, and as that to which the plate itself was to be attached. But in these directions the plate is first described, as being the most significant part of the head-dress. For a similar transposition, shewing the strictly practical character of the narrative, see on xxxv. 11.

engravings of a signet] See on *v.* 11.

HOLINESS TO THE LORD] This inscription testified in express words the holiness with which the High-priest was invested in virtue of his sacred calling.

37. *a blue lace*] The plate was fastened upon a blue band or fillet, so tied round the mitre as to shew the plate in front.

the mitre] According to the derivation of the Hebrew word, and from the statement in *v.* 39, this was a twisted band of linen coiled into a cap, to which the name *mitre*, in its original sense, closely answers, but which, in modern usage, would rather be called a *turban*.

38. *bear the iniquity of the holy things*] The Hebrew expression "to bear iniquity" is applied either to one who suffers the penalty of sin (*v.* 43; Lev. v. 1, 17, xvii. 16, xxvi. 41, &c.), or to one who takes away the sin of others (Gen. l. 17; Lev. x. 17, xvi. 22; Num. xxx. 15; 1 S. xv. 25, &c. See on Gen. iv. 13). In several of these passages the verb is rightly rendered to *forgive*.—The iniquity which is spoken of in this place does not mean particular sins actually committed, but that condition of alienation from God in every earthly thing which makes reconciliation and consecration needful. Cf. Num. xviii. 1. It belonged to the High-priest, as the chief atoning mediator between Jehovah and His people (see on *v.* 36), to atone for the holy things that they might be "accepted before the Lord" (cf. Lev. viii. 15, xvi. 20, 33, with the notes): but the common priests also, in their proper functions, had to take their part in making atonement (Lev. iv. 20, v. 10, x. 17, xxii. 16; Num. xviii. 23, &c.).

39. *embroider the coat of fine linen*] This garment appears to have been a long tunic, or cassock. Josephus says that it was worn next the skin, that it reached to the feet, and that it had closely fitting sleeves ('Ant.' III. 7. § 2). The verb translated *embroider* (*shābatz*, a word of very rare occurrence) appears ra-

40 ¶ And for Aaron's sons thou
shalt make coats, and thou shalt make
for them girdles, and bonnets shalt
thou make for them, for glory and for
beauty.

41 And thou shalt put them upon
Aaron thy brother, and his sons with
him; and shalt anoint them, and
† consecrate them, and sanctify them,
that they may minister unto me in
the priest's office.

42 And thou shalt make them
linen breeches to cover † their nakedness; from the loins even unto the
thighs they shall † reach:

43 And they shall be upon Aaron,
and upon his sons, when they come
in unto the tabernacle of the congregation, or when they come near
unto the altar to minister in the
holy *place;* that they bear not iniquity, and die: *it shall be* a statute
for ever unto him and his seed after
him.

† Heb. *fill their hand.*

† Heb. *flesh of their nakedness.*

† Heb. *be.*

---

ther to mean **weave in diaper work.** The tissue consisted of threads of one and the same colour diapered in checkers, or in some small figure. According to xxxix. 27 such tissue was woven by the ordinary weaver, not by the skilled weaver. (See on xxxv. 35; Gesen. 'Thes.' p. 1356; Fürst, 'Lex.' s.v. Cf. Wilkinson, 'Pop. Account,' Vol. II. p. 86.) It has been inferred from *vv.* 40, 41, and from xxxix. 27, that this and the other linen garments of the High-priest, with the exception of the mitre, did not differ from the dress of the common priests mentioned in the next verse. See Lev. vi. 10; Ezek. xliv. 17.

the mitre of fine linen] See on *v.* 37.

the girdle of needlework] **the girdle of the work of the embroiderer** (xxvi. 1, xxxv. 35). The word translated *girdle* is a different one from that so rendered in *v.* 8 (see note). The name here used (*abnet*) has been supposed to be a Persian word (Gesenius), but it is more likely to be an Egyptian one (Fürst, Brugsch, Birch). It was embroidered in three colours (xxxix. 29). Josephus says that its texture was very loose, so that it resembled the slough of a snake, that it was wound several times round the body, and that its ends ordinarily hung down to the feet, but were thrown over the shoulder when the priest was engaged in his work.

40. *Aaron's sons*] The common priests are here meant. See on *v.* 4. The girdle worn by them is here called by the same name as that of the High-priest (*abnet*), and was probably of the same make. Cf. xxxix. 29. Instead of the mitre consisting of a coil of twisted linen, the common priests wore **caps** of a simple construction which, according to a probable explanation of the name, seem to have been cup-shaped. They were however of fine texture and workmanship (xxxix. 28). The word *bonnet* is, in our present English, less suitable than **cap.** The description of the head-dress of the priests given by Josephus ('Ant.' III. 3. § 6) perhaps indicates a change of form in his day. Cf. on *v.* 7.

for glory and for beauty] See *v.* 2 and the following note.

41—43. The dress of white linen was the strictly sacerdotal dress common to the whole body of priests (Ezek. xliv. 17, 18). These were "for glory and for beauty" not less than *the golden garments* (as they were called by the Jews) which formed the High-priest's dress of state (*v.* 2). The linen suit which the High-priest put on when he went into the Most Holy place on the Day of Atonement, appears to have been regarded with peculiar respect (Lev. xvi. 4, 23; cf. Exod. xxxi. 10), though it is nowhere stated that it was distinguished in its make or texture, except in having a girdle (*abnet*) wholly of white linen, instead of a variegated one.—It may here be observed that the statement in Josephus, that the High-priest wore his golden garments only when he went into the Most Holy place ('Bel. Jud.' v. 5. § 7) is an obvious mistake: the reading is probably corrupt (see Hudson's note).—The ancient Egyptian priests, like the Hebrew priests, wore nothing but white linen garments in the performance of their duties (Herod. II. 37, with Wilkinson's note; Hengst. 'Egypt and the Books of Moses,' p. 145).

43. *in unto the tabernacle*] **into the Tent.** See on xxvi. 1.

that they bear not iniquity, and die] See on *vv.* 35, 38.

NOTE on CHAP. XXVIII. 30.

ON THE URIM AND THE THUMMIM.

I. *Their names.* II. *They were previously known, and distinct from the Breastplate.* III. *Their purpose and history.* IV. *Their origin.* V. *Theories.*

I.

The expression *the Urim and the Thummim* (אֶת־הָאוּרִים וְאֶת־הַתֻּמִּים) appears to mean *the Light and the Truth.* The primary meaning of the latter term is *perfection.* The form of the words is plural; but, according to the Hebrew idiom, this does not necessarily imply a plural sense. The rendering of the LXX. is, ἡ δήλωσις καὶ ἡ ἀλήθεια; that of Symmachus, φωτισμοὶ καὶ τελειότητες; that of the Vulgate, *Doctrina et Veritas*. The other ancient versions substantially agree with one or other of these. In most modern versions, except Luther's (*Licht und Recht*) and de Wette's (*das Licht und die Wahrheit*), the words are untranslated.

II.

From the way in which they are spoken of in Ex. xxviii. 30 and in Lev. viii. 8, compared with Ex. xxviii. 15—21, it would appear, taking a simple view of the words, that the Urim and the Thummim were some material things, and that they were separate from the Breastplate itself, as well as from the gems that were set upon it. It would seem most probable that they were kept in the bag of the Breastplate (Ex. xxviii. 16). And from the definite article being prefixed to each of the names, from their not being described in any way, and from their not being mentioned in the record of the construction of the Breastplate (xxxix. 21), it seems most likely that they were something previously existing and familiarly known. It is true that the Samaritan text says that Moses was *to make* them: but even if we accept this very weak authority, when the statement is compared with the fact that there is no direction given as to form or material, it leaves us to infer that they were no novelty as regards their use.

III.

The purpose of the Urim and the Thummim is clearly enough indicated in Num. xxvii. 21; 1 S. xxviii. 6; and also (as they were evidently regarded as belonging to the Ephod) in 1 S. xxiii. 9—12, xxx. 7, 8, cf. xxii. 14, 15. We are warranted in concluding that they were visible things of some sort by which the will of Jehovah, especially in what related to the wars in which His people were engaged, was made known, and that from this time they were preserved in the bag of the Breastplate of the High-priest, to be borne "upon his heart before the LORD continually" (Ex. xxviii. 30). They were formally delivered by Moses to Aaron (Lev. viii. 8), and subsequently passed on to Eleazar (Num. xx. 28, xxvii. 21). They were esteemed as the crowning glory of the Tribe of Levi (Deut. xxxiii. 8). There is no instance on record of their being consulted after the time of David. They were certainly not in use after the Captivity; and it seems to have become a proverb in reference to a question of inextricable difficulty, that it should not be solved "till there stood up a priest with Urim and Thummim" (Ezra ii. 63; Neh. vii. 65; cf. Hos. iii. 4).—Such seem to be all the particulars that can be gathered immediately, or by easy inference, from Holy Scripture, regarding the nature, purpose, and history of the Urim and the Thummim.

IV.

Since the time of Spencer, the opinion has prevailed to a great extent that the Urim and the Thummim were wholly, or in part, of Egyptian origin. With this opinion is connected the notion that they were two small images of precious stone, which appears to have taken its rise from a passage in Philo; τὸ δὲ λογεῖον τετράγωνον διπλοῦν κατεσκευάζετο, ὡσανεὶ βάσις, ἵνα δύο ἀρετὰς ἀγαλματοφορῇ, δήλωσίν τε καὶ ἀλήθειαν ('Vit. Mos.' III. 11). But may not the symbol of the two virtues in the fancy of Philo have been rather the two sides of the *Choshen* than two actual images? Philo's use of the verb ἀγαλματοφορεῖν in other connections may tend to confirm this view. See 'de Confus. Ling.' c. 13; 'de Mundi Opif.' c. 23; but still more to the point is a passage in which he says that the two webs of the *Choshen* were called *Revelation and Truth*.—Ἐπὶ δὲ τοῦ λογείου διττὰ ὑφάσματα καταποικίλλει, προσαγαρεύων τὸ μὲν δήλωσιν τὸ δὲ ἀλήθειαν ('de Monarch.' II. 5. See also 'Legis Alleg.' III. 40, where he substitutes σαφήνεια for δήλωσις). But it is alleged that a close analogy is furnished by the image of sapphire (*lapis lazuli*, see on Ex. xxviii. 18) called *Truth*, that was suspended by a gold chain on the breasts of the Egyptian Judges, with which they touched the lips of acquitted persons (Diod. Sic. I. 48, 75; Ælian, 'Var. Hist.' XIV. 34). That such a custom as this was of old standing in Egypt, is rendered very probable by certain pictures of great antiquity in which the image is represented as a double one, bearing the symbols of *Truth and Justice*. The deity endowed with this dual character was called *Thmei*, and with this name some have connected the word *Thummim*, (Wilkinson, II. p. 205). But this etymology is entirely rejected by Egyptian scholars.—The Egyptian origin of the Urim and the Thummim has been advocated by Spencer, Gesenius, Knobel, Fürst, Hengstenberg, Plumptre (in Smith's 'Dict.' s. v.) and others.

But an argument on the other side seems to be furnished by the connection of the *Teraphim* with the Urim and the Thummim, which may be traced in the Old Testament. It has been suggested on very probable ground that the Teraphim may have been employed as an unauthorized substitute for the Urim and the Thummim[1]. Now we know that the Teraphim belonged to patriarchal times,

[1] See Judg. xvii. 5, xviii. 14, 17, 20; Hos. iii. 4; and, as rightly rendered in the margin, 2 K. xxiii. 24; Ezek. xxi. 21; Zech. x. 2: to these may be added, as it stands in the Hebrew, 1 S. xv. 23.

to the Semitic race, and to regions remote from Egypt (see Gen. xxxi. 19, &c.). Is not the supposition as easy that the Urim and the Thummim took the place of what must have been familiarly known to the Patriarchs, and which appear, in a renewal of the old degraded form, to have been in later times confounded with them, as that they were adopted from the Egyptians?

V.

As to the form and material of the Urim and the Thummim, and as to the mode in which they were consulted by the High-priest, there have been many conjectures, some of them very wild and startling. It would be out of place here to go at length into a subject in which there is so little to limit or to regulate the field of conjecture, that anything like certainty is beyond the reach of hope; but the inquiry must not be entirely passed over. We may first observe that the different views which have been taken are based on three distinct theories:—

1. That the Divine Will was manifested through the Urim and the Thummim by some physical effect addressed to the eye or the ear.

2. That they were some ordained symbol which, when the High-priest concentrated his sight and attention on it, became a means of calling forth the prophetic gift.

3. That they were some contrivance for casting lots.

1. Josephus, who identified the stones of the Breastplate with the Urim and the Thummim, says that they signified a favourable answer to the question proposed by shining forth with unusual brilliancy. He adds that they had not been known to exhibit this power for 200 years before his time ('Ant.' III. 8. § 9). As regards the mode of the answer, several Jewish, and many Christian, writers, have followed him. The rabbinists adopted the notion, and shewed their usual tendency by exaggerating it. They said that the answer was communicated in detail by particular letters in the inscriptions on the stones shining out in succession, so as to spell the words[1].—Spencer, supposing that the Urim and the Thummim were two images, or Teraphim, imagined that an angel was commissioned to speak through the lips of one of them with an audible voice ('de Leg. Hebr.' lib. III. c. v. § 3). Prideaux and others have supposed that an audible voice addressed itself from the Mercy-seat as the High-priest stood before it wearing the Breastplate on his breast ('Connection,' &c., book I.).

2. Some of those who have held the second theory have conceived that the High-priest used to fix his eyes on the gems of the Breastplate until the spirit of Prophecy came upon him and gave him utterance. Others have conjectured that the object of his contemplation was not the gems themselves, but some distinct object with sacred associations, such as a gold plate or gem of some kind inscribed with the name JEHOVAH, attached to the outside of the Breastplate. This theory, in some form, is adopted by the Targum of Palestine, Theodoret, Lightfoot, Kalisch and many others; but it is most fully reasoned out by Plumptre in Smith's 'Dictionary.'

3. Michaelis, Jahn and others, have supposed that the Urim and the Thummim might have been three slips, one with *yes* upon it, one with *no*, and the third plain, and that the slip taken out of the pocket of the Breastplate at hap-hazard by the High-priest was regarded as giving the answer to the question proposed.—Gesenius and Fürst have adopted Spencer's notion, that they were two images, but supposed that they were used in some mode of casting lots.—Winer, following Züllig, imagined that the Urim were diamonds cut in the form of dice, and that the Thummim were rough diamonds (according to the meaning of the word, *entire*) with some sort of marks engraved on them, which the High-priest, when he sought for an answer, took out of the bag and threw down on a table in the Sanctuary, drawing a meaning from the mode in which they fell.

But the theory itself is not necessarily involved in these hollow and vain conjectures as to the material instruments which may have been employed. No attempted explanation seems to be more in accordance with such analogy as the history of the Israelites affords, or more free from objection, than that the Urim and the Thummim were some means of casting lots. That the Lord should have made His will known to His people by such means may indeed run counter to our own habits of thought. But we know that appeals to lots were made under divine authority by the chosen people on the most solemn occasions[2]. The divine will was manifested by circumstances in themselves of as little note, or of as little external connection with the question at issue, as the dampness or the dryness of a fleece laid on the ground (Judg. vi. 36—40). It must have been a truth commonly recognized by the people that though "the lot was cast into the lap, the whole disposing thereof was of the Lord" (Prov. xvi. 33).—The practice of casting lots was not wholly discontinued till it was exer-

[1] See Sheringham's note on *Yoma*, in Surenhusius, Vol. II. p. 251, and the notes of Drusius and Cartwright on Ex. xxviii. 30 in the 'Crit. Sac.'

[2] Lev. xvi. 8; Num. xxvi. 55; Josh. vii. 14—18, xiii. 6, xviii. 8; 1 S. xiv. 41, 42; Acts i. 26.

cised in completing the number of the twelve Apostles (Acts i. 26). It seems worthy of remark, that the Urim and the Thummim appear to have fallen into disuse as the prophetic office became more distinct and important in and after the reign of David; and that we hear nothing of the casting of lots in the Apostolic History after the day of Pentecost, when the Holy Ghost was given to lead believers into all truth. In each case, the lower mode of revelation appears to give way to the higher[1].

[1] It has been objected that there is nothing in the etymology of the names of the Urim and the Thummim to justify the conjecture that they were connected with casting lots. But the words in their proper meaning probably referred to the result obtained (*i.e.* the knowledge of the divine will) rather than to the mere material instruments employed.

CHAPTER XXIX.

1 *The sacrifice and ceremonies of consecrating the priests.* 38 *The continual burnt offering.* 45 *God's promise to dwell among the children of Israel.*

AND this *is* the thing that thou shalt do unto them to hallow them, to minister unto me in the priest's office: [a]Take one young bullock, and two rams without blemish,

[a Lev. 8. 2. & 9. 2.]

2 And unleavened bread, and cakes unleavened tempered with oil, and wafers unleavened anointed with oil: *of* wheaten flour shalt thou make them.

3 And thou shalt put them into one basket, and bring them in the basket, with the bullock and the two rams.

4 And Aaron and his sons thou shalt bring unto the door of the tabernacle of the congregation, and shalt wash them with water.

5 And thou shalt take the garments, and put upon Aaron the coat, and the robe of the ephod, and the ephod, and the breastplate, and gird him with the curious girdle of the ephod:

6 And thou shalt put the mitre upon his head, and put the holy crown upon the mitre.

7 Then shalt thou take the anointing [b]oil, and pour *it* upon his head, and anoint him.

[b chap. 30. 25.]

8 And thou shalt bring his sons, and put coats upon them.

9 And thou shalt gird them with girdles, Aaron and his sons, and †put the bonnets on them: and the priest's office shall be theirs for a perpetual statute: and thou shalt †[c]consecrate Aaron and his sons.

[† Heb. *bind.*] [† Heb. *fill the hand of.*] [c chap. 28. 41.]

10 And thou shalt cause a bullock to be brought before the tabernacle of the congregation: and [d]Aaron and his sons shall put their hands upon the head of the bullock.

[d Lev. 1. 4.]

11 And thou shalt kill the bullock before the LORD, *by* the door of the tabernacle of the congregation.

12 And thou shalt take of the blood of the bullock, and put *it* upon the horns of the altar with thy finger, and pour all the blood beside the bottom of the altar.

13 And [e]thou shalt take all the fat that covereth the inwards, and ‖the caul *that is* above the liver, and the

[e Lev. 3. 3.] [‖ *It seemeth by anatomy, and the Hebrew doctors, to be the midriff.*]

CHAP. XXIX.

THE CONSECRATION OF THE PRIESTS.

1—37.

The account of the consecration of Aaron and his sons, in accordance with the directions contained in this chapter, is given in Lev. viii., ix. The details of the ceremonies involve many important references to the Law of the Offerings contained in Lev. i.—vii. Most of the notes on these details are therefore given under the narrative of the consecration in Leviticus.

1, 2, 3. See on Lev. viii. 2, 26.

2. *cakes unleavened tempered with oil*] These are called *cakes of oiled bread* in Lev. viii. 26. See on Lev. ii. 4.

4. *door of the tabernacle*] **entrance of the tent.** See on Lev. viii. 3.

wash them] See on Lev. viii. 6.

5, 6. See on Lev. viii. 7, 8, 9; Exod. xxviii. 7, 8, 31—39, xxxix. 30.

6. *the holy crown*] See on xxxix. 30.

7. *the anointing oil*] See Lev. viii. 10—12; Exod. xxx. 22—25.

8. See on Lev. viii. 13; cf. Exod. xxxix. 41.

10—14. See on Lev. viii. 14—17; cf. Lev. iv. 3.

two kidneys, and the fat that *is* upon
them, and burn *them* upon the altar.
14 But the flesh of the bullock,
and his skin, and his dung, shalt thou
burn with fire without the camp: it
is a sin offering.
15 ¶ Thou shalt also take one
ram; and Aaron and his sons shall
put their hands upon the head of
the ram.
16 And thou shalt slay the ram,
and thou shalt take his blood, and
sprinkle *it* round about upon the altar.
17 And thou shalt cut the ram in
pieces, and wash the inwards of him,
and his legs, and put *them* unto his
pieces, and ‖ unto his head. (‖ Or, *upon.*)
18 And thou shalt burn the whole
ram upon the altar: it *is* a burnt offering unto the LORD: it *is* a sweet
savour, an offering made by fire unto
the LORD.
19 ¶ And thou shalt take the
other ram; and Aaron and his sons
shall put their hands upon the head
of the ram.
20 Then shalt thou kill the ram,
and take of his blood, and put *it* upon
the tip of the right ear of Aaron, and
upon the tip of the right ear of his
sons, and upon the thumb of their
right hand, and upon the great toe of
their right foot, and sprinkle the blood
upon the altar round about.
21 And thou shalt take of the blood
that *is* upon the altar, and of the
anointing oil, and sprinkle *it* upon
Aaron, and upon his garments, and
upon his sons, and upon the garments
of his sons with him: and he shall
be hallowed, and his garments, and
his sons, and his sons' garments with
him.
22 Also thou shalt take of the ram
the fat and the rump, and the fat that
covereth the inwards, and the caul
above the liver, and the two kidneys,
and the fat that *is* upon them, and
the right shoulder; for it *is* a ram of
consecration:
23 And one loaf of bread, and one
cake of oiled bread, and one wafer
out of the basket of the unleavened
bread that *is* before the LORD:
24 And thou shalt put all in the
hands of Aaron, and in the hands of
his sons; and shalt ‖ wave them *for* a (‖ Or, *shake to and fro.*)
wave offering before the LORD.
25 And thou shalt receive them of
their hands, and burn *them* upon the
altar for a burnt offering, for a sweet
savour before the LORD: it *is* an offering made by fire unto the LORD.
26 And thou shalt take the breast
of the ram of Aaron's consecration,
and wave it *for* a wave offering before
the LORD: and it shall be thy part.
27 And thou shalt sanctify the
breast of the wave offering, and the
shoulder of the heave offering, which
is waved, and which is heaved up, of
the ram of the consecration, *even* of
that which *is* for Aaron, and of *that*
which is for his sons:
28 And it shall be Aaron's and his
sons' by a statute for ever from the
children of Israel: for it *is* an heave
offering: and it shall be an heave
offering from the children of Israel of
the sacrifice of their peace offerings,
even their heave offering unto the
LORD.
29 ¶ And the holy garments of
Aaron shall be his sons' after him, to
be anointed therein, and to be consecrated in them.
30 *And* † that son that is priest in († Heb. *he of his sons.*)
his stead shall put them on seven days,

15—18. See on Lev. viii. 18—21.

19—28. See on Lev. viii. 22—29.

27. On Waving and Heaving, first mentioned in their connection with the ceremonies of the Altar in this chapter, see preface to Leviticus. It should be noticed that the right shoulder (rather perhaps *the right leg*, see Lev. vii. 32) was to be formally presented to the priests (*vv.* 22, 24), in order to make a recognition of the Law of the Heave-offering, though, on this special occasion, it was not to be eaten like an ordinary heave-offering, but to be made part of the burnt-offering. (*v.* 25.)

28. This law is repeated Lev. vii. 34. Cf. Lev. x. 14, 15; Num. vi. 20.

29, 30. See on Lev. viii. 30, 33.

when he cometh into the tabernacle
of the congregation to minister in the
holy *place*.
31 ¶ And thou shalt take the ram
of the consecration, and seethe his
flesh in the holy place.
32 And Aaron and his sons shall
eat the flesh of the ram, and the
Lev. 8. *f* bread that *is* in the basket, *by* the
att. 12. door of the tabernacle of the congregation.
33 And they shall eat those things
wherewith the atonement was made,
to consecrate *and* to sanctify them:
but a stranger shall not eat *thereof*,
because they *are* holy.
34 And if ought of the flesh of the
consecrations, or of the bread, remain
unto the morning, then thou shalt
burn the remainder with fire: it shall
not be eaten, because it *is* holy.
35 And thus shalt thou do unto
Aaron, and to his sons, according to
all *things* which I have commanded
thee: seven days shalt thou consecrate
them.
36 And thou shalt offer every day
a bullock *for* a sin offering for atonement: and thou shalt cleanse the altar,
when thou hast made an atonement
for it, and thou shalt anoint it, to
sanctify it.
37 Seven days thou shalt make an
atonement for the altar, and sanctify
it; and it shall be an altar most holy:
whatsoever toucheth the altar shall be
holy.
38 ¶ Now this *is that* which thou
shalt offer upon the altar; *g* two *g* Numb.
lambs of the first year day by day 28. 3.
continually.
39 The one lamb thou shalt offer
in the morning; and the other lamb
thou shalt offer at even:
40 And with the one lamb a tenth
deal of flour mingled with the fourth
part of an hin of beaten oil; and the
fourth part of an hin of wine *for* a
drink offering.
41 And the other lamb thou shalt
offer at even, and shalt do thereto according to the meat offering of the
morning, and according to the drink
offering thereof, for a sweet savour,
an offering made by fire unto the
LORD.

31—34. See on Lev. viii. 31, 32.

33. *a stranger*] **one of another family**, *i.e.* in this case, one not of the family of Aaron. The Hebrew word (*zār*) is the same as is used xxx. 33, Deut. xxv. 5.

35, 36. See on Lev. viii. 33, 35.

37. See on Lev. viii. 11.

The Continual Burnt-offering.

38—46.

38. *this is that which thou shalt offer*] The primary purpose of the national Altar is here set forth. On it was to be offered "the continual Burnt-offering" (*v.* 42), consisting of a yearling lamb with its meat-offering and its drink-offering, and this was to figure the daily renewal of the consecration of the nation. The victim slain every morning and every evening was an acknowledgment that the life of the people belonged to Jehovah, and the offering of meal was an acknowledgment that all their right works were His due (see on Lev. ii.); while the incense symbolized their daily prayers. (See on xxx. 6—8.)

39. *at even*] Literally, *between the two evenings*. See on xii. 6.

40. *a tenth deal*] *i.e.* the tenth part of an Ephah; it is sometimes called an Omer (Exod. xvi. 36; Num. xxviii. 5. See on Lev. xxiii. 13). The Ephah seems to have been rather less than four gallons and a half (see on Lev. xix. 36); and the tenth deal of flour may have weighed about 3 lbs. 2 oz.

an hin] The word *hin*, which here first occurs, appears to be Egyptian. The measure was one-sixth of an ephah. The quarter of a hin was therefore about a pint and a half. See on Lev. xix. 36.

beaten oil] *i.e.* oil of the best quality. See on xxvii. 20.

wine for a drink-offering] The earliest mention of the Drink-offering is found in connection with Jacob's setting up the stone at Bethel (Gen. xxxv. 14). But it is here first associated with the rites of the Altar. The Law of the Drink-offering is stated Num. xv. 5 sq. Nothing whatever is expressly said in the Old Testament regarding the mode in which the wine was treated: but it would seem probable, from the prohibition that it should not be poured upon the Altar of Incense (Exod. xxx. 9), that it used to be poured on the Altar of Burnt-offering. Josephus ('Ant.' III. 9. § 4) says that it was poured round the Altar (περὶ τὸν βωμόν): it may have been cast upon it in the same way as the blood of the Burnt-

42 *This shall be* a continual burnt
offering throughout your generations
at the door of the tabernacle of the
congregation before the LORD: where
I will meet you, to speak there unto
thee.
43 And there I will meet with the
‖ Or, Israel. children of Israel, and ‖ *the tabernacle*
shall be sanctified by my glory.
44 And I will sanctify the tabernacle of the congregation, and the
altar: I will sanctify also both Aaron
and his sons, to minister to me in the
priest's office.
h Lev. 26. 12. 2 Cor. 6. 16 45 ¶ And [h] I will dwell among the
children of Israel, and will be their
God.
46 And they shall know that I *am*
the LORD their God, that brought
them forth out of the land of Egypt,
that I may dwell among them: I *am*
the LORD their God.

CHAPTER XXX.

1 *The altar of incense.* 11 *The ransom of souls.* 17 *The brasen laver.* 22 *The holy anointing oil.* 34 *The composition of the perfume.*

AND thou shalt make an altar to
burn incense upon: *of* shittim
wood shalt thou make it.
2 A cubit *shall be* the length thereof, and a cubit the breadth thereof;
foursquare shall it be: and two cubits
shall be the height thereof: the horns
thereof *shall be* of the same.
3 And thou shalt overlay it with
pure gold, the † top thereof, and the † Heb. the roof.
† sides thereof round about, and the
horns thereof; and thou shalt make † Heb. walls.
unto it a crown of gold round about.
4 And two golden rings shalt thou
make to it under the crown of it, by
the two † corners thereof, upon the † Heb. ribs.
two sides of it shalt thou make *it;* and

---

offering and the Peace-offering (see on Lev. i.), or at its foot (ἐς θεμέλια), Ecclus. i. 15. This appears to agree with the patriarchal usage mentioned Gen. xxxv. 14.

42. *at the door of the tabernacle*] **at the entrance of the Tent.**

43. *the (tabernacle) shall be sanctified*] The word *tabernacle* is certainly not the right one to be here supplied. From the context it may be inferred that what is meant is the spot in which Jehovah promises to meet with the assembly of His people, who were not admitted into the *Mishkān* itself, as the priests were (see xxv. 22); that is, the Holy Precinct between the Tabernacle and the Altar. See Lev. x. 17, 18.—This verse should be rendered, **And in that place will I meet with the children of Israel, and it shall be sanctified with my glory.**

44, 45. The purpose of the formal consecration of the Sanctuary and of the priests who served in it was, that the whole nation which Jehovah had set free from its bondage in Egypt might be consecrated in its daily life, and dwell continually in His presence as "a kingdom of priests and an holy nation."

46. Cf. Gen. xvii. 7.

CHAP. XXX.

The Altar of Incense.

1—10. (xxxvii. 25—28, xl. 26, 27.)

This passage would seem naturally to belong to ch. xxv., where directions are given for the whole of the furniture of the Tabernacle, except the Altar of Incense. No satisfactory reason appears for its occurrence in this place. In the lists of the articles (xxxi. 8, xxxv. 15), and in the record of their construction (xxxvii. 25—28), and of their arrangement in the Sanctuary (xl. 26, 27), the Altar of Incense is mentioned in due order. It should however be observed, that the instructions here given respecting it are distinguished from those relating to the other articles in ch. xxv. in as far as they comprise directions for the mode in which it was to be used (*vv.* 7—10).

The Altar was to be a casing of boards of shittim wood (see on xxv. 5), 18 inches square and three feet in height (taking the cubit as 18 inches), entirely covered with plates of gold. Four "horns" were to project upwards at the corners like those of the Altar of Burnt-offering (xxvii. 2). A moulding of gold was to run round the top. On each of two opposite sides there was to be a gold ring through which the staves were to be put when it was moved from place to place.

3. *a crown of gold*] **a moulding of gold.** See on xxv. 11.

4. *by the two corners thereof*] The Hebrew word does not mean *corners*. See margin. The sense of the first part of the verse appears to be: *And two gold rings shalt thou make for it under its moulding; on its two sides shalt thou make them* (*i.e.* one ring on each side). So de Wette, Knobel, Schott, Wogue. The Ark and the Shewbread Table had each four rings, two for the pole on each side; but the Incense Altar, being shorter,

they shall be for places for the staves
to bear it withal.
5 And thou shalt make the staves
of shittim wood, and overlay them
with gold.
6 And thou shalt put it before the
vail that *is* by the ark of the testimony,
before the mercy seat that *is* over the
testimony, where I will meet with
thee.
7 And Aaron shall burn thereon
† sweet incense every morning: when
he dresseth the lamps, he shall burn
incense upon it.
8 And when Aaron ‖ lighteth the
lamps † at even, he shall burn incense
upon it, a perpetual incense before the
LORD throughout your generations.
9 Ye shall offer no strange incense
thereon, nor burnt sacrifice, nor meat
offering; neither shall ye pour drink
offering thereon.
10 And Aaron shall make an atonement upon the horns of it once in a
year with the blood of the sin offering
of atonements: once in the year shall
he make atonement upon it throughout your generations: it *is* most holy
unto the LORD.
11 ¶ And the LORD spake unto
Moses, saying,
12 [a] When thou takest the sum of
the children of Israel after † their number, then shall they give every man a
ransom for his soul unto the LORD,
when thou numberest them; that
there be no plague among them, when
thou numberest them.

† Heb. *incense of spices.*
‖ Or, *setteth up.* Heb. *causeth to ascend.*
† Heb. *between the two evens.*
[a] Numb. i. 2, 5.
† Heb. *them that are to be numbered.*

---

was sufficiently supported by a single ring on each side, without risk of its being thrown off its balance.

6. The place for the Altar of Incense was outside the vail, opposite to the Ark of the Covenant and between the Candlestick on the south side and the Shewbread Table on the north (xl. 22—24). It appears to have been regarded as having a more intimate connection with the Holy of Holies than the other things in the Holy Place (see 1 K. vi. 22; Rev. viii. 3; also Heb. ix. 4, if we are to identify it with the θυμιατήριον there mentioned, see on Lev. xvi. 12); and the mention of the Mercy-seat in this verse, if we associate with it the significance of incense as figuring the prayers of the Lord's people (Ps. cxli. 2; Rev. v. 8, viii. 3, 4), seems to furnish additional ground for an inference that the Incense Altar took precedence of the Table of Show-bread and the Candlestick.

7. *the lamps*] See on xxvii. 21.

burn incense] The word here and elsewhere applied to the burning of incense is the same as that used xxv. 37. See note.

7, 8. The offering of the Incense accompanied that of the morning and evening sacrifice. The two forms of offering symbolized the spirit of man reaching after communion with Jehovah, both in act and utterance, according to the words of the Psalmist, "Let my prayer be set forth before thee as incense; and the lifting up of my hands as the evening sacrifice." Ps. cxli. 2.

9. By this regulation, the symbolism of the Altar of Incense was kept free from ambiguity. Atonement was made by means of the victim on the Brazen altar in the court outside; the prayers of the reconciled worshippers had their type within the Tabernacle.

10. See on Lev. xvi. 18, 19.

shall he make atonement] rather, **shall atonement be made.**

The Ransom of Souls.

11—16. (xxxviii. 25—28.)

11, 12. The materials for the textile work, the wood, the gold, and the bronze, were to be the free-will offerings of those who could contribute them (xxv. 2, xxxv. 21 sq.). But the silver was to be obtained by an enforced capitation on every adult male Israelite, the poor and the rich having to pay the same (*v.* 15). Hence, in the estimate of the metals collected for the work (xxxviii. 24—31) the gold and the bronze are termed *offerings* (strictly, **wave-offerings**, see preface to Leviticus), while the silver is spoken of as "the silver of them that were numbered." But this payment is brought into its highest relation in being here accounted a spiritual obligation laid on each individual, a tribute expressly exacted by Jehovah. Every man of Israel who would escape a curse (*v.* 12) had in this way to make a practical acknowledgment that he had a share in the Sanctuary, on the occasion of his being recognised as one of the covenanted people (*v.* 16).—Silver was the metal commonly used for current coin. See Gen. xxiii. 16.

12. *When thou takest the sum of the children of Israel*] The silver must have been contributed at this time, along with the other materials, since it was used in the Tabernacle, which was completed on the first day of the first month of the second year after coming

13 This they shall give, every one that passeth among them that are numbered, half a shekel after the shekel of the sanctuary: ([b]a shekel *is* twenty gerahs:) an half shekel *shall be* the offering of the LORD.

[b] Lev. 27. 25. Numb. 3. 47. Ezek. 45. 12.

14 Every one that passeth among them that are numbered, from twenty years old and above, shall give an offering unto the LORD.

15 The rich shall not †give more, and the poor shall not †give less than half a shekel, when *they* give an offering unto the LORD, to make an atonement for your souls.

† Heb. *multiply.* † Heb. *diminish.*

16 And thou shalt take the atonement money of the children of Israel, and shalt appoint it for the service of the tabernacle of the congregation; that it may be a memorial unto the children of Israel before the LORD, to make an atonement for your souls.

17 ¶ And the LORD spake unto Moses, saying,

18 Thou shalt also make a laver *of* brass, and his foot *also of* brass, to wash *withal:* and thou shalt put it between the tabernacle of the congregation and the altar, and thou shalt put water therein.

19 For Aaron and his sons shall wash their hands and their feet thereat:

---

out of Egypt (xl. 17). But the command to take the complete census of the nation appears not to have been given until the first day of the second month of that year (Num. i. 1). On comparing the words of Exod. xxx. 12 with those of Num. i. 1—3, we may perhaps infer that the first passage relates to a mere counting of the adult Israelites at the time when the money was taken from each, and that what the latter passage enjoins was a formal enrolment of them according to their genealogies and their order of military service.

a ransom for his soul] What the sincere worshipper thus paid was at once the fruit and the sign of his faith in the goodness of Jehovah, who had redeemed him and brought him into the Covenant. (See Introd. note to ch. xxv.) Hence the payment is rightly called a *ransom* in as much as it involved a personal appropriation of the fact of his redemption. On the word *soul*, see on Lev. xvii. 11.

that there be no plague] *i.e.* that they might not incur punishment for the neglect and contempt of spiritual privileges. Cf. 1 Cor. xi. 27—30; and the Exhortation in our Communion Service.

13. *half a shekel*] The probable weight of silver in the half-shekel would now be worth about 1*s.* 3½*d.* (See on Exod. xxxviii. 25.) *Gerah* is, literally, a *bean*, probably the bean of the carob or locust-tree (Aben-Ezra). It was used as the name of a small weight, as our word *grain* came into use from a grain of wheat. The purpose of the definition of the shekel here given is not quite certain. It might seem to countenance the rabbinical notion that there were two kinds of shekel, the shekel of the Sanctuary consisting of twenty gerahs, and the common shekel. (See on xxxviii. 24.) But it is more likely that the weight is defined rather for the sake of emphasis, to intimate that the just value should be given precisely. The words in question might rather be rendered: "half a shekel after the shekel of the sanctuary, **twenty gerahs to the shekel; the half shekel shall be the offering** (Heb. *terumah*, as in *vv.* 14, 15; see xxv. 2) **to Jehovah.**"

15. Every Israelite stood in one and the same relation to Jehovah. See on *vv.* 11, 12.

16. *tabernacle of the congregation*] **Tent of meeting.**

a memorial unto the children of Israel] The silver used in the Tabernacle was a memorial to remind each man of his position before the Lord, as one of the covenanted people.

The Laver of Brass.

17—21. (xxxviii. 8.)

18. *a laver of brass*] The bronze for the Laver and its foot was supplied from the bronze mirrors of the women "who assembled at the door of the tabernacle." The women seem to have voluntarily given up these articles of luxury (see on xxxviii. 8). Bronze mirrors were much used by the ancient Egyptians. Wilkinson, Vol. II. p. 345. No hint is given as to the form of the Laver. It may have been made with an immediate view to use of the simplest and most convenient form. The Brazen Sea and the ten Lavers that served the same purpose in the Temple of Solomon, were elaborately wrought in artistic designs and are minutely described (1 K. vii. 23—29).

tabernacle of the congregation] **Tent of meeting.**

19. *wash their hands and their feet*] Whenever a priest had to enter the Tabernacle, or to offer a victim on the Altar, he was required to wash his hands and his feet; but on certain solemn occasions he was required to bathe his whole person (xxix. 4; Lev. xvi. 4). The Laver must also have furnished the water for washing those parts of the victims that needed cleansing (Lev. i. 9).

20 When they go into the tabernacle of the congregation, they shall
wash with water, that they die not;
or when they come near to the altar
to minister, to burn offering made by
fire unto the LORD:
21 So they shall wash their hands
and their feet, that they die not: and
it shall be a statute for ever to them,
even to him and to his seed throughout their generations.

22 ¶ Moreover the LORD spake
unto Moses, saying,
23 Take thou also unto thee principal spices, of pure myrrh five hundred *shekels*, and of sweet cinnamon
half so much, *even* two hundred and
fifty *shekels*, and of sweet calamus two
hundred and fifty *shekels*,
24 And of cassia five hundred *shekels*, after the shekel of the sanctuary,
and of oil olive an [c] hin:

[c] chap. 29. 40.

---

20. *tabernacle of the congregation*] **Tent of meeting.**

that they die not] See on xxviii. 35.

to burn offering made by fire unto the LORD] Literally, *to send up in fire an offering to Jehovah.* The verb is the same as in *v.* 7 and xxv 37.

The Holy Anointing Oil.

22—33. (xxxvii. 29.)

23. *principal spices*] *i.e.* the best spices.

pure myrrh] There cannot be much doubt as to the identity of this substance from its name in different languages (Hebrew, *mōr;* Arabic, *murr;* Greek, σμύρνα; Latin, *myrrha*). It is a gum which comes from the stem of a low, thorny, ragged tree, that grows in Arabia Felix and Eastern Africa, called by botanists *Balsamodendron myrrha.* The word here rendered *pure*, is literally, *freely flowing*, an epithet which is explained by the fact that the best myrrh is said to exude spontaneously from the bark (Plin. 'H. N.' XII. 35; Theophrast. 'de Odorib.' 29), while that of inferior quality oozes out in greater quantity from incisions made in the bark. On the estimation in which myrrh was held, see Cant. i. 13; Matt. ii. 11; on its use as a perfume, Ps. xlv. 8; Prov. vii. 17; Cant. v. 5; and on its use in embalming, John xix. 39. This is the first mention of it in the Hebrew text of the Old Testament, but in our version it is named by mistake in Gen. xxxvii. 25, xliii. 11.

five hundred shekels] Probably rather more than 15¼ lbs. See on xxxviii. 24.

sweet cinnamon] This substance is satisfactorily identified, like the preceding one, on account of its name (Heb. *Kinnamon;* Gr. κινάμωμον; Lat. *cinnamomum*). It is obtained from a tree allied to the laurel that grows in Ceylon and other islands of the Indian Ocean, known in Botany as the *Cinnamomun zeylanicum.* It is the inner rind of the tree dried in the sun. The origin of the name appears to be found in the Malay language (Ritter, Knobel), Herodotus says that the word is Phœnician, but this means no more than that the Greeks learned it from the Phœnicians. It is probable that Cinnamon was imported from India in very early times by the people of Ophir, and that it was brought with other spices from the south part of Arabia by the trading caravans that visited Egypt and Syria. Hence, even in later times, Cinnamon and other Indian spices were spoken of as productions of the land of the Sabæans (Strabo, XVI. pp. 769, 774, 778). If we accept this explanation, the mention of these spices in Exodus may be taken as the earliest notice we have connected with commerce with the remote East. Cinnamon is elsewhere mentioned in the Scriptures only, Prov. vii. 17; Cant. iv. 14; Rev. xviii. 13.

two hundred and fifty shekels] Probably about 7 lbs. 14 oz. See on xxxviii. 24.

sweet calamus] The word rendered calamus (*kanēh*) is the common Hebrew name for a *stalk*, *reed*, or *cane* (Gen. xli. 5; 1 K. xiv. 15; Ezek. xli. 8). The **fragrant cane** (or *rush*) here spoken of is mentioned in Isa. xliii. 24, in Jer. vi. 20 (where it is called in the Hebrew "**the good cane** from a far country"), and in Cant. iv. 14; Ezek. xxvii. 19, where it is called simply **cane**. It was probably what is now known in India as the Lemon Grass (*Andropogon schoenanthus*). Aromatic reeds were known to the ancients as the produce of India and the region of the Euphrates (Xenophon, 'Anab.' I. 5, § 1; Diosc. 'Mat. Med.' I. 16). The statements that such reeds were produced in the neighbourhood of Libanus (Theophr. 'H. P.' IX. 7; 'C. P.' VI. 18; Polybius, V. 45), near the Lake of Gennesaret (Strabo, XVI. p. 755) and in the Land of the Sabæans (Strabo, XVI. p. 778; cf. Diod. II. 49), may be regarded as some of the many mistakes which have arisen from confounding the country from which a commodity is obtained with that of its original production.

24. *cassia*] The Hebrew name (*kiddāh*) is found elsewhere only in Ezek. xxvii. 19, where it is associated, as it is here, with sweet cane. The word rendered *cassia* in Ps. xlv. 8 is a different one, but it is probable that the same substance is denoted by it. Most of the ancient versions, and all modern authorities, seem to be in favour of *cassia* being the true rendering of *kiddāh*. Cassia is the inner bark

25 And thou shalt make it an oil of holy ointment, an ointment compound after the art of the [1]apothecary: it shall be an holy anointing oil.

[1] Or, *perfumer.*

26 And thou shalt anoint the tabernacle of the congregation therewith, and the ark of the testimony,

27 And the table and all his vessels, and the candlestick and his vessels, and the altar of incense,

28 And the altar of burnt offering with all his vessels, and the laver and his foot.

29 And thou shalt sanctify them, that they may be most holy: whatsoever toucheth them shall be holy.

30 And thou shalt anoint Aaron and his sons, and consecrate them, that *they* may minister unto me in the priest's office.

31 And thou shalt speak unto the children of Israel, saying, This shall be an holy anointing oil unto me throughout your generations.

32 Upon man's flesh shall it not be poured, neither shall ye make *any other* like it, after the composition of it: it *is* holy, *and* it shall be holy unto you.

33 Whosoever compoundeth *any* like it, or whosoever putteth *any* of it upon a stranger, shall even be cut off from his people.

34 ¶ And the LORD said unto Moses, Take unto thee sweet spices, stacte, and onycha, and galbanum;

---

of an Indian tree (*Cinnamonum cassia*), which differs from that which produces cinnamon in the shape of its leaves and some other particulars. It bears a strong resemblance to cinnamon, but it is more pungent, and of coarser texture. It was probably in ancient times, as it is at present, by far less costly than cinnamon, and it may have been on this account that it was used in double quantity.

an hin] Probably about six pints. See on Lev. xix. 36.

25.] *an oil of holy ointment*] rather, **a holy anointing oil.**

after the art of the apothecary] According to Jewish tradition, the essences of the spices were first extracted, and then mixed with the oil (Otho, 'Lex. Rabb.' p. 486). That some such process was employed is probable from the great proportion of solid matter compared with the oil. The preparation of the Anointing Oil, as well as of the Incense, was entrusted to Bezaleel (xxxvii. 29), and the care of preserving it to Eleazar the son of Aaron (Num. iv. 16). In a later age, it was prepared by the sons of the priests (1 Chro. ix. 30).

26—31.] Cf. xl. 9—15. See on Lev. viii. 10—12.

26. *tabernacle of the congregation*] **Tent of meeting.**

29.] See on xxix. 37.

32. *upon man's flesh*] *i.e.* on the persons of those that were not priests who might employ it for such anointing as was usual on festive occasions (Ps. civ. 15; Prov. xxvii. 9; Matt. vi. 17, &c.).

33. *a stranger*] **one of another family.** See on xxix. 33. The Holy Anointing Oil was not even to be used for the anointing of a king. See on 1 K. i. 39.

cut off from his people.] See on Gen. xvii. 14, Exod. xxxi. 14, and Lev. vii. 20.

The Holy Incense.

34—38. (xxxvii. 29.)

34.] The Incense, like the Anointing Oil, consisted of four aromatic ingredients.

stacte] The Hebrew word is *nataph* (*i.e. a drop*), which occurs in its simple sense in Job xxxvi. 27. Our version and the Vulgate have adopted the word used by the LXX. (στακτή), which, like the Hebrew, may denote anything that drops, and was applied to the purest kind of myrrh that drops spontaneously from the tree (see on *v.* 23). But the substance here meant, which is nowhere else mentioned in the Old Testament, is generally supposed to be the gum of the Storax-tree (*Styrax officinalis*) found in Syria and the neighbouring countries. The gum was burned as a perfume in the time of Pliny ('H. N.' XII. 40). But it seems by no means unlikely that the *stacte* here mentioned was the gum known as Benzoin, or Gum Benjamin, which is an important ingredient in the incense now used in churches and mosks, and is the produce of another storax-tree (*Styrax benjoin*) that grows in Java and Sumatra. See on *v.* 23. It may be observed that the liquid storax of commerce is obtained from quite a different tree known to botanists as *Liquidambar syraciflua.*

onycha] Heb. *shechēleth* (which appears to mean a *shell*, or *scale*), LXX. ὄνυξ, Vulg. *onycha.* The word does not occur in any other place in the Old Testament. The Greek word was not only applied to the well-known precious stone, the onyx, from its resemblance to the human nail, but to the horny operculum, or cap, of a shell. The operculum of the strombus, or wing-shell, which

these sweet spices with pure frankincense: of each shall there be a like
weight:
35 And thou shalt make it a perfume, a confection after the art of
† Heb. *salted.* the apothecary, †tempered together,
pure *and* holy:
36 And thou shalt beat *some* of it
very small, and put of it before the
testimony in the tabernacle of the
congregation, where I will meet with
thee: it shall be unto you most
holy.
37 And *as for* the perfume which
thou shalt make, ye shall not make
to yourselves according to the composition thereof: it shall be unto thee
holy for the LORD.

---

abounds in the Red Sea, is said to be employed at this day in the composition of perfume, and to have been used as a medicine in the Middle Ages under the name of *Blatta Byzantina*. Pliny, most likely referring to the same substance with imperfect knowledge, speaks of a shell called *onyx* that was used both as a perfume and a medicine ('H. N.' XXXII. 46; cf. Dioscorides, 'Mat. Med.' II. 11). Its identification with the *shecheleth* of the text seems probable. Saadia uses the word *ladanum*, the name of the gum of the Lada tree (see Plin. 'H. N.' XII. 37). Bochart, on weak ground, imagined that bdellium (Gen. ii. 12) was meant. See Bochart, 'Op.' Vol. III. p. 803; Gesen. 'Thes.' p. 1388.

galbanum] Heb. *chelbenāh;* LXX. χαλβάνη; Vulg. *galbanum*. It is not mentioned elsewhere in the Old Testament. No doubt has been raised as to its identity. Galbanum is now well known in medicine as a gum of a yellowish brown colour, in the form of either grains or masses. It burns with a pungent smell which is agreeable when it is combined with other smells, but not else. It is imported from India, Persia, and Africa; yet, strange to say, the plant from which it comes is not yet certainly known. (See 'English Cyclo.' s. v.)

pure frankincense] Heb. *lebonah;* LXX. λίβανος; Vulg. *thus*. This was the most important of the aromatic gums. Like myrrh, it was regarded by itself as a precious perfume (Cant. iii. 6; Matt. ii. 11), and it was used unmixed with other substances in some of the rites of the Law (Lev. ii. 1. 15, v. 11, vi. 15, &c.). The Hebrew name is improperly rendered *incense* in our Version in Isa. xliii. 23, lx. 6, lxvi. 3; Jer. vi. 20, xvii. 26, xli. 5. It is certain that the supplies of it, as well as of the other spices, were obtained from Southern Arabia (Isa. lx. 6, Jer. vi. 20. Cf. 1 K. x. 1, 2, 10, 15; 2 Chro. ix. 9. 14). The Greek and Latin writers in general speak of its being produced in that region. But they evidently knew but little of the subject, as their descriptions of the plant producing it differ greatly from each other. (Plin. 'H. N.' VI. 32, XII. 31; Diod. Sic. II. 49, V. 41; Theophrast. 'de Plant.' IX. 1; Arrian, 'Perip.' with Stuck's note, p. 49; Dioscor. I. 82; Strabo, XVI. p. 774. Cf. p. 782.) The tree from which it is obtained is not found in Arabia, and it was most likely imported from India by the Sabæans, like Cinnamon, Cassia, and Calamus (see on *v.* 23). The tree is now known as the *Boswellia serrata*, or *B. thurifera*, and grows abundantly in the highlands of India, where its native name is *Salai*. The native name of the gum is *olibanum*, and its Arabic name, *looban:* the Hebrew and Greek names seem to have been taken directly from the Arabic. The frankincense of commerce is a different substance, the resin of the spruce and of some other kinds of fir.

35. *after the art of the apothecary*] The four substances were perhaps pounded and thoroughly mixed together, and then fused into a mass.

tempered together] With this rendering, most Versions, modern as well as ancient, and many of the best critics, agree. But, according to its etymology, the Hebrew might mean *seasoned with salt*, or (as it stands in the margin) *salted*. It is thus explained in the Talmud, which has been followed by Maimonides, de Wette, Gesenius, Herxheimer, Kalisch, and Keil. It is urged that this accords with the law that every offering should be accompanied by salt (Lev. ii. 13). But this law appears to refer only to the offerings of what was used as food (see note in loc., and on Lev. xxiv. 7), and Knobel has well observed that the use of salt in incense is contrary to all known analogy, since no such combination is known to have been made in the incense of any people.—Josephus speaks of the incense of the Temple as consisting of thirteen ingredients, but he does not state what they were ('B. J.' V. 5. § 5). A list of them is however given by Maimonides. A change may have been made in the composition in later times.

36. A portion of the mass was to be broken into small pieces and put "before the testimony;" that is opposite to the Ark of the Covenant, on the outside of the vail, conveniently near the Golden Altar on which it was to be lighted. (See on *v.* 6, and on xl. 20.) It may be observed that the incense thus brought into relation with the Ark was styled "most holy," while the Oil is no more than "holy," *v.* 32.

37, 38. Cf. *vv.* 32, 33. The Holy Incense, like the Holy Anointing Oil, was to be

38 Whosoever shall make like unto that, to smell thereto, shall even be
cut off from his people.

CHAPTER XXXI.

1 *Bezaleel and Aholiab are called and made meet for the work of the tabernacle.* 12 *The observation of the sabbath is again commanded.* 18 *Moses receiveth the two tables.*

AND the LORD spake unto Moses,
saying,
2 See, I have called by name Bezaleel the [a] son of Uri, the son of
Hur, of the tribe of Judah:

[a] 1 Chron. 2. 20.

3 And I have filled him with the
spirit of God, in wisdom, and in understanding, and in knowledge, and in
all manner of workmanship,
4 To devise cunning works, to work
in gold, and in silver, and in brass,
5 And in cutting of stones, to set
them, and in carving of timber, to
work in all manner of workmanship.
6 And I, behold, I have given with
him Aholiab, the son of Ahisamach,
of the tribe of Dan: and in the hearts
of all that are wise hearted I have put

---

kept in the Sanctuary, exclusively for the service of Jehovah.

CHAP. XXXI.

The Call of Bezaleel and Aholiab.
1—11. (xxxv. 30—35.)

2—6. This solemn call of Bezaleel and Aholiab is full of instruction. Their work was to be only that of handicraftsmen. Every thing that they had to do was prescribed in strict and precise detail. There was to be no exercise for their original powers of invention, nor for their taste. Still it was Jehovah Himself who called them by name to their tasks, and the powers which they were now called upon to exercise in their respective crafts, were declared to have been given them by the Holy Spirit. (See on xxviii. 3.) Thus is every effort of skill, every sort of well-ordered labour, when directed to a right end, brought into the very highest sphere of association.

3. *the spirit of God*] Literally, *a spirit of Elohim.* Mr Quarry ('Genesis,' &c. pp. 271—275) endeavours to prove that this expression has a lower meaning than *the spirit of Jehovah* (which stands in our Bible, "the spirit of the LORD"), and he would rather translate it, "a divine spirit." The definite article is wanting in the Hebrew in both cases. Mr Quarry however conceives that the distinction lies in the fact that Jehovah is a proper name, while Elohim is an appellative. But there is certainly no fair ground to infer any difference of meaning from the general use of the two phrases in the sacred text. It is the spirit of Elohim who inspires Balaam (Num. xxiv. 2), Azariah, the son of Oded (2 Chro. xv. 1), and Zechariah, the son of Jehoiada (2 Chro. xxiv. 20), in their prophetic utterances; while it is the Spirit of Jehovah who inspires the Judges for their work as leaders of the people. (Judg. iii. 10, vi. 34, xi. 29.) The Spirit of Jehovah who inspired Saul (1 S. x. 6) is the same as is more frequently called the Spirit of Elohim (1 S. x. 10, xi. 6, &c.). The terms would thus seem to be strictly equivalent.

wisdom] The Hebrew word is derived from a root of which the meaning is *to judge* or *decide.* It is used to denote the proper endowment of the ruler (2 S. xiv. 20; Is. xix. 11), and that of the prophet (Ezek. xxviii. 3, 4; Dan. v. 11); the highest exercise of the mind in a general sense (Job ix. 4, xi. 6, xii. 12, xv. 8), and, as in this place, the prime qualification of the workman in any manner of work. (Exod. xxviii. 3, xxxi. 6, xxxv. 10, 25, 26, 31, 35, xxxvi. 1, 2, &c.) It is, in fact, that "right judgment in all things" for which we specially pray on Whitsun-day. LXX. σόφια; Vulg. *sapientia.*

understanding] The Hebrew word is from a root that signifies *to discern*, or *discriminate;* it denotes the perceptive faculty. LXX. σύνεσις; Vulg. *intelligentia.*

knowledge] *i.e.* experience, a practical acquaintance with facts. LXX. ἐπιστήμη; Vulg. *scientia.*

in all manner of workmanship] *i.e.* not only in the intellectual gifts of wisdom, understanding and knowledge, but in dexterity of hand.

4. *to devise cunning works*] Rather, **to devise works of skill.** The Hebrew phrase is not the same as that rendered "cunning work" in respect to textile fabrics in xxvi. 1.

4—6. There appears to be sufficient reason to identify Hur, the grandfather of Bezaleel, with the Hur who assisted Aaron in supporting the hands of Moses during the battle with Amalek at Rephidim (Ex. xvii. 10), and who was associated with Aaron in the charge of the people while Moses was on the mountain (Ex. xxiv. 14). Josephus says that he was the husband of Miriam ('Ant.' III. 2. §4; VI. § 1). It is thus probable that Bezaleel was related to Moses. He was the chief artificer in metal, stone and wood; he had also to perform the apothecary's work in the composition of the Anointing Oil and the Incense (xxxvii. 29). He had precedence of all the artificers, but Aholiab appears to have had the entire charge of the textile work (xxxv. 35, xxxviii. 23).

wisdom, that they may make all that
I have commanded thee;
7 The tabernacle of the congregation, and the ark of the testimony,
and the mercy seat that *is* thereupon,
and all the †furniture of the tabernacle, † Heb. *vessels.*
8 And the table and his furniture,
and the pure candlestick with all his
furniture, and the altar of incense,
9 And the altar of burnt offering
with all his furniture, and the laver
and his foot,
10 And the cloths of service, and
the holy garments for Aaron the
priest, and the garments of his sons,
to minister in the priest's office,
11 And the anointing oil, and
sweet incense for the holy *place:* according to all that I have commanded
thee shall they do.
12 ¶ And the LORD spake unto
Moses, saying,
13 Speak thou also unto the children of Israel, saying, Verily my
sabbaths ye shall keep: for it *is* a
sign between me and you throughout your generations; that *ye* may
know that I *am* the LORD that doth
sanctify you.
14 [b] Ye shall keep the sabbath [b] chap. 20. 8.
therefore; for it *is* holy unto you: Deut. 5. 12.
every one that defileth it shall surely Ezek. 20. 12.
be put to death: for whosoever doeth
any work therein, that soul shall be
cut off from among his people.
15 Six days may work be done;

---

6. *all that are wise hearted*] See on xxviii. 3.

7. *tabernacle*] **Tent**, in both places. *of the congregation*] **of meeting**.

8. *the table and his furniture*] xxv. 23—30. *the pure candlestick*] That is, the candlestick of pure gold; xxv. 31—40. *the altar of incense*] xxx. 1—10.

9. *the altar of burnt offering*] xxvii. 1—8. *the laver*] xxx. 17—21.

10. *And the cloths of service*] Rather, **And the garments of office**; that is, the distinguishing official garments of the High-priest. LXX. στολαὶ λειτουργικαί. With this agree, more or less clearly, the Syriac, Vulg., Targums, Saadia, Luther, Cranmer, both the Geneva Versions, de Wette, Zunz, Knobel, Kalisch, &c. The three kinds of dress mentioned in this verse appear to be the only ones which were peculiar to the Sanctuary. They were: (1) The richly adorned state robes of the High-priest (see xxviii. 6—38, xxxix. 1 sq.). (2) The "holy garments" of white linen for the High-priest, worn on the most solemn occasion in the year (see Lev. xvi. 4; Ex. xxviii. 39). (3) The garments of white linen for all the priests, worn in their regular ministrations (see xxviii. 40, 41).—From the connection in which the expression rendered "cloths of service" here occurs, and a comparison of this verse with xxxix. 1, it seems strange that any doubt should have arisen as to its meaning. But some Jewish writers have supposed that the wrapping cloths are denoted which are mentioned Num. iv. 6, 7, 11, &c., and our translators appear to have held some similar notion. Gesenius imagined that the inner curtains of the Tabernacle are meant. But neither of these interpretations appears to be supported by a single ancient authority, nor can either of them be well reconciled with the expression, "to do service in the holy place" (xxxv. 19, xxxix. 1, 41). Cf. xxviii. 35.

The Penal Law of the Sabbath.

12—17. (xxxv. 2, 3.)

In the Fourth Commandment the injunction to observe the Seventh Day is addressed to the conscience of the people (see on xx. 8): in this place, the object is to declare an infraction of the Commandment to be a capital offence. The two passages stand in a relation to each other similar to that between Lev. xviii. xix. and Lev. xx. See note on Lev. xviii. 24.—Considering the weighty bearing of the Sabbath upon the Covenant between Jehovah and His people, a solemn sanction of its observance might well form the conclusion of the string of messages which Moses was to deliver on this occasion. But from the repetition of the substance of these verses in the beginning of ch. xxxv. it seems likely (as many commentators have observed) that the penal edict was specially introduced as a caution in reference to the construction of the Tabernacle, lest the people, in their zeal to carry on the work, should be tempted to break the divine Law for the observance of the Day. In this chapter, the edict immediately follows the series of directions given to Moses on Sinai for the work; in ch. xxxv. Moses utters it before he repeats any of the directions to the people.

13. *a sign between me and you*, &c.] Cf. *v.* 17: Ezek. xx. 12, 20. See on Exod. xx. 8.

14. *put to death*] This Law was very soon put into operation in the case of the man who gathered sticks upon the Sabbath-

but in the seventh *is* the sabbath of rest, † holy to the LORD: whosoever doeth *any* work in the sabbath day, he shall surely be put to death.

† Heb. *holiness.*

16 Wherefore the children of Israel shall keep the sabbath, to observe the sabbath throughout their generations, *for* a perpetual covenant.

17 It *is* a sign between me and the children of Israel for ever: for [c] *in* six days the LORD made heaven and earth, and on the seventh day he rested, and was refreshed.

c Gen. 1. 31. & 2. 2.

18 ¶ And he gave unto Moses, when he had made an end of communing with him upon mount Sinai, [d] two tables of testimony, tables of stone, written with the finger of God.

d Deut. 9. 10.

CHAPTER XXXII.

1 The people, in the absence of Moses, cause Aaron to make a calf. 7 God is angered thereby. 11 At the intreaty of Moses he is appeased. 15 Moses cometh down with the tables. 19 He breaketh them. 20 He destroyeth the calf. 22 Aaron's excuse for himself. 25 Moses causeth the idolaters to be slain. 30 He prayeth for the people.

AND when the people saw that Moses delayed to come down out of the mount, the people gathered themselves together unto Aaron, and said unto him, [a] Up, make us gods, which shall go before us; for *as for*

a Acts 7. 40.

---

day. Death was inflicted by stoning. Num. xv. 35.

cut off from among his people] This is distinctly assigned as a reason why the offender should, or might, be put to death. The passage seems to indicate the distinction between the meaning of the two expressions, *to be cut off from the people*, and *to be put to death*. He who was cut off from the people had, by his offence, put himself out of the terms of the Covenant, and was an outlaw. (See on Lev. xviii. 29.) On such, and on such alone, when the offence was one which affected the well-being of the nation, as it was in this case, death could be inflicted by the public authority.

17. *was refreshed*] Literally, *he took breath*. Cf. xxiii. 12; 2 S. xvi. 14. The application of the word to the Creator, which occurs nowhere else, is remarkable.

18. The directions for the construction of the Sanctuary and its furniture being ended, the Tables of Stone which represented the Covenant between Jehovah and His people, and which, when covered with the Mercy-seat were to give the Sanctuary its significance, are now delivered to Moses in accordance with the promise xxiv. 12; cf. xxxii. 15, 16.

The history of what relates to the construction of the Sanctuary is here interrupted, and is taken up again chap. xxxv. 1.

CHAP. XXXII.—XXXIV.

THE GOLDEN CALF. THE COVENANT AND THE TABLES BROKEN AND RENEWED.

The exact coherence of the narrative of all that immediately relates to the construction of the Sanctuary, if we pass on immediately from ch. xxxi. to ch. xxxv., might suggest the probability that these three chapters originally formed a distinct composition. This suggestion is in some degree strengthened, if we take account of some part of the subject matter of ch. xxxiv. (see on xxxiv. 12—27). But this need not involve the question of the Mosaic authorship of the three chapters. The main incidents recorded in them follow in due order of time, and are therefore in their proper place as regards historical sequence.

The Golden Calf, xxxii. 1—6.

The people had, to a great extent, lost the patriarchal faith, and were but imperfectly instructed in the reality of a personal unseen God. Being disappointed at the long absence of Moses, they seem to have imagined that he had deluded them and had probably been destroyed amidst the thunders of the mountain (xxiv. 15—18). They accordingly gave way to their superstitious fears and fell back upon that form of idolatry that was most familiar to them (see on *v.* 4). The narrative of the circumstances is more briefly given by Moses at a later period in one of his addresses to the people (Deut. ix. 8—21, 25—29, x. 1—5, 8—11). It is worthy of remark that Josephus, in his very characteristic chapter on the giving of the Law ('Ant.' III. 5), says nothing whatever of this act of apostasy, though he relates that Moses twice ascended the mountain, and renews his own profession that he is faithfully following the authority of the Holy Scriptures. Philo speaks of the calf as an imitation of the idolatry of Egypt, but he takes no notice of Aaron's share in the sin ('Vit. Mos.' III. 19. 37).

1. *unto Aaron*] The chief authority during the absence of Moses was committed to Aaron and Hur (xxiv. 14).

make us gods] The substantive (*elohim*) is plural in form and may denote *gods*. But according to the Hebrew idiom, the meaning need not be plural, and hence the word is used as the common designation of the true God (Gen. i. 1, &c. See on xxi. 6). It here denotes a god, and should be so rendered

this Moses, the man that brought us
up out of the land of Egypt, we wot
not what is become of him.
2 And Aaron said unto them, Break
off the golden earrings, which *are* in
the ears of your wives, of your sons,
and of your daughters, and bring *them*
unto me.
3 And all the people brake off the
golden earrings which *were* in their
ears, and brought *them* unto Aaron.
[b] Psal. 106. 19. 1 Kings 12. 28. 4 [b] And he received *them* at their
hand, and fashioned it with a graving
tool, after he had made it a molten
calf: and they said, These *be* thy
gods, O Israel, which brought thee
up out of the land of Egypt.
5 And when Aaron saw *it*, he built
an altar before it; and Aaron made
proclamation, and said, To morrow
is a feast to the LORD.
6 And they rose up early on the
morrow, and offered burnt offerings,
and brought peace offerings; and the
[c] people sat down to eat and to drink, [c] 1 Cor. 10. 7.
and rose up to play.
7 ¶ And the LORD said unto Moses,
[d] Go, get thee down; for thy [d] Deut. 9. 12.

(Saadia and most modern interpreters). It is evident that what the Israelites asked for was a visible god. Our version follows the LXX., Vulg., &c.

2. *Break off the golden earrings*] It has been very generally held from early times, that Aaron did not willingly lend himself to the mad design of the multitude; but that, when overcome by their importunity, he asked them to give up such possessions as he knew they would not willingly part with, in the hope of putting a check on them (Augustin. 'Quæst.' 141; Theodoret. 'Quæst.' 66). Assuming this to have been his purpose, he took a wrong measure of their fanaticism, for all the people made the sacrifice at once (*v.* 3). His weakness, in any case, was unpardonable and called for the intercession of Moses (Deut. ix. 20). According to a Jewish tradition found in the later Targums, Aaron was terrified by seeing Hur, his colleague in authority (xxiv. 14), slain by the people because he had ventured to oppose them.

4. *And he received...a molten calf*] The Hebrew is somewhat difficult. The following rendering represents the sense approved by most modern critics;—*and he received the gold at their hand and collected it in a bag and made it a molten calf* (Bochart, Gesenius, Rosenmüller, Fürst, Knobel, Kurtz, &c. with the later Targums). Our version is supported by the LXX., Onkelos, Luther, de Wette, Keil, &c. Other interpreters conceive the latter part of the passage to mean that Aaron *shaped the gold in a mould* (or, *after a pattern*) *and made it a molten calf* (Saadia, Syriac, Vulgate, Aben-Ezra, Michaelis, Zunz, Herx., &c.).

a molten calf] The word *calf* may mean a yearling ox. The Israelites must have been familiar with the ox-worship of the Egyptians; perhaps many of them had witnessed the rites of Mnevis at Heliopolis, almost on the borders of the Land of Goshen, and they could not have been unacquainted with the more famous rites of Apis at Memphis. It is expressly said that they yielded to the idolatry of Egypt while they were in bondage (Josh. xxiv. 14; Ezek. xx. 8, xxiii. 3, 8). The earliest Jewish tradition derives the golden calf from an Egyptian origin (Philo, 'Vit. Mos.' III. 19). It seems most likely that the idolatrous tendency of the people had been contracted from the Egyptians, but that it was qualified by what they still retained of the truths revealed to their forefathers. In the next verse, Aaron appears to speak of the calf as if it was a representative of Jehovah—"To-morrow is a feast to the LORD." They did not, it should be noted, worship a living Mnevis, or Apis, having a proper name, but only the golden type of the animal. The mystical notions connected with the ox by the Egyptian priests may have possessed their minds, and, when expressed in this modified and less gross manner, may have been applied to the LORD, who had really delivered them out of the hand of the Egyptians. Their sin then lay, not in their adopting another god, but in their pretending to worship a visible symbol of Him whom no symbol could represent. The close connection between the calves of Jeroboam and this calf is shewn by the repetition of the formula, "which brought thee up out of the land of Egypt" (1 Kings xii. 28).

These be thy gods] **This is thy god.** See on *v.* 1.

5. *a feast to the LORD*] See on *v.* 4.

6. See 1 Cor. x. 7). Hengstenberg, Kurtz and others have laid a stress upon the similarity of what is briefly described in the words, "the people sat down to eat and drink, and rose up to play," to certain rites of the Egyptians spoken of by Herodotus (II. 60. III. 27). But such orgies were too common amongst ancient idolaters for the remark to be of much worth.

The trial of Moses as a Mediator.

7—35.

The faithfulness of Moses in the office that had been entrusted to him was now to be put

people, which thou broughtest out of
the land of Egypt, have corrupted
themselves:
8 [e] They have turned aside quickly
out of the way which I commanded
them: they have made them a molten calf, and have worshipped it, and
have sacrificed thereunto, and said,
These *be* thy gods, O Israel, which
have brought thee up out of the land
of Egypt.
9 And the LORD said unto Moses,
[f] I have seen this people, and, behold,
it *is* a stiffnecked people:
10 Now therefore let me alone, that
my wrath may wax hot against them,
and that I may consume them: and I
will make of thee a great nation.
11 [g] And Moses besought [†] the
LORD his God, and said, LORD, why
doth thy wrath wax hot against thy
people, which thou hast brought forth
out of the land of Egypt with great
power, and with a mighty hand?
12 [h] Wherefore should the Egyptians speak, and say, For mischief
did he bring them out, to slay them
in the mountains, and to consume
them from the face of the earth?
Turn from thy fierce wrath, and repent of this evil against thy people.
13 Remember Abraham, Isaac, and
Israel, thy servants, to whom thou
swarest by thine own self, and saidst
unto them, [i] I will multiply your seed
as the stars of heaven, and all this
land that I have spoken of will I give
unto your seed, and they shall inherit
it for ever.
14 And the LORD repented of the
evil which he thought to do unto his
people.

[e] Deut. 9. 8.
[f] chap. 33. 3. Deut. 9. 13.
[g] Psal. 106. 23.
† Heb. *the face of the LORD.*
[h] Numb. 14. 13.
[i] Gen. 12. 7. & 15. 7. & 48. 16.

---

to the test. It was to be made manifest whether he loved his own glory better than he loved the brethren who were under his charge; whether he would prefer that he should himself become the founder of a "great nation," or that the LORD's promise should be fulfilled in the whole people of Israel. As in the trial of Abraham, the object to be attained was not that He who knows the hearts of all men might be assured that the servant whom He had chosen was true and stedfast, but that the faith of the servant might be strengthened and instructed, by its being made known to him what power had been given to him to resist temptation. This may have been especially needful for Moses, in consequence of his natural disposition. See Num. xii. 3; cf. Ex. iii. 11. With this trial of Moses may be compared the third temptation which the evil one was permitted to set before our Saviour. Matt. iv. 8—10.

Moses was tried in a twofold manner. The trial was at first based on the divine communication made to him in the mount respecting the apostasy of the people: on this occasion, he rejects the offer of glory for himself and intercedes for the nation; the exercise was a purely spiritual one, apart from visible fact, and no answer is given to his intercession (see on *v.* 14). But in the second case, stirred up as he was by the facts actually before his eyes, after he had unflinchingly carried out the judgment of God upon the persons of the obstinate idolaters, he not only again intercedes for the nation, but declares himself ready to sacrifice his own salvation for them (*v.* 32). It is thus that the hearts of God's saints in all ages are strengthened beforehand, by inward struggles that are witnessed by no human eye, to fight the battle when outward trials come upon them.—If the wonderful narrative in this passage should appear to any thoughtful reader incoherent or obscure, let him read it again and again and apply to it the key of his own spiritual experience.

On another occasion in the history, when the people had rebelled on account of the report of the ten spies, the trial of Moses' faithfulness was repeated in a very similar manner (Num. xiv. 11—23).

8. *These be thy gods...have brought*] **This is thy god, O Israel, who has brought—**

10. *let me alone*] But Moses did not let the LORD alone; he wrestled, as Jacob had done, until, like Jacob, he obtained the blessing (Gen. xxxii. 24).

12. *repent of this evil*] See on *v.* 14.

13. See Gen. xv. 5, 18, xxii. 17, xxxii. 12.

14. This states the fact that was not revealed to Moses till after his second intercession when he had come down from the mountain and witnessed the sin of the people (*vv.* 30—34). He was then assured that the Lord's love to His ancient people would prevail. God is said, in the language of Scripture, to repent, when his forgiving love is seen by man to blot out the letter of His judgments against sin (2 Sam. xxiv. 16; Joel ii. 13; Jonah iii. 10, &c.); or when the sin of man seems to human sight to have disappointed the purposes of grace (Gen. vi. 6; 1 Sam. xv. 35, &c.). As they exist in the

15 ¶ And Moses turned, and went
down from the mount, and the two
tables of the testimony *were* in his
hand: the tables *were* written on both
their sides; on the one side and on
the other *were* they written.
hap. 31. 16 And the [k] tables *were* the work
of God, and the writing *was* the writing of God, graven upon the tables.
17 And when Joshua heard the
noise of the people as they shouted,
he said unto Moses, *There is* a noise
of war in the camp.
18 And he said, *It is* not the voice
of *them that* shout for mastery, neither
is it the voice of *them that* cry for
Heb. [†] being overcome: *but* the noise of *them*
akness. *that* sing do I hear.
19 ¶ And it came to pass, as soon
as he came nigh unto the camp, that
he saw the calf, and the dancing: and
Moses' anger waxed hot, and he cast
the tables out of his hands, and brake
them beneath the mount.
Deut. 9. 20 [l] And he took the calf which they
had made, and burnt *it* in the fire, and
ground *it* to powder, and strawed *it*
upon the water, and made the children
of Israel drink *of it*.
21 And Moses said unto Aaron,
What did this people unto thee, that
thou hast brought so great a sin upon
them?
22 And Aaron said, Let not the
anger of my lord wax hot: thou
knowest the people, that they *are set*
on mischief.
23 For they said unto me, Make
us gods, which shall go before us: for
as for this Moses, the man that brought
us up out of the land of Egypt, we
wot not what is become of him.
24 And I said unto them, Whosoever hath any gold, let them break *it*
off. So they gave *it* me: then I cast
it into the fire, and there came out
this calf.
25 ¶ And when Moses saw that
the people *were* naked; (for Aaron
had made them naked unto *their* [†] Heb.
shame among [†] their enemies:) *those that rose up*
26 Then Moses stood in the gate *against them.*

Eternal Father, wrath and love are essentially ONE, however they may appear to thwart each other to carnal eyes. The awakened conscience is said *to repent*, when, having felt its sin, it feels also the divine forgiveness: it is at this crisis that God, according to the language of Scripture, repents towards the sinner. Thus the repentance of God made known in and through the One true Mediator reciprocates the repentance of the returning sinner, and reveals to him Atonement.

17, 18. Moses does not tell Joshua of the divine communication that had been made to him respecting the apostasy of the people, but only corrects his impression by calling his attention to the kind of noise which they are making.

19. Though Moses had been prepared by the revelation on the Mount, his righteous indignation was stirred up beyond control when the abomination was before his eyes.

20. We need not suppose that each incident is here placed in strict order of time. What is related in this verse must have occupied some time and may have followed the rebuke of Aaron. Moses appears to have thrown the calf into the fire to destroy its form and then to have pounded, or filed, the metal to powder, which he cast into the brook (Deut. ix. 21). He then made the Israelites drink of the water of the brook. The act was of course a symbolical one. The idol was brought to nothing and the people were made to swallow their own sin (cf. Mic. vii. 13, 14). It seems idle to speculate, as many interpreters have done (Rosenmüller, Davidson, Kurtz, &c.), on the means by which the comminution of the gold was effected.

21. Moses, in grave irony, asks Aaron whether the people had offended him in any way to induce him to inflict such an injury on them as to yield to their request.

22. *my lord*] The deference here shown to Moses by Aaron should be noticed. His reference to the character of the people, and his manner of stating what he had done (*v.* 24), are very characteristic of the deprecating language of a weak mind.

23. *Make us gods*] **Make us a god.**

25. *naked*] Rather, **unruly**, or *licentious*. So the LXX., Onk., Syriac, and nearly all critical authorities.

shame among their enemies] Cf. Ps. xliv. 13; Deut. xxviii. 37; Ps. lxxix. 4.

26—29.] The Tribe of Levi, Moses' own Tribe, now distinguished itself by immediately returning to its allegiance and obeying the call to fight on the side of Jehovah. We need not doubt that the 3000 who were slain were those who persisted in resisting Moses: we may perhaps conjecture that they were

of the camp, and said, Who *is* on the
LORD's side? *let him come* unto me.
And all the sons of Levi gathered
themselves together unto him.
27 And he said unto them, Thus
saith the LORD God of Israel, Put
every man his sword by his side, *and*
go in and out from gate to gate
throughout the camp, and slay every
man his brother, and every man his
companion, and every man his neighbour.
28 And the children of Levi did
according to the word of Moses: and
there fell of the people that day about
three thousand men.
29 ‖For Moses had said, †Conse-
crate yourselves to day to the LORD,
even every man upon his son, and
upon his brother; that he may bestow upon you a blessing this day.
30 ¶ And it came to pass on the
morrow, that Moses said unto the
people, Ye have sinned a great sin:
and now I will go up unto the LORD;
peradventure I shall make an atonement for your sin.
31 And Moses returned unto the
LORD, and said, Oh, this people have
sinned a great sin, and have made
them gods of gold.
32 Yet now, if thou wilt forgive
their sin—; and if not, blot me, I
pray thee, out of thy book which thou
hast written.
33 And the LORD said unto Moses,
Whosoever hath sinned against me,
him will I blot out of my book.
34 Therefore now go, lead the
people unto *the place* of which I have
spoken unto thee: behold, mine Angel
shall go before thee: nevertheless in
the day when I visit I will visit their
sin upon them.

‖ Or, *And Moses said, Consecrate yourselves to day to the LORD, because every man* hath been *against his son, and against his brother, &c.*
† Heb. *Fill your hands.*

---

such as contumaciously refused to drink of the water of the brook (*v.* 20). The spirit of the narrative forbids us to conceive that the act of the Levites was anything like an indiscriminate massacre. An amnesty had first been offered to all in the words, "Who is on the LORD's side?" Those who were forward to draw the sword were directed not to spare their closest relations or friends; but this must plainly have been with an understood qualification as regards the conduct of those who were to be slain. Had it not been so, they who were on the LORD's side would have had to destroy each other. We need not stumble at the bold, simple way in which the statement is made. The Bible does not deign to apologise for itself; and hence at times it affords occasion to gainsayers, who shut their eyes to the spirit while they are captiously looking at dissevered fragments of the letter.

29. *Consecrate yourselves to day to the LORD*] The margin contains the literal rendering. Our version gives the most probable meaning of the Hebrew (see Lev. viii. 22, 27), and is supported by the best authority. The Levites were to prove themselves in a special way the servants of Jehovah, in anticipation of their formal consecration as ministers of the Sanctuary, by manifesting a self-sacrificing zeal in carrying out the divine command, even upon their nearest relatives (cf. Deut. x. 8). Kurtz, adopting the rendering of the Targums, supposes that what the Levites were commanded to do was to offer sacrifices upon the Altar to expiate the blood which they were directed to shed. But this interpretation cannot be well reconciled with the Hebrew, and it is hard to imagine that expiation could be required for what was done in direct obedience to the command of the LORD. It may be added that the Sin-offering, the only kind of sacrifice that would be suitable on such a hypothesis, had not yet been instituted.

31. *returned unto the LORD*] *i.e.* he again ascended the Mount.

gods of gold] **a god of gold.**

32. For a similar form of expression, in which the conclusion is left to be supplied by the mind of the reader, see Dan. iii. 15; Luke xiii. 9, xix. 42; John vi. 62; Rom. ix. 22.—For the same thought, see Rom. ix. 3. It is for such as Moses and St Paul to realize, and to dare to utter, their readiness to be wholly sacrificed for the sake of those whom God has entrusted to their love. This expresses the perfected idea of the whole Burnt-offering.

thy book] The figure is taken from the enrolment of the names of citizens. This is its first occurrence in the Scriptures. See Ps. lxix. 28; Isa. iv. 3; Dan. xii. 1; Luke x. 20; Phil. iv. 3; Rev. iii. 5, &c.

33, 34. Each offender was to suffer for his own sin. On xx. 5 cf. Ezek. xviii. 4, 20. Moses was not to be taken at his word. He was to fulfil his appointed mission of leading on the people towards the Land of Promise.

34. *mine Angel shall go before thee*] See on xxiii. 20, and xxxiii. 3.

35 And the LORD plagued the
people, because they made the calf,
which Aaron made.

CHAPTER XXXIII.

1 *The Lord refuseth to go as he had promised with the people.* 4 *The people murmur thereat.* 7 *The tabernacle is removed out of the camp.* 9 *The Lord talketh familiarly with Moses.* 12 *Moses desireth to see the glory of God.*

AND the LORD said unto Moses,
Depart, *and* go up hence, thou
and the people which thou hast brought
up out of the land of Egypt, unto the
land which I sware unto Abraham, to
Isaac, and to Jacob, saying, [a] Unto [a] Gen. 12.
thy seed will I give it: 7.
2 [b] And I will send an angel before [b] Deut. 7.
thee; and I will drive out the Ca- 22.
naanite, the Amorite, and the Hittite, Josh. 24.
and the Perizzite, the Hivite, and the 11.
Jebusite:
3 Unto a land flowing with milk
and honey: for I will not go up in
the midst of thee; for thou *art* a [c] stiff- [c] chap. 32.
necked people: lest I consume thee 9.
in the way. Deut. 9. 13.

---

in the day when I visit, &c.] This has been supposed to refer to the sentence that was pronounced on the generation of Israelites then living, when they murmured on account of the report of the ten spies, that they should not enter the land (Num. xiv.). On that occasion they were charged with having tempted God "these ten times" (*v.* 22). But though the LORD visited the sin upon those who rebelled, yet He "repented of the evil which He thought to do unto His people." He chastised the individuals, but did not take His blessing from the nation.

35. *and the LORD*] **Thus Jehovah.**

CHAP. XXXIII.

The Conference between Jehovah and His mediator is continued in this Chapter. It had been conceded to Moses that the nation should not be destroyed (see xxxii. 10 sq.), and that he should lead them on towards the place of which the LORD had spoken (see xxxii. 34). But the favour was not to be awarded according to the terms of the original promise (xxiii. 20—23). The Covenant on which the promise was based had been broken by the people. Jehovah now therefore declared that though His Angel should go before Moses (xxxii. 34) and should drive out the heathen from the land, He would withhold His own favouring presence, *lest he should consume them in the way* (xxxiii. 2, 3). Thus were the people forcibly warned that His presence could prove a blessing to them only on condition of their keeping their part of the covenant (see on *v.* 3). If they failed in this, His presence would be to them "a consuming fire" (Deut. iv. 24). The people, when they heard the Divine message, mourned and humbled themselves, stripping off their accustomed ornaments in accordance with the command (*vv.* 4—6). Moses now appointed a religious service of a peculiar kind, dedicating a Tent pitched at some distance from the camp, as a meeting-place for Jehovah and himself (*vv.* 7—11). Here he again intercedes with persevering fervour until he obtains the answer, "My presence shall go with thee, and I will give thee rest" (*v.* 14; see note). He then dares to reason on this answer and to prove its necessity, as one man might discuss terms with another (*v.* 11). The answer is at last given in a still clearer and more gracious form: "I will do this thing also that thou hast spoken: for thou hast found grace in my sight, and I know thee by name" (*v.* 17). Having proved himself worthy of his calling as a mediator, both in vindicating the honour of Jehovah and in his self-sacrificing intercession with Jehovah for the nation, he is rewarded by a special vision of the Divine nature: Jehovah reveals Himself to him in His essential character to the utmost point that such revelation is possible to a finite being (*vv.* 18—23).

2. See on iii. 8.

3. *milk and honey*] See on iii. 8.

for I will not go up in the midst of thee] This is the awful qualification with which the possession of the promised Land might have been granted: Jehovah Himself was not to go before the people. According to the Targums, it was the *shekinah* that was to be withheld (see on xiv. 19, 20). Hengstenberg supposes that the Angel promised in xxiii. 20—23 was "the Angel of Jehovah," κατ' ἐξοχήν, the Second Person of the Trinity, in whom Jehovah was essentially present, the same whom Isaiah called "the Angel of His presence" (lxiii. 9) and Malachi, "the Angel of the Covenant" (iii. 1); but that the Angel here mentioned was an ordinary Angel, one commissioned for this service out of the heavenly host (Christology, Vol. I. p. 107). It should however be noted that this Angel is expressly spoken of as *the Angel of Jehovah* in xxxii. 34. But in whatever way we understand the mention of the Angel in this passage as compared with xxiii. 20, the meaning of the threat appears to be that the nation should be put on a level with other nations, to lose its character as the people in special covenant with Jehovah (see on *v.* 16).—On the name *Angel*

4 ¶ And when the people heard these evil tidings, they mourned: and no man did put on him his ornaments.
5 For the LORD had said unto Moses, Say unto the children of Israel, Ye *are* a stiffnecked people: I will come up into the midst of thee in a moment, and consume thee: therefore now put off thy ornaments from thee, that I may know what to do unto thee.
6 And the children of Israel stripped themselves of their ornaments by the mount Horeb.
7 And Moses took the tabernacle, and pitched it without the camp, afar off from the camp, and called it the Tabernacle of the congregation. And it came to pass, *that* every one which sought the LORD went out unto the tabernacle of the congregation, which *was* without the camp.
8 And it came to pass, when Moses went out unto the tabernacle, *that* all the people rose up, and stood every man *at* his tent door, and looked after Moses, until he was gone into the tabernacle.
9 And it came to pass, as Moses entered into the tabernacle, the cloudy pillar descended, and stood *at* the door

---

of Jehovah, see on Gen. ii. 1. Hengstenberg's arguments have been elaborately answered by Kurtz, 'Hist of O. C.' Vol. I. § 50 (2), and Vol. III. § 14 (3).

lest I consume thee in the way] See introd. note to this chap. St Augustine speaks of the mystery that Jehovah should declare Himself to be less merciful than His Angel (Quæst. 150). It would seem that the presence of Jehovah represented the Covenant with its penalties as well as its privileges. See preceding note.

4—6. See introd. note.

5. *I will come up...consume thee*] By far the greater number of versions put this conditionally; **If I were to go up for one moment in the midst of thee, I should consume thee** (see *v.* 3). This rendering seems best to suit the context. Our translators follow the earlier English versions, which are supported by the Syriac, Vulg. and Luther.

that I may know, &c.] **and I shall know** *by that* **what to do unto thee.** That is, by that sign of their repentance Jehovah would decide in what way they were to be punished.

6. *by the mount Horeb*] **from mount Horeb** *onwards*. The meaning, according to all the best authorities, appears to be that they ceased to wear their ornaments from the time they were at Mount Horeb.

The Temporary Tent of Meeting.

7—11.

7. *the tabernacle*] The original word signifies **the Tent.** The only word in the Old Testament which ought to be rendered *tabernacle* (*mishkān*) does not occur once in this narrative (see on xxvi. 1). What is here called The Tent has been understood in three different ways. It has been taken to denote:

1. The Tabernacle constructed according to the pattern showed to Moses in the Mount (our version and the earlier English ones, several Jewish authorities, Knobel, &c.). But if we are in any degree to respect the order of the narrative, the Tabernacle was not made until after the events here recorded (see xl. 2).

2. An old sanctuary, or sacred tent, which the Israelites had previously possessed (Michaelis, Rosenmüller, &c.). But it is incredible that such a structure should not have been spoken of elsewhere, had it existed.

3. A tent appointed for this temporary purpose by Moses, very probably the one in which he was accustomed to dwell. According to the Hebrew idiom, the article may stand for the possessive pronoun, and thus it is most likely that the right rendering is, *his tent*. This is by far the most satisfactory interpretation (LXX., Syriac, Jarchi, Aben-Ezra, Drusius, Grotius, Geneva French, Kurtz, Wogue, &c.).

pitched it without the camp, afar off from the camp] This tent was to be a place for meeting with Jehovah, like the Tabernacle which was about to be constructed. But in order that the people might feel that they had forfeited the Divine presence (see xxv. 8), **the Tent of meeting** (as it should be called, see on xxvii. 21, and Note at the end of Chap. xl.) was placed "afar off from the camp," and the Mediator and his faithful servant Joshua were alone admitted to it (*v.* 11).

8. *the tabernacle*] **the Tent.**

at his tent door] **at the entrance of his tent** (see on xxvi. 36). The people may have stood up either out of respect to Moses, or from doubt as to what was going to occur. But as soon as the cloudy pillar was seen, they joined in worship (*v.* 10).

9. *as Moses entered...talked with Moses*] "As Moses entered into **the Tent**, the cloudy

of the tabernacle, and *the* LORD talked
with Moses.
10 And all the people saw the cloudy
pillar stand *at* the tabernacle door:
and all the people rose up and worshipped, every man *in* his tent door.
11 And the LORD spake unto Moses
face to face, as a man speaketh unto
his friend. And he turned again into
the camp: but his servant Joshua, the
son of Nun, a young man, departed
not out of the tabernacle.
12 ¶ And Moses said unto the
LORD, See, thou sayest unto me, Bring
up this people: and thou hast not let
me know whom thou wilt send with
me. Yet thou hast said, I know thee
by name, and thou hast also found
grace in my sight.
13 Now therefore, I pray thee, if
I have found grace in thy sight, shew
me now thy way, that I may know
thee, that I may find grace in thy
sight: and consider that this nation
is thy people.
14 And he said, My presence shall
go *with thee*, and I will give thee
rest.
15 And he said unto him, If thy
presence go not *with me*, carry us not
up hence.
16 For wherein shall it be known
here that I and thy people have found
grace in thy sight? *is it* not in that
thou goest with us? so shall we be
separated, I and thy people, from all
the people that *are* upon the face of the
earth.
17 And the LORD said unto Moses,
I will do this thing also that thou hast
spoken: for thou hast found grace in
my sight, and I know thee by name.
18 And he said, I beseech thee,
shew me thy glory.

---

pillar **came down and stood at the entrance of the Tent and talked with Moses**" (LXX., Vulg., Onk., de Wette, Knobel, &c.). *The Cloudy pillar* is the proper nominative to the verb *talked* (cf. xiii. 21, xix. 9, xxiv. 16, xl. 35).

10. *the tabernacle door*] **the entrance of the Tent.**

rose up and worshipped] or, *began to worship.* The people by this act gave another proof of their penitence.

in his tent door] **at the entrance of his tent.**

11. *face to face*] The meaning of these words is limited by *v.* 20, see note; cf. also Num. xii. 8; Deut. iv. 12.

Joshua] See on xvii. 9.

the tabernacle] **the Tent.**

The Mediator is rewarded.

12—13.

12. *let me know whom thou wilt send with me*] Jehovah had just previously commanded Moses to lead on the people and had promised to send an Angel before him (*v.* 2, xxxii. 34). Moses was now anxious to know who the Angel was to be.

I know thee by name] The LORD had called him by his name, iii. 4; cf. Isa. xliii. 1, xlix. 1.

found grace] xxxii. 10, &c.

13. *thy way*] He desires not to be left in uncertainty, but to be assured, by Jehovah's mode of proceeding, of the reality of the promises that had been made to him.

14.] Ewald considers that this verse should be read interrogatively, "Must my presence go with thee, and shall I give thee rest?" This rendering may make the connection more simple; but it appears to be supported by no other authority. See on xxxiv. 9.

rest] This was the common expression for the possession of the promised Land. Deut. iii. 20; Josh. i. 13, 15, xxii. 4, &c.; cf. Heb. iv. 8.

15, 16] Moses would have preferred that the people should forego the possession of the Land and remain in the wilderness, if they were to be deprived of the presence of Jehovah, as the witness for the Covenant, according to the original promise. It was this which alone **distinguished** (rather than "separated") them from other nations, and which alone would render the Land of Promise a home to be desired.

17. Cf. *v.* 13. His petition for the nation, and his own claims as a mediator, are now granted to the full.

18. *shew me thy glory*] The faithful servant of Jehovah, now assured by the success of his mediation, yearns, with the proper tendency of a devout spirit, for a more intimate communion with his Divine Master than he had yet enjoyed. He seeks for something surpassing all former revelations. He had talked with the LORD "face to face as a man speaketh unto his friend" (*v.* 11; cf. Deut. xxxiv. 10), but it was in the Cloudy pillar: he, and the people with him, had seen "the glory of the LORD," but it was in the form of "devouring fire" (xvi. 7. 10, xxiv. 16, 17):

19 And he said, I will make all
my goodness pass before thee, and I
will proclaim the name of the LORD
before thee; [d]and will be gracious to [d] Rom. 9. 15.
whom I will be gracious, and will shew
mercy on whom I will shew mercy.
20 And he said, Thou canst not see
my face: for there shall no man see
me, and live.
21 And the LORD said, Behold,
there is a place by me, and thou shalt
stand upon a rock:
22 And it shall come to pass, while
my glory passeth by, that I will put
thee in a clift of the rock, and will
cover thee with my hand while I pass
by:
23 And I will take away mine hand,
and thou shalt see my back parts: but
my face shall not be seen.

CHAPTER XXXIV.

1 *The tables are renewed.* 5 *The name of the LORD proclaimed.* 8 *Moses intreateth God to go with them.* 10 *God maketh a covenant with them, repeating certain duties of the first table.* 28 *Moses after forty days in the mount cometh down with the tables.* 29 *His face shineth, and he covereth it with a vail.*

AND the LORD said unto Moses,
[a]Hew thee two tables of stone [a] Deut. 10. 1.
like unto the first: and I will write
upon *these* tables the words that were
in the first tables, which thou brakest.
2 And be ready in the morning,
and come up in the morning unto

---

he had even beheld the "similitude" of the LORD in a mystical sense (Num. xii. 8). But he asks now to behold the face of Jehovah in all its essential glory, neither veiled by a cloud nor represented by an Angel.

19, 20] But his request could not be granted in accordance with the conditions of human existence. The glory of the Almighty in its fulness is not to be revealed to the eye of man. A further revelation of the Divine goodness was however possible. Jehovah was to reveal Himself as the gracious One, whose mercy in forgiving iniquity included, and brought into harmony, all the claims of justice (xxxiv. 6, 7; see on xxxii. 14). The promise here given was to be fulfilled on the morrow, when the mediator was to receive the twofold reward of his spiritual wrestling; the covenant was to be renewed with the nation according to its original terms, and he himself was to be permitted to penetrate more deeply into the mysteries of the Divine nature than had ever before been granted to mortal man.

It was vouchsafed to St Paul, as it had been to Moses, to have special "visions and revelations of the Lord" (2 Cor. xii. 1—4). He was "caught up into the third heaven" and heard "unspeakable words which it is not *possible* for a man to utter." But he had, also like Moses, to find the narrow reach of the intellect of man in the region of Godhead. It was long after he had heard the unspeakable words in Paradise that he spoke of the Lord as dwelling "in the light which no man can approach unto, whom no man hath seen nor can see" (1 Tim. vi. 16). He knew of the Mediator greater than Moses (Heb. iii. 5, 6), who being "in the bosom of the Father" had declared Him in a higher sense than He had been declared to Moses, but still it remains true that "no man hath seen God at any time" (John i. 18). However intimate may be our communion with the Holy One, we are still, as long as we are in the flesh, "to see through a glass darkly," waiting for the time when we shall see, with no figure of speech, "face to face" (1 Cor. xiii. 12). Then we know "that we shall be like him, for we shall see him as he is" (1 John iii. 2). It was in a tone of aspiration lower than that of Moses or St Paul, that St Philip said, "Lord, shew us the Father" (John xiv. 8).

19. *will be gracious to whom I will be gracious, and will shew mercy on whom I will shew mercy*] Jehovah declares His own will to be the ground of the grace which He is going to shew the nation. St Paul applies these words to the election of Jacob in order to overthrow the self-righteous boasting of the Jews (Rom. ix. 15).

20. Cf. xix. 21. Such passages as this being clearly in accordance with what we know of the relation of spiritual existence to the human senses, shew how we are to interpret the expressions "face to face" (*v.* 11), "mouth to mouth" (Num. xii. 8), and others of the like kind. See especially xxiv. 10, 11; Isa. vi. 1; and cf. John xiv. 9.

21—23.] The conjectures and traditions on the place of this vision, inconclusive as they must be, are given by Robinson, 'Bib. Res.' Vol. I. p. 153.

CHAP. XXXIV.

The Covenant and the Tables are renewed—The second revelation of the Divine Name to Moses.

1—10.

1. *Hew thee*] See *v.* 4. The former tables are called "the work of God," xxxii. 16.

the words that were in the first tables, which thou brakest] These were "the words

mount Sinai, and present thyself there
to me in the top of the mount.
3 And no man shall [b]come up with
thee, neither let any man be seen
throughout all the mount; neither let
the flocks nor herds feed before that
mount.
4 ¶ And he hewed two tables of
stone like unto the first; and Moses
rose up early in the morning, and went
up unto mount Sinai, as the LORD had
commanded him, and took in his hand
the two tables of stone.
5 And the LORD descended in the
cloud, and stood with him there, and
proclaimed the name of the LORD.

[b] chap. 19. 12.

6 And the LORD passed by before
him, and proclaimed, The LORD, The
LORD God, merciful and gracious,
longsuffering, and abundant in goodness and truth,
7 Keeping mercy for thousands,
forgiving iniquity and transgression
and sin, and that will by no means
clear *the guilty*; [c]visiting the iniquity
of the fathers upon the children, and
upon the children's children, unto the
third and to the fourth *generation*.
8 And Moses made haste, and
bowed his head toward the earth, and
worshipped.
9 And he said, If now I have found

[c] chap. 20. 5. Deut. 5. 9. Jer. 32. 18.

---

of the covenant, the ten commandments" (*v.* 28); see Deut. iv. 13, ix. 10, 11, x. 1, 4, and especially Deut. v. 6—22. These passages would seem to leave no room for doubt that what we recognize as the Ten Commandments were inscribed on the second as well as the first pair of Tables. But Göthe, in one of his early works, started the notion that what was written on these Tables was the string of precepts, which may be reckoned as Ten, contained in this chap. *vv.* 12—26. Falsely regarding the Mosaic Covenant as essentially narrow and exclusive, he could not see how an expression of universal morality like the Ten Commandments of Ex. xx. could possibly have formed its basis. Hitzig has taken a similar view. Hengstenberg ('Pent.' Vol. II. p. 31) and Kurtz ('Old Cov.' III. 182) have answered Hitzig at length.—Ewald holds that the Tables mentioned in this verse contained the original Ten Commandments, but that the tables spoken of in *v.* 28 were distinct ones, on which Moses engraved this string of precepts. But this seems an utterly gratuitous supposition.

3. These are similar to the instructions given on the first occasion. See xix. 12, 13.

6, 7. This was the second revelation of the name of the God of Israel to Moses. The first revelation was of Jehovah as the self-existent One, who purposed to deliver His people with a mighty hand (iii. 14); this was of the same Jehovah as a loving Saviour who was now forgiving their sins. The two ideas that mark these revelations are found combined, apart from their historical development, in the Second Commandment, where the Divine unity is shewn on its practical side, in its relation to human obligations (cf. xxxiv. 14). Both in the Commandment and in this passage, the Divine Love is associated with the Divine Justice; but in the former there is a transposition to serve the proper purpose of the Commandments, and the Justice stands before the Love. This is strictly the legal arrangement, brought out in the completed system of the ceremonial Law, in which the Sin-offering, in acknowledgment of the sentence of Justice against sin, was offered before the Burnt-offering and the Peace-offering (see pref. to Leviticus). But in this place the truth appears in its essential order; the retributive Justice of Jehovah is subordinated to, rather it is made a part of, His forgiving Love (see on xxxii. 14). The visitation of God, whatever form it may wear, is in all ages working out purposes of Love towards all His children. The diverse aspects of the Divine nature, to separate which is the tendency of the unregenerate mind of man and of all heathenism, are united in perfect harmony in the Lord Jehovah, of whom the saying is true in all its length and breadth, "God is love" (1 Joh. iv. 8). It was the sense of this in the degree to which it was now revealed to him that caused Moses to bow his head and worship (*v.* 8). But the perfect revelation of the harmony was reserved for the fulness of time when "the Lamb slain from the foundation of the world" was made known to us in the flesh as both our Saviour and our Judge.—Moses quotes the words here pronounced to him in his supplication after the rebellion that arose from the report of the ten spies (Num. xiv. 18).

9. Moses had been assured of the pardon of the people and the perfect restoration of the Covenant (xxxiii. 14, 17): he had just had revealed to him, in a most distinguished manner, the riches of the Divine forgiveness. Yet now, in the earnest travail of his spirit, he supplicates for a repetition of the promise, adding the emphatic petition, that Jehovah would take Israel for his own inheritance (ch. xv. 17). This yearning struggle after assurance

grace in thy sight, O Lord, let my
Lord, I pray thee, go among us; for
it *is* a stiffnecked people; and pardon
our iniquity and our sin, and take us
for thine inheritance.
d Deut. 5. 2. 10 ¶ And he said, Behold, [d] I
make a covenant: before all thy people I will do marvels, such as have
not been done in all the earth, nor in
any nation: and all the people among
which thou *art* shall see the work of
the LORD: for it *is* a terrible thing
that I will do with thee.
11 Observe thou that which I
command thee this day: behold, I
drive out before thee the Amorite,
and the Canaanite, and the Hittite,
and the Perizzite, and the Hivite,
and the Jebusite.
e chap. 23. 32. Deut. 7. 2. 12 [e] Take heed to thyself, lest thou
make a covenant with the inhabitants
of the land whither thou goest, lest
it be for a snare in the midst of thee:
13 But ye shall destroy their altars,
† Heb. *statues*. break their † images, and cut down
their groves:
14 For thou shalt worship no other
god: for the LORD, whose name *is*
f chap. 20. 5. Jealous, *is* a [f] jealous God:
15 Lest thou make a covenant
with the inhabitants of the land, and
they go a whoring after their gods, and
do sacrifice unto their gods, and *one*
call thee, and thou eat of his sacrifice;
16 And thou take of [g] their daugh- g 1 Kings 11. 2.
ters unto thy sons, and their daugh-
ters go a whoring after their gods,
and make thy sons go a whoring after
their gods.
17 Thou shalt make thee no molten gods.
18 ¶ The feast of [h] unleavened h chap. 23. 15.
bread shalt thou keep. Seven days
thou shalt eat unleavened bread, as I
commanded thee, in the time of the
month Abib: for in the [i] month Abib i chap. 13. 4.
thou camest out from Egypt.
19 [k] All that openeth the matrix *is* k chap. 22. 29.
mine; and every firstling among thy Ezek. 44. 30.
cattle, *whether* ox or sheep, *that is male*.
20 But the firstling of an ass thou
shalt redeem with a ‖ lamb: and if ‖ Or, *kid*.
thou redeem *him* not, then shalt thou
break his neck. All the firstborn of
thy sons thou shalt redeem. And
none shall appear before me [l] empty. l chap. 23. 15.
21 ¶ [m] Six days thou shalt work, m chap. 23. 12.
but on the seventh day thou shalt Deut. 5. 12.
rest: in earing time and in harvest Luke 13. 14.
thou shalt rest.

---

is like the often-repeated utterance of the heart, when it receives a blessing beyond its hopes, "can this be real?" These words of Moses wonderfully commend themselves to the experience of the prayerful spirits of all ages.—A hint may perhaps be gathered from this verse in favour of reading the verbs in xxxiii. 14 (see note) affirmatively rather than interrogatively.

10. *marvels*] These marvels are explained in the following verse. Cf. Deut. vii. 1, &c.

Conditions of the Covenant.

11—27.

11. The names of the nations are the same as occur in the first promise to Moses in iii. 8.

12—27. The precepts contained in these verses are, for the most part, identical in substance with some of those which follow the Ten Commandments and are recorded in "the Book of the Covenant" (xx.—xxiii.; see xxiv. 7). Such a selection of precepts in this place, connected with the account of the restored Covenant and the new Tables, may tend to support the probability that chapters xxxii., xxxiii., xxxiv. originally formed a distinct composition. See introd. note to xxxii.

12. See on xxiii. 32, 33.

13. See on xxiii. 24.

cut down their groves] See Note at the end of the Chap.

14. See on xx. 5.

15, 16] An expansion of *v.* 12 (cf. Deut. xxxi. 16). The unfaithfulness of the nation to its Covenant with Jehovah is here for the first time spoken of as a breach of the marriage bond. The metaphor is, in any case, a natural one, but it seems to gain point, if we suppose it to convey an allusion to the abominations connected with heathen worship, such as are spoken of Num. xxv. 1—3. Cf Lev. xvii. 7, xx. 5, 6; Num. xiv. 33.

15. *eat of his sacrifice*] See Num. xxv. 2.

17. *molten*] See on xx. 4.

18. See xxiii. 15.

19. See on xiii. 2, 12 and Lev. xxvii. 26.

20. See xiii. 13.

shall appear before me empty] See xxiii. 15.

21. See xx. 9, xxiii. 12. There is here added to the Commandment a particular cau-

[n] chap. 23. 16. 22 ¶ [n] And thou shalt observe the
feast of weeks, of the firstfruits of
wheat harvest, and the feast of in-
† Heb. *revolution of the year.* gathering at the † year's end.
[o] chap. 23. 14, 17. Deut. 16. 16. 23 ¶ [o] Thrice in the year shall all
your men children appear before the
Lord God, the God of Israel.
24 For I will cast out the nations
before thee, and enlarge thy borders: neither shall any man desire
thy land, when thou shalt go up to
appear before the LORD thy God
thrice in the year.
[p] chap. 23. 18. 25 [p] Thou shalt not offer the blood
of my sacrifice with leaven; neither
shall the sacrifice of the feast of the
passover be left unto the morning.
26 The first of the firstfruits of
thy land thou shalt bring unto the
house of the LORD thy God. Thou
[q] chap. 23. 19. Deut. 14. 21. shalt not seethe a [q] kid in his mother's milk.
27 And the LORD said unto Moses,
[r] Deut. 4. 13. Write thou [r] these words: for after
the tenor of these words I have made
a covenant with thee and with Israel.
28 [s] And he was there with the [s] chap. 24. 18. Deut. 9. 9.
LORD forty days and forty nights;
he did neither eat bread, nor drink
water. And he wrote upon the tables
the words of the covenant, the ten
† commandments. † Heb. *words.*
29 ¶ And it came to pass, when
Moses came down from mount Sinai
with the two tables of testimony in
Moses' hand, when he came down
from the mount, that Moses wist not
that the skin of his face shone while
he talked with him.
30 And when Aaron and all the
children of Israel saw Moses, behold,
the skin of his face shone; and they
were afraid to come nigh him.
31 And Moses called unto them;
and Aaron and all the rulers of the
congregation returned unto him: and
Moses talked with them.
32 And afterward all the children of
Israel came nigh: and he gave them
in commandment all that the LORD
had spoken with him in mount
Sinai.

---

tion respecting those times of year when the land calls for most labour.—The old verb *to ear* (*i.e.* to plough) is genuine English. Though it appears to be cognate with the Latin *arare*, it is certainly not derived from it. The English verb is found Gen. xlv. 6, in Shakespeare ('Rich. II.' III. 2; 'Ant. and Cleo.' I. 4), and elsewhere.

22. See xxiii. 16.

23. See xxiii. 14, 17.

24. *for I will cast out*] See xxiii. 23.

enlarge thy borders] See xxiii. 31; Deut. xii. 20.

neither shall any man desire, &c.] This is the only place in which the promise is given to encourage such as might fear the consequences of obeying the Divine Law in attending to their religious duties. But cf. xxiii. 27.

25, 26.] See xxiii. 18, 19.

27. *Write thou*] Moses is here commanded to make a record in his own writing of the preceding precepts (see on *vv.* 12—27). The Book of the Covenant was written in like manner (xxiv. 4, 7).—On the words "he wrote," in the next verse, see note.

Moses receives the New Tables, comes down from the Mount, and converses with the people.

28—35.

28. Cf. xxiv. 18.

he wrote] According to Hebrew usage, the name of Jehovah *may* be the subject of the verb; that it must be so, is evident from *v.* 1. Cf. xxxii. 16.

29. *the two tables of testimony*] Cf. xxxi. 18.

the skin of his face shone] Cf. Matt. xvii. 2. The brightness of the Eternal Glory, though Moses had witnessed it only in a modified manner (xxxiii. 22, 23), was so reflected in his face, that Aaron and the people were stricken with awe and feared to approach him until he gave them words of encouragement. The Hebrew verb *kāran*, to *shine*, is connected through a simple metaphor with *keren*, a *horn;* and hence Aquila and the Vulgate have rendered the verb *to be horned.* The latter part of the verse in the Vulg. is, *et ignorabat quod cornuta esset facies sua ex consortio sermonis Domini.* From this use of the word *cornuta* has arisen the popular representation of Moses with horns on his forehead.

33—35. St Paul refers to this passage as shewing forth the glory of the Law, though it was but a "ministration of condemnation," and was to be done away, in order to enhance the glory of the Gospel, "the ministration of the spirit," which is concealed by no vail from the eyes of believers, and is to last for ever (2 Cor. iii. 7—15).

33 And *till* Moses had done speaking with them, he put [t] a vail on his
face.

[t] 2 Cor. 3. 13.

34 But when Moses went in before the LORD to speak with him, he
took the vail off, until he came out.
And he came out, and spake unto
the children of Israel *that* which he
was commanded.

35 And the children of Israel saw
the face of Moses, that the skin of
Moses' face shone: and Moses put
the vail upon his face again, until he
went in to speak with him.

---

33. *And till Moses had done*] Our translators give what may seem to be the easiest sense of the original by supplying the word *till*. But the Hebrew rather requires that **when**, not *till*, should be inserted; and this agrees better with *v.* 35 (so the LXX., Vulg., the Targums, Syriac, Saadia, and nearly all modern versions, not excepting Luther and Cranmer). If we adopt this rendering, Moses did not wear the vail when he was speaking to the people, but when he was silent. See on *v.* 35.

34. *Moses went in*] *i.e.* to the Tent of meeting.

35. Our version accords with the Hebrew and all the ancient versions, except the Vulgate, which has this remarkable rendering, for which it is difficult to account unless we may suppose it to represent a different reading in the original:—*videbant faciem egredientis Moysi esse cornutam; sed operiebat ille rursus faciem suam, siquando loquebatur ad eos.* It has been suggested that if we may imagine St Paul to have had such a reading in his mind, it would simplify the use he makes of the passage in 2 Cor. iii. 12—15. But it is not necessary to resort to any such supposition, since St Paul's application of the narrative may be well explained as referring to the simple fact that it was distinctive of the old dispensation that a vail should conceal the glory. There was no occasion to notice the particular that Moses did not wear the vail just in the act of speaking.

NOTE ON CHAP. XXXIV. 13.

THE GROVES.

This is the first reference to what is commonly known as grove-worship. The original word for *grove* in this connection is אֲשֵׁרָה (*ashērāh*), a different one from that so rendered in Gen. xxi. 33 (אֵשֶׁל, *ēshel*). Our translators have followed the sense given in most of the passages in which the word occurs by the LXX., Vulg., and Saadia, and which has been adopted by most Jewish authorities, by Luther, and other modern translators. It was supposed that what the Law commands is the destruction of groves dedicated to the worship of false deities. The allusions to such groves in classical writers are familiar enough. The connection of sacred groves and trees with the worship of the powers of nature may be traced very generally amongst the ancient nations of Asia and Europe (see Humboldt, 'Cosmos,' Vol. II. p. 95, Sabine's translation). But there appear to be insuperable difficulties in the way of thus rendering *ashērāh*. Since the times of Selden and Spencer most critics have taken the word to denote either a personal goddess or some symbolical representation of one.

The following conclusions seem to be fairly deduced from the references to the subject in the Old Testament:

(1) According to the most probable derivation of the name the *ashērāh* represented something that was upright, which was fixed, or planted, in the ground; hence, if it was not a tree, it must have been some sort of upright pillar or monument.

(2) It was formed of wood, and when it was destroyed it was cut down and burned (Deut. vii. 5; Judg. vi. 25, 26; 2 K. xxiii. 6, 15). It might be made of any sort of wood. See note on Deut. xvi. 21.

(3) That it could not be a grove appears from an *ashērāh* having been set up "under every green tree" in Judah in the time of Rehoboam (1 K. xiv. 23), and in Israel in the time of Hoshea (2 K. xvii. 10); from an *ashērāh idol* (not "an idol in a grove," as it stands in our version) having been destroyed and burnt near the brook Kidron by Asa (1 K. xv. 13; 2 Chr. xv. 16); and from a carved image of *the ashērāh* having been set up in the Temple by Manasseh (2 K. xxi. 7), which was brought out by Josiah and burnt and stamped to powder (2 K. xxiii. 6).

The worship of *ashērāh* is found associated with that of Baal (Judg. iii. 7; 1 K. xviii. 19, 2 K. xxi. 3; xxiii. 4), like that of Astarte, or *Ashtoreth* (עַשְׁתֹּרֶת) (Judg. ii. 13, x. 6; 1 S. vii. 4). Hence it has been inferred by de Wette and others that *Ashērāh* was another name for Astarte. This opinion might seem to be countenanced by the LXX. in

2 Chron. xv. 16 (where the Vulgate has *simulacrum Priapi*), and by the Vulgate in Judg. iii. 7. But it has been proved that the words have no etymological connection with each other, and are not likely to have had the same denotation. Movers, resting his main argument upon 2 K. xxiii. 13—15, conceived them to be the names of two distinct deities. On the whole, the most probable result of the inquiry seems to be that while Astarte was the personal name of the goddess, the *ashērāh* was a symbol of her, probably in some one of her characters, wrought in wood in some conventional form. If we suppose it to have symbolized her as a goddess of nature, the conjecture that its form resembled that of the sacred tree of the Assyrians, with which we have become familiar from the monuments of Nineveh[1] (see Fergusson, 'Nineveh and Persepolis,' p. 299), gains something in probability.

It has been supposed, on what seems to be good ground, that the image, or rather **pillar** (מַצֵּבָה, *matzēvāh*), spoken of here and elsewhere in the same connection, was a stone pillar, set up in honour of Baal, as the *Ashērāh* was a wooden pillar, set up in honour of Astarte (1 K. xiv. 23; 2 K. xvii. 10, xviii. 4, &c.). But Gesenius rightly observes that these monuments may have lost in later times their original meaning as regards Baal and Astarte, as the *hermæ* of the Greeks did in regard to Hermes. They probably became connected with a debased and superstitious worship of Jehovah, like the figure of the calf (see on xxxii. 4). This perhaps explains the need of the prohibition that an *ashērāh* should be placed near the Altar of Jehovah. See Deut. xvi. 21. (Selden, 'de Diis Syr.' p. 343 sq.; Spencer, 'de Leg. Heb.' lib. II. c. xxvii. §1; Gesenius, 'Thes.' and 'Handwörterbuch,' s.v.; Fürst, 'Lex.' s. v.; Movers, 'Phönizier,' I. p. 560; Keil on 1 Kings xiv. 23.)

[1] It has been conjectured from the sculptured figures that this was an upright stock which was adorned at festive seasons with boughs, flowers, and ribbons. Such might have been the *ashērāh*.

CHAPTER XXXV.

1 *The sabbath.* 4 *The free gifts for the tabernacle.* 20 *The readiness of the people to offer.* 30 *Bezaleel and Aholiab are called to the work.*

AND Moses gathered all the congregation of the children of Israel together, and said unto them,
These *are* the words which the LORD
hath commanded, that *ye* should do
them.
2 [a] Six days shall work be done, (a chap. 20. 9. Lev. 23. 3. Deut. 5. 12. Luke 13. 14.)
but on the seventh day there shall be
to you † an holy day, a sabbath of rest († Heb. *holiness.*)
to the LORD: whosoever doeth work
therein shall be put to death.
3 Ye shall kindle no fire throughout
your habitations upon the sabbath day.
4 ¶ And Moses spake unto all the
congregation of the children of Israel,
saying, This *is* the thing which the
LORD commanded, saying,
5 Take ye from among you an of-
fering unto the LORD: [b] whosoever *is* (b chap. 25. 2.)
of a willing heart, let him bring it, an
offering of the LORD; gold, and silver, and brass,
6 And blue, and purple, and scarlet,
and fine linen, and goats' *hair*,
7 And rams' skins dyed red, and
badgers' skins, and shittim wood,
8 And oil for the light, and spices
for anointing oil, and for the sweet
incense,
9 And onyx stones, and stones to
be set for the ephod, and for the
breastplate.
10 And every wise hearted among
you shall come, and make all that the
LORD hath commanded;
11 [c] The tabernacle, his tent, and (c chap. 26. 31.)
his covering, his taches, and his boards,
his bars, his pillars, and his sockets,

CHAP. XXXV. The narrative of what relates to the construction of the Sanctuary is now resumed from xxxi. 18.

Moses delivers to the people the messages on the supply of materials for the Sanctuary.

1—19.

1. Moses here addresses the whole people. See xxv. 1; cf. on Lev. viii. 3. On *v.* 2 see on xxxi. 12.

3. This prohibition is here first distinctly expressed, but it is implied xvi. 23.

10. *wise hearted*] See on xxviii. 3.

11. See on xxvi. 1—37. It has been already observed that in the instructions for making the Sanctuary, the Ark of the Covenant, as the principal thing belonging to it, is mentioned first; but in the practical order of the work, as it is here arranged, the

12 The ark, and the staves thereof,
with the mercy seat, and the vail of
the covering,
13 The table, and his staves, and
all his vessels, and the shewbread,
14 The candlestick also for the
light, and his furniture, and his lamps,
with the oil for the light,
[d] chap. 30. 1. 15 [d] And the incense altar, and his
staves, and the anointing oil, and the
sweet incense, and the hanging for
the door at the entering in of the
tabernacle,
[e] chap. 27. 1. 16 [e] The altar of burnt offering,
with his brasen grate, his staves, and
all his vessels, the laver and his foot,
17 The hangings of the court, his
pillars, and their sockets, and the
hanging for the door of the court,
18 The pins of the tabernacle, and
the pins of the court, and their cords,
19 The cloths of service, to do
service in the holy *place*, the holy
garments for Aaron the priest, and
the garments of his sons, to minister
in the priest's office.
20 ¶ And all the congregation of
the children of Israel departed from
the presence of Moses.
21 And they came, every one whose
heart stirred him up, and every one
whom his spirit made willing, *and*
they brought the LORD's offering to
the work of the tabernacle of the congregation, and for all his service, and
for the holy garments.
22 And they came, both men and
women, as many as were willing
hearted, *and* brought bracelets, and
earrings, and rings, and tablets, all
jewels of gold: and every man that
offered *offered* an offering of gold unto
the LORD.
23 And every man, with whom
was found blue, and purple, and
scarlet, and fine linen, and goats' *hair*,
and red skins of rams, and badgers'
skins, brought *them*.
24 Every one that did offer an offering of silver and brass brought the
LORD's offering: and every man, with
whom was found shittim wood for any
work of the service, brought *it*.
25 And all the women that were

Tabernacle with its Tent and covering come first. See on xxv. 10—16.

12. On the Ark and the Mercy Seat, see on xxv. 10—22.

the vail of the covering] The second Hebrew word is not the same as that in the preceding verse, which is rendered *covering*, and denotes the Covering of the Tent (see on xxvi. 14): but it is the one used for the entrance curtains (see on xxvi. 36, xxvii. 16). The same phrase occurs Ex. xxxv. 12, xl. 21; Num. iv. 5.

13, 14. See on xxv. 23—38.

15. *the incense altar*] See on xxx. 1

the anointing oil] See on xxx. 22—33.

the sweet incense] See on xxx. 34—38.

the hanging for the door] **the entrance curtain.** See on xxvi. 36, xxvii. 16.

16. *the altar of burnt offering*] See on xxvii. 1—8.

the laver] See on xxx. 18—21.

17. See on xxvii. 9—18.

18. These were the tent-pins and cords of the Tent of the Tabernacle and those of the pillars of the Court. See Note at the end of Ch. xxvi. The word *Tabernacle* (*mishkān*) is here used for the full name, **the Tabernacle of the Tent of meeting** (see xl. 2, 6, 29, note on xxvi. 1, &c.). It denotes the entire structure.

19. *the cloths of service to do service in the holy place*] Rather;—**the garments of office to do service in the Sanctuary,** &c. See on xxxi. 10.

21. See on xxv. 2.

22. *bracelets*] Rather, **brooches.**

earrings] The Hebrew word signifies a ring, either for the nose (Prov. xi. 22; Isa. iii. 21) or for the ear (xxxii. 2; Gen. xxxv. 4; Judg. viii. 24). That ear-rings, not nose-rings, as some have imagined, are here meant is confirmed by what we know of early Hebrew and Egyptian customs. See Gen. xxxv. 4; Wilkinson, 'Pop. Acc.' I. p. 145, II. p. 338.

rings] **signet rings.**

tablets] It is not certain what the Hebrew word denotes. Gesenius and others have taken it for *gold beads;* but Fürst, with more probability, for **armlets**, in accordance with the Ancient Versions. It is most likely that all the articles mentioned in this verse were of gold. The indulgence of private luxury was thus given up for the honour of the LORD. Cf. xxxviii. 8.

23, 24. See on xxv. 3, 4, 5.

25. See on xxv. 4.

wise hearted did spin with their hands,
and brought that which they had spun,
both of blue, and of purple, *and* of
scarlet, and of fine linen.
26 And all the women whose heart
stirred them up in wisdom spun goats'
hair.
27 And the rulers brought onyx
stones, and stones to be set, for the
ephod, and for the breastplate;
chap. 30. 23. 28 And [f]spice, and oil for the light,
and for the anointing oil, and for the
sweet incense.
29 The children of Israel brought
a willing offering unto the LORD,
every man and woman, whose heart
made them willing to bring for all
manner of work, which the LORD
had commanded to be made by the
hand of Moses.
30 ¶ And Moses said unto the
chap. 31. 2. children of Israel, See, [g]the LORD
hath called by name Bezaleel the son
of Uri, the son of Hur, of the tribe of
Judah;
31 And he hath filled him with the
spirit of God, in wisdom, in understanding, and in knowledge, and in all
manner of workmanship;
32 And to devise curious works, to
work in gold, and in silver, and in brass,
33 And in the cutting of stones,
to set *them*, and in carving of wood,
to make any manner of cunning work.
34 And he hath put in his heart
that he may teach, *both* he, and Aholiab, the son of Ahisamach, of the
tribe of Dan.
35 Them hath he filled with wisdom of heart, to work all manner of
work, of the engraver, and of the
cunning workman, and of the embroiderer, in blue, and in purple, in
scarlet, and in fine linen, and of the
weaver, *even* of them that do any work,
and of those that devise cunning work.

---

27. See on xxviii. 9—20. The precious stones and spices were contributed by the rulers, who were more wealthy than the other Israelites.

28. See on xxx. 22—38.

29. Cf. *v.* 21. Observe the emphatic repetition.

30. Cf. xxxi. 2

31. Cf. xxxi. 3.

32. *to devise curious works*] **to devise works of skill.** Cf. xxxi. 4.

33 *to make any manner of cunning work*] **to work in all manner of works of skill.**

34. "And he hath put **it into his heart to teach, both into his heart and into Aholiab's,**" &c.—They were qualified by the Lord not only to work themselves, but to instruct those who were under them.

35. *of the engraver*] **of the artificer.** The branches of work committed to Bezaleel are here included under the general term **the work of the artificer**: they are distinctly enumerated *vv.* 32, 33 and xxxi. 4, 5. But what was under the charge of Aholiab is here for the first time clearly distinguished into the work of **the skilled weaver**, that of the embroiderer, and that of the weaver.

the cunning workman] **the skilled weaver**, literally, *the reckoner*. He might have been so called because he had nicely to count and calculate the threads in weaving figures in the manner of tapestry or carpet. His work was chiefly used in the curtains and vail of the Tabernacle, in the Ephod and the Breastplate (xxvi. 1, 31, xxviii. 6, 15, &c.). It is generally called "cunning work" in our version, but the name is unfortunately not restricted to it.

the embroiderer] He worked with a needle, either shaping his design in stitches of coloured thread, or in pieces of coloured cloth sewn upon the groundwork. His work was employed in the **entrance curtains** of the Tent and the court, and in the girdle of the High-priest (xxvi. 36, xxvii. 16, xxviii. 39).—The Hebrew root *rākam* = to work with a needle, has survived in Arabic, but is not found in Syriac, nor in the Targums. It is a curious fact that through the Arabic have come from the same Semitic root the Spanish *recamare* and the Italian *ricamare*.

the weaver] He appears to have worked in the loom in the ordinary way with materials of only a single colour. The tissues made by him were used for the Robe of the Ephod and its binding and for the coats of the priests (xxviii. 32, xxxix. 22, 27). The distinctions in the kinds of work mentioned in this and the two preceding notes are clearly expressed in the LXX. and are in accordance with Jewish tradition (Bähr, 'Symb.' I. p. 266; Gesenius, 'Thes.' p. 1310).

As the names of the three classes of workers are in the masculine gender, we know that they denote men, while the spinners and dyers were women (*v.* 25). From what we know of the proficiency

CHAPTER XXXVI.

1 The offerings are delivered to the workmen. 5 The liberality of the people is restrained. 8 The curtains of cherubims. 14 The curtains of goats' hair. 19 The covering of skins. 20 The boards with their sockets. 31 The bars. 35 The vail. 37 The hanging for the door.

THEN wrought Bezaleel and
Aholiab, and every wise hearted
man, in whom the LORD put wisdom
and understanding to know how to
work all manner of work for the service of the sanctuary, according to all
that the LORD had commanded.
2 And Moses called Bezaleel and
Aholiab, and every wise hearted man,
in whose heart the LORD had put
wisdom, *even* every one whose heart
stirred him up to come unto the work
to do it:
3 And they received of Moses all
the offering, which the children of
Israel had brought for the work of the
service of the sanctuary, to make it
withal. And they brought yet unto
him free offerings every morning.
4 And all the wise men, that wrought
all the work of the sanctuary, came
every man from his work which they
made;
5 ¶ And they spake unto Moses,
saying, The people bring much more
than enough for the service of the
work, which the LORD commanded
to make.
6 And Moses gave commandment,
and they caused it to be proclaimed
throughout the camp, saying, Let
neither man nor woman make any
more work for the offering of the
sanctuary. So the people were restrained from bringing.
7 For the stuff they had was sufficient for all the work to make it,
and too much.
8 ¶ [a] And every wise hearted man [a] chap. 26. 3, 4.
among them that wrought the work
of the tabernacle made ten curtains
of fine twined linen, and blue, and
purple, and scarlet: *with* cherubims
of cunning work made he them.
9 The length of one curtain *was*
twenty and eight cubits, and the
breadth of one curtain four cubits:
the curtains *were* all of one size.
10 And he coupled the five curtains
one unto another: and *the other* five
curtains he coupled one unto another.
11 And he made loops of blue on
the edge of one curtain from the selvedge in the coupling: likewise he
made in the uttermost side of *another*
curtain, in the coupling of the second.
12 [b] Fifty loops made he in one [b] chap. 26. 10.
curtain, and fifty loops made he in the
edge of the curtain which *was* in the
coupling of the second: the loops held
one *curtain* to another.
13 And he made fifty taches of
gold, and coupled the curtains one
unto another with the taches: so it
became one tabernacle.

---

of the textile arts in Egypt in early times, we need not wonder at the exact division of labour among the Hebrews which the use of the terms in this verse indicates.—It is remarkable in regard to the other arts of construction, that the workman in each of them was called by the general name *artificer* (in Hebrew, literally, *one who cuts*) added to the name of the material in which he worked: thus the carpenter was called **an artificer in wood**; the smith, **an artificer in iron**; the mason, or the lapidary (xxviii. 11), **an artificer in stone**.—The view given in these notes of the three kinds of workers in textile fabrics, is substantially that of Gesenius, Bähr, Fürst, Winer and others. But Knobel and Keil take a different view respecting the embroiderer, and consider that he worked not with a needle but with a loom of some peculiar kind.

CHAP. XXXVI.

Bezaleel, Aholiab, and their assistants are set to work.

1—7.

1. See on xxxi. 3.

4. *the wise men*] *i.e.* the skilful men. See on xxxi. 3.

3, 5—7. See on xxv. 2.

The Tabernacle is made.

8—38.

8—13. See on xxvi. 1—6.

8. *made he them*] Rather, **were they made.** A corresponding change should be made in most of the verses in this Chapter. See on xxxvii. 1—5.

14 ¶ And he made curtains *of* goats' *hair* for the tent over the tabernacle: eleven curtains he made them.

15 The length of one curtain *was* thirty cubits, and four cubits *was* the breadth of one curtain: the eleven curtains *were* of one size.

16 And he coupled five curtains by themselves, and six curtains by themselves.

17 And he made fifty loops upon the uttermost edge of the curtain in the coupling, and fifty loops made he upon the edge of the curtain which coupleth the second.

18 And he made fifty taches *of* brass to couple the tent together, that it might be one.

19 And he made a covering for the tent *of* rams' skins dyed red, and a covering *of* badgers' skins above *that*.

20 ¶ And he made boards for the tabernacle *of* shittim wood, standing up.

21 The length of a board *was* ten cubits, and the breadth of a board one cubit and a half.

22 One board had two tenons, equally distant one from another: thus did he make for all the boards of the tabernacle.

23 And he made boards for the tabernacle; twenty boards for the south side southward:

24 And forty sockets of silver he made under the twenty boards; two sockets under one board for his two tenons, and two sockets under another board for his two tenons.

25 And for the other side of the tabernacle, *which is* toward the north corner, he made twenty boards,

26 And their forty sockets of silver; two sockets under one board, and two sockets under another board.

27 And for the sides of the tabernacle westward he made six boards.

28 And two boards made he for the corners of the tabernacle in the two sides.

29 And they were †coupled beneath, and coupled together at the head thereof, to one ring: thus he did to both of them in both the corners.

† Heb. *twinned.*

30 And there were eight boards; and their sockets *were* sixteen sockets of silver, †under every board two sockets.

† Heb. *two sockets, two sockets under one board.*

31 ¶ And he made [c] bars of shittim wood; five for the boards of the one side of the tabernacle,

[c] chap. 25. 28. & 30. 5.

32 And five bars for the boards of the other side of the tabernacle, and five bars for the boards of the tabernacle for the sides westward.

33 And he made the middle bar to shoot through the boards from the one end to the other.

34 And he overlaid the boards with gold, and made their rings *of* gold *to be* places for the bars, and overlaid the bars with gold.

35 ¶ And he made a vail *of* blue, and purple, and scarlet, and fine twined linen: *with* cherubims made he it of cunning work.

36 And he made thereunto four pillars *of* shittim *wood*, and overlaid them with gold: their hooks *were of* gold; and he cast for them four sockets of silver.

37 ¶ And he made an hanging for the tabernacle door *of* blue, and purple, and scarlet, and fine twined linen, †of needlework;

† Heb. *the work of a needle-worker,* or, *em-broiderer.*

38 And the five pillars of it with their hooks: and he overlaid their chapiters and their fillets with gold: but their five sockets *were of* brass.

14—18. See on xxvi. 7—13.

19. See on xxvi. 14.

20—34. See on xxvi. 15—29.

22. *equally distant one from another*] **set in order one against another.** See xxvi. 17.

27. *for the sides*] **for the back.** See xxvi. 22.

33. *to shoot through the boards*] rather, **to reach across the boards.** See xxvi. 28.

35, 36. See on xxvi. 31, 32.

37. *an hanging for the tabernacle door*] **an entrance curtain for the entering of the Tent.** See on xxvi. 36.

38. *their chapiters and their fillets*] **their capitals and their connecting rods.**

CHAPTER XXXVII.

1 The ark. 6 The mercy seat with cherubims. 10 The table with his vessels. 17 The candlestick with his lamps and instruments. 25 The altar of incense. 29 The anointing oil and sweet incense.

a chap. 25. 10.

AND Bezaleel made [a]the ark *of* shittim wood: two cubits and a half *was* the length of it, and a cubit and a half the breadth of it, and a cubit and a half the height of it:

2 And he overlaid it with pure gold within and without, and made a crown of gold to it round about.

3 And he cast for it four rings of gold, *to be set* by the four corners of it; even two rings upon the one side of it, and two rings upon the other side of it.

4 And he made staves *of* shittim wood, and overlaid them with gold.

5 And he put the staves into the rings by the sides of the ark, to bear the ark.

b chap. 25. 17.

6 ¶ And he made the [b]mercy seat *of* pure gold: two cubits and a half *was* the length thereof, and one cubit and a half the breadth thereof.

7 And he made two cherubims *of* gold, beaten out of one piece made he them, on the two ends of the mercy seat;

‖ Or, *out of, &c.* ‖ Or, *out of, &c.*

8 One cherub ‖on the end on this side, and another cherub ‖on the *other* end on that side: out of the mercy seat made he the cherubims on the two ends thereof.

9 And the cherubims spread out *their* wings on high, *and* covered with their wings over the mercy seat, with their faces one to another; *even* to the mercy seatward were the faces of the cherubims.

10 ¶ And he made the table *of* shittim wood: two cubits *was* the length thereof, and a cubit the breadth thereof, and a cubit and a half the height thereof:

11 And he overlaid it with pure gold, and made thereunto a crown of gold round about.

12 Also he made thereunto a border of an handbreadth round about; and made a crown of gold for the border thereof round about.

13 And he cast for it four rings of gold, and put the rings upon the four corners that *were* in the four feet thereof.

14 Over against the border were the rings, the places for the staves to bear the table.

15 And he made the staves *of* shittim wood, and overlaid them with gold, to bear the table.

16 And he made the vessels which *were* upon the table, his [c]dishes, and his spoons, and his bowls, and his covers ‖to cover withal, *of* pure gold.

c chap. 25. 29.

‖ Or, *to pour out withal.*

17 ¶ And he made the [d]candlestick *of* pure gold: *of* beaten work made he the candlestick; his shaft, and his branch, his bowls, his knops, and his flowers, were of the same:

d chap. 25. 31.

18 And six branches going out of the sides thereof; three branches of the candlestick out of the one side thereof, and three branches of the candlestick out of the other side thereof:

19 Three bowls made after the

These rods united the heads of the pillars, like the connecting rods of the Court (xxvii. 10). Neither these nor the capitals are mentioned in the instructions in xxvi. 37. See Note at the end of Ch. xxvi.

Chap. XXXVII.

The Furniture of the Tabernacle is made. 1—29.

1—5. See on xxv. 10—16 and on xxxv. 11. It has been observed that the Ark, as the most precious thing made for the Sanctuary, is expressly spoken of as the workmanship of Bezaleel himself. The expression here is quite free from ambiguity; but to prevent misunderstanding, it may be well to observe that in chap. xxxvi. 8, 10, 11, 12, 13, 14, 16, 17, 18, 19, 20, &c., and elsewhere, there is no nominative expressed in the Hebrew, and the verb is used indefinitely, as in the German phrase with *man* and the French one with *on*. In translating into English, it would be better in such cases to use the passive voice. See on xxxvi. 8.

6—9. See on xxv. 17—22.

7. *beaten out of one piece*] See on **xxv. 18.**

10—16. See on xxv. 23—30.

17—24. See on xxv. 31—39.

fashion of almonds in one branch, a knop and a flower; and three bowls made like almonds in another branch, a knop and a flower: so throughout the six branches going out of the candlestick.

20 And in the candlestick *were* four bowls made like almonds, his knops, and his flowers:

21 And a knop under two branches of the same, and a knop under two branches of the same, and a knop under two branches of the same, according to the six branches going out of it.

22 Their knops and their branches were of the same: all of it *was* one beaten work *of* pure gold.

23 And he made his seven lamps, and his snuffers, and his snuffdishes, *of* pure gold.

24 *Of* a talent of pure gold made he it, and all the vessels thereof.

[e] chap. 30. 1. 25 ¶ [e]And he made the incense altar *of* shittim wood: the length of it *was* a cubit, and the breadth of it a cubit; *it was* foursquare; and two cubits *was* the height of it; the horns thereof were of the same.

26 And he overlaid it with pure gold, *both* the top of it, and the sides thereof round about, and the horns of it: also he made unto it a crown of gold round about.

27 And he made two rings of gold for it under the crown thereof, by the two corners of it, upon the two sides thereof, to be places for the staves to bear it withal.

28 And he made the staves *of* shittim wood, and overlaid them with gold.

29 ¶ And he made [f]the holy anointing oil, and the pure incense of sweet spices, according to the work of the apothecary. [f] chap. 30. 35.

CHAPTER XXXVIII.

1 *The altar of burnt offering.* 8 *The laver of brass.* 9 *The court.* 21 *The sum of that the people offered.*

AND [a]he made the altar of burnt offering *of* shittim wood: five cubits *was* the length thereof, and five cubits the breadth thereof; *it was* foursquare; and three cubits the height thereof. [a] chap. 27. 1.

2 And he made the horns thereof on the four corners of it; the horns thereof were of the same: and he overlaid it with brass.

3 And he made all the vessels of the altar, the pots, and the shovels, and the basons, *and* the fleshhooks, and the firepans: all the vessels thereof made he *of* brass.

4 And he made for the altar a brasen grate of network under the compass thereof beneath unto the midst of it.

5 And he cast four rings for the four ends of the grate of brass, *to be* places for the staves.

6 And he made the staves *of* shittim wood, and overlaid them with brass.

7 And he put the staves into the rings on the sides of the altar, to bear it withal; he made the altar hollow with boards.

8 ¶ And he made the laver *of* brass, and the foot of it *of* brass, of

---

25—28. See on xxx. 1—10.
29. See on xxx. 22—38.

CHAP. XXXVIII.

The Brazen Altar, the Laver, and the Court are made.

1—20.

1—7. See on xxvii. 1—8.

8. *the laver*] See on xxx. 18—21. It appears that the metal for this laver was supplied by women, who gave up their bronze mirrors, such as were commonly used in Egypt and elsewhere (Wilkinson, 'Pop. Acc.' II. p. 336). This is generally approved by critics as the simple meaning of the Hebrew, and it agrees with the ancient versions and the Targums. The other interpretations—one, that the laver was furnished with mirrors for the use of the women who served in the Sanctuary (Michaelis, Bähr); and another, that its sides were adorned with figures in relief of women ranged in a religious procession (Knobel)—only deserve notice from the learning and reputation of their authors. The women who assembled **at the entrance of the Tent of meeting** were most probably devout women who loved the public service of religion. The giving up their mirrors for the use of the Sanctuary was a fit sacrifice for such women to make (cf. on

‖ Or, *brasen glasses.* † Heb. *assembling by troops.*

the ‖ lookingglasses of *the women*
† assembling, which assembled *at* the
door of the tabernacle of the congregation.
9 ¶ And he made the court: on the
south side southward the hangings of
the court *were of* fine twined linen, an
hundred cubits:
10 Their pillars *were* twenty, and
their brasen sockets twenty; the hooks
of the pillars and their fillets *were of*
silver.
11 And for the north side *the hang-*
ings were an hundred cubits, their pillars *were* twenty, and their sockets of
brass twenty; the hooks of the pillars
and their fillets *of* silver.
12 And for the west side *were* hangings of fifty cubits, their pillars ten,
and their sockets ten; the hooks of
the pillars and their fillets *of* silver.
13 And for the east side eastward
fifty cubits.
14 The hangings of the one side *of*
the gate were fifteen cubits; their pillars three, and their sockets three.
15 And for the other side of the
court gate, on this hand and that hand,
were hangings of fifteen cubits; their
pillars three, and their sockets three.
16 All the hangings of the court
round about *were* of fine twined linen.
17 And the sockets for the pillars
were of brass; the hooks of the pillars
and their fillets *of* silver; and the overlaying of their chapiters *of* silver; and
all the pillars of the court *were* filleted
with silver.
18 And the hanging for the gate of
the court *was* needlework, *of* blue, and
purple, and scarlet, and fine twined
linen: and twenty cubits *was* the
length, and the height in the breadth
was five cubits, answerable to the hangings of the court.
19 And their pillars *were* four, and
their sockets *of* brass four; their hooks
of silver, and the overlaying of their
chapiters and their fillets *of* silver.
20 And all the [b] pins of the taber- [b] chap. 27. 19.
nacle, and of the court round about,
were of brass.
21 ¶ This is the sum of the tabernacle, *even* of the tabernacle of testimony, as it was counted, according to
the commandment of Moses, *for* the
service of the Levites, by the hand of
Ithamar, son to Aaron the priest.
22 And Bezaleel the son of Uri, the
son of Hur, of the tribe of Judah,
made all that the LORD commanded
Moses.
23 And with him *was* Aholiab, son
of Ahisamach, of the tribe of Dan, an
engraver, and a cunning workman,
and an embroiderer in blue, and in
purple, and in scarlet, and fine linen.
24 All the gold that was occupied

---

xxxv. 22). We know from the instance of Anna (Luke ii. 36) that pious women, in later ages, used to spend much time within the precincts of the Temple. But there seems to be but weak ground for the notion of Hengstenberg and others that these women ever formed a regularly constituted order, like the widows, or deaconesses, of the early Church, and the Nazarites for life in the time of the Prophets (Lam. iv. 7; Amos ii. 11). Hengstenberg conceives that Moses made no specific law on the subject because the institution had been adopted from the customs of the Egyptian temples. The only passages quoted from the Old Testament in support of the existence of such an order of women are 1 Sam. ii. 22, Lam. ii. 21 (Hengst. 'Egypt,' &c. p. 184).

9—20. See on xxvii. 10—19.

18. *the height in the breadth was five cubits*] The meaning seems to be that the height of the curtain answered to the breadth of the stuff of which it was formed; *i.e.* five cubits. See xxvii. 18.

The sum of the metals used in the Sanctuary. 21—31.

21. "This is the **reckoning** of the Tabernacle, **the Tabernacle of the Testimony** (see on xxv. 16) **as it was reckoned up** according to the *commandment* of Moses, by the service of the Levites, by the hand of Ithamar," &c. The weight of the metals was taken by the Levites, under the direction of Ithamar.

23. *an engraver*] **an artificer.**—*a cunning workman*] **a skilled weaver.** See on xxxv. 35.

24. *of the holy place*] Rather, **of the Sanctuary.** The gold was employed not only in the Holy Place, but in the Most Holy

for the work in all the work of the
holy *place*, even the gold of the offering, was twenty and nine talents, and
seven hundred and thirty shekels, after
the shekel of the sanctuary.
25 And the silver of them that were
numbered of the congregation *was* an
hundred talents, and a thousand seven
hundred and threescore and fifteen
shekels, after the shekel of the sanctuary:
26 A bekah for † every man, *that is*,
half a shekel, after the shekel of the
sanctuary, for every one that went to
be numbered, from twenty years old
and upward, for six hundred thousand
and three thousand and five hundred
and fifty *men*.
27 And of the hundred talents of
silver were cast the sockets of the
sanctuary, and the sockets of the vail;
an hundred sockets of the hundred
talents, a talent for a socket.
28 And of the thousand seven

† Heb. *a poll.*

Place and in the entrance to the Tent (xxxvi. 38).

the gold of the offering] **the gold of the wave offering** (see pref. to Leviticus).

talents...the shekel of the sanctuary] The Shekel was the common standard of weight and value with the Hebrews: but what its weight was in early times, as compared with our standard, is a matter on which there has been much difference of opinion. There is however no particular reason to suppose that the Hebrew standard underwent much alteration in the course of ages; and in regard to later times, we have three distinct elements of calculation which lead to a tolerably harmonious result. (*a*) According to the rabbinists, the shekel weighed 320 barley grains, which are equal to about 214 English grains, the weight of which was originally taken from a grain of wheat. (*b*) There are several silver shekels in existence coined in the Maccabean times (see 1 Macc. xv. 6), and, making allowance for wear, each of these appears to have weighed 220 grains. (*c*) The LXX., when they do not retain the original name in the form σίκλος, render it by δίδραχμον (Gen. xxiii. 15; Ex. xxi. 32, xxx. 13, 15; Lev. xxvii. 3; Num. iii. 47, &c.): they also render *bekah*, the half shekel, by δραχμή (see *v.* 26). Now the Macedonian didrachmon, with which they must have been familiar, weighed 218 grains. It hence appears that we cannot be far wrong in estimating the shekel at 220 English grains (just over half an ounce avoidupois) and its value in silver as 2*s.* 7*d.*—The statement of Josephus ('Ant.' III. 8. § 2), that the shekel was equal to four Attic drachms (252 grains) is evidently a rough estimate: and still further from accuracy is his turning the fifty shekels of 2 K. xv. 20 into fifty drachms ('Ant.' IX. 11. § 1)—A question is raised as to the meaning of the term, "a shekel of the sanctuary." The rabbinists speak of a common shekel of half the weight of the shekel of the sanctuary. But there is no sufficient reason to suppose that such a distinction existed in ancient times, and the Shekel of the Sanctuary (or, *the Holy Shekel*) would seem to denote no more than an *exact* Shekel, "after the king's weight" (2 S. xiv. 26), "current money of the merchant" (Gen. xxiii. 16).

In the reign of Joash, a collection similar to the one here mentioned, apparently at the same rate of capitation, was made for the repairs of the Temple (2 Chron. xxiv. 9). The tax of later times, called *didrachma* (Matt. xvii. 27), which has often been connected with this passage of Exodus, and which was recognized by our Lord as having the same solemn meaning as this payment of half a shekel, was not, like this one and that of Joash, a collection for a special occasion, but a yearly tax for the support of the Temple, of a whole shekel (δίδραχμον).—See on xxx. 13.

The Talent (Heb. *kikkār*, LXX. τάλαντον) contained 3000 shekels, as may be gathered from *vv.* 25, 26. According to the computation here adopted, the Hebrew Talent was 94$\frac{2}{7}$ lbs. avoirdupois. The Greek (Æginetan) Talent, from which the LXX. and most succeeding versions have taken the name *talent*, was 82$\frac{1}{4}$ lbs. The original word, *kikkār*, would denote a circular mass, and nearly the same word, *kerker*, was in use amongst the Egyptians for a mass of metal cast in the form of a massive ring with its weight stamped upon it.

26. *A bekah*] Literally, *a half*: the words "half a shekel," &c. appear to be inserted only for emphasis, to enforce the accuracy to be observed in the payment. See on xxx. 13, where there is a similar expression, and cf. xxx. 15.—Respecting the capitation and the numbering of the people, see on xxx. 12. There must have been, in addition to the sum of the half shekels, the free-will offerings of silver (see xxxv. 24), of which no reckoning is here made. They may perhaps have been amongst what was returned to the donors as being more than enough (xxxvi. 7).

27. *sockets*] **bases.** See on xxvi. 19.

28. The hooks, chapiters and fillets here spoken of belonged to the pillars of the Court. See xxvii. 10, 17.

hundred seventy and five *shekels* he made hooks for the pillars, and overlaid their chapiters, and filleted them.

29 And the brass of the offering *was* seventy talents, and two thousand and four hundred shekels.

30 And therewith he made the sockets to the door of the tabernacle of the congregation, and the brasen altar, and the brasen grate for it, and all the vessels of the altar,

31 And the sockets of the court round about, and the sockets of the court gate, and all the pins of the tabernacle, and all the pins of the court round about.

CHAPTER XXXIX.

1 *The cloths of service and holy garments.* 2 *The ephod.* 8 *The breastplate.* 22 *The robe of the ephod.* 27 *The coats, mitre, and girdle of fine linen.* 30 *The plate of the holy crown.* 32 *All is viewed and approved by Moses.*

AND of the blue, and purple, and scarlet, they made cloths of service, to do service in the holy *place*,

---

30. *sockets to the door of the tabernacle of the congregation*] **bases for the entrance of the Tent of meeting.** See xxvi. 37.

the brasen altar] See xxvii. 1—8.

31. *the sockets of the court*] See xxvii. 10, 17.

the pins of the tabernacle ... the pins of the court] See on xxvii. 19.

According to the estimate of the shekel that has here been adopted, the weight of the metals mentioned in this chapter would be nearly as follows, in avoirdupois weight:—

Gold,	1 ton	4 cwt.	2 qrs.	13 lbs.
Silver,	4 tons	4 cwt.	2 qrs.	20 lbs.
Bronze,	2 tons	19 cwt.	2 qrs.	11 lbs.

The value of the gold, if pure, in our money would be £175075. 13*s.*, and of the silver £38034. 15*s.* 10*d.* The quantities of the precious metals come quite within the limits of probability, if we consider the condition of the Israelites when they left Egypt (see introd. note to Exod. and on xxv. 3), and the object for which the collection was made. There is no reasonable ground to call in question the substantial accuracy of the statements of Strabo (XVI. p. 778) and Diodorus (III. 45) regarding the great stores of gold collected by the Arab tribes near the Ælanitic Gulf, and they were probably still more abundant at this time when the tribes must have come into frequent contact with the Israelites. There may be no trace of native gold in those regions at present; but the entire exhaustion of natural supplies of the precious metals is too familiarly known to need more than a bare notice in this place (see 'Bib. Atlas' of the S. P. C. K. p. 38). Bähr, Knobel and others have remarked that the quantities collected for the Tabernacle are insignificant when compared with the hoards of gold and silver collected in the East in recent, as well as ancient, times. In communities in which there is not much commercial stir, and in consequence not much use for a circulating medium, the precious metals will be more readily accumulated either for a great national object, as in this case, or for the gratification of a ruler. The enormous wealth of the sovereigns, and also of the temples, of India, a century ago, taking the most moderate statements, may furnish examples. As instances in ancient times, we may refer to the accounts of gold in the temple of Belus (Diod. Sic. II. 9; cf. Herodot. I. 183); of the wealth of Sardanapalus (Ctesias, edit. Bähr, p. 431); and of the spoils taken by Cyrus (Plin. 'H. N.' XXXIII. 15, 47) and by Alexander (Diod. Sic. XVII. 66). All reasonable allowance may be made for exaggeration in these statements, and the argument, in its connection with well ascertained facts, will still be left amply strong enough for our purpose. For more examples, see Bähr, 'Symbolik,' I. p. 259; Knobel on Ex. xxv. and xxxviii.

It is worthy of notice that silver, in the time of Homer, appears to have been more precious than gold amongst the Greeks (Gladstone, 'Juventus Mundi,' p. 531). The treasures of Thrace and Laurium were then unknown. But it seems to have been otherwise with the Asiatic nations. The word *silver* (according to Pictet) is Sanscrit. This would tend to shew that the metal was known to the Aryan race before the Germanic nations migrated to the West. The forefathers of the Greeks and Romans probably lost all knowledge of it, and when they again met with it, they gave it quite a different name (*ἀργύριον, argentum*). This same argument may be applied to other metals. But what distinguishes silver is, that it was at first obtained by the people of Southern Europe from sparing, and, perhaps, distant sources. We know that the quantity of silver at Rome was very greatly increased by the contributions obtained in the Punic Wars (Niebuhr, 'Hist. of Rome,' Vol. III. p. 613). By this time Spain had begun to yield its supply. The Hebrews and Egyptians probably obtained the metal in the earliest times both from Asia and Africa.

CHAP. XXXIX.

The Priests' Dresses are made.

1—31.

1. See on xxviii. 5. The fine linen is omitted in this verse, but is mentioned in the next.

[a chap. 31. 10. & 35. 19.] and [a]made the holy garments for Aaron; as the LORD commanded Moses.

2 And he made the ephod *of* gold, blue, and purple, and scarlet, and fine twined linen.

3 And they did beat the gold into thin plates, and cut *it into* wires, to work *it* in the blue, and in the purple, and in the scarlet, and in the fine linen, *with* cunning work.

4 They made shoulderpieces for it, to couple *it* together: by the two edges was it coupled together.

5 And the curious girdle of his ephod, that *was* upon it, *was* of the same, according to the work thereof; *of* gold, blue, and purple, and scarlet, and fine twined linen; as the LORD commanded Moses.

[b chap. 28. 9.] 6 ¶ [b]And they wrought onyx stones inclosed in ouches of gold, graven, as signets are graven, with the names of the children of Israel.

7 And he put them on the shoulders of the ephod, *that they should be* stones for a [c]memorial to the children of Israel; as the LORD commanded Moses. [c chap. 28. 12.]

8 ¶ And he made the breastplate *of* cunning work, like the work of the ephod; *of* gold, blue, and purple, and scarlet, and fine twined linen.

9 It was foursquare; they made the breastplate double: a span *was* the length thereof, and a span the breadth thereof, *being* doubled.

10 And they set in it four rows of stones: *the first* row *was* a ‖sardius, a topaz, and a carbuncle: this *was* the first row. [‖ Or, *ruby*.]

11 And the second row, an emerald, a sapphire, and a diamond.

12 And the third row, a ligure, an agate, and an amethyst.

13 And the fourth row, a beryl, an onyx, and a jasper: *they were* inclosed in ouches of gold in their inclosings.

14 And the stones *were* according to the names of the children of Israel, twelve, according to their names, *like* the engravings of a signet, every one with his name, according to the twelve tribes.

15 And they made upon the breastplate chains at the ends, *of* wreathen work *of* pure gold.

16 And they made two ouches *of* gold, and two gold rings; and put the two rings in the two ends of the breastplate.

17 And they put the two wreathen chains of gold in the two rings on the ends of the breastplate.

18 And the two ends of the two wreathen chains they fastened in the two ouches, and put them on the shoulderpieces of the ephod, before it.

19 And they made two rings of gold, and put *them* on the two ends of the breastplate, upon the border of it, which *was* on the side of the ephod inward.

20 And they made two *other* golden rings, and put them on the two sides of the ephod underneath, toward the forepart of it, over against the *other* coupling thereof, above the curious girdle of the ephod.

21 And they did bind the breastplate by his rings unto the rings of the

---

cloths of service] more properly, **the garments of office.** On these and the Holy Garments, see on xxxi. 10.

2. *the ephod*] See on xxviii. 6 sq.

3. *the gold*] See on xxviii. 5.

with cunning work] **with work of the skilled weaver.** See on xxvi. 1, xxxv. 35.

5. *the curious girdle*] See on xxviii. 8.

6, 7. See on xxviii. 9—12.

8. *the breastplate*] See on xxviii. 15, 16.

10—13. On the precious stones, see on xxviii. 17—20.

13. *in their inclosings*] Rather, **in their settings.** See on xxviii. 11, 17.

15. *chains at the ends, of wreathen work*] **chains of wreathen work twisted.** See on xxviii. 14.

16. See on xxviii. 13, 23.

19. See on xxviii. 26, 27.

20. "And they made **two rings of gold** and put them on the two **shoulder-pieces of the Ephod, low down in the front of it, near the joining, above the band for fastening it.**" See on xxviii. 27.

21. See on xxviii. 28.

ephod with a lace of blue, that it might
be above the curious girdle of the
ephod, and that the breastplate might
not be loosed from the ephod; as the
LORD commanded Moses.
22 ¶ And he made the robe of the
ephod *of* woven work, all *of* blue.
23 And *there was* an hole in the
midst of the robe, as the hole of an
habergeon, *with* a band round about
the hole, that it should not rend.
24 And they made upon the hems
of the robe pomegranates *of* blue, and
purple, and scarlet, *and* twined *linen*.
[d] chap. 28. 33. 25 And they made [d]bells *of* pure
gold, and put the bells between the
pomegranates upon the hem of the
robe, round about between the pomegranates;
26 A bell and a pomegranate, a bell
and a pomegranate, round about the
hem of the robe to minister *in*; as the
LORD commanded Moses.
27 ¶ And they made coats *of* fine
linen *of* woven work for Aaron, and
for his sons,
28 And a mitre *of* fine linen, and
[e] chap. 28. 42. goodly bonnets *of* fine linen, and [e]linen
breeches *of* fine twined linen,
29 And a girdle *of* fine twined
linen, and blue, and purple, and scarlet,
of needlework; as the LORD commanded Moses.
30 ¶ And they made the plate of
the holy crown *of* pure gold, and wrote
upon it a writing, *like to* the engrav-
[f] chap. 28. 36. ings of a signet, [f]HOLINESS TO
THE LORD.
31 And they tied unto it a lace
of blue, to fasten *it* on high upon
the mitre; as the LORD commanded
Moses.
32 ¶ Thus was all the work of the
tabernacle of the tent of the congregation finished: and the children of
Israel did according to all that the
LORD commanded Moses, so did they.
33 ¶ And they brought the tabernacle unto Moses, the tent, and all his
furniture, his taches, his boards, his
bars, and his pillars, and his sockets,
34 And the covering of rams' skins
dyed red, and the covering of badgers'
skins, and the vail of the covering,
35 The ark of the testimony, and
the staves thereof, and the mercy seat,
36 The table, *and* all the vessels
thereof, and the shewbread,
37 The pure candlestick, *with* the
lamps thereof, *even with* the lamps to
be set in order, and all the vessels
thereof, and the oil for light,
38 And the golden altar, and the
anointing oil, and † the sweet incense, † Heb. *the incense of sweet spices.*
and the hanging for the tabernacle
door,
39 The brasen altar, and his grate
of brass, his staves, and all his vessels,
the laver and his foot,
40 The hangings of the court, his
pillars, and his sockets, and the hanging for the court gate, his cords, and
his pins, and all the vessels of the service of the tabernacle, for the tent of
the congregation,
41 The cloths of service to do service in the holy *place*, and the holy
garments for Aaron the priest, and his
sons' garments, to minister in the
priest's office.
42 According to all that the LORD
commanded Moses, so the children of
Israel made all the work.
43 And Moses did look upon all
the work, and, behold, they had done
it as the LORD had commanded, even
so had they done it: and Moses blessed
them.

22—26. See on xxviii. 31—35.

27. See on xxviii. 40, 41.

28. *a mitre*] See on xxviii. 37.

bonnets] See on xxviii. 40.
breeches] See on xxviii. 42.

29. *a girdle*] See on xxviii. 40.

30. *the holy crown of pure gold*] Cf. xxix. 6. See on xxviii. 36.

HOLINESS TO THE LORD] See on xxviii. 36.

The whole work of the Sanctuary is submitted to Moses and approved.

32—43.

33—38. See on xxxv. 11—15, and on xxvi. 1.

39, 40. See on xxxv. 16—18.

41. See *vv.* 1, 27, xxxi. 10.

CHAPTER XL.

1 *The tabernacle is commanded to be reared,* 9 *and anointed.* 13 *Aaron and his sons to be sanctified.* 16 *Moses performeth all things accordingly.* 34 *A cloud covereth the tabernacle.*

AND the LORD spake unto Moses,
saying,
2 On the first day of the first
month shalt thou set up the tabernacle
of the tent of the congregation.
3 And thou shalt put therein the
ark of the testimony, and cover the
ark with the vail.
4 And [a]thou shalt bring in the table, and set in order †the things that
are to be set in order upon it; and
thou shalt bring in the candlestick,
and light the lamps thereof.
5 And thou shalt set the altar of
gold for the incense before the ark of
the testimony, and put the hanging of
the door to the tabernacle.
6 And thou shalt set the altar of
the burnt offering before the door of
the tabernacle of the tent of the congregation.
7 And thou shalt set the laver between the tent of the congregation
and the altar, and shalt put water
therein.
8 And thou shalt set up the court
round about, and hang up the hanging at the court gate.
9 And thou shalt take the anointing oil, and anoint the tabernacle, and
all that *is* therein, and shalt hallow it,
and all the vessels thereof: and it shall
be holy.
10 And thou shalt anoint the altar
of the burnt offering, and all his vessels, and sanctify the altar: and it
shall be an altar †most holy.
11 And thou shalt anoint the laver
and his foot, and sanctify it.
12 And thou shalt bring Aaron
and his sons unto the door of the
tabernacle of the congregation, and
wash them with water.
13 And thou shalt put upon Aaron the holy garments, and anoint
him, and sanctify him; that he may
minister unto me in the priest's office.
14 And thou shalt bring his sons,
and clothe them with coats:
15 And thou shalt anoint them,
as thou didst anoint their father, that
they may minister unto me in the
priest's office: for their anointing shall
surely be an everlasting priesthood
throughout their generations.

[a] chap. 26. 35.
† Heb. *the order thereof.*
† Heb. *holiness of holinesses.*

CHAP. XL.

Moses is commanded to arrange the holy things, and to anoint them and the priests.

1—11.

2. *On the first day of the first month*] See *v.* 17.

4. *the things that are to be set in order*] The directions given in Lev. xxiv. 5—9 are here presupposed, and must have been issued before this chapter was written.

5. *before the ark*] See on xxx. 6.

the hanging of the door to the tabernacle] **the curtain at the entrance of the Tabernacle.**

6. *before the door of the tabernacle of the tent of the congregation*] **before the entrance of the Tabernacle of the Tent of meeting.**

7, 8. See Note at the end of Ch. xxvi. § VI.

8. *hang up the hanging*] **hang up the entrance curtain.**

9—11. The directions to anoint and consecrate the Tabernacle and the Priests had been previously given xxx. 26—31. They are here repeated in a summary form. The anointing is described Lev. viii. 10—12.

9. *vessels*] **utensils** The name includes the whole of the furniture of the Tabernacle. See on xxvii. 19.

10. *vessels*] **utensils.**

most holy] In the preceding verse the Tabernacle and its utensils are said to be rendered *holy* by the anointing; the Altar and its utensils are here, and in xxx. 10, said to be *most holy.* The term *most holy* must not in this case be taken as expressing a higher degree of holiness than that which belonged to the Tabernacle; it is only used for emphasis, as a caution (it has been conjectured) in reference to the position of the Altar exposing it to the chance of being touched by the people when they assembled in the Court, while they were not permitted to enter the Tabernacle. The Tabernacle itself, with all that belonged to it, is called *most holy* in xxx. 29.

12. *the door of the tabernacle of the congregation*] **the entrance of the Tent of meeting.** The directions in *vv.* 12—15 had been previously given xxix. 4—9, xxx. 30; the ceremony is described Lev. viii. 5, 6.

16 Thus did Moses: according to
all that the LORD commanded him,
so did he.

17 ¶ And it came to pass in the
first month in the second year, on the
[b] Numb. 7. 1. first *day* of the month, *that* the [b] tabernacle was reared up.

18 And Moses reared up the tabernacle, and fastened his sockets, and
set up the boards thereof, and put
in the bars thereof, and reared up his
pillars.

19 And he spread abroad the tent
over the tabernacle, and put the covering of the tent above upon it; as
the LORD commanded Moses.

20 ¶ And he took and put the
testimony into the ark, and set the
staves on the ark, and put the mercy
seat above upon the ark:

21 And he brought the ark into
the tabernacle, and [c] set up the vail of [c] chap. 35. 12.
the covering, and covered the ark of
the testimony; as the LORD commanded Moses.

22 ¶ And he put the table in the
tent of the congregation, upon the
side of the tabernacle northward, without the vail.

23 And he set the bread in order
upon it before the LORD; as the
LORD had commanded Moses.

Moses puts the Tabernacle in order.
17—33.

17. *on the first day of the month*] That is, on the first of the month Nisan (xii. 2, xiii. 4), one year, wanting fourteen days, after the departure of the Israelites from Egypt. They had been nearly three months in reaching the foot of Mount Sinai (xix. 1); Moses had spent eighty days on the mountain (xxiv. 18, xxxiv. 28), and some time must be allowed for what is related in chap. xxiv., as well as for the interval between the two periods which Moses spent on the mountain (xxxiii. 1—23). The construction of the Tabernacle and its furniture would thus appear to have occupied something less than half a year. Bleek's objection to this period as too short for the completion of such a work ('Introd. to O. T.' Vol. I. p. 247) is worth nothing if we duly consider the interest which the whole people must have felt in it, and the nature of the structure, so unlike one of solid masonry.

19. The tent cloth was spread over the tabernacle cloth, and the covering of skins was put over the tent cloth. See xxvi. 1, 6, 11, 14; and Note at the end of Ch. xxvi. § II.

20. *the testimony*] *i.e.* the Tables of stone with the Ten Commandments engraved on them (see xxv. 16, xxxi. 18). Nothing else is said to have been put into the Ark. These were found there by themselves in the time of Solomon (1 K. viii. 9; 2 Chron. v. 10). The Pot of Manna was "laid up before the testimony" (Ex. xvi. 34); Aaron's rod was also placed "before the testimony" (Num. xvii. 10); and the Book of the Law was put at "the side of the Ark" (Deut. xxxi. 26). The expression "before the testimony" appears to mean the space immediately in front of the Ark. Most interpreters hold that the Pot of Manna and Aaron's rod were placed between the Ark and the Vail. It is however said in the Epistle to the Hebrews that the Ark contained "the golden pot that had manna, and Aaron's rod that budded, and the tables of the covenant" (ix. 4). From this statement, and from the mode of expression in Kings and Chronicles (which appears to indicate that the fact of the Ark's containing nothing at that time but the Tables was unexpected), it would seem that the other articles were at some period put within the Ark; and this accords with some rabbinical traditions. It has however been conjectured that "before the testimony" may mean the space within the Ark, at the back of which the Tables are supposed to have been placed. But from a comparison of Ex. xxx. 36 with xl. 5, it appears that the two expressions "before the testimony," and "before the ark of the testimony," are equivalent and denote the space in front of the Ark, even extending to the outside of the Vail. Besides this, it is plain that Aaron's Rod, when it was brought "before the testimony," was merely restored to the place "before the Lord in the tabernacle of witness," where it was first placed along with the other rods (Num. xvii.; cf. *v.* 7 with *v.* 10). These considerations, added to the presumption from Ex. xxv. 16, xl. 20, that nothing but the Tables were put into the Ark, seem to afford sufficient evidence that the articles in question were not at first placed within it, but in front of it. It is very probable that the pot and the rod had been put into the Ark before it was taken by the Philistines, but that they were not sent back with the Ark and the Tables. 1 Sam. iv. 11, vi. 11.

the mercy seat] See on xxv. 21.

21. *the vail of the covering*] See on xxxv. 12.

22—24. See on xxv. 23—29, and Lev. xxiv. 5—9.

23. *he set the bread in order*] Moses performed these priestly functions (see on xxviii. 1) of setting the Bread on the Table, lighting

24 ¶ And he put the candlestick in the tent of the congregation, over against the table, on the side of the tabernacle southward.

25 And he lighted the lamps before the LORD; as the LORD commanded Moses.

26 ¶ And he put the golden altar in the tent of the congregation before the vail:

27 And he burnt sweet incense thereon; as the LORD commanded Moses.

28 ¶ And he set up the hanging *at* the door of the tabernacle.

29 And he put the altar of burnt offering *by* the door of the tabernacle of the tent of the congregation, and offered upon it the burnt offering and the meat offering; as the [d] LORD commanded Moses.

[d] chap 30. 9.

30 ¶ And he set the laver between the tent of the congregation and the altar, and put water there, to wash *withal*.

31 And Moses and Aaron and his sons washed their hands and their feet thereat:

32 When they went into the tent of the congregation, and when they came near unto the altar, they washed; as the LORD commanded Moses.

33 And he reared up the court round about the tabernacle and the altar, and set up the hanging of the court gate. So Moses finished the work.

34 ¶ [e] Then a cloud covered the tent of the congregation, and the glory of the LORD filled the tabernacle.

[e] Numb. 9. 15. 1 Kings 8. 10.

35 And Moses was not able to enter into the tent of the congregation, because the cloud abode thereon, and the glory of the LORD filled the tabernacle.

36 And when the cloud was taken up from over the tabernacle, the children of Israel † went onward in all their journeys:

† Heb. *journeyed*

37 But if the cloud were not taken up, then they journeyed not till the day that it was taken up.

38 For the cloud of the LORD *was* upon the tabernacle by day, and fire was on it by night, in the sight of all the house of Israel, throughout all their journeys.

---

the Lamps (*v.* 25), burning Incense (*v.* 27), and offering the Daily Sacrifice (*v.* 29), before the holy things with which they were performed were anointed. The things had been made expressly for the service of Jehovah, by His command, and in this fact lay their essential sanctity, of which the anointing was only the seal and symbol. Aaron and his sons, on similar ground, having had the divine call, took part in the service of the Sanctuary as soon as the work was completed (*v.* 31). But Moses took part with them, and most likely took the lead, until they were consecrated and invested (Lev. viii.) and publicly set apart for the office. See on Lev. viii. 14.

26. *before the vail*] that is, opposite to the Ark, in the middle between the Table of Shewbread on the North and the Candlestick on the South (see on xxx. 36).

28. *set up the hanging*, &c.] **put up the curtain at the entrance to the Tabernacle.**

29. *by the door*] **at the entrance.** It is here evident that the term denoted a broad space in front of the Tabernacle. See Plan, p. 378.

31, 32. See xxx. 18—21.

33. *set up the hanging*] **put up the curtain.** See on xxvi. 36.

The glory of the Lord is manifested on the completed work.

34—38.

34, 35. On the distinction between the Tent as the outer shelter and the Tabernacle as the *dwelling-place* of Jehovah, which is very clear in these verses, see on xxvi. 1. The glory appeared as a light within and as a cloud on the outside.

35. Cf. the entrance of the High-priest into the Holy of Holies on the Day of Atonement, Lev. xvi. 2, 13. For special appearances of this glory in the Tabernacle, see Num. xiv. 10, xvi. 19, 42; cf. Ex. xvi. 10; 1 K. viii. 10, 11.

36—38. This is more fully described Num. ix. 15—23, x. 11, 12, 34.

The Tabernacle, after it had accompanied the Israelites in their wanderings in the wilderness, was most probably first set up in the Holy Land at Gilgal (Josh. iv. 19, v. 10, ix. 6, x. 6, 43). But before the death of

Joshua, it was erected at Shiloh (Josh. xviii. 1, xix. 51). Here it remained as the national Sanctuary throughout the time of the Judges (Josh. xviii. 8, xxi. 2, xxii. 19; Judg. xviii. 31, xxi. 19; 1 S. i. 3, iv. 3). But its external construction was at this time somewhat changed, and *doors*, strictly so called, had taken the place of the entrance curtain (1 S. iii. 15): hence it seems to have been sometimes called *the Temple* (1 S. i. 9, iii. 3), the name by which the structure of Solomon was afterwards commonly known. After the time of Eli it was removed to Nob in the canton of Benjamin, not far from Jerusalem (1 S. xxi. 1—9). From thence, in the time of David, it was removed to Gibeon (1 Chro. xvi. 39, xxi. 29; 2 Chro. i. 3; 1 K. iii. 4, ix. 2). It was brought from Gibeon to Jerusalem by Solomon (1 K. viii. 4). After this, it disappears in the narrative of Scripture. When the Temple of Solomon was built, "the Tabernacle of the Tent" had entirely performed its work; it had protected the Ark of the Covenant during the migrations of the people until they were settled in the Land, and the promise was fulfilled, that the Lord would choose out a place for Himself in which His name should be preserved and His service should be maintained (Deut. xii. 14, 21, xiv. 24).

In accordance with its dignity as the most sacred object in the Sanctuary, the original Ark of the Covenant constructed by Moses was preserved and transferred from the Tabernacle to the Temple. The Golden Altar, the Candlestick and the Shewbread table were renewed by Solomon. They were subsequently renewed by Zerubbabel, and lastly by the Maccabees (see on xxv. 23). But the Ark was preserved in the Temple until Jerusalem was taken by the forces of Nebuchadnezzar (2 Chro. xxxv. 3; Jer. iii. 16). It was never replaced in the Second Temple. (Jos. 'Bell. Jud.' v. 5. § 5; Tacitus, 'Hist.' v. 9). According to a rabbinical tradition, its place was occupied by a block of stone.

NOTE ON CHAP. XL.

ON THE SANCTUARY AS A WHOLE.

I. *The Altar and the Tabernacle.* II. *Names of the Tabernacle.* III. *Order of the Sacred things.* IV. *The Ark and its belongings.* V. *Allegorical explanations.* VI. *Originality of the Tabernacle.*

I.

The two chief objects within the Court were the Brazen Altar and the Tabernacle. As sacrificial worship was no new thing, there is nothing said or intimated as to the purpose of the Altar, either in the instructions for the Sanctuary or in the record of its completion[1]. The intention was merely to provide a *single* Altar of suitable construction for the offerings of the whole nation in such juxtaposition with the Tabernacle as to suit the order of the inspired ritual.

But the Tabernacle was an entirely new matter belonging to the dispensation of the Mosaic Covenant. Its purpose was therefore distinctly set forth at this time. It was to be the symbolical dwelling-place of Jehovah, where He was to meet with His people or their representatives. His own words were: "Let them make me a sanctuary that I may dwell among them."—"I will meet you, to speak there unto thee, and there will I meet with the Children of Israel[2]."

II.

The name most frequently given to the Tabernacle in our Version is, "The Tabernacle (or Tent[3]) of the congregation[4]." But the latter word in Hebrew (מוֹעֵד) signifies *meeting*, in its most general sense, and is always used without the article. The better rendering of the name is **The Tabernacle** (or **The Tent**) **of meeting**, and the idea connected with it is that of Jehovah meeting with either Moses, or the priests, or (in only a few cases[5]) with the people gathered into a congregation at the entrance of the Tent. The English translation is not supported by the old Versions, nor by the best critical authorities. The complete designation is given as "the Tabernacle of the Tent of **meeting**." Ex. xl. 1, 29, &c.

The Tabernacle is also called, **The Tabernacle** (or **The Tent**) **of the Testimony**[6]. Now this designation evidently relates to the Tabernacle as the depository of the Testimony[7], that is, the Tables of the Law. It has been preferred by the LXX. (ἡ σκηνὴ τοῦ μαρτυρίου) and the Vulgate (*tabernaculum testimonii*), to render not only the Hebrew, which strictly answers to it, but also the name in more common use, which means The Tabernacle of **meeting**. It occurs in the New Testament, Acts vii. 44; Rev. xv. 5.

[1] Ex. xxvii. 1—8, xxxviii. 1—7. See note on Ex. xx. 24.

[2] Ex. xxv. 8, xxix. 42, 43. See also Ex. xxvii. 21, xxviii. 12.

[3] On the words *Tabernacle* and *Tent*, in some cases used indifferently for the whole structure, see on xxvi. 1.

[4] Ex. xxvii. 21, xxviii. 43, xxix. 4, 10, 11, 30, xxx. 16, 18, 20, 36, xxxi. 7, xxxv. 21, xl. 2, 6, 7, 12; Lev. i. 1, 3, 5, &c. &c.

[5] Lev. viii. 3, 4; Num. x. 3; cf. Ex. xxxiii. 7.

[6] The Hebrew word (עֵדוּת), in this connection, always has the article. Ex. xxxviii. 21; Num. i. 50, 53, ix. 15, x. 11, xvii. 7, 8, xviii. 2.

[7] See Note on Ex. xx. 1—17, § V.

The second name, of itself, suggests that the Tabernacle owed its character and significance to the Ark with its sacred contents and the Mercy-seat that covered it. Above the Mercy-seat, in a concentrated sense, was the spot where Jehovah communed with His people[1]. The furniture of the Holy Place held a subordinate position, and all its symbolism pointed to the truth which had its deepest and fullest expression in the Ark. In the form and materials of the Tabernacle itself there appears to have been nothing, either in its wood-work or its curtains, but what was most convenient for the arrangement and protection of the holy things and most becoming for beauty. It was in fact a regal Tent[2], in which the Ark symbolized the constant presence of Jehovah, who now condescended to dwell amongst the people whom He had redeemed.

III.

The order in which the chief facts connected with the construction of the Sanctuary are related in the sacred narrative, closely corresponds with the essential relation in which the several parts stand to each other. The Ten Commandments are uttered by the voice of Jehovah from the summit of Mount Sinai, with every circumstance that can show their solemn importance[3]: a short practical compendium of the Law, called the Book of the Covenant[4], is written out by Moses for the occasion: after the Covenant is sealed by sprinkling on the people the blood of Burnt-offerings and Peace-offerings, a mysterious manifestation of the Divine presence is made to Moses, Aaron and the Elders[5]: Moses is then summoned to the Mount and receives instructions first for making the Ark that was to contain the tables of the Ten Commandments with the Mercy-seat that was to cover them[6], next for the holy things that were to be placed in the Holy Place, and not till then, for the Tabernacle with its Tent and its Covering[7]: after this, the Brazen Altar and the Court are described[8], and directions are given for the consecration of those who had to minister at the Altar and the Tabernacle[9]: what may be regarded as a supplementary section relating to the Golden Altar[10] and some other things, is followed by the appointment of the workmen and a repetition of the Law for the observance of the Sabbath-day[1]. These practical instructions being completed, the precious gift of the Tables of the Law is put into the hands of Moses[2]. This arrangement of the particulars is the more noticeable, because the articles are named in reversed order in the account of the construction of the work[3].

IV.

The Ten Commandments conveyed no new revelation in the details of their subject matter. Every duty enjoined in them may be found expressed in no obscure terms in the earlier portion of the Pentateuch. But the old truths were now for the first time embodied and proclaimed to the people in connection with their lately recovered freedom. Hence they were put into new relations with other truths, and were combined with them in expressing the will of Jehovah. The tables of the Testimony did not however, by themselves, form the central point of the Sanctuary. It required the complete Ark that contained them, with the Mercy-seat that covered them, to convey the true meaning of the Covenant that was based on the name of Jehovah as it was revealed to Moses[4].

We may regard then the sacred contents of the Tabernacle as figuring what was peculiar to the Covenant of which Moses was the Mediator, the closer union of God with Israel and their consequent election as "a kingdom of priests, an holy nation[5]:" while the Brazen Altar in the Court not only bore witness for the old sacrificial worship by which the Patriarchs had drawn nigh to God, but formed an essential part of the Sanctuary, signifying, by its now more fully developed system of Sacrifices[6] in connection with the Tabernacle, those ideas of Sin and Atonement, which were first distinctly brought out by the revelation of the Law and the sanctification of the nation[7].

V.

Keeping strictly to the conclusions that appear clearly to follow from the sacred narrative, there seems to be neither occasion nor place for those allegorical explanations of the Tabernacle which are so often found in commentators, both Jewish and Christian. Philo[8], Josephus[9], Theodoret[10], Jerome[11], with other Fathers, and some of the Rabbinists, supposed

1 Ex. xxv. 22.
2 See Note on chap. xxvi.
3 Ex. xix, xx.
4 See on Ex. xx. 22.
5 Ex. xxiv. According to the Epistle to the Hebrews, the Book was sprinkled as well as the people; see Heb. ix. 19.
6 See on Ex. xxv. 10—16.
7 See Note on Ex. xxvi.
8 Ex. xxvii.
9 Ex. xxviii, xxix.
10 See on Ex. xxx. 1.

1 Ex. xxxi. 1—17. 2 Ex. xxxi. 18.
3 Ex. xxxvi, xxxvii.
4 Ex. xxxiv. 6, 7. See Note on ch. xx. § VI.
5 Ex. xix. 6.
6 See Lev. i.—vii.
7 See notes on Lev. iv.
8 'Vit. Mos.' III. 6.
9 'Ant.' III. 7. § 7. Cf. 'Bel. Jud.' v. 5. § 4, where the same explanation is applied to the Temple.
10 'Quæst. in Exod.' 60.
11 'Epist.' LXIV. § 9.

that the structure was a type of the material universe of heaven and earth which the Lord had created as an abode for Himself. It appears however that no two of these writers agree together in the application of this theory to the several parts. Bähr[1], following in this general track, has elaborated with curious ingenuity an explanation of almost every recorded particular in the description of Moses.—In other lines of speculation, the Tabernacle has been taken as a symbol of human nature (Luther), and as a prophetic type of the Christian Church (Cocceius).

VI.

It has been usual, especially since the time of Spencer, to seek out parallels from heathen antiquity for the Tabernacle itself, but more particularly for the Ark of the Covenant. The Tabernacle has been compared with several moveable temples of which there are notices in ancient writers, the most remarkable of which seems to be "the Sacred Tent" (*ἡ ἱερὰ σκηνή*) of the Carthaginians mentioned by Diodorus[2].

The Ark of the Covenant has been most generally likened to the arks, or moveable shrines, which are represented on Egyptian monuments[3]. The Egyptian arks were carried in a similar manner by poles resting on men's shoulders, and some of them had on the cover two winged figures not unlike what we conceive the golden Cherubim to have been. Thus far the similarity is striking. But there were points of great dissimilarity. Between the winged figures on the Egyptian arks there was placed the material symbol of a deity, and the arks themselves were carried about in religious processions, so as to make a show in the eyes of the people. We know not what they contained. As regards the Ark of the Covenant, the absence of any symbol of God was one of its great characteristics. It was never carried in a ceremonial procession: when it was moved from one place to another, it was closely packed up, concealed from the eyes even of the Levites who bore it[4]. When the Tabernacle was pitched, the Ark was never exhibited, but was kept in solemn darkness. Rest, it is evident, was its appointed condition. It was occasionally moved out of its place in the Holy of Holies, but only as long as the nation was without a settled capital, and had something of the character of an army on the march. During this period it accompanied the army on several occasions[1]. But it had been foretold that the time should come when the Sanctuary was to be fixed[2], and when this was fulfilled, we are told that "the Ark had rest[3]." It was never again moved till the capture of Jerusalem by the forces of Nebuchadnezzar[4]. Not less, we may fairly suppose, was it distinguished from all other arks in the simple grandeur of its purpose: it was constructed to contain the plain text of the Ten Commandments written on stone in words that were intelligible to all.

Such resemblances to foreign patterns as have been mentioned are without doubt interesting; but it should always be kept in view that they are extremely superficial. The Israelites could hardly have been in contact with the Egyptians for so long a period without learning much of their arts and customs. It is most likely that they were in the habit of using the same tools and modes of construction. In order to attain a given end they probably used similar mechanical contrivances. There are certain points of likeness in the descriptions of Moses and what we know of Egyptian art, which would clearly prove that the Israelites had dwelt in Egypt[5]. But on the whole, it seems wonderful that there is so little in the Sanctuary to remind us of any foreign association. Besides such distinctions as might naturally be ascribed to the difference between an idol's temple and a structure meant to express the Covenant between the unseen Lord and His people, there is in the Tabernacle an originality, both in its general arrangement and in its details, which is by far more striking than any resemblance that may be traced between it and heathen models.

[1] 'Symbolik,' Vol. I. p. 75.

[2] Lib. XX. 65: others are mentioned by Knobel.

[3] Wilkinson, 'Pop. Acc.' Vol. I. p. 267.—The articles in Smith's and Kitto's Dictionaries.—Smith, 'The Pentateuch,' p. 260, &c. &c.—On the arks of other ancient nations, see Bähr, 'Symbolik,' Vol. I. 399, and Knobel, p. 262.

[4] Num. iv. 5, 6, 19, 20.

[1] 1 S. iv. 3, xiv. 18; 2 S. xi. 11.

[2] Deut. xii. 10, 11.

[3] 1 Chro. vi. 31; cf. xvi. 1.

[4] See concluding note on Exod. xl.—It is strange that Knobel and others should regard such occasions as are described Josh. vi. 8, 2 S. vi. 12—16, as of the nature of ceremonial processions.

[5] Hengstenberg has not stated the argument too confidently in his 'Egypt and the Books of Moses,' but he has certainly brought some very fanciful instances to its support.

NOTE ON THE ROUTE OF THE ISRAELITES FROM RAMESES TO SINAI. F. C. C.

(Chaps. XVI. XVII. XIX.)

The commentary on the first nineteen chapters of Exodus had been some time in print, when the results of the survey of the western districts of the Sinaitic peninsula were communicated to the writer. Some conclusions to which he had been led by the researches of travellers, of which the fullest account is given in Ritter's work on Sinai and Palestine (see Band 1. p. 517—638), were materially affected by the information which he received from Captain Wilson, of the Royal Engineers, who with Captain Palmer, R. E., conducted the survey, and from the Rev. F. W. Holland, who accompanied the expedition, and had previously spent much time in exploring the Peninsula, of which he has prepared a valuable map, published by the Geographical Society.

The first part of the route, from Rameses to Elim, is not affected by these new sources of information, and the notes remain untouched. It may, however, be convenient to touch briefly on this portion in order to present a clear and connected view of the circumstances which may have determined the direction of the march. The first two days' march brought the Israelites from Rameses to Etham. Rameses was the general name of the district in the time of Jacob; the principal city built by the Israelites was probably situate on the ancient canal at some distance from the frontier. Etham was on the edge of the wilderness, at the point where the road towards Palestine branched off; and the direction of the journey was turned southwards, towards the encampment by the sea at Baal-zephon. See xii. 37, xiii. 20, xiv. 2, 3. Etham, which is probably identical with Pithom, is held by the writer of this note to correspond to the ancient Heroopolis, the frontier city of Egypt, near the southern extremity of Lake Timsah. The journey from this place to Suez would occupy sufficient time for a communication to be made to Pharaoh, and for the rapid march of his army[1]. The Israelites

[1] The subjoined sketch, prepared by the Rev. S. Clark, shows the route of the Israelites from Rameses to 'Ayún Músa, and the probable extent of the Red Sea north of its present bed in the time of Moses. Mr Clark identifies Etham with a spot near Serapeum.

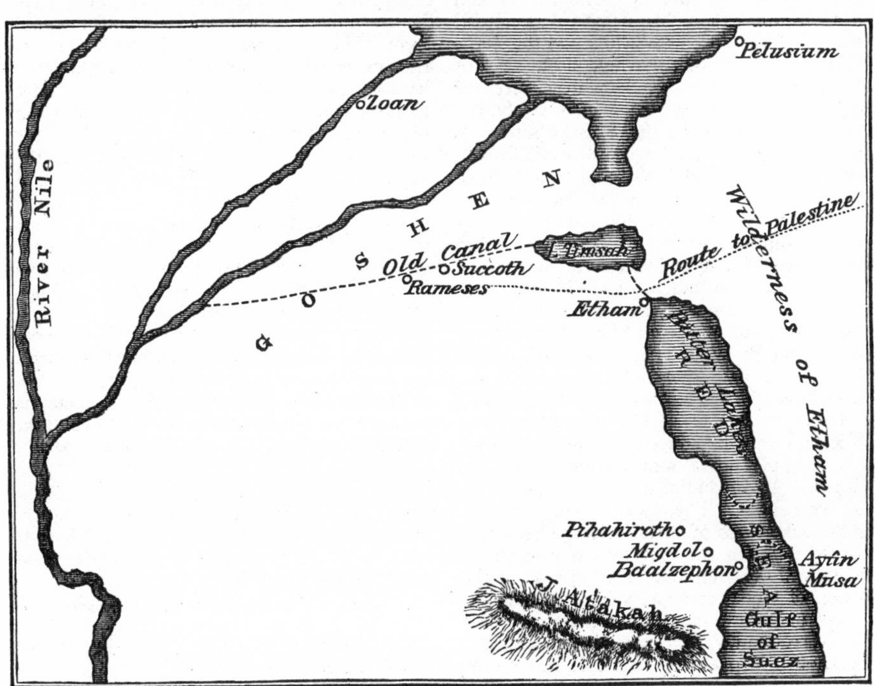

must have had a considerable start in order to reach the encampment of Suez before they were overtaken, but they could scarcely have been so near to Suez when at Etham as the site fixed upon by Robinson would bring them, or the passage could have been effected without interruption. That passage took place, as nearly all modern critics admit, near Suez, where sands of considerable extent were passable when "the Lord caused the sea to go back by a strong east wind," which blew all the night; see c. xiv. 21. After crossing the sea the Israelites would naturally make their first station at ʿAyún Músa, where they would find an ample supply of water: passing thence by Marah they reached Elim, when they encamped under the palm-trees, by the waters. Elim is generally identified with the Wady Gharandel. It is probable that the Israelites remained there several days and then advanced to the station on the Red Sea, near the headland called Ras-Selima, or, as in the map, Ras Abu Zenimeh.

The difference of opinions as to the course pursued by the Israelites up to this point is limited to questions of secondary importance; but from Elim two principal routes lead to Sinai, one by El Markha and Wady Feiran, the other, less circuitous, through a succession of Wadys on the north-east. Both these routes are reported by Captain Wilson, R.E. to be practicable even for a large host like that of the Israelites: the former is the more easy of transit; the latter has the advantage of an abundant supply of excellent water at the beginning of the journey. At the one end of the route it may be regarded as settled that the station by Ras-Selima was the starting-point, if not for the whole host, yet for the head-quarters of the Israelites. At the other extremity the reasons which will be adduced appear to prove that Ras Sufsafeh was the summit from which the Law was delivered, and the Wady er Rahah the wilderness of Sinai on which the people were assembled to hear it.

The facts stated in Exodus and in the itinerary in Numbers xxxiii. are these. The first station was in the wilderness of Sin, which lay between Elim and Sinai. The people remained there some days: we find no complaint of want of water, but they suffered from want of food, and were supplied first with quails and then with manna. From this wilderness they advanced, encamping first at Dophkah, then at Alush; thence they went to Rephidim, where they found no water until it was supplied by a miracle from the rock of Horeb. At Rephidim they were attacked by the Amalekites. Their next encampment was in the wilderness of Sinai. Some fifteen days elapsed between the first encampment in the wilderness of Sin and their arrival at the Mount of God: compare xvi. 1, and xix. 1.

We may first consider the claims of the more direct route, advocated with great ability by Knobel, whose view has been adopted by Keil, and is accepted in the foot-notes of this commentary. It has been fully described by Burckhardt, Robinson and other travellers, whose accounts are generally corroborated by Captains Wilson and Palmer and by Mr Holland.

From Ras Abu Zenimeh this route passes through several Wadys to a wide undulating plain, the Debbet er Ramleh. This desert is identified by Knobel with the wilderness of Sin. It corresponds in many striking particulars with the accounts of that wilderness: bare, wild, and desolate, it would offer no refreshment to the Israelites after their first long and laborious march. It lies, properly speaking, between Elim and the Sinaitic group in which greenstone and porphyry take the place of the sandstone of the desert. The word Debbet moreover corresponds exactly in meaning to Sin[1]; and at Wady Nasb, the first station on this route, there is a copious supply of water: a circumstance which, combined with the supply of quails and manna, gives a probable reason for the delay of some days in this wilderness. From Wady Nasb the road passes by Sarábít el Khadim. At this place the Egyptians worked mines of great extent, and the remains of buildings with numerous inscriptions prove that it was occupied by an Egyptian colony before the time of Moses. The existence of this settlement presents conflicting arguments for and against the selection of this route by Moses. On the one hand it may be reasoned that he would avoid coming into contact with Egyptians, especially since this must have been a military station, and a conflict would seem inevitable, since the sojourn in the district extended over some days. On the other hand it is admitted that the Egyptians would keep the entire route from Ras Selima in good order, and take great care to protect the sources of water: nor considering that the whole colony, as Captain Wilson states, could not consist of more than 1000 men, is it at all probable that they would attempt to arrest the advance of the vast host of the Israelites; especially if, as may be assumed, they had received information of the destruction of Pharaoh's host in the Red Sea.

The road from Sarábít el Khadim is extremely rough; but, as military authorities affirm, not impracticable even for light waggons, such as the Israelites probably used. Dophkah is assumed by Knobel to be in the Wady Sih, both names having the same meaning[2]. Alush,

[1] Freytag, in his Arabic lexicon, s. v. explains the former to mean "arena æquabilis et plana," the latter Sin, or Sinin, "arena elatior et longius protensa per regionis superficiem," a most exact description of this district.

[2] سيح, *sih*, flowing waters, the same being the meaning of دفق, *dafaka*, from which דפקה was probably derived.

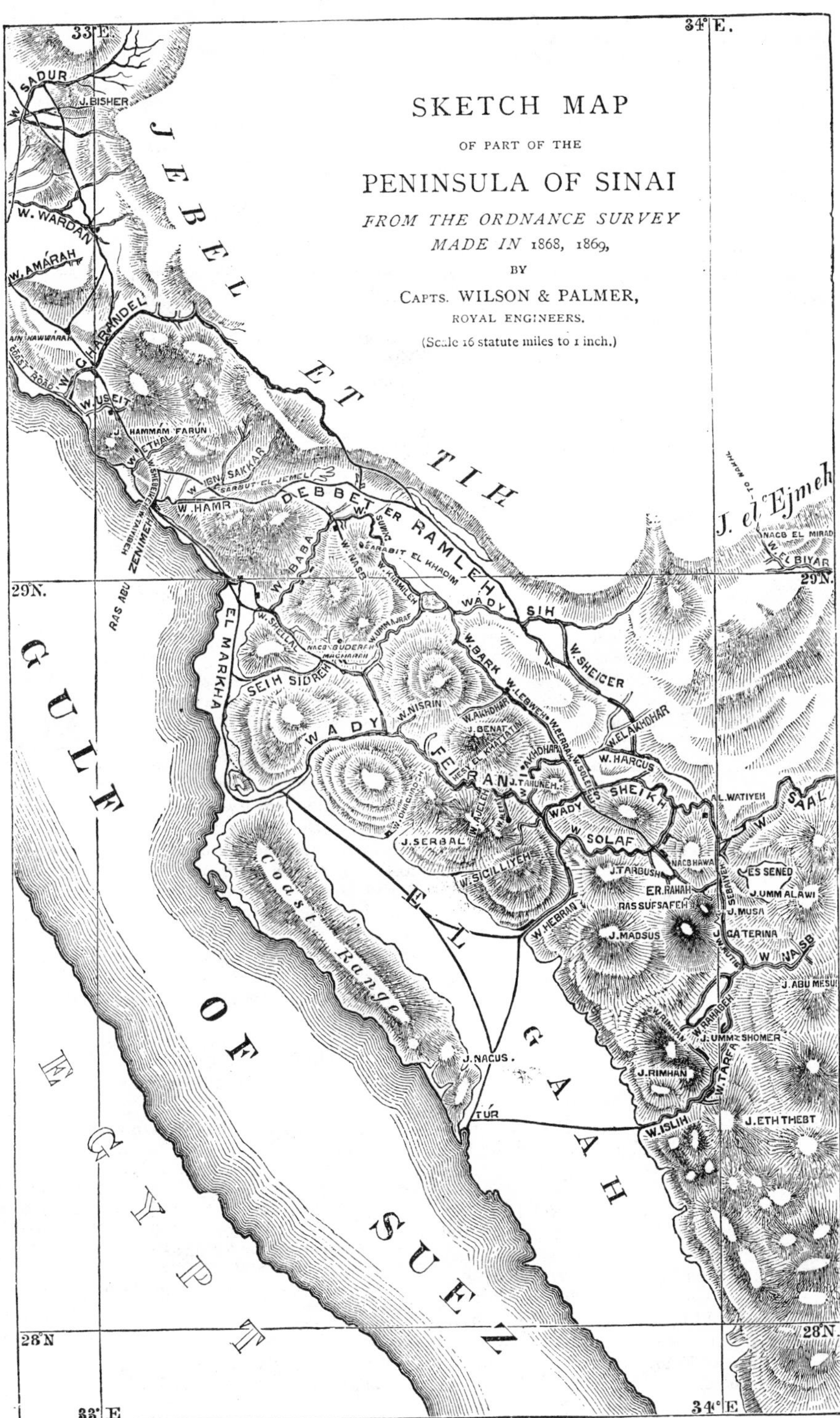

Country through which the Israelites must have passed on their way to Mount Sinai.

according to the same critic, may be the Wady el 'Esh, where there is a spring of good water: a journey of two hours from this point ends in the Wady es Sheikh.

The correspondence of the sites and even of the names on this route, and of the circumstances of the journey, presents a strong if not conclusive argument in its favour, nor is the argument affected by any discoveries made in the late survey. The notes on the text are therefore left in their original form; the writer still retaining, though with some diffidence in face of the opinions of the explorers, his conviction that Knobel is right, so far as this part of the route is concerned.

We have now to consider the other main route. The first day's journey from Ras Abu Zenimeh southwards leads through a narrow slip of barren sand to the open plain of El Markha. From this a Wady at once opens on the east, leading to the Wady Feiran. This route is most unlikely to have been selected by the Israelites: it would have brought them into contact with Egyptians in a district occupied by that people for centuries, nor do the narrow passes present any features corresponding to the wilderness of Sin. On the south, however, a very even and tolerably wide tract of desert land extends through El Markha, and at its southern extremity, by a sudden turn eastwards, through the Wady Feiran just described. This tract is identified by the conductors of the survey and by Mr Holland with the wilderness of Sin. They consider it to be the route which Moses would naturally have followed having once reached the station by Ras Selima. The chief objection to this view is that there are no springs of water in the district; to which it is answered that the Israelites who had waggons (see Num. vii. 3) and oxen would of course bring with them a supply, which might suffice for a rapid march until they reached the upper part of the Wady Feiran. The march however was not rapid, since there was a considerable delay, probably a whole week, in the wilderness of Sin. The route then passes north east of Mount Serbal, till it meets the Wady Sheikh, from which point two routes lead to Er Rahah and Ras-Sufsafeh; the one direct, but rough at the upper end; the other circuitous, but well adapted for the march and encampment of the Israelites. In Wady es Sheikh about midway this route meets the upper route previously described.

The question on which the explorers differ is one of great importance. It touches the site of Rephidim, where the Israelites first suffered for want of water, and where they defeated the Amalekites. Captains Wilson and Palmer hold that the battle was fought in the Wady Feiran, under Mount Serbal. Mr. Holland places Rephidim at the pass of Al Watíyeh, at the eastern end of Wady es Sheikh, to the north of the point where it joins the Wady ed Deir, which leads to Sinai.

If indeed the Israelites passed through Wady Feiran, it seems improbable that they should not have come into collision with the natives. From El Hesweh it is a well-watered district, winding for a considerable distance through defiles which could be easily defended by a people who had been trained for warfare by centuries of fierce struggles with the Egyptians: on the adjoining highlands towards Jebel Serbal remains of curious buildings, which undoubtedly belong to a very ancient period, still attest the presence of a numerous population along this route[1]. The site of the battle with the Amalekites is fixed by Captain Wilson near the ancient city of Feiran. The hill on which Moses witnessed the combat is supposed by Dr Stanley, 'S. and P.' p. 41, to be the rocky eminence which commands the palm-grove, on which in early Christian times stood the church and palace of the bishops of Paran. Captain Wilson holds it to be the Jebel Tahûneh, on the opposite side of the Wady. The whole of the Wady Feiran may have been cleared of the Amalekites by the decisive victory; after which the Israelites halted some time, with their head-quarters under the palm-groves, when they were visited by Jethro. This view assumes the identification of the Mount of God where Moses encamped in the wilderness, c. xviii. 5, with Mount Serbal, a conjecture of Ritter's which seems open to grave objection, since the Mount of God in Exodus is in all probability the group of Sinai, and the term "wilderness" is scarcely applicable to the palm-groves of Feiran. From this place the Israelites might have proceeded to the Wady er Rahah, either by Wady es Sheikh, the longer route, but presenting no impediments; or by the W. Solaf, which though rugged in part is not impracticable, and in Captain Wilson's opinion would most probably have been pursued.

Mr Holland, on the other hand, believes that the Israelites passed through the Wady Feiran without encountering opposition, and that they then traversed the Wady es Sheikh; Rephidim he places at the pass, called El

[1] Mr Holland describes them in a paper read at the Church Congress, 1869. After careful examination he came to the conclusion that they were probably the tombs and store-houses of the ancient Amalekites. They evidently were the work of a large and powerful people who inhabited the peninsula at a very early period. There are indications that they were, to some extent, an agricultural, as well as a pastoral people, a point of great importance in its bearings upon the probable condition of the neighbourhood of Mount Sinai at the time of the Exodus. See Introduction, p. 245. The Egyptian names of the old inhabitants were Anu and Mentu.

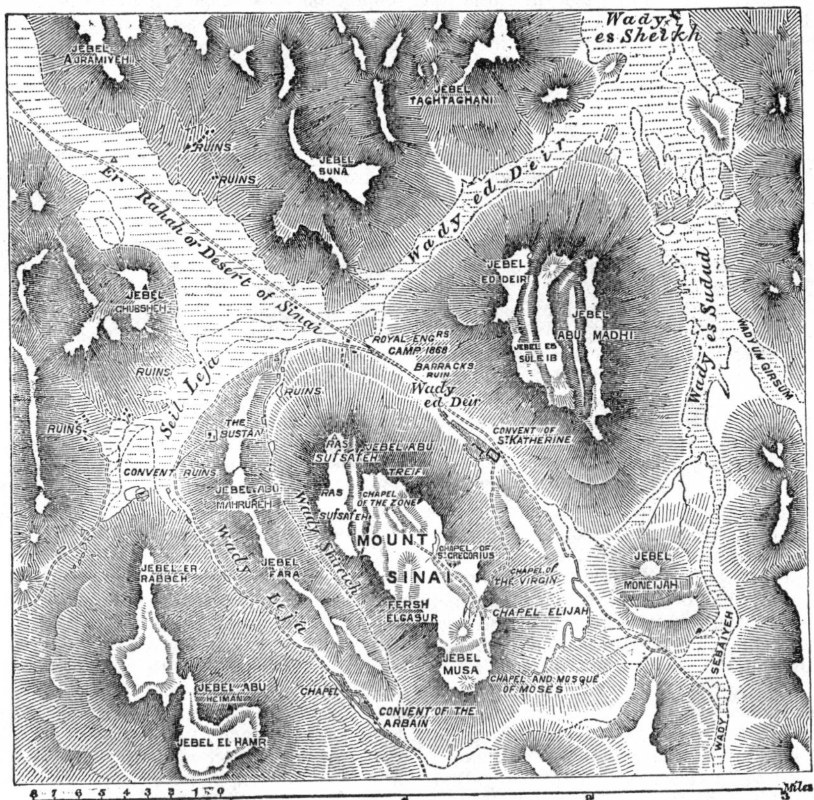

Group of Mount Sinai from the Ordnance Survey[1].

Watíyeh; it is shut in by perpendicular rocks on either side. The Amalekites holding this defile would be in a position of great strength: and their choice of this point for the attack is well accounted for, supposing the Israelites to have reached it without previous molestation. It commands the entrance to the Wadys surrounding the central group of Sinai, on and about which the Bedouins pasture their flocks during the summer. All the requirements of the narrative appear to be satisfied by this assumption. On the north is a large plain destitute of water for the encampment of the Israelites; there is a conspicuous hill to the north of the defile commanding the battle-field, presenting a bare cliff, such as we may suppose the rock to have been which Moses struck with his rod. On the south of the pass is another plain sufficient for the encampment of the Amalekites, within easy reach of an abundant supply of water. At the foot of the hill on which Moses most probably sat, if this be Rephidim, the Arabs point out a rock, which they call "the seat of the prophet Moses."

Taking all points into consideration we feel constrained to adopt one of the following alternatives. If, as the explorers hold, the Israelites passed through the Wady Feiran, the conflict with the Amalekites must have taken place on the spot fixed upon by Captains Wilson

[1] The engravings which accompany this note were supplied by General Sir Henry James, F.R.S.

The first is an accurate representation of a raised model of that group, together with the adjoining Wadys, which is at the Topographical department. The model is on the scale of six inches to the mile, and represents the natural features in their true proportions.

The other is taken from a photograph, which represents the northern end of the Sinaitic group, with Ras-Sufsafeh in the centre, and the extensive plain of the Wady Rahah in front.

and Palmer. If however the battle field was at El Watiyeh the Israelites may have reached it by the upper route, which meets the lower about midway in the Wady es Sheikh. The arguments appear to the writer to preponderate in favour of this view, which accepts all the facts ascertained by the Expedition of Survey, and presents a series of coincidences of great weight in the settlement of the question.

From this point the writer accepts without hesitation the conclusion to which all the persons concerned in the Survey unanimously arrive touching the encampment of the Israelites in the wilderness of Sinai. The representation of the Sinaitic group here given will enable the reader to judge of the weight of the arguments which led to that conclusion.

The opinion which formerly appeared to the writer to be sustained by the strongest evidence identified Jebel Musa with the peak of Sinai. This view was advocated by Ritter. He supposed that on the south of Jebel Musa there is a plain of great extent, the Wady Sebaîyeh, in which the Israelites could assemble in front of the mount. The pyramidal height of Jebel Musa is described as rising over it like a monolithic wall of granite, a sheer precipice of 2000 feet; on the summit the mosque, the Christian chapel, and even the so-called stone of Moses, are seen distinctly from the plain; which Wellsted, Vol. II. p. 34, describes in terms which might have seemed conclusive.

"We crossed a large plain terminating in a broad and extensive valley. It has been objected to the identification of Jebel Musa with Mount Sinai, that the narrow valleys and ravines contiguous to it could not have contained the immense multitude of Israelites. *In this valley however there is more than ample space for them:* while at the same time at its termination Mount Sinai stands forth in naked majesty." A traveller who spent some time in the neighbourhood lately informed the writer of this note that the description is quite accurate, and that it is the only plain where the host could have been assembled. Tischendorf, who notices the extent of the plain, specially adapted for so great an event, observes that "the situation supplies an excellent illustration of the words in c. xix. 12, 'that ye go not up unto the mount, nor touch the border of it;' for in this plain the mountain can be touched in the literal sense, rising sheer from the plain, standing before the eye from base to summit as a whole;" and again, "Seldom could one so properly be said to stand at the nether part of the mount as in the plain at the foot of Sinai looking upwards to the granite summit 2000 feet high."

The view of Jebel Musa is admitted to be singularly striking. Lepsius says of the ascent that it lies between vast heights and rocks of the wildest and grandest character, giving the impression of an approach to a spot of historical interest. The ascent from the chapel of Elijah occupies about three-quarters of an hour to the summit, a height of 7,530 to 7,548 feet. On the top is a level space 70 or 80 feet in width. Travellers give different accounts of the view from this spot. Seetzen and Burckhardt could see nothing; when they visited it the whole district was covered with a dense mist. Robinson speaks slightingly of the effect: and Ruppell says that the view is shut in by higher mountains on all sides except the north, on which he looked over a vast expanse including the desert of Er Ramleh, which is identified in these notes with the wilderness of Sin. Wellsted, however, who explored the district with unusual care, gives a most impressive description of the view. Vol. II. p. 97. He ascended the mount in very clear weather in January 1833, and took accurate trigonometrical measurements over an extent of 90 miles. "The view comprehends a vast circle. The gulphs of Suez and Akaba were distinctly visible, and from the dark blue waters of the latter the island of Tiran, sacred to Isis, rears itself. Mount Agrib on the other side points to the land of bondage. Before me is St Catherine, its bare conical peak now capped with snow. In magnificence and striking effect few parts of the world can surpass the wild naked scenery everywhere met with in the mountain-chain which girds the sea-coast of Arabia. Several years wholly passed in cruising along its shores have rendered all its varieties familiar to me, but I trace no resemblance to any other in that before me: it has a character of its own. Mount Sinai itself and the hills which compose the district in its immediate vicinity, rise in sharp, isolated conical peaks. From their steep and shattered sides huge masses have been splintered, leaving fissures rather than valleys between their remaining portions. These form the highest part of the range of mountains that, spread over the peninsula, are very generally in the winter months covered with snow, the melting of which occasions the torrents which everywhere devastate the plains below. The peculiarities of its conical formation render this district yet more distinct from the adjoining heights which appear in successive ridges beyond it, while the valleys between them are so narrow that they can scarcely be perceived. No villages and castles as in Europe here animate the picture: no forests, lakes, or falls of water break the silence and monotony of the scene. All has the appearance of a vast and desolate wilderness either grey, or darkly brown, or wholly black. Few who stand on the summit of Mount Sinai, and gaze from its fearful height upon the dreary wilderness below, will fail to be impressed with the fitness of the whole scene for the sublime and awful dispensation, which an almost universal tradition declares to have been revealed there." Schubert's description, quoted by Ritter, 'Sinai,' p. 587, fully corroborates this account. "The summit of the mount was reached, a holy place to the mightier half of the nations of the earth, to Jews, Moslems and Christians. The view from its height of 7000 feet extends over a circle of more than 360 miles in diameter, and 1600 miles in circumference: a rugged outline of a desert panorama of terrible beauty under the blue vault of the purest and brightest heaven of Arabia. No other place comes near to it in all this. On the east and west the eye catches glimpses of the girdle of sea which encircles the highlands of the Peninsula: beyond it are seen the ranges of Arabian and Egyptian heights. In the space between no green meadow, no cultivated field, no wood, no brook, no village, no Alpine hut. Only storm and thunder resound in the wilderness of Sinai, else for ever silent: a chain of rock standing as on the third day of creation when as yet there was no grass, no tree upon the earth: a mass of granite, unmingled with later formations; none of its abrupt deep ravines are filled up with sandstone, or chalk, or other alluvial deposits: strata of Greywacke and Basalt run like black veins for leagues through its walls and peaks. Here on such a spot as this was the law given, which pointed to Christ by whom it was fulfilled."

The accuracy of these descriptions is borne out by the accounts of other travellers. Thus Henniker quoted by Dr Stanley, 'S. P.' p. 12: "The view from Jebel Musa (where the particular aspect of the infinite complication of jagged peaks and varied ridges is seen with the greatest perfection) is as if Arabia Petræa were an ocean of lava, which, whilst its waves were running mountains high, had suddenly stood still."

Unfortunately for this hypothesis the raised model, from which the plan is taken, proves that the valley immediately below Jebel Musa could not have held a considerable portion of the Israelites; it is, as Dean Stanley describes it, rough, uneven, and narrow. It is proved, moreover, that there is no level plain in the Wady Sebaiyeh on which the Israelites could be assembled within sight of the summit of Jebel Musa, which however is visible at many points between the entrance of the Wady (which lies to the south-east) and its farthest end, a distance of nearly seven miles. This circumstance, which rests on the authority of military surveyors, seems conclusive. Jebel Musa, the loftiest and grandest summit of the group, may have been included in the tremendous manifestations of divine power, but the announcement of the Law must have taken place elsewhere.

On the northern extremity however there is a concurrence of circumstances in favour of Ras Sufsafeh. At its foot lies the plain Wady ed Deir extending to the north-east, meeting the Wady es Sheikh, which has been above

The Mountains of Sinai, Ras Sufsafeh in the centre. The foreground is the extensive plain of *Wady Rahah.*
(Photograph by the Ordnance Survey.)

identified with Rephidim, and immediately in front the far wider plain Er Rahah; to the left a plain of greater extent than was previously supposed, the Seil Leja. From every part of these two Wadys the granite rock of Ras Sufsafeh is distinctly visible, and there is space for the entire host of the Israelites, taking the highest calculation of their numbers. This fact, of cardinal importance in the question, is attested by the military officers who conducted the survey.

Indeed Sir Henry James concurs with those officers in the opinion that no spot in the world can be pointed out which combines in a more remarkable manner the conditions of a commanding height, and of a plain in every part of which the sights and sounds described in Exodus would reach an assembled multitude of more than two million souls. The description of Ras Sufsafeh, the central height in the subjoined engraving, taken from the photographs, presents many remarkable coincidences; and though inferior in height to the peak of Jebel Musa, it satisfies the main conditions of the narrative.

Dean Stanley, 'S. P.' p. 42—44, has drawn out, with his usual felicity of expression, the most striking characteristics of the scenery. He observes that the existence of such a plain in front of such a cliff is so remarkable a coincidence with the sacred narrative, as to furnish a strong internal argument, not only of its identity with the scene, but of the scene itself having been described by an eye-witness. He then dilates upon other not less impressive circumstances. The awful and lengthened approach as to some natural sanctuary; the plain not broken and narrowly shut in, like almost all others in the range, but presenting a long retiring sweep against which the people could remove and stand afar off; the cliff rising like a huge altar in front of the whole congregation, and visible against the sky in lonely grandeur from end to end of the whole plain, the very image of the "mount that might be touched," and from which the "voice" of God might be heard far and wide over the stillness of the plain below, widened at that point to the utmost extent by the confluence of all the contiguous valleys; the place where beyond all other parts of the Peninsula is the adytum withdrawn as if in the end of the world from all the stir and confusion of earthly things. We are also indebted to Dean Stanley for noting other details which are fully borne out by the late exploration, and scarcely leave room for doubt as to the exact point of the delivery of the Law. A small eminence at the entrance of the convent valley is marked by the name of Aaron, from which he is believed to have witnessed the festival of the golden calf; a tradition which fixes the locality of the encamption on Wady Rahah. Two other points meet here and nowhere else; first Moses is described as descending the mountain without seeing the people, the shout strikes the ear of his companion before they ascertain the cause; the view breaks on him suddenly as he draws nigh to the camp, and he throws down the tables and dashes them in pieces "beneath the mount:" now any one descending the mountain path by which Ras Sufsafeh is accessible (according to Captain Wilson in three-quarters of an hour to a practised mountaineer) through the oblique gullies which flank it, would hear the sounds borne through the silence of the plain, but would not see the plain itself until he emerged from the lateral Wady; and when he did so he would be immediately under the precipitous cliff of Sufsafeh. The brook which came down from the mount is probably identified with that which flows through the Seil Leja.

Taking all these circumstances into consideration it seems impossible to resist the conclusion that the Law was delivered on Ras Sufsafeh, to the Israelites encamped in the plain below.

ESSAY I.

ON THE BEARINGS OF EGYPTIAN HISTORY UPON THE PENTATEUCH.

1. SOURCES of Egyptian history. 2. General results. 3. List of Pharaohs from 12th to 20th Dynasty. 4. Time of Abram's visit; objections and proofs; Story of the two Brothers; Benihassan; Story of Saneha; presents to Abram. 5. Time of Joseph; invasion of Hyksos; inquiry into Manetho's statements; era of Set Nubte. 6. Apepi or Apophis not the Pharaoh of Joseph. 7. Connection of 12th Dynasty with On. 8. Tomb of Chnumhotep; Egyptian nomes. 9. Egyptian irrigation; labyrinth under Amenemha III. 10. Probable condition of the Israelites under the Hyksos. 11. Inquiry into date of Exodus. 12. Amosis or Aahmes I., a new king, a conqueror, builder of ports, &c., employs forced labourers. 13. Chronology, dates examined. 14. Last year of Thotmes II.; probable date of the Exodus. 15. Amenophis I. 16. Thotmes I. 17. Thotmes II.; events of reign; character of Queen Hatasou. 18. Campaigns of Thotmes III. concluded 40 years after decease of Thotmes II. 19. Objections considered. 20. Amenophis II. and Thotmes IV. 21. Amenophis III. and the Queen Tei. 22. Religious revolution in Egypt. 23. Statements of Manetho, Cheremon, Lysimachus, and Diodorus. 24. The identification of Rameses II. with the Pharaoh of Moses considered. 25. State of Palestine under the early Judges. 26. Campaigns of Seti I. against the Cheta. 27. Rameses II., length of reign, first campaign in Syria. 28. Fortresses built or enlarged. 29. Employment of Aperu identified with Hebrew captives. 30. Alliance of Rameses with Cheta. 31. State of Palestine described in Egyptian Papyrus. 32. State of Goshen at the same time incompatible with occupation by Israelites. 33. Reign of Merneptah; events and dates coincide with the first hypothesis in this Essay. 34. Rameses III.

(1.) OUR knowledge of early Egyptian history is derived chiefly from monumental inscriptions and papyri, which have been deciphered within the last few years: partly also from fragments of Manetho, and from the accounts of Greeks who visited Egypt after the close of the Old Testament history.[1]

The historical notices drawn from the last source have little independent value. Facts of importance, corroborated by modern researches, are recorded by Herodotus, Diodorus, and other Greeks, but they are mixed with legends, disfigured by manifest forgeries, and their statements, so far as regards the chronology, are irreconcileable with contemporary inscriptions.

The fragments of Manetho[2] have a higher value. He was a priest, conversant with the literature of ancient Egypt, and had access to monuments which, under the Ptolemies, were for the most part in a state of perfect preservation. The original history perished at a very early period, and is only known from extracts in Josephus. The catalogue of Kings begins with gods, and continues through thirty dynasties of mortals, ending with Nectanebo 343 B.C. The list is derived from authentic sources, but there are numerous errors and mis-statements attributable in part to the ignorance or carelessness of transcribers. This remark applies to names, but still more to dates, which are seldom confirmed, and often contradicted, by the monuments.[3]

The facts drawn from old Egyptian docu-

[1] The principal object of this dissertation is to bring the latest discoveries to bear upon biblical questions, reference is therefore seldom made to works of great value already well known to all students. It is right to observe that it was printed in 1868; a few references have been made in the notes, and two or three in the text, to works which have appeared before the last revision in 1870.

[2] The best account of Manetho is given by Rev. H. Browne in Kitto's 'Cyclopædia.' All the fragments are to be found in the first volume of Bunsen's 'Egypt.' The extracts in Josephus are taken from the Αἰγυπτιακά; the catalogue of dynasties is preserved by Syncellus, 800 A.D., in two widely-differing recensions, one from the lost 'Chronographia' of Julius Africanus, 220 A.D., the other from the 'Chronicon' of Eusebius, of which we have now the Armenian version.

[3] The regnal years of many kings are deter-

ments are of the highest importance. Some refer to past transactions, and are chiefly valuable as showing what view the Egyptians took of their ancient history, more especially of the succession and character of their ancient kings.[4] Other inscriptions relate to contemporary events, which they describe for the most part in highly coloured and inflated language, but apparently without careless or wilful misstatement of the facts.

(2.) From these monuments the history of a large portion of the ancient and middle empire, with which alone we are now concerned, has been constructed, though not without long intervals of partial or total obscurity. The earliest part of that history has lately been investigated with great care, and the results given in a work by M. de Rougé,[5] to which reference will frequently be made in the following pages. The names of nearly all the Pharaohs of the first six dynasties have been found, together with notices which prove the extent and complete organisation of their kingdom.

The interval between the sixth and the eleventh dynasties is of uncertain duration. No light is thrown upon it by contemporary monuments. M. de Rougé[6] considers it probable that "the royal families placed here in the lists of Manetho do but represent sovereigns of a part of the country, contemporary with other Pharaohs."

The twelfth dynasty again stands out in clear and strong relief. The Pharaohs were lords of all Egypt; their monuments represent the highest development of sculpture and architecture, and the main events of their reigns are recorded in numerous inscriptions. Some facts of importance have also been lately ascertained in reference to the early kings of the thirteenth dynasty, proving that they too were masters of all Egypt, and therefore that the invasion of the Shepherd kings could not have taken place at the time formerly assumed by Lepsius.[7]

The interval between the fourth king of the thirteenth dynasty and the last of the seventeenth is a period of confusion and disturbance. The monuments supply no data by which the order of events and the chronology can be determined, or even probably conjectured. That Egypt during that time was invaded by the Hyksos, who were masters of the north, has been proved by the researches of M. Mariette: part of the country appears to have been governed throughout the period by contemporary dynasties, ending with Rasekenen; but the most complete list of the ancestors of Seti I. gives the name of no Pharaoh between Amenemha, the last king but one of the twelfth dynasty, and Aahmes, or Amosis, the first of the eighteenth.

From the beginning of the eighteenth dynasty, when the Hyksos were expelled by Aahmes I., the monumental history of Egypt is tolerably complete; the succession of nearly all the Pharaohs and the principal events in the reigns of the most distinguished are distinctly recorded. The chronology, however, is uncertain; the regnal years are often found on the monuments, but without even an approximation to completeness; with one exception, to be noticed presently, no general era, or computation of lengthened periods, is based on the authority of ancient inscriptions.

(3.) The subjoined list embraces the whole period within which the Israelites and their ancestors are assumed by any scholars to have been in contact with Egypt before or soon after the settlement in Canaan.

12th Dynasty.—Amenemha, Osirtasin I., Amenemha II., Osirtasin II., Osirtasin III., Amenemha III., Amenemha IV., and a Queen, Ra-Sebek-Nefrou.

13th Dynasty.—A series of Pharaohs bearing a general name, Sebek-hotep.

14th to 17th Dynasty.—Hyksos, and Egyptians; the last of the Hyksos, Apepi, or Apophis; the last of the contemporary Egyptians, Ta-aaken Rasekenen.

18th Dynasty. — Aahmes I. (Nefertari Queen), Amenhotep I., Thotmes I. (Aahmes Regent), Thotmes II., Thotmes III., Amenhotep II., Thotmes IV., Amenhotep III., Amenhotep IV. (who took the name Khun-Aten), three other kings not recognised as legitimate, Horemheb.

19th Dynasty.—Rameses I., Seti I., Rameses II., Merneptah I, Seti II. or Merneptah II., Amemmeses, Siptah, and Tauser.

20th Dynasty.—Rameses III., twelve kings bearing the name Rameses with special designations.

(4.) The first contact with Egypt is generally admitted,[8] and may be here assumed to have

mined from contemporary inscriptions. The discrepancies in Manetho are so numerous that they can scarcely be accounted for by errors of transcription.

[4] The two most important documents referring to the past are the Turin Papyrus (published by Lepsius, 'Auswahl,' 1842, and 'Kœnigsbuch,' 1858), and the list of kings lately discovered in the temple of Abydos by M. Mariette. It is printed in the 'Zeitschrift,' 1864, by M. de Rougé, 'Recherches,' pl. ii., and by M. Mariette, 'Fouilles,' vol. ii. It represents Seti I., accompanied by his son Rameses II., in the act of rendering homage to seventy-six of his ancestors, beginning with Mena or Menes.

[5] 'Recherches sur les Monuments qu'on peut attribuer aux six premières Dynasties de Manethon.' Paris, 1866.

[6] 'Recherches,' p. iv. This statement is again made in M. de Rougé's 'Exposé de l'État actuel des Études égyptiennes,' 1867. See p. 17.

[7] See M. de Rougé, 'Recherches,' pp. vi. vii.

[8] Lepsius is the only exception. All other scholars in England, France, and Germany, are

taken place before the eighteenth dynasty: the first question to be considered is whether the visit of Abram, and the immigration of the Israelites, are to be referred to the period of disturbance and general misery which followed the invasion of the Hyksos, and lasted till their expulsion, or to the earlier period when Egypt was united and prosperous under its native sovereigns.

The natural impression made by the narrative in the Book of Genesis would certainly be that the transactions which it sets before us so fully and distinctly, belong to the earlier period. The account of Abram's visit (Gen. xii. 10-20) is very brief, but it evidently represents Egypt as in a condition of great prosperity. It was the resort of foreigners in times of famine. Pharaoh and his princes are rich and luxurious, nor are there any indications of war or intestine troubles.

It has, however, been argued that some facts in this short narrative point rather to the habits of a nomad and half-savage race, than to the polished and civilised Pharaohs of the ancient empire. It is urged that representations of camels are not found on Egyptian monuments; but they formed part of the property which Abram acquired by the favour of Pharaoh. It is, however, known that long before that period the Pharaohs were masters of a large part of the Peninsula of Sinai, and of the intervening district, nor is it likely that they would have kept up their communications without using the 'ships of the desert.' Camels were not likely to be represented on the sepulchral monuments at Benihassan,[9] far from the frontiers of Egypt: they were not used in the interior of the country, and were probably regarded as unclean.

Two objections of more importance rest on the supposed habits and feelings of the early Egyptian kings: late discoveries have converted these objections into strong arguments in favour of the earlier date.

The fear which Abram felt lest his wife should be taken from him, and that he should be slain for her sake, would seem to indicate wild and savage habits, such as can scarcely be attributed to native Egyptians. But in the story of the two brothers,[10] the Pharaoh of the time, acting on the advice of his counsellors, sends two armies to fetch a beautiful woman by force and then to murder her husband. The story is full of wild superstitions, but the portraiture of manners is remarkably simple and graphic, and it unquestionably represents the feelings of the Egyptians at the time of their highest civilisation. It belongs to the age of Rameses II., and the act is attributed not to a tyrant and oppressor, but to a Pharaoh beloved by his people, and passing into heaven at his decease.

Another curious coincidence has been pointed out by M. Chabas, 'Les Papyrus hiératiques de Berlin,' p. xiv. In a very ancient papyrus of Berlin, referring to the 12th dynasty, the wife and children of a foreigner are confiscated as a matter of course, and become the property of the king. M. Chabas observes, "C'est ainsi qu'à une époque probablement un peu postérieure à celle des événements que raconte notre papyrus, Abraham se vit enlever sa femme Sarai, qui fut placée dans la maison du Roi."

It is again objected that Abram was not likely to be admitted into the presence, much less into the favour, of a native Egyptian king, whereas a nomad of kindred origin and similar habits might willingly receive him.

We have, however, two distinct and absolute proofs that under the twelfth dynasty a personage of the race, habits, and position of Abram would be welcomed under such circumstances as those described in Genesis.

In the sepulchral monuments at Benihassan, and in the tomb of the Governor of the province, a man of the highest rank, nearly related to the reigning Pharaoh, Osirtasin II., is found one of the most interesting and best known pictures of the ancient empire. It represents the arrival of a nomad chief, with his family and dependents, to render homage and seek the protection of the prince. These foreigners are called Amu,[11] a name which was given

so far agreed, they place the visit of Abraham before the eighteenth dynasty. Dr. Ebers places the visit of Abraham before the Hyksos, and that of Joseph some time after their expulsion. This involves, according to his calculations, an interval of some eight or ten centuries between Abraham and Joseph. The arguments by which he shows that neither could have visited Egypt during the Hyksos period corroborate the position taken in this dissertation. Dr. Ebers' work, 'Ægypten und die Bücher Moses,' published a few months since, reached me after this dissertation was ready for the press. Reference will be made to it in the notes.

[9] We have no other monuments which represent the habits of Egypt under the twelfth dynasty. There are no representations of camels on monuments of the Ptolemaic or the Roman period, when they were of course well known to the Egyptians. Ebers supposes that it was contrary to the rules of Egyptian art to represent these uncouth forms. This is possible, but scarcely probable, since the giraffe and other strange animals are common on the monuments. It is more probable that they were held unclean.

[10] This curious story, the earliest fiction in existence, is among the select Papyri in the British Museum: it is called the Papyrus d'Orbiney: a fac-simile is published by the Trustees of the Museum: it contains nineteen pages of hieratic writing, remarkably clear and legible: the style is simple, and presents fewer difficulties than any similar document. It has been translated in part by Mr. Goodwin, Mr. Le Page Renouf, and M. de Rougé. The story abounds throughout with illustrations of the narrative in the Pentateuch.

[11] The word is applied to pastoral nomads,

specially to the native tribes on the north-west of Egypt and in Palestine of Semitic descent. The chief is called the Hak, or prince, corresponding to Sheich, as used chiefly of heads of tribes: his name is Abshah.[12] The features of the family, their colour, and their costume, a rich tunic, or "coat of many colours," are thoroughly Semitic. It is to be observed also that, although they are represented as suppliants, making lowly obeisance, and bringing the customary gifts, yet the prince receives them as persons of some distinction: a scribe who presents them holds a tablet describing their number and purpose, and a slave behind the governor bears his sandals, which were only taken off on ceremonial occasions.

Not less striking is the evidence drawn from one of the oldest papyri in existence, lately translated by Mr. Goodwin. He calls it the Story of Saneha: the events which it relates belong to the reigns of the first two kings of the twelfth dynasty, Amenemha and Osirtasin. Saneha (*i.e.* son of the Sycomore, a name probably given or assumed on his adoption by the Egyptians) was, like the chief above described, an Amu; he was not only received into the service of the Pharaoh, but rose to high rank, and, even after a long residence as a fugitive in a foreign land, he was restored to favour, made "a counsellor among the officers, set among the chosen ones: precedence is accorded to him among the courtiers, he is installed in the house of a prince, and prepares his sepulchre among the tombs of the chief officers." Mr. Goodwin points out the resemblance between this narrative and the history of Abraham; but it proves something more, for it shows that to an Egyptian of that early age the circumstances in the history of Abraham and of Joseph which are often regarded as improbable would appear most natural, facts if not of frequent, yet of certain occurrence.

M. Chabas, in a treatise on the same papyrus, observes—"Ce narrateur devint le favori de ce monarque (*sc.* Asirtasin) et fut pendant quelque temps préposé à l'administration de l'Égypte, *pour en développer les ressources.* Ce détail nous rappelle le rôle que, selon l'Écriture, Pharaon attribua au patriarche Joseph."

It may also be argued that such a reception was far less likely to be accorded to either of these Patriarchs at any later period. The little that is positively known of the Hyksos, the masters of Tanis, indicates a certain harshness and even ferocity of character;[13] nor after their expulsion were the kings either of the eighteenth or nineteenth dynasty likely to look with favour upon foreigners bearing, as may be probably inferred, a close resemblance to them in features and language. The presents too which the Pharaoh made to Abram include sheep, oxen, asses, and slaves, all of which are frequently represented on the early monuments, and specially at Benihassan,[14]—a fact the more important to be noticed since V. Bohlen and others ventured to deny that either sheep or asses were common in Egypt: the ass was looked upon as unclean under the middle and later Empire, as Typhonian, and would not probably have been presented to a favoured stranger. The omission of horses is remarkable. The Hyksos, admitted to be Arabians, probably brought the horse into Egypt, and no animal was more prized by the later Pharaohs; but it was wholly unknown, so far as we can judge from the monuments, to the Egyptians of the twelfth or any earlier dynasty.[15]

In fact, the notices of Abram's visit to Egypt agree so entirely with all that is certainly known of the Egyptians under the twelfth dynasty, and differ in so many material points from what is known from the monuments or early tradition of the Hyksos, and of the Middle Empire, that critics of very opposite schools have concurred in adopting the earlier date, notwithstanding the difficulty presented by their acceptance of the chronology of Manetho as given by Africanus or Josephus. For my own part I regard it as all but cer-

and specially those of Arabia and Palestine. It is an Egyptian word, derived from Amu , a herdsman's scourge. The word Shasous, which will occur frequently, is also applied to nomads, but probably with reference to their wandering habits, equivalent to Bedouins. Hyksos is not the name of a people, but of the dynasty, and probably means Prince of the Shasous. M. Chabas objects to this etymology, but it is generally accepted, and rests on strong grounds.

12 Some have thought that the name is identical with Abraham, an opinion which is undoubtedly incorrect; but there is a very remarkable resemblance between the names, both in form and meaning: since "shah" means sand, and "raham" means multitude. When Abshah was received, Abraham would not be rejected.

13 This alludes particularly to the hard, sullen features, wholly unlike those of Egyptian princes, found on the lately-discovered monuments which represent the Hyksos at Tanis. See 'Rev. Archéologique,' 1861, p. 105. Dr. Ebers gives the head of the Sphinx from M. Mariette, l. c. 208.

14 Sheep are represented on the Pyramids—in one inscription 3208 as the property of an individual. Asses of great size and beauty are found in many pictures at Benihassan. I believe, but may be mistaken, that they occur comparatively seldom on the monuments of later periods.

15 V. Bohlen infers from this omission that Genesis could not have been written by an author conversant with Egyptian manners. The true inference is that he describes exactly what took place at the time which he gives an account of. It is very probable that horses were first introduced under the 12th dynasty, after the reign of Osirtasin. From that time the intercourse with Asia appears to have been constant.

tain that Abraham visited Egypt in some reign between the middle of the eleventh and the thirteenth dynasty, and most probably under one of the earliest Pharaohs of the twelfth.

(5.) The history of Joseph belongs to a period about two centuries later.[16] The duration of the twelfth dynasty is estimated at 213 years; and as the monuments were numerous and complete in Manetho's time, it is probable that the regnal years are drawn from them, and that the numbers are tolerably correct. It has been lately proved beyond all doubt that the invasion of the Hyksos could not have taken place immediately afterwards, as was formerly supposed. Colossal figures of great beauty, and inscriptions, have been found at Tanis, the head-quarters of the Hyksos, which prove that the fourth king of the thirteenth dynasty was still in undisturbed possession of that city; and monumental notices of even later kings are found, both at Tanis and in other parts of Egypt, scarcely reconcileable with the presence of the Arabian invaders.[17]

So far as the monuments and other Egyptian documents are concerned, we are at liberty to place the visit of Joseph either towards the end of the twelfth dynasty, the earlier portion of the thirteenth, or under the first Hyksos.

We are bound to give special attention to this last alternative; it was maintained by all ancient writers, and is accepted, with few but important exceptions, by modern critics. Thus Syncellus: "It is asserted unanimously by all that Joseph ruled over Egypt in the time of Apophis:" Eusebius, speaking of the seventeenth (Shepherd) dynasty, says *κατὰ τούτους Αἰγυπτίων βασιλεὺς Ἰωσὴφ δείκνυται.* This unanimous consent, however, refers only to Josephus and to those who drew their information exclusively from his account of Manetho's work. It depended wholly upon chronological calculations, and it is of course quite clear that, if the Shepherd dynasty had lasted some 800 years, all the narrative in Genesis would have fallen within it.

This necessitates a brief inquiry into the grounds for the statements in Manetho.

We have first an account of a dynasty of six Shepherd kings: their names in Josephus are Salatis, Beon, Apachnas, Apophis, Jannes, Assir. The general accuracy of this list may be admitted, transposing one name only, viz., Apophis, who is known to have been the last of the Shepherd kings. The late discoveries of M. Mariette at Tanis have given us contemporary authority for the first name. It is Semitic, old Arabian probably (Σάλατις = שַׁלִּיט mighty, ruler), but the Egyptians transcribe it accurately and give the full title, with the invariable adjuncts of Egyptian etiquette, "the Good Deity, star of both worlds, Son of the Sun, Set Shalti,[18] beloved by Sutech, Lord of Avaris." So that Salatis, the first of the Shepherd dynasty, assumed at once the state and title of the Pharaohs, and at least claimed to be sovereign of all Egypt. The second name Beon or "Benon," the more correct reading of Africanus, is also found.[19] Like many other words it has probably the same meaning[20] in Semitic and Egyptian, Son of the Eye, *i.e.* the beloved one. The order of the three last names is proved by the Turin Papyrus, and by the well-ascertained position of Apophis.

Up to this point we have a solid foundation; six kings, foreigners, two bearing Semitic names, and recognised by ancient Egyptian documents. The duration of the dynasty may have been between two and three centuries.

But in addition to these kings, Manetho, according to Josephus, states that a dynasty or dynasties of Shepherds ruled over all Egypt upwards of 500 years. Africanus gives two dynasties, one lasting 284 years, the other 518. For this statement, however, no evidence is adduced. Not a single name is given by Josephus. The Turin Papyrus has no indication of the dynasty. The monuments are absolutely silent. The statement, indeed, is in glaring contradiction to the fact that Salatis was the first and Apophis the last of the Shepherd kings. It involves an admission of the most improbable of all assumptions, for which not a shadow of resemblance can be found in ancient or modern history,—an assumption that, after a total suspension of the national life lasting from five to ten centuries, after a complete overthrow of their government, institutions, and religion, the Egyptians reverted to the exact point of civilisation in which the invaders found them, speaking and writing their own language without a trace of foreign infusion,[21] worshipping the old gods with the old rites, retaining their old theology,

---

[16] The dates are not certain, but Isaac was born some years after Abraham's visit to Egypt, lived 180 years (Gen. xxxv. 28), and died before Joseph was sold by his brethren.

[17] See M. de Rougé, 'Recherches,' p. vii. We owe these important facts to M. Mariette.

[18] The group is noticeable . It is found also in a mutilated form in the Turin Papyrus.

[19] In the Papyrus Sallier 1, pl. 1, l. 7.

[20] בן עין. The Egyptian is Beben-an, which Dr. Ebers derives from Ben, "son," and "*an*," the eye. The Egyptians have the well-known Hebrew and classical term, "child of the eye" for "darling."

[21] The strong infusion of Semitic belongs to the age of Rameses II. The inscriptions of the eighteenth dynasty are nearly free from it. A very remarkable confirmation of the above statements is found in the account of the mummy of Aah-hotep, mother of Ahmes I., given by M. Mariette, 'Musée de Boulaq,' p. 254:—"L'Égypte est revenue sous la xviime dynastie avec la plus singulière persistance au style de la xime."

and recognising in the descendants of their old Pharaohs the inheritors of all their titles and prerogatives. It seems quite incredible that such a statement should have been adopted, as adopted it has been by critics remarkable for sagacity, and some for caution approaching to scepticism. It is the only ground for the assumption that Joseph must needs have visited Egypt while it was under the dominion of the Hyksos.

We do not attach much importance to the chronology of this remote period, so far as it rests on Egyptian documents: it is to a great extent conjectural, and incapable of proof or disproof. But it is a remarkable fact that the only inscription on Egyptian monuments of any age which mentions an era distinct from the regnal year of the actual sovereign, is found on a monument referring to the Hyksos. The importance of this inscription was pointed out by M. de Rougé,[22] and it has been carefully examined by M. Chabas. The personage who set up the tablet was an official of high rank, Governor of Tanis under Rameses II. The date which he gives is the four hundredth year from the era of Set Nubte, *i.e.* Set the golden, under the reign of a Hyksos king, Set-aa-Pehti, *i.e.* Set the mighty and victorious. There is of course a wide field for conjecture here. The reign of Rameses was a very long one (see further on, p. 464), and the Hyksos king is not positively identified. We may consider it as almost certain that the Egyptian governor, a descendant of the Hyksos, believed that 400 years had elapsed between the era of Set and some year in the reign of Rameses. When, again, we consider the analogy of all ancient eras, and the natural course of events, we are all but forced to infer that this era must coincide with the formal recognition of Set as the chief object of worship to the dynasty. If the Papyrus Sallier were our only authority, that recognition might be assigned to Apophis; but the late discovery of the style and title of the first of the Shepherd Kings, Salatis the beloved of Set,[23] proves that the establishment of Set worship at Tanis was far more ancient, contemporary in fact with the inauguration of the Shepherd dynasty.

The inferences from these facts tally very remarkably with the chronology which upon the whole appears to be best supported by Biblical and documental evidence. The end of the reign of Rameses is most probably about 1340 B.C. From this, 400 years would bring us to the middle of the eighteenth century, about 1750 B.C. The expulsion of the Hyksos being taken about 1500, we have thus 250 years for their dynasty, and 250 more would bring us to the time of Abraham. Such arguments are of course open to objections, nor are they given here as conclusive, but they have weight when they harmonize with a system resting on wholly independent grounds. One point at least is clear: if the date is accepted it involves a considerable reduction in the length of the period assigned by Lepsius and Brugsch to the dynasties preceding the age of Rameses.

(6.) But the name of Apophis is specially mentioned as that of the king by whom Joseph was received. The question whether this is possible or probable may now be decided by the positive evidence of contemporary inscriptions,[24] and of the ancient papyrus, Sallier I.

We know now that Apophis was the contemporary of Rasekenen, the immediate predecessor of Aahmes I., and that Aahmes captured Avaris, the capital or chief fortress of Apophis, and afterwards drove out all the adherents of the hostile dynasty, pursuing them as far as Palestine.

This fact is conclusive. Joseph was a very young man when he came first under the notice of Pharaoh, and lived to an advanced age, 110 years, the utmost limit, as has been lately shown,[25] of Egyptian life. He would therefore have long outlived Apophis, but no one supposes that he could have lived a prosperous and powerful man after the extermination of the dynasty by which he was raised to the highest rank in the state. Nor do other notices of the Pharaoh of Joseph at all accord with what is known of Apophis.

Apophis was not, properly speaking, Lord of all Egypt. Upper Egypt was governed by an independent dynasty; and the very terms which describe the extent of his influence prove the limits of his dominion. Rasekenen, his antagonist, retained possession of the Thebaid to the end of his life, and buildings of great extent were erected by him in Memphis and Thebes after the termination of a successful campaign against Apophis.[26] The

[22] 'Revue Archéologique,' Feb. 1864. M. Mariette sent a copy to the same Review, March, 1865. M. Chabas has two articles on it printed in the 'Zeitschrift,' April and May, 1865. The tablet was found in a mass of ruins in the sanctuary of the great temple at San, *i.e.* Tanis.

[23] It is probable that Set-aa-pehti, *i.e.* Set the mighty and victorious, was either the Egyptian translation of the Semitic Set-Shalt, Set the mighty ruler, or a second title borne in accordance with Egyptian usage.

[24] The inscriptions are found in the sepulchres of officers who served under Ra-sekenen and the first Pharaohs of the eighteenth dynasty. They are given by Lepsius, 'Denkmäler,' and have been explained by M. de Rougé (whose treatise on the tomb of Aahmes marked a crisis in the advance of Egyptian studies), and are quoted repeatedly in M. Brugsch's 'Histoire d'Égypte.'

[25] By Mr. Goodwin, in the second part of the 'Mélanges égyptologiques' of M. Chabas. The argument is good for Egypt, not for the patriarchs, living the simple life and breathing the pure air of the desert.

[26] See Brugsch, 'Die Geographie des alten

Pharaoh of Joseph was certainly in a different position.

We have also evidence touching the general condition of Egypt under the dynasty or which Apophis was the most powerful king, and to whose reign the notice specially applies. The account given by Manetho of their devastations is probably exaggerated. It is certain that they did not deface the monuments to the extent which is generally supposed. The pyramids, the obelisk at Heliopolis, colossal figures and inscriptions even at Tanis (see above), and monuments in Middle and Upper Egypt, still bear witness in their favour. The Labyrinth in the Fayoum, and the great temples at Memphis and Heliopolis, were certainly left by them uninjured. Still the impression made by their ravages upon the Egyptians was profound: the name by which they were designated means pestilential deadly enemies.[27] From an inscription at Karnak,[28] we find that, under the nineteenth dynasty, when the Egyptians would describe a period of dreadful calamity, they could find no precedent so strong and apt as that of the Shepherd Kings. "One had not seen anything like it even in the time of the kings of Lower Egypt, when the land of Egypt was in their power, when wretchedness prevailed, in the time when the kings of Upper Egypt had not power to repel them." The account in the Papyrus Sallier I. quite agrees with this, showing that the reign of Apophis was cruel and oppressive throughout, and occupied towards the end, as we have seen, by an internecine war.

Again, no fact about Apophis is more certain than that he repudiated the national religion.[29] The testimony of the Papyrus Sallier is clear and explicit: "the King Apepi adopted Sutech as his God, he did not serve any God which was in the whole land." Sutech, or Set, in later ages the representative of the evil principle Typhon, is identified, and was certainly confounded with Baal of the Phœnicians. The only monument[30] on which the name of Apophis is found calls him "the beloved of Sutech:" an appellation, as we have seen, borne by the first Shepherd king, and probably common to all the dynasty. If we accept the probable tradition of Porphyry ('de Abst.' II, 55), that Aahmes I. suppressed human sacrifices offered under the Shepherd kings at Heliopolis, the form of worship must have been Typhonian, and in all probability of Phœnician origin.[31]

Each and all of these points are quite irreconcileable with the account in Genesis. The Pharaoh of Joseph was unquestionably Lord of all Egypt: the country was in a state of great prosperity: the religion, all the usages and institutions of the Pharaoh and his courtiers, were those of ancient Egypt. There is not a single fact[32] in the history of Joseph which is not illustrated by the inscriptions and sculptures of the best and most prosperous periods of Egypt; not one which gives the least indication of the predominance of a foreign religion, habits, or race.[33]

The question, however, still remains, if Joseph did not enter Egypt when the Shepherds were there, did his visit and the immigration of the Israelites take place before or after that period? We may assume that it did not occur at a later time. With very few exceptions, critics agree that the Israelites were in Egypt at the accession of the eighteenth dynasty. If before, we have still to inquire at what time.

This part of the inquiry is beset with considerable difficulties. We have no means of ascertaining the duration of the interval between the last sovereign of the twelfth dynasty and the invasion of the Shepherds. The titles of forty-eight kings of the thirteenth dynasty are given in the papyrus of Turin; and the names of three of them bear a very remark-

Ægyptens,' p. 180. M. Chabas in a treatise, 'Les Pasteurs en Égypte,' published within the last two months, assumes that three Pharaohs bore the name Ra-sekenen, Ra the conqueror. If this were granted, it would leave all other arguments untouched.

27 See M. Chabas, 'Mél. égypt.,' i.

28 See 'Revue Archéologique' for July and August, 1867. M. de Rougé gives a full account of the inscription, which has been lately published by M. Duemichen, 'Historische Inschriften.' I observe that the reference to the Shepherd kings is adopted by Dr. Ebers, 'Ægypten,' &c., p. 207.

29 The name Apepi, the Egyptian form of the word, signifies the great serpent, the enemy of Ra and Osiris. It was probably given to this king, or assumed by him, to mark his antagonism to the old national religion. It has, however, been shown by M. de Rougé, 'Recherches,' p. 9 and p. 45, that the worship of Sutech, or Set, as the tutelary god of lower Egypt, dates from the ancient empire. The peculiarity of Apepi, and probably of his predecessors, would seem to be his exclusive devotion to this deity, who represented force and destruction.

30 The inscription is given by Burton, 'Excerpta Hieroglyphica,' at San (*i.e.* Tanis), No. 7, pl. xv.; and by Brugsch, 'Geog. Inschr.,' p. 88, No. 576. Like Salatis, Apepi takes the style of a legitimate Pharaoh.

31 Sutech is identified with Baal in numerous inscriptions, and is represented specially as the chief deity of the Cheta, masters of northern Syria under the nineteenth dynasty.

32 This statement is strongly corroborated by the work of Dr. Ebers.

33 It must be remembered that in Joseph's time the Egyptians would not eat with shepherds; they were an abomination to them. This, of itself, is almost, if not quite, conclusive against the supposition that he was at the court of a Shepherd king. M. Chabas has shown this to be a true and monumental designation of the invaders.

able resemblance to the name given by Pharaoh to Joseph.[34] There appear to be good grounds for the opinion that they were driven out of Lower Egypt, and retained a partial and precarious hold on Middle or Upper Egypt within a century or two after their accession; and if so, Joseph, at the latest, may have lived under one of the early kings, such as the Sebekhotep, whose colossal statue in the Louvre belongs to the best age of Egyptian art, and evidently also to a period of unbroken prosperity.

It is however scarcely possible to resist the impression made by monuments of the twelfth dynasty, which seem to connect the history of Abraham, as we have already seen (p. 446), and still more specially that of Joseph, with this most important and interesting period of Egypt.

(7.) We have the fact that the princes of this great dynasty stood in very special relation to On or Heliopolis. The temple there was built by Osirtasin I., whose name and official title, Osirtasin Cheperkara, stand out in clear and perfect characters on the oldest and most beautiful obelisk of Egypt, still standing at On, the only but certain evidence of the magnificence of the temple. The priest of that city and temple, judging from the general usage of the ancient Pharaohs,[35] was in all probability a near relative of the sovereign. We have abundant notices on the monuments of that dynasty which agree with the intimations of Genesis; proving, on the one hand, that the forms of worship were purely Egyptian, and, on the other hand, that the fundamental principles which underlie those forms, and which belong, as we may not doubt, to the primeval religion of humanity, were still distinctly recognised, although they were blended with speculation and superstitious errors:[36] they were moreover associated with a system which, on many essential points, inculcated a sound and even delicate morality. In the priest of On a Shepherd king would have seen the antagonist of his own special superstition, the last man in Egypt whom he would have brought into connection with his favourite and prime minister: to an Osirtasin and to Joseph himself the alliance would present every inducement of policy, interest, and suitableness.

(8.) The tombs at Benihassan have already supplied us with illustrations of the history of Abraham, which are equally applicable to that of Joseph. The inscriptions, which describe the character of Chnumhotep (a near relative and favourite of Osirtasin I. and his immediate successor), and the recorded events of his government, remind the reader irresistibly of the young Hebrew. It is said of him[37] "he injured no little child: he oppressed no widow: he detained for his own purpose no fisherman: took from his work no shepherd: no overseer's men were taken. There was no beggar in his days: no one starved in his time. When years of famine occurred he ploughed all the lands of the district producing abundant food: no one was starved in it: he treated the widow as a woman with a husband to protect her." The mention of famine, and of unusual precautions to guard against its recurrence, together with other obvious traits of resemblance, led some critics a few years since to see in Chnumhotep the Egyptian original of Joseph. At present the antecedents and connections of that personage are too well known to admit of any confusion; but the probability must be admitted that a king, belonging to a dynasty which sought and rewarded such characteristics in the great officers of state, should have advanced Joseph to a position such as the Bible describes, such too as the old Egyptian papyrus already quoted (p. 446) shows to have been then within the reach of a foreigner.

(9.) There are still more specific reasons for fixing on this period. According to Genesis, one permanent consequence of the visitation was a new division of all Egypt, a redistribution of the land and property: probably, as is pointed out by the Bishop of Ely,[38] a necessary and politic measure, after the complete break-down of the ancient system. Now we are told by Herodotus and Diodorus that an ancient Egyptian king so divided the lands, and that the same system continued to their time. This king must evidently have belonged to a native dynasty: had the division been made by a foreigner and invader, it

---

[34] Viz. Zaf., *i.e.* food. See note on the name Zafnath Paaneah.

[35] See M. de Rougé, 'Recherches,' p. 34. Nearly all the chief priests bear the titles Suten sa or Suten rech — son, grandson, or relative of the king. Ewald justly observes that Heliopolis was, so to speak, the true sacerdotal city and university of Northern Egypt. Geschichte, ii., p. 51.

[36] See especially Lepsius, 'Ælteste Texte des Todtenbuchs.' The earliest known text of the seventeenth chapter of the Ritual belongs to the eleventh dynasty. Its importance is recognised as the most ancient statement of Egyptian views as to the origin and government of the universe. It undoubtedly indicates the previous existence of a pure Monotheism, of which it retains the great principles, the unity, eternity, self-existence of the unknown Deity. Each age witnessed some corruption and amplification of the ancient religion, and corresponding interpolations of the old texts. The very earliest has several glosses, and the text taken apart from them approaches very nearly to the truth as revealed in the Bible.

[37] Lepsius, 'Denkmäler,' ii. pl. 122. Dr. Birch, who gives an interlinear translation in Bunsen's 'Egypt,' vol. v. p. 726-729.

[38] See notes on Genesis.

would have been swept away when the line of the so-called legitimate Pharaohs was restored. Those two historians indeed attribute the division to the sovereign called Sesostris by Herodotus, and Sesoosis by Diodorus: an appellation which was afterwards appropriated to Rameses II., or perhaps to his father, Seti I. But it is well known that the exploits of the great sovereigns who preceded Rameses II. were transferred to him by popular tradition:[39] it is certain also that the division into nomes, and the exemption of the priestly lands from taxation, were anterior to him by many centuries. The system appears to have been coeval with the monarchy, certainly with the pyramids, but in all probability was modified, and extended, if not completed, under the great Pharaohs of the twelfth dynasty. No occasion can be pointed out more likely to have suggested it, and to have enabled the Pharaoh to accomplish it, than that described in Genesis.

Again, we learn from Egyptian sources that, under Amenemha III., in some respects the greatest king of this noble dynasty, whose reign is separated from the first by an interval of some two centuries (see above), a work of extraordinary magnitude and importance was undertaken and completed: one that proves at once the terror caused by the previous liability to famines, and the enormous resources, skill, and forethought of the Pharaoh. Amenemha III. first established a complete system of dykes, canals, locks, and reservoirs, by which the inundations of the Nile were henceforth regulated.[40] The immense artificial lake of Mœris in the Fayoum was made by his orders; it communicated with the Nile by a canal, received the overflowing waters at the time of the inundation, and secured the complete irrigation of the adjoining nomes in the dry season. M. Linant de Bellefonds,[41] to whose industry and ability we are indebted for ascertaining the exact site and extent of this lake, observes that the restoration of this magnificent work would be one of the greatest benefits that could be conferred on modern Egypt. Under Amenemha III. also the great labyrinth, the most stupendous work of that great age, was erected. This building was probably connected with the same series of events: it consisted of a vast number of halls and buildings, in which the representatives of the Egyptian nomes were assembled periodically to consult on subjects of national interest; and certainly not without a special view to the conservation of a system which afforded the best—indeed the only real—security against the recurrence of the most formidable calamity to which this people could be exposed. At no period would an Egyptian king have such special reasons for undertaking these works: at none would he have such peculiar opportunities of carrying them into effect—the reasons enforced by the seven years of famine, and the means supplied by the reconstruction of the territorial organisation, which placed the whole resources of the nation at the disposal of this Pharaoh.[42]

In the absence of positive evidence for or against any hypotheses, these coincidences may justify us in regarding it at least as a very probable conjecture that the visit of Abraham may have taken place under the first king of the dynasty, and that of Joseph under Amenemha III., the Pharaoh who is represented on the lately-discovered table of Abydos as the last great king of all Egypt in the ancient empire, and, as such, receiving divine honours from his descendant Rameses.

(10.) But if Joseph and the Israelites were received and treated with great favour by the native dynasty, it may seem improbable that they should have remained undisturbed under the Shepherd kings. We have of course no conclusive evidence either for or against the objection; but we have facts enough to show that it is quite possible that they may have occupied a relative position under the foreigners not differing widely from that in which the invasion found them. There can be no doubt that the invaders directed their assaults at once against the great cities of Egypt; both to enrich themselves with the spoil, and to secure their dominion over the lands. We may also feel pretty confident that they overthrew the national forms of worship, although, as we have above shown,

[39] Josephus expressly states that Manetho gives the name of Sesostris to the third king of the twelfth dynasty, whom he represents as conqueror of Asia. The researches of M. Mariette have lately shown that Rameses II. was in the habit of appropriating the exploits of his predecessors, and substituting his own name on the monuments (see below, p. 465). This evil habit was adopted by his son Merneptah.

[40] See Brugsch, 'Histoire d'Égypte,' p. 69. Lepsius found a Nilometer of Amenemha and several accurate notices of the height of the inundations under the twelfth and thirteenth dynasties at Semneh and Kumme.

[41] 'Mémoire sur le Lac Mœris:' Alexandrie, 1843. Mœris is not the name of a king, but he Egyptian word "mer," a lake or reservoir. Fayoum is the Arabic corruption of the Coptic ϕιομ, an old Egyptian word, "the sea." According to Ptolemy, near the lake was a place called Bakkhis or Banchis. M. Brugsch identifies this with a place called Pi-aneh, "the house of life," which is found on the monuments in connexion with Sebek, the tutelary deity of the district. See 'Geographie des Alten Ægyptens,' p. 233. This name has a special interest for its bearing upon Joseph's Egyptian name Zafnath Paaneah, "the food of life."

[42] The copper mines at Wady Mughara were worked under this prince; there is a curious notice of the expedition in Brugsch, 'H. E.,' p. 69. See also 'Introduction' to Exodus.

there is no evidence that they destroyed or defaced the temples. The Israelites, then a small colony lately established, would offer no temptation to their cupidity; no buildings, no temples, no elaborate ritual which could provoke their animosity. It must also be borne in mind that all historians are agreed that the invasion of the Hyksos was most probably preceded by peaceful visits of the chieftains of Arabia and the adjoining districts of Palestine, of which we have numerous traces in early monuments; from them they may have learned at once to appreciate the riches of Egypt, and to ascertain the state of the country. The jealousy with which such visitors were watched is distinctly noted in Genesis: every nomad company might be suspected of a desire to see the nakedness—that is, to spy the assailable approaches to the land; a jealousy of which also we have distinct notices in the story of Saneha and the inscriptions of Benihassan. But when the fathers of those invaders visited Egypt in the time of the great famine, which, as we know from other documents,[43] would draw them, with their flocks and herds, to the frontier, the person with whom they were brought into contact, and for whom they would feel the deepest reverence, was the master of the granaries, the distributor of food. Joseph could not be unknown by name or by character to the early Hyksos, who were little likely to disturb the kindred and descendants of the man to whom they were indebted for their lives. It is also evident that the rapid multiplication of the Israelites might be favoured by the withdrawal of the native princes from their immediate neighbourhood: they would be relieved from a superintendence ever vigilant and suspicious. It is not, however, necessary to assume any special favour shown to the Israelites by the Shepherds; the absence of any motive for cruel and oppressive treatment is obvious, and suffices for the removal of all objection on this score to the historical combination we have proposed.

(11.) We are now in a position to consider the question at what period in Egyptian history the Exodus took place. Some points of importance may be assumed as all but certain, there being no difference of opinion between Egyptologers. (1.) At whatever period the Israelites came into Egypt, they were settled in the district assigned to them when the first sovereign of the eighteenth dynasty conquered and expelled the Shepherd dynasty. (2.) The Exodus is admitted to have taken place under the eighteenth or nineteenth dynasty, under which is a question to be settled, but certainly under the one or the other. (3.) The dates referring to this period are still generally uncertain, they rest on doubtful calculations; it may suffice to quote the words of M. de Rougé, adopted by M. Chabas, 'Mélanges égyptologiques,' ii. p. 112: "On restera dans la limite du probable en plaçant Seti I. vers 1500, et le commencement de la 17e dynastie vers le 18e siècle. Mais il n'y aurait nullement à s'étonner si l'on s'était trompé de *deux cents ans* dans cette estimation, tant les documents sont viciés dans l'histoire, ou incomplets sur les monuments." In a work of great interest and importance published lately by M. Chabas, he reiterates this assertion, and rejects all the dates derived from astronomical notices. *See* 'Voyage d'un Égyptien,' p. 26.[44] This uncertainty must always be borne in mind: the dates derived from Egyptian monuments may be implicitly relied upon so far as they go, but, with one exception already noticed, they never refer to any general epoch, and do not supply materials for a complete chronological arrangement of events under either of the dynasties with which we are at present concerned.

Egyptian scholars have hitherto been divided between two opinions, some recognising in Aahmes, or Amosis, the first sovereign of the eighteenth dynasty, the first persecutor of the Israelites, and in one of his descendants the Pharaoh of the Exodus; others regarding the third sovereign of the nineteenth dynasty, *i.e.* Rameses II., the Sesostris of the Greeks, and his son Merneptah, or his grandson Seti, as the contemporaries of Moses. We will examine the grounds on which each of these opinions rests; and proceeding in order of time will first inquire into the claims of the eighteenth dynasty

(12.) The circumstances under which Aahmes I. the Amosis of Josephus, obtained possession of Lower Egypt, make it extremely probable that he should have adopted such measures towards the Israelites as are described in the beginning of Exodus.

His accession constitutes one of the most important epochs in Egyptian history; with it terminates the broken and confused period of the ancient Empire; with it begins a continuous series of events under successive dynasties. Previous to his accession, or shortly afterwards, he married an Ethiopian Princess, Nefertari, whose name and portrait are found on many monuments,[45] in which she

43 See the account of the admission of Edomites under Merneptah, infra, p. 486.

44 A single clear notice of a solar eclipse would settle a vast number of questions. M. Chabas has completely shown that hitherto none has been found (see 'Zeitschrift,' May, 1868). On the various attempts to establish a system on astronomical calculations, see Mr. Browne in Kitto's 'Cyclopædia,' vol. iii. p. 52.

45 One of the most striking portraits of Nefertari is the first plate in the third volume of Lepsius' 'Denkmäler.' See also a coloured tablet in the British Museum. She is there represented as jet black, but not with negro features. She was probably of the higher Nubian race. It has been observed that the portraits of the earlier

is represented as a personage of singular distinction, daughter, wife, sister, and mother of kings, and worshipped centuries after her death as a tutelary deity. It is inferred, with great probability, that this alliance with Ethiopia, which under the ancient empire had furnished large contingents of auxiliary troops to Egypt,[46] supplied Aahmes with resources which enabled him soon after his accession to undertake an expedition against the Northern dynasty. That expedition was completely successful: it terminated the struggle. A contemporary inscription on the tomb of one of his chief officers (the naval captain Ahmes), gives an account of the siege of Avaris, of a battle fought in its vicinity, and of the capture of that city, the stronghold of Apepi. It also informs us that the expulsion of the enemy was followed by an expedition to the borders of Canaan, when Sarouhen was taken by storm.[47]

It is at once clear that the expressions used in Exodus to describe the Pharaoh by whom the Israelites were first persecuted, apply, in the fullest and most literal sense, to this sovereign. To the people of the greater part of Egypt, and most especially to the inhabitants of the North, he was emphatically "a new king:" of him it might be said, as of no native king, succeeding without a struggle (as was most especially the case of Rameses II.), "he arose up over" Egypt; he was, in the true sense of the word, like the Norman William, *a conqueror*. The name of Joseph, whether as a minister of the ejected dynasty, or of one more ancient than that, would probably be unknown to him. Nor can there be any reasonable doubt as to the feelings with which a king in his position must have regarded the Israelites. There is no question as to his finding them in Goshen; that is admitted by all.[48] They were there as the subjects, apparently the favoured subjects, of the expelled dynasty, under whom they retained undisturbed possession of the richest district of Egypt, commanding the western approach to the very heart of the land. The first point that would naturally strike him would be their number (Exod. i. 9), which, after the expulsion of his enemies, would bear an alarming proportion to the native population of the Delta. A prudent man under such circumstances would not be likely to provoke rebellion by proceeding to extremities, but nothing is more probable than that he should do just what Moses tells us the new king actually did, deal with them craftily, prevent their increase, utilise their labour, and cut off all communication with foreigners. The most advantageous employment which would suggest itself would of course be the construction of strongly-fortified depositaries of provisions and arms near the eastern frontier. The line of fortresses was enlarged and strengthened by Rameses II., but that king was not the original founder. Traces are found which prove the existence both of the canal and of several forts under the ancient empire.[49] One of these forts, bearing the name Pa-chtum en Zaru, is mentioned in the monumental annals of Thotmes III. It is identified by M. Brugsch with the Pithom of the Exodus.[50] The name signifies "the fortress of foreigners or sojourners," *i.e.* a fortress either built by foreigners or assigned to immigrants as a

---

kings of the dynasty bear distinct traces of black blood. Rosellini gives a portrait of Amenophis I. (whom, however, he confounds with Aahmes), in which he is represented as a black. 'Monum. R.,' pl. xxix. At Karnak there is a representation of the shrine of Nefertari borne by twelve priests; she is there associated with Rameses II., after an interval of some three centuries.

46 M. de Rougé gives a very curious account of the organisation of a negro army, under Pepi, of the sixth dynasty. As in our Indian possessions, these alien troops were drilled and commanded by native Egyptians. See 'Recherches,' p. 123.

47 This is a very important point. It shows the inaccuracy of the account given by Josephus from Manetho, and, before this inscription was known, adopted by Egyptian scholars, viz., that the war between upper and lower Egypt continued to the third or fourth reign of the eighteenth dynasty. There can be no question as to the correctness of the contemporary inscription. Ptolemy, a priest of Mendes, quoted by Apion (ap. Clem. Alex. 'Sor.,' 1, 21, p. 178, ed. Potter), says of Amosis that he *κατέσκαψε τὴν Αὔαριν*. He was better informed than Manetho. M. de Rougé justly claims the credit of having proved this capital point (question capitale). See the 'Report on Egyptian Studies' for 1867, p. 18; and compare M. Chabas, 'Les Pasteurs en Egypte,' 1868, where the whole inscription is translated.

48 *E.g.* by M. de Rougé, Brugsch, &c.

49 An officer who fled from Egypt in the reign of Osirtasin speaks of a wall which the king had built to keep off the Sakti, *i.e.* Asiatic invaders. See the story of Saneha; and Chabas, 'Voyage d'un Égyptien,' p. 293; and on the Sakti, p. 321. Dr. Ebers, l. c. p. 81, entirely corroborates the view taken by the writer. He shows that the line, previously existing, must have been strengthened by one of the earliest kings of the eighteenth dynasty, and completed in all probability by the fortress, called the fort, or the "close" of Zar. The word rendered "fort," viz. chetem, is retained in Coptic, as ϣⲧⲙ̀, or ⲧⲱⲙ, to shut. This fort is very specially the key of Egypt, *ἡ κλεὶς τῆς Αἰγύπτου*, the frontier station for the armies of the Pharaohs, and for Asiatic immigrants.

50 This identification is not accepted by M. Chabas, who gives another and more probable etymology for the Hebrew Pithom, viz. the sanctuary of Tum. But it is probable, indeed all but certain, that the fortress and the sanctuary were contiguous, and formed together the principal rendezvous of the Egyptian troops and foreign embassies on the frontier. On the name Raamses, see infra, under Rameses.

residence.[51] We learn from Genesis that Raamses was the name of the district in the time of Jacob, and from the Egyptian monuments that one of the sons of Aahmes was named Rames; probable grounds are thus found for the designation of the second fort built at the same time. It is also well known that during the latter part of his reign Aahmes was occupied in building and repairing the cities of Northern Egypt. In an inscription lately deciphered,[52] dated in his twenty-second year, certain Fenchu are stated to be employed in the transport of blocks of limestone from the quarries of Rufu (the Troja of Strabo) to Memphis and other cities. These Fenchu are unquestionably aliens, either mercenaries or forced labourers. According to Brugsch, the name means "bearers of the shepherd's staff;" and he describes their occupation as precisely corresponding to that of the Israelites.[53] No proper name for the Israelites is found on the monuments of the eighteenth dynasty;[54] during which period all Egyptologers admit their presence in Egypt: they could certainly not be designated more exactly whether we regard the name or the occupation of these Fenchu.

(13.) It has been shown that little dependence can be placed on systems of Egyptian chronology, yet it may be observed that either of those which are most generally accepted is quite reconcileable with this hypothesis.

Two dates, which differ very widely, are given, not as certain, but approximative and probable.

Brugsch, following Lepsius, fixes the accession of Aahmes I. at 1706 B.C. This would be in very near accordance with Hebrew history if the dates drawn from notices in the Book of Judges were accepted in preference to that given in 1 Kings vi. The last year of Thotmes II., which, as will be shown, is very probably that of the Exodus, falls on the same system in 1647 B.C. Now, the interval between the building of the Temple, about 1010 A.C., and the Exodus, is calculated to amount to 638 years by the advocates of the longer chronology: certainly a most remarkable coincidence, the more so since neither Brugsch nor the other Egyptian chronologers adopt that date for the Exodus.

The other date, given also approximately, is 1525 B.C. for Aahmes I., and 1463 for the last year of Thotmes II. This accords pretty nearly with the shorter interval of 480 years given in 1 Kings vi. 1.

This later date has been lately supported in a very remarkable way by a discovery which, if it could be absolutely relied upon, would settle the chronology.[55] Thotmes III. built a temple at Elephantine: it has been destroyed within the last few years by the natives, but on one stone found near the ruins the name of the king is distinctly read; on another stone is an inscription stating that the 28th of the month Epiphi was the festival of the rising of Sothis, *i. e.* Sirius. From this M. Biot calculates the date, which he fixes as 1445 B.C. Now the reign of Thotmes III. lasted about forty-eight years; the temple was probably built towards the end of his reign, which up to the last seven years was occupied in foreign warfare; we should thus get the date from 1485 to 1492 for the last year of Thotmes II.,

---

51 This is a point of considerable importance, brought out by Brugsch in the third volume of the 'Geographische Inschriften,' p. 21. He says, "I believe that I am nearer than formerly to the trace of the meaning of this name. The old Egyptian Zaru, or Zalu, is evidently related to the Coptic ⲭⲱⲓⲗⲓ, whence ⲣⲉⲙⲭⲱⲓⲗⲓ, peregrinus, advena."

52 See Brugsch, 'Zeitschrift' for November, 1867.

53 Brugsch observes, "With this name are designated the pastoral and nomad tribes of Semitic origin, who lived in the neighbourhood of Egypt, and who are to be thought of as standing to Egypt in the same relation as the Jews," l. c. p. 92. This is the more important since Brugsch does not connect the narrative of Exodus with this period.

54 On the name "Aperu," supposed to represent Hebrews, see further on. It is found first in papyri of a later date, under the nineteenth dynasty.

55 This date has given occasion to much controversy. It is utterly irreconcileable with the system of some chronologers. Lepsius at once met it with the assumption that the Egyptian sculptor committed the error of adding a line, the effect of which would be to alter the calculations to the extent of 130 years. He was followed by Bunsen, and, though with some misgiving, by Brugsch. If any answer were needed, it might be given in the words of M. de Rougé: "Ce n'est pas ainsi qu'on peut lever une difficulté de cette gravité : le monument aujourd'hui à Paris est comme gravure de la plus grande beauté; il appartient du reste à l'époque où les inscriptions présentent la correction la plus parfaite." See also M. Chabas, M.E. ii. p. 18. A more serious objection has since been raised and defended with great ability by M. Chabas. The inscription which gives the official name of Thotmes III., and that which gives the name of the month on which the calculation is based, are on different stones, and cannot be proved to refer to the same date. The latter may possibly refer to additions to the temple. M. Chabas writes with a strong bias, so much so that he even attempts to explain away the well-known phrase for the coming forth or heliacal rising of Sothis; and Mr. Goodwin, a very high authority, does not consider that he has proved his points. In the present state of the question, all that we are entitled to assume is that the inscriptions may probably refer to the same time, viz. that of the erection of the temple, and give a date which presents a very striking coincidence with that taken from the statement in 1 Kings vi.

a date exactly in accordance with that derived from 1 Kings vi. 1.[56]

In the present state of inquiry it is sufficient to point out the singular accordance between two very different systems of Biblical and Egyptian chronology, whichever may be ultimately adopted.

(14.) Assuming for the present that the persecution of the Israelites began under Aahmes I., the question still remains under which of his successors the Exodus took place. In the absence of monumental evidence the question cannot be decisively settled, but there appear to be substantial grounds for the conclusion that it occurred at the close of the reign of Thotmes II.

The length of the interval between the accession of Aahmes I. and of Thotmes III. cannot be accurately determined. The calculations of Brugsch (which are quite irrespective of our question) give an interval of eighty-one years. According to Josephus, Manetho gives 100 years 5 months for the period between the expulsion of the shepherds and the accession of the Pharaoh whom he calls Mephramuthosis. These dates are wholly uncertain, each recension of Manetho giving different numbers; but the interval probably extended over one hundred years. This coincides very closely with the period required by the Scriptural narrative: some years elapsed before the birth of Moses, eighty years between his birth and the Exodus.

(15.) The events of the succeeding reigns under which Moses must have lived, assuming the correctness of this hypothesis, accord with inferences suggested by the brief narrative of Exodus, and also with notices in Josephus, which though of a legendary character may have some foundation in facts. On the death of Aahmes the government appears to have been in the hands of Nefertari, the Ethiopian princess, either as sovereign, or more probably as regent.[57] Little was known of Amenophis (or Amenhotep) her son, until the following facts were elicited from contemporary monuments. Ahmes, the naval officer already mentioned, went with Amenophis in an expedition into Ethiopia against an insurgent chieftain. The expedition was successful. Josephus gives a long and evidently legendary account of an expedition of Moses into Ethiopia. As a member of the royal household, the adopted child of the King's sister, he would naturally accompany his master; while gratitude to his benefactress would of course give additional impetus to his efforts against an Ethiopian rebel. Amenophis was undoubtedly an able and prosperous king, leaving a great name, and worshipped as a god in after ages.

The circumstances which led to the flight of Moses may have taken place at the close of this reign.[58] Syncellus mentions a tradition that Moses left the court after the death of Amosis and of his daughter, whom he calls Pharie: it is more probable that this occurred some years later, since Moses could not have reached manhood when Aahmes died. At the death of Amenophis he would be about forty. It has been represented as improbable that the adopted son of Pharaoh's daughter found no protector when he slew an Egyptian subject, a most unreasonable objection even if the princess were still living; her death would of course leave him friendless.

(16.) During the reign of Thotmes I., Moses, on this supposition, must have been in Midian, but the events are not without bearings upon his history. The reign was one of great prosperity. The complete subjugation of the district between Upper Egypt and Nubia Proper is attested by the inscirption previously quoted and by another found by the Prussian expedition on the rock opposite the island of Tombos.[59] The latter years of his reign[60] were employed in a war of greater interest. We learn from the sepulchral inscription already mentioned that he invaded Mesopotamia, won a great victory, and brought back an immense number of captives. A great advance was thus made in the condition of Egypt. Its

[56] A very curious corroboration of this hypothesis may be drawn from some calculations of Mr. Goodwin in the 'Zeitschrift' for 1867, p. 78. He shows that, if certain data are admitted, one of the following dates would fall within the reign of Thotmes III., viz. 1481, 1480, 1479, 1478. He says, "According to the system of some of the chronologists this would suit the reign of Thotmes III." It certainly suits that chronology of the Bible which appears most probable to the writer of this Essay. On grounds quite independent of the astronomical calculation, he would have us go back 120 years, and take 1601, 1600, 1599, 1598 as the date, fixing the accession of Thotmes III. as 1623, 1622, 1621, or 1620. This, as he points out, agrees very nearly with the date of Brugsch, viz. 1625 A.C. It certainly agrees also with the system of those chronologers who adopt the longer interval.

[57] It is an obvious conjecture that such an association may have had some influence upon the feelings of Moses when in later years he married an Ethiopian.

[58] All the recensions of Manetho give thirteen years for Chebron, *i.e.* Nefertari (see above), and twenty-one for Amenophis. Moses is said to have been forty years old at the time of his flight. The coincidence of dates is perfect, as he was in all probability born a few years before the death of Aahmes.

[59] Ethiopia was henceforth governed by princes of the blood royal. A list of twenty, bearing the style Prince Royal of Cush, beginning with this reign, is drawn from the monuments. The first bears the name Me-Mes, an odd coincidence. See 'Exc.' on Moses.

[60] The duration of the reign is uncertain; the monuments give no information, and the dates of Manetho are in utter confusion.

permanent resources were increased by the acquisition of Nubia, the land of gold,[61] and henceforth we find the Pharaohs in possession of numerous chariots, which, though not unknown,[62] are not represented on early monuments. We have here every indication of national greatness.

(17.) On the death of Thotmes I. the government was once more for some years in the hands of a woman. His wife and sister Aahmes,[63] called Amessis by Josephus, was regent or sovereign, according to Manetho, for upwards of twenty years. Thotmes II.[64] showed energy in the beginning of his reign; he carried on a successful war against the Shasous, the nomad tribes on the north-eastern frontier. No other notice is found of his acts on the monuments. His reign was probably short and certainly inglorious. The following facts are however certain from contemporary monuments.[65] He was married to his sister Hatasou;[66] after his decease, of which the circumstances are unknown, she succeeded him as Queen Regnant. His death was immediately followed by a general revolt of the confederated nations on the north of Palestine, which had been conquered by his father: no attempt was made to recover the lost ascendancy of Egypt until the 22nd year of Thotmes III.

Certainly no conjunction of circumstances can be conceived which would adjust itself more naturally to the Scriptural narrative, if we assume that the Exodus took place at this time. In a history drawn entirely from public inscriptions and monuments, no one would expect to find records of events humiliating to the national pride: a period of heavy and disgraceful calamity would present but a blank.[67] Now the reigns of all other early kings in this great dynasty were prosperous and glorious, filled with great events attested by numerous monuments. This king succeeded to a great place; his first years were brilliant, he cleared his frontiers: there is no indication of rebellion or of foreign invasion, and yet the last years are a complete blank: there is a sudden and complete collapse:[68] he dies, no son succeeding: his throne is long occupied by a woman: and no effort is made to regain the former possessions of Egypt for more than twenty years. We have ample space for the events which preceded the Exodus; we find the conditions presupposed in the accounts of the mission of Moses, and the results which might have been anticipated from calamities which, though not sufficient to crush the nation, would cripple its resources, and for a time subdue its spirit.

Assuming for the present the truth of this hypothesis, we may consider what might be the probable course of events. On the return of Moses from Midian, in the eightieth year of his age, and therefore towards the close of the reign of Thotmes II., he found the Pharaoh in lower Egypt, probably at Zoan (see Psalm lxxviii. 12), *i.e.* Tanis, or as the Egyptians call it Avaris, the city captured by his ancestor. The residence of the court for a great part of the year would naturally be in that district. The upper country was quiet after the conquest of Nubia, whereas the territory occupied by the Israelites required watching, and the neighbouring Shasous, or Bedouins, caused constant alarms. The character of the king as described in Exodus was at once weak and obstinate, cruel and capricious,

[61] Nub is the well-known Egyptian name for gold.

[62] The war chariot of Aahmes I. is expressly mentioned in the inscription at Elkab.

[63] In these reigns there are several instances of marriages between brother and sister. M. de Rougé observes that it does not appear to have been a custom under the early Pharaohs.—'Recherches,' p. 62.

[64] The joint reigns of Amesses and Mephres, or Misaphris, are computed at thirty-five or thirty-three years in the tables of Bunsen, from Josephus and Africanus. Eusebius omits both Thotmes I. and Amesses. We may not place any reliance on the numbers of Manetho, but they were probably taken from old monuments, and, though often corrupted and distorted, may occasionally be correct. In this case they coincide very strikingly with the narrative of Exodus, allowing an interval of some forty years between the decease of Amenophis and of Thotmes II.

[65] According to the monuments, Thotmes II., his wife Hatasou, and Thotmes III., were children of the same parent or parents. If the joint reigns of Amesses and Thotmes II. extended over thirty years, or even a much shorter period, Thotmes III. could not have been the son of Thotmes I., since he was a mere child at the death of Thotmes II. He is represented as a boy of some ten or twelve years old, sitting on the knees of Hatasou, on the monuments. If we might assume that Thotmes II. and his wife were children of Thotmes I. and Amesses, and that Thotmes III. was a son of Amesses by another husband, this would meet the difficulty. It is certain that Thotmes II. was son of Thotmes I. See 'Denkmäler,' iii. pl. xvi. a. l. 7.

[66] This is probably the true reading of the name, which means "chief of the illustrious." The phonetic value of one of the signs is disputed by Mr. Goodwin, but is shown to be correct by Renouf and Lauth.

[67] M. de Rougé, speaking of the name Aperu (see further on), observes, "C'est la seule trace que la captivité d'Israel aura laissée probablement sur les monuments : il n'est pas à penser que les Égyptiens y aient jamais consigné ni le souvenir des plaies, ni celui de la catastrophe terrible de la Mer Rouge ; car leurs monuments ne consacrent que bien rarement le souvenir de leurs défaites." See also the memoir lately published (1869), 'Moïse et les Hébreux,' p. 2.

[68] M. Brugsch says strongly and truly, "as it seems, all that had been previously conquered was completely lost.—'Geographie,' i. p. 54.

such a character as is calculated to provoke or accelerate great national calamities. Nor can we lose sight altogether of the queen. She was a very remarkable woman, daughter, sister, and wife of kings, with the antecedents of her mother and grandmother, both of whom had been regents, and she was able to retain the government of the nation during the prolonged minority of the greatest and most energetic king of the dynasty. Such a woman may well have helped her brother and husband to "harden his heart," after each ague fit of misgiving and terror. That she was a woman of strong religious prejudices is proved by her own inscriptions: as such she could not but be revolted by the insults heaped upon the soothsayers, priests, temples, and idols of Egypt. When her heart was crushed by the loss of her first-born son, we can conceive the mingled feelings which would send her to the king, if not to suggest, yet to strengthen his resolution to make one more effort to save his kingdom from disgrace, and to avenge the long series of calamities upon Israel.[69] These are of course but conjectures, but they rest upon facts distinctly recorded on contemporary Egyptian monuments, and they harmonize thoroughly with the narrative of Exodus.

The history of the next reign supplies some remarkable coincidences.

(18.) Thotmes III. remained in reluctant subjection to his sister at least seventeen years.[70] On taking possession of the throne he defaced her titles on the monuments, and reckoned his own reign from the death of his predecessor, without any notice of the intervening period. It may be inferred from this that her rule was distasteful to the people, associated, it may be, with national disasters. It is certain that during her regency there was a general revolt and confederacy of the nations on the north-west of Egypt from Palestine to Mesopotamia.

It was not until the twenty-second year of his reign—a date, as will appear, of singular importance in this inquiry—that Thotmes III. began a series of expeditions unparalleled for extent and grandeur in Egyptian history.[71]

The following facts are clearly proved.

The king left Zaru, or Pithom, early in the year, and advanced without encountering any opposition to Sarouhen on the southern frontier of Palestine. He was detained by the siege of Gaza, which he took early in the spring of the following year. On the 16th of Pachon, early in March, at a fort named Souhem, he heard of the advance of the allied kings of all the districts between the Euphrates and the Mediterranean. The decisive battle was fought at Megiddo, the earliest and one of the most important of the conflicts in that great battle-field of Western Asia. The allies were completely defeated, the dead covered the plain, horses and chariots[72] in vast numbers were taken, and on the following day the chiefs, who had fled to Megiddo, came to offer submission and tributes, consisting of gold, silver, bronze, lapis-lazuli, coffers of precious metals, chariots plated with gold and silver, magnificent vases of Phœnician workmanship, a harp of bronze inlaid with gold, ivory, perfumes, and wine. The proofs of an advanced civilisation in the nations then dominant in Palestine accord with all the representations in Scripture. The point, however, of main importance in the present inquiry is that the power of the confederacy which gave unity and strength to the people of Canaan was completely broken by Thotmes III., just seventeen years before the date when, on the hypothesis we are now considering, the Israelites entered Palestine.

The incursions of Thotmes continued without intermission during this interval. We have accounts of repeated invasions of Phœnicia, conquests over the Rutens[73] in Mesopotamia, where the king established a fortress or military colony: we find the great names of Assur, Babel, Nineveh, Shinear, the Remenen, or Armenians, and most frequently of the Cheta, the sons of Heth, the Hittites of Scripture.[74]

---

[69] The inscriptions on her obelisk, the most beautiful now remaining at Thebes, give a strong impression of this queen's character. She speaks of her favour with Ammon, boasts of her gracious and popular manners, and is represented in this, and also in other monuments, in masculine attire, including *a beard*. See the inscriptions in the 'Zeitschrift' for 1865, p. 34, and Brugsch, 'Recueil,' ii. p. 79.

[70] Dr. Birch finds a higher date for the joint government, twenty-one years.

[71] A full account of these expeditions was inscribed on the walls of a temple dedicated to Ammon after his last return to Egypt. They are given by Lepsius in the 'Denkmäler,' vol. iii., and in the 'Auswahl;' some are published by Brugsch, 'Recueil,' and by M. de Rougé, 'Étude sur divers monuments du règne de Toutmès III,' 1861. Mr. Birch first encountered, and to a great extent overcame, the formidable difficulties of decipherment and translation. His labours, and those of M. de Rougé and Brugsch, have made them accessible to students.

[72] 892 chariots are mentioned; a very curious coincidence with the statement in Judges v., where we are told that Jabin, in the same battle-field, had 900 chariots.

[73], Rutennu, as M. Chabas has proved, designates the northern Syrians. The name may be read Lutennu, or even Ludennu, and is identified with Lud by M. de Rougemont, 'Age du Bronze.' The presence of Egyptians in Mesopotamia under the eighteenth dynasty, and in the time of Thotmes III., is proved by scarabæi found at Arban, on the Cabus, a tributary of the Euphrates.

[74] M. Chabas denies the identity of the Hittites with the Cheta, chiefly on philological grounds, since the names, of which several are given, indi-

One object was steadily pursued by the king during these campaigns. In accordance with the ancient policy of the Pharaohs,[75] but as it would seem because such a measure was especially important at that time, and probably one main motive for the repeated razzias, Thotmes brought an immense number of captives into Egypt. These are his own words:[76] "I made a great offering to Ammon in recognition of the first victory which he granted me, filling his domain with slaves, to make him stuffs of various materials, to labour and cultivate the lands, to make harvests, to fill the habitation of Father Ammon."[77] At Abd el Kurna, in the temple before mentioned, there is a well-known picture of such captives employed in making bricks. It is an admirable illustration of the labours of the Israelites, whom it was formerly supposed to represent: the inscription, however, states that they are "captives taken by his Majesty to build the temple of his Father Ammon."

We have now to call special attention to this fact. The wars of Thotmes III. were terminated by the complete overthrow of all his foes in Syria and Mesopotamia in the fortieth year of his reign. No question is raised about this date. But according to our present hypothesis this took place exactly forty years after the Exodus, immediately before the entrance of the Israelites into Palestine.

They would then have found the country in a state of utter prostration. With the exception of such strongholds as might be retained by the Egyptians to command the road into Syria, the petty kings would keep each his own fortress, with no common head, no powerful ally, accustomed to see their neighbours and kinsmen beaten and subjugated, and, though warlike, well supplied with arms, and occupying forts well-nigh impregnable,[78] yet habituated to defeat, and liable, as the Scriptural narrative describes them, to wild fits of panic at the approach of a new foe. If again, as there is reason to believe, the kings of Bashan, and other districts east of the Jordan, were among the confederates defeated on his first invasion by Thotmes, it would account for their exhaustion, and the extreme terror of the princes of Midian and Moab.[79]

(19.) It may be asked how could the Israelites during that period escape the notice of the king? It is certain that the high road, always followed by the Egyptian armies, ran along the coast of the Mediterranean till it turned off towards Megiddo. The Israelites were in the desert of Tih, a district not easily accessible and offering no temptation to a conqueror whose energies were concentrated in a desperate war. Had they remained in the peninsula of Sinai they would have been within his reach, for its western district was subject to Egypt from a very early period.[80] It is possible that their flight might have been one motive for an expedition which, as we learn from an inscription in the Wady Mughara, was undertaken by the forces of Hatasou and Thotmes in the sixteenth year of their joint reign.

A far more serious objection rests on the improbability that the powerful kings of the eighteenth and nineteenth dynasties would have permitted the invasion or the continued occupation of Palestine by the Israelites.

We might answer in the first place that this objection applies to every other date suggested by chronologers. The very latest date assumes that the Exodus took place under the son or grandson of Rameses II., and that the Israelites passed the Jordan in the time of Rameses III. But that Pharaoh was one of the most powerful sovereigns of Egypt, and it is certain that his descendants, the princes of the twentieth dynasty, retained command of the communications by land and water with Mesopotamia. This is proved by

---

cate a different origin. Most Egyptologers, however, retain the older view, which is defended by very convincing arguments by M. de Rougé. It is confirmed also by the Assyrian inscriptions, which make the Khati or Hatti occupy the country between the Mediterranean and Carchemish, their frontier city in the times of Tiglath Pileser I., see Rawlinson's 'Ancient Monarchies,' vol. ii. pp. 315, 317, and Menant, 'Syllabaire Assyrien,' p. 155, who identifies them with the Hittites. The identification of the Remenen is proposed by Brugsch.

75 We have a very early record of this policy in the reign of Pepi, of the sixth dynasty. See M. de Rougé, 'Recherches,' p. 128.

76 See Brugsch, 'Recueil de Monuments Égyptiens,' vol. i. p. 53.

77 See Brugsch, 'Recueil,' i. p. 53.

78 The history of the siege of Gaza, which lasted more than a year, may account for the Egyptians leaving so many cities untouched, retaining a partial or entire independence. This applies to campaigns under the nineteenth and twentieth dynasties.

79 This gives a peculiar force and suitableness to the words of Balaam, twice repeated, "God brought them out of Egypt. He hath, as it were, the strength of an unicorn." Num. xxiii. 22, xxiv. 8.

80 The intercourse between Egypt and the west of the peninsula began under Snefru, the last Pharaoh of the third dynasty. He defeated the Anu, the ancient inhabitants, and founded a colony at the Wady Mughara. The most ancient monument in existence records this event. The copper-mines there were worked under Chufu (Cheops) and other sovereigns of the fourth and following dynasties. We read of a formal inspection by Pepi. See M. de Rougé, 'Recherches,' pp. 7, 30, 31, 42, 81, 115. The mines were worked under Amenemha, twelfth dynasty, and the influence or sovereignty of Egypt continued unbroken till long after the Exodus. M. Chabas shows that under the twentieth dynasty the communications were regularly carried on.

an inscription of great interest and importance, well known to Egyptian scholars, which belongs to the reign of Rameses XII., towards the close of the dynasty. M. de Rougé[81] says, "Elle suppose une domination encore incontestée sur la Mesopotamie, des relations amicales entre les princes d'Asie et le Pharaon, ainsi que des routes habituellement parcourues par le commerce." However it may be accounted for, it is certain that during the whole period between Joshua and Rehoboam the Israelites were not disturbed in the possession of the strongholds of Palestine, although the Pharaohs, as we have just seen, retained an undisputed supremacy in Western Asia up to the time of Samuel or Saul.

There are, however, facts, which, though seldom noticed, are sufficiently obvious, and may enable us to understand the policy of the Pharaohs.

It is clear, even from the history of the campaigns of Thotmes III., that at the end of each campaign the Egyptians withdrew their forces altogether from the countries which they overran, content with the plunder, and especially the capture of prisoners, with the submission of the chiefs, and the tributes which they were secure of exacting. This might be a result of the constitution of the Egyptian armies. The Calasirians and Hermotybians, the warrior caste, had settled homes to which they would certainly choose to return, probably each year after the subsidence of the inundation, when their labours would be required for the cultivation of the fields. We have no trace of permanent occupancy of foreign stations, excepting one in Mesopotamia, another at the copper-mines in the Wady Mughara, and perhaps of a few fortresses on the route through Syria. A rapid campaign directed against the nations to the north of Palestine, who were in a state of chronic insurrection, and threw off the yoke at every opportunity, would give an Egyptian king neither the leisure nor the inclination to assail the strongholds occupied by the Israelites. It must also be borne in mind that the Israelites attacked the most powerful enemies of Egypt, the Hittites and Amorites, and that, whereas their conquest certainly did not result in the establishment of a formidable empire, it was an effectual check to the restoration and consolidation of the powers which Thotmes had overthrown. We do not find notices of many incursions under the immediate successors of Thotmes. That which is recorded, under Amenophis II., appears from the inscription[82] to have been carried on by sea. The three invasions under the nineteenth and twentieth dynasties, by Seti I., Rameses II., and Rameses III., had each the same general object, and was pursued on the same system and with the same general results, although as we shall find presently a considerable number of Israelites were probably carried into captivity by the two last-named kings.

If the date which is here assumed be correct, we shall expect that those events which are ascertained from later Egyptian monuments of the eighteenth and nineteenth dynasties will harmonise with it. An absolute contradiction would be fatal to the hypothesis, which of course will be materially strengthened by general and special coincidences.

(20.) The reign of Thotmes III. was followed by a period of great prosperity. The supremacy of Egypt in Western Asia was unbroken, certainly during the two following reigns. Is this general statement compatible with the conquest of Palestine by the Israelites? To answer this question we must look closely at the events in each reign, not forgetting that, as we have already shown, a general supremacy was undoubtedly retained from the accession of the nineteenth to the termination of the twentieth dynasty: that is throughout the period which all chronologers hold to have extended to the end of the book of Judges.

Immediately after the accession of Amenophis II. he undertook an expedition against the Rutens. He appears to have advanced as far as Nineveh; he certainly returned to Egypt with the trophies of a great victory. An inscription at Amada in Nubia, quoted by M. Brugsch, 'H. E.,' p. 111, and by M. Chabas, 'Voyage d'un Égyptien,' p. 194, states that this king slew seven princes of the confederates at Tachis (a city in Syria), and that "they were hung head downwards on the prow of his Majesty's ship."

These facts are of considerable importance. They show that the whole energies of the Pharaohs were directed against the confederates on the north of Palestine, whose defeat and prostration would of course effectually prevent them from marching into Palestine either to support their allies, or to avenge

---

[81] 'Journal Asiatique,' 5th series, vol. viii. p. 204.

[82] The word used in reference to the invasions of Asia in the reigns of Amenophis II. and III., is , which indicates a naval expedition. See 'Denkmäler,' iii. pl. 82. M. Chabas, who quotes the inscription, 'Voyage d'un Égyptien,' p. 194, refers, of course by oversight, to Amenophis I. It is a point of much importance in this inquiry to have this intimation of the transport of troops to Phœnicia by water. It is more than probable that the Egyptians had a considerable navy under the vigorous administration of the early kings of this dynasty. We have, in fact, the representation of the transport of chariots and horses on ships in the tomb of Ahmes at El Kab, which belongs to this very period. See Rosellini, M. C., pl. cx., and Duemichen, 'Fleet of an Egyptian Queen,' taf. xxviii. 5.

their fall before Joshua. The mention of the ship of war has a special interest. It is obvious that, as the Pharaohs were the undisputed masters of the sea after the conquest of Phœnicia under Thotmes III., the most ready and effectual way of transporting their troops would be by ships.[83] We have not sufficient data to prove that they did adopt this mode of carrying on their communications, but there are other indications which make it extremely probable. The word used in the inscriptions which record invasions of Asia under Amenophis III. is specially if not exclusively used of naval expeditions. (See note 82.) It has been shown very lately by a contemporary inscription that at a far earlier period, under the sixth dynasty, the Pharaoh Pepi sent large forces by sea against the Herusha, probably Asiatics. See De Rougé, 'Recherches,' p. 126. The rapid march of an Egyptian army along the coast of Palestine some seven or eight years after the passage over the Jordan would not present any considerable difficulty, directed as it was against the confederates of the Amorites, but every semblance of a difficulty disappears if the expedition was by sea.

Under Thotmes IV. we have no notice of Asiatic war. The tributes were probably paid without any further attempt at resistance during that reign, which, though undistinguished and probably short, does not appear to have been a period of disturbance.[84]

(21.) The reign of Amenophis III. was long and prosperous. His supremacy in Syria and Mesopotamia was uncontested; but though the inscriptions speak of expeditions into the Soudan, and of tributes brought from all nations, there is no indication of Asiatic warfare. It was a period of almost uninterrupted peace. There is no probability that the struggles in Palestine would have attracted the attention or called for the interposition of a monarch engaged in magnificent works which surpass in beauty and rival in extent those which were completed under any succeeding dynasty.

There are, however, facts which may perhaps justify a conjecture that the relations between Egypt and the Israelites underwent some modification in the interval after the occupation of Palestine which corresponds to this period. In 1 Chron. iv. 17, we read that Mered, of the tribe of Judah, founded two families, one by an Egyptian wife Bithia, who is called a daughter of Pharaoh. This family was settled at Eshtemoa, on the hilly district of Judah, south of Hebron, now Isemna; the ruins indicate the site of a considerable city. The exact place of Ezra, the father of Mered, in the genealogy is uncertain, but it belongs apparently to the second generation from Caleb. Now we have the fact that Amenophis III. was married to a very remarkable personage who was not of royal parentage and not an Egyptian by creed. Under her influence Amenophis IV., her son (whose strongly marked features have a Semitic, not to say Jewish character),[85] completely revolutionised the religion of Egypt, more especially attacking its most loathsome form, the phallus-worship of Khem. The names of this princess, Tei, and of her parents, Iuaa and Tuaa, bear a singularly near resemblance to that of Mered's wife.[86]

(22.) However this may be, the few known facts of Egyptian history from the accession of Amenophis IV., or Khu-n-Aten (*i.e.* Glory of the Sunbeam), are readily adjusted to the early annals of the Judges. For a few years the ascendancy of Egypt in Mesopotamia was unimpaired. The Rutens and their allies were kept in submission; no indication of an occupation of Palestine by Egypt or its opponents is to be found: then comes a time of internal struggle and confusion, during which all the Asiatics threw off the yoke. We have here a place for the invasion of Cushan Rishathaim, the King of Mesopotamia; which must have taken place about a century after the death of Joshua. The

[83] It is to be observed that the current of the Riviera di Ponente runs along the Delta and thence to the coast of Palestine or Syria, carrying with it so much of the Nile mud as to fill up the harbours. The sea voyage would be easy and rapid. We find notice of the transport of corn from Egypt to the land of the Kheta under Merneptah. 'Histor. Ins.,' iii. 24.

[84] Some scholars hold that the Exodus took place at the close of this reign. This theory is supported by ingenious arguments, but is scarcely reconcileable with the condition of Egypt at the beginning of the next reign, nor does it present the coincidences which are drawn from the reign of Thotmes II. and his successors.

[85] The most striking portraits of this king are in Prisse, 'Monuments,' pl. x., and in the 'Denkmäler III.;' all the portraits have the strongest character of individuality, wild, dreamy, fanatic, with features in some points unlike those of his predecessors, and approaching closely to the Hebrew type. Ewald recognises and attaches much importance to the traces of an attempt to introduce a more spiritual form of religion at this period: see 'Geschichte,' v. I. ii., p. 51, note, 2nd edition.

[86] In Egyptian, [hieroglyphs]. The name Bithia, exactly transcribed, would be [hieroglyphs]. The name of the father of Tei, [hieroglyphs], Iua, is markedly Jewish. See the inscription in Brugsch, 'Geographische Inscriften,' i., taf. ix., No. 333. In a work lately published (1868), 'The Fleet of an Egyptian Queen,' M. Duemichen points out the resemblance and apparent connection between Aten and אדון, Lord, observing that the hieroglyphic group is certainly used with reference to this Semitic name of God. See explanation of pl. iii.

growth of the power of the Moabites, and of the nomads bearing the general denomination of Shasous in Egyptian, of Amalek, Edom, Ammon, &c., in Hebrew, was a natural result of the expulsion of the Mesopotamians on the one side, and the prostration of Egypt on the other.[87] In the mean time the Cheta were gradually acquiring the ascendancy from Cilicia to the Euphrates,[88] occupying the strongholds in Syria, and encroaching gradually on the borders of Palestine, a position which, notwithstanding repeated and triumphant invasions of their own territory, they occupied during the whole period of the nineteenth and apparently also the twentieth dynasties.

The duration assigned by M. Brugsch to the eighteenth dynasty from the decease of Thotmes III. is about 100 years. The corresponding period, on the hypothesis we are now considering, brings us near to the occupation of Palestine by Eglon King of Moab. It will be observed that, although the results of comparison of Egyptian and Hebrew annals are, and must be to a great extent conjectural, inasmuch as no direct or distinct notice of the events preceding the Exodus or following the occupation of Palestine by the Israelites is found on Egyptian monuments, and no notice of Egyptian history occurs in the books of Joshua, Judges, and Samuel, yet the conjectures rest on data established beyond all contradiction. They do not profess to do more than show that the two series of events dovetail, and mutually sustain and explain each other: the coincidences, whether they be held complete and convincing or not, are unsought; they forced themselves on the writer's attention, and gradually led him to give a decided preference to the hypothesis which has been here defended, over that which is at present generally supported by Egyptian scholars.

(23.) We have now to consider what arguments favourable or unfavourable to this hypothesis are drawn from Manetho and other documents known to us through the medium of Greek. Here we must carefully distinguish between facts borne out by contemporary monuments, and statements which, whether correctly or incorrectly represented by the translators and epitomizers, are contradicted or not corroborated by such authority.

The Exodus is assumed by all ancient chronologers, who derived their information from Egyptian sources, to have taken place under the eighteenth dynasty.[89] Josephus, who regards the expulsion of the Hyksos to be but a confused tradition of the departure of the Israelites, places it under the first king whom he calls Tethmosis; Africanus, who follows Ptolemy the Mendesian, under Amos, *i.e.* Amosis, or Aahmes. Eusebius brings the transaction lower down, but still long before the nineteenth dynasty, viz. under Achencherses or Achencheres, *i. e.* probably Khunaten, the son of Amenophis III. This opinion is said by Syncellus to be avowedly in contradiction to all other authorities. Eusebius was probably led to it by the evident indications of great disturbances under that reign, and by the tradition that emigrations of considerable extent took place soon afterwards.[90]

Passing to Manetho's own statements, we find that he represents the kings of the Thebaid and of Upper Egypt as engaged in a great and long-continued warfare with the Hyksos: he asserts that the king, Misphragmuthosis, drove them out of all the other districts in Egypt, and confined them within the vast enclosure of Avaris. His son Tethmosis besieged the city with an immense army, and, being unable to capture it, made a treaty with them, permitting their departure: they are said to have gone forth with their furniture and their cattle, forming a host not less than 240,000 in number, then to have traversed the desert between Egypt and Syria, and at last, fearing the Assyrians, at that time masters of Asia, to have settled in Judæa, where they built the city of Jerusalem.

Setting the account which has been given in these pages side by side with the statement of Manetho, we see at once the character of his history, and the corroboration which it supplies to what has been advanced.

(1) A war of considerable duration was carried on between the kings of Upper Egypt and the Shepherds. Here Manetho and the monuments agree. (2) The king whom Manetho calls Misphragmuthosis achieved great successes in war, but did not capture Avaris. It is true that the Shepherds were attacked by the first king of the dynasty, but untrue that Avaris was not captured by him. Here we have a partial agreement, but the name of the king is not correct. (3) Certain enemies of the Egyptians were in possession of a limited district under his successor. The monuments are silent, but from the Pentateuch we know that the Israelites occupied Goshen at this time, as nearly all Egyptian scholars agree. (4) These enemies left Egypt by permission, traversed Syria, and occupied Palestine. Their forces amounted to 240,000. The monuments are silent. We have the Scriptural account with scarcely a variation.

---

[87] It is also to be remarked that the Rutens, or Assyrians, were so weakened towards the end of the eighteenth dynasty that they lost the ascendancy; a fact sufficiently explained by the overthrow of Cushan Rishathaim.

[88] See Brugsch, 'H. E.,' p. 127, and M. Chabas, 'Voyage,' p. 325.

[89] All the passages are collected in the first volume of Bunsen's 'Egypt.'

[90] Viz. the expulsion of Danaus and his settlement at Argos. See the statement of Diodorus, p. 462.

The principal inference bearing on our present subject is that all these notices refer to the same period, viz. the early years of the eighteenth dynasty.

In another work Manetho gives what may have been in his time the Egyptian account of the Exodus: it is utterly worthless, and, as nearly all critics have observed, was evidently invented by a person who had the Scripture narrative before him.[91] It represents the Israelites as lepers, and identifies Moses with Osarsiph,[92] a priest of Heliopolis, evidently Joseph. The Egyptian king, in whose reign the enemies first made themselves masters of all Egypt, committing atrocities far beyond those attributed to the Hyksos, is called Amenophis. According to this strange figment, Amenophis committed his son Sethos, called also Rhamses, to the charge of some private individual, and retired into Ethiopia, whence he returned with a great army, and finally ejected the lepers and their allies the Shepherds from Egypt, pursuing them unto the borders of Syria.

All names and events are here in hopeless confusion: but each name and each event is found, though under very different circumstances, either in Egyptian or in sacred history. Osarsiph and Moses, the character of the Mosaic law, the prevalence of leprosy, the connection of Osarsiph with Heliopolis, are taken from Scripture: the names of Avaris, Amenophis, Sethos, Rhamses, from Egyptian monuments. The expulsion of the Shepherds by an Egyptian king with forces brought from Ethiopia is, as we have seen, historical. Amenophis himself, the son of Amosis, made an expedition into Ethiopia. There was a religious aspect of the struggle between the Shepherds and the Egyptians. No inference of any value can be drawn from the whole narrative in favour of either hypothesis now under consideration. On the one side the names of Sethos and Rameses would point to the nineteenth dynasty, but it is scarcely conceivable that a man having the least acquaintance with Egyptian history should have confounded Sethos and his son, or have represented Amenophis as the father of Sesostris. On the other side, the name of Amenophis would point distinctly to the eighteenth dynasty, and the whole narrative might get into the shape which it here assumes, if the facts above proved, and the combinations which we have assumed, had been manipulated by an Egyptian priest under the Ptolemies.

The story told by Chæremon (see Josephus c. Apion, i. 32) is a modification of this. The Israelites are led by Moses and Joseph, whose Egyptian names are said to be Tisithen and Peteseph.[93] They join an army of 300,000 men, whom Amenophis had left at Pelusium, because he did not wish to bring them into Egypt. Amenophis retreated into Ethiopia, where he had a son named Mepenes, who, when he became a man, drove the Jews into Syria, and recalled his father Amenophis from Ethiopia.

An extract from Lysimachus, given also by Josephus, is a mere corruption of the Scriptural narrative, invented under the Ptolemies. It names Bocchoris (B.C. 721) as the Pharaoh of the Exodus: a striking instance of contemptuous disregard of all historical probabilities.

Diodorus has two accounts:[94] in one (c. xxxiv. 1) the adherents of Antiochus Sidetes represent the Jews as a despicable race expelled from Egypt, hateful to the gods on account of foul cutaneous diseases; in the other (c. xl. 1) he relates that in ancient times a pestilence which raged in Egypt was ascribed to the wrath of the gods on account of the multitude of aliens who with their strange worship were offensive to the gods of the land. The aliens were therefore expelled. The most distinguished among them betook themselves to Greece and other adjoining regions, among whom were Danaus and Cadmus. The main body, however, retired into the country afterwards called Judæa, which at that time was a desert. This colony was led by Moses.

From what source Diodorus derived this latter statement is quite uncertain, but the colouring is Egyptian. It undoubtedly points to an earlier period than the nineteenth dynasty; most probably to that assigned by Eusebius to the emigration into Palestine and Greece, viz. the latter reigns of the eighteenth dynasty.

As a general result from this part of our inquiry, we find that, with two exceptions, all the names and transactions noticed by Manetho, and by Greek writers, whether heathen or Christian, harmonise with the course of events under the eighteenth dynasty. One exception is simply noticeable for its absurdity, bringing the Exodus down to the eighth century and the twenty-fourth dynasty: the other is more important since it introduces the names of Sethos and Rameses, but under circumstances and in a relationship which evince either an entire ignorance or a wilful perversion of the best known facts of Egyptian history.

One argument remains of which the importance will not be questioned. Critics of the most opposite schools who have carefully

---

91 See Browne, 'Ordo Sæclorum,' p. 581.

92 There is an evident reference to one or both of Joseph's names. The last syllable, Siph, answers to seph, and also to Zaf, food. Osir means rich, powerful, &c.; Osersiph, rich in food.

93 Seph, the last syllable of Joseph's Hebrew, and the first of his Egyptian name, seems to have left a permanent impression, and that a very natural one, as meaning "food." See Essay II.

94 See Browne, 'Ordo Sæclorum,' p. 584.

considered the bearings of the facts drawn from Egyptian sources upon the narrative of Exodus, concur in the conclusion that the accession of the eighteenth dynasty was the beginning of the persecution, and that the Exodus took place in some reign before the accession of the nineteenth. Thus Knobel, Winer, and Ewald.

(24.) We have now to consider whether the facts, admitted by all Egyptologers and attested by monuments and other documents of unquestionable authority, which appertain to the history of the 19th dynasty, accord with the hypothesis here adopted, or whether we should acquiesce in the conclusion to which eminent scholars have been led;[95] that which identifies Rameses II. with the first persecutor of the Israelites, and places the Exodus under his son Merneptah. It may be well to say at once that the reader might accept that conclusion without repugnance: on certain conditions it may be reconciled with the narrative of Exodus, which some at least of its chief supporters accept as an authentic document, if not as the production of Moses. It is, however, a question to be determined not by authority, but by circumstantial evidence. It is now universally admitted that no monuments of this or of any other period make mention of the events which preceded or immediately followed the departure of the Israelites.[96] In the following pages every fact bearing upon this question will be fairly and fully stated, together with the arguments on both sides.

(25.) We have first to inquire into the known or probable condition of Palestine during the interval between the early Judges and the time of Deborah and Barak. It is an interval of considerable duration, extending over some two centuries, if we take the numbers in the book of Judges literally,[97] and covering certainly as much time as is occupied by the annals of Egypt between Amenophis III. and the later kings of the nineteenth dynasty.

During the whole of that period it is distinctly stated that the Israelites were not in exclusive possession of Palestine; they dwelt among the Canaanites, Hittites, and Amorites, and Perizzites, and Hivites, and Jebusites. (Judges iii. 5.) Many of the most important strongholds were occupied by these nations, including nearly all those which are mentioned in the records of Seti and Rameses II.[98] Generally speaking, the open country was retained by the Amorites, against whose iron chariotry the Israelites could not make head even in Judah (Judges i. 19). The whole district from the southern frontier upward belonged to them, and was apparently called, as we find it even in inscriptions of the twentieth dynasty, the land of the Amorites.[99] This was the case even when the land was at rest: in some portions of Palestine the Israelites brought the inhabitants into partial subjection and made them tributaries, but the process was slow, alternating with many disasters, and not completed until a very late period, long after that which is now under consideration. When the Israelites were themselves brought under subjection the whole country was in a state described incidentally in the song of Deborah: the highways were unoccupied, the villages ceased, there was war in the gates, *i.e.* the strongholds were blockaded; while not a spear or shield was to be seen among 40,000 in Israel (Judges v. 6).

It is clear therefore that an Egyptian army traversing Palestine at any part of this time would not encounter Israelitish forces in the open field: Israel had no chariotry, no horses, and would not be concerned with expeditions which were invariably directed against its own enemies in Syria.[100]

We have now to remark the very exact correspondence between the Hebrew and

---

[95] M. de Rougé says in his 'Report on Egyptian Studies,' 1867, p. 27, "Les rapports de temps et de noms ont fait penser à M. de Rougé que Ramesès II. devait être considéré également comme le Pharaon sous lequel Moïse dut fuir l'Égypte et dont le très-long règne força le législateur futur des Hébreux à un très-long exil. À défaut d'un texte précis qui manque dans la Bible, cette conjecture rend bien compte des faits, et elle a été généralement adoptée." It has in fact been adopted by Egyptian scholars in Germany, France, and England. The sobriety and reserve with which M. de Rougé states this conjecture, to which he attaches great value, stand out in strong contrast to the confidence with which it is maintained as a proved fact by most of his followers.

[96] See the statement of M. de Rougé quoted above, note 67.

[97] The numbers in Judges iii. are a long but uncertain time from the conquest under Joshua, x, Cushan Rishathaim, 8 years; peace, 40 years; Eglon, 18 years; rest, 80 years; Philistines, x; *i.e.* $146 + x + x$. Brugsch calculates the interval between Amenophis III. and Merneptah at 200 years. The elements of uncertainty on both sides are considerable, but the general correspondence is noteworthy.

[98] *E.g.*, Jerusalem, Bethshean, Taanach, Dor, Megiddo, Zidon, Bethshemesh, Bethanath. Gaza and the other four cities in the district were evidently recovered during this period by the Philistines. Compare Judges i. 18 with iii. 3 and 31. In the inscriptions of the nineteenth dynasty, I cannot find any Palestinian city which the book of Judges represents as occupied by Israelites in the period after the conquest.

[99] See *e.g.* Duemichen, 'Hist. Inschriften,' pl. xxviii., xxix.

[100] The strongholds which the Egyptians, under Seti and Rameses II., had occasion to attack, and some of which they appear to have garrisoned, were, with scarcely an exception, in the possession of Canaanites or Hittites. See note 98.

Egyptian notices of the power predominant in Western Asia.

The Assyrians, called Rutens by the Egyptians, were masters of the north of Syria, and of all the countries extending from Cilicia to Mesopotamia, when that district was invaded by the early kings of the eighteenth dynasty.[101] Their influence in the confederacy opposed to Egypt was gradually superseded. Up to the time when Seti I. invaded Syria, *i.e.* according to our computation about 150 years after the Exodus, they were the leaders of the confederacy, which was then broken, dispersed, and for a season crushed by repeated defeats. M. Chabas observes (p. 328) that under Rameses II. they disappear altogether, they are not even mentioned in the great campaign of his 5th year. Their name is found on a small number of monuments belonging to later reigns, but there is no indication that they had recovered their former importance.

In accordance with this we find that their last appearance in Palestine was soon after its occupation by the Israelites, when Cushan Rishathaim was finally expelled by Othniel the nephew of Caleb.

Nothing more probable than that such an event should have occurred under the eighteenth dynasty (see above, p. 460); its occurrence at the late period which the acceptance of the other chronological system would involve is inconceivable.

In place of the Rutens or Assyrians we find the Cheta in possession of Syria at the accession of Seti I. The identification of this people with the Hittites of Scripture has been questioned, chiefly on philological grounds,[102] by M. Chabas; but is still generally admitted by Egyptian scholars, and appears to rest on very sufficient evidence. It is certain that the Hittites, Canaanites, Zidonians, and Amorites, formed part of the confederacy opposed to Seti and Rameses II. We learn from the book of Judges (i. 26) that the country north of Palestine was called the land of the Hittites, that Phœnicia retained its independence, and further, that at the close of the period the whole country was in subjection to Jabin King of Canaan, the captain of whose host was "Sisera,[103] which dwelt in Harosheth of the Gentiles."

Taking now the contemporary history of Egypt derived exclusively from public inscriptions, we have the following coincidences:—

(26.) In the first year of his reign Seti marched against the Shasous, who at that time occupied, or were masters of, the countries from Pithom to Pakanana.[104] He defeated them with great slaughter, and advanced into Mesopotamia. On a second invasion he again traversed the territory occupied by the Shasous and took several forts.

The word Shasous, as we have before seen, was a general denomination for the warlike tribes who at various times overran Palestine. About the time which the synchronism of Egyptian and Hebrew history, on our hypothesis, assigns to Seti and the Israelites, we find Eglon King of Moab in combination with the children of Ammon and Amalek, master of the country. At any time within the period, as we have also observed, the opponents whom the Pharaohs would encounter in Palestine would come under the same general designation.

The fortresses named in the inscriptions which refer to this campaign were one and all occupied by the enemies of Israel.

The Shasous conquered by Seti were in alliance with the Syrians and the Rutens: both mentioned as foes or oppressors of the Israelites.

The great object of Seti and his successor was to conquer Syria, and to occupy its principal city called Kadesh, which is probably identified by Egyptologers with Edessa, or Ems, on the Orontes.

At the close of this reign Egypt was dominant in Syria, and held some fortresses, but the power of the Cheta was unbroken, and we have no traces whatever of a permanent occupation of Palestine. As in the time of Shamgar, the Israelites were in the state described as that of Seti's foes in the inscriptions, either hidden in caves or entrenched in inaccessible strongholds.[105] The principal effect of the invasion, so far as the Hebrews were concerned, would be a diminution in the power and resources of their foes.

The transactions in the reign of Rameses II. will require very special attention. We shall best arrive at a conclusion by considering each point in detail which may tell for or against either hypothesis.

(27.) Rameses Merammon, the Sesostris[106] of

---

101 For proofs see M. Brugsch, 'H. E. and G.,' and the dissertation by M. Chabas, 'Voyage d'un Égyptien,' p. 318-332.

102 *I.e.*, from the comparison of Chetan names (of which seventeen are preserved in the treaty between Rameses II. and Khetasar) with the names of Hittites found in the Bible.

103 The name is evidently *Chetan;* it has the most marked characteristic of the names collected by M. Chabas (see note 74), viz. the termination Sera or *Sar:* see further on.

104 It is questioned whether this means a fort in Syria or Canaan.

105 See Brugsch, 'Recueil I.,' pl. xlv. e: "throwing away their bows they fled to *caves* in terror from his majesty." The word "caves" here is Hebrew, [hieroglyphs], magaratha = בערות.

106 This is generally held, but is not certain. Dr. G. Ebers doubts whether Herodotus does not refer the name to Seti I., and suggests that the hieroglyphic group may perhaps be read Sesetres, or Sesetresu, which comes very near Sesostris. See 'Egypten und die Bücher Moses,' i. p. 79. 1868.

the Greeks, succeeded Seti I. It was supposed until very lately that he was very young, a mere lad, on his accession; but the researches of M. Mariette[107] have brought to light the curious and interesting fact that he had been associated with his father from infancy in the royal dignity, and that he had been admitted to the full prerogatives of a Pharaoh long before the death of Seti: in the first year after that event he is represented as surrounded with a family of twenty-seven princes and as many princesses. This is important in its bearings on Egyptian chronology. There is no doubt that he reigned full sixty-seven years, a date found lately on a monument at Tanis, but from what epoch the year is dated remains uncertain; probably from an epoch long anterior to his father's decease.[108] The argument is of still more importance in its bearing upon another biblical question. Of no king in the whole series of Pharaohs could it be asserted, in such direct contradiction of well-known facts, that he was a *new king*, rising up over Egypt: of none can it be proved more certainly that he did not at once make an entire change in the policy of this kingdom. The argument upon which much stress is laid, viz. that his lengthened reign accords with the notices in Exodus, falls with the assumption that he outlived his father some sixty-seven years.

In the 5th year of his sole reign Rameses invaded Syria. In the neighbourhood of Kadesh, on the Orontes, he defeated the confederates, who as usual had revolted when their conqueror died. The battle would almost seem to be the only one in which the king distinguished himself; it is described on numerous monuments, and forms the subject of what is called the epic poem of Pentaour.[109] The campaign was successful: one of the most important results for this inquiry was the capture, and perhaps the occupation, of some fortresses in Palestine. We have the name of Sharem, or Shalem; it is doubtful whether this is to be identified with Jerusalem; if so, it was, as we know, long after the conquest, in possession of the Jebusites; Maram and Dapur, in the land of the Amorites, are also mentioned; Bethanath, still occupied by Canaanites (see Judges i. 33); and lastly Askelon. The notices of Askelon in Judges show that it was taken at first by the Israelites (i. 18), and imply probably that it came again into the occupation of the Philistines some time later, perhaps in the time of Shamgar. See Judges iii. 31.

So far the argument remains stationary. The condition of Palestine under Rameses continues as under Seti, quite in agreement with that which we find in the 3rd chapter of Judges; Egypt commanding the high roads, occupying some fortresses taken principally from the Canaanites, but concentrating its forces and developing all its energies in its attempt to retain supremacy in Syria. We should of course expect to find among the numerous prisoners of war brought back by Rameses some Israelites, if, as we have assumed, they were then dwelling, though not dominant, in the land.

(28.) It was after the king's return to Egypt that the events occurred upon which the hypothesis rests that he reduced the Israelites of Goshen to bondage. Diodorus relates that he constructed a line of fortifications from Pelusium to Heliopolis. It is, however, proved by the monuments that such a line existed under the ancient empire, and that it had been enlarged and strengthened by his father Seti. It is also known that in the latter years of his reign Rameses effaced his father's name and substituted his own on many of the principal constructions of Egypt;[110] still there can be no reasonable doubt that he employed vast numbers of captives in the fortresses which

---

[107] 'Fouilles exécutées en Égypte, en Nubie, et au Soudan, d'après les ordres de S. A. le Viceroi d'Égypte, par Auguste Mariette Bey.' Paris, 1867. The second volume, in two parts, contains text and plates; the first volume is not yet published. The most important inscription, from the temple at Abydos, has been carefully analysed by M. Maspero, 1867. It belongs to the first year of the sole reign of Rameses II., who is represented as associated from his infancy with his father, and formally crowned while yet a boy. Compare Maspero, p. 29, with Mariette, p. 15. Mariette's work throws an unexpected and curious light on the character of Rameses, and on the state of Egyptian art towards the end of his reign. In the earlier inscriptions Rameses expresses the highest veneration and gratitude to his father; in the latter he effaces the name of Seti, and substitutes his own. The earlier portions of the building and inscriptions are remarkable for beauty and breadth of style; the later sculptures are incorrect, and the style detestable. See 'Fouilles,' especially p. 99. Since this note was printed, M. Mariette has withdrawn the volume here quoted from circulation, and substituted another, in which much valuable matter is suppressed.

[108] This materially affects the argument to which M. de Rougé has always attached special importance (see above, note 95). Moses could not have been born until some years after the beginning of the persecution, *i.e.*, according to M. de Rougé, Brugsch, and others, after the Syrian campaign; when Rameses is now proved to have been at least in the maturity of middle life. We thus lose the space of eighty years required by the Biblical narrative before the Exodus.

[109] This curious and important document was first explained and afterwards translated by M. de Rougé, M. Chabas, and Mr. Goodwin. The translation in Brugsch, 'Histoire d'Égypte,' p. 140, is that of M. de Rougé. The original exists in a hieratic papyrus, Sallier III., in the Select Papyri of the British Museum, and more or less complete in hieroglyphic inscriptions at Karnak and Abu Simbel.

[110] See note [107].

he enlarged, or erected on the banks of the great canal, now called the Wady Tumilat. Among these fortresses two are mentioned specially, the fort of Zaru and Pe-Ramesses. These are assumed by Brugsch to be the Pithom and Rameses of Exodus. The question is fully discussed in another part of this work. Here it is enough to observe that these two cities or forts existed previously. That which Brugsch calls Pithom, but of which the true name in Egyptian is Pa-Chetem en Zalou, was at least as old as the time of Thotmes III. Pithom itself, the Pa-Tum of the inscriptions, the Πάτουμος of Herodotus, may have been, and probably was, in its immediate neighbourhood, but it is nowhere mentioned in connexion with Rameses. The case is much stronger for the other city.[111] Pa-Ramessou, or A-Ramessou, *i.e.* the residence of Rameses, was undoubtedly enlarged by this king: it was a city of the highest importance, the capital of a rich district, the residence of the sovereign, where he received foreign embassies, reviewed his troops, and held a magnificent court. Still it is proved by contemporary documents that it was not founded by Rameses. In the fifth year of his reign, before the great works for the defence of the frontier were constructed, Rameses received the ambassadors of the Cheta in this city, which, according to M. Brugsch, is mentioned by name in the reign of Seti.[112]

Considering, however, the great importance of this citadel, to which additions were made continually under this reign, we should expect that a large number of captives would be employed in the works, and among the captives brought into Egypt at the end of the Syrian campaign Israelites would naturally be looked for. Although it was the usual policy of Rameses to employ prisoners in the parts of his dominions most remote from their own country, there were obvious reasons why this system should be departed from in their case: there was a grim irony, quite in keeping with Egyptian character, in reducing Israelites to servitude on the scene of their forefathers' oppression; and their escape, difficult under all circumstances, could be, and, as we shall see, actually was, guarded against by measures of peculiar stringency.

(29.) Now, that Israelites were actually employed then and there has been, though not really proved, yet shown to be so probable that nearly all Egyptian scholars accept it as a fact. M. Chabas[113] first called attention to the circumstance that the Egyptian word "Aperu" corresponds very closely to "Hebrews," the name by which the Israelites were perhaps best known to foreigners. The transcription is not quite accurate: the letter "p" is by no means the proper representation of the Hebrew "b," nor have I found any conclusive example of a substitution;[114] but the general acquiescence of Egyptologers may be regarded as a sufficient ground for admitting the identification.

Still the question remains whether these Hebrews were in the condition described in Exodus, inhabitants of the district in which

---

[111] The identity of this city with Rameses is the main, in fact the only substantial argument for making Moses the contemporary of Rameses II. Even were it admitted that the name, in the exact form which it takes in Exodus, was first given by Rameses, the argument, though strong, would not be conclusive, for all hold that the names of places may have been altered at successive revisions of the Pentateuch, the new and well-known name being substituted for the old, when a modern editor would give a note. The argument, moreover, has no weight at all when urged by critics who suppose that the Pentateuch was written after the Israelites were connected with Egypt under Solomon, or later. In that case the names of the district and city would of course have been taken from actual usage. I believe the truth to be as stated in the text.

[112] Brugsch, 'H. E.,' p. 156.

[113] See 'Melanges Egyptologiques,' i. p. 42-54, and ii., on Rameses and Pithom.

[114] After a repeated examination of the Semitic names transcribed on Egyptian documents, I find no instance upon which full reliance can be placed. Many names occur in which the B is represented by the Egyptian homophones. The Egyptian "p" represents the "ph" of the Hebrews. Mr. Birch concurs in this statement. The word , Aper, or Apher, occurs in the annals of Thotmes III. twice in an inscription at Karnak. See M. de Rougé, 'Album Photographique,' pl. lii., and is transcribed by M. de Rougé, עפרה. The exact and proper transcription of the Aperu would be עפרי, not עברי. A still stronger objection, which seems indeed insurmountable, is suggested by one account of these Aperu. In the inscription at Hamamat, under Rameses IV. (see further on), they are called Aperu n na petu Anu, *i.e.* Aperu of the Anu. The Anu are often mentioned as a warlike race in Nubia, who rebelled frequently against the Pharaohs. They are here written with a group which always represents bowmen, whether auxiliaries or enemies.

The inference is almost irresistible that these Aperu, and, if these, the others also, were Nubians, condemned to work in the quarries. See Brugsch, 'Geog. Inschriften,' iii. p. 77; and on the Anu, see the 'Excursus II.,' article Anamim. It seems after all doubtful whether Aperu is a proper name, or simply denotes workmen. Maspero says that they were, as one knows, the servants of the temple. 'Essai,' p. 22. Neither Birch nor Brugsch give this in their Dictionaries, but the etymology points to such a meaning, "Aper, to supply or prepare," and Maspero is a good authority. Aperu is given as a variant of Shennin, attendants in the Ritual, c. lxxviii. 37.

they were employed, or prisoners of war. The former alternative is generally assumed: a close examination of the original documents seems decidedly to point to the latter.

Four Egyptian documents give an account of these Aperu. Two belong to the reign of Rameses II. They are official documents of very peculiar interest. One of them was written by a certain Kawisar, an officer of the commissariat at Pa-Ramesson. He reports that he has executed his orders, which were to distribute corn to the soldiers and to the Aperu, or Apuriu, who are employed in drawing stones for the great Bekken (*i.e.* fortified enclosure) of Pa-Ramesson: the corn was delivered to a general of mercenary troops; the distribution was made monthly. In another report (which however does not mention the Aperu) he speaks of large supplies of fish for the city.

The obvious inference from this account would seem to be that persons employed in such labours, fed by rations, and under military superintendence, were captives, and not inhabitants of the district.[115] The name "Kawisar" resembles the well-known names of Cheta: Chetan officers are found in the service of Rameses, and such a man was peculiarly qualified for the office, both as a natural enemy of the Hebrews and as familiar with their language.[116]

The second document has special claims to attention, since M. Chabas has shown that it is probably the original report addressed by a scribe Keniamen to an officer of high rank, the Kazana, or General Hui,[117] of the household of Rameses. It proves that strict injunctions were given to provide food for the officers of the garrison and also for the "Aperu" who drew stones for the Pharaoh Rameses Merammon in a district south of Memphis.

This is a strong corroboration of the conclusion that, if Israelites, they were prisoners of war. The Israelites of the Exodus, from first to last, are represented as forced to labour in their own district under Egyptian taskmasters, who were certainly not soldiers, and with a complete national organization of superintendents.

The other documents complete the argument. Aperu were employed in considerable numbers in reigns which all admit to be posterior to the Exodus. In a document of great importance, of which M. Chabas gives an account (see 'Voyage d'un Égyptien,' p. 211), we find a body of 2083 Aperu residing upon a domain of Rameses III. under the command of officers of rank called Marinas: from the signs attached to these names it is evident that they were not subjects but captives.[118] Here, again, the inference is natural that they were brought by Rameses III. on his return from a campaign in Syria. (See further on.) Another notice (see note 114) is found under Rameses IV.: 800 Aperu were employed in the quarries of Hamamat, accompanied, as in all the cases where they are mentioned, by an armed force, generally a detachment of mercenaries. With regard to the Aperu in both reigns, M. Chabas supposes that they may have remained after the Exodus as mercenaries. It may be so; if so, the same explanation would apply to the Aperu under Rameses II.; but it scarcely agrees with the descriptions of their condition, and it seems very improbable that any considerable number of Israelites should have wished or dared to stay, or that their presence would have been tolerated by the Egyptians at all for a long time after the Exodus.

It is to be observed that in every case, far from wishing to diminish the numbers of these labourers, the Egyptian kings took great pains for their maintenance; they were valuable as slaves, not objects of suspicion as disaffected and dangerous subjects.

(30.) Reverting now to the condition of Western Asia, we find that during the latter years of this reign the Cheta retained their position as the dominant power in Syria. In the twenty-first year of Rameses he made a formal treaty[119]

---

[115] This inference is in fact the first which would suggest itself to a scholar looking at any of these documents. M. Brugsch observes (in the third part of his great work on Egyptian Geography, published in 1860, see p. 77), "This name, as the determinative shows, evidently belonged to a foreign people, who had been taken prisoners in the Egyptian campaigns, and condemned to work in the quarries, a custom noticed by all ancient writers on Egypt, and especially with reference to Rameses II."

[116] In the 'Mél. Egypt.' M. Chabas assumes that the name is Semitic. He has since taken much pains (see 'Voy. E.', pp. 326-330) to prove that the Chetan names are altogether of a different origin. The argument stands good in the form above proposed, whichever view is taken.

[117] M. Chabas treats this as a proper name. M. de Rougé shows that it is equivalent to קָצִין, and means general of cavalry. See 'Revue Archéologique,' Août, 1867. The name Hui is Egyptian, and is found under the ancient empire. This does not support Dr. Ebers' statement, that the cavalry was always under the management of Semitics in this time. See 'Ægypten,' &c., p. 229.

[118] In addition to the stake, which denotes foreigners or slaves, they have for a determinative "a leg in a trap." This is used sometimes for dwellers in general; but the proper meaning, as given by Birch ('Dict. Hier.'), is "entrap, ravish, trample;" and Ebers gives the same meaning to the word which is used in this passage.

[119] This curious document is printed in Brugsch's 'Recueil.' It has been translated, first by Brugsch, and lately by M. Chabas, 'Voyage d'un Égyptien.' Among the terms is one, to which both parties evidently attached great im-

with Chetasar, their king; both parties treating on terms of equality and pledging themselves to perpetual amity. The alliance was confirmed by the marriage of Rameses with the daughter of Chetasar. Between two great powers thus evenly balanced Palestine might be, and probably was, in a state of comparative tranquillity for a period corresponding with the uncertain interval between Eglon and Shamgar. At the close of that interval, which would cover the time of Rameses and extend into the reign of Merneptah, the sacred history represents the south of Palestine as occupied, for the first time after the Exodus, by the Philistines, and the north completely subjugated by Jabin King of Canaan.

(31.) Notices are found in papyri of this period which give some notion of the state of Palestine. The most important is that which was first analysed by Mr. Goodwin, and has since been translated and explained with remarkable ingenuity and learning by M. Chabas.[120] It recites the adventures of an officer of cavalry employed, as it would seem, on a mission into Syria towards the end of the reign of Rameses II. Whether the adventures are real, or, as M. de Rougé[121] and others maintain, the narrative is fictitious, composed for the instruction of students preparing for military service, may be uncertain, but the notices, so far as they go, are valuable, and were probably derived from persons who had been engaged in the campaigns of Rameses. A considerable number of names have been identified, some with certainty, others with more or less of probability, with cities well known from the Scriptural narrative. It is, however, to be remarked, that of these a very small proportion, and those for the most part very doubtful, belong to the interior of Palestine: and that these lie almost exclusively on the high-road, followed, as we have before seen, by the Egyptian armies. The traveller is represented in the first part of the narrative as proceeding at once to Syria,[122] where the transactions occur which occupy the greater part of the story.[123] That country was held by the Cheta, but it was in a state of general disorganisation, overrun by Shasous, and the supremacy of Egypt was evidently recognised. On his return the officer crossed the Jordan, and touched apparently at some places[124] in the north of Palestine; this part of the journey was beset by almost insurmountable difficulties: the country seems to have been almost impassable to a charioteer; until he entered Megiddo (which, as we before saw, was in possession of the Canaanites in the time of the early Judges) he had to encounter the Shasous, from whom he escapes by a precipitate flight, not without serious detriment to his person and property. The description reminds the reader of all the notices in the book of Judges which refer to periods when the Israelites were driven to their fastnesses, or hiding in caves, while the open country, or the passes, were infested by robber hordes from the adjoining deserts. At Joppa, where the authority of Egypt appears to be recognised, the journey seems to come to an end. No mention is made of Israelites in this papyrus, none indeed was to be expected:[125] the only designation for the inhabitants with whom the officer came into contact was Shasous—that which the Egyptians gave to all the nomad and pastoral tribes, probably including the Hebrews, who occupied the countries between their frontiers and Syria.

(32.) One point of great importance in reference to this and the succeeding reigns, in which the events recorded in Exodus are so generally assumed to have occurred, remains to be considered. The collection of papyri in the British Museum, of which the principal have been published by the trustees, belong for the most part to this period. They were written either under Rameses II. or his immediate successors. They indicate a very considerable development of Egyptian literature. The writing is legible, and the composition includes a varied treatment of many distinct subjects, giving a tolerably complete idea of the social and political condition of the people, especially of those employed in the district adjoining Pa-Ramesson. It was quite natural to expect that, if the Israelites were settled in Goshen, or had been very lately expelled, when those documents were written, some notices of them would be found, some allusions at least to the events preceding the Exodus. Accordingly a writer,[126] to whose industry and ingenuity we are indebted for some of the first attempts to decipher and

portance, viz. the mutual extradition of fugitives. Stress is laid upon this as bearing upon the narrative in Exodus, but with little cause: it was a condition not likely to be omitted, under any circumstances, between the owners of immense numbers of slaves and the rulers of disaffected districts.

[120] Under the attractive title, 'Voyage d'un Égyptien en Syrie, en Phénicie, en Palestine, &c., au 14me siècle avant notre ère.' 1866.

[121] See 'Revue Archéologique,' Août, 1867, p. 100, note 1.

[122] This is noticed by M. Chabas, p. 96; it accords with the view above stated, that the communications between Egypt and Syria were most commonly by sea.

[123] At least three sections, from p. 18 to p. 23.

[124] The places named in the first part of the fourth section are in great confusion, and, though evidently Palestinian, are not clearly identified.

[125] M. Chabas ('Voyage,' p. 220) draws an argument against the presence of Israelites from the mention of camels as used for food; but the explanation of the passage is doubtful, and the Shasous named in it were nomads of the desert, who, as M. Chabas observes, ate camel's flesh.

[126] Mr. Dunbar Heath, 'Papyri of the Exodus.'

explain the select papyri, believed, and for a time persuaded others, that he found abundance of such notices. He speaks of a true, original, and varied picture of many of the very actors in the Exodus, a Jannes mentioned five times, a Moses twice, a Balaam son of Zippor, and the sudden and mysterious death of a prince royal, &c. Since his work was written all the passages adduced by him have been carefully investigated,[127] and every indication of the presence of the Israelites has disappeared. The absence of such indications supplies, if not a conclusive, yet a very strong argument against the hypothesis which they were adduced to support. It may be added that the descriptions of that part of Egypt which had been occupied by the Israelites happen to be both full and graphic in these documents, and they represent it as remarkably rich, fertile, and prosperous, the centre of an extensive commerce, occupied by a vast native population, a land of unceasing festivities and enjoyment, such as the district might well be some centuries after the departure of the Israelites, such as it certainly was not during the period of their cruel persecution, and of the long series of plagues which fell on their oppressors.

(33.) We now come to the reign of Merneptah, in which M. Brugsch, and many distinguished scholars, consider that the Exodus took place. Merneptah succeeded his father Rameses II., and is said to have reigned twenty years.[128] The notices of this Pharaoh in M. Brugsch's 'Histoire d'Égypte' are but scanty; few monuments were erected in his reign; even his father's tomb was left unfinished; and the indications of a decline in art, and exhaustion of national resources observable towards the close of his father's reign, are numerous and strong. There are not, however, on the monuments, or in the papyri of that period, any notices of internal disturbances towards the end of his reign; it can be shown that the eastern frontier was vigilantly guarded, and nomad tribes admitted under due precautions to feed their cattle in the extensive district occupied by the herds of Pharaoh.[129]

The beginning of this reign was, however, signalised by the complete discomfiture of an invasion, which presents some points of peculiar interest in reference to general history as well as to our present inquiry.[130] The names of the confederates are partly African (not negro, but Libyan), and partly Asiatic or European; if M. de Rougé's conclusions are admitted, they consisted of Tyrrhenians or Etrurians, Siculi, Sardinians, Achæans, and Lycians, the first appearance of these well-known names in history. None of the names here mentioned enter into the register of ancient people given in the tenth of Genesis.[131] They were therefore evidently unknown to Moses, who must, however, have had his attention specially drawn to them had he returned to Egypt at that time. The ravages committed by these invaders on the north-west of Egypt are described in language which has an important bearing on a point already discussed; "nothing," the king says, "has been seen like it even in the times of the kings of lower Egypt, when the whole country was in their power and reduced to a state of desolation."

Merneptah appears to have conducted the campaign with considerable ability: he boasts of the supplies of corn by which he saved his people in some districts from perishing by famine, and of a successful incursion into the enemies' territories: unlike the Pharaoh of the Exodus, who led his own army and perished with it in the Red Sea,[132] but like Louis XIV., of whom the reader is constantly reminded in this ostentatious period, Merneptah did not expose his sacred person to the chances of war: "his grandeur was chained to the bank of the river by the divine command." The result was a complete victory, the enemies were driven out of Egypt, vast numbers of prisoners and spoils of great value rewarded the conquerors, obelisks were erected to commemorate the event, and the customary self-laudations of the Pharaoh were accepted and echoed by a grateful people. M. de Rougé observes that the terms in which the Egyptian writer[133] de-

---

127 See Mr. Goodwin's article in the 'Cambridge Essays' for 1858. This remarkable essay attracted little notice in England, but made an epoch in one of the most difficult and important branches of Egyptian studies. This opinion is completely confirmed by M. Chabas and M. de Rougé, 'Moïse et les Hébreux,' p. 6.

128 This is quite uncertain: different recensions of Manetho give nineteen and forty years. The highest regnal year in Egyptian documents is the seventh.

129 See 'Excursus II.,' p. 1. The passage here referred to is quoted and translated by M. Chabas, 'Mél. Égypt.,' ii. p. 155, from the papyrus in the British Museum, Anastasi vi. pl. iv. l. 13.

130 M. de Rougé gives a full account of the inscription at Karnak (since published by M. Duemichen) which describes this invasion. See 'Revue Archéologique,' Juillet et Août, 1867. The general tenour was known to M. Brugsch; see 'H. E.,' p. 172. The identifications of M. de Rougé are maintained with equal learning and acuteness, and, as I have observed (since this note was written), they are for the most part accepted by Dr. Ebers, p. 154.

131 It is more than probable that every name in that register was known in Egypt, in Phœnicia, or Assyria, before Moses wrote; names not mentioned by him were first known in Egypt under the nineteenth dynasty. If the register had been written under the kings, as M. Ewald assumes, the absence of these great names is inconceivable.

132 See notes on Exodus.

133 'Revue Archéologique,' l. c. M. Rougé

scribes his triumph are in striking opposition to the severity with which late historians have judged his character.

M. Brugsch lays some stress on an inscription which proves that Merneptah lost a son who is named on a monument at Tanis.[134] This he connects with the death of Pharaoh's first-born; but it is evident from that inscription that Merneptah lived some time after his son's death, certainly a longer time than can be reconciled with the account in Exodus.

The little that is actually known of the later years of this Pharaoh militates against the assumption that they were disturbed by a series of tremendous losses. The papyri written about that time or a few years later represent the district of Rameses or Goshen as enjoying peace and remarkable prosperity (see above), and there is reason to believe that the Cheta and Egypt were still in alliance (see the last note): a state of affairs which ensured peace on the eastern frontier.

On the other hand, the facts thus made known, and the probable inferences from them, harmonise with the account of the condition of Palestine in Judges iii. and iv. Jabin, king of Canaan, obtained the complete mastery of the north at the close of the period. The designation of this king is obscure; Canaan can scarcely be the name of the whole country or of the whole people descended from the son of Ham. It is possible that Jabin may have taken his title from the great fortress in the north, Pakanana, of which mention is repeatedly made in the campaigns of Seti and Rameses II., retaining that title after his occupation of Hazor. In that case he was a Cheta, whether or not we are to identify that people with the Hittites. The name of the captain of his host, Sisera, is still more striking. It bears the closest possible resemblance to the principal Chetan names in the treaty with Rameses, of which one main characteristic is the termination Sar (see note 103). Sisera's position is altogether peculiar, and the most natural explanation of it is that he was the chief of the confederates of Syria, and as such commanding the forces of Jabin. The number of chariots, 900, as I have already remarked, corresponds most remarkably with the 892 taken by Thotmes III., after defeating the confederates of Syria on the same battle-field of Megiddo.

The important question of dates has still to be considered. The chronology even of this comparatively late period may still be regarded as open to question: but at present nearly all, if not all, Egyptian scholars consider it certain that the year 1320 occurred in the reign of Merneptah. This rests on calculations too lengthy and difficult to be here discussed: the agreement of scholars may suffice, especially as no one assigns an earlier date to the reign. But we have thus very little more than 300 years, at the utmost 320, between the Exodus and the building of the temple. When we deduct from this number the 40 years in the wilderness and some 30 years up to the death of Joshua on the one hand, and on the other at least 100 from the death of Eli to the building of the temple, we get only 150 years for the whole period of the Judges, including the long government of Eli: little more in short than 100 years for the interval between Joshua and Eli. The events which the most sceptical criticism accepts as historical can by no possibility be compressed within so limited an interval: 200 years is the very least that any manipulation of the narrative can elicit for those transactions; the contradiction is fatal either to the hypothesis of Egyptologers or to the Hebrew records, *i.e.* either to a conjecture resting on coincidences which scarcely bear a searching criticism, or to written documents which all scholars admit to contain a series of authentic transactions. On the other hand, if the reign of Merneptah be assumed to coincide, as we have shown to be probable, with the ascendancy of the Chetan Jabin or Sisera, we have as elsewhere a very near approximation to complete agreement: Hebrew chronologers fixing the date of the temple building at 1010, and the defeat of Jabin somewhere about 1320.[135]

(34.) Little is known of the interval between Merneptah and Rameses III.: that it was a period of weakness and disturbance is tolerably certain, and as such it may supply arguments for either hypothesis, for the Israelites would be left in peace whether they were in the wilderness or in Palestine: if the calculations of Brugsch and other scholars can be depended upon, the duration of the interval was some 33 years, nor can there be much room for doubt, since the dates of Merneptah and Ra-

---

translates the passage addressed to Merneptah, 'Bonheur extrême dans ton retour à Thèbes en vainqueur. On traine ton char avec les mains. Les chefs garrottés sont devant toi, et tu vas les conduire à ton père Amon, mari de sa mère.' Anastasi, iv. pl. v. l. 1, 2.

[134] The defunct prince is represented in the act of offering a libation and incense to Suteh, the god of Avaris. The deity wears a crown exactly resembling that of the Chetan king. It is curious, and may indicate special amity between Merneptah and that family, with which his own was nearly connected: he may have been a son of the Chetan princess married by Rameses II. in the twenty-second year of his reign.

[135] This odd coincidence is unsought. The dates, 1340 for Jabin, 1320 for Barak, are given by Browne, 'Ordo Sæclorum,' p. 281. Thenius, 'Exegetisches Handbuch,' vol. iii. p. 469, gives 1429 for the death of Joshua, adding, "Von da bis 1188 Othniel, Ehud, Jair, Deborah und Barak, Gideon, Abimelech, Thola, Jair" (a misprint for Jephtha). This leads nearly to the same conclusion, and gives ample scope for the events of the scriptural narrative.

meses III. are generally accepted. The importance of this calculation will be shown presently.

Rameses III. was the last Egyptian king whose reign was signalised by great victories in Syria. The events are recorded in numerous inscriptions at Medinet Abou, published by M. Duemichen: a manuscript of great extent in the possession of Mr. Harris[136] has not yet been printed, but the contents so far as can be ascertained confirm the inscriptions, especially in the historical details. The first years were occupied by wars with the same confederation of Libyans and Mediterraneans who had been repulsed by Merneptah: these wars began in the fifth and were terminated in the twelfth year of his reign. We have, moreover, notices of an expedition into Syria in the eighth year, probably in the interval between two campaigns in Africa. A decisive battle was fought in Northern Syria, in which the Cheta are represented as undergoing a complete defeat.[137] A long list of places attacked or taken in this campaign is given by M. Brugsch ('Geographische Inschriften,' vol. ii. p. 75), and some are identified with names well known in Scripture. Of these by far the larger number belong to Syria,[138] and the general result from the notices of the war in the inscription would seem to be that this Pharaoh, like his predecessors, traversed Palestine rapidly,[139] not diverging from the usual high road, nor losing time in the siege of strongholds occupied by a people who were certainly not confederates of his formidable enemies. Among the conquered chiefs represented on the walls of Medinet Abou are found the king of the Cheta and the king of the Amorites: from other notices it is known that both designations at that period belong to the district north of Palestine.

Bringing these facts to bear upon the two hypotheses, we observe that, on the assumption that the Exodus took place under Merneptah, the campaign of Rameses III. would exactly coincide with the entrance of Joshua: and inasmuch as this king reigned at least twenty-six years,[140] the conquest of Canaan would have been begun and nearly completed while his ascendancy was undisputed. The improbability is obvious.

On the other hand, we have the following indications in support of the opposite hypothesis. Accepting the Aperu as Hebrews, we find that a considerable number, evidently prisoners of war, were employed on the royal domain in this reign, and in the quarries of Hamamat under his immediate successor (see note 114). We observe also that after the overthrow of Jabin the peace of Palestine was undisturbed, as might be expected after the discomfiture of the Chetan confederacy, when the Pharaohs were occupied with the internal affairs of Egypt.[141] The outbreak of the Midianites, described in the sixth of Judges, took place some years later, and was probably a result of the increasing weakness of the monarchy. It will be remembered, however, that the general ascendancy of Egypt in Syria and Mesopotamia was unimpaired to the very end of the twentieth dynasty, an era which, according to all systems of chronology, synchronises with the termination of the period embraced in the book of Judges. Palestine in the mean time went through a series of alternate struggles and successes. That Israel was not crushed or absorbed by the great empires between whom its little territory lay, and by whom it was ultimately subjugated, may be attributed, under God's providence, to their mutual rivalry and nearly balanced power; it was frequently overrun by nomad hordes and conterminous nations, Midianites, Amalekites, Ammonites, and Philistines; but the character of the people was gradually matured, and prepared for the vast development of its resources and institutions under

136 This is one of the most beautiful and interesting of existing papyri; it may be hoped that it will be ere long in the British Museum, and published and translated by Dr. Birch, a scholar to whom Egyptian students are under the very deepest obligation.

137 Rameses III. employed a large fleet in this war, and of course transported the greater part of his forces into Syria by sea. See Brugsch and De Rougé.

138 The only names which are held to belong to Palestine proper are each and all questionable: Jamnia, Azer, Duma, Hebron, alone are identified by Brugsch; the last is more probably the name of a city often mentioned in the inscriptions referring to Northern Syria. A repeated examination of the names in this list, and of those which occur in Duemichen's inscriptions, confirm my impression that Rameses did not occupy Palestine either before or after his Syrian campaign; some few places he may probably have captured on his way. If, however, Chibur or Hebron be the city in Judæa, it would be a strong argument that Rameses III. found the Hebrews there; the Canaanitish name was Kirjath Arba; the old name given at its first building before Abraham, was probably restored after the conquest.

139 The Philistines were in possession of their five cities in the time of Rameses III., and are represented among his captives: see Brugsch, 'G. I.,' ii. pl. xi. This agrees with the notices of a considerable advance of the Philistines in Judges iii. They probably retook the cities which had been conquered by Joshua.

140 The date 26 is found in the Serapeum of Memphis: Brugsch, 'H. E.,' p. 193.

141 Numerous inscriptions and some papyri prove that Rameses III. and his successors were employed in developing the resources of Egypt, and in building palaces and temples. Rameses IV., his son, boasts that he had erected as many monuments in a few years as Rameses II. had done in his long reign. M. de Rougé, 'Études égypt.,' p. 29.

Saul, David, and Solomon, in whose reigns it vindicated its claim to equality with the contemporary empires in Africa and Asia.

It would be too much to expect that the conclusions to which the writer of this dissertation has been irresistibly led will be accepted by those who are satisfied with a system which rests on the authority of many great names; but the greatest care has been taken throughout to separate the facts, which are positively ascertained, from the inferences which must to a certain extent vary according to the state of the reader's mind, his judgment, or his prepossessions. Those facts are stated with all possible care, and with as much of completeness as is compatible with the limits of an Excursus. They have been submitted to the judgment of scholars, and have an independent value; nor, although every year brings important additions to our knowledge of the texts and of their interpretation, is it to be feared that what has hitherto been gained will be overthrown, or the fair and legitimate inferences be considerably modified. The truth of the scriptural narrative does not need such support, but some important links are supplied; the series and meaning of events are better understood in the light thrown upon them by contemporary documents which present coincidences and suggest combinations hitherto unknown, or imperfectly appreciated, by the students of Holy Writ.

Since this Essay was printed, two points of great importance to the argument have been illustrated. (1.) In the work lately published by Duemichen, 'The Fleet of an Egyptian Queen from the seventeenth century before our Era,' we have an account of an expedition into Poumt, *i.e.* Arabia. It proves that a considerable navy was fitted out early under the 18th dynasty; on one plate (xxviii.) the gradual improvement in ship-building is shown by drawings from the 6th, 12th, 17th, and 18th dynasties; on two ships the transport of horses and chariots is represented. (2.) M. Lieblein has published in the last number of the 'Revue Archéologique' (October, 1868) a letter to M. de Rougé, in which he gives very strong reasons for bringing down the date of Rameses II. to the twelfth century. Without accepting all his conclusions, we can scarcely resist the impression that the lowest date hitherto assigned to the 18th dynasty is remarkably confirmed by his arguments. See also 'Zeitschrift,' 1869, p. 122, where the same writer fixes the date of Rameses II. at 1134 B.C. This argument, however, rests on genealogical calculations, which are always open to objection.

The writer has lately ascertained that the copper-mines in the peninsula of Sinai were not worked by the Egyptians from the time when they obtained supplies of copper from Syria, *i.e.* from the reign of Tothmosis I.[142] to the seventeenth year of Tothmosis III., when an expedition was sent under military escort—the last occasion on which the presence of Egyptians is noticed. There were therefore no Egyptians settled on the peninsula at the date assigned to the Exodus in this Essay. This important fact is established, though without reference to the Exodus, in an essay by Dr. Gensler, in the Egyptian 'Zeitschrift,' for October and November, 1870.

---

[142] This transcription now appears to the writer preferable to that which has been adopted in these Essays.

A SUMMARY VIEW OF THE TRANSACTIONS ATTESTED BY EGYPTIAN MONUMENTS, AND OF THEIR CONNECTION WITH HEBREW HISTORY.

Dynasties.	Transactions known from Contemporary Monuments.	Connection with Scriptural History.	
		According to this Excursus.	According to Brugsch and others.
XIIth Dynasty: seven Pharaohs, from Amenemha I. to Amenemha IV., and a queen regnant.	A period of great prosperity; foreigners, especially from Western Asia, received and promoted under the early kings; and under the later kings works of extraordinary magnitude executed to secure the irrigation of Egypt, and to guard against the recurrence of famine.	Abraham received and favoured. Joseph saves Egypt from famine; the Pharaoh master of the resources of Egypt.	
XIIIth to XVIIth Dynasty:	The early Pharaohs still masters of Egypt. Invasion of the Hyksos. Salatis master of Avaris, *i.e.* Tanis, or Zoan. Egypt divided: the worship of Set, Sutech, or Baal, established by the Hyksos in the north; wars between the Theban dynasty and Apepi or Apophis, the last king of the Hyksos.	The Israelites in Goshen rapidly increasing and occupying the whole district, but in a condition of dependence, or partial servitude.	Abraham in Egypt under the Hyksos. Joseph minister of Apophis.
XVIIIth Dynasty: Aahmes I. (Amosis)	Aahmes I. or Amosis captures Avaris and expels the Hyksos. Buildings of great extent undertaken or completed with the aid of forced labourers or mercenaries. The worship of the Theban deities re-established.	Beginning of a systematic persecution of the Israelites, who are employed as forced labourers in restoring or building forts and magazines in their own district.	The Israelites are supposed to remain during the whole period of the 18th dynasty in undisturbed possession of the district of Goshen.
Nefertari.	The Egyptian Queen, a Nubian by birth, possessed of great influence, both before and after the death of Aahmes.	Moses saved and adopted by an Egyptian princess.	
Amenotep I. or Amenophis.	Expeditions into Ethiopia: the Queen-sister in power; succeeding as Regent.	Flight of Moses into Midian.	
Thotmes I.	Expeditions into Nubia and Mesopotamia; immense increase of the Egyptian power.		
Thotmes II. and Hatasou.	First part of the reign prosperous; no indication of foreign or intestine war; latter part of the reign a blank, followed by a general revolt of the confederates in Syria. Hatasou, queen regnant, and retaining power for seventeen or twenty-two years.	Return of Moses, the Exodus, destruction of Pharaoh and his army.	

Dynasties.	Transactions known from Contemporary Monuments.	Connection with Scriptural History. According to this Excursus.	Connection with Scriptural History. According to Brugsch and others.
Thotmes III.	First attempt to recover the ascendancy in Syria in the 22nd year. Wars: repeated incursions into Palestine, Phœnicia, Syria, and Mesopotamia, terminating in the fortieth year of this reign.	The Israelites in the wilderness; entrance into Palestine of Joshua in the fortieth year after the Exodus.	
Amenotep (Amenophis) II.	Expedition into Syria by sea: overthrow of the confederated nations to the north of Palestine.	Progress of the Israelites in Palestine.	
Thotmes IV.	A reign without notable occurrences.		
Amenotep III.	A prosperous reign; supremacy maintained in Syria and Mesopotamia: no intimations of warfare in Palestine: the Queen Tei of foreign origin favours a new and purer form of religion.		
Amenotep IV. or Khu-en-Aten. Princes not considered legitimate.	The religious revolution completed: followed by a period of disturbance and exhaustion.	Cushan Rishathaim in Palestine.	
Horemheb.	End of eighteenth dynasty.		
XIXth Dynasty: Rameses I.	No considerable events; notices of war with the Cheta, who from this time are dominant in Syria.	The interval between Cushan Rishathaim, and Jabin, extends to the latter reigns in this dynasty. Palestine remains, to a great extent, in the possession of the Amorites and other people of Canaan; sometimes overrun by neighbouring people, and towards the close of the period subject to the Philistines in the south, and the Cheta, or Hittites, in the north.	
Seti I.	The Shasous or Nomads from Egypt to Syria, and the Cheta and nations of Mesopotamia, broken and subdued by a series of invasions. The empire reaches its highest point of civilisation and power.		
Rameses II.	During many years Rameses II. is co-regent with his father with royal dignity. On his accession as sole monarch, he invades Syria, defeats the Cheta, with whose king, however, he afterwards contracts an alliance on equal terms, marrying his daughter. Captives are employed in great numbers in building, restoring, or enlarging fortresses, cities, and temples; among them Aperu at Pa-Rameses and Memphis. The reign lasts sixty-seven years, but the date of its commencement, whether from his father's death, or his admission to royalty, is uncertain.		First beginning of the persecution of the Israelites; the birth, early life, and exile of Moses.
Merneptah.	Beginning of reign signalised by victory over Libyan and Mediterranean invaders: no expeditions into Asia: general state of amity with the Cheta: eastern frontier of Egypt carefully guarded: indications of unbroken peace and prosperity in the district about Pa-Rameses.	..	The plagues of Egypt, followed by the Exodus.

Dynasties.	Transactions known from Contemporary Monuments.	Connection with Scriptural History.	
		According to this Excursus.	According to Brugsch and others.
Seti II., Siptah; is close of XIXth Dynasty.	A period not distinguished by foreign wars: letters, however, flourish, and the nation appears to be peaceful and contented.	Palestine in a state of depression, Philistines in the south, Jabin in the north; revolt against Jabin, overthrow of Sisera, war against Jabin continued for some years.	The Israelites in the wilderness.
XXth Dynasty: Rameses III.	A long series of successful wars in Africa and Asia: Palestine traversed, Syria invaded, and the Cheta overthrown. The reign lasts at least twenty-seven years. Aperu employed on the royal domains.	Israelites recover possession of Palestine after the overthrow of Jabin.	The conquest of Palestine begun under Joshua.
Rameses IV.	A peaceful reign occupied chiefly in great buildings. Aperu, captives of war, employed in the quarries.		
Rameses V. to XI.	A period of uncertain duration, the reigns generally short and undistinguished.	The events recorded in the book of Judges after the time of Deborah and Barak.	The entire series of events from the passage over the Jordan to the close of the book of Judges.
Rameses XII.	In this reign the Egyptians retain an acknowledged pre-eminence in Syria and Mesopotamia.		
Rameses XIII.	Close of the twentieth dynasty.		

ESSAY II.

ON EGYPTIAN WORDS IN THE PENTATEUCH.

ONE important result of late Egyptian researches is the establishment of a complete system of transcription of Hebrew and Egyptian characters. At present no doubt remains as to the exact correspondence of the Hebrew letters with phonetic signs, or groups of common occurrence in papyri and monumental inscriptions. An attempt will be here made to bring this result to bear upon the transcription and explanation of the names, titles, and other words of Egyptian origin in the Pentateuch.[1] In the first place, the Hebrew word will be represented in those Egyptian characters which are accepted by all Egyptologers as the exact, and for the most part the invariable, equivalents. In the next place, the meaning of the Egyptian words thus represented will be investigated. In no case will any doubtful transcription be admitted: nor will any meaning be proposed for which conclusive authority cannot be produced from monuments or papyri of the 18th, 19th, and 20th dynasties, or from still earlier periods. If the interpretation thus elicited give a clear, complete, and satisfactory meaning, one in perfect accordance with the context, and the evident intention of the writer of the Pentateuch, there can be no question as to its value, whether in regard to the bearings upon the exegesis of the Book or upon the question of authorship. It is highly improbable that any Hebrew born and brought up in Palestine, within the period extending from the Exodus to the accession of Solomon, would have had the knowledge of the Egyptian language which will thus be shown to have been possessed by the writer; it is certain that no author would have given the words without any explanation, or even indication, of their meaning, had he not known that his readers would be equally familiar with them.

The following table, which gives the Hebrew characters and the corresponding phonetic signs or letters in Egyptian, will enable the reader to judge for himself of the accuracy of the transcription. The transcription in Roman characters is that which has been lately proposed by M. de Rougé, and accepted by Lepsius, Brugsch, and other Egyptologers. See 'Zeitschrift für Ægyptische Sprache,' &c., 1866.

Hebrew	Egyptian.	Conventional Transcription.	The nearest equivalent in ordinary characters.
א	, , or	ȧ, or a	a
ב		b	b
ג		ḳ	g
ד		ṭ	d
ה		h	h
ו	,	u	u
ח	, or	ḥ, or χ	h, or ch, hard
ט		+ t	t, or th
י	, or	ī	i, or ee
כ		k	k
ל		l, or r	l, or r
מ		m	m
נ		n	n
ס		s	s
ע	or	ā	a, o, or ao
פ	or	p, or f	p, ph, or f
צ	or	ṫ	z, or ts
ק		ḳ	k
ר		r	r
ש	, or	ṡ	sh, or s
ת	or	t	th, or t

In addition to the phonetic letters in this list there are many homophones, and syllabic signs, representing the combination of two or more letters. Full lists of these are given by Mr. Birch in the first and last volumes of the latest edition of Bunsen's 'Egypt;' and by M. de Rougé, in the 'Chrestomathie,' now in course of publication. These signs will be explained when they occur in this excursus: they are especially important in

[1] This Essay was printed in 1868. Since that time Dr. Ebers' work has appeared, to which allusion is occasionally made in the notes.

reference to the names of places and official designations.

It must be borne in mind that the vowels are of secondary importance both in Hebrew and Egyptian. They might be disregarded in the transcription were it not that certain affinities between some consonants and vowels are observable in both languages.

The first name in the Bible of purely Egyptian origin, form, and meaning, is Pharaoh.

פַּרְעֹה

The vocalisation and diacritic points show that the Hebrews read this Par-aoh, not Pa-raoh. This is important, since the name, whatever it might signify, was well known as the proper official designation of the kings of Egypt, and its correct pronunciation must have been familiar to the translators of the Pentateuch, and probably also to the punctuators of the Bible. The cuneiform inscriptions have the same division, Pir-u, not Pi-ru.

The transcription gives one of these forms: (*Pa Ra*), or, adopting a syllabic form of very common occurrence, *i. e.* Per, or Phar, פר, and the elongated form which more exactly represents עה, we have (Par-aoh), or one of the ordinary variants of this well-known word.

The first of these transcriptions gives a clear and not improbable meaning, viz., 'The Sun.' Ra is the well-known designation of the sun from sunrise to sunset; and it is certain that the King of Egypt was regarded as the favourite or living representative of Ra: the question is, whether this was the usual and formal designation of the king, recognised by his subjects and known to foreigners.

Several arguments are used in support of this assumption.

1. From a very early period, long before the Hebrews came into contact with the Egyptians, the sign ⨀, pronounced Ra, was the first and most prominent word in the cartouche, or ring, which contained the official name of every Pharaoh, that is, the name which he assumed at his accession.

But this word was not read apart from the other words in the ring, in most cases it was read at the end, not at the beginning of the designation; it had not the article prefixed, and could not therefore be pronounced Pa Ra, or Pharaoh.

2. The king is always called Si Ra, son of Ra. This designation comes between the two rings. It is very ancient, being first borne by Chafra or Chephren. See M. de Rougé, 'Recherches,' p. 56.

But this is in reality an argument against the assumption. The king was not likely to be called both Son of Ra, and The Ra.

3. The word Pa Ra actually occurs as a title of Merneptah Hotephima, the son of Rameses II., in a contemporary papyrus, Anastasi, VI. Pl. v. l. 2.

The sovereign, living, sound, and mighty, *the good Sun* of the whole land.

But "the good Sun" here is not a title, properly speaking. It is simply one of the numerous epithets applied by the Egyptians to their king; a fact sufficiently evident from the addition of the adjective good.[2] The title in this passage is the first word , however, that may be read and explained.

4. A stronger argument is drawn from the Papyrus Rollin (No. 1888), which gives an account of the trial and execution of a sorcerer under Rameses III. It is explained by M. Chabas, in his curious and valuable work, 'Le Papyrus magique d'Harris.' He writes thus (p. 173, n. 2), " , Pera, le Soleil, Memph. ϕρα, Heb. פרעה, designation ordinaire des rois d'Egypt." This seems conclusive, considerng the high authority which always attaches to M. Chabas' opinion. It must, however, be observed that no other passage is adduced, nor, so far as I am aware, can be adduced, in support of the statement that it is the ordinary designation of the sovereign; and in this passage the word is understood by Mr. Deveria, and by M. Pleyte (who has lately published the papyrus) to mean "the Sun God," to whom the frustration of the sorcerer is attributed.[3] It is true that the kings of Egypt were called "Horus," or the "Crowned Hawk" (the Sun God, as symbol of victory), a title taken at their accession, and borne upon their standard; but this was equivalent to the epithet Si Ra, Son of Ra, and constitutes, therefore, an argument against the assumption, which, if not disproved, must be regarded as not proven.

We have now to consider the other and well-known form, , more commonly as above, in the title of Merneptah, . If the transcription Per-ao, or Phar-ao, can be relied upon, of which we have presently to consider the evidence, the proof of the identity of the title with Pha-

[2] Thus Rameses II. is called "Ra, the life of the world," not as an appellation, but an epithet. Mariette, 'Abydos,' pl. 18, l. 36.

[3] Mr. Goodwin observes, "I am now convinced that Pa-Ra in the Rollin Papyrus means the Sun, or God, and not, as I supposed ten years ago when I first deciphered that papyrus, the king or Pharaoh." Mr. Goodwin's remarks, quoted in these notes, are taken from a letter lately received on this Essay, which was forwarded to him by the writer in 1868.

raoh will be conclusive, for the following reasons:—

The regular title of the King of Egypt, the title, *i. e.*, as distinguished from honorary epithets, by which it is always accompanied, is , written also , and , or . These forms occur very frequently under the ancient Empire, in the inscriptions of the Denkmæler of Lepsius, and in those examined and illustrated by M. de Rougé, 'Recherches sur les Monuments qu'on peut attribuer aux six premières Dynasties de Manéthon.' The simpler form is more commonly found in the earlier inscriptions. On monuments of the 19th and following dynasties the latter is almost exclusively used. The meaning of the group is not questioned, viz., the great house, or the great double house, *i. e.*, the royal palace: nor is it doubted that it stands absolutely for the sovereign. It is further to be observed that whenever the sovereign is spoken of as such, not by his proper name, or by his distinctive official name, this and no other designation is found. In official letters, in reports and in treaties, this designation generally precedes the proper and official names: in narratives, when the name of the king is not given, it is used precisely in the same way as Pharaoh in the Bible.[4] There can be no doubt but that this was the title which to Egyptians and foreigners represented the person of the king.

It is perhaps difficult to present the full force of this argument; but no one can look through the Papyrus D'Orbiney, or other papyri of the 19th and 20th dynasties, without feeling that, so far as the usage is concerned, we have in this group the exact equivalent of Pharaoh. It is the group which would necessarily be used if Genesis were translated into ancient Egyptian. Pharaoh alone would represent to a Hebrew the central group in the Egyptian formula:—"His majesty *the Sovereign*, full of life, health, and might."

But the transcription presents a difficulty, which for a long time prevented Egyptian scholars from recognising the identity of the designations. The group is undoubtedly equivalent to פי, or "Pi" in the names of cities, as in Pithom, Pihahiroth, &c. M. de Rougé, however, and M. Brugsch, men of the highest eminence among Egyptologers, whose authority on such a point is especially important, hold that the original and proper pronunciation of was "per," or "pere," in Hebrew פר.[5] It is possible that the r, by the common process of phonetic decay, was gradually disused in a word of common occurrence, but it may have been, and probably was, retained in a title of such dignity, especially as it preceded the vowel sound "a o."

Another difficulty is presented by the dual form. If actually represented two distinct houses, it would be read either Pere pere' or Pere-ti; but as representing not a numerical dual, but a form of majesty, the old pronunciation might be, and probably was, retained unchanged. M. Brugsch (D. H., p. 452) gives several instances which seem to prove that though the sign of the house-plan is doubled, it was pronounced in the singular. However this may be, it is a sufficient answer to the objection that the original form, as we have already seen, the form most commonly found in inscriptions unquestionably much older than the Pentateuch, was [6], of which the nearest possible transcription in Hebrew is פרעה, Pharaoh.

Another argument, which may be regarded as conclusive, has been adduced by M. C. Lenormant, and Professor Lauth, a distinguished Egyptologer. It is clear that

---

[4] The word occurs ten times in seven lines of the Papyrus D'Orbiney, from p. x. l. 9, to p. xi. l. 4. It has almost invariably the addition of , living, sound, and mighty; and is generally preceded by "honef," his majesty.

[5] See 'Chrestomathie Égyptienne,' p. 79, and 'Dictionnaire Hieroglyphique,' pp. 452, 482-3. This is questioned by M. Page Renouf, a very high authority; but a reference to Mr. Birch's Dictionary, in Bunsen's 'Egypt,' vol. v. p. 464, will shew the invariable connection between and , and one variant at least of for points in the same direction. I believe M. de Rougé to be, as usual, right in his conclusion. See also M. Chabas, 'Pap. Mag. Harris,' p. 48, and 'Mél. Ég.' ii. p. 204. The group is found in ancient inscriptions, and proves the phonetic value of the shorter form. Mr. Goodwin observes, "there can be no doubt that was originally par:" he adds, "I agree with your remark that in such a title the pronunciation would very probably be retained."

[6] Thus, for instance, M. de Rougé renders sutèn rech (*i.e.*, near relative, perhaps grandson), du Pharaon, 'Rech.' p. 97. Numerous inscriptions in the Denkmæler, Abt. II., leave no doubt as to the usage. I find that Dr. Ebers adopts the same view, and considers it as unquestionably correct, p. 264. Thus also Duemichen, who gives an example from the time of Thotmes III. See 'Fleet of an Egyptian Queen,' pl. vi.

this transcription exactly explains the assertion of Horapollo, 1, 61; viz. that οἶκος μέγας, "the great house," is the true meaning of the hieroglyphic group which formally represents the Egyptian king, and which therefore is the equivalent of the Hebrew Pharaoh.

Other derivations of the word have been proposed, more or less unsatisfactory. The late Duke of Northumberland suggested that it might be identified with the Uræus (in Egyptian [hieroglyphs], ārāt), the basilisk on the diadem of every Pharaoh. To this the objections are insuperable. The transcription is inexact; the word is never found as a royal designation; and when the sign stands alone it represents a female deity.

The identification with the Coptic ⲡⲟⲩⲣⲟ was natural. It is the general designation of a king; but it appears to represent Pa-Oer, a word constantly employed in the texts to represent a prince, whether native or foreign, but which is never applied to the Pharaoh. Mr. Birch has lately shown the writer two passages in the 5th volume of the Denkmæler, pl. 53, in which [hieroglyphs], or [hieroglyphs], appears to stand for Pharaoh. It would seem, however, to be a proper name, not a title or general designation.

פּוֹטִיפֶרַע, Potiphera,
and
פּוֹטִיפַר, Potiphar.

The first part of both names is admitted to correspond to the Egyptian [hieroglyphs], Pa-ti, "the given," *i. e.*, a person devoted to, dependent upon, &c. Instances are given by Champollion (not in the Grammar, but in the Précis), and by Rosellini, who says that the form occurs frequently in the name [hieroglyphs], Patipara, of which פוטיפרע is an exact transcription. The name signified "devoted to Ra," the most natural designation for the High Priest of On or Heliopolis, the head-quarters of Sun worship. This derivation is well known and universally accepted. It may perhaps be used as an additional argument that [hieroglyphs], Pa Ra, represented the Sun-God, not the Sovereign.

The other name presents more difficulty. Gesenius and others assume that Potiphar is simply an abbreviation or a variant of Potiphera. This is very improbable. The transcription of Egyptian words in Hebrew is now admitted by scholars to be exceedingly accurate, and the omission of the characteristic letter ā, [hieroglyph], ע, would be without a parallel. The meaning of the word must be "devoted to Par," or Phar. If the transcription of [hieroglyph], פר, Phar, be accepted (see above), Potiphar would signify devoted to, or dependent upon the house or palace, and would be written in Egyptian [hieroglyphs] Though this name does not occur in the texts it seems to be in accordance with the usage of the language,[7] and is a very suitable designation for the captain of Pharaoh's bodyguard. The priest thus takes his name from the deity to whose service he is attached, the courtier from his master's house.

אָסְנַת

Asenath, wife of Joseph.

The first syllable may be transcribed by [hieroglyphs], the exact phonetic equivalent, or by either of two well-known groups [hieroglyphs], "as,"[8] or [hieroglyphs], the name of Isis, which has the same phonetic value.

The second part may be read [hieroglyphs], with the determinative [hieroglyph] or any of the numerous variants. It represents the goddess Neit, or Neith, the Athene of Greece.

The combination of these transcriptions, whichever is adopted, gives a clear meaning in accordance with Egyptian usage.

As-Neit would mean favourite of Neith, or Minerva: the word "as" signifies precious, sacred, or consecrated.

[hieroglyphs] would mean Isis-Neith. The double name seems strange, but it was not uncommon in Egypt thus to combine the names of two Deities in one proper name. The first example of a man's name taken from

---

[7] We have χerp-pere, mer-pere = house-steward, major-domo: common titles under the ancient empire. I must add that Mr. Goodwin does not admit the probability of this transcription, which needs the support of ancient inscriptions.

[8] Mr. Goodwin has lately proposed a different reading for this sign, viz., "sheps," and he is followed by Brugsch; but both M. Le Page Renouf and Professor Lauth have since *proved* that "as" is the true value in the older texts. See 'Zeitschrift für Ægyptische Sprache,' &c., 1868, pp. 42 and 45. Thus also Maspero, 'Essai,' p. 16. Since this was printed, I have observed [hieroglyphs] as a variant in Mariette's 'Fouilles d'Abydos.' Mr. Goodwin now says he can only admit that the group is a polyphone, and may have both values. He adds that he considers the combination Isis Neit supplies a much more plausible explanation.

the gods, given by Champollion in the Grammar, p. 135, combines the two divine names Hor Phre, a second in the same page combines Chons and Thot. It is a strong argument in support of this explanation that a Priest of On would naturally give to his daughter the name of a Deity specially connected with the locality. The principal objects of worship, next to the Sun-God, were Seb and Nut (not Neit), who were honoured as the parents of Osiris and *Isis*, the two tutelary Deities. See Brugsch 'Geographische Inschriften,' vol. i. p. 255. Isis moreover was a name commonly given to women, and most likely to be borne by a daughter of Potiphera. It is also to be remarked that there was a close connection between Isis and Neith. Isis was worshipped at Sais in the temple of Neith, under the name As-ta-oert, Isis the Great. See Brugsch, l. c., p. 245.

The connection of Joseph with this family would seem to have had lasting and very serious consequences. Asenath may, or may not, have adopted her husband's faith—probably she did so; but, like the wives of Jacob, she may not have separated herself altogether from her father's influence, or have cast away altogether the traditional superstitions of her family. It is natural to refer the idolatry of the Ephraimites to this origin. Mnevis, the black bull, was worshipped at On as a local Deity, the living representative of the God Tum, the unseen principle and first cause of all existence.

The question whether a priest of On would be disposed to give his daughter to a Hebrew, the favourite and prime minister of Pharaoh, ought not to be regarded as a difficulty. There was nothing to create a scruple. The worship of Jehovah was certainly not known at that age to Egyptians in its exclusive character. Foreigners, especially of Semitic origin, were received with honour, and raised to the highest rank by the greatest sovereigns of the ancient Empire,[9] and the descendant of Abraham, who had been admitted to the intimacy of a former Pharaoh, would be acknowledged as of noble birth. The circumcision of Joseph would be a strong recommendation: it was a sign of consecration and purity to which the Egyptian priests attached peculiar importance. If the rite were previously known as an Egyptian custom, more especially in priestly and royal families, it would mark Joseph both to Pharaoh and Potiphar as specially qualified for the alliance. If it were previously unknown, no person was more likely than Joseph to have introduced it among the Egyptians; and this is possibly the true solution of an acknowledged difficulty The first distinct representation of the rite is found on a monument of the 19th dynasty, long after the time of Joseph: two sons of Rameses II. are pictured as undergoing it. See M. Chabas' art. in 'Revue Archéologique,' 1861, p. 298. The word [hieroglyphs], "sabu" (which is translated "circumcise" by Champollion, and after him by Mr. Birch, D. H.), is not found with that sense in any ancient inscription.[10] A passage in the 'Funeral Ritual' (c. xvii. l. 23, ed. Leps.) is supposed by M. de Rougé to refer to circumcision, but the meaning is very doubtful, nor if his explanation were accepted, would it be conclusive: for although portions of the chapter are undoubtedly older than Joseph, the passage is a gloss of doubtful antiquity, and is omitted in the ancient copy lately published by M. Lepsius. See 'Aelteste Texte, Sarkophag 1 des Mentuhotep,' pl. 1, l. 16, 17.

צפנת פענח

Zaphnath Paaneah.—Gen. xli. 45.

The history of the attempts to explain this designation of Joseph is curious and instructive. The most natural process before the hieroglyphic inscriptions were deciphered was to compare the Hebrew form with the Coptic: no explanation was derived from this source which was generally satisfactory to scholars, and most interpreters resorted to the Septuagint, which gives several forms all differing from the Hebrew. Gesenius holds that the Hebrew writer must have modified the Egyptian words in order to bring them into accordance with his own language: a singular assumption, since the word is completely inexplicable in Hebrew. It will be found that an exact transcription of the Hebrew letters gives a clear sense in Egyptian.

The word stands thus—

[hieroglyphs], z f n t p ānch.

[9] This curious fact is proved beyond all doubt by the 'Story of Saneha,' a hieratic papyrus of extreme antiquity, lately translated by Mr. Goodwin. See especially pp. 39 and 43. It is also to be observed that Saneha, Son of the Sycomore, was a name probably given to the foreigner on his adoption by the Egyptians.

[10] M. Brugsch gives no such meaning in his dictionary. Mr. Goodwin adds, in the letter lately received by me; the meaning adopted by Birch from Champollion's Dictionary is probably based only on the Copic ⲥⲉⲃⲓ, and is of little authority. Ebers gives another word [hieroglyphs] or [hieroglyphs], which he translates "circumcise." Brugsch and Birch have no such meaning, nor do I find any example. A stronger but not conclusive argument is drawn from the well-known hieroglyphic for *mt*. The representations, however, to which Ebers alludes, and the mummies which have been examined, are much later than the time of Joseph.

The letter ץ is invariably transcribed by or , and most commonly by the latter. is the nearest form for ף, could only be represented in Hebrew by נת or נט; and in the Pentateuch is generally transcribed by ת, as in Pithom and Asenath. No doubt can be entertained about the remaining letters: all scholars would accept the identification of the Egyptian word here given with the Hebrew. In fact every letter in this transcription rests on the unanimous authority of Egyptian scholars, and is confirmed by a vast number of unmistakable words in ancient inscriptions and papyri.

The meaning is quite clear. The first syllable "zaf," is a word of very common occurrence, both in this simple form, and with explanatory signs called determinatives, as a "bushel," or a "widgeon," indicating abundance.[11] Its well-ascertained meaning is "food," especially "corn," or "grain," in general. A few instances will show this usage, and serve to illustrate the biblical account of Joseph's position. Under the early dynasties of the ancient empire the officer of state who received the tributes in kind and had the superintendence of the public granaries bore the title "master of the house of ('zaf' or 'zafa') provisions." M. de Rougé gives the names of three officers who bore this title. Ptah-ases, the son-in-law of a Pharaoh of the 4th dynasty, Chafra or Chefren, was called "mer set zafa," which M. de Rougé renders "chargé de la maison des provisions de bouche." This remark on the office is important, the more so since he does not connect the word with the history of Joseph. "Les tributs versés en nature rendaient cette fonction très importante, ainsi qu'on peut le voir par l'histoire de Joseph."[12] The grandson and chief minister of Nepherkara bore the same title, l. c. p. 86. Another great official of the same early age held the three offices, master of the arsenals, of the Treasury, and of the depôts of provisions, "zaf." De Rougé renders the last title, "chef des lieux des offrandes, des denrées," p. 87. From the last passage it is also clear that the granaries throughout Egypt were under the superintendence of one great officer of state. M. de Rougé observes, "Ces trois titres pouvaient constituer une sorte de ministère des finances."

The next word , "nt" is the preposition "of," used very commonly on the early monuments. Two examples may be found in Egyptian words quoted by M. de Rougé on the last passage which has been discussed.

The meaning of "Anch" is not questioned. It signifies "life," or with the article it may mean "the living." Thus one name of Memphis is ta-anch for the land of life or of the living.[13]

The meaning, therefore, of the whole name, the only meaning which it could bear to an Egyptian, and of course to a Hebrew of the age of Moses, is "the food of life" or "the food of the living." No question can be raised as to the appropriateness of this designation: it only remains to show that the word "zaf" was likely to be applied to a person. To this it is a complete answer that it occurs in the rings of three Pharaohs of the 13th dynasty. See Brugsch, 'Histoire d'Égypte,' pl. viii., nos. 162, 164, and 167; or Lepsius, 'Königsbuch,' taf. xix. 282, 284.[14]

We have now to consider the remarkable reading of the Septuagint. The Egyptian was a living language, though it had undergone considerable modifications, when the Pentateuch was translated, and it is evident from Jerome's account that the Jews in Egypt attached a definite meaning to the word ψονθομ φανηχ, which on their authority he renders salvator mundi. The latter part corresponds with the interpretation above given. Life, or the living, is the equivalent of "the world." The first part is more difficult to explain. The transcription of ψονθ would give , p-sont, *i.e.*, "foundation." It might possibly be used in the sense of "support," "sustentation;" but I am not aware that any example of such a meaning can be adduced.[15]

---

[11] This complete form is . The last two signs are not phonetic; they represent a widgeon or duck, and bread.

[12] See 'Recherches,' p. 69.

[13] Jablonski, 'Opuscula,' tom. i. p. 210, suggests from the Coptic ϫⲱϥ ⲛⲧⲉ ⲡⲉⲛⲉϥ, caput mundi; La Crozius, ϫⲱϥ ⲛⲧⲉ ⲡⲱⲛϧ, thus agreeing with the transcription here given so far as the last part is concerned. There can, however, be no doubt that represents צף; whereas the phonetic value of the Egyptian sign for head differs from it considerably.

[14] The transcription of Brugsch is more accurate, . Traces of the word are found in other rings, probably also in the name of a Pharaoh of much earlier date. See De Rougé, 'Recherches,' p. 155. In choosing the name, Pharaoh might possibly have had some regard to the name Joseph; seph and zaph bear a near resemblance.

[15] Gesenius renders the word "the support of life;" but the imperfect knowledge of hiero

Another transcription of the Greek form may be suggested; one more exact, since it retains the consonants without any modification.

, Psntmnānch.

The meaning would be "he who gives joy to the world." This name has a strong Egyptian colouring. It occurs precisely in the same form as that of a royal favourite under the 5th dynasty, , sntm het, or, as M. de Rougé reads, "senotem het," "delighting the heart." The example shows, also, that the construction is correct: "senotem" is a transitive form, and does not require or admit a preposition. It may be observed that the same root occurs in the names of two princes of the 21st dynasty. (See Brugsch, H. E., Pl. xiv., Nos. 299 and 302.)

One or other of these forms may have been before the minds of the Greek translator—probably the latter; but the reading of the LXX is uncertain, and there is no reason whatever for departing from the simple, intelligible, and well-ascertained sense of the words which is elicited by transcription of the Hebrew.

אַבְרֵךְ

This word, which Gesenius (Thes. *s. v.*) calls "vox perdubia," has never had a satisfactory explanation. It is admitted to be Egyptian, though, as usual, Gesenius supposes that it was modified in the transcription in order to give it a Hebrew character. The explanation suggested by Rosellini, and adopted by Gesenius, is ⲁⲡⲉⲣⲉⲕ, *i.e.* incline or bow the head. This, however, is inadmissible. The transposition of the two words ⲣⲉⲕ and ⲁⲡⲉ is not in accordance with old Egyptian usage. ⲁⲡⲉ may possibly be the true sound of the hieroglyphic for head (see De Rougé, 'Recherches,' p. 91, n. 2.), but it would not be correctly transcribed by אַב. ⲣⲉⲕ is not found in the sense "bow" or "incline" in old Egyptian.

The exact transcription is .

If this give a meaning exactly applicable, there can be no need of further inquiry.

The context tells us, not, as is commonly assumed, that a herald went before Joseph, addressing the people, but "they cried before him," *i. e.* the people or the attendants shouted out with reference to Joseph, "Abrek."

But ab-rek is the imperative, and the emphatic imperative, of the verb "Ab," which is a word specially used in reference to public demonstrations of rejoicing. Thus, in an inscription of Rameses II. we find *Ab*-sen-nek, "they rejoice before thee:" and in another of later date, "the world is in a state of rejoicing," in *Ab* ni. The termination "rek" is equivalent to the Hebrew לָךְ, as M. Chabas has pointed out in explaining the word mai-rek, *i. e.* come.[16] 'Voyage d'un Égyptien,' p. 285.

The chief objection to this explanation is that the verb is in the singular number, addressing an individual, not a multitude. But it seems quite natural that the attendants should address Joseph, calling upon him to rejoice, together with all the people, in his deliverance and exaltation. Some support may be found for this explanation in the fact that subject princes address the Pharaoh in the same form, hotep-rek. See the vignette to the Stèle Pianchi in Mariette's 'Fouilles d'Abydos.'

Another transcription, which comes very near to the Hebrew, would give Ab Rekh, *i. e.* "pure" and "wise:" but it is unlikely to have been used as an exclamation.[17]

מֹשֶׁה, Moses.

In examining the form which this name would properly assume in Egyptian, we must bear in mind the following points:—1. The letter שׁ is generally represented by *i. e.* sh and its homophones, but in very ancient transcriptions, and specially in monuments of the 18th and 19th dynasties, it corresponds in proper names to , s. Thus we find , Āstharta, for עַשְׁתֹּרֶת,

glyphics in his time led him to the error of identifying "sont" with , to which it bears no real resemblance. I have since found the name Sont-ur, *i.e.* the "great foundation," as that of a high priest at Thebes. See Mariette, 'Fouilles,' pl. vii. l. 12. The LXX. may therefore have meant to represent Pa-sont-om-Paanch (om = ϯ *i.e.* am, or ami), belonging to the support of the world. A good sense, but not so good as that given by the Hebrew. Mr. Goodwin considers the transcription of the LXX, which is given above, to be very probable. He translates it "making life pleasant," which is equivalent in meaning. He observes also that the article in old Egyptian would not have been written, but probably it was often supplied in reading and speaking. This applies to the preceding account of the Hebrew form.

[16] It is especially used in exclamations, thus: harek—stand up, see 'Br. D. H.', p. 814, equivalent to "up with you." The form occurs repeatedly in the texts.

[17] In the 'Æg. Zeitschrift'. for 1869, p. 1869, the Egyptian Ap-Rech, i.e. Chief of the Wise. The transcription is not accurate, p for b, and ch for k.

, Askelna, for אשקלון, Askalon, and , Pulistha, for פלשת. M. Brugsch, a high authority in all such questions, gives ס or ש as the corresponding letters to the Egyptian (See 'Geographische Inschriften,' p. 15). This is a point of importance, considering the remarkable accuracy of the transcriptions in the Pentateuch.

2. The final letter ה is adequately represented by a vowel sound, either \\ = *i*, or more commonly by , *u*, corresponding to the Hebrew ו.

3. The vowel sound in *Mo* is not represented either in Hebrew or Egyptian, but in the transcription a preference should be given to the vowel *o*, which appears from Coptic and Greek to be associated with the consonants *Ms*.

4. It is also to be observed that Moses undoubtedly lays the stress on the verb "draw out," not on the noun "water." The name in Egyptian ought to bear the sense "drawn out," "brought forth." The verb may have borne the same sense in Hebrew also (a fact of extremely common occurrence), but if the writer knew Egyptian he certainly would not have chosen a word for which that language does not supply a natural interpretation.

Among transcriptions which are probable or possible, one exactly fulfils all these conditions. The word , *m s u*, unquestionably corresponds in form to the Hebrew, letter for letter, on the principles laid down above. The vowel sound, which is required for the first syllable, may be assumed to have been *o*, and this for several reasons. The syllable occurs in many names of the 18th dynasty, and is always transcribed by Manetho or his Greek translators by *mos;* thus we find Amosis and Thotmosis.

The question of equal importance as to the meaning remains to be answered.

The explanation, suggested first as it would seem by Gesenius (Thes. *s. v.*) "child" or "son," is quite accurate so far as it goes. Mesu, or Moses, undoubtedly does bear that signification, and may be rendered exactly by "son." But if we had no other information as to the original and common sense of the verb from which it is derived, this interpretation, which contradicts the statement in Exodus, would present an insuperable difficulty, unless we were satisfied with the usual evasion that the word was altered so as to adapt it to a Hebrew etymology. The difficulty, however, is entirely removed when the original meaning, as well as usage, of the word in Egyptian is examined. In his 'Hieroglyphic Dictionary' M. Brugsch shows that the sense "drawing out" is the original one. It is taken from the work of the potter (p. 705). It there means "produce," "bring forth," and, as M. Brugsch affirms in another passage (p. 698), the derivation of משה from the Hebrew root משה, traxit, extraxit, suitably also in the sense "extraxit e ventre matris," would preserve the true sense of the Egyptian.[18]

The word used by Moses may of course be Semitic; although it must be observed that it occurs only in this passage, and in one other which is evidently taken from it, Ps. xviii. 17 (repeated 2 Sam. xxii. 17); but at any rate it is so exceedingly rare that we can best account for its selection by Moses by the supposition that it came exceedingly near to, or exactly represented, the Egyptian. It is far from improbable that it was, in fact, a simple transcription of words, which must have been perfectly intelligible to the Israelites of that age. What the Egyptian princess said—and her words were not likely to be forgotten or misrepresented by her adopted son—was this: "I give him the name Moses—'brought forth'—because I brought him forth from the water."[19]

The probability that this was actually the Egyptian name of Moses comes very near a certainty when we learn that it was very common under the Middle Empire. In the select papyri (Anastasi, vi. p. 3, l. 4)[20] it occurs as the names of a keeper of goats, the superintendent of the "house of measures," where corn was measured or weighed. It was also borne by a prince of the blood-royal of Egypt who held the office of Viceroy of Nubia under the nineteenth dynasty. There is no reason for identifying either of these persons with Moses, but the coincidences with the biblical history and with the legends in Josephus and other writers are curious. This ascertained use of the word appears to give it a very decided preference over two other senses suggested by a faithful transcription. The

---

[18] A family of words closely resembling, or identical with, משה משה, is found in Egyptian. See Brugsch D. H., p. 711, *s. v.*

[19] In the Egyptian the translation would run thus:

Au set hi tat naf pa rañ Mesu em tat pe-un mesna su emta pa mu.

[20] See Brugsch, D. H., p. 1162.

word *i.e.* māsi, in the sense "to bring," is common, not only as the instances given by Birch and Brugsch would lead us to suppose, in reference to tributes, but to the simple transfer of objects.[21] It would be quite intelligible in Egyptian were we to read, "She called his name *Masi*, saying because I brought (māsi) him out of the waters." It is, however, doubtful whether such a proper name would be in accordance with Egyptian usage. Again, it might be possible, with our present knowledge of Egyptian, to give a more plausible etymology derived from the word "water," than either of those which Jablonski and other scholars formerly proposed. The phonetic value of the group is admitted to be Mu, or Mo, and , shī, denotes a child. Mo-shi, a water-child, would not be an impossible transcription or rendering, were it justified by Egyptian usage. Still it is clear that the stress is laid, not on the noun, but on the verb, and there appears no reason to depart from the simple and natural explanation which has been given above.

It may, however, appear to require some additional evidence that Moses should have used an Egyptian word, or have selected, to say the least, a very unusual Hebrew word to represent it. Here we may call attention to a fact which has hitherto been unnoticed. In that part of the narrative which deals specially with Egyptian matters, words are constantly used which are either of Egyptian origin or common to Hebrew and Egyptian. The following instances are taken from one verse, that in which Moses gives the history of his exposure. His mother made him an ark of bulrushes. The word "ark," תבה (of which Rödiger says, "falsi sunt, qui etymon in linguis Semiticis quærerent), is admitted to be Egyptian. It is, indeed, very common in the sense "chest" or "coffer," also in the sense "cradle," , teb, with several variants. (Birch D. N., p. 5359; Br. D.H., 1628.) The Septuagint retains the Hebrew θίβιν, doubtless as a well-known Egyptian word. The material of which this ark was made is called גמא. Brugsch ('Dict. Hier.,' p. 145.) identifies this word with the Coptic ⲕⲁⲙ, "juncus quo fiunt funes." Brugsch shows, moreover, that it was specially used for making the light boats of the Nile. He gives the word ⲕⲁⲙ, papyrus myopea, p. 1452. See also p. 2320, where a basket of green papyrus (kam nat) is mentioned.

Again, "when she made it, she *daubed* it with *slime*." The word חמר is used in the original both for the process and the material. This corresponds exactly with the original meaning and use of the Egyptian word , which has the same letters, though, as is very commonly the case, in a different order. The Hebrew is ch-m-r, the Egyptian m-r-ch. Brugsch ('Dict. Hier.,' p. 769) says, "Die Grundbedeutung der Wurzel Merh. ist 'beschmieren, bestreichen, überzeichen etwas mit einem feuchten gegenstande." Mr. Goodwin has very lately shown the identity of the words. "The root appears again in ⲁⲙⲣⲏϩⲉ, ⲁⲙⲃⲣⲉϩⲓ, bitumen, pitch, in Hebrew חמר."—'Zeits.,' 1867, p. 86. Whether Moses had this word in mind may, of course, be questioned, but it is evidently the most suitable that could be suggested.

The next word, "pitch," is common to Hebrew and Egyptian. זפת, , or , sft. The Egyptian word is very common; the Hebrew occurs only twice in the Bible, but is well known in Arabic, and was probably common to Egyptian and Hebrew.

Jochebed then placed the ark in "the flags." The Hebrew is סוף, for which no plausible etymology has been suggested, nor is the word found in any Semitic language. It answers, however, very nearly to the Egyptian name for a species of papyrus found in marshy places and on the banks of rivers. The word was written either (Sallier, 1, 4, 9), *i.e.*, tufi, or , also to be read "tufi." The Coptic equivalent is ϫⲟⲟϥ, which indicates a predominance of the sibilant sound common to dentals. It seems probable that it was also written with , "z," both because of the Coptic form, and because , "tzet" (which seems to be an abbreviation), also means papyrus. In that case "tufi" would be translated "zufi" = סוף. The identification of the Egyptian and Hebrew is so probable as to approximate to a certainty. In the last number of Brugsch's Dictionary, published since this was printed, I find that he also identifies tufi, ϫⲟⲟⲩϥ and סוף, p. 1580.

Lastly, we read "by the river's brink." על שפת היאר. The form and meaning are Egyptian. It is well known that יאר is

[21] It is used for bringing a harp to a man in a tavern. See 'Stele Pianchi ap. Brugsch, D. H.', p. 157. Brugsch writes the word Masib, but Birch gives Masi, which seems correct. The leg is not phonetic, but determinative.

Egyptian. The Nile has two names: the sacred name Hapi, and the common name, meaning "river," which is here exactly transcribed [hieroglyphs] Aor. The word שׂפה, *i. e.* "lip," for "brink," is sufficiently common in Hebrew, but it is interesting to find in a papyrus of the 19th dynasty precisely the same word with the same meaning. "I sat down by the *lip* of the river, [hieroglyphs]" *i. e.* "spot Atur." Atur is another form of "Aor." The same idiom occurs in the 'Funeral Ritual,' c. ii. 3, l. 2.

It would be very difficult to resist the impression that this verse was written by a man equally familiar with both languages, or, on the other hand, to admit the possibility that coincidences coming so near together were purely accidental, as they must have been in the mouth of a Palestinian Jew.

One more instance of equal interest is taken from the 1st chapter of Exodus, ver. 11. We there read that the Egyptians set שׂרי מסים, "sari massim," over Israel. The words are both common in Hebrew, but they are also common in Egyptian, and precisely in the same signification. Birch gives [hieroglyphs], mās, tribute. 'Dictionary of Hieroglyphics,' *s. v.* The official name "ser" is still more striking. It is common in the sense "chieftain," but we find it specially applied to the officer appointed by Tothmosis III. to superintend the work of captives employed in making bricks. In the inscription on the well-known picture which represents the processes, we find the proper official designation of the overseers,[22] who were armed with heavy whips, and also of the chief superintendent. He is called [hieroglyphs][23], of which the Hebrew שׂר, "ser," is the exact transcription. His rank is denoted by the long staff, and by the determinative, viz. the head and neck of a giraffe. Had this title occurred first under the 19th dynasty it might have been regarded as Semitic (for a vast number of military and civil titles were then introduced into Egypt); but occurring, as it does, under the 18th dynasty, it is unquestionably Egyptian. It is found, indeed, in inscriptions far more ancient, *e. g.* under Pepi of the 6th dynasty. See De Rougé, 'Recherches,' p. 118. We have, in any case, a proof that in relating Egyptian transactions Moses either used the native Egyptian word, or that he adopted the Hebrew word which expressed it most exactly both in meaning and form.

פִּתֹם, Pithom. This city was formerly identified by Brugsch with the fort of Djar, *Pachtum* n Zar. This was a point of importance, since it is certain that that fort or city was in existence early in the 18th dynasty, before the accession of Tothmosis III., the grandson of Amosis I., to whom its erection may be unhesitatingly ascribed. The fortress in question is shown, on grounds which appear conclusive, to have been known at a later period by the name Heroopolis, near the ruins of Mukfar, or Abn Kasheb. See Brugsch, 'Geographie des Alten Ægyptens,' p. 263. The word Pithom, however, does not correspond to the Egyptian form with sufficient accuracy, and it is now admitted to be identical with [hieroglyphs], Pe-tum, the house, *i. e.* dwelling or temple of Tum. Still the conclusions drawn by Brugsch do not lose their interest, since it has lately been shown that this place was in the immediate vicinity of the fortress, and was in all probability built at the same time as the adjoining sanctuary, giving name to the whole set of edifices, or it might have been a second name of the same place. Thus On is called Pitum, with the same meaning, "house of Tum." This is probably the true explanation. The passage translated by M. Chabas, 'Mét. Égypt.,' ii., p. 155, shows that certain nomads of Atema (or, as the name should be transcribed, Edom) applied to the guards of Merneptah Hotephima, the son of Rameses, for permission to feed their cattle in the district adjoining the fortress, to which that sovereign had then given his own name. The place of conference was the great reservoir at Pithom. From this we learn that Pithom was on the frontier of the desert. The name here used for reservoir in the papyrus is Semitic, [hieroglyphs], as Chabas transcribes it Bere-koavota, *i. e.* ברכות, cisterns or reservoirs: a curious illustration of the biblical narrative, built as the place was by Israelites, and probably occupied by them up to the date of the Exodus. In the time of Merneptah there is no indication of their presence, nor is it at all probable that had the Delta at that time been in the state supposed by Brugsch (see 'Histoire d'Égypte,' p. 174), the king would have admitted a nomad tribe into the district.

אֵתָם, Etham. Exod. xiii. 20. The transcription of this name comes exceedingly near to Pithom. , A-tum, Pitum. The meaning is

---

22 [hieroglyphs] The meaning of the group is the head work-givers, the eye denoting superintendence.

23 In the eleventh line of the inscription, which is read from right to left. See Brugsch, 'Histoire d'Égypte,' p. 106.

identical, [hieroglyph] *i.e.* A, and [hieroglyph] per, mean "house," "dwelling," and are applied indifferently as designations of one and the same locality: thus Pi Ramessu and A-Ramessu (Chab., 'Mél. Ég.') Etham and Pithom are to be rendered "house of Tum." The site of Etham was on the extreme border of the desert, such, as we have seen, must have been the site of Pithom. The identification of the two names which M. Chabas ('Voy. Ég.,' p. 286) proposes as probable, may therefore be regarded as all but certain. The LXX. give Ὀθόμ, or Ὀθώμ, for Etham. This represents the Egyptian exactly, for the [hieroglyph] corresponds generally to O. In Numbers xxxiii. 6, 7, they give Βουθάν, or, as it should be read, Βουθάμ. The Βου, as in the well-known Busiris for Pe-bsiri, represents the Egyptian [hieroglyph] (not the article, but the group for "house" or Pe): this corroborates the argument for the identification.

The derivation proposed by Jablonski, and accepted by Forster, viz. At-iom, *not-sea*, may illustrate the shifts to which men of learning were formerly driven by their ignorance of the ancient language of Egypt.

רַעְמְסֵס, Gen. xlvii. 11; רַעְמְסֵס, Exod. i. 11. In the former passage the name "Rameses" is that of a district; in the latter, "Raamses," it is the name of a city. The pointing of the former name is preferable. The first syllable רע is the exact transcription of [hieroglyph], Ra, the well-known name of the Sun-God. The second part of the word, מסס, represents with equal fidelity the Egyptian [hieroglyph], "meses." This latter part is a reduplicated form of the very common word [hieroglyph], "mes," a child. It occurs in the name Rameses, which was borne by two Pharaohs of the 19th, and by all the kings of the 20th dynasty. In the name of the sovereign the meaning of the word is either "Ra begat," or "Ra begat him." Hence it is inferred that the name both of the district and of the city must have been derived from that of the king.

It is, however, clear that the writer of the Pentateuch represents the name as that of the district at the time of its occupation by the Israelites, that is, at a time admitted by all to be ages before the 19th dynasty. Had the passage in Genesis occurred in a papyrus of the age of the Exodus, it would have been held as a sufficient proof that the name must have been ancient; nor is there any reason to doubt the statement, or to suppose that the name was simply given as that by which the district was known at the time when Moses wrote. The only question is whether it was a name likely to be given to a place or district at an early age, in accordance with Egyptian usage.

Late researches have shown that "Ra," the first part of the word, entered very commonly into names of places, districts, and cities under the ancient empire: far more commonly than at a later period. Thus we find, from inscriptions in the tomb of Tei (son-in-law of a Pharaoh of the 5th dynasty, An, or Ranuser), that not less than four cities, or districts, in his government were called Ra-asket, Ra-shephet, Ra-Seket, and Ra-hotep (De Rougé, 'Recherches,' p. 94; see also p. 72, where M. de R. observes that the frequent notices of Ra have been much overlooked). Under a preceding Pharaoh we meet with Ra-heb, *i.e.*, festival of Ra; this was a royal residence. Such names might be expected to be found very frequently in the country about On, which was called Pe-Ra, Es-Ra, Nes-Ra, and Aa-Ra. (See Brugsch, 'Geog.,' Nos. 1213, 1214.)

Ra-meses may therefore well have been the old name of the district: whether it represents the original form, "Ra-messon," with the sense "Ra the self-begetting," an ancient appellation of Ra in the Ritual; or Ra-meses, "Ra the creator, former, or begotten," a sense equally suitable and harmonizing with Egyptian notions; or "Ra-mesu," children of Ra. The Egyptians called themselves children of Ra, *i.e.*, Ra-mesu, from the earliest times; it was probably their characteristic name as distinguished from foreigners: this appears from a well-known inscription on the tomb of Seti Merneptah, the father of Rameses II. A city, of which the site is unknown, bore the name Mis-Ra:[24] nor is it at all improbable that this is connected with the name given to the Egyptians in the Bible, viz., Mizraim.[25] That some district should have borne the name, and, if any district, that which was peculiarly associated with the earliest forms of Sun worship, presents no improbability,[26] nothing which can justify us in questioning the accuracy of Moses.

The same arguments apply to the name of the city of Rameses. It was a name very naturally given to the capital of the district. The certain fact that Rameses II. gave his own name to a fortress of considerable extent in this district, as well as to others in different parts of Egypt, has been regarded by Egyptologers as a

---

[24] See Brugsch, 'Geog.,' No. 1517.

[25] This has been suggested by M. Rougemont, 'Age de Bronze,' and is supported by M. Rheinisch. Dr. Ebers rejects, but does not disprove, the identification. In an Essay lately published by Mr. Birch, on the trilingual inscription of San, he observes that Mizraim is supposed by some to represent the common Egyptian word for Egypt, viz. ta-meri. This requires two transpositions, mer-ta and met-ra.

[26] This is, in fact, admitted even by M. Chabas, 'Mél. égypt.,' ii. p. 125.

conclusive proof that it could not have borne the name previously. It should, however, be observed that Moses does not call the city, or arsenal, Pi Ramessu, but simply Rameses. The word Pi, or its equivalent *A*, signifying house or residence, so far as I can ascertain, is never omitted in the Egyptian designations of places named after the king. It is found in all the names given by M. Chabas, 'Mél. Ég.,' ii. p. 126. It is extremely unlikely that it should have been omitted by Moses in the very same sentence in which he gives the full and accurate transcription of Pithom. Again, the name which the fortress bore after its enlargement by Rameses was invariably that of the Sovereign, who is not called in Egyptian documents Rameses simply, but Rameses Meiamon, or Meramon. This is not conclusive, but it adds some weight to the argument. It is known, moreover, that the fortress was in existence at the beginning of the reign of Rameses, and apparently bearing the name Rameses.[27] In addition to these facts we find that Amosis, or Aahmes, to whom the building of several cities in the Delta is attributed by contemporary monuments, gave the name "Rames" to one of his own sons. It has been observed above, that in the names of early kings, the Greeks transcribe Mes by Moses, which points to a duplicate *s* in Egyptian. It may not be assumed that the name of the city was taken from this prince, but the probability that the same, or that a similar name should be given to both at the same time, is sufficiently obvious. It may be added that Ramesses was likely to be the true name of one of the treasure cities built by Aahmes, because the king was a restorer of the worship of Ra. He was a great builder, and had special reasons for fortifying the Eastern district, which previously bore the name Rameses. It is also certain that Egyptian cities often took their name from a district, in which case the prefix "Pi" is not used[28]

One argument of great weight remains to be considered. The city of Rameses Meiamon, with its parks, lakes, and the whole adjoining district, was the centre of a great Egyptian population, a place of festivities; whereas, at the time described in the Pentateuch, the two fortresses built by the Israelites were in the district which they occupied, and of which there is no indication whatever that they were dispossessed. In the time of Rameses it was a rich, fertile, and beautiful district, described as the abode of happiness, where all alike, rich and poor, lived in peace and plenty; but in the time of Moses it was the abode of a suffering race, resounding not with the jubilant shouts of Egyptians, but with the groans and execrations of an oppressed population. A stronger contrast can scarcely be drawn than that of the state of the district at the Exodus and that which it presented under Rameses II. and his successors.

פִּיהַחִירֹת, Pihahiroth. It is not certain that the word is Egyptian. If so, it may, like some other names, have been adopted and modified either by the Israelites or other Semitic occupants of the district. There appear to be indications of the name in one of the Select Papyri (Anast. iii. 1, 2), in which the scribe Penbesa gives an account of a visit of Rameses to the adjoining district. The passage is translated by M. Chabas, 'Mél. Égypt.,' ii. p. 133. Garlands of flowers were sent from a place called [hieroglyphs], *i.e. Pehir:* from the determinatives, it appears that the place was on a river or reservoir. Chabas, however, connects the word [hieroglyphs] "hir," with the Hebrew חור. We may, therefore, translate Pihahiroth (regarding it as partly Egyptian, partly Semitic) "the house of wells, the watering-place in the desert."

M. Brugsch, however, compares Pihahiroth with the name of a place called "Pehuret," but of which nothing is known. 'Geog.,' p. 298.

גֹּשֶׁן. There can be no doubt that this name is Egyptian, although, as the Israelites occupied the district during the whole period of their sojourn, the form may have been modified. No probable interpretation is supplied by the Coptic, nor does any name exactly corresponding to Goshen appear on the monuments. It is, however, to be remarked that three Egyptian nomes, situate in the Delta, and extending over great part of the district of Goshen, bore each a name beginning with the word *Ka*, *i. e.* a bull. This word would be represented in Hebrew by the first syllable of Goshen. The Egyptian for bull is written either with [hieroglyph] or [hieroglyph] (see Birch, D. H., p. 417, [hieroglyphs], *ga*), and the regular transcription of [hieroglyph] ([hieroglyph] being a homophone) is ג, *g*. The vowel sound is vague, but the Greek transcription of Ka-kem is κωχώμη. See Brugsch, 'Geographie,' Index. We may accept "go" as the transcription of the first syllable without any hesitation. That of the second remains doubtful.

If, again, we can depend upon the transcription of M. Brugsch, the name of the 12th

---

[27] Brugsch, 'Histoire d'Égypte,' p. 156. "Les papyrus mentionnent ces deux endroits existants déjà sous Sethos I. par leurs noms égyptiens."

[28] Thus the fortress of Zar is found without the prefix in numerous inscriptions. See Brugsch, 'Geog.,' p. 260, and Nos. 1263, 1267, taf. xlvii. Dr. Haigh suggests that a synonym of Zar may be read Ka-sen, or Kashen; but his arguments are not very satisfactory. See 'Zeits.' 1861, p. 47.

nomos in Lower Egypt was Ka-she, of which the Hebrew transcription would be נשה. This comes exceedingly near to the form now in question. The Egyptian ideographs to which Brugsch gives this phonetic value, represent a bull and a leaping calf.[29] See Brugsch, 'Geographie des Alten Ægyptens,' p. 253. The name of the principal city in the district was She-nefer, *i.e.* "the sacred calf," a name which has an obvious and striking bearing upon the history of the Israelites. From another notice it is proved that this city, Neter-she, was situate in a district adjoining that of which *Zar* was the capital. But Zar, or, as it is written more fully, "the fortress of Zar," was close to Pithom, and was formerly identified with it by Brugsch. So that there is sufficient reason to assume that the Egyptian name of the district may have been pronounced Goshe. It is of course possible that the name Goshen may have represented to the Israelites an adjoining district beginning with the word Ka; or that some name even nearer than "Goshe" may have been in use. Ka-kem, *i.e.* the black bull, appears to have been the origin of the LXX. and Coptic ⲔⲈⲤⲈⲘ. The monumental inscriptions in Lower Egypt are scanty.

The bull represented in the names of these districts was Mnevis, worshipped specially at On as the living representative of Tum, the unknown principle and source of all existence. See Brugsch, *l. c.*

גרשם. Gershom. Moses explains this name to mean a sojourner in a strange land, Exodus ii. 22. Gesenius finding no Hebrew authority for this meaning of שם, assumes a double error, viz. that the writer took שם, "there," to be the equivalent of a strange land, and that he was ignorant of the true derivation from גרש, banished. The Egyptian gives a complete etymology. The first syllable is common to both languages: גר is the exact equivalent and transcription of [hieroglyphs] or [hieroglyphs], dweller, or sojourner. The word is preserved in Coptic in the form ϪⲰⲒⲖⲒ, in which Ϫ = [hieroglyph] and λ = [hieroglyph]. Moses, as we have seen, usually takes a word common to both languages. The second syllable שם is pure Egyptian, retained in the Coptic in the common word ϢⲈⲘⲘⲞ, shemmo, a foreigner, or a foreign land. Thus in this passage the Coptic version of ארץ נכריה, a foreign land, is ⲞⲨⲔⲀϨⲒ Ⲛ ϢⲈⲘⲘⲞ. The meaning to an Egyptian would be exactly what the Hebrew expresses "a dweller in a foreign land." The Coptic, according to Brugsch, D. H., is the equivalent of "shumer," a bow, used commonly as the hieroglyphic of "foreigners."

Genesis xli. 2, אחו, LXX. ἄχει, Coptic ⲀϪⲒ. The word has long been recognised as Egyptian. It occurs only in this passage and in Job viii. 11, where it is used in parallelism with גמא (see above, p. 485), and described as a water plant. The old Egyptian corresponds exactly, [hieroglyphs], as a verb to be green, to grow and flower. The determinative points to herbage by a stream. Another form of the word [hieroglyphs], *aχu*, is used for reeds, rushes, &c. The radical meaning is bright luxuriant growth.

[29] The leaping calf is the D. of *Ab*, "thirst." I do not find the value assigned to it by Brugsch.

In the Introduction to Exodus the attention of scholars was specially called to a list of words taken from the first fifteen chapters of Exodus, which contain the history of the transactions in Egypt. They are either ἅπαξ λεγόμενα, or peculiar to the Pentateuch, occurring, if at all elsewhere, only in the Psalms of later date, which recapitulate the history. Nearly all are words which are found in Egyptian documents of unquestioned antiquity, either older or not much later than Moses.

C. i. 7. שרץ. In Pentateuch only, except in Psalm cv., taken from this passage, the root is found in Arabic and Æthiopic. The Egyptian [hieroglyphs] s written with all the dentals, *e.g.*, with [hieroglyph], which is the exact equivalent of צ.[1] It exactly corresponds to the Æthiopian ሠረጸ, pullulavit; the [hieroglyph] represents the impulsive mood, equivalent to Hiphil. This accounts for שרץ being followed by the objective of the object produced.

פרה, not an uncommon word, but far more frequently found in the Pentateuch (nineteen times) than elsewhere (eleven times altogether): the Eg. root is per, *i.e.*, come forth, grow abundantly, corn and all kinds of grain.

11. שרי מסים, see above, p. 486.

13. בפרך occurs once only, Ez. xxxiv. 4 out of the Pent.

16. האבנים, the two stones. The meaning is purely conjectural; there is no trace of the expression in Hebrew, or of the usage to which it is supposed to refer to Palestine. The root [hieroglyph], ben, is found

[1] Thus de Rougé, Chr. p. 103. Br. D. H. s. v.

in many derivatives in Egyptian; it has the sense to roll, twist, turn, &c.; also to produce, engender. Brugsch connects it with אופן. Possibly it may have some connexion with the very doubtful Hebrew.

C. ii. 3. תבה, ark. 27 times in the Pentateuch, not found elsewhere. It is only used of the ark of Noah, and of the cradle of Moses. It has no Semitic root or equivalent, the Arabic being derived entirely from this passage. In Egyptian it is a common word in the sense of chest, coffer, and *cradle*.

גמא, a word found in Job and Isaiah; but from Egyptian, see above.

זפת, pitch, occurs twice only out of Pentateuch, Isaiah xxxiv. 9; xxxv. 9: common in Egyptian, see above. יאר, the Nile, long known as Egyptian.

5. רחץ, wash, a common word, but used in Egyptian rakat, and recht in the same sense.

10. משה, "to draw forth," only here and in the 18th Psalm; no satisfactory etymology in Semitic, but common in the form mesu, and with variants in the sense bring forth, draw forth, &c. See above.

16. רהט, once only in Cant. i. 17.

iii, 2. סנה, only in Exodus and Deut.; shown in note *ad loc.* to be Egyptian in the sense "thorny acacia."

7. תבן, straw, common in the Pentateuch, rare elsewhere. In Egyptian tebn means "chaff." Pap. Sall. 4, p. 5. קש, stalk, not uncommon in Hebrew, but Egyptian in exactly the same form and sense.

9. שעה, look to, trust in; very rare in this sense. שדי occurs nine times in Pent., thirty times in Job, very rare in later books.

vi. 25. The father-in-law and the son of Eleazer both bear Egyptian names, Putiel, "devoted to El." Phineas occurs under Rameses II.

vii. 3. On the names of magicians and sorcerers see note on this chapter, at the end.

להט, ἁ. λ., and v. 22, לט, correspond to Egyptian words for magic and medical formulæ.

27. צפרדע, zeparda, frog; only found in Exodus and in one Psalm taken from it. It is a purely local name, adopted by the Arabs in Egypt. The radicals of which it is composed occur in a modified form in the Egyptian for "tadpole," hefennu, or hefenr: [hieroglyphs], and [hieroglyphs], which Brugsch renders "tadpoles," giving as the Arabic equivalent ولد ضفدع the young dofda. The word has also the secondary meaning 100,000 or an indefinite number. The interchange of aspirates and sibilants is common, indeed regular in Zend and Sanscrit, in Greek and Latin. Another word comes even nearer, [hieroglyphs], tsfdt, which has the exact correspondents of צ, ף, and ד; the word means snake or "viper," but appears to be generic for reptiles. It is to be observed also that [hieroglyphs], hefed, means to squat; a very probable etymology.

19. אגם: found in Isaiah, but uncommon. No satisfactory etymology is given, nor does the word occur in the same sense in the cognate languages. In this passage four words are given, rivers, streams, agammim, and generally every reservoir or collection of water. "Agam" may be assumed to be a well known local term. I find no exact Egyptian equivalent, and the Hebrews probably modified that which they adopted. But [hieroglyphs], chnum, le puits, la citerne, Brugsch, D. H., p. 1100, would answer the conditions of an exact correspondence in sense, and resemblance in sound. A well 120 cubits deep is mentioned in an inscription quoted p. 246. Another word occurs in the Ritual, 99, 26, which comes nearer in form, viz., Achem, which is mentioned in connexion with the Nile, but the meaning is uncertain.

viii. 3. The combination of these words, shown above to be probably Egyptian, is remarkable, שרץ היאר צפרדעים. It is an instance of the custom of Moses, in describing Egyptian events, to use words either purely Egyptian or common to the two languages.

תנור, oven. The word is not uncommon, but occurs more frequently in the Pentateuch than elsewhere. The etymology is uncertain. The Coptic ⲑⲣⲓⲣ, or ⲧⲣⲓⲣ, comes very near; the permutation of ⲣ and ⲛ is common. The Egyptian supplies "*nennu*," to bake or roast, D. H., p. 784, and "hir," an oven; combined, the two words give all the elements, but the connection is scarcely probable. The old Egyptian must have had a form from which the Coptic certainly, and probably the Hebrew also, was derived.

14. חמר, in the sense "heap," is peculiar to this passage.

16. כנים: the word occurs six times in this passage, and nowhere else, except in Ps. cv. 31, which is taken from it. No probable Hebrew root is suggested, nor is the word extant in the Semitic dialects. The Arabic Chaldee and Syriac translators use a word quite distinct from it. The Egyptian has no name for an insect corresponding to this, but it has the root "ken," [hieroglyphs], in the sense force and abundance, a sense which in one word is developed into multitudinous [hieroglyphs], one of the commonest words in the language; and in another,

[hieroglyphs], takes the sense plague, calamity, &c. The Coptic has ϫⲛⲉ, percussit. This sense is further determined in one variant by the sign [hieroglyph], which associates the plague with a bad smell and corruption. One passage quoted by Brugsch is curious, since it points to a periodical visitation: "The year did not bring the plague (ken) at the usual time." This quotation gives a peculiar force to the exclamation of Pharaoh's magicians, "It is the finger of God:" they recognised it as a severe visitation. The word is identified by Brugsch with the Egyptian [hieroglyphs], chenemms, the mosquito. It is retained in the Coptic ϣⲟⲗⲙⲉ, κώνωψ, culex. See D. H., p. 1103.

21. הערב: the word occurs nowhere but in the description of this plague, seven times here, and twice in Psalms lxxviii. 45, and cv. 31. The Semitic root ערב is very common, but is nowhere connected with insects or a plague of any kind. A late Egyptian word, [hieroglyphs], Abeb, *i. e.* a beetle, resembles the Hebrew in form, and is connected with several words, ⲁϥ, ⲁⲃ, ⲁⲁⲃ, which represent species of flies: as for instance [hieroglyphs], D. H., p. 183, Champollion Gr., p. 74, which evidently denotes a venomous fly. It is possible either that the Hebrews, adopting the Egyptian word, accommodated it to their own common root, or that the middle letter ר may have been, for the same reason, substituted for ב in the transcription. The oldest forms of ר and ב, *i.e.*, are scarcely distinguishable; and even in the Samaritan, which adds a line to the b, they are easily confused. The Coptic Pentateuch uses the word af, ⲛⲓⲁϥ, adding ⲛⲟⲩϩⲟⲣ, "dog," to express the κυνόμυια of the LXX. This conjecture is somewhat confirmed by the affinity thus brought out with זבוב, the fly, especially "the fly that is in the uttermost parts of the rivers of Egypt," Isaiah vii. 18.

23. פדות, separation, not found elsewhere in this sense: it is from Semitic.

ix. 8. פיח, ἅ. λ. Gesenius derives it from פוח = נפח. If this probable connection be correct, the word would be common to the Egyptian and Hebrew, nef, nefu, to breathe, or blow.

כבשן occurs only in the Pentateuch. The Arabic has قبس, ignem extudit, which may, or may not, be the root. No Semitic etymology is satisfactory. The Chaldee, Syriac, and Arabic employ a different word. I find no Egyptian equivalent; the nearest in form and sense is [hieroglyphs], χabs, a burning lamp. Perhaps [hieroglyphs], to bake, of which כפן would be the transcription, may have had a variant nearer to the Hebrew. The word is used in a late variant in the sense of baking bricks, or more probably "using a lime kiln." A curious word lately discovered by Mr. Birch, very probably gives the true form [hieroglyphs], kabusa, in Coptic ϫⲃⲃⲉⲥ, ἄνθραξ, carbo. 'Egypt. Zeitschrift,' 1868, p. 121. Mr. Birch writes ϫⲁⲓⲃⲉⲥ; Peyron gives ϫⲃⲃⲉⲥ; and ϫⲃⲉⲥ.—Lex. Copt. This meets the two conditions of agreement in sense and radical letters.

9. אבק, "fine dust," is a very rare word, twice in the Pentateuch, four times in later books.

שחין, A. V. boils. The word occurs in Job ii. 7, and in reference to Hezekiah. Gesenius compares the Arabic سخن, to be hot, used specially of fever heat: but the word never occurs in connection with eruptions. A Coptic MS., quoted by Peyron, renders this and the word פרח which follows ϫⲛⲟⲩϥ ⲃⲉⲣⲃⲉⲣ, in which the radical letters partly correspond with the Hebrew, ϫ often = ש. Possibly the Egyptian came nearer still. The true derivation, however, appears to be ϩⲱϩ, prurire, of which the Egyptian form was [hieroglyphs], to scratch, a word which occurs frequently in early papyri. The exact transcription is χaku. A variant somewhat nearer probably existed, or the Hebrews may have adopted and modified it, substituting, as in many words, sh for χ, and ch for k.

פרח. = ⲃⲉⲣⲃⲉⲣ, see last note.

אבעבעת, ἅ. λ. The assumed root, בוע, is not extant. Egyptian has [hieroglyphs] bābā, Cop. ⲃⲉⲃⲉ, overflow. The א presents no difficulty.

15. כחד, cut off. In this sense it occurs once in Zechariah, otherwise only here and in Job iv. 7; xv. 28; xxii. 20. The Coptic ⲕⲱⲣⲩ cædere, abscindere, is connected with the root [hieroglyphs], כח. [hieroglyphs], cut, [hieroglyphs], engrave, carve; still nearer is ϭⲉⲧϭⲱⲧ, concidere, cædere.

31. פשתה, flax, a common word, is probably Egyptian. No satisfactory Semitic

etymology is proposed; the Arabic has فشر, to which Fuerst gives the sense "carminari," without authority as it would seem: nor is the meaning assigned to it by Gesenius supported by Arabic Lexicographers. A glance at Freytag will show how utterly unconnected the meaning is with flax. Gesenius observes that it is found in Avicenna. I believe that in Syriac and Arabic it is merely a derivative meaning. Gesenius observes that the word does not occur in any Semitic dialect. He had good reason to reject the conjectures of Forster; he would probably not have hesitated to adopt the etymology suggested by the Egyptian [hieroglyphs], Pek, flax, linen, and linen stuffs. It is a very common word, known first from the Rosetta stone. The change of "k" to "sh" is normal. Brugsch, p. 515, compares it with פשתה.

נבעל ἁ. λ. The assumed root נבע does not occur in any Semitic dialect. In Egyptian [hieroglyphs], gabu, blossom, corresponds very nearly. 'D. H.,' p. 755.

32. כסמת, "spelt," occurs very seldom. The Arabic which resembles it is uncommon, كرسنة; it is used by Saddia in translating Is. xxviii. 25. Freytag gives كرسنة, vicia, vetch, but without a root, and it evidently is a strange word, probably a compound word, and of Egyptian origin. [hieroglyphs], sim, Coptic ⲥⲓⲙ, is a general name for herbs, and is used in the Coptic Version of v. 25. A compound word of uncertain meaning, but denoting some vegetable food, is found in the 'Ritual,' c. 124, 4: [hieroglyphs], chersemau, which corresponds very nearly to the Hebrew grain [hieroglyphs], kemetta, or kemdut, written also [hieroglyphs], means a kind of corn, represented [hieroglyph] on the Sarcophagus of Seti; Bon., p. 2, B. l. 43; B. 43; D. H., p. 1497.

32. אפילת, ἁ. λ. No Semitic root is found; that suggested by Gesenius is unsatisfactory, أفل has the sense deficit, latuit, whence G. elicits the meaning, late in season, tender. In Egyptian [hieroglyphs], pirt, or pilt. Brugsch renders the word "jeunes plantes qui viennent de pousser," the exact meaning of the Hebrew.

xii. 11. פסח, passover. The Semitic derivations are doubtful, see note *in loc.* The Egyptian [hieroglyphs], pesh-t, corresponds very nearly in form, and exactly in meaning and construction. Champollion, Gr., p. 446, gives two examples, to extend the arms or wings over a person, protecting him.

15. שאר, leaven; the word occurs only in this chapter. Gesenius compares סיר, to boil. In Egyptian [hieroglyphs], with variants pronounced seri, means "seethe," "seething pot." It is connected with seru, cheese, or buttermilk. There can be little doubt of the connexion with the Hebrew, and the Egyptian probably supplies the true root. חמץ, leavened dough, does not occur in the same sense out of the Pentateuch, unless it be in Amos iv. 5, when it seems rather to mean "spoil." The Coptic has ϩⲙⲙϫ, acid, which, corresponding with it exactly in form and nearly in sense, implies an Egyptian root; but it may be taken from the Arabic. The Egyptian for fermentation does not seem to be connected with it, [hieroglyphs], stf; which is represented by the Coptic ⲥⲃⲏⲧⲉ, see Chabas 'Mél.' ii. p. 219; though the radical letters might be brought under the common law of transmutation between aspirants and sibilants.

22. סף, basin, or, according to some, "threshold," see note *in loc.* The latter sense is somewhat confirmed by the Eg. [hieroglyphs], sep, a step, or threshold.

Considerable additions may be made to this list, which will probably form the basis of a separate treatise. Enough has been said to show that Moses habitually uses words which existed in Egyptian, and for the most part cannot be shown to have a true Semitic etymology.

Since the preceding pages were finally revised for the press the writer has received the 'Journal Asiatique' for March and April, 1870. It contains an article by M. Harkavy, entitled, "Les Mots Égyptiens de la Bible." It does not include proper names. In some important points the writer has the satisfaction of finding his conclusions supported by this Egyptologer, who appears not to have seen these Essays, which were sent to Paris towards the end of last year.

The following derivations are partly new and of much interest.

Gen. xli. 43. M. Harkavy adopts Ap-rech, chief of the Rech, or men of learning; a derivation noticed above, p. 483. He defends the transcription of *p* by *b*, and *ch* by *k*, and certainly shows that in words common to Hebrew and Egyptian they are sometimes interchanged. He gives also what appears to be the true equivalent of כנים, see above, p. 491, viz. Chenemms.

Gen. xli. 2, Achu. The same derivation as that given above.

xli. 8. Chartummim, magicians. In a note, p. 109, M. Harkavy observes: "Un savant distingué, qui a lu notre travail, remarque qu'il avait pensé au radical *tem* qui signifie prononcer, énoncer, avec la particule *cher*. L'initiale *cher* forme en effet des titres avec d'autres mots." The reader will find this derivation stated and defended in the note at the end of Exodus, c. vii., p. 279. It was mentioned by the writer to some scholars both in England and Paris, by whom it was approved.

טנא, tena, a sacred basket. The derivation has been given in note on Exod. xvi.

Exod. vii. 11, 22. Mr. Harkavy derives לט להט from Rech-chet, a magician, or man of learning. The writer prefers the etymology proposed, p. 276.

Gen. xlix. 5, מכרות, rendered habitation, probably equivalent to Macher, a granary.

Gen. xii. et passim, "Pharaoh." The derivation proposed above is defended.

Gen. xli. 45. Zaphnath Paaneh. M. Harkavy gives the same value to the first syllable, Zaph, food, and to the word Paaneh, life. For the middle syllable he proposes net, saviour. The transcription given above still appears preferable to the writer, who is glad to find M. H. in accord with him in regard to the more important terms, food and life.

The derivations of Shesh and Pak, fine linen, have been already noted.

LEVITICUS

INTRODUCTION

I. LEVITICUS, that is, the Levitical Book (LXX. Λευιτικόν, Vulg. *Leviticus*), is the name by which this portion of the Law of Moses has always been called by the Hellenistic Jews and the Christian Church. But according to the text of the Masorites, it does not appear certain that the Book was originally named, or in any way regarded by them, as a whole. It would rather seem that they reckoned it simply as ten out of the fifty-four sections into which the entire Book of the Mosaic writings is divided. The ten Sections are as follow:—

Sect. 24,	Chap.	i.—vi. 7.
" 25,	"	vi. 8—viii.
" 26,	"	ix.—xi.
" 27,	"	xii. xiii.
" 28,	"	xiv. xv.
" 29,	"	xvi.—xviii.
" 30,	"	xix. xx.
" 31,	"	xxi.—xxiv.
" 32,	"	xxv. xxvi. 2.
" 33,	"	xxvi. 3—xxvii.

Each Section, in accordance with rabbinical custom, is named from the word, or phrase, with which it commences. Section 24 is called *Vayikra* (ויקרא), which means, "and he (the LORD) called." But it appears that the Rabbinical Jews in the time of S. Jerome used the Pentateuchal division, and gave to each of the five Books the name of its first section[1]. The modern Jews apply the title *Vayikra* both to the whole book of Leviticus, and, in its more strict sense, to Sect. 24 of the Pentateuch.

As regards its subject matter, Leviticus is closely connected with Exodus at its commencement and with Numbers at its conclusion. The first link of connection is clearly shewn by the fact that while the directions for the Consecration of the priests are given in Exodus, the Consecration itself is narrated in Leviticus in nearly the same words, changing the tense of the verbs. See prel. note to Ex. xxix.

The Book however has a certain claim to unity from so large a portion of it being occupied with instructions for the service of the Sanctuary. It is true that much matter of the same kind is found in Exodus and Numbers. But Leviticus differs from those Books in in its general exclusion of historical narrative. The only historical portions are the accounts of the Consecration of the priests, with the deaths of Nadab and Abihu (ch. viii.—x.), and of the punishment of the blasphemer (xxiv. 10—23).

II. As regards the question of authorship, most, even of those who hold a different opinion on the other books of the Pentateuch, ascribe it in the

[1] Hieron. 'Prologus Galeatus.'

main to Moses. The theories which are counter to its Mosaic origin are so much at variance with each other—no two of them being in anything like substantial agreement—that it does not seem worth while to notice them in this place.

Leviticus has no pretension to systematic arrangement as a whole, nor does it appear to have been originally written all at one time. Some repetitions occur in it[1]; and in many instances, certain particulars are separated from others with which, by the subject-matter, they are immediately connected[2]. There appear to be in Leviticus, as well as in the other Books of the Pentateuch, præ-Mosaic fragments incorporated with the more recent matter[3]. There are also passages which may probably have been written by Moses on previous occasions and inserted in the places they now occupy when the Pentateuch was put together. It is by no means unlikely that there are insertions of a later date which were written, or sanctioned, by the Prophets and holy men who, after the Captivity, arranged and edited the Scriptures of the Old Testament[4]. The fragmentary way in which the Law has been recorded, regarded in connection with the perfect harmony of its spirit and details, may tend to confirm both the unity of the authorship of the Books in which it is contained, and the true inspiration of the Lawgiver.

III. In the following table, the contents of the Book of Leviticus are shewn in the order in which they occur.

LAWS FOR THE ALTAR.........	i.—vii.
Laws addressed to the people Burnt-offerings, i. Meat-offerings, ii. Peace-offerings, iii. Sin-offerings, iv. 1—v. 13. Trespass-offerings, v. 14—vi. 7.	i.—vi. 7.
Laws addressed to the priests Burnt-offerings, vi. 8—13. Meat-offerings, vi. 14—23. Sin-offerings, vi. 24—30. Trespass-offerings, vii. 1—7. Meat-offerings, Peace-offerings, &c. 8—21.	vi. 8—vii. 21
Laws addressed to the people Fat and blood not to be eaten, vii. 22—27. The priests' portions of the Peace-offerings, vii. 28—38.	vii. 22—38.
The Consecration of the Priests (cf. Ex. xxix.)..................	viii.
Aaron and his sons enter upon their office........................	ix.
Nadab and Abihu are punished	x. 1—20.
The laws of clean and unclean animal food	xi.
Purification after child-birth ...	xii.
The Leprosy .... Examination of suspected cases, xiii. 1—44. Exclusion of lepers from the camp. xiii. 45, 46. The Leprosy in clothing and leather, xiii. 47—59. The cleansing and restoration of the healed leper, xiv. 1—32. The Leprosy in a house, xiv. 33—53. Conclusion, xiv. 54—57.	xiii. xiv.
Purifications on account of secretions..........................	xv.
The Day of Atonement	xvi.
The slaughtering of animals for food..............................	xvii.
Unlawful marriages..............	xviii. 1—18.
Abominable lusts..................	xviii. 19—30.
Precepts on duties	xix.
Precepts on duties, for the most part with punishments prescribed	xx.
Precepts on holiness for the priests	xxi. xxii. 16.
Choice of victims for the Altar, and rules for eating the flesh of the Peace-offerings	xxii. 17—33.
The days of Holy Convocation and the Festivals in their connection with agriculture.......	xxiii.
The Lamps and the Shewbread for the Sanctuary..............	xxiv. 1—9.
The blasphemer punished, with an interpolation on retribution	xxiv. 10—23.
The Sabbath year, and the Jubilee in connection with the rights of the poor..............	xxv.
Promises and Threatenings for the nation........................	xxvi.
Vows	xxvii.

[1] For examples, compare Lev. xi. 39, 40 with xxii. 8; and Lev. xix. 9 with xxiii. 22. But on some of the most considerable alleged cases of mere repetition in the Pentateuch, see notes on ch. xx. xxiii.

[2] See *e.g.* Prel. notes to ch. xii. and ch. xv.; note on xiii. 39; also xix. 5—8, xxii. 17—25.

[3] See Introd. Note to Ex. xx. 22; notes on Lev. xxiii. xxv.

[4] We seek in vain for any clear internal evidence of such interpolations in Leviticus. But the probability of their existence may be easily admitted, taking account of the literary habits of past ages, before the spirit of modern criticism had introduced a curious desire to appropriate every sentence to its author. On the objections to Mosaic authorship which have been based on passages relating to the future history of the nation, see Note after Chap. xxvi. and cf. notes on Ex. xxiii. 20, 31.

IV. The Ritual of the Sacrifices.

The instructions respecting the offerings for the Altar contained in Leviticus are given, like most of the other portions of the Law, in a more or less disjoined and occasional way. They were recorded with a view to the guidance of those who were practically conversant with the service of the Tabernacle. They do not as they stand furnish a methodical statement for the information of those who are strangers to the subject. A compact and systematic sketch of the ritual of the Altar, may therefore well form part of an Introduction to the study of this Book.

§ i. In regard to the whole sacrificial system of the Hebrew Law, it is most necessary that we should keep in view that it was intended for a people already brought into covenant with the living God, and that every sacrifice was assumed to have a vital connexion with the spirit of the worshipper. A Hebrew Sacrifice, like a Christian Sacrament, possessed the inward and spiritual grace, as well as the outward and visible sign. The mere empty form, or the feeling of an opus operatum, was as alien to the mind of an enlightened Israelite who brought his gift to the Altar, as it is to the well instructed Christian who comes to the Table of the Lord. This fact will be found not obscurely intimated in the words of the Law itself. But it is most clearly expressed by the sacred writers in later ages, when it became necessary that they should remind their backsliding countrymen of the truth[1].

It may however be supposed that to those who came to the Sanctuary in sincerity and truth, a sacrifice may have borne a very different amount of meaning, according to the religious conditions of their minds. One may have come in devout obedience to the voice of the Law, with little more than a vague sense that his offering in some way expressed his own spiritual wants, and that the fact that he was permitted to offer it, was a sacramental pledge of God's good will and favour towards him. But to another, with clearer spiritual insight, the lessons conveyed in the symbols of the Altar must have all converged with more or less distinctness towards the Lamb slain from the foundation of the world[2], Who was to come in the fulness of times that He might fulfil all righteousness[3], and realize in the eyes of men the true Sin-offering, Burnt-offering, and Peace-offering; Who has now been made sin for us, though He knew no sin, that we might be made the righteousness of God in Him[4], Who has given Himself for us an offering and a sacrifice to God for a sweet-smelling savour[5], Who is our peace that He might bring us nigh by His blood[6], our very Paschal Lamb which has been slain for us[7], to the end that by eating His flesh and drinking His blood we might have eternal life[8].

The Classification of Offerings.

§ ii. The general name for what was formally given up to the service of God was *korbān* (קרבן), which exactly answers to the English words, *offering* and *oblation*. It is rendered by δῶρον (gift) in the Septuagint[9]. Under this name were included what was paid for the maintenance of the Priests and Levites in the shape of first-fruits and tithes[10], whatever was contributed for the endowment of the Sanctuary[11], and whatever offerings were brought to be sacrificed on the Altar. The last, which alone belong to our present purpose, may be thus classed:—

Offerings for the Altar.

Animal.	*Vegetable.*
1 Burnt-offerings,	1 Meat- and Drink-offerings for the Altar in the Court.
2 Peace-offerings,	2 Incense and Meat-offerings for the Holy Place within the Tabernacle.
3 Sin-offerings.	

Besides the three ordinary classes of animal sacrifices, there were several

[1] Ps. xl. 6; l. 8—15; Prov. xxi. 3; Is. i. 11—15; Jer. vii. 21—23; Hos. vi. 6; Mic. vi. 7, 8. Cf. 1 Sam. xv. 22; Matt. v. 23, 24.

[2] Rev. xiii. 8.
[3] Matt. iii. 15.
[4] 2 Cor. v. 21.
[5] Eph. v. 2.
[6] Eph. ii. 13, 14.
[7] 1 Cor. v. 7.
[8] Joh. vi. 54.
[9] Cf. Mark vii. 11.
[10] Lev. ii. 12; xxvii. 30; Num. xviii. 12, 26.
[11] Num. vii. 3; xxxi. 50.

offerings which were peculiar in their nature, such as the Paschal lamb[1], the Scape goat[2], and the Red heifer[3]. There was also the sort of Peace-offering called *Chagigah*, connected mainly with the Passover, and apparently referred to in the Law, though not mentioned by name[4], the Firstlings[5], and the Tithe animals[6].

The offerings for the Altar were (1) public sacrifices, offered at the cost and on behalf of the community (such as the victims offered in the morning and evening service of the Sanctuary and in the public festivals)[7], and (2) private sacrifices which were offered either by express enactment of the Law on particular occasions, or by the voluntary devotion of the sacrificer. It will be seen that the first three chapters of Leviticus relate entirely to private voluntary offerings[8]. But it may be observed that the mode of conducting a sacrifice of any given kind was nearly the same, whether it was a public or a private one. The main points of exception were that in the public sacrifices the priests, or the Levites, did what was else done by the person who brought the offering, or by those who were employed by him; and, according to the Mishna[9], that the laying of the hand upon the head of the victim was required in the public sacrifices only in particular cases, which are specified in the Law[10].

The Animal Sacrifices.

§ iii. The external distinction between the three classes of animal sacrifices may be thus broadly stated:—the Burnt-offering was wholly burnt upon the Altar; the Sin-offering was in part burnt on the Altar, and in part, either given to the priests or burnt outside the camp; and the Peace-offering was shared between the Altar, the priests and the sacrificer. This formal difference is immediately connected with the distinctive meaning of each kind of sacrifice. See § xvi.

The names by which the animal sacrifices are called in the Hebrew text are as follows:—

The general name is *zebach* (זבח), that is, a slaughtered animal. In the English Bible it is commonly rendered sacrifice, but sometimes offering. It is opposed to *minchāh* (מנחה), literally, a gift[11], which denotes a vegetable-offering, called in our version a Meat-offering.

The Burnt-offering is called *'olāh* (עלה), that which ascends, or *ishsheh* (אִשֶּׁה), that which is burnt; it is also occasionally called *kāleel* (כליל), that which is whole, because the whole victim was given to the altar. In our version, *'olāh* is rendered "burnt-offering," or "burnt sacrifice," and *kāleel*, "whole burnt sacrifice[12]."

The Peace-offering is called *shelem* (שלם), that is peace, or concord. The Thank-offering, a Peace-offering made under certain conditions[13], was called *tōdāh* (תודה), a thanksgiving.

The Sin-offering was called *chattāth* (חטאת), strictly either a sin, or punishment for sin.

The Trespass-offering which, as regards its meaning, was a kind of Sin-offering always accompanied by a pecuniary fine, was called *āshām* (אשם) *i.e.* a forfeit[14].

The Selection of Animals for Sacrifice.

§ iv. Five animals are named in the Law as suitable for sacrifice, the ox, the sheep, the goat, the dove and the pigeon. It is worthy of notice that these were all offered by Abraham in the great sacrifice of the Covenant. The divine command was, "Take me an heifer of three years old, and a she-goat of three years old, and a ram of three years old, and a turtledove and a young pigeon[15]." These animals are all clean according to

[1] Ex. xii. 3.
[2] Lev. xvi. 10.
[3] Num. xix. 2.
[4] See Num. x. 10; Deut. xvi. 2.
[5] Ex. xiii. 12, 13.
[6] Lev. xxvii. 32.
[7] Ex. xxix. 38—44; Num. xxviii. xxix.
[8] See Lev. i. 2; ii. 1, &c.
[9] Menach, ix. 7.
[10] Lev. iv. 15; xvi. 21; 2 Chron. xxix. 23. See Outram, I. xv. § 7.

[11] Ps. xl. 6; Jer. xvii. 26; Dan. ix. 27. See on Lev. ii. 1.
[12] Deut. xxxiii. 10; Ps. li. 19. The words used by the Septuagint are ὁλοκαύτωμα, ὁλοκαύτωσις and ὁλοκάρπωμα; and by the Vulgate, *holocaustum*.
[13] See on Lev. vii. 11, 12.
[14] See on Lev. v. 14.
[15] Gen. xv. 9.

the division into clean and unclean which was adopted in the Law[1], but which had its origin in remoter ages[2]. They are also the most important of those which are used for food and are of the greatest utility to man. The three kinds of quadrupeds were domesticated in flocks and herds[3] and were recognized as property, making up in fact a great part of the wealth of the Hebrews before they settled in the Holy Land. It would thus appear that three conditions met in the sacrificial quadrupeds; (1) they were clean according to the Law; (2) they were commonly used as food; and, being domesticated, (3) they formed a part of the home wealth of the sacrificers. If there were any birds which were domesticated by the Israelites in the time of Moses, they were most probably the dove and the pigeon, for dove-cots and pigeon-houses have been from very early times common appendages to the houses of the Holy Land and the neighbouring countries[4]. But even if it could be proved that the doves and the pigeons used in sacrifice were wild, and did not therefore fulfil the last-mentioned condition of the sacrificial quadrupeds, it would make no real difficulty, since it appears that, in the regular sacrifices, birds were accepted only from the poor who possessed no other clean animals which they could offer[5]. It is not in the least probable that the domestic fowl was known in Western Asia till after the time of Solomon[6].

"The roebuck and the hart" (more properly, the gazelle and the deer), though they were clean and were commonly used for food[7], were not offered in sacrifice, most probably because they were not domesticated nor regarded as property: the camel and the ass, though they were domesticated, were not offered because they were unclean[8]. These instances, as well as the exclusion from the vegetable offerings of grapes, figs, pomegranates, honey and milk, contradict the notion of Bähr and others, that the materials for sacrifice were chosen mainly because they were the chief natural productions of the land. The view of Philo[9], which has been adopted by some in modern times, that the animals were chosen on account of their mild and tractable disposition, is sufficiently answered by referring to the habitual tempers of the bull, the goat and the ram, which are so plainly recognized in Scripture[10].

Every animal offered in sacrifice was to be perfect, without spot or blemish. It was to have neither disease nor deformity of any kind[11]. An exception was however made in regard to a limb out of proportion in a victim for a Free-will offering, which was an inferior sort of Peace-offering[12]. A male animal was required in most offerings[13].

The age of the victims was, for the most part, limited. It would seem to have been a primitive law that no animal was to be sacrificed which was less than a week old[14]. The four-footed animals offered by Abraham were three years old[15]. These may be taken in a general way as the two limits of the ages of the animals offered in sacrifice. The case of a victim of seven years old in Judg. vi. 25 must be regarded as exceptional, having a peculiar significance of its own.

The ox was sacrificed either as a calf (עגל *'ēgel*), which might be a year old[16],

[1] Lev. xi.; Deut. xiv.

[2] Gen. vii. 2.

[3] Lev. i. 2.

[4] Josephus, 'Bell. Jud.' v. 4. § 4. See Tristram, 'Nat. Hist.' p. 212.

[5] Lev. v. 7. See note on Lev. i. 14.

[6] See note on Neh. v. 18. Smith's 'Dict.' III. 1575. Ducks and geese appear to have abounded in ancient Egypt, but the Israelites could hardly have had them in considerable numbers in the Wilderness. That the ancient Egyptians were acquainted with the common fowl rests on no earlier testimony than Plutarch's. See Wilkinson, 'Pop. Account,' &c. Vol. I. p. 250.

[7] Deut. xii. 15, 22, xiv. 5, xv. 22; 1 Kings iv. 23. Cf. on Lev. xi. 7.

[8] Amongst the Gentile nations, the camel was offered in sacrifice by the Arabians, the horse by the Hindoos, the swine by the Greeks, Romans and Egyptians, the goose and other domestic birds by the Egyptians.

[9] 'De Victimis,' cap. I. De Maistre, Hengstenberg, &c.

[10] See Ps. xxii. 12; Jer. xxxi. 18; Jer. 4. 8; Dan. viii. 3, 4, 5, 6, 7. Cf. also Note after Lev. xi. § II.

[11] Lev. xxii. 18—25.

[12] See Lev. vii. 16, 17, xxii. 23.

[13] See on Lev. i. 3.

[14] Ex. xxii. 30; Lev. xxii. 27.

[15] Gen. xv. 9.

[16] Micah vi. 6. Cf. on Ex. xxxii. 4; Lev. ix. 2, 3, 8.

or as a bull (פר *par*) from one to three years old[1].

In like manner, the sheep was offered either as a lamb of a year old or under, or as a young sheep from one to three years old. But a single name (כבש *kebes*, or כשׂב *keseb*, different forms of the same word) for these is found in the Law. The age in the case of the lamb is expressly defined[2]. Our version has lamb in some places where sheep would, according to common usage, be more appropriate[3].

The same custom was most likely followed in regard to the age of the goat. But there appear to have been two breeds of goats, one shaggy and the other smooth-haired, distinguished in sacrificial use, but mistaken in our version for distinctions of age[4].

The Presentation and Slaughter of the Victims.

§ v. It was the duty of the man who offered a private sacrifice to lead with his own hands the victim into the court of the Sanctuary, and to "offer it before the Lord," that is, formally to present it to the priest in front of the Tabernacle[5]. It is said that a priest selected for the service first carefully examined the animal to see that it was without spot or blemish. The sacrificer then laid, or rather pressed, his hand upon its head. According to some Jewish traditions, both hands were used, as they were by the priest on the head of the Scape goat[6]. Nothing is said in the Law of the imposition of hands being accompanied by any form of prayer or confession. The confession made by the High priest over the Scape goat[7] was evidently peculiar; and the confessions spoken of in connection with the Sin-offerings[8] were evidently made before the sacrificial ceremony had commenced, and had nothing immediately to do with the imposition of hands. But according to the Rabbinists the sacrificer always uttered a prayer or confession of some sort while his hand rested on the head of the victim, except in the case of Peace-offerings[9]. There does not appear to have been an imposition of hands in the sacrifices of birds[10]: nor, according to the Mishna, was there any in the sacrifice of the Paschal lamb, or in the offering of any of the public sacrifices, except the Scape goat and the Sin-offering for the people[11].

The regular place for slaughtering the animals for Burnt-offerings, Sin-offerings and Trespass-offerings, was the north side of the Altar[12]. Tradition tells us that before the sacrificer laid his hand upon the head of the victim, it was bound by a cord to one of the rings fixed for the purpose on the north side of the Altar[13], and that at the very instant when the words of the prayer, or confession, were ended, the fatal stroke was given[14]. The Peace-offerings and the Paschal lambs, might, it would seem, be slain in any part of the court[15].

If we take the text of Leviticus in its most obvious meaning as our guide, the person who brought the sacrifice had to slay it[16]. But some Jewish authorities state that this was the duty of the priest or an assistant[17]. The Hebrew idiom is not free from ambiguity[18]. It is however most likely that the duty devolved on the sacrificer, but that he could employ a deputy who might be a priest or not[19]. In the public sacrifices, and on certain peculiar occasions in later times, the priests, or the Levites, were appointed

[1] See on Lev. ix. 3; Lev. iv. 3, viii. 2; xvi. 3, &c.

[2] Ex. xii. 5, xxix. 38; Lev. ix. 3, xii. 6 (see note), xxiii. 12, 18, &c.

[3] Lev. iii. 7, iv. 32, xiv. 10, xxiii. 12, &c.—The words lamb, ewe, and sheep, are also often employed to translate *seh* (שֶׂה), which would be more fairly represented by *one of the flock*, that is, either sheep or goat. See Lev. v. 7, xii. 8, xxii. 23, 28, xxvii. 26, &c.

[4] See on Lev. iv. 23.

[5] See note on Lev. i. 3.

[6] Lev. i. 4, xvi. 21.

[7] Lev. xvi. 21.

[8] See on Lev. v. 5.

[9] Maimonides, 'Corban,' III. 15. Otho, 'Rab. Lex.' p. 634. Outram, I. c. 15.

[10] Otho, p. 658.

[11] Lev. iv. 15. 'Menach,' IX. 7.

[12] Lev. i. 11; vi. 25; vii. 2. On the arrangement of the court, see Note after Ex. xxvi. § VI.

[13] Mishna, 'Middoth,' III. 5.

[14] Otho, p. 634.

[15] Cf. Lev. i. 11 with iii. 2. Mishna, 'Zebach,' v. 6.

[16] See Lev. i. 5, &c. &c.

[17] Philo, 'De Victimis,' cap. 5. Otho, p. 634.

[18] See on Ex. xxxvii. 1.

[19] Cf. 2 Chron. xxx. 17.

to do it[1]. The mode of killing appears not to have differed from that of slaughtering animals for food. The throat was cut while a priest or assistant held a bowl under the neck to receive the blood[2]. The sacrificer, or his assistant, then flayed the victim and cut it into pieces[3], probably while the priest was engaged in disposing of the blood.

Up to this point the ritual was the same for all sacrifices of quadrupeds, whether they were destined to be Burnt-offerings, Peace-offerings, or Sin-offerings, except in the license allowed in the case of Peace-offerings as to the place of slaughter, and, according to tradition, in the prayer accompanying the imposition of hands. But from this point a very important divergence takes place, and the distinctive mark of each kind of offering comes into view. The treatment of the blood was the same in the Burnt-offering, the Peace-offering, and the Trespass-offering, but it was peculiar in the Sin-offering: the burning of certain parts on the Altar was the same in the Sin-offering, the Trespass-offering, and the Peace-offering, but the burning of the whole was peculiar to the Burnt-offering: the sacrificial meal was peculiar to the Peace-offering.

The Treatment of the Blood.

§ vi. In sacrificing the Burnt-offerings[4], the Peace-offerings[5] and the Trespass-offerings[6], we read that the priests were to "bring the blood and sprinkle the blood round about upon the altar." In the Sin-offerings, the priest had to take some of the blood with his finger and put it upon the horns of the Altar of Burnt-offering, and to pour out what remained at the bottom of the Altar. This was all that was required for the blood of the Sin-offering for one of the common people, or for a ruler[7]. But in the Sin-offering for the Congregation and that for the High-priest[8], in addition to these two processes, the High-priest himself had to bring a portion of the blood into the Sanctuary, to sprinkle it with his finger seven times before the vail[9], and to put some of it upon the horns of the Altar of incense[10].

Now there are here to be distinguished four different modes of disposing of the blood. In regard to the three of these which belong to the Sin-offering, our version exactly represents the original:—(1) the putting the blood with the finger upon the horns of the two Altars, (2) the sprinkling it with the finger before the vail, and (3) the pouring out of what remained at the base of the Altar of Burnt-offering. But as regards the blood of the other offerings, which it is said the priests were to "sprinkle round about upon the altar," our translation may mislead. The Hebrew verb (*zārak*, זרק) is a quite different one from that rendered *sprinkle* (*hizzāh*, הזה), in reference to the blood of the Sin-offering: and as *zārak* is applied to the whole of the blood of the victim, it must evidently denote a more copious way of disposing of the blood than is expressed by our word *sprinkling*. While *hizzāh* is used for what was done with the finger, or a bunch of hyssop, *zārak* is applied to an action performed with the bowl[11] in which the blood of the victim was received as it flowed from the carcase. The verb is to be understood in the sense of *casting abroad*, so as to make the liquid cover a considerable surface. The two Hebrew words are clearly distinguished in the Septuagint and Vulgate. They render *zārak* by προσχεῖν and *fundere;* and *hizzāh* by ῥαίνειν and *aspergere.* But almost all modern versions confound the words.

The Mishna tells us that the great Altar of the Temple was furnished with two holes at its south-west corner through which the blood ran into a drain which conveyed it to the Cedron. There must have been some arrangement of this kind for taking the blood away from the Altar in the Wilderness. We are further told that in casting the blood

[1] Lev. iv. 4. xvi, 11, 15; 2 Chron. xxix. 24, 34, &c.

[2] L'Empereur, notes to 'Middoth,' cap. III. Carpzov. 'Mantissa de Sacrif.' p. 712. Philo, 'De Victimis,' cap. 5. See on Lev. ix. 9, xvii. 3.

[3] Lev. i. 5, 6, &c.

[4] Lev. i. 5, 11.

[5] Lev. iii. 2, 8, 13.

[6] Lev. vii. 2. On the relation of the Trespass-offering to the Sin-offering, see on Lev. v. 14.

[7] Lev. iv. 25, 30.

[8] note Lev. iv. 3.

[9] See note Lev. iv. 6.

[10] Lev. iv. 5—7, 16—18.

[11] The name of this bowl was *mizrāk* (מזרק), which is immediately formed from the verb *zārak*. See Ex. xxvii. 3; Num. iv. 14, vii. 13; Note after Lev. xvii., &c.

"round about upon the altar," it was the custom to throw it in two portions, one at the north-eastern corner and the other at the south-western, so as to wet all the four sides[1]. In accordance with this statement, it has been very generally held[2] that it was intended that the blood should be diffused over the walls of the Altar; and this seems to be confirmed by what is said of the blood of the bird for a burnt-offering—"the blood thereof shall be wrung out at the side of the altar[3]."—But it is urged, on the other hand[4], that it is improbable that the blood should have been suffered, as it must thus have been, to run down upon the bank or ledge round the Altar, on which the officiating priests stood. It has been conjectured that it was cast upon the margin of the top of the Altar in such a way as to flow round the space occupied by the fire. This is of course conceivable, if a channel was provided to conduct the blood round the four sides, inclining towards the openings at the south-western corner[5].

The Burning on the Altar.

§ vii. When the blood was disposed of, the skin removed, and the animal cut into pieces, the sacrificer, or his assistant, washed the entrails and feet[6]. In the case of a Burnt-offering, all the pieces were then taken to the Altar and salted in accordance with the command, "with all thine offerings thou shalt offer salt[7]." It is said that the salting took place on the slope of the Altar[8]. The priest next piled the pieces on the Altar, in order, with the wood, upon the fire which he had previously made up[9]. The expression "in order[10]" is understood by the Jewish writers to signify that the pieces were to be placed in the pile, so as to stand in the same relation to each other as they did in the living animal[11]. The hind limbs were probably put at the base of the pile, then the entrails and other viscera with the fat, then the fore limbs, with the head at the top.—It should here be remarked that a peculiar word is uniformly applied to the action of the fire of the Altar, one which means rather to send up in smoke than to consume. See on Lev. i. 9.

The Fat and its Accompaniments.

§ viii. The parts burned upon the Altar of the Peace-offering, the Sin-offering and the Trespass-offering, were the same in each case. They consisted mainly of the internal fat, the "sweet fat," or suet[12]. The Hebrews called this fat *chēlev* (חלב)[13], and distinguished it from the fat which is diffused in the flesh, which was called *mishmān* (מִשְׁמָן), or *shāmeen* (שָׁמֵן)[14]. The Law strictly forbad that the *chēlev* should ever be eaten: "It shall be a perpetual statute ...that ye eat neither fat (*chēlev*) nor blood[15]." On the contrary, it was allowed to eat the other fat[16].—It is remarkable that another word, *peder* (פדר), is used to denote the fat of the Burnt-offering which was burned along with the flesh, not exclusively selected for the Altar like the *chēlev* of the other sacrifices[17].

The portions burned are briefly summed up as "the fat, and the kidneys, and the caul above the liver[18];" but they are generally described more in detail in this way[19]—

1. "The fat that covereth the inwards;" that is, the caul or great omentum, a transparent membrane which has upon it a net-work of fatty tissue.

2. "The fat that is upon the inwards," the small lumps of suet found upon the intestines of healthy animals.

3. "The two kidneys with the fat that is on them which is by the flanks."

1 'Middoth,' III. 2. Otho, p. 636.
2 Outram, Carpzov., Bähr, Knobel, Keil, &c. with the general voice of rabbinical traditions. Otho, p. 635; Outram, I. c. XVI. § 2.
3 Lev. i. 15.
4 By Kurtz and Hofmann.
5 This may have some countenance from the words of Philo ('de Vict.' c. 6), and of the Vulgate, Lev. i. 11.
6 See note on Lev. i. 9.
7 Lev. ii. 13; Ezek. xliii. 24; Mark ix. 49.
8 Otho, p. 637. See on Lev. i. 11; Ex. xxvii. 5.
9 See note Lev. vi. 13.
10 Lev. i. 7, 8, 12, vi. 12; cf. xxiv. 8.

11 Maimon. ap. Outram, I. 16.
12 See Richardson's 'Dict.' s. *Suet*.
13 Ex. xxix. 13, 22; Lev. iii. 4, 10, 15, iv. 9, vii. 4, &c.
14 Num. xiii. 20; Ps. lxxviii. 31; Is. x. 16, xxx. 23, &c.
15 Lev. iii. 17.
16 See Neh. viii. 10.
17 Lev. i. 8, 12; viii. 20. On the meaning of *peder*, see Gesenius, 'Thes.'
18 Lev. ix. 10.
19 Ex. xxix. 13, 22; Lev. iii. 4, 10, 15, iv. 9, vii. 4, viii. 16, &c.

4. "The caul above the liver." There is a doubt as to the part which is here designated. The Hebrew word rendered caul is *yōthereth* (יותרת), which appears to be derived from a root signifying to abound or to spread over. The two interpretations of the word which have found most favour appear to have taken their rise from the different renderings of the Septuagint and the Vulgate. It is translated by the former, ὁ λοβὸς ὁ ἐπὶ τοῦ ἥπατος, and, in other places, ὁ λοβὸς τοῦ ἥπατος. It has hence been supposed by many critics[1] to mean the great upper lobe of the liver. But this lobe is a part of the liver, and cannot therefore properly be said to be "above the liver." The word has been rendered by the Vulgate *reticulum jecoris*, a name which answers very well to the membrane covering the upper part of the liver, sometimes called the small omentum. This is taken to be what is here meant by the greater number of modern critics and translators[2]. A third opinion, of less authority, is that which is given in the margin of our Bible, that the word means the midriff, or diaphragm, the broad muscle which forms the division between the abdomen and the thorax. On the whole, it must be admitted that the question as to what *yothereth* really denotes has not been satisfactorily settled, though much learning has been expended on it[3].

5. When the offering was a sheep, the fat tail which characterizes several breeds of sheep, was added[4].

On the significance of burning the fat, see on Lev. iii. 17.

On the Priests' Portions.

§ ix. The parts of the victims which regularly fell to the priests were:—

Of the Burnt-offerings, only the hide[5], the whole of the flesh being consigned to the Altar.

Of the Peace-offerings, the breast and the right shoulder (or leg), which might be eaten by the priests and their families in any unpolluted place. The hide appears to have been retained by the sacrificer[6].

Of the Sin-offerings and the Trespass-offerings, the whole of the flesh (except the fat portions burnt on the Altar), and probably the hide. The flesh could only be eaten within the precinct of the Tabernacle. It was distinguished from the "holy" flesh of the Peace-offerings as being "most holy[7]."

As regards the two portions of the flesh of the Peace-offerings which were assigned to be "Aaron's and his sons' by a statute for ever from the children of Israel[8]," and which probably, from the great number of Peace-offerings which were offered, furnished them with their chief supply of animal food, it appears certain that one was what we call the breast or brisket, but there is a doubt as to the other. The Hebrew word *shōk* (שׁוק) means leg rather than shoulder. In rendering it shoulder in this connection, our translators have the authority of the LXX., Vulg., and Onkelos. But wherever the word occurs in other parts of the Old Testament, with a single exception, our own version, (in agreement with the LXX. and Vulg.) takes it for the leg or hip[9]. Josephus, in speaking of the priests' portions, mentions the leg[10]. But the regular word for shoulder *zerōa'* (זרוע) is used in Num. vi. 19 and Deut. xviii. 3. The leg is generally regarded as the choicer joint of the two, but Sir Gardiner Wilkinson says that shoulder was preferred by the ancient Egyptians[11]. Many recent critics are inclined to the opinion that it was the right leg which was given to the priests; but the question is not satisfactorily settled.

Connected with the priests' breast and shoulder is the inquiry as to the two ceremonies called *waving* and *heav-*

[1] Philo, Josephus, Saadia, Bochart, Gesenius, Bähr, Schott, Ewald, Kalisch.

[2] Luther, the English Version, Nic. Fuller, Fürst, De Wette, Knobel, Bunsen, Kurtz, Keil, Zunz, Herxheimer, Luzzatto, Wogue.

[3] See Nic. Fuller, 'Misc. Sacr.' V. 14. Bochart, 'Hieroz.' II. 45. Gesenius, 'Thes.' *sub voce*. Knobel on Lev. iii. 4, &c. &c.

[4] See on Lev. iii. 9.

[5] Lev. vii. 8.

[6] Lev. vii. 31, 32, x. 14. Note on vii. 8.

[7] Lev. vi. 26, vii. 6; Note after Ex. xxvi. § v. Cf. Ezek. xlii. 13. On the peculiar holiness of the flesh, see on Lev. vi. 25.

[8] Ex. xxix. 28. Cf. 2 Chron. xxx. 22—24, xxxv. 7, 8.

[9] Deut. xxviii. 35; Judg. xv. 8; Prov. xxvi. 7; Cant. v. 15; Isa. xlvii. 2. The exception is 1 Sam. ix. 24. The Mishna in one place at least seems to favour the same view. 'Cholin,' x. 4, with Bartenora's note

[10] Κνήμη, 'Ant.' III. 9, § 2.

[11] Note on Herodot. II. 39.

ing. The shoulder, which belonged to the officiating priest, was heaved, and the breast, which was for the common stock of the priests in general, was waved before the Lord[1]. Each process appears to have been a solemn form of dedicating a thing to the use of the Sanctuary. The term strictly rendered Heave-offering (*terūmāh*, תרומה) appears to be used in as wide a sense as *korbān*, for offerings in general. It is so applied to all the gifts for the construction of the Tabernacle[2]. That rendered Wave-offering (*tenūphāh*, תנופה) is not so broadly applied, but it is used to denote the gold and bronze that were contributed for the same purpose[3]: it is also applied to the Levites as dedicated to the divine service[4]. From the clearly marked distinction between the heave shoulder and the wave breast, it can hardly be doubted that the terms, in their proper meaning, referred to two distinct forms of dedication. The verb from which *terūmāh* is derived, signifies to lift up, that from which *tenūphāh* comes, to move repeatedly either up and down, or to and fro. The Rabbinists say that heaving was a moving up and down, waving a moving to and fro[5]. But, as waving appears to have been the more solemn process of the two, it was probably, in accordance with its derivation[6], a movement several times repeated, while heaving was simply a lifting up once.

The Meat-offerings and the Drink-offerings.

§ x. On the Meat-offerings (rather Vegetable-offerings) in general, see Lev. ii. with the notes.

On the Drink-offerings, see on Ex. xxix. 40.

Every Burnt-offering and Peace-offering was accompanied by a Meat-offering and a Drink-offering. There is no mention of this in Leviticus. The quantities of flour, oil and wine were thus proportioned to the importance of the victims[7]:—

With a bullock:

Flour.	*Oil.*	*Wine.*
$\frac{3}{10}$ of an ephah.	$\frac{1}{2}$ of a hin.	$\frac{1}{2}$ of a hin.

With a ram:

Flour.	*Oil.*	*Wine.*
$\frac{2}{10}$ of an ephah.	$\frac{1}{3}$ of a hin.	$\frac{1}{3}$ of a hin.

With a young sheep or goat:

Flour.	*Oil.*	*Wine.*
$\frac{1}{10}$ of an ephah.	$\frac{1}{4}$ of a hin.	$\frac{1}{4}$ of a hin.

The whole of the Meat-offerings and Drink-offerings, with the exception of what was burnt, or poured, on the Altar, fell to the lot of the priests. Lev. ii. 3.

The Sin-offering and the Trespass-offering were sacrificed without either Meat-offering or Drink-offering.

The Public-offerings.

§ xi. On the daily Burnt-offerings, see Ex. xxix. 38—42.

On the offerings for the Day of Atonement and the Great Festivals, see Lev. xvi. xxiii. and Num. xxviii. xxix.

V. Historical Development of Sacrifice.

§ xii. In the earliest record of sacrifice the name given in common to the animal and vegetable offerings is *minchāh* (*i. e.* a gift), which the Law afterwards restricted to the vegetable-offerings[8]. It is said that "Cain brought of the fruit of the ground an offering (*minchāh*) unto the Lord. And Abel, he also brought of the firstlings of his flock and of the fat thereof. And the Lord had respect unto Abel and to his offering (*minchāh*); but unto Cain and his offering (*minchāh*) he had not respect." Gen. iv. 3—5. We are told nothing, and from the narrative itself we can infer nothing, as to the mode in which the offerings were made, except that the fat[9] (*chēlev*) appears to have been treated as a distinct part of the offering of Abel.

The sacrifices of Noah after the flood consisted of Burnt-offerings of clean

[1] Ex. xxix. 26, 27; Lev. vii. 32—34.

[2] Ex. xxv. 2. See also Num. v. 9; Deut. xii. 6, &c.

[3] Ex. xxxv. 22, xxxviii. 24, 29.

[4] Num. viii. 11.

[5] Carpzov. 'App. Crit.' p. 709.

[6] The Hebrew verb is applied to such actions as using a saw, or other tool, Ex. xx. 25; Josh. viii. 31; Isa. x. 15, xxx. 28, &c. For instances of waving, see Lev. xxiii. 11. 17.

[7] Num. xv. 5 sq., xxviii. 5 sq.; Ex. xxix. 40. On the measures here named, see Lev. xix. 36.

[8] See § iii.

[9] See § viii.

beasts and birds offered upon an altar[1]. The historian tells us on this occasion that the Lord smelled "a sweet savour," using for the first time the phrase which came into current use in reference to the Burnt-offerings and whatever portions of the other sacrifices were offered on the altar[2].

The Covenant sacrifice of Abraham[3] consisted of one of each of the five animals which the Law afterwards recognized as fit for sacrifice[4]. This is the earliest instance of an offering being formally commanded by the Lord and of its matter being prescribed. But the cutting in twain of the four-footed victims appears to mark it as a peculiar rite belonging to a personal covenant[5], and to distinguish it from the classes of sacrifices ordained by the Law.

In none of the other references to sacrifice in the life of Abraham is there an indication of any kind of offering except the Burnt-offering. He built an altar at Shechem, another between Beth-el and Ai, a third at Hebron and a fourth at Beersheba. At two of these we are told that he "called upon the name of the Lord," but there is no mention of any particular act of sacrifice[6].

Among the different aspects under which the offering up of Isaac may be viewed, this is perhaps the one which most directly connects it with the history of sacrifice. Abraham had still one great lesson to learn. He did not clearly perceive that Jehovah did not require his gifts. The Law had not yet been given which would have suggested this truth to him by the *single* victim appointed for the Burnt-offering and for the Sin-offering, and by the sparing handful of the Meat-offering[7]. To correct and enlighten him, the Lord tempted him to offer up as a Burnt-offering, his most cherished possession, the centre of his hopes. The offering, had it been completed, would have been an actual gift to Jehovah, not a ceremonial act of worship: it would have been not an outward and visible sign of an inward and spiritual grace, but a stern reality in itself[8]. Isaac was not, as regards his father's purpose, in any proper sense a symbol or representative. Nor is there any hint that would justify us in making the voluntary submission of Isaac a significant part of the transaction. The act of the patriarch in giving up his own flesh and blood was an analogue rather than a type of the sacrifice of the Great High Priest who gave up Himself as a victim. In order to instruct Abraham that the service of the Altar fulfilled its purpose in being the expression of the spiritual condition of the worshipper, the Lord Himself provided a ram which was accepted instead of the beloved son. He had already made the offering of himself in his ready faith and obedience; the acceptable means for expressing this fact was appointed in the "ram caught in a thicket by his horns."

Isaac, as his father had done, "built an altar and called upon the name of the Lord" at Beersheba[9]. Jacob built at Shechem an altar that he called El-elohe-Israel (*i.e.* the God, the God of Israel), and another at Bethel, which he called El-Bethel (*i.e.* the God of Bethel)[10].

The sacrifices offered by Jacob at Mizpeh when he parted with Laban, and at Beersheba when he was taking his last farewell of the Land of Promise[11], appear to have been strictly Peace-offerings.

There is no reference to the offering of sacrifice during the sojourn of the Israelites in Egypt. But that the rite was familiarly known to them in connection with the worship of Jehovah, appears from Moses alleging as a reason for taking them out of Egypt, that they might hold a festival and offer sacrifices unto the LORD[12].

Jethro offered both Burnt-offerings and Peace-offerings when he met Moses and the Israelites. This seems to show that sacrificial worship of substantially the same kind was common to the two great

[1] Gen. viii. 20, 21.

[2] Lev. i. 9, ii. 2, 9, 12, iii. 5, &c. The fat portions of the Sin-offering formed no exception, see Lev. iv. 31.

[3] Gen. xv. 9—17.

[4] See § iv.

[5] See on Gen. xv. 8. Cf. Jer. xxxiv. 18, 19.

[6] Gen. xii. 7. 8, xiii 4, 18, xxvi. 25. Cf. xxi. 33.

[7] Lev. ii. 2, &c.

[8] Cf. Micah vi. 7.

[9] Gen. xxvi. 25.

[10] Gen. xxxiii. 20, xxxv. 1, 7. See notes in loc.

[11] Gen. xxxi. 54, xlvi. 1.

[12] Ex. iii. 18, v. 1, 3, 8, 17.

branches of the Semitic stock[1].—The sacrifices of Balaam were Burnt-offerings of oxen and rams, Num. xxiii. 2, 3, 6, 15.—Those of Job were Burnt-offerings (Job i. 5, xlii. 7, 8); but the language used respecting them is distinguished by the mention of a particular that will be noticed presently[2].

§ xiii. We thus see that if we take the narrative of Scripture for our guide, the most ancient sacrifices were Burnt-offerings. There is a reference in the very earliest instance to the fat of the victim; no reference whatever, throughout the patriarchal age, to the blood. The Burnt-offering must have had the very same significance in the case of Noah's sacrifices, when the Lord is said to have smelled "a sweet savour," as it had under the Law. The Peace-offering is not mentioned till a later period of patriarchal history, in connection with a more advanced development of social life. The order in which the kinds of sacrifice are placed by Moses in the first chapters of Leviticus is in agreement with this historical succession as it is traced in the Pentateuch[3].

It would seem to follow that the radical idea of sacrifice is to be sought in the Burnt-offering rather than in the Peace-offering, or in the Sin-offering. Assuming that the animal brought to the Altar represented the person of him who offered it, the act of sacrifice from the very first figured the ascent of the reconciled and accepted creature to Jehovah. According to the strict meaning of the Hebrew, as shown in the name by which the Burnt-offering was commonly called[4], signifying that which ascends, as well as in the verb uniformly applied to the act of burning on the Altar, the flesh was spoken of not as destroyed by burning, but as sent up in the fire like incense towards heaven[5]. It was in this way that the believer confessed the obligation of surrendering himself, body, soul and spirit, to the Lord of heaven and earth who had been revealed to him. The truth expressed then in the whole Burnt-offering is the unqualified self-sacrifice of the person. "The keynote of all the sacrificial systems is the same; self-abdication and a sense of dependence on God are the feelings which gifts and victims strive to express[6]."

In the Peace-offerings of the patriarchal age, before the institution of a national priesthood, there is no reason to doubt that, as in the Peace-offerings of the Law, certain portions of the victim were burned upon the altar, and that the remainder of the flesh was eaten by the offerer, and those who were associated with him by participation in the spirit of the sacrifice. The method of the Peace-offering in its great features would so far answer to the earliest recorded heathen sacrifices, in which the thighs, enveloped in the caul and masses of fat, were the chief portions burnt upon the altar, while the other parts of the victim furnished materials for a feast[7]. It may however be doubted whether the fat in the Homeric sacrifices had any special significance, since we find the fat of animals employed to cover the body of Patroclus on the pyre merely in order that the corpse might be consumed more quickly and completely[8]. The whole Burnt-offering does not appear to be distinctly named in any Greek writer before the time of Xenophon[9], though it may probably have been offered in much earlier times.

§ xiv. In the scriptural records there is no trace either of the Sin-offering, or of any special treatment of the blood of victims, before the time of Moses. We cannot however imagine a single act of sacrifice to have been performed since the first transgression, without a consciousness of sin in the mind of the worshipper. Earnest devotion to a Holy God in a fallen creature must necessarily include a sense of sin and unworthiness. It is not to be imagined that Noah made his offerings at the foot of Ararat, without the sin of past generations being present to his mind, ac-

[1] Ex. xviii. 12. See note in loc.
[2] See § xiv.
[3] See on Lev. ii. 1.
[4] *'olāh*, see § iii.
[5] See on Lev. i. 9.

[6] Thomson, 'Bampton Lectures,' p. 40.
[7] Hom. 'Il.' I. 458, II. 421, XI. 770; Æsch. 'Prom.' 496; Soph. 'Antig.' 1010, &c. In 'Il.' I. 315 there is no reference to a feast.
[8] 'Il.' XXIII. 168.
[9] See 'Anab.' VII. 8. § 4; 'Cyrop.' VIII. 3. 24.

companied by awe at the thought that he was a brother of the same race, with a consciousness of the same tendencies to evil in his own heart. In the account of the sacrifices of Job, the idea of atonement is expressly connected with the Burnt-offerings[1]. But the feeling which most prominently found its expression in the Burnt-offerings of Noah, must have been of a different kind. The sense of present deliverance, of thankfulness deeper than words, of complete self-surrender to the solemn bond now laid upon him in the Covenant, must rather have been figured in the victims which were sent up in the flame of the Altar as a sweet savour to Jehovah.

There is certainly no countenance whatever to be found in the Scriptures for the notion of de Maistre[2] and other writers of more recent date, that the fire of the Altar symbolized retribution for sin.

§ xv. The first instance of the blood of a sacrifice being noticed in any way occurs in the account of the institution of the Passover[3]. It is there commanded that the blood of the Paschal lamb should be sprinkled on the door posts of the houses of the Israelites, as a mark that the destroyer might not enter when he was smiting the firstborn of the Egyptians. No further hint is given of its sacrificial meaning.

The next notice of blood is in connexion with the Burnt-offerings and Peace-offerings of the Covenant of Sinai[4]. Moses having built an altar and twelve pillars, according to the twelve tribes of Israel, at the foot of the mountain "sent young men of the children of Israel, which offered burnt offerings and sacrificed peace-offerings of oxen unto the Lord," and "took half the blood and put it in basons; and half of the blood he sprinkled (threw[5]) on the altar." After reading the Book of the Covenant, the people giving their assent to it, he took the blood in the basons and "sprinkled (threw) it on them, and said, Behold the blood of the covenant which the Lord hath made with you concerning all these words." Cf. Heb. ix. 19, 20, xiii. 20. On this occasion we find the first mention of *throwing* the blood upon the Altar which became the established mode in the Burnt-offerings, Peace-offerings, and Trespass-offerings, but not in the Sin-offerings[6].

With this rite should be compared the use of the blood of the Ram of consecration which was offered in the Consecration of the priests after the Law of the offerings had been given. The ram was essentially a Peace-offering, though it was in some respects peculiar. The greater part of its blood was thrown upon the Altar, but a portion of it was taken by Moses to be put on the persons of the priests and to be sprinkled upon their garments[7].

It should be observed that the treatment of the blood in these two ceremonies was very different from that which was practised in the Sin-offerings. Here a portion of the blood was applied to the persons of those who were especially concerned in the sacrifice, while the remainder was thrown upon the Altar: in the Sin-offering, a portion was offered to the LORD by being put upon the horns of the Altar, and on certain occasions, by being sprinkled within the Tabernacle, while the rest was merely poured away at the base of the Altar[8].

We are left in no doubt as to the sacrificial meaning of the blood. As the material vehicle of the life of the victim, it was the symbol of the life of the offerer. In contrast with the flesh and bones it expressed in a distinct manner the immaterial principle which survives death. This is distinctly assigned as the reason for its appointed use in the rites of atonement[9]. In the two cases of Consecration (and probably in the case of the Paschal lamb) the blood of the sacrifice appears to have stood for the collective life of those who were to be consecrated. Having been accepted by Jehovah in the presentation of the victim before the Altar, it expressed, in the earlier instance, that the life of the chosen nation, and, in the latter in-

[1] Job i. 5, xlii. 7, 8. Cf. Lev. i. 4; see also § xvi.

[2] 'Éclaircissement sur les sacrifices,' p. 234.

[3] Ex. xii. 7, 22, 23.

[4] Ex. xxiv. 4—8. See notes in loc.

[5] The blood was not sprinkled but cast forth out of the basons. See § vi.

[6] See § vi.

[7] See Lev. viii. 23, 24, 30.

[8] Lev. iv. 6, 7, 17, 18, 25, &c. xvi. 18, &c.

[9] See Lev. xvii. 11, with the note.

stance, that the life of the priests in their official calling, had been made holy; and now in the drops applied to their persons it symbolized that the consecrated life was given back to them in order that it should be devoted to the service of the Lord.

It is evident that in these instances the ideas of Consecration and Dedication are signified, rather than the idea of Atonement. Had the Covenant sacrifice at Mount Sinai been a solitary instance, it might indeed be supposed that, the Sin-offering not having as yet been instituted, atonement was ascribed to the blood of the Burnt-offering, as it appears to have been in the sacrifices of Job. But in the Consecration of the priests any such notion is precluded. In this ceremony a Sin-offering was the *first* victim offered, and its blood was passed by for that of the Peace-offering[1]. We are therefore brought to the conclusion that "the blood of the covenant[2]" was, both in form and significance, the blood of the Burnt-offering and the Peace-offering, not that of the Sin-offering[3].

§ xvi. The Sin-offering is to be regarded as a creation of the Law. It was the voice of the Law that awakened the distinct consciousness of sin in the individual mind[4]. This clearer development of the nature of man's struggle upon the earth required to be embodied in a new form. The institution of the Sin-offering appears in this way as a necessary consequence of the giving of the Law.

In the perfected sacrificial system, the three classes of offerings are to be regarded as representing distinct aspects of divine truth connected with man's relation to Jehovah. But it is important to observe that in no sacrifice was the idea of the Burnt-offering left out. Of every victim which was offered an appointed portion was sent up to Jehovah in the flame of the Altar: the ashes of "the continual Burnt-offering" of the morning and evening service were never quenched[5]. The central idea of sacrificial worship was thus kept constantly on view. On the other hand, the truth that every sacrifice, for the Israelite to whom the Law had been revealed, must be based upon Atonement, is declared in the words that his Burnt-offering "shall be accepted for him to make atonement for him[6]."

The natural order of victims in the sacrificial service of the Law was, first the Sin-offering, then the Burnt-offering, and last the Peace-offering[7]. This answers to the spiritual process through which the worshipper had to pass. He had transgressed the Law, and he needed the atonement signified by the Sin-offering: if his offering had been made in truth and sincerity, he could then offer himself to the Lord as an accepted person, as a sweet savour, in the Burnt-offering[8]; and in virtue of this acceptance, he could enjoy communion with the Lord and with his brethren in the Peace-offering. But when the occasion was one in which the consideration of personal holiness was subordinate to that of the consecration of the nation, as was the case in the offerings of the princes at the dedication of the Altar, and in the rite for reconsecrating the Nazarite who had been ceremonially, not morally, defiled, the order was changed and the Burnt-offering was sacrificed before the Sin-offering[9].

The main additions made to the ritual of sacrifice by the Levitical Law consisted in the establishment of one national Altar[10], the institution of the national Priesthood[11], and all those particulars that were peculiar to the Sin-offerings and the Trespass-offerings.

While therefore the essential idea of all sacrifice continued to be the same which had been conveyed in the Burnt-offer-

[1] Lev. viii. 14, 22, 23.

[2] Hebr ix. 18—22, x. 29, &c.

[3] The only other instances in which the Law speaks of the application of the blood of animals to the person, are in Lev. xiv. 7, 14; where see the notes.

[4] Rom. iii. 20, vii. 7. See 'Note on the Ten Commandments' after Ex. xx. 1—17. § v.

[5] See Exod. xxix. 31—42. The importance of the fact here noticed is shown in the expressions used in Lev. iii. 5 (see note), iv. 35, vi. 9, 12, &c.

[6] Lev. i. 4.

[7] See Lev. viii. 14—22, ix. 8—14, 15—22, xii. 8, xiv. 19, 20.

[8] See Ps. li. 19.

[9] Num. vi. 14, vii. 15—17, &c. Cf. Ezek. xlv. 17.

[10] See 'Note on the Sanctuary as a whole' after Ex. xl.

[11] See preliminary note to Ex. xxviii.

ings and Peace-offerings of the patriarchal ages, the Sin-offering embodied the expression of a distinct idea in order to meet the more complicated aspect of human nature, which had been revealed by the giving of the Law on Mount Sinai. The fullest and most intense setting forth of the relation which grace was to produce between the LORD and the worshipper was still reserved for the Burnt-offering. But as the knowledge of personal sin had been more clearly unveiled in the Law, the believer became conscious that sin was separating him from Jehovah, and that it must be removed before he could attain to a state of acceptance[1]. Sinner as he felt himself to be, the Law allowed him to bring his victim to the door of the Tabernacle, to present it before the LORD, to slay it, and to cut it in pieces. So far the ceremony was his own act: so far it was the same with the Sin-offering as with the Burnt-offering and the Peace-offering. But now came the necessity of a mediator, of one who had been consecrated to perfect the work for him. The priest took the victim thus far prepared entirely out of the hands of the worshipper. This was done, according to the Law, with the Burnt-offering as well as with the Sin-offering; but it is evident that the meaning of the priest's taking part in the ceremony belonged with more peculiar significance to the latter[2]. When the sacrifice was a Sin-offering, the first duty of the priest was in certain prescribed cases to sprinkle a portion of the blood within the Tabernacle, and in all cases to put some of the blood upon the horns of one of the Altars. It has been conjectured that, as the horns were the highest part of the Altar, this act signified a near approach to the Lord of heaven, in token that the offering was approved, and that acceptance was ready for the offerer. He then had to place in the fire of the Altar the fat portions of the victim which were acknowledged as a "sweet savour" to the LORD[3]. The penitent worshipper had now recovered his position by the atonement of the Sin-offering, as one who might claim acceptance; but the full expression of self-dedication as a condition was still looked for at his hands in another sacrificial act, in offering his whole Burnt-offering.

With the exception of the parts which, in all the animal offerings, were assigned to the Altar, the whole of the flesh of the Sin-offering was given for the use of the priests as the servants of the Sanctuary. It was removed from all ordinary use or contact, it could be eaten by the priests only within the holy precinct, it was pronounced "most holy," because the offering the life which had dwelt in it upon the horns of the Altar had specially consecrated it to the purpose of atonement[4].

But an Israelite who had studied the Divine Law must have perceived a mystery and a contradiction in the perfectness and freedom from guilt of the animal which he brought as his Sin-offering. On the one hand he must have felt that an offering without blemish was the only one which could be fit for the Altar of Jehovah: on the other hand, he must have felt that it could not fairly represent himself, in his actual condition, as bringing his offering expressly because he was burdened with the consciousness of sin and imperfection[5]. He must also have learned from the language of the Law, in prescribing what part of the ceremony was to be performed by the priest, that he could not be his own atoner. He was told that the priest should "make atonement for him[6]." In these particulars, which in spite of prophetic teaching must have been difficult and obscure to him, we can now clearly trace the forecast shadows of the spotless Saviour who was to come, to stand for the sinful race as its head, to make the offering of Himself as both priest and victim, to perfect the work of redemption by Himself, and so to enter into the presence of God for us as a sweet savour[7].

§ xvii. It was not merely by the institution of another kind of sacrifice that the Law set forth its new development of the history of man's spiritual struggle;

[1] See 'Note on The Ten Commandments' (Exod. xx.) § v.

[2] See Lev. iv. 24—26, 34, 35, v. 6, 8—10; cf. vii. 29, 30, also note on vi. 25.

[3] Lev. iv. 31.

[4] See on Lev. vi. 25. Cf. xvii. 11.

[5] Ps. li. 17.

[6] Lev. iv. 20, 26, v. 6, vi. 7, xii. 8, &c. &c.

[7] Heb. x. 19, 20, 21.

it carried out the same lesson still more fully by an addition to the great ceremonial observances of the year. The three festivals of Unleavened bread, Pentecost, and Tabernacles, with the Feast of trumpets and the New moons, may have been based upon patriarchal usages, whatever additional meaning they may have received from Moses[1]. But the Day of Atonement took its rise in the working out of the Law itself. Its ceremonial was a showing forth in distinct analytical detail of the truth which was compendiously expressed in the single rite of the Sin-offering[2].

§ xviii. A different view from that here given of the fundamental idea of sacrifice, and of the relation in which the Sin-offering stood to the entire sacrificial system, has been very generally held. It has been said that "the first word of the *original* man was probably a prayer, and the first action of *fallen* man a sacrifice[3]." In accordance with this view the key to the idea of sacrifice has been supposed to be given in the passage that sets forth the sacrificial significance of the blood in making atonement—"I have given it to you upon the altar to make an atonement for your souls[4]." Expiation has thus been regarded as the essential meaning of sacrifice. But, as we have seen, the blood seems not to have been recognized in the patriarchal sacrifices; it held but a very subordinate place under the Law in the Burnt-offering and the Peace-offering, no place at all in the Meat-offering. It has been said, not without reason, that sacrifices "might have been offered by man even before the fall as certainly as it was his duty to devote himself to God, to thank Him for His benefits, and to vow to walk in His ways[5]." We may take still higher ground. If we accept the expression, "the Lamb slain from the foundation of the world[6]" as actually denoting the highest truth of which ceremonial sacrifice is the symbol, the Son of God Himself realized the meaning of the Burnt-offering before the actual development of sin in the world.

Hengstenberg appears to be right in objecting to the line which has been taken by de Maistre[7], von Lasaulx, and others, in endeavouring to trace in the records of heathen sacrifice the significance of the blood of victims as an atonement for sin. Instances may indeed be easily found of blood having been regarded as a propitiation to a hostile demon, or as a healing charm; but we seem to seek in vain for an instance in which the blood, as the natural symbol of the soul, was offered as an atoning sacrifice[8].

§ xix. Another view, widely different from the one that has just been mentioned, has been revived by some modern biblical critics[9]. It has been imagined that the first sacrifices were entirely eucharistic and consisted wholly of vegetable substances. This was the notion of Plato[10], Porphyry[11], and other heathen philosophers. Many, starting from nearly the same ground of thought, have conceived that the first sacrifices were Peace-offerings connected with social feasts, such as are described in Homer[12]. It is needless to point out that these theories are directly opposed to the historical development of the subject in the Pentateuch; hardly necessary to observe that the Burnt-offering and the Sin-offering could never have originated in any mere eucharistic service, unless we are to regard them as gross corruptions of the original institution[13].

[1] See notes on Lev. xxiii.

[2] See notes on Lev. xvi.

[3] Von Lasaulx, 'Die Sühnopfer der Griechen und Römer und ihr verhältniss zu dem einen auf Golgotha,' p. 1.

[4] Lev. xvii. 11.

[5] Hengstenberg, 'The Sacrifices of Holy Scripture,' in Clark's Theological Library.

[6] Rev. xiii. 8. Cf. 1 Pet. i. 18—20.

[7] 'Éclaircissement,' &c. p. 232.

[8] See on Lev. xvii. 11. In the instance of the ancient Persians, on which de Maistre (p. 260) and others have strongly rested, in which the blood seems to be clearly recognized as the symbol of the soul, we are told that the victim was cut into pieces, the flesh being distributed amongst the worshippers, and that the blood (ψυχή) was given up to God as the only part he would accept (Strabo, XV. p. 732). But, though neither altar nor fire appears to have been used, the ideas here expressed are surely those of the Burnt-offering and the Peace-offering rather than of the Sin-offering.

[9] Especially by Knobel.

[10] 'De Legg.' VI. 22. [11] 'De Abst.' II. 5, 27.

[12] See § xiii.

[13] Plutarch seems to have perceived this difficulty. He supposed that the first offerings were of vegetables, but imagined that animal sacrifices were instituted at the command of an oracle. 'Sympos.' VIII. 8, 3.

THE THIRD BOOK OF MOSES,

CALLED

LEVITICUS.

CHAPTER I.

1 *The burnt offerings.* 3 *Of the herd,* 10 *of the flocks,* 14 *of the fowls.*

AND the LORD called unto Moses, and spake unto him out of the tabernacle of the congregation, saying,

2 Speak unto the children of Israel, and say unto them, If any man of you bring an offering unto the LORD, ye shall bring your offering of the cattle, *even* of the herd, and of the flock.

3 If his offering *be* a burnt sacrifice

THE OFFERINGS FOR THE ALTAR.
CHAP. I—VII.

CHAP. I. **1.** *the LORD*] In the Hebrew text of Leviticus, JEHOVAH is the name by which God is always called, except when the word *Elohim* is used with a possessive pronoun, so as to designate Him as the God of the chosen people (Lev. ii. 13; xi. 45; xviii. 21; xix. 12, 14, 32, &c.). Neither *Adonāi* nor *Shaddai* occur throughout the book. (See on Exod. vi. 3.)

the tabernacle of the congregation] Rather, **the Tent of meeting.** See on Ex. xl. § II. When JEHOVAH was about to give His people the law of the Ten Commandments (Exod. xix. 3) He called to Moses from the top of Mount Sinai in thunders and lightnings and a thick cloud. When He was now about to give them the laws by which their formal acts of worship were to be regulated, He called to Moses out of the Tabernacle which had just been constructed at the foot of the mountain. The promise which He had made to Moses was now fulfilled:—"And there I will meet with thee, and I will commune with thee from above the mercy seat, from between the cherubims, which are upon the ark of the testimony, of all things which I will give thee in commandment unto the children of Israel" (Exod. xxv. 22).

2. *Speak unto the children of Israel*] The directions for the different kinds of sacrifice contained in ch. i. 2—iii. 17, are addressed to the people, and contain such instructions as were required for persons who voluntarily offered sacrifice (see Introd. § ii.). There are other directions concerning each sort of offering, formally addressed to the priests in ch. vi. 8—vii. 21. It is important to observe that these first instructions are addressed expressly to the individual who felt the need of sacrifice on his own account. They were not delivered through the priests, nor had the officiating priest any choice as to what he was to do. He was only to examine the victim to see that it was perfect (xxii. 17—24), and to perform other strictly prescribed duties. The act of offering was to be voluntary on the part of the worshipper, but the mode of doing it was in every point defined by the Law. The presenting of the victim at the entrance of the Tabernacle was in fact a symbol of the free will submitting itself to the Law of the Lord. The obligation to offer lay beyond the sphere of the mere ceremonial law. Such acts of sacrifice are to be distinguished from the public offerings, and those ordained for individuals on special occasions (see on iv. 2), which belonged to the religious education of the nation.

offering] Heb. *korbān.* (See Introd. § ii.)

ye shall bring your offering of the cattle, even of the herd, and of the flock] Our version here follows the LXX., the Vulg., and Luther. But the Hebrew text should rather be rendered, **If any man of you bring an offering to Jehovah from the beasts, from the herd or from the flock ye shall bring your offering.** The purpose of the words is to define which kinds of beasts are to be offered. (See Introd. § ii.) The expression answers to that respecting birds in *v.* 14, and that respecting vegetable offerings ch. ii. 1.

THE BURNT-OFFERINGS. i. 3—17.

The Burnt-offering from the Herd.
i. 3—9.

3. *burnt sacrifice*] Heb. *'olāh.* See Introd. § iii.

of the herd, let him offer a male without blemish: he shall offer it of his
own voluntary will at the door of the
tabernacle of the congregation before
the LORD.
[a] Exod. 29. 10. 4 [a]And he shall put his hand upon
the head of the burnt offering; and it
shall be accepted for him to make
atonement for him.
5 And he shall kill the bullock
before the LORD: and the priests,
Aaron's sons, shall bring the blood,
and sprinkle the blood round about
upon the altar that *is by* the door of
the tabernacle of the congregation.
6 And he shall flay the burnt offering, and cut it into his pieces.
7 And the sons of Aaron the priest
shall put fire upon the altar, and lay
the wood in order upon the fire:
8 And the priests, Aaron's sons,
shall lay the parts, the head, and the
fat, in order upon the wood that *is* on
the fire which *is* upon the altar:
9 But his inwards and his legs
shall he wash in water: and the

---

a male without blemish] See Introd. § iv. Males were required in most offerings, as the stronger sex which takes precedence of the other. But females were allowed in Peace-offerings (Lev. iii. 1, 6), and were expressly prescribed in the Sin-offerings of the common people. (Lev. iv. 28, 32, v. 6.)

of his own voluntary will] The English version is supported by Grotius and several of the older critics. But most interpreters, ancient and modern, give it the meaning, *for his acceptance;* that is, that he may be accepted. The latter part of the verse might be thus translated: **at the entrance of the Tent of meeting shall he offer it that he may be accepted before Jehovah.** (See on *v.* 4.) The Hebrew phrase here used is rightly translated in several places in our Bible (Exod. xxviii. 38; Lev. xxii. 20, 21, xxiii. 11, &c.), but in others, it is rendered as it is here. (Lev. xix. 5, xxii. 19, 29.)

at the door of the tabernacle of the congregation] Wherever these words occur they should be rendered, **at the entrance of the Tent of meeting.** See preceding note. The place denoted is that part of the court which lay in front of the Tabernacle, in which stood the brazen Altar and the laver, and where alone sacrifices could be offered. See Note on Ex. xxvi. § VI.

4. *And he shall put his hand upon the head of the burnt offering*] The ceremony appears never to have been omitted in the private sacrifices of quadrupeds (see on *v.* 10 and Introd. § v.). By it the sacrificer identified himself with his victim. Introd. § xvi.

and it shall be accepted] The word here used belongs to the same root as that in *v.* 3, to which it evidently answers.

to make atonement for him] This phrase belongs more especially to the Sin-offerings and the Trespass-offerings. (Lev. iv. 20, 26, 31, 35, v. 16, 18, vi. 7, &c.) It is not used in reference to the Peace-offerings, and but rarely in reference to the Burnt-offerings. It should be noticed that it is here introduced in close connection with the imposition of hands by the worshipper, not, as it is when it refers to the Sin-offering, with the special functions of the priest, iv. 26, 35. See Introd. §§ xiv, xvi.

5. *And he shall kill the bullock*] See Introd. § v.

the bullock] Strictly, *the son of the bull*, a common Hebrew periphrasis for a young ox. (See Introd. § iv.) In like manner young pigeons are called in the Hebrew *sons of the pigeon.* (Lev. i. 14, v. 7, 11, xii. 6, &c.)

before the LORD] *i.e.* before the Tabernacle.

sprinkle the blood] Rather, **throw the blood.** See Introd. § vi.

by the door of the tabernacle] **at the entrance of the Tent.**

6. *And he shall flay*] The sacrificer, or his assistant, had to skin and cut up the victim. The hide was the perquisite of the officiating priest. (Lev. vii. 8.)

his pieces] That is, its proper pieces, the parts into which it was usual for a sacrificed animal to be divided.

7. *the sons of Aaron*] *i.e.* the common priests.

put fire upon the altar] Knobel observes that this must specifically refer to the first Burnt-offering on the newly constructed Altar. The rule was afterwards to be, "The fire shall ever be burning upon the altar; it shall never go out," Lev. vi. 13.

8. It would seem that the parts of the victim were then salted by the priest in conformity with the rule, "with all thine offerings thou shalt offer salt" (Lev. ii. 13; Ezek. xliii. 24; Mark ix. 49), and placed in order with the wood upon the altar. See Introd. § vii.

the fat] See Introd. § viii.

9. *his inwards and his legs shall he wash in water*] The parts which were washed appear not to have been the whole of the vis-

priest shall burn all on the altar, *to*
be a burnt sacrifice, an offering made
by fire, of a sweet savour unto the
LORD.

10 ¶ And if his offering *be* of the
flocks, *namely*, of the sheep, or of the
goats, for a burnt sacrifice; he shall
bring it a male without blemish.

11 And he shall kill it on the
side of the altar northward before the
LORD: and the priests, Aaron's sons,
shall sprinkle his blood round about
upon the altar.

12 And he shall cut it into his
pieces, with his head and his fat: and
the priest shall lay them in order on

---

cera, with the whole of the legs; but only the stomach and bowels, and the feet, divided from the carcase at the knee-joint. The Septuagint has τὰ ἐγκοίλια καὶ οἱ πόδες, and the Vulgate, *intestina et pedes*. With these agree Onkelos, Philo, Josephus, and most modern authorities.

the priest shall burn] The verb here translated *burn* (*biktīr*), is applied exclusively to the burning of the incense, of the lights of the Tabernacle, and of the offerings on the Altar. The primary meaning of its root seems to be *to exhale odour* (Gesen., Fürst). It is in some places rendered in the margin of our Bible, "to cause to ascend" (Exod. xxx. 8; Lev. xxiv. 2, &c.). The word for burning in a common way is a quite different one (*sāraph*), and this is applied to the burning of those parts of victims which were burned without the camp (Lev. iv. 12, 21; Num. xix. 5, &c.). The importance of the distinction is great in its bearing on the meaning of the Burnt-offering (see Introd. § xiii.). The substance of the victim was regarded not as something to be consumed, but as an offering of sweet-smelling savour sent up in the flame to Jehovah. The two words are distinguished in the LXX., the Vulg., Geneva Fr., De Wette, Herxh., and other versions. Mr Sharpe renders the sacrificial word "to burn as incense."

a burnt sacrifice, an offering made by fire] There is no tautology in the original, which might be rendered *an offering sent upwards*, *a sacrifice made by fire*.

a sweet savour] The expression, *a sweet savour unto Jehovah*, is applied to offerings of all kinds which were burnt upon the altar, but it finds its fullest application in the whole Burnt-offering. (Lev. ii. 12, iii. 5, 16, iv. 31; Num. xv. 7, 10, &c.) It may be regarded as belonging more especially to the Burnt-offerings, as the phrase, *to make atonement*, belongs more especially, but not exclusively, to the Sin-offerings. See on *v.* 4.

The Burnt-offering from the Flock.
i. 10—13.

10. *of the flocks*] The directions for the sheep or the goat are more briefly given than those for the bullock. There is no mention made of the presentation of the victim in the court of the Sanctuary (*v.* 3), of the imposition of hands, or of the flaying. The place of slaughter is however more clearly defined (*v.* 11). But there is no good reason to doubt that the victims were all treated in the same manner in these respects.—The LXX. add the words, καὶ ἐπιθήσει χεῖρα τὴν ἐπὶ τὴν κεφαλὴν αὐτοῦ. The Burnt-offering of the sheep must have been that with which the people were most familiar in the daily morning and evening service. Ex. xxix. 38—42.

of the goats] It would seem that sheep were preferred for sacrifice when they could be obtained, except in some special Sin-offerings in which goats were required, such as that of the ruler and the high-priest, and the Sin-offering with the Scape-goat of the Day of atonement (Lev. iv. 23, ix. 3, xvi. 5). Maimonides says that the public Burnt-offerings could be only of bullocks or sheep, not of goats ('Corban,' I. 15); and Theodoret probably preserves a genuine Jewish tradition when he says that it was the duty of him who had a lamb for the Passover to slaughter it, but that if he had not a lamb he might slay a kid. ('Quæst. in Exod.' 24.)

11. *northward before the LORD*] That is, on the north side of the altar. This was the appointed place for killing the Burnt-offerings, the Sin-offerings, and the Trespass-offerings. (Lev. iv. 24, 29, 33, vii. 2.) Nothing is said in the Pentateuch regarding the place where the Peace-offerings were to be slain, but the Mishna tells us that they might be slain in any part of the court. (See on iii. 2.)—There has been a strange divergence of opinion regarding the reason of this rule. Some suppose that it was because the north is the region of sunless gloom (Tholuck); others, that it was in accordance with a primitive notion, that God's dwelling-place was in the north, traces of which are supposed to exist in the position of the table of shew-bread (the bread of the presence) (Exod. xxvi. 35); and in several passages of Scripture (Ps. xlviii. 2; Is. xiv. 13; Ezek. i. 4); also in the Hindoo Puranas and the apocryphal book of Enoch (see Ewald, *Alterthümer*, p. 48). But it may have been an arrangement of mere practical convenience. On the west side of the Altar stood the laver; on the east side was the place of ashes (see on *v.* 16), and the south side, where appears to have been the slope by which the priests went up to the

the wood that *is* on the fire which *is*
upon the altar:
13 But he shall wash the inwards
and the legs with water: and the
priest shall bring *it* all, and burn *it*
upon the altar: it *is* a burnt sacrifice,
an offering made by fire, of a sweet
savour unto the LORD.
14 ¶ And if the burnt sacrifice for
his offering to the LORD *be* of fowls,
then he shall bring his offering of
turtledoves, or of young pigeons.
15 And the priest shall bring it
unto the altar, and ‖wring off his
head, and burn *it* on the altar; and
the blood thereof shall be wrung out
at the side of the altar:
16 And he shall pluck away his
crop with ‖his feathers, and cast it
beside the altar on the east part, by
the place of the ashes:
17 And he shall cleave it with the
wings thereof, *but* shall not divide *it*
asunder: and the priest shall burn it
upon the altar, upon the wood that *is*
upon the fire: it *is* a burnt sacrifice,
an offering made by fire, of a sweet
savour unto the LORD.

‖ Or, *pinch off the head with the nail.*

‖ Or, *the filth thereof.*

CHAPTER II.

1 *The meat offering of flour with oil and incense,* 4 *either baken in the oven,* 5 *or on a plate,* 7 *or in a fryingpan,* 12 *or of the firstfruits in the ear.* 13 *The salt of the meat offering.*

AND when any will offer a meat
offering unto the LORD, his of-

Altar (Joseph. 'Bell. Jud.' v. 5. § 6), must have been left clear for thoroughfare. The north side must, therefore, have been the most convenient for slaughtering the victims. (Rosenmüller, Knobel, Kurtz, Keil.) See Note after Ex. xxvi. § VI.

The Burnt-offering of the Dove or the Pigeon. i. 14—17.

14. *of turtledoves, or of young pigeons*] The offering of a bird was permitted to one who was too poor to offer a quadruped. (Cf. v. 7—11, xii. 8.) But in certain rites of purification birds were appointed for all, whatever might be their circumstances. See xv. 14, 29; Num. vi. 10. It is to be noticed that there is a limitation of the age of the pigeons, but none in regard to the doves. This may, perhaps, be accounted for from the natural habits of the birds. It would seem that the species which are most likely to have been the sacrificial dove and pigeon are the common turtle, *Turtur auritus*, and the blue-rock pigeon, sometimes called the Egyptian rock-pigeon, *Columba Schimperi*, which is always called *the pigeon* by the Arabs. The latter bears a considerable resemblance to our stock-dove, and is considerably larger than the turtle. Now the turtles come in vast flocks (Cant. ii. 11, 12; Jer. viii. 7), with great regularity, in the early part of April, and for a portion of the year the full-grown birds can be easily taken by nets or other contrivances; but as the season advances they wholly disappear. The pigeons, on the contrary, do not leave the country. They have three or four broods in the year, and, in common with the doves and other pigeons, they hatch two eggs at a time, and no more. The adult birds are very wild and rapid of flight, and it is almost impossible to obtain them without fire-arms. But their nests, with young ones in them, may be easily found at any season of the year. (Tristram, 'Land of Israel,' pp. 446, 509; 'Nat. Hist. of the Bible,' p. 213.) Hence it would appear, that when turtledoves could not be obtained nestling pigeons were accepted as a substitute.

15. *And the priest shall bring*] The mode of sacrificing the bird was simple. The marginal rendering agrees with the Mishna ('Zebach,' VI. 5). In the Sin-offering of birds the blood was sprinkled on the side of the Altar. See Lev. v. 9.

16. *his crop with his feathers*] Our version here follows the LXX., the Vulg., and Luther, and agrees with some of the modern Jewish versions. But the weight of authority is in favour of the marginal rendering (Onkelos, the Syriac, Gesenius, De Wette, Fürst, Knobel, &c.). It is most probable that the feathers were burnt with the body, and that the wings, mentioned in *v.* 17, were not mutilated.

the place of the ashes] It is said that the ashes were daily removed from the Altar (except on certain holy days) and thrown into a heap on its eastern side. (Mishna, 'Tamid,' II. 2, with the notes.) It would appear that when the heap became inconveniently large, they were removed in vessels appropriated to the purpose (see Exod. xxvii. 3) to a spot without the camp, designated as the place "where the ashes are poured out." (Lev. iv. 12, vi. 11.)

17. *a burnt sacrifice*, &c.] See on *v.* 9.

THE MEAT-OFFERINGS.

CHAP. II. **1.** *a meat offering*] The two Hebrew words thus rendered are the same which in *v.* 4 are better translated **an oblation of a meat-offering** (*korbān minchāh*). The

fering shall be *of* fine flour; and he
shall pour oil upon it, and put frankincense thereon:
2 And he shall bring it to Aaron's
sons the priests: and he shall take
thereout his handful of the flour
thereof, and of the oil thereof, with
all the frankincense thereof; and the
priest shall burn the memorial of it
upon the altar, *to be* an offering made
by fire, of a sweet savour unto the
LORD:
3 And [a] the remnant of the meat of- [a] Ecclus. 7. 31.
fering *shall be* Aaron's and his sons':
it is a thing most holy of the offerings of the LORD made by fire.

---

latter word (*minchāh*) signifies literally *a gift;* and it appears to have been applied specially to what was given by an inferior to a superior (Gen. xxxii. 18—20, xliii. 11; Judg. iii. 15; 1 S. x. 27). It was sometimes used for any sort of offering to the Lord, in the same sense as *korbān* (Gen. iv. 3, 4; 1 S. ii. 17; Isa. i. 13, &c.). But in the technical language of the Law, Minchah regularly denoted the vegetable offerings as distinguished from the animal offerings (see Introd. § iii.). Luther rendered it food-offering (*Speis-opfer*), and our translators followed him, applying the word meat, according to old usage, as a general term for food. Vegetable-offering or Meal-offering would be a more convenient rendering.

It may seem strange that the Minchah is here introduced between the Burnt-offering and the Peace-offering. The order in which the kinds of offering are named agrees with their development in order of time. The Burnt-offering and the Minchah answer to the first two offerings on record (Gen. iv. 3, 4; Amos v. 22). It may be added that they appear to be cognate in the simplicity of their meaning. (See Introd. § xii.)

It has been supposed that the Minchah was never offered but when it accompanied an animal sacrifice (Bähr, Kurtz, Bonar). But the mode in which it is spoken of in this verse, in *v.* 2, vi. 14, Num. v. 15, and elsewhere, would seem to leave but little doubt that it was, on occasions, offered as a distinct sacrifice. The Drink-offering (which is mentioned nowhere in Leviticus, except in chap. xxiii.), on the other hand, appears never to have been offered by itself. The laws of the Drink-offering and the Minchah, when offered as accompaniments of the Burnt-offering and the Peace-offering, are given Num. xv. 1—12.

Salt (*v.* 13) and oil (see Note at the end of the chap.) were ingredients in every Minchah, but leaven and honey were wholly excluded from them (*v.* 11).

Three kinds of Minchah are here mentioned; (1) fine flour with frankincense, *vv.* 1—3; (2) cakes and wafers of fine flour, *vv.* 4—8; (3) parched grains of the first gathered corn, with frankincense, *vv.* 14—16. Of each of them a small portion was burnt on the Altar "for a memorial," and the remainder was given to the priests. The offerings of flour belonged to the priests at large, but those of cakes and wafers to the officiating priests, vii. 9, 10.—Instructions to the priests regarding the Minchahs are given vi. 14—23.

The Offering of Fine flour, 1—3.

1. *fine flour*] That is, finely bolted flour of wheat. See Ex. xxix. 2; LXX. σεμίδαλις; Vulg. *simila*. It was probably always presented in a bowl. The Minchahs of the princes at the dedication of the Tabernacle were presented in bowls of silver, Num. vii. 13.

oil] See Note at the end of the chapter.

frankincense] See on Ex. xxx. 34.

2. This verse might rather be rendered, "And he shall bring it to Aaron's sons, the priests; **and the** (officiating) **priest shall take from it a handful of its flour and its oil with all its frankincense, and this shall he burn as its memorial upon the Altar,**" &c.

memorial] The English word literally answers to the Hebrew (*azkārāh*), which was the regular name not only for the portion of the Minchah which was burnt on the Altar (*vv.* 9, 16, v. 12, vi. 15; Num. v. 26), but for the frankincense which was laid upon the Shewbread (Lev. xxiv. 7). The LXX. call it τὸ μνημόσυνον, the word which is applied to the prayers and alms of Cornelius, Acts x. 4. This application of the Greek word seems well to illustrate the meaning of the *azkārāh*. Cf. on Ex. xxx. 8.

3. *a thing most holy*] Literally, *a holy of holies*. As there was a distinction between the places dedicated to the divine service into holy and most holy (Ex. xxvi. 33), so was there a similar distinction in what was offered to Jehovah. All offerings were *holy*, including the portions of the Peace-offerings which were eaten by the laity; but that was *most holy* of which every part was devoted either to the Altar, or to the use of the priests. Such were the Minchahs (*v.* 10, vi. 16, x. 12), the Shewbread (Lev. xxiv. 9), the incense (Ex. xxx. 36), and the flesh of the Sin- and Trespass-offerings (Lev. vi. 17, 18, vii. 1, 6, x. 17, xiv. 13; Num. xviii. 9, 10). Every son of Aaron, even he who had a bodily defect and could not perform any priestly office, was permitted "to eat the bread of his God, both of the most holy and of the holy," Lev. xxi. 22. The most holy sacrificial

4 ¶ And if thou bring an oblation
of a meat offering baken in the oven,
it shall be unleavened cakes of fine
flour mingled with oil, or unleavened
wafers anointed with oil.
5 ¶ And if thy oblation *be* a meat
offering *baken* ‖ in a pan, it shall be *of*
fine flour unleavened, mingled with
oil.
6 Thou shalt part it in pieces, and
pour oil thereon: it *is* a meat offering.
7 ¶ And if thy oblation *be* a meat
offering *baken* in the fryingpan, it shall
be made *of* fine flour with oil.
8 And thou shalt bring the meat
offering that is made of these things
unto the LORD: and when it is presented
unto the priest, he shall bring
it unto the altar.
9 And the priest shall take from
the meat offering [b] a memorial thereof,
and shall burn *it* upon the altar: *it is*
[c] an offering made by fire, of a sweet
savour unto the LORD.
10 And that which is left of the
meat offering *shall be* Aaron's and his
sons': *it is* a thing most holy of the
offerings of the LORD made by fire.
11 No meat offering, which ye shall
bring unto the LORD, shall be made

‖ Or, *on a flat plate*, or, *slice*.

[b] ver. 2.

[c] Exod. 29. 18.

---

food was eaten in "the holy place," that is the precinct of the Tabernacle, probably in the priests' lodgings. See Note after Ex. xxvi. § V.: but the priests' portion of the Peace-offerings might be eaten by the priests and their families in any "clean place" (x. 12—14). It should however be observed that the term *most holy* is not always used strictly in accordance with this distinction. See on Ex. xl. 10: cf. also Ex. xxix. 37, and Lev. xxvii. 28.

The offerings of Cakes and Wafers.
4—10.

The four kinds of bread and the three cooking utensils which are mentioned in this section were probably such as were in common use in the daily life of the Israelites; and there appears no reason to doubt that they were such as are still used in the East.—There is no indication of any difference in the significance of the different offerings. The variety was most likely permitted to suit the circumstances of the worshippers. The fine flour and oil, with its frankincense (*v.* 1), seems to have been the most costly of the Minchahs, and the most liberal in quantity: cf. Num. vii. 13. The cakes and wafers mentioned in *v.* 4 would require that the offerer should at least possess an oven. The "pan" and the "frying pan" (*vv.* 5, 7) may have been the common cooking implements of the poorest of the people.

4. *oven*] This was most likely a portable vessel of earthenware. It was liable to be broken (see xi. 35). Its shape may have been like the oven represented in Wilkinson (Vol. I. p. 176, fig. 20[y]), a truncated cone about 3 ft. 6 in. high, and 1 ft. 6 in. diameter. Similar jars are now used for the same purpose by the Arabs. After the vessel has been thoroughly heated by a fire lighted in the inside, the cakes are placed within it, and the top is covered up until they are sufficiently baked. Meantime the outside of the vessel is turned to account. Dough rolled out very thin is spread over it, and a sort of wafer is produced considerably thinner than a Scotch oat-cake. Harmer, 'Observations,' Vol. I. p. 476. Such wafers are a common accompaniment of an Arab meal. Tristram, 'Land of Israel,' p. 262. Both cakes and wafers are mentioned Ex. xxix. 2. The cakes, from the apparent derivation of their Hebrew name, are supposed to have been pricked like our biscuits. The word aptly rendered *wafer* signifies something spread out.

5. *a pan*] Rather, as in the margin, **a flat plate**. It was probably of earthenware, like the oven. In later times it was sometimes of iron (Ezek. iv. 3). The Bedouins use such a plate of earthenware, which they call *tajen*, a name that seems to be identical with τήγανον, the word here used by the LXX. Robinson, 'Bib. Res.' I. p. 485: Harmer, 'Observations,' I. p. 477.

6. *part it in pieces*] The Hebrew word for *part* signifies to **break**, not to cut. The Bedouins are in the habit of breaking up their cakes when warm and mixing the fragments with butter when that luxury can be obtained. Robinson, II. p. 118.

7. *fryingpan*] Rather, **pan**. The word, according to the best authorities (Maimonides, Gesenius, Knobel, Fürst, &c.), signifies a vessel deeper than a fryingpan, and its derivation seems to show that it was commonly used for boiling. Jewish tradition assigns a lid to it (Mishna, 'Menach.' v. 8). It may have been a *pan* or *pot* used either for baking or for boiling. It should however be observed that the word *baken* in this verse and *v.* 5 rests on no authority, but is supplied by our translators. It is possible that the cakes here spoken of were boiled in oil. It can hardly be doubted that the LXX. and the Vulgate are wrong in translating the word ἐσχάρα and *craticula*.

with leaven: for ye shall burn no
leaven, nor any honey, in any offering of the LORD made by fire.
12 ¶ As for the oblation of the firstfruits, ye shall offer them unto the
LORD: but they shall not †be burnt
on the altar for a sweet savour.
13 And every oblation of thy meat
offering [d]shalt thou season with salt;
neither shalt thou suffer the salt of
the covenant of thy God to be lacking
from thy meat offering: with all thine
offerings thou shalt offer salt.
14 And if thou offer a meat offer
ing of thy firstfruits unto the LORD,
thou shalt offer for the meat offering
of thy firstfruits green ears of corn
dried by the fire, *even* corn beaten out
of full ears.
15 And thou shalt put oil upon it,

† Heb. *ascend.*

[d] Mark 9. 49.

11, 12. *As for the oblation of the firstfruits*] Rather, **As an oblation of firstfruits.** The words refer to the leaven and honey mentioned in *v.* 11 which might be offered amongst the firstfruits and tithes (Deut. xxvi. 2, 12; cf. 2 Chro. xxxi. 5): leaven was also a regular constituent in the bread of the Thank-offering (vii. 13) and in the Pentecostal loaves (xxiii. 17). The exclusion of honey from the offerings of the Altar appears to have had the same meaning as the exclusion of leaven. We know that honey was used in ancient times to produce fermentation in the preparation of vinegar (Plin. 'Hist. Nat.' XI. 15, XXI. 48); and there is reason to believe that the same use of it was made by the Hebrews (Buxtorf, 'Lex. Talm.' p. 500). The leaven commonly used was, as it still is in many countries, a small piece of fermented dough. Fermentation of all kinds seems to furnish an apt symbol of the working of corruption in the human heart. See Schöttgen, 'Hor. Heb.' p. 597. This was perceived by the Romans: Aul. Gell. 'Noct. Att.' X. 15; Plut. 'Quæst. Rom.' c. 109. Compare the language of S. Paul, 1 Cor. v. 6—8.

13. *with all thine offerings thou shalt offer salt*] Not only every Minchah, but every animal offering was to be accompanied by salt. Considering the emphatic form of this command, and the importance subsequently ascribed to it (Ezek. xliii. 24; Mark ix. 49, 50), it is remarkable that this appears to be the only reference to salt in the ceremonial Law. On Ex. xxx. 35 (where some suppose that salt is mentioned) see note. The significance of it, as a sacrificial symbol, is set forth in the expression "the salt of the covenant of thy God" (cf. Num. xviii. 19; 2 Chro. xiii. 5). It was the one symbol which was never absent from the Altar of Burnt-offering, showing the imperishableness of the love of Jehovah for His people. In its unalterable nature, it is the contrary of leaven. The Arabs are said to retain in common use the expression, "a covenant of salt," and the respect they pay to bread and salt in their rites of hospitality is well known. Cf. Ezra iv. 14. In heathen sacrifices its use seems to have been all but universal. Pliny says, after praising its virtues in food and medicine, *maxime tamen in sacris intelligitur auctoritas, quando nulla conficiuntur sine mola salsa.* 'H. N.' XXXI. 41. The *mola salsa* was meal mixed with salt, which was either sprinkled on the head of a victim about to be slain (Cicero, 'de Div.' II. 16; Virg. 'Ecl.' VIII. 82; Hor. II. Sat. III. 200; Festus s. *mola;* Val. Max. II. 5, § 5; Pseudo-Didymus in Hom. 'Il.' I. 449); or offered in place of a more costly offering (Hor. III. Od. XXIII. 20). Cf. Lev. v. 11.

The Minchah of Firstfruits.
14—16.

The place of these instructions may suggest that they were added to the chapter as a supplement.—There is certainly no sufficient ground to suppose, with the rabbinists and modern Jewish authorities, that this Minchah differed from the others in being a national offering, identical with the offering of the Wave-sheaf prescribed xxiii. 10: it seems to be the same kind of offering as is mentioned Num. xviii. 12, 13.

14. *green ears of corn*] Rather, "**fresh** ears of corn;" that is, corn just ripe, freshly gathered. Parched corn, such as is here spoken of, is a common article of food in Syria and Egypt, and was very generally eaten in ancient times. Cf. xxiii. 14; Josh. v. 11; 1 S. xvii. 17, xxv. 18; 2 S. xvii. 28, &c.

beaten out] Not rubbed out by the hands, as described in Luke vi. 1, but bruised or crushed so as to form groats.

The meaning of the Minchahs appears to be much more simple than that of the animal sacrifices. This is indicated by the simplicity of the only name by which they are designated (see on *v.* 1). The Minchah, as a sacrifice, was something surrendered to God, which was of the greatest value to man as a means of living. It might thus seem to be merely eucharistic. But it should not be overlooked that the grain had been modified, and made useful, by man's own labour. Hence it has been supposed that the Minchah expressed a confession that all our good works are wrought in God and are due to Him.—On the Great Minchah of the Shewbread, see Ex. xxv. 30.—On the Drink-offerings, see on Ex. xxix. 40; Lev. xxiii. 18.

and lay frankincense thereon: it *is* a meat offering.

16 And the priest shall burn the memorial of it, *part* of the beaten corn thereof, and *part* of the oil thereof, with all the frankincense thereof: *it is* an offering made by fire unto the LORD.

NOTE on CHAP. II. 1.

ON THE SYMBOLICAL USE OF OIL.

There were three principal uses of oil familiar to the Hebrews. (1) It was employed to anoint the surface of the body in order to mollify the skin, to heal injuries, and to strengthen the muscles (Ps. civ. 15, cix. 18, cxli. 5; Isa. i. 6; Mic. vi. 15; Luke x. 34; Mark vi. 13; Jam. v. 14, &c.): (2) it was largely used as an ingredient of food (Num. xi. 8; 1 K. xvii. 12; 1 Chro. xii. 40; Ezek. xvi. 13, 19; Hos. ii. 5, &c.); and (3) it was commonly burned in lamps (Ex. xxv. 6; Matt. xxv. 3, &c.).—In each of these uses it may be taken as a fit symbol of divine grace. It might figure it as conferring on each believer the strength and faculties required to carry on his work (1 Cor. xii. 4); as supporting and renewing him day by day with fresh supplies of life (1 Cor. iii. 16, Tit. iii. 5); and as giving light, comfort, and guidance into all truth (Job xxxii. 8; John xiv. 16, xv. 26).

There was what closely answered to each of the ordinary uses of oil in the different modes in which it was employed in the Sanctuary. It was used for anointing the priests and the holy things, it served as food in the Minchahs, and it was what kept alive the lights in "the pure candlestick," "the lamp of God" (1 S. iii. 3) in the holy place. In the first of these applications in the Sanctuary, oil served no practical purpose; it was simply typical, and it is in this connection that it bears its highest significance. As if to keep this significance in view, the mode in which it was added to the Minchah seems to be spoken of as an anointing (see *vv.* 1, 15, 16). In the language of both the Old and the New Testaments, the figurative references to oil most frequently turn upon this meaning. See Isa. lxi. 1; 2 Cor. i. 21; 1 Joh. ii. 20, 27; Heb. i. 9, &c. Its most perfect application is found in the words MESSIAH and CHRIST as the names of Him whose anointing was the gift of the Spirit without measure, Joh. iii. 34. On the anointing of the holy things, see on viii. 11.—On the holy anointing oil, see Ex. xxx. 22—33.

The offering of oil on the Altar involved an acknowledgment on the part of the worshipper that his spiritual gifts were from Jehovah and belonged to Him. It was in this that it became specially connected with the Minchah. See the preceding note.

CHAPTER III.

1 *The peace offering of the herd,* 6 *of the flock,* 7 *either a lamb,* 12 *or a goat.*

AND if his oblation *be* a sacrifice of peace offering, if he offer *it* of the herd; whether *it be* a male or female, he shall offer it without blemish before the LORD.

2 And he shall lay his hand upon the head of his offering, and kill it *at* the door of the tabernacle of the congregation: and Aaron's sons the priests

THE PEACE-OFFERINGS.

The Peace-offering from the Herd.
1—5.

CHAP. III. **1.** The Peace-offering (like the Burnt-offering, i. 3, and the Minchah, ii. 1) is here spoken of as if it was familiarly known before the giving of the Law. See Introd. § xii. The Sin-offering and the Trespass-offering are introduced in a different manner (iv. 1, v. 1, &c.). It would also seem that the alternative of a male or a female was in accordance with old usage. There is no specified limitation in respect to age, such as there is in the cases of the Burnt-offering and the Sin-offering. The point of this first injunction is that the animal should be "without blemish."

peace offering] This rendering of the Hebrew is in accordance with the ancient versions and seems preferable to "thank-offering," which occurs in several places in the margin of our Bible, and has been used by Luther and many modern translators. Thank-offering appears to be the right name for a subordinate class of Peace-offerings. See on vii. 12.

2. *at the door of the tabernacle of the congregation*] **at the entrance of the Tent of meeting.** See on i. 3. We are not told on which side of the Altar, as we are in reference to Burnt-offerings and Sin-offerings (i. 11, iv. 24, 29, vii. 2). As a matter of convenience, it is likely that all victims were usually slaughtered in one place: but, as the Peace-offerings were sometimes very numerous,

shall sprinkle the blood upon the altar
round about.
3 And he shall offer of the sacrifice
of the peace offering an offering made
by fire unto the LORD; [a]the ‖fat that
covereth the inwards, and all the fat
that *is* upon the inwards,
4 And the two kidneys, and the fat
that *is* on them, which *is* by the flanks,
and the ‖caul above the liver, with the
kidneys, it shall he take away.
5 And Aaron's sons shall burn it on
the altar upon the burnt sacrifice,
which *is* upon the wood that *is* on the
fire: *it is* an offering made by fire, of
a sweet savour unto the LORD.
6 ¶ And if his offering for a sacrifice of peace offering unto the LORD
be of the flock; male or female, he
shall offer it without blemish.
7 If he offer a lamb for his offering, then shall he offer it before the
LORD.
8 And he shall lay his hand upon
the head of his offering, and kill it
before the tabernacle of the congregation: and Aaron's sons shall sprinkle
the blood thereof round about upon
the altar.
9 And he shall offer of the sacrifice
of the peace offering an offering made
by fire unto the LORD; the fat thereof, *and* the whole rump, it shall he
take off hard by the backbone; and
the fat that covereth the inwards, and
all the fat that *is* upon the inwards,
10 And the two kidneys, and the
fat that *is* upon them, which *is* by the
flanks, and the caul above the liver,
with the kidneys, it shall he take
away.
11 And the priest shall burn it upon
the altar: *it is* the food of the offering made by fire unto the LORD.
12 ¶ And if his offering *be* a goat,
then he shall offer it before the LORD.
13 And he shall lay his hand upon
the head of it, and kill it before the
tabernacle of the congregation: and
the sons of Aaron shall sprinkle the

[a] Exod. 29. 22.
‖ Or, *suet*.
‖ Or, *midriff over the liver*, and *over the kidneys*.

---

a licence was probably permitted in respect of them when occasion required it. See on i. 11.

shall sprinkle] Rather, **shall throw**. See Introd. § vi.

3, 4. On the parts of the Peace-offerings, the Sin-offerings and the Trespass-offerings which were put on the Altar, see Introd. § viii.

5. *upon the burnt sacrifice*] This is the right rendering, and it appears to mean, upon the ashes of the continual Burnt-offering (Ex. xxix. 38), in accordance with Lev. vi. 12, "and the priest shall burn wood on it (*i.e.* the Altar) every morning, and lay the burnt-offering in order upon it; and he shall burn thereon the fat of the peace-offerings." But the same phrase is rendered "according to the offerings made by fire," &c. in iv. 35, v. 12, giving a different sense to the preposition. Knobel and some other modern interpreters adopt the latter interpretation.

The Peace-offering from the Flock.
6—15.

7. *a lamb*] **a sheep.** The word signifies a full-grown sheep, in its prime. The same Hebrew word is frequently rendered *sheep* in our version. Gen. xxx. 32; Lev. i. 10, vii. 23. See on *v.* 1; Introd. § iv.

8. See notes on i. 4, 5.

9. *the whole rump*] It should be rendered **the whole fat tail.** The substantive (*aleyāh*) has this meaning in Arabic. It occurs nowhere in the Hebrew Bible except in this connection. (Ex. xxix. 22; Lev. vii. 3, viii. 25, ix. 19.) The ancient translators in general, and Josephus, have taken the word to denote the tail, but the LXX. in this place and two others have rendered it by ὀσφύς, the loin. There is no doubt that what is meant is the tail of the kind of sheep well known in the East, and in Africa, called by naturalists *Ovis laticaudata*. (Robinson, 'Bib. Res.' I. p. 477. Tristram, 'Nat. Hist.' p. 143.) Mr Fellowes describes the tail as "an apron of rich marrowy fat extending to the width of the hind-quarters and often trailing on the ground." ('Asia Minor,' p. 10.) Dr Russell says that the tails often weigh 15lbs. and even as much as 50lbs. when they have been increased by artificial fattening ('Nat. Hist. of Aleppo,' II. p. 147). It appears that a custom has existed from early times of attaching the heavy tail to a small truck to save the animal from the pain occasioned by its trailing on the ground (Herodot. III. 113. Mishna, 'de Sabb.' V. 4.) The whole tail was to be taken off "hard by the backbone," where the pad of fat commences.

11. *burn it*] See on i. 9.

the food of the offering, &c.] See on *v.* 16.

blood thereof upon the altar round
about.
14 And he shall offer thereof his
offering, *even* an offering made by fire
unto the LORD; the fat that covereth
the inwards, and all the fat that *is*
upon the inwards,
15 And the two kidneys, and the
fat that *is* upon them, which *is* by the
flanks, and the caul above the liver,
with the kidneys, it shall he take
away.
16 And the priest shall burn them
upon the altar: *it is* the food of the
offering made by fire for a sweet
savour: [b] all the fat *is* the LORD's.

[b] chap. 7. 25.

17 *It shall be* a perpetual statute
for your generations throughout all
your dwellings, that ye eat neither fat
nor [c] blood.

[c] Gen. 9. chap. 7. 2 & 17. 14.

CHAPTER IV.

1 The sin offering of ignorance, 3 for the priest, 13 for the congregation, 22 for the ruler, 27 for any of the people.

AND the LORD spake unto Moses,
saying,
2 Speak unto the children of Israel,
saying, If a soul shall sin through
ignorance against any of the commandments of the LORD *concerning things*
which ought not to be done, and shall
do against any of them:

---

12. When the alternative is permitted, the sheep always takes precedence of the goat. See on i. 10. Birds were not accepted as Peace-offerings, most probably because they were, by themselves, insufficient to make up a sacrificial meal.

16. *it is the food of the offering made by fire for a sweet savour: all the fat is the LORD's*] This might rather be rendered, **as food of an offering made by fire for a sweet savour, shall all the fat be for Jehovah.** So de Wette, Zunz, Herxh., &c. In this expression, our bodily taste and smell furnish figures of the satisfaction with which the LORD accepts the appointed symbols of the true worship of the heart. All that was sent up in the fire of the Altar, including the parts of the Sin-offering (iv. 31), as well as the Burnt-offering (i. 9, &c.), was accepted for "a sweet savour:" but the word *food* may here have a peculiar fitness in its application to the Peace-offering, which served for food also to the priests and the offerer, and so symbolized communion between the LORD, His ministers, and His worshippers. The omission of the word *food* in connection with the Burnt-offering in ch. i. is at least worthy of remark. Cf. xxi. 6, 17, 21, 22, xxii. 11; Num. xxviii. 2, &c.

17. *a perpetual statute*, &c.] This is repeated with increased emphasis as regards the fat, vii. 23—25.

fat] *i.e.* the suet and the marrowy fat of the tail. See Introd. § viii. The significance of offering fat to Jehovah appears to consist in the fact that its proper development in the animal is, in general, a mark of perfection. This is immediately connected with what seems to be its purpose in the body. "Its remarkable absorption in certain cases of disease and of deficiency of proper food, seems to point it out as a source of nutriment of which the animal economy may avail itself on emergency; and accordingly in cases of emaciation or atrophy it is the first substance which disappears." Todd's 'Cyclopædia of Physiology,' Vol. I. p. 232.

blood] See on xvii. 11.

throughout...your dwellings] The meaning is that the suet is neither to be eaten in sacrificial meals in the Sanctuary, nor in ordinary meals in private houses.

On the classification of Peace-offerings, on the Meat-offerings and Drink-offerings which accompanied them, and on the portions awarded to the priests, see vii. 11—21; Num. xv. 2—11. On the *Chagigah*, a sort of social feast allied to the Peace-offering, which forms the subject of a treatise of the Mishna, and is supposed to be alluded to Deut. xiv. 26, xvi. 2; 2 Chro. xxx. 22, 24; John xviii. 28, see notes in loc. and Smith's 'Dict.' II. p. 717.

THE SIN-OFFERINGS.

iv. 1—v. 13.

CHAP. IV. 1, 2. *And the LORD spake unto Moses, saying, Speak unto the children of Israel*] This formula answers to that which introduces the three previous chapters as a whole (i. 1, 2). It is the commencement of a distinct section of the Law. See following note.

2. *If a soul shall sin*] The Sin-offering was a new thing, instituted by the Law. (See Introd. § xvi.) The older kinds of sacrifice (see iii. 1) when offered by individuals were purely voluntary: no special occasions were prescribed when they were to be offered. Hence the form, "If any man of you bring," &c., i. 2, cf. ii. 1, iii. 1. But it was plainly commanded that he who was conscious that he had committed a sin should bring his Sin-offering. Each of these offerings and of the Trespass-offerings is accordingly introduced

3 If the priest that is anointed do
sin according to the sin of the people;
then let him bring for his sin, which
he hath sinned, a young bullock without blemish unto the LORD for a sin
offering.
4 And he shall bring the bullock
unto the door of the tabernacle of the
congregation before the LORD; and
shall lay his hand upon the bullock's
head, and kill the bullock before the
LORD.
5 And the priest that is anointed
shall take of the bullock's blood, and
bring it to the tabernacle of the congregation:

6 And the priest shall dip his finger
in the blood, and sprinkle of the blood
seven times before the LORD, before
the vail of the sanctuary.
7 And the priest shall put *some* of
the blood upon the horns of the altar
of sweet incense before the LORD,
which *is* in the tabernacle of the congregation; and shall pour [a] all the blood [a] chap. 5. 9.
of the bullock at the bottom of the
altar of the burnt offering, which *is*
at the door of the tabernacle of the
congregation.
8 And he shall take off from it all
the fat of the bullock for the sin offering; the fat that covereth the inwards,

---

by a definition of the circumstance which renders the sacrifice necessary. The antecedent condition for Sin-offerings in general is here stated; for particular cases, see iv. 3, 13, 22, 27, v. 1—15.

sin through ignorance] **Sin through error**; that is, through straying from the right way. See Note at the end of the chapter.

The Sin-offering for the High-priest. 3—12.

3. *the priest that is anointed*] The High-priest was thus called because he alone of the priests was anointed on the head in consecration. Ex. xxix. 7; Lev. viii. 12, xxi. 10. On the anointing of the other priests see note on viii. 13. The High-priest is generally called in Leviticus the Anointed priest (iv. 5, 16, vi. 22, xvi. 32). He is called the High-priest (strictly *the great* priest) Lev. xxi. 10; Num. xxxv. 25, 28; Josh. xx. 6; and in later times, the Chief-priest (2 K. xxv. 18; 2 Chro. xix. 11).

The gradation of the Sin-offerings is remarkable. It was not like the choice offered to meet cases of poverty, v. 7—13, xii. 8, &c. It might seem that the distinction addressed itself more pointedly to each individual according to his rank and consequent responsibility. That there is nothing akin to it in the Trespass-offering seems to have arisen from the latter having had a less direct relation to the conscience, and a closer connection with the amount of harm that had been done by the offence for which atonement was sought. See on v. 14.

according to the sin of the people] Rather, **to** *bring* **guilt on the people.** These words have been supposed to limit the occasion of this Sin-offering to the offences of the High-priest in his official capacity (Lev. x. 17; Mal. ii. 7, 8) as the head of the nation (Knobel, Keil, Herxh.). But on the other hand it has been fairly urged that the whole nation is concerned in every transgression of its representative.

4. See on i. 3, 4.

5. The presentation of the victim, the imposition of hands and the slaughtering of all the Sin-offerings were the same as in the other sacrifices (see Introd. § v.). The difference lay in the treatment of the blood. In the inferior Sin-offerings the officiating priest smeared some of the blood on the horns of the Altar of Burnt-offering (*vv.* 25, 30, 34), while in this offering for the High-priest, and in that for the nation, the High-priest himself sprinkled the blood seven times within the Tabernacle and smeared it on the horns of the Altar of incense (*vv.* 6, 7, 17, 18). Compare the sprinklings on the Day of Atonement, xvi. 14, 19. The different modes of sprinkling appear to have marked successive degrees of consecration in advancing from the Altar of Burnt-offering to the presence of Jehovah within the vail.

6. *before the vail of the sanctuary*] This is generally understood to mean the floor of the holy place in front of the vail (Onk., Luther, Knobel, Keil, and others). It is, however, objected that the priests in this case would tread on the blood (Kurtz, Kalisch, &c.); and the LXX. and Vulgate may rather countenance the notion that the sprinkling was on the vail itself (*κατὰ τὸ καταπέτασμα—contra velum*). But the quantity sprinkled with the finger must have been very small, and the area it would occupy of the floor might have been easily left untrodden.

7. *pour all the blood*] The Hebrew word for pour (*shāphak*) is not like that in i. 5, &c. See Introd. § vi. The meaning is, that all the blood that was left after the sprinkling and the smearing should be disposed of in such a manner as to suit the decorum of divine service. It had no sacrificial significance.

at the door of the tabernacle of the congregation] See on i. 3.

8. *the fat*] See Introd. § viii.

and all the fat that *is* upon the inwards,
9 And the two kidneys, and the fat
that *is* upon them, which *is* by the
flanks, and the caul above the liver,
with the kidneys, it shall he take
away,
10 As it was taken off from the
bullock of the sacrifice of peace offerings: and the priest shall burn them
upon the altar of the burnt offering.
11 [b] And the skin of the bullock, and
all his flesh, with his head, and with his
legs, and his inwards, and his dung,
12 Even the whole bullock shall he
carry forth [†] without the camp unto a
clean place, where the ashes are poured
out, and [c] burn him on the wood with
fire: [†] where the ashes are poured out
shall he be burnt.
13 ¶ And if the whole congregation
of Israel sin through ignorance, [d] and
the thing be hid from the eyes of the
assembly, and they have done *somewhat against* any of the commandments of the LORD *concerning things*
which should not be done, and are
guilty;
14 When the sin, which they have
sinned against it, is known, then the
congregation shall offer a young bullock for the sin, and bring him before
the tabernacle of the congregation.
15 And the elders of the congregation shall lay their hands upon the
head of the bullock before the LORD:
and the bullock shall be killed before
the LORD.
16 And the priest that is anointed
shall bring of the bullock's blood to
the tabernacle of the congregation:
17 And the priest shall dip his

[b] Exod. 29. 14. Numb. 19. 5.
[†] Heb. *to without the camp.*
[c] Heb. 13. 11.
[†] Heb. *at the pouring out of the ashes.*
[d] chap. 5. 2, 3, 4.

---

10. *shall burn*] See on i. 9.

12. *Even the whole bullock shall he carry forth*] The Hebrew verb strictly signifies *shall cause to go forth*. Or, according to a common Heb. idiom (see on Ex. xxxvii. 1—5), it might be rendered, *the whole bullock shall be carried forth* (cf. Lev. xvi. 27). Our verb *carry*, in the active voice, was however rightly used by our translators in this connection, according to the old usage. Thus Nebuchadnezzar "carried away all Jerusalem, and all the princes, and all the mighty men of valour, ten thousand captives," 2 K. xxiv. 14; and Jacob "carried away all his cattle" from Padan-aram, Gen. xxxi. 18. See also 2 K. xvii. 6, xviii. 11, xxv. 11; 2 Chro. xxxvi. 6; Jer. xxxix. 7, &c. The word was so used very frequently by the writers of the last century. A recent critic, overlooking these simple facts, has imagined that the words mean that the High-priest himself had to carry the whole bullock a distance which is estimated at three-quarters of a mile, and has drawn an argument from his own mistake to prove the statement fictitious.—There is a solemn reference to the burning of the flesh of the Sin-offering without the camp, Heb. xiii. 11—13.

a clean place, where the ashes are poured out] The spot outside the camp to which the ashes were conveyed from the side of the Altar (i. 16). It was a place free from impurities, not like those referred to xiv. 40, 45. The flesh, though it was burned in an ordinary way, and not sent up in the fire of the Altar (see on i. 9), was not to be confounded with carrion, but was associated with the remains of the sacrifices.—The priests could not eat the flesh of this victim or of that offered for the sin of the congregation, as they ate that of other Sin-offerings, because they were in these cases in the position of offerers. The same rule was observed in regard to the Meat-offering of the priests, vi. 23. It was only of the Peace-offering that the offerer himself could partake. See on x. 17, 18, xvi. 27; Heb. xiii. 11.

The Sin-offering for the Congregation.
13—21.

13. *congregation...assembly*] Each of the Hebrew words signifies the people in a collected body. It does not appear that there is any difference between them in the connection in which they are here used. Cf. Num. xv. 24, 26.

sin through ignorance] See Note at the end of the chapter.

14. *When the sin...is known*] Such a case seems to have been that related 1 S. xiv. 31—35.

15. In this case the imposition of hands is performed by the elders in behalf of the nation. But in other respects the rites were performed by the High-priest in the same manner as in the Sin-offering for himself. According to the Mishna this and the Scape-goat were the only public acts of sacrifice in which there was the imposition of hands ('Menach,' IX. 7), while it was observed in all private sacrifices. See on i. 4. If this is correct, there was no such observance in the continual Burnt-offering nor in the Festival offerings.

16. *the priest that is anointed*] See on *v.* 3.

17. See *v.* 6.

finger *in some* of the blood, and sprinkle *it* seven times before the LORD, *even* before the vail.

18 And he shall put *some* of the blood upon the horns of the altar which *is* before the LORD, that *is* in the tabernacle of the congregation, and shall pour out all the blood at the bottom of the altar of the burnt offering, which *is at* the door of the tabernacle of the congregation.

19 And he shall take all his fat from him, and burn *it* upon the altar.

20 And he shall do with the bullock as he did with the bullock for a sin offering, so shall he do with this: and the priest shall make an atonement for them, and it shall be forgiven them.

21 And he shall carry forth the bullock without the camp, and burn him as he burned the first bullock: it *is* a sin offering for the congregation.

22 ¶ When a ruler hath sinned, and done *somewhat* through ignorance *against* any of the commandments of the LORD his God *concerning things* which should not be done, and is guilty;

23 Or if his sin, wherein he hath sinned, come to his knowledge; he shall bring his offering, a kid of the goats, a male without blemish:

24 And he shall lay his hand upon the head of the goat, and kill it in the place where they kill the burnt offering before the LORD: it *is* a sin offering.

25 And the priest shall take of the blood of the sin offering with his finger, and put *it* upon the horns of the altar of burnt offering, and shall pour out his blood at the bottom of the altar of burnt offering.

26 And he shall burn all his fat upon the altar, as the fat of the sacrifice of peace offerings: and the priest shall make an atonement for him as concerning his sin, and it shall be forgiven him.

27 ¶ And if † any one of the † common people sin through ignorance, while he doeth *somewhat against* any

† Heb. *any soul.* † Heb. *people of the land.*

---

18. *the altar...in the tabernacle*] *i.e.* the Altar of incense (cf. *v.* 7).

20. *the bullock for a sin-offering*] "The bullock for **the** sin-offering," *i.e.* for his own sin-offering, *v.* 3.

21. See on *v.* 12.

The Sin-offering for the Ruler.
22—26.

22. *ruler*] The Hebrew word denoted either the head of a tribe (Num. i. 4—16), or the head of a division of a tribe (see Num. xxxiv. 18; cf. Josh. xxii. 30). It is variously rendered in our Bible by *prince* (Gen. xvii. 20, xxiii. 6; Num. i. 16, 44, vii. 2, 3, 10, 16, &c.), by *ruler* (Ex. xvi. 22, xxii. 28, &c.), by *captain* (Num. ii. 3, 5, 7, &c.), by *chief* (Num. iii. 24, 30, 32; 2 Chro. v. 2, &c.), by *governor* (2 Chro. i. 2).

through ignorance] See on *v.* 2.

23. *Or if his sin*] Rather, **And if** his sin.

come to his knowledge] *i.e.* when he has become conscious of his sin.

a kid of the goats] Strictly, a shaggy buck of the goats, that is, a **shaggy he-goat**. Our version seems to stand almost alone in rendering the Heb. *sa'eer* by kid. The word literally means a rough shaggy goat, in distinction from a smooth-haired he-goat, *'attud*, Gen. xxxi. 10, 12; Num. vii. 17, 23, 83, &c. *Sa'eer* occurs Lev. ix. 3, xvi. 5, xxiii. 19; Num. vii. 16, &c. It is rendered *devil*, Lev. xvii. 7, 2 Chro. xi. 15; *satyr*, Isa. xiii. 21, xxxiv. 14; *rough goat*, Dan. viii. 21; and is applied to Esau, Gen. xxvii. 11. Bochart supposed *sa'eer* and *'attud* to represent varieties of breed, and this seems most probable, see *v.* 28; but Knobel supposes the first to denote an old goat with a beard, and the latter a younger one. The *sa'eer* was the regular Sin-offering at the yearly Festivals, Lev. xvi. 9, 15, xxiii. 19; Num. xxviii. 15, 22, 30, xxix. 5, 16, &c., and at the consecration of the priests, Lev. ix. 3, 15, x. 16, while the *'attud* appears to have been generally offered for the other sacrifices, Ps. l. 9, 13, lxvi. 15; Isa. l. 11, xxxiv. 6; &c. Ezek. xxxix. 18, &c.

24. *where they kill the burnt-offering*] On the north side of the Altar. See on i. 11.

25. *the horns of the altar of burnt-offering*] See on *v.* 5.

The Sin-offering for one of the People.
27—35.

27. *any one of the common people*] Literally, any one of the people of the land. These words are so rendered Lev. xx. 2, 4; 2 K. xi. 18, 19, xvi. 15. It was the ordinary designation of the people, as distinguished from the priests and the rulers.

of the commandments of the LORD
concerning things which ought not to
be done, and be guilty;
28 Or if his sin, which he hath
sinned, come to his knowledge: then
he shall bring his offering, a kid of the
goats, a female without blemish, for
his sin which he hath sinned.
29 And he shall lay his hand upon
the head of the sin offering, and slay
the sin offering in the place of the
burnt offering.
30 And the priest shall take of the
blood thereof with his finger, and put
it upon the horns of the altar of burnt
offering, and shall pour out all the
blood thereof at the bottom of the
altar.
[e] chap. 3. 14. 31 And [e] he shall take away all the
fat thereof, as the fat is taken away
from off the sacrifice of peace offerings; and the priest shall burn *it* upon
[f] Exod. 29. 18. the altar for a [f] sweet savour unto the
LORD; and the priest shall make an
atonement for him, and it shall be forgiven him.
32 And if he bring a lamb for a
sin offering, he shall bring it a female
without blemish.
33 And he shall lay his hand upon
the head of the sin offering, and slay
it for a sin offering in the place where
they kill the burnt offering.
34 And the priest shall take of the
blood of the sin offering with his finger,
and put *it* upon the horns of the altar
of burnt offering, and shall pour out
all the blood thereof at the bottom of
the altar:
35 And he shall take away all the
fat thereof, as the fat of the lamb is
taken away from the sacrifice of the
peace offerings; and the priest shall
burn them upon the altar, according
to the offerings made by fire unto the
LORD: and the priest shall make an
atonement for his sin that he hath committed, and it shall be forgiven him.

---

28. *Or if his sin*] **And if** his sin.

a kid of the goats] **A shaggy she-goat.** The word is the feminine of *sa'er*, *v.* 23.

31. *for a sweet savour*] See on i. 9.

32. *a lamb*] Rather, **a sheep**; one between one and three years old. See on iii. 7. Introd. § iv. Three points are to be observed in regard to the victims for Sin-offerings.—The common people had to offer a female, as the less valuable animal; they might present either a sheep or a goat to suit their convenience, while the rulers had always to offer a male-goat: and the goat was preferred to the sheep, unlike the victim for a Peace-offering or a Burnt-offering.

35. *according to the offerings made by fire*] Rather, **upon** the offerings made by fire. See on iii. 5.

It should be observed, that the Sin-offerings were not accompanied by Meat-offerings or Drink-offerings. See Num. xv. 3—11.

NOTE on CHAP. IV. 2.

ON SINNING THROUGH IGNORANCE.

This verse defines the kind of sin for which Sin-offerings were accepted. In the abridged rules for sin-offerings in Numbers xv. this kind of sin is contrasted with that which cut off the perpetrator from among his people (cf. *v.* 22 with *v.* 30). The two classes are distinguished in the language of our Bible as sin through ignorance and presumptuous sin. The distinction is clearly recognized Ps. xix. 12, 13 and Heb. x. 26, 27. It seems evident that the classification thus indicated refers immediately to the relation of the conscience to God, not to outward penalties, nor, immediately, to outward actions. The presumptuous sinner, literally he who sinned "with a high hand," might or might not have committed such a crime as to incur punishment from the civil law: it was enough that he had with deliberate purpose, rebelled against God (see Prov. ii. 13—15), and *ipso facto* was "cut off from among his people" and alienated from the divine covenant (see on Ex. xxxi. 14; Lev. vii. 20; cf. Matt. xii. 31; 1 Joh. v. 16). But the other kind of sin, that for which the Sin-offering was appointed, was of a more complicated nature. It appears to have included the entire range of "sins, negligences and ignorances" for which we are accustomed to ask forgiveness. It is what the Psalmist spoke of, "Who can understand his errors? Cleanse thou me from secret faults." When he examined his heart, he found his offences multiply to such extent that he felt them to be beyond calculation, and so prayed to be cleansed from those which were concealed not only from others, but from himself. It was not the outward form of the offence which determined the class to which it belonged. It might have been merely an indulgence of sinful thought. Or, on the other hand, it might have been a gross offence in its external aspect (see v. 1, 4, vi. 2, 3, 5); but if it was not clearly premeditated as a sin, if the offender now felt himself amenable to Jehovah and recognized the Covenant, becoming thereby the more conscious of his sin, he might bring the symbol of his repentance to the Altar, and the priest was to make atonement for him.

If we accept this view, the designation of "sin through ignorance" cannot be the right one. The Hebrew word rendered in our version "ignorance" comes from a root which signifies to err or go astray (see Ps. cxix. 67) (שׁגג, *shāgag*). The substantive is rendered error, Eccles. v. 6, x. 5, and used with a preposition, as an adverb, unawares, Num. xxxv. 11, 15; Josh. xx. 3, 9; it seems strictly to denote inadvertence. It is true that the writer of the Ep. to the Hebrews has ἀγνόημα in the same sense (Heb. ix. 7). But ἀγνόημα and ἄγνοια are used in Hellenistic Greek not merely to denote sins of ignorance but as general words for offences. (LXX. Gen. xxvi. 10; 2 Chro. xxviii. 15; Lev. xxii. 14. See Schl. 'Lex. in LXX.' Schweighæuser, 'Lex. Polyb.') The rendering, *through inadvertence*, would substantially agree with most of the versions ancient and modern. The LXX. have ἀκουσίως: the old Italic has *imprudenter*. Our translators followed the Vulgate and Onkelos.

It should however be observed that Sin-offerings were required not only when the conscience accused the offender of having yielded to temptation, but sometimes for what were breaches of the Law committed strictly in ignorance (v. 17, iv. 14, 23, 28), and sometimes on account of ceremonial pollution. They are thus to be regarded as protests against everything which is opposed to the holiness and purity of the divine Law. They were, in short, to be offered by the worshipper as a relief to the conscience whenever he felt the need of atonement.

The notion of Ebrard (on Heb. *v.* 1—10), and others, that the priest had to decide whether each particular case which came before him was one for which a Sin-offering was available, seems to be quite hostile to the idea of the Mosaic ritual and to what we know of the functions of the priesthood.

CHAPTER V.

1 *He that sinneth in concealing his knowledge*, 2 *in touching an unclean thing*, 4 *or in making an oath*. 6 *His trespass offering, of the flock*, 7 *of fowls*, 11 *or of flour*. 14 *The trespass offering in sacrilege*, 17 *and in sins of ignorance*.

AND if a soul sin, and hear the
voice of swearing, and *is* a witness, whether he hath seen or known *of it;* if he do not utter *it*, then he shall bear his iniquity.
2 Or if a soul touch any unclean
thing, whether *it be* a carcase of an unclean beast, or a carcase of unclean cattle, or the carcase of unclean creeping things, and *if* it be hidden from him; he also shall be unclean, and guilty.
3 Or if he touch the uncleanness
of man, whatsoever uncleanness *it be* that a man shall be defiled withal, and it be hid from him; when he knoweth *of it*, then he shall be guilty.

CHAP. V. 1—13] The subject of the Sin-offering is continued in this chapter to *v.* 14. See on *vv.* 6, 7. Special occasions are mentioned on which Sin-offerings are to be made with a particular confession of the offence for which atonement is sought (*v.* 5). These Sin-offerings are thus brought into a class clearly distinguished by this additional form from those prescribed in the preceding chapter.

1. *hear the voice of swearing*] Rather, "hear the voice **of adjuration**." The case appears to be that of one who has been put upon his oath as a witness by a magistrate and fails to utter all he has seen and heard (cf. Prov. xxix. 24; Numb. v. 21; Matt. xxvi. 63). The fabrication of what is false in giving evidence is not here mentioned (see Deut. xix. 16—19).

2, 3. Cases of ceremonial uncleanness.—If a person took immediate notice of his pollution from either of these sources, simple forms of purification were provided for him. Lev. xi. 24, 25, 28, 39, 40, xv. 5, 8, 21; Num. xix. 11, 22. But if the thing was "hid from him," either through forgetfulness or indifference, so that purification had been neglected, a Sin-offering was required. There had of course in such a case been a guilty negligence. But on the essential connection between impurity and the Sin-offering, see Note after ch. xv.

4 Or if a soul swear, pronouncing with *his* lips to do evil, or to do good, whatsoever *it be* that a man shall pronounce with an oath, and it be hid from him; when he knoweth *of it*, then he shall be guilty in one of these.

5 And it shall be, when he shall be guilty in one of these *things*, that he shall confess that he hath sinned in that *thing*:

6 And he shall bring his trespass offering unto the LORD for his sin which he hath sinned, a female from the flock, a lamb or a kid of the goats, for a sin offering; and the priest shall make an atonement for him concerning his sin.

7 And if † he be not able to bring a lamb, then he shall bring for his trespass, which he hath committed, two turtledoves, or two young pigeons, unto the LORD; one for a sin offering, and the other for a burnt offering.

† Heb. *his hand cannot reach to the sufficiency of a lamb.*

8 And he shall bring them unto the priest, who shall offer *that* which *is* for the sin offering first, and [a] wring off his head from his neck, but shall not divide *it* asunder:

[a] chap. i. 15.

9 And he shall sprinkle of the blood of the sin offering upon the side of the altar; and the rest of the blood shall be wrung out at the bottom of the altar: it *is* a sin offering.

10 And he shall offer the second *for* a burnt offering, according to the ‖ manner: and the priest shall make an atonement for him for his sin which he hath sinned, and it shall be forgiven him.

‖ Or, *ordinance.*

11 ¶ But if he be not able to bring two turtledoves, or two young pigeons, then he that sinned shall bring for his offering the tenth part of an ephah of fine flour for a sin offering; he shall put no oil upon it, neither shall he put *any* frankincense thereon: for it *is* a sin offering.

12 Then shall he bring it to the priest, and the priest shall take his handful of it, [b] *even* a memorial thereof, and burn *it* on the altar, [c] according to the offerings made by fire unto the LORD: it *is* a sin offering.

[b] chap. 2. 2.
[c] chap. 4. 35.

13 And the priest shall make an atonement for him as touching his sin that he hath sinned in one of these,

---

4. The case of rash or forgotten oaths.—

pronouncing] Rather **idly speaking** (Ps. cvi. 33). The reference is to an oath to do something uttered in recklessness or passion and forgotten as soon as uttered.

5. The confession of the particular offence here spoken of appears to be no part of the sacrificial ceremony. Cf. Num. v. 6, 7. It is not therefore to be confounded with the general prayer or confession which, according to Jewish tradition, accompanied the imposition of hands on the head of the victim. See Introd. § v.

6. *his trespass-offering*] Rather, **as his forfeit**, that is, whatever is due for his offence. In it's old use, *forfeit* seems to have answered exactly to the Heb. *āshām*, meaning either an offence, or the penalty for an offence. See the quotations in Richardson's Dict. The word *āshām* is generally translated Trespass-offering, and that rendering might have conveyed the sense here had not the term Trespass-offering become the current designation for a distinct kind of Sin-offering mentioned in the next section (see on *v.* 14).

a lamb or a kid of the goats] **a sheep** (iv. 32) **or a shaggy she-goat** (iv. 23).

7—10. See i. 14—16, xii. 8. In the larger offerings of the ox and the sheep, the fat which was burnt upon the Altar represented, like the Burnt-offering, the dedication of the worshipper; in this case, the same meaning was conveyed by one of the birds being treated as a distinct Burnt-offering (See Introd. § xvi.). According to Josephus ('Ant.' III. 9. § 3) and the Mishna ('Zebach,' VI. 4) the body of the bird for the Sin-offering was eaten by the priests, like the flesh of the larger Sin-offerings.

7. *a lamb*] **one of the flock**, either a sheep or a goat. See Introd. § iv.

for his trespass, which he hath committed] **as his forfeit for the sin he hath committed.**

11. *tenth part of an ephah*] *i.e.* "the tenth deal;" probably less than half a gallon. See on xix. 36. This Sin-offering of meal was distinguished from the ordinary Minchah by the absence of oil and frankincense. Cf. the absence of the Meat- and Drink-offerings in the animal Sin-offerings.

12. *according to the offerings made by fire*] Rather, **upon the Burnt-offerings.** See on Lev. iii. 5.

and it shall be forgiven him: and *the*
remnant shall be the priest's, as a meat
offering.
14 ¶ And the LORD spake unto
Moses, saying,
15 If a soul commit a trespass, and
sin through ignorance, in the holy
things of the LORD; then he shall
bring for his trespass unto the LORD
a ram without blemish out of the
flocks, with thy estimation by shekels
of silver, after the shekel of the sanctuary, for a trespass offering:
16 And he shall make amends for
the harm that he hath done in the
holy thing, and shall add the fifth part
thereto, and give it unto the priest:
and the priest shall make an atonement for him with the ram of the
trespass offering, and it shall be forgiven him.
17 ¶ And if a [d]soul sin, and commit any of these things which are forbidden to be done by the commandments of the LORD; though he wist
it not, yet is he guilty, and shall bear
his iniquity.
18 And he shall bring a ram without blemish out of the flock, with thy
estimation, for a trespass offering, unto
the priest: and the priest shall make
an atonement for him concerning his
ignorance wherein he erred and wist
it not, and it shall be forgiven him.
19 It *is* a trespass offering: he hath
certainly trespassed against the LORD.

[d] chap. 4. 2.

CHAPTER VI.

1 The trespass offering for sins done wittingly. 8 The law of the burnt offering, 14 and of the meat offering. 19 The offering at the consecration of a priest. 24 The law of the sin offering.

AND the LORD spake unto Moses,
saying,
2 If a soul sin, and commit a
trespass against the LORD, and lie

THE TRESPASS-OFFERINGS.

v. 14.—vi. 7.

14. The Trespass-offerings as they are described in this section and in vii. 1—7, are clearly distinguished from the ordinary Sin-offerings in these particulars:—

(1) They were offered on account of offences which involved an injury to some person (it might be the LORD Himself) in respect to property. See *v.* 16, vi. 4, 5.

(2) They were always accompanied by a pecuniary fine equal to the value of the injury done, with the addition of one-fifth. It has hence been proposed that they should be called "Fine-offerings." Cf. Num. v. 5—8.

(3) The treatment of the blood was more simple. It was disposed of in the same way as the blood of the Burnt-offerings and the Peace-offerings, none of it being put on the horns of the Altar.

(4) The victim was a ram, instead of a female sheep or goat.

(5) There was no such graduation of offerings to suit the rank or circumstances of the worshipper as is set forth iv. 3—35, v. 7—13, xii. 8, xiv. 21, 22.

It appears from the treatment of the blood that the Trespass-offering had less intimate connection with the conscience than the Sin-offering; and, from the absence of any graduation to suit the circumstances of the sacrificer, that it was regarded with a strict reference to the material injury inflicted. See on iv. 3.

15. *commit a trespass*] Rather, **perpetrate a wrong.** The word (*ma'al*) is different from that rendered trespass elsewhere in these chapters (*āshām*).

through ignorance] **through inadvertence.** See Note on iv. 2.

in the holy things of the LORD] The reference is to a failure in the payment of first-fruits, tithes or fees of any kind connected with the public service of religion by which the Sanctuary suffered loss; cf. Num. v. 6—8.

shekel of the sanctuary] See on Exod. xxxviii. 24.

17, 18. It has been conjectured that the Law of the Trespass-offering was first laid down in regard to frauds on the Sanctuary. It is here expanded so as to include all wrongs which could be compensated for by money. On the form of the law cf. iv. 2, 13, 27.

17. *these things*] It should be "**the** things."

though he wist it not] Ignorance of the Law, or even of the consequences of the act at the time it was committed, was not to excuse him from the obligation to offer the sacrifice.

18. *his ignorance*] **his inadvertence.**

CHAP. VI. **1.** In the Hebrew Bible *vv.* 1—7 form part of Ch. v. It is evident that they ought to do so. See on *v.* 7. Our translators unfortunately adopted the division of the LXX. Cf. on vii. 1.

2. *commit a trespass against the LORD*] **perpetrate a wrong against Jehovah.**

unto his neighbour in that which was delivered him to keep, or ‖ in † fellowship, or in a thing taken away by violence, or hath deceived his neighbour;

‖ Or, *in dealing.* † Heb. *putting of the hand.*

3 Or have found that which was lost, and lieth concerning it, and [a] sweareth falsely; in any of all these that a man doeth, sinning therein:

[a] Numb. 5. 6.

4 Then it shall be, because he hath sinned, and is guilty, that he shall restore that which he took violently away, or the thing which he hath deceitfully gotten, or that which was delivered him to keep, or the lost thing which he found,

5 Or all that about which he hath sworn falsely; he shall even [b] restore it in the principal, and shall add the fifth part more thereto, *and* give it unto him to whom it appertaineth, ‖ in the day of his trespass offering.

[b] chap. 5. 16. ‖ Or, *in the day of his being found guilty.* Heb. *in the day of his trespass.*

6 And he shall bring his trespass offering unto the LORD, a ram without blemish out of the [c] flock, with thy estimation, for a trespass offering, unto the priest:

[c] chap. 5. 15.

7 And the priest shall make an atonement for him before the LORD: and it shall be forgiven him for any thing of all that he hath done in trespassing therein.

8 ¶ And the LORD spake unto Moses, saying,

9 Command Aaron and his sons, saying, This *is* the law of the burnt offering: It *is* the burnt offering, ‖ because of the burning upon the altar all night unto the morning, and the fire of the altar shall be burning in it.

‖ Or, *for the burning.*

10 And the priest shall put on his linen garment, and his linen breeches shall he put upon his flesh, and take up the ashes which the fire hath consumed with the burnt offering on the altar, and he shall put them beside the altar.

See on v. 15. The law expressed in its most compendious way in v. 17 is here carried out into detail. The distinct heading, "And the Lord spake" (*v.* 1), may suggest that it was written down somewhat later by way of explanation, or comment on v. 17, and inserted in its right place when the book of Leviticus was put together. The connection into which the offences named are here brought, placed the mulct which the civil law would have exacted (see Exod. xxii. 7—15, &c.) in direct relation with sacrificial devotion to Jehovah.

5. *in the day of his trespass offering*] The restitution was thus to be associated with the religious act by which the offender testified his penitence.

7. This is the proper conclusion of ch. v. See on *v.* 1.

The confusion which prevailed amongst the older critics regarding the distinction between the Trespass-offering and the ordinary Sin-offering was without doubt connected with the false division of the chapters in the LXX. and other versions. It was imagined that ch. v. 1—13 (which relates to the Sin-offering) related to the Trespass-offering. Neither Jewish traditions, nor the rendering of the old versions, throw much light on the subject. Josephus ('Ant.' III. 9. § 3), and Philo ('de Vict.' XI.) conceive that the Sin-offering was offered for open transgressions, the Trespass-offering for what was known only to the conscience of the offender: this view has been adopted by Reland and others. Many have supposed, with some countenance from the LXX., that the distinction was based upon that between sins of omission and sins of commission (Grotius, Michaelis, &c.). For the best views of the old state of the controversy, see Carpzov. "App. Crit." p. 707, Bähr, 'Symbolik,' II. p. 400.

INSTRUCTIONS ON THE OFFERINGS FOR THE PRIESTS. vi. 8—vii. 21.

9. *Command Aaron and his sons*] The Directions on sacrifices in previous chapters were intended for the guidance and instruction of those who brought their gifts to the Altar (see i. 2, IV. 2); those which follow were for the guidance of the priests who officiated at the Altar.

On the Burnt-offering and the Meat-offering. 8—18.

9. *It is the burnt offering, because of the burning upon the altar*, &c.] Rather, "**This, the Burnt-offering, shall be upon the fire on the Altar** all night unto the morning." This refers to the continual Burnt-offering which represented its class. See Exod. xxix. 38—46, with the notes. Introd. § xvi.

10. *linen garment*, &c.] See Ex. xxviii. 41—43.

which the fire hath consumed with the burnt-

11 And he shall put off his garments, and put on other garments, and carry forth the ashes without the camp unto a clean place.

12 And the fire upon the altar shall be burning in it; it shall not be put out: and the priest shall burn wood on it every morning, and lay the burnt offering in order upon it; and he shall burn thereon the fat of the peace offerings.

13 The fire shall ever be burning upon the altar; it shall never go out.

[d] chap. 2. 1. Numb. 15. 4.

14 ¶ [d] And this *is* the law of the meat offering: the sons of Aaron shall offer it before the LORD, before the altar.

15 And he shall take of it his handful, of the flour of the meat offering, and of the oil thereof, and all the frankincense which *is* upon the meat offering, and shall burn *it* upon the altar *for* a sweet savour, *even* the [e] memorial of it, unto the LORD.

[e] chap. 2. 9.

16 And the remainder thereof shall Aaron and his sons eat: with unleavened bread shall it be eaten in the holy place; in the court of the tabernacle of the congregation they shall eat it.

17 It shall not be baken with leaven. I have given it *unto them for* their portion of my offerings made by fire; it *is* most holy, as *is* the sin offering, and as the trespass offering.

18 All the males among the children of Aaron shall eat of it. *It shall be* a statute for ever in your generations concerning the offerings of the LORD made by fire: [f] every one that toucheth them shall be holy.

[f] Exod. 29. 37.

19 ¶ And the LORD spake unto Moses, saying,

20 This *is* the offering of Aaron and of his sons, which they shall offer unto the LORD in the day when he is anointed; the tenth part of an [g] ephah of fine flour for a meat offering perpetual, half of it in the morning, and half thereof at night.

[g] Exod. 16. 36.

21 In a pan it shall be made with oil; *and when it is* baken, thou shalt bring it in: *and* the baken pieces of the meat offering shalt thou offer *for* a sweet savour unto the LORD.

22 And the priest of his sons that

---

offering] Rather, **to which the fire hath consumed the Burnt-offering.**

beside the altar] See on i. 16.

11. *clean place*] See iv. 12.

12. *burn thereon the fat*] The verb is different from that applied to the burning of the wood. See i. 9.

13. *The fire shall ever be burning*] This was a symbol of the never-ceasing worship which Jehovah required of His people. It was essentially connected with their acts of sacrifice, and was therefore clearly distinguished from the sacred fire of Vesta, that of the Persians, and of other heathen peoples with which it has often been compared.

14—18. These directions might relate to Minchahs in general. See ii. 1—10. But some would refer them more especially to the daily Minchahs mentioned Ex. xxix. 40, 41.

15. Cf. ii. 2.

16. *with unleavened bread it shall be eaten*] This should be, **it shall be eaten unleavened.**

in the holy place] See Note after Ex. xxvi. § v.

18. *All the males*] See xxi. 22.

The High-Priest's Minchah. 19—23.

20. *in the day when he is anointed*] See on iv. 3. As this must refer to a rite in the consecration of the High-priest, Aaron's sons here spoken of (as in *v.* 22) must be the succession of High-priests who succeeded him. See on Ex. xxviii. 4. The day of this offering was probably the eighth day of the ceremony of consecration (viii. 35, ix. 1), when the High-priest appears to have entered upon the duties of his office.

a meat offering perpetual] Jewish tradition is in favour of these words implying that this Minchah was offered by the High-priest as a daily rite from the time of his consecration (Philo, 'de Vict.' 15; Jos. 'Ant.' III. 10. § 7, Ecclus. xlv. 14; Saadia, Mishna, 'Menach,' IV. 5, xi. 3). This view is defended on probable grounds by Delitzsch (on Heb. vii. 27), Kurtz and others. But some understand the word *perpetual* to refer to the observance of the law at every time of consecration, and suppose the ceremony to have been performed but once by each High-priest. Knobel, Kiel, Kalisch.

21. *In a pan*] Rather, **Upon a flat plate.** See on ii. 5.

is anointed in his stead shall offer it:
it is a statute for ever unto the LORD;
it shall be wholly burnt.
23 For every meat offering for the
priest shall be wholly burnt: it shall
not be eaten.
24 ¶ And the LORD spake unto
Moses, saying,
25 Speak unto Aaron and to his
sons, saying, This *is* the law of the
sin offering: In the place where the
burnt offering is killed shall the sin
offering be killed before the LORD: it
is most holy.
26 The priest that offereth it for sin
shall eat it: in the holy place shall it
be eaten, in the court of the tabernacle of the congregation.
27 Whatsoever shall touch the flesh
thereof shall be holy: and when there
is sprinkled of the blood thereof upon
any garment, thou shalt wash that
whereon it was sprinkled in the holy
place.
28 But the earthen vessel where-
in it is sodden [h] shall be broken: and [h] chap. 11. 33.
if it be sodden in a brasen pot, it
shall be both scoured, and rinsed in
water.
29 All the males among the priests
shall eat thereof: it *is* most holy.
30 [i] And no sin offering, whereof [i] Heb. 13. 11
any of the blood is brought into the
tabernacle of the congregation to reconcile *withal* in the holy *place*, shall
be eaten: it shall be burnt in the fire.

CHAPTER VII.

1 *The law of the trespass offering,* 11 *and of the peace offerings,* 12 *whether it be for a thanksgiving,* 16 *or a vow, or a freewill offering.* 22 *The fat,* 26 *and the blood, are forbidden.* 28 *The priests' portion in the peace offerings.*

LIKEWISE this *is* the law of the
trespass offering: it *is* most holy.

---

22. *it shall be wholly burnt*] Literally, *it shall ascend in fire as a whole Burnt-offering.* The noun is *kāleel.* See Introd. § iii.

23. *it shall not be eaten*] Cf. *v.* 30. No sacrificer could eat of his own offering except in the case of the Peace-offerings. See on iv. 12.

On the Sin-Offering. 24—30.

25. *Where the burnt offering is killed*] See on i. 11.

it is most holy] On this phrase see ii. 3. Much has been written on the grounds of the peculiar sanctity of the flesh of the Sin-offering, as set forth in *vv.* 26—30. The key to the subject must, it would seem, be found in those words of Moses to the priests, in which he tells them that God required them to eat the flesh, in order that they might "bear the iniquity of the congregation, to make atonement for them before the Lord" (Lev. x. 17). The flesh of the victim, which represented the sinner for whom atonement was now made, was to be solemnly, and most exclusively, appropriated by those who were appointed to mediate between the sinner and the Lord. The far-reaching symbolism of the act met its perfect fulfilment in the One Mediator who took our nature upon Himself and was essentially "victima sacerdotii sui, et sacerdos suæ victimæ" (S. Paulinus). For a fuller treatment of the subject, see Thomson, 'Bampton Lectures,' Lect. III.; Hengstenberg, 'Sacrifices of Holy Scripture,' p. 379; Kurtz, 'Sacrificial Worship,' p. 239; Bähr, 'Symbolik,' Vol. I. p. 386.

28. *the earthen vessel*] Unglazed pottery would absorb some of the juices of the meat: cf. xi. 33, 35, where the case is of a vessel polluted, not, as here, of one made holy. In neither case could the vessel be put to any other purpose.

30. This refers to the Sin-offering for the High-priest and the Congregation (iv. 5—7, 16—18) and the Sin-offering of the Day of Atonement (xvi. 27). The priests were of course participants in all these as sacrificers. The law mentioned in the note on *v.* 23 would therefore apply here. Cf. Heb. xiii. 11.

to reconcile withal] The same word is generally rendered "to make atonement for."

the holy place] This denotes here the outer apartment of the Mishkan. See Ex. xxvi. 33; note on Lev. x. 18.

Instructions for the Priests continued. vii. 1—21.

CHAP. VII. 1—10. In the LXX. these verses are part of Chap. vi. This is evidently the better arrangement. Our Bible follows the Hebrew here, and the LXX. in the commencement of Chap. vi. (see on vi. 1), in both cases for the worse.

On the Trespass-offering. 1—7.

1. *Likewise*] Rather, **And**, as in *v.* 11. The law of the Trespass-offering is here placed as co-ordinate with that of the Sin-offering (vi. 25—30) and that of the Peace-offerings (vii. 11—21).

it is most holy] Cf. *v.* 7, and see on vi. 25.

2 In the place where they kill the
burnt offering shall they kill the trespass offering: and the blood thereof
shall he sprinkle round about upon
the altar.
3 And he shall offer of it all the
fat thereof; the rump, and the fat
that covereth the inwards,
4 And the two kidneys, and the
fat that *is* on them, which *is* by the
flanks, and the caul *that is* above
the liver, with the kidneys, it shall he
take away:
5 And the priest shall burn them
upon the altar *for* an offering made
by fire unto the LORD: it *is* a trespass offering.
6 Every male among the priests
shall eat thereof: it shall be eaten in
the holy place: it *is* most holy.
7 As the sin offering *is*, so *is* the
trespass offering: *there is* one law for
them: the priest that maketh atonement therewith shall have *it*.
8 And the priest that offereth any
man's burnt offering, *even* the priest
shall have to himself the skin of the
burnt offering which he hath offered.
9 And all the meat offering that
is baken in the oven, and all that
is dressed in the fryingpan, and ‖ in
the pan, shall be the priest's that of- ‖ Or, *on the flat plate*, or, *slice*.
fereth it.
10 And every meat offering, mingled with oil, and dry, shall all the
sons of Aaron have, one *as much* as
another.
11 And this *is* the law of the sacrifice of peace offerings, which he
shall offer unto the LORD.
12 If he offer it for a thanksgiving, then he shall offer with the
sacrifice of thanksgiving unleavened
cakes mingled with oil, and unleavened wafers anointed with oil, and
cakes mingled with oil, of fine flour,
fried.
13 Besides the cakes, he shall offer
for his offering leavened bread with
the sacrifice of thanksgiving of his
peace offerings.
14 And of it he shall offer one out

2—7. See on v. 14. In *v.* 2 "sprinkle" should rather be **cast**. Introd. § vi. There is no mention here of the placing the hands on the head of the victim, but it is not likely (as Knobel and others have conjectured) that that rite was omitted. We may infer that such a point of difference between this and the Sin-offering, had it existed, would have been expressly mentioned.—Cf. on i. 10. It is worthy of remark that all the details regarding the parts put on the Altar are repeated for each kind of sacrifice, because the matter was one of paramount importance. See Introd. § xvi.

On the Burnt-offering and the Meat-offering.

8—10.

8. *the skin of the burnt-offering*] It is most likely that the skins of the Sin-offering and the Trespass-offering also fell to the lot of the officiating priest. The point is probably noticed in regard to the Burnt-offering alone, because all the rest of the victim was consigned to the Altar. In accordance with this view the Mishna says that the skins of the most holy victims were all given to the priests, those of the less holy (*i. e.* the Peace-offerings) were retained by the sacrificer. ('Zebach,' XII. 3).

9, 10. All that was left of every sort of Minchah after the offering of the *azkārāh* (ii. 2) belonged to the priests. But the remains of those that were baked or fried (see on ii. 4, 5, 7) belonged to the officiating priest, those of the others to the priests in general.

On the Peace-offerings.

11—21.

11. On the mode of offering the victim, see iii. 1—17. On the omission of the place of slaughter, as compared with vi. 25, vii. 2, see on iii. 2.—What is here added, relates to the accompanying Minchah, the classification of Peace-offerings into (1) Thank-offerings, (2) Vow-offerings and (3) Voluntary-offerings, and the conditions to be observed by the worshipper in eating the flesh. The portions for the priests are mentioned in a distinct section, *vv.* 28—36. Cf. with this section xxii. 17—25.

12. *for a thanksgiving*] That is, a Thank-offering for mercies received. On the three kinds of Minchah which formed parts of the offering, see ii. 4—11, viii. 26.

13. *for his offering*] The leavened bread was a distinct offering, not a part of the sacrifice for the Altar as the Minchahs were, of which the *azkārāh* was burned. See ii. 2, 9, 11.

of the whole oblation *for* an heave offering unto the LORD, *and* it shall be the priest's that sprinkleth the blood of the peace offerings.

15 And the flesh of the sacrifice of his peace offerings for thanksgiving shall be eaten the same day that it is offered; he shall not leave any of it until the morning.

16 But if the sacrifice of his offering *be* a vow, or a voluntary offering, it shall be eaten the same day that he offereth his sacrifice: and on the morrow also the remainder of it shall be eaten:

17 But the remainder of the flesh of the sacrifice on the third day shall be burnt with fire.

18 And if *any* of the flesh of the sacrifice of his peace offerings be eaten at all on the third day, it shall not be accepted, neither shall it be imputed unto him that offereth it: it shall be an abomination, and the soul that eateth of it shall bear his iniquity.

19 And the flesh that toucheth any unclean *thing* shall not be eaten; it shall be burnt with fire: and as for the flesh, all that be clean shall eat thereof.

20 But the soul that eateth *of* the flesh of the sacrifice of peace offerings, that *pertain* unto the LORD, [a] having his uncleanness upon him, even that soul shall be cut off from his people.

[a] chap. 15. 3.

21 Moreover the soul that shall touch any unclean *thing*, *as* the uncleanness of man, or *any* unclean beast, or any abominable unclean *thing*, and eat of the flesh of the sacrifice of peace offerings, which *pertain* unto the LORD, even that soul shall be cut off from his people.

22 ¶ And the LORD spake unto Moses, saying,

23 Speak unto the children of Israel, saying, [b] Ye shall eat no manner of fat, of ox, or of sheep, or of goat.

[b] chap. 3. 17.

24 And the fat of the † beast that dieth of itself, and the fat of that

† Heb. *carcase*.

---

14. *out of the whole oblation*] Rather, **out of each offering.** That is, one loaf or cake out of each kind of Meat-offering was to be a heave-offering (Introd. § ix) for the officiating priest. According to Jewish tradition, there were to be ten cakes of each kind of bread in every Thank-offering. The other cakes were returned to the sacrificer. In other Meat-offerings what was not put upon the Altar belonged to the priests. See *vv.* 9, 10, ii. 3, 10.

sprinkleth] **casteth forth.**

16. The Vow-offering appears to have been a Peace-offering vowed upon a certain condition; the Voluntary-offering, one offered as the simple tribute of a devout heart rejoicing in peace with God and man offered on no external occasion (cf. xxii. 17—25). Hengstenberg would identify the latter with the Thank-offering, and thus make but two classes of Peace-offerings. But this seems to be at variance with the distinction laid down in *vv.* 15, 16. That distinction marks these two kinds as inferior to, as well as distinct from, the Thank-offering, which in xix. 5—8 is called the Peace-offering *par excellence.*

18, 19. It was proper that the sacrificial meat should not be polluted by any approach to putrefaction. But Theodoret and many later commentators have supposed that the rule in regard to the Peace-offerings was in part, at least, intended to exclude the operation of a mean-spirited economy. This may have furnished the ground for the distinction between the Thank-offerings and the others. The most liberal distribution of the meat of the offering, particularly amongst the poor who were invited to partake, would plainly be becoming when the sacrifice was intended especially to express gratitude for mercies received. (Philo, Abarbanel, &c.)

21. *unclean beast*] That is, carrion of any kind. To touch an ass or a camel when alive would not have communicated pollution. See Note after ch. xi.

shall be cut off] See on Ex. xxxi. 14. It is here used as a stronger expression than "shall bear his iniquity" (*v.* 18), which is equivalent to, shall incur guilt.

INSTRUCTIONS FOR THE PEOPLE, 22—38.

On the fat and the blood, 22—27.

23. *Speak unto the children of Israel*] This is emphatically addressed to the people. The same command is succinctly given in iii. 17. Cf. xvii. 10. The subject may be introduced here as an especial caution for those who partook of the Peace-offerings. They were not to eat in their own meal what belonged to the Altar of Jehovah, nor what was the perquisite of the priests. See *vv.* 33—36.

fat] Heb. *chēlev*, **suet.** Introd. § viii.

24. Cf. xvii. 15, xxii. 8.

which is torn with beasts, may be used
in any other use: but ye shall in no
wise eat of it.
25 For whosoever eateth the fat of
the beast, of which men offer an offering made by fire unto the LORD, even
the soul that eateth *it* shall be cut off
from his people.
c Gen. 9. 4. chap. 3. 17. & 17. 14. 26 [c] Moreover ye shall eat no manner of blood, *whether it be* of fowl or
of beast, in any of your dwellings.
27 Whatsoever soul *it be* that eateth any manner of blood, even that
soul shall be cut off from his people.
28 ¶ And the LORD spake unto
Moses, saying,
29 Speak unto the children of Israel, saying, He that offereth the sacrifice of his peace offerings unto the
LORD shall bring his oblation unto the
LORD of the sacrifice of his peace
offerings.
30 His own hands shall bring the
offerings of the LORD made by fire,
the fat with the breast, it shall he bring,
d Exod. 29. 24. that [d] the breast may be waved *for* a
wave offering before the LORD.
31 And the priest shall burn the fat
upon the altar: but the breast shall be
Aaron's and his sons'.
32 And the right shoulder shall ye
give unto the priest *for* an heave
offering of the sacrifices of your peace
offerings.
33 He among the sons of Aaron,
that offereth the blood of the peace
offerings, and the fat, shall have the
right shoulder for *his* part.
34 For the wave breast and the
heave shoulder have I taken of the
children of Israel from off the sacrifices of their peace offerings, and have
given them unto Aaron the priest and
unto his sons by a statute for ever
from among the children of Israel.
35 ¶ This *is the portion* of the anointing of Aaron, and of the anointing
of his sons, out of the offerings of the
LORD made by fire, in the day *when*
he presented them to minister unto
the LORD in the priest's office;
36 Which the LORD commanded
to be given them of the children of
Israel, in the day that he anointed
them, *by* a statute for ever throughout
their generations.
37 This *is* the law of the burnt
offering, of the meat offering, and of
the sin offering, and of the trespass
offering, and of the consecrations, and

---

25. This restriction included not merely the sacrificial fat of the animals which were actually brought to the Altar, but that of all animals of the same kinds which were slain for food, which were all to be offered before the Lord in the court. See xvii. 6. But it probably did not include the fat of animals which were eaten but not sacrificed, such as the roebuck and the hart. See on xi. 7.

26. *no manner of blood*] The prohibition of blood was more absolute and inclusive than that of fat for obvious reasons. See on Lev. xvii. 10.

On the Priests' portions of the Peace-offering. 28—34.

29, 30. He who brought a Peace-offering was, with his own hands, to present the parts destined for the Altar and for the priests. In the Sin-offering the priest appears to have taken a more active part: iv. 25, 26. Introd. xvi.

30. *a wave-offering*] See Introd. § ix.

32. *the right shoulder*] See Introd. § ix. The shoulder which was heaved, was for the officiating priest; the breast which was waved, for the priests in general and their families: *v.* 31. Cf. x. 14, 15. In Deut. xviii. 3, the shoulder, the two cheeks, and the maw are mentioned as the due of the priest, but not the breast. The Mishna ('Cholin,' x. 1) explains this apparent discrepancy by referring the law in Deuteronomy to animals slaughtered for food in the court (Lev. xvii. 3, 4), that in Leviticus to the sacrifices of the Altar.

Conclusion of the Law of the Offerings. 35—38.

35, 36. Whether this passage refers only to the wave-breast and the heave-shoulder (Knobel, Keil), or to all that belonged to the priests of the sacrifices, is not very important. The latter is the more probable. Cf. Num. xviii. 8—10.

35. *the portion of the anointing*] Rather, **the appointed share.** So Syriac, Saadia, and most modern critics. Our version follows the LXX., Vulg., Onk. So also in Num. xviii. 8.

37, 38. This is the formal conclusion of the whole section, i—vii.

37. *of the consecrations*] That is, of the

of the sacrifice of the peace offerings;

38 Which the LORD commanded
Moses in mount Sinai, in the day that
he commanded the children of Israel
to offer their oblations unto the LORD,
in the wilderness of Sinai.

CHAPTER VIII.

1 Moses consecrateth Aaron and his sons. 14 Their sin offering. 18 Their burnt offering. 22 The ram of consecrations. 31 The place and time of their consecration.

AND the LORD spake unto Moses,
saying,

2 [a]Take Aaron and his sons with
him, and the garments, and [b]the anointing oil, and a bullock for the sin
offering, and two rams, and a basket
of unleavened bread;

[a] Exod. 28. 2, 4. [b] Exod. 30. 24.

3 And gather thou all the congregation together unto the door of the
tabernacle of the congregation.

4 And Moses did as the LORD
commanded him; and the assembly
was gathered together unto the door
of the tabernacle of the congregation.

5 And Moses said unto the congre-

---

sacrifices which were to be offered in the Consecration of the priests. See Ex. xxix.

38. *wilderness of Sinai*] Cf. Ex. xix. 1, Num. i. 1 sq., xxvi. 63, 64.

THE SERVICE OF THE SANCTUARY INAUGURATED. Ch. viii. ix. x.

This is the only historical portion of the Book of Leviticus, with the exception of the short narrative of the execution of the blasphemer, xxiv. 10—23. The commandment to appoint Aaron and his sons to the priesthood, with directions for the preparation of the official dresses and for the mode of consecration, had been given in connection with the instructions respecting the construction and arrangement of the Tabernacle and its furniture, Ex. xxviii. 1—43, xxix. 1—37, xl. 9—16. But the ceremonial could not be properly carried out until the Law of the Offerings had been laid down, as it was necessary that each kind of sacrifice to be offered on the occasion should be duly defined.

THE CONSECRATION OF THE PRIESTS AND OF THE SANCTUARY AND ALTAR. viii. 1—36.

2. *a bullock...two rams...a basket*] The definite article should be placed before each of these words. **The bullock—the two rams—the basket** of unleavened bread are thus specifically mentioned in the Hebrew text as the offerings for which directions are given in Ex. xxix. 1—3. This shews the coherence of this part of Leviticus with the latter part of Exodus. The basket of unleavened bread used on this occasion appears, from *v.* 26 and Ex. xxix. 2, 3, 23, to have contained three sorts of bread; cakes or loaves of the ordinary unleavened bread; cakes of oiled bread, rather, **oil bread**, which appears to have been kneaded with oil (see Ex. xxix. 2, and note on Lev. ii. 4); and oiled wafers (see on ii. 4, 6). Rabbinical tradition says there were six cakes of each sort.

3. *gather thou all the congregation together unto the door of the tabernacle of the congregation*] **gather all the assembly together towards the entrance of the Tent of meeting** [see Note on Ex. xl. § II]. The word here rendered congregation is the same which is rendered assembly in *v.* 4. See on iv. 13. Keil and others suppose that "all the congregation" means the nation represented by its elders. But it appears that the whole body of the people were summoned on this occasion, though the elders may probably have occupied the first places. The elders are specially called together in an unequivocal manner to receive directions to provide the first sacrifices for the nation to be offered by the newly consecrated priests (ix. 1), and the body of the people afterwards assemble as they do here (ix. 5).—The spot designated was the portion of the court in front of the Tabernacle (see on i. 3). **Towards** this space the people were commanded to assemble to witness the great national ceremony of the Consecration of the priesthood, the solemn setting apart of one of their families, the members of which were henceforth to stand as mediators between them and Jehovah in carrying out the precepts of the ceremonial law. Those who could do so, may have come into the court, and a great number of others may have occupied the heights which overlooked the enclosure of the court. As the series of ceremonies was repeated every day during a week (*v.* 33), it is natural to suppose that some of the people attended on one day and some on another.

This is one of the passages which have presented a difficulty to the mind of a living writer, who strangely imagines that the ceremony was "to be performed inside the Tabernacle itself, and could only, therefore, be seen by those standing at the door." See on *v.* 33. The number who could be thus favoured at one time he calculates at not more than nine! On such ground he rejects the narrative as a fiction.

4. *unto the door*, &c.] **towards the entrance.** See the preceding note.

Exod. 29. gation, [c]This *is* the thing which the
LORD commanded to be done.
6 And Moses brought Aaron and
his sons, and washed them with water.
7 And he put upon him the coat,
and girded him with the girdle, and
clothed him with the robe, and put
the ephod upon him, and he girded
him with the curious girdle of the
ephod, and bound *it* unto him therewith.
8 And he put the breastplate upon
Exod. him: also he [d]put in the breastplate
. 30. the Urim and the Thummim.
9 And he put the mitre upon his
head; also upon the mitre, *even* upon
his forefront, did he put the golden
plate, the holy crown; as the LORD
[e]commanded Moses. [e] Exod. 28.
10 And Moses took the anointing 39, &c.
oil, and anointed the tabernacle and all
that *was* therein, and sanctified them.
11 And he sprinkled thereof upon
the altar seven times, and anointed
the altar and all his vessels, both the
laver and his foot, to sanctify them.
12 And he [f]poured of the anointing [f] Ecclus.
oil upon Aaron's head, and anointed 45. 15.
him, to sanctify him. Psal. 133. 2.
13 And Moses brought Aaron's
sons, and put coats upon them, and
girded them with girdles, and [†]put [†] Heb.
bonnets upon them; as the LORD *bound.*
commanded Moses.

---

5. *This is the thing which the* LORD *commanded to be done.*] This refers to Ex. xxviii. 1—43, xxix. 1—37, xl. 9—16.

The Cleansing, Investing and Anointing. 6—13.

6. *washed them with water*] Moses caused them to bathe entirely (cf. xvi. 4), not merely to wash their hands and feet, as they were to do in their daily ministrations. See Ex. xxx. 19. This bathing, which the High-priest had also to go through on the Day of Atonement, was symbolical of the spiritual cleansing required of all (2 Cor. vii. 1), but especially of those who had to draw near to God to make reconciliation for the sins of the people (Heb. vii. 26; Matt. iii. 15).

7—9. On the parts of the High-priest's dress, with the breastplate and the Urim and the Thummim, see notes on Exod. xxviii.

9. *the holy crown*] The golden plate of the mitre was so called as the distinctive badge of the High-priest's consecration. See xxi. 12.

10—12.] Moses first anointed with the holy oil the Tabernacle (*mishkān*, not *ohel*, see Note on Ex. xxvi. § I.) and all that was therein, that is, the Ark of the Covenant, the Table of Shewbread, the Candlestick and the Golden Altar, with all the articles that belonged to them; he then sprinkled the Altar of Burnt-offering with the oil seven times and anointed it, with all its utensils, and the Laver with its foot; last of all, he poured some of the oil on the head of Aaron, and conferred on him "the crown of the anointing oil of his God," Lev. xxi. 12. The oil is spoken of as running down upon Aaron's beard and his garments to their skirts in Ps. cxxxiii. 2.

10. On the holy anointing oil, see Ex. xxx. 23—25.

11. *sprinkled...the altar seven times*] The Altar of Burnt-offering was distinguished by this sevenfold sprinkling with the holy oil. Cf. xvi. 14, 19. The number of the Covenant was thus brought into connection with those acts of sacrifice by which the Covenant between Jehovah and the worshipper was formally renewed and confirmed.

On the symbolical use of oil, see Note after Chap. ii. As investing the priest with official garments was a recognition before men of the official position of the person (see on Ex. xxviii. 3), the anointing him with oil was an acknowledgment that all fitness for his office, all the powers with which he would rightly fulfil its duties, must come from the Lord.

In the anointing of the Sanctuary with its contents and of the Altar with its utensils the same idea evidently held its place. As Aaron was sanctified by the act, so were they sanctified (*vv.* 10, 11, 12). The pouring the oil on the head of Aaron stands in the narrative as the culmination of the ceremony of anointing. All the holy things had been made after the heavenly patterns shewed to Moses in the mount (Ex. xxv. 40, Heb. ix. 23), and each of them was intended by divine wisdom to convey a spiritual meaning to the mind of man. They were means of grace to the devout worshipper. The oil poured upon them was a recognition of this fact, and at the same time it made them holy and set them apart from all profane and ordinary uses. On kindred grounds, though to express another idea, the Altar was to be sanctified also by blood. See on *v.* 15.—With the anointing of the holy things of the Sanctuary may be compared the anointing of memorial stones. Gen. xxviii. 18, xxxv. 14.

13. *Aaron's sons*] These were the common priests. On the articles of dress, see Ex. xxviii. 40. Nothing is here, or in Ex. xxix.

g Exod. 29. 1.

14 g And he brought the bullock for the sin offering: and Aaron and his sons laid their hands upon the head of the bullock for the sin offering.

15 And he slew *it;* and Moses took the blood, and put *it* upon the horns of the altar round about with his finger, and purified the altar, and poured the blood at the bottom of the altar, and sanctified it, to make reconciliation upon it.

7—9, said of the anointing of the common priests, though it is expressly commanded, Ex. xxviii. 41, xl. 15, and is evidently implied as a fact, Lev. vii. 36, x. 7, Num. iii. 3. The simplest and best mode of explaining this appears to be to regard as the only anointing of the common priests the process described in *v.* 30, where it is said that Moses, at a later period of the ceremony of Consecration, sprinkled them, as well as Aaron himself, with the holy oil mixed with the blood of the Peace-offering. Many however would make a distinction between sprinkling with oil and anointing, and are inclined to follow the Jewish traditions, according to which the common priests were anointed immediately after their investiture, but the oil, instead of being poured upon the head as in the case of the High-priest, was only smeared on the forehead with the finger. Keil, Wordsworth, Selden, 'de Succ. in Pontif.' II. 9; Reland, 'Ant.' II. 5, 7; Carpzov. 'App. Crit.' p. 67. Some have held that the distinction lay in the fact that while each succeeding High-priest was anointed, the common priests were regarded as anointed once for all on this occasion in the persons of the immediate sons of Aaron. Outram, I. v. 7.—It is evidently assumed that the High-priest had a distinct anointing belonging peculiarly to his office in his common designation in Leviticus (see on Lev. iv. 3). But it would seem that the anointing of the common priests consisted in some rite common to them and the High-priest (Ex. xl. 15), and this can answer only to the sprinkling mentioned in *v.* 30. The same view seems to accord with a comparison of the expression regarding the High-priest, "the crown of the anointing oil of his God is upon him," Lev. xxi. 12, with that regarding the common priests, "the anointing oil of the Lord is upon you," Lev. x. 7.

The Sacrifices of Consecration.

14—36.

Moses as the mediator of the Covenant of the Law (Gal. iii. 19, Heb. viii. 6) was called to perform the priestly functions, in consecrating those on whom henceforth those functions were to devolve, and in inaugurating the legal order of sacrifices. In the same capacity he had performed the daily service of the Sanctuary from the day of the setting up of the Tabernacle and the Altar. See on Ex. xl. 23. The Sin-offering was now offered for the first time. The succession in which the sacrifices followed each other on this occasion, first the Sin-offering, then the Burnt-offering, and lastly the Peace-offering, has its ground in the meaning of each sacrifice, and became the established custom in later ages. See Introd. § xvi. But there are several points in which the mode of sacrificing the Sin-offering and the Peace-offering here described differed from the ordinary instructions of the Law. These differences were evidently designed to adapt the sacrifices to their special object as parts in the rite of Consecration.

14—17. Cf. the directions for the regular Sin-offering of the High-priest, iv. 3—12.

15. *And he slew it*] If we take this to refer to Moses he took on himself one of the duties generally performed by the sacrificer, though Aaron and his sons had pressed their hands upon the head of the victim. (See Introd. § v., cf. on *v.* 19.)

15—17. This Sin-offering was sacrificed in the usual manner as regards the blood and the fat. See iv. 25, 30, 34. But what was peculiar in it was that the flesh was not eaten, and though none of the blood was sprinkled in the Tabernacle, or put on the horns of the Altar of incense, as in the sacrifice of the Sin-offerings for the High-priest and the nation, the flesh was yet carried outside the camp to be consumed, *v.* 17. This burning does not therefore fall under the rule that "the bodies of those beasts whose blood is brought into the Sanctuary by the High-priest for sin are burned without the camp," Heb. xiii. 11; cf. Lev. x. 18. The ground of this distinction may be seen in the note on iv. 12. The flesh of the Sin-offering could not be eaten by any but a legally consecrated priest (on vi. 25). Moses therefore could not eat of it himself, though he was, for the occasion, performing the duties of a priest. Those whom he was consecrating could not eat it, not only because they were not yet duly installed, but because the sacrifice was offered on their behalf, and the body of the victim stood to them in the same relation as that of the regular Sin-offering afterwards stood to the High-priest.

15. *purified the altar...sanctified it, to make reconciliation upon it*] Atonement was thus made for the Altar itself as well as for the priests. The Altar had been sanctified by the

16 And he took all the fat that *was*
upon the inwards, and the caul *above*
the liver, and the two kidneys, and
their fat, and Moses burned *it* upon
the altar.
17 But the bullock, and his hide,
his flesh, and his dung, he burnt with
fire without the camp; as the LORD
od. 29. [h] commanded Moses.
18 ¶ And he brought the ram for
the burnt offering: and Aaron and his
sons laid their hands upon the head
of the ram.
19 And he killed *it;* and Moses
sprinkled the blood upon the altar
round about.
20 And he cut the ram into pieces;
and Moses burnt the head, and the
pieces, and the fat.
21 And he washed the inwards and
the legs in water; and Moses burnt
the whole ram upon the altar: it *was*
a burnt sacrifice for a sweet savour,
and an offering made by fire unto the
LORD; as the LORD commanded
Moses.
22 ¶ And [i]he brought the other [i] Exod. 29.
ram, the ram of consecration: and 31.
Aaron and his sons laid their hands
upon the head of the ram.
23 And he slew *it;* and Moses took
of the blood of it, and put *it* upon the
tip of Aaron's right ear, and upon the
thumb of his right hand, and upon
the great toe of his right foot.
24 And he brought Aaron's sons,
and Moses put of the blood upon the
tip of their right ear, and upon the
thumbs of their right hands, and upon the great toes of their right feet:
and Moses sprinkled the blood upon
the altar round about.

---

anointing oil (*v.* 11) like the priests who were to officiate at it; it was now, like them, sanctified by blood. The anointing with oil consecrated it for its special purpose in the service of Jehovah, but it was now anointed with blood as an acknowledgment of the alienation of all nature, in itself, from God, and the need of a reconciliation to Him of all things by blood. Col. i. 20; Heb. ix. 21, 22. See on Ex. xxviii. 38 and on Lev. xvii. 11.

16. See Introd. § viii.

17. *burnt with fire without the camp*] See on iv. 12.

18—21. Atonement having been made, Aaron and his sons were now permitted, by the laying on of their hands, to make themselves one (see Introd. § xiii.) with the victim, which was to be sent up to Jehovah as "a burnt sacrifice for a sweet savour, an offering made by fire unto the Lord." There was no peculiarity in the mode of offering this sacrifice. All was done strictly according to the ritual (i. 3—9), except that Moses performed the duties of the priest.

19. *And he killed it*] **And it was slain.** See Introd. § v. So in *v.* 23.

sprinkled, &c.] Rather, **cast upon the Altar.** See Introd. § vi.

21. *legs*] See on i. 9.

burnt] See on i. 9.

22 *the ram of consecration*] The sacrifice of this ram was by far the most peculiar part of the whole ceremony. There was something marked in the fact of the victim being a ram. An ordinary Peace-offering might be either male or female, from the herd or from the flock, iii. 1, 6. But a ram was enjoined in this case, as it was also in the Peace-offerings for the nation, ix. 4, cp. *v.* 8; for the princes of the tribes, Num. vii. 17, and for the Nazarite, Num. vi. 14, 17. It is here called "the other ram," as being the second of the two rams mentioned in *v.* 2. The words rightly translated the "ram of consecration" may be literally rendered *the ram of the fillings*, and the name has been supposed to have reference to the ceremony in which Moses fills the hands of the priests; see *v.* 27. Luther calls it the ram of the fill-offering (*Füllopfer*). But the LXX. has ὁ κριὸς τῆς τελειώσεως, the old Italic, *aries perfectionis*, and St Augustin, *sacrificium consummationis*. The renderings of the Targums, the Syriac, and Saadia all mean "the ram of completion." The offering was in the highest sense *the sacrifice of completion* or *fulfilling*, as being the central point of the consecrating rite. The final perfection of the creature is Consecration to the LORD. With the τελείωσις of the LXX. in this connection may be compared the use which the writer of the Epistle to the Hebrews makes of the derivatives of τέλος: ii. 10, v. 9, vii. 28, x. 14, xii. 23.

23, 24. Before **casting forth the blood round the Altar** in the usual manner, Moses took a portion of the blood and put some of it on the right extremities of each of the priests. This, being performed with the blood of the Peace-offering, has been supposed to figure the readiness of the priest who is at peace with Jehovah to hear with the ear and obey the divine word, to perform

25 And he took the fat, and the
rump, and all the fat that *was* upon
the inwards, and the caul *above* the
liver, and the two kidneys, and their
fat, and the right shoulder:
26 And out of the basket of unleavened bread, that *was* before the
LORD, he took one unleavened cake,
and a cake of oiled bread, and one
wafer, and put *them* on the fat, and
upon the right shoulder:
[k] Exod. 29. 24, &c. 27 And he put all [k] upon Aaron's
hands, and upon his sons' hands, and
waved them *for* a wave offering before
the LORD.
28 And Moses took them from off
their hands, and burnt *them* on the
altar upon the burnt offering: they
were consecrations for a sweet savour:
it *is* an offering made by fire unto
the LORD.
29 And Moses took the breast, and
waved it *for* a wave offering before
the LORD: *for* of the ram of con-
secration it was Moses' [l] part; as the [l] Exod. 29. 26.
LORD commanded Moses.
30 And Moses took of the anointing oil, and of the blood which *was*
upon the altar, and sprinkled *it* upon
Aaron, *and* upon his garments, and
upon his sons, and upon his sons'
garments with him; and sanctified
Aaron, *and* his garments, and his
sons, and his sons' garments with
him.
31 ¶ And Moses said unto Aaron
and to his sons, Boil the flesh *at* the
door of the tabernacle of the congre-
gation: and there [m] eat it with the [m] Exod. 29. 32.
bread that *is* in the basket of consecrations, as I commanded, saying,
Aaron and his sons shall eat it.
32 And that which remaineth of
the flesh and of the bread shall ye
burn with fire.
33 And ye shall not go out of the

---

with the hand the sacred duties of his office, and to walk with the feet in the way of holiness. Had the ceremony been, as some have supposed, a symbolical cleansing of the natural powers of the priest, it seems more likely that it would have been performed with the blood of the Sin-offering than with that of the Peace-offering. (See Introd. § xv.). In the case of the cured Leper the same parts were touched with the blood of the Trespass-offering. See Lev. xiv. 14—17.

25—28. In the rite of filling the hands of the priests, Moses took the portions of the victim which usually belonged to the Altar, with the right shoulder (or leg; see Introd. § ix.), placed upon them one cake of each of the three kinds of unleavened bread contained in the basket (see on *v.* 2), and then put the whole first upon the hands of Aaron and in succession upon the hands of his sons, in each case, according to Jewish tradition, putting his own hands under the hands of the priest, moving them backwards and forwards, so as to wave the mass to and fro. See Introd. § ix. He then offered them on the Altar as a Burnt-offering.

In this remarkable ceremony the gifts of the people appear to have been made over to the priests, as if in trust, for the service of the Altar. The articles were presented to Jehovah and solemnly waved in the hands of the priests, but not by their own act and deed. The mediator of the Law, who was expressly commissioned on this occasion, was the agent in the process.

25. *the rump*] **The fat-tail.** See on iii. 9.

26. *unleavened cake*, &c.] See on *v.* 2.

29. The heave-shoulder was the ordinary perquisite of the officiating priest (Introd. § ix.), but the wave-breast appears to have been awarded to Moses as the servant of Jehovah now especially appointed for the priestly service.

30. In the instructions for the ceremony of Consecration in Exod. xxix. the sprinkling with the mingled blood and oil is mentioned immediately after the casting forth of the blood of the Peace-offering upon the Altar. See Exod. xxix. 21. But in its practical order the ceremony of Consecration was concluded with this ceremony. Whether it was the only anointing performed on the common priests or not, see on *v.* 13. The sprinkling was on their garments as well as their persons, because it belonged to them in reference to the office with which they had been formally invested by putting on the garments. (See on Exod. xxviii. 3.) The union of the two symbols of the atoning blood and the inspiring unction appears to be a fit conclusion of the entire rite.

31, 32. The prohibitions that none but the priests must eat of the flesh (Exod. xxix. 33), and that none but unleavened bread should

door of the tabernacle of the congregation *in* seven days, until the days
of your consecration be at an end:
Exod. · 35· for [n] seven days shall he consecrate
you.

34 As he hath done this day, *so*
the LORD hath commanded to do, to
make an atonement for you.

35 Therefore shall ye abide *at* the
door of the tabernacle of the congregation day and night seven days, and
keep the charge of the LORD, that ye
die not: for so I am commanded.

36 So Aaron and his sons did all
things which the LORD commanded
by the hand of Moses.

CHAPTER IX.

1 *The first offerings of Aaron, for himself and the people.* 8 *The sin offering,* 12 *and the burnt offering for himself.* 15 *The offerings for the people.* 23 *Moses and Aaron bless the people.* 24 *Fire cometh from the Lord, upon the altar.*

AND it came to pass on the eighth
day, *that* Moses called Aaron
and his sons, and the elders of Israel;

2 And he said unto Aaron, [a] Take [a] Exod.
thee a young calf for a sin offering, 29. 1.
and a ram for a burnt offering, without blemish, and offer *them* before the
LORD.

3 And unto the children of Israel
thou shalt speak, saying, Take ye a
kid of the goats for a sin offering;
and a calf and a lamb, *both* of the first
year, without blemish, for a burnt
offering;

4 Also a bullock and a ram for
peace offerings, to sacrifice before the
LORD; and a meat offering mingled
with oil: for to day the LORD will
appear unto you.

5 ¶ And they brought *that* which
Moses commanded before the tabernacle of the congregation: and all the
congregation drew near and stood before the LORD.

6 And Moses said, This *is* the thing
which the LORD commanded that ye
should do: and the glory of the LORD
shall appear unto you.

---

be eaten with it, distinguished this from an ordinary sacrificial meal on the flesh of a Peace-offering, of which any invited guest might partake, and in which ordinary leavened bread might be eaten. See vii. 13.

33—36. The rites of Consecration were to last a whole week, and thus, like the longer of the annual festivals, were connected in an emphatic manner with the sabbatical number of the Covenant. During this period the priests were not to leave the holy precinct for the sake of any worldly business, and the whole series of ceremonies, including the sacrifice of the Ram of Consecration, was to be gone through on each day. Cf. Ex. xxix. 35, 36, 37.

33. *ye shall not go out of the door of the tabernacle*] Rather, **ye shall not go away from the entrance of the Tent.** With this agree Cranmer, the Geneva Bible, &c. The meaning is evidently that they were not to go out of the court, as is more clearly expressed in *v.* 35. The authorized version appears to have misled a recent writer (to whom reference has already been made) into the notion that the consecration was "performed inside the Tabernacle itself." See on *v.* 3.

shall he consecrate you, &c.] Rather, **shall ye be consecrated.** So Vulg., Syriac, Saadia, &c. On the original idiom, see on Ex. xxxvii. 1. Cf. *v.* 19. On the word *consecrate,* see on *v.* 22.

35. *at the door of the tabernacle*] See on *v.* 33.

that ye die not] See on Exod. xxviii. 35.

CHAP. IX.

THE PRIESTS ENTER UPON THEIR OFFICE.
ix. 1—24.

1—6. *on the eighth day*] That is, on the first day after the week of Consecration.

2. *a young calf*] Literally, *a calf, the son of a bull.* See on i. 5. The meaning is not "a young calf," but **a bull calf** which might have been what we should call a yearling ox.

3. *a kid of the goats*] **a shaggy he-goat.** See on iv. 23.

both of the first year] Literally, sons of a year. See on xii. 6. This is the only instance in which the age of *a calf* is prescribed. The age of sheep and goats for sacrifice is very commonly stated. Exod. xxix. 38; Lev. xii. 6; Num. xxviii. 3, 9, 11, &c. Introd. § iv. The clear distinction between the words *'egel = calf,* and *par = ox,* may sufficiently account for this difference in usage.

4. *mingled with oil*] Rather, **with oil poured over it.** The offering was of the sort described ii. 1, consisting of fine flour with oil and frankincense.

6. *the glory of the LORD*] Cf. Exod. xvi. 7. See *v.* 23.

7 And Moses said unto Aaron, Go
unto the altar, and offer thy sin offering, and thy burnt offering, and make
an atonement for thyself, and for the
people: and offer the offering of the
people, and make an atonement for
them; as the LORD commanded.
8 ¶ Aaron therefore went unto the
altar, and slew the calf of the sin offering, which *was* for himself.
9 And the sons of Aaron brought
the blood unto him: and he dipped
his finger in the blood, and put *it* upon
the horns of the altar, and poured
out the blood at the bottom of the
altar:
10 But the fat, and the kidneys,
and the caul above the liver of the sin
offering, he burnt upon the altar; as
the LORD commanded Moses.
11 And the flesh and the hide he
burnt with fire without the camp.
12 And he slew the burnt offering;
and Aaron's sons presented unto him
the blood, which he sprinkled round
about upon the altar.
13 And they presented the burnt
offering unto him, with the pieces
thereof, and the head: and he burnt
them upon the altar.
14 And he did wash the inwards
and the legs, and burnt *them* upon the
burnt offering on the altar.
15 ¶ And he brought the people's
offering, and took the goat, which *was*
the sin offering for the people, and

Aaron offers sacrifice for himself.
7—14.

Moses now commands Aaron first to offer the sacrifices for himself and then those for the people. It is to be remarked that Aaron offers no Peace-offering for himself. The Sin-offering and the Burnt-offering have a more strict connexion with the person of the sacrificer: the Peace-offering, with its sacrificial feast, connects him as a reconciled believer with his brethren as well as with Jehovah. It appears therefore to have been enough that he should participate in the Peace-offerings of the Consecration, viii. 31, and in the two Peace-offerings about to be sacrificed for the people.

Aaron's Sin-offering being a calf was of inferior dignity to the Sin-offering of the Consecration ceremony, which was a bullock (viii. 14), and to that which the High-priest was commanded on subsequent occasions to offer for his own sins (iv. 3). This offering was probably regarded not so much as a sacrifice for his own actual sins as a typical acknowledgment of his sinful nature and of his future duty to offer for his own sins and those of the people. Heb. v. 3, vii. 27. That this offering and the Burnt-offering had some such broad and official signification as this, seems to be shewn in the words of Moses in *v.* 7, "offer thy Sin-offering, and thy Burnt-offering, and make an atonement for thyself and for the people: and offer the offering for the people, and make an atonement for them." The Septuagint has "make an atonement for thyself and thy house," (περὶ σεαυτοῦ καὶ τοῦ οἴκου σοῦ), but the meaning of the Hebrew text is plainly in accordance with our own version. It was a striking acknowledgment of the true character of the Levitical Priesthood, that the very first official act of the anointed priest should be to offer a sacrifice for his own sinful nature. "The law maketh men High-priests which have infirmity; but the word of the oath, which was since the law, maketh the Son, who is consecrated (in the margin, *perfected*, see on viii. 22) for evermore." Heb. vii. 28.

9. Aaron did not take the blood into the Tabernacle according to the ordinary Law of the Sin-offerings for the High-priest and for the people (iv. 5, 6, 7, 16, 17, 18), but he put some of it upon the horns of the brazen Altar, as in the sacrifice of the other Sin-offerings (iv. 25, 30, 34), and as Moses had done in the Sin-offering of the Consecration ceremony, viii. 15. The probable reason of this was that he had not yet been formally introduced as the High-priest into the Holy Place of the Tabernacle. See on *v.* 23.

brought the blood] They most likely held the basons in which the blood was received as it ran from the victim, and then handed them to their father. Introd. § v.

11. See iv. 11, 12.

12—14. In offering his Burnt-sacrifice, Aaron and his sons took the same respective parts as they had done in the Sin-offering, observing the Law in all particulars, i. 3—9.

12. *sprinkled*] rather **cast**, Introd. § vi.

13. *with the pieces thereof*] Rather, **piece by piece**, literally, according to its pieces.

No Meat-offering is said to have been offered with Aaron's own Burnt-offering. The Meat-offering may however have been made as a thing of course without being mentioned, or possibly the law of Num. xv. 3, 4, may not yet have been in full force.

Aaron offers the sacrifices for the People.
15—23.

In this first complete series of offerings made by the High-priest, the sacrifices take

slew it, and offered it for sin, as the
first.
16 And he brought the burnt offering,
and offered it according to the ‖manner.
17 And he brought the meat offering, and †took an handful thereof, and
burnt *it* upon the altar, [b]beside the
burnt sacrifice of the morning.
18 He slew also the bullock and
the ram *for* a sacrifice of peace offerings, which *was* for the people: and
Aaron's sons presented unto him the
blood, which he sprinkled upon the
altar round about,
19 And the fat of the bullock and
of the ram, the rump, and that which
covereth *the inwards*, and the kidneys,
and the caul *above* the liver:
20 And they put the fat upon the
breasts, and he burnt the fat upon the
altar:
21 And the breasts and the right
shoulder Aaron waved *for* a wave
offering before the LORD; as Moses
commanded.
22 And Aaron lifted up his hand
toward the people, and blessed them,
and came down from offering of the
sin offering, and the burnt offering,
and peace offerings.
23 And Moses and Aaron went
into the tabernacle of the congregation, and came out, and blessed the
people: and the glory of the LORD
appeared unto all the people.
24 And [c]there came a fire out
from before the LORD, and consumed
upon the altar the burnt offering and
the fat: *which* when all the people
saw, they shouted, and fell on their
faces.

‖ Or, *ordinance.*
† Heb. *filled his hand out of it.*
[b] Exod. 29. 38.
[c] Gen. 4. 4. 1 Kings 18. 38. 2 Chron. 7. 1. 2 Macc. 2. 10, 11.

---

their appointed order; first, the Sin-Offering to make atonement, the Burnt-offering, to signify the surrender of the body, soul and spirit to Jehovah in heaven; and lastly the Peace-offering, to show forth the communion vouchsafed to those who are justified and sanctified. Introd. § xvi.

15. *the sin offering for the people*] In the regular Sin-offering for the people the High-priest offered also for his own sins as the head of the nation, and hence he was not allowed to eat of the flesh, which was burned without the camp (iv. 21). But on this occasion, as the priests had already offered a Sin-offering for themselves, the sacrifice was exclusively for the people, and the ordinary law should have taken effect, that they should eat the appointed portions of the victim (vi. 26). In consequence of their failing to do this, they were rebuked by Moses. (See x. 16—18.)

as the first] That is, as his own Sin-offering.

16. *according to the manner*] Rather as in the margin. He offered the Burnt-offering of the yearling calf and lamb, observing the Law in ch. i.

17. *the meat-offering*] See ii. 1, 2; vi. 14—16.

burnt sacrifice of the morning] See Ex. xxix. 39; also, Lev. iii. 5.

18. *sprinkled*] **cast**, Introd. § vi.

20. *the breasts*] *i.e.* the briskets of the bullock and the ram, vii. 30; Introd. § ix.

21. *right shoulder*] On the ceremony of waving, see Introd. § ix.

Nothing is said of the Meat-offering. See on *v.* 13.

22. Aaron having completed the offerings, before he came down from the stage surrounding the Altar on which the priests used to stand to officiate (see on Exod. xxvii. 8), turns toward the people, and blesses them; probably using the form which became the established one for the priests (Num. vi. 24—26), and which is still maintained in the synagogues (Stanley, *Jewish Church*, II. p. 419).

Aaron is inducted into the Tabernacle.
ix. 23—24.

23. Aaron, having now gone through the cycle of priestly duties connected with the Brazen Altar, accompanies Moses into the **Tent of Meeting**. It was reasonable that Moses, as the divinely appointed leader of the nation, should induct Aaron into the Tabernacle.

blessed the people] This joint blessing of the mediator of the Law and the High-priest was the solemn conclusion of the Consecration and Inauguration. (Cf. Solomon's blessing the people, 2 Chron. vi. 3—12.) According to one tradition the form used by Moses and Aaron resembled Ps. xc. 17. But another form is given in the Targum of Palestine, "May your offerings be accepted, and may the Lord dwell among you and forgive you your sins."

23—24. *the glory of the LORD appeared... there came a fire out from before the LORD*] Cf. Exod. xvi. 10, xl. 34; Num xiv. 10, xvi. 19, xx. 6; 2 Chron. vii. 1, &c. St Augustine characteristically says, "Quid dixerit, *a Domino*, quæri potest, utrum quia nutu et voluntate Domini factum est, an ab eo loco ignis exiit ubi erat arca testimonii. Non

CHAPTER X.

1 *Nadab and Abihu, for offering of strange fire, are burnt by fire.* 6 *Aaron and his sons are forbidden to mourn for them.* 8 *The priests are forbidden wine when they are to go into the tabernacle.* 12 *The law of eating the holy things.* 16 *Aaron's excuse for transgressing thereof.*

AND [a]Nadab and Abihu, the sons [a] Num. 4. & 26. 61. 1 Chron. 24. 2.
of Aaron, took either of them
his censer, and put fire therein, and
put incense thereon, and offered strange
fire before the LORD, which he commanded them not.

2 And there went out fire from the

---

enim in loco aliquo ita est Dominus, quasi alibi non sit." 'Quæst. in Lev.' xxx.

24. The very ancient Jewish tradition has been widely adopted that the sacred fire of the Altar originated in this divine act, and that it was afterwards preserved on the Altar of the Tabernacle until the dedication of the Temple, when fire again "came down from heaven, and consumed the burnt-offering and the sacrifices; and the glory of the Lord filled the house" (2 Chron. vii. 1). Some Jewish authorities allow that this sacred fire became extinct when the Babylonians sacked Jerusalem; but others say that it was miraculously kept alive during the captivity and restored to its use on the Altar of the second Temple by Nehemiah. 2 Macc. i. 19—22. See Fagius *in loc.*; Bochart, 'Hieroz.' II. 35.—But according to the sacred narrative the Altar-fire had been lighted in a natural way before this occasion. It had burned the morning and evening sacrifices (Exod. xl. 29) and the sacrifices of Consecration (Lev. viii. 16, 21, 28); and Aaron had previously employed it on this day for the offerings for himself and the people (*vv.* 10, 13, 14, 17, 20). It is evident that the fire of the morning sacrifice was burning at the time when the special sacrifices for the occasion were offered (see *v.* 17). It would therefore seem that the fire which "came out from before the Lord" manifested itself, according to the words of *v.* 24, not in kindling the fuel on the Altar, but in the sudden consuming of the victim. For the like testimony to the acceptance of a sacrifice, see Judg. vi. 21, xiii. 19, 20; 1 K. xviii. 38; 1 Chron. xxi. 26, and probably Gen. iv. 4. The phrase *to turn a sacrifice to ashes*, became equivalent to *accepting it* (Ps. xx. 3, see margin). The fire of the Altar was maintained in accordance with Lev. vi. 13,

CHAP. X.

The events recorded in this chapter must have occurred immediately after the offering of the sacrifices of inauguration, on the evening of the same day. See *v.* 19.

Nadab and Abihu are stricken: the priests are forbidden to mourn for them.

X. 1—7.

1. *Nadab and Abihu*] The two elder sons of Aaron (Exod. vi. 23, Num. iii. 2), who were amongst those invited to accompany Moses when he was going up Mount Sinai, but who were "to worship afar off," and not "come near the Lord." Exod. xxiv. 1, 2.

censer] See on Exod. xxv. 38.

strange fire] The particular offence which was perpetrated by Nadab and Abihu has been a subject of much discussion. The greater number of commentators, Jewish as well as Christian, have supposed that the "strange fire" was common fire, not taken from the holy fire of the Altar. See on ix. 24. But it should be observed that no law is found in the Pentateuch to forbid the burning of incense by means of ordinary fire: it is only for a single occasion in the year that the High-priest is commanded to fill his censer with coals from the Altar, Lev. xvi. 12. Some suppose that the offence lay in breaking the commandment of Exod. xxx. 9, and burning "strange incense," that is incense not prepared according to the instructions given in Exod. xxx. 34—38. Others have suggested that they offered incense at an unauthorized time, that is, not at either of the hours of the daily service: and this is favoured by the order of the narrative. Many have connected their sin with the prohibition of the use of wine and strong drink to those engaged in the service of the Sanctuary (see *vv.* 9, 10), and have supposed that they performed their sacred office in a state of intoxication [Targum of Palestine, de Lyra, Patrick, Rosenmüller, Herxheimer, Wordsworth]. But the outward point of their offence is evidently expressed in the term "strange fire." This may very probably mean that the incense was lighted at an unauthorized time. And we may reasonably unite with this the supposition that they were intoxicated, as well as the conjecture of Knobel's, that they made their offering of incense an accompaniment to the exultation of the people on the manifestation of the glory of the Lord, ix. 24. As they perished not within the Tabernacle, but in front of it, it seems likely that they may have been making an ostentatious and irreverent display of their ministration to accompany the shouts of the people, on their way towards the Tabernacle. The offence for which they were immediately visited with outward punishment was thus a flagrant outrage on the solemn order of the divine service, while the cause of their offence may have been their guilty excess.

before the LORD] These words might denote the whole space between the Ark of the Cove-

LORD, and devoured them, and they died before the LORD.

3 Then Moses said unto Aaron, This *is it* that the LORD spake, saying, I will be sanctified in them that come nigh me, and before all the people I will be glorified. And Aaron held his peace.

4 And Moses called Mishael and Elzaphan, the sons of Uzziel the uncle of Aaron, and said unto them, Come near, carry your brethren from before the sanctuary out of the camp.

5 So they went near, and carried them in their coats out of the camp; as Moses had said.

6 And Moses said unto Aaron, and unto Eleazar and unto Ithamar, his

---

nant and the Brazen Altar, both that within the Tabernacle and that without it. Cf. i. 5. The death of Nadab and Abihu occurred outside the Tabernacle "before the Sanctuary," *v.* 4. See the preceding note.

2. *fire from the LORD*] "The fire which had just before sanctified the ministry of Aaron as well pleasing to God, now brought to destruction his two eldest sons because they did not sanctify Jehovah in their hearts, but dared to perform a self-willed act of worship; just as the same Gospel is to one a savour of life unto life, and to another a savour of death unto death." 2 Cor. ii. 16. (Keil.) On the patristic applications of the sin of Nadab and Abihu, see especially Irenæus. 'Adv. Her.' IV. 43. Cyprian, 'de Unit. Ecc.' XVIII. Theod. 'Quæst. in Lev.' IX. Hesych. *in loc.* &c.

3. Moses now declares to Aaron the meaning of this visitation, and the father "holds his peace," not daring to gainsay the righteous judgment of Jehovah. Cf. Psalm xxxix. 9. His silence on this occasion may be compared with his reasonable and natural expostulation with Moses when his surviving sons are rebuked for not having eaten the flesh of the Sin-offering. *v.* 19.

I will be sanctified in them that come nigh me, and before all the people I will be glorified] The priests are often designated as those who draw near to the Lord (Exod. xix. 22; Num. xvi. 5; Ezek. xlii. 13; xliii. 19). If the verbs in this passage are rendered as reflexive rather than as passive it makes the connection with what had just happened more strict;—**I will sanctify myself in them that come near to me** (i.e. the priests), **and I will glorify myself before all the people.** [So de Wette, Luzzato, Keil, &c.] The Hebrew forms here used (like the kindred ones in many other languages ancient and modern) were originally reflexive, but came to be as commonly employed in a passive sense. The words used by Moses on this occasion are not found elsewhere in the Pentateuch: it has been supposed that they had been previously spoken to Moses, but that he had not committed them to writing. [St Augustin, 'Quæst. in Lev.' 31.] But the sense is implied in such passages as Exod. xix. 22, xxviii. 41, xxix. 1, 44.

4. Mishael and Elzaphan, the first cousins of Aaron (Exod. vi. 22), are selected by Moses to convey the bodies of Nadab and Abihu out of the camp, and, as we may presume, to bury them, probably because they were the nearest relations who were not priests. It has been conjectured by Blunt that they were the men who could not keep the Passover when it was observed on the 14th of Nisan at the beginning of the second year after the Exodus, because they were "defiled by the dead body of a man," and on whose account "the little Passover," to be observed on the 14th of the second month, Zif, was first instituted. Num. ix. 6. Blunt's 'Undesigned Coincidences,' I. 14.

brethren] *i.e.* near relations, as in Gen. xiii. 8, xiv. 16, xxix. 12, 15, &c.

from before the sanctuary] See on *v.* 1.

5. *coats*] The long white tunics, which were the most characteristic part of the priest's dress. See on Exod. xxviii. 40, 41. Life had been extinguished as if by a flash of lightning, but neither the bodies nor the dresses were destroyed.

6, 7. Aaron and his two surviving sons are forbidden to show the accustomed signs of mourning, or to leave the Court of the Tabernacle in order to attend the funeral, because, from their office, they were especially concerned as consecrated priests in outwardly maintaining the honour of Jehovah. They were to bear visible testimony to the righteousness of the punishment of Nadab and Abihu, lest they themselves should incur guilt by seeming personally to participate in the sin which had been committed. The claims of natural relationship were superseded by this consideration. The people, on the other hand, as not formally standing so near to Jehovah, were permitted to "bewail the burning which the Lord had kindled," as an acknowledgment that the nation had a share in the sin of its priests. (1 Cor. xii. 26.) It should be observed that the ground of the priests being forbidden to mourn on this particular occasion, appears not to be merely the same as that on which the general law was based prohibiting the High-priest from mourning even for his nearest relation, which was evidently designed to keep him entirely out of the way of defilement. See Lev. xxi. 10, 11.

sons, Uncover not your heads, neither
rend your clothes; lest ye die, and
lest wrath come upon all the people:
but let your brethren, the whole house
of Israel, bewail the burning which
the LORD hath kindled.
7 And ye shall not go out from
the door of the tabernacle of the congregation, lest ye die: for the anointing oil of the LORD *is* upon you.
And they did according to the word
of Moses.
8 ¶ And the LORD spake unto
Aaron, saying,
9 Do not drink wine nor strong
drink, thou, nor thy sons with thee,
when ye go into the tabernacle of the
congregation, lest ye die: *it shall be* a
statute for ever throughout your generations:
10 And that ye may put difference
between holy and unholy, and between
unclean and clean;
11 And that ye may teach the
children of Israel all the statutes which
the LORD hath spoken unto them by
the hand of Moses.
12 ¶ And Moses spake unto Aaron,
and unto Eleazar and unto Ithamar,
his sons that were left, Take the meat

---

6. *Uncover not your heads*] Our version follows the LXX. and Vulgate. The word rendered "uncover" signifies, *to set free—to let go loose*. It was a custom to cut off or pluck out the hair as a sign of grief (Ezra ix. 3; Job i. 20; Is. xv. 2; Jer. xli. 5, xlviii. 37), and it has been supposed that this mode of uncovering the head is what is here meant. But it was also a custom to let the hair grow long and fall loosely over the head and face (xiii. 45; 2 Sam. xv. 30, xix. 4); and this is most likely what is expressed by the Hebrew word in this connection. The weight of authority is on this side. The substance of the command would thus be that they should not let the hair go dishevelled. It is so rendered by Saadia and others.—Rending the clothes in front so as to lay open the breast was one of the commonest manifestations of grief. Gen. xxxvii. 29, xliv. 13; 2 S. i. 11; Job i. 20; Joel ii. 13, &c. &c. The garments as well as the persons of the priests were consecrated; this appears to be the reason of the prohibition of these ordinary signs of mourning. Cf. Lev. xxi. 10.

lest ye die] See on Exod. xxviii. 35.

7. *out from the door*] **away from the entrance.** See on i. 3 and viii. 33.

the anointing oil...is upon you] See viii. 30. The holy oil, "the oil of gladness," Ps. xlv. 7, Heb. i. 9, as the symbol of the Holy Spirit, the Spirit of Life and immortality and joy, was the sign of the priests being brought near to Jehovah. See Note after ch. ii. It was therefore in its meaning connected both with the ground of the general law which forbad the High-priest ever to put on signs of mourning on account of death (xxi. 10—12), and with the more special reason for the prohibition on this occasion.

The priests are forbidden to drink wine, when officiating. x. 8—11.

9—11. This restraint is to be understood as relating to the entire cycle of priestly functions. When the priest was on duty he was to abstain from wine and strong drink, lest he should commit excess and so become disqualified for carrying out the precepts of the ceremonial Law.

9. *strong drink*] Heb. *shekār*, LXX. σίκερα (Luke i. 15). The Hebrew word is used as a general name for intoxicating drinks, including wine, Num. xxviii. 7. But it is more frequently employed as it is here, to denote strong drinks of any kind (the *vina ficticia* of Pliny) except wine made from the grape. St Jerome says that the Hebrews applied the name *shekār* to any drink prepared from wheat, barley (like the beer of the Egyptians, Herod. II. 77; Diod. I. 20), millet, the juice of apples, or dates. Hieron. in Is. xxviii. 7; Pliny, 'H. N.' xiv. 19.

lest ye die] See *v.* 6.

10. The Hebrew word rendered "holy" (*kodesh*) has no etymological relation to that rendered "unholy" (*chol*). The first denotes what is consecrated to the service of the Sanctuary, the latter, all which is not so consecrated and should therefore be called **common** rather than "unholy."

unclean] That is, what occasions defilement by being touched or eaten. All else is reckoned as *clean*. Cf. Acts x. 14.

11. That is, "that you may, by your example in your ministrations, preserve the minds of the Israelites from confusion in regard to the distinctions made by the divine Law."

The priests' share in the Meat-offerings and Peace-offerings. 12—15.

12—15. Moses now reminds the priests of the laws regarding the portions of the offerings which were awarded to them (vi. 16 18, 26, 29, &c.), probably in the way of warning in connection with what had just happened. This connection is the more plain, if we suppose that Nadab and Abihu had

offering that remaineth of the offerings
of the LORD made by fire, and eat it
without leaven beside the altar: for it
is most holy:
13 And ye shall eat it in the holy
place, because it *is* thy due, and thy
sons' due, of the sacrifices of the
LORD made by fire: for so I am commanded.
[b] Exod. 29. 24. 14 And [b]the wave breast and heave
shoulder shall ye eat in a clean place;
thou, and thy sons, and thy daughters
with thee: for *they be* thy due, and
thy sons' due, *which* are given out of
the sacrifices of peace offerings of the
children of Israel.
15 The heave shoulder and the
wave breast shall they bring with the
offerings made by fire of the fat, to
wave *it for* a wave offering before the
LORD; and it shall be thine, and thy
sons' with thee, by a statute for ever;
as the LORD hath commanded.
16 ¶ And Moses diligently sought
the goat of the sin offering, and, behold, it was burnt: and he was angry
with Eleazar and Ithamar, the sons of
Aaron *which were* left *alive*, saying,
17 Wherefore have ye not eaten
the sin offering in the holy place, seeing
it *is* most holy, and *God* hath given it
you to bear the iniquity of the congregation, to make atonement for them
before the LORD?
18 Behold, the blood of it was not
brought in within the holy *place:* ye
should indeed have eaten it in the holy
place, [c]as I commanded. [c] chap. 6. 26.

---

indulged to excess in the Drink-offerings (see on *v.* 1). The argument would thus be, that as such meals were appointed in honour of Jehovah Himself, they ought to be conducted with due reverence and discretion.

12. *the meat-offering that remaineth*] See ii. 3.

beside the altar] What is called "the holy place" in *v.* 13: it should be rather, **a holy place**, any part of the holy precinct, as distinguished from a merely "clean place" (*v.* 14), either within or without the court of the Tabernacle. Cf. on *v.* 17.

most holy] See on ii. 3.

14. *wave breast and heave shoulder*] Introd. § ix.

thy sons and thy daughters] The priests' portions of the Peace-offerings were *holy*, but not *most holy*, and any member of their families, either male or female, might partake of them.

15. *wave offering*] Introd. § ix.

The Priests rebuked on account of the flesh of the Sin-offering. 16—20.

The Law had expressly commanded that the flesh of those Sin-offerings the blood of which was not carried into the Sanctuary should belong to the priests, and that it should be eaten by them alone in a holy place. See on ii. 3. The Sin-offerings of which the blood was carried into the Sanctuary were those for the High-priest and for the people, iv. 5, 16. But on this occasion, though the Sin-offering which had been offered by Aaron was for the people (ix. 15), its blood was not carried into the Tabernacle. See ix. 9, x. 18. The priests might therefore have too readily supposed that their eating the flesh, or burning it, was a matter of indifference. A doubt was in some way raised in the mind of Moses as to the fact, and he "diligently sought the goat of the Sin-offering, and, behold, it was burnt." In his rebuke he tells them that the flesh of the Sin-offering is given to the priests "to bear the iniquity of the congregation to make atonement for them before the Lord." The appropriation of the flesh by the priests is thus made an essential part of the act of atonement. See on vi. 25.

16. *the goat of the sin offering*] See ix. 15.

it was burnt] It was consumed by fire in an ordinary way, not in the fire of the Altar. See on i. 9.

Eleazar and Ithamar] Aaron is not mentioned, perhaps because it was the appointed duty of his sons to see to the sacrificial meals. But in his apology he appears to acknowledge that he participated in the offence.

17. *in the holy place*] *i.e.* within the holy precinct. See on *v.* 12.

to bear the iniquity] See on Exod. xxviii. 38; Lev. vi. 25.

18. *the holy place*] "The holy *place*," as it is called in our version, within the Tabernacle (see Exod. xxvi. 33, xxviii. 29, &c.) into which the blood was carried, is regularly called in Hebrew, simply, *the Holy* (as the innermost chamber is called *the Holy of Holies*), the adjective being used substantively; while the precinct in which the flesh of the Sin-offering was eaten is generally called in full *the Holy Place*, the substantive being expressed. But in this verse, in the second sentence, the usual Hebrew name of the former is given to the latter, to give point to the sense.—In a translation the ambiguity, which is awkward in many places, would be avoided by uniformly

19 And Aaron said unto Moses, Behold, this day have they offered their sin offering and their burnt offering before the LORD; and such things have befallen me: and *if* I had eaten the sin offering to day, should it have been accepted in the sight of the LORD?

20 And when Moses heard *that*, he was content.

CHAPTER XI.

1 *What beasts may*, 4 *and what may not be eaten.* 9 *What fishes.* 13 *What fowls.* 29 *The creeping things which are unclean.*

AND the LORD spake unto Moses and to Aaron, saying unto them,

---

calling one **the Holy precinct**, and the other **the Holy place.**

19. Aaron's apology appears to amount to this;—"Behold this very day, in which we have done our part in sacrificing Sin-offerings and Burnt-offerings to the Lord, this great calamity has befallen me. Could it have been well-pleasing to the Lord if those who have been so humbled as I and my sons have been by the sin of our relations and the divine judgment, had feasted on the most holy flesh of the Sin-offering?" He and his sons would seem to have been bowed down by a sense of self-humiliation and awe suggested by the fearful example which they had witnessed and by grief at the loss of their kindred. This working of natural feeling seems to be sufficient to account for their abstinence and for Aaron's words.—There is another view of the subject which may just be noticed. It has been conceived that Moses suspected that the priests had shrunk from eating the flesh of the Sin-offering as something awful containing the nature of a curse; that they might have been swayed by a superstitious notion derived from Egypt that the Sin-offering was a sort of Typhonic sacrifice (Ewald, Kurtz, &c.). But any such theory as this is quite gratuitous. Moses simply charges the priests with an obvious transgression of the Law.

It has been said that Aaron might have alleged in vindication of himself the Law that the carcase of the people's Sin-offering should be burned without the camp (Lev. iv. 21); and an argument has been based on this, that the narrative is inconsistent with the earlier chapters of Leviticus, and must have been written by a different author (Knobel). But it has been shown that this offering was sacrificed in a peculiar relation, in behalf of the people, *apart from the priest* (on ix. 15), and the flesh was therefore under the same conditions as that of the ordinary Sin-offering (see vi. 26). Aaron was not blamed for burning the flesh of his own Sin-offering of the calf (see ix. 2), because, being offered on his behalf, it fell under the Law of Lev. iv. 21. On the holiness of the flesh of the Sin-offering, see on vi. 25.

20. *he was content*] Moses admitted Aaron's plea, but it is not stated whether he was conscious that he had himself spoken hastily and now conceded the point at issue (as we find him doing on another occasion, in reference to the settlement of the two tribes and a half, Num. xxxii. 6), allowing that the priests had done what was in itself right, as S. Augustin, the later Targums, Kurtz, and others, interpret the passage; or whether he yielded out of sympathy with Aaron's natural feelings. The latter alternative is perhaps the more probable one.

CHAP. XI.

CLEAN AND UNCLEAN ANIMAL FOOD. 1—47.

Preliminary Note.

This chapter contains directions to regulate the animal food of the Israelites, and to keep them from defilement by contact with any sort of dead flesh which they were not permitted to eat. The instructions appear to have been given in the way which was most convenient, and most generally intelligible, at the time. Some animals are prohibited in easily defined classes; while others, with which the people were probably familiar as articles of food that had been eaten by themselves or were eaten by their neighbours, are forbidden in detail. The same rules are given with no important variations of meaning in Deut. xiv.

Of quadrupeds, those only might be eaten which completely divide the hoof and chew the cud, *vv.* 3—8.

Of fish, all those might be eaten which have both scales and fins, but no others, *vv.* 9—12.

Of birds, nineteen are prohibited by name which appear to comprise types of all sorts of birds of prey, along with the bat, which was classed as a bird, *vv.* 13—19.—From the words of Deut. xiv. 11, 20 we may infer that all birds which do not belong to the kinds here mentioned were to be regarded as clean.

Of flying insects, those only which are furnished with two long legs for leaping, like the grasshopper, were permitted to be eaten. *vv.* 20—23.

Of creeping things, or vermin (see on *v.* 20), including small quadrupeds, such as rats and mice, with reptiles, worms, mollusks and crawling insects, none might be eaten. *vv.* 29—38, *vv.* 41—44. The kinds of these are enumerated in *v.* 42, and eight of them are distinguished by name in *vv.* 29, 30.

No flesh could be lawfully eaten by an

2 Speak unto the children of Israel,
[a] Deut. 14. 4. Acts 10. 14. saying, [a]These *are* the beasts which
ye shall eat among all the beasts that
are on the earth.
3 Whatsoever parteth the hoof, and
is clovenfooted, *and* cheweth the cud,
among the beasts, that shall ye eat.
4 Nevertheless these shall ye not
eat of them that chew the cud, or of
them that divide the hoof: *as* the
camel, because he cheweth the cud,
but divideth not the hoof; he *is* unclean unto you.
5 And the coney, because he cheweth the cud, but divideth not the hoof;
he *is* unclean unto you.

Israelite, or even touched without defilement, unless it was that of a clean animal which had been properly slaughtered (*vv.* 8, 11, 24, 25, 27, 28, 31, 39, 40). On slaughtering, see xvii. 3—7, 13, 14.

It was unconditionally forbidden to taste the flesh of any unclean animal (*vv.* 8, 13, 41, 42, 47); but if anyone ate of the flesh of a clean animal which had not been properly slaughtered, he was to purify himself. See on *vv.* 39, 40.

It may be observed that the words of the Law are not so strong regarding the unclean quadrupeds as they are regarding the unclean fish, birds and creeping things. The flesh of the former is simply declared to be unclean (*vv.* 4—8, 26—28), that is, unfit for the food of the people of Jehovah (see on x. 10); but the flesh of the others is pronounced to be not only unclean but "an abomination," something to be cast away (*vv.* 10, 11, 12, 13, 20, 23, 41, 42, 43). See on *vv.* 41—43. It is not however clear that the different expressions mark any practical difference.

[On the grounds of this law, see Note at the end of the Chapter.]

CHAP. XI. 1. This is one of the places in Leviticus in which Jehovah speaks to Moses and Aaron conjointly. Others are xiii. 1, xv. 1. The High-priest, in regard to the legal purifications, is treated as coordinate with the legislator.

The Clean and Unclean Quadrupeds. 2—8.

2. *These are the beasts*, &c.] This should rather be "These are the **animals which ye may eat out of** all the beasts;" that is, out of the larger creatures, the quadrupeds, as distinguished from birds and reptiles. See Gen. i. 24.

3. *parteth the hoof, and is clovenfooted*]. Rather, **is clovenfooted and completely separates the hoofs.**

4. *divideth not the hoof*] The toes of the camel are divided above, but they are united below in a sort of cushion or pad resting upon the hard bottom of the foot, which is "like the sole of a shoe." Bell 'On the Hand,' p. 94. The Moslems eat the flesh of the camel, and it is the most esteemed of the animals which they offer in sacrifice, the others being the cow, the goat, and the sheep (Lane's 'Modern Egyptians,' I. p. 134; 'Hedàya,' IV. p. 81; 'Koran,' Sura XXII.). The flesh and milk were eaten by the ancient Arabians, as we learn from St Jerome ('Adv. Jov.' II. 7). The flesh is however said not to be wholesome (Tennent's 'Ceylon,' I. p. 76).

5. *the coney*] In Hebrew, *shāphān, i.e.* the hider. Bruce appears to have been right in his conjecture that this is the animal called by the Southern Arabs *thofun* (the same word as *shaphān*), and by the Arabs in Syria and Palestine, *weber*. Naturalists call it *Hyrax Syriacus*. It is "about the size of a well-grown rabbit, with short ears, round head, long plantigrade foot, no tail, and nails instead of claws. With its weak teeth and short incisors, there seem few animals so entirely without the means for self-defence. But 'the stony rocks are a refuge for the coneys' (Prov. xxx. 26, Ps. civ. 18), and tolerably secure they are in such rocks as these (near Ain Feshkhah on the shore of the Dead Sea). No animal ever gave us so much trouble to secure." Tristram, 'Land of Israel,' p. 250. It is said to be more common in the Sinaitic Peninsula than in the Holy Land. The animal seems to bear some resemblance to the guinea-pig or the marmot, and in its general appearance and habits it might easily be taken for a rodent. But Cuvier discovered that it is, in its anatomy, a true pachyderm, allied to the rhinoceros and the tapir, inferior to them as it is in size. Its physiology is peculiarly interesting. See 'Penny Cyclo.' and the Duke of Argyll's 'Reign of Law,' p. 264; with Rödiger in Gesenius' 'Thes.' p. 1467. The LXX. render *shāphān* by χοιρογρύλλιος, a porcupine. Luther, following Jewish authorities, took it for a rabbit, and the English translators took the same line in translating it by *coney*, the ordinary old English name for a rabbit; but it is very doubtful whether the rabbit was known in South-Western Asia in ancient times.—Bochart supposed the name to denote the jerboa, an animal that abounds in the Holy Land, but which does not suit the Scripture notices of the *shāphān*, as it lives in the sand and not in the rocks. See on *v.* 29.

he cheweth the cud] Not one of the animals which have been taken for the *shāphān* (nor the hare mentioned in the next verse) chews the cud in the proper sense of the words. They have not the peculiar stomach of the true ruminants, which is essential to the act

6 And the hare, because he cheweth the cud, but divideth not the hoof; he *is* unclean unto you.

[b] 2 Mac. 6. 18.

7 And [b]the swine, though he divide the hoof, and be clovenfooted, yet he cheweth not the cud; he *is* unclean to you.

8 Of their flesh shall ye not eat, and their carcase shall ye not touch; they *are* unclean to you.

---

of rumination. But the Hyrax has the same habit as the hare, the rabbit, the guinea-pig, and some other rodents, of moving its jaws when it is at rest as if it was masticating. Mr Tristram says, "It is quite sufficient to watch the creature working and moving its jaws, as it sits in a chink of the rocks, to understand how anyone writing as an ordinary observer, and not as a comparative anatomist, would naturally thus speak of it; and this apart from the question whether the Hebrew word signifies anything more than re-chew." 'Land of Israel,' p. 251. The Hebrew phrase, according to its etymology, certainly does refer rather to the act of coughing up the half-masticated food than to that of moving the jaws. But by a process common enough in all languages, its meaning became expanded, and the rodents and pachyderms, which have the habit of grinding with their jaws, were familiarly spoken of as ruminating animals, as the bat was reckoned amongst birds because it flies (see *v.* 19), and as we might speak of whales and their congeners as fish, when there is no occasion for scientific accuracy. It was not the object of the legislator to give a scientific classification of animals nor formally to ground the law upon the facts of mastication and dividing the hoof. He had merely to furnish the people with a ready index by which they could recognise certain animals the flesh of which, for some reason, was not to be eaten. See Note at the end of this Chapter. It was enough for his purpose, in laying down a practical rule for the people, that the Hyrax and the hare with other animals allied to them were commonly known to move their jaws in the same manner as the ox, the sheep and the camel. The limits of the prohibition could in no way have been rendered more easily intelligible. See Prel. Note. It may also be observed that these creatures were excluded from the clean animals by the rule subsequently given in *v.* 27, as being comprised within "whatsoever goeth upon his paws." They are mentioned here only by way of illustration to enforce the caution that no beast should be regarded as clean which does not completely divide the hoof as well as chew the cud. The flesh of the Hyrax is said to be eaten by the Arabs of Mount Sinai, but not by the Moslems in general.

6. *the hare*] See the preceding note. There is no reasonable doubt as to the identity of the animal: the name (*arnebeth*) is the same in Arabic and other cognate languages. The Moslems have the express permission of their prophet to eat the flesh of the hare ('Hedàya,' IV. p. 75; Lane, I. 135); and the Arabs avail themselves of it, but according to Dr Russell (Vol. I. p. 158), not the Turks of Aleppo. The Parsees are said to abstain from it. Forbes, 'Orient. Mem.' II. p. 138. According to Cæsar, its flesh was not eaten by the ancient Britons ('de Bell. Gal.' V. 12).

7. *the swine, though he divide the hoof, and be clovenfooted*] Rather, "the swine, **though it is clovenfooted and completely separates the hoofs.**" See on *v.* 3. Of all the quadrupeds of which the Law forbids the flesh to be eaten, the pig seems to have been regarded as the most unclean. Is. lxv. 4, lxvi. 3, 17; 2 Macc. vi. 18, 19. Several other nations have agreed with the Hebrews in this respect. Though pigs were sacrificed by the ancient Egyptians at the yearly festival of the Moon and Bacchus, and their flesh on that occasion was eaten by the people, they were regarded at all other times with the utmost aversion, and swineherds were banished from society: the priests appear never to have eaten of their flesh, nor even to have taken part in sacrificing it. Herodot. II. 47, 48; Ælian, 'Hist. Anim.' X. 16; Joseph. 'Cont. Ap.' II. 14. The Brahmin is degraded immediately who intentionally tastes swine's flesh. 'Menu,' V. 19. The ancient Arabians held the animal in no better esteem. Solinus, XXXIII. 4; Hieron. 'Adv. Jov.' II. 7. Swine's flesh is singled out from the forbidden flesh of other animals by the Koran and named in several places along with "the flesh of that which dies of itself, and blood." Suras II., V., VI., XVI, &c. And according to the Moslem laws, the flesh of men and that of swine are the only kinds of flesh which cannot be rendered pure by *zabbah*, that is, by cutting the throat according to a prescribed form. 'Hedàya,' IV. pp. 62—75. See note after ch. xvii. The dirty habits and uncouth form of the creature may have no doubt tended to bring it into disrepute. There is a curious passage to this effect, too long for quotation, in Lactantius, 'Institut.' IV. 17. But a very general notion has prevailed that its flesh is unwholesome, especially in warm climates. According to a Jewish proverb, it promotes leprosy. Manetho speaks to the same purpose (ap. Ælian, 'H. A.' X. 16; cf. Tacitus, 'Hist.' V. 4), and there seems good reason to believe that it has under certain circumstances a tendency to produce diseases of the skin. Michaelis, 'Laws of Moses,'

9 ¶ These shall ye eat of all that
are in the waters: whatsoever hath
fins and scales in the waters, in the
seas, and in the rivers, them shall
ye eat.
10 And all that have not fins and
scales in the seas, and in the rivers, of
all that move in the waters, and of
any living thing which *is* in the waters,
they *shall be* an abomination unto you:
11 They shall be even an abomination unto you; ye shall not eat of
their flesh, but ye shall have their
carcases in abomination.
12 Whatsoever hath no fins nor
scales in the waters, that *shall be* an
abomination unto you.
13 ¶ And these *are they which* ye
shall have in abomination among the
fowls; they shall not be eaten, they

III. p. 230. Lord Clyde forbad the use of swine's flesh in the Indian army on sanitary grounds. Tennent's 'Ceylon,' I. p. 76. Sir Gardiner Wilkinson says, "the reason of the meat not being eaten (by the Egyptians) was its unwholesomeness, on which account it was forbidden to the Jews and Moslems; and the prejudice naturally extended from the animal to those who kept it, as at present in India and other parts of the East, where a Hindoo (that is, one of high caste) or a Moslem is, like an ancient Egyptian, defiled by the touch of a pig, and looks with horror on those who tend it and eat its flesh." Note on 'Herodotus,' II. 47. See also Lane, 'Mod. Egypt.' I. p. 134. Much curious learning has been expended on the causes of the disesteem in which the pig has been held amongst Eastern nations, by Spencer, 'De Leg. Heb.' I. 7, § 4, and by Bochart, 'Hieroz.' II. 57.

It should be noticed that the law regarding quadrupeds is given in a positive form in Deut. xiv. 3, 4, 5, "Thou shalt not eat any abominable thing. These are the beasts which ye shall eat: the ox, the sheep, and the goat," &c. Then follow seven names which appear to belong to the roebuck, the gazelle and four other kinds of antelope, with the wild sheep. (See notes in loc.) These most likely constituted the game with which the Israelites were familiar in the Wilderness and on the borders of the Holy Land. Cf. Lev. xvii. 13.

The Clean and Unclean Fish, 9—12.
(Deut. xiv. 9, 10.)

9. The rule here is simple and comprehensive. Any fish, either from salt water or fresh, might be eaten if it had both scales and fins, but no other creature that lives in the waters. Shellfish of all kinds, whether mollusks or crustaceans, and cetaceous animals, were therefore prohibited, as well as fish which appear to have no scales, like the eel.

Fish were generally forbidden to the Egyptian priests, but were largely eaten by the rest of the people. Wilkinson, I. p. 322; Porphyry, 'De Abstin.' IV. 7. The eel was held sacred in several parts of Egypt, and was not eaten. Sir Gardiner Wilkinson supposes that "the reason of its sanctity, like that of the Oxyrhynchus, was owing to its being unwholesome; and the best way of preventing its being eaten was to assign it a place among the sacred animals of the country," II. 192. This theory however is not easily reconciled with the consecration of such animals as the ox and the sheep; or of the fish called *Lepidotus*, which had large scales and must have been a wholesome fish, whether it was allied to the salmon, the carp, or the perch. See 'Herod.' II. 72; Wilkinson's 'Ancient Egypt.' II. p. 192. The modern Egyptians consider all fish without scales to be unwholesome. Lane, I. p. 135. The Moslem law, like the Hebrew, forbids the eating of shellfish, mollusks of all kinds, and, according to the best authorities, of seals and other marine beasts. "No animal that lives in water is lawful except fish." 'Hedàya,' IV. 75. It is said that Numa Pompilius made a law that no scaleless fish should be offered in sacrifice, though, if we are to trust the tradition in the form in which it has reached us, not in consequence of their being looked upon as impure. Plin. 'H. N.', XXXII. 10. Festus refers to a similar law (s. v. *pollucere*), and states that any fish having scales might be sacrificed except the Scarus.

There is probably a reference to the distinction between clean and unclean fishes in Matt. xiii. 48. See Trench 'on the Parables,' p. 137. The scaleless fish which most abounds in the Sea of Galilee is the Silurus; of those which have scales, some of the most abundant are the chub, the barbel and the bream. Robinson, 'Physical Geography of the Holy Land,' p. 182; Tristram, 'Land of Israel,' pp. 426, 428, 435, 575.

The Unclean Birds, 13—19.

No general rule is given for the distinction between clean and unclean birds, but there is merely a list of twenty which are prohibited, nothing being said of those which might be eaten. See Prel. Note. It will be seen that, as far as they can be identified, the birds here mentioned are such as live upon animal food. The Mishna ('Cholin,' III. 6) lays it down as a rule that every bird is unclean which strikes its talons into its prey; and quotes one authority which puts into the same class every bird which divides its toes equally in climb-

are an abomination: the eagle, and
the ossifrage, and the ospray,
14 And the vulture, and the kite
after his kind;
15 Every raven after his kind;
16 And the owl, and the night
hawk, and the cuckow, and the hawk
after his kind,

---

ing, like the parrot and woodpecker. The distinction between birds in the Moslem law appears similarly to hinge upon their food. 'Hedàya,' IV. 74. According to Porphyry, the Egyptian priests also followed the same rule. 'De Abstin.' IV. 7. The list of species here given is evidently not intended to be an exhaustive one. It is likely that the birds which are distinguished by name were those which the Israelites might have been tempted to eat, either from their being easy to obtain, or from the example of other nations, and which served as types of the entire range of prohibited kinds.—In the notes which follow, the Hebrew names are, in general, followed by the names in the Septuagint and the Vulgate.

13. *the eagle*] *nesher;* ἀετός; *aquila.* Rather, **the great vulture.** It has been generally taken for the golden eagle, which is commonly called the king of birds. But Mr Tristram seems to prove that the bird which is meant is the Griffon Vulture, *Vultur fulvus*, called by the Arabs, *Nisr.* "The identity of the Hebrew and Arabic terms can scarcely be questioned. However degrading the substitution of the ignoble vulture for the royal eagle may at first sight appear in many passages, it must be borne in mind that the griffon is in all its movements and characteristics a majestic and royal bird, the largest and most powerful which is seen on the wing in Palestine, and far surpassing the eagle in size and power." Smith's 'Dict.' and 'Land of Israel,' p. 447. In Micah i. 16, baldness is ascribed to the *nesher*, which certainly does not belong to the eagle, but is appropriate to the griffon vulture. The Egyptians are known to have ranked the vulture as the first amongst birds. The *nesher* is mentioned 2 S. i. 23; Ps. ciii. 5; Prov. xxiii. 5, &c.

the ossifrage, and the ospray] The latter of these English words is but a corruption of the former, though they are used to distinguish different birds. The Hebrew words are *peres* and *'ozneeyāh.* The first, *peres*, is exactly rendered in its etymological sense by *ossifrage*, *i.e.* the bone-breaker, and the bird known as the ossifrage is probably the one here denoted. Smith's 'Dict.' s. v. It is sometimes called the lamergeyer, and by naturalists, *Gypaetus barbatus*, the bearded vulture. It is the rival of the griffon in strength and size, but is a much rarer bird. The other, *'ozneeyāh*, may be either the ospray, or sea-eagle (*Pandion Haliaëtus*), in accordance with the rendering of the Septuagint, ἁλιαίετος; or the short-toed eagle, *Circaëtus gallicus*, which feeds upon reptiles. Smith's 'Dict.'

14. *the vulture*] *dāāh;* γύψ; *milvus.* Rather, **the kite.** The English version has followed the Septuagint, but the Vulgate appears to be more correct. The Arabic name for a kite is *dayah*, the same as this Hebrew word. The species denoted is probably the black kite, *Milvus ater*, the gregarious habits of which agree with the mode in which the *dāyāh* is mentioned Isaiah xxxiv. 15. Tristram, 'Land of Israel,' p. 204.

the kite] *ayāh;* ἴκτιν; *vultur.* The Septuagint and our version are here probably more correct than the Vulgate. See on *v.* 18. The **red kite,** *Milvus regalis*, which is remarkable for its piercing sight, to which reference is made where the same bird is named in Job xxviii. 7, is supposed to be the bird here meant. Tristram in Smith's 'Dict.' The words "after his kind," might include all allied species.

15. *Every raven after his kind*] The names of the raven and the birds allied to it, in many languages, appear to be formed by onomatopœia, from the cry of the birds. Heb. *'orēb;* κόραξ; *corvus;* Germ. *rabe;* English, *raven*, *crow*, *rook.* There can be no doubt that the whole family of corvidæ are here designated. The raven, the rook, the crow and the jackdaw are very abundant in the neighbourhood of Jerusalem. 'Land of Israel,' p. 184. The raven and the crow are forbidden to be eaten by the Moslem law, but not rooks which feed on grain. 'Hedàya,' Vol. IV. p. 74.

16. *the owl*] *bath haya'anāh;* στρουθὸς; *struthio.* Most probably, **the ostrich.** The Hebrew name appears to mean "the daughter of greediness" (Gesenius), but others explain it as "the daughter of wailing" (Fürst). It is rendered ostrich in the margin in Job xxx. 29, Is. xxxiv. 13, xliii. 20, in agreement with the Septuagint, the Vulgate, the Targums, the Syriac, and Saadia. Though the name is formally feminine, it is to be taken to denote the species, and not necessarily, as some have imagined, the hen-bird. The flesh of the ostrich is eaten by some of the Arabs, but not by all. An African people called Struthophagi (ostrich-eaters), are mentioned by Strabo and other writers (Knobel). Our translators appear to have been misled in rendering the word in the text by the notion that *ya'anāh* means *shouting*, which they thought applied best to the owl. Neither Luther, Cranmer, nor the Geneva translators fell into the same mistake.

17 And the little owl, and the cormorant, and the great owl,

18 And the swan, and the pelican, and the gier eagle,

night hawk] *tachmās* (literally, the violent one); γλαύξ; *noctua*. Rather, **the owl**. Some high authorities, rejecting the ancient versions, suppose the male ostrich to be intended, on the ground of the Arabs calling him by a name having the same meaning, and take *bath haya'anāh* exclusively for the female bird (Bochart, Gesenius). But it may be doubted whether the Hebrews gave radically different names to the male and female of the same species, except in the case of domesticated or familiarly known animals, like our own bull and cow, horse and mare, ram and ewe. By some *tachmās* has been taken for the cuckoo, from its well-known violence towards the eggs and the young of other birds (Knobel, Keil), and by some Jewish authors for the swallow (Saadia, Targ. Pal.). But it appears reasonable on the whole to follow the ancient versions, and to understand the word as denoting some species of owl, of ferocious habits, such as the *Strix orientalis* of Hasselquist. See Hasselquist, 'Travels,' p. 196.

the cuckow] *shāchaph*; λάρος; *larus*. Probably, **the gull**. There seems to be nothing to favour the claims of the cuckoo. The Greek name denotes a gull, and it is likely that some sea-bird is meant. See Lewysohn, 'Die Zoologie des Talmuds,' § 223. The Hebrew word is found nowhere else but in Deut. xiv. 15. Bochart and Gesenius are inclined to identify *shāchaph* with the κέπφος of Aristotle, the storm petrel. It may perhaps be "the light and elegant Andouini's gull" (*Larus Andouni*), which abounds on the shores of Syria (Tristram, 'Land of Israel,' p. 102, &c.), and is certainly a more likely bird to be the object of a prohibition than the storm petrel, which is so seldom seen on land.

the hawk after his kind] *neets*; ἱέραξ; *accipiter*. There is no reason to question that the whole family of hawks is here intended.

17. *the little owl*] *kos*; νυκτίκοραξ; *bubo*. Mr Tristram has no hesitation in identifying this with the small owl, *Athene meridionalis*, "which stands out on the coins of old Athens, the emblem of Minerva, dignified, yet occasionally grotesque, in its motions; with all the gravity, yet without the heaviness, of the owls of our own woods and towers; and it is the only kind universally distributed and everywhere common and familiar in Syria, Greece, and the Levant." 'Land of Israel,' p. 68. It is "the owl of the desert" mentioned in Ps. cii. 6.

the cormorant] *shālāk* (*i.e.* the diver); καταράκτης; *mergulus*. The name occurs only here and in Deut. xiv. 17. The καταῤῥάκτης is mentioned by Aristotle ('Hist. Anim.' IX. 13, &c.), and has been supposed to be the gannet (*Sula bassana*). But it is doubted whether the gannet is to be found in or near Syria. It is as likely to have been the common cormorant (*Phalacrocorax carbo*), which is often seen in Syria, and occasionally visits the Sea of Galilee.

the great owl] *yanshuph*; Deut. xiv. 16; Is. xxxiv. 11. Our version is most likely right. The bird was probably the horned owl (*Bubo maximus*), well known in Egypt (Wilkinson, I. 249). According to the LXX., as its text stands (see the next note), the Vulg., and Onkelos, the *yanshuph* was the ibis, the sacred bird of the Egyptians, *Ibis religiosa*, which, although it is not found in Palestine, must have been familiar to the Hebrews in the wilderness. But the habits of the ibis do not agree with the reference to the *yanshuph* in Is. xxxiv. 11. The best Jewish authorities agree with our version (Lewysohn, § 188). The etymology of the name may connect it either with the twilight (Bochart), or with the act of puffing out the breath (Knobel). Either meaning would accord with the habits of the great owl.

18. *the swan*] *tinshemeth*. Our version follows the authority of the LXX. and Vulg. according to the present order of the texts. (κύκνος, *cygnus*.) But a more probable rendering is **the ibis**.—By comparing the Septuagint, the Vulgate, Onkelos, and the Hebrew text here and in Deut. xiv. 16, 17, and the various readings of the LXX., it becomes evident that the order of the names has been disturbed in the versions. There is a similar disturbance, though not such a complicated one, in verses 5 and 6. It appears highly probable that the word intended by the LXX. to answer to *tinshemeth* is ἶβις (as it stands in Deut. xiv. 16), and that the right bird is the *Ibis religiosa* mentioned in the preceding note. It is an unclean feeder, by no means good for food. It is difficult to suppose that the swan could have been reckoned amongst unclean birds: the LXX. and Vulg. were most likely wrong in introducing it anywhere into this list.—The name *tinshemeth* belongs to another unclean animal, most likely the chameleon. See on *v.* 30.

the pelican] *kāāth*; πελεκὰν; *onocratalus*; Deut. xiv. 17; Ps. cii. 6; Is. xxxiv. 11; Zeph. ii. 14. In the latter two places our version has cormorant in the text, but pelican in the margin. Two species of pelican are known in the Levant, *Pelicanus onocratalus* and *P. crispus*. There is reason to suppose that pelicans were formerly by far more numerous than they are at present, though they are

19 And the stork, the heron after her kind, and the lapwing, and the bat.

20 All fowls that creep, going upon *all* four, *shall be* an abomination unto you.

---

frequently seen now on the upper Jordan. See 'The Rob Roy on the Jordan,' p. 286.

the gier eagle] *rāchām*. The bird here mentioned is most likely **the Egyptian vulture** (*Neophron percnopterus*), called *racham* by the modern Arabs. It is a bird of unprepossessing appearance and disgusting habits, but fostered by the Egyptians as a useful scavenger. Hasselquist has a lively description of its appearance and habits, p. 195. It is doubtful, according to the present state of the text, by what word the LXX. intended to render *rāchām*. All the best authorities appear to identify it with the Egyptian vulture.

19. *the stork*] *chaseedāh*; *ἐρωδιὸς*; *herodius*; Job xxxix. 13 (see the margin); Zech. v. 9. The Hebrew name appears to be derived from a root which signifies affection, and this answers to the well-known character of the stork in respect to its love of its offspring. The common white stork (*Ciconia alba*) is not so abundant in the Holy Land and the East as the black stork (*Ciconia nigra*).—Tristram, 'Land of Israel,' pp. 438, 539; 'Nat. Hist.' p. 244: but it was well-known in Egypt (Wilk. I. p. 25).—The word used by the Septuagint denotes, and has most likely furnished with its name, the common *heron*. See Ducange, sub *herodius*. The heron was a bird of omen with the ancient Greeks ('Iliad,' x. 274). As it is said to be very fond of its young and abounds in Palestine (Tristram, pp. 456, 587) as well as Egypt, it might perhaps answer as well as the stork to the meaning of *chaseedāh*; and if we accept it we should be able to account for the Septuagint not using the familiar word for the stork, πελαργός. But as regards the scope of the prohibition, to whichever of the birds in question the name strictly belongs, the two allied species would most likely here be included under it.

the heron] *anāphāh*; *χαραδριὸς*; *charadrius*. Rather, **the great plover**. Our version and the earlier English translators have followed a weak rabbinical authority in rendering *ānāphah* by *heron*. See Lewysohn, § 200. Luther, following other Jewish authorities, has translated it by *jay*. The derivation of the Hebrew name is doubtful (see Fürst). The word of the Septuagint denotes some bird of which the name was a proverb for greediness amongst the Greeks (see Liddell and Scott). It is identified on pretty safe ground with the great or thick-kneed plover (*Charadrius œdicnemus*), a bird widely diffused in Europe, Asia, and North Africa, and well known to the ancient Egyptians (Wilkinson, I. p. 251). It lives on coarse food such as slugs, worms, frogs and toads. The *Charadrius* had magical qualities ascribed to it by the Egyptians. Heliodorus, 'Æthiop.' Lib. III.

the lapwing] *dukiphath*; *ἔποψ*; *upupa*. Rather **the hoopoe**. Our translators have followed the older English versions with no good authority. The Hebrew name cannot be satisfactorily explained (Fürst). There appears to be no reason for preferring any rendering to that of the Septuagint, the hoopoe (*Upupa epops*). Its peculiar cry or whoop is expressed in its name in most languages. It lives upon insects, and it is often found in Syria. Its flesh is said to be very good. But the bird has been generally regarded with superstitious feelings from early times, especially by the Egyptians. Ælian, 'H. A.' x. 16. Aristoph. 'Av.' 94. Mr Tristram says, "The Arabs have a superstitious reverence for this bird, which they believe to possess marvellous medicinal qualities, and they call it 'the doctor.' Its head is an indispensable ingredient in all charms and in the practice of witchcraft." The Bedouins are said to believe that it is inhabited by the spirits of the departed. 'Penny Cyclo.' Art. *Upupidæ*. Rabbinical authorities take the *dukiphath* for some kind of grouse. Lewysohn, § 267. But it is highly improbable that any bird allied to the grouse should have been deemed unclean.

the bat] *'hatalleph*; *νυκτερὶς*; *vespertilio*. There is no doubt that the bat is the animal here intended (see Fürst). Luther and Cranmer with some of the rabbinists have however preferred the swallow. The word *'hatalleph* signifies a creature which flies in the dark. It is mentioned along with the mole as symbolical of darkness, Isaiah ii. 20. It is reckoned in this place amongst birds in accordance with popular notions, as the coney and the hare are placed amongst ruminants. See on *v.* 5.

Creeping things, 20—23.

The word rendered creeping things (*sheretz*) is applied to insects (*vv.* 20—23), reptiles, and small land animals of different kinds (see *v.* 29). In a general way, it may be regarded as coextensive with our word *vermin*. It is derived from a verb which signifies not only to creep, but to teem, or bring forth abundantly (Gen. i. 21, viii. 17; Exod. viii. 3; Ps. cv. 30), and so easily came to denote creatures which are apt to abound, to the annoyance of mankind.

20. *All fowls that creep, going upon all four*] This should rather be, "**All creeping things which have wings,** going

21 Yet these may ye eat of every
flying creeping thing that goeth upon
all four, which have legs above their
feet, to leap withal upon the earth;
22 *Even* these of them ye may eat;
the locust after his kind, and the bald
locust after his kind, and the beetle
after his kind, and the grasshopper
after his kind.
23 But all *other* flying creeping
things, which have four feet, *shall be*
an abomination unto you.

---

upon all four." It has been considered that the words refer to the bat, spoken of in the preceding verse, and not to insects which have more than four legs (Gesenius). But it is not certain that the Hebrew expression, "going upon all four," is to be taken in its literal sense. It may be a general expression for walking upon feet with the body in a horizontal position (so far like a quadruped), as distinguished from flying, leaping or crawling. The Jewish writers appear thus to have understood the phrase here and in *v.* 23: they considered that it refers to such creatures as the fly and the wasp (see Targum of Palestine, and R. Levi quoted by Drusius).

21. *legs above their feet, to leap withal upon the earth*] There are three families of orthopterous insects furnished with a pair of long legs for leaping, distinguished by the name *Saltatoria.* The common cricket, the common grasshopper, and the migratory locust, may be taken as types of these three families. Several species of these creatures are eaten in the East at this day. They are formally permitted to be used as food by the Moslem law, 'Hedàya,' IV. p. 75. They are dressed in different ways. For the most part, they are thrown alive into boiling water with salt in it, and the heads, wings, and legs are pulled off. The bodies are then either roasted on hot plates, baked in ovens, stewed, or fried in butter, for immediate use, or dried and smoked to be kept in store. They are eaten either with salt or with spice and vinegar. The inhabitants of Senegal grind them, when dried, to powder, and mix them with flour to make cakes of the mixture. According to Hasselquist the Arabs of Mecca treat them in the same manner, p. 232. They are eaten by some of the Bedouin tribes, but not by all (Robinson, 'B. R.' Vol. II. p. 204). In Eastern Arabia, according to Mr Palgrave, a large reddish-brown locust is esteemed as a peculiar delicacy (Vol. II. p. 138). In some of the Arabian markets locusts are sold in a dried state either by measure, or by number, strung upon threads. Pliny speaks of a nation of Ethiopians who used to live entirely upon them ('H. N.' VI. 35. See also Arist. 'H. A. V.' 30; Aristoph. 'Acharn.' 1116; Solinus, XXX. 8). The field-cricket and the cicada are eaten by the native peoples of Western America (Lord, 'At home in the Wilderness,' p. 250).

22. *the locust*] *arbeh*; βροῦχος; *bruchus:* more frequently and more correctly rendered in the LXX. ἀκρίς: the βροῦχος was a wingless insect. Theophrastus, Fragm. 14. 4. *Arbeh* appears to be the name of one species of the migratory locusts, which are those best known in the East as the most destructive and the most generally eaten by the Arabs. There are three distinct species, called by naturalists *Œdipoda migratoria*, *Acrydium peregrinum*, and *Acrydium lineola*. The *arbeh* is the one commonly mentioned in the Old Testament. See Ex. x. 4; Job xxxix. 20; Ps. lxxviii. 46, cv. 34; Joel i. 4, &c. &c.

bald locust] *sol'ām*; ἀττάκη; *attacus.* It is not mentioned elsewhere. The Hebrew name seems to be identical with the Egyptian name for the locust (Brugsch). There is no evidence to identify it with any known species. Our version has called it "the bald locust," in accordance with a mere rabbinical fancy. (See Drusius in loc.) It may have been one of the two migratory species mentioned above.

the beetle] *chargol*; ὀφιομάχης; *ophiomachus.* Neither is this mentioned elsewhere in the Old Testament. There seems to be no authority for calling it "the beetle." It must certainly be some species of the *Saltatoria.* No one of them appears to have been noticed which, from its enmity to the serpent, could have any claim to the name given in the Septuagint. The Mishna mentions the *chargol*, and says that its eggs were worn in the ears of women as a sort of charm. 'De Sabb.' VI. 10.

the grasshopper] *chāgāb*; ἀκρίς; *locusta.* This is mentioned Num. xiii. 33; 2 Chron. vii. 13; Eccles. xii. 5; Is. xl. 22. That this was one of the destructive locusts, is evident from 2 Chron. vii. 13; and that it is one of the smaller ones, is probable from Num. xiii. 33; Ecc. xii. 5.

In the uncertainty of identifying these four creatures, it has been suggested that some of the names may belong to locusts in an imperfect state of development; but this can hardly meet the case, since the larva of any insect would necessarily be unclean according to *v.* 42. Most versions in modern languages, including the older English versions, have taken a safer course than our translators, by retaining the Hebrew names. The Geneva Bible wisely adds in the margin, "These were certain kinds of grasshoppers which are not now properly known."

23. *four feet*] See on *v.* 20.

In the law given in Deut. xiv. 19, flying

24 And for these ye shall be unclean: whosoever toucheth the carcase
of them shall be unclean until the even.
25 And whosoever beareth *ought*
of the carcase of them shall wash his
clothes, and be unclean until the even.
26 *The carcases* of every beast
which divideth the hoof, and *is* not
clovenfooted, nor cheweth the cud,
are unclean unto you: every one that
toucheth them shall be unclean.
27 And whatsoever goeth upon his
paws, among all manner of beasts that
go on *all* four, those *are* unclean unto
you: whoso toucheth their carcase
shall be unclean until the even.
28 And he that beareth the carcase
of them shall wash his clothes, and be
unclean until the even: they *are* unclean unto you.
29 ¶ These also *shall be* unclean
unto you among the creeping things
that creep upon the earth; the weasel,
and the mouse, and the tortoise after
his kind,
30 And the ferret, and the chame-

---

insects are prohibited without qualification. Locusts are not mentioned as an exception, but they must have been so understood. That they were actually eaten by the Jews, we know from the case of St John the Baptist. This is of itself sufficient to confute the inference of Knobel, that the permission to eat locusts was withdrawn when Deuteronomy was written.

Contact with the carcases of unclean animals. 24—28.

The law is here laid down regarding contact with the dead bodies, (1) of unclean insects; (2) of quadrupeds unclean because they do not ruminate and divide the hoof; and (3) of quadrupeds unclean because they walk on their toes. See on *v.* 27. Whoever merely touched a carcase of either of these creatures was to be unclean until the evening of the day, but whoever carried one, was, besides this, to wash his clothes. If the due purification was omitted at the time, through negligence or forgetfulness, a Sin-offering was required. See on v. 2.

26. *every one that toucheth them*] *i.e.* not the living animals, but their carcases.

27. *goeth upon his paws*] Like the dog, cat, and all beasts of prey. These are included in the preceding class of those which do not ruminate and divide the hoof, but they appear to be mentioned for emphasis.

Unclean Creeping things, and the Pollution of domestic Utensils. 29—43.

29. *These also shall be unclean*, &c.] "The creeping things" (see on *vv.* 20—23) which are here named are most likely those which were occasionally eaten.

the weasel] *choled*; γαλῆ; *mustela*; so the Targums. The word *choled* occurs nowhere else in the O. T. According to its etymology, it would denote an animal that glides, or slips away. There can be no doubt that the Mishna uses it for a weasel, or some such animal, when it speaks of a creature which catches birds by the head or poll ('Cholin,' III. 4. See also 'Taharoth,' IV. 2; Buxt. 'Lex. Tal.' 756; Lewysohn, § 135). These authorities are strong in favour of the weasel. But Mr Tristram is inclined to follow Bochart in taking *choled* for the same as the Arabic *khlunt* or *khald*, which denotes the mole. 'Land of Israel,' p. 186. The regular Hebrew name for the mole appears to be *chephar*, Is. ii. 20.

the mouse] *akbār*; μῦς; *mus*. 1 S. vi. 4; Is. lxvi. 17. The word is said to mean a *waster of fields*. It has been supposed to be the jerboa or "jumping mouse" (*Dipus Ægyptius*) that abounds in Egypt and Syria, which is sometimes eaten and is very destructive to grain. Bochart, Gesenius, Knobel; see Hasselquist, p. 186. But Mr Tristram with great probability conjectures that *'akbār* may be the equivalent of the Arabic *farah*, which is applied to any small rodent.

the tortoise] *tzāb*. Rather, **the great lizard**. The Septuagint calls it *the land-crocodile* (which is mentioned by Herodotus, IV. 192, where see Sir G. Wilkinson's note), and the other ancient versions simply *the crocodile*. It is not mentioned elsewhere in the O. T. Bochart considers the Hebrew word to be allied to the Arabic *dhab*, the name of a large lizard, often two feet long, which abounds in Egypt and Syria. Tristram identifies it with the *Uromastix spinipes* ('Nat. Hist.' p. 255). According to Hasselquist, its flesh is dried by some of the Eastern nations as a charm or medicine, which in past ages was sent to Venice and Marseilles as an article of commerce. He adds that the Arabs make broth of its fresh flesh, p. 220. St Jerome, who calls it the land-crocodile, says that the Syrians in his time were accustomed to eat its flesh, 'Adv. Jovin.' II. 7, p. 334. Some have taken *tzab* for the toad. Lewysohn, § 281.

30. *the ferret*] *anākāh*; μυγάλη; *mygale*. Rather, **the gecko**. The Hebrew word appears to mean the squeaker or croaker. While the Septuagint and the Vulgate identify this with the shrew mouse, the Eastern versions take it on better ground for some sort of lizard. Bochart, Gesenius, Knobel, and Tris-

leon, and the lizard, and the snail, and
the mole.
31 These *are* unclean to you among
all that creep: whosoever doth touch
them, when they be dead, shall be unclean until the even.
32 And upon whatsoever *any* of
them, when they are dead, doth fall,
it shall be unclean; whether *it be*
any vessel of wood, or raiment, or
skin, or sack, whatsoever vessel *it be*,
wherein *any* work is done, it must
be put into water, and it shall be
unclean until the even; so it shall be
cleansed.
33 And every earthen vessel, whereinto *any* of them falleth, whatsoever
is in it shall be unclean; and [c] ye shall [c] chap 6. 28.
break it.
34 Of all meat which may be eaten,
that on which *such* water cometh shall
be unclean: and all drink that may be
drunk in every *such* vessel shall be
unclean.
35 And every *thing* whereupon *any*
part of their carcase falleth shall be
unclean; *whether it be* oven, or ranges
for pots, they shall be broken down:
for they *are* unclean, and shall be unclean unto you.

---

tram agree with the latter. Rosenmüller supposes it to be the gecko (*Lacerta gecko*), which makes a noise something like the croaking of a frog, and has feet of a peculiar construction which enable it to walk on ceilings. It often intrudes into dwelling-rooms. The animal is not named in any other passage of the O. T.

the chameleon] *koach.* Our translators have here followed the Septuagint, Vulgate and Targums. But a word, to be noticed lower down, has better claims to denote the chameleon. Knobel, comparing *koach* with the Arab word *keek*, with κοάξ, the word by which Aristophanes represents the croaking of frogs, and the Latin *coaxare*, supposes it to denote **the frog**. According to its supposed etymological sense (the strong one) it might fairly belong to the frog, from the great muscular power which that animal exhibits in leaping. Gesenius, Robinson and Keil prefer to apply it to one of the Monitors, especially the *Lacerta Nilotica.*

the lizard] *letāāh;* ἀσκαλαβώτης; *stellio.* All the ancient versions take this to be a newt or lizard of some kind. The Septuagint identifies it with the gecko mentioned above. It may rather be one of the Monitors mentioned in the preceding note. The Talmud appears to use the word as a general name for lizards. Lewysohn, § 272.

the snail] *chomet;* σαῦρα; *lacerta.* Our version here follows the Targum of Palestine and most Jewish authorities. The old versions in general take *chomet* for a **lizard** of some kind. The word appears to come from a root which signifies to lie flat. Some have supposed that the slow-worm (*Anguis fragilis*) is intended, which forms a link between the snakes and the lizards. The proper Hebrew word for "the snail" is *shavlūl.* Ps. lviii. 8.

the mole] Rather, **the chameleon**; *tinshemeth* (*i.e.* the breather or inflater); ἀσπάλαξ; *talpa.* The same Hebrew name is applied to a bird in *v.* 18. The ancient versions agree with ours in rendering the word *mole*, in this place. It is however supposed by most modern critics to denote the chameleon, to which the name might belong either from the old notion that it lives upon air or from its well-known habit of inflating the body when it is excited (Bochart, Gesenius, Knobel, Keil, Herxheimer, Tristram). Its flesh was supposed by the ancients to possess medicinal virtues. Pliny, 'H. N.' XXVIII. 29.

31. *when they be dead*] That is, whether they had died naturally or had been killed. Cf. *v.* 39.

32—35. These regulations seem to be given in consequence of its being more probable that the bodies of the animals which are mentioned in *vv.* 29, 30 should accidentally come into contact with cooking apparatus and other domestic furniture than the bodies of the other unclean animals. It may also have served as an emphatic caution in connection with the use that might have been made of such creatures in gravy or soup, "the broth of abominable things," Is. lxv. 4. The rule can hardly be intended to intimate, as some Jewish and other commentators (Maimonides, Kurtz, &c.) have imagined, that their flesh would communicate a peculiar degree of pollution, beyond that spoken of in *vv.* 11, 12, 13.

32. *vessel of wood...whatsoever vessel*] **utensil** rather than vessel. The word here and in *v.* 33 is a term of wide meaning like the Greek σκεῦος. See on Ex. xxvii. 19.

33. *earthen vessel*] See on vi. 28; cf. *v.* 34.

35. *oven, or ranges for pots*] The word here used for oven is *tanur*, the name for the earthenware oven in common use. See on Lev. ii. 4. The word rendered "ranges for pots" is a peculiar one, in the dual number. It has been conjectured to mean either an excavated fireplace, fitted to receive a pair of ovens (Kimchi, Gesenius, Rosenmüller, Herxheimer), a vessel consisting of two parts, like

36 Nevertheless a fountain or pit,
† *wherein there is* plenty of water, shall
be clean: but that which toucheth
their carcase shall be unclean.

† Heb. *a gathering together of waters.*

37 And if *any part* of their carcase
fall upon any sowing seed which is to
be sown, it *shall be* clean.
38 But if *any* water be put upon
the seed, and *any part* of their carcase
fall thereon, it *shall be* unclean unto
you.
39 And if any beast, of which ye
may eat, die; he that toucheth the
carcase thereof shall be unclean until
the even.
40 And he that eateth of the carcase of it shall wash his clothes, and
be unclean until the even: he also
that beareth the carcase of it shall
wash his clothes, and be unclean until
the even.
41 And every creeping thing that
creepeth upon the earth *shall be* an
abomination; it shall not be eaten.
42 Whatsoever goeth upon the
belly, and whatsoever goeth upon *all*
four, or whatsoever † hath more feet

† Heb. *doth multiply feet.*

among all creeping things that creep
upon the earth, them ye shall not eat;
for they *are* an abomination.
43 Ye shall not make your † selves
abominable with any creeping thing
that creepeth, neither shall ye make
yourselves unclean with them, that ye
should be defiled thereby.

† Heb. *souls.*

44 For I *am* the LORD your God:
ye shall therefore sanctify yourselves,
and [d] ye shall be holy; for I *am* holy:
neither shall ye defile yourselves with
any manner of creeping thing that
creepeth upon the earth.

[d] chap. 1[9]. 2. & 20. [7]. 1 Pet. 1. 1[6].

45 For I *am* the LORD that bringeth
you up out of the land of Egypt, to
be your God: ye shall therefore be
holy, for I *am* holy.
46 This *is* the law of the beasts,
and of the fowl, and of every living
creature that moveth in the waters,
and of every creature that creepeth
upon the earth:
47 To make a difference between
the unclean and the clean, and between
the beast that may be eaten and the
beast that may not be eaten.

---

a stewpan and its cover (Knobel, Keil, the Targums), or a support to serve as a trevit (LXX.), perhaps like a pair of andirons. Mr Palgrave speaks of a contrivance found in the remoter parts of Arabia which may illustrate and confirm the last of these conjectures. He describes it as "an open fireplace hollowed in the ground-floor, with a raised stone border, and dog-irons for the fuel, and so forth, just like what may be seen in Spain and some old English manor-houses." 'Travels in Arabia,' Vol. I. p. 50.

36. That is, whatever touched the carcase, in the act of removing it, or otherwise, became unclean.

37, 38. If the seed had been wetted it would imbibe the pollution. The exemption applied exclusively to dry grain which was to be used for seed. That which was to be eaten required purification like other things.

39, 40. The carcase of a clean beast which had not been properly slaughtered (cf. Lev. xvii. 15) was under the same conditions, as regards mere contact, as the dead body of an unclean beast. But the eating of its flesh is treated as what might possibly occur, and the terms of purification for him who had eaten are given. This may have been to meet the probability of the body of an ox, a sheep, or a goat, being recovered from a wild beast and, from need or economy, eaten by its owner. See on xvii. 11, 15, 16.

41—43. But all "creeping things" are unconditionally forbidden, because "they are an abomination." In like manner the prohibitions to eat of the other unclean animals are expressed without condition, *vv.* 8, 11, 13. The command is, not that he who may eat of them should purify himself, but that they should not be eaten at all.

42. *Whatsoever goeth upon the belly*] That is, all footless reptiles, and mollusks, such as snakes of all kinds, snails, slugs, and worms. *Whatsoever goeth upon all four;* that is, of "creeping things," or vermin; such as the weasel, the mouse or the lizard. See on *vv.* 20—23. *Whatsoever hath more feet;* all insects, except the locust family (*v.* 22), myriapods, spiders, and caterpillars.

One letter in the Hebrew word which is rendered *belly* in this verse is said by the Jews to be the middle letter of the Pentateuch, and is printed in the Hebrew Bibles in a larger type than the rest.

44, 47. Then follows, in immediate connection with the prohibition of creeping things, a setting forth of the spiritual ground on which the distinction between clean and unclean is based. Cf. x. 10, xx. 25, 26; 1 Peter i. 15, 16.

NOTE on CHAP. XI. 2—30.

ON THE DISTINCTION BETWEEN CLEAN AND UNCLEAN IN RESPECT TO FOOD.

I. *The distinction made by the Law a special mark of the chosen people.* II. *Different theories of the details.* III. *The primary distinction, that between Life and Death.* IV. *Conditions of animal food.* V. *The distinction on its practical side not peculiar to the Law.* VI. *The wisdom of it on sanitary grounds.* VII. *In what was the Mosaic Law of distinction peculiar?*

I. The object of this law is declared in *vv.* 43, 47, and is emphatically repeated in ch. xx. 24—26, "I am the Lord your God, which have separated you from other people. Ye shall therefore put difference between clean beasts and unclean, and between unclean fowls and clean: and ye shall not make your souls abominable by beast, or by fowl, or by any manner of living thing that creepeth on the ground, which I have separated from you as unclean. And ye shall be holy unto me: for I the Lord am holy, and have severed you from other people, that ye should be mine."

The basis of the obligation to maintain the prescribed distinction is thus declared to be the call of the Hebrews to be the peculiar people of Jehovah. It was to be something in their daily life to remind them of the Covenant which distinguished them from the nations of the world. It might so become an apt type of the call itself, the clean animals answering to the Israelites and the unclean to the Gentiles. St Peter's vision of the vessel like a sheet knit at the four corners, "wherein were all manner of foorfooted beasts of the earth, and wild beasts, and creeping things, and fowls of the air" (Acts x. 12), appears to recognize it in this way. It was at that time made known to the apostle that the revelation, which had broken down the middle wall of partition between Jew and Gentile, had pronounced every creature of God to be clean; that every creature of God is good, and nothing to be refused, if it be received with thanksgiving (1 Tim. iv. 4); that it is not that which goeth into the mouth which defileth a man, but that which cometh out of the mouth. Matt. xv. 11. The elect people were no longer to be tied by the letter of the Law in regard to their food, but were to be left to the exercise of a regenerated judgment. They were to learn that the kingdom of God is not eating, or abstaining, from meats and drinks; but righteousness, and truth, and peace, and joy in the Holy Ghost. Rom. xiv. 17.

II. Various opinions have been formed as to what considerations directed the line by which clean animals were separated from unclean.

It has been held, (1) That the food forbidden was such as was commonly eaten by the neighbouring nations, and that the prohibition served as a check to keep the people away from social intercourse with the Gentiles[1]. (2) That the flesh of certain animals from which the Egyptians abstained, because they held it to be sacred, was pronounced clean, and treated as common food; and that the flesh of other animals, which was associated with the practice of magic, was abominated as unclean, in order that the Israelites might in their daily life bear a testimony against idolatry and superstition[2]. (3) That it is impossible to refer the line of demarcation to anything but the arbitrary will of God[3]. (4) But the notion which has been accepted with most favour is that the distinction is based wholly or mainly upon symbolical ground. By some it has been connected with the degradation of all creation through the fall of man. The apparent reflection of moral depravity in the disposition of some animals has been identified in rather a loose way with the unclean creatures of the Law[4]. Following in the wake of many of the Fathers, or perhaps rather turning their figurative language into formal interpretation, some modern critics have attached symbolism also to the particulars in the form and physiology of animals, from which rules are laid down for distinguishing the classes of clean and unclean animals. The cloven hoof, standing firmly on the ground, and yet well adapted for locomotion, has been taken as a figure of the standing in the world and the walk in the road of life of the believer: the ruminating process is regarded as intended to remind the Israelites of the duty of forming a habit of meditating again and again on the divine counsels (Josh. i. 8). As the fins of a fish are intended to raise it out of the mud in which such creatures as the eel dwell, so prayer and faith are meant to raise the soul out of darkness and pollution[5]. (5) Many have considered that the prohibition of the unclean animals was based mainly or entirely upon sanitary grounds, their flesh being regarded as unwholesome[6].

[1] Davidson, 'Int. to O. T.' I. 258.

[2] Origen, 'Cont. Cels.' IV. p. 225. See on Lev. xi. 18, 19, 29.—It is surprising to find Ewald imagining that the Israelites ate oxen and other animals out of ridicule of the idolatry of those animals by the Egyptians. 'Hist. of Israel,' I. p. 573. Beef was eaten by the Egyptians as freely as by the Israelites. Wilkinson, I. p. 166.

[3] Cunæus, 'de Rep. Heb.' II. 24 in 'Critici Sacri.'

[4] Barnabas, 'Ep.' ch. X. Aristæus in Euseb. 'Prep. Evan.' VIII. 9. Jones of Nayland, 'Zoologia Ethica.' Keil.

[5] See Kurtz, 'Sac. Worship,' pp. 28, 20.

[6] Maimon. 'Mor. Nev.' III. 48. Spencer, 'de

The different views which have been held on the subject are discussed at length by Spencer and by Michaelis. We may briefly remark, in regard to the First view we have stated, that the animal food of the ancient Egyptians and Arabians appears to have been, with but little exception, the same as that of the Israelites[1]: in regard to the Second, that the clean ox, sheep, goat, and stag were amongst the animals which were held as most sacred by the Egyptians. On the Third nothing need be said, except that it is arbitrary and unsatisfactory In regard to the Fourth, it is strange that its advocates should overlook the facts that the morose and sulky bull and the capricious goat are clean, while the patient camel and the hare are unclean; and that the hoof of the unclean horse and the foot of the unclean camel seem to be better adapted to symbolize the outward life of the faithful believer than the foot of the ox or the sheep.

III. In order to come to anything like a satisfactory conclusion on the subject, it seems necessary to look more strictly than some have done at the way in which this law was regarded in the practical life of the Hebrews. The division which was the foundation of the law was not one of *living* animals. Uncleanness, as such, belonged to no creature while it was alive. The Hebrew treated his camel and his ass with as much care as he did his ox or his sheep, and came into contact with them as freely. And further, regarding them as authorized symbols of spiritual truth, the Lion and the Eagle were in the vision of the prophet coordinate with the Ox and the Man, Ezek. i. 10. But according to the whole spirit of the Law, as well as its letter, every dead body, whether of a human being, of an animal clean or unclean, if it had died of itself or had been killed in a common way, was a polluted thing, not to be touched. We have thus brought before us the great opposition between Life and Death. As every living animal was clean, so every dead animal, in its natural condition, was unclean.

IV. But it was necessary to make provision for human food. The Law therefore pointed out those animals which Divine wisdom decided to be the best for the purpose; and it ordained that, when they were required as food, they should be slaughtered in a particular manner and sanctified by being brought to the door of the Tabernacle (Lev. xvii. 3—6). They thus became ceremonially excepted from the general taint of death. The blood, in which was "the life of the flesh" (Lev. xvii. 11, see note), was carefully drawn off from the meat, which having been presented before Jehovah, was endowed with a new relation. It was made clean and fit to be the food of Jehovah's people. See Note after ch. xvii.

V. The distinction between clean and unclean animals was no new thing at the time of the giving of the Law. It had been recognized before the flood and immediately afterwards (Gen. vii. 2, 3, viii. 20). But we are not told how far the patriarchal rule coincided with the Mosaic.

The chief part of the animal food of cultivated nations has in all ages and in all parts of the world been taken from the same kinds of animals. The ruminating quadrupeds, the fishes with fins and scales, the gallinaceous birds and other birds which feed on vegetables, are evidently preferred by the general choice of mankind. Where there has been no prescribed law the common usage has tended to the same practical result. The ancient Gentile laws on the subject, as far as we are acquainted with them, are, with very inconsiderable exceptions, in agreement with this law of Moses. The Egyptian priests, we are told, abstained from the flesh of all solid-hoofed quadrupeds, all which have toes and all which have not horns; from birds of prey and from fish[1]. The Parsees are said to reject the flesh of all beasts and birds of prey and of the hare. The ancient Arabians, though, like the modern Moslems, they ate the flesh of the camel, carefully abstained from pork (see notes on *vv.* 4, 7). According to the Moslem law, all beasts and birds of prey, the ass, the mule, and (in the judgment of the best authorities) the horse, all insects except locusts, and all animals living in the water except true fish, are prohibited[2]. The Brahmin rule is based upon an appeal to a certain divine law which is infringed in the ordinary facts of nature. It is assumed to be right that only the higher creature should eat the flesh of the lower. When, as in the case of beasts and birds of prey, an animal feeds upon another in the same rank with itself, the order is disturbed, and its flesh becomes impure and unfit for the food of the Brahmin. Menu says, "for the sustenance of the vital spirit, Brahmâ created all this animal and vegetable system; and all that is moveable or immoveable that spirit devours. Things which do not move are eaten by creatures with locomotion; toothless animals, by animals with teeth; those without hands, by those to whom hands are given; and the timid, by the bold. He who eats according to (this) law commits no sin, even though every day he taste the flesh of such animals as may lawfully be tasted; since both the animals which may be eaten, and those who eat them, were equally created by Brahmâ[3]". It would seem that the flesh of the cow, from which nearly all modern Hindoos

'Leg. Heb.' I. ch. 7. Michaelis, 'Laws of Moses,' No. CCII., &c.

[1] See below, § V.

[1] Chæremon, quoted by Porphyry, 'De Abst.' IV. 7.

[2] 'Hedàya,' Vol. IV. p. 74.

[3] 'Institutes of Menu,' ch. V. 28—35.

strictly abstain, was originally not excepted from the lawful diet of the Brahmins[1]. But beasts of prey, quadrupeds which have solid hoofs and those which have five toes (except the hare and a few others), the tame pig, carnivorous birds, webfooted birds, the heron, the raven, the parrot, and fish of all kinds, appear to have been expressly prohibited from the earliest times[2].

VI. It cannot be doubted that the distinction which is substantially recognized by these different nations is in agreement with the laws of our earthly life. All experience tends to shew that the animals generally recognized as clean are those which furnish the best and most wholesome sorts of food. The instinct of our nature points in the same direction. Every one dislikes the snake and the toad. No one likes the form and habits of the pig[3]. We shrink from the notion of eating the flesh of the hyæna or the vulture. When we are told of our fellow-creatures eating slugs, snails and earthworms, and accounting the grubs found in rotten wood a peculiar delicacy[4], the feeling of disgust which arises within us would not seem to be the offspring of mere conventional refinement. This conclusion is not invalidated by the fact that our own repugnant feelings have been subdued in the case of the oyster and the pig. In regard to the distinction as it is laid down in the Mosaic Law, Cyril appears to be amply justified in saying that it coincides with our natural instinct and observation[5].

It has indeed been alleged by modern critics that the Law "cannot be supposed to have a dietetic object." (Kurtz, Keil, &c.) But this is surely taking a very contracted view of the subject. He who gave the Law to Moses created the earth with all that it contains and man who lives upon it. It cannot have been beneath Him or His chosen servant to instruct His people to live in accordance with the harmony of which He is the author, and to obey His laws whether they relate to the body or the spirit.

VII. But if the distinction of animals laid down by Moses agreed in the main with that recognized by other nations than the Hebrews, we may ask what just claim has this law to the distinctive character ascribed to it in Lev. xi. 43—47, xx. 25, 26? In what way was it essentially connected with the separation of Israel from the nations of the world? The answer appears to be this;—the ordinance of Moses was for the *whole* nation. It was not, like the Egyptian law, intended for priests alone; nor like the Hindoo law, binding only on the twice-born Brahmin; nor like the Parsee law, to be apprehended and obeyed only by those disciplined in spiritual matters. It was a law for the people, for every man, woman and child of the race chosen to be "a kingdom of priests, an holy nation" (Exod. xix. 6). It was to be one of the foreshadows of the higher spiritual equality of the better seed of Abraham which was in later ages pronounced "a chosen generation, a royal priesthood, an holy nation, a peculiar people." 1 Pet. ii. 9; cf. Is. lxi. 6, also 1 Cor. x. 17.

[1] Colebrooke, quoted in 'The Hindoos,' published by Knight, ch. VIII.

[2] Menu, v. 11—18.

[3] See note on Lev. xi. 7.

[4] See Hieron. 'adv. Jovin.' II. 7.

[5] 'Cont. Jul.' IX. p. 316.

CHAPTER XII.

1 *The purification of women after childbirth.* 6 *Her offerings for her purifying.*

AND the LORD spake unto Moses,
saying,
2 Speak unto the children of Israel,
saying, If a [a]woman have conceived
seed, and born a man child: then she
shall be unclean seven days; according
to the days of the separation for
her infirmity shall she be unclean.
3 And in the [b]eighth day the flesh
of his foreskin shall be circumcised.
4 And she shall then continue in
the blood of her purifying three and

[a] chap. 15. 19.

[b] Luke 2. 21. John 7. 22.

CEREMONIAL PURIFICATIONS.

CHAPTERS XII.—XV.

The Purifications of the Law fall under three heads; (i) those for defilement arising from secretions; (ii) those for the Leprosy; (iii) those for pollution from corpses. The first and second classes are described in these chapters; the last, as relates to human corpses, in Num. xix., and as relates to the bodies of dead animals, in Lev. xi. 24—28, 31—40.

CHAPTER XII.

PURIFICATION AFTER CHILD-BIRTH.

It would seem that this chapter would more naturally follow the fifteenth. See Prel. Note to ch. xv.

1. *unto Moses*] The Lawgiver is now again addressed alone, not along with Aaron, as in the preceding chapter and the following one.

2. *according to*, &c.] Rather, "**the same as the days of separation.**" Her un-

thirty days; she shall touch no hallowed
thing, nor come into the sanctuary,
until the days of her purifying be fulfilled.
5 But if she bear a maid child, then
she shall be unclean two weeks, as in
her separation: and she shall continue
in the blood of her purifying threescore and six days.
6 And when the days of her purifying are fulfilled, for a son, or for a
† Heb. *a son of his year.* daughter, she shall bring a lamb †of
the first year for a burnt offering,
and a young pigeon, or a turtledove,
for a sin offering, unto the door of
the tabernacle of the congregation,
unto the priest:
7 Who shall offer it before the
LORD, and make an atonement for
her; and she shall be cleansed from
the issue of her blood. This *is* the
law for her that hath born a male or
a female.
8 [c]And if †she be not able to [c] Luke 2. 24.
bring a lamb, then she shall bring † Heb. *her hand find not sufficiency of.*
two turtles, or two young pigeons;
the one for the burnt offering, and
the other for a sin offering: and the
priest shall make an atonement for
her, and she shall be clean.

---

cleanness was accounted to be of the same degree as that described xv. 19 sq.

3. On circumcision, see Gen. xvii. 10, 13.

4. During the first period of seven days the mother was called "unclean" and communicated defilement to whomever, or to whatever, she touched. During the second period of thirty-three days she was said to be "in the blood of her purifying." Her impurity at this time was not infectious, but she was restrained from joining in the public religious services. It should be observed that the Levitical law ascribed impurity exclusively to the Mother, in no degree to the Child. See Note after ch. xv.

5. No very satisfactory reason appears to have been given for this doubling of each of the two periods. Some of the Fathers, and several modern writers, conceive that it was intended to remind the people of the fact that woman represents the lower side of human nature, and was the first to fall into temptation. 1 Tim. ii. 13—15; 1 Pet. iii. 7. But to whatever reason it is to be assigned, a notion appears to have prevailed amongst the ancients that the mother suffers for a longer time after the birth of a girl than after the birth of a boy. According to Hippocrates and Aristotle, the period required for the restoration of her health in the one case was thirty days, and in the other, it was forty or forty-two days. This notion may have been connected with a general custom of observing the distinction as early as the time of Moses. Arist. 'Hist. An.' VII. 3, § 2; 4, § 3; Hippoc. Vol. I. p. 392, edit. Kuhn; Hesychius in loc.

6—8. The purification of the mother is completed by a sacrificial act which expressed an acknowledgment of sin and a dedication of herself to Jehovah. The same was done by those who were purified from their issues (xv. 14, 15, 29, 30); and, with the addition of a Trespass-offering, by the cleansed Leper (xiv. 12—20), and the reconsecrated Nazarite (Num. vi. 11, 12). Every complete act of sacrificial worship under the Law began with a Sin-offering. See Introd. § xvi. That there is nothing emphatic in the Sin-offering in connection with childbirth (as some have imagined) is evidently shewn not only by these parallel cases, but by the inferiority of the victim for a Sin-offering compared with that for the Burnt-offering, the first being a bird, the other a lamb.—The Virgin Mary availed herself of the liberty which the Law allowed to the poor, and offered the inferior Burnt-offering, Luke ii. 24.

6. *of the first year*] Literally, as in the margin, *the son of his year;* cf. xiv. 10. This expression is supposed to mean one less than a year old, while *the son of a year* is one that has just completed its first year.

8. *a lamb*] Rather, **one of the flock;** either a sheep or a goat, Heb. *seh*; in *v.* 6, the word is *kebes*. See Introd. § IV.

two turtles, or two young pigeons] See on i. 14.

she shall be clean] Uncleanness was generally ascribed to childbirth, according to the usages of the most ancient nations. The Hindoo law pronounced the mother of a newborn child to be impure for forty days, required the father to bathe as soon as the birth had taken place, and debarred the whole family for a period from religious rites, while they were to "confine themselves to inward remembrances of the Deity:" in a Brahmin family this rule extended to all relations within the fourth degree, for ten days, at the end of which they had to bathe. According to the Parsee law, the mother and child were bathed, and the mother had to live in seclusion for forty days, after which she had to undergo other purifying rites. The Arabs are said, by Burckhardt, to regard the mother as unclean for forty days.

The ancient Greeks suffered neither childbirth, nor death, to take place within consecrated places: both the mother and child were bathed, and the mother was not allowed to approach an altar for forty days. The term of forty days, it is evident, was generally regarded as a critical one for both the mother and the child.—The day on which the Romans gave the name to the child, the eighth day for a girl and the ninth for a boy, was called *lustricus dies*, "the day of purification," because certain lustral rites in behalf of the child were performed on the occasion, and some sort of offering was made. The Amphidromia of the Greeks was a similar lustration for the child, when the name was given, probably between the seventh and tenth days (Menu, v. 62; Ayeen Akbery, Vol. II. p. 556; Zend Avesta, ap. Bähr; Thucyd. III. 104; Eurip. 'Iph. Taur.' 382; Callim. 'Hym. ad Jov.' 16, 'Hym. ad Del.' 123; Censorin. 'De Die Nat.' cap. xi. p. 51; Celsus, II. 1; Festus, s. *Lustrici Dies*, with the note in Lindemann II. 480; Smith, 'Dict. of Antiquities,' s. *Amphidromia*). On the essential distinction of the Mosaic purification, see Note at the end of ch. xv.

CHAPTERS XIII. XIV.

THE LAWS RELATING TO LEPROSY.

Preliminary Note on the Character of the Disease.

I. *Importance of the subject.* II. *Names of the Disease.* III. *Its nature.* IV. *The Tuberculated variety.* V. *The Anæsthetic variety.* VI. *Each form recognized by the ancients.* VII. *Subordinate varieties.* VIII. *Is it incurable?* IX. *Is it hereditary?* X. *Is it endemic?* XI. *What circumstances foster it?* XII. *Is it contagious?*

I. The Leprosy is the most terrible of all the disorders to which the body of man is subject. There is no disease in which hope of recovery is so nearly extinguished. From a commencement slight in appearance, with but little pain or inconvenience, often in its earlier stage insidiously disappearing and reappearing, it goes on in its strong but sluggish course, generally in defiance of the efforts of medical skill, until it reduces the patient to a mutilated cripple with dulled or obliterated senses, the voice turned to a croak, and ghastly deformity of features. When it reaches some vital part it generally occasions what seem like the symptoms of a distinct disease (most often Dysentery), and so puts an end to the life of the sufferer.

Its mode of selecting its victims has something of the same mysterious deliberation as its mode of attack. It passes on slowly from country to country and from race to race, as little checked by variations of climate as by artificial remedies. If the type of disease is in some degree modified in different countries, or in particular cases, by local circumstances or constitutional peculiarities, it never fails to have its own way in the general character of the effect produced. From the time of Moses till the coming of Christ we know that it prevailed amongst the Hebrew race. At this time, that race, as a whole, does not seem to be especially subject to it. It has moved off and has in turn visited almost every other branch of the human family. On the most superficial view of the subject, it would seem that no disease could so well deserve to be singled out by Divine wisdom as the object of special laws[1].

Owing to the happy exemption in modern times of the greater part of Europe from the dreadful scourge, as well as to the lurking secrecy of its own nature, the subject in its bearing on the Levitical law has been beset with doubts until within the last few years. Our information respecting it was incoherent and unsatisfactory, being mainly derived from the insulated and imperfect reports of individual observers in distant lands, not one of whom had well examined a sufficient number of cases to furnish ground for fair generalization. Even to this day, the great question as to the disease being contagious cannot be answered with well-grounded confidence. It was not until the appearance of a Report on the Leprosy in Norway, drawn up under the sanction of the government by Dr Danielssen, chief physician of the leper hospital at Bergen, and Prof. Boeck (published in Paris, 1848), that there were materials for treating the inquiry in a methodical way. Recent medical writers, especially Mr Erasmus Wilson and Dr A. T. Thomson, have added some important observations. Mr Wilson has devoted a chapter of his book 'On Diseases of the Skin' to the illustration of Lev. xiii. (4th edit. p. 384). But since the publication that work, the College of Physicians have issued a series of questions regarding the nature of Leprosy, its prevalence, and its treatment, to which answers have been received from the best qualified persons in above fifty places on the shores of the Mediterranean, in India, China, our African and North American colonies and the West Indies: from these answers a Report has been drawn up. Mr E. Atkinson of Leeds, formerly surgeon to the Jews' hospital at Jerusalem, collected a valuable body of observations, in his visits to the leper houses from 1856 to 1860, with which the writer has been favoured in manuscript. Chiefly from these sources the information

[1] See Note on xiii. 45, 46.

contained in the following notes respecting the nature and symptoms of the disease has been drawn[1]. Not only the explanation of the Levitical law, but the importance which the Leprosy assumes in the history of the human race, and of the Israelites in particular, may justify the space which is here given to the subject.

II. Much confusion has arisen from the ambiguity of the name in popular use. The Hebrew word for the disease to which the Law relates is *tzāra'ath* (צרעת) or *nega' tzāra'ath* (נגע צרעת). In the English Bible *tzāra'ath* is always rendered Leprosy, *nega' tzāra'ath*, a plague of Leprosy. From its derivation, *tzāra'ath* has nearly the same meaning as *nega'*, *i.e.* a stroke. But *tzāra'ath* became the specific name of the disease, and is nowhere found in any other sense, except in so far as it is applied to a disease with similar aspect in Lev. xiii. 12. See note. *Nega'*, on the contrary, is a general name for plague, stroke, or wound. Gen. xii. 17; Deut. xvii. 8; 2 Chron. vi. 28; Ps. xxxviii. 11, lxxxix. 32; Is. liii. 8, &c. From the way in which its visitation was regarded, *nega'* is, however, frequently applied to it without *tzāra'ath*, as *stroke* is applied to paralysis among ourselves. Lev. xiii. 17, 22, 32, &c.

It is now considered by all the best authorities that *tzāra'ath* does not denote the disease which is more properly called the Leprosy[2], but that which is known to physicians as the Elephantiasis. As the right distinction in applying the names was clearly observed by the Greek and Latin medical writers[3], and as both the Elephantiasis and the Leprosy must have been familiarly known in Egypt, it is remarkable that the LXX. should have adopted λέπρα as the rendering of *tzāra'ath*. To them must be ascribed the fact that *Leprosy* has become the established scriptural name and that by which the disease was universally known in the middle ages.

It seems worth while to observe that Elephantiasis is often popularly used as the name of a disease, properly called *Bucnemia*, or, from the place in which it was first known to prevail, "the Barbadoes leg." Its distinguishing mark is an enlargement of the leg, and it is wanting in the more important features of the disease of which it sometimes usurps the name[4].

III. Elephantiasis is now considered by most observers to be quite distinct in its nature from any of those diseases with which it has often been supposed to be connected, such as the Lepra vulgaris, Psoriasis, Syphilis, Yaws, &c.[5] Its character seems indeed to be more strongly individualized than that of almost any other malady. Its origin is ascribed to "an animal poison generated in or received into the blood, accumulated therein probably by a process analogous to fermentation." (Wilson.) This poison primarily affects either the skin, by depositing in it a peculiar albuminous substance, or the nerves and nervous centres, at last destroying them so as to take away sensation. In this way, two forms of elephantiasis are distinguished, the *Tuberculated Elephantiasis*, and the *Anæsthetic* or *Non-tuberculated Elephantiasis*[6]. Some of the most obvious external effects of these forms, in well-marked cases, bear such different aspects that they might easily be taken to belong to two entirely distinct maladies. But the identity of their origin appears to be clearly proved by several facts. In many cases, the characteristic features of the two forms are combined[7]; instances occur in which one form changes entirely into the other[8]; and in hereditary transmission, the parent is sometimes afflicted with one form and the child with the other[9].

The numbers in brackets prefixed to the particulars described in the two following paragraphs are referred to in the notes on those expressions in Lev. xiii. which the particulars appear to illustrate.

IV. (1) The Tuberculated Elephantiasis is the more common form. It generally first shews itself by inflamed patches in the skin, on the face, ears or hands, of a dull red or purplish hue, from half an inch to two inches in diameter. (2) These soon change to a brownish or bronze colour, with a metallic or oily lustre, and a clearly-defined edge, and in this state they often remain for several weeks or months. (3) In some cases these external symptoms disappear altogether, and after a while again shew themselves. (4) By degrees the discoloured surface becomes hard, and rises here and there into tubercles at first reddish, but afterwards either bronzed or white. The scarf skin often scales off. The hardness and rising result from a thickening of the true skin by the injection of albuminous matter. (5) After another period, of weeks, or months, or even of years, many of the tubercles subside and leave a kind of cicatrix, thinner than the surrounding skin, which may remain either bronzed or white. (6) The tubercles which do not subside, or which break out again, may vary from the size of a pea to that of a pigeon's egg; and after continuing, it may be for years, with no external change, they ulcerate, discharging a whitish matter. The ulcers often eat into the

[1] To these may be added, 'Notes on the Leper Hospital at Granada,' by Dr Webster, in the 'Medico-Chirurgical Transactions,' Vol. XLIII.

[2] The proper Leprosy (*Lepra vulgaris*) is a disease of a different and much more superficial nature. See on xiii. 12.

[3] See § VI.

[4] 'Report of the College of Physicians,' p. viii.

[5] 'Report,' pp. xli., lxviii.

[6] 'Report,' p. lxix.

[7] 'Report,' pp. ix., xi., xv., &c.

[8] 'Report,' p. lxiv.

[9] 'Report,' p. lxviii., &c.

muscle till they expose the bones, or, occasionally, heal over and leave hard white cicatrices. (7) Should there be any hair on the tubercles, it either falls off, or turns white, and the hair of the head and eyebrows mostly disappears[1]. From the gradual swelling of the features the face assumes a sort of lion-like or satyr-like aspect, which suggested the names which have been sometimes applied to the disease, *Leontiasis* and *Satyriasis*. The change on the surface of the skin has given rise to other names, in more modern times, such as the Black Leprosy, and the Humid Leprosy. "When the disease is fully formed, the distorted face, and the livid, encrusted and ulcerated tubercles, the deformed, sightless and uncovered eyes, the hoarse, whispering voice, the fœtid breath and cutaneous excretion, the contorted joints, which are often buried in or absolutely dislocated by tubercles, the livid patches on those parts of the body not yet tuberculous, all form a picture which is not exceeded in the horror of its features by any other disease" (Dr A. T. Thomson). (8) The disease for the most part creeps on with irresistible progress until it attacks some vital organ and occasions death.

V. (1) The Anæsthetic Elephantiasis often commences in the forehead (see 2 Chron. xxvi. 19, 20), with shining white or copper-coloured patches and vesicles, technically called *bullæ*, which are developed suddenly without pain, soon burst, and discharge a milk-like matter. (2) An inflamed ulcerated surface is left, which is very tender, but heals after a time and leaves a smooth, white, insensible cicatrix without hair. The hair in some cases returns, but it is always white and fine. For a period, sometimes of years, fresh crops of bullæ arise. (3) The disease soon attacks the joints of the fingers and toes, and afterwards those of the larger limbs, which drop off bone by bone. In some cases the bones appear to be absorbed. The ulcers heal with wonderful celerity and completeness. It is said that amputation by Elephantiasis will often "bear comparison with the most finished performance of the surgeon." (4) The limbs which are affected but do not ulcerate become at last so completely devoid of sensation that portions of them may be burned, cut, or nibbled off by mice, without the person being conscious of it. (5) The face never becomes so utterly deformed as in Tuberculated Elephantiasis, but the skin is, for the most part, tightly strained over the features with a mummy-like aspect, the eyelids droop, tears continually flow, and the lower lip hangs down and exposes the teeth and gums. The taste, sight and smell fail, but the voice is not affected. (6) The eyebrows and lashes, and the other hair, generally fall or become white. (7) The progress of the disease is even much slower than that of Tuberculated Elephantiasis, and its fatal termination is not so nearly certain. The average duration of life after the first appearance of the disease in the one is ten years, in the other nearly twenty, or, in India, above thirty years[2]. In each of the two forms death is mostly preceded by an attack of Dysentery. See § I. (8) Anæsthetic Elephantiasis is sometimes called the Joint evil, and sometimes the Dry Leprosy: but it is still more frequently known as the White Leprosy, and under that name is confounded with what is more properly called the Leprosy, to which it bears, in its early stages, a superficial resemblance. See § II., and notes on Lev. xiii. 12, 38.

VI. Both these forms of Elephantiasis were well known to the ancient physicians and were accurately described by them, but they were treated as separate diseases. Aretæus and Celsus have well described the Tuberculated form under the name *Elephantiasis*. Celsus has described the Anæsthetic form under the name of *Vitiligo alba* or λεύκη. He has associated it, but not confounded it (as many moderns have done), with the common white Leprosy, which he calls by the name ἀλφός, the word which the LXX. have rightly used in Lev. xiii. 39. Herodotus also, with better knowledge than some of his commentators, distinguishes λεύκη from λέπρα (the latter appears to be the same as the ἀλφός of Celsus), both of which were regarded as unclean by the ancient Persians, not distinguished as they were in the Mosaic law[3].

VII. It has appeared desirable thus far to discriminate the two forms of Elephantiasis in order to explain the references to particular symptoms in this chapter of Leviticus. At this present time, that which prevails by far the most, especially in Egypt and Syria, is the Tuberculated form. But it should be kept in view that the two in a great number of cases work together (see § III.); and, as it did in the days of Moses, the disease appears occasionally in an ambiguous form on some one part of the body, with but little or no tendency to spread. One variety (*Morphæa alba*) sometimes affects a single limb with "a dead pearl-like whiteness." Mr Wilson likens the thigh of one of his patients to "a piece of beautiful white marble sculpture[4]." This reminds one of the hand of Moses, "leprous as snow," Ex. iv. 6, and of the application of the same expression to the leprosy of Miriam, Num. xii. 10, and to that of Gehazi, 2 K. v. 27. Other local varieties, to which reference appears to be made in the Law, will be noticed in the notes on Lev. xiii. 29—40. In some rare cases, the Tuberculated Ele-

[1] See on Lev. xiii. 3.

[2] 'Report,' p. lxv.; 'Abstract of Replies,' p. 116.

[3] Aretæus, p. 174 sq., edit. Kühn; Celsus, lib. III. p. 25; Festus, s. *Vitiligo*, with Lindemann's note, p. 742; Herodot. I. 138.

[4] 'Diseases of the Skin,' p. 376.

phantiasis becomes acute, the tubercles rapidly rise and become ulcerated, and the disease runs its course in a few weeks[1]. This may perhaps explain Job ii. 7, 8.

VIII. Medical skill appears to have been more completely foiled by Elephantiasis than by any other malady. That the Israelites regarded it as beyond the reach of natural remedies has been inferred from the words of the king of Israel, "Am I God to kill and to make alive, that this man doth send unto me to recover a man of his leprosy?" 2 K. v. 7. The ancient physicians prescribed treatment for it, but it appears to have been commonly regarded as incurable in the times of Cyril and Augustin[2]. Of modern physicians, a great number express themselves with entire hopelessness in regard to Tuberculated Elephantiasis; but the Anæsthetic form seems to be in some degree amenable to remedies and regimen. It has however been observed that, from the false shame usually felt by those who are afflicted with it, the disease in either form is rarely seen by the physician until it has passed the stage in which remedies might be applied with hope of success. Change of climate and habit of living, with certain medicines, chiefly preparations of iron, iodine and arsenic, seem to have done good in some cases[3]. The disease appears at times to stop of itself and to lie dormant for years, and some spontaneous cures are recorded[4]. It is a fact worthy of notice, that the people of Jerusalem and its neighbourhood do not send pure Anæsthetic cases to the leper houses, because they believe them to be curable (Mr Atkinson).

IX. It cannot reasonably be doubted that Elephantiasis is hereditary. (Cf. 2 K. v. 27.) There are families in which it has been handed down for ages. The lepers of New Brunswick afford a remarkable instance. The disease was brought into the settlement by a French emigrant family named Bredau, originally from St Malo. Of the twenty-two inmates of the leper house, every one is related by blood to that unfortunate stock[5]. It however frequently skips over a generation, and affects only one or two members of a family. The children of leprous parents are in infancy as fair, and seem to be as healthy, as others. The morbid symptoms generally make their first appearance about the age of puberty, and the work of destruction then creeps on until the comely child becomes a disfigured and mutilated man. But there are many cases in which the malady first appears in more advanced life, when there seems to be no hereditary transmission. Of 213 cases examined in Norway, 189 proved to be hereditary, and 24 of spontaneous origin. In Crete, out of 122 cases, 76 were hereditary, and 46 spontaneous[6].—It is a well-established fact that in almost all places where the disease prevails, there are many more men affected with it than women.

X. The attachment of Elephantiasis to particular races may be regarded as subordinate to its hereditary transmission. The prevalence of the disease appears to be much more dependent on local or special circumstances than on race, which evidently does not circumscribe the instances of its spontaneous appearance. The evidence bearing on these points is remarkable. In Syria, Elephantiasis still keeps its ground, but it is said to be unknown among the Jews who live there[7]; Mr Atkinson, however, saw a *single* Jew leper at Jerusalem. No leper of Jewish race has been known for many years to die in the Presidency of Bombay, where the number of lepers is perhaps as great as in any part of the world. At Aden, where Arabs, Hindoos and Parsees all suffer from the disease, the Jews enjoy the same immunity as the Europeans[8]. Lower Egypt, the old seat of Elephantiasis, maintains its unhappy distinction in spite of the change in the races which inhabit it; but there it prevails more among the Jews than among the Arabs. As was probably the case in ancient times, in and near this same region, the Anæsthetic form more affects the Jews, and the Tuberculated form, the Arabs[9]. In Crete, where there are supposed to be a thousand lepers, it spares no race, but the Greeks have it in the most aggravated degree. It has been observed that in Crete, Cyprus and Scio, the Moslems are less subject to it than the Christians, and their exemption is ascribed to their abstaining from pork, and using frequent ablutions[10]. In the West Indies, the blacks and coloured races are the most affected, while the Jews appear to suffer in the next degree, and in some parts of Jamaica they suffer more than any[11]. The native races of India, and the Chinese, appear at the present time to be more subject to the disease than any other peoples. In the Presidency of Bombay, and the Deccan, there are villages in which the lepers exceed one per cent. of the population[12]. There are 900 in the leper asylum at Canton, and 2,500 are supposed to

[1] Wilson, p. 342.

[2] Cyril, 'Glaph. in Lev.' p. 36; August. 'Serm. ad Pop.' 78.—Aretæus (p. 341) considered that there was hope of cure if the disease was taken in its early stage, but that when advanced it was incurable. In accordance with the best results of modern experience, he chiefly recommended as remedies baths and attention to diet.

[3] 'Report,' pp. liv.—lvi., lxxi.

[4] 'Report,' pp. liv.—lvi., lxxi., lxxii.; Wilson, pp. 337, 338, 355.

[5] 'Report, 'Abstract of Replies,' p. 6.

[6] 'Report,' pp. xxxix., xli., lxvii.; 'Abstract of Replies,' p. 64.

[7] 'Report. Abstract,' 54—57. Cf. 'Report,' pp. xxix., lxvi.

[8] 'Abstract,' p. 110.

[9] 'Abstract,' p. 53.

[10] 'Abstract,' pp. 55—65.

[11] 'Report,' p. xxix.; 'Abstract,' pp. 9—15

[12] 'Abstract,' p. 112, &c.

be getting their living in the city as beggars and pedlars[1].

XI. The inquiry into the circumstances which may produce or foster Elephantiasis is connected with its local distribution. It was in Norway that it was first observed that the disease prevails most on the seacoast, where the people live chiefly upon fish. Extensive observations have since been made elsewhere, and it may be considered as well established, that those communities who live mainly upon fish, and those whose chief meat is the flesh of ill-fed pigs, are the most subject to Elephantiasis. The tendency is aggravated where the fish and pork are generally salted. The Jews of Jamaica, among whom the disease prevails, eat more fish than any other part of the population[2]. On the importance of these facts, as regards our present purpose, see notes on Lev. xi. 7, 9—12. Oil used as food in excess, or in a rancid state, also appears to encourage the disease[3].

An impression has prevailed that Elephantiasis prevails more amongst the poor than amongst those who are in comfortable circumstances. The habits of living which poverty is apt to engender might seem to make this reasonable. But there are some strong testimonies on the other side respecting the Jews of Jamaica and Constantinople, and respecting other races, in Mauritius, Tobago, and elsewhere: and it has been remarked that a large proportion of the lepers who are in good circumstances are kept out of sight, so that their number is probably underrated. The evidence from Barbadoes seems to favour the conclusion that Tuberculated Elephantiasis prevails equally amongst all classes, but that the Anæsthetic form is more common amongst the poor[4].

XII. But the question whether Elephantiasis is contagious or not, is the one of most peculiar interest in connection with the Levitical law. The Committee of the College of Physicians consider that the weight of evidence is decidedly on the negative side[5]. The freedom with which lepers often live with others in the closest domestic relation indicates that common opinion practically takes the same view. Several surgeons are said to have wounded themselves in the dissection of leprous bodies, without suffering any characteristic injury[6]. But many of those who have replied to the Leprosy Committee affirm their belief that the disease is contagious in a certain stage, when the ulcers are running[7]. It is evident that, if the disease is contagious, a very rare and critical concurrence of circumstances is required to develope the contagion. But it should not be overlooked that the contagiousness of a disease cannot be disproved by the multitude of escapes, if there are a few well-attested and well-observed facts in its favour. It cannot, at any rate, be doubted that the few Englishmen who have suffered from Elephantiasis have always, or nearly always, associated with leprous people, or lived in leprous countries[8]. The case of Dr Robertson, who while superintending the leper house in the Seychelles islands became a leper, is a very important one[9].—The recent investigations have not tended to confirm the popular opinion which in different ages has assigned the origin of cases of Leprosy to irregularities of life[10].

We have thus far given an outline of those particulars in the nature of the disease in question, which seem most likely to throw light upon the reasons and the forms of this portion of the Levitical law. Some few further details, which seem to be referred to in the text, will be given in the notes.—On the mode in which lepers have been treated in different ages and nations, see Note after chap. xiii. We believe that it will be found that modern observations and science not only tend to set forth the Divine wisdom which directed the mind of Moses, but that they also shew the precision of the terms used in the Law. It should however be carefully observed that the particular features of the disease which are here mentioned are those belonging to its earlier stages, at the time when its actual presence is more or less doubtful[11]. The object of these directions was to enable the priests to decide upon such cases. That the Israelites were familiar with the horrors of its more matured development is sufficiently shewn by Num. xii. 12, and, probably, by Job ii. 7, 8[12].

[1] 'Abstract,' p. 77.

[2] See 'Abstract of Replies,' from Norway, New Brunswick, China, Japan, India, Mauritius, &c. 'Report,' p. lxviii, and Dr Webster's 'Notes on the Granada Hospital.'

[3] 'Report,' p. lxvii. 'Abstract of Replies,' from Smyrna, Crete, the Ionian Islands.

[4] 'Abstract,' pp. 30, 31. [5] 'Report,' p. vii.

[6] 'Abstract,' pp. 32, 86, &c. Wilson, p. 356. But see on the other side Mr Wilson's cases described in the Appendix, pp. 235, 239; and 'Notes on the Granada Hospital.'

[7] 'Abstract,' pp. 25, 32, 36, 67, 77, 108.

[8] 'Observations,' by Mr Wilson, in the Appendix to the Report, p. 231. 'Notes on the Granada Hospital.'—An excellent observer in Mauritius, in a private letter, states that he has personally known only two Europeans affected with the disease. Each of these had married Creole women, apparently free from disease, but they have left leprous children.

[9] 'Abstract,' p. 90.

[10] See Theod. 'Quæst. in Lev.' 21; Otho, 'Rabb. Lex.' p. 367. 'Report,' pp. xli., xlii.

[11] A recent writer speaks of "the confused and imperfect account of the leprosy given in Leviticus." A more careful perusal of the text might have shewn him that Moses does not pretend to give *an account* of the disease, which must have been familiar enough, in its great features, to those for whose immediate use he wrote.

[12] Origen was most probably right in calling the disease of Job Elephantiasis. 'Cont. Cels.' p. 305.

CHAPTER XIII.

1 *The laws and tokens whereby the priest is to be guided in discerning the leprosy.*

AND the LORD spake unto Moses and Aaron, saying,
2 When a man shall have in the
skin of his flesh a ‖ rising, a scab, or
bright spot, and it be in the skin of
his flesh *like* the plague of leprosy;
then he shall be brought unto Aaron
the priest, or unto one of his sons the
priests:
3 And the priest shall look on
the plague in the skin of the flesh:
and *when* the hair in the plague is
turned white, and the plague in sight
be deeper than the skin of his flesh,
it *is* a plague of leprosy: and the
priest shall look on him, and pronounce him unclean.
4 If the bright spot *be* white in
the skin of his flesh, and in sight *be*
not deeper than the skin, and the hair
thereof be not turned white; then the
priest shall shut up *him that hath* the
plague seven days:
5 And the priest shall look on
him the seventh day: and, behold,
if the plague in his sight be at a
stay, *and* the plague spread not in
the skin; then the priest shall shut
him up seven days more:

‖ Or, *swelling*.

CHAPTER XIII.

THE SIGNS OF LEPROSY, 1—44.

1. Both Moses and Aaron are now addressed. See on xii. 1.

The first marks of the Disease. 2—8.

2. *the skin of his flesh*] This expression is found nowhere but in this chapter. The word rendered *skin* (*'ōr*) is commonly used for the external skin either of man or of an animal. See Ex. xxxiv. 29; Job vii. 5; Lev. iv. 11, vii. 8, &c. Mr Wilson has inferred from the nature of the case that, in this connection, the phrase "skin of his flesh" denotes the cuticle or scarf skin, as distinguished from the cutis or true skin. He observes that one of the most important distinctions between Elephantiasis and other diseases which outwardly resemble it in its early stages, is that it affects the cutis rather than the cuticle. See Prel. Note to this chap., § III., § IV. 4. We are thus to understand the expression in the next verse, and elsewhere in the chapter, "deeper than the skin of his flesh," as, **below the scarf skin.**

[1]*rising*—[2]*scab*—[3]*bright spot*] The Hebrew words thus fairly rendered according to their derivation, are used only in reference to the Leprosy. They are repeated in the same order in xiv. 56. They seem to be technical names applied to the common external signs of incipient Elephantiasis: (1) either the Tubercle of the Tuberculated form or the Bulla of the Anæsthetic (Prel. Note § IV. 4, § V. 1), (2) the Cicatrix (§ IV. 5, § V. 2), and (3) the Glossy patch (§ IV. 2, § V. 1). The rendering of the LXX., though it is rather loose, appears to countenance this view of the words, which are summed up as, a symptomatic or shining scar—οὐλὴ σημασίας ἢ τηλαυγής.—The references on the word *scab*, in the margin of the later editions of our Authorized Version, belong more properly to verse 18, where the original word is different. See on *v.* 18.

like the plague of leprosy] **like a stroke of Leprosy.** There is no article.

3. *the hair in the plague is turned white*] The sparing growth of very fine whitish hair on leprous spots in the place of the natural hair, appears to have been always regarded as a characteristic symptom (Prel. Note, § IV. 7, § V. 6). Dr Davison, after carefully examining nearly a hundred lepers in Madagascar, says: "The hairs upon the part become yellow and stunted, and after a time fall off, leaving the hair bulbs empty and enlarged, especially on the face, so as to present *one of the most diagnostic signs* of the malady." (Appendix to 'Report,' p. 221.) Wilson speaks of the diseased hair as "so fine as to be hardly perceptible." Celsus, in reference to the Anæsthetic Elephantiasis, speaks of it as like pale down (in eaque albi pili sunt, et lanuginis similes). The "yellow thin hair" is mentioned in *v.* 30. The Arabs are said to regard a case of Elephantiasis as curable, if dark hairs are found on the spots. (Forskal, quoted by Keil.) It should however be kept in view that the hair of the head, even when this is not the part of the body visibly diseased, generally falls; and, if it returns, it is always whitish; see on *vv.* 29—37: sometimes the hair is white in patches. Hence a white head was regarded by the ancients as a common sign of the disease. Æschylus, 'Choeph.' 276; Æschines, 'Epist.' I.; Aristotle, 'Hist. An.' III. 10, § 5.

the plague in sight be deeper than the skin of his flesh] **the stroke appears to be deeper than the scarf skin.** See on *v.* 2. This symptom, along with the whitish hair, at once decided the case to be one of Leprosy.

4. *bright spot...not deeper than the skin*] See Prel. Note, § IV. 2, § V. 1.

5. *and the plague spread not*] Rather, **advance not**, so as to shew that the disease is under the cuticle and to assume the defined

6 And the priest shall look on
him again the seventh day: and, behold, *if* the plague *be* somewhat dark,
and the plague spread not in the skin,
the priest shall pronounce him clean:
it *is but* a scab: and he shall wash his
clothes, and be clean.
7 But if the scab spread much
abroad in the skin, after that he
hath been seen of the priest for his
cleansing, he shall be seen of the
priest again:
8 And *if* the priest see that, behold, the scab spreadeth in the skin,
then the priest shall pronounce him
unclean: it *is* a leprosy.
9 ¶ When the plague of leprosy is
in a man, then he shall be brought
unto the priest;
10 And the priest shall see *him*:
and, behold, *if* the rising *be* white in
the skin, and it have turned the hair
white, and *there be* †quick raw flesh
in the rising;
11 It *is* an old leprosy in the skin
of his flesh, and the priest shall pronounce him unclean, and shall not
shut him up: for he *is* unclean.
12 And if a leprosy break out a-
broad in the skin, and the leprosy
cover all the skin of *him that hath*
the plague from his head even to his
foot, wheresoever the priest looketh;
13 Then the priest shall consider:

† Heb. *the quickening of living flesh.*

---

edge and the glossy surface that are characteristic of leprous spots. See on *v.* 2 and Prel. Note, § IV. 2. The old English versions, instead of "spread not," have "grow not," and this rendering is more in accordance with the LXX. and Vulgate. The Hebrew verb (*pāsah*) occurs nowhere but in this and the following chapter. It is applied only to the progress made by a spot of Leprosy, and there is no reason why its meaning should be restricted to superficial extension.

6. *somewhat dark*] Rather, **somewhat dim**: that is, if the spot is dying away, or wanting either in the gloss or in the clearly defined outline by which leprous spots are distinguished. Prel. Note, § IV. 2.

spread not] *i.e.* **advance not.**

it is but a scab] If it was a mere common scab, not the result of Leprosy, the man had to wash his clothes in order that he might appear no longer as a leper.

7. *spread much abroad in the skin*] Rather, **advance much in the skin.**

seen of the priest for his cleansing] The purport of these words is doubtful. They probably mean "seen by the priest and pronounced clean." Taken in this way, they would refer to the visit of the suspected leper to the priest at the end of the second week. The direction here given would thus bear on a recurrence of the morbid symptoms after the case had been discharged (Prel. Note, § IV. 3). So Vulg., Luther, Geneva Fr. and Eng., Rosenmüller, Herxh., Luzzatto, Wogue. We are thus left to draw the inference that if, at the end of the first week, the spot was seen to have advanced, the person was at once declared a leper (cf. *v.* 32). But some have taken the words to mean "seen by the priest with a view to be pronounced clean" (de Wette, Knobel, Keil). Our Version has, perhaps rightly, preserved the ambiguity of the original. The Law according to the explanation here preferred regards the sentence of the priest as provisional, holding good only till the symptoms may appear to resume their progress. Cf. *v.* 35.

8. *spreadeth*] **advances.** See on *v.* 5.

Case of confirmed Leprosy. 9—11.

When the disease had become confirmed before the patient was brought to the priest, which might occur either through mistake, indifference, the natural unwillingness to undergo examination, or the rapid progress of the stroke (Prel. Note. § VII., § VIII.), the man was at once pronounced unclean.

10. *if the rising be white*] Rather, **if there be a white rising.** The term very probably denotes the white Bulla of Anæsthetic Elephantiasis when it has re-appeared. Prel. Note, § V. 1, 2.

quick raw flesh in the rising] The margin gives the literal rendering. The symptom here denoted exhibits a more advanced stage of the disease than those that have been previously mentioned. The expression might denote an ulcer or open sore with fungous granulations (or "proud flesh") appearing in it. If this is not the meaning, it may possibly be referred to that excessive tenderness (*hyperæsthesia*) which, especially in Anæsthetic Elephantiasis, affects the surface before it becomes insensible. Prel. Note, § V. 2, cf. § IV. 6. The interpretation of the LXX. and the Mishna, which some have adopted, that an insulated spot of sound flesh in the midst of a Tubercle is meant, must be a mistake.

Case of the Common Leprosy. 12—17.

If a great part of the surface of the body had turned white, with none of the proper symptoms of Elephantiasis, the man was to be pronounced clean. But if, after he had been discharged by the priest, ulceration made its appearance, he was to be regarded as a leper

and, behold, *if* the leprosy have covered all his flesh, he shall pronounce *him* clean *that hath* the plague: it is all turned white: he *is* clean.

14 But when raw flesh appeareth in him, he shall be unclean.

15 And the priest shall see the raw flesh, and pronounce him to be unclean: *for* the raw flesh *is* unclean: it *is* a leprosy.

16 Or if the raw flesh turn again, and be changed unto white, he shall come unto the priest;

17 And the priest shall see him: and, behold, *if* the plague be turned into white; then the priest shall pronounce *him* clean *that hath* the plague: he *is* clean.

18 ¶ The flesh also, in which, *even* in the skin thereof, was a boil, and is healed,

19 And in the place of the boil there be a white rising, or a bright spot, white, and somewhat reddish, and it be shewed to the priest;

20 And if, when the priest seeth it, behold, it *be* in sight lower than the skin, and the hair thereof be turned white; the priest shall pronounce him unclean: it *is* a plague of leprosy broken out of the boil.

21 But if the priest look on it, and, behold, *there be* no white hairs therein, and *if* it *be* not lower than the skin, but *be* somewhat dark; then the priest shall shut him up seven days:

22 And if it spread much abroad in the skin, then the priest shall pronounce him unclean: it *is* a plague.

23 But if the bright spot stay in his place, *and* spread not, it *is* a

---

unless the ulceration proved to be but temporary.

12. *the leprosy*] The Hebrew word *tzāra'ath* appears to be here used with the same sort of breadth as *Leprosy*, in modern times, and *Vitiligo*, in ancient times. The disease indicated appears to be that now known as *Lepra vulgaris*, the common White Leprosy, or Dry Tetter. Prel. Note, § II., § VI. Cf. on *v.* 39. It first shews itself in reddish pimples, the surface of which becomes white and scaly, spreading in a circular form till they meet each other and cover large patches of the body. It scarcely affects the general health, and for the most part disappears of itself, though it often lasts for years.

from his head even to his foot, wheresoever the priest looketh] The first appearance of the Lepra vulgaris may take place in any part of the body, especially however at the larger joints of the limbs; but the spots of Elephantiasis are almost always first seen on those parts which are habitually exposed, the face, ears and hands.

16. *raw flesh*] See on *v.* 10. The existence of an open sore on the white surface might, it would seem, prove to be either the ulceration of Elephantiasis complicated with the milder disease, as described in *v.* 14, or a sore of a common sort that would soon heal.

Special cases of Leprosy. 18—28.

The first case of this sort is spoken of in *vv.* 18—23. The Hebrew word *shechīn* (*v.* 18), rendered "boil," is of doubtful origin. The most probable rendering of it here and in most other places is **ulcer**: so the LXX. and Vulg. It is applied (1) to the "boil" of Hezekiah, which might have been an abscess or carbuncle, Is. xxxviii. 21; 2 K. xx. 7; (2) to the "boils" of Job, Job ii. 7, 8; (3) to the "boils breaking forth with blains" (*i.e.* pustules) of the Egyptians, Ex. ix. 9; and (4) to "the botch of Egypt," Deut. xxviii. 27, 35. In these latter instances, but especially in the second and fourth, it would seem highly probable that the word expresses the ulcers of Elephantiasis: so Gesenius and Fürst As Elephantiasis has certainly been from early times a characteristic disease of Egypt, see Note on xiii. 45, 46, § I., and as its nature is so dreadful, it seems most likely that it should be the first named of the diseases to which the Egyptians were subject in such a list as that given in Deut. xxviii. 27. Admitting this, there is probably reference to the special action of Anæsthetic Elephantiasis, "the Joint evil," in *v.* 35 of the same chapter: "The LORD shall smite thee in the knees, and in the legs, with a sore botch that cannot be healed."

19—21. The passage appears to refer to one of the ordinary modes in which Elephantiasis is now known to reappear when tubercles, bullæ or glossy spots, white or reddish, appear in the scar of an ulcer. Prel. Note, § IV. 5, 6, § V. 2.

20. *lower than the skin*] Rather, **reaching below the scarf skin.** See on *v.* 2. The same correction should be made in *v.* 21. As compared with the word *deeper. vv.* 3. 4, &c., the word *lower* might justly represent the Hebrew. It would seem, however, that no distinction of meaning is intended.

boil] Rather, **ulcer.** Heb. *shechīn.*

burning boil; and the priest shall
pronounce him clean.
24 ¶ Or if there be *any* flesh, in
the skin whereof *there is* † a hot burning, and the quick *flesh* that burneth
have a white bright spot, somewhat
reddish, or white;
25 Then the priest shall look upon it: and, behold, *if* the hair in
the bright spot be turned white, and
it *be in* sight deeper than the skin; it
is a leprosy broken out of the burning: wherefore the priest shall pronounce him unclean: it *is* the plague
of leprosy.
26 But if the priest look on it,
and, behold, *there be* no white hair
in the bright spot, and it *be* no lower
than the *other* skin, but *be* somewhat
dark; then the priest shall shut him
up seven days:
27 And the priest shall look upon
him the seventh day: *and* if it be
spread much abroad in the skin, then
the priest shall pronounce him unclean: it *is* the plague of leprosy.
28 And if the bright spot stay in
his place, *and* spread not in the skin,
but it *be* somewhat dark; it *is* a
rising of the burning, and the priest
shall pronounce him clean: for it *is*
an inflammation of the burning.
29 ¶ If a man or woman have a
plague upon the head or the beard;

† Heb. *a burning of fire.*

---

somewhat dark] Rather, **somewhat dim.**

22. *spread much abroad*] Rather, **advance much.** See on *v.* 7.

plague] i.e. *the stroke of leprosy.* Prel. Note, § II.

23. *a burning boil*] Rather, **the scar of the ulcer**; literally, *the burn of the ulcer.*

The second special case of Leprosy is spoken of in *vv.* 24—28. The main question here is, what is denoted by "a hot burning"? The Hebrew is literally rendered in the margin. The greater number of commentators, Jewish as well as Christian, take it as a burn, in the simple sense of the word. Some suppose it to be a Carbuncle. It may perhaps denote a place previously affected by any sort of inflammation resulting either from disease or injury. Such a spot may be either more liable to leprous development, or liable to be affected by the disease in such a peculiar way as to claim distinct notice. It should be observed that in each of the two special cases which have been mentioned, only a single period of quarantine is appointed, instead of the two periods which were provided when the disease came in its usual course.

24. The sense of this verse in accordance with the view we have given might be thus expressed:—*Or if there be flesh of which the skin has been affected by severe inflammation, and the sore of the inflammation has become a glossy spot, somewhat reddish or white.*

26. *no lower than the other skin*] The word *other* is here out of place. The Hebrew is the same as in *v.* 20, and means, **not beneath the scarf skin.**

somewhat dark] Rather, **somewhat dim.** See on *v.* 6.

27. *spread much abroad*] Rather, **have made much advance.** See on *v.* 5.

28. This verse might perhaps be rendered:—*And if the glossy spot continues unchanged and makes no advance in the skin, and is rather indistinct* (see on *v.* 6), *it is the mark of the inflammation, and the priest shall pronounce him clean, for it is the* (*mere*) *hurt of inflammation.*

The Leprosy upon the Head or Chin. 29—37.

The Leprosy which made its appearance amongst the hair of the head or of the beard, was formally distinguished from the Leprosy in other parts of the body (see also ch. xiv. 54), and was called *nethek*, which our translators have rendered a scall, or a dry scall. As *scall* is the name for another disease not allied to the Leprosy, it would have been better to retain the original word. The chief features of the disease are the same as those of ordinary Elephantiasis, the morbid affection of the entire depth of the skin and the yellow or whitish hairs. It is a true Elephantiasis, and is recognised by modern writers under the name of *Morphœa alopeciata*, or the Fox mange. It usually appears in one or two circular patches, from which the hair falls off either suddenly or by degrees. The hair sometimes appears again of its natural colour, and the disease is then subdued. See *v.* 37. But if the hair returns, as it often does, while the disease is advancing, it appears whitish and impoverished. A common seat of the *nethek* in adult men is the chin. It is sometimes permanent for life, but it more frequently passes away after a period of months or years (Wilson, p. 383). The ancients called this form of Elephantiasis, *Lichen.* Pliny uses the specific name, *Mentagra*, *i.e.* the beard evil, and describes an aggravated variety of it, which he says first appeared in the beard, often spread over the face, and at times over the breast and hands. It was brought into Italy from Asia in the time of Tiberius. The Lichen men-

30 Then the priest shall see the
plague: and, behold, if it *be* in sight
deeper than the skin; *and there be*
in it a yellow thin hair; then the
priest shall pronounce him unclean:
it *is* a dry scall, *even* a leprosy upon
the head or beard.
31 And if the priest look on the
plague of the scall, and, behold, it
be not in sight deeper than the skin,
and *that there is* no black hair in
it; then the priest shall shut up *him
that hath* the plague of the scall seven
days:
32 And in the seventh day the
priest shall look on the plague: and,
behold, *if* the scall spread not, and
there be in it no yellow hair, and
the scall *be* not in sight deeper than
the skin;
33 He shall be shaven, but the
scall shall he not shave; and the
priest shall shut up *him that hath* the
scall seven days more:
34 And in the seventh day the
priest shall look on the scall: and,
behold, *if* the scall be not spread in
the skin, nor *be* in sight deeper than
the skin; then the priest shall pronounce him clean: and he shall wash
his clothes, and be clean.
35 But if the scall spread much in
the skin after his cleansing;
36 Then the priest shall look on
him: and, behold, if the scall be
spread in the skin, the priest shall
not seek for yellow hair; he *is* unclean.
37 But if the scall be in his sight
at a stay, and *that* there is black
hair grown up therein; the scall is
healed, he *is* clean: and the priest
shall pronounce him clean.
38 ¶ If a man also or a woman
have in the skin of their flesh bright
spots, *even* white bright spots;
39 Then the priest shall look: and,
behold, *if* the bright spots in the skin
of their flesh *be* darkish white; it *is* a
freckled spot *that* groweth in the
skin; he *is* clean.
40 And the man whose † hair is

† Heb. *head is pilled.*

---

tioned by Æschylus, in which the hair round the temples turned white, was probably of the same kind, still more aggravated, and was that which in the time of Æschines afflicted the people of Delos. Æsch. 'Choeph.' 276, Æschines, 'Ep.' I., Aretæus, p. 181, Plin. 'H. N.' XXVI. 2.

29. *a plague*] See Prel. Note, II.

30. *if it be in sight deeper than the skin*] **if it appears to be deeper than the scarf skin.** See on *v.* 5. The same correction is required in *vv.* 32, 34, 35, 36.

a yellow thin hair] The indefinite article should be omitted. See on *v.* 3.

31. *there is no black hair in it*] More probably, **there is no yellow hair in it.** In order to make sense with the context, we must either (1) change the copulative conjunction into an adversative one, so as to read, *if the spot is not seen to be deeper than the cuticle and yet there is no black hair in it.* This would imply that the presence of dark hair (see on *v.* 3) would be needful in order to save the person from quarantine (Drusius, several Jewish authorities, De Wette, Herxheimer); or (2) omit the negative before black. This would mean that the person should be shut up on account of the suspicious aspect of the spot, although it might appear only on the surface and the hair on it had not yet changed colour (Vulgate); or (3) read *yellow* instead of *black* (Septuagint, Luther, Knobel, Keil). This last gives the best sense, and it is likely that the LXX. and the old Italic represent the original reading of the Hebrew.

32. We must infer that if the diseased spot had advanced at the end of the first week, the person was immediately pronounced unclean. See on *v.* 7.

37. *be in his sight at a stay*] **does not alter in appearance.**

The Freckled spot. 38, 39.

39. *freckled spot*] The original word, *bōhak*, is said to be still used by the Arabs for a superficial skin disease, neither dangerous nor contagious. It appears that the Eastern and Southern Arabs call it *baras*, while they call Elephantiasis *djedam*. Palgrave, Vol. II. p. 34. Burton, Vol. II. p. 182. The LXX. use ἀλφός in this place. Prel. Note, VI. If *v.* 12 refers to the Lepra vulgaris, as seems most probable, the Hebrew *bōhak* may denote some kind of *Eczema*, a skin disease of a somewhat similar external character. (Wilson, p. 165.)

These verses (38, 39) seem to intrude between the Leprosy of the hairy head and that of the bald head. They would seem more in their natural place between *vv.* 17, 18.

fallen off his head, he *is* bald; *yet is*
he clean.
41 And he that hath his hair
fallen off from the part of his head
toward his face, he *is* forehead bald:
yet is he clean.
42 And if there be in the bald
head, or bald forehead, a white reddish sore; it *is* a leprosy sprung up in
his bald head, or his bald forehead.
43 Then the priest shall look upon it: and, behold, *if* the rising of
the sore *be* white reddish in his bald
head, or in his bald forehead, as the
leprosy appeareth in the skin of the
flesh;
44 He is a leprous man, he *is* unclean: the priest shall pronounce him
utterly unclean; his plague *is* in his
head.
45 And the leper in whom the
plague *is*, his clothes shall be rent,
and his head bare, and he shall put
a covering upon his upper lip, and
shall cry, Unclean, unclean.
46 All the days wherein the plague
shall be in him he shall be defiled;
he *is* unclean: he shall dwell alone;
[a]without the camp *shall* his habita- [a] Numb. 5. 2.
tion *be*. 2 Kings 15. 5.
47 ¶ The garment also that the
plague of leprosy is in, *whether it be* a
woollen garment, or a linen garment;
48 Whether *it be* in the warp, or
woof; of linen, or of woollen; whether in a skin, or in any †thing made † Heb.
of skin; *work of.*
49 And if the plague be greenish
or reddish in the garment, or in the
skin, either in the warp, or in the
woof, or in any †thing of skin; it *is* † Heb.
a plague of leprosy, and shall be shewed *vessel,* or, *instrument.*
unto the priest:
50 And the priest shall look upon
the plague, and shut up *it that hath*
the plague seven days:

The Leprosy in the Bald head. 40—44.

Baldness was no mark of unclean disease: but when signs which might be those of Elephantiasis appeared in a bald head, they were to be dealt with as in other cases. According to Jewish tradition, there were two periods of quarantine assigned for this form of Leprosy as in that of the hairy head. Mishna, 'Negaim,' x. 10.

42. *sore*] Rather, **stroke**. The word here and in *v.* 43 is *nega'*, which elsewhere in this and the next chapter is rendered plague. Prel. Note II.

43. *rising of the sore*] Rather **rising of the stroke**. See Prel. Note IV. 4.

The law for the Confirmed Leper. 45, 46.

45. The leper was to carry about with him the usual signs of mourning for the dead. Cf. Ezek. xxiv. 17; Lev. x. 6. He was to mourn for himself as one over whom death had already gained the victory. See Note at the end of the chap.

his head bare] Rather, "his head **neglected**." See on Lev. x. 6.

Unclean, unclean] Cf. Lam. iv. 14, 15.

46. *dwell alone*] More properly, **dwell apart**; that is, separated from the people.

without the camp] Cf. Num. v. 2—4, xii. 14, 15; 2 K. vii. 3, xv. 5; Luke xvii. 12. According to the Mishna, a leper polluted everything in the house which he entered. A separate space used to be provided for lepers in the Synagogues ('Kelim,' I. 4; 'Negaim,' XIII. 11, 12).

LEPROSY IN CLOTHING AND LEATHER.

CHAPTER XIII. 47—59.

47. *The garment*] Rather, **The clothing**, in a general sense of material. The word should be thus rendered throughout this section. The ordinary dress of the Israelites in the wilderness was probably like that of the Egyptians described by Herodotus (II. 81), consisting of a linen tunic with a fringe (Num. xv. 38) and a woollen cloak or blanket thrown on in colder weather. Wool and flax were the great materials for clothing also in later times (Hos. ii. 9; Prov. xxxi. 13). They could not be spun together. See on xix. 19.

47, 48. The meaning of these verses may be thus given:—*And the clothing in which there is a stroke of Leprosy, whether the stroke is in clothing of wool or in clothing of linen; or in yarn for warp or in yarn for woof, either for linen clothing or for woollen clothing; or in a skin of leather or in any article made of leather.*—The warp and the woof here and in *vv.* 49, 51, 52, 53, 56, cannot mean, as is implied in our version, the constituent parts of woven cloth. The original words would as well denote *yarn prepared for warp* and *yarn prepared for woof*, and the connection evidently requires this sense. So De Wette, Knobel, Keil, Wogue.

49, 51, 53. *either in the warp*] This expression in all these verses should be, "**or** in the

51 And he shall look on the plague on the seventh day: if the plague be spread in the garment, either in the warp, or in the woof, or in a skin, *or* in any work that is made of skin; the plague *is* a fretting leprosy; it *is* unclean.

52 He shall therefore burn that garment, whether warp or woof, in woollen or in linen, or any thing of skin, wherein the plague is: for it *is* a fretting leprosy; it shall be burnt in the fire.

53 And if the priest shall look, and, behold, the plague be not spread in the garment, either in the warp, or in the woof, or in any thing of skin;

54 Then the priest shall command that they wash *the thing* wherein the plague *is*, and he shall shut it up seven days more:

55 And the priest shall look on the plague, after that it is washed: and, behold, *if* the plague have not changed his colour, and the plague be not spread; it *is* unclean; thou shalt burn it in the fire; it *is* fret inward,† *whether* it *be* bare within or without.

† Heb. *whether it be bald in the head thereof, or in the forehead thereof.*

56 And if the priest look, and, behold, the plague *be* somewhat dark after the washing of it; then he shall rend it out of the garment, or out of the skin, or out of the warp, or out of the woof:

57 And if it appear still in the garment, either in the warp, or in the woof, or in any thing of skin; it *is* a spreading *plague:* thou shalt burn that wherein the plague *is* with fire.

58 And the garment, either warp, or woof, or whatsoever thing of skin *it be*, which thou shalt wash, if the plague be departed from them, then it shall be washed the second time, and shall be clean.

59 This *is* the law of the plague of leprosy in a garment of woollen or linen, either in the warp, or woof, or any thing of skins, to pronounce it clean, or to pronounce it unclean.

---

warp." *In the warp* is coordinate with *in the clothing*, &c. See preceding note.

52. For the same reason, in this verse, "whether warp" should be "**or** warp."

51. *a fretting leprosy*] *i.e.* a malignant or corroding Leprosy. What was the nature of the Leprosy in clothing, which produced greenish or reddish spots, cannot be precisely determined. It was most likely destructive mildew, perhaps of more than one kind. Knobel and others are inclined to connect it with stains from leprous ulcers in the flesh. But there are no known facts to confirm this.

56. *somewhat dark*] Rather "somewhat **faint**."

57, 58, 59. *either*, in each of these verses, should be **or**. See on *vv.* 47, 49.

It should be noticed that no religious or symbolical rite is prescribed for Leprosy in clothing. The priest had only to decide whether the process of decay was at work in the article presented to him and to pronounce accordingly. Compare the Leprosy in houses, xiv. 33—53.

NOTE on CHAP. XIII. 45, 46.

ON THE TREATMENT OF LEPERS AND THE GROUNDS OF THE LAWS RESPECTING THEM.

I. *The Leprosy in Egypt.* II. *The way in which Lepers have been regarded.* III. *Their treatment according to the Law.* IV. *The Leprosy in Europe.* V. *Segregation of Lepers.* VI. *Its probable effects.* VII. *Objects of the Law respecting Leprosy.* VIII. *The Law was not cruel.*

I. Egypt was regarded in ancient times as the great seat of Elephantiasis. Lucretius says that the disease originated on the banks of the Nile, and Pliny repeats the statement, calling Egypt "genetrix talium vitiorum[1]." We know that the Israelites in Egypt lived upon nearly the same food as the Egyptians (Num. xi. 5; cf. Prel. Note, § XI.). We thus seem to have reason to infer that the disease must have prevailed considerably amongst the Hebrews while they were in Egypt. The legend repeated in a later age, which connects the Leprosy with the departure of the Israelites[2], may not be wholly with-

[1] Lucret. VI. 1112; Plin. 'H.N.' XXVI. 3, 5.

[2] Diod. Sic. Vol. II. p. 542; Tacitus, 'Hist.' V. 3, 4; Justin XXXVI. 2; Joseph. 'Ant.' III. 11. § 4; Chæremon and Manetho, quoted by Josephus, 'Cont. Ap.' I. 26, 32, 34.

out an element of truth in that form in which it is given by Manetho. The king of Egypt is said to have driven out from the country a multitude of Egyptian lepers along with the Israelites. If any such expulsion of lepers took place about the time of the Exodus, it seems very likely that a number of them joined the "mixed multitude," which travelled into the Wilderness along with the Israelites (Ex. xii. 38). That the people were in danger from Leprosy, and were very familiar with it, cannot be doubted, from the prominence which Moses has given to it in the Law.

II. The separation of Lepers from the familiar intercourse of social life has been common to nearly all nations and ages. The effect of the malady in disfiguring its victims, with the dread of contagion, whether justly founded or not (see Prel. Note to ch. xiii. § XII.), might sufficiently account for this practice. But at the same time must be noticed the all but universal impression that the Leprosy, above all other diseases, comes upon man as an irresistible stroke of superhuman power, either in the way of punishment for personal sin or of an infliction with some definite purpose. This natural suggestion was confirmed and realized upon several occasions in the history of the Israelites. A stroke of Leprosy was the mark of the divine displeasure at the slow faith of Moses, at the contumacy of Miriam, at the dishonesty of Gehazi, and at the impious presumption of Uzziah. One of the denunciations against Joab, on account of the death of Abner, was that his children should be lepers[1].

The ancient Persians did not allow their lepers to enter a city nor to have any dealings with other men, and they excluded foreign lepers from their country. According to Herodotus, they regarded the disease as a penalty for some offence committed against the Sun: according to the Zendavesta, it was a scourge sent by Ahriman. They had forms of prayer to be used by the devout when they happened to meet a leper[2]. The Greek writers speak of Leprosy as an infliction from Phœbus[3]. Aretæus says that lepers were avoided by all men, even their nearest relations, and that most of them withdrew into solitudes (p. 183). The Arabs will not sleep near a leper, nor eat with him, nor contract marriage with a family in which the Leprosy is known to exist. (Burckhardt, quoted by Knobel.) In China the disease is commonly spoken of as a retribution for sin, and lepers are excluded from society as objects of disgust and aversion: they often commit suicide, and there is a proverb common amongst Chinese lepers, "to die is to become clean:" intermarriage with leprous families is forbidden, though it sometimes takes place. In Japan, Madagascar and New Zealand, the disease is looked upon in the same light, and lepers are treated in nearly the same manner[4].

III. We are told in the Law that the lepers, during the period of their uncleanness, were to dwell apart, and to have their habitation without the camp. Though thus excluded from general intercourse with society, it is not likely that they ceased to be objects of sympathy and kindness, such as they now are in those Christian and Moslem countries in which the Leprosy prevails. That they associated together in the Holy Land, as they do at present, is evident from 2 K. vii. 3; Luke xvii. 12. It has been conjectured that a habitation was provided for them outside of Jerusalem, on the hill Gareb, which is mentioned only in Jer. xxxi. 40. It is mostly identified with Bezetha (Gesenius, Winer), the northern hill, which was brought within the city by the wall built by Agrippa. The name *Gareb* means, "the scabby hill;" and, assuming this to denote the hill of the lepers, it is supposed to be appropriately associated with Goath (on rather insecure ground identified with Golgotha), "the hill of the dead," and Tophet, "the valley of the dead bodies," as making up the three polluted spots that were to be purged and included within the limits of the renovated Holy City, according to the vision of Jeremiah[5].

IV. A few facts from the history of the Leprosy in Europe will not be out of place. Some of the varieties of Elephantiasis were known in Greece in the fourth century A.C., and probably in the fifth. But the disease appears not to have made its way into western Europe till the time of Pompey, when it was brought into Italy from Egypt. It is said to have disappeared soon afterwards, but it is likely that it lingered on from this time without spreading much[6]. A canon of the Council of Compiegne, A.D. 759, allows Leprosy to be a ground for divorce (Fleury). During the Crusades, in the eleventh and twelfth centuries, the disease appears to have spread all over Europe. At this time the public care of lepers was left exclusively to the ecclesiastical authorities[7]. At Constantinople, in the twelfth century,

[1] Ex. iv. 6; 2 K. v. 27; 2 Chron. xxvi. 19, 20; 2 S. iii. 29; Deut. xxiv. 8, xxviii. 27, with note on Lev. xiii. 18.

[2] Herodot. I. 138; Ctesias, 'Pers.' 41, with Bähr's note, p. 181.

[3] Æschylus, 'Choeph.' 276; Æschines, 'Ep.' I.

[4] 'Replies to the Leprosy Committee,' pp. 76, 79, 221, 223.

[5] Hengstenberg, 'Christology,' Vol. II. p. 450.

[6] Æschyl. 'Choeph.' 271; Æschines, 'Epist.' I.; Pliny, 'H. N.' XXVI. 1—5; Celsus, III. 25.

[7] After the rise of the Franciscan Order, they made lepers the object of their particular care. St Francis himself expressed his thankfulness that he had overcome his repugnance to come into contact with Leprosy. 'Monum. Francisc.' Appendix, p. 562.

lepers were admitted into the churches, and mixed in social life without restraint[1]. But in other places they were shut out of the churches, and did not mix in society. At the third Lateran Council, A.D. 1179, it was decreed, that wherever there was a sufficient number of lepers they should have a church, a priest, and a cemetery of their own, and that lepers should be exempted from paying tithe (Fleury). A similar canon was passed at the Synod of Westminster, A.D. 1200[2]. In the fifteenth century an ecclesiastical form was used, by which lepers were cut off from general intercourse, and were bound to wear a peculiar dress. On this ground, according to a canon passed at Nougarot, in Armagnac, A.D. 1290, they could not be brought before lay tribunals (Fleury). When a monk was stricken with Leprosy funeral obsequies were performed over him in the convent chapel, and he was taken in a sort of funeral procession to the abode of his relations (Ducange, s. *Leprosi*). In England the Leprosy was common from the tenth century to the beginning of the sixteenth[3]. Leper homes were numerous, but as most of them were found to be empty in the reign of Edward VI. they were destroyed, or turned to some other purpose[4]. The disease lingered longer in Scotland. A thanksgiving was celebrated in Shetland in 1742, on account of the disappearance of the Leprosy in the islands; but a Shetland leper survived in Edinburgh till 1798[5]. On the continent of Europe lepers became less numerous from the fifteenth century, but the disease maintained its ground in the northern maritime parts. In 1641 Evelyn saw "divers leprous poor creatures dwelling in solitary huts," between Delf and the Hague, who were supported by charity[6]. It would seem that in Iceland, and on the coast of Norway, Elephantiasis has rather increased during the present century; and the Anæsthetic form is more frequent there than elsewhere, unless some parts of India may be excepted. The disease appears to be slowly disappearing in the south of Spain[7].

V. The countries in which the Leprosy is known to have prevailed for the longest period are Egypt and Syria. No provision appears to have been made in Egypt for the segregation of lepers. In Syria, on the contrary, leper houses have existed from time immemorial, and it can hardly be unreasonable to connect this fact with the operation of the Law of Moses continued from age to age, even if we do not rest upon the conjecture regarding the appropriation of the hill Gareb (see § III.). There are at present such homes at Jerusalem, Damascus, Nablus and Ramleh. We are indebted to Mr Atkinson for the following particulars relating to the home at Jerusalem. It consists of a row of huts enclosed by a wall just within the south gate of the city. The lepers are maintained in part by a fund left by a pious Mussulman, but mainly by alms. Parties of four or five take their stand to beg at certain spots outside the city. Their receipts are equally shared. One of their number is appointed as Sheikh by the Pacha of Jerusalem to transact the business of the community. They are exempt from taxes. They are bound to reside within their quarter, but they are free to go into the city and to receive visits from their friends. The distinction between Christian and Moslem is wholly disregarded in their intercourse amongst themselves (cf. Luke xvii. 16). In 1860 the home contained 24 males and 9 females; all the latter were married except one. One of the women was in good health, and appeared to have suffered originally only from the Lepra vulgaris; but having been pronounced a leper, she could not be liberated owing to the want of some such provision as the purification of the Levitical Law. Compare the case of Simon the leper, Matt. xxvi. 6; Mark xiv. 3.

In modern times, since Elephantiasis has been more carefully observed, the segregation of lepers has become general. In the replies to the Committee of the College of Physicians it

1 Balsamon, ap. Suicer, s. Λεπρός.

2 Johnson's 'Canons,' Vol. II. p. 91, edit. 1851.—A small opening which is found in some old churches near the altar has been supposed to have been used to hand out the consecrated elements to leprous communicants, as they knelt outside. But this matter is involved in doubt. See 'Archæological Journal,' Vol. IV. p. 314.

3 The gradual disappearance of the disease in England may be curiously traced in our literature. In Lydgate's 'Testament and Complaint of Creseide,' published in Speght's and other early editions of Chaucer, the most striking features of Elephantiasis are described in clear and graphic terms, and Creseide has to dwell as "a lazarous" in a "leper lodge," and to go about begging with "a cup and clapper." (See Nares' 'Glossary,' s. *Clapdish*.) The writer must have been familiar with what he describes. Shakspeare speaks of the Leprosy, but applies the name to a different disease. Milton does not mention it, even in that terrible vision of the diseases to come upon mankind which Michael sets before Adam. 'P. L.' XI. 470 sq.

4 The largest leper house in England is said to have given the name to the village of Burton-lazars in Leicestershire. There were six in London; of which one, according to Pennant, occupied the site of St James's palace. Dugdale has given a list of eighty-five in different parts of England; but his list is far from complete.

5 Simpson, 'Antiquarian Notices of Leprosy,' quoted by Wilson.

6 'Diary' Vol. I. p. 18. See also Howell's 'Letters,' Bk. I. § 2, Letter 13.

7 Dr Webster's 'Notes on the Leper Hospital at Granada.'—There is a paper on the 'Geographical Distribution of Leprosy at the present time,' by Dr Gavin Milroy, in the Appendix to the 'Report on Leprosy' by the College of Physicians, p. 227.

is very generally recommended as the best way of checking the advance of the disease. Some striking facts bearing on this point are adduced. In Madagascar, the law has been relaxed within the last few years and the number of lepers has increased. The law has been stringently enforced at New Brunswick and the number has diminished. In most cases in which a diminished prevalence of the disease is reported, it is said to be connected with the same cause. Segregation has however been pronounced by the Committee as most probably inoperative in checking the progress of the disease[1]. It must of course be admitted that, from the nature of the malady, the results of any agencies to resist its operation can only be estimated by long and widely-spread observation.

VI. But without insisting on the probability that the Leprosy is, under certain rare conditions, contagious[2], it is obvious that segregation must have a salutary tendency in checking intermarriage between lepers and others. The Mosaic Law must have had this effect to the same extent as the modern usage of segregation. We know however that the disease continued to infest the Hebrew race as long as they dwelt in their own land, though probably in a diminishing degree. It is worthy of remark that the Jews at this day are much affected by Leprosy in the West Indies and in Egypt, while they are as free from it as any race in Syria, India and Europe. But whatever may be the state of existing facts, it is difficult to imagine that the exclusion of lepers from common intercourse, maintained during a very long period, can have failed to help in relieving the race of its terrible burden.

VII. Michaelis, in accordance with his general views of the Mosaic legislation, regarded the laws respecting Leprosy as based entirely upon sanitary considerations and the desirableness of keeping unsightly objects out of the way of common concourse: and on this ground he takes the rites enjoined for the healed leper as meant for little more than artificial sanctions to impress the minds of the people. Such a theory is neither consistent with the integrity of the Legislator nor with the dignity of the Law. But some writers seem to have erred in a contrary direction by denouncing a regard to sanitary results as unworthy of "an ambassador of God." (Cf. Note after ch. xi. § vi.) To believe that the Law took cognizance of the instincts which are common to our nature, and that its enactments were such as tended to promote the material benefit of the chosen people, in accordance with the dictates of sound political wisdom, is in nowise inconsistent with the belief that it also comprised a Spiritual meaning distinguishing it from ordinary legislation. The teaching of that which is invisible by means of visible objects cannot be less efficient when it consists in an appeal to real analogies in nature than when the sensible objects of illustration are arbitrarily chosen on account of their mere external appearance. The healing of the soul by the forgiveness of sins was revealed by the Son of God through the visible fact of the healing of the body. See Matt. ix. 2. In like manner, the proper treatment of Leprosy as a disease of the body became a type of the proper treatment of sin, not through a mere resemblance which might recommend itself to the fancy, but through the Law being an inspired interpretation of the Truths of nature.

That the Leprosy was entitled to the distinction with which it was treated in the ceremonial Law is indeed most obvious. Disease is the usher of death. Every sort of disease should convey a lesson not only to him that suffers from it, but to him that witnesses it. But it is evident that there could be no arrangement to make every case of disease bear its formal testimony, which would be feasible or compatible with the material welfare of the people. The malady which was most palpably expressive of the nature common to all disease became therefore the fit subject of special ordinances superadded to, or rather grafted upon, the sanitary regulations. The leper is one in whom it may be said "death lives" during the period of his leprous existence: he has been called "a walking tomb" (*sepulchrum ambulans*), "a parable of death." It was the sight first of a decrepit old man, then of a horribly deformed Leper, and lastly of a putrid corpse, which, according to the legend, confirmed Gótama Buddha in his resolution to retire from a world full of decay and death in order to lead the life of an ascetic. Hardy, 'Manual of Buddhism,' p. 154. The leper was thus the best parable in the world of the sin of which death was the wages; not the less so because his suffering might have been in no degree due to his own personal deserts. He bore about with him at once the deadly fruit and the symbol of the sin of his race. Ex. xx. 5. As his body slowly perished, first the skin, then the flesh, then the bone, and fell to pieces while yet the animal life survived, he was a terrible picture of the gradual corruption of the spirit wrought by sin. The best of all types of the healing of the Spirit, was the healing of the Leper. In his formal Cleansing, Consecration, and Atonement by sacrifice (see notes on xiv. 9—20), the ministers of the Sanctuary bore public witness that he was restored to the blessing of communion with his brethren and with Jehovah. Hence when the Son of God proved His divine mission by healing the lepers (Matt. xi. 5) He did not excuse them from going to the priest to "offer for the cleansing these things which Moses commanded" (Mark i. 44; Luke v. 14) "for a testimony to the people," Matt. viii. 4.

[1] 'Report,' p. vii.
[2] See Preliminary Note to ch. xiii., § XII.

How closely the Hebrews associated the Leprosy with Death is expressly shewn by the signs of mourning which the leper had to wear (Lev. xiii. 45), by Miriam being spoken of "as one dead" (Num. xii. 12), and by the words of Josephus, that the Law excludes lepers from civil life, as being "in no wise different from the dead"—νεκροῦ μηδὲν διαφέροντας[1].

The lower symbolical bearing of the law of Leprosy—that which related to Cleansing, as distinguished from Consecration (see on Lev. xiv. 9)—comes out in strong relief in what relates to that which was termed the Leprosy, in materials for clothing and shelter. The name appears to have been applied to certain processes of decay of which we cannot ascertain the precise nature (Lev. xiii. 47—59, xiv. 33—53). The rites ordained for cleansing evidently point to an analogy between that which slowly corrodes dead matter and the action of the poison of Leprosy on the body of man.

VIII. It has been objected that the treatment of lepers according to the Law was an inhuman confusion between sin and misfortune. It may seem that the leper had to endure a legal punishment in addition to the stroke of disease[2]. It was indeed, in itself, a hard condition that lepers were excluded from the Sanctuary. But the lesson which their disease was intended by Divine wisdom to teach the nation, could not be made complete without this. Not that the Leper was merely made use of for the sake of others: the lesson was for himself as well as for them, hard as it may have been for him to apply it. If he accepted it in faith and submission, though the ordinary means of grace were straitened for him, he might still have the spiritual satisfaction that he was fulfilling an ordained purpose of Self-sacrifice in acquiescing from his heart in the full meaning of the Divine Law. This mode of regarding the position of the outcast leper is remarkably shewn in a very ancient and widely-accepted interpretation of Isaiah liii. 4, according to which the prophet foresaw the Messiah *esteemed as a Leper, smitten of God, and afflicted* (*quasi leprosum et percussum a Deo et humiliatum.* Vulgate). This rendering has the authority of Symmachus, Aquila, St Jerome, Procopius, and many moderns.

But it may fairly be questioned whether the regulations of the Law lessened in any degree the amount of natural enjoyment of which the Leprosy left its victim capable. When we consider the loathsome outward effects of the disease, the consciousness in the leper that he was a marked and stricken man, and the fact that he was for the most part in no need of those attentions which relieve and solace ordinary invalids, he might have found his burden greater and more galling in the common intercourse of life than in the position marked out for him by the Law. If he was cut off from society which he might else have enjoyed, he was less frequently reminded that he was an object of aversion to his neighbours, and he probably had a much larger share of unqualified sympathy[3].

[1] 'Ant.' III. 11, § 3.—On the connection between the Leprosy and sin, see especially Theodoret, 'Quæst. in Lev.' xvi.; Hesych. *in loc.*; Cyril. Alex. 'Glaph.' *in loc.*

[2] Tertullian answers Marcion on this point, 'Adv. Marc.' IV. 35.

[3] This view of the effect of segregation on the happiness of lepers is strikingly confirmed by Mr Atkinson (MS. notes), Dr Webster ('Notes on the Hospital at Granada'), and in several of the Replies to the Leprosy Committee.

CHAPTER XIV.

1 *The rites and sacrifices in cleansing of the leper.* 33 *The signs of leprosy in a house.* 43 *The cleansing of that house.*

AND the LORD spake unto Moses,
saying,
2 This shall be the law of the leper
in the day of his cleansing: He [a]shall [a] Matt. 8. 2. Mark 1. 40. Luke 5. 12.
be brought unto the priest:
3 And the priest shall go forth out
of the camp; and the priest shall look,
and, behold, *if* the plague of leprosy
be healed in the leper;
4 Then shall the priest command

CHAP. XIV.

THE PURIFICATION OF THE LEPER. 1—32.

1. *unto Moses*] The directions for the Purification are addressed to Moses alone, those for the Examination to Moses and Aaron conjointly, xiii. 1.

The Leper was excluded not only from the Sanctuary but from the Camp. The ceremony of restoration which he had to undergo was therefore twofold. The first part, performed outside the camp, entitled him to come within and to mix with his brethren, 3—9. The second part, performed in the court of the Tabernacle and separated from the first by an interval of seven days, restored him to all the privileges of the Covenant with Jehovah, 10—32.

The Rites performed without the Camp. 3—7.

2, 3. The priest had to go to the entrance

to take for him that is to be cleansed
two ‖birds alive *and* clean, and cedar
wood, and scarlet, and hyssop:

‖Or, sparrows.

5 And the priest shall command
that one of the birds be killed in an
earthen vessel over running water:

---

of the camp at a time agreed on to meet and examine the cured Leper.

4. *two birds*]. Our translators have inserted in the margin, "or sparrows," in accordance with the rendering of the Vulgate. There is no reason to doubt that the Hebrew word *tzippōr*, evidently formed from the sound of chirping or twittering, may often denote a sparrow (Ps. lxxxiv. 3, civ. 17, &c.); but it is for the most part used for a bird in the general sense. Gen. vii. 14, xv. 10; Deut. iv. 17, &c.—This ceremony of the two birds has been very generally regarded by Commentators as a sacrifice in the proper sense of the word, like the two goats of the Day of Atonement. On the objections to this, see Note at the end of the chapter.

cedar wood, and scarlet, and hyssop] These, with the two birds and the spring water, were employed in cleansing the leprous house in precisely the same manner as they were on this occasion. See *vv.* 49, 51, 52. In burning the Red heifer (Num. xix. 6), they were all three cast into the fire and burnt with the victim instead of being dipped in the blood. Hyssop was used in sprinkling the blood of the Paschal lamb upon the doorposts and lintels of the Israelites in the observance of the Passover in Egypt (Exod. xii. 22), and in sprinkling the water of purification on a tent, a person or a vessel polluted by the touch of a dead body, Num. xix. 18. The scarlet and the hyssop, as well as the water mixed with the blood of victims, are mentioned by the writer of the Epistle to the Hebrews (ix. 19, 20), as having been used by Moses in sprinkling the Book of the Covenant and the people, though only the blood is named in Ex. xxiv. 6. From these passages we may infer that the three substances were used as the common materials in rites of purification. How far their natural qualities may have recommended them for this purpose, will be seen in the following notes. In their being burned with the Red heifer (Num. xix. 6), their symbolical import was simply expressed by their presence in the fire. But they seem to have been generally employed as instruments in the act of sprinkling. See the next three notes. Their full meaning in its deepest relation is brought out in the expression of the Psalmist, "Purge me with hyssop (the name here represents the whole rite) and I shall be clean," li. 7.

cedar wood] According to the Mishna, this was a stick of cedar a cubit in length. 'Negaim,' XIV. 6. But the name cedar appears to have been given by the ancients not only to the well-known Cedar of Lebanon, but to a Juniper (*Juniperus oxycedrus*), and it is almost certainly this which is here meant. It should be distinguished from the juniper with the fragrant wood of which we are familiar as "the pencil cedar" (*Juniperus Bermudiana*), the qualities of which are somewhat similar. We are told by Pliny that the wood was burnt in temples as incense before the time of the Trojan war. Its smoke was probably used as a disinfectant. The resin or turpentine obtained from it (κεδρία, *cedria*) was employed to preserve various substances from decay, and in its application to books it made the name cedar into a common proverb for literary immortality (Horat. 'A.P.' 332; Ovid. 'Trist.' I. 'El.' I. 7; Martial, III. 'Epig.' II. 7; Pers. 'Sat.' I. 42). It was applied by the Egyptians to preserve dead bodies from decay. It preserved clothes from moth. The wood itself of this Juniper is so enduring that it was spoken of as everlasting, and the statues of deities were often made of it. Cf. Is. xl. 20. Medicines were made of the turpentine which were used in Elephantiasis and other skin diseases. Herodot. II. 87; Theophrastus, see Schneider's 'Index rerum,' s. v. κέδρος; Plin. 'H. N.' XIII. 1, 11, XVI. 21, 76, § 1, 79, XXIV. 11; Dioscorides, 'Mat. Med.' I. 105 with Kühn's note; cf. Is. xl. 19; Suicer, s. v. κέδρος, § III. These testimonies make sufficiently clear the meaning which was given to the cedar wood in its ceremonial use, and especially in cleansing the leper.

scarlet] If we may trust to the Mishna this was a "tongue," or band, of twice-dyed scarlet wool, with which the living bird, the hyssop, and the cedar wood were tied together when they were dipped into the blood and water. 'Negaim,' XIV. 1, with the notes. The scarlet wool is generally supposed to express the rosy colour which is associated with health and vital energy. (Bähr, Kurtz, Keil, &c.) It is worth notice that scarlet is used by the prophets with a contrary signification. Isa. i. 18; Nahum ii. 3. The Mishna says that "a tongue of scarlet" was attached to the horns of the Scapegoat when he was sent into the wilderness. Lev. xvi. 22.

hyssop] See Ex. xii. 22. It is very doubtful what plant is meant. The Hebrew name is *ezōb*, and that used by the LXX. ὕσσωπος. It is generally admitted that it cannot be the plant now called hyssop (*Hyssopus officinalis*), which appears to have been unknown in ancient Syria and Egypt. It is by no means certain to what plant the Greeks gave the name ὕσσωπος. The references to the Hyssop of the Scriptures would seem to require (1) that the plant should be found in Egypt, the desert, and the Holy Land; (2) that it should grow

6 As for the living bird, he shall
take it, and the cedar wood, and the
scarlet, and the hyssop, and shall dip
them and the living bird in the blood
of the bird *that was* killed over the
running water:
7 And he shall sprinkle upon him
that is to be cleansed from the leprosy
seven times, and shall pronounce him
clean, and shall let the living bird
loose †into the open field.
8 And he that is to be cleansed
shall wash his clothes, and shave off
all his hair, and wash himself in water,
that he may be clean: and after that
he shall come into the camp, and
shall tarry abroad out of his tent
seven days.
9 But it shall be on the seventh
day, that he shall shave all his hair
off his head and his beard and his eyebrows, even all his hair he shall shave
off: and he shall wash his clothes,
also he shall wash his flesh in water,
and he shall be clean.
10 And on the eighth day he shall
take two he lambs without blemish,
and one ewe lamb †of the first year
without blemish, and three tenth deals
of fine flour *for* a meat offering,
mingled with oil, and one log of oil.
11 And the priest that maketh *him*

† Heb. *upon the face of the field.*

† Heb. *the daughter of her year.*

---

amongst stones and upon walls, and that it should be of low growth, so as to furnish a contrast when compared with the Cedar of Lebanon (1 K. iv. 33); (3) that it should have a stem capable of forming a stick of considerable length (Joh. xix. 29); and (4) that it should have such qualities as might fit it for use in the rites of purification.—The Jewish authorities, most of the older critics and some recent ones, are inclined to identify the *ezōb* of the Old Testament with some species of marjoram (*Origanum Ægyptiacum* or *O. Syriacum*). Several other well-known plants, most of them possessing aromatic, detergent, or disinfecting properties, such as rosemary, southernwood, thyme, and lavender, have been suggested. But no one of these is capable of producing a sufficiently long stick, to which the sponge could have been attached when it was raised to the lips of our Saviour. Bochart, who identifies the *ezōb* with marjoram of some kind, is in consequence driven to suppose that the Evangelist spoke of a different plant bearing the same Greek name. On the whole, it must be admitted that no single plant appears to meet all the conditions which Scripture seems to require so well as the Caper plant (*Capparis spinosa*), the claims of which were advanced by the late Prof. J. Forbes Royle. It grows freely in all the countries bordering on the Mediterranean Sea. One of the names that the Arabs give it is *asuf*, which comes very close to the Hebrew word. It is mentioned by Dean Stanley as a "bright green creeper, which climbs out of the fissures of the rocks." It commonly grows in the most barren soil, on rocks, ruins, and walls. Its stem will often furnish a stick of considerable length. Its cleansing virtues as a medicine, and its use in the treatment of ulcers and diseases of the skin allied to Leprosy, are noticed by Pliny ('H. N.' xx. 59). See a paper, 'On the Hyssop of Scripture,' by Prof. J. Forbes Royle, in the 'Journal of the Asiatic Society,' Vol. VIII.; Stanley, 'S. and P.' p. 21; Smith's 'Dict.' s. v.—The Jews say that the sprig of hyssop used for sprinkling was eight or nine inches in length. Maimon. in 'Negaim,' XIV. 6. It has been conjectured that the scarlet band was used to tie the hyssop upon the cedar, so as to make a sort of brush, such as would be convenient for sprinkling.

5. *running water*] Literally, living water, *i.e.* water fresh from the spring (Gen. xxvi. 19), such as was used with the ashes of the Red heifer for the water of purification. Num. xix. 17.

7. *seven times*] The seal of the Covenant, expressed in the number seven, was renewed in sprinkling him who, during his Leprosy, had lived as an outcast.

9. He was again reminded of the number of the Covenant by the seventh day of his exclusion from domestic life, on which he had to wash and to cut off his hair more thoroughly than he had been previously required to do.

he shall be clean] What was strictly the Purification of the leper was completed within the week of his first entrance into the camp, while he was still excluded from the Sanctuary, and from his own abode. That which followed was a Consecration, by which he was reinstated in his position as one of the "holy nation" (Ex. xix. 6). Hence the ceremonial bore a strong resemblance to that of the Consecration of Aaron and his sons to the priesthood (Lev. viii.). The points of distinction will be noticed below.

The Rites within the Court. 10—32.

10, 11. On the eighth day, the cleansed leper had to bring to the priest who had received him into the camp two **young rams** from one to three years old (not lambs), a ewe lamb in her first year (see xii. 6), three tenth parts of an ephah (something over ten

clean shall present the man that is to
be made clean, and those things, before
the LORD, *at* the door of the tabernacle of the congregation:
12 And the priest shall take one he
lamb, and offer him for a trespass
[b] Exod. 29. 24. offering, and the log of oil, and [b]wave
them *for* a wave offering before the
LORD:
13 And he shall slay the lamb in
the place where he shall kill the sin
offering and the burnt offering, in the
[c] chap. 7. 7. holy place: for [c]as the sin offering *is*
the priest's, *so is* the trespass offering:
it *is* most holy:
14 And the priest shall take *some*
of the blood of the trespass offering,
and the priest shall put *it* upon the
tip of the right ear of him that is to
be cleansed, and upon the thumb of
his right hand, and upon the great toe
of his right foot:
15 And the priest shall take *some*
of the log of oil, and pour *it* into the
palm of his own left hand:
16 And the priest shall dip his right
finger in the oil that *is* in his left
hand, and shall sprinkle of the oil
with his finger seven times before the
LORD:
17 And of the rest of the oil that
is in his hand shall the priest put upon
the tip of the right ear of him that
is to be cleansed, and upon the thumb
of his right hand, and upon the great
toe of his right foot, upon the blood
of the trespass offering:
18 And the remnant of the oil that
is in the priest's hand he shall pour
upon the head of him that is to be
cleansed: and the priest shall make
an atonement for him before the
LORD.
19 And the priest shall offer the
sin offering, and make an atonement
for him that is to be cleansed from
his uncleanness; and afterward he
shall kill the burnt offering:
20 And the priest shall offer the
burnt offering and the meat offering

---

pints and a-half) of fine flour mingled with oil, and a log (about half-a-pint, see on xix. 35) of oil. The priest presented both the man and his offerings to Jehovah **at the entrance of the Tent of meeting.** See on i. 3.

12. *a wave offering*] One of the young rams was taken by the priest for a Trespass offering, and, along with the log of oil, was solemnly made over to Jehovah by the ceremony of waving. This Trespass-offering, with its blood and the oil, must be regarded as the main feature in the ceremony. There appears to be no other case in which an entire victim was waved before Jehovah. Introduct. § IX. The Levites are spoken of as "a wave offering," Num. viii. 11—15 (see margin). The man in this case, represented by his Trespass-offering, was dedicated as a Wave-offering in like manner.

13. The Trespass-offering was sacrificed in the usual manner. See Note at the end of this chapter.

it is most holy] See on vi. 25, cf. vii. 7.

14. The priest applied the blood of the Trespass-offering to the person of the cleansed Leper, in the same way as the blood of the Ram of Consecration was applied to the priests, and with the same significance. See Lev. viii. 23. It is said that a portion of the blood was caught by the priest in the palm of his hand as it ran from the victim. It was no doubt applied with the finger. 'Negaim,' XIV. 8.

15—17. Having sprinkled seven drops of the oil in succession towards the entrance of the Tabernacle, the priest touched with the oil the spots on the person of the cleansed Leper, which he had already stained with the blood of the Trespass-offering. The sevenfold sprinkling of the oil before the Sanctuary, in addition to the waving of it, seems to have been intended to consecrate it to represent the spiritual gift (see Note after Lev. ii.) consequent upon the Covenant, the sealing of which had been figured by the sacramental blood of the offering.

17. *him that is to be cleansed*] Rather, **of him that has been cleansed.** The Hebrew would bear either rendering, but the fact spoken of here is a completed one; see on *v.* 9. The same correction is needed *v.* 19.

18. *pour*] More properly, **put;** literally, *give.* The quantity left in the hand could hardly have been sufficient to pour.

19. *the sin offering*] *i.e.* the ewe lamb, *v.* 10.
him that is to be cleansed] See on *v.* 17.

19, 20. The work of the priest connected with the Trespass-offering and the oil brought the cleansed Leper into that position upon the altar: and the priest shall make an atonement for him, and he shall be clean.

21 And if he *be* poor, and †cannot get so much; then he shall take one lamb *for* a trespass offering †to be waved, to make an atonement for him, and one tenth deal of fine flour mingled with oil for a meat offering, and a log of oil;

† Heb. *his hand reach not.*
† Heb. *for a waving.*

22 And two turtledoves, or two young pigeons, such as he is able to get; and the one shall be a sin offering, and the other a burnt offering.

23 And he shall bring them on the eighth day for his cleansing unto the priest, unto the door of the tabernacle of the congregation, before the LORD.

24 And the priest shall take the lamb of the trespass offering, and the log of oil, and the priest shall wave them *for* a wave offering before the LORD:

25 And he shall kill the lamb of the trespass offering, and the priest shall take *some* of the blood of the trespass offering, and put *it* upon the tip of the right ear of him that is to be cleansed, and upon the thumb of his right hand, and upon the great toe of his right foot:

26 And the priest shall pour of the oil into the palm of his own left hand:

27 And the priest shall sprinkle with his right finger *some* of the oil that *is* in his left hand seven times before the LORD:

28 And the priest shall put of the oil that *is* in his hand upon the tip of the right ear of him that is to be cleansed, and upon the thumb of his right hand, and upon the great toe of his right foot, upon the place of the blood of the trespass offering:

29 And the rest of the oil that *is* in the priest's hand he shall put upon the head of him that is to be cleansed, to make an atonement for him before the LORD.

30 And he shall offer the one of the turtledoves, or of the young pigeons, such as he can get;

31 *Even* such as he is able to get, the one *for* a sin offering, and the other *for* a burnt offering, with the meat offering: and the priest shall make an atonement for him that is to be cleansed before the LORD.

32 This *is* the law *of him* in whom *is* the plague of leprosy, whose hand is not able to get *that which pertaineth* to his cleansing.

33 ¶ And the LORD spake unto Moses and unto Aaron, saying,

34 When ye be come into the land of Canaan, which I give to you for a

---

in which he could avail himself of the accustomed law of sacrifice as one completely restored. The ewe lamb was now offered in his behalf as a Sin-offering, one of the young rams as a Burnt-offering, and the fine flour mingled with oil as a Meat-offering. From the mode in which the Meat-offering is here mentioned, it seems evident that it constituted a distinct sacrifice. See on ii. 1.

21—23. A cleansed Leper who was poor might bring birds for the Sin- and Burnt-offerings (cf. on i. 14), and one-tenth of an ephah of fine flour instead of three-tenths; but no alteration was permitted in the Trespass-offering or in the log of oil, which constituted the characteristic part of the ceremony of Consecration. The directions respecting these in *vv.* 24—29 are repeated from *vv.* 12—18.

It may be observed that the consecrating rites for the priests (ch. viii.), which bore most resemblance to those for the cleansed Leper, differed from them in the following particulars:—(1) In the order in which they were performed: the blood was put upon the priest after the sacrifice of the Sin- and Burnt-offerings, it was put upon the cleansed Leper before these sacrifices. (2) In the character of the victim from which the consecrating blood was taken: the Ram of Consecration partook of the nature of a Peace-offering (Lev. viii. 22), the Leper was touched with the blood of a Trespass-offering. (3) In the oil for anointing and the mode of using it: the priest was anointed on his garments as well as his person with the holy oil of the Sanctuary (Lev. viii. 12, 30), the cleansed Leper only on specified parts of his person, with common oil supplied by himself.

THE LEPROSY IN THE HOUSE. 33—53.

33. *Moses and...Aaron*] This law is addressed to them conjointly, that relating to human Leprosy to Moses alone.

34. *When ye be come into the land of Ca-*

possession, and I put the plague of
leprosy in a house of the land of your
possession;
35 And he that owneth the house
shall come and tell the priest, saying,
It seemeth to me *there is* as it were a
plague in the house:
36 Then the priest shall command
that they ‖ empty the house, before
the priest go *into it* to see the plague,
that all that *is* in the house be not
made unclean: and afterward the
priest shall go in to see the house:
37 And he shall look on the plague,
and, behold, *if* the plague *be* in the
walls of the house with hollow strakes,
greenish or reddish, which in sight
are lower than the wall;
38 Then the priest shall go out of
the house to the door of the house,
and shut up the house seven days:
39 And the priest shall come again
the seventh day, and shall look: and,
behold, *if* the plague be spread in the
walls of the house;
40 Then the priest shall command
that they take away the stones in
which the plague *is*, and they shall
cast them into an unclean place without the city:
41 And he shall cause the house
to be scraped within round about, and
they shall pour out the dust that they
scrape off without the city into an
unclean place:
42 And they shall take other stones,
and put *them* in the place of those
stones; and he shall take other morter, and shall plaister the house.
43 And if the plague come again,
and break out in the house, after that
he hath taken away the stones, and
after he hath scraped the house, and
after it is plaistered;
44 Then the priest shall come and
look, and, behold, *if* the plague be
spread in the house, it *is* a fretting
leprosy in the house: it *is* unclean.
45 And he shall break down the
house, the stones of it, and the
timber thereof, and all the morter of
the house; and he shall carry *them*
forth out of the city into an unclean
place.
46 Moreover he that goeth into the
house all the while that it is shut up
shall be unclean until the even.
47 And he that lieth in the house
shall wash his clothes; and he that
eateth in the house shall wash his
clothes.
48 And if the priest † shall come
in, and look *upon it*, and, behold,
the plague hath not spread in the
house, after the house was plaistered:
then the priest shall pronounce the
house clean, because the plague is
healed.
49 And he shall take to cleanse
the house two birds, and cedar wood,
and scarlet, and hyssop:
50 And he shall kill the one of
the birds in an earthen vessel over
running water:

‖ Or, *prepare.*

† Heb. *in coming in shall come in, &c.*

---

naan] This section is separated from that on Leprosy in clothing (xiii. 47—59) with which it would seem to be naturally connected, and is placed last of all the laws concerning Leprosy, probably on account of its being wholly prospective. While the Israelites were in the Wilderness, the materials of their dwellings were of nearly the same nature as those of their clothing, and would be liable to the same sort of decay. They were therefore included under the same law.

I put the plague] Jehovah here speaks as the Lord of all created things, determining their decay and destruction as well as their production. Cf. Isa. xlv. 6, 7; Jonah iv. 7; Matt. xxi. 20.

36. The removal of the furniture shews that the law of the Leprosy in the house was not based on the fear of infection.

37. *hollow strakes, greenish or reddish,...in sight lower than the wall*] Rather, **depressed spots of dark green or dark red, appearing beneath** (the surface of) **the wall.** See Note at end of the chapter.

49—53. This ceremony with the two birds is exactly the same as that performed on behalf of the healed Leper outside the camp or city (*vv.* 3—6).

49. *cleanse the house*] Strictly, *purge the house from sin.* The same word is used in *v.* 52; and in *v.* 53 it is said, "and make an atonement for it." Cf. Exod. xxix. 36, Ezek. xliii. 22, where the Hebrew is the same. Such language must of course be used figuratively

51 And he shall take the cedar
wood, and the hyssop, and the scarlet,
and the living bird, and dip them in
the blood of the slain bird, and in the
running water, and sprinkle the house
seven times:
52 And he shall cleanse the house
with the blood of the bird, and with
the running water, and with the living bird, and with the cedar wood,
and with the hyssop, and with the
scarlet:
53 But he shall let go the living
bird out of the city into the open
fields, and make an atonement for the
house: and it shall be clean.
54 This *is* the law for all manner
of plague of leprosy, and [d] scall, [d] chap. 13. 30.
55 And for the leprosy of a gar-
ment, and of a house,
56 And for a rising, and for a
scab, and for a bright spot:
57 To teach † when *it is* unclean, † Heb. *in the day of the unclean, and in the day of the clean.*
and when *it is* clean: this *is* the law
of leprosy.

---

when it is applied to things, not to persons. See Note at the end of the chapter.

54—57. These verses are a formal conclusion to the laws of Leprosy contained in chaps. xiii., xiv. The technical names of the first external symptoms of Leprosy of the person are repeated in *v.* 56 from xiii. 2.

NOTES on CHAP. XIV.

I. ON THE TWO BIRDS OF THE HEALED LEPER. *vv.* 4—7.

These birds were provided by the priest for the man. They were not, like the offerings for the Altar, brought by the man himself (cf. *v.* 4 with *v.* 10), they were not presented nor brought near the Sanctuary, nor was any portion of them offered on the Altar. It has been usual with commentators, Jewish and Christian, ancient and modern, to liken them to the two goats of the Day of Atonement. But it should be kept in view that the resemblance is only on the surface. It seems hardly to extend beyond the fact that the two creatures in each case go to make up a single type. The significance of the two goats is obviously sacrificial, and holds a quite different place in the scope of the ceremony to which it belongs See on xvi. 8. The slain goat was a Sin-offering, the slain bird was no sacrifice at all; the Scape-goat typically bore away a burden of sin, the bird let loose figured a man restored to freedom.

The older Jewish writers allegorized each particular connected with the two birds in such a way that Maimonides condemns all their explanations as inconsistent with the spirit of the Hebrew Law, and gives up the matter in despair. Abarbanel appears to have come near to the truth in taking the ceremony as symbolizing, in its immediate bearing, no more than the renewed health of the Leper. The living bird, according to him, represented the restored vigour and freedom of the vital functions; the cedar wood, the flesh redeemed from decay and putrefaction; the scarlet, the purged blood giving the hue of health to the complexion; and the hyssop, deliverance from the fetor which is characteristic of the disease. The details of a restoration to health and freedom appear to be well expressed in the whole ceremony. Each of the birds represented the Leper. They were to be of a clean kind, because they stood for one of the chosen race. The death-like state of the Leper during his exclusion from the camp was expressed by the killing of one of the birds. The living bird was identified with the slain one by being dipped in his blood mixed with the spring water that figured the process of purification, while the cured Leper was identified with the rite by having the same water and blood sprinkled over him. The bird then liberated leaves behind him all the symbols of the death disease and of the remedies associated with it, and is free to enjoy health and social freedom with his kind.

The natural image thus presented to the mind easily suggests the way in which St Paul speaks of the better resurrection—"Therefore we are buried with him by baptism into death: that like as Christ was raised up from the dead by the glory of the Father, even so we also should walk in newness of life." The Fathers, especially Origen, Cyril, Theodoret and Hesychius, have freely followed out this thought. Many modern writers have taken the same line. Bochart has enumerated eighteen particulars in which the ceremony appears to supply figures of spiritual truth connected with our redemption. ('Opera,' Vol. III. p. 151.) If regarded merely as figures of speech and kept within proper bounds, such applications are allowable. But they do not come within the legitimate range of scriptural interpretation. They should not be permitted to divert our minds from the obvious scope of this particular observance of the Law, the meaning of which was realized in visible fact, and which should not be placed on the same ground as the rites of the Altar, which pointed directly and exclusively to spiritual antitypes. If we fail to observe this distinction, we lose the edifying lesson conveyed by the two parts of the Leper's restoration to his position as one of the chosen people, confusing what properly belonged to the outside of the Camp with that which could only be performed within the court of the Sanctuary.

II. On the Trespass-offering of the Leper. *vv.* 12—18.

The sacrifice of a Trespass-offering formed a point of resemblance between the consecration of the Leper and the reconsecration of the Nazarite who had incurred defilement by contact with the dead; but the latter was not touched with the blood of the victim. In his case, as in that of the priests, a Sin-offering and a Burnt-offering were sacrificed before the Consecration. After directing the priest to offer in the defiled Nazarite's behalf the two birds for Sin- and Burnt-offerings, the words of the Law are;—"for that he sinned by the dead, and shall hallow his head that same day. And he shall consecrate unto the LORD the days of his separation, and shall bring a lamb of the first year for a trespass-offering." Num. vi. 11, 12.

As regards the sequence of the rites, it is obvious that the starting-point of the Leper was different from that either of the Priest or of the Nazarite. Though the Nazarite had been defiled in respect to his Nazarite vow, he had in no degree lost his position as an Israelite. In his national relation he stood on a par with a son of Aaron before he was consecrated: both were in the full sense members of the priestly people. The Consecration of the priest was to qualify him for the service of the Altar; that of the Nazarite, to distinguish him from his brethren as a devoted person. But the Leper was in a very different position. He had to begin the ceremony, not indeed quite as an alien—for he was a circumcised son of Israel and had been readmitted into the camp by a formal act—but as one cut off from his people on account of personal defilement, with whom the Covenant with Jehovah required to be resealed. Until this was done, until his Consecration had taken place, he could not bring as an accepted worshipper the offerings which were to testify his sense of sin, his devotion of body, soul and spirit to Jehovah, and his faith in atonement by sacrifice.

The Peace-offering seems to have been the natural Consecration-sacrifice for the priest. The blood of no other victim could have been so clearly significant of the work of him who was to administer the symbols of reconciliation between Jehovah and His people. But the connection between the Trespass-offering of the Consecrations of the defiled Nazarite and the cleansed Leper is not quite so obvious.

We have seen that the Trespass-offering appears to have been a forfeit for the violated rights of others, whether of Jehovah as the head of the nation or of a fellow mortal. See on Lev. v. 14 seq. It related more immediately to the consequence of sin than to sin itself in the heart of the sinner. Now this perhaps brings us to a point at which we can see the reason of the connection of the Trespass-offering with these two Consecrations. The Trespass-offering, though it was not immediately connected with the special personal sin of the Nazarite or the Leper, expressed the share which each bore of the consequence of sin in general; it bore witness that disease and death and the defilements connected with them (see Note after ch. xv.) are the wages of sin for the whole race.

The notion of Keil that the Trespass-offering was not sacrificed in its proper signification; and that of Knobel, that it was a forfeit for the Leper's non-attendance at the Sanctuary, seem to be not worth much.

III. On the Leprosy in the House. *vv.* 33—53.

Many of the old commentators, and some of later times, have imagined that the house Leprosy (as well as the Leprosy in clothing) was in some way connected with the human disease. The prevailing Jewish notion seems to have been that it was something peculiar to the Holy Land, and to the time of the Law, divinely purposed as a punishment for an evil tongue. It was regarded as a first warning; if it did not take effect, the Leprosy attacked the garments; and if the transgressor still persisted, he was smitten with the disease in his person[1]. The Targum of Palestine, with rather more aptness, makes it a visitation on a house that has been built by means of unjust gains.

It seems, however, more probable that it was some form of ordinary decay which was familiarly known. Some have considered that the object of the law respecting it was chiefly or wholly practical utility, in order to secure for the Israelites sound and wholesome houses[2]. That it may have tended towards this end, by inducing a care in the selection of materials and a habit of keeping the house clean and in good repair, is probable. But the form in which the law is expressed in *vv.* 49, 53, appears to intimate that its meaning was primarily symbolical. Leprosy in the person, above all other affections of living bodies, represented decay and corruption. Decay in all material substances has a common ground. In everything it is the dissolution, the falling to pieces, of that which is naturally one. But decay in what covers the body and what

[1] Maimon. 'More Nev.' III. 47. Abarbanel and others quoted by Patrick.

[2] Michaelis, 'L. of M.' Vol. III. p. 303. Davidson, 'Introd. to O. T.' Vol. I. p. 260.

shelters it must bear the nearest relationship to the decay of the body itself. The Leprosy in houses, the Leprosy in clothing, and the terrible disease in the human body, were representative forms of decay which taught the lesson that all created things, in their own nature, are passing away, and are only maintained for their destined uses during an appointed period, by the power of Jehovah. See Note after chap. xiii. § VII.

Several of the Fathers have applied the Leprosy in the house as an apt figure to illustrate the histories of the Jewish nation and of the Christian Church. See Theod. 'Quæst. in Lev.' xviii.; Cyril, 'Glaph.' *in loc.*; Hieron. in Zeph. i. 13; Hesychius *in loc.*

CHAPTER XV.

1 *The uncleanness of men in their issues.* 13 *The cleansing of them.* 19 *The uncleanness of women in their issues.* 28 *Their cleansing.*

AND the LORD spake unto Moses
and to Aaron, saying,
2 Speak unto the children of Israel, and say unto them, When any
man hath a ‖ running issue out of ‖ Or, *running of the reins.*
his flesh, *because of* his issue he *is*
unclean.
3 And this shall be his uncleanness in his issue: whether his flesh
run with his issue, or his flesh be
stopped from his issue, it *is* his uncleanness.
4 Every bed, whereon he lieth
that hath the issue, is unclean: and
every † thing, whereon he sitteth, † Heb. *vessel.*
shall be unclean.
5 And whosoever toucheth his bed
shall wash his clothes, and bathe *himself* in water, and be unclean until
the even.
6 And he that sitteth on *any* thing
whereon he sat that hath the issue
shall wash his clothes, and bathe *himself* in water, and be unclean until
the even.
7 And he that toucheth the flesh of
him that hath the issue shall wash his
clothes, and bathe *himself* in water,
and be unclean until the even.
8 And if he that hath the issue
spit upon him that is clean; then he
shall wash his clothes, and bathe *himself* in water, and be unclean until
the even.
9 And what saddle soever he rideth
upon that hath the issue shall be unclean.
10 And whosoever toucheth any
thing that was under him shall be
unclean until the even: and he that
beareth *any of* those things shall wash
his clothes, and bathe *himself* in water, and be unclean until the even.
11 And whomsoever he toucheth
that hath the issue, and hath not
rinsed his hands in water, he shall
wash his clothes, and bathe *himself*
in water, and be unclean until the
even.
12 And the [a] vessel of earth, that [a] chap 6. 28.
he toucheth which hath the issue,
shall be broken: and every vessel of
wood shall be rinsed in water.
13 And when he that hath an issue
is cleansed of his issue; then he shall
number to himself seven days for his
cleansing, and wash his clothes, and
bathe his flesh in running water, and
shall be clean.
14 And on the eighth day he shall
take to him two turtledoves, or two
young pigeons, and come before the

CHAPTER XV.

UNCLEANNESS FROM SECRETIONS. 1—33.

This chapter would seem to take its place more naturally before the Twelfth, with the subject of which it is immediately connected. Cf. especially xii. 2 with xv. 19. It stands here between two chapters, with neither of which has it any close connection.

1. This law is addressed to Moses and Aaron.

2. *running issue*] See Jos. 'Ant.' III. 11, § 3; Maimon., Note on 'Zabim,' II. 2, &c., &c.

13. The mere cessation of the issue does not make him clean: he must wait seven days, and then bathe and wash his clothes preparatory to his offering sacrifice (*vv.* 13, 14). As long as the cause of his uncleanness continued, he communicated a degree of pollution to any person or thing with which he might come into contact.—On the distinction between earthen and wooden utensils (*v.* 12), see on vi. 28, xi. 33, 35.

LORD unto the door of the tabernacle of the congregation, and give them unto the priest:

15 And the priest shall offer them, the one *for* a sin offering, and the other *for* a burnt offering; and the priest shall make an atonement for him before the LORD for his issue.

16 And if any man's seed of copulation go out from him, then he shall wash all his flesh in water, and be unclean until the even.

17 And every garment, and every skin, whereon is the seed of copulation, shall be washed with water, and be unclean until the even.

18 The woman also with whom man shall lie *with* seed of copulation, they shall *both* bathe *themselves* in water, and be unclean until the even.

19 ¶ And if a woman have an issue, *and* her issue in her flesh be blood, she shall be † put apart seven days: and whosoever toucheth her shall be unclean until the even.

† eb. *her ara- n.*

20 And every thing that she lieth upon in her separation shall be unclean: every thing also that she sitteth upon shall be unclean.

21 And whosoever toucheth her bed shall wash his clothes, and bathe *himself* in water, and be unclean until the even.

22 And whosoever toucheth any thing that she sat upon shall wash his clothes, and bathe *himself* in water, and be unclean until the even.

23 And if it *be* on *her* bed, or on any thing whereon she sitteth, when he toucheth it, he shall be unclean until the even.

24 And if any man lie with her at all, and her flowers be upon him, he shall be unclean seven days; and all the bed whereon he lieth shall be unclean.

25 And if a woman have an issue of her blood many days out of the time of her separation, or if it run beyond the time of her separation; all the days of the issue of her uncleanness shall be as the days of her separation: she *shall be* unclean.

26 Every bed whereon she lieth all the days of her issue shall be unto her as the bed of her separation: and whatsoever she sitteth upon shall be unclean, as the uncleanness of her separation.

27 And whosoever toucheth those things shall be unclean, and shall wash his clothes, and bathe *himself* in water, and be unclean until the even.

28 But if she be cleansed of her issue, then she shall number to herself seven days, and after that she shall be clean.

29 And on the eighth day she shall take unto her two turtles, or two young pigeons, and bring them unto the priest, to the door of the tabernacle of the congregation.

30 And the priest shall offer the one *for* a sin offering, and the other *for* a burnt offering; and the priest shall make an atonement for her be-

---

16—18. Most of the ancient religions made a similar recognition of impurity and of the need of purification. On the Babylonians, Egyptians, Greeks and Romans, see Herodot. I. 198, II. 64; Strabo, XVI. p. 745; Hesiod. 'Op. et Dies' 731; Eurip. 'Ion' 150; Pers. 'Sat.' II. 15; Tibull. Lib. II. I. I. On the Hindoos, 'Menu' V. 63. On the Parsees, Zendavesta ap. Bähr; 'Symb.' II. p. 466. On the Moslems, Koran, IV, V. See also a remarkable passage in Porph. 'de Abst.' IV. 7, 20.

17. *every garment*] Cf. Jude *v.* 23.

19—24. From the commencement of the period uncleanness was to last seven days, 20—23.

24. This must refer to an unexpected occurrence. Intercourse during the acknowledged period was a heavy crime, and was to be punished by "cutting off." Lev. xviii. 19, xx. 18; Ezek. xviii. 6. It is so regarded in the Hindoo, Parsee, and Moslem Laws. 'Menu,' IV. 40, V. 8; 'Koran' II.; 'Hedáya,' Vol. IV. p. 103, II. 620; Bähr, II. p. 466; cf. Porph. 'De Abst.' II. 50.

25—30. If the period was irregular, the uncleanness was in all respects equal to that of him who had an issue (*vv.* 2—15), each state being one of disease. See Note at the end of the chapter, § ii.

fore the LORD for the issue of her uncleanness.

31 Thus shall ye separate the children of Israel from their uncleanness; that they die not in their uncleanness, when they defile my tabernacle that *is* among them.

32 This *is* the law of him that hath an issue, and *of him* whose seed goeth from him, and is defiled therewith;

33 And of her that is sick of her flowers, and of him that hath an issue, of the man, and of the woman, and of him that lieth with her that is unclean.

31—33. This solemn admonition is addressed to Moses and Aaron, see *v.* 1.

31. *my tabernacle*] Strictly, *my dwelling-place* (*mishkān*), as in Lev. viii. 10, xvii. 4, xxvi. 11. The word rendered "tabernacle" elsewhere in Leviticus is properly **Tent** (*ōhel*). See on Ex. xxvi. 1.

NOTE on CHAPS. XII.—XV.

ON THE PURIFICATIONS OF THE LAW IN GENERAL.

i. Legal pollution was not in any mode or degree connected with the personal sin of the individual by whom it was occasioned or contracted. It originated only in certain physical conditions. The corpse of a saint was as impure as that of the most degraded criminal, and any human corpse communicated even a greater degree of impurity by contact or approximation than the body of an animal. The Law made no distinction between the Leprosy which an unoffending child inherited from its parents and that which might have been inflicted as a visitation for crime.

We have already had occasion to speak of the strong light in which the Law places the difference between Life and Death. Note after chap. xi. It has also been observed that the defilement of the Leprosy arose from the Leper being regarded as already amongst the dead. Note after chap. xiii. § VII. The conclusion follows that two out of the three kinds of pollution obviously hinge upon the idea of the uncleanness of Death. A question remains as to the defilement resulting from the secretions. Why should those mentioned in the Law be distinguished from the other secretions of the body?

It has been assumed that, as human life ends in corruption, leaving behind an unclean corpse, so it must begin in corruption. The sinfulness of human nature would thus be represented by the uncleanness of its two poles, Birth and Death (Bähr). But this, which refers immediately to purification after childbirth, falls to the ground as an explanation, if we consider that it was not the newborn child who was recognized as unclean, but its mother[1]. The defilement of childbirth is thus brought into close relationship with the defilements mentioned in ch. xv.

The inquiry into the meaning of this sort of uncleanness must, it would seem, remain involved in a share of that mystery which shrouds the whole of the subject with which it is connected. The best clue we can get towards a solution appears to be that furnished by such passages as Gen. iii. 16, Rom. vii. 24, viii. 21, in connexion with that feeling of shame which is common to all human beings not entirely debased, of which we gather the history from Gen. ii. 25, iii. 7, 10, 11.

ii. All need of purification without doubt took its rise in a sense of the sinfulness of man. Legal uncleanness would not else have excluded the person from participation in the service of the Sanctuary. But the connection between sin and uncleanness is not immediate. The connecting links between them are the disease and death which are the offspring of sin. The pains of childbirth and the suffering of death were the two sentences pronounced by God upon mankind after the first sin[2]. The case seems to be strengthened by the fact that the diseased conditions of uncleanness (xv. 2, 25), compared with the healthy ones, are treated as if they had a double ground of pollution; they alone require sacrificial atonement. The conclusion then appears to be reasonable that all the rites of purification were intended to remind the Israelite that he belonged to a fallen race and that he needed a Purification and Atonement which he could not effect for himself.

It is worthy of remark that the same causes of uncleanness have been generally recognized by the ancient nations. Some authorities on this point as to details have been given in the preceding notes. It would seem that the law of purifications, in its three great lines of application (see note before ch. xii.), coincides with the suggestions of the common instinct, or of the common tradition, of the human race.

iii. But it is important to observe in the way of contrast with what completeness and

[1] See on xii. 4, 6—8.

[2] Gen. ii. 17, iii. 16, 19; Rom. v. 12; Heb. ii. 14, 15; 1 Tim. ii. 15.

logical consistency the Law of Moses treats the subject, and how it raises it above the level of natural feeling to a higher sphere. When the Law in later ages was misrepresented by the rabbinical teachers, its logical distinctions were crumbled away, and attention to minute artificial rules became the badge of the self-righteous Jew. The deep significance of the ceremonial purifications was confounded with the mere forms, not necessarily with the reality, of cleanliness. Hence came in the washing of hands and "of cups and pots, brazen vessels and of tables." Mark vii. 2—8. Just the same kind of confusion is to be traced in all the Gentile systems of purification. The Hindoos, for example, put into the same category of pollution a corpse, an outcast for deadly sin, and a newborn child with all its relations within a certain degree of consanguinity, which is specially extended beyond the common limits for the Brahmin[1]. But the rules of the Moslems bear a yet closer outward resemblance to those of the rabbinical Jews denounced by our Saviour[2].

[1] 'Menu,' v. 62, 85; note on Lev. xii. 8.
[2] See Koran v.; Lane, 'Mod. Egypt.' ch. III.

The original character of the Mosaic law of purifications is remarkably shewn in its belonging to every member of the nation without distinction, so testifying to his position before Jehovah (cf. Note after chap. xi. § VII.), and by its clearness and practical method. In all cases, a period of uncleanness was defined—in ordinary defilements, either one day or seven days—at the end of which a formal washing of the person, and in certain prescribed instances of the clothes also, was to take place. The purifying rite could thus never be hurried so as to impair its solemnity; the person was to have time to realize the sense of his uncleanness. It could not, like most of the Gentile purifications, be performed immediately when the occasion for it occurred, as if the object were mainly to cleanse the flesh. But above all, it should be observed that every Levitical purification of a graver kind culminated in a Sin-offering and a Burnt-offering sacrificed to Jehovah according to the general law of sacrificial worship. And the atoning act of the priest gave its meaning not merely to the single occasion on which the sacrifices were offered, but to every rite of purification, whether great or small, which was prescribed by the Law.

CHAPTER XVI.

1 *How the high priest must enter into the holy place.* 11 *The sin offering for himself.* 15 *The sin offering for the people.* 20 *The scapegoat.* 29 *The yearly feast of the expiations.*

AND the LORD spake unto Moses after [a] the death of the two sons of Aaron, when they offered before the LORD, and died; ([a] chap. 10. 1, 2.)

2 And the LORD said unto Moses, Speak unto Aaron thy brother, that he [b] come not at all times into the holy *place* within the vail before the mercy seat, which *is* upon the ark; that he die not: for I will appear in the cloud upon the mercy seat. ([b] Exod. 30. 10. Heb. 9. 7.)

3 Thus shall Aaron come into the holy *place*: with a young bullock for a sin offering, and a ram for a burnt offering.

CHAP. XVI.

THE DAY OF ATONEMENT. 1—34.

The Day of Atonement, or, as it is in the Hebrew, the Day of Atonements (*Yōm Kippurim*), is called by the Rabbins *Yōma*, *i.e.* the Day, which is the title of the treatise on it in the Mishna. Philo calls it "the Festival of Fasting," and St Luke (probably) "the Fast." See Acts xxvii. 9. The purpose of the observance of the day is expressly stated in the Law: "to make an atonement for the children of Israel for all their sins (and uncleanness) once a year." See *vv.* 34 and 16.—Cf. with this chap., xxiii. 26—32.

1. The instructions for observing this day seem naturally to follow the laws of Sacrifices and Purifications. See on *vv.* 33, 34. The chapter would on this ground appear to hold its proper place. The reference to the death of Nadab and Abihu is not therefore to be regarded as a resuming of the historical narrative from ch. x. 20, but as a notice of the occasion on which the instructions were given, well calculated to add point and emphasis to the solemn admonition to the High priest in the second verse. The death of his sons, for drawing nigh to Jehovah in an unauthorized manner, was to serve as a warning to Aaron himself never to transgress in this respect.

2. *the holy place within the vail*] See Ex. xxvi. 33; Heb. ix. 3.

the cloud] Cf. Ex. xvi. 10, xix. 9, xl. 34; Num. ix. 15; 1 K. viii. 10. See *v.* 13.

the mercy seat] See Note on Ex. xxv. 17.

3. *Thus*] More strictly, **With this**; that is, with the offerings about to be mentioned.

holy place] This name here denotes **the Sanctuary**, the whole sacred enclosure, the

4 He shall put on the holy linen coat, and he shall have the linen breeches upon his flesh, and shall be girded with a linen girdle, and with the linen mitre shall he be attired: these *are* holy garments; therefore shall he wash his flesh in water, and *so* put them on.

5 And he shall take of the congregation of the children of Israel two kids of the goats for a sin offering, and one ram for a burnt offering.

6 And Aaron shall offer his bullock of the sin offering, which *is* for himself, and [c] make an atonement for himself, and for his house.

[c] Heb. 7.

7 And he shall take the two goats, and present them before the LORD *at* the door of the tabernacle of the congregation.

---

court of the Tabernacle. The offerings were for Aaron and his sons, supplied by himself. See *v.* 6.

4. In preparing for the ordinary ministrations the priest had to wash only his feet and hands; Ex. xxx. 19—21, xl. 31. But the High priest when he changed his dress on this day was required **to bathe himself**. This was done when he resumed his "golden garments" (Ex. xxviii.), as well as on this occasion. See *v.* 24. According to Jewish tradition the High priest himself in his golden garments had, on this day, and for the previous week, to offer the regular daily sacrifices, and to perform the other sacerdotal duties of the Sanctuary, which were usually performed by a common priest.—The dress of white linen, which he now put on, appears to have been like the ordinary dress of the common priests, except in the substitution of a linen mitre for the bonnet (or **cap**), and of a plain linen girdle for the variegated one. Ex. xxviii. 40—43, with notes. The mitre still distinguished him as the High priest, and the plain white girdle was in exact keeping with the other parts of the dress. It has been supposed by many that this white dress was worn by the High priest to mark that he reduced himself on this occasion to the level of a common priest, as an act of humiliation becoming the character of the Day of Atonement. It is alleged that he could have worn these peculiar garments only as a humbled penitent asking for forgiveness when he offered the Sin-offering for himself, *v.* 6. (Several Jewish authorities, quoted by Drusius, Cyril Alex., a Lapide, Grotius, Rosenmüller, Knobel, Kurtz, &c.) But it seems to be justly urged against this: (1) that the dress, though it was like that of the common priests in being white, was still distinguished by the insignia of the High-priesthood; (2) that these garments are emphatically called *holy* (*vv.* 4, 32), in virtue, it would seem, of their special significance, not merely in the same sense as the golden garments, which were consecrated by the anointing oil, Ex. xxviii. 2, xxix. 21; Lev. viii. 30; (3) that even admitting that they were intended to assimilate to the dress of the common priests, they were not the more symbolical of humiliation, for this dress was appointed "for glory and beauty" as much as the golden garments of the High priest. See Ex. xxviii., cf. *v.* 2 with *v.* 40; (4) and, above all, that whiteness never appears to have been connected by the Hebrews with mourning or penitence; on the contrary, all the evidence we have appears to make it significant of triumphant holiness. See Eccles. ix. 8; Ezek. ix. 2, x. 2; Dan. x. 5, xii. 6; Matt. xvii. 2, xxviii. 3; Mark ix. 3; Luke ix. 29; Rev. iii. 4, iv. 4, vi. 11, xix. 14, &c. &c. Hence it seems most probable that the High priest, in preparing to enter the Holy of holies, attired himself in spotless white as a token of the holiness without which none, in a spiritual sense, can enter the divine presence. So Origen, Hesychius, Keil, Wogue. He thus became a more distinct foreshadow of the greater High Priest, who is "holy, harmless, undefiled, separate from sinners;" who has once for all "entered into that within the vail," Heb. vii. 26, vi. 19, 20. This significance belonged to the High priest only in his official capacity as mediator: in his own person he had infirmity, and was required "to offer up sacrifice, *first* for his own sins, and then for the people's." Heb. vii. 27. See on ix. 7—14. On the same ground it was that, although as a mediator he had to enter the Most Holy place, as sinful flesh he needed the cloud of incense as a vail to come between him and the holiness of Jehovah. See *v.* 13.

5. *take of the congregation*] The two goats for the Sin-offering for the people, and the ram for their Burnt-offering, were to be supplied at the public cost, as the Sin-offering and the Burnt-offering for the priests were to be supplied by the High priest. See *v.* 3.

two kids of the goats] This should be, **two shaggy he-goats.** See on iv. 23. According to the Mishna these were to be of the same colour, size, and value ('Yoma,' VI. 1).

6. *shall offer*] Rather, **shall present,** as in *vv.* 7, 10, &c. The word expresses the formal act of placing the victims in front of the entrance of the Tabernacle. Introd. § v.

for himself, and for his house] That is, for himself as the High priest and all the common priests. Cf. on ix. 7—14.

8 And Aaron shall cast lots upon
the two goats; one lot for the LORD, † Heb. *Azazel.*
and the other lot for the †scapegoat.
9 And Aaron shall bring the goat
upon which the LORD's lot †fell, and † Heb. *went up.*
offer him *for* a sin offering.
10 But the goat, on which the lot
fell to be the scapegoat, shall be presented alive before the LORD, to make
an atonement with him, *and* to let
him go for a scapegoat into the wilderness.
11 And Aaron shall bring the bullock of the sin offering, which *is* for
himself, and shall make an atonement
for himself, and for his house, and
shall kill the bullock of the sin offering which *is* for himself:
12 And he shall take a censer full
of burning coals of fire from off the
altar before the LORD, and his hands
full of sweet incense beaten small, and
bring *it* within the vail:
13 And he shall put the incense
upon the fire before the LORD, that
the cloud of the incense may cover
the mercy seat that *is* upon the testimony, that he die not: [d] Heb. 9. 13.
14 And [d]he shall take of the blood & 10. 4.
of the bullock, and [e]sprinkle *it* with [e] chap. 4. 6.

---

8. The two goats formed a single Sin-offering, *v.* 5. In order duly to bring out the meaning of the sacrifice it was necessary that the act of a living being should be performed after death. See on *v.* 22 As this could not possibly be visibly set forth with a single victim, two were employed, as in the case of the birds in the rite for the healed leper. See Note after chap. xiv. The two goats were presented together before Jehovah. Up to this point they were on a par, and to decide which of them should die recourse was had to casting lots. See Note on Ex. xxviii. 30, § V. 3.

for the scapegoat] Rather, **for Azazel.** In the uncertainty which exists respecting the meaning of the original word, it would be better to retain it in the text of our Bible. It thus appears in the Geneva French, Junius and Tremellius, and nearly all modern critical translations, Jewish and Christian. The word has no article in Heb., and is probably a proper name. See Note at the end of the chapter.

9. *offer him for a sin offering*] Rather, "**present him** for a sin offering." Cf. *v.* 6. The goat was not to be offered on the Altar until after the sacrifice of the High priest's Sin-offering, *vv.* 11—14. It should be observed that *vv.* 9, 10 merely speak of the purposes for which the two goats were destined. The practical directions respecting them, in which the required details are given, will be found in verses 15, 16, 20—22.

10. *on which the lot fell to be the scapegoat*] Rather, **on which the lot 'for Azazel' fell.**

an atonement with him] Different opinions have been held as to the meaning of the original words. It is most probable that they express that the goat "for Azazel" was to be considered as taking his part along with the other goat in the great symbol of atonement. The words of our version thus appear fairly to represent the Hebrew.

for a scapegoat into the wilderness] Rather, "**to Azazel**, into the Wilderness."

11—25. It is important, in reference to the meaning of the Day of Atonement, to observe the order of the rites as they are described in these verses. (1) The Sin-offering for the priests (*v.* 11). (2) The High priest enters the First time, within the vail, with the incense (*vv.* 12, 13). (3) He enters the Second time with the blood of the priest's Sin-offering (*v.* 14). (4) The sacrifice of the goat "for Jehovah" (*v.* 15). (5) The High priest enters the Third time within the vail with the blood of the goat (*v.* 15). (6) The atonement for **the Tent of meeting** (note on *v.* 16). (7) The atonement for the Altar of Burnt-offering in the court (*vv.* 18, 19). (8) The goat sent away to **Azazel** (*vv.* 20—22). (9) The High priest bathes himself and resumes his golden garments (*vv.* 23, 24). (10) The Burnt-offerings for the High priest and the people, with the fat of the two Sin-offerings, offered on the Altar (*vv.* 24, 25). (11) The accessory sacrifices mentioned Num. xxix. 8—11 (see on Lev. xxiii. 20), appear now to have been offered. (12) According to Jewish tradition, the High priest again resumed his white dress and entered a Fourth time within the vail to fetch out the censer and the bowl ('Yoma,' VIII. 4).

12. *a censer*] See on Ex. xxv. 38. Literally, **the censer.** According to the Mishna, a golden censer was used on this occasion. If the English version is right in Heb. ix. 4, it is what is there called θυμιατήριον. See in loc. and on Ex. xxx. 6. It is here called by the LXX. τὸ πυρεῖον.

the altar before the LORD] *i.e.* the Altar of Burnt-offering on which the fire was always burning.

sweet incense] See Exod. xxx. 34—36.

13. *the cloud of the incense*] See on Ex. xxx. 7, 8.

mercy seat that is upon the testimony] See Note on Ex. xxv. 17.

14. *and he shall take of the blood*] The High priest must have come out from the

his finger upon the mercy seat eastward; and before the mercy seat shall he sprinkle of the blood with his finger seven times.

15 ¶ Then shall he kill the goat of the sin offering, that *is* for the people, and bring his blood within the vail, and do with that blood as he did with the blood of the bullock, and sprinkle it upon the mercy seat, and before the mercy seat:

16 And he shall make an atonement for the holy *place*, because of the uncleanness of the children of Israel, and because of their transgressions in all their sins: and so shall he do for the tabernacle of the congregation, that †remaineth among them in the midst of their uncleanness.

† Heb. *dwelleth.*

17 *f* And there shall be no man in the tabernacle of the congregation when he goeth in to make an atonement in the holy *place*, until he come out, and have made an atonement for himself, and for his household, and for all the congregation of Israel.

f Luke 1. 10.

18 And he shall go out unto the altar that *is* before the LORD, and make an atonement for it; and shall take of the blood of the bullock, and of the blood of the goat, and put *it* upon the horns of the altar round about.

19 And he shall sprinkle of the blood upon it with his finger seven times, and cleanse it, and hallow it from the uncleanness of the children of Israel.

20 ¶ And when he hath made an

Most Holy place to fetch the blood, leaving the censer smoking within, and then have entered again within the vail. According to the most probable interpretation of the verse, it would appear that he sprinkled the blood seven times upon the Mercy seat, **on its east side** (not "eastward"), and then seven times upon the floor in front of it (so Knobel, Keil, and others). If the Mercy seat may be regarded as an Altar, the holiest one of the three, on this one occasion in the year atonement was thus made for it, as for the other Altars, with sacrificial blood (Ewald, Kurtz, &c.). But the Jewish writers in general, and some others, do not think that the Mercy seat itself was touched with the blood, and would render the preposition *over against* (not "upon") the Mercy seat. Josephus says that the blood was sprinkled first upon the ceiling and then upon the floor of the Most Holy place ('Ant.' III. 10, § 3). Cf. on iv. 6.

15. Having completed the atonement in the Holy of holies on behalf of the priests, the High priest has now to do the same thing on behalf of the people.

16. By "the holy *place*" appears to be here meant the place within the vail, the Holy of holies. The first part of the verse thus refers to the rites already performed.

tabernacle of the congregation] **Tent of meeting.** Atonement was now to be made for the Tabernacle as a whole. The sense is very briefly expressed, but there seems to be no room to doubt that the High priest was to sprinkle the blood of each of the victims before the Altar of incense, as he had done before the Mercy seat within the vail. Josephus so understood the matter. 'Ant.' III. 10. § 3. That the High priest had on this occasion also to touch with blood the horns of the Altar of incense appears from Ex. xxx. 10.

that remaineth among them in the midst of their uncleanness] A nearly similar expression is used in *v.* 19 regarding the Brazen altar. The most sacred earthly things which came into contact with the nature of man needed from time to time to be cleansed and sanctified by the blood of the Sin-offerings which had been taken into the presence of Jehovah. See on Ex. xxviii. 38.

18. *the altar that is before the LORD*] Some of the rabbins, and others, have taken this for the Golden altar (Bähr, Knobel, &c.). But the words, "he shall go out," in connection with *vv.* 16, 17, would intimate that he was to go out of the Tabernacle into the Court. That the designation may properly belong to the Brazen altar, is proved by *v.* 12. See Ex. xxix. 11, 12; Lev. i. 5. So Josephus, 'Ant.' III. 10. § 3. The order of the ceremony required that atonement should first be made for the Most Holy place with the Mercy seat, then for the Holy place with the Golden altar, and then for the Altar in the court. See *vv.* 20, 33. The horns of the Brazen altar were touched with the blood, as they were in the ordinary Sin-offerings. Lev. iv. 25, 30, 34. Cf. Ezek. xliii. 19—22; Heb. ix. 21, 22.

of the blood of the bullock, and of the blood of the goat] The Jewish tradition is that, for this purpose, some of the blood of the two victims was mingled together in a basin.

19. *upon it*] The Hebrew is here exactly represented. The blood may have been sprinkled either on the top or the side of the Altar. In reference to the sprinkling of the Mercy seat, in *v.* 14, the front, or east side, is distinctly expressed.

end of reconciling the holy *place*, and the tabernacle of the congregation, and the altar, he shall bring the live goat:

21 And Aaron shall lay both his hands upon the head of the live goat, and confess over him all the iniquities of the children of Israel, and all their transgressions in all their sins, putting them upon the head of the goat, and shall send *him* away by the hand of †a fit man into the wilderness:

22 And the goat shall bear upon him all their iniquities unto a land †not inhabited: and he shall let go the goat in the wilderness.

23 And Aaron shall come into the tabernacle of the congregation, and shall put off the linen garments, which he put on when he went into the holy *place*, and shall leave them there:

24 And he shall wash his flesh with water in the holy place, and put on his garments, and come forth, and offer his burnt offering, and the burnt offering of the people, and make an atonement for himself, and for the people.

25 And the fat of the sin offering shall he burn upon the altar.

26 And he that let go the goat for the scapegoat shall wash his clothes, and bathe his flesh in water, and afterward come into the camp.

† Heb. *a man of opportunity.*

† Heb. *of separation.*

20—22. Not until the atonement by blood of the holy places on behalf of the priests and the people had been accomplished, was the High priest to complete the Sin-offering of the two goats by sending the living one into the Wilderness. See on *vv.* 11—25.

21. *confess over him*] According to the Mishna, the form of confession used on this occasion in later times was:—"O Lord, thy people, the house of Israel, have transgressed, they have rebelled, they have sinned before thee. I beseech thee now absolve their transgressions, their rebellion and their sin that they have sinned against thee, as it is written in the law of Moses thy servant, that on this day he shall make atonement for you to cleanse you from all your sins, and ye shall be clean." 'Yoma,' VI. 2.

a fit man] Literally, *a timely man*, or, *a man at hand.* Tradition says that the man was appointed for this work the year before.

22. *shall bear upon him all their iniquities unto a land not inhabited*] Literally, **unto a place cut off**, or (as in the margin) a place "of separation."—The Jewish tradition that the goat was hooted and goaded away and at last thrown down a precipice ('Yoma,' VI. 4; Otho, 'Rab. Lex.' p. 220), must be a corrupt fable utterly alien to the true idea of the rite.

It is evident that the one signification of the ceremony of this goat was the complete removal of the sins which were confessed over him. See Note on Azazel at the end of the chapter, §§ III. IV. The atonement for the sins committed had been signified by the blood of the slain goat: peace had so been made with Jehovah. Still the sins were facts, their consequences remained. That which Milton has so naturally put into the mouth of our first parent, is the burden, and may be the snare, of every believer who feels that he has sinned;—

"But past who can recal, or done undo?
Not God omnipotent, nor fate—"

Heathen literature shews emphatically how the thought has haunted the human mind in different ages. See Soph. 'Trach.' 742; Arist. 'Ethic.' VI. 2; Hor. III. 'Od.' xxix. 45. We know that the mercy of God does nothing by halves. The spiritual restoration of the reconciled sinner is perfect before Him. Ps. li. 7, ciii. 12; Isa. i. 18. But it is in accepting this truth that the believer needs special help. Temptation continues to assail his heart, the sense of sin abides with him, and is apt to seem to him in itself to be sin. No symbol could so plainly set forth the completeness of Jehovah's acceptance of the penitent, as a Sin-offering in which a life was given up for the Altar, and yet a living being survived to carry away all sin and uncleanness. The truth of atonement was involved in every Sin-offering; but it was only in the offering of the two goats in this great annual rite that the expression of it was carried out into complete detail. The declared object of the observance was that the Israelites might be "clean from all their sins before the Lord," *v.* 30. Cf. Ps. ciii. 10—12; Isa. liii. 6, 11, 12; Micah vii. 19; Joh. i. 29; Heb. ix. 28; 1 Pet. ii. 24.

26—28. Both he who led away the goat and he who burned the parts of the Sin-offerings had to purify themselves. It was probably a rule that those who went out of the camp during a religious solemnity incurred uncleanness. Many however suppose that pollution was communicated by contact with the Scape-goat and with the flesh of the Sin-offering. But there is no hint of this kind in reference to the flesh which was burnt of the Sin-offerings given in ch. iv. *vv.* 12, 21. Cf. also vi. 27, and Note on Azazel at the end of this chapter, § IV.

g chap. 6. 30. Heb. 13. 11.

27 [g]And the bullock *for* the sin offering, and the goat *for* the sin offering, whose blood was brought in to make atonement in the holy *place*, shall *one* carry forth without the camp; and they shall burn in the fire their skins, and their flesh, and their dung.

28 And he that burneth them shall wash his clothes, and bathe his flesh in water, and afterward he shall come into the camp.

29 ¶ And *this* shall be a statute for ever unto you: *that* in the seventh month, on the tenth *day* of the month, ye shall afflict your souls, and do no work at all, *whether it be* one of your own country, or a stranger that sojourneth among you:

30 For on that day shall *the priest* make an atonement for you, to cleanse you, *that* ye may be clean from all your sins before the LORD.

31 It *shall be* a sabbath of rest unto you, and ye shall afflict your souls, by a statute for ever.

32 And the priest, whom he shall anoint, and whom he shall †consecrate to minister in the priest's office in his father's stead, shall make the atonement, and shall put on the linen clothes, *even* the holy garments:

† Heb. *fill his hand.*

33 And he shall make an atonement for the holy sanctuary, and he

---

27. *shall burn in the fire*] That is, **consume with fire**, not burn sacrificially. See on i. 9, iv. 12; Heb. xiii. 11.

29. *seventh month, on the tenth day*] The month Ethanim or Tisri, as being the seventh in the Sacred year, has been called the Sabbatical month. On the first day was celebrated the Feast of Trumpets, Lev. xxiii. 24, the tenth day was the Day of Atonement, and on the fourteenth day the Feast of Tabernacles commenced. Ex. xxiii. 16; Note on Lev. xxiii. 24.

afflict your souls] In chap. xxiii. 27—32, the direction as to the mode in which the people were to observe the Day of Atonement is expanded, and sanctioned by a sentence of cutting off from the nation whoever transgressed it. It was to be a day of Holy Convocation of the strictest observance (see on xxiii. 7), a Sabbath of rest in which no work whatever was to be done from evening to evening, that is, from the evening of the 9th to the evening of the 10th day. The expression "to afflict the soul," appears to be the old term for fasting; but its meaning evidently embraces, not only abstinence from food, but that penitence and humiliation which give scope and purpose to the outward act of fasting. The specific word for abstinence (*tzum*) is not found in the Pentateuch, but often occurs in the Prophets and Historical books. The Day of Atonement was the only public fast commanded by the Law of Moses. On fasts observed in later times, see Zech. viii. 19, &c., and on those of the Pharisaic Jews, which were multiplied to twenty-nine annual, and two weekly fasts, see Reland, 'Antiq.' p. 270.

a stranger that sojourneth among you] Rather, **the foreigner who dwelleth among you**. See on Ex. xx. 10. The meaning is, one of foreign blood, who dwelt with the Israelites, had abjured false gods, and had become familiarly known to his neighbours. The Kenites appear to have been foreigners of this kind (Judg. iv. 11, &c.); and, in the next age, the Gibeonites (Josh. ix.). It is not improbable that a considerable portion of the "mixed multitude" of Ex. xii. 38 (cf. *v.* 48) might have taken a similar position. As he had the blessing and protection of the Law (Num. xxxv. 15; Josh. xx. 9; Deut. x. 18; Lev. xix. 10, xxiii. 22, xxiv. 22), the foreigner was bound to obey its statutes. He had to observe the Sabbath (Ex. xx. 10, xxiii. 12), the Day of Atonement, abstinence from blood (Lev. xvii. 10), and the law of marriage (Lev. xviii. 26). He was subject to the ordained punishments for the worship of Molech (Lev. xx. 2), and for blasphemy (Lev. xxiv. 16). He could partake in the festivities of Pentecost and the Feast of Tabernacles (Deut. xvi. 11, 14). He could offer Burnt-offerings and Peace-offerings (Lev. xvii. 8, xxii. 18) and Sin-offerings (Num. xv. 29). The Law expressly states that he could not take part in the Passover, unless he was circumcised. Ex. xii. 48, Num. ix. 14. We may infer that this condition, expressed exclusively in regard to the great national festival, applied to some other of his religious privileges.

32. *whom he shall anoint—whom he shall consecrate*] **who shall be anointed—who shall be consecrated.** See on iv. 3: on the form of expression, see on Ex. xxxvii. 1—5.

the holy garments] See on *v.* 4.

33, 34. There is here a summary of what was done on the Day of Atonement. Its purpose was to signify Atonement for the whole of the children of Israel, from the High priest to the lowest of the people.

It has been held that the atonement of this day related to all the sins committed by the people for which atonement had not been

shall make an atonement for the tabernacle of the congregation, and for the altar, and he shall make an atonement for the priests, and for all the people of the congregation.

34 And this shall be an everlasting statute unto you, to make an atonement for the children of Israel for all their sins [h]once a year. And he did as the LORD commanded Moses.

[h] Exod. 30. 10. Heb. 9. 7.

duly made at the Altar in the course of the past year (Knobel, Keil, Herxheimer). But it would rather seem that the Day was intended as an occasion for expressing more completely than could be done in the ordinary sacrifices the Spiritual truth of Atonement, with a fuller acknowledgment of the sinfulness and weakness of man and of the corruptible nature of all earthly things, even of those most solemnly consecrated and devoted to the service of God. It belonged to its observances especially to set forth, by the entrance of the High priest into the Holy of holies, that Atonement could only be effected before the throne of Jehovah Himself (cf. Matt. ix. 6; Mark ii. 7—10; Heb. iv. 16, &c.); and, by the goat sent into the Wilderness, that the sins atoned for were not only forgiven, but carried wholly away. See on *v.* 22. The rites were not in any proper sense supplemental, but were a solemn gathering up, as it were, of all other rites of atonement, so as to make them point more expressively to the revelation to come of God's gracious purpose to man in sending His Son to be delivered for our offences, and to rise again for our justification; to be our great High Priest for ever after the order of Melchisedec, and to enter for us within the vail (Rom. iv. 25; Heb. vi. 20). The Day of Atonement expanded the meaning of every Sin-offering, in the same way as the services for Good Friday and Ash Wednesday expand the meaning of our Litany days throughout the year, and Easter Day, that of our Sundays.

34. *And he did as the* LORD *commanded Moses*] There is a similar notice of the first observance of the Passover at the conclusion of the instructions respecting it. Ex. xii. 50.

The modern Jews are said to observe the Day of Atonement by the slaughter of a fowl. See Buxtorf's 'Synagoga Judaica,' chap. XXVI.; Dr McCaul's 'The Old Paths,' No. 36.—The external form of the ceremony of the goat set free may have been, as many have supposed, pre-Mosaic. But the Law must have given it a new and distinct meaning in making it part of the great Sin-offering of the year. See Introd. §§ xvi. xvii.

NOTE on CHAP. XVI. 8.

ON AZAZEL.

I. *Origin of the word.* II. *Is it the name of a Personal being?* III. *The function of the Goat sent away.* IV. *His typical character.* V. *Names of the Evil one.* VI. *Other explanations of Azazel.*

I. The word *'azāzēl* (עֲזָאזֵל) occurs nowhere in the Old Testament except in this chapter. What is denoted by it, is a question to which no very certain answer can be given. The best modern scholars consider its most probable derivation to be from a root in use in Arabic, but not in Hebrew, signifying *to remove*, or *to separate*. They are equally agreed as to the word expressing the destination to which the goat was sent, not (as in our Version) the goat itself. The etymology suggested by Buxtorf and the earlier critics, according to which the word answered to our own "scape-goat," is now almost universally rejected.

II. The acceptance of Azazel as the name of a personal being placed in opposition to Jehovah, seems to be the only mode of justifying the relation in which the two lots stood to each other. Upon this a great majority of critics, ancient as well as modern, are agreed. But different views have been held regarding the nature of this personal being. The Syriac version appears to give to Azazel the sense of *the mighty God* (*Deus fortissimus*), which may be supported by an explanation of the etymology not wholly improbable. This notion has been adopted by Le Moyne and ingeniously carried out so as to make Azazel denote God as the God of power in His relation to the Gentiles, as distinguished from Jehovah, revealed as the God of grace to the chosen people[1]. The greater number of critics are however inclined to take Azazel as the name of an evil spirit to whom the goat was sent. It is considered that the name itself, signifying the entirely separate one, one dwelling in banishment, is in favour of this meaning (Knobel, Hengstenberg, &c.). That the Hebrews were familiar with the notion of evil spirits making their abode in desert places is evident from Is. xiii. 21, xxxiv. 14 (cf. on Lev. xvii. 7); Matt. xii. 43; Luke viii. 27; Rev. xviii. 2. Several Jewish traditions point to the same conclusion. The name Azalzel, easily corrupted from Azazel, is applied to a fallen angel in the book of Enoch, which was most likely written by a Jew about

[1] Carpzov, 'App. Crit.' p. 439.

40 A.C. Some of the rabbinists identify Azazel with Sammael, the name given by the Jews to the angel of death, the chief of the devils[1].—Origen expressly says that Azazel denoted the devil ('Cont. Cels.' lib. VI. p. 305).

III. Taking then Azazel as the evil one, the important question remains, in what capacity was the goat dismissed to him? Was he sent as a sacrifice, to bribe, or mollify him? (Spencer, Gesenius, Rosenmüller, &c.) Against this it is justly urged, that the two goats formed together one Sin-offering, and as such had been presented to Jehovah: and also that anything like the worship, by sacrifice or otherwise, of an evil spirit was forbidden by the whole spirit of the Law.—Or, is the strange notion to be entertained that the goat was sent out with his symbolical burden of sin, as if to vex the devil, "to deride and to triumph over him" in his own dominion? (Witsius, Hengstenberg, Kurtz.)—May not the matter be rather put in this way, in accordance with the sense given in the preceding notes? It is evident that the goat sent away could not stand in the same relation to Azazel as the other did to Jehovah. Having been presented to Jehovah before the lots were cast, each goat stood in a sacrificial relation to Him. The casting of lots was an appeal to the decision of Jehovah (cf. Josh. vii. 16, 17, xiv. 2; Prov. xvi. 33; Acts i. 26, &c.); it was therefore His act to choose one of the goats for His service in the way of ordinary sacrifice, the other for His service in carrying off the sins to Azazel. The idea to be set before the Israelites was the absolute annihilation, by the atoning sacrifice, of sin as a separation between Jehovah and His people, the complete setting free of their consciences. See note on *v.* 22. This was expressed in later times by the Psalmist; "As far as the east is from the west, so far hath he removed our transgressions from us" (ciii. 12); and by the Prophet: "He will subdue our iniquities; and thou wilt cast all their sins into the depths of the sea." Micah vii. 19. By this expressive outward sign the sins were sent back to the author of sin himself, "the entirely separate one," who was banished from the realm of grace.

IV. The removal of the sins which had been atoned for could only be effected by means as holy, as much belonging to Jehovah, as those which had been employed in the atonement itself. They were not, as in the case of the Sin-offering, put upon the head of the goat by the offerers, nor by the elders of the people as their representatives (see Lev. iv. 15); but by the High priest in his holy white robes lately come from the presence of Jehovah in the innermost Sanctuary, presenting the signs of his mediatorial character in the strongest light. The goat itself could not have lost the sacred character with which it had been endued in being presented before Jehovah. It was, as much as the slain goat, a figure of Him who bore our griefs and carried our sorrows, on whom the Lord laid the iniquity of us all (Is. liii. 4, 6), that we might become a sanctified Church to be presented unto Himself, not having spot or wrinkle or any such thing (Eph. v. 26, 27).

The Fathers in general speak of each goat as a figure of our Saviour. (Cyril Alex., Theodoret, Hesychius, Jerome.) But they do not agree with the view which has been given as to the destination of the living goat. Regarding the animal as a type of the risen Saviour, Cyril supposed the place to which he was sent to represent Heaven to which Christ was to ascend: Theodoret, taking the same general view, conceived it to symbolize *the impassibility of the divine nature* (τὸ ἀπαθὲς τῆς θεότητος), upon which the sins were cast and lost all their virulence. Cyril, 'Glaph.' p. 374; Theod. 'Quæst. in Lev.' XXII.

V. We do not see the practical end of such inquiries as have occupied the attention of so many critics regarding the identity or non-identity of Azazel with the serpent of Genesis iii., with Satan, with the Egyptian Typhon, or with some other recognized aspect of the evil spirit[2]. Our spiritual enemy has never been made known to us by a proper name. We can only here and there trace the mention of him in the Scriptures until his personality becomes most clearly developed in his struggle with the Son of God; but even then he has no stedfast name. He is called the serpent (Gen. iii; Rev. xii. 9), the enemy or fiend, ("Satan," Job i. 6; Zech. iii. 1, 2; Rev. xii. 9, xx. 2), the accuser, or slanderer (Matt. iv. 10; Luke x. 18; Rom. xvi. 20; Rev. xii. 9, &c. &c.), the tempter (Matt. iv. 3; 1 Thess. iii. 5), the prince of this world (John xii. 31, xiv. 30, xvi. 11), the prince of the power of the air (Eph. ii. 2), the destroyer (Rev. ix. 11; cf. Job xxvi. 6; Prov. xxvii. 20, where the same Hebrew word [אֲבַדּוֹן, *abaddōn*] is used), and the Jews called him by the name of the Philistine god, Beelzebub (Matt. x. 25; Luke xi. 15, &c.). In this place he appears to be called by a name which was no doubt præ-Mosaic (as Gesenius and Ewald have remarked), with a very apposite meaning. This variety of designation in different ages, and under different circumstances of development, may tend to shew in what a practical way the idea of one who is a rebel against God and a spiritual enemy to man naturally arises in the human mind. It tends to prove the important fact that the belief in the existence of such a being, through a succession of ages, has not been dependent on the tradition of a name.

[1] Buxt. 'Syn. Jud.' c. XXVI; 'Lex. Talm.' p. 1495. Rosenmüller, on Lev. xvi. 8.

[2] Gesen. 'Thes.' p. 1012. Ewald, 'Alterthüm.' 403. Hengstenberg, 'Egypt and the Books of Moses,' p. 170. Kurtz, 'S. W.' 402, &c.

VI. The other chief explanations of the word *'azāzēl* may be briefly noticed.

(1) The word has been taken as a verbal substantive signifying, with its preposition, *for complete removal* (Bähr, Winer, Tholuck, &c.). As a formal explanation of the Hebrew word, this is of very recent authority, but it may have some countenance from the rendering of the Septuagint in two out of the four places in which *'azāzēl* occurs (*vv.* 10, 26), and still more from the Old Italic, which reads "ad dimissionem."

(2) It has been understood to signify some mountainous desert place. Saadia, several Jewish writers quoted by Vatablus, Bochart, Carpzov, Reland, Le Clerc, &c. But this notion is opposed to *vv.* 10, 21, in which the desert is distinguished from Azazel in such a way as hardly to admit of one being the explanation of the other.

(3) Azazel has been taken as a designation of the goat itself, by the ancient Greek versions (but the LXX. is not consistent in this respect in *vv.* 10, 26), the Vulgate, Luther, the English Version, &c. The word used by the Septuagint in *v.* 8 (ἀποπομπαῖος) can only be taken in an active sense = *the averter of ills*, *averruncus*, not as it is by several of the Fathers, as *the goat dismissed*. Symmachus has, *the goat that departs* (ἀπερχόμενος), Theodotion, *the goat sent away* (ἀφιέμενος), Aquila, *the goat set free*, strictly "the scapegoat" (ἀπολελυμένος), and the Vulgate, *caper emissarius*. Josephus agrees in sense with the Septuagint. But the construction of the Hebrew is certainly not in favour of these renderings, nor of Azazel being in any sense applied to the goat as a proper name.—If on one of the lots the prepositional prefix ל has the ordinary sense of *for* or *to*, it is not likely that, on the other, it would mean, *appointed to be*. The inconsistency which our translators have fallen into in following the Vulgate, may be seen in *v.* 10.

CHAPTER XVII.

1 *The blood of all slain beasts must be offered to the Lord at the door of the tabernacle.* 7 *They must not offer to devils.* 10 *All eating of blood is forbidden,* 15 *and all that dieth alone, or is torn.*

AND the LORD spake unto Moses, saying,
2 Speak unto Aaron, and unto his
sons, and unto all the children of Israel, and say unto them; This *is* the
thing which the LORD hath commanded, saying,
3 What man soever *there be* of the
house of Israel, that killeth an ox, or
lamb, or goat, in the camp, or that
killeth *it* out of the camp,
4 And bringeth it not unto the
door of the tabernacle of the congregation, to offer an offering unto the
LORD before the tabernacle of the

CHAP. XVII.

The leading topic of this chapter is the blood of animals; what it is, why it should be held sacred, how it should be treated in the processes of daily life. The subject evidently has a connection with what goes before, as an explanation of why blood should be an object of chief significance on the Altar, and especially in the rites of the Day of Atonement, in which its meaning was brought into its holiest, highest association.—But this chapter in its immediate bearing on the daily life of the Israelites stands as the first of four (xvii.—xx.), which set forth practical duties, directing the Israelites to walk, not in the way of the heathen, but according to the ordinances of Jehovah.

ON SLAYING ANIMALS FOR FOOD.
1—16.

1, 2. The Legislator is now commanded to address the whole of the people as well as the priests. The subject-matter of the laws here expressed is one in which the ordinary life of the people was brought into immediate relation to the priests'.

All animals are to be slaughtered before the Tabernacle. 3—7.

3, 4. Every domesticated animal that was slain for food was a sort of Peace-offering (*v.* 5): the Mishna says that the shoulder, the cheeks, and the paunch of each animal so slaughtered was given to the priests ('Cholin,' x. 1, see on vii. 32). This law, though it expressed a great principle (see on *v.* 7), was only provisional in its practical bearing. It could only be kept as long as the children of Israel dwelt in their camp in the Wilderness. The restriction was removed before they settled in the Holy Land, where their numbers and diffusion over the country would have rendered its strict observance impossible. See Deut. xii. 15, 16, 20—24. On the mode of slaughtering see Note at the end of the Chapter.

3. *lamb*] **Sheep.** See on iii. 7.

4. Rather "And bringeth it not unto **the entrance of the Tent of meeting to offer it as an offering before the Tabernacle** (*i.e.* the dwellingplace) **of Jehovah,**" &c. See on Ex. xxvi. 1: Lev. i. 3.

LORD; blood shall be imputed unto that
man; he hath shed blood; and that man
shall be cut off from among his people:
5 To the end that the children of
Israel may bring their sacrifices, which
they offer in the open field, even that
they may bring them unto the LORD,
unto the door of the tabernacle of the
congregation, unto the priest, and offer
them *for* peace offerings unto the LORD.
6 And the priest shall sprinkle the
blood upon the altar of the LORD *at*
the door of the tabernacle of the con-
gregation, and burn the fat for a [a] sweet a Exod. 29. 18. chap. 4. 31.
savour unto the LORD.
7 And they shall no more offer
their sacrifices unto devils, after whom
they have gone a whoring. This
shall be a statute for ever unto them
throughout their generations.
8 ¶ And thou shalt say unto them,
Whatsoever man *there be* of the house
of Israel, or of the strangers which
sojourn among you, that offereth a
burnt offering or sacrifice,
9 And bringeth it not unto the

---

blood shall be imputed unto that man] *i.e.* he has incurred guilt in shedding blood in an unlawful manner.

cut off] See on Ex. xxxi. 14.

5. *sacrifices*] The Hebrew is *zebāchim*, *i.e.* slain beasts or beasts for slaughter. See Introd. § iii. St Augustin ('Quæst. in Lev.' 56) understood *vv.* 3—6 to refer to ceremonial sacrifices. The older versions (with our own) seem to countenance this. But the connection justifies most of the modern interpreters in applying the words to animals slaughtered for food. See the heading in our Bible. The whole verse might be rendered: **In order that the children of Israel may bring their beasts for slaughter, which they (now) slaughter in the open field, even that they may bring them before Jehovah to the entrance of the Tent of meeting unto the priests, and slaughter them as Peace-offerings to Jehovah.**

6. *sprinkle*] *i.e.* **cast forth.** See Introd. § vi.

burn] See on i. 9.

fat] *i.e.* the suet. See Introd. § viii.

7. *offer their sacrifices*] The words might be rendered, **sacrifice their beasts for slaughter.** See on *v.* 5.

unto devils] The word *sā'eer* denotes a shaggy goat. See on iv. 23. But it is sometimes employed, as here, to denote an object of heathen worship or a demon dwelling in the deserts. 2 Chron. xi. 15; Is. xiii. 21, xxxiv. 14. The worship of the goat, accompanied by the foulest rites, prevailed at Mendes in Lower Egypt. Herodot. II. 46; Strabo, XVII. p. 802; Ælian, 'Hist. An.' VII. 19: other authorities are given by Bochart, 'Hieroz.' lib. II. c. 53. The Israelites may have been led into this snare while they dwelt in Egypt. See Hengstenberg, 'Egypt,' &c. p. 203. Cf. Josh. xxiv. 14, 15; Ezek. xxiii. 8, 9, 21. There is however no evidence to shew that the slaughter of animals, in the way here alluded to, formed any part of the goat worship of Egypt. On the other hand, the ancient Persians slew victims in honour of their deities in the open fields. Herodot. I. 132; Strabo, XV. p. 732. There is a reference in the Koran to the practice of the heathen Arabs of calling on false gods in the act of slaughter. Sura V., with Sale's note. Cf. Mishna, 'Cholin,' II. 8. See also Palgrave, 'Arabia,' Vol. I. p. 10. The ordinances of Menu do not approve of any flesh being eaten which has not been offered to a deity. Ch. V. §§ 23, 32, 34, 39, 41, 52. These customs seem to bear clear traces of a primeval habit in regard to taking the life of animals for food, which the Israelites at this time were in some form or other tempted to invest with idolatrous associations. It might be better, following the hint furnished by Is. xiii. 21, xxxiv. 14, to render the expression, **to the evil spirits of the desert.** Luther has, *to field devils*.

But this law for the slaughtering of animals was not, as some have suggested (*e.g.* Hävernick, 'Pent.' p. 299), merely to exclude idolatry from the chosen nation. It had a more positive and permanent purpose. It bore witness to the sanctity of life; it served to remind the people of the solemnity of the grant of the lives of all inferior creatures made to Noah (Gen. ix. 2, 3); it purged and directed towards Jehovah the feelings in respect to animal food which seem to be common to man's nature; and it connected a habit of thanksgiving with the maintenance of our human life by means of daily food. 1 Tim. iv. 3—5. Having acknowledged that the animal belonged to Jehovah, the devout Hebrew received back its flesh as Jehovah's gift. Cf. Note after Chap. xi. §§ III. IV.

No Sacrifice to be offered except in the Court.

8, 9.

The precept is here put into a negative form which has already been expressed positively in regard to each kind of sacrifice in detail. Ch. i. ii. iii., &c. Cf. Deut. xii. 2.

door of the tabernacle of the congregation, to offer it unto the LORD;
even that man shall be cut off from
among his people.
10 ¶ And whatsoever man *there*
be of the house of Israel, or of the
strangers that sojourn among you,
that eateth any manner of blood; I
will even set my face against that soul
that eateth blood, and will cut him off
from among his people.
11 For the life of the flesh *is* in
the blood: and I have given it to you
upon the altar to make an atonement
for your souls: for it *is* the blood *that*
maketh an atonement for the soul.
12 Therefore I said unto the children of Israel, No soul of you shall
eat blood, neither shall any stranger
that sojourneth among you eat blood.
13 And whatsoever man *there be*
of the children of Israel, or of the
strangers that sojourn among you,
†which hunteth and catcheth any beast † Heb.
or fowl that may be eaten; he shall *that hunteth any*
even pour out the blood thereof, and *hunting.*
cover it with dust.
14 For *it is* the life of all flesh; the
blood of it *is* for the life thereof: therefore I said unto the children of Israel,
[b] Ye shall eat the blood of no manner [b] Gen. 9. 4.
of flesh: for the life of all flesh *is* the

---

8. *the strangers which sojourn*] **the foreigners who dwell.** See on xvi. 29.

or sacrifice] That is, a slaughtered offering of any kind, generally a Peace-offering. See Introd. § iii.

9. *cut off*, &c.] See Ex. xxxi. 14.

Blood not to be eaten, and why. 10—14.

The prohibition to eat blood is repeated in seven places in the Pentateuch, Gen. ix. 4; Lev. iii. 17, vii. 26, 27, xvii. 10—14, xix. 26; Deut. xii. 16, 23, 24, xv. 23. But in this passage the ground of the law is stated more fully than elsewhere.

11. This verse should rather be rendered;—**For the soul of the flesh is in the blood; and I have ordained it for you upon the Altar, to make atonement for your souls; for the blood it is which makes atonement by means of the soul.** See Note at the end of the chapter.

the life of the flesh is in the blood] The word here translated life (*nephesh*) is the same which is twice rendered **soul** in the latter part of the verse. This is one of the places which the English translators, from Wickliffe to the most recent, with Luther, de Sacy, Diodati, Luzzatto and others, have entangled in difficulty owing to the vague use which they have made of the word *soul*. The ancient versions, with Leo Juda, Junius and Tremellius, the Geneva French and the recent German versions, consistently follow the original. See Note at the end of the chap.

I have given it to you upon the altar] These words (as Kurtz has observed) preclude any superstitious notion that there was atoning virtue in the blood itself. It had a natural fitness to express a truth and was therefore the symbol chosen by Divine wisdom for use upon the Altar.

for it is the blood that maketh an atonement for the soul] Our translators have followed the LXX., the Vulgate, the Targums and Luther. A few modern critics take the same course. But the more exact rendering of the Hebrew is that given above. So Bähr, Zunz, Kurtz, Knobel, Keil, Herxheimer, &c.

12. There are two distinct grounds given for the prohibition of blood as food: first, its own nature as the vital fluid; secondly, its consecration in sacrificial worship. We have already noticed that the prohibition of fat (suet) was distinguished from that of blood by its being grounded *simply* on its consecration to a peculiar use on the Altar and its being limited to the suet of the animals which were offered in sacrifice. See on vii. 25. It would seem that it was in virtue of this distinction that the Apostles decided to retain only the restriction regarding blood, confirmed as it is by the primeval prohibition, Gen. ix. 4.—The Mahometans, in like manner, abstain from blood but not from fat. See Note on *v.* 3.—St Augustin, in connection with the saying of our Lord, "Except ye eat my flesh and drink my blood," &c., remarks, "quærendum igitur quid significet, quod homo prohibetur in lege sanguinem manducare, eumque Deo fundere jubetur." 'Quæst. in Lev.' 57.

13. *beast or fowl*] See on xi. 7. The same rule was laid down for the blood of domesticated animals when at a later period they were no longer required to be slaughtered in the court. Deut. xii. 15, 16, 22—24. See Note on *v.* 11 at the end of the chapter.

14. Rather, **For the soul of all flesh is its blood with its soul** (*i.e.* its blood and soul together): **therefore spake I to the children of Israel, Ye shall not eat the blood of any flesh, for the soul of all flesh is its blood**, &c. The two Geneva versions, Zunz, Knobel, Herxheimer, &c. See Note on *v.* 11.

blood thereof: whosoever eateth it
shall be cut off.
15 And every soul that eateth †that
which died *of itself*, or that which
was torn *with beasts*, *whether it be* one
of your own country, or a stranger,
he shall both wash his clothes, and
bathe *himself* in water, and be unclean until the even: then shall he
be clean.
16 But if he wash *them* not, nor bathe
his flesh; then he shall bear his iniquity.

† Heb. *a carcase.*

---

15. Cf. Ex. xxii. 31; Lev. xi. 39 (see note), xxii. 8; Deut. xiv. 21. This law appears to be grounded on the fact that the body of an animal killed by a wild beast, or which has died of itself, still retains a great portion of its blood. The importance ascribed to this law in later times may be seen 1 S. xiv. 32—35; Ezek. iv. 14, xliv. 31, and still more in the Apostolic decision regarding "things strangled," which are pointedly connected with blood, Acts xv. 20. See Note on *v.* 3 at the end of the chapter.

a stranger] **a foreigner**, dwelling with the Israelites.—In Ex. xxii. 31 we find that such carcases were to be given to the dogs. On the apparent modification of this law in Deut. xiv. 21, see note *in loc.*

15, 16. The sanction of this law is less peremptory than that of the law against the eating of blood. See on *v.* 12. The latter was "cutting off from among his people" (*vv.* 10, 14); the former, only the penalty of an easy form of purification. See on xi. 39, 40. But if the prescribed rite of purification had been neglected, a Sin-offering was required. See on v. 2, 3.

NOTES on CHAP. XVII.

I. ON THE SLAUGHTERING OF ANIMALS. *v.* 3.

The same mode of slaughter appears to have been followed by the Hebrews, the Egyptians, and the Arabs. As regards the mere slaying the animal, there is no trace of any difference in the mode, whether it was intended for ordinary food or for a sacrifice. It should be observed that, amongst the Semitic nations above all others, the taking the life of an animal, especially of an animal of a kind which might be offered in sacrifice, has always been regarded as a solemn act, partaking of a somewhat religious character. There is a treatise on the subject in the Mishna, entitled 'Cholin[1],' and one in the Hedàya[2], entitled 'Zabbah,' which show the importance attached to the matter in Jewish and Arab traditions. The method of slaughter may be clearly gathered from these treatises. The three points kept in view were, that the process should be as expeditious as possible, that the least possible suffering should be inflicted on the creature, and that the blood should flow out of the carcase in the most speedy and thorough manner. The animal, if a large one, was thrown down by hobbling. The slayer was provided with a sword or long knife which he drew across the throat, at one stroke cutting through the windpipe, the gullet, and the large blood-vessels of the neck. The least tearing of the flesh, owing to a notched or blunt weapon, or to clumsy manipulation, rendered the carcase unclean[3]. In some ancient Egyptian pictures this method is shown. In one of those given by Wilkinson, a man is holding up by the horns the head of the dying ox, while an attendant is removing in basins the blood as it runs from the neck[4]. There is no reason to doubt that this picture accurately represents the mode pursued in the court of the Tabernacle.

The verse of the Koran which speaks on the subjects of this chapter is worth quoting: "That which dieth of itself, and blood, and swine's flesh, and all that hath been sacrificed under the invocation of any other name than that of God, and the strangled, and the killed by a blow or by a fall or by goring, and that which hath been eaten by beasts of prey (unless ye make it clean by giving the death stroke yourselves), and that which hath been sacrificed on blocks of stone, are forbidden to you[5]." The "blocks of stones" are such as were set up for the purpose by the pagan Arabs[6]. All Moslems appear to reckon flesh as carrion, unless *Bismillah* (*i.e.* 'in the name of God') is pronounced when the throat of the animal is cut, or, in the case of game, when the gun is fired, or the leash of the dog slipped[7]. The strictness, even of the most

[1] See also Philo, 'de Victimis,' c. v. and L'Empereur's Notes on 'Middoth,' c. III.

[2] Vol. IV. p. 62, sq.

[3] The present Jews observe precisely the same rules. It would seem that skill in the slaughtering of an animal was as little degrading to the ancient Israelite as the skill of a sportsman is amongst ourselves. Dean Stanley makes a striking remark in connection with the Passover of the modern Samaritans which bears on this subject. 'Jewish Church,' Vol. II. p. 412.

[4] 'Popular Account,' I. p. 175.

[5] Sura v., Rodwell's translation, p. 631.

[6] Sale's note; cf. Burton, 'Arabia,' Vol. III. p. 303.

[7] 'Hedàya,' IV. p. 64; Lane's 'Modern Egyp-

degraded of them, in this respect is remarkable. Mr Speke, in his African journey, found that his Arab attendants would not eat the flesh of any animal which had been shot, unless they had cut its throat in due form before its death.

II. On the Life in the Blood. *v.* 11.

There are three words relating to the constitution of man in the Old Testament, and three corresponding ones in the New Testament, which it seems desirable to notice in their connection with this subject. Olshausen, in his 'Opuscula,' has treated the words at length as far as the New Testament is concerned, has satisfactorily vindicated the consistency and clearness of the sacred writers, and has traced out the way in which confusion respecting them has crept into theological language. It will perhaps be sufficient for our purpose thus to mark the difference between the words in question; (1) *chay* (חי), ζωή, *vita*, denoting Life, as opposed to death[1]: (2) *nephesh* (נפש), ψυχή, *anima*, the Soul, as distinguished from the body; the individual life either in man or beast, whether united to the body during life (*chay*), or separated from the body after death; observe the expression "living soul," Gen. ii. 7: (3) *ruach* (רוח) πνεῦμα, spiritus, the Spirit, that which is opposed to the flesh, Rom. viii. 6; Gal. v. 17; 1 Pet. iii. 18, and is distinguished from the life of the flesh; the highest element in man, that which, in its true condition, holds communion with God (Rom. viii. 4, 5, 6). Some of the passages in the New Testament which, if read in the original, the Vulgate, Erasmus, Beza, or the Geneva French, illustrate the distinction which now claims our attention are, Matt. vi. 25, x. 28, 39, xvi. 25, 26; Mark viii. 35; Luke xii. 22, 23; 1 Cor. xv. 44; 1 Thess. v. 23; Heb. iv. 12: while several of these in our version exemplify the confusion of which we have spoken.

The words *nephesh* and ψυχή, like the English *soul*, were, however, occasionally used for *person*. Gen. xlvi. 18; Lev. ii. 1 (in Hebrew), iv. 2, v. 1, 15; Acts vii. 14, xxvii. 37, &c. Compare the use of our word *body* in the Prayer-Book Ps. liii. 1, and in the compounds, *nobody*, *anybody*, &c. *Nephesh* is even used in some cases where we should rather use *dead body*, Num. v. 2, vi. 11, ix. 6, 10, &c.

The soul (*nephesh*) has its abode in the blood as long as life lasts. In *v.* 14, the Soul is identified with the Blood, as it is in Genesis ix. 4. Deut. xii. 23[2]. That the Blood is rightly thus distinguished from all other constituents of the body is acknowledged by the highest authorities in physiology. "It is the fountain of life (says Harvey), the first to live, and the last to die, and the primary seat of the animal soul; it lives and is nourished of itself, and by no other part of the human body." John Hunter inferred that it is the seat of life, because all the parts of the frame are formed and nourished from it. "And if (says he) it has not life previous to this operation, it must then acquire it in the act of forming; for we all give our assent to the existence of life in the parts when once formed." Milne Edwards observes that, "if an animal be bled till it falls into a state of syncope, and the further loss of blood is not prevented, all muscular motion quickly ceases, respiration is suspended, the heart pauses from its action, life is no longer manifested by any outward sign, and death soon becomes inevitable; but if, in this state, the blood of another animal of the same species be injected into the veins of the one to all appearance dead, we see with amazement this inanimate body return to life, gaining accessions of vitality with each new quantity of blood that is introduced, by-and-bye beginning to breathe freely, moving with ease, and finally walking as it was wont to do, and recovering completely." Art. *Blood.* 'Cyclopædia of Anatomy and Physiology.' See also Stevens' "Observations on the Blood," p. 119. The more or less distinct traces of the recognition of blood as the vehicle of life to be found in the Greek and Roman writers are collected—perhaps without sufficient discrimination—by Von Lasaulx ('Die Sühnopfer der Griechen und Römer,' &c.), and by de Maistre ('Eclaircissement sur les Sacrifices'). The knowledge of the ancients on the subject may indeed have been based on the mere observation that an animal loses its life when it loses its blood. But it may deepen our sense of the wisdom and significance of the Law of Moses to know that the fact which it sets forth so distinctly and consistently, and in such pregnant connection, is so clearly recognized by modern scientific research.

tians,' I. 134. Cf. Baker, 'Nile Tributaries,' pp. 137, 202; Speke, pp. 66, 230, 513.

[1] Gen. i. 20, 24, ii. 7; Deut. xxx. 15, 19; Prov. xviii. 21.

[2] It should be noted that the LXX. and the Vulg. are consistent in rendering the Hebrew words *chay* and *nephesh* in this chap. and elsewhere.

CHAPTER XVIII.

1 *Unlawful marriages.* 19 *Unlawful lusts.*

AND the Lord spake unto Moses, saying,
2 Speak unto the children of Israel,

and say unto them, I am the LORD
your God.
3 After the doings of the land of
Egypt, wherein ye dwelt, shall ye
not do: and after the doings of the
land of Canaan, whither I bring you,
shall ye not do: neither shall ye walk
in their ordinances.
4 Ye shall do my judgments, and
keep mine ordinances, to walk therein: I *am* the LORD your God.
5 Ye shall therefore keep my sta-
tutes, and my judgments: [a]which if a — [a] Ezek. 20. 11.
man do, he shall live in them: I *am* — Rom. 10. 5.
the LORD. — Gal. 3. 12.

6 ¶ None of you shall approach to
any that is †near of kin to him, to un- — † Heb. *remainder of his flesh.*
cover *their* nakedness: I *am* the LORD.
7 The nakedness of thy father, or
the nakedness of thy mother, shalt
thou not uncover: she *is* thy mother;
thou shalt not uncover her nakedness.
8 [b]The nakedness of thy father's — [b] chap. 20. 11.
wife shalt thou not uncover: it *is* thy
father's nakedness.
9 The nakedness of thy sister, the
daughter of thy father, or daughter of
thy mother, *whether she be* born at
home, or born abroad, *even* their nakedness thou shalt not uncover.

CHAP. XVIII.

OF UNLAWFUL MARRIAGES AND LUSTS. 1—30.

2. *I am the LORD your God*] This formula, or the shorter one, *I am the LORD*, occurs also in *vv.* 4, 5, 6, 21, 30. Cf. xi. 44, 45. It is found several times in the chapters that follow. Its frequent repetition in these parts of the Law may be intended to keep the Israelites in mind of their Covenant with Jehovah in connection with the common affairs of life, in which they might be tempted to look at legal restrictions in a mere secular light. It is but sparingly used in the laws that refer to the observances of religion. Cf. note on *vv.* 24—30.

3. *the land of Egypt—the land of Canaan*] See note on 24—30.

5. *statutes*] **ordinances**. The same Heb. word is thus rendered in *v.* 4.

which if a man do, he shall live in them] If a man keeps the ordinances and judgments of the Divine Law, he shall not be "cut off from his people" (cf. *v.* 29), he shall gain true life, the life which connects him with Jehovah through his obedience. Ezek. xx. 11, 13, 21; Luke x. 28; Rom. x. 5; Gal. iii. 12.

Unlawful Marriages. 6—18.

6. *near of kin*] The Hebrew phrase means literally, *flesh of his body*. The term strictly taken would express all blood relations (as there is no limitation in the original answering to "near") and no others; but it was evidently used to denote those only who came within certain limits of consanguinity, together with those who by affinity were regarded in the same relationship. The rendering of the LXX. is worthy of note—ἄνθρωπος πρὸς πάντα οἰκεῖα σαρκὸς αὐτοῦ οὐ προσελεύσεται.

to uncover...nakedness] *i.e.* to have intercourse. The immediate object of this law was to forbid incest.

7—18. See Note at the end of the chapter.

7. *The nakedness of thy father, or the nakedness*, &c.] The Hebrew conjunction is copulative, not adversative. It might be rendered *and*, or rather, **even**; that is, which belongs to both parents as being "one flesh." Gen. ii. 24; cp. *vv.* 8, 14. These prohibitions are addressed to men and not to women, as is shewn by the concluding words of the verse having reference only to the mother.

8. Cf. the case of Reuben, Gen. xxxv. 22, xlix. 3, 4; St Paul speaks of intercourse with a stepmother as an abomination "not so much as named among the Gentiles," *i.e.* among the Greeks. 1 Cor. v. 1.

thy father's nakedness] See on *v.* 7.

9. *thy sister*] What was here spoken of was the distinguishing offence of the Egyptians. See Note on *v.* 30 at the end of the chapter.

born at home, or born abroad] The alternative thus expressed has been taken to mean;—(1) legitimate or illegitimate; (2) the illegitimate daughter of the father or the illegitimate daughter of the mother; (3) the daughter of the father by a previous marriage (*born at home*), or the daughter of the mother by a previous marriage (*born abroad*, that is, *in another house*). But the phrase might be taken in a broader sense so as to embrace all of these alternatives.—According to the third explanation, the connection prohibited would be that with an elder half-sister. Whether the rule regarding a half-sister by the father was observed by the old Hebrews has been questioned from the instance of Abraham, Gen. xx. 12, where Michaelis ('Laws of Moses,' Art. CX.) and many others take the word sister in its strict sense. But Jewish tradition is probably right in giving a wider meaning to the word *sister* (like *brother* Gen. xiii. 8, xiv. 16), and in regarding Sarah as the niece of

10 The nakedness of thy son's daughter, or of thy daughter's daughter, *even* their nakedness thou shalt not uncover: for theirs *is* thine own nakedness.

11 The nakedness of thy father's wife's daughter, begotten of thy father, she *is* thy sister, thou shalt not uncover her nakedness.

12 [c]Thou shalt not uncover the nakedness of thy father's sister: she *is* thy father's near kinswoman.

13 Thou shalt not uncover the nakedness of thy mother's sister: for she *is* thy mother's near kinswoman.

14 [d]Thou shalt not uncover the nakedness of thy father's brother, thou shalt not approach to his wife: she *is* thine aunt.

15 [e]Thou shalt not uncover the nakedness of thy daughter in law: she *is* thy son's wife; thou shalt not uncover her nakedness.

16 [f]Thou shalt not uncover the nakedness of thy brother's wife: it *is* thy brother's nakedness.

17 Thou shalt not uncover the nakedness of a woman and her daughter, neither shalt thou take her son's daughter, or her daughter's daughter, to uncover her nakedness; *for* they *are* her near kinswomen: it *is* wickedness.

18 Neither shalt thou take ‖a wife to her sister, to vex *her*, to uncover her nakedness, beside the other in her life *time*.

19 [g]Also thou shalt not approach unto a woman to uncover her nakedness, as long as she is put apart for her uncleanness.

20 Moreover thou shalt not lie carnally with thy neighbour's wife, to defile thyself with her.

21 And thou shalt not let any of thy seed [h]pass through *the fire* to [i]Molech, neither shalt thou profane the name of thy God: I *am* the LORD.

c chap. 20. … d chap. 20. … e chap. 20. … f chap. 20. …

‖ Or, one *wife to another*.

g chap. 20. 18.

h chap. 20. 2. 2 Kings 23. 10.

i Called, Acts 7. 43, *Moloch*.

Abraham. Jos. 'Ant.' I. 6. § 5. See on Gen. xi. 29, xx. 12.

11. It is not easy to determine in what way the meaning of this verse is to be distinguished from that of *v.* 9. But however the details are to be made out, it is obvious that the purpose of *vv.* 9, 11 is emphatically to forbid connection with sisters and half-sisters in whatever way the relationship may come.

12. *thy father's sister*] The instance of Amram and Jochebed (Exod. vi. 20) seems to shew that marriage with an aunt was not considered wrong by the Israelites when they were in Egypt.

16. *thy brother's wife*] That is, if she had children. See Deut. xxv. 5. On the question regarding the inference drawn from this prohibition that it is unlawful to marry the sister of a deceased wife, see Note on *vv.* 7—18 at the end of the chapter, § iv. The law here expressed was broken by Antipas in his connection with Herodias. But the argument to prove that St John the Baptist appealed to this law rather than to the seventh Commandment (see Beda, 'Hist. Ecc.' Lib. I. c. 27), appears to be based on an unsupported assumption that the first husband of Herodias was dead at that time. See Joseph. 'Ant.' XVIII. 5. § 1.

17. It is here forbidden that a man should have connection with both a woman and her daughter, or with both a woman and her granddaughter. The former prohibition is repeated in Deut. xxvii. 23. The rule might have had immediate reference to the relationship incurred by concubinage or irregular intercourse. The Mussulman law, in adopting the rule, applies it expressly in this way, and declares intercourse to be "a principle or cause of a mutual participation of blood between the parties concerned in it." 'Hedàya,' Vol. I. pp. 81, 485. Cf. Amos ii. 7; 1 Cor. vi. 16. It cannot be doubted that the prohibition includes the mother, the daughter and the granddaughter, of either a wife or a concubine. See note on *v.* 6. It should be noticed that incest with a daughter is forbidden only in this indirect manner, while the other very near relationships are distinctly mentioned. See Note at the end of the chapter.

18. *to vex her*] Literally, to *bind* or *pack together*. The Jewish commentators illustrate this by the example of Leah and Rachel. See Note at the end of the chapter.

Unlawful Lusts. 19—23.

19. *her uncleanness*] Cf. xx. 18.

20. *thy neighbour's wife*] Cf. Exod. xx. 14; Deut. v. 18, &c. See on xx. 10.

21. *pass through the fire to Molech*] Strictly, *pass through to Molech*. This is the earliest mention of Molech. See on xx. 2—5.

22 Thou shalt not lie with mankind, as with womankind: it *is* abomination.

k chap. 20. 15.

23 [k]Neither shalt thou lie with any beast to defile thyself therewith: neither shall any woman stand before a beast to lie down thereto: it *is* confusion.

24 Defile not ye yourselves in any of these things: for in all these the nations are defiled which I cast out before you:

25 And the land is defiled: therefore I do visit the iniquity thereof upon it, and the land itself vomiteth out her inhabitants.

26 Ye shall therefore keep my statutes and my judgments, and shall not commit *any* of these abominations; *neither* any of your own nation, nor any stranger that sojourneth among you:

27 (For all these abominations have the men of the land done, which *were* before you, and the land is defiled;)

28 That the land spue not you out also, when ye defile it, as it spued out the nations that *were* before you.

29 For whosoever shall commit any of these abominations, even the souls that commit *them* shall be cut off from among their people.

30 Therefore shall ye keep mine ordinance, that *ye* commit not *any one* of these abominable customs, which were committed before you, and that ye defile not yourselves therein: I *am* the LORD your God.

---

22. The ancient Persian law sternly condemned this offence ('Vendid.' VIII. 10, ap. Knobel). Also the Hindoo law ('Menu,' XI. 174, 175), and the Koran, VII. 78—80

23. The story of Pasiphae may furnish proof that the early Greeks abhorred this offence. The Hindoo law punishes it severely 'Menu,' XI. 17, 'Gentoo Laws,' p. 280. The Moslem law condemns it. 'Hedàya,' II. p. 27.—On the abominations of ancient Egypt, see on xvii. 7.

it is confusion] See on xix. 19.

Conclusion. 24—30.

24—30. The land designed and consecrated for His people by Jehovah (Lev. xxv. 23) is here impersonated, and represented as vomiting forth its present inhabitants, in consequence of their indulgence in the abominations that have been mentioned. The iniquity of the Canaanites was now full. See Gen. xv. 16; cf. Isaiah xxiv. 1—6. The Israelites in this place, and throughout the chapter, are exhorted to a pure and holy life, on the ground that Jehovah, the Holy One, is their God and that they are His people. Cf. xix. 2. It is upon this high sanction that they are peremptorily forbidden to defile themselves with the pollutions of the heathen. The only punishment here pronounced upon individual transgressors is, that they shall "bear their iniquity" and be "cut off from among their people." We must understand this latter phrase as expressing an *ipso facto* excommunication or outlawry, the divine Law pronouncing on the offender an immediate forfeiture of the privileges which belonged to him as one of the people in Covenant with Jehovah. See on Exod. xxxi. 14, and on Lev. xx. 17. The same purely spiritual sanction is applied to the string of statutes in the next chapter. But in chapter xx. special external punishments are allotted to the offences which have been previously named. The course which the Law here takes seems to be first to appeal to the conscience of the individual man on the ground of his relation to Jehovah, and then to enact such penalties as the order of the state required, and as represented the collective conscience of the nation put into operation. See xx. 26.

NOTES on CHAP. XVIII.

I. ON THE LIST OF PROHIBITED DEGREES. *vv.* 7—18.

i. The relations mentioned or evidently implied in these verses are:—

Relations by blood.

Mother, *v.* 7.
Sister and half-sister, *vv.* 9, 11.
Granddaughter, *vv.* 10, 17.
Aunt, paternal and maternal, *vv.* 12, 13.
Daughter, *v.* 17 (see note).

Relations by affinity, through marriage or carnal connection.

Wife's or concubine's mother }
Wife's or concubine's daughter } *v.* 17
Wife's or concubine's granddaughter }
"A wife to her sister." See Note on *v.* 18.

Relations by affinity, through the marriage of near blood relations.

Stepmother, *v.* 8.
Father's brother's wife, *v.* 14.
Son's wife, *v.* 15.
Brother's wife, *v.* 16.

ii. The other passages in the Law relating to this subject are:—

Lev. xx. 11, 12, 14, 17, 19, 20, 21. In these verses certain punishments are appointed for particular kinds of unlawful connection. By the inclusive law in *v.* 29 of chapter xviii. all who perpetrated incest were to be "cut off from among their people." But it is enacted in ch. xx. that when the crime was committed with a mother, stepmother, or daughter-in-law, a sentence of death should be passed upon both the offenders (xx. 11, 12): when with the daughter or the mother, of either a wife or a concubine, they were to be burned (xx. 14, see note): when with a sister or half-sister, they were to be "cut off in the sight of their people" (xx. 17, see note). For incest with an uncle's wife, or a brother's wife, no external punishment is specified, but they were to bear their sin and to be childless (see on xx. 20). The wife of a mother's brother is here included in the term "uncle's wife:" in *v.* 14 of chapter xviii. the father's brother's wife only is mentioned.

Deut. xxii. 30. The rule regarding the mother and stepmother is repeated in its shortest form.

Deut. xxv. 5—10. By this law, commonly known as "the Levirate law," when brethren were dwelling together, if one died leaving a widow without children the single brother was required, under a certain penalty, to marry her. Cf. Matt. xxii. 24.

Deut. xxvii. 20, 22, 23. In the Commination, which was to be proclaimed on taking possession of the Holy Land, curses were comprised on those who committed incest with a mother, a stepmother, a sister, a half-sister, or a mother-in-law. The mother-in-law is here distinctly mentioned for the first time in connection with the law of incest. She is however implied in xviii. 17 and in xx. 14.

iii. It is considered by most critics that neither of these statements, nor the whole of them together, can be intended to present a complete list of the proscribed relationships. The grandmother and the niece (see on *v.* 9) are certainly omitted. The daughter and the full sister are not expressly mentioned, though they are necessarily implied in *vv.* 9, 17. It would seem that, in accordance with the pervading practical character of the Mosaic statutes, such details were given, or repeated, from time to time, as the occasion required, the general principle of the law having been expressed in *v.* 6.

iv. From the order in which the particulars are given, and from the use of the expression "near of kin" in *v.* 6, there would seem to have been a general recognition of the maxim that the relationships of the husband devolved on the wife, and those of the wife upon the husband. This is distinctly put as regards the husband's relations concerning the stepmother in the expression, "it is thy father's nakedness" (*v.* 8), and in similar expressions concerning the brother's wife and the uncle's wife (xviii. 16, xx. 20, 21). But yet there is undoubtedly in Lev. xxi. 1—4 a clear distinction recognized between relations by blood and relations by affinity. And it has been argued that, as the wife lost her family name, acquired the civil rights of her husband's family, and, if a priest's daughter, lost the privileges she had as such (see Lev. xxi. 3, xxii. 12), though the husband's relations might have become the wife's, the wife's relations did not, in the full sense, become the husband's. It may be added that the Levirate marriage (Deut. xxv. 5—10) very clearly proves that, even in the case of the wife, the relationship with her husband's kindred was not by any means so stringent as that with her near blood relations, with whom connection could under no circumstances be permitted.

II. On Marriage with two Sisters. *v.* 18.

i. *Meaning of the words "a wife to her sister."* ii. *Not a prohibition of Polygamy.* iii. *The Ecclesiastical question.*

i. The rule, as it here stands, would seem to bear no other meaning than that a man is not to form a connection with his wife's sister, while his wife is alive. It appears to follow that the Law permitted marriage with the sister of a deceased wife. A limitation being expressly laid down in the words, "beside the other in her lifetime," it may be inferred that, when the limitation is removed, the prohibition loses its force, and permission is implied.

The testimony of the Rabbinical Jews in the Targums, the Mishna and their later writings; that of the Hellenistic Jews in the Septuagint and Philo ('de Spec. Legg.' III. 5); that of the early and mediæval Church in the old Italic, the Vulgate, with the other early versions of the Old Testament, and in every reference to the text in the Fathers and Schoolmen, are unanimous in supporting, or in not in any wise opposing, the common rendering of the passage. This interpretation appears indeed to have stood its ground unchallenged from the third century before Christ to the middle of the sixteenth century after Christ[1].

But a different version of the words rendered "a wife to her sister" was given by Junius and Tremellius (A.D. 1575), was

[1] See 'Ancient interpretation of Leviticus xviii. 18,' by Dr McCaul: 'Report of the Commissioners on the Law of Marriage,' p. 152.

treated with some allowance by Drusius (about A.D. 1600), found its way into the margin of our authorized version and into the margin of the Geneva French, and has been adopted more recently in the 'Berlenburger Bibel.' In our margin, the words "one wife to another" are offered as an alternative for, "a wife to her sister." The command would thus be turned into a prohibition of polygamy.

ii. It is quite true that the phrase in question, and the corresponding one, *a man to his brother*, are used idiomatically in Hebrew in cases in which the words are not applied in their primary sense but as Pronouns. But this idiomatic use appears regularly to follow a plural antecedent, and involves necessarily, not the sense merely of *one* added on to another *single one* (which is what would be required here), but a distributive and reciprocal sense, answering to, *each one to another*. It is so applied to the loops of the curtains of the tabernacle, to the tenons of the boards, in Ex. xxvi. (*vv.* 3, 5, 6, 17), and to the wings of the cherubim in Ezek. i. *vv.* 11, 23. See Robinson, quoted by McCaul, p. 59. The suggested interpretation in this place in Leviticus is rendered still more improbable by the fact that the words are the same as are used elsewhere throughout this chapter for *wife* and *sister*.

If the grammatical argument were less clear, the acceptance of the verse as a prohibition of polygamy would be obviously at variance with the laws in Ex. xxi. 7—11, and Deut. xxi. 15—17, which direct the mode for regulating a family in which there are more than one wife; to say nothing of the cases of Elkanah, David, Joash (2 Chro. xxiv. 3) and others, which are never called in question as breaches of the Law. By these instances, and by the warning for the king, Deut. xvii. 17, it would appear that the Law, while it restricted and even discouraged polygamy, certainly permitted it to exist.

iii. It must be kept in view that our business here is only to inquire what the Law of Moses actually says. The great practical questions relating to the obligation of Christians and to the alteration which has been proposed in the English law of marriage, have been argued at large, and may be well determined, upon other grounds. The Ecclesiastical rule which we have to obey rests upon a basis of its own, and the weighty arguments drawn from the conditions of social life may be deemed sufficient to support our law as it exists; but with these we have here nothing to do.

There is however a question which has been, in the eyes of some, almost identified with the practical inquiry, which affects in an important degree the light in which we are to regard this portion of the Mosaic law in whatever way we may interpret Lev. xviii. 18. Are the prohibitions contained in this chapter, in all their details, binding upon Christians? The affirmative has been strongly insisted on in modern times. Our Reformers were very decided on this point[1]. It has been contended that the Levitical table of prohibitions in all its details is as much a part of the moral law as, "Thou shalt not commit adultery," or any other of the Ten Commandments.

The Fathers in general, most of the Schoolmen and the mediæval Church, took different ground. They considered that while the great principles of the law of incest must ever be binding upon mankind, the limits to which their application should be carried out were not absolutely fixed, and might have been determined by Moses with a view to the particular circumstances and condition of the Hebrew nation. The testimony of St Basil, strongly as he was opposed to marriage with the sister of a deceased wife, is remarkable on this head. He declares that the Mosaic law of Prohibited degrees does not bind Christians more than the law of Circumcision; but he considers that the marriages in question are unlawful because man and wife are one, and the sister in law is to be regarded in the same light as the sister by blood[2].

Every particular prohibition actually contained in the Mosaic Law has however been generally acknowledged in the Church. But the tendency of ecclesiastical authorities, up to the time of the Reformation, was to multiply prohibitions. To give a few examples—St Augustin, in setting forth the reasons of laws against connections with near relations upon natural and social grounds, strongly objects to marriages between cousins[3]. Marriages between first cousins were forbidden by a law of Theodosius, which was revoked by Arcadius and Honorius A.D. 405. St Gregory (A.D. 590) forbad all marriages that came within the fourth degree of relationship. The Council of London assembled by Lanfranc A.D. 1075, prohibited anyone from marrying one of his own kindred, or one of the kindred of a deceased wife, within the seventh degree, and this law was reenacted in 1102 and 1126. In the Council of Westminster A.D. 1200, a man was forbidden to marry any relation of a deceased wife; and by the same canon, a godson was forbidden to marry the daughter of his godfather. This state of the Ecclesiastical law, along with the abomination of frequent dispensations which it entailed, probably occasioned a reckless revulsion in some minds of which traces may be seen in the

[1] See especially 'Reformatio Legum,' p. 47, edit. 1850.

[2] Ep. CXCVII. 'ad Diodotum.' The argument against the obligation of Christians to obey the letter of the Law is carried out by Jeremy Taylor, 'Ductor Dub.' Bk. II. ch. ii, and by Archdn. Hare, in his Charge for 1849, entitled, 'The True Remedy for the evils of the Age.'

[3] 'De Civ. Dei,' XV. 16. The passage is very striking.

controversy regarding the divorce of Henry VIII. Our Reformers were perhaps on this account driven more formally to entrench themselves behind the authority of the text of Leviticus, although they were obliged to supplement it in some particulars in constructing their own table for practical use.

III. On the Prohibited Degrees among the Gentile Nations. *v.* 30.

The excellence of the law contained in this chapter of Leviticus is shown in a strong light if contrasted with the abominations and irregularities in the usages of the most cultivated nations of antiquity.

The Egyptians and the Persians appear to have indulged in connections with near relations to a greater degree than any other civilized nations. In Egypt marriage with a full sister was permitted in very early times[1]. The custom was handed down in the royal family from the Pharaohs to the Ptolemies, and seems to have been continued till the termination of the latter dynasty with Cleopatra and her brother[2]. The prevalence of the custom is shown in the sculptures in both Lower and Upper Egypt[3]. The Medes and Persians were in the habit of marrying their mothers from the earliest ages. Eastern tradition ascribes the origin of this to Nimrod, and makes it coeval with the rise of the Magian religion[4]. But marriage with a sister appears to have been unknown in Persia till the time of Cambyses[5]. Later writers freely ascribe all other kinds of incest to the Persians[6]; but that with a mother continued to be their distinguishing opprobrium[7].

The Greeks and Romans, especially the latter, were in very early times much stricter in this branch of morality. The stories of Œdipus and Hippolytus sufficiently show the abhorrence in which connections with mothers and stepmothers were held[8]. Marriages with sisters were condemned as barbarous and unholy[9], although Solon permitted marriage with a half-sister by the father, and Lycurgus that with a half-sister by the mother[10]. Marriages between an uncle and niece appear to have been common at Sparta[11]. The old Roman custom was to avoid marriage with a blood relation, even with a first cousin. From the second century A.C. marriages between uncles and nieces, and between cousins, were tolerated[12]; but they were very infrequent, and those between uncles and nieces were disgraceful till after the middle of the first century A.D., when Claudius set the example by marrying Agrippina[13].

By the Brahmin law the twice-born man was not permitted to marry any woman who came within the sixth degree of relationship, either on the father's or on the mother's side, or was known by her family name to belong to the same stock. Incest with a mother was punished by death with frightful torture; that with a sister, aunt, or niece, by severe penance[14]. The ancient Arabs are said to have been very lax[15]; but the Moslem law is based upon the Hebrew, and adds to the prohibited degrees, nieces, foster-mothers and foster-sisters[16].

It seems worthy of remark that in early ages incestuous connections appear to have been avoided for the most part from instinctive repugnance ruling the general practice, rather than from positive statutes. The moral of the stories of Œdipus and Hippolytus must have been rooted in the Greek mind before there were positive laws on the subject. When Claudius wished to marry his niece he satisfied himself that he could carry out his purpose without breaking any express law. When it was made lawful at Athens and Sparta to marry half-sisters, and at Rome to marry cousins and nieces, the people showed themselves very backward in availing themselves of the license. It may also be observed in connection with this operation of a common instinct that several of the instances which have been adduced show in a very marked manner the observance in heathen nations to have been stricter in early ages than in later ones. The Persians and Medes seem at first to have made incestuous marriages only with mothers; but from the time of Cambyses they began to throw off all restraint. The Romans began with peculiar strictness, and became lax at a late period and by slow degrees. The histories of the family of Augustus and of the Herods sadly show how entirely the old strictness yielded at last to the opposite extreme.

1 Diod. Sic. I. 27.

2 Dio. Cass. XLII. 44.

3 Wilkinson, 'Pop. Account,' Vol. II. p. 224.

4 Selden, 'de Jure Gent.' lib. V. cap. 11, p. 552.

5 Herodot. III. 31. When Cambyses consulted his wise men on his intention to marry his sister, they replied that they could not find a law permitting a man to marry his sister, but they found one to allow a king to do as he liked.

6 Philo, 'de Sp. Legg.' III. 3; Hieron. 'adv. Jovin.' II. 7, &c.

7 Catullus, 'Carm.' XC.

8 See also Virgil, 'Æn.' X. 389.

9 Eurip. 'Androm.' 174; Aristoph. 'Ran.' 850; Plato, 'de Legg.' VIII. 6.

10 Philo, 'de Sp. Legg.' III. 4. Cimon availed himself of Solon's law in marrying Elpinice.

11 Herodot. V. 39, 48, cf. VII. 239, VI. 71.

12 Liv. XLII. 34; Cic. 'pro Cluent.' V.

13 Plut. 'Quæst. Rom.' p. 76, edit. Reiske; Tacit. 'Annal.' XII. 5, 6; Sueton. 'Claud.' XXVI.

14 'Menu,' III. 5, XI. 104, 171, sq.

15 Freytag, 'Einleitung,' ap. Rodwell, p. 532.

16 Koran, Sura IV. 20, sq.; 'Hedàya,' Vol. I. p. 76.

CHAPTER XIX.

A repetition of sundry laws.

AND the LORD spake unto Moses, saying,
2 Speak unto all the congregation
of the children of Israel, and say unto
[a] ch. 11. 44. & 20. 7. 1 Pet. 1. 16. them, [a]Ye shall be holy: for I the
LORD your God *am* holy.
3 ¶ Ye shall fear every man his
mother, and his father, and keep my
sabbaths: I *am* the LORD your God.
4 ¶ Turn ye not unto idols, nor
make to yourselves molten gods: I
am the LORD your God.
5 ¶ And if ye offer a sacrifice of
peace offerings unto the LORD, ye
shall offer it at your own will.
6 It shall be eaten the same day ye
offer it, and on the morrow: and if
ought remain until the third day, it
shall be burnt in the fire.
7 And if it be eaten at all on the
third day, it *is* abominable; it shall
not be accepted.
8 Therefore *every one* that eateth
it shall bear his iniquity, because he
hath profaned the hallowed thing of
the LORD: and that soul shall be cut
off from among his people.
9 ¶ And [b]when ye reap the har- [b] chap. 23. 22.
vest of your land, thou shalt not
wholly reap the corners of thy field,
neither shalt thou gather the gleanings of thy harvest.
10 And thou shalt not glean thy
vineyard, neither shalt thou gather
every grape of thy vineyard; thou
shalt leave them for the poor and
stranger: I *am* the LORD your God.
11 ¶ Ye shall not steal, neither
deal falsely, neither lie one to another.
12 ¶ And ye shall not [c]swear by [c] Exod. 20. 7. Deut. 5. 11. Matt. 5. 33. James 5. 12.
my name falsely, neither shalt thou
profane the name of thy God: I *am*
the LORD.
13 ¶ [d]Thou shalt not defraud thy [d] Ecclus. 10. 6.
neighbour, neither rob *him:* the wages
of him that is hired shall not abide
with thee all night until the morning.
14 ¶ Thou shalt not curse the

CHAP. XIX.

A REPETITION OF SUNDRY LAWS. 1—37.

2. *Ye shall be holy: for I the* LORD *your God am holy*] These words express the key-note to the whole book of Leviticus, being addressed as they are not to the priests, or the rulers, or the saintly few, but to the whole nation. Cf. xi. 45; xx. 7, 26; Ex. xix. 6.—There does not appear to be any systematic arrangement in the laws which follow; but it is evident that they were intended as guards to the sanctity of the elect people, enforcing common duties by immediate appeal to the highest authority. Cf. on xviii. 24—30.

3. Ex. xx. 8, 12, xxxi. 13, 14. The two laws repeated here are the only ones in the Decalogue which assume a positive shape, all the others being introduced by the formula, "Thou shalt not."—These express two great central points, the first belonging to natural law and the second to positive law, in the maintenance of the well-being of the social body of which Jehovah was the acknowledged king.

4. Ex. xx. 4, xxxiv. 14—17; see on Lev. xxvi. 1.

5. *ye shall offer it at your own will*] Rather, **ye shall offer it that you may be accepted.** See on i. 3.

6—8. See on vii. 15—18. Of the rules relating to holy things this was perhaps one of those most likely to be transgressed by the people, and hence the propriety of its being repeated in this place.

9, 10. This law is expressed more fully, Deut. xxiv. 19—21. As regards the grain harvest it is repeated in connection with the Feasts of Weeks, Lev. xxiii. 22. It was a charitable provision that related to every sort of grain and fruit. The word rendered "grape" in *v.* 10 signifies rather **fallen fruit** of any kind; and the word rendered "vineyard" may also be applied to **a fruit garden** of any kind. Cf. Deut. xxiii. 24.—*the poor* is the poor Israelite—*the stranger* is properly **the foreigner**, who could possess no land of his own in the land of Israel. See on xvi. 29; cf. *vv.* 33, 34. Like the law in *vv.* 23—25 (on which see note) this was prospective in its actual operation.

11, 12. The meaning of the eighth Commandment is here expanded into the prohibition of (1) theft, (2) cheating (cf. vi. 2, 3, 4), (3) falsehood. When the act of deception was aggravated by an oath the third Commandment was of course broken as well as the eighth. Ex. xx. 7, 15.

13, 14. The aphorism in *v.* 11 forbids injuries perpetrated by craft; this one, those perpetrated by violence or power, the conversion of might into right. In *v.* 13 "de-

deaf, [e] nor put a stumblingblock before
the blind, but shalt fear thy God: I
am the LORD.
15 ¶ [f] Ye shall do no unrighteousness in judgment: thou shalt not
respect the person of the poor, nor
honour the person of the mighty: *but*
in righteousness shalt thou judge thy
neighbour.
16 ¶ Thou shalt not go up and
down *as* a talebearer among thy people:
neither shalt thou stand against the
blood of thy neighbour: I *am* the
LORD.
17 ¶ [g] Thou shalt not hate thy
brother in thine heart: [h] thou shalt in
any wise rebuke thy neighbour, ‖ and
not suffer sin upon him.
18 ¶ Thou shalt not avenge, nor
bear any grudge against the children
of thy people, [i] but thou shalt love thy
neighbour as thyself: I *am* the LORD.
19 ¶ Ye shall keep my statutes.
Thou shalt not let thy cattle gender
with a diverse kind: thou shalt not
sow thy field with mingled seed: neither shall a garment mingled of linen
and woollen come upon thee.

[e] Deut. 27. 18.
[f] Exod. 23. 3. Deut. 1. 17. & 16. 19. Prov. 24. 23. James 2. 9.
[g] 1 John 2. 11.
[h] Matt. 18. 15. Ecclus. 19. 13.
‖ Or, *that thou bear not sin for him.*
[i] Matt. 5. 43. & 22. 39. Rom. 13. 9. Gal. 5. 14. James 2. 8.

---

fraud" should rather be, **oppress**. The rule given in the latter clause is expressed at more length Deut. xxiv. 14, 15; cf. James v. 4. The meaning of *v.* 14 appears to be, *Thou shalt not utter curses to the deaf because he cannot hear thee, neither shalt thou put a stumbling-block in the way of the blind because he cannot see thee* (cf. Deut. xxvii. 18), *but thou shalt remember that though the weak and poor cannot resist, nor the deaf hear, nor the blind see, God is strong, and sees and hears all that thou doest.* Cf. Job xxix. 15. The principle is brought into connection with the law of the Jubilee in Lev. xxv. 17, 36, 43.

15, 16. In the administration of justice there is to be no respect of persons. Judgment is not to be warped, either out of pity to the poor or to win favour with the rich: nor is it to be based upon idle tale-bearing (cf. Ex. xxiii. 1—3, 8). The meaning of the latter clause of *v.* 16 is not quite so clear. The expression, to "stand against the blood of thy neighbour," has been generally understood to mean, to put his life in danger by standing up as his accuser. But most of the recent Jewish versions follow the Talmud in giving another sense to the words, which it appears the Hebrew will bear: *Thou shalt not stand by idly when thy neighbour's life is in danger.* So Zunz, Luzzatto, Herxheimer, Leeser, Wogue.—Whichever interpretation we adopt, from the connection in which the passage stands, it may be inferred that the clause prohibits that which might interfere with the course of justice.

17, 18. The Israelite was not to conceal hatred in his heart towards his brother. When injured he was to admonish the offender at once, and not to incur sin by retaining any feeling of unkindness. Cf. Matt. xviii. 15 sq. The words *not suffer sin upon him*, should rather be, **not bear sin on his account**; that is, either by bearing secret ill-will (Ephes. iv. 26), or by encouraging him to sin in withholding due rebuke. Rom. i. 32. All feeling of vengeance or grudge was precluded by the commandment, "Thou shalt love thy neighbour as thyself." Cf. Matt. xxii. 39; Luke x. 27; Rom. xiii. 9; Gal. v. 14; James ii. 8, &c.

19. This law is substantially repeated Deut. xxii. 9, 10, 11. The distinctions which God has established in the physical order of the world were thus to be kept in view in accordance with the original law of creation. Gen. i. 11, 12, 21, 24, 25. The observance also of deeply rooted conventional distinctions, in which "use becomes second nature" (φύσις), is similarly connected with moral obligation in Deut. xxii. 5; cf. 1 Cor. xi. 14, 15.

linen and woollen] The original word thus rendered (*sha'atnez*) is a peculiar one. It is found only here and in Deut. xxii. 11, where it is rendered "of divers sorts," and the ordinary Hebrew words for woollen and linen which there follow it are in this place assumed by our translators to be an equivalent term. But *sha'atnez* appears to be a Coptic word and to mean *spurious* or *adulterated* (Gesenius, Fürst, Knobel, &c.); LXX. κίβδηλος. The mention of mixed woollen and linen in Deuteronomy only furnishes an illustrative example and is not a rendering of *sha'atnez.*—But there is a difficulty in reconciling this law with the combination of wool and linen used in the dress of the High priest. On Ex. xxviii. 4. Some of the Jews suppose that this law was made only for the laity; others refer to the rabbinical maxim that the Lord could at pleasure dispense with His own law. It may however be conjectured that the rule was not intended to forbid the weaving of different kinds of yarn into one piece where each material could be distinctly seen, but only the spinning into one thread two or more different materials. This may perhaps indicate the meaning of *sha'atnez* as denoting such tissues as linsey woolsey. It should be noticed that the flax is spoken of in Exodus as

20 ¶ And whosoever lieth carnally
with a woman, that *is* a bondmaid,
‖ betrothed to an husband, and not at
all redeemed, nor freedom given her;
‖ she shall be scourged; they shall not
be put to death, because she was not
free.
21 And he shall bring his trespass offering unto the LORD, unto the
door of the tabernacle of the congregation, *even* a ram for a trespass offering.
22 And the priest shall make an
atonement for him with the ram of
the trespass offering before the LORD
for his sin which he hath done: and
the sin which he hath done shall be
forgiven him.
23 ¶ And when ye shall come into
the land, and shall have planted all
manner of trees for food, then ye shall
count the fruit thereof as uncircumcised: three years shall it be as uncircumcised unto you: it shall not be
eaten of.
24 But in the fourth year all the
fruit thereof shall be † holy to praise
the LORD *withal.*
25 And in the fifth year shall ye
eat of the fruit thereof, that it may
yield unto you the increase thereof:
I *am* the LORD your God.
26 ¶ Ye shall not eat *any thing*
with the blood: neither shall ye use
enchantment, nor observe times.
27 [k] Ye shall not round the corners
of your heads, neither shalt thou mar
the corners of thy beard.
28 Ye shall not [l] make any cuttings in your flesh for the dead, nor

‖ Or, *abused by any.* Heb. *reproached by,* or, *for man.*
‖ Or, *they.* Heb. *there shall be a scourging.*
† Heb. *holiness of praises to the LORD.*
k chap. 21. 5.
l Deut. 14. 1.

---

spun by itself, xxvi. 1, xxvii. 16, xxxvi. 8, xxxix. 24, &c.

20. *betrothed to an husband*] Rather, **who has been betrothed to a man.** The reference appears to be to a bondwoman who has been betrothed to a fellow-servant by her master. Death was the punishment for unfaithfulness in a betrothed woman in other cases. Deut. xxii. 23, 24.

she shall be scourged] Literally, *there shall be a chastisement.* Our version follows the Targums. But a better rendering is that of the LXX., Vulg., Syriac and many recent versions, **they shall be chastised.** The Trespass-offering was especially due from the man as having not only sinned with the woman, but inflicted an injury on the rights of the master. See on v. 14.

23—25. When a fruit-tree of any kind was planted, its produce was to be deemed imperfect and unfit for presentation to Jehovah for the first three years. In the fourth year its fruit was presented in the Sanctuary (see Deut. xxvi. 2), and the tree was thus sanctified in a way which bore an analogy to the circumcision of one of the chosen race. Cf. "the vine undressed," literally, *the Nazarite vine.* Lev. xxv. 5, 11. Not until the fifth year was the owner permitted to eat of the fruit. In regard to its spiritual lesson, this law may be compared with the dedication of the first-born of beasts to Jehovah. Ex. xiii. 12, xxxiv. 19. Though in practical operation it could be only prospective, like the law of gleaning in *vv.* 9, 10, its meaning in a moral point of view was plain, and tended to illustrate the spirit of the whole Law.

I am the LORD] See on xviii. 2, xix. 2.

26—28. Certain heathen customs, several of them connected with magic, are here grouped together. The prohibition to eat anything *with the blood* (strictly, *upon the blood,*) may indeed refer to the eating of meat which had not been properly bled in slaughtering, and would thus take its ground only on the general prohibition of blood. Lev. vii. 26, xvii. 10; Deut. xii. 23; cf. 1 S. xiv. 32, 33. But it is not improbable that there may be a special reference to some sort of magical or idolatrous rites. Cf. Ezek. xxxiii. 25. See Spencer, Lib. I. c. VIII. § 1.

observe times] It is not clear whether the original word refers to the fancied distinction between lucky and unlucky days, to some mode of drawing omens from the clouds, or to the exercise of "the evil eye."

27. *round the corners of your heads*] It is supposed that this may allude to such a custom as that of the Arabs described by Herodotus. They used to shew honour to their deity Orotal by cutting the hair away from the temples in a circular form (III. 8). Cf. on Jer. ix. 26.

mar the corners of thy beard] Cf. xxi. 5; Jer. xlviii. 37. It has been conjectured that this also relates to a custom which existed amongst the Arabs (see Plin. 'H. N.' VI. 32), but we are not informed that it had any idolatrous or magical association. As the same, or very similar customs, are mentioned in connexion with cuttings in the flesh for the dead in ch. xxi. 5, in Deut. xiv. 1, as well as here, it would appear that they may have been signs of mourning. See Herodotus, II. 36.

28. *cuttings in your flesh for the dead*] Cf. xxi. 5; Deut. xiv. 1; Jer. xvi. 6, xlviii. 37, &c. Amongst the excitable races of the East

print any marks upon you: I *am* the
LORD.
† Heb. *profane.* 29 ¶ Do not † prostitute thy daughter, to cause her to be a whore; lest
the land fall to whoredom, and the
land become full of wickedness.
30 ¶ Ye shall keep my sabbaths,
and reverence my sanctuary: I *am*
the LORD.
31 ¶ Regard not them that have
familiar spirits, neither seek after
wizards, to be defiled by them: I *am*
the LORD your God.
32 ¶ Thou shalt rise up before the
hoary head, and honour the face of
the old man, and fear thy God: I *am*
the LORD.
33 ¶ And [m] if a stranger sojourn *m* Exod. 22. 21.
with thee in your land, ye shall not
‖ vex him. ‖ Or, *oppress.*
34 [n] *But* the stranger that dwelleth *n* Exod. 12. 48, 49.
with you shall be unto you as one
born among you, and thou shalt love
him as thyself; for ye were strangers
in the land of Egypt: I *am* the LORD
your God.
35 ¶ Ye shall do no unrighteous- *o* Prov. 11. 1. & 16. 11. & 20. 10.
ness in judgment, in meteyard, in
weight, or in measure.
36 [o] Just balances, just † weights, a † Heb. *stones.*

---

this custom appears to have been very common. Xenoph. 'Cyrop.' III. 1. 13, III. 3. 67; Herodot. IV. 71, &c. The Persians, Abyssinians, Bedouins, and many other nations still practise it.

print any marks] This appears to refer to the process of tattooing, in which different devices are formed by perforations in the cuticle, and ink, or some other coloured substance, is rubbed over them so as to leave a permanent mark. It was probably practised in ancient Egypt, as it is now by the lower classes of the modern Egyptians (Lane, ch. I.). This, as well as the other practices here named, appears to have been connected with superstitious notions. See Mishna, 'Makkoth,' III. 6, with Bartenora's note; Theodoret, 'Quæst. in Lev.' XXVIII. But any voluntary disfigurement of the person was in itself an outrage upon God's workmanship, and might well form the subject of a law.

29. This command would seem to refer to common prostitution as well as to that mentioned Deut. xxiii. 17, which is connected with idolatrous rites.

30. Cf. *v.* 3, xxvi. 2.

31. The devotion of faith, which would manifest itself in obedience to the commandment to keep God's Sabbaths and to reverence his Sanctuary (*v.* 30), is the true preservative against the superstition which is forbidden in this verse. The people whose God was Jehovah were not to indulge those wayward feelings of their human nature which are gratified in magical arts and pretensions. Cf. Isa. viii. 19.

them that have familiar spirits] The word thus rendered is supposed to signify *bottles*. So the Talmud, Gesenius, Fürst. This application of the word is supposed to have been suggested by the tricks of ventriloquists, within whose bodies it was fancied that spirits used to speak. Hence the LXX. use the word, ἐγγαστρίμυθοι. See Theod. 'Quæst. in Lev.' XXIX. The word which here and in some other places appears to denote the person practising the art, is in other cases used for the familiar spirit which he pretended to employ in order to consult, or to raise, the spirits of the dead. See 1 S. xxviii. 7, 8.

wizard] The English word literally answers to the Hebrew, being equivalent to *a knowing man*, or, *a cunning man*. See Lev. xx. 6, 27; Deut. xviii. 11; cf. Exod. xxii. 18.

32. The outward respect due to old age is here immediately connected with the fear of God. Prov. xx. 29; 1 Tim. v. 1. The ancient Egyptians, like the Lacedemonians and the old Romans, appear to have been exemplary in this respect (Herodot. II. 80; 'Aul. Gell.' II. 15), as were, and are to this day, most of the eastern nations: 'Menu,' II. 120, 121, 122; Lane's 'Modern Egyptians,' ch. VIII. XIII. &c.

33, 34. *the stranger*] **the foreigner.** See on xvi. 29. In Ex. xxii. 21, xxiii. 9, the Israelite was forbidden on the same ground—that he had himself been a foreigner in Egypt—to oppress the foreigner; but he is now commanded to treat him without reserve like a brother, to love him as himself. See on Ex. xxiii. 23. The word "*But*," supplied at the beginning of *v.* 34, is needless and rather obscures the meaning.

35, 36. In all kinds of exchanges, strict justice was to be observed. The Ephah is here taken as the standard of dry measure, and the Hin (see on Ex. xxix. 40) as the standard of liquid measure. Cf. Ezek. xlv. 10—12. Two very different estimates of the capacities of these measures have been formed. From the statements of Josephus, who compares the Hebrew measures with the Greek ('Ant.' III. 9. § 4, VIII. 2. § 9, &c.), the Ephah, or Bath, contained above eight gallons and a half, and the Hin (which was a sixth part of the Ephah), rather less than one gallon and a half. But according to the rabbinists, who make

just ephah, and a just hin, shall ye
have: I *am* the LORD your God,
which brought you out of the land of
Egypt.
37 Therefore shall ye observe all
my statutes, and all my judgments,
and do them: I *am* the LORD.

CHAPTER XX.

1 *Of him that giveth of his seed to Molech.* 4 *Of him that favoureth such an one.* 6 *Of going to wizards.* 7 *Of sanctification.* 9 *Of him that curseth his parents.* 10 *Of adultery.* 11, 14, 17, 19 *Of incest.* 13 *Of sodomy.* 15 *Of beastiality.* 18 *Of uncleanness.* 22 *Obedience is required with holiness.* 27 *Wizards must be put to death.*

AND the LORD spake unto Moses,
saying,
2 [a] Again, thou shalt say to the [a] chap. 18. 21.
children of Israel, Whosoever *he be*
of the children of Israel, or of the

---

the contents of a hen's egg their standard, the Ephah did not hold quite four gallons and a half, and the Hin not quite six pints. The Log was a twelfth part of the Hin. The latter estimate is to be preferred on grounds of probability.—For the moral duty here enjoined, cf. Deut. xxv. 13—16; Prov. xi. 1, xvi. 11, xx. 10; Ezek. xlv. 10; Micah vi. 10, 11; Amos viii. 5.

36. *I am the LORD your God*, &c] A full stop should without doubt precede these words. They introduce the formal conclusion to the whole string of precepts in this chapter, which are all enforced upon the ground of the election of the nation by Jehovah who had delivered them from the bondage of Egypt. Cf. on *v.* 2.

CHAP. XX.

PUNISHMENTS APPOINTED FOR CERTAIN CRIMES. 1—27.

Respecting the relation in which this chapter stands to chapters xviii. and xix. see on xviii. 24—30. The crimes which are condemned in those chapters on purely spiritual ground, the absolute prohibition of Jehovah, have here special punishments allotted to them as offences against the well-being of the nation.

2—5. Molech, literally, *the King*, called also Moloch, Milcom, and Malcham, whose rites are here so severely condemned, was known in later times as "the abomination of the Ammonites," when Chemosh was the abomination of the Moabites, and Astarte the abomination of the Sidonians. Solomon dedicated to each one of these deities a high place (see on xxvi. 30), most probably at the corner of Jerusalem which overlooked the valley of Hinnom. See Stanley, 'Jewish Church,' II. p. 390. These were destroyed and defiled by Josiah. 1 K. xi. 5, 7; 2 K. xxiii. 10, 13. Molech was called Adrammelech by the Sepharvites. 2 K. xvii. 31. He appears to have been *the fire-god* of the eastern nations; related to, and sometimes made identical with, Baal, *the sun-god.* The impious custom with which his name is mainly connected was called in full, *passing children through the fire to Molech*, sometimes elliptically (as in the Hebrew text of Lev. xviii. 21), *passing them through to Molech;* or, omitting the name of the god, *passing them through the fire.* In this place the children are spoken of as *given to Molech.* According to a Jewish tradition of very light authority, the deity was worshipped under the form of a brazen image, having the head of an ox, with the arms extended to receive the babe, who was in some way there subjected to the action of fire. A brass image of the god Kronos, said to have been used in this manner by the Carthaginians, is described by Diodorus Siculus (XX. 14), which seems to have furnished the rabbinists with the suggestion. But the nature of this rite, and of what others there may have been connected with the name of Molech, is very doubtful. The practices appear to have been essentially connected with magical arts; probably also with unlawful lusts (see *vv.* 5, 6; xviii. 20, 21; Deut. xviii. 10, 11; 2 K. xvii. 17, xxi. 6; 2 Chron. xxxiii. 6; Ezek. xxiii. 37), and with some particular form of profane swearing; see *v.* 3, xviii. 21; cf. Zeph. I. 5.—It is a question whether the child who was passed through the fire to Molech was destroyed or not; whether he was regarded as a propitiatory sacrifice, or as the object of a rite imagined to be in some way beneficial to him. Maimonides and the Jewish authorities in general appear to take the latter view. On the other hand, there is express mention of burning children as sacrifices. Ps. cvi. 37, 38; Is. lvii. 5; Jer. vii. 31, xix. 5; Ezek. xvi. 21, xxiii. 39. The sacrifice of his son by the king of Moab (2 K. iii. 27) was probably performed to the Moabite god, Chemosh, whose worship, it may reasonably be supposed, was of similar nature to that of Molech. But however the question is decided in reference to later times, we may perhaps conjecture, from the context in which it is here mentioned, that the rite in the time of Moses belonged to the region rather of magic than of definite idolatrous worship, and that it may have been practised as a lustral charm, or fire-baptism, for the children of incest and adultery. Its connection with the children of Ammon, the child of incest, may be worth noticing in reference to this suggestion. It should be recollected that Idolatry and Magic of all kinds are closely connect-

strangers that sojourn in Israel, that
giveth *any* of his seed unto Molech;
he shall surely be put to death: the
people of the land shall stone him
with stones.
3 And I will set my face against
that man, and will cut him off from
among his people; because he hath
given of his seed unto Molech, to defile my sanctuary, and to profane my
holy name.
4 And if the people of the land do
any ways hide their eyes from the man,
when he giveth of his seed unto Molech, and kill him not:
5 Then I will set my face against
that man, and against his family, and
will cut him off, and all that go a
whoring after him, to commit whoredom with Molech, from among their
people.
6 ¶ And the soul that turneth after
such as have familiar spirits, and after
wizards, to go a whoring after them,
I will even set my face against that
soul, and will cut him off from among
his people.
[b] chap. 11. 44. & 19. 2. 1 Pet. 1. 16. 7 ¶ [b]Sanctify yourselves therefore,
and be ye holy: for I *am* the LORD
your God.
[c] Exod. 21. 17. Prov. 20. 20. Matt. 15. 4. 8 And ye shall keep my statutes,
and do them: I *am* the LORD which
sanctify you.
9 ¶ [c]For every one that curseth his
father or his mother shall be surely
put to death: he hath cursed his father or his mother; his blood *shall be*
upon him.
10 ¶ And [d]the man that commit- [d] Deut. 22. 22. John 8. 4.
teth adultery with *another* man's wife,
even he that committeth adultery with
his neighbour's wife, the adulterer and
the adulteress shall surely be put to
death.
11 [e]And the man that lieth with [e] chap. 18. 8.
his father's wife hath uncovered his
father's nakedness: both of them shall
surely be put to death; their blood
shall be upon them.
12 And if a man lie with his daughter in law, both of them shall surely
be put to death: they have wrought
confusion; their blood *shall be* upon
them.
13 [f]If a man also lie with man- [f] chap. 18. 22.
kind, as he lieth with a woman, both
of them have committed an abomination: they shall surely be put to death;
their blood *shall be* upon them.
14 And if a man take a wife and
her mother, it *is* wickedness: they
shall be burnt with fire, both he and
they; that there be no wickedness
among you.
15 [g]And if a man lie with a beast, [g] chap. 18. 23.
he shall surely be put to death: and
ye shall slay the beast.
16 And if a woman approach unto

---

ed, and are always apt to run into each other, while true Faith is equally opposed to both of them. See on Exod. xxii. 18. Bacon reckons as two "declinations from religion," "*idolatry*, when we worship false gods, supposing them to be true; and *witchcraft*, when we adore false gods,. knowing them to be wicked and false." 'Advancement of Learning,' Bk. II.—In connection with this subject the matter collected by Brand, in his accounts of May day and Midsummer day, is of interest, 'Popular Antiquities,' Vol. I.

2. *strangers that sojourn*] **foreigners who dwell.** See xvi. 29.

people of the land] *i.e.* native Hebrews. See iv. 27.

stone him with stones] The commonest form of capital punishment. It was probably preferred as being the one in which the execution was the act of the whole congregation.

3. *defile my sanctuary*] *i.e.* pollute the people as identified with their Sanctuary. Cf. xv. 31; Num. xix. 13, &c.

6. Cf. *v.* 27 and on xix. 31.

7, 8. Cf. xi. 45, xviii. 4, 5, xix. 2, xx. 22—26, &c.

9. Ex. xxi. 17; Deut. xxvii. 16; Matt. xv. 4; Mark vii. 10.

10. xviii. 20; Ex. xx. 14; Deut. xxii. 22.

11. See Note I. after chap. xviii.

13. Cf. xviii. 22; Deut. xxiii. 17.

14. *burnt with fire*] Cf. Gen. xxxviii. 24. It is inferred, on very probable ground, that the burning under the sentence of the Law took place after the death of the criminal by stoning, or strangling. See the case of Achan, Josh. vii. 25. Cf. Lev. xxi. 9. The Targum of Palestine says that the offenders in this case were destroyed by molten lead being poured down their throats. But this is utterly improbable. On the nature of the offence see on xviii. 17.

15, 16. xviii. 28; Deut. xxvii. 21.

any beast, and lie down thereto, thou
shalt kill the woman, and the beast:
they shall surely be put to death;
their blood *shall be* upon them.
17 And if a man shall take his
sister, his father's daughter, or his
mother's daughter, and see her nakedness, and she see his nakedness; it *is*
a wicked thing; and they shall be cut
off in the sight of their people: he
hath uncovered his sister's nakedness;
he shall bear his iniquity.
[h] chap. 18. 19. 18 [h] And if a man shall lie with a
woman having her sickness, and shall
† Heb. *made naked.* uncover her nakedness; he hath † discovered her fountain, and she hath
uncovered the fountain of her blood:
and both of them shall be cut off
from among their people.
19 And thou shalt not uncover the
nakedness of thy mother's sister, nor
of thy father's sister: for he uncovereth his near kin: they shall bear their
iniquity.
20 And if a man shall lie with his
uncle's wife, he hath uncovered his
uncle's nakedness: they shall bear their
sin; they shall die childless.
21 And if a man shall take his
† Heb. *a separation.* brother's wife, it *is* † an unclean thing:
he hath uncovered his brother's na-
kedness; they shall be childless.
22 ¶ Ye shall therefore keep all
[i] chap. 18. 26. my [i] statutes, and all my judgments,
and do them: that the land, whither
[k] chap. 18. 25. I bring you to dwell therein, [k] spue
you not out.
23 And ye shall not walk in the
manners of the nation, which I cast
out before you: for they committed
all these things, and [l] therefore I ab- [l] Deut. 9. 5.
horred them.
24 But I have said unto you, Ye
shall inherit their land, and I will
give it unto you to possess it, a land
that floweth with milk and honey: I
am the LORD your God, which have
separated you from *other* people.
25 [m] Ye shall therefore put differ- [m] chap. 11. 2. Deut. 14. 4.
ence between clean beasts and un-
clean, and between unclean fowls
and clean: and ye shall not make
your souls abominable by beast, or
by fowl, or by any manner of living
thing that ‖ creepeth on the ground, ‖ Or, *moveth.*
which I have separated from you as
unclean.
26 And ye shall be holy unto me:
[n] for I the LORD *am* holy, and have [n] ver. 7. chap. 19. 2. & 20. 7. 1 Pet. 1. 15.
severed you from *other* people, that
ye should be mine.
27 ¶ [o] A man also or woman that [o] Deut. 18. 11. 1 Sam. 28. 7.
hath a familiar spirit, or that is a
wizard, shall surely be put to death:
they shall stone them with stones:
their blood *shall be* upon them.

CHAPTER XXI.

1 *Of the priests' mourning.* 6 *Of their holiness.* 8 *Of their estimation.* 7, 13 *Of their marriages.* 17 *The priests that have blemishes must not minister in the sanctuary.*

AND the LORD said unto Moses,
Speak unto the priests the sons

---

17. *cut off in the sight of their people*] See on Ex. xxxi. 14. But the more full expression here used probably refers to some special form of public excommunication, accompanied, it may be, by expulsion from the camp.

18. Cf. xviii. 19. See xii. 2; xv. 19.

19. *bear their iniquity*] See on Ex. xxviii. 38.

20. *they shall die childless*] This may mean either that the offspring should not be regarded as lawfully theirs, nor be entitled to any hereditary privileges (St Augustin, Hesychius, Michaelis), or that they should have no blessing in their children (see authorities quoted by Drusius).

21. Cf. on xviii. 16.

22—26. The ground is here again stated on which all these laws of holiness should be obeyed. See on xviii. 24—30.

24. Cf. Ex. iii. 8, 17, xiii. 5, xxxiii. 3, &c.

25, 26. The distinction between clean and unclean for the whole people, and not for any mere section of it, was one great typical mark of "the kingdom of priests, the holy nation." See Note after chap. xi. § VII.

25. *any manner of living thing that creepeth*] Rather, **any creeping thing**; that is, any vermin. See on xi. 20—23. The reference in this verse is to dead animals, not to the creatures when alive. See Note after chap. xi. § III.

27. See on xix. 31.

of Aaron, and say unto them, There
shall none be defiled for the dead
among his people:
2 But for his kin, that is near unto
him, *that is*, for his mother, and for
his father, and for his son, and for
his daughter, and for his brother,
3 And for his sister a virgin, that
is nigh unto him, which hath had
no husband; for her may he be defiled.
4 *But* ‖ he shall not defile himself,
being a chief man among his people,
to profane himself.
5 [a] They shall not make baldness
upon their head, neither shall they
shave off the corner of their beard,
nor make any cuttings in their flesh.
6 They shall be holy unto their
God, and not profane the name of
their God: for the offerings of the
LORD made by fire, *and* the bread
of their God, they do offer: therefore
they shall be holy.

‖ Or, *being an husband among his people, he shall not defile himself* for his wife, &c.

[a] chap. 19. 27.

THE LAWS OF HOLINESS FOR THE PRIESTS.
xxi. 1. xxii. 16.

CHAP. XXI. 1—15. The priests were to maintain a peculiarly high standard of legal purity in their family relations because it was their office to offer sacrifices to Jehovah. *vv.* 6, 8, 15. The common priest was not merely required, like the rest of the people, to purify himself when he had become defiled by contact with the dead, but he was to avoid such defilement in all cases except those of the nearest relationship, *vv.* 2, 3; the High priest was not to incur it in any case, *v.* 11. The common priest was not permitted to marry a prostitute, a woman of lost character, nor a divorced woman, *v.* 7: the High priest could marry no one but a virgin of Hebrew blood, *vv.* 13, 14. The priest's family was to be a model of purity, and unchastity in a priest's daughter was punished with marked severity, *vv.* 4 (see note), 9.

2—3. Cf. Ezek. xliv. 25.—*his kin* (Heb. *sheer*, see xviii. 6), *that is near unto him*] The relations here mentioned are those that would make up one household with the priest himself and his wife, in the case of his being a married man, see on *v.* 4. The presence of a corpse defiled the tent, or house, and all those who entered it, Num. xix. 14. On the apparent approach of the death of one of these near relations, the common priest was not obliged to leave the house, but might remain and take part in the funeral. The High priest, on such an occasion, must have had either to leave the house, or to remove the sick person; see *v.* 11.

4. The meaning of this verse is doubtful. Our translation is supported by Onkelos, Leo Juda, Rosenmüller, Zunz, Luzzatto, Wogue, &c. The sense seems to be that, owing to his position in the nation, he is not to defile himself in any cases except those named in *vv.* 2, 3; these two verses may indeed be read parenthetically, omitting the interpolated "*But*" in *v.* 4. Some understand that the priest was not to mourn *even for a ruler of his people* (Syriac, Vulgate, &c.). The LXX. appear to have followed a different reading of the text (approved by Fürst) which would mean, *he shall not defile himself for a moment.* Some modern critics approve the explanation in the margin of our version; but that the priests were permitted to mourn for their wives appears from the prohibition to Ezekiel on a special occasion. See Ezek. xxiv. 16.

5. These prohibitions were also given to the people at large. See xix. 27, 28; Deut. xiv. 1. —The testimonies which Knobel and several of the older commentators have collected to show that the priests of the Egyptians, Greeks, Romans and other ancient nations avoided funerals and contact with the dead, afford but an imperfect parallel to these Levitical laws concerning the priests. The sense of the uncleanness of dead bodies was common to those nations and has its origin in human nature. See Note after ch. xv. Wherever this feeling was recognized in a ceremonial usage, the priest, from his office, would naturally be expected to observe the highest standard of purity. But the laws which regulated the priesthood of the chosen people had a deeper basis than this. They had to administer a Law of Life. See Notes after ch. xi. § III, and after ch. xv. § i. St Cyril truly observes that the Hebrew priests were the instruments of the divine will for averting death, that all their sacrifices were a type of the death of Christ, which swallowed up death in victory, and that it would therefore have been unsuitable that they should have the same freedom as other people to become mourners. 'Glaphyra' in Lev. p. 430.

6. *the offerings of the* LORD *made by fire, and the bread of their God*] The word here and in *v.* 8 rendered *bread*, is the same as is rendered *food* iii. 11, 16, &c., and *meat* in xxii. 11. The reader of the English Bible should keep in view that *bread*, *meat*, and *food*, were nearly equivalent terms when our translation was made, and represent no distinctions that exist in the Hebrew. Cf. on ii. 1. On

7 They shall not take a wife *that is* a whore, or profane; neither shall they take a woman put away from her husband: for he *is* holy unto his God.

8 Thou shalt sanctify him therefore; for he offereth the bread of thy God: he shall be holy unto thee: for I the LORD, which sanctify you, *am* holy.

9 ¶ And the daughter of any priest, if she profane herself by playing the whore, she profaneth her father: she shall be burnt with fire.

10 And *he that is* the high priest among his brethren, upon whose head the anointing oil was poured, and that is consecrated to put on the garments, shall not uncover his head, nor rend his clothes;

11 Neither shall he go in to any dead body, nor defile himself for his father, or for his mother;

12 Neither shall he go out of the sanctuary, nor profane the sanctuary of his God; for the crown of the anointing oil of his God *is* upon him: I *am* the LORD.

13 And he shall take a wife in her virginity.

14 A widow, or a divorced woman, or profane, *or* an harlot, these shall he not take: but he shall take a virgin of his own people to wife.

15 Neither shall he profane his seed among his people: for I the LORD do sanctify him.

16 ¶ And the LORD spake unto Moses, saying,

17 Speak unto Aaron, saying, Whosoever *he be* of thy seed in their generations that hath *any* blemish, let him not approach to offer the ‖ bread of his God. ‖ Or, *food*.

18 For whatsoever man *he be* that hath a blemish, he shall not approach: a blind man, or a lame, or he that hath a flat nose, or any thing [b] superfluous, [b] chap. 22. 23.

19 Or a man that is brokenfooted, or brokenhanded,

20 Or crookbackt, or ‖ a dwarf, or that hath a blemish in his eye, or be scurvy, or scabbed, or hath his stones broken; ‖ Or, *too slender*.

---

the expression "bread of their God," see on iii. 16.

7. *profane*] The word probably means a woman who has been seduced, or, according to some Jewish authorities, one of illegitimate birth.—The wife of a common priest might be a widow, or the daughter of a foreigner, if she was not an idolater, and in these respects the priests were only under the same restraint as the people. Deut. vii. 3. A somewhat stricter rule for the priests' marriages was revealed to the prophet in later times, Ezek. xliv. 22.

8. *Thou shalt sanctify...he shall be holy unto thee*] The people of Israel are now addressed. They are commanded to regard the priests, who perform for them the service of the Altar, as holy in respect of their office.

9. *burnt with fire*] See on xx. 14. The offence was forbidden to the laity, but not visited with external punishment. See xix. 29.

10. *upon whose head the anointing oil was poured*] Cf. "the crown of the anointing oil of his God is upon him," *v.* 12. It was the distinguishing mark of the anointing of the High priest, that the holy oil was poured on his head like a crown, viii. 12; cf. iv. 3, x. 7. See on iv. 3.

uncover his head] rather, **let his hair be dishevelled.** See on x. 6.

11. See on *vv.* 2, 3.

12. *go out of the sanctuary*] *i.e.* not for the purpose to which reference is here made. The words do not mean, as some have imagined, that his abode was confined to the Sanctuary. See on Ex. xxv. 8.

15. *profane his seed*] *i.e.* by a marriage which was not in keeping with the holiness of his office.

16, 24. One of the family of Aaron who was deformed or disfigured in any way, though he was not permitted to perform priestly functions, was allowed to share the sacrificial meat and bread and to dwell with his brethren. See vi. 16. He was not treated as an outcast, but enjoyed his privileges as a son of Aaron, except in regard to active duties.

17. *in their generations*] *i.e.* **in future generations.**

to offer the bread of his God] See on *v.* 6.

20. *a dwarf*] This is the most probable rendering. The LXX., Onkelos, Vulg., and Saadia, take it for blear-eyed. The etymology of the word would rather express one who is small and wasted, either short, as in the text,

21 No man that hath a blemish of
the seed of Aaron the priest shall
come nigh to offer the offerings of
the LORD made by fire: he hath a
blemish; he shall not come nigh to
offer the bread of his God.
22 He shall eat the bread of his
God, *both* of the most holy, and of
the holy.
23 Only he shall not go in unto
the vail, nor come nigh unto the
altar, because he hath a blemish; that
he profane not my sanctuaries: for I
the LORD do sanctify them.
24 And Moses told *it* unto Aaron,
and to his sons, and unto all the children of Israel.

CHAPTER XXII.

1 *The priests in their uncleanness must abstain from the holy things.* 6 *How they shall be cleansed.* 10 *Who of the priest's house may eat of the holy things.* 17 *The sacrifices must be without blemish.* 26 *The age of the sacrifice.* 29 *The law of eating the sacrifice of thanksgiving.*

AND the LORD spake unto Moses,
saying,
2 Speak unto Aaron and to his
sons, that they separate themselves
from the holy things of the children of Israel, and that they profane not my holy name *in those*
things which they hallow unto me:
I *am* the LORD.
3 Say unto them, Whosoever *he be*
of all your seed among your generations, that goeth unto the holy
things, which the children of Israel
hallow unto the LORD, having his
uncleanness upon him, that soul shall
be cut off from my presence: I *am*
the LORD.
4 What man soever of the seed of
Aaron *is* a leper, or hath a †run- † Heb. *running of the reins.*
ning issue; he shall not eat of the
holy things, until he be clean. And chap. 15. 2.
whoso toucheth any thing *that is*
unclean *by* the dead, or a man whose
seed goeth from him;
5 Or whosoever toucheth any creeping thing, whereby he may be made
unclean, or a man of whom he may
take uncleanness, whatsoever uncleanness he hath;
6 The soul which hath touched

---

or slender, as in the margin. It is hardly likely that dwarfishness would be overlooked in this enumeration. So the Syriac and most critical authorities.

scurvy or scabbed] These words most probably include all affected with any skin disease.

22. See on ii. 3, vi. 25.

23. *sanctuaries*] The places peculiarly holy, including the Most holy place, the Holy place, and the Altar.

This law is of course to be regarded as one development of the great principle that all which is devoted to the service of God should be as perfect as possible of its kind. Respecting the mode in which the details of the law were expanded by the rabbinists, see Selden, 'de Succ. in Pont.' c. v.

CHAP. XXII.

Laws of holiness for the Priests, continued. 1—16.

1—9. No one of the sons of Aaron who was in any way ceremonially unclean was permitted to partake of the sacrificial food, or even to touch it. The commonest form of purification is here repeated.

2. "Speak unto Aaron and to his sons that they **so abstain from touching** the holy things of the children of Israel **which they consecrate unto me**, that they profane not my holy name." When they are to abstain is explained in the following verses.

the holy things] *i.e.* the sacrificial food of all kinds. See xxi. 22.

I am the LORD] See on xviii. 2. This law related to the daily life and the ordinary food of the priests (*v.* 7). The occurrence of the formula here is therefore no exception to the general rule that it is for the most part introduced as a sanction to what relates to common life as distinguished from formal religious observances.

3. *cut off from my presence*] *i.e.* excluded from the Sanctuary.. See xx. 17.

4. *until he be clean*] See xv. 13.

unclean by the dead] Num. xix. 22.

whose seed, &c.] xv. 16.

5. *creeping thing, whereby he may be made unclean*] *i.e.* dead vermin. xi. 29, 31, 43, xx. 25. Dead vermin seem to be singled out in this way, because they are so much more liable to be met with accidentally than the dead bodies of other creatures.

or a man of whom, &c.] xv. 5, 7, 19.

6. *The soul*] Rather, **the person.** See Note II. after chap. xvii.

any such shall be unclean until even, and shall not eat of the holy things, unless he wash his flesh with water.

7 And when the sun is down, he shall be clean, and shall afterward eat of the holy things; because it *is* his food.

8 [a]That which dieth of itself, or is torn *with beasts*, he shall not eat to defile himself therewith: I *am* the LORD.

[a] Exod. 22. 31. Ezek. 44. 31.

9 They shall therefore keep mine ordinance, lest they bear sin for it, and die therefore, if they profane it: I the LORD do sanctify them.

10 There shall no stranger eat *of* the holy thing: a sojourner of the priest, or an hired servant, shall not eat *of* the holy thing.

11 But if the priest buy *any* soul †with his money, he shall eat of it, and he that is born in his house: they shall eat of his meat.

† Heb. *with the purchase of his money.*

12 If the priest's daughter also be *married* unto †a stranger, she may not eat of an offering of the holy things.

† Heb. *a man a stranger.*

13 But if the priest's daughter be a widow, or divorced, and have no child, and is returned unto her father's house, [b]as in her youth, she shall eat of her father's meat: but there shall no stranger eat thereof.

[b] chap. 10. 14.

14 ¶ And if a man eat *of* the holy thing unwittingly, then he shall put the fifth *part* thereof unto it, and shall give *it* unto the priest with the holy thing.

15 And they shall not profane the holy things of the children of Israel, which they offer unto the LORD;

16 Or ‖suffer them to bear the iniquity of trespass, when they eat their holy things: for I the LORD do sanctify them.

‖ Or, *lade themselves with the iniquity of trespass in their eating.*

17 ¶ And the LORD spake unto Moses, saying,

18 Speak unto Aaron, and to his sons, and unto all the children of Israel, and say unto them, Whatsoever *he be* of the house of Israel, or of the strangers in Israel, that will offer his oblation for all his vows, and for all his freewill offerings, which they will offer unto the LORD for a burnt offering;

---

unclean until even] cf. xi. 24, xv. 5.

8. The law relating to the eating of carrion is here repeated with special reference to the priests. The pollution in them would be an aggravated one, inasmuch as they would have to forego their sacred functions. Cf. Ezek. iv. 14, xliv. 31. The general prohibition occurs Ex. xxii. 31; Lev. xi. 39, xvii. 15.

9. *lest they bear sin for it*] The priests whom Jehovah sanctified were to observe his commandments, lest they should call down upon themselves a sentence of death. Cf. Ex. xxviii. 35; Lev. viii. 35; Num. xviii. 32. When the Israelite offended in a similar manner by eating of the Peace-offering with his uncleanness upon him, he was to be "cut off from amongst his people." vii. 20.

10. *stranger*] **one of another family**; that is, not of the family of Aaron. Heb. *zār*. See on Ex. xxix. 33.—The sojourner was a neighbour, or visitor, who might eat of ordinary food as an invited guest.

11. This shows how completely a purchased bondsman was incorporated into the household. See on Ex. xxi. 2, 20, 21.

12. *a stranger*] **one of another family.**

14. *unwittingly*] **inadvertently.** The same Hebrew word as is rendered "through ignorance." See Note after chap. iv. The value of the holy thing, with the addition of one-fifth, was given to the priest according to the law of the Trespass-offering. See on v. 14.

15, 16. These verses are rather difficult. Their meaning appears to be:—*The holy things of the children of Israel which are heaved before Jehovah* (see Introd. § ix.) *shall not be profaned; and they shall incur a sin of trespass who eat of their holy things* (*so as to profane them*). The words may have been intended either as a general admonition referring to the whole passage, *vv.* 2—14, or as having special reference to the duty of the priests to prevent the laity from eating the sacrificial food to their injury, as enjoined in *v.* 14.

THE CHOICE OF VICTIMS FOR THE ALTAR. 17—33.

18. It devolved on the priest to see that these rules were observed; but they are here addressed to the people as well as to the priests.

strangers in Israel] **foreigners dwelling in Israel.** See on Ex. xx. 10; Lev. xvi. 29.

for all his vows, and for all his freewill offerings] **for any manner of vow, or for any manner of freewill offering.**

19 *Ye shall offer* at your own will
a male without blemish, of the beeves,
of the sheep, or of the goats.
eut. 15. 20 [c] *But* whatsoever hath a blemish,
7. 1. *that* shall ye not offer: for it shall not
be acceptable for you.
21 And whosoever offereth a sacrifice of peace offerings unto the
LORD to accomplish *his* vow, or a
freewill offering in beeves or ‖ sheep,
it shall be perfect to be accepted;
there shall be no blemish therein.
22 Blind, or broken, or maimed,
or having a wen, or scurvy, or scabbed, ye shall not offer these unto
the LORD, nor make an offering by
fire of them upon the altar unto the
LORD.
, kid. 23 Either a bullock or a ‖ lamb that
ap. 21. hath any thing [d] superfluous or lacking in his parts, that mayest thou
offer *for* a freewill offering; but for
a vow it shall not be accepted.
24 Ye shall not offer unto the LORD
that which is bruised, or crushed, or
broken, or cut; neither shall ye make
any offering thereof in your land.
25 Neither from a stranger's hand
shall ye offer the bread of your God
of any of these; because their corruption *is* in them, *and* blemishes *be*
in them: they shall not be accepted
for you.
26 ¶ And the LORD spake unto
Moses, saying,
27 When a bullock, or a sheep, or
a goat, is brought forth, then it shall
be seven days under the dam; and
from the eighth day and thenceforth
it shall be accepted for an offering
made by fire unto the LORD.
28 And *whether it be* cow or ‖ ewe, ‖ Or, *she goat.*

---

19. *Ye shall offer at your own will a male*] Rather, **That it may be accepted for you it shall be a male.** See on i. 3. The same Hebrew phrase occurs in *vv.* 20, 21, 27, where the sense is correctly given, and in *v.* 29, where the same mistake is made here.

21. *sheep*] Rather, **cattle of the flock,** including sheep and goats. Introd. § iv.

22. *broken*] *i.e.* broken-limbed, or lame. Cf. xxi. 19, Deut. xv. 21. Cf. xxi. 20.

23. *lamb*] **one of the flock.**

superfluous or lacking] That is, with a limb too large or too small. Cf. xxi. 18. According to several of the ancient versions the latter term means having its ears or tail cropped.—On the Freewill- and Vow-offerings, see vii. 16.

24. The reference here is to animals emasculated by different methods. Cf. Aristot. 'H. N.' IX. 37, § 3; Columella, Lib. VII. ch. 11, and Drusius in loc.; cf. Deut. xxiii. 2.

neither shall ye make any offering thereof in your land] The words supplied in our version in italics have the authority of the Syriac version and Saadia, and their sense is approved by Knobel and others. But the literal meaning of the passage is, **and this shall ye not do in your land.** So the LXX., Targums, Vulgate and most modern versions. It appears to have been understood by the Jews as a prohibition of the mutilation of animals. Joseph. 'Ant.' IV. 8. § 40; Drusius *in loc.*

25. *a stranger's hand*] The word here rendered *stranger*, is not the same as that in *vv.* 10, 18: it means literally, *the son of the unknown.* The question is whether the resident foreigner (*geer;* see on Ex. xx. 10; Lev. xvi. 29, cf. Num. xv. 14) is meant, or one dwelling in another land who desired to show respect to the God of Israel. See 1 Kings viii. 41. Wogue and the rabbinists with good reason take the latter alternative. The Hebrew certainly appears to favour this interpretation. So understood, the passage is one of those which indicate the beneficent breadth with which the Law was administered. See on Ex. xx. 10, xxiii. 23; Lev. xv. 29, &c.

27. No victim was to be offered in sacrifice until it was a week old. The meaning of this law appears to be that the animal should realize a distinct existence in becoming less dependent on its mother and able to provide for its own wants. Cf. Ex. xxii. 30. The Romans observed a rule of similar purport, that a young pig should not be pure for sacrifice till the fifth day, a sheep or a goat until the eighth day, nor a calf till the thirtieth day: a great authority among the priests said that no ruminating animal should be offered till it had become *bidens.* See Plin. 'H. N.' VIII. 77. Whether the term *bidens*, which occurs so frequently in reference to the sacrifices of the Romans, denoted an animal in which two teeth had just developed themselves, or one which had teeth in both jaws, has been doubted, but the latter is more probable. Festus, with the note in Lindemann, p. 305; Facciolati, s. v. Knobel supposes that *bidens* was equivalent to the Hebrew, *son of his year;* that is, a lamb less than a year old, but of which its teeth were developed; see on xii. 6. Regarding the limitation of the age of victims, see Introd. § iv.

[e] Deut. 22. 6. ye shall not kill it [e]and her young
both in one day.
29 And when ye will offer a sacrifice of thanksgiving unto the LORD,
offer *it* at your own will.
30 On the same day it shall be
[f] chap. 7. 15. eaten up; ye shall leave [f]none of it
until the morrow: I *am* the LORD.
31 Therefore shall ye keep my
commandments, and do them: I *am*
the LORD.
32 Neither shall ye profane my
[g] chap. 10. 3. holy name; but [g]I will be hallowed
among the children of Israel: I *am*
the LORD which hallow you,
33 That brought you out of the
land of Egypt, to be your God: I
am the LORD.

CHAPTER XXIII.

1 *The feasts of the Lord.* 3 *The sabbath.* 4 *The passover.* 9 *The sheaf of firstfruits.* 15 *The feast of Pentecost.* 22 *Gleanings to be left for the poor.* 23 *The feast of trumpets.* 26 *The day of atonement.* 33 *The feast of tabernacles.*

AND the LORD spake unto Moses,
saying,

---

28. This law appears to have been intended to remind the Israelites of the sacredness of the relation between the parent and its offspring. Of the same nature would seem to have been the prohibition to take a bird's nest containing the mother with its young. Deut. xxii. 6, 7. Some suppose that it was on the same ground that it was forbidden to seethe a kid in its mother's milk. Cf. on Ex. xxiii. 19.

ewe] **a female of the flock**, either a sheep or a goat, Introd. § iv.

29. *offer it at your own will*] **offer it so that it may be accepted for you.** See on *v.* 19.

30. Cf. vii. 15, xix. 6.

31—33. A solemn conclusion to the whole chapter. Cf. xviii. 29, 30, xix. 37.

32. Cf. *v.* 9, x. 3, xi. 44, 45, xviii. 21, xix. 12.

33. xi. 45, xix. 36, xxv. 38, Num. xv. 41.

CHAP. XXIII.

THE FESTIVALS.

The Pentateuch does not contain any one complete account of the Festivals. But each of the longer passages relating to the subject appears to have a method of its own bearing upon some particular object of the Legislator at the time it was published. Those of them which embrace the widest range of information are this chapter of Leviticus and Chaps. xxviii. xxix. of Numbers. It may be observed that a part of this chapter, *vv.* 39—43, does not fall immediately within the practical scope of the preceding larger portion, *vv.* 1—38, relating to the days of Holy Convocation: in its form as well as in its matter it constitutes a distinct section. But the 44th verse serves as a general conclusion to the whole chapter.

THE DAYS OF HOLY CONVOCATION AND THE RELATION OF THE ANNUAL FEASTS TO THE AGRICULTURE OF THE YEAR. 1—38.

Preliminary Note.

I. The specified times for public worship according to the Law were; (1) The daily Morning and Evening sacrifices, sometimes called "the continual Burnt-offering." (2) The weekly Sabbath. (3) The day of the New Moon. (4) The "set feasts" (Num. xxix. 39) or appointed times of annual observance, of which there were five, the Passover, the day of Pentecost, the feast of Trumpets, the day of Atonement, and the feast of Tabernacles. 1 Chr. xxiii. 30, 31; 2 Chr. viii. 13, xxxi. 3; Neh. x. 33; Isaiah i. 13, 14. For each of these occasions special sacrifices were appointed. The whole of them are therefore mentioned in the passage of the Law which prescribes in detail the festival sacrifices, Num. xxviii. xxix. and in no other single passage. They are severally named, Num. xxviii. 3, 9, 11, 16, 26, xxix. 1, 7, 12.

The weekly Sabbaths, and certain days in the appointed times of annual observance, were distinguished as "days of holy convocation." To determine and to classify the days of Holy Convocation, appears to be the main object of this section (see *v.* 2). It certainly is not, as some have imagined, to be regarded as "a calendar" of the Hebrew worship. It contains no mention of the New Moons (which were not days of Holy Convocation), nor of the Morning and Evening service spoken of in Num. xxviii.

The general word rendered "feasts" in our version, *vv.* 2, 4, 37, &c., is *mō'adim*, which signifies literally **appointed times.** The three festivals, (often called the Great Festivals), Passover, Pentecost and Tabernacles, to which the name *chag*, i.e. a *feast* or *rejoicing*, properly belongs (*vv.* 6, 34, 39, 41), were distinguished by the attendance of the male Israelites at the national Sanctuary. Hence they are enumerated with the formula, "Three times in the year all thy males shall appear before the Lord God," Exod. xxiii. 17, xxxiv. 23; Deut. xvi. 16. In later times they were called by the rabbins "pilgrimage feasts." It is worthy of note that the Hebrew word is identical with the Arabic *haj*, the name of the pilgrimage to Mecca, from which comes the well-known word for a pilgrim, *haji.*

2 Speak unto the children of Israel, and say unto them, *Concerning*
the feasts of the LORD, which ye
shall proclaim *to be* holy convoca-
tions, *even* these *are* my feasts. [a Exod. 20. 9.]
3 [a]Six days shall work be done: [Deut. 5. 13.]
but the seventh day *is* the sabbath [Luke 13. 14.]
of rest, an holy convocation; ye shall
do no work *therein*: it *is* the sabbath
of the LORD in all your dwellings.
4 ¶ These *are* the feasts of the
LORD, *even* holy convocations, which
ye shall proclaim in their seasons.
5 [b]In the fourteenth *day* of the [b Exod. 12. 18.]
first month at even *is* the LORD'S [Numb. 28. 17.]
passover.

Besides the order of the days of Holy Convocation, we have in this section an account of the peculiar offerings of grain which marked the commencement and the termination of the grain harvest, *vv.* 9—21. Taking account of this particular, along with the suspension of labour commanded on the days of Holy Convocation, this section sets forth for practical guidance the relation in which **the appointed times** of the LORD, weekly as well as annual, stood to the ordinary occupations of the people.

II. There is no explanation given in the Law of the meaning of the term "holy convocation." We can only determine what it denoted by inference. The most probable conclusion is that the days of Holy Convocation were occasions for sabbatical rest for the whole people, and that they owed their name to gatherings for religious edification, which, in later times, were probably held in every town and village in the Holy Land. These meetings might have been like those held in the Synagogues which were established after the Captivity. See Note on the Sabbath day (Exod. xx.), § 1. There were in the course of the year, besides the weekly Sabbaths, seven days of Holy Convocation, the first and last days of the Feast of Unleavened bread, the first day of the Feast of Tabernacles and the day following the Feast, the day of Pentecost, the Day of Atonement, and the Feast of Trumpets. Ex. xii. 16; Num. xxviii. 18, 25, 26, xxix. 1, 12, 35. There was a distinction between them as regards strictness of observance. On the weekly Sabbath and on the Day of Atonement no work of any kind was to be done (*vv.* 3, 28). But on the days of Holy Convocation in the great festivals and on the Feast of Trumpets, "servile work" only was prohibited. See on *v.* 7.

It has been very generally supposed that a Holy Convocation was a πανήγυρις, a solemn assembly of the people at the national Sanctuary, according to the formula used in reference to the three great festivals (Hupfeld, Knobel, Kurtz, Davidson, &c.). But we know that there was no central gathering of the people of this kind either on the weekly Sabbath, on the Day of Atonement, or at the feast of Trumpets. It may be added that the notion is obviously inconsistent with the command in which the general attendances of the people at the Sanctuary are limited to *three* occasions in the year. Ex. xxiii. 17, &c.

2. *Concerning the feasts*, &c.] The latter part of this verse might rather be rendered: **The appointed times of Jehovah which ye shall proclaim as Holy Convocations, these are my appointed times.** Cf. *v.* 37.

3. The Sabbath is in like manner placed before the annual appointed times in Ex. xxxiv. 21—23; Ex. xxiii. 12, 14; and Num. xxviii. 9 sq. The seventh day had been consecrated as **the Sabbath of Jehovah**, figuring His own rest; it was the acknowledged sign of the Covenant between God and His people. See on Ex. xx. As such it properly held its place at the head of the days of Holy Convocation.

in all your dwellings] Most of the Jewish writers explain this to mean, *either in the Holy Land or out of it*. The expression may certainly be taken in its broadest sense. Cf. *v.* 14.

4. This verse might be rendered: **These appointed times of the Lord are Holy Convocations which ye shall proclaim at their appointed season**: *i.e.* as the year comes round. The recurrence of the Sabbatical number in the annual days of Holy Convocation—two at the Passover, two at the feast of Tabernacles, with the day of Pentecost, the feast of Trumpets, and the Day of Atonement—should be noticed.

5—8. In these verses, the Passover, or Paschal Supper, and the feast of Unleavened Bread, are plainly spoken of as distinct feasts. See Ex. xii. 6, 15, 17; Num. xxviii. 16, 17. Joseph. 'Ant.' III. 10. § 5. The two days of Holy Convocation strictly belonged to the latter. But the two names, in common usage, became convertible.

5. *the fourteenth day of the first month at even*] According to the Hebrew mode of reckoning the 15th day of the month began on the evening of the 14th. The paschal lamb was slain *between the two evenings* (see on Ex. xii. 6), an interval of time in which the two days seem to have been regarded as overlapping each other. The day of Holy Convocation with which the feast of Unleavened bread commenced (*v.* 7) was the 15th, and

6 And on the fifteenth day of the same month *is* the feast of unleavened bread unto the LORD: seven days ye must eat unleavened bread.

7 In the first day ye shall have an holy convocation: ye shall do no servile work therein.

8 But ye shall offer an offering made by fire unto the LORD seven days: in the seventh day *is* an holy convocation: ye shall do no servile work *therein*.

9 ¶ And the LORD spake unto Moses, saying,

10 Speak unto the children of Israel, and say unto them, When ye be come into the land which I give unto you, and shall reap the harvest thereof, then ye shall bring a ‖ sheaf of the firstfruits of your harvest unto the priest:

‖ Or, *handful*. Heb. *omer*.

11 And he shall wave the sheaf before the LORD, to be accepted for you: on the morrow after the sabbath the priest shall wave it.

---

that with which it terminated was the 21st. Cf. Num. xxviii. 16, 17.

6. *feast*] Heb. *chag*. See prel. Note.

unleavened bread] See on Ex. xii. 15.

7. *no servile work*] Literally, no work of labour, no work that belongs to one's worldly calling, such as labour in agriculture or handicraft. A licence was permitted for the preparation of food, which is fully expressed in Ex. xii. 16. This licence was not granted on the weekly Sabbath, or on the Day of Atonement. On them it was not lawful to do work of any sort, not even to kindle a fire. Ex. xx. 10, xxxv. 3; Lev. xxiii. 28, 30. For all the details of the Passover, see Notes on Ex. xii. xiii.

8. *an offering made by fire*] The sacrifices here meant are the two young bullocks, the ram and the seven sheep, with their Meat-offerings, and the goat for a Sin-offering, which were offered on each of the seven days of the feast. Num. xxviii. 19—24. See on *v.* 20 of this chap. As there is no mention made of these offerings in Exodus, it has been inferred that they formed a departure from the original simplicity of the primitive feast as described in Ex. xxiii., &c. (Hupfeld, Davidson). But it is in accordance with analogy to suppose that sacrifices may have been offered, according to usage, on each day of the feast before specific directions for them were actually written in the Law.

9—22. These verses contain a distinct command regarding the religious services immediately connected with the grain harvest, given by anticipation against the time when the people were to possess the Promised Land.

The First Sheaf of the Harvest. 9—14.

This is the only place in the Law in which the offering of the First Sheaf is mentioned. But in Josh. v. 11 there is a reference to the prohibition connected with it which is prescribed in *v.* 14.

10. *sheaf*] The original word, *ōmer*, means either a sheaf (Deut. xxiv. 19; Ruth ii. 7, 15, &c.), or a measure, the "tenth deal" of an Ephah, being something more than four fifths of a gallon (Ex. xvi. 16, 18, 36; Lev. xix. 35, 36). Our version is probably right in this place. So LXX., Philo ('de Sept.' 20), Vulg., Luther, Gesenius, Fürst, de Wette, &c. The offering which was waved was most likely a small sheaf of barley, the grain which is first ripe. The first fruits of the wheat harvest were offered seven weeks later in the Loaves of Pentecost. See *vv.* 15—17. The two offerings thus figure the very commencement and the completion of the grain harvest; cf. Ruth i. 22, ii. 23. But Josephus, the Mishna, with the Rabbinists and most of the recent Jewish translators, take the offering to have been not a sheaf, but a measure of the freshly ground barley meal. Josephus and the Mishna describe it as a regular Meat-offering with its oil and its frankincense offered in the usual way. Jos. 'Ant.' III. 10, § 5; Mishna, 'Menach.' x. 2—6; Buxtorf, 'Lex. Chald.' p. 1628. If the grain was ground, or mixed with oil and frankincense, and if a handful was offered on the Altar (as Josephus says), it seems unaccountable that nothing of the kind is hinted at in this place, while the Loaves of Pentecost are fully described in *v.* 17.

11. *wave the sheaf*] See Introd. § iv.

to be accepted for you] See on i. 3.

on the morrow after the sabbath] It is most probable that these words denote the 16th of Abib, the day after the first day of Holy Convocation (see on *vv.* 5—8), and that this was called *the Sabbath of the Passover*, or, *the Sabbath of Unleavened bread*. The word Sabbath is similarly applied to the Day of Atonement in *v.* 32. That the day on which the Sheaf was offered was the 16th of the month, and the "Sabbath" here spoken of was the 15th, is in accordance with the LXX., Philo, Josephus, the Mishna, the Targums, and the Rabbinists in general. The reason of the offering being made on this particular day may have been that the cutting of the Sheaf

12 And ye shall offer that day when ye wave the sheaf an he lamb without blemish of the first year for a burnt offering unto the LORD.

13 And the meat offering thereof *shall be* two tenth deals of fine flour mingled with oil, an offering made by fire unto the LORD *for* a sweet savour: and the drink offering thereof *shall be* of wine, the fourth *part* of an hin.

14 And ye shall eat neither bread, nor parched corn, nor green ears, until the selfsame day that ye have brought an offering unto your God: *it shall be* a statute for ever throughout your generations in all your dwellings.

15 ¶ And [c] ye shall count unto you from the morrow after the sabbath, from the day that ye brought the sheaf of the wave offering; seven sabbaths shall be complete:

16 Even unto the morrow after

[c] Deut. 16. 9.

---

formed a part of the ceremony; and, as the formal commencement of the practical work of harvest (cf. Deut. xvi. 9), it was less suitable for the day of Holy Convocation than for the first of the days of less solemn observance, on which, according to Jewish tradition, ordinary work was permitted under certain limitations.—There has however been a difference of opinion regarding the day from early times. The Karaite Jews, and the Sadducees before them, held that the name *Sabbath* could denote nothing but the weekly sabbath, in this place as well as in *v.* 15; see note. They therefore held that the day here spoken of was the weekly Sabbath which happened to fall within the week of the Passover. See Mishna, 'Menach.' x. 3, with Maimonides' note; Lightfoot on Luke vi. 6.—It has been imagined in recent times that the commencement of the year and the time of the feast were so arranged that the day of the Paschal supper, the 14th of Abib, and the last day of the feast, the 21st, coincided with the weekly Sabbath (Hitzig, Hupfeld, Knobel, Kurtz). On this hypothesis, the Sheaf was offered either on the 22nd of the month, after the conclusion of the feast (Hitzig, Hupfeld), or on the 15th, that is the first day of Holy Convocation (Knobel, Kurtz). But this arrangement would involve a disturbance of the year, which would end with a broken week, and a still more serious dislocation of the Sabbath-day by no means consistent with its peculiar sanctity, unless we adopt the very unreasonable supposition that the Hebrew year consisted of twelve months of exactly four weeks.—Wogue suggests that the day of the ceremony was not determined with any fixed relation to the Passover, but that it was the day following the Sabbath whenever the barley happened to be ripe, according as the season was later or earlier.—The subject of this note derives interest from its probable connection with Luke vi. 1. See note *in loc.*

12—13. These offerings, which expressly belonged to the ceremony of the First sheaf, are not mentioned in Num. xxviii. See on *vv.* 8 and 20.

13. *two tenth deals*] Two omers, or tenth parts of an ephah, about a gallon and three quarters. See on xix. 36. The usual Meat-offering to accompany a sheep was a single omer. Ex. xxix. 40; Num. xv. 4, xxviii. 19—21. A greater liberality in this respect was appropriate in a harvest feast.

an offering made by fire] Rather, **a sacrifice**. The offering was made in the same way as the private Meat-offering of fine flour (Lev. ii. 1), a handful being thrown on the Altar and the remainder given to the priests.

drink offering] This and *vv.* 18, 37 are the only places in the book of Leviticus in which Drink-offerings are mentioned. See Gen. xxxv. 14; Exod. xxix. 40; Introd. § x.

14. *bread...parched corn...green ears*] These are the three forms in which grain was commonly eaten. We find from Josh. v. 11, that this direction was observed at Gilgal in the first celebration of the Passover after the entrance into the Holy Land. On the proper rendering of that verse, see note. The offering before Jehovah of the Sheaf marked the first month of which the old name *Abib* signified "the month of green ears." The produce of the land for the year was consecrated to Jehovah by this act, and it was now given back to His people for their free use.

The Day of Pentecost, 15—22.

The accustomed introductory formula (see *vv.* 1, 9) is not repeated for Pentecost owing to the close connection between Pentecost and the offering of the Sheaf. The latter, though it was connected by the time of its observance with the Passover, was more intimately related in its nature to Pentecost. The meanings of the Sheaf and of the Wave loaves were concentrated in the period of the grain harvest.

15. *the morrow after the sabbath*] See on *v.* 11.

seven sabbaths] More properly, **seven weeks**. The sense answers to Deut. xvi. 9. The term in its plural form rendered "complete" could hardly be predicated of Sabbath-days in the computation of a series of weeks. The word Sabbath, in the language of the New

the seventh sabbath shall ye number
fifty days; and ye shall offer a new
meat offering unto the LORD.
17 Ye shall bring out of your habitations two wave loaves of two
tenth deals: they shall be of fine
flour; they shall be baken with leaven;
they are the firstfruits unto the LORD.
18 And ye shall offer with the
bread seven lambs without blemish
of the first year, and one young bullock, and two rams: they shall be
for a burnt offering unto the LORD,
with their meat offering, and their
drink offerings, *even* an offering made
by fire, of sweet savour unto the
LORD.
19 Then ye shall sacrifice one kid
of the goats for a sin offering, and
two lambs of the first year for a
sacrifice of peace offerings.
20 And the priest shall wave them
with the bread of the firstfruits *for*
a wave offering before the LORD,
with the two lambs: they shall be
holy to the LORD for the priest.

Testament as well as the Old, is used, by a simple metonymy, for *week* (Lev. xxv. 8; Matt. xxviii. 1; Luke xviii. 12, &c.).

16. *seventh sabbath*] **seventh week**. The morrow after the seventh week was of course the fiftieth day after the conclusion of a week of weeks. It may be observed that the day has no proper name given to it in this chapter of Leviticus. It is only spoken of as a day of Holy Convocation for the offering of the two Loaves with their accompanying sacrifices. The word "Pentecost" used in the heading of the chapter is found only in the Apocrypha and the New Testament, Tobit ii. 1; 2 Macc. xii. 32; Acts ii. 1, xx. 16; 1 Cor. xvi. 8. The day is called in the Old Testament, "the feast of harvest" (Ex. xxiii. 16), "the feast of weeks," "the feast of the first fruits of wheat harvest" (Ex. xxxiv. 22; Deut. xvi. 10), and "the day of the first fruits" (Num. xxviii. 26). It was commonly called by the Jews in later times, *'atzereth*, a word which will be explained in the note on *v.* 34.

17. *out of your habitations two wave loaves*, &c.] These were loaves of leavened household bread, of wheat flour (Exod. xxxiv. 22), such as were commonly eaten. The word translated "habitations" does not, however, strictly mean houses, but places of abode in a general sense. It seems here to denote the land in which the Israelites were to dwell so as to express that the flour was to be of home growth. But Calvin and a Lapide supposed that each householder had to bring to the Sanctuary two loaves. The Vulgate rather favours this view, rendering the passage, "Ex omnibus habitaculis vestris." The Hebrew will, however, hardly bear such an interpretation, which is improbable in the nature of things: it is most unlikely that such a mass of leavened bread should have been presented to the priests at once. Each loaf was to contain a "tenth deal" (probably four-fifths of a gallon) of fine flour. The two Loaves were to be merely waved before Jehovah and then to become the property of the priests. Introd. § ix. No bread containing leaven could be offered on the Altar, Lev. ii. 11. The object of this offering seems to have been to present to the Lord the best produce of the earth in the actual condition in which it is most useful for the support of human life. It thus represented in the fittest manner the thanksgiving which was proper for the season. The Loaves appear to be distinctively called "the first fruits **for Jehovah**." Compare the language used in reference to the First sheaf in *v.* 10. The references to First fruits in the New Testament, Rom. xi. 16; 1 Cor. xv. 20, 23; James i. 18; Rev. xiv. 4, &c., would seem to be most aptly applied to the Loaves of Pentecost. As these Loaves offered before Jehovah sanctified the harvest of the year, so has "Christ the first fruits" sanctified the Church, which, in its union with Him as the First fruits, becomes also the Sanctifier of the world. See the services for Whitsuntide. The references in the margin of the more recent editions of our Bible to *v.* 11 of this chapter, would seem to belong more strictly to the words **first fruits for Jehovah** in this 17th verse.

18. *seven lambs...of the first year*] More properly, **seven sheep of a year old**, not like the lamb in *v.* 12. Introd. § iv.

young bullock] **a young bull**, it might be from one to three years old. Introd. § iv.

their meat offering, and their drink offerings] Introd. § x.

19. *one kid of the goats*] Properly, **a shaggy he-goat**. See on iv. 23.

two lambs of the first year] **two sheep of a year old.**

20. The meaning appears to be, "The priest shall wave the two sheep (of the Peace-offering) with the bread of the First fruits (the two Pentecostal loaves) for a wave-offering to Jehovah."—When living creatures were *waved* before Jehovah, it is said that they were led to and fro before the Tabernacle according to an established form, Introd. § ix.

21 And ye shall proclaim on the
selfsame day, *that* it may be an holy
convocation unto you: ye shall do
no servile work *therein*: *it shall be*
a statute for ever in all your dwellings throughout your generations.
d chap. 19. 22 ¶ And [d]when ye reap the har-
9. vest of your land, thou shalt not
make clean riddance of the corners
e Deut. 24. of thy field when thou reapest, [e]nei-
19. ther shalt thou gather any gleaning
of thy harvest: thou shalt leave them
unto the poor, and to the stranger: I
am the LORD your God.
23 ¶ And the LORD spake unto
Moses, saying,
24 Speak unto the children of Is-
rael, saying, In the [f]seventh month, f Numb.
in the first *day* of the month, shall 29. 1.
ye have a sabbath, a memorial of
blowing of trumpets, an holy convocation.

The victims prescribed in *vv.* 18, 19 to be offered "with the bread," differ from those which are prescribed for "the day of the first-fruits" in Num. xxviii. 26, 27. In the latter statement, there are two young bulls and one ram, instead of the one young bull and the two rams here mentioned. The seven young sheep and the one goat are the same in each place. If (with Bähr, Winer, Ewald, Knobel) we suppose the statements to relate to the same set of sacrifices, there is an inexplicable discrepancy. But most of the Jewish authorities, and many others, consider that the offerings in Num. were to be offered in addition to those here mentioned. (Mishna, 'Menach.' IV. 3; Josephus, Kurtz, Keil, &c.) This seems to be confirmed by a comparison of the forms of expression used in *v.* 18 and in Num. xxviii. 19; and still more by the statement of the offerings to accompany the special rites of the Day of Atonement, Lev. xvi. 11—25, compared with the offerings of the Day itself, which are distinctly connected with the Daily sacrifice, Num. xxix. 11. It would indeed seem that the sacrifices prescribed in Num. xxviii. xxix. were offered as additions to the continual Burnt-offering, while all those mentioned in this chapter accompanied the rites peculiar to each festival, and formed more strictly essential parts of them.

21. *the selfsame day*] The feast of Weeks was distinguished from the two other great annual feasts by its consisting, according to the Law, of only a single day. But in later times it is said that during the following six days the Israelites used to bring their offerings to the Temple, and to give the week something of a festal character in the suspension of mourning for the dead. Mishna, 'Moed Katan,' III. 6, with the notes.

22. The repetition of the Law given in xix. 9, 10, and reiterated Deut. xxiv. 19, is appropriately connected, as far as grain is concerned, with the thanksgiving for the completed grain harvest. In like manner, the laws regarding the oppression of the poor given in Lev. xix. and in Ex. xxii. are repeated in connection with the Jubilee in chapter xxv. 14—17, 35, 36, &c.

poor] *i.e.* the poor Israelite.

stranger] **foreigner.** See xvi. 29.—Cf. Deut. xvi. 10—12.

I am the LORD your God] See on xviii. 2.

The Feast of Trumpets. 23—25.

24. *a sabbath*] This feast was one of the days of Holy Convocation of ordinary observance. See on *vv.* 7, 11. The word in this verse, and also in *v.* 39, is *shabbāthōn*, not *shabbāth*, the proper Hebrew form of "sabbath." The same word is used in the phrase *shabbāth shabbāthōn*, which is rightly rendered "sabbath of rest" *v.* 32, xvi. 31, xxv. 4; Ex. xxxi. 15, xxxv. 2. *Shabbāthōn*, by itself, as in this place, should rather be rendered **a sabbatical rest.**—In this verse and in Num. xxix. 1, the only places in the Old Testament where the festival is named, the word rendered "blowing of trumpets," means literally *shouting*. There is no mention of trumpets in the Hebrew text of the Law in connection with the day. We know from Num. x. 10, that the silver trumpets of the Sanctuary were blown at all the festivals, including the New moons, and, as a matter of course, on this occasion, which was the chief festival of the New moon. There is however no reason to doubt the tradition that the day was distinguished by a general blowing of trumpets throughout the land, and that the kind of trumpet generally used for the purpose was the *shophār* (which it seems might have been either the horn of an animal or a cornet of metal), such as was used at Sinai (Ex. xix. 16), and on the Day of Jubilee. See on xxv. 9. It must have differed in this respect from the ordinary festival of the New moon when the long straight trumpet of the temple alone was blown. See on Num. x. 2; Ex. xxv. 23. In the modern service of the Synagogue, Psalm lxxxi. is used at the feast of Trumpets. It is however doubted by Gesenius and others whether that Psalm does not more properly belong to one of the feasts celebrated at the Full moon, either the Passover or the feast of Tabernacles, the word

25 Ye shall do no servile work
therein: but ye shall offer an offering
made by fire unto the LORD.
26 ¶ And the LORD spake unto
Moses, saying,
27 [g] Also on the tenth *day* of this
seventh month *there shall be* a day
of atonement: it shall be an holy
convocation unto you; and ye shall
afflict your souls, and offer an offering made by fire unto the LORD.
28 And ye shall do no work in that
same day: for it *is* a day of atonement, to make an atonement for you
before the LORD your God.
29 For whatsoever soul *it be* that
shall not be afflicted in that same
day, he shall be cut off from among
his people.
30 And whatsoever soul *it be* that
doeth any work in that same day,
the same soul will I destroy from
among his people.
31 Ye shall do no manner of
work: *it shall be* a statute for ever
throughout your generations in all
your dwellings.
32 It *shall be* unto you a sabbath of
rest, and ye shall afflict your souls:
in the ninth *day* of the month at
even, from even unto even, shall ye
† celebrate your sabbath.
33 ¶ And the LORD spake unto
Moses, saying,
34 Speak unto the children of Israel, saying, [h] The fifteenth day of
this seventh month *shall be* the feast
of tabernacles *for* seven days unto the
LORD.
35 On the first day *shall be* an

g chap. 16. 30. Numb. 29. 7.

† Heb. *rest.*

h Numb. 29. 12. John 7. 37.

---

rendered "new moon" in *v.* 3 being of doubtful meaning. See note *in loc.*

seventh month] The festival was observed on the first day of the Seventh month, called by the Jews in later times Tisri, but in the Old Testament Ethanim, 1 K. viii. 2. According to the uniform voice of tradition it was the first day of the Civil year (see Note at the end of chap.) in use before the Exodus, and was observed as the festival of the New year. Philo, 'de Sept.' 19; Mishna, 'Rosh Hash.' I. 1. The general opinion of the Rabbinists has been that it was a commemoration of the creation of the world (see Buxt. 'Lex. Talm.' 2667), when "all the sons of God shouted for joy." Job xxxviii. 7. But Philo, with some others, Jews as well as Christians, regarded this day, rather than the day of Pentecost (see Note at the end of chap.), as the anniversary of the giving of the Law. Philo, 'de Sept.' 22. Theodoret, 'Quæst. in Lev.' 32.

The Day of Atonement. 26—32.

27. The tenth of Tisri, that is from the evening of the ninth day of the month to that of the tenth (*v.* 32), was ordained to be the great Day of Atonement which was to be, like the Sabbath, a day of Holy Convocation of strictest observance, in which no sort of work was to be done. On the peculiar rites of the Day, see ch. xvi.

Also] The Hebrew word is not merely copulative, but emphatic. It might rather be rendered, **Surely.**

afflict your souls] See on xvi. 29.

an offering made by fire] *i.e.* the whole of the appointed sacrifices.

31. *in all your dwellings*] See on *v.* 14; also iii. 17.

32. *sabbath of rest*] See on *v.* 24.

celebrate] The marginal rendering is more correct.

The Feast of Tabernacles. 33—36.

34. *seven days*] Like the Passover, the feast of Tabernacles commenced at the Full moon, on the fifteenth of the month, and lasted for seven days. The first day only was a day of Holy Convocation. But the week of the feast was followed by an eighth day, forming strictly no part of it (*v.* 36, Num. xxix. 35; Neh. viii. 18), which was a day of Holy Convocation, and appears to have been generally distinguished by the name '*'atzereth*' in our version, "solemn assembly," *v.* 36. See Num. xxix. 35; 2 Chron. vii. 9; Neh. viii. 18. The same word is applied to the last day of the Passover, Deut. xvi. 8, and to a religious assembly in a general sense, 2 Kings x. 20; Is. i. 13; Jer. ix. 2; Joel i. 14. The Jews in later times so called the day of Pentecost; see on *v.* 16. There is a difference of opinion as to the meaning of the word. From its derivation it appears strictly to denote *a closing festival*, and this rendering has the authority of the Septuagint, Buxtorf, Fürst, Wogue and others. The term in this sense might of course be applied with propriety to the last day of the Passover, as in Deut. xvi. 8, with still more fulness of meaning to the day of Pentecost as the close of the Pentecostal season, but with the most perfect fitness to the day after the week of the feast of Tabernacles, as the conclusion of the series of yearly festivals. Philo, 'de Sept.' 24; Theodoret,

holy convocation: ye shall do no
servile work *therein*.
36 Seven days ye shall offer an offering made by fire unto the LORD:
on the eighth day shall be an holy
convocation unto you; and ye shall
offer an offering made by fire unto
† Heb. day of *restraint*. the LORD: it *is* a †solemn assembly; *and* ye shall do no servile work
therein.
37 These *are* the feasts of the
LORD, which ye shall proclaim *to be*
holy convocations, to offer an offering made by fire unto the LORD, a
burnt offering, and a meat offering, a
sacrifice, and drink offerings, every
thing upon his day:
38 Beside the sabbaths of the
LORD, and beside your gifts, and
beside all your vows, and beside all
your freewill offerings, which ye give
unto the LORD.
39 Also in the fifteenth day of the
seventh month, when ye have gathered in the fruit of the land, ye
shall keep a feast unto the LORD
seven days: on the first day *shall*
be a sabbath, and on the eighth day
shall be a sabbath.
40 And ye shall take you on the
first day the †boughs of goodly trees, † Heb. *fruit*.
branches of palm trees, and the
boughs of thick trees, and willows
of the brook; and ye shall rejoice
before the LORD your God seven
days.

'Quæst. in Lev.' 32. We are not told that the *'atzereth* was one of the days of Holy Convocation of strict observance; servile work only appears to have been prohibited. This seems to furnish an objection to our marginal rendering "day of restraint," (which has the support of Rosenmüller and Herxheimer). The rendering in the text "solemn assembly," agrees with Onk., the Vulg., Gesenius and de Wette. In the Law the word appears always to hold its specific meaning. In its general application to solemn assemblies it is only found in the later Scriptures. Whether the *'atzereth* was "that great day of the feast" mentioned John vii. 37, see note *in loc.*

36. *an offering made by fire*] See *v.* 8. The succession of sacrifices prescribed in Num. xxix. 12—38 (see on *v.* 20), which forms such a marked feature in the feast of Tabernacles, tends to show the distinctness of the *'atzereth* from the festal week. On each of the eight days, including the *'atzereth*, a shaggy he-goat was offered for a Sin-offering. But on each of the seven days of the festival itself the Burnt-offering consisted of two rams, fourteen lambs of a year old, with a number of young bulls, beginning with thirteen on the first day, but diminishing by one on each successive day till, on the seventh, the number was reduced to seven. The whole number of bulls sacrificed during the week thus amounted to seventy. But on the *'atzereth* the Burnt-offering consisted of only one bull, one ram and seven lambs. The other particulars relating to the feast of Tabernacles will come under our notice in the notes on *vv.* 39 sq.

37, 38. The meaning appears to be; *these are the yearly appointed times on which ye shall hold Holy Convocations and offer to Jehovah sacrifices, in addition to the Sabbath offerings* (Num. xxviii. 9, 10) *and to all your voluntary offerings*. Cf. Num. xxix. 39.

FURTHER INSTRUCTIONS REGARDING THE FEAST OF TABERNACLES. 39—43.

39. *Also*] Rather, **Surely.** See on *v.* 27. The mode in which the feast of Tabernacles is here reintroduced, after the mention of it in *vv.* 34—36, may suggest that this passage originally formed a distinct document. The feast is evidently spoken of as if it had not been mentioned before. If we admit this, the connection of the subject-matter seems to be quite clear. The passage serves as a supplement to the previous notice of the feast, and shows the place which it held in reference to the yearly cycle.

when ye have gathered in] **when ye gather in.** See on Ex. xxiii. 16.

the fruit of the land] *i.e.* the produce, including the grain, the olives, the vintage and the fruits of all kinds. The time of year so indicated would answer in the Holy Land to the beginning of October.

a feast] Heb. *chag*. See Preliminary note.

a sabbath] In each place, the Hebrew is *shabbāthōn*, **a sabbatical rest.** See on *v.* 24.

40. It is doubtful what were "the boughs of goodly trees" and "the boughs of thick trees." In the first term, the marginal rendering **fruit** is certainly better than *boughs*. The word rendered "goodly trees" (Heb. *hādār*) is so understood, in a generic sense, by the LXX., Vulg., Gesenius, Fürst, de Wette, Knobel. But Josephus ('Ant.' XIII. 13. § 5), the Targums and the Rabbinists in general, treat the word as denoting specifically the

41 And ye shall keep it a feast unto the LORD seven days in the year. *It shall be* a statute for ever in your generations: ye shall celebrate it in the seventh month.

42 Ye shall dwell in booths seven days; all that are Israelites born shall dwell in booths:

43 That your generations may know that I made the children of Israel to dwell in booths, when I brought them out of the land of Egypt: I *am* the LORD your God.

44 And Moses declared unto the children of Israel the feasts of the LORD.

Citron, while most of the recent Jewish translators, and Josephus himself in another place, 'Ant.' III. 10. § 4, retain the original word. In the second term (Heb. *'ābōth*) the rendering "thick trees" has the support of the LXX., Vulg., Gesenius, de Wette, Fürst, Knobel, and is favoured by the etymology of *'ābōth*, according to which it would signify a kind, or kinds, of trees with thick, or pleached, foliage. The Targums, and those who have followed them, must evidently be wrong in taking it for the myrtle, since the myrtle is distinctly named along with these same "thick trees" in Neh. viii. 15. The modern Jews generally retain the original word without explanation, as they do *hādār*. There is a well-supported tradition which throws some light on the subject, though it leaves the "thick trees" in uncertainty. It is said that every Israelite at the feast of Tabernacles carried in one hand a bundle of branches (called, in rabbinical Hebrew, *lulāb*), and in the other a citron. The lulab would seem to have comprised the boughs of palm-trees, "thick trees," and willows here named, while the fruit of the *hādār* must have been the citron. Jos. 'Ant.' III. 10. § 4, XIII. 13. 15; 2 Macc. x. 6, 7; Mishna, 'Succah,' cap. III. The boughs mentioned by Nehemiah, of the olive, the pine (rather the wild olive), the myrtle, the palm and the *'aboth*, appear to have been used for covering the huts in which the Israelites lived during the festival. See on *v.* 42; Neh. viii. 15, 16.

42. *Ye shall dwell in booths seven days*] The word rendered "booth" (Heb. *sukkāh*) denotes a shed such as is used for cattle (Gen. xxxiii. 17), a mean dwelling (Is. i. 8; Job xxvii. 18), a bower of branches, as in this place (Job xxxviii. 40; Jonah iv. 5), or the huts of soldiers (2 S. xi. 11; 1 K. xx. 12, 16). According to Jewish tradition, what were used at the feast of Tabernacles were strictly *tabernacula*, structures of boards, with a covering of boughs. Such structures are now erected at this festival by the Jews in some parts of Europe. Certain conditions for their construction are laid down in the Mishna, but their forms might vary considerably. 'Succah,' I. II.; Stauben, 'La Vie Juive en Alsace,' p. 170. It should be noticed that the huts were inhabited only during the seven days of the festival, not on the *'atzereth*. In later times it appears they were set up in such parts of Jerusalem as afforded convenient space for them. Neh. viii. 16. See Note at the end of the Chapter.

all that are Israelites born] The omission of the foreigners in this command is remarkable. Perhaps the intention was that on this joyous occasion they were to be hospitably entertained as guests. Cf. Deut. xvi. 14.

43. *that I made the children of Israel to dwell in booths, when I brought them out of the land of Egypt*] See Note at the end of the Chapter.

44. *feasts*] **appointed times**. See on *v.* 2. This verse is a conclusion to the whole chapter. See Prel. Note.

NOTES on CHAP. XXIII.

I. ON THE PENTECOST. *vv.* 15—22.

The other chief passages in the Law relating to the feast of Weeks are Ex. xxiii. 16; Num. xxviii. 26—31; Deut. xvi. 9—12. But here only is the offering of the Pentecostal loaves mentioned, unless it is they which are designated "the first of the firstfruits," Ex. xxiii. 19 (see note); and "the firstfruits," Ex. xxxiv. 26.

The true connection between the offering of the First Sheaf and the Passover may perhaps be traced in Josh. v. 10—12. The Passover was the great national commemoration of the deliverance from Egypt which was to lead on to the settlement of the Israelites in the Promised Land as its crowning result. The first offering of the Sheaf seems to be implied in the narration of what occurred at Gilgal, when the people ate of the "corn of the land on the morrow after the Passover." See on *v.* 14. From this time, the complete festival, including the Paschal Lamb, the Unleavened Bread, and the First Sheaf, was to remind them how they had been set free and preserved in the Wilderness until they could eat of the produce of the Land which Jehovah had given to them. But the connection between the First Sheaf and the feast of Weeks, as marking the beginning and the end of the grain harvest, is of a more obvious kind. The two observances sanctified the interval between them, the whole period of harvest, "the Pentecostal season." Jewish tradition has preserved some curious traces of the general recognition of this by the Hebrew race. Buxtorf, 'Syn. Jud.' p. 440; Stauben, 'Vie Juive en Alsace,' p. 124; Mills, 'The Modern Jews,' p. 207. Philo calls the offering of the First Sheaf "the prelude to a greater festival," *i.e.* Pentecost. The Rabbinists called the Day of Pentecost *'atzereth* (see on *v.* 35), as the last day of Holy Convocation of the Pentecostal season. Mishna, 'Rosh Hash.' I. 2; 'Chag,' II. 4; Joseph. 'Ant.' III. 10, § 6. The two loaves of the Day of Pentecost bore to the people the same message regarding Jehovah as the words of the Psalmist, "He maketh peace in thy borders, He filleth thee with the finest of the wheat," Ps. cxlvii. 14. Theodoret speaks of Pentecost as a memorial of the promise of the possession of the Holy Land. 'Quæst. in Lev.' 32.

The tradition that the feast of Weeks was intended to commemorate the giving of the Law on Mount Sinai appears first in the Fathers of the fourth century. When it had been inferred from Ex. xix. that the day must have nearly coincided with the fiftieth day after the Exodus, the day on which the gift of the Law marked Israel as an organized nation might have been easily connected with the day on which the gift of the Holy Spirit united the believers in Jesus of Nazareth into a Church. S. Jerom. Ep. ad Fabiolam M. XII.; S. Aug. 'Contr. Faust.' XXXII. 12. It is, however, most probable that a Jewish tradition to the same effect existed before the fourth century. The general acceptance of the notion by the Jews of later ages (Maimon. 'More Nev.' III. 41; Buxt. 'Syn. Jud.' p. 438; Schoettgen, 'Hor. Heb.' Act. II. 1) cannot easily be reconciled with the supposition that it originated with the Fathers of the Church.

We may perhaps be allowed to conjecture that it was because the day of Pentecost was regarded as, in a sense, the birth-day of the Church, that St Paul was so careful to keep it after his conversion. Acts xx. 16; 1 Cor. xvi. 8. The entire Pentecostal season, the period between Easter and Whitsuntide, became in an early age the ordinary time for the baptism of converts (Hessey, 'Bampton Lectures,' p. 88), as the harvest season of the Church, answering to the harvest season of the Land according to the old Law.

II. On the Civil Year. *v.* 24.

There is no direct reference to the months in the Old Testament which, by itself, would lead us to suppose that the Israelites used any other year than that beginning with the month Abib (Ex. xiii. 4, cf. xii. 2; Deut. xvi. 1), which, after the Captivity, was called Nisan (Neh. ii. 1; Est. iii. 7). Hence the existence of a Civil year, as distinct from the Sacred year, has been sometimes treated as a modern fiction. Smith's 'Dict.' I. p. 359. But the form of expression in Ex. xii. 2, the commencement of the Sabbatical and Jubilee years in the month Ethanim, or Tisri, the traditions of both the rabbinical and Alexandrian Jews, and the fact that the New moon festival of Tisri is the only one—not excepting that of Nisan—which is distinguished by peculiar observance, seem to bear sufficient testimony to a more ancient computation of time than that instituted by Moses in connection with the Passover. Another argument is furnished by Ex. xxiii. 16. See note.

Keeping in view the enumeration of the holy days in this chapter of Leviticus (*vv.* 4—27), and that in the law of festival sacrifices in Numbers (xxviii. xxix.), we may perceive a simple arrangement which appears to connect the yearly observances at once with the order of the natural year and with the Sabbatical idea. It was the Hebrew custom to speak of the year as divided into two seasons, Summer and Winter (Gen. viii. 22; Ps. lxxiv. 17; Zech. xiv. 8), and to designate the produce of the earth in general as the fruits of Summer (Jer. viii. 20, xl. 10—12; Mic. vii. 1). The only months specified in this enumeration of the festivals are the first of the sacred year, Abib, "the month of green ears," the commencement of Summer, and the seventh, Ethanim, "the month of flowing streams" (Gesenius), the first month of Winter. Under these months the set times are arranged in two groups. In the Summer half-year we find the Passover linked on by the offering of the First sheaf followed by the Week of weeks to the feast of perfected First fruits at Pentecost; in the half-year of Winter, grouped within a single month, are the feast of Trumpets, the Day of Atonement, and the feast of Tabernacles, with the *'atzereth*, or "concluding festival" of the year. See on *v.* 34. Thus each season was consecrated by its appropriate observances. That the Seventh month should have come to be regarded by the Jews with peculiar respect as "the Sabbatical month," appears to be natural from the place which it holds as the seventh in the Sacred year, from its lunar cycle commencing with an extraordinary New moon festival, and from its comprising such a large proportion of holy days, especially the Day of Atonement, to say nothing of the ancient dignity which probably belonged to it as the First month in the patriarchal year.

It is worthy of remark that both the Spring feast in Abib and the Autumn feast in Ethanim appropriately commenced at the Full moon in their respective months.

III. On the Meaning of the Feast of Tabernacles. *v.* 43.

Objection is made to the statement in *v.* 43 on the ground that the kind of habitation used by the Israelites in the wilderness is never called in the history *sukkāh*, a booth (see on xxiii. 42), but always *ōhel*, that is, a tent of skins or cloth. See Ex. xvi. 16, xxxiii. 8, 10; Lev. xiv. 8; Num. xi. 10, xvi. 26, xix. 18; Deut. v. 30, xi. 6, &c., &c. This circumstance seems to show that the *primary* object of the booths could not have been to remind the Israelites of the tents in which their fathers had encamped in the Wilderness. It is indeed alleged that some of the dwellers in the Wilderness at this day shelter themselves in huts or bowers, and that the Israelites may have done so in some part of their wanderings. But neither this, nor the fact that *sukkāh* is sometimes used for the hut or tent of a soldier in an encampment (2 S. xi. 11; 1 K. xx. 12, 16), can bring the title of the feast into direct agreement with the course of the historical narrative. The people were accustomed to hear of their fathers dwelling in tents, not in booths, and all the Hebrew words used in reference to moving the camp in the Wilderness strictly belong to tents (Hupfeld). It is not therefore likely that the Lawgiver would call the festival "the festival of Booths" if it had been first instituted to keep the Israelites in mind of the camp in the Wilderness.—Once indeed, in later times, the term *ōhel* is connected with the feast of Tabernacles (Hos. xii. 9).

The original idea of the festival plainly appears to be expressed in the name applied to it in Exodus, "the feast of Ingathering," the celebration of harvest-home, when the fruits of the earth were gathered in. See on Ex. xxiii. 16; cf. xxxiv. 22. As the feast of Ingathering the festival may have been observed in the land of Goshen, and it may there have been the custom for the parties keeping holiday to meet in bowers set up for the occasion, such as were used in the Summer and Autumn festivals of other nations. (See Ovid 'Fast.' III. 523; Tibullus, I. 'Eleg.' I. 24; 'Festus' s. *umbræ*.) The practice is familiar in the East, and it is one which might naturally arise anywhere. But the feast of Tabernacles was solemnly recognized by the Law as one of the three great festivals at which every male Israelite was to present himself before Jehovah at the Sanctuary. Ex. xxiii. 16, xxxiv. 22, 23. It was in its nature a joyous occasion, the most joyous of all the feasts, the one which was named *par excellence*, "the feast." See Deut. xvi. 13—15; 1 K. viii. 2, 65; Ezek. xlv. 25; Zech. xiv. 16. In the wandering life in the Wilderness its proper significance as the feast of Ingathering must have been rather in prospect and retrospect than in the actual present; but its jubilant character may have been kept up. Now the *sukkāh* in which the Israelite kept the feast, and the *ōhel* which was his ordinary abode in the wilderness, had this in common—they were temporary places of sojourn, they belonged to camp-life. The seven days of abode in the booths of the festival was thus a fair symbol of the forty years of abode in tents in the Wilderness. The feast might well become the appointed memorial of this period of their history for the ages to come, and Hosea, in the passage to which reference has been made, might easily use the word *tent*, immediately suggesting the historical connection, rather than *booth*, the one strictly belonging to the feast.—In like manner the feast of Weeks was endowed with a meaning certainly not immediately connected with its original institution, being recognized as a memorial of the bondage of Egypt. See Deut. xvi. 11, 12. This may possibly have had reference to the hard toil of harvest which was past, and now rewarded with the blessing of a store of provision. There is a still nearer parallel in the case of the weekly Sabbath being appointed to remind the people of their deliverance from Egypt. See Note on the Sabbath-day, § v., Ex. xx.—A kindred connection between the year of Release with the Exodus is indicated, Deut. xv. 15.

The substance of the lesson of the feast of Tabernacles as expressed in this verse may however have had a deeper ground than any mere material resemblance existing between the *sukkāh* and the *ōhel*. No time in the year could be so suitable for the Israelites to be reminded of the wonderful providence which had fed and sheltered them in the Wilderness, where they had no land to call their own, and where there was neither harvest nor gathering into barns nor vintage, as the season in which they offered thanksgiving to Jehovah for the fruits of the ground and consecrated the crops newly stored in. In this way the transition from nomadic to agricultural life, which took place when the people settled in the Holy Land, must have tended to fulfil the meaning of the feast of Tabernacles. From that time the festival called to mind their long and weary wanderings in contrast with the plenty and comfort of settled possession. The parallel between this change in the condition of the people and the transferring of the centre of national worship from the Tabernacle to the Temple, may have been the reason of the connection of the Dedication of the first and second Temples, and of the Encænia of the Maccabees, with the feast of Tabernacles. See 1 K. viii. 2, 65; Jos. 'Ant.' VIII. 4. § 5; Neh. viii. 13—18; 2 Macc. x. 5—8.

The popular character of the festival, and its connection with the Dedication of the Temple of Solomon, were probably what induced Jeroboam to set up an imitation of it in the inauguration of the false worship at Bethel. 1 K. xii. 32, 33.

On the reading of portions of the Law during the feast of Tabernacles in the Sabbatical year, see Deut. xxxi. 10—13; and on the references to the festival in the New Testament, see John vii. 37, viii. 12.

CHAPTER XXIV.

1 *The oil for the lamps.* 5 *The shewbread.* 10 *Shelomith's son blasphemeth.* 13 *The law of blasphemy.* 17 *Of murder.* 18 *Of damage.* 23 *The blasphemer is stoned.*

AND the LORD spake unto Moses,
saying,
2 Command the children of Israel,
that they bring unto thee pure oil
olive beaten for the light, †to cause
the lamps to burn continually.
3 Without the vail of the testimony, in the tabernacle of the congregation, shall Aaron order it from
the evening unto the morning before the LORD continually: *it shall*
be a statute for ever in your generations.
4 He shall order the lamps upon
[a] the pure candlestick before the LORD
continually.
5 ¶ And thou shalt take fine flour,
and bake twelve [b] cakes thereof: two
tenth deals shall be in one cake.
6 And thou shalt set them in two
rows, six on a row, upon the pure
table before the LORD.
7 And thou shalt put pure frankincense upon *each* row, that it may
be on the bread for a memorial, *even*
an offering made by fire unto the
LORD.

† Heb. *to cause to ascend.*

[a] Exod. 31. 8.

[b] Exod. 25. 30.

CHAP. XXIV.

THE OIL FOR THE LAMPS—THE SHEWBREAD.

1—9.

As setting forth a part of the duty of the laity in the maintenance of public worship, this section may have a connection with the preceding chapter. The oil for the lamps of the Tabernacle and the meal for the Shewbread were to be offerings from the Congregation, like the meal for the Pentecostal Loaves, xxiii. 17. The instructions regarding the oil (*vv.* 2, 3) are almost a verbal repetition of Ex. xxvii. 20, 21, except that "Aaron and his sons" are mentioned in Exodus, and in this place (*v.* 3) only Aaron. It appears that the responsibility of keeping up the lights rested on the High-priest, but the actual service might be performed, on ordinary occasions, by the common priests. Cf. on xvi. 4.

2. *to cause the lamps to burn*] See on i. 9.

4. *the pure candlestick* See Ex. xxv. 31—39, xxxi. 8.

5—9. The Shewbread is mentioned Ex. xxv. 30, xxxv. 13, xxxix. 36; 2 Chron. xiii. 11, &c. It is not in this place designated by its peculiar name. The purpose of the passage is to give instructions for its preparation and treatment. Our translators have followed Luther in their use of the name Shewbread. Wickliffe, following the LXX. and Vulg., has "Bread of the Proposition;" that is, *the Bread which is set forth.* The Hebrew name might fairly be rendered **Bread of the presence.**

5. *two tenth deals shall be in one cake*] Each cake or loaf was to contain two tenths of an ephah, about six pounds and a quarter (see on Ex. xxix. 40; Lev. xix. 36) of fine flour. The material was the same, both in quality and in quantity, with that of each one of the Wave-loaves of Pentecost (xxiii. 17). The word rendered *cake* is the same as occurs ii. 4, vii. 12, viii. 26, &c., and appears to be regularly applied to loaves of unleavened bread. Some imagine the Shewbread to have been leavened, like the Pentecostal loaves (Knobel, &c.). But Jewish tradition (see Joseph. 'Ant.' III. 6. § 6—10, § 7; Mishna, "Menach." V. 1) and most authorities of all ages take the opposite view. Since the bread was brought into the Holy place (which was not the case with the Pentecostal bread) it almost certainly came under the general law of the Meat-offerings, which excluded the use of leaven (ii. 11). In the service of the Temple the preparation and arrangement of the cakes were committed to the Levites (1 Chron. ix. 32, xxiii. 29; 2 Chron. xiii. 11.).

6. *two rows, six in a row*] Rather, **two piles, six in a pile.** The Hebrew word might denote either *row* or *pile.* But the measure of the Table, two cubits long by one broad, in connection with the bulk of the loaves, and the testimony of Josephus who must have known the usage in the second Temple ('Ant.' III. 6, § 6), favour the notion that the bread stood in two piles.—On the Table, see Ex. xxv. 23—30.

7. *pure frankincense*] The LXX. adds *salt*, which probably represents the true reading and accords with the Law that no Meat-offering was to be offered without salt (ii. 13).

for a memorial] Our version here gives what appears to be the true sense of the Hebrew, in opposition to the most ancient versions and some modern authorities, which apply the words *for a memorial* to the Shewbread itself, not to the frankincense. The frankincense as a memorial, or *azkārāh* (like the handful of the Meat-offering, ii. 2), was most likely cast upon the Altar-fire as "an offering made by fire unto the Lord," when the bread was removed from the Table on the Sabbath-day (*v.* 8; 1 S. xxi. 6; cf. Mishna,

8 Every sabbath he shall set it in
order before the LORD continually,
being taken from the children of Israel by an everlasting covenant.
9 And it shall be Aaron's and his
sons'; [e]and they shall eat it in the
holy place: for it *is* most holy unto
him of the offerings of the LORD
made by fire by a perpetual statute.
10 ¶ And the son of an Israelitish
woman, whose father *was* an Egyptian, went out among the children
of Israel: and this son of the Israelitish *woman* and a man of Israel
strove together in the camp;
11 And the Israelitish woman's son
blasphemed the name *of the LORD*,
and cursed. And they brought him
unto Moses: (and his mother's name
was Shelomith, the daughter of Dibri,
of the tribe of Dan:)
12 And they [d]put him in ward,
[†]that the mind of the LORD might
be shewed them.

[e] Exod. 29. 33. chap. 8. 31. Matt. 12. 4.

[d] Numb. 15. 34.

† Heb. *to expound unto them according to the mouth of the LORD.*

'Menach.' XI. 7). The frankincense was put into small gold cups, one of which was placed upon each pile of bread. (See on Ex. xxv. 23—30.)

8. *being taken from the children of Israel*] Each cake represented the offering of a Tribe.

9. See on ii. 3. It could have been only by a stretch of the Law that Ahimelech gave a portion of the Shewbread to David and his men, on the ground that they were free from ceremonial defilement. 1 Sam. xxi. 4—6; Matt. xii. 4.

Nothing is said in Scripture that throws any direct light upon the specific meaning of the Shewbread. But there seems no reasonable doubt that it was a true Meat-offering, with its frankincense, its Drink-offering (see on Ex. xxv. 29), and its salt (see on *v.* 7). The peculiar form in which it was offered, especially in its being brought into the Tabernacle and in its consisting of Twelve loaves, distinguish it as an offering made on behalf of the nation. See on Ex. xxv. 30.—Bähr has ingeniously carried out the theory that the loaves were intended for a symbolical manifestation of the Holy One in His Sanctuary as the Bread of Life, as the supporter both of the spiritual and the bodily life of His faithful people. John vi. 47—51; Matt. iv. 4; Deut. viii. 3; see 'Symbolik,' I. p. 425. But sufficient objection to this view seems to be furnished by the facts that the loaves were taken "from the children of Israel," not in any way presented to them; and that the symbolism on which it is based would be better expressed by One loaf than by Twelve loaves. See 1 Cor. x. 17.—Spencer and other critics of his school have actually supposed that the setting forth of the Shewbread Table was a symbolical meal offered to Jehovah, like the *Lectisternium* of the Romans, in which food used to be placed before the statues of the gods.

THE BLASPHEMER—THE LAW OF BLASPHEMY AND OTHER PENAL LAWS ENACTED. 10—23.

This section appears to stand by itself. The place it holds may have been determined by the mere time of the incident related in it. The Legislator had, it seems, just completed a topic: the incident, with the law suggested by it, was probably recorded at once and suffered to keep its place, as not severing any important connection.

The blasphemer was the son of a Hebrew woman of the tribe of Dan by an Egyptian father. He had come out of Egypt with the children of Israel, and must have been under the ordinary conditions of a resident foreigner. See xvi. 29. He happened to have a quarrel with an Israelite, and in the course of altercation he used some blasphemous expression. See on *v.* 16. It was revealed to Moses that blasphemy was to be punished by stoning, and that this and all penal laws were to be carried out not only against Israelites, but against resident foreigners (*v.* 22). The laws against murder and violence appear to be here introduced in the way of illustration. The purpose of *vv.* 17—22 would thus be to ratify with the utmost distinctness the maxim of the Law which rendered foreigners amenable to all penalties and restrictions. Cf. Ex. xii. 49; Num. ix. 14, xv. 15, 16: notes on Ex. xx. 10; Lev. xvi. 29.—The rabbinists have filled out this narrative of the son of Shelomith in a curious manner. They say that the father of the young man was the Egyptian slain by Moses (Ex. ii. 11), that he was the taskmaster under whom the husband of Shelomith worked, and that Moses found him smiting the man whom he had injured and put to shame. It is added that the quarrel in which the young man was engaged arose out of a claim set up by him to have his abode in the camp of the Danites [see Num. ii. 2], not being content to remain in the quarters appropriated to foreigners (Targum of Palestine and authorities quoted by Selden, 'de Syned.' II. c. I. § 2).

11. *blasphemed the name of the LORD, and cursed*] See on *v.* 16.

12. Selden (*u. s.*) supposes that the offender had already been pronounced guilty by the rulers [see Ex. xviii. 21, 22], and that the case

13 And the LORD spake unto Moses, saying,

14 Bring forth him that hath cursed without the camp; and let all that heard *him* [e]lay their hands upon his head, and let all the congregation stone him.

[e] Deut. 13. 9. & 17. 7.

15 And thou shalt speak unto the children of Israel, saying, Whosoever curseth his God shall bear his sin.

16 And he that blasphemeth the name of the LORD, he shall surely be put to death, *and* all the congregation shall certainly stone him: as well the stranger, as he that is born in the land, when he blasphemeth the name *of the LORD*, shall be put to death.

17 ¶ [f]And he that †killeth any man shall surely be put to death.

18 And he that killeth a beast shall make it good; †beast for beast.

19 And if a man cause a blemish in his neighbour; as [g]he hath done, so shall it be done to him;

20 Breach for breach, eye for eye, tooth for tooth: as he hath caused a blemish in a man, so shall it be done to him *again*.

21 And he that killeth a beast, he shall restore it: and he that killeth a man, he shall be put to death.

22 Ye shall have [h]one manner of law, as well for the stranger, as for one of your own country: for I *am* the LORD your God.

23 ¶ And Moses spake to the chil-

[f] Exod. 21. 12. Deut. 19. 21.
† Heb. *smiteth the life of a man.*
† Heb. *life for life.*
[g] Exod. 21. 24. Deut. 19. 21. Matt. 5. 38.
[h] Exod. 12. 49.

---

was referred to Moses in order that the punishment might be awarded by the divine decree. No law had as yet been enacted against blasphemy except by implication. See Ex. xxi. 17, xxii. 28.

14. *lay their hands upon his head*] The simplest view seems to be that the witnesses, by this act, were to protest against the impiety of the criminal, symbolically laying the guilt upon his head. The two elders in the story of Susanna are said to do the same, not after condemnation, but in bringing their charge against the accused before the people, *v.* 34. Cf. the washing of hands, Deut. xxi. 6; Matt. xxvii. 24. The act has been, certainly with no good reason, connected with the sacrificial imposition of hands, and understood to be a solemn dedication of the offender to death by his accusers. Kurtz, 'S. W.' § 47; cf. on xxvii. 28.

let all the congregation stone him] See on xx. 2.

16. *he that blasphemeth the name of the LORD*] It should be observed that the words "of THE LORD," are here translated from the original, not, as in *v.* 11, and in the latter part of this verse, inserted by the translators. The verb, according to all the best critical authorities, denotes *to revile*: but Jewish interpreters in general, with the countenance of the LXX. and the Targums, understand it to mean no more than *to utter distinctly*. Hence the rabbinists based on this verse the notion that it is not lawful to speak the name which appears in some places in our version as JEHOVAH, but is, for the most part, rendered "the LORD." On the mode in which the Jews have evaded the use of the name, see Buxtorf, 'Lex. Talmud.' p. 2432. Its true pronunciation is irretrievably lost, owing to its vowel points having been shifted. Most is perhaps to be said in favour of the uncouth form JAHVE. See Martineau's preface to Ewald's 'History,' p. xviii. When the name is referred to in rabbinical writings, it generally stands as simply "the name," or "the name of four letters" (*tetragrammaton*), "the great and terrible name," &c. It is remarkable that this habit has practically kept its hold upon most modern versions of the Bible, Christian as well as Jewish. The Septuagint render the name by ὁ Κύριος, the Vulgate, by *Dominus*, and nearly all English translators, by "THE LORD," distinguished by capital letters. Luther, the Italian translators, and some of the French, use words with the same meaning. Others of the French versions, and the modern Jewish versions in general, have "the Eternal," or some equivalent word. Jehovah is retained by Junius and Tremellius, Schott, de Wette, &c.

stranger] i.e **foreigner**. See on xvi. 29.

17. Cf. *v.* 21. See Ex. xxi. 12; Num. xxxv. 30, 31; Deut. xix. 11, 12.

18. Cf. *v.* 21. See Ex. xxi. 33, 34. The law expressed in this verse is more broadly given than in Exodus.

19, 20. See on Ex. xxi. 22—25.

cause a blemish] *i.e.* inflict a bodily injury.

21. An emphatic repetition of *vv.* 17, 18.

22. *one manner of law*] The Hebrew word rendered "law" is *mishpat*, i.e. *judicial law*.

stranger] **foreigner**.

I am the LORD] See on xviii. 2.

dren of Israel, that they should bring
forth him that had cursed out of the
camp, and stone him with stones.
And the children of Israel did as the
LORD commanded Moses.

CHAPTER XXV.

1 *The sabbath of the seventh year.* 8 *The jubile in the fiftieth year.* 14 *Of oppression.* 18 *A blessing of obedience.* 23 *The redemption of land.* 29 *Of houses.* 35 *Compassion of the poor.* 39 *The usage of bondmen.* 47 *The redemption of servants.*

AND the LORD spake unto Moses
in mount Sinai, saying,
2 Speak unto the children of Israel, and say unto them, When ye
come into the land which I give you,
then shall the land †keep [a] a sabbath († Heb. *rest.* a Exod. 23. 10.)
unto the LORD.
3 Six years thou shalt sow thy
field, and six years thou shalt prune
thy vineyard, and gather in the fruit
thereof;
4 But in the seventh year shall be
a sabbath of rest unto the land, a
sabbath for the LORD: thou shalt
neither sow thy field, nor prune thy
vineyard.
5 That which groweth of its own
accord of thy harvest thou shalt not
reap, neither gather the grapes †of († Heb. *of thy separation.*)
thy vine undressed: *for* it is a year
of rest unto the land.
6 And the sabbath of the land shall
be meat for you; for thee, and for
thy servant, and for thy maid, and
for thy hired servant, and for thy
stranger that sojourneth with thee,
7 And for thy cattle, and for the
beast that *are* in thy land, shall all
the increase thereof be meat.
8 ¶ And thou shalt number seven
sabbaths of years unto thee, seven
times seven years; and the space of
the seven sabbaths of years shall be
unto thee forty and nine years.
9 Then shalt thou cause the trum-
pet †of the jubile to sound on the († Heb. *loud of sound.*)
tenth *day* of the seventh month, in

CHAPTER XXV.

THE SABBATICAL YEAR AND THE YEAR OF JUBILEE. 1—55.

Preliminary Note.

The Sabbatical year and the year of Jubilee belong to that great Sabbatical system which runs through the religious observances of the Law. They were solemnly connected with the sacred Covenant. But it is important to observe that they were distinguished by no religious ceremonies, they were accompanied by no act of religious worship. There were no sacrifices, nor Holy Convocations, belonging to them. In their distinctive aspect they may be said to rest upon moral rather than upon formally religious ground. It is not therefore without reason that they are here set apart from the set times which fell strictly within the sphere of religious observances.

The Sabbatical year. 1—7.

2. *keep a sabbath unto the LORD*] See on Ex. xxiii. 11.

3. *vineyard*] Rather, **fruit-garden**. The Hebrew word is a general one for a plantation of fruit-trees. See on Lev. ix. 10.

4. *a sabbath of rest*] Heb. *shabbath shabbātōn*. See on xxiii. 3.

neither sow thy field] The express prohibition of sowing and reaping, and of pruning and gathering, affords a presumption in favour of the Sabbatical year beginning, like the year of Jubilee (*v.* 9), in the first month of the Civil year, the seventh of the Sacred year, when the land was cleared of the crops of the preceding year. See on Ex. xxiii. 16, and Note 'On the Civil year' after chap. xxiii.

5. *thy vine undressed*] That is, *unpruned*; literally, *thy Nazarite vine*, the figure being taken from the unshorn locks of the Nazarite. Num. vi. 5; cf. Tibullus, I. 'El.' VII. 34.

6. *the sabbath of the land shall be meat for you*] That is, the produce of the untilled land (its "increase" *v.* 7) shall be food for the whole of you in common, rich and poor without distinction, Ex. xxiii. 11.

the stranger that sojourneth with thee] **the foreigner who dwelleth with thee.**

7. *the beast*] **the living creature.**

The year of Jubilee. 8—55.

8—13. The Land was to be divided by lot among the families of the Israelites when the possession of it was obtained. Num. xxv. 52—56, xxxiii. 54, &c. At the end of every seventh sabbatical cycle of years, in the year of Jubilee, each field or estate that might have been alienated was to be restored to the family to which it had been originally allotted.

8. *seven sabbaths of years*] **seven weeks of years.**

9. *cause the trumpet of the jubile to sound*] Rather, **cause the sound of the cornet to go through** (the land). The word

the day of atonement shall ye make
the trumpet sound throughout all
your land.
10 And ye shall hallow the fiftieth
year, and proclaim liberty throughout *all* the land unto all the inhabitants thereof: it shall be a jubile
unto you; and ye shall return every
man unto his possession, and ye shall
return every man unto his family.
11 A jubile shall that fiftieth year
be unto you: ye shall not sow, nei-

Jubilee does not occur in this verse in the Hebrew. The trumpet is the *shophār*, *i.e.* the cornet, *buccina*, either the horn of some animal or a tube of metal shaped like one. The Mishna says that the horn of the chamois or wild goat was used on this occasion. 'Rosh Hash.' III. 5. See on xxiii. 24; cf. Num. x. 2. Keil has well remarked that as the sound of the cornet (see on *v.* 10) was the signal of the descent of Jehovah when He came down upon Sinai to take Israel into Covenant with Himself (Ex. xix. 13, 16, 19, xx. 18), so the same sound announced, at the close of the great Day of Atonement, the year which restored each Israelite to the freedom and the blessings of the Covenant.—The word *shophār* is rendered "shawm" in the Prayer-Book version of Ps. xcviii. 7.

the tenth day of the seventh month, in the day of atonement] It seems most likely that the blast of the cornets took place in the evening, after the Evening sacrifice, when the solemn rites of Atonement were concluded. The contrast between the humbling quiet of the day and the sudden outpouring of the sound which proclaimed the year of freedom, must have been very impressive. Nothing, however, could be more appropriate than that freedom should be declared just after the great national act of humiliation and reconcilement with Jehovah. It has been conjectured that the cornets were blown in every priest's city, or wherever a priest might be living (Bähr), but according to tradition they were blown by any of the people "throughout all the land."

10. *the fiftieth year*]. If this means the fiftieth year, beginning to reckon from the first year after the preceding Jubilee, since the forty-ninth year must have been a Sabbatical year, two fallow years must have come together (see *v.* 11). This seems unlikely. But it is probable that the Jubilee coincided with each seventh Sabbatical year. It might, in this case, have been called the fiftieth, reckoning it as the last of a series of which the first was the preceding Jubilee. A tendency may be traced in many languages in reference to periods of time to include the starting point as the first unit in the series. It may be seen in the mode in which such words and phrases are used as *πενταετηρίς*, *τριετηρίς*, *quinquennalia*, *nundinæ*, *huitaine*, *quinzaine*, or *quinzejours*, *quindici giorni*, *acht Tage*, *the octave of a festival* (cf. Luke ix. 28; Joh. xx. 26), &c., &c. With this agree some early Jewish traditions, and the opinions of Scaliger, Usher, Petavius, Rosenmüller and others. Cf. notes on *vv.* 11, 18—22.—It must, however, be admitted that the question is a difficult one, and the greater number of Jewish authorities, as well as of the more recent critics, are in favour of the fiftieth year, taking the expression in the sense with which we are more familiar.

it shall be a jubile unto you] Except in the English Bible the word is commonly spelt *jubilee.* Like the *jubilæus* of the Vulgate, it was intended to represent the Hebrew, *jōbeel.* The form found in Cranmer's Bible, "jubelye," must have been derived from *jubilæus.* But our translators, with the Genevan, probably meant "jubile," to come more closely to the Hebrew, and to be pronounced as a dissyllable, as if spelt *jubil.*—The word *jōbeel* was taken by several early authorities (Josephus, S. Jerome, Theodoret, with some support from the Septuagint) to mean *liberty*, or, *the act of setting free.* But the word first occurs Ex. xix. 13, where it certainly cannot have any such meaning, and where it is rendered in our version, "trumpet," marg. "cornet." It most probably denotes the sound of the cornet, not the cornet itself. Cf. Josh. vi. 5. Various opinions have been formed regarding its derivation. Some of the Rabbinists imagined it to be identical with a word said to exist in old Arabic, signifying a ram, or a ram's horn. It has been regarded as an onomatopoetic word, like the Latin *jubilare*, to shout for help, and *jubilum*, an outcry (Gesenius). It is worth while to observe that our word, *jubilant*, though derived from the Latin verb, rather takes its meaning from the Hebrew substantive. But a very probable conjecture, approved by the best authorities, connects *jobeel* with the root *jābal*, to flow abundantly, which by a familiar metaphor might be applied to sound. The word has been discussed at length by Bochart ('Hieroz.' I. c. 43), Carpzov ('App. Crit.' p. 447), Gesenius ('Thes.' p. 561), and Kranold ('De Jubil.' p. 11).

11. See on *v.* 10. Hupfeld and others have so estimated the improbability of one fallow year succeeding another that they have been disposed to reject this verse as spurious. They imagine that tillage did not cease in the Jubilee. But the difficulty disappears if we suppose the Jubilee to have coincided with the seventh Sabbatical year. Cf. on *vv.* 18—22.

ther reap that which groweth of itself
in it, nor gather *the grapes* in it of
thy vine undressed.
12 For it *is* the jubile; it shall be
holy unto you: ye shall eat the increase thereof out of the field.
13 In the year of this jubile ye
shall return every man unto his possession.
14 And if thou sell ought unto
thy neighbour, or buyest *ought* of
thy neighbour's hand, ye shall not
oppress one another:
15 According to the number of
years after the jubile thou shalt buy
of thy neighbour, *and* according unto
the number of years of the fruits he
shall sell unto thee:
16 According to the multitude of
years thou shalt increase the price
thereof, and according to the few-
ness of years thou shalt diminish the
price of it: for *according* to the number *of the years* of the fruits doth he
sell unto thee.
17 Ye shall not therefore oppress
one another; but thou shalt fear thy
God: for I *am* the LORD your God.
18 ¶ Wherefore ye shall do my
statutes, and keep my judgments,
and do them; and ye shall dwell in
the land in safety.
19 And the land shall yield her
fruit, and ye shall eat your fill, and
dwell therein in safety.
20 And if ye shall say, What shall
we eat the seventh year? behold, we
shall not sow, nor gather in our increase:
21 Then I will command my blessing upon you in the sixth year, and
it shall bring forth fruit for three
years.
22 And ye shall sow the eighth
year, and eat *yet* of old fruit until the
ninth year; until her fruits come in
ye shall eat *of* the old *store*.
23 ¶ The land shall not be sold
‖for ever: for the land *is* mine; for
ye *are* strangers and sojourners with
me.
24 And in all the land of your possession ye shall grant a redemption
for the land.
25 ¶ If thy brother be waxen
poor, and hath sold away *some* of
his possession, and if any of his kin
come to redeem it, then shall he redeem that which his brother sold.
26 And if the man have none to

‖ Or, *to be quite cut off.* Heb. *for cutting off.*

---

vine undressed] See on *v.* 5.

14—17. The principle on which the law of Jubilee, as it regards the land, was based, is expressed in *vv.* 23, 24. The land belonged to Jehovah, and it was He who allotted it amongst the families of Israel for their use. No estate could therefore be alienated in perpetuity, by any human authority, from the family to whose lot it might fall. But the usufruct, or lease, of a portion might be sold at any time for a period extending to the next Jubilee.

14. *sell ought*] That is, any piece of ground.

oppress one another] Rather, **overreach one another.**

15, 16. *the number of years of the fruits*] *i. e.* according to the number of harvests. The average value of a yearly crop might of course be estimated, and the Sabbatical years were to be deducted from the series.

17. *oppress one another*] See on *v.* 14.

18—22. It has been conjectured that these verses are out of their proper place, that they relate to the Sabbatical year, not to the year of Jubilee, and that they should be read immediately after the seventh verse (Ewald, Hupfeld, Knobel, Davidson). But if the Jubilee coincided with the seventh Sabbatical year, the conjecture is needless. See on *vv.* 10, 11.

18, 19. *in safety*] That is, secure from famine, xxvi. 5.

23, 24. See on 14—17.

23. *sold for ever*] Marg. "*for cutting off*," or, "*to be quite cut off;*" in modern phrase, sold in perpetuity.

strangers] **foreigners**, who had become residents. See on Ex. xx. 12; Lev. xvi. 29.

24. *grant a redemption for the land*] *i. e.* grant power to recover the land to the original holder who had parted with it.

25. *If thy brother be waxen poor*] It would seem that the Israelites were expected never to part with their land except under the pressure of poverty. The answer of Naboth to Ahab expressed the feelings which must have been thus fostered, "The Lord forbid it me that I should give the inheritance of my fathers to thee." 1 K. xxi. 3.

redeem it, and †himself be able to redeem it;

† Heb. *his hand hath attained and found sufficiency.*

27 Then let him count the years of the sale thereof, and restore the overplus unto the man to whom he sold it; that he may return unto his possession.

28 But if he be not able to restore *it* to him, then that which is sold shall remain in the hand of him that hath bought it until the year of jubile: and in the jubile it shall go out, and he shall return unto his possession.

29 And if a man sell a dwelling house in a walled city, then he may redeem it within a whole year after it is sold; *within* a full year may he redeem it.

30 And if it be not redeemed within the space of a full year, then the house that *is* in the walled city shall be established for ever to him that bought it throughout his generations: it shall not go out in the jubile.

31 But the houses of the villages which have no wall round about them shall be counted as the fields of the country: †they may be redeemed, and they shall go out in the jubile.

† Heb. *redemption belongeth unto it.*

32 Notwithstanding the cities of the Levites, *and* the houses of the cities of their possession, may the Levites redeem at any time.

33 And if ‖a man purchase of the Levites, then the house that was sold, and the city of his possession, shall go out in *the year of* jubile: for the houses of the cities of the Levites *are* their possession among the children of Israel.

‖ Or, one *of the Levites redeem* them.

34 But the field of the suburbs of their cities may not be sold; for it *is* their perpetual possession.

35 ¶ And if thy brother be waxen poor, and †fallen in decay with thee; then thou shalt †relieve him: *yea, though he be* a stranger, or a sojourner; that he may live with thee.

† Heb. *his hand faileth.*
† Heb. *strengthen.*

---

28. *in the jubile it shall go out*] *i.e.* it shall be set free in the Jubilee.

30. *not go out*] The reason of this law may have been that most of the houses in cities were occupied by artificers and traders whose wealth did not consist in lands, many of whom were foreigners who could not hold land in the country (Bähr).

32—34. The purchaser of a Levite's house was in fact only in the condition of a tenant at will, while the fields attached to the Levitical cities could never be alienated, even for a time.

32. *Notwithstanding the cities*, &c.] Rather, **And concerning the cities of the Levites, the houses, &c.** See Num. xxxv. 2; Josh. xxi. 2 sq.

33. *if a man purchase of the Levites*] More properly, **If one of the Levites redeems a house in the city**, &c. See next note. The meaning appears to be, if a Levite (in accordance with the law in *v.* 25) redeems a house which has been sold to a person of a different tribe by another Levite, it is to revert in the Jubilee to the latter Levite as its original possessor. (So Rosenmüller, De Wette, Kranold, Herxheimer, &c.) The verse thus secures the original tenure to each individual Levite.—Our version follows the Targums, Saadia, and several other Jewish authorities, and has some support from the LXX. and the Syriac.—The Vulgate inserts a negative, "Si redemptæ (sc. ædes) non fuerint." This of course involves a different reading of the Hebrew text: it is preferred by Ewald and Knobel.

the house...and the city of his possession] These words seem to be a hendiadys for **the house in the city of his possession.** So LXX., Kranold, de Wette, &c.

Regarding the application of the law of Jubilee to lands dedicated to the service of the Sanctuary, see xxvii. 16—25.

The law of Servitude. 35—55.

In connection with the bearing of the Jubilee on personal freedom, the general law regarding servants is here set forth. The principle which was to limit and modify the servitude of Hebrew servants is expressed and repeated *vv.* 38, 42, 55.

35. This verse might rather be rendered, **And if thy brother** (an Israelite) **becomes poor and falls into decay with thee, thou shalt assist him and let him live with thee like a resident foreigner.** So the LXX, the Targums, the Vulgate, Saadia, Luther, Knobel, Luzzatto, &c. Though he had parted with his land he was not to be regarded as an outcast, but was to be treated with the same respect and consideration as a resident foreigner who, like him, could pos-

[b] Exod. 22. 25. Deut. 23. 19. Prov. 28. 8. Ezek. 18. 8. & 22. 12.

36 [b]Take thou no usury of him,
or increase: but fear thy God; that
thy brother may live with thee.
37 Thou shalt not give him thy
money upon usury, nor lend him thy
victuals for increase.
38 I *am* the LORD your God,
which brought you forth out of the
land of Egypt, to give you the land
of Canaan, *and* to be your God.

[c] Exod. 21. 2. Deut. 15. 12. Jer. 34. 14.

39 ¶ And [c]if thy brother *that*
dwelleth by thee be waxen poor, and
be sold unto thee; thou shalt not
†compel him to serve as a bondservant:
40 *But* as an hired servant, *and* as
a sojourner, he shall be with thee,
and shall serve thee unto the year of
jubile:

† Heb. *serve thyself with him with the service, &c.*

41 And *then* shall he depart from
thee, *both* he and his children with
him, and shall return unto his own
family, and unto the possession of his
fathers shall he return.
42 For they *are* my servants,
which I brought forth out of the land
of Egypt: they shall not be sold †as
bondmen.

† Heb. *with the sale of a bondman.*

43 [d]Thou shalt not rule over him
with rigour; but shalt fear thy God.

[d] Ephes. 6. 9. Col. 4. 1.

44 Both thy bondmen, and thy
bondmaids, which thou shalt have,
shall be of the heathen that are round
about you; of them shall ye buy
bondmen and bondmaids.
45 Moreover of the children of the
strangers that do sojourn among you,
of them shall ye buy, and of their families that *are* with you, which they
begat in your land: and they shall be
your possession.
46 And ye shall take them as an
inheritance for your children after
you, to inherit *them for* a possession;
†they shall be your bondmen for ever:
but over your brethren the children
of Israel, ye shall not rule one over
another with rigour.

† Heb. *ye shall serve yourselves with them.*

47 ¶ And if a sojourner or stranger
†wax rich by thee, and thy brother
that dwelleth by him wax poor, and
sell himself unto the stranger *or* sojourner by thee, or to the stock of
the stranger's family:
48 After that he is sold he may be

† Heb. *his hand obtain, &c.*

---

sess no land, but could accumulate property and live in comfort as a free man. See on Ex. xx. 10; Lev. xvi. 29. In *vv.* 39, 40 the same rule is addressed to masters in reference to Hebrews who had become their bond-servants. Cf. xix. 10, xxiii. 22, xxiv. 22; Neh. v. 1—13.

37. *lend him thy victuals for increase*] *i.e.* supply him with food for thy own profit.

39, 40. The law had already provided that no Israelite who had become bound to serve another could be forced to continue more than six years in servitude, Ex. xxi. 2. But in the year of Jubilee every Hebrew servant could claim liberty for himself and his family, without respect to his period of service, at the same time that he recovered his share in the land (*v.* 41). See on Ex. xxi. 5, 6. The law appears harmoniously to supplement the earlier one in Exodus. It was another check applied periodically to the tyranny of the rich. Cf. Jer. xxxiv. 8—17. Ewald gratuitously considers that the earlier law had become obsolete before the law of Jubilee was promulgated. 'Altert.' p. 421.

43. *fear thy God*] Jehovah was the Lord and Master of His people. To treat a Hebrew as a slave was therefore to interfere with the rights of Jehovah. Cf. Rom. xiv. 4.

44—46. Property in foreign slaves, who might be handed down from father to son, is here distinctly permitted. It was a patriarchal custom. See Gen. xvii. 12. Such slaves might be captives taken in war (Num. xxxi. 6 sq.; Deut. xx. 14), those consigned to slavery for their crimes, or those purchased of foreign slave-dealers. The price of a slave is supposed to have varied from thirty to fifty shekels. See Ex. xxi. 32; Lev. xxvii. 3, 4; Zech. xi. 12, 13; Matt. xxvi. 15. It was the object of Moses, not at once to do away with slavery, but to discourage and to mitigate it. Kidnapping was punished with death (Ex. xxi. 16). The slave was encouraged to become a proselyte (Ex. xii. 44). He might be set free (Ex. xxi. 26, 27). Special rules were laid down for the security of his life and limbs (Ex. xxi. 20, 21, 26, 27). The Law would not suffer it to be forgotten that the slave is a man, and protected him in every way that was possible at the time against the injustice or cruelty of his master. See notes on Ex. xxi.

46. *your bondmen for ever*] *i.e.* they were not necessarily to be released in the Sabbatical year nor the Jubilee.

47—54. *a sojourner or stranger*] Rather, **a foreigner who has settled among**

redeemed again; one of his brethren
may redeem him:
49 Either his uncle, or his uncle's
son, may redeem him, or *any* that is
nigh of kin unto him of his family
may redeem him; or if he be able, he
may redeem himself.
50 And he shall reckon with him
that bought him from the year that
he was sold to him unto the year of
jubile: and the price of his sale shall
be according unto the number of
years, according to the time of an
hired servant shall it be with him.
51 If *there be* yet many years *behind*, according unto them he shall give
again the price of his redemption out
of the money that he was bought for.
52 And if there remain but few
years unto the year of jubile, then he
shall count with him, *and* according
unto his years shall he give him again
the price of his redemption.
53 *And* as a yearly hired servant
shall he be with him: *and the other*
shall not rule with rigour over him
in thy sight.
54 And if he be not redeemed ‖ in
these *years*, then he shall go out in
the year of jubile, *both* he, and his
children with him.
55 For unto me the children of
Israel *are* servants; they *are* my servants whom I brought forth out of
the land of Egypt: I *am* the LORD
your God.

‖ Or, *by these* means.

---

you. Ex. xx. 10; Lev. xvi. 29. So Knobel, Wogue, &c. The extreme period of servitude in this case was probably six years, as when the master was a Hebrew (Ex. xxi. 2).

54. *in these years*] More properly, **by one of these means.**

55. Cf. *vv.* 38, 42.

NOTES on CHAP. XXV.

I. ON THE SABBATICAL YEAR.

vv. 1—7.

In Exodus, the Sabbatical year is called "the seventh year" (xxiii. 10), and in Deuteronomy, "the year of release" (xxxi. 10, cf. xv. 1). In this passage and in Exodus it is represented merely as a period of rest for the land, during which the ownership of the soil was practically in abeyance and the chance produce (which in the climate of the Holy Land must have been very considerable) was at the service of all comers. There was to be neither sowing nor reaping, neither planting, pruning, nor gathering. What Day and Night are to man and beast, that Summer and Winter are to the soil; and hence as man had his Sabbath every seventh day, so the land was to have its Sabbath every seventh year. See on Ex. xxiii. 11. But we are informed in Deuteronomy xv. that all debtors were to be released from their obligation. Whether their debts were wholly cancelled, or the claims upon them were only suspended during the year, see notes *in loc.*

The rest is here spoken of simply as a rest of the land. It must have debarred a great part of the people from their accustomed occupations. But there appears to be no sufficient reason to suppose, as some have done, that the rest, or the recreation, of the people formed any essential part of the design of the Legislator. One effect of the institution may indeed have been to keep alive and encourage occupations which were not purely agricultural, such as trade, various kinds of handicraft, the chase and the care of cattle. It is also (as Carpzov and Ewald have conjectured) not improbable that schools, and instruction of all kinds both for young and old, were carried on during the year with more than ordinary energy and system. The reading of the Law at the feast of Tabernacles in every Sabbatical year may have been connected with this. See Deut. xxxi. 10—13.

But the great material advantage of the institution must have been the increased fertility of the soil from its lying fallow one year out of seven, at a time when neither the rotation of crops nor the art of manuring were understood. It must also have kept up a salutary habit of economy in the storing of corn. Cf. Gen. xli. 48—56. Its great Spiritual lesson was that there was no such thing as absolute ownership in the land vested in any man, that the soil was the property of Jehovah, that it was to be held in trust for Him, and not to be abused by overworking, but to be made the most of for the good of every creature which dwelt upon it. Theodoret, 'Quæst.' 35. The land was Jehovah's (*v.* 23), and the declared purpose of the law is explained in the words that it should "rest and lie still, that the poor of the people may eat, and what they leave the beasts of the field shall eat." Ex. xxiii. 11. The weekly Sabbath bore witness to the equality of the people in regard to the Covenant with Jehovah, of which the whole Sabbatical institution was the symbol (see Note on the Sabbath-day, Ex. xx. § vi.): the restored distribution of the Land in the year of Jubilee testified that every Israelite had originally an equal claim to the possession of the Land of Promise (see the following Note): but the Sabbatical rest of the soil bore even a broader meaning; it declared that every dweller in the land, the hired servant, the foreigner, the cattle, even the wild animals, had an acknowledged claim of their own on its produce. The different Sabbatical observances of the Law thus concur in pointing to that state of things which would have followed the first Sabbath of Creation, had not sin and its consequences brought disorder amongst the creatures of God. Gen. i. 31.

It would appear from 2 Chr. xxxvi. 20, 21, that the Sabbatical year was neglected during seventy sabbatical cycles, 490 years, which must have included the period of the Monarchy. Cf. Lev. xxvi. 34, 35, 43, where the obligation to maintain the institution is made the subject of solemn admonition. But after the Captivity, there are found several historical notices which imply its observance. The Jews were exempted from tribute in the Sabbatical year by Alexander the Great (Jos. 'Ant.' XI. 8. § 6), and by Julius Cæsar (Jos. 'Ant.' XIV. 10. § 6). The inhabitants of Bethsura could not stand out when besieged by Antiochus Epiphanes, because they had no store of provisions owing to the Sabbatical year (1 Macc. vi. 49), and the inhabitants of Jerusalem suffered from the like cause when they were besieged by Herod (Jos. 'Ant.' XIV. 16. § 2, XV. 1. § 2).

The originality of the Sabbatical year, as well as of the year of Jubilee, is very striking. There seems to be nothing like either of them to be fairly traced in any ancient legislation. See the following Note.

II. On the Jubilee.

vv. 8—33.

Josephus ('Ant.' XIII. 2. § 3) says that debts were remitted in the Jubilee as they were in the year of Release. Deut. xv. 2. But there is no hint of this in the Law. Some of the Rabbinists expressly deny it.

There is no direct historical statement of the observance of the Jubilee on any one occasion, either in the Old Testament or elsewhere. The only mention of it in the Law, except in this chapter and in xxvii. 16—25, is in the narrative regarding the daughters of Zelophehad, Num. xxxvi. 4. See note. There appears to be reference to its operation in Ruth iv. 3 sq. But in the deficiency of more direct testimony, some critics have doubted (Michaelis, Winer), and others have denied (Kranold, Hupfeld), that it was ever actually observed. The Rabbinists however, and Josephus ('Ant.' III. 12. § 3), affirm that it was observed up to the Captivity, and some of them say that it was restored after the return. The statement of Diodorus Siculus that the Jews could not sell their estates (Tom. II. p. 544), has been quoted to prove that it was maintained in operation in his time. Ewald and others have urged that nothing is proved by the absence of any distinct statement regarding its observance, and that the allusions to it in the Prophets are sufficiently clear and numerous to show that the people were practically familiar with its operation. See Isa. lxi. 1, 2; cf. v. 7—10; Ezek. xlvi. 17; Jer. xi. 23, xxiii. 12, xlviii. 44. In these passages in Jeremiah it is assumed, on what seems to be probable ground, that the "year of visitation" means the law of the Jubilee enforced in the restoration of ill-gotten gains to those from whom they had been taken. In Jer. xxxii. 6—12, Ewald traces the restored working of the law which had taken place in the reign of Josiah. 'Alterthümer,' p. 424. If there is any reference to the Jubilee in Neh. v. 1—13 (especially compare *vv.* 3, 4 with *v.* 11), the institution must have been recognized and partially reestablished immediately after the return from the Captivity.

There appears to be no trace of anything like the restoration of family estates in the Jubilee in the customs of other ancient nations. Strabo's statement regarding the Dalmatians (to which some have referred) is merely that they redistributed their lands every eighth year (lib. VII. p. 315). Regarding the statement of Plutarch, that Lycurgus made an equal division of the land amongst the Spartans, Mr Grote seems to prove clearly that it was a mistake. 'History of Greece,' Vol. II. p. 530. Taking it as a whole, the Jubilee as instituted by Moses appears to be without parallel in the history of the world.

Looking at the law of the Jubilee from a simply practical point of view, its operation must have tended to remedy those evils which are always growing up in the ordinary conditions of human society. It prevented the permanent accumulation of land in the hands of a few, and periodically raised those whom fault or misfortune had sunk into poverty to a position of competency. It must also have tended to keep alive family feeling, and helped to preserve the family genealogies. It has been conjectured that the public tables of genealogy were corrected in each Jubilee year, in order to meet the dying out of some families and the multiplication of others (Michaelis, Ewald).

But in its more special character, as a law given by Jehovah to His peculiar people, it was a standing lesson to those who would rightly regard it, on the terms upon which the enjoyment of the Land of Promise had been conferred upon them. All the land belonged to Jehovah as its supreme Lord, every Israelite as His vassal belonged to Him. The voice of the Jubilee horns, twice in every century, must have proclaimed the equitable and beneficent social order appointed for the people, as the silver trumpets of the Sanctuary had ten days before (if we may trust the tradition; see on xxiii. 24), called to mind the perfect physical order of the world on the eve of the first Sabbath, when "God saw everything that he had made, and behold it was very good." They who saw that all physical and social order must be the reflection of spiritual realities, who waited for "the consolation of Israel," were so led to look for that acceptable year of Jehovah which was to bring comfort to all that mourned, in which the slavery of sin was to be abolished and the true liberty of God's children was to be proclaimed. Luke ii. 25; Isa. lxi. 2; Luke iv. 19; Acts iii. 21; Rom. viii. 19—23; 1 Pet. i. 3, 4.

CHAPTER XXVI.

1 *Of idolatry.* 2 *Religiousness.* 3 *A blessing to them that keep the commandments.* 14 *A curse to those that break them.* 40 *God promiseth to remember them that repent.*

YE shall make you [a] no idols nor
graven image, neither rear you
up a ‖ standing image, neither shall
ye set up *any* ‖ image of stone in
your land, to bow down unto it: for
I *am* the LORD your God.

[a] Exod. 20. 4. Deut. 5. 8. & 16. 22. Psal. 97. 7.
‖ Or, *pillar.*
‖ Or, *figured stone.* Heb. *a stone of picture.*

2 ¶ [b] Ye shall keep my sabbaths,
and reverence my sanctuary: I *am*
the LORD.
3 ¶ [c] If ye walk in my statutes,
and keep my commandments, and do
them;
4 Then I will give you rain in
due season, and the land shall yield
her increase, and the trees of the field
shall yield their fruit.
5 And your threshing shall reach

[b] chap. 19. 30.
[c] Deut. 28. 1.

CHAPTER XXVI.

This chapter appears to contain a formal conclusion of the Book of Leviticus, the twenty-seventh chapter being a distinct Appendix.

COMMAND TO MAINTAIN THE PUBLIC WORSHIP OF JEHOVAH.

According to the Jewish arrangement, in both the Hebrew text and the Targums, these two verses form part of the preceding chapter. Their connection either with chap. xxv. or with chap. xxvi. is not very close. They might form a section by themselves.

1. *idols*] Literally, *things of nought.* xix. 4; Heb. *eleelim.* There appears to have been a play on the similarity in sound of this word to *Elohim.* Cf. 1 Cor. viii. 4.

graven image] See on Exod. xx. 4.

standing image] Either an upright statue, or a pillar, such as an obelisk or a Celtic menhir. The same word denotes simply a memorial stone. Gen. xxviii. 18, xxxv. 14; Ex. xxiv. 4. But here and elsewhere it expresses a stone set up for an idolatrous purpose. Ex. xxiii. 24, xxxiv. 13; Deut. vii. 5, xvi. 22; 2 K. iii. 2, &c.

image of stone] The phrase is not found elsewhere.—Other names for objects of false worship occur in *v.* 30.

2. Repeated from xix. 30. The public worship of Jehovah required, first, the exclusion of all visible symbols of deity as well as of all idolatrous objects, and next, the keeping holy of the times and the place appointed by the Law for His formal service. The word Sabbaths must here include the whole of the set times. See xxiii. 3. Note on the Sabbath-day, § VI. Ex. xx. This and the previous verse include the substance of the first four commandments of the Decalogue.

PROMISES AND THREATENINGS. 3—45.

As "the Book of the Covenant" (Ex. xx. 22—xxiii. 33) concludes with promises and warnings (Ex. xxiii. 20—33), so does this collection of laws contained in the Book of Leviticus. But the former passage relates to the conquest of the Land of Promise, this one to the subsequent history of the nation. The longer similar passage in Deuteronomy (xxvii.—xxx.) is marked by broader and deeper promises and denunciations having immediate reference not only to outward consequences, but to the spiritual death incurred by transgressing the Divine will.

Promises for Obedience. 3—13.

4. *rain in due season*] The periodical rains, on which the fertility of the Holy Land so much depends, are here spoken of. There are two wet seasons, called in Scripture the former and the latter rain. Deut. xi. 14; Jer. v. 24; Joel ii. 23; Hos. vi. 3; Jam. v. 7. The former or Autumn rain commences after the autumnal equinox and falls in heavy showers in November and December. Then generally follows a period with occasional light showers, and in March the latter or Spring rain comes on, which is precarious in quantity and duration, and rarely lasts more than two days. Job xxix. 23; Prov. xvi. 15; Robinson, 'Phy-

unto the vintage, and the vintage
shall reach unto the sowing time: and
ye shall eat your bread to the full,
d Job 11. 19. and [d]dwell in your land safely.
6 And I will give peace in the
e Job 11. 19. land, and [e]ye shall lie down, and none
† Heb. *cause to cease.* shall make *you* afraid: and I will †rid
evil beasts out of the land, neither
shall the sword go through your land.
7 And ye shall chase your enemies, and they shall fall before you
by the sword.
f Josh. 23. 10. 8 And [f]five of you shall chase an
hundred, and an hundred of you shall
put ten thousand to flight: and your
enemies shall fall before you by the
sword.
9 For I will have respect unto
you, and make you fruitful, and multiply you, and establish my covenant
with you.
10 And ye shall eat old store, and
bring forth the old because of the
new.

11 [g]And I will set my tabernacle g Ezek. 37. 26.
among you: and my soul shall not
abhor you.
12 [h]And I will walk among you, h 2 Cor. 6. 16.
and will be your God, and ye shall
be my people.
13 I *am* the LORD your God,
which brought you forth out of the
land of Egypt, that ye should not be
their bondmen; and I have broken
the bands of your yoke, and made
you go upright.
14 ¶ [i]But if ye will not hearken i Deut. 28. 15.
unto me, and will not do all these Lam. 2. 17.
commandments; Mal. 2. 2.
15 And if ye shall despise my statutes, or if your soul abhor my judgments, so that ye will not do all my
commandments, *but* that ye break my
covenant:
16 I also will do this unto you; I
will even appoint †over you terror, † Heb. *upon you.*
consumption, and the burning ague,
that shall consume the eyes, and

---

sical Geog. of the H. L.' p. 263; Tristram, 'Nat. Hist.' p. 30 sq.

5. Cf. xxv. 21, 22; Amos ix. 13.

safely] That is, in security from famine, xxv. 19; Joel ii. 19, 26.

6. Cf. Job xi. 18, 19; Ps. cxlvii. 14; Ezek. xxxiv. 25—28.

lie down] *i.e.* repose in comfort.

evil beasts] *i.e.* beasts of prey and destructive vermin. Cf. Isa. xxxv. 9; Ezek. v. 17, xiv. 15.

sword] Ezek. xiv. 17, xxi. 3, 4.

8. *five of you shall chase*] A proverbial mode of expression for superiority in warlike prowess. Deut. xxxii. 30; Josh. xxiii. 10; Isa. xxx. 17.

9. *establish my covenant*] All material blessings were to be regarded in the light of seals of the "everlasting covenant." Gen. xvii. 4—8.

10. *bring forth the old because of the new*] Rather, **clear away the old before the new**; that is, in order to make room for the latter. Cf. xxv. 22.

11. *my tabernacle*] A more suitable rendering here would be **my abode**. Heb. *mishkān*. See on Ex. xxvi. 1.

12, 13. Ch. xxv. 38; Ex. vi. 6—8, xxix. 45, 46.

13. *yoke*] Jer. ii. 20; Ezek. xxxiv. 27.

The Five Warnings for Disobedience. 14—32.

16, 17. The ministers of chastisement which Jehovah threatens to appoint over his people if they break the covenant are (1) Disease, (2) Famine, (3) Defeat.

16. *terror*] Literally, *trembling*. The same Hebrew word is rendered *trouble*, Ps. lxxviii. 33; Isa. lxv. 23. It can hardly be here, as Knobel and Keil take it, a general word for *the objects of terror*, specified in the words that follow it. It seems rather to denote that terrible affliction, an anxious temperament, the mental state ever at war with Faith and Hope. This might well be placed at the head of the visitations on a backslider who had broken the Covenant with his God. "The wicked flee when no man pursueth: but the righteous are bold as a lion." Prov. xxviii. 1; cf. *v.* 17; Job xxiv. 17; Ps. xxiii. 4.

consumption, and the burning ague] The Hebrew words here used occur nowhere else except Deut. xxviii. 22. The first comes from a root signifying *to waste away;* the latter, from one signifying *to kindle a fire.* Consumption is common in Egypt and some parts of Asia Minor, but it is more rare in Syria. Fevers of different kinds are the commonest of all diseases in Syria and all the neighbouring countries. The terms are probably to be taken in a general sense for any wasting disease and any inflammatory disease. **Fever** (as in Deut. xxviii. 22) would be better than *burning ague*, being less specific. The oppo-

cause sorrow of heart: and ye shall sow your seed in vain, for your enemies shall eat it.

17 And I will set my face against you, and ye shall be slain before your enemies: they that hate you shall reign over you; and [k] ye shall flee when none pursueth you.

[k] Prov. 28. 1.

18 And if ye will not yet for all this hearken unto me, then I will punish you seven times more for your sins.

19 And I will break the pride of your power; and I will make your heaven as iron, and your earth as brass:

20 And your strength shall be spent in vain: for your land shall not yield her increase, neither shall the trees of the land yield their fruits.

21 ¶ And if ye walk ‖ contrary unto me, and will not hearken unto me; I will bring seven times more plagues upon you according to your sins.

‖ Or, *at all adventures with me*, and so ver. 24.

22 I will also send wild beasts among you, which shall rob you of your children, and destroy your cattle, and make you few in number; and your *high* ways shall be desolate.

23 And if ye will not be reformed by me by these things, but will walk contrary unto me;

24 [l] Then will I also walk contrary unto you, and will punish you yet seven times for your sins.

[l] 2 Sam. 22. 27. Psal. 18 26.

25 And I will bring a sword upon you, that shall avenge the quarrel of *my* covenant: and when ye are gathered together within your cities, I will send the pestilence among you; and ye shall be delivered into the hand of the enemy.

26 *And* when I have broken the staff of your bread, ten women shall bake your bread in one oven, and they shall deliver *you* your bread again by weight: and ye shall eat, and not be satisfied.

27 And if ye will not for all this hearken unto me, but walk contrary unto me;

---

site promise to the threat contained in this verse is given Ex. xv. 26, xxiii. 25.

consume the eyes] See 1 Sam. ii. 33; Job xi. 20.

cause sorrow of heart] Literally, *cause the soul to pine away.*

your enemies shall eat it] Cf. Deut. xxviii. 33, 51; Job xxxi. 8; Jer. v. 17, &c.

17. *they that hate you*, &c.] Cf. Ps. cvi. 41.

ye shall flee when none pursueth you] This may be connected with "the terror" in *v.* 16; see note: cf. Prov. xxviii. 1.

18—43. Four further stages of severity are mentioned in succession in these verses which were to be reserved. Cf. *vv.* 18, 21, 24, 28.

18. *for all this*] *i.e.* for all the afflictions in *vv.* 16, 17.

seven times] The sabbatical number is here proverbially used to remind the people of the Covenant. Cf. Gen. iv. 15, 24; Ps. lxxix. 12; Prov. xxiv. 16; Luke xvii. 4.

19, 20. THE SECOND WARNING is utter sterility of the soil. Cf. Ezek. xxxiii. 28, xxxvi. 34, 35.

21, 22. THE THIRD WARNING is the multiplication of destructive animals, &c. Cf. Ezek. v. 17, xiv. 15; Judg. v. 6, 7; Isa. xxxiii. 8.

22. *which shall rob you of your children*] Literally, **make you childless.**

23—26. THE FOURTH WARNING. Jehovah now places Himself as it were in a hostile position towards His rebellious people. He will avenge the outraged cause of His Covenant, by the sword, pestilence, famine and captivity.

26. *And when I have broken*, &c.] Our translators should not have inserted the copulative here, and the preceding verse should terminate only with a semicolon, so as to be more closely connected with this one.—"To break the staff of bread," was a proverbial expression for cutting off the supply of bread, the staff of life. Ps. cv. 16; Ezek. iv. 16, v. 16, xiv. 13, cf. Isa. iii. 1. The supply was to be so reduced that one oven would suffice for baking the bread made by ten women for ten families, and when made it was to be dealt out in sparing rations by weight. See 2 K. vi. 25; Isa. iii. 1; Jer. xiv. 18; Lam. iv. 9; Ezek. iv. 16, v. 12; Hos. iv. 10; Mic. vi. 14.

27—33. THE FIFTH WARNING. If they should still persist in their sinful course they should be so reduced by famine that they should eat the flesh of their children, *v.* 29. See 2 K. vi. 28, 29; Jer. xix. 8, 9; Lam. ii.

28 Then I will walk contrary unto
you also in fury; and I, even I, will
chastise you seven times for your sins.
29 [m]And ye shall eat the flesh of
your sons, and the flesh of your
daughters shall ye eat.
30 And I will destroy your high
places, and [n]cut down your images,
and cast your carcases upon the carcases of your idols, and my soul shall
abhor you.
31 And I will make your cities
waste, and bring your sanctuaries unto desolation, and I will not smell the
savour of your sweet odours.
32 And I will bring the land into
desolation: and your enemies which
dwell therein shall be astonished at
it.
33 And I will scatter you among
the heathen, and will draw out a
sword after you: and your land shall
be desolate, and your cities waste.

[m] Deut. 28. 53.

[n] 2 Chron. 34. 7.

34 Then shall the land enjoy her
sabbaths, as long as it lieth desolate,
and ye *be* in your enemies' land; *even*
then shall the land rest, and enjoy her
sabbaths.
35 As long as it lieth desolate it
shall rest; because it did not rest in
your sabbaths, when ye dwelt upon it.
36 And upon them that are left
alive of you I will send a faintness
into their hearts in the lands of their
enemies; and the sound of a †shaken
leaf shall chase them; and they shall
flee, as fleeing from a sword; and they
shall fall when none pursueth.
37 And they shall fall one upon
another, as it were before a sword,
when none pursueth: and ye shall
have no power to stand before your
enemies.
38 And ye shall perish among the
heathen, and the land of your enemies shall eat you up.

† Heb. *driven.*

20, iv. 10; Ezek. v. 10; Joseph. 'B. J.' v. 10. § 3; cf. Deut. xxviii. 53:—the abominations of idolatry were to be destroyed in the land, and the carcases of their worshippers should be cast upon them, *v.* 30; see 2 K. xxiii. 16; Ezek. vi. 4:—their cities should be laid waste, the Sanctuary itself with its sacred contents should be destroyed and the savour of their sacrifices would be rejected, *v.* 31; see 2 K. xxv. 9; Ps. lxxiv. 6, 7:—the land should be brought to such entire desolation, that their enemies themselves should be astonished at it, wondering at the great effect of their own hostile efforts, and the people themselves should be scattered among the heathen, *vv.* 32, 33; see Ps. xliv. 11; Jer. ix. 16 sq.; Ezek. v. 1—17; cf. Deut. iv. 27; xxviii. 37, 64.

27. *for all this*] See *v.* 18.

30. *high places*] See Note at the end of the chapter.

your images] The original word (*chammānim*) is derived from one of the names of the sun, and in the margin of our Bible it is rendered *sun images*, 2 Chro. xiv. 5; Isa. xvii. 8; Ezek. vi. 4, &c. It was rightly thus taken by the older commentators to denote monuments of some kind dedicated to the sun. Gesenius ('Thes.' p. 489) seems to prove satisfactorily from Phœnician inscriptions that the word was commonly applied to images of Baal and Astarte, the god of the sun and the goddess of the moon. This exactly explains 2 Chro. xxxiv. 4 sq.

idols] Heb. word (*gillūlim*) literally means things which could be rolled about, such as a block of wood or a lump of dirt. It was no doubt a name given in derision. Cf. Isa. xl. 20, xliv. 19; 2 K. i. 2. The word idol, like image, is used by our translators to render several different Hebrew words with distinct meanings. See *v.* 1; Deut. xxix. 17; 1 K. xv. 12; 2 Chro. xv. 8; Zech. x. 2, &c.

31. *sanctuaries*] The holy places in the Tabernacle and the Temple. Ps. lxviii. 35. Cf. Ps. lxxiv. 7.

I will not smell the savour, &c.] See i. 9. Cf. Isa. i. 13.

Results of the Visitations upon the Land and the People. 33—38.

33—38. One immediate consequence of the scattering of the people among the heathen would be that the land would be left to rest, and so far would expiate the long-continued breach of the Sabbatical law, to which the Legislator looked forward, *vv.* 34, 35. See on xxv. 6. Cf. 2 Chro. xxxvi. 21.—A connection may possibly here be traced with *v.* 2 of this chapter.

35. More literally: **All the days of its desolation shall it rest that time which it rested not in your Sabbaths while ye dwelt upon it.** That is, the periods of rest of which the land had been deprived would be made up to it.

38. *the land of your enemies shall eat you up*] Num. xiii. 32; Ezek. xxxvi. 13.

39 And they that are left of you
shall pine away in their iniquity in
your enemies' lands; and also in the
iniquities of their fathers shall they
pine away with them.
40 If they shall confess their iniquity, and the iniquity of their fathers, with their trespass which they
trespassed against me, and that also
they have walked contrary unto me;
41 And *that* I also have walked
contrary unto them, and have brought
them into the land of their enemies;
if then their uncircumcised hearts be
humbled, and they then accept of the
punishment of their iniquity:
42 Then will I remember my covenant with Jacob, and also my covenant with Isaac, and also my covenant
with Abraham will I remember; and
I will remember the land.
43 The land also shall be left of
them, and shall enjoy her sabbaths,
while she lieth desolate without them:
and they shall accept of the punishment of their iniquity: because, even
because they despised my judgments,
and because their soul abhorred my
statutes.
44 And yet for all that, when they
be in the land of their enemies, [o] I will [o] Deut. 4.
not cast them away, neither will I 31. Rom. 11.
abhor them, to destroy them utterly, 26.
and to break my covenant with them:
for I *am* the LORD their God.
45 But I will for their sakes remember the covenant of their ancestors, whom I brought forth out of the
land of Egypt in the sight of the
heathen, that I might be their God:
I *am* the LORD.
46 These *are* the statutes and
judgments and laws, which the LORD
made between him and the children
of Israel in mount Sinai by the hand
of Moses.

The Covenant may still be restored.
39—45.

39. *iniquity*] The Hebrew word is rendered "iniquity" here, in *v.* 40, v. 1, 17, xvi. 22, &c.; "punishment of iniquity," in *vv.* 41, 43; and "punishment" in Gen. iv. 13, &c. The meaning here is, **in the punishment of their iniquity**, and, in the next clause, **in the punishment of the iniquity of their fathers.** In the next verse the same Heb. word is properly represented by "iniquity." Our translators have in several places put one of the English words in the text and the other in the margin. Gen. iv. 13, xix. 15; 2 K. vii. 9; Ps. lxix. 27, &c. The primary meaning of the Hebrew word is *iniquity*, but the language of Scripture does not make that trenchant division between *sin* and *punishment* which we are accustomed to do. Sin is its own punishment, having in itself, from its very commencement, the germ of death. "Sin, when it is finished, bringeth forth death." Jam. i. 15; Rom. ii. 5, v. 12. See on *v.* 41.

iniquities of their fathers] See on Ex. xx. 5.

40. *trespass*] The Hebrew word (*ma'al*, see on v. 15) signifies an injury inflicted on the rights of a person, as distinguished from a sin or iniquity regarded as an outrage of the Divine law. Every wrong act is of course both a sin and a trespass against God. In this place Jehovah takes the breach of the Covenant as a personal trespass.

41. *uncircumcised hearts*] The outward sign of the Covenant might be preserved, but the answering grace in the heart would be wanting. Acts vii. 51; Rom. ii. 28, 29; Jer. vi. 10, ix. 26; cf. Col. ii. 11.

accept of the punishment of their iniquity] Literally, *enjoy their iniquity*. The figure is a bold one, but not difficult of explanation, if we keep in view the full sense of the Hebrew word for *iniquity*. See on *v.* 39. The word here and in *v.* 43 rendered "accept" in this phrase, is the same as is rendered "enjoy" in the expression, "the land shall enjoy her sabbaths." The antithesis in *v.* 43 is this: *The land shall enjoy her sabbaths—and they shall enjoy the punishment of their iniquity.* The meaning is, that the land being desolate shall have the blessing of rest, and they having repented shall have the blessing of chastisement. So the LXX and Syriac. The feelings of a devout captive Israelite are beautifully expressed in Tobit xiii. 1—18.

44, 45. Cf. Jer. xxx. 10—24.

46. These words are generally taken as concluding the Book of Leviticus. See preliminary note. It has, however, been doubted whether this verse does not, in a stricter sense, answer to xxv. 1, so as to indicate that chapters xxv. and xxvi. form a section by themselves. Some suppose that this may add point to the fact that the neglect of the Sabbatical year is the most prominent subject of admonition in this chapter, while the rules for its observance are a chief topic in ch. xxv.

NOTFS on Chap. xxvi.

I. On the High Places.

v. 30.

The name "High places" exactly represents the Hebrew word (במות, *bāmōth*) according to its etymology, and agrees with the Vulgate and the Targums. But the LXX. and the old Italic here and elsewhere in the Pentateuch have στῆλαι and *tituli* (monuments). In the Historical Books, however, the LXX. use τὰ ὑψηλά or τὰ ὕψη, and in the Prophets, βωμοί. The other ancient versions generally have words answering to *altars*, or *fanes*. There is no doubt that the word here denotes elevated spots dedicated to false worship (see Deut. xii. 2), and especially, it would seem, to that of Baal (Num. xxii. 41; Josh. xiii. 17). Such spots were however employed and approved for the worship of Jehovah, not only before the building of the Temple, but afterwards. Judg. vi. 25, 26, xiii. 16—23; 1 S. vii. 10, xvi. 5; 1 K. iii. 2, xviii. 30; 2 K. xii. 3; 1 Chro. xxi. 26, &c. There seems to have been a widely spread tendency in early times to select hills as places for public devotion. Xen. 'Memorab.' III. 8. § 10; cf. Herodot. I. 131. The spots which have the oldest religious association in most regions are on elevated ground. The Acropolis and the Capitol are examples. Most druidical monuments are similarly situated. The three altars built by Abraham at Shechem, between Bethel and Ai, and at Mamre, appear to have been on heights, and so was the Temple. It must be evident that the High places which were denounced in the Law were those which had idolatrous or superstitious associations.

We may see how superstitious notions may be connected by those who profess a higher faith with spots once devoted to idolatry in such peoples as the Bretons in reference to their dolmens and menhirs. It is likely that the Israelites were in like manner led astray in reference to the places which had been dedicated by the old inhabitants of the Holy Land to heathen worship. See on xx. 2, and Note on the Groves, Ex. xxxiv. 13.

The High places in the Holy Land may thus have been divided into those dedicated to the worship of Jehovah, and those which had been dedicated to idols. It was of course contrary to the letter of the Law that sacrifice should be offered at any place except the national Sanctuary, whether it was the Tabernacle at Shiloh or the Temple at Jerusalem. But the restraint took effect only by degrees. The public worship of Jehovah was still permitted at the High places even by Kings who desired to serve Him. 2 K. xiv. 4, xv. 35; 2 Chro. xv. 17, &c. It would seem as if there was a constant struggle going on. The High places polluted by idol worship were of course to be wholly condemned. They were probably resorted to only to gratify a degraded superstition. See on xix. 31, xx. 2—5. The others might have been innocently used for prayer and religious teaching as the Synagogues were in a later age. But the temptation appears to have been too great for the temper of the people. They offered sacrifice and burnt incense on them; and hence thorough reformers of the national religion, such as Hezekiah and Josiah, removed the High places altogether. 2 K. xviii. 4, xxiii. 5.

II. On the Mosaic Origin of Chap. XXVI.

i. *Objections on the score of Style;* ii. *and of Subject matter.* iii. *Conjectural dates.* iv. *In what sense a Prophecy.* v. *Distinguishing character of the Mosaic Legislation.*

i. The late origin of this twenty-sixth chapter has been strongly urged, on the grounds of both its style and its subject-matter. That the style differs from that of the great part of the Book of Leviticus is obvious. But, without going into details, it may be asked whether its mode of expression, in its main features, does not resemble that Prophetic style which appears to have been common to all ages of Hebrew literature: and whether the two styles in Leviticus are more dissimilar than the different styles of many a writer, in various languages, who has had to write under different impulses and with different objects.

ii. As regards the argument from the subject-matter, it is mainly based upon *vv.* 34, 35, 43, in which it is declared that the land shall enjoy her Sabbaths, while the people are scattered among the heathen. It is assumed that Moses could not have foreseen that the Sabbatical year would be neglected, and that the passages in question could have been written only by one who had actually witnessed the shortcomings of the Israelites in this particular. It is urged that this is, of itself, sufficient to give to the entire paragraph (Lev. xxvi. 3—45) the stamp of a period much later than the Mosaic.

iii. A late writer considers that a clue is furnished to the date of the composition by a comparison of *v.* 30 with 2 K. xxiii. 14, 16. In the former we read, "And I will cast your carcases upon the carcases of your idols;" and in the latter it is said that Josiah "brake in pieces the images, and cut down the groves, and filled their places with the bones of men," and also that "he took the bones out of the sepulchres and burned them upon the altar, and polluted it." This "novel mode of pollution" is suppossd to have originated from reading the book found in the Temple by Hilkiah, 2 K. xxii. 8, which must have been the Pentateuch. The critic is therefore willing to admit that the chapter in question must have been written before the reign of Josiah: while from arguments derived mainly from the style, he would ascribe it to a writer who is supposed to have lived about A.C. 880.

But if the argument which has been stated is worth anything, it surely proves that the passage in Leviticus must have been written before the reign of Jeroboam (A.C. 976—955), when the man of God uttered the prediction that the altar in Bethel should be polluted in the very manner fulfilled by Josiah, 1 K. xiii. 2.

Ewald is inclined to place its date considerably lower, towards the end of the eighth or the beginning of the seventh century, but still long before the Captivity. ('Geschichte,' I. p. 156.)

All the reasoning advanced to prove the late date of the composition of this chapter assumes that the writer knew as matter of fact that the law of the Sabbatical year had been neglected, and that he put forth his admonition to the people in the guise of old threatenings and promises by the Legislator.

Now if we take the references to the neglect of the Sabbatical year as necessarily based upon existing fact, it must be fair that we should take in the same way the references to the scattering among the heathen *vv.* 32, 41, 44. It is not easy to see how any solid foundation can be obtained for the main argument for the lateness of the composition, unless we bring it down below the reign of Josiah to the period of the Captivity, A.C. 606. Neither of the dates which have been conjectured appears to be late enough to be in harmony with the theory upon which they are chiefly based.

iv. But the chapter is not to be taken as a foretelling, either real or pretended, of special facts. It is indeed an inspired Prophecy, in the true sense of the word, an utterance of the Spirit regarding the present and the future. But there seems to be no one point which renders it necessary for us to suppose that distinct occurrences of actual fact, either present or to come, were in the mind of the writer. The succession of visitations spoken of *vv.* 18—43 is (as Keil has observed) not to be regarded in a historical light, as setting forth occurrences in their order of time. Its object is rather to furnish illustrations of the idea of the Divine judgments unfolding themselves in a way naturally answering to the progressive development of sin. We know from the history that the disobedience of the nation did not go on without intermission. Periods of recovery intervened, so that renewed blessings alternated from time to time with fulfilled threatenings. But the Covenant was outraged more and more flagrantly, as each sinful period took its turn, until at last ungodliness gained the upper hand, and the full measure of punishment was poured out upon the reprobate race.

v. Moses knew the human heart, and he was acquainted with the temper and disposition of his own people. Like our Saviour Himself in delivering the Sermon on the mount, the Legislator knew that his words would be but imperfectly obeyed. He could not have been blind in this matter. Insight will always beget foresight. He knew that such a law as that of the Sabbatical year would run counter to the selfishness and avarice of the people. He expected the result which later writers had to record in history. He was not so ignorant of the position which the nation would hold, after his own work was done, in reference to the natural features of the Promised Land and in relation to the great neighbouring states, as to fail to foresee, in such outline as is here given, the manner in which their disobedience and degradation would be punished. Cf. on Ex. xxiii. 11, 20, 31.

The highest laws are not to be regarded as useless because they are certain to be generally neglected. The Hebrew Law in regard to sacrifices, attendances at the Temple and the Holy Convocations, was perhaps, even in ordinary times, as much neglected as the rules of the Christian Church are in our day. The proportion of Israelites who failed to maintain a strict observance of religious rites may have been as small as the proportion of baptized Christians who partake of the Holy Communion. The obligation in each case has the same sanction; the heart of man was not more amenable to it then than it is now. But the Law was not foiled of its purpose. It was intended to represent human duty in its relation to divine holiness, to show forth and reprove human weakness, not to stoop to it (Rom. vii. 10—14). Its requirements were not lowered to the probabilities of man's conduct. It was not, like the legislation of ordinary states, intended primarily to meet the exigencies of existing facts and to keep offenders in order. Its purpose was to help and instruct the best of the people, not merely to chastise the worst. Other legislators have taken their starting points from human facts: Moses took his from the character and purpose of God.

CHAPTER XXVII.

1 *He that maketh a singular vow must be the Lord's.* 2 *The estimation of the person.* 9 *Of a beast given by vow.* 14 *Of a house.* 16 *Of a field, and the redemption thereof.* 28 *No devoted thing may be redeemed.* 32 *The tithe may not be changed.*

AND the LORD spake unto Moses,
saying,
2 Speak unto the children of Israel,
and say unto them, When a man shall
make a singular vow, the persons *shall*
be for the LORD by thy estimation.

3 And thy estimation shall be of
the male from twenty years old even
unto sixty years old, even thy estimation shall be fifty shekels of silver,
after the shekel of the sanctuary.
4 And if it *be* a female, then thy
estimation shall be thirty shekels.
5 And if *it be* from five years old
even unto twenty years old, then thy
estimation shall be of the male twenty
shekels, and for the female ten shekels.
6 And if *it be* from a month old
even unto five years old, then thy
estimation shall be of the male five
shekels of silver, and for the female
thy estimation *shall be* three shekels
of silver.
7 And if *it be* from sixty years old
and above; if *it be* a male, then thy
estimation shall be fifteen shekels, and
for the female ten shekels.
8 But if he be poorer than thy estimation, then he shall present himself before the priest, and the priest
shall value him; according to his
ability that vowed shall the priest
value him.
9 And if *it be* a beast, whereof men
bring an offering unto the LORD, all
that *any man* giveth of such unto the
LORD shall be holy.
10 He shall not alter it, nor change
it, a good for a bad, or a bad for a
good: and if he shall at all change

CHAP. XXVII.

OF THE COMMUTATION OF VOWS AND DUES.

The position which this chapter holds after the formal conclusion, xxvi. 46, suggests that it is of a supplementary character. There seems however no reason to doubt its Mosaic origin.

The nature of a Vow is set forth Deut. xxiii. 21, 22: it was an obligation to Jehovah voluntarily incurred. Cf. Num. xxx. 2; Ps. xv. 4; Prov. xx. 25; Eccles. v. 4, 5. A broken Vow required a Sin-offering, Lev. v. 4—6. —The law for Vows made by women is given Num. xxx. 2—16.

The Commutation of Vows.

2—25.

Things of any kind which a man, under the impulse of religious feeling, either in the way of thankfulness for blessings received, or of supplication for something desired, had vowed to dedicate to the service of the Sanctuary, in the ordinary way, might be redeemed according to a fixed mode of valuation.

2—3. The meaning of the latter part of the second verse and the beginning of the third appears to be, **When a man makes a special vow which concerns thy valuation of persons to Jehovah, if thy estimation shall be of the male,** &c. The expression "thy estimation" is addressed either to Moses or to the priest (*v.* 12): it denoted a legal valuation. See next note.

2—8. The vow of a Person was perhaps most frequently made in cases of illness or danger. A man might dedicate himself, his wife, his child, or his bondservant, on condition of recovery or deliverance. This might have been an old custom; but the Law ordained that he who had taken such a vow should pay a sum of money to the Sanctuary, determined according to the age and sex of the person. That the redemption of the person in money was what the Law reckoned on in the kind of vow here spoken of, appears from the form of the expression (*v.* 2), and from the reduction of the ransom-money permitted to meet the circumstances of a poor man (*v.* 8). If the actual service of the individual had been contemplated, the poor man who had been dedicated would simply have had to do his work for the Sanctuary.—It would hence seem that there can be no reference here to such vows as Hannah's regarding her offspring (1 S. i. 11), or as that which Absalom pretended to have taken (2 S. xv. 8). It would, moreover, be contrary to the spirit of these, as well as of the Nazarite vow described Num. vi., that the option of commuting them should be allowed.

3—7. The relative values of the persons appear to be regulated according to an estimate of the probable value of their future work:—

	Male.	Female.	
From a month to five years	5	3	shekels.
From five years to twenty	20	10	,,
From forty years to sixty	50	30	,,
Sixty years and more	15	10	,,

Regarding the shekel of the sanctuary, see Ex. xxxviii. 24.

8. *if he be poorer than thy estimation*] **too poor (to pay) thy valuation.** Cf. v. 7, 11.

9—13. A clean animal which had been vowed was "holy" (*v.* 10), and could only be sacrificed. It could neither be redeemed nor changed. But an unclean animal, such as a camel or an ass, was either sold for the value which the priest set on it, or could be

beast for beast, then it and the exchange thereof shall be holy.
11 And if *it be* any unclean beast,
of which they do not offer a sacrifice unto the LORD, then he shall present the beast before the priest:
12 And the priest shall value it,
whether it be good or bad: †as thou
valuest it, *who art* the priest, so shall
it be.
13 But if he will at all redeem it,
then he shall add a fifth *part* thereof
unto thy estimation.
14 ¶ And when a man shall sanctify his house *to be* holy unto the
LORD, then the priest shall estimate
it, whether it be good or bad: as
the priest shall estimate it, so shall
it stand.
15 And if he that sanctified it will
redeem his house, then he shall add
the fifth *part* of the money of thy
estimation unto it, and it shall be
his.
16 And if a man shall sanctify unto
the LORD *some part* of a field of his
possession, then thy estimation shall
be according to the seed thereof: ‖an
homer of barley seed *shall be valued*
at fifty shekels of silver.
17 If he sanctify his field from the
year of jubile, according to thy estimation it shall stand.
18 But if he sanctify his field after
the jubile, then the priest shall reckon
unto him the money according to the
years that remain, even unto the year
of the jubile, and it shall be abated
from thy estimation.
19 And if he that sanctified the
field will in any wise redeem it, then
he shall add the fifth *part* of the money
of thy estimation unto it, and it shall
be assured to him.
20 And if he will not redeem the
field, or if he have sold the field to
another man, it shall not be redeemed
any more.
21 But the field, when it goeth
out in the jubile, shall be holy unto
the LORD, as a field devoted; the possession thereof shall be the priest's.
22 And if *a man* sanctify unto the
LORD a field which he hath bought,
which *is* not of the fields of his possession;

† Heb. *according to thy estimation, O priest, &c.*

‖ Or, *the land of an homer, &c.*

---

redeemed for its value with one-fifth added. Cf. v. 16, vi. 5.—The apostrophe to the priest in *v.* 12 is worthy of note.

14, 15. The law respecting the vow of a house was the same as that of an unclean animal. It is most likely that this relates to houses in the country (xxv. 31), which were under the same general law as the land itself, with a right of redemption for the inheritor till the next Jubilee. See on *vv.* 17—19. For houses in walled towns the right of redemption lasted for only one year, xxv. 29.

14. *sanctify*] *i.e.* vow to devote.

16. *some part of a field of his possession*] Rather, **a part of the land of his inheritance.**

the seed thereof] *i.e.* the quantity of seed required to sow it properly. This was the mode in which the value of a certain area was to be estimated.

a homer] The Homer was ten Ephahs (Ezek. xlv. 11); it must therefore have been something above $5\frac{1}{2}$ bushels. See Lev. xix. 36.

17—19. If the possession was surrendered from one Jubilee to the next, for a field which required a homer of barley to sow it, fifty shekels (probably £6. 9*s.* 2*d.*; see on Ex. xxxviii. 24), with the addition of one-fifth, made up the price of redemption.

20, 21. If the field was not redeemed before the next Jubilee, it lapsed to the priests in perpetuity. On the word "devoted" (*chērem*), see on *v.* 28.—The meaning of the words, "or if he have sold the field to another man," is not clear. They may refer to a case in which a man might have fraudulently sold his interest in a field and appropriated the price after having vowed it to the Sanctuary (Knobel); or to one in which a man retained the use of the field, fulfilled his vow by paying as a yearly rent a due proportion of the redemption money (see on 22—24), and then parted with his interest to another for the sake of acquiring some ready money (Keil).

22—24. If a man vowed the worth of his interest in a field which he had purchased, the transaction was a simple one. He had to pay down at once ("in that day," *v.* 23) the calculated value to the next Jubilee. In this case, the field reverted at the Jubilee to the original owner, who, it is likely, had the same right of redeeming it from the priests during the interval, as he had previously had of redeeming it from the man to whom he had sold it, in accordance with xxv. 23—28. The

23 Then the priest shall reckon
unto him the worth of thy estimation, *even* unto the year of the jubile:
and he shall give thine estimation in
that day, *as* a holy thing unto the
LORD.
24 In the year of the jubile the
field shall return unto him of whom
it was bought, *even* to him to whom
the possession of the land *did belong*.
25 And all thy estimations shall be
according to the shekel of the sanctuary: [a] twenty gerahs shall be the
shekel.
26 ¶ Only the † firstling of the
beasts, which should be the LORD'S
firstling, no man shall sanctify it;
whether *it be* ox, or sheep: it *is* the
LORD'S.
27 And if *it be* of an unclean beast,
then he shall redeem *it* according to
thine estimation, and shall add a fifth
part of it thereto: or if it be not redeemed, then it shall be sold according to thy estimation.
28 [b] Notwithstanding no devoted
thing, that a man shall devote unto
the LORD of all that he hath, *both* of
man and beast, and of the field of his
possession, shall be sold or redeemed:
every devoted thing *is* most holy unto
the LORD.
29 None devoted, which shall be
devoted of men, shall be redeemed;
but shall surely be put to death.
30 And all the tithe of the land,
whether of the seed of the land, *or* of
the fruit of the tree, *is* the LORD'S:
it is holy unto the LORD.
31 And if a man will at all redeem
ought of his tithes, he shall add thereto the fifth *part* thereof.

[a] Exod. 30. 13. Numb. 3. 47. Ezek. 45. 12.
† Heb. *firstborn, &c.*
[b] Josh. 6. 19.

---

regulation for the payment of the exact sum to be made in this case in ready money is supposed to furnish ground for inference that, in redeeming an inherited field, the money was paid to the priests year by year, and hence the fairness of the addition of one-fifth to the total sum as interest (*v.* 19).

25. On the Shekel and the Gerah, see Ex. xxx. 13, xxxviii. 24.

The Redeeming of Firstlings. 26, 27.

The firstborn of oxen and sheep already belonged to Jehovah (Ex. xiii. 2, xxii. 30), and could not therefore be made the objects of vows. But the firstling of an unclean animal, such as an ass or a camel, could be redeemed according to the ordinary rate (*vv.* 11, 13), or sold for its value. Cf. Num. xviii. 15, 18. It might seem that the earlier law in Exodus (xiii. 13, xxxiv. 20), which required that the firstborn of an ass was to be either redeemed with a sheep or put to death, is here modified for the advantage of the Sanctuary. A change of circumstances may have rendered this alteration expedient. The priesthood and the regular service of the Tabernacle were now established and needed support. There was nothing in the change at variance with the spirit of the older law.

26. *sheep*] **one of the flock.** Introd. § iv.

27. *shall redeem it*] Rather, **shall deliver it.** The Hebrew word is different from that in the second part of the verse, and appears to have a less special meaning. See *v.* 29.

Of things Devoted under a Ban. 28, 29.

28, 29. But nothing of his possessions that a man might devote to Jehovah under a ban (see next note), whether it was a human creature, or beast, or land, could be either redeemed or sold. Whatever was devoted under ban was to be regarded as entirely consecrated to Jehovah. Any live creature so devoted was to be put to death.

28. The word rendered "devoted thing" is *chērem*, as in *v.* 21. The primary meaning is something cut off, or shut up. Its specific meaning in the Law is, that which is cut off from common use and given up in some sense to Jehovah, without the right of recal or commutation. It is applied to a field wholly appropriated to the Sanctuary in *v.* 21, and to whatever was doomed to destruction, 1 S. xv. 21; 1 K. xx. 42. The phrase, "most holy unto the Lord," is here predicated of whatever is devoted under a ban, but it more commonly and strictly belongs to the holiest class of offerings for the Altar and the Sanctuary. See on ii. 3. Our translators have often rendered the word by "cursed," or "a curse," which in some places may convey the right sense, but it should be remembered that the terms are not identical in their compass of meaning. Deut. vii. 26; Josh. vi. 17, 18, vii. 1; Isa. xxxiv. 5, xliii. 28, &c. Cf. Gal. iii. 13.

of man and beast] See Note at the end of this chapter.

29. *redeemed*] Rather, **delivered.** See on *v.* 27.

32 And concerning the tithe of the
herd, or of the flock, *even* of whatsoever passeth under the rod, the tenth
shall be holy unto the LORD.
33 He shall not search whether
it be good or bad, neither shall he
change it: and if he change it at all,
then both it and the change thereof
shall be holy; it shall not be redeemed.
34 These *are* the commandments,
which the LORD commanded Moses
for the children of Israel in mount
Sinai.

The Commutation of Tithes. 30, 33.

30, 31. Cf. 13, 27.

32, 33. The tenth of sheep and oxen, like the firstling, *v.* 26, was neither to be redeemed nor changed, according to the same rule as was laid down for the clean animal that had been vowed, *v.* 10.

32. *whatsoever passeth under the rod*] According to rabbinical tradition, the animals to be tithed were enclosed in a pen, and a they went out one by one at the opening, every tenth animal was touched with a rod dipped in vermilion. Cf. Jer. xxxiii. 13; Ezek. xx. 37.

For a more full explanation of what relates to tithes, see on Gen. xiv. 20, xxviii. 22; Num. xviii. 20—32; Deut. xiv. 22, 28.

34. The Conclusion. Cf. xxvi. 46.

NOTE on CHAP. XXVII. 28.

ON THE DEVOTED THING.

i. This passage has often been alleged in proof that the Law of Moses permitted human sacrifices. It has been applied in this way to the case of Jephthah and his daughter. (See on Judg. xi. 30.) But such an inference is at once precluded by the exact limitation of the beasts which were to be offered in sacrifice. The right rendering of Lev. i. 2 is, "If any man of you bring an offering to Jehovah from the beasts, from the Herd or from the Flock shall ye bring your offering." There is moreover a clear recognition of man as one of the creatures which were not to be offered in sacrifice in Ex. xiii. 13, xxxiv. 20; Num. xviii. 15.

ii. The word *chērem* (חרם) has been explained in the note under the text. There is no good reason to doubt that its application to man is made exclusively in reference to one rightly doomed to death and, in that sense alone, given up to Jehovah. The feeling of the sacredness of Life has its seat in the depth of the human heart. This feeling may work blindly, and exhibit itself in diverse ways. But in an enlightened mind it becomes a clear conviction that all Life belongs to God, and is claimed by Him. Every animal sacrifice is an expression of this truth. The Law of Moses recognizes it in a marked manner in the regulation for the slaughter of animals for food. Lev. xvii. When human life is in question, the impression is beyond comparison stronger and more distinct. To destroy a life is in fact to give it back to God. The putting to death either of a criminal or an enemy, if it is anything more than an indulgence of vengeance, is to be regarded in this light. The man who, in a right spirit, either carries out a sentence of just doom on an offender, or who, with a single eye to duty, slays an enemy in battle, must regard himself as God's servant rendering up a life to the claim of the Divine justice. Rom. xiii. 4. It was in this way that Israel was required to destroy the Canaanites at Hormah (Num. xxi. 2, 3; cf. Deut. xiii. 12—18), and that Samuel hewed Agag in pieces before the Lord (1 S. xv. 33). In all such instances a moral obligation rests upon him whose office it is to take the life. He has to look upon the object of his stroke as under a ban to the Lord. Cf. Deut. xx. 4; Gal. iii. 13. This is the only ground on which the destruction of human life is to be justified. When this ground is clearly ascertained, the duty of him who is called to act refers to the forfeit of the individual life. There can therefore be neither redemption nor commutation.

iii. It is evident that the righteousness of this law is not involved in the sin of rash or foolish vows, such as Saul's (1 S. xiv. 24) or Jephthah's (Judg. xi. 30). A man through wilfulness or blindness may be betrayed into a dilemma in which he has to choose between breaking his vow, or breaking the Divine law in some other way. Such a difficulty is radically the same in all ages and circumstances, and has to be met under the same sort of moral conditions, of whatever kind the oath may be.

iv. It seems hardly needful to add that sacrifice, as it is represented both in the Law and in the usage of the Patriarchs, is something very different from consecration under a ban, though a thing to be sacrificed might come under the designation of *chērem* in its wider sense. See on xxvii. 28. The sacrifice was always the offering up of the innocent life of a creature chosen and approved without spot or blemish.

The offering was made, not by any constraint involved in the nature of things, but as a free act of worship. In either case, indeed, a life was given up to God. But the mode, the purpose, and the meaning were as distinct as possible. In heathen systems the two ideas were often confounded. Criminals or captives were the most frequent human victims offered on the altar. But the teaching of the Old Testament on this head is perfectly clear. There was no trace of this confusion even in the mind of Abraham, when he was preparing to make his great sacrifice. He had been led on to offer Isaac to the Lord as his best and most perfect possession. But the voice from heaven saved him from carrying out his purpose at the cost of other principles of righteousness on which he needed to be instructed. See Introd. § xii.

The subject of this note is elaborately treated by Selden, 'de Jure Gent.' Lib. IV. cap. vi.—xi. See also Waterland, 'Scripture Vindicated,' Works, Vol. IV. p. 226 sq.

NUMBERS

INTRODUCTION.

§ 1. *Title.*

THE title commonly given to this Book (LXX. Ἀριθμοί, Vulg. *Numeri*) is evidently suggested by the two numberings of the people recorded in it in chapters i. and xxvi. The Jews sometimes designate it after their ordinary mode by its first word *Vayedabber*, or more frequently by its first distinctive word *Bemidbar*.

§ 2. *Contents.*

The book narrates the history of the Israelites during their sojourn in the wilderness from the completion of the law-giving at Sinai, Lev. xxvii. 34, to their mustering in the Plains of Moab for actual entry into the Land of Promise. Its contents may be divided into four parts:—

(1) Preparations for the break up of the encampment at Sinai, and for marching on Canaan; i. 1—x. 10.

(2) The march from Sinai to the borders of Canaan, and repulse by the Canaanites; x. 11—xiv. 45.

(3) A notice of various occurrences and enactments belonging to the thirty-eight years of penal wandering in the desert; xv. 1—xix. 22.

(4) The history of the last year spent in the wilderness, the fortieth after the Exodus; xx. 1—xxxvi. 13.

The incidents are generally given in their chronological order, except in the third part. The five chapters comprised in this part deal with a long period, from which only isolated episodes are given; and of these the dates can only be conjectured; see introductory notes to xv. and xvi., and note on xx. 1. In this and other parts of the book several ordinances are added to the Sinaitic code, and these are apparently introduced in their historical connexion with the circumstances which gave occasion for them.

§ 3. *Chronology.*

(1) The narrative commences with "the first day of the second month of the second year after they were come out of Egypt," i. 1; and the death of Aaron at the first encampment during the final march on Canaan (xx. 22) took place in the first day of the fifth month of the fortieth year (xxxiii. 38).

(2) Between these two dates therefore intervene no less than thirty-eight years and three months (cf. Deut. ii. 14), the long and dreary period of tarrying in the wilderness till the disobedient generation had wasted away. Cf. xiv. 27—35. On the history of these years, see notes on xx. 1; and on xxxiii. 19.

(3) The solemn rehearsal of the Law contained in Deuteronomy was commenced by Moses after the overthrow of Sihon and Og, in the beginning of the

eleventh month of the fortieth year (Deut. i. 3, 4).

(4) We have consequently from the death of Aaron to the opening of Deut. a space of exactly six months, in which all the events narrated in the fourth part of the Book of Numbers, from xx. 1 to the end, would seem to have occurred, with the probable exception of the defeat of the king of Arad mentioned below.

(5) Those events are many and remarkable. After the tedious years of suspense were once passed the history of the chosen people hurries on, not without a sort of dramatic propriety, to a crisis. Crowded as this space is, it yet has room enough for the incidents which are here assigned to it.

(6) The first month of the six was passed at the foot of mount Hor in mourning for Aaron (xx. 29). But it is likely that during this month a part of the host was engaged in revenging upon the king of Arad the molestation inflicted by him on the Israelites during their journey from Kadesh to Mount Hor; see introductory note to xx. and on xxi. 1.

(7) Next ensued the journey "from Mount Hor by the way of the Red Sea to compass the land of Edom," xxi. 4; and this being about 220 miles to the brook Zered (cf. on xxi. 12) would be accomplished within four weeks.

(8) The appearance of the host in the plains of Moab brought them into the neighbourhood of Sihon, king of the Amorites. The policy pursued by him of resisting the progress of Israel with all his forces (xxi. 23) caused his overthrow to be speedy and total; as was also for like reasons that of Og king of Bashan. The two battles at Jahaz and Edrei probably took place both within a fortnight; *i.e.* towards the middle of the third of the six months in question.

(9) The issue of the conflict with the Amorite kings determined Balak to send for Balaam (xxii. 2). The distance from Moab to the nearest point of the Euphrates is about 350 miles, and Pethor (cf. on xxii. 5) may have been yet more distant. But as Balak was urgent in the matter (cf. xxii. 16), and could of course command all facilities for travelling, two months would amply suffice for his ambassadors to go and return twice over; and for the delivery by Balaam of his prophecies (xxii—xxiv). No doubt during these weeks the Israelites were engaged in completing and consolidating their conquest of Gilead and Bashan.

(10) We have thus a margin of at least six weeks left, during which occurred the seduction of Israel by the wiles of the Midianites, and the consequent plague (xxv.); the second numbering of the people in the plains of Moab (xxvi.); and the war upon the Midianites (xxxi.).

(11) It is accordingly in full consistency that the death of Moses is spoken of xxxi. 2, in connexion with the Midianitish war, and as following close upon it; and that Balaam after quitting Balak had not yet returned home when that war occurred, and was taken captive amongst the Midianites; see on xxxi. 8.

(12) There is no weight in the allegation that Moses in Deut. iii. 4—14 speaks of the conquest of Gilead and Bashan as long past. See notes on that place.

§ 4. *Authorship and Date of Composition.*

These two points are of course closely connected; and a determination of the former brings the question about the latter within narrow limits.

In common with the preceding books and Deuteronomy, Numbers has usually and from the most ancient times been regarded as in substance at least the work of Moses. The grounds for still maintaining this opinion as regards the Pentateuch generally have been stated and discussed in the Introduction to this volume. It remains only to inquire here whether the Book of Numbers, particularly considered, contributes any items to the argument on the one side or the other, and what value is to be attached to them.

(1) The catalogue of the stations or encampments during the journeyings from Egypt to the plains of Moab (xxxiii.) is specially assigned to Moses in the

text, "Moses wrote it by the commandment of the Lord," *v.* 2. The great antiquity of this catalogue is universally admitted. Bleek, *e.g.* ('Einleitung,' pp. 225, 227) esteems it "perhaps the earliest record relating to the journey of the Israelites through the wilderness;" and as "a list which may very well have been written down by an actor in the events." But to admit thus much of one important chapter, so minute in details, and so intimately connected with the general story, establishes a strong probability that other portions of the book are of the same age and authorship.

(2) The intermixture in this book of narrative and legislative matter is one of its characteristic features. The enactments too follow in most cases hard upon acts or emergencies which evidently led up to them. See *e.g.* introductory notes to v. ix. xix. xxx. and xxxvi.; and notes on xv. 22, 24, 32. The legislation of Sinai was completed in Leviticus, but the prolonged exclusion of the people from their future homes involved some regulations not originally provided (*e.g.* those respecting purification "when a man dieth in a tent" xix. 14); and further experience suggested some others of a supplementary or explanatory character (*e.g.* those of xv. 4 sqq.; xxx. 1—16; and xxxvi. 1—13, on which see notes). These are almost always in this book recorded in a living connexion with incidents from which it is wholly impossible to sever them, from which they draw their occasion and their meaning. Evidently the alternations of historical and legislative portions reflect the order of actual transaction. This feature is exactly one which belongs to the work of a contemporary annalist.

(3) The argument stated in the Introd. to the Pentateuch, p. 15, that the author had an intimate acquaintance with Egypt, may be strikingly illustrated from Numbers. The purifications of the priests (viii. 7 sqq.), the trial of jealousy (v. 11—35), the ordinance of the red heifer (xix. 1—10), are all adaptations from Egyptian rites; the language of the people in xi. 5, 6 bespeaks a personal relish of Egyptian dainties; the antiquarian note about Hebron, xiii. 22, indicates a knowledge of Egyptian history. References to the exodus from Egypt and the circumstances of it are frequent; *e. g.* iii. 13, xiv. 19, xv. 41, &c.

(4) The statements of this book abound in evidences (cf. Introd. to Pent., p. 17), that the writer and those with whom he lived were still in the desert. One direct illustration (in xix. 14) has been referred to above. The regulations for encamping and marching (ii., ix. 16 sqq., x. 1—28), and especially the solemn invocation of Moses contained in x. 35, 36, on the occasion of the removing and resting of the Ark, should be also noted. The directions respecting the transport of the Tabernacle in iii. and iv. belong to the nomadic life of the desert, and were consequently but of a temporary obligation. It is thus that an apparent inconsistency as to the age and service of the Levites between viii. 24—26 and iv. 3, 23 is to be explained; see the note on the former passage. It is obvious also that proximity to the Tabernacle is tacitly assumed throughout such laws as those of vi. and xix., as it is in many of those given in Leviticus. This proximity existed only whilst the people were in the wilderness. The presence of the Ark in the Tabernacle too is presupposed throughout the book; but the Ark, after its capture by the Philistines in the days of Eli (1 S. iv.), never again had a place within the Tabernacle. It is obviously to be inferred that Numbers was written before that capture.

(5) There are topographical statements in the book which cannot have been written after the days of Moses. Such is the notice xxi. 13, that "Arnon is the border of Moab, between Moab and the Amorites." The Amorites had clearly not been dispossessed by the two tribes and a half (xxxii.) when this remark was made. So too the settlements of those tribes in the Amorite territory were not in fact adjusted in all respects as originally designed by Moses and described in xxxii. 34 sqq. See note there, and cf. on Joshua xiii. 15 sqq. A later narrator would surely not gratuitously vary in such details from the facts before him. In the delineation (xxxiv.) of the boundaries of the Promised Land

far more territory is assigned to the Israelites than they ever permanently occupied, and less than they occasionally ruled over. A historian of later times would hardly ascribe to his people without explanation or qualification districts which in fact they did not possess; a romancer of such times, drawing an imaginary frontier, would certainly not have left out of it the renowned city of Damascus, especially after carrying his border-line almost round this district (see on xxxiv. 7 sqq.), and in view of the fact that the city and its territory were in the dominions of David and Solomon and afterwards of Jeroboam II.

(6) The various communications purporting to be from God to Moses are so worded and often of such a nature (cf. *e.g.* xiv. 11—26), that unless we go the length of denying their historical character altogether, we must admit them to have been recorded by the very person who received them. They are also so interwoven with the historical and legislative elements of the book that the whole composition must in reason be accepted or rejected together.

(7) No other person than Moses has been or can be named with anything like probability, or even plausibility, as the author. Various conjectures have indeed been hazarded by rationalist critics, but all of them are devoid of evidence, and some of them particularly unlikely, such is *e.g.* the suggestion that Samuel wrote this book, which includes amongst its most striking features the rebellion of Korah. Now Samuel was descended from Korah (see on xxvi. 11), and it is incredible, especially when we remember how keenly the Jew appropriates the acts of his ancestors, that Samuel, if we could suppose him to invent a story at all, would devise one which represents his own forefathers and their kinsmen as flagrant rebels against God and against the great national hero, God's prophet, and as miraculously destroyed for their sin.

Thus the notes of time, the tenor of the contents, no less than the direct assertions of the text itself, converge upon the conclusion that Moses is properly spoken of as the writer of the Book of Numbers.

It may however be quite consistently allowed that Moses availed himself in some cases of pre-existing materials, whether documentary or traditional, and combined in his narrative the results of information obtained from others (cf. Introd. to Genesis, p. 21); and this fact is a sufficient explanation of the use in certain passages of words or groups of words, and grammatical forms, which are not found or found but rarely, in other parts of the book. Nor is there any reason to believe that Moses wrote at one time the whole of what he may have himself contributed to this book. On the contrary it seems in parts to be composed out of memoranda, originally made at intervals ranging over thirty-eight years. If then the style and diction are found to vary in different parts of the book, this by no means disproves the unity of its authorship. The same writer may write very differently at different dates. The phenomena of this kind in Numbers are not however of great importance, and have been in principle sufficiently discussed in the Introd. to the Pentateuch. It is manifest indeed that we have in xxi. 14, 17, 27 an incorporation of matter not of the writer's own production; and the long and deeply interesting episode of Balaam (xxii—xxiv) is a yet more important example. Whether that prophet spoke in Hebrew or Aramaic cannot be determined. Some critics have detected an Aramaic cast in parts of his "parables;" but there is at any rate no improbability in the supposition that a man of his attainments could speak any or all of the dialects, and these were only dialects of the same great tongue, then current between the peninsula of Sinai and the Euphrates; and Hebrew would certainly be understood by the Moabites, to whom he directly addressed himself. The Moabite stone of course belongs to a date from five to six centuries later than that of Numbers, but it proves, if proof were needed, that the vernacular tongue of Moab was substantially the same with that of Israel nine hundred years before the Christian era, as it doubtless had been from the most ancient times. On the mode in which his prophecies probably became known to Moses, see on xxiv. 25, and xxxi. 8.

It is likely indeed that this book, as others, underwent after it left the hands of its composer a revision, or perhaps more than one revision, in which here and there later elements were introduced. These indeed cannot have been of any great bulk, and some passages have been quoted as instances which may well be otherwise explained. On the parenthetic verse xii. 3 (*e.g.*) a Lapide observes: "videntur hæc post Mosen ab aliquo alio scriptore hagiographo, qui hæc ejus diaria digessit, esse addita et intexta;" but see note on the verse.

The indications of interpolation in xiii. xiv. and xvi. are of another kind, and more convincing. It seems apparent that xiv. 39 connects itself not with *v.* 38 but with *v.* 25 of that chapter; and we notice in certain groups of verses included in the chapters xiii. and xiv. that Caleb only is named as labouring to still the people, *i.e.* in xiii. 30 sqq., xiv. 11—25; whilst in other groups Joshua is combined with him, *i.e.* in xiv. 6—10, 26—39. In the former, too, Caleb is mentioned without the addition of his father's name; in the latter we have always "Caleb the son of Jephunneh," as well as "Joshua the son of Nun." These facts, as well as the repetitions and want of consecutiveness apparent in the chapters as they stand, render it likely that a later and independent, but not inconsistent account, has been interwoven with the earlier one. The passages introducing the name of Joshua would seem to be the inserted ones, and they were added perhaps for the purpose of putting on express record what would seem to have been tacitly assumed in the original narrative, namely, that Joshua, Moses' chosen attendant and successor, was not one of the murmurers. Chapter xxxii. presents some similar characteristics to xiii. and xiv. The *vv.* 31, 32 in it repeat *vv.* 25—27, and *vv.* 9—15 may be compared with xiv. 6—10, and *v.* 30. But the alleged traces of interpolation here are not demonstrative.

On the tokens of supplementary insertion in xvi., see note at end of that chapter.

The objections which have been based upon particular passages, and urged against ascribing the book to Moses, are insignificant both in number and weight. Some of them will be found sufficiently dealt with in the notes on the passages themselves; see *e.g.* notes on xii. 3, xv. 32. Great stress has been laid upon the citation, in xxi. 14, of "the book of the wars of the Lord." Critics have pronounced it incredible that such a work should be extant in the days of Moses, and have alleged further that the chapter quotes it as belonging to bygone times. But in the months which closed Moses' life, when great events succeeded each other rapidly, and scenes and circumstances were ever changing, the songs commemorative of Israel's triumphs would soon become historical. Moreover "the book of the wars of the Lord" would probably commence with His noble works done in Egypt for the fathers of those who vanquished Sihon and Og.

Again, it has been urged that the occurrence of the word *prophet* and its cognate verb in this book (*e.g.* xi. 29, xii. 6) is a sign of a later date than that of Moses, because we are told in 1 S. ix. 9, "He that is now called a Prophet was beforetime called a Seer." It is hence inferred that Numbers must have been written at a period later than that indicated by the "now" of the Book of Samuel, since the term "prophet" is evidently familiar to the writer. But this argument is based upon a misapprehension of the passage in 1 Sam. It is not asserted there that the word "prophet" (*nabhi*) was unknown in earlier times, but simply that the personage consulted by the people in their emergencies was, after the days of Samuel, known as "the prophet," whereas formerly he was called "the seer" (*roëh*). The sense of the passage comes out more clearly in the LXX., τὸν προφήτην ἐκάλει ὁ λαὸς ἔμπροσθεν, ὁ βλέπων. The LXX. apparently read *ha'am* for *ha-yōm;* and probably this is the true reading (see note in 1 Sam. l. c.). The reason why the term "prophet" was disused in the days of the later Judges may be inferred from what is said 1 S. iii. 1: "the word of the Lord was precious in those days." In other words there was no "prophet" properly so called; no one who spoke under direct inspiration and supernatural impulse; nor apparently had there been any such since Deborah, *i.e.* for about a century and a half. Hence the people naturally ceased to speak of "the prophet," and called those to whom they resorted for advice by the name of "seer," which does not imply any miraculous gift, but simply superior penetration and intelligence. (See the analysis of the use and meaning of the words *nabhi*, *roëh*, and of *chozeh*, which also is important in this connexion, by Professor R. Payne Smith, 'Bampton Lectures' for 1869, pp. 46 sqq.). With Samuel the prophetical order was restored, and perpetuated through "the Schools of the Prophets." And the members of this higher and more gifted order often, probably generally, discharged in addition to their proper functions those also which previously had devolved upon "the seer." Hence the latter, both in name and person, ceased to occupy the prominent position he had long enjoyed, and was accordingly less frequently mentioned. In fact, after the days of Samuel, the word "seer" (*roëh*) occurs only twice, viz. in 2 S. xv. 27; 2 Chron. xvi. 7, 10. The term "prophet," on the contrary, became common and colloquial. But it was not now first coined. It only regained the currency which it had had in the days of Moses (cf. Ex. vii. 1), and even in earlier times (cf. Gen. xx. 7). The fact then that the word "prophet" is found in Numbers cannot prove that the book was written after the times of the Judges. Clericus on Gen. xx. 7 has summed up the facts as regards this word very neatly: "Hæc vox temporibus Mosis usitata erat, Judicum tempore desiit, inde iterum renata est."

We conclude then with confidence that nothing has been as yet alleged which disturbs the generally accepted views respecting the authorship of this book. It is in substance the work of Moses; and whilst many portions of it were probably committed to writing for years before the whole was completed, yet the concluding chapters were not written until towards the close of the fortieth year after the exodus.

The Book of Numbers was allotted in the early arrangements for this Commentary to the Rev. J. F. Thrupp, M.A. Vicar of Barrington, and late Fellow of Trinity College, Cambridge. Mr Thrupp was one of the first to send to the editor the results of his labours, but died in 1867, before his work could be revised and adjusted with that of his colleagues. His papers on this book were most considerately placed by his representatives at the disposal of the editor, and were by him intrusted to the Rev. T. E. Espin to be prepared for the press. As the work proceeded it was found necessary to change and remodel the notes as left by Mr Thrupp far more than was originally proposed, and ultimately to re-write the most of them. The scale eventually adopted for the foot-notes was much smaller than that on which Mr Thrupp had worked; and the conclusions finally reached were upon several controverted points (*e.g.* the site of Kadesh, see note at end of chapter xiii.) different from those which had recommended themselves to Mr Thrupp five or six years ago. The Rev. T. E. Espin must therefore with the editor be regarded as responsible for the notes on Numbers contained in this volume, though in writing them he has had throughout important aid from Mr Thrupp's copious and learned annotations. The chief portions which now remain as Mr Thrupp penned them are portions of the foot-notes to chapters xxii.—xxv., and many of the geographical and topographical remarks and illustrations, especially those in chapter xxxiv.

THE FOURTH BOOK OF MOSES,

CALLED

NUMBERS.

CHAPTER I.

1 God commandeth Moses to number the people. 5 The princes of the tribes. 17 The number of every tribe. 47 The Levites are exempted for the service of the Lord.

AND the LORD spake unto Moses
in the wilderness of Sinai, in the
tabernacle of the congregation, on the
first *day* of the second month, in the
second year after they were come out
of the land of Egypt, saying,
Exod. 0. 12. 2 [a]Take ye the sum of all the congregation of the children of Israel,
after their families, by the house of
their fathers, with the number of *their*
names, every male by their polls;
3 From twenty years old and upward, all that are able to go forth to
war in Israel: thou and Aaron shall
number them by their armies.
4 And with you there shall be a
man of every tribe; every one head
of the house of his fathers.
5 ¶ And these *are* the names of the
men that shall stand with you: of *the*
tribe of Reuben; Elizur the son of
Shedeur.
6 Of Simeon; Shelumiel the son
of Zurishaddai.
7 Of Judah; Nahshon the son of
Amminadab.
8 Of Issachar; Nethaneel the son
of Zuar.
9 Of Zebulun; Eliab the son of
Helon.
10 Of the children of Joseph: of
Ephraim; Elishama the son of Ammihud: of Manasseh; Gamaliel the
son of Pedahzur.
11 Of Benjamin; Abidan the son
of Gideoni.
12 Of Dan; Ahiezer the son of
Ammishaddai.
13 Of Asher; Pagiel the son of
Ocran.
14 Of Gad; Eliasaph the son of
Deuel.
15 Of Naphtali; Ahira the son of
Enan.

CHAP. I. 1—4. A month had passed away since the setting up of the tabernacle (Ex. xl. 2, 17); and the Sinaitic legislation was now complete (cf. Lev. xxvii. 34).

The labour involved in taking the census had already been partially anticipated. An order had been issued some months before, that, whenever the sum of the Israelites was taken, every person numbered should offer an atonement-money of half-a-shekel, to be applied for the service of the tabernacle (Ex. xxx. 11 sqq.). Before the construction of the tabernacle was complete, such a poll-offering had been actually received (Ex. xxxviii. 25—28). The accordance of numerical results shows that the present census was based, not upon any fresh registration of individuals, but upon that which necessarily accompanied the previous collection of the offerings. From the round numbers in which the results are given, we may infer that the offerings had been tendered by the people in groups, and these probably determined by kindred. If certificates of registration were furnished to such groups, the new census might be easily carried out by means of these documents, and got through, as seems suggested by *v.* 18, in a single day. But while, for the purpose of the poll-offering, it sufficed to note merely the number of persons, it was now required to enrol them "after their families, by the house of their fathers." The former registration too had been superintended by the Levites (see Ex. xxxviii. 21 and note); but now (*v.* 4) an assessor is to be named for each tribe to act in the business with Moses and Aaron; for the purpose now in view was not religious only. The census now taken would serve as a basis for various civil and military arrangements.

5—16. The selection of the Princes of the Tribes appears from *v.* 4 to have been made under divine direction; but probably, as *v.* 16 seems to suggest, they were for the most part the same persons as those chosen a few months previously at the counsel of Jethro, Ex. xviii. 21—26. Of those here named Nah-

16 These *were* the renowned of the congregation, princes of the tribes of their fathers, heads of thousands in Israel.

17 ¶ And Moses and Aaron took these men which are expressed by *their* names:

18 And they assembled all the congregation together on the first *day* of the second month, and they declared their pedigrees after their families, by the house of their fathers, according to the number of the names, from twenty years old and upward, by their polls.

19 As the LORD commanded Moses, so he numbered them in the wilderness of Sinai.

20 And the children of Reuben, Israel's eldest son, by their generations, after their families, by the house of their fathers, according to the number of the names, by their polls, every male from twenty years old and upward, all that were able to go forth to war;

21 Those that were numbered of them, *even* of the tribe of Reuben, *were* forty and six thousand and five hundred.

22 ¶ Of the children of Simeon, by their generations, after their families, by the house of their fathers, those that were numbered of them, according to the number of the names, by their polls, every male from twenty years old and upward, all that were able to go forth to war;

23 Those that were numbered of them, *even* of the tribe of Simeon, *were* fifty and nine thousand and three hundred.

24 ¶ Of the children of Gad, by their generations, after their families, by the house of their fathers, according to the number of the names, from twenty years old and upward, all that were able to go forth to war;

25 Those that were numbered of them, *even* of the tribe of Gad, *were* forty and five thousand six hundred and fifty.

26 ¶ Of the children of Judah, by their generations, after their families, by the house of their fathers, according to the number of the names, from twenty years old and upward, all that were able to go forth to war;

27 Those that were numbered of them, *even* of the tribe of Judah, *were* threescore and fourteen thousand and six hundred.

28 ¶ Of the children of Issachar, by their generations, after their families, by the house of their fathers, according to the number of the names, from twenty years old and upward, all that were able to go forth to war;

29 Those that were numbered of them, *even* of the tribe of Issachar, *were* fifty and four thousand and four hundred.

30 ¶ Of the children of Zebulun, by their generations, after their families, by the house of their fathers, according to the number of the names,

---

shon, prince of Judah, was brother-in-law of Aaron (Ex. vi. 23), and ancestor of King David. Elishama, prince of Ephraim, was grandfather of Joshua (1 Chron. vii. 26, 27). The peers of men like these, though nothing has been in fact preserved to us respecting them, were no doubt intitled, amongst their fellows, to the epithet "renowned," *v.* 16.

17—19. See on *vv.* 1—4.

20—46. In eleven tribes the number enrolled consists of complete hundreds. This is in all likelihood to be explained by the fact that the census was taken principally for military purposes (cf. *vv.* 3, 20). Hence the enrolment would naturally be arranged by hundreds, fifties, &c. (cf. 2 K. i. 9, 11, 13). Supernumerary units would in such a calculation be left to balance the losses from physical unfitness for service, and from casualties of various kinds; and the general result would thus fairly exhibit the available military strength of the nation. It is not a little remarkable however that here the tribe of Gad, *v.* 25, and (xxvi. 7) at the later census, the tribe of Reuben, yield odd decades over their hundreds. Can this be accounted for by the pastoral, and consequently nomadic, habits of these tribes? This cause might render it difficult to bring all their members together at once for a census. Judah already takes precedence of his brethren in point of numbers (cf. Gen. xlix. 8); and Ephraim of Manasseh (cf. Gen. xlviii. 19, 20).

from twenty years old and upward, all
that were able to go forth to war;
31 Those that were numbered of
them, *even* of the tribe of Zebulun,
were fifty and seven thousand and four
hundred.
32 ¶ Of the children of Joseph,
namely, of the children of Ephraim,
by their generations, after their families,
by the house of their fathers, according
to the number of the names,
from twenty years old and upward, all
that were able to go forth to war;
33 Those that were numbered of
them, *even* of the tribe of Ephraim,
were forty thousand and five hundred.
34 ¶ Of the children of Manasseh,
by their generations, after their families,
by the house of their fathers, according
to the number of the names,
from twenty years old and upward, all
that were able to go forth to war;
35 Those that were numbered of
them, *even* of the tribe of Manasseh,
were thirty and two thousand and two
hundred.
36 ¶ Of the children of Benjamin,
by their generations, after their families,
by the house of their fathers, according
to the number of the names,
from twenty years old and upward, all
that were able to go forth to war;
37 Those that were numbered of
them, *even* of the tribe of Benjamin,
were thirty and five thousand and four
hundred.
38 ¶ Of the children of Dan, by
their generations, after their families,
by the house of their fathers, according
to the number of the names, from
twenty years old and upward, all that
were able to go forth to war;
39 Those that were numbered of
them, *even* of the tribe of Dan, *were*
threescore and two thousand and seven
hundred.
40 ¶ Of the children of Asher, by
their generations, after their families,
by the house of their fathers, according
to the number of the names, from
twenty years old and upward, all that
were able to go forth to war;
41 Those that were numbered of
them, *even* of the tribe of Asher, *were*
forty and one thousand and five hundred.
42 ¶ Of the children of Naphtali,
throughout their generations, after
their families, by the house of their
fathers, according to the number of
the names, from twenty years old
and upward, all that were able to go
forth to war;
43 Those that were numbered of
them, *even* of the tribe of Naphtali,
were fifty and three thousand and four
hundred.
44 These *are* those that were numbered,
which Moses and Aaron numbered,
and the princes of Israel, *being*
twelve men: each one was for the
house of his fathers.
45 So were all those that were numbered
of the children of Israel, by the
house of their fathers, from twenty
years old and upward, all that were
able to go forth to war in Israel;
46 Even all they that were numbered
were six hundred thousand and
three thousand and five hundred and
fifty.
47 ¶ But the Levites after the tribe
of their fathers were not numbered
among them.
48 For the LORD had spoken unto
Moses, saying,

47—54. The Levites were appointed to the charge of the Tabernacle, and were therefore not entered on the general muster rolls. Hence when a census of this tribe takes place, iii. 15, xxvi. 62, *all* the males are counted from a month old and upward, and not, as in the other tribes, those only who were of age for service in the field.

48. *had spoken*] Render **spake**, for the formal appointment is only now made. The Levites had indeed already acted as assistants to the Priests (cf. Ex. xxxviii. 21), being the tribesmen of Moses and Aaron. Their zeal against the worshippers of the golden calf (Ex. xxxii. 26—29; Deut. xxxiii. 8 sqq.) gave them a distinct position, and led to their receiving as their reward the dignity to which they are now first expressly named, though reference to their future office appears previously in Lev. xxv. 32 sqq.

49 Only thou shalt not number the tribe of Levi, neither take the sum of them among the children of Israel:

50 But thou shalt appoint the Levites over the tabernacle of testimony, and over all the vessels thereof, and over all things that *belong* to it: they shall bear the tabernacle, and all the vessels thereof; and they shall minister unto it, and shall encamp round about the tabernacle.

51 And when the tabernacle setteth forward, the Levites shall take it down: and when the tabernacle is to be pitched, the Levites shall set it up: and the stranger that cometh nigh shall be put to death.

52 And the children of Israel shall pitch their tents, every man by his own camp, and every man by his own standard, throughout their hosts.

53 But the Levites shall pitch round about the tabernacle of testimony, that there be no wrath upon the congregation of the children of Israel: and the Levites shall keep the charge of the tabernacle of testimony.

54 And the children of Israel did according to all that the LORD commanded Moses, so did they.

CHAPTER II.

The order of the tribes in their tents.

AND the LORD spake unto Moses and unto Aaron, saying,

2 Every man of the children of Israel shall pitch by his own standard, with the ensign of their father's house: †far off about the tabernacle of the congregation shall they pitch.

† Heb. *over against.*

3 And on the east side toward the rising of the sun shall they of the standard of the camp of Judah pitch throughout their armies: and Nahshon the son of Amminadab *shall be* captain of the children of Judah.

4 And his host, and those that were numbered of them, *were* threescore and fourteen thousand and six hundred.

5 And those that do pitch next unto him *shall be* the tribe of Issachar: and Nethaneel the son of Zuar *shall be* captain of the children of Issachar.

6 And his host, and those that were numbered thereof, *were* fifty and four thousand and four hundred.

7 *Then* the tribe of Zebulun: and Eliab the son of Helon *shall be* captain of the children of Zebulun.

8 And his host, and those that were

CHAP. II. **1—34.** Order of the tribes in their tents, and on the march.

2. *by his own standard, with the ensign of their father's house*] The "standard" (*degel*) marked the division, or camp (cf. *vv.* 9, 16, 24, 31); the "ensign" (*oth*) the family. There would thus be four "standards" only, one for each "camp" of three tribes. We have no certain information what was the structure and what the devices of the "standards." The word is derived from a root signifying "to glitter," or "lighten afar" (Rosenm., Fürst, &c.); and probably points to a solid figure or emblem mounted on a pole, such as the Egyptians used (see Wilkinson, 'Ancient Egyptians,' I. 294 sqq.). Tradition appropriates the four cherubic forms (Ezek. i. 26, x. 1; Rev. iv. 4 sqq.), the lion, man, ox, and eagle, to the camps of Judah, Reuben, Ephraim, and Dan respectively; and this, as to the first, has a certain support from Gen. xlix. 9 (cf. Rev. v. 5), and as to the third, from Deut. xxxiii. 17.

far off] Rather as the word may be and often is rendered elsewhere, **over against**; *i.e.* facing the tabernacle on every side. The distance was perhaps 2000 cubits: cf. Josh. iii. 4.

3—9. *on the east side*] The post of honour, in front of the curtain of the Tabernacle, and corresponding to the position occupied by Moses, Aaron, and the Priests in the Levites' camp, is assigned to Judah, with Issachar and Zebulun, also descendants of Leah. Judah, as the strongest tribe in point of numbers, is appointed also to lead the van on the march.

3. *Nahshon the son of Amminadab shall be captain of the children of Judah*] Cf. 1 Chron. xxvii. 16—22, where the "princes" or "rulers" of the Twelve Tribes at a far later date are again named. Each tribe had thus an organization complete for certain purposes in itself. Accordingly we sometimes read of wars waged by separate tribes or groups of tribes; *e.g.* Josh. xvii. 15 sqq.; Judg. iv. 10.

numbered thereof, *were* fifty and seven thousand and four hundred.

9 All that were numbered in the camp of Judah *were* an hundred thousand and fourscore thousand and six thousand and four hundred, throughout their armies. These shall first set forth.

10 ¶ On the south side *shall be* the standard of the camp of Reuben according to their armies: and the captain of the children of Reuben *shall be* Elizur the son of Shedeur.

11 And his host, and those that were numbered thereof, *were* forty and six thousand and five hundred.

12 And those which pitch by him *shall be* the tribe of Simeon: and the captain of the children of Simeon *shall be* Shelumiel the son of Zurishaddai.

13 And his host, and those that were numbered of them, *were* fifty and nine thousand and three hundred.

14 Then the tribe of Gad: and the captain of the sons of Gad *shall be* Eliasaph the son of Reuel.

15 And his host, and those that were numbered of them, *were* forty and five thousand and six hundred and fifty.

16 All that were numbered in the camp of Reuben *were* an hundred thousand and fifty and one thousand and four hundred and fifty, throughout their armies. And they shall set forth in the second rank.

17 ¶ Then the tabernacle of the congregation shall set forward with the camp of the Levites in the midst of the camp: as they encamp, so shall they set forward, every man in his place by their standards.

18 ¶ On the west side *shall be* the standard of the camp of Ephraim according to their armies: and the captain of the sons of Ephraim *shall be* Elishama the son of Ammihud.

19 And his host, and those that were numbered of them, *were* forty thousand and five hundred.

20 And by him *shall be* the tribe of Manasseh: and the captain of the children of Manasseh *shall be* Gamaliel the son of Pedahzur.

21 And his host, and those that were numbered of them, *were* thirty and two thousand and two hundred.

22 Then the tribe of Benjamin: and the captain of the sons of Benjamin *shall be* Abidan the son of Gideoni.

23 And his host, and those that were numbered of them, *were* thirty and five thousand and four hundred.

24 All that were numbered of the camp of Ephraim *were* an hundred thousand and eight thousand and an hundred, throughout their armies. And they shall go forward in the third rank.

25 ¶ The standard of the camp of Dan *shall be* on the north side by their armies: and the captain of the children of Dan *shall be* Ahiezer the son of Ammishaddai.

26 And his host, and those that

10—16. Next in order, and south of the Tabernacle, comes the tribe that bore the name of Reuben, Leah's eldest son; and associated therewith Simeon, the second of the descendants of Leah, and Gad, the eldest of the descendants of Leah's handmaid Zilpah.

14. *Reuel*] Doubtless an error of transcription for the Deuel of i. 14, which in fact is read here in several MSS. and Versions.

17. See on iii. 14—39, x. 17.

18—24. The third camp, which had its place westward of the Tabernacle, consists of the tribe of Ephraim, with the kindred tribes of Manasseh and Benjamin, all descended from Rachel. These three tribes all obtained adjoining allotments when Canaan was divided, and are accordingly spoken of as associated, Ps. lxxx. 2, "Before Ephraim, Benjamin, and Manasseh, stir up thy strength."

25—31. The fourth division, which encamped north of the Tabernacle, is named after Dan, the eldest of Jacob's children by the handmaids. This powerful tribe, the second of all in number, brought up the rear on the march. With it are joined the remaining tribes, Asher and Naphtali, sprung from the handmaids Zilpah and Bilhah.

The following plan shows the entire arrangement of the camp as gathered from this and the next chapter. Some place the four leading tribes in the centre each of its own side; but the scheme here given seems more probable

were numbered of them, *were* threescore and two thousand and seven hundred.

27 And those that encamp by him *shall be* the tribe of Asher: and the captain of the children of Asher *shall be* Pagiel the son of Ocran.

28 And his host, and those that were numbered of them, *were* forty and one thousand and five hundred.

29 ¶ Then the tribe of Naphtali: and the captain of the children of Naphtali *shall be* Ahira the son of Enan.

30 And his host, and those that were numbered of them, *were* fifty and three thousand and four hundred.

31 All they that were numbered in the camp of Dan *were* an hundred thousand and fifty and seven thousand and six hundred. They shall go hindmost with their standards.

32 ¶ These *are* those which were numbered of the children of Israel by the house of their fathers: all those that were numbered of the camps throughout their hosts *were* six hundred thousand and three thousand and five hundred and fifty.

33 But the Levites were not numbered among the children of Israel; as the LORD commanded Moses.

34 And the children of Israel did according to all that the LORD commanded Moses: so they pitched by their standards, and so they set forward, every one after their families, according to the house of their fathers.

---

from the order in which the tribes were to set out on the march.

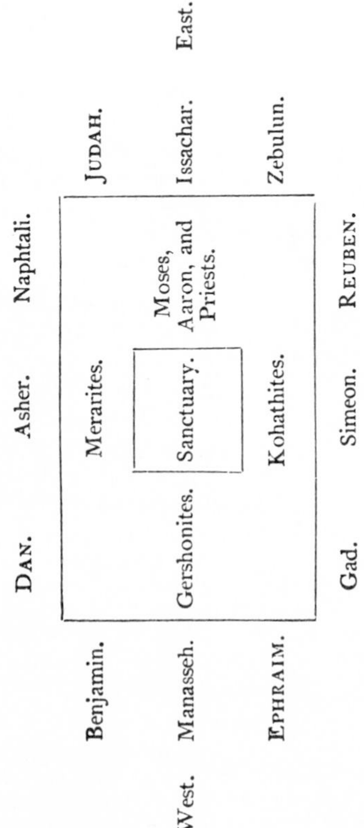

32—34. Such was the ideal form of the encampment in the wilderness: a form reproduced in the square court with which the Temple was eventually surrounded, and in the vision of the heavenly city as seen by Ezek. xlviii. 20; and by St John, Rev. xxi. 16; cf. Rev. xx. 9. Thus the camp of God's earthly people was divinely ordered so as to set forth the completeness of His Church; and to illustrate by its whole arrangement, which was determined by the Tabernacle in the centre, both the dependance of all on God, and the access which all enjoyed to God.

It is to be observed however that the collocation of the tribes is only prescribed in general terms. The actual form of the encampment would no doubt, whilst observing this arrangement generally, vary in different places according to local exigencies. At Sinai itself, *e.g.* the granite cliffs which hemmed in the host on every side would render it impossible for the tents to be pitched on any symmetrical plan; whilst in the Plains of Moab, where a long halt was made, the camp might on the other hand lie "four-square," or nearly so; for the line of encampment from Beth-Jesimoth to Abel Shittim (cf. xxii. 1, and note) would extend nearly five miles.

The area of the camp might be about three square miles. Polybius (VI. 27), describing the camps of the Roman armies, tells us that a space of about one-sixth of a square mile sufficed for twenty thousand men, and allowed ample room for streets, officers' quarters, accommodation for horses, &c., with a vacant space of two hundred feet behind the rampart all round. It must be remembered that the two million Israelites were living together in families, and therefore would not occupy so much ground as a like number of warriors.

CHAPTER III.

1 The sons of Aaron. 5 The Levites are given to the priests for the service of the tabernacle, 11 instead of the firstborn. 14 The Levites are numbered by their families. 21 The families, number, and charge of the Gershonites, 27 of the Kohathites, 33 of the Merarites. 38 The place and charge of Moses and Aaron. 40 The firstborn are freed by the Levites. 44. The overplus are redeemed.

THESE also *are* the generations of Aaron and Moses in the day *that* the LORD spake with Moses in mount Sinai.

2 And these *are* the names of the sons of Aaron; Nadab the [a] firstborn, and Abihu, Eleazar, and Ithamar.

3 These *are* the names of the sons of Aaron, the priests which were anointed, † whom he consecrated to minister in the priest's office.

4 [b] And Nadab and Abihu died before the LORD, when they offered strange fire before the LORD, in the wilderness of Sinai, and they had no children: and Eleazar and Ithamar ministered in the priest's office in the sight of Aaron their father.

5 ¶ And the LORD spake unto Moses, saying,

6 Bring the tribe of Levi near, and present them before Aaron the priest, that they may minister unto him.

7 And they shall keep his charge, and the charge of the whole congregation before the tabernacle of the congregation, to do the service of the tabernacle.

8 And they shall keep all the instruments of the tabernacle of the congregation, and the charge of the children of Israel, to do the service of the tabernacle.

9 And thou shalt give the Levites unto Aaron and to his sons: they *are* wholly given unto him out of the children of Israel.

10 And thou shalt appoint Aaron and his sons, and they shall wait on their priest's office: and the stranger that cometh nigh shall be put to death.

11 And the LORD spake unto Moses, saying,

12 And I, behold, I have taken the Levites from among the children of Israel instead of all the firstborn that openeth the matrix among the children of Israel: therefore the Levites shall be mine;

13 Because [c] all the firstborn *are* mine; *for* on the day that I smote all the firstborn in the land of Egypt I hallowed unto me all the firstborn

[a] Exod. 6. 23.
† Heb. *whose hand he filled.*
[b] Lev. 10. 1. chap. 26. 61. 1 Chron. 24. 2.
[c] Exod. 13. 2. Lev. 27. 26. chap. 8. 16. Luke 2. 23.

CHAP. III. 1. *These also are the generations of Aaron and Moses*] The term "generations" is strictly a technical word (cf. note on Gen. ii. 4; and Gen. v. 1, vi. 9, &c.; Ruth iv. 18). It does not point to birth and origin so much as to downward history and development. Hence the "generations" of a person are commonly introduced, as in the text, at a crisis, when either a signal and accomplished fulfilment of the Divine counsels is to be indicated; or a stage has been reached which establishes a basis for a fulfilment to be narrated at large in the sequel. Hence it is that the "generations" now given, though entitled those of Aaron and Moses (Aaron standing first as the elder brother), turn out really to be those of Aaron only. The personal dignity of Moses, though it gave him rank as at the head of his tribe, was not hereditary. He had, and desired to have (Ex. xxxii. 10; Num. xiv. 12), no successor in his office but the distant Prophet like unto himself (Deut. xviii. 18). Aaron however was, as this chapter shows, the ancestor of a regular succession of Priests.

3. *whom he consecrated*] *i.e.* whom Moses consecrated, or literally as marg., whose "hand he filled," by conferring their office upon them: Lev. viii. 1 sqq.

5—13. Actual dedication of the Levites for the functions already assigned, i. 47—50; and that in lieu of the firstborn (*vv.* 11—13); who, although originally designated according to patriarchal precedent for the more especial service of God, and having perhaps (cf. Ex. xxiv. 5 and note) even actually officiated therein, could from the first be redeemed by an equivalent (cf. Ex. xiii. 2, 12, 13).

The concluding words of *v.* 13 are better thus expressed: **Mine shall they be, mine, the LORD's.** So also at *vv.* 41, 45.

7. *keep his charge, and the charge of the whole congregation*] *i.e.* so assist him that the obligations incumbent on him and on the congregation may be fulfilled.

12, 13. On the subject of the firstborn see notes on *vv.* 40—43 and on *vv.* 44—51.

in Israel, both man and beast: mine
shall they be: I *am* the LORD.
14 ¶ And the LORD spake unto
Moses in the wilderness of Sinai,
saying,
15 Number the children of Levi
after the house of their fathers, by
their families: every male from a
month old and upward shalt thou
number them.
16 And Moses numbered them according to the †word of the LORD, as
he was commanded.
17 [d]And these were the sons of
Levi by their names; Gershon, and
Kohath, and Merari.
18 And these *are* the names of
the sons of Gershon by their families; Libni, and Shimei.
19 And the sons of Kohath by
their families; Amram, and Izehar,
Hebron, and Uzziel.
20 And the sons of Merari by their
families; Mahli, and Mushi. These
are the families of the Levites according to the house of their fathers.
21 Of Gershon *was* the family of
the Libnites, and the family of the
Shimites: these *are* the families of the
Gershonites.
22 Those that were numbered of
them, according to the number of all
the males, from a month old and upward, *even* those that were numbered
of them *were* seven thousand and five
hundred.
23 The families of the Gershonites shall pitch behind the tabernacle
westward.
24 And the chief of the house of
the father of the Gershonites *shall be*
Eliasaph the son of Lael.
25 And the charge of the sons of
Gershon in the tabernacle of the congregation *shall be* the tabernacle, and

[d] Gen. 46. 11. Exod. 6. 16. chap. 26. 57. 1 Chron. 6. 1.
† Heb. *mouth.*

the tent, the covering thereof, and
the hanging for the door of the tabernacle of the congregation,
26 And the hangings of the court,
and the curtain for the door of the
court, which *is* by the tabernacle, and
by the altar round about, and the cords
of it for all the service thereof.
27 ¶ And of Kohath *was* the family of the Amramites, and the family
of the Izeharites, and the family of the
Hebronites, and the family of the Uzzielites: these *are* the families of the
Kohathites.
28 In the number of all the males,
from a month old and upward, *were*
eight thousand and six hundred, keeping the charge of the sanctuary.
29 The families of the sons of Kohath shall pitch on the side of the
tabernacle southward.
30 And the chief of the house of
the father of the families of the Kohathites *shall be* Elizaphan the son of
Uzziel.
31 And their charge *shall be* the
ark, and the table, and the candlestick, and the altars, and the vessels
of the sanctuary wherewith they minister, and the hanging, and all the
service thereof.
32 And Eleazar the son of Aaron
the priest *shall be* chief over the chief
of the Levites, *and have* the oversight
of them that keep the charge of the
sanctuary.
33 ¶ Of Merari *was* the family of
the Mahlites, and the family of the
Mushites: these *are* the families of
Merari.
34 And those that were numbered
of them, according to the number of
all the males, from a month old and
upward, *were* six thousand and two
hundred.

14—39. Enumeration of the Levites after their three families, and allotment to each family of its special station and duty. Of these, the Kohathites (*vv.* 27—32), the kinsmen of Moses and Aaron, and the most numerous, have the most important charge confided to them, that of the Ark, the Altars, and the more especially sacred furniture generally.

26. *the cords of it*] *i.e.* of the Tabernacle, not of the hangings of the Court; for these, with their cords and other fittings, belonged to the charge of the Merarites. So too the expression *the service thereof* refers to the Tabernacle, of which more particularly the Gershonites have the care.

35 And the chief of the house of the father of the families of Merari *was* Zuriel the son of Abihail: *these* shall pitch on the side of the tabernacle northward.

36 And †*under* the custody and charge of the sons of Merari *shall be* the boards of the tabernacle, and the bars thereof, and the pillars thereof, and the sockets thereof, and all the vessels thereof, and all that serveth thereto,

† Heb. *the office of the charge*

37 And the pillars of the court round about, and their sockets, and their pins, and their cords.

38 ¶ But those that encamp before the tabernacle toward the east, *even* before the tabernacle of the congregation eastward, *shall be* Moses, and Aaron and his sons, keeping the charge of the sanctuary for the charge of the children of Israel; and the stranger that cometh nigh shall be put to death.

39 All that were numbered of the Levites, which Moses and Aaron numbered at the commandment of the LORD, throughout their families, all the males from a month old and upward, *were* twenty and two thousand.

40 ¶ And the LORD said unto Moses, Number all the firstborn of the males of the children of Israel from a month old and upward, and take the number of their names.

41 And thou shalt take the Levites for me (I *am* the LORD) instead of all the firstborn among the children of Israel; and the cattle of the Levites instead of all the firstlings among the cattle of the children of Israel.

42 And Moses numbered, as the LORD commanded him, all the firstborn among the children of Israel.

43 And all the firstborn males by the number of names, from a month old and upward, of those that were numbered of them, were twenty and two thousand two hundred and threescore and thirteen.

---

39. *twenty and two thousand*] The aggregate of the three families makes the total 22,300: thus

Gershonites...	7500:	*v.* 22.
Kohathites ...	8600:	*v.* 28.
Merarites.....	6200:	*v.* 34.
	22300	

It is apparent however that the number 22,000 is the basis on which the commutation with the First-born of the Twelve Tribes is in fact made to depend (*vv.* 43—46). The actual total of the male Levites (22,300) seems therefore to be tacitly corrected by the subtraction of 300 from it. The Talmud, followed by the Jewish Commentators generally, and by Hävern., Bp. Wordsw., &c. regards these 300 as representing those who, being first-born themselves in the Tribe of Levi, could not be available to redeem the first-born in other tribes. They will be of course the first-born of Levi within the year which had elapsed since the command was issued; see on *vv.* 40—43. Cf. *v.* 13, and Ex. xiii. 1, 2. The fact that the deduction is made without remark is perhaps explained by the observation of Baumgarten (in loc.), that the purport of the passage is to point out the relation between the tribe of Levi and the other tribes, and not to give prominence to restrictions or qualifications in the redemptive virtue assigned to the Levites. It is enough for the writer in this context to note that 22,000 is the numerical factor furnished by the tribe for the reckoning. Modern commentators generally (Mich., Knob., Kurtz, Keil, &c.) have assumed an error in the Hebrew text. And, to insert a single letter (reading in *v.* 28 שלש for שש) would exhibit the number of the Kohathites as 8300, instead of 8600, and remove the difficulty. Other slight alterations of a similar kind have been suggested; but there is no warrant in ancient MSS., or Versions, for any emendation of the text in this place.

It is noteworthy that the tribe of Levi is shown by this census to have been by far the smallest of any of the thirteen of the other tribes. The least numerous, Manasseh, contained 32,200 fighting men; whilst all the males of the Levites, from a month old and upwards, did not reach that total within ten thousand. No doubt, however, many of those reckoned amongst the other tribes were servants or dependants, and not pure Israelites; whilst none but actual descendants of Levi would be dedicated to the service of the Tabernacle.

40—43. Numbering of the first-born males throughout the Twelve Tribes in order to effect the exchange commanded, *v.* 12.

The result (*v.* 43) shows a total of 22,273.

44 ¶ And the LORD spake unto Moses, saying,
45 Take the Levites instead of all the firstborn among the children of Israel, and the cattle of the Levites instead of their cattle; and the Levites shall be mine: I *am* the LORD.
46 And for those that are to be redeemed of the two hundred and threescore and thirteen of the firstborn of the children of Israel, which are more than the Levites;
47 Thou shalt even take five shekels apiece by the poll, after the shekel of the sanctuary shalt thou take *them*: ([e]the shekel *is* twenty gerahs:)
48 And thou shalt give the money, wherewith the odd number of them is to be redeemed, unto Aaron and to his sons.
49 And Moses took the redemption money of them that were over and above them that were redeemed by the Levites:
50 Of the firstborn of the children of Israel took he the money; a thousand three hundred and threescore and five *shekels*, after the shekel of the sanctuary:
51 And Moses gave the money of them that were redeemed unto Aaron and to his sons, according to the word of the LORD, as the LORD commanded Moses.

e Exod. 30. 13. Lev. 27. 25. chap. 18. 16. Ezek. 45. 12.

CHAPTER IV.

1 *The age and time of the Levites' service.* 4 *The carriage of the Kohathites, when the priests have taken down the tabernacle.* 16 *The charge of Eleazar.* 17 *The office of the priests.* 21 *The carriage of the Gershonites.* 29 *The carriage of the Merarites.* 34 *The number of the Kohathites,* 38 *of the Gershonites,* 42 *and of the Merarites.*

This when compared with the number of male adults (603, 550, cf. ii. 32) is disproportionately small, the usual proportion of first-born sons to a total male population being about one in four. The explanation is that the law of Ex. xiii. 1, 2, prescribed a dedication of those only who should be first-born *thenceforward*. (So Vitringa, Scott, Keil, Bp. Wordsw., Herxheimer, &c.) This seems implied in the very language used, "Sanctify unto Me the first-born, whatsoever openeth (not *hath opened*) the womb," Ex. xiii. 2, 11, 12: by the ground which God is pleased to assign (iii. 13, viii. 17) for making this claim: by the fact that the special duties of the first-born had reference to a ritual which, at the time of the Exodus, had yet to be revealed: and by the inclusion in the command of the first-born of cattle, which obviously must mean those *thereafter* first-born, for we cannot imagine that an inquisition amongst the flocks and herds was made at the exodus to discover for immediate sacrifice the first-born already in existence.

Hence the real difficulty is to explain how the first-born sons, amongst two millions of persons in a single year, could have been so many as is stated in the text; and it must be admitted, notwithstanding the well-known and often very remarkable fluctuations in statistics of this sort, that some unusual causes must have been concerned. Such, not to mention the Divine Blessing, may be found in the sudden development of national energies which would immediately ensue on the exodus. Before that event, the miserable estate of the people during their bondage, and especially the inhuman order for the destruction of their first-born, would check very seriously the ratio of marriages and births; and this ratio would naturally, when the check was removed, exhibit a sudden and striking increase. Commentators adduce some auxiliary arguments: *e.g.* Keil, from statistics argues, that amongst the Jews the proportion of male births is usually very large. In truth, however, we have no sufficient data for entering into statistical discussions upon the subject; and it is obvious that inferences drawn from the statistics of ordinary and settled communities are not altogether relevant to a case so peculiar in many ways as that laid before us in the Pentateuch.

44—51. The excess in the number of first-born males found amongst the twelve tribes is redeemed by money at a rate which henceforth became the fixed one (xviii. 16; Lev. xxvii. 6) for such redemption.

This redemption money would perhaps be exacted from the parents of the *youngest* children of the 22,273, they being in the case most nearly approaching that of those who would pay the tax for the redemption of the first-born in future. The cattle of the Levites was doubtless taken in the gross as an equivalent for the first-born cattle of the other tribes, which of course, no less than the first-born of men, belonged to the Lord; and in future would have to be redeemed (xviii. 15; Deut. xv. 19).

CHAP. IV. Particulars of the service of the Levites according to their three families, *vv.* 1—33; and numbering of the men between 30 and 50 years of age of each family severally (*vv.* 34—49).

AND the LORD spake unto Moses and unto Aaron, saying,

2 Take the sum of the sons of Kohath from among the sons of Levi, after their families, by the house of their fathers,

3 From thirty years old and upward even until fifty years old, all that enter into the host, to do the work in the tabernacle of the congregation.

4 This *shall be* the service of the sons of Kohath in the tabernacle of the congregation, *about* the most holy things:

5 ¶ And when the camp setteth forward, Aaron shall come, and his sons, and they shall take down the covering vail, and cover the ark of testimony with it:

6 And shall put thereon the covering of badgers' skins, and shall spread over *it* a cloth wholly of blue, and shall put in the staves thereof.

7 And upon the [a]table of shewbread they shall spread a cloth of blue, and put thereon the dishes, and the spoons, and the bowls, and covers to ‖cover withal: and the continual bread shall be thereon:

[a] Exod. 25. 30.

‖ Or, *pour out withal.*

8 And they shall spread upon them a cloth of scarlet, and cover the same with a covering of badgers' skins, and shall put in the staves thereof.

9 And they shall take a cloth of blue, and cover the [b]candlestick of the light, and his lamps, and his tongs, [c]and his snuffdishes, and all the oil vessels thereof, wherewith they minister unto it:

[b] Exod. 25. 31.

[c] Exod. 25. 38.

10 And they shall put it and all the vessels thereof within a covering of badgers' skins, and shall put *it* upon a bar.

11 And upon the golden altar they shall spread a cloth of blue, and cover it with a covering of badgers' skins, and shall put to the staves thereof:

12 And they shall take all the instruments of ministry, wherewith they minister in the sanctuary, and put *them* in a cloth of blue, and cover them with a covering of badgers' skins, and shall put *them* on a bar:

13 And they shall take away the ashes from the altar, and spread a purple cloth thereon:

14 And they shall put upon it all the vessels thereof, wherewith they minister about it, *even* the censers, the fleshhooks, and the shovels, and the ‖basons, all the vessels of the altar; and they shall spread upon it a covering of badgers' skins, and put to the staves of it.

‖ Or, *bowls.*

15 And when Aaron and his sons have made an end of covering the sanctuary, and all the vessels of the sanctuary, as the camp is to set forward; after that, the sons of Kohath shall come to bear *it*: but they shall not touch *any* holy thing, lest they die. These *things are* the burden of the sons of Kohath in the tabernacle of the congregation.

1—20. Service of the Kohathites, who take precedence because they take charge of "the most holy things."

4. *about the most holy things*] Omit the word "about," which is unnecessarily supplied. The sense is, "this is the charge of the sons of Kohath, the most holy things:" *i.e.* the Ark of the Covenant, the Table of Shew-bread, the Candlestick, and the Golden Altar, as appears from the verses following, together with the furniture pertaining thereto. Particular directions are laid down as to the preparation of these for being transported when the camp set forward, and strict injunction given that none but the Priests were to take part in that duty. After the Priests had covered the most holy things and made them ready according to the rules here prescribed, then only were the Kohathites to lift their burden (*v.* 15). It appears, from a comparison of *vv.* 16, 28, and 33, that the ministry of the Kohathites was superintended by Eleazar, the elder of the two surviving sons of Aaron; as was that of the two other families by Ithamar.

6. *wholly of blue.*] Cf. on Ex. xxv. 4. The third and external covering of the Ark only was to be of this colour. The Table of shew-bread had (*v.* 8) an outer wrapping of scarlet; the Altar (*v.* 13) one of purple.

put in the staves] Rather probably "put the staves thereof in order." These were never taken out of the golden rings by which the Ark was to be borne (see Ex. xxv. 14, 15), but would need adjustment after the process described in *vv.* 5 and 6, which would be likely to disturb them.

16 ¶ And to the office of Eleazar the son of Aaron the priest *pertaineth* the oil for the light, and the [d] sweet incense, and the daily meat offering, and the [e] anointing oil, *and* the oversight of all the tabernacle, and of all that therein *is*, in the sanctuary, and in the vessels thereof.

[d] Exod. 30. 34.
[e] Exod. 30. 23.

17 ¶ And the LORD spake unto Moses and unto Aaron, saying,

18 Cut ye not off the tribe of the families of the Kohathites from among the Levites:

19 But thus do unto them, that they may live, and not die, when they approach unto the most holy things: Aaron and his sons shall go in, and appoint them every one to his service and to his burden:

20 But they shall not go in to see when the holy things are covered, lest they die.

21 ¶ And the LORD spake unto Moses, saying,

22 Take also the sum of the sons of Gershon, throughout the houses of their fathers, by their families;

23 From thirty years old and upward until fifty years old shalt thou number them; all that enter in † to perform the service, to do the work in the tabernacle of the congregation.

† Heb. *to war the warfare.*

24 This *is* the service of the families of the Gershonites, to serve, and for ‖ burdens:

‖ Or, *carriage.*

25 And they shall bear the curtains of the tabernacle, and the tabernacle of the congregation, his covering, and the covering of the badgers' skins that *is* above upon it, and the hanging for the door of the tabernacle of the congregation,

26 And the hangings of the court, and the hanging for the door of the gate of the court, which *is* by the tabernacle and by the altar round about, and their cords, and all the instruments of their service, and all that is made for them: so shall they serve.

27 At the † appointment of Aaron and his sons shall be all the service of the sons of the Gershonites, in all their burdens, and in all their service: and ye shall appoint unto them in charge all their burdens.

† Heb. *mouth.*

28 This *is* the service of the families of the sons of Gershon in the tabernacle of the congregation: and their charge *shall be* under the hand of Ithamar the son of Aaron the priest.

29 ¶ As for the sons of Merari, thou shalt number them after their families, by the house of their fathers;

30 From thirty years old and upward even unto fifty years old shalt thou number them, every one that entereth into the † service, to do the work of the tabernacle of the congregation.

† Heb. *warfare.*

31 And this *is* the charge of their burden, according to all their service in the tabernacle of the congregation; [f] the boards of the tabernacle, and the bars thereof, and the pillars thereof, and sockets thereof,

[f] Exod. 26. 15.

32 And the pillars of the court round about, and their sockets, and their pins, and their cords, with all

---

20. *to see when the holy things are covered*] Render: **to see the holy things for an instant.** The expression means literally "as a gulp," *i.e.* for the instant it takes to swallow. Cf. Job vii. 19.

21—28. To the Gershonites is consigned the transport of all the hangings, curtains, and coverings of the tabernacle. They are superintended by Ithamar, Aaron's younger son, who had already had the oversight of the Tabernacle in its construction (Ex. xxxviii. 21). Thus readily do the permanent offices of the leaders of the Israelite community spring out of the duties which, under the emergencies of the first year of the Exodus, they had been led, from time to time, to undertake.

23. *enter in to perform the service*] Lit. as marg. "to war the warfare," or, as the same phrase in part is rendered, *v.* 3, "enter into the host to serve." The language is military. The service of God is a sacred warfare (viii. 24, 25).

29—33. The Merarites are also placed under the orders of Ithamar; and to them the transport of the pillars, boards, and more solid parts of the tabernacle is consigned.

their instruments, and with all their service: and by name ye shall reckon the instruments of the charge of their burden.

33 This *is* the service of the families of the sons of Merari, according to all their service, in the tabernacle of the congregation, under the hand of Ithamar the son of Aaron the priest.

34 ¶ And Moses and Aaron and the chief of the congregation numbered the sons of the Kohathites after their families, and after the house of their fathers,

35 From thirty years old and upward even unto fifty years old, every one that entereth into the service, for the work in the tabernacle of the congregation:

36 And those that were numbered of them by their families were two thousand seven hundred and fifty.

37 These *were* they that were numbered of the families of the Kohathites, all that might do service in the tabernacle of the congregation, which Moses and Aaron did number according to the commandment of the LORD by the hand of Moses.

38 And those that were numbered of the sons of Gershon, throughout their families, and by the house of their fathers,

39 From thirty years old and upward even unto fifty years old, every one that entereth into the service, for the work in the tabernacle of the congregation,

40 Even those that were numbered of them, throughout their families, by the house of their fathers, were two thousand and six hundred and thirty.

41 These *are* they that were numbered of the families of the sons of Gershon, of all that might do service in the tabernacle of the congregation, whom Moses and Aaron did number according to the commandment of the LORD.

42 ¶ And those that were numbered of the families of the sons of Merari, throughout their families, by the house of their fathers,

43 From thirty years old and upward even unto fifty years old, every one that entereth into the service, for the work in the tabernacle of the congregation,

44 Even those that were numbered of them after their families, were three thousand and two hundred.

45 These *be* those that were numbered of the families of the sons of Merari, whom Moses and Aaron numbered according to the word of the LORD by the hand of Moses.

46 All those that were numbered of the Levites, whom Moses and Aaron and the chief of Israel numbered, after their families, and after the house of their fathers,

47 From thirty years old and upward even unto fifty years old, every one that came to do the service of the ministry, and the service of the burden in the tabernacle of the congregation,

48 Even those that were number-

---

32. *by name ye shall reckon the instruments*] This direction, which occurs only in reference to the charge of the Merarites, imports apparently that "the instruments" were to be assigned, no doubt, by Ithamar and his immediate assistants, to their bearers singly, and nominatim. These "instruments" comprised the heavier parts of the Tabernacle; and the order seems intended to prevent individual Merarites choosing their own burden, and so throwing more than the proper share on others.

34—49. Numbering of the Levites after their families according to the command of *vv.* 1—3. This numbering exhibits of males between 30 and 50 years of age:

Family of Kohath	2750
Family of Gershon ...	2630
Family of Merari	3200
	8580

This number corresponds well with the total of 22,000, which the whole tribe reaches, iii. 39: but the number of Merarites available for the sacred service bears an unusually large proportion to the total number of males of that family, which is (iii. 34) 6200.

ed of them, were eight thousand and
five hundred and fourscore.

49 According to the commandment of the LORD they were numbered by the hand of Moses, every
one according to his service, and according to his burden: thus were
they numbered of him, as the LORD
commanded Moses.

CHAPTER V.

1 The unclean are removed out of the camp. 5 Restitution is to be made in trespasses. 11 The trial of jealousy.

AND the LORD spake unto Moses,
saying,

2 Command the children of Israel,
that they put out of the camp every
[a] Lev. 13. 3. [a]leper, and every one that hath an
[b] Lev. 15. 2. [b]issue, and whosoever is defiled by
[c] Lev. 21. 1. the [c]dead:

3 Both male and female shall ye
put out, without the camp shall ye
put them; that they defile not their
camps, in the midst whereof I dwell.

4 And the children of Israel did
so, and put them out without the
camp: as the LORD spake unto Moses, so did the children of Israel.

5 ¶ And the LORD spake unto
Moses, saying,

6 Speak unto the children of Is-
rael, [d]When a man or woman shall [d] Lev. 6
commit any sin that men commit, to
do a trespass against the LORD, and
that person be guilty;

7 Then they shall confess their sin
which they have done: and he shall
recompense his trespass [e]with the [e] Lev. 6.
principal thereof, and add unto it the
fifth *part* thereof, and give *it* unto
him against whom he hath trespassed.

8 But if the man have no kinsman
to recompense the trespass unto, let
the trespass be recompensed unto the
LORD, *even* to the priest; beside the
ram of the atonement, whereby an
atonement shall be made for him.

9 And every ‖offering of all the ‖ Or, *heave of-*
holy things of the children of Israel, *fering.*
which they bring unto the priest,
shall be his.

10 And every man's hallowed
things shall be his: whatsoever any
man giveth the priest, it shall be [f]his. [f] Lev. 10. 12.

11 ¶ And the LORD spake unto
Moses, saying,

CHAP. V. Now that the nation was regularly organized, the sacred tribe dedicated, and the sanctuary with the tokens of God's more immediate Presence provided with its proper place and attendants in the camp, it remained to attest and to vindicate, by modes in harmony with the spirit of the theocratical law, the sanctity of the people of God. This accordingly is the general purpose of the directions given in this and the next chapter. Thus the congregation of Israel was made to typify the Church of God, within which, in its perfection, nothing that offends can be allowed to remain (cf. St Matt. viii. 22; Rev. xxi. 27).

1—4. Removal of unclean persons out of the camp. The precepts respecting ceremonial defilements had been already laid down, Lev. xiii. and xv., excepting that arising from contact with a corpse, which occurs in Num. xix. (cf. however Lev. xi. 24, and xxi. 1). They are now first fully carried out; and hardly could have been so earlier, during the hurry and confusion which must have attended the march out of Egypt, and the encampments which next followed.

5—10. Law of restitution. In case of wrong against another recompense is prescribed, and the rule is based on the principle that such wrong doing is also "a trespass against the Lord," and so an infringement of the sanctity of the congregation: cf. Lev. v. 5 sqq., vi. 5 sqq., to which passages this appears supplementary.

6. *commit any sin that men commit*] Lit. "commit one of all the transgressions of man." The A. V. however probably gives the sense correctly, though some (Luth., Patrick, Rosenm., &c.) render "sins *against* men."

7. *recompense his trespass*] *i.e.* make restitution to the person whom he has injured.

8. *whereby an atonement shall be made for him*] Lit. "which shall clear him of guilt as to it," *i.e.* as to the trespass.

10. *And every man's hallowed things shall be his*] *i.e.* the priest's. The heave offerings (*v.* 9) and dedicatory offerings (*e.g.* first-fruits) were to be the perquisite of the officiating priests.

11—31. The trial of jealousy. Along with other ordinances intended at once to indicate and to secure the sanctity of God's people, is now given an ordeal which should remove the very suspicion of adultery from amongst them. As this crime is peculiarly defiling, and destructive of the very founda-

12 Speak unto the children of Israel, and say unto them, If any man's
wife go aside, and commit a trespass
against him,
13 And a man lie with her carnally, and it be hid from the eyes of
her husband, and be kept close, and
she be defiled, and *there be* no witness
against her, neither she be taken *with
the manner;*
14 And the spirit of jealousy come
upon him, and he be jealous of his
wife, and she be defiled: or if the
spirit of jealousy come upon him, and
he be jealous of his wife, and she be
not defiled:
15 Then shall the man bring his
wife unto the priest, and he shall
bring her offering for her, the tenth
part of an ephah of barley meal; he
shall pour no oil upon it, nor put frankincense thereon; for it *is* an offering
of jealousy, an offering of memorial,
bringing iniquity to remembrance.
16 And the priest shall bring her
near, and set her before the LORD:
17 And the priest shall take holy
water in an earthen vessel; and of
the dust that is in the floor of the
tabernacle the priest shall take, and
put *it* into the water:
18 And the priest shall set the woman before the LORD, and uncover
the woman's head, and put the offering of memorial in her hands, which
is the jealousy offering: and the priest
shall have in his hand the bitter water
that causeth the curse:
19 And the priest shall charge her
by an oath, and say unto the woman,
If no man have lain with thee, and if
thou hast not gone aside to uncleanness ‖ † *with another* instead of thy
husband, be thou free from this bitter
water that causeth the curse:
20 But if thou hast gone aside *to
another* instead of thy husband, and if
thou be defiled, and some man have
lain with thee beside thine husband:
21 Then the priest shall charge
the woman with an oath of cursing,
and the priest shall say unto the woman, The LORD make thee a curse
and an oath among thy people, when
the LORD doth make thy thigh to
† rot, and thy belly to swell;
22 And this water that causeth
the curse shall go into thy bowels, to
make *thy* belly to swell, and *thy* thigh
to rot: And the woman shall say,
Amen, amen.
23 And the priest shall write these
curses in a book, and he shall blot
them out with the bitter water:

‖ Or, being *in the power of thy husband.*

† Heb. *under thy husband.*

† Heb. *fall.*

---

tions of social order, the whole subject is dealt with at a length proportionate to its importance. The process prescribed has been lately strikingly illustrated from the Egyptian 'Romance of Setnau,' translated by Brugsch, which though itself comparatively modern (of the third century B.C.), yet refers to the time of Rameses the Great, and may therefore well serve to illustrate the manners and customs of the Mosaic times. "In the story, Ptahneferka takes a leaf of papyrus, and on it copies out every word of a certain magical formula. He then dissolves the writing in water, drinks the decoction, and knows in consequence all that it contained." See Smith, 'Pent.' I. 297, 298; 'Revue Archéol.' Sept. 1867, pp. 161 sqq. This then, like several other ordinances, was adopted by Moses from existing and probably very ancient and widely spread institutions.

15. The details given here are significant. The offering was to be of the fruits of the earth, but of the cheapest and coarsest kind, barley (cf. 2 K. vii. 1, 16, 18) representing the abased condition of the suspected woman. It was, like the sin-offering (Lev. v. 11), to be made without oil and frankincense, the symbols of grace and acceptableness. The woman herself stood whilst making her offering with head uncovered, in token of her shame.

17. *holy water*] No doubt from the laver which stood near the altar, Ex. xxx. 18 sqq.

the dust that is in the floor of the tabernacle] To set forth the fact that the water was indued with extraordinary power by Him that dwelt in the Tabernacle. Dust is an emblem of a state of condemnation (Gen. iii. 14; Micah vii. 17).

19. *gone aside to uncleanness with another instead of thy husband*] Render, **been faithless to**, literally "gone astray from" **thy husband by uncleanness**; cf. Hos. iv. 12.

23. *blot them out with the bitter water*] Rather, **wash them into the bitter water**; in order to transfer the curses into

24 And he shall cause the woman to drink the bitter water that causeth the curse: and the water that causeth the curse shall enter into her, *and become* bitter.

25 Then the priest shall take the jealousy offering out of the woman's hand, and shall wave the offering before the LORD, and offer it upon the altar:

26 And the priest shall take an handful of the offering, *even* the memorial thereof, and burn *it* upon the altar, and afterward shall cause the woman to drink the water.

27 And when he hath made her to drink the water, then it shall come to pass, *that*, if she be defiled, and have done trespass against her husband, that the water that causeth the curse shall enter into her, *and become* bitter, and her belly shall swell, and her thigh shall rot: and the woman shall be a curse among her people.

28 And if the woman be not defiled, but be clean; then she shall be free, and shall conceive seed.

29 This *is* the law of jealousies, when a wife goeth aside *to another* instead of her husband, and is defiled;

30 Or when the spirit of jealousy cometh upon him, and he be jealous over his wife, and shall set the woman before the LORD, and the priest shall execute upon her all this law.

31 Then shall the man be guiltless from iniquity, and this woman shall bear her iniquity.

CHAPTER VI.

1 *The law of the Nazarites.* 22 *The form of blessing the people.*

AND the LORD spake unto Moses, saying,

---

the water. The action was in this case purely symbolical, but travellers speak of the natives of Africa as still habitually seeking to obtain the full force of a written charm by drinking the water into which they have washed it.

24. *shall cause the woman to drink*] Thus was symbolized both her full acceptance of the hypothetical curse (cf. Ezek. iii. 1—3; Jer. xv. 16; Rev. x. 9), and its actual operation upon her if she should be guilty (cf. Ps. cix. 18). The direction in this verse is anticipatory; for the woman's offering was taken from her, and offered, before the water was actually given her to drink, *vv.* 25, 26.

26. *the memorial thereof*] The part of the offering burnt, as in Lev. ii. 2, &c. The Hebrew for it is not that which is translated "memorial" in *v.* 15.

27. *it shall come to pass*] The solemnity of the oath, and the awe-inspiring ritual which accompanied it, might of themselves suffice to deter a woman from taking it, unless she were supported by the consciousness of innocence. But the ingredients of the drink given to her were not in themselves noxious; and could only produce the effects here described by a special interposition of God, such as is promised so continually as the ultimate sanction of all the precepts of Moses. We do not read of any instance in which this ordeal was resorted to: a fact which may be explained either (with the Jews) as a proof of its efficacy, since the guilty could not be brought to face its terrors at all, and avoided them by confession; or more probably by the license of divorce tolerated by the law of Moses. Since a husband could put away his wife at pleasure, a jealous man would naturally prefer to take this course with a suspected wife rather than to call public attention to his own shame by having recourse to the trial of jealousy. The Talmud states that the trial lapsed into disuse forty years before the destruction of Jerusalem; and that because the crime of adultery was so common amongst men that God would no longer inflict the curses here named upon women (cf. Hos. iv. 14).

The trial by Red Water, which bears a general resemblance to that here prescribed by Moses, is still in use amongst the tribes of Western Africa. (See Kitto's 'Encycl.' ed. Alexander, Art. Adultery, and reff. to travellers therein.) There is no evidence to show whether this usage sprang from imitation of the law of Moses, or whether Moses himself, in this as in other things, engrafted his ordinance upon a previously existing custom. There is no doubt however that the managers of the ordeal in Africa prepare the Red Water so as to secure the result which they may desire from the experiment.

CHAP. VI. **1—21.** Law of the Nazarite. The previous chapter has provided for the exclusion from the pale of God's people of certain forms of guilt and defilement. The present one offers an opening to that zeal for God which, not content with observing what is obligatory, seeks for higher and stricter modes of self-dedication. Thus the law of the Nazarite is appropriately added to other enactments which concern the sanctity of the holy nation. That sanctity found its highest expression in the Nazarite vow, which was the voluntary adoption for a time of obligations

2 Speak unto the children of Israel,
and say unto them, When either man
or woman shall ‖separate *themselves* to
vow a vow of a Nazarite, to separate
themselves unto the LORD:
3 He shall separate *himself* from
wine and strong drink, and shall drink
no vinegar of wine, or vinegar of
strong drink, neither shall he drink
any liquor of grapes, nor eat moist
grapes, or dried.
4 All the days of his ‖separation
shall he eat nothing that is made of
the †vine tree, from the kernels even
to the husk.
5 All the days of the vow of his
separation there shall no *a*rasor come
upon his head: until the days be fulfilled, in the which he separateth *him-*
self unto the LORD, he shall be holy,
and shall let the locks of the hair of
his head grow.
6 All the days that he separateth
himself unto the LORD he shall come
at no dead body.
7 He shall not make himself unclean for his father, or for his mother,
for his brother, or for his sister, when
they die: because the †consecration of
his God *is* upon his head.
8 All the days of his separation he
is holy unto the LORD.
9 And if any man die very suddenly by him, and he hath defiled the

‖ Or, *make themselves Nazarites.*

‖ Or, *Nazariteship.*

† Heb. *vine of the vine.*

a Judg. 13. 5. 1 Sam. 1. 11.

† Heb. *separation.*

resembling, and indeed in some particulars exceeding, those under which the Priests were placed. It is obvious, from the manner in which the subject is introduced in *v.* 2, that the present enactments do not institute a new kind of observance, but only regulate one already familiar to the Israelites. The illustrations of the subject which have been adduced from Egyptian and other heathen customs (cf. Bilmar, in 'Stud. und Kritik.' 1864) must however be admitted to be vague and partial.

2. *separate themselves to vow a vow of a Nazarite, to separate themselves*] Rather probably, "shall solemnly vow a vow," as LXX., μεγάλως εὔξηται εὐχήν. Two different Hebrew words are in the A. V. rendered by "separate;" and the former of them, as in Judg. xiii. 19, is probably meant only to qualify the word next following.

a Nazarite] This term signifies "separated," *i.e.* as the words following show, "unto God" (cf. Judg. xiii. 5). It is used in a general sense, Gen. xlix. 26; Lev. xxv. 5, 11; Deut. xxxiii. 16; Lam. iv. 7; but became, as it is used in A. V., a technical term at an early date; cf. Judg. xiii. 5, 7, xvi. 17. It should in strictness be written *Nāzirite.* The accepted spelling has no doubt prevailed amongst Christians from its being supposed that this vow is referred to in St Matt. ii. 23.

3. *liquor of grapes*] *i.e.* a drink made of grape-skins macerated in water.

4. *from the kernels even to the husk*] A sour drink was made from the stones of unripe grapes; and cakes were also made of the husks. These latter appear from Hos. iii. 1 (see note there) to have been regarded as a delicacy. These regulations forbid the Nazarite using wine or any other product into which the vine or its fruit enters. The Priests were also forbidden to taste wine whilst engaged in the sacred functions (Lev. x. 9—11). This interdict figures that separation from the general society of men to which the Nazarite for the time was consecrated. The Flamen Dialis amongst the Romans was forbidden to touch a vine, or even to walk under one.

5. The second rule prohibits the Nazarite from cutting his hair during the period of his vow. The hair is to be regarded as the symbol of the vital power at its full natural development. Generally amongst the Jews the abundance of the hair was considered to betoken physical strength and perfection (cf. 2 S. xiv. 25, 26), and baldness was regarded as a grave blemish, which exposed a man to ridicule, and even disqualified him for admission to priestly functions (cf. Lev. xxi. 20 note, xiii. 40 sqq.; 2 K. ii. 23; Is. iii. 24). Thus the free growth of the hair on the head of the Nazarite represented the dedication of the man with all his strength and powers to the service of God.

6—8. The third rule of the Nazarite interdicted him from contracting any ceremonial defilement even under circumstances which excused such defilement in others: cf. especially Lev. xxi. 1—3, where the discharge of the last duties to deceased kinsmen is permitted to the ordinary priests under specified conditions, though forbidden here to Nazarites as it was to the High Priest, Lev. xxi. 10, 11. On the uncleanness caused by contact with a corpse, cf. xix. 11 sqq.; Lev. v. 2; xi. 24 sqq. It is of course assumed that all other ceremonial defilements were to be shunned by the Nazarites: cf the directions given to Samson's mother, Judg xiii. 4 sqq.

7. *the consecration of his God*] *i.e.* the unshorn locks: cf. Lev. xxv. 5, 11, where the vine, left during the Sabbatical year untouched by the hand of man, either for pruning or for vintage, is called simply a "Nazarite."

head of his consecration; then he shall shave his head in the day of his cleansing, on the seventh day shall he shave it.

10 And on the eighth day he shall bring two turtles, or two young pigeons, to the priest, to the door of the tabernacle of the congregation:

11 And the priest shall offer the one for a sin offering, and the other for a burnt offering, and make an atonement for him, for that he sinned by the dead, and shall hallow his head that same day.

12 And he shall consecrate unto the LORD the days of his separation, and shall bring a lamb of the first year for a trespass offering: but the days that were before shall †be lost, because his separation was defiled.

† Heb. *fall.*

13 ¶ And this *is* the law of the Nazarite, when the days of his separation are fulfilled: he shall be brought unto the door of the tabernacle of the congregation:

14 And he shall offer his offering unto the LORD, one he lamb of the first year without blemish for a burnt offering, and one ewe lamb of the first year without blemish for a sin offering, and one ram without blemish for peace offerings,

15 And a basket of unleavened bread, cakes of fine flour mingled with oil, and wafers of unleavened bread anointed with oil, and their meat offering, and their drink offerings.

16 And the priest shall bring *them* before the LORD, and shall offer his sin offering, and his burnt offering:

17 And he shall offer the ram *for* a sacrifice of peace offerings unto the LORD, with the basket of unleavened

---

9—12. Prescriptions to meet the case of involuntary defilement contracted by a Nazarite. In case of a sudden death taking place "by him" (*i.e.* in his presence), the Nazarite had to undergo the ordinary process of purification commanded for others (cf. xix. 11, 12, and Lev. v. 6 sqq.), and also besides to offer a trespass offering as "having sinned in the holy things of the Lord" (cf. Lev. v. 15 sqq.); and that of a kind peculiar to this case. Moreover his hair was to be shaved, and the days of his dedication to be recommenced, those that had been observed previously to his defilement being regarded as lost.

13—21. Ceremonies on the completion of the Nazarite vow.

13. *when the days of his separation are fulfilled*] The tenor of these words seems to imply that perpetual Nazariteship was unknown in the days of Moses. On the other hand, however, Moses does not expressly require that limits should be assigned to the vow; and the examples of Samson, Samuel, and John the Baptist, show that it was in later times undertaken for life, and that parents could even devote their future children to it (1 S. i. 11). The Jewish doctors recognize two classes of perpetual Nazarites, the "Samson Nazarites" who were not bound by the rules laid down in *vv.* 9—11, and the "ordinary perpetual Nazarites," who were allowed to poll their hair when too heavy. The exemption of the Samson Nazarite is inferred from Judg. xv. 16, where Samson wields the jawbone of the dead ass, yet is not recorded to have brought any sacrifice afterwards. These dispensations have no countenance from the chapter before us. Another rule imposed by the administrators of the law, that no Nazarite vow should be taken for less than thirty days, is reasonable. To permit the vow to be taken for very short periods, would diminish its solemnity and estimation.

14. *his offering*] *i.e.* the offering of which particulars follow immediately. From the rationale of these sacrifices (cf. Lev. viii., ix.) it would seem that the sin-offering (cf. Lev. iv. 32 sqq.), though named second, was in practice offered first, being intended to expiate involuntary sins committed during the period of separation. The burnt-offering (Lev. i. 10 sqq.) denoted the self-surrender on which alone all acceptableness in the Nazarite before God must rest; the peace-offerings (Lev. iii. 12 sqq.) expressed thankfulness to God by whose grace the vow had been fulfilled.

15. *their meat offering, and their drink offerings*] *i.e.* the ordinary meat and drink-offerings which were subsidiary to the other offerings required in *v.* 14 (cf. Ex. xxix. 40, 41; Num. xxviii. 9 sqq.; Lev. ii. 4, vii. 12 sqq.); and additional to the basket of unleavened bread, the cakes and the wafers specially prescribed in the beginning of this verse to be brought by the Nazarite. The offerings required on the completion of the Nazarite vow thus involved considerable expense, and it was regarded as a pious work to provide the poor with the means of making them (cf. Acts xxi. 23 sqq.; Joseph. 'Antiq.' XIX. 6. 1; 1 Macc. iii. 49).

bread: the priest shall offer also his
meat offering, and his drink offering.
[b] Acts 21. 24. 18 [b] And the Nazarite shall shave
the head of his separation *at* the door
of the tabernacle of the congregation,
and shall take the hair of the head of
his separation, and put *it* in the fire
which *is* under the sacrifice of the
peace offerings.
19 And the priest shall take the
sodden shoulder of the ram, and one
unleavened cake out of the basket,
and one unleavened wafer, and shall
put *them* upon the hands of the Nazarite, after *the hair of* his separation
is shaven:
20 And the priest shall wave them
for a wave offering before the LORD:
[c] this *is* holy for the priest, with the [c] Exod. 29. 27.
wave breast and heave shoulder: and
after that the Nazarite may drink
wine.
21 This *is* the law of the Nazarite
who hath vowed, *and of* his offering
unto the LORD for his separation, beside *that* that his hand shall get: according to the vow which he vowed,
so he must do after the law of his
separation.
22 ¶ And the LORD spake unto
Moses, saying,
23 Speak unto Aaron and unto his

---

18. *shave the head*] As the Nazarite had during his vow worn his hair unshorn in honour of God, so when the time was complete it was natural that the hair, the symbol of his vow, should be cut off, and offered to God at the sanctuary. The burning of the hair "in the fire under the sacrifice of the peace offering," represented the eucharistic communion with God obtained by those who realized the ideal which the Nazarite set forth. The Nazarite vow is only one of many illustrations of the religious significance associated with the hair in ancient times and in very diverse countries. St Paul is said to have "shorn (the word should rather be 'polled') his head in Cenchrea because he had a vow," Acts xviii. 18; where the "vow" can hardly be that of a Nazarite, though that mentioned, Acts xxi. 23 sqq. (see notes on these places), no doubt was so. The many and various observances connected with the hair may be traced back to the estimation attached to a profuse growth of it. Peleus ('Il.' XXIII. 142 sqq.) dedicates a lock of Achilles' hair and vows to shear it on the safe return of his son from the Trojan war. Achilles after the death of Patroclus cuts off this sacred lock, and in course of the funeral rites places it in the hand of his dead friend. Other like observances may be noticed, Æsch. 'Choeph.' 7; Eurip. 'Bacchæ,' 494. Similar customs were known to the Romans; cf. Suet. 'Nero,' 12; Martial, IX. 17, 3; Seneca, 'Herc. Fur.' 855; Lucan, 'Pharsal.' V. 6, 3. Examples are found of vows symbolized by particular modes of cropping or partially shaving off the hair, as amongst the Egyptians, Herod. II. 65. The casting of hair from the forehead of victims into the flame as an earnest of the sacrifice about to be offered is mentioned, 'Il.' XIX. 254; Virgil, 'Æn.' VI. 245. Very apposite to the text is Koran, II. 192, "Perform the pilgrimage, and shave not your heads until your offering reaches the place of sacrifice;" and Morier, 'Second Journey into Persia,' p. 117, "After the birth of a son, if the parent be in distress, or the child be sick.... the mother makes a vow that no razor shall come upon the child's head for a certain time, or for life, cf. 1 Sam. i. 11. If the child recovers, and the vow be but for a time, so that the mother's vow be fulfilled, then she shaves his head at the end of the time prescribed, makes an entertainment, collects money and other things from her relations, which are sent as Nezers (offerings) to the mosque." Further illustrations are given by Winer, 'Realw.' Art. 'Nasiräer.'

20. *the priest shall wave them*] *i.e.* by placing his hands under those of the Nazarite: cf. on Lev. vii. 28 sqq.

21. *beside that that his hand shall get*] Lit. "his hand grasps." The Nazarite, in addition to the offerings prescribed above, was to present free-will offerings according to his means.

22—27. The priestly blessing: cf. Ecclus. xxxvi. 17. The blessing gives as it were the crown and seal to the whole sacred order, by which Israel was now fully organized, as the people of God, for the march to the Holy Land. It is appointed as a solemn form to be used by the priests exclusively, and in this function their office as it were culminates (cf. Lev. ix. 22). The duties thus far assigned to them and their assistants have had reference to the purity, order, and sanctity of the nation. This whole set of regulations is most suitably and emphatically closed by the solemn words of benediction, in which God vouchsafes to survey as it were (cf. Gen. i 31) the whole theocratic system created by Himself for man's benefit, and pronounces it very good. Accordingly a formula is provided by God Himself, through which from time to time,

sons, saying, On this wise ye shall
bless the children of Israel, saying
unto them,
24 The LORD bless thee, and keep
thee:
25 The LORD make his face shine
upon thee, and be gracious unto thee:
26 The LORD lift up his countenance upon thee, and give thee peace.
27 And they shall put my name
upon the children of Israel; and I
will bless them.

CHAPTER VII.

1 The offering of the princes at the dedication of the tabernacle. 10 Their several offerings at the dedication of the altar. 89 God speaketh to Moses from the mercy seat.

AND it came to pass on the day
that Moses had fully [a] set up [a] Exod. 40. 18.
the tabernacle, and had anointed it,
and sanctified it, and all the instruments thereof, both the altar and all
the vessels thereof, and had anointed
them, and sanctified them;

---

as His people by obedience place themselves in true and right relationship to Him, the authorized mediators may pronounce and communicate His special blessing to them. The Jewish tradition therefore that this blessing was given at the close of the daily sacrifice is at least in accordance with its character and tenor. It will be observed that the text does not appoint the occasion on which it is to be used.

The structure of the blessing is remarkable. It is rhythmical; consists of three distinct parts, in each of which the Most Holy Name stands as nominative; it contains altogether twelve words, excluding the Sacred Name itself; and mounts by gradual stages to that Peace which forms the last and most consummate gift which God can give His people.

From a Christian point of view, and comparing the counterpart Benediction of 2 Cor. xiii. 14 (cf. Is. vi. 3; Matt. xxviii. 19), it is impossible not to see shadowed forth the Doctrine of the Holy Trinity. And the three several sets of terms correspond fittingly to the office of the Persons in their gracious work in the redemption of man.

24. *The LORD bless thee, and keep thee*] The second clause here, as in the other three verses, defines more closely the general tenor of the preceding one. The singular number, which is observed throughout, indicates that the blessing is conferred on Israel *collectively*.

25. *make his face shine*] This is an enhancement of the preceding benediction. "The face of God" imports not merely God's good will in general, but His active and special regard. With the "face" or "eye of the Lord" accordingly is connected alike the judicial visitation of the wicked (cf. Ps. xxxiv. 17), and His mercies to the righteous (Ps. iv. 6).

26. *lift up his countenance upon thee*] *i.e.* specially direct His thought and care towards thee: cf. 2 K. ix. 32, and similar phrases Gen. xliii. 29, xliv. 21. Through such loving providence alone could the peace of God in which the blessing closes be given.

27. *put my name upon the children of Israel*] *i.e.* pronounce my Sacred Name over them in blessing them. Maimonides states that the Sacred Name has never been used even in the solemn benediction of the sanctuary since the death of Simon the Just.

and I will bless them] *i.e.* the children of Israel, not, as some, the Priests. The words import that God will give effect to the benediction pronounced by the Priests.

CHAP. VII. This and the two next chapters narrate the closing events which happened during the stay at Sinai.

The present chapter describes the presentation of gifts by the Princes of the Tribes at the dedication of the Tabernacle.

1. *on the day that*] *i.e.* "at the time that," cf. Gen. ii. 4. The presentation of the gifts in fact occupied twelve days, as the sequel shows. The "Princes" were apparently first elevated to official dignity in connexion with the numbering of the people (cf. i. 1—16). Their offering of gifts then was made after that census, and of course before the breaking up of the encampment at Sinai, *i.e.* between the first and the twentieth days of the second month in the second year: cf. i. 1. The anointing of the Tabernacle here referred to had no doubt taken place in the course of the first month, Ex. xl. 17, Lev. viii. 10 sqq., and had occupied eight days of that month, Lev. viii. 33. The enactments set forth in the Chapters from Lev. x. to Numb. vi. inclusive, were doubtless promulgated at various times between the consecration of the Tabernacle and the departure from Sinai, but are for convenience set out connectedly. The contents of the present chapter are accordingly placed after them; and all the more properly, since part of the gifts consisted of the wagons and oxen by which the Tabernacle and its furniture could be conveyed in the ensuing marches. The order pursued throughout is justly noted as one which would naturally suggest itself to a narrator who was contemporary with the events.

2 That the princes of Israel, heads
of the house of their fathers, who
† Heb. who stood. *were* the princes of the tribes, [†]and
were over them that were numbered,
offered:
3 And they brought their offering
before the LORD, six covered wagons,
and twelve oxen; a wagon for two of
the princes, and for each one an ox:
and they brought them before the tabernacle.
4 And the LORD spake unto Moses, saying,
5 Take *it* of them, that they may
be to do the service of the tabernacle
of the congregation; and thou shalt
give them unto the Levites, to every
man according to his service.
6 And Moses took the wagons and
the oxen, and gave them unto the
Levites.
7 Two wagons and four oxen he
gave unto the sons of Gershon, according to their service:
8 And four wagons and eight oxen
he gave unto the sons of Merari, according unto their service, under the
hand of Ithamar the son of Aaron the
priest.
9 But unto the sons of Kohath
he gave none: because the service of
the sanctuary belonging unto them
was that they should bear upon their
shoulders.
10 ¶ And the princes offered for
dedicating of the altar in the day that
it was anointed, even the princes offered their offering before the altar.
11 And the LORD said unto Moses, They shall offer their offering,
each prince on his day, for the dedicating of the altar.
12 ¶ And he that offered his offering the first day was Nahshon the son
of Amminadab, of the tribe of Judah:
13 And his offering *was* one silver
charger, the weight thereof *was* an
hundred and thirty *shekels*, one silver
bowl of seventy shekels, after the shekel of the sanctuary; both of them
were full of fine flour mingled with
oil for a [b]meat offering: b Lev. 2. 1.
14 One spoon of ten *shekels* of
gold, full of incense:
15 One young bullock, one ram,
one lamb of the first year, for a burnt
offering:
16 One kid of the goats for a [c]sin c Lev. 4. 23.
offering:
17 And for a sacrifice of peace offerings, two oxen, five rams, five he
goats, five lambs of the first year:
this *was* the offering of Nahshon the
son of Amminadab.
18 ¶ On the second day Nethaneel
the son of Zuar, prince of Issachar,
did offer:
19 He offered *for* his offering one
silver charger, the weight whereof
was an hundred and thirty *shekels*,
one silver bowl of seventy shekels,
after the shekel of the sanctuary;
both of them full of fine flour mingled with oil for a meat offering:
20 One spoon of gold of ten *shekels*, full of incense:

---

3. *covered wagons*] The qualifying word of this phrase is rendered "litter," Is. lxvi. 20; and some (Gesen., De Wette, &c.) prefer to render "litter wagons:" *i.e.* litters which were not on wheels, but borne by two oxen, one in front and one behind. Such conveyances would probably be more convenient than wheeled wagons in the rough country to be traversed.

7—9. To the Gershonites, who had to transport the hangings and coverings of the tabernacle, two wagons are assigned: to the Merarites, who had the charge of the solid parts of the tabernacle, four wagons. The furniture and vessels the Kohathites were to carry on their own shoulders. Compare iii. 25, 26, 31, 36, 37.

12—83. The several princes make their offerings in the order assigned to the tribes, ch. ii. It was doubtless the tribes themselves which presented these gifts through their chiefs. The twelve offerings are strictly alike, and had no doubt been arranged and prepared previously. They were offered however on twelve separate days, and the narrative describing each severally at length with unaltered language, reflects somewhat of the stately solemnity which marked the repetition of the same ceremonial day by day. Of course the sacrifices brought by each prince were offered on the day on which they were presented; the chargers, bowls, and spoons being preserved for the future use of the Sanctuary.

21 One young bullock, one ram,
one lamb of the first year, for a burnt
offering:
22 One kid of the goats for a sin
offering:
23 And for a sacrifice of peace offerings, two oxen, five rams, five he
goats, five lambs of the first year:
this *was* the offering of Nethaneel the
son of Zuar.
24 ¶ On the third day Eliab the
son of Helon, prince of the children
of Zebulun, *did offer:*
25 His offering *was* one silver
charger, the weight whereof *was* an
hundred and thirty *shekels*, one silver
bowl of seventy shekels, after the shekel of the sanctuary; both of them
full of fine flour mingled with oil for
a meat offering:
26 One golden spoon of ten *shekels*, full of incense:
27 One young bullock, one ram,
one lamb of the first year, for a
burnt offering:
28 One kid of the goats for a sin
offering:
29 And for a sacrifice of peace offerings, two oxen, five rams, five he
goats, five lambs of the first year:
this *was* the offering of Eliab the son
of Helon.
30 ¶ On the fourth day Elizur the
son of Shedeur, prince of the children of Reuben, *did offer:*
31 His offering *was* one silver
charger of the weight of an hundred
and thirty *shekels*, one silver bowl of
seventy shekels, after the shekel of the
sanctuary; both of them full of fine
flour mingled with oil for a meat offering:
32 One golden spoon of ten *shekels*, full of incense:
33 One young bullock, one ram,
one lamb of the first year, for a burnt
offering:
34 One kid of the goats for a sin
offering:
35 And for a sacrifice of peace offerings, two oxen, five rams, five he
goats, five lambs of the first year:
this *was* the offering of Elizur the
son of Shedeur.

36 ¶ On the fifth day Shelumiel
the son of Zurishaddai, prince of the
children of Simeon, *did offer:*
37 His offering *was* one silver
charger, the weight whereof *was* an
hundred and thirty *shekels*, one silver
bowl of seventy shekels, after the shekel of the sanctuary; both of them
full of fine flour mingled with oil for
a meat offering:
38 One golden spoon of ten *shekels*, full of incense:
39 One young bullock, one ram,
one lamb of the first year, for a burnt
offering:
40 One kid of the goats for a sin
offering:
41 And for a sacrifice of peace offerings, two oxen, five rams, five he
goats, five lambs of the first year:
this *was* the offering of Shelumiel the
son of Zurishaddai.
42 ¶ On the sixth day Eliasaph
the son of Deuel, prince of the children of Gad, *offered:*
43 His offering *was* one silver
charger of the weight of an hundred
and thirty *shekels*, a silver bowl of
seventy shekels, after the shekel of the
sanctuary; both of them full of fine
flour mingled with oil for a meat offering:
44 One golden spoon of ten *shekels*, full of incense:
45 One young bullock, one ram,
one lamb of the first year, for a burnt
offering:
46 One kid of the goats for a sin
offering:
47 And for a sacrifice of peace offerings, two oxen, five rams, five he
goats, five lambs of the first year:
this *was* the offering of Eliasaph the
son of Deuel.
48 ¶ On the seventh day Elishama
the son of Ammihud, prince of the
children of Ephraim, *offered:*
49 His offering *was* one silver
charger, the weight whereof *was* an
hundred and thirty *shekels*, one silver
bowl of seventy shekels, after the shekel of the sanctuary; both of them
full of fine flour mingled with oil for
a meat offering:

50 One golden spoon of ten *shekels*, full of incense:
51 One young bullock, one ram,
one lamb of the first year, for a burnt
offering:
52 One kid of the goats for a sin
offering:
53 And for a sacrifice of peace offerings, two oxen, five rams, five he
goats, five lambs of the first year:
this *was* the offering of Elishama the
son of Ammihud.
54 ¶ On the eighth day *offered*
Gamaliel the son of Pedahzur, prince
of the children of Manasseh:
55 His offering *was* one silver
charger of the weight of an hundred
and thirty *shekels*, one silver bowl of
seventy shekels, after the shekel of
the sanctuary; both of them full of
fine flour mingled with oil for a meat
offering:
56 One golden spoon of ten *shekels*, full of incense:
57 One young bullock, one ram,
one lamb of the first year, for a burnt
offering:
58 One kid of the goats for a sin
offering:
59 And for a sacrifice of peace offerings, two oxen, five rams, five he
goats, five lambs of the first year:
this *was* the offering of Gamaliel the
son of Pedahzur.
60 ¶ On the ninth day Abidan
the son of Gideoni, prince of the children of Benjamin, *offered:*
61 His offering *was* one silver
charger, the weight whereof *was* an
hundred and thirty *shekels*, one silver
bowl of seventy shekels, after the shekel of the sanctuary; both of them
full of fine flour mingled with oil for
a meat offering:
62 One golden spoon of ten *shekels*, full of incense:
63 One young bullock, one ram,
one lamb of the first year, for a burnt
offering:
64 One kid of the goats for a sin
offering:
65 And for a sacrifice of peace offerings, two oxen, five rams, five he
goats, five lambs of the first year:
this *was* the offering of Abidan the
son of Gideoni.
66 ¶ On the tenth day Ahiezer
the son of Ammishaddai, prince of
the children of Dan, *offered:*
67 His offering *was* one silver
charger, the weight whereof *was* an
hundred and thirty *shekels*, one silver
bowl of seventy shekels, after the shekel of the sanctuary; both of them
full of fine flour mingled with oil for
a meat offering:
68 One golden spoon of ten *shekels*, full of incense:
69 One young bullock, one ram,
one lamb of the first year, for a burnt
offering:
70 One kid of the goats for a sin
offering:
71 And for a sacrifice of peace offerings, two oxen, five rams, five he
goats, five lambs of the first year:
this *was* the offering of Ahiezer the
son of Ammishaddai.
72 ¶ On the eleventh day Pagiel
the son of Ocran, prince of the children of Asher, *offered:*
73 His offering *was* one silver
charger, the weight whereof *was* an
hundred and thirty *shekels*, one silver
bowl of seventy shekels, after the shekel of the sanctuary; both of them
full of fine flour mingled with oil for
a meat offering:
74 One golden spoon of ten *shekels*, full of incense:
75 One young bullock, one ram,
one lamb of the first year, for a burnt
offering:
76 One kid of the goats for a sin
offering:
77 And for a sacrifice of peace offerings, two oxen, five rams, five he
goats, five lambs of the first year:
this *was* the offering of Pagiel the son
of Ocran.
78 ¶ On the twelfth day Ahira
the son of Enan, prince of the children of Naphtali, *offered:*
79 His offering *was* one silver
charger, the weight whereof *was* an
hundred and thirty *shekels*, one silver

bowl of seventy shekels, after the shekel of the sanctuary; both of them full
of fine flour mingled with oil for a
meat offering:
80 One golden spoon of ten *she-*
kels, full of incense:
81 One young bullock, one ram,
one lamb of the first year, for a burnt
offering:
82 One kid of the goats for a sin
offering:
83 And for a sacrifice of peace offerings, two oxen, five rams, five he
goats, five lambs of the first year:
this *was* the offering of Ahira the son
of Enan.
84 This *was* the dedication of the
altar, in the day when it was anointed, by the princes of Israel: twelve
chargers of silver, twelve silver bowls,
twelve spoons of gold:
85 Each charger of silver *weighing*
an hundred and thirty *shekels*, each
bowl seventy: all the silver vessels
weighed two thousand and four hundred *shekels*, after the shekel of the
sanctuary:
86 The golden spoons *were* twelve,
full of incense, *weighing* ten *shekels*
apiece, after the shekel of the sanctuary: all the gold of the spoons *was*
an hundred and twenty *shekels*.
87 All the oxen for the burnt offering *were* twelve bullocks, the rams
twelve, the lambs of the first year
twelve, with their meat offering: and
the kids of the goats for sin offering
twelve.
88 And all the oxen for the sacrifice of the peace offerings *were* twenty
and four bullocks, the rams sixty, the
he goats sixty, the lambs of the first
year sixty. This *was* the dedication
of the altar, after that it was anointed.
89 And when Moses was gone into
the tabernacle of the congregation to
speak with ‖him, then he heard the ‖ That is,
voice of one speaking unto him from *God.*
off the mercy seat that *was* upon the
ark of testimony, from between the
two cherubims: and he spake unto
him.

CHAPTER VIII.

1 *How the lamps are to be lighted.* 5 *The consecration of the Levites.* 23 *The age and time of their service.*

AND the LORD spake unto Moses,
saying,
2 Speak unto Aaron, and say unto [a] Exod.
him, When thou [a]lightest the lamps, 25. 37. & 40. 25.

84—88. If a silver shekel be taken, roughly, as weighing 2·5 of a shilling, and a golden shekel 1·15 of a sovereign, the intrinsic worth, by weight, of each silver charger will be 325*s*., of each bowl 175*s*., of each golden spoon 230*s*. Consequently the aggregate worth, by weight, of the whole of the offerings will be £438. But the real worth of such a sum, when measured by the prices of clothing and food at that time, must have been vastly greater. It must not be forgotten too that the Tabernacle itself had been recently constructed at a vast cost.

89. *tabernacle of the congregation*] Rather **of meeting**, cf. Ex. xxix. 42 and note.

with him] *i.e.* as marg. with God, not (as some) with himself. The name of God is implied in the phrase "tabernacle of meeting."

he heard the voice of one speaking] Rather **he heard the voice speaking**, or **conversing**. The proper force of the Hebrew participle (Hithpael, as in 2 S. xiv. 13; Ezek. ii. 2, xliii. 6) would be given if we render, "he heard the voice making itself as speaking." The effect was as though Moses was audibly addressed by another person: how this effect was produced we are not told.

Thus was the promise of Ex. xxv. 20—22 (on which see notes) fulfilled; and that as an immediate response on the part of God to the cheerful readiness with which the tribes had made their offerings, and supplied everything needful for the Holy Place and its service (cf. Lev. ix. 23, 24, and notes). All being now complete as God had appointed, and the camp purified from defilements, God meets Moses the mediator of the people, not as before on the peak of Sinai far away, but in their very midst, in the dwelling-place which He henceforth vouchsafed to tenant.

CHAP. VIII. **1—4.** These verses enjoin the actual lighting of the lamps on the Golden Candlestick. This was now to be done to set forth symbolically the peculiar presence which God had now (cf. vii. 89) actually established amongst His people. The workmanship, arrangements, and ritual of the Candlestick and its Lamps have been already discussed, Ex. xxv. 31 sqq., xxvii. 20 sqq., xxxvii. 17 sqq., xl. 24, 25; where see notes.

the seven lamps shall give light over against the candlestick.

3 And Aaron did so; he lighted the lamps thereof over against the candlestick, as the LORD commanded Moses.

[b] Exod. 25. 31.

4 [b]And this work of the candlestick *was of* beaten gold, unto the shaft thereof, unto the flowers thereof, *was*

[c] Exod. 25. 18.

[c]beaten work: according unto the pattern which the LORD had shewed Moses, so he made the candlestick.

5 ¶ And the LORD spake unto Moses, saying,

6 Take the Levites from among the children of Israel, and cleanse them.

† Heb. *let them cause a rasor to pass over, &c.*

7 And thus shalt thou do unto them, to cleanse them: Sprinkle water of purifying upon them, and †let them shave all their flesh, and let them wash their clothes, and *so* make themselves clean.

8 Then let them take a young bullock with his meat offering, *even* fine flour mingled with oil, and another young bullock shalt thou take for a sin offering.

9 And thou shalt bring the Levites before the tabernacle of the congregation: and thou shalt gather the whole assembly of the children of Israel together:

10 And thou shalt bring the Levites before the LORD: and the children of Israel shall put their hands upon the Levites:

11 And Aaron shall †offer the Levites before the LORD *for* an †offering of the children of Israel, that †they may execute the service of the LORD.

† Heb. *wave.*

† Heb. *wave offering.*

† Heb. *they may be to execute, &c.*

12 And the Levites shall lay their

---

2. *over against the candlestick*] Cf. Ex. xxv. 37 and note.

5—22. Ordination of the Levites to the duties already prescribed for them in chaps. iii., iv. This could only take place after the formal exchange of the Levites for the first-born (iii. 44—51); and probably stands here in its proper chronological order.

The "consecration" of the Priests is recorded Lev. viii. The distinction between that ceremony and the less solemn "purification" (cf. *v.* 21) of the Levites is marked. The Levites are simply sprinkled with water, have to wash their clothes, and to shave their flesh (*v.* 7); and then are offered (*vv.* 10, 11) to God on behalf of the people. There is no "washing" with water, anointing, or sprinkling with the blood of a consecrating sacrifice (Lev. viii. 6, 22, 30). These rites of purification are similar to those incumbent on the priests of Egypt: see 'Introd. to Pentateuch,' p. 15.

7. *water of purifying*] Lit. "sin water:" *i.e.* water to cleanse from sin. This water was no doubt that taken from the laver or the sanctuary, which was used by the Priests for purification before they went into the tabernacle to minister (cf. v. 17; Ex. xxx. 18 sqq.). The water used for cleansing the leper (Lev. xiv. 5) was prepared in a peculiar manner for that single purpose; as was also the water of separation, ch. xix.; neither could be available for such a purpose as the inauguration of the Levites.

The "sprinkling" of so large a body of men could have been only general. The tokens of individual purification were, however, to be exhibited by each of them through the shaving of the body and washing the clothes; on which ceremonies and their import see Lev. xiv. 8 and notes.

8. The two bullocks were "to make an atonement for the Levites," and therefore are presented in their name. These offerings are similar to those prescribed Lev. viii. 14 sqq. at the consecration of the priests, except that the burnt-offering was on that occasion a ram. The larger victim corresponds to the larger number of the Levites.

10. *the children of Israel*] *i.e.* through the heads of their tribes, who here, as elsewhere (cf. vii. 2), no doubt acted for their tribesmen. This act, the distinguishing feature of the ceremony, represented the transfer to the Levites of the sacred duties originally incumbent on the whole people.

11. *Offer...offering*] Lit. here and in *vv.* 13, 15, "wave," and "wave-offering," as marg. How this was to be done is not determined. Most likely Aaron pointed to the Levites, and then waved his hands as in ordinary cases of making this offering. The multitude of the Levites seems to preclude the other modes suggested; *e.g.* causing them to march backwards and forwards before the Altar, or taking them round it. The ceremony of waving indicated (cf. Lev. vii. 30 and note) that the offering was dedicated to God, and, again, by grant from Him withdrawn for the use of the priests. It was therefore aptly used at the inauguration of the Levites.

hands upon the heads of the bullocks: and thou shalt offer the one *for* a sin offering, and the other *for* a burnt offering, unto the LORD, to make an atonement for the Levites.

13 And thou shalt set the Levites before Aaron, and before his sons, and offer them *for* an offering unto the LORD.

14 Thus shalt thou separate the Levites from among the children of Israel: and the Levites shall be [d] mine.

[d] chap. 3. 45.

15 And after that shall the Levites go in to do the service of the tabernacle of the congregation: and thou shalt cleanse them, and offer them *for* an offering.

16 For they *are* wholly given unto me from among the children of Israel; instead of such as open every womb, *even instead of* the firstborn of all the children of Israel, have I taken them unto me.

17 [e] For all the firstborn of the children of Israel *are* mine, *both* man and beast: on the day that I smote every firstborn in the land of Egypt I sanctified them for myself.

[e] Exod. 13. 2. chap. 3. 13. Luke 2. 23.

18 And I have taken the Levites for all the firstborn of the children of Israel.

19 And I have given the Levites *as* † a gift to Aaron and to his sons from among the children of Israel, to do the service of the children of Israel in the tabernacle of the congregation, and to make an atonement for the children of Israel: that there be no plague among the children of Israel, when the children of Israel come nigh unto the sanctuary.

† Heb. *given.*

20 And Moses, and Aaron, and all the congregation of the children of Israel, did to the Levites according unto all that the LORD commanded Moses concerning the Levites, so did the children of Israel unto them.

21 And the Levites were purified, and they washed their clothes; and Aaron offered them *as* an offering before the LORD; and Aaron made an atonement for them to cleanse them.

22 And after that went the Levites in to do their service in the tabernacle of the congregation before Aaron, and before his sons: as the LORD had commanded Moses concerning the Levites, so did they unto them.

23 ¶ And the LORD spake unto Moses, saying,

24 This *is it* that *belongeth* unto the Levites: from twenty and five years old and upward they shall go in † to wait upon the service of the tabernacle of the congregation:

† Heb. *to war the warfare of, &c.*

---

13. *And thou shalt set*] The copula might perhaps be better rendered "thus" in this place than in the beginning of the next verse. The *vv.* 13—15 reiterate the commands of *vv.* 6 sqq., and point to the rite as directly preparatory to the Levites going in "to do the service of the tabernacle."

16. *the firstborn of all the children of Israel*] Hebr. more emphatically, "the firstborn of every one of, &c."

19. *make an atonement for the children of Israel*] *i.e.* by performing those services which were due from the children of Israel; the omission of which by the children of Israel would but for the interposition of the Levites have called down wrath from God.

That there be no plague] Cf. i. 53. The institution of the Levites was an extension of that mediatorial system which the people themselves, terrified at the direct manifestations to them of the Divine Presence, desired, Deut. v. 25. The office of Moses, of the Priests, and, finally, of the Levites, was to interpose after rules and limits laid down by God Himself between Him and the people. The substitution of the Levites for the firstborn is suggested to us here as an act of mercy on the part of God; for the firstborn, had they had to discharge their duties in person, would assuredly have fallen into omissions or transgressions of the prescribed order, such as would have drawn down those judicial visitations by which God taught Israel the reverence due to Him. Even the Priests and Levites themselves were not always sufficiently heedful and reverent. Cf. Lev. x. 1 sqq.; Num. xvii.; 2 Sam. vi. 6 sqq.

21. *were purified*] Rather, **purified themselves**; *i.e.* by shaving their flesh and washing their clothes, as directed in *v.* 7.

23—26. Period of the Levites' service.

24. *twenty and five years old and upward*] But in iv. 3, 23, 30, the limit is fixed at *thirty* years instead of twenty-five. The directions

25 And from the age of fifty years
they shall †cease waiting upon the
service *thereof*, and shall serve no
more:

† Heb. *return from the warfare of the service.*

26 But shall minister with their
brethren in the tabernacle of the congregation, to keep the charge, and
shall do no service. Thus shalt thou
do unto the Levites touching their
charge.

CHAPTER IX.

1 *The passover is commanded again.* 6 *A second passover. allowed for them that were unclean or absent.* 15 *The cloud guideth the removings and encampings of the Israelites.*

AND the LORD spake unto Moses
in the wilderness of Sinai, in the
first month of the second year after
they were come out of the land of
Egypt, saying,
2 Let the children of Israel also
keep *a*the passover at his appointed
season.
3 In the fourteenth day of this
month, †at even, ye shall keep it in
his appointed season: according to all
the rites of it, and according to all the
ceremonies thereof, shall ye keep it.
4 And Moses spake unto the children of Israel, that they should keep
the passover.
5 And they kept the passover on
the fourteenth day of the first month
at even in the wilderness of Sinai:

a Exod. 12. 1, &c. Lev. 23. 5. chap. 28. 16. Deut. 16. 2.

† Heb. *between the two evenings.*

---

there given however are temporary, and refer to the transport of the Tabernacle during the journeyings in the wilderness; those of this place are permanent, and determine the ordinary and regular obligations of the Levites with respect to the service. The pulling down, erection, and conveyance of the Tabernacle and its furniture would require the services of able-bodied and careful men in their prime; and the number of Levites between 30 and 50 might well suffice for those duties. After the people were settled in Canaan, and the Levites dispersed over the whole land in their cities, the somewhat larger number which the law now before us would afford was necessary. This number indeed proved to be insufficient, even though the Tribe had considerably increased (1 Chron. xxiii. 3), when David reorganized and developed the whole ritual of the law; and accordingly amongst his last acts he extended the period of the Levites' service by causing it to commence at 20 years of age (1 Chron. xxiii. 24—28). And this David is expressly stated to have done because the Levites had no longer to carry the Tabernacle and the vessels (1 Chr. xxiii. 26); and, consequently, younger men might now undertake the office. This rule continued in force from the time of David downwards (cf. 2 Chron. xxxi. 17; Ezra iii. 8).

to wait upon the service] Cf. iv. 23 and note).

CHAP. IX. 1—5. Passover at Sinai. This, as being kept in the first month, was prior in time to the numbering of ch. i. 1 sqq., and to the other events narrated in this book. It is, however, recorded here as introductory to the ordinance of *vv.* 6—14 in this chapter respecting the supplementary Passover, the observance of which was one of the last occurrences during the halt at Sinai.

From the terms of the institution of the Passover (Ex. xii. 25, xiii. 5—10), it would appear that the next celebration of it was designed to be after the settlement in Canaan. As, however, the anniversary of the Feast occurred before the wilderness was traversed, a special command of God is given to meet the case; and had it not been for the subsequent rebellion of the people they would have been "brought into the land of the Canaanites" before this festival came round a third time.

5. As to the manner in which this exceptional Passover was observed we are only informed generally in *v.* 3 that the Israelites conformed to "all the rites and ceremonies" of it. Probably, in some details, the present Passover differed both from the one kept at the Exodus itself and from all subsequent ones. The direction of Ex. xii. 17 ("they shall take of the blood and strike it on the two side posts, &c.") could obviously not be carried out in the letter whilst the people were dwelling in tents; and indeed may, together with the whole command to kill the Paschal victim at home, be regarded as superseded by Lev. xvii. 3—6, enforced as regards the Passover in particular by Deut. xvi. 5 sqq.

But if the blood of the Paschal victims was sprinkled by the Priests upon the altar, it may be asked how Aaron, Eleazar, and Ithamar, the only Priests at this time, could discharge this duty within the time prescribed, "between the two evenings:" cf. Ex. xii. 6. The number of victims must of course have been great; but it has been much overstated by those who estimate it to have reached many scores of thousands. To eat a morsel of the Paschal victim satisfied the commemorative purposes of the Festival, as the Jewish authorities remark; and calculations as to the

according to all that the LORD commanded Moses, so did the children of
Israel.
6 ¶ And there were certain men,
who were defiled by the dead body of
a man, that they could not keep the
passover on that day: and they came
before Moses and before Aaron on
that day:
7 And those men said unto him,
We *are* defiled by the dead body of a
man: wherefore are we kept back,
that we may not offer an offering of
the LORD in his appointed season
among the children of Israel?
8 And Moses said unto them,
Stand still, and I will hear what the
LORD will command concerning you.
9 ¶ And the LORD spake unto
Moses, saying,
10 Speak unto the children of Israel, saying, If any man of you or of
your posterity shall be unclean by
reason of a dead body, or *be* in a
journey afar off, yet he shall keep the
passover unto the LORD.
11 The fourteenth day of the second month at even they shall keep
it, *and* eat it with unleavened bread
and bitter *herbs*.
12 They shall leave none of it un-
to the morning, [b]nor break any bone [b] Exod. 12. 46.
of it: according to all the ordinances John 19. 36.
of the passover they shall keep it.
13 But the man that *is* clean, and
is not in a journey, and forbeareth
to keep the passover, even the same
soul shall be cut off from among his
people: because he brought not the
offering of the LORD in his appointed
season, that man shall bear his sin.
14 And if a stranger shall sojourn
among you, and will keep the passover unto the LORD; according to the
ordinance of the passover, and according to the manner thereof, so shall he
do: [c]ye shall have one ordinance, [c] Exod. 12. 49.
both for the stranger, and for him
that was born in the land.
15 ¶ And [d]on the day that the [d] Exod. 40. 34.
tabernacle was reared up the cloud
covered the tabernacle, *namely*, the
tent of the testimony: and at even
there was upon the tabernacle as it
were the appearance of fire, until the
morning.

---

number of lambs required to supply the two million of Israelites with a meal are therefore irrelevant. Neither was it necessary that all the victims should be lambs: cf. Ex. xii. 5. The Priests were no doubt assisted at this time, as afterwards (cf. 2 Chron. xxx. 16, xxxv. 11) by the Levites. In such points of detail the administrators of the law of Moses would here, as elsewhere, have, from the nature of the case, power to order what might be requisite to carry the law into effect. Josephus, 'Bell. Jud.' VI. 9. 3, speaks of the blood of 256,000 victims having been in his days sprinkled on the altar within three hours.

6. *certain men*] Probably (cf. Blunt's 'Script. Coincidences,' pp. 62—65) Mishael and Elizaphan, who buried their cousins, Nadab and Abihu, within a week of this Passover (Lev. x. 4, 5). None would be more likely to make this inquiry of Moses than his kinsmen, who had defiled themselves by his express direction.

11. *The fourteenth day of the second month*] The later Jews speak of this as the Little Passover. Coming, as it did, a month after the proper Passover, it afforded ample time for a man to purify himself from legal defilement, as also to return from any but a very distant journey. It was in conformity with the spirit of this ordinance that Hezekiah, at the opening of his reign, celebrated the Great Passover in the second month, being unable to complete the sanctification of the temple and priesthood against the regular season of the feast (2 Chron. xxix., xxx.).

12. *according to all the ordinances*] *i.e.* those relating to the passover-lamb, not those concerning the feast; for the Little Passover lasted, according to the Jews, only one day; nor was it held to be needful that at it leaven should be put away out of the houses.

15—20. The signals given by God for marching and for halting.

15. *on the day that the tabernacle was reared up*] Cf. Ex. xl. 34, which is evidently referred to in this verse. The phenomenon first appeared at the Exodus itself, Ex. xiii. 21, 22; it is now again more particularly described in connexion with the journeyings which are to be narrated in the sequel of the book.

the tabernacle, namely, the tent of the testimony] On these words see note at end of chapter.

16 So it was alway: the cloud covered it *by day*, and the appearance of fire by night.

17 And when the cloud was taken up from the tabernacle, then after that the children of Israel journeyed: and in the place where the cloud abode, there the children of Israel pitched their tents.

18 At the commandment of the LORD the children of Israel journeyed, and at the commandment of the
1 Cor. 10. LORD they pitched: [e]as long as the cloud abode upon the tabernacle they rested in their tents.

Heb. prolonged.
19 And when the cloud †tarried long upon the tabernacle many days, then the children of Israel kept the charge of the LORD, and journeyed not.

20 And *so* it was, when the cloud was a few days upon the tabernacle; according to the commandment of the LORD they abode in their tents, and according to the commandment of the LORD they journeyed.

21 And *so* it was, when the cloud
†abode from even unto the morning, † Heb. *was.*
and *that* the cloud was taken up in the morning, then they journeyed: whether *it was* by day or by night that the cloud was taken up, they journeyed.

22 Or *whether it were* two days, or a month, or a year, that the cloud tarried upon the tabernacle, remaining thereon, the children of Israel
[f]abode in their tents, and journeyed [f] Exod. 40.
not: but when it was taken up, they 36, 37.
journeyed.

23 At the commandment of the LORD they rested in the tents, and at the commandment of the LORD they journeyed: they kept the charge of the LORD, at the commandment of the LORD by the hand of Moses.

---

20. *And so it was, when*, &c.] Rather, **And there was also when, &c.** (cf. for the Hebrew, Neh. v. 2, 3, 4). As the preceding verse had contemplated a time when the cloud tarried many days, so there were also occasions on which it tarried but few days.

21. *And so it was, when*, &c.] Rather, **And there was also when the cloud abode from even unto morning, and the cloud was taken up in the morning, and they journeyed:** see on *v.* 20.

22. *a year*] The Hebrew expression is "days," which idiomatically denotes a year in Lev. xxv. 29. But in the present passage the ancient translators, whom some follow, understood it to mean simply "a longer time." It probably is equivalent to "a full period," though not necessarily the period of a year.

NOTE on CHAP. IX. 15.

1. In *v.* 15 the words "namely the tent of the testimony" are obviously added to the word "tabernacle" (משכן), in order to describe the phenomenon more accurately. The passage would literally run "the cloud covered the tabernacle towards the tent of the testimony" (לאהל העדת); *i.e.* the cloud did not cover the whole structure, court and all, but only the portion of it in which the Ark was placed, including perhaps the holy place as well as the holy of holies.

2. As the ark was termed "the Ark of Testimony" (cf. Ex. xxv. 16, 21, 22) because the testimony (*i.e.* the decalogue) was placed in it, so in like manner the inclosure which contained the Ark itself was termed the "tent of the testimony" or "witness:" as in the passage before us, and in xvii. 4, 8, xviii. 2.

3. The same portion of the structure seems properly to be indicated by the phrase אהל מועד, "tent of the congregation," or more properly "of meeting;" cf. note at the end of Ex. xl.

4. The phrase "tabernacle of testimony" (משכן העדת), seems (cf. i. 50, x. 11) to import generally the whole structure.

5. The A. V. generally translates משכן and אהל by "tabernacle" and "tent" respectively; but in Num. xvi. 42, 43 (in the Hebrew Bible, xvii. 7, 8) the latter word is represented by "tabernacle," as it is also in the repeated translation of אהל מועד by "tabernacle of the congregation," in Num. iii. Respecting the structure and arrangements of the Tabernacle full information is given in the notes on Ex. xxvi. and xl.

CHAPTER X.

1 *The use of the silver trumpets.* 11 *The Israelites remove from Sinai to Paran.* 14 *The order of their march.* 29 *Hobab is intreated by Moses not to leave them.* 33 *The blessing of Moses at the removing and resting of the ark.*

AND the LORD spake unto Moses, saying,

2 Make thee two trumpets of silver; of a whole piece shalt thou make them: that thou mayest use them for the calling of the assembly, and for the journeying of the camps.

3 And when they shall blow with them, all the assembly shall assemble themselves to thee at the door of the tabernacle of the congregation.

4 And if they blow *but* with one *trumpet*, then the princes, *which are* heads of the thousands of Israel, shall gather themselves unto thee.

5 When ye blow an alarm, then the camps that lie on the east parts shall go forward.

6 When ye blow an alarm the second time, then the camps that lie on the south side shall take their journey: they shall blow an alarm for their journeys.

7 But when the congregation is to be gathered together, ye shall blow, but ye shall not sound an alarm.

8 And the sons of Aaron, the priests, shall blow with the trumpets; and they shall be to you for an ordinance for ever throughout your generations.

9 And if ye go to war in your land against the enemy that oppresseth you, then ye shall blow an alarm with the trumpets; and ye shall be remembered before the LORD your God, and ye shall be saved from your enemies.

10 Also in the day of your gladness, and in your solemn days, and in the beginnings of your months, ye shall blow with the trumpets over your burnt offerings, and over the sacrifices of your peace offerings; that they may be to you for a memorial before your God: I *am* the LORD your God.

CHAP. X. 1—10. The Silver Trumpets. These, as employed in signalling the movements of the Camp, are here mentioned among other preliminaries for the impending journeys. Occasion is taken to describe the various uses of the Trumpets. It is not necessary to suppose that the Trumpets were now first appointed by God. Indeed, reference is made to them Lev. xxv. 9.

2. The trumpet (*khatsotserah*) was a straight instrument, differing in this respect from the curved horn or cornet (*keren*, *shophar*); yet the latter is frequently rendered "trumpet" in the English Version, when the two instruments are not mentioned together. The Jewish trumpet is described (Joseph. 'Ant.' III. 12. 6) as "a little less than a cubit in length; the tube narrow, a little thicker than a flute, and just wide enough to permit the performer to blow it; while it terminated, like other trumpets, in the form of a bell." Such instruments are represented, among the other spoils of the temple, on the Arch of Titus. See on Ex. xxv. 23. From Egyptian monuments it appears that the Jewish trumpet was copied from that used in the armies of the Pharaohs, &c. (see Wilkinson's 'Manners and Customs of the Ancient Egyptians,' II. pp. 260 sqq.). The shape of the cornet bespeaks its pastoral origin. At first it was a simple ram's horn (Josh. vi. 4); and the metal instrument of later times preserved the original shape.

5. *blow an alarm*] *i.e.* a long continuous peal. Cf. *v.* 7, *ye shall blow, but not sound an alarm: i.e.* blow in short, sharp notes not in a continuous peal.

6. *the second time*] The LXX. introduces here a third and a fourth alarm as signals for the west and north camps. No express mention of these is found in the Hebrew text, but we may infer that they were actually used.

8. *the sons of Aaron*] As the trumpets were emblematic of the voice of God the Priests only were to use them. At this time there were only two "sons of Aaron;" but in later times, when the number of priests was greater, more trumpets were used; we read of seven in the reign of David, 1 Chron. xv. 24; of a hundred and twenty in that of Solomon, 2 Chron. v. 12.

9. For examples of the employment of trumpets in war cf. xxxi. 6; Josh. vi.; 2 Chron. xiii. 12, 14, xx. 28. By this employment was signified the dependence of God's people on His aid.

10. *in the day of your gladness*] Cf. xxix. 1; Lev. xxiii. 24; 2 Chron. xxix. 27; Ezra iii. 10; Neh. xii. 35, 41; Ps. lxxxi. 3.

I am the LORD your God] Rather, **even before me, the LORD your God.** The words do not form a separate period as in A.V.

11 ¶ And it came to pass on the twentieth *day* of the second month, in the second year, that the cloud was taken up from off the tabernacle of the testimony.

12 And the children of Israel took their journeys out of the wilderness of Sinai; and the cloud rested in the wilderness of Paran.

13 And they first took their journey according to the commandment of the LORD by the hand of Moses.

14 ¶ [a] In the first *place* went the standard of the camp of the children of Judah according to their armies: and over his host *was* [b] Nahshon the son of Amminadab.

[a] chap. 2. 3.
[b] chap. 1. 7.

15 And over the host of the tribe

---

11. At this point commences the second great division of the book, extending to the close of chapter xiv. Cf. Introd. § 2. The remaining verses of the present chapter narrate the actual break up of the camp at Sinai and the order of the march.

12. *took their journeys*] Lit. "journeyed after their journeys," cf. Ex. xvii. 1.

the wilderness of Paran] This tract comprised about one-third of the entire extent of the peninsula, which lies between Egypt and Canaan, and is the eastern half of the great limestone plateau, which constitutes the centre of that peninsula. It was bounded on the north by the Canaanitish frontier; on the west by the Brook or River of Egypt, which parted it from the other half of the plateau, the Wilderness of Shur; on the south by the great sand-belt, which sweeps across the peninsula in a northwardly-concave line, from gulf to gulf, and forms a broad demarcation between it and the cliffs of Sinai; and on the east by the northern portion of the Elanitic gulf, and by the great valley of the Arabah, which divides it from the mountains of Edom. The Wilderness of Zin (to be carefully distinguished from that of Sin), forming the immediate boundary of Canaan (xxxiv. 3), was its north-eastern extremity; and it is thus that Kadesh is indifferently spoken of as in the Wilderness of Zin, or in that of Paran (xiii. 26, xx. 1, &c.). Indeed, in 1 Sam. xxv. 1, even parts of the south of Canaan seem to be included under the name of Paran. But this name has now disappeared from the tract in question, which, in common with the rest of the plateau of which it forms a part, is known under the general name of et-Tîh, "the Wandering;" a name also specially applied to the range of hills that mark its southern edge. It must not be confounded with a district which could never have been included within it, the well-known and beautiful Wâdy Feirân, deriving its name from the early Christian city on which, through some unexplained cause, the name Pharan was bestowed. But a genuine trace of it may perhaps be found in the Phara, marked in the Roman tables of the fourth century as a station on the road between the heads of the two gulfs, 120 Roman miles from the western and 50 from the eastern extremity (compare Ritter, I. pp. 69 and 428 sqq. Clark's Transl.).

The Wilderness of Paran is, on the whole, to European eyes, a blanched and dreary waste; intersected by watercourses, almost always dry except in the rainy season, and crossed by low ranges of horizontal hills which relieve but little the general monotony of its appearance. It does not exhibit the savage and frightful desolation of the Arabah; but neither, on the other hand, is it enlivened by the fertile valleys to be found amid the granite mountains of Sinai. Its soil is mostly strewn with pebbles, through which a slight coating of vegetation struggles; yet here and there level plains may be found in it of rich red earth fit for culture, or valleys abounding in shrubs and trees, and offering coverts for hares. It has been remarked that vegetation is readily produced wherever the winter rains do not at once run to waste (see Burckhardt, pp. 148 sqq.; Rogers, 'Mosaic Records,' Art. 130). But this vegetation has probably been long on the decrease, and is still decreasing, principally from the reckless destruction of trees for charcoal, and the aspect of the wilderness has been proportionately deteriorated thereby: see Introd. to Exodus, pp. 245, 246.

Towards this wilderness the Israelites now advanced on their march from Sinai to Canaan, unaware as yet that on its wastes the next eight and thirty years of their existence would be spent. They did not actually enter it till they had crossed the sand-belt: it is therefore mentioned here by anticipation. Their earliest halting-places, Kibroth-hattaavah and Hazeroth, were not within its limits (xi. 35, xii. 16). For the direction of their march see on xi. 35.

13. *And they first took their journey*, &c.] Rather, **And they journeyed** (or, set forth) **in the order of precedence according to** (*i.e.* established by) **the commandment of the LORD**, &c. The meaning of the Hebrew word for "first" is determined by its use in the following verse, where it applies to the camp of Judah going before the rest. This order of precedence is described in *vv.* 14—28.

14. *according to their armies*] Cf. i. 3. There were three tribal hosts in each camp; and each tribe had of course its subdivisions.

of the children of Issachar *was* Nethaneel the son of Zuar.
16 And over the host of the tribe
of the children of Zebulun *was* Eliab
the son of Helon.
17 And the tabernacle was taken
down; and the sons of Gershon and
the sons of Merari set forward, bearing the tabernacle.
18 ¶ And the standard of the camp
of Reuben set forward according to
their armies: and over his host *was*
Elizur the son of Shedeur.
19 And over the host of the tribe
of the children of Simeon *was* Shelumiel the son of Zurishaddai.
20 And over the host of the tribe
of the children of Gad *was* Eliasaph
the son of Deuel.
21 And the Kohathites set forward,
bearing the [c] sanctuary: and ‖ *the other*
did set up the tabernacle against they
came.
22 ¶ And the standard of the camp
of the children of Ephraim set forward according to their armies: and
over his host *was* Elishama the son of
Ammihud.
23 And over the host of the tribe
of the children of Manasseh *was* Gamaliel the son of Pedahzur.
24 And over the host of the tribe
of the children of Benjamin *was* Abidan the son of Gideoni.
25 ¶ And the standard of the camp
of the children of Dan set forward,
which was the rereward of all the
camps throughout their hosts: and
over his host *was* Ahiezer the son of
Ammishaddai.
26 And over the host of the tribe
of the children of Asher *was* Pagiel
the son of Ocran.
27 And over the host of the tribe
of the children of Naphtali *was* Ahira
the son of Enan.
28 † Thus *were* the journeyings of
the children of Israel according to
their armies, when they set forward.
29 ¶ And Moses said unto Hobab,
the son of Raguel the Midianite,
Moses' father in law, We are journeying unto the place of which the
LORD said, I will give it you: come
thou with us, and we will do thee
good: for the LORD hath spoken good
concerning Israel.
30 And he said unto him, I will

[c] chap. 4. 4.
‖ That is, *the Gershonites and the Merarites:* See ver. 17.
† Heb. *These.*

---

17. The command had been, in general terms, that the Levites, with the tabernacle, should occupy the central place in the line of march, after the camps of Judah and Reuben, ii. 17. But convenience now necessitated, if not a modification of this order, at least a more precise determination of the method of executing it. The appointed place of the tabernacle, in the midst of the host, was represented during the march by the ark, the holy vessels, &c. carried by the Kohathites; the actual structure of the tabernacle was borne in advance by the Gershonites and Merarites, immediately behind the camp of Judah; so as to be set up ready against the arrival of the sacred utensils borne by the Kohathites. See *v.* 21, and cf. chs. ii., iv.

21. *the sanctuary*, &c.] *i.e.* the holy furniture which remained when the tabernacle was taken down.

29. *Hobab, the son of Raguel the Midianite, Moses' father in law*] The form Raguel, for Reuel (Exod. ii. 18), has needlessly been perpetuated in the A. V. from the Latin; the names are one in Hebrew (so, Gaza and Azzah, Ai and Hai, &c.). Reuel was probably not identical with Jethro: see on Ex. ii. 18. It seems evident too that Hobab was in fact the brother-in-law, not the father-in-law, of Moses, and the Hebrew word translated in A. V. "father-in-law," signifies simply any relation by marriage, as does the Greek γαμβρός: see on Ex. ii. 18. Hobab is described as the "son of Reuel;" and the desire of Moses to obtain his services as guide through the wilderness indicates that he was younger than Moses' father-in-law could now have been. It is stated in Exod. xviii. 27 that Jethro quitted the Israelites, before they reached Sinai, to return to his own land; whilst it appears from the passage now before us compared with Judges i. 16, iv. 11, that Hobab eventually accompanied them, and obtained a settlement with them in the land of Canaan (so Joseph., Bertheau, Keil, &c.). Hobab and Jethro may have been brethren and sons of Reuel. The other solution that Jethro and Hobab were the same person, Jethro ("excellency") being his official title, though adopted by many authorities ancient and modern, seems less probable. More improbable still is the suggestion that Reuel, Jethro, and Hobab are all three appellations of one individual.

not go; but I will depart to mine
own land, and to my kindred.
31 And he said, Leave us not, I pray
thee; forasmuch as thou knowest how
we are to encamp in the wilderness, and
thou mayest be to us instead of eyes.
32 And it shall be, if thou go with
us, yea, it shall be, that what goodness
the LORD shall do unto us, the
same will we do unto thee.

33 ¶ And they departed from the
mount of the LORD three days' journey:
and the ark of the covenant of
the LORD went before them in the
three days' journey, to search out a
resting place for them.
34 And the cloud of the LORD *was*
upon them by day, when they went
out of the camp.
35 And it came to pass, when the

The Mahometan legends neither expressly identify nor yet distinguish between Jethro, Reuel, and Hobab. The Shu'eib of whom they speak, corresponds on the whole rather to the early host and father-in-law than to the subsequent companion of Moses; though his name has locally connected itself with a watercourse running westward into the Jordan opposite Jericho, as well as with one of the ravines at Sinai, and with a cave on the eastern shores of the eastern branch of the Red Sea. But even were these legends more definite, they could hardly carry weight in regard to the question before us.

31. *thou mayest be to us instead of eyes*] *i.e.* mayest discern what is needful for us: a proverbial expression still in use in the East. The narrative gives no more exact description of the services expected from Hobab. The divine guidance of the Pillar of the cloud would not render superfluous the human conductor who could indicate the spots where water, fuel, and pasture might be found, the dangers from hurricanes, and the localities infested by robbers. Probably indeed the Pillar prescribed only the general direction of the journey. Nor would it be according to the general analogy of God's dealings had He miraculously rendered His people independent of such aids from human experience and sagacity as were within their reach.

33. *three days' journey*] Probably a technical expression for such a distance as could not be traversed in a single day, and therefore not without intervals of encampment and due provision: cf. Gen. xxx. 36; Exod. iii. 18, v. 3, viii. 27, xv. 22. The technical use of the phrase "Sabbath-day's journey" for another average distance, Acts i. 12, is similar. Even were the expression strictly interpreted it would remain to be noted that three days of Jewish reckoning are not necessarily more than one whole day and two fragments of days. The end of this stage, where the tabernacle was first re-erected, and the square encampment formed, was apparently Kibroth-hattaavah: see xi. 24, 34, xxxiii. 16.

the ark of the covenant of the LORD went before them] From *v.* 21 and ii. 17 it would appear that the usual place of the Ark during the march was in the midst of the host. It was evidently an exceptional case when, in Josh. iii. the Ark preceded the people into the bed of the Jordan. Nevertheless some, especially among the Jewish commentators, attending only to the position of the Ark at the commencement of that miraculous passage, deem that the first march from Sinai was also similarly exceptional, it being for the occasion carried before the host. Others, as Keil, view the present verse as furnishing the key to the true interpretation of the earlier notices: they hold that the Ark, as distinguished from the sanctuary, went always in advance. They insist on the intimate connexion between the Ark as God's throne and the cloud of His presence, which latter we know to have preceded the host on its long line of march. Cf. Exod. xiii. 21, xiv. 19. But the better view is that of Bp. Patrick, that the words "went before them" do not here imply local precedence. The phrase, or its equivalent, is used of a leader going out in command of his troops, xxvii. 17; Deut. xxxi. 3; 1 Sam. xviii. 16; 2 Chron. i. 10; who of course would not necessarily go before them in a local sense. Thus the Ark may well be said to have gone at the head of the Israelites, when it was borne solemnly in their midst as the outward embodiment of the Presence whose sovereign word was their law. That the divine cloud remained with the Ark as they journeyed is not asserted, and the tenor of the next verse seems against it; as also is the fact that, when the tabernacle was reared, the cloud rested over, not within, the tabernacle.

a resting place] Lit. "rest." It is commonly understood of each successive encampment; or, in particular, of the first encampment. Yet the term would hardly be here employed, did it not carry with it a higher meaning, pointing to the promised rest of Canaan, for which the Israelites were now in full march, and from the speedy enjoyment of which no sentence of exclusion as yet debarred them. Cf. Deut. i. 33; Ps. xxxii. 8; Ezek. xx. 6.

ark set forward, that Moses said,
[d] Rise up, LORD, and let thine enemies be scattered; and let them that
hate thee flee before thee.
36 And when it rested, he said,
Return, O LORD, unto the †many
thousands of Israel.

d Psal. 68. 1, 2.
† Heb. *ten thousand thousands.*

CHAPTER XI.

1 *The burning at Taberah quenched by Moses' prayer.* 4 *The people lust for flesh, and loathe manna.* 10 *Moses complaineth of his charge.* 16 *God divideth his burden unto seventy elders.* 31 *Quails are given in wrath at Kibroth-hattaavah.*

AND *when* the people ‖complained,
†it displeased the LORD: and
the LORD heard *it;* [a] and his anger
was kindled; and the fire of the LORD
burnt among them, and consumed
them that were in the uttermost parts
of the camp.
2 And the people cried unto Moses; and when Moses prayed unto
the LORD, the fire †was quenched.
3 And he called the name of the
place ‖Taberah: because the fire of
the LORD burnt among them.
4 ¶ And the [b] mixt multitude that
was among them †fell a lusting: and
the children of Israel †also wept again,
and said, [c] Who shall give us flesh to eat?
5 We remember the fish, which
we did eat in Egypt freely; the cucumbers, and the melons, and the
leeks, and the onions, and the garlic:
6 But now our soul *is* dried away:
there is nothing at all, beside this
manna, *before* our eyes.

‖ Or, *were as it were complainers.*
† Heb. *it was evil in the ears of, &c.*
a Psal. 78. 21.
† Heb. *sunk.*
‖ That is, *A burning.*
b As Exo. 12. 38.
† Heb. *lusted a lust.*
† Heb. *returned and wept.*
c 1 Cor. 10. 6.

35, 36. Each forward movement and each rest of the Ark was made to bear a sacramental character. The one betokened the going forth of God against his enemies; the other, His gathering of His own people to himself: the one was the pledge of victory, the other the earnest of repose. The verb in *v.* 36 is best taken transitively (with Maurer, Gesen. &c.): "Restore" (*i.e.* to the land which their fathers sojourned in), "O LORD, the ten thousands of the thousands of Israel." (Cf. Psalm lxxxv. 4, where the verb in the Hebrew is the same.)

CHAP. XI. This and the following three chapters recount the successive rebellions of the Israelites after their departure from Sinai; culminating in that by which they brought upon themselves the sentence of personal exclusion from the land of promise. Incidentally the narrative furnishes some details of the northward march.

1—3. Burning at Taberah.

1. *And when the people complained, it displeased the LORD*] Render, **And the people were as those that complain of evil in the ears of the LORD**: *i.e.* they murmured against the privations of the march.

the fire of the LORD] Probably lightning: cf. Ps. lxxviii. 21. The cases xvi. 35 and Lev. x. 2 seem to be different.

in the uttermost parts] Rather, **in the end**. The fire did not reach far into the camp. It was quickly quenched at the intercession of Moses.

3. *Taberah*] (*i.e.* "burning"): not the name of a station, and accordingly not found in the list given in xxxiii., but only of the spot where the fire broke out. This incident might seem (cf. *v.* 34) to have occurred at the station called, from another still more terrible event which shortly followed, Kibroth-hattaavah (so Keil and Del., Clark, 'Bible Atlas,' p. 24); see on Deut. ix. 22.

4—35. Occurrences at Kibroth-hattaavah.

4. *the mixt multitude*] (Hebrew, *hasaphsuph*, a word which occurs here only). The word resembles our "riff-raff," and denotes a mob of people scraped together. It refers here to the multitude of strangers of Ex. xii. 38, who had followed the Israelites from Egypt.

wept again] *i.e.* as they had done before. Cf. Ex. xvi. 2 sqq.

5. *We remember the fish*, &c.] The natural dainties of Egypt are set forth in this passage with the fullness and relish which bespeak personal experience. Fish, garlic, onions, melons (especially water-melons), and cucumbers, abound in modern Egypt, and are used as staple articles of food. The first three were not less common in ancient Egypt (see Herod. II. 125, and especially Hengstenberg, 'Egypt and the Books of Moses,' ch. VII.).

leeks] The Hebrew word (*kâtsîr*) is the ordinary term for grass (cf. Ps. civ. 14, cxlvii. 8, &c.); and Hengstenberg l. c. strongly advocates the same rendering in this place. He identifies the *kâtsîr* with a kind of clover freely eaten in Egypt at the present day. The LXX. however, the writers of which must have been well acquainted with the diet customary in the country in question, renders "leeks" (πράσα); and this is followed by most authorities ancient and modern. Leeks were unquestionably much eaten in Egypt. Cf. Plin. 'Nat. Hist.' XIX. 33.

d Exod. 16. 14, 31. 7 And [d] the manna *was* as corian-
† Heb. der seed, and the † colour thereof as
eye of it as the eye of. the colour of bdellium.
8 *And* the people went about, and
gathered *it*, and ground *it* in mills, or
beat *it* in a mortar, and baked *it* in
pans, and made cakes of it: and the
taste of it was as the taste of fresh oil.
9 And when the dew fell upon the
camp in the night, the manna fell
upon it.
10 ¶ Then Moses heard the people
weep throughout their families, every
man in the door of his tent: and the
anger of the LORD was kindled greatly; Moses also was displeased.
11 And Moses said unto the LORD,
Wherefore hast thou afflicted thy servant? and wherefore have I not found
favour in thy sight, that thou layest
the burden of all this people upon
me?
12 Have I conceived all this people? have I begotten them, that thou
shouldest say unto me, Carry them in
thy bosom, as a nursing father beareth the sucking child, unto the land
which thou swarest unto their fathers?
13 Whence should I have flesh to
give unto all this people? for they
weep unto me, saying, Give us flesh,
that we may eat.
14 I am not able to bear all this
people alone, because *it is* too heavy
for me.
15 And if thou deal thus with me,
kill me, I pray thee, out of hand, if I
have found favour in thy sight; and
let me not see my wretchedness.
16 ¶ And the LORD said unto Moses, Gather unto me seventy men of
the elders of Israel, whom thou knowest to be the elders of the people, and
officers over them; and bring them
unto the tabernacle of the congregation, that they may stand there with
thee.
17 And I will come down and
talk with thee there: and I will take
of the spirit which *is* upon thee, and

---

onions] The staple food of the labourers at the pyramids: Herod. II. 125. These vegetables, which grew large in size and mild in flavour, were in various forms one of the most common dishes of the Egyptians.

garlic] Cf. Herod. l. c.

6. *there is nothing at all, beside this manna, before our eyes*] Heb. "Nought at all have we except that our eyes are unto this manna;" *i. e.* "Nought else have we to expect beside this manna." Cf. on the phrase, "to have the eyes towards," Ps. xxv. 15.

7—9. On the manna see on Ex. xvi.; on bdellium Gen. ii. 12. The description of the manna seems inserted in order to illustrate the unreasonableness of the people in disliking it.

10. *throughout their families*] The weeping was general; every family wept: cf. Zech. xii. 12.

every man in the door of his tent] The weeping was public and unconcealed.

11—15. The complaint and remonstrance of Moses may be compared with Gen. xviii. 23 sqq., and more appositely with 1 K. xix. 4 sqq.; Jonah iv. 1—3. The meekness of Moses (cf. xii. 3) sank under vexation into despair. The language shows us how imperfect and prone to degeneracy are the graces of the best saints on earth, as the forbearing answer of God manifests His readiness to heed and answer the sincere pouring out of the heart to Him, even though its utterances be passionate and unmeasured. For certainly Moses could not justly say that God had laid "the burden of all this people" upon him. Moses had ample direction and help from God. Such a trait as that exhibited in this passage would not have been attributed to Moses by tradition.

16. *seventy men of the elders of Israel*] Seventy elders had also gone up with Moses to the Lord in the mount, Ex. xxiv. 1, 9. On the historical and symbolical significance of this number see note there. Seventy is accordingly the number of colleagues assigned to Moses to share his burden with him; and to enable them for their office the spirit of the Lord was poured upon them. This appointment is totally distinct from that of the Captains or Rulers, Exod. xviii. 21 sq. and Deut. i. 9 sqq. (see note). To it, however, the Jews trace the origin of the Sanhedrim, and rightly, if we regard the Mosaic college as the prototype on which the Sanhedrim was modelled after the end of the monarchy. Subsequent notices (xvi. 25; Josh. vii. 6, viii. 10, 33, ix. 11, xxiii. 2, xxiv. 1, 31) of "the Elders" (not of *all* the elders, as in Ex. iv. 29, xii. 21, xviii. 12) make no mention of the number seventy; yet so connect the Elders with the government of Israel as to point to the fact that the appointment now made was not a

will put *it* upon them; and they shall
bear the burden of the people with
thee, that thou bear *it* not thyself
alone.
18 And say thou unto the people,
Sanctify yourselves against to morrow, and ye shall eat flesh: for ye
have wept in the ears of the LORD,
saying, Who shall give us flesh to eat?
for *it was* well with us in Egypt:
therefore the LORD will give you flesh,
and ye shall eat.
19 Ye shall not eat one day, nor
two days, nor five days, neither ten
days, nor twenty days;
20 *But* even a †whole month, until
it come out at your nostrils, and it be
loathsome unto you: because that ye
have despised the LORD which *is*
among you, and have wept before
him, saying, Why came we forth out
of Egypt?
21 And Moses said, The people,
among whom I *am*, *are* six hundred
thousand footmen; and thou hast
said, I will give them flesh, that they
may eat a whole month.
22 Shall the flocks and the herds
be slain for them, to suffice them?
or shall all the fish of the sea be gathered together for them, to suffice
them?
23 And the LORD said unto Moses,
[e]Is the LORD's hand waxed short?
thou shalt see now whether my word
shall come to pass unto thee or not.
24 ¶ And Moses went out, and
told the people the words of the LORD,
and gathered the seventy men of the
elders of the people, and set them
round about the tabernacle.
25 And the LORD came down in a
cloud, and spake unto him, and took
of the spirit that *was* upon him, and
gave *it* unto the seventy elders: and
it came to pass, *that*, when the spirit
rested upon them, they prophesied,
and did not cease.
26 But there remained two *of the*
men in the camp, the name of the
one *was* Eldad, and the name of the
other Medad: and the spirit rested
upon them; and they *were* of them
that were written, but went not out
unto the tabernacle: and they prophesied in the camp.
27 And there ran a young man,
and told Moses, and said, Eldad and
Medad do prophesy in the camp.
28 And Joshua the son of Nun,

† Heb. *month of days.*

e Isai. 50. 2. & 59. 1.

merely temporary one. The Council of the Elders however would seem to have soon fallen into desuetude. We find no traces of it in the days of the Judges and the Kings; nor is it easy to see how such an institution would have worked along with the forms and modes of monarchical government prevalent in the ancient East. Cf. note on Deut. xvii. 8.

elders of the people, and officers over them] In English idiom, "elders and officers of the people." Both elders and officers appear in Egypt, Ex. iii. 16, v. 6 sqq. The former had headed the nation in its efforts after freedom; the latter were the subordinate, though unwilling, agents of Egyptian tyranny. The two classes no doubt were working together; and from those who belonged to either, perhaps from those who were both elders and officers, the council of seventy was to be selected.

17. *I will take of the spirit which is upon thee*] Render rather *separate from the spirit* &c.; *i.e.* they shall have their portion in the same divine gift which thou hast.

25. *they prophesied*] *i.e.* under the extraordinary impulse of the Holy Ghost they uttered forth the praises of God, or declared His Will. Cf. 1 Sam. xix. 22 sqq. The Hebrew word here used (*hithnabbé*) imports etymologically "they were caused to pour forth."

and did not cease] Render, **and added not** (on the Hebrew word cf. Deut. v. 22): *i.e.* they prophesied at this time only and not afterwards. The sign was granted on the occasion of their appointment to accredit them in their office; it was not continued, because their proper function was to be that of government not prophesying.

26. *of them that were written*] *i.e.* enrolled amongst the Seventy. The expression points to a regular appointment duly recorded and permanent.

went not out unto the tabernacle] The reason of this can only be conjectured. It was not ceremonial uncleanness, since that (cf. v. 2) would have excluded them from the camp altogether.

27. *a young man*] Heb. "the young man;" *i.e.* the attendants collectively; cf. on Ex. iv. 20.

the servant of Moses, *one* of his young
men, answered and said, My lord
Moses, forbid them.

29 And Moses said unto him, Enviest thou for my sake? would God
that all the LORD's people were prophets, *and* that the LORD would put
his spirit upon them!

30 And Moses gat him into the
camp, he and the elders of Israel.

Exod. 16. 31 ¶ And there went forth a [f]wind
Psal. 78. from the LORD, and brought quails
from the sea, and let *them* fall by the
Heb. camp, [†]as it were a day's journey on
it were the way of a day. this side, and as it were a day's journey on the other side, round about
the camp, and as it were two cubits
high upon the face of the earth.

32 And the people stood up all that
day, and all *that* night, and all the
next day, and they gathered the quails:
he that gathered least gathered ten
homers: and they spread *them* all
abroad for themselves round about the
camp.

33 And while the [g]flesh *was* yet [g] Psal. 78. 31.
between their teeth, ere it was chew-
ed, the wrath of the LORD was kindled against the people, and the LORD
smote the people with a very great
plague.

34 And he called the name of that
place [‖]Kibroth-hattaavah: because ‖ That is, *The graves of lust.*
there they buried the people that
lusted.

35 *And* the people journeyed from
Kibroth-hattaavah unto Hazeroth; [†] Heb. *they were in, &c.*
and [†]abode at Hazeroth.

---

29. *Enviest thou for my sake?*] (Cf. St Mark ix. 38 sqq.). The other members of the Seventy had been with Moses (cf. *vv.* 16, 24, 25) when the gift of prophecy was bestowed on them. They received "of the spirit that was upon him," and exercised their office visibly through and for him. Eldad and Medad prophesying in the camp seemed to Joshua to be acting independently, and so establishing a separate centre of authority.

31. *a wind*] That is, as Ps. lxxviii. 26 intimates, though in a poetical form of expression, the south-east wind, which blew from the neighbouring Elanitic gulf of the Red Sea.

quails] Cf. Ex. xvi. 13.

let them fall by the camp] Rather "threw them upon or over the camp." The meaning is that the quails were borne by the wind upon the encampment and into its neighbourhood. LXX. correctly ἐπέβαλεν ἐπὶ τὴν παρεμβολήν. Cf. Ps. lxxviii. 27, 28.

round about] *i.e.* "on both sides of:" cf. Ex. vii. 24.

two cubits high upon the face of the earth] Omit the word "high" supplied by the A. V., and render **about two cubits above the face of the ground**: *i.e.* the quails, wearied with their long flight, flew about breast high, and were easily secured by the people. So Vulg. "volabant in aere duobus cubitibus altitudine super terram." The quail habitually flies with the wind, and low: "Aurâ vehi volunt, propter pondus corporum. Coturnix terrestris potius quam sublimis." Plin. 'N. H.' x. 23.

32. *ten homers*] On the homer, the largest measure of capacity used by the Hebrews, cf. Lev. xxvii. 16. The quantity of the quails indicated by the statements of the text is prodigious, and must be recognised as miraculous. But large flocks of birds, so numerous as to darken the sky, have been seen by modern travellers in the same district (Stanley, 'Sinai and Pal.' p. 82). The people had met with quails before in the desert: cf. Ex. xvi. 13, note and reff.

they spread them all abroad for themselves] In order to salt and dry them (cf. Herod. II. 77).

33. *ere it was chewed*] Better, **ere it was consumed**, as all the ancient translators understood it. Such a supply of food would last many days. Indeed God had told them that they should eat flesh "a whole month," until it came out at their nostrils, and was loathsome unto them (*v.* 20).

smote the people] Ancient naturalists assert that the quail feeds and fattens on herbs which are poisonous to man, and regarded the bird as unwholesome for food. Cf. Lucr. IV. 642:

"Præterea nobis veratrum est acre venenum,
At capris adipes et coturnicibus auget:"

and Plin. x. 23. Further illustrations are given, Bochart, II. 657. But Dr G. M. Humphry, Professor of Anatomy in the University of Cambridge, reports in a letter communicated to the writer (Dec. 21, 1870), that "in instances in which the contents of the quail's stomach have been examined after death only common grass and other seeds have been found." He adds however that the free partaking of quails, or indeed of any other bird, "for a whole month," *v.* 20, by a people lusting for flesh, would be likely to be attended with injurious consequences, especially under the circumstances in which the Israelites then were. Thus the plague with which God smote the people is to be regarded, as are miracles in many other cases, as a Divine interference enhancing a pre-exist-

CHAPTER XII.

1 *God rebuketh the sedition of Miriam and Aaron.* 10 *Miriam's leprosy is healed at the prayer of Moses.* 14 *God commandeth her to be shut out of the host.*

AND Miriam and Aaron spake
against Moses because of the
‖ Or, Cushite. ‖ Ethiopian woman whom he had married: for he had † married an Ethio- † Heb. *taken.*
pian woman.
2 And they said, Hath the LORD
indeed spoken only by Moses? hath
he not spoken also by us? And the
LORD heard *it*.
3 (Now the man Moses *was* [a] very [a] Ecclu 45. 4.

---

ing cause. The surfeit in which the people indulged, as described in *v.* 32, of itself disposed them to sickness. God's wrath, visiting the gluttonous through their gluttony, aggravated natural consequences into a supernatural visitation.

35. *journeyed from Kibroth-hattaavah*] They had probably, for the sake of the quails, continued at Kibroth-hattaavah longer than they otherwise would have done. Their lust, and God's indulgence of it, had been their hindrance. After a month's delay the punishment which had overtaken them would make them remove the more readily from the Encampment of Death; and, accordingly, the divine signal of the lifting of the cloud was given for their forward march.

Hazeroth] This place has been identified by Burckhardt and others with "Ain el Hadherah," a fountain some forty miles N.E. of Sinai. This, however, lies too much to the east of the proper route of the Israelites, and is approached by a route from Sinai, which offers no fitting site for Kibroth-hattaavah. With more probability Laborde locates Hazeroth at "El Ain," a place famous, as its name imports, for its spring; situated some fifteen miles northward of Ain el Hadherah; and in the route which the host must apparently have adopted; *i.e.* that by the Wady es Zŭlakeh (cf. Stanley, 'Sinai,' p. 84; Clark's 'Bible Atlas,' p. 24). Mr Clark, however, regards El Ain as identical with Kibroth-hattaavah, removing Hazeroth many miles still further on the march northwards, to Bir-eth-Themed. These are mere conjectures, and, in the instances before us, are the more precarious, as the name Hazeroth (= "inclosures") is of the sort that almost always serves more places than one, and is as suitable to a district as to a particular spot. It is probable, from its mention along with other places on the sea-shore, that the "Hazeroth" of Deut. i. 1 is not the same as the one now before us. El Ain, from its natural advantages, must certainly have formed one of the halting-places in the earlier stages of the march from Sinai, whether it be identified with Kibroth-hattaavah or Hazeroth. It is here that several valleys converge around springs, which, from their copiousness, render this the great oasis of the eastern side of the whole peninsula. On the route of the Israelites from Hazeroth see notes on xii. 16 and xxxiii. 18.

CHAP. XII. 1—15. Rebellion of Miriam and Aaron against Moses. Miriam, as a prophetess (cf. Ex. xv. 20, 21) no less than as the sister of Moses and Aaron, took the first rank amongst the women of Israel; and Aaron may be regarded as the ecclesiastical head of the whole nation. But instead of being grateful for these high dignities they presumed upon them, just as the Levites afterwards did on theirs (cf. xvi. 9), and went on to challenge the special vocation of Moses and the exclusive authority which God had assigned to him. This envious feeling had probably rankled in their minds for some time, but was now provoked to open outbreak by the recent (see next note) marriage of Moses, the circumstances of which touched the female susceptibilities of Miriam. She probably considered herself as supplanted, and that too by a foreigner. It is evident that she was the instigator, from the fact that her name stands conspicuously first (*v.* 1), and that the punishment (*v.* 10) fell on her alone. Aaron was misled this time by the urgency of his sister, as once before (Ex. xxxii.) by that of the people.

1. *the Ethiopian* (Heb. "Cushite") *woman whom he had married*] This can hardly be Zipporah, who was not an Ethiopian but a Midianite (cf. Ex. ii. 21). And even if we regard the term Cushite as one which Miriam applied to the wife of Moses in contempt, because of her dark colour, it is highly improbable that Miriam could now have brought up in reproach a marriage which Moses had contracted half a century at least previously, and before his special call by God. It is far more likely that Zipporah was dead, and that Miriam in consequence expected to have greater influence than ever with Moses. Her disappointment at his second marriage would consequently be very great.

On Cush, always, when translated at all, rendered by A.V. "Ethiopia" (*e.g.* Ps. lxviii. 31; Is. xliii. 3), cf. Gen. ii. 13, x. 6, and notes.

The marriage of Moses with a woman descended from Ham was not prohibited, so long as she was not of the stock of Canaan; cf. Ex. xxxiv. 11—16; but it would at any time have been offensive to that intense nationality which characterized the Jews. The Christian Fathers note in the successive marriage of Moses with a Midianite and an Ethiopian a foreshadowing of the future extension to the

meek, above all the men which *were*
upon the face of the earth.)
4 And the LORD spake suddenly
unto Moses, and unto Aaron, and
unto Miriam, Come out ye three unto
the tabernacle of the congregation.
And they three came out.
5 And the LORD came down in
the pillar of the cloud, and stood *in*
the door of the tabernacle, and called
Aaron and Miriam: and they both
came forth.
6 And he said, Hear now my words:
If there be a prophet among you, *I*
the LORD will make myself known
unto him in a vision, *and* will speak
unto him in a dream.
7 My servant Moses *is* not so,
[b] Heb. 3. 2. [b]who *is* faithful in all mine house.
[c] Exod. 33. 11. 8 With him will I speak [c]mouth
to mouth, even apparently, and not
in dark speeches; and the similitude
of the LORD shall he behold: wherefore then were ye not afraid to speak
against my servant Moses?
9 And the anger of the LORD was
kindled against them; and he departed.
10 And the cloud departed from
off the tabernacle; and, behold, Miriam *became* leprous, *white* as snow:
and Aaron looked upon Miriam, and,
behold, *she was* leprous.
11 And Aaron said unto Moses,
Alas, my lord, I beseech thee, lay not
the sin upon us, wherein we have
done foolishly, and wherein we have
sinned.
12 Let her not be as one dead, of
whom the flesh is half consumed
when he cometh out of his mother's
womb.

Gentiles of God's covenant and its promises (cf. Ps. xlv. 9 sqq.; Cant. i. 4 sqq.); and in the murmuring of Miriam and Aaron a type of the discontent of the Jews because of such extension: cf. St Luke xv. 29, 30.

2. *Hath the LORD indeed spoken only by Moses?*] *i.e.* Is it merely, after all, by Moses that the LORD hath spoken?

3. *the man Moses was very meek*] These words have been, with no little insensibility to the finer traits of the passage, often regarded as words which Moses himself could not have penned; and accordingly have been cited sometimes as indicating an interpolation, sometimes as proof that the book is not Mosaic. When we regard them as uttered by Moses not "*proprio motu*," but under the direction of the Holy Spirit which was upon him (cf. xi. 17), they exhibit a certain "objectivity," which is a witness at once to their genuineness and also to their inspiration. There is about these words, as also about the passages in which Moses no less unequivocally records his own faults (cf. xx. 12 sqq.; Ex. iv. 24 sqq.; Deut. i. 37), the simplicity of one who bare witness of himself, but not to himself (cf. St Matt. xi. 28, 29). The words are inserted to explain how it was that Moses took no steps to vindicate himself, and why consequently the Lord so promptly intervened. Proposals to substitute "miserable" (Palfrey) or "afflicted" (Dr W. Smith) in the text instead of "meek" are needless, and if the original word will bear such rendering it certainly does not solicit it. The Hebrew word occurs frequently in the Psalms, is usually rendered by "meek" or "humble," and is frequently applied by the writers to themselves and their associates. Cf. Ps. x. 17; xxii. 27.

4, 5. *suddenly*] In wrath, *v.* 9.

7. *faithful in all mine house*] *i.e.* approved by me as my vicegerent in the general administration and government of my people. "My whole house," as distinguished from any particular department of it: cf. on the expression "house" as denoting God's covenant people, Hebr. iii. 6, "whose house are we;" and cf. the whole passage Hebr. iii. 1—6.

8. *mouth to mouth*] *i.e.* without the intervention of any third person or thing: cf. Ex. xxxiii. 11, Deut. xxxiv. 10.

even apparently] Lit. **and as an appearance**: an apposition to elucidate the words preceding. Moses received the word of God direct from Him and plainly, not through the medium of dream, vision, parable, dark saying, or such like; cf. Ex. xxxiii. 11, Deut. xxxiv. 10.

the similitude of the LORD shall he behold] "No man hath seen God at any time," St John i. 18: cf. 1 Tim. vi. 16, and especially Ex. xxxiii. 20 sqq. It was not therefore the Beatific Vision, the unveiled essence of the Deity, which Moses saw on the one hand. Nor was it, on the other hand, a mere emblematic representation, as in Ezek. i. 26 sqq., Dan. vii. 9, or an Angel sent as a messenger. It was the Deity Himself manifesting Himself so as to be cognizable to mortal eye. The special footing on which Moses stood as regards God (cf. Deut. xviii. 18, 19, and note), the "Gradus Mosaicus" of theologians, is here laid down in detail, because it at once demonstrates that the supremacy of Moses rested on the

13 And Moses cried unto the LORD,
saying, Heal her now, O God, I beseech thee.

14 ¶ And the LORD said unto Moses, If her father had but spit in her face, should she not be ashamed seven days? let her be [d]shut out from the camp seven days, and after that let her be received in *again*.

d Lev. 13. 46.

15 And Miriam was shut out from the camp seven days: and the people journeyed not till Miriam was brought in *again*.

16 And afterward the people removed from Hazeroth, and pitched in the wilderness of Paran.

CHAPTER XIII.

1 *The names of the men who were sent to search the land.* 17 *Their instructions.* 21 *Their acts.* 26 *Their relation.*

AND the LORD spake unto Moses,
saying,

2 Send thou men, that they may search the land of Canaan, which I give unto the children of Israel: of every tribe of their fathers shall ye send a man, every one a ruler among them.

3 And Moses by the commandment of the LORD sent them from the wilderness of Paran: all those men *were* heads of the children of Israel.

4 And these *were* their names: of the tribe of Reuben, Shammua the son of Zaccur.

5 Of the tribe of Simeon, Shaphat the son of Hori.

6 Of the tribe of Judah, Caleb the son of Jephunneh.

---

distinct appointment of God, and also that Miriam in contravening that supremacy had incurred the penalty proper to sins against the theocracy (cf. Trench, 'On the Miracles,' pp. 212—216).

12. *as one dead*] "Leprosy was nothing short of a living death, a poisoning of the springs, a corrupting of all the humours of life; a dissolution little by little of the whole body, so that one limb after another actually decayed and fell away." Trench, 'Miracles,' p. 213. Cf. notes on Lev. xiii.

13. *Heal her now, O God, I beseech thee*] A slight and probable alteration of the Hebrew punctuation (*al* for *el*) affords the rendering, "Oh not so; heal her now, I beseech thee:" so Knobel and others.

14. *If her father*] *i.e.* if her earthly parent had treated her with contumely (cf. Deut. xxv. 9) she would feel for a time humiliated, how much more when God has visited her thus?

seven days] Cf. Lev. xiii. 4, 5.

16. *the wilderness of Paran*] See on x. 12.

CHAP. XIII.—The fourth and crowning rebellion of the Israelites on their first northward march took place in the summer of the second year from the Exodus (cf. Introd. § 3. and note on *v.* 20 of this chap.), on the return of the spies from Canaan. The account of it occupies two entire chapters.

1. *And the LORD spake*] The mission of the spies was first suggested by the Israelites themselves, Deut. i. 22 and note.

2. *every one a ruler*] So in *v.* 3, "all those men were heads, &c.;" that is, heads of houses or families; for a comparison of the list with that of i. 5 sqq. shews that they were not the princes of the tribes, though the words rendered "prince" and "ruler" are, in Hebrew, the same.

3. *from the wilderness of Paran*] More particularly from Kadesh in the wilderness of Paran: cf. *v.* 26 and xxxii. 8.

4—15. Cf. i. 5—15. The tribe of Zebulun (*v.* 10) is out of its natural place, which is next after Issachar, and last of those descended from Leah; as also is that of Benjamin (*v.* 9), inserted between Ephraim and Manasseh. There can be little doubt that the original order has been disturbed by errors of transcription. It may be conjectured too in *v.* 7 that the name of the father of Igal has dropped out of the text, and that the words following Igal belong to the next verse. They probably served to introduce the name of the spy from the tribe of Ephraim, and should run thus, "Of the sons of Joseph, of the tribe of Ephraim, &c.:" cf. *v.* 11.

The tribe of Levi being already set apart for the service of the Tabernale did not furnish a representative on this occasion.

Of the names here given those of Joshua and Caleb alone are otherwise known to us.

6. *Caleb*] Called, xxxii. 12, and twice in Josh. xiv., "the Kenezite." Kenaz, cf. Gen. xxxvi. 11, 15, was the name of one of the "dukes of Edom." In the genealogy of the family of Caleb given 1 Chron. ii. we find also other Edomitish names: *e.g.* Shobal: cf. 1 Chron. ii. 50, 52 with Gen. xxxvi. 20, 23. It has on these grounds been conjectured that the family of Caleb was of Edomite extraction, and was incorporated into the tribe of Judah. It must be remembered however that

7 Of the tribe of Issachar, Igal the son of Joseph.

8 Of the tribe of Ephraim, Oshea the son of Nun.

9 Of the tribe of Benjamin, Palti the son of Raphu.

10 Of the tribe of Zebulun, Gaddiel the son of Sodi.

11 Of the tribe of Joseph, *namely*, of the tribe of Manasseh, Gaddi the son of Susi.

12 Of the tribe of Dan, Ammiel the son of Gemalli.

13 Of the tribe of Asher, Sethur the son of Michael.

14 Of the tribe of Naphtali, Nahbi the son of Vophsi.

15 Of the tribe of Gad, Geuel the son of Machi.

16 These *are* the names of the men which Moses sent to spy out the land. And Moses called Oshea the son of Nun Jehoshua.

17 ¶ And Moses sent them to spy out the land of Canaan, and said unto them, Get you up this *way* southward, and go up into the mountain:

18 And see the land, what it *is*; and the people that dwelleth therein, whether they *be* strong or weak, few or many;

19 And what the land *is* that they dwell in, whether it *be* good or bad; and what cities *they be* that they dwell in, whether in tents, or in strong holds;

20 And what the land *is*, whether it *be* fat or lean, whether there be wood therein, or not. And be ye of good courage, and bring of the fruit of the land. Now the time *was* the time of the firstripe grapes.

Israel and Edom were of kindred origin, and that therefore the use of similar names by the two peoples is not surprising.

16. *And Moses called Oshea....Jehoshua*] It is most probably, though not necessarily to be inferred from the text, that Moses did this first at this time. The earlier employment of the name (Ex. xvii. 9, xxiv. 13, &c.) by which Oshea became henceforth known is natural in one who wrote after "Joshua" had passed into current use. The original name however is still used Deut. xxxii. 44.

Oshea, Hoshea, or Hosea, the name also of the last king of Israel and the first minor prophet, means "deliverance" or "salvation." To this Moses added a syllable containing the sacred name, Jehovah or Jah: thus intimating that salvation was from God, and by the hand of him who bore the title of "God's salvation." Jehoshua was contracted in later Hebrew (cf. Neh. viii. 17) into Jeshua: the Vulg. writes Josua or Josue; LXX. Ἰησοῦς. On the name see Bp. Pearson on the Creed, Art. 2.

17. *southward*] Rather "by the negeb, or south-country" (from *nāgav* "to be dry"); a well-defined tract of territory forming the southernmost and least fertile portion of the land of Canaan and of the subsequent inheritance of Judah. It extended northward from Kadesh to within a few miles of Hebron, and from the Dead Sea westward to the Mediterranean (cf. especially Josh. xv. 21—32). The characteristic features of this region, long unrecognized, have been elucidated in a recent monograph by Rev. Edward Wilton, "The Negeb, or 'South Country' of Scripture," London, 1863; and see also Mr Clark's 'Bible Atlas,' pp. 11, 12, where the several physical divisions of the Holy Land, remarkable in themselves, are characterized and shown to be constantly apparent in the Old Test. The Negeb is frequently mentioned in Scripture; and it is also three times enumerated, by its Hebrew name, with the Egyptian article prefixed, in the list of places conquered by Shishak hieroglyphically engraven on the walls of Karnak (see Brugsch, 'Geographische Inschriften,' II. p. 69).

into the mountain] The hill-country of southern and central Canaan, mostly within the borders of Judah and Ephraim. It commences a few miles south of Hebron, and extending northward to the plain of Jezreel, runs out eventually north-westward into the sea in the headland of Carmel.

19. *in tents*] *i.e.* in open unwalled villages.

20. *And be ye of good courage, and bring*, &c.] Rather, perhaps, **And take boldly**, &c.

the time...of the firstripe grapes] The first grapes ripen in Palestine in July and August: the vintage is gathered in September and October. This indication of date tallies with what we should have inferred from the previous narrative. For the Israelitish host had quitted Sinai on the 20th day of the second month (x. 11), or about the middle of May: since then they had spent a month at Kibroth-hattaavah and a week at Hazeroth, and had accomplished, in all, from 150 to 200 miles of march: it therefore must have been at least the beginning of July, and may have been a month later, when the spies were despatched into the land of promise.

21 ¶ So they went up, and search-
ed the land from the wilderness of
Zin unto Rehob, as men come to
Hamath.

22 And they ascended by the south,
and came unto Hebron; where Ahiman, Sheshai, and Talmai, the children of Anak, *were*. (Now Hebron
was built seven years before Zoan in
Egypt.)

23 [a]And they came unto the ‖brook
of Eshcol, and cut down from thence
a branch with one cluster of grapes,
and they bare it between two upon a
staff; and *they brought* of the pomegranates, and of the figs.

24 The place was called the ‖brook
‖Eshcol, because of the cluster of
grapes which the children of Israel
cut down from thence.

[a] Deut. 1. 24.

‖ Or, *valley*.

‖ Or, *valley*.

‖ That is, *A cluster of grapes*.

---

21. *the wilderness of Zin*] The north-eastern portion of the wilderness of Paran. The spring of Kadesh lay within it; and from Kadesh on the west it probably stretched away to the Arabah on the east (see on x. 12, xxxiv. 3 sqq.)

unto Rehob] Probably the Beth-rehob of Judg. xviii. 28, near Dan-Laish; and apparently to the north of it, since it gave its name to a Syrian kingdom (2. S. viii. 3), and must thus have lain without the territory occupied by the Israelites It may perhaps be identified with the village Khurbeh or Khureibeh, between Bâniâs and Hasbeiya.

as men come to Hamath] By the "entrance of Hamath," the assigned boundary of the inheritance of Israel (cf. on xxxiv. 8), is to be understood the southern approach to Hamath, from the plain of Cœle-Syria, lying between those two ranges of Lebanon called Libanus and Antilibanus. A low screen of hills connects the northernmost points of these two ranges; and through this screen the Orontes bursts from the upper Cœlesyrian hollow into the open plain of Hamath. (Stanley, 'S. and P.' p. 399.) Its approximate place in the map is in latitude 34° 20′; and it lies south-west of Riblah, which was itself within the Hamath territory (2 K. xxiii. 33, &c.). A different view of the entrance of Hamath is taken by Robinson ('B. R.' III. 551, and 568, 569) and Porter ('Damascus,' pp. 332 sqq. &c.). They understand it of the western approach to Hamath, from the Mediterranean, and make it the interval which separates the northern end of Lebanon from the mountains of the Nusairîyeh. But this is less probable; and even Robinson virtually admits that in the present passage the southern approach to Hamath must be intended.

22. *by the south*] By the south-country, cf. *v*. 17.

Ahiman, Sheshai, and Talmai, the children of Anak] The progenitor of the Anakim was Arba "the father of Anak" (Josh. xv. 13), from whom the city of Hebron took its name of Kirjath-Arba. The name Anak denotes "long necked;" and though here the name of a race may originally have been that of a chieftain, yet Ahiman, Sheshai, and Talmai were probably not individual warriors, but names of three tribes of the Anakim. Hence we find them still in existence half a century later, when Caleb, who now brought tidings of them, became their eventual destroyer (Josh. xv. 14).

Now Hebron was built seven years before Zoan in Egypt] Knobel is probably right in explaining the somewhat abrupt introduction of this parenthesis by the supposition that these two cities had a common founder, and were built, or perhaps, at least in the case of Zoan (Tanis, see on Ex. v. 1) rebuilt, by the Hyksos, to which nations, once the conquerors of Egypt, the Anakim perhaps belonged. The Hyksos fortified and garrisoned Zoan as a defence of their Eastern frontier.

23. *the brook of Eshcol*] This is generally identified with the rich valley immediately to the north of Hebron; described by Robinson as producing the largest and best grapes in all Palestine, besides pomegranates, figs, apricots, quinces, and other fruits, in abundance. A fountain in it, lying within a mile of the city, is said by Van de Velde to be still known as Ain Eskâly. The valley was, in all likelihood, originally named after one of the three chiefs who were confederate with Abraham (Gen. xiv. 24); but, as often came to pass, the Israelites, wittingly or unwittingly, took up in a new and significant sense the name which they found; and to them the valley thus became the Valley of the Cluster.

they bare it between two upon a staff] Reland ('Palest.' 351, apud Rosenm. Scholia in loc.) narrates, on the authority of an eyewitness, that bunches of grapes are found in Palestine of ten pounds weight: Schulzius had seen them two pounds heavier than this: Ignatius of Rheinfelden speaks of clusters an ell long: Tobler, of individual grapes as large as plums. Kitto ('Phys. Hist. of Palestine,' p. 330) states that a bunch of grapes of enormous size was produced at Welbeck from a Syrian vine, and sent as a present in 1819 from the Duke of Portland to the Marquis of Rockingham. It weighed nineteen pounds, and was conveyed to its destination, more than twenty miles distant, on a staff by four labourers, two of whom bore it in rotation.

25 And they returned from searching of the land after forty days.
26 ¶ And they went and came to
Moses, and to Aaron, and to all the
congregation of the children of Israel,
unto the wilderness of Paran, to Kadesh; and brought back word unto
them, and unto all the congregation,
and shewed them the fruit of the land.
27 And they told him, and said,
We came unto the land whither thou
sentest us, and surely it floweth with
[b] Exod. 33. 3. [b]milk and honey; and this *is* the fruit
of it.
28 Nevertheless the people *be* strong
that dwell in the land, and the cities
are walled, *and* very great: and moreover we saw the children of Anak
there.
29 The Amalekites dwell in the
land of the south: and the Hittites,
and the Jebusites, and the Amorites,
dwell in the mountains: and the Canaanites dwell by the sea, and by the
coast of Jordan.
30 And Caleb stilled the people
before Moses, and said, Let us go up
at once, and possess it; for we are
well able to overcome it.
31 But the men that went up with
him said, We be not able to go up
against the people; for they *are* stronger than we.
32 And they brought up an evil
report of the land which they had
searched unto the children of Israel,
saying, The land, through which we
have gone to search it, *is* a land that
eateth up the inhabitants thereof; and
all the people that we saw in it *are*
†men of a great stature. † Heb. *men of statures.*
33 And there we saw the giants,
the sons of Anak, *which come* of the
giants: and we were in our own sight
as grasshoppers, and so we were in
their sight.

---

25. *after forty days*] They had no doubt in this time explored the whole land. It was however with the southern part that the Israelites expected to have to deal immediately: and accordingly it is that which is particularly referred to in the following verses, Hebron and its vicinity above all.

26. *to Kadesh*] See Note at the end of chapter.

28. *the cities are walled*] The annals of the patriarchal times do not suggest such a condition of things in Canaan as is here described. No doubt the repeated invasions of the Egyptians (see Essay on Egyptian History, § 25) had compelled the Canaanites to entrench themselves in those fortifications which afterwards, as the book of Joshua shows, were the element of their greatest strength.

29. *The Amalekites*] See on xiv. 25.

the Canaanites] *i.e.* those of the Phenician race: the word is here used in its narrow sense: cf. Gen. x. 15—18.

32. *a land that eateth up*, &c.] *i.e.* it is a land which from its position is exposed to incessant attacks from one quarter and another, and so its occupants must be always armed and watchful (cf. Lev. xxvi. 38, which however does not furnish a strict parallel). In fact the early annals of Canaan, though very fragmentary, afford evidences of various and extensive invasions, wars of extermination, &c.: cf. xxi. 27, 28; Deut. ii. 20, &c.

On the combination of two originally independent but consistent supplementary narratives in this chapter, cf. Introd. § 4. 7.

NOTE on CHAP. XIII. 26.

unto the wilderness of Paran, to Kadesh] (1) Kadesh is in the foot-notes identified with Ain-el-Weibeh, which lies in the Arabah, about ten miles north of the place in which Mount Hor abuts on that valley. Here the Wady el Ghuweir opens into the low grounds, and affords an access, by far the best, indeed the only one practicable for an army, through the mountain country of Edom, to the north-west: cf. on xx. 14 and 17. It was this doubtless which the ambassadors of Moses, sent from Kadesh to the king of Edom, described xx. 17 as "the king's highway." At Ain-el-Weibeh are three fountains issuing from the chalky rock. Probably in ancient times the water supply here, as elsewhere throughout the Sinaitic Peninsula, was more copious than at present, and the place accordingly of greater importance. Yet even now Ain-el-Weibeh is the most frequented watering-place in the Arabah. See Robinson, 'B. R.' II. 173—176. Robinson's identification of Ain-el-Weibeh as the ancient Kadesh has been generally accepted by English geographers as the most probable, *e.g.* by Mr Clark in his 'Bible Atlas,' pp. 24—26, by

Wordsworth, Porter, &c.; and by some also amongst the Germans.

(2) Yet so difficult has it been found to group satisfactorily all the passages in which mention is made of Kadesh round this or any other one spot, that some commentators and geographers (after Reland) have assumed that two distinct places must be supposed to bear the name in the Bible: and they observe that we have mention of Kadesh and of Kadesh Barnea; of Kadesh in the wilderness of Paran, and of Kadesh in that of Zin; and also of Meribah Kadesh.

And no doubt the appellation, which is equivalent to Holy Place, or Sanctuary, is one which was in fact borne by several localities; see below, § 8. But it seems clear, nevertheless, that one and the same locality throughout is intended in the Old Testament by these three names. For the encampment from which the spies were dispatched and to which they returned is called Kadesh in xiii. 26, but Kadesh Barnea in xxxii. 8, as it is also in Deut. ix. 23, Josh. xiv. 6, 7. (On the term "Barnea" see note on xxxii. 8.) It is further clear, on comparing Ezek. xlvii. 19, xlviii. 28 with Num. xxxiv. 4, Josh. xv. 3 and Deut. xxxii. 51, that Meribah Kadesh is the same as Kadesh Barnea. Kadesh appears to have been the name of a city, xx. 16; is doubtless the Kedesh mentioned Josh. xv. 23 as one of the "uttermost cities of Judah toward the coast of Edom southward;" was on the south border of Judah, xxxiv. 4; and was evidently a leading landmark in the boundary line. The name of the city was extended, as was often the case, to the district around it, hence "the wilderness of Cades," Ps. xxix. 8: cf. Deut. xxxii. 51. That Kadesh is sometimes assigned to the wilderness of Paran (*e.g.* xii. 16, xiii. 3 compared with xiii. 26), and sometimes to that of Zin (xiii. 21, xx. 1, xxxiii. 36), is explained by the fact that the name of Zin was given to the northernmost portion of the great desert of Paran in which Kadesh lay: see on x. 12, xiii. 21.

(3) It is further apparent on comparing Num. xii. 16 with xxxiii. 18, and then referring to xiii. 3, 21, and 26, that the same encampment which is described in chap. xiii. as at Kadesh is in the catalogue of stations in xxxiii. named Rithmah.

(4) The ancient name of Kadesh seems, Gen. xiv. 7 (where see note), to have been En-mishpat, "well of judgment." This may perhaps point to the place as being not only a religious centre, but one also where litigation was wont to be determined. And the priestly and judicial functions were and are often combined in the East. Rithmah is however probably descriptive of a district, and is derived (see note on xxxiii. 18) from the broom which abounded thereabouts. Possibly the name Rithmah was more particularly associated with the encampment in this portion of the desert which took place during the first march towards Canaan, Num. xxxiii. 18, and was given in order to distinguish it from a second encampment, also near Kadesh, and therefore in the same district, though not necessarily on the same spot, which occurred in the fortieth year, Num. xxxiii. 38.

(5) The criteria for determining the situation of Kadesh are the following:

(*a*) It is described by Moses in the embassy sent to the king of Edom as "a city in the uttermost of thy border," Num. xx. 16. But at that time the territory of Edom consisted only of Mount Seir, Deut. ii. 4, and Mount Hor was the western limit of it towards the Arabah, Num. xx. 22, 23, xxxiii. 37.

(*b*) In Deut. i. 2 the distance from Horeb to Kadesh is described as eleven days' journey "by the way of Mount Seir;" and in *v.* 19 of the same chapter the same journey to Kadesh is described as made "through all that great and terrible wilderness by the way of the mountain of the Amorites." By the "mountain of the Amorites" is to be understood most probably (cf. Judg. i. 36) the white calcareous ridge near 2000 feet high in places which skirts the Arabah on the west, and is by it separated from Mount Seir.

(*c*) It would further seem from xx. 22 and xxxiii. 37, that Kadesh was only one march distant from Mount Hor.

(*d*) And Kadesh was north of Mount Hor; for the host marched from the former to the latter as the first stage in their tedious journey, when denied a passage through the defiles of Mount Seir, they turned away and went southwards to compass the land of Edom: cf. Num. xx. 21, 22; Deut. ii. 8.

(*e*) Kadesh was situated on low ground, at least on ground low as compared with that in its neighbourhood. For the spies are repeatedly and consistently spoken of as "going up" to search the land (cf. xiii. 21, 22): and the land itself is described as "the mountain," xiii. 17: cf. xiv. 40, 42, 44, 45.

These conditions are all of them satisfied if we assume that Kadesh is the modern Ain-el-Weibeh: and then the route by which the host made their first rash and disastrous invasion of Canaan (xiv. 40 sqq.) would be that through the steep pass of es Safâh or es Sufâh: see on xiv. 45, and xxxiv. 3—5.

(6) The objections urged against this view are, that Ain-el-Weibeh is at present a spot of no great importance, and that there is near it no remarkable cliff such as seems implied in the narrative of Moses' disobedience, xx. 7 sqq. The former objection has been already answered in the first paragraph of this note: the latter seems of little weight, since the high cliffs at the mouth of the Wady el Ghuweir are certainly in the neighbourhood of Ain-el-Weibeh, and were in front of the host when it was proposing to march eastward through Mount Seir. We may add, that the word

sela used of the cliff at Kadesh, on which stress has been laid (cf. Stanley 'S. and P.' p. 95), is employed Judg. vi. 20 to describe the rock on which Gideon laid his offering, which can hardly have been a cliff.

(7) Other travellers have suggested Ain Hasb, some twelve miles north of Ain-el-Weibeh; others Ain esh Shehâbeh, fifteen miles to the south-west; little is known of these places; the latter seems too far away to the south to have been in the frontier of Judah; the former, though but little known, satisfies the leading conditions of the texts in which Kadesh is mentioned, as well as does Ain-el-Weibeh.

(8) Thus much can hardly be said for the claim of el-Ain, more than 70 miles away to the westward, though advocated by Messrs. Rowlands and Williams ('Holy City,' I. 463 sqq.), by Mr Wilton ('Negeb,' pp. 79, 80); by many German geographers and commentators, Ritter, Tuch, Kurtz, &c.; and in particular by the original writer of the notes on Numbers for this Commentary, Mr Thrupp. The principal argument in favour of this site is that it is said to be called Kudes or Kadeis or Gadis, and that there is in its neighbourhood a plain bearing the name Abu Retemet, which recalls the Rithmah of xxxiii. 18. But the root from which Kadesh is derived appears to have, and to have had from ancient times, a wide range as a topographical term. We have, *e.g.* El Kuds, the Arabic name of Jerusalem; Kedesh of Naphtali, Josh. xix. 37, the modern Kedes (cf. Robinson, 'B. R.' III. 366 sqq.); Kadisha, "the sacred stream," the name of a Phœnician river, Stanley, 'S. and P.' p. 269, Porter, 'Damascus,' pp. 301 sqq.; Kaditha, a village in the same district, Robinson, 'B. R.' II. 444; Kadessa or Cadessah, given as another name of Madurah by Bertou and others (cf. Robinson, 'B. R.' II. 179 note); Cadish in Syria, frequently named in early Egyptian annals, and identified by Brugsch with Emesa, the modern Hums. Others have found traces of the same name in Elusa, now El Khalaseh: and lastly the map engraved by Kiepert for the last edition of Robinson's 'B. R.' gives, after Abeken, a Jebel el Kudeis in the western part of the desert. Robinson indeed denies (see foot-notes in I. 189, and II. 194) that El Ain has the name of Kudes or Kadeis at all, and thinks that Rowlands mistook for Kudes the name Kudeirat, which is given to El Ain after a tribe of Arabs that water there. But even if Rowlands be right as to the name, its occurrence at El Ain would prove nothing, since it occurs elsewhere repeatedly, and probably in ancient times was given to many places which do not now bear it.

(9) Again, Rithmah, like Abu Retemet, "Broom Plain," no doubt derived its name from the broom-plant, *retem*. But names suggested by peculiarities of vegetation are of constant occurrence in the nomenclature of the Peninsula of Sinai; and the broom is the largest and most conspicuous shrub of the Desert, growing thickly in the watercourses in many parts. It probably gave a name to many localities; and Robinson in fact, 'B. R.' I. 84, visited a Wady Retâmeh abounding in the retem, on his journey between Suez and Sinai, about a day's march from the latter.

Altogether then the resemblance of the names Kudes and Retemet to the Kadesh and Rithmah of the Pentateuch, and even the occurrence of both of them in the same locality, are far from conclusive of the question.

(10) And it is obvious that El Ain satisfies none of the criteria stated above (§ 5) for determining the site of the ancient Kadesh. It is described (Num. xx. 16) as "a city in the uttermost of the border" of Edom. So too Mount Hor is said to be "in the edge of the land of Edom," Num. xxxiii. 37; and the Hebrew term in the two passages is the same. Yet El Ain lies far away to the west, more than seventy miles in a direct line from Mount Hor, and sixty from the nearest spur of Mount Seir. El Ain then could not by any stretch of language be said to be "in the border" or "edge" of the land of Edom. The territory of Edom did not in the days of Moses extend beyond the Arabah to the west (Stanley, 'S. and P.' p. 94, note; Clark's 'Bible Atlas,' p. 26).

Moreover, if Kadesh be identified with El Ain, it cannot be explained how Moses came to journey thither by the "way of Mount Seir," see above, § 5 *b*. "The way of Shur" was his proper course, as the map demonstrates. And even had he unaccountably chosen the very circuitous course by Mount Seir, why, when he was at Mount Seir, close to the defiles through which he desired to obtain a passage, and near to the chief city and head-quarters of the king of Edom, should he journey away far to the west before sending the embassy mentioned in Num. xx. 14—17; and since he had to come back again to Mount Hor, inflict thus on the host a gratuitous march and counter-march of near 150 miles?

It has been remarked above, § 5 *e*, that Kadesh was situated on ground distinctly lower than that which lay in front of the host when it first reached the border of Canaan. But El Ain is on high ground; from it the spies must have gone *down* rather than *up* towards Hebron.

(11) Lastly, the territory allotted to Judah (see Josh. xv. 21—47) seems to have included the whole of the Negeb, or South Country. But a boundary-line drawn through El Ain towards "the river of Egypt" would cross the middle of the Negeb, and so cut off a portion of the promised inheritance. The true Kadesh, then, which was unquestionably a border city (cf. Num. xxxiv. 3—5), must have

been situated more to the south than El Ain is, had it lain in this part of the Desert at all.

(12) Others (*e.g.* Stanley, 'S. and P.' pp. 94 sqq.) have identified Kadesh with Petra; and the Syriac and Chaldee Version uniformly replace Kadesh in the Scripture narrative by Rekem, the Aramaic name of Petra. The Targums render Kadesh Barnea by Rekem-Giah, *i. e.* "Rekem of the Ravine." The word Petra itself recalls the cliff (*sela*) which Moses smote, Num. xx. 8—11; drawing from it the second miraculous supply of water; and the fact that the word used of the rock at Kadesh is *sela*, and not, as in the narrative of former like miracles, Ex. xvii. 6, the more ordinary word *tsur* is, no doubt, noteworthy. There appears, too, 2 K. xiv. 7, to have been a city in Edom called Selah, which possibly was Petra. And Jerome ('Onom.' s.v.) connects Kadesh with Petra: "Cades Barnea in deserto quæ conjungitur civitate Petræ in Arabia." And lastly, the gorge in which Petra is bears the name of Wady Musa, as having been cleft by Moses' rod.

(13) Such coincidences are striking; but Petra lies too far southwards to have been in the frontier of Judah; it is not a city "in the uttermost of the border" of Edom, but is rather in the heart of Edom, far in the defiles through which the Israelites vainly sought a passage: and moreover it is in the very skirts of Mount Hor, whereas Num. xxxiii. 37 speaks of an encampment at Kadesh, and then of a separate and distinct one at Mount Hor.

(14) Whilst therefore it must remain as yet doubtful what precise spot is the Kadesh of Scripture, yet it seems clear on the whole that traces of this famous sanctuary must be looked for in the neighbourhood suggested by Robinson, that of Ain-el-Weibeh.

(15) If the arguments contained in § 3 of this note be correct, it will be apparent that two separate encampments of the host are named after Kadesh. The first, the Rithmah of the catalogue in Num. xxxiii. 18, 19, took place in the middle of the summer, in the second year after the exodus, see on xiii. 20; the latter in the first month of the fortieth year, see on xx. 1. On the former occasion the people abode in Kadesh for some, perhaps many months. For it was here that they expected for forty days the return of the spies, xiii. 25; and here Moses and the Tabernacle remained, xiv. 44: whilst the people, though sentenced by God to wander in the desert, attempted notwithstanding to occupy the land of rest. And after their repulse by the Canaanites, they spent, as it seems, Deut. i. 45, 46, "many days," the usual Hebrew idiom for any long period, in vain endeavours to obtain remission of their sentence. Eventually this prolonged encampment at Kadesh was broken up; and the people "compassed Mount Seir many days," Deut. ii. 1: *i.e.* roamed in the wilderness of Paran until the generation of murmurers was wasted away. To this long and dreary period must be assigned the seventeen stations enumerated Num. xxxiii. 19—36; on which see note on *v.* 19 of that chapter. Finally, the host was re-assembled at Kadesh early in the fortieth year (cf. xx. 1 and note), and was evidently again encamped here for a period of from three to four months: cf. xx. 1 with xx. 22—28, and xxxiii. 38. Here it was that Miriam died and was buried, *ibid.*: here that the people mustered in full strength for the final march on Canaan, soon exhausted the natural supplies of water, xx. 2 sqq., and were given to drink from the rock smitten by the rod of Moses: here that sentence was pronounced on Moses and Aaron for their sin, xx. 12, 13; and from hence that the messengers were dispatched to the king of Edom, xx. 14 sqq. After the return of the messengers the people turned away from Edom, quitted Kadesh for the last time, and after a halt at Mount Hor occasioned by the death of Aaron, proceeded by the marches set forth xxxiii. 41—49 round the borders of Edom to the Plains of Moab.

(16) It is possible that the memorable events which happened at Kadesh during the years covered by the book of Numbers first made the spot famous, and that the name of Kadesh was bestowed upon it because of the long continuance there of the Tabernacle with its priests and services.

After the settlement in Canaan the energies and interests of the nation found channels far away from the sterile and remote district of the northern Arabah. Kadesh seems gradually to have lapsed into obscurity, and to have become, what it probably was originally, nothing more than a watering place for the nomadic tribes of the Desert. The latest allusion to it by name in the Jewish annals is in Judith i. 9. Josephus does not mention it at all.

CHAPTER XIV.

1 *The people murmur at the news.* 6 *Joshua and Caleb labour to still them.* 11 *God threateneth them.* 13 *Moses persuadeth God, and obtaineth pardon.* 26 *The murmurers are deprived of entering into the land.* 36 *The men who raised the evil report die by a plague.* 40 *The people that would invade the land against the will of God are smitten.*

AND all the congregation lifted
up their voice, and cried; and
the people wept that night.
2 And all the children of Israel
murmured against Moses and against
Aaron: and the whole congregation
said unto them, Would God that we

had died in the land of Egypt! or
would God we had died in this wilderness!
3 And wherefore hath the LORD
brought us unto this land, to fall by
the sword, that our wives and our
children should be a prey? were it
not better for us to return into
Egypt?
4 And they said one to another,
Let us make a captain, and let us return into Egypt.
5 Then Moses and Aaron fell on
their faces before all the assembly of
the congregation of the children of
Israel.
6 ¶ And Joshua the son of Nun,
and Caleb the son of Jephunneh,
which were of them that searched the
land, rent their clothes:
7 And they spake unto all the company of the children of Israel, saying,
The land, which we passed through
to search it, *is* an exceeding good
land.
8 If the LORD delight in us, then
he will bring us into this land, and
give it us; a land which floweth with
milk and honey.
9 Only rebel not ye against the
LORD, neither fear ye the people of
the land; for they *are* bread for us:
their †defence is departed from them, († Heb. *shadow.*)
and the LORD *is* with us: fear them
not.
10 But all the congregation bade
stone them with stones. And the
glory of the LORD appeared in the
tabernacle of the congregation before
all the children of Israel.
11 ¶ And the LORD said unto Moses, How long will this people provoke me? and how long will it be
ere they believe me, for all the signs
which I have shewed among them?
12 I will smite them with the pestilence, and disinherit them, and will
make of thee a greater nation and
mightier than they.
13 ¶ And [a]Moses said unto the ([a] Exod. 32. 12.)
LORD, Then the Egyptians shall
hear *it*, (for thou broughtest up this
people in thy might from among
them;)
14 And they will tell *it* to the inhabitants of this land: *for* they have
heard that thou LORD *art* among this
people, that thou LORD art seen face ([b] Exod. 13. 21.)
to face, and *that* [b]thy cloud standeth
over them, and *that* thou goest be-

CHAP. XIV. 5. *Then Moses and Aaron fell on their faces*] Already Caleb had endeavoured to still the people before Moses (xiii. 30); already Moses himself (Deut. i. 29 sqq.) had endeavoured to recall the people to obedience. After the failure of these efforts Moses and Aaron cast themselves down in solemn prayer before God (cf. xvi. 22); and the appearance of the glory of the LORD in the tabernacle of the congregation (*v.* 10) was the immediate answer.

9. *their defence*] Lit. "their shadow," *i.e.* their shelter as from the scorching sun: an Oriental figure. Cf. Is. xxx. 2, 3, xxxii. 2.

12. *and disinherit them*] By the proposed extinction of Israel the blessings of the covenant would revert to their original donor.

13—17. The syntax of these verses is singularly broken. Moses describes himself (Ex. iv. 10, see note) as "not a man of words," and as "slow of speech, and of a slow tongue." These defects would be apt to embarrass him doubly in an exigency like the present. And, just as does St Paul when deeply moved, Moses presses his arguments one on the other without pausing to ascertain the grammatical finish of his expressions. He speaks here as if in momentary apprehension of an outbreak of God's wrath, unless he could perhaps arrest it by crowding in every topic of deprecation and intercession that he could summon on the instant. His appeal, preserving its native ruggedness, may be paraphrased thus: "And if then the Egyptians shall hear how, after bringing up this people by Thy might from amongst them,—and if they shall tell the inhabitants of the land what they have heard, how that Thou, LORD, wast among this people, Thou who art seen, O Lord, face to face of them, and whose cloud resteth over them, and who goest before them in a pillar of cloud by day and in a pillar of fire by night;—and if then Thou shalt kill this people as one man, and so the nations which have heard the fame of Thee shalt tell and say, Because the LORD was not able to bring this people into the land which He sware unto them, therefore He hath slain them in the wilderness:—Now therefore, I beseech Thee, let the power of my Lord be great, &c."

fore them, by day time in a pillar of a
cloud, and in a pillar of fire by
night.
15 ¶ Now *if* thou shalt kill *all* this
people as one man, then the nations
which have heard the fame of thee
will speak, saying,
[c] Deut. 9. 28. 16 Because the LORD was not [c] able
to bring this people into the land
which he sware unto them, therefore he hath slain them in the wilderness.
17 And now, I beseech thee, let the
power of my Lord be great, according
as thou hast spoken, saying,
[d] Exod. 34. 6. 18 The LORD *is* [d] longsuffering, and
Psal. 103. 8. of great mercy, forgiving iniquity and
transgression, and by no means clear-
[e] Exod. 20. 5. & 34. 7. ing *the guilty*, [e] visiting the iniquity of
the fathers upon the children unto the
third and fourth *generation*.
19 Pardon, I beseech thee, the iniquity of this people according unto
the greatness of thy mercy, and as
thou hast forgiven this people, from
Egypt even ‖ until now. ‖ Or, *hitherto.*
20 And the LORD said, I have pardoned according to thy word:
21 But *as* truly *as* I live, all the
earth shall be filled with the glory of
the LORD.
22 Because all those men which
have seen my glory, and my miracles,
which I did in Egypt and in the wilderness, and have tempted me now
these ten times, and have not hearkened to my voice;
23 † Surely they shall not see the † Heb. *If they see the land.*
land which I sware unto their fathers,
neither shall any of them that provoked me see it:
24 But my servant [f] Caleb, be- [f] Josh. 14. 6.
cause he had another spirit with him,
and hath followed me fully, him will
I bring into the land whereinto he
went; and his seed shall possess it.

---

18. Cf. Ex. xxxiv. 6, 7.

20. *I have pardoned*] God consents to preserve the nation; but sentences the rebels to personal exclusion from Canaan.

21—23. Render: **But as truly as I live, and as all the earth shall be filled with the glory of the LORD;** (*v.* 22) **all those men,** &c.; (*v.* 23) **shall not see,** &c. The Hebrew particle (*chî*), erroneously rendered "because" in A. V., introduces (as often in such forms) the substance of the oath to which the preceding verse gave the introduction. The particle in beginning of *v.* 23 signifies merely "not." Cf. Deut. xxxii. 40 and note.

22. *these ten times*] Ten is the number which imports completeness. Cf. Gen. xxxi. 7. The sense is that the measure of their provocations was now full: the day of grace was at last over. The Rabbins however take the words literally, and enumerate ten several occasions on which the people had tempted God since the Exodus.

24. *my servant Caleb*] Caleb only is mentioned here as also in xiii. 30 sqq. Both passages probably form part of the matter introduced at a later period into the narrative of Moses, and either by Joshua or under his superintendence. Hence the name of Joshua is omitted, and his faithfulness together with its reward are taken for granted. In *vv.* 30, 38, both names are mentioned together; and these verses in all likelihood belong to the same original composition with *vv.* 6—10. See Introd. § 7.

It is noteworthy also that no express mention is made of Moses and Aaron as exempt from the sentence: though their inclusion in it only took place long subsequently (cf. xx. 12). But such exemption is perhaps implied in the fact that God speaks to them (*v.* 26) whilst giving judgment upon the "evil congregation." Eleazar too, who had already entered on the duties of the priesthood (iv. 16, &c.), and therefore was doubtless more than twenty years old, survived to assist Joshua in allotting Canaan to the victorious tribes, Josh. xiv. 1. But as the tribe of Levi had no representative amongst the twelve spies (cf. xiii. 4—15), it was not included with the "all that were numbered" of *v.* 39 (cf. i. 46, 47), so its exception from the judgment seems self-evident.

The exceptions then were on the whole neither few nor inconsiderable; and the fact that only one of them is named, *v.* 30, whilst yet the language is emphatically general, should serve as a warning against the common assumption that the words of Scripture can have no limitations except such as are actually expressed.

Ps. xc., which is entitled "a Prayer of Moses," has been most appropriately regarded as a kind of dirge upon those sentenced thus awfully by God to waste away in the wilderness.

25 (Now the Amalekites and the
Canaanites dwelt in the valley.) To
morrow turn you, and get you into
the wilderness by the way of the Red
sea.
26 ¶ And the LORD spake unto
Moses and unto Aaron, saying,
27 How long *shall I bear with* this
evil congregation, which murmur
against me? I have heard the murmurings of the children of Israel, which
they murmur against me.
[g chap. 26. 65. & 32. 10.] 28 Say unto them, [g] *As truly as* I
live, saith the LORD, as ye have spoken
in mine ears, so will I do to you:
29 Your carcases shall fall in this
[h Deut. 1. 35.] wilderness; and [h] all that were numbered of you, according to your whole
number, from twenty years old and
upward, which have murmured against
me,
[† Heb. *lifted up my hand.*] 30 Doubtless ye shall not come into the land, *concerning* which I † sware
to make you dwell therein, save Caleb the son of Jephunneh, and Joshua
the son of Nun.
31 But your little ones, which ye
said should be a prey, them will I
bring in, and they shall know the
land which ye have despised.
32 But *as for* you, your carcases,
they shall fall in this wilderness.
33 And your children shall ‖ wan- [‖ Or, *feed.*]
der in the wilderness forty years, and
bear your whoredoms, until your carcases be wasted in the wilderness.
34 After the number of the days
in which ye searched the land, *even*
[i] forty days, each day for a year, shall [i Psal. 95. 10. Ezek. 4. 6]
ye bear your iniquities, *even* forty
years, and ye shall know my ‖ breach [‖ Or, *altering of my purpose.*]
of promise.
35 I the LORD have said, I will
surely do it unto all this evil congregation, that are gathered together
against me: in this wilderness they

---

25. *Now the Amalekites and the Canaanites dwelt in the valley*] These words are best understood as the continuation of the answer of God to Moses: **And now the Amalekites and the Canaanites are dwelling** (or abiding) **in the valley: wherefore turn you,** &c." (that so ye be not smitten before them). Some difficulty has been occasioned by the fact that in *vv.* 43—45 these tribes are represented rather as dwelling on the hill. The Syriac version alters the passage before us accordingly; but such procedure is unnecessary. What was in one respect a valley, or rather, as the Hebrew term *ēmek* implies, a broad sweep between hills, might in another respect be itself a hill, as lying on the top of the mountain-plateau. Such was precisely the case with the elevated plain on which the conflict of the disobedient Israelites with the Amalekites and Canaanites eventually ensued (see on *v.* 45). This was perhaps the very plain which had long been known as one of the seats of the Amalekites, the "country (or field) of the Amalekites," by which, centuries back, the invader had pursued his march from Kadesh to the Amorite city of Hazezon-tamar (Gen. xiv. 7); the "field" (1 S. xxvii. 5, Heb.) in which lay the city of Ziklag, if that be, as is probable (see Wilton, 'The Negeb,' pp. 206—209) identical with the modern Kaslûj. The text speaks of this district as tenanted, generally, by the Amalekites and Canaanites. The former term points to the nomad bands that roved through its open pastures: the latter, here taken in its wider sense, to the Amorites of the neighbouring cities (comp. *v.* 45 with Deut. i. 44), who probably lived in league with the Amalekites.

To morrow] Not necessarily the next day, but an idiom for "hereafter," "henceforward:" Ex. xiii. 14, Josh. iv. 6, &c.

by the way of the Red sea] That is, apparently, of the eastern or Elanitic gulf. Respecting the course of the subsequent wanderings see xxxiii. 20—36, and notes.

30. *save Caleb...and Joshua*] Cf. xxxii. 11, 12.

32. *But as for you, your carcases,* &c.] Rather, **But your carcases, even yours, shall fall,** &c.

33. *your whoredoms*] Their several rebellions had been so many acts of faithless departure from the Lord who had taken them unto himself. And as the children of the unchaste have generally to bear in their earthly careers much of the disgrace and the misery which forms the natural penalty of their parents' transgression; so here the children of the Israelites, although suffered to hope for an eventual entry into Canaan, were yet to endure, through many long years' wandering, the appropriate punishment of their fathers' wilfulness.

34. *my breach of promise*] In Hebrew this is one word, found elsewhere only in Job xxx. 10 (where A. V. renders "occasions"): and here best rendered perhaps, "my withdrawal," "my turning away."

shall be consumed, and there they shall die.

36 And the men, which Moses sent to search the land, who returned, and made all the congregation to murmur against him, by bringing up a slander upon the land,

37 Even those men that did bring up the evil report upon the land, [k]died by the plague before the LORD.

k 1 Cor. 10. 10. Heb. 3. 17. Jude 5.

38 But Joshua the son of Nun, and Caleb the son of Jephunneh, *which were* of the men that went to search the land, lived *still*.

39 And Moses told these sayings unto all the children of Israel: and the people mourned greatly.

40 ¶ And they rose up early in the morning, and gat them up into the top of the mountain, saying, Lo, [l]we *be here*, and will go up unto the place which the LORD hath promised: for we have sinned.

l Deut. 1. 41.

41 And Moses said, Wherefore now do ye transgress the commandment of the LORD? but it shall not prosper.

42 Go not up, for the LORD *is* not among you; that ye be not smitten before your enemies.

43 For the Amalekites and the Canaanites *are* there before you, and ye shall fall by the sword: because ye are turned away from the LORD, therefore the LORD will not be with you.

44 But they presumed to go up unto the hill top: nevertheless the ark of the covenant of the LORD, and Moses, departed not out of the camp.

45 Then the Amalekites [m]came down, and the Canaanites which dwelt in that hill, and smote them, and discomfited them, *even* unto Hormah.

m Deut. 1. 44.

CHAPTER XV.

1 *The law of the meat offering and the drink offering.* 13, 29 *The stranger is under the same law.* 17 *The law of the first of the dough for an heave offering.* 22 *The sacrifice for sin of ignorance.* 30 *The punishment of presumption.* 32 *He that violated the sabbath is stoned.* 37 *The law of fringes.*

AND the LORD spake unto Moses, saying,

2 [a] Speak unto the children of Is-

a Lev. 23. 10.

---

44. *they presumed to go up*] Rather perhaps "they despised" (*i.e.* the warning of Moses just given), "so as to go up, &c." Cf. Deut. i. 41—43, and note.

45. *unto Hormah*] Lit. "the Hormah:" *i.e.* "the banning," or "ban-place." This name, of which we find the history in xxi. 3, is here used by anticipation. The mention of it in Josh. xii. 14 as the seat of a Canaanitish king marks it as a city of importance. Its site is disputed. Its earlier name, Zephath, Judg. i. 17, has been compared with that of the ascent es-Safâh on the south-eastern frontier of Canaan (Robinson, 'B. R.' II. p. 198, foot-note: see on xxxiv. 3 sqq.): and it was probably by this steep pass (Nakb es Safâh, see on xxxiv. 3—5) that the Israelites quitted the Arabah for the higher ground. See note at end of ch. xiii., and Robinson, II. 180—182, and 194. Rowlands identifies Zephath with Sebâta, which lies further to the west, about 25 miles north of Ain Kadeis. Sebâta was visited by Rev. C. H. Palmer late in the year 1869. Its ruins are very extensive, including three churches and a tower. There is an Arab saying "Greater ruins than El-Aujeh and El-Abdeh there are none, save only Sebâta, which is grander than either." Near this city, and protecting it from a very commanding position, is a ruined fortress called El-Meshrifeh, furnished with escarpments, bastions, and strong towers, which Mr Palmer supposes to have been the site of the "Watch-tower" in question. (See Quarterly Statement of Palestine Exploration Fund, No. VI. March 31 to June 30, 1870, pp. 315, 316.) Yet it must be observed that the name Sebâta or Esbâta has not, in Arabic (cf. Seetzen, III. p. 44), the resemblance to Zephath which the English orthography suggests. And in fact later notices of the city (1 S. xxx. 30, 1 Chron. iv. 30) seem to shew that, of its two names, Hormah was that which survived. Perhaps its real site was some miles east of Sebâta at the ruins called Rakhmah (or Rukhama), a name which in Hebrew letters is an anagram of Hormah. If so, we can, notwithstanding our imperfect knowledge of the surrounding region, trace the progress of the Israelite invaders. The direction of their line of march would be N. N. W., from the Arabah. Continuing onward past Rakhmah or Hormah, it would lead them into the extensive plain now known as es-Serr or es-Sîr, the Seir of Deut. i. 44. A further progress of 20 miles along this plain would have brought them to the royal city of Arad (see xxi. 1, Josh. xii. 14), still bearing its ancient designation though in ruins. But their enemies, warned of their approach, waited

rael, and say unto them, When ye
be come into the land of your habitations, which I give unto you,
3 And will make an offering by fire
unto the LORD, a burnt offering, or
b Lev. 22. 21. a sacrifice [b]in [†]performing a vow, or
† Heb. *separating.* in a freewill offering, or in your solemn feasts, to make a [c]sweet savour
c Exod. 29. 18. unto the LORD, of the herd, or of the
flock:
d Lev. 2. 1. 4 Then [d]shall he that offereth his
offering unto the LORD bring a meat
offering of a tenth deal of flour mingled with the fourth *part* of an hin of
oil.
5 And the fourth *part* of an hin of
wine for a drink offering shalt thou
prepare with the burnt offering or
sacrifice, for one lamb.
6 Or for a ram, thou shalt prepare
for a meat offering two tenth deals of
flour mingled with the third *part* of
an hin of oil.
7 And for a drink offering thou
shalt offer the third *part* of an hin of
wine, *for* a sweet savour unto the
LORD.
8 And when thou preparest a bullock *for* a burnt offering, or *for* a
sacrifice in performing a vow, or peace
offerings unto the LORD:
9 Then shall he bring with a bullock a meat offering of three tenth
deals of flour mingled with half an
hin of oil.
10 And thou shalt bring for a
drink offering half an hin of wine, *for*
an offering made by fire, of a sweet
savour unto the LORD.
11 Thus shall it be done for one
bullock, or for one ram, or for a
lamb, or a kid.
12 According to the number that
ye shall prepare, so shall ye do to
every one according to their number.
13 All that are born of the country
shall do these things after this manner,
in offering an offering made by fire,
of a sweet savour unto the LORD.
14 And if a stranger sojourn with

---

for them probably under the command of the king of Arad on the plain, and there defeated them. From the statement that they were driven back only to Hormah it would seem that the country between that and Kadesh remained in their possession.

CHAP. XV. The contents of the next five chapters must apparently be referred to the long period of wandering to which (xiv. 33) the people were condemned. See Introd. § 3. Chapter xx. introduces us at once to the transactions belonging to the second encampment at Kadesh in the fortieth year after the Exodus.

The chapter now before us lays down certain ordinances. These will be seen, as we proceed, to be connected with the circumstances of the time in which, as their position indicates, they were promulgated.

1—21. Ordinances respecting the meat-, drink-, and heave-offerings.

2. *When ye be come into the land of your habitations*] After the account of the rebellion and of the discomfiture at Kadesh, the main interest of the history descends on the Israelites of the younger generation. To them is conveyed in these words the hope that the nation should yet enter into the land of promise. The ordinances that follow are more likely to have been addressed to adults than to children; and we may therefore assume that at the date of their delivery the new generation was growing up, and the period of wandering drawing towards its close. During that period the meat-offerings and drink-offerings prescribed by law had been probably intermitted by reason of the scanty supply of corn and wine in the wilderness. The command therefore to provide such offerings was a pledge to Israel that it should possess the land which was to furnish the wherewithal for them.

4—12. The meat-offering is treated of Lev. ii. No mention is there made of any drink-offering; yet from scattered notices (Ex. xxix. 40, Lev. xxiii. 14) it appears to have been an ordinary accessory to the former. Now however it is prescribed that a meat-offering and a drink-offering of definite measure shall accompany every sacrifice. This measure is apparently the same as had been customary already. The lambs of the morning and evening sacrifice had been each accompanied from the first by one tenth deal of flour, a quarter of a hin of oil, and the like of wine (Ex. xxix. 40); and these measures are now prescribed for every lamb, though double that quantity of flour was (Lev. xxiii. 13) prescribed as an adjunct to the wave-sheaf. Larger measures are prescribed for a ram, and still larger for a bullock. If more than one animal be sacrificed, the proper measures must be used with each.

you, or whosoever *be* among you in
your generations, and will offer an
offering made by fire, of a sweet savour unto the LORD; as ye do, so he
shall do.
15 [e] One ordinance *shall be both*
for you of the congregation, and also
for the stranger that sojourneth *with
you*, an ordinance for ever in your
generations: as ye *are*, so shall the
stranger be before the LORD.
16 One law and one manner shall
be for you, and for the stranger that
sojourneth with you.
17 ¶ And the LORD spake unto
Moses, saying,
18 Speak unto the children of Israel, and say unto them, When ye
come into the land whither I bring
you,
19 Then it shall be, that, when ye
eat of the bread of the land, ye shall
offer up an heave offering unto the
LORD.
20 Ye shall offer up a cake of the
first of your dough *for* an heave offering: as *ye do* the heave offering of the
threshingfloor, so shall ye heave it.
21 Of the first of your dough ye
shall give unto the LORD an heave
offering in your generations.
22 ¶ And if ye have erred, and
not observed all these commandments,
which the LORD hath spoken unto
Moses,
23 *Even* all that the LORD hath
commanded you by the hand of
Moses, from the day that the LORD
commanded *Moses*, and henceforward
among your generations;
24 Then it shall be, if *ought* be
committed by ignorance † without the
knowledge of the congregation, that
all the congregation shall offer one
young bullock for a burnt offering,
for a sweet savour unto the LORD,
with his meat offering, and his drink
offering, according to the ‖ manner,
and one kid of the goats for a sin
offering.
25 And the priest shall make an
atonement for all the congregation of

[e] Exod. 12. 49. chap. 9. 14.

† Heb. *from the eyes.*

‖ Or, *ordinance.*

---

15. *as ye are, so shall the stranger be,* &c.] The meaning is, "as with you, so shall it be with the stranger, &c."

18. *When ye come into the land*] Cf. on *v.* 2. The general principle under which the ordinance of this and the three verses following comes is laid down Ex. xxii. 29, xxiii. 19. It had already been exemplified in the offering of the "firstfruits, green ears of corn," Lev. ii. 14; that of "the sheaf of firstfruits," Lev. xxiii. 9 sqq.; and that of the "two wave loaves," ibid. *v.* 17. It is now enjoined in addition that a similar offering be made of the first dough of the year. These offerings having been waved or heaved before the Lord (xviii. 24) became the perquisite of the priests. Cf. Neh. x. 37; Ezek. xliv. 30.

20, 21. *dough*] Or perhaps, "coarse meal." The Hebrew word occurs elsewhere only at Neh. x. 37, Ezek. xliv. 30, where the reference is to this ordinance.

as ye do the heave offering of the threshing-floor] Of this, unless it be the same with the dried green ears of Lev. ii. 14, nothing is said elsewhere.

22—31. Ordinances respecting sins of ignorance and sins of presumption.

22. *And if ye have erred*] The heavy punishments which had already overtaken the people might naturally give rise to apprehensions for the future, especially in view of the fact that on the approaching entrance into Canaan the complete observance of the Law in all its details would become imperative on them. To meet such apprehensions a distinction is emphatically drawn between sins of ignorance and those of presumption: and the people are reminded that for the former an atonement is provided. Cf. Lev. iv. 13 sqq. The passage deals separately with imperfections of obedience which would be regarded as attaching to the whole nation (*vv.* 22—26), such as *e.g.* dereliction of a sacred duty on the part of a ruler; and those of individuals (*vv.* 27—30).

24. *without the knowledge of the congregation*] lit. as marg. "*from* the eyes of the congregation." The words point to an error of omission which escaped notice at the time: *i.e.* to an oversight.

one young bullock] The reference here is to sins of omission: cf. *v.* 22, "if ye have erred, and not observed all these commandments." In Lev. l. c. the reference is to sins of commission. Accordingly there is some difference in the ritual. There the bullock was treated as a sin-offering, here as a burnt-offering. With the burnt-offering however is to be joined the kid of sin-offering (cf. Lev. iv. 23) as an atonement for the sin of him or them who had occasioned the lapse on the part of the people at large.

the children of Israel, and it shall be
forgiven them; for it *is* ignorance:
and they shall bring their offering, a
sacrifice made by fire unto the LORD,
and their sin offering before the LORD,
for their ignorance:
26 And it shall be forgiven all the
congregation of the children of Israel, and the stranger that sojourneth
among them; seeing all the people
were in ignorance.
f Lev. 4. 27. 27 ¶ And [f] if any soul sin through
ignorance, then he shall bring a she
goat of the first year for a sin offering.
28 And the priest shall make an
atonement for the soul that sinneth
ignorantly, when he sinneth by ignorance before the LORD, to make an
atonement for him; and it shall be
forgiven him.
29 Ye shall have one law for him
† Heb. doeth. that † sinneth through ignorance, *both
for* him that is born among the chil-
dren of Israel, and for the stranger
that sojourneth among them.
30 ¶ But the soul that doeth *ought*
† Heb. with an high hand. † presumptuously, *whether he be* born
in the land, or a stranger, the same
reproacheth the LORD; and that soul
shall be cut off from among his people.
31 Because he hath despised the
word of the LORD, and hath broken
his commandment, that soul shall utterly be cut off; his iniquity *shall be*
upon him.
32 ¶ And while the children of
Israel were in the wilderness, they
found a man that gathered sticks upon the sabbath day.
33 And they that found him gathering sticks brought him unto Moses and Aaron, and unto all the congregation.
34 And they put him [g] in ward, g Lev. 24. 12.
because it was not declared what
should be done to him.
35 And the LORD said unto Moses, The man shall be surely put to
death: all the congregation shall stone
him with stones without the camp.
36 And all the congregation brought
him without the camp, and stoned
him with stones, and he died; as the
LORD commanded Moses.
37 ¶ And the LORD spake unto
Moses, saying,
38 Speak unto the children of Is-
rael, and bid [h] them that they make h Deut. 22. 12. Matt. 23. 5.
them fringes in the borders of their
garments throughout their generations, and that they put upon the
fringe of the borders a ribband of blue:

---

30. *presumptuously*] The original (cf. margin, and Ex. xiv. 8) imports something done wilfully and openly; in case of a sin against God it implies that the act is committed ostentatiously and in bravado: cf. the French "haut la main."

reproacheth the LORD] Rather **revileth** or **blasphemeth** the LORD: cf. Ezek. xx. 27.

32. *And while the children of Israel were in the wilderness*] Moses mentions here, as is his wont (cf. Lev. xxiv. 10—16), the first open transgression and its punishment in order to exemplify the laws which he is laying down. The offence of Sabbath-breaking was one for which there could be no excuse. This law at least might be observed even in the wilderness. The notice of time *while the children of Israel were in the wilderness* is thus no token that the narrative was written when the people were no longer there. On the contrary it is properly introduced here to contrast the ordinance of the Sabbath, given some time ago, Ex. xxxi. 14, and daringly violated in the case before us, with the series of ordinances first given in this very chapter. The latter were not obligatory until after the settlement in Canaan: the former was obligatory already. Transgression of it was therefore a presumptuous sin, and was punished accordingly.

34. *it was not declared what should be done to him*] Death had indeed been assigned as the penalty (Ex. xxxi. 14, xxxv. 2); but it had not been determined how that death was to be inflicted. On the Hebrew word translated here "declare," cf. Lev. xxiv. 12, Neh. viii. 8.

37—41. Ordinance of the fringes.

38. *that they put upon the fringe of the borders a ribband of blue*] Render **that they add to the fringes of the borders** (or **corners**) **a thread of blue**: cf. Deut. xxii. 12, where the word translated "fringes" is a different one but with the same general sense. These fringes are considered by Wilkinson to be of Egyptian origin ('Anc. Egypt,' II. 321, 322). The ordinary outer Jewish garment was a quadrangular piece of cloth like a modern plaid, to the corners of which, in

39 And it shall be unto you for a
fringe, that ye may look upon it, and
remember all the commandments of
the LORD, and do them; and that ye
seek not after your own heart and
your own eyes, after which ye use
to go a whoring:
40 That ye may remember, and
do all my commandments, and be
holy unto your God.
41 I *am* the LORD your God,
which brought you out of the land of
Egypt, to be your God: I *am* the
LORD your God.

CHAPTER XVI.

1 *The rebellion of Korah, Dathan, and Abiram.* 23 *Moses separateth the people from the rebels' tents.* 31 *The earth swalloweth up Korah, and a fire consumeth others.* 36 *The censers are reserved to holy use.* 41 *Fourteen thousand and seven hundred are slain by a plague for murmuring against Moses and Aaron.* 46 *Aaron by incense stayeth the plague.*

NOW [a]Korah, the son of Izhar, [a] chap. 27. 3.
the son of Kohath, the son of Ecclus. 45. 18.
Levi, and Dathan and Abiram, the Jude 11.
sons of Eliab, and On, the son of
Peleth, sons of Reuben, took *men:*
2 And they rose up before Moses,
with certain of the children of Israel,
two hundred and fifty princes of the
assembly, [b]famous in the congrega- [b] chap. 26. 9.
tion, men of renown:
3 And they gathered themselves
together against Moses and against
Aaron, and said unto them, †*Ye take* † Heb.
too much upon you, seeing all the It is *much for you.*

conformity with this command, a tassel was attached. Each tassel had a conspicuous thread of deep blue, this colour being doubtless symbolical of the heavenly origin of the commandments of which it was to serve as a memento. Tradition determined that the other threads should be white,—this colour being an emblem of purity (cf. Is. i. 18). The arrangement of the threads and knots, to which the Jews attached the greatest importance, was so adjusted as to set forth symbolically the 613 precepts of which the Law was believed to consist. In our Lord's time the Pharisees enlarged their fringes (Matt. xxiii. 5) in order to obtain reputation for their piety. In later times however the Jews have worn the fringed garment (*tālīth*) of a smaller size and as an under dress. Its use is however still retained, especially at morning prayer in the Synagogue.

39. *that ye seek not*] Rather, *that ye wander not.*

41. May be connected with the preceding, and thus rendered: *Unto me the LORD your God, which brought you out of the land of Egypt, to be your God: even unto me, the LORD your God.*

CHAP. XVI. Rebellion of Korah and his company. This narrative is regarded even by Ewald, Knobel, &c. as possessing the characteristics attributed by them to the oldest documents. It has also, as will be noted in the course of it, remarkable internal tokens of historical truth. See these latter more fully developed by Blunt, 'Undesigned Coin.' pp. 15—79. The date of the transaction contained in it cannot be determined, but *vv.* 13, 14 probably point to a period not much later than that of the rebellion at Kadesh. At any rate this chapter does not necessarily rank chronologically after the one preceding.

1. *Korah, the son of Izhar*] "Son" here is equivalent to descendant, as often in the Bible. Amram and Izhar were brothers, cf. Ex. vi. 18, and thus Korah was connected by distant cousinship with Moses and Aaron. Though being a Kohathite, he was of that division of the Levites which had the most honourable charge, yet as Elizaphan, who had been made "chief of the families of the Kohathites" (iii. 30), belonged to the youngest branch descended from Uzziel (cf. iii. 27), Korah probably regarded himself as injured; and therefore took the lead in this rebellion which bears always his name in particular: cf. *vv.* 5, 6, xxvi. 9; Jude 11.

Dathan and Abiram...On] Of these, On is not again mentioned. He probably withdrew from the conspiracy. These three were Reubenites; and were probably discontented because the birthright had been taken away from their ancestor (cf. Gen. xlix. 3 and note), and with it the primacy of their own tribe amongst the tribes of Israel. The Reubenites encamped near to the Kohathites (cf. ii. 25 and note), and "thus the two families were conveniently situated for taking counsel together" (cf. Blunt, p. 76). One pretext of the insurrection probably was to assert the rights of primogeniture,—on the part of the Reubenites against Moses, on the part of Korah against the appointment of Uzziel.

took men] The original has simply "took;" what they took is not said. See note at end of chapter.

2. *two hundred and fifty princes of the assembly*] These appear to have belonged to the other tribes, as is implied in the statement (xxvii. 3) that Zelophehad the Manassite was "not in the company of Korah."

congregation *are* holy, every one of
them, and the LORD *is* among them:
wherefore then lift ye up yourselves
above the congregation of the LORD?
4 And when Moses heard *it*, he
fell upon his face:
5 And he spake unto Korah and
unto all his company, saying, Even
to morrow the LORD will shew who
are his, and *who is* holy; and will
cause *him* to come near unto him:
even *him* whom he hath chosen will
he cause to come near unto him.
6 This do; Take you censers, Korah, and all his company;
7 And put fire therein, and put
incense in them before the LORD to
morrow: and it shall be *that* the man
whom the LORD doth choose, he *shall*
be holy: *ye take* too much upon you,
ye sons of Levi.
8 And Moses said unto Korah,
Hear, I pray you, ye sons of Levi:
9 *Seemeth it but* a small thing unto
you, that the God of Israel hath separated you from the congregation of
Israel, to bring you near to himself
to do the service of the tabernacle of
the LORD, and to stand before the
congregation to minister unto them?
10 And he hath brought thee near
to him, and all thy brethren the sons
of Levi with thee: and seek ye the
priesthood also?
11 For which cause *both* thou and
all thy company *are* gathered together
against the LORD: and what *is* Aaron,
that ye murmur against him?
12 ¶ And Moses sent to call Dathan and Abiram, the sons of Eliab:
which said, We will not come up:
13 *Is it* a small thing that thou
hast brought us up out of a land that
floweth with milk and honey, to kill
us in the wilderness, except thou
make thyself altogether a prince over
us?
14 Moreover thou hast not brought
us into a land that floweth with milk
and honey, or given us inheritance of
fields and vineyards: wilt thou †put † Heb.
out the eyes of these men? we will *bore out.*
not come up.
15 And Moses was very wroth,
and said unto the LORD, [c]Respect not [c] Gen. 4. 4.
thou their offering: I have not taken
one ass from them, neither have I
hurt one of them.
16 And Moses said unto Korah,
Be thou and all thy company before
the LORD, thou, and they, and Aaron,
to morrow:

---

3. *all the congregation are holy*] Cf. Ex. xix. 6. The real attack of Korah was doubtless upon the authority of the family of Aaron over the Levites. Cf. *v.* 10. His object was not to abolish the distinction between the Levites and the people, but to win priestly dignity for himself and his kinsmen. But this ultimate design is masked for the present in order to win support from the Reubenites by putting forward claims to spiritual equality on behalf of every Israelite.

8. *ye sons of Levi*] Moses addresses Korah, but speaks in the plural, both as including the Levites of Korah's faction and also in order to intimate that he was aware of the real motives of the Levite conspirators (cf. note on *v.* 3).

9. *Seemeth it but a small thing unto you,* &c.] The "seemeth" is not in the original. Render thus: **Is it too little for you,** *i.e.* "is it less than your dignity demands?"

11. The words of Moses in his wrath are broken. Literally the verse runs: "Wherefore against the LORD (not against Aaron) thou and all thy company who are gathered together, and Aaron, what is he, that ye murmur against him?" Cf. the parallel reproof of Ananias by St Peter, Acts v. 3, 4. The Aaronic priesthood was of divine appointment; and thus in rejecting it, the conspirators were really rebelling against God.

13. *Is it a small thing that thou hast brought us up out of a land that floweth with milk and honey?*] With perverse contempt for the promises Dathan and Abiram designate Egypt by the terms appropriated elsewhere to the land of Canaan. But in fact an exchange of taunts was being carried on between the parties; the "ye take too much upon you" of Moses in *v.* 7, is his reproof of the like words used by the conspirators in *v.* 3, and their "is it a small thing" in the verse before us is but the echo of his words in *v.* 9.

14. *wilt thou put out the eyes of these men?*] *i.e.* "blind them to the fact that you keep none of your promises;" equivalent to "throw dust in their eyes."

17 And take every man his censer, and put incense in them, and bring ye before the LORD every man his censer, two hundred and fifty censers; thou also, and Aaron, each *of you* his censer.

18 And they took every man his censer, and put fire in them, and laid incense thereon, and stood in the door of the tabernacle of the congregation with Moses and Aaron.

19 And Korah gathered all the congregation against them unto the door of the tabernacle of the congregation: and the glory of the LORD appeared unto all the congregation.

20 And the LORD spake unto Moses and unto Aaron, saying,

21 Separate yourselves from among this congregation, that I may consume them in a moment.

22 And they fell upon their faces, and said, O God, the God of the spirits of all flesh, shall one man sin, and wilt thou be wroth with all the congregation?

23 ¶ And the LORD spake unto Moses, saying,

24 Speak unto the congregation, saying, Get you up from about the tabernacle of Korah, Dathan, and Abiram.

25 And Moses rose up and went unto Dathan and Abiram; and the elders of Israel followed him.

26 And he spake unto the congregation, saying, Depart, I pray you, from the tents of these wicked men, and touch nothing of theirs, lest ye be consumed in all their sins.

27 So they gat up from the tabernacle of Korah, Dathan, and Abiram, on every side: and Dathan and Abiram came out, and stood in the door of their tents, and their wives, and their sons, and their little children.

28 And Moses said, Hereby ye shall know that the LORD hath sent me to do all these works; for *I have* not *done them* of mine own mind.

29 If these men die †the common death of all men, or if they be visited after the visitation of all men; *then* the LORD hath not sent me.

† Heb. *as every man dieth*

30 But if the LORD †make a new thing, and the earth open her mouth, and swallow them up, with all that *appertain* unto them, and they go down quick into the pit; then ye shall understand that these men have provoked the LORD.

† Heb. *create a creature.*

31 ¶ [d]And it came to pass, as he had made an end of speaking all these words, that the ground clave asunder that *was* under them:

[d] chap. 2 3. Deut. 11. Ps. 106.

32 And the earth opened her mouth, and swallowed them up, and their houses, and all the men that *appertained* unto Korah, and all *their* goods.

33 They, and all that *appertained* to them, went down alive into the pit, and the earth closed upon them: and they perished from among the congregation.

---

24. *from about the tabernacle of Korah, Dathan, and Abiram*] Render, **Dwelling of Korah**, &c. The tent of Korah, as a Kohathite, stood on the south side of the tabernacle of the Lord; and those of Dathan and Abiram, as Reubenites, in the outer line of encampment on the same side: cf. on *v.* 2. Yet though the tents of these three were thus contiguous the narrative, whilst not going into detail, suggests to us that they did not share the same fate. Korah and his company who dared to intrude themselves on the priestly office were destroyed by fire from the Lord at the door of the tabernacle of the Lord, *v.* 35; the Reubenites, who had reviled Moses for the failure of the promises about the pleasant land, were suddenly engulfed whilst standing at their own tent-doors in the barren wilderness (*vv.* 31—33). The A.V. then is inaccurate in the heading of this chapter, where it states, "31, The earth swalloweth up Korah, and a fire consumeth others." Cf. xxvi. 10, 11, and note. This real and obviously undesigned coincidence between the statement made in those verses and that of these is happily drawn out by Blunt, pp. 78, 79.

27. *stood in the door of their tents*] Apparently in contumacious defiance.

32. *all the men that appertained unto Korah*] Lit. "all unto Korah;" *i.e.* not his sons, for we read xxvi. 11, "the children of Korah died not," but all belonging to him who had associated themselves with him in this rebellion.

34 And all Israel that *were* round about them fled at the cry of them: for they said, Lest the earth swallow us up *also*.

35 And there came out a fire from the LORD, and consumed the two hundred and fifty men that offered incense.

36 ¶ And the LORD spake unto Moses, saying,

37 Speak unto Eleazar the son of Aaron the priest, that he take up the censers out of the burning, and scatter thou the fire yonder; for they are hallowed.

38 The censers of these sinners against their own souls, let them make them broad plates *for* a covering of the altar: for they offered them before the LORD, therefore they are hallowed: and they shall be a sign unto the children of Israel.

39 And Eleazar the priest took the brasen censers, wherewith they that were burnt had offered; and they were made broad *plates for* a covering of the altar:

40 *To be* a memorial unto the children of Israel, that no stranger, which *is* not of the seed of Aaron, come near to offer incense before the LORD; that he be not as Korah, and as his company: as the LORD said to him by the hand of Moses.

41 ¶ But on the morrow all the congregation of the children of Israel murmured against Moses and against Aaron, saying, Ye have killed the people of the LORD.

42 And it came to pass, when the congregation was gathered against Moses and against Aaron, that they looked toward the tabernacle of the congregation: and, behold, the cloud covered it, and the glory of the LORD appeared.

43 And Moses and Aaron came before the tabernacle of the congregation.

44 ¶ And the LORD spake unto Moses, saying,

45 Get you up from among this congregation, that I may consume them as in a moment. And they fell upon their faces.

46 ¶ And Moses said unto Aaron, Take a censer, and put fire therein from off the altar, and put on incense, and go quickly unto the congregation, and make an atonement for them: for there is wrath gone out from the LORD; the plague is begun.

47 And Aaron took as Moses commanded, and ran into the midst of the congregation; and, behold, the plague was begun among the people: and he put on incense, and made an atonement for the people.

48 And he stood between the dead and the living; and the plague was stayed.

---

35. *there came out a fire from the LORD*] *i.e.* As appears from the similar case Lev. x. 1—7, the fire came out from the sanctuary or the altar.

37. *Eleazar*] Not Aaron himself, because as high-priest, and as one of those that offered incense (*v.* 17), it was not meet that he should be defiled by going among the dead.

scatter thou the fire yonder] That is, "afar off." As the censers were not to be used again for censers, so the coals on them were to be used no more for kindling the incense to be offered before the Lord. Yet neither of them could fittingly be employed for common purposes. The censers therefore were beaten into plates for the altar; the coals scattered at a distance.

38. *these sinners against their own souls*] That is, "against their own lives." By their sin they had brought destruction upon themselves.

45. *they fell upon their faces*] In inter cession for the people; cf. *v.* 22, xiv. 5.

46. *a censer*] Rather **the censer.** *i.e.* that of the High-priest which was used by him on the Great Day of Atonement: cf. Lev. xvi. 12; Heb. ix. 4. It appears from Lev. x. 1, that each priest had also his own censer, no doubt for the daily incense offering: Ex. xxx. 1—8. Korah and his company had probably provided themselves with censers in emulation of the priests: cf. *v.* 6, Ezek. viii. 11.

and go] Or perhaps, "And carry it."

make an atonement for them] The effectual intercession of Aaron in behalf of the people was the best answer to the reproaches of those that disparaged his dignity.

49 Now they that died in the
plague were fourteen thousand and
seven hundred, beside them that died
about the matter of Korah.

50 And Aaron returned unto Moses unto the door of the tabernacle
of the congregation: and the plague
was stayed.

---

48. *He stood between the dead and the living; and the plague was stayed*] A striking proof of the efficacy of that very Aaronic priesthood which the rebels had presumed to reject. The incense offering which had brought down destruction when presented by unauthorized hands, now in the hand of the true priest is the medium of instant salvation to the whole people. Aaron by his acceptable ministration and his personal self-devotion foreshadows emphatically in this transaction the perfect mediation and sacrifice of Himself made by Christ.

NOTE on CHAP. XVI. 1.

The Jerusalem Targum supplies עצה (counsel) as the accusative after ויקח. If this be accepted, and the verb referred, as from its being first in the sentence and in the singular number, seems necessary, to Korah, then ודתן may be "with Dathan" (cf. ומשה, *v.* 18). The translation will then run: "And Korah . . . took counsel apart with Dathan and Abiram, &c." Various other renderings, less satisfactory, have been offered. LXX. gives ἐλαλήσε, which certainly does not answer to our present text. Accordingly emendations have been proposed, and for ויקח have been suggested ויקהל, ויקשר, ויקם; of which the last corresponds in a general way to the rendering of Onkelos (אתפליג "he separated himself"), and to that of the Syriac Version. The Arab. is equivalent to "he drew near." The ancient translators with these exceptions seem to have had our present text before them; and to have followed it, though with different interpretations. The Vulgate omits the word altogether. Probably however the difficulty of construction arises from an after insertion of the mention of Dathan and Abiram, and of their insurrection against Moses, into the original narrative of the sedition of Korah. This narrative would run naturally as follows:

ויקח קרח בן־יצהר בן־קהת בן־לוי מבני ישראל חמשים ומאתים וג׳

"Now Korah, the son of Izhar, the son of Kohath, the son of Levi, took of the children of Israel two hundred and fifty, &c." In it, moreover, Korah and his company would be naturally represented as gathering themselves together against Aaron as well as against Moses, *v.* 3. But in the expansion of this narrative with a view of making it comprise the account of the proceedings of Dathan and Abiram, it became important to mark that the outcry of the latter was directed against Moses alone; hence the introduction of the opening words of *v.* 2.

CHAPTER XVII.

1 *Aaron's rod among all the rods of the tribes only flourisheth.* 10 *It is left for a monument against the rebels.*

AND the LORD spake unto Moses, saying,
2 Speak unto the children of Israel, and take of every one of them
a rod according to the house of *their*
fathers, of all their princes according
to the house of their fathers twelve
rods: write thou every man's name
upon his rod.
3 And thou shalt write Aaron's
name upon the rod of Levi: for one
rod *shall be* for the head of the house
of their fathers.
4 And thou shalt lay them up in
the tabernacle of the congregation
before the testimony, [a]where I will
meet with you.
5 And it shall come to pass, *that*

[a] Exod. 25. 22.

CHAP. XVII. Further vindication (*vv.* 1—11) of the priestly authority of Aaron.

2. Cf. Ezek. xxxvii. 16, sqq.

3. *thou shalt write Aaron's name upon the rod of Levi*] The Levites had taken part in the late outbreak. It was therefore necessary to vindicate the supremacy of the house of Aaron over them; and accordingly his name was written on the rod of Levi, although being the son of Kohath, the *second* son of Levi (Ex. vi. 16, sqq.), he would not be the natural head of the tribe.

4. *before the testimony*] See on *v.* 10.

the man's rod, whom I shall choose,
shall blossom: and I will make to
cease from me the murmurings of
the children of Israel, whereby they
murmur against you.
6 ¶ And Moses spake unto the
children of Israel, and every one of
their princes gave him †a rod apiece, † Heb. *a rod for one prince, a rod for one prince.*
for each prince one, according to
their fathers' houses, *even* twelve
rods: and the rod of Aaron *was*
among their rods.
7 And Moses laid up the rods before the LORD in the tabernacle of
witness.
8 And it came to pass, that on
the morrow Moses went into the
tabernacle of witness; and, behold,
the rod of Aaron for the house of
Levi was budded, and brought forth
buds, and bloomed blossoms, and
yielded almonds.
9 And Moses brought out all the
rods from before the LORD unto all
the children of Israel: and they
looked, and took every man his rod.
10 ¶ And the LORD said unto Mo-
ses, Bring [b]Aaron's rod again before [b] Heb. 9. 4.
the testimony, to be kept for a token
against the †rebels; and thou shalt † Heb. *children of rebellion.*
quite take away their murmurings
from me, that they die not.
11 And Moses did *so:* as the LORD
commanded him, so did he.
12 And the children of Israel spake
unto Moses, saying, Behold, we die,
we perish, we all perish.
13 Whosoever cometh any thing
near unto the tabernacle of the LORD
shall die: shall we be consumed with
dying?

CHAPTER XVIII.

1 *The charge of the priests and Levites.* 9 *The priests' portion.* 21 *The Levites' portion.* 25 *The heave offering to the priests out of the Levites' portion.*

AND the LORD said unto Aaron,
Thou and thy sons and thy

---

6. *even twelve rods*] Possibly the two tribes of the children of Joseph were reckoned together, as in Deut. xxvii. 12. But as these two tribes had separate princes, and it was with the names of the princes that the rods were marked (*v.* 2), it is more probable that the whole number of rods was twelve exclusively of Aaron's, as the Vulgate expressly renders ("fuerunt virgæ duodecim absque virga Aaron").

8. *yielded almonds*] Or rather "ripened almonds," *i.e.* "brought forth ripe almonds." Probably different portions of the rod shewed the several stages of the process of fructification through which those parts which had advanced the furthest had passed. The name almond in Hebrew denotes the "waking-tree," the "waking-fruit;" and is applied to this tree, because it blossoms early in the season. It serves here, as in Jer. i. 11, 12, to set forth the speed and certainty with which, at God's will, His purposes are accomplished. So again the blossoming and bearing of Aaron's rod, naturally impotent when severed from the parent tree, may signify the profitableness because of God's appointment and blessing of the various means of grace (the priesthood, the sacraments), which of themselves and apart from Him could have no such efficacy. The incidents of this marvel are then by no means arbitrary. It is instructive to compare Is. iv. 2, xi. 1, liii. 2; Jer. xxxiii. 6; Zech. vi. 12.

10. *the testimony*] *i.e.* The Two Tables of the Law; cf. Ex. xxv. 16. No doubt the rod lay in front of the Tables within the Ark. It appears, 1 Kings viii. 9, that in the days of Solomon there was nothing in the ark save the two Tables. Aaron's rod then was probably lost when the Ark was taken by the Philistines.

12, 13. A new section should begin with these verses. They are connected retrospectively with chap. xvi.; and form the immediate introduction to ch. xviii. The people were terror-stricken by the fate of the company of Korah at the door of the tabernacle; followed up by the plague in which so many thousands of their numbers had perished. Presumption passes by reaction into despair. Was there any approach for them to the tabernacle of the Lord? Was there any escape from death, except by keeping aloof from his presence? The answers are supplied by the ordinances that follow; ordinances which testified that the God of judgment was still a God of grace and of love.

CHAP. XVIII. The priesthood of Aaron having been thus confirmed, the functions of his family and of the Levites are now finally and completely regulated; and definite provision made for their maintenance. The directions given in *vv.* 1—24, as more immediately pertaining to the office of the priests, are addressed by God directly to Aaron.

1. *the iniquity of the sanctuary*] *i.e.* Guilt of the offences which an erring people

father's house with thee shall bear the iniquity of the sanctuary: and thou and thy sons with thee shall bear the iniquity of your priesthood.

2 And thy brethren also of the tribe of Levi, the tribe of thy father, bring thou with thee, that they may be joined unto thee, and minister unto thee: but thou and thy sons with thee *shall minister* before the tabernacle of witness.

3 And they shall keep thy charge, and the charge of all the tabernacle: only they shall not come nigh the vessels of the sanctuary and the altar, that neither they, nor ye also, die.

4 And they shall be joined unto thee, and keep the charge of the tabernacle of the congregation, for all the service of the tabernacle: and a stranger shall not come nigh unto you.

5 And ye shall keep the charge of the sanctuary, and the charge of the altar: that there be no wrath any more upon the children of Israel.

[a] chap. 3. 45.

6 And I, behold, I have [a]taken your brethren the Levites from among the children of Israel: to you *they are* given *as* a gift for the LORD, to do the service of the tabernacle of the congregation.

7 Therefore thou and thy sons with thee shall keep your priest's office for every thing of the altar, and within the vail; and ye shall serve: I have given your priest's office *unto you as* a service of gift: and the stranger that cometh nigh shall be put to death.

8 ¶ And the LORD spake unto Aaron, Behold, I also have given thee the charge of mine heave offerings of all the hallowed things of the children of Israel; unto thee have I given them by reason of the anointing, and to thy sons, by an ordinance for ever.

9 This shall be thine of the most holy things, *reserved* from the fire: every oblation of theirs, every meat offering of theirs, and every sin offering of theirs, and every trespass offering of theirs, which they shall render unto me, *shall be* most holy for thee and for thy sons.

10 In the most holy *place* shalt thou eat it; every male shall eat it: it shall be holy unto thee.

11 And this *is* thine; the heave offering of their gift, with all the

---

would be continually committing against the majesty of God, when brought into contact, through the ordinances, with the manifestations of His presence. Cf. Ex. xxviii. 38; also viii. 19, and note.

the iniquity of your priesthood] As the priests themselves were but men, they could no more than others abide it, if God were extreme to mark what was done amiss. An atonement was consequently ordained for them (Lev. xvi.); and they were strengthened to bear the iniquity of their own unintentional offences, by being entrusted with the ceremonial means of taking it away. The word "bear" has, in the Old Testament, this double sense of "enduring" and "removing;" but in the person of Christ, who atoned by His own endurance, the two are in effect one.

2. *that they may be joined*] An allusion to the name Levi, which signifies "being joined." The old name is, in fact, taken up with a new meaning; the Levites became, by virtue of their office, a Levi indeed: cf. Eph. ii. 13, sqq.

unto thee] The priests ministered to the Lord: the Levites to the priests.

4. *a stranger*] *i.e.* every one not a Levite. So, *v.* 7, it denotes every one who was not a priest: cf. iii. 10, xvi. 40.

6, 7.] Inasmuch as the Lord proceeds after this to speak of the portion assigned to the priests for their maintenance, He takes occasion here, beforehand, to instruct them that the office which they fill, and the help which they enjoy, are gifts from Him, and are to be viewed as such.

8. *by reason of the anointing*] Recent commentators render "for a portion." See on Lev. vii. 35.

10. *In the most holy place*] Rather, "among the most holy things;" as in iv. 4: *i.e.* "As the most holy of things shalt thou eat it." Accordingly only the males of the priestly families could eat of the things here specified. On the contrary, of the heave and wave offerings described in the next verse, both males and females of these families might partake.

wave offerings of the children of Is-
b Lev. 10. 4. rael: I have given them unto [b]thee,
and to thy sons and to thy daughters
with thee, by a statute for ever:
every one that is clean in thy house
shall eat of it.
† Heb. *fat.* 12 All the †best of the oil, and
all the best of the wine, and of the
wheat, the firstfruits of them which
they shall offer unto the LORD, them
have I given thee.
13 *And* whatsoever is first ripe in
the land, which they shall bring unto
the LORD, shall be thine; every one
that is clean in thine house shall
eat *of* it.
c Lev. 27. 28. 14 [c]Every thing devoted in Israel
shall be thine.
d Exod. 13. 2. 15 Every thing that openeth [d]the
& 22. 29. matrix in all flesh, which they bring
Lev. 27. 26. unto the LORD, *whether it be* of men
chap. 3. 13. or beasts, shall be thine: nevertheless the firstborn of man shalt thou
surely redeem, and the firstling of
unclean beasts shalt thou redeem.
16 And those that are to be redeemed from a month old shalt thou
e Exod. 30. 13. redeem, according to thine estima-
Lev. 27. 25. tion, for the money of five shekels,
chap. 3. 47. after the shekel of the sanctuary,
Ezek. 45. 12. [e]which *is* twenty gerahs.

17 But the firstling of a cow, or
the firstling of a sheep, or the firstling of a goat, thou shalt not redeem; they *are* holy: thou shalt
sprinkle their blood upon the altar,
and shalt burn their fat *for* an offering made by fire, for a sweet savour
unto the LORD.
18 And the flesh of them shall be
thine, as the [f]wave breast and as the f Exod. 29. 26.
right shoulder are thine.
19 All the heave offerings of the
holy things, which the children of
Israel offer unto the LORD, have I
given thee, and thy sons and thy
daughters with thee, by a statute
for ever: it *is* a covenant of salt
for ever before the LORD unto thee
and to thy seed with thee.
20 ¶ And the LORD spake unto
Aaron, Thou shalt have no inheritance in their land, neither shalt
thou have any part among them:
[g]I *am* thy part and thine inheritance g Deut. 10. 9.
among the children of Israel. & 18. 2.
21 And, behold, I have given the Josh. 13. 14, 33.
children of Levi all the tenth in Ezek. 44. 28.
Israel for an inheritance, for their
service which they serve, *even* the
service of the tabernacle of the congregation.

---

15. *surely redeem...redeem*] A stronger expression is intentionally used in reference to the redemption of the firstborn of man than in reference to that of unclean beasts. For the rule as to the former admitted of no exception: the owner of the latter, if unwilling to redeem, might destroy the beasts (Ex. xiii. 13, xxxiv. 20). Usually of course he would redeem them, but in the case of a diseased or maimed animal he might well be excused from making a payment for that which, if redeemed, would be worthless. As to the mode of redemption of unclean beasts, it had been originally enjoined that the firstling of an ass should be redeemed with a lamb. But the owner of the beast might not be always able to provide a lamb, especially in the wilderness, and the liability was accordingly commuted (Lev. xxvii. 27). Into all the details of this the present ordinances do not enter. Their object is not so much to prescribe accurately to the people what should be paid, as to assign to the priests their various revenues.

16. *according to thine estimation*] Cf. Lev. v. 15, xxvii. 27, and notes.

18. *as the wave breast and as the right shoulder are thine*] This reference to the earlier legislation of Ex. xxix. 26—28 (eventually modified by Deut. xviii. 3) seems to indicate that the ordinance in question belongs to a comparatively early period of the years of wandering.

19. *a covenant of salt*] Cf. 2 Chron. xiii. 5. Covenants were ordinarily cemented in the East by the rites of hospitality; of which salt was the obvious token, entering as it does into every article of diet. It indicates perpetuity: cf. Lev. ii. 13, and note.

20. *I am thy part and thine inheritance*] Cf. Deut. x. 9.

21. *all the tenth in Israel*] Cf. Lev. xxvii. 30—33. The dedication of the tithe had however been handed down from patriarchal times. See Deut. Introd. § IV. Abraham paid tithes to Melchizedek: Jacob had promised the tithe of all wherewith God blessed him if he should return in peace to his father's house. But now first the Lord's tithes are assigned to the Levites for their support. The payment of tithes

22 Neither must the children of
Israel henceforth come nigh the tabernacle of the congregation, lest they
bear sin, †and die.
23 But the Levites shall do the
service of the tabernacle of the congregation, and they shall bear their
iniquity: *it shall be* a statute for ever
throughout your generations, that a-
mong the children of Israel they have
no inheritance.
24 But the tithes of the children
of Israel, which they offer *as* an
heave offering unto the LORD, I have
given to the Levites to inherit: therefore I have said unto them, Among
the children of Israel they shall have
no inheritance.
25 ¶ And the LORD spake unto
Moses, saying,
26 Thus speak unto the Levites,
and say unto them, When ye take
of the children of Israel the tithes
which I have given you from them
for your inheritance, then ye shall
offer up an heave offering of it for
the LORD, *even* a tenth *part* of the
tithe.
27 And *this* your heave offering
shall be reckoned unto you, as though
it were the corn of the threshing-
floor, and as the fulness of the winepress.
28 Thus ye also shall offer an
heave offering unto the LORD of all
your tithes, which ye receive of the
children of Israel; and ye shall give
thereof the LORD's heave offering to
Aaron the priest.
29 Out of all your gifts ye shall
offer every heave offering of the
LORD, of all the †best thereof, *even*
the hallowed part thereof out of it.
30 Therefore thou shalt say unto
them, When ye have heaved the
best thereof from it, then it shall be
counted unto the Levites as the
increase of the threshingfloor, and as
the increase of the winepress.
31 And ye shall eat it in every
place, ye and your households: for
it *is* your reward for your service in
the tabernacle of the congregation.
32 And ye shall bear no sin by
reason of it, when ye have heaved
from it the best of it: neither shall
ye pollute the holy things of the
children of Israel, lest ye die.

† Heb. *to die.*

† Heb. *fat.*

---

to them is recognized in Neh. x. 37, xii. 44; Tobit i. 7. Whether the Levites received the tithes of live stock as well as of produce seems doubtful. In no passage is there distinct mention of the former being theirs; and as a large number of animals must have been required for the public sacrifices, it is probable that the tithes of live stock were used for this purpose.

22. *lest they bear sin, and die*] Heb. "To bear sin, and die;" which would be the consequence of their approach.

23. *bear their iniquity*] The words are ambiguous. They probably refer to the iniquity of the people; who would, had they approached the tabernacle have fallen, from their proneness to transgress, into overt acts of offence. Against such a result they were, through the ministrations of the Levites, mercifully protected. Cf. *v.* 1, and Lev. xix. 17.

24. *as an heave offering*] Here only are the tithes described as a heave-offering; though in *v.* 26 the priestly tithes are also to be dedicated to their purpose by the ceremony of heaving them to the Lord. It is possible that all that is meant is that the tithes, being solemnly set apart for sacred purposes, became virtually a heave-offering, like the gifts for the Tabernacle. Ex. xxv. 2. There is no reason to think that the tithes were in fact heaved or waved before the Lord, though they were appropriated just as were those offerings that were heaved or waved.

25—32. Command as to the tithe of the Levitical tithe. This command, as enjoining perquisites of Aaron and his family, is addressed to Moses as the head of the whole nation, not to Aaron, who would be directly interested in it.

27. *shall be reckoned unto you*] Or, **by you**, as the same phrase means also at the close of Ex. xii. 16. The Levites were, of their tithes, to pay tithe to the priests, just as other Israelites paid tithe to the Levites.

29. *Out of all your gifts*] The spirit of this law would extend to all the revenues of the Levites, and we may thus assume that of the increase of their cattle, as well as of their tithes, a tithe was paid by them for the Lord's service.

32. *neither shall ye pollute, &c.*] Rather, **and by not polluting the holy things of the children of Israel, ye shall not**

CHAPTER XIX.

1 *The water of separation made of the ashes of a red heifer.* 11 *The law for the use of it in purification of the unclean.*

AND the LORD spake unto Moses and unto Aaron, saying,
2 This *is* the ordinance of the law which the LORD hath commanded, saying, Speak unto the children of Israel, that they bring thee a red heifer without spot, wherein *is* no blemish, *and* upon which never came yoke:
3 And ye shall give her unto Eleazar the priest, that he may bring her [a]forth without the camp, and *one* shall slay her before his face:

[a] Heb. 13. 11.

---

die. The words are words of comfort and assurance; and form a fitting conclusion to the legislation of the chapter.

CHAP. XIX. Ordinances respecting purification from the uncleanness of death.

The association of death with sin (Gen. ii. 17) sufficiently explains the ideas on which these ordinances are based. The principle that death and all pertaining to it, as being the manifestation and result of sin, are defiling, and so lead to interruption of the living relationship between God and His people, is not now introduced for the first time, nor is it at all peculiar to the Mosaic law. It was, on the contrary, traditional amongst the Israelites from the earliest times, is assumed in various enactments made already (cf. v. 2, ix. 6, sqq.; Lev. x. 1, 7, xi. 8, 11, 24, xxi. 1, sqq.), and is traceable in various forms amongst many nations of antiquity: *e.g.* the Egyptian priests were obliged to shun graves, funerals and funeral feasts (Porph. 'de Abst.' II. 50): the Persian Zendavesta has rules of remarkable strictness and particularity on the subject (cf. Bähr, 'Symbol.' II. 466, 467, reff.); and these were even exceeded by the rules prevailing amongst the Indians, both ancient and modern (cf. Knobel, note *in loc.*): like ideas are found amongst the Romans (cf. Plutarch, 'Sulla,' 35; Virgil, 'Æn.' VI. 228, sqq.; and Festus, 'apud Kn.' *in loc.*; and Bähr, II. 471), and Greeks (cf. Eurip. 'Alcest.' 97, sqq., 'Helen.' 1450, sqq., 'Iph. Taur.' 380, sqq.; Thucyd. III. 104).

The *tapu*, or uncleanness, regarded amongst the Maories of New Zealand as attaching to the man who has handled the dead, is such that not only can he not enter any house, or come in contact with any person or thing, without defiling it, but he may not even put forth his hands to the food which he himself eats (see 'Old New Zealand,' by a Pakeha Maori, pp. 122 sqq.).

The rites of purifying prescribed amongst these various nations trace points of similarity to those laid down in this chapter; and indeed sprinklings and washings would naturally form a part in them all (cf. ch. viii. 7). Moses then adopted, here as elsewhere, existing and ancient customs, with significant additions, as helps in the spiritual education of his people.

The ordinance was probably given at this time because the plague which happened (xvi. 46—50) about the matter of Korah had spread the defilement of death so widely through the camp as to seem to require some special measures of purification, more particularly as the deaths through it were in an extraordinary manner the penalty of sin. Occasion is accordingly taken to introduce a new ordinance on the whole subject, which might serve to re-assure the affrighted people at the time, supply a ready means of relief from this sort of uncleanness for the future, and by the typical character of its new elements provide a vehicle for important instruction as to a more real Atonement afterward to be revealed. That the ordinance of the red heifer in fact produced a deep impression appears from its introduction with characteristic variations into the Koran, the second Sura of which is entitled "the Heifer."

1. *unto Moses and unto Aaron*] Unto Aaron as well as unto Moses, because the ordinance was intended not merely for future observance, but also for immediate necessities.

2. *a red heifer*] "Red, in order to shadow forth man's earthly body, even as the name Adam bears allusion to the red earth of which man's body was fashioned" (Theodoret, 'Qu. in Num.' 35). Others less appositely regard the colour as an emblem of life: others again of sin (cf. Is. i. 18). The female sex of the victim perhaps denoted that the offering was only of secondary import: it was an offering not for actual sin, but only for ceremonial defilement.

without spot, wherein is no blemish] As with sin-offerings generally, Lev. iv. 3.

upon which never came yoke] So here and in Deut. xxi. 3, 1 S. vi. 7, in the case of female victims. In that of male victims this condition was not imposed: it can therefore hardly bear a typical meaning. Female cattle were not commonly employed in ploughing, and were perhaps therefore deemed to be marred if so used.

3. *unto Eleazar*] Cf. xvi. 37. The work would necessarily require a priest; yet as it rendered him unclean for the day, the high-priest was relieved of it.

without the camp] The defilement was viewed as transferred to the victim that was to be offered for its removal. Under these circumstances the victim, like the defiled persons themselves, would be removed outside the camp. So too those that had to do with the

4 And Eleazar the priest shall take of her blood with his finger, and [b]sprinkle of her blood directly before the tabernacle of the congregation seven times:

b Heb. 9. 13.

5 And *one* shall burn the heifer in his sight; [c]her skin, and her flesh, and her blood, with her dung, shall he burn:

c Exod. 29. 14. Lev. 4. 11, 12.

6 And the priest shall take cedar wood, and hyssop, and scarlet, and cast *it* into the midst of the burning of the heifer.

7 Then the priest shall wash his clothes, and he shall bathe his flesh in water, and afterward he shall come into the camp, and the priest shall be unclean until the even.

8 And he that burneth her shall wash his clothes in water, and bathe his flesh in water, and shall be unclean until the even.

9 And a man *that is* clean shall gather up the ashes of the heifer, and lay *them* up without the camp in a clean place, and it shall be kept for the congregation of the children of Israel for a water of separation: it *is* a purification for sin.

10 And he that gathereth the ashes of the heifer shall wash his clothes, and be unclean until the even: and it shall be unto the children of Israel, and unto the stranger that sojourneth among them, for a statute for ever.

11 ¶ He that toucheth the dead body of any †man shall be unclean seven days.

† Heb. *soul.*

12 He shall purify himself with

---

heifer were unclean until evening, just as if they had touched a defiled man (*v.* 22). The Jewish traditionary practice, subsequently to the building of the temple at Jerusalem, was to slay the heifer on the Mount of Olives, eastward from the temple across the valley of the Kidron. Here the priest was able, through the open eastern gate of the temple-court, to behold the sanctuary in the direction of which he was to sprinkle the heifer's blood (*v.* 4). The particular pollution to be remedied by this ordinance was the indirect one resulting from contact with tokens and manifestations of sin, not the direct and personal one arising from actual commission of sin. So too the sinless Antitype had to bear the reproach of associating with sinners (St Luke v. 30, xv. 2). And as the red heifer was expelled from the precincts of the camp, so was the Saviour cut off in no small measure during His Life from the fellowship of the chief representatives of the Theocracy, and put to death outside Jerusalem between two thieves. Cf. Heb. xiii. 11, 12.

5. *her skin, and her flesh*, &c.] The defilement, being external, extended to the whole body of the animal: hence the propriety of burning the victim entire and everything connected with it.

6. *cedar wood, and hyssop, and scarlet*] As in case of leprosy: Lev. xiv. 4, 6, 49. All three were associated with purification. Cedar-wood, when burnt, gave forth an odour regarded as counteractive to corruption and death. Hence it was burnt at funerals, and the resin of it was used in embalming. Plin. 'Nat. Hist.' XVI. 21, 76, and XXIV. 11; Herod. II. 87. Hyssop was a well-known detergent. The scarlet dye (which stands in Lev. xiv. between the other two, and which thus seems to have an emblematical meaning not radically different from theirs) was employed in medicine for strengthening the heart. It may also be viewed as pointing by its colour to the healing blood of Christ.

9. *water of separation*] In viii. 7, the water of purification from sin is in the Hebrew, "water of sin." So that which was to remedy a state of legal separation is here called "water of separation."

10. *he that gathereth the ashes*] The ashes were to be gathered by one who had taken no previous part in the work to be performed, and so was still clean. But the execution of his task rendered him equally unclean with the others. For the defilement of the people, previously transferred to the heifer, was regarded as concentrated in the ashes. The sprinkling of the ash-water upon any unclean person was the individual application of that purification which had already been provided, or rather effected, for all.

11—22. The provision for purification from defilement is supplemented by a definite determination of various degrees of uncleanness. One practical effect of thus attaching defilement to a dead body, to all that touched it, &c., would be to insure early burial, and to correct a practice not uncommon in the East, of leaving the dead to be devoured by the wild beasts. That these ordinances were promulgated in the wilderness appears from the references to "the tent" in *v.* 14. It may be asked, therefore, how would these directions be construed when the people came to dwell in settled and more spacious

it on the third day, and on the seventh day he shall be clean: but if he purify not himself the third day, then the seventh day he shall not be clean.

13 Whosoever toucheth the dead body of any man that is dead, and purifieth not himself, defileth the tabernacle of the LORD; and that soul shall be cut off from Israel: because the water of separation was not sprinkled upon him, he shall be unclean; his uncleanness *is* yet upon him.

14 This *is* the law, when a man dieth in a tent: all that come into the tent, and all that *is* in the tent, shall be unclean seven days.

15 And every open vessel, which hath no covering bound upon it, *is* unclean.

16 And whosoever toucheth one that is slain with a sword in the open fields, or a dead body, or a bone of a man, or a grave, shall be unclean seven days.

17 And for an unclean *person* they shall take of the †ashes of the burnt heifer of purification for sin, and †running water shall be put thereto in a vessel:

eb. st.

eb. ing water s shall given.

18 And a clean person shall take hyssop, and dip *it* in the water, and sprinkle *it* upon the tent, and upon all the vessels, and upon the persons that were there, and upon him that touched a bone, or one slain, or one dead, or a grave:

19 And the clean *person* shall sprinkle upon the unclean on the third day, and on the seventh day: and on the seventh day he shall purify himself, and wash his clothes, and bathe himself in water, and shall be clean at even.

20 But the man that shall be unclean, and shall not purify himself, that soul shall be cut off from among the congregation, because he hath defiled the sanctuary of the LORD: the water of separation hath not been sprinkled upon him; he *is* unclean.

21 And it shall be a perpetual statute unto them, that he that sprinkleth the water of separation shall wash his clothes; and he that toucheth the water of separation shall be unclean until even.

22 And whatsoever the unclean *person* toucheth shall be unclean; and the soul that toucheth *it* shall be unclean until even.

CHAPTER XX.

1 *The children of Israel come to Zin, where Miriam dieth.* 2 *They murmur for want of water.* 7 *Moses smiting the rock bringeth forth water at Meribah.* 14 *Moses at Kadesh desireth passage through Edom, which is denied him.* 22 *At mount Hor Aaron resigneth his place to Eleazar, and dieth.*

THEN came the children of Israel, *even* the whole congrega-

---

abodes? Michaelis hazards an opinion that the defilement would only reach to that apartment of the house in which the death had occurred. The LXX., with whom modern Jewish usage coincides, replacing the word "tent" by "house" (*οἰκία*), imply that what was law for the one was law also for the other.

CHAP. XX. This and the next chapter narrate the journey of the people from Kadesh round Mount Seir to the heights of Pisgah, near the Jordan, and the various incidents connected with that journey. A list of the several marches is given xxxiii. 37—41. They formed the third and last stage of the progress of Israel from Sinai to Canaan, and took place in the fortieth year of the Exodus.

The incidents are apparently not narrated in a strictly chronological order, for the attack of king Arad (xxi. 1) no doubt took place during the march from Kadesh to Mount Hor (xxxiii. 37—40), and before the host had by turning away southwards (xx. 21, xxi. 4) relieved the king from his apprehensions. Indeed the leading purpose of ch. xx. seems to be to narrate the loss by the people of their original leaders before their entrance into the land of promise. On the chronology of this period see Introd. § 3.

1. *even the whole congregation*] The A.V. rightly marks the expression as emphatic by inserting the word "even." The words occur before in xiii. 26, and xiv. 1, at the commencement of the tedious period of penal wandering. Their use again now serves to mark its close, and points to a re-assembling of the people for the purpose of at last

tion, into the desert of Zin in the first month: and the people abode in Kadesh; and Miriam died there, and was buried there.

---

resuming the advance to the promised land. The long 38 years which intervene are almost a blank (see Introd. § 2); they can hardly be said to form a portion of the history of God's people at all, for the covenant though not cancelled was in abeyance. A veil is accordingly thrown by Moses over this dreary interval, during which the rebellious generation was wasting away. But the words before us seem to hint, what is in itself natural and likely, that the "congregation" was during these years broken up. No doubt round the Tabernacle there continued an organized camp consisting of the Levites and others, which was moved from time to time up and down the country. But there was no longer any reason for the coherence of the whole people in mass, and we may accordingly believe that they were scattered over the face of the wilderness of Paran, and led a nomadic life as best suited the pasturage of the cattle. It is thus that the modern Bedouins maintain very large flocks and herds in these same deserts. "On one occasion," says Mr J. L. Porter (cited in 'Mosaic Records" by Mr B. B. Rogers, p. 67, note, 2nd Edit. 1865), "I rode for two successive days through the flocks of a section of the Anazeh tribe, and the encampment of the chief was then at a noted fountain, thirty miles distant, at right angles to my course; yet the country was swarming with men and women, boys and girls, looking after the cattle." He adds with special reference to the Israelites, "The camp would be a mere nucleus. Yet as being the head-quarters of the nation, containing the Tabernacle, the priests, and the chiefs, and forming the rallying point for the warriors, it was the only place with which the sacred historian is concerned." Thus the encampments named xxxiii. 18—36 would be various spots at which in the course of these years the Tabernacle was for a time pitched; and possibly in *v.* 22, "Kehelathah" ("assembling"), and *v.* 25, "Makheloth" ("assemblies"), may be names bestowed because of some extraordinary though temporary gatherings of the Israelites there.

We can hardly doubt that during the year's sojourn at Sinai there would be a dispersion of the people for the purpose of foraging; and it is obvious how pertinent are the above considerations, based as they are upon the suggestions of the text and the known habits of oriental nations, to the difficulties which have been raised as to the means of subsistence for the multitudes of Israel in the wilderness.

Although it is no part of the plan of Scripture to give details on this subject, yet one or two incidental notices throw light upon it. It is evident *e.g.* from Deut. ii. 26—29, that the Israelites had traffic in provisions with surrounding tribes; indeed the regular highway of the caravans from the East to Egypt, and *vice versâ*, lay across the Desert of the Wandering; and from Ps. lxxiv. 14 it appears to have been the belief of a later generation that fish were occasionally at least to be had, no doubt from the gulf of Akabah, on which was the encampment, xxxiii. 35, and where it may have been for years. (Cf. Hengstenb. on Ps. lxxiv.; Rogers, 'Mosaic Rec.' p. 134.) Nothing too is better ascertained than the fact that the resources of the whole district were in ancient times vastly greater than they now are. The traces of a population, fertility, and wealth, that have long passed away, are found by every traveller; cf. Burckhardt, pp. 469, 495, &c.; Stanley, 'Sinai,' pp. 24, sqq., and several authorities there quoted; Ewald, 'Hist. of Israel,' Vol. I. p. 620 and note (English transl. by Martineau); and see further in Introd. to Exodus, pp. 245, 246. The language used in Deut. i. 19, viii. 15, &c., respecting the hardships of the journey through the wilderness, belongs more particularly to the latest marches in the fortieth year through the Arabah (see on xxi. 4), rather than to the whole period of the wanderings; and is such as would naturally suggest itself to one who entered after toilsome wayfaring upon the fertile pastures of Gilead and Bashan.

The Israelites also had doubtless these natural resources supplemented where needful by miraculous aid. We can hardly think that the manna, or the occasional bestowal of quails, or of water, which are actually recorded were the only facts of the kind that took place. Rather are those facts mentioned as examples, selected because of some special instruction wrapped up in the particular instances. The whole guidance of Israel through the wilderness is constantly referred to God's special and immediately superintending care: Deut. viii. 4, sqq., xxix. 5; Neh. ix. 21; Is. lxiii. 11—14; Amos ii. 10, &c. It is probable indeed, and seems remarkably suggested by the language of many later references, that the miraculous supply of water for the people and their cattle was, as in this ch., *vv.* 8, 11, and earlier at Rephidim on the march to Sinai (Ex. xvii. 1 sqq.), so elsewhere, one of God's frequent mercies to them; cf. Judges v. 4 sqq.; Ps. lxviii. 7 sqq. Compare also the glowing language of Isaiah, evidently foretelling God's future graciousness to His people in terms borrowed from the past in chs. xxxv. 1, sqq., xli. 17, sqq., xliii. 16, sqq., xlix. 9—10, and Hos. ii. 14, sqq. This whole subject is well handled by Mr Rogers, 'Mos. Records,' pp. 142, sqq., who illustrates also from various travellers "the magical effect" of a supply of water in any part of the peninsula. It must

2 And there was no water for the
congregation: and they gathered themselves together against Moses and
against Aaron.
3 And the people chode with Moses, and spake, saying, Would God
chap. 11. that we had died [a]when our brethren
died before the LORD!
Exod. 17. 4 And [b]why have ye brought up
the congregation of the LORD into
this wilderness, that we and our cattle should die there?
5 And wherefore have ye made us
to come up out of Egypt, to bring
us in unto this evil place? it *is* no
place of seed, or of figs, or of vines,
or of pomegranates; neither *is* there
any water to drink.
6 And Moses and Aaron went from
the presence of the assembly unto
the door of the tabernacle of the
congregation, and they fell upon their
faces: and the glory of the LORD
appeared unto them.
7 ¶ And the LORD spake unto
Moses, saying,
8 Take the rod, and gather thou
the assembly together, thou, and
Aaron thy brother, and speak ye
unto the rock before their eyes; and
it shall give forth his water, and
thou shalt bring forth to them water
out of the rock: so thou shalt give the
congregation and their beasts drink.
9 And Moses took the rod from
before the LORD, as he commanded
him.
10 And Moses and Aaron gathered the congregation together before
the rock, and he said unto them,
Hear now, ye rebels; must we fetch
you water out of this rock?

---

be added too that the Israelites, from their sojourn in Egypt, were familiar with artificial irrigation, and well able to husband and turn to account all available supplies of water, whether ordinary or extraordinary.

Yet though God's extraordinary bounty was thus still vouchsafed to them, it is probable that this period was, amongst the perishing generation at all events, one of great religious declension, or even apostasy. To it must no doubt be referred such passages as Ezek. xx. 15 sqq.; Amos v. 25 sqq.; Hosea ix. 10.

into the desert of Zin] Cf. x. 12, xxxiv. 3, sqq. and notes. The place of encampment was no doubt adjacent to the spring of Kadesh. On the former occasion they probably encamped on the more level ground of the wilderness of Paran to the west; but now, for some reason unknown to us, on the hills of the wilderness of Zin to the east. Hence perhaps the difference of the terms used in reference to these two encampments at Kadesh (cf. xii. 16, xiii. 26; also xxxiii. 36, with *ib.* 18, and note).

in the first month] Of the fortieth year of the Exodus; see Introduction, § 3.

and the people abode in Kadesh] These words are, perhaps, through some private theory of the history of the wanderings, ignored by Josephus and by the later Targums. But being represented in the older versions, they are doubtless genuine.

Miriam died there, and was buried there] Eusebius mentions that in his day her sepulchre was still shewn, apparently either at Petra or not far from it ('Onom.' apud Hieron. s.v. Cades-barne). No sepulchre is now shewn as Miriam's either at Petra or elsewhere; and Josephus ('Ant.' IV. 4. § 6) places her sepulchre on a mountain named Zin.

2—6. Complaints of the people for want of water. The spring of Kadesh (cf. on xiii. 26), near which they were probably encamped, was no doubt wholly insufficient for the wants of so great a concentrated multitude. The language of the murmurers is noteworthy. It has the air of a traditional remonstrance handed down from the last generation. Cf. xiv. 2, sqq.; Ex. xvii. 3.

6. *they fell upon their faces*] Cf. xiv. 5, &c.

8. *Take the rod*] Not the budding rod of xvii. 5, but that with which the miracles in Egypt had been wrought (Ex. vii. 8, sqq., 19, sqq., viii. 5, sqq., &c.), and which had been used on a similar occasion at Rephidim, Ex. xvii. 5, sqq. This rod, as the memorial of so many Divine interpositions, was naturally laid up in the Tabernacle, and is accordingly, *v.* 9, described now as taken by Moses "from before the Lord."

the rock] Heb. *sela*, **cliff**; a different word from *zur*, by which the "rock" in Horeb is designated.

10. *ye rebels*] See note at end of chapter.

must we fetch, &c.] The later Targumists, and many recent comm. render, "Can we fetch," &c.; and view the words as words of doubt. But other passages of Scripture (cf. xxvii. 14; Deut. xxxii. 51, 52; Ps. cvi. 33) do not bear out the view that it was in doubt of God's succouring power that the "unbelief" (*v.* 12) of Moses and Aaron con-

11 And Moses lifted up his hand, and with his rod he smote the rock twice: and the water came out abundantly, and the congregation drank, and their beasts *also*.

12 ¶ And the LORD spake unto Moses and Aaron, Because ye believed me not, to sanctify me in the eyes of the children of Israel, therefore ye shall not bring this congregation into the land which I have given them.

c Ps. 106. 32, &c.
‖ That is, *Strife*.

13 *c*This *is* the water of ‖Meribah; because the children of Israel strove with the LORD, and he was sanctified in them.

14 ¶ And Moses sent messengers from Kadesh unto the king of Edom, Thus saith thy brother Israel, Thou knowest all the travel that hath †befallen us:

† Heb. *found*

15 How our fathers went down into Egypt, and we have dwelt in Egypt a long time; and the Egyptians vexed us, and our fathers:

16 And when we cried unto the LORD, he heard our voice, and sent an angel, and hath brought us forth out of Egypt: and, behold, we *are* in Kadesh, a city in the uttermost of thy border:

17 Let us pass, I pray thee, through thy country: we will not pass through the fields, or through the vineyards, neither will we drink *of* the water of the wells: we will

---

sisted; nor is it likely that they who had wrought the miracle at Rephidim would be staggered when bidden to do a like thing again. The A. V. has therefore rightly retained the older interpretation.

11. *he smote the rock twice*] The command, *v.* 8, was "Speak ye unto the rock." The act of smiting, and especially with two strokes, indicates violent irritation on the part of Moses; as does also his unseemly mode of addressing the people: "Hear now, ye rebels." The form too of the question, "must *we*, &c.," directs the people not, as ought to have been the case, to God as their deliverer, but to Moses and Aaron personally. In fact the faithful servant of God, worn out by the reiterated perversities of the people, at last breaks down; and in the actual discharge of his duty as God's representative before Israel, acts unworthily of the great function entrusted to him. Thus Moses did not "sanctify God in the eyes of the children of Israel." Aaron might have checked the intemperate words and acts of Moses, and did not. Hence God punishes both by withdrawing them from their work for Him, and handing over its accomplishment to another.

13. *the water of Meribah*] *i.e.* "Strife." The place is called "Meribah in Kadesh," xxvii. 14, and "Meribah-Kadesh," Deut. xxxii. 51, to distinguish it from the "Meribah" of Ex. xvii. 2, sqq. The fact of this addition to the common name, and the diverse circumstances of the two cases, shew that we have not here another version of the same occurrence; nor in forty years is it surprising that scarcity of water should be repeatedly recorded in the annals of the wanderings through the wilderness. Indeed the same want is mentioned again in the very next ch., *v.* 5.

and he was sanctified in them] An allusion doubtless to the name "Kadesh" (holy), which though not now bestowed, acquired a new significance from the fact that God here indicated His own sanctity, punishing Moses and Aaron who had trespassed against it.

14. Cf. Judg. xi. 16, 17. It appears from comparing xx. 1 with xxxiii. 38, that the host must have remained in Kadesh some three or four months. No doubt time was required for re-organization. It may be also that they proposed, as 38 years previously, to invade Canaan from this quarter, but were prevented by obstacles of which they had for a time reason to hope for the removal. The passage of Egyptian troops through the west and south of Canaan might be such an obstacle. Eventually however they were, for reasons which we can but conjecture, moved round to the eastern frontier, through the territory of Moab. In order to gain the banks of Jordan by the shortest route they had to march nearly due east from Kadesh, and pass through the heart of the Edomitish mountains. These are lofty and precipitous, traversed by two or three narrow defiles, of which one (the Wady Ghuweir) only is practicable for an army. Hence the necessity of the request *v.* 17.

Thus saith] Cf. Deut. ii. 4, and reff.

thy brother] An appeal to the Edomites to remember and renew the old kindnesses of Jacob and Esau, Gen. xxxiii. 1—17.

It appears from Judg. xi. 17 that a similar request was addressed to the Moabites.

16. *an angel*] Cf. Ex. xiv. 19. The term is to be understood as importing generally the supernatural guidance under which Israel was.

a city in the uttermost of thy border] On Kadesh see note at end of ch. xiii.

go by the king's *high* way, we will not turn to the right hand nor to the left, until we have passed thy borders.

18 And Edom said unto him, Thou shalt not pass by me, lest I come out against thee with the sword.

19 And the children of Israel said unto him, We will go by the high way: and if I and my cattle drink of thy water, then I will pay for it: I will only, without *doing* any thing *else*, go through on my feet.

20 And he said, Thou shalt not go through. And Edom came out against him with much people, and with a strong hand.

21 Thus Edom refused to give Israel passage through his border: wherefore Israel turned away from him.

22 ¶ And the children of Israel, *even* the whole congregation, journeyed from [d] Kadesh, and came unto mount Hor.

[d] chap. 33. 37.

23 And the LORD spake unto Moses and Aaron in mount Hor, by the coast of the land of Edom, saying,

24 Aaron shall be gathered unto his people: for he shall not enter into the land which I have given unto the children of Israel, because ye rebelled against my † word at the water of Meribah.

† Heb. *mouth.*

25 [e] Take Aaron and Eleazar his son, and bring them up unto mount Hor:

[e] chap. 33. 38. Deut. 32. 50.

26 And strip Aaron of his garments, and put them upon Eleazar his son: and Aaron shall be gathered *unto his people*, and shall die there.

27 And Moses did as the LORD commanded: and they went up into mount Hor in the sight of all the congregation.

28 And Moses stripped Aaron of his garments, and put them upon Eleazar his son; and [f] Aaron died there in the top of the mount: and Moses and Eleazar came down from the mount.

[f] Deut. 10. 6. & 32. 50.

29 And when all the congregation saw that Aaron was dead, they mourned for Aaron thirty days, *even* all the house of Israel.

---

17. *by the king's high way*] Heb. "by the king's way." In *v.* 19 the word used (*mesillah*) denotes a causeway or raised road, adapted for military purposes. To such the name "imperial road" (*derb es-sultân*) is in the East still often given. Moses doubtless sought a passage by the Wady Ghuweir, leading eastward through the heart of the mountains of Edom to the table-land above; see on *v.* 14. This valley has still excellent pasture and many springs.

20. *And Edom came out against him*] The Israelites, without awaiting at Kadesh the return of their ambassadors, commenced their eastward march. At the tidings of their approach the Edomites mustered their forces to oppose them; and on crossing the Arabah they found their ascent through the mountains barred. The notice of this is inserted here to complete the narrative; but in order of time it comes after the march of *v.* 22.

22. *mount Hor*] On the name see Note at end of chapter. The topographical remark in *v.* 23, that this mountain is "by the coast" (*i.e.* border) "of the land of Edom" (xxxiii. 37), the authority of Josephus ('Ant.' iv. 4. 7), and constant tradition identify Mount Hor as the modern Jebel Harun, situated on the eastern side of the Arabah, and close to Petra. This striking mountain, rising on a dark red bare rock, to a height of near 5000 feet above the Mediterranean, is remarkable far and near for its two summits, on one of which is still shown a small square building, crowned with a dome, called the Tomb of Aaron (Stanley, 'S. and P.' p. 86, Ritter, I. 448, Eng. Transl.). The host was doubtless encamped in the Arabah below (at a place called Moseroth or Mosera, xxxiii. 30; Deut. x. 6), whilst Aaron and his companions ascended the mountain "in the sight of the congregation" (*v.* 27). Though Hor unquestionably lay within the territory of Edom, yet there could be no unfriendly trespass in the mere ascent of its barren heights by the three leaders of the host, especially whilst a friendly reply to their peaceful message (*v.* 14), was expected.

26. *of his garments*] The priestly garments, wherewith he had invested him, Lev. viii. 7—9.

put them upon Eleazar] By way of solemn transference of Aaron's office to him, cf. 1 Kings xix. 19.

27. *in the sight of all the congregation*] The congregation could not however witness the actual transaction on the mountain-top. Thus in his death as in his life (ch. xvii.) is Aaron's dignity guarded by God. The transference of his office to his son, at the command of God and by the hand of Moses, sets forth in act the will of God for the continuance of the High Priesthood, notwithstanding the mortality of its successive inheritors (Hebr. vii. 23); and also its subordination to him who came invested with direct authority from God.

29. *Aaron was dead*] Cf. xxxiii. 37—39; Deut. x. 6.

NOTES on CHAP. XX. 10, 22.

10. Heb. המֹּרִים. This is probably the word used by our Lord in the Sermon on the Mount, St Matt. v. 20, and rendered rather after the sound than the sense by the Greek *μωρέ*. For the verb מרה seems to be a word designed, like murmur, and the German "murren," to echo its own sense; and to mean in in the first place "to complain fretfully;" hence "to be refractory," "to rebel," as in *v.* 24 of this chapter. The words Marah and Meribah are cognate.

22. Hor has been immemorially treated as a proper name, yet it is probably only an archaic form of הַר, the common Hebrew term for "mountain" (Gesen., Fürst. sub. v.). Hence it is applied, xxxiv. 7, to a summit of Mount Lebanon, where the LXX. renders *ad verbum*, *τὸ ὄρος τὸ ὄρος*. It affords too the only example in the Bible in which the proper name comes first; for "Hor, the mountain," would exhibit the order of the words in the original. It is probable that the proper import of the expression הֹר הָהָר is simply "summit of the mountain;" as is noted by Jerome ('Ep. ad Fabiolam') in remarking upon this passage of Numbers: "Legi potest, Ascendit Aaron sacerdos in montis montem." So Jarchi *in loc.* "Mons fuit super montem, veluti pomum parvum super pomum magnum." Mount Hor in fact "rises like a huge castellated building from a lower base" (Stanley, 'S. and P.' p. 86). The mountain intended xxxiv. 7 was probably one of similar outline.

CHAPTER XXI.

1 *Israel with some loss destroy the Canaanites at Hormah.* 4 *The people murmuring are plagued with fiery serpents.* 7 *They repenting are healed by a brasen serpent.* 10 *Sundry journeys of the Israelites.* 21 *Sihon is overcome,* 33 *and Og.*

AND *when* [a] king Arad the Canaanite, which dwelt in the south, heard tell that Israel came by the way of the spies; then he fought against Israel, and took *some* of them prisoners.

[a] chap. 40.

CHAP. XXI. **1.** *king Arad the Canaanite*] Rather, "**the Canaanite, the king of Arad.**" See on xiv. 45. Arad stood on a small hill, now called Tel-Arad (Rob. II. 101, 201), 20 miles south of Hebron. (Euseb. 'Onom.' s. v. Ἀράμα). Human habitations have now disappeared from the spot; but a ruined reservoir remains, and fragments of pottery are still found there.

in the south] See on xiii. 17, 22.

by the way of the spies] *i.e.* Through the desert of Zin, the route which the spies sent out by Moses 38 years before had adopted; cf. xiii. 21. On the expression, which is not free from difficulty, see note at end of chapter.

he fought against Israel] This, as has been already observed (cf. xx. 1, and note), can hardly have taken place after the death of Aaron. The king of Arad cannot be supposed to have waited until the host had marched more than sixty miles away from his borders to Mount Hor, and was in full march further away, before attacking them; nor can the Israelites, on the other hand, have laid aside their journey towards Canaan, retraced their steps into the wilderness of Zin, and returned to Kadesh in order to invade Arad, which lay north of that place. The attack of the king was most probably made just when the camp broke up from Kadesh, and the ultimate direction of the march was not as yet pronounced. The words, "when the king . . . heard tell that Israel came by the way of the spies," seem to hint that the king of Arad apprehended that the invasion of Canaan would be attempted from the same quarter as before, xiv. 40—45, and determined to take the offensive, and try to drive back his enemies ere they reached his territory. The insult was no doubt avenged as soon as the host was ready for action. The order of the narrative in these chapters, as occasionally elsewhere in this book (cf. on ix. 1, &c.), is not that of time, but of subject-matter; and the war against Arad is introduced here as the first of the series of victories gained under Moses, which the historian now takes in hand to narrate.

2 And Israel vowed a vow unto
the LORD, and said, If thou wilt
indeed deliver this people into my
hand, then I will utterly destroy their
cities.
3 And the LORD hearkened to the
voice of Israel, and delivered up
the Canaanites; and they utterly
destroyed them and their cities: and
he called the name of the place ‖ Hormah.

‖ That is, *Utter destruction.*

4 ¶ And they journeyed from
mount Hor by the way of the Red
sea, to compass the land of Edom:
and the soul of the people was much
‖ discouraged because of the way.
5 And the people spake against
God, and against Moses, Wherefore have ye brought us up out of
Egypt to die in the wilderness? for
there is no bread, neither *is there*
any water; and [b] our soul loatheth
this light bread.

‖ Or, *grieved.* Heb. *shortened.*

[b] chap. 11. 6.

6 And [c] the LORD sent fiery serpents among the people, and they
bit the people; and much people of
Israel died.
7 ¶ Therefore the people came

[c] Wisdom 16. 1, 5. 1 Cor. 10. 9.

---

3. *he called the name of the place*] Render, **the name of the place was called.** The transitive verb here is, by a common Hebrew idiom, equivalent to an impersonal one.

Hormah] *i.e.* "Ban." On the site of this place see xiv. 45, and note. In Judges i. 17, we read that the men of Judah and Simeon "slew the Canaanites that inhabited Zephath, and utterly destroyed it;" and further, that "the name of the city was called Hormah." But it does not follow that the name "Hormah" was first bestowed in consequence of the destruction of the place in the time of the Judges, and that in Numbers its occurrence is a sign of a post-Mosaic date of composition. The text of Num. xxi. 3 informs us that this aggression of the king of Arad was repelled, and avenged by the capture and sack of his cities; and that the Israelites "banned" them (cf. Lev. xxvii. 28, 29). But it was not the plan of the Israelites in the time of Moses to remain in this district. They therefore marched away south-eastward; and no doubt for the time the Canaanites resumed possession, and restored the ancient name (Zephath). But Joshua again conquered the king of this district, and finally in the time of the early Judges the ban of Moses and his contemporaries was fully executed. We have therefore in the passage before us the history of the actual origin of the name "Hormah."

4. *And they journeyed*] Their direct route to Moab through the valleys of Edom being closed against them (xx. 20, 21), they were now compelled to seek a circuitous one by marching round the mountain fastnesses. Their course lay down the Arabah; between the limestone cliffs of the Tih on the west, and the granite range of Mount Seir on the east, until, a few hours north of Akaba (Ezion-Geber) the Wady Ithm opened to them a gap in the hostile mountains, allowed them to turn to their left, and to march northwards towards Moab (Deut. ii. 3). Cf. Ritter, 'S. and P.' Vol. I. p. 75 (Clark's Transl.). They were thus for some days (see on xxii. 1) in the Arabah, a mountain plain of loose sand, gravel, and detritus of granite, which though sprinkled with low shrubs, especially near the mouths of the wadys and the courses of the winter-torrents, furnishes extremely little either of food or water, and is moreover often troubled by sand-storms from the shore of the gulf (see Ritter, I. 53 sqq. Eng. Transl.). Hence "the soul of the people was much discouraged because of the way."

5. *this light bread*] *i.e.* this vile, contemptible bread. The Hebrew word is derived from a root signifying "to be light," and so "to be mean," "despised," &c. Cf. the Horatian "et spondere levi pro paupere," 'A. P.' 423

6. *fiery serpents*] The epithet (Deut. viii. 15, Is. xiv. 29, xxx. 6) denotes the inflammatory effect of their bite. So in Greek writers we read of the διψάς (Nicander, 'Theriaca,' 334), a poisonous snake whose bite caused intense thirst; of the πρηστήρ and the καύσων (Ælian, 'Nat. An.' vi. 51), names which point in like manner to fever, swelling, and inflammation. The peninsula of Sinai, and not least, the Arabah, abounds in venomous reptiles of various kinds, which may well be described in such terms. V. Schubert travelling in this district remarks: "In the afternoon they brought us a very mottled snake of large size, marked with fiery red spots and wavy stripes, which belonged to the most poisonous species, as the formation of its teeth clearly showed. According to the Bedouins, these snakes, which they greatly dreaded, were very common in that neighbourhood," II. 406: see also Burckhardt, p. 499. Alexander in crossing Gedrosia lost many men through the serpents which sprang upon those passing by from the sand and brushwood (Strabo xv. 723). Strabo also remarks the dangers of this kind to which travellers in the Peninsula of Sinai were exposed (xvi. 759).

to Moses, and said, We have sinned,
for we have spoken against the LORD,
and against thee; pray unto the
LORD, that he take away the serpents from us. And Moses prayed
for the people.
8 And the LORD said unto Moses,
Make thee a fiery serpent, and set
it upon a pole: and it shall come to
pass, that every one that is bitten,
[d] 2 Kings 18. 4. John 3. 14. when he looketh upon it, shall live.
9 And [d]Moses made a serpent of
brass, and put it upon a pole, and
it came to pass, that if a serpent had
bitten any man, when he beheld the
serpent of brass, he lived.
10 ¶ And the children of Israel set
forward, and [e]pitched in Oboth. [e] chap. 33. 43.
11 And they journeyed from O-
both, and pitched at ‖ Ije-abarim, in ‖ Or, *Heaps of Abarim.*
the wilderness which *is* before Moab,
toward the sunrising.
12 ¶ From thence they removed,
and pitched in the valley of Zared.

---

8. *Make thee a fiery serpent*] *i.e.* a serpent resembling in appearance the reptiles which attacked the people. The resemblance was of the essence of the symbolism (cf. 1 Sam. vi. 5). As the brazen serpent represented the instrument of their chastisement, so the looking unto it at God's word denoted acknowledgment of their sin, longing for deliverance from its penalty, and faith in the means appointed by God for healing. The typical import of this incident, indicated by the Saviour Himself (St John iii. 14, 15), has been very copiously treated of by the Christian Fathers and commentators. In the serpent of brass, harmless itself, but made in the image of the creature that is accursed above others (Gen. iii. 14), they rightly see a figure of Him who though "holy, harmless, undefiled, separate from sinners" (Heb. vii. 26), was yet "made sin" (2 Cor. v. 21), and "made a curse" (Gal. iii. 13) for us. And the eye of faith fixed on Him beholds, as in his day and degree did the stricken Israelite in the wilderness, the manifestation at once of the deserts of sin, of its punishment imminent and deprecated, and of the method of its remission devised by God Himself.

The explanations of certain commentators that the brazen serpent was set forth by Moses as an emblem of healing by the medical art; as a form of amulet to be copied and worn; as a reminiscence of Egyptian serpent-worship, &c., are obviously unworthy and beside the mark, and are rebuked by Wisd. xvi. 7. Cf. 2 Kings xviii. 4.

10, 11. *Oboth*] At the opening in the hills now known as Wady-el-Ithm, the route of the Israelites took a sharp turn, and ran thenceforward in a north-easterly direction. After a march of about fifty miles they would reach the line of the present pilgrim route between Mekka and Damascus; and along this, or nearly so, their march must for some distance have lain. The earlier stations in this part of their journey were Zalmonah and Punon (xxxiii. 41, 42). Oboth was north of Punon, east of the northern part of Edom, and is pretty certainly the same as the present pilgrim halting-place el-Ahsa. The name denotes "holes dug in the ground for water," being the plural of the term *ob* or *obah*, which appears in Arabic as *weibeh*. The term *hasy*, of which *ahsa* is the plural, has the same meaning; and thus the modern station corresponds to the ancient both in name and place. The brook Wady-el-Ahsa, which, rising near the spot, runs north-westwards into the southern bay of the Dead Sea, is the boundary between the modern provinces of Jebâl and Kerak, as it probably was in ancient times between Edom and Moab. On advancing further north, therefore, the Israelites would find themselves in the "wilderness" or pasture-land to the east of Moab. Here they encamped, on the border of Moab, at Iim, a name which signifies "ruinous heaps" (xxxiii. 45); called here more fully, Ije-abarim, or Iim of Abarim, to distinguish it from another Iim in south-western Canaan (Josh. xv. 29). The name Abarim, usually rendered "further regions," but perhaps better rendered "coast regions," is more particularly applied to the hills immediately facing Jericho (xxvii. 12, xxxiii. 47, 48; Deut. xxxii. 49), and denotes generally, as we may gather from Jer. xxii. 20 (where it is erroneously rendered "passages"), the whole upland country on the east of the Jordan. The Greek equivalent of the name is Perea, familiar to us through the writings of Josephus. The Syriac Version, by a peculiar punctuation of the word represented in A. V. by "Abarim," gives to it the sense "Hebrews." The same name would thus stand "Ije of the Hebrews;" as if the people had left their names with this place of their encampment.

12. *the valley of Zared*] Rather the **brook** or watercourse of Zared; more properly written **Zered.** It is to be identified with the present Wady Ain Franjy, the main upper branch of Wady Kerak. This was the first westward-flowing brook that crossed the line of march. As such, it marked an era in their progress; and the summons to them to

13 From thence they removed, and pitched on the other side of Arnon, which *is* in the wilderness that cometh out of the coasts of the Amorites: for Arnon *is* the border of Moab, between Moab and the Amorites.

14 Wherefore it is said in the book of the wars of the LORD, ‖What he did in the Red sea, and in the brooks of Arnon,

‖ Or, *Vaheb in Suphah.*

15 And at the stream of the brooks that goeth down to the dwelling of Ar, and †lieth upon the border of Moab.

† Heb. *leaneth.*

16 And from thence *they went* to Beer: that *is* the well whereof the LORD spake unto Moses, Gather the people together, and I will give them water.

17 ¶ Then Israel sang this song, †Spring up, O well; ‖sing ye unto it:

† Heb. *Ascend.* ‖ Or, *answer.*

---

cross it is still preserved to us in Deut. ii. 13. The word *Zered* signifies "osier;" and, remarkably enough, the name Wady Safsâf, Willow Brook, still clings to the tributary which unites with Wady Ain Franjy below Kerak. Possibly one of these is identical with the "brook of the willows," of Isaiah xv. 7.

13. *on the other side of Arnon*] The Arnon, now the Wady Môjeb, is an impetuous torrent; the most important of all the streams which run into the Dead Sea from the east. The Israelites probably crossed the principal branch of the stream, now known as Seil Saideh. For their course lay through the "wilderness" or pasture-ground, and east of a range of hills which here runs in the form of the quadrant from south-west to north-east.

Arnon is the border of Moab, between Moab and the Amorites] *i.e.* between the territory which remained to the Moabites, and that which the Amorites had wrested from them, *v.* 26. On the former the Israelites did not set foot (Deut. ii. 9): the latter, as will hereafter appear, they triumphantly traversed. It seems here implied that the Moabitish territory no longer extended to the north of the Arnon or of that branch of it which the Israelites crossed. They could therefore without scruple follow the most direct course towards Dibon (xxxiii. 45); marching north-westward along the northern bank of Arnon, and taking advantage of the break which it makes in the neighbouring hills, to pass through them to the territory on the west. See on this *v.* Introd. § 4.

14. *the book of the wars of the LORD*] Of this book nothing is known except what may be gathered from the passage before us. It was apparently a collection of sacred odes commemorative of that triumphant progress of God's people which this chapter records. From it is taken the ensuing fragment of ancient poetry relating to the passage of the Arnon, and probably also the Song of the Well, and the Ode on the Conquest of the Kingdom of Sihon (*vv.* 17, 18, 27—30). The allusion to this book cannot supply any valid argument against the Mosaic authorship of Numbers; see Introd. § 4.

What he did in the Red sea, &c.] The words which follow to the end of the next verse are a reference rather than a quotation. Contemporaries who had "the Book of the Wars of the Lord" at hand, could of course supply the context. In the absence of such help we can only conjecture the sense of the words before us; which are a mere fragment of a strophe, probably even grammatically incomplete, without either verb or nominative. The A.V. follows the ancient Jewish division and interpretation of the clauses. The Marg. however, suggests a better sense; and, supplying some such verb as "conquered," the words would run "He" (*i.e.* the Lord) "conquered Vaheb in Suphah, the brooks, &c." See Note at the end of the chapter.

15. *to the dwelling of Ar*] Ar (cf. *v.* 28, Is. xv. 1, and Note at end of the chapter) was on the bank of the Arnon, lower down the stream than where the Israelites crossed. And near the spot where the upper Arnon (Seil Saideh) receives the tributary Nahaliel (*v.* 19), there rises, in the midst of the meadow-land between the two torrents, a hill covered with what are doubtless the ruins of the ancient city. The place was first visited by Burckhardt. A neighbouring aqueduct testifies to its former importance. The peculiarity of the site points to it as the "city that is in the midst of the river," Josh. xiii. 9, 16; cf. Deut. ii. 36, and note. It had been, perhaps, heretofore the chief city of the Moabites; it now marked the limit of their territory; and it was hither accordingly that the king of Moab went to welcome Balaam (xxii. 36, and note). It was respected by the Israelites (Deut. ii. 9, 29), as being still a frontier city of Moab, although it lay on the northern bank of what was elsewhere the boundary stream; but it had not escaped the ravages of the Amorites in the recent war (*v.* 28).

16. *Beer*] That is, "Well." Probably the one afterward known as Beer-elim, the "well of heroes," Is. xv. 8.

17, 18. This song, recognized by all authorities as dating from the earliest times,

18 The princes digged the well,
the nobles of the people digged it,
by *the direction of* the lawgiver, with
their staves. And from the wilderness
they went to Mattanah:
19 And from Mattanah to Nahaliel: and from Nahaliel to Bamoth: † Heb.
20 And from Bamoth *in* the val- *field.*
ley, that *is* in the †country of Moab, ‖ Or, *The hill.*
to the top of ‖ Pisgah, which looketh ‖ Or, *The wil-*
toward ‖ Jeshimon. *derness.*

---

and suggested apparently by the fact that God in this place gave the people water not from the rock, but by commanding Moses to cause a well to be dug, bespeaks of itself the glad zeal, the joyful faith, and the hearty co-operation amongst all ranks, which at the time possessed the people. In after time it may well have been the water-drawing song of the maidens of Israel.

18. *by the direction of the lawgiver*] Render **with the lawgiver's sceptre**; *i.e.* under the direction and with the authority of Moses; cf. on the Hebrew word Gen. xlix. 10, and note.

And from the wilderness they went to Mattanah] The "wilderness" comprised all the district east of the hills mentioned in the note on *v.* 13: Mattanah was the first station on the west. It has not been identified with certainty. Eusebius makes it the Maschana of his day, which lay on the Arnon, 12 miles from some known town, perhaps Dibon.

19. *Nahaliel*] *i.e.* "brook of God." The name is still approximately preserved in that of Wady Enkheileh, which unites with Seil Saideh to form Wady Môjeb (see on *v.* 15). The Israelites must have crossed the stream not much above Ar.

Bamoth] Otherwise Bamoth-baal, "the high places of Baal," xxii. 41: mentioned in connexion with Dibon in Josh. xiii. 17, and Is. xv. 2. Mesha in recording his triumphs on the Moabite stone speaks of himself as having "rebuilt" Beth-Bamoth. It had no doubt been destroyed in the struggles which would seem to have been constant between the Moabites and the tribes of Reuben and Gad. The halt here described as made at Bamoth is identical with that connected, xxxiii. 45, with Dibon-gad, for it appears from Josh. xiii. 17 that Dibon and Bamoth-Baal were neighbouring towns. The words of the next verse describe the encampment as at "Bamoth in the valley" or "in the ravine." Immediately north of Dibon, and within two miles of it, in the centre of the valley of Wady Wâleh, a northern tributary of the Arnon, rises a detached knoll, of no great height, upon the right bank of the rivulet. On its summit are the remains of a very large quadrangular platform, constructed of rude stones laid together without cement. It was visited by Irby and Mangles; and to them the thought first suggested itself that this might be one of the altars of the high places. The spot is still in some measure consecrated, and paltry votive offerings hang around a tomb on its summit. Should it be objected that from this site Balaam could hardly have gazed on the Israelites in their encampment opposite Jericho (xxii. 41), the answer is that "Bamoth in the ravine" did not necessarily constitute the whole of the "Bamoth" round Dibon: there may have been other high places to the west, where stand the ruins Keraum Abu el-Hossein, or on part of Jebel Attârus.

20. *in the country of Moab*] Rather, **in the field of Moab**: the upland pastures, or, as travellers have described them, flat downs, which are intersected by the ravine of Wady Wâleh. These, as also "the plains of Moab" (xxii. 1), had now passed to the Amorites, and it was from the latter that Israel wrested them.

From Dibon the Israelites proceeded to Almon-diblathaim, or rather "Almon-toward-Diblathaim;" cf. xxxiii. 46. The neighbouring town, by means of which this place was distinguished from Almon on the west of the Jordan (Josh. xxi. 18), was probably the Beth-diblathaim of Jer. xlviii. 22, where Mesha, according to the Moabite inscription, built a temple; but the sites of both are unknown.

to the top of Pisgah, which looketh toward Jeshimon] (Or, "the waste.") In xxxiii. 47, this encampment is described as "in the mountains of Abarim before Nebo." Pisgah was a ridge of the Abarim mountains, westward from Heshbon; Nebo, a town on or near that ridge (xxxii. 3, 38), and apparently lying on its western slope, inasmuch as the Israelite encampment on the height was "before," *i.e.* to the east of, Nebo. A ruined village of the name Neba has been mentioned by travellers as still existing in those parts (cf. Robinson, 'B. R.' I. 570, note), and from the latest account seems to be on the most elevated of the crests, due west of Baal-meon (xxxii. 38), and three miles south-west of Heshbon (Tristram, 'Land of Israel,' p. 535). From the summit of Pisgah the Israelites gained their first view of the wastes of the Dead Sea and of the valley of the Jordan. It was hither, moreover, that Moses subsequently again ascended, to view, before his death, the land of promise. The interest attaching to the spot, and the need of a convenient name

f Deut. 2. 27. Judg. 11. 19.
21 ¶ And [f] Israel sent messengers
unto Sihon king of the Amorites,
saying,
22 Let me pass through thy land:
we will not turn into the fields, or
into the vineyards; we will not drink
of the waters of the well: *but* we will
go along by the king's *high* way, until we be past thy borders.
g Deut. 29. 7.
23 [g] And Sihon would not suffer
Israel to pass through his border: but
Sihon gathered all his people together, and went out against Israel into
the wilderness: and he came to Jahaz,
and fought against Israel.
h Josh. 12. 2. Ps. 135. 11. Amos 2. 9.
24 And [h] Israel smote him with the
edge of the sword, and possessed his
land from Arnon unto Jabbok, even
unto the children of Ammon: for the
border of the children of Ammon *was*
strong.
25 And Israel took all these cities:
and Israel dwelt in all the cities of
the Amorites, in Heshbon, and in
all the † villages thereof. † Heb. *daughters*.
26 For Heshbon *was* the city of
Sihon the king of the Amorites, who
had fought against the former king
of Moab, and taken all his land out
of his hand, even unto Arnon.
27 Wherefore they that speak in
proverbs say, Come into Heshbon,

---

for it, has led Christians often to designate it as "Nebo," rather than as "the mountain of, or near to, Nebo;" but the latter is the correct appellation (Deut. xxxii. 49, xxxiv. 1); and in Scripture, even to the latest times, "Nebo," alone, denoted only the town (Is. xv. 2; Jer. xlviii. 1, 22). And indeed the uniform, peakless character of the ridge of Pisgah renders it unlikely that its different portions would be distinguished otherwise than by the names of adjacent villages.

21—24. Having chronicled without interruption the progress of the Israelites through the Amoritish territory, Moses now goes back to relate the story of the conflict by which their way had been opened. The town which gave its name to the battlefield, and which grateful memories converted in after times into a Levitical city, lay, according to Eusebius, between Dibon and Medeba; to the east of the route followed by the non-combatants; and in a country as yet unexplored by modern travel.

24. *unto Jabbok*] Now Wâdy Zerka: cf. Gen. xxxii. 22. In its early course it runs eastward under Rabbah of the Children of Ammon, always in ancient days one of the strongest fortresses of the East. Hence it curves northward and westward to within a few miles of Gerasa. Thence it flows westward, and reaches the Jordan, 45 miles north of the Arnon. It was between Rabbah and Gerasa that it formed the Ammonite boundary. The territory westward from it, through which the direct route between those two places lies, and which had probably been wrested from the Ammonites by the Amorites (see Josh. xiii. 25; Judg. xi. 13), is, though now one vast pasture, covered with the ruined sites of former cities, and must once have been thickly peopled. The eastern territory, to which in the days of Moses the Ammonites were restricted, and through which the Mekka pilgrim-road now passes, remains as yet almost unvisited by Europeans.

for the border of the children of Ammon was strong] These words are intended to explain what had prevented Sihon from carrying his conquests further: he had paused, no doubt, before the fortress of Rabbah. The Israelites had a different reason for respecting the Ammonitish territory. (Cf. Deut. ii. 19 sqq.)

25. *Heshbon*] Now Heshbân, a ruined city, due east of the point where the Jordan enters the Dead Sea; conspicuous from all parts of the high plateau on which it stands, but concealed, like the rest of the plateau, from the valley beneath.

26. *all his land*] Evidently that to the north of the Arnon alone is intended:—an example of the limitation with which the biblical statements must be sometimes understood; and which may be legitimately assumed in many cases where no direct proof of it can be furnished.

27. *Wherefore*] The word of the historian introducing the song which follows.

they that speak in proverbs] The original has for these words only one, a participle from a verb which signifies "to place side by side," and so "to draw comparisons." The word (*hammo'shleym*) is in fact almost equivalent to "the poets;" for *mashal* and its derivatives serve as general terms, not restricted to any one poetic style amongst the Hebrews. The word supplies the title of the Book of Proverbs itself; and is used of the parable proper as in Ezek. xvii. 2; of the prophecies of Balaam, xxiii. 7—10, xxiv. 3—9, &c.; of a taunting song of triumph over fallen Babylon in Is. xiv. 4 sqq., an instance very similar to the one before us. The Hebrew Poetry is essentially sententious and gnomic in character, and its

let the city of Sihon be built and
prepared:
28 For there is a fire gone out
of Heshbon, a flame from the city
of Sihon: it hath consumed Ar of
Moab, *and* the lords of the high places
of Arnon.
29 Woe to thee, Moab! thou art
[i] 1 Kings 11. 7, 33. undone, O people of [i]Chemosh: he
hath given his sons that escaped, and
his daughters, into captivity unto Sihon king of the Amorites.
30 We have shot at them; Heshbon is perished even unto Dibon,
and we have laid them waste even unto
Nophah, which *reacheth* unto Medeba.
31 ¶ Thus Israel dwelt in the land
of the Amorites.
32 And Moses sent to spy out
Jaazer, and they took the villages
thereof, and drove out the Amorites
that *were* there.
33 ¶ [k]And they turned and went [k] Deut. 3. 1.
up by the way of Bashan: and Og & 29. 7.

---

style is based on antithesis, in words, or sense. The verb in question then expresses the genius of that poetry very accurately.

29. *Chemosh*] The national god of the Moabites (cf. Jer. xlviii. 7, 13, 46), who are called after him "the people of Chemosh." The name probably means "Vanquisher," or "Master;" see Note at end of the chapter. The worship of Chemosh was introduced into Israel by Solomon, 1 K. xi. 7; 2 K. xxiii. 13. It was no doubt to Chemosh that Mesha, king of Moab, offered up his son as a burnt-offering: 2 K. iii. 26, 27, where see notes.

30. *We have shot at them*] Others "we have burned them:" see Note at end of the chapter.

Which reacheth unto] Rather **with fire unto Medeba.**

The Ode itself may be exhibited thus:

Come ye to Heshbon,
Built and established be the city of Sihon:
For a fire is gone forth from Heshbon,
A flame from the city of Sihon,
It hath consumed Ar of Moab,
And the lords of the Bamoth of Arnon.
Woe to thee, Moab! Thou art undone, O people of Chemosh!
His sons he hath rendered fugitives, and yielded his daughters into captivity
To the king of the Amorites, Sihon!
But we have shot at them—perished is Heshbon—unto Dibon:
We have wasted unto Nophah, with fire unto Medeba.

In the first six lines (*vv.* 27, 28) the poet imagines for the Amorites a song of exultation for their victories over Moab, and for the consequent glories of Heshbon, their own capital. In the next three lines (*v.* 29) he himself joins in this strain; which now becomes one of half-real, half-ironical compassion for the Moabites, whom their idol Chemosh was unable to save. But in the last two lines (*v.* 30) a startling change takes place; and the new and decisive triumph of the poet's own countrymen is abruptly introduced; and the boastings of the Amorites fade utterly away. The structure of these two lines is of a thoroughly Hebrew cast, the words being put, for the sake of symmetry, into an order by which the syntax is disguised: they would otherwise run thus, "We have shot at them unto Dibon; we have wasted with fire unto Nophah and unto Medeba: Heshbon (*i.e.* the pride of Heshbon, as capital of the Amorites) is perished." Of all these towns Heshbon was the northernmost, and therefore, to the advancing Israelites, the last to be reached. For Dibon, see on xxxii. 34. Medeba, now Mâdeba, was 4 miles south-east of Heshbon. It appears from 1 Chron. xix. 7, 15, to have been a fortified place in the reign of David. And the Moabite inscription informs us that Medeba was seized and held by Omri and his successors, no doubt as a fortress through which the obedience of the surrounding district might be insured. Nophah is unknown, unless it be Arneibah, 10 miles east south-east of Medeba.

32. *Jaazer*] To be identified probably with the ruins Sîr or es-Sîr, 10 miles north-east of Heshbon. They consist of a castle and a large walled pool (Seetzen, II. p. 318); the latter being probably the "sea" of Jer. xlviii. 32. The city gave its name to the territory around it (xxxii. 1; cf. Josh. xiii. 25; 2 S. xxiv. 5). The occupation of it by the Israelites virtually completed their conquest of the Amorite kingdom; and prepared the way for the pastoral settlements in it which they not long after established (xxxii. 35).

33. *And they turned and went up by the way of Bashan*] In these apparently unimportant words is contained the record of the Israelitish occupation of Gilead north of the Jabbok; a territory which, though peopled, like southern Gilead, by the Amorites (Deut. iii. 9; Josh. ii. 10, &c.), formed part of the domain of Og king of Bashan, who was himself of a different race (Deut. iii. 2; Josh. xii. 5, xiii. 11). The occupation was effected by the Machirites of Manasseh (xxxii. 39).

the king of Bashan went out against
them, he, and all his people, to the
battle at Edrei.
34 And the LORD said unto Moses, Fear him not: for I have delivered him into thy hand, and all his
135. people, and his land; and [l]thou shalt
do to him as thou didst unto Sihon
king of the Amorites, which dwelt at
Heshbon.
35 So they smote him, and his
sons, and all his people, until there
was none left him alive: and they
possessed his land.

We are not told whether they were led thither by express warrant of God, or whether their advance upon Bashan was provoked by Og and his people.

at Edrei] Now Edhra'âh, vulgarly Der'a; situate on a branch of the Jarmuk. This river is not mentioned in Scripture, but formed the boundary between Gilead and Bashan. The identification of Edrei rests on the frontier position of the site, on the modern name, and on the testimony of Eusebius; but it is only recently that the explorations of Wetzstein ('Reisebericht,' pp. 47, 8) have disclosed the fact that the original city was subterranean, and that its streets may still be seen running in all directions beneath the present inhabited town, which is built on the ground above. Some with less probability, especially since the discoveries just mentioned, would seek Edrei 10 miles further north, in the extensive and commanding ruins bearing the name of Edhr'a, like the other (see Porter, 'Damascus,' pp. 271 sqq., and 'Dict. of Bible,' s. v. Edrei). The battle of Edrei was followed by the conquest of all Og's dominions, Deut. iii. 4. The carrying off of one remarkable trophy to Rabbah (Deut. iii. 11) suggests that the Ammonites may have taken part with the Israelites in this war.

NOTES on CHAP. XXI. 1, 14, 15, 29, 30.

1. *by the way of the spies*] This rendering is supported by Vulg. and most Jewish and modern authorities; the noun אתרים being regarded as identical with the תרים of xiv. 6 with a prosthetic א. This explanation, though conjectural, is on the whole the most probable. The LXX. (followed by Saad., Gesen., Dathe, Maurer, &c.) make the word in question a proper name, ὁδὸν Ἀθαρείμ; but no traces of such a name have ever been discovered elsewhere. Aramaic etymology suggests "by the way of the places;" Arabic, "by way of the tracks" or "monuments."

14. The rendering adopted by our version after Jarchi, Vulg. and most Jewish authorities, assumes (1) that והב is here written for יהב, and is a verb signifying "dedit," "fecit;" and (2) that סופה is a form of סוף, and this itself an elliptical expression for ים־סוף, the sea of weed, the Red Sea. On the latter part of the second assumption see on Deut. i. 1.

Both assumptions are now generally regarded as untenable.

Whilst the full import of words so entirely fragmentary must remain uncertain, it is allowed by nearly all modern commentators that והב must be a proper name marked in the usual way by את as in the accusative case, and co-ordinate with "the brooks of Arnon" which follow. The LXX. would seem to have had a slightly different reading, זהב for והב, for it, taking the word as a proper name, translates Ζωόβ.

The verb must be supplied in some such way as is suggested in the foot-note.

סופה is in all likelihood a proper name also, and denotes the district, perhaps an alluvial one remarkable for its reeds and water-flags, in which Vaheb was situated (cf. on Deut. i. 1).

Some, however (Gesen., Keil, Wordsw., &c.), regard it as a common noun from the verb סוף "to destroy," and translate "in a storm," or "whirlwind," in which sense the word occurs Job xxi. 18, and with the same prep. ב in Nah. i. 3. The sense would thus be: "In a storm the Lord conquered Vaheb, and the brooks, &c."

Another modern rendering, altering the accepted punctuation, but respecting ordinary grammatical laws, gives the sense thus:

"Vaheb in Suphah did He conquer, and the brooks;
Arnon and the outpouring of the brooks,
That goeth down, &c."

15. Many modern scholars, after the example of Reland, have regarded Ar as the same with Rabbath-Moab or Areopolis, the ruins of which, still bearing the name Rabbah, lie 10 miles south of the Arnon. The distinction between Ar and Rabbah was in recent times first brought out by Hengstenberg ('Geschichte Bileams,' p. 234 sqq.); but he fell into the error which Ritter, who otherwise followed him, avoided, of supposing Areopolis to be the classical name of the former rather than of the latter city. Jerome, it is true, in his commentary on Is. xv., asserts the identity of Ar with Areopolis; but has probably no better ground for so doing than the fact that the two words are the same in their first syllable. Eusebius, in his article on Ar in the 'Onomasticon,' drops no hint of the identity in question, though he speaks freely of Areopolis elsewhere in that work (s. vv. Arnon, Agallim, Arina, Moab). On the contrary, he distinctly implies that Areopolis was the same with Rabbath-Moab (s. v. Moab). This Rabbah of Moab is itself not mentioned in the Bible; it was perhaps a city of late growth.

29. The derivation and significance of the name Chemōsh (כְּמוֹשׁ) are uncertain. The most probable conjecture is that adopted by Gesen., who refers it to the root כָּבַשׁ, "to vanquish," "to subdue;" the labial letters מ and ב being, as they often are, interchanged. This derivation is to some extent supported by the joint mention of Chemosh with Molech and with Milcom, 1 Kings xi. 5—8, 2 Kings xxiii. 13. These names, as also the Malcham of Zeph. i. 5, are evidently only dialectical varieties of one title; and they have a similar sense to the other title of Baal, and to that of Chemosh according to the probable explanation suggested above; *i.e.* "Lord," "King," "Master," &c. From 2 Kings xvii. 16, 17, and xxi. 5, 6, it would seem that Molech and Baal were worshipped with the same rites; and regarded as in effect the same deity.

Other less probable derivations are, that of Fürst, 'Lex.,' who derives Chemosh from כמשׁ "to burn," or "glow," the Arabic قبس, and regards him as the "Fire-God;" that of Hyde, repeated by Rosenm. and Winer from خموش; "culex," which would identify Chemosh with the "Baal-zebub" of 2 Kings i. 2: cf. *Ζεὺς ἀπόμυιος*, Pausan. V. 14. 2; and that of Clericus from كمس, "celer fuit," which would represent Chemosh as the "Sun-god."

Attempts have been made to identify Chemosh with various deities of other nations: *e.g.* with Saturn, the planet of ill-omen, a hypothesis based on the Jewish tradition that Chemosh was worshipped under the image of a black star; and with Ares or Mars, because he is represented on coins of Areopolis (the ancient Rabbath) as an armed warrior (Eckhel, 'Doct. Num. Vet.' III. 394). Jerome on Isa. xv. 1, derives the name Areopolis itself from Ἄρεος πόλις, a derivation however which is certainly erroneous; see last note.

Recent inquiries have however more and more suggested the opinion that the different names assigned to the heathen deities of ancient Oriental Mythology are in origin and principle nothing more than the recognition separately of the attributes belonging to the one supreme God. These in the progress of corruption and superstition were attached one by one to idols of various names; and became localized usually upon special occasions and circumstances and with various rites in different places. Thus the diverse names Chemosh, Ashtoreth, Baal, Molech, &c. would seem to point to one central, original, comprehensive conception of which these several cults represent portions and depravations. Of this idea the Moabite stone has furnished a new and very striking illustration. It makes mention, in connection with the capture of Nebo, of a god called "Ashtar-Chemosh." This title at once connects the Moabite religion with the Phœnician, in which Ashtar, the masculine form of Astarte or Ashtoreth, represents one side (*i.e.* the male) of the creative and reproductive power which is conceived to be one of the leading attributes of God.

It would thus seem probable that Chemosh, in one at least of the manifestations in which the Moabites venerated him, was connected with the androgynous deities of Phœnicia. Amongst them we have not only Ashtar, the masculine form of Astarte and identified with Baal; but Astarte herself is spoken of as "the King," "the Sun God," "the Face of Baal," &c.; see Schlottmann, "Die Inschrift Eshmunazar's," p. 143: and 'Die Siegesäule Mesa's,' p. 28 sqq. (cf. the "Venus Victrix" and "Venus Amathusia," "eadem mas et fœmina," of classical art and literature). It is probably because Baal was frequently worshipped as an androgynous deity, and not by way of contempt (as has been commonly supposed), that the name has the feminine article several times in LXX.: *e.g.* Hos. ii. 8; Zeph. i. 4; Tobit i. 5; cf. Rom. xi. 4.

Accordingly the worship of Chemosh assumed various forms in different places, and was accompanied by a ritual appropriate to the special attribute to be praised or propitiated. As the god of War and Victory he exacted human sacrifices: cf. 2 Kings iii. 26, 27; and Mesha on the Moabite stone declares himself, after taking Ataroth, if that be (as seems probable) the proper name which has to be replaced in line xi. of the Inscription, to have killed all the warriors for the well-pleasing of Chemosh and Moab, and to have taken out of the city all the spoil and dedicated it also to Chemosh: cf. the precisely similar treatment of Jericho by Joshua, Josh. vi. 17, 18; and see Dr Ginsburg, "The Moabite Stone," p. 34. As the lord of productiveness he is probably identical with Baal-peor, as Jerome 'in Jovin,' I. 12, long ago surmised (פעור "aperire"). It was the licentious rites connected with the Moabite worship in its last-named development which led to the transgression of Israel mentioned in Num. xxv. 1—3; Josh. xxii. 17; and gave occasion to such protective enactments as that of Deut. xxii. 5, where see note. He was probably also worshipped as "the Sun God;" and it is likely that the remark of Eusebius,

'Onom.' s. v. Ἄριυα, is to be thus explained; for he states that the god of the people of Areopolis (*i.e.* Ar Moab) was Ariel; a word which in Ezek. xliii. 15, at least (if not elsewhere) appears according to Gesen., Fürst, &c. to signify "the fire," or "hearth of God."

30. ונירם, the first word in this verse, has been very variously rendered; its punctuation is anomalous; and the ancient authorities (*e.g.* LXX., Vulg., Onkelos, the Arabic and Syriac Versions) generally regarded it as a noun, and are followed by Clericus and Rosenm.; though they differ amongst themselves as to its meaning. Modern commentators and grammarians are agreed that the word is a verb, the first person pl. Imp. Kal of ירה with the suffix of third person pl., the termination ם being written as in Ex. xxix. 30, for ם.

Of the sense assigned to the verb in this place by the A. V., "to shoot," examples will be found in Gesen. The same sense is adopted by Maurer, Schröder, Dathe, &c. Others (Keil, Wordsw., &c.) prefer the secondary sense of the verb, "to throw down," of which an example occurs Ex. xv. 4. Ewald however ('Ausf. Lehrbuch der Heb. Sprache,' p. 424 note), and Fürst ('Lex.' s.v. ירה), connect the word with ארה, and translated "to burn." This sense has support from the Arabic, and suits well with the sequel of the verse.

The word נשים, first pers. pl. Hiph. Imperf. from נשה, has also the suffix of the third person pl. in an irregular form; cf. Ewald, 'Ausf. Lehr. der Hebr. Spr.' p. 628.

In the conclusion of the verse the reading אשר yields no satisfactory sense, and the ר is marked by the Masoretes with a circle over it as suspicious. Commentators generally, both ancient and modern, have adopted the reading אש, which the LXX., the Samaritan Text and version have evidently followed.

CHAPTER XXII.

1 *Balak's first message for Balaam is refused.* 15 *His second message obtaineth him.* 22 *An angel would have slain him, if his ass had not saved him.* 36 *Balak entertaineth him.*

AND the children of Israel set forward, and pitched in the plains
of Moab on this side Jordan *by* Jericho.
2 ¶ And Balak the son of Zippor
saw all that Israel had done to the
Amorites.
3 And Moab was sore afraid of

CHAP. XXII. With this chapter begins the fourth and last division of the Book (see Introd. § 2), comprising fourteen chapters. In them are narrated the events which befell Israel whilst encamped in the plains of Moab, and certain instructions and arrangements are laid down by Moses with reference to their actual entry upon the promised inheritance, from which they were now separated only by the Jordan.

The first three chapters of this division record the appearance and prophecies of Balaam: see note at end of the chapter.

1. *the plains*] Heb. *araboth;* the word is the plural of that which is used to denote the whole depressed tract along the Jordan and the Dead Sea, and onward, where it is still called the Arabah (cf. on xxi. 4), to the Elanitic gulf. Near the mouth of the Jordan this tract is about eleven miles across, a breadth of from four to five miles being on the eastern bank. The space occupied by the Israelitish camp consisted, in the main, of a large and luxuriant oasis upon this bank, slightly raised above the barren flat, sultry because sheltered by the Peræan hills which bear up the fertile plateau above, and watered by the brooks which, descending from those hills, run westward across the plain into the Jordan (see Tristram, 'Land of Israel,' pp. 528 sqq.). It commenced on the south at Beth-jeshimoth, "house of the wastes," close to the Dead Sea: thence it covered the sites of the future cities Beth-ram (in A.V. "Beth-aram"), now er-Râmeh (Josh. xiii. 27), and Beth-haran, now Beit-haran, (xxxii. 36): and terminated northwards at Abel-shittim, the "acacia-meadow." This place is no longer to be distinguished by its peculiar vegetation, for acacias are now common to the whole district around, but is doubtless to be sought along the brook that flows past the ruins of Keferein. These reach upwards from the plain to a small rocky slope above, and probably represent the ancient city of Abila, to which the meadow eventually gave its name (Jos. 'Ant.' IV. 8. 1, V. 1. 1). Immediately north of the camp was Nimrah or Beth-nimrah, now Nimrûn (xxxii. 3, 36). Josephus mentions four of these cities together; viz. Bethennabris (Beth-nimrah, Abila (Abel), Julias, *i.e.* Betharamphtha (Beth-ram, in Aramaic Beth-rametha), and Besemoth (Beth-jeshimoth). 'B. J.' IV. 7.

of Moab] See on xxi. 20.

on this side Jordan by Jericho] Rather, **across the Jordan of Jericho**, *i.e.* that part of Jordan which skirted the territory of Jericho. This form of expression indicates the site of the camp in its relation to the well-known city of Jericho. On the phrase "on this side Jordan" see on Deut. i. 1.

2. *Balak the son of Zippor*] The way in which he is mentioned in *v.* 4, and the ex-

the people, because they *were* many:
and Moab was distressed because of
the children of Israel.
4 And Moab said unto the elders
of Midian, Now shall this company
lick up all *that are* round about us,
as the ox licketh up the grass of the
field. And Balak the son of Zippor *was* king of the Moabites at that
time.
a Josh. 24, 9. 5 [a]He sent messengers therefore
unto Balaam the son of Beor to
Pethor, which *is* by the river of the
land of the children of his people, to
call him, saying, Behold, there is a
people come out from Egypt: behold,
† Heb. eye. they cover the † face of the earth, and
they abide over against me:
6 Come now therefore, I pray
thee, curse me this people; for they
are too mighty for me: peradventure
I shall prevail, *that* we may smite
them, and *that* I may drive them out
of the land: for I wot that he whom
thou blessest *is* blessed, and he whom
thou cursest is cursed.
7 And the elders of Moab and
the elders of Midian departed with
the rewards of divination in their
hand; and they came unto Balaam,
and spake unto him the words of
Balak.
8 And he said unto them, Lodge
here this night, and I will bring you
word again, as the LORD shall speak
unto me: and the princes of Moab
abode with Balaam.
9 And God came unto Balaam,
and said, What men *are* these with
thee?
10 And Balaam said unto God,
Balak the son of Zippor, king of
Moab, hath sent unto me, *saying*,
11 Behold, *there is* a people come
out of Egypt, which covereth the
face of the earth: come now, curse
me them; peradventure † I shall be † Heb. *I shall prevail in fighting against him.*
able to overcome them, and drive
them out.
12 And God said unto Balaam,
Thou shalt not go with them; thou
shalt not curse the people: for they
are blessed.
13 And Balaam rose up in the

---

pression in xxi. 26 ("former king of Moab"), suggest that Balak was not the hereditary king, and that a change of dynasty had taken place. The later Targums make Balak a Midianite; and not improbably. His father's name, Zippor, "Bird," reminds us of those of other Midianites, *e.g.* Oreb, "Crow," Zeeb, "Wolf." Possibly the Midianitish chieftains had taken advantage of the weakness of the Moabites after the Amoritish victories to establish themselves as princes in the land, as the Hyksos had done in Egypt; possibly they had been imposed upon the Moabites by Sihon; cf. Josh. xiii. 21.

3. *was distressed because of*] Lit. "shrank from before them," in terror.

5. *Balaam the son of Beor*] See Note at end of the chapter.

Pethor, which is by the river of the land of the children of his people] Rather, **which was on the river** (*i.e.* the Euphrates, so called here and elsewhere by pre-eminence), **in his native land.** For "his people" some ancient authorities read "Ammon," but wrongly: the Ammonitish territory did not stretch to the Euphrates. On Pethor, see Note at end of the chapter.

7. *Rewards of divination*] Heb. "divinations," rightly interpreted in 2 Pet. ii. 15, by "the wages of unrighteousness." So in 2 Sam. iv. 10, the Hebrew word for "good tidings" denotes the reward of such tidings.

8. *this night*] It was either in dream or in nightly vision that Balaam expected his communications. His eventual compliance with Balak's request suggests an unfavourable interpretation of his conduct on this occasion. He must surely have known that God's blessing was on the people with whose marvellous march forth from Egypt he was acquainted, and from whom he had himself probably learned much. And his reply to the messengers next morning (*v.* 13), betrays the desire to venture to the utmost of that which God would not forbid rather than to carry out God's will in hearty sincerity.

12. *Thou shalt not go with them; thou shalt not curse the people*] The meaning is substantially: "Thou shalt not go with them to curse the people." In Hebrew, two clauses of which the one is logically subordinate to the other, often appear as coordinate. So in the Second Commandment, "Thou shalt not make . . . thou shalt not bow down to them;" *i.e.* "Thou shalt not make ... in order to bow down to them."

morning, and said unto the princes
of Balak, Get you into your land:
for the LORD refuseth to give me
leave to go with you.
14 And the princes of Moab rose
up, and they went unto Balak, and
said, Balaam refuseth to come with us.
15 ¶ And Balak sent yet again
princes, more, and more honourable
than they.
16 And they came to Balaam, and
said to him, Thus saith Balak the son
† Heb. *Be not thou letted from, &c.* of Zippor, †Let nothing, I pray thee,
hinder thee from coming unto me:
17 For I will promote thee unto
very great honour, and I will do
whatsoever thou sayest unto me:
come therefore, I pray thee, curse
me this people.
18 And Balaam answered and said
[b] chap. 24. 13. unto the servants of Balak, [b]If Balak
would give me his house full of silver
and gold, I cannot go beyond the
word of the LORD my God, to do
less or more.

19 Now therefore, I pray you,
tarry ye also here this night, that I
may know what the LORD will say
unto me more.
20 And God came unto Balaam
at night, and said unto him, If the
men come to call thee, rise up, *and*
go with them; but yet the word
which I shall say unto thee, that
shalt thou do.
21 And Balaam rose up in the
morning, and saddled his ass, and
went with the princes of Moab.
22 ¶ And God's anger was kindled
because he went: and the angel of
the LORD stood in the way for an
adversary against him. Now he was
riding upon his ass, and his two servants *were* with him.
23 And [c]the ass saw the angel of [c] 2 Pet. 2 16.
the LORD standing in the way, and Jude 11.
his sword drawn in his hand: and
the ass turned aside out of the way,
and went into the field: and Balaam
smote the ass, to turn her into the way.

---

15. *And Balak sent yet again*, &c.] Balak, like the ancient heathen world generally, not only believed in the efficacy of the curses and incantations of the soothsayers, but regarded their services as strictly venal. So the favours of the gods themselves were likewise considered as purchasable (cf. Plin. 'Nat. Hist.' XXVIII. 4). Hence Balak, when his first offer was declined, infers at once that he had not bid high enough, and sends "princes more and more honourable," with richer presents than before. And the terms of Balaam's answer as reported to the king ("Balaam refuseth to come") would seem to invite the construction actually put on them by Balak.

19. *ye also*] *i.e.* as the other envoys before you. The spirit in which Balaam acted displays itself now more clearly. There was no ground for expecting different directions from God on the matter than those already given.

20. *rise up, and go with them*] God's first command to Balaam, *v.* 12, verbally two-fold ("thou shalt not go with them;" "thou shalt not curse, &c."), was one and simple in effect. He was bidden absolutely to reject the request of the princes of Moab. Had Balaam possessed a sincere spirit of obedience, he would have found in these first instructions a final decision upon the matter. His hypocritical importunity with God when the fresh messengers came from Balak demonstrate his aversion to God's declared will. Thenceforward he was no longer on probation for the dignity of being God's loyal ambassador, but was degraded to the meaner function of an unwilling instrument. Accordingly he is provided with new instructions. Origen observes that had Balaam been worthy God would have put His word in his heart; but as that heart was occupied by the lust of gain, the word was put in the prophet's mouth only. The spirit of God's dealings with Balaam is rightly exhibited in this remark, though the sense of the Scripture phrase, "to put a word in the mouth" is hardly so (cf. Deut. xviii. 18). On the character of Balaam, see Bp. Butler's well-known Sermon, and that of Dr J. H. Newman, 'Parochial Sermons,' Vol. IV.

22. *the angel of the LORD stood in the way for an adversary against him*] *i.e.* The angel that led the Israelites through the wilderness (Ex. xiv. 19, &c.), and subsequently appeared as the Captain of the LORD'S host to Joshua (Josh. v. 13). In desiring to curse Israel, Balaam was fighting against Israel's Leader. The presence of the angel in his path was designed to open his eyes, blinded by sin, to the real character of his course of conduct.

24 But the angel of the LORD stood in a path of the vineyards, a wall *being* on this side, and a wall on that side.

25 And when the ass saw the angel of the LORD, she thrust herself unto the wall, and crushed Balaam's foot against the wall: and he smote her again.

26 And the angel of the LORD went further, and stood in a narrow place, where *was* no way to turn either to the right hand or to the left.

27 And when the ass saw the angel of the LORD, she fell down under Balaam: and Balaam's anger was kindled, and he smote the ass with a staff.

28 And the LORD opened the mouth of the ass, and she said unto Balaam, What have I done unto thee, that thou hast smitten me these three times?

29 And Balaam said unto the ass, Because thou hast mocked me: I would there were a sword in mine hand, for now would I kill thee.

30 And the ass said unto Balaam, *Am* not I thine ass, †upon which thou hast ridden ‖ever since *I was* thine unto this day? was I ever wont to do so unto thee? And he said, Nay.

31 Then the LORD opened the eyes of Balaam, and he saw the angel of the LORD standing in the way, and his sword drawn in his hand: and he bowed down his head, and ‖fell flat on his face.

32 And the angel of the LORD said unto him, Wherefore hast thou smitten thine ass these three times? behold, I went out †to withstand thee, because *thy* way is perverse before me:

† Heb. *who hast ridden upon me.*
‖ Or, *ever since thou* wast, &c.
‖ Or, *bowed himself.*
† Heb. *to be an adversary unto thee.*

---

24. *in a path of the vineyards*] *i.e.* in a path shut in by vineyard-walls on each side. The progress from the road through the open field (*v.* 23) to that walled in, and thence to the strait place, where there was no room to turn (*v.* 26), shews that Balaam was approaching a city, no doubt that which was the goal of his journey.

28. *And the LORD opened the mouth of the ass*] The account of this occurrence can hardly have come from any one else than Balaam himself, and may perhaps have been given by him to the Israelites after his capture in the war against Midian. Cf. on xxxi. 8. That which is here recorded was apparently perceived by him alone amongst human witnesses. For though his two servants were with him (*v.* 22), and the envoys of Balak also (*v.* 35), yet the marvel does not appear to have attracted their attention. The cries of the ass would seem then to have been significant to Balaam's mind only (so St Greg. Nyss. 'de Vita Mosis,' *sub finem*). God may have brought it about that sounds uttered by the creature after its kind became to the prophet's intelligence as though it addressed him in rational speech. Indeed to an augur, priding himself on his skill in interpreting the cries and movements of animals, no more startling warning could be given than one so real as this, yet conveyed through the medium of his own art; and to a seer pretending to superhuman wisdom no more humiliating rebuke can be imagined than to teach him by the mouth of his own ass. These, the special significances of the transaction, would be missed entirely if we were to suppose (as Maimonides apud Grotius *in loc.*, Bauer, Tholuck, and especially Hengstenberg, 'Geschichte Bileams,' pp. 48 sqq.) that the whole passed in a vision, Balaam being by the power of God cast into an ecstatic state. And the words "the Lord opened, &c." clearly indicate that it was on the ass not on the prophet that the Divine Hand was more immediately laid. On the other hand, the opinion that the ass actually uttered with the mouth articulate words of human speech (though still defended by Baumgarten, Von Gerlach, Wordsw. &c.); or even that the utterance of the ass was so formed in the air as to fall with the accents of man's voice on Balaam's ears (a Lapide *in loc.*), seems irreconcileable with Balaam's behaviour. Balaam was indeed labouring under derangement, induced by his indulgence of avarice and ambition, and this too aggravated at the moment by furious anger; yet it seems scarcely conceivable that he could actually have heard human speech from the mouth of his own ass, and even go on as narrated in *vv.* 29, 30, to hold a dialogue with her, and show no signs of dismay and astonishment.

31. *and he saw the angel of the LORD*] The angel was outwardly visible, as in Ex. xiv. 19, and was thus now seen by Balaam, as before by the ass; yet was visible with such limitation that he was not beheld by any others. Beyond this we know not the manner or conditions of his appearance.

32. *is perverse*] Rather, **is headlong.**

33 And the ass saw me, and turned
from me these three times: unless she
had turned from me, surely now also
I had slain thee, and saved her alive.
34 And Balaam said unto the angel
of the LORD, I have sinned; for I
knew not that thou stoodest in the
way against me: now therefore, if it
†displease thee, I will get me back
again.

† Heb. *be evil in thine eyes.*

35 And the angel of the LORD said
unto Balaam, Go with the men: but
only the word that I shall speak unto thee, that thou shalt speak. So
Balaam went with the princes of Balak.
36 ¶ And when Balak heard that
Balaam was come, he went out to
meet him unto a city of Moab, which
is in the border of Arnon, which *is* in
the utmost coast.
37 And Balak said unto Balaam,
Did I not earnestly send unto thee to
call thee? wherefore camest thou not
unto me? am I not able indeed to
promote thee to honour?
38 And Balaam said unto Balak,
Lo, I am come unto thee: have I
now any power at all to say any
thing? the word that God putteth
in my mouth, that shall I speak.
39 And Balaam went with Balak,
and they came unto ‖Kirjath-huzoth.
40 And Balak offered oxen and
sheep, and sent to Balaam, and to the
princes that *were* with him.
41 And it came to pass on the
morrow, that Balak took Balaam, and
brought him up into the high places
of Baal, that thence he might see the
utmost *part* of the people.

‖ Or, *A city of streets.*

The Hebrew word is a rare one, occurring only once again, in a verbal form, Job xvi. 11, but its sense seems clear from that of the cognate Arabic word. Cf. St Peter's words, 2 St Pet. ii. 16, "the madness of the prophet."

35. *Go with the men*] A command, not a permission merely. Cf. on *v.* 20. Balaam, no longer a faithful servant of God, was henceforth overruled in all his acts so that he might subserve the Divine purpose as an instrument.

36. *a city of Moab*] Or, **Ir-Moab**; probably the same with Ar-Moab, see on xxi. 15. As Balaam in his journey would avoid the districts occupied by the Israelites, he must have approached this city from the east, by the course of the Nahaliel; and in the name Balû'a, still borne by one of the upper branches of this stream, there is perhaps a reminiscence of the name of the prophet.

39. *Kirjath-huzoth*] *i.e.* "city of streets." From the context, apparently within Balak's dominions, and therefore south of the Arnon. Hardly however far south, for from it, on the morrow, the company proceeded to Bamoth-baal, which lay north of the Arnon. It was probably a place of importance, and possibly that of Balak's residence. As such it is perhaps mentioned in an endorsement on an Egyptian papyrus now in the British Museum (Anastasi III.), dating, as would seem, from the reign of Merneptah. That endorsement, according to the translation of it given in Heath's 'Exodus Papyri,' p. 89, is to the effect that on a certain day of a certain year "there set out a mission to Baal (or Bal) son of Zippor of Huzoth, which he appointed to Hor." The papyrus is mutilated at the name Bal, which may have answered more fully to Balak than now appears. Brugsch confirms the above rendering as regards the personal names, but takes the city not for Huzoth, but for Gaza ('Geogr. Inschr.' II. p. 32). However this may be, all the conditions implied as to the site of Kirjath-huzoth in the Scriptural notice of it are satisfied by the ruins of Shîhân, 4 miles west by south of the site assigned to Ar or Ir. They stand on a slight but insulated eminence, and form a conspicuous object to all the country round (see Irby and Mangles, p. 141, who wrongly write the name "Sheikh Harn;" also Burckhardt, p. 375, and De Saulcy). And this is probably the site intended in the later Targums, which speak of Kirjath-huzoth as "the great city which is the city of Sihon, which is Birosha."

41. *the high places of Baal*] *i.e.* Bamoth-baal: see on xxi. 19, 20.

that thence he might see] Rather, **and thence he saw.**

NOTE on CHAP. XXII. 5.

Balaam the son of Beor] The character of this extraordinary man has to be inferred almost exclusively from the ensuing narrative, but has been very variously estimated. It seems however probable that he was from the first a worshipper in some sort of the true

God; and doubtless had learned some elements of pure and true religion in his home in the far east, the cradle of the ancestors of Israel, "whence Abraham had emigrated, and where Nahor and that branch of Terah's family remained," Blunt, 'Undes. Coin.' p. 85; and where we know, from various notices, that remains of patriarchal tradition long lingered. Such superior knowledge doubtless conduced to Balaam's reputation as a prophet, whilst it was not clear and coherent enough to deter him from employing as a trade the arts of the heathen sorcerer. The recent dealings of God with Israel, which had produced a profound sensation amongst all neighbouring peoples (Ex. xv. 14, xviii. 1 sqq.; Josh. ii. 9 sqq.) could not be unknown to Balaam; and indeed the intercourse between Mesopotamia and Egypt, as indeed amongst the peoples of the East generally (cf. Blunt, § 23), was considerable and continuous in those times. He had, we may be sure, inquired into the past history, and present hopes of this remarkable nation; and we find him accordingly using language which reflects that of the Jewish records (cf. xxiii. 12, and Gen. xiii. 16, xxiv. 9, and Gen. xlix. 9), and implies a knowledge of the promises made to their forefathers. Above all we find him employing on occasion the most Holy Name. He noted and believed in the signs and wonders which ushered in the new dispensation; and, by profession a diviner, he coveted a share in those marvellous powers which he saw associated with it. But, like Simon Magus, he sought spiritual gifts for worldly purposes. Though prophesying, doubtless even before the ambassadors of Balak came to him, in the name of the true God, yet prophecy was still to him as before a mere business, not a religion. The summons of Balak proved to be a crisis in his career. It gave opportunity for immediate contact with God's people, for closer intercourse with God Himself, and thus for attaining that fulness of prophetic gifts and dignity, to which he would seem to have aspired. But nearness to God, and keen prophetic illumination, could not of themselves reclaim the worldly heart nor convert the stubborn will. He yet loved the wages of unrighteousness (cf. Soph. 'Antig.' 1055, τὸ μαντικὸν γὰρ πᾶν φιλάργυρον γένος), and strove for sake of them to break away from the line of conduct distinctly prescribed to him by God. When his perversity was at length overborne by irresistible influence from on high, and the gold and honours of Balak seemed to be finally lost, he became reckless and desperate; and, as if in defiance, counselled the evil stratagem by which he hoped to compass indirectly that ruin of God's people which he had been withheld from working otherwise. He thus, like Judas and Ahithophel, set in motion a train of events which involved his own destruction. This explanation of Balaam's character, which was first brought out clearly by Hengstenberg ('Geschichte Bileams'), and has been adopted by Kurtz, 'Hist. of Old Covenant,' III. 389 sqq., Keil, Reinke ('Beiträge,' IV. 179—287), &c. is more consistent with the various facts apparent in the narrative than is either of the other contradictory views which have been offered. On the one hand Philo, Josephus, and most of the Jewish authorities, with Origen, St Ambrose, St Augustine, Lyranus, a Lapide, &c., regard Balaam as "prophetam non Dei sed diaboli," who was compelled by God against his will to bless when he would fain both then and always have cursed. This view was the one generally accepted by the earlier Christian Fathers, who in their antagonism to the heathen world would naturally find great difficulty in recognising that combination of genuine enlightenment from God with Gentile witchcraft which seems nevertheless apparent in Balaam, and gives to his character that inconsistency and complexity which so strangely mark it. And the combination was indeed one which could not last. The two elements of it were essentially incompatible, and Balaam had in the event to make his choice between them. But the chapters before us exhibit him at the critical juncture when he stood partly on the domain of Gentile magic, and partly upon that of true revealed religion and prophecy; and deliberately proposed to maintain his ground upon both. Balaam knew and confessed the Lord (Jehovah) when the ambassadors of Balak first came to him (xxii. 8), and was not backward in professing obedience before the king himself. He describes himself as one who "heard the words of God," "had the knowledge of the Most High," "saw the vision of the Almighty." Obviously then he was not a mere heathen wizard.

The other and opposite view maintained by Tertullian and Jerome, followed by Rupertus Duitius, Deyling, Buddeus, &c., is that Balaam was a holy man and a true prophet who fell through avarice and ambition. Yet when summoned by Balak he resorts, as of course, to the heathen art of augury (xxiii. 3, 5, xxiv. 1), and is styled (Josh. xiii. 22) "the soothsayer" (*hakkosem*), a word never used in the Bible in other than an unfavourable sense. "Soothsaying" is expressly forbidden (Deut. xviii. 10), is characterised always as a deadly sin (1 Sam. xv. 23; 2 Kings xvii. 17; Ezek. xiii. 23), and as the mark of a false prophet (Ezek. xiii. 9; Jer. xiv. 14, &c.). Accordingly the "kosem" is distinguished from the true prophet, Is. iii. 2. This view then, which possibly originated from a Jewish conjecture, that Balaam is identical with the Elihu of the book of Job, may unhesitatingly be dismissed.

The name Balaam (LXX. Βαλαάμ; Joseph. Βάλαμος; more correctly Bileam, after the Hebrew pointing), is derived from *bala*, "to devour," with a formative syllable attached; and signifies "destroyer," or "glutton." Less probable is the derivation "bala-am," "destroyer of the people."

In Gen. xxxvi. 32, we read of "Bela son of Beor," the first king of Edom. The name "Beor" (בער "to burn up") is identical with that of the father, or possibly ancestor, of the prophet; and "Balaam" is in the original identical with "Bela" except in having the afformative. The coincidence seems too remarkable to be quite accidental, as Knobel, Ewald, and others have hastily pronounced it. Does it point to a dynasty from Balaam's native country, on the banks of the great river, reigning in patriarchal times over tribes on the south-east of Canaan?

The name Beor is written Bosor (Βοσόρ), 2 Pet. ii. 15, and this implies an original בצור, an Aramaic equivalent for the Hebrew בעור, the Aramaic ע often taking the place of the Hebrew צ. The form possibly became familiar to St Peter during his residence at Babylon, and suggests the probability that Aramaic traditions were still current respecting Balaam at the Christian era, and on the banks of the Euphrates. Philo, writing at a slightly earlier date in Egypt, describes Balaam as an adept in every branch of soothsaying, who attained wide renown by his successful predictions of natural phenomena, such as drought, inundations, pestilence, &c. 'De Vita Mosis,' I. Other widely spread traditions identify him with Lokman, whose fables are a familiar portion of Arabic literature, the Æsop of the East, and by some regarded as identical with Æsop himself. Lokman (cf. Koran, XXXI.), whose name, like Balaam's, means "devourer," is described in Arabic writers as the son of Bâ'ûra, *i.e.* Beor. The Hebrew book of Henoch states that Balaam was called in Arabic Loknin, possibly a misreading for Lokman. See especially on these names, the Introduction to Derenbourg's Edition of Lokman's Fables, § II. 'De la personne de Loqman' (Asher, Berlin and London, 1850).

The names Balaam, Beor, Lokman are such as would be given by popular dread to wizards whose curses were regarded as destructive; a dread which it would be the interest of the magicians themselves to encourage. "Balaam the son of Beor" was probably of a family in which the mantic art was hereditary.

The exact situation of Pethor is uncertain. Balaam came "from the mountains of the east" (xxiii. 7), *i.e.* from Aram, or (Deut. xxiii. 4) from Mesopotamia; and Pethor therefore cannot be placed very far down the river. It was probably, as its name (derived apparently from פתר, *pathar*, signifying "to open" or "reveal," and used of the interpretation of dreams, Gen. xli. 8) indicates, a head-quarters of the oriental Magi (respecting whom, see on Dan. ii. 2, St Matt. ii. 1), who were wont to congregate in particular spots (Strabo, XVI. 1). Pethor (LXX. Φαθοῦρα) is identified by Knobel with Φαθοῦσαι ('Zosim.' III. 14), a place some considerable distance south of Circesium; and with the Βέθαυνα of Ptolemy, V. 18. 6. Both these names Knobel conjectures to be corruptions of Pethor, and identifies the place with عانة, *Anah*, a name in the Arabic of similar signification with Pethor in Hebrew. Anah ("Anatha," 'Ammian. Marcell.' xxiv. 1. 6), is described in Ritter, 'Erdk.' xi. 716 sqq., and appears to have been situated partly on one side of the river, partly on the other, and partly on an island in the river, in a fertile and well-protected vale, which has certainly for ages been the seat of a very ancient heathen cultus. No better centre could be found for influencing alike the Arabian tribes on the east, and the Aramaic tribes on the west bank of the great river.

CHAPTER XXIII.

1, 13, 28 *Balak's sacrifice.* 7, 18 *Balaam's parable.*

AND Balaam said unto Balak, Build me here seven altars, and prepare me here seven oxen and seven rams.

2 And Balak did as Balaam had spoken; and Balak and Balaam offered on *every* altar a bullock and a ram.

3 And Balaam said unto Balak, Stand by thy burnt offering, and I will go: peradventure the LORD will come

---

CHAP. XXIII. 1. *Build me here seven altars*, &c.] It may be inferred from this that Balaam, after the general custom of the heathen, had been wont to preface his divinations by sacrifice. Diodorus notes (II. 29), that it was by sacrifice and incantation that the Chaldeans sought to avert calamity and to produce prosperity. In the number of the altars regard was probably had to the number of the then known planets. Yet Balaam evidently intended his sacrifice as an offering to the true God.

3. *will come to meet me*] Balaam apparently expected to mark some phenomenon in the sky or in nature below, which he would be

to meet me: and whatsoever he sheweth me I will tell thee. And ‖he
went to an high place.
4 And God met Balaam: and he
said unto him, I have prepared seven
altars, and I have offered upon *every*
altar a bullock and a ram.
5 And the LORD put a word in
Balaam's mouth, and said, Return
unto Balak, and thus thou shalt speak.
6 And he returned unto him, and,
lo, he stood by his burnt sacrifice, he,
and all the princes of Moab.
7 And he took up his parable, and
said, Balak the king of Moab hath
brought me from Aram, out of the
mountains of the east, *saying*, Come,
curse me Jacob, and come, defy
Israel.
8 How shall I curse, whom God
hath not cursed? or how shall I defy,
whom the LORD hath not defied?
9 For from the top of the rocks I
see him, and from the hills I behold
him: lo, the people shall dwell alone,
and shall not be reckoned among the
nations.
10 Who can count the dust of
Jacob, and the number of the fourth
part of Israel? Let †me die the

‖ Or, *he went solitary.*

† Heb. *my soul*, or, *my life.*

---

able, according to the rules of his art, to interpret as a portent. It was for such "auguries" (not as A. V. "enchantments") that he now departed to watch; cf. xxiv. 1.

an high place] Heb. *shephi*, "a bare place on the hill," or "a scar;" as opposed to the *bamah*, the high place, with its grove of trees.

4. *God met Balaam*] God (in the original "Elohim," though the context both before and after has "Jehovah;" cf. Introduction to Genesis pp. 24, 25) served His own purposes through the arts of Balaam, and manifested his will through the agencies employed to seek it, dealing thus with Balaam in an exceptional manner. For to God's own people auguries were forbidden (Lev. xix. 26).

I have prepared seven altars] The sacrifices offered are alleged by Balaam as a ground for looking that God on His part would do what was expected and desired by the donor. The spirit of these words is thoroughly that of a heathen worshipper expecting in all his devotions his "quid pro quo:" cf. on xxii. 15.

Balaam's first "Parable" may be exhibited, somewhat more accurately than it is given in the A. V., thus:—

"From Aram hath Balak brought me,
The king of Moab from the mountains of the east,
Saying, Come, curse me Jacob,
And come, menace Israel.
How shall I curse whom God hath not cursed?
Or how shall I menace whom God hath not menaced?
For from the top of the rocks I see him,
And from the hills I behold him:
Lo, it is a people that dwelleth alone,
And that is not reckoned among the nations.
Who can count the dust of Jacob,
And the number of the offspring of Israel?
Let me die the death of the righteous,
And be my last estate like his!"

7. *Aram*] This term, which signifies simply "highland," denotes the whole elevated region, from the north-eastern frontier of Palestine to the Euphrates and the Tigris. The country between these streams was specially designated "Aram-naharaim," or "Aram of the two rivers;" the Greeks called it Mesopotamia; and here, according to Deut. xxiii. 4, was Balaam's home. Cf. on xxii. 5.

9. *For from the top of the rocks*, &c.] The "for" indicates the constraint under which Balaam felt himself. He had been met by God in his own way; from the cliff he had watched for the expected augury; and by the light of this he here interprets, according to the rules of his art, the destiny of Israel. His first parables are, however, not strictly predictions; nor is it till he abandons his auguries (xxiv. 1), and has the future revealed to him in inward vision from God (ib. 4), that he rises into the foreteller of that which should yet come to pass.

dwell alone] *i.e.* apart from others, undisturbed by their tumults, and therefore in safety and just security. Cf. the same idea in the blessing of Moses, Deut. xxxiii. 28, "Israel then shall dwell in safety alone;" also in Jer. xlix. 31, Micah vii. 14, and perhaps also in Ps. iv. 8. This tranquillity was realized by the Israelites so long as they clave to God as their shelter and protection. But the inward "dwelling alone" was the indispensable condition of the outward "dwelling alone," and so soon as the influence of the heathen world affected Israel internally, the external power of heathenism prevailed also (Hengstenberg). Balaam himself, when he eventually counselled the attempt to tempt the people into sin, acted upon the knowledge that God's blessing and Israel's prosperity depended essentially on faithfulness to God.

10. *the fourth part of Israel*] *i.e.* even each one of the four camps into which the

death of the righteous, and let my
last end be like his!
11 And Balak said unto Balaam,
What hast thou done unto me? I
took thee to curse mine enemies,
and, behold, thou hast blessed *them*
altogether.
12 And he answered and said,
Must I not take heed to speak that
which the LORD hath put in my
mouth?
13 And Balak said unto him,
Come, I pray thee, with me unto
another place, from whence thou
mayest see them: thou shalt see but
the utmost part of them, and shalt
not see them all: and curse me them
from thence.
14 ¶ And he brought him into the
‖ Or, *The hill.* field of Zophim, to the top of ‖ Pisgah, and built seven altars, and offer-
ed a bullock and a ram on *every*
altar.
15 And he said unto Balak, Stand
here by thy burnt offering, while I
meet *the* LORD yonder.
16 And the LORD met Balaam,
and [a] put a word in his mouth, and [a] chap. 22. 35.
said, Go again unto Balak, and say
thus.
17 And when he came to him, behold, he stood by his burnt offering,
and the princes of Moab with him.
And Balak said unto him, What hath
the LORD spoken?
18 And he took up his parable,
and said, Rise up, Balak, and hear;
hearken unto me, thou son of Zippor:
19 God *is* not a man, that he
should lie; neither the son of man,
that he should repent: hath he said,
and shall he not do *it?* or hath he
spoken, and shall he not make it
good?
20 Behold, I have received *commandment* to bless: and he hath blessed; and I cannot reverse it.
21 He hath not beheld iniquity in

---

host of Israel was divided (see ch. ii.), seemed to swarm with innumerable multitudes. Possibly Balaam could only see one camp. On the rendering see note at end of the chapter. Balaam bears testimony in this verse to the fulfilment of the promises Gen. xiii. 16, xxviii. 14, and that in terms borrowed from the promises themselves.

the righteous] *i.e.* not Israel, whose "death" could not suitably be spoken of, but "the righteous" ancestors of Israel, who "died in faith, not having received the promises, but having seen them afar off," Heb. xi. 13. With their histories Balaam was doubtless familiar (see last note), particularly with that of Abraham, "the righteous man" whom God had "raised up from the east and called to his foot" (Is. xli. 2).

let my last end be like his] Render rather "last estate," for the reference is not so much to the act of death, as to all that followed upon it—to the future, in which the name and influence of the deceased person would be perpetuated. The change from the plural to the singular number, as in this verse, is frequent in Hebrew poetry.

11—13. The cliff from which Balaam had watched for the augury (*v.* 3) had probably commanded a wider view than the spot on which the altars had been built (*v.* 1, cf. xxii. 41). Balak therefore seems to hope that the prophet's words, "Who can count the dust of Jacob," reflected the impression conveyed by the scene before him at the moment of the augury; and so that the sight of a mere few straggling Israelites in the utmost part of the camp might induce a different estimate of their resources and prospects.

14. *the field of Zophim*] Or "of watchers." It lay upon the top of Pisgah, north of the former station, and nearer to the Israelitish camp; the greater part of which was, however probably concealed from it by an intervening spur of the hill. Beyond the camp Balaam's eye would pass on to the bed of the Jordan. It was perhaps a lion coming up in his strength from the swelling of that stream (cf. Jer. xlix. 19) that furnished him with the augury he awaited, and so dictated the final similitude of his next parable.

20. *I have received commandment to bless*] Literally, "I have received to bless." The reason of his blessing lay in the augury which he acknowledged, and in the divine overruling impulse which he could not resist, not in any "commandment" in words.

21—23. These verses may be better rendered as follows:—

"No iniquity can one descry in Jacob,
And no distress can one see in Israel:
The LORD his God is with him,
And the shout of a king is in his midst.
God brought them forth out of Egypt: his
strength is like that of a wild bull.

Jacob, neither hath he seen perverseness in Israel: the LORD his God *is*
with him, and the shout of a king *is*
among them.
b chap. 24. 8. 22 [b]God brought them out of
Egypt; he hath as it were the
strength of an unicorn.
23 Surely *there is* no enchantment
|| Or, *in*. ||against Jacob, neither *is there* any
divination against Israel: according
to this time it shall be said of Jacob and of Israel, What hath God
wrought!
24 Behold, the people shall rise up
as a great lion, and lift up himself as
a young lion: he shall not lie down
until he eat *of* the prey, and drink
the blood of the slain.
25 ¶ And Balak said unto Balaam,
Neither curse them at all, nor bless
them at all.
26 But Balaam answered and said
unto Balak, Told not I thee, saying,
All that the LORD speaketh, that I
must do?
27 ¶ And Balak said unto Balaam,
Come, I pray thee, I will bring thee
unto another place; peradventure it
will please God that thou mayest
curse me them from thence.

Verily there is no augury against Jacob,
And no soothsayer's token against Israel:
In due time shall it be told to Jacob and
Israel what God doeth!

21. The words which the A. V. here renders "iniquity" and "perverseness" are found together again Ps. x. 7, xc. 10, and elsewhere; and import wickedness together with that tribulation which is its proper result.

the shout] The word is used, Lev. xxiii. 24, to describe the sound of the silver trumpets. The "shout of a king" will then refer to the jubilant sounds by which the presence of the Lord as their king amongst them was celebrated by Israel.

22. *God*] The name of God with which this verse begins, and which recurs at the close of *v.* 23, is not the ordinary *Elohim*, but *El*, which implies more particularly His might.

an unicorn] Render rather, **a wild bull**, and see Note at end of the chapter.

23. *enchantment ... divination*] More strictly "augury" and "soothsayer's token" (οἰωνισμὸς and μαντεία, LXX.): on the former word cf. *v.* 3; the latter (*kesem*) imports any kind of omen that was superstitiously observed. "Soothsayer" (*kōsem*) is the term applied to Balaam, Josh. xiii. 22.

The verse intimates that the seer was at last, through the overruling of his own auguries, compelled to own what, had he not been blinded by avarice and ambition, he would have discerned before—that there was an indisputable interference of God on Israel's behalf, against which all arts and efforts of man must prove vain. The margin gives "in" for "against" after LXX., Targums, &c. The original will bear either rendering; and the sense suggested by margin (*i.e.* that the soothsayer's art was not practised in Israel) would doubtless be strictly true (cf. Lev. xix. 26), though perhaps hardly so apt from the mouth of Balaam, just after his vain attempt to employ soothsaying against Israel, as that of our present text.

according to this time it shall be said of Jacob] Rather **in due time it shall be told to Jacob**, &c. The sense that God will, through His own divinely appointed means (*e.g.* the Urim and Thummim), reveal to Israel, as occasion may require, His will and purposes.

24. *as a great lion*] See on *v.* 14.

28. *the top of Peor*] Its position, northward from Pisgah, along the Abarim heights, is approximately determined by the extant notices of Beth-peor. This village adjoined the "ravine" (Heb. *gai*), which is (Deut. iii. 29, iv. 46) connected with the Israelite encampment, and (Deut. xxxiv. 6) with the burial-place of Moses. The place retained its name, and is described by Eusebius as six miles from Livias (*i.e.* Bethram, see on xxii. 1), on the ascent towards Heshbon. The ravine of Beth-peor was consequently that which runs down from near Heshbon eastward past Beth-ram; especially, perhaps, its northern tributary branch. This is a rough and narrow dell, watered at its bottom by an abundant spring that gushes from beneath the enclosing rocks, and is overshadowed by the gnarled and twisted boughs of some of the largest terebinths that the Holy Land contains (Tristram, 'Land of Israel,' p. 542). A hermit's cave—perhaps originally sepulchral—may be seen in one side of the ravine: at its upper extremity are the ruins of a town which most travellers designate as Na'ûr; Eli Smith, as Tâ'ûr. The Arabic form of Peor would be Fa'ûr; and the other names may possibly be but corruptions of this.

Jeshimon] Or **the waste**, in the great valley below, where stood Beth-jesimoth, "the house of the wastes." See on xxii. 1.

28 And Balak brought Balaam unto the top of Peor, that looketh toward Jeshimon.
29 And Balaam said unto Balak, Build me here seven altars, and prepare me here seven bullocks and seven rams.
30 And Balak did as Balaam had said, and offered a bullock and a ram on *every* altar.

NOTES on CHAP. XXIII. 10, 22.

10. *The fourth part of Israel*] The word רבע is perhaps rather to be rendered "progeny," as Rashi, Saad., Samar., Vulg., &c. The LXX. has δήμους, which probably represents a reading רבת. The A.V. has the support of Onkelos and the Palestine Targum. The sense thus given, though adopted by Keil, Bp. Wordsworth, and other modern commentators, savours somewhat of that proneness to excessive minuteness which marks Jewish exegesis; and the former rendering suits better the poetical character of the passage.

22. The term "unicorn" was adopted by our translators from LXX., which renders the Hebrew ראם by μονοκέρως. It is obvious however from Deut. xxxiii. 17, where see note, that the animal in question was two horned, for Moses compares the house of Joseph for its warlike strength to a ראם, and the twin tribes of Ephraim and Manasseh are represented by the two mighty horns of the beast. The ראם must not be confounded with the "wild ox" of Deut. xiv. 5, or the "wild bull" of Is. li. 20, where see notes. The latter is the oryx, a species of antelope. The animal named by Balaam in the text as an apt symbol of the strength of Israel is now extinct, and is the *Bos primigenius* of naturalists, the Auerochs of old Germans, the Urus of Cæsar, who gives a formidable account of its size, strength, speed, and ferocity, 'De Bello Gallico,' IV. 29. Accordingly it is employed to figure forth the unsparing fierceness of enemies, Ps. xxii. 21; Is. xxxiv. 7; its tall horns represent exaltation and established prosperity; it is also spoken of Job xxxix. 9—12 as intractable and untameable. See an excellent article, Tristram, 'Natural History of the Bible,' pp. 146—150.

CHAPTER XXIV.

1 *Balaam, leaving divinations, prophesieth the happiness of Israel.* 10 *Balak in anger dismisseth him.* 15 *He prophesieth of the Star of Jacob, and the destruction of some nations.*

AND when Balaam saw that it pleased the LORD to bless Israel, he went not, as at other [a]times, [†]to seek for enchantments, but he set his face toward the wilderness.

[a] chap. 23. 3, 15. [†] Heb. *to the meeting of enchantments.*

2 And Balaam lifted up his eyes, and he saw Israel abiding *in his tents* according to their tribes; and the spirit of God came upon him.
3 [b]And he took up his parable, and said, Balaam the son of Beor hath said, and the man [†]whose eyes are open hath said:
4 He hath said, which heard the words of God, which saw the vision of the Almighty, falling *into a trance*, but having his eyes open:

[b] chap. 23. 7, 18. [†] Heb. *who had his eyes shut*, but now open.

CHAP. XXIV. 1. *toward the wilderness*] *i.e.* to the plains of Moab, where Israel was encamped. The verse indicates that Balaam, in despair of being permitted to attain his own and Balak's purpose through his art, no longer looked for auguries; but simply "lifted up his eyes," *i.e.* gazed over the camp of Israel that stretched before him, and allowed the spectacle to work its own influence upon him.

3. *whose eyes are open*] *i.e.* opened in inward vision, to discern things that were hidden from ordinary beholders.

4. *falling into a trance, but having his eyes open*] On the "eyes open," see note at end of the chapter.

The "falling" of which Balaam speaks was (as Vulg. implies: "qui cadit, et sic aperiuntur oculi") the condition under which the inward opening of his eyes took place. Balaam had (cf. xxii. 8, 19) sought in time past to learn the will of God through inward visions as well as by "auguries." The "falling" is not that of one awestruck by the surpassing glory revealed to him, as was that of Daniel (viii. 17), and St John (Rev. i. 17). Rather does it indicate the force of the Divine inspiration overpowering the seer, as Saul (1 Sam. xix. 24) was overpowered, and stripped off his clothes before Samuel, and "fell" or "lay down naked all that day and all that night." The faithful prophets of the Lord do not appear to have been subject to these violent illapses. In Balaam and in Saul the word

5 How goodly are thy tents, O Jacob, *and* thy tabernacles, O Israel!
6 As the valleys are they spread
forth, as gardens by the river's side,
as the trees of lign aloes which the
LORD hath planted, *and* as cedar trees
beside the waters.
7 He shall pour the water out of
his buckets, and his seed *shall be* in
many waters, and his king shall be
higher than Agag, and his kingdom
shall be exalted.
[c] chap. 23. 22. 8 [c] God brought him forth out of
Egypt; he hath as it were the
strength of an unicorn: he shall eat
up the nations his enemies, and shall
break their bones, and pierce *them*
through with his arrows.
[d] Gen. 49. 9. 9 [d] He couched, he lay down as a
lion, and as a great lion: who shall
stir him up? Blessed *is* he that blesseth thee, and cursed *is* he that curseth
thee.
10 ¶ And Balak's anger was kindled against Balaam, and he smote
his hands together: and Balak said
unto Balaam, I called thee to curse
mine enemies, and, behold, thou hast
altogether blessed *them* these three
times.
11 Therefore now flee thou to thy
place: I thought to promote thee
unto great honour; but, lo, the LORD
hath kept thee back from honour.
12 And Balaam said unto Balak,
Spake I not also to thy messengers
which thou sentest unto me, saying,
13 If Balak would give me his

---

of God could only prevail by first subduing the alien will, and overpowering the bodily energies which the will ordinarily directs.

6. *as the valleys*] or **brooks**; with reference possibly to the four parallel brooks, running westward into the Jordan, over which the camp of Israel stretched, and by which the dispositions of its various parts must have been to some extent determined (see on xxii. 1).

as gardens by the river's side] Balaam's language here reflects rather the famous artificial gardens along the banks of his own river, the Euphrates, than the landscape actually before him.

as the trees of lign aloes which the LORD hath planted] The latter words contain an apparent reference to Paradise (cf. Gen. ii. 8). The aloe, imported from China and the far distant east, furnished to the ancients one of the most fragrant and precious of spices; cf. Ps. xlv. 8, "All thy garments smell of myrrh, aloes, and cassia;" Prov. vii. 17.

as cedar trees besides the waters] *i.e.* as the noblest of trees branching forth in the fairest of situations: an image of majestic beauty, as that of the last verse was of rare fecundity.

7. *He shall pour the water*] Rather **he shall stream with water.**

out of his buckets] Lit. "from his two buckets." Balaam's native soil was ordinarily irrigated by water fetched from the neighbouring Euphrates, and carried in buckets suspended from the two ends of a pole. Water in the East is the first essential of all fertility. Thus the metaphor would import that Israel should have his own exuberant and unfailing channels of blessing and plenty. But the prep. may in this phrase, as in the latter half of the verse, be the sign of comparison; and the passage would thus signify: "He shall flow with water more plentifully than his buckets:" *i.e.* Israel himself, abundantly fertilized, shall abound to others even beyond what himself has received. The words would thus be predictive of the future benefits which, through the means of Israel, were to accrue to the rest of the world.

in many waters] *i.e.* enjoy the benefit of various and copious waters. Cf. Jer. x. 13.

Agag] The name, apparently hereditary (cf. 1 S. xv.) to the chieftains of Amalek, means "high" (cf. the English "Hugh") or, as Arabic analogy suggests, "fiery." It was probably of the royal race of the Agags that Haman, "the Agagite," (Esth. iii. 1), the bitter enemy of the Jews in later times, was descended. The words point to the Amalekite kingdom as highly prosperous and powerful at the time (cf. *v.* 20); but as to be far excelled by the future glories of Israel. The Amalekites never in fact recovered their crushing defeat by Saul, 1 S. xv. 2 sqq., though they appear again as foes to Israel in the reign of David, 1 S. xxvii. and xxx. The remnant of them was destroyed in the reign of Hezekiah, 1 Chron. iv. 43.

8. The earlier part of this verse is repeated from xxiii. 22; but is followed up, as in *v.* 7, by words of prediction which are wanting in the earlier parable.

his enemies] Literally, and here more appropriately, "those that beset him round."

break their bones] Rather (as LXX. and older interpreters) "**suck** their bones;" *i.e.* empty them of their marrow.

11. *flee thou*] Rather, **haste thou**; cf.

house full of silver and gold, I cannot
go beyond the commandment of the
LORD, to do *either* good or bad of
mine own mind; *but* what the LORD
saith, that will I speak?
14 And now, behold, I go unto
my people: come *therefore*, *and* I will
advertise thee what this people shall
do to thy people in the latter days.
15 ¶ And he took up his parable,
and said, Balaam the son of Beor
hath said, and the man whose eyes
are open hath said:
16 He hath said, which heard the
words of God, and knew the knowledge of the most High, *which* saw
the vision of the Almighty, falling
into a trance, but having his eyes open:
17 I shall see him, but not now:
I shall behold him, but not nigh:
there shall come a Star out of Jacob,
and a Sceptre shall rise out of Israel,
and shall ‖smite the corners of Moab,
and destroy all the children of Sheth.
18 And Edom shall be a possession, Seir also shall be a possession

‖ Or, *smite through the princes of Moab.*

---

for the word Gen. xxvii. 43; Cant. viii. 14. No threat is implied.

14. *I will advertise thee*] Literally, according to the Hebrew, "I will advise thee." It has been surmised, especially amongst the Jewish interpreters, that the reference is to "the counsel of Balaam" alluded to xxxi. 16. The Vulg. actually alters the text to this sense, "dabo consilium quid populus tuus populo huic faciat." Some have supposed that the particulars of this advice have dropped out of the succeeding context, or been purposely withheld as communicated to Balak in secret. The A.V. is however most probably right; the word "advise" is here equivalent to "advertise," and refers to the ensuing prophecy.

16. *and knew the knowledge of the most High*] With the addition of these words, which point to the greater importance and the more distinctly predictive character of what follows, the introduction to this last parable is the same as that to the preceding one.

17. *I shall see him, but not now*, &c.] Better, **I see him, though he be not now: I behold him, though he be not nigh.** The tenses are as in xxiii. 9. Balaam there spoke of what he saw in fact with the bodily eye; here he describes what is actually before him in inward vision.

him] *i.e.* the prince, represented in the succeeding words by the star and sceptre. On these the prophetic gaze of Balaam is fixed, not on the people encamped on the plain beneath him. The use of the pronoun to stand for a person not yet named is common in Oriental, especially Arabic, poetry.

a Star] The star has amongst all nations served as a symbol of regal power and splendour: cf. Virgil, 'Ecl.' IX. 47, Ecce Dionæi processit Cæsaris astrum; Hor. 'Od.' I. xii. 47, Micat inter omnes Julium sidus. The birth and future glory of great monarchs were believed by the ancients to be heralded by the appearance of stars or comets: *e.g.* those of Mithridates in Justin, 'Hist.' XXXVII. 2; of Alexander the Great, Curtius, IX. 6, 8; cf. Suet. 'Jul. Cæs.' LXXXVIII. and the line of Æschylus, 'Agam.' 6, λαμπροὺς δυνάστας, ἐμπρέποντας αἰθέρι. The same idea recurs in Scripture, Is. xiv. 12; Dan. viii. 10; Rev. i. 16, 20, ii. 1, ix. 1. How current it was amongst the Jews, and accepted too as a well understood emblem of the Messiah in particular, is strikingly illustrated by the fact that the well-known pretender in the reign of Hadrian adopted the name of Bar-cochab, *i.e.* son of a star.

the corners of Moab] Literally, "the two sides of Moab," *i.e.* the length and breadth of the land: cf. Jer. xlviii. 45.

destroy all the children of Sheth] Rather, "overthrow the sons of tumult," *i.e.* the warriors of Moab, whose valour and fierceness is frequently referred to elsewhere (cf. Ex. xv. 15; Is. xv. 4, xvi. 6, &c.). The word *sheth* is connected with the word *shaon* used in the parallel passage, Jer. xlviii. 45; and the phrase *b'ne shaon* is there rightly translated "tumultuous ones," or more literally in marg., "children of noise." (So Gesen., Keil, Fürst, Maurer, Reinke, &c.) The A.V. has followed the LXX., Vulg., and the ancient Versions generally in taking the word *sheth* here as a proper name; and so too one or two modern scholars, *e.g.* Winzer, who conjectures that it is the name of a Moabitish king. Jewish authorities (Onk., Rashi, &c.) refer the word to Seth the son of Adam, and regard the phrase "sons of Sheth" as equivalent to "all mankind." Thus the passage would import that "he," *i.e.* the ruler that should arise out of Israel, "should rule all mankind." The verb however will not bear the sense "rule;" and on the whole the passage of Jeremiah, so manifestly borrowed from this, seems decisive as to its import.

18. *Seir*] The older name of the mountain-land, south of Moab, and east of the Arabah, which the Edomites inhabited, Gen. xxxvi. 8;

for his enemies; and Israel shall do valiantly.

19 Out of Jacob shall come he
that shall have dominion, and shall

Deut. ii. 1, &c. The southern portion of it is still called esh-Sherâh, perhaps a corruption of the older name.

19. *have dominion*] *i.e.* acquire, exercise, and keep dominion.

destroy him that remaineth of the city] *i.e.* shall destroy those of every city that had previously escaped. The phrase is peculiar to this place. It tersely describes a conqueror who first defeats his enemies in battle, and then hunts out the fugitives till he has cut off all of every place. (Cf. 1 K. xi. 16.)

With this verse ends the first "parable" of Balaam's last prophetical utterance. It fulfils the Prophet's promise in *v.* 14 to foretell to Balak what should befall his people at the hands of Israel; and adds also, *v.* 18, that Edom should share the fate of Moab. There can be no doubt that the victories of David were a partial accomplishment of these predictions, and the terms in which they are mentioned (cf. 2 S. viii. 2, 13, 14, reading in 13 "Edomites" instead of "Syrians," see note; 1 K. xi. 15, 16; Ps. lx. 8) seem to carry on their face a reference to the passage before us.

It is however no less clear that these victories do not exhaust the import of Balaam's predictions. For he emphatically promises to Israel a complete and permanent conquest of Moab and Edom; and no such conquest was achieved by David or any of his successors. Indeed in the days of the Judges, Eglon king of Moab conquered Jericho, and held the southern tribes of Israel in subjection (see Judg. iii. 12 sqq., and notes); Ehud delivered his own land from the Moabites; but we do not read of his conquering them in theirs. Hence Saul again found the Moabites in hostility 1 S. xiv. 47; David effected for a time a complete subjugation of Moab; but the yoke would seem to have been thrown off again at the disruption. The Moabite stone informs us that they were again subdued by Omri, and oppressed by him and his successors for 40 years. It records also the success of the revolt of Mesha, alluded to 2 K. i. 1 and iii. 4, 5. Henceforth the Moabites, though defeated by Joram (2 K. iii. 21 sqq.), succeeded in maintaining their independence, and in the reign of Joash appear (2 K. xiii. 20) even to have waged offensive war against Israel. They were eventually conquered by John Hyrcanus, B.C. 129, and merged in the Jewish state. So too the Edomites revolted under Solomon (1 K. xi. 14 sqq.); and under Joram again, and more successfully (2 K. viii. 20); and though defeated by Amaziah (2 K. xiv. 7) and by Uzziah (2 K. xiv. 22), were never again completely subjugated. Indeed in the reign of Ahaz (2 Chr. xxviii. 17) they invaded Judah.

Accordingly we find in the prophets the strain of Balaam taken up, often with a manifest re-echo of his very words, and the threats of destruction against Moab and Edom, together with the promises of dominion to Jacob over them repeated, centuries of course after the time of David: cf. as to Moab Is. xv., xvi. 1—5, xxv. 10 sqq.; Amos ii. 1; Zeph. ii. 8 sqq.; and as to Edom, Is. xxxiv. 5 sqq., lxiii. 1—6; Jer. xlix. 7 sqq.; Lam. iv. 21, 22; Ezek. xxv. 12 sqq.; Amos ix. 11, 12; Obad. 17 sqq. Both are included together in Is. xi. 14, a prophecy of similar import as to these two peoples with that of Balaam in the text.

It is further apparent that Edom and Moab are named by Balaam, as they are also by the prophets (cf. *e.g.* Is. xi. 14), not for their own sake merely, but as representatives of the heathen nations (*goyeem*, cf. xxiv. 8) who were hostile to the Theocracy. As Jacob then figures as a constant type of the kingdom of Messiah in the prophets, so too do Edom and Moab of the enemies of that kingdom; and in the threatened ruin of Edom and Moab is indicated the eventual destruction of all that resist the kingdom of God in its power.

The adoption of the name of Bar-cochab by the leader of the last rebellion of the Jews in the reign of Hadrian (cf. on *v.* 17) is an undeniable proof that Balaam's magnificent promises were regarded by the Jews themselves at that time as yet awaiting fulfilment, though the people of Moab had then long vanished from the theatre of history. It was on the faith of his people in their glorious future, as sketched out by Balaam, that the pretender traded; and their disappointment, when their hopes were belied by his defeat, was marked by their altering his surname to Bar-coziba, *i.e.* "Son of Falsehood."

The Star and Sceptre of the prophecy too, like the "Sceptre" and "Lawgiver" of Gen. xlix. 10, point naturally rather to a line of princes than to an individual; or rather are emblems of the kingdom of Israel generally. Thus the victories of David and his successors, generation after generation over Edom and Moab, are unquestionably recurring and progressive accomplishments of what Balaam foretold; but after all of them the prophecy yet reaches forward to some further and culminating accomplishment; and that too in "the latter days," *v.* 14, the ordinary prophetic designation for the time of the Messiah (cf. Dan. x. 14).

To a Christian the connection between the star and sceptre of Balaam and the star of the king of the Jews, which the wise men saw,

destroy him that remaineth of the
city.
20 ¶ And when he looked on
Amalek, he took up his parable, and
said, Amalek *was* ‖the first of the nations; but his latter end ‖*shall be* that
he perish for ever.
21 And he looked on the Kenites,

‖ Or, *the first of the nations that warred against Israel.*

Exod. 17. 8.

‖ Or, shall be *even to destruction.*

St Matt. ii. 2, is self-evident. As they were "wise men from the east," so was Balaam also a "wise man from the east" (cf. xxiii. 7); and the tradition that they were, if not descendants, yet fellow-countrymen, of Balaam, and occupied in pursuits kindred to his, is probable enough.

Nor is it any valid objection to urge that Balaam could not possibly have shared in the hopes of such a kingdom of God, dominant over all heathen and adverse peoples, as is seen here to be implied in what he said: The faithful and holy prophets of God themselves did not always comprehend the full bearings of the predictions which the Spirit of God delivered through them (cf. 1 St Pet. i. 11). In Balaam, whose mind and will were alien from the tenor of that which his lips spake, this was doubtless far more decidedly the case. The true and final scope of his words must be sought, not in the sense he would himself probably have assigned to them, but in that which was beyond question permanently associated with them by God's people from that time forward.

20. *when he looked*] *i.e.* in spirit, as he saw the star, *v.* 17.

Amalek] Cf. Gen. xxxvi. 12 and note.

was] Rather **is**. The copula supplied should be in the present tense.

the first of the nations] *i.e.* pre-eminent amongst the neighbouring nations: cf. the same expression Amos vi. 1. Hence the force of the words, *v.* 7, "higher than Agag," *i.e.* than the king of this powerful nation. This rank, due to the warlike prowess of the tribe, Balaam contrasts with its approaching downfall and extinction. The Amalekites attacked Israel soon after their passage through the Red Sea, Ex. xvii. 8, and defeated their first attempt at an invasion of Canaan, Num. xiv. 45. The sense given by the margin, "first amongst the nations that warred against Israel," though supported by the Targums and some modern Commentators (*e.g.* Herxheimer, Keil), is forced, and fails to bring out the antithesis on which Balaam lays stress. That preferred by Rosenm., Ewald, Maurer, &c., "first = most ancient of the nations," is contradicted by the genealogies of Genesis xxxvi. 12, according to which the Amalekites are a branch of the Edomites.

21. *the Kenites*] First mentioned, Gen. xv. 19, as one of the tribes whose territory was promised to Abraham. In Judg. i. 16, where we read of them as moving with the children of Judah, to establish themselves in the pastures south of Arad, Moses' father-in-law is spoken of as a Kenite; cf. Judg. iv. 11. It appears then, since Moses' father-in-law was a prince or priest of Midian (Exod. ii. 15 sqq.), that the Kenites must have been of Midianitish extraction, and so descended from Abraham through Keturah, Gen. xxv. 2.

But it seems unlikely that the Kenites of Gen. xv. 19, who were to be dispossessed by the descendants of Abraham, are identical with those of whom Balaam speaks, and who were, because of good offices rendered at the time of the Exodus, always regarded as kinsmen and friends by Israel (cf. 1 S. xv. 6, xxvii. 10). It is probable rather that the Kenites of Gen. xv. 19 were a Canaanitish people, who derived their name from the city Kain, which fell eventually within the borders of the tribe of Judah (Josh. xv. 27); and that the descendants of Hobab, who appear in Judg. i. 16 as making war in this very district, possessed themselves of this city, and with it of the name Kenite also. This they would seem to have already done when Balaam uttered his prediction; and in the next verse it is, as the margin correctly indicates, not of the Kenite, but of Kain the city, that he speaks. Nor is it surprising to find them in possession of their new abode in the promised land, while the Israelites were yet in their tents. It may well be that this roving band of Midianites had already entered Canaan, perhaps along the shores of the Dead Sea, and by routes impracticable for the huge host of Israel, and had, as a kind of advanced guard, made beginning of the conquest of the country.

From 1 Chr. ii. 54, 55, we learn that the Rechabites were a branch of the Kenites; and the name Salmaites, always given to the Kenites in the Targums, connects them with Salma, the son of Caleb, there mentioned. Jer. xxxv. shews how tenaciously, for many centuries, they held fast the nomadic habits of their race.

Strong is thy dwelling place, and thou puttest thy nest in a rock] Render, **Strong** (or firm) **be thy dwelling-place, and put thou thy nest in the rock** (or cliff). In the Hebrew there is a play on the words *ken*, "nest," and *Kain*, the name of the Kenites' abode. This nest in the cliff might be the city of Hazazon-tamar or Engedi, if that be (as is likely) the "city of palm-trees," from which they went subsequently up, Judg. i. 16. But there is another site, about ten miles south

and took up his parable, and said, Strong is thy dwellingplace, and thou puttest thy nest in a rock.

22 Nevertheless †the Kenite shall be wasted, ‖until Asshur shall carry thee away captive.

† Heb. *Kain.*
‖ Or, *how long shall it be ere Asshur carry thee away captive*

---

of Engedi, to which Balaam's words would be more appropriate, on the summit of the cliff rising perpendicularly from the level of the western shore of the Dead Sea, where was afterwards built the city of Masada, the scene of the closing tragedy of the Jewish-Roman war. It is not likely that such a natural fortress would ever have been unoccupied, or even excluded from a place in the list of the cities of Judah. Nor is there any site in the Holy Land which a rude but warlike people might more fittingly designate as either Ken, the Nest, or Kain, the Possession.

22. *Nevertheless the Kenite shall be wasted,* &c.] Render, **For Kain shall surely not be destroyed** (lit. "be for destruction") **until Asshur,** &c.: cf. note at end of chapter. The words are not, as they appear in A. V., a prediction of evil to the Kenites, but a promise, on the contrary, of safety to be long continued to them. The assurance of Moses to Hobab, "what goodness the Lord shall do unto us, the same will we do unto thee" (cf. x. 32), is in substance endorsed by Balaam. Another and later pledge of Divine favour was granted to those who helped to conduct Israel to his inheritance; see Jer. xxxv. 19; and, in fact, they shared the fortune of God's chosen people until the Captivity.

23. *when God doeth this*] The eventual carrying away of the allies of Israel by Assyria presented itself to Balaam as the ruin of all peace and safety upon earth. His thoughts were fixed on the fates of those whom he knew; and if even the Kenites might not be spared in the end, who then might? One prediction was however yet wanting, and is next given, viz. that the conquerors of the Kenites should fare no better than the Kenites themselves.

24. *Chittim*] *i.e.* Cyprus, the nearest of the western islands, the only one visible from Palestine, and so the representative to Balaam and to Israel of all those unknown western regions across the Mediterranean Sea, from which were at length to come the conquerors of the mighty empires of the East. Cf. Is. xxiii. 1, 12; Jer. ii. 10. The Vulgate rendering is remarkable, "Venient in trieribus de Italiâ." In Dan. xi. 30 however Chittim appears to be equivalent to Italy: the Targums render it so several times.

Eber] *i.e.* not as Vulg. and LXX., "the Hebrews," but generally the descendants of Shem. Of these Asshur was one (cf. Gen. x. 21, 22), and is here specified by name, since the Assyrians attained, in the empires of Babylon and Nineveh, to an extraordinary grandeur, and were destined to a most signal and irretrievable fall.

he also] *i.e.* the conqueror of Asshur and Eber who should come across the sea. The pronoun cannot refer to Asshur (as Knobel), from which word it is in syntax disconnected; nor yet to Eber, whose fate has been already announced along with that of Asshur. To the downfall of Asshur and of Eber there is obviously added that of another, and, in earthly might, greater empire; but as the historical events which unroll themselves before the Prophet's spirit become more distant in time, they become also less determinate in outline. It is not revealed whence the blow should come that should overthrow in its turn the power that prevailed over the great monarchies of the East.

It is evident that the prophecy now before us extends its view far beyond the latest date that has ever been assigned for the composition of the Pentateuch, and even for the closing of the volume of the Old Testament. The "ships of Chittim" were naturally referred, in the days of the Maccabees, to the Macedonian invasion of Asia (cf. 1 Macc. i. 1, and viii. 5); nor is it easy to see how any event of less magnitude can adequately interpret the broad prediction of affliction to Asshur and Eber. The bearing of this part of the prophecy is perhaps adequately represented in the well-known "ut valesceret Occidens," *i.e.* from the West should come a power before which the conquerors of the East should be subdued. But beyond this we have a clear intimation that the Western Empire itself, which was at its zenith long after the last of the Old Testament writers had lived and died, should "perish for ever." It is not surprising that those who reject all actual prediction of future events should have proposed, though without a shadow of proof, to regard *vv.* 23, 24 as a later addition to the prophecy of Balaam.

25. *returned to his own place*] Not to his own land, for he remained amongst the Midianites to plot by new means against the people of God, and to perish in his sin (xxxi. 8, 16 (where see notes); Rev. ii. 14). The phrase, which is of frequent recurrence (cf. *e.g.* Gen. xviii. 33, xxxi. 55; 1 S. xxvi. 25; 2 S. xix. 39), is idiomatic, meaning merely that Balaam went away whither he would.

23 And he took up his parable,
and said, Alas, who shall live when
God doeth this!
24 And ships *shall come* from the
coast of Chittim, and shall afflict
Asshur, and shall afflict Eber, and he
also shall perish for ever.
25 And Balaam rose up, and went
and returned to his place: and Balak
also went his way.

NOTES on CHAP. XXIV. 3, and 22.

3. *The man whose eyes were open*] Literally "the man opened of eye." The expression is further explained in the next verse "falling into a trance, but having his eyes open," where the word for "open" is, however, a different and common one.

The margin gives a different rendering to the word שתם, rendered in the text by "open," and, referring the phrase to Balaam's past blindness as to God's purpose, renders "who had his eyes shut." Others, adopting the same sense, "shut," refer the term, and so far more correctly, to the prophet's present state. Balaam would thus be described as having the outward and bodily vision closed against all external things, whilst the inner sense was, on the contrary, ecstatically active.

The word שתם is very rare. The only other example of it in the Bible is in the parallel phrase, *v.* 15. Hence the doubt about its signification. Gesen. ('Thes.' s. v.) prefers, though not very decidedly, the sense "closed." So Vulg. ("obturatus"), De Wette, Hupfeld, Keil, Hengst., &c. The other rendering, "unclosed," is however preferable; and is adopted by Jewish authorities generally; by LXX. (ἀληθινῶς ὁρῶν), Saad., Maurer, Fürst, Wogue, Knobel, &c. The passage of the Mishna, 'Abod. Sar.' chap. v. (Surenhusius, 'Mishna.' IV. pp. 385 sqq.) seems decisive. There שתם and סתם are repeatedly used together to express the unstopping and closing again of a wine-jar.

22. *Nevertheless the Kenite shall be wasted, until Asshur shall carry thee away captive*] Marg. "how long shall it be ere Asshur carry thee away captive?"

The rendering of the passage depends upon the sense assigned to the particles כי אם, translated "nevertheless" in A.V., and עד־מה translated by "until."

To the former two particles in combination the sense of "only" is assigned in this verse by Ewald, 'Ausf. Lehr.' p. 847, as in Gen. xl. 14, and in several other passages; and the sense would thus be "only is the Kenite for destruction then when, &c."

But it is probable that we ought in this case to dissociate the particles, as is in effect done in the Targums of Jerusalem and Palestine, and by Rashi, and give to each its own proper force. The כי will thus be equivalent to "for," and the אם have, as in xiv. 23, and often, the strong negative sense which it bears in oaths; cf. Ewald, 'Ausf. Lehr.' p. 846. So substantially Keil.

Of the other two particles מה is ordinarily and in classical Hebrew interrogative; and the phrase עד־מה would mean, as in margin, "how long?" But such a sense, though retained here by some commentators, does not suit the construction; and the particle מה on which the question turns is employed by Balaam, xxiii. 2 and xxiii. 23, in a non-interrogative sense. In his mouth this use must be regarded as an Aramaism; and an Aramaism is a token of the Hebrew in which it occurs being of a very early or a very late date (cf. on Gen. xlix. 10). Examples of similar uses of מה in Chaldee will be found Dan. ii. 22, 28, iv. 32. Thus the phrase עד־מה will mean in effect, as it is correctly rendered by A. V. "until." So as regards these latter two particles Keil; and as to the general effect of the passage Knobel.

Render therefore "for Kain shall surely not be for destruction until Asshur, &c."

CHAPTER XXV.

1 *Israel at Shittim commit whoredom and idolatry.* 6 *Phinehas killeth Zimri and Cozbi.* 10 *God therefore giveth him an everlasting priesthood.* 16 *The Midianites are to be vexed.*

AND Israel abode in [a] Shittim, and
the people began to commit
whoredom with the daughters of
Moab.
2 And they called the people unto

[a] chap. 33. 49.

CHAP. XXV. 1. *Shittim*] An abbreviation for Abel-shittim; see on xxii. 1.

the people began to commit, &c.] The records of the neighbouring cities of the plain, and the circumstances of the origin of Moab, Gen. xix. 30 sqq., suggest that the people amongst whom Israel was now thrown were more than ordinarily licentious.

2. *And they called*] *i.e.* "the daughters of Moab called:" the verb, and the ensuing "their," being in Hebrew feminine.

the sacrifices of their gods: and the
people did eat, and bowed down to
their gods.
3 And Israel joined himself unto
Baal-peor: and the anger of the
LORD was kindled against Israel.
4 And the LORD said unto Moses,
[b] Deut. 4. 3. [b]Take all the heads of the people,
Josh. 22. 17. and hang them up before the LORD
against the sun, that the fierce anger
of the LORD may be turned away
from Israel.
5 And Moses said unto the judges
of Israel, Slay ye every one his men
that were joined unto Baal-peor.
6 ¶ And, behold, one of the children of Israel came and brought unto
his brethren a Midianitish woman in
the sight of Moses, and in the sight
of all the congregation of the children
of Israel, who *were* weeping *before*
the door of the tabernacle of the congregation.
7 And [c]when Phinehas, the son of [c] Ps. 106. 30.
Eleazar, the son of Aaron the priest, 1 Mac. 2. 54.
saw *it*, he rose up from among the
congregation, and took a javelin in
his hand;
8 And he went after the man of
Israel into the tent, and thrust both
of them through, the man of Israel,
and the woman through her belly.
So the plague was stayed from the
children of Israel.
9 And [d]those that died in the [d] 1 Cor. 10. 8.
plague were twenty and four thousand.
10 ¶ And the LORD spake unto
Moses, saying,

---

3. *joined himself*] *i.e.* by taking part in the sacrificial meals as described in the last verse. Cf. Exod. xxxiv. 15; 1 Cor. x. 18. The phrase is repeated, *v.* 5; Ps. cvi. 28. The LXX. and Vulg. render "was initiated;" and correctly as to the effect of the acts described. The worship of Baal was attended with the grossest impurity, indeed partly consisted in it. Cf. Hos. iv. 14, ix. 10; also the worship of Mylitta, Herod. I. 187.

Baal-peor] *i.e.* the Baal worshipped at Peor, the place mentioned xxiii. 28. Hence the god himself is styled "Peor" in *v.* 18, xxxi. 16; Josh. xxii. 17; and the spot "Beth-peor," "house of Peor," Deut. iii. 29, iv. 46. Baal-peor is probably to be identified with Chemosh; see notes on xxi. 29, and xxxii. 37, 38.

4. *Take all the heads of the people*] *i.e.* assemble the chiefs of the people to thee. Cf. "took men," xvi. 1.

hang them] *i.e.* those who had joined themselves to Peor. It appears from the command given by Moses in the next verse that the offenders were to be first slain by the hands of "the judges of Israel," and afterwards hung up "against the sun" (*i.e.* publicly, openly; cf. 2 Sam. xii. 12) as an aggravation of their punishment. This would be done by impaling the body or fastening it to a cross. Cf. Deut. xxi. 23, note, and 2 Sam. xxi.

5. *Slay ye every one his men*] The judges were each to kill the offenders belonging to his own jurisdiction.

6. *a Midianitish woman*] Lit. "the Midianitish woman," the particular one by whom he had been enticed. From *v.* 15 it appears that she was the daughter of Zur, who was a "head over a people, and of a chief house in Midian," and is mentioned xxxi. 8 as one of the five kings of Midian that afterwards perished by the hands of the Israelites. Her high rank proves that Zimri had not fallen in with her by mere chance, but had been deliberately singled out by the Midianites as one whom they must at any price lead astray. The example of Zimri is doubtless recorded as one of the most memorable and characteristic in itself, as well as because it gave the impulse to the act of Phinehas, *vv.* 7, 8.

weeping before the door of the tabernacle] The plague (*v.* 9) had doubtless already broken out among the people. The more god-fearing had already assembled at the door of the Tabernacle of God (cf. Joel ii. 15—17) to intercede for mercy, when Zimri committed the fresh and public outrage just described.

8. *into the tent*] Heb. *hakkubbah:* the word with the article attached to it has passed through the Arabic and Spanish into our language as "alcove." It denotes anything arched: here, the inner recess in the tent, fashioned archwise (cf. the Latin "fornex," Juv. III. 156), and appropriated as the sleeping-chamber and women's apartment.

the plague was stayed] No plague had as yet been mentioned; but it appears from the next verse, and from God's words in *v.* 11, that a divinely sent pestilence was raging until the wrath of God was appeased by the act of Phinehas. The term "plague" may however be understood to include the slaughter wrought upon the offenders by "the judges," *v.* 5. (Cf. for such sense of the Hebrew word, 1 Sam. iv. 17; 2 Sam. xvii. 9.)

9. *twenty and four thousand*] St Paul (1 Cor. x. 8) says "three and twenty thou-

e Ps. 106. 30.

11 ᵉPhinehas, the son of Eleazar,
the son of Aaron the priest, hath
turned my wrath away from the children of Israel, while he was zealous
for my sake among them, that I consumed not the children of Israel in
my jealousy.

f Ecclus. 45. 24. 1 Mac. 2. 54.

12 Wherefore say, ᶠBehold, I give
unto him my covenant of peace:
13 And he shall have it, and his
seed after him, *even* the covenant of
an everlasting priesthood; because he
was zealous for his God, and made an
atonement for the children of Israel.
14 Now the name of the Israelite
that was slain, *even* that was slain
with the Midianitish woman, *was*
Zimri, the son of Salu, a prince of a
† chief house among the Simeonites.
15 And the name of the Midianitish woman that was slain *was* Cozbi, the daughter of Zur; he *was* head
over a people, *and* of a chief house in
Midian.

† Heb. *house of a father.*

---

sand," following probably the Jewish tradition which deducted one thousand as the number slain by the hands of their brethren.

11. *hath turned my wrath away*] So *v.* 13 he is said to have "made an atonement for the children of Israel." The signal example thus made by Phinehas of a leading offender was accepted by God as an expiation (lit. in *v.* 13 "covering;" see on the typical significance Lev. i. 4), and the exterminating wrath which had gone forth against the whole people was arrested. Cf. the case of Achan, Josh. vii. and Ps. cvi. 30, "Then stood up Phinehas, and executed judgment, and so the plague was stayed."

The act of Phinehas must be regarded as exceptional. It was an extraordinary deed of vengeance, justified by the singular atrocity of the crime which provoked it. The later Jews rightly appreciated its character, though, whilst guarding the application of a dangerous precedent by minute conditions, they lost the spirit of it, when they founded on it and on the similar act of Samuel (1 Sam. xv. 33) the "jus zelotyparum;" *i.e.* the right accorded to every Jew to punish summarily any gross and flagrant breach of Divine law committed in his presence. Cf. the act of Mattathias (1 Macc. ii. 24 sqq.) in slaying a man about to sacrifice publicly on an idolatrous altar, and the praise bestowed upon it *v.* 26, "Thus dealt he zealously for the law of God, like as Phinees did unto Zambri the son of Salom." The stoning of St Stephen (Acts vii.) has been quoted as an application of the "jus zelotyparum." Our Lord's expulsion of the traffickers from the Temple is another, characterized however by abstinence from all violence beyond what was necessary to vindicate the law.

The act of Phinehas was not done under the commission of Moses given *v.* 5. Phinehas was not one of the "chiefs" or "judges;" and had he been so, could only have been warranted in slaying offenders of his own tribe of Levi. Nor is there any evidence, unless it be found in the approval of the deed afterwards, that he was bidden by extraordinary command of God to do it. It was its own justification. Its merit consisted in the evidence it gave that his heart was right before God. He was, to quote the text of *v.* 11 *ad literam*, "zealous with God's zeal," and abhorred the presumptuous wickedness of Zimri, as God abhorred it. He therefore risked his own life by dealing according to their deserts with two influential and defiant evil doers; and his act, done in the face of Moses and the people, and for them, was accepted by God as a national atonement. How thoroughly the nation adopted the deed is manifest by the conspicuous position from henceforth assigned to Phinehas (cf. xxxi. 6; Josh. xxii. 13 sqq.), and by the fame which attached to him and it ever afterwards. On the public and civil aspects of the subject see Bp Sanderson's Sermon on Ps. cvi. 30, 'Works,' Oxford Ed., II. 240 sqq.; on the more personal and private, Bp Andrewes' Sermon on the same text, Andrewes' Sermons, 'Lib. of Anglo-Cath. Theol.' V. 223.

12. *my covenant of peace*] Equivalent to "the covenant of my peace." God establishes with Phinehas in particular that covenant which He had made generally with all his people; and among its blessings peace is specially mentioned, because of the peace between God and the congregation which Phinehas had brought about. The assurance of peace with God is appropriately bestowed on the man who had regained this peace for others. As an additional gift there is assigned to him and his seed for ever the office of peace-making, the legitimate function of the priesthood (cf. Eph. ii. 14); and the covenant was thus to him a covenant not only of peace but of life (cf. Mal. ii. 5). It is not the high-priesthood that is here exclusively intended: to this Phinehas had not as yet succeeded, for his father Eleazar was still alive. Yet after he had become high-priest, the office, with a short interruption from the days of Eli to those of David, when for unknown reasons it was filled by the descendants of his uncle Ithamar, was perpetuated in the line of Phinehas; nor indeed is it known to have departed from that line again until the

16 ¶ And the LORD spake unto
Moses, saying,
[g] chap. 31. 2. 17 [g]Vex the Midianites, and smite
them:
18 For they vex you with their
wiles, wherewith they have beguiled
you in the matter of Peor, and in the
matter of Cozbi, the daughter of a
prince of Midian, their sister, which
was slain in the day of the plague for
Peor's sake.

CHAPTER XXVI.

1 *The sum of all Israel is taken in the plains of Moab.* 52 *The law of dividing among them the inheritance of the land.* 57 *The families and number of the Levites.* 63 *None were left of them which were numbered at Sinai, but Caleb and Joshua.*

AND it came to pass after the
plague, that the LORD spake
unto Moses and unto Eleazar the son
of Aaron the priest, saying,
2 Take the sum of all the congre-
gation of the children of Israel, [a]from [a] chap. 1. 3.
twenty years old and upward, through-
out their fathers' house, all that are
able to go to war in Israel.
3 And Moses and Eleazar the
priest spake with them in the plains
of Moab by Jordan *near* Jericho,
saying,
4 *Take the sum of the people*, from
twenty years old and upward; as the
LORD [b]commanded Moses and the [b] chap. 1. 1.
children of Israel, which went forth
out of the land of Egypt.
5 ¶ [c]Reuben, the eldest son of Is- [c] Gen. 46. 8. Exod. 6. 14. 1 Chron. 5. 1.
rael: the children of Reuben; Hanoch,
of whom cometh the family of the Ha-

---

typical priesthood of the sons of Aaron was merged in the actual priesthood of the Saviour of mankind.

17. *Vex the Midianites*] On the relations between the Midianites and the Moabites, cf. xxii. 2 and note. As the Israelites are to "vex the Midianites" alone, it may be inferred that though the licentious rites of the Moabites had furnished the occasion, yet it was the Midianites in particular that had been the active agents in corrupting the people. Cf. on *v.* 1; and, for the execution of this command, ch. xxxi.

CHAP. XXVI. *Census in the Plains of Moab.*

This mustering of the Tribes was immediately preparatory to the war against Midian, and to the invasion of Canaan which shortly followed. With a view also to an equitable allotment of the land to be conquered (cf. *v.* 54) the numbers of the several tribes are taken according to their families.

1. *after the plague*] These words serve to show approximately the date at which the census was taken, and intimate the reason for the great decrease in numbers which was found to have taken place in certain tribes. Cf. Deut. iv. 3 and on *v.* 5 of this chapter.

3, 4. There is an ellipsis in the beginning of *v.* 4, which is probably rightly supplied by the English Version from *v.* 2. The LXX. takes the last clause of *v.* 4 as a kind of title to the catalogue which follows in this sense: And the children of Israel which went forth from the land of Egypt were those whose names follow.

5 sqq. The tribes are mentioned in the same order as in the earlier census, ch. i., except that Manasseh here precedes Ephraim; probably as being now the larger tribe. The following table shows the numbers of the tribes at each census:

	At Sinai.	In the Plains of Moab.
Reuben	46,500	43,730
Simeon	59,300	22,200
Gad	45,650	40,500
Judah	74,600	76,500
Issachar	54,400	64,300
Zebulun	57,400	60,500
Ephraim	40,500	32,500
Manasseh	32,200	52,700
Benjamin	35,400	45,600
Dan	62,700	64,400
Asher	41,500	53,400
Naphtali	53,400	45,400

Seven of the tribes, of which are the three belonging to the camp of Judah, shew an increase of numbers; and five, among whom are the three belonging to the camp of Reuben, shew a decrease. The greatest increase of any one tribe is in Manasseh: see on xxxii. 42. The most remarkable decrease is in Simeon, which now shews less than half its former strength. To this tribe Zimri, the chief offender in the recent transgression, belonged (xxv. 14). Probably his tribesmen generally had followed his example, and had accordingly suffered most severely in the plague. See further on *v.* 12. In the parting blessing of Moses, uttered at no great interval from this date, the tribe of Simeon alone is omitted. Respecting the round numbers which the census shews, see on Deut. xxxiii. On the odd thirty in the tribe of Reuben see i. 20 sqq. and the note.

Each tribe is, in the ensuing catalogue, represented as subdivided into certain chief fami-

nochites: of Pallu, the family of the
Palluites:
6 Of Hezron, the family of the
Hezronites: of Carmi, the family of
the Carmites.
7 These *are* the families of the
Reubenites: and they that were
numbered of them were forty and
three thousand and seven hundred
and thirty.
8 And the sons of Pallu; Eliab.
9 And the sons of Eliab; Nemuel,
and Dathan, and Abiram. This *is*
that Dathan and Abiram, *which were*
famous in the congregation, who
chap. 16. [d]strove against Moses and against
Aaron in the company of Korah,
when they strove against the LORD:
10 And the earth opened her
mouth, and swallowed them up together with Korah, when that company died, what time the fire devoured two hundred and fifty men: and
they became a sign.
11 Notwithstanding the children
of Korah died not.
12 ¶ The sons of Simeon after
their families: of Nemuel, the family
of the Nemuelites: of Jamin, the
family of the Jaminites: of Jachin,
the family of the Jachinites:
13 Of Zerah, the family of the
Zarhites: of Shaul, the family of the
Shaulites.
14 These *are* the families of the
Simeonites, twenty and two thousand
and two hundred.
15 ¶ The children of Gad after
their families: of Zephon, the family
of the Zephonites: of Haggi, the fa-

---

lies. The families of all the tribes, excluding the Levites, number fifty-seven. The ancestral heads after whom these families are named correspond nearly with the grandchildren and great-grandchildren of Jacob, enumerated in Gen. xlvi. Both lists consist mainly of grandchildren of Jacob, both contain also the same two grandchildren of Judah, and the same two grandchildren of Asher. It appears then that the document in Genesis must be regarded as a list, not of those who went down in their own persons with Jacob into Egypt, but of those whose names were transmitted to their posterity of the date of the Exodus as the heads of Israelitish houses, and who may thus be reckoned the early ancestors of the people. It is not necessary to regard each house as consisting of actual lineal descendants only; or yet as comprising always all the descendants of the ancestor whose name it bears. In some cases, probably, families attached themselves to more powerful households to which they were akin, and became merged in them, and so lost all separate name and place. It is likely, *e.g.* that Dan had many children, and many branches of descendants, notwithstanding that they were all comprised, by estimation, in the family of the one son known to us. In other cases, where new families sprang up and took their name from leaders of a younger generation, the family named after the older ancestor would consist only of such remnant of his descendants as had not become incorporated in the younger families; *e.g.* in the tribe of Ephraim the Shuthalhites appear to have absorbed the Eranites, although the latter were actually descended, through Eran, from Shuthelah. A variety of circumstances would naturally tend to bring into prominence some branches of the same parent stock, and to throw others into the background.

10. *together with Korah*] *i.e.* they were engulphed at the same time that Korah perished; for Korah himself appears to have died amongst the two hundred and fifty incense offerers at the door of the Tabernacle, not with Dathan and Abiram (cf. on xvi. 32 and 35).

11. *the children of Korah died not*] Cf. *v.* 58. Samuel the prophet was of this family according to 1 Chr. vi. 22 sqq.; and Heman, "the king's seer," 1 Chr. xxv. 5, the first of the three Levites to whom David intrusted the management of the vocal and instrumental music of the Temple services, 1 Chr. vi. 33. Several of the Psalms appear from the titles to have been composed for the sons of Korah: cf. titles of Ps. xlii., xliv., xlv., &c.

12. *Nemuel*] So 1 Chron. iv. 24. In Gen. xlvi. 10, Ex. vi. 15, Jemuel. The variation, like other similar ones which follow, seems due merely to error of transcription.

Jamin] So in Gen. xlvi. 10, Ex. vi. 15. In 1 Chron. iv. 24, Jarib.

The earlier list enumerates Ohad among the sons of Simeon. As this name does not appear either here or in Chronicles, it is probable that his family had become extinct. They may have been carried off in the recent plague: possibly were "the chief house among the Simeonites," of which Zimri had been prince.

13. *Zerah*] So in Chronicles; but in Gen. list Zohar, with a different initial letter.

15—18. *Zephon; Ozni; Arod.*] In Gen. xlvi. 16, Ziphion; Ezbon; Arodi.

mily of the Haggites: of Shuni, the
family of the Shunites:
16 Of Ozni, the family of the
Oznites: of Eri, the family of the
Erites:
17 Of Arod, the family of the
Arodites: of Areli, the family of the
Arelites.
18 These *are* the families of the
children of Gad according to those
that were numbered of them, forty
thousand and five hundred.
[e] Gen. 38. 2, &c. & 46. 12. 19 ¶ [e] The sons of Judah *were* Er
and Onan: and Er and Onan died in
the land of Canaan.
20 And the sons of Judah after
their families were; of Shelah, the family of the Shelanites: of Pharez, the
family of the Pharzites: of Zerah, the
family of the Zarhites.
21 And the sons of Pharez were;
of Hezron, the family of the Hezronites: of Hamul, the family of the
Hamulites.
22 These *are* the families of Judah according to those that were
numbered of them, threescore and
sixteen thousand and five hundred.
23 ¶ *Of* the sons of Issachar after
their families: *of* Tola, the family of
the Tolaites: of Pua, the family of
the Punites:
24 Of Jashub, the family of the
Jashubites: of Shimron, the family of
the Shimronites.
25 These *are* the families of Issachar according to those that were
numbered of them, threescore and four
thousand and three hundred.
26 ¶ *Of* the sons of Zebulun after
their families: of Sered, the family of
the Sardites: of Elon, the family of
the Elonites: of Jahleel, the family
of the Jahleelites.
27 These *are* the families of the
Zebulunites according to those that
were numbered of them, threescore
thousand and five hundred.
28 ¶ The sons of Joseph after
their families *were* Manasseh and
Ephraim.
29 Of the sons of Manasseh: of
[f] Machir, the family of the Machirites: and Machir begat Gilead: of Gilead *come* the family of the Gileadites. [f] Josh. 17. 1.
30 These *are* the sons of Gilead:
of Jeezer, the family of the Jeezerites: of Helek, the family of the
Helekites:
31 And *of* Asriel, the family of
the Asrielites: and *of* Shechem, the
family of the Shechemites:
32 And *of* Shemida, the family of
the Shemidaites: and *of* Hepher, the
family of the Hepherites.
33 ¶ And [g] Zelophehad the son of [g] chap. 27. 1.
Hepher had no sons, but daughters:
and the names of the daughters of
Zelophehad *were* Mahlah, and Noah,
Hoglah, Milcah, and Tirzah.
34 These *are* the families of Manasseh, and those that were numbered of them, fifty and two thousand
and seven hundred.

23—25. *Pua*] Heb. Puvah, as in Gen. xlvi. 13. Slightly otherwise in 1 Chron. vii. 1. *Jashub:* so in Chronicles; but in Genesis *Job. Shimron:* so in Genesis; in Chronicles *Shimrom.*

29. *Gilead*] He was the grandfather of Zelophehad (xxvii. 1), and belonged therefore to a generation which had now quite passed away. Amid some confusion, occasioned by the manner in which the records were copied, the genealogy of 1 Chron. vii. 14 sqq. reveals to us the fact that either the mother or grandmother of Gilead was an Aramite. For this reason doubtless he was named after the territory which formed the frontier between Aram and Canaan, the territory wherein Laban the Aramite and Jacob the inheritor of the promises had finally parted. (Gen. xxxi. 25, 47.) These associations probably suggested the special allotment in the district of Gilead to the Machirites (xxxii. 40), as being the district from which their ancestress had sprung, and which had given its name to the head of their families. It was, however, only a small part of the territory usually known as Gilead that was occupied by any of the Manassite families: their inheritance in that direction was, in the main, the land of Bashan. For the further use of Gilead as a personal name, see Judg. xi. 1, 2. Gen. xliv. gives no record of the names of the children of Manasseh and Ephraim.

35 ¶ These *are* the sons of Ephraim after their families: of Shuthelah, the family of the Shuthalhites: of
Becher, the family of the Bachrites:
of Tahan, the family of the Tahanites.
36 And these *are* the sons of
Shuthelah: of Eran, the family of the
Eranites.
37 These *are* the families of the
sons of Ephraim according to those
that were numbered of them, thirty
and two thousand and five hundred.
These *are* the sons of Joseph after
their families.
38 ¶ The sons of Benjamin after
their families: of Bela, the family of
the Belaites: of Ashbel, the family of
the Ashbelites: of Ahiram, the family
of the Ahiramites:
39 Of Shupham, the family of the
Shuphamites: of Hupham, the family
of the Huphamites.
40 And the sons of Bela were Ard
and Naaman: *of Ard*, the family of
the Ardites: *and* of Naaman, the
family of the Naamites.
41 These *are* the sons of Benjamin
after their families: and they that
were numbered of them *were* forty
and five thousand and six hundred.
42 ¶ These *are* the sons of Dan
after their families: of Shuham, the
family of the Shuhamites. These
are the families of Dan after their
families.
43 All the families of the Shuhamites, according to those that were
numbered of them, *were* threescore
and four thousand and four hundred.
44 ¶ *Of* the children of Asher
after their families: of Jimna, the
family of the Jimnites: of Jesui, the
family of the Jesuites: of Beriah, the
family of the Beriites.
45 Of the sons of Beriah: of Heber, the family of the Heberites:
of Malchiel, the family of the Mal-
chielites.
46 And the name of the daughter
of Asher *was* Sarah.
47 These *are* the families of the
sons of Asher according to those that
were numbered of them; *who were*
fifty and three thousand and four
hundred.
48 ¶ *Of* the sons of Naphtali after
their families: of Jahzeel, the family
of the Jahzeelites: of Guni, the family of the Gunites:
49 Of Jezer, the family of the Je-
zerites: of Shillem, the family of the
Shillemites.
50 These *are* the families of Naphtali according to their families: and
they that were numbered of them
were forty and five thousand and four
hundred.
51 These *were* the numbered of
the children of Israel, six hundred
thousand and a thousand seven hundred and thirty.
52 ¶ And the LORD spake unto
Moses, saying,
53 Unto these the land shall be di-
vided for an inheritance according to [h] chap. 33. 54.
the number of names.
54 [h] To many thou shalt † give the † Heb. *multiply his inheritance.*
more inheritance, and to few thou
shalt † give the less inheritance: to † Heb. *diminish his inheritance.*
every one shall his inheritance be

38—41. The list of Benjamite families does not accord with the list in Genesis. See note on Gen. xlvi. 21; and on 1 Chron. vii. 6—12. The names Shupham and Hupham appear in Gen. xlvi. 21 as Muppim and Huppim; in 1 Chron. vii. 12 as Shuppim and Huppim, in 1 Chron. viii. 5 as Shephuphan and Huram.

42. *Shuham*] Elsewhere Hushim (Gen. xlvi. 23; 1 Chron. vii. 12).

44—47. The names of the Asherites correspond to those of Gen. xlvi. 17, except that the Ishuah of that list is wanting. The name is possibly due to an error of a transcriber, whose eye, after he had copied three letters of the following name Isui, reverted to the final letter of the preceding Jimnah. Sarah (*v.* 46) is merely another form of the name Serah of Gen. *l.c.*

51. The total number of the male adult Israelites, exclusive of the Levites, is 601, 730; shewing a decrease of 1820 from the number at Sinai. Yet the present census would have exhibited an increase had it not been for the recent plague.

given according to those that were
numbered of him.
55 Notwithstanding the land shall
i chap. 33. 54. Josh. 11. 23. & 14. 2. be [i]divided by lot: according to the
names of the tribes of their fathers
they shall inherit.
56 According to the lot shall the
possession thereof be divided between
many and few.
k Exod. 6. 16, 17, 18, 19. 57 ¶ [k]And these *are* they that
were numbered of the Levites after
their families: of Gershon, the family
of the Gershonites: of Kohath, the
family of the Kohathites: of Merari,
the family of the Merarites.
58 These *are* the families of the
Levites: the family of the Libnites,
the family of the Hebronites, the
family of the Mahlites, the family of
the Mushites, the family of the Korathites.
And Kohath begat Amram.
59 And the name of Amram's wife
l Exod. 2. 2. & 6. 20. *was* [l]Jochebed, the daughter of Levi,
whom *her mother* bare to Levi in
Egypt: and she bare unto Amram
Aaron and Moses, and Miriam their
sister.
60 And unto Aaron was born
Nadab, and Abihu, Eleazar, and
Ithamar.
61 And [m]Nadab and Abihu died, m Lev. 10. 2. chap. 3. 4. 1 Chron. 24. 2.
when they offered strange fire before
the LORD.
62 And those that were numbered
of them were twenty and three thousand,
all males from a month old and
upward: for they were not numbered
among the children of Israel, because
there was no inheritance given them
among the children of Israel.
63 ¶ These *are* they that were
numbered by Moses and Eleazar the
priest, who numbered the children of
Israel in the plains of Moab by Jordan
near Jericho.
64 But among these there was not
a man of them whom Moses and
Aaron the priest numbered, when
they numbered the children of Israel
in the wilderness of Sinai.
65 For the LORD had said of them,
They [n]shall surely die in the wilderness. n chap. 14. 28. 1 Cor. 10. 5, 6.
And there was not left a
man of them, save Caleb the son of
Jephunneh, and Joshua the son of
Nun.

---

56. *According to the lot*, &c.] The general situation, though not the extent of the various tribal territories, was to be determined by lot. The land therefore could not be mapped out into territories till after the lots had been drawn. This method was doubtless adopted not only in order to preclude jealousies and disputes, but also that the several tribes might regard the territories as determined for them by God Himself: cf. Prov. xvi. 33.

58. Of these Levite families, the Libnites belonged to the branch of Gershon, the Hebronites and Korathites or more correctly Korahites (Heb. "the Korhite family," *i.e.* the family of Korah), to that of Kohath, and the Mahlites and Mushites to that of Merari: see iii. 21, 27, 33, xvi. 1. Of the other families named in ch. iii. the Shimites would seem to be now extinct, or to have been incorporated with the Libnites; and the Uzzielites, if they still survived, in like manner with another of the Kohathite families. The Izeharites of iii. 27 were probably now all known as Korathites, Korah being the son of Izhar; and of the Amramites, who consisted of Moses and Aaron and their descendants, with Miriam, we have an account in the ensuing verses.

59. *whom her mother bare*] Literally "whom she bare;" the subject is wanting and the verb is in the feminine gender. The text is probably imperfect here. See Note at end of the chapter.

62. The total number of male Levites, 23,000, shews an increase of 1000 on the number at Sinai (iii. 39). It is doubtless to be taken as a round number; and, as before, includes the male children from a month old and upward, as well as the male adults.

64. *there was not a man*] Indeed it appears from Deut. ii. 14—15 that the generation numbered at the former census had perished before the host crossed the brook Zered. Eleazar is here accounted as one of the enumeration: see *v.* 63, and cf. xiv. 24 and note.

NOTE on Chap. xxvi. 59.

The mode of filling up the ellipse adopted by the A. V., though supported by most authorities ancient and modern, is merely conjectural. It is too quite without parallel; for in 1 Kings i. 6 quoted by Ewald, 'Ausf. Lehr.' § 294, and Keil, as a similar case, the missing name can easily be supplied from the preceding verse. It seems most likely that several words have fallen out of the text in this place. On comparing the Levite families here named with iii. 18—20, Ex. vi. 17 sqq., those of Shimei and Uzziel are omitted; and the latter family at any rate was neither extinct nor obscure: cf. Ex. vi. 22, Lev. x. 4. Moreover Jochebed the mother of Moses could not be strictly the daughter of Levi, for three centuries must have intervened between the death of Levi and the birth of Moses, see on Ex. ii. 1. Amram and Jochebed were then descendants of Levi, probably seven or eight generations removed. Michaelis, Geddes, and Boothroyd take the Hebrew pronoun אתה as a proper name, "whom Atha bare:" Knobel, after Vulg., Jarchi, Onk., Arab. &c., proposes to alter the pointing, and to take the verb as a passive "who was born." In the face of the strong probability that the text is very imperfect, and in the absence of means for restoring it, conjectures as to what the proper sense may be are wholly useless.

CHAPTER XXVII.

1 *The daughters of Zelophehad sue for an inheritance.* 6 *The law of inheritances.* 12 *Moses, being told of his death, sueth for a successor.* 18 *Joshua is appointed to succeed him.*

THEN came the daughters of
[a]Zelophehad, the son of Hepher, the son of Gilead, the son of
Machir, the son of Manasseh, of the
families of Manasseh the son of Joseph: and these *are* the names of his
daughters; Mahlah, Noah, and Hoglah, and Milcah, and Tirzah.

2 And they stood before Moses,
and before Eleazar the priest, and
before the princes and all the congregation, *by* the door of the tabernacle
of the congregation, saying,

[a] chap. 26. 33. Josh. 17. 3.

Chap. XXVII. The command given xxvi. 52 sqq. to divide the land among the people "according to the number of the tribes of their fathers," suggests the petition of the daughters of Zelophehad now brought before Moses (*vv.* 1—6); and the decision in this case leads to a general enactment respecting the right of inheritance when a man died and left only daughters behind him. This law is afterwards supplemented by certain restrictions as to the marriage of such heiresses (xxxvi). It is obvious that these successive enactments grew out of emergencies which presented themselves when the questions connected with the taking possession of Canaan came actually to be encountered, and hold thus their natural place and order in the closing chapters of Numbers. The preparations for taking possession of the land being thus completed, the approaching death of Moses, who was not to enter it (xx. 12), is announced (*vv.* 12—14), and his successor solemnly appointed (*vv.* 15—23).

1. *the daughters of Zelophehad, the son of Hepher, the son of Gilead*] Cf. on xxvi. 29.

It does not appear that women in Israel had, up to the present time, enjoyed any distinct right of inheritance. Yet a father, whether sons had been born to him or not, had the power, either before or at his death, to cause part of his estate to pass to a daughter; in which case her husband married into her family rather than she into his, and the children were regarded as of the family from which the estate had come. Thus Machir, ancestor of Zelophehad, although he had a son Gilead, left also, as is probable, an inheritance to his daughter, the wife of Hezron of the tribe of Judah, by reason of which their descendants, among whom was Jair, were reckoned as belonging to the tribe of Manasseh (1 Chron. ii. 21 sqq., Num. xxxii. 41). Thus Sheshan also, who had no sons, married his daughter to his Egyptian servant Jarha, and so had by them a long line of posterity (1 Chron. ii. 34 sqq.). Other eastern nations had like customs. The daughters of Laban complain of having no "portion or inheritance in their father's house" (Gen. xxxi. 14), intimating apparently that Laban might have given them such had he so pleased, and thus bound their husband by ties that would have prevented him leaving his father-in-law. So of the daughters of Job it is specially noted that "their father gave them inheritance among their brethren" (Job xlii. 15).

2. *by the door of the tabernacle of the congregation*] The place of solemn assembly of the elders; for when in xi. 16, 26, they are said to go out to the tabernacle, it is the entrance of the tabernacle that is meant (compare xii. 4 and 5). It was however hardly to the seventy elders that the daughters of Zelo-

[b] chap. 14. 35. & 26. 64, 65.

3 Our father [b]died in the wilderness, and he was not in the company
of them that gathered themselves together against the LORD in the company of Korah; but died in his own
sin, and had no sons.
4 Why should the name of our
father be [†]done away from among
his family, because he hath no son?
Give unto us *therefore* a possession
among the brethren of our father.
5 And Moses brought their cause
before the LORD.
6 ¶ And the LORD spake unto
Moses, saying,
7 The daughters of Zelophehad
speak right: thou shalt surely give
them a possession of an inheritance
among their father's brethren; and
thou shalt cause the inheritance of
their father to pass unto them.
8 And thou shalt speak unto the
children of Israel, saying, If a man
die, and have no son, then ye shall
cause his inheritance to pass unto his
daughter.
9 And if he have no daughter,
then ye shall give his inheritance
unto his brethren.
10 And if he have no brethren,
then ye shall give his inheritance
unto his father's brethren.
11 And if his father have no brethren, then ye shall give his inheritance unto his kinsman that is next
to him of his family, and he shall
possess it: and it shall be unto the
children of Israel a statute of judgment, as the LORD commanded Moses.
12 ¶ And the LORD said unto Moses, [c]Get thee up into this mount
Abarim, and see the land which I have
given unto the children of Israel.
13 And when thou hast seen it,
thou also shalt be gathered unto thy
people, as [d]Aaron thy brother was
gathered.
14 For ye [e]rebelled against my
commandment in the desert of Zin,
in the strife of the congregation, to
sanctify me at the water before their
eyes: that *is* the [f]water of Meribah
in Kadesh in the wilderness of Zin.
15 ¶ And Moses spake unto the
LORD, saying,
16 Let the LORD, the God of the
spirits of all flesh, set a man over the
congregation,
17 Which may go out before

† Heb. *diminished.*

[c] Deut. 3[2]. 49.

[d] chap. 2[0]. 24.

[e] chap. 20. 24.

[f] Exod. 1[7]. 7.

---

phehad made suit; but rather to the princes, the heads of tribes and of families, who were making the census under the superintendence of Moses and Eleazar.

3. *but died in his own sin*] *i.e.* perished under the general sentence of exclusion from the land of promise passed on all the older generation, but limited to that generation alone. It had been declared at the period of that sentence (xiv. 31) that "their little ones should enter in, to know the land which their fathers had despised;" and by virtue of this declaration the daughters of Zelophehad claim that their father's sin should not be visited upon them. There would have been less ground for the claim had Zelophehad shared in any of the other special rebellions; for it was the general rule of God's government in such cases that the children should bear the consequences of their fathers' iniquity.

4. *Give unto us*] As representing our father; that so he, through us his representatives, may enjoy a like inheritance with his brethren.

12. *mount Abarim*] The host had crossed these heights already on its march (xxi. 20 and note); and it was from them too that Balaam had made his second attempt to curse the people (xxiii. 14).

Moses' charge to Joshua, Deut. xxxi. 23, must have been subsequent to the appointment of Joshua recorded in this chapter. It is probable then that the commands now given to Moses stand in their proper chronological place here. Moses' ascent of the mount and his death there are recorded, Deut. xxxii. 48 sqq., xxxiv. 1—4. The closing scenes of his life, the war against Midian, and the rehearsal of the law in Deut., which occupy the rest of the Pentateuch, appear thus to be narrated in the order in which they occurred.

14. *that is the water of Meribah*, &c.] These words look like a gloss; and possibly found their way into the text though originally written in the margin.

16. *the God of the spirits of all flesh*] An acknowledgment that man, who is but flesh (cf. Gen. vi. 3), is of himself helpless; and "lives and moves and has his being" in God (cf. Acts xvii. 28): hence suitably em-

them, and which may go in before
them, and which may lead them out,
and which may bring them in; that
the congregation of the LORD be not
as sheep which have no shepherd.

18 ¶ And the LORD said unto
Moses, Take thee Joshua the son of
Nun, a man in whom *is* the spirit,
and lay thine hand upon him;

19 And set him before Eleazar the
priest, and before all the congregation; and give him a charge in their
sight.

20 And thou shalt put *some* of
thine honour upon him, that all the
congregation of the children of Israel
may be obedient.

21 And he shall stand before
Eleazar the priest, who shall ask
counsel for him [g]after the judgment (g Exod. 28. 30.)
of Urim before the LORD: at his
word shall they go out, and at his
word they shall come in, *both* he,
and all the children of Israel with
him, even all the congregation.

22 And Moses did as the LORD
commanded him: and he took Joshua, and set him before Eleazar the
priest, and before all the congregation:

23 And he laid his hands upon
him, and gave him a charge, as the
LORD commanded by the hand of
Moses.

CHAPTER XXVIII.

1 *Offerings are to be observed.* 3 *The continual burnt offering.* 9 *The offering on the sabbath,* 11 *on the new moons,* 16 *at the passover,* 26 *in the day of firstfruits.*

AND the LORD spake unto Moses,
saying,

2 Command the children of Israel,
and say unto them, My offering, *and*
my bread for my sacrifices made by
fire, *for* †a sweet savour unto me, († Heb. *a savour of my rest.*)

---

ployed here to introduce an entreaty that God would not leave the congregation without a guide and leader, and in xvi. 22 as preface to an intercession that the whole people should not suffer for the sin of a few.

18. *in whom is the spirit*] (Cf. Gen. xli. 38.) Joshua was endowed by God with the requisite spiritual qualifications for the office. Moses however was to lay his hands upon him, both in order to confer formal and public appointment, and also, as it would seem from Deut. xxxiv. 9 ("Joshua was full of the spirit of wisdom, for Moses had laid his hands upon him"), to confirm and strengthen the spiritual gifts already bestowed. The previous reception of the inner grace did not dispense with that of the outward sign; cf. the case of Cornelius, Acts x. 44—48; and St Paul's baptism after his miraculous conversion, Acts ix. 18.

20. *of thine honour*] *i.e.* of thy dignity and authority. Joshua was constituted forthwith vice-leader under Moses, by way of introduction to his becoming chief after Moses' death. The transference of this honour to Joshua is not parallel to the communication of the spirit which rested upon Moses to the seventy elders in xi. 17, 25; for though Moses, in elevating Joshua to his new office, did not part with any of his own spiritual gifts, he yet necessarily shared henceforward with another that power which hitherto he had exercised alone.

21. *And he shall stand before Eleazar the priest,* &c.] Joshua was thus to be inferior to what Moses had been. For Moses had enjoyed the privilege of unrestricted direct intercourse with God: the other, like all future rulers of Israel, was to ask counsel mediately, through the high-priest, and those means of enquiring of God wherewith the high-priest was entrusted. Such counsel Joshua seems to have omitted to seek when he concluded his hasty treaty with the Gibeonites. Joshua ix. 3 sqq.

judgment of Urim] See on Exod. xxviii. 30.

CHAP. XXVIII. Ordinance of the daily offering (*vv.* 1—8); and of the Sabbath (*vv.* 9—10), monthly (*vv.* 11—15), and festal offerings (*vv.* 16—31). The daily offering had been already commanded (Ex. xxix. 38), and no doubt additional offerings had become customary on festivals. But no such elaborate system as is here prescribed was or could possibly have been observed in the wilderness: cf. Deut. xii. 8, 9. The regulations of this and the next chapter therefore point to the immediate prospect of that settlement in Canaan which alone could enable the Israelites to obey them. Cf. the ordinances in ch. xv.

2. *My offering, and my bread,* &c.] Or, **my offering, even my bread,** &c. The word for offering is here *korban* (cf. St Mark vii. 11), a term in itself of quite general import, but often especially applied, as apparently in this instance, to the meat-offering which accompanied the sacrifices. This meat-offering connected itself, from its very nature, with the life of the Israelites in Canaan, not with their life in the wilderness; and it was annexed to

shall ye observe to offer unto me in
their due season.
3 And thou shalt say unto them,
[a]This *is* the offering made by fire
which ye shall offer unto the LORD;
two lambs of the first year without
spot †day by day, *for* a continual
burnt offering.
4 The one lamb shalt thou offer
in the morning, and the other lamb
shalt thou offer † at even;
5 And a tenth *part* of an ephah
of flour for a [b]meat offering, mingled
with the fourth *part* of an [c]hin of
beaten oil.
6 *It is* a continual burnt offering,
which was ordained in mount Sinai
for a sweet savour, a sacrifice made
by fire unto the LORD.
7 And the drink offering thereof
shall be the fourth *part* of an hin
for the one lamb: in the holy *place*
shalt thou cause the strong wine to
be poured unto the LORD *for* a drink
offering.
8 And the other lamb shalt thou
offer at even: as the meat offering
of the morning, and as the drink
offering thereof, thou shalt offer *it*,
a sacrifice made by fire, of a sweet
savour unto the LORD.
9 ¶ And on the sabbath day two
lambs of the first year without spot,
and two tenth deals of flour *for* a
meat offering, mingled with oil, and
the drink offering thereof:
10 *This is* the burnt offering of
every sabbath, beside the continual
burnt offering, and his drink offering.
11 ¶ And in the beginnings of
your months ye shall offer a burnt
offering unto the LORD; two young
bullocks, and one ram, seven lambs
of the first year without spot;
12 And three tenth deals of flour
for a meat offering, mingled with

[a] Exod. 29. 38.
† Heb. *in a day.*
† Heb. *between the two evenings.*
[b] Lev. 2. 1.
[c] Exod. 29. 40.

---

the animal sacrifices as a token that the people must dedicate to God their property and the fruits of their labour as well as their own persons. See on xv. and Lev. xxi. 6.

3—8. The daily offering, as already enjoined at Sinai, Ex. xxix. 38—42. It is peculiar to the present passage that the liquor of the drink-offering is described in *v.* 7 as "strong wine;" Heb. *shechar*, a term usually employed to describe strong drink other than wine (*e.g.* Lev. x. 9). The Targum here understands it of old wine. But the explanation probably is that the Israelites in the wilderness had, in their lack of wine, substituted *shechar* made from barley for it. Of barley they had doubtless been able to grow sufficient for their needs. They had thus observed the spirit, though not the letter of the ordinance, and their practice hitherto would naturally betray itself in the language now employed by Moses. There are but few injunctions in the Pentateuch respecting drink-offerings. They are named in Lev. only in chap. xxiii.; and seem generally to be assumed rather than specified. From the present passage we gather that they were to be offered by being poured "in the holy place," not, as some render, "with a holy vessel." It has been inferred, from Josephus, 'Antiq.' III. 10, and Ecclus. l. 15, that they were poured round the foot of the altar. Others (Kurtz 'Sacrificial Worship of the Old Testament,' pp. 301—303, Clark's Transl.) maintain that the drink-offering was poured on the altar, and so upon the flesh of the sacrifice by which the altar was covered. In favour of this view Ex. xxx. 9 is referred to, which by forbidding effusion on the altar of incense seems to recognize it on the altar of sacrifice.

9—10. The Sabbath-offering, not previously enjoined, consisted of two lambs, properly accompanied, in addition to the regular daily offering.

11—15. The new-moon offering also is here commanded for the first time. The observance of the new moon had been enjoined at Sinai when the directions were given for making the silver trumpets, x. 10. That they were observed by the Israelites in later times appears from various notices, *e.g.* 1 Sam. xx. 5; 2 Kings iv. 23; 1 Chr. xxiii. 31; Col. ii. 16. The offering consisted of two bullocks, a ram, and seven lambs, accompanied as prescribed in xv. 1—12. There was added a goat as a sin-offering; and this, though mentioned last, would seem in fact to have been offered first, since in all actually recorded cases the sin-offering invariably preceded the burnt-offering (Ex. xxix; Lev. v, viii, ix, xiv, xvi). A more definite interpretation was put by this ordinance upon that of xv. 22—26. The sin-offering, which had been there contemplated in cases where a sin had been committed ignorantly without the knowledge of the congregation, was henceforth not to be offered merely at discretion, as circumstances might seem to require, but to be regularly repeated, not less frequently than once a month.

oil, for one bullock; and two tenth deals of flour *for* a meat offering, mingled with oil, for one ram;

13 And a several tenth deal of flour mingled with oil *for* a meat offering unto one lamb; *for* a burnt offering of a sweet savour, a sacrifice made by fire unto the LORD.

14 And their drink offerings shall be half an hin of wine unto a bullock, and the third *part* of an hin unto a ram, and a fourth *part* of an hin unto a lamb: this *is* the burnt offering of every month throughout the months of the year.

15 And one kid of the goats for a sin offering unto the LORD shall be offered, beside the continual burnt offering, and his drink offering.

[d] Exod. 12. 18. Lev. 23. 5.

16 [d]And in the fourteenth day of the first month *is* the passover of the LORD.

17 And in the fifteenth day of this month *is* the feast: seven days shall unleavened bread be eaten.

[e] Lev. 23. 7.

18 In the [e]first day *shall be* an holy convocation; ye shall do no manner of servile work *therein:*

19 But ye shall offer a sacrifice made by fire *for* a burnt offering unto the LORD; two young bullocks, and one ram, and seven lambs of the first year: they shall be unto you without blemish:

20 And their meat offering *shall be of* flour mingled with oil: three tenth deals shall ye offer for a bullock, and two tenth deals for a ram;

21 A several tenth deal shalt thou offer for every lamb, throughout the seven lambs:

22 And one goat *for* a sin offering, to make an atonement for you.

23 Ye shall offer these beside the burnt offering in the morning, which *is* for a continual burnt offering.

24 After this manner ye shall offer daily, throughout the seven days, the meat of the sacrifice made by fire, of a sweet savour unto the LORD: it shall be offered beside the continual burnt offering, and his drink offering.

25 And on the seventh day ye shall have an holy convocation; ye shall do no servile work.

26 ¶ Also in the day of the firstfruits, when ye bring a new meat offering unto the LORD, after your weeks *be out*, ye shall have an holy convocation; ye shall do no servile work:

27 But ye shall offer the burnt offering for a sweet savour unto the LORD; two young bullocks, one ram, seven lambs of the first year;

28 And their meat offering of flour mingled with oil, three tenth deals

---

16—25. The Passover offering was the same as that of the new moon, and was repeated on each of the seven days of the festival, thus marking the importance and the solemnity of the occasion. The details of the offering had not been previously prescribed; but the command for an holy convocation on the first and last days of the festival appears in Lev. xxiii. 7, 8.

26—31. The festival offering at the season of firstfruits was to be offered on one day only; and was the same with that of the new moon and passover. It nearly though not entirely accords with the sacrificial offering prescribed Lev. xxiii. 18 sqq., as an accompaniment to the offering of the loaves of firstfruits. There and here the sin-offering is the same, and the seven lambs of the burnt-offering also. But instead of the two bullocks and one ram of Numbers, two rams and one bullock, with the further addition of two lambs for a peace-offering, are specified in Leviticus. The discrepancy in the number of bullocks and rams is due perhaps to a corruption of the text; and the peace-offering, as being merely an ordinary concomitant of the wave-loaves, might be on this very account omitted from the passage before us, which prescribes only the general offerings of the festival, and not the special ones connected with any particular ceremony observed at it. It is unlikely that two extensive sets of sacrifices, nearly identical in their details, should have been offered on the same day, and yet that the command enjoining each should make no reference to the other. The distinction between the two is indeed recognised by Josephus ('Ant.' III. 10. 6), who, however, in computing the aggregate of the animals specified in the two passages errs as to the number of rams. But his statement probably represents only his own opinion: and even the practice of the Jews

unto one bullock, two tenth deals unto
one ram,
29 A several tenth deal unto one
lamb, throughout the seven lambs;
30 *And* one kid of the goats, to
make an atonement for you.
31 Ye shall offer *them* beside the
continual burnt offering, and his meat
offering, (they shall be unto you without
blemish) and their drink offerings.

CHAPTER XXIX.

1 *The offering at the feast of trumpets,* 7 *at the day of afflicting their souls,* 13 *and on the eight days of the feast of tabernacles.*

AND in the seventh month, on the
first *day* of the month, ye shall
have an holy convocation; ye shall
do no servile work: [a]it is a day of [a] Lev. 23.
blowing the trumpets unto you. 24.
2 And ye shall offer a burnt offering for a sweet savour unto the
LORD; one young bullock, one ram,
and seven lambs of the first year
without blemish:
3 And their meat offering *shall be*
of flour mingled with oil, three tenth
deals for a bullock, *and* two tenth
deals for a ram,
4 And one tenth deal for one lamb,
throughout the seven lambs:
5 And one kid of the goats *for* a
sin offering, to make an atonement
for you:
6 Beside the burnt offering of the
month, and his meat offering, and
the daily burnt offering, and his meat
offering, and their drink offerings, according unto their manner, for a sweet
savour, a sacrifice made by fire unto
the LORD.
7 ¶ And [b]ye shall have on the [b] Lev. 16.
tenth *day* of this seventh month an 29. & 23. 27.
holy convocation; and ye shall afflict
your souls: ye shall not do any work
therein:
8 But ye shall offer a burnt offering unto the LORD *for* a sweet savour;
one young bullock, one ram, *and* seven
lambs of the first year; they shall be
unto you without blemish:
9 And their meat offering *shall*
be of flour mingled with oil, three
tenth deals to a bullock, *and* two
tenth deals to one ram,
10 A several tenth deal for one
lamb, throughout the seven lambs:
11 One kid of the goats *for* a sin
offering; beside the sin offering of
atonement, and the continual burnt
offering, and the meat offering of it,
and their drink offerings.
12 ¶ And on the fifteenth day of
the seventh month ye shall have an
holy convocation; ye shall do no servile work, and ye shall keep a feast
unto the LORD seven days:

---

after the captivity would not be decisive as to the true meaning of the Mosaic law.

CHAP. XXIX. **1—6.** Ordinance of the Feast of Trumpets. This was to be observed on the opening day of that month within which the Great Day of the Atonement and the Feast of Tabernacles fell (cf. Lev. xxiii. 23 sqq.). The offering consisted of one bullock, one ram, and seven lambs, with a goat for a sin-offering, in addition to the usual new-moon offering (cf. xxviii. 11), and to the regular daily offering. The special offering for the day anticipated that of the Great Day of Atonement.

7—11. The offering on the Great Day of Atonement was the same with that just specified. The sin-offering included in this offering was independent of the sin-offerings which formed the great ceremonies of the day, as described in Lev. xvi. It differed from the offering made on the days of the Passover, and on the day of first-fruits, inasmuch as it included only one bullock instead of two. The reason of this distinction is not certain. Possibly since the bullock was preeminently the animal of agriculture, the offering of bullocks on God's altar was most in keeping at those feasts dedicated more especially to an acknowledgment of the blessings bestowed in the realm of nature. Such was, peculiarly, the aim of the Feast of Tabernacles, when the offering of a very large number of bullocks was commanded; cf. *v.* 13. The day of Atonement had a very different signification; and on it one bullock only was offered for the people; though another was enjoined as a sin-offering for the priest (cf. Lev. xvi. 11 sqq.).

12—34. Feast of Tabernacles: cf. Lev. xxiii. 33 sqq. The offerings required at this feast were the largest of all. They amounted to fourteen rams, ninety-eight lambs, and no less than seventy bullocks; being twice as many lambs and four times as many bullocks as enjoined for the Passover. The Feast of Taber-

13 And ye shall offer a burnt offering, a sacrifice made by fire, of a sweet savour unto the LORD; thirteen young bullocks, two rams, *and* fourteen lambs of the first year; they shall be without blemish:

14 And their meat offering *shall be of* flour mingled with oil, three tenth deals unto every bullock of the thirteen bullocks, two tenth deals to each ram of the two rams,

15 And a several tenth deal to each lamb of the fourteen lambs:

16 And one kid of the goats *for* a sin offering; beside the continual burnt offering, his meat offering, and his drink offering.

17 ¶ And on the second day *ye shall offer* twelve young bullocks, two rams, fourteen lambs of the first year without spot:

18 And their meat offering and their drink offerings for the bullocks, for the rams, and for the lambs, *shall be* according to their number, after the manner:

19 And one kid of the goats *for* a sin offering; beside the continual burnt offering, and the meat offering thereof, and their drink offerings.

20 ¶ And on the third day eleven bullocks, two rams, fourteen lambs of the first year without blemish;

21 And their meat offering and their drink offerings for the bullocks, for the rams, and for the lambs, *shall be* according to their number, after the manner:

22 And one goat *for* a sin offering; beside the continual burnt offering, and his meat offering, and his drink offering.

23 ¶ And on the fourth day ten bullocks, two rams, *and* fourteen lambs of the first year without blemish:

24 Their meat offering and their drink offerings for the bullocks, for the rams, and for the lambs, *shall be* according to their number, after the manner:

25 And one kid of the goats *for* a sin offering; beside the continual burnt offering, his meat offering, and his drink offering.

26 ¶ And on the fifth day nine bullocks, two rams, *and* fourteen lambs of the first year without spot:

27 And their meat offering and their drink offerings for the bullocks, for the rams, and for the lambs, *shall be* according to their number, after the manner:

28 And one goat *for* a sin offering; beside the continual burnt offering, and his meat offering, and his drink offering.

29 ¶ And on the sixth day eight bullocks, two rams, *and* fourteen lambs of the first year without blemish:

30 And their meat offering and their drink offerings for the bullocks, for the rams, and for the lambs, *shall be* according to their number, after the manner:

31 And one goat *for* a sin offering; beside the continual burnt offering, his meat offering, and his drink offering.

32 ¶ And on the seventh day seven bullocks, two rams, *and* four-

---

nacles was especially one of thankfulness to God for the gift of the fruits of the earth, and the quantity and the nature of the offerings (see on *vv.* 7—11) were determined accordingly.

32. *on the seventh day seven bullocks*] By this coincidence, as also by the total amount (seventy) of the bullocks sacrificed during the feast, stress is laid on the number seven, the holy symbolical covenant number, by way of intimation that the mercies of the harvest accrued by virtue of God's covenant. It would seem that the number of bullocks sacrificed on the preceding days of the feast (thirteen on the first day, *v.* 13, twelve the second day, *v.* 17, &c.) is adjusted simply to obtain the coincidence before us on the seventh day. Bähr however ('Symb.' II. p. 616) sees in the gradually decreasing number a reference to the moon, which was full on the first day of the feast, and of course was waning during the after days; Knobel regards the same arrangement as marking the transition to the non-festal months of the year which followed this feast: whilst Bishop Wordsworth conjectures that the gradual evanescence of the law till the time of its absorption in the Gospel is here presignified in the law itself.

teen lambs of the first year without blemish:

33 And their meat offering and their drink offerings for the bullocks, for the rams, and for the lambs, *shall be* according to their number, after the manner:

34 And one goat *for* a sin offering; beside the continual burnt offering, his meat offering, and his drink offering.

35 ¶ On the eighth day ye shall
[c] Lev. 23. 36. have a [c] solemn assembly: ye shall do no servile work *therein:*

36 But ye shall offer a burnt offering, a sacrifice made by fire, of a sweet savour unto the LORD: one bullock, one ram, seven lambs of the first year without blemish:

37 Their meat offering and their drink offerings for the bullock, for the ram, and for the lambs, *shall be* according to their number, after the manner:

38 And one goat *for* a sin offering; beside the continual burnt offering, and his meat offering, and his drink offering.

39 These *things* ye shall ‖ do unto ‖ Or, *offer*
the LORD in your set feasts, beside your vows, and your freewill offerings, for your burnt offerings, and for your meat offerings, and for your drink offerings, and for your peace offerings.

40 And Moses told the children of Israel according to all that the LORD commanded Moses.

CHAPTER XXX.

1 *Vows are not to be broken.* 3 *The exception of a maid's vow.* 6 *Of a wife's.* 9 *Of a widow's, or her that is divorced.*

AND Moses spake unto the heads of the tribes concerning the children of Israel, saying, This *is* the thing which the LORD hath commanded.

2 If a man vow a vow unto the LORD, or swear an oath to bind his soul with a bond; he shall not

---

35—38. The feast of tabernacles was closed by an eighth day solemnity: see on Lev. xxiii. 36. The offerings prescribed for it were the same with those appointed for the Feast of Trumpets and the Day of Atonement. The solemnities of the month thus terminated, as a whole, with the same sacrifices with which, three weeks before, they had been introduced; and the Day of Atonement, even though succeeded by the rejoicings of the Feast of Tabernacles, thus left its impress on the whole month. Cf. on *vv.* 1—6.

39. *for your burnt offerings*] It is grammatically uncertain whether these and the succeeding words are to be connected with "vows and free-will offerings," or with the offerings "in the set feasts," or with both. But since in this and the last chapter no peace-offerings are required at the set feasts, it would seem that the reference is to the free-will offerings only.

CHAP. XXX. **1—16.** The regulations here laid down respecting the validity and obligation of vows appropriately follow those given in the preceding context respecting sacrifices, since a large proportion of vows would always relate to the presentation of such offerings. Rules had already been given (Lev. xxvii,) for the estimation of things vowed to God. It is probable that this fresh legislation dealing specially with vows made by persons in a state of tutelage, was occasioned by some case of practical difficulty that had recently arisen; and it is addressed by Moses to "the heads of the tribes" *v.* 1, who would in their judicial capacity have to determine questions on these subjects; and would also represent the class specially interested in obtaining relief, where they might think fit to claim it, from vows made by persons in their families who had no independent means. Four examples are taken: (1) that of a maid in her father's house, *vv.* 3—5; (2) that of a woman betrothed though not yet married, *vv.* 6—9; (3) that of a widow or divorced woman, *v.* 9; (4) that of a wife in her husband's house (*vv.* 10—14). Other instances (*e. g.* that of a vow made by a widow) are not mentioned, but would obviously be determined by the principles laid down in those here given.

There is no provision in the chapter for annulling vows made by boys and young men; from which it has been inferred that the vows of males were in all cases and circumstances binding.

2. *vow a vow unto the LORD, or swear an oath to bind his soul with a bond*] The "vow" (Heb. *neder*) was positive; the "bond" (Heb. *issar*) negative or restrictive. By a vow a man engaged to dedicate something to God, or to accomplish some work for Him: by a bond he debarred himself from some privilege or enjoyment. A vow involved an obligation to do: a bond, an obligation to forbear doing.

† Heb. *profane.*

†break his word, he shall do according to all that proceedeth out of his
mouth.
3 If a woman also vow a vow unto the LORD, and bind *herself* by a
bond, *being* in her father's house in
her youth;
4 And her father hear her vow,
and her bond wherewith she hath
bound her soul, and her father shall
hold his peace at her: then all her
vows shall stand, and every bond
wherewith she hath bound her soul
shall stand.
5 But if her father disallow her
in the day that he heareth; not any
of her vows, or of her bonds wherewith she hath bound her soul, shall
stand: and the LORD shall forgive
her, because her father disallowed her.
6 And if she had at all an husband, when † she vowed, or uttered
ought out of her lips, wherewith she
bound her soul;
7 And her husband heard *it*, and
held his peace at her in the day
that he heard *it*: then her vows
shall stand, and her bonds wherewith
she bound her soul shall stand.
8 But if her husband disallowed
her on the day that he heard *it*;
then he shall make her vow which
she vowed, and that which she uttered with her lips, wherewith she
bound her soul, of none effect: and
the LORD shall forgive her.
9 But every vow of a widow, and
of her that is divorced, wherewith
they have bound their souls, shall
stand against her.
10 And if she vowed in her husband's house, or bound her soul by
a bond with an oath;
11 And her husband heard *it*, and
held his peace at her, *and* disallowed
her not: then all her vows shall
stand, and every bond wherewith she
bound her soul shall stand.
12 But if her husband hath utterly made them void on the day he

† Heb. *her vows were upon her.*

The Nazarite vow however is called in vi. 2 *neder*, because though including certain abstinences it contained also the positive element; for the Nazarite was bound to let his hair grow.

3. *being in her father's house in her youth*] Modern Jewish authorities teach that the control here given to the parent ceased when the girl attained the age of twelve years. There is however no trace of such limitation. It was not ordinarily till her betrothal or marriage, that the female passed (some suppose by purchase) from the power of her father to that of her husband (compare Michaelis, 'Laws of Moses,' Art. 83).

4. *hear her vow*] It would almost necessarily be brought to his knowledge when the time for the performance of it arrived, if not sooner.

5. *the LORD shall forgive her*] *i.e.* shall remit the obligation. Cf. the use of the same verb in 2 K. v. 18.

6. *And if she had at all an husband, when she vowed*, &c.] Rather, **And if she shall at all be an husband's, and her vows shall be upon her, or a rash utterance of her lips, wherewith she hath bound her soul.** The "at all" intimates that the case of a girl betrothed but not yet actually married is here especially contemplated. Among the Jews the ceremony of betrothal was hardly less important than that of marriage, which, in the case of a virgin, it usually preceded by ten months or a year. After betrothal, a woman continued to reside, till the period of her marriage arrived, in her father's house; but her property was from that time forward vested in her husband, and she was so far regarded as personally his, that an act of faithlessness to him was, like adultery, punishable with death (Deut. xxii. 23, 24). Hence his right to control her vows even before he actually took her home as his wife. The vows might have been made either previously or subsequently to betrothal; but in either case her future husband, under whose control she passed with these vows upon her, might disallow them. It would seem that even the father's express sanction of his unbetrothed daughter's vow did not affect the husband's power, after her betrothal, of disallowing it. To have given the father a power to ratify it absolutely might have either involved a wrong to a future husband, or else have interfered with the girl's prospects of marriage.

uttered ought out of her lips] Lit. "the rash utterance of her lips." The word here used is not found elsewhere, and imports an utterance made without reflection. The allusion to such rash vows indicates perhaps that they were not uncommon; perhaps it was a case of this kind which led to legislation on the whole subject.

heard *them*; *then* whatsoever proceeded out of her lips concerning her
vows, or concerning the bond of her
soul, shall not stand: her husband
hath made them void; and the LORD
shall forgive her.
13 Every vow, and every binding
oath to afflict the soul, her husband
may establish it, or her husband may
make it void.
14 But if her husband altogether
hold his peace at her from day to
day; then he establisheth all her
vows, or all her bonds, which *are*
upon her: he confirmeth them, because he held his peace at her in the
day that he heard *them*.
15 But if he shall any ways make
them void after that he hath heard
them; then he shall bear her iniquity.
16 These *are* the statutes, which
the LORD commanded Moses, between a man and his wife, between
the father and his daughter, *being yet*
in her youth in her father's house.

CHAPTER XXXI.

1 The Midianites are spoiled, and Balaam slain. 13 Moses is wroth with the officers, for saving the women alive. 19 How the soldiers, with their captives and spoil, are to be purified. 25 The proportion whereby the prey is to be divided. 48 The voluntary oblation unto the treasury of the Lord.

AND the LORD spake unto Moses,
saying,
2 [a]Avenge the children of Israel [a] chap. 25. 17.
of the Midianites: afterward shalt
thou [b]be gathered unto thy people. [b] chap. 27. 13.
3 And Moses spake unto the peo-
ple, saying, Arm some of yourselves
unto the war, and let them go against
the Midianites, and avenge the LORD
of Midian.

CHAP. XXXI. The command of xxv. 17 is now ordered to be executed, and a war of vengeance against Midian is undertaken. This war and the transactions connected with it are narrated in this chapter; and would seem to have occurred immediately before those closing addresses of Moses to the people which form the book of Deuteronomy. See Introd. § III. 10, 11. The result of this war completed and secured the conquest of the promised land east of Jordan.

2. *the Midianites*] The Moabites are not included. It would thus seem that it was the Midianites, and they only, who deliberately set themselves to work the corruption of Israel.

3. *Avenge the LORD of Midian*] The very words in which the command is given show that the war against the Midianites was no ordinary one. It was indeed less a war than the execution of a divine sentence against a most guilty people. The Midianites had corrupted, and, so far as in them lay, ruined God's people, body and soul; and had done this knowing, as after the overruling by God of Balaam's attempts to curse Israel they must have known, that in doing it they were openly rebelling against God. From God then a no less open retribution overtakes them. The employment in this work of so small a number of Israelites as 12,000 (*v.* 4) against the whole numerous nation of Midian; the selection of an equal number from each tribe irrespective of its warlike strength; the appointment of Phineas, famous for his zeal against the very sin to which the Midianites had tempted Israel, to take the lead in the war with "the holy instruments and trumpets" (*v.* 6); and the extraordinary preservation (*v.* 49) of all those engaged; are tokens that on this occasion, no less than when the cities of the plain were destroyed by fire from heaven, the hand of God directed the stroke. It is but analogous to His general dealings to scourge the Midianites through the instrumentality of their own victims.

Doubtless there were many amongst the Midianites who were personally guiltless as regards Israel. But the rulers deliberately adopted the counsel of Balaam against Israel, and their behests had been but too readily obeyed by their subjects. The sin therefore was national, and the retribution could be no less so. And such a judgment must necessarily fall on the whole people indiscriminately. It is also in this particular case obvious that to spare the male children would have prepared for Israel in a few years a nation of implacable foes.

No doubt a general license to slay at pleasure could hardly have been given without demoralizing those employed. But the commission of the Israelites in the text must not be so conceived. They had no discretion to kill or to spare. They were bidden to exterminate without mercy, and brought back to their task (*v.* 14) when they shewed signs of flinching from it. The discharge of a painful duty like this would no more necessarily tend to make the Israelites cruel than a military execution does our own soldiers. It was however a preparation for other duties of the like kind which awaited them; a proof by experiment that they had no alternative in such matters except to

† Heb. *A thousand of a tribe, a thousand of a tribe.*

4 † Of every tribe a thousand, throughout all the tribes of Israel, shall ye send to the war.

5 So there were delivered out of the thousands of Israel, a thousand of *every* tribe, twelve thousand armed for war.

6 And Moses sent them to the war, a thousand of *every* tribe, them and Phinehas the son of Eleazar the priest, to the war, with the holy instruments, and the trumpets to blow in his hand.

7 And they warred against the Midianites, as the LORD commanded Moses; and they slew all the males.

8 And they slew the kings of Midian, beside the rest of them that were slain; *namely*, [c] Evi, and Rekem, and Zur, and Hur, and Reba, five kings of Midian: Balaam also the son of Beor they slew with the sword.

c Josh. 13. 21.

9 And the children of Israel took *all* the women of Midian captives, and their little ones, and took the spoil of all their cattle, and all their flocks, and all their goods.

10 And they burnt all their cities wherein they dwelt, and all their goodly castles, with fire.

11 And they took all the spoil, and all the prey, *both* of men and of beasts.

12 And they brought the captives, and the prey, and the spoil, unto Moses, and Eleazar the priest, and unto the congregation of the children of Israel, unto the camp at the plains of Moab, which *are* by Jordan *near* Jericho.

13 ¶ And Moses, and Eleazar the priest, and all the princes of the congregation, went forth to meet them without the camp.

14 And Moses was wroth with the officers of the host, *with* the captains over thousands, and captains over hundreds, which came from the † battle.

† Heb. *host of war.*

---

fulfil the commands of God; an awful but doubtless salutary manifestation, as was afterwards the slaughter of the Canaanites, to which that of Midian is in all essential respects similar (cf. on Josh. x. Note at end of chapter), of God's wrath against sin; and a type of the future extermination of sin and sinners from His kingdom. See on the whole subject Hengstenberg, 'Authentie,' II. 471 sqq.; Reinke, 'Beiträge,' I. 351; Graves, 'On Pentateuch,' Part III. Lecture I.; Macdonald, 'On the Pentateuch,' II. 60 sqq.

5. *were delivered*] Or, "were told off." The Hebrew word is used in *v.* 16 in a somewhat different sense, but is not found elsewhere. Cf. on *v.* 16.

6. *Phinehas*] He was marked out as the fitting director of the expedition by his conduct (cf. ch. xxv.) in the matter of Zimri and Cozbi.

with the holy instruments, and the trumpets] Or rather, "with the holy instruments, to wit, the trumpets," for the trumpets themselves seem to be the instruments intended.

8. *And they slew...that were slain*] Our translators have not exhibited the distinction between the two Hebrew words here employed. Render thus: **And the kings of Midian they put to death, beside those that fell in the battle; namely,** &c. From which it would seem that beside these five, put to death after the battle, there were other Midianitish kings who perished fighting; and also that Balaam did not fall in battle, but was judicially executed. From Josh. xiii. 21 it appears that the five chieftains here mentioned were vassals of Sihon the Amorite. Cf. on xxii. 2. The name of one of them, Rekem, was bestowed by the Jews of later times upon the city of Petra; the coincidence is however in all likelihood accidental. On Balaam cf. on xxiv. 25.

10. *their goodly castles*] Render rather, both here and in Gen. xxv. 16, **hamlets.** The LXX. renders ἐπαύλεις, "pastoral enclosures." The word is derived from a word (*tōr*) signifying "a row" or "range" (cf. Ezek. xlvi. 23); and probably indicates those collections of rude dwellings, made of stones piled one on another and covered with tent-cloths, which are used by the Arabs to this day; and which are frequently mentioned as *douars* in narratives of the French campaigns in Algeria. These dwellings would be formed usually in a circle. Cf. the word "Hazeroth," and note on xi. 35.

11. *all the spoil, and all the prey*] The latter word refers to the captives and live-stock: the former to the ornaments and other effects. In 1 Sam. xv. 19 however the Amalekite live-stock is included under the general term of "spoil."

12. *by Jordan near Jericho*] Literally "by the Jericho Jordan." Cf. on xxii. 1.

15 And Moses said unto them, Have ye saved all the women alive?

16 Behold, [d] these caused the children of Israel, through the [e] counsel of Balaam, to commit trespass against the LORD in the matter of Peor, and there was a plague among the congregation of the LORD.

[d] chap. 25. 2.
[e] 2 Pet. 2. 15.

17 Now therefore [f] kill every male among the little ones, and kill every woman that hath known man by lying with † him.

[f] Judg. 21. 11.
† Heb. *a male.*

18 But all the women children, that have not known a man by lying with him, keep alive for yourselves.

19 And do ye abide without the camp seven days: whosoever hath killed any person, and [g] whosoever hath touched any slain, purify *both* yourselves and your captives on the third day, and on the seventh day.

[g] chap. 19. 11, &c.

20 And purify all *your* raiment, and all † that is made of skins, and all work of goats' *hair*, and all things made of wood.

† Heb. *instrument*, or, *vessel of skins.*

21 ¶ And Eleazar the priest said unto the men of war which went to the battle, This *is* the ordinance of the law which the LORD commanded Moses;

22 Only the gold, and the silver, the brass, the iron, the tin, and the lead,

23 Every thing that may abide the fire, ye shall make *it* go through the fire, and it shall be clean: nevertheless it shall be purified with the water of separation: and all that abideth not the fire ye shall make go through the water.

24 And ye shall wash your clothes on the seventh day, and ye shall be clean, and afterward ye shall come into the camp.

25 ¶ And the LORD spake unto Moses, saying,

26 Take the sum of the prey † that was taken, *both* of man and of beast, thou, and Eleazar the priest, and the chief fathers of the congregation:

† Heb. *of the captivity.*

27 And divide the prey into two parts; between them that took the war upon them, who went out to battle, and between all the congregation:

28 And levy a tribute unto the LORD of the men of war which went out to battle: one soul of five hundred, *both* of the persons, and of the beeves, and of the asses, and of the sheep:

29 Take *it* of their half, and give *it* unto Eleazar the priest, *for* an heave offering of the LORD.

30 And of the children of Israel's half, thou shalt take one portion of fifty, of the persons, of the beeves, of the asses, and of the ‖ flocks, of all manner of beasts, and give them unto the Levites, which keep the charge of the tabernacle of the LORD.

‖ Or, *goats.*

31 And Moses and Eleazar the priest did as the LORD commanded Moses.

32 And the booty, *being* the rest of the prey which the men of war had caught, was six hundred thousand and seventy thousand and five thousand sheep,

---

16. *caused...to commit trespass*] On this verse see Note at end of the chapter.

19. *and your captives*] Their captivity rendered them to some extent a constituent part of the Israelitish people. Like the warriors therefore they needed purification.

on the third day, and on the seventh day] According to the law set forth in xix. 12.

22. *brass*] Render **copper**: Cf. on Gen. *v.* 22. The verse is curious as illustrating the variety of metals in use at this early date for domestic purposes. All these metals were common in Egypt centuries before the date of the Exodus.

29. *an heave-offering*] Render simply **an offering**, and cf. on xviii. 24. The verb from which the word here rendered "heave-offering" is derived, is rightly translated "levy" in *v.* 28.

32. Render rather, "And the prey" (*i.e.* the live prey, the word being the same as in *v.* 11) "in addition to the plunder which the men of war seized, &c." The "plunder" of this verse is that named "spoil" in *v.* 11, and described more particularly in *v.* 50.

The numbers of sheep, beeves, asses, and persons taken are given in this and following verses in round thousands. Hence the Lord's

33 And threescore and twelve thousand beeves,

34 And threescore and one thousand asses,

35 And thirty and two thousand persons in all, of women that had not known man by lying with him.

36 And the half, *which was* the portion of them that went out to war, was in number three hundred thousand and seven and thirty thousand and five hundred sheep:

37 And the LORD's tribute of the sheep was six hundred and threescore and fifteen.

38 And the beeves *were* thirty and six thousand; of which the LORD's tribute *was* threescore and twelve.

39 And the asses *were* thirty thousand and five hundred; of which the LORD's tribute *was* threescore and one.

40 And the persons *were* sixteen thousand; of which the LORD's tribute *was* thirty and two persons.

41 And Moses gave the tribute, *which was* the LORD's heave offering, unto Eleazar the priest, as the LORD commanded Moses.

42 And of the children of Israel's half, which Moses divided from the men that warred,

43 (Now the half *that pertained unto* the congregation was three hundred thousand and thirty thousand *and* seven thousand and five hundred sheep,

44 And thirty and six thousand beeves,

45 And thirty thousand asses and five hundred,

46 And sixteen thousand persons;)

47 Even of the children of Israel's half, Moses took one portion of fifty, *both* of man and of beast, and gave them unto the Levites, which kept the charge of the tabernacle of the LORD; as the LORD commanded Moses.

48 ¶ And the officers which *were* over thousands of the host, the captains of thousands, and captains of hundreds, came near unto Moses:

49 And they said unto Moses, Thy servants have taken the sum of the men of war which *are* under our †charge, and there lacketh not one man of us. † Heb. *hand.*

50 We have therefore brought an oblation for the LORD, what every man hath †gotten, of jewels of gold, chains, and bracelets, rings, earrings, and tablets, to make an atonement for our souls before the LORD. † Heb. *found.*

51 And Moses and Eleazar the priest took the gold of them, *even* all wrought jewels.

52 And all the gold of the †offering that they offered up to the LORD, of the captains of thousands, and of the captains of hundreds, was sixteen thousand seven hundred and fifty shekels. † Heb. *heave offering.*

---

tribute (*vv.* 29, 37, 38, &c.), being the five-hundredth part of the half, comes out also in round numbers. Probably indeed this tribute, set apart at the time, formed the basis of the subsequent record; and upon it the warriors' share, and the general totals, were calculated by multiplication. The enormous amount both of live stock and of personal ornament was characteristic of the Midianites. When they invaded Israel in the days of the Judges, their wealth was still of the same kind (Judg. vi. 5, viii. 24 sqq.). The Bedouins, notwithstanding their wild nomadic life, retain their ancestral love of finery to this present day.

49. *there lacketh not one man of us*] There is no mention of any resistance on the part of the Midianites. Probably they were routed by a sudden attack. The Israelites saw in this a proof that the Lord had been with them in the work, and hence the free-will oblation of *v.* 50.

50. *chains*] *i.e.* "armlets," as in 2 Sam. i. 10.

rings] Specially, "finger-rings," or "seal-rings;" cf. Ex. xxxv. 22.

tablets] Worn suspended from the neck; see *ibid.*

to make an atonement for our souls before the LORD] Cf. Ex. xxx. 11—16. The atonement was not for any special offence committed (which would have called for a sacrifice of blood-shedding), but rather like the half-shekel given at the census in Ex. *l. c.*, was an acknowledgment of having received undeserved mercies. These, if unacknowledged, would have entailed guilt on the soul.

52. *sixteen thousand seven hundred and fifty shekels*] In value about 20,000*l.* See on vii. 84 sqq.

53 (*For* the men of war had taken
spoil, every man for himself.)
54 And Moses and Eleazar the
priest took the gold of the captains
of thousands and of hundreds, and
brought it into the tabernacle of the
congregation, *for* a memorial for the
children of Israel before the LORD.

---

53. This verse seems to imply that the soldiers, as distinct from the officers (cf. *v.* 49), did not make any offering from their plunder. Of course besides the gold there would be much spoil of less precious materials; see *vv.* 20, 22.

NOTE on CHAP. XXXI. 16.

The word here (מסר) is the one to which attention was drawn at *v.* 5. It means literally "to deliver," or "give;" and so to communicate or teach. Arab. مسر, eduxit, prodire fecit, incitavit, Freytag. Here the passage more closely rendered would run: "became to the children of Israel for a cause" (or "incitement," Dr Lee, 'Lex.' sub v.) "of treachery to the Lord."

CHAPTER XXXII.

1 *The Reubenites and Gadites sue for their inheritance on that side Jordan.* 6 *Moses reproveth them.* 16 *They offer him conditions to his content.* 33 *Moses assigneth them the land.* 39 *They conquer it.*

NOW the children of Reuben
and the children of Gad had a
very great multitude of cattle: and
when they saw the land of Jazer, and
the land of Gilead, that, behold, the
place *was* a place for cattle;
2 The children of Gad and the
children of Reuben came and spake
unto Moses, and to Eleazar the priest,
and unto the princes of the congregation, saying,
3 Ataroth, and Dibon, and Jazer,
and Nimrah, and Heshbon, and Elealeh, and Shebam, and Nebo, and Beon,
4 *Even* the country which the
LORD smote before the congregation
of Israel, *is* a land for cattle, and thy
servants have cattle:
5 Wherefore, said they, if we
have found grace in thy sight, let this
land be given unto thy servants for
a possession, *and* bring us not over
Jordan.
6 ¶ And Moses said unto the children of Gad and to the children of
Reuben, Shall your brethren go to
war, and shall ye sit here?
7 And wherefore † discourage ye † Heb. *break.*
the heart of the children of Israel
from going over into the land which
the LORD hath given them?
8 Thus did your fathers, when I
sent them from Kadesh-barnea to see
the land.
9 For ª when they went up unto ª chap. 13. 24.
the valley of Eshcol, and saw the
land, they discouraged the heart of

CHAP. XXXII. The record of the last war to the east of the Jordan is followed by the assignment of the lands already conquered to the tribes of Reuben and Gad and to certain families of the tribe of Manasseh.

1. *the land of Jazer*] Cf. on xxi. 32. This district, although included in the land of Gilead, seems to have had especial attractions for the Israelitish settlers; and hence possibly the previous and special notice of its occupation after the victory of Jahaz. It was moreover the first district in Gilead which the Israelites invaded.

a place for cattle] All travellers in Gilead, the modern Belka, bear witness to its richness as compared with the country to the west of the Jordan. Its general character is that of an upland pasture, undulating and thickly timbered. In the last respect its northern portions excel its southern; but for fertility of soil the southern province is preferred by the Arabs, in whose lips it has passed into a proverb: "Thou canst not find a country like the Belka." Cf. Tristram, 'Land of Israel,' p. 541 sqq.

3. Respecting the places here mentioned see on *vv.* 34—38. Shebam is the same with Shibmah: Beon with Baal-meon.

8. *your fathers*] The generation of the Exodus was now substantially extinct. Cf. xxvi. 64, 65.

Kadesh-barnea] On the site of Kadesh, see Note at end of ch. xiii.: on Barnea, see Note at end of this chapter.

the children of Israel, that they should
not go into the land which the LORD
had given them.
10 And the LORD's anger was kindled the same time, and he sware,
saying,
11 Surely none of the men that
came up out of Egypt, [b]from twenty
years old and upward, shall see the
land which I sware unto Abraham,
unto Isaac, and unto Jacob; because
they have not [†]wholly followed me:
12 Save Caleb the son of Jephunneh the Kenezite, and Joshua the
son of Nun: for they have wholly
followed the LORD.
13 And the LORD's anger was kindled against Israel, and he made them
wander in the wilderness forty years,
until all the generation, that had done
evil in the sight of the LORD, was
consumed.
14 And, behold, ye are risen up
in your fathers' stead, an increase of
sinful men, to augment yet the fierce
anger of the LORD toward Israel.
15 For if ye turn away from after
him, he will yet again leave them in
the wilderness; and ye shall destroy
all this people.
16 ¶ And they came near unto
him, and said, We will build sheepfolds here for our cattle, and cities for
our little ones:
17 But we ourselves will go ready
armed before the children of Israel,
until we have brought them unto
their place: and our little ones shall
dwell in the fenced cities because of
the inhabitants of the land.
18 We will not return unto our
houses, until the children of Israel
have inherited every man his inheritance.
19 For we will not inherit with
them on yonder side Jordan, or forward; because our inheritance is fallen
to us on this side Jordan eastward.
20 ¶ And [c]Moses said unto them,
If ye will do this thing, if ye will go
armed before the LORD to war,
21 And will go all of you armed
over Jordan before the LORD, until
he hath driven out his enemies from
before him,
22 And the land be subdued before the LORD: then afterward ye
shall return, and be guiltless before
the LORD, and before Israel; and
this land shall be your possession before the LORD.
23 But if ye will not do so, behold, ye have sinned against the
LORD: and be sure your sin will find
you out.
24 Build you cities for your little
ones, and folds for your sheep; and
do that which hath proceeded out of
your mouth.
25 And the children of Gad and
the children of Reuben spake unto
Moses, saying, Thy servants will do
as my lord commandeth.
26 Our little ones, our wives, our
flocks, and all our cattle, shall be
there in the cities of Gilead:
27 [d]But thy servants will pass over,
every man armed for war, before the
LORD to battle, as my lord saith.
28 So concerning them Moses commanded Eleazar the priest, and Joshua the son of Nun, and the chief
fathers of the tribes of the children of
Israel:

[b] chap. 14. 28, 29.
[†] Heb. *fulfilled after me.*
[c] Josh. 1. 13.
[d] Josh. 4. 12.

---

12. *the Kenezite*] Cf. 1 Chron. iv. 13 sqq.; and ch. xiii. 6 and note.

19. *on yonder side Jordan...on this side Jordan*] The expressions in the Hebrew differ but slightly (*me-eber lay-yarden—me-eber hay-yarden*). And in *v.* 32 the latter is actually used of the district west of Jordan, though here applied to that east of it. The terms are therefore used with some laxity (cf. on Deut. i. 1), and are here accordingly defined by the addition of "forward" and "eastward" respectively.

23. *be sure your sin will find you out*] Lit. "know ye of your sin that it will find you out." Moses implies that their sin would eventually bring its own punishment along with it.

27. *before the LORD*] *i.e.* immediately in front of the sacred tokens of the Lord's presence; cf. x. 18—21.

28. *Moses commanded*] Moses gives the necessary instructions to those intrusted with the duty of making the partition (cf. xxxiv. 17 sqq.). It was only when the nine and a

29 And Moses said unto them, If
the children of Gad and the children
of Reuben will pass with you over
Jordan, every man armed to battle,
before the LORD, and the land shall
be subdued before you; then ye shall
give them the land of Gilead for a
possession:
30 But if they will not pass over
with you armed, they shall have possessions among you in the land of
Canaan.
31 And the children of Gad and
the children of Reuben answered,
saying, As the LORD hath said unto
thy servants, so will we do.
32 We will pass over armed before
the LORD into the land of Canaan,
that the possession of our inheritance
on this side Jordan *may be* ours.
33 And [e] Moses gave unto them, [e] Deut. 3.
even to the children of Gad, and to 12. Josh. 13
the children of Reuben, and unto half & 22. 4.
the tribe of Manasseh the son of Joseph, the kingdom of Sihon king of
the Amorites, and the kingdom of
Og king of Bashan, the land, with
the cities thereof in the coasts, *even*
the cities of the country round about.
34 ¶ And the children of Gad
built Dibon, and Ataroth, and Aroer,
35 And Atroth, Shophan, and Jaazer, and Jogbehah,
36 And Beth-nimrah, and Beth-
haran, fenced cities: and folds for
sheep.

---

half tribes received their inheritance in western Canaan, that the two tribes and a half, having fulfilled the conditions required of them, formally entered into possession of Gilead and Bashan, *v.* 32; cf. Deut. iii. 12—20. Then too, no doubt, the boundaries of their respective allotments were determined.

33. *half the tribe of Manasseh*] This half tribe, consisting, as appears from *vv.* 39 sqq., of the families of Machir, is here mentioned for the first time. It would seem that Moses, when assigning to the pastoral tribes the inheritance which they desired, took opportunity at the same time to appropriate to these Manassites specially the district they had already subdued. Thus the whole of the conquered country was provisionally disposed of, and the forwardness and valour of the Machirites rewarded. It seems clear from *v.* 39 and Josh. xvii. 1, that the claims of the Machirites arose simply out of their exploits.

34—36. Settlements formed forthwith by the Gadites. The cities here named fall into three groups.

34. The leading city of the first group is *Dibon*, cf. xxi. 30; called, from the possession which the Gadites now took of it, Dibon-gad, xxxiii. 45, 46. It lay four miles north of the Arnon; and its extensive ruins still bear the name Dhîbân. It was here that the Moabite stone was discovered by the Rev. T. Klein, in 1868. According to a very probable restoration of two letters missing at the end of the first line of the inscription on the stone, Chemoshgad (= "he whose good fortune is Chemosh," cf. Baal-gad, Josh. xi. 17), the father of Mesha, was a Dibonite. Dibon is reckoned as a Reubenite town, Josh. xiii. 9; whilst in Isa. xv. 2 and Jer. xlviii. 18, 22, it is spoken of as Moabite. Occupied on the first acquisition of the territory by the Gadites, and assigned by Joshua to the Reubenites, it was eventually recaptured by the Moabites, in whose hands it remained. *Ataroth*, *i.e.* "crowns," now the ruin Attârûs, on the hill to which it gives its name, was seven miles north-west of Dibon. *Aroer*, now Arâir, also in ruins, lay between Dibon and the Arnon, on the brink of the precipitous ravine through which that torrent flows. It must not be confounded with the Aroer which fell permanently to the Gadites, in front of Rabbath-Ammon, Josh. xiii. 25.

35. *Atroth, Shophan*] Write **Atroth-Shophan**, *i.e.* Atroth, or Ataroth of Shophan, or "of the burrow." The addition is made to distinguish this Ataroth from the one named in the verse preceding, from which it was probably not far distant. The four cities now named may be styled the Dibon settlement.

Jaazer] Or Jazer. See on *v.* 1. This city with the neighbouring *Jogbehah*, now Jebeiha, a ruined place seven miles to the north-east, formed the second group.

36. The third Gadite settlement lay in the valley of the Jordan, to the west of the preceding, with which it may possibly have been connected. It comprised the cities of *Beth-nimrah*, otherwise Nimrah, and *Beth-haran:* see, for both, on xxii. 1. The latter of these lay within the ground covered by the Israelitish camp, and therefore can hardly have been occupied by the Gadites till the host crossed the Jordan.

The Jaazer and Jordan settlements were eventually confirmed to the Gadites as part of their inheritance, which from them stretched away northwards. But their Dibon settle-

37 And the children of Reuben built
Heshbon, and Elealeh, and Kirjathaim,
38 And Nebo, and Baal-meon,
(their names being changed,) and
Shibmah: and †gave other names unto the cities which they builded.
39 And the children of [f]Machir the
son of Manasseh went to Gilead, and
took it, and dispossessed the Amorite
which *was* in it.
40 And Moses gave Gilead unto
Machir the son of Manasseh; and he
dwelt therein.
41 And [g]Jair the son of Manasseh
went and took the small towns thereof, and called them Havoth-jair.

† Heb. *they called by names the names of the cities.*
[f] Gen. 50. 23.
[g] Deut. 3. 14.

---

ment, which was cut off from the others, must have passed into the possession of Reuben: see Josh. xiii. 16, 17.

37, 38. The Reubenites established themselves more compactly than the Gadites. Their central city was the old Amoritish capital, Heshbon: see on xxi. 25. They occupied also *Elealeh*, now el-'Al, a mile to the north-east; *Nebo*, probably three miles to the south-west (see on xxi. 20); and *Baal-meon*, now apparently Myûn (see Burckhardt, p. 365), nearly two miles to the south. The names of the last two cities they endeavoured to change, probably on account of their idolatrous character. Of Nebo, Jerome (on Isa. xv. 2) says: "In Nebo erat Chamos idolum consecratum, quod alio nomine Baal-phegor appellatur." It was retaken by Mesha, circ. 895 B.C., as the Moabite stone records; and hence we find it spoken of by Isaiah, xv. 2, and by Jeremiah, xlviii. 1, as a Moabite town: cf. on xxi. 29. Beon (*v.* 3), or Beth-meon (Jer. xlviii. 23), may be the name by which Baal-meon was replaced. The cities, however, still bore in the days of the prophets their old designations; cf. Is. xv. 2, Ezek. xxv. 9. Baal-meon indeed would seem to have fallen into the hands of the Moabites before the days of Mesha, who speaks of himself as having there built a temple, no doubt to Chemosh, and as having fortified the town. He would seem to have made it the stronghold from which as a basis he operated in his later conquests. See Schlottmann, 'Die Siege. Mesas,' pp. 16, 17. Of the remaining two cities of the Reubenite settlement, *Kirjathaim*, which is mentioned between Elealeh and Nebo, has been sought three miles south of Heshbon, in the ruins known as et-Teim. The ancient name, which signifies "the double city," may perhaps by a false etymology have been written Kir-iathaim, have lost its initial syllable in course of time, and been corrupted into its modern form. According to Eusebius Kiriathaim is to be found in the site now called Kureiyat, on the mountain, close to Ataroth; but this would have lain within the southern Gadite settlement, and would not have been occupied as yet by the Reubenites. Lastly, *Shibmah*, more properly Sibmah, famous at a later period for its vines, cf. Isa. xvi. 8, still leaves the trace of its name in the ruins es-Sameh, four miles east of Heshbon. Thus all these Reubenite cities clustered round Heshbon; and, allowing a fair space round each, the extent of the Reubenite settlement would be about one-tenth of the extent of their eventual inheritance. They probably at the partition retained all these cities with the exception of Heshbon itself, which, passing to the Levites, was thenceforth reckoned as within the tribe of Gad.

It is obvious that neither the Reubenites nor the Gadites were the founders of the cities of which they thus took possession, and which the text describes them as "building." They probably fortified them, for the first time or afresh, so as to render them places of safety for their families during the campaigns on the other side of the Jordan; and provided them with all conveniences for their flocks and herds.

39. *the children of Machir*] Machir, the son of Manasseh, was long since dead: even his sons had been brought up upon Joseph's knees (Gen. l. 23). But the renown acquired by his descendants raised his family almost to the dignity of a tribe; and the Machirites are in the next verse styled Machir, just as the children of Judah, or of Ephraim are often spoken of as Judah or Ephraim. So in Judg. v. 14 Machir is coupled with Ephraim and Zebulun.

went] *i.e.* "had gone:" the statement is preparatory to the ensuing record of the grant to them of the land they had won.

Gilead] More strictly part of north Gilead; which, though inhabited by the Amorites, had belonged to the kingdom of Og. Respecting this use of the name Gilead for the territory of the Machirites, see on xxvi. 29.

41. *Jair*] On his pedigree cf. on xxvii. 1. He was, through his father's mother, a descendant of Machir, though not of Gilead; but while reckoned, on her account, a Manassite, he traced up his ancestry in the male line to the more illustrious family of Judah. His own exploits—he was the conqueror of Argob, Deut. iii. 14—gave new lustre to his name; and the fame of the family is attested by the history of Jair the Israelitish judge, doubtless a descendant; perhaps also by the mention of Jairus, St Luke viii. 41, the ruler of the synagogue at the neighbouring city of Capernaum.

42 And Nobah went and took Kenath, and the villages thereof, and called it Nobah, after his own name.

Havoth-jair] That is, the villages, or rather groups of tents, or "kraals," of Jair. The term probably springs from an Arabic root, signifying "to collect;" and suggests that the "towns" in question had peculiar characteristics. The original "havoth-jair" were twenty-three in number, 1 Chron. ii. 22: in the days of the younger Jair, to whom they probably descended by inheritance, they either had increased to thirty, or were reckoned at that round number, Judg. x. 4. The western Israelites had however but an imperfect knowledge of this district, which was moreover crowded with towns. The Arabs reckon more than 1000 now deserted towns in the Hauran alone. (See Buckingham and Seetzen, in Knobel, in loc.) Hence the appellation Havoth-jair was sometimes extended to more distant portions of the Machirite domain; to Argob with its threescore fortified cities, the very reverse, in their structure, of "havoth;" and to Kenath, of which, *v.* 42, not Jair but Nobah was the conqueror (see Deut. iii. 14; Josh. xiii. 30; 1 Chron. ii. 23). This inaccuracy as to a remote district may be illustrated by our use of the name Connaught, originally the territory of the sept of the McNaughts, but now denoting the whole western province of Ireland.

42. *Nobah*] Scripture mentions him no more, but he is the hero of various extravagant legends in the Samaritan Book of Joshua; which may possibly in part have sprung out of authentic local traditions.

Kenath] Now Kenawât, an important site near the southern extremity of the tract el-Lejah, and on the western slopes of the mountains of the Haurân. Its ruins, chiefly however of the Roman era, attest its former grandeur; and extend for about a mile along the precipitous bank of a deep and wild ravine. The country round is richly wooded. The city is apparently called Nobah after its conqueror in Judg. viii. 11; but this name, as in other cases, fell ere long into disuse, and the old name has held its ground to this day.

The notices, both Scriptural and traditional, of the conquest of north-eastern Gilead and Bashan by the Machirites, plainly intimate that it was effected by a few chiefs of great military prowess, who overran rapidly a far larger district than they could colonize. The tribe of Manasseh was the least numerous of all at Sinai, and only stood sixth in the census recently held (chap. xxvi.); yet it eventually received on the west of Jordan a territory as large on the average as fell to the other tribes, beside the district here allotted to the Machirites. The father of Jair, however, Segub, was of the tribe of Judah (1 Chron. ii. 21, 22, cf. ch. xxvii. 1, and note); and it is likely that the Manassite leaders induced many of the more adventurous of this, and some possibly of other tribes, to join them in their enterprise against Bashan. The remarkable notice in Josh. xix. 34 (see note) points to a settlement of the children of Judah as then existing in the very district in question; and thus too the fact, recorded Josh. xix. 9, that the main body of the tribe of Judah proved insufficient to occupy the inheritance assigned to them, may be accounted for.

It appears from Josh. xiii. 13 (see note) that the Machirites did not exterminate the whole population of this district. Probably they destroyed (cf. xxi. 35) only the dominant heathen tribe through which Og held sway, and merely put to tribute the subject race or races, as Og had done before. The conquest of the district east of Jordan seems never to have been so effectually accomplished as that on the other side. It was indeed no part of the inheritance originally promised (cf. xxxiv. 1—15), and was first swept away by the storm of heathen invasion (1 Chr. v. 26).

During the troublous times of the Judges the eastern Manassites rendered good service to the nation; cf. Judg. v. 14. Gideon, and probably Jephthah, were of this tribe, and reflect in a later generation the warlike and adventurous spirit which Jair and Nobah exhibited in the days of Moses. On the contrary, the apathy of the pastoral tribes of Reuben and Gad is more than once censured (Judg. v. 15—17, viii. 4—9).

NOTE on Chap. xxxii. 8.

Kadesh Barnea. The meaning of the term Barnea is uncertain. In xxxiv. 4 the LXX. renders Κάδης τοῦ Βαρνή, which suggests the notion that Barnea was regarded as a man's name. Elsewhere however the LXX. gives Κάδης Βαρνή. Fürst proposes, בר־נוע = "Son of Wandering:" *i.e.* Bedouin. But the word בר in the sense of "Son" does not occur in the Pentateuch. Others prefer to take בר as from ברר, and render it "country" or "land," as it is probably to be rendered in Job xxxix. 4. The other half of the word

(נוע) is derived from a word signifying to "move to and fro," or "to be shaken." Possibly the name carries the tradition of some great natural convulsion which happened in the district. Have we an allusion to Barnea, understood according to the last derivation, in Ps. xxix. 8: "The Lord shaketh the wilderness of Cades"? The Hebrew word however there used is not נוע.

CHAPTER XXXIII.

1 *Two and forty journeys of the Israelites.* 50 *The Canaanites are to be destroyed.*

THESE *are* the journeys of the
children of Israel, which went
forth out of the land of Egypt with
their armies under the hand of Moses
and Aaron.

2 And Moses wrote their goings
out according to their journeys by
the commandment of the LORD: and
these *are* their journeys according to
their goings out.

[a] Exod. 12. 3 And they [a]departed from Ra-
37. meses in the first month, on the fifteenth day of the first month; on the
morrow after the passover the children of Israel went out with an high
hand in the sight of all the Egyptians.

4 For the Egyptians buried all
their firstborn, which the LORD had
smitten among them: upon their gods
also the LORD executed judgments.

5 And the children of Israel removed from Rameses, and pitched in
Succoth.

[b] Exod. 13. 6 And they departed from [b]Suc-
20. coth, and pitched in Etham, which *is*
in the edge of the wilderness.

7 And they removed from Etham,
and turned again unto Pi-hahiroth,
which *is* before Baal-zephon: and
they pitched before Migdol.

8 And they departed from before
Pi-hahiroth, and [c]passed through the [c] Exod. 15.
midst of the sea into the wilderness, 2.
and went three days' journey in the
wilderness of Etham, and pitched in
Marah.

9 And they removed from Marah,
and [d]came unto Elim: and in Elim [d] Exod. 15.
were twelve fountains of water, and 27.
threescore and ten palm trees; and
they pitched there.

10 And they removed from Elim,
and encamped by the Red sea.

11 And they removed from the
Red sea, and encamped in the [e]wil- [e] Exod. 16.
derness of Sin. 1.

12 And they took their journey
out of the wilderness of Sin, and encamped in Dophkah.

13 And they departed from Dophkah, and encamped in Alush.

14 And they removed from Alush,
and encamped at [f]Rephidim, where [f] Exod. 17.
was no water for the people to 1.
drink.

15 And they departed from Rephi-
dim, and pitched in the [g]wilderness [g] Exod. 19.
of Sinai. 1.

CHAP. XXXIII. 1—49. The history of the Wandering in the Desert is closed by a list of the places occupied by the Israelite encampment from the exodus to the arrival at the Jordan. This list was written out by Moses at God's command (*v.* 2), doubtless as a memorial of God's providential care for His people throughout this long and trying period. On it see Introd. § 4.

3. *Rameses*] See on Ex. i. 11 and xii. 37.

4. *buried*] Rather, **were burying.**

5. *Succoth*] See on Ex. xii. 37.

6. *Etham*] Cf. on Ex. xiv. 2.

8. *Pi-hahiroth*] Hebr. "Hahiroth;" but perhaps only by an error of transcription. The omitted "pi" is however only a common Egyptian prefix. See on Ex. xiv. 2.

wilderness of Etham] *i.e.* that part of the great wilderness of Shur which adjoined Etham: cf. on Ex. xv. 22 and ch. x. 12. The list of stations up to that at Sinai agrees with the narrative of Exodus except that we have here mentioned (*v.* 10) an encampment by the Red Sea, and two others, Dophkah and Alush (*vv.* 12—14), which are there omitted. On these places, and on the route followed by the Israelites from the Red Sea to Sinai, see on Ex. xv. Note at end of chapter.

16 And they removed from the
h chap. 11. 34. desert of Sinai, and pitched [h]at ‖Ki-
‖ That is, The graves of lust. broth-hattaavah.
17 And they departed from Ki-
i chap. 11. 35. broth-hattaavah, and [i]encamped at
Hazeroth.
18 And they departed from Hazeroth, and pitched in Rithmah.
19 And they departed from Rithmah, and pitched at Rimmon-parez.
20 And they departed from Rimmon-parez, and pitched in Libnah.
21 And they removed from Libnah, and pitched at Rissah.
22 And they journeyed from Rissah, and pitched in Kehelathah.
23 And they went from Kehelathah, and pitched in mount Shapher.
24 And they removed from mount
Shapher, and encamped in Haradah.
25 And they removed from Haradah, and pitched in Makheloth.
26 And they removed from Makheloth, and encamped at Tahath.
27 And they departed from Tahath, and pitched at Tarah.
28 And they removed from Tarah,
and pitched in Mithcah.
29 And they went from Mithcah,
and pitched in Hashmonah.
30 And they departed from Hash-
monah, and [k]encamped at Moseroth. k Deut. 10. 6.

16, 17. See on xi. 35.

18. *Rithmah*] The name of this station is derived from *retem*, the broom-plant, the "juniper" of the A.V.; see on xiii. 26. This must be the same encampment as that which is said, xiii. 26, to have been at Kadesh.

19. *Rimmon-parez*] Or rather **Rimmon-perez**, *i.e.* "Rimmon (*i.e.* the Pomegranate) of the Breach." The term *perez* is used either of hostile irruption (Ps. cxliv. 14) or (cf. Perez-uzzah, 2 Sam. vi. 8) of the outbreak of God's wrath (Job xvi. 14). Possibly the encampment of Rimmon-perez witnessed some signal manifestation of Divine anger. It may have been here that the sedition of Korah occurred.

From this verse to *v.* 36 the stations named are those visited during the years of penal wandering. The determination of their positions is difficult, because during this period there was no definite line of march pursued. Some identifications are rendered probable by modern research, which may hereafter suggest others. All indications thus far seem to show that the Israelites during this period did not overstep the boundaries of the Wilderness of Paran (as defined x. 12), except to pass along the adjoining valley of the Arabah. Over the ridges of Paran then it is probable that for many years the people spread, while the tabernacle and organized camp moved about from place to place amongst them (cf. on xx. 1).

20. *Libnah*] Probably the Laban of Deut. i. 1 (where see note), and situated on or near either the Elanitic gulf or the Arabah. The name is perhaps preserved, though in a corrupted form, in el-Beyâneh, the designation of a part of the mountain-plateau and adjacent valley, on the west of the Arabah, north of Ezion-geber. The Hebrew name signifies "whiteness:" the modern Arabic, "the distinct." It is by some connected with the white poplar tree, which possibly grew abundantly in the neighbourhood. If so derived, this and the two preceding names of stations have been all suggested by some natural feature of vegetation. See Stanley, 'S. and P.' p. 521.

21. *Rissah*] This may perhaps be identified with the Rasa of the Roman tables; which, being about 30 miles from Elath on the road to Jerusalem, must have lain on the plateau of the wilderness, near to the hill now known as Râs-el-Kâ'a, "Head of the plain," north-west of Ezion-geber, and west or south-west of el-Beyâneh.

22. *Kehelathah*] *i.e.* "assembling." The name was evidently given to the station by the Israelites themselves; and is not likely to have been locally preserved. See on xx. 1.

23. *mount Shapher*] Probably either the hill now known as Jebel-esh-Shureif, about 40 miles north-west of Râs-el-Kâ'a (see on ver. 21); or else that known as Jebel-Sherâfeh, a rocky promontory on the western shore of the Elanitic gulf, near the southern limit of the Tîh. The former is, from its position, the more likely (see von Schubert, II. p. 372).

24. *Haradah*] Probably Wâdy-el-Kharâizeh, about 15 miles south-east of Jebel-esh-Shureif.

25. *Makheloth*] "Assemblies" or "congregations:" a kindred name to Kehelathah, *v.* 22.

28. *Mithcah*] The name (= "sweetness:" cf. with *Marah* = "bitterness") probably points to the excellence of the water at this station.

29. *Hashmonah*] Probably the Heshmon of Josh. xv. 27, one of "the uttermost cities of the tribe of the children of Judah toward the coast of Edom southward;" and which therefore, like another of the same cities,

31 And they departed from Moseroth, and pitched in Bene-jaakan.
32 And they removed from Bene-jaakan, and encamped at Hor-hagidgad.
33 And they went from Hor-hagidgad, and pitched in Jotbathah.
34 And they removed from Jotbathah, and encamped at Ebronah.

Kedesh, may well have lain without the natural frontier of the Holy Land, in the extreme north of the wilderness. Such is the actual situation of the fountain Ain Hasb, in the north-west of the Arabah; where there is said to be a natural pool filled with sweet living water, surrounded by much verdure, and with traces of ruins (Robinson, 'Bib. Res.' II. 119; Wilton, 'Negeb,' pp. 121 sqq.).

30. *Moseroth*] For this plural form of the name we have, Deut. x. 6, the simple Moserah (A. V. *Mosera*). It would seem from that passage that the station lay in the neighbourhood of the mountain on which Aaron died; cf. on xx. 22. It was perhaps opposite to it, on the western side of the Arabah, under the mountain-bluff, now known as el-Makrâh. Some have thought indeed that the name is perpetuated in that of the hill Maderah, much further north, an isolated mount of singular shape, forming the point of separation between Wady-el-Fikreh and the lower portion of Wady-el-Marrah (see on xxxiv. 3 sqq.). This hill is about a mile in circumference, steep, and perfectly bare. It consists in part of a brittle mixture of chalk and sandstone, in part of strata of earth, which might, by reason of their colour and formation, be easily taken for ashes baked together. At its foot lie an astonishing quantity of large lens-shaped stones, such as are also found near the southern extremity f the Dead Sea. Arab tradition relates that a city once stood on this spot, and that for the sins of its inhabitants it was destroyed by the fall of these stones from heaven (Seetzen, III. pp. 14 sqq.); or, according to another account, that the earth engulphed the inhabitants alive, and that the hill subsequently rose up as a monument of God's displeasure. It is remarkable enough that the name Moserah itself signifies chastisement. Yet the resemblance of the names Maderah and Moserah is not strong enough to warrant our setting aside the tradition which fixes the scene of Aaron's death further south; and the principal interest of the Arab stories relating to the place lies in the reminiscences which they may contain of the destruction of Sodom and of the fate of Dathan and Abiram.

31. *Bene-jaakan*] *i.e.* "the children of Jaakan;" in Deut. x. 6 "Beeroth (*i.e. the wells*) of the children of Jaakan." It is there stated that "the children of Israel took their journey from Beeroth of the children of Jaakan to Mosera;" whilst here Mosera, or Moseroth, is placed first. There is nothing improbable in the supposition that the Israelites during their long wanderings visited these places twice, though Moses in this succinct list of stations names each of them only once. The order here given (Moseroth, Bene-jaakan) is perhaps that followed in the first march toward Canaan; whilst the reverse order of Deut. x. 6 (Bene-jaakan, Mosera) may have been adopted in the fortieth year when the march was differently directed. The verse in Deut. is however evidently a fragment, and probably a gloss; and its authority consequently uncertain.

Bene-jaakan] like many places in the east, derives its name from a tribe once settled in it. Jaakan, or Akan, was a Horite, of the race of the old inhabitants of Mount Seir, Gen. xxxvi. 27, 1 Chron. i. 42; and the wells of his tribe may have been those to which they repaired after their expulsion by the Edomites from their earlier homes. They may be identical with the wells of sweet water now known as el-Mayein, which, lying up high among the hills, more than 60 miles due west of Mount Hor, would be likely to be visited by the Israelites either immediately before or after their encampment at Moserah. Schwarz conjectures that the name Jaakan may itself be perpetuated, in a corrupted form, in en-Nâkah, "the she-camel," the designation now bestowed upon the important mountain to which the wells el-Mayein are contiguous.

32. *Hor-hagidgad*] If the initial Hebrew letter be *Kheth* (as in Tex. Recep., Syr., and later Targum) the name will denote "the Cavern of Gidgad;" if *He* (as some few MSS., Samaritan text, earlier Targ., LXX., Vulg. read) it will denote "the Summit of Gidgad" (see on xx. 22). In Deut. x. 7 we read simply Gudgodah or Gudgod. The corresponding Arabic term *jedjad* signifies a hard and level tract, and would be strictly applicable to the summit of one of the mountain-ranges in the wilderness. Some, misled by the English orthography of the Arabic, have thought to find this station in Wady Ghadhâghidh, "the Valley of Diminutions," about forty-five miles north-north-west of the head of the Elanitic gulf; but there is no real correspondence in the letters of this name to those of Gidgad.

33. *Jotbathah*] *i.e.* "Goodness:" in Deut. x. 7, "Jotbath (Hebr. *Jotbathah*), a land of rivers of waters." This place is perhaps to be identified with Wady Tâbah, six miles

35 And they departed from Ebronah, and encamped at Ezion-gaber.
36 And they removed from Ezion-
gaber, and pitched in the [l] wilderness
of Zin, which *is* Kadesh.
37 And they removed from [m] Kadesh, and pitched in mount Hor, in
the edge of the land of Edom.
38 And [n] Aaron the priest went up
into mount Hor at the commandment of the LORD, and died there,
in the fortieth year after the children of Israel were come out of the
land of Egypt, in the first *day* of the
fifth month.
39 And Aaron *was* an hundred
and twenty and three years old when
he died in mount Hor.
40 And [o] king Arad the Canaanite,
which dwelt in the south in the land
of Canaan, heard of the coming of
the children of Israel.
41 And they departed from mount
[p] Hor, and pitched in Zalmonah.
42 And they departed from Zalmonah, and pitched in Punon.

[l] chap. 20. 1.
[m] chap. 20. 22.
[n] chap. 20. 25. Deut. 32. 50.
[o] chap. 21. 1, &c.
[p] chap. 21. 4.

---

south-west of the head of the Elanitic gulf; where is a broad plain running down to the sea, containing many palm-trees and tamarisks, and well supplied with water (see Burckhardt, p. 507; also Laborde, and Robinson, 'B. R.' I. 160, who writes the name Tâba').

34. *Ebronah*] *i. e.* "passage." This station apparently lay on the shore of the Elanitic gulf, at a point where the ebb of the tide left a ford across. Hence the later Targum renders the word "fords."

35. *Ezion-gaber*] More properly **Ezion-geber**, *i.e.* "giant's backbone." The earlier half of this name is preserved to us, though the English orthography conceals the correspondence of the Hebrew and Arabic forms, in that of Wâdy Ghadhyân, a valley running eastward into the Arabah some miles north of the present head of the Elanitic gulf. A salt marsh which here overspreads a portion of the Arabah may be taken as indicating the limit to which the sea anciently reached; and we may thus infer the existence here in former times of an extensive tidal haven, at the head of which the city of Ezion-geber stood. The mouth of the haven was guarded, on the eastern side, by the no less well-known city of Elath: on the western side, directly opposite to Elath, was probably the site of Ebronah (*v.* 35). The name occurs on an Egyptian papyrus of the 19th Dynasty—as that of a fortress of some importance under Rameses II. See Chabas, "Voyage d'un Egyptien," p. 284. He says, "Aszium. C'est ainsi que les Arabes nomment de nos jours un petit groupe de huttes ombragées par des palmiers, situées à l'extremité septentrionale du Bahr Agabah." It was at Ezion-geber that from the time of Solomon onward the Jewish navy was constructed (1 Kings ix. 26, xxii. 49). Its importance naturally decreased as the haven was destroyed by that gradual retirement of the water, of which other examples have been observed by travellers along the shores of the Red Sea. The site of the city was unknown to Josephus, who, with disregard of all probability, transferred it more than four hundred miles further south, to the Egyptian port of Berenice ('Ant.' VIII. 6. 4). Yet at the end of the fourth century of our era we still find it mentioned, under the name "Ad Dianam," evidently a Latin corruption of the Arabic Ghadhyân, as a station on the Roman road between Aila (Elath) and Rasa (see on *v.* 21), sixteen Roman miles from each; and as marking the point at which the branch road ran off, by the east of Mount Seir, to Petra. Later mention is made of Ezion by two Arabian geographers, Makrîzy and Muhammed Ibn Ahmed (Ritter, XIV. pp. 52—4); but as they give the name in its Jewish rather than in its Arabic form, it is likely that their acquaintance with it was purely historical.

37—40. See on xx. 22—xxi. 3; and respecting the chronology, Introd. § 3. The notice that Aaron was a hundred and twenty-three years old at his death in the fortieth year of the Exodus accords with the notice of Ex. vii. 7, that he was eighty-three years old when he stood before Pharaoh.

41. *Zalmonah*] No doubt a station on the march from Kadesh round the land of Edom. The name has by some been derived from *zelem*, "image;" and this has been assigned as the place where the brazen serpent was set up. Von Raumer thinks it the same with Ma'ân, otherwise Alam Ma'ân, east of Petra, one of the largest villages on the Mekka pilgrim-route, well supplied with water and surrounded by gardens and vineyards; where the Israelites might, like the pilgrims of the present day, have conveniently trafficked with the inhabitants for provisions.

42. *Punon*] By Eusebius and Jerome, in the 'Onomasticon,' identified with the Pinon of Gen. xxxvi. 41, which they regard as the name of a ducal city rather than of a person;

43 And they departed from Punon, and pitched in Oboth.

44 And they departed from Oboth, and pitched in ‖Ije-abarim, in the border of Moab.

‖ Or, *Heaps of Abarim.*

45 And they departed from Iim, and pitched in Dibon-gad.

46 And they removed from Dibon-gad, and encamped in Almon-diblathaim.

47 And they removed from Almon-diblathaim, and pitched in the mountains of Abarim, before Nebo.

48 And they departed from the mountains of Abarim, and pitched in the plains of Moab by Jordan *near* Jericho.

49 And they pitched by Jordan, from Beth-jesimoth *even* unto ‖ *q* Abel-shittim in the plains of Moab.

‖ Or, *The plains of Shittim.* *q* chap. 25. 1.

50 ¶ And the LORD spake unto Moses in the plains of Moab by Jordan *near* Jericho, saying,

51 Speak unto the children of Israel, and say unto them, *r* When ye are passed over Jordan into the land of Canaan;

r Deut. 7. 1. Josh. 11. 2.

52 Then ye shall drive out all the inhabitants of the land from before you, and destroy all their pictures, and destroy all their molten images, and quite pluck down all their high places:

53 And ye shall dispossess *the inhabitants of* the land, and dwell therein: for I have given you the land to possess it.

54 And *s* ye shall divide the land by lot for an inheritance among your families: *and* to the more ye shall †give the more inheritance, and to the fewer ye shall †give the less inheritance: every man's *inheritance* shall be in the place where his lot falleth; according to the tribes of your fathers ye shall inherit.

s chap. 26. 53. † Heb. *multiply his inheritance.* † Heb. *diminish his inheritance.*

55 But if ye will not drive out the inhabitants of the land from before you; then it shall come to pass, that those which ye let remain of them *shall be* *t* pricks in your eyes, and thorns in your sides, and shall vex you in the land wherein ye dwell.

t Josh. 23. 13. Judg. 2. 3.

56 Moreover it shall come to pass, *that* I shall do unto you, as I thought to do unto them.

---

and further with the Phæno of their own day, a place notorious as the penal abode of convicts who were sent thither to labour in the neighbouring copper-mines. This identification is corroborated by the form Φινών in LXX. The place lay between Petra and Zoar, probably near the Roman road which connected those places. As this road, which is still visible (see Irby and Mangles, p. 115), ran considerably to the right of what would have been the direct line of march, it may be that Phæno lay east of, rather than within, the territory of Edom. It is there that we should naturally seek for Punon; and if the pilgrim-station el-Ahsa represent the ancient Oboth (see on xxi. 10), the site of Punon may coincide with that of Kala'at Aneizeh, intermediate to el-Ahsa and Ma'ân. Seetzen, when at Maderah, learnt the existence of a ruined castle Fenân (III. p. 17), which Arabic form of name would correspond to the Hebrew Punon; but the locality of this castle is not as yet ascertained.

43—47. See on xxi. 10—20.

46. *Dibon-gad*] This halt was apparently the same as that which in xxi. 19 bears the name of Bamoth: see note there.

48, 49. See on xxii. 1.

50—xxxvi. 13. This last portion of the book concludes the record of the long wandering of the people by certain directions respecting that conquest and allotment of the Promised Land, with which the wandering terminated. These regulations are divided into two sections by the re-insertion at xxxv. 1 of the introductory formula with which xxxiii. 50 opens. Of these portions the former contains commands concerning, (1) the extermination of the Canaanitish nations, xxxiii. 50—56: (2) the boundaries of the Promised Land, xxxiv. 1—15: (3) the names of the men who should allot the land, xxxiv. 16—29.

50—56. The expulsion of the Canaanites and the destruction of their monuments of idolatry had been already enjoined, Ex. xxiii. 24, 33, xxxiv. 13; and *v.* 54 is substantially a repetition from xxvi. 53—55. But the solemn warning of *vv.* 55, 56 is new. A call for it had been furnished by their past transgressions

CHAPTER XXXIV.

1 *The borders of the land.* 16 *The names of the men which shall divide the land.*

AND the LORD spake unto Moses,
saying,
2 Command the children of Israel,
and say unto them, When ye come
into the land of Canaan; (this *is* the
land that shall fall unto you for an
inheritance, *even* the land of Canaan
with the coasts thereof:)
[a] Josh. 15. 1. 3 Then [a]your south quarter shall
be from the wilderness of Zin along
by the coast of Edom, and your south
border shall be the outmost coast of
the salt sea eastward:
4 And your border shall turn from
the south to the ascent of Akrabbim,
and pass on to Zin: and the going
forth thereof shall be from the south
to Kadesh-barnea, and shall go on to
Hazar-addar, and pass on to Azmon:
5 And the border shall fetch a
compass from Azmon unto the river
of Egypt, and the goings out of it
shall be at the sea.

---

in the matter of Baal-peor, by their imperfect fulfilment, at the first, of Moses' orders in the Midianitish war; and perhaps by the indulgence of the Machirites to those whom they conquered in Bashan (cf. on xxxii. 42).

CHAP. XXXIV. The next section, (*vv.* 1—15, see on xxxiii. 50) treats of the boundaries of the land of inheritance; which will be seen greatly to exceed those of the territory actually conquered. On the limits of the Holy Land, see further on Gen. xv. 18—21; Ex. xxiii. 31; Deut. xi. 24.

2. *the land of Canaan*] The name Canaan is here restricted to the territory west of the Jordan.

3—5. Render: **Then your south quarter shall extend from the wilderness of Zin which resteth upon the side of Edom. And your south border shall start from the extremity of the salt sea on the east; and your border shall turn on the south to Maaleh-akrabbim, and shall pass on toward Zin, and the extent of its reach on the south shall be to Kadesh-barnea; and it shall reach forth thence to Hazar-addar, and shall pass on to Azmon, and from Azmon the border shall turn to the river of Egypt, and its reach shall be to the sea.**

The first few words set forth in general terms the southern boundary, which is more exactly described in the following sentence. The details of its course are more fully given, Josh. xv. 1—4; for the southern confines of Judah there described were in effect the southernmost portion of Canaan. These accounts will be best illustrated by a description, based upon the explorations of modern travellers, of the nature of the boundary.

It commenced at the Dead Sea. Of the broad and desolate valley by which the depressed bed of that sea, shut in by cliffs on both sides, is protracted toward the south, the first few miles, comprised under the general name of the Ghôr, present little else than a tract of marshy jungle. A deep narrow glen, descending from the south-west, enters this tract at its south-west corner; it is called Wâdy-el-Fikreh, bearing, perhaps, in its name the only remaining vestige of the ancient city of Epicærus. The course of this valley forms the natural division between the land of promise and the desert. On its left side, as one ascends it, the hills are, though utterly barren, comparatively low; but on the right it is flanked all the way by a steep mountain-wall varying from about 700 to 1000 feet in height, to the north of which rise ranges of much greater elevation. The route from Petra to Hebron mounts this precipice at a point about fourteen miles from the mouth of Wady el-Fikreh, by a long winding track, appropriately designated the "Pass of the Bare Rock," Nakb es-Safâh; and attesting by its difficulty how formidable was the rampart which the land of Canaan here presented to an invader. About three miles further up the valley, on its left bank, stands the isolated hill of Maderah (see on xxxiii. 30), rising, citadel-like, in the form of a truncated cone, to a height of about 500 feet. Here the head of the watercourse of Wady el-Fikreh is reached. But the valley itself is continued in the same south-western direction, under the name of Wady el-Marrah; the watercourse of which, passing south of the hill of Maderah, runs eastward, not like Wady el-Fikreh into the Ghôr, but into the higher level of the Arabah. The upper part of Wady el-Marrah is, however, grander and more striking than Wady el-Fikreh. Not only do the hills of Canaan rise as precipitously and in greater elevation on the right, jutting forth in huge irregular promontories or bastions of naked rock; but on the other side, the hills of the wilderness (which in this part are known as Jebel el-Marrah) become more lofty, and present in their terrific ruggedness an aspect which English travellers describe as

6 And *as for* the western border, ye shall even have the great sea for a border: this shall be your west border.

7 And this shall be your north border: from the great sea ye shall point out for you mount Hor:

8 From mount Hor ye shall point

---

that of a confused chaos of matter once in a boiling state and whilst so suddenly solidified. To the French traveller Callier the great depth of the valley appeared extraordinary in a district where the watercourses are often so shallow as to be scarcely recognizable. The direction of this valley continues nearly straight for about ten miles above Maderah, up to a wild ascent on the Canaanitish side called Nakb Kareb. In this we may recognize, by the resemblance of name, the ancient Maaleh-akrabbim or "Scorpion Pass." The literal Arabic rendering of Akrabbim, "scorpions," would be Akârib; and to this the modern name of the ascent comes very near. Here the Wady el-Marrah turns southward, and probably loses itself among the hills, which remain as yet unexplored. Those hills must have belonged to "the wilderness of Zin;" and Kadesh-barnea (see note at end of Chapter xiii.), which is "in the wilderness of Zin," will be, as the text implies, the southernmost point of the southern boundary. That wilderness however was probably of wide extent, and comprised the whole rugged mountain region south of Wady el-Marrah and Wady el-Fikreh, as far east as the Arabah. If this be so, it was separated by the Arabah only from the mountains of Edom; and might thus be fairly described in the text as resting upon the side or flank of the latter territory. It is possible that it may have derived its name from an Edomitish city. On the declivity of a commanding hill, within the ancient territory of Edom, there yet stands an important village bearing the name Dhâna, which, in its Arabic orthography, corresponds etymologically to Zin. Burckhardt wrongly regarded Dhâna as the Thana or Thoana of Ptolemy; which should however rather be identified with the modern eth-Thawâneh (cf. Robinson, 'B. R.' II. 168). There seems no just reason why a neighbouring part of the wilderness across the Arabah might not be named from this in the same way that a part of the wilderness east of the Red Sea was named from the Egyptian city of Etham (see on xxxiii. 8). And if the wilderness of Zin, although not strictly belonging to Edom, were yet thus regarded as connected with it, the fact would help to account for the way in which the southern cities of Judah are described as lying "toward the coast of Edom" (Josh. xv. 21).

From Kadesh, if we regard it as identical with the present Ain el-Weibeh, westward to the River, or Brook of Egypt, now Wady el-Arîsh (see on x. 12), is a distance of about seventy miles. In this interval the book of Numbers names two points of the boundary-line: Hazar-addar and Azmon. The book of Joshua for Hazar-addar substitutes Hezron and Addar (A. V. *Adar*), the former being perhaps the general name of a district of *Hazers*, or nomad hamlets (see on Deut. ii. 23), of which Addar was one: and, before carrying the line to Azmon, speaks of its turning to "the Karkaa" (see on Josh. xv. 3). That so many points are named in so short a line is due perhaps to the familiarity which the Israelites had acquired with the district during the period of their encampment at Kadesh. It is probable, though from geographical rather than etymological considerations, that Hazar-addar is to be sought at Ain el-Kudeirât, on the northern side of the ridge which here forms the natural demarcation between Canaan and the desert. The fountain is still the source of fertility to the neighbouring fields. Azmon is identified in the later Jewish Targum with Kesam, the modern Kasâimeh, a group of springs situate in the north of one of the gaps in the ridge, and a short distance west of Ain el-Kudeirât.

The junction of the boundary line with "the River of Egypt," will fall near the spot now called el-Kasaby. Here that important watercourse, coming down from the south, bends suddenly to the west, and forms a deep and narrow gorge between the last-mentioned ridge on the north, and the mountain Helâl on the south. Its ultimate direction, after emerging from this gorge, is north-west; and it enters "the great sea" at the point where was eventually built the frontier city of Rhinocorura, now el Arîsh.

6. *for a border*] Literally, "with its border;" *i.e.* "with the border which it makes."

7—9. The northern border. On the "mount Hor," cf. on xx. 22. Here the name denotes the whole western crest of Mount Lebanon, eighty miles in length, commencing east of Zidon, and terminating with the point immediately above the entrance of Hamath (cf. on xiii. 21). To the southern end of this range a frontier-line would have to be drawn from the Mediterranean Sea; and some illustration of the description in the text may be gained from the circumstance that the great river between Tyre and Zidon, along whose westward bend such a line might be drawn, still bears a name, Kâsimîyeh, *i.e.*

out *your border* unto the entrance of
Hamath; and the goings forth of the
border shall be to Zedad:
9 ¶ And the border shall go on to
Ziphron, and the goings out of it
shall be at Hazar-enan: this shall be
your north border.
10 And ye shall point out your
east border from Hazar-enan to Shepham:
11 And the coast shall go down
from Shepham to Riblah, on the east
side of Ain; and the border shall de-
scend, and shall reach unto the †side † Heb. *shoulder.*
of the sea of Chinnereth eastward:
12 And the border shall go down
to Jordan, and the goings out of it
shall be at the salt sea: this shall be
your land with the coasts thereof
round about.

"boundary-stream." It is possible indeed (see Josh. xix. 28, &c.) that the border was intended to comprise Zidon as well as Tyre; but this is not clear; and neither of them was in fact ever acquired by Israel. The more northern portion of the Phenician plain was not within the limits, though the entire district of Cœle-Syria, between the western and eastern ranges of Lebanon, was so. Yet this district did not fall into possession of the Israelites till the days of David and Solomon; and even then they ruled over it rather than occupied it. The extreme point in the northern border of the land, as laid down by Moses, was the city of Zedad, now a large village, still bearing its ancient name (Sadad), about thirty miles east of the entrance of Hamath. Hence the border turned back south-westward to Ziphron, now Zifrân. This place, not to be confounded with ez Za'ferâneh, near Hamath, has not been as yet visited by modern travellers, but is reported to lie about forty miles north-east of Damascus, near the road to Palmyra, and to contain extensive ruins. It is probable that from Ziphron to Hazar-enan, "the fountain village," the course of the border would be still south-westward or westward; and there is no place with which Hazar-enan may be better conjecturally identified than with Ayûn ed-Dara, a fountain situate in the very heart of the great central chain of Antilibanus; the loftiest peaks of which rise up in stern grandeur around on every side (Porter, 'Damascus,' pp. 332 sqq. Its position in Van de Velde's map is lat. 33° 49', long. 36° 12', and ruins are marked at the spot). The eastern portion of the northern border thus formed a great north-eastward loop, so as to include all the declivities, both western and eastern, of the northern part of the Antilibanus range; returning however to the crest of that range at Hazar-enan, and thus excluding the plain of Damascus together with the valleys which descend toward it.

10—12. The eastern border, as here described, must be understood to commence at that point from which the boundary line pursued an uninterruptedly southward course; and its general direction may be determined from the physical features of the country, notwithstanding some uncertainty as to details. It ran at first along the mountain crest. Shepham, the first point after Hazar-enan, is unknown. Of the next, all that is certain is that it could not have been Riblah in the land of Hamath, which lay outside the northern border described in the preceding verses. But probably the true name in this passage is not Riblah at all. The Hebrew letters of the word, disengaged from the Jewish vowel-marks, are HRBLH; and if the final *h* be "*He* locale" (our English "ward"), the name may then be read Har-bel (LXX. 'Αρβηλά), *i.e.* "the Mountain of Bel;" the Har-baal-hermon of Judg. iii. 3. Bel, for Baal, is merely an Aramaism (cf. Is. xlvi. 1), and was probably the form employed by the Aramaic population that dwelt in those districts. No more striking landmark could be set forth than the summit of Hermon, the southernmost and by far the loftiest peak of the whole Antilibanus range, rising to a height of ten thousand feet, and overtopping every other mountain in the Holy Land; yet not so inaccessible but that it was crowned by heathen zeal with a sanctuary of Baal, of which the ruins, consisting of foundations of walls and of heaps of hewn stones, still remain. Should however the phrase "go down from Shepham" be deemed inconsistent with the greater elevation of Hermon, the landmark before us may still be identified with one of those numerous sanctuaries with which both ancient testimony and modern exploration shew the sides as well as the summit of the mountain to have been covered. In any case it is unlikely that the landmark named Judg. iii. 3 would be omitted here. This is here described as "on the east side of Ain," literally "the Ain," *i.e.* fountain. This Ain is understood by Jerome and the later Targums of the fountain of the Jordan; and it is in the plain at the south-western foot of Hermon that the two most celebrated sources of that river, those of Daphne and of Paneas, are situate, while from the western slopes of the same mountain there issue the streams by which its remaining and longest branch is fed.

The border next descended to the "sea of Chinnereth," better known by its later name

13 And Moses commanded the
children of Israel, saying, This *is* the
land which ye shall inherit by lot,
which the LORD commanded to give
unto the nine tribes, and to the half
tribe:
chap. 32. 14 [b]For the tribe of the children
sh. 14. 2, of Reuben according to the house of
their fathers, and the tribe of the children of Gad according to the house
of their fathers, have received *their*
inheritance; and half the tribe of Manasseh have received their inheritance:

15 The two tribes and the half
tribe have received their inheritance
on this side Jordan *near* Jericho eastward, toward the sunrising.
16 And the LORD spake unto Moses, saying,
17 These *are* the names of the
men which shall divide the land unto
you: [c]Eleazar the priest, and Joshua [c] Josh. 19.
the son of Nun. 51.
18 And ye shall take one prince of
every tribe, to divide the land by inheritance.

---

of Gennesaret, which is suppossd to be only a corruption of Chinnereth. It is not described as following the line of the Jordan; and the intention was probably that it should run parallel to it, along the line of hill about ten miles further east, bending so as to strike the lake on its north-east side or shoulder. It may be that the Manassite leaders had already overrun some of the ground which it would thus comprise (see on xxxii. 42); but that the inheritance of Naphtali was not bounded by the Jordan on the east may be inferred from the sites of some of the Naphtalite cities, as Hazor and Migdal-el (Josh. xix. 36, 38), as well as from the assertion of Josephus ('Ant.' V. 22). On the other hand, from the Lake of Gennesaret to the Dead Sea, the Jordan would have formed the natural frontier, had not the territory of Gilead been already assigned to the pastoral tribes.

10. *point out your border*] Lit. "measure off," or "mark out."

12. *with the coasts thereof round about*] *i.e.* as defined by its coasts, or borders, round about.

14, 15. *have received their inheritance*] Cf. on xxxii. 28, 33. The territory on the east of the Jordan had been assigned, as a whole, to Reuben, Gad, and Machir, though not yet partitioned among them.

on this side Jordan near Jericho] Literally, "on this side of the Jericho Jordan," as at xxii. 1, xxvi. 3, 63, xxxiii. 48, 50. The expression here is remarkable, because applied not, as elsewhere, to a limited space, but to the whole territory of the two-and-a-half tribes. Yet it is appropriate enough, for it was by the passage of the Jordan at Jericho that all the remaining inheritance would have to be reached. It is too, geographically, more accurate than would have been the simple phrase "on this side of the Jordan," for (cf. on *vv.* 10—12) the Jordan did not divide the western and eastern tribes throughout the whole of its course. It may be here observed that the effect of the conquest on the east of the Jordan would, had the whole of the promised territory fallen into Israelitish possession, have been not only to add greatly to the extent of the Israelitish domain, but also to environ on three sides the territory of Damascus. Historically this was never brought to pass till Damascus itself became tributary to Israel, and probably the settlement of so many of the Israelites in Gilead and Bashan was not without its influence in inducing the rest to view the southern expanse of Canaan as sufficient for their needs, and so to leave Hermon, Cœle-Syria, and Zedad, unconquered.

16—29. Appointment of princes from the Ten Tribes to divide the land just described. The positions of the several inheritances were to be determined by lot; but their dimensions were proportioned to the wants of the tribes to which they fell. Thus the limits of each were to be marked out after the lot had determined to which tribe it belonged, and for the due and fair adjustment of the limits the presence of a representative from each tribe was requisite. Of the representatives now selected through Moses beforehand, who were all princes, *i.e.* heads of chief families, in their respective tribes (see on xiii. 2), Caleb alone, of the tribe of Judah, is otherwise known to us (see on xiii. 4 sqq.). The order in which the tribes are named is peculiar to this passage. If they be taken in pairs, Judah and Simeon, Benjamin and Dan, Manasseh and Ephraim, Zebulun and Issachar, Asher and Naphtali, the order of the pairs agrees with the order in which the allotments in the Holy Land, taken also in couples, followed each other in the map from south to north. Moreover, these pairs are formed of two tribes otherwise mutually connected, except only that which consists of Benjamin and Dan; and even these two had been next each other in the order of march, and probably were still contiguous in their encampments (see on ch. ii.).

19 And the names of the men *are*
these: Of the tribe of Judah, Caleb
the son of Jephunneh.
20 And of the tribe of the children
of Simeon, Shemuel the son of Ammihud.
21 Of the tribe of Benjamin, Elidad the son of Chislon.
22 And the prince of the tribe of
the children of Dan, Bukki the son
of Jogli.
23 The prince of the children of
Joseph, for the tribe of the children of Manasseh, Hanniel the son
of Ephod.
24 And the prince of the tribe of
the children of Ephraim, Kemuel the
son of Shiphtan.
25 And the prince of the tribe of
the children of Zebulun, Elizaphan
the son of Parnach.
26 And the prince of the tribe of
the children of Issachar, Paltiel the
son of Azzan.
27 And the prince of the tribe of
the children of Asher, Ahihud the
son of Shelomi.
28 And the prince of the tribe of
the children of Naphtali, Pedahel the
son of Ammihud.
29 These *are they* whom the LORD
commanded to divide the inheritance
unto the children of Israel in the land
of Canaan.

CHAPTER XXXV.

1 *Eight and forty cities for the Levites with their suburbs, and measure thereof.* 6 *Six of them are to be cities of refuge.* 9 *The laws of murder.* 31 *No satisfaction for murder.*

AND the LORD spake unto Moses
in the plains of Moab by Jordan
near Jericho, saying,
2 [a]Command the children of Israel, that they give unto the Levites
of the inheritance of their possession
cities to dwell in; and ye shall give
also unto the Levites suburbs for the
cities round about them.
3 And the cities shall they have to
dwell in; and the suburbs of them
shall be for their cattle, and for their
goods, and for all their beasts.
4 And the suburbs of the cities,
which ye shall give unto the Levites,
shall reach from the wall of the city
and outward a thousand cubits round
about.
5 And ye shall measure from without the city on the east side two
thousand cubits, and on the south
side two thousand cubits, and on the
west side two thousand cubits, and
on the north side two thousand cubits; and the city *shall be* in the
midst: this shall be to them the
suburbs of the cities.
6 And among the cities which ye
shall give unto the Levites *there shall*

[a] Josh. 21. 2.

CHAP. XXXV. 1—xxxvi. 13. These chapters constitute the second division of those final regulations which complete the book: cf. on xxxiii. 50. They contain (1) the appointment of cities for the residence of the Levites, *vv.* 1—8; (2) the nomination of Cities of Refuge, *vv.* 9—34; (3) enactments, supplementary to those of xxviii. 6 sqq., and relating to the marriage of heiresses, xxxvi. 1—13.

2. *suburbs*] Render rather (with Gesen., Knob., Keil, &c.) "pasture-grounds."

3. *for their cattle, and for their goods, and for all their beasts*] More strictly, "for their large cattle, for their sheep and goats, and for all their beasts whatsoever they be."

5. *from without the city*] Render, **without the city**. The demarcation here intended would run parallel to the wall of the city, outside which it was made. The object was apparently to secure that the preceding provision should be fairly and fully carried out. The "suburb" would thus extend for a distance of a thousand cubits, or nearly one-third of a mile from the wall. There might be danger, especially with the irregular forms which the sites of cities might assume, and with the physical obstacles presented by the surrounding ground, that neighbouring proprietors would deem the suburb sufficient if it measured a thousand cubits in some directions, not in others; in which case it might be occasionally restricted to a very small area. To guard against this, it was ordained that the suburb should, alike on north, south, east, and west, present, at a distance of a thousand cubits from the wall, a front not less than two thousand cubits in length; and, by joining the extremities of these measured fronts according to the nature of the ground, a sufficient space for the Levites would be secured.

[b] Deut. 4. 41. Josh. 20. 2. & 21. 3. † Heb. *above them ye shall give.*

be [b]six cities for refuge, which ye
shall appoint for the manslayer, that
he may flee thither: and † to them ye
shall add forty and two cities.
7 *So* all the cities which ye shall
give to the Levites *shall be* forty and
eight cities: them *shall ye give* with
their suburbs.
8 And the cities which ye shall
give *shall be* of the possession of the
children of Israel: from *them that
have* many ye shall give many; but
from *them that have* few ye shall give
few: every one shall give of his cities
unto the Levites according to his inheritance which † he inheriteth.

† Heb. *they inherit.*

9 ¶ And the LORD spake unto
Moses, saying,
10 Speak unto the children of Israel, and say unto them, [c]When ye
be come over Jordan into the land
of Canaan;
11 Then ye shall appoint you cities
to be cities of refuge for you; that
the slayer may flee thither, which
killeth any person † at unawares.
12 And they shall be unto you
cities for refuge from the avenger;
that the manslayer die not, until he
stand before the congregation in judgment.
13 And of these cities which ye

[c] Deut. 19. 2. Josh. 20. 2.

† Heb. *by error.*

---

6. *among the cities*] The construction here is confused and irregular. See Note at end of the chapter.

The general sense however is plain; viz. that the Levitical cities shall be forty-eight altogether, of which six shall be Cities of Refuge, for the purposes described in *vv.* 9—34. The passage might be rendered thus: "As to the cities which ye shall give to the Levites, ye shall give six cities, &c."

The Levitical cities were in an especial manner the Lord's, and therefore the places of refuge, where the manslayer might remain under the protection of a special institution devised by Divine mercy, were appropriately selected from amongst them. No doubt also the Priests and Levites would be fittest persons to administer the law in the doubtful cases which would be sure to occur: cf. on *v.* 24.

8. *from them that have many ye shall give many*, &c.] Nine cities were eventually given to the Levites from the large joint inheritance of Judah and Simeon; three were taken from the territory of Naphtali, and the other tribes gave each four apiece.

10. *When ye be come over Jordan*] The three cities on the east of the Jordan were afterwards set apart by Moses himself, Deut. iv. 41—43. See on Deut. xix. 8 sqq.

12. *the avenger*] Heb. *goel*, a term of which the original import is uncertain. The very obscurity of its etymology testifies to the antiquity of the office which it denotes. That office rested on the principle of Gen. ix. 6, "whoso sheddeth man's blood, by man shall his blood be shed." In an unsettled state of society the execution of justice was necessarily left in private hands. The lowest stage of national development is where every one assumes the right of avenging alleged misdeeds at his discretion; and it was therefore already an upward step when prevailing custom restricted this right to certain persons, who, although wielding no public authority, were yet invested, *ipso facto*, for the time being, with a public character. It was in such a spirit that the unwritten code of the east conceded to the nearest kinsman of a murdered man the right of avenging the blood that had been shed. He was permitted to kill the murderer, without notice, openly or secretly, wheresoever he might find him. Such rude justice necessarily involved grave evils. It gave no opportunity to the person charged with crime of establishing his innocence; it recognized no distinction between murder, manslaughter, and accidental homicide; it perpetuated family blood-feuds, the avenger of blood being liable to be treated in his turn as a murderer by the kinsman of the man whom he had slain. These grievances could not be removed as long as there was no central government strong enough to vindicate the law; but they might be mitigated; and to do this was the object of the institution in the text: an institution already promised in general terms by God, Ex. xxi. 13.

Among the Arab tribes, who are under the control of no central authority, the practice of blood-revenge subsists in full force to the present day. The law of the Koran limits the right of demanding satisfaction to cases in which a man has been unjustly smitten, and forbids the kinsman of the deceased to avenge his blood on any other than the actual murderer. But these restrictions are generally disregarded in practice by the Arabs.

12. *the congregation*] *i.e.* local court, consisting of the elders of the city (Josh. xx. 4). Two terms (*kāhal* and *eydah*) are rendered "congregation" in the A. V. The former word denotes properly the general assembly of the people; the latter, which is here employed,

shall give six cities shall ye have for refuge.

14 Ye shall give three cities on this side Jordan, and three cities shall ye give in the land of Canaan, *which* shall be cities of refuge.

15 These six cities shall be a refuge, *both* for the children of Israel, and for the stranger, and for the sojourner among them: that every one that killeth any person unawares may flee thither.

[d] Exod. 21. 14.

16 [d] And if he smite him with an instrument of iron, so that he die, he *is* a murderer: the murderer shall surely be put to death.

† Heb. *with a stone of the hand.*

17 And if he smite him † with throwing a stone, wherewith he may die, and he die, he *is* a murderer: the murderer shall surely be put to death.

18 Or *if* he smite him with an hand weapon of wood, wherewith he may die, and he die, he *is* a murderer: the murderer shall surely be put to death.

19 The revenger of blood himself shall slay the murderer: when he meeteth him, he shall slay him.

20 [e] But if he thrust him of hatred, or hurl at him by laying of wait, that he die;

[e] Deut. 19. 11.

21 Or in enmity smite him with his hand, that he die: he that smote *him* shall surely be put to death; *for* he *is* a murderer: the revenger of blood shall slay the murderer, when he meeteth him.

22 But if he thrust him suddenly [f] without enmity, or have cast upon him any thing without laying of wait,

[f] Exod. 21. 13.

23 Or with any stone, wherewith a man may die, seeing *him* not, and cast *it* upon him, that he die, and *was* not his enemy, neither sought his harm:

24 Then the congregation shall judge between the slayer and the revenger of blood according to these judgments:

25 And the congregation shall deliver the slayer out of the hand of the revenger of blood, and the congregation shall restore him to the city

---

means simply any appointed gathering; and so, though occasionally used for the general assembly, is used with propriety here of a select representative body.

16. *instrument of iron*] *i.e.* a tool; iron was not at this date used for arms. Cf. note on Deut. iii. 11.

19. *when he meeteth him*] Provided, of course, it were without a city of refuge.

20. *But*] Rather, **now**. This and the following verses limit the application of *vv.* 16—19 to cases in which a man has slain with malice aforethought. It had, *e.g.* been laid down in *v.* 17 that to hurl a stone at another and cause his death thereby was murder; yet *v.* 23 declares this not to be murder if he who hurled the stone sought not thereby his neighbour's harm. The sense of *vv.* 16—25 might then be exhibited thus: "whereas it is laid down that to take another man's life by any means soever is murder, and exposes the murderer to the penalty of retaliation; now therefore be it known that, if the deed be done in enmity, it is in truth very murder, and the murderer shall be slain; but if it be not done in enmity, then the congregation shall interpose to stay the avenger's hand."

24. *shall judge between*] *i.e.* shall authoritatively intervene so as to protect the slayer from the avenger. It is the case of the innocent slayer that is here contemplated. The expression "to judge" often denotes not the mere hearing of the cause but the actual redress of the wrong sustained (*e.g.* Ps. x. 18). It is evident that in a doubtful case there would necessarily have to be a judicial decision as to the guilt or innocence of the person who claimed the right of asylum; as is indeed implied in *v.* 12.

25. *and he shall abide in it*] Thus the homicide was safe only within the walls of his city of refuge. He became therefore a virtual exile from his home; was debarred from the tillage of his paternal fields, and lost the revenues which would have accrued from such tillage. The city which afforded him shelter was in some measure a place of confinement to him. The provisions here made serve to mark the gravity of the act of manslaughter, even when not premeditated; and the inconveniences attending on them fell, as is right and fair, upon him who committed the deed.

unto the death of the high priest] The atoning death of the Saviour cast its shadow before

of his refuge, whither he was fled: and he shall abide in it unto the death of the high priest, which was anointed with the holy oil.

26 But if the slayer shall at any time come without the border of the city of his refuge, whither he was fled;

27 And the revenger of blood find him without the borders of the city of his refuge, and the revenger of blood kill the slayer; † he shall not be guilty of blood:

† Heb. *no blood shall be to him.*

28 Because he should have remained in the city of his refuge until the death of the high priest: but after the death of the high priest the slayer shall return into the land of his possession.

29 So these *things* shall be for a statute of judgment unto you throughout your generations in all your dwellings.

30 Whoso killeth any person, the murderer shall be put to death by the [g] mouth of witnesses: but one witness shall not testify against any person *to cause him* to die.

g Deut. 17. 6. & 19. 15. Matt. 18. 16. 2 Cor. 13. 1. Heb. 10. 28.

31 Moreover ye shall take no satisfaction for the life of a murderer, which *is* † guilty of death: but he shall be surely put to death.

† Heb. *faulty to die.*

32 And ye shall take no satisfaction for him that is fled to the city of his refuge, that he should come again to dwell in the land, until the death of the priest.

33 So ye shall not pollute the land wherein ye *are*: for blood it defileth the land: and † the land cannot be cleansed of the blood that is shed therein, but by the blood of him that shed it.

† Heb. *there can be no expiation for the land.*

34 Defile not therefore the land which ye shall inhabit, wherein I dwell: for I the LORD dwell among the children of Israel.

---

on the statute-book of the Law and on the annals of Jewish history. The High-Priest, as the head and representative of the whole chosen family of sacerdotal mediators, as exclusively entrusted with some of the chief priestly functions, as alone privileged to make yearly atonement within the Holy of Holies, and to gain, from the mysterious Urim and Thummim, special revelations of the will of God, was, preeminently, a type of Christ. And thus the death of each successive high-priest presignified that death of Christ by which the captives were to be freed, and the remembrance of transgressions made to cease. Whether at each high-priest's death all existing blood-feuds were to terminate, even in those cases in which no shelter had been sought in a city of refuge, is not stated. No doubt, however, the merciful provisions of this law would ameliorate general practice in many particulars which the letter of its ordinance did not reach.

30. *by the mouth of witnesses*] *i. e.* two witnesses, at the least (cf. Deut. xvii. 6, &c.). The provisions of this and the following verses protect the enactments of this chapter from abuse. The Cities of Refuge were not intended to exempt a criminal from deserved punishment, as did the asylums of the Greeks and Romans, and the sanctuaries of mediæval Europe.

31. *no satisfaction*] Rather **ransom**, as in Ex. xxi. 30, where see note. In the Koran the acceptance of ransom is expressly sanctioned; nay, blood-revenge seems to be contemplated only as a last resource, after the demand for pecuniary compensation has been refused. The Arabs vary in their practice in reference to this matter. Some will waive the right of retaliation on receipt of a fine, others account the acceptance of such blood-money as dishonourable (see Niebuhr, 'Travels' I. pp. 28—31). The permission to make compensation for murders undoubtedly mitigates, in practice, the system of private retaliation; but it does so by sacrificing the principle which is the basis of that retaliation itself. Resting ultimately upon the law of God, that, "whosoever sheddeth man's blood, by man shall his blood be shed," it bids men rest content with a convenient evasion of that law, and converts the authority given to men to act as God's ministers, in taking life for life, into a warrant for enabling the kinsmen of a murdered man to make gain out of his murder.

32. *for him that is fled to the city of his refuge*] A fine for an accidental homicide is forbidden; for though not so derogatory to the primeval law as a fine for murder, it would equally cause the kinsman to profit by that which he ought to deplore, and would defeat the higher object of the various provisions of the law of refuge, especially in their typical bearing.

34. *for I the LORD dwell*, &c.] An emphatic protest against all enactment or relaxation of laws by men for their own private convenience.

NOTE on Chap. xxxv. 6.

The A. V. is probably wrong in taking the particle אֶת as a preposition. It appears to be only the sign of the accusative. The writer intending to add a verb governing "cities," omits to do so amongst the various clauses with which he proceeds; and then in *v.* 8 resumes once more with "cities" instead of completing the construction of *v.* 6. The three verses are really one sentence.

CHAPTER XXXVI.

1 *The inconvenience of the inheritance of daughters* 5 *is remedied by marrying in their own tribes,* 7 *lest the inheritance should be removed from the tribe.* 10 *The daughters of Zelophehad marry their father's brothers' sons.*

AND the chief fathers of the families of the children of Gilead,
the son of Machir, the son of Manasseh, of the families of the sons of
Joseph, came near, and spake before
Moses, and before the princes, the
chief fathers of the children of Israel:
2 And they said, [a]The LORD com- [a] chap. 27. 1.
manded my lord to give the land for Josh. 17. 3.
an inheritance by lot to the children
of Israel: and my lord was commanded by the LORD to give the inheritance of Zelophehad our brother unto
his daughters.
3 And if they be married to any of
the sons of the *other* tribes of the
children of Israel, then shall their
inheritance be taken from the inheritance of our fathers, and shall be
put to the inheritance of the tribe
† whereunto they are received: so († Heb. *unto whom they shall be.*)
shall it be taken from the lot of our
inheritance.
4 And when the jubile of the children of Israel shall be, then shall
their inheritance be put unto the inheritance of the tribe whereunto they
are received: so shall their inheritance be taken away from the inheritance of the tribe of our fathers.
5 And Moses commanded the children of Israel according to the word
of the LORD, saying, The tribe of the
sons of Joseph hath said well.
6 This *is* the thing which the
LORD doth command concerning the
daughters of Zelophehad, saying, Let
them † marry to whom they think († Heb. *be wives.*)
best; [b]only to the family of the tribe ([b] Tob. 1. 9)
of their father shall they marry.
7 So shall not the inheritance of
the children of Israel remove from
tribe to tribe: for every one of the
children of Israel shall † keep himself († Heb. *cleave to the, &c.*)
to the inheritance of the tribe of his
fathers.
8 And every daughter, that pos-
sesseth an inheritance in any tribe of
the children of Israel, shall be wife
unto one of the family of the tribe of
her father, that the children of Israel
may enjoy every man the inheritance
of his fathers.
9 Neither shall the inheritance remove from *one* tribe to another tribe;
but every one of the tribes of the

Chap. XXXVI. 1—13. Provisions for preventing any portion of the inheritance of one tribe passing to another through the marriage of an heiress. The necessity for regulating this arose out of the ordinance of xxviii. 6—11, which permitted the daughters of an Israelite dying without male issue to inherit their father's property. And as it was on the suit of the daughters of Zelophehad that that earlier ordinance had been promulgated, so now it was on the suit of the chiefs of the Machirites, of whom Zelophehad had been one, that a supplemental enactment is made, directing that heiresses should marry within their own tribe. The Machirites doubtless foresaw the loss which, but for the provisions of the text, would be likely to fall on their tribal inheritance.

4. *be taken away*] *i.e.* be permanently taken away. The jubilee year, by not restoring the estate to the tribe to which it originally belonged, would in effect confirm the alienation. There were, moreover, cases in which it would not merely confirm it, but even cause it. A tribe might have purchased an heiress' estate, in order to prevent the loss of it at her marriage; the jubilee would annihilate the title of the purchaser, without annihilating the transfer of the rights of the vendor to her husband; and to him the estate would thus eventually pass. The Machirites in effect represent that the jubilee, as the law at present stood, would certainly not avail to benefit them in the case in question, but rather might positively injure them.

children of Israel shall keep himself
to his own inheritance.
10 Even as the LORD commanded
Moses, so did the daughters of Zelophehad:
11 [c]For Mahlah, Tirzah, and
Hoglah, and Milcah, and Noah, the
daughters of Zelophehad, were married unto their father's brothers' sons:
12 *And* they were married [†]into
the families of the sons of Manasseh the son of Joseph, and their inheritance remained in the tribe of the
family of their father.
13 These *are* the commandments
and the judgments, which the LORD
commanded by the hand of Moses
unto the children of Israel in the
plains of Moab by Jordan *near* Jericho.

[c] chap. 27. 1.

† Heb. *to some that were of the families.*

---

11. *unto their father's brothers' sons*] Or more generally, "unto the sons of their kinsmen." Though the Hebrew term *dod* ordinarily denotes a father's brother, yet it is not always so restricted; *e.g.* in Jer. xxxii. 12 it seems to mean an uncle's son, a cousin-german.

13. *the commandments and the judgments*] Cf. Deut. vi. 1.

DEUTERONOMY

INTRODUCTION.

I. THE ordinary name of the book is derived, through the LXX. (Δευτερονόμιον) and Vulgate (*Deuteronomium*), from the one sometimes employed by the Jews, *mishneh hattōrah*, "repetition of the law." This name was probably suggested by the text xvii. 18, in which the expression *mishneh hattōrah hazzōth*, rendered in A.V. "a copy of this law," was anciently construed as referring to Deuteronomy only. This is probably not the right sense of the phrase, (see note *in loc.*), but the title borrowed from it indicates correctly enough the character and contents of the book. From another point of view some of the Rabbinical writers have styled Deuteronomy *sepher tōcakhōth*, "the Book of Reproofs," see on i. 1; whilst others denoted this as they did the other books of Scripture by the first two Hebrew words occurring in it, *elleh hadd'bhārim*.

II. The contents of Deuteronomy consist (1) of three addresses to the people delivered by Moses in the eleventh month of the fortieth year after the Exodus (chapters i.—xxx.); and (2) of certain final acts and words of Moses, viz. the solemn appointment of his successor (xxxi.), his Song (xxxii.), and Blessing (xxxiii.), which together with the account of his death (xxxiv.) form an appropriate conclusion to the book and to the whole Pentateuch.

The bulk of Deuteronomy thus consists of the three addresses, the first contained in i. 6—iv. 40; the second in v. 1—xxvi. 19; the third in xxvii. 1—xxix. 29. Of these the first (i. 6—iv. 40) is introductory and preparatory. In it Moses reminds the people of the protecting guidance under which they had passed from the bondage of Egypt to the border of the Promised Land where they then stood, and of their own repeated acts of ingratitude and rebellion against God, which had been punished by their long wandering in the desert. He conjures them to take warning from the past, and to resolve henceforth on a strict obedience, that so they might not lose the blessings which were now just within their reach. The second, and by far the longest speech (v. 1—xxvi. 19) carries the exhortation into details. It contains a practical exposition of the whole law in its incidence on the people, and dwells earnestly, as the several precepts are reviewed, on the sanctions of reward and punishment annexed to them by God. This portion commences with a rehearsal of the Ten Commandments (v. 6—21), the basis and essence of the whole Mosaic system, and proceeds to develope and apply more particularly the principles of the First Table (v. 22—xi. 32). Next follows, in what may be described as the second half of the speech (xii. 1—xxvi. 32), a declaration and enforcement of various particular statutes and regulations. These, though handled with that freedom of arrangement which suits the purposes of the orator, yet group themselves on the whole into (1) laws concerning religion (xii. 1—xvi. 17); (2) laws concerning the administration of justice, the powers and privileges of public officers, &c. (xvi. 18—xxi. 23); and (3) laws relating to private and social rights and duties (xxii. 1—xxvi. 19). The third speech (xxvii.—xxx.) relates to the solemn renewal of the covenant which is directed in it, and recites severally and emphatically the Blessings and the Cursings which will follow respectively upon observance and breach of the law.

The second and much the shorter part of the book, containing the thirty-first and three following chapters, was probably added to the rest by Joshua, or some other duly authorized prophet or leader of the people, after the death of Moses. Its characteristics are discussed in the notes on those chapters. The three addresses which constitute seven-eighths of the contents of Deuteronomy present some marked features requiring general notice here.

These addresses reflect very clearly the circumstances which attended their delivery. They were spoken within the space of a very few days. It was on the tenth day of the first month of the forty-first year after the exodus that the people passed over the Jordan, and commenced the conquest of Canaan under Joshua (Josh. iv. 19). Thirty days had been previously spent in the mourning after the death of Moses (Deut. xxxiv. 8). On the other hand, the commencement of the first of the three addresses is expressly fixed by Deut. i. 3 for the first day of the eleventh month in the fortieth year. It is thus evident that the delivery of these speeches, and likewise the utterance of the Song and Blessing, and the transaction of the closing events of Moses' life, must all be placed chronologically in the first ten days of that eleventh month.

III. Accordingly the speeches exhibit an unity of style and character which is strikingly consistent with such circumstances. They are pervaded by the same vein of thought, the same tone and tenor of feeling, the same peculiarities of conception and expression. They exhibit matter which is neither documentary nor traditional, but conveyed in the speaker's own words.

Their aim is strictly hortatory; their style earnest, heart-stirring, impressive, in passages sublime, but throughout rhetorical; they keep constantly in view the circumstances then present and the crisis to which the fortunes of Israel had at last been brought. Moses had before him not the men to whom by God's command he delivered the law at Sinai, but the generation following which had grown up in the wilderness. Large portions of the law necessarily stood in abeyance during the years of wandering; and of his present hearers many must have been strangers to various prescribed observances and ordinances, and those not unimportant ones (see on Josh. v. 2 sqq., and notes and reff.). Now however on their entry into settled homes in Canaan a thorough discharge of the various obligations laid on them by the covenant would become imperative; and it is to this state of things that Moses addresses himself. He speaks to hearers neither wholly ignorant of the law, nor yet fully versed in it. Much is assumed and taken for granted in his speeches; again, on other matters he goes into detail, knowing that instruction in them was needed. Sometimes too opportunity is taken of promulgating regulations which are supplementary or auxiliary to those of the preceding books; some few modifications suggested by longer experience or altered circumstances are now made; and the whole Mosaic system is completed by the addition of several enactments in chapters xii.—xxvi. of a social, civil, and political nature. These would have been wholly superfluous during the nomadic life of the desert; but now when the permanent organization of Israel as a nation was to be accomplished, they could not be longer deferred. Accordingly the legislator, at the command of God, completes his great work by supplying them. Thus he provides civil institutions for his people accredited by the same Divine sanctions as had been vouchsafed to their religious rites.

IV. It is then not quite accurate to speak of Deuteronomy as merely a recapitulation of things commanded and done in the preceding books; nor yet as properly a compendium and summary of the law. Large and important sections of the Mosaic code are unnoticed in the book. Still less is it a manual compiled for the instruction of those wholly ignorant of the law. The phrase used in i. 5 (see note on i. 3—5) exactly indicates both the task which Moses undertook in the closing month of his life, and the relation of this book to the preceding ones. Having long ago propounded his formal legislative decrees, he now undertakes to explain and elucidate them; he develops their spirit and aim; he endeavours to impress on those for whom they were designed the advantages of observing, and the evils of neglecting them. It is thus quite in keeping that the various commandments are given in Deuteronomy as injunctions of Moses, and not, as before, directly in the name of God. Deuteronomy is an authoritative and inspired commentary on the Law; serving in some respects also as a supplement and codicil to it[1].

The preceding books displayed Moses principally in the capacity of legislator or annalist. Deuteronomy sets him before us in that of a prophet. And he not only warns and teaches with an authority and energy which the sublimest pages of the Four Greater Prophets cannot surpass, but he delivers some of the most notable and incontrovertible predictions to be found in the Old Testament. The prophecy in xviii. 18 (see note) respecting the prophet like unto himself had no doubt its partial verifications in successive ages, but its terms are satisfied in none of them. The prospect opened by it advances continually until it finds its rest in the Messiah, who stands alone as the only complete counterpart of Moses, and the greater than he. Chapter xxviii. furnishes another and no less manifest example. The punishments there denounced are so minutely and pointedly specified, and were on record, whatever opinion be adopted about the age and authorship of Deuteronomy, so many centuries before the destruction of the Jewish Commonwealth by the Romans which so strikingly realized them, that the argument derived from such prediction and fulfilment cannot be gainsayed or evaded. It is true that the whole prophecy is conditional. The people had blessings as well as cursings set before them, and might choose whichever they would (xxx. 19). But there is throughout ch. xxviii., as in other passages (*e.g.* xxix.) where this alternative is set forth, a far greater stress and fulness apparent in the penal clauses; and thus there is contained in the very prophecy itself on its first delivery a clear foretokening of the future result. Indeed Moses, in xxxi. 29 sqq. expressly says that the people would after his death so act as to bring these judgments upon themselves. And his Song in xxxii. indicates vividly a long series of transgressions and consequent retributions, ending in the rejection of Israel by God. Beyond this however lies a distant epoch when mercy should eventually triumph over justice, and embrace the Gentile no less than the Jew within the blessings of the Covenant (xxxii. 43, see note). Thus does Moses, in the very act of completing his own institutions, foretell the eventual termination of them, and their absorption into a wider range of dispensations. Thus did the great legislator both himself gain some glimpses of the vast future which lay behind the enactments he was commissioned to deliver, and put on record also both promises and threats which could not but excite amongst his people expectations and speculations as to the form which the events thus foreshadowed by him would take. Deuteronomy is then, as St Jerome (Ep. ad Paulinum, Opera, Vol. III. p. 3, Edit. Paris, 1546) describes it, "Secunda lex et evangelicæ legis præparatio. Nonne sic habet ea quæ priora sunt ut tamen nova sunt omnia de veteribus?"

V. As regards authorship it is generally allowed that Deuteronomy must, in substance, have come from one hand. The Song and the Blessing have indeed been

[1] The Synopsis Sacræ Scripturæ ascribed to St Athanasius describes very clearly the relation of Deuteronomy to the preceding books: *ἐν αὐτῷ Μωυσῆς δευτεροῖ καὶ διεσάφησε πάντα προειρημένα, ἔν τε τῇ Ἐξόδῳ, καὶ τῷ Λευιτικῷ, καὶ τοῖς Ἀριθμοῖς, νομιμά τε καὶ δικαιώματα καὶ προστάγματα· καὶ ὑπομιμνήσκεται πάλιν τὸν λαὸν ἵνα φυλάξῃ αὐτά.* Athanasii Opera, Vol. II. p. 71. Paris Edit. 1627.

regarded by some as independent poems which the writer found and incorporated into his work. But on the whole the processes applied by many writers so freely to the rest of the Pentateuch, the processes of disintegration and partition of contents amongst a number of supposed writers of different dates, have been admitted to be not applicable to Deuteronomy. The book in fact presents, the last four chapters excepted, an undeniable unity in style and treatment; it is cast, so to speak, in one mould; its literary characteristics are such that we cannot believe the composition of it to have been spread over any long period of time.

These facts are in full accord with the traditional view which ascribes the book to Moses. This view however many modern critics and commentators unhesitatingly reject. These writers are too generally agreed that the author of Deuteronomy, whoever he was, did not write any large portions of the preceding books, though some think that he was the one who reduced them to their present shape, and completed his work by adding to it this original composition. It is indeed asserted to be "one of the most certain results of modern criticism" (Colenso, 'Pent.' Vol. III. § 863), that Deuteronomy was written in the later period of the Jewish monarchy; and consequently long after the main part of the Pentateuch, to which it forms a kind of appendix or peroration.

Yet several scholars who have adopted this self-same method of investigation, and who have a high reputation for learning and acuteness, have maintained, on the contrary, that Deuteronomy is more ancient than any other part of the Pentateuch. They observe that the legislative element in Deuteronomy is exhibited in a simpler and more subjective form than in the preceding books, and hold that the matter-of-fact and systematic prescriptions of Exodus and Leviticus were evolved at a later date out of the prophetic discourses of Deuteronomy. Views of this sort have been maintained by Van Bohlen, Vater, Vatke, George, Reuss, and by Dr S. Davidson in Horne's 'Introduction,' Vol. II. (1856), though he has subsequently abandoned that view in his Introd. to the Old Test. (1862). It is true that other authorities of the same school have treated this decision with scanty respect; but how little warrant there is, on the principles of the so-called "higher criticism at least, for this summary" judgment, is apparent by the fact that Kuenen, whose work on the Pentateuch is one of the most recent and by no means the least learned, whilst not yet adopting outright the opinion of Van Bohlen, &c., confesses that "gradually the conviction has settled on his mind that there is more truth in the views of these last than is recognized by the defenders of the former view." (Kuenen on the 'Pentateuch,' translated by Colenso, pp. 192, 193.) More recently still Kalisch in his commentary on Leviticus, Part I. published in 1867, whilst allowing that "the author of Deuteronomy had before him full outlines of the narrative and legislation of the three middle books" of the Pentateuch, is nevertheless decidedly of opinion that "the elaborate system" of sacrifices, &c. laid down in Leviticus was developed on the basis afforded by Deuteronomy; and of course rejects on the whole the views of those "who claim a higher antiquity" for those middle books, pp. 44 sqq.

In truth no more convincing proof could be afforded that the method of criticism in question is untrustworthy than the results of its application to Deuteronomy. The older scholars, Gesenius, de Wette, Ewald, Bleek, &c. unhesitatingly affirmed that Deuteronomy was written long after the rest of the Pentateuch was extant in its present shape. The newer school sees no less certainly in Deuteronomy the primæval quarry out of which the writers concerned in the production of the preceding books drew their materials.

Out of this conflict of opinions one inference may safely be drawn. The allegation so positively made that the very style of Deuteronomy betrays its late origin is arbitrary and baseless. No doubt the book is written in a very different manner from the preceding ones; yet the parallelisms between it and them both in ideas and expressions are neither few nor insignificant (cf. for instance Deut. xxviii. with Lev. xxvi. throughout), as any one who will turn to the references in the margin and notes for a few consecutive chapters will easily ascertain. And the fact that the book consists mainly of three speeches addressed by Moses to the people in immediate view of his own death and their entrance into Canaan sufficiently explains its literary characteristics. Naturally the matter thus orally set forth is given in more sustained, flowing, and rhetorical language than would be employed when laws were to be promulgated, passing events chronicled, or ancient transactions, already perhaps enshrined in tradition or document, incorporated into a connected historical work. It is to be observed also that all the classes of archaisms, whether in vocabulary or grammatical forms, which have been pointed out as characteristic of the Hebrew of the Pentateuch (see Introd. to Pent. pp. 18, 19) are found in Deuteronomy, and some of them frequently.

The writings of Jeremiah often strikingly recall passages of Deuteronomy. The prophet repeatedly employs words and phrases which are characteristic of Deuteronomy. Numerous illustrations and examples are given by Colenso on 'Pent.' § 556; and there is also at times (the reff. given in margin and notes to Deut. xxviii. and xxxii. will supply illustrations) a remarkable similarity of general style and treatment. These resemblances are neither few nor insignificant. It is needless in this place to demonstrate their existence and importance, which are now admitted on all hands. The question to be considered here is, how are they to be accounted for?

Those who regard Deuteronomy as the work of Moses can explain them at once. The priest of Anathoth would have made the Law his study from his childhood, and his modes of thought and expression would naturally be greatly influenced by that law, and more so than those of the non-priestly prophets. Of all parts of the Pentateuch Deuteronomy would in the calamitous days of Jeremiah come home to the prophet's mind with most frequency and force. The sins which Deuteronomy specially denounces were in Jeremiah's days most rife and gross in Israel; the retributive judgments denounced as a consequence in the same book were lighting on the people before his eyes; topics of comfort there were none except those splendid though distant promises which in spite of its predominating tone of warning and threatening break so wonderfully through the prophecies of Deuteronomy (see above, § IV.). What wonder then that Jeremiah's utterances should so often sound like an echo of Deuteronomy; that his denunciations, as did those of his contemporary Huldah (cf. 2 Kings xxii. 16 sqq. with Deut. xxix. 2 sqq.), should fall into the strains of this book; or that his topics of consolation should recall the reassuring words with which (*e.g.* in xxx.) the severity of God's judgment is tempered even in the law?

It would be a yet stronger reason why this of all the then existing sacred writings should have exerted a special influence on Jeremiah if the book discovered in his days in the Temple by the High Priest Hilkiah, and brought again to the knowledge of the king and people after having been banished from public sight and use for nearly sixty years during the two preceding reigns, were ascertained to be the book of Deuteronomy only[1]. But if we hold the other view, that "the book of the law" found by Hilkiah in the house of the Lord (2 Kings xxii. 8) was the original copy of the Pentateuch deposited by order of Moses in the ark (cf. Deut. xxxi. 9. 26), as the peculiar expression used about it 2 Chron. xxxiv. 14 (where see note), certainly seems to suggest, yet even so the narrative of 2 Kings xxii. xxiii. makes it apparent that it was Deuteronomy above all portions of the law which pricked the consciences of king and people. For Deut. xxviii. and xxix. seem plainly to be referred to in 2 Kings xxii. 13, 16, 17, xxiii. 2, 3, &c.; and the special measures

[1] St Chrysostom clearly regarded "the book of the law" found by Hilkiah as identical with Deuteronomy; for, speaking of the destruction of many sacred books at the Captivity, he proceeds: *Καὶ τί λέγω περὶ τῆς αἰχμαλωσίας; Καὶ γὰρ πρὸ τῆς αἰχμαλωσίας πολλὰ ἠφάνιστο βιβλία, τῶν Ἰουδαίων εἰς ἐσχάτην ἀσέβειαν ἐξοκειλάντων. Καὶ δῆλον ἐκ τοῦ τέλους τῆς τετάρτης τῶν Βασιλειῶν· τὸ γὰρ Δευτερονόμιον μόλις που εὕρηται ἐν κοπρίᾳ κατακεχωσμένον.* (Chrysost. Op. X. 54, ed. Bened.).

of reform actually adopted by Josiah are those enjoined by Deuteronomy, and more fully and emphatically there than anywhere else (cf. 2 Kings xxiii. 5—25, with Deut. xii. 2, 3; xvi. xviii., &c.). It is probable too that Jeremiah and Hilkiah were related[1]; and it is at any rate certain that they were friends and fellow-labourers in the restoration of religion effected under Josiah; and thus the prophet would be one of the very first to be informed of Hilkiah's discovery as he would naturally be one of the most intensely moved by it[2]. The coincidences then between Deuteronomy and the prophecies of Jeremiah are only what might be expected from the known circumstances of Jewish history. Their existence, so far from furnishing any kind of argument against the Mosaic origin of the Pentateuch, rather suggests confirmation of the traditional view. All the circumstances considered it would have been *pro tanto* a reason for misgivings about the authenticity of Deuteronomy if a great prophet of the times and in the circumstances of Jeremiah had not manifested much of the spirit and power of Deuteronomy.

Further, whilst the language of Jeremiah unquestionably indicates an acquaintance with the book of Deuteronomy, it is yet apparent, if linguistic considerations are to decide, that the author of Deuteronomy and of the prophecies

[1] Jeremiah speaks of himself as "the son of Hilkiah." But this was hardly Hilkiah the High-priest; for had he been so, he would have been so styled: and the priests of Anathoth were (1 Kings ii. 26) of the house of Abiathar, which had been deposed from the high-priesthood by Solomon. The name Hilkiah too was common. But when we note (cf. Jer. xxxii. 7, with 2 Kings xxii. 14) that Shallum the uncle of Jeremiah was apparently the husband of Huldah the prophetess, and that Ahikam, Jeremiah's protector (Jer. xxvi. 24) was with Huldah one of Hilkiah's coadjutors in the work of reform (2 Chron. xxxiv. 20), it seems likely that there was some affinity between the prophet and the High-priest.

[2] It has not been deemed necessary to discuss the coarse hypothesis of Von Bohlen, although it was not long ago revived in this country, that Hilkiah wrote the book of Deuteronomy himself, and then pretended to have discovered it as an autograph of Moses in the Temple. This view has been latterly discarded as untenable even by the most advanced adherents of "modern criticism:" see *e.g.* Davidson, 'Introd. to O. T.' pp. 385, 386.

which pass under the name of Jeremiah were neither identical nor contemporary. The resemblances between the two books are on the surface, easy to notice, and at first sight are very striking. A more minute scrutiny of the language of the writings under comparison will make it manifest that whilst there is in various passages of the later document a distinct imitation or repetition of the earlier[1], yet that the two are in date, associations, idioms, and vocabulary as distinct as any two other writers in the Old Testament. After the complete and exhaustive discussion of this subject by Kœnig ('Altestamentl. Studien,' Part II.) which has never been and cannot be answered, lengthened argument on this point is needless[2]. The

[1] This is in fact one of the characteristics of Jeremiah, who frequently reproduces both the thoughts and words of older prophets.

[2] Phrases and words of constant use in Jeremiah are absent from Deut. altogether: *e.g.* נאם־יהוה and נאם אדני, which are found above a hundred times in Jeremiah. Had these phrases been familiar to the writer of Deut. he could hardly have altogether omitted to use them. The like may be said of the phrase "The word of the Lord came to me," which with slight variations is frequent in Jeremiah; also of the expressions "Lord of hosts" (*Sabaoth*), "house of Jacob," and "house of Israel." The expressions "virgin of Israel," "the virgin daughter of my people," &c., are again and again used by the prophet figuratively for the whole nation, and are not so used in Deut.; on the contrary the first of them occurs in Deut. xxii. 19, in its primary sense. The favourite combination of the prophet "to root out, and to pull down, and to destroy, and to throw down, and to plant, &c." (cf. Jer. i. 10 with marginal references) is not found in Deut., suitable as it is to the themes handled in that book; and the like remark is true of the other combination "the sword, the famine, and the pestilence," found repeatedly in Jer. Cf. xiv. 18, xviii. 21, xxi. 7, 9. &c.

On the contrary in Deut. the writer constantly speaks of and to the people as "Israel" simply, which Jeremiah never does: the phrase he so constantly uses of observing the law, "hear and do" (cf. *e.g.* Deut. v. 27) is strange to Jeremiah; the Deuteronomistic phrase "to cleave to the Lord" (cf. *e.g.* Deut. x. 20) is not found in Jer. though it would often have suited his purpose well. The phrases לפני יהוה and its cognates (see Deut. i. 45, vi. 25, &c.), and the expressions "to be afraid of the face of," and others connected with such verbs as to "fear" and "to make to fear" (see Deut. i. 17, xviii. 22, &c.) do not occur in Jer., but with like ideas other words are used. The passages in Deut. which refer to the exodus and the wonderworks which accompanied it are so many and conspicuous as to be a distinct trait of the book. The later prophet handles the same subject once in a

priest of Anathoth reproduced in many particulars the warnings and the teachings of Moses; and under circumstances different in some respects but remarkably similar in others, had a like prophetical burden from God laid upon him to deliver to the people. The view of the Jews that Jeremiah was "the prophet like unto Moses" of Deuteronomy xviii. 15 (cf. St John i. 20 sqq.), is rather short of the truth than wide of it.

Various texts from the book have been adduced as proofs that it was not composed by the author of the books preceding it. These contain deviations from the earlier narrative, additions to it, or assumed inconsistencies with it; and have been alleged both from the legislative and from the historical contents of the book. No doubt some of these are important, and require careful consideration and explanation; but upon the whole list one or two general remarks must be made.

Be it noted in the first place that there is nothing in Deuteronomy which positively contradicts anything in the earlier books. This is now generally admitted (*e.g.* by Von Lengerke and Davidson); and it is an important admission, for it can be demonstrated that the author of Deuteronomy had the preceding books before him with their contents as we now have them, and knew them well[1]. How then is it credible that the Deuteronomist "was a late writer who composed his work centuries after the rest of the Pentateuch was written, and passed it off as a Mosaic document?" For such a forger would certainly have anxiously removed all such seeming discrepancies as those in question; and when combining his new work with the old would have brought the two into a self-evident harmony, either by making the necessary modifications in his own materials, or by erasures from the pre-existing ones. The very occurrence then of the phenomena in question, arising on a comparison of Deuteronomy with Exodus, Leviticus, and Numbers, striking as those phenomena are, and just because they are striking, is a *prima facie* token of authenticity. No one but the original legislator and historian would deal with his subject in this free and independent spirit.

Again, many of the supposed contradictions vanish or admit of easy explanation if we bear in mind the circumstances under which the speeches contained in

similar strain, but then with very different phraseology: cf. Deut. iv. 34, xi. 2, 3, xvii. 19, xxvi. 8, &c. with Jer. xxxii. 20, 21. The phrases characteristic of Deut. respecting the unity of the Sanctuary are only found in one or two passages of the prophet where he is evidently alluding to Deut. (cf. Deut. xii. 5, 14, 18, &c., xiv. 23, 24, 25, xv. 20, &c., with Jer. vii. 7, 12).

Similar results appear from comparing the two books in respect of grammatical peculiarities, such as inflections, syntax, &c.; *e.g.* the pronoun of the 3rd person is in Deut. almost always הם, in Jer. המה: in Deut. we have repeatedly בעת ההוא, in Jer. always בעת ההיא; in Jer. the dative with the prep. ל stands several times instead of the accusative with את, in Deut. never: in Jer. the use of the infinitive absolute followed by the finite verb with the conj. ו is very frequent and characteristic: in Deut. it is very rare; and the same infinitive, which is commonly used by Jer. in other peculiar turns of expression (*e.g.* vii. 13, 25, xi. 7, xii. 17, &c.) is not found at all so used in Deut.

The Aramaisms in Jer. are very numerous and of very various kinds; Aramaic words, Aramaic meanings of words, Aramaic inflexions, terminations, constructions, &c. These, as all writers on Jeremiah who discuss the original text admit, indicate that the Hebrew of his day was no longer pure and sound. Such peculiarities are altogether wanting in Deut. with the exception of the Aramaisms alleged in xxxii and xxxiii. These are however not many in number, nor are they all unquestionable; they are too to be explained on quite a different principle from that which applies to the many and manifest Aramaisms of Jeremiah.

It will be understood that the above are only a few selected by way of example from the copious lists of Kœnig, who has examined and compared the language of the two books thoroughly, chapter by chapter, almost verse by verse.

[1] There are repeated references expressed or implied to laws already given: cf. Deut. xviii. 2 with Num. xviii. 20: Deut. xxiv. with Lev. xiii. and xiv.: Deut. xiv. 3—20 with Lev. xi.: Deut. xvi. with Ex. xxxiv. 22, Lev. xxiii. 15, 16, 34, 39: Deut. xxii. 9—11 with Lev. xix. 19, &c. The language in which the same transactions are described is often borrowed from the earlier books or evidently modelled after them; cf. Deut. ix. 12 with Ex. xxxii. 7, 8: Deut. vii. 20 with Ex. xxiii. 28: Deut. vii. 22 with Ex. xxiii. 29, 30. In fact, as Davidson (Introd. to O. T. I. 389) allows, "almost every chapter presents some indication, however slight, that written documents" (*i.e.* the four preceding books) "were employed by him." A very numerous and absolutely convincing list of references in Deut. to the preceding books and citations from them is given by Kœnig, 'Alt. Studien.' II. 126—146.

this book were delivered. The legislation about Tithes is a most important instance. Lev. xxvii. 30—34 prescribes that a tenth of all the produce of animals and of the land should be the Lord's; and Num. xviii. 20 sqq. appropriates this tenth for the support of the Levites; who again are to give a tenth of their tenth for the maintenance of the priests, Num. xviii. 26 sqq. But in Deut. xii. 6, 17, the tithes, evidently from *v.* 17 the vegetable ones, are alluded to as one of the sources from which the sacrificial meals at the sanctuary are to be supplied: in xiv. 22 sqq. strict levying of this tithe is enjoined, and commutation of it provided for where the sanctuary was far away, with a view to the money being applied to the same sacrificial feasts: in xiv. 28, 29 directions are given for holding in every third year a feast off this tithe at home instead of at the Sanctuary; and finally in xxvi. 12 sqq. a solemn form of declaration and prayer is prescribed which is to be rehearsed before the Lord in each third year when the cycle of tithe obligations would be completed. These regulations of Deuteronomy (see the foot-notes on the passages) undoubtedly are altogether different from those of the preceding books upon the subject, but they are neither inconsistent with them, nor do they supersede them. They refer one and all not to the general and first tithe of all produce both animal and vegetable, but to the second and additional tithe taken on the increase of the field only. This latter was not for the maintenance of the priests and Levites, but for the celebration of the sacred feasts, in each first and second year at the Sanctuary, in the third year at home. The priests and Levites were indeed to be invited to partake, as in each third year were the stranger, the fatherless, and the widow; but the purpose of these meals (cf. the agapæ of the New Test.), which are not instituted by Deuteronomy, but only regulated, was not to furnish a maintenance for the priests and Levites, but to promote charity and brotherly feeling, and to gather the religious life and associations of the people round the Sanctuary (see on xi. 5). There appears to be no express mention in Deuteronomy of the first tithe, out of which the priests and Levites were to be supported. This as of familiar and established, we might say primæval, obligation (cf. Gen. xiv. 20, xxviii. 22) is taken for granted on all hands. Yet the reason for which the first tithe was appointed by God to the Levites is mentioned x. 9, xviii. 1, 2; and no doubt that Levitical tithe was understood to be meant by the repeated declaration respecting Levi, that "the Lord is his inheritance:" for the tithe is emphatically "the Lord's:" cf. Lev. xxvii. 30 sqq.; Num. xviii. 20, 21; Mal. iii. 8[1].

Connected with this subject is that of the relative position of the priests and Levites as exhibited in the other books and in Deuteronomy. In the three middle books of the Pentateuch the priests are, it is said, carefully distinguished from the Levites; the duties of the latter are subordinate, such as erecting and taking down the Tabernacle, carrying it and its furniture, &c.; in short the Levites are to minister to the priests (Num. iii. 5 sqq., and iv.) as the priests to God (Ex. xxviii. 1, xxix. 1, etc.). But in Deuteronomy no such distinction between the two orders is observed. On the contrary, language applied in the earlier books to the priests only is used of the Levites, and functions limited before to the former are now assigned to the latter also: cf. Deut. x. 8, 9, where the duty of blessing the people is assigned to the tribe of Levi, with Num. vi. 23—27, where the same duty seems limited to the priests

[1] Some commentators insist that one and the same tithe must be meant throughout Lev., Num., and Deut. (so Knobel, Ewald, Davidson, Colenso, &c.); and infer from the discrepancies which arise on this assumption between the last book and the former a difference of authorship, date, &c. But how could the Deuteromist expect his work to be received as Mosaic whilst allowing such a glaring inconsistency to remain between his own precepts and those of the earlier legislation? Nor is it possible to regard Deut. as providing a substitute for an earlier tithe system which had fallen into abeyance. To meet the wants of the Levites merely by occasional feasts to which they were to be invited, would be to mock their poverty rather than to relieve it. Moreover, the second and third tithe (which was but another application of the second tithe in each third year) were as a matter of fact paid by the later Jews in addition to the first tithe: see on xxvi. 12.

alone: and Deut. xviii. 7, where "ministering in the name of the Lord" is attributed to the Levite, with Ex. xxviii. xxix. where this office is referred to as a priestly one. It is noted too that in the earlier books the priests are spoken of as the "sons of Aaron," never "the sons of Levi;" in Deuteronomy, on the contrary, we do not read of "sons of Aaron," but always of "sons of Levi," or "Levites," or "priests the Levites." Finally, Deuteronomy when noticing (xi. 6) the rebellion of Korah, Dathan and Abiram, significantly omits the name of the Levite Korah, though he was evidently the ringleader. From all this the inference is confidently drawn that the marked distinction which obtained in early times between the priests, the sons of Aaron, and the other Levites, had by the date of "the Deuteronomist" disappeared; and that in his eyes Korah committed no sin in "seeking the priesthood." It is further inferred, that this important elevation of the status of the Levite, which is nowhere commented upon in the historical books but simply appears from the language of Deuteronomy as an accomplished fact, can only have taken place gradually and in a long series of years; and that consequently Deuteronomy was written very much later than the date which belongs to Exodus and the two following books[1]. "It is," it has been said, "impossible to believe that any writer should have so suddenly changed his form of expression in such a case as this, in the very short interval of a few days or weeks at most, between the last act recorded in the book of Numbers and the first in Deuteronomy."

In reply it is to be noted, in the first place, that the description of the priests as the "sons of Aaron" does not occur in the latter part of Numbers at all, but only in the first fourteen chapters. Now Num. i.—xiv. belong to the second year of the Exodus; Deuteronomy to the fortieth. Consequently there is, according to the narrative of these two books themselves, not a very short interval, but a space of more than thirty-eight years in which this change of phraseology might have obtained currency.

But in truth the change in question is readily explained without supposing that the priests were at all less generally styled "sons of Aaron" at the time of the conquest of Canaan than they were at that of the exodus. Moses in Deuteronomy is not prescribing the several functions and privileges of the various orders of clergy, as he has to do in the preceding books. He is addressing the people, and when he has occasion to mention the clergy it is only in a general way, in reference broadly to their relation and duties towards the body of the nation. Hence he (as does also the writer of the Book of Joshua, cf. Josh. iii. 3, viii. 33) very naturally disregards for the time the difference of orders amongst the clergy, which was not to his purpose, and ascribes priestly and Levitical functions indifferently to the tribe of Levi,—to which as the priests were of course Levites these functions really belonged. So too in xi. 7 (where see note) no mention is made of Korah because it was to the rebellions of the people against God, and not to that of the Levites against the priesthood, that Moses wished his hearers to attend (see notes on xi. 7, and Num. xvi. 1). The discrepancies therefore between Deuteronomy and the earlier books are in this particular superficial only. They are at once explained by the familiar consideration that he who speaks to a large and mixed audience will take care, if he knows his business, to shun irrelevant details and distinctions. It is however incidentally made apparent that the difference between the priests and Levites was quite understood by the writer of Deuteronomy; see *e.g.* on xviii. 1.

Other particular objections are discussed in the notes upon the several passages which have suggested them: *e.g.* that based on the prescription of Num. xviii. 17 respecting the firstlings when compared with Deut. xv. 19 sqq., is dealt with in the latter passage; that on the supposed abstraction in Deuteronomy of certain perquisites allowed to the Le-

[1] It is worth while to note that the alleged identification of priests and Levites in Deut. is brought forward by George as a proof that Deut. is much older than the middle books of the Pentateuch; the division of the sacred caste into priests and Levites, which is recognized in Exodus and Numbers, being assumed to be a later development: cf. Bähr, 'Symb.' II. p. 7.

vites by the earlier legislation in the note on xviii. 3; that on the supposed allusion to Solomon's temple in xi. 5; that on the enactments respecting a king and a prophetical order in the notes at the end of chapters xvii. and xviii. No doubt several of the enactments in Deuteronomy are not found in the preceding books. But these additions do not betray another and a later hand than that which gave the original code. They are one and all such as are supplementary or explanatory of earlier laws, and might well be suggested by a short experience of the working of those laws; or such as would have been premature or impracticable during the wandering in the wilderness, but became necessary when the people was about to settle down in Canaan: cf. note at the beginning of ch. xii. on xii. 7. The occurrence of such enactments in Deuteronomy, and there first, is in thorough harmony with the time and circumstances set forth in the book itself as belonging to its composition.

In like manner the alleged historical inconsistencies between this book and the earlier narrative are apparent only and not real (see *e.g.* on i. 9—15, i. 22, 23, ix. 1, &c.): and the total omission of large portions of the Sinaitic legislation is easily intelligible when we bear in mind the purpose which the orator in Deuteronomy had in view. It is particularly to be noted that the laws passed over in this book are more especially those pertaining to the offices of the priests and Levites. And these are precisely the topics which it would be needless for one addressing the general assembly of the people to expound or insist upon.

It is indeed possible that some or perhaps all of the archæological and topographical remarks which are interwoven in several places (see *e.g.* ii. 10—12, and 20—23, iii. 9) are insertions made by a later reviser, perhaps a much later reviser, after the book was complete: see the notes on those passages. But on the other hand it is quite in the manner of very ancient writers to interrupt the thread of their narrative by parentheses of this character, and to introduce them as abruptly as Moses does. The pages of Herodotus furnish many illustrations of this (see the remarks in Rawlinson's 'Herod.' I. 29, 125, and notes). It must be remembered that foot-notes are an invention of modern times. An ancient historian embodied incidental remarks, references, and illustrations in his text; nor would one who at a subsequent period undertook to re-edit an ancient work regard himself as taking any unwarrantable liberty if he added here and there any incidental notice or short explanation in a parenthetic form which might be useful to his own contemporaries. And it seems hardly likely that Moses would himself digress into such topics in the course of an address to the people, though there would be no improbability in believing that he did so when writing a history. Hence it is on the whole not unlikely that the passages in question were, as Prideaux long ago maintained, see 'Connexion,' (Part I. Book V. §§ 3 and 4), glosses added by Ezra, who would certainly regard himself as fully authorized thus to interpolate. But the question as to the Mosaic authorship of the book is not affected by any conclusion which may be formed about such isolated passages.

On the whole then the assertions of some modern critics as to the spuriousness of Deuteronomy, though very positive, appear when sifted to rest upon most insufficient arguments. The alleged anachronisms, discrepancies, and difficulties admit for the most part of easy and complete explanation; and no serious attempt has ever been made by these critics to meet the overwhelming presumption drawn from the unanimous and unwavering testimony of the ancient Jewish church and nation that Moses is the author of this book. The whole of this part of the argument, though enough of itself to outweigh many difficulties even were they insoluble, is almost always passed over by the critics *sub silentio.*

It must be added too that Deuteronomy has in a singular manner the attestation of the Apostles and of our Lord. St Paul in Romans x. and xv. argues from it at some length, and expressly quotes it as written by Moses; St Peter and St Stephen (Acts iii. 22, vii. 37) refer to the promise of "a Prophet like unto" Moses, and regard it as given, as it professes to be, by Moses himself; our Lord, wielding "the sword of the Spirit which is the word of God" against the open assaults of Satan, thrice resorts to Deuteronomy for the texts with which He repels the tempter, St Matt. iv. 4—10. It is in vain to urge in reply that the inspiration of the Apostles, and even the indwelling of the Spirit "without measure" in the Saviour, would not necessarily preserve them from mistakes on such subjects as the authorship of ancient writings, or to fortify such assertions by remarking that our Lord as the Son of Man was Himself ignorant of some things. Even were we warranted in inferring from St Luke ii. 52, St Mark xiii. 32, that some things were not known to the Lord as the Son of Man, because His human faculties must have been finite, yet the answer overlooks the important distinction between ignorance and error. To be conscious that much truth lies beyond the range of the intelligence is compatible with the perfection of the creature, which of course must be finite perfection (cf. Butler, 'Anal.' Part I. ch. v., Vol. I. pp. 95 sqq. Oxford Ed. of Butler's Works): but to be deceived by the fraud of others and to fall into error, is not so. To assert then that He who is "the Truth" believed Deuteronomy to be the work of Moses and quoted it expressly as such, though it was in fact a forgery introduced into the world seven or eight centuries after the exodus, is in effect, even though not in intention, to impeach the perfection and sinlessness of His nature, and seems thus to gainsay the first principles of Christianity.

THE FIFTH BOOK OF MOSES,

CALLED

DEUTERONOMY.

CHAPTER I.

1 *Moses' speech in the end of the fortieth year, briefly rehearsing the story* 6 *of God's promise,* 13 *of giving them officers,* 19 *of sending the spies to search the land,* 34 *of God's anger for their incredulity,* 41 *and disobedience.*

THESE *be* the words which Moses spake unto all Israel on this
side Jordan in the wilderness, in the
plain over against ‖the Red *sea*, be- ‖ Or, *Zuph.*
tween Paran, and Tophel, and Laban,
and Hazeroth, and Dizahab.

CHAP. I. **1, 2.**—These *vv.* are prefixed as a connecting link between the contents of the preceding books and that of Deut. now to follow.

1. *These be the words*] The clause is retrospective, as the geographical data which follow indicate, and serves to connect Deut. with the preceding book. The Hebrew pronoun (*elleh*, *these*), when used without the copulative *and*, generally refers exclusively to what follows (see on Gen. ii. 4). But here it serves, as in Lev. xxvi. 46, and perhaps Deut. xxix. 1, where see note, to point a clause conclusive of the preceding and introductory to the succeeding context. The sense of the passage might be given thus: "The discourses of Moses to the people up to the eleventh month of the fortieth year" (cf. *v.* 3) "have now been recorded." The general term "words" is used in order to include the various kinds of communications made by Moses to the people, laws, speeches, commands, &c. The proper names which follow seem to belong to places where "words" of remarkable importance were spoken. They are by the Jewish commentators referred to the spots which witnessed the more special sins of the people, and the mention of them here is construed as a pregnant rebuke. The Book of Deut. is known amongst the Jews as "the book of reproofs;" cf. Introd. § I.

on this side Jordan] Render rather **beyond Jordan**, as the same Hebrew phrase is translated iii. 20 and 25: and as the LXX. and the versions generally have it. A. V. has "on this side Jordan" also in Num. xxii. 1 (where see note); Deut. i. 5, iii. 8, &c.: but one rendering ought to be followed throughout. The phrase (*b'eber hay-yarden*) means literally "at the side or passage of Jordan." It was a standing designation for the district east of Jordan, and in times when Greek became commonly spoken in the country was exactly represented by the proper name Peræa. It was used quite irrespectively of the actual position of the speaker or writer (just as "seawards" or "from the sea" was used for "west," cf. Ex. x. 19); had probably been settled by the usage of the Canaanites in very early times; and passed from them to the patriarchs and the Jews generally. Yet alongside of this conventional sense the natural one is still found; and the phrase is used of both sides of the river: in Gen. l. 10, 11; Josh. ix. 1, &c., of Cisjordanic territory: in Num. xxii. 1, xxxii. 32, of Transjordanic; and even in the same chapter is used first of one and then of the other: see Deut. iii. 8, 20, 25. The immediate context will usually determine the sense of the phrase, which is thus in itself ambiguous; but often some qualifying addition is made to determine it (cf. *e.g.* iv. 41; Josh. xxii. 7). In Num. xxxii. 19, the Transjordanic tribes use a phrase nearly identical with the one before us first of their own territory and then of that of their brethren; but add terms to explain their meaning. It is evident, from a mere inspection of the passages in which the phrase is used, that no inferences at all can be drawn from it as to whether the writer of Deut. dwelt on the one side of Jordan or the other.

in the wilderness, in the plain] These terms assign broadly the localities referred to in the preceding books. The former term (*midbār*) denotes the desert of Arabia generally; the latter (*arābāh*) the sterile tract which stretches along the lower Jordan to the Dead Sea, and is continued thence to the Gulf of Akaba. In this *v.* and ii. 8 ("the way of the plain") it is the southern portion of this depressed tract which is meant.

over against the Red Sea] Render: **over against Suph.** Here the A. V. (cf. on Num. xxi. 14) supplies "Sea." But though

2 (*There are* eleven days' *journey*
from Horeb by the way of mount
Seir unto Kadesh-barnea.)
3 And it came to pass in the fortieth year, in the eleventh month, on
the first *day* of the month, *that* Moses
spake unto the children of Israel, according unto all that the LORD had
given him in commandment unto
them;
4 [a] After he had slain Sihon the [a] Numb. 21. 24.
king of the Amorites, which dwelt
in Heshbon, and Og the king of
Bashan, which dwelt at Astaroth in
Edrei:
5 On this side Jordan, in the land

---

the Red Sea (Hebr. *yam suph*) is often called simply "the Sea," yet "Suph" without "Sea" must be a proper name, especially as the full expression "yam suph" occurs *v.* 40. "Suph" is most probably the pass *es Sufah* near Ain-el-Weibeh described by Robinson ('Bib. Researches,' II. 181 sqq.: see also on Num. xiii. 26; § 5 of Note at end of chapter), or some place in the neighbourhood. Thus, the Maaleh-acrabbim of Josh. xv. 3 is the shortest (cf. on Num. xxxiv. 4), and anciently was the most frequented path from the Arabah, the plain mentioned in the last note, through the mountains to Hebron. It commands an extensive view, and the district beneath it, which may have been signalized by some deeds or words of Moses, is probably meant by the expression "over against Suph."

between Paran and Tophel] Of these places Tophel is by general consent identified as the Tufileh of Robinson ('Bib. Res.' II. 570), the Tafyle of Burckhardt (p. 402 sqq.). Saadia writes "Tufal." It is still a considerable place,—some little distance S. E. of the Dead Sea. "Numerous springs and rivulets (ninety-nine, according to the Arabs,) the waters of which unite below, render the vicinity of the town very agreeable. It is surrounded by large plantations of fruit-trees: apples, apricots, figs, pomegranates, and olive- and beech-trees of a large species are cultivated in great numbers" (Burckhardt, l. c.). It is naturally, therefore, selected as a landmark. Paran being assigned here as the western limit of a district is probably the Mount Paran of xxxiii. 2; or a city of the same name mentioned by Euseb., Jer. and several modern geographers, near the mountain. The name is familiar in the phrase "wilderness of Paran;" cf. Gen. xiv. 6, xxi. 21; Num. x. 12 and note.

and Laban] With this and the two following names we must understand the preposition "in:" and regard them as adding three more to those already mentioned as memorable. Laban is generally identified with Libnah (Num. xxxiii. 20, see Note): the latter being the same word in the fem. form.

Hazeroth] *i.e.* "inclosures" (cf. on ii. 23), probably not identical with the place of the same name mentioned Num. xi. 35; where see note.

Dizahab] *i.e.* region of gold; LXX. καταχρύσεα. The name suggests the idea of gold-mines; and Jerome ('De Situ et Nom. Loc. Heb.' s. v. Cata ta chrysea) says "sunt montes auri fertiles in deserto." Cf. Ewald, 'History of Israel,' p. 466 (translated by Martineau), and foot-note. Nothing can be ascertained of the place except that it was one of the earlier stations after the people left Sinai. Knobel identifies it with Kibroth-hattaavah. It can hardly be the modern Dahab, which is out of the way on the Gulf of Akaba.

2. *There are eleven days' journey...unto Kadesh*] Kadesh (see on Num. xiii. 26) is named as the southern point of the Promised Land. In this *v.*, as in the first, the mind of the reader seems directed to the past history. It was but eleven days' journey from the Mountain of the Covenant to the Promised Land; yet in the fortieth year the chosen people were still in the wilderness.

Horeb] On this name and its relation to Sinai, see on Ex. iii. 1.

3—5. The time and place at which the following exhortations were addressed to the people, are now defined; cf. iv. 44—49. In *v.* 5 too the nature of Moses' address is indicated. He "began," or better perhaps "undertook," to "declare this law:" *i.e.* explain and elucidate it. Such is the force of the Hebrew verb (*beer*), a word implying the pre-existence of the matter on which the process is employed, and so the substantial identity of the Deuteronomic legislation with that of the previous books.

4. *Astaroth*] On this place cf. Gen. xiv. 5, and note.

in Edrei] These words should, to render the sense clear, come next after "slain." The battle in which Sihon and Og were defeated took place at Edrei.

5. *in the land of Moab*] Cf. xxix. 1. More accurately in Num. xxxiii. 48, "in the plains of Moab by Jordan near Jericho." This district had formerly been occupied by the Moabites, and retained its name from them: but had been conquered by the Amorites. Cf. Num. xxi. 26.

of Moab, began Moses to declare this
law, saying,
6 The LORD our God spake unto
us in Horeb, saying, Ye have dwelt
long enough in this mount:
7 Turn you, and take your journey, and go to the mount of the
Amorites, and unto †all *the places*
nigh thereunto, in the plain, in the
hills, and in the vale, and in the
south, and by the sea side, to the land
of the Canaanites, and unto Lebanon,
unto the great river, the river Euphrates.
8 Behold, I have †set the land before you: go in and possess the land
which the LORD sware unto your fathers, [b]Abraham, Isaac, and Jacob,
to give unto them and to their seed
after them.
9 ¶ And I spake unto you at that
time, saying, I am not able to bear
you myself alone:
10 The LORD your God hath multiplied you, and, behold, ye *are* this day
as the stars of heaven for multitude.
11 (The LORD God of your fathers make you a thousand times so
many more as ye *are*, and bless you,
as he hath promised you!)

† Heb. *all his neighbours.*

† Heb. *given.*

[b] Gen. 15. 18. & 17. 7, 8.

---

declare] Render **explain**: and see on *vv.* 3—5 above. LXX. διασαφῆσαι: Vulg. *explanare.*

6. The first and introductory address of Moses to the people is here commenced. It extends to iv. 40, and is divided from the second discourse by the *vv.* iv. 41—49, which are obviously of a different character from those which precede and follow them. Addressing the people on the very threshold of the Promised Land, Moses summarily recalls to them the manifold proofs they had experienced of the care and the faithfulness of God towards them, and the manifold instances of their own perverseness and rebellion. These their sins had shut them out during a whole generation from the inheritance covenanted to be given to their fathers. The warning is thus most effectively pointed,—that they should not by new transgressions debar themselves from those blessings which even now lay before their eyes; and the way is appropriately prepared for that recapitulation and re-inforcement of the law of the covenant, which it is the main purpose of Deuteronomy to convey.

7. *to the mount of the Amorites*] *i.e.* to the mountain district occupied by the Amorites, reaching into the Negeb, and part of the territory assigned to the tribe of Judah. The Amorites, as the leading people of Canaan, here stand for the nations of that country generally (see *v.* 44); and "the mountain of the Amorites and the places nigh thereunto," (or more literally, "all its neighbours"), denote the whole district, which is more particularly specified in the concluding part of the verse.

9—15. This appointment of the "captains" (cf. Ex. xviii. 21 sqq.) must not be confounded with that of the Elders in Numb. xi. 16 sqq. The former would number 78,600; the latter were seventy only. The time and place, and indeed the transactions themselves, were quite different. The only common point between the two lies in the complaint of Moses, *v.* 12, which bears some verbal resemblance to Numb. xi. 14 and 17. But, as in both cases, the grievance Moses had was of the same kind, there is no reason why he should not express it in the like terms. It is, in fact, a characteristic of the speech of early times, and one exemplified in every ancient record, to employ the same or similar combinations of words for like occasions, instead of inventing new combinations for each. Such similarities afford no proof whatever of the writers having other like passages in view. Very ancient languages had not that variety and flexibility of expression which belong to the modern languages of Western Europe.

It has been observed, that in Exodus the appointment of the captains is described as made before the giving of the Law at Sinai; here it seems to be placed immediately before the people departed from Horeb, *i.e.* a year later. But it is obvious that Moses is only touching on certain parts of the whole history, and with a special purpose. God had given them a promise, and willed them to enter on the enjoyment of it. Moses too had done his part, and had provided for the good government and organization of their greatly increased multitudes. All was ready for the full accomplishment of the promises before the camp broke up from Horeb. The order of statement is here rather suggested by the purposes of the speaker than by the facts. But it is nevertheless quite correct in the main point, which is that this important arrangement for the good government of the people took place before they quitted Horeb to march direct to the Promised Land. This fact sets more clearly before us the perverseness and ingratitude of the people, to which the orator next passes; and shows, what he

12 How can I myself alone bear
your cumbrance, and your burden,
and your strife?
† Heb. *Give.*
13 †Take you wise men, and understanding, and known among your
tribes, and I will make them rulers
over you.
14 And ye answered me, and said,
The thing which thou hast spoken *is*
good *for us* to do.
15 So I took the chief of your
tribes, wise men, and known, and
† Heb. *gave.*
†made them heads over you, captains
over thousands, and captains over
hundreds, and captains over fifties,
and captains over tens, and officers
among your tribes.
16 And I charged your judges at
that time, saying, Hear *the causes*
[c] John 7. 24.
between your brethren, and [c]judge
righteously between *every* man and
his brother, and the stranger *that is*
with him.
[d] Lev. 19. 15. chap. 16. 19. 1 Sam. 16. 7. Prov. 24. 23. † Heb. *acknowledge faces.*
17 [d]Ye shall not †respect persons
in judgment; *but* ye shall hear the
small as well as the great; ye shall
not be afraid of the face of man; for
the judgment *is* God's: and the cause
that is too hard for you, bring *it* unto
me, and I will hear it.
18 And I commanded you at that
time all the things which ye should
do.
19 ¶ And when we departed from
Horeb, we went through all that
great and terrible wilderness, which
ye saw by the way of the mountain
of the Amorites, as the LORD our
God commanded us; and we came to
Kadesh-barnea.
20 And I said unto you, Ye are
come unto the mountain of the Amorites, which the LORD our God doth
give unto us.
21 Behold, the LORD thy God
hath set the land before thee: go up
and possess *it*, as the LORD God of
thy fathers hath said unto thee; fear
not, neither be discouraged.
22 ¶ And ye came near unto me
every one of you, and said, We will
send men before us, and they shall
search us out the land, and bring us
word again by what way we must go
up, and into what cities we shall
come.
23 And the saying pleased me
well: and [e]I took twelve men of you, [e] Numb. 13. 3.
one of a tribe:
24 And [f]they turned and went up [f] Numb. 13. 24.

---

was anxious to impress, that the fault of the 40 years' delay rested only with themselves.

Similar reasons explain the omission of Jethro's counsel, which led to the nomination of the captains. It was beside the present purpose to enter into such particulars.

19. *that great and terrible wilderness*] Cf. viii. 15. This language is by no means applicable to the whole peninsula of Sinai, even in its present deteriorated state: see on Num. xx. 1. It is however quite such as men would employ after having passed with toil and suffering through the worst part of it, the southern half of the Arabah: see on Num. xxi. 4; and more especially when they had but recently rested from their marches in the plain of Shittim, the largest and richest oasis in the whole district: see on Num. xxii. 1, and cf. Tristram, 'Land of Israel,' pp. 528, 529.

22, 23. Cf. Numb. xiii. 1, 2. There is no real discrepancy between these passages. The plan of sending the spies originated with the people; and, as in itself a reasonable one, it approved itself to Moses; was submitted to God, and sanctioned by Him; and carried out under special Divine direction. The orator's purpose in this chapter is to bring before the people emphatically their own responsibilities and behaviour. It is therefore important to remind them, that the sending of the spies, which led immediately to their murmuring and rebellion, was their own suggestion.

It is frivolous to object that the generation which had sinned thus was dead; and that Moses was addressing men who had had no concern in the events to which he is referring. That this fact was present to the speaker's mind is clear from *vv.* 34, 35; nay, it was the very aim he had in view, to warn the present generation not to follow their fathers in their perversity, and so defraud themselves of the promised blessing, as their fathers had done. It is but natural that Moses, who had been the leader of the congregation all along, should, when addressing it collectively, treat it as the same which he had brought forth from Egypt, and had now, for the second time, conducted to the threshold of the Promised Land.

The following *vv.* to the end of the

into the mountain, and came unto
the valley of Eshcol, and searched it
out.
25 And they took of the fruit of
the land in their hands, and brought
it down unto us, and brought us word
again, and said, *It is* a good land
which the LORD our God doth give
us.
26 Notwithstanding ye would not
go up, but rebelled against the commandment of the LORD your God:
27 And ye murmured in your
tents, and said, Because the LORD
hated us, he hath brought us forth
out of the land of Egypt, to deliver
us into the hand of the Amorites, to
destroy us.
28 Whither shall we go up? our
† Heb. *melted.* brethren have † discouraged our heart,
saying, The people *is* greater and
taller than we; the cities *are* great
and walled up to heaven; and moreover we have seen the sons of the
[g] Numb. 13. 28. [g] Anakims there.
29 Then I said unto you, Dread
not, neither be afraid of them.
30 The LORD your God which
goeth before you, he shall fight for
you, according to all that he did for
you in Egypt before your eyes;
31 And in the wilderness, where
thou hast seen how that the LORD
thy God bare thee, as a man doth
bear his son, in all the way that ye
went, until ye came into this place.
32 Yet in this thing ye did not believe the LORD your God,
33 [h] Who went in the way before [h] Exod. 13. 21.
you, to search you out a place to
pitch your tents *in*, in fire by night,
to shew you by what way ye should
go, and in a cloud by day.
34 And the LORD heard the voice
of your words, and was wroth, and
sware, saying,
35 [i] Surely there shall not one of [i] Numb. 14. 29.
these men of this evil generation see
that good land, which I sware to give
unto your fathers,
36 Save Caleb the son of Jephunneh; he shall see it, and to him will
I give the land that he hath trodden
upon, and to his children, because he
hath † wholly followed the LORD. † Heb. *fulfilled to go after.*
37 [k] Also the LORD was angry with
me for your sakes, saying, [l] Thou also [k] Numb. 20. 12. & 27. 14.
shalt not go in thither.
38 *But* Joshua the son of Nun, [l] chap. 3. 26. & 4. 21. & 34. 4.
which standeth before thee, he shall
go in thither: encourage him: for he
shall cause Israel to inherit it.

---

chapter give a condensed statement, the fuller account being in Numb. xiii. and xiv., of the occurrences which led to the banishment of the people for 40 years into the wilderness. The facts are treated with freedom, as by one familiar with them, addressing those no less so, yet in consistency with the more strictly historical record of Numbers.

37, 38. The sentence on Moses was not passed on occasion of the rebellion of the people at Kadesh, but at Meribah, some thirty-seven years later. This, as having happened not many months previously, was well known to those whom he was addressing. The general tenor of the discourse has led to its being parenthetically mentioned here. The faithfulness of God, the trespasses of the people, these are the key-notes throughout. In stating the sentence of God on the rebellious generation, the preacher naturally names the only exceptions to it. The name of Joshua leads on at once to his appointment to the leadership of the people, now just about to take effect. And so Moses naturally alludes to the cause why he himself is to be set aside. The fact that, in the midst of judgment, a future leader was provided to put them in possession of the promises, illustrates the faithfulness of God; and the description of Moses' sentence, as "for your sakes," no less illustrates the perversity of the people, to which alone the ultimate blame of all these calamities rolls back. See further on iii. 26. Ps. cvi. 32, 33, is strikingly parallel with the passage before us: "They angered God also at the waters of strife, so that it went ill with Moses for their sakes: because they provoked his spirit, so that he spake unadvisedly with his lips." Moses also was culpable in the matter, and his fault is set forth unshrinkingly; cf. xxxii. 51. There is then no suppression of anything out of reverence for God's extraordinary messenger, nor any real inconsistency between this passage and Num. xx. 10 sqq., much less any proof that we have here another independent and wholly different narrative of the transactions at Meribah. Moses simply dwells on the side of

39 Moreover your little ones, which
ye said should be a prey, and your
children, which in that day had no
knowledge between good and evil,
they shall go in thither, and unto
them will I give it, and they shall
possess it.
40 But *as for* you, turn you, and
take your journey into the wilderness
by the way of the Red sea.
41 Then ye answered and said unto me, [m] We have sinned against the
LORD, we will go up and fight, according to all that the LORD our God
commanded us. And when ye had
girded on every man his weapons of
war, ye were ready to go up into the
hill.
42 And the LORD said unto me,
Say unto them, Go not up, neither
fight; for I *am* not among you; lest
ye be smitten before your enemies.
43 So I spake unto you; and ye
would not hear, but rebelled against
the commandment of the LORD, and
† went presumptuously up into the hill.
44 And the Amorites, which dwelt
in that mountain, came out against
you, and chased you, as bees do, and
destroyed you in Seir, *even* unto
Hormah.
45 And ye returned and wept before the LORD; but the LORD would
not hearken to your voice, nor give
ear unto you.
46 So ye abode in Kadesh many
days, according unto the days that ye
abode *there*.

[m] Numb. 14. 40.

† Heb. *you were presumptuous, and went up*

---

the facts which was to his purpose; he aims at pricking the conscience of the people.

41. *ye were ready to go up into the hill*] Rather, perhaps, "ye made light of going up;" *i.e.* "ye were ready to attempt it as a trifling undertaking." On the Hebrew verb here used, see note at the end of the chapter. *V.* 43, "ye went presumptuously," or better, "were presumptuous and went," as margin, shows the issue of this spirit in action: Cf. Numb. xiv. 44, where however the Hebrew words are different.

44. *the Amorites*] In Numb. xiv. 45, it is "the Amalekites and the Canaanites," who are said to have discomfited them. The Amorites, as the most powerful nation of Canaan, lend their name here, as in other passages, to the Canaanitish tribes generally. Cf. *e.g. vv.* 7 and 19 of this chapter. The more lengthy and precise narrative of Numbers gives details here, as elsewhere, which are disregarded as unimportant to his purpose by the speaker in Deut.

as bees do] The same comparison will be found, Iliad XVI. 259 sqq.

in Seir] Cf. Numb. xiv. 45 and note.

46. *ye abode in Kadesh many days*] On this long stay cf. Introd. to Numbers, § 3, and note on Num. xx. 1.

NOTE on CHAP. I. 41.

The Hebrew word rendered in A. V. "ye were ready" is the Hiphil of הִין. It is ἅπαξ λεγόμενον, and about its precise sense there has always been much difference of opinion. Gesenius says ('Lex.' s. v.) "in hoc verbo interpretando in alia omnia abibant veteres interpretes."

Modern commentators have for the most part connected the Hebrew word with the Arabic هان, "lenis, facilis fuit," which in the fourth conjugation has the sense "despexit, vilipendit." This would give the rendering suggested in the note, "ye made light of going up;" which is adopted by Dathe, Gesen., Knob., Fürst, Keil, Schultz, &c. It cannot however be regarded as more than a probable rendering. None of the ancient versions or comm. adopt it; and it is remarkable that Saadia translates הון by بادر, in conj. 3, *i.e.* "prævenit," "festinavit;" whereas هان, a familiar word, solicited by the very letters of the Hebrew verb, would have been an obvious equivalent, if it were an equivalent at all.

The LXX. renders the word by συναθροισθέντες: (συναθροισθέντες ἀνεβαίνετε εἰς τὸ ὄρος). This sense, and possibly that of the Vulg., "instructi armis," would seem to have been derived, by a very forced inference certainly, from the root הון, in the sense of "abundance," "facultates."

The A. V. follows Jarchi, Abenezra, Vatablus, &c., and assumes that the verb הון is cognate with הן, "ecce;" and signifies strictly "ecce nos, parati sumus ascendere," &c. Cf. the German "bejahen;" the Arabic ألا. This view has been again recently put forward by Wogue; but seems somewhat farfetched.

CHAPTER II.

1 *The story is continued, that they were not to meddle with the Edomites,* 9 *nor with the Moabites,* 17 *nor with the Ammonites,* 24 *but Sihon the Amorite was subdued by them.*

THEN we turned, and took our
journey into the wilderness by
the way of the Red sea, as the LORD
spake unto me: and we compassed
mount Seir many days.
2 And the LORD spake unto me,
saying,
3 Ye have compassed this mountain long enough: turn you northward.
4 And command thou the people,
saying, Ye *are* to pass through the
coast of your brethren the children
of Esau, which dwell in Seir; and
they shall be afraid of you: take ye
good heed unto yourselves therefore:
5 Meddle not with them; for I will
not give you of their land, † no, not
so much as a foot breadth; [a] because
I have given mount Seir unto Esau
for a possession.
6 Ye shall buy meat of them for
money, that ye may eat; and ye shall
also buy water of them for money,
that ye may drink.
7 For the LORD thy God hath
blessed thee in all the works of thy
hand: he knoweth thy walking through
this great wilderness: these forty years
the LORD thy God *hath been* with
thee; thou hast lacked nothing.
8 And when we passed by from
our brethren the children of Esau,
which dwelt in Seir, through the way
of the plain from Elath, and from
Ezion-gaber, we turned and passed by
the way of the wilderness of Moab.
9 And the LORD said unto me,
‖ Distress not the Moabites, neither

† Heb. *even to the treading of the sole of the foot.*
[a] Gen. 36. 8.
‖ Or, *Use no hostility against Moab.*

CHAP. II. **1—3.** The people were at Kadesh in the second year of the Exodus (Num. xiii. 26, where see Note at the end of the chapter), and are again spoken of as being there at the close of the thirty-eight years' wandering, and in the fortieth of the Exodus (Num. xx. 1). *V.* 1 seems to refer in general terms to the long years of wandering, the details of which were not to Moses' present purpose. The command of *vv.* 2 and 3 relates to their journey from Kadesh to Mount Hor (Num. xx. 22; xxxiii. 37), and directs their march round the south extremity of Mount Seir, so as to "compass the land of Edom" (Judges xi. 18; Num. xxi. 4), and so northwards towards the Arnon, *i.e.* "by the way of the wilderness of Moab," *v.* 8. This circuitous path was followed because of the refusal of the Edomites to allow the people to pass through their territory.

4. From Num. xx. 18—20, it appears that the Edomites made formidable preparations to resist the passage of the Israelites through the midst of their land; they did not, however, and probably dared not, resist the passage of the host along their eastern frontier, which is, as compared with that towards the Arabah, open and defenceless.

5. *I have given mount Seir to Esau*] Though the descendants of Esau were conquered by David (2 Sam. viii. 14), and "all they of Edom became David's servants," yet they were not dispossessed of their land, and in the reign of Jehoshaphat they regained their independence (2 Kings viii. 20—22).

6. The Edomites, though they refused to allow passage through their land, did not decline to sell the people necessary provisions (*v.* 29); and indeed would, as we may infer from *v.* 4, be afraid to irritate them by doing so.

buy water] Literally "dig water:" *i.e.* purchase permission to dig for water.

8. *And when we passed by*] These words imply the failure of the attempt made to pass directly through the territory of Edom: cf. Num. xx. 20, 21.

from Elath, and from Ezion-gaber] For Ezion-geber, see Num. xxxiii. 35. Elath is mentioned again in connexion with it, 1 Kings ix. 26: "Solomon made a navy of ships in Ezion-geber, which is beside Eloth, on the shore of the Red Sea, in the land of Edom." From this it would appear that Elath was the better known place of the two. Elath, in Greek Αἰλών and Αἰλανή, is at the northern extremity of the eastern arm of the Red Sea, and gives to that arm the name of the Elanitic Gulf. The town has now a small castle with a garrison under the viceroy of Egypt; and, like the gulf, bears the name of Akaba. Its sole importance lies at present in its being on the route of the annual caravan of pilgrims from Cairo to Mecca. The word Elath or Eloth means "trees;" and is still justified by the grove of palm-trees at Akaba. (Cf. Stanley, 'Sinai and Palestine,' p. 84.)

9. The Moabites and the Ammonites (*v.* 19) being descended from Lot, the nephew of Abraham (Gen. xix. 30—38), were, like the Edomites, kinsmen of the Israelites.

contend with them in battle: for I
will not give thee of their land *for*
a possession; because I have given
Ar unto the children of Lot *for* a
possession.
10 The Emims dwelt therein in
times past, a people great, and many,
and tall, as the Anakims;
11 Which also were accounted
giants, as the Anakims; but the Moabites call them Emims.
12 [b]The Horims also dwelt in
Seir beforetime; but the children of
Esau [†]succeeded them, when they
had destroyed them from before them,
and dwelt in their ‖stead; as Israel
did unto the land of his possession,
which the LORD gave unto them.
13 Now rise up, *said I*, and get
you over [c]the ‖brook Zered. And
we went over the brook Zered.
14 And the space in which we
came from Kadesh-barnea, until we
were come over the brook Zered,
was thirty and eight years; until all
the generation of the men of war
were wasted out from among the host,
as the LORD sware unto them.
15 For indeed the hand of the
LORD was against them, to destroy
them from among the host, until they
were consumed.
16 ¶ So it came to pass, when all
the men of war were consumed and
dead from among the people,
17 That the LORD spake unto me,
saying,
18 Thou art to pass over through
Ar, the coast of Moab, this day:
19 And *when* thou comest nigh
over against the children of Ammon,
distress them not, nor meddle with
them: for I will not give thee of
the land of the children of Ammon
any possession; because I have given
it unto the children of Lot *for* a possession.
20 (That also was accounted a
land of giants: giants dwelt therein
in old time; and the Ammonites call
them Zamzummims;
21 A people great, and many, and

[b] Gen. 36. 20.
† Heb. *inherited them.*
‖ Or, *room.*
[c] Numb. 21. 12.
‖ Or, *valley.*

10—12. For the Emims and the Horims see Gen. xiv. 5 and 6: for the Anakims, Num. xiii. 22.

The archæological notices in these verses, which obviously break the sense of the context (see next note), have every appearance of being a gloss. See the Note at the end of the chapter.

13. *Now rise up*, said I, *and get you over the brook Zered.*] The words, "said I," introduced by our translators at the last revision, and not found in the Hebrew, should be dropped. The words "rise up, and get you over the brook Zered" connect themselves with *v.* 9, and form the conclusion of what God said to Moses. The intermediate *vv.* must be regarded, if allowed to stand in the text, as parenthetic. Moses resumes the narrative in his own words in what immediately follows: "And we went over the brook Zered."

14. Before they passed the Zered, "the generation of the men of war," which came out of Egypt, had passed away. Thus was fulfilled the sentence of Num. xiv. 23, that none of these men should see the land which God sware unto their fathers. From the high ground, on the other side of the Zered, if we identify it with the Wady Kerek (see Num. xxi. 12), a distant view of the Promised Land might have been obtained; and according to Seetzen, even Jerusalem can be seen in clear weather.

16—19. From the brook Zered the people passed on "by the way of the wilderness of Moab," *i.e.* leaving the country occupied by Moab on their left, until they came to the Arnon, which formed at that time the northern boundary of Moab, and separated Moab from the Amorites and the Ammonites. At the Arnon they would, in their line of march, come upon the territories of Sihon, and consequently "nigh over against" (*v.* 19) those of the Ammonites, who dwelt to the East of Sihon's kingdom. The mention of the Ammonites leads to the insertion (*vv.* 20—23) of some particulars respecting the ancient inhabitants of these districts, and their extermination.

20—23. These *vv.*, like *vv.* 10—12 (see note), are in all likelihood an addition made by a later reviser. See the Note at the end of the chapter.

20. *Zamzummims*] A giant race usually identified, from the similarity of name, with the Zuzims of Gen. xiv. 5. It would give probability to this conjecture if we could be sure that the 'Ham' of that verse is the name of the chief city of the Zuzims (see note in loc.); since 'Ham' might then be, as Tuch, Clark ('Bible Atlas,' p. 8), and others

tall, as the Anakims; but the LORD destroyed them before them; and they succeeded them, and dwelt in their stead:

22 As he did to the children of Esau, which dwelt in Seir, when he destroyed the Horims from before them; and they succeeded them, and dwelt in their stead even unto this day:

23 And the Avims which dwelt in Hazerim, *even* unto Azzah, the Caphtorims, which came forth out of Caphtor, destroyed them, and dwelt in their stead.)

24 ¶ Rise ye up, take your journey, and pass over the river Arnon: behold, I have given into thine hand Sihon the Amorite, king of Heshbon,
† Heb. *begin, possess.* and his land: † begin to possess *it*, and contend with him in battle.

25 This day will I begin to put the dread of thee and the fear of thee upon the nations *that are* under the whole heaven, who shall hear report of thee, and shall tremble, and be in anguish because of thee.

26 ¶ And I sent messengers out of the wilderness of Kedemoth unto Sihon king of Heshbon with words of peace, saying,

27 [d]Let me pass through thy land: [d] Numb. 21. 21, 22.
I will go along by the high way, I will neither turn unto the right hand nor to the left.

28 Thou shalt sell me meat for money, that I may eat; and give me water for money, that I may drink: only I will pass through on my feet;

29 (As the children of Esau which dwell in Seir, and the Moabites which dwell in Ar, did unto me;) until I shall pass over Jordan into the land which the LORD our God giveth us.

30 But Sihon king of Heshbon would not let us pass by him: for the LORD thy God hardened his spirit, and made his heart obstinate, that he might deliver him into thy hand, as *appeareth* this day.

31 And the LORD said unto me, Behold, I have begun to give Sihon and his land before thee: begin to

---

suppose, the root of the name given to the chief city of the Ammonites, Rabbath-Ammon.

23. *the Avims which dwelt in Hazerim, even unto Azzah*] Read **Gaza**, of which Azzah is the Hebrew form. "Hazerim" is not strictly a proper name, but means "villages," or "enclosures," probably such as are still common in the East. A piece of ground is surrounded with a rude fence, in the midst of which the tents may be pitched, and the cattle tethered at night in safety from marauders. The Avims are no doubt identical with the Avites of Joshua xiii. 3, and possibly connected with the Ava of 2 Kings xvii. 24. We have perhaps another trace of them in Avim, the name of a Benjamite town, Josh. xviii. 23. As their district appears to have been included in the promise (Josh. xiii.) it seems probable that they belonged to the original Canaanitish population; and as the words "from the south," with which Josh. xiii. 4 begins, belong apparently to the preceding verse, it would appear that the Avites dwelt in the extreme southern district of the land. Their name is added as a sort of appendage in this passage of Joshua to those of the five powerful cities which formed the confederacy of the Philistines. The Avims were doubtless a scattered remnant of a conquered people living in their "hazerim" in the neighbourhood of Gerar. The word, which means "ruins," seems itself expressive of their fallen estate.

It has been inferred, from the mention of the Avites in Joshua *l. c.*, that their conquest by the Caphtorims cannot have taken place till the days of the Judges at the earliest, and that the passage before us is consequently of later date than Moses. The passage has indeed the appearance of a note which has improperly found its way into the text: see on *vv.* 10—12. But it is unlikely that the Caphtorims, whenever their invasion may have been, extirpated the Avites utterly; and the character of the notice in Joshua xiii. 3, 4 suggests that the Avites were even then dependent on the Philistines (*i.e.* the Caphtorims), and consequently that the conquest had taken place long before.

LXX. identifies the Avims and the Hivites, rendering both Εὐαῖοι. The names are however radically different in Hebrew.

the Caphtorims] See note on Gen. x. 14.

26. *Kedemoth*] This town was afterwards assigned to the Reubenites (Josh. xiii. 18): it was (1 Chron. vi. 79) one of the cities out of that tribe given to the Levites. Its name signifies "easternmost parts."

29. Cf. xxiii. 3, 4, and note.

possess, that thou mayest inherit his
land.
[e] Numb. 21. 23.
32 [e] Then Sihon came out against
us, he and all his people, to fight at
Jahaz.
33 And the LORD our God delivered him before us; and we smote
him, and his sons, and all his people.
34 And we took all his cities at
that time, and utterly destroyed † the
men, and the women, and the little
ones, of every city, we left none to
remain:
† Heb. *every city of men, and women, and little ones.*
35 Only the cattle we took for a
prey unto ourselves, and the spoil of
the cities which we took.
36 From Aroer, which *is* by the
brink of the river of Arnon, and
from the city that *is* by the river,
even unto Gilead, there was not one
city too strong for us: the LORD our
God delivered all unto us:
37 Only unto the land of the children of Ammon thou camest not, *nor*
unto any place of the river Jabbok,
nor unto the cities in the mountains,
nor unto whatsoever the LORD our
God forbad us.

---

34. *utterly destroyed the men, and the women, and the little ones, of every city*] Render, **laid under ban every inhabited city, both women and children.** See Note at the end of the chapter.

36. *Aroer, which is by the brink of the river of Arnon*] Aroer stood on the north bank of the river, and was assigned (Josh. xiii. 9, 16) to the tribe of Reuben, of which it formed the most southerly city. Burckhardt in 1852 found the ruins, which still bear the name Ara'yr, on the edge of a cliff overlooking the river. 'Travels,' pp. 372—374. Mesha in the 26th line of the Moabite stone records that "he built Aroer and made the road over the Arnon." No doubt the city was restored and probably re-fortified by Mesha after his successes over king Ahaziah. If the latter words of the line above quoted are correctly interpreted by Nöldeke, Ginsburg, &c., as importing that Mesha bridged over the valley of the Arnon at this place, the work was a gigantic one. The width across is great (it is described by Burckhardt as "about two hours"); the valley is deep, and the descent to it abrupt. In Roman times it was spanned by a viaduct the ruins of which still remain, and which was probably built on the lines of the original structure of Mesha. It must not be confounded with "Aroer, which is before Rabbah" (Josh. xiii. 25). This latter place was "built," *i.e.* rebuilt, by the Gadites (Num. xxxii. 34); belonged to that tribe; and was consequently far to the north of the Arnon. A third Aroer in the tribe of Judah is mentioned 1 Sam. xxx. 28.

and from the city that is by the river] Literally, "in the river." The situation is more distinctly described Joshua xiii. 9, 16, as "*in the midst* of the river." The words are not a further description of Aroer, which was *on the brink* of the valley, not *in the midst of it.* They point to Ar Moab, named in *v.* 18, which is "the dwelling of Ar" of Num. xxi. 15; where see note and reff.

NOTES on CHAP. II. 10—12, 20—23, and 34.

The two groups of ethnological notices contained in these passages have been long ago suspected to be insertions from a later hand: so Kennicott, Geddes, Boothroyd; and see Rosenm. *in loc.* The reasons for this opinion are certainly weighty.

(1) The removal of both from the narrative not only does not injure it, but greatly add to its directness and effectiveness. It is impossible not to see that *v.* 13 closely belongs to *v.* 9, and when the two are read consecutively it is difficult to escape the conviction that that was their original relation. The A. V. indeed unwarrantably attributes the order given in *v.* 13 to Moses by interpolating the words "said I." But *v.* 13 clearly gives the close of the Divine behest begun in *v.* 9. Similarly the *vv.* 20—23 interrupt, not quite so harshly but as manifestly, a similar direction of God to Moses commenced in *vv.* 17 sqq., and of which *vv.* 24, 25 are the conclusion. They are properly marked in A. V. as parenthetic: but it is certainly little after the manner of Moses to break in upon the communications of God to him with parentheses; and it seems somewhat unsuitable to regard these fragments of ancient history as portions of what God revealed.

(2) The words "as Israel did unto the land of his possession," taken in their natural sense, refer to the conquest of Canaan as a past transaction. The explanations offered, *e.g.* that the passage is prophetical, that it refers to the territories of Sihon and Og only, &c., are not satisfactory.

(3) The observation that the *vv.* in ques-

tion are germane to the purpose of the narrative is true, but does not of itself prove that they formed originally integral portions of it. *Vv.* 10—12 are obviously introduced in explanation of the statement that "Ar was given to the children of Lot." God destroyed from before the children of Lot mighty nations, as He did the nations of Canaan before the Israelites. Therefore the Israelites were not to disturb the Moabites, who had the same title to Ar as Israel to Canaan. Like reasons are adduced, *vv.* 20—23, for not molesting the Ammonites. But the reasons are antiquarian details which could hardly be necessary for Moses and his contemporaries, but are exactly such as a later and learned historian would desire to put on record by way of confirming and illustrating the general assertion of *vv.* 9 and 19, that God had "given their land to the children of Lot."

(4) It is evident however that the two sets of *vv.*, if introduced long after the days of Moses, were not intended to be passed off as part of the original text. No attempt was made to interweave them closely into the context, or to accommodate the phraseology of them to the circumstances of the fortieth year after the exodus. They contain exactly such matter as a modern editor might have given in explanatory foot-notes: but which a Jewish reviser, if duly authorized, would feel warranted in writing along with his text. Substantially then we may regard them as glosses, perhaps contributed by Ezra.

34. The A. V. renders here, "utterly destroyed the men, and the women, and the little ones of every city." The interpretation of the passage turns upon (1) the proper sense of the word מתם; (2) the true syntax. In neither particular can the decision arrived at by our translators be now maintained.

For (1) מתם is obviously connected with מות, and does not mean adult males as distinct from other human beings, but "mortals," "men," generally. Indeed in the present text the adult males seem excluded by the nature of the case, for they had perished in battle, *v.* 33, and the special aim of the verse is to record how the Israelites completed the work of slaughter by afterwards destroying the non-combatants. The word occurs again in a strictly parallel passage, iii. 6. The A. V. has rendered the word correctly in Job xxiv. 12 ("Men groan from out of the city"), though there too (as here) it should be taken as dependent upon עיר, and the passage rendered "from the city of men (*i.e.* the inhabited city) they raise a cry." In Judg. xx. 48 the word occurs with a different punctuation in a context similar in tenor to Deut. ii. 34, iii. 6, and describing the utter destruction of the Benjamites. But there can be no doubt that the pointing of מתם there ought to be the same as it is here, and indeed (cf. Rosenm., Gesen.) the Peshito, many ancient editions, and some MSS. so exhibit it. The LXX. has one and the same rendering for the word in the three passages: *i.e.* ἑξῆς. In the passage before us the LXX. renders ἐξωλοθρεύσαμεν πᾶσαν πόλιν ἑξῆς καὶ τὰς γυναῖκας καὶ τὰ τέκνα, and reads apparently מְתֹם in all three cases, regarding it as a substantive = "integritas" (connected with תמם, see Fürst, s. v. מתם). The occurrence of the word four times in construction with עיר is noteworthy. The phrase seems to have been a common one, and the sense, "city of mortals," *i.e.* "inhabited city," is apposite and etymologically satisfactory. (So after some discussion Gesen. eventually renders, 'Thes.' s. v. מתם: and Wogue.)

But (2) the A. V. in Deut. ii. 34, iii. 6, has disregarded the true syntax. The three nouns מתם, הנשים, הטף are certainly not coordinate. The omission of the article with the first of them, and its insertion before the other two, shows this, as does also the accentuation. The sense therefore clearly is, "we destroyed every inhabited city, both women and little ones;" the latter clause being added by way of fuller explanation.

CHAPTER III.

1 The story of the conquest of Og king of Bashan. 11 The bigness of his bed. 12 The distribution of those lands to the two tribes and half. 23 Moses' prayer to enter into the land. 26 He is permitted to see it.

THEN we turned, and went up
[a] Numb. 21. 33, &c. chap. 29. 7. the way to Bashan: and [a] Og
the king of Bashan came out against
us, he and all his people, to battle at
Edrei.
2 And the LORD said unto me,
Fear him not: for I will deliver him,
and all his people, and his land, into
thy hand; and thou shalt do unto
him as thou didst unto [b] Sihon king [b] Numb. 21. 24.
of the Amorites, which dwelt at Heshbon.
3 So the LORD our God delivered
into our hands [c] Og also, the king of [c] Numb. 21. 33.
Bashan, and all his people: and we
smote him until none was left to him
remaining.
4 And we took all his cities at
that time, there was not a city which
we took not from them, threescore

cities, all the region of Argob, the kingdom of Og in Bashan.
5 All these cities *were* fenced with high walls, gates, and bars; beside unwalled towns a great many.
6 And we utterly destroyed them, as we did unto Sihon king of Heshbon, utterly destroying the men, women, and children, of every city.
7 But all the cattle, and the spoil

CHAP. III. 4. *threescore cities*] Cf. *vv.* 12—15. No doubt these are identical with the "Bashan-havoth-jair," *i.e.* cities of Jair in Bashan, of *v.* 14: and with "the towns of Jair" in Bashan of the same number in Josh. xiii. 30; 1 K. iv. 13; and 1 Chr. xi. 23. See on Num. xxxii. 41.

all the region of Argob] The Hebrew word here rendered "region," means literally *rope* or *cable;* and though undoubtedly used elsewhere in a general topographical sense for *portion* or *district* (*e.g.* Josh. xvii. 5), has a special propriety in reference to Argob, with which it is connected wherever that term is used, *i.e.* in this *v.*, and in *vv.* 13 and 14, and 1 K. iv. 13. The name Argob means (according to Gesen.) *stone-heap*, and is paraphrased by the Targums, *Trachonitis*, or "the rough country;" both titles, like the modern *Lejah*, designating, with the wonted vigour of Hebrew topographical terms, the more striking features of the district. The Argob is described as an island of black basaltic rock, oval in form, measuring sixty miles by twenty, rising abruptly to the height of from twenty to thirty feet from the surrounding plains of Bashan. Its borders are compared to a rugged shore-line; hence its description in the text as "the girdle of the stony country," would seem peculiarly appropriate.

"The physical features of the Lejah," says Porter ('Travels,' II. pp. 241, 242), "present the most singular phenomena I have ever witnessed. It is wholly composed of black basalt rock, which appears to have in past ages issued from innumerable pores in the earth in a liquid state, and to have flowed out on every side until the plain was almost covered. Before cooling, its surface was agitated by some fearful tempest or other such agency; and it was afterwards shattered and rent by internal convulsions and vibrations. The cup-like cavities from which the liquid mass was projected are still seen; and likewise the wavy surface a thick liquid generally assumes which cools while flowing. There are in many places deep fissures and yawning gulfs, with rugged broken edges, while in other places are jagged heaps of rock that seem not to have been sufficiently heated to flow, but were forced upward by a mighty agency, and rent and shattered to their centre. The rock is filled with little pits and protuberances like air-bubbles: it is as hard as flint, and emits a sharp metallic sound when struck." Yet "this forbidding region is thickly studded with deserted cities and villages," and many of them, from the extraordinary solidity of their structure, are still standing almost uninjured. See a paper by Mr C. G. Graham "On the Ancient Bashan and the cities of Og," in 'Cambridge Essays for 1858.' The rocky labyrinth of the Argob in fact offers natural fastnesses which are almost impregnable, and which compensated, by the security they offered, for the many inconveniences of the site.

5. *All these cities were fenced with high walls, gates, and bars*] Lit. "double gates and a bar." The stone doors of Bashan, whether as ancient as the days of Og or not, have excited the amazement of every traveller who has visited the country. "The streets are perfect," says Mr Graham, 'Cambridge Essays for 1858,' p. 160, "the walls perfect, and, what seems most astonishing, the stone doors are still hanging on their hinges, so little impression has been made during these many centuries on the hard and durable stone of which they were built." The doors are described by Mr Porter ('Travels,' II. 22, 23), as "formed of slabs of stone, opening on pivots which are projecting parts of the stone itself, and working in sockets in the lintel and threshold." He mentions one, in a house, "so large that camels could go in and out with ease." The height of the doors in general points to a race of great stature. Mr Graham remarks (*l. c.*), "We could not help being impressed with the belief that had we never known anything of the early portion of Scripture history before visiting this country, we should have been forced to the conclusion that its original inhabitants, the people who had constructed these cities, were not only a powerful and mighty nation, but individuals of greater strength than ourselves." Mr Graham remarks "on the crowding together of the towns" as "one of the first peculiarities" which he remarked in visiting the district. A recent traveller, Mr D. W. Freshfield ('Travels in the Central Caucasus,' &c. London, 1869), has indeed called in question the correctness of the conclusions arrived at by Mr Porter and Mr Graham respecting the age and origin of these cities. But his examination of them seems to have been but hurried, and he himself admits the great antiquity of some of the buildings. Many of them, especially in the larger towns, which were those visited by Mr Freshfield, have evidently been altered in comparatively modern times, and others erected beside and amongst them. These facts sufficiently explain the

of the cities, we took for a prey to
ourselves.
8 And we took at that time out
of the hand of the two kings of the
Amorites the land that *was* on this
side Jordan, from the river of Arnon
unto mount Hermon;
9 (*Which* Hermon the Sidonians
call Sirion; and the Amorites call
it Shenir;)
10 All the cities of the plain, and
all Gilead, and all Bashan, unto Salchah and Edrei, cities of the kingdom
of Og in Bashan.
11 For only Og king of Bashan
remained of the remnant of giants;

---

occurrence amongst the remains of Greek inscriptions and Saracenic ornaments, as has been pointed out by Mr Porter in the Preface to his second edition of 'Five Years in Damascus' (London, 1870); in which (under date March, 1870) he makes some strictures on Mr Freshfield's remarks.

The *vv.* before us then, far from reflecting, as some have fancied, the tone of one speaking as of events in a far distant past, represent the lively impressions made by the spectacle of a memorable victory won in a very remarkable territory. Before they approached Edrei the Israelites had traversed either a limestone district where the abodes of men were often artificial caves, or a rich pasture land such as the plains destitute of rock and stones, which stretch to the foot of the Argob. All at once they came on the marvellous barrier of rocks amidst which Edrei and the other of the sixty cities were perched; built of black stone as hard as iron, defended by the Rephaim, and ruled over by the giant-king Og. Had Og remained within his fortifications it was humanly speaking impossible for the Israelites to have vanquished him. Such was the dread he inspired, that God (*v.* 2) gave special encouragement to Moses, "Fear him not." It would seem (Joshua xxiv. 12) that the hornet was sent into these impregnable cities by God, and so Og and his people were driven forth into the open field (*v.* 1), where they were overthrown by Moses and the Israelites in a pitched battle opposite Edrei. This signal victory and its circumstances evidently impressed the people deeply at this time, and its memory, as the Psalms attest, lingered for ages after in the national mind.

9. *Which Hermon the Sidonians call Sirion; and the Amorites call it Shenir*] Hermon is the southern and culminating point of the range of Lebanon. "It is both physically and politically a grand central point in the geography of Syria and Palestine. From it are derived all the most noted rivers—the Jordan, whose fountains are fed by its eternal snows; the Abana and Pharpar, 'rivers of Damascus;' the Orontes, which swept past the walls of the classic and Christian Antioch; and the Leontes. All the great ancient kingdoms of the country also converged at Hermon—Bashan, Damascus, Syria, Israel. It was also the religious centre of primæval Syria. Its Baal sanctuaries not only existed but gave it a name before the Exodus." (Porter in Kitto's 'Encycl.' sub voce *Hermon.*) Hence the careful specification of the various names by which the mountain was known. The Sidonian name of it might easily have become known to Moses through the constant traffic which had gone on from the most ancient times between Sidon and Egypt. Syria was repeatedly traversed in all directions by the Egyptian armies from the accession of the 18th dynasty downwards. The transcription of Semitic words in the papyri of the 19th dynasty is remarkably complete. Dean Stanley observes, 'Sinai and Palestine," pp. 403, 404, "The several names in the text, as also that of Sion, iv. 48, and not less the modern appellations of it, are all descriptive. Rising with its grey snow-capped cone to a height of about 9500 feet it is visible from most parts of the promised land, and even from the depths of the Jordan valley and the shores of the Dead Sea. Hence it was Sion 'the upraised;' or 'Hermon' 'the lofty peak;' or 'Shenir' and 'Sirion,' the glittering 'breastplate' of ice; or above all, 'Lebanon' the 'Mont Blanc' of Palestine; the 'White Mountain' of ancient times; the mountain of the 'Old White-headed Man' (Jebel es Sheykh), or 'the mountain of ice' (Jebel eth Tilj), in modern times."

10. *Salchah*] Cf. Josh. xii. 5; 1 Chr. v. 11, where it is named as belonging to the tribe of Gad. The modern Salchah of Burckhardt; Sarchad of Robinson; Sulkhad of Porter, who visited it in 1853, and describes it, 'Five Years in Damascus,' 2nd edit. pp. 248 sqq., lies seven hours' journey to the south-east of Bostra or Bozrah of Moab. As the eastern border city of the kingdom of Bashan it was no doubt strongly fortified. Mr Graham describes it in 'Cambridge Essays for 1858,' p. 156: "Above the town, and built upon a hill, one of the last off-shoots from the mountains of Bashan, is a strong castle, which occupies one of the most commanding positions imaginable. It is just on the very edge of the Desert, and a foe from whichever direction he might come could be seen almost a day's journey off."

Edrei] Cf. on Num. xxi. 33.

11. *of the remnant of giants*] Or Rephaim: see on Gen. xiv. 5 and xv. 20.

behold, his bedstead *was* a bedstead
of iron; *is* it not in Rabbath of the
children of Ammon? nine cubits *was*
the length thereof, and four cubits
the breadth of it, after the cubit of
a man.

12 And this land, *which* we possessed at that time, from Aroer, which
is by the river Arnon, and half mount
[d] Numb. Gilead, and [d] the cities thereof, gave
32. 33. Josh. 13. 8, I unto the Reubenites and to the
&c. Gadites.

13 And the rest of Gilead, and
all Bashan, *being* the kingdom of Og,
gave I unto the half tribe of Manasseh; all the region of Argob, with
all Bashan, which was called the land
of giants.

14 Jair the son of Manasseh took
all the country of Argob unto the
coasts of Geshuri and Maachathi;
and called them after his own
name, Bashan-[e] havoth-jair, unto this [e] Numb.
day. 32. 41.

---

a bedstead of iron] The "iron" was probably the black basalt ("eisenstein") of the country, which not only contains a large proportion, about 20 per cent., of iron, but was actually called iron, and is still so regarded by the Arabians. So too Pliny, 'Nat. Hist.' XXXVI. 11: "Invenit Egyptus in Ethiopia quem vocant basalten ferrei coloris atque duritiæ. Unde et nomen ei dedit." Iron was indeed both known and used, principally for tools (see *e.g.* xix. 5 and note), at the date in question by the Semitic people of Palestine and the adjoining countries; see Wilkinson, 'A. E.' II. pp. 154 sqq., Rougemont, 'L'Age du Bronze,' p. 189; but bronze was the ordinary metal of which weapons, articles of furniture, &c. were made.

The word translated "bedstead" (*eres*) is derived from a root signifying "to unite" or "bind together," and so "to arch" or "cover with a vault." Its cognate forms in Arabic and Syriac have parallel significations. The word may then certainly mean "bier," and perhaps does so in this passage. (So Knob., Winer, Von Lengerke, &c.) Modern travellers have discovered in the territories of Og sarcophagi as well as many other articles made of the black basalt of the country.

is it not in Rabbath of the children of Ammon?] Probably after the defeat and death of Og at Edrei the remnant of his army fled into the territory of the friendly Ammonites, and carried with them the corpse of the giant king. It is not necessary to suppose from *v.* 3 (cf. Num. xxi. 35) that there were absolutely no survivors at all of Og's people. Rabbah was not captured by the Israelites till the time of David, 2 Sam. xii. 29; but it is not likely that this remarkable relic would remain at Rabbah unknown to them. There is no necessity to suppose, with Ewald, that the Ammonites were allies of Israel against Og; nor, with Schultz, that they took the opportunity of making an inroad on Og's territory on the flank whilst he was engaged with Israel in front.

after the cubit of a man.] *i.e.* after the usual and ordinary cubit. Cf. Is. viii. 1, "take thee a roll, and write in it with a man's pen," Rev. xxi. 17, "a hundred and forty and four cubits, according to the measure of a man:" *i. e.* counted as men are wont to count. The words are added to the number of cubits in order to exclude the idea that a smaller cubit than usual was intended. The bedstead or sarcophagus would thus be from thirteen to fourteen feet long: but was of course considerably larger than the body of the man for whom it was designed.

14. *of Geshuri and Maachathi*] Render, **of the Geshurite and Maachathite;** and see Josh. xii. 5 and xiii. 11.

The Geshurites here mentioned are not to be confounded with those mentioned in Joshua xiii. 2, who, as appears from that place, and more clearly from 1 Sam. xvii. 8, were neighbours of the Philistines. The Geshurites here in question are frequently named in connection with Bashan, and their territory, if not included within Bashan, evidently adjoined it. Though (1 Chron. ii. 23) Jair the son of Manasseh "took Geshur," yet (Josh. xiii. 13) the Geshurites were not expelled, but dwelt among the Israelites. Probably they occupied some corner of the impregnable district of Argob, with which they are here connected. Hence we read (2 Sam. xv. 8) of "Geshur in Aram" or "in the high ground," rendered in A.V. Syria. The Geshurites maintained themselves, probably as a tributary principality, even in the times of the kings. David married Maachah "the daughter of Talmai king of Geshur" (2 Sam. iii. 3), and was by her the father of Absalom.

Maachathi] The mention of this people both here and in Joshua xii. and xiii. *l. c.* with the Geshurites points to a connection between the peoples; and this, since the name Maachah was borne by the daughter of Talmai king of Geshur, may have been more than a local one. Like Geshur, Maachah is connected with Aram (1 Chron. xix. 6, 7); and had a king in later times who allied himself with the Ammonites against David. The

15 And I gave Gilead unto Machir.
16 And unto the Reubenites and
unto the Gadites I gave from Gilead
even unto the river Arnon half the
valley, and the border even unto the
river Jabbok, *which is* the border of
the children of Ammon;
17 The plain also, and Jordan, and
the coast *thereof*, from Chinnereth
even unto the sea of the plain, *even*
‖ Or, *under the springs of Pisgah*, or, *the hill*. the salt sea, ‖ under Ashdoth-pisgah
eastward.
18 ¶ And I commanded you at
that time, saying, The LORD your
God hath given you this land to pos-
f Numb. 32. 20. sess it: *f* ye shall pass over armed
before your brethren the children of
† Heb. *sons of power*. Israel, all *that are* † meet for the war.
19 But your wives, and your little
ones, and your cattle, (*for* I know
that ye have much cattle,) shall abide
in your cities which I have given you;
20 Until the LORD have given
rest unto your brethren, as well as
unto you, and *until* they also possess the land which the LORD your
God hath given them beyond Jordan:
and *then* shall ye *g* return every man *g* Josh. 22. 4.
unto his possession, which I have given
you.
21 ¶ And *h* I commanded Joshua *h* Numb. 27. 18.
at that time, saying, Thine eyes have
seen all that the LORD your God hath
done unto these two kings: so shall
the LORD do unto all the kingdoms
whither thou passest.
22 Ye shall not fear them: for
the LORD your God he shall fight for
you.

---

exact position of Maachah like that of Geshur cannot be ascertained; but was no doubt amongst the fastnesses which lay between Bashan and the kingdom of Damascus, and on the skirts of mount Hermon.

unto this day] This expression, frequent in Genesis, is not found in Exodus and the two following books. It may be a gloss inserted here by an after hand, but it does not as used in the Bible necessarily imply that the time spoken of as elapsed is long. It amounts to no more than our "until now." In Josh. xxii. 3 it denotes the few months during which the two tribes and a half had assisted their brethren in the conquest of the land westward of Jordan: and in Josh. xxiii. 9, refers to the period that had passed from the beginning of the victories of the Israelites to the close of Joshua's life. It may then be used in the text to denote the duration to the time then present of what had been already some months accomplished. Moses dwells, *vv.* 13, 14, on the completeness of that part of the conquest which had been achieved; and winds up his accumulation of particulars, "all Bashan," "all Argob," &c., with the statement that Jair had so thoroughly made himself master of the cities of the district as that they were now currently known by his name.

16. *from Gilead even unto the river Arnon half the valley, and the border even unto the river Jabbok*] The words "and the border," *i.e.* "and its border," belong, as in Num. xxxiv. 6, to the preceding context. The sense is that the Reubenites and Gadites were to possess the district from the Jabbok on the north to the Arnon on the south, including the middle part of the valley of the Arnon, and the territory ("coast" or "border") thereto pertaining. Thus these tribes who had "much cattle," *v.* 19, were provided with free access to the water, and with the valuable though narrow strip of green pasture along the side of the brook. The gorge of Arnon, about eighty miles in length, is for the most part about two miles wide. So in the next *v.* the words "and the coast," lit. "the boundary," are added similarly to the Jordan, and mean that the valley and bank on their own side of the stream were included in the portion of the two tribes.

the border of the children of Ammon] The Jabbok in its earlier course divided the two tribes from the Ammonites, in its later from Bashan.

17. *under Ashdoth-pisgah*] It is doubtful whether these words form a proper name or not. The word (*ashdōth*) is translated "springs" iv. 49, and Josh. x. 40 and xii. 8, though in Josh. xii. 3 it is again treated as a proper name. It is derived from a root signifying "to pour forth," and signifies "the pourings forth" of the torrents, *i.e.* the ravines down which the torrents find their way to the low grounds. Thus the words may signify "under the slopes of Pisgah towards the east," and are added to define somewhat more accurately the portion of the Arabah allotted to the two tribes.

On "Pisgah" or "*the* Pisgah," for the word is always used with the article, and may (as marg.) be rendered "the hill:" see Num. xxi. 20.

23 And I besought the LORD at
that time, saying,
24 O Lord GOD, thou hast begun
to shew thy servant thy greatness,
and thy mighty hand: for what God
is there in heaven or in earth, that can
do according to thy works, and according to thy might?
25 I pray thee, let me go over,
and see the good land that *is* beyond
Jordan, that goodly mountain, and
Lebanon.
26 But the LORD [i]was wroth with
me for your sakes, and would not
hear me: and the LORD said unto
me, Let it suffice thee; speak no
more unto me of this matter.
27 Get thee up into the top of
‖ Pisgah, and lift up thine eyes westward, and northward, and southward,
and eastward, and behold *it* with thine
eyes: for thou shalt not go over this
Jordan.
28 But charge Joshua, and encourage him, and strengthen him: for he
shall go over before this people, and
he shall cause them to inherit the land
which thou shalt see.
29 So we abode in the valley over
against Beth-peor.

[i] Numb. 20. 12. chap. 1. 37.

‖ Or, *the hill.*

CHAPTER IV.

1 *An exhortation to obedience.* 41 *Moses appointeth the three cities of refuge on that side Jordan.*

NOW therefore hearken, O Israel, unto the statutes and unto the judgments, which I teach you,
for to do *them*, that ye may live, and

25. *that goodly mountain*] *i.e.* that mountainous district. The flat districts of the East are generally scorched, destitute of water, and therefore sterile: the hilly ones, on the contrary, are of more tempered climate, and fertilized by the streams from the high grounds. It was, more especially perhaps to the mind of one who had wandered so long in the desert, part of the attractions of the promised land that it was a mountain country. Cf. xi. 11, "but the land whither ye go to possess it is a land of hills and valleys, and drinketh water of the rain of heaven."

The whole of this prayer of Moses is very characteristic. The longing to witness further manifestations of God's goodness and glory, and the reluctance to leave unfinished an undertaking which he had been permitted to commence, are striking traits in his character: cf. Ex. xxxii. 32 sq., xxxiii. 12, 18 sq.; Num. xiv. 12 sq.

26. *the LORD was wroth with me for your sakes*] Here, as in i. 37 and iv. 21, the sin of the people is stated to be the ground on which Moses' prayer is denied. In Num. xxvii. 14 and in Deut. xxxii. 51 the transgression of Moses and Aaron themselves is assigned as the cause of their punishment. The reason why one side of the transaction is put forward in this place, and the other elsewhere, is evident. *Here* Moses is addressing the people, and mentions the punishment of their leaders as a most impressive warning to them. And that the first and principal fault was with the people is clear. Cf. Num. xx. 1—13; and on ch. i. 37, 38. In ch. xxxii. and Num. xxvii., God is addressing Moses, and visits on him, as is fitting, not the sin of the people but his own.

29. *So we abode in the valley over against Beth-peor*] Beth-peor, *i.e.* the house of Peor, no doubt derived its name from a temple of the Moabite god Peor which was there situated. It was no doubt near to Mount Peor (Num. xxiii. 28), and also to the valley of the Jordan. A notice in Eusebius places it in the Wady Heshban, which has yet to be explored by modern travellers. In this valley the people must have been encamped some time. Here it was, apparently, that the transactions recorded in Num. xxviii—xxxiv. took place; here too the several discourses of Moses, preserved to us in this book, were delivered; and somewhere in it (xxxiv. 6) he was buried.

The *v.* before us marks a break in the discourse, as does the similar verse at the end of ch. ii. Moses hitherto had made mention of the great acts of God on behalf of his people, and reminded them of their own ill return for His mercies. The next chapter, though still belonging to the introductory portion of the book, passes on to different topics.

CHAP. IV. After thus briefly reviewing the past, Moses proceeds in the present chapter to matter of a directly didactic and hortatory kind. His topics arise clearly and forcibly out of the historical incidents he had been rehearsing. God had done great things for the people in the way both of mercies and chastisements. Their duty thenceforward, and their interest also, were plain—to abide firmly by the covenant into which they had entered with Him. "Now therefore hearken, O Israel, unto the statutes, &c." *v.* 1 sqq. This general entreaty is pointed by special mention and enforcement of the fundamental principles of

go in and possess the land which
the LORD God of your fathers giveth
you.
chap. 12. 2 [a] Ye shall not add unto the
[3]2. Josh. 1. 7. word which I command you, nei-
Prov. 30. ther shall ye diminish *ought* from it,
[6.] Rev. 22. that ye may keep the commandments
18. of the LORD your God which I command you.
3 Your eyes have seen what the
Numb. 25. 4, &c. LORD did because of [b] Baal-peor: for
all the men that followed Baal-peor,
the LORD thy God hath destroyed
them from among you.
4 But ye that did cleave unto the
LORD your God *are* alive every one
of you this day.
5 Behold, I have taught you statutes and judgments, even as the
LORD my God commanded me, that
ye should do so in the land whither
ye go to possess it.
6 Keep therefore and do *them*;
for this *is* your wisdom and your
understanding in the sight of the
nations, which shall hear all these
statutes, and say, Surely this great
nation *is* a wise and understanding
people.
7 For what nation *is there so* great,
who *hath* God *so* nigh unto them, as
the LORD our God *is* in all *things that*
we call upon him *for?*
8 And what nation *is there so* great,
that hath statutes and judgments *so*
righteous as all this law, which I set
before you this day?
9 Only take heed to thyself, and
keep thy soul diligently, lest thou
forget the things which thine eyes
have seen, and lest they depart from
thy heart all the days of thy life:
but teach them thy sons, and thy
sons' sons;
10 *Specially* the day that thou
stoodest before the LORD thy God
in Horeb, when the LORD said unto
me, Gather me the people together,
and I will make them hear my words,
that they may learn to fear me all
the days that they shall live upon the
earth, and *that* they may teach their
children.
11 And ye came near and stood
under the mountain; and the [c] moun- [c] Exod. 19. 18.
tain burned with fire unto the † midst † Heb. *heart.*
of heaven, with darkness, clouds, and
thick darkness.
12 And the LORD spake unto
you out of the midst of the fire: ye

---

the whole covenant (*vv.* 9—40), the spiritual nature of the Deity, His exclusive right to their allegiance, His abhorrence of idolatry in every form, His choice of them for His elect people. These same teachings are much more copiously and elaborately insisted on in Moses' third and last address ch. xxvii—xxx. (Cf. Introd. § II.); and appear in this one in the form of prelude and introduction to the fuller treatment which awaits them hereafter. Yet they follow so naturally on the history just narrated, that the orator could not, so to say, pass from it, even for a time, without pausing to urge them, through a few weighty sentences, in their more obvious bearings.

10, 11. Render, **at the time that thou stoodest**, &c. (11) **then ye came near**, &c. The word "specially" is needlessly introduced in the A. V., and the Hebrew word rendered "the day" is merely an adverbial accusative; equivalent to "at what time;" and introduces a new sentence which is continued in the *vv.* 11—13. Moses, exhorting to heedful observance of the law, strives to renew the impressions of that tremendous scene which attended its promulgation at Sinai.

12 sqq. The following *vv.* are designed to proscribe idolatry in all its manifestations. The corrupt worship of the ancient Oriental nations may probably be traced back in its ultimate analysis to two roots or principles, the deification of ancestors or national leaders, and veneration of the powers of nature. The former is perhaps to be recognized in the idolatry of Terah (Josh. xxiv. 2); of Laban (Gen. xxxi. 19, 30, 32); and of Jacob's household (Gen. xxxv. 2). From this ancestral corruption of the true religion, Abraham, "the father of the faithful," was probably called away. To guard against it, as is commonly supposed, the sepulchre of Moses was kept secret from the people: (ch. xxxiv. 6; but see note *in loc.*). Not unconnected with this tendency to hero-worship was perhaps the idolatry practised in reference to Gideon's ephod (Judg. viii. 27); the worship of the brazen serpent in later times (2 Kings xviii. 4); and the teraphim of Micah (Judg. xvii. 4, 5). The other kind of idolatry, nature-worship,

heard the voice of the words, but
saw no similitude; † only *ye heard* a † Heb. *save a voice.*
voice.
13 And he declared unto you his
covenant, which he commanded you
to perform, *even* ten commandments;
and he wrote them upon two tables
of stone.
14 ¶ And the LORD commanded
me at that time to teach you statutes and judgments, that ye might
do them in the land whither ye go
over to possess it.
15 Take ye therefore good heed
unto yourselves; for ye saw no manner of similitude on the day *that* the
LORD spake unto you in Horeb out
of the midst of the fire:
16 Lest ye corrupt *yourselves*, and
make you a graven image, the similitude of any figure, the likeness of
male or female,
17 The likeness of any beast that
is on the earth, the likeness of any
winged fowl that flieth in the air,
18 The likeness of any thing that
creepeth on the ground, the likeness
of any fish that *is* in the waters beneath the earth:
19 And lest thou lift up thine eyes
unto heaven, and when thou seest
the sun, and the moon, and the stars,
even all the host of heaven, shouldest
be driven to worship them, and serve
them, which the LORD thy God hath
‖ divided unto all nations under the ‖ Or, *imparted*
whole heaven.
20 But the LORD hath taken you,
and brought you forth out of the iron
furnace, *even* out of Egypt, to be unto
him a people of inheritance, as *ye are*
this day.
21 Furthermore the LORD was
angry with me for your sakes, and
sware that I should not go over Jordan, and that I should not go in

---

was widely spread through the East, and forms in various aspects and degrees an element in the religious sentiment of Arabians, Phœnicians, Persians, Chaldees, and Egyptians. Hero-worship exhibited itself in the practice of setting up images of human form as household gods (Penates), or as local and civic divinities: a practice forbidden by *v.* 16. Nature-worship in its baser shapes is seen in the Egyptian idolatry of animals and animal figures, condemned in *vv.* 17, 18: whilst its less ignoble flights, the worship of the sun, moon, and stars, are forbidden in *v.* 19. The latter was practised by the ancient Persians (Herod. I. 131), and by other oriental nations who rejected anthropomorphic idolatry. It was formally introduced and made popular in Israel only, as it seems, in the times of the later kings; but it cannot have been unknown to Moses and the Jews of his times, since it was undoubtedly practised by many of the tribes with whom they had come in contact. The great legislator then may be regarded as taking in the passage before us a complete and comprehensive survey of the various forms of idolatrous and corrupt worship practised by the surrounding oriental nations, and as particularly and successively forbidding them every one. The chosen people of God are not to regard with superstitious reverence one of their own race, male or female: nor to fall into the low nature-worship of which they had seen so much in Egypt, and to which they had once since, in the sin of the golden calf, shown a bias; nor yet to be beguiled by the more subtle cosmic religionism of some of the Syrian tribes with which on their march they had made acquaintance. These did not indeed make gods for themselves; but they "worshipped and served the creature more than the Creator," addressed themselves to inferior objects, not to Him Himself, and so were idolaters still. God is not to be worshipped under any visible image and form, whether made by man for the purpose, or created by Himself for man's service. God had been manifested to them through no media of shape and figure: through no such media was He therefore to be sought.

19. *which the LORD thy God hath divided unto all nations*] *i.e.* "whose light God has distributed to the nations for their use and benefit, and which therefore being creatures ministering to man's convenience must not be worshipped as man's lords." So Targg., Jarchi, Saad., Jerome, Bp. Wordsworth, &c. Others regard this passage as importing that God had allotted the heavenly bodies to the heathen for worship, and that His own people therefore must not worship them. This sense, though current as long ago as the time of Justin Martyr ('D. cum Tryph.' § 55 and 121, and Clemens Alex. 'Strom.' VI. 14), and preferred by many modern critics (Knobel, Keil), is by no means apposite.

21. Cf. iii. 26, and note.

unto that good land, which the LORD
thy God giveth thee *for* an inheritance:
22 But I must die in this land,
I must not go over Jordan: but ye
shall go over, and possess that good
land.
23 Take heed unto yourselves,
lest ye forget the covenant of the
LORD your God, which he made
with you, and make you a graven
image, *or* the likeness of any *thing*,
which the LORD thy God hath forbidden thee.
d chap. 9. 3. Hebr. 12. 29. 24 For the [d] LORD thy God *is* a
consuming fire, *even* a jealous God.
25 ¶ When thou shalt beget children, and children's children, and ye
shall have remained long in the land,
and shall corrupt *yourselves*, and make
a graven image, *or* the likeness of any
thing, and shall do evil in the sight of
the LORD thy God, to provoke him
to anger:
26 I call heaven and earth to witness against you this day, that ye
shall soon utterly perish from off the
land whereunto ye go over Jordan to
possess it; ye shall not prolong *your*
days upon it, but shall utterly be destroyed.
27 And the LORD shall scatter you
among the nations, and ye shall be
left few in number among the heathen, whither the LORD shall lead you.
28 And there ye shall serve gods,
the work of men's hands, wood and
stone, which neither see, nor hear,
nor eat, nor smell.
29 But if from thence thou shalt
seek the LORD thy God, thou shalt
find *him*, if thou seek him with all
thy heart and with all thy soul.
30 When thou art in tribulation,
and all these things † are come upon † Heb. *have found thee.*
thee, *even* in the latter days, if thou
turn to the LORD thy God, and shalt
be obedient unto his voice;
31 (For the LORD thy God *is* a
merciful God;) he will not forsake
thee, neither destroy thee, nor forget
the covenant of thy fathers which he
sware unto them.
32 For ask now of the days that
are past, which were before thee,
since the day that God created man
upon the earth, and *ask* from the one
side of heaven unto the other, whether there hath been *any such thing*
as this great thing *is*, or hath been
heard like it?
33 Did *ever* people hear the voice
of God speaking out of the midst of
the fire, as thou hast heard, and live?
34 Or hath God assayed to go *and*
take him a nation from the midst of
another nation, by temptations, by
signs, and by wonders, and by war,
and by a mighty hand, and by a
stretched out arm, and by great terrors, according to all that the LORD
your God did for you in Egypt before
your eyes?
35 Unto thee it was shewed, that
thou mightest know that the LORD he
is God; *there is* none else beside him.
36 Out of heaven he made thee
to hear his voice, that he might instruct thee: and upon earth he shewed thee his great fire; and thou
heardest his words out of the midst
of the fire.

25–28. The warnings against idolatry are enforced by distinct prediction of the terrible punishments which would ensue on commission of it. Cf. with these verses Lev. xxvi. 33—40, and chap. xxviii. 64 sqq.

29—40. Unwilling, as it might seem, to close his discourse with words of terror, Moses makes a last appeal to them in these *vv.* in a different strain. He calls on them to cleave steadfastly to God because God had given them evidences of His Deity and His power such as had been vouchsafed to no others; and had worked and would still work no less singular deliverances for them, having chosen them out to be His own people.

34. *by temptations*] Cf. vii. 18, 19, and xxix. 2, 3. From a comparison of these passages it appears that we must refer the word "temptations" (as does Gesen.), not to the tribulations and persecutions undergone by the Israelites, but to the plagues miraculously inflicted on the Egyptians. By these plagues the might of God and the obstinacy of Pharaoh were at once tested and manifested.

37 And because he loved thy fathers, therefore he chose their seed
after them, and brought thee out in
his sight with his mighty power out
of Egypt;
38 To drive out nations from before thee greater and mightier than
thou *art*, to bring thee in, to give
thee their land *for* an inheritance, as
it is this day.
39 Know therefore this day, and
consider *it* in thine heart, that the
LORD he *is* God in heaven above, and
upon the earth beneath: *there is* none
else.
40 Thou shalt keep therefore his
statutes, and his commandments,
which I command thee this day, that
it may go well with thee, and with
thy children after thee, and that thou
mayest prolong *thy* days upon the
earth, which the LORD thy God giveth thee, for ever.
41 ¶ Then Moses severed three
cities on this side Jordan toward the
sunrising;
42 That the slayer might flee thither, which should kill his neighbour
unawares, and hated him not in times
past; and that fleeing unto one of
these cities he might live:
43 *Namely*, [e]Bezer in the wilder- [e] Josh. [2]
ness, in the plain country, of the 8.
Reubenites; and Ramoth in Gilead,
of the Gadites; and Golan in Bashan,
of the Manassites.
44 ¶ And this *is* the law which
Moses set before the children of Israel:
45 These *are* the testimonies, and

---

37. *he chose their seed after them*] Lit. "*his* seed after *him*." Though Moses begins the *v.* by setting forth the love of God to the "fathers" of the nation as the foundation of His election of their posterity (cf. ix. 5 and x. 15), yet he proceeds in the singular number to speak of "*his* seed after *him*." The assumption of corruption in the text is quite arbitrary. Speaking of the love of God to their fathers in general, Moses has more especially in mind that one of them who was called "the Friend of God" (St James ii. 23); and instinctively, so to say, constructs the sentence accordingly.

brought thee out in his sight] Lit. "by His face." *i.e.* by the might of His personal presence: cf. Exod. xxxiii. 14, where God promises to Moses "My presence (lit. 'my face') shall go with thee."

41—43. Many of the older commentators (*e.g.* Calmet, Houbigant, &c.), unable to see any propriety or relevancy in these *vv.* as at present placed, have regarded them as an interpolation. There is however no reason to depart from the view suggested alike by their contents and context. The *vv.* preceding are clearly the conclusion, as those succeeding are the exordium, of a distinct and complete discourse. These *vv.*, then, are inserted between the two simply for the reason to which they themselves call attention ("*Then* Moses severed three cities," &c.); *i.e.* the fact narrated took place historically after Moses spoke the one discourse and before he delivered the other. In thus severing the three cities of refuge Moses carried out a previous command of God, Num. xxxv. 14; and so followed up his exhortations to obedience by setting a punctual example of it, as far as opportunity was given him.

43. *Bezer in the wilderness, in the plain country*] On the "wilderness," see chap. i. 1. "In the plain country," lit. "in the land of the *Mishor*." The word means a level tract of land; but when used, as here and in iii. 10, Josh. xiii. 9, &c. with the article, seems to be a proper name, as it is treated by the LXX. It denotes the smooth downs of Moab, which reach from the Jordan eastward of Jericho far into the desert of Arabia, and which form a striking contrast alike to the rugged country west of the river, and to the higher and remarkable districts belonging to Bashan northwards.

Bezer is, with little certainty, identified with Bostra, or (1 Macc. v. 36) Bosor.

Ramoth in Gilead] Identical with Ramoth Mizpeh, Josh. xiii. 26; where see note.

Golan] Described by Jerome after Eusebius as "villa prægrandis;" it subsequently gave the name of Gaulonitis to a district of some extent east of the sea of Galilee and north of the Hieromax; but the exact site of the city is uncertain.

44—49. These *vv.* would be more properly assigned to the next chapter. They are intended to serve, not as a conclusion to the first introductory and preparatory discourse which has been recorded (Rosenmüller), but as the announcement and introduction of the one now to be commenced. *V.* 44 gives a kind of general title to the whole of the weighty address, including in fact the central part and substance of the

the statutes, and the judgments, which Moses spake unto the children of Israel, after they came forth out of Egypt,

46 On this side Jordan, in the valley over against Beth-peor, in the land of Sihon king of the Amorites, who dwelt at Heshbon, whom Moses and the children of Israel [f] smote, after they were come forth out of Egypt:

Numb. 1. 24. hap. 1. 4.

47 And they possessed his land, and the land [g] of Og king of Bashan, two kings of the Amorites, which *were* on this side Jordan toward the sunrising;

Numb. 1. 33. hap. 3. 3.

48 From Aroer, which *is* by the bank of the river Arnon, even unto mount Sion, which *is* Hermon,

49 And all the plain on this side Jordan eastward, even unto the sea of the plain, under the [h] springs of Pisgah.

h chap. 3. 17.

CHAPTER V.

1 *The covenant in Horeb.* 6 *The ten commandments.* 22 *At the people's request Moses receiveth the law from God.*

AND Moses called all Israel, and said unto them, Hear, O Israel, the statutes and judgments which I speak in your ears this day, that ye may learn them, and [†] keep, and do them.

† Heb. *keep to do them.*

2 [a] The LORD our God made a covenant with us in Horeb.

a Exod. 19. 5.

3 The LORD made not this covenant with our fathers, but with us, *even* us, who *are* all of us here alive this day.

---

book, which now follows in twenty-two chapters; cf. Introd. § 11. These chapters may be divided into two groups, the former consisting of ch. v.—xi., the latter of ch. xii.—xxvi. inclusive. The former division commences with a repetition of the Ten Words, which appropriately occupy here, not less than at their first announcement in Exodus, the forefront of the whole legislative system as its leading and essential principles. Amongst these Ten Words the first two might, under the circumstances, be justly regarded as "first and great commandments;" and Moses accordingly makes application of them in some detail to his audience, mingling warnings and exhortations, through six chapters (vi.—xi.). The second division (xii.—xxvi.) recounts the principal laws and regulations which the people were to observe in the land of their inheritance. In *v.* 45 this "law" (*thōrah*) is summarily described as consisting of "testimonies, statutes, and judgments:" *i.e.* commandments considered first as manifestations or attestations (*eydōth*) of the will of God; next as duties of moral obligation (*khŭkim*), and, thirdly, as precepts securing the mutual rights of men (*mishpātim*). See on these last two words Levit. xviii. 4, 5. This statement of the contents of the succeeding portion of the book is accompanied by a notice of time and place: "after they came forth out of Egypt," lit., and more accurately, "*in* their coming forth:" *i.e.* whilst they were yet on their march from the house of bondage to the Promised Land; but "in the land of Sihon," *v.* 46; and so when they had already received the first fruits of those promises, the full fruition of which was to be consequent on their fulfilment of that covenant now again about to be rehearsed to them in its leading features.

48. *mount Sion, which is Hermon*] See note on iii. 9. The name Zion (cf. Ps. xlviii. 2) connected with Jerusalem is quite differently spelt in the original from the Sion of the text.

CHAP. V. Moses now proceeds with the Deuteronomy or Second Law itself: *i.e.* with that recapitulation of the Sinaitic code in all its more important features which was suggested at once by the fact that the generation to which it was originally given was now dead; by the change which was about to be accomplished in the circumstances of Israel through their actual entrance and settlement in the land of promise; and by the approaching decease of the great lawgiver who had been the mediator of the covenant, and whose authority had hitherto been available for its explanation and enforcement.

1. *And Moses called all Israel, and said*] This more emphatic introductory formula instead of the simpler and ordinary "And Moses said," points to the publicity and importance of the discourse which follows.

3. *The LORD made not this covenant with our fathers, but with us, even us, who are all of us here alive this day*] The "fathers" here intended are, as in iv. 37, the patriarchs, Abraham, Isaac, and Jacob. With them God did indeed make a covenant, but not the particular covenant now in question. The responsibilities of this later covenant, made at Sinai by the nation as a nation, attached in their day and generation to those whom Moses was addressing.

4 The LORD talked with you face
to face in the mount out of the midst
of the fire,
5 (I stood between the LORD and
you at that time, to shew you the
word of the LORD: for ye were afraid
by reason of the fire, and went not up
into the mount;) saying,
[b] Exod. 20. 6 ¶ [b] I *am* the LORD thy God,
2, &c. Lev. 26. 1. which brought thee out of the land
Psal. 81. 10. of Egypt, from the house of † bondage.
† Heb. *servants.* 7 Thou shalt have none other gods
before me.
8 Thou shalt not make thee *any*
graven image, *or* any likeness *of any*
thing that *is* in heaven above, or that
is in the earth beneath, or that *is* in
the waters beneath the earth:
9 Thou shalt not bow down thyself unto them, nor serve them: for
I the LORD thy God *am* a jealous
God, [c] visiting the iniquity of the fa- [c] Exod.
thers upon the children unto the third 7.
and fourth *generation* of them that
hate me,
10 [d] And shewing mercy unto thou- [d] Jer.
sands of them that love me and keep 18.
my commandments.
11 Thou shalt not take the name
of the LORD thy God in vain: for the
LORD will not hold *him* guiltless that
taketh his name in vain.
12 Keep the sabbath day to sanctify it, as the LORD thy God hath
commanded thee.
13 Six days thou shalt labour, and
do all thy work:
14 But the seventh day *is* the
[e] sabbath of the LORD thy God: *in* [e] Gen.
it thou shalt not do any work, thou, 2. Heb. 4.

---

4 & 5. The participle "saying" at the end of *v.* 5 depends on the verb "talked" in *v.* 4. The intermediate part of *v.* 5 is therefore parenthetic, as marked in the A. V. It appears from *vv.* 22—25 and from iv. 11, 12, that the Ten Words were uttered "with a great voice" to the assembly from the awful summit of the Mount itself; whilst the other precepts were communicated to the people through the agency of Moses. It appears from Exod. xix. 9, 17, 20, 24, that whilst the people remained in the lower parts of the mountain, Moses was from the first called apart to God on the top of it. No doubt whilst the great voice sounded forth the "Ten Words," he still remained there, either to convey more certainly and exactly what was uttered to the people standing far off in consternation, or, as is suggested by Exod. xx. 9, to authenticate his mission. Even then, as regards the Decalogue, the statement of *v.* 5 has its application. Moses "stood between the Lord and them" whilst it was delivered; and perhaps it was (Exod. xix. 19) addressed directly to Moses, though in accents audible to the assembly beneath. Thus was the Law, including even the "Ten Words" "in the hand of a mediator" (Gal. iii. 19). The diversity and the separation of the parties to the Covenant, indicated all along by the intervention of Moses, became still more conspicuous after that the Lord, at the request of the terrified people (*v.* 27), ceased to speak so that they could hear Him for themselves.

6—21. Repetition of the Ten Commandments. On the variations between the Commandments as given here and in Exod. xx., also on the different modes of dividing the Commandments, and distributing them between the Two Tables, and other questions connected with the Decalogue, see Exod. xx. and notes at the end of that chapter.

Moses here adopts the Ten Words as a ground from which he may proceed to reprove, warn, and exhort; and repeats them, as is natural, where literal accuracy is not to the purpose, with a measure of freedom and adaptation. Our Lord (St Mark x. 19) and St Paul (Eph. vi. 2, 3) deal similarly with the same subject; as indeed preachers in all ages have done. It is important, however, to note, that in the course of thus freely quoting the law, Moses thrice refers his hearers, to the statutes of God themselves, *vv.* 12, 15, 16, "as the Lord thy God hath commanded thee;" *i.e.* commanded from Sinai. It is thus apparent that speaker and hearers recognized a statutory and authoritative form of the laws in question, which, because it was familiar to both parties, needed not to be reproduced with verbal fidelity.

12—15. In stating the purposes of the Sabbath ordinance Moses introduces a few words, originally applied in the same connexion, from Exod. xxiii. 12: and the exhortation to observe the Sabbath and allow their time of rest to servants is pointed by reminding the people that they too were formerly servants themselves. The bondage in Egypt and the deliverance from it are not assigned as grounds for the institution of the Sabbath, which is of far older date (see on Gen. ii. 3), but rather as suggesting motives for the religious observance of that institution. The exodus was an entrance into rest from the

nor thy son, nor thy daughter, nor
thy manservant, nor thy maidservant,
nor thine ox, nor thine ass, nor any
of thy cattle, nor thy stranger that
is within thy gates; that thy manservant and thy maidservant may rest
as well as thou.
15 And remember that thou wast
a servant in the land of Egypt, and
that the LORD thy God brought thee
out thence through a mighty hand
and by a stretched out arm: therefore
the LORD thy God commanded thee
to keep the sabbath day.
16 ¶ Honour thy father and thy
mother, as the LORD thy God hath
commanded thee; that thy days may
be prolonged, and that it may go well
with thee, in the land which the LORD
thy God giveth thee.
[f] Matt. 5. 17 [f] Thou shalt not kill.
21. [g] Luke 18. 18 [g] Neither shalt thou commit
20. [h] Rom. 13. adultery.
9. 19 [h] Neither shalt thou steal.
20 Neither shalt thou bear false
witness against thy neighbour.
21 [i] Neither shalt thou desire thy [i] Rom. 7.
neighbour's wife, neither shalt thou 7.
covet thy neighbour's house, his field,
or his manservant, or his maidservant,
his ox, or his ass, or any *thing* that *is*
thy neighbour's.
22 ¶ These words the LORD
spake unto all your assembly in the
mount out of the midst of the fire,
of the cloud, and of the thick darkness, with a great voice: and he
added no more. And he wrote them
in two tables of stone, and delivered
them unto me.
23 And it came to pass, when ye
heard the voice out of the midst of
the darkness, (for the mountain did
burn with fire,) that ye came near
unto me, *even* all the heads of your
tribes, and your elders;
24 And ye said, Behold, the LORD
our God hath shewed us his glory

---

toils of the house of bondage, and is thought even to have occurred on the Sabbath-day. Hence arose special and national obligations with respect to the Sabbath, on which it is exactly within the scope of Moses' purpose in Deuteronomy to insist.

16. The blessing of general well-being is here annexed to the keeping of the fifth Commandment, as well as that of long life, which alone is found in the parallel passage of Exodus. The insertion, however, is no real addition to the promise, but only an amplification of its expression, intended to serve the homiletic purposes of the speaker. Long life would present itself to the Jewish mind as one element of well-being, and a very important one. Here too Moses refers his hearers back to the command of God in Exodus.

21. The tenth Commandment, as here given, varies in three particulars from that in Exodus.

(1) In Exod. the *house* is mentioned first, the *wife* second: in Deut. the reverse.

(2) In Deut. a different word is used in reference to wife, ("thou shalt not *desire*," *thakmōd*, "thy neighbour's wife"); and in reference to the other objects, ("neither shalt thou covet," *hithavveh*, "thy neighbour's house, &c.")

(3) In Deut. the "field" is added to the list of objects specifically forbidden to be desired.

The first two variations are explained by the general character of the passage before us. The express mention of the "field" amongst the forbidden objects seems very natural in one who was speaking with the partition of Canaan amongst his hearers directly in view. The LXX. has brought about an uniformity as regards the second variation by altering the text of Exodus after that of Deuteronomy; the Samaritan Pentateuch by altering Deuteronomy after Exodus.

22. *he added no more.*] Lit. "He did not add:" *i.e.* He spoke no more with the great voice directly to the people, but addressed all other communications to them through Moses. The expression (*lō yāsaph:* cf. Num. xi. 25) points to the occurrence as one that was not repeated. This unique and sublime phenomenon, followed up by the inscription of the Ten Words on the Two Tables by the finger of God, marks not only the holiness of God's Law in general, but the special eminence and permanent obligation of the Ten Words themselves as compared with the rest of the Mosaic enactments. The giving of the Two Tables did not take place until Moses had been on the Mount forty days and forty nights, as appears from the fuller account of ix. 9—12.

23—33. These *vv.* contain a much fuller narrative of the events described in Exod. xx. 18—21. The reply of God to the request

[k] Exod. 19. 19. and his greatness, and [k] we have
heard his voice out of the midst of
the fire: we have seen this day that
God doth talk with man, and he
[l] chap. 4. 33. [l] liveth.
25 Now therefore why should we
die? for this great fire will consume
† Heb. *add to hear.* us: if we † hear the voice of the
LORD our God any more, then we
shall die.
26 For who *is there of* all flesh,
that hath heard the voice of the living
God speaking out of the midst of the
fire, as we *have*, and lived?
27 Go thou near, and hear all that
the LORD our God shall say: and
speak thou unto us all that the LORD
[m] Exod. 20. 19. our God shall [m] speak unto thee; and
we will hear *it*, and do *it*.
28 And the LORD heard the voice
of your words, when ye spake unto
me; and the LORD said unto me, I
have heard the voice of the words
of this people, which they have spoken
unto thee: they have well said all
that they have spoken.
29 O that there were such an
heart in them, that they would fear
me, and keep all my commandments
always, that it might be well with
them, and with their children for
ever!
30 Go say to them, Get you into
your tents again.
31 But as for thee, stand thou here
by me, and I will speak unto thee
all the commandments, and the statutes,
and the judgments, which thou
shalt teach them, that they may do
them in the land which I give them
to possess it.
32 Ye shall observe to do therefore
as the LORD your God hath
commanded you: ye shall not turn
aside to the right hand or to the left.
33 Ye shall walk in all the ways
which the LORD your God hath commanded
you, that ye may live, and
that it may be well with you, and *that*
ye may prolong *your* days in the land
which ye shall possess.

CHAPTER VI.

1 *The end of the law is obedience.* 3 *An exhortation thereto.*

NOW these *are* the commandments,
the statutes, and the
judgments, which the LORD your
God commanded to teach you, that
ye might do *them* in the land whither
ye † go to possess it: † Heb. *pass over.*
2 That thou mightest fear the
LORD thy God, to keep all his statutes
and his commandments, which
I command thee, thou, and thy son,
and thy son's son, all the days of thy
life; and that thy days may be prolonged.
3 ¶ Hear therefore, O Israel, and
observe to do *it;* that it may be
well with thee, and that ye may increase
mightily, as the LORD God

---

of the people (*vv.* 28—31) is omitted altogether in the historical summary of Exodus. Here it is important to the speaker's purpose to call attention to the fact that it was on their own entreaty that he had taken on him to be the channel of communication between God and them. God approved (*v.* 28) the request of the people, because it showed a feeling of their own unworthiness to enter into direct communion with God. The terrors of Sinai had done their work. They had awakened the consciousness of sin.

CHAP. VI. Moses having rehearsed the Decalogue, and reminded the people of the awful circumstances by which its Divine origin and authority were accredited, proceeds next to set forth more particularly and to enforce those cardinal and essential doctrines of it, the nature and attributes of God, and the fitting mode of honouring and worshipping Him. Two objects are indicated (*vv.* 2, 3) as sought by the lawgiver in thus expounding anew these important duties. He aims at awakening a holy fear of God in the heart of his people, a fear which shall manifest itself in steadfast fulfilment of the Covenant; and he seeks no less the temporal prosperity of Israel, which is shown as a certain result upon such fidelity. Thus the glory of God and the welfare of man are seen to be the grand ends he has in view.

1. *the commandments*] Lit. "commandment," for the noun is singular. It is thus equivalent to the "thorah" of iv. 44, and is explained in the context as consisting of "statutes and judgments."

of thy fathers hath promised thee, in
the land that floweth with milk and
honey.
4 Hear, O Israel: The LORD our
God *is* one LORD:
5 And [a] thou shalt love the LORD
thy God with all thine heart, and
with all thy soul, and with all thy
might.
6 And [b] these words, which I command thee this day, shall be in thine
heart:

[a] chap. 10. 12. Matt. 22. 37. Mark 12. 30. Luke 10. 27.
[b] chap. 11. 18.

7 And thou shalt † teach them diligently unto thy children, and shalt
talk of them when thou sittest in
thine house, and when thou walkest
by the way, and when thou liest down,
and when thou risest up.
8 And thou shalt bind them for a
sign upon thine hand, and they shall
be as frontlets between thine eyes.
9 And thou shalt write them upon
the posts of thy house, and on thy
gates.

† Heb. *whet*, or, *sharpen*.

---

3. *in the land*] There is no prep. in the Hebrew. It seems better to regard the words "the land, &c." simply as an explanatory clause. **According as the Lord the God of thy fathers promised thee a land flowing with milk and honey.**

4. *Hear, O Israel: the* LORD *our God is one* LORD] These words form the beginning of what is termed the *Shama* ("Hear") in the Jewish Services, and belong to the daily Morning and Evening office. They may indeed be termed the Creed of the Jews. Their expression is in the original singularly terse and forcible. "Jehovah our Elohim, Jehovah one." Their very brevity opens them to different constructions: *e.g.* "the Lord is our God, the Lord alone:" "the Lord our God, namely, the Lord, is one:" "the Lord, the Lord only, is our God." The rendering of A. V. is on all grounds the best.

This weighty text contains far more than a mere declaration of the unity of God as against polytheism; or of the sole authority of the revelation He had made to Israel as against other pretended manifestations of His will and attributes. It asserts that the Lord God of Israel is absolutely God, and none other. He, and He alone, is Jehovah the absolute, uncaused God; He who had by His election of them made Himself known to Israel.

The last letter of the first and last words of this verse are *majuscula* in the original, *i.e.* written larger than the ordinary size: being the ninth and tenth which are so written in the Hebrew of the Scriptures. These two *majuscula* form together a word signifying "witness." It is uncertain how this difference in writing originated. It may be intentional, but of late date. It is construed by the Jewish commentators as highly significant. In this place it is held to import that the utterance of this verse is to be accounted a witness for the faith; or that God is a witness of the sincerity and earnestness of him who utters it.

5. As there is but one God, and that God Israel's God, so Israel must love God unreservedly and entirely. The specification "with all thine heart, and with all thy soul, and with all thy might," is intended to include every faculty that can possibly come in question. The "heart" is mentioned as the seat of the understanding; the "soul" as the centre of will and personality; the "might" as representing the outgoings and energies of all the vital powers.

The command of the text cannot be surpassed in comprehensiveness by any which God can give or man receive. The New Testament itself can require no more than this total self-surrender of man's being to his Maker. It is then a very imperfect conception of the scope of the text, and not less so of the nature of the service required from God's people of old, to limit it to outward and ceremonial obedience (as Olsh. on St Matt. xxii. 37). The Gospel differs from the law not so much in replacing an external and carnal service of God by an inward and spiritual one, as in supplying new motives and peculiar assistances for the attainment of that Divine love which was from the first and all along enjoined as "the first and great commandment."

8 and 9. Here as elsewhere Moses turns to account usages widely spread in his times, and still common in the East. The ancient Egyptians commonly wore amulets of various kinds; some, "consisting of words written on folds of papyrus tightly rolled up and sown in linen," have been found at Thebes (Wilkinson, 'A.E.' III. 364); and the modern Egyptians still continue the practice (Lane, 'Mod. Egypt,' I. 338). The "pillows," spoken of Ezek. xiii. 18 as "sown to armholes" were probably amulets of an idolatrous character. The wearing of amulets engraved with a sacred symbol or motto, and the inscribing of texts of the Koran on buildings, have been noticed by many modern travellers. By adopting and regulating this custom Moses provides at once a check on superstition and a means of keeping the

10 And it shall be, when the
LORD thy God shall have brought
thee into the land which he sware
unto thy fathers, to Abraham, to
Isaac, and to Jacob, to give thee great
and goodly cities, which thou build-
edst not,
11 And houses full of all good
things, which thou filledst not, and
wells digged, which thou diggedst not,
vineyards and olive trees, which thou
[c] chap. 8. 9, 10, &c. plantedst not; [c] when thou shalt have
eaten and be full;
12 *Then* beware lest thou forget
the LORD, which brought thee forth
out of the land of Egypt, from the
† Heb. *bondmen*, or, *servants*. house of † bondage.
13 Thou shalt [d] fear the LORD thy
[d] chap. 10. 12, 20. & 13. 4. God, and serve him, and shalt swear
by his name.
14 Ye shall not go after other gods,
of the gods of the people which *are*
round about you;
15 (For the LORD thy God *is* a
jealous God among you) lest the
anger of the LORD thy God be kindled against thee, and destroy thee
from off the face of the earth.
16 ¶ [e] Ye shall not tempt the
LORD your God, [f] as ye tempted *him*
in Massah.
[e] Matt. 4. 7. [f] Exod. 17. 2.
17 Ye shall diligently keep the
commandments of the LORD your
God, and his testimonies, and his
statutes, which he hath commanded
thee.
18 And thou shalt do *that which*
is right and good in the sight of the
LORD: that it may be well with thee,
and that thou mayest go in and possess the good land which the LORD
sware unto thy fathers,
19 To cast out all thine enemies
from before thee, as the LORD hath
spoken.
20 *And* when thy son asketh thee

---

divine law in memory. On the "frontlets" (*tōtaphōth*), the "phylacteries" of the New Test. (St Matt. xxiii. 5), see on Exod. xiii. 16. On *v.* 9 and xi. 20 is based the Jewish usage of the *Mezuzah*. This word denotes properly a door-post, as it is rendered here and Ex. xii. 7, 22, 23, xxi. 6, &c. Amongst the Jews however it is the name given to the square piece of parchment, inscribed with Deut. vi. 4—9 and xi. 13—21, which is rolled up in a small cylinder of wood or metal, and affixed to the right-hand post of every door in a Jewish house. The pious Jew touches the Mezuzah on each occasion of passing, or kisses his finger, and says in Hebrew Ps. cxxi. 8, "The Lord shall preserve thy going out," &c. See Ginsburg in Alexander's Edit. of Kitto's Encyc. article *Mezuzah*.

10—25. Having stated thus emphatically their primary duty towards God, Moses goes on to add warnings and cautions. The pertinence and the necessity of these are derived from the existing circumstances of the case. The Israelites were on the point of quitting a nomad life, in which they had lived in a great degree aloof from other nations, for a fixed and settled abode in the midst of them; were exchanging a condition of comparative poverty, in which they possessed nothing except what they carried, for "great and goodly cities, houses full of all good things," &c. There was then before them a double danger; that namely of a God-forgetting worldliness, and that of a false tolerance of the idolatries practised by those about to become their neighbours. The former error Moses strives to guard against in the *vv.* before us; the latter in vii. 1—11.

13. *and serve him, and shalt swear by his name.*] The LXX. here has "Him only shalt thou serve, and to Him shalt thou cleave, and by His Name shalt thou swear." The addition of μόνῳ, clearly implied in the Hebrew, was probably made simply in order to bring out the sense more forcibly. In this particular the LXX. is followed by St Matt. iv. 10. The clause "to Him shalt thou cleave" is borrowed from the parallel passage x. 20, which the LXX. gives word for word the same as the verse before us.

The command "to swear by His Name" is not inconsistent with the Lord's injunction St Matt. v. 34, "Swear not at all." Moses refers to legal swearing, our Lord to swearing in common conversation. It is not the purpose of Moses to encourage the practice of taking oaths, but to forbid that when taken they should be taken in any other name than that of Israel's God. The oath involves an invocation of Deity, and so a solemn recognition of Him whose name is made use of in it. Hence it comes peculiarly within the scope of the commandment Moses is enforcing.

20—25. These *vv.* describe more particularly the command already given, *v.* 7, "thou shalt teach these words, &c."

Ieb. † in time to come, saying, What *mean*
morrow. the testimonies, and the statutes, and
the judgments, which the LORD our
God hath commanded you?
21 Then thou shalt say unto thy
son, We were Pharaoh's bondmen
in Egypt; and the LORD brought us
out of Egypt with a mighty hand:
22 And the LORD shewed signs
Ieb. and wonders, great and † sore, upon
il. Egypt, upon Pharaoh, and upon all
his household, before our eyes:
23 And he brought us out from
thence, that he might bring us in, to
give us the land which he sware unto
our fathers.
24 And the LORD commanded us
to do all these statutes, to fear the
LORD our God, for our good always,
that he might preserve us alive, as *it*
is at this day.
25 And it shall be our righteousness, if we observe to do all these
commandments before the LORD our
God, as he hath commanded us.

CHAPTER VII.

1 *All communion with the nations is forbidden,* 4 *for fear of idolatry,* 6 *for the holiness of the people,* 9 *for the nature of God in his mercy and justice,* 17 *for the assuredness of victory which God will give over them.*

WHEN the [a] LORD thy God [a] chap. 31. 3.
shall bring thee into the land
whither thou goest to possess it, and
hath cast out many nations before
thee, the Hittites, and the Girgashites,
and the Amorites, and the Canaanites, and the Perizzites, and the Hivites, and the Jebusites, seven nations
greater and mightier than thou;
2 And when the LORD thy God
shall deliver them before thee; thou
shalt smite them, *and* utterly destroy
them; [b] thou shalt make no cove- [b] Exod. 23. 32.
nant with them, nor shew mercy & 34. 12.
unto them:
3 Neither shalt thou make marriages with them; thy daughter thou
shalt not give unto his son, nor his
daughter shalt thou take unto thy son.
4 For they will turn away thy son
from following me, that they may
serve other gods: so will the anger of
the LORD be kindled against you, and
destroy thee suddenly.
5 But thus shall ye deal with
them; ye shall destroy their altars,
and break down their † images, and † Heb. *statues,*
cut down their groves, and burn their or, *pillars.*
graven images with fire. [c] chap. 14. 2.
6 [c] For thou *art* an holy people & 26. 19.

---

25. *it shall be our righteousness*] Lit. "righteousness shall be to us;" *i.e.* God will esteem us righteous and deal with us accordingly. The LXX. renders "there shall be mercy (ἐλεημοσύνη) to us:" and similarly the Vulgate, "God shall be merciful to us:" as if to guard against the tenet of "justification by works." The word translated "righteousness" is the same as in the famous passage Gen. xv. 6; rendered in the New Testament by δικαιοσύνη; but often in the LXX. as here by ἐλεημοσύνη. It is often found in a context where it probably means *liberality, beneficence,* &c. (see Gesenius' Thesaurus, s. v.); but there is no need in this *v.* to depart from the ordinary and proper signification. Moses from the very beginning has made the whole "righteousness of the law" to depend so entirely on a right state of the heart, in one word, on faith, that there can be no real inconsistency between the *v.* before us taken thus strictly and properly, and the principle of "justification by faith only."

CHAP. VII. 1—11. See on vi. 10. Moses proceeds to forewarn Israel against a false toleration of idolatry. Commerce with the idolatrous nations amongst which they were about to live might easily render them dangerously familiar with superstitions and abominations, against which it was a primary purpose of the whole legislation to raise up a witness and a protest. Hence the stringency of the command given *vv.* 2—5, and repeated *vv.* 23—26, to excommunicate the idolatrous nations and all belonging to them, and to exterminate their degraded worship with all its appliances. The renewal of the promises in *vv.* 12 sqq. is but set forth as supplying a motive for the more zealous and effectual execution of these duties; and thus the destruction of idolatry and idolaters within the sacred precincts of the chosen people appears as the leading topic of this part of Moses' discourse. The words and phrases employed will be found parallel to various passages of the preceding books given in the margin.

5. *cut down their groves*] Render **their idols of wood**: the reference is to the wooden trunk used as a representation of Ashtaroth; see on *v.* 13 and xvi. 21.

[d] Exod. 19. 5. unto the LORD thy God: [d] the LORD
1 Pet. 2. 9. thy God hath chosen thee to be a
special people unto himself, above all
people that *are* upon the face of the
earth.
7 The LORD did not set his love
upon you, nor choose you, because
ye were more in number than any
people; for ye *were* the fewest of all
people:
8 But because the LORD loved
you, and because he would keep the
oath which he had sworn unto your
fathers, hath the LORD brought you
out with a mighty hand, and redeemed you out of the house of bondmen, from the hand of Pharaoh king
of Egypt.
9 Know therefore that the LORD
thy God, he *is* God, the faithful
God, which keepeth covenant and
mercy with them that love him and
keep his commandments to a thousand generations;
10 And repayeth them that hate
him to their face, to destroy them:
he will not be slack to him that
hateth him, he will repay him to his
face.
11 Thou shalt therefore keep the
commandments, and the statutes, and
the judgments, which I command
thee this day, to do them.
12 ¶ Wherefore it shall come to
pass, [†] if ye hearken to these judg- † Heb. *because.*
ments, and keep, and do them, that
the LORD thy God shall keep unto
thee the covenant and the mercy
which he sware unto thy fathers:
13 And he will love thee, and bless
thee, and multiply thee: he will also
bless the fruit of thy womb, and the
fruit of thy land, thy corn, and thy
wine, and thine oil, the increase of
thy kine, and the flocks of thy sheep,
in the land which he sware unto thy
fathers to give thee.
14 Thou shalt be blessed above all
people: [e] there shall not be male or [e] Exod. 23. 26, &c.
female barren among you, or among
your cattle.
15 And the LORD will take away
from thee all sickness, and will put [f] Exod. 9. 14.
none of the [f] evil diseases of Egypt, & 15. 26.

---

7. *the fewest of all people.*] Moses is here referring to the ground or motive from which the election of Israel was originally made. Though it might have seemed suitable that the God of the universe should choose to Himself the mightiest nation of any, yet God had not so acted. He chose to Himself Israel, when as yet but a single family, or rather a single person, Abraham; though there were already numerous nations and powerful kingdoms in the earth. It is then no inconsistency in Moses to describe Israel as rivalling the stars of heaven for multitude (i. 10, x. 22); since such increase had taken place because of the very blessing of God here spoken of.

9, 10. *repayeth them that hate him to their face*] *i.e.* punishes His enemies in their own proper persons, much as in Ex. xxxiii. 14. The phrase "to their faces" has been variously understood: "openly, manifestly" (Grotius, Michaelis): "instantly," "statim" (Vulgate, Vater, &c.). Dathe connects it closely with the following "to destroy them," and renders "qui vero rependat sui osoribus præsentissima pernicie:" the word "faces" being taken as equivalent to a reciprocal pronoun, "to their own very selves." Better perhaps Rosenm. "whilst still alive."

13. *flocks of thy sheep*] (*Ashterōth tsōnechā*). Render rather **the ewes of thy sheep**. So Gesen. *femellæ gregem propagantes.* The phrase is found again xxviii. 4, 18, 51; but is peculiar to Deut. The former of the Hebrew words composing it is the plural form of Ashtoreth the well-known name of the "goddess of the Sidonians" (1 K. xi. 5). This goddess, called by the classical writers Astarte, and identified with Venus, represented the fruitfulness of nature; cf. xvi. 21 and note. The name Ashtaroth is found on early Egyptian monuments: see Brugsch, 'Recueil,' I. pl. 3.

15. *evil diseases of Egypt, which thou knowest,*] There seems to be here not so much a reference to the plagues inflicted miraculously by God on Egypt (cf. Ex. xv. 26), as to the terrible diseases with which above other countries Egypt was infested. Pliny (Nat. Hist. XXVI. 1) calls it "the mother of worst diseases," Wagner ('Naturgesch. des Menschen,' II. 270, quoted by Schultz on this place), "a focus of contagious sicknesses." Cf. xxviii. 27, 35. It is not without significance that Egypt, which represents in Scripture the world as contrasted with the Church, should thus above other lands lie under the power of disease and death.

which thou knowest, upon thee; but will lay them upon all *them* that hate thee.

16 And thou shalt consume all the people which the LORD thy God shall deliver thee; thine eye shall have no pity upon them: neither shalt thou serve their gods; for that *will be* a [g] snare unto thee.

[g] Exod. 23. 33.

17 If thou shalt say in thine heart, These nations *are* more than I; how can I dispossess them?

18 Thou shalt not be afraid of them: *but* shalt well remember what the LORD thy God did unto Pharaoh, and unto all Egypt;

19 The great temptations which thine eyes saw, and the signs, and the wonders, and the mighty hand, and the stretched out arm, whereby the LORD thy God brought thee out: so shall the LORD thy God do unto all the people of whom thou art afraid.

20 [h] Moreover the LORD thy God will send the hornet among them, until they that are left, and hide themselves from thee, be destroyed.

[h] Exod. 23. 28. Josh. 24. 12.

21 Thou shalt not be affrighted at them: for the LORD thy God *is* among you, a mighty God and terrible.

22 And the LORD thy God will † put out those nations before thee by little and little: thou mayest not consume them at once, lest the beasts of the field increase upon thee.

† Heb. *pluck off.*

23 But the LORD thy God shall deliver them † unto thee, and shall destroy them with a mighty destruction, until they be destroyed.

† Heb. *before thy face.*

24 And he shall deliver their kings into thine hand, and thou shalt destroy their name from under heaven: there shall no man be able to stand before thee, until thou have destroyed them.

25 The graven images of their gods [i] shall ye burn with fire: thou [k] shalt not desire the silver or gold *that is* on them, nor take *it* unto thee, lest thou be snared therein: for it *is* an abomination to the LORD thy God.

[i] chap. 12. 3. [k] Josh. 7. 1, 21. 2 Mac. 12. 40.

26 Neither shalt thou bring an abomination into thine house, lest thou be a cursed thing like it: *but* thou shalt utterly detest it, and thou shalt utterly abhor it; [l] for it *is* a cursed thing.

[l] chap. 13. 17.

CHAPTER VIII.

An exhortation to obedience in regard of God's dealing with them.

ALL the commandments which I command thee this day shall ye observe to do, that ye may live, and multiply, and go in and possess the land which the LORD sware unto your fathers.

2 And thou shalt remember all the way which the LORD thy God led thee these forty years in the wilderness, to humble thee, *and* to prove thee, to know what *was* in thine

---

22. Cf. Ex. xxxiii. 29, 30.

25. *thou shalt not desire the silver or gold that is on them*] The silver and gold with which the statues of the gods were overlaid. St Paul is probably alluding to this command Rom. ii. 22, ("Thou that abhorrest idols, dost thou commit sacrilege?"), and his accusation of the Jew thus shows that the prohibition of the text was a very necessary one.

lest thou be snared] As by the rich ephod made by Gideon: cf. Judg. viii. 27.

CHAP. VIII. To the cautions of the last chapter, directed against the risk of a lapse into idolatry through association with it, another no less pertinent and necessary caution is now to be added. The long wandering in the wilderness had been designed, amongst other purposes, to teach God's people humility and a self-distrusting reliance on Him for the supply of their necessities. For this end had Israel long been kept where the ordinary means of providing for their bodily life and safety were insufficient, and where their own exertions could have availed but little (*vv.* 3—6, 15, 16): and had been preserved by the special providence of God. But this extraordinary dispensation was now to end. They were about to take possession of a fertile land where their daily wants would be satisfied from the bounty of nature in the usual way (*vv.* 7—10). But as the former discipline was needed, so now when it was about to be removed, a warning against forgetting its teachings is seasonable. God as really pro-

heart, whether thou wouldest keep
his commandments, or no.
3 And he humbled thee, and suffered thee to hunger, and fed thee
with manna, which thou knewest
not, neither did thy fathers know;
that he might make thee know that
[a] Matt. 4. 4. man doth [a] not live by bread only,
Luke 4. 4. but by every *word* that proceedeth
out of the mouth of the LORD doth
man live.
[b] Neh. 9. 21. 4 [b] Thy raiment waxed not old
upon thee, neither did thy foot swell,
these forty years.
5 Thou shalt also consider in thine
heart, that, as a man chasteneth his
son, *so* the LORD thy God chasteneth
thee.
6 Therefore thou shalt keep the
commandments of the LORD thy God,
to walk in his ways, and to fear him.
7 For the LORD thy God bringeth thee into a good land, a land
of brooks of water, of fountains and

---

vided for them the wealth and abundance of Canaan as He had done the manna of the desert (*vv.* 17, 18).

3. *but by every word that proceedeth out of the mouth of the LORD*] Lit. "every outgoing of the mouth of the Lord." Cf. xxix. 5, 6. The term "word" is inserted by A. V. after the LXX., which is followed by St Matt. and St Luke. On the means of subsistence available to the people during the wandering, see on Num. xx. 1. "Bread" in this verse stands for the ordinary means of earthly sustenance in general. Those means in the case of Israel were withheld, and new ones by God's almighty word and will substituted. Thus was the lesson taught, that it is not nature which nourishes man, but God the Creator by and through nature: and generally that God is not tied to the particular channels through which He is ordinarily pleased to work.

4. *Thy raiment waxed not old upon thee, neither did thy foot swell, these forty years.*] Cf. xxix. 5, "Your clothes are not waxen old upon you, and thy shoe is not waxen old upon thy foot." These words in a passage like the present, where the speaker is not so much narrating historically as alluding for hortatory purposes to God's care of them in the desert, may signify no more than that "God so amply provided for them all the necessaries of life, that they were never obliged to wear tattered garments, nor were their feet injured for lack of shoes or sandals."

Of course they had clothes, it would seem in abundance (cf. Exod. xii. 34, 35), at the beginning of the forty years; and equally of course some sources of supply during them. They had abundance of sheep and oxen, and so must have had much material for clothing always at command; and no doubt also carried on a traffic in these, as in other commodities, with the Moabites and the nomadic tribes of the desert. Such ordinary supplies must not be shut out of consideration, as regards the raiment of the chosen people, as they cannot in the similar question regarding their victual: cf. on Num. xx. 1. It may have been that these natural sources were on occasions supplemented by extraordinary providences of God, as was undoubtedly the case with their food. So substantially Calmet, Kurtz, Keil, Wogue, &c. The Jewish commentators, in bondage as elsewhere to the letter, construe the *v.* as meaning that the raiment of the Israelites did not wear out in their wanderings, and as implying even that the clothes of the children grew with their growth. So too Justin Mar. 'Dial. cum Tryph.' § 131 *sub fin.* The lesson of *v.* 3, which it is the object of Moses to impress, comes out sufficiently without such suppositions.

swell] On this word see Note at end of chapter.

7—9. On the ancient fertility of Canaan, see on Ex. iii. 8. In these *vv.* is implied a contrast, which in the parallel passage xi. 10, 11, is expressed, between Palestine and Egypt. The latter depends entirely on its single river; without the Nile, and the utmost use of the waters of the Nile, Egypt would be a desert. But Palestine is well distinguished not merely as "a land of wheat and barley, and vines and fig-trees and pomegranates, of oil-olive and honey," but emphatically as "a good land, a land of brooks of water, of fountains and depths that spring out of plains and mountains;" "not as the land of Egypt, where thou sowedst thy seed, and wateredst it with thy foot, as a garden of herbs," but a land of "mountains and plains which drinketh water of the rain of heaven." This mountainous character, this abundance of water both from natural springs and from the clouds of heaven, in contradistinction to the one uniform supply of the great river, this abundance of "milk" from its "cattle on a thousand hills," of "honey" from its forests and its thymy shrubs, was absolutely peculiar to Palestine amongst the civilized nations of the East.—Feeble as its brooks might be, though, doubtless, they were then far more frequently and fully filled than now, yet still it was the

depths that spring out of valleys and
hills;
8 A land of wheat, and barley, and
vines, and fig trees, and pomegranates;
a land † of oil olive, and honey;
9 A land wherein thou shalt eat
bread without scarceness, thou shalt
not lack any *thing* in it; a land whose
stones *are* iron, and out of whose hills
thou mayest dig brass.
10 [c] When thou hast eaten and
art full, then thou shalt bless the
LORD thy God for the good land
which he hath given thee.
11 Beware that thou forget not
the LORD thy God, in not keeping
his commandments, and his judgments, and his statutes, which I command thee this day:
12 Lest *when* thou hast eaten and
art full, and hast built goodly houses,
and dwelt *therein*;
13 And *when* thy herds and thy
flocks multiply, and thy silver and
thy gold is multiplied, and all that
thou hast is multiplied;
14 Then thine heart be lifted up,
and thou forget the LORD thy God,
which brought thee forth out of the
land of Egypt, from the house of
bondage;
15 Who led thee through that
great and terrible wilderness, *wherein
were* fiery serpents, and scorpions,

† Heb. *of olive tree of oil.*

[c] chap. 6. 11, 12.

---

only country where an Eastern could have written as does the Psalmist: "He sendeth the springs into the valleys, which run among the mountains." Those springs too, however short-lived, are remarkable for their copiousness and beauty.

The physical characteristics and advantages of a country like Palestine must have been quite strange to Israel at the time Moses was speaking: cf. note on iii. 25. It is significant that Deut. should abound more than the earlier books in praises of the fertility and excellence of the promised land. "Such a topic at an earlier period would have increased the murmurings and impatience of the people at being detained in the wilderness: whereas now it encouraged them to encounter with more cheerfulness the opposition they must must meet with from the inhabitants of Canaan." (Dean Graves on the Pentateuch, pp. 45, 46.)

8. *vines,*] The abundance of wine in Syria and Palestine is dwelt upon in the Egyptian records of the campaigns of Thotmosis III. In Egypt itself but little wine is produced. The country has not the slopes suitable for vineyards, and the overflow of the Nile occurs about the season when grapes would ripen. The Mareotic wine would seem however to have been prized (Hor. 'Od.' I. XXXVII. 14), and came to perfection in Egypt apparently for one principal reason which forbad the successful cultivation of grapes in general, viz. the fatness of the soil.

"Sunt Thasiæ vites, sunt et Mareotides albæ
Pinguibus hæ terris habiles, levioribus illæ."
Virg. 'Georg.' II. 92, 93.

The production of wine has in later times gradually ceased in Palestine, cf. Ritter, "Pal." IV. 185 (Clark's Transl.), except in some parts of the south where there is a considerable Jewish and Christian population, *e.g.* near Bethlehem: cf. Stanley, "S. and E." p. 164, and Hebron, Robinson "Bibl. Res." II. 80, 81.

9. *a land whose stones are iron, and out of whose hills thou mayest dig brass*] For *brass* read **copper**: cf. on Gen. iv. 22. We have a highly poetical description of mining operations Job xxviii. 1—11. Mining does not seem to have been extensively carried on by the Jews, though it certainly was so by the Canaanitish peoples displaced by them; see Rougemont, 'L'Age du Bronze,' pp. 188 sqq. Traces of iron and copper works have been discovered by modern travellers on Lebanon (Volney, 'Travels,' II. 438); and many parts of the country, *e.g.* the district of Argob (see notes on iii. 4), contain iron-stone in abundance. The brass, iron, &c. used for Solomon's temple were probably either the spoils of war (2 Sam. viii. 8, &c.), or imported.

15. *Who led thee through that great and terrible wilderness*, wherein were *fiery serpents, and scorpions, and drought, where* there was *no water*] The insertions made by our translations seem to carry the construction needlessly away from that of the original. The words rendered "fiery serpents" and "scorpions," singular nouns in the Hebrew, stand grammatically in apposition with "wilderness." The word rendered drought (*tsimmāon*) means "a dry place or land;" and should be closely connected with the clause following. That clause literally rendered would run, "a dry land to which there were no waters." The passuge might be more accurately rendered thus: "who brought thee through that great and terrible wilderness, the

and drought, where *there was* no
water; [d]who brought thee forth water (d Numb. 20. 11.)
out of the rock of flint;
16 Who fed thee in the wilderness
with [e]manna, which thy fathers knew (e Exod. 16. 15.)
not, that he might humble thee, and
that he might prove thee, to do thee
good at thy latter end;
17 And thou say in thine heart,
My power and the might of *mine*
hand hath gotten me this wealth.
18 But thou shalt remember the
LORD thy God: for *it is* he that
giveth thee power to get wealth, that
he may establish his covenant which
he sware unto thy fathers, as *it is*
this day.
19 And it shall be, if thou do at
all forget the LORD thy God, and
walk after other gods, and serve them,
and worship them, I testify against
you this day that ye shall surely
perish.
20 As the nations which the LORD
destroyeth before your face, so shall
ye perish; because ye would not be
obedient unto the voice of the LORD
your God.

---

fiery serpent, and the scorpion, and the dry land where are no waters." On the fiery serpents see on Num. xxi. 6.

16. *to do thee good at thy latter end*] This is presented as the result of God's dealings. The people had been suffered to hunger (*v.* 3) and fed with manna in order that God might prove them. But this trial was not laid on them arbitrarily, but as a moral discipline qualifying for the blessings which God designed ultimately to bestow. The "humbling" and "proving" are exhibited as God's immediate purpose:—the "doing good" to Israel as the eventual issue. The expression "at thy latter end" conveys somewhat more than "at length," "in future." The settlement of Israel in Canaan was the end and climax of the Mosaic dispensation, to which the sojourn in Egypt, the wandering in the desert, and the arrangements of the law, all led up. "Thy latter end" is then the later, and for the purpose in hand, final epoch in the national life to which all that had gone before was preparatory and introductory. The wilderness was to the Jewish Church analogous to the Cross, Canaan to the Crown.

NOTE on *v.* 4.

The Hebrew word rendered "swell" in A. V. only occurs again in Neh. ix. 21, where it is quoted from the present passage. This rendering proposed by Jarchi, is followed by Gesen., Fürst, Keil and the majority of authorities. The Hebrew verb seems certainly connected with the noun בצק, dough; and used Ex. xii. 34, 39, and elsewhere; and probably through the idea of the swelling which accompanies fermentation. The LXX. renders the word before as ἐτυλώθησαν, *i.e.* "became callous," in this place; though in the parallel passage of Neh. it has διεῤῥάνησαν. Vulg. "pes tuus non est subtritus." Onk Saad. and other Versions render "unshod," "naked:" all these senses except the first appear to be conjectures as to the sense of the word drawn from the context.

CHAPTER IX.

Moses dissuadeth them from the opinion of their own righteousness, by rehearsing their several rebellions.

HEAR, O Israel: Thou *art* to
pass over Jordan this day, to
go in to possess nations greater and
mightier than thyself, cities great and
fenced up to heaven,
2 A people great and tall, the children of the Anakims, whom thou
knowest, and *of whom* thou hast heard

CHAP. IX. **1—29.** Moses has been warning his hearers against that form of pride which claims victory as the fruit of human might only. He now goes on naturally to caution them against another and subtler aspect of the same sin, that namely which sees in success only the reward of one's own righteousness. The real causes are therefore set forth of God's dealings as to the Promised Land, (1) the wickedness of the Canaanitish nations, and (2) free grace towards Israel. The lesson is exactly that of Eph. ii. 8, "By

[a] Numb. 13. 28.

say, Who can stand before [a] the children of Anak!

3 Understand therefore this day, that the LORD thy God *is* he which goeth over before thee; *as* a [b] consuming fire he shall destroy them, and he shall bring them down before thy face: so shalt thou drive them out, and destroy them quickly, as the LORD hath said unto thee.

[b] chap. 4. 24. Heb. 12. 29.

4 Speak not thou in thine heart, after that the LORD thy God hath cast them out from before thee, saying, For my righteousness the LORD hath brought me in to possess this land: but for the wickedness of these nations the LORD doth drive them out from before thee.

5 Not for thy righteousness, or for the uprightness of thine heart, dost thou go to possess their land: but for the wickedness of these nations the LORD thy God doth drive them out from before thee, and that he may perform the word which the LORD sware unto thy fathers, Abraham, Isaac, and Jacob.

6 Understand therefore, that the LORD thy God giveth thee not this good land to possess it for thy righteousness; for thou *art* a stiffnecked people.

7 ¶ Remember, *and* forget not, how thou provokedst the LORD thy God to wrath in the wilderness: from the day that thou didst depart out of the land of Egypt, until ye came unto this place, ye have been rebellious against the LORD

8 Also in Horeb ye provoked the

---

grace are ye saved through faith; and that not of yourselves; it is the gift of God: not of works, lest any man should boast."

Moses points his admonition by reminding them of their repeated rebellions in past times, *vv.* 7, 8; 22, 23, &c.; and dwells especially on their apostasy at Horeb (*vv.* 8—21). This was so flagrant that it was only his own earnest intercessions which averted the destruction of the people, and won at length from God a renewal of the forfeited pledges of the Covenant (*vv.* 25—29; x. 1—11).

In referring to these circumstances Moses here, as elsewhere, has regard not so much to the order of time as to that of subject. (Cf. note on i. 9—15.) He inserts *e.g.* mention of the provocations at Taberah, Massah, Kibroth-hattaavah and Kadesh-barnea (*vv.* 22, 23), in the very midst of the narrative respecting the idolatry at Horeb and his own conduct in reference thereto. The like reasons, convenience and fitness to his argument, sufficiently explain the variations observable when the statements of this chapter are minutely compared with those of Exod. xxxii.—xxxiv. There is no real discrepancy, much less contradiction. Sometimes the more particular history of Exodus is condensed; as in *vv.* 26—29, where the substance of Moses' intercessions on two occasions (Ex. xxxii. 11—13, xxxiv. 9) is summed up in one statement: at other times circumstances not in Exodus are set forth here, because they are such as enhance the impressiveness of the admonitions Moses was uttering; *e.g.* the fact is put forward that Moses fasted for *two* periods of forty days (*vv.* 9 and 18), *one* such fast only being expressly named in Exodus; as is also his special intercession for Aaron (*v.* 20). In these variations we have nothing more or other than such treatment of facts as is usual and warrantable enough between parties personally acquainted with the matters in question; a treatment which implies and assumes a knowledge of the facts in both speaker and hearer, and which therefore, there being no fear of misleading, can dispense with minute specifications of time, place, and circumstance.

3. *Understand therefore*] Render **And thou shalt know.** The verb is not to be taken as an imperative, but as simply continuing the announcement of *v.* 1, "Thou art to pass over Jordan &c.; and thou shalt know &c."

so shalt thou drive them out, and destroy them quickly] This is not inconsistent with vii. 22, "thou mayest not consume them at once," though the word here rendered "quickly" is the same as that there translated "at once." In the former passage the Israelites are warned not to expect that God would bring about an instant annihilation of the Canaanites: the word there employed ("consume," *callōth*) has clearly this force, and the reason why no such annihilation was to take place is assigned there, "lest the beasts of the field increase upon thee." Here Moses urges the people to trust in God's covenanted aid; since He would then make no delay in so destroying the nations attacked by them as to put them into enjoyment of the promises, and in doing so as fast as was for the well-being of Israel itself.

8. *Also in Horeb ye provoked the LORD*] Rather "*even* in Horeb:" the conjunction here

LORD to wrath, so that the LORD
was angry with you to have destroyed
you.
9 When I was gone up into the
mount to receive the tables of stone,
even the tables of the covenant which
[c] Exod. 24. 18. & 34. 28. the LORD made with you, then [c] I
abode in the mount forty days and
forty nights, I neither did eat bread
nor drink water:
[d] Exod. 31. 18. 10 [d] And the LORD delivered unto
me two tables of stone written with
the finger of God; and on them *was*
written according to all the words,
which the LORD spake with you in
the mount out of the midst of the
fire in the day of the assembly.
11 And it came to pass at the end
of forty days and forty nights, *that*
the LORD gave me the two tables
of stone, *even* the tables of the covenant.
12 And the LORD said unto me,
[e] Exod. 32. 7. [e] Arise, get thee down quickly from
hence; for thy people which thou
hast brought forth out of Egypt have
corrupted *themselves;* they are quickly
turned aside out of the way which I
commanded them; they have made
them a molten image.
13 Furthermore the LORD spake
unto me, saying, I have seen this
people, and, behold, it *is* a stiffnecked
people:
14 Let me alone, that I may destroy them, and blot out their name
from under heaven: and I will make
of thee a nation mightier and greater
than they.
15 So I turned and came down
from the mount, and the mount
burned with fire: and the two tables
of the covenant *were* in my two
hands.
16 And I looked, and, behold, ye
had sinned against the LORD your
God, *and* had made you a molten
calf: ye had turned aside quickly out
of the way which the LORD had commanded you.
17 And I took the two tables, and
cast them out of my two hands, and
brake them before your eyes.
18 And I fell down before the
LORD, as at the first, forty days and
forty nights: I did neither eat bread,
nor drink water, because of all your
sins which ye sinned, in doing wickedly in the sight of the LORD, to provoke him to anger.
19 For I was afraid of the anger
and hot displeasure, wherewith the
LORD was wroth against you to destroy you. But the LORD hearkened
unto me at that time also.
20 And the LORD was very angry
with Aaron to have destroyed him:
and I prayed for Aaron also the same
time.
21 And I took your sin, the calf
which ye had made, and burnt it
with fire, and stamped it, *and* ground
it very small, *even* until it was as
small as dust: and I cast the dust

(as often) introduces a special example of a general statement. The time and circumstances made the apostasy at Horeb particularly inexcusable.

18. *I fell down before the LORD, as at the first*] Moses interceded for the people before he came down from the mountain the first time: Ex. xxxii. 11—13. This intercession is only briefly alluded to in this *v.* Afterwards he spent another forty days on the mountain in fasting and prayer to obtain a complete restitution of the covenant: Ex. xxxiv. 28. It is this second forty days, and the intercession of Moses made therein (cf. Ex. xxxiv. 9), that is more particularly brought forward here and in *vv.* 25—29. There is no inconsistency between the two accounts.

20. *And the LORD was very angry with Aaron to have destroyed him*] Israel could not boast even that its heads and representatives continued faithful. Aaron had been already designated for the high-priestly functions; but he fell away with the rest of the people. It was due then solely to the grace of God and the intercession of Moses that Aaron himself and his promised priesthood with him were not cut off; just as at a later time, when Aaron had actually to die for a new sin Israel owed it still to the same causes that Eleazar was substituted and the high priesthood perpetuated (x. 6, Num. xx. 25 sqq. and note).

thereof into the brook that descended
out of the mount.
f Numb. 22 And at [f]Taberah, and at [g]Mas-
11. 1, 3. g Exod. 17. sah, and at [h]Kibroth-hattaavah, ye
7. h Numb. provoked the LORD to wrath.
11. 34. 23 Likewise when the LORD sent
you from Kadesh-barnea, saying, Go
up and possess the land which I have
given you; then ye rebelled against
the commandment of the LORD your
God, and ye believed him not, nor
hearkened to his voice.
24 Ye have been rebellious against
the LORD from the day that I knew
you.
25 Thus I fell down before the
LORD forty days and forty nights,
as I fell down *at the first*; because
the LORD had said he would destroy
you.
26 I prayed therefore unto the
LORD, and said, O Lord GOD, destroy
not thy people and thine inheritance,
which thou hast redeemed through
thy greatness, which thou hast brought
forth out of Egypt with a mighty
hand.
27 Remember thy servants, Abraham, Isaac, and Jacob; look not
unto the stubbornness of this people, nor to their wickedness, nor to
their sin:
28 Lest the land whence thou
broughtest us out say, [i]Because the i Numb.
LORD was not able to bring them 14. 16.
into the land which he promised
them, and because he hated them,
he hath brought them out to slay
them in the wilderness.
29 Yet they *are* thy people and
thine inheritance, which thou broughtest out by thy mighty power and by
thy stretched out arm.

CHAPTER X.

1 *God's mercy in restoring the two tables,* 6 *in continuing the priesthood,* 8 *in separating the tribe of Levi,* 10 *in hearkening unto Moses' suit for the people.* 12 *An exhortation unto obedience.*

AT that time the LORD said unto
me, [a]Hew thee two tables of a Exod. 34.
stone like unto the first, and come 1.
up unto me into the mount, and
make thee an ark of wood.
2 And I will write on the tables
the words that were in the first tables
which thou brakest, and thou shalt
put them in the ark.
3 And I made an ark *of* shittim
wood, and hewed two tables of stone
like unto the first, and went up into
the mount, having the two tables in
mine hand.
4 And he wrote on the tables, ac-

---

22. *Taberah...Kibroth-hattaavah*] The "burning" which gave to the place the name of Taberah, occurred on the outer edge of the camp; Num. xi. 1, see note. It happened however whilst the people were encamped at the station afterwards termed Kibroth-hattaavah, from another judgment inflicted there for another rebellion. Taberah was then the name of a spot in or near the station of Kibroth-hattaavah, and accordingly is not named in the list of encampments given Num. xxxiii. 16. The separate mention of the two is however here appropriate; for each place and each name was a memorial of an act of rebellion. The instances in this and the next *v.* are not given in order of occurrence. The speaker for his own purposes advances from the slighter to the more heinous proofs of guilt. The transpositions by which some editors have attempted to reduce these statements into conformity with chronology are, when the nature of the language before us is considered, alike needless and unauthorized.

CHAP. X. 1—11. These *vv.* are closely connected with the preceding chapter, and state very briefly the results of that intercession of Moses recorded ix. 25—29. They present not only the grant of the second tables of the Covenant (*vv.* 1—5) but the institution and regulation of the priestly (*v.* 6) and Levitical (*vv.* 8, 9) services, and even the permission to march onward and take possession of the promised land (*v.* 11), as all consequent upon Moses' intervention. Thus effectively does Moses close his admonition against spiritual pride by reminding the people how all their blessings and privileges, forfeited by apostasy as soon as bestowed, were only now their own by a new and most unmerited act of grace on the part of God, won from Him by the self-sacrificing mediation of Moses himself (*v.* 10).

1—5. *come up unto me into the mount, and make thee an ark of wood,* &c.] The order for making the ark and tabernacle was evidently

cording to the first writing, the ten
† commandments, which the LORD
spake unto you in the mount out of
the midst of the fire in the day of
the assembly: and the LORD gave
them unto me.

† Heb. *words.*

5 And I turned myself and came
down from the mount, and put the
tables in the ark which I had made;
and there they be, as the LORD commanded me.
6 ¶ And the children of Israel
took their journey from Beeroth of
the children of Jaakan to [b] Mosera:
[c] there Aaron died, and there he was
buried; and Eleazar his son ministered in the priest's office in his
stead.

[b] Numb. 33. 30. [c] Numb. 20. 28.

7 From thence they journeyed
unto Gudgodah; and from Gudgodah to Jotbath, a land of rivers of
waters.
8 ¶ At that time the LORD separated the tribe of Levi, to bear the
ark of the covenant of the LORD,
to stand before the LORD to minister
unto him, and to bless in his name,
unto this day.
9 [d] Wherefore Levi hath no part
nor inheritance with his brethren;
the LORD *is* his inheritance, according as the LORD thy God promised
him.
10 And I stayed in the mount,
according to the ‖ first time, forty
days and forty nights; and the LORD

[d] Numb. 18. 20.

‖ Or, *former days.*

---

given before the apostasy of the people (Ex. xxv. sqq.); and the tables were not put in the ark until the completion and dedication of the tabernacle (Exod. xl.). But here as elsewhere (cf. on ix. 1) Moses connects transactions closely related to each other and to his purpose without regard to the order of occurrence.

6. *Beeroth of the children of Jaakan*] This place is identical with the Bene-jaakan of Num xxxiii. 31, where see note.

Mosera] The *Moseroth* of Num. xxxiii. 31, where see note.

there Aaron died] *i.e.* whilst the people were encamped at Mosera or Moseroth. In xxxii. 50 as well as in Num. xx. 25 sqq. Mount Hor is assigned as the place of Aaron's death. It is plain then that Moserah was in the neighbourhood of Mount Hor; and this is confirmed by other notices of the locality. See note on Numbers *l.c.* Aaron did not die in the camp, neither, from the nature of the case, could the camp be pitched actually on Mount Hor. It was of course located on the slopes or at the foot of the mount; more precisely at Moserah. Thence Moses, Aaron, and Eleazar "went up into Mount Hor in the sight of the congregation," and "Aaron died there in the top of the mount" (Num. xx. 27—28).

Eleazar his son ministered in...his stead] The appointment of Eleazar to minister in place of Aaron, as in *vv.* 1—3 the restitution of the Decalogue, and in *vv.* 8, 9 the establishment of the ministry of the Levites, is referred to in proof of the completeness and fullness of the reconciliation effected between God and the people by Moses. Though Aaron was sentenced to die in the wilderness for his sin at Meribah, yet God provided for the perpetuation of the high-priesthood, so that the people should not suffer. Cf. ix. 20 and note.

7. *Jotbath, a land of rivers of waters*] Parenthetical mention is made of the two journeys which next followed Aaron's death; and with the same theme apparently in view. God showed that His care and love of His people were not diminished because of the sin and consequent death of the first solemnly appointed and official mediator, Aaron. God led them from the spot where they had witnessed Aaron's departure to a land of rest and refreshment. It is possible however that these two *vv.* may be, as may some other notices of a like character, a gloss: cf. note on ii. 10—12, and 20—23. The words "at that time" in *v.* 8 certainly connect themselves with *v.* 5 and not with *v.* 7. Jotbath is the Jotbathah of Num. xxxiii. 33, where see note.

8. *At that time*] *i.e.* that of the encampment at Sinai, as the words also import in *v.* 1. Throughout the passage the time of the important events at Sinai is kept in view, and is reverted to as each incident is brought forward by Moses, alluded to sufficiently for his purpose, and dismissed.

As the priests were of the tribe of Levi, their special duties, as well as those belonging to the other Levites, may generally be assigned to that tribe in contradistinction to the other eleven. It was properly the priest's office to bless (Num. vi. 22 sqq.), and to minister before the Lord (ch. xviii. 5), whilst the non-priestly family of Kohath (Num. iv. 15) had the duty of bearing the ark. But Moses is evidently here speaking of the election by God of the tribe of Levi at large, priests and others also, for His own service. On the passages in

hearkened unto me at that time
also, *and* the LORD would not destroy thee.

11 And the LORD said unto me,
Arise, [†] take *thy* journey before the † Heb. *in journey.*
people, that they may go in and pos-
sess the land, which I sware unto
their fathers to give unto them.

12 ¶ And now, Israel, what doth
the LORD thy God require of thee,
but to fear the LORD thy God, to
walk in all his ways, and to love him,
and to serve the LORD thy God
with all thy heart and with all thy
soul,

13 To keep the commandments of
the LORD, and his statutes, which
I command thee this day for thy
good?

14 Behold, the heaven and the
heaven of heavens *is* the LORD'S thy
God, [e] the earth *also*, with all that e Psal. 24. 1.
therein *is*.

15 Only the LORD had a delight
in thy fathers to love them, and he
chose their seed after them, *even* you
above all people, as *it is* this day.

16 Circumcise therefore the foreskin of your heart, and be no more
stiffnecked.

Deut. relating to the priests and Levites, see Introd. § v. and Note at end of chap. xviii.

12 sqq. After these emphatic warnings against self-righteousness the principal topic is resumed from ch. vi., and this division of the discourse is drawn to a conclusion in the next two chapters by a series of direct and positive exhortations to a careful fulfilment of the duties prescribed in the first two of the Ten Words. Pride having been shown to be utterly out of place in those who had so often provoked God, and who owed their all to God's forgiveness and Moses' intreaties, it remains for Israel to make such return as is possible for God's undeserved mercies, by loving and fearing Him and diligently keeping his commandments. Both for love and fear of Him abundant cause is drawn from His past dealings with Israel: from His condescension to their fathers (*vv.* 14, 15), and to themselves in their distress (*vv.* 18, 19); and from His great acts for them and against their enemies (*v.* 22: xi. 1 sqq.). Finally Moses reminds them of the consequences which await their conduct; prosperity and success if they be faithful, misfortune and sorrow if otherwise (xi. 13—25). The alternative is solemnly and distinctly set before them, and the choice committed to themselves (xi. 26 sqq.).

12. *And now, Israel*, &c.] *i.e.* "Since all that thou hast is thus shown to be of mere grace, without desert of thine own."

what doth the LORD *thy God require*, &c.] A noteworthy demand. God has in the Mosaic law positively commanded many things. These however relate to external observances, which if need be can be enforced. But love and veneration cannot be enforced, even by God himself. They must be spontaneous. Hence, even under the law of ordinances where so much was peremptorily laid down, and omnipotence was ready to compel obedience, those sentiments, which are the spirit and life of the whole, have to be, as they here are, invited and solicited.

14. *heaven of heavens*] Cf. 1 K. viii. 27; Ps. cxlviii. 4. The phrase is an exhaustive one like sæcula sæculorum, αἰῶνες τῶν αἰώνων; and imports all which can be included under the name of heaven. Cf. St Paul's record that he had been "caught up to the third heaven," 2 Cor. xii. 2. The declaration that "heaven and the heaven of heavens is the Lord's" warns Israel that this authority is not local and circumscribed; that He was not in any way bound to make election of Israel, but did so (*v.* 15) of His own free grace.

16. *Circumcise therefore the foreskin of your heart, and be no more stiffnecked*] On circumcision see Gen. xvii., Note at end of chapter. This *v.* points to the spiritual import of circumcision. Circumcision must not be regarded as a rite adopted principally for sanitary reasons, and incorporated into the ritual of Moses by way of securing its regular observance. Nor is it enough to regard circumcision as representing merely the purity of heart and life required of those who would dedicate themselves to God. Circumcision was rather designed to set forth the truth which lies at the very basis of revealed religion, and which requires to be recognized as a preliminary to the saving reception of revealed truth, that man is by nature "very far gone from original righteousness," and in a state of enmity to God. The peremptory requirement of circumcision as the sacrament of admission to the privileges of the chosen people denoted that this opposition must be taken away ere man could enter into covenant with God; and the peculiar nature of the rite itself indicated the origin and cause of that opposition, and marked that element of our nature which is the most guilty and fallen. It was through the flesh that man first sinned;

17 For the LORD your God *is* God of gods, and Lord of lords, a great God, a mighty, and a terrible, which *f* regardeth not persons, nor taketh reward:

18 He doth execute the judgment of the fatherless and widow, and loveth the stranger, in giving him food and raiment.

19 Love ye therefore the stranger: for ye were strangers in the land of Egypt.

20 *g* Thou shalt fear the LORD thy God; him shalt thou serve, and to him shalt thou *h* cleave, and swear by his name.

21 He *is* thy praise, and he *is* thy God, that hath done for thee these great and terrible things, which thine eyes have seen.

f 2 Chron. 19. 7. Job 34. 19. Acts 10. 34. Rom. 2. 11. Gal. 2. 6. Eph. 6. 9. Col. 3. 25. 1 Pet. 1. 17.

g chap. 6. 13. Matt. 4. 10. Luke 4. 8.

h chap. 13. 4.

22 Thy fathers went down into Egypt *i* with threescore and ten persons; and now the LORD thy God hath made thee *k* as the stars of heaven for multitude.

i Gen. 4[6]. 27. Exod. 1[.5].

k Gen. 1[5]. 5.

CHAPTER XI.

1 *An exhortation to obedience,* 2 *by their own experience of God's great works,* 8 *by promise of God's great blessings,* 16 *and by threatenings.* 18 *A careful study is required in God's words.* 26 *The blessing and curse is set before them.*

THEREFORE thou shalt love the LORD thy God, and keep his charge, and his statutes, and his judgments, and his commandments, alway.

2 And know ye this day: for *I speak* not with your children which have not known, and which have not seen the chastisement of the LORD

---

as it is also in the flesh, its functions, lusts, &c., that man's rebellion against God chiefly manifests itself still. It was fitting therefore that the symbol which should denote the removal of this estrangement from God should be wrought in the body. Moses then fitly follows up the command "to circumcise the heart" with the warning "to be no more stiffnecked." His meaning is that they should lay aside that obduracy and perverseness towards God for which he had been reproving them, which had led them into so many transgressions of the covenant and revolts from God, and which was especially the very contrary of that love and fear of God required by the first two of the Ten Commandments. Similarly, xxx. 6, circumcision of the heart is spoken of as a necessary condition of loving God; and on the other hand the epithet "uncircumcised" is applied to the heart, lips, &c. Lev. xxvi. 41; Jer. iv. 4; Ezek. xliv. 9; Acts vii. 51, &c., to denote the native incapacity of the members of the body for God's service. The language associated with circumcision in the Bible distinguishes the use made of this rite in the Jewish religion from that found amongst certain heathen nations. Circumcision was practised by those nations, and as a religious rite; but not by any, the Egyptians probably excepted, at all in the Jewish sense and meaning. It is found *e.g.* amongst the Phœnicians; but as one of a class of usages, human sacrifices being another example, which were designed to appease a deity representing the powers of death and destruction, and supposed therefore to delight in human privation and suffering.

The grounds on which Circumcision was imposed as essential by the Law are the same as those on which Baptism is required in the Gospel. The latter in the New Testament is strictly analogous to the former under the Old; cf. Col. ii. 11, 12.

17, 18. *For the LORD your God is God of gods, and Lord of lords,* &c.] The demand for a surrender on the part of Israel of that refractoriness towards God to which they were prone, is followed up by an admonition respecting His majesty and omnipotence. As He sums up in Himself all power and might, He will not (*v.* 17) accept sacrifices or gifts (cf. Ps. li. 16) to win His favour, nor will He tolerate resistance, either against Himself or (*v.* 18) against those whom He takes into His protection.

18. The uncircumcised heart is ever proud, hard, selfish. The call to put it away is naturally coupled therefore with an admonition that though "God be high, yet hath He respect unto the lowly," and with an injunction to "love the stranger, as God had loved them when strangers in Egypt." Thus would it be shown that they had circumcised their hearts indeed (cf. 1 St John iii. 10, 17, and iv. 20).

CHAP. XI. **1.** *keep his charge*] Cf. Levit. viii. 35.

2. *And know ye this day: for I speak not with your children which have not known, and which have not seen the chastisement of the LORD your God, his greatness,* &c.] Render: **And own ye this day (for I have not to do with your children which have not known and which have not seen) the**

your God, his greatness, his mighty
hand, and his stretched out arm,
3 And his miracles, and his acts,
which he did in the midst of Egypt
unto Pharaoh the king of Egypt, and
unto all his land;
4 And what he did unto the army
of Egypt, unto their horses, and to
their chariots; how he made the
water of the Red sea to overflow
them as they pursued after you, and
how the LORD hath destroyed them
unto this day;
5 And what he did unto you in
the wilderness, until ye came into
this place;

[a] Numb. 16. 31. & 27. 3. Ps. 106. 17.

6 And [a] what he did unto Dathan and Abiram, the sons of Eliab,
the son of Reuben: how the earth
opened her mouth, and swallowed
them up, and their households, and
their tents, and all the ‖ substance
that † *was* in their possession, in the
midst of all Israel:

‖ Or, *living substance which followed them.* † Heb. *was at their feet.*

7 But your eyes have seen all the
great acts of the LORD which he did.
8 Therefore shall ye keep all the
commandments which I command you
this day, that ye may be strong, and
go in and possess the land, whither ye
go to possess it;
9 And that ye may prolong *your*
days in the land, which the LORD
sware unto your fathers to give unto
them and to their seed, a land that
floweth with milk and honey.
10 ¶ For the land, whither thou
goest in to possess it, *is* not as the
land of Egypt, from whence ye came
out, where thou sowedst thy seed,
and wateredst *it* with thy foot, as a
garden of herbs:

---

chastisement of the LORD, his greatness, &c. The word "chastisement" is evidently the accusative governed by the verb at the beginning of the *v.*, rendered "know" in A. V. The colon placed after "day" should therefore be removed, and the words between the verb and its accusative placed in parenthesis as above. The ellipse in the parenthetic words, supplied in the A. V. by the insertion of "I speak," is better filled up as above, understanding a common Hebrew phrase (*haddābhār hahoo*): so Schultz, Keil, and Del., Bp. Wordsworth, &c. With the words "which have not known and which have not seen," it is easy from the context to supply a clause equivalent to "what ye have known and seen."

The "chastisement" consisted in the many mighty acts, both of punishment and mercy, through which God had guided them from Egypt to the borders of the Promised Land. This loving discipline Moses calls on them to recognize and lay to heart: and in this and the following four *vv.* he specifies some leading instances of its exercise.

6. *And what he did unto Dathan and Abiram, the sons of Eliab, the sons of Reuben*] It has been noted that Korah and the Levites who took part with him are not mentioned here, though in Num. xvi. "Korah and his company" took a leading part in the rebellion. It may be added that the name of "On, the son of Peleth" (cf. Num. xvi. 1) is omitted also. But in a mere allusion such as that before us, and made too in the presence of eyewitnesses of the facts, it was superfluous to give all the names of the leaders in "the gainsaying." The omission of Korah and the Levites seems intelligible enough when we remember that Moses was addressing and admonishing, not the Levites, but the congregation at large. The rebellion of Korah evidently included an attack on both the ecclesiastical and civil arrangements of Moses; see note on Num. xvi. The former were assailed by Korah and certain of the Levites, the latter by Dathan, Abiram, and On, with 250 other "princes of the assembly" (Num. xvi. 2). This latter was the only portion of the sedition which it was relevant to Moses' present purpose to name; and he therefore naturally omits the former.

all the substance that was in their possession] Render, **every living thing which followed them.** Literally, "every living thing at their feet." The expression does not mean their goods, which would be included in their "households and tents," but their followers, described Num. xvi. 32 as "all the men that appertained to Korah."

10. Another motive for fidelity is added, viz. the entire dependence of the Promised Land upon God for its fertility. It was "a land flowing with milk and honey;" yet this its richness was not, as was that of Egypt, the reward of human skill and labour, but was, on the contrary, the gift of God simply and entirely; the effect of "the former and the latter rains" sent by Him. The spiritual significance of these and many other such peculiarities of the Promised Land must not be overlooked.

Egypt and Canaan are distinguished in this and the following verses, by certain of their

11 But the land, whither ye go
to possess it, *is* a land of hills and
valleys, *and* drinketh water of the
rain of heaven:
12 A land which the LORD thy
† Heb. *seeketh.* God †careth for: the eyes of the
LORD thy God *are* always upon it,
from the beginning of the year even
unto the end of the year.
13 ¶ And it shall come to pass, if
ye shall hearken diligently unto my
commandments which I command you
this day, to love the LORD your God,
and to serve him with all your heart
and with all your soul,
14 That I will give *you* the rain
of your land in his due season, the
first rain and the latter rain, that thou
mayest gather in thy corn, and thy
wine, and thine oil.
15 And I will †send grass in thy † Heb. *give.*
fields for thy cattle, that thou mayest
eat and be full.
16 Take heed to yourselves, that
your heart be not deceived, and ye
turn aside, and serve other gods, and
worship them;
17 And *then* the LORD's wrath be
kindled against you, and he shut up
the heaven, that there be no rain,
and that the land yield not her fruit;
and *lest* ye perish quickly from off
the good land which the LORD giveth
you.
18 ¶ Therefore shall ye lay up
these my words in your heart and
in your soul, and [b]bind them for a [b] chap. 6. 8.
sign upon your hand, that they may
be as frontlets between your eyes.
19 [c]And ye shall teach them your [c] chap. 4. 10. & 6. 7.

---

most remarkable physical traits. Canaan as a mountainous country (cf. on iii. 25) was well watered, but by the rains of heaven, on which it absolutely depended for its crops. Without the autumn rain to quicken the newly sown seed, and the spring rain to give the grain bulk and substance, the harvest of Palestine would totally fail. Nor, from the configuration of the country, could artificial irrigation do anything to remedy this dependence. Hence it was a land on which, so long as God's people were faithful and consequently prosperous, "the eyes of God" would always be: *i.e.* He would supply at each successive season (cf. *vv.* 14, 15) the needful conditions of productiveness. But Egypt, fit emblem here as elsewhere of the world of nature in distinction from the world of grace, though of course deriving its all ultimately from the Giver of all good things, yet directly and immediately owed its riches and plenty to human ingenuity and capital. It enjoyed no rain worth speaking of, but drew its water supply from the annual overflowing of the Nile. This only lasts about a hundred days; but is rendered available for agricultural purposes throughout the year by an elaborate and costly system of tanks, canals, forcing machines, &c. To these mechanical appliances allusion is made in this verse: "Egypt where thou sowedst thy seed, and wateredst it with thy foot." The inhabitants of Egypt probably watered "with the foot" in two ways, viz. by means of tread-wheels working sets of pumps, and by means of artificial channels connected with reservoirs, and opened, turned, or closed by the feet. Both methods are still in use in Egypt and other similar districts of country. On the former see Hengstenberg, 'Auth.' I. 435. Of the latter Bp. Daniel Wilson (*e.g.*) speaks, writing from Mayaveram on a visitation tour; he journeyed (1835) through "rice-fields, waving with their green mass of blade-grass, every field soaked and floated. Literally they 'sow amidst many waters,' 'cast their bread (corn) upon them,' 'water them with their foot,' which removes the petty embankmeut when they let in the stream; whilst 'the sending out thither the feet of the ox and the ass' is perpetually seen." Bp. Wilson's 'Journal, Letters,' p. 35. Cf. Virgil, 'Georgic,' I. 106 sqq.:

satis fluvium inducit rivosque sequentes,
Et quum exustus ager morientibus æstuat herbis,
Ecce supercilio clivosi tramitis undam
Elicit; illa cadens raucum per lævia murmur
Saxa ciet, &c.

14. *the first rain and the latter rain*] The Hebrew nouns are here rendered in sense rather than in letter. The former, derived from a verb signifying *to cast forth* or *to sprinkle*, is the proper term for the autumn rain, falling about the time of sowing, and which may be named "the former," as occuring in the early part of the Hebrew civil year, viz. in October and November. The other word (*malkōsh*), derived from a verb signifying "to be late," or "to gather in the late fruits," is applied to the spring rain, which falls in March and April, because it fits the earth for the ingathering of harvest. Between these two wet periods, and except them, there was little or no rain in Canaan. Rain in harvest time (cf. 1 Sam. xii. 17, 18) was so rare as to be regarded as portentous.

children, speaking of them when thou
sittest in thine house, and when thou
walkest by the way, when thou liest
down, and when thou risest up.
20 And thou shalt write them upon the door posts of thine house, and
upon thy gates:
21 That your days may be multiplied, and the days of your children,
in the land which the LORD sware
unto your fathers to give them, as the
days of heaven upon the earth.
22 ¶ For if ye shall diligently keep
all these commandments which I command you, to do them, to love the
LORD your God, to walk in all his
ways, and to cleave unto him;
23 Then will the LORD drive out
all these nations from before you, and
ye shall possess greater nations and
mightier than yourselves.
Josh. 1. 24 [d]Every place whereon the soles
of your feet shall tread shall be yours:
from the wilderness and Lebanon,
from the river, the river Euphrates,
even unto the uttermost sea shall
your coast be.
25 There shall no man be able to
stand before you: *for* the LORD your
God shall lay the fear of you and
the dread of you upon all the land
that ye shall tread upon, as he hath
said unto you.
26 ¶ Behold, I set before you this
day a blessing and a curse;
27 [e]A blessing, if ye obey the com- [e] chap. 28.
mandments of the LORD your God, 2.
which I command you this day:
28 And a [f]curse, if ye will not [f] chap. 28.
obey the commandments of the LORD 15.
your God, but turn aside out of the
way which I command you this day,
to go after other gods, which ye have
not known.
29 And it shall come to pass, when
the LORD thy God hath brought thee
in unto the land whither thou goest
to possess it, that thou shalt put [g]the [g] chap. 27.
blessing upon mount Gerizim, and 13. Josh. 8. 33.
the curse upon mount Ebal.
30 *Are* they not on the other side
Jordan, by the way where the sun
goeth down, in the land of the Canaanites, which dwell in the champaign over against Gilgal, beside the
plains of Moreh?

---

21. *as the days of heaven upon the earth*] These words are grammatically connected with the verb "multiplied" in the beginning of the *v.* The sense is: "Keep the covenant faithfully, and so your own and your children's days be multiplied as long as the heaven covers the earth." The promise of Canaan to Israel then was a *perpetual* promise, but also a *conditional* one.

24. *Every place whereon the soles of your feet shall tread shall be yours*] This promise is restricted by the words following to certain limits: viz. the desert of Arabia on the south; Lebanon on the north; the Mediterranean on the west; the Euphrates on the east (cf. Gen. xv. 18; Josh. i. 3, 4). Before the word Lebanon must apparently be understood the preposition "from."

29. *thou shalt put the blessing upon mount Gerizim*] Lit. thou shalt *give*, *i.e.* give utterance to it.

The word *Gerizim* is probably derived from a root (*gāraz*), to shear or cut off. It can however hardly (as Rosenm. and others) have been bestowed on the mountain because it grew large crops, and so found much employment for the sickle. Mount Gerizim was and is as barren as Ebal (see Robinson, II. 276 sqq.): and was probably selected as the hill of benediction because it was the southernmost of the two, the south being the region, according to Hebrew ideas, of light, and so of life and blessing. On the ceremony of the solemn benediction and commination, see xxvii. 14 sqq:

30. *Are they not on the other side Jordan, by the way where the sun goeth down, in the land of the Canaanites, which dwell in the champaign over against Gilgal, beside the plains of Moreh?*] The situation of the mountains is here described more accurately. The words "by the way where the sun goeth down," should run, **beyond the road of the west**; *i.e.* on the further side of the main track which ran from Syria and Damascus to Jerusalem and Egypt through the centre of Palestine. This is called "the way of the west" in contrast to the other main route from Damascus to the south which passed through the district east of Jordan. The portion of this western road which lies between Jerusalem and Nablous is described in Ritter, 'Palestine,' IV. 293 sqq. (Clark's Transl.). Robinson on his way from Acre to Jerusalem passed over the same portion, and describes the road as skirting Ebal and Gerizim.

31 For ye shall pass over Jordan
to go in to possess the land which the
LORD your God giveth you, and ye
shall possess it, and dwell therein.

h chap. 5. 32

32 And ye shall observe [h] to do all
the statutes and judgments which I
set before you this day.

CHAPTER XII.

1 *Monuments of idolatry are to be destroyed.* 5 *The place of God's service is to be kept.* 15, 23 *Blood is forbidden.* 17, 20, 26 *Holy things must be eaten in the holy place.* 19 *The Levite is not to be forsaken.* 29 *Idolatry is not to be inquired after.*

THESE *are* the statutes and judgments, which ye shall observe
to do in the land, which the LORD
God of thy fathers giveth thee to possess it, all the days that ye live upon
the earth.

Traces of the ancient road, which is still a much frequented track, were noticed in many places by Robinson: see "Bibl. Res." III. 127 sqq. The further specifications of the verse apply only indirectly to Ebal and Gerizim. "Gilgal" and "the plains (rather, **the oaks**, cf. on Gen. xii. 6) of Moreh," are added to define more particularly the section of Canaanites intended. The fact that the whole district in question is clearly placed by these local notes beyond the main central road of Palestine, ought to have precluded the charges of anachronism brought forward on the assumption that the Gilgal here named is Gilgal by Jericho, which only received its name in the time of Joshua (Josh. v. 9).

The purpose of Moses is to mark the situation of two mountains which were to be the scene of a very remarkable function of his ritual. He describes them first as beyond Jordan, on the banks of which Israel then was; next, as beyond the well-known high road through the country; next, as in the land occupied by certain Canaanites "over against Gilgal, and beside the oaks of Moreh." These latter were apparently familiar to the people from the history of Abraham (cf. Gen. xii. 6), and were in the neighbourhood of Sichem: obviously therefore the Gilgal by Jericho is out of the question in the case before us. Whether Deuteronomy was or was not written after the time of Joshua, the writer of this verse did not and could not intend to refer to a place on the edge of the Jordan, such as the Gilgal of Joshua v. 9, but to one in the neighbourhood of Moreh and Sichem, some thirty-five miles distant at least.

Bearing these things in mind it seems impossible to doubt that the Gilgal of this verse is to be found in the Jiljûlieh of Robinson ('Bibl. Researches,' III. pp. 138, 139), a large village about twelve miles south of Gerizim. Jiljûlieh is on the brow of a lofty range of hills, and would be very appropriately assigned as a landmark. It is called "Gilgoul" by Ritter, 'Pal.' IV. 268 (Clark's Transl.). It may also have been the Gilgal from which Elijah and Elisha "went down" to Bethel (2 K. ii. 1, 2); and which is repeatedly named in the history of those prophets. The Gilgal mentioned Josh. xii. 23 as a capital of certain nations, seems to have been a *third* place bearing this descriptive and so not uncommon name. See note there.

CHAP. XII. Having thus rehearsed the Decalogue and enforced its leading principles, Moses now passes on to apply those principles to the ecclesiastical, civil, and social life of the people. Fourteen chapters are thus occupied. In proceeding through them many particulars will be noticed which are peculiar to the law as given in Deut.; and even in laws repeated from the earlier books various new circumstances and details are introduced. This is but natural. The Sinaitic legislation was nearly forty years old, and had been given under conditions of time place, and circumstance now distant from, the present ones. The promised land was in sight, the lawgiver himself was about to be withdrawn, and his institutions were at length about to be put into full effect. Moses in ripeness of wisdom and experience now completes his office by enlarging, explaining, modifying, and supplementing, under Divine guidance and sanction, the code which under the like authority he had in earlier days promulgated. Yet the Sinaitic system, so far from being set aside or in any way abrogated, is on the contrary throughout presupposed and assumed. Its existence and authority are taken as the starting-point of what is here prescribed, and an accurate acquaintance with it on the part of the people is taken for granted. It is too much to say that the details of chaps. xii.—xxvi. can be at all satisfactorily grouped in order round the precepts of the Decalogue; but the allusions to it are so frequent that we can readily see how here, as in other parts, the book of Deuteronomy is a kind of commentary upon the Decalogue, and an application of it. Yet the particulars into which Moses enters, with the daily life and walk of his own people in their future home before his mind, are such that the prescriptions in these chapters are for the most part purely national; they belong to the ceremonial and civil rather than to the moral elements of his system.

Moses fitly begins with regulations pertaining to the worship of the Israelites during their settled life in Canaan.

chap. 7. 2 [a] Ye shall utterly destroy all the
places, wherein the nations which ye
Or, inherit. shall ‖possess served their gods, upon
the high mountains, and upon the hills,
and under every green tree:
Judg. 2. 3 And [b] ye shall † overthrow their
Heb. break down. altars, and break their pillars, and
burn their groves with fire; and ye
shall hew down the graven images of
their gods, and destroy the names of
them out of that place.
4 Ye shall not do so unto the LORD
your God.
5 But unto the place which the
LORD your God shall [c] choose out of [c] 1 Kin. 8.
all your tribes to put his name there, 29. 2 Chron. 7.
even unto his habitation shall ye seek, 12.
and thither thou shalt come:

1—7. On the command to destroy the places and monuments of idolatrous worship, see on vii. 5.

3. *their groves*] Render **their idols of wood**: and see on xvi. 21.

4. *Ye shall not do so unto the LORD your God*] *i.e.* "The idolaters set up their altars and images on any high hill, and under every green tree at their pleasure, but *ye* shall not do so; the Lord Himself shall determine the spot for your worship, and there only shall ye seek Him." The religion of the Canaanites was human; its modes of worship were of man's devising. It fixed its holy places on the hills in the vain thought of being nearer heaven, or in deep groves where the silence and gloom might overawe the worshipper. But such superstitious appliances were not worthy of the true religion. God had in it revealed Himself to men, and manifested amongst them His immediate presence and power. It followed of course that the machinery of idolatry must thenceforward be swept away; and that God thus come down amongst men, would Himself assign the sanctuary and the ritual of His own service.

5. *But unto the place which the LORD your God shall choose out of all your tribes to put his name there, even unto his habitation shall ye seek, and thither thou shalt come*] The A. V. here follows the syntax and punctuation of the ordinary Hebrew text. Others regard the word rendered "unto his habitation" as a verb infinitive, and connect it with the preceding; "to put his name there, that he might dwell there:" Vulg. "ut ponat nomen suum ibi et habitet in eo;" cf. *v.* 11. "To put his name there:" *i.e.* to manifest to men His Divine Presence. The Targumists rightly refer to the Shechinah. The expression "put His Name," comprehends however all the various modes in which God vouchsafed to reveal Himself and His attributes to men. God is present everywhere by His power; but is present "per præsentiam gratiæ" only where He has covenanted to be so; as He is "per præsentiam gloriæ" to the Angels and Saints in Heaven.

The purpose of the command of the text is to secure the unity, and through unity the purity of the worship of God. That there should be one national centre for the religion of the people was obviously essential to the great ends of the whole dispensation. Had fanciful varieties of worship such as Polytheism delighted in been tolerated, the Israelites would soon have lapsed into idolatry, and the deposit of the true faith and knowledge of God would have been, humanly speaking, hopelessly lost. There are not wanting in their history examples which demonstrate their proneness to this corruption as soon as the precepts of the text were relaxed or neglected: *e.g.* that of Gideon, Judg. viii.; of Micah, Judg. xviii.; of Jeroboam, 1 K. xiii. Hence the emphasis and reiteration with which in this chapter, and elsewhere in Deut., "will-worship" is forbidden, and the outward religious life of the people gathered strictly round the authorized sanctuary.

The prescription before us is not altogether new. Its principle is clearly laid down Ex. xx. 24, simultaneously with the very first promulgation of the Law at Sinai. Its practice was secured during the journeyings through the wilderness by the enactment Levit. xvii. 1—7, which forbad the offering of sacrifices elsewhere than "at the door of the tabernacle of the congregation." But the detection and suppression of unlawful worship was comparatively easy whilst the whole nation was organized in one camp. Now that the two tribes and a half were established beyond Jordan, and the rest were soon to be scattered in their settled homes over the whole face of the promised land, the opportunities and the temptations for setting up idol shrines, and for devising private rites, would be much greater. As a natural and necessary consequence, the command before us is repeated with more point and stringency, and is guarded on every side from infringement.

The words "the place which the LORD shall choose to put his name there" suggest Jerusalem and Solomon's Temple to our minds. But though spoken as they were by a Prophet, and interpreted as they are by the Psalms (*e.g.* Ps. lxxviii. 67—69), they have a proper application to the Temple, yet they must not be referred exclusively to it. Jarchi names Shiloh as the spot indicated; and Jeremiah (vii. 12), speaking in the name of the Lord, calls Shiloh "my place, where I

6 And thither ye shall bring your burnt offerings, and your sacrifices, and your tithes, and heave offerings of your hand, and your vows, and your freewill offerings, and the firstlings of your herds and of your flocks:

7 And there ye shall eat before the LORD your God, and ye shall rejoice in all that ye put your hand unto, ye and your households, wherein the LORD thy God hath blessed thee.

---

set my name at the first." The text in truth does not import that God would always from the first choose one and the same locality "to put His Name there," but that there would always be a locality so chosen by Him; and that thither the people must bring their sacrifices, and not offer them at their pleasure or convenience elsewhere.

Neither does the text forbid the offering of sacrifices to God at other places than the one chosen by Him "to put His Name there" on proper occasions and by proper authority. Moses himself, ch. xxvii. 5, 6, enjoins the erection of a stone altar on Mount Ebal for burnt offerings to be offered on the day of commination: and we read of sacrifices offered at various places by Judges, Prophets, Kings, and others, and accepted by God. Gideon, *e.g.* offered a burnt offering at Jehovah Shalom in Ophrah (Judg. vi. 24 sqq.); Manoah did the like at the suggestion of the angel who appeared to him, no doubt near his own home (Judg. xiii. 16 sqq.); Solomon in Gibeon, where "the Lord appeared to him" (1 Kings iii. 4, 5); Elijah on Mount Carmel, and that after the erection of the temple (1 Kings xviii. 31 sqq.), &c. Yet these were no transgressions of the command of the text, much less can we infer from them that the worshippers knew nothing of such a command. Clearly the several places in question were *for the particular purpose and occasion* as really "chosen by God to put His Name there," as were Shiloh or Jerusalem for ordinary purposes and occasions. In short, the text prohibits sacrifices at any other locality than that which God should appoint for the purpose. It is no contravention of it that He should not only choose a site for the national sanctuary, and for the regular worship of His people, but should also specially direct on extraordinary emergencies sacrifices to be brought to Him elsewhere.

6. *thither shall ye bring your burnt offerings, and your sacrifices*] The various kinds of sacrificial gifts are here specified, in order to enforce the order that each and every one of them is to be offered at the Sanctuary, and nowhere else. Some have objected that this command cannot possibly have been ever carried out, at all events until in later days the territory which owned obedience to it was narrowed to the little kingdom of Judah. No doubt the necessity for making some kinds of offerings (*e.g.* the trespass-offerings) must under the statutes of Levit. v. and vi. have arisen very frequently. Can it have been imperative on every one who contracted ceremonial uncleanness to rid himself of it on each occasion by journeying, perhaps from distant Dan, or the further side of Jordan, to Shiloh or Jerusalem to offer the prescribed sacrifices? Let it be noted that the dimensions of the difficulty have been sometimes over-estimated. Even Dan, the furthest point of the land, was less than 100 miles from Jerusalem. This fact shows that the rule requiring all the males to go up to the Capital at the three great feasts was by no means impracticable because of distance, even when the twelve tribes were united in one kingdom, especially as these feasts all occurred in the summer months, when travelling is easy. But in these and in other precepts Moses doubtless takes much for granted. He is here, as elsewhere, regulating and defining more precisely institutions which had long been in existence, as to many details of which custom, as in our own law both of Church and State, superseded the necessity of specific enactment. No doubt the people well understood what Maimonides expressly tells us in reference to the matter, namely, that where immediate payment could not be made, the debt to God was to be reserved until the next great feast, and then duly discharged. Nor need we doubt that the commutation of the tithes allowed, xiv. 24, 25, was extended, as indeed would follow from the nature of the case and from the parallel directions about the redemption of things not presented to God in kind (*e.g.* Num. xviii. 15), to any or all of the offerings here enumerated, as occasion might require. The thing specially to be observed was that no kind of sacrifice was to be offered except at the sacred spot fixed by God for its acceptance. The reserving of an offering until it could be made at this spot was in some cases necessary if this command was to be kept: and where necessary was no doubt lawful.

7. *And there ye shall eat*, &c.] To the injunction that the sacrifices and other offerings to God were to be made only at the Sanctuary is here added another, that the feasts which accompanied certain offerings were to be also held in the same place. This command is here given for the first time in a peremptory form. Whilst the people formed but one camp the sacrificial meal would naturally take

8 Ye shall not do after all *the*
things that we do here this day, every
man whatsoever *is* right in his own
eyes.
9 For ye are not as yet come to
the rest and to the inheritance, which
the LORD your God giveth you.
10 But *when* ye go over Jordan,
and dwell in the land which the LORD
your God giveth you to inherit, and
when he giveth you rest from all your
enemies round about, so that ye dwell
in safety;
11 Then there shall be a place
which the LORD your God shall
choose to cause his name to dwell
there; thither shall ye bring all that
I command you; your burnt offerings,
and your sacrifices, your tithes, and
the heave offering of your hand, and
all † your choice vows which ye vow † Heb. *the choice of your vows*
unto the LORD:
12 And ye shall rejoice before the
LORD your God, ye, and your sons,
and your daughters, and your menservants, and your maidservants, and
the Levite that *is* within your gates;
forasmuch as [d] he hath no part nor [d] chap. 10. 9.
inheritance with you.
13 Take heed to thyself that thou
offer not thy burnt offerings in every
place that thou seest:
14 But in the place which the
LORD shall choose in one of thy tribes,
there thou shalt offer thy burnt offerings, and there thou shalt do all that
I command thee.
15 Notwithstanding thou mayest
kill and eat flesh in all thy gates,
whatsoever thy soul lusteth after, ac-

---

place at the spot where the victim was slain and offered, as was the custom amongst all other nations. But when the people lived in dwellings far asunder from one another and from the Sanctuary, there was need to enjoin precisely the same thing as to the sacrificial meals which was ruled as to the sacrifices themselves.

It is not here specified which of the eight kinds of offerings enumerated furnished the wherewithal for a feast to the offerers, and which not. This, as so much in various parts of the book, is presumed to be known. The burnt-offerings *e.g.* were wholly consumed on the altar; and the sin-offerings too were in certain cases wholly burnt, though not on the altar only (Lev. iv. 21). These sacrifices therefore left nothing for the worshippers to partake of. Comparing *vv.* 17, 18, we learn that the presentation of the tithes and the firstlings was also associated with a feast. This however is not instituted by Moses here, nor indeed anywhere else. It makes its appearance incidentally as a custom. All that is said of it is that it shall take place, like other such feasts, at the Sanctuary. The firstlings (Num. xviii. 15—18) are assigned to the priests, the tithes to the Levites (Num. xviii. 21 sqq.). On the participation of the people in the feasts made upon the firstlings and tithes, see xv. 19—23 sqq., and on Lev. 8 sqq. Moses points out that heretofore they had not observed the prescribed order in their worship, because during their migratory life in the wilderness it had been impossible to do so. During their wanderings there were doubtless times when the tabernacle was not set up for days together, and when the daily sacrifice (Num. xxviii. 1), together with many other ordinances, were necessarily omitted. It is not too much to say, in face of the fact (Josh. v. 5 sqq.) that circumcision itself had been for many years neglected, that the whole system was imperfectly acted upon up to the death of Moses, and important parts of it left altogether in abeyance. This consideration must be carefully borne in mind throughout Deut. It illustrates the necessity for a repetition of very much of the Sinaitic legislation, and suggests the reason why some parts are so urgently reiterated and impressed, whilst others are left unnoticed. The speaker has in view throughout the state of religion and its observances amongst his hearers. He warns them in the *vv.* before us that as they were now about to quit their unsettled mode of life, God's purpose of choosing for Himself a place to set His Name there would be executed, and the whole of the sacred ritual would consequently become obligatory. The rest and safety of Canaan is significantly laid down, *vv.* 10, 11, as the indispensable condition and basis for an entire fulfilment of the law: the perfection of righteousness coinciding thus with the cessation of wanderings, dangers, and toils.

12. *hath no part nor inheritance with you*] Cf. *v.* 19 and xiv. 27, xvi. 11, 14. On the allusions in Deut. to the condition of the Levites see Introduction, § v.

15. In Levit. xvii. 3—6, the people had been forbidden under any circumstances to slay any animal except "at the door of the tabernacle of the congregation." This prohibition was designed (*v.* 7) to cut off all pretexts and opportunities for those private and idolatrous rites to which the people were

cording to the blessing of the LORD thy God which he hath given thee: the unclean and the clean may eat thereof, as of the roebuck, and as of the hart.

[e] chap. 15. 23.

16 [e]Only ye shall not eat the blood; ye shall pour it upon the earth as water.

17 ¶ Thou mayest not eat within thy gates the tithe of thy corn, or of thy wine, or of thy oil, or the firstlings of thy herds or of thy flock, nor any of thy vows which thou vowest, nor thy freewill offerings, or heave offering of thine hand:

18 But thou must eat them before the LORD thy God in the place which the LORD thy God shall choose, thou, and thy son, and thy daughter, and thy manservant, and thy maidservant, and the Levite that *is* within thy gates: and thou shalt rejoice before the LORD thy God in all that thou puttest thine hands unto.

[f] chap. 14. 27. Ecclus. 7. 31.
† Heb. *all thy days.*

19 [f]Take heed to thyself that thou forsake not the Levite †as long as thou livest upon the earth.

[g] Gen. 28. 14. chap. 19. 8.

20 ¶ When the LORD thy God shall enlarge thy border, [g]as he hath promised thee, and thou shalt say, I will eat flesh, because thy soul longeth to eat flesh; thou mayest eat flesh, whatsoever thy soul lusteth after.

21 If the place which the LORD thy God hath chosen to put his name there be too far from thee, then thou shalt kill of thy herd and of thy flock, which the LORD hath given thee, as I have commanded thee, and thou shalt eat in thy gates whatsoever thy soul lusteth after.

22 Even as the roebuck and the hart is eaten, so thou shalt eat them: the unclean and the clean shall eat *of* them alike.

† Heb. *be strong.*

23 Only †be sure that thou eat not the blood: for the blood *is* the life; and thou mayest not eat the life with the flesh.

24 Thou shalt not eat it; thou shalt pour it upon the earth as water.

25 Thou shalt not eat it; that it may go well with thee, and with thy children after thee, when thou shalt do *that which is* right in the sight of the LORD.

26 Only thy holy things which thou hast, and thy vows, thou shalt take, and go unto the place which the LORD shall choose:

27 And thou shalt offer thy burnt offerings, the flesh and the blood, upon the altar of the LORD thy God: and the blood of thy sacrifices shall be poured out upon the altar of the LORD thy God, and thou shalt eat the flesh.

28 Observe and hear all these words which I command thee, that it may go well with thee, and with thy children after thee for ever, when thou doest *that which is* good and right in the sight of the LORD thy God.

† Heb. *inheritest,* or, *possessest them.*

29 ¶ When the LORD thy God shall cut off the nations from before thee, whither thou goest to possess them, and thou †succeedest them, and dwellest in their land;

---

prone, as well as to gather their sacrificial worship round one centre. In the chapter before us the latter essential object is insisted on even more emphatically. A reason for this increased emphasis may be seen in the fact that the prohibition against slaying animals for food elsewhere than at the Sanctuary had necessarily now to be relaxed. It could not be maintained when the people were dispersed in their homes from Dan to Beersheba. Whilst then a stringent injunction is laid down that the old rule must be adhered to as regards animals slain in sacrifice, yet permission is given to slaughter at home what was necessary for the table. Such meat not having been dedicated to God could be partaken of by "clean and unclean," and at home. The ceremonial distinctions did not apply in such cases, any more than to "the roebuck" (or gazelle) "and hart," animals allowed for food but not for sacrifice.

21. *If the place...be too far from thee*] Rather, "*Because*, or *since*, the place will be too far from thee." The allowance given in *vv.* 15, 16 is repeated, and the reason of it assigned.

27. *the blood...shall be poured out upon the altar*] Cf. on Lev. i. 5.

30 Take heed to thyself that thou
be not snared †by following them,
after that they be destroyed from before
thee; and that thou inquire not
after their gods, saying, How did
these nations serve their gods? even
so will I do likewise.
31 Thou shalt not do so unto the
LORD thy God: for every †abomination
to the LORD, which he hateth,
have they done unto their gods; for
even their sons and their daughters they
have burnt in the fire to their gods.
32 What thing soever I command
you, observe to do it: [h] thou shalt not
add thereto, nor diminish from it.

† Heb. *after them.*

† Heb. *abomination of the.*

[h] chap. 4. 2. Josh. 1. 7. Prov. 30. 6. Rev. 22. 18.

CHAPTER XIII.

1 *Enticers to idolatry,* 6 *how near soever unto thee,* 9 *are to be stoned to death.* 12 *Idolatrous cities are not to be spared.*

IF there arise among you a prophet,
or a dreamer of dreams, and
giveth thee a sign or a wonder,
2 And the sign or the wonder
come to pass, whereof he spake unto
thee, saying, Let us go after other
gods, which thou hast not known,
and let us serve them;

---

30. *Take heed to thyself that thou be not snared by following them, after that they be destroyed from before thee*] This caution is based upon the notion generally entertained in the ancient heathen world, that each country had its own tutelary deities whom it would be perilous to neglect (θεοὶ ἐπιχώριοι); cf. 1 K. xx. 23; 2 K. xvii. 26. Hence even in conquered districts the worship of the local deities was wont to be scrupulously maintained. But Israel was to shun such superstitions.

CHAP. XIII. The admonition of the closing verse of the last chapter, to observe the whole of God's commands without addition or subtraction, introduces a new series of warnings intended to serve as a further safeguard against violation of these duties. The true modes and forms of worship have been laid down: the next step is to legislate against the authors and abettors of false ones. Such tempters are not to be spared, even though (*vv.* 1—5) their teaching be confirmed by miracles: or (*vv.* 6—12) they be nearly allied by kindred or friendship: or (*vv.* 12—19) be supported in their apostasy by a whole city.

1. *a prophet, or a dreamer of dreams*] Cf. Num. xii. 6. The "prophet" received his revelations by vision or direct oral communication; "the dreamer of dreams" through the medium of a dream. Balaam "fell into a trance, yet had his eyes open," Num. xxiv. 16: St Paul was "caught up to the third heaven, and heard unspeakable words," 2 Cor. xii. 2 sqq. Nathan received the word of the Lord in the night (2 Sam. vii. 4). All these in various ways had the will of God made known to them as "prophets." Such revelations are different in kind from the less direct ones made by dreams; as *e.g.* to King Solomon, 1 Kings iii. 5; to Joseph, St Matt. ii. 13. On the occurrence of the word "prophet" (*nābhī*) in the Pentateuch, erroneously regarded by some as a mark of late origin, see Introd. to Numbers, § 4.

2. *And the sign or the wonder come to pass*] The people are warned not to listen to the seducer even should he show signs and wonders to authenticate his doctrine. The Lord had said "Thou shalt have none other Gods but Me." A prophet is here supposed who invites the people "to go after other Gods." To such a one no credit is under any circumstances to be given. The standing rule of faith and practice had been laid down once for all. That the people were to hold fast. The prophet who propounded another rule could only be an impostor.

We need not then suppose that Moses is putting an impossible case by way of enforcing his words, as St Paul does Gal. i. 6; nor yet that the prophet in question is one who was originally a true prophet, and obtained authority by his miracles as such, but was afterwards drawn away into apostasy.

In ch. xviii. 18 sqq. Israel is led to expect that God will hereafter send prophets to speak in His name: and the accomplishment of their predictions is laid down as a proof (*vv.* 21, 22) of their authority. But the context renders it clear that the case supposed is not the one before us in this chapter. *Here* a prophet is spoken of who teaches in plain contradiction to the received and accredited standards of truth by advocating a distinct apostasy: *there* the prophet is assumed to recognize those standards, and to be *primâ facie* within the limits of the religious system authorized by God as to doctrine and mission.

The Jews applied *vv.* 2—5 to Christ and His followers, as though their teaching aimed at bringing about a revolt from the law of Moses. But the Gospel is not only no contradiction or abolition of the law, but is its complement and fulfilment, and was always presented in that light by Christ and His Apostles. The Jews ought then, instead of endeavouring to stone Christ and His disciples as men who sought to draw them away to apostasy (cf. St John viii. 58, 59), rather to have given heed to the command of ch. xviii., and "hearkened

3 Thou shalt not hearken unto the
words of that prophet, or that dreamer of dreams: for the LORD your God
proveth you, to know whether ye love
the LORD your God with all your
heart and with all your soul.
4 Ye shall walk after the LORD
your God, and fear him, and keep his
commandments, and obey his voice,
and ye shall serve him, and [a]cleave
unto him.
5 And that prophet, or that dreamer of dreams, shall be put to death;
because he hath †spoken to turn *you*
away from the LORD your God,
which brought you out of the land of
Egypt, and redeemed you out of the
house of bondage, to thrust thee out
of the way which the LORD thy God
commanded thee to walk in. So shalt
thou put the evil away from the midst
of thee.
6 ¶ If thy brother, the son of thy
mother, or thy son, or thy daughter,
or the wife of thy bosom, or thy
friend, which *is* as thine own soul,
entice thee secretly, saying, Let us go
and serve other gods, which thou hast
not known, thou, nor thy fathers;

[a] chap. 10. 20.

† Heb. *spoken revolt against the LORD.*

7 *Namely*, of the gods of the people which *are* round about you, nigh
unto thee, or far off from thee, from
the *one* end of the earth even unto the
other end of the earth;
8 Thou shalt not consent unto
him, nor hearken unto him; neither
shall thine eye pity him, neither shalt
thou spare, neither shalt thou conceal
him:
9 But [b]thou shalt surely kill him;
thine hand shall be first upon him to
put him to death, and afterwards the
hand of all the people.
10 And thou shalt stone him with
stones, that he die; because he hath
sought to thrust thee away from the
LORD thy God, which brought thee
out of the land of Egypt, from the
house of †bondage.
11 And [c]all Israel shall hear, and
fear, and shall do no more any such
wickedness as this is among you.
12 ¶ If thou shalt hear *say* in one
of thy cities, which the LORD thy
God hath given thee to dwell there,
saying,
13 *Certain* men, ‖the children of
Belial, are gone out from among you,

[b] chap. 17. 7.

† Heb. *bondmen.*

[c] chap. 17. 13.

‖ Or, *naughty men.*

---

to the words spoken" in the name of the God of Israel, because they were supported by the accomplishment of those signs and wonders which the preachers took in hand.

3. *the LORD your God proveth you*] Cf. viii. 2; Gen. xxii. 1.

5. *that prophet, or that dreamer of dreams, shall be put to death*] Cf. *vv.* 9, 10. The context and parallel passages (cf. ch. xvii. 7; Lev. xx. 2) indicate that there was to be a regular judicial procedure, and that the manner of the execution was to be by stoning. In this the community was to take its part in order to show its horror at the crime, and to clear itself of complicity therein.

The text has been commonly brought forward by Roman Catholic commentators to justify the capital punishment of heretics in the Church: and by others (*e.g.* Calvin *in loc.*) as proving that such punishment must be inflicted by the magistrate. But such application of it overlooks not only the different "manner of spirit" of which the Gospel is (St Luke ix. 55); but also the fact that such obligation attached to the Jewish magistrate simply and solely because he had to administer the law of a theocracy. God was pleased to place Himself for the time in a relation to Israel analogous to that of an earthly sovereign to an earthly people. Consequently His worship and the laws of that polity, whilst not ceasing to be duties of religion, were also matters of civil law. To bring in the worship of another God was therefore not merely to lead away God's people into error, it was to seduce them from their loyalty to their rightful prince and ruler. It was in a word high treason, and to be punished accordingly. So too the concealment of attempts to bring in apostasy was "misprision of treason." But with the cessation of the theocracy heresy ceased to be *ipso facto* punishable as a crime against the state.

6. Michaelis observes that the omissions in this enumeration seem to imply that no one was bound to impeach father, mother, or husband.

12, 13. *If thou shalt hear say in one of thy cities, which the LORD thy God hath given thee to dwell there, saying, Certain men, the children of Belial, are gone out from among you*] *i.e.* "when one city hears concerning another;" or more strictly "when ye in one city hear, &c." In this duty, essential as it was to the very exist-

and have withdrawn the inhabitants
of their city, saying, Let us go and
serve other gods, which ye have not
known;
14 Then shalt thou inquire, and
make search, and ask diligently; and,
behold, *if it be* truth, *and* the thing
certain, *that* such abomination is
wrought among you;
15 Thou shalt surely smite the inhabitants of that city with the edge of
the sword, destroying it utterly, and
all that *is* therein, and the cattle
thereof, with the edge of the sword.
16 And thou shalt gather all the
spoil of it into the midst of the street
thereof, and shalt burn with fire the
city, and all the spoil thereof every
whit, for the LORD thy God: and it
shall be an heap for ever; it shall not
be built again.
17 And there shall cleave nought — ‖Or, *devoted.*
of the ‖cursed thing to thine hand:
that the LORD may turn from the
fierceness of his anger, and shew thee
mercy, and have compassion upon
thee, and multiply thee, as he hath
sworn unto thy fathers;
18 When thou shalt hearken to
the voice of the LORD thy God, to
keep all his commandments which I
command thee this day, to do *that
which is* right in the eyes of the LORD
thy God.

---

ence of the Mosaic commonwealth, city was to keep jealous watch over city, as man over man. The clause "which the Lord thy God hath given thee to dwell in" significantly reminds them that the real ownership of their dwellings rested in the Lord (cf. Lev. xxv. 23), and that they, the mere tenants, must not allow His property to become a centre of rebellion against His just authority.

13. *children of Belial*] In xv. 9 the word Belial is rendered in our translation by the adj. "wicked;" as it is also in Nahum i. 11. In Ps. xviii. 4, "floods of ungodly men," is literally "floods of Belial." In the thirteen other places in which the word occurs, all being in the historical books, it is treated consistently in the A. V. as a proper name. The LXX. and most ancient versions render it by ἄνομος, παράνομος, and their cognates. St Paul, 2 Cor. vi. 15, uses the word Belial (Greek Βελίαρ) as equivalent to Satan. Beliar is no doubt equivalent to Belial; and probably this use of the word as a proper name originated with the Apostle. The word means *worthlessness*, *quod nullius frugis est*, *nequitia*. The expression "sons of worthlessness" is similar to many others in Hebrew: *e.g.* "sons of strength," "years," &c.

16. *every whit, for the LORD thy God*]. Render: **"as a whole offering to the Lord thy God:"** see the Note at end of the chapter.

NOTE on CHAP. XIII. 16.

Every whit] The Hebrew word here is כליל derived from a verb כלל, "to make circular," or "complete." The word is properly an adj. signifying "perfect" or "entire;" and may no doubt be used adverbially as it is in Is. ii. 18. The A.V. in thus taking it has the support of the Versions generally; but the words following "for the Lord thy God" do not fit aptly to this sense, and indeed should rather run "unto the Lord thy God." This addition, which evidently must be closely connected with כליל, certainly suggests the other sense of the word, found also in xxxiii. 10, "whole offering," ὁλοκαύτωμα. The word כליל is applied to offerings whether of corn or the flesh of animals provided they were wholly burnt; cf. Lev. vi. 22, 23; Deut. xxxiii. 10. As a synonym for the more common עלה, it is sometimes used in apposition to or further explanation of עלה, *e.g.* 1 S. vii. 9; Ps. li. 19. The rendering suggested in the foot-note is that of the Mishna, and other Jewish authorities· cf. Gesen., Fürst, Keil, Knobel, &c.

CHAPTER XIV.

1 *God's children are not to disfigure themselves in mourning.* 3 *What may, and what may not be eaten,* 4 *of beasts,* 9 *of fishes,* 11 *of fowls.* 21 *That which dieth of itself may not be eaten.* 22 *Tithes of divine service.* 23 *Tithes and firstlings of rejoicing before the Lord.* 28 *The third year's tithe of alms and charity.*

YE *are* the children of the LORD
your God: [a]ye shall not cut — [a] Lev. 19. 28.
yourselves, nor make any baldness
between your eyes for the dead.
2 [b]For thou *art* an holy people un- — [b] chap. 7. 6. & 26. 18.
to the LORD thy God, and the LORD
hath chosen thee to be a peculiar peo-

ple unto himself, above all the nations that *are* upon the earth.

3 ¶ Thou shalt not eat any abominable thing.

4 [c]These *are* the beasts which ye shall eat: the ox, the sheep, and the goat,

5 The hart, and the roebuck, and the fallow deer, and the wild goat, and the ‖pygarg, and the wild ox, and the chamois.

6 And every beast that parteth the hoof, and cleaveth the cleft into two

[c] Lev. 11. 2, &c.

‖ Or, *bison*. Heb. *dishon*.

CHAP. XIV. Not only was open idolatry to be sternly suppressed (ch. xiii.), but the whole life and walk of the people were to be regulated with continual regard to that character which God designed to impress upon them. The words "ye are the children of the Lord your God" which introduce this chapter, suggest the principle which underlies its precepts. It was unbeseeming their dignity and privileges to disfigure themselves in mourning (*vv.* 1, 2), as the heathen which have no hope; or to defile themselves by eating "any abominable thing" (*vv.* 3—22); on the contrary they were to honour God and act worthily of their special relationship to Him by holy meals at the sanctuary; meals associated with charity to the needy (*vv.* 23—29).

1, 2. *make any baldness between your eyes*] *i.e.* by shaving the forepart of the head and the eyebrows. The practices here named were common amongst the heathen, and seem to be forbidden, not only because such wild excesses of grief would be inconsistent in those who as children of a heavenly Father had prospects beyond this world, but also because these usages themselves arose out of idolatrous notions. The mourners inflicted wounds and privations on themselves, as the priests of Baal (1 K. xviii. 28) cut themselves with knives, by way of propitiating deities to whom human suffering and woe were regarded as acceptable.

The Roman law of the Ten Tables had restrictions (borrowed from Solon; see Cicero, 'De Leg.' II. 25) very similar to those of the text and its parallel passages.

3—21. Moses follows up the general injunction against eating "any abominable thing" by specifying particularly what creatures may and what may not be used as food. The restrictions laid down are substantially repeated from the parallel passages of Levit. (where see notes), but not without noteworthy variation. Three classes of creatures are here referred to, quadrupeds (*vv.* 4—9), fishes (*vv.* 9 and 10), and fowls (*vv.* 11—21); a fourth class, reptiles, is omitted, though carefully dealt with in Levit. xi. 29, 30, where eight species of it are forbidden: on the other hand, the locust and certain other insects are enumerated as clean Levit. xi. 22, but are not named in this chapter. Both omissions are probably to be explained by the time and circumstances of the speaker. The reptiles of the promised land, into which the people were about to enter, were not such as they would be likely to think of eating; whilst the locust and the other insects, allowed as food in the earlier book, and probably of occasional importance as such in the wilderness, could be but of small account to those who had their fields and vineyards in Canaan. The example of John the Baptist (St Matt. iii. 4) shows us of itself that the omission of locusts from the list of clean animals in this place was not supposed to exclude them. So too in *v.* 19 "every creeping thing that flieth" is simply forbidden; and the qualification of Levit. xi. 20, that such of this class as "have legs above their feet to leap" may nevertheless be eaten, is omitted. On the border of the promised land, and in a repetition of laws which he desired particularly to impress, this permission is passed over as of no moment. Here too the kinds of clean quadrupeds are specified by name as well as in general characteristics, obviously because the diet of the people would for the future mainly be drawn from this class. In Levit. xi. 3 sqq., whilst they had yet many years of life in the desert before them, it was enough to lay down the law as regards quadrupeds in general terms.

4. *the ox, the sheep, and the goat*] These are probably named first as being the animals used for sacrifice. In the next *v.* follow the wild animals which might lawfully be eaten, though not sacrificed.

5. *The hart*] *i.e.* the ordinary kind of deer; other and less common species come after.

fallow deer] Rather perhaps antelope. The word is derived from a root signifying "to be red."

the pygarg] Hebr. *dīshōn*, a species of antelope or gazelle.

wild ox] Hebr. *thō*, translated Is. li. 20 "wild bull;" to be carefully distinguished from the *re'em:* cf. Num. xxiii. 22 and note. The "tho" is also a kind of antelope. The etymology of the name points to its swiftness in running. The LXX. render oryx. Both the pygarg and the oryx are named Herod. IV. 192.

chamois] Hebr. *zamer;* LXX. the camelopard, *i.e.* the giraffe. The giraffe however is not a native of Palestine. It is therefore more likely to be another species of antelope. Its name is derived from a root signifying "to leap."

claws, *and* cheweth the cud among
the beasts, that ye shall eat.
7 Nevertheless these ye shall not
eat of them that chew the cud, or
of them that divide the cloven hoof;
as the camel, and the hare, and the
coney: for they chew the cud, but
divide not the hoof; *therefore* they
are unclean unto you.
8 And the swine, because it divideth the hoof, yet cheweth not the
cud, it *is* unclean unto you: ye shall
not eat of their flesh, nor touch their
dead carcase.
[d] Lev. 11. 9. — 9 ¶ [d]These ye shall eat of all that
are in the waters: all that have fins
and scales shall ye eat:
10 And whatsoever hath not fins
and scales ye may not eat; it *is* unclean unto you.
11 ¶ *Of* all clean birds ye shall eat.
12 But these *are they* of which ye
shall not eat: the eagle, and the ossifrage, and the ospray,
13 And the glede, and the kite,
and the vulture after his kind,
14 And every raven after his kind,
15 And the owl, and the night
hawk, and the cuckow, and the hawk
after his kind,
16 The little owl, and the great
owl, and the swan,
17 And the pelican, and the gier
eagle, and the cormorant,
18 And the stork, and the heron
after her kind, and the lapwing, and
the [e] bat. — [e] Lev. 11. 19.
19 And every creeping thing that
flieth *is* unclean unto you: they shall
not be eaten.
20 *But of* all clean fowls ye may eat.
21 ¶ Ye shall not eat *of* any thing
that dieth of itself: thou shalt give
it unto the stranger that *is* in thy
gates, that he may eat it; or thou
mayest sell it unto an alien: for thou
art an holy people unto the LORD thy
God. [f]Thou shalt not seethe a kid — [f] Exod. 23. 19. & 34. 26.
in his mother's milk.
22 Thou shalt truly tithe all the
increase of thy seed, that the field
bringeth forth year by year.

---

7. *the hare*] See on Levit. xi. 6.

12. The birds here named are the same as those in Lev. xi. 13 sqq. (where see note), except that in 13 "the glede" (*rāāh*) is added. The "vulture" (*dayyāh*) of *v.* 13 is no doubt the same as the (*dāāh*) of Lev. xi. 14.

21. *Ye shall not eat of anything that dieth of itself: thou shalt give it to the stranger*, &c.] The prohibition is repeated from Levit. xxii. 8: the directions as to the disposal of the carcase are peculiar to Deut. Their motive is clear. To have forbidden the people either to eat themselves that which had died, or to allow any others to do so, would have involved loss of property, and consequent temptation to an infraction of the command. The permissions now for the first time granted would have been useless in the wilderness. During the forty years' wandering there could be but little opportunity of selling such carcases; whilst non-Israelites living in the camp would in such a matter be bound by the same rules as the Israelites (Levit. xvii. 15, and xxiv. 22). "The stranger that is in thy gates" will be the uncircumcised proselyte, or in the language of later Judaism "the proselyte of the gate." Such a one would stand midway between the "proselyte of righteousness," who was circumcised and a "debtor to do the whole law," and "the alien," who had no concern whatever in the national religion. It would seem, on comparing this *v.* with Levit. xvii. 15, that greater stringency is here given to the requirement of abstinence from that which had died of itself. In the earlier book the eating of such flesh involved merely uncleanness until the evening; here it is absolutely interdicted. Probably on this, as on so many other points, allowance was made for the circumstances of the people. Flesh meat was no doubt often scarce in the desert. It would therefore have been a hardship to forbid entirely the use of that which had not been killed. Now however when the plenty of the promised land was before them, the modified toleration of this unholy food is withdrawn.

22. *Thou shalt truly tithe all the increase of thy seed*] These words recall in general terms the command of the earlier legislation respecting tithes (cf. Lev. xxvii. 30, Num. xviii. 27) but refer more particularly to the second or festival tithe, which was an exclusively vegetable one: see Introd. § 5. So Keil, Schultz, Lange, &c., and the Jewish authorities generally. One computation of the increase of the field would of course serve for both the Levitical tithe of Lev. xxvii., so far as it consisted of that increase, and for the other tithe to be applied to the feasts at the sanctuary, or in each third year at home, as directed in this

23 And thou shalt eat before the
LORD thy God, in the place which
he shall choose to place his name
there, the tithe of thy corn, of thy
wine, and of thine oil, and the firstlings of thy herds and of thy flocks;
that thou mayest learn to fear the
LORD thy God always.
24 And if the way be too long for
thee, so that thou art not able to
carry it; *or* if the place be too far
from thee, which the LORD thy God
shall choose to set his name there,
when the LORD thy God hath blessed
thee:
25 Then shalt thou turn *it* into
money, and bind up the money in
thine hand, and shalt go unto the
place which the LORD thy God shall
choose:
26 And thou shalt bestow that
money for whatsoever thy soul lusteth
after, for oxen, or for sheep, or for
wine, or for strong drink, or for what-
† Heb. *asketh of thee.* soever thy soul † desireth: and thou
shalt eat there before the LORD thy
God, and thou shalt rejoice, thou,
and thine household,
27 And [g] the Levite that *is* within [g] chap. 12. 19.
thy gates; thou shalt not forsake him;
for he hath no part nor inheritance
with thee.
28 ¶ At the end of three years
thou shalt bring forth all the tithe of
thine increase the same year, and shalt
lay *it* up within thy gates:
29 And the Levite, (because he
hath no part nor inheritance with
thee,) and the stranger, and the fatherless, and the widow, which *are*
within thy gates, shall come, and
shall eat and be satisfied; that the
LORD thy God may bless thee in all the
work of thine hand which thou doest.

CHAPTER XV.

1 The seventh year a year of release for the poor. 7 It must be no let of lending or giving. 12 An Hebrew servant, 16 except he will not depart, must in the seventh year go forth free and well furnished. 19 All firstling males of the cattle are to be sanctified unto the Lord.

AT the end of [a] *every* seven years [a] Lev. 25. 2, 4.
thou shalt make a release.

---

passage: cf. on *vv.* 28, 29. One tenth would belong to the Levites, the second tenth would remain at the disposal of the landowner for the purposes so earnestly commended to him in Deut. xii. 6, 7, 17—20 (see notes), and in this passage. These purposes are minutely classified and regulated in the Mishna. Thus altogether one-fifth part of the annual produce would be claimed for religious hospitable and charitable employments; and this, considering the various charges met out of it, would not be an unreasonably burdensome impost. See on Gen. xli. 34, xlvii. 26, and Winer, 'Realwört,' (Article, *Zehent*), and Saalschütz, 'Mos. Recht,' I. 354 sqq., who however regard the festival tithe as levied upon the nine portions that remained after the Levitical tithe had been subtracted, and not as a full tenth of all the produce. The tithes are only named here in passing, as are also the firstlings, in order to introduce certain directions respecting the sacred meals which were celebrated out of them. The firstlings come on for more special treatment in xv. 19 sqq.

28, 29. Cf. on xxvi. 12. It is only necessary to observe here that the tithe thus directed in the third year to be dispensed in charity at home, though called by the Jewish authorities "the third tithe," was not paid in addition to that in other years bestowed on the sacred meals, but was substituted for it. This is plainly implied in the text. The three years would count from the Sabbatical year, and Moses accordingly goes on to legislate in reference to that important year in the beginning of the next chapter. In the Sabbatical year there would of course be neither payment of tithe nor celebration of the feasts at the Sanctuary. In the third and sixth years of the septennial cycle the feasts would be superseded by the private hospitality enjoined in the verses before us.

28. *all the tithe*] LXX. πᾶν τὸ ἐπιδέκατον: Vulg. "aliam decimam," *i.e.* the second tithe: see above.

CHAP. XV. The regulations for the relief of the necessitous by means of the triennial tithe are followed up in this chapter by others of a similar tendency. *Vv.* 1—11 prescribe a Year of Release; *vv.* 12—18 the manumission of Hebrew slaves; *vv.* 19—23 the appropriation of the firstlings of cattle, which had already (xii. 6; xiv. 23) been designated as offerings to be made by the people for sacred and charitable purposes.

1—11. The Year of Release is no doubt identical with the Sabbatical Year of the earlier legislation; on which see Exod. xxiii. 10 sqq., and Levit. xxv. 2 sqq.; the word "release" of this passage being indeed fundamentally the same word as is used in refer-

2 And this *is* the manner of the
release: Every † creditor that lend-
eth *ought* unto his neighbour shall
release *it*; he shall not exact *it* of
his neighbour, or of his brother; because it is called the LORD's release.
3 Of a foreigner thou mayest exact *it again*: but *that* which is thine
with thy brother thine hand shall
release;
4 ‖ Save when there shall be no
poor among you; for the LORD shall
greatly bless thee in the land which
the LORD thy God giveth thee *for* an
inheritance to possess it:
5 Only if thou carefully hearken
unto the voice of the LORD thy God,
to observe to do all these commandments which I command thee this
day.
6 For the LORD thy God blesseth
thee, as he promised thee: and [b] thou
shalt lend unto many nations, but
thou shalt not borrow; and thou shalt
reign over many nations, but they
shall not reign over thee.
7 ¶ If there be among you a poor
man of one of thy brethren within
any of thy gates in thy land which
the LORD thy God giveth thee, thou

† Heb. *master of the lending of his hand.*

‖ Or, *To the end that there be no poor among you.*

[b] chap. 28. 12.

---

ence to the land Exod. xxiii. 11. The command of the older legislation is here amplified. Not only is the land to have its "release" or "rest" for the year, but the debt also. The obvious reference of this passage to that of Exod. seems to render it most probable (as Rosenm., Bähr, 'Symb.' II. 570; Saalschütz, Keil, Knobel, Schultz, &c., maintain), in spite of a consensus of Jewish authorities to the contrary, that the release in question must have been for the year, not total and final. As the land was during this year to keep sabbath, so the debt was to stand over; but neither of the one nor the other would the usufruct be lost in perpetuity to the owner. It seems further clear that the release had reference only to loans (see especially *v.* 2); and to loans lent because of poverty (cf. *vv.* 4, 7). Apparently therefore that a debt contracted *e.g.* by purchase of goods, would not come under this law. It would seem, however, notwithstanding these qualifications, and the fact that the release did not extend at all to foreigners, that the law was found too stringent for the avarice of the people; for it was one of those which the Rabbis "made of none effect by their traditions." A gloss attributed to Hillel permitted the judges to authorize a creditor to enforce his claim even during the year of release. (See Smith's 'Dict. of the Bible,' III. 1074.) This fact, as well as the references in the later books to the year of release and the laws associated with it, shows that the ordinances of Moses now before us were sufficiently well understood, though too much disregarded in the later days of the Jewish commonwealth. (Cf. Is. lxi. 1, 2; Jer. xxxiv. 8—17.)

2. *manner of the release*] Cf. the similar phrase xix. 4; 1 K. ix. 15.

he shall not exact it of his neighbour, or of his brother] Lit. "he shall not urge or press his neighbour and his brother." The latter words are added to explain who is meant by the neighbour: *i.e.* not one who lives near, but an Israelite as opposed to a foreigner.

because it is called the LORD's release] Render **because proclamation has been made of the Lord's release.** The verb is impersonal, and implies (cf. xxxi. 10) that "the solemnity of the year of release" has been publicly announced.

3. *Of a foreigner thou mayest exact it*] The foreigner would not be bound by the restriction of the Sabbatical year, and therefore would have no claim to its special remissions and privileges. He could earn his usual income in the seventh as in other years, and therefore is not exonerated from liability to discharge a debt any more in the one than the others.

4. *Save when there shall be no poor among you; for the LORD shall greatly bless thee*] Rather perhaps "no poor with thee," *i. e.* concerned in the transaction. See Note at end of chapter. There is no inconsistency between this and *v.* 11, in which it is affirmed that "the poor shall never cease out of the land." The meaning seems simply to be "Thou must release the debt for the year, except when there be no poor person concerned, a contingency which may happen, for the Lord shall greatly bless thee." Thus it was lawful to call in a loan (one contracted *e.g.* for such purposes as the purchase of land, carrying on commerce &c.) when the borrower could refund it without impoverishment. The reasonableness of the limitation of the release is obvious. If no lender could recover his money during the year of release the unscrupulous debtor might have enriched himself at the expense of his, perhaps less wealthy, neighbour. The general object of these precepts, as also of the year of Jubilee and the laws respecting inheritance, is to prevent the total ruin of a needy man, and his disappearance from the families of Israel by the sale of his patrimony.

shalt not harden thine heart, nor shut
thine hand from thy poor brother:
[c] Matt. 5. 42. 8 [c] But thou shalt open thine hand
Luke 6. 34. wide unto him, and shalt surely lend
him sufficient for his need, *in that*
which he wanteth.
9 Beware that there be not a
† Heb. *word.* † thought in thy † wicked heart, say-
† Heb. *Belial.* ing, The seventh year, the year of
release, is at hand; and thine eye be
evil against thy poor brother, and thou
givest him nought; and he cry unto
the LORD against thee, and it be sin
unto thee.
10 Thou shalt surely give him, and
thine heart shall not be grieved when
thou givest unto him: because that
for this thing the LORD thy God
shall bless thee in all thy works, and
in all that thou puttest thine hand unto.
11 For the poor shall never cease
out of the land: therefore I command
thee, saying, Thou shalt open thine
hand wide unto thy brother, to thy
poor, and to thy needy, in thy land.
[d] Exod. 21. 2. 12 ¶ *And* [d] if thy brother, an He-
Jer. 34. 14. brew man, or an Hebrew woman, be
sold unto thee, and serve thee six
years; then in the seventh year thou
shalt let him go free from thee.
13 And when thou sendest him out
free from thee, thou shalt not let him
go away empty:
14 Thou shalt furnish him liberally out of thy flock, and out of thy
floor, and out of thy winepress: *of*
that wherewith the LORD thy God
hath blessed thee thou shalt give unto
him.
15 And thou shalt remember that
thou wast a bondman in the land of
Egypt, and the LORD thy God redeemed thee: therefore I command
thee this thing to day.
16 And it shall be, if he say unto
thee, I will not go away from thee;
because he loveth thee and thine house,
because he is well with thee;
17 [e] Then thou shalt take an aul, [e] Exod. 21. 6.
and thrust *it* through his ear unto the
door, and he shall be thy servant for
ever. And also unto thy maidservant
thou shalt do likewise.
18 It shall not seem hard unto
thee, when thou sendest him away
free from thee; for he hath been
worth a double hired servant *to thee*,
in serving thee six years: and the
LORD thy God shall bless thee in all
that thou doest.

---

9. *Beware that there be not a thought in thy wicked heart*] Render, **that there be not a wicked word in thy heart.** The word *belial*, worthlessness, (cf. xiii. 13, and note) is used emphatically in place of an adjective, and is in apposition grammatically to "word," not, as suggested by A. V., to "heart." The original is very forcible, "that there be not in thy heart a word which is worthless, ness."

14. *Thou shalt furnish him liberally*] The verb in the Hebrew is remarkable. It means "thou shalt lay on his neck," "adorn his neck with thy gifts." The LXX. and Vulg. express the end and purpose of the command; ἐφόδιον ἐφοδιάσεις, "dabis viaticum."

12—18. Regulations of a similarly beneficent tenor with those respecting debtors are now laid down respecting Hebrew servants. The commands here are repeated from Exod. xxi. 2—6, with amplifications characteristic of Deut. In the earlier code mention is made only of the manservant, here of the maidservant also (*v.* 12): there the command is simply to manumit after six years of service; now it is further required (*vv.* 13, sqq.) that liberal provision should be made for launching the freedman on an independent course of life. The release of the servant is connected with the Sabbatical principle though not with the Sabbatical year. That release was to take place after six years of bondage in all cases. The injunction is introduced here only because it is, like that of the Sabbatical year, one of those designed for the benefit of the poor. It is noteworthy also that the prospect of a gift of this sort, the amount of which was left at the master's discretion, would be likely to encourage diligence and faithfulness during the years of servitude.

17. *thou shalt take an aul*] Thus bored ears were made a badge of slavery, and so became ignominious. This would discourage the wearing of ear-rings, which are often in the East regarded as amulets.

18. *he hath been worth a double hired servant to thee, in serving thee six years*] Render, rather perhaps, "double the hire of a hireling has he earned thee by serving thee six years:" *i.e.* such a servant has earned twice as much as a common hired labourer would have done in

[f Exod. 34. 19.] 19 ¶ [f] All the firstling males that
come of thy herd and of thy flock
thou shalt sanctify unto the LORD
thy God: thou shalt do no work with
the firstling of thy bullock, nor shear
the firstling of thy sheep.
20 Thou shalt eat *it* before the
[g Lev. 22. 20. chap. 17. 1. Ecclus. 35. 12.] LORD thy God year by year in the
place which the LORD shall choose,
thou and thy household.
21 [g] And if there be *any* blemish
therein, *as if it be* lame, or blind,
or have any ill blemish, thou shalt
not sacrifice it unto the LORD thy
God.
22 Thou shalt eat it within thy
gates: the unclean and the clean *person shall eat it* alike, as the roebuck,
and as the hart.
23 [h] Only thou shalt not eat the [h chap. 12. 16, 23.]
blood thereof; thou shalt pour it upon
the ground as water.

---

the same time. So substantially Saad., Rashi, Rosenm., Wogue, &c. The clause is however somewhat obscure and difficult. Literally it runs, "double the hire of a hireling hath he served thee during six years." Schultz, Knob., Keil, &c., understand this to mean "he has done so much that if you had had to keep a day labourer in place of him, the cost to you would have been twice as great."

19—23. The command to dedicate the firstborn to God, as a memorial of the destruction of the firstborn of the Egyptians, is one of the very earliest regulations of the Mosaic ritual (Ex. xiii. 11 sqq.). The directions of the preceding legislation (see Num. xviii. 15 sqq.) are here assumed, with the injunction added, that the animals thus set apart to God (*v.* 19) were not to be used by their owners for their earthly purposes. It is further allowed that firstborn animals which had a blemish should be regarded as exceptions, and instead of being given to God might be used as food (*vv.* 21, 22). The application of the firstborn of cattle is here directed as in xii. 6, 17 and xiv. 23: they are to be consumed in the sacred feasts at the Sanctuary.

It has been pointed out that the flesh of the firstlings is given (Num. xviii. 18) to the priest, whilst in the passage before us, as in xii. 6, 17, and xiv. 23, the same flesh is assigned as the wherewithal for the sacred feasts which the offerer and his household were to celebrate at the Sanctuary. The inconsistency is apparent only. Num. xviii. 18, in assigning the priest's portion, prescribes as regards the firstborn, "the flesh of them shall be thine, as the wave breast and the right shoulder are thine:" *i.e.* shall be thine on the like terms and conditions as the wave breast and right shoulder are so. This can scarcely mean, as some (Kalisch, Hengstenberg) have thought, that only those portions of the firstlings were to go to the priests, the rest remaining the property of the offerer for a sacrificial meal; it rather directs that the flesh of the firstlings was to be disposed of by the priests in the same manner as the wave breast and heave shoulder. The appropriation of these, the priests' portions, is seen from Levit. vii. 15, 16. They were to be employed in a sacrificial feast which had to be held on the day of the making of the offering, or on the next day, and of course at the Sanctuary. In the case of the firstlings the priests would have the whole of the victim to consume thus at once, and at certain seasons no doubt many victims at once. Under these circumstances the priest would naturally invite the offerers to partake in the feast for which such abundant provision was made; and indeed would feel it a duty to do so. The presentation of the firstlings is spoken of Ex. xiii. 15 as a sacrifice; and a sacrificial meal on the flesh of the victim, in which the offerer and those associated with him partook, was an established part of the system and ritual of sacrifice. In the case of the firstborn, where all the flesh was the perquisite of the priests, the offerer could only have his share in such meal on the invitation of the priests; an invitation which we may be sure would never be withheld, and which is regarded in the text accordingly as a matter of course if not of right. We must remember that the expectation of sharing in the feast on the firstlings would tend to encourage their being regularly brought in by the people; and that under no circumstances would the priests be allowed to sell any portion of them. Any flesh of such offerings remaining till the third day had to be burnt (Lev. vii. 17). It is to be noted too that Moses in the text is addressing the whole people—priests, Levites, and laity. The general direction then that the firstlings should be brought to the Sanctuary and there consumed in a sacred meal seems on the whole sufficiently accordant with the earlier legislation on the same offerings. Cf. Keil on Deut. xii. 6 and 7, from whom this note is principally taken.

NOTE on CHAP. XV. 4.

Save when there shall be no poor] The sense suggested in the foot-note is adopted by Gerhard, several Commentators quoted in Poole's Synopsis, Rosenm. ("nisi fortasse pauperes non sint"), Maurer, Michaelis, Dathe, &c.; and seems on the whole the preferable one. The particles אפס כי are thus taken much in the same sense as in Amos ix. 8, "except that," "saving that." The "save when" of the A. V. brings out the force of the clause more clearly than "save that," but the meaning is substantially the same. Knobel insists that the clause gives an absolute promise that there should be no poverty in Israel. But no writer would set forth such a promise and then six verses afterwards flatly contradict himself: cf. *v.* 11. Others regard the words as giving a conditional promise, which was not accomplished because of Israel's disobedience. But the statement in *v.* 11 that "the poor should never cease out of the land," is not announced as a penalty for sin. The rendering of margin is supported by the Syr., Bp. Wordsworth and others. But no passage has been alleged in which אפס כי has this telic force; on the contrary these particles, as the root of אפס determines, always have a limiting force: cf. Num. xiii. 28; Judg. iv. 9. Several modern Comm. (Keil, Schultz, Lange, &c.) take the clause as an imperative, "only let there not be &c.;" so taken however its connexion with what follows is awkward and obscure.

CHAPTER XVI.

1 *The feast of the passover*, 9 *of weeks*, 13 *of tabernacles*. 16 *Every male must offer, as he is able, at these three feasts*. 18 *Of judges and justice*. 21 *Groves and images are forbidden*.

[a] Exod. 12. 2, &c.
OBSERVE the [a] month of Abib,
and keep the passover unto the
LORD thy God: for [b] in the month of [b] Exod. 13. 4.
Abib the LORD thy God brought thee
forth out of Egypt by night.
2 Thou shalt therefore sacrifice the
passover unto the LORD thy God, of
the flock and the herd, in the [c] place [c] chap. 12. 5.
which the LORD shall choose to place
his name there.

CHAP. XVI. Moses continues in this chapter the review of the religious ordinances to be observed by the people in Canaan. Prominent amongst these were the three great festivals, of Passover, Pentecost, and Tabernacles. The regulations respecting them given in the earlier books (Ex. xii., Lev. xxiii., Num. xxviii. and xxix.) are assumed, and the feasts themselves touched upon only so far as present circumstances required. The treatment throughout presupposes the hearers to be well informed as to the ordinances in question, and only needing to have their attention drawn to certain particulars as to which reiteration might seem advisable, or changes called for. The cardinal point on which the whole of the prescriptions here before us turn is evidently the same as has been so often insisted on in the previous chapters, viz. the concentration of the religious services of the people round one common Sanctuary. The prohibition against observing these great feasts, the three annual epochs in the sacred year of the Jew, at home and in private, is reiterated in a variety of words no less than six times in the first sixteen verses of this chapter (2, 6, 7, 11, 15, 16). Hence it is easy to see why nothing is here said of the other holy days. No doubt the Great Day of Atonement (Lev. xxiii. 26 sqq.), and the Feast of Trumpets (Lev. xxiii. 23 sqq.), are as positively enjoined by Moses as are the three Festivals mentioned in the present chapter: but it was no part of the observances of either of those days that all the males should "appear before the Lord." Those days might be regularly observed by the faithful without the necessity of their going to the central Sanctuary for the purpose; and so could furnish no occasion for enforcing that peculiar and leading topic of Deuteronomy, the observance of a national and visible unity in faith and worship.

1—8. The Feast of Passover (Ex. xii. 1—27; Num. ix. 1—14; Lev. xxiii. 1—8). A re-enforcement of this ordinance was the more necessary because its observance had clearly been intermitted for thirty-nine years (see on Josh. v. 10). One passover only had been kept in the wilderness, that recorded in Num. ix., where see notes. Various Jewish authorities observed that the passover was not designed to be kept regularly until after the settlement in Canaan (see Exod. xii. 25, xiii. 5). The same remark may be made of the Feast of Pentecost (see Lev. xxiii. 10).

2. *sacrifice the passover*] *i.e.* offer the sacrifices proper to the feast of the passover, which lasted seven days. The word passover here is used in a general sense for the passover offerings, as in St John xviii. 28, "that they might eat the passover," *i.e.* the passover offerings. The passover itself in the strictest sense was a lamb or a kid (Exod. xii. 5); but the slaying of this on the fourteenth day of the month at even was but the inauguration of a large number of sacrifices appointed for the days following (Num. xxviii. 17—24; 2 Chron. xxxv. 7). These sacrifices, strictly the passover offerings (*happesāchim*), were often by the Jews spoken of, together with the paschal

[d] Exod. 12. 5. 3 [d] Thou shalt eat no leavened
bread with it; seven days shalt thou
eat unleavened bread therewith, *even*
the bread of affliction; for thou camest
forth out of the land of Egypt in
haste: that thou mayest remember
the day when thou camest forth out
of the land of Egypt all the days of
thy life.
[e] Exod. 34. 5. 4 [e] And there shall be no leavened
bread seen with thee in all thy coast
seven days; neither shall there *any*
thing of the flesh, which thou sacri-
ficedst the first day at even, remain
all night until the morning.
‖ Or, *kill.* 5 Thou mayest not ‖ sacrifice the
passover within any of thy gates, which
the LORD thy God giveth thee:
6 But at the place which the LORD
thy God shall choose to place his
name in, there thou shalt sacrifice the
passover at even, at the going down
of the sun, at the season that thou
camest forth out of Egypt.
7 And thou shalt roast and eat *it*
in the place which the LORD thy God
shall choose: and thou shalt turn in
the morning, and go unto thy tents.
8 Six days thou shalt eat unleavened bread: and on the seventh
day *shall be* a † solemn assembly to † Heb. *restraint.*
the LORD thy God: thou shalt do no
work *therein.*
9 ¶ [f] Seven weeks shalt thou num- [f] Lev. 23. 15.
ber unto thee: begin to number the
seven weeks from *such time as* thou
beginnest *to put* the sickle to the corn.
10 And thou shalt keep the feast
of weeks unto the LORD thy God
with ‖ a tribute of a freewill offering ‖ Or, *sufficiency.*

---

lamb that inaugurated them, as simply the Pascha or Passover. It is clear that the word passover is thus used in the passage before us from what follows immediately in the next *v.*, "thou shalt eat no leavened bread with it: seven days shalt thou eat unleavened bread therewith:" *i.e.* with the passover. Now the passover in the narrowest sense, *i.e.* the lamb or kid, had to be consumed on the first evening, *v.* 4. That therefore with which they were to eat unleavened bread seven days is the passover in the wider sense, the paschal offerings which continued to be offered throughout the week. Hence the direction to "sacrifice the passover of the flock and the herd," *i.e.* of small cattle and oxen, is no variation of the ordinance of Exod. xii. 5. The rite of the paschal lamb is presupposed throughout, and the command of the present passage is to bring the other paschal offerings "of the flock and of the herd" to the place which the Lord should choose. In the latter part of *v.* 4 and the following *vv.* Moses passes, as the context again shows, into the narrower sense of the word passover.

7. *thou shalt roast*] Lit. **Thou shalt cook it.** The word (*bāshal*) means generally to prepare food by cooking. Ordinarily it is applied to boiling: but it may be used, as here and in 2 Chron. xxxv. 13, of roasting also. The previous rules about the passover being assumed, no Jew would think of cooking it in any other way than by fire.

thou shalt turn in the morning, and go unto thy tents] *i.e.* after the Paschal Supper in the courts or neighbourhood of the Sanctuary was over, they might disperse to their several lodgings. These would of course be within a short distance of the Sanctuary, because the other paschal offerings were yet to be offered day by day for seven days, and the people would remain to share them; and especially to take part in the holy convocation on the first and seventh of the days. The expression "unto thy tents," means simply "to thy dwellings," as in 1 K. viii. 66. The use of "tents" as a synonym for "dwellings" (cf. Is. xvi. 5) is a trace of the original nomadic life of the people.

9—13. Feast of Weeks; and *vv.* 13—17, Feast of Tabernacles. As regards these holy seasons nothing is here added to the rules given in Levit. and Num. except the clauses so often recurring in Deut. and so characteristic of it, which restrict the public celebration of the festivals to the Sanctuary, and enjoin that the enjoyments of them should be extended to the Levites, widows, orphans, &c. It is obviously for the sake of urging these two last-mentioned points that any allusion is here made at all to the two feasts.

9. *begin to number the weeks from such time as thou beginnest to put the sickle to the corn*] Lit. "upon the beginning of the sickle to the corn;" *i.e.* from the beginning of corn harvest. This could not be (Lev. xxiii. 14, 15) until the presentation of the first-fruits of the new harvest before God on "the morrow after the sabbath" in the Passover week, *i.e.* the sixteenth of Nisan; and accordingly the fifty days were counted from this "beginning of the sickle to the corn," or lawful commencement of harvest, on the second of the seven days of unleavened bread.

of thine hand, which thou shalt give
unto the LORD *thy God*, according as
the LORD thy God hath blessed thee:
11 And thou shalt rejoice before
the LORD thy God, thou, and thy
son, and thy daughter, and thy manservant, and thy maidservant, and the
Levite that *is* within thy gates, and
the stranger, and the fatherless, and
the widow, that *are* among you, in
the place which the LORD thy God
hath chosen to place his name there.
12 And thou shalt remember that
thou wast a bondman in Egypt: and
thou shalt observe and do these statutes.
13 ¶ Thou shalt observe the feast
of tabernacles seven days, after that
thou hast gathered in thy † corn and † Heb. *floor and thy winepress.*
thy wine:
14 And thou shalt rejoice in thy
feast, thou, and thy son, and thy
daughter, and thy manservant, and
thy maidservant, and the Levite, the
stranger, and the fatherless, and the
widow, that *are* within thy gates.
15 Seven days shalt thou keep a
solemn feast unto the LORD thy God
in the place which the LORD shall
choose: because the LORD thy God
shall bless thee in all thine increase,
and in all the works of thine hands,
therefore thou shalt surely rejoice.

16 ¶ [g] Three times in a year shall [g] Exod. 23. 14. & 34. 23.
all thy males appear before the LORD
thy God in the place which he shall
choose; in the feast of unleavened
bread, and in the feast of weeks, and
in the feast of tabernacles: and [h] they [h] Ecclus. 35. 4.
shall not appear before the LORD
empty:
17 Every man *shall give* † as he is † Heb. *according to the gift of his hand.*
able, according to the blessing of the
LORD thy God which he hath given
thee.
18 ¶ Judges and officers shalt thou
make thee in all thy gates, which the
LORD thy God giveth thee, throughout thy tribes: and they shall judge
the people with just judgment.
19 Thou shalt not wrest judgment; thou shalt not respect persons,
[i] neither take a gift: for a gift doth [i] Exod. 23. 8.
blind the eyes of the wise, and pervert
the ‖ words of the righteous. ‖ Or, *matters.*
20 † That which is altogether just † Heb. *Justice, justice.*
shalt thou follow, that thou mayest
live, and inherit the land which the
LORD thy God giveth thee.
21 ¶ Thou shalt not plant thee a
grove of any trees near unto the altar
of the LORD thy God, which thou
shalt make thee.
22 [k] Neither shalt thou set thee up [k] Lev. 26. 1.
any ‖ image; which the LORD thy ‖ Or, *statue*, or, *pillar.*
God hateth.

18—22. These *vv.* are closely connected in subject with the following chapter; and form with that and the four next chapters a proper lesson in the Synagogue service-book. They introduce certain directions for the administration of justice and the carrying on of the civil government of the people in Canaan. See on Judg. iii. 7. During the lifetime of Moses, he himself, specially inspired and guided by God, was sufficient, with the aid of the subordinate judges appointed at a very early period of the people's independence (cf. Ex. xviii. 13 sqq.), for the duties in question; and the more so because the nation had thus far lived in encampment together, and so within a small compass. But now when Moses was to be withdrawn, and the people would soon be scattered up and down the land of Canaan, regular and permanent provision must be made for civil and social order and good government. To such provision Moses now addresses himself; and with a statesmanlike foresight, not only arranges for immediate exigencies, but leaves room within his plan for ideas and wants which as yet lay in the far distant future.

21. *Thou shalt not plant thee a grove of any trees*] Render, **Thou shalt not plant for thee any tree as an idol**: literally "as an Asherah," *i.e.* an image of Astarte or Ashtaroth, the Phœnician goddess: cf. on vii. 13. The word is rendered "groves" by A. V. also in vii. 5, xii. 3; Ex. xxxiv. 13; Judg. vi. 25. This rendering is adopted after LXX., Saad., and many ancient authorities, but cannot be maintained, for the word is connected with various verbs (*e.g.* "to make," 1 K. xiv. 15; "to set up" or "erect," 2 K. xvii. 10; 2 Chron. xxxiii. 19; "to build," 1 K xiv. 23) which are quite inapplicable to a grove. The wooden idol in question was the stem of a tree, stripped of its boughs, set upright in the ground, and rudely carved with emblems.

CHAPTER XVII.

1 *The things sacrificed must be sound.* 2 *Idolaters must be slain.* 8 *Hard controversies are to be determined by the priests and judges.* 12 *The contemner of that determination must die.* 14 *The election,* 16 *and duty of a king.*

THOU shalt not sacrifice unto the LORD thy God *any* bullock, or ‖ sheep, wherein is blemish, *or* any evilfavouredness: for that *is* an abomination unto the LORD thy God.

‖ Or, *goat.*

2 ¶ If there be found among you, within any of thy gates which the LORD thy God giveth thee, man or woman, that hath wrought wickedness in the sight of the LORD thy God, in transgressing his covenant,

3 And hath gone and served other gods, and worshipped them, either the sun, or moon, or any of the host of heaven, which I have not commanded;

4 And it be told thee, and thou hast heard *of it*, and inquired diligently, and, behold, *it be* true, *and* the thing certain, *that* such abomination is wrought in Israel:

5 Then shalt thou bring forth that man or that woman, which have committed that wicked thing, unto thy gates, *even* that man or that woman, and shalt stone them with stones, till they die.

6 [a] At the mouth of two witnesses, or three witnesses, shall he that is worthy of death be put to death; *but* at the mouth of one witness he shall not be put to death.

7 The hands of the witnesses shall be first upon him to put him to death, and afterward the hands of all the people. So thou shalt put the evil away from among you.

[a] Numb. 35. 30. chap. 19. 15. Matt. 18. 16. John 8. 17. 2 Cor. 13. 1. Heb. 10. 28.

8 ¶ If there arise a matter too hard for thee in judgment, between blood and blood, between plea and plea, and between stroke and stroke, *being* matters of controversy within thy gates: then shalt thou arise, and get thee up into the place which the LORD thy God shall choose;

9 And thou shalt come unto the

CHAP. XVII. **1.** This *v.* belongs in subject to the last chapter. It prohibits once more (cf. xv. 21) that form of insult to God which consists in offering to Him a blemished sacrifice.

any evil-favouredness] Render **any evil thing.** The reference is to the faults or maims enumerated Lev. xxii. 22—24.

2—7. The detection and punishment of idolatry, as leading duties of the magistrate, are again enjoined (cf. xiii sqq.) with special reference to the legal forms to be adopted, *vv.* 5—7. The sentence is to be carried into effect at "the gates" (cf. on Gen. xix. 1) of the town in which the crime is committed; because, as "all the people" were to take a part, an open space would be requisite for the execution. Note the typical and prophetical aspect of the injunction; cf. Acts vii. 58; Hebr. xiii. 12. It is quite in keeping with the time and circumstances of Deut. that we should find here the expression "unto the gates" instead of the "without the camp" of the earlier books; cf. Lev. xxiv. 14; Num. xv. 35. On the requirement of two witnesses see reff. in margin. The accuser however might himself be one of the two. The obligation laid on the witnesses (*v.* 7) on whose testimony sentence of death should be passed, to take the lead in the execution of it, is calculated to ensure their sincerity and truthfulness, and to deter from false witness.

8—13. The transition is obvious from the enactments respecting a leading class of capital crimes to those respecting obscure or complicated cases. These *vv.* do not, strictly speaking, provide for a court of appeal. No provision for appeals in the proper sense is found in the laws of Moses. The cases in question are, like those to be brought before Moses in person according to the suggestion of Jethro (Ex. xviii. 23—27), such as the inferior judges did not feel able to decide satisfactorily, and which accordingly they remitted to their superiors.

The Supreme Court is referred to in very general terms as sitting at the Sanctuary, *v.* 8, and as consisting of "the priests the Levites, and the judge that shall be in those days," *v.* 9. "The judge" would no doubt usually be a layman, and thus the court would contain both an ecclesiastical and a civil element. In like manner Moses and Aaron (Num. xv. 33), and after Aaron's death Moses and Eleazar (Num. xxvii. 2), seem to have acted as judges in chief whilst the people were still in the wilderness. Jehoshaphat, when (2 Chron. xix. 4—11) "he brought the people back unto the Lord God of their fathers," organized his judicial system very closely upon the lines here laid down. He "set judges in the land throughout all the fenced cities of Judah," *i.e.* local courts, as is enjoined Deut. xvi. 18, and appointed the chief priest and "Zebadiah

priests the Levites, and unto the judge
that shall be in those days, and inquire; and they shall shew thee the
sentence of judgment:
10 And thou shalt do according to
the sentence, which they of that place
which the LORD shall choose shall
shew thee; and thou shalt observe to
do according to all that they inform
thee:
11 According to the sentence of
the law which they shall teach thee,
and according to the judgment which
they shall tell thee, thou shalt do:
thou shalt not decline from the sentence which they shall shew thee, *to*
the right hand, nor *to* the left.
12 And the man that will do presumptuously, †and will not hearken
unto the priest that standeth to minister there before the LORD thy God,

† Heb. *not to hearken.*

or unto the judge, even that man shall
die: and thou shalt put away the evil
from Israel.
13 And all the people shall hear,
and fear, and do no more presumptuously.
14 ¶ When thou art come unto
the land which the LORD thy God
giveth thee, and shalt possess it, and
shalt dwell therein, and shalt say, I
will set a king over me, like as all the
nations that *are* about me;
15 Thou shalt in any wise set *him*
king over thee, whom the LORD thy
God shall choose: *one* from among
thy brethren shalt thou set king over
thee: thou mayest not set a stranger
over thee, which *is* not thy brother.
16 But he shall not multiply horses
to himself, nor cause the people to
return to Egypt, to the end that he

---

the son of Ishmael, the ruler of the house of Judah" to be a central and supreme court at Jerusalem. On the judicial institutions of the Jews in general, see Note at end of chapter.

9. *the priests the Levites*] This expression, as also the similar one "the priests the sons of Levi," is equivalent to "the Levitical priests," and is found in Deut. and Josh. (cf. *v.* 18, xviii. 1, xxi. 5; Josh. iii. 3, &c.), instead of "the sons of Aaron" of Exodus and the two following books. See on it, Introd. § V.

14—20. The provisions for a supreme court of justice carry the writer on to the consideration of a contingency which nearly concerns this part of his polity, that of his people wishing to set a king over them. The king, if appointed, would of course gather round himself the functions of judicature and administration which are treated of in this part of the book; and his election, duties and responsibilities are thus naturally and appositely spoken of here. On the inferences drawn from these verses as to the date of Deut. see Note at end of chapter. It is only necessary to observe here that the choice of a king is not, like that of judges and officers, xvi. 18, enjoined, but simply permitted. The reason of this is obvious. Provision for the due administration of justice is essential: that justice should be dispensed through monarchical forms is not so; and is accordingly only recognized as an arrangement which might probably result on the settlement and consolidation of the people in Canaan.

14. No encouragement is given to the desire, natural in an Oriental people, for monarchical government; but neither is such desire blamed, as appears from the fact that conditions are immediately laid down upon which it may be satisfied.

I will set a king over me] Cf. 1 S. viii. 5, 19.

15. The king, like the judges and officers (cf. xvi. 18), is to be chosen by the people; but their choice is to be in accordance with the will of God, and to be made from amongst "their brethren." Cf. 1 S. ix. 15, x. 24, xvi. 12; 1 K. xix. 16. Neither the manner of the election, nor the channel through which the Divine will would be manifested, are specified. The former point, in this as in other such cases, is taken as sufficiently provided for by the usual customs of the people; the latter is appropriately left indeterminate. God would make His choice evident, and this was all that needed to be intimated. In fact a prophet was usually commissioned, as in the examples above cited; though in the case of Solomon the decision of the Lord was directly communicated to David also. Cf. 1 Chron. xxii. 10.

thou mayest not set a stranger over thee] The Jews extended this prohibition to all offices whatsoever; cf. Jer. xxx. 21; and naturally attached the greatest importance to it: whence the significance of the question proposed to our Lord, "Is it lawful to give tribute to Cæsar?" St Matt. xx. 17. A Gentile head for the Jewish people, which it was a main aim of the law to keep peculiar and distinct from others, was an anomaly.

should multiply horses: forasmuch as
the LORD hath said unto you, Ye
shall henceforth return no more that
way.
17 Neither shall he multiply wives
to himself, that his heart turn not
away: neither shall he greatly multiply to himself silver and gold.
18 And it shall be, when he sitteth upon the throne of his kingdom,
that he shall write him a copy of this
law in a book out of *that which is*
before the priests the Levites:
19 And it shall be with him, and
he shall read therein all the days of
his life: that he may learn to fear

---

16. *he shall not multiply horses to himself, nor cause the people to return to Egypt, to the end that he should multiply horses*] The horse was not anciently used in the East for purposes of agriculture or travelling, but ordinarily for war only. He appears constantly in Scripture as the symbol and embodiment of fleshly strength and the might of the creature; cf. Ps. xx. 7, xxxiii. 16, 17, cxlvii. 10; Job xxxix. 19 sqq., and is sometimes significantly spoken of simply as "the strong one," cf. Jer. viii. 16. The spirit of the prohibition therefore is that the king of Israel must not, like other earthly potentates, put his trust in costly and formidable preparations for war, but in God who "saves not by horses nor by horsemen," Hos. i. 7.

Canaan being a mountainous country was not suited for the breeding and training of horses. Egypt was the principal source whence the nations of western Asia drew their supplies of this animal: cf. 1 K. x. 28, 29; and horses and chariots figure constantly as most important elements in the armies of the Pharaohs; cf. Ex. xiv. 5 sqq.; 2 K. vii. 6. The Assyrians likewise excelled in this arm (cf. 2 K. xviii. 23; Habak. i. 8; Nah. iii. 3), and it was the natural resource of the later kings of Judah, themselves weak in cavalry, to seek to balance the superiority of the Assyrians in this respect by alliances with the Egyptians. This policy of worldly wisdom is often and emphatically condemned by the prophets; cf. Is. xxx. 1, xxxvi. 9; Ezek. xvii. 15; and in the very spirit of the text. Egypt everywhere in Scripture stands as the antithesis to the theocratic covenant and kingdom on earth. "To cause the people to return to Egypt" would be to reverse that great and beneficent wonderwork of God which inaugurated the Mosaic covenant, the deliverance from the bondage of Egypt; and to bring that about of set purpose which God threatens (xxviii. 68) as the sorest punishment for Israel's sin. The multiplication of horses could not take place, as experience in Solomon's reign showed, without constant traffic with Egypt and consequent intercourse with the Egyptians; and this it was important for the purposes of the Mosaic law to prevent (cf. Ex. xiii. 17; Jer. xlii. 14 sqq.; Hos. xi. 5).

17. *Neither shall he multiply wives to himself*] Cf. Ex. xxxiv. 16: where, however, (as in Deut. vii. 3, 4) the warning is rather against intermarriage with idolatrous nations which might by their example seduce the chosen people from the faith, than as here, against excessive multiplication of wives. The latter sin would lead to sensuality, and so to an apostasy no less fatal in effect than downright idolatry. This rule, like the others, abridges to the ruler of Israel liberties usually enjoyed without stint by the kings of the East. It does not forbid polygamy, but inordinate polygamy. The Targum of Jonathan interprets it as limiting the king to eighteen wives. The restriction, however lax to Christian notions, was in the days of Moses unprecedented; and demanded a higher standard in the king of Israel than was looked for amongst his equals in other nations.

neither shall he greatly multiply to himself silver and gold] In this third, as in the other two prohibitions, excess is forbidden. Vast accumulation of treasure could hardly be effected without oppression; nor when effected fail to produce pride and a "trust in uncertain riches," 1 Tim. vi. 17.

18. *he shall write him a copy of this law*] This prescription is every way a remarkable one. Philo and other Jewish commentators understand it as binding the king to transcribe the law with his own hand. The spirit of the rule however seems only to require that the king should have a copy written for him (so Saad., Keil, Knobel, &c.). It is in striking consistency with the dignity which everywhere throughout the Mosaic legislation surrounds the chosen people of God, that even if they will be "like as all the nations about," and be governed by a king, care should nevertheless be taken that he shall be no Oriental despot. He is to be of no royal caste, but *one from among thy brethren;* he is to bear himself as a kind of "primus inter pares," his heart *not being lifted up above his brethren*, *v.* 20; he is, like his subjects, to be bound by the fundamental laws and institutions of the nation, and obliged, as they were, to do his duty in his station of life with constant reference thereto. The spirit of the text is that of St Matt. xxiii. 9. It is noteworthy too that none of the kings of Israel appears in character of a legislator.

a copy of this law] The A. V. reproduces exactly the sense of the Hebrew, and the ex-the LORD his God, to keep all the words of this law and these statutes, to do them:

20 That his heart be not lifted up above his brethren, and that he turn not aside from the commandment, *to* the right hand, or *to* the left: to the end that he may prolong *his* days in his kingdom, he, and his children, in the midst of Israel.

---

pression is generally and correctly explained as importing the whole Pentateuch, or at any rate the legal portion of the Pentateuch. A knowledge of Exodus and the two following books would indeed be even more essential to the king than that of Deuteronomy, which is to so great an extent a hortatory comment on them and supplement to them. The LXX. renders "*τὸ δευτερονόμιον τοῦτο*"; and the Vulg. "Deuteronomium legis hujus." The Talmud understands *two* copies, making *mishneh* equivalent to "duplum."

in a book out of that which is before the priests the Levites] Cf. xxxi. 9 sqq. and 24 sqq. and notes.

NOTES on CHAP. XVII. 8—13, and 14—17.

We have no means of determining questions of detail connected with the judicial institutions of the ancient Jews. The words of this passage and of xix. 17, 18 intimate that the chief priest and the judge had each assessors or assistants; and the last-cited one seems to assign the inquiry into fact specially to the judges. "The priests the Levites" would naturally be regarded as more particularly entrusted with the duty of interpreting and expounding the law of God.

Yet distinctions of a legal character, such as that between questions of law and questions of fact, would not be drawn with nicety in the days of Moses. Some such distinctions, *e.g.* that between ecclesiastical, civil, and criminal causes, would be to some extent inapplicable under a theocracy.

Three sorts of functionaries appear in the Pentateuch as taking part in the administration of justice: (1) "the Elders;" (2) "the Judges" (שפטים, once Ex. xxi. 22 פלילים); (3) "the Officers" (שטרים).

For the basis of the whole system we must go back to the patriarchal institution of "the Elders." Cf. on Num. xi. 16. In this as in other parts of his legislation Moses, strictly speaking, originates little, but regulates and develops what was in its germs already present in the social system and habits of his people. "The Elders" of Israel are mentioned before the Exodus, Ex. iii. 18; and appear also amongst the Egyptians, Gen. l. 7, as they do indeed amongst Oriental nations commonly, from the dawn of history to the present time. They are in the Pentateuch identical with "the heads of the people" and "chief of the tribes," who so often come forward either by themselves or their deputies, in the course of the wandering, as representatives of the nation at large.

It is clear that on the first emancipation of the people from Egypt, Moses united in his own person the judicial as well as the other principal theocratical functions. As the organization of the nation proceeded, Moses on the counsel of Jethro appointed a large number of inferior judges, who accordingly are distinguished from "the Elders," though perhaps chosen from amongst them: (cf. Exod. xviii. 21 sqq.; and ch. i. 13, 15, 16, and xxi. 2). The college of Elders however seems to have retained the adjudication of certain cases (cf. xxi. 19, xxii. 15, xxv. 8), probably cases of a domestic nature. The Elders of Jezreel (1 K. xxi.) play a conspicuous part in the judicial murder of Naboth; but we can hardly infer from such a transaction, especially in Ahab's kingdom, that they ordinarily and regularly exercised powers of this sort.

"The Officers" too (Shoterim) are found as well as "the Elders" before the Exodus: Ex. v. 10, where see note. Subsequently they are mentioned with "the Elders" (Num. xi. 16), and with "the Judges" (ch. xvi. 18); from which last place it appears that they were in some way concerned in the administration of justice. In Josh. viii. 33 and xxiv. 1 "the Elders, Officers, and Judges" are enumerated severally.

The Rabbinists find in the text the Greater and Lesser Sanhedrim. No doubt the Lesser Sanhedrim corresponded in functions with the local court provided in xvi. 18, as did the Greater with the supreme court of xvii. 8 (cf. St Matt. v. 22); but the Sanhedrim in the strict and proper sense was only instituted after the return from the exile. The Talmud, differing herein from Josephus, speaks of the Lesser Sanhedrim as containing twenty-three members.

It would seem likely, from the wording of xvi. 18 (cf. i. 13 and Josh. iv. 1), that the various officers concerned in the administration of justice were, to some extent at least, chosen by popular election. Of the mode however in which this was done as well as of many other particulars, such as the qualifications required in those to be elected, we have no information. The directions given on the whole subject in chapters xvi. and xvii. are of the most general kind. The language is in truth more that of one alluding to customs and institutions already existing and well known, than of one founding new ones by legislation. But it is quite arbitrary to assert (Riehm, Kuenen) that the writer cannot but have had before him the judicial reforms of Jehoshaphat (2 Chron. xix.). A far more apposite explanation is furnished by those (as Keil) who remind us that Moses had before him no disorganized mob, but a nation already in possession of civil and religious institutions; institutions indeed such as have for ages sufficed of themselves for the purposes of many an Oriental community. It was enough therefore for Moses to lay down broadly the general principles to be kept in view and the larger outlines to be followed in working these out, leaving details to be evolved as circumstances and the natural development of the nation might suggest. Here as elsewhere the Mosaic Code is designed for a free and independent people, and leaves scope for that national energy which will not fail to provide itself with organization according to emergencies. The New Testament treats the Christian Church in a strictly analogous manner on the like classes of subjects, such as discipline, government, &c. *Ends* are set forth; *means* left largely to the discretion of the rulers of the Church in different ages and countries. The continuity of the Church has been unbroken from the days of the Apostles to the present; yet there are many debateable questions as to what were ecclesiastical usages and arrangements in Apostolic days. How much more must this be expected as to the far more ancient institutions of the Jewish theocracy, which have been too swept away entirely once and again by overwhelming national calamity, and have now been for eighteen hundred years extinct!

vv. 14—17.

This passage is one of the most important amongst those brought forward by certain critics as proofs that Deuteronomy was not written until the time of the later kings. The positions assumed by these critics (*e.g.* Vater, De Wette, Von Bohlen, Ewald, Riehm, Colenso, &c., and even Winer, 'Real Wörterb.' s. v. *Kœnig*) may be thus stated:

(1) It is inconceivable that Moses, who died more than three centuries before regal government was introduced in the person of Saul, can have made mention of a king as these *vv.* do; especially as the principles and tenor of his legislation are decidedly not monarchical.

(2) In the narrative of the appointment of Saul, 1 S. viii—xii., there is no reference whatever to these provisions of Deuteronomy. Yet had these been then extant either Samuel must have quoted them when speaking of "the manner of the king," chap. viii. and xii., or the people have alleged them in vindication or excuse of their desire to have a king. But, on the contrary, Samuel charges it on the people as a great wickedness that they had asked a king; and the people themselves admit their guilt in the matter, 1 S. xii. 17—19.

(3) The prohibitions against accumulation of horses, wives, and treasure, are evidently suggested by the history of Solomon; cf. 1 K. x. 26—29 and xi. 1—4.

(4) The reference to the traffic in horses with Egypt points to the times of the later kings of Judah; cf. Is. ii. 7, xxxvi. 9; Jer. ii. 18, 36, xlii. 15—19, &c.

On these grounds it is argued that the passage was certainly penned long after the date of Moses, and indeed subsequently to the reign of Solomon, and most probably in the age of Jeremiah.

But it may be answered:

(1) Even if we exclude from the question Moses' supernatural gifts, he may very probably have contemplated such a contingency as Israel wishing at some time or other for a king, and especially have thought it likely, as the text presents it, when the people had settled themselves in the promised land. When we consider that the experience of Moses, wide as it no doubt was, would probably fail to afford a single instance of any settled community governed otherwise than by a monarch, we might fairly argue that it is more surprising that he should have founded any other polity and expected that polity to endure, as he does, than to find him entertaining the supposition that Israel might wish to be governed as all other nations were.

If the institutions of Moses are non-monarchical, yet neither have they any greater affinity for other special forms of civil government. The main purposes of his law are religious and theocratical; and these are carefully secured by enactment. But they could be attained as well under kings as under prophets like Moses, generals like Joshua, or judges like Samuel; and accordingly no definite polity was by Divine authority imposed on the Jews in perpetuity.

Neither is the passage before us the only one of the Pentateuch in which allusion seems made to kings of Israel. Cf. Gen. xvii. 16, xxxvi. 31, xlix. 10; Ex. xxii. 28; Num. xxiv. 17; Deut. xxviii. 36. It is not too much to say that the presage of royalty to come pervades every part of the early annals of the people.

(2) In reply to the second position, it is to be remembered that a direct and formal quotation of an earlier book in a later is not at all in the manner of the Old Testament writers. Yet the request of the people (1 S. viii. 5), "Make us a king to judge us like all the nations," is preferred in terms very like those employed Deut. xvii. 14. Is the resemblance accidental? It is hard to think so

when we find Samuel, in presenting Saul to the people as "him whom the Lord hath chosen," 1 S. x. 24, employing again the words of this verse of Deut.; and in his exhortation, 1 S. xii. 14, reproducing the tone, phraseology, and rhetorical accumulation of clauses which are characteristic features of Deut. (cf. Deut. i. 26, 43, ix. 7, 23, &c.). It is therefore too much to say that no allusion to the passage of Deut. before us can be found in 1 S. viii.—xii.

(3) Neither is it correct to assume that Samuel condemned the demand for a king as in itself a sin. As in so many other parts of Scripture, so in the language ascribed to God 1 S. x. 18, 19, and to Samuel 1 S. xii. 17, misconception arises from insulating particular verses, and construing them irrespectively of the context. When we duly note that God, 1 S. viii. 7, enjoined Samuel "to hearken to the voice of the people in all that they say," it is not possible to regard the demand in question as one which the sacred writer thought absolutely wicked. In truth it is plain, upon a survey of the whole transaction, that it was not the mere desire of a king which is blamed, but the time and circumstances under which that desire was manifested. It might *e.g.* have been innocent to have brought forward a scheme for a regal government at the death of the divinely appointed judge, and in the absence of any directions from God respecting a successor. But the people desired to set aside Samuel, a man who had the special approval of the Divine head of the theocracy, and upon a pretext "Behold thou art old," (1 S. viii. 5), which can hardly have been sincere, seeing that Samuel lived to take a leading part in public affairs for some thirty-five years afterwards; and in distrust of God's will and power to interpose for their succour (1 S. xii. 12) against the attack of Nahash, king of the Ammonites. The allegation against the sons of Samuel (1 S. viii. 3 sqq.) was valid ground for remonstrance, but not for setting aside one whom the people themselves did not dare to deny to have been as uncorrupt as he was able and diligent in his duties (1 S. xii. 1—5). It is in short evident that the demand for a king arose partly out of that culpable proneness towards imitation of heathen nations which so often led the people into error; partly out of a peevish impatience at certain abuses of a remediable and temporary character; and partly out of a want of faith in time of trial. For these reasons the demand for a king was sinful at the time it was made, and became doubly so when persisted in against the remonstrances of God's prophet (1 S. viii. 10 sqq.); and though God bade Samuel to "hearken unto the voice of the people," yet (Hos. xiii. 11) "He gave them a king in His anger." There is therefore, on the whole, no real repugnance between the narrative in 1 S. viii.—xii. and the passage o Deut. before us.

(4) The similarity between our passage of Deut. and 1 K. x. 26—29, xi. 1—5 cannot be gainsayed. The only open (literary) question is whether the writer of Deut. had the passage of Kings before him, or the writer of Kings that of Deut. The broad reasons on which we decide for the latter alternative are set out in the Introduction. Here we may note that it is clear that the writer of 1 K. had in view not only Deut. xvii. but also Deut. vii. 3, 4, and Ex. xxxiv. 16.

Nothing can be plainer than that the intention of the author of 1 K. in x. 26 sqq. is to trace the backsliding of Solomon to his disregard amidst his prosperity of the wholesome restraints imposed by the Divine law. This intention comes out explicitly in xi. 2; but it is no less perceptible, though implied, in the preceding context; and there is nothing in that context which the writer can have had in view except our passage of Deut.

(5) The allegation that the restrictions laid on the supposed king by Deut. reflect the ideas of a later age, is simply arbitrary. The excesses forbidden to the king of Israel were those in which eastern potentates were wont to indulge; nor, supposing Moses to have thought of a king at all, is anything more in keeping with the general spirit of his legislation than that he should have sought to guard against some of the more obvious and ordinary abuses of Oriental despotism.

(6) The caution against "causing the people to return to Egypt" (Deut. xvii. 16), is thoroughly consistent with the character and circumstances of Moses. Again and again do we read of the people longing for the land they had left behind (cf. Ex. xvi. 3; Num. xi. 5); and they once actually proposed to "make a captain and return to Egypt" (Num. xiv. 4). But after the glorious reigns of David, Solomon, and others, the building of the Temple, and the long annals of Israel as an independent nation, it would have been preposterous to mention such a thing as replanting the Jews in Egypt.

(7) Equally absurd would it have been in the days of the later kings to forbid the choice of an alien as king. No one would have thought of such an appointment whilst the seed royal was prolific in several branches.

(8) The rules laid down in Deut. xvii. respecting the kingdom do not therefore bear the marks of a date long after that of Moses, but rather the contrary. It is a striking illustration of the peremptory spirit in which arguments on this subject are manufactured, that we find Riehm coupling this passage with Deut. xxviii. 68, and finding in the two evidence of a treaty by which Manasseh furnished infantry to the Egyptian king Psammetichus in return for horses. According to Diodorus (I. 66), and Herod. (I. 152), Psam-

metichus hired soldiers from Arabia and Asia Minor; but there is not a single historical trace of the supposed treaty in any writer sacred or secular; and no mention of Judea at all in the historians referred to.

(9) We may add that it is quite unintelligible how and why a later writer, desiring to pass under the name of Moses, could have penned a passage exhibiting the peculiarities of the one under consideration. He could not have designed it as an example of the prophetical powers of the great lawgiver of Israel, for it is so vaguely and generally conceived as to look rather like a surmise than a prediction. Nor could he have intended to insert by it a kind of sanction of royalty in the Mosaic legislation; for it contains rather a toleration of that mode of government than an approval of it. Neither would he have thought of subjecting his imaginary king to rules which must have sounded, in part at least, little less than absurd to his own contemporaries, and which are in themselves such as no one in his (supposed) time and circumstances can naturally be thought to have invented.

CHAPTER XVIII.

1 *The Lord is the priests' and Levites' inheritance.* 3 *The priest's due.* 6 *The Levite's portion.* 9 *The abominations of the nations are to be avoided.* 15 *Christ the Prophet is to be heard.* 20 *The presumptuous prophet is to die.*

THE priests the Levites, *and* all
the tribe of Levi, [a]shall have no
part nor inheritance with Israel: they
[b]shall eat the offerings of the LORD
made by fire, and his inheritance.

[a] Numb. 18. 20. chap. 10. 9.
[b] 1 Cor. 9. 13.

2 Therefore shall they have no inheritance among their brethren: the
LORD *is* their inheritance, as he hath
said unto them.
3 ¶ And this shall be the priest's
due from the people, from them that
offer a sacrifice, whether *it be* ox or
sheep; and they shall give unto the
priest the shoulder, and the two cheeks,
and the maw.
4 The firstfruit *also* of thy corn, of

CHAP. XVIII. Whilst speaking of the guides and rulers of the people the legislator could not wholly omit the priests, the Levites, and the prophets, though his description of the ecclesiastical life of the nation had led him already to treat copiously of their office and duties. Accordingly he now summarily repeats, with some supplementary additions, from his former enactments what were to be their privileges and position after the settlement in Canaan; beginning with the priests (*vv.* 3—5), and Levites (*vv.* 6—8), the ordinary ministers of religion and expositors of the law of God; and proceeding, in contrast with the false pretences of the heathen seers (*vv.* 9—14), to promise that the true God would not fail in extraordinary emergencies to afford the needful instruction as to His will and way. Accordingly the prophets are (*vv.* 15—22) formally accredited as instruments through which the divine Head of the Theocracy would from time to time exercise His superintendence and control.

1. *The priests the Levites*, and *all the tribe of Levi*] The word *and*, inserted by our translators, weakens the force of the original. The absence of conjunctions in the Hebrew, and its climax from the particular to the general, are emphatic; the effect might be given thus: "there shall not be to the priests, the Levites, yea the whole tribe of Levi, any inheritance, &c." This is thus forcibly laid down by way of basis for the enlargement made in the subsequent verses of the emoluments of the priests and Levites; and serves to suggest the need, probably already ascertained, of some addition to their allowance.

and his inheritance] *i.e.* God's inheritance, that which in making a grant to His people of the Promised Land with its earthly blessings He had reserved for Himself; more particularly the sacrifices, or as they are here termed "firings," and the holy gifts, such as tithes and firstfruits (so Vulg. "oblationes"). These were God's portion (κλῆρος) of the substance of Israel; and as the Levites were His portion of the persons of Israel, it was fitting that the Levites should be sustained from these. The words of *vv.* 1 and 2 are evidently suggested by Num. xviii. 20 sqq.; cf. also Deut. x. 9; Josh. xiii. 14, 33; and on the principle here laid down, 1 Cor. ix. 13, 14.

3—5. Separate allusion is now made to the two parts of the tribe of Levi, the priests (*vv.* 3—5) and the Levites (*vv.* 6—8). The perquisites here named are clearly (*v.* 3) assigned to the priests as distinct from the Levites; the corresponding mention of privileges belonging specifically to the latter coming in due order, *v.* 6 sqq. On the bearing of these *vv.* upon the relations between the priests and Levites as exhibited in Deuteronomy, see Note at end of chapter.

the shoulder, and the two cheeks, and the maw]

thy wine, and of thine oil, and the
first of the fleece of thy sheep, shalt
thou give him.
5 For the LORD thy God hath
chosen him out of all thy tribes, to
stand to minister in the name of the
LORD, him and his sons for ever.
6 ¶ And if a Levite come from
any of thy gates out of all Israel,
where he sojourned, and come with
all the desire of his mind unto the
place which the LORD shall choose;
7 Then he shall minister in the
name of the LORD his God, as all his
brethren the Levites *do*, which stand
there before the LORD.
8 They shall have like portions to
eat, beside †that which cometh of the
sale of his patrimony.
9 ¶ When thou art come into the

† Heb. *his sales by the fathers.*

For *maw* read **stomach**. The part intended is the fourth stomach of ruminating animals in which the digestion is completed. This was regarded as one of the richest and choicest parts (so LXX. ἤνυστρον, Vulg. "ventriculus," Keil, Schultz, &c.). On the provision for the priest here made and its relation to that of Levit. vii. 31—34, see Note at end of chapter. As the animal slain may be considered to consist of three principal parts, head, feet, and body, a portion of each is by the regulation in question to be given to the priest, thus representing the consecration of the whole; or, as some ancient commentators think, the dedication of the words, acts, and appetites of the worshipper to God.

Jewish authorities (Philo, Joseph., the Talmud) regard the regulation as applicable to animals slain at home for food. But not only the phraseology ("offer a sacrifice"), but the utter impossibility of transporting these pieces from various parts of the country to the residences of the priests, seems to forbid such a sense. Keil is probably right in understanding the text to refer to peace-offerings, and animals killed for the sacrificial meals held in connection with the peace-offerings.

4. The law of firstfruits is repeated from Num. xviii. 12, 13 for the purpose of adding thereto "the first fleece of the sheep."

5. *him and his sons for ever*] A plain reference to the original appointment of Aaron and his sons to the priesthood.

6—8. Allusion is now made to the Levites specifically so called, *i.e.* to the non-priestly Levites, in contrast with "the priest" who "with his sons" is mentioned *vv.* 3 and 5.

These *vv.* presuppose that part of the Levites only will be in residence and officiating at the place of the Sanctuary, the others of course dwelling at their own homes in the Levitical cities; cf. Num. xxxv. 2 sqq. But if any Levite out of love for the service of the Sanctuary chose to resort to it when he might reside in his own home, he was to have his share in the maintenance which was provided for those ministering in the order of their course.

6. *any of thy gates...where he sojourned*] The various administrative duties discharged by Levites (*e.g.* that of Shoterim, cf. xvii. 8 sqq. and note) would necessarily lead to many individuals of them "sojourning" from time to time in various parts of the land, and often in other than Levitical cities; and indeed as these cities were scattered up and down amongst the tribes, and were the only regular dwellingplaces of the tribe of Levi, the members of that tribe may be said, in contrast with the others, to be "sojourners" altogether.

7. *he shall minister in the name of the LORD his God*] The duty of the Levites was to assist the priests; and this subordinate ministration is expressed in Num. iii. 6 by the same Hebrew word as is here used.

8. *They shall have like portions to eat*] Lit. "part like part shall they eat:" *i.e.* the new-comer and those already in attendance. Due provision had been made in the preceding legislation for the maintenance of the ministers at the Sanctuary. All that now needed to be done was to secure the volunteer his share in it.

beside that which cometh of the sale of his patrimony] Marg. more literally "his sales by the fathers." The wording of the original is singular and difficult (see Note at end of chapter). A great variety of interpretations has been proposed, yet there seems little doubt about the real meaning. The Levites had indeed "no part nor inheritance with Israel," but they might individually possess property, and in fact often did so. Thus Abiathar (1 K. ii. 26) owned certain "fields," and Jeremiah (xxxii. 7 sqq.) bought a field of his uncle. The law, Levit. xxv. 33, 34, forbids the sale of the pastures belonging in common to the Levites as such, but private property might of course be disposed of at the pleasure of the owner. The Levite who desired to settle at the place of the Sanctuary would probably sell his patrimony when quitting his former home. The text directs that he should, notwithstanding any such private resources, duly enjoy his share of the perquisites provided for the ministers at the sanctuary, and as he was "waiting at the altar" should be "partaker with the altar" (1 Cor. ix. 13).

land which the LORD thy God giveth
thee, thou shalt not learn to do after
the abominations of those nations.
10 There shall not be found among
you *any one* that maketh his son or
[c] Lev. 18. 21. his daughter [c] to pass through the fire,
or that useth divination, *or* an ob-
server of times, or an enchanter, or a
witch,
[d] Lev. 20. 27. 11 [d] Or a charmer, or a consulter
with familiar spirits, or a wizard, or a
[e] 1 Sam. 28. 7. [e] necromancer.
12 For all that do these things *are*
an abomination unto the LORD: and
because of these abominations the
LORD thy God doth drive them out
from before thee.
‖ Or, *upright*, or, *sincere*. 13 Thou shalt be ‖ perfect with the
LORD thy God.
14 For these nations, which thou
‖ Or, *inherit*. shalt ‖ possess, hearkened unto observers of times, and unto diviners: but
as for thee, the LORD thy God hath
[f] John 1. 45. Acts 3. 22. & 7. 37. not suffered thee so *to do*.
15 ¶ [f] The LORD thy God will
raise up unto thee a Prophet from the
midst of thee, of thy brethren, like
unto me; unto him ye shall hearken;
16 According to all that thou de-
siredst of the LORD thy God in Horeb in the day of the assembly, saying,
[g] Let me not hear again the voice of [g] Exod. 20. 19.
the LORD my God, neither let me see
this great fire any more, that I die not.
17 And the LORD said unto me,
They have well *spoken that* which
they have spoken.
18 [h] I will raise them up a Prophet [h] John 1. 45. Acts 3. 22. & 7. 37.
from among their brethren, like unto
thee, and will put my words in his
mouth; and he shall speak unto them
all that I shall command him.
19 And it shall come to pass, *that*
whosoever will not hearken unto my
words which he shall speak in my
name, I will require *it* of him.
20 But the prophet, which shall
presume to speak a word in my name,
which I have not commanded him to
speak, or that shall speak in the name
of other gods, even that prophet shall
die.

9—14. Passing on to speak of the prophets, the legislator begins by enumerating and prohibiting the various superstitions by which the heathen nations of Canaan had sought to explore the future and to test the will of the Deity.

10. *maketh his son or his daughter to pass through the fire*] *i.e.* to Moloch; cf. Levit. xviii. 21 and note. The practice was probably in some way connected with soothsaying.

that useth divination] Cf. Num. xxiii. 23 and note.

observer of times] Cf. Lev. xix. 26 and note.

enchanter] Or serpent-charmer; cf. Lev. l.c.

witch] Rather sorcerer, as in Ex. vii. 11; see note there.

11. *a charmer*] *i.e.* one who fascinates and subdues noxious animals or men, such as the famous serpent-charmers of the East. Cf. especially Ps. lviii. 4, 5. The word is derived from a root signifying to bind or ban.

a consulter with familiar spirits] Cf. Lev. xix. 31, xx. 6.

a wizard] Cf. Lev. l. c.

necromancer] Literally "one who interrogates the dead." And it might be better to restore the literal rendering in the A. V., for the term "necromancer" seems to be equivalent to the "consulter with familiar spirits," named above. The purpose of the text is obviously to group together all the known words belonging to the practices in question; cf. 2 Chron. xxxiii. 6.

13. *Thou shalt be perfect with the LORD thy God*] On the word *perfect* cf. Gen. xvii. 1; Job i. 1. The sense is that Israel was to keep the worship of the true God wholly uncontaminated by idolatrous pollutions.

15—19. On this passage see Note at end of chapter.

15. *a Prophet*] Cf. St John i. 45, v. 45—47. On the Hebrew word (*nābhī*) see Introd. to Numbers, § 4.

unto him ye shall hearken] Cf. St Matt. xvii. 5.

16. *in the day of the assembly*] Cf. Chap. ix. 10 and Ex. xx. 19.

18. *like unto thee*] Cf. Heb. iii. 2 sqq.

he shall speak unto them all that I shall command him] Cf. St John iv. 25, viii. 28, xii. 49, 50, and reff.

19. *I will require it of him*] In Acts iii. 23, "shall be destroyed from among the people;" see note there.

20. *the prophet, which shall presume*, &c.] Cf. xiii. 1—5 and notes; and Jer. xxviii. 15—17.

21 And if thou say in thine heart, How shall we know the word which the LORD hath not spoken?

22 When a prophet speaketh in the name of the LORD, if the thing follow not, nor come to pass, that *is* the thing which the LORD hath not spoken, *but* the prophet hath spoken it presumptuously: thou shalt not be afraid of him.

---

21. *And if thou say in thine heart, How, &c.*] The passage evidently assumes such an occasion for consulting the prophet as was usual amongst the heathen, *e.g.* an impending battle or other such crisis (cf. 1 K. xxii. 11), in which his veracity would soon be put to the test. Failure of a prediction is set forth as a sure note of its being "presumptuous." But from xiii. 2 sqq. we see that the fulfilment of a prediction would not decisively accredit him who uttered it: for the prophet or dreamer of dreams who endeavoured on the strength of miracles to seduce to idolatry was to be rejected and punished. Nothing therefore *contrary* to the revealed truth of God was to be accepted under any circumstances.

NOTES on CHAP. XVIII. 3, 8, 15—18.

On *v.* 3.

The command given in *vv.* 1 and 2 that the priests and Levites should have no inheritance in Canaan as the other tribes had, is clearly repeated, indeed almost verbatim, from Numbers. Neither can it fairly and consistently be denied that the provision here made has in view the regulations of the earlier books on the subject: cf. Ex. xxix. 26—28; Lev. vii. 31—34, and x. 12—15; Num. vi. 20, and xviii. 11—18. Yet in those passages throughout the portions assigned to the priest are "the wave-breast and the heave-shoulder," or more properly "heave-leg." Here, on the contrary, the priest is to have "the shoulder," *i.e.* the fore-quarter (זרע), not apparently the same with the "heave-shoulder" (שוק) of Lev. vii. 34; the two jaws or cheeks; and "the maw," LXX. *ἤνυστρον*. By the latter is usually and correctly understood the lower or fourth stomach of ruminant animals, which was esteemed as a dainty by the ancients. Cf. Gesen. 'Thesaur.' s. v.

The question is whether the portions assigned to the priest in this place are so in *substitution* for those named Lev. vii., or in *addition* thereto?

The former view is taken by a large class of commentators, who regard the provision here made for the priests as much more slender than that in the earlier books, and see in the difference a token that Deut. was written at a late date, when the Levitical priesthood had declined in estimation, and had to be content with reduced revenues.

But the following considerations must be borne in mind: (1) The passage opens, *vv.* 1 and 2, by emphatically presenting the priests and Levites as standing in need of some special provision after the settlement in Canaan had assigned possessions of land to the other tribes. (2) That certain perquisites hitherto enjoyed by the priests would fail after the necessary abolition (cf. ch. xii. 15) of the command given in Levit. xvii. to slay animals nowhere save at the door of the Tabernacle. (3) "The shoulder" and "the maw" were not esteemed inferior pieces, but on the contrary amongst the choicest. (4) That *v.* 4 incontrovertibly provides a new item of income for the priests, viz. "the first fleece of thy sheep," cf. Num. l. c. (5) A distinction seems clearly intended between "the firings of the Lord and His inheritance" in *v.* 1, which would include "the wave breast and the heave shoulder," and "the priests' due from the people," *v.* 3, *i.e.* the shoulder, the cheeks, and the maw, which were to be given by the people to the priest out of their own portion or "inheritance." (6) It appears historically that in later times the priest had a recognized claim to some other portions of the victims slain than the wave-breast and heave-shoulder; cf. 1 S. ii. 13—16 and note.

On the whole then there seems to be nothing in the passage to point to a lower estimation of the priests than that suggested by the preceding books; nor can it fairly be regarded as substituting for the more generous allowance of old laws a scantier provision, the best that later and less religious days admitted of. On the contrary its tenor and contents clearly point to the conclusion (adopted by Keil, Schultz, Wordsworth, &c.), that "the shoulder, cheeks, and maw" were to be given by the people to the priests *in addition to* those portions claimed by the laws of Levit. as belonging to the Lord. Just so (cf. Num. vi. 19, 20) the Nazarite, when the days of his separation were complete, had to give to the priest "the sodden shoulder" (*i.e.* the fore-quarter) in addition to "the wave-breast and the heave-shoulder."

On *v.* 8.

The words לבד ממכריו על האבות, though their general sense seems clear (see foot-note), are in a grammatical point of view perplexing. The anomalies contained in them are such as to suggest a suspicion that the text is corrupt. (1) לבד everywhere else when used as a prep. is accompanied by מן. Possibly, as Wogue suggests, the מן is here omitted because of the double מ of the word following. (2) The expression ממכריו על is without parallel and hardly intelligible. Wogue compares with it the French idiom "vendre sur son bien." (3) The words על האבות must evidently be an elliptical expression for על בית אבתיו, which would mean "at the house of his fathers."

On *vv.* 15—18.

The ancient Fathers of the Church have generally regarded our Lord as the Prophet promised in these *vv.*; and this view has been adopted by most Lutheran Commentators as well as by many Roman Catholics and Anglicans.

On the contrary many of the mediæval Jewish authorities (Maimonides, Kimchi, Lipmann, &c.) refer it to the prophetical order at large, denying any reference, or at least any special reference, to the Messiah. Yet it is evident from the New Testament alone that the Messianic interpretation was the accredited one amongst the Jews at the beginning of the Christian era. Setting aside passages such as St Luke xxiv. 27; St John i. 21 and 45, in which it is perhaps uncertain whether Deut. xviii. 15 sqq. is alluded to at all, or at least whether it alone is so, it is certainly directly cited Acts iii. 22 sqq. and vii. 37. On it no doubt the Samaritans, who received the Pentateuch only, grounded their expectation of a Messiah; cf. St John iv. 25; nor can our Lord Himself, when He declares that Moses "wrote of Him" (St John v. 45—47), be supposed to have any other words in view than these, the only words in which Moses, speaking in his own person, gives any prediction of the kind. In these passages no attempt is made to prove the Messianic interpretation, nor any to challenge it. It is taken for granted on all hands. Polemical considerations would therefore seem in this, as in some other passages, to have induced later Jewish interpreters to depart from the judgment of their forefathers.

Yet though the Messianic interpretation is thus correct, and even primarily intended, yet it seems of itself not to be exhaustive of the pregnant clauses before us. The tenor of the passage considered as a whole points to a series of prophets to be raised up as the exigencies of God's people might require as no less promised here, than is the One Divine Teacher to Whom they all gave witness. For

(1) The passage occurs amidst a series of regulations concerning the *orders* of rulers, civil and spiritual, by which the people were to be governed when settled in Canaan. In such a connexion it seems anomalous to refer the *vv.* before us to an individual exclusively.

(2) The passage is introduced by prohibitions of those "curious arts" by which the heathen sought to pry into futurity. Upon these interdicts is based a promise, the purport of which is to assure the people that all needful instruction and guidance shall be vouchsafed to them in their necessities by God Himself. But to refer Israel to a single Teacher in the distant future would not be to the purpose.

(3) To the promise Moses adds a denunciation of false prophets, and gives a test by which they might be detected. It seems then that he must in what precedes have been speaking not of a single true prophet, but of true prophets generally. Could any reference to such a contingency as that indicated in *vv.* 10—20 be suitable, or even admissible, if the context were applicable to Christ simply and exclusively?

(4) If this passage points solely to the Person of the Messiah, then the prophets are left, so far as the Law is concerned, without any recognition. Considering the important part which devolved on the prophetical order in the after history of the chosen people, and in the development and regulation of the Theocracy, this seems highly improbable.

Whilst then the reference to the Messiah must not be excluded, but rather maintained, as pre-eminently designed in the *vv.* before us, yet they seem to have a further, no less evident if subsidiary, reference to a prophetical order which should stand from time to time, as Moses had done, between God and the people; which should make known God's will to the latter; which should by its presence render it unnecessary either that God should address the people directly, as at Sinai (*v.* 16, and cf. chap. v. 25 sqq.); or that the people themselves in lack of counsel should resort to the superstitions of the heathen. It was the undeniable fulfilment of this promise which lent point to the rebuke of Elijah (2 K. i. 3, 6, 16): "Is it not because there is not a God in Israel that ye go to inquire of Baalzebub?" &c., and to the reproach of Amos, when he recounts this amongst the mercies of God (ii. 11): "And I raised up of your sons for prophets," &c. The result is well summed up in Poole's 'Synopsis:' "Ita de Prophetis ut simul de Christo præcipue et primario intelligendum."

It is argued indeed that none of the prophets could be fairly said to be "like unto" Moses; and xxxiv. 10; Num. xii. 6—8; Hebr. iii. 2, 5 are quoted in corroboration. Moses, it is urged, had no successor, in his character of legislator, or in the directness and nearness of his approach to God, except the Messiah. But the expression "like unto," *vv.* 15 and 18, hardly refers to particulars like these, and in fact finds its explanation by what follows in *v.* 18; "I will put my words in his mouth, and he shall speak unto them all that I shall command him." This explanation embodies an ordinary formula for describing the Divine communications to the prophets (cf. Num. xxiii. 5, 16; Is. li. 16; Jer. i. 9, &c.); and intimates that the future prophet was to be "like unto" Moses not necessarily in all respects, but in that now in question, viz. that he should be intermediate betwixt God and the people.

The arguments which incline us to extend the scope of the passage beyond the Person of Christ, are decisive against those who limit it to any other individual: *e.g.* David, Jeremiah (Abarbanel), or Joshua (Jarchi, Abenezra). This last view was current amongst the Jews in the time of St Augustine (cf. 'contr. Faust.' XVI. 19), and has received countenance from some modern expositors (Clericus, Ammon, &c.). Yet if the words could point solely to any one person, it would seem obvious that Joshua could not be he, since the promise is *for the future*, and Joshua had already been designated as Moses' successor (Num. xxvii. 18, 23).

The word "Prophet" (נביא) is probably here a "collective noun." "The writer regards the prophets as belonging the one to the other; or as a whole, which includes the successors of Moses, as the post-Mosaic embassy of God; and so uses the singular." Knobel *in loc.* Examples of "collective nouns" are זרע Gen. i. 15; יושב Gen. iv. 20; אב Ex. iii. 6; נצר Num. xi. 27: and מלך in the preceding chapter *vv.* 14—20 appears equivalent to the kings of Israel generally. The word נביא itself seems so used Dan. ix. 24.

The passage thus appears to contemplate, as its secondary though still momentous sense, a succession of prophets, not necessarily an uninterrupted succession, but one which should never fail in Israel's emergency. And even if it bore no further import than this it would yet *a fortiori* have a reference to the Messiah, though not to Him alone. For in proportion as we see in Him the characteristics of the Prophet most perfectly exhibited, so must we regard the promise of Moses as in Him most completely accomplished. But in fact, in the words before us Moses gives promise both of a prophetical order, and of the Messiah in particular as its chief; of a line of prophets culminating in one eminent individual. This view is supported more or less decidedly by Origen and Theodoret, by Corn. a Lapide, Menoch., Tirinus, Calvin, Grotius, Scholz, Hävern., Keil, Schultz; and especially by Reinke in a copious treatise, 'Beitr. zur Erklärung des A. T.' IV. 289—352; nor can the view of Hengstenberg, 'Christologie des A. T.' I. 110—124, be regarded as substantially different.

The question whether Moses himself had consciously in view the Person in Whom his words would find their ultimate accomplishment has nothing really to do with the exegesis of the passage. The maxim "nihil potest esse in scripto quod non in scriptore," cannot be admitted when applied to writings presupposed to be divinely inspired. We may well believe that the grammatical form of the words (the singular number of the leading noun, and the singular suffix) was overruled so as to suggest to the reflective and inquiring the expectation of One in Whom they would be most signally realized. The promise of Gen. iii. 15 presents in this as in other characteristics a striking resemblance to that here before us. Both are instances of prophecies which have had what Lord Bacon calls "springing and germinant accomplishments," *i. e.* which had partial though real accomplishments from age to age, but which awaited in the Messiah that crowning fulfilment in which their sense would be exhausted.

CHAPTER XIX.

1 *The cities of refuge.* 4 *The privilege thereof for the manslayer.* 14 *The landmark is not to be removed.* 15 *Two witnesses at the least.* 16 *The punishment of a false witness.*

1 WHEN the LORD thy God
[a] hath cut off the nations, (a chap. 12. 29.)
whose land the LORD thy God giveth
thee, and thou †succeedest them, and († Heb. *inheritest* or, *possessest.*)
dwellest in their cities, and in their
houses;
2 [b] Thou shalt separate three cities (b Exod. 21. 13. Numb. 35. 10. Josh. 20. 2.)
for thee in the midst of thy land,
which the LORD thy God giveth thee
to possess it.

CHAP. XIX. This and the next two chapters contain enactments designed to protect human life, and to impress its sanctity on Israel.

With *vv.* 1—13, which relate to the cities of refuge, cf. Ex. xxi. 13, and Num. xxxv. 9—34. The laws here given are in some particulars supplementary to those of the last-named passage.

1, 2. The three cities of refuge for the district east of Jordan had been already named. Moses now directs that when the territory on the west of Jordan had been conquered, a like allotment of three other cities in it should be made. This was done accordingly; cf. Josh. xx. 1 sqq.

3 Thou shalt prepare thee a way,
and divide the coasts of thy land,
which the LORD thy God giveth thee
to inherit, into three parts, that every
slayer may flee thither.
4 ¶ And this *is* the case of the
slayer, which shall flee thither, that
he may live: Whoso killeth his neighbour ignorantly, whom he hated not
† Heb. *from yesterday the third day.* †in time past;
5 As when a man goeth into the
wood with his neighbour to hew
wood, and his hand fetcheth a stroke
with the axe to cut down the tree,
† Heb. *iron.* and the †head slippeth from the †helve,
† Heb. *wood.* and †lighteth upon his neighbour, that
† Heb. *findeth.* he die; he shall flee unto one of those
cities, and live:
6 Lest the avenger of the blood
pursue the slayer, while his heart is
† Heb. *smite him in life.* hot, and overtake him, because the
way is long, and †slay him; whereas
† Heb. *from yesterday the third day.* he *was* not worthy of death, inasmuch
as he hated him not †in time past.

7 Wherefore I command thee, saying, Thou shalt separate three cities
for thee.
8 And if the LORD thy God [c]en- [c] chap. 12. 20.
large thy coast, as he hath sworn
unto thy fathers, and give thee all the
land which he promised to give unto
thy fathers;
9 If thou shalt keep all these
commandments to do them, which I
command thee this day, to love the
LORD thy God, and to walk ever in
his ways; [d]then shalt thou add three [d] Josh. 20. 7.
cities more for thee, beside these three:
10 That innocent blood be not
shed in thy land, which the LORD
thy God giveth thee *for* an inheritance, and *so* blood be upon thee.
11 ¶ But if any man hate his
neighbour, and lie in wait for him,
and rise up against him, and smite
him †mortally that he die, and fleeth † Heb. *in life.*
into one of these cities:
12 Then the elders of his city shall

---

3. *Thou shalt prepare thee a way*] It was the duty of the Senate to make the roads that led to the cities of refuge convenient by repairing them annually in the month Adar and removing every obstruction. No hillock was left, no river over which there was not a bridge; and the road was at least two and thirty cubits broad. At cross-roads there were posts bearing the words *Refuge*, *Refuge*, to guide the fugitive in his flight. See Surenhusius, Mishna, Vol. IV. 279. It seems as if in Is. xl. 3 sqq. the imagery were borrowed from the preparation of the ways to the cities of refuge.

5. *with the axe*] Lit. "with the iron." Note the employment of iron for tools, and cf. on iii. 11.

slippeth] On this word cf. xxviii. 40.

8, 9. The *three cities more* cannot, as Knobel, Hengstenberg, &c. maintain, be the same as those alluded to in *vv.* 2 and 7. Rather is provision here made for the anticipated enlargement of the borders of Israel to the utmost limits promised by God, from the river of Egypt to the Euphrates (Gen. xv. 18; Ex. xxiii. 31, and notes). This promise, owing to the sins of the people, received but a late fulfilment after David had conquered the Philistines, Syrians, &c.; and a transient one, for many of the conquered peoples regained independence on the dissolution of Solomon's empire. And in several districts the native inhabitants, though rendered tributary, were never dispossessed. Had Israel "succeeded" to the heathen, and "dwelt in their place" throughout all the regions assigned by God's covenant with their fathers, the nine cities of refuge, which are contemplated by the passage before us, would certainly have been needed. That nine cities and not six only are provided by the *vv.* before us is the opinion of the Jewish authorities generally, of Lyra, Gerhard, Keil, Schultz, &c. It is obvious that such a passage as this could not have been penned in the times to which rationalist critics are wont to assign Deut. No one living in those times would think of treating as a future contingency ("if the Lord thy God enlarge," &c.) an extension of territory which, at the date in question, had in fact taken place long ago and been subsequently forfeited.

11—13. Cf. Num. xxxv. 12, 24; Josh xx. 6 sqq. The elders are to act as the leaders and administrators of the people at large, *i.e.* of "the congregation," with whom the adjudication respecting the guilt of the manslayer would ultimately rest.

In these *vv.* the directions respecting the preparation of the roads to the cities of refuge, the provision of additional cities in case of an extension of territory, and the intervention of the elders as representing the congregation, are peculiar to Deut. and supplementary to the laws on the same subject given in the earlier books.

send and fetch him thence, and deliver him into the hand of the avenger
of blood, that he may die.
13 Thine eye shall not pity him,
but thou shalt put away *the guilt of*
innocent blood from Israel, that it
may go well with thee.
14 ¶ Thou shalt not remove thy
neighbour's landmark, which they of
old time have set in thine inheritance,
which thou shalt inherit in the land
that the LORD thy God giveth thee
to possess it.
15 ¶ [e]One witness shall not rise
up against a man for any iniquity, or
for any sin, in any sin that he sinneth: at the mouth of two witnesses,
or at the mouth of three witnesses,
shall the matter be established.
16 ¶ If a false witness rise up
against any man to testify against
him ‖ *that which is* wrong;

[e] chap. 17. 6. Numb. 35. 30. Matt. 18. 16. John 8. 17. 2 Cor. 13. 1. Heb. 10. 28.

‖ Or, *falling away.*

17 Then both the men, between
whom the controversy *is*, shall stand
before the LORD, before the priests
and the judges, which shall be in
those days;
18 And the judges shall make
diligent inquisition: and, behold,
if the witness *be* a false witness,
and hath testified falsely against his
brother;
19 [f]Then shall ye do unto him, as
he had thought to have done unto his
brother: so shalt thou put the evil
away from among you.
20 And those which remain shall
hear, and fear, and shall henceforth
commit no more any such evil among
you.
21 And thine eye shall not pity;
but [g]life *shall go* for life, eye for eye,
tooth for tooth, hand for hand, foot
for foot.

[f] Prov. 19. 5, 9. Dan. 6. 24.

[g] Exod. 21. 23. Lev. 24. 20. Matt. 5. 38.

---

14. As a man's life so his means of livelihood are to be held sacred; and in this connection a prohibition is inserted against removing a neighbour's landmark: cf. xxvii. 17; Prov. xxii. 28, xxiii. 10.

they of old time] Rather perhaps, "thy fathers," as LXX.; Vulg. *priores*, as the word also probably means in Is. lxi. 4. The enactment simply forbids the removal of the landmarks set up by those who should distribute the land after the conquest. The facts that the words immediately following refer to the land as yet to be acquired, ought to have precluded the allegation of Vater, Davidson, &c., that the *v.* presupposes a long abode in Canaan.

15. The rule laid down xvii. 6 as to capital charges is extended here to all accusations before a court of justice.

16—21. The passage refers generally to the crime of bearing false witness, denounced so repeatedly in the Decalogue and elsewhere; cf. Ex. xxiii. 1; Lev. xix. 16. If any traces of this crime should appear in the course of judicial proceedings, the matter was to be brought before the supreme court (cf. on xvii. 9); and the false witness on conviction punished after the rule of the lex talionis. According to the Rabbins the testimony of a single witness was in civil cases so far admitted as to oblige the accused person to purge himself by oath; in criminal cases such unsupported testimony was not only to be utterly rejected, but the person who tendered it punished for a breach of the law given in *v.* 15. But these *vv.* do not refer to the *number* of witnesses at all, but simply prescribe how a case of false witness is to be dealt with.

16. *testify against him that which is wrong*] Marg. more literally, "a falling away." The word (*sārāh*) is used xiii. 5 to signify apostasy: but here is no doubt to be understood in the wider sense of any departure from the law.

17. *both the men, between whom the controversy is*] *i.e.* the parties to the original suit, one of whom has brought forward a false witness; not (as Keil) the accused and the false witness. The supreme court is directed to summon the plaintiff and defendant, and through their evidence, and such other as might be obtained, try the suspected witness, *v.* 19; cf. Ex. xxiii. 1.

stand before the LORD, before the priests and the judges] *i.e.* before the supreme court held, as provided in chap. xvii., at the Sanctuary. The judges stood as God's representatives; to lie to them was to lie to Him. The crime of false witness therefore was to be tried on this account, as well perhaps as because of its intrinsic gravity and difficulty, in His more immediate presence.

19. Cf. Prov. xix. 5, 9; Dan. vi. 24.

21. On the lex talionis, which was observed in principle not in letter by the Jewish courts, see Ex. xxi. 23, 24.

CHAPTER XX.

1 The priest's exhortation to encourage the people to battle. 5 The officers' proclamation who are to be dismissed from the war. 10 How to use the cities that accept or refuse the proclamation of peace. 16 What cities must be devoted. 19 Trees of man's meat must not be destroyed in the siege.

WHEN thou goest out to battle against thine enemies, and
seest horses, and chariots, *and* a people more than thou, be not afraid of
them: for the LORD thy God *is* with
thee, which brought thee up out of
the land of Egypt.
2 And it shall be, when ye are
come nigh unto the battle, that the
priest shall approach and speak unto
the people,
3 And shall say unto them, Hear,
O Israel, ye approach this day unto
battle against your enemies: let not
your hearts †faint, fear not, and do — † Heb. *tender.*
not †tremble, neither be ye terrified — † Heb. *make haste.*
because of them;
4 For the LORD your God *is* he
that goeth with you, to fight for you
against your enemies, to save you.
5 ¶ And the officers shall speak
unto the people, saying, What man
is there that hath built a new house,
and hath not dedicated it? let him go
and return to his house, lest he die in
the battle, and another man dedicate it.
6 And what man *is he* that hath
planted a vineyard, and hath not *yet*
†eaten of it? let him *also* go and re- — † Heb. *made it common:* See Lev. 19. 23.
turn unto his house, lest he die in the
battle, and another man eat of it.
7 [a] And what man *is there* that — [a] chap. 24. 5.
hath betrothed a wife, and hath not
taken her? let him go and return
unto his house, lest he die in the battle, and another man take her.
8 And the officers shall speak further unto the people, and they shall
say, [b] What man *is there that is* fear- — [b] Judg. 7. 3.
ful and fainthearted? let him go and
return unto his house, lest his breth-
ren's heart †faint as well as his heart. — † Heb. *melt.*
9 And it shall be, when the offi-
cers have made an end of speaking
unto the people, that they shall make
captains of the armies †to lead the — † Heb. to be *in the head of the people.*
people.

CHAP. XX. Reverence for human life and that which tends to preserve it was the motive of the laws given in the last chapter. The same is the basis of those in this chapter. Even in time of war forbearance was to be exercised both in respect of the Israelites themselves who are levied for war (*vv.* 1—9): in respect of the enemy (*vv.* 10—15), the Canaanitish nations alone excepted (16—18): and in respect of the property of the vanquished (*vv.* 19, 20). These requirements sound indeed but small to Christian ears; but when the ferocity and mercilessness of Oriental wars in ancient times are recollected, Moses may well in this as in other respects be thought to have carried his demands on the self-control of the people to the utmost they could then bear.

1. *horses, and chariots*] The most formidable elements of an Oriental host, which the Canaanites possessed in great numbers; cf. Josh. xvii. 16; Judg. iv. 3; 1 S. xiii. 5. Israel could not match these with corresponding forces (cf. xvii. 16 notes and reff.), but having the God of battles on its side, was not to be dismayed by them. This topic of encouragement, not less than the language put into the mouth of the priest *vv.* 3, 4, assumes that every such war had the sanction of God, and was consequently just.

2. *the priest*] Not the High Priest, but one appointed for the purpose, and called, according to the Rabbins, "the Anointed of the War:" hence perhaps the expression of Jer. vi. 4, &c. "to prepare" (lit. consecrate) war. Thus Phinehas went with the warriors to fight against Midian, Num. xxxi. 6; cf. 1 S. iv. 4, 11; 2 Chron. xiii. 12.

4. *the LORD your God is he that goeth with you, to fight for you*] Cf. i. 30, iii. 22; Josh. xxiii. 10, &c.

5. *the officers*] *i.e.* the Shoterim, on whom see on Ex. v. 10.

dedicated it] Cf. Neh. xii. 27; Ps. xxx. title. The expression is appropriate, because various ceremonies of a religious kind were customary amongst the Jews on taking possession of a new house. The immunity conferred in this *v.* lasted (Joseph. 'Ant.' IV. 8. 41), like that in *v.* 7 (cf. xxiv. 5), for a year.

6. *hath not yet eaten of it*] Hebrew as marg. "hath not made it common." The fruit of newly planted trees was set apart from common uses for four years (Lev. xix. 23 sqq.).

9. *they shall make captains of the armies to lead the people*] Marg. more literally "in the head of the people." The meaning is that

10 ¶ When thou comest nigh unto a city to fight against it, then proclaim peace unto it.

11 And it shall be, if it make thee answer of peace, and open unto thee, then it shall be, *that* all the people *that is* found therein shall be tributaries unto thee, and they shall serve thee.

12 And if it will make no peace with thee, but will make war against thee, then thou shalt besiege it:

13 And when the LORD thy God hath delivered it into thine hands, thou shalt smite every male thereof with the edge of the sword:

14 But the women, and the little ones, and [c] the cattle, and all that is in the city, *even* all the spoil thereof, shalt thou † take unto thyself; and thou shalt eat the spoil of thine enemies, which the LORD thy God hath given thee.

15 Thus shalt thou do unto all the cities *which are* very far off from thee, which *are* not of the cities of these nations.

16 But of the cities of these people, which the LORD thy God doth give thee *for* an inheritance, thou shalt save alive nothing that breatheth:

17 But thou shalt utterly destroy them; *namely*, the Hittites, and the Amorites, the Canaanites, and the Perizzites, the Hivites, and the Jebusites; as the LORD thy God hath commanded thee:

18 That they teach you not to do after all their abominations, which they have done unto their gods; so should ye sin against the LORD your God.

19 ¶ When thou shalt besiege a city a long time, in making war against it to take it, thou shalt not destroy the trees thereof by forcing an axe against them: for thou mayest eat of them, and thou shalt not cut them down (‖ for the tree of the field *is* man's *life*) † to employ *them* in the siege:

20 Only the trees which thou knowest that they *be* not trees for meat, thou shalt destroy and cut them down; and thou shalt build bulwarks against the city that maketh war with thee, until † it be subdued.

[c] Josh. 8. 2.

† Heb. *spoil.*

‖ Or, *for, O man, the tree of the field* is *to be employed in the siege.*

† Heb. *to go from before thee.*

† Heb. *it come down.*

---

the "officers" (see on *v.* 5) should then subdivide the levies, and appoint leaders of the smaller divisions thus constituted. See Note at end of the chapter.

10—20. Directions intended to prevent wanton destruction of life and property in sieges.

10. Cf. 2 S. xx. 18—20. It appears from this *v.* that when towns surrendered peaceably not even the armed men in it were to be put to death: and from the following *vv.* that in those taken by storm males only might be killed.

13. *smite every male*] Cf. Num. xxxi. 7.

14. *the spoil of thine enemies*] Cf. Josh. viii. 2, xxii. 8.

15—18. Such forbearance, however, was not to be shown towards the Canaanitish nations, which were to be utterly exterminated; cf. vii. 1—4.

16. *thou shalt save alive nothing that breatheth*] *i.e.* kill every human being. The command did not apply to beasts as well as men; cf. Josh. xi. 11 and 14.

19. *thou shalt not cut them down (for the tree of the field is man's life) to employ them in the siege*] The A. V. here follows the interpretation of Abenezra. The words of the parenthesis may be more literally rendered "for man is a tree of the field," *i.e.* has his life from the tree of the field, is supported in life by it: cf. xxiv. 6. The parenthesis itself may be compared with xii. 9. On this difficult passage see Note at the end of the chapter.

man's life] *i.e.* the sustenance and support of life. The phrase is used again xxiv. 6, ("No man shall take the nether or the upper millstone to pledge, for he taketh a man's life to pledge") but the Hebrew there has "life" only, whilst here it has "man" only. The A. V. however seems on the whole to exhibit correctly the sense of the passage. See Note at the end of the chapter. The Egyptians seem invariably to have cut down the fruit-trees in war. Thus in the 30th year of Thotmes III. the king invaded the Rutens, "coupant tous ses arbres et détruisant son blé," Brugsch, 'Hist. d'Egypte,' p. 101; and ages before this in an expedition against the Herusha, probably a people of Asia, the army of Pepi, of the VIth dynasty, cut down the fig trees and the vines. De Rougé, "Recherches sur les Monuments de l'Egypte," p. 125. (These references have been supplied by the Editor, Rev. Canon Cook.)

20. *cut them down*] Cf. Jer. vi. 6.

until it be subdued] Marg. literally "come down." On the word cf. xxviii. 52.

NOTES on Chap. xx. 9, and on 19, 20.

v. 9.

The word "captains" (שרי) in this *v.* may grammatically be either subject or object. The A. V. takes it to be the latter, after LXX., Onkelos, Saad., Keil, Knobel, Wogue, &c. The other construction is however adopted by Vulg., Syr., Masius, Clericus, Schultz, &c., and would give the sense "the captains at the head of the people shall array them." But no instance can be produced of the verb פקד being used without an object; and שרי, if the subject of the sentence, ought to have the article.

vv. 19, 20.

The A. V. assumes a parenthesis in the former of these *vv.*; but a large class of commentators reject this expedient, and connect the latter clauses of the *v.* 19 closely with the immediately preceding context. Of these some (the LXX., Jarchi, Clericus, Ewald, Knobel, Keil) render the clauses in question as interrogative: "For is the tree of the field a man that it should be besieged before thee?" But this sense requires, as its advocates generally allow, an alteration in the punctuation, the substitution of ה interrogative (*i.e.* הֲ) for the article (הָ) in the word האדם. Others arrive at much the same sense by carrying on a negative from the preceding words: "For the tree of the field is not a man to go before thee (*i. e.* stand as an adversary to thee) in the siege." This rendering, though favoured by old expositors of weight (the Vulgate, Onkelos, Abarbanel, Luther, Grotius), has deservedly been neglected by the moderns. The interpolation of the negative from the earlier part of the verse is harsh, and unexampled, and the natural order of the words, according to which האדם is clearly the subject, is inverted. To command a fruit-tree to be spared because it is "not a man," seems absurd, and irrelevant also, since the same might be said of trees which are not "trees for meat."

Our margin (so de Dieu) suggests a fourth view. Taking the ה as the sign of the vocative, it gives the sense of the latter part of the verse thus; "for, O man, the tree of the field is to be employed in the siege." But, passing by the fact that ה "cum vi exclamandi" is out of place in didactic and plain prose narration, the criticism of Frommann (apud Rosenmüller 'Scholia' and Barrett's 'Synopsis' *in loc.*) seems convincing; viz. that since the command to cut down unproductive trees is given clearly and expressly in the next *v.*, it is not likely that Moses should have given an otiose, and it might be added obscure, repetition of it in this.

Schroeder ('Janua Hebr.' *in loc.*) ingeniously proposes to remove the Athnakh from its present place after תכרת to a new position after האדם, and to render thus: "thou shalt not cut down them (*i. e.* the trees) but men only."

On the whole it seems best to retain the rendering of the A. V. In face of the fact that *v.* 20 manifestly deals with the case of trees that are "not for meat," it seems natural to regard the trees spoken of in *v.* 19 as those which are for meat. So substantially render Abenezra, Frommann, Rosenmüller, Dathe, Vater, Baumgarten, Schultz, Herxheimer, &c.

CHAPTER XXI.

1 *The expiation of an uncertain murder.* 10 *The usage of a captive taken to wife.* 15 *The firstborn is not to be disinherited upon private affection.* 18 *A stubborn son is to be stoned to death.* 22 *The malefactor must not hang all night on a tree.*

IF *one* be found slain in the land
which the LORD thy God giveth
thee to possess it, lying in the field,
and it be not known who hath slain
him:
2 Then thy elders and thy judges
shall come forth, and they shall measure unto the cities which *are* round
about him that is slain:
3 And it shall be, *that* the city

Chap. XXI. The sanctity of human life is still the leading thought; cf. the introductory words to chapters xix. and xx.; and where a corpse is found "lying in the field, and it be not known who hath slain him," the whole land is regarded as guilty before God (*v.* 8) until a solemn rite of expiation be gone through. *Vv.* 1—9 of this chapter prescribe the mode and form of this expiation; which from the nature of the case could have place only when the people were settled in Canaan, and so is prescribed first in Deuteronomy.

2. *thy elders and thy judges*] *i.e.* the elders and judges of the neighbouring cities; cf. Joseph. 'Ant.' IV. 8. The elders represented the citizens at large, the judges the magistracy, whilst "the priests the sons of Levi," *v.* 5, *i.e.* some priests from the nearest priestly town, were likewise to be at hand. Thus all classes were represented at the purging away

which is next unto the slain man, even the elders of that city shall take an heifer, which hath not been wrought with, *and* which hath not drawn in the yoke;

4 And the elders of that city shall bring down the heifer unto a rough valley, which is neither eared nor sown, and shall strike off the heifer's neck there in the valley:

5 And the priests the sons of Levi shall come near; for them the LORD thy God hath chosen to minister unto him, and to bless in the name of the LORD; and by their †word shall every controversy and every stroke be *tried:*

† Heb. *mouth.*

6 And all the elders of that city, *that are* next unto the slain *man*, shall wash their hands over the heifer that is beheaded in the valley:

7 And they shall answer and say, Our hands have not shed this blood, neither have our eyes seen *it.*

8 Be merciful, O LORD, unto thy people Israel, whom thou hast redeemed, and lay not innocent blood †unto thy people of Israel's charge. And the blood shall be forgiven them.

† Heb. *in the midst.*

9 So shalt thou put away the *guilt of* innocent blood from among you, when thou shalt do *that which is* right in the sight of the LORD.

10 ¶ When thou goest forth to war against thine enemies, and the LORD thy God hath delivered them into thine hands, and thou hast taken them captive,

11 And seest among the captives a beautiful woman, and hast a desire unto her, that thou wouldest have her to thy wife;

12 Then thou shalt bring her home to thine house; and she shall shave her head, and ‖pare her nails;

‖ Or, *suffer to grow.* Heb. *make,* or, *dress.*

13 And she shall put the raiment of her captivity from off her, and shall

---

of that blood-guiltiness which until removed attached to the whole community.

3. *an heifer, which hath not been wrought with*] The requirements as regards place and victim are symbolical. The heifer represented the murderer, so far at least as to die in his stead, since he himself could not be found. As bearing his guilt then the heifer must be one which was of full growth and strength, and had not yet been ceremonially profaned by human use (cf. Ex. xx. 25). The Christian commentators find here a type of Christ and of His sacrifice for man: but the heifer was not strictly a sacrifice or sin-offering. The transaction was rather figurative, and was so ordered as to impress the lesson of Gen. ix. 5. When the real culprit escaped justice there must be at least a symbolical infliction of the due penalty, ere the innocent blood could be deemed to be expiated. According to the Rabbinists (see Saalschütz, 'Mos. Recht.' p. 548) the murderer, if subsequently apprehended, would be liable to his proper punishment, notwithstanding the performance of this legal expiation.

4. *rough valley*] On these words see Note at end of chapter.

eared] *i.e.* ploughed, as in 1 S. viii. 12; Is. xxx. 24. The word is derived from the Latin "arare," and is in frequent use by English writers of the fifteenth and two following centuries: cf. *e.g.* Skakespeare, 'Ant. and Cleop.' I.

"Menecrates and Menas, famous pirates,
Make the sea serve them, which they ear and plough
With keels."

strike off the heifer's neck] Rather, "break its neck," as the same word is rendered Ex. xiii. 13. The mode of killing the victim distinguishes this lustration from the sin-offering, in which there would be of course shedding and sprinkling of the blood.

5. The presence of the priests seems required as the representatives of their order in the state. They would also see that the rite was regularly performed, and accredit it when it had been so. They do not appear to have any direct part assigned them in it, perhaps in order to mark more clearly that no sacrifice, properly so called, was being offered.

10 sqq. The regulations which now follow in the rest of this and throughout the next chapter bring out the sanctity of various personal rights and relations fundamental to human life and society. Mere existence, which has been guarded in the laws preceding, is valueless unless with it be secured also the use and enjoyment of its blessings and privileges.

10—14. The usage of a captive taken to wife. The war supposed here is one against the neighbouring nations after Israel had utterly destroyed the Canaanites, cf. vii. 3, and taken possession of their land: cf. on xxi.

12. *pare her nails*] Marg. "make" or "dress" or "suffer to grow." Our trans-

remain in thine house, and bewail her
father and her mother a full month:
and after that thou shalt go in unto
her, and be her husband, and she shall
be thy wife.
14 And it shall be, if thou have no
delight in her, then thou shalt let her
go whither she will; but thou shalt
not sell her at all for money, thou
shalt not make merchandise of her,
because thou hast humbled her.
15 ¶ If a man have two wives,
one beloved, and another hated, and
they have born him children, *both*
the beloved and the hated; and *if*
the firstborn son be hers that was
hated:
16 Then it shall be, when he maketh his sons to inherit *that* which he
hath, *that* he may not make the son
of the beloved firstborn before the son
of the hated, *which is indeed* the firstborn:
17 But he shall acknowledge the
son of the hated *for* the firstborn, by
giving him a double portion of all
†that he hath: for he *is* the beginning
of his strength; the right of the firstborn *is* his.

† Heb. *that is found with him.*

18 ¶ If a man have a stubborn and
rebellious son, which will not obey
the voice of his father, or the voice of
his mother, and *that*, when they have
chastened him, will not hearken unto
them:
19 Then shall his father and his
mother lay hold on him, and bring
him out unto the elders of his city,
and unto the gate of his place;
20 And they shall say unto the elders of his city, This our son *is* stubborn and rebellious, he will not obey
our voice; *he is* a glutton, and a
drunkard.
21 And all the men of his city
shall stone him with stones, that he
die: so shalt thou put evil away from
among you; and all Israel shall hear,
and fear.
22 ¶ And if a man have commit-

---

lators appear to have been uncertain of the exact sense. The Christian expositors both ancient and modern have generally adopted the rendering given by A. V.: the Jewish for the most part prefer the opposite one given in the first place by the margin. The question must be determined by our view of the general purpose of these directions. We can scarce doubt that the shaving the head (a customary sign of purification, Lev. xiv. 8; Num. viii. 7), and the putting away "the garment of her captivity," must be designed to signify the translation of the woman from the state of a heathen and a slave to that of a wife amongst the covenant people. Consistency seems then to require that she should "pare," not "suffer to grow," her nails; and thus, so far as possible, lay aside all belonging to her condition as an alien. This rendering of the word is strongly supported by 2 S. xix. 24. The Rabbins consider that the intention of the legislator is to deform the woman, and so deter the man from an alliance which was not to be encouraged though it might be under regulations permitted; an idea quite against the spirit of the passage.

13. *bewail her father and her mother a full month*] This is prescribed from motives of humanity, that the woman might have time and leisure to detach her affections from their natural ties, and prepare her mind for new ones.

14. *thou shalt not make merchandise of her*] Rather, **thou shalt not constrain her**: lit. "treat her with constraint," or "treat her as a slave." The same form occurs again xxiv. 7, and there only, and apparently in the same sense. Selling the woman had been forbidden just before.

15—17. On the rights of primogeniture see Gen. xxv. Moses did not originate these rights, but recognized them, since he found them pre-existing in the general social system of the East. Paternal authority could set aside these rights on just grounds (Gen. xxvii. 33), but is forbidden here to do so from mere partiality.

18—21. The incorrigible son, whom milder measures failed to reclaim, was to be denounced by his parents to "the elders;" and stoned at the gate of the city (cf. on the place of execution xvii. 5). The Elders acted as magistrates in causes of a domestic character (cf. note on xvi. 18). The formal accusation of parents against a child was to be received without inquiry, as being its own proof. Thus the just authority of the parents is recognized and effectually upheld (cf. Ex. xx. 12, xxi. 15, 17; Lev. xx. 9), but the extreme and irresponsible power of life and death, conceded by the law of Rome and other heathen nations, is withheld from the Israelite father. In this, as in the last law, provision is made against the abuses of a necessary authority.

ted a sin worthy of death, and he be to be put to death, and thou hang him on a tree:

23 His body shall not remain all night upon the tree, but thou shalt in any wise bury him that day; (for [a]he that is hanged *is* [†]accursed of God;) that thy land be not defiled, which the LORD thy God giveth thee *for* an inheritance.

[a] Gal. 3. 13.
† Heb. *the curse of God.*

22, 23. Command has been given to "put away evil" by the death of the offender. A caution follows as to the fulfilment of the command. If the criminal, as a further punishment, were condemned to be hanged, which would only be after death (see Note at end of chapter), then the body was not to "remain all night upon the tree," because that instead of cleansing the land would defile it anew (cf. Josh. viii. 29, x. 26).

23. *he that is hanged is accursed of God*] Cf. Gal. iii. 13, and Note at end of chapter.

NOTES on CHAP. XXI. 4, and 23.

v. 4.

The words נחל איתן have been by most modern commentators (Gesenius, Knobel, Keil, Schultz, &c.) and by some few Jewish ones (*e.g.* Maimonides, Abarbanel) rendered "a constant, or perennial stream." This sense is supported by Amos v. 24, where A. V. renders the words "a mighty stream;" as well as by the primary sense of the word איתן (cf. Jer. xlix. 19, l. 44); but the sequel of the *v.* which specifies that the נחל shall be one that is "neither eared" (*i.e.* worked, ploughed) "nor sown," seems against it. For a perennial stream of course could not be eared or sown. The A. V. therefore has correctly adhered to the ancient rendering, which is that of LXX., Vulg., Onkelos, Saadia, and of Wogue, amongst later authorities. The word נחל means sometimes a torrent, sometimes a gorge or valley. In Gen. xxvi. 17, 19, *e.g.* it must evidently be rendered as here simply "valley." The word איתן primarily meaning "firm," "strong;" applied to a valley would import "barren" or "rocky:" cf. Num. xxiv. 21.

v. 23.

There were four methods of execution in use amongst the ancient Jews; stoning (Ex. xvii. 4; Deut. xiii. 10, &c.), burning (Lev. xx. 14; xxi. 9), the sword (Ex. xxxii. 27), and strangulation. The latter, though not named in Scripture, is regarded by the Rabbins as the most common, and the proper one to be adopted when no other is expressly enjoined by the law. Suspension, whether from cross, stake, or gallows, was not used as a mode of taking life, but in cases of peculiar atrocity was sometimes added after death as an enhancement of punishment; and according to the Rabbins for the crimes of idolatry and cursing God only (cf. Saalschütz, 'Mos. Recht,' p. 461). Pharaoh's chief baker (Gen. xl. 19) was hanged after being put to death by the sword; and similarly Joshua appears (Jos. x. 26) to have dealt with the five kings who made war against Gibeon (cf. also Josh. viii. 29; 1 S. xxxi. 10; 2 S. xxi. 6, 9, 12). The command Num. xxv. 4, 5, appears to mean that the rebels should be first slain and then impaled or nailed to crosses; the word translated "hang" there (הוקע) being diverse from the one (תלוי) in the passage of Deut. before us, and signifying *to be torn or dislocated* (cf. Ges. and Fürst *sub v.* and note on Num. l. c.).

The grounds of the emphatic detestation expressed in the text against him that is hanged are variously stated; and will depend in some degree on the exact rendering of the words. For as Professor Lightfoot ('on Galatians,' p. 150) observes, in an important note on this text, "the case attached to קללת may denote either the person who pronounces the curse, as Judg. ix. 57, or the person against whom the curse is pronounced, as Gen. xxvii. 13; in other words, it represents either a subjective or an objective genitive. As we assign one or other sense therefore to the dependent case, we get two distinct interpretations" (or rather classes of interpretation). These are

(1) "He that is hanged is accursed by God:" a rendering adopted in substance by the LXX., Vulg., Syr.; by St Paul, Gal. iii. 13; and, as might be expected in consequence, by nearly all Christian translators and commentators. The purport of the passage would then be: "Bury him that is hanged out of the way before evening: his hanging body defiles the land; for God's curse rests on it." The curse of God is probably regarded as lying on the malefactor because from the fact of his being hanged he must have been guilty of a peculiarly atrocious breach of God's covenant. Such an offender could not remain on the face of the earth without defiling it (cf. Lev. xviii. 25, 28; Num. xxxv. 34). Therefore after the penalty of his crime had been inflicted, and he had hung for a time as a public example, the holy land was to be at once and entirely delivered from his presence. The notion of a physical pollution of the land from the unseemly consequences of lengthened exposure on the gibbet (Michaelis, 'Mos. Recht') seems unsuitable.

(2) "He that is hanged is a curse (*i.e.* an insult, injury or mockery) to God." This rendering has been, according to Professor Lightfoot, 'Galatians,' l. c., "the popular Jewish interpretation at all events from the second century of the Christian era." It is not however supported by the ancient Targum of Onkelos, or that of Palestine, or by Saadia. Its idea is well explained by Jarchi *in loc.* (edit. Breithaupt): "Suspensio est vilipensio sive contemptus regis cælestis, quoniam homo factus est ad similitudinem imaginis ejus." With which may be compared the reason (Deut. xxv. 3) assigned for limiting the number of stripes to forty. The explanation of others (Saalschütz, 'Mos. Recht,' p. 461), that the continued suspension of the body would be profaneness towards God because it would keep in sight and in mind the sin for which the malefactor suffered, is unlikely; and not less so that other which referring to the etymology rather than the usage of קללת (from קלל "to be light"), renders "quia alleviatio Dei suspensus; hoc est quando reus suspensus est hoc Deo sufficit, et alleviatur ira ejus" (apud Gerhard, p. 1286). Other Jews (Onk., Saad., &c.) consider "a curse of God" to be equivalent to "because he cursed God," that being a crime for which hanging after death was especially adjudicated. But this, as Bishop Patrick (*in loc.*) observes, though a reason for hanging the malefactor, is no reason why he should be taken down from the gallows.

On the whole there can be no doubt that the former rendering, that of LXX., and followed by St Paul, is the original and correct one; yet the other construction, fairly supported as it is by grammar and analogy, not without some (though comparatively late) Jewish authority, and followed also by a few Christian commentators (Masius, Menochius, Grotius, &c.), deserves at least discussion. It is however neglected by the moderns generally (*e.g.* Knobel, Keil, Schultz).

On the quotation of this text by St Paul, Gal. iii. 13, and his application of it, see note on that place.

The supposition of St Jerome, that this text had been tampered with by the Jews, seems grounded only on the omission by St Paul of the words "of God." Yet all MSS. and LXX. have these words. See note on Gal. l.c.

CHAPTER XXII.

1 *Of humanity toward brethren.* 5 *The sex is to be distinguished by apparel.* 6 *The dam is not to be taken with her young ones.* 8 *The house must have battlements.* 9 *Confusion is to be avoided.* 12 *Fringes upon the vesture.* 13 *The punishment of him that slandereth his wife.* 20, 22 *Of adultery,* 25 *of rape,* 28 *and of fornication.* 30 *Incest.*

[a] Exod. 23. 4.

THOU [a]shalt not see thy brother's ox or his sheep go astray,
and hide thyself from them: thou
shalt in any case bring them again
unto thy brother.
2 And if thy brother *be* not nigh
unto thee, or if thou know him not,
then thou shalt bring it unto thine
own house, and it shall be with thee
until thy brother seek after it, and
thou shalt restore it to him again.
3 In like manner shalt thou do
with his ass; and so shalt thou do
with his raiment; and with all lost
thing of thy brother's, which he hath
lost, and thou hast found, shalt thou
do likewise: thou mayest not hide
thyself.
4 ¶ Thou shalt not see thy brother's ass or his ox fall down by the
way, and hide thyself from them:
thou shalt surely help him to lift *them*
up again.
5 ¶ The woman shall not wear
that which pertaineth unto a man,
neither shall a man put on a woman's

CHAP. XXII. On the general character of the contents of this chapter see on xxi. 10. The cases stated and provided for in *vv.* 1—12 seem selected by way of example, and belong, according to our notions, rather to ethics than to law. It is noteworthy that no penalty is annexed to the breach of these regulations. No doubt it would be the duty of the "officers" (xvi. 18) and the elders in the several cities to enforce their observance.

1—4. Cf. Ex. xxiii. 4, 5, of which these verses are an expansion.

5. *that which pertaineth unto a man*] *i.e.* not only his dress but all that specially pertains distinctively to his sex; arms, domestic and other utensils, &c., σκεύη ἀνδρὸς LXX. The word (*c'ley*) is frequently used in this comprehensive sense, for "things" or "articles" generally; cf. Ex. xxv. 39; Lev. xi. 32, xiii. 49; Is. lxi. 10, &c. Colenso is in error in stating, § 741, that it is used in the above sense only in this passage and in Ex. xxii. 7.

The design of this and the cognate laws in *vv.* 9—11 is moral. Cf. Seneca, 'Epist.' 122

garment: for all that do so *are* abomination unto the LORD thy God.
6 ¶ If a bird's nest chance to be
before thee in the way in any tree,
or on the ground, *whether they be*
young ones, or eggs, and the dam sitting upon the young, or upon the
eggs, thou shalt not take the dam
with the young:
7 *But* thou shalt in any wise let
the dam go, and take the young to
thee; that it may be well with thee,
and *that* thou mayest prolong *thy*
days.
8 ¶ When thou buildest a new
house, then thou shalt make a battlement for thy roof, that thou bring
not blood upon thine house, if any
man fall from thence.
9 ¶ Thou shalt not sow thy vineyard with divers seeds: lest the †fruit
of thy seed which thou hast sown,
and the fruit of thy vineyard, be defiled.
10 ¶ Thou shalt not plow with an
ox and an ass together.
11 ¶ [b] Thou shalt not wear a garment of divers sorts, *as* of woollen and
linen together.
12 ¶ Thou shalt make thee [c] fringes
upon the four †quarters of thy vesture,
wherewith thou coverest *thyself*.
13 ¶ If any man take a wife, and
go in unto her, and hate her,
14 And give occasions of speech
against her, and bring up an evil
name upon her, and say, I took this
woman, and when I came to her, I
found her not a maid:
15 Then shall the father of the
damsel, and her mother, take and
bring forth *the tokens of* the damsel's
virginity unto the elders of the city in
the gate:
16 And the damsel's father shall say
unto the elders, I gave my daughter
unto this man to wife, and he hateth
her;
17 And, lo, he hath given occasions of speech *against her*, saying,
I found not thy daughter a maid;
and yet these *are the tokens of* my
daughter's virginity. And they shall
spread the cloth before the elders of
the city.
18 And the elders of that city shall
take that man and chastise him;
19 And they shall amerce him in
an hundred *shekels* of silver, and give
them unto the father of the damsel,

† Heb. *fulness of thy seed.*

[b] Lev. 19. 19.

[c] Numb. 15. 38.

† Heb. *wings.*

"Nonne videntur contra naturam vivere qui commutant cum fœminis vestem?" And

"Quem præstare potest mulier galeata pudorem
Quæ fugit a sexu?" Juv. 'Sat.' VI. 252.

The distinction between the sexes is natural and divinely established, and cannot be neglected without indecorum, and consequent danger to purity. There is an Epistle of St Ambrose on this text and subject (IV. Ep. 15): cf. 1 Cor. xi. 3—15. The supposition of Maimon., followed by Spencer, 'De Leg. Heb.' and others, that reference is here made to certain practices in the idolatrous festivals, is ill supported.

6—8. These precepts are designed to cultivate a spirit of humanity. With *vv.* 6 and 7 cf. Lev. xxii. 28; ch. xxv. 4; and 1 Cor. ix. 9, 10. On *v.* 6 Gerhard appositely quotes Phocylides:

μήδε τις ὄρνιθας καλιῆς ἅμα πάντας ἑλέσθω
μητέρα δ' ἐκπρολίπῃς, ἵν' ἔχῃς πάλι τῆσδε νεόττους.

8. The roofs of houses in Palestine were flat and used for various domestic purposes: for drying linen or flax, Josh. ii. 6; for walking upon to take the air, 2 Sam. xi. 2; for prayer, Acts x. 9 &c. A battlement then was almost a necessary protection. It was to be, according to the Rabbins, at least two cubits high.

9—11. On these prohibitions cf. Lev. xix. 19. They seem all founded on the aversion to mixtures which characterizes several parts of the law of Moses. The one of *v.* 10 may be dictated also by humanity. The ox and the ass being of such different size and strength, it would be cruel to the latter to yoke them together. These two animals are named as being those ordinarily employed in agriculture; cf. Is. xxxii. 20.

12. Cf. Num. xv. 38 and note. Several commentators however understand this *v.* to refer not to wearing apparel but to the coverlet of the bed, and regard the *fringes* as strings or ribbons intended for sake of decency to tie the coverlet to the bed posts or corners of the bed. So Houbigant, Horsley, Geddes, Schultz, &c.

13—29. Certain laws respecting marriage.

18. *chastise him*] *i.e.* according to the Rabbins with stripes, not to exceed forty.

because he hath brought up an evil
name upon a virgin of Israel: and she
shall be his wife; he may not put her
away all his days.
20 But if this thing be true, *and*
the tokens of virginity be not found
for the damsel:
21 Then they shall bring out the
damsel to the door of her father's
house, and the men of her city shall
stone her with stones that she die:
because she hath wrought folly in Israel, to play the whore in her father's
house: so shalt thou put evil away
from among you.
[d] Lev. 20. 10. 22 ¶ [d] If a man be found lying
with a woman married to an hus-
band, then they shall both of them
die, *both* the man that lay with the
woman, and the woman: so shalt thou
put away evil from Israel.
23 ¶ If a damsel *that is* a virgin
be betrothed unto an husband, and
a man find her in the city, and lie
with her;
24 Then ye shall bring them both
out unto the gate of that city, and
ye shall stone them with stones that
they die; the damsel, because she
cried not, *being* in the city; and the
man, because he hath humbled his
neighbour's wife: so thou shalt put
away evil from among you.
25 ¶ But if a man find a betrothed damsel in the field, and the man
‖ force her, and lie with her: then ‖ Or, *take strong hold of her.*
the man only that lay with her shall
die:
26 But unto the damsel thou shalt
do nothing; *there is* in the damsel
no sin *worthy* of death: for as when
a man riseth against his neighbour,
and slayeth him, even so *is* this
matter:
27 For he found her in the field,
and the betrothed damsel cried, and
there was none to save her.
28 ¶ [e] If a man find a damsel *that* [e] Exod. 22. 16.
is a virgin, which is not betrothed,
and lay hold on her, and lie with her,
and they be found;
29 Then the man that lay with
her shall give unto the damsel's father
fifty *shekels* of silver, and she shall
be his wife; because he hath humbled
her, he may not put her away all his
days.
30 ¶ [f] A man shall not take his [f] Lev. 18. 8.
father's wife, nor discover his father's
skirt.

CHAPTER XXIII.

1 *Who may or may not enter into the congregation.* 9 *Uncleanness to be avoided in the host.* 15 *Of the fugitive servant.* 17 *Of filthiness.* 18 *Of abominable sacrifices.* 19 *Of usury.* 21 *Of vows.* 24 *Of trespasses.*

HE that is wounded in the stones,
or hath his privy member cut
off, shall not enter into the congregation of the LORD.

---

19. *an hundred shekels*] The fine was to be paid to the father, because the slander was against him principally as the head of the wife's family. If the damsel were an orphan the fine, according to the Rabbins, reverted to herself. The false charge might have arisen from a wanton desire to contract another marriage, and would thus be punished by the withdrawal of the right of divorce (cf. xxiv. 1, 2); or from an avaricious desire to appropriate the damsel's dowry, which was rebuked by the fine of a hundred shekels. The amount was twice as much as had to be paid by a seducer, cf. *v.* 29. False witness in other cases was punished on the principle of the "lex talionis" (cf. xix. 16 sqq.). The fact that the penalties attached to bearing false witness against a wife are fixed and comparatively light indicates, as St Augustine observes ('Quæstiones in Deut.' XXXIII.), the low estimation and position of the woman under the law.

29. The case of rape here mentioned is not identical with that of seduction provided for Ex. xxii. 16, 17. The ravisher has necessarily to marry his victim and to pay a fine.

30. Cf. xxvii. 20; Lev. xviii. 8 and xx. 11; 1 Cor. v. 1 and 13.

father's skirt]. Cf. Ruth iii. 9; Ezek. xvi. 8.

CHAP. XXIII. From the domestic relations the lawgiver now passes on to enjoin sanctity and purity in the congregation of Israel as a whole, and to lay down certain rights and duties of citizenship.

1—8. Exclusion of five classes of persons from the congregation of the Lord.

1. On the two classes named here cf. Lev. xxi. 17—24. The exclusion is however here

2 A bastard shall not enter into the congregation of the LORD; even to his tenth generation shall he not enter into the congregation of the LORD.

a Neh. 13. 1.

3 [a]An Ammonite or Moabite shall not enter into the congregation of the LORD; even to their tenth generation shall they not enter into the congregation of the LORD for ever:

4 Because they met you not with bread and with water in the way, when ye came forth out of Egypt; and [b]because they hired against thee Balaam the son of Beor of Pethor of Mesopotamia, to curse thee.

b Numb. 22. 5, 6.

5 Nevertheless the LORD thy God would not hearken unto Balaam; but the LORD thy God turned the curse into a blessing unto thee, because the LORD thy God loved thee.

6 Thou shalt not seek their peace nor their † prosperity all thy days for ever.

† Heb. *good.*

7 ¶ Thou shalt not abhor an Edomite; for he *is* thy brother: thou shalt not abhor an Egyptian; because thou wast a stranger in his land.

8 The children that are begotten of them shall enter into the congregation of the LORD in their third generation.

---

carried, in the case of persons mutilated or maimed as described in the text, further than in Lev. Such persons are not to be admitted at all into the commonwealth of Israel. Cf. Lev. xxii. 24. Amongst the Gentiles eunuchs held offices of the greatest trust. Under the theocracy, as exhibiting in their persons a mutilation of that human nature which was made in God's image, they were rejected from the covenant entirely. They could however be proselytes (cf. Acts viii. 27). The Old Test. itself foretells (Is. lvi. 3—5) the removal of this ban when under the kingdom of Messiah the outward and emblematic perfection and sanctity of Israel should be fulfilled in their inner meaning by the covenanted presence and work of the Holy Spirit in the Church.

2. *A bastard*] On this word see Note at end of chapter.

even to his tenth generation] *i.e.*, see next *v.* and Neh. xiii. 1, *for ever.* Ten is the number of perfection and completeness.

3—5. Fourthly and fifthly the Ammonite and the Moabite are for ever disqualified from admission to Israel. In this connection it seems not unlikely that there is a tacit reference to the incestuous origin of the forefathers of these nations, cf. Gen. xix. 30—38, though other reasons for the exclusion are given *vv.* 4 and 5. These reasons would be fresh in the minds of those to whom Moses was speaking, and would naturally occur to him as instances of that resistance to the Theocracy which was to be punished by perpetual rejection from its blessings. Cf. Neh. xiii. 1, 2; Lam. 1. 10. Saalschütz (p. 691) remarks that this law forbids only the naturalization of those against whom it is directed. It does not forbid their dwelling in the land; and seems to refer rather to the nations than to individuals. It was not understood at any rate to interdict marriage with a Moabitess; cf. Ruth i. 4, iv. 13. Ruth however and her sister were doubtless proselytes. Such a law would certainly never have suggested itself to the mind of a writer after the times of David, whose great-grandmother was a Moabitess.

4. *Because they met you not with bread*] Cf. ii. 29. This offence was common to the two; the next one, the hiring of Balaam, seems, from Num. xxii. 5 sqq., to have been the act of the king of Moab only. But the Moabites and the Ammonites are to be regarded as clans of the same stock rather than as two independent nations (see Smith's 'Dict. of the Bible,' s. v. *Ammon*), and as acting together in this as they did in other matters. Cf. 2 Chron. xx. 1.

6. *Thou shalt not seek their peace nor their prosperity*] Literally, "nor their good:" *i.e.* thou shalt not invite them to be on terms of amity with thee (cf. xx. 10 sqq.), nor make their welfare thy care: cf. Ezra ix. 12. There is here no injunction to hatred or retaliation: cf. on the contrary ii. 9 and 19. Later history contains frequent record of hostility between Israel and the Ammonites (cf. Judg. xi.; 1 S. xi.; 2 S. x. and xii. 26—31; 2 Chron. xx. &c.); and the Moabites (Judg. iii. 12 sqq.; 1 S. xiv. 47; 2 S. viii. 2; 2 Chron. xx. &c.).

7, 8. The Edomite, as descended from Esau a twin brother of Jacob, and the Egyptian, as of that nation which had for long shewn hospitality to Joseph and his brethren, were not to be objects of abhorrence. The Edomites had indeed shewn themselves unfriendly to Israel in refusing a passage through their land (cf. Num. xx. 18 sqq.), but had not actively resisted them, and the tie of kindred was therefore to be respected (cf. ii. 8). The oppression of the Egyptians was perhaps regarded as the act of the Pharaohs rather than the will of the people (Schultz aptly refers to Ex. xi. 2, 3); and at any rate was not to cancel the memory of preceding hospitality.

9 ¶ When the host goeth forth against thine enemies, then keep thee from every wicked thing.

10 ¶ If there be among you any man, that is not clean by reason of uncleanness that chanceth him by night, then shall he go abroad out of the camp, he shall not come within the camp:

11 But it shall be, when evening † cometh on, he shall wash *himself* with water: and when the sun is down, he shall come into the camp *again*.

† Heb. *urneth oward.*

12 ¶ Thou shalt have a place also without the camp, whither thou shalt go forth abroad:

13 And thou shalt have a paddle upon thy weapon; and it shall be, when thou † wilt ease thyself abroad, thou shalt dig therewith, and shalt turn back and cover that which cometh from thee:

† Heb. *ittest lown.*

14 For the LORD thy God walketh in the midst of thy camp, to deliver thee, and to give up thine enemies before thee; therefore shall thy camp be holy: that he see no † unclean thing in thee, and turn away from thee.

† Heb. *nakedness of any thing.*

15 ¶ Thou shalt not deliver unto his master the servant which is escaped from his master unto thee:

16 He shall dwell with thee, *even* among you, in that place which he shall choose in one of thy gates, where it † liketh him best: thou shalt not oppress him.

† Heb. *is good for him.*

17 ¶ There shall be no ‖ whore of the daughters of Israel, nor a sodomite of the sons of Israel.

‖ Or, *sodomitess.*

18 Thou shalt not bring the hire of a whore, or the price of a dog, into the house of the LORD thy God for any vow: for even both these *are* abomination unto the LORD thy God.

19 ¶ [c] Thou shalt not lend upon usury to thy brother; usury of money, usury of victuals, usury of any thing that is lent upon usury:

[c] Exod. 22. 25. Lev. 25. 36. Ps. 15. 5.

20 Unto a stranger thou mayest lend upon usury; but unto thy brother thou shalt not lend upon usury: that the LORD thy God may bless thee in all that thou settest thine hand to in the land whither thou goest to possess it.

21 ¶ [d] When thou shalt vow a vow unto the LORD thy God, thou shalt not slack to pay it: for the LORD thy God will surely require it of thee; and it would be sin in thee.

[d] Eccles. 5. 4.

22 But if thou shalt forbear to vow, it shall be no sin in thee.

23 That which is gone out of thy

---

8. *in their third generation*] *i.e.* the great-grandchildren of the Edomite or Egyptian alien: cf. Ex. xx. 5.

9—14. The sanctity of the camp is to be preserved even in time of war. Amongst others the ordinary rules of morality and religion were then relaxed:

> "Nulla fides pietasque viris qui castra sequuntur." Lucan, x. 407.

but Israel on the contrary, as needing at such a time more especially the divine help, was more especially to shun "every wicked thing," *v.* 9. The special significance of this expression is shewn in the *vv.* following. The whole passage obviously refers not to the encampments of the nation whilst passing from Egypt through the wilderness, but to future warlike expeditions sent out from Canaan.

13. *upon thy weapon*] The word rendered "weapon" occurs in this form only in this passage. The LXX. (ἐπὶ τῆς ζωνῆς) and the Vulg. would seem to have followed another reading. The words should rather be rendered "besides thy weapon."

15, 16. The case in question is that of a slave who fled from a heathen master to the holy land. It is of course assumed that the refugee was not flying from justice, but only from the tyranny of his lord. Our English law is in this point identical with the Mosaic.

17. Cf. Lev. xix. 29. Prostitution was a common part of religious observances amongst idolatrous nations, especially in the worship of Ashtoreth or Astarte: cf. Herod. I. 199.

18. Another Gentile practice, connected with the one alluded to in the preceding verse, is here forbidden. The word *dog* is figurative (cf. Rev. xxii. 15), and equivalent to the "sodomite" of the *v.* preceding. Cf. Micah i. 7; Baruch vi. 43.

19, 20. Cf. Ex. xxii. 25 sqq.; Lev. xxv. 36, 37.

lips thou shalt keep and perform; *even* a freewill offering, according as thou hast vowed unto the LORD thy God, which thou hast promised with thy mouth.

24 ¶ When thou comest into thy neighbour's vineyard, then thou mayest eat grapes thy fill at thine own pleasure; but thou shalt not put *any* in thy vessel.

25 When thou comest into the standing corn of thy neighbour, [e] then thou mayest pluck the ears with thine hand; but thou shalt not move a sickle unto thy neighbour's standing corn.

[e] Matt. 12. 1. Mark 2. 23. Luke 6. 1.

21—23. Cf. Ex. xxii. 29; Num. xxx. 2; Eccles. v. 4, 5; and the general laws of vows in Lev. xxvii.

24, 25. Cf. St Matt. xii. 1; St Luke vi. 1. The commands of Deut. xxiv. 19, 20 are of like spirit.

NOTE on CHAP. XXIII. 2.

The Hebr. word (ממזר), which only occurs again Zech. ix. 6, is of uncertain root and sense. See Gesen. s. v. The LXX. renders ἐκ πόρνης, Vulg. *de scorto natus*, and so Saad., Syr., &c. Yet it seems unlikely, since concubinage was tolerated and seduction but lightly punished under the law, that bastards in the widest sense of the term could have been excluded from the congregation. The modern Jews in fact do not so exclude them. The Rabbins therefore are probably right when they interpret the word as denoting only those born of incest or adultery. This sense, adopted by Keil, Wogue, and apparently by the author of the Book of Wisdom iii. 16, suits the context, and the probably true derivation from מזר, Arab. مزر, "to be foul" or "corrupt." Such persons spring from a connection which is against the order of nature and God.

CHAPTER XXIV.

1 *Of divorce.* 5 *A new married man goeth not to war.* 6, 10 *Of pledges.* 7 *Of manstealers.* 8 *Of leprosy.* 14 *The hire is to be given.* 16 *Of justice.* 19 *Of charity.*

WHEN a [a] man hath taken a wife, and married her, and it come to pass that she find no favour in his eyes, because he hath found † some uncleanness in her: then let him write her a bill of † divorcement, and give *it* in her hand, and send her out of his house.

[a] Matt. 5. 31. & 19. 7. Mark 10. 4.
† Heb. *matter of nakedness.*
† Heb. *cutting off.*

2 And when she is departed out of his house, she may go and be another man's *wife.*

3 And *if* the latter husband hate her, and write her a bill of divorcement, and giveth *it* in her hand, and sendeth her out of his house; or if the latter husband die, which took her *to be* his wife;

4 Her former husband, which sent her away, may not take her again to be his wife, after that she is defiled; for that *is* abomination before the LORD: and thou shalt not cause the land to sin, which the LORD thy God giveth thee *for* an inheritance.

5 ¶ [b] When a man hath taken a new wife, he shall not go out to war, † neither shall he be charged with any

[b] chap. 20. 7.
† Heb. *not any thing shall pass upon him.*

CHAP. XXIV. In this and the next ch. certain particular rights and duties, domestic, social, and civil, are treated of. The cases brought forward have often no definite connexion, and seem selected in order to illustrate the application of the great principles of the law in certain important events and circumstances.

1—5. The relations of man and wife.

1—4. Of divorce. On these verses and on the subject to which they relate, see note at end of chapter; and cf. Jer. iii. 1; St Matt. v. 31, 32 and xix. 3—9. The colon in middle of *v.* 1 and the full stops placed at the end of *vv.* 1 and 2 should be removed, and the four verses, which contain only one sentence, rendered thus: **If a man hath taken a wife &c., and given her a bill of divorcement; and** (*v.* 2) **if she has departed out of his house and become another man's wife; and** (*v.* 3) **if the latter husband hate her, then** (*v.* 4) **her former husband, &c.**

5. Cf. xx. 7. There however the be-

business: *but* he shall be free at home
one year, and shall cheer up his wife
which he hath taken.
6 ¶ No man shall take the nether
or the upper millstone to pledge: for
he taketh *a man's* life to pledge.
7 ¶ If a man be found stealing
any of his brethren of the children of
Israel, and maketh merchandise of
him, or selleth him; then that thief
shall die; and thou shalt put evil away
from among you.
Lev. 13. 8 ¶ Take heed in [c] the plague of
leprosy, that thou observe diligently,
and do according to all that the
priests the Levites shall teach you:
as I commanded them, *so* ye shall observe to do.
9 Remember what the LORD thy
Numb. 12. 10. God did [d] unto Miriam by the way,
after that ye were come forth out of
Egypt.
Heb. lend the loan of any thing to, &c. 10 ¶ When thou dost † lend thy
brother any thing, thou shalt not go
into his house to fetch his pledge.
11 Thou shalt stand abroad, and
the man to whom thou dost lend
shall bring out the pledge abroad unto
thee.
12 And if the man *be* poor, thou
shalt not sleep with his pledge:
13 In any case thou shalt deliver
him the pledge again when the sun
goeth down, that he may sleep in his
own raiment, and bless thee: and it
shall be righteousness unto thee before the LORD thy God.
14 ¶ Thou shalt not oppress an
hired servant *that is* poor and needy,
whether he be of thy brethren, or of
thy strangers that *are* in thy land
within thy gates:
15 At his day [e] thou shalt give *him* [e] Lev. 19. 13. Tob. 4. 14.
his hire, neither shall the sun go down
upon it; for he *is* poor, and † setteth † Heb. *he lifteth his soul unto it.*
his heart upon it: lest he cry against
thee unto the LORD, and it be sin
unto thee.
16 The [f] fathers shall not be put [f] 2 Kin. 14. 6. 2 Chron. 25. 4. Jer. 31. 29, 30. Ezek. 18. 20.
to death for the children, neither shall
the children be put to death for the
fathers: every man shall be put to
death for his own sin.
17 ¶ Thou shalt not pervert the
judgment of the stranger, *nor* of the
fatherless; nor take a widow's raiment to pledge:
18 But thou shalt remember that

---

trothed man is spoken of; here the newly married. The command here given was designed to endear the marriage tie, as the one last preceding was to prevent a frivolous rupture of it.

6. A precept of like tenor with that in Ex. xxii. 25, 26.

7. Cf. Ex. xxi. 16.

maketh merchandise of him] Rather, **constrain him**, *i.e.* treat him as a slave. See on xxi. 14.

8, 9. On the laws relating to leprosy see Lev. xiii. and xiv. On Miriam's rebellion see Num. xii. 10 sqq. The leprosy was "the symbol of sin, most often the theocratic punishment, the penalty for sins committed against the theocracy, as in the cases of Miriam, of Gehazi, of Uzziah" (Abp. Trench 'On the Miracles,' p. 215). The allusion to Miriam, who disobeyed the ordinances of God and was punished with leprosy for her rebellion, serves to point the injunction of *v.* 8.

10—15. Warnings against oppression of the poor.

10—13. Cf. Ex. xxii. 25—27. The creditor is forbidden to enter his debtor's dwelling, and to seize as security what he might think sufficient. He is to stand without, and leave it to the debtor to bring forth that which he could best spare. No doubt the creditor would have the right to judge whether the pledge offered were adequate or not. *Vv.* 12, 13 assume, what would be constantly the case in Palestine, that the poor debtor would have nothing to offer for pledge except his wearing apparel.

13. *it shall be righteousness unto thee*] Cf. vi. 25; Prov. xix. 17; Dan. iv. 27.

14, 15. Repeated and enlarged from Lev. xix. 13. Cf. xv. 9; St James v. 4.

16. A caution addressed to earthly judges. God, by right of his Sovereignty over all mankind, "jure dominii non pœnæ" (Grotius), threatens to visit the sins of the fathers upon the children (cf. on Ex. xx. 5); but in the dispensation of earthly justice the maxim must hold "pœna caput sequitur." Amongst other Oriental nations the family of a criminal was commonly involved in his punishment (cf. Esth. ix. 13, 14: Herod. III. 19). In Israel it was not to be so; cf. 2 K. xiv. 6; 2 Chron. xxv. 4. See also Jer. xxxi. 29, 30; Ezek. xviii. 20 and notes.

17. Cf. Ex. xxii. 21, 22, xxiii. 9.

thou wast a bondman in Egypt, and
the LORD thy God redeemed thee
thence: therefore I command thee to
do this thing.

g Lev. 19. 9. & 23. 22.

19 ¶ g When thou cuttest down
thine harvest in thy field, and hast
forgot a sheaf in the field, thou shalt
not go again to fetch it: it shall be
for the stranger, for the fatherless,
and for the widow: that the LORD
thy God may bless thee in all the
work of thine hands.
20 When thou beatest thine olive
tree, † thou shalt not go over the
boughs again: it shall be for the
stranger, for the fatherless, and for
the widow.

† Heb. *thou shalt not bough it after thee.*

21 When thou gatherest the grapes
of thy vineyard, thou shalt not glean
it † afterward: it shall be for the
stranger, for the fatherless, and for
the widow.

† Heb. *after thee.*

22 And thou shalt remember that
thou wast a bondman in the land of
Egypt: therefore I command thee to
do this thing.

---

18. Cf. Lev. xix. 33, 34.

19—22. Repeated in substance from Lev. xix. 9 sq. and xxiii. 22. The motive assigned *v.* 22 is the same as in *v.* 18 and xvi. 12.

NOTE on CHAP. XXIV. 1—4.

The A. V. is undoubtedly wrong in placing a full stop at the end of *vv.* 1 and 2. The four *vv.* form only one sentence, the first three being the protasis, &c., *v.* 4 the apodosis as is exhibited in the foot-note. Thus *v.* 4 lays down the law in the supposed case. So the LXX. and the large majority of commentators. It is thus evident that Moses neither institutes nor enjoins divorce. The exact spirit of the passage is given in our Lord's words to the Jews, St Matt. xix. 8; "Moses because of the hardness of your hearts suffered you to put away your wives." Not only does the original institution of marriage as recorded by Moses, Gen. ii. 24, set forth the perpetuity of the bond, but the *vv.* before us plainly intimate that divorce, whilst tolerated for the time, contravenes the order of nature and of God. The divorced woman who marries again is "defiled," *v.* 4, and is grouped in this particular with the adulteress; cf. Lev. xviii. 20. Our Lord then was speaking according to the spirit of the law of Moses when He declared, St Matt. xix. 9, "Whoso marrieth her that is put away doth commit adultery." He was speaking too not less according to the mind of the Prophets, cf. Mal. ii. 14—16. But Moses could not absolutely put an end to a practice which was traditional, and common to the Jews with other Oriental nations. His aim is therefore to regulate and thus to mitigate an evil which he could not extirpate. He enacts therefore in the passage before us (1) that divorce must take place not as heretofore, at the arbitrary will and pleasure of the husband, and by mere word of mouth, but upon reason given and by means of a written and formal document; (2) that the divorced wife who had married a second time shall never return to her first husband. The tendency of these laws is obvious. The former would enforce the preparation of a regular and legal instrument, which, from the nature of the case, would require time and the intervention of public authority to attest its sufficiency and its due execution. Thus a certain delay would necessarily take place, giving opportunity for reconsideration; and the interposition of the magistrates would prevent many frivolous complaints from being treated as grounds for divorce. The other law would admonish the parties that the divorce once consummated would be irreparable, and ought not therefore to be brought about rashly and lightly. It must be added too that Moses withholds the right of divorce altogether where a man slanders his wife as unchaste (xxii. 13—19), or seduces her before marriage (xxii. 28, 29).

The import of the expression "some uncleanness" (ערות דבר, lit. "the nakedness or shame of a thing,") has been variously explained. It was a well-known theme of disputation between the schools of Hillel and Shammai. The former explained it, as the Pharisees (St Matt. xix. 3) seem to have done, in a general manner, as equivalent to anything which made the woman unacceptable to her husband. And this certainly seems borne out by what is said in *v.* 3, where it appears that the second husband might divorce merely on grounds of personal dislike. The other and rival interpreters regard the terms, which are used also in the preceding ch., *v.* 14, as applicable to nothing short of immodest conduct or grave physical defect. Adultery is clearly out of the question, since that was a capital crime (cf. xxii. 20—22). Whichever school be right it is clear that the legislator felt himself constrained to leave in the husband's hands large powers as regards divorce. Humane restraints and conditions are however imposed on the exercise of that power, and the rights of the wife on her side are not forgotten. It appears from Ex. xxi. 10 that the maid sold to be "a servant," *i.e.* purchased by a man to be a wife, could quit her husband, or master, if he did not perform his duties towards her; and we can hardly doubt that the inferences drawn in much variety by the Jewish doctors (cf. Saalschütz, 'Mos. Recht,' pp. 806, 807 and notes), as to the circumstances under which a wife could enforce divorce, are in the main correct. The freewoman would certainly not be in a worse position than is secured in Ex. l.c. for the bondwoman. Our Lord's words too (St Mark x. 11 and 12) seem to imply that the right of divorce existed equally on both sides. Yet no doubt the initiation of divorce by the wife was extremely rare in the East. It was not however unknown, at any rate in later times, for Salome, the sister of Herod, divorced her husband; cf. Joseph. 'Ant.' XV. 7, and XVIII. 5, 4.

It appears that if the divorced wife did not contract a new marriage her husband might take her back. This has been the immemorial practice of the Jews; and there is certainly nothing to bar it in the passage before us or elsewhere in the law; on the contrary, the spirit of the enactments of Moses is certainly to encourage the preservation of the original tie; the prohibition of re-union in *v.* 4 is limited expressly to the case where a second marriage had been contracted.

CHAPTER XXV.

1 *Stripes must not exceed forty.* 4 *The ox is not to be muzzled.* 5 *Of raising seed unto a brother.* 11 *Of the immodest woman.* 13 *Of unjust weights.* 17 *The memory of Amalek is to be blotted out.*

IF there be a controversy between
men, and they come unto judgment, that *the judges* may judge them;
then they shall justify the righteous,
and condemn the wicked.
2 And it shall be, if the wicked
man *be* worthy to be beaten, that
the judge shall cause him to lie down,
and to be beaten before his face,
according to his fault, by a certain
number.
3 [a] Forty stripes he may give him, [a] 2 Cor. 11. 24.
and not exceed: lest, *if* he should
exceed, and beat him above these
with many stripes, then thy brother [b] 1 Cor. 9. 9.
should seem vile unto thee. 1 Tim. 5. 18.
4 ¶ [b] Thou shalt not muzzle the † Heb. *thresheth.*
ox when he † treadeth out *the corn.*
5 ¶ [c] If brethren dwell together, [c] Matt. 22. 24.
and one of them die, and have no Mark 12. 19.
child, the wife of the dead shall not Luke 20. 28.

CHAP. XXV. **1—3.** Punishment by stripes.

1, 2. These verses form grammatically only one sentence, of which *v.* 2 is the apodosis, as the LXX. correctly gives it. Remove therefore the full stop at end of *v.* 1, and render thus: (1) **If there be a controversy between men, and they come to judgment, and the judges judge them, and justify the righteous and condemn the wicked;** (2) **then it shall be**, &c.

1. *justify the righteous*] On the expression, cf. Ex. xxiii. 7; Prov. xvii. 15.

2. *worthy to be beaten*] Lit. "a son of beating," *i.e.* deserving stripes: cf. a like idiom, iii. 18: 1 S. xx. 31.

Scourging is named as a penalty Lev. xix. 20. The beating here spoken of would be on the back with a rod or stick (cf. Prov. x. 13, xix. 29, xxvi. 3).

3. *Forty stripes he may give him, and not exceed*] The Jews to keep within the letter of the law fixed 39 stripes as the maximum (cf. 2 Cor. xi. 24). Forty signifies the full measure of judgment (Keil) cf. Gen. vii. 12; Num. xiv. 33, 34; but the reason for the limitation is rather to be sought in what is added here, "lest thy brother should seem vile unto thee." The son of Israel was not to be lashed like a slave at the mercy of another. The judge was always to be present to see that the law in this particular was not overpassed.

4. Cf. 1 Cor. ix. 9; 1 Tim. v. 18; and Hos. x. 11. In other kinds of labour the oxen were usually muzzled. When driven to and fro over the threshing-floor in order to stamp out the grain from the chaff, they were to be allowed to partake of the fruits of their labours. The figurative sense of this command is drawn out by St Paul l.c. The Greeks and other heathen frequently treated their labouring animals with great inhumanity, putting sharp bits in their mouths, or keeping them for a long time without drink, before employing them on the threshing-floor. Another inhuman method of preventing them from eating whilst on the threshing-floor is mentioned by Ælian, 'Hist. An.' IV. 25. The expression βοῦς ἐπὶ σωρῷ was proverbial. (Cf. Bochart, 'Hieroz.' II. 40.) The practice of threshing by oxen has retained its hold in the East, as has likewise the humane rule of the text.

marry without unto a stranger: her
‖ husband's brother shall go in unto
her, and take her to him to wife, and
perform the duty of an husband's
brother unto her.

‖ Or, *next kinsman.*

6 And it shall be, *that* the firstborn which she beareth shall succeed
in the name of his brother *which is*
dead, that his name be not put out of
Israel.

7 And if the man like not to take
his ‖ brother's wife, then let his brother's wife go up to the gate unto
the elders, and say, [d] My husband's
brother refuseth to raise up unto his
brother a name in Israel, he will not
perform the duty of my husband's
brother.

‖ Or, *next kinsman's wife.*
[d] Ruth 4. 7.

8 Then the elders of his city shall
call him, and speak unto him: and
if he stand *to it*, and say, I like not
to take her;

9 Then shall his brother's wife
come unto him in the presence of the
elders, and loose his shoe from off his
foot, and spit in his face, and shall
answer and say, So shall it be done
unto that man that will not build up
his brother's house.

10 And his name shall be called in
Israel, The house of him that hath
his shoe loosed.

5—10. Law of levirate marriage. The law on this subject is not peculiar to the Jews, but is found (see on Gen. xxxviii. 8) in all essential respects the same amongst various Oriental nations, ancient and modern, and exists at present amongst the South African tribes (Colenso, 'Pent.' § 754); amongst the Arabians (Burckhardt, 'Notes,' I. 112); amongst the Druses (Volney, 'Travels,' II. 80); and amongst the tribes of the Caucasus, (Haxthausen's 'Transcauçasia,' p. 403). It is obvious from Gen. xxxviii., where it appears as familiar and recognized on all hands, that Moses did not originate it; and in fact the rules in these *vv.*, like those upon divorce, do but incorporate existing immemorial usages, and introduce various wise and politic limitations and mitigations of them. The root of the obligation here imposed upon the brother of the deceased husband lies in the primitive idea of childlessness being a great calamity (cf. Gen. xvi. 4, and note), and extinction of name and family one of the greatest that could happen (cf. ix. 14; Ps. cix. 12—15). To avert this the ordinary rules as to inter-marriage are in the case in question (cf. Lev. xviii. 16) set aside. The obligation was onerous (cf. Ruth iv. 6), and might be repugnant; and it is accordingly considerably reduced and restricted by Moses. It did not lie at all unless the brethren "dwell together:" *i.e.* unless they were neighbours. The surviving brother from a distant home was not to be expected to fetch the widow, or perhaps widows, and household, and take them to himself. It would seem (Ruth ii. 20, iii. 9) that the office in such cases devolved on the next neighbouring kinsman; or perhaps the term "brethren" *v.* 5 is to be understood in its more general sense as equivalent to "kinsmen." The fact that these arrangements were well understood superseded the necessity of minutely ruling such points. Moses permits escape from the marriage altogether, therein introducing apparently a new relaxation, if any brother-in-law preferred to submit to reproach; *vv.* 7, 8. In other words, the duty is recognized as one of affection for the memory of the deceased; it is not one which could be enforced at law. That it continued "in viridi observantia" down to the Christian era is apparent from St Matt. xxii. 25 sq., and the parallel passages in St Mark and St Luke.

5. *no child*] Lit. "no son." But the existence of a daughter would clearly suffice, and so the Rabbins have always understood. The daughter would inherit the name and property of the father; cf. Num. xxvii. 1—11.

9. *loose his shoe from off his foot*] In token of taking from the unwilling brother all right over the wife and property of the deceased. Planting the foot on a thing was an usual symbol of lordship and of taking possession (cf. Gen. xiii. 17; Josh. x. 24), and loosing the shoe and handing it to another in like manner signified a renunciation and transfer of right and title (cf. Ruth iv. 7, 8). Ps. lx. 8, and cviii. 9, are also to be noted here, if the expression "over Edom will I cast out my shoe," is rightly understood by the Jewish authorities generally to mean "of Edom will I take possession." Burckhardt ('Notes on the Bedouins,' I. 113) states that when a Bedouin husband divorces a runaway wife, he usually says: "she was my slipper, I have cast her off." The widow here is directed herself, as the party slighted and injured, to deprive her brother-in-law of his shoe.

spit in his face] According to the Rabbins "*before* his face." The Hebrew will bear this sense, but cf. Num. xii. 14. The action of course is intended to aggravate the disgrace conceived to attach to the conduct of the man.

10. *The house of him that hath his shoe loosed*] Equivalent to "the house of the bare-

11 ¶ When men strive together one with another, and the wife of the one draweth near for to deliver her husband out of the hand of him that smiteth him, and putteth forth her hand, and taketh him by the secrets:

12 Then thou shalt cut off her hand, thine eye shall not pity *her*.

13 ¶ Thou shalt not have in thy bag † divers weights, a great and a small.

Heb. *stone and stone.*

14 Thou shalt not have in thine house † divers measures, a great and a small.

Heb. *n ephah nd an phah.*

15 *But* thou shalt have a perfect and just weight, a perfect and just measure shalt thou have: that thy days may be lengthened in the land which the LORD thy God giveth thee.

16 For all that do such things, *and* all that do unrighteously, *are* an abomination unto the LORD thy God.

Exod. 17.

17 ¶ [e] Remember what Amalek did unto thee by the way, when ye were come forth out of Egypt;

18 How he met thee by the way, and smote the hindmost of thee, *even* all *that were* feeble behind thee, when thou *wast* faint and weary; and he feared not God.

19 Therefore it shall be, when the LORD thy God hath given thee rest from all thine enemies round about, in the land which the LORD thy God giveth thee *for* an inheritance to possess it, *that* thou shalt blot out the remembrance of Amalek from under heaven; thou shalt not forget *it*.

CHAPTER XXVI.

1 *The confession of him that offereth the basket of firstfruits.* 12 *The prayer of him that giveth his third year's tithes.* 16 *The covenant between God and the people.*

AND it shall be, when thou *art* come in unto the land which the LORD thy God giveth thee *for*

---

footed one." To go barefoot was a sign of the most abject condition; cf. 2 S. xv. 30.

11, 12. The last law laid certain burdensome obligations on men for the preservation of the families of their brethren. It is now followed up by another, which imposes a severe penalty on a woman who by a shameless act should endanger or take away the hope of offspring from a man; cf. Ex. xxi. 22. The act in question was probably not rare in the times and countries for which the law of Moses was designed. It is of course to be understood that the act was wilful, and that the prescribed punishment would be inflicted according to sentence of the judges. This is the only mutilation prescribed by the Law of Moses, unless we except the retaliation prescribed as a punishment for the infliction on another of bodily injuries, Lev. xxiv. 19, 20. But that law would seldom be carried out in the letter.

13—19. Of duties towards our neighbour those which occur most frequently will be to the legislator the most important. That of honesty in trade is therefore emphatically enforced once more in conclusion (cf. Lev. xix. 35, 36). It is noteworthy that John the Baptist puts the like duties in the forefront of his preaching (cf. St Luke iii. 12 sqq.); and that "the Prophets" (cf. Ezek. xlv. 10—12; Amos viii. 8; Mic. vi. 10, 11) and "the Psalms" (Prov. xvi. 11, xx. 10, 23), not less than "the Law," specially insist on them. Every part of Scripture in fact gives much prominence to these duties.

13. *divers weights*] Lit. "a stone and a stone;" *i.e.* stones of unequal weights, the lighter to sell with, the heavier to buy with. So in Ps. xii. 2 "a heart and a heart" means "a double-heart." Stones were used by the Jews instead of brass or lead for their weights, as less liable to lose anything through rust or wear.

15. *that thy days may be lengthened in the land*] Cf. iv. 26, v. 16.

17—19. Over against those duties which are summed up in the words "thou shalt love thy neighbour as thyself," there stand however for the Jew another set of an opposite nature towards the enemies of God and His kingdom. It was not after the spirit or mission of the Law (cf. St Luke ix. 55, 56) to aim at overcoming inveterate opposition by love and by attempts at conversion. The law taught God's hatred of sin and of rebellion against Him by enjoining the extinction of the obstinate sinner. The Amalekites were a kindred people (Gen. xxxvi. 15, 16); and living as they did in the peninsula of Sinai, they could not but have well known the mighty acts God had done for His people in Egypt and the Red Sea; yet they manifested from the first a persistent hostility to Israel (cf. Ex. xvii. 8, and note; Num. xiv. 45). They provoked therefore the sentence

an inheritance, and possessest it, and dwellest therein;

2 That thou shalt take of the first of all the fruit of the earth, which thou shalt bring of thy land that the LORD thy God giveth thee, and shalt put *it* in a basket, and shalt go unto the place which the LORD thy God shall choose to place his name there.

3 And thou shalt go unto the priest that shall be in those days, and say unto him, I profess this day unto the LORD thy God, that I am come unto the country which the LORD sware unto our fathers for to give us.

4 And the priest shall take the basket out of thine hand, and set it down before the altar of the LORD thy God.

5 And thou shalt speak and say before the LORD thy God, A Syrian ready to perish *was* my father, and he went down into Egypt, and sojourned there with a few, and became there a nation, great, mighty, and populous:

---

here pronounced, which was executed at last by Saul, 1 S. xv.

CHAP. XXVI. The rehearsal of rights and duties, public and private, terminates in this chapter with two liturgical enactments. These have a clear and close reference to the whole of the preceding legislation, and form a most appropriate and significant conclusion to it. On the performance of its part of that covenant, which the previous books and chapters have set forth, Israel was to be put in possession of God's promises. When these should be realized (*v.* 1) each Israelite is directed, for himself personally and also as one of the covenant people, to make solemn acknowledgment in deed and symbol of God's faithfulness, by presentment of a basket filled with firstfruits, and in word by recitation of the solemn formula prescribed *v.* 3 and *vv.* 5—10. This thanksgiving is so worded as to express the entire dependence of the offerer and his nation upon God's grace and mercy for all they had and all they were, and to check the self-righteous temper which might under a covenant of works be expected to develop itself.

But the continuance of God's blessings was contingent on Israel's obedience. The occasion of the third tithe (*v.* 12) is accordingly appointed as one for making solemn declaration and profession on the part of each Israelite that he personally had acquitted himself of the several obligations laid by the law upon him (*vv.* 13, 14), and for prayer based upon that avowal that God on His side would be pleased still to bless His faithful people (*v.* 15).

2. *thou shalt take of the first of all the fruit of the earth*] As the fruit was visible proof of their being in possession of the land, so the presentation of the first of their fruit to God was an act of confession that they owed that blessing to Him.

On the subject of Firstfruits see note on Lev. xxiii. 10 sqq.

The firstfruits here in question are to be distinguished alike from those offered in acknowledgment of the blessings of harvest (cf. Ex. xxii. 29; Lev. xxiii. 10—17) at the feasts of Passover and Pentecost, and also from the offerings prescribed Num. xviii. 8 sqq. The latter consisted of *preparations* from the produce of the earth, such as oil, flour, wine, &c.; whilst those here meant are of the raw produce: the former were national and public offerings, those of this chapter are private and personal ones. The whole of the firstfruits belonged to the officiating priest.

On the mode in which this duty of presenting the firstfruits was actually performed see note on Lev. l. c.

5. *A Syrian ready to perish was my father*] The reference is shown by the context to be to Jacob, as the ancestor in whom particularly the family of Abraham began to develop into a nation (cf. Is. xliii. 22, 28, &c.). Jacob is called *a Syrian* (lit. Aramæan), not only because of his own long residence in Syria with Laban (Gen. xxix.—xxxi.), as our Lord was called a Nazarene because of his residence at Nazareth, but because he there married and had his children (cf. Hos. xii. 12); and might be said accordingly to belong to that more than to any other land. The designation of Jacob as a Syrian, found here only, has led some of the Targums and Versions, also Luther, and others, to render very differently, understanding the Syrian to be Laban; "A Syrian was destroying, or almost destroyed, my father:" "Syrus persequebatur patrem meum," Vulg. But this sense of the word (*ābhad*) is unparalleled. The rendering of LXX. (Συρίαν ἀπέβαλεν ὁ πατήρ μου) is singular, and irreconcileable with the present punctuation. Others render the word (*ābhad*) "wandering," as in Ps. cxix. 176 (so Gesen. 'Thesaur.,' Rosenm., Maurer, &c.). They refer, as against the rendering adopted by A. V., to the fact that Jacob, though he led a nomadic life, was yet wealthy and powerful. Our rendering of the word is

6 And the Egyptians evil entreated
us, and afflicted us, and laid upon us
hard bondage:
7 And when we cried unto the
LORD God of our fathers, the LORD
heard our voice, and looked on our
affliction, and our labour, and our oppression:
8 And the LORD brought us forth
out of Egypt with a mighty hand,
and with an outstretched arm, and
with great terribleness, and with signs,
and with wonders:
9 And he hath brought us into this
place, and hath given us this land,
even a land that floweth with milk
and honey.
10 And now, behold, I have brought
the firstfruits of the land, which thou,
O LORD, hast given me. And thou
shalt set it before the LORD thy God,
and worship before the LORD thy
God:
11 And thou shalt rejoice in every
good *thing* which the LORD thy God
hath given unto thee, and unto thine
house, thou, and the Levite, and the
stranger that *is* among you.
12 ¶ When thou hast made an end
of tithing all the tithes of thine increase the third year, *which is* [a] the
year of tithing, and hast given *it* unto
the Levite, the stranger, the fatherless, and the widow, that they may
eat within thy gates, and be filled;
13 Then thou shalt say before the
LORD thy God, I have brought away
the hallowed things out of *mine* house,
and also have given them unto the
Levite, and unto the stranger, to the
fatherless, and to the widow, according to all thy commandments which
thou hast commanded me: I have not
transgressed thy commandments, neither have I forgotten *them*:
14 I have not eaten thereof in my
mourning, neither have I taken away
ought thereof for *any* unclean *use*, nor
given *ought* thereof for the dead: *but*
I have hearkened to the voice of the

[a] chap. 14. 28.

---

however supported by Job xxix. 13; Prov. xxxi. 6, &c.; and as regards the fact, seems sufficiently sustained by the narrative of Gen. xxxi.; cf. xxxv. 3, xlii. 2, xliii. 2, 8, &c.

went down into Egypt] Cf. Gen. xlvi.

became there a nation] Cf. ch. vii. 7.

6 and 7. Cf. Ex. i., ii., and iv.

8. *the LORD brought us forth*] Cf. Ex. xii., xiii.

with signs, and with wonders] Cf. iv. 34.

9. *a land that floweth with milk and honey*] Cf. Ex. iii. 8.

11. *thou shalt rejoice*, &c.] Cf. xii. 7, 12, xvi. 11.

12. Each third year the second or vegetable tithe, instead of being taken as in other years to the Sanctuary, was to be employed at home in hospitality and charity (cf. xiv. 28, 29). The LXX. exactly give the true sense in this verse, τὸ δεύτερον ἐπιδέκατον δώσεις τῷ Λευίτῃ κ.τ.λ. But this third year's tithe, though really only the ordinary second tithe diversely applied, is usually called the third tithe (Tobit i. 7, 8; Joseph. 'Ant.' IV. 8. 22). The seventh year being Sabbatical, and no tithes being payable in it (cf. Ex. xxiii. 10 sqq.), the "third year, the year of tithing" here alluded to, would be each third and sixth of the septennial cycle. As in each of these years the whole triennial series of tithe obligations would have been completed, the Israelite is appropriately called upon, "when he had made an end of tithing the third year," to make solemn profession before God that he had discharged each and all as they fell due, and applied them as the law appointed. A strict fulfilment of the onerous and complicated tithe obligations was a leading part of the righteousness of the Pharisees: cf. St Matt. xxiii. 23.

The Jewish doctors, in full conformity with the spirit of this passage, required the faithful Israelite on the Preparation Day of Passover in each fourth and seventh year solemnly to examine himself whether he had faithfully and punctually paid all the sacred dues in the three preceding years, and to make restitution and satisfaction for all shortcomings. On the last day of Passover, at evening sacrifice, the pilgrim before he returned home was to recite before God the avowal and prayer, *vv.* 13—15 (cf. Dr Ginsburg in Kitto's 'Encycl.' art. 'Tithe:' and on the whole subject of Tithes cf. Introd. § 5).

14. *I have not eaten thereof in my mourning*] When the Israelite would be unclean, cf. Lev. vii. 20, xxi. 1 sqq.

neither have I taken away ought thereof for any unclean use] Rather perhaps, "I have not separated any of them when unclean." Vulg. very closely, "nec separavi ea in qualibet immunditia."

LORD my God, *and* have done according to all that thou hast commanded me.

[b] Isai. 63. 15.
15 [b]Look down from thy holy habitation, from heaven, and bless thy people Israel, and the land which thou hast given us, as thou swarest unto our fathers, a land that floweth with milk and honey.

16 ¶ This day the LORD thy God hath commanded thee to do these statutes and judgments: thou shalt therefore keep and do them with all thine heart, and with all thy soul.

17 Thou hast avouched the LORD this day to be thy God, and to walk in his ways, and to keep his statutes, and his commandments, and his judgments, and to hearken unto his voice:

[c] chap. 7. 6.
18 And [c]the LORD hath avouched thee this day to be his peculiar people, as he hath promised thee, and that *thou* shouldest keep all his commandments;

19 And to make thee high above all nations which he hath made, in praise, and in name, and in honour; and that thou mayest be an holy people unto the LORD thy God, as he hath spoken.

CHAPTER XXVII.

1 *The people are commanded to write the law upon stones,* 5 *and to build an altar of whole stones.* 11 *The tribes divided on Gerizim and Ebal.* 14 *The curses pronounced on mount Ebal.*

AND Moses with the elders of Israel commanded the people, saying, Keep all the commandments which I command you this day.

2 And it shall be on the day [a]when ye shall pass over Jordan unto the land which the LORD thy God giveth [a] Josh. 4.

---

nor given ought thereof for the dead] Others, as perhaps LXX. (τῷ τεθνηκότι), "to the dead," with reference apparently to the superstitious custom of placing food on or in tombs (cf. Juv. 'Sat.' v. 85, "feralis cœna"). Probably however it is the funeral expenses, and more especially the usual feast for the mourners, which are meant (cf. Jer. xvi. 7; Ezek. xxiv. 17; Hos. ix. 4; Tob. iv. 17). The dedicated things were to be employed in glad and holy feasting, not therefore for funeral banquets, for death and all associated with it was regarded as unclean.

15. Cf. Is. lxiii. 15; lxvi. 1.

16—19. A brief and earnest exhortation by way of conclusion to the second and longest discourse of the book. The people is reminded that its troth was plighted to God, as God's covenant was on His part established towards them. Moses entreats them therefore to be faithful, that God too might manifest His faithfulness in exalting them as He had promised.

17. *Thou hast avouched*] Lit. "made to say:" the word occurs in this form only in this and next *v.* The sense is: "Thou hast given occasion to the Lord to say that He is thy God," *i.e.* by promising that He shall be so. Cf. Ex. xxiv. 7; Josh. xxiv. 14—25.

18. Cf. Ex. xix. 5, 6, notes and reff.

19. Cf. Jer. xiii. 11, xxxiii. 9.
an holy people] Cf. vii. 6, and reff.

CHAP. XXVII. The law having been reiterated with special reference to the circumstances of the people when settled in the promised land, Moses in a third discourse, contained in chapters xxvii.—xxx., proceeds more specially to dwell on its sanctions. In these chapters he sets before Israel in striking and elaborate detail the blessings which would ensue upon faithfulness to the covenant, and the curses which disobedience would involve. The xxviith chapter introduces this portion of the book by enjoining the erection of a stone monument on which the law should be inscribed as soon as the people took possession of the promised inheritance (*vv.* 1—10); and by next prescribing the liturgical form after which the blessings and cursings should be pronounced (*vv.* 11—26).

1—10. The erection of the stones as here prescribed "on the day when Israel passed over Jordan unto the land which the LORD gave him," and the inscription of the law on those stones, was a symbolical act declaring on the part of the people that they took possession of the land by virtue of their covenant with God, and on condition of their own faithfulness thereto. These acts, as also the preservation of the two tables in the ark of the covenant (cf. xxxi. 26), were witness against the people in case they should break their vows.

1. *Moses with the elders*] The elders are no doubt associated with Moses here because he was near the end of his office, and henceforth it would devolve on them to require what was due to God.

2. *on the day when ye shall pass over Jordan*] The expression "on the day" is used here, as

thee, that thou shalt set thee up great
stones, and plaister them with plaister:
3 And thou shalt write upon them
all the words of this law, when thou
art passed over, that thou mayest go
in unto the land which the LORD thy
God giveth thee, a land that floweth
with milk and honey; as the LORD
God of thy fathers hath promised
thee.
4 Therefore it shall be when ye be
gone over Jordan, *that* ye shall set up
these stones, which I command you
this day, in mount Ebal, and thou
shalt plaister them with plaister.
5 And there shalt thou build an altar unto the LORD thy God, an altar
of stones: [b]thou shalt not lift up *any*
iron *tool* upon them.
6 Thou shalt build the altar of the
LORD thy God of whole stones: and
thou shalt offer burnt offerings thereon
unto the LORD thy God:
7 And thou shalt offer peace offerings, and shalt eat there, and rejoice
before the LORD thy God.

[b] Exod. 20. 25. Josh. 8. 31.

---

so often (*e.g.* Gen. ii. 4; Num. iii. 1), in a broad sense, and is equivalent to "at the time when." Vulg. "cum transieritis Jordanem." Cf. in *v.* 3, *when thou art passed over*, and *v.* 4, *when ye be gone over*. In fact the command was carried out by Joshua (viii. 30—35), as soon after the passage of Jordan as circumstances permitted (cf. notes there).

thou shalt set thee up great stones, and plaister them with plaister] The stones here named are not those of which the altar (*v.* 4) was to be built, but are to serve as a separate monument witnessing to the fact that the people took possession of the land by virtue of the law inscribed on them and with an acknowledgment of its obligations.

3. *And thou shalt write upon them all the words of this law*] Thus attesting at once their duty and their resolve to observe that which themselves thus placed in durable record. Cf. the injunction to the king, xvii. 18. It is evident that the design is to set forth *all* the obligations of the people on their side of the covenant; hence we must not restrict the expression *all the words of this law* (cf. Josh. i. 8; viii. 34) to the Decalogue, since that was but a summary and abridgment of those obligations, nor would the "great stones" of *v.* 2 be required to contain the Decalogue only; nor yet to the following blessings and cursings, which certainly could not be properly described by the words of the text; nor yet to the book of Deut. only. The words can only mean all the laws revealed from God to the people by Moses. In these would not be included the historical, didactic, ethnological, and other non-legislative matter comprised in the Pentateuch, but simply its legal enactments, regarded by the Jews as six hundred and thirteen in number. The exhibition of laws in this manner on stones, pillars, or tablets, was familiar to the ancients. Knobel quotes Apollodorus in the Scholiast on Aristoph. 'Nub.' 447: οἱ ἀρχαῖοι λίθους ἱστάντες εἰώθεσαν τὰ δόξαντα ἐν αὐτοῖς ἀναγράφειν: and Polyb. XXVI. 1. 4, who uses παραβῆναι τὰς στήλας as a kind of proverbial expression. The laws were probably graven in the stone, as are for the most part the Egyptian hieroglyphics, the "plaister" being afterwards added to protect the inscription from the weather.

4. *in mount Ebal*] Cf. xi. 29; Josh. viii. 30. The Samaritan Pentateuch and Version read here *Gerizim* instead of Ebal; and are followed by Kennicott, Semler, Geddes, Boothroyd, Colenso, &c. But the Hebrew MSS. and all ancient versions, except the Samaritan (even LXX. which follows elsewhere the Samaritan very closely), are unanimous, and far outweigh the authority of the Samaritan. The original text was probably, as nearly all modern authorities hold, altered in order to lend a show of scriptural sanction to the Samaritan temple on Mount Gerizim.

The erection of the altar, the offering thereon burnt offerings and peace offerings (*vv.* 6, 7), the publication of the law in writing, form altogether a solemn renewal of the covenant on the entrance of the people into the promised land, and recall the ceremonies observed on the original grant of the covenant at Sinai. And Ebal, the mount of cursing, was the fitting spot on which to celebrate them. For the curses were the penalties under which the children of Israel bound themselves to keep the law. Suitably also was the same place selected as that in which were to be set up both the monumental stones containing the law, and the altar at which the covenant was to be renewed. We must note too the fact that *vv.* 15 sqq. set out verbatim the curses only, the blessings being omitted. The law because of man's sinfulness brings on him first and chiefly a curse; cf. xxxi. 16, 17; Gal. iii. 10.

5. *thou shalt not lift up any iron tool upon them*] Cf. Ex. xx. 25.

6, 7. *burnt offerings...peace offerings*] As on the establishment of the covenant at Sinai. Cf. Ex. xxiv. 5.

8 And thou shalt write upon the
stones all the words of this law very
plainly.
9 ¶ And Moses and the priests the
Levites spake unto all Israel, saying,
Take heed, and hearken, O Israel;
this day thou art become the people
of the LORD thy God.
10 Thou shalt therefore obey the
voice of the LORD thy God, and do
his commandments and his statutes,
which I command thee this day.
11 ¶ And Moses charged the people the same day, saying,
12 These shall stand upon mount
Gerizim to bless the people, when ye
are come over Jordan; Simeon, and
Levi, and Judah, and Issachar, and
Joseph, and Benjamin:
13 And these shall stand upon
mount Ebal †to curse; Reuben, Gad,
and Asher, and Zebulun, Dan, and
Naphtali.
14 ¶ And *c*the Levites shall speak,
and say unto all the men of Israel
with a loud voice,
15 Cursed *be* the man that maketh
any graven or molten image, an abomination unto the LORD, the work of
the hands of the craftsman, and putteth *it* in *a* secret *place*. And all the
people shall answer and say, Amen.
16 Cursed *be* he that setteth light
by his father or his mother. And all
the people shall say, Amen.
17 Cursed *be* he that removeth his
neighbour's landmark. And all the
people shall say, Amen.

† Heb. *for a cursing.*

c Dan. 9. 11.

9, 10. An appeal for attention, made apparently because of the special importance of what follows.

11—26. Form and manner of the solemn blessing and cursing. These had already been prescribed xi. 29, 30, and were carried out by Joshua; cf. Josh. viii. 32—35: where see notes. The solemnity was apparently designed only for the single occasion on which it actually took place.

12, 13. The tribes appointed to stand on Gerizim to bless the people all sprang from the two wives of Jacob, Leah and Rachel. All the four tribes which sprang from the handmaids Zilpah and Bilhah are located on Ebal. But in order, as it would seem, to effect an equal division two tribes are added to the latter from the descendants of the wives, that of Reuben, probably because he forfeited his primogeniture, Gen. xlix. 4; and of Zebulun, apparently because he was the youngest son of Leah.

The transaction presents itself as a solemn renewal of the covenant made by God with Abraham and Isaac, but more especially with Jacob and his family. Accordingly the genealogical basis of the "twelve patriarchs" (cf. Acts vii. 12), the sons of Jacob, is here assumed. The tribes of Ephraim and Manasseh are merged in the name of Joseph, their father; and Levi, although the tribe is so often spoken of in this book as having for secular purposes no part or lot with his brethren (cf. xiv. 27, xviii. 1, 2), regains on this occasion his place collaterally with the others. And thus whilst "the Levites" are in *v.* 14 appointed to utter aloud, and no doubt in chorus, the communication and the benediction, we find nevertheless, *v.* 12, Levi amongst the tribes which had to make response. "The Levites" of *v.* 14 are no doubt "the priests the Levites" (cf. Josh. viii. 33), in whom the ministerial character attaching to the tribe was more particularly manifested. The rest of the tribe of Levi would stand side by side with the others to occupy its own place in ratifying the covenant by its "Amen." It is noteworthy that the group of tribes which stood on Gerizim far exceeded the other in numbers and in importance, thus perhaps indicating that even by the Law the blessing should at length prevail.

15. The arrangements of this striking solemnity are more nearly indicated in Josh. viii. 32 sqq.: where see notes. The "Amen" attested the conviction of the utterers that the sentences to which they responded were true, just, and certain: so in Num. v. 22, and in our own Commination Office, which is modelled after this ordinance of Moses.

15—26. Twelve curses against transgressions of the covenant. The first eleven are directed against special sins which are selected by way of example, the last comprehensively sums up in general terms and condemns all and every offence against God's law.

Cursed be the man that maketh any graven or molten image] Cf. iv. 16, v. 8; Ex. xx. 4, 23; Lev. xxvi. 1.

putteth it in a secret place] This and the other maledictions seem especially to aim at those forms of guilt which could be most easily screened from human justice.

16. Cf. xxi. 18; Lev. xix. 3.

17. Cf. xix. 14 and reff.

18 Cursed *be* he that maketh the
blind to wander out of the way. And
all the people shall say, Amen.
19 Cursed *be* he that perverteth
the judgment of the stranger, fatherless, and widow. And all the people
shall say, Amen.
20 Cursed *be* he that lieth with his
father's wife; because he uncovereth
his father's skirt. And all the people
shall say, Amen.
21 Cursed *be* he that lieth with any
manner of beast. And all the people
shall say, Amen.
22 Cursed *be* he that lieth with his
sister, the daughter of his father, or
the daughter of his mother. And all
the people shall say, Amen.
23 Cursed *be* he that lieth with his
mother in law. And all the people
shall say, Amen.
24 Cursed *be* he that smiteth his
neighbour secretly. And all the people shall say, Amen.
[d] Ezek. 22. 12. 25 [d]Cursed *be* he that taketh reward to slay an innocent person. And
all the people shall say, Amen.
26 [e]Cursed *be* he that confirmeth [e] Gal. 3. 10.
not *all* the words of this law to do
them. And all the people shall say,
Amen.

CHAPTER XXVIII.

1 *The blessings for obedience.* 15 *The curses for disobedience.*

AND it shall come to pass, [a]if thou [a] Lev. 26. 3.
shalt hearken diligently unto the
voice of the LORD thy God, to observe *and* to do all his commandments
which I command thee this day, that
the LORD thy God will set thee on
high above all nations of the earth:
2 And all these blessings shall come
on thee, and overtake thee, if thou
shalt hearken unto the voice of the
LORD thy God.
3 Blessed *shalt* thou *be* in the city,
and blessed *shalt* thou *be* in the field.
4 Blessed *shall be* the fruit of thy
body, and the fruit of thy ground,
and the fruit of thy cattle, the increase of thy kine, and the flocks of
thy sheep.
5 Blessed *shall be* thy basket and ‖ Or, *dough*, or, *kneading-troughs.*
thy ‖store.

---

18. Cf. Lev. xix. 14.

19. Cf. xxiv. 17 and reff.

20. Cf. xxii. 30.

21. Cf. Lev. xviii. 23, xx. 15.

22. Cf. Lev. xviii. 9, xx. 17.

23. Cf. Lev. xviii. 17, xx. 14.

24. Cf. xix. 11 sqq.

25. Cf. Ex. xxiii. 7, 8.

26. Cf. xxviii. 15; Ps. cxix. 21; Jer. xi. 3. The blessings, as has been already observed, are not given. No doubt when the solemnity was enacted by Joshua they ran *mutatis mutandis* in the same formula as the curses, and they were probably (as the Mishna says, see Surenhusius, 'Mish.' III. 262) delivered alternately with the several corresponding curses: "Blessed is he that maketh not any graven image," &c.

CHAP. XXVIII. Having enjoined the solemn rehearsal of the blessings and the cursings, Moses next enlarges upon them, and describes in detail their effect and import. His object is of course to impress upon his hearers clearly and fully the momentous consequences of their own acts, whether for good or for evil. A comparison of this chapter with Ex. xxiii. 20—23 and Lev. xxvi. will shew how he here resumes and amplifies the promises and threats already set forth in the earlier records of the law. The blessings are declared in fourteen *vv.*; the curses require nearly four times as many. Thus here again the curse is the more conspicuous feature in the law. The language rises in this chapter to the sublimest strains, especially in the latter part of it; and the prophecies respecting the dispersion and degradation of the Jewish nation in its later days are amongst the most remarkable in scripture. They are plain, precise, and circumstantial; and the fulfilment of them has been literal, complete, and undeniable. Dean Jackson, 'On the Creed,' I. 27—30, draws out the argument derivable from this particular prophecy with fulness and care, and applies it to establish the inspiration and authority of scripture.

1—14. The Blessing. As in the closing words of the exposition of the Law, xxvi. 19, so here, exaltation is promised to Israel on condition of obedience. The condition is very emphatically stated at the beginning (*vv.* 1, 2), middle (*v.* 9), and close (*vv.* 13, 14) of this portion of the discourse; and the several blessings enumerated appear as directly consequent on its performance. The six repetitions of the word "blessed" introduce the particular forms which the blessing would take in the various relations of life.

6 Blessed *shalt* thou *be* when thou
comest in, and blessed *shalt* thou *be*
when thou goest out.

7 The LORD shall cause thine enemies that rise up against thee to be
smitten before thy face: they shall
come out against thee one way, and
flee before thee seven ways.

8 The LORD shall command the
‖ Or, *barns.* blessing upon thee in thy ‖store-
houses, and in all that thou settest
thine hand unto; and he shall bless
thee in the land which the LORD thy
God giveth thee.

9 The LORD shall establish thee an
holy people unto himself, as he hath
sworn unto thee, if thou shalt keep
the commandments of the LORD thy
God, and walk in his ways.

10 And all people of the earth
shall see that thou art called by the
name of the LORD; and they shall be
afraid of thee.

[b] chap. 30. 9, &c. 11 And [b]the LORD shall make thee
‖ Or, *for good.* plenteous ‖in goods, in the fruit of thy
† Heb. *belly.* †body, and in the fruit of thy cattle,
and in the fruit of thy ground, in the
land which the LORD sware unto thy
fathers to give thee.

12 The LORD shall open unto thee
his good treasure, the heaven to give
the rain unto thy land in his season,
and to bless all the work of thine
[c] chap. 15. 6. hand: and [c]thou shalt lend unto many
nations, and thou shalt not borrow.

13 And the LORD shall make thee
the head, and not the tail; and
thou shalt be above only, and thou
shalt not be beneath; if that thou
hearken unto the commandments of
the LORD thy God, which I command thee this day, to observe and to
do *them*:

14 And thou shalt not go aside
from any of the words which I command thee this day, *to* the right hand,
or *to* the left, to go after other gods
to serve them.

15 ¶ But it shall come to pass,
[d]if thou wilt not hearken unto the [d] Lev. 26. 14.
voice of the LORD thy God, to ob- Lam. 2. 17.
serve to do all his commandments Mal. 2. 2.
and his statutes which I command Baruch 1. 20.
thee this day; that all these curses
shall come upon thee, and overtake
thee:

16 Cursed *shalt* thou *be* in the city,
and cursed *shalt* thou *be* in the field.

17 Cursed *shall be* thy basket and
thy store.

18 Cursed *shall be* the fruit of thy
body, and the fruit of thy land, the
increase of thy kine, and the flocks of
thy sheep.

19 Cursed *shalt* thou *be* when thou
comest in, and cursed *shalt* thou *be*
when thou goest out.

20 The LORD shall send upon thee
cursing, vexation, and rebuke, in all † Heb. *which thou*
that thou settest thine hand unto †for *wouldest do.*

---

5. *Blessed shall be thy basket*] The word translated "basket" (*tene*) occurs only again in xxvi. 2, where its sense is determined alike by the connexion and by the immemorial practice of the Jews. The basket or bag was a customary means in the East for carrying about whatever might be needed for personal uses; cf. St John xiii. 29; Juv. 'Sat.' III. 14, "Judæis, quorum cophinus fœnumque supellex."

store] Rather **kneading-trough**, as the word is properly rendered in Ex. viii. 3 and xii. 34. Others render "what was left;" so LXX. Vulg. and Luther. But see note on Ex. xii. 34. The blessings here promised relate, it will be observed, to private and personal life: in *v.* 7 those which are of a more public and national character are brought forward.

6. Cf. Ps. cxxi. 8.

8. *storehouses*] The Hebrew word (*āsām*) is Aramaic, and only used here and in Prov. iii. 10. See Gesen. s. v.

9. *as he hath sworn unto thee*] The oath with which God vouchsafed to confirm His promises to the patriarchs (cf. Gen. xxii. 16; Heb. vi. 13, 14) contained by implication these gifts of holiness and eminence to Israel (cf. Ex. xix. 5, 6).

13. Cf. *v.* 44.

15—68. The Curses.

15—19. The Blessings are promised in six forms (*vv.* 3—6) as rewards of obedience, and the results of the contrary conduct are set forth in manner and number corresponding. The special modes in which these threats should be executed are described in five groups of denunciations, *vv.* 20—68.

20—26. First series of judgments. The curse of God should rest on all they do, and to do, until thou be destroyed, and until thou perish quickly; because of the wickedness of thy doings, whereby thou hast forsaken me.

21 The LORD shall make the pestilence cleave unto thee, until he have consumed thee from off the land, whither thou goest to possess it.

[e] Lev. 26. 16.

22 [e] The LORD shall smite thee with a consumption, and with a fever, and with an inflammation, and with an extreme burning, and with the ‖ sword, and with blasting, and with mildew; and they shall pursue thee until thou perish.

‖ Or, *drought.*

23 And thy heaven that *is* over thy head shall be brass, and the earth that *is* under thee *shall be* iron.

24 The LORD shall make the rain of thy land powder and dust: from heaven shall it come down upon thee, until thou be destroyed.

25 The LORD shall cause thee to be smitten before thine enemies: thou shalt go out one way against them, and flee seven ways before them: and shalt be † removed into all the kingdoms of the earth.

† Heb. *for a removing.*

26 And thy carcase shall be meat unto all fowls of the air, and unto the beasts of the earth, and no man shall fray *them* away.

27 The LORD will smite thee with the botch of Egypt, and with the emerods, and with the scab, and with the itch, whereof thou canst not be healed.

28 The LORD shall smite thee with madness, and blindness, and astonishment of heart:

29 And thou shalt grope at noonday, as the blind gropeth in darkness, and thou shalt not prosper in thy ways: and thou shalt be only op-

---

should issue in manifold forms of disease, in famine, and in defeat in war.

20. *cursing*] Cf. Mal. ii. 2.

vexation] Rather **confusion**: the word is used (vii. 23; 1 S. xiv. 20) for the panic and disorder with which the curse of God smites His foes.

21. *the pestilence*] The word is a general term (cf. Lev. xxvi. 25; Hab. iii. 5); the painful symptoms and concomitants of the pestilence are set forth in the next verse.

22. *with a consumption, and with a fever*] Cf. Lev. xxvi. 16. The Hebrew words occur only in these two places.

with the sword] Others "drought" or "heat." But see Note at end of chapter.

with blasting, and with mildew] The same words occur together Amos iv. 9. They are derived from roots signifying respectively "to be black," "to be yellow." The former denotes (cf. Gen. xli. 23) the result of the scorching east wind, the latter that of an untimely blight falling on the green ear, withering it and marring its produce.

23. Cf. Lev. xxvi. 19.

24. When the heat is very great the atmosphere in Palestine is often filled with dust and sand; the wind is a burning sirocco, and the air comparable to the glowing heat at the mouth of a furnace. Cf. Robinson, 'B. R.' II. 123.

25. *The LORD shall cause thee to be smitten before thine enemies*] Cf. Lev. xxvi. 17, 37; Is. xxx. 17.

shalt be removed] Lit. "shall be for a removing." The threat differs from that of Lev. xxvi. 33, which refers to a dispersion of the people amongst the heathen. Here it is meant that they should be tossed to and fro at the will of others, driven from one country to another without any certain settlement. Israel should be, so to speak, a ball for all the kingdoms of the earth to play with (Schultz). Contrast v. 10; and for the word cf. Jer. xv. 4, xxiv. 9; Ezek. xxiii. 46, &c.

26. Cf. Ps. lxxix. 2, 3. This was looked upon with the greatest horror; cf. Joseph. 'Bell. Jud.' IV. 5. 6; Sophocles, 'Antig.' 26 sqq.

27—37. Further working of the curse of God on the body, soul, and outward circumstances of the sinners.

27. *the botch of Egypt*] Rather **boil**, as the word is translated in Ex. ix. 9, where see note.

the emerods] Cf. 1 S. v. 6, 9. The Hebrew word signifies tumours merely.

with the scab (cf. Lev. xxi. 20), *and with the itch*] Various forms of the loathsome skin diseases which are common in Syria and Egypt.

28. Mental maladies shall be added to those sore bodily plagues, and should (29—34) reduce the sufferers to powerlessness before their enemies and oppressors.

madness] LXX. παραπληξία: cf. Jer. xxv. 16—18.

blindness] Most probably mental blindness; cf. Lam. iv. 14; Zeph. i. 17; 2 Cor. iii. 14, sqq.

astonishment] Cf. Jer. iv. 9.

29. *thou shalt grope*] Cf. Is. lix. 10.

pressed and spoiled evermore, and no man shall save *thee.*

30 Thou shalt betroth a wife, and another man shall lie with her: thou shalt build an house, and thou shalt not dwell therein: [f]thou shalt plant a vineyard, and shalt not †gather the grapes thereof.

31 Thine ox *shall be* slain before thine eyes, and thou shalt not eat thereof: thine ass *shall be* violently taken away from before thy face, and †shall not be restored to thee: thy sheep *shall be* given unto thine enemies, and thou shalt have none to rescue *them.*

[f] chap. 20. 6.
† Heb. *profane,* or, *use it as common meat.*
† Heb. *shall not return to thee.*

32 Thy sons and thy daughters *shall be* given unto another people, and thine eyes shall look, and fail *with longing* for them all the day long: and *there shall be* no might in thine hand.

33 The fruit of thy land, and all thy labours, shall a nation which thou knowest not eat up; and thou shalt be only oppressed and crushed alway:

34 So that thou shalt be mad for the sight of thine eyes which thou shalt see.

35 The LORD shall smite thee in the knees, and in the legs, with a sore botch that cannot be healed, from the sole of thy foot unto the top of thy head.

36 The LORD shall bring thee, and thy king which thou shalt set over thee, unto a nation which neither thou nor thy fathers have known; and there shalt thou serve other gods, wood and stone.

37 And thou shalt become [g]an astonishment, a proverb, and a byword, among all nations whither the LORD shall lead thee.

38 [h]Thou shalt carry much seed out into the field, and shalt gather *but* little in; for the locust shall consume it.

[g] 1 Kin. 9. 7. Jer. 24. 9. & 25. 9.
[h] Mic. 6. 15. Hag. 1. 6.

39 Thou shalt plant vineyards, and dress *them,* but shalt neither drink *of* the wine, nor gather *the grapes;* for the worms shall eat them.

40 Thou shalt have olive trees throughout all thy coasts, but thou shalt not anoint *thyself* with the oil; for thine olive shall cast *his fruit.*

41 Thou shalt beget sons and daughters, but †thou shalt not enjoy them; for they shall go into captivity.

42 All thy trees and fruit of thy land shall the locust ‖consume.

43 The stranger that *is* within thee shall get up above thee very high; and thou shalt come down very low.

44 He shall lend to thee, and thou

† Heb. *they shall not be thine.*
‖ Or, *possess.*

---

no man shall save thee] Cf. Lam. v. 8.

30. *Thou shalt betroth a wife*] Cf. Jer. viii. 10.

thou shalt build an house] Cf. Amos v. 11; Micah vi. 15; Zeph. i. 13.

shalt not gather the grapes thereof] Lit. "use it as common," or profane it; cf. xx. 6, and note.

31. *shall not be restored*] Lit. "return."

32. *Thy sons and thy daughters shall be given unto another people*] Cf. 2 Chron. xxix. 9.

there shall be no might in thine hand] Keil renders "thy hand shall not be towards God." The rendering of A. V. is preferable; cf. Gen. xxxi. 29 and note.

33. Cf. Neh. ix. 36, 37; Jer. v. 17.

35. Cf. *v.* 27 and Is. i. 6.

36. *and thy king*] Cf. note on xvii. 14.

38—48. The curse is described as working on every kind of labour and enterprise, until it had accomplished the total ruin of the nation, and its subjection to its enemies.

38. Cf. Mic. vi. 15; Hag. i. 6; Joel i. 4.

39. *worms*] *i.e.* the vine-weevil, the convolvulus of Pliny, 'Nat. Hist.' XVII. 47, and Cato, 'de Re Rustica,' chap. 95, who prescribe elaborate precautions against its ravages. Plautus, 'Cistell.' IV. 2, calls it "involvulus:" ("*La.* Imitatur nequam bestiam, et damnificam. *Ph.* Quamnam amabo? *La.* Involvulum, quæ in pampini folio intorta, implicat se"). Bochart, 'Hieroz.' Part II. Lib. IV. ch. 27, identifies this worm with that called ἴξ or ἶψ by the Greeks.

40. *thine olive shall cast his fruit*] Render **shall fall off.** See Note at end of chapter.

41. *they shall go into captivity*] Cf. Lam. i. 5.

42. *shall the locust consume*] Lit. "possess," a word in this connection even more forcible.

43, 44. Contrast *vv.* 12 and 13.

shalt not lend to him: he shall be the
head, and thou shalt be the tail.
45 Moreover all these curses shall
come upon thee, and shall pursue
thee, and overtake thee, till thou be
destroyed; because thou hearkenedst
not unto the voice of the LORD thy
God, to keep his commandments and
his statutes which he commanded thee:
46 And they shall be upon thee for
a sign and for a wonder, and upon thy
seed for ever.
47 Because thou servedst not the
LORD thy God with joyfulness, and
with gladness of heart, for the abundance of all *things;*
48 Therefore shalt thou serve thine
enemies which the LORD shall send
against thee, in hunger, and in thirst,
and in nakedness, and in want of all
things: and he shall put a yoke of
iron upon thy neck, until he have
destroyed thee.
49 The LORD shall bring a nation
against thee from far, from the end
of the earth, *as swift* as the eagle
flieth; a nation whose tongue thou
shalt not † understand; († Heb. *hear.*)
50 A nation † of fierce counte- († Heb. *strong of face.*)
nance, which shall not regard the
person of the old, nor shew favour
to the young:
51 And he shall eat the fruit of
thy cattle, and the fruit of thy land,
until thou be destroyed: which *also*
shall not leave thee *either* corn, wine,
or oil, *or* the increase of thy kine, or
flocks of thy sheep, until he have destroyed thee.
52 And he shall besiege thee in
all thy gates, until thy high and
fenced walls come down, wherein
thou trustedst, throughout all thy
land: and he shall besiege thee in
all thy gates throughout all thy land,
which the LORD thy God hath given
thee.
53 And *i* thou shalt eat the fruit (*i* Lev. 26. 29. 2 Kin. 6. 29. Lam. 4. 10. Baruch 2. 3.)
of thine own † body, the flesh of thy († Heb. *belly.*)
sons and of thy daughters, which the
LORD thy God hath given thee, in
the siege, and in the straitness, wherewith thine enemies shall distress thee:
54 *So that* the man *that is* tender
among you, and very delicate, his eye
shall be evil toward his brother, and
toward the wife of his bosom, and
toward the remnant of his children
which he shall leave:
55 So that he will not give to any
of them of the flesh of his children
whom he shall eat: because he hath
nothing left him in the siege, and in
the straitness, wherewith thine enemies shall distress thee in all thy
gates.
56 The tender and delicate woman among you, which would not
adventure to set the sole of her foot
upon the ground for delicateness and

---

46. *for ever*] Yet "the remnant" (Rom. ix. 27, xi. 5) would by faith and obedience become a holy seed.

47. Cf. Neh. ix. 35—37; ch. xxxii. 15.

48. Cf. Jer. xxviii. 14.

49—58. The calamities and horrors which should ensue when Israel should be subjugated, as was denounced in the preceding *vv.*, by its foreign foes.

49. *The LORD shall bring a nation against thee from far*] This, as other features of the description (cf. Jer. iv. 13, v. 15; Lam. iv. 19; Hab. i. 8), apply undoubtedly to the Chaldeans, and in a degree to other nations also whom God raised up as ministers of vengeance upon apostate Israel (*e.g.* the Medes, cf. Is. xiii. 17, 18). But it only needs to read this part of the denunciation, and to compare it with the narrative of Josephus, 'De Bell. Jud.' VI. to see that its full and exact accomplishment took place in the wars of Vespasian and Titus against the Jews, as indeed the Jews themselves generally admit.

49. *the eagle*] The Roman ensign; cf. St Matt. xxiv. 28.

50. *A nation of fierce countenance*] Lit. "strong or firm of face." So in the prediction of the Roman power, Dan. viii. 23. Cf. Prov. vii. 13, xxi. 29.

52. *And he shall besiege thee*] This part of the prophecy received various minor fulfilments before the crowning accomplishment of it by the Romans. Cf. 2 K. vi. and xxv.

53. Cf. Lev. xxvi. 29 and reff.; 2 K. vi. 28, sqq.

54. *his eye shall be evil*] *i.e.* grudging; cf. xv. 9.

tenderness, her eye shall be evil toward the husband of her bosom, and
toward her son, and toward her
daughter,
† Heb. *afterbirth.*
57 And toward her †young one
that cometh out from between her
feet, and toward her children which
she shall bear: for she shall eat them
for want of all *things* secretly in the
siege and straitness, wherewith thine
enemy shall distress thee in thy gates.
58 If thou wilt not observe to do
all the words of this law that are
written in this book, that thou mayest fear this glorious and fearful name,
THE LORD THY GOD;
59 Then the LORD will make thy
plagues wonderful, and the plagues of
thy seed, *even* great plagues, and of
long continuance, and sore sicknesses,
and of long continuance.
60 Moreover he will bring upon
thee all the diseases of Egypt, which
thou wast afraid of; and they shall
cleave unto thee.
61 Also every sickness, and every
plague, which *is* not written in the
book of this law, them will the LORD
† Heb. *cause to ascend.*
†bring upon thee, until thou be destroyed.
62 And ye shall be left few in
number, whereas ye were [k]as the stars
k chap. 10. 22.
of heaven for multitude; because thou
wouldest not obey the voice of the
LORD thy God.
63 And it shall come to pass, *that*
as the LORD rejoiced over you to do
you good, and to multiply you; so the
LORD will rejoice over you to destroy
you, and to bring you to nought; and
ye shall be plucked from off the land
whither thou goest to possess it.
64 And the LORD shall scatter
thee among all people, from the one
end of the earth even unto the other;
and there thou shalt serve other gods,
which neither thou nor thy fathers
have known, *even* wood and stone.
65 And among these nations shalt
thou find no ease, neither shall the
sole of thy foot have rest: but the
LORD shall give thee there a trembling heart, and failing of eyes, and
sorrow of mind:
66 And thy life shall hang in doubt
before thee; and thou shalt fear day
and night, and shalt have none assurance of thy life:
67 In the morning thou shalt say,
Would God it were even! and at
even thou shalt say, Would God it
were morning! for the fear of thine

---

57. *And toward her young one*] The word translated "young one" means "afterbirth;" and this verse is probably to be taken as setting forth the reason why "the delicate woman" would have an "evil eye" toward her husband: *i.e.* she would grudge him his share. "Idque ob secundinam suam et ob filios" (Rosenm.). The Hebrew text in fact suggests an extremity of horror which the A. V. fails to exhibit. Cf. 2 K. vi. 29; and Josephus, 'De Bell. Jud.' VI. 3. 4.

58—68. Ultimate issues of the curse in the uprooting of Israel from the promised land, and its dispersion amongst other nations.

58. *in this book*] *i.e.* in the book of the Law, or the Pentateuch in so far as it contains commands of God to Israel. Deut. is included, but not exclusively intended. So *v.* 61; cf. xxvii. 3 and note, xxxi. 9 and note.

this glorious and fearful name] Cf. Ex. vi. 3; Lev. xxiv. 11, sqq.

60. *all the diseases of Egypt*] Cf. vii. 15 and note.

62. *ye shall be left few in number*] See the same threat iv. 27.

ye were as the stars of heaven] Cf. x. 22; Neh. ix. 23.

63. *rejoiced over you to do you good*] Cf. xxx. 9; Jer. xxxii. 41.

rejoice over you to destroy you] Cf. Prov. i. 26.

64. *the LORD shall scatter thee*] Cf. iv. 27, 28; Lev. xxvi. 33; Neh. i. 8; Jer. xvi. 13; Ecclus. xlviii. 15; Joseph. 'De Bell. Jud.' VI. 9. 2.

65. Cf. Lev. xxvi. 36; Amos ix. 4.

66. *thy life shall hang in doubt before thee*] Lit. "thy life shall be hanging before thee," *i.e.* shall be hanging as it were on a thread, and that before thine own eyes. The Fathers (Iren. 'Adv. Hær.' IV. 23, V. 23; Tertullian, 'Contr. Jud.' XI.; Lactant. 'de Ver. Sap.' IV. 18; Athanas. 'de Incar.' XXXV. and others) regard this passage as suggesting in a secondary or mystical sense Christ hanging on the cross, as the life of the Jews who would not believe in Him.

67. Cf. Job vii. 4.

heart wherewith thou shalt fear, and for the sight of thine eyes which thou shalt see.

68 And the LORD shall bring thee into Egypt again with ships, by the way whereof I spake unto thee, Thou shalt see it no more again: and there ye shall be sold unto your enemies for bondmen and bondwomen, and no man shall buy *you*.

---

68. *bring thee into Egypt again with ships*] This is the climax. As the exodus from Egypt was as it were the birth of the nation into its covenant relationship with God, so the return to the house of bondage is in like manner the death of it. The mode of conveyance, "in ships," is added to heighten the contrast. They crossed the sea from Egypt with a high hand, the waves being parted before them. They should go back again cooped up in slave-ships. Cf. Hosea viii. 13, ix. 3.

by the way whereof I spake unto thee, Thou shalt see it no more again] An explanation, not of the words "in ships," but of the preceding threat that they should be brought back to Egypt; cf. xvii. 16. With the *v.* cf. Jer. xlii. and xliii.; Hos. viii. 13, ix. 3.

there ye shall be sold] Rather, "there shall ye offer yourselves, or be offered for sale." This denunciation was literally fulfilled on more than one occasion: most signally when many thousand Jews were sold into slavery and sent into Egypt by Titus (cf. Joseph. 'De Bell. Jud.' VI. 9. 2); but also under Hadrian, when numbers were again sold at Rachel's grave. Cf. Jerome on Jer. xxxi.

no man shall buy you] *i.e.* no one shall venture even to employ you as slaves, regarding you as accursed of God, and to be shunned in everything.

NOTES on CHAP. XXVIII. 22, and 40

v. 22.

The rendering "drought," "heat," is supported by Samar., Vulg., Luth., Geddes, Gesen., &c., but would seem to require a change in the pointing; cf. Gen. xxxi. 40. The A. V. is supported by LXX. (φόνῳ), Saad., and the majority of authorities of all kinds. The judgment of drought too is introduced in what immediately follows.

v. 40.

The verb ישׁל is best taken with Fürst, Gesen., Knobel, and most authorities as the Kal. Fut. of נשׁל, used intransitively. Keil however, with Schultz and some others, hold it to be the Niphal of another verb שׁלל, and the sense would thus be "shall be spoiled or plundered." A like difference of opinion exists on xix. 5, where a form occurs which probably belongs to the same verb.

CHAPTER XXIX.

1 *Moses exhorteth them to obedience, by the memory of the works they have seen.* 10 *All are presented before the Lord to enter into his covenant.* 18 *The great wrath on him that flattereth himself in his wickedness.* 29 *Secret things belong unto God.*

THESE *are* the words of the covenant, which the LORD commanded Moses to make with the children of Israel in the land of Moab, beside the covenant which he made with them in Horeb.

CHAP. XXIX. This and the following chapter contain the address of Moses to the people on the solemn renewal of the covenant. The people were now on the borders of the promised land, ready to enter in and take possession of that which God on His side had stipulated. It was fitting therefore that in doing so they should once more on their side recognize the obligations under which they were laid. The renewal of the covenant in the land of Moab did not consist in any revision or alteration of stipulations, nor in a repetition of the sacrifices and the blood-sprinkling (cf. Ex. xxiv.), with which the compact was ratified at Sinai. These acts remained still valid, and all that was necessary was a declaration on the part of God that His promises and purposes towards them still continued in force; and on the part of the people a new and solemn profession of their duties, and a vow to discharge them. This it was the more incumbent on them to make, and on Moses to require, because thus far, as Moses reminded them in ch. i., they had repeatedly broken their engagements to God.

After making appeal to God's past mercies (*vv.* 1—9), Moses summons the people to pledge themselves anew to the covenant (*vv.* 10—15), denouncing once more rejection of them by God in case of their apostasy (*vv.* 16—29); but promising restoration upon their repentance (xxx. 1—14). Finally he

2 ¶ And Moses called unto all Israel, and said unto them, [a]Ye have seen all that the LORD did before your eyes in the land of Egypt unto Pharaoh, and unto all his servants, and unto all his land;

[a] Exod. 19. 4.

3 The great temptations which thine eyes have seen, the signs, and those great miracles:

4 Yet the LORD hath not given you an heart to perceive, and eyes to see, and ears to hear, unto this day.

5 And I have led you forty years in the wilderness: your clothes are not waxen old upon you, and thy shoe is not waxen old upon thy foot.

6 Ye have not eaten bread, neither have ye drunk wine or strong drink: that ye might know that I *am* the LORD your God.

7 And when ye came unto this place, Sihon the king of Heshbon, and Og the king of Bashan, came out against us unto battle, and we smote them:

8 And we took their land, and gave it for an inheritance unto the Reubenites, and to the Gadites, and to the half tribe of Manasseh.

9 [b]Keep therefore the words of this covenant, and do them, that ye may prosper in all that ye do.

[b] chap. 4. 6. Josh. 1. 7. 1 Kin. 2. 2.

10 ¶ Ye stand this day all of you before the LORD your God; your captains of your tribes, your elders, and your officers, *with* all the men of Israel,

11 Your little ones, your wives, and thy stranger that *is* in thy camp, from the hewer of thy wood unto the drawer of thy water:

12 That thou shouldest †enter into

† Heb. *pass.*

---

solemnly sets before them the blessing and the curse, and adjures them to choose the blessing (*vv.* 15—20).

1. This *v.* is added to the last chapter in the Hebrew text of most editions; and so Gedd., Knob., Schultz, Wogue, and the Jewish authorities generally, who regard it, and probably correctly (cf. the very similar case Lev. xxvi. 46), as a recapitulation. The division of the A. V. is however that of LXX. and Vulg.

2. Cf. Ex. xix. 4.

3. *The great temptations*] Cf. iv. 34, vii. 19.

4. *Yet the LORD hath not given you an heart to perceive, and eyes to see, and ears to hear*] Ability to understand the things of God is the gift of God (cf. 1 Cor. ii. 14); yet man is not guiltless if he lacks that ability. The people had it not because they had not felt their want of it, nor asked for it. God makes a like complaint of the people *v.* 29; as does St Paul in later days, 2 Cor. iii. 14, 15. It is needless either to turn the passage interrogatively (as Clericus) "hath God given?" or (with Grotius and others, after Maimonides) to explain "given" as really meaning "received;" "non accepistis cor intelligens." Cf. Is. vi. 9, 10, lxiii. 9, 10, 17; Ezek. xii. 2; St Matt. xiii. 14, 15; St John viii. 43; Acts xxviii. 26, 27.

5. *And I have led you forty years*] Cf. i. 3, viii. 2.

your clothes are not waxen old] Cf. viii. 4 and note.

6. Cf. viii. 3. Moses passes imperceptibly into an address as from God Himself, on Whose behalf he was standing before the people; so in xi. 13, 14.

7. Cf. ii. 32, iii. 1.

8. Cf. iii. 12, 13.

9. Cf. iv. 6; Josh. i. 7.

that ye may prosper] Literally "that ye may act wisely;" so perhaps in xxxii. 29; Josh. i. 7; 1 K. ii. 3. The connexion of the two ideas of wisdom in conduct and prosperity in circumstances is noteworthy.

10—15. Summons to enter anew into the Covenant.

10. *your captains of your tribes, your elders, and your officers, with all the men of Israel*] The A. V. here follows the LXX. But the Hebrew strictly construed runs thus: **your captains, your tribes, your elders, and your officers, every man of Israel.** The word "tribes" apparently denotes all not in office.

11. The covenant was national, and therefore embraced all the elements which make up the nation. The "little ones" would of course be represented by their parents or guardians; the absent (*v.* 15) by those present; nor were the servants and proselytes to be excluded (cf. Acts ii. 39). The text is fairly alleged in justification of the Church's practice of admitting little ones into covenant with God by baptism, and accepting promises made on their behalf by sponsors.

thy stranger] LXX. "the proselyte." Cf. Ex. xii. 38, 48.

the hewer of thy wood] Cf. Josh. ix. 21 sqq.

covenant with the LORD thy God,
and into his oath, which the LORD
thy God maketh with thee this day:
13 That he may establish thee to
day for a people unto himself, and
that he may be unto thee a God, as
he hath said unto thee, and as he hath
sworn unto thy fathers, to Abraham,
to Isaac, and to Jacob.
14 Neither with you only do I
make this covenant and this oath;
15 But with *him* that standeth here
with us this day before the LORD our
God, and also with *him* that *is* not
here with us this day:
16 (For ye know how we have
dwelt in the land of Egypt; and how
we came through the nations which
ye passed by;
17 And ye have seen their abominations, and their †idols, wood and
stone, silver and gold, which *were*
among them:)
18 Lest there should be among
you man, or woman, or family, or
tribe, whose heart turneth away this
day from the LORD our God, to go
and serve the gods of these nations;
lest there should be among you a root
that beareth ‖gall and wormwood;
19 And it come to pass, when he
heareth the words of this curse, that
he bless himself in his heart, saying, I
shall have peace, though I walk in
the ‖imagination of mine heart, to
add †drunkenness to thirst:
20 The LORD will not spare him,
but then the anger of the LORD and

† Heb. *dungy gods.*

‖ Or, *a poisonful herb.* Heb. *rosh.*

‖ Or, *stubbornness.*

† Heb. *the drunken to the thirsty.*

---

15. *with him that is not here with us*] *i.e.*, as the Jews explain, posterity; which throughout all generations was to be taken as bound by the act and deed of those present and living.

16—29. The appeal just made is enforced by another warning against apostasy, and declaration of the fearful judgments which would follow upon it.

16, 17. These *vv.* are not parenthetic as in the A. V. *V.* 18 stands in close connexion, not with *v.* 15, but with what immediately precedes. The people is reminded (*vv.* 16, 17) of what it had itself witnessed, in Egypt and on its journey, of the vileness of idolatry, and that experience is urged (*v.* 18) as a motive for shunning that heinous sin.

17. *idols*] Marg. "dungy gods;" *i.e.* clods or stocks which can be rolled about; cf. Lev. xxvi. 30.

18. *whose heart turneth away*] Cf. xi. 16.

lest there should be among you a root that beareth gall and wormwood] The word (*rōsh*) here and in xxxii. 32 rendered "gall," is in Hos. x. 4 translated "hemlock." It is the name of a plant of intense bitterness, and (cf. Hos. x. 4) of quick growth; and is therefore repeatedly used in conjunction with "wormwood" (cf. Jer. ix. 15, Lam. iii. 19; Amos vi. 12), to express figuratively the nature and effects of sin (cf. Acts viii. 23; Heb. xii. 15). The Hebrew word means "a head," and is no doubt descriptive of the plant, which grew to a tuft. Some identify the herb with colocynth, others with tares, Gesen., more probably, with the poppy. Hence the "water" (*i.e.* juice) "of gall" (Jer. viii. 14, xxiii. 15) would be opium. This would explain its employment in the stupefying drink given to criminals at the time of execution (cf. Ps. lxix. 21; St Matt. xxvii. 34), and the use of the word as synonymous with poison (cf. xxxii. 33; Job xx. 16).

wormwood] Hebr. (*laanāh*) derived from a root signifying "to detest" or "curse." The plant (absinthium) is sufficiently familiar. It is used to denote metaphorically the distress and trouble which result from sin, and is translated by the LXX. here πικρία; in Jerem. ὀδύνη and ἀνάγκη. Cf. the passages quoted above, and Amos v. 7; Rev. viii. 11. In Amos vi. 12 this word is rendered "hemlock."

"The root that beareth gall and wormwood," means in this place any person lurking amongst them who is tainted with apostasy.

19. *And it come to pass,...that he bless himself in his heart, saying, I shall have peace, though I walk in the imagination of mine heart*] The marg. for "imagination" has more correctly "stubbornness." The word is derived from a root (*shārar*) signifying "to twist into a cord," and so "to resolve" or "determine." The subst. here used is not found except in combination with "heart" (Ps. lxxxi. 12; Jer. iii. 17 and elsewhere), and imports hardness or stedfast determination of the heart. The particle rendered in A. V. "though" may retain its ordinary sense, "for" or "because." "It is well with me, for I am living in the self-will of my mind: *i.e.* my 'summum bonum' is in following my own will and way." Cf. on the thought Jer. xxiii. 17. The secret and presumptuous sinner is meant who flatters himself that he will remain undetected and unpunished, since he follows his own devices and prospers. Cf. Ps. lxxiii. 11 sqq.

to add drunkenness to thirst] On this difficult and proverbial phrase, see Note at the end

his jealousy shall smoke against that
man, and all the curses that are written in this book shall lie upon him,
and the LORD shall blot out his name
from under heaven.
21 And the LORD shall separate
him unto evil out of all the tribes of
Israel, according to all the curses of
the covenant that †are written in this
book of the law:
22 So that the generation to come
of your children that shall rise up
after you, and the stranger that shall
come from a far land, shall say, when
they see the plagues of that land, and
the sicknesses †which the LORD hath
laid upon it;
23 *And that* the whole land thereof
is brimstone, and salt, *and* burning,
that it is not sown, nor beareth, nor
any grass groweth therein, [c]like the
overthrow of Sodom, and Gomorrah,
Admah, and Zeboim, which the LORD
overthrew in his anger, and in his
wrath:
24 Even all nations shall say,
[d]Wherefore hath the LORD done thus
unto this land? what *meaneth* the heat
of this great anger?
25 Then men shall say, Because
they have forsaken the covenant of
the LORD God of their fathers, which
he made with them when he brought
them forth out of the land of Egypt:
26 For they went and served other
gods, and worshipped them, gods whom
they knew not, and ‖*whom* he had not
†given unto them:
27 And the anger of the LORD was
kindled against this land, to bring
upon it all the curses that are written
in this book:
28 And the LORD rooted them out
of their land in anger, and in wrath,
and in great indignation, and cast
them into another land, as *it is* this
day.
29 The secret *things belong* unto
the LORD our God: but those *things*
which are revealed *belong* unto us and
to our children for ever, that *we* may
do all the words of this law.

† Heb. *is written.*

† Heb. *wherewith the LORD hath made it sick.*

[c] Gen. 19. 24, 25.

[d] 1 Kin. 9. 8. Jer. 22. 8.

‖ Or, who *had not given to them* any portion.

† Heb. *divided.*

---

of the chapter. The sense is probably: "so that the sated soul hurry away with itself that other soul which longs for the forbidden sin."

The sense of the whole passage from *v.* 16 onward to *v.* 20 may be exhibited thus: "Ye have seen the abominations of idolatry amongst the heathen. Do you therefore look diligently that there be no secret idolater amongst you; a root of bitterness to all about him. Let there be no one, I say, who when he hears the curses of the law against this sin, flatters himself, saying within himself, 'All will be well, for I walk unmolested in my own self-chosen path;' and thus acting, not only takes his own fill of sin, but destroys likewise every tempted brother within his reach; for the LORD will not spare him," &c.

20. Though the secret idolater may escape human justice, he shall not escape the judgment of God. Cf. Ezek. xiv. 7, 8. More literally the *v.* would run: "the LORD will not pardon him," &c.

the anger of the LORD and his jealousy shall smoke] Cf. Ps. lxxiv. 1, lxxix. 5.

blot out his name] Cf. ix. 14.

21. *that are written*] Marg. correctly **that is written**: the participle agrees with "covenant."

22, 23. The baleful effects of the "root of bitterness" are described. It would defile and ruin the whole land.

23. The description is borrowed from the local features of the Dead Sea and its vicinity. The towns of the vale of Siddim were fertile and well watered (cf. Gen. xiii. 10) until devastated by the wrath of God (Gen. xix. 24, 25). The ruin of Israel and its land should be of the like sort (cf. Lev. xxvi. 31, 32; Ps. cvii. 34; Zeph. ii. 9). The desolate state of Palestine at present, and the traces of former fertility and prosperity, are attested by every traveller. See *e.g.* Keith's 'Land of Israel,' chaps. 3, 4, and 5.

24. Cf. 1 K. ix. 8, 9; Jer. xxii. 8, 9.

26. *whom he had not given unto them*] Cf. iv. 19 and note.

27. Cf. Dan. ix. 11—15.

28. *and cast them into another land*] See on these words Note at end of chapter.

29. *The secret things belong unto the LORD our God*] This *v.* seems to be added, not (as some take it) by way of an expression of pious submission on the part of those who give their answer to the questions proposed in *v.* 24, but rather as a solemn admonition on the part of Moses, in order to close the series of blessings and cursings which he has delivered. The sense seems to be this: "The future, when and how these good and evil things will take effect, it lies with the Lord our God to determine; it pertains not to man's sphere and duty. His revealed will is that which we must carry out." The 17th of our Articles of Religion concludes with much the same sentiment. The words "unto us and to our children" are in the Hebr. distinguished by "puncta extraordinaria," in order no doubt to draw attention to them. Nor is this without reason. For that "they and their children" should act upon the revealed will of God was the aim and end of the whole law.

NOTES on Chap. xxix. 19, and 28.

v. 19.

Many and various interpretations have been given of these words. It is to be noted however that (1) the two words translated "drunkenness" and "thirst" are strictly two feminine adjectives; (2) the former adj., "the drunken," seems to belong to the subject of the verb, the other being marked by the usual particle as the object; (3) the verb (ספה), though sometimes meaning "to add," is always (*e.g.* xxxii. 23) in this sense associated with a prep. (על), which is here wanting; and therefore the other sense which the verb undoubtedly has also, and which suits the present context well, viz. "to take away," "consume," or "destroy" (cf. Gen. xviii. 23; Num. xvi. 26; Is. vii. 20), is in this place to be preferred; (4) that the subst. to be supplied for the two adjectives seems in this connexion evidently to be "person" or "soul" (*nephesh*). The words would then appear to mark the result of the conduct of the sinner whose hardihood has been set forth in the context preceding; and to mean "so that the soul that is drunken with sin carry away that which thirsts for sin." The presumptuous sinner is described as congratulating himself that all is and will be well with him, since he acts as pleases him best; and thus, himself "drinking iniquity like water" (cf. Job xv. 16), he corrupts and destroys others who are thirsting or prone to it. So Maurer, and substantially Schultz, Wogue. &c. Other renderings are given by Rosenm., who prefers to supply the subst. "land," and to treat the whole as a sort of proverbial expression: "that the watered and the thirsty soil may be destroyed together;" *i.e.* that there may be a general and sweeping ruin. But this seems farfetched.

v. 28.

The Hebr. word (*yashlīchem*) is written with a great lamed, and with yod defective. The former letter is the first in the word (*l'ōlām*), "for ever;" the latter used as a numeral signifies "ten." In the mode of writing is supposed to be mystically signified the perpetual rejection of the Ten tribes. Buxtorf, 'Masoret. Com.' XIV.

CHAPTER XXX.

1 *Great mercies promised unto the repentant.* 11 *The commandment is manifest.* 15 *Death and life are set before them.*

AND it shall come to pass, when
all these things are come upon
thee, the blessing and the curse, which
I have set before thee, and thou shalt
call *them* to mind among all the nations, whither the LORD thy God
hath driven thee,
2 And shalt return unto the LORD
thy God, and shalt obey his voice according to all that I command thee
this day, thou and thy children, with
all thine heart, and with all thy soul;
3 That then the LORD thy God
will turn thy captivity, and have com-

CHAP. XXX. Yet the rejection of Israel and the desolation of the promised inheritance were not to be the close of God's dispensations. Were this so the good purposes of God would have been defeated, and the promise have been brought at last to nought. But such a result is impossible (cf. Num. xxiii. 19; Rom. xi. 1 and 29). The closing words of the address therefore are words of comfort and promise. So when Moses had previously (iv. 29 sqq.; Lev. xxvi. 40 sqq.) denounced the judgments of God against apostasy, he adds similar predictions of the eventual conversion and restoration of Israel. (Cf. 1 K. viii. 46—50.)

1—10. The chastisements of God would lead the nation to repent, and thereupon God would again bless them.

2. *And shalt return*] Cf. Neh. i. 9.

3. *will turn thy captivity*] Will change or put an end to thy state of captivity or distress; not (as some) "bring back thy captives," a rendering refuted by the use of the phrase in Job xlii. 10. (Cf. Ps. xiv. 7, lxxxv.

passion upon thee, and will return
and gather thee from all the nations,
whither the LORD thy God hath scattered thee.

[a] Neh. i. 9.

4 [a]If *any* of thine be driven out
unto the outmost *parts* of heaven,
from thence will the LORD thy God
gather thee, and from thence will he
fetch thee:

5 And the LORD thy God will
bring thee into the land which thy
fathers possessed, and thou shalt possess it; and he will do thee good, and
multiply thee above thy fathers.

6 And the LORD thy God will circumcise thine heart, and the heart of
thy seed, to love the LORD thy God
with all thine heart, and with all thy
soul, that thou mayest live.

7 And the LORD thy God will put
all these curses upon thine enemies,
and on them that hate thee, which
persecuted thee.

8 And thou shalt return and obey
the voice of the LORD, and do all his
commandments which I command
thee this day.

9 [b]And the LORD thy God will [b] chap. 28. 11.
make thee plenteous in every work of
thine hand, in the fruit of thy body,
and in the fruit of thy cattle, and in
the fruit of thy land, for good: for
the LORD will again rejoice over thee
for good, as he rejoiced over thy fathers:

10 If thou shalt hearken unto the
voice of the LORD thy God, to keep
his commandments and his statutes
which are written in this book of the
law, *and* if thou turn unto the LORD
thy God with all thine heart, and
with all thy soul.

11 ¶ For this commandment which
I command thee this day, it *is* not
hidden from thee, neither *is* it far
off.

2; Jer. xxx. 18.) The rendering of the LXX. is significant; "the Lord will heal thy sins."

The promises of this and following *vv.* had no doubt their partial fulfilments in the days of the Judges; but the fact that various important features of them are repeated in Jer. xxxii. 37 sqq., and in Ezek. xi. 19 sqq., xxxiv. 13 sqq., xxxvi. 24 sqq., shews us that none of these was regarded as exhausting the promises. In full analogy with the scheme of prophecy we may add that the return from the Babylonian Captivity has not exhausted their depth. The New Testament takes up the strain (*e.g.* Rom. xi.), and foretells the restoration of Israel to the covenanted mercies of God. True these mercies shall not be, as before, confined to that nation. The "turning again of the captivity" will be when Israel is converted to Him in Whom the Law was fulfilled, and who died "not for that nation only," but also that he might "gather together in one the children of God that were scattered abroad" (St John xi. 51, 52). Then shall there be "one fold and one shepherd" (St John x. 16). But whether the general conversion of the Jews shall be accompanied with any *national* restoration, any recovery of their ancient prerogatives as the chosen people; and further, whether there shall be any local replacement of them in the land of their fathers, may be regarded as of "the secret things" which belong unto God (xxix. 29); and so indeed our Lord Himself teaches us (Acts i. 6, 7). The letter of the *vv.* before us and of the parallel passages seems indeed to point to both a national and a local return of Israel. On the other hand, in this very passage *v.* 6 seems plainly to intimate that in the Kingdom of the Messiah the ceremonies and ordinances at any rate shall reach that accomplishment in which the outward sign shall be superseded by the thing signified; cf. Rom. ii. 29. And God's purpose may be similar as regards the promises. The restoration here foretold may be realized, and the promises to Abraham (Gen. xvii. 6, &c.) most abundantly fulfilled to Israel, yet not to the Israel "according to the flesh" merely, but to that spiritual Israel whose Promised Land is not narrowed to an earthly Canaan. To us however the exact import of the prophecies respecting the future of the Jews must remain as yet, as was the similar inquiry respecting the Messianic prophecies in pre-Messianic days (cf. 1 Pet. i. 11), matter of reverent search and discussion only.

4. Cf. Neh. i. 9.

6. *circumcise thine heart*] Cf. x. 16; Jer. xxxii. 39 sqq.; Heb. viii. 10.

9. *rejoice over thee for good*] Cf. xxviii. 63; Jer. xxxii. 41.

10—20. The law which thus bears with it blessings for the faithful, and woes for the disobedient, has been brought home to Israel (*vv.* 10—14), so that ignorance of its requirements cannot be pleaded; hence (*vv.* 15—20) life and death, good and evil, are solemnly set before the people for their own

[c] Rom. 10. 6, &c.

12 [c]It *is* not in heaven, that thou
shouldest say, Who shall go up for us
to heaven, and bring it unto us, that
we may hear it, and do it?
13 Neither *is* it beyond the sea,
that thou shouldest say, Who shall
go over the sea for us, and bring it
unto us, that we may hear it, and
do it?
14 But the word *is* very nigh unto
thee, in thy mouth, and in thy heart,
that thou mayest do it.
15 ¶ See, I have set before thee
this day life and good, and death and
evil;
16 In that I command thee this
day to love the LORD thy God, to
walk in his ways, and to keep his
commandments and his statutes and
his judgments, that thou mayest live
and multiply: and the LORD thy God
shall bless thee in the land whither
thou goest to possess it.
17 But if thine heart turn away,
so that thou wilt not hear, but shalt
be drawn away, and worship other
gods, and serve them;
18 I denounce unto you this day,
that ye shall surely perish, *and that*
ye shall not prolong *your* days upon
the land, whither thou passest over
Jordan to go to possess it.
19 [d]I call heaven and earth to re- [d] chap. 4. 26.
cord this day against you, *that* I have
set before you life and death, blessing
and cursing: therefore choose life,
that both thou and thy seed may live:
20 That thou mayest love the
LORD thy God, *and* that thou mayest
obey his voice, and that thou mayest

---

choice; and an earnest exhortation to choose the better part concludes the address.

11—14. The immediate purpose of this passage is to encourage the people by reminding them that all necessary instruction had been placed within their reach. God had on His side done all that was possible to make the knowledge of His will and the performance of it easy to Israel: cf. Isa. xlv. 19, and especially Rom. x. 6 sqq. The passage is not cited by St Paul strictly either according to the Hebr. or the LXX. Yet we must not consider it as quoted by him merely in the way of illustration, much less as accommodated to suit the purposes of the argument on hand, regardless of its significance in its own context. We have in Rom. an authoritative interpretation of what the words of Moses do really and principally if not obviously signify. The Prophet spake, the Apostle expounded, by one and the selfsame Spirit. Those who believe this will not question the authority, and consequently not the correctness, of the sense assigned by the latter to the words of the former. It is nothing to the purpose to inquire how far the ideas assigned to the words by St Paul were present to the mind of Moses. At any rate what is here predicated by Moses of the law finds its practical issue only under the Gospel. The law may give "line upon line, and precept upon precept," yet where the heart is unrenewed actual fulfilment of it will still be far off and unattainable. It is then only by "the word of faith" (Rom. x. 8) that the objective nearness and facility of the commandment are realized by man; and that which is so feasible *per se* (cf. Mic. vi. 8) becomes practicable in fact to us. Thus "the righteousness which is of faith" is really and truly described in these words of the law, and under St Paul's guidance we affirm was intended so to be. For the simplicity and accessibility which Moses here attributes to the law of God neither are nor can be experimentally found in it except through the medium of faith; even though outwardly and in the letter that law be written out for us so "that he may run that readeth," and be set forth in its duties and its sanctions as plainly as it was before the Jews by Moses. The seeming ease of the commandment, and its real impossibility to the natural man, form part of the qualifications of the law to be our schoolmaster to bring us unto Christ. See further on Rom. l. c.

11. *hidden from thee*] Rather, **too hard for thee**, as the same Hebrew word is rendered, xvii. 8.

neither is it far off] Cf. St Luke xvii. 21.

13. The paraphrase of this *v.* in the Jer. Targ. is noteworthy, and should be compared with St Paul's rendering in Rom. x. 7: "Neither is the law beyond the great sea, that thou shouldest say, Oh that we had one like Jonah the prophet who could descend into the depths of the sea and bring it to us!"

14. *in thy mouth, and in thy heart*] Cf. vi. 6, xi. 18—20.

15—20. Last appeal to the people to choose the better of the alternatives set before them.

15. Cf. xi. 26, 27.

18. Cf. iv. 26; viii. 19.

cleave unto him: for he *is* thy life,
and the length of thy days: that
thou mayest dwell in the land which
the LORD sware unto thy fathers, to
Abraham, to Isaac, and to Jacob, to
give them.

CHAPTER XXXI.

1 *Moses encourageth the people.* 7 *He encourageth Joshua.* 9 *He delivereth the law unto the priests to read it in the seventh year to the people.* 14 *God giveth a charge to Joshua,* 19 *and a song to testify against the people.* 24 *Moses delivereth the book of the law to the Levites to keep.* 28 *He maketh a protestation to the elders.*

AND Moses went and spake these
words unto all Israel.
2 And he said unto them, I *am*
an hundred and twenty years old this
day; I can no more go out and come
in: also the LORD hath said unto me,
[a] Numb. 20. 12. chap. 3. 27. [a]Thou shalt not go over this Jordan.
3 The LORD thy God, he will go
over before thee, *and* he will destroy
these nations from before thee, and
thou shalt possess them: *and* Joshua,
he shall go over before thee, [b]as the [b] Numb. 27. 21.
LORD hath said.
4 And the LORD shall do unto
them as he did to Sihon and to Og,
kings of the Amorites, and unto the
land of them, whom he destroyed.
5 And [c]the LORD shall give them [c] chap. 7. 2.
up before your face, that ye may do
unto them according unto all the
commandments which I have commanded you.
6 Be strong and of a good courage,
fear not, nor be afraid of them: for
the LORD thy God, he *it is* that doth
go with thee; he will not fail thee,
nor forsake thee.
7 ¶ And Moses called unto Joshua,
and said unto him in the sight of all
Israel, Be strong and of a good courage: for thou must go with this people unto the land which the LORD
hath sworn unto their fathers to give
them; and thou shalt cause them to
inherit it.
8 And the LORD, he *it is* that doth

---

20. *that thou mayest love the LORD*] Cf. vi. 5. Love stands first as the essential and only source of obedience.

he is thy life] Or, as Jer. Targ., LXX., Luth., &c., "that" (*i.e.* "to love the Lord,") "is thy life;" *i.e.* the condition of thy life and of its prolongation in the promised land. Cf. iv. 40, xxxii. 47. With the passage as it stands in A. V. cf. Ps. xxvii. 1; St John xi. 25, xvii. 3; 1 John v. 20.

CHAP. XXXI. Certain last acts and arrangements of Moses in view of his death.

1. *Moses went and spake*] The word "went" must not be pressed, as in *e.g.* the Targum of Palestine, "Mosheh went into the tabernacle of the house of instruction and spake." This verb is frequently in Hebrew as in English prefixed to another verb with a kind of redundancy; cf. Ex. ii. 1; Job i. 4, and is so used here.

2. *I am an hundred and twenty years old*] The forty years of the wandering had passed since Moses, then fourscore years old, "spake unto Pharaoh," Ex. vii. 7. Cf. xxxiv. 7.

I can no more go out and come in] Render: **I shall not longer be able to go out and come in**: LXX. correctly οὐ δυνήσομαι ἔτι κ.τ.λ. Thus there is no inconsistency with xxxiv. 7. Moses here adverts to his own age as likely to render him in future unequal to the active discharge of his office as leader of the people: the writer of the xxxivth chapter, one of Moses' contemporaries, remarks of him that up to the close of life "his eye was not dim, nor his natural force abated;" *i.e.* that he was to the last, in the judgment of others, in full possession of faculties and strength. It is therefore needless, with Patrick, Ainsworth, &c., to render the clause following thus: "*for* the LORD hath said," &c. The phrase "to go out and come in" generally means "to discharge my duties amongst you:" cf. Num. xxvii. 17; 1 K. iii. 7.

Thou shalt not go over this Jordan] Cf. iii. 27.

3. *he will go over before thee*] Cf. ix. 3.

and Joshua, he shall go over before thee] Cf. i. 37 sq., and iii. 28.

6. Cf. i. 29, vii. 18; Josh. x. 25.

he will not fail thee, nor forsake thee] Cf. Josh. i. 5; Heb. xiii. 5.

7, 8. Moses hands over to Joshua that office as leader of the people, to which Joshua had already been designated (i. 38; Num. xxvii. 23). He assigns also to the Levitical priests and the elders, as the ecclesiastical and civil heads of the nation, the responsibility of teaching the law and enforcing its observance (*vv.* 10—13). Both these were symbolical acts, designed to mark the responsibility of the parties concerned after the death of Moses. It is therefore not at all inconsistent that

go before thee; he will be with thee,
he will not fail thee, neither forsake
thee: fear not, neither be dismayed.

9 ¶ And Moses wrote this law, and
delivered it unto the priests the sons
of Levi, which bare the ark of the
covenant of the LORD, and unto all
the elders of Israel.

10 And Moses commanded them,
saying, At the end of *every* seven
years, in the solemnity of the [d]year
of release, in the feast of tabernacles,

[d] chap. 15. 1.

11 When all Israel is come to appear before the LORD thy God in the
place which he shall choose, thou
shalt read this law before all Israel in
their hearing.

12 Gather the people together,
men, and women, and children, and
thy stranger that *is* within thy gates,
that they may hear, and that they
may learn, and fear the LORD your
God, and observe to do all the words
of this law:

13 And *that* their children, which
have not known *any thing*, may hear,
and learn to fear the LORD your God,
as long as ye live in the land whither
ye go over Jordan to possess it.

14 ¶ And the LORD said unto Moses, Behold, thy days approach that
thou must die: call Joshua, and present yourselves in the tabernacle of
the congregation, that I may give him
a charge. And Moses and Joshua
went, and presented themselves in the
tabernacle of the congregation.

15 And the LORD appeared in the

Moses should appear, in the short interval which has yet to elapse before he is actually withdrawn, as in full possession of his own authority. The duties of Joshua as his successor, and those here devolved upon the priests and elders, could, from the nature of the case, only require to be in fact discharged by them when the event which rendered the transfer of those duties necessary had taken place.

9. *Moses wrote this law, and delivered it unto the priests*] This simply means that Moses now consigned to the charge of the priests the law which he had written. The first clause, though connected with the following one by "and," is (as often in Hebrew) subordinate to it. The point to be noted is that Moses now formally intrusted the law, which at God's command he had promulgated, and with the exception of the concluding clauses (see *v.* 24) had already written out, to those who should be the regular and official guardians and teachers of it in future. He evidently did not actually transfer "the book," *v.* 24, from his own hands to theirs until he had completed the writing as there described.

the priests the sons of Levi] Cf. *v.* 25 and xvii. 18.

10. *the year of release*] Cf. xv. 1 and note.

feast of tabernacles] Cf. Lev. xxiii. 34.

11. *When all Israel is come to appear before the LORD*] Cf. xvi. 16. The actual discharge of this duty is recorded Neh. viii. 1 sqq.

thou shalt read this law] Cf. Josh. viii. 34, 35; 2 K. xxiii. 2; Neh. viii. 1 sqq. It is not to be supposed that the whole of the Pentateuch was read, nor does the letter of the command require that it should be so. This reading could not be primarily designed for the information and instruction of the people, since it only took place once in seven years; but was evidently a symbolical transaction, intended, as so many others were, to impress on the people the conditions on which they held possession of their privileges and blessings. For such purposes a solemn and public reading of lessons out of the book of the Law (*i.e.* the Pentateuch) was all that was needed; and it is left by the text to the Jewish Church to rule details, such as when during the eight days of the Feast of Tabernacles the reading should take place, who should read, and what portion of the law. From Neh. viii. 18 it appears that Ezra "read in the book of the law of God" day by day during the feast; but later Jewish practice has confined the reading to the first day of the feast, and to certain portions of Deuteronomy only. In after times the Jewish rule assigned this duty to the High Priest or King, who was expected to perform it in the Temple before the whole congregation (*v.* 12).

14—23. Moses and Joshua summoned to the tabernacle that God might "give Joshua a charge," *i.e.* the command which is given (perhaps in substance only) in *v.* 23, where see note. This is the first occasion on which the tabernacle of the congregation is mentioned in Deuteronomy. This will not appear remarkable when we remember that the book thus far has consisted almost exclusively of addresses made by Moses to the people, and that the bulk of these is legislative matter. The transaction recorded in these *vv.* may be regarded as the solemn inauguration of Joshua to the office to which he had some time before (Num. xxvii. 23 sqq.) been called, and his

tabernacle in a pillar of a cloud: and
the pillar of the cloud stood over the
door of the tabernacle.

16 ¶ And the LORD said unto Moses, Behold, thou shalt †sleep with
thy fathers; and this people will rise
up, and go a whoring after the gods
of the strangers of the land, whither
they go *to be* among them, and will
forsake me, and break my covenant
which I have made with them.

17 Then my anger shall be kindled
against them in that day, and I will
forsake them, and I will hide my face
from them, and they shall be devoured, and many evils and troubles shall
†befall them; so that they will say
in that day, Are not these evils
come upon us, because our God *is*
not among us?

18 And I will surely hide my face
in that day for all the evils which they
shall have wrought, in that they are
turned unto other gods.

19 Now therefore write ye this
song for you, and teach it the children
of Israel: put it in their mouths, that
this song may be a witness for me
against the children of Israel.

20 For when I shall have brought
them into the land which I sware
unto their fathers, that floweth with
milk and honey; and they shall have
eaten and filled themselves, and wax-
en fat; then will they turn unto other
gods, and serve them, and provoke
me, and break my covenant.

21 And it shall come to pass, when
many evils and troubles are befallen
them, that this song shall testify †a-
gainst them as a witness; for it shall
not be forgotten out of the mouths of
their seed: for I know their imagination which they †go about, even now,
before I have brought them into the
land which I sware.

22 ¶ Moses therefore wrote this
song the same day, and taught it the
children of Israel.

23 And he gave Joshua the son of
Nun a charge, and said, [e] Be strong
and of a good courage: for thou shalt
bring the children of Israel into the
land which I sware unto them: and
I will be with thee.

24 ¶ And it came to pass, when
Moses had made an end of writing
the words of this law in a book, until
they were finished,

25 That Moses commanded the

† Heb. *lie down.*

† Heb. *find them.*

† Heb. *before.*

† Heb. *do.*

[e] Josh. 1. 6.

---

recognition in it by God, which were manifested by his being summoned into the tabernacle with Moses whilst the Lord appeared in the pillar of cloud (cf. Num. xi. 25, xii. 5).

16. God announces to Moses the future apostasy of the people. This is done in the presence of Joshua that the latter might be fully aware of the danger and strive in his day to avert it. This he faithfully did (cf. Josh. xxiv. 31); but we find him in his own last address to Israel repeating (Josh. xxiii. 15, 16) the self-same prediction and warning.

sleep with thy fathers] Hebr. as margin "lie down." The same word is used in the same sense in the very ancient Phœnician Inscription of Eshmunazar.

go a whoring] Cf. Ex. xxxiv. 15; Judg. ii. 17.

forsake me, and break my covenant] Cf. xxxii. 15; Judg. ii. 12 sqq.

17. *hide my face from them*] Cf. xxxii. 20; Is. viii. 17 and lxiv. 7; Ezek. xxxix. 23.

19. Because of what has been foretold *vv.* 16—18 Moses and Joshua ("write ye") are commanded to write the song of Moses (xxxii. 1—43), and to teach it to the children of Israel that it might be "a witness for God against them:" *i.e.* an attestation from their own mouths at once of God's benefits, their own duties, and their deserts when they should fall away.

20. *waxen fat*] Cf. xxxii. 15; Neh. ix. 25; Hos. xiii. 6.

21. *it shall not be forgotten*] Being in verse it would be the more easily learned and kept in memory. The use of songs for such didactic purposes was not unknown to the legislators of antiquity; cf. Plato, 'de Leg.' II. (Vol. II. p. 656, edit. Steph.); and was familiar to theologians of later times; cf. Socr. 'Hist. Eccl.' VI. 8; and St Paul, Col. iii. 16, "teaching and admonishing one another in psalms and hymns and spiritual songs."

their imagination which they go about, even now] Cf. Amos v. 25 sqq.

23. *he gave*] *i.e.* the Lord gave: cf. on *v.* 14.

Be strong] Cf. *v.* 7.

24—30. Moses completes the writing out of the book of the law, and directs it to be placed by the ark of the Covenant.

Levites, which bare the ark of the covenant of the LORD, saying,

26 Take this book of the law, and put it in the side of the ark of the covenant of the LORD your God, that it may be there for a witness against thee.

27 For I know thy rebellion, and thy stiff neck: behold, while I am yet alive with you this day, ye have been rebellious against the LORD; and how much more after my death?

28 ¶ Gather unto me all the elders of your tribes, and your officers, that I may speak these words in their ears, and call heaven and earth to record against them.

29 For I know that after my death ye will utterly corrupt *yourselves*, and turn aside from the way which I have commanded you; and evil will befall you in the latter days; because ye will do evil in the sight of the LORD, to provoke him to anger through the work of your hands.

30 And Moses spake in the ears of all the congregation of Israel the words of this song, until they were ended.

CHAPTER XXXII.

1 *Moses' song, which setteth forth God's mercy and vengeance.* 46 *He exhorteth them to set their hearts upon it.* 48 *God sendeth him up to mount Nebo, to see the land, and die.*

GIVE ear, O ye heavens, and I will speak; and hear, O earth, the words of my mouth.

2 My doctrine shall drop as the

---

24. *writing the words of this law in a book*] "To write in a book" simply means "to commit to writing." A later word for "book" (*sepher*) is "roll," or "roll of a book:" cf. Jer. xxxvi. 23, and ibid. *vv.* 2, 4: Ps. xl. 7. The "book" here spoken of would contain the whole Pentateuch up to *v.* 24 of this chapter (see note there); and be "the book of Moses," called generally by the Jews "the law:" cf. St Matt. xxii. 40: Gal. iv. 21, &c.

25. *the Levites, which bare the ark*] *i.e.* as in *v.* 9, "the priests the sons of Levi." The non-priestly Levites could not so much as enter the Sanctuary or touch the ark (cf. Num. iv. 15). Though in the journeys through the wilderness the ark was borne by the non-priestly Kohathites, yet on occasions of a more solemn and public character it was carried by the priests themselves (Josh. iii. 3 sqq., iv. 9, 10, vi. 6, 12, viii. 33; 1 K. viii. 3).

26. *put it in the side of the ark*] Rather, **by the side of the ark.** The two tables of the Decalogue were *in* the ark, 1 K. viii. 9; the book of the law was to be laid up in the Holy of Holies close by the ark of the covenant, probably in a chest. Cf. 2 K. xxii. 8. This was not so much a provision for the safe custody of the volume, nor yet an attestation of its divine authority, though it served both these ends also, as a witness or protest against their breach of the covenant, of which the ark was a symbol, by idolatry. Cf. Dr Pusey's 'Daniel,' pp. 306, 307.

27. *how much more after my death*] With these words Moses appears to have handed over the book written and completed by him (*v.* 24) to the priests. It would seem then that what is actually intended to be taken as transcribed by Moses in person ends in this place with *v.* 23, and that *v.* 24 and the rest of the book (with the exception of the Song, *v.* 19) must be regarded as a kind of appendix added after Moses' death by another hand; though the Blessing is of course to be regarded as a composition of Moses. Cf. Introduction, § II.

28—30. Gathering of the elders and officers and the whole congregation by order of Moses that he might rehearse the ode to them. The elders and officers would be specially charged with the duty of making the people learn the ode.

28. *call heaven and earth to record*] Cf. xxx. 19, xxxii. 1.

29. *in the latter days*] Cf. iv. 30.

CHAP. XXXII. **1—43.** Song of Moses. On general questions connected with this Song see Note at the end of the chapter.

The contents have been very diversely distributed into heads by the commentators. It is obvious that minute and artificial divisions of the matter are inapplicable to a poetical composition like this. One of the most simple and satisfactory arrangements is that suggested by Kamphausen. Regarding *vv.* 1—3 as the introduction, and *v.* 43 as the conclusion, he groups the main contents of the song under three heads, viz. (1) *vv.* 4—18, the faithfulness of God, the faithlessness of Israel; (2) *vv.* 19—33, the chastisement and the need of its infliction by God; (3) *vv.* 34—42, God's compassion upon the low and humbled state of His people.

1—3. Introduction.

1. Heaven and earth are invoked, as in iv. 26, xxx. 19, xxxi. 28, 29 (cf. Isa. i. 2;

rain, my speech shall distil as the dew,
as the small rain upon the tender herb,
and as the showers upon the grass:
3 Because I will publish the name
of the LORD: ascribe ye greatness
unto our God.
4 *He is* the Rock, his work *is* perfect: for all his ways *are* judgment:
a God of truth and without iniquity,
just and right *is* he.
5 †They have corrupted themselves,
‖their spot *is* not *the spot* of his children: *they are* a perverse and crooked generation.
6 Do ye thus requite the LORD, O
foolish people and unwise? *is* not he
thy father *that* hath bought thee?
hath he not made thee, and established thee?
7 ¶ Remember the days of old,
consider the years of †many generations: ask thy father, and he will
shew thee; thy elders, and they will
tell thee.
8 When the most High divided to
the nations their inheritance, when
he separated the sons of Adam, he
set the bounds of the people according
to the number of the children of
Israel.
9 For the LORD's portion *is* his
people; Jacob *is* the †lot of his inheritance.
10 He found him in a desert land,

† Heb. *He hath corrupted to himself.*
‖ Or, that they are *not his children*, that is *their blot.*

† Heb. *generation and generation.*

† Heb. *cord.*

Jer. ii. 12, xxii. 29), in order to impress on the hearers the importance of what is to follow.

2. *My doctrine shall drop*] Or perhaps (as LXX., Vulg., &c.) "Let my doctrine drop."

4—14. Here follows the main body of the Song, commencing with a contrast drawn between the faithfulness of God and the perfidy of Israel.

4. *He is the Rock, his work is perfect*] Rather, **the Rock, perfect is His work.** The term Rock stands absolutely as the first and leading word. This epithet, repeated no less than five times in the Song, (*vv.* 15, 18, 31, 37), represents those attributes of God which Moses is seeking to enforce, immutability and impregnable strength. Cf. the expression "the stone of Israel," Gen. xlix. 24; and 1 S. ii. 2; Ps. xviii. 2; Isa. xxvi. 4 and xxx. 29; Matt. xvi. 18; John i. 42. The Hebrew word *tsōr* is frequently used in compounding proper names, of the Mosaic time, *e.g.* Num. i. 5, 6, 10, ii. 12, iii. 35, &c. Our translators have elsewhere rendered it according to the sense ("everlasting strength," "the Mighty One," &c.); in this chapter they have rightly adhered to the letter throughout.

5. The other side of the picture is now brought forward with a brevity and abruptness which strikingly enforces the contrast.

They have corrupted themselves, &c.] The verb is in the singular. Render, "It" (*i.e.* "the perverse and crooked generation" understood from the context) "hath corrupted itself before Him (cf. Isa. i. 4); they are not His children, but their blemish:" *i.e.* the generation of evil-doers cannot be styled God's children, but rather the shame and disgrace of God's children. On the words *their spot*, &c., see the Note at the end of the chapter.

a perverse and crooked generation] Cf. Matt. xvii. 17; Luke ix. 41.

6. *foolish people and unwise*] Cf. iv. 6; Ps. xc. 12.

is not he thy father that hath bought thee] Rather perhaps "hath acquired thee for his own," or "possessed thee:" and on the word see note on Gen. xiv. 19, &c., Ps. lxxiv. 2; Isa. lxiii. 16; Acts xx. 28; 1 Pet. ii. 9 ("a peculiar people;" marg. "a purchased people"), and reff.

7. *days*] The plural form of this noun is archaic, and occurs only here and in the Psalm attributed to Moses, Ps. xc. 15. In both places too it is in combination with "years."

8. *When the most High divided*, &c.] That is, whilst nations were being constituted under God's providence, and the bounds of their habitation determined under His government (cf. Acts xvii. 26), He had even then in view the interests of His elect, and reserved a fitting inheritance "according to the number of the children of Israel;" *i.e.* proportionate to the wants of their population. The LXX. instead of "according to the number of the children of Israel," has "according to the number of the angels of God;" following apparently not a different reading, but the Jewish notion that the nations of the earth are seventy in number (cf. Gen. x.), and that each has its own guardian angel (cf. Ecclus. xvii. 17). This rendering, which thus curiously preserves the general sense, whilst signally departing from the letter, was possibly suggested by an apprehension that the literal one might prove invidious to the many Gentiles who would read the Greek version.

9. *the LORD'S portion*] Cf. Ex. xv. 16, xix. 5 and reff.

and in the waste howling wilderness;
he ‖led him about, he instructed him, ‖ Or, *compassed him about.*
he kept him as the apple of his eye.
11 As an eagle stirreth up her nest,
fluttereth over her young, spreadeth
abroad her wings, taketh them, beareth them on her wings:
12 *So* the LORD alone did lead
him, and *there was* no strange god
with him.
13 He made him ride on the high
places of the earth, that he might eat
the increase of the fields; and he
made him to suck honey out of the
rock, and oil out of the flinty rock;
14 Butter of kine, and milk of
sheep, with fat of lambs, and rams
of the breed of Bashan, and goats,
with the fat of kidneys of wheat; and
thou didst drink the pure blood of the
grape.
15 ¶ But Jeshurun waxed fat, and
kicked: thou art waxen fat, thou art
grown thick, thou art covered *with*
fatness; then he forsook God *which*
made him, and lightly esteemed the
Rock of his salvation.
16 They provoked him to jealousy
with strange *gods*, with abominations
provoked they him to anger.
17 They sacrificed unto devils, ‖ not ‖ Or, which were *not* God.
to God; to gods whom they knew
not, to new *gods that* came newly up,
whom your fathers feared not.

10—14. These *vv.* set forth in figurative language the helpless and hopeless state of the nation when God took pity on it, and the love and care which He bestowed on it. The illustration of a man ready to perish in the desert (cf. xxvi. 5), though sufficiently obvious to one writing in the East, is probably chosen because God did in fact lead the people through the desert of Arabia, but it is not the design of the passage to rehearse events historically.

10. *in the waste howling wilderness*] Lit. "in a waste, the howling of a wilderness," *i.e.* a wilderness in which wild beasts howl. The word for waste is that used Gen. i. 2, and there rendered "without form."

apple of his eye] Cf. Ps. xvii. 8; Prov. vii. 2.

11. *As an eagle*] Cf. Ex. xix. 4.

spreadeth abroad her wings] These words begin the apodosis. The "so," which A. V. supplies at the next *v.*, should be inserted here. The sense is, "so He spread out His wings, took them up," &c. The *v.* is thus an expansion of the figure employed in Ex. l. c.

12. *So the LORD*] Omit "so." The sentence is independent.

with him] *i.e.* with God. The Lord alone delivered Israel; Israel therefore ought to have served none other than Him.

13. *He made him ride on the high places*] *i.e.* gave Israel possession of those commanding positions which carry with them dominion over the whole land. Cf. xxxiii. 29.

made him to suck honey out of the rock, and oil] *i.e.* the blessing of God enabled Israel to draw the richest provision out of spots naturally unproductive. The wild bees however hived and the olives flourished in the rocky soil of Canaan. Cf. Ex. iii. 8, and note.

14. *breed of Bashan*] Bashan was famous for its cattle. Cf. Ps. xxii. 12; Ezek. xxxix. 18.

fat of kidneys of wheat] *i.e.* the finest and most nutritious wheat. The fat of the kidneys was regarded as being the finest and tenderest, and was therefore specified as a part of the sacrificial animals which was to be offered to the Lord: cf. Ex. xxix. 13, &c.

the pure blood of the grape] Render, **the blood of the grape** (cf. Gen. xlix. 11), **even wine.** The Hebrew word means "foaming" or "fermenting," and seems (cf. Isa. xxvii. 2) a poetical term for wine.

15. *Jeshurun*] This word, found again only in xxxiii. 5, 26, and Isa. xliv. 2, is not a diminutive but an appellative (from *yāshar* "to be righteous"); and describes not the character which belonged to Israel in fact, but that to which Israel was called. Cf. Num. xxiii. 21. The prefixing of this epithet to the description of Israel's apostasy contained in the words next following is full of keen reproof.

Rock of his salvation] Cf. *v.* 4.

16. *They provoked him to jealousy*] The language is borrowed from the matrimonial relationship, as in xxxi. 16; Exod. xxxiv. 14, 15 (reff.); Isa. liv. 5; Jer. ii. 25, and frequently in the Prophets.

17. *devils*] Render, **destroyers;** and also in Ps. cvi. 37. The root is common to the Shemitic languages (cf. its use Ps. xci. 6), and means "to waste" or "hurry away violently." Its application here to the false gods points to the trait so deeply graven in all heathen worship, that of regarding the deities as malignant, and needing to be propitiated by human sufferings.

not to God] Rather, "not-God," *i.e.* which were not God; see margin.

whom your fathers feared not] Cf. xiii. 7, xxix. 25.

18 Of the Rock *that* begat thee
thou art unmindful, and hast forgotten
God that formed thee.
19 And when the LORD saw *it*, he
‖ Or, *despised.* ‖ abhorred *them*, because of the pro-
voking of his sons, and of his daugh-
ters.
20 And he said, I will hide my face
from them, I will see what their end
shall be: for they *are* a very froward
generation, children in whom *is* no
faith.
21 They have moved me to jealousy with *that which is* not God;
they have provoked me to anger with
their vanities: and [a] I will move them [a] Rom. 10. 9.
to jealousy with *those which are* not a
people; I will provoke them to anger
with a foolish nation.
22 For a fire is kindled in mine
anger, and ‖ shall burn unto the low- ‖ Or, *hath burned.*
est hell, and ‖ shall consume the earth ‖ Or, *hath consumed.*
with her increase, and set on fire the
foundations of the mountains.
23 I will heap mischiefs upon them;
I will spend mine arrows upon them.
24 *They shall be* burnt with hunger, † Heb. *burning coals.*
and devoured with † burning heat, and

19—33. God's decree of rejection; the terrible accomplishment of it; and the reasons which led to its severity and to its eventual mitigation.

19. The anger of God at the apostasy of His people is stated in general terms in this *v.*; and the results of it described, in words as of God Himself, in the next and following *vv.* These consisted negatively in the withdrawal of God's favour (*v.* 20), and positively in the infliction of a righteous retribution.

And when the LORD *saw it, he abhorred them, because of,* &c.] The rendering, "And the Lord saw it, and from provocation (*i.e.* from being provoked) rejected his sons," adopted by Keil, Knobel, &c., seems easier than that of A.V., but has no support in the ancient Targums or Versions.

daughters] The women had their full share in the sins of the people. Cf. Isa. iii. 16 sqq., xxxii. 9 sqq.; Jer. vii. 18, xliv. 15 sqq.

20. Cf. xxxi. 17, 18.

I will see what their end shall be] Cf. Gen. xxxvii. 20 ad fin.

21. *They have moved me to jealousy*] Cf. *v.* 16. God would mete out to them the same measure as they had done to Him. Though chosen by the one God to be His own, they had preferred idols, which are no gods. So therefore would He prefer to His people that which was no people. As they had angered Him with their vanities, so would He provoke them by adopting in their stead those whom they counted as nothing. Cf. Hos. i. 10; Rom. x. 19; 1 Pet. ii. 10. The force of the passage turns on the antithesis between two sets of terms, viz. "not-God," and "vanities" (or "nothingnesses") on the one side; and "not a people," and "a foolish nation," on the other. Now the first pair of terms (not-God, and vanities) must clearly be taken strictly in a theological, and (so to say) technical sense, and denotes the privation of those blessings which in the phraseology of Scripture would be described by such words as God, Truth, Being, &c. Hence the second and contrasted set of terms, "not a people," and "a foolish nation," cannot mean a barbarous or inhuman people, such as the Chaldeans (Rosenm., Maur., Kamph., &c.), but such a people as not being God's, would, from the theological point of view, not be accounted a people at all (cf. Eph. ii. 12; 1 Pet. ii. 10). And the "foolish nation" is such as is destitute of that which alone can make a really "wise and understanding people" (Deut. iv. 6), the knowledge of the revealed word and will of God; and therefore, though perhaps wise in this world's wisdom, is foolishness before God (cf. 1 Cor. i. 18—28).

The epithets "not a people," and "foolish nation," represent very faithfully the estimation in which the Jews held all others than themselves (cf. Ecclus. l. 25, 26). When therefore St Paul asserts that Israel in this passage had forewarning of the call of the Gentiles, he is assuredly only declaring its real import. God announces His resolve to repay the faithlessness of the Jews by withdrawing their privileges, and conferring them on those whom the Jews despised. The ultimate result, that by the call of the Gentiles Israel should be provoked to emulation, and so eventually be saved also, is not here brought forward. It lies amongst those mysteries of the distant future which the Gospel was to bring to light. Moses, the minister of the Law, goes on to utter in glowing language the threatenings of God against the apostates.

22. Cf. Jer. xv. 14, xvii. 4; Lam. iv. 11.

23. *I will spend mine arrows*] Cf. *v.* 42; Ps. vii. 12, 13, xlv. 5.

24. *burning heat*] *i.e.* the fever of a pestilential disease. On the "four sore judgments," famine, plague, noisome beasts, the sword, cf. Lev. xxvi. 22; Jer. xv. 2; Ezek. v. 17, xiv. 21.

with bitter destruction: I will also
send the teeth of beasts upon them,
with the poison of serpents of the dust.
25 The sword without, and terror
† within, shall † destroy both the young
man and the virgin, the suckling *also*
with the man of gray hairs.

† Heb. *from the chambers.*
† Heb. *bereave.*

26 I said, I would scatter them into
corners, I would make the remembrance of them to cease from among
men:
27 Were it not that I feared the
wrath of the enemy, lest their adversaries should behave themselves
strangely, *and* lest they should say,
‖ Our hand *is* high, and the LORD
hath not done all this.
28 For they *are* a nation void of

‖ Or, *Our high hand, and not the LORD, hath done all this.*

counsel, neither *is there any* understanding in them.
29 O that they were wise, *that* they
understood this, *that* they would consider their latter end!
30 How should [b]one chase a thousand, and two put ten thousand to
flight, except their Rock had sold
them, and the LORD had shut them up?

b Josh. 23. 10.

31 For their rock *is* not as our
Rock, even our enemies themselves
being judges.
32 For their vine ‖ *is* of the vine of
Sodom, and of the fields of Gomorrah: their grapes *are* grapes of gall,
their clusters *are* bitter:

‖ Or, is worse *than the vine of Sodom, &c.*

33 Their wine *is* the poison of
dragons, and the cruel venom of asps.

---

26. *I would scatter them into corners*] Rather, **I would utterly disperse them.** See Note at end of the chapter.

27. *Were it not that I feared the wrath of the enemy*] Rather, **Were it not that I apprehended the provocation of the enemy,** *i.e.* that I should be provoked to wrath when the enemy ascribed the overthrow of Israel to his own prowess and not to my judgments. So Vitringa, Keil, Wogue, &c. The Hebrew noun (*caas*) is used in the same sense as the cognate verb in *v.* 21. On the general sense of the passage cf. Ezek. xx. 9, 14, 21. Moses employs a like argument in interceding with God for Israel, ix. 28, 29.

behave themselves strangely] Rather, **misunderstand it,** *i.e.* mistake the cause of Israel's ruin.

28 sqq. The reason why such severity was needed is noted and dwelt upon, the discourse passing almost imperceptibly into words of Moses' own.

29. Cf. Isa. xlvii. 7; Lam. i. 9.

30. *their Rock*] *i.e.* the Lord, Israel's true Rock, *v.* 4, as the parallel clause which follows makes clear. Some commentators wrongly refer the expression here to the false gods, to which however it certainly is applied in the next *v.* But the purpose of Moses here is evidently to shew that the defeat of Israel would be due to the fact that God, their strength, had abandoned them because of their apostasy.

31. *their rock...our Rock*] *i.e.* the false gods of the heathen to which the apostate Israelites had fallen away, on the one side; and God, the true Rock, in which Moses and the faithful trust, on the other side. The change in the application of the term "their rock," rightly marked in the A. V. by the withdrawal of the capital from the substantive, is sudden; but the sense is settled by the antithesis on which the *v.* turns, and which is sharpened by the very suddenness of the interchange in the pronouns. In the next *v.* the pronoun "their" reverts to its usual sense in the whole passage, and denotes the apostate Israelites.

our enemies] The enemies of Moses and the faithful Israelites; the heathen, more specially those with whom Israel was brought into collision, whom Israel was commissioned to "chase," but to whom, as a punishment for faithlessness, Israel was "sold," *v.* 30. Moses leaves the decision, whether "their rock" or "our Rock" is superior, to be determined by the unbelievers themselves. For examples we have the testimony of the Egyptians, Ex. xiv. 25; of Balaam in Num. xxiii. and xxiv.; of the Philistines: cf. also Josh. ii. 9 sqq.; 1 S. iv. 8 and v. 7 sqq.; 1 K. xx. 28. That the heathen should thus be constrained to bear witness to the supremacy of Israel's God heightens the folly of Israel's apostasy.

judges] The Hebrew word is a very rare and undoubtedly archaic one, occurring only Ex. xx. 22.

32. *their vine*] *i.e.* the nature and character of Israel: cf. for similar expressions Ps. lxxx. 8, 14; Jer. ii. 21; Hos. x. 1. This and the following verses must not (with Schultz, Volck, &c.) be referred to the heathen enemies of Israel. Such a digression upon the faults of the heathen is quite foreign to the purpose of the Song.

Sodom...Gomorrah] Here, as elsewhere, and often in the prophets, emblems of utter depravity: cf. Isa. i. 10; Jer. xxiii. 14.

gall] Cf. xxix. 18.

34 *Is* not this laid up in store with
me, *and* sealed up among my treasures?
35 To me *belongeth* [c] vengeance,
and recompence; their foot shall slide
in *due* time: for the day of their calamity
is at hand, and the things that
shall come upon them make haste.
36 For the LORD shall judge his
people, and repent himself for his servants,
when he seeth that *their* † power
is gone, and *there is* none shut up, or left.
37 And he shall say, Where *are* their
gods, *their* rock in whom they trusted,
38 Which did eat the fat of their
sacrifices, *and* drank the wine of their
drink offerings? let them rise up and
help you, *and* be † your protection.
39 See now that I, *even* I, *am* he,
and *there is* no god with me: [d] I kill,
and I make alive; I wound, and I
heal: neither *is there any* that can deliver
out of my hand.

[c] Ecclus. 28. 1. Rom. 12. 19. Heb. 10. 30.
† Heb. *hand.*
† Heb. *an hiding for you.*
[d] 1 Sam. 2. 6. Tob. 13. 2. Wisd. 16. 13.

40 For I lift up my hand to heaven,
and say, I live for ever.
41 If I whet my glittering sword,
and mine hand take hold on judgment;
I will render vengeance to
mine enemies, and will reward them
that hate me.
42 I will make mine arrows drunk
with blood, and my sword shall devour
flesh; *and that* with the blood of
the slain and of the captives, from the
beginning of revenges upon the enemy.
43 ‖ [e] Rejoice, O ye nations, *with*
his people: for he will avenge the
blood of his servants, and will render
vengeance to his adversaries, and will
be merciful unto his land, *and* to his
people.
44 ¶ And Moses came and spake
all the words of this song in the ears
of the people, he, and ‖ Hoshea the son
of Nun.

‖ Or, *Praise his people, ye nations.* Or, *Sing ye.*
[e] Rom. 15. 10.
‖ Or, *Joshua*

34—43. God's purpose to have mercy on His people when chastised and humbled. The declaration is introduced by an assertion that God's plan had been all along fixed, and that its execution was therefore sure and rapidly approaching. On the language of *v.* 34, cf. Job xiv. 17; Hos. xiii. 12.

35. *their foot shall slide*] Cf. Ps. xxxviii. 17, xciv. 18. These words should not, as in the A.V., stand as a distinct clause. They are closely connected with the preceding. The passage should rather be rendered: "Vengeance is mine and recompence, at the time when their foot slideth."

36. *the LORD shall judge his people*] Cf. Ps. cxxxv. 14; 1 Pet. iv. 17.

repent himself for] Rather, **have compassion upon.** The *v.* declares that God's judgment of His people would issue at once in the punishment of the wicked, and in the comfort of the righteous.

none shut up, or left] On this proverbial phrase, see the Note at end of the chapter.

38. *let them rise up*] Cf. Jer. ii. 28.

39. *I, even I, am he, and there is no god with me*] The words interpolated in the A. V., though necessary for the idiom of the English, somewhat mar the force of the shorter original. The LXX. has ἐγώ εἰμι καὶ οὐκ ἔστι Θεὸς πλὴν ἐμοῦ. Cf. Isa. xli. 4, xlviii. 12; Joh. viii. 24, xviii. 5.

I kill, and I make alive] Cf. 1 S. ii. 6; 2 K. v. 7.

I wound, and I heal] Cf. Job v. 18; Hos. vi. 1.

neither is there any that can deliver out of my hand] Cf. Isa. xliii. 13; Hos. v. 14.

40—42. These *vv.* are closely connected. The full stop in the A. V. at end of *v.* 40 should be removed, and the passage should run thus: **For I lift up my hand to heaven and say, As I live for ever, if I whet,** &c. On *v.* 40, in which God is described as swearing by Himself, cf. Isa. xlv. 23; Jer. xxii. 5; Heb. vi. 17. The lifting up of the hand was a gesture used in making oath. Cf. Gen. xiv. 22; Rev. x. 5, 6.

40. *I live for ever*] "The Lord liveth" was an usual formula in swearing. Cf. Num. xiv. 21; 1 S. xiv. 39, 45; Jer. v. 2.

41. *I will render vengeance*] Having taken the work in hand, I will thoroughly and terribly avenge myself. Here begins the apodosis of the sentence, the substance of the oath.

42. *from the beginning of revenges upon the enemy*] Render, **from the head** (*i.e.* the chief) **of the princes of the enemy.** See Note at end of the chapter.

43. *Rejoice, O ye nations, with his people*] Render rather, **O ye nations, praise His people;** and see the Note at end of the chapter. The A. V. however follows LXX., as does St Paul when citing the passage, Rom. xv. 10.

Nor does the rendering of the LXX. differ greatly in effect from that above suggested. For the heathen, here called upon to laud God's people, can only be required to do

45 And Moses made an end of
speaking all these words to all Israel:
f chap. 6. 6. & 11. 18. 46 And he said unto them, [f] Set
your hearts unto all the words which
I testify among you this day, which
ye shall command your children to
observe to do, all the words of this
law.
47 For it *is* not a vain thing for
you; because it *is* your life: and
through this thing ye shall prolong
your days in the land, whither ye go
over Jordan to possess it.
g Numb. 27. 12. 48 [g] And the LORD spake unto
Moses that selfsame day, saying,
49 Get thee up into this mountain
Abarim, *unto* mount Nebo, which *is*
in the land of Moab, that *is* over
against Jericho; and behold the land
of Canaan, which I give unto the children of Israel for a possession:
50 And die in the mount whither
thou goest up, and be gathered unto
thy people; as [h] Aaron thy brother *h* Numb. 20. 25, 28. & 33. 38.
died in mount Hor, and was gathered
unto his people:
51 Because [i] ye trespassed against *i* Numb. 20. 12, 13. & 27. 14.
me among the children of Israel at
the waters of ‖ Meribah-Kadesh, in ‖ Or, *Strife* at *Kadesh.*
the wilderness of Zin; because ye
sanctified me not in the midst of the
children of Israel.
52 Yet thou shalt see the land before *thee;* but thou shalt not go thither
unto the land which I give the children of Israel.

---

so when they have themselves received a share of God's mercies "to His land and to His people," and had cause therefore themselves to "rejoice with His people." It is apparent also that, since the praise is to be addressed, in the first instance, to "His people," and not directly to God Himself, the "mercies" must be regarded as overflowing to the rejoicing Gentiles through and from the Jews. Nor can we imagine such praise to be bestowed by the Gentiles upon the Jews for such "mercies," whilst the Jews were themselves excluded from the same. It seems then that, in this profound passage, there is shadowed forth the purpose of God to overrule (1) the unbelief of the Jews to the bringing in of the Gentiles; and (2) the mercy shewn to the Gentiles to the eventual restoration of the Jews (cf. Rom. xi. 25—36).

The Song closes then, as it began *vv.* 1—3, with an invitation to praise; and has reached, through a long series of Divine interpositions, the grandest theme for it in this call to the Gentiles, now heathen no more, to rejoice over God's restored people, the Jews.

44—52. These verses were, no doubt, added by the author of the supplement to Deut. See Introd., § II. *Vv.* 48 sqq. repeat the command already given, Num. xxvii. 12 sqq.

44. *Hoshea*] Cf. Num. xiii. 16.

46. Cf. vi. 6, xi. 18.

47. *because it is your life*] Cf. xxx. 20.

49. *this mountain Abarim, unto mount Nebo*] Cf. Num. xxi. 10, 20, and notes.

52. *Yet thou shalt see the land*] Cf. Heb. xi. 13.

NOTES on CHAP. XXXII; and on *vv.* 5, 26, 33, 36, 42, and 43.

NOTE on ch. xxxii.

Those who deny that Moses is the author of Deuteronomy, of course include this chapter in their statements. As regards it, however, the further and special question has been raised whether it is from the same hand, be it of Moses or of any other, as the rest of the book in which it is placed. That there is nothing in its length and structure to prove a late origin has been in effect shown by the remarks on the other Song of Moses given in Ex. xv.: cf. Introduction to Exodus, p. 239. Many modern critics (Ewald, Knobel, Bleek, Kamphausen, Davidson, &c.) have however confidently maintained that this Song was first written in the days of the Kings, subsequent to the revolt of Jeroboam, and was inserted by the still later "Deuteronomist" in his compilation. They maintain this as regards the Song because of the characteristics (1) of its style, (2) of its ideas.

1. That the Song differs signally in diction and idiom from the preceding chapters is obvious, but proves nothing. That a lyrical passage should be conceived in modes of thought wholly unlike those which belong to narrative or exhortation, and be uttered in different phraseology, is ordinary and natural. The same general traits distinguish the choruses of a Greek play from its dialogue.

There are in the Song notwithstanding numerous coincidences both in thoughts and words with other parts of the Pentateuch, and especially with Deut. Some of these have been pointed out in the notes on the successive verses. A long list of them is given by Colenso, 'Pentateuch,' § 799. Many no doubt are unimportant, but others are not so; and their critical weight altogether is more than enough to outweigh the presumption, in itself not very grave, of a difference of authorship drawn from a difference of style.

The occurrence of Aramaisms in the Song is alleged by Kamph. and others (*e.g.* שדים *v.* 17; תשי from שיה *v.* 18; אפאיהם *v.* 26; אזלת *v.* 36). Of these and other instances given, some are questioned by recent critics (see *e.g.* the note on *v.* 26); and even were all certain, they would not furnish conclusive proof of the date assigned by Ewald, Kamph., &c.. For the canon laid down by Koenig, 'Alttest. Studien,' II. 8, "Aramaisms in a book of Scripture are a token either of a very early or very late composition," is now generally accepted. In poetry particularly Aramaisms were used, as are archaisms in the poetry of all languages, long after they had ceased to be vernacular (see Bleek, 'Introduction to the Old Testament,' Vol. I. § 39 (edit. Venables); Keil, 'Introd. to the Old Testament,' Part I. ch. II, § 13 (edit. Clark). The Aramaisms in question then are compatible with a Mosaic origin of the Song, and possibly also with one dating after the reign of Hezekiah; but they can hardly be so with the date suggested by Knobel, the reign of Ahab, *i.e.* the tenth century B.C.

The resemblances between Ps. xc. and Deut. xxxii. have been rightly regarded as important. Cf. especially the expression "the Rock," with *v.* 1 of the Psalm; and Deut. xxxii. 7 with *vv.* 1 and 15 of the Psalm; also *vv.* 4 and 36 of the former with *vv.* 16 and 13 of the latter. The manner and turn of thought of the Psalm are certainly also similar to those of the Song (see Delitzsch on Ps. xc.). Now Bleek, remarking ('Introduction to Old Testament,' Vol. II. p. 234, edit. Venables) on the superscription of the Psalm, which calls it "A Prayer of Moses," says: "There is no authentic reason for denying to the lawgiver the authorship of this Psalm, and at all events it bears the stamp of very great antiquity." Ewald also grants the last part of this statement.

Kamph. however himself seems practically to admit the insufficiency of the argument drawn from style, when he says, p. 247, "If the composition of Deuteronomy by Moses, of which many learned men are still convinced, could really stand as established, then naturally the question about the authenticity of our Song would be decided in the traditional sense."

(2) Of arguments against the Mosaic authorship belonging to the second class, many resolve themselves ultimately into a mere rejection of prophecy as such. The Song has reference to a state of things which did not ensue until long after the days of Moses. It is thence inferred at once that it could not have been written by him. Such assumptions need not be here discussed.

But some (*e.g.* Kamph.) who will not reject prophecy *in toto*, are nevertheless convinced that the Song must have originated at a far later epoch than that of Moses. It sets forth, they observe, a religious and political aspect of affairs which did not arise until after the disruption in the reign of Rehoboam, and even the decline of the Monarchy of the Ten Tribes; its whole tenor of ideas and associations is of some such era; its very theme and scope is the restoration of a right relationship of God's people to Him, a relationship which is assumed to have been interrupted by the faithlessness of the human party in the covenant. Now the topics of Isaiah and the prophets following him are the very same.

In reply it must be said that other parts of Deuteronomy and the Pentateuch no less distinctly contemplate an apostasy (*e.g.* Deut. xxviii.; Lev. xxvi.), and that therefore the mere fact of such being referred to in this chapter proves nothing as to it in particular. Further, the apostasy is really named here in general and highly poetical terms; terms certainly not so definite as those employed in other parts of the Pentateuch on the same subject. The exhibition of the apostasy in the Song, not as a possible but as an accomplished event, is in the manner common to the prophets. They treat a Future presented to their inspired gaze whilst they write or speak, as though it were a real living Present; and hence "the prophetic present" has passed into a well-understood and technical term.

The like remarks apply to the political allusions. No doubt these assume that the people has passed through an era of prosperity and success, and has reached one of disaster and subjugation. Yet the description contains no single trait which can fairly be said to imply a personal knowledge either of the Syrian or Assyrian victories over Israel. Indeed the fact (remarked by Knobel), that the close of the Song holds out to Israel, and, be it noted, not to a portion of Israel, but emphatically to Israel as a whole, a lively hope of revenge and recovery, seems, on the ground of "the higher criticism" at least, to refute at once the usual hypothesis of the critics of that school themselves; for in the closing years of the kingdom of Samaria such triumphs could hardly be dreamed of by any discerning patriot against the overwhelming might of Assyria. And yet it is just to those years that they ascribe the origin of the Song.

It is to be observed that the blessings annexed in the Song to faithfulness, whether named as promises or performances, are those which recur so commonly in Deuteronomy, and which must have been in the closing months of Moses' life perpetually in his mind; those namely connected with the Promised Land. On the other hand, the promises which emerge in the later times, and which cluster round the "Son of David," who should restore again all things to Israel, are wholly absent.

The "objectivity" of the Song is justly referred to by Schultz and others as one of its most remarkable traits. Now there is no more universal or striking characteristic of the most ancient poetry of every nation than this.

It may be added that, exhibiting as it does in series, God's preventing mercies, His people's faithlessness and ingratitude, God's consequent judgments, and the final and complete triumph of the Divine counsels of grace, it forms the summary of all later Old Testament prophecies, and gives as it were the framework upon which they are laid out. Here as elsewhere the Pentateuch presents itself as the foundation of the religious life of Israel in after times.

If once we admit the possibility that Moses might foresee the future apostasy of Israel, it is scarce possible to conceive how such foresight could be turned to better account by him than by the writing of this Song. In style rugged, sententious, and incisive; abounding in pregnant metaphors, and bold contrasts; impassioned in earnestness; and built up with a very careful attention to rhythm, no strain could be more likely to strike the imagination or to fasten on the memory of an Eastern people or better calculated to attain the specific purpose announced as aimed at in its composition: see xxxi. 19 sqq. Its currency would be a standing protest against apostasy; a protest which might well check waverers, and warn the faithful that the revolt of others was neither unforeseen nor unprovided for by Him in whom they trusted.

That this Ode must on every ground take the very first rank in Hebrew poetry is universally allowed. The rationalist critics however have no better explanation to offer about its origin than that "the Deuteronomist," a compiler supposed to be living in the years immediately preceding the Babylonish captivity, "found" it, an anonymous document of more than a century old, the production of some forgotten author belonging to the northern kingdom, and incorporated it into his work, inventing by way of accounting for its insertion the statements of xxxi. 16—30. Such a conjecture is most unlikely on the face of it; and is a supposition such surely as no one would maintain about this splendid poem, unless he had adopted it on grounds other than those found in the Song itself, and had to defend it to the utmost at all hazards.

"The Song of Moses" has furnished a theme for several monographs; amongst the most noteworthy of which are Vitringa, 'Commentarius ad Canticum Mosis' (1734); Dathe, 'Dissertatio in Canticum Mosis' (1769); Ewald, 'Das grosse Lied in Deuteronomium' ('Jahrb. der Bibl. Wissenschaft,' 1857); Volck, 'Mosis Canticum Cygneum,' Nordlingen, 1861; Kamphausen, 'Das Lied Moses,' Leipzig, 1862.

v. 5.

The word "spot" or "blemish" (מום) appears to have a moral signification here as Prov. ix. 7; Job xi. 15; 2 Pet. ii. 13. The rendering of margin, though supported by Abenez., Philippson, &c., is intolerably harsh; others (Rosenm., Baumg., Schultz, &c.) treat the whole passage as interrogative, and carry on the subject from the preceding verse, "Has He" (*i.e.* God) "acted corruptly towards him? No: His children themselves are their own disgrace." But this does not suit the tenor of the context. Others (Lowth, Donald., &c.) render "their spot" (*i.e.* the defiling infection of their sin) "has corrupted before Him children not" (*i.e.* no longer) "His"; but this inversion of the order of the words is unwarrantable. Ewald and Fürst assign quite another sense: "His notsons have violated their oath to Him." They give however no example of מום in the sense of "oath" from the Hebrew, and the illustrations from the Arabic are not convincing. On the whole, though the passage is difficult, no better version has yet been offered than that suggested in the foot-note; which is substantially that adopted by Knob., Keil, Schröder, &c. The variations of the ancient versions suggest the suspicion that the text in this *v.* is and has long been corrupt.

v. 26.

LXX. διασπερῶ αὐτούς. The Hebrew word here is ἅπαξ λεγ., and is taken by the English Version after most ancient authorities as a denominative from פאה. The modern Hebraists (Gesen., Fürst, &c.) however regard it as an independent root, found also in פה and Arab. فاه (cf. Gk. φη-μι, Lat. *fa-ri*), and meaning to "breathe" or "blow." Hence it means "ceu vento dispergam eos," Gesen. 'Thes.'

v. 36.

This phrase is proverbial (cf. 1 K. xiv. 10, xxi. 21; 2 K. ix. 8), and based on a paronomasia (עצור ועזוב). Its general sense is clear: it means "all men of all sorts;" and its literal force is correctly given in the A. V., though the word translated "left" might perhaps as well be rendered "set free." Its original and proper significance has however been uncertain from very early times. The best explanation of it is probably that of De Dieu, which has analogies in the Arabic, and is followed by Dathe, Baumg., Delitzsch, Keil, Knob., &c., who regard it as originally meaning "married and single" (cf. the German *ledig*): others (Rosenm., Gesen., De Wette, &c.) suggest "bond and free," or "confined and at large:" others (Kimchi and some

Jewish authorities) "precious" (and so shut up and guarded), and "vile" (and so neglected): others (Fürst, &c.) "he who is restrained and he who is his own master," which is substantially identical with that of Kamph., "he who is not of full age, and he who is so, and therefore is independent:" *alii alia.*

v. 42.

The LXX. [ἀπὸ κεφαλῆς ἀρχόντων ἐχθρῶν] adopts the rendering suggested in the foot-note. So Vater, Gesen., Maur., Kamph., Fürst, Wogue, &c. This rendering is strongly supported by the Hebrew of Judg. v. 2 (see note). Others indeed (Cappellus, Vitringa, Knobel, Keil, Schröder, Volck, &c.) render the word פרע by "hair," as in Num. vi. 5; cf. Lev. xxi. 10; and thus the passage would run: "from the hairy head of the enemy;" cf. Ps. lxviii. 21. The word פרע is however here in the plural. Either way the clause connects itself with the verbs in the preceding clauses: "I will make my arrows drunk with blood, and my sword shall devour flesh; with (or from) the blood of the slain, and with (or from) the chief of the princes." The rendering of the A.V., in this place and Judg. v. 2, cannot be maintained.

v. 43.

The word "with" is supplied by the A.V., as by the LXX. εὐφράνθητε ἔθνη μετὰ τοῦ λαοῦ αὐτοῦ, but needlessly. The translation of the words, however, which has been variously given, must depend upon that of the verb, הרנינו. This verb in Kal and Piel means "to sound;" and also "to rejoice," or "to utter praise;" and transitively "to laud," "praise," or "rejoice in" (cf. for Kal, Isa. lxi. 7; for Piel, Ps. li. 16). The intransitive senses of the verb in Kal and Piel are found also in its Hiphil forms (*e.g.* Job xxix. 13; Ps. xxxii. 11). There can then be no doubt that the transitive sense, though it does not actually occur, is admissible in Hiphil; and we have, in all likelihood, an example of it in the words before us. (So Vulg., "Laudate gentes populum ejus;" Samar., and many Jewish authorities; Dathe, Baumg., Schultz, Volck, Herx., Knob., Schröder, Wogue, &c.) Other renderings are (1) "O ye nations, cause His people to rejoice" (Alting, Vater, &c.); (2) "O ye nations, who are His people, rejoice" (Aquila, Theodot., Luther, Rosenm., Ewald, Maur., Gesen., Fürst, &c.). But of these two the former does not suit the context, no reason being assigned in it why "the nations" should cause joy to God's people; the latter is objectionable, because it assumes an apposition between עמו and גוים, which terms are generally (though not universally) contradistinguished, and here seem to be especially so from the tenor of the whole Song (cf. *v.* 21), and from the difference of number in the nouns.

CHAPTER XXXIII.

1 *The majesty of God.* 6 *The blessings of the twelve tribes.* 26 *The excellency of Israel.*

AND this *is* the blessing, wherewith Moses the man of God
blessed the children of Israel before
his death.
2 And he said, The LORD came
from Sinai, and rose up from Seir
unto them; he shined forth from

CHAP. XXXIII. Blessing of Moses. For general remarks, see Note at end of chapter.

The Blessing contains (1) an Introduction, *vv.* 1—5; (2) the Benedictions pronounced on the Tribes individually, *vv.* 6—25; (3) a Conclusion, *vv.* 26—29.

It was no doubt spoken by Moses, probably on the same day and to the same assembly as the Song (xxxii. 1—43), as soon as he received the renewed notice of his approaching decease (xxxii. 48), and just before he ascended Mount Nebo. Like the Blessing of Jacob (Gen. xlix.), to which it has an intimate though independent correspondence throughout, it is the solemn farewell of the earthly head of the race. A comparison with Gen. l. c. will shew how the blessings uttered by Moses over the several Tribes partly repeat, partly enlarge and supplement, and sometimes modify or even reverse, the predictions of the dying Jacob. The characteristics of the Blessing are such as distinctly suit the place which it occupies in the Pentateuch, both as to time and circumstance.

This chapter, in striking contrast with the last, is pervaded by a tone of happy augury. It is indeed fitting to use auspicious words in a leave-taking; but the total absence of warning and reproof has been rightly noted as indicating that Moses is here speaking of the ideal Israel, of the people of God as they might and would have been but for their perverseness, rather than foretelling what would in fact be the fate and fortunes of the Twelve Tribes. As then the Song sets forth the calamities with which God's justice will visit Israel's fall, so does the Blessing describe the glory and greatness which would from His mercy crown Israel's faithfulness. The Song and the Blessing are therefore correspondent, and mutually supplementary. The form into which the Blessing is thrown exhibits the several tribes co-operating, each according to its peculiar characteristics and

mount Paran, and he came with ten
thousands of saints: from his right
hand *went* †a fiery law for them.
3 Yea, he loved the people; all his
saints *are* in thy hand: and they sat
down at thy feet; *every one* shall receive of thy words.
4 Moses commanded us a law, *even*
the inheritance of the congregation of
Jacob.
5 And he was king in Jeshurun,
when the heads of the people *and*
the tribes of Israel were gathered together.
6 ¶ Let Reuben live, and not die;
and let *not* his men be few.

† Heb. *a fire of law.*

---

circumstances, for the accomplishment of the national mission.

1—5. Introduction.

1. *Moses the man of God*] The same title is given to Moses, Josh. xiv. 6, and in the heading of Ps. xc. Cf. 1 S. ix. 6; 1 K. xii. 22. The "man of God" in the Old Testament is one who is favoured with direct revelations, but not necessarily an official Prophet (*nābhī*). The occurrence of the title here is no doubt a token that the Blessing was not, as was the Song, transcribed by Moses himself. Cf. xxxi. 22.

Moses when he spoke it had no doubt his coadjutor (cf. xxxi. 14 sqq.) and successor Joshua by his side, who also shared in the prophetic spirit by which the Blessing was dictated.

2—5. The glorious giving of the Law from Sinai, and appointment thereby of Israel to be God's peculiar people. The blessings of the individual tribes spring out of God's mercies to the nation, and hence are introduced as they are summed up (*vv.* 26—29) by an eulogy of the great privileges pertaining to Israel as a whole.

2. *The LORD came from Sinai, and rose up from Seir*, &c.] By "Seir" is to be understood the mountain-land of the Edomites, and by "mount Paran" (cf. on Num. x. 12) the range which forms the northern boundary of the desert of Sinai. Thus the *v.* forms a poetical description of the vast arena upon which the glorious manifestation of the Lord in the giving of the Covenant took place. The passage is imitated Judg. v. 4, 5, and Hab. iii. 3, where Teman is synonymous with Seir. Cf. also Ps. lxviii. 7, 8.

with ten thousands of saints] Render, **from amidst ten thousands of holy ones**: lit. from myriads of holiness, *i.e.* holy angels; cf. Zech. xiv. 5. See Note at end of the chapter.

3. *he loved the people*] Lit. "the peoples," *i.e.* the Twelve Tribes, not the Gentiles. The latter sense, suggested by some, is here out of place.

all his saints are in thy hand] The term saints refers to God's chosen people just before spoken of. Cf. vii. 18, 21; Ex. xix. 6; Dan. vii. 18, 21. The change from the third to the second person, or vice versa, is not uncommon in Hebrew poetry. Cf. xxxii. 15; Ps. xlix. 15—19. The explanation suggested by Wordsw. after Vater, Keil, &c., "all the holy angels wait upon Him," seems less suitable to the tenor of the context.

4. *Moses commanded us a law*] Though Moses probably did not transcribe this Blessing, yet he probably uttered these words, although he himself is thus referred to in the third person. The inspired writers, speaking less their own words and in their own person than in the name and words of the Spirit which moved them, frequently refer to themselves in this objective way: cf. Num. xii. 3; Judg. v. 15; Ps. xxi. throughout. In the word "us" Moses identifies himself with the people. Cf. Hab. iii. 19; Joh. xix. 24.

5. *he was king*] Rather, **he became king**, *i.e.* the Lord, not (as Abenez., Vatabl., Luth., &c.) Moses, who is never spoken of as a "king."

Jeshurun] Cf. xxxii. 15.

6—25. Blessings of the Tribes individually.

6. Reuben.

let not his men be few] Lit. "a number." The negative particle is supplied in the A. V. from the preceding context, and, so far as concerns the sense, rightly. The term "a number" means "a small number," such as could be easily counted. Cf. iv. 27; Gen. xxxiv. 30. The *v.* thus promises that the tribe shall endure and prosper, and its tenor is in contrast with that of Gen. xlix. 3, 4. Yet it must be noted that the tribe had decreased since the Exodus, cf. Num. i. 21 with xxvi. 7; and also that in later times its numbers, even when counted with the Gadites and the half of Manasseh, were fewer than that of the Reubenites alone at the census of Num. i. (Cf. 1 Chron. v. 18). The blessing of the text seems therefore to be so worded as to carry with it a warning. The Reubenites took possession of the southern portion of the land conquered east of Jordan, a large and fertile district without determinate boundary towards the Euphrates. Occupied with their herds and flocks, they appear, soon after the days of Joshua, to have lost their early energy. They could not be roused to take

7 ¶ And this *is the blessing* of Judah: and he said, Hear, LORD, the voice of Judah, and bring him unto his people: let his hands be sufficient for him; and be thou an help *to him* from his enemies.

[a] Exod. 28. 30.

8 ¶ And of Levi he said, [a] *Let* thy Thummim and thy Urim *be* with thy holy one, whom thou didst prove at Massah, *and with* whom thou didst strive at the waters of Meribah;

9 Who said unto his father and to his mother, I have not seen him; neither did he acknowledge his brethren, nor knew his own children: for they have observed thy word, and kept thy covenant.

10 ‖ They shall teach Jacob thy

‖ Or, *Let them teach, &c.*

their part in the national rising against Jabin (cf. Judg. v. 15, 16); they dissipated their strength in distant expeditions, carried sometimes as far as the Euphrates, and undertaken no doubt to provide pastures for their multiplying flocks (cf. 1 Chron. v. 9, 10, 18 sqq.); and they do not seem to have cared to complete the conquest of the territory of which they took possession after the victories over Sihon and Og: cf. Num. xxxii. and notes. No judge, prophet, or national hero arose out of this tribe; and, as the recently discovered Moabite stone proves, the cities assigned to the Reubenites by Joshua were for the most part wrested, partly or wholly, from them by the Moabites, with whom they in all likelihood became gradually much intermixed. (See Schlottmann, 'Die Siegesäule Mesa's, pp. 36 sqq.)

The tribe of Simeon, which would according to the order of birth come next, though of course comprehended in the general blessing bestowed upon the whole people, *vv.* 1—5 and 26—29, is not here named. This omission is explained by reference to the words of Jacob concerning Simeon, Gen. xlix. 7. This tribe with Levi was to be "scattered in Israel." The fulfilment of this prediction was in the case of Levi so ordered as to carry with it honour and blessing; but no such reversal of punishment is granted to Simeon. Rather had this latter tribe added new sins to those which Jacob denounced (cf. Num. xxv.). Accordingly, though very numerous at the Exodus, it had surprisingly diminished before the death of Moses; cf. Num. i. 22, 23 with Num. xxvi. 12—14; and found eventually an adequate territory within the limits of Judah. Cf. Josh. xix. 2—9. The tribe is mentioned as making certain conquests along with Judah, Judg. i. 17; and is probably "the remnant of the people" spoken of, 1 K. xii. 23, as constituting, together with Judah and Benjamin, the forces of Rehoboam. In later history the families of the Simeonites were not only still extant, but made certain conquests in the south, 1 Chro. iv. 24 sqq., and 39—43.

7. Judah.

bring him unto his people] Jacob (Gen. xlix. 8, 9) had predicted glorious success in war to this tribe. Moses now, taking up, as it were, the promise of Jacob, prays that Judah, marching forth at the head of the tribes, might ever be brought back in safety and victory; and intimates that God would grant help to accomplish this. (So substantially Onkel., Saad., Hengst., Keil, &c.) It is obvious that the words "bring him unto his people" cannot have the sense attached to them by the rationalist commentators, "bring back the tribes," *i.e.* the ten tribes which revolted under Jeroboam "to him."

8—11. Levi.

The blessing of Levi, like that of Judah, is addressed to God as a prayer.

thy Thummim and thy Urim] *i.e.* "thy Right and thy Light:" cf. on Ex. xxviii. 30.

thy holy one] *i.e.* Levi, regarded as the representative of the whole priestly and levitical stock which sprang from him. Hence, in the *vv.* following, the blessing proceeds in the plural form. The contrast between the tone of this passage and that of Gen. xlix. 5—7 is remarkable. Though the prediction of Jacob respecting the dispersion of this tribe held good, yet it was so overruled as to issue in honour and reward. The recovery of God's favour is to be traced to the faithfulness with which Moses and Aaron, who came of this tribe, served God in their high offices; and to the zeal and constancy which conspicuous persons of the tribe (*e.g.* Phinehas, Num. xxv. 11 sqq.), and the whole tribe itself (cf. Ex. xxxii. 26), manifested on critical occasions in supporting the leaders of the people. The same reasons led to Levi's being selected for the special service of God in the Sanctuary, ch. x. 8 sqq., and Num. viii. 5 sqq.; and for the office of instructing their brethren in the knowledge of the Law. On *Massah*, cf. Ex. xvii. 1—7; on *Meribah*, Num. xx. 1—13. The two events thus alluded to, the one occurring at the beginning, the other towards the end of the forty years' wandering, serve to represent the whole series of trials by which God proved and exercised the faith and obedience of this chosen tribe. In conformity with the spirit of the chapter, the facts that Moses and Aaron failed under the trial at Kadesh (cf. Num. xx.), and that some of the Levites were concerned in the rebellion of Korah (Num. xvi.), are passed over in silence.

9. *Who said unto his father and to his mother*] Cf. St Matt. x. 37; St Luke xiv. 26.

‖ Or, *let them put incense.* † Heb. *at thy nose.*

judgments, and Israel thy law: ‖they
shall put incense †before thee, and
whole burnt sacrifice upon thine altar.
11 Bless, LORD, his substance, and
accept the work of his hands: smite
through the loins of them that rise
against him, and of them that hate
him, that they rise not again.
12 ¶ *And* of Benjamin he said, The
beloved of the LORD shall dwell in
safety by him; *and the LORD* shall
cover him all the day long, and he
shall dwell between his shoulders.
13 ¶ And of Joseph he said, [b] Blessed of the LORD *be* his land, for the
precious things of heaven, for the dew,
and for the deep that coucheth beneath,
14 And for the precious fruits
brought forth by the sun, and for the
precious things †put forth by the
†moon,

[b] Gen. 49. 25.

† Heb. *thrust forth.* † Heb. *moons.*

15 And for the chief things of the
ancient mountains, and for the precious things of the lasting hills,
16 And for the precious things of
the earth and fulness thereof, and *for*
the good will of him that dwelt in the
bush: let *the blessing* come upon the
head of Joseph, and upon the top of
the head of him *that was* [c] separated
from his brethren.
17 His glory *is like* the firstling of
his bullock, and his horns *are like* the
horns of unicorns: with them he shall
push the people together to the ends
of the earth: and they *are* the ten
thousands of Ephraim, and they *are*
the thousands of Manasseh.
18 ¶ And of Zebulun he said, Rejoice, Zebulun, in thy going out; and,
Issachar, in thy tents.
19 They shall call the people unto
the mountain; there they shall offer

[c] Gen. 49. 26.

---

11. *smite through the loins*] Rather, **smite the loins**, *i.e.* the seat of their strength.

12. Benjamin.

he shall dwell between his shoulders] *i.e.* be supported by God as a son who is carried by his father; cf. i. 31. The change of subject in this *v.* is not rare in Hebrew, cf. *e.g.* 2 S. xi. 13, and is here the less difficult, because the suffix throughout the passage has but one reference, viz. to God. Benjamin was specially beloved of his father (Gen. xxxv. 18, xliv. 20); Moses now promises no less love to him from God Himself. To refer the words, "He shall dwell, &c." to God and to explain them of the Temple, which was afterwards built in the land of this tribe, as many commentators do, is farfetched and harsh.

13—17. Joseph, including Ephraim and Manasseh.

The resemblance of this blessing to that pronounced on the same tribes by Jacob (cf. Gen. xlix. 25 and 26) is obvious both in thoughts and words; and in both the exuberant fertility of the large districts allotted to the descendants of Joseph is a leading feature. Yet the words of Moses are far from being a mere reproduction of Jacob's. The patriarch dwells with emphasis on the severe conflicts which these tribes would undergo (cf. Gen. xlix. 23, 24); the lawgiver seems to look beyond, and to behold the two tribes triumphant and established in their power. The utterances respecting Ephraim and Manasseh in these *vv.* are such as are wholly unlikely to have proceeded from a writer of the kingdom of Judah, at the time assigned by the rationalist critics for the composition of Deut.

17. *His glory is like the firstling of his bullock*] Render rather: "The first-born of his" (*i.e.* Joseph's) "bullock is his glory." (So substantially Onkel., Maurer, Knobel, &c.) The reference here is not to Joseph, nor to Joshua, nor to Jeroboam II., but to Ephraim, who was raised by Jacob to the honours of the firstborn (Gen. xlviii. 8), and is here likened to the firstling of Joseph's oxen, *i.e.* of Joseph's offspring, the singular noun (*shōr*) being taken collectively. The ox is a common emblem of power and strength; cf. Gen. xlix. 6, margin, and note; Ps. xxii. 12; Jer. xlvi. 20; Amos iv. 1.

unicorns] Render, **a wild bull**. Cf. Num. xxiii. 22 and note.

the ten thousands of Ephraim, and...the thousands of Manasseh] Cf. Gen xlviii. 19; 1 S. xviii. 7, 8.

18, 19. Zebulun and Issachar.

Cf. Gen. xlix. 13—15, the substance of which is forcibly repeated; and, like Jacob, Moses places first the younger of the two tribes. Zebulun possessed a commodious seashore, and the fisheries of the Lake of Tiberias: and was therefore to thrive by commerce, and to rejoice in his "going out," *i.e.* in his mercantile enterprises. Issachar possessed a fertile inland district, and would therefore dwell at home and prosper in agriculture. Both tribes distinguished themselves in the contest with Jabin; cf. Judg. v. 14, 15, 18: and of Zebulun it is particularly noted

sacrifices of righteousness: for they
shall suck *of* the abundance of the
seas, and *of* treasures hid in the sand.
20 ¶ And of Gad he said, Blessed
be he that enlargeth Gad: he dwelleth
as a lion, and teareth the arm with
the crown of the head.
21 And he provided the first part
for himself, because there, *in* a portion of the lawgiver, *was he* † seated;
and he came with the heads of the
people, he executed the justice of the
LORD, and his judgments with Israel.

† Heb. *cieled.*

22 ¶ And of Dan he said, Dan *is* a
lion's whelp: he shall leap from Bashan.
23 ¶ And of Naphtali he said, O
Naphtali, satisfied with favour, and
full with the blessing of the LORD:
possess thou the west and the south.
24 ¶ And of Asher he said, *Let*
Asher *be* blessed with children; let
him be acceptable to his brethren, and
let him dip his foot in oil.
25 ‖ Thy shoes *shall be* iron and
brass; and as thy days, *so shall* thy
strength *be*.

‖ Or, Under *thy shoes* shall be *iron.*

---

that it produced the officers and tacticians who led and marshalled the host which vanquished Sisera: see on Judg. v. 14, and cf. 1 Chron. xii. 33.

19. *unto the mountain*] Cf. Ex. xv. 17.

sacrifices of righteousness] Sacrifices offered by the righteous, and therefore well pleasing to God. Cf. Ps. iv. 5, li. 19.

treasures hid in the sand] The riches of the seas in general. It is noteworthy however that the sand of these coasts was specially valuable in the manufacture of glass (cf. Tac. 'Hist.' v. 7; Pliny 'H. N.' v. 17; XXXVI. 65; Joseph. 'B. J.' II. 10. 2); and glass was a precious thing in ancient times: cf. Job xxviii. 17. The murex too, from which the precious purple dye was extracted, was found here. A typical reference to the conversion of the Gentiles is strongly suggested by Isa. lx. 5, 6, 16, and lxvi. 11, 12.

20, 21. Gad.

20. *Blessed be he that enlargeth Gad*] *i.e.* blessed be God who shall grant to Gad a spacious territory; cf. the blessing of Shem, Gen. ix. 26.

the arm with the crown] Rather, **yea, the crown.** The warlike character of this tribe is shewn by their leading the van in the long campaigns of Joshua; cf. Josh. iv. 12, 13, xxii. 1—4; by the acts of Jehu, 2 K. ix. x.; by 1 Chro. v. 18—22, and xii. 8 sqq.

21. *the first part for himself*] The first fruits of the conquest made by Israel were assigned to Gad and Reuben by Moses at their own request. Cf. Num. xxxii.

because there, in a portion of the lawgiver, was he seated] Render rather, **because there was the leader's portion reserved,** *i.e.* there was reserved the fitting portion for Gad as a leader in war. See Note at end of the chapter.

and he came with the heads of the people] *i.e.* he joined the other leaders to fulfil the commands of God respecting the conquest of Canaan. Cf. Num. xxxii. 17, 21, 32; Josh. i. 14, iv. 12. Moses regards the promise of the Gadites to do this as already redeemed.

22. Dan.

he shall leap from Bashan] *i.e.* be like a lion which leaps forth from his covert in Bashan. Cf. Song of S. iv. 8. There is no historical reference, as *e.g.* to the conquest of Dan-Laish, Josh. xix. 47.

23. Naphtali.

satisfied with favour] Cf. Gen. xlix. 21 and note. The idea suggested in both passages is similar.

the west and the south] The territory of Naphtali was situated in the north-west of Canaan; and the words should therefore evidently be taken, as in the Hebrew they often are, and as LXX. and other Versions suggest, as referring not to geographical position, but to natural characteristics. Render therefore "the sea and the sunny district." The possession of Naphtali included nearly the whole west coast of the Sea of Galilee, the Lake of Merom, the modern *Bahr el Huleh*, and the well-watered district near to the springs of Jordan. It contained some of the grandest scenery and some of the most fertile land in Palestine. Josephus speaks of the shore of Gennesaret as "an earthly paradise" ('B. J.' III. 3. 2); and Porter, 'Handbook for Syria,' as "the garden of Palestine." The modern name for this district *Belad Besharah*, ("land of good tidings") is significant. The climate in the lower levels towards the waters of Merom is exceedingly hot, peculiarly suited for tropical productions. Fruits ripen here much earlier than in other parts of the country: see Robinson 'B. R.' II. 434 sqq.; Tristram 'Land of Israel' p. 583; Burckhardt, 'Syria,' pp. 40 sqq.

24, 25. Asher.

Let Asher be blessed with children; and *let him be acceptable to his brethren*] These words should rather perhaps be rendered (with Keil. Knobel, Wogue, &c.), "Blessed above the sons" (*i.e.* of Jacob = most blessed amongst

26 ¶ *There is* none like unto the God of Jeshurun, *who* rideth upon the heaven in thy help, and in his excellency on the sky.

27 The eternal God *is thy* refuge, and underneath *are* the everlasting arms: and he shall thrust out the enemy from before thee; and shall say, Destroy *them*.

[d] Jer. 23. 6.

28 [d] Israel then shall dwell in safety alone: the fountain of Jacob *shall be* upon a land of corn and wine; also his heavens shall drop down dew.

29 Happy *art* thou, O Israel: who *is* like unto thee, O people saved by the LORD, the shield of thy help, and who *is* the sword of thy excellency! and thine enemies ‖ shall be found liars unto thee; and thou shalt tread upon their high places.

‖ Or, *shall be subdued.*

---

the sons of Jacob) "be Asher; let him be the favoured one of his brethren," *i.e.* the one favoured of God.

25. *Thy shoes*] See the Note at end of the chapter. The *v.* preceding had described the plenty with which this tribe should be blessed under the figure of dipping the foot in oil (cf. Job xxix. 6); and this *v.* continues the figure, and represents the strength and firmness of Asher to be as if he were shod with iron and brass. Cf. Rev. i. 15. The territory of this tribe probably contained iron and copper. Cf. viii. 9.

as thy days, so shall thy strength be] The original here has two words only, of which the latter is not found elsewhere. On it see the Note at the end of the chapter. The sense is "thy strength shall be continued to thee as long as thou shalt live: thou shalt never know feebleness and decay."

26—29. Conclusion.

God's glory and power, and the consequent safety and prosperity of God's people, form the climax, as they do the basis, of the Blessing which the lawgiver has to pronounce.

26. *There is none like unto the God of Jeshurun*] Rather, as the punctuation of the original requires, **There is none like unto God, O Jeshurun.**

27. *thy refuge*] Rather, "dwellingplace." Cf. Ps. xc. 1, xci. 9.

28. *Israel then shall dwell in safety alone: the fountain of Jacob shall be upon a land of corn and wine*] The A. V. does not preserve the symmetry of the clauses, so marked in the original here as throughout. Render rather, "Israel shall dwell in safety; alone shall the fountain of Jacob be; in a land," &c. The rendering "eye of Jacob" (Vulg., &c.) yields no apt sense, unless the words be closely connected with the following context ("oculus Jacob in terra frumenti," &c., Vulg.), and such a construction is forbidden by the rhythmical structure of the clauses above referred to. On the phrase "fountain of Jacob," cf. Ps. lxviii. 26; Isa. xlviii. 1.

29. *be found liars unto thee*] Perhaps rather "cringe before thee." The verb means to shew a feigned or forced obedience: cf. Ps. xviii. 45 and note, and Ps. lxvi. 2.

thou shalt tread upon their high places] *i.e.* occupy the commanding positions in their land, and so have it in subjection. Cf. xxxii. 13; Isa. xxxvii. 24.

NOTES on CHAP. XXXIII.; and on *vv.* 2, 21, and 25.

NOTE on ch. xxxiii.

Many modern critics have argued that the Blessing of the Tribes cannot be really Mosaic on the same general grounds of style, literary characteristics, &c. as have been brought forward in reference to the Song of Moses. It is needless to repeat, from the Note at the end of ch. xxxii., the answers already made to objections of this kind.

It has however been specially objected to the Blessing, that its contents in various places betray on the face of them an origin far later in date than the days of Moses. There are, it is urged, unquestionable allusions in what is said of several of the Tribes to the different districts in Canaan which they occupied after the conquests of Joshua: *e.g.* in the Blessing of Zebulun and Issachar, *v.* 19; of Naphtali, *v.* 23; of Asher, *vv.* 24, 25. These allusions have been by some attributed to that prophetic foresight which Moses undoubtedly possessed. Yet they may be probably explained without reference to it. For the location of the several tribes was fixed in a general way before the time at which the Blessing is represented as spoken (cf. Num. xxxiv. 16, and note); and Moses, as having lived for many years at the very borders of Canaan and in frequent intercourse with its inhabitants and their neighbours, must undoubtedly have possessed some knowledge of the topography of the country which was to be the future home of his people. The allusions in question are of a general kind, and quite consistent in character with a knowledge so acquired. It has been asserted also that *v.* 5 contains a reference to a monarchical form of government; that *v.* 7, in which Moses prays, "Hear, Lord, the voice of Judah, and bring him to his people," is an aspiration for the reunion under the sceptre of Judah of the kingdom divided under Rehoboam (Graf, Von Lengerke, Ewald, &c.); that *v.* 12 must be explained as an allusion to the Temple, &c. These objections rest on erroneous interpretations of particular verses, and are sufficiently answered in the notes on those verses. The utter uncertainty of the grounds on which such objections rest, is demonstrated by the very diverse and totally inconsistent conclusions deduced from them. Thus Knobel refers the Blessing to the days of David, whilst Graf, followed by Bleek ('Introduction to Old Testament,' Vol. I. p. 335 sqq., Eng. Transl.), proposes the reign of Jeroboam II. (B.C. 825—785). The main reason for selecting this particular period is the admission, which the critics are constrained to make, that the Blessing must have been composed at a time when all the Twelve Tribes were still abiding in their places in Canaan, and enjoying a high degree of material prosperity. But the reign of Jeroboam II. hardly satisfies these conditions. That time was certainly marked by considerable recovery, but such passages as 2 K. xiv. 26, and the tenor of the utterances of Amos respecting the condition of the northern kingdom at this very date, are inconsistent with any such happy circumstances as the Blessing confessedly supposes. Indeed it is little likely that the two tribes and a half on the east of Jordan ever recovered from the calamities inflicted by Hazael; cf. 2 K. x. 32 sqq. Still more improbable is the opinion of Maurer and Hoffmann, who place the Blessing in the days of Jehoiachin (B.C. 599), and explain *v.* 7 as referring to the large number of Jews who were then carried away from Jerusalem to Babylon (cf. 2 K. xxiv. 10 sqq.).

As against the various dates suggested subsequent to the disruption under Rehoboam, it is to be noted that there is not the slightest trace of a reference to any of those bloody civil dissensions and disorders, nor to any of those foreign wars and frequent defeats from Syrians and other neighbouring nations, which befell the people, or some one or more of its tribes in the years following that disruption, and which continued, with but little intermission, in the northern kingdom at least, until the captivity. The Blessing speaks throughout of peace and plenty. These facts have obliged Knobel to admit that the Blessing cannot have been composed later than the beginning of David's reign. His own arguments ought in consistency to have carried him further, and led him to place it much earlier. For it is impossible on his own principles to explain how the disasters, apostasies, and confusion of the latter part of Saul's reign, and still more those of the times of the Judges, could have happened at a date not long preceding that in which the Song was penned.

There is therefore no substantial reason in the contents of the Blessing for questioning that conclusion to which many verbal characteristics of the chapter point, viz. that it is by the same author as chapter xxxii., to which it has an evident relationship (see Note at beginning of chapter), *i.e.* by Moses.

On this chapter the following special treatises may be mentioned: W. A. Teller, 'Notae criticae' in Gen. xlix. Deut. xxxiii. &c., and 'Uebersetzung des Segens Jacob und Mosis,' Halle, 1766; A. G. Hoffman, 'Comm. in Mosis Benedictionem,' in Keil's 'Analekten,' IV. 2, Jena, 1823; K. H. Graf, 'Der Segen Mosis,' Leipzig, 1857; L. Diestel also ('Der Segen Jakob's,' Braunschweig, 1853) has many valuable remarks on this chapter.

v. 2.

with ten thousands of saints] The prep. (מִן) can hardly mean "with," as A. V. renders (after LXX., Vulg., Luth., and others). The notion that the angels took an active part in the covenant making at Sinai, though in itself a correct one (cf. Ps. lxviii. 17; Acts vii. 53; Gal. iii. 19; Heb. ii. 2), and one on which the Jews specially dwell as proof of the superiority of the Law to all other dispensations, is not found in the original words of this passage. They rather represent God as *quitting* heaven, where He dwells amidst the hosts of the angels (cf. 1 K. xxii. 19; Job i. 6), and descending in majesty to earth (cf. Mic. i. 3). The "ten thousands of saints" cannot in such a context mean the hosts of the Israelites (as Cler., Dathe, Winz., &c.). Fürst ('Lex.' s. v. רבבה) proposes to point as in xxxvii. 51, and to treat these words as a proper name "from Meribah."

from his right hand went a fiery law for them] The A. V. here follows Vulg., Saad., Luther, and many other authorities both ancient and modern. But the original has (see marg.) not, as the rendering of the A. V. would seem to require, "a law of fire" (*i.e.* "a fiery law"), but "a fire of law" (אש דת), *i.e.* apparently, "a fire which was a law." Accordingly Gesenius suggests that the reference is not to the lightnings of Sinai, but to the pillar of fire Ex. xiii. 21, "columna ignis quæ legi esset iis." So De Wette, Maur., Dathe, &c.

Several Hebrew MSS. however write the words in question as one. The chief reason advanced by some (Keil, Fürst, &c.) for preferring this reading is, that דת is not properly a Hebrew word, but one imported in later times from the Chaldee, which (it is said) derived it from the Persian. The word certainly occurs in Hebrew only in Ezra and

Esther; but Hävernick ('Introduction to Old Testament,' pp. 146, 147, edit. Clark) argues with some force that it is an old Hebrew word, connected with דין and דון, which, like other archaisms, held its ground in poetry, as in the present passage, after it had fallen into disuse in prose. But the authority of all kinds for the reading אשדת is considerable. The LXX. (ἐκ δεξιῶν αὐτοῦ ἄγγελοι μετ' αὐτοῦ) probably had it; for their ἄγγελοι seems to be this Hebrew word considered as a plural noun, and connected with שדר.

Yet if this probable reading be accepted, further questions arise as to its pointing and meaning. Amongst the best suggestions may be named that of Böttcher (approved substantially by Gesen., Knob., Keil, &c.), who writes "ishdeth," and renders the word "fire-darting," treating it as a noun fem. sing.; and that of Fürst, who compares Josh. xii. 3 and 8, and regards it as a proper name, or a description of a locality (Lexicon, s. v.).

v. 21.

The word מחקק is used here as in Judg. v. 9; Isa. xxxiii. 22. The fem. subst. with masc. adj. as Gen. iv. 10, xlix. 15. So Graf, Delitzsch, Johlson, Schröder, &c. The rendering of A. V. can only mean that Gad in fact firmly established himself in the territory assigned to him by Moses. But the words are introduced by "because," and are intended to explain why Gad "provided the first part for himself." This explanation is not given by the rendering in question, though adopted also by Rosenm., Gesen., &c. The Jewish authorities (*e.g.* Onkel., Jarchi) and Fürst, with Diest., Baumg., and other moderns, refer the passage to the grave of Moses, though differing somewhat as to the precise rendering of the words. So Vulg., "quod in parte suâ doctor esset repositus." But such a sense seems unsuited to the context; and in fact from xxxiv. 1—5, compared with Josh. xiii. 20, it would seem that the place where Moses died and was buried was in the country of Reuben.

v. 25.

The Hebrew word מנעלך is ἅπ. λεγ., and by several, both ancient and modern (Onk., Saad., Gesen., Maur., Keil, Schröd., &c.), is rendered "thy bars." The root נעל means to "fasten" or "bind," as is clear from the Arabic نعل, and numerous cognate forms. But the force of the root is almost equally exhibited in either rendering. That of A.V. on the whole seems best.

v. 25.

The Hebrew word דבא here used is again ἅπ. λεγ., and is variously rendered. Vulg. with Jerus. Targum, "senectus tua;" others (Rosenm., Gesen., Keil, Maur., Graf, Diest., and most moderns), "thy rest;" Fürst ('Lex.' s. v. דבא) "riches, affluence." The A. V., follows the majority of ancient authorities.

CHAPTER XXXIV.

1 *Moses from mount Nebo vieweth the land.* 5 *He dieth there.* 6 *His burial.* 7 *His age.* 8 *Thirty days' mourning for him.* 9 *Joshua succeedeth him.* 10 *The praise of Moses.*

AND Moses went up from the
plains of Moab unto the moun-
‖ Or, *the hill.* tain of Nebo, to the top of ‖ Pisgah,
that *is* over against Jericho. And
[a] chap. 3. 27. 2 Mac. 2. 4. the LORD [a] shewed him all the land
of Gilead, unto Dan,
2 And all Naphtali, and the land
of Ephraim, and Manasseh, and all the
land of Judah, unto the utmost sea,
3 And the south, and the plain of
the valley of Jericho, the city of palm
trees, unto Zoar.
4 And the LORD said unto him,
[b] This *is* the land which I sware un- [b] Gen. 12. 7. & 13. 15.
to Abraham, unto Isaac, and unto
Jacob, saying, I will give it unto thy
seed: I have caused thee to see *it*
with thine eyes, but thou shalt not go
over thither.

CHAP. XXXIV. Death and Burial of Moses.

1. *mountain of Nebo*] Cf. xxxii. 49 sqq. and reff.

all the land of Gilead, unto Dan] This can hardly be the Dan (Dan-Laish) of Judg. xviii. 27 sqq., which was not in Gilead. It is probably a town of this name which stood in the north of Peræa; perhaps the same as Dan-jaan, 2 S. xxiv. 6, and the Dan of Gen. xiv. 14, where see note.

2. *utmost sea*] Cf. xi. 24.

3. *unto Zoar*] At the southern extremity of the Dead Sea. Cf. Gen. xix. 22.

4. *I have caused thee to see it*] The sight thus afforded to Moses, like that of "all the kingdoms of the world in a moment of time," Luke iv. 5, was no doubt supernatural. Yet it was not imaginary only, but a real view of the land, obtained perhaps through an extraordinary enhancement of the dying lawgiver's power of vision.

5 ¶ So Moses the servant of the LORD died there in the land of Moab, according to the word of the LORD.

6 And he buried him in a valley in the land of Moab, over against Beth-peor: but no man knoweth of his sepulchre unto this day.

7 ¶ And Moses *was* an hundred and twenty years old when he died: his eye was not dim, nor his †natural force †abated.

† Heb. *moisture.* † Heb. *fled.*

8 ¶ And the children of Israel wept for Moses in the plains of Moab thirty days: so the days of weeping *and* mourning for Moses were ended.

9 ¶ And Joshua the son of Nun was full of the spirit of wisdom; for Moses had laid his hands upon him: and the children of Israel hearkened unto him, and did as the LORD commanded Moses.

10 ¶ And there arose not a prophet since in Israel like unto Moses, whom the LORD knew face to face,

11 In all the signs and the wonders, which the LORD sent him to do in the land of Egypt to Pharaoh, and to all his servants, and to all his land,

12 And in all that mighty hand, and in all the great terror which Moses shewed in the sight of all Israel.

---

5. *according to the word of the LORD*] Lit. "at the mouth of the Lord," which the Rabbins explain "by a kiss of the Lord." But the sense of the phrase is clear, cf. Gen. xlv. 21. Vulg. correctly "jubente Domino." It denotes that Moses died, not because his vital powers were exhausted, but at the sentence of God, and as a punishment for his sin. Cf. xxxii. 51.

6. *he buried him*] *i.e.* God buried him. The penalty of Moses' sin was fully paid by his death; and this signal honour conferred on him after death was, doubtless, designed to sustain the lawgiver's authority, which without it might have been impaired with the people in consequence of his punishment.

no man knoweth of his sepulchre] Hardly lest the grave of Moses should become an object of superstitious honour, for the Jews were not prone to this particular form of error. Bearing in mind the appearance of Moses at the Transfiguration (St Matt. xvii. 1—10), and what is said by St Jude, *v.* 9, we may conjecture that Moses after death passed into the same state with Enoch and Elijah; and that his sepulchre could not be found because he was shortly translated from it.

9. *spirit of wisdom*] Cf. Isa. xi. 2. The practical wisdom (φρόνησις) of the ruler is specially meant.

10. *there arose not a prophet since in Israel*] Words like these can only have been written some time, but not necessarily a long time, after the death of Moses. They refer more particularly to the wonders wrought by the hand of Moses at the Exodus and in the desert; and do but reecho the declaration of God Himself, Num. xii. 6 sqq. They may naturally enough be attributed to one of Moses' successors, writing perhaps soon after the settlement of the people in Canaan.